THE ENCYCLOPEDIA OF
THE
MUSICAL THEATRE

GÄNZL, Kurt Friedrich [GALLAS, Brian Roy] (b Wellington, 15 February 1946).

New-Zealand born, of Viennese stock, Kurt Gänzl studied law and classics at Canterbury University (MA [Hons] 1967) whilst at the same time building a career as a radio and concert vocalist. At the age of 21 he joined the New Zealand Opera Company as a basso soloist and, when that company curled up, moved to London where he soon swapped the operatic world for a life in the musical theatre. Over the next twenty years, he worked in almost every area of the musical theatre, at first as a performer, then as a talent agent and finally as a casting director both for musicals and plays in London's West End and for musical and operatic productions in Europe, America and Australia.

In 1986 his first book on the musical theatre, the 2-volume history of *The British Musical Theatre*, was published. Greeted as 'one of the great works of cultural reference', it was awarded the Roger Machell Prize for the year's best performing-arts book and the British Library Association's McColvin Medal for the outstanding reference work (any subject) of its season. In the four succeeding years, he followed this with *Gänzl's Book of the Musical Theatre*, commissioned as a companion volume to Kobbé's famous opera guide, with the story of the making of Andrew Lloyd Webber's musical in *The Complete 'Aspects of Love'*, and with a survey of recorded musicals, *The Blackwell Guide to the Musical Theatre on Record*, before retiring from the office-bound part of his double life to devote himself full-time to the compilation of *The Encyclopedia of the Musical Theatre*.

THE ENCYCLOPEDIA OF
The
Musical Theatre

A-K

KURT GÄNZL

SCHIRMER BOOKS
An Imprint of Macmillan Publishing Company
New York

Maxwell Macmillan Canada
Toronto

This American edition published in 1994 by Schirmer
Books, An Imprint of Macmillan Publishing Company.

Schirmer Books
An Imprint of Macmillan Publishing Company
866 Third Avenue
New York, NY 10022

First published in Great Britain by
Blackwell Publishers
108 Cowley Road
Oxford OX4 1JF
UK

Macmillan Publishing Company is part of the Maxwell
Communications Group of Companies.

Library of Congress Catalog Card Number: 93-48237

Printed in the United States of America.

Printing number
    3   4   5   6   7   8   9   10

Library of Congress Cataloging-in-Publication Data

Gänzl, Kurt.
The encyclopedia of the musical theatre/Kurt Gänzl. –
American ed.
        p.   cm.
Includes bibliographical references.
ISBN 0-02-871445-8 : $150.00
1. Musicals – Encyclopedias.   I. Title.
ML102.M88G3   1994   93-48237
                                       CIP
                                       MN

This book is printed on acid-free paper

Contents

Introduction

When I was in the long-drawn-out process of compiling my first musical-theatre book, *The British Musical Theatre*, in the 1980s, I became an habitué of second-hand bookstores, ephemera fairs and flea-markets, buying up anything and everything that might yield information on, and/or insight into all those shows and people I was writing about but had never seen. When that book was published in 1986 I found myself with a huge amount of musical-theatre scores, sheet music, libretti, lyric-books, photos, programmes and other material on my hands. I was caught. It didn't go quietly into the basement, it got shelves built for it and it became a 'collection'. It was (and is) actually quite a remarkable collection of material on the British musical stage (1865–1985), but unfortunately – or fortunately, depending on how you look at it – it did what collections are inclined to do. It expanded round the edges. I unearthed a splendid set of 19th-century American musical-comedy scores in a damp hotel in New York and suddenly I was a no-holds-barred collector of pre-war American material. I was unable to resist a carton of French programmes and 200 libretti in what looked as if it was nothing but a niçoise newsagent's shop, the heaps of operettic playbills and photos to be found in Vienna's much-regretted Kunst und Kultur Markt on the banks of the Donau canal, and all that marvellous Hungarian sheet-music that used to sell for next to nothing in Budapest. I ended up with the collector's equivalent of omnivorousness, and my interests expanded every time the 'collection' did.

I had a splendid time playing and singing my way through all this international cornucopia of theatre music, reading the sometimes hilarious, sometimes teeth-curling texts – old, very old and new – arranging the programmes in rows of folders like colourful stamps in a philatelist's album and scouring them for rising and/or repeated names or unexpected credits. And all the time my curiosity was being aroused – I wanted to know as much about these non-British shows and all these writers whose work I was gradually discovering as I'd found out about the people and plays of Britain over the course of my previous ten years of study.

It wasn't, at this stage, a case of putting anything in print. I'd done my 'big book' and its equally 'big' backlog of preparatory work, and I wasn't counting on getting involved in another. A man has only so many decades in his life. This time I wanted my information straight, complete and nicely assembled and tabulated by someone else, thank you. Only it wasn't that easy. Although there had been a number of more or less detailed surveys of musical-theatre activity in one particular period and/or city (Bruyas on Paris, Bordman on New York, Bauer on Vienna, and others more anecdote- than fact-orientated), as well as a number of sometimes more, sometimes less reliable lexicons and theatrical *Who's Who*ses from various nations, containing little or lots of biographical details on writers and players, there wasn't one hold-all volume of international musical-theatre data to which I could go for full-scale lists of names, dates, places, figures, facts and explanations. Worse. Even when you put together all the material from all the best published books – and that's supposing you could actually get hold of them all – there were still some notable and sizeable gaps. I grumbled about all this to Gerald Bordman, the Boswell of Broadway, I grumbled to Stanley Green, who had started out to do exactly that kind of book in his own *Encyclopaedia of the Musical* but had been forced by a sad chauvinism on the part of the powers-that-publish to limit himself to 20th-century New York in scope, I grumbled suggestively to operetta expert Andrew Lamb who, I knew, had done a great deal of original work gathering together all sorts of information on, in particular, Continental musicians, and to several other stars of the international fraternity of theatre scholars, and not one of them said enthusiastically, 'What a good idea, I'll do that'. They, without exception, said 'What a good idea. I'm doing such and such this year, and such and such next year ... why don't you do it?'. Perhaps, by that time, the memory of the efforts involved in compiling *The British Musical Theatre* had faded a touch. But I took a deep breath, took it on, and, over the past six years – with time off for a few such-and-suches of my own (*Gänzl's Book of the Musical Theatre, The Complete 'Aspects of Love', The Blackwell Guide to the Musical Theatre on Record*) – most of my time has been spent getting these two volumes together.

What you will find in these pages is my best throw at putting together the sort of work that I missed: a compilation of such material on two or three thousand of the most important (and even some of the less important) and interesting people and plays of the musical stage as I have been able to gather whilst digging and diving my way around the world's libraries, archives and flea-markets over the past few years. I'd like to think that in many or even most cases I've been able to put together something like a complete musical-theatre worklist for the writers and composers involved. And I'm pretty sure I've turned out a reasonably thorough picture of the musical-theatre careers of the performers listed (I soon found that any attempt to include every job of every player was impossible, especially in countries with a repertoire system) and of the principal shows of the 19th- and 20th-century musical stage. But I know that these things are neverending. There is always more information out there, in Nuremberg, in Lyon or in Atlantic City, forgotten shows and probably discreditable credits that will have got through my net. I know, because I found so much of this kind of material on my travels, and because fresh information kept and keeps on coming in, steadily, week upon week. However, the flow eventually came down to a steady but definite trickle, so – after some two final, concentrated years of get-it-all-together work on this project – I thought the time had come to stop fiddling with the 40 disks' worth of articles and lists covering my desk, shelves and floors before they and their tiniest details became a real obsession, sandpaper them up and put the result between covers.

The main reason that the job has taken me so long is that I decided early on, with what turned out to be a painful bravado, that wherever possible I wouldn't take anyone else's word for anything. I was going to go back to primary sources for my information: to the programmes, newspapers and magazines of the countries and the eras with which I was dealing. The British end of things was easily managed, thanks to that huge collection of material which I'd put together in the 1980s, but, as far as was humanly and financially possible, the rest of the world needed to be covered in the same way. So off I set.

I sailed across the Atlantic on a cargo ship and spent more than three American months blinking through microfilm files of *The New York Dramatic Mirror*, *The New York Times* and *Variety*, delving about at length in the vast private collection of American music and scripts gathered by Gerry Bordman whilst he was writing his *American Musical Theatre* and *Companion to the American Theatre*, in the magnificent music archive that is the Rokahr Family Library in Los Angeles, and dipping into material – with all sorts of surprising results – in libraries, museums and newspaper offices from Millersville to Baltimore to Philadelphia. I took a train to Austria and stayed five weeks under the kindly eye of Frau Széles in Vienna's quaint Pension Quisisana in the Windmühlgasse, only a few hundred metres from the house where my father was born, spending my days going – one by one – through the remarkable collection of playbills and programmes in the archives of the Oester-reichisches Theater Museum. Every opening hour (and some that weren't) was spent frantically pounding the information I gleaned onto my trusty Toshiba T1200, all the time trying head-achingly to make sure that, in the sixth or seventh hour of a working day, a slip of a tired finger didn't make a 19 into a 29, or cause a letter or a figure to drop out of its proper place. Next, I paddled down the river to Budapest, where Frau Széles had arranged for me to be looked after by her friend Frau Erdéi, and the Magyar Színházi Intézet and its fine archive of theatre material was awaiting me. My studies there were cut a little short when a transport strike threatened to turn into something graver, and I (carrying more than 20 kilos of elderly Hungarian sheet music on my back) slogged 3 kilometres through Budapest's deserted – apart from the odd soldier – streets to the station, to get what looked like being the last train out of town for the duration. It took me 32 hours, clutching the Toshiba and the music, to get back to Nice ... just in time to miss the last bus that would take me the final 20 kilometres to my apartment in St Paul de Vence. My neighbour, Carolanne, drove down in her pyjamas to rescue a verging-on-the-snuffling voyager.

Not long after recovering from this heroic cavalcade, I headed on to Australia and, there, five weeks glued to more microfilm machines in the State Library and a swift visit to the theatre archives in Canberra allowed me – simply by once more going day by day through contemporary newspapers – to compile a list of all the musical productions played in Melbourne and Sydney since theatre began down under. Sydney was the scene of one of my most memorable moments spent in the search of a missing piece of information: zooming round the 17 hectares of the beautiful cliffside Waverley cemetery in the car of a helpful workman who – out of the thousands of graves – was, with no map, able to pinpoint the last resting place of Johnnie Sheridan. Somehow, it didn't really matter that, when we found it, the stone didn't actually give me the date I was after.

And each time, when the work was done, I hurried back to my hungry computers in St Paul to copy out and consolidate.

Needless to say, once I really began to try to put order into the mass of information gobbled up in my peregrinations, I soon found that there was an almost unending list of things I'd failed to note down on the way round. Bertrand the St-Paulois postman is now quite used to the parade of parcels with foreign stamps he delivers to 'le fou néo-zélandais' who appears in town for a few months of light-through-the-night working sessions before disappearing off once more to other parts of the world and other, doubtless equally unspeakable, occupations. Those foreign stamps are quite varied, for my network of scholarly pals and friendly library professionals from Budapest and Buar to Croydon and Sydney have done wonders in answering my all-too-frequent howls for help.

In London, Andrew Lamb has spent months of lunchtimes in the national archives tracing birth, death and marriage certificates for dozens and dozens of actors and writers who have 'sheltered' their real name, their age and just about everything else you can imagine, in a remarkable bit of detective work. He's found all sorts of those little jigsaw-pieces of information that go to make up a well-wrapped dossier: the whatever-happened-to of Edward Jakobowski, the once-famous composer of *Erminie*, which the combined efforts of Bordman, Green, Gänzl and the American libraries system had failed, in spite of a long search, ever to discover; the facts on the star whose autobiography neglects to mention that her parents were indeed married, but only eight years after the date she doesn't admit was that of her birth; and many and many another birth date which is one (why?), three, five or eight years further back in time than those admitted by their subjects. In New York, Richard Norton has scoured the libraries and delved into his own mighty musical-theatre collection for answers to the faxes-full of queries on shows from Davidson, Milwaukee or Albany, NY (and even New York, NY) that have zoomed regularly across the Atlantic; in Budapest, Dr György Székely has spent hours putting the accents right on my misspelt Hungarian and digging up information on ancient (and modern) first performances in a city which must, then as now, be the most musical-theatre-minded centre in the world, and Támas Gajdó has taken time off from editing his own Hungarian theatre lexicon to dig through the theatre museum's files, filleting out the musical-theatre stories of which the strike deprived me and translating them into French (our language of communication). Vienna's Gerti Fischer has kept me endlessly supplied with packages of Austrian answers, Jacques Derouet in Poitiers has led my French helpers in turning up bits and pieces on early French productions, Rudolf Maeder in Switzerland has taken chunks out of my 'Help! List, Germany', Louise Grant in London has turned up regularly with theatre programmes which I would have thought were unfindable, and Hollywood's Hank Moonjean and London's Kevin Gough-Yates have kept an eye on my film-associated references. And, all the time, the phone calls and the envelopes of photocopies have just kept and still keep coming from all corners of the globe ('Kurt? Rida Johnson Young graduated from high school in 1882 – I have her graduation list. Her given birth date would mean she was 13. Not possible. She's lied by at least three years. By the way, her name then was just Ida ...' 'Kurt, I have a score by Jean Gilbert for you, it's called *Der Gauklerkönig* ... but it isn't on your worklist ...').

Finally, on 12 December 1992, the deadline fell. A deputation from Blackwell descended on St Paul, and the print-out of those 40 full-to-meltdown-point disks was packed up into a bevy of suitcases and knapsacks and plastic bags, and carried off to Oxford to be put through the first stages of being made into a book. Or two books. These two books. Along with the text went some 300 photographs that I'd gathered up to accompany the written part of the book. Rather than choose all of these from the shows' first stagings, photos of which have been reproduced regularly over the years, I've purposely picked some that I hope will be new to you, pictures taken from regional theatres and international productions. This at least partly on the principle that the musical theatre's real powerbases are not in London's West End, in Vienna, Paris or on Broadway, but in the thousands of theatres around the world that play the shows after they've been created in the main centres and that are very largely responsible for their continued life. As in the case of the text, you get what I've got, been got or given (for which very much thanks to all the long list of collections, collectors, theatres and theatrical photographers concerned, and especially to Peter Joslin who organized the whole photographic side of the book). I hope you'll find them interesting, and a touch refreshing.

Well, that's the 'why' and the 'how' of this work. Now for the 'what'. Way back in 1986, when, having decided to go for it, I sat down to set up the parameters for the (one-volume) *Encyclopedia of the Musical Theatre*, I decided that, in spite of its title, it had, for practical reasons, to be limited to a coverage of the plays and the people involved in the mainstream of Western musical theatre and, more specifically, to those parts of that musical-theatre tradition which were internationally played and popular. Thus, for example, there is only occasional reference to the Spanish and Italian musical stages, even though both countries have produced fine, durable and popular works for their own home audiences. The Russian musical theatre and that of the other former Eastern bloc countries, similarly, have an almost negligible place. And there are, alas for my chauvinism, only three New Zealand entries.

I selected as my principal areas of concentration that handful of countries and traditions which have been the most productive of original musical plays for the world's stages in the last 150 years: France, Austria, Britain, the United States of America and Hungary. To these, I added Australia, which, having virtually no home product of its own, has, during those 150 years, sat on the other side of the world from the main production centres, picking and choosing a fascinating microcosm (and not as micro- as all that) of musical theatre for its stages, and Germany, which if it had only a brief hour of glory as a supplier to international stages, has both supplemented the Austrian tradition in a manner impossible to ignore and is showing interesting signs of producing more new works – if as yet mostly copycat ones – than any other area in the 1990s.

Having established my geographical area, I then had to set up that almost-impossibly-fuzzy-edged parameter of what 'musical theatre' was to mean for the purposes of this work. As I did in *The British Musical Theatre*, I have chosen to stick with the area I know about. I deal only with the book musical. That is to say, I cover the original musical play in all its shapes, forms and sizes – any original piece with a continuous libretto, lyrics and music, whether it be a sung-through five-act romantic operetta, a Germanic Posse with a half-dozen numbers, or a little farcical piece illustrated by some tap-dancing high-jinks and a tiny bookful of squeaked-out excuses for songs. I draw my line around that area, and in doing so I regretfully – but necessarily – exclude from my survey all such contiguous and/or related forms of musico-theatre entertainment as opera, pantomime (in both the original and the Anglo-Christmas senses of the word), revue, compilation shows, paste-up musicals (mostly), dance shows, concerts, music hall/variety/vaudeville and so forth, as well as musical film and television. This doesn't mean that there is no mention of these areas in the book. They just aren't the subject of the book. Many of the people who worked/work in what I call the musical theatre also operated/operate in these associated areas of the entertainment business and their contributions there are, naturally, noted. But they are noted in the wings of the main stage of the work.

Selecting my headwords – the people and the plays to whom and which I was going to devote space – was the same thought-provoking job that it always is. Every time you put together a work which is not all-embracing, which involves a selection of subject matter, almost anyone and everyone who comes near it manages to find something that you have decided not to include that they think – for a variety of reasons and with varying degrees of indignation – should have been put in. All I can say is, I have put in the pieces and people that this long-time lover of the worldwide musical stage thinks should be there. Folks are welcome to disagree ... and they can put their favourite 'missing' ones in their encyclopedias.

I have set out to deal with, first and foremost, the most successful, most prolific and most extensively heard writers and composers for the musical stages of the countries under survey and, in parallel, the most successful, interesting and – the three things are not always compatible – the most widely travelled shows. I have added to this backbone of the work details on those artists who led/have led the fullest and most interesting lives on the musical stage, as well as on a limited number of producers and a very small representative group of creative personnel – directors, choreographers and designers. The ultimate accent, however, is on those two areas that originally prompted me to put the book together – the writers and their shows.

Two of my main and original criteria in picking the headwords were, firstly, that writers, shows and performers who were seen and heard in more than one of my countries should have preference and place here over those which were of interest only in a single centre, and that – for all the folk concerned – a full career in the musical theatre was of more relevance than just one or two appearances, no matter how starry, on the musical stage. Where performers are concerned, I have also leaned heavily towards those players who created rôles in new musicals, which means that there is a distinct bias towards those artists who were active in each centre in the period of its creative pre-eminence. By the same token, you won't find in these pages entries on Favourite Flops, no matter how well-known their authors or stars. Although it is undoubtedly important to a detailing of a writer's career to note his unsuccessful work along with his hits, the description and dissection of failed shows in themselves is a job that's been splendidly done – with the kind of gusto that suits this 'special taste' – by others.

Of course, it goes without saying that all the criteria with which I started out got bent a little here and there on the way through the compilation, as criteria always do, but since this was a one-man book, rather than one made up of an editor and contributors, I was able just to let it happen. I didn't bother arguing with myself. If a score or a script, a personality or an author appealed to me particularly, I didn't stop myself from popping in a few words about it or him. If I was fascinated, perhaps other folk might be too. As a result, the 'final' headword list with which I'd started out got intermittent additions as work progressed. But it also got a certain number of deletions. There were some people and shows I would have liked to have included but on whom/which I was unable to find out the necessary. In spite of all my best efforts, and those of my 'network', there were scores and libretti which defied the finding. And although most of the dead people supplied the information I asked for splendidly, a disappointing handful of live ones (and live ones with agents) proved to be less forthcoming. So, the final list that you see here developed by a kind of natural selection.

At the end of the day, I have ended up with this – nearly 3,000 articles in two volumes – smugly accepted by a publisher who had always said that I'd never limit myself to one, but who did smile a little stiffly when I at one stage mumbled 'three' – which I hope cover the people and plays of the international musical theatre of the last few generations as fully and as accurately as can be done in two volumes.

Here is perhaps the place to say that when I have not been able to find a piece of information – a date or place of birth or death, a date or place of a production – I have simply left the gap. I have not, as I (dare I say it?) suspect one recent book of reference of doing, taken flying guesses in order to fill in a hole. When in doubt, I have left out (either the fact, or even the article) or used that most useful of devices – the question mark.

Of course, even now when the text has gone out of my hands, and I am under threat of having my PCW cut off if I start sticking any more extra bits of material into the thing when it's trying to be page proofs, the parcels will keep on coming. Having started so many folk chasing so many facts and doing so many flea-markets all around the world, even the past isn't going to stop – as I am supposed to have – on 12 December 1992. Whilst the present rolls inevitably on. But I wouldn't want them to stop. Published or not, the more information I can gather, the happier I'll be. So I'd be delighted to hear (c/o Blackwell Publishers, 108 Cowley Rd, Oxford OX4 1JF, England; or c/o Schirmer Books, 866 Third Avenue, New York, NY 10022) from all and any specialists on the area that I have covered, and from all and any musical-theatre fans who have extra material (primary sources only, please!) to add to what I've been able to put together. Perhaps someone in America knows what happened to Mizzi Hajós, to Evelyn Herbert and Robert Halliday, to Emmy Wehlen or to that fabulous creature called 'The Only Leon'? Perhaps there is a real, live list of the hundred opérettes Vincent Scotto is said to have written (but of which no one, when pressed, is able to give me the titles) hidden in the archive of a Marseille music publisher, or records of a bundle of other quick-flop try-outs like *Page Mr Cupid*, *The Love School* or *Cocktail* to be found in the newspaper and programme files at Wilkes-Barre, Pa. Perhaps there are other descendants of the famous folk of the past – like the Mrs Nash I met in Millersville, Pa, who turned out to have been Miss Ascher, daughter of Leo – who have music, texts, pictures and memories to share. And there must be mines of information in centres such as San Francisco, Chicago, Prague, Stettin, Hamburg, Lyon and Marseille, none of which I've yet been able to visit, and whose busy musical-theatre history has not, to my knowledge, ever been detailed between covers. A jigsaw-puzzle never gives its full effect until it is completed – and I'd love to complete each and every one of the jigsaws that go to make up this book (and the ones which had to be omitted) before they carry me away. All and any help in this respect would be very gratefully received.

For the moment, however, I'm putting it all aside, and I'm going off to be musical-theatrically 'dried out'. I've this little farm in the outish-backs in New Zealand which doesn't have a fax, or a computer, or a piano, or a record player (CD? what's that?), or mains water. Or even a bookshelf. So even if someone's discovered whatever happened to Marie Halton, it'll have to keep till the spring...

KURT GÄNZL

Air New Zealand, between St Paul de Vence, France, and Tophouse, New Zealand
24 and 26 December 1992 (amazing what the international date-line does to you...)

Organization of the encyclopedia

Alphabetization

Entries are arranged in a single alphabetical sequence, using a letter-by-letter system, as follows

MANNEQUINS
DER MANN MIT DEN DREI FRAUEN
MANNSCHAFT AN BORD
MANNSTÄDT, William
MAN OF LA MANCHA

For alphabetization purposes, the following conventions have been followed:
- the definite and indefinite articles A, The, L', Le, La, Les, Das, Der, Die etc. are ignored where they appear at the beginning of show headwords.
- the Scots or Irish prefixes 'Mac', 'Mc' and 'M' are all treated as if they were spelt out 'Mac'.
- all accented letters are treated as English unaccented letters.

Cross references appear as follows:

MAYTIME   *see* WIE EINST IM MAI

with the large capital letter indicating the letter under which the entry may be found.

Introductory and supplementary sections to people entries

The articles are written and ordered under the name in which their subject was active in the theatre. When that name is simply an easily shortened version of the subject's real full name, the rest of that real name is given in square brackets: for example,

BROWN, Jon[athan Frederick]

When the bold headword is not simply a shortened form of the real full name or when the nom de théâtre/nom de plume is not that with which the subject was born, the real full name (where known) is given separately, again in square brackets. For example,

BROWN, John [BROWN, Jonathan Frederick]
BROWN, John [BRAUNSTEIN, Johann Friedrich]

The name is followed by the places and dates of birth and death, where known, in parentheses. For example,

(b London, 6 February 1933; d unknown)

On a number of occasions, a birth year is included but is marked with a query. This is generally where a death certificate or obituary has given the subject's age at death, but a birth certificate and/or date has not been found to confirm that information. For example,

(b Paris, ?1946; d Nice, 10 August 1980).

The bibliographies given at the end of entries include a representative selection of biographies, autobiographies or other significant literature devoted to the subject. I have not attempted to list every published work – not least because many of the people who have the most works written about them are those whose principal activity was not the musical theatre.

Introductory and supplementary sections to show entries

The introductory sections to show entries give the title (and subtitle where relevant) under which the show was normally played, followed by any considerably used alternative title, then the credits as given on the playbill, and the date and place of the first production. As in the worklists that appear at the end of people articles (see below), this information refers to the first metropolitan performance. In the case of modern works, the date of the official 'first night', rather than that of the first preview performance, is given. Out-of-town try-out dates are shown only when there is an appreciable gap between the initial out-of-town production and any later metropolitan production, or when the show failed to find its way to town at all. For example,

> **NO, NO, NANETTE** Musical comedy in 3 acts by Frank Mandel, Otto Harbach and Irving Caesar based on *My Lady Friends* by Mandel and Emil Nyitray (and *Oh, James!* by May Edgington). Music by Vincent Youmans. Garrick Theater, Detroit, 23 April 1923; Harris Theater, Chicago, 7 May 1923; Globe Theater, New York, 16 September 1925.

The supplementary sections at the end of the show entries consist of a record of the dates and places of the first productions of the show in what, for the purposes of this book, are treated as the 'main centres' (Berlin, Budapest, London, Melbourne, New York, Paris, Sydney, Vienna) other than that in which it was first performed. When the show was, on these occasions, given in France, Austria, Britain, America, Australia, Hungary or Germany under a title other than its original, the altered or translated title is given, along with the date and place of the production. For example,

> Austria: Theater in der Josefstadt 15 May 1952; France: Théâtre Marigny *Feu d'artifice* 1952; UK: Bristol Old Vic *Oh, My Papa!* 2 April, Garrick Theatre, London 17 July 1957
> Recordings: selection (Ariola-Eurodisc); selection in English (Parlophone EP)

Mention is also made of films and recordings of, and books on, individual shows. I have made no attempt to give details of recordings, as labels and serial numbers of recordings vary from country to country and a complete list of all the show recordings in question would fill a vast volume. I have merely tried to indicate which of the shows dealt with can be found on record, at least some of the labels that have been responsible for those recordings, and whether 'original cast' or foreign-language recordings are included amongst them. Similarly, I have mentioned books only in the rare instances where a book is wholly, or very largely, devoted to the show in question.

Authors' and composers' worklists

The worklists attached to the articles on librettists, lyricists and composers are intended to include all of each writer's credited works for the book musical theatre.

Works for which a writer was not credited on the playbills are not included, and neither are works written for such adjacent musical and theatrical areas as opera, ballet, pantomime and revue.

The original works in the list are given in chronological order of their first production.

When a show has been played under more than one title, the title in bold type is the title under which its main metropolitan run was given, with alternative titles in italic type in parentheses. Titles discarded in try-out are noted as 'ex-'. For example,

> 1988 **Ain't Broadway Grand** (ex- *Mike*)

Post-metropolitan changes of title are indicated by the prefix 'later-'. Where the title change was part of a significant rewrite, the rewrite will have a separate entry as 'revised version of [original title]'.

The year and title of the piece are followed by the names of the writer's credited collaborators on the show in question, in the order: composer(s)/lyricist(s)/librettist(s). Writers who collaborated with the writer in his or her area are shown by a 'w' indicating 'with'. Thus (Smith/w Brown/w Green) would mean that the person who is the subject of the article worked on the show's lyrics with Brown and its book with Green, and the music was by Smith. The names of the subject's collaborators are given in full on their first mention in a worklist, and thereafter by surname only except where a duplicated surname could lead to confusion, such as in the case of contemporaneous text-writers H B Smith, R B Smith and E Smith. Any variants occurring in a show's author/composer credits are included in square brackets. Major revisions of a show are credited separately in the worklist.

In the case of short works only, the names of the authors are followed by an indication such as '1 act' or '3 scenes'. Otherwise all works are 'full-length' pieces (in the loosest possible meaning of the term when some works from the 19th-century days of very long evenings are in question) in a minimum of two acts.

Each original work entry on the worklist ends with the place and date of the first metropolitan performance. In the case of modern works, the date of the official 'first night' rather than that of the first preview performance is used. Out-of-town try-out dates are shown only when there is an appreciable gap between the initial out-of-town production and any later metropolitan production, or when the show failed to find its way to town at all. In the case of shows initially staged in other cities and subsequently remounted in what, for the purposes of this book, are accounted the 'main centres' (Berlin, Budapest, London, Melbourne, New York, Paris, Sydney, Vienna), both dates are given. When the theatre in which the show's première is given is not based in the city that may be regarded as being/having been the writer's base, the name of the city is included alongside the theatre. So, for example, a Vienna-centred author will be credited with works at the Carltheater, the Theater an der Wien or the Raimundtheater without further elaboration, but for productions at the Theater am Gärtner-platz, Munich, the Népszinház, Budapest, or the Thalia-Theater, Berlin, the cities would be specified. For example,

1890 **Erminy** (*Erminie*) German version w Heinrich von Wald-berg (Carltheater)
1890 **Der bleiche Gast** (Josef Hellmesberger, Zamara/w von Waldberg) Carl-Schultze Theater, Hamburg 6 September

Shows which are not the original work of the writer in question, but simply adaptations of a musical originally written and produced by other writers in another language, are listed under the year of their production in the version by the subject of the worklist. The year is followed by the title given to the piece in the subject's adaptation, followed in parentheses by the title of the original piece in its original language, a description of the nature of the adaptation (where applicable) and the theatre where the adaptation was first staged. For example,

1889 **Capitän Wilson** (*The Yeomen of the Guard*) German version w Carl Lindau (Carltheater)

On the occasions where I have been unable to trace or to confirm that a show credited to a writer was in fact produced, rather than just being announced for production, I have listed the title at the end of the worklist under the heading 'Other titles attributed'. Conversely, shows which were definitely produced, but for which my details are incomplete, are included in the worklist, with their details as complete as I have been able to make them. Any dubious dates, places or credits are indicated with a question mark, thus, ?1849.

Occasionally circumstances arose which could not be adequately dealt with by the arrangements described above. In these cases, it has been my main care simply to make whatever the situation and credits might be as clear as possible without clinging too unbendingly to a 'standard' layout.

KURT GÄNZL

Abbreviations

(X) ad (Y)	the work of (X) adapted by (Y), adapter
add	additional
aka	also known as
(X) arr (Y)	the work of (X) arranged by (Y), arranger
b	born
ch	choreographed by, choreographer
d	died
Eng	English/England
fr	from
Fr	French/France
Frln	Fräulein
Ger	German/Germany
Hun	Hungarian/Hungary
jr	junior
Lat	Latin
lib	libretto
ly	lyric(s)
md	musical director
mus	music
nd	no date known
np	no place known
posth	posthumous
rev	revival
scr	screenplay
Sp	Spanish/Spain
sq/sqq	and that/those following
sr	senior
t/o	takeover (of a rôle)
UK	United Kingdom
u/s	understudy
USA	United States of America

A

AARONS, Alex[ander] A (b Philadelphia, 1891; d Beverly Hills, 14 March 1943).

If he spread himself less flamboyantly than his father, the irrepressible Alfred Aarons, and did not attempt to double in musical composition, Alex Aarons had a considerably more significant career as a producer than his parent. At first involved in the garment trade, holding a controlling interest in the 5th Avenue menswear store Croydons Ltd by his mid-twenties, he nevertheless had an early finger in showbusiness through an association with playwright Frederick Jackson. He made his entry on to Broadway (with 'considerable aid' from his father) with *La La Lucille* (ex- *Your Money or Your Wife*), a show written by Jackson and sporting the young George Gershwin's first attempt at a musical comedy score, in 1919. Although the early years brought several failures, including the small-scale *Oui Madame*, one of only a very few Victor Herbert musicals never to make it into New York, and Vincent Youmans's rewrite of the British musical comedy hit *A Night Out* (1925 w Edward Laurillard), Jackson's Fred and Adele Astaire show *For Goodness' Sake* (1922), which the younger Aarons presented both in America and, as *Stop Flirting*, in Britain (w George Grossmith, Pat Malone and Alfred Butt), soon gave him a first taste of international success.

Aarons's most noble productions were mounted in a decade-long partnership with Vinton Freedley, who had earlier been an actor in his musical comedy companies. During the late 1920s and the early 1930s they produced Gershwin's *Lady, Be Good!* (1924), *Tip-Toes* (1925), *Oh, Kay!* (1926), *Funny Face* (1927), *Treasure Girl* (1928), *Girl Crazy* (1930) and *Pardon My English* (1933), De Sylva, Brown and Henderson's highly successful boxing musical *Hold Everything!* (1928) which, in spite of its low profile in later years, gave the partnership its most substantial Broadway run of all on its original production, Rodgers and Hart's *Spring Is Here* (1929) and *Heads Up!* (1929), and *Here's Howe* (1928). The partners, however, cannily renounced the less than successful melodrama with music, *Singin' the Blues* (1931), soon after its opening and it finished its short life being run as a co-operative by its cast.

Most of the partnership's later productions were staged at the Alvin Theater, which Aarons and Freedley had built in 1927 at the peak of their success (and christened with the combined first syllables of their Christian names), and in which, after years headquartered at the New Amsterdam Theater, they made their Broadway base. However, several losing productions and the onset of the Depression found them obliged to sell their theatre and, after their staging of the unfortunate *Pardon My English* at the Majestic Theater, the partnership split up and Aarons withdrew definitively from the production arena.

His name surfaced occasionally thereafter, attached to abortive Broadway projects, but what activity he maintained was centred largely on film. He worked at Metro and RKO, and with the A & S Lyons agency in California, and his last involvement with the musical world was when he was taken on by Warner Brothers in an assistant capacity on the Gershwin biopic *Rhapsody in Blue*, ultimately brought out, after his death, in 1945.

AARONS, Alfred E (b Philadelphia, 16 November 1865; d New York, 16 November 1936).

Alfred Aarons began his life in the Philadelphia theatre as a callboy, worked in the box office at Gilmore's Central Theater at the age of fifteen, and set up as a dramatic and vaudeville agent, with an office in that city's Walnut Street, at sixteen. In 1890 he left his home town and headed for New York where he opened an agency office on Broadway before moving on to become, successively, house manager of J M Hill's Standard Theater, a booker for Koster and Bial's Music Hall, and the manager of Oscar Hammerstein's Manhattan Opera House Roof Garden. During these years, the young man also began to write songs, and he had an early composing success with a ragtime piece called 'Rag Time Liz', played in Koster and Bial's entertainment *In Gotham* (1898). He also supplied a number for the successful soubrette Josephine Hall (Mrs Aarons) to sing in Charles Frohman's production of *The Girl from Maxim's* (1899, w Richard Carle, 'Honi Soit Qui Mal y Pense').

Aarons made his first venture as a producer when he took Herrmann's Theater to stage a season of vaudeville, and then, in 1900, launched out both as a composer and as a producer of musical comedy with a piece called *Mam'selle 'Awkins*, written in collaboration with an old Koster and Bial's pal, comedian Richard Carle. The show's 35 Broadway performances were prelude to a touring life which was sufficient to encourage Aarons to persevere. In partnership with David Henderson, he took a lease on George Krause's new Schley Music Hall on 34th Street, rechristened it the Savoy Theater, and produced a second home-made musical, *The Military Maid*, with a libretto by proven dramatist George V Hobart (though said to be 'from the French').

The Military Maid had just a handful of Broadway performances, but Aarons's confidence was such that he soon bought Henderson out of his share in their lease, only to be quickly booted out of his theatre for not paying the rent. Within a year he went bankrupt to the tune of $27,000 after attempting to jump on the then fast-rolling British bandwagon, by producing Ivan Caryll's *The Ladies' Paradise* at no less a venue than the Metropolitan Opera House. This made-for-the-English-provinces piece, starring Miss Hall and Carle, was thoroughly overproduced and, lost in

1

its surroundings, folded after 14 performances. This setback, however, did not stop Aarons producing, nor did it stop him writing. *My Antoinette* (a touring rewrite of *The Ladies' Paradise*, tarted up with some Aarons songs) and *The Knickerbocker Girl* (played by Miss Hall for two Broadway weeks) did nothing, however, to restore his colour and he did little better when F C Whitney produced his *A China Doll* (1904), an oddly old-fashioned piece about an automaton, which fared fairly on the road but was exposed as very weak stuff when it was brought into New York.

His next piece, *The Pink Hussars* (1905), was a collaboration with the respected composer Julian Edwards, but by the time it got to town Aarons was billed as producer only (F C Whitney had originally sent the piece out) and Edwards was given full credit for the score of what was now called *His Honor the Mayor* (1906). With this piece, however, Aarons finally found success, and *His Honor the Mayor*, with its variety-based combination of girls, songs and fun, proved a good touring proposition, pleased summer theatre-goers in New York for 104 performances, and played two return engagements over the following seasons, with Blanche Ring starring and with an ever-changing set of songs. His *The Girl from Yama* served for several seasons on the road, but another producing essay with Edwards's *Miss Molly May* (1909), starring the glamorous soprano Grace La Rue, was less forthcoming.

Aarons subsequently spent a period on the staff of Abe Erlanger's more substantial production outfit, where he is credited with having contributed largely to the development of that office's very efficacious touring booking system, but he resigned from time to time to take further turns as an independent manager (his last own show to play Broadway, *The Deacon and the Lady* w Louis Werba, Harry Archer's maiden *The Pearl Maiden* w Rube Welch, etc). In 1925 he resigned for the last time, apparently after a quarrel with Erlanger, and announced that he would produce the American version of Lehár's *Frasquita* with opera diva Geraldine Farrar starring. Although he did not bring this project to fruition (and it was a disaster for those who did), he had occasional success in these latter years, during which he produced several rather more up-market musicals, such as George Gershwin's *Tell Me More!* (1925) and Sigmund Romberg's *My Princess* (1927), in between stints working as manager of the Broadhurst Theater and at the New Amsterdam Theater.

1900 **Mam'selle 'Awkins** (w Herman Perlet/Richard Carle) Victoria Theater 26 February
1900 **The Military Maid** (George V Hobart) Savoy Theater 8 October
1901 **My Antoinette** (*The Ladies' Paradise*) revised version with additional music by Aarons (w Carle, M E Rourke, Edward Abeles, George Totten Smith)
1901 **The Liberty Belles** (w Aimé Lachaume, A Baldwin Sloane, Clifton Crawford et al/Harry B Smith) Madison Square Theater 30 September
1903 **The Knickerbocker Girl** (Totten Smith) Herald Square Theater 15 June
1904 **A China Doll** (H B Smith, Robert B Smith) Majestic Theater 19 November
1905 **The Pink Hussars** (later *His Honor the Mayor*) (w Julian Edwards/Charles J Campbell, Ralph M Skinner) Chicago Opera House 23 October; New York Theater, New York 28 May 1906
1907 **[The Girl from] Yama** (R B Smith/Totten Smith) Walnut Street Theater, Philadelphia 4 November
1908 **The Hotel Clerk** (R B Smith) Walnut Street Theater, Philadelphia 27 April
1910 **The Deacon and the Lady** (Totten Smith) New York Theater 4 October

ABARBANELL, Lina (b Berlin, 3 February 1879; d New York, 6 January 1963).

The daughter of a conductor, the young Lina Abarbanell made her first stage appearances at Berlin's Residenztheater (1985), playing in both opera and Operette. She fulfilled engagements at Posen, Königsberg and at Berlin's Neues Königliches Opernhaus, and scored a personal success in the title-rôle of the German version of the Gaiety musical *A Runaway Girl* (*Daisy*, 1900), before being contracted by Karczag to play leading parts at Vienna's Theater an der Wien. She appeared there as Sáffi in *Der Zigeunerbaron* and as Adele in *Die Fledermaus*, and created the rôles of Lucy Handsome in Gustav Wanda's *Die Dame aus Trouville* (1902), Clara in Lehár's maiden work, *Wiener Frauen* (1902), the prima donna, Bianca Testa, in Ziehrer's *Der Fremdenführer* (1902), Lili in Alfred Grünfeld's *Der Lebermann* (1903) and the leading feminine part of the wild little Oculi in Eysler's highly successful *Bruder Straubinger* (1903). She also appeared at the Überbrettl cabaret theatre performing character songs.

Abarbanell went to America in 1905, under contract to Gustav Amberg, and, after appearing in his German-language musical productions at the Irving Place Theater (Hanni in *Frühlingsluft*, Denise in *Nitouche*, Lieutenant von Vogel in *Jung Heidelberg*) and also in light opera at the Metropolitan Opera House (Gretel in *Hansel and Gretel*), she made her first appearance in the English-language theatre when she was seen on Broadway as the Princess Ilsa in Reginald De Koven's comic opera, *The Student King* (1906).

She took the title-rôle of the first American touring production of *The Merry Widow* and succeeded to the rôle on Broadway (1908), starred on the road in the small-scale British musical *The White Chrysanthemum* (1907, Sybil) and in Henry Savage's production of Eysler's *The Love Cure* (*Künstlerblut* 1909, Nellie Vaughan), and scored her biggest success on the Broadway stage in the title-rôle of Harbach and Hoschna's remusicked version of the Continental hit *Madame Sherry* (1910, Yvonne). She subsequently appeared in the title-rôle of the unsuccessful *Miss Princess* (1912, Princess Polonio) and in the equally short-lived Harold Orlob musical *The Red Canary* (1914, Jane), took the soubrette rôle of Molly Seamore in a revival of *The Geisha* (1913) and starred in Chicago's *Molly and I* (1915), but her only other successful starring rôle in a Broadway musical was that of the Princess Manja in the American production of Cuvillier's *Flora Bella* (1916).

She then moved on to playing character rôles in straight and, occasionally, musical theatre. In 1926 she replaced Madeleine Baxter as Elsie Dayly in a weak musical called *Happy Go Lucky* in time for its Broadway opening, won what notices the piece got, and was promptly herself replaced, but she returned again as the devious Princess von Auen in the short-lived *The Silver Swan* (1929) and, one last time, as Frau Schlitzl in *The Well of Romance* (1930), alongside Norma Terris and Howard Marsh.

Following her retirement from the stage she continued

an involvement in the musical theatre as a member of producer Dwight Deere Wiman's staff, acting as a casting director, talent scout and an adviser on musical productions, notably those with a Continental background.

ABBACADABRA Musical fantasy in 2 acts by Alain and Daniel Boublil. Music by Björn Ulvaeus, Benny Andersson and Stig Anderson. Lyric Theatre, Hammersmith, London, 8 December 1983.

A fairytale musical for children of the television generation. Snow White, Pinocchio, Cinderella, Bluebeard, Aladdin, Alice and the Little Prince are released from their pages by three tots to do battle with the fairy Carabosse – who, in this version, is the hostess of a TV cooking programme – to the accompaniment of the relyricked melodies of such Abba hit songs as 'Money, Money, Money' (which became Pinocchio's 'Mon nez, Mon nez'), 'Dancing Queen' ('The Carabosse Super-Show') and 'Thank You for the Music'. Originally issued as a concept recording featuring Fabienne Thibeault, Daniel Balavoine, Plastic Bertrand and *Les Misérables* originals Maurice Barrier and Marie-France Roussel in its cast, the show was later adapted to the stage by David Wood and Don Black (add material by Ulvaeus and Mike Batt) and mounted by Cameron Mackintosh as a 1983 London Christmas entertainment. The cast included Elaine Paige as the Witch, Michael Praed, B A Robertson and Finola Hughes. It was revived for a second season the following year.

Recordings: original concept recording (WEA), Dutch version (DIL), English cast recordings (Epic, 45rpm)

ABBOTT, George [Francis] (b Forestville, NY, 25 January 1887).

For many years the doyen of the Broadway stage, George Abbott had an outstanding and unparalleledly long career in the theatre, not least in the musical theatre. He made a start in 1913 both as a playwright (*Head of the Family, Man in the Manhole*), and as an actor (*The Misleading Lady*), but concentrated over the following years largely on a performing career. An early connection with the musical theatre came when he appeared as the Second Yeomen in *The Yeomen of the Guard* at the 48th Street Theater in 1915.

Abbott rejoined the ranks of the playwrights when he collaborated with James Gleason on the authorship of the comedy *The Fall Guy* (Eltinge Theatre, 1925), and over the next decade he compounded that success almost annually with a regular stream of new plays, written usually in collaboration. His two major credits from this period were *Broadway* (Broadhurst Theater, 1926), a gangster play illustrated with popular period songs which Abbott, here making his Broadway début as a director, doctored into an international success, and the racing comedy *Three Men on a Horse* (w John Cecil Holm, Playhouse, 1935) which later became regarded as a classic representative of its kind and its period. *Three Men on a Horse* was subsequently made twice into a musical, first as *Banjo Eyes* (Vernon Duke/John Latouche/Joe Quillan, Izzy Ellison, Hollywood Theater, 25 December 1941) with Eddie Cantor in the starring rôle, and again as *Let it Ride!* (Jay Livingstone, Ray Evans/Abram S Ginnes, Eugene O'Neill Theater, 12 October 1961), but in neither case with equivalent success.

Abbott's first venture into the musical theatre was as a director, a function which he had fulfilled with considerable success since the production of *Broadway*, notably with Hecht and MacArthur's famous show-business comedy *Twentieth Century* (1932), a show on which he also made his first venture as a producer. That directorial début was, however, not on what have might been thought of as a normal first musical for a director of plays: it was a mammoth spectacular, Billy Rose's production of Rodgers and Hart's oversized circus musical *Jumbo* (1935). Abbott continued his association with Rodgers and Hart the following year when he not only directed but collaborated with them on the authorship of the dance musical *On Your Toes*. The three teamed up again on *The Boys from Syracuse* (1938, also producer), for which Abbott took a solo credit for the libretto, adapted from Shakespeare's *A Comedy of Errors*, and he subsequently produced and directed the next two Rodgers and Hart shows, *Too Many Girls* (1939) and *Pal Joey* (1940), without on these occasions being ostensibly involved in the construction of the libretti.

During this period, Abbott had also had further play successes, both as an author and as a director, but from this time on he concentrated, in both of these departments, very largely on the musical stage. As in the case of his plays, his libretti were almost always written either in a collaboration or as adaptations of an existing play or novel. *Where's Charley?* (1948), curiously compounded from Brandon Thomas's comedy *Charley's Aunt* for Frank Loesser, and two musicalized novels, *The Pajama Game* (1954) and *Damn Yankees* (1955), with songs by the short-lived team of Adler and Ross, gave him his most significant international successes, although *Fiorello!* (1959), a musical comedy based on the life of New York's Mayor La Guardia, also found success on home ground. *A Tree Grows in Brooklyn*, based on Betty Smith's novel, had a quieter but happy life and *New Girl in Town*, a musical version of Eugene O'Neill's *Anna Christie*, also found a good Broadway run.

From the 1960s, however, his writing was less blessed with success and, after the indifferent *Tenderloin* (1960) and 87 performances of *Flora, the Red Menace* (1965), musical versions of *Anastasia* (*Anya*, 1965) and Shakespeare's *Twelfth Night* (*Music Is*, 1976) counted their runs in days. In 1989 he was credited with the libretto and co-direction (w Donald Saddler) of a musical version of Mary Shelley's *Frankenstein* tale mounted at off-Broadway's York Theater in what must be the only example of a musical written by a centenarian.

Abbott directed all his own musicals, but also staged a number of others, including several major hits of the 1940s and 1950s. These included *Best Foot Forward* (1941, which he produced and on which he seems to have had an uncredited share in the libretto, written by *Three Men on a Horse*'s John Cecil Holm), *Beat the Band* (1942, also producer), the memorable revusical *On the Town* (1944), *Billion Dollar Baby* (1945), *Beggar's Holiday* (1946), *Barefoot Boy with Cheek* (1947), *High Button Shoes* (1947), *Look Ma, I'm Dancin'* (1948, also producer), the highly successful Ethel Merman vehicle *Call Me Madam* (1950), *Wonderful Town* (1953), Rodgers and Hammerstein's *Me and Juliet* (1953) and the comical fairytale *Once Upon a Mattress* (1959). The most successful of these were, however, not those staged under his own management and a brief revival of *On Your Toes* in 1954 virtually marked the end of his career as a musical-comedy producer.

In 1962–3 he directed the Broadway and London productions of the enormously successful *A Funny Thing Happened on the Way to the Forum*, and subsequently staged *Fade Out – Fade In* (1964), *How Now, Dow Jones* (1967), *The Education of H*Y*M*A*N K*A*P*L*A*N* (1968) and *The Fig Leaves are Falling* (1969) for Broadway. He was already in his eighties when he staged a short-lived revival of *The Pajama Game* at the Lunt-Fontanne Theater in 1973, but he made his last Broadway appearance very much more successfully when he directed and co-produced a second revival of *On Your Toes* (Virginia Theater, 1983 and Palace Theatre, London, 1984).

Abbott entered films as early as the 1920s both as an author (notably with *Broadway*) and as a director. He directed the film version of *Too Many Girls* (1940) and acted as producer on Hollywood's versions of *The Pajama Game* (1957) and *Damn Yankees* (1958).

1936 **On Your Toes** (Richard Rodgers/Lorenz Hart/w Rodgers, Hart) Imperial Theater 11 April

1938 **The Boys from Syracuse** (Rodgers/Hart) Alvin Theater 23 November

1948 **Where's Charley?** (Frank Loesser) St James Theater 11 October

1951 **A Tree Grows in Brooklyn** (Arthur Schwartz/Dorothy Fields/w Betty Smith) Alvin Theater 19 April

1954 **The Pajama Game** (Richard Adler, Jerry Ross/w Richard Bissell) St James Theater 13 May

1955 **Damn Yankees** (Adler, Ross/w Douglass Wallop) 46th Street Theater 5 May

1957 **New Girl in Town** (Bob Merrill) 46th Street Theater 14 May

1959 **Fiorello!** (Jerry Bock/Sheldon Harnick/w Jerome Weidman) Broadhurst Theater 23 November

1960 **Tenderloin** (Bock/Harnick/w Weidman) 46th Street Theater 17 October

1965 **Flora, the Red Menace** (John Kander/Fred Ebb/w Robert Russell) Alvin Theater 11 May

1965 **Anya** (Robert Wright, George Forrest/w Guy Bolton) Ziegfeld Theater 29 November

1976 **Music Is** (Adler/Will Holt) St James Theater 20 December

1986 **Tropicana** (Robert Nassif/Peter Napolitano) Musical Theater Works 29 May

1989 **Frankie** (Joseph Turrin/Gloria Nissenson) York Theater 6 October

Autobiography: *Mister Abbott* (Random House, New York, 1963)

THE ABC, or Flossie the Frivolous Musical comedy in 2 acts by 'Richard Henry' (H Chance Newton and Richard Butler). Music by 'Graban' (Granville Bantock), Gustave Chaudoir et al. Grand Theatre, Wolverhampton, 21 March 1898.

Written by the successful burlesque team of 'Richard Henry' with the purpose of providing music-hall star Marie Lloyd with her only stage rôle, *The ABC* was partly composed by Granville Bantock, then a musical director for touring musical-comedy companies but later distinguished as a serious composer and administrator. It had a brief touring life before Miss Lloyd returned to her more natural habitat, the music halls.

ÁBRAHÁM, Pál [Paul] (b Apatin, Hungary, 2 November 1892; d Hamburg, 6 May 1960). The most successful of the Continental composers who attempted to blend traditional European and modern trans-Atlantic styles in the musical theatre of the pre-Hitler years.

After first following studies in the serious musical field, an area in which he also made his earliest attempts as a composer, Ábrahám turned his attention progressively towards lighter music and particularly towards the works of Broadway's songwriters and what was then called jazz. In 1927, he became conductor and house composer at Budapest's principal musical house, the Fővárosi Operett-színház, and there he contributed songs and incidental music to several musical shows of varying kinds, notably an up-to-date score – some original, some borrowed (the credits included the names of Gus Kahn, Harry Akst, de Sylva, Brown and Henderson, Benny Davis and Sidney Holden) and some arranged tunes – for the entertainment *Zenebona*. *Zenebona* won him his first good notices ('a young composer who will make his mark') and the show won a transfer to Vienna under the title *Spektakel* (ad Hans Adler, Paul Frank, Johann Strauss-Theater, 3 October 1928).

Ábrahám confirmed this success with a 1928 *Jazz-Kabaré* and, most effectively, with the 1928 operett *Az utolsó Verebély lány*, a musicalization of the Gábor Drégely comedy hit *Kisasszony férje* (1915) which would in other hands become a Broadway musical as *Little Miss Bluebeard* (1923). *Az utolsó Verebély lány* won considerable hometown success and later earned several revivals.

Ábrahám also provided the score for a musical version of the French farce *La Fille et le garçon*, produced at the Magyar Színház, before he left Budapest in 1930 and moved to Berlin. There he composed the score for what would be his most internationally successful work, *Viktória*. This colourful Hungarian-Japanese piece which combined a dark romanticism and some lightly jazzy dance music in its score, was produced in Budapest later in the same year and subsequently went on to productions in Leipzig, Berlin and Vienna (1930), London (1931), Paris (1933), Australia and many other overseas cities. It has remained a regularly produced favourite in the European musical theatre repertoire and is one of the few pieces of its period and place to win revivals more than half a century on.

The following year, Ábrahám's *Die Blume von Hawaii*, an even more exotic piece which put an Al Jolson-style blackface entertainer alongside its operettic South Pacific lovers, confirmed this initial success, and *Ball im Savoy*, produced in Berlin in 1932, gave him a third consecutive hit. Like *Viktória*, both these pieces won international productions, recordings and, in Germany, films, and both have continued to find further productions up to the present day. *Die Blume von Hawaii*'s imitation American cabaret number, 'My Golden Baby', even became a song success in America itself, as sung by Donald Peers.

Obliged to leave Hitler's Germany at the height of his newly acquired fame, Ábrahám settled in Vienna where, over the next few years, he had three further new Operetten produced without, however, finding the success he had won with his earlier pieces. *Märchen im Grand-Hotel*, a musical version of Alfred Savoir's *La Grande-Duchesse et le garçon d'étage* (Théâtre de l'Avenue, Paris, 15 May 1924 and later to be the basis for Hollywood's *Here Is My Heart*), was seen 65 times at the Theater an der Wien, the oriental *Dschainah* played 57 times at the same house, and the sporting musical *Roxy und ihr Wunderteam* just twice more.

Ábrahám then moved back to Budapest which he had continued to supply with music for such pieces as the comedy with songs *Viki* and the musical comedy *Történnek még csodák* during his absences. A major revival of *Az utolsó Verebély lány* and László Szűcs's production of *Mese a Grand-Hotelben* (aka *A nagyhercegnő és a pincér*) at the Kamara Színház, with Hungarian film favourite Irén Ágay as the grand-duchess of the title, prefaced the production of several new and successful operetts. *3:1 a szerelem javára* with Rózsi Bársony and Oskar Dénes, who had made international successes in *Ball im Savoy*, played for a splendid 73 performances at the Royal Színház. It was followed by *Julia*, with Hanna Honthy as the lady in question and, finally, *Fehér hattyú*, a First-World-War tale of a ballerina's affair with the Grand Duke Constantin, in which another major local star, Sári Fedák, appeared.

Politics once more caught up with the composer, however, and soon he moved on again, leaving Hungary and fleeing to France, where a version of his Vienna piece *Roxy und ihr Wunderteam*, done over by French hands to the extent of including the latest British hit song 'The Lambeth Walk' in the score, was produced at the Théâtre Mogador as *Billy et son équipe*. But, as he continued on to Cuba and, finally, to America, the composer's output faltered and soon ceased altogether. During his years in America the man who had not long since been hailed as one of the coming composers of the European musical theatre, eked out an insecure living as a pianist, and an attempt at a musical play, *Tambourin*, written with fellow exile Alfred Grünwald and 'William J Blake', failed to make it to the stage. In the mid-1950s a movement was mounted in Germany to secure recognition for Ábrahám and his work. This ultimately resulted in the composer returning to Europe where, after several ill and unhappy years, he died in 1960.

The best of Ábrahám's work was produced in a period of some three years between 1930 and 1932 when his three enduring Operetten and the most successful of his film musical scores, *Die Privatsekretärin* (1931) in which Renate Müller memorably performed his 'Ich bin ja heut' so glücklich'/'Today I Am So Happy', all appeared. His music was highly regarded in its time and, alongside the heavily romantic later works of Lehár, his happily showy mixture of operettic elements and fashionable jazzy and South American rhythms proved both theatrically colourful and musically effective, if unlikely to appeal to conservatives.

An Operette in 14 scenes entitled *Wintermelodie*, with a score credited to Ábrahám and libretto by Ladislaus Fodor, was produced at the Landestheater, Salzburg 12 February 1978.

1928 **Zenebona** (László Lakatos, István Bródy) Fővárosi Operett-színház 2 March
1928 **Az utolsó Verebély lány** (Gábor Drégely, Imre Harmath) Fővárosi Operettszinház 13 October
1929 **Szeretem a feleségem** (André Birabeau, Georges Dolley ad Adorján Stella) Magyar Színház 15 June
1930 **Viktória** (aka *Viktoria und ihr Husar*) (Imre Földes, Harmath) Király Színház 21 February
1931 **Die Blume von Hawaii** (Földes ad Alfred Grünwald, Fritz Löhner-Beda) Stadttheater, Leipzig 24 July
1932 **Ball im Savoy** (Grünwald, Löhner-Beda) Grosses Schauspielhaus, Berlin 23 December
1934 **Märchen im Grand-Hotel** (Grünwald, Löhner-Beda) Theater an der Wien, Vienna 29 March
1935 **Viki** (Harmath/Adorján Bónyi) Magyar Színház 26 January
1935 **Történnek még csodák** (Imre Halász, István Békeffy) Magyar Színház 20 April
1935 **Dschainah, das Mädchen aus dem Tanzhaus** (Grünwald, Löhner-Beda) Theater an der Wien, Vienna 20 December
1936 **3:1 a szerelem javára** (Harmath/László Szilágyi, Dezső Kellér) Royal Színház 18 December
1937 **Roxy und ihr Wunderteam** (Grünwald, Hans Weigl) Theater an der Wien, Vienna 25 March
1937 **Júlia** (Harmath/Földes) Városi Színház 23 December
1938 **Fehér hattyú** (Földes) Városi Színház 23 December

ABSCHIEDSWALZER Operette in 2 acts by Hubert Marischka and Rudolf Österreicher. Music by Ludwig Schmidseder. Wiener Bürgertheater, Vienna, 8 September 1949.

Viennese diplomat Ferry Kornegg (Walter Müller) has been engaged for three years to the singer Anita (Friedl Loor), daughter of the celebrated painter Georg Ferdinand Waldmüller (Hubert Marischka). However, the two have an argument, he sends her a letter breaking off their engagement, and soon ends up down the river in Hungary celebrating a new engagement with pretty little Thussy von Szómary (Waltraut Haas). Papa Waldmüller, who has begun a painting of the wedding of Anita and Ferry, to be called 'Hochzeit in Petersdorf', zips back and forth between Vienna and Hungary, and manages affairs so that the pair are finally reunited. Thussy gets personable compensation in the form of Ferry's cousin Laczi (Franz Marischka) and a dowry, and the piece finishes with a staged representation of the completed painting 'Hochzeit in Petersdorf'.

Marischka, now in his 'elder character' period, supplied himself with an effective rôle, and songwriter Schmidseder's attractive, if traditional score, which included the farewell waltz of the title, 'Tanz mit mir ein Walzer', at the head of a number of other waltzes and foxtrots, was an effective illustration to both the Viennese and the Hungarian scenes. The show had a successful first run at the Bürgertheater before going on to other productions in both Austria and Germany.

Germany: Städtische Bühnen, Augsburg 15 March 1953

ACE OF CLUBS Musical play in 2 acts by Noël Coward. Cambridge Theatre, London, 7 July 1950.

An uncharacteristic Coward musical, in which the author dipped into the then fashionable sleazy venues and petty gangster milieux of contemporary London for his characters and action, *Ace of Clubs* mixed the romance of a club singer (Pat Kirkwood) and a sailor (Graham Payn) with a tale about some stolen jewels. The score of the show was a movable one and it had, in fact, been attached to a rather different libretto which as, variously, *Over the Garden Wall*, *Hoi Polloi* and *Come Out to Play*, had failed to find a producer at a period when Coward's fortunes were at less than their peak.

If, hoist on the petard of its author's own reputation, the show did not make a genuine success in its London production (211 performances), it nevertheless turned up its quota of durable revue-style songs: the satirical 'Three Juvenile Delinquents', mocking the weakness of contemporary courts, Miss Kirkwood's cabaret songs 'Josephine' and 'Chase Me, Charlie', Payn's lilting 'Sail

'Away', which would later turn up again in the show of the same title, and the brittle, pasted-in 'I Like America' which subsequently served its writer well in his cabaret act. Miss Kirkwood's pretty 'I'd Never, Never Know' proved the most successful of the lyric music, as soprano Sylvia Cecil, who provided the genuine vocal values in the show in the co-starring rôle of the club owner, was left short of appreciable material.

Recording: original cast (part record *Noël Coward: the Great Shows*) (EMI)

ACHARD, Marcel (b Sainte-Foy-lès-Lyon, 5 July 1899; d Paris, 4 September, 1974).

A successful playwright of comedies (*Jean de la lune, Patate* etc) and a member of the Académie française, Achard dipped on several occasions into the musical theatre, providing the libretto to *La P'tite Lili*, in which Edith Piaf made a venture into the musical theatre, and authoring an adaptation of the famous screenplay *Some Like It Hot*, played at the Théâtre du Châtelet as *La Polka des lampions* with considerable success. He also wrote a less happy piece for the same house which, based on the life of author Eugène Sue, was entitled *Eugène le Mystérieux* on the excuse that Sue had written *Mystères de Paris*. The show's run of 116 performances placed it well behind a musicalization of that same work made a century earlier, Serafino de Ferrari's Venetian opera buffa *Pipele* (Teatro San Benedetto, 25 November 1855).

Achard scripted the film *Valse de Paris*, doing to Offenbach's life what *Das Dreimäderlhaus* had done to Schubert, and Hollywood to many another writer and composer, with the usual minuscule amount of care for things factual. Pierre Fresnay portrayed the composer in memorable style through Achard's invented love affair between Offenbach and Hortense Schneider (Yvonne Printemps). He was also adapter and director of the Hollywood French versions of *Die lustige Witwe* (1934) and *Folies-Bergère* (1935).

Achard's play *Voulez-vous jouez avec moi?* (1923) was musicalized in America as *Come Play With Me* (Dana Suesse/ad Tamara Geva, Halla Stoddard), produced at the York Playhouse 30 April 1959 with Liliane Montevecchi in the principal rôle.

1951 **La P'tite Lili** (Marguerite Monnot) Théâtre de l'ABC 10 March
1961 **La Polka des lampions** (Gérard Calvi) Théâtre du Châtelet 15 December
1964 **Eugène le Mystérieux** (Jean-Michel Damase) Théâtre du Châtelet 7 February

Biography: Lorcey, J: *Marcel Achard* (Editions France Empire, Paris, 1977)

ACKLAND, Joss (b London, 29 February 1928). After an early career spent largely in repertory theatre, followed by a period in South Africa variously as a tea-planter and an actor, Ackland joined Britain's Old Vic company in 1958. His first musical appearance in London came when, as associate director of the Mermaid Theatre, he played the part of Sotmore in their 1962 revival of *Lock Up Your Daughters*. In 1966 he was top-billed in the title-rôle of *Jorrocks* at the New Theatre, scoring a notable personal success as the singing version of the most famous hunting man of English literature.

His next musical rôle – in a career largely devoted to

straight theatre, film and television – was as Fredrik Egermann in the London production of *A Little Night Music* (1975), but his most memorable singing part came in 1978 when he created the rôle of Juan Peron to the Eva of Elaine Paige in *Evita* at the Prince Edward Theatre. In 1983 he appeared as Romain Gary in the unfortunate National Theatre biomusical of *Jean Seberg*, and in 1985 played a lip-smacking musical Captain Hook to the *Peter Pan* of Bonnie Langford in the first London performances of the American musical-comedy version of Barrie's play.

Autobiography: *I Must Be In There Somewhere* (Hodder & Stoughton, London, 1989)

L'ACQUA CHETA Operetta in 3 acts by Augusto Novelli based on his play of the same name. Lyrics by Angelo Nessi. Music by Giuseppe Pietri. Teatro Nazionale, Rome, 27 November 1920.

One of the most successful Italian operettas of its period, *L'acqua cheta* was adapted by Novelli from his successful 1908 play of the same name. The 'still waters' of that title refer to little Florentine Ida (Jole Pacifici) who, in comparison with her sister, Anita (Mimy Aylmer), is a picture of quiet modesty. However, the still waters really do run deep in this case, and Ida has a lover called Alfredo with whom, in the course of the evening, she tries to elope. The elopement is discovered by the comical stable-lad, Stinchi (Enrico Dezan), and the carpenter, Cecco (Vannutelli), but, when all is sung and done, the marriage still takes place.

A piece in a warmly rustic vein, *L'acqua cheta* was illustrated by a delightfully melodic and suitably Italianate score, which ranged from the Mascagani-like tones of its prelude and the beautiful Trio di ricamo (Embroidery trio) to the blatantly catchy sound of the popular canzone. The lively, swinging ensemble 'O com'è bello guidare i cavalli' for Stinchi and Cecco proved the most popular single number.

Recording: selection (Cetra)

THE ACT (ex- *Shine It On*) Musical in 2 acts by George Furth. Lyrics by Fred Ebb. Music by John Kander. Majestic Theater, New York, 29 October 1977.

The Act was mounted as a vehicle for singing and cinema star Liza Minnelli, cast in the rôle of Michelle Craig, a faded film star on the comeback trail as a nightclub singer at Las Vegas's Miramar Hotel. The rôle gave her the chance to perform a series of Kander/Ebb songs made to her measure. Pieces such as 'Shine it On', 'The Money Tree' and 'City Lights' allowed the star to open up in her audience's favourite, stinging style, 'Arthur in the Afternoon' provided a comical moment, and the evening as a whole fulfilled its purpose as a singing, dancing, barnstorming showcase. It also brought its fair share of controversy, notably when it was revealed that the star was leaning even more than had become generally accepted on the use of pre-recorded playback tapes, and then when she took to not playing at all. The Shubert/Feuer and Martin production played 233 Broadway performances.

Recording: original cast (DRG)

ADAM, Adolphe [Charles] (b Paris, 24 July 1803; d Paris, 3 May 1856). Influential producer and composer at the dawning of the modern musical theatre age.

Along with his compatriots Daniel Auber and François Boïeldieu, Adolphe Adam was one of the most successful musicians of the opéra-comique genre, the most sophisticated of the forms of light musical theatre which held the world's stages in the decades prior to the coming of the opéra-bouffe and a more frankly high-spirited style of popular lyric theatre.

Adam's first theatre piece, the one-act *Pierre et Catherine*, was produced at the Opéra-Comique in 1829 and, of the 52 other opéras-comiques large and small which followed, pieces such as *Le Châlet* (1834), *Le Postillon de Longjumeau* (1836), *Le Brasseur de Preston* (1838), *Le Roi d'Yvetot* (1842), *Giralda, ou la nouvelle Psyche* (1850) and *Si j'étais roi* (1852) become internationally played favourites. Several of his shorter works, notably *Les Pantins de Violette* (1856) and *La Poupée de Nuremberg* (1852), were near enough in temperament to the later opérette genre to remain around and share bills and repertoires with the early Offenbach and Hervé works both in France and abroad, whilst the humorous libretto to *Giralda* proved its viability in a later age, subsequently reset as a late 19th-century comic opera by Britain's Bucalossi under the title *Manteaux Noirs* (1882) and by Hungary's Jenő Sztojanovits as *A kis molnárné* (1892).

Adam unsuccessfully founded a Théâtre Lyrique in 1847, but a second attempt in the same vein in 1851 was a splendid success. Under the management of Adam himself, and later under the direction of Carvalho, it provided in the 17 years of its existence a production base for such not-so-desperately-grand operas as *Faust, Mireille, Roméo et Juliette, Les Pêcheurs de perles* and *La Jolie Fille de Perth* by the younger French composers, such almost-opérettes as Aimé Maillart's *Les Dragons de Villars* (1856), and a host of one-act opéras-comiques of which a number were headed in style and subject matter towards the less formal operettic manners of the coming age.

Today Adam is principally remembered for his ballet music, *Giselle*, but he holds an important place in theatre history as one of the principal precursors of the modern musical theatre.

Memoirs: *Souvenirs d'un musicien* (Michel Lévy, Paris, 1857), *Derniers souvenirs d'un musicien* (Michel Lévy, Paris, 1859); Biography: Pougin, A: *Adolphe Adam: sa vie, sa carrière, ses memoires artistiques* (Charpentier, Paris, 1876)

ADAM ET ÈVE

ADAM ET ÈVE   Opérette fantastique in 4 acts by Raoul Toché and Ernest Blum. Music by Gaston Serpette. Théâtre des Nouveautés, Paris, 6 October 1886.

The Parisian extravaganza *Adam et Ève* opened in the Garden of Eden, where Satan (Jules Brasseur) outwits the good spirit Adramalec (Berthelier) and gets Ève (Louise Théo) and Adam (Albert Brasseur) to taste the apple. The guilty Adramalec is condemned to celibacy until his fault is expiated and Adam and Ève have been brought back together. The remaining three acts took in episodes in Ancient Rome (Adamis and Eva), in brigandland Spain (Adamos, the brigand trying to carry off a Spanish Eva) and finally in contemporary France, where the modern artist Saint-Adam finally whisks his Ève away from the clutches of old Baron Sataniel and, thus, releases Adramalec from his painful situation. Marie Lantelme (later the subject of a mysterious death in the Rhine), Mlle

Decrozat and Marguerite Deval were amongst the other ladies of the various eras.

The appearance of Théo as the original Eve, opening the show in the 'nude' (with strategically placed ivy), a lively and well-reviewed Serpette score, and a spectacular production contributed towards a first run of 63 consecutive Paris performances. The show was later produced in Budapest (ad Emil Makai, Dezső Bálint) for a successful run of 31 performances with Gabi Bardi as Eve.

Adam and Eve have been the subject of, or excuse for, a number of other stage works since the days of the mystery plays. An operatic *Adam und Eva* (Theile/C Richter) opened Hamburg's first opera-house in 1678, a Posse mit Gesang, *Adam und Eva*, composed by Carl Binder appeared at the Carltheater in 1859 (25 September), a Schwank mit Gesang by Wilhelm Jacoby and L André played under the same title at Mainz in 1884 (14 December), and an Operette by Hugo Wittmann and Julius Bauer, composed by Carl Weinberger, was produced at the Carltheater, 5 January 1899. Like the French work, this *Adam und Eva* (*Die Seelenwanderung*), wandered through the ages, beginning in an Indian paradise, with Alexander Girardi as its Adam and American soubrette Marie Halton as Eva, and parading its stars through impersonations of Joseph and Mme Potiphar, Sokrates and Xanthippe, and Don Quixote and Dulcinea, under the eye of an ever-disguised, comical Mercury (Siegmund Natzler), before finishing on a present-day backstage episode. It played 52 performances.

Amongst the other musical stage pieces to depict the primal couple have been Cuvillier's one-act opérette *Avant-hier matin* (1905), the opening episode of the three-part Broadway musical *The Apple Tree* (1966), and the 1990 London *Children of Eden* which, in deference to current sensibilities, presented a white Adam (Martin Smith) paired with a black Eve (Shezwae Powell). Paris's *Pom-Pom* (Théâtre de la Potinière, 1928) also visited the Garden of Eden.

Hungary: Népszinház *Ádám és Éva* 10 January 1902

AN ADAMLESS EDEN

AN ADAMLESS EDEN   Comic operetta in 1 act by Savile Clark. Music by Walter Slaughter. Opera Comique, London, 13 December 1882.

An operetta written by men for the all-women troupe run by conductor/composer Lila Clay, *An Adamless Eden* necessarily told of the failure of such a society. The women who have got together and sworn to avoid the 'tyranny of men' soon begin to cheat, and Eden is foresworn.

A successful London season as part of the programme of Miss Clay's company, with Emily Cross, Emma D'Auban and Miss Amalia amongst the foolish ladies and Linda Verner as one of the triumphant men, was followed by several tours, and several productions in America. The first of these was seen at Broadway's Comedy Theater in 1884, played by M B Leavitt's company with Marie Sanger, Pauline Hall, Topsy Venn and Venie Burroughs amongst the cast. A repeat Broadway season was played at the 3rd Avenue Theater in 1885 (1 June), and the show was seen played by ladies' companies in vaudeville programmes and theatres throughout the country for several years.

USA: Comedy Theater 24 November 1884

ADAMS, Frank R[amsey] (b Morrison, Ill, 7 July 1883; d White Lake, Mich, 8 October, 1963). Chicago-based Adams led an eclectic writing career, finding success as a journalist (*Tribune, Examiner, Daily News* etc), an author and novelist, a film scenarist and, in his twenties, as a busy librettist and lyricist for the musical theatre.

As a twenty-year-old student at the University of Chicago, he combined with fellow student Will M Hough on the book and lyrics to a musical, *His Highness the Bey*, with a musical score composed by the already established Joe Howard. Produced at the little local La Salle Theater, the show found a considerable success and, over the following years, the trio's bright, easy-going and, not infrequently, interestingly original musical shows built up some mighty Chicago runs and a lively following on the road. *The Umpire* (1905), *The Time, the Place and the Girl* (1906), *The Girl Question* (1907), and *A Stubborn Cinderella* (1908) proved the most widely appreciated of the set, but not even these, in spite of their years of success around the country, were able to establish themselves in New York where what had become regarded as the native Chicago musical was looked upon with some disdain.

The team's producer Mort Singer was encouraged by the apparent development of Chicago as a strong production centre to build the Princess Theater to permit the staging of additional productions. The new theatre was opened successfully with *A Stubborn Cinderella* in 1908, but the second Howard/Adams/Hough show to play the Princess, *The Prince of To-night* (1909), was the first of the team's nine collaborations to date to win only a lukewarm reception, in spite of the fact that it contained the only song from any of these shows to become a standard. 'I Wonder Who's Kissing Her Now', although presented and published as the work of Adams, Hough and Joe Howard, was later proved to have been composed by the young Harold Orlob.

Orlob joined the team officially for the 1909 *The Flirting Princess*, without producing a second hit song, and the team went further with interpolations in their 1910 *Miss Nobody from Starland* before Howard split from the group. It was, in any case, becoming clear that the vein which had proved so fruitful over the past half-dozen years had begun to run dry.

While his erstwhile partners went their separate ways, Adams abandoned the musical theatre and spent the remainder of his career in alternative writing fields. He provided more than 30 screenplays for early Hollywood films, including such ventures as the Tarzan films and *The Ten Commandments*, and authored a long list of novels. He returned to the theatre rarely, winning one further musical credit when the La Salle Theater management decided to get him to turn his play *Molly and I* into a musical for Lina Abarbanell before its opening night and making a last appearance on a musical playbill when a story of his was adapted by William Cary Duncan and Lewis Allen Browne as the libretto for the flop *Princess April* in 1924 (Ambassador Theater 1 December).

1904 **His Highness the Bey** (Joe Howard/w Will M Hough) La Salle Theater, Chicago 21 November
1905 **The Isle of Bong-Bong** (Howard/w Hough) La Salle Theater, Chicago 14 March
1905 **The Land of Nod** (Howard/w Hough) Opera House, Chicago 17 June; New York Theater, New York 1 April 1907

1905 **The Umpire** (Howard/w Hough) La Salle Theater, Chicago 2 December
1906 **The Time, the Place and the Girl** (Howard/w Hough) La Salle Theater, Chicago 20 August; Wallack's Theater, New York 5 August 1907
1907 **The Girl Question** (Howard/w Hough) La Salle Theater, Chicago 24 August; Wallack's Theater, New York 3 August 1908
1908 **The Honeymoon Trail** (Howard/w Hough) La Salle Theater, Chicago 23 March
1908 **A Stubborn Cinderella** (Howard/w Hough) Princess Theater, Chicago 31 May; Broadway Theater, New York, 25 January 1909
1909 **The Prince of To-night** (Howard/w Hough) Princess Theater, Chicago 9 March
1909 **The Golden Girl** (Howard/w Hough) La Salle Theater, Chicago 16 March
1909 **The Goddess of Liberty** (Howard/w Hough) Princess Theater, Chicago 15 August; Weber's Theater, New York 22 December 1909
1909 **The Flirting Princess** (Harold Orlob, Howard/w Hough) La Salle Theater, Chicago 1 November
1910 **Miss Nobody From Starland** (Howard/w Hough) Princess Theater, Chicago 31 January
1911 **The Heartbreakers** (Orlob, Melville Gideon/w Hough) Princess Theater, Chicago 30 May
1915 **Molly and I** (Louis Hirsch) La Salle Theater, Chicago 31 August

ADAMS, Lee [Richard] (b Mansfield, Ohio, 14 August 1924). Lyricist to a pair of Broadway hits.

Whilst continuing early work in newspaper, magazine, TV and radio journalism, the young Lee Adams began a song-writing collaboration with composer Charles Strouse which led to a series of published songs, special material for television and nightclub performers of the early 1950s and, from 1954, contributions to theatrical revue. From writing stage material for a summer resort in the Adirondacks, they progressed to the New York theatre, where they placed material in Ben Bagley's *The Littlest Revue* (1956) and *Shoestring '57*, *The Ziegfeld Follies of 1956* and *Catch a Star* before joining a third habitué of the off-Broadway revue, librettist Michael Stewart, to write a full-scale musical.

Bye Bye Birdie (1960), which kidded the newish rock and roll craze, won its authors a Tony Award, racked up a 607-performance Broadway run, and proved a sizeable international success ('Kids', 'Put on a Happy Face', 'A Lot of Livin' to Do'). The Adams–Strouse team followed up with the scores for seven further musicals over the next two decades or so. Of these, *Applause*, a musicalization of the screenplay *All About Eve* and its source novel, which starred Lauren Bacall in a first-rate Broadway-Big-Momma rôle, proved the most generally successful (Tony Award), whilst New York and London also welcomed a musical version of the play *Golden Boy* with Sammy Davis jr featured as a black singing version of Clifford Odets's ill-fated boxer.

All American (1962), with a libretto by Mel Brooks and a cast headed by Ray Bolger, and a musical version of the Superman comic strips (predating the widely publicized modern films of the same subject) both found some adherents but insufficient audiences, but an effort to bring a singing, dancing Queen Victoria to the London stage in *I and Albert* foundered nastily. Two later shows, the last an attempt to mount a sequel to *Bye Bye Birdie*, were first-week failures. Adams's more recent collaborations with Albert Hague and Mitch Leigh produced an adaptation of an O Henry story entitled *Flim Flam*, and a musical biography of Mike Todd mounted in Philadelphia in 1988, and remounted (as *Ain't Broadway Grand*) in New Fairfield, Connecticut, in 1992, prior to Broadway.

Non-theatre work has included film and television material, including the theme song to the television series *All in the Family*.

1960 **Bye Bye Birdie** (Charles Strouse/Michael Stewart) Martin Beck Theater 14 April
1962 **All American** (Strouse/Mel Brooks) Winter Garden Theater 19 March
1964 **Golden Boy** (Strouse/Clifford Odets, William Gibson) Majestic Theater 20 October
1966 **It's a Bird It's a Plane It's Superman** (Strouse/David Newman, Robert Benton) Alvin Theater 29 March
1970 **Applause** (Strouse/Adolph Green, Betty Comden) Palace Theater 30 March
1972 **I and Albert** (Strouse/Jay Presson Allen) Piccadilly Theatre, London 6 November
1978 **A Broadway Musical** (Strouse/William F Brown) Lunt-Fontanne Theater 21 December
1981 **Bring Back Birdie** (Strouse/Stewart) Martin Beck Theater 5 March
1987 **Flim-Flam** (Albert Hague/Milburn Smith)
1988 **Ain't Broadway Grand** (ex-*Mike*) (Mitch Leigh/Thomas Meehan) Walnut Street Theater, Philadelphia 26 March; Lunt-Fontanne Theater, New York 18 April 1993

ADDIO GIOVINEZZA Operetta in 3 acts by Camasio and Oxilia. Music by Giuseppe Pietri. Politeama Goldoni, Livorno, 20 January 1915; Teatro Diana, Rome, 20 April 1915.

Pietri's earliest operetta success, and one of the most attractive and enduring pieces from the happiest years of the Italian musical theatre, *Addio giovinezza* was written in the warmly folky manner of the zarzuela rather than the glitzy revusical style currently invading the musical theatre. Its characters, too, came from the everyday world which zarzuela writers favoured. The little modista, Dorina, falls in love with the student, Mario, who is a lodger in her home, but the young lad, discovering life, seems to be more likely to appreciate the charms of the worldly Elena. Eventually, of course, Mario graduates and says 'addio' to his youthful flings, and Dorina says goodbye, too, to 'giovinezza' and to 'amor'.

Pietri's attractively simple music illustrated the tale aptly. The score, which opened and closed with a quote from 'Gaudeamus', mixed almost light-operatic moments with jaunty student and dancing ones, but it was the former group which produced the favourite pieces: a wistful solo for Dorina, with a gentle echo of *Cavalleria Rusticana* to it ('Non vedo, non senti'), and the unhurriedly waltzing duo for Mario and Dorina ('Tu m'ami, è già qualcosa'). A second waltz duo, with Elena ('Ma lei non è curioso'), was in a less romantic vein, whilst a jaunty quintet with imitation trumpets, a duo for Dorina and the soubret-comic, Leone, and marches and choruses in the student style went to make up the contrasting moments.

Recording: selection (part record) (EDM)

ADE, George (b Kentland, Ind, 9 February 1866; d Brook, Ind, 16 May 1944).

A highly reputed comic writer who worked as a journalist on the Chicago *Record* between 1890 and 1900 before moving into the theatre, Ade evinced a particular interest in popular slang, a subject on which he wrote analytically whilst also making active use of its jauntier phrases in his successful 'Fables in Slang' (subsequently filmed as a series of shorts by Essanay) and, later, in his books, plays and libretti.

Ade made his theatrical début, somewhat diffidently, with the libretto for the San Francisco musical *The Night of the Fourth*. By the time it made its brief New York appearance, his name had slipped from the bill. However, when Henry Savage commissioned him to write a musical for the Chicago stage, in tandem with the young English composer Alfred Wathall, he produced the colourful and successful *The Sultan of Sulu* and, finding the work both lucrative and appealing, began to devote more conscientious energies to the musical stage, at first in Chicago and then further East.

Of his three initial pieces for Chicago, *The Sultan of Sulu* and *The Sho-Gun* both cashed in on the standard English musical-comedy formula – a tale of dashing home-town boys and girls, plonked down in exotic and scenery-worthy locations amid curious foreigners and, in particular, comico-threatening potentates, illustrated by bright music and low comedy – and both were highly successful. *The Sultan of Sulu* was clearly recognized as amongst the best of the American musical comedies of the period, whilst *The Sho-Gun* was played as far afield as Hungary (where, curiously, its libretto was attributed to cast member Clyde McKinley) and both pieces survived for many years on the American touring circuits. The third piece, *Peggy from Paris*, yielded little to either, clocking up 16 weeks in Chicago and 15 in Boston before a fair New York showing during which one critic opined that, although uneven, its best bits were the best musical comedy yet to have come out of the native American popular lyric theatre.

Ade established himself, simultaneously, as an author of straight plays, scoring particular successes with *The County Chairman* (1903) and *The College Widow* (1904), but he subsequently found most of his best results with musical pieces: two vehicles for popular impersonator-cum-soubrette Elsie Janis – *The Fair Co-Ed*, set in the same college precincts as *The College Widow*, and *The Slim Princess* – and one for the top comedy team of Montgomery and Stone (*The Old Town*). He also authored a musical, *The City Chap* (1910), with a score by Benjamin Hapgood Burt, for Purdue University, and a musical comedy, *The Hermits on Main Street* (23 May 1921, music: Milton Lusk) to be played at the Hermit's Club Frolic at Cleveland's Opera House. He eventually renounced the stage, and retired to spend his winters in Florida and summers on his Indiana farm.

The College Widow was later used as the source for the successful musical *Leave it to Jane* (Longacre Theater, 28 August 1917, Jerome Kern/P G Wodehouse, Guy Bolton).

1900 **The Night of the Fourth** (Max Hoffman/J Sherrie Matthews) San Francisco August; Victoria Theater, New York 21 January 1901
1902 **The Sultan of Sulu** (Alfred G Wathall) Studebaker Theater, Chicago 11 March; Wallack's Theater, New York 29 December

1903 **Peggy from Paris** (William Lorraine) Studebaker Theater, Chicago 31 January; Wallack's Theater, New York 10 September
1904 **The Sho-Gun** (Gustav Luders) Studebaker Theater, Chicago 4 April; Wallack's Theater, New York 29 December
1909 **The Fair Co-Ed** (Luders) Knickerbocker Theater 1 February
1910 **The Old Town** (Luders) Globe Theater 10 January
1911 **The Slim Princess** (Leslie Stuart/w Henry Blossom) Globe Theater 2 January

Biography: Kelly, F C: *George Ade, Warmhearted Satirist* (Bobbs-Merrill, Indianapolis, 1947)

ADLER, Richard (b New York, 3 August 1921). Songwriter of a pair of major hits of the Broadway 1950s.

The son of a musician, Adler had no regular musical training himself but, in the years following a wartime navy stint, he turned his hand to writing songs. In 1950, he teamed up with singer-songwriter Jerry Ross, who had had little more success than Adler in getting his work placed anywhere that it might be significantly heard. Together the two wrote words and music for the radio programmes *Broadway Scrapbook* and *Stop the Music* as well as some special material for various artists, and as a result came to the notice of Frank Loesser. Promoted by Loesser, Adler and Ross had their first song hit with 'From Rags to Riches', sung by Tony Bennett and nearly 20 years later re-popularized by Elvis Presley, and they then moved into the theatre to provide the songs, first, for the revue *John Murray Anderson's Almanac* (1953), and then for two highly successful Broadway musicals. *The Pajama Game* (1954) and *Damn Yankees* (1955) were both played internationally after long Broadway runs; each produced a pair of hit songs ('Hey There', 'Hernando's Hideaway', 'Heart', 'Whatever Lola Wants'), and both became Hollywood films.

After Ross's premature death in 1955, Adler worked principally in television (*The Gift of the Magi, Little Women, Olympus 7-0000*) and in commercials, returning to the theatre, after a mooted musical version of Somerset Maugham's *Of Human Bondage* failed to eventuate, only for the short-lived *Kwamina* (1961), *A Mother's Kisses* (1968), which folded prior to Broadway, and *Music Is* (1976), a quick-failure musical version of *Twelfth Night*. He subsequently turned to orchestral and instrumental writing (*Memory of Childhood, Retrospective, Yellowstone, Wilderness Suite, The Lady Remembers*).

Adler, who had ventured early into production, also co-produced a 1973 remounting of *The Pajama Game* and the Richard Rodgers musical *Rex* (1976), both without success.

He was married for a period to vocalist Sally Ann Howes, and his son from an earlier marriage, Christopher Adler (b October 1955; d New York, 30 November 1984), wrote for the variety show *Shirley Maclaine on Broadway* (1984, w Marvin Hamlisch), for the one-man show *Herman van Veen: All of Him*, and was the lyricist for the unsuccessful musical *Jean Seberg* (Hamlisch/Julian Barry, National Theatre, London, 1983, 'based on an original idea by Christopher Adler').

1954 **The Pajama Game** (w Jerry Ross/George Abbott, Richard Bissell) St James Theater 13 May
1955 **Damn Yankees** (w Ross/Abbott, Douglas Wallop) 46th Street Theater 5 May

1961 **Kwamina** (Robert Alan Arthur) 54th Street Theater 23 October
1968 **A Mother's Kisses** (Bruce Jay Friedman) Shubert Theater, New Haven 23 September
1976 **Music Is** (Will Holt, Abbott) St James Theater 20 December

Autobiography: *You Gotta Have Heart* (Donald I Fine, New York, 1990)

ADONIS Burlesque [a perversion of common sense] in 2 acts by Edward E Rice and William Gill (later credited to Gill and Henry E Dixey). Original music by E E Rice. Selected music 'cheerfully contributed by Beethoven, Audran, Suppé, Planquette, Offenbach, Strauss, Mozart, Haydn, Dave Braham, John Eller, Henry Sator and many others too numerous to individualize'. Hooley's Theater, Chicago, 6 July 1884; Bijou Theater, New York, 4 September 1884.

The most successful pasticcio burlesque/extravaganza of the early American musical theatre, *Adonis* took the familiar subject matter so effectively used, in particular, in the libretto to the Viennese Operette *Die schöne Galathee* (itself borrowed from Massé's comic opera *Galathée*) and gave it the kind of everything-including-the-kitchen-sink burlesque treatment favoured in the 1870s and early 1880s. In this version, the statue which comes to life is not a beautiful maiden, but Adonis (Henry E Dixey), a delectable lad with nude knees. Like Galathee, he is lusted after by everyone who comes in his path, beginning with his sculptress, Talamea (Lillie Grubb), and her patroness, the Duchess of Area (Jennie Reiffarth), but his own fancies settle on the extremely simple, broad-beamed Rosetta Turke (Amelia Summerville). He gambols through a variety of disguises in his flight from the lusty ladies of the cast, from the villainous Marquis de Baccarat (Herbert Gresham, also director), and in pursuit of Rosetta, but it all finally gets too much for him, and like Galathee, Niobe and all his other theatrical predecessors in the stone-to-flesh stakes, he turns back into a statue for a bit of peace and quiet.

The principal raison d'être of *Adonis* was to allow Dixey the opportunity to indulge in a series of songs, dances, disguises and impersonations – including a lengthy impression of everybody's favourite impersonee, Henry Irving – and his initial success in Chicago, followed by an even greater one when the show was taken to New York, earned him the right to expand and elasticize his rôle at will. The most effective musical part of this expansion was the song 'It's English, You Know', one of several composed by Rice ('I'm O'Donohue from Nowhere', 'The Wall Street Broker') to be added to the original score of pasticcio songs in which Dixey introduced himself, to the strains of Arthur Sullivan's *Iolanthe* music, as 'A Most Susceptible Statue'. Rice's song became both a hit of the time and a popular catchphrase and was promptly lifted by other artists to be interpolated into other pasticcio shows.

The season spent by *Adonis* in Chicago meant that, in contrast to most pieces of the time, the show arrived in New York in a thoroughly worked-in condition. There the slick and funny entertainment, Dixey's handsome face, wavy forelock and (apparently) naked thighs, all put to good use in a star part made to order, helped *Adonis* to an immense popularity and a very long run. It scored a famous Broadway first when the 500th New York performance was reached on 7 January 1886, and another when the record-breaking last was seen on 17 April (603 performances) before the cast – still headed by Dixey, Gresham and Misses Summerville and Grubb, and with Annie Alliston now playing the Duchess of Area, set off for England and a season at the Gaiety Theatre.

London, however, had no need for old-fashioned burlesque (Gaiety supremo Hollingshead called *Adonis* simply 'a variety show'), especially at a theatre which had just hosted the red-hot 'new burlesque' *Little Jack Sheppard*, nor for yet another imitation of Henry Irving (people had been 'doing' him in London eternally). *Adonis* moved out of the Gaiety after 105 summer-season performances to disappointing houses, leaving the new manager, George Edwardes, to replace it with a success which would outscore even the long-run record won by Dixey on Broadway: the comedy opera *Dorothy*.

Dixey and his show (for which he was now billed as part-author, alongside Rice as 'composer'), however, still had plenty of life in them. If London didn't want them, America did. Dixey reprised *Adonis* off and on for two decades, returning for brief visits to Broadway in September 1886 (5th Avenue Theater), 1888 (Star Theater, 12 November), 1892 (Casino Theater, 18 April), 1894 (Palmer's Theater, 7 May) and 1899 (Bijou Theater, 9 May) as part of his touring schedule.

In Australia, what seem to have been the only performances of what was clearly a much personalized version of *Adonis* were played by the supreme female impersonator Francis Leon, appearing for once in something other than a skirt for a half of a programme which was completed by his well-known interpretation of the predatory widow in *His Grace the Duke*.

At the height of its fame, *Adonis* suffered that fate of only the most famous of burlesques – it was itself burlesqued both as *A-Donis* (Fred Solomon/H M Pitts, 1887) and, in minstrelized form, as a burnt-cork extravaganza called *Black Adonis*.

UK: Gaiety Theatre 31 May 1886; Australia: Nugget Theatre, Melbourne 1885

AFGAR, ou Les Loisirs andalous Opérette in 2 acts by André Barde and Michel Carré fils. Music by Charles Cuvillier. Théâtre des Capucines, Paris, 2 April 1909.

Barde and Carré's libretto left little doubt as to what the Andalous did with their 'loisirs'. In their story, the sultan Afgar (Armand Berthez), unable, after years of over-exertion, to fulfil his haremic duties, appoints a particularly handsome captive (Henri Defreyn) to deputize and, at peril of impaling, to repopulate the land with little Afgars. However, in their years of marital deprivation, the ladies of the harem, headed by Zaydée (Marguerite Deval), have made themselves alternative arrangements. The young Don Juan finds himself first balked and then, when Zaydée turns amorous at the same time that his own fiancée Isilda turns up as the newest addition to the harem, in a nicer dilemma. His problems are solved only when Afgar regains his virility, leaving Don Juan and his Isilda to escape to less hectic climes.

The tale was set to a Cuvillier score which was often curiously un-French in tone. It was neither in the style of the turn-of-the-century French opérette, nor of the song-writers' musical comedy which would soon take over the Paris stage, but hovered somewhere in between. Several of the numbers – solos and ensembles – had a seeming tinge of the English to them: at moments Cuvillier's often pretty but rarely adventurous melodies held echoes of Daly's theatre. At Daly's, however, the music was never set to lyrics as wickedly witty as those of André Barde.

Afgar proved highly successful entertainment at the little Théâtre des Capucines, from where it moved liberally into provincial theatres and, eventually, overseas productions. Ten years on, following Cuvillier's London triumph with *The Lilac Domino*, C B Cochran produced *Afgar* (ad Fred Thompson, Worton David) in Britain with Alice Delysia starred as Zaydée in a version which had, not unexpectedly, undergone some severe textual whitewashing. The songs (lyrics: Douglas Furber), mostly by Cuvillier – some old, some new, some *Afgar* – included Irving Berlin's 'You'd Be Surprised' and Fred Fisher's 'Dardanella' amongst the successful interpolations performed by Delysia for 300 performances. Baritone Harry Welchman (Don Juan jr), John Humphries (Afgar), newcomer Marie Burke (Isilda) and Lupino Lane (Coucourli) completed the star team of a show in which all that was left for the Lord Chamberlain to object to was the dress worn by the dancer Mona Païva.

Morris Gest, who had recently run uncomfortably into officialdom over his highly sexed production of the Pierre Louÿs-based extravaganza *Aphrodite*, took up Cochran's production and exported it, Delysia, Lane and W H Rawlins (Afgar) to America. There, with its now less recognizable score heavily added to by Tierney and Joseph McCarthy ('Why Don't You?' etc), and local cast-members Irving Beebe (Don Juan jr) and Frances Cameron (Isilda) in support, *Afgar* achieved another good run (171 performances).

The show returned to Paris, in 1919 at the Théâtre Antoine, and in 1947 it was brought back again at the little Théâtre Monceau under the management of Gil Roland and Pierre Jourdan, in a new version by Jean de Letraz, with the two managers featuring themselves alongside Catherine Gay (Zaydée), Andrée Grandjean (Isilda), a speciality belly dancer and a piano accompaniment.

UK: London Pavilion 17 September 1919; USA: Central Theater 8 November 1920

L'AFRICAINE, or The Queen of the Cannibal Islands Operatic burlesque in 5 scenes by F C Burnand. Music by Frank Musgrave. Strand Theatre, London, 18 November 1865.

The second of Burnand and Musgrave's original British opéras-bouffes, *L'Africaine* – burlesquing Meyerbeer's opera – was a little more substantial than the first, *Windsor Castle*, but built and written on the same extravagant lines. Thomas Thorne played the heroine, Selika, in nigger-minstrel blackface, the comedians J D Stoyle and David James were Vasco da Gama and Nelusko, and the theatre's principal boy, Miss Raynham, was Don Pedro, in a piece which Burnand evolved in such a way as to include each of the artists' special turns alongside a score which ranged from the burlesque operatic to the bones.

L'Africaine proved a great success for the Swanborough family's Strand Theatre (88 performances), leading to the hope that a British school of original musical burlesques in the vein of Offenbach's greatest triumphs might develop

11

there. However, having been innovative, the Swan-boroughs found that their public apparently preferred familiar music as the accompaniment to their burlesques, and they returned to the old habit of decorating their entertainments with popular tunes. Although they later revived *L'Africaine* (Strand Theatre, 15 April 1876), there were but few further original musical pieces produced under their régime.

USA: Euclid Avenue Opera House, Cleveland 22 February 1876

DIE AFRIKAREISE Operette in 3 acts by Richard Genée and Moritz West. Music by Franz von Suppé. Theater an der Wien, Vienna, 17 March 1883.

The initial production of *Die Afrikareise* followed not only behind Suppe's own greatest successes (*Boccaccio*, *Gasparone*, *Donna Juanita*), but also right behind the Theater an der Wien's overwhelming triumph with the first run of Millöcker's *Der Bettelstudent* and, although it was unable to come up to the level of success of these enduring shows, it nevertheless had a respectable first run of a month in Vienna and won a number of further productions.

Genée and West's story dealt with a dubious adventurer called Miradello (Alexander Girardi) who, stranded penni-less in Cairo, is paid to pose as the husband of Titania Fanfani (Karoline Finaly) when that lady needs to produce a husband in order to claim her inheritance of two million local crowns. However, her uncle, Fanfani Pasha (Karl Blasel), who is supposed to deliver, has squandered the money and, as part of his attempts to hide the fact, whisks the couple away to his villa. Miradello's sweetheart Tessa (Marie-Theresia Massa) and her mother Buccametta (Therese Schäfer) turn up, Titania falls in love with a Bedouin chief, Antarsid (Josef Joseffy), and all sorts of amorous and kidnapping complications ensue before the right couples are paired up. The naughty Pasha suffers the traditional operettic fate of his kind and is lumbered with the garrulous Buccametta.

Following its original Vienna run, the piece was pro-duced in Germany – playing in Nuremberg, Lübeck, Teplitz and Stettin before finding a spot in the repertoire at the Friedrich-Wilhelmstädtisches Theater in Berlin – and in Hungary (ad Lajos Evva, Jenő Rákosi). It was par-ticularly well received in America, at first in a German-language production mounted at the Thalia Theater with no less a star than Marie Geistinger playing Titania along-side Alexander Klein (Miradello), Ernst Schütz (Antarsid), Emma Seebold (Tessa) and Thaller (Fanfani), and then in John and James Duff's English-language production. Marie Conron (Titania), Charles Stanley (Fanfani), A L King (Antarsid) and Mae St John (Tessa) played alongside Klein, repeating his rôle in English, for just under three months of a season enlivened by the English-language début of Emma Seebold who, having played Tessa at the Thalia, apparently now took turns at playing both Titania and Antarsid.

A Trip to Africa returned to Broadway's Standard Theater in 1887 (11 April) when Lillian Russell starred as Titania in a high-powered cast including J H Ryley (Fan-fani), Eugene Oudin (Antarsid), C W Dungan (Miradello) and Zelda Seguin (Buccametta) for a five-week season, in 1889 at the German-language Terrace Garten, and again as late as 1898 when the Castle Square Opera Company

included it in their repertoire season. In this production the young Raymond Hitchcock appeared as Fanfani Pasha, with the unrisen Frank Moulan in the tiny rôle of the peddler Nakid, first played in America by ex-D'Oyly Carte man Fred Clifton.

Die Afrikareise was revived in Vienna in a revised version, with a new libretto by Fritz Lunzer, at the Wiener Bürger-theater (14 June 1924) with Grete Holm (Titania), Fritz Imhoff (Miradello), Robert Nästlberger (Antarsid) and Bruno Wiesner (Fanfani) and another remade version was produced at Berlin's Theater des Volkes in 1936 (ad Arthur Bauckner, Andreas Zeltner) under the title *Aben-teuer in Afrika* (17 October).

Germany: Saison Theater, Nuremberg 10 June 1883, Friedrich-Wilhelmstädtisches Theater, Berlin 30 January 1884; Hung-ary: Népszinház *Afrikautazó* 25 September 1883; USA: Thalia-Theater (Ger) 27 December 1883, Standard Theater *A Trip to Africa* 23 November 1884

AFTER THE BALL Musical play (operette) in 3 (later 2) acts by Noël Coward, based on Oscar Wilde's *Lady Windermere's Fan*. Globe Theatre, London, 10 June 1954.

Coward's musical adaptation of Wilde's popular play suffered badly from the remoulding that was made due to its casting: Mary Ellis, cast as the pivotal Mrs Erlynne, proved over-parted vocally, leading to her rôle being musi-cally cut on the run in to London, while what had been, in the play, the peripheral rôle of Mr Hopper (Graham Payn) was unsuitably enlarged, and Seamus Locke, the dashing Irish tenor, proved no actor in what should have been the important rôle of Darlington. Many squalls and alterations after its out-of-town opening, the show reached London to a lukewarm reception and an indifferent run of 188 per-formances. Like Coward's other less-than-successful stage works, the show nevertheless had its takeaway gems: the comical 'A Little Something on a Tray', and 'Why Is It Always the Woman Who Pays?', Payn's tongue-in-cheek chanty, and the melodious 'I Knew That You Would Be My Love' sung by Lord and Lady Windermere (Peter Graves, Vanessa Lee), but the piece as a whole proved to have only a little appeal.

USA: Lambertville, NJ, 2 August 1955
Recording: original cast (Philips)

AFTER THE GIRL Revusical comedy in 2 acts by Paul Rubens. Lyrics by Percy Greenbank and Paul Rubens. Music by Paul Rubens. Gaiety Theatre, London, 7 Feb-ruary 1914.

The last of the 'Girl' musicals at the Gaiety Theatre, this semi-plotless entertainment showed the rising influence of the newly fashionable variety-revue shows both in its style and its subtitle. With George Edwardes ill and dying, his stage director Pat Malone took over the effective production of this Paul Rubens musical which was, in essence, little more than a series of song, dance and comedy scenes strung together around the character of Miss Doris Pitt (Isobel Elsom) as she was – for various reasons, or none at all – chased by much of the rest of the cast (Lew Hearn and Bonita, Mabel Sealby, Mlle Caumont, Guy Le Feuvre, Willie Stephens) through various picturesque Continental towns. In spite of plenty of lavish production detail and some competent work in Rubens's script and songs, *After the Girl* – with none of the old Gaiety big names in its bill – failed to catch on with

Plate 1. **After the Ball**: *Peter Graves and Vanessa Lee as the musical Lord and Lady Windermere.*

London audiences and closed after 105 performances, ending an era at the Gaiety Theatre.

The show did, however, win itself productions in areas where Gaiety shows had become popular fare, including a mounting in Australia where Thelma Raye was featured as Doris and her pursuers included veteran Maggie Moore as Mrs Pitt.

Australia: His Majesty's Theatre, Sydney 7 August 1915

AGES AGO   Musical legend in 1 act by W S Gilbert. Music by Frederic Clay. Gallery of Illustration, London, 22 November 1869.

A short comic piece written by Gilbert and Clay for the German Reed family entertainment at the Gallery of Illustration, *Ages Ago* featured a scene in which the ancestral paintings of Castle Cockalcckic came to life to point out to penniless Columbus Hebblethwaite (Arthur Cecil) where he might find the proof of his ownership of the castle. Gilbert later reused the conceit in his full-length *Ruddigore*. Reed himself played Sir Ebenezer Tare, Fanny Holland his daughter and Hebblethwaite's beloved, Rose, Mrs Reed was the housekeeper Mistress Maggie McMotherly and Edward Connell the servant, Angus McTavish, all four doubling as the paintings in the central scene.

Set with a delightful comic operetta score, *Ages Ago* proved to be one of the German Reeds' greatest successes and it was played for several seasons as part of their entertain-

ment (Gallery of Illustration (abridged) 11 July 1870, St George's Hall 20 April 1874, 21 November 1882) whilst also getting showings in America and Australia, where it was played, as in London, in a double bill with *Cox and Box*. The most recent London performance was given by Morley Opera at King's College 4 and 6 June 1988.

USA: Bijou Theater 31 March 1880; Australia: Victoria Hall, Sydney 3 February 1882

AGGIUNGI UN POSTO A TAVOLA   Musical comedy in 2 acts by Pietro Garinei, Sandro Giovannini and Iaia Fiastri based on *After Me the Deluge* by 'David Forrest'. Music by Armando Trovaioli. Teatro Sistina, Rome, 8 December 1974.

The most widely successful of the many musical plays produced by Italy's Garinei and Giovannini, *Aggiungi un posto a tavola* (bring up a chair to the table) was based on an English novel following the religious and amorous predicaments of a pretty priest (Johnny Dorelli) summoned by the ringing off-stage voice of God (Renato Turi) to be the Noah of the 20th century. In spite of unbelievers, headed by the local low comedy mayor (Paolo Panelli) and distracting temptations of the flesh as represented by ingénue Clementina (Daniela Goggi), he builds his ark and ultimately manages to save the world from a second inundation.

The show's Italian production broke every local record with a run of 630 performances, and Spain (*El Diluvio que viene* ad Giorgi, Damasco), Mexico and South America (Chile, Argentine, Venezuela, Brazil) took with a vigorous will to the show's priestly comedy and catchy melodies, its on-stage construction of a vast ark, and its final visitation by a dove loosed from the gallery. The show went down less well in less Latin countries, particularly in Britain (ad 'David Forrest', Leslie Bricusse), where the celibacy of the priesthood, as represented again by Dorelli until a street accident had him replaced by Australian Andrew Sharp and then by Germany's Freddy Quinn, was hardly a burning topic, and where some of its other comedy, staging and translation seemed too unsophisticated.

Quinn starred in a production in Germany (where Garinei and Giovannini's works found regular productions), which was entitled *Himmel Arche und Wolkenbruch* (ad Peter Turrini, Olympia Gineri, Peter Orthofer), whilst Vienna's Theater an der Wien took a change from its run of British and American musicals to mount *Evviva amico*. The show was revived in Italy in 1990.

Austria: Theater an der Wien *Evviva amico* 1976; Germany: Lubeck *Himmel Arche und Wolkenbruck*; UK: Adelphi Theatre *Beyond the Rainbow* 9 November 1978

Recordings: original cast (CGD, 2 records), London cast (MCA), Spanish cast (EMI/Regal, 2 records), Mexican cast (EMI, 2 records), Italian revival cast (CGD, 2 records)

AHLERS, Anny   (b Hamburg, 21 December 1907; d London, 26 March 1933).

Born into a circus family, Anny Ahlers first went on the stage at the age of four. After juvenile appearances in Hamburg and, following the war, in Vienna, she worked as a chorus dancer and then a singer, graduated to small rôles, and made her earliest adult appearances in Hamburg as an 18-year-old Venus in *Orpheus in der Unterwelt* and in Krefeld in the title-rôle of *Gräfin Mariza*.

The red-haired, blue-eyed singer then progressed to

Breslau where she made a considerable success in the rôle of Amy in the original production of Künneke's *Lady Hamilton*, and she was subsequently introduced to Vienna as a leading lady in the title-rôle of a revival of Fall's *Madame Pompadour* and to Berlin as Barberina in Erik Charell's spectacular Strauss pasticcio *Casanova* (1928). She played in Vienna in 1929–30 in revivals of *Die Bajadere* (Odette) and *Der lustige Krieg* (Violetta), in the Vienna productions of *Das Veilchen vom Montmartre* (Ninon) and *Hotel Stadt-Lemberg* (Anna), then at Berlin's Metropol-theater in the title-rôle of *Viktoria und ihr Husar*, in *Der Zarewitsch*, as the original Princess Laya in Ábrahám's *Die Blume von Hawaii*, in *Der Vogelhändler*, and opposite Richard Tauber as the heroine of the Johann Strauss pasticcio *Der Lied der Liebe*. She also appeared on the musical screen as *Die Marquise von Pompadour* (1931).

In 1932 she went to London to play Jeanne, the title-rôle of the revised version of Millöcker's *Gräfin Dubarry* (*Die Dubarry*) created in Berlin by Gitta Alpár. She scored a great personal success, but 11 months into the show's long run, the 26-year-old star committed suicide by throwing herself from the window of her Duchess Street lodgings.

AIMÉE, Marie [TRONCHON, Marie Aimée] (b Algiers, 1852; d Paris, 2 October 1887). French actress and singer who became America's foremost star of opéra-bouffe.

The young Mlle Aimée is said to have made her first theatrical appearance in Rio de Janeiro at the age of 14, but before long she was to be seen starring on the stages of Paris. As a teenager, she created the lead ingénue rôles of Princess Girandole in Delibes's *La Cour du Roi Pétaud* (1869) and Fiorella in Offenbach's *Les Brigands* (1869) at the Théâtre des Variétés where she became amorously linked with the manager, Eugène Bertrand. She starred opposite José Dupuis as Loïse in *Le Beau Dunois* (1870) and replaced the temperamental Hortense Schneider during rehearsals in the title-rôle of Margot in the first production of Offenbach's relatively unsuccessful *La Boulangère a des écus*. Following this incident Schneider was credited with the famous pun against Bertrand, 'Beaucoup lui sera pardonné parce qui'il a ... Aimée'.

Aimée toured through Europe and then, carried on the crest of the opéra-bouffe wave and sped on her way by the Franco-Prussian war, she took an engagement to play opéra-bouffe in America. She made her début at New York's Grand Opera House on 21 December 1870, under the management of Messrs Grau and Chizzola, as Boulotte in *Barbe-Bleue*. The new French star was greeted with great acclaim and thereafter she toured America widely and continuously through the 1870s, at the head of her own company, with a large repertoire of opéras-bouffes and -comiques. The company made regular visits to New York to perform the latest pieces and a quick-changing bill of former favourites and wandered to the limits of the continent ('Mlle Aimée's receipts during eight weeks in Havana amounted to 107,000 dollars, and in Mexico, in seven weeks, to 59,000 dollars in gold ...') as Aimée established herself, by her regular presence and her superior comic abilities,

Plate 2. **Marie Aimée**: *America's queen of the opéra-bouffe stage.*

as the country's foremost star of the opéra-bouffe genre.

She made several return visits to France and, having lost some of the fortune she had amassed in America in trying to run theatres in Brussels and Rouen, once more crossed the Atlantic to recoup her losses. Finally, after having, for more than a decade, performed to her American audiences only in French, she got up one English song, 'Pretty as a Picture', to add some necessary novelty to her performance. Then, when the opéra-bouffe fashion had thoroughly died, she ventured out in a comedy called *Mam'selle* specially constructed to her needs by G H Jessop and William Gill. She was able to use what should have been the springboard to a second career for only a short while, for she developed cancer and returned to France for surgery. There, after two years of struggle against the disease, she died at the age of 35.

Tending to the then fashionably well-rounded, Aimée combined a useful singing voice with a light and breezy comedy style which led Odell to describe her as 'the most arch, the most piquant, the most attractive of all the artists in [the opéra-bouffe] line seen on the American stage ...' Another contemporary declared 'one of the most consummate and artistic bits of comedy acting ever witnessed in this country was Aimée's singing of the drinking song in *La Périchole*'. In France, however, unlike Paola Marié or Anna Judic, with whom she competed successfully abroad, she was never considered a star, and the failure of the first production of *La Boulangère* was charged largely to her lack of personality and presence at its centre.

Aimée's American repertoire included, at various periods, Offenbach's *La Grande-Duchesse de Gérolstein*, *Barbe-Bleue*, *Les Brigands*, *La Périchole*, *La Boulangère a des écus*, *La Belle Hélène*, *La Jolie Parfumeuse*, *Madame Favart*, *La*

Vie parisienne, Lischen et Fritzchen, Le Pont des soupirs, Geneviève de Brabant, La Princesse de Trébizonde and *Les Géorgiennes,* Lecocq's *Fleur de thé, Les Cent Vierges, Giroflé-Girofla, La Marjolaine, La Petite Mariée, Le Petit Duc, La Princesse des Canaries* and *La Fille de Madame Angot,* Hervé's *Le Petit Faust, L'Oeil crevé* and *La Belle Poule,* Planquette's *Les Cloches de Corneville,* Maillart's *Les Dragons de Villars,* Johann Strauss's frenchified *La Reine Indigo,* Suppé's *Boccaccio,* Balfe's *The Bohemian Girl* and Vasseur's *La Timbale d'Argent,* a good number of which she introduced to American audiences. She also introduced Bizet's 'Habanera' to America, before *Carmen* as a whole had been played on the left-hand side of the Atlantic.

ALADDIN

The story of Aladdin and his Wonderful Lamp originated in the collection of oriental tales known as the Arabian Nights' Entertainment. The boy with the genii seems to have been first seen on the musical stage in Denmark, but his first appearance in the English-language theatre was, to all evidence, in a pantomime at Covent Garden, on Boxing Day of 1788, in a version of the story dramatized by John O'Keefe with music by William Shield. The tale was thereafter used as the basis for a number of British theatre pieces including an unsuccessful 'fairy opera in three acts' with a score by Henry Bishop (Drury Lane 29 April 1826). Continental authors and composers also took to the subject around the same time, and amongst the musical *Aladdins* which appeared in the early part of the 19th century were Nicolas Isouard's opera *Aladin, ou La Lampe merveilleuse* (6 February 1822 Paris Opéra), Wenzel Müller's spectacular four-act magical comic opera *Die Wunderlampe* (1810 Prague), Adalbert Gyrowetz's one-act Vienna Singspiel *Aladin, oder Die Wunderlampe* (7 February 1819 Hoftheater), an opera by Luigi Ricci produced in Naples in 1825, and yet another by Gustave Räder mounted in 1855 at Dresden (*Aladin, oder Die Wunderlampe* 4 March).

As the age of burlesque got under way, the spectacular fairy stories of the Arabian Nights fell into the hands of the specialists of that genre and were developed by them into adventures which were much more humorous than dreadful and magical. Gilbert a' Beckett's *Aladdin, or The Wonderful Lamp in a New Light* (Princess's Theatre 1844) and Albert Smith's *Aladdin* for the Lyceum Theatre were the earliest efforts of the kind, but H J Byron's Strand Theatre burlesque *Aladdin, or The Wonderful Scamp* (1 April 1861), which introduced the characters of Widow Twankay and Prince Pekoe into the original fairytale for the first time as part of a version which made great play with the terms of the tea trade, largely surpassed all previous *Aladdins* in popularity. From that time onwards, Byron's version of the tale became the standard *Aladdin,* and his burlesque was widely used in the latter decades of the century as a first part for Christmas pantomimes. The tale was, nevertheless, also used as the subject for other British burlesques, notably Frank Green's 1874 piece, Robert Reece's Gaiety Theatre *Aladdin* (24 December 1881) and the pasticcio which Lydia Thompson and her blondes and their imitators toured through America in the 1870s, as well as for such American novelties as the 1895 *Aladdin Jr* (W H Batchelor, Jesse Greer, W F Glover/ J Cheever Goodwin, Broadway Theater 6 April).

In France, Hostein produced a spectacular féerie by Adolphe d'Ennery and Hector Crémieux under the title *Aladin, ou La Lampe merveilleuse* (music: A de Groot, 3 October 1863, 102 performances) at the newly opened Théâtre du Châtelet, and a Danish 'adventure-opera' composed by Christian Horneman appeared in Copenhagen in 1888 (18 November), but by far the most substantial light musical theatre *Aladdin* of the second half of the 19th century was Alfred Thompson's opéra-bouffe *Aladdin II* composed by Hervé and produced at London's Gaiety Theatre (23 December 1870) and subsequently at Paris's Théâtre des Folies-Dramatiques (*Le Nouvel Aladin*).

The 20th century brought several other musicals using the elements of the tale of the magic lamp, including John Philip Souza's *Chris and the Wonderful Lamp* (1 January 1900, Victoria Theater, New York), the Gaiety Theatre extravaganza *The New Aladdin* (29 September 1906) with a score by Ivan Caryll and Lionel Monckton, Caryll's highly successful *Chin-Chin,* produced at New York's Globe Theater (20 October 1914) with Montgomery and Stone starred, Rip's Parisian art-nouveau 'opérette féerie' with music by Willy Redstone and décors by Bakst (Théâtre Marigny, 21 May 1919), Cole Porter's television musical (1958) subsequently staged at the London Coliseum (1959), Sandy Wilson's *Aladdin* for the Lyric, Hammersmith (21 December 1979), and the Italian musical show *Accendiamo la Lampada* (30 December 1979), but in spite of this proliferation of genie-in-the-lamp pieces it is as a British pantomime subject that *Aladdin* has principally survived its two centuries on the stage.

ALADDIN II, or An Old Lamp in a New Light   Operatic extravaganza in 5 scenes by Alfred Thompson. Music by Hervé. Gaiety Theatre, London, 23 December 1870.

John Hollingshead's first venture with an original musical at the Gaiety Theatre, which had relied for the two years of its existence on pasticcio entertainments and French shows, was written by Alfred Thompson, the theatre's 'resident' playwright, who had contributed to the very first Gaiety bill in 1868, and the French composer Hervé, whose *Chilpéric* and *Le Petit Faust* had been among the first big opera-bouffe hits in London. A cleverly plotted burlesque version of the favourite tale, it featured star comedians Johnnie Toole and Nellie Farren in its principal roles of the nasty shopkeeper-magician, Ko-kli-ko, and the umpteenth lad called Aladdin whom he has taken on as shopboy, hoping to find a descendant of the original boy who can lead him to the famous lamp of old. Toole's catchphrase 'Still I am not happy' became the saw of the town and the show scored sufficient success for it to be taken on tour in Toole's repertoire and later re-presented for a second run at the Gaiety (24 February 1872). A Paris production (ad Hervé) folded prematurely through the fault of an amateurish management.

Thompson was later credited as the author of an *Arabian Nights* mounted at the Chicago Opera House (4 June 1887) and again at New York's Standard Theater (12 September 1887) which was, in fact, a version of *Aladdin.* Hervé had no credit, so presumably the piece was not – musically at least – *Aladdin II.*

The villain's name, Ko-kli-ko, a borrowing from the French stage where it had been heard just months previously in L'Eveillé's opérette *Le Fils à Ko-kli-ko*

Plate 3. **Aladdin II**: *Nellie Farren as 'son of Aladdin' in the Gaiety Theatre's early British musical comedy.*

(Folies-Marigny, 10 September 1869) was probably a forerunner of W S Gilbert's ultimately more famous Ko-ko (*The Mikado*).

France: Folies-Nouvelles *Le Nouvel Aladin* 16 December 1871

À LA JAMAÏQUE Opérette in 2 acts by Raymond Vincy. Music by Francis Lopez. Théâtre de la Porte Saint-Martin, Paris, 24 January 1954.

Another success from the Vincy/Lopez mill, *À la Jamaïque* was a vehicle for the comedienne Jane Sourza who starred as one Annie Krushen, a sometime charcutière from Saint-Antoine who has become the happy heiress to a chain of American snack bars. Annie's only remaining problem in life is to find a man – for, in spite of 18 engagements, she hasn't yet got one to the altar. This is because none of the 18, in the run-up to matrimony, has proven to have the qualities Annie so appreciates in the heroes of the romantic novels of Maxime de Saint-Maxient (Jacques Moret), and she's sent them away with a snack-bar as a consolation prize. This largesse worries Annie's business manager, Siméon Legrand (Pasquali), who promptly decides to wed Annie himself and enlists the help of the novelist with the promise of a share in the spoils. Annie, of course, ends up wedding her author, but not before a sexy Jamaican called Manoël Martinez (Jacques de Mersan) has played red herring and dragged everyone off to his island for a splash of traditional second-act scenery, some Caribbean-flavoured dances and songs, and a few quiproquos involving Manoël's lady friend Olivia (Maria Candido), a private detective called Peter Noster (Rogers), his Rita-Hayworthy assistant Gilda (Gisèle Robert) and others.

Lopez decorated *À la Jamaïque*'s jolly tale with a predictable set of numbers, the Porte Saint-Martin stage held the 'grand spectacle' of the piece well, and the result was a run of nearly a year and a half before Mlle Sourza went off to put a version of the show on celluloid. Mlle Robert repeated her stage rôle on the screen, and the other principal rôles were taken by Luis Mariano (Manoël), Darry Cowl (Peter Noster), Fernand Sardou (Legrand) and Orbal (Saint-Maxient).

The show remained amongst the Lopez revivables, and it was subsequently given a fresh showing in Paris in a revival at the Théâtre de la Renaissance as well as continuing to turn up in provincial productions with regularity up to the present day.

Recording: film cast star (EP) (HMV)

ALBERY, Donald [Arthur Rolleston] (Sir) (b London, 19 June 1914; d Monte Carlo, 14 September 1988). British producer and theatre-owner whose list of hits included a number of musicals.

Donald Albery was a descendant of a famous theatrical family, headed by the author James Albery (1838–1889) and his wife Mary Moore (1862–1931). It was she, Mrs/Lady Charles Wyndham *en secondes noces*, who, by carrying on the operation of the significant theatrical holdings originally run by Wyndham (London's Criterion, Wyndham's and New Theatres), consolidated what was to be the firm subsequently run by her son, Bronson Albery, and then by his son, Donald.

Although the Criterion, Wyndham's and the New were conceived and operated as playhouses, each was occasionally sublet to house musical pieces under the Wyndham régime – *Bilberry of Tilbury*, *All Abroad*, *The White Chrysanthemum* (Criterion), *The Girl Behind the Counter* (Wyndham's), *Amasis*, *The Laughing Husband* (New) – and, similarly, in a family which was known generally for its considerable activities on the 19th-century straight stage, some contribution to the musical stage was to be found.

James Albery himself, best known as the author of such pieces as the ubiquitous *Two Roses* and the English version of *Pink Dominos*, was also responsible for a not-very-successful musical 'romantic legend' in rhyming couplets called *Oriana* (Globe Theatre, 1873, music: Frederic Clay) and the 'fairy spectacular extravaganza' *The Will of Wise King Kino*, played at the Princess's Theatre later the same year, as well as a short operetta *The Spectre Knight* (1878, music: Alfred Cellier) which the young D'Oyly Carte produced to supplement the original *The Sorcerer* and *HMS Pinafore* at the Opera Comique. Mary Moore's elder sister, Haidée Crofton, who was to have a good second-string career as a performer in the musical theatre, succeeded to the rôle of Hebe in the same *HMS Pinafore*.

Under the management of Bronson Albery, the theatre group continued to house principally plays, but they chalked up the longest single run in their history when Wyndham's Theatre took in the small-scale musical *The Boy Friend* (1954) for what turned out to be a memorable run of 2,084 performances.

Donald himself began in the theatre at a young age, acting as wartime manager of the Sadler's Wells ballet between 1941 and 1945, but it was 1953 before he began a career as a producer. His ventures were eclectic, often unusual, often adventurous, and included such pieces as Graham Greene's *The Living Room* (1953) and Beckett's *Waiting for Godot* (1955) as well as Anouilh's *The Waltz of the Toreadors* and the play *Gigi* (1956). He produced his first musical (w Neil Crawford) when he transferred *Grab Me a Gondola* (1956) from Windsor's Theatre Royal to the West End, and followed up with an unfortunate musical version of Max Beerbohm's *Zuleika Dobson* (*Zuleika*, 1957) before striking a major hit with the English version of *Irma la Douce* (London, 1958, and New York, 1960).

A close working connection with the Theatre Royal, Stratford East, where Joan Littlewood had established her Theatre Workshop, resulted in his making the transfer of a number of notable plays from that venue (*A Taste of Honey* (1959), *The Hostage* (1959)) as well as two successful and widely differing musicals: the excellent *Make Me an Offer*, and the lively, amateurish *Fings Ain't Wot They Used T'Be*. His major success, however, came with a musical originally destined for Stratford, but which outgrew that intention: Lionel Bart's piece of musical Dickens, *Oliver!* (1960), which ran for six years at the New Theatre prior to being performed around the world.

In 1962 Albery took over from his father at the head of the theatre group, adding a fourth house to their holdings with the purchase of the Piccadilly Theatre, the only freehold property of the set. He had another fine success with the revue *Beyond the Fringe*, but subsequent musical ventures were less profitable: the oversized *Blitz!* (1962) held up for 16 months, but a production of the American musical *Fiorello!* (1962) failed at the Piccadilly, *The Perils of Scobie Prilt* (1963) closed out of town and a tacky rip-off of *La Cagnotte* called *Instant Marriage* (1964) stayed on for a run simply to occupy the Piccadilly Theatre, where *Man of La Mancha* (1968, 1969) proved much better if less long-lived fare.

Whilst the play successes continued (*Entertaining Mr Sloane* (1964), *The Prime of Miss Jean Brodie* (1966) etc), two further musicals by *Make Me an Offer*'s David Heneker, *Jorrocks* (1966) and *Popkiss* (1972), brought more pleasure than profit, and a transfer of the ragged *Mandrake* (1970) from the Bristol Old Vic, brought neither, ending Albery's musical theatre career on an atypically downbeat but typically intuitive production.

He retired in 1978, selling his firm to Associated Newspapers Ltd with his son Ian (b 1939) left in charge, and with the New Theatre now rechristened, in honour of his father, the Albery Theatre. Subsequent financial dealings saw the firm, the theatres and Ian Albery change hands again in the 1980s.

Biography: (family) Trewin, W: *All on Stage: Charles Wyndham and the Alberys* (Harrap, London, 1980)

ALBINI, Felix [ALBINI, Srećko] (b Zupanje, 20 December 1869; d Agram (Zagreb), 18 April 1933).

The Croatian composer Albini trained in Vienna and in Graz, where he had his earliest engagement as a conductor, and he made his first attempt at stage writing in the field of opera (*Marion* w Milan Smrekar, Kroatisches Theater, Zagreb, 1901). However, he found more significant success when he turned to the lighter musical field. His first Operette, *Der Nabob*, was played for 18 performances at Vienna's Carltheater in 1905 with Ferdinand

Pagin and Therese Loewe in the featured rôles, and was also subsequently staged in Budapest (*Az indiai nábob* Budai Színkör, 2 July 1910, ad Emil Tabori), whilst his *Madame Troubadour* (1907), a version of the French comedy *La Petite Marquise*, first produced in Zagreb, was later seen in Germany (Stadttheater, Leipzig, 27 November 1908) and in an English-language production sponsored by the Shuberts in America (Lyric Theater, 10 October 1910 ad Joseph W Herbert, aka *The Little Parisienne*). Albini composed the score for a musical version of Charles Dickens's *A Christmas Carol* (*Ein Weihnachtsabend*) produced in Vienna in 1906, but his greatest success came with the 1908 Leipzig piece, *Baron Trenck [der Pandur]*, which went on from its German première to productions in Austria, Hungary, Britain and America.

Albini subsequently became director of the Opera at Zagreb and, although he continued to write ballet and choral music and songs, from that time he closed down his career as a composer of Operette.

1905 **Der Nabob** (Leopold Krenn) Carltheater 23 September
1906 **Die kühle Blonde** 1 act Apollotheater 31 March
1906 **Ein Weinachtsabend** (Max Foges) Wiener Colosseum 21 December
1907 **Madame Troubadour** (Bela Jenbach, Richard Pohl) National-Theater, Agram 7 April
1908 **Baron Trenck [der Pandur]** (A M Willner, Robert Bodanzky) Stadttheater, Leipzig 15 February; Stadttheater, Vienna 29 October 1909
1909 **Die kleine Baronesse** (Bodanzky) 1 act Apollotheater 31 March
1909 **Die Barfusstänzerin** (Jenbach) Altes Theater, Leipzig 28 August

ALDREDGE, Theoni V[achlioti] [VACHLIOTI, Theoni Athanasiou] (b Salonika, Greece, 1932). Greek-born artist who became one of Broadway's most successful costume designers in the 1960s and 1970s.

Trained at the Goodman Memorial Theater, Chicago, Mrs Aldredge participated in her first production there in 1950 and subsequently designed clothes for a number of regional play productions before moving to New York in 1957. One of her earliest Broadway assignments was on Geraldine Page's costumes for *Sweet Bird of Youth* (1959). She has since designed some 150 Broadway shows, moving into the musical theatre for the first time with *Anyone Can Whistle* (1964), *Hot September* (1965) and *Skyscraper* (1965), and clothed several notable successes, including *A Chorus Line* (1975), as part of a long association with Joseph Papp and the New York Shakespeare Festival.

Amongst the other musicals she has costumed in recent years are *Annie* (1977, Tony Award), *Barnum* (1980, Tony Award), *42nd Street* (1980), *Woman of the Year* (1981), *La Cage aux Folles* (1983), *Merlin* (1983), *Chess* (London, 1986), *Ziegfeld* (London, 1988), *Gypsy* revival (1989), *Annie 2* (1989) and *Nick and Nora* (1991).

She has also designed for film (*The Great Gatsby*, Academy Award), television, opera and ballet.

ALEXANDRA Operett in 3 acts by Ferenc Martos. Music by Albert Szirmai. Király Színház, Budapest, 25 November 1925.

Alexandra can probably be considered the most internationally successful of Szirmai's operetts, given the amount of travelling that the various versions of the show did. However, the alterations made during the piece's travels beyond Hungary and around the world were considerable, and most of the foreign versions of the show owed only a small debt to the original composer.

The Russian Grand-Duchess Alexandra (Erzsi Péchy) is to be married to the King of Illyria (Dezső Kertész). However on the day that the ship comes to collect her, Russian revolution breaks out and Alexandra is forced into a hurried wedding with the captain of the ship, Torelli (Jenő Nádor), so that, as an Illyrian citizen, she may safely depart. It is a marriage which, two acts later, stands good. Árpád Latabár (Count Szuvarov), Márton Rátkai (Prince Károly) and Nusi Somogyi supplied the humorous moments as supporting aristocrats.

Szirmai's music was of his best, the romantic leads being particularly well supplied with the two waltz-refrained duos 'Rözsák közt' and 'Túl az üveghegyek kék ködén' which were the heart of the score. They were pieces with excitingly unobvious verses, and refrains which became only a little less inventive largely because tied to the familiar 3/4 pattern. A splendid guards' march for solo and chorus, which rattled exhilaratingly along at a rate more like a step-dance, the usual dance-based Hungarian-style soubret pieces ('Csókolj meg szép babám') and the almost crooning praises of 'Kicsi feleség' (little wife) went to make up the highlights of a score of conventional proportions, but of well above average quality.

Clayton and Waller's London production of *Princess Charming* was the first foreign version of *Alexandra* to hit the boards. Anything as realistic as Russia and its revolution was unthinkable on the London musical stage, so Russia went out of the window and Ruritania stepped in. Winnie Melville (later Evelyn Laye) was Princess Elaine of Novia, John Clarke was Torelli, and adaptors Arthur Wimperis and Lauri Wylie worked in the rôle of Albert Chuff, an insurance man, for chief comic W H Berry. George Grossmith played Christian II of Sylvania and Alice Delysia was one sexy Wanda Navaro. Additional numbers were credited to Russell Bennett and producer Jack Waller (two apiece), but by the time Kalmar and Ruby's 'Babyin' You' and Phil Charig's 'Why Do You Roll those Eyes?' (both Delysia/Berry), Stransky's 'Kisses' (Laye/Clarke), Hirsch's 'Learn to Smile' (Laye) and Weston and Lee's comedy songs 'Ninepence a Week' and 'Not Old Enough to be Old' (Berry) had been inserted, little beyond Szirmai's concerted music was left, for all that he had sole musical billing. The resultant patchwork of a show, however, ran for 362 performances before going to the country.

Soon after the London opening, a rather less adulterated *Alexandra* (ad Paul Frank, Peter Herz) was mounted by Erich Müller at the Johann Strauss-Theater in Vienna. Emmi Kosáry starred as Alexandra alongside Gisa Kolbe (Krackowianskaja), Robert Nästlberger (Cäsar, ex-Torelli), Fritz Imhoff (Prince Karl Maria), Max Brod (Suwarov) and Manfred Kempel (King) through a fair run of 77 performances.

Italy saw its version of the show as *Mascherine russe* (which means they must have at least avoided Ruritania) but Australia's J C Williamson Ltd preferred to take up London's version of *Princess Charming* for its season in Sydney in 1928 with Cecil Kellaway (Chuff), Kathryn Reece (Elaine), Reginald Dandy (Torelli), Peter Gaw-

thorne and Olive Sloane featured, and again, in Melbourne, nearly a decade later (Her Majesty's Theatre, February 1937) with Albert Frith, Romola Hansen and Herbert Browne in the lead rôles. Broadway went one step further and remade the British remake (ad Jack Donahue, ballets by Albertina Rasch, add mus Arthur Schwartz, add ly Arthur Swanstrom, interpolated numbers Robert Dolan and Walter O'Keefe). Director Bobby Connolly and Swanstrom's production featured a cast including Evelyn Herbert and Robert Halliday in the romantic leads, and Grossmith, Victor Moore (now called Irving Huff) and Jeanne Aubert in comic support. A show which was very little of *Alexandra* if rather more of *Princess Charming* flopped in 56 performances.

Alexandra was, however, no longer Szirmai's even in a tiny part when the film version of *Princess Charming*, made in Britain by Gainsborough Films, with Miss Laye, Grossmith, Yvonne Arnaud and Max Miller starring, appeared in 1934. This time, all his music had gone, and only Ruritania and Albert Chuff – as impersonated by Miller – remained.

UK: Palace Theatre *Princess Charming* 21 October 1926; Austria: Johann Strauss-Theater 5 November 1926; Australia: Her Majesty's Theatre, Sydney *Princess Charming* 12 May 1928; USA: Imperial Theater *Princess Charming* 13 October 1930; Film: Gainsborough Films *Princess Charming* 1934
Recording: selection (part record) (Qualiton)

ALGERIA Musical play in 2 acts by Glen Mac-Donough. Music by Victor Herbert. Broadway Theater, New York, 31 August 1908.

Many years before *The Desert Song* was a twinkle in anyone's eye, Broadway librettist Glen MacDonough wandered into the operettic north African desert with the tale of *Algeria*. Zoradie (Ida Brooks Hunt), the Sultana of the Barakeesh, a powerful desert tribe, develops a passion for the pseudonymous author of the poem 'Rose of the World' and determines to seek him out. When the comedians (Harry Tighe, Toby Lyons, Randall Davey) have been disposed of as candidates, the right man turns out to be the French Captain de Lome (George Leon Moore), commander of the Oasis of Sidi Ahmoud and nephew of the Governor General (William Pruette). The romantic tale was perforated with comedy from the trio of deserters, and from Mr and Mrs Billings F Cooings from Paterson, New Jersey (Florence Nash, Eugene P Arnold), and with soubrettery from Millicent Madison MD (Harriet Burt), an American girl practising medicine in the Middle East.

Herbert decorated this book with a score that included two numbers as good as anything he had written: the soaring melody of Zoradie's 'Rose of the World', brought back with pounding meaningfulness in the dramatic first-act finale, and her Eastern-rhythmic 'Twilight in Barakeesh'. The hero lilted out the much-used conceit that 'Love Is Like a Cigarette', the soubrette hinted that you should 'Ask Her While the Band Is Playing' and Pruette's star status meant that there were two basso numbers in the dozen that made up the score.

However, in spite of the score, Frank McKee's production of *Algeria* was not well liked, and after 49 performances it was closed. Lew Fields, however, realized that there was something there worth saving. He took up the piece, had the libretto rewritten a little, and revived the show as *The Rose of Algeria* at the Herald Square Theater the following season (20 September 1909). Since the original stars, Miss Brooks Hunt and Pruette, were currently triumphing in the leading rôles of Broadway's *The Chocolate Soldier*, he replaced them with Lillie Herlein and the other famous bass of the comic opera circuits, Eugene Cowles. Frank Pollock was the poetic hero, and the score little altered. The alterations were insufficient to allow more than 40 performances, and some fine music went to waste.

ALIAS, Charles   (b France, 184–?; d London, 11 May 1921). The most famous name in British theatrical costumery in the second half of the 19th century.

The son of a French doctor, the young Alias fought alongside his father in the Franco-Prussian war where he is said to have lost the sight in one eye. He visited Britain and the Philharmonic Theatre, Islington, shortly afterwards as a dresser with the French dance troupe, Les Clodoches, and there he met and married Miss Price, the theatre's costumier. Although Alias had no experience in the theatre, he joined his wife in setting up the freelance firm of M et Mme Alias & Co, sometimes designing and manufacturing, or more often just making up from the designs of such artists as Wilhelm or Faustin, the costumes for an ever-extending series of musical shows.

The Aliases made their mark in the West End when they provided the costumes for the original London production of *La Fille de Madame Angot* (1873), and thereafter they costumed, either wholly or partly, many of London's most important musical productions including the burlesques at the Gaiety Theatre (*The Bohemian G'yurl*, *Little Dr Faust*, *Gulliver*, *Il Sonnambulo*, *Pretty Esmeralda* etc), the Royalty (*Madcap*, *Pluto* etc), and the Strand (*The Lying Dutchman*, *L'Africaine*, *Nemesis*, *Loo*, *Antarctic*, *Champagne*, *The Baby*, *Intimidad*), Gilbert's early *Tospyturveydom* and *Princess Toto*, Gilbert and Sullivan premières at the Opera Comique (*The Pirates of Penzance*) and the Savoy (*Iolanthe*), the vast spectaculars at the Alhambra (*La Poule aux oeufs d'or* etc) and, most noticeably, the long string of French opéras-bouffes and opéras-comiques which were produced in Britain in the 1870s and 1880s. These included the record-breaking *Les Cloches de Corneville* (for which the costume bill amounted to an unheard-of £300), *Les Noces d'Olivette*, *La Famille Trouillat* (*La Belle Normande*), *Le Jour et la nuit* (*Manola*), *La Timbale d'argent* (*The Duke's Daughter*), *La Marjolaine*, *Les Prés St Gervais* and most of the long string of adaptations from the French made by Alias's close friend Henry Farnie, and produced by Alexander Henderson.

Alias maintained a close connection with his homeland. His home at 48 Soho Square became well known as a first stopping place for Frenchmen new to London and a congenial gathering place for theatricals, and he as a useful and friendly intermediary in various theatrical dealings between London and Paris. Hervé, Planquette, Chassaigne, Audran and Lecocq were all guests at Soho Square and the little costumier was said to have been instrumental in the brothers Mansell bringing Hervé and his *Chilpéric* (1870) to London, and thus helping set off the craze for opéra-bouffe which dominated the 1870s musical theatre in England. He also encouraged Planquette to work with H B Farnie on an original musical for Britain – the result of which was the enduring *Rip van Winkle*.

Alias & Co prospered in the 1880s, having a major success with their new costumes for the transferred version of the amazing *Dorothy*, and on into the 1890s by which stage they had become largely costume-makers rather than designers. Alias himself had by this time become one of the 'characters' of the London theatre, always anxiously asking 'What time de répétition générale?' as an opening approached, but always punctually ready with the show's costumes on dress-rehearsal night.

When Mme Alias died, Charles remarried and continued the business with his new wife, Mme Marie Wallet Floret from the Paris Opéra wardrobe, up to his death.

ALI BABA   [and the Forty Thieves]

One of the 19th-century favourites amongst the tales transferred to the stage from the Arabian Nights' Entertainment, *Ali Baba* became popular, most particularly in Britain, as an extravaganza and pantomime subject. It was, however, at first played as a genuine melodrama, and was seen at Drury Lane as early as 1806 before, like other such tales of cavalier gore, it turned from being drama to becoming a favourite topic for pantomime and burlesque.

Gilbert a' Beckett ventured an early extravaganza *Open Sesame, or a Night with the Forty Thieves* for the Lyceum, whilst Planché, H J Byron and the brothers Brough were among the collaborators on a memorable version of *The Forty Thieves* for the Brough Memorial Fund at the same house in 1860. Byron's highly successful Strand Theatre burlesque *Ali Baba and the Thirty Nine Thieves* (*in accordance with the Author's habit of 'taking one off'*) produced in 1863 was, like its definitive *Aladdin* counterpart, much used as a pantomime first part in the decades that followed. Lydia Thompson's company played an H B Farnie *Forty Thieves* all around America, and other *Ali Baba* burlesques included Robert Reece's *Ali Baba à la mode* (Gaiety Theatre 1872) and *The Forty Thieves* (Gaiety Theatre 1880) in Britain, and a heap of touring variants of Farnie's piece long played by bundles of burlesque blondes in the American regions.

Cherubini (Paris Opéra, 1833 to a libretto by no less authors than Scribe and Mélesville), Bottesini (Lyceum 1871) and Max Brauer (*Morgiane*, Karlsruhe 1899) each produced operatic *Ali Babas*, whilst, in the musical theatre, France hosted a Cogniard brothers spectacular *Ali Baba, ou Les Quarante Voleurs* at the Cirque-Nationale (24 October 1853) at the same time that Ernest Dubreuil's drama of the same title was playing at the Théâtre Beaumarchais, and later an 1872 opérette by Adolphe Nibelle, *Les Quatre-Cents Femmes d'Ali Baba*, Berlin had an *Almazinde, oder der Höhle Sesam* as early as 1814, Britain the 1901 Terry's Theatre musical *The Thirty Thieves* (clearly hit by rising costs) and America a Harry B Smith *Ali Baba jr, or Morgiana and the Forty Thieves* (w Franklyn W Lee, John Gilbert, music: W H Batchelor et al) and Cheever Goodwin's Chicago burlesque-spectacular *Ali Baba*, retitled *An Arabian Girl and the Forty Thieves* (1899) for its seasons on Broadway. Each of these diverged somewhat from the original tale, as did Johann Strauss's setting of a version of the tale as *Indigo und die vierzig Räuber*.

Lecocq's 1887 opérette à grand spectacle, *Ali-Baba*, played first in Brussels (Théâtre de l'Alhambra 11 November 1887) and later, in a revised version, in Paris (Théâtre de l'Eden, November 1889, Théâtre de la Gaîté-Lyrique February 1927), and Munich (Theater am Gärtnerplatz 10 November 1888), actually spared the robbers from their traditional fate in the jars of oil, but that clemency was not extended to the male chorus of the most successful of all *Ali Baba*s, the famous British wartime hit *Chu Chin Chow*.

On this occasion, author–producer–star Oscar Asche embroidered the character of the glamorous spy Zahrat al-Kulub onto the traditional story in order to make a rôle for his non-singing wife, Lily Brayton, introduced increased romantic and spectacular elements, and redistributed some of the other well-known features of the original tale with as easy a hand as had some of the burlesque writers, while still retaining all the main parts of the original tale.

In recent times, *Ali Baba* has lost its place as a British pantomime subject, perhaps partly because of its explicit demand for a chorus of 40 thieves, unthinkable under modern salary conditions.

ALIBERT, Henri [ALLIBERT, Henri] (b Carpentras, ?1889; d Marseille, January 1951). French singer turned librettist who made himself a star with a series of jolly musical comedies in the 1930s.

The dark, sharp-faced little southerner, who began life apprenticed to a pastry-cook, had a slow beginning to his career as a performer. After several years working in the provinces, subsisting largely on imitations of the famous, he ultimately took the first steps towards success as a comic actor and singer in Paris, when he was engaged in 1919 at the Eldorado. His first appearance there was in the rôle of a cabaret singer in *Le Crime du Bouif*. He subsequently appeared at the Alhambra and the Empire, in an act which often included the songs of his father-in-law, Vincent Scotto.

The success of the Marseillais plays of Marcel Pagnol and of southern-flavoured revue, *La Revue marseillaise*, which played for two seasons at the Moulin de la Chanson, persuaded Alibert (libretto), René Sarvil (lyrics) and Scotto (music) to venture a musical comedy in the same 'midi' style. Their first attempt with what they called an opérette-revue, *Au pays du soleil*, was produced at the Moulin de la Chanson in 1931 with Alibert in the central rôle of a callow and comical marseillais. This light-hearted, unpretentious fare with its jolly, simple story, catchy music-hall songs and midi accents proved a perfect complement to the lush opérettes à grand spectacle again becoming popular in Paris. The show was a hit, and Alibert was lifted into the major star category.

The same formula was followed successfully during the 1930s in *Trois de la marine*, *Zou! le midi bouge*, *Un de la Canebière*, *Les Gangsters du Château d'If* and *Le Roi des galéjeurs*, and Alibert subsequently appeared in his popular marseillais persona in revue (*Paris-Marseille*, *C'est tout le midi* etc), in several musical shows composed by his habitual conductor, Georges Sellers (*Ma belle Marseillaise*, *Le Port du soleil*), and in such films as *Titin de Martigues* (Scotto/Sarvil), *Un Soir à Marseille* (Sellers/Sarvil) and *L'Affaire du grand hôtel* (Scotto/Vincy). In parallel, he became a favourite recording star for the Pathé label, notably with the songs from his shows and films ('Sur le plancher des vaches', 'Adieu, Venise provençale', 'Le Plus Beau Tango du monde', 'Les Pescadous', etc).

Alibert was director of Paris's Théâtre des Deux-Ânes

from 1931 to the time of his death, and also, for a time, of the Théâtre des Variétés, where he played a repertoire featuring marseillais opérette and Pagnol's plays.

Several of his marseillais opérettes-revues, notably *Un de la Canebière*, which contains the most popular collection of songs in the series, are still performed in France more than half a century after their first appearances.

1931 **Au pays du soleil** (Vincent Scotto/René Sarvil) Moulin de la Chanson 22 October
1933 **Trois de la marine** (Scotto/Sarvil) Nouvel-Ambigu 20 December
1934 **Zou! le midi bouge** (aka *Arènes Joyeuses*) (Scotto/Sarvil) Alcazar
1935 **Un de la Canebière** (Scotto/Raymond Vincy, Sarvil) Théâtre des Célestins, Lyon 14 October; Théâtre des Variétés 3 April 1936
1936 **Les Gangsters du Château d'If** (Scotto) Théâtre des Célestins, Lyon 10 November; Théâtre des Variétés 30 January 1937
1936 **Le Roi des galéjeurs** (Scotto) Théâtre des Célestins, Lyon; Théâtre des Variétés 16 September
1946 **Les Gauchos de Marseille** (Scotto/Sarvil) Théâtre des Variétés

ALICE IN WONDERLAND

Lewis Carroll's Alice books, *Alice in Wonderland* (1865) and *Through the Looking Glass* (1872), have been the subject of a large number of adaptations for the musical stage. Far and away the most successful of these was the earliest, a version written by H Savile Clarke with a musical score by Walter Slaughter and produced as a Christmas entertainment at London's Prince of Wales Theatre in 1886. Lewis Carroll himself had a hand in the casting of little Phoebe Carlo as the first stage Alice, and designer Lucien Besche reproduced Tenniel's famous illustrations in his stage designs. This *Alice in Wonderland* was revived for 18 further Christmas seasons in the West End, most notably in 1900 when Ellaline Terriss appeared as a not terribly juvenile Alice with Seymour Hicks in the principal comedy rôle as the Mad Hatter.

Subsequent English-language *Alice*s have been consistently less successful. A 1903 *Through the Looking Glass* at London's New Theatre found little favour, and Eva Le Gallienne's *Alice in Wonderland* (Civic Repertory Theater, New York, 12 December 1932 with Florida Frebus, music: Richard Addinsell), revived in 1947 by the American Repertory Theater (International Theater, New York 28 May, 100 performances), a fresh Clemence Dane/Richard Addinsell adaptation (Scala 1943), a France Pole/John Sacco piece which came out at the same time as the Walt Disney animated film of *Alice in Wonderland*, a Felicity Douglas/Dave King *Alice Through the Looking Glass* (Prince's Theatre 1954) and a string of lesser attempts all failed to come up to the first version.

Sweden's Stefan Roos produced a version of the tale in 1968, and in 1978 a French Alice appeared when the Opéra Royal de Wallonie produced a two act opérette-féerie by Paul Francy at the Théâtre de Liège (19 October), but the most substantial modern Alice, originally produced by Vinnette Carroll and New York's Urban Arts Theater, on the wave of hope engendered by the success of *The Wiz*, was also the most substantial flop. It closed out of town at Philadelphia's Forrest Theater in 1978 (31 May, music: Micki Grant) and failed again, under the title *Never*

Jam Today (music: Bert Keyes and Bob Larimer) at the Longacre Theater in 1979 (31 July). A modernized *Alice* at Britain's Leeds Playhouse and a German *Nachtkind* (1982) and *Alice* (Thalia-Theater, Hamburg, 19 December 1992) used Carroll's story and characters in a free fashion, but regional and suburban theatres in Britain and elsewhere continue to produce fresh musical versions of the tale in a more or less traditional fashion (*The Adventures of Alice*, Farnham 1985, a John Wells/Colin Davis *Alice in Wonderland* at the Lyric, Hammersmith 1986 etc), in spite of the piece's apparent unsuitability for the stage.

Alice has also appeared, rather more happily, on musical film, both in the famous Walt Disney animated version of 1951 and, with human actors, in a 1972 British version which featured the young Fiona Fullerton as Alice, and on television. An American NBC *Alice Through the Looking Glass* of 1966, with songs by Moose Charlap and Elsie Simmons, featured Judi Rolin as Alice alongside Robert Coote, Nanette Fabray, Agnes Moorehead, Roy Castle, Jimmy Durante and Jack Palance.

Recording: TV cast (RCA Victor)

ALIX, Victor (b 1890; d 1968)

Alix was the composer of several successful featherweight Parisian musical comedies of the 1920s and early 1930s, including the oriental tale of *You-You*, and a successful musical version of Romain Coolus's comedy *Les Bleus de l'amour* (a double-meaning title, referring to both the beginners in love, and the bruises of love) mounted at the Théâtre de l'Avenue with Paul Villé and Henri Defreyn featured. The little ten-handed *Mon amant* was produced by Max Danset with the same stars – Villé turning Machiavellian to stop Defreyn having an affair with his wife (Marguerite Deval) – and, later the same year, a second piece written with Coolus, *Boby chéri*, did well enough in its original season at the Scala to warrant a revival in 1934.

In the spirit of the times, Alix indulged in the foxtrot, the shimmy, and even the beguine, alongside the more traditional waltz rhythms and couplets in which he was apparently more at home.

1921 **Princesse Lily** (Jean-Claude Vaumousse) Théâtre des Variétés 12 June
1922 **You-You** (Jane Ardot, Jacques Sirrah) Théâtre de l'Apollo 25 February
1922 **Lulu** (Alain Monjardin) Caen 29 December
1923 **Pincette** (Ardot, Paidlon) La Fauvette-Concert 21 September
1926 **Les Bleus de l'amour** (Blanche Alix, Henry Jacques/Romain Coolus) Théâtre de l'Avenue April
1932 **Mon amant** (Ardot/Henry Darcourt, Maurice Lupin) Théâtre de la Potinière 1 April
1932 **Boby chéri** (Ardot/Coolus) Théâtre de la Scala 13 December

ALLEGRO Musical play in 2 acts by Oscar Hammerstein II. Music by Richard Rodgers. Majestic Theater, New York, 10 October 1947.

In *Allegro*, Hammerstein abandoned the highly coloured American operetta style of story he had used so effectively in *Oklahoma!* and *Carousel* for a different kind of small-town, small-people tale – one which came to its climax not, like the other two shows, in a murder, but in a bit of common or garden infidelity.

Joe (William Ching) and Marjorie (Annamary Dickie) Taylor give birth to baby Joe. Joe grows up (John Battles), goes to college, becomes a doctor, marries Jenny, the girl back home (Roberta Jonay), moves on to a better if less genuine job in the city and to a higher kind of life. Then, when his socially ambitious wife turns out to be a two-timer, he chucks in the big city and heads back to where he started to take up real doctoring again.

The various events of the life of Dr Joe Taylor, played out in front of a simple set of drops, were linked in the telling by a narrating ensemble who welcomed the baby ('Joseph Taylor Jr'), saw him through his first steps ('One Foot, Other Foot') and his marriage ('To Have and to Hold'/'Wish Them Well') to the final call of his mother to 'Come Home'. In between, Rodgers and Hammerstein's principal songs were sung largely by supporting characters. Lisa Kirk as Dr Joe's loving nurse concluded that 'The Gentleman is a Dope' for not seeing what his wife is up to, Gloria Wills as his college flirt sang 'So Far', mother and father Taylor suggested conventionally, and not only of their son, that 'A Fellow Needs a Girl', whilst Joe jr serenaded the girl back home in 'You Are Never Away' and waxed moral in the show's title-song.

Several of the songs won some popularity, but *Allegro* proved too long on sanctimoniousness and too short on fun and colour to succeed in the same way that the two previous Rodgers and Hammerstein shows had done. The Theatre Guild's production ran through 315 Broadway performances – more than many contemporary shows, but insufficient to get it into the black – before going on the road. It was not picked up by overseas producers, and it remains one of the few comparatively forgotten parts of the Rodgers and Hammerstein opus, although the famous names attached to it have won it several outings, notably in a production at the Goodspeed Opera House in 1968.

Recording: original cast (RCA)

ALL THE KING'S HORSES Romantic musical comedy in 2 acts by Frederick Herendeen based on the play by Lawrence Clarke. Music by Edward Horan. Shubert Theater, New York, 30 January 1934.

All the King's Horses was a *Prisoner of Zenda*-esque piece which had Guy Robertson starred as a movie star called Donald MacArthur who deputizes for his look-alike, King Rudolf of Langenstein, long enough for the King to go off for a jolly time in Paris and for MacArthur to have a nice affair with Queen Erna (Nancy McCord).

Following its 120 performances on Broadway, *All the King's Horses* was shipped to Hollywood where it was filmed, with Mary Ellis and Carl Brisson, and, eventually, an altered story and different songs. It was then taken up for London by Joe Sacks who had it again rewritten, by Archie Menzies, with a 'happy' ending and a new title, *Royal Exchange*. This time the rollicking King was knocked off, allowing his stand-in to happily wed his Queen. In London, Carlos Gavalia (as he was now called) was played by a real live movie star in the person of Ramon Novarro, who starred alongside D'Oyly Carte veteran Charles Walenn, Eddie Foy and Doris Kenyon. Novarro got devastatingly bad notices, and the show closed in one week.

UK: His Majesty's Theatre *Royal Exchange* 6 December 1935

ALMA, WO WOHNST DU? Vaudeville in 3 acts 'adapted by Adolf Philipp from the play by Paul Hervé'. Music by 'Jean Briquet' and Adolf Philipp. Wintergarten 'Zum schwarzen Adler', New York, 25 October 1909; Weber's Theater, New York, 26 August 1910.

Quite where the successful musical *Alma, wo wohnst du?* originated is a mystery veiled behind a mass of phoney credits. Jean Briquet never existed and it is a fair bet that Paul Hervé didn't either. Both names were undoubtedly used to cover the fact that Adolf Philipp, the guiding factotum of the New York German-language theatre, was both author and composer of the show which he mounted with his Deutsch-Amerikanische Ensemble in 1909. He also starred alongside Hedwig von Ostermann as the Alma of whom the title asked the address.

Whether Philipp's work was wholly or partly original or borrowed is another question. His plot was certainly far from new. Alma was an apparently irresistible young lady dangled by interested parties in front of poor Pierre Le Peach to tempt him to break the conditions of a musical-comedy will. She was also saucy enough to win the show a great success amongst German-speaking gentlemen of New York, and the following season the piece was translated into English by George V Hobart and produced in a regular Broadway house by Joe Weber as *Alma, Where Do You Live?* It was subtitled 'a lyrical comedy', the fake credits were still in place, and Kitty Gordon starred as Alma, with John McCloskey as Pierre, and Charles A Bigelow as chief comic.

The press consensus was that Hobart had done a splendid job in cleaning up the naughty French original, which of course wasn't French or original in the sense they were meaning at all, and that Philipp's score, featuring a 'Hush the Bogie' number about 'The Boogie Boo', a Tom-Cat song encouraging the girls to come out and 'Love Me' and more conventional pieces for the two stars recalling 'Childhood Days', exploring 'The Land of the Beautiful Dream' and waltzing with *Merry Widow* abandon to 'Kiss Me, My Love', fitted it perfectly. The consensus was not, however, shared by quite all of the show's public. One viewer laid a complaint against the show's morals, obliging Mayor Gaynor to an enquiry which came out with the usual 'in the ear of the beholder' kind of answer and did absolutely no harm to the show's box-office.

Alma, Where Do You Live? was one of the biggest hits of the vintage 1910–11 season, outrunning *Naughty Marietta* comprehensively, equalling *Madame Sherry* and giving best only to the hugely successful *The Pink Lady*. It totalled 232 Broadway performances before going on the road and Philipp remounted the original German-language version at his new 57th Street Theater in the 1912–13 season (17 April 1913). When she had done touring the show at length, the now spicily celebrated Miss Gordon had a small-scale sequel written to measure, and went on the vaudeville stage playing *Alma's Return* (1914).

The credits for the show got even more tangled when the German version of *Alma* ('a Parisian vaudeville in 3 acts') was taken up back in Berlin. When the piece appeared on the stage of the Luisen-Theater (17 October 1911), still credited to Paul Hervé as adapted by Herr Philipp, she had been equipped with a fresh score by Walter Kollo with lyrics by Louis Taufstein. It was that score which was later heard in Vienna (Lustspieltheater

17 November 1911) when Annie Dirkens appeared as the luscious Alma alongside Gustav Maran (Theobald Simonet), Gisela Werbezirk (Louise Parfait) and Louis Holzer (Pierre Roussant) in Josef Jarno's Austrian production of a show which wasn't quite the *Alma, wo wohnst du?* that had begun its life in New York and which, in spite of a hugely successful life, still hadn't been seen in its professed city of origin.

ALPÁR, Gitta (b Budapest, 5 February 1900; d Los Angeles, 17 February 1991).

The Hungarian coloratura soprano, daughter of a Budapest cantor, made early appearances in her home town both in opera – as Gilda (*Rigoletto*) at the Budapest Operaház (1923) – and in Operette, starring at the Király Színház as the heroine of *Három a kislány* (*Das Dreimäderlhaus*). She sang thereafter for some years only in grand opera, including periods at Munich (1925–7) and at Berlin's Staatsoper (1927–30), winning particular praise for her Violetta in *La Traviata*, and guested at Covent Garden in 1929 as Sophie in *Der Rosenkavalier*, in a useful career, but one which brought her none of the adulation she would later find when she returned to the musical theatre.

It was in 1930 that she made that return, to create the rôle of Viktória in *Viktória* at Budapest's Fővárosi Operett-színház and again, in German, in Leipzig. As a result of her huge personal success as the Hungarian heroine of Pál Ábrahám's piece, she was swiftly cast in the part of the Princess Elisabeth, opposite Richard Tauber, in the première of Lehár's *Schön ist die Welt* (Metropoltheater, Berlin 1930) and repeated that success. She subsequently appeared in Berlin as Violette in *Das Veilchen vom Montmartre*, in *Der Bettelstudent*, and the following year took on her most famous rôle as Jeanne Dubarry in the reworked version of Millöcker's *Gräfin Dubarry* staged at the Admiralspalast as *Die Dubarry*. She repeated that rôle in Hungary but, after starring as Catherine the Great in *Kaiserin Katharina* and in Ábrahám's subsequent *Ball im Savoy* (1932, Madeleine) in Berlin, the prima donna who had become accepted as the natural successor to Fritzi Massary in the hearts of critics and public was forced from Germany by the early strains of anti-Semitism.

She appeared in Vienna as the star of Miklós Brodszky's *Die verliebte Königin* (1934), paired with Owen Nares in a Hollywood film version of *Die Dubarry*, *I Give My Heart* (1935), and returned to Budapest as *A szerelmes királynő* (*Die verliebte Königin*) and again as Marie-Antoinette in Károly Komjáti's attempt to repeat the *Dubarry* recipe in *Antoinette* (1938). In 1936 she was announced to appear in London in a Brodszky musical with a text by James Bridie and A P Herbert, but ultimately London audiences saw her instead in Brodszky and Herbert's Coronation revue *Home and Beauty* (1937) alongside Binnie Hale and Nelson Keys.

Alpár thereafter based herself in America where she appeared in several other films, and was seen in 1941 in a John Murray Anderson revue, but the career which had promised so stunningly in pre-Nazi Germany never again took off in the same way.

ALTON, Robert [HART, Robert Alton] (b Bennington, Vt, 28 January 1897; d Hollywood, Calif, 12 June 1957).

After a first career as a chorus dancer, Alton became a dance assistant and subsequently a choreographer in his own right, beginning his list of Broadway credits with the dances for the 1933 Winter Garden show *Hold Your Horses*. Amongst the musicals for which he subsequently created the dances were *Anything Goes* (1934), *Leave It To Me!* (1938), *Dubarry Was a Lady* (1939), *Too Many Girls* (1939), *Panama Hattie* (1940), *Pal Joey* (1940), *By Jupiter* (1942), the 1952 revival of *Pal Joey* (also 'production supervisor'), *Hazel Flagg* (1953) and *Me and Juliet* (1953) as well as several editions of the *Ziegfeld Follies* and a number of other revues. For the Fats Waller musical *Early to Bed* (1943), and the Carol Channing vehicle *The Vamp* (1955) he acted as both director and choreographer.

Alton went to Hollywood for the first time in 1935 to direct the Goldwyn Girls sequences in *Strike Me Pink*, and he later spent a considerable period at MGM (1944–53), and choreographed musical sequences for film versions of *Good News* (1947), *Annie Get Your Gun* (1950), *Show Boat* (1951) and *Call Me Madam* (1953) as well as such films as *The Harvey Girls*, *The Ziegfeld Follies*, *Till the Clouds Roll By*, *The Pirate*, *Easter Parade*, *The Barkleys of Broadway*, *The Belle of New York*, *White Christmas* and *There's No Business Like Show Business*. He also directed the movies *Merton of the Movies* (1947) and *Pagan Love Song* (1950).

ALT-WIEN Operette in 3 acts by Gustav Kadelburg and Julius Wilhelm. Music taken from the works of Josef Lanner, arranged by Emil Stern. Carltheater, Vienna, 23 December 1911.

Pretty Lini (Mizzi Zwerenz) lives happily at the beer-house run by her stepfather, Andreas Johann Nepomuk Stöckl (Karl Schöpfer). She entertains the customers with her songs, she has her beloved Franz (Josef König), and some good, jolly friends like Alois Nussberger, the inn's chucker-out (Richard Waldemar). But one day the police-officer Prohaska (Karl Wallner) comes, bringing the Graf Lepold von Tutzing-Garatshausen (Karl Blasel), his sister Philomene (Therese Löwe), his niece Felizitas (Dora Keplinger), and the news that Lini is the nobleman's daughter, the long-lost Countess Hortense. Transported to the Tutzing mansion, Lini finds herself ill at ease in her new home, and when she invites all her friends in for a party in the style she is used to, her new family are aghast. She runs away back to her papa Stöckl and, when the wetnurse finally admits that she lied in order to cover the fact that the noble baby had died, Lini is able to go back to being just the little queen of the 'Zum braunen Hirschen'.

The music of the Strauss family had been arranged and rearranged as the scores for pasticcio Operetten for many years (*Frühlingsluft*, *Das Schwaberl aus dem Wienerwald*, *Das Teufelsmädel*, *Die weisse Fahne* etc), and it was only a matter of time before someone got around to moving on to the melodies of Josef Lanner, the other great Viennese dance composer of the same period, as the raw material for a major Operette. Emil Stern, musical director of the Carltheater, put together 16 musical pieces which largely featured the above-the-title Frln Zwerenz and, to a lesser extent, Frln Keplinger (the manager's wife). Lini took part in each of the five numbers of the first act (Couplets with Stöckl, duos with the Baron Seespitz, with Franz, a waltz ensemble with Nussberger and a finale) and had her big solo moment with the Alt-Wienermarsch 'Ich bin nun

Komtesse' in Act Two where she also shared a Zepperl-polka with her lofty relations, and a Busserlwalzer with Franz. In the final act, a Gespenster-Quartett (w Nussberger, Stöckl, Franz) led up to the final Couplets, led by Lini and Franz. Felizitas featured a solo to open the second act ('Junges Lieben') and two duos with Seespitz.

Alt-Wien proved a real success for the Carltheater, running for 159 performances in its first series and remaining in their repertoire for more than a decade. In 1913 that company, which had already guested *Alt-Wien* at Ronacher in Vienna, introduced the original version to Budapest when they played it in a season at the Király Színház, hard on the heels of an Hungarian version (ad Adolf Mérei) which switched the action to Budapest and changed the title to *A régi Pest*. The show was also a considerable success on German stages, but it was not played further afield. In 1944 a revised and modernized version of the piece (ad Alexander Steinbrecher) was produced at Vienna's Raimundtheater (21 April) as typical 'good old days' entertainment for the last days of the war.

Another piece under the same title, written by Eduard Wagner, was produced at the Graz Stadttheater in 1910.

Germany: ?1912; Hungary: Budapesti Színház *A régi Pest* 28 September 1912, Király Színház (Ger) May 1913

AMADI, Madame [TREMAINE, Annie]. Gaiety Theatre soubrette who became one of London's favourite musical character ladies.

Annie Tremaine led a career as a vocalist in the music halls until John Hollingshead hired her as a member of his original Gaiety Theatre company. She appeared on the first night at the Gaiety as Albert in W S Gilbert's burlesque *Robert the Devil* (1868) and thereafter continuously, for four years, in the personality mezzo-soprano rôles in such of the house's burlesques and comic operas as *Aladdin II* (Karamel), *The Beggar's Opera* (Lucy), *The Waterman* (Wilhelmina), *Thespis* (Daphne), *Cinderella the Younger* (Pamela), *The Forty Thieves* (Hassarac), and the English versions of *La Princesse de Trébizonde* (Zanetta), *La Belle Hélène* (Orestes), *Fra Diavolo* (Lady Allcash) and *Zar und Zimmermann* (Widow Brown), as well as in straight comedy.

In the 1880s and 1890s, having changed her name to suit her second career, she became one of the foremost London players of musical 'heavy' character rôles, appearing in many comic operas, amongst which two pieces played in Paris by Thérésa – the title rôle of *La Boulangère a des écus* (Margot) and *La Belle Normande* (ie *La Famille Trouillat*, Margot) – *The Merry War* (Artemisia), *Our Diva* (Madame Jacob), *Mynheer Jan* (Donna Tralara), *Marjorie* (Lady Alicia), *Captain Thérèse* (La Chanoinesse), *The Golden Web* (Mistress Pamela Patch), *Cigarette* (Comtesse de Montrouget), *The Queen of Brilliants* (Mme Englestein), and *The Taboo* (Wattatauka).

LES AMANTS DE VENISE Opérette à grand spectacle in 2 acts by Henri Varna, Marc-Cab and René Richard based on the books *Le Pont des soupirs* and *Les Amants de Venise* by Michel Zevaco. Music by Vincent Scotto. Théâtre Mogador, Paris, 5 December 1953.

One of the most successful of Henri Varna's Théâtre Mogador series of romantic musical spectacles, *Les Amants de Venise* took 17 scenes of Venetian splendour to follow the 16th-century captain and Doge's son, Roland Candiano (Marcel Merkès), through his problems with a malefic Council of Ten, led by the horrid Altieri (Jacques Harden), who want to stop him wedding the unaristocratic Leonore Dandolo (Paulette Merval). A villainous police-chief (Raymond Danjou), a venal courtesan (Lola Maddalena), a hired assassin (Alexandre Rignault) and a flock of pigeons can do nothing to stop Candiano conquering all opposition by the strength of his sword and a ringing baritone. Jacky Piervil and Jacqueline Mille provided the soubret element, the Ballets de France and Oleg Koby the dance, and the late Vincent Scotto the suitably romantic large-house score, completed shortly before his death.

The piece ran for two full seasons at the Mogador, went to the country, and reappeared in Paris, with Merkès and Merval again heading the cast, for a second run in 1966 (26 November). The baddies were headed by Jean-Jacques Steen, Pierre Plessis and Catherine Bréa, Huguette Duval and Michel Dunand were the soubrets, and Varna himself appeared in the rôle of the Cardinal, as *Les Amants de Venise* added almost another year of performances to its Parisian total before making its way into the repertoire of the provincial houses.

Recordings: selection with original stars (Odéon, CBS)

AMASIS, an Egyptian Princess   Comic opera in 2 acts by Frederick Fenn. Music by Philip Michael Faraday. New Theatre, London, 9 August 1906.

This veritable comic opera, an hilarious piece of Ancient Egyptian nonsense about a Prince who accidentally kills a yowling but definitely sacred cat, appeared, from a combination of writers with no West End credits, in the hands of a management (Louis Calvert) which did not know how to handle such a potential success. Surprised and delighted reviews hailed the piece as a worthy follower of the Gilbert and Sullivan tradition, but the authors and manager got themselves embroiled in theatre trouble, plagiarism suits and internal wranglings and, in the end, the show was closed down after 200 performances with its creators in both financial and personal problems.

The soprano song 'Little Princess, Look Up', as introduced by Ruth Vincent in the piece's title-rôle, became a favourite with recording and concert artists, but, although pictures of the now very stout Rutland Barrington in a preposterous wig and of Lauri de Frece, as the keeper of the royal crocodiles, cuddling his charges in the same way he would make merry with a lobster a decade later in *The Maid of the Mountains* remained in people's memories, the show did not establish itself as it might have following its exciting start. Only the Orient saw it, when the indefatigable Maurice Bandmann snatched it up for his ravenous Asian and Pacific repertoire company.

AMBIENT, Mark   (b Rastrick, 20 June 1860; d Brighton, 9 August 1937). Theatrical wannabe, who (with some help) set up the best musical play of the Edwardian age.

Cambridge-educated Ambient tried his hand at both acting (at the Princess's with Wilson Barrett) and songwriting ('The Old Soldiers', 'Chorus, Gentlemen', 'Love's Return', 'Golden Lilies') without finding any notable success, but did a little better as a writer for the stage. A song 'Comme ça', with music by Edward Solomon, made some

effect in the Gaiety burlesque *Don Juan* (1893), whilst his 'Boots' (Meyer Lutz) as performed by Letty Lind and several numbers written for Harry Monkhouse's touring show *Pat* also proved mildly popular. He also had several plays presented, including *Oh Susannah!* (1897), a London success with Louie Freear starred, and *A Little Ray of Sunshine* (1899) with W S Penley, as well as a botched version of Audran's musical comedy *L'Oncle Célestin*, staged with indifferent results in 1895 at the Trafalgar Square Theatre under the title *Baron Golosh*. He worked with Francis Money-Coutts, a wealthy amateur writer who hired himself co-authors and composers (including Albéniz, introduced to him by Ambient) in order to get his works on the stage, and together they turned out an unproduced musical (music: Edward Solomon) called *A.D. 3000*, and another piece, *The Shepherd Lord* (w Albéniz), apparently produced in Barcelona. He also joined Coutts and his money as part of the syndicate which, for several years, ran the Lyric Theatre before stumbling into receivership.

Ambient frequented, in particular, the important theatrical group which lived and drank in Brighton and his connection there with Robert Courtneidge led him to suggest to the producer an idea for an original musical. Courtneidge accepted the outline, but since Ambient – not the most stable of characters – proved unable to come up with a script, he paired him with his house writer, Alexander M Thompson, who was ultimately responsible for much of the libretto of the show which was to become *The Arcadians*, the classic musical comedy of its era. Courtneidge duly included Ambient in his writing team for the subsequent *The Light Blues* (1915–16), a disastrous flop which all but put the producer out of business and which ended the would-be author's connection with the musical theatre.

1892 **Pat** (John Crook, Alfred Lee et al/w Frederick Wood/George Roberts, Harry Monkhouse) Aquarium, Yarmouth 1 August 1892

1895 **Baron Golosh** (*L'Oncle Célestin*) English version w Meyer Lutz, Leslie Stuart et al (Trafalgar Square Theatre)

1909 **The Arcadians** (Howard Talbot, Lionel Monckton/Arthur Wimperis/w Alexander M Thompson) Shaftesbury Theatre 28 April

1915 **The Light Blues** (Talbot, Herman Finck/Adrian Ross/ w Jack Hulbert) Prince of Wales Theatre, Birmingham 13 September/Shaftesbury Theatre 14 September 1916

AMECHE, Don   [AMICI, Dominic Felix] (b Kenosha, Wis, 31 May 1908)

Best known as the leading man of a run of 1930s and 1940s films (including an appearance as a singing D'Artagnan in *The Three Musketeers* in 1939), Ameche appeared, later in his career, in major rôles in several stage musicals. He was the leading man of *Silk Stockings* (1955, Steve Canfield), in which he romanced the sternly Russian Hildegarde Neff to the strains of 'Paris Loves Lovers', and insisted on 'All of You', he co-starred with Elaine Stritch as madcap movie mogul, Max Grady, in the cinema burlesque *Goldilocks* (1958), and passed briefly by as the Chinese father of *Thirteen Daughters* (1961) and as the titular Henry Orient of the 1967 *Henry, Sweet Henry*.

Outside New York, he was seen in *I Married an Angel* (1964) and as Jimmy Smith in *No, No, Nanette* (1972), and in a long and varied career on television (*Don's Musical*

Playhouse 1951 etc), in a TV version of *High Button Shoes* (NBS 1956).

In 1940 he appeared on film in the rôle of composer Edward Solomon, the paramour of Lillian Russell.

AMERICA'S SWEETHEART Musical comedy in 2 acts by Herbert Fields. Lyrics by Lorenz Hart. Music by Richard Rodgers. Broadhurst Theater, New York, 10 February 1931.

America's Sweetheart was a filmland musical written by Fields, Rodgers and Hart and flavoured by their own recent experiences in newly talking and singing Hollywood. Geraldine (Harriette Lake ie Ann Sothern) and Michael (Jack Whiting) go west to become silent movie stars. She succeeds, he gets left in her wake, and then sound comes and their positions are reversed. The show's songs did not include any which would become part of the Rodgers and Hart songbook, but a depression-time marriage proposal to music, 'I've Got Five Dollars', won some popularity. However, even without hit songs, Laurence Schwab and Frank Mandel's production of *America's Sweetheart* proved popular enough to run for 135 performances on Broadway.

Another musical with the same title centred on a very different kind of sweetheart. Alfred Uhry and John Weidman's *America's Sweetheart* (music: Robert Waldman, Hartford Stage, Hartford, Conn, 5 March 1985) was the story of criminal Al Capone.

L'AMOUR MASQUÉ Comédie musicale in 3 acts by Sacha Guitry. Music by André Messager. Théâtre Edouard VII, Paris, 15 February 1923.

A small-cast (seven principals and a chorus of ten), free verse play in Guitry's most urbanely humorous style, *L'Amour masqué* was designed as a vehicle for, and decorated with a set songs of songs mostly for, Mme Guitry (Yvonne Printemps). Those songs were composed to Guitry's lyrics by the doyen of elegant, old-style musical theatre composers, 70-year-old André Messager.

Elle (Mlle Printemps), although suitably 'protected' by not one but two gentlemen, the Baron (Urban) and the Maharadjah (Pierre Darmant), has fallen in love, with all the rapture of her 20 years, with a photograph of an unknown young man which she has passionately stolen from her photographer's studio. When a dashing, greying gentleman (Guitry, playing 15 years older than his veritable age), who resembles the portrait unmistakably, comes to investigate, she makes him promise to bring his son to a masked dance that evening. At the ball, her two disguised servants (Marthe Ferrare, Marie Dubas) efficaciously distract the two official lovers, whilst she wins herself the willing original of the photograph. In the hectic events of the morning after, she realizes that her new, true lover is nobody's son but her previous day's visitor himself, 24 elegant years after his photograph session.

Messager's score was a perfect complement to this witty and often satirical little romantic idyll of the belles années and the beau monde, and it produced one of his most enduring single songs in the heroine's first-act 'J'ai deux amants'. Saying goodbye to her teens, she laughingly describes her financially satisfying arrangement with the Baron and the Maharadjah, wondering mockingly over the stupidity of men to the celebrated refrain 'Mais, mon Dieu, que c'est bête, un homme...'. Amongst her other songs, the celebration of her 'Vingt ans!' and her uncomplicated summing up of her own appeal, 'Elle est charmante', stood out. The more flagrantly comic songs were the province of the two lovers. The Baron described with horror his wife's adventure with a young dancing partner, in tango time ('Valentine a perdu la tête'), and cockily assured the disguised maid that 'J' n'aime pas les bonnes', whilst the Maharadjah's gobbledegook lovemaking (not translated, for once, by his omnipresent interpreter), was a highlight of the entertainment. The rôle of Lui also had some musical sections, which Guitry spoke through the small accompanying orchestra.

L'Amour masqué scored a fine Parisian success before Guitry and Mlle Printemps moved on to other successes, leaving it behind, but it returned to Paris, at the Palais-Royal, in 1970 with Jean Marais (Lui), Arlette Didier (Elle) and Jean Parèdes featured, and an orchestra conducted by the composer Georges van Parys. A German-language version (ad Robert Blum) was produced by its adaptor as a late-night entertainment at Vienna's Modernes Theater in 1924 with Lea Seidl and Otto Storm featured in the Guitrys' rôles, but no one seems yet to have been game to adapt Guitry's exquisite lines into English.

Austria: Modernes Theater 2 February 1924

Recording: 1970 revival cast (Decca), original star excerpts on *Les Triomphes d'Yvonne Printemps* (EMI)

L'AMOUR MOUILLÉ Opéra-comique in 3 acts by Jules Prével and Armand Liorat. Music by Louis Varney. Théâtre des Nouveautés, Paris, 25 January 1887.

Allegedly based, at least in part, on an ode by Anacreon, Liorat and Prével's libretto for *L'Amour mouillé* was nevertheless set in the 16th century, in a city on the shores of the Ionian sea. A statue of Cupid, left by the Greeks during one of their occupations of Tarento, arouses the curiosity of the local teenage girls. None of them, including the Princess Lauretta (Mlle Darcelle), who is about to be married off to the foolish Ascanio (Guy), knows what 'love' is, and when they read that this, his representative, shoots kindly people with his arrows, they decide to throw the statue in the sea. They are aghast when a man arises from the waves. They think he is the God of Love, but he is in fact shipwrecked Prince Carlo of Syracuse (Maria Nixau) and, after two acts of quiproquos it is he who will marry Lauretta. The comical content of the piece was supplied by the politically and nuptially machinating Pampinelli (Jules Brasseur) and his rosy wife, Catarina (Marie Desclauzas), who rediscovers the love of her earlier life in the person of the prince's secretary, Cascarino (Albert Brasseur).

With the rôle of the Prince being played by a soprano en travesti, the bulk of Varney's attractive score was written for female voices. Carlo's serenade 'Prisonnier dans sa cage' and its connected waltz duo 'P'tit fi! petit mignon!' (w Lauretta) proved one of the lyric highlights of the evening, alongside the heroine's pretty barcarolle ('Il pleuvait et le vent soufflait'), her legend of 'L'Amour mouillé', and the comical song of Catarina who, in order to help Cascarino escape trouble, hides him in a barrow and pretends to go back to her old career as 'La marchande d'oranges'. Cascarino had two comedy numbers and shared a duet,

25

but otherwise the 19 numbers (excluding finales) of the score were devoted to the ladies.

With two celebrated comedians such as Brasseur and Mme Desclauzas at the head of the bill, *L'Amour mouillé* was, predictably, a great success on its production at the Nouveautés. It was played 140 times en suite for its first run, and subsequently reprised at the Athénée-Comique. It was, oddly, only exported a decade later, but its foreign productions, though numerous, had little success, whether in the German language (ad Heinrich Bolten-Bäckers) or in the English version, produced by Tom B Davis at London's Lyric Theatre. Intended there as the producer's successor to his highly successful first venture with *Little Miss Nobody*, the show was produced with much splendour, a cast including Evie Greene (Carlo), Kate Cutler (Catarina), John Le Hay (Pampinelli) and Jessie Huddlestone (Lauretta), and some interpolated songs by Paul and Walter Rubens. In spite of cuts, changes, the importation of some French dancers and a title change to the theoretically more accessible *Cupid and the Princess*, what appeared an essentially old-fashioned piece failed to take in London and closed after less than three forced months.

In Vienna, Alexandrine von Schönerer's staging of *Der verregnete Amor*, with Frln Frey (Carlo), Marie Ottmann (Lauretta) and Karl Blasel (Pampinelli) was taken off after three performances, whilst Lajos Máko and Emil Makai's Hungarian version did little better.

An earlier musical, a one-act piece also entitled *L'Amour mouillé* and apparently based on an 1850 play of the same title, was produced at the Paris Fantaisies-Parisiennes in 1868 (30 May). Jules Barbier and Arthur de Beauplan were the librettists and the score was composed by E de Hartog.

Austria: Theater an der Wien *Der verregnete Amor* 18 November 1897; Germany: Leipzig *Der Liebesgott* 29 January 1898; UK: Lyric Theatre aka *Cupid and the Princess* 5 April 1899; Hungary: Budai Színkör *Megázott ámor* 16 June 1899

LES AMOURS DE DON JUAN Opérette à grand spectacle in 2 acts by Henri Varna, Marc-Cab and René Richard. Music by Jean Morata. Additional music by Pauline Zevaco. Théâtre Mogador, Paris, 23 December 1955.

Henri Varna's Théâtre Mogador successor to the lush *Les Amants de Venise*, *Les Amours de Don Juan* brought the stars of the previous show, Marcel Merkès and Paulette Merval, back in another richly spectacular large-stage production. He played a descendant of the famous rake, thrown out of Spain for his sins, and gallivanting round the world in search of sex (Mlle Merval as Antonia) and scenery. A score by Spanish composer Juan Morata began in 'Le Soleil Catalan' where 'Un Appel de castagnettes' gave local colour and, after he had said 'Adieu, mon Espagne', opened up into a series of romantic numbers ('Mon premier amour', 'Viens, mon coeur est à toi', 'Ne dites pas "je t'aime"' etc) and the occasional bit of local colour. The star team headed the production through most of its 18 months' run with the support of soubrets Eddy Rasimi and Frédérique.

Recording: original cast (Odéon)

ANATEVKA *see* FIDDLER ON THE ROOF

ANDALOUSIE Opérette à grand spectacle in 2 acts by Albert Willemetz and Raymond Vincy. Music by Francis Lopez. Théâtre de la Gaîté-Lyrique, Paris, 25 October 1947.

One of the most successful of the series of postwar musicals authored by Vincy (and, in this case, Willemetz) and Lopez, *Andalousie* adhered closely to the classic formula which had been so successful in their first big hit, *La Belle de Cadix*. There was a big, central tenor rôle made to feature the earlier show's star, Luis Mariano, who was again paired with a soprano sweetheart and supported by a contrasting soubret pair, a rival-in-love baritone, and some minor comedy characters, all embroiled in a story where romance, comedy and a touch of drama were mixed with a mise-en-scène which, whilst allowing plenty of colour, did not rely on its grand spectacle as its principal attraction, as did too many Parisian musical shows a few years later.

The poor Andalusian pot-seller Juanito (Mariano) makes himself a name as a bull-fighter and, promising to return, rich and famous, to his beloved Dolores (Marina Hotine), he sets sail to take up a contract in Caracas. To the annoyance of the dashing rebel Rodriguez Valiente (Pierre Faure), he attracts the attentions of the Viennese soprano Fanny Miller (Sophia Botény), who intercepts his letters home, leaving the disappointed Dolores to give up waiting and take a job as a saucy singer. When Juanito arrives home, triumphant, with Fanny following in his wake, he is horrified, and Valiente venges himself for Frln Miller's indifference by taking up with the Spanish girl. Things come to a peak when the desperate Juanito almost lets himself be gored in the ring. Fanny admits her deception and returns with Valiente (now – thanks to a little revolution – promoted President) to Venezuela, leaving the lovers to a happy ending.

The parallel comic tale concerned little Pépé (Maurice Bacquet), who spends the evening gathering together all the impossible items needed for the gipsy love potion which will win him Pilar (Gise Mey), a señorita who is determined to wed only the man predicted to her by a local fortune-teller. Pépé follows Juanito to Venezuela, as does a curious little fellow called Baedecker (O'Brady) who has this crazy idea of writing travel guide books. They get mixed up with a large South American with a larger knife (Metairie) and suffer many a vagary before their happy ending is reached.

Lopez's score was a blatantly tuneful one. The tenor ran the gamut, entering as 'Le Marchand d'alacarazas', swearing his love for Dolores ('Je veux t'aimer d'un amour merveilleux') and his country ('Andalucia mia') in throbbing tones, challenging the bull ('Olé Torero'), arriving home rhythmically to 'C'est la fête à Seville' and pouring out his troubled heart to 'Santa Maria' in a pre-fight prayer, whilst the soprano had one of Lopez's prettiest waltz tunes in the tipsy 'Ça fait tourner la tête', sung by Dolores as she nervously sips an unaccustomed sherry whilst awaiting her staged rendez-vous with Valiente. The baritone song ('Seul, je vais par tous les chemins') and the soubret pieces were a touch less effective than their *Belle de Cadix* equivalents, but the sum total was a score which was as good as anything of its time and place.

Andalousie confirmed the success of *La Belle de Cadix* with a 12-month run at the Gaîté-Lyrique before heading for the provinces and other French-speaking parts of the world. A film version, with Mariano and Baquet teamed with Carmen Sevilla and Liliane Bert, was produced by

Robert Vernay in 1950, and the show returned to Paris in 1954 for a season (Gaîté-Lyrique, August) with Rudi Hirigoyen, Baquet and Mlles Mey (Dolores), Arta Verlen and Doris Marnier featured. Since that date, *Andalousie* has been regularly reprised in French provincial theatres.

Film: Robert Vernay, L Lucia 1951
Recordings: original cast recordings compiled (EMI-Pathé), selections (Odéon, Philips, CBS) etc

ANDERSEN, Hans Christian (b Odense, 2 April 1805; d nr Copenhagen, 4 August 1875).

Storyteller Hans Andersen made several attempts as an operatic librettist, adapting Scott's *The Bride of Lammermoor* for Ivar Bredal (before the appearance of Donizetti's version), Gozzi's *Il Corvo* for J P E Hartmann (1832), and Manzoni's *I promessi sposi* for Franz Gläser (1849) as well as supplying the original text for the successful one-act *Liden Kristin* (Hartmann, 1846) and several plays with music. It is, however, not those pieces but the tales which made him famous which have won him his place in the theatre, providing the subject matter for numerous entertainments of all kinds, all around the world.

There have been Danish operatic versions of his stories of *The Match Girl* (*Pigen med svovlstikkerne*), *The Princess and the Pea* (*Prinsessen paa aerten*), *The Emperor's Nightingale* (*Nattergallen*) and *The Emperor's New Clothes* (*Kejserens nye klaeder*), the Hungarian composer Ede Poldini composed a one-act *A csavargó és királylány* on *The Swineherd and the Princess* (1903) and Igor Stravinsky produced, with his *Rossignol* (1914), what is probably the most substantial piece of musical Andersen. In the English-language theatre, Charles Villiers Stanford composed an operatic *The Travelling Companion* whilst Ernst Toch set a *Die Prinzessin auf der Erbse*, later played as *The Princess and the Pea* in New York (1936).

On the light musical stage, *Ib and Little Christina*, originally presented as a play by Martin Harvey, was adapted as a London musical by Basil Hood, given a score by Franco Leoni, and played at the Savoy Theatre (14 November 1901), whilst a version of *The Swineherd and the Princess* (Royalty Theatre 19 December 1901) was given a seasonal production the same year. A piece called *Little Hans Andersen* (Adelphi Theatre, London, 1903, Walter Slaughter/Basil Hood) tried out four years earlier at Terry's Theatre as *Hans Andersen's Fairytales* introduced *The Emperor's New Clothes*, *Ole-Luk-Oie*, *The Red Shoes*, *The Princess and the Swineherd*, *The Tinder Box* and *The Little Mermaid* in the course of its action. An operettic version of *The Emperor's New Clothes* was composed by the Swedish Charles Kjerulf and produced in Stockholm in November 1889, and *The Princess and the Pea* was apparently put to contribution for an unlikely sounding Czech piece, *König Blaubart und die Prinzessin auf der Erbse*, written and composed by Maria Günther and staged in Prague in 1896. Vienna's Theater an der Wien presented a *Die wilden Schwäne* (ad Feld), with a score by Adolf Müller, 8 October 1871, which was billed as a 'féerie nachdem gleichnamigen Märchen Andersens', whilst *The Travelling Companion* became *Wanderhansel* (mus: Max Clarus) in Braunschweig in 1914 (Hoftheater, 5 December).

Vienna's Ronacher and Carltheater presented a piece by L Novak, J Kvapil and Emil Kläger, with a score by Oskar Nedbal, under the title *Andersen* (1914), in which Karl Hübner appeared as Andersen through seven scenes of his tales, but the major stage depiction of Andersen as a character came in a 1974 musical, *Hans Andersen*, based on Frank Loesser's score to the hugely successful Danny Kaye film, *Hans Christian Andersen*, and with a libretto built round a fictionalized life of the writer. Produced at the London Palladium (Loesser/Tommy Steele, Beverly Cross), it was subsequently revived and played widely through the British provinces. Another *Hans Andersen*, written by Irene Mann and adapted by Kurt Huemer and Sepp Tatzel, was produced at Vienna's Raimundtheater in 1986 (8 February).

Amongst the post-war musicals based on Andersen's works, the most widely successful has been the witty American *Once Upon a Mattress*, like Norbert Schulz and Dolly Hardt's *Die Prinzessin auf der Erbse* (Berlin 28 November 1954), another version of *The Princess and the Pea*. Versions of *The Emperor's Nightingale* have come from Poland (Ernst Bryll/Piotr Hertel), Germany (Hans Schanzara/Herbert Hennies Cologne 31 December 1947) and America and Britain (Charles Strouse, New York 1982, Buxton Festival 1982), whilst David Wood authored a children's musical version of *The Tinderbox* (Worcester 26 December 1967), a piece which was also the basis of the German musical *Der Soldat und das Feuerzeug* (Thomas Bürkholz/Heinz-Martin Benecke). *The Little Match Girl* was seen at London's Orange Tree Theatre as *Scraps* (27 December 1977) and subsequently televised.

Autobiography: *The Story of my Life* (1855); Biography: Bain, R N: *Hans Christian Andersen, a Biography* (1895)

ANDERSON, Arthur (d 1942). Songwriter and adapter, prominent before and during the war in the London theatre.

After having made his first venture into the musical theatre with the lyrics to a flop musical version of *The Lady of Lyons*, Anderson moved on to success when he wrote lyrics and part-libretti for two Frank Curzon productions, *The White Chrysanthemum* and *The Girl Behind the Counter*, and the lyrics to *Butterflies*, the attractive musical version of W J Locke's whimsical play *The Palace of Puck*.

He subsequently adapted and/or relyricked a good number of Continental musical plays for the English stage, but otherwise concentrated largely on non-theatre songwriting, for a while as part of a group which also included James Tate, Clifford Harris, Valentine, Ord Hamilton and Donovan Parsons. He scored a song success with 'Somewhere in France With You' (w Tate, Valentine 1918), and lyricked interpolated numbers in such pieces as *A Night Out*, *Jenny*, *His Girl*, *The Last Waltz* ('Nur eine Nacht' ad as 'Just For a While'), and a revival of *The Maid of the Mountains*.

In 1916 he had one further original success with a vaudevillesque piece called *Toto* which toured for several seasons after its original West End run, and was seen as far afield as Budapest.

1901 **Melnotte, or The Gardener's Bride** (Frank E Tours/Herbert Shelley) Coronet Theatre 30 September
1905 **The White Chrysanthemum** (Howard Talbot/w Leedham Bantock) Criterion Theatre 31 August
1906 **The Girl Behind the Counter** (Talbot/w Bantock) Wyndham's Theatre 21 April

1908 **Butterflies** (J H Robertson/w T H Read/W J Locke) Apollo Theatre 12 May

1910 **Two Merry Monarchs** (Orlando Morgan/w Hartley Carrick/w George Levy) Savoy Theatre 10 March

1911 **Nightbirds** (*Die Fledermaus*) English lyrics (Lyric Theatre) and as *The Merry Countess* (New York, 1912)

1912 **Darby and Joan** (*Brüderlein fein*) English version (London Coliseum)

1912 **The Daring of Diane** (*Die süssen Grisetten*) English version (Tivoli)

1912 **Two Little Brides** (*Schneeglöckchen*) American version w Harold Atteridge, J T Powers (Casino Theater, New York)

1912 **The Grass Widows** revised version of *Two Little Brides* w Hartley Carrick (Apollo Theatre)

1912 **The H'arum Lily** (*Abenteuer in Harem*) English version w Carrick (London Pavilion)

1913 **The Marriage Market** (*Leányvásár*) English version w Adrian Ross, Gladys Unger (Daly's Theatre)

1914 **The Joy Ride Lady** (*Autoliebchen*) English version w Carrick (New Theatre)

1916 **Toto** (Archibald Joyce, Merlin Morgan/Gladys Unger) Duke of York's Theatre 19 April

1917 **The Beauty Spot** (James Tate/Clifford Harris, Valentine/w P-L Flers) Gaiety Theatre 22 December

1924 **Springtime** (*Frühling*) 1 act English version (Empire Theatre)

ANDERSON, [James] Maxwell (b Atlantic, Pa, 15 December 1888; d Stamford, Conn, 28 February 1959).

A highly regarded and successful American playwright (*What Price Glory?* w Laurence Stallings, *Winterset*, *High Tor*, *Key Largo*, *Anne of the Thousand Days* etc), Anderson collaborated on two Broadway musicals with a purposefully left-wing political bias with composer Kurt Weill. In *Knickerbocker Holiday*, the first and more successful of the pair, he notably composed the lyric to the show's take-out tune 'September Song'. The second, *Lost in the Stars*, was a musical theatre adaptation of the South African novel *Cry, the Beloved Country*. Both reached the cinema screen in their musical versions, *Knickerbocker Holiday* in 1944 and *Lost in the Stars* in 1974.

The 1980 off-Broadway musical *Elizabeth and Essex* (York Theater, Doug Katsaros/Richard Engquist/Michael Stewart, Mark Bramble, 16 performances) was based on Anderson's play *Elizabeth the Queen* (1920), whilst his *High Tor* was adapted as a television film musical, with a score by Arthur Schwartz, in 1956.

1938 **Knickerbocker Holiday** (Kurt Weill) Barrymore Theater 19 October

1949 **Lost in the Stars** (Weill) Music Box Theater 30 October

Biography: Clark, B: *Maxwell Anderson: The Man and His Plays* (Samuel French, New York, 1933), Shivers, A S: *The Life of Maxwell Anderson* (Stein & Day, New York, 1983)

ANDERSON, Percy (b ?Hendon, 1851; d Crondall, Hants, 30 October 1928). One of Britain's most effective costume designers for the Victorian and Edwardian stage.

Percy Anderson made his début as a designer for the theatre with the majority of the costumes for the comic opera *The Lady of the Locket* (1885), composed by his friend William Fullerton, and staged with much splendour at the new Empire Theatre under the management of actor John Shine and John Hollingshead. These costumes were designed and made with a lavishness and individuality uncommon in the theatre of the time (in a large cast, each chorister's clothes were separately designed) and Ander-

son won extended critical approval for his 'rich and gorgeous dresses.' His array of variously shaded crimson Venetian costumes earned him acclaim as the first theatrical designer to use other than the primary colours which had been de rigueur on the British stage in the age of gas lighting.

Anderson quickly became one of the foremost costume designers in the British musical theatre, being engaged by George Edwardes for the costumes of the internationally successful series of Gaiety Theatre new burlesques from *Monte Cristo jr* in 1886 to *Carmen-up-to-Data* in 1890, by D'Oyly Carte for the original *The Gondoliers*, *The Yeomen of the Guard*, *The Nautch Girl* and the latter day Savoy Theatre comic operas, and for Edwardes's four greatest products from Daly's Theatre, *The Geisha* (1896), *A Greek Slave* (1898), *San Toy* (1899) and *A Country Girl* (1902). He also designed a number of American productions.

During the first decade of the 20th century, whilst venturing into all areas of theatre, including the designs for a complete *Ring of the Nibelungs* in Germany, Anderson designed regularly for Edwardes and other musical managements in Britain and in America, including amongst his work Edward German's *Merrie England* and *A Princess of Kensington*, Ivan Caryll's Napoleonic *The Duchess of Dantzic*, the Gaiety musicals *The Girls of Gottenberg* and *Havana*, and the daffodil-drenched *The Belle of Brittany*.

In 1916 he designed the costumes for the spectacular production of *Chu Chin Chow* at His Majesty's Theatre, and followed up with such pieces as *A Southern Maid* at Daly's, the beautifully staged *Monsieur Beaucaire* with Maggie Teyte, the vast Comstock and Gest New York spectacular *Aphrodite*, and Oscar Asche's dazzling pageant *Mecca/Cairo*. In his 75th year he designed Künneke's *Riki-Tiki* for the Gaiety Theatre.

ANDERSSON, Benny (b Stockholm, 16 December 1946).

A member of the highly popular singing group Abba, Andersson collaborated with fellow member Björn Ulvaeus on the composition of the songs which the group took to the top of the charts ('Dancing Queen', 'Knowing Me Knowing You', 'The Name of the Game', 'Take a Chance on Me', 'The Winner Takes It All' etc). Their music formed the basis of three juvenile pasticcio made-for-records shows compiled in France, one of which was staged in Britain, before they collaborated with librettist/lyricist Tim Rice on the musical *Chess* ('I Know Him So Well', 'Heaven Help My Heart', 'One Night in Bangkok').

1983 **Abbacadabra** (Alain Boublil, Daniel Boublil ad Don Black, David Wood) Lyric Theatre, Hammersmith, London 8 December)

1986 **Chess** (w Ulvaeus/Tim Rice) Prince Edward Theatre, London 14 May

ANDREWS, Julie [WELLS, Julia Elizabeth] (b Walton-on-Thames, 1 October 1935). Stage and screen singing star of the 1950s and 1960s.

A child soprano in variety and pantomime, Julie Andrews appeared in the 1947 revue *Starlight Roof* singing Ambroise Thomas's coloratura aria 'Je suis Titania'. She was seen as principal girl in the London Palladium pantomime of 1953 and was subsequently cast in the ingénue rôle of Polly Browne in the American reproduction of the London success, *The Boy Friend* (1954).

She created the rôle of Eliza Doolittle in *My Fair Lady* (1956) on Broadway, introducing 'I Could Have Danced All Night', 'Show Me', 'Wouldn't It Be Loverly' and 'Just You Wait, Henry Higgins', and repeated her triumphant American success opposite Rex Harrison and Stanley Holloway in London's production of the show (1958), before going on to star in Lerner and Loewe's subsequent *Camelot* (1960), playing Queen Guenevere ('Take Me to the Fair', 'The Simple Joys of Maidenhood' etc) to the King Arthur of Richard Burton. Her success in musical theatre was mirrored in musical film where she appeared in the title-rôles of *Mary Poppins* (Academy Award, 1964), *Thoroughly Modern Millie* (1967) and, most notably, as Maria von Trapp in the blockbusting film version of *The Sound of Music* (1965, 'I Have Confidence', 'Something Good'). She also impersonated Gertrude Lawrence in a filmland biography entitled *Star!* (1968) and appeared in television musical versions of *High Tor* (1956) and *Cinderella* (1957).

Coolly attractive with a clear, effortless soprano tied to utterly undistorted sung English, Andrews has chosen to spend the last 30 years as a film and television actress and had not appeared in the musical theatre since *Camelot* until taking part in the compilation show *Putting It Together* at the Manhattan Theater Club in 1993.

Biography: Cottrell, J: *Julie Andrews: The Story of a Star* (Barker, London, 1968), Windeler, R: *Julie Andrews* (Putnam, New York, 1970) etc

AND SO TO BED
Comedy in 3 acts by J B Fagan with music and lyrics by Vivian Ellis. New Theatre, London, 17 October 1951.

A musical version of Fagan's highly successful play (Queen's Theatre, 6 September 1926) on the fictional flirtations of the historical Samuel Pepys and King Charles II, planned around comic Leslie Henson in the latter days of his career, *And So to Bed* allowed the star to show off a different side of his comic persona from the energetically frog-faced efforts which had made him a favourite. Cast as the unfortunately amorous diarist, caught up in an embarrassing situation with Mistress Knight (Jessie Royce Landis), the mistress of the King (Keith Michell), Henson had a comic rôle of fine farcical potential which required, and got, none of the ad lib gagging usually inserted by musical comedians into their rôles.

Ellis's accompanying music was written in an elegant period style, ranging from madrigal to rigadon and jig, and had the air of being more an extended score of incidental songs and music, of a ballad opera nature, than the musical part of a modern musical play.

In spite of the fact that Henson's traditional audience had problems accepting him in a different style of rôle, Jack de Leon's production of *And So to Bed* had a fine West End run of 323 performances. The show was subsequently revised and made into more of a regular musical comedy to be taken on tour with Henson supported by the popular singing team of Ann Ziegler and Webster Booth as Mistress Knight and the King.

A British television musical version of *And So to Bed*, with a score by Cyril Ornadel, was produced by ITV under the title *Pepys*.

Recording: original cast recordings compiled on WRC

ANGEL FACE
Musical farce in 3 acts by Harry B Smith based on the play *Some Baby* by Zellah Covington and Jules Simonson. Lyrics by Robert B Smith. Music by Victor Herbert. Colonial Theater, Chicago, 8 June 1919; Knickerbocker Theater, New York, 29 December 1919.

George Lederer's production of Victor Herbert's *Angel Face* did not have a smooth life. An adaptation of the play *Some Baby* (1915), originally played at the Fulton Theater with Francine Larrimore, Frank Lalor and Emma Janvier featured in its cast, it had a plot based on a rejuvenating elixir into which a certain number of singing-dancing young couples were eased. Marguerite Zender was Betty, the ingenuous-looking lass of the musical's title, anxious to entrap the sculptor Arthur Griffin (Tyler Brooke), who is, at the outset, engaged to her older sister, Vera (Minerva Grey). On the comical side George Schiller played a Professor Barlow, who thinks his elixir has turned the comical Tessie (Emilie Lea) into a baby. John F Young was a would-be musical comedy writer, and vaudeville's Jack Donahue topped up the principal cast as a correspondence-school detective called Slooch. The cast was equipped with a Victor Herbert score which included a medley of his old hits, and one new one: 'I Might Be Your Once-In-A-While'.

The show opened in Chicago where it was well received, but it was stopped in its tracks by an actors' strike. It was re-routed to Philadelphia and Boston and, having twice changed comedienne en route (Ada Meade giving way to first Adele Rowland and then Emilie Lea), it landed on Broadway six months after its première only to be shunted out after a 57-performance season because the theatre was otherwise booked. It went profitably touring, but attracted further complications when one of the original play's producers sued the other two, claiming they had unilaterally sold off the musical rights and he hadn't been paid.

Angel Face had its worst time, however, when Norman J Norman produced it in London with Winifred Barnes in the title rôle, alongside Brooke, Mabel Sealby, Eric Blore and George Gregory. It won what were reported as 'the most adverse press criticisms for some time' and came off after 13 performances.

UK: Strand Theatre 11 October 1922

ANIMAL CRACKERS
Musical comedy in 2 acts by George S Kaufman and Morrie Ryskind. Music and lyrics by Bert Kalmar and Harry Ruby. 44th Street Theater, New York, 23 October 1928.

A third stage vehicle for the Marx Brothers, following their successes with *I'll Say She Is* and *The Cocoanuts*, *Animal Crackers* had the four comedians performing their special brand of comedy in and around a little plot about a painting stolen from the Long Island home of richly endowed Mrs Rittenhouse (Margaret Dumont). Groucho Marx played the part of the celebrated explorer, the solar-topeed Captain Spalding, who sets out to track down the thief and recover the picture, yet the authors still managed to get him into an elaborate period costume to impersonate King Louis in an encounter with Madame Dubarry. Chico was the suitably Italianate musico Emanuel Ravelli, Zeppo was one Jamison, and Harpo sported knickers and top-hat as The Professor, bumbling around in the dark and a simultaneous thunderstorm to remove the not-so-very-crucial picture from its place. Alice Wood completed the principal line-up as ingénue Miss Arabella Rittenhouse.

The short musical score which crept in amongst the clowning included 'Watching the Clouds Roll By', 'The Long Island Low Down' and 'Who's Been Listening to My Heart?', but the song success of the piece was Groucho Marx's entrance number, 'Hooray for Captain Spalding' (and his reply 'Hello, I Must Be Going').

Animal Crackers proved a good vehicle for the team. Hailed as an 'uproarious slapstick comedy... a new fury of puns and gibes...' for what were undoubtedly 'the maddest troupe of comedians of the day... nihilists [who provide] vulgar mountebankery [with] bewildering, passing, stinging thrusts at everything in general, including themselves', it played a Broadway run of 191 performances, following which the brothers put their performances down on film.

It was barely a musical film, as one new song, 'Why Am I So Romantic?' replaced almost all of the rest of the stage score – except, of course, 'Hooray for Captain Spalding'. It was, as the stage show was, a zany comedy show equipped with musical parts which filled a very secondary place. Being so wholly made-to-measure for the Marxes, *Animal Crackers* had little life beyond its original production, but it was given a showing, in a version stiffened with further (mostly) Kalmar/Ruby songs at Washington's Arena Stage in 1982 (8 May), and another at Connecticut's Goodspeed Opera House in 1992 (23 September).

Film: Paramount 1930

ANKLES AWEIGH

ANKLES AWEIGH Musical comedy in 2 acts by Guy Bolton and Eddie Davis. Lyrics by Dan Shapiro. Music by Sammy Fain. Mark Hellinger Theater, New York, 18 April 1955.

Following on behind, and in the same style as the same authors' successful *Follow the Girls*, *Ankles Aweigh* was a 'musical comedy' which, in an era where the romantic musical play had become the fashion, thoroughly deserved that description. Jane Kean played a Hollywood starlet called Wynne and Mark Dawson her navy-airman newly wed husband, who spent the evening attempting to consummate their marriage on what was supposed to be a nice, peaceful honeymoon. The smidgin of plot, decorated by lashings of mostly cheerfully low comedy, skated from one picturesque Mediterranean location to another in what was described as 'a story about a movie company on location in Italy, some American sailors, intrigue, misunderstandings, strumpets in Morocco, a stolen code, an interrupted honeymoon etc'. The leading lady's sister, Betty Kean (they shared the top billing) paired with Lew Parker in support as Elsey and Dinky.

The four featured players largely cornered the music of the show, which ranged from the enthusiastic 'Kiss Me and Kill Me with Love' to the heroine's assertion that 'Nothing Can Replace a Man' and the strange wish to 'Walk Like a Sailor'. The number-three lady, Betty George, as Lucia indulged in the 'Headin' for the Bottom Blues'.

The show's cheerful ingenuousness provoked such comments from the serious-minded as 'imagine that nothing interesting has developed in the field of musical comedy for the last ten or fifteen years... it leaves off where modern musical comedy began, [with] the worn-out

staples of show business that presumably were laid away in the store-house a long time ago'. However, there were sufficient folk about who just liked a good, low, fun time for Anthony Brady Farrell's production to run through 176 Broadway performances without managing to repeat the success won by *Follow the Girls* at home and abroad.

A revival of a revised version (ad Charles Busch) was mounted at the Goodspeed Opera House, Connecticut 13 July 1988.

Recording: original cast (Decca, AEI)

ANNE OF GREEN GABLES Musical in 2 acts by Donald Harron based on the novel by Lucy Maud Montgomery. Lyrics by Donald Harron and Norman Campbell (later also Mavor Moore, Elaine Campbell). Music by Norman Campbell. Confederation Centre Theatre, Charlottetown, Canada, August 1965.

L M Montgomery's 1908 Canadian novel, *Anne of Green Gables*, a popular favourite with young lady readers through the years, was twice translated to the large screen (silently in 1919 with Mary Miles Minter, 1934 with Anne Shirley) before Donald Harron and Norman Campbell wrote a television musical version which was produced in Canada in 1956. Nearly a decade later, that version was re-adapted and extended into a full-length stage musical, and produced at Charlottetown, in the area where the events of the novel take place.

Anne is sent from an orphanage to live with Matthew and Marilla Cuthbert, who had intended to adopt a boy to help on their farm. Used to sticking up for herself, she has run-ins with the local busybody and with some chaffing fellow students, but wins friends both in school and at home as she works her way towards the top of the class, at the expense of rival Gilbert Blythe. By the final curtain all hearts, on stage and off, are Anne's.

Three seasons at Charlottetown prefaced showings around Canada for the show, and in 1969 Canadian producer Bill Freedman mounted the show in London. Polly James played Anne, with Hiram Sherman and Barbara Hamilton as her adoptive 'parents', through a run of 319 West End performances. *Anne of Green Gables* was subsequently seen for 16 performances at New York's City Center, and has continued to win hardy annual productions in Canada.

UK: New Theatre 16 April 1969; USA: City Center 21 December 1971
Recordings: London cast (CBS), Charlottetown revival 1984 (Ready)

ANNIE Musical in 2 acts by Thomas Meehan based on the cartoon strip *Little Orphan Annie* by Harold Gray. Lyrics by Martin Charnin. Music by Charles Strouse. Goodspeed Opera House, East Haddam, Conn, 10 August 1976; Alvin Theater, New York, 21 April 1977.

Beloved, since 1924, by readers of *The Chicago Tribune* and by other newspaper comic-strip devotees around the world, mop-headed, pinafore-frocked Little Orphan Annie made her way on to the musical stage for the first time, half a century on, at Connecticut's Goodspeed Opera House, at that time the breeding-ground of several successful new musicals.

Annie (Kristin Vigard) is an outspoken little orphan who unsuccessfully runs away from the home presided over by the grotesque Miss Hannigan (Maggie Task) into the big, wide world that is New York City. Her second escape is luckier. She succeeds in getting herself chosen to be the un-owned child whom exorbitantly rich and powerful Daddy Warbucks (Reid Shelton) will conscience-salvingly treat to a moneyed Christmas. Warbucks falls under the insistent charm of the little girl, and promises to help her find the parents who, she is sure, would come back for her if they could. He even gets not only the President of the United States but the National Broadcasting Corporation in on the act. Alas, the only candidates who pass the test turn out to be Miss Hannigan's rascally brother and his moll in greedy disguise. Little Orphan Annie really is an orphan, but by the final curtain she has found herself a fine replacement father in Daddy Warbucks.

Strouse and Charnin's songs helped bring the cartoon characters off the page without ever making the mistake of making them too three-dimensional. Little Annie dreamed of her missing family ('Maybe'), joined her orphan friends asserting 'It's the Hard-Knock Life', stormed out her optimistic hopes for 'Tomorrow' in one of the show's most takeable-away tunes and joined in the jolly hymn in praise of 'NYC', whilst the personnel of the radio Hour of Smiles gave forth with a catchy pastiche of old radioland in 'You're Never Fully Dressed Without a Smile'. Two of the piece's most effective songs, however, were late arrivals in the score: Miss Hannigan's venomously frightened description of what 'Little Girls' do to her nervous equilibrium, and the greasy song-and-dance trio in which she joins her accomplices in dreaming of 'Easy Street'.

Mike Nichols's Broadway production followed eight months behind the original provincial staging. Shelton repeated his portrayal of bald-headed Daddy Warbucks – a rôle which was to go on to force many an actor to have his head shaven to chime with the original cartoon – alongside Dorothy Loudon as Miss Hannigan and Andrea McArdle, promoted from minor orphanhood at Goodspeed to the title-rôle, tricked out in the curly red wig and white-collared and -cuffed red dress which would be the uniform of countless Annies. Sandy Faison played Warbucks's secretary, Grace Farrell, Robert Fitch and Barbara Erwin were the phoney parents, and there was of course, Sandy, the dog, a familiar character from the original cartoon strip, to provide the 'animal' to go with the 'child'.

The show hit the spot precisely, and was quickly established as a hit of the first degree, with an appeal which went well beyond the family groups which might have seemed at first to be its natural audience. Nichols's production stayed for 2,377 performances on Broadway as *Annie* moved on to multiple productions and translations around the world, even in countries where *The Chicago Tribune* and Little Orphan Annie had never been heard of.

Michael White's London mounting – a reproduction of the Broadway version, staged by lyricist Charnin – imported Miss McArdle to recreate her Annie alongside Stratford Johns (Daddy Warbucks) and Sheila Hancock (Miss Hannigan), and once again the piece scored a major success, remaining more than three and a half years (1,485 performances) at the West End's Victoria Palace before moving on to the road, and to widespread productions in provincial houses. It returned to London for a Christmas season in 1982–3 (20 December, Adelphi Theatre, 66 performances), but took little heed of the season elsewhere.

Most of Britain's producing regional theatres have staged *Annie* at one time or another.

Australia carried on the run of successful English-language *Annie*s with J C Williamson Ltd's production, starring top Australian names Hayes Gordon (Warbucks), Jill Perryman (Miss Hannigan) and Nancye Hayes (Lily) alongside the Annie of Sally-Anne Bourne, with New Zealand, Ireland and South Africa following suit, whilst the show was translated for productions in Mexico and Spain (Teatro Principe, Madrid 25 September 1981), in Denmark (Aalborg Theatre 10 December 1981), Japan and Germany at the head of a very long list of foreign versions.

A film version produced by Columbia in 1982, with Albert Finney (Warbucks), Carol Burnett (Miss Hannigan), Tim Curry (Rooster), Anne Reinking (Lily), Bernadette Peters (Grace) and Aileen Quinn as an Annie chosen after a much-publicized international search, put in five alternative songs – losing 'NYC' amongst others – and proved much less popular than the stage show.

In an age where successful films breed sequels like rabbits, this most successful of theatre shows attempted the same trick. *Annie 2*, subtitled 'Miss Hannigan's Revenge', proved a lemming. It featured Dorothy Loudon, repeating her original part in the sub-title-rôle with Danielle Finlay as Annie, as it followed the harridan's attempts to win Daddy Warbucks's (Harve Presnell) contest for a wife and mother to his new daughter. Written by the same team as the original, it was mounted at the Kennedy Center, Washington (4 January 1990), but did not make the announced move to its 1 March 1990 opening at Broadway's Marquis Theater. However, there was to be an *Annie* 2ª. A rewritten musequel entitled *Annie Warbucks* was produced at Chicago's Marriot Lincolnshire Theater on 9 February 1992 and proceeded from there towards a Broadway opening at the Neil Simon Theater. The tale was once again that of the search by Warbucks (Presnell) for a mother for his child, but Miss Hannigan was no longer in on the action. Once again it blew out prior to reaching New York.

Annie succeeded *Li'l Abner* and Bruce Bairnsfather's *The Better 'Ole* as the most successful musical theatre piece written around a newspaper cartoon. They had had many predecessors on the American musical stage over almost a century, of which a handful, such as Victor Herbert's *Little Nemo* (115 performances) and a stage musical of *Buster Brown* (95 performances) had some success, but by and large cartoon-to-musical results had not been encouraging. The folk of *Hogan's Alley* were amongst the earliest to make the trip to the singing stage, showing up as musical comedy characters on the touring circuits in the mid 1890s (People's Theater 12 October 1896) alongside the equally out-of-town *McFadden's Row of Flats* (People's Theater 27 September 1897). In the early years of the 20th century Gus Hill's stage musical of *Alphonse and Gaston* (Metropolis Theater 20 December 1902) and others of *The Katzenjammer Kids* (3rd Avenue Theater 26 November 1900), *The Happy Hooligan* (Metropolis Theater 10 March 1902) *Mickey Finn* (3rd Avenue 4 May 1903) and, more substantially, of *The New York Herald*'s *Fluffy Ruffles* (W T Francis/Wallace Irwin/J J McNally, Criterion Theater 7 September 1908) proved short-lived.

George McManus's *The Newlyweds and their Baby*

(Majestic Theater 22 March 1909, John W Bratton, Nat Ayer/Paul West, Seymour Brown/Aaron Hoffman, West) proved no happier a source than the same author's *Panhandle Pete* (Metropolis Theater 10 September 1906) and his more famous *Bringing Up Father*. This strip was used for a series of touring shows, including *Bringing up Father in Ireland* (Seymour Furth/Nat Leroy Lyric Theater 30 March 1925) and *Bringing up Father [at the Seashore]* (Lyric Theater 6 April 1925 Seymour Furth/R F Carroll/Edward Hutchinson, Leroy) in America as well as for *Patsy from Paris* (Maidstone 1927, Louis Jerome/George Arthurs) in England. Another comic strip series of shows which, similarly, spent most of its life in the boondocks was a set based on the *Mutt and Jeff* characters. *The Dingbat Family* (John Bratton/Mark Swan, Paterson NJ 28 October 1912) and *Keeping Up* based on the 'Pop, Mom and ...' cartoons in the *Globe* (Crescent, Brooklyn 1925) were others which did not hit the highlights. The Shubert production of *My Boy Friend* (Parsons Theater, Hartford 1 December 1924) based on Jack Lait's 'Gus the Bus' cartoon was seen in Boston but not on Broadway.

In more recent times, the world-famous Superman was brought to the stage in *It's a Bird It's a Plane It's Superman* (29 March 1966), a piece composed, like *Annie*, by Charles Strouse, the Charles M Schulz 'Peanuts' strip served as the basis for two musicals – the generally successful *You're a Good Man, Charlie Brown* (Clarke Gesner/John Gordon Theater 80 St Marks 7 March 1967) and *Snoopy* (Larry Grossman/Hal Hackady Little Fox Theater, San Francisco 9 December 1975) whilst Britain turned out stage versions of the Scots *Oor Wullie* (Overground Theatre 20 December 1978), and the *Daily Mail*'s *Andy Capp* (Aldwych Theatre 28 September 1982, 99 performances), with Tom Courtenay as its slobbish hero. Osbert Lancaster's devastating Maudie Littlehampton was given stage life by David Wood in *Maudie* (Thorndike Theatre, Leatherhead 12 November 1974).

Another musical entitled *Annie*, this one dealing with a lady from the Moral Rearmament Group, was produced at that group's Westminster Theatre, London, in 1967 (William Reed/Alan Thornhill 27 July, 398 performances).

UK: Victoria Palace 3 May 1978; Australia: Her Majesty's Theatre, Melbourne 25 October 1978; Germany: Landestheater, Detmold 20 December 1980; Film: Columbia Pictures 1982

Recordings: original cast (Columbia), London cast (CBS), Australian cast (Festival), Spanish cast (Bocaccio), Danish cast (Polydor), film soundtrack (Columbia), French soundtrack (Rastar) etc

ANNIE DEAR Musical comedy in 3 acts by Clare Kummer based on her play *Good Gracious Annabelle*. Music by Sigmund Romberg and Clare Kummer. Times Square Theater, New York, 4 November 1924.

Mrs Kummer's *Good Gracious Annabelle* (Republic Theater 31 October 1916) was apparently originally written as a hopeful libretto, but it ended up being produced by Arthur Hopkins as a straight play (although the authoress-songwriter did manage to sneak in one song, 'Other Eyes', for her heroine) with considerable Broadway success (111 performances). Only eight years later was the now highly rated playwright's first hit turned into the musical it had been intended as, under the aegis of Florenz Ziegfeld, as a vehicle for Billie Burke, in Lola Fisher's rôle of Annabelle.

A sort of a modern variation on the Prince-and-Princess-in-disguise theme decorated with snazzy chat and a bundle of complexities about mining shares, mistaken identities and masquerades, it had for its heroine a dizzy lass called Annie (Miss Burke) who, having fled from her rough country husband immediately after a curious teenage marriage, runs daffily through her allowance, gets mixed up in a divorce and hides as a billionaire's cook to avoid both sets of consequences. On the way she falls in love with the mine-owner John Ralston (Marion Green), rival of her ever-intoxicated employer (Ernest Truex), who turns out to be none other than the man she married. He'd got educated, rich and shaved his beard off, so she didn't recognize him.

Romberg and Miss Kummer (six numbers) supplied a lightweight score, suited to the rather more sophisticated than usual dialogue, and Ziegfeld interpolated some outrageous extravagances into the drawing-room-comedy-sized piece, and consequently came to words with the shocked author. *Annie Dear* (which had been called simply *Annie* on its way into town) was received very warmly and played on Broadway for 103 performances.

ANNIE GET YOUR GUN Musical comedy in 2 acts by Herbert and Dorothy Fields. Music and lyrics by Irving Berlin. Imperial Theater, New York, 16 May 1946.

The idea of a musical comedy based on the career of semi-legendary sharpshooter Annie Oakley was first mooted by Herbert and Dorothy Fields, as a potential vehicle for singing star Ethel Merman. The Fields took the project to Rodgers and Hammerstein, at that time riding very high with *Oklahoma!* and *Carousel* as writers, but also active as producers of other people's works. This one – and the star envisaged – didn't fit into the romantic musical-play mode in which the pair were then writing, but the combination of librettists, subject and star appealed mightily to their producing instincts. They took the venture on, and added to the team the most outstanding composer they could come up with: Jerome Kern. However, before *Annie Oakley* got off the ground, Kern died. Irving Berlin, who had wandered away from the world of the book musical, was persuaded by the producers to take his place.

Outback lassie Annie Oakley (Miss Merman) is as naïve as they come, but she can put two bullets through a bird on the wing without blinking. It is a talent which wins her a job in the Wild West show toured by Buffalo Bill Cody (William O'Neal) but which offends the masculinity of the show's handsome shooting star, Frank Butler (Ray Middleton), and damps the prospect of a romance between the pair. Unable to handle the situation, Frank finally quits and goes to the opposition show, but that way neither of them is happy and neither show prospers. A merger is proposed, but that old pride gets in the way again, and it is only when wise old Sitting Bull (Harry Bellaver) gently shows the unthinking Annie that she can win herself a stubborn man by losing a shooting match, that the happy ending finally arrives.

Berlin's score proved to be full of winning numbers. Annie's singing rôle was huge. She chortled through the music-hally tale of the folks back home who are used to 'Doin' what Comes Natur'lly', bewailed the fact that 'You Can't Get a Man With a Gun', belted her little brother and sisters to sleep with 'A Moonshine Lullaby', hailed the

Plate 4. **Annie Get Your Gun**: *Suzi Quatro's apple-cheeked Annie goes Indian for the benefit of Chief Sitting Bull (Berwick Kaler).*

simple life in 'Sun in the Morning', and whooped through her induction into Sitting Bull's tribe in 'I'm an Indian Too'. Romance touched her hopefully for 'They Say That Falling in Love Is Wonderful' and 'I Got Lost in His Arms', but business won out as she faced up to challenge Frank with a gun declaring 'Anything You Can Do (I can do better)' at the end of an evening where one hit number had followed another with barely a breath-space. Frank, too, had his hits, both in the duets with Annie, and also with the rueful ballad 'My Defences Are Down' and his tuneful serenade to the sugary ideal of 'The Girl That I Marry', whilst the supporting characters got a peep-in in a pair of light-footed duets ('Who Do You Love, I Hope?', 'I'll Share It All With You') for the soubret pair (Anne Nyman, Kenny Bowers) and with a rousing affirmation that 'There's No Business Like Show Business' as Buffalo Bill and his advance manager, Charlie Davenport (Marty May) pointed out the joys of barnstorming to the inexperienced Annie.

Annie Get Your Gun was a huge success. Rodgers and Hammerstein's Broadway production ran for 1,147 performances and, while it ran, the show began to make its way round the world. Emile Littler's London production,

featuring Dolores Gray (Annie), Bill Johnson (Frank), Wendy Toye (Winnie) and Irving Davies (Tommy), arrived in town within weeks of two other major hits, *Oklahoma!* and *Bless the Bride*, giving the West End one of the liveliest injections of entertainment it had had in years as London theatre-folk lined up argumentatively to support one new show or another. C B Cochran himself sabotaged *Bless the Bride*'s run, and, if *Oklahoma!* lasted a little longer than *Annie Get Your Gun*, the latter show, housed in the vastness of the London Coliseum, undoubtedly welcomed the larger number of customers in the course of its 1,304 West End performances.

As in London, Australia's *Annie Get Your Gun* didn't cast a star, it made one. Variety performer Evie Hayes was J C Williamson Ltd's choice for Annie Oakley, teamed with Webb Tilton as Frank and with former Savoy star Claude Flemming as Buffalo Bill. When the piece opened in Melbourne, just a few weeks after London's première, she and the show scored the kind of sensational long-running hit that Australia was at that time unused to seeing. Ten months in Melbourne were followed by 12 more (425 performances) at Sydney's Theatre Royal (27 August 1948), with June Clyde spelling Miss Hayes, prior to a

33

New Zealand tour, a second round in Australia in 1952 and regular reappearances thereafter.

Earl Covert who took a stint as leading man in this production was also Frank Butler to the Annie of Mary Martin in the first American touring company, which set out on the road soon after the British and Australian premières and ran through more than 18 months. The London run was also followed by an extensive tour, whilst 1950 saw the production of a film version (originally begun with Judy Garland, but ultimately starring Betty Hutton opposite Howard Keel as Frank) and a French production, mounted by Maurice Lehmann at the huge Théâtre du Châtelet (ad André Mouëzy-Éon, Albert Willemetz). The first Broadway musical to have been produced in Paris since the French capital's love affair with the works of Romberg, *Annie du Far-West* featured Lily Fayol, Marcel Merkès, Pierjac (Cossard ie Charlie), Jane Montange (Dolly) and Jack Claret (Tommy) through a 316-perform-ance run which was, however, considered a little disappointing.

The show was one of the first modern American musi-cals to break into the German-language theatre, following close behind the ground-breaking *Kiss Me, Kate* when it was produced at Vienna's Volksoper (ad Marcel Prawy) in 1957. Berlin followed this lead some years later when Heidi Brühl and Robert Trehy starred in a Theater des Westens production (ad Robert Gilbert), and Scandanavia and most other areas where the light musical theatre was popular, as well as one or two where it wasn't, also saw versions of the show.

Annie Get Your Gun became an often-played favourite in the American musical comedy repertoire, as Billie Worth, Martha Raye, Betty Jane Watson, Ginger Rogers, Debbie Reynolds and other musical stars all took their turns as sometimes not-so-young Annies, but the first major revival in New York did not come until 20 years after the original production. Miss Merman starred once more, alongside the Frank Butler of Bruce Yarnell, Benay Venuta (the screen Dolly) and Bellaver repeating his Sitting Bull in a Music Theatre of Lincoln Center production (31 May 1966) which was also seen on the road and briefly at the Broadway Theater (21 December 1966). For this produc-tion, the piece was reorganized and the rôles of Annie and Frank made even more prominent by the suppression of the soubrets and their two numbers. Berlin provided an additional number for the two stars, 'An Old-Fashioned Wedding'.

London waited 40 years for its revival, and it too got the revised version when a scaled-down Chichester Festival Theatre production starring Suzi Quatro and Eric Flynn and with Edmund Hockridge featured in the rôle of Buf-falo Bill was brought to the Aldwych Theatre (29 July 1986). Just half a dozen years later the West End got a second helping of the show when a Plymouth Theatre Royal production, featuring Kim Criswell, John Diedrich, Meg Johnson and Leon Greene was taken briefly in to the Prince of Wales Theatre (25 November 1992).

UK: London Coliseum 7 June 1947; Australia: Her Majesty's Theatre, Melbourne, 20 July 1947; France: Théâtre du Châtelet *Annie du Far-West* 19 February 1950; Austria: Volk-soper 27 February 1957; Germany: Theater des Westens *Annie, schiess los!* 5 September 1963; Film: MGM 1950

Recordings: original cast (Decca), New York 1966, revival cast (RCA), German cast (Philips), London cast 1986 (First Night), Swedish cast (Sonet), film soundtrack (MGM) etc

ANTIGNY, Blanche d' [ANTIGNY, Marie Ernestine d'] (b Martizay, Indre, 9 May 1840; d Paris, 28 June 1874).

The decidedly tall, fairly blonde and very shapely Mlle d'Antigny ('cette grande, bonne et belle fille blonde, respirant la force et la santé, jetant la gaieté à pleines mains' [Arsène Houssaye]), the daughter of a provincial carpenter, was 14 years old and a Parisian shopgirl when she found her first 'protector'. He carried her off to Bucharest before she abandoned him, gallivanted about a while with gipsies, and then found another gentleman with whom she returned to Paris. She worked at the Cirque d'Hiver and the Bal Mabille as a dancer and a model, and appeared at the Porte Saint-Martin as a non-speaking Helen of Troy in d'Ennery's *Faust* before she attracted the amorous attention of the Russian tsarist police chief, Mesentzov. Whisked off to live in luxury in Wiesbaden and St Petersburg, she discovered a further ambition and took a bet that she could, if she would, dethrone Hortense Schneider as the reigning queen of the Paris opéra-bouffe stage and of all the off-stage activity that went with that crown.

Her policeman let her go and try, and thus lost her for, after a few singing and acting lessons and a couple of rôles at the Palais-Royal (*Danaë et sa bonne*, *Les Mémoires de Mimi Bamboche*, 1868), she was cast hastily in the star rôle of the tempestuous Frédégonde in Hervé's *Chilpéric* (1868) when the originally slated Julia Baron fell ill. She trium-phed along with the show. Her bet was, to all intents and purposes, won. She confirmed her success as Marguerite in the same composer's *Le Petit Faust*, played in his *L'Oeil crevé* (where an unkind journalist remarked, apparently without real justification, that 'ses diamants jouaient mieux qu'elle') and became the delight of the Parisian gentlemen of her day to whom, at the dawn of the 1870s, she was the reigning beauty of the French stage and its adjacent demi-monde. She played further rôles at the Palais-Royal and at the Folies-Dramatiques, Hamburg saw her as Offenbach's Métella (*La Vie parisienne*) and London had its opportunity to gaze at (and listen to) her when the Folies-Dramatiques company visited the old Globe Theatre in 1872 to perform *L'Oeil crevé* (Fleur de Noblesse) and *Chilpéric* (Frédé-gonde). When the preferred, if not necessarily richest, of her lofty series of lovers foundered financially and vanished, she hurried out of town, ending up in Cairo where she appeared in opéra-bouffe and soon attracted the Khedive himself.

She was only 34 years of age when she died in Paris in 1874, but there was little doubt that she had well and truly lived.

ANTONY, F [NIKOLOWSKY, Anton] (b Vienna, 7 April 1855; d Vienna, 17 January 1916).

Viennese playwright and sometime house author at the Theater in der Josefstadt, whose twenty-five years of writ-ing for the stage brought forth a sizeable body of work including a large number of Possen, both musical and musicless. A fruitful collaboration with Carl Lindau pro-duced a number of original pieces for the musical stage and also 'Viennese versions' of a number of others, from Adolf Philipp's New York-German *Across the Big Pond* (aka

From Across the Pond, New York in Wort und Bild) to a parody of *Die lustige Witwe*.

One of his own works was adapted by Rudolf Lothar as the libretto to the Eugen d'Albert comic opera *Die verschenkte Frau* (Troppau, 3 February 1912).

1886 **Der Aprilnarr** (Karl Kleiber/w Carl Lindau) Theater in der Josefstadt 13 April

1886 **Der Stabstrompeter** Viennese version w Lindau and music by Hanns Krenn (Theater in der Josefstadt)

1887 **Wien bleibt Wien** (Hanns Krenn/ad w Lindau) Theater in der Josefstadt 1 October

1888 **Nigerls Reise nach Paris** (Krenn) Theater in der Josefstadt October

1889 **Der dumme Augustin** (Julius Stern/w Anton Maurer) Theater in der Josefstadt 23 October

1890 **Ein alter Hallodri** (Kleiber/w Heinrich Thalboth) Theater in der Josefstadt 4 October

1890 **Die flotten Weiber von Wien** (Kleiber/w Leon Treptow) Theater in der Josefstadt 5 December

1891 **Wien im XX Jahrhundert** (Ernst Reiterer) Carltheater 5 September

1892 **Unser Volk unter Waffen** (Kleiber/w Lindau, Thalboth) Theater in der Josefstadt 17 September

1893 **Die Arbeit hoch** (Alexander Krakauer/w W Fresking) Raimundtheater 4 December

1894 **Die Deutschmeister sind da** (Karl Bergen) Theater in der Josefstadt 31 March

1894 **Der Herr Bigelhofer** (aka *Ein Wiener in Amerika*) (Reiterer/w E Prudens) Carltheater 8 October

1895 **Wiener Touristen** (Karl Kappeller/w Lindau) Theater in der Josefstadt 2 March

1896 **Die Liebe auf ersten Blick** (Leopold Kuhn) Theater an der Wien 9 May

1896 **Der Hungerleider** Viennese version w music by Roth (Theater an der Wien)

1896 **Flotte Geister** (Max von Weinzierl) Raimundtheater 25 January

?1897 **Der Zauberlehrling** (Josef Bayer/w Max Kalbeck, Eugen Negue)

1900 **Die bessere Hälfte** (Paul Mestrozzi) Kaiser-Jubiläums Theater 10 October

1903 **Herz ist Adutt** (Mestrozzi) Kaiser-Jubiläums Theater 18 January

1903 **Gaudeamus Igitur** (Mestrozzi) Kaiser-Jubiläums Theater 24 January

1903 **Der Bräutigam vom Himmel** (Georg Klammer) Jantsch-theater 21 October

1904 **Café Pascha** (Mestrozzi/w Emil Norini) Kaiser-Jubiläums Theater 30 January

1904 **Das goldene Handwerk** (Mestrozzi/w Fresking) Kaiser-Jubiläums Theater 12 November

1905 **Das Schwalbennest** (Henri Hirschmann/Maurice Ordonneau ad Maurice Rappaport) Viennese version Venedig in Wien

1905 **Ausser Rand und Band** (Paul Lincke/w Lindau) 1 act Danzers Orpheum 4 November

1905 **Auf's in Orpheum** (Viktor Holländer/Julius Freund) Viennese version w Lindau (Danzers Orpheum)

1906 **Die drei Engel** (Hellmesberger/w Lindau) Venedig in Wien 4 May

1906 **Das Scheckbuch des Teufels** (*Le Carnet du Diable*) German version w Lindau and add mus Maximilan Steiner (Danzers Orpheum)

1906 **Einer, der sich zu helfen weiss** (Richard Fronz) Bürgertheater 2 September

1906 **Über'm grossen Teich** (*Across the Big Pond*) Viennese version w Lindau and mus Ziegler (Theater an der Wien)

1907 **Der lustiger Witwer** (Julius Freund) Viennese version w Lindau and mus M Steiner (Danzers Orpheum)

1907 **Monte Carlo** (Ludwig Roman Ehmel/w Lindau) Neues Operetten-Theater, Leipzig 7 April

1907 **Die kleine Prinzessin** (Bela von Ujj/w Lindau) Venedig in Wien 5 May

1907 **Eine Sensation** (von Ujj/w Lindau) 3 scenes Danzers Orpheum 20 December

1908 **Unser Franz** (Ludwig Gothov-Grüneke) Raimundtheater 31 October

1908 **Der Prinz von Marokko** (Ehmel) 1 act Munich

1909 **Drei Stunden Leben** (von Ujj/w Lindau) 1 act Apollotheater 1 November

1909 **Am Gänselhäusel** (Franz Ziegler) Raimundtheater 14 November

1910 **Wann der Auerhahn balzt** (Ziegler/w Ziegler) Raimundtheater 3 April

1910 **Die verhexte Wienerstadt** (*The New Aladdin*) German version w Lindau (Venedig in Wien)

1913 **Das haben die Mädchen so gern** (Ernst Wolf et al/Friedrich Alfred Löbl et al/w K Elberg) Wiener Bürgertheater 22 March

ANYONE CAN WHISTLE Musical in 2 acts by Arthur Laurents. Lyrics and music by Stephen Sondheim. Majestic Theater, New York, 4 April 1964.

Having worked together on *West Side Story* and *Gypsy*, librettist Arthur Laurents and lyricist Stephen Sondheim, who had recently made his composing mark as the songwriter of the highly successful *A Funny Thing Happened on the Way to the Forum*, came together again on *Anyone Can Whistle*. Angela Lansbury starred as Cora Hoover Hooper, hereditary boss of a bankrupted town, who, with the help of Police Chief Magruder (James Frawley), Comptroller Schub (Gabriel Dell) and Treasurer Cooley (Arnold Soboloff), sets up a phoney therapeutic fountain to attract dumb money. When a group of mentally handicapped, under the care of Nurse Fay Apple (Lee Remick), come to partake, troubles begin. Energetic Dr Hapgood (Harry Guardino) arrives to move along events and to pair off with Nurse Apple in the midst of a confusing saga of sanity and insanity.

The score provided a title number, sung by Miss Remick, which proved both extractable and popular, but Kermit Bloomgarden's and Diana Krasny's production of a show which, wilfully meaningful, also came across too often as distasteful and/or tasteless, survived only nine performances. It nevertheless won a number of college productions in America and, with the swelling of Sondheim's status in later years, was finally given a British provincial production in 1986 with Pip Hinton (Cora), Michael Jayes (Hapgood) and Marilyn Cutts (Fay) heading the cast.

UK: Everyman Theatre, Cheltenham 21 August 1986
Recording: original cast (Columbia).

ANYTHING GOES Musical in 2 acts by Guy Bolton and P G Wodehouse. Revised version by Howard Lindsay and Russel Crouse. Music and lyrics by Cole Porter. Alvin Theater, New York, 21 November 1934.

Along with the more operettic *Kiss Me, Kate, Anything Goes* remains the most popular and most often performed of the list of musical comedies for which Cole Porter supplied the songs, proving yet again (if it needed proving) that a show rebuilt hastily, considerably, and late can often do as well or better than one carefully and respectfully lifted from the original page to the stage.

Producer Vinton Freedley – previously co-producer of *Girl Crazy* – had planned *Bon Voyage*, book by Bolton and Wodehouse, songs by Porter, starring *Girl Crazy*'s Ethel Merman, William Gaxton, Victor Moore and Bettina Hall, and directed by Howard Lindsay, for the 1934–5 Broadway season. But the Bolton/Wodehouse libretto, the final act of which set its group of seafaring bon-voyagers afloat in a disastrous and comical shipwreck, did not meet with the producer's approval. The real-life sinking of the *S.S. Morro Castle* gave Freedley the excuse needed to dump it (and win some publicity), and Lindsay was seconded to get another book made, built around the already hired and hierarched stars, and around Porter's songs.

In the short weeks before rehearsals were due to begin, the new script was written by Lindsay and then Theatre Guild publicity man, Russel Crouse. Miss Merman was cast as an evangelist-turned-nightclub-singer (unlikely, perhaps, but there was a song called 'Blow, Gabriel, Blow' to cope with) with a yen for a smart young man (Gaxton) who is, in turn, all of a fluster about a lovely daughter of biggish business (Miss Hall), destined for a dynastical marriage not with a Prince, but with a more flourishing business. Moore was given a splendidly suitably rôle as an aspiring but low-rated 'public enemy' without the ability to rise to Number One, who spent much of the evening disguised as a reverend, and the shipboard scenery of the original script was accommodated by having almost the whole of the action take place during an Atlantic crossing.

In his pursuit of the lovely Hope Hampton, Billy Crocker stows away on the ship bearing her to Britain and a marriage with Sir Evelyn Oakleigh (Leslie Barrie). Whilst trying to change his fair lady's mind about her hand, he goes through any number of disguises and tricks to avoid detection, not only as himself, but as the criminal whose ticket he has been loaned by a subordinate criminal, who is himself disguised as a minister. Chanteuse Reno Sweeney helps him out, even though she fancies Billy for herself, and is ultimately rewarded with the left-over Lord when the business situation changes, and Billy's persistence wins him the hand of Hope.

The songs of what was ultimately called *Anything Goes* included gems for each of the stars. Miss Merman had the lioness's share, topped by the catalogue song 'I Get a Kick Out of You' (a number left over from an aborted piece written for E Ray Goetz and called *Stardust*) and the powerful 'Blow, Gabriel, Blow' as well as two more typical and topical Porter pieces, a second catalogue, 'You're the Top' (with Gaxton), and the newly written title-song 'Anything Goes'. Gaxton and Miss Hall had the mellow 'All Through the Night', she slunk through the admission of 'The Gypsy in Me', and Moore twittered out his advice to 'Be Like the Bluebird'. There was even fine material left behind: Gaxton's 'Easy to Love' went before opening, and a sizzling piece advising 'Buddie, Beware', originally sung by Miss Merman, survived only a short while after opening, being cut to make way for yet more topicalities in an extra reprise of 'I Get a Kick Out of You'. The old title-song, 'Bon Voyage' survived, counter-melodied, for the ensemble.

Although there were changes, additions and rewrites on the road to town, *Anything Goes* was never in trouble, and once it opened it was always going to be a success. It was still on the way to the end of its first run of 420 Broadway performances when C B Cochran – who, far from seeking the kind of pre-production plays for his score that modern musicals do, had actually injuncted Carroll Gibbons's Orpheans from playing Porter's *Anything Goes* songs at the Savoy Hotel – mounted his edition at London's Palace Theatre. Although the press had originally reported that Leslie Howard was to play Billy and Leslie Henson was to take Moore's rôle, alongside French cabaret and theatre star Jeanne Aubert, the lady, sumptuously dressed as Reno (now nationalistically called Lagrange instead of Sweeney), was teamed with Jack Whiting as Crocker, Adele Dixon as Hope, Sydney Harcourt as the despairingly criminal Moon-Face Mooney, and Peter Haddon in his well-known noodle performance as Sir Evelyn. In the style of the time, a harmony group, the Four Admirals, was engaged to perform the fine shanty 'There'll Always Be a Lady Fair'. Once again, the producer must have been glad to have lost that *Bon Voyage* shipwreck, for Ivor Novello's sinking ship in Drury Lane's *Glamorous Night* had been the scenic sensation of the season. *Anything Goes* didn't do quite as well as the Novello piece, but it played a smart 261 performances in London before going on the road.

Australia's version, featuring Harry Langdon, Lillian Pertka, Charles Norman and Robert Coote did not, however, do well at all. It proved something of a disappointment as it ran its course in six Sydney and seven Melbourne (Her Majesty's Theatre, 11 April 1936) weeks.

The show did not, apparently, attract any takers outside the English-speaking theatre but after the songwriter's death the growing fashion for Porter's works provoked revivals both in America and Britain. A revised version of the show was mounted at off-Broadway's Orpheum Theater in 1962 (15 May, 239 performances), featuring Hal Linden (Billy), Eileen Rodgers (Reno) and Mickey Deems (Moon-Face) and, in the beginning of a sad trend, a number of extraneous Porter numbers from other sources, and then in Britain when the extremely young Cameron Mackintosh sponsored a 1969 London staging with James Kenney as Billy and Marian Montgomery as Reno (Saville Theatre 18 November) and an even larger helping of Porter pops. It failed in 27 performances.

The most important revival, however, came in 1987. Timothy Crouse (son of Russel) and John Weidman reorganized the libretto sufficiently to retain 'It's D'Lovely' and 'Friendship' from the last round's tackings-in, to bring back some of the show's outcuts (whilst keeping most of the original score), and to add some other Porter spare parts. Howard McGillin (Billy), Patti LuPone (Reno), Bill McCutcheon (Moon-Face) and Kathleen Mahoney-Bennett (Hope) featured and the resultant show was launched at New York's Vivian Beaumont Theater (19 October 1987). It was a fine success there, going on to a run of nearly two years and 804 performances and setting in motion a round of productions of this particular version of the show. A touring company, with Mitzi Gaynor at its head, went out on the American road in 1989 and, in the same year, *Anything Goes* was mounted both in London (Prince Edward Theatre, 4 July 1989) with McGillin, Elaine Paige and comedian Bernard Cribbins starred, and in Australia, where local star Geraldine Turner blew Gabriel right out through the flies and encouraged Australians to be more receptive than they had to the show's first-round production.

Plate 5. **Anything Goes**: *William Gaxton (Billy) and Benay Venuta (Reno) were the first to take Cole Porter's merry musical comedy to the American touring circuits.*

Rather different from this official new *Anything Goes* was another American production of the same period which cast the rôle of Reno Sweeney as a man, and had Billy rejecting an invitation to the gay life for the caresses of Hope. This version drew the disapproval of the establishment, but the ease with which the part changed sex with no harm (and even some advantage) to the show's story and songs was such as to point up the androgynous nature and appeal of this popular kind of rôle. As in the original text, the male Reno ended the night on the arm of the English lord.

A German version of *Anything Goes* (ad Rolf Merz, Gerhard Hagen) was first produced at Kaiserslautern in 1981, and the 1987 version was also later played in German, notably in a production at Berlin's Theater des Westens (29 January 1993) featuring Hartwig Rudolz, Helen Schneider and Ralf Wolter.

A film version, which used only four numbers from the original show alongside four new ones, was produced in 1936. Bing Crosby played Billy alongside Miss Merman, in her original rôle, with Charles Ruggles at the head of the comedy, a dubbed Ida Lupino as juvenile girl and Margaret Dumont and Richard Carle in support. Another film, under the same title, but bearing little resemblance to the stage show beyond its use of five of its songs, appeared in 1956 with Crosby teamed up with Zizi Jeanmaire, Donald O'Connor and Mitzi Gaynor.

UK: Palace Theatre 14 June 1935; Australia: Theatre Royal, Sydney 8 February 1936; Germany: Pfalztheater, Kaiserslautern *Anything Goes – Alles OK* 10 February 1981; Film: Paramount 1936

Recordings: original Broadway and London casts assembled (Smithsonian), London cast included on *Cole Porter in London* (WRC), New York 1962 revival (Epic), New York cast 1987 (RCA), London cast 1989 (First Night), Australian cast (EMC), film soundtrack 1956 (Decca) etc

DIE APACHEN Operette in 3 acts by Ignaz M Welleminsky and Ralph Benatzky. Music by Ralph Benatzky. Apollotheater, Vienna, 20 December 1920.

A piece evolved around the then fashionable scenes of deliciously 'canaille' Parisian low life, *Die Apachen*, like the famous sado-masochistic apache dance, and like other pieces set in such marginal areas, sugared the milieu and its characters up to make nothing but a pretty entertainment, with an 'apache' hero who was little more than a jolly scamp.

Like all the best operettic heros, Romain Tierce (Louis Treumann) is not really a true-born Paris street-thief, but an aristocrat fallen on hard times, who has turned to banditry to restore the family fortunes. His victim is a self-made but unattractive bourgeois who makes sausages and who has a highly attractive wife who, in her turn, has jewels. Tierce poses as a Duke in order to relieve the wife of the jewels and the sausage-maker of his wife, only to have the real Duke turn up. Our hero dupes the gendarmerie and, in the third act, leads everyone off to the Pyrénées for some scenery and a happy ending.

Josef König, Betty Myra, Olga Bartos-Trau and Rudolf Kumpa supported the evening's overwhelming star, and *Die Apachen*, equipped, of course, with a centrepiece Apache Dance at the heart of its light, Viennesey and (for the time) unsyncopated score, did well enough in its Vienna season to attract attentions from Britain and from

America. An American staging apparently foundered on its way to Broadway, but London's Wylie–Tate organization brought *The Apache* (adapted by Dion Titheradge) to the London Palladium, with dancer and ex-sportsman Carl Brisson starred as Romain Tierce, Shaun Glenville as merchant Redingote, Adrienne Brune as his wife Marian and Dorothy Ward as Lallage. The dances – including 'a sensational new apache dance by Carl Brisson and his sister Tilly' – were arranged by Edward Dolly (brother of the more famous sisters), the costumes by Dolly Tree, there were the odd song by Kollo ('Is Love Worthwhile') and Leslie Sarony ('Cuckoo'), by Wottitz ('Parlez-vous français?') and Reesen ('Let Me Hold Your Hand, Dear'), and the combination pleased London for a run of 166 performances.

UK: London Palladium *The Apache* 15 February 1927

APAJUNE, DER WASSERMANN Operette in 3 acts by F Zell and Richard Genée. Music by Carl Millöcker. Theater an der Wien, Vienna, 18 December 1880.

When pretty Romanian Natalitza (Karoline Finaly) and her Marcu (Alexander Girardi) have celebrated their wedding, the steward Alexandri (Carl Adolf Friese) insists that she go to the castle to pay her respects to their overlord, Graf Alamir Prutschesko (Felix Schweighofer). Marcu knows what that means, and, accompanied by his friends Manolle Ritschano (Ernst Schütz) and Joza (Ausim), all three disguised as girls, he also heads for the castle. Whilst Ritschano makes rendez-vous with Prutschesko's step-daughter, Jlinka (Frln Rafael), Natalitza holds the itchy-fingered Count at bay with the old tale of Apajune, the watersprite, who watches over newly-wed girls. Prutschesko dresses up as Apajune to pursue his seigneurial way but, instead of coming back to Natalitza, he runs into Marcu who promptly throws him in his own river. When the Gräfin Heloise (Therese Schäfer), who can hardly stay deaf to all this activity, starts asking questions, her husband is obliged not only to let Natalitza and Marcu go, but also Ritschano and Jlinka. Apajune has looked after his own.

The third of Millöcker's out-and-out Operetten, following the successful *Das verwunschene Schloss* and the less fortunate *Gräfin Dubarry*, *Apajune* gave the composer another signal success. The piece stood up very favourably alongside the Theater an der Wien's other major production of the year, Johann Strauss's *Das Spitzentuch der Königin*, and was played for a more than respectable month over Christmas and the New Year period, remaining in the theatre's repertoire for the two following seasons for a total of 45 performances. It was quickly exported, being played in the months following its première both in Germany and in Budapest (ad Lajos Evva, Jenő Rákosi) where it was the first of Millöcker's Operetten to be seen. A year later it was mounted at New York's German-language Thalia Theater with Jenny Stubel (Natalitza), Adolf Link (Prutschesko) and Alexander Klein (Marcu), and the first English version was played on Broadway by Emilie Melville's company with the manageress starred as Natalitza alongside the Prutschesko of William Gilbert and the Marco of Tom Casselli. It played just three weeks, but the show was later repeated on Broadway by John McCaull's troupe (Casino Theater 16 January 1885) with Mathilde Cottrelly and Francis Wilson (Prutschesko) featured, and the German house heard Geistinger as Natalitza in 1884. *Apajune* had a number of subsequent productions in Germany and it was also played in Prague, Zagreb and other middle-European centres in the first years following its production.

In 1903, *Apajune* was given a revival at the Carltheater (24 September) with Louis Treumann (Prutschesko) and Mizzi Günther (Natalitza), the following year to become famous as the originators of *Die lustige Witwe*, and Carl Streitmann (Marcu) heading the cast. It was played as a supporting piece in the repertoire during some six months, but the revival re-established the show, and the star pair brought it back again in 1910 at the Johann Strauss-Theater (30 April) where it ran for a straight month.

Germany: Pressburg 21 February 1881, Friedrich-Wilhelmstädtisches Theater, Berlin 10 December 1881; Hungary: Népszinház *Apajune a vizitünder* 4 March 1881; USA: Thalia Theater 13 January 1882; Bijou Theater *Apajune the Water Sprite* 25 February 1882

APPLAUSE Musical in 2 acts by Adolph Green and Betty Comden based on the screenplay *All About Eve* by Joseph L Mankiewicz and the story *The Wisdom of Eve* by Mary Orr. Lyrics by Lee Adams. Music by Charles Strouse. Palace Theater, New York, 30 March 1970.

Applause was an adaptation for the musical stage of the story of the cult film *All About Eve* (1950), in which the covertly ambitious Anne Baxter pulled stardom from under the feet of the established actress played by Bette Davis. The musical version presented Penny Fuller as Eve Harrington, the harmless-looking fan who becomes the inseparable Girl Friday of theatre favourite Margo Channing (Lauren Bacall), and then gradually works, plots and sleeps her way from backstage to centre-stage and, ultimately, into the new starring rôle that Margo knows was to have been hers. It is some consolation to the older woman that she can see in this disgustingly determined creature something of herself, 20 years earlier, and that, forced from the limelight, she can take a more measured view of her career and of her life with Bill (Len Cariou), whom Eve failed to seduce on her stairway to the stars.

Star-billed Miss Bacall got the lioness's share of the musical score ('But Alive', 'Welcome to the Theater', 'Hurry Back', 'Something Greater' etc, plus a share in a piece which used the film's most famous line 'Fasten Your Seatbelts [it's going to be a bumpy night]' as an opening line) but, since the show represented in the story of *Applause* was not a musical but a play, the plotline moved outside the main story for its production numbers. It found them in the café frequented by those members of Broadway choruses who foregather in each others' company after work, late into the night. It was one of these numbers, the title-song describing the unparalleled jolt an artist gets from 'Applause', which, as performed by Bonnie Franklin and the show's dancers, became the musical highlight of the evening. A similarly-titled song expressing much the same sentiment and written by Burton Lane and Ira Gershwin had previously been heard in the film *Give a Girl a Break* (1953), performed by Gower Champion and Debbie Reynolds, but this one took on better.

Joe Kipness and Lawrence Kasha (w Nederlander Productions and George Steinbrenner III) produced *Applause* on Broadway in a staging by choreographer Ron Field, here taking the director's chair for the first time (Tony Award), and scored a fine success with a run of 896 performances at the Palace Theater. Some imaginative recasting saw the star succeeded during the run by Anne Baxter, who had been the film Eve, and then by red-headed celluloid seductress Arlene Dahl. Miss Bacall headed the subsequent touring company before leaving the road to Eleanor Parker, Patrice Munsel and Eva Gabor and moving to London to star in Bernard Delfont's and Alexander H Cohen's West End version. Angela Richards was Eve and Sheila O'Neill did the show-stealing in 'Applause' through 382 performances. *Applause* went on to be played in Europe in German and Spanish versions (ad Julie Kaufmann) and it was also televised by CBS (15 March 1973) with Miss Bacall and Miss Fuller repeating their original rôles and Larry Hagman as Bill.

UK: Her Majesty's Theatre 16 November 1972; Germany: Bühnen der Hansestadt, Lübeck 2 May 1975
Recording: original cast (ABC)

APPLE BLOSSOMS Musical play in a prologue and 2 acts by William Le Baron based on *Un Mariage sous Louis XV* by Alexandre Dumas. Music by Fritz Kreisler and Victor Jacobi. Globe Theater, New York, 7 October 1919.

One of the most successful shows of the 1919–20 Broadway season, *Apple Blossoms* followed the way successfully signalled by the German *Maytime* in the romantic Continental operetta style and won, if not as outstanding a result as that show, a run of 256 New York performances and a good touring afterlife. Its libretto was announced as being based on Alexandre Dumas's *Un Mariage sous Louis XV*, but there was little more than the theme of arranged marriage and its consequences that was recognizably Dumas in William Le Baron's non-period, thoroughly romantic and unsuggestive libretto. John Charles Thomas and Wilda Bennett starred as Philip Campbell and Nancy Dodge, a young pair who get wed to please their relatives, but agree that they will carry on their respective love affairs all the same. Philip contrives to let Nancy see the good-for-little Dickie Stewart (Percival Knight) whilst he continues to sigh after pretty widow Anne Merton (Florence Shirley). However, by the time the final curtain has been reached the married couple have decided to be a proper husband and wife.

The show was equipped with a score made up of half a dozen pieces by Hungarian ex-patriate Victor Jacobi, and slightly more from violinist-composer Fritz Kreisler. Not unexpectedly, Kreisler got the publicity whilst the composer of *Szibill* and *Leányvásár* supplied the best songs: the leading pair's duo 'You Are Free' and Philip's 'Little Girls, Goodbye' (a title dangerously near to the 'Goodbye, Girls, I'm Through' of a few seasons earlier). There were two dance numbers – one from each composer – for the young Fred and Adele Astaire in supporting rôles as 'Molly' and 'Johnny', whilst Kreisler's most successful contribution turned out to be the waltz-song 'Who Can Tell?', later recycled into the popular 'Stars In Your Eyes', and given a second theatrical showing in the violinist's later Operette *Sissi* ('Ich war so gern einmal verliebt').

THE APPLE TREE Musical in 3 acts by Sheldon Harnick, Jerry Bock and Jerome Coopersmith based on stories by Mark Twain, Frank Stockton and Jules Feiffer.

Lyrics by Sheldon Harnick. Music by Jerry Bock. Shubert Theater, New York, 18 October 1966.

Three one-act musical plays of very diverse styles and subjects, with a tenuous linking theme of temptation, *The Diary of Adam and Eve*, *The Lady or the Tiger?* and *Passionella* made up an evening's entertainment, under the umbrella title *The Apple Tree*, which was about as different from its authors' then still-running *Fiddler on the Roof* as could be.

The Diary of Adam and Eve, based on a Mark Twain novella, introduced a very human Adam (Alan Alda) and Eve (Barbara Harris) who become ordinary, everyday folk after the Fall and the birth of the first baby. Larry Blyden played the snake, lubriciously tempting the outgoing Eve to 'Forbidden Fruit' and the jiggery Alda puzzled endearingly over his child, deciding for want of better references that 'It's a Fish'.

In *The Lady or the Tiger?*, a musicalization of the Frank Stockton tale famous for its cliff-hanger ending, Miss Harris played the Princess Barbara, caught in compromising position with a Captain of the Guard (Alda) who is, as a result, condemned to the arena. But it is Barbara who is in the no-win situation. She has to indicate which of two doors he must open – one releases a man-eating tiger, the other a beautiful lady. Unlike Sydney Rosenfeld's 1888 full-scale musical adaptation of the same tale, this one maintained the famous lack of an ending. You never find out what is behind the door the lady chooses. (Rosenfeld's lady, by the way, chose the tiger – but when the door was opened it had been poisoned, so ...).

The humanity of the first play and the classic comedy of the second were replaced by campy extravagance in the Jules Feiffer Cinderella tale which ended the evening. Miss Harris played a little drab who dreams of being a dyed-blonde Hollywood dolly called Passionella, paired off with the equally plastic, black-leathered rocker, Flip (Alda). Then she wakes up. Blyden topped the piece, gushing over the lady that 'You Are Not Real'.

The Apple Tree played 463 Broadway performances and, helped by its unextravagant size, has since received a number of further productions both as a whole piece or, occasionally, of just one of its three rather unequal portions, in America, Canada and in Europe. The German version (ad Max Colpet) underlined the evening's soi-disant theme a little more obviously by calling itself *Die Versuchung* (temptation).

A further musical version of *The Lady or the Tiger?* was brought from London's fringe Orange Tree Theatre to the West End's Fortune Theatre in 1976. The neighbouring Overground Theatre Company later produced *The Apple Tree* with Ken Caswell, Jonathan Rowe and Lesley Duff.

Germany: *Die Versuchung* 6 February 1969; UK: Overground Theatre, London March 1980
Recording: original cast (Columbia), etc.

THE ARABIAN NIGHTS

The collection of tales known as the *Arabian Nights Entertainment* or *The Thousand and One Nights*, introduced to European readers in Antoine Gallard's French version in the early years of the 18th century and in a full English version by Edward William Lane in 1839, proved a long and highly fruitful source of subjects for extravaganzas, pantomimes and all other forms of musical theatre. The most popular tales were those of *Aladdin* and *Ali Baba*, both of which were the bases for many major musical productions, but a number of the other tales were also widely used.

Abu Hasan, or The Sleeper Awakened, successfully taken as a subject for an opera by Weber in 1811, was burlesqued by Francis Talfourd (St James Theatre, 1854) and Arthur O'Neil (Charing Cross Theatre, 1869), played as *The Cockney Caliph* (1866), and as *Abou or the Sleeper Awakened* (1885) and was taken as comic opera material both for Luscombe Searelle's *Bobadil* (Sydney, 1884) and, most memorably, for Basil Hood and Arthur Sullivan's *The Rose of Persia* (1899). The French opérette *La Dormeuse éveillée* (1883) also professed to have had its roots in the tale.

The tale of *Prince Camaralzaman* and his Princess Badoura, highly popular in the mid-19th century, served as the basis for the Broughs' *Camaralzaman and Badoura* (Haymarket Theatre, 1848), Bellingham and Best's 1865 *Prince Camaralzaman* at the Olympic, and further burlesques by Byron (1871) and Burnand (1884), whilst *Ganem, Slave of Love* was used as the topic of a long popular Francis Talfourd extravaganza, first mounted at the Olympic Theatre in 1852 and subsequently seen throughout the English-speaking theatre world.

Sindbad the Sailor was long popular as a pantomime hero in Britain, and also led a number of extravaganzas, notably H B Farnie's piece for Lydia Thompson, played in both Britain and America, and two further American pieces: Harry B Smith's spectacular and long-running version with music by W H Batchelor (Garden Theater 27 June 1892), and, most notably, the Al Jolson vehicle, a not very Arabian Nights piece with a basic score by Romberg and a whole swatch of popular songs as incidental numbers, produced at the Winter Garden Theater 14 February 1918.

The brothers Brough also authored a burlesque which was eventually simply called *The Arabian Nights* (Haymarket Theatre, 1850) in which Priscilla Horton, James Bland and J B Buckstone, in 'an entirely new translation taken an immense way from the original Arabic', told of – in the words of its original title – 'the second Calendar who was turned into an ape and the Queen of Beauty who had to fight with a genie', and the evocative title of *The Arabian Nights* and its derivatives have been used since for such pieces as Alfred Thompson's 1888 Chicago *Arabian Nights*, the Viennese Johann Strauss pasticcio *Tausend und eine Nacht* (1906), and the American extravaganza *Arabian Nights* (Carmen Lombardo, John Jacob Loeb/George Marion jr), a piece borrowing elements from *Sindbad* and *Aladdin* and mounted as a spectacular for several seasons at the Jones Beach marine theatre in the 1950s.

Recording: Jones Beach cast (Decca)

ARANYVIRÁG Operett in 3 acts by Ferenc Martos. Music by Jenő Huszka. Király Színház, Budapest, 6 November 1903.

Jenő Huszka followed up his great success with *Bob herceg* with a new vehicle for that show's star, Sári Fedák, in the title-rôle of *Aranyvirág* (gold-flower), the work selected to open Budapest's new musical theatre, the Király Színház, in 1903.

Elza Szamosi and Károly Ferenczy were Ellen Stone and Harry Gould, a pair of American (multi)-millionaires (the adjective and the noun were, at this time, operettically inseparable) out for a slummy, sexy time in turn-of-the-century Naples. Ellen decides to do the thing in style. She changes clothes and places with the street-dancer known as 'Aranyvirág' and sets her sights on the girl's sailor lover, Beppo (Géza Vécsei), whilst Harry swans around town with the dressed-up dancer on his arm. Beppo and the lazzarone of Naples aren't fooled. In fact, they take the whole thing poorly and no one gets much joy out of the charade. Finally the Americans get bored with their fruitless fun and head off back to the land of the dollar.

Izsó Gyögyi played the Count Daniló Potyoviev, and the locals were headed by Zsofi Csatay as Tina, Zsigmond Torma (Silvio) and Arthur Csiszér (Carlo). The show proved a fine success and, if it endured less well ultimately than several of Huszka's other pieces it was nevertheless revived at the Király Színház in 1907 (8 May).

L'ARBRE DE NOËL Féerie nouvelle in 3 acts by Arnold Mortier, Albert Vanloo and Eugène Leterrier. Music by Charles Lecocq. Théâtre de la Porte Saint-Martin, Paris, 6 October 1880.

L'Arbre de Noël was a vast, spectacular fairy-tale piece in 30 scenes, the cloths painted by no less an artist than Jules Chéret, which followed such performers as Zulma Bouffar (Bagatelle), Ange Milher (Oscar de Pulna), Alexandre (Eucalyptus), Gobin (Popoff) and Alice Reine (Fridolin) and a corps of 180 dancers on their four-hour journey to the Land of Christmas. Going ever for the best, it was musically decorated by Lecocq who provided all the traditional accoutrements of the féerie, from a children's chorus, ballets and parades to genuine prima donna solos, as an accompaniment to the display of scenic art and mass dancing which was the key to the entertainment.

A grand success on its Parisian production (100th performance 28 December 1880), the piece was taken up for further productions elsewhere in Europe, beginning in Vienna (ad uncredited) where a rather reduced 15-scene *Der Weihnachtsbaum, oder der Schatzgräber* was given a new score by Louis Roth and played a fine season of 70 performances, and in Berlin where *Der Schatzgräber*'s original score was 'adapted' rather than replaced by Gustav Lehnhardt. An Hungarian version (ad Béla J Fái) was later played in Budapest.

Austria: Theater an der Wien *Der Weihnachtsbaum* 6 May 1881; Germany: Berlin *Der Schatzgraber* 1881; Hungary: Népszinház *A karácsonyfa* 16 October 1881

THE ARCADIANS Fantastic musical play in 3 acts by Mark Ambient and Alexander M Thompson. Lyrics by Arthur Wimperis. Music by Lionel Monckton and Howard Talbot. Shaftesbury Theatre, London, 29 April 1909.

Perhaps the most complete of all the British Edwardian musical comedies, *The Arcadians* mixed the light romantic and the broadly comic, the picturesque and the spectacular, the musically literate and the music-hall, in doses which caught not only the fancy of its time, but also the imagination of decades. The idea for the show was initiated by the odd little man-about-town and strivingly occasional writer, Mark Ambient, who, finding himself incapable of developing it, took his outline to producer Robert Courtneidge. Courtneidge put his crony and in-house writer Alex Thompson to fleshing out Ambient's

tale, and handed the musical part to lyricist Arthur Wimperis, who had worked effectively on an earlier hit, *The Dairymaids*, for him, and to two of the most successful theatre composers of the age, Lionel Monckton and Howard Talbot.

The libretto had errant aviator James Smith (Dan Rolyat), a second-rate London hotelier, bailing out of his aeroplane over Arcadia, an idyllic area somewhere near the North Pole, where truth is beautiful and the lie unknown. When the noble savages who inhabit the place catch Smith in an untruth they are horrified. They dip him in the Well of Truth, changing him into 'Simplicitas, an Arcadian', and decide to accompany him back to the dreadful city of London to spread their message of truth and beauty amongst the English. Amongst a bevy of philanderings and colourful events at Askham racetrack and at Smith's Arcadian Restaurant, built to capitalize on the craze started by his newfound friends and his own popularity in his new guise, the lovers of truth and beauty are defeated in their purpose and return to Arcadia, leaving London to its wicked old ways.

It was a story which gave the opportunity for plenty of the gentle social satire popular in musical plays of the time, and also for a flock of songs and dances. Phyllis Dare, in the rôle of an incidental Irish lassie, described herself enduringly as 'The Girl with the Brogue' and joined with juvenile hero Harry Welchman in chatting obliquely about the 'Charming Weather' and in deciding to meet at 'Half Past Two'. Alfred Lester, in the comedy rôle of the lugubrious jockey, Doody, made a hit with a glum number about 'My Motter' which was, impossibly, 'always merry and bright', Dan Rolyat as Simplicitas sang saucily about the ladies chasing him 'All Down Piccadilly', and the dark-eyed and pixie-faced Florence Smithson in the rôle of the most vocal Arcadian, Sombra, used her dazzling light coloratura soprano to introduce 'The Pipes of Pan' and 'Arcady is Always Young'. There was also some particularly attractive and well-written ensemble music in a score that included a half-dozen pieces which would become musical-comedy standards. During the course of the shows's initial run a number of new songs were tried (and Lester took to singing a verse of his 'Motter' song in French) but only a couple, Miss Smithson's 'The Call of Arcady' and a topical dance piece called 'The Two-Step', added for Maud Thornton and Harry Ray to boost the show's dance content, were retained for any time.

Gloriously staged under Courtneidge's own direction, *The Arcadians* was an instant success, and it settled in at the Shaftesbury Theatre for a run of more than two years (809 performances). By the time it closed, it had already been seen in a highly successful Broadway production, and in cities as far apart as Melbourne, Bombay and Vienna. America's *Arcadians*, mounted by Charles Frohman at the Liberty Theater and subsequently transferred to the Knickerbocker, starred Frank Moulan (Simplicitas), Ethel Cadman (Sombra), Julia Sanderson (Eileen), Alan Mudie (Jack) and comedienne Connie Ediss in an enlarged version of the rôle of the 'abandoned' Mrs Smith and ran for 193 performances, whilst Clarke and Meynell's Australian production, with Maie Sydney (Sombra), William Cromwell (Simplicitas), Essie Perrin (Eileen) and Tom Walls (Doody) proved equally successful, being brought back the following season with Winnie O'Connor starred and

Plate 6. **The Arcadians**: *'The Deuce' wins the race, saves the situation, and brings Simplicitas (Dan Rolyat) on-stage for the show's second-act curtain.*

establishing the show as firmly in the southern hemisphere as it already was in the northern.

Vienna's version (ad Oskar Friedmann, Fritz Lunzer) of *Die Arkadier*, with Olga Barco-Franck (Sombra), Josef Joseffy (Simplicitas) and Annie Dirkens (Ella, ex-Eileen) which boasted mendaciously '1000 performances in London!' in its advertising, was played at the large music-hall Ronacher, bookended between a flamenco act and an English song-and-dance turn, and took a pause after the first act to allow the audience to have supper. Germany, however, decided on its own *Arcadians*. Julius Freund 'adapted' the libretto, Rudolf Nelson composed a new score and the resultant piece was mounted at the Berlin Metropoltheater (27 April 1912) under the title *Schwindelmeier et cie.*

In 1913 *Les Arcadiens* (ad Charles Quinel, Max Dearly) accomplished the rare feat for an anglophone musical of being played in Paris, with Dearly starring as Simplicitas in another music-hall venue, the Olympia, and, only two years later, it returned for a second London season (Shaftesbury Theatre 20 May 1915). The show became a feature of the British touring circuits, appearing regularly in the provinces for over 30 years, whilst overseas productions continued, and in 1927 its story line and its spectacular scenes (including a second-act finale which brought Simplicitas on stage on the back of a live horse) proved strong enough to warrant it being made into a silent film. In 1984 it was given a major regional revival in Britain under the aegis of Stewart Trotter at the Northcott Theatre, Exeter, where it proved to have lost none of its attractions with the passing of the years.

USA: Liberty Theater 17 January 1910; Australia: Theatre Royal, Melbourne 26 March 1910; Austria: Ronacher *Die Arkadier* 24 February 1911; France: L'Olympia *Les Arcadiens* 3 April 1913; Film: Gaumont British 1927 (silent)

Recordings: selections (Columbia, MFP)

ARC DE TRIOMPHE   Play with music in 3 acts by Ivor Novello. Lyrics by Christopher Hassall and Ivor Novello. Music by Ivor Novello. Phoenix Theatre, London, 9 November 1943.

A lesser Novello work, built to showcase the star of *The Dancing Years*, Mary Ellis, *Arc de Triomphe* traced the professional and amorous career of a French opera-singer through the theatre and the war in much the same way that *The Lisbon Story* was doing simultaneously, on a larger scale and with more success, at the London Hippodrome. The music for *Arc de Triomphe* had an unusual first public playing when it was tried out by orchestra leader Geraldo during a Middle East tour of British army posts, but the score contained little of Novello's better work and only 'Dark Music', sung in the show by Elisabeth Welch in a very incidental rôle, proved to have any lasting value. Enemy action and Novello's conviction on rationing charges hastened the show's closure after a six-months' run.

Recording: original cast (part record *Ivor Novello*) (EMI)

ARCHER, Harry E   [AURACHER, Harry] (b Creston, Iowa, 21 February 1888; d New York, 23 April 1960).

Auracher, as he was at first known, was educated at Michigan Military Academy before going on to study music at Princeton University and Knox, and he was 23

LE PLUS FORMIDABLE SUCCÈS ACTUEL

I LOVE YOU

FOX-TROT CHANTÉ

MUSIQUE DE
HARRY ARCHER

PAROLES DE
R. NAZELLES

PRIX
1 FR 50

CHANTÉ PAR
PIERRE LAMY

Plate 7. **Harry Archer**'s Little Jessie James *song went round the world – even becoming (allowing for a touch of hype) 'le plus formidable succès actuel' in France.*

years old when his first musical comedy, *The Pearl Maiden*, was produced by Aarons and Welch at Broadway's New York Theater. His music was set to an old-fashioned comic opera libretto about jiggery-pokery on a South Seas island, delivered by a cast headed by long-qualified stars Jefferson de Angelis and Flora Zabelle, and the whole misguided affair lasted just 24 performances.

Archer worked as a musician, leading his own jazz band and playing as a member of others, including that of Paul Whiteman, and he continued at the same time to compose for the theatre, turning out the scores to the Kitty Gordon vehicle *Love for Sale*, the revue which started out as *Frivolities of 1919* and became *Frivolities of 1920* (w William B Friedlander, Tom Johnstone) by the time it reached the 44th Street Theater, and the Clark and McCullough revue *Peek-a-boo* (1921). Then, more than a decade after his first ephemeral Broadway musical comedy, he returned with the songs for the brightly farcical and highly successful musical play *Little Jessie James*. Following its Broadway run, versions of *Little Jessie James* were produced in Britain, Germany and Hungary and its hit song 'I Love You' (made into a Paris hit by Pierre Lamy and reused in the film *The Sun Also Rises*) gave Archer the biggest single song success of his career.

The 1922 *Paradise Alley*, a more conventional, old-fashioned musical comedy, was brought to town in 1924, after *Little Jessie James*'s success, and played 64 performances there prior to an Australian season, but there was much more future in Archer's continued collaboration with his hit show's librettist, Harlan Thompson, on a series

of further small-scale musical farces. Although Lyle Andrews's production of their *My Girl* was considered too undersized – it had, after all, only one set – for the New York papers to send their first-string critics to its opening, it won both fine notices from those who did go and a 291-performance run at the little Vanderbilt Theater. Andrews followed it with *Merry, Merry* ('Little Girl', 'I Was Blue', 'It Must Be Love'), another piece built on similarly economic and comically play-orientated lines, which confirmed the writers' success with both critics and public (176 performances).

By the time of Louis Werba's mounting of their *Twinkle, Twinkle* (add scenes and numbers by Harry Ruby and Bert Kalmar), a 167-performance success with Joe E Brown in its starring rôle, one journal was able to announce that although the piece was 'a little less intimate than when their works were staged at the Vanderbilt ... in certain circles the honors, mantles and emoluments of the Princess Theater team of Bolton, Woodhouse and Kern have more or less definitely been assigned [to Thompson and Archer]'.

The mantle did not stay on their shoulders even as long as it had on those of their predecessors. Phil Morris and H C Greene's production of the 1928 *Just a Minute* saw the end of the four-show run of success (80 performances), and the end of Archer's career on Broadway. Although he contributed the odd song thereafter to such pieces as *Sweet and Low* (1930) and wrote music for the revue *Shoot the Works* and off-Broadway's *Entre Nous*, he provided no more scores to the musical comedy stage. Many years later, he attempted to bring back a new and revised version of *Little Jessie James*, but the attempt foundered.

A composer of catchy, lightly jazzy music which was an ideal accompaniment to the modern, farcical tales supplied by his librettist, Archer never succeeded in becoming fashionable and, in spite of a run of success which at least challenged that of the still much-talked-of little shows at the Princess Theater a few years earlier, he is now virtually forgotten.

1912 **The Pearl Maiden** (Earle C Anthony, Arthur F Kales) New York Theater 22 January
1915 **Love for Sale** (w Tom Johnstone, Will B Johnstone, Jack Wilson)
1922 **Paradise Alley** (w Carle Carlton, Adorjan Ötvös/Howard Johnson/Charles W Bell, Edward Clark) Providence, RI, 18 September; Casino Theater, New York, 31 March 1924
1923 **Little Jessie James** (Harlan Thompson) Longacre Theater 15 August
1924 **My Girl** (Thompson) Vanderbilt Theater 24 November
1925 **Merry, Merry** (Thompson) Vanderbilt Theater 24 September
1926 **Twinkle, Twinkle** (Thompson) Liberty Theater 16 November
1928 **Just a Minute** (Walter O'Keefe/H C Greene) Ambassador Theater 8 October
1935 **Entre Nous** (w Richard Lewine/W B Johnstone) 30 December

ARIZONA LADY Operette in 2 acts by Alfred Grünwald and Gustav Beer. Music by Emmerich Kálmán. Stadttheater, Berne, 14 February 1954.

Independent, no-nonsense rancher Lona Farrell takes an unwilling fancy to the new cowboy, Roy Dexter, who has tamed her brilliant horse 'Arizona Lady'. However, thanks to a rash bet, she has no choice but to marry the sheriff, Harry Sullivan, when the horse is beaten in a race because of a girth sabotaged by a rich racing rival who is actually head of a bandit gang. In spite of kidnapping, gangstering and the arrival in mid-plot of a sexy dancer, 'Arizona Lady' wins the Kentucky Derby and the Sheriff renounces his claims on Lona in favour of Roy at the final curtain. The traditional comedy was supplied by Nelly, a travelling pedlar, and the comical and kidnapped cowboy, Chester.

The basic plot of the piece was one that had been well used in turn-of-the-century racing musical comedies, touched up this time with bits of *La Fanciulla del West* and plonked down in *Oklahoma!* country, and Kálmán's score had equally little to do with the 1950s, being laid out in traditional Viennese Operette fashion with its tenor and soprano leads and its supporting soubrets who, amongst them, performed virtually the entire solo music. The heroine's attractive opening song 'War's nicht schön' was a rangy piece with Hungarian tones, the soubrette's 'Wer führt mich heut zum Tanzen aus?' with its dancing rhythms and above-the-stave finish was a far cry from 'I Cain't Say No' and, if the hero's kleine Cowboylied with its exhortation 'Singende Cowboy reite' and celebrating 'mein Song, mein Pferd und ich' had something of the Hollywood cowboy song in its lazy triplets, it was in the minority. There were, however, some moments such as the first-act finale in which the hero tunefully serenaded Arizona ('Hier ist alles Okay') which showed more obvious, if not simply 'borrowed', trans-Atlantic musical theatre influences.

Arizona Lady, completed by the composer's son Charles, was Kálmán's last staged work, produced in Berne the year after his death and subsequently seen in Germany.

Germany: Städtische Bühnen, Augsburg 26 October 1954

ARKELL, Reginald ['Billy'] (b Lechlade, Glos, 14 October 1882; d Cricklade, 1 May 1959).

A prolific author of magazine articles, light verse, novels and plays, the first of which (*Columbine*) was produced in 1913, Billy Arkell began to write lyrics and, later, libretti for the musical theatre and revue after the war. His first contribution, in 1921, was to the touring musical comedy *Kiki*, but he subsequently collaborated on the libretti and/or lyrics for the English versions of *Der letzte Walzer*, *Frasquita*, *Toi c'est moi*, *Mädi* and *Paganini*, supplied the English libretto for Kurt Weill's unfortunate *Der Kuhhandel* (*A Kingdom for a Cow*), and was involved in four shows for singing star José Collins in her post-Daly's Theater period.

Amongst his revue material (*Jumble Sale*, *Life*, *London's Potinière Revue*, *Savoy Follies*) the highly successful British schoolboy's retelling of history, *1066 and All That* (music: Alfred Reynolds), was a particular and long-running success.

1921 **Kiki** (Herman Finck/Martin Henry) Ramsgate 7 March
1921 **Now and Then** (Philip Braham/J Hastings Turner, George Graves) Vaudeville Theatre 17 September
1922 **The Last Waltz** (*Der letzte Walzer*) English version w Robert Evett (Gaiety Theatre)
1923 **Catherine** (*Die Siegerin*) English version w Fred de Grésac (Gaiety Theatre)
1924 **Our Nell** (H Fraser Simson/Harry Graham/w Louis N Parker) Gaiety Theatre 16 April
1924 **Frasquita** English version w de Grésac (Prince's Theatre)
1927 **The Blue Train** (*Mädi*) English version w Dion Titheradge (Prince of Wales Theatre)
1934 **Gay Deceivers** (*Toi c'est moi*) English version (Gaiety Theatre)
1935 **A Kingdom for a Cow** (*Der Kuhhandel*) English version w Desmond Carter (Savoy Theatre)
1935 **Paganini** English version w A P Herbert (Lyceum)
1937 **The Laughing Cavalier** (Wainwright Morgan/w Stafford Byrne) Adelphi Theatre 19 October

ARLEN Harold [ARLUCK, Hyman] (b Buffalo, NY, 15 February 1905; d New York, 23 April 1986). Screen and stage songwriter whose numbers have survived better than the shows which housed them.

Arlen started his life in the music world as a sometime jazz player and singer and as a revue and musical theatre rehearsal pianist. During this period, whilst working on the Vincent Youmans musical *Great Day!*, he even appeared briefly on the pre-Broadway stage. Before long he turned his hand to song-writing and scored an initial success with the number 'Get Happy' (w Ted Koehler), introduced by Ruth Etting in *The 9:15 Revue* (1930). Arlen and Koehler continued their partnership through a series of scores and songs for Harlem's Cotton Club shows – 'Between the Devil and the Deep Blue Sea' (1931), 'I've Got the World on a String' (1932), 'Stormy Weather' (1933) – and for Broadway revues (*Earl Carroll Vanities*, *Americana*, *Life Begins at 8:40* w E Y Harburg, Ira Gershwin) before the composer moved on to Hollywood where he had already been represented by the inclusion of his 'It's Only a Paper Moon' (w Harburg, Billy Rose) in the film of the musical *Take a Chance* (1933).

From 1934 Arlen provided songs for 24 feature films through more than two decades. These included *Let's Fall in Love* (1934, 'Let's Fall in Love' w Koehler), *The Wizard of Oz* (1939, 'Over the Rainbow' [Academy Award], 'Follow the Yellow Brick Road' etc., w Harburg), *Blues in the Night* (1941, 'Blues in the Night' w Johnny Mercer), *Star-Spangled Rhythm* (1942, 'That Old Black Magic' w Mercer), *The Sky's the Limit* (1943, 'One for my Baby' w Mercer), *Cabin in the Sky* (1943, additional numbers), *Here Come the Waves* (1944, 'Ac-cent-tchu-ate the Positive'), *Four Jills in a Jeep* (1944, 'How Blue the Night' w Jimmy McHugh), *Up in Arms* (1944, 'Now I Know' w Koehler), *Casbah* (1948, 'Hooray for Love' w Leo Robin), *A Star is Born* (1954, 'The Man That Got Away' w Ira Gershwin) and *I Could Go On Singing* (1963).

Arlen's first ventures in the field of the book musical, one with Jack Yellen in the cutesy college musical *You Said It* and another with librettists Lindsay and Crouse and lyricist E Y ('Yip') Harburg in a hotch-potch vehicle for comedian Ed Wynn called *Hooray For What!*, won little attention. However, he had considerably more success and a long Broadway run with the *Oklahoma!*-clone period piece *Bloomer Girl*, and created his best – if not most theatrically successful – theatre score in 1946 with the splendid Cotton Club-sounding *St Louis Woman* ('Any Place I Hang My Hat Is Home', 'Come Rain or Come Shine', 'Legalize My Name'). The 1950s brought two further black-cast musicals in the short-lived but still liked *House of Flowers*, with Pearl Bailey, Juanita Hall and Dionne Warwick, and the custom-made and rather plastic *Jamaica*, starring Lena Horne. He made his last contribution to the Broadway stage with the songs for an unsuccessful adaptation of Edna Ferber's period epic *Saratoga*.

Arlen has also been represented on the stage by various theatrical versions of *The Wizard of Oz* using the film score which have been played at venues as disparate as Britain's Royal Shakespeare Theatre and New York's Radio City Music Hall, and his list of favourite songs has been plundered on many occasions for compilation shows.

1931 **You Said It** (Jack Yellen/Sid Silvers, Yellen) 46th Street Theater 19 January

1937 **Hooray for What!** (E Y Harburg/Howard Lindsay, Russel Crouse) Winter Garden Theater 1 December

1942 **The Wizard of Oz** (with score from film and original stage versions) Muncipal Opera, St Louis

1944 **Bloomer Girl** (Harburg/Sig Herzig, Fred Saidy) Shubert Theater 5 October

1946 **St Louis Woman** (Johnny Mercer/Countee Cullen, Arna Bontemps) Martin Beck Theater 30 March

1954 **House of Flowers** (Truman Capote) Alvin Theater 30 December

1957 **Jamaica** (Harburg/Saidy) Imperial Theater 31 October

1959 **Saratoga** (Mercer/Morton da Costa) Winter Garden Theater 7 December

Biography: Jablonski, E: *Harold Arlen: Happy with the Blues* (Doubleday, New York, 1961)

ARLETTE   Opérette in 3 acts by Claude Roland and L Bouvet. Music by Jane Vieu. Galeries Saint-Hubert, Brussels, 28 October 1904.

First produced in Belgium, Mme Vieu's opérette told of a playboy Prince who is duty bound to marry money for sake of his country. In the end, he does nothing of the sort. He abdicates and marries his unrich sweetheart, whilst the rich girl who had been designated to be queen weds his ambitious and now crown-worthy cousin instead.

The Belgian production was followed by a provincial French one, but the show did not move to Paris. It was, however, somewhat surprisingly, picked up more than a decade later by London's Grossmith/Laurillard combine and, heavily adapted for British consumption, produced in London in 1917. A half-dozen British writers, including director Austen Hurgon, ensured that the *Arlette* staged in London finally bore little resemblance to its original. Of the 19 musical pieces in the new score, only two owed their music to Mme Vieu, the rest being written to order by Ivor Novello and Guy Le Feuvre. The Novello/Clifford Grey song 'On the Staff' provided a comical hit for the rising comedian Stanley Lupino who, alongside the nominal stars, Winifred Barnes and *Merry Widow* hero Joseph Coyne, assured a 255-performance run for the little Ruritanian piece.

Novello clearly nurtured fond memories of *Arlette*, for many years later he supplied a complete score for a piece called *How Do, Princess?* (Manchester, 16 March 1936) credited to George Arthurs as 'based on an adaptation by Jose H Levy', directed by Christopher Fry and with additional numbers by Maurice Dixon. *How Do, Princess?* was the libretto of *Arlette*, retranslated, readapted and rescored. There was no sign of Mme Vieu.

France: Grand Théâtre, Angers 15 February 1906; UK: Shaftesbury Theatre 6 September 1917

DER ARME JONATHAN   Operette in 3 acts by Hugo Wittmann and Julius Bauer based on *Les Deux Anglais* by P-F Merville. Music by Carl Millöcker. Theater an der Wien, Vienna, 4 January 1890.

The most successful Operette of the latter part of Carl Millöcker's career, *Der arme Jonathan* was based by librettists Wittmann and Bauer on the French comedy *Les Deux Anglais* (Odéon, Paris 3 July 1817), an item in the Odéon repertoire for well over half a century, and supplied an outstanding rôle for Alexander Girardi, the star of the Theater an der Wien (and the rest of Vienna), as Jonathan, the comical little cook to eccentric Boston millionaire Vandergold (Rudolf del Zopp).

The world-weary Vandergold decides to give away all his possessions and shoot himself, and at the same time the penniless and homeless little cook, whom he has sacked, embarks, for the very opposite reasons, on the same deadly plan. But, instead, the two come to an agreement. Vandergold ignores all his fawning friends and hangers-on and, making Jonathan the recipient of all his goods and chattels, he disappears. The two have effectively changed places, but they have a pact that should it not work out they will get together again, with their revolvers, and finish what they almost started. They agree on a musical signal for the eventuality. Jonathan and his Molly (Therese Biedermann) go off to lead the high life in Monte Carlo and there they meet Harriet (Ottilie Collin), the little medical student whom Vandergold cherished, now a famous singer under the management of the perky Tobias Quickly (Sebastian Stelzer). Harriet is not really happy, any more than Jonathan and Molly are, whilst Vandergold, who stayed alive only in the hope of winning Harriet, now thinks she has fallen for Jonathan and, utterly miserable, decides to call in his plan. Fortunately, he cannot remember the piece of music, for in the end he gets both his Harriet and his fortune back, Jonathan being only too happy to get rid of the responsibilities of wealth and become a cook once more.

Millöcker's score was unfailingly tuneful in both solo and in ensemble, its hits coming with the jaunty and plot-worthy 'Willst du mein Liebster sein', introduced by Harriet in the first act and repeated at the end of the third, and even more notably with Girardi's obligatory waltz, 'Ich bin der arme Jonathan', sung by the star as his entrance in the first act and again as a closer. Harriet, the prima donna, skittered through pages of coloratura on the top lines of the ensembles and finales, but the score of *Der arme Jonathan* was based firmly on the comical. The second act gave the soubrette her chance in a lively song ('Wir reisen im ganzen Italien') and in a showy duet, with orchestral imitations, with Jonathan ('Der Mann in allen guten Ehen'), whilst the comedian playing Tobias had two numbers, and the tenor Vandergold, returning from his heartbroken wanderings in the last act, had a jolly, marked sailor song.

Der arme Jonathan was an unequivocal success. It was played 54 times consecutively under Alexandrine von Schönerer's management at the Theater an der Wien, and was repeated over the next year or so more than 50 further times. It passed its hundredth performance 2 April 1891 with Girardi now paired with Ilka Pálmay (Molly), and remained in the repertoire until 1896. Within a fortnight of its première the piece was on stage in Berlin, and within two months Budapest's Népszinház opened its version (ad Béla J Fái, Ferenc Rajna) featuring Pál Vidor (Jonathan),

Aranka Hegyi (Harriet) and the queen of the Budapest stage, Luisa Blaha, as Molly, and made an enormous success. *Der arme Jonathan* was played throughout Central Europe (Zagreb, Prague, Basel, Bucharest etc), in Scandanavia and Russia (28 March 1890) all within months of the first performance, and America saw its first *Poor Jonathan* (ad by J A Jackson, R A Weill) in October the same year. Produced by Rudolf Aronson and John McCaull at the Casino Theater, with Jeff de Angelis (Jonathan), Fanny Rice (Molly), Harry MacDonough (Rubygold), Edwin Stevens (Tobias) and Lillian Russell (Harriet) starring, it proved the biggest success that theatre had had in a number of years, playing seven months and 208 performances on Broadway before heading for the road. In the meanwhile, the original German version had also come on display at New York's Amberg Theater with Josef Brakl (Jonathan), Paula Loewe (Molly), Adolf Philipp (Vandergold) and Emma Seebold (Harriet) starred, and it too proved a favourite.

Australia saw *Poor Jonathan* the following year, when Clara Merivale's company introduced it in Melbourne with the manageress playing Harriet to the Jonathan of Jack Leumane, the Vandergold of W H Woodfield and the Molly of Ida Osborne. Britain, however, ignored the piece until well after the American success and, when Horace Sedger staged a version at the Prince of Wales Theatre in 1893, he had a new libretto written (ad C H E Brookfield, Harry Greenbank) which situated the piece in Britain, busied itself mainly with topical jokes, and cut some of Millöcker's music, replacing it with extra numbers by a young composer currently trying to break in to the West End musical scene, Isaac Albéniz. Harry Monkhouse, Annie Schuberth and the Savoy's Jessie Bond starred in this botched version which was a palpable and salutory failure.

Der arme Jonathan had its first significant Vienna revival at the Johann Strauss-Theater in September 1910, with Louis Treumann as Jonathan and Mizzi Freihardt as Molly (35 performances), it was given a purposeful Nazi working-over by Heinz Hentschke and Günther Schwenn for a 1939 revival at Berlin's Admiralspalast (add mus Josef Rixner), and was played both in the repertoire at the Volksoper in 1952 and, in yet another reworking, at Munich's Theater am Gärtnerplatz in 1959. Latterly, however, with the comedy musical falling out of fashion, it has slipped from the schedules.

A film version was produced by UFA Films with Lizzi Waldmüller and Rudi Godden featured.

Germany: Friedrich-Wilhelmstädtisches Theater 16 January 1890; Hungary: Népszinház *Szegény Jonathan* 14 March 1890; US: Casino Theater 14 October 1890, Amberg Theater (Ger) 2 January 1891; Australia: Opera House, Melbourne *Poor Jonathan* 4 June 1891; UK: Prince of Wales Theatre *Poor Jonathan* 15 June 1893; Film: UFA
Recording: selection (part record) (Vienna Disc)

ARMONT, Paul [PETROCOCCHINO, Dimitri] (b Rostov, Russia, 1874; d Paris, 2 March 1943)

The author of many successful vaudevilles and comedies (and the occasional drama) for the French stage, Armont was known as the playwright who had never written a word of any of his plays. Solely an 'ideas' man, a brilliant constructor of comedy plots and scenes, he left the actual dialogue of his works to his collaborators, most often Nicolas Nancey or Marcel Gerbidon. Armont ventured only once into the world of the musical comedy when he co-authored the 1932 hit *Un soir de reveillon*, but his plays proved fertile material for librettists and he was represented across the world by musicalized versions of his biggest hits.

In America his *Jeunes Filles de palaces* (w Marcel Gerbidon, Théâtre de la Madeleine 5 May 1925) was turned into *The French Doll* for Irene Bordoni (Lyceum Theater 20 February 1922), *Souris d'hôtel* (w Gerbidon, Fémina 13 October 1919) was made into Ivan Caryll's *The Hotel Mouse* (aka *Little Miss Raffles*) and Anita Loos transformed *L'École des cocottes* into the 1964 *Go-Go Loves You*. In Britain *Théodore et cie* (w Nicolas Nancey, Paul Gavault, Théâtre des Nouveautés 29 September 1909) became the hit Gaiety musical *Theodore and Co.* (Ivor Novello, Jerome Kern/Adrian Ross, Clifford Grey/H M Harwood, George Grossmith, 19 September 1916), *Le Truc du Brésilien* (w Nancey) made up into a second hit for the same management in *Yes, Uncle!* (Prince of Wales Theatre 29 December 1917) and *Le Zèbre* (w Nancey, Théâtre des Nouveautés 3 December 1910), a major success as *The Glad Eye* on English stages, was turned into both the touring *Kiki* (Herman Finck/Reginald Arkell, Martin Henry Palace, Ramsgate 7 March 1921) and the metropolitan *Up with the Lark* (Adelphi Theatre 25 August 1927).

No sources were given for Ralph Benatzky's Armont and Gerbidon-based musical *Pariserinnin* (Theater in der Josefstadt 7 May 1937) nor for the Hungarian musicals *Papucs* (1933, w Gerbidon, ad Sándor Lestayán music: Michael Krazsnay Krausz) produced at the Pesti Színház 18 November, and *Szabo a kastelyban* (w Léopold Marchand, ad Zsolt Harsányi, music: Alexander Steinbrecher) mounted at the Vigszinház in 1937 (7 October). However, the latter piece reached a wider audience when – attached to a different score – it became the Hollywood musical *Tell Me Tonight*.

1932 **Un soir de reveillon** (Raoul Moretti/Jean Boyer/w Marcel Gerbidon) Théâtre des Bouffes-Parisiens

ARMS AND THE GIRL

Musical comedy in 2 acts by Herbert and Dorothy Fields and Rouben Mamoulian based on the play *The Pursuit of Happiness* by Lawrence Langner and Armina Marshall. Music by Morton Gould. 46th Street Theater, New York, 2 February 1950.

A Theatre Guild production of a musical based on a play by its own executives, *Arms and the Girl* featured Nanette Fabray as the girl who takes up arms in an American-Revolution tale of spying and romance. The romance was represented by the French star of *Bless the Bride*, Georges Guétary, who sang of his ideals in a Germanic 'A Cow and a Plow and a Frau', whilst Pearl Bailey featured as a black servant with a pair of songs which dropped almost every final consonant in sight ('There Must Be Somethin' Better Than Love', 'Nothin' for Nothin''). The show was a 134-performance failure.

The same title was used earlier, in Britain, for a comic operette in two scenes, written by Austen Hurgon with music by Richard Fall (London Hippodrome, 29 April 1912). Hippodrome manager Albert de Courville attemped to build up the variety programmes at his theatre by introducing substantial small musicals which he commissioned or adapted from composers such as Leoncavallo, Heinrich Reinhardt and Leo and Richard Fall. With favourite comic G P Huntley, American soprano May de Sousa and the Gaiety's Jean Aylwin top-billed, backed by a chorus of 65 and an orchestra of 42, *Arms and the Girl* proved to have insufficient pull and de Courville soon changed his policy.

Recording: original cast, US musical (Decca, Columbia)

ARNAUD, Yvonne (b Bordeaux, 20 December 1892; d London, 20 September 1958).

Trained principally as a pianist, Mlle Arnaud made an early success as an actress and vocalist when she appeared alongside Gertie Millar in the rôle of the French Princess Mathilde, created by Elsie Spain, in *The Quaker Girl* at London's Adelphi Theatre at the age of 19. The following year she starred as Suzanne in the London version of Jean Gilbert's *Die keusche Susanne*, (*The Girl in the Taxi*) at the Lyric Theatre, a rôle which she repeated several times over the following years, and followed up as Zara in Oscar Straus's *Love and Laughter* and in the lead rôles of the British versions of Eysler's *Der lachende Ehemann* (*The Girl Who Didn't*, Etelka von Basewitz) and Gilbert's *Fräulein Tralala* (*Mlle Tralala, Oh! Be Careful*, Noisette) in 1915.

She subsequently appeared in French rôles in two successful post-war musicals, *Kissing Time* (1919, Georgette St Pol) and *The Naughty Princess* (*La Reine s'amuse*, 1920, Chiquette), before abandoning the musical stage for a distinguished career in the straight theatre.

Mlle Arnaud was married to librettist C M S (Hugh) McLellan.

Biography: 'Malet, O': *Marraine: a portrait of my godmother* (Heinemann, London, 1961)

ARNE, Thomas [Augustine] (b London, 28 May 1710; d London, 5 March 1778). One of the most important figures of the English-language musical theatre in the latter years of the 18th century.

Intended by his father for a more worldly career, the young Arne studied music secretly and made his first contributions to the musical theatre with songs for the opera *Rosamond*, composed to a text by Joseph Addison and produced at Lincoln's Inn Fields (7 March 1733), and with music for a version of Henry Fielding's famous burlesque *Tom Thumb the Great* (originally produced in 1730) and other works from musical farce to pantomime. Over the next decade he supplied much incidental music for such masques as Thomas Bridges's *Dido and Aeneas* (1733), Milton's *Comus* (1738), Congreve's *The Judgement of Paris* (1740), Alfred Mallet's *Britannia* (1743) and the royal production of *Alfred* (1740, 'Rule Britannia'), and for revivals of classic plays, notably the Drury Lane productions of Shakespeare ('Blow, blow, thou winter wind', 'When Daisies Pied' etc), and also composed a short opera *The Blind Beggar of Bethnal Green* (libretto: Robert Dodsley, Theatre Royal, Drury Lane, 3 April 1741).

In the mid-1740s, whilst working as musical director at the Theatre Royal, Drury Lane, he made further forays in the lighter genre with the score to Colley Cibber's comic opera *The Temple of Dulness* and Shirley's burlesque *King Pepin's Campaign*, and composed the version of Shakespeare's 'Where the Bee Sucks' which has survived 250 years as standard as part of an incidental score to *The Tempest*. However, his most fruitful period came in the 1760s when, now the musical head of the Covent Garden Theatre, he produced not only the most successful English opera of the time, *Artaxerxes* (2 February 1762 Drury Lane, Metastasio ad), but also his two most enduring light works, the comic operas *Thomas and Sally* and *Love in a Village*. The latter piece, whose 43 musical portions included 19 original numbers by Arne, has been noted as the landmark musical show in which the ballad-opera format of a score made up of borrowed rather than specially composed music was first significantly broken away from.

During the 1770s he wrote further works in all fields from different levels of opera (*Olimpiade*, *Achilles in Petticoats*) and oratorio to incidental music (*Caractacus*), comic opera (*The Rose*), burletta (*The Golden Pippin*) and musical farce (*May Day*), without again finding the very large success of his three principal works.

Arne was given an honorary Doctorate of Music by Oxford University in 1759.

His sister, Susannah Maria (1714–1766, Mrs Theophilus Cibber) was a successful actress and vocalist, and his son Michael Arne (?1741–1786), best known for his melody to the song 'The Lass With the Delicate Air', also composed for the theatre.

1733 **Tom Thumb the Great** (aka *The Opera of Operas*) (Henry Fielding) Haymarket Theatre 31 May
1736 **The Fall of Phaeton** (Prichard) Theatre Royal, Drury Lane 28 February
1739 **A Hospital for Fools** (James Miller) Theatre Royal, Drury Lane 15 November
1745 **The Temple of Dulness** (Colley Cibber) Theatre Royal, Drury Lane 17 January
1745 **King Pepin's Campaign** (William Shirley) Theatre Royal, Drury Lane 15 April
1760 **Thomas and Sally, or the Sailor's Return** (Isaac Bickerstaff) Covent Garden Theatre 28 November
1762 **Love In a Village** (Bickerstaff) Covent Garden Theatre 8 December
1764 **The Guardian Outwitted** (Arne) Covent Garden Theatre 12 December
1769 **Tom Jones** (w Joseph Reed) Covent Garden Theatre 14 January
1772 **The Sot** (aka *Squire Badger*) (Henry Fielding ad Arne) His Majesty's Theatre 16 March
1772 **The Cooper** (*Le Tonnelier*) (ad Arne) His Majesty's Theatre 10 June
1772 **The Rose** (Arne) Theatre Royal, Drury Lane 2 December
1773 **The Golden Pippin** (pasticcio arr/Kane O'Hara) Covent Garden Theatre 6 February
1775 **May Day, or the Little Gipsy** (David Garrick) Theatre Royal, Drury Lane 28 October
1776 **Phoebe at Court** (Arne) King's Theatre 22 February

Biography: Langley, H: *Doctor Arne* (Cambridge, 1938)

ARNOLD, Charles see HANS THE BOATMAN

ARNOLD, Franz [HIRSCH, Franz] (b Znim bei Bromberg, 28 April 1878; d London, 29 September 1960) Berlin actor, playwright, librettist and sometime producer.

Although a Franz Arnold is credited with the text on Waldemar Wendland's 1904 *Der Negerlein* and again with the Posse *Ach, die Kerls* in 1910, this Arnold is said (by himself) to have made his début as a dramatist with the successful play *Die spanische Fliege* in 1912, and he supplied – or seems to have supplied – one musical comedy text to successful composer Jean Gilbert (again, confusingly, the

'Arnold' author of Gilbert's *Das Fräulein von Amt* is apparently not him, as sometimes credited, but actor-playwright Ernst Arnold before he began a writing collaboration with fellow performer-writer and director Ernst Bach. It was a collaboration that would produce a long series of successful works for both the musical and non-musical stage.

The pair supplied texts to Walter Kollo (*Die Königin der Nacht*), Gilbert, Hugo Hirsch (the highly successful *Der Fürst von Pappenheim* and *Dolly*) and a number of the other principal songwriters of the wartime and post-wartime Berlin theatre up until Bach's death in 1929. Even thereafter, their work got international exposure, notably in Britain where their farce *Hurra! Eine Junge* became a major London comedy hit under the title *It's a Boy*, and was later used as the basis for the long-running musical comedy *Blue for a Boy*.

Arnold and Bach were strongly represented on the British musical stage for, although their names appeared but rarely on a playbill, it was one of their pieces – apparently the Hugo Hirsch musical *Der Fürst von Pappenheim* – that was made over as a vehicle for Jack Buchanan under the title *Toni* (1924) at the beginning of a series of adaptations for the English musical stage. It seems that whatever it was that became *Strandszerelem* in Hungary was the play that was musicalized for Leslie Henson as *Nice Goings On*, whilst the piece that had been adapted to the comic stage as *The Whole Town's Talking*, after being the subject of an abortive Arthur Freed musical, *A Pair o' Fools*, in America (25 January 1926), was turned into the musical comedy *Oh! You Letty* (Palace Theatre 8 December 1937), and the partners also had a credit on the flop *The Girl from Cooks* (Gaiety Theatre 1 November 1927), a piece with a tortuous pedigree and a half-Jean Gilbert score which may – or may not – have had something to do with their musical *Die Fahrt ins Glück*.

Hungary was no more precise than Britain in billing its Bach/Arnold musical comedy sources, but several unspecified plays by the pair were also adapted to the musical stage in Budapest. Their names appeared on the 1914 *Ezüstpille* (ad Andor Gábor, mus: Albert Szirmai) produced at the Vígszinház 9 May 1914, the Magyar Színház's *Jó firma* (ad Jenö Molnár, mus arr Mihály Nádor 5 June 1930) and *Strandszerelem* (ad Harmath) played at the Fővárosi Nyári Operettszinház 10 July 1929.

After Bach's death Arnold collaborated on a number of pieces with Emil Golz (*Hulda Pessl in Venedig*, *Epsteins Witwe*, *Frau Pick in Audienz* etc), before quitting Germany to settle in London where he became a naturalized British citizen. There his Operette *Jack of Hearts*, unproduced in its original German, was mounted unsuccessfully at Drury Lane as *Rise and Shine* and on the road as *Darling You*.

1910 **Ach, die Kerls** (Julius Einödshofer/w Heinz Saltenburg) Theater Sanssouci 29 October
1913 **Tsching Bum!** (Rudolf Hartmann) Ernst-Drucker-Theater April
1914 **Woran wir denken** (Jean Gilbert/w Walter Turszinksy) Metropoltheater 25 December
1916 **Die Fahrt ins Glück** (Gilbert/w Ernst Bach) Theater des Westens 2 September
1917 **Neptun auf Reisen** (Rudolf Nelson/w Bach) Apollotheater January
1919 **Fräulein Puck** (Walter Kollo/w Bach) Volkstheater, Munich 25 June

1921 **Die Königin der Nacht** (Kollo/w Bach) Neues Operetten-Theater 2 September
1923 **Der Fürst von Pappenheim** (Hugo Hirsch/w Bach) Deutsches Künstlertheater 16 February
1923 **Dolly** (Hirsch/Rudolf Bernauer/w Bach) Deutsches Künstlertheater 16 October
1924 **Die vertauschte Frau** (Kollo/w Bach) Operettenhaus am Schiffbauerdamm 22 December
1925 **Olly Polly** (Kollo/w Bach) Neues Theater am Zoo 3 September
1928 **Arme Ritter** (Kollo/w Bach) Volkstheater, Munich 22 September
1934 **Lieber, reich – aber glücklich** (Kollo/w Bach) Johann Strauss-Theater, Vienna 11 May
1935 **Frauen haben das gerne** (Kollo/w Bach) Residenzbühne 17 December
1936 **Rise and Shine** (aka *Darling You*) (*Jack of Hearts*) (Robert Stolz et al/Robert Gilbert/ad Desmond Carter, Harry Graham) Theatre Royal, Drury Lane, London 7 May

ARNOLD, Tom [ARNOLD, Thomas Charles] (b Richmond, Yorks, 19 August 1893; d London, 2 February 1969). Prolific British producer of musicals for both London and the touring circuits over more than 20 years.

Arnold spent his earliest working years as a clerk in the de Frece music-hall organization and later in a variety agency office before he began his operation as a producer of touring revues, pantomimes and the occasional made-for-touring musical comedy (*Love and Laughter* (1924), *Oh Patsy* (1926) etc) in the early- and mid-1920s. In the 1930s he began taking out full-scale post-London tours of more significant musicals such as *Waltzes From Vienna*, *The Merry Widow*, *Anything Goes*, *The Crest of the Wave*, *Give Us a Ring* with Flanagan and Allen, *Balalaika*, *Operette*, *Wild Oats*, *Me and my Girl* and *The Fleet's Lit Up* as well as a heavy complement of revues, pantomimes and ice shows, gaining in the process a reputation as a lavish producer of large-scale musical shows.

His first significant West End success came with the production of Novello's *The Dancing Years* in 1939, a production which his acumen and knowledge of provincial theatre salvaged and turned into a hit when the war closed down the Theatre Royal, Drury Lane, and evicted the new musical. After a triumphant and well-organized wartime tour, *The Dancing Years* returned to London for the long run it had previously been denied.

Arnold produced all of Novello's subsequent musicals (*Arc de Triomphe*, *Perchance to Dream*, *King's Rhapsody*, *Gay's the Word*), as well as the successful series of Cicely Courtneidge vehicles (*Full Swing*, *Something in the Air*, *Under the Counter*, *Gay's the Word*), Noel Gay's wartime *Present Arms* (1940), *The Land of Smiles* with Tauber (1942), Cole Porter's *Panama Hattie* and Coward's *Ace of Clubs* (1950) – occasionally in partnership with Lee Ephraim and/or Emile Littler. He also kept up a continuing presence in the provinces with a wide range of musical shows, produced either alone or with Bernard Delfont, which included revivals of the classics *Monsieur Beaucaire* (1943) and *The Duchess of Dantzic* (1943), *Hit the Deck* (1944), Zeller's *The Birdseller* (*Der Vogelhändler*) (1947) and a new Swedish musical, *Serenade* (1948), unwisely advertised as Scandanavia's answer to *Oklahoma!*.

After a limited activity on the musical front in the 1950s, he returned, in partnership with Delfont, to produce three new musicals in the 1960s – *Pickwick* (1963), *Our Man*

Crichton (1964) and *Maggie May* (1964) – as well as the London representation of Broadway's *Little Me* (1964).

Following his death, his production office maintained a limited and intermittent action and was involved with such productions as the children's musical *The Water Babies* (1973) and a revival of *The King and I* (1980) at the London Palladium.

ARONSON, Rudolf (b New York, 8 April 1856; d New York, 4 February 1919). New York's principal producer of the all-consuming European comic opera in the 1880s.

At first prominent in the musical and theatrical world as the very young manager of the Metropolitan Concert Hall in New York, Aronson was still in his mid-twenties when he capitalized and built the oriental-looking Casino Theater on New York's Broadway and 39th Street and became its first manager. The theatre opened with a production of Johann Strauss's *The Queen's Lace Handkerchief* in 1882 and quickly became established as the city's leading house for quality musical theatre. At first, Aronson ran the house in collaboration with John McCaull, whose comic opera company provided much of the product staged there (*Prince Methusalem, La Princesse de Trébizonde, Der Bettelstudent, The Merry War, Falka, Le Petit Duc*), but the two managers soon fell out over McCaull's insistence on artistic control, and he departed leaving Aronson to run the house alone.

In his first decade of operation Aronson mounted or housed an impressive list of exclusively imported musical plays including *Polly, Billee Taylor, Nanon, Die Fledermaus, Amorita* (*Pfingsten in Florenz*), *The Gipsy Baron* (*Der Zigeunerbaron*), *Ermine, The Commodore* (*La Créole*), *The Marquis* (*Jeanne, Jeannette et Jeanneton*), *Madelon* (*La Petite Mademoiselle*), *Nadgy* (*Les Noces improvisées*), *The Yeomen of the Guard, The Brigands, The Drum Major* (*La Fille du tambour-major*), *La Grande-Duchesse de Gérolstein*, a piece advertised as Francis Chassaigne's *The Brazilian, La Fille de Madame Angot, Poor Jonathan* (*Der arme Jonathan*), *Apollo* (*Das Orakel*), *Indigo* (*Indigo und die vierzig Räuber*), *The Tyrolean* (*Der Vogelhändler*), *Cavalleria Rusticana, Uncle Célestin* (*L'Oncle Célestin*), *The Child of Fortune* (*Das Sonntagskind*) and *The Vice Admiral* (*Der Vizeadmiral*). Of these, by far the most successful single production was the English show, *Erminie*, which proved to be unchallengeably the longest-running comic opera of the 19th-century Broadway stage and which was revived at the Casino several times in later years. Aronson also opened the first roof-garden theatre in New York, on the Casino Theater roof (1883), a feature that was subsequently copied by a number of other houses, looking to catch the kind of trade that was seeking some light (and often late) entertainment as an adjunct to food and drink.

In 1893 his term at the Casino came to an end. Some of the company's stockholders called in the receivers and Aronson, who had been precariously balancing the theatre's affairs in a way all too common in the theatre world, found himself dispossessed. The theatre he had created was passed over to Thomas Canary and George Lederer at a rent of $38,000 pa. Aronson fought back, and was temporarily restored to 'his' theatre, but not for long. He continued to mount occasional productions – he was responsible for the 1900 Broadway version of *Wiener Blut*

(*Vienna Life*) – but to all intents and purposes his career as a producer was done.

Later Aronson became a booker in Europe for American theatres, was rumoured to be involved in land speculation in Puerto Rico, and announced the building of a Casino Theater in Los Angeles, a project which came to nothing.

Alongside his managerial activities, Aronson was also a prolific composer of, mainly, orchestral music, but he also ventured into comic opera and produced one of his own works, *The Rainmaker of Syria* at the Casino in 1894. It failed, but librettist Sydney Rosenfeld had it tarted up by musical director Ludwig Englander and sent on the road as *The Woman King, or the Royal Prize* (Miner's Theater, Newark, NJ 20 November 1893). He is also credited with a *Sweet Sixteen* (1883) and a *Captain Kidd* (1883) which, if they made it to the stage, certainly did not get a showing on Broadway.

1894 **The Rainmaker of Syria** (aka *The Woman King*) (Sydney Rosenfeld) Casino Theater 25 September

Autobiography: *Theatrical and Musical Memoirs* (McBride, Nast, New York, 1912)

ARRIETA [y Corera], [Pascual Juan] Emilio (b Puente la reina, 21 October 1823; d Madrid, 11 February 1894).

Musically trained at the Conservatoire in Milan, Arrieta at first tried his hand at writing operas. His *Ildegonda* was played in Milan in 1845, and later in Madrid and Lisbon, and *La conquista de Granada* (also known as *Isabella la catolica*) was produced in Madrid in 1850 and again in 1855 before the composer moved on to composing lighter pieces.

Under the influence of his Italian training, both in so far as form and style were concerned, Arrieta wrote a considerable number of full-length pieces at a time when most Spanish composers were concentrating on the genero chico, or short zarzuela, and his most successful single work was *Marina*, a two-act piece to a text by Francisco Camprodón, first produced in 1855 (Teatro del Circo 21 September) and later extended by its composer and the librettist Miguel Ramos Carrión into a three-act opera. *Llamada y tropa* (libretto: Antonio Garcia Guttierez, Teatro del Circo 8 March 1861), *La guerra santa* (lib: de Larra, Enrico Perez Eserich, Teatro Zarzuela 4 March 1879) and the short *El Grumete* (lib: Guttierez, Teatro del Circo 17 June 1853) were amongst others of his successful pieces from a list which also included *Al Amanecer* (1851), *El Domino Azul* (1853), *La estrella de Madrid* (1853), *La Carceria real* (1854), *La dama del rey* (1855) *Guerra muerte* (1855), *La hija de la providence* (1856), *El sonambulo* (1856), *El planeta Venus* (1858), *Azon Visconti* (1858), *Quien manda manda* (1859), *Los circasianos* (1860), *Un ayo para el niño* (1861), *Dos coronas* (1861), *Al agente de matrimonios* (1862), *La tabernesa de Londres* (1862), *Un trono y un desengano* (1862), *La vuelta del corsario* (1863), *De tal palo tal astilla* (1864) *Cadenas de oro* (1864), *El toque de animas* (1864), *La insula Barataria* (1864), *El capitan negrero* (1865), *El conjuro* (1866), *Un sarao y una soirée* (1866), *La suegra del diabolo* (1867), *Los enemigos-domestico* (1867), *Los novios de Teruel* (1867), *El figle enamorado* (1867) *A la humanidad doliente* (1868), *Los misterios del Parnaso* (1868), *Los progresos del amor* (1868), *Las fuentes del Prado* (1870), *De Madrid a Biarritz* (1870), *El potosi submarino* (1870), *El molin contra equilache* (1871), *La sota de espadas* (1871), *La manzanas de oro* (1873), *Un viaje a Cochinchina* (1875), *Entre el alcade e el rey* (1875), *El amor enamorado* (1880), *San Franco di Sena* (1883), *El guerrillero* (1855 w Caballero, Ruperto Chapí) etc.

ARTHUR, Beatrice [FRANKEL, Bernice] (b New York, 13 May 1926).

A deep-voiced American character actress widely familiar through her television appearances in *Maude* and *The Golden Girls*, Miss Arthur appeared as Lucy Brown in the 1954 off-Broadway *The Threepenny Opera*, played in the *Shoestring Revues*, in *Seventh Heaven* (1955, Mme Suze) and the 1960 reprise of *Gay Divorce* (Hortense). The most memorable part of her musical theatre career came, however, in the 1960s when she created the roles of Yente, the matchmaker, in *Fiddler on the Roof* (1964) and best-friend Vera Charles ('Bosom Buddies') in *Mame* (1966). A 1968 show, *A Mother's Kisses* (Meg), in which she was top-billed, folded on the road.

She was married to director Gene Saks (b New York, 8 November 1921) whose musical theatre credits include *Half a Sixpence* (1965), *Mame* (1966), *A Mother's Kisses* (1966), *The Prince of Grand Street* (1978), *Home Again* (1979) and *Rags* (1986).

ARTHURS, George (b Manchester, 13 April 1875; d Harrow, 14 March 1944). Songwriter whose work ranged from the music-hall to the musical comedy.

After making an early living as an accountant in his native Manchester, Arthurs found his first musical and theatrical success as a lyricist for the music halls. His most enduring efforts in this field included 'I Want to Sing in Opera', written in collaboration with Worton David for Wilkie Bard, the wailing serenade to 'Josh-u-a' (w Bert Lee) as originally performed by Clarice Mayne, Whit Cunliffe's 'A Different Girl Again', and 'A Little of What You Fancy [Does You Good]' (w Fred W Leigh), connected forever to the name of Marie Lloyd. He also wrote intermittently for the theatre, to which he contributed, often in collaboration, lyrics and libretti for musicals and songs and sketches for revue (*Hullo, Tango* etc).

Arthurs's first venture into the London musical theatre was with some 'additional lyrics' for *The Belle of Mayfair* and *Havana*, both composed by fellow Mancunian Leslie Stuart. He subsequently supplied texts and/or songwords for a number of the Hippodrome and Pavilion revues, for some of the one-act operettas then played in the bigger revue houses, and also for such other revues as *Honeymoon Express* at the Oxford (1914), *The Whirl of the Town* at the London Palladium (1915), *We're All In It* (1916) and *Seeing Life* (1917). He contributed to the words of the rewritten-readapted German musical comedy *Oh! Be Careful* (ex-*Mlle Tralala*, 1915), but his most substantial contribution to the book musical came between 1917 and 1919 when he co-wrote libretti and lyrics for four West End shows, the most successful of which were the long-running Leslie Henson vehicle *Yes, Uncle!*, fabricated from the French comedy *Le Truc du Brésilien*, and his adaptation of the famous comedy *La Petite Chocolatière* as *The Girl for the Boy* as a showcase for Gina Palerme. Both *Yes, Uncle!* (Theatre Royal, Melbourne 12 June 1920) and *The Girl for the Boy*

(Tivoli, Melbourne 18 September 1920) got showings on both sides of the world.

Arthurs also placed songs in the American productions of several book shows, notably *The Echo* ('I'm Waiting for Kate' w David), what remained of Winterberg's *Die Dame in Rot*, ('Cupid Never Wrote the Alphabet' w David), *The Girl behind the Counter* ('Anytime You're Passing By' w C W Murphy), and Leo Fall's *The Dollar Princess* ('I Can Say Truly Rural' w David, sung by Will West) and *Die Sirene* ('I Want to Sing in Opera').

His later musical comedy work, in the 1920s and 1930s, was confined to touring shows, of which the easy-going *Archie*, toured liberally in Britain, also made it to productions in Australia (Princess Theatre, Melbourne 7 November 1925, St James Theatre, Sydney 5 November 1927).

1904 **A Chinese Idyll** (E C Brierley/w J Gar Kiddie/Fred Danvers) Grand Theatre, Stalybridge 18 July
1904 **The Belle of the Orient** (Paul Knox, James W Tate/w Clifford Harris, J B Peterman) 3 scenes Islington Empire 18 July
1910 **The White Knight** (Julian Wilson) 1 act Crouch End 6 September
1912 **Maison Décolleté** (*Décolleté et cie*) 1 act English version (London Pavilion)
1913 **An Arabian Night** (Wilson) 1 act 18 August
1914 **Dora's Doze** (Louis Hirsch) 1 act London Palladium 6 July
1915 **The Magic Touch** (Leon Bassett/w Charles Danvers) 1 act Walthamstow Palace 18 January
1915 **Go to Jericho** (w Hirsch, Fred Godfrey) 1 act Oxford Theatre 22 February
1915 **Million Dollar Girl** (Louis Jerome) 1 act Victoria Palace 16 May
1917 **Sugar** (Jerome/Lauri Wylie, Alfred Parker) 1 act Oxford Theatre 16 July
1917 **Sugar Baby** (Grace Vernon/Harry M Vernon) 1 act Victoria Palace
1917 **Suzette** (Max Darewski/w Austen Hurgon) Globe Theatre 29 March
1917 **Arlette** English version w Ivor Novello, Guy LeFeuvre, Adrian Ross, Clifford Grey and Hurgon (Shaftesbury Theatre)
1917 **Yes, Uncle!** (Nat D Ayer/Grey/w Hurgon) Prince's Theatre
1919 **The Girl for the Boy** (Howard Carr, Bernard Rolt/w Percy Greenbank/w Hurgon et al) Duke of York's Theatre 23 September
1921 **Peri, the Slave of Love** (William Neale) Wolverhampton 21 February
1923 **Biffy** (Gil Roy/Vera Beringer, William Ray) tour
1924 **Archie** (Haydn Wood, Jack Waller/w Worton David) Grand Theatre, Hull 28 July
1927 **Patsy From Paris** (L Jerome) Palace, Maidstone 14 March
1928 **Tipperary Tim** (Joseph Tunbridge/w Arthur Field) Alhambra Theatre, Bradford 6 August
1930 **Wild Rose** (Kennedy Russell/David Fairweather/w Worton David) tour
1936 **How Do, Princess** revised *Arlette* (Novello) Manchester 16 March

AN ARTIST'S MODEL Comedy with music in 2 acts by Owen Hall. Lyrics by Harry Greenbank. Music by Sidney Jones. Daly's Theatre, London, 2 February 1895.

Following the great success of *A Gaiety Girl*, which had been transferred from its production venue at the Prince of Wales Theatre into Daly's Theatre during its run, George Edwardes commissioned from its authors and composer another show in the same new line of modern-dress musical comedy as a follow-up. *A Naughty Girl* was intended to feature Lottie Venne in a rôle similar to that in which she had scored in *A Gaiety Girl*, and (following the ups and downs the producer had experienced with the American soubrette Marie Halton) Letty Lind, the town's favourite dancing and sort-of-singing ingénue, was tabbed to take the title-rôle in a farcical piece centred around the high jinks of this stock 'romp-of-the-school' character in the fleshpots of Paris. The whole piece was, of course, to be told in the frothy, smart society manner which had helped make such a hit of the earlier show.

Plans for the show were turned on their head, however, when the hugely popular Marie Tempest returned to London from a triumphant stay in America, and Edwardes signed her for the new show. There was no question of ousting Lottie Venne from the cast, so librettist Jimmy Davis ('Owen Hall') was simply given instructions to write in a large co-starring role for Miss Tempest. His intelligent answer to this problem was to invent a whole second plot: the tale of a former artist's model, now a rich widow, and her former lover, a poor Parisian artist (a role allotted to Miss Tempest's *Dorothy* and *Red Hussar* co-star Hayden Coffin) chary, under the circumstances, of attempting to renew their youthful romance. This plot was interwoven with the jaunts and japes of madcap Daisy Vane and the cavalcade of her guardian and other susceptible Britons through Paris.

The enforced rewrite turned out to be the best thing that could have happened to the show. The new portion (which annexed the show's title, now *An Artist's Model)* turned out to be the heart of the entertainment, the old portion the decoration and the light relief, in a musical which provided a fine variety of humour and romance, and of lyrical solos and ensembles and character songs in Sidney Jones's score. Lottie Venne scored with a knowing point number 'The Lady Wasn't Going That Way', but the most notable public favourites amongst the songs proved to be a dainty song-and-dance piece for Letty Lind telling the fable of 'The Gay Tom Tit', and 'The Laughing Song' as put over by the dashingly darkish Maurice Farkoa, and subsequently recorded many times by him as the most successful of all early 78rpm show song recordings.

An Artist's Model set the pattern for one of the most successful series of musicals in theatre history. The two-headed arrangement, with Coffin and Miss Tempest featured in a strong singing romantic partnership, and Miss Lind and, later, other comedy performers heading the equally important soubret and comic portion of the piece, remained standard at Daly's Theatre where, with Edwardes at the helm, Owen Hall, Harry Greenbank and Sidney Jones provided, during the next decade, several of the most enduring shows of the period: *The Geisha*, *A Greek Slave* and *San Toy*. After its 392 performances at Daly's and in an enforced transfer to the Lyric Theatre, *An Artist's Model* went on the road, at first with Maud Boyd and Leonard Russell starred in Edwardes's Number One Company, and then in many subsequent, and later lesser, companies.

Al Hayman and Charles Frohman mounted a Broadway version of *An Artist's Model* with Australian star Nellie Stewart in Miss Tempest's rôle and an otherwise largely London cast including Marie Studholme (Daisy), Farkoa, and John Coates (Rudolph) through 56 performances, but the show did not go further afield. It took the next of the Daly's shows, *The Geisha*, to wake the world up to what was going on at Edwardes's theatre.

USA: Broadway Theater 23 December 1895

ASCHE, Oscar [HEISS, John Stanger] (b Geelong, Australia, 26 June 1872; d Marlow, Bucks, 23 March 1936).

Born in Australia, the big, barrel-chested Asche made his stage career in Britain, establishing himself as an actor in mostly Shakespearian rôles under the management of F R Benson and of Herbert Beerbohm Tree at London's His Majesty's Theatre. It was also with Tree that he had his first experience as a director, on Stephen Phillips's popular drama *Ulysses*. Asche subsequently played several seasons under his own management, taking some of the principal heroic rôles in the standard repertoire as well as those in which his physique rendered him particularly effective, from Falstaff and Attila the Hun to Hajj the Beggar in Edward Knoblock's eastern tale, *Kismet*. He also made several forays into the field of authorship, and collaborated with F Norreys Connell on the play *Count Hannibal* (1910).

Asche appeared on the music-hall stage as *Hajj* in a musical scena written for him by Knoblock, but he made his full-scale entry into the musical theatre in 1916 when he wrote, directed and starred in the rather *Kismet*-like spectacular musical piece *Chu Chin Chow* ('Anytime's Kissing Time', 'The Cobbler's Song'), produced by his old master, Tree, and his wife and co-star, Lily Brayton, at His Majesty's Theatre. This version of the Arabian Nights tale of Ali Baba and the 40 thieves, rewritten to give Asche and Miss Brayton starring rôles of the kind best suited to them as the robber chieftain and his vengeful slave girl, was directed by Asche in a lavishly dramatic and picturesque fashion, and it became one of the favourite entertainments of the First World War, running on at its London base for an unprecedented 2,235 performances over five years. It made a huge profit for all concerned and notably for Asche who, although his chronic inability to manage money had made him unable to invest in the show as a producer, had won a large share in its running profits by taking as his director's fee a percentage on the show's box-office.

The greatest rival to *Chu Chin Chow* during its five years' run was another musical in which Asche had a hand, this time as director only: *The Maid of the Mountains* at Daly's Theatre. The spectacular aspect of *Chu Chin Chow* had played a very large part in its success and *The Maid of the Mountains*' striking and expansive production, designed and staged by Asche, was once again an important element of a stage piece which proved extraordinarily popular with wartime audiences. Asche proved himself to have a sure touch with the theatrically highly-coloured, both visually and dramatically, and these two great successes were followed by other similarly lavish productions (*A Southern Maid*, *Frasquita*, *Cleopatra*, *The Swordsman*) which made him a reputation as the foremost director of the large-scale musical of his time.

There was, however, little further success for him as an author. *Chu Chin Chow* was succeeded by another Eastern extravaganza called *Mecca* (a title subsequently censored into *Cairo*) in which an original story of some ingenuity was evolved to give Asche and Miss Brayton a second chance to appear in the same kind of rôles they had played so effectively in *Chu Chin Chow*. It had some success as a dance and scenery piece on Broadway and in London, and was played for a season in Australia, without anywhere rivalling its predecessor, but an attempt to produce a grandiose piece in the Olde English vein, *The Good Old Days*, was a disastrous failure.

Beset by financial troubles which were only partly alleviated by his wife's secure management of her affairs, Asche found success more and more difficult to achieve in his later days and his last work as both a director and performer was in some of the more pretentiously amateurish musical would-be spectaculars of his time (*The White Camellia*, *El Dorado*, *Kong*).

Asche also appeared on the musical screen, being seen in the British film of *Two Hearts in Waltz Time* (1934) shortly before his death.

1916 **Chu Chin Chow** (Frederic Norton) Her Majesty's Theatre 31 August

1919 **Eastward Ho!** (Grace Torrens, John Ansell/w Dornford Yates) Alhambra Theatre 9 September

1920 **Mecca** (aka *Cairo*) (Percy Fletcher) Century Theater, New York, 4 October

1925 **The Good Old Days** (Fletcher) Gaiety Theatre 27 October

Autobiography: *Oscar Asche: His Life, by Himself* (Hurst & Blackett Ltd, London, 1929)

ASCHER, Leo (b Vienna, 17 August 1880; d New York, 25 February 1942). Composer of a long list of musical plays for the Austrian and German stages, whose career was ended by the rise of Nazism.

Educated for a career in the legal world, Leo Ascher qualified as a Doctor of Law, but he carried on his musical studies to such effect that, at the age of 26, he had his first Operette, *Vergeltsgott*, a comical piece written to a text by Victor Léon, produced at the Theater an der Wien. It won some success there, and went on to subsequent productions in Germany (*Der Bettelgraf*) and Hungary (*A koldusgróf*), confirming the young composer in the career he would follow. In the years that followed, Ascher turned out numerous songs and scores for the little Operetten played at Gabor Steiner's Danzers Orpheum and Venedig in Wien summer theater, and at the Kabarett Fledermaus, where he became, for a time, musical director. Amongst these, the locally-coloured *Vindobona, du herrliches Stadt* proved the most popular, and several were given productions in Hungarian versions (*A Palatinus lány* 3 September 1910, *Ostrómallapot* 30 January 1912, *Rampsenit* October 1912).

The more substantial *Die arme Lori*, produced at the Raimundtheater in 1910 with Carl Streitmann, Vera Schwarz and Gerda Walde heading the cast, was given only a few en suite performances before going into the repertoire, but two years later the same house mounted the composer's most successful piece to date. The charming *Hoheit tanzt Walzer*, with Betty Fischer in its title-rôle, had a magnificent first run of 230 performances, and, in all, played more than 350 performances at the Raimundtheater between 1912 and 1914 before going on to productions further afield.

His *Was tut man nicht alles aus Liebe* topped 50 nights at Ronachers (50th performance 27 January 1915) before, similarly, going on to other productions, including a heavily botched one on Broadway, whilst *Botschafterin Leni*,

Plate 8. Leo Ascher's *long list of Austrian hits was boosted further by a run of successful musicals, including* Egon und seine Frauen, *for the Berlin stage of the 1910s.*

mounted at the Theater in der Josefstadt, also progressed to further productions (57 performances at the Berlin Thalia-Theater in 1920-1, *Kotnyeles naccsága* in Hungary) after its initial 41 nights, but it was the middle years of the war which brought the composer his other biggest successes, both in Berlin and in Vienna.

Ascher combined with Berlin's favourite Posse authors, Jean Kren and Bernhard Buchbinder, on the pretty *Der Soldat der Marie* (1916), with which Kren opened his newly acquired Neues Operettenhaus to enormous success, and the team also got a seven months' Berlin run out of the 'musikalischer Schwank' *Egon und seine Frauen* (1917), another lively musical piece with a score made up of marches, waltzes and polkas, not to mention a Rhineländer and a ländler. In Vienna, in the same year, *Bruder Leichtsinn*, which followed the 112 performances of the local production of *Der Soldat der Marie* into the Wiener Bürgertheater, was played for 176 performances with a cast headed by longtime stars Streitmann and Joseffy, before going on to a major success in Hungary under the title *Heja-huja báró*.

By the end of the war, Ascher was established on German, Austrian and Hungarian fronts as one of the most fruitful composers of the musical stage. In the post-war years, however, his new pieces, without ever demeriting, did not quite find the same storming success. *Was Mädchen traumen* had a fine run of over 100 performances at the Raimundtheater, outpointing the five and a half weeks of *Zwölf Uhr Nachts!*. *Der Künstlerpreis* followed its season at the Apollotheater by going on to be seen in Germany (Horst-Theater am Sophienblatt 11 January 1920) and in

Hungary (*Uldöz a pénz*, Budapesti Színház 15 May 1923), whilst *Prinzessin Friedl* had three months' run in Berlin and *Baronesschen Sarah*, a musical adaptation of Nötzler's *Im Klubsessel*, slightly less.

Another Thalia-Theater piece, *Ein Jahr ohne Liebe*, followed a three-and-a-half-month run in Berlin with a production at the Wiener Stadttheater later the same year, the Viennese *Sonja* played 55 performances at the Carltheater, *Das Amorettenhaus*, originally produced in Hamburg, was later seen at Baden-bei-Wien (7 March 1926), and *Ich hab' dich Lieb...* had a first run of 62 performances at the Raimundtheater.

Fair runs with *Ninon am Scheideweg* in Berlin, the Singspiel *Frühling im Wienerwald* in Vienna and *Bravo, Peggy!*, produced in Leipzig before being mounted at Volksoper, as well as two film scores (*Purpur und Waschblau*, 1931, *Mein Leopold*, 1932) led to Ascher's final work, *Um ein bisschen Liebe*, for a European stage on which he had been featured for some 30 years, before he joined the Jewish exodus which would drain Central Europe of almost all its operettic talent in the 1930s. He settled in America, and was working there on an English version of *Um ein bisschen Liebe* when he died in 1942.

In spite of his popularity in Austria, Germany and Hungary, Ascher's works were little heard in the rest of the world. A Carlo Lombardo pasticcio of his works was mounted in Italy as *La regina della fonografo* whilst what purported to be a version of *Was tut man nicht alles aus Liebe* was played on Broadway as *Follow Me* (Casino Theater 29 November 1916) with numbers by Sigmund Romberg, Harry Tierney and Robert B Smith comprising most of the score, and Anna Held singing 'Oh, Johnny, Oh'. *Hoheit tanzt Walzer* was played at New York's Irving Place Theater in German: renamed *Princess Tralala* it was published in English, but apparently not produced.

1905 **Vergeltsgott** (aka *Der Bettlerklub*) (Victor Léon) Theater an der Wien 14 October
1907 **Es gibt nur a Kaiserstadt** (Leopold Krenn) 3 scenes Danzers Orpheum 27 September
1908 **Die grüne Redoute** (Julius Brammer, Alfred Grünwald) 1 act Danzers Orpheum 26 March
1908 **Die kleine Manicure** (Brammer, Grünwald) 1 act Parisiana
1909 **Die arme Lori** (Krenn) Raimundtheater 12 March
1909 **Hut ab!** (Edmund Skurawy, S B Tellheim) 1 act Venedig in Wien 28 May
1909 **Ein Belagerungszustand** (August Neidhart) 1 act Kabarett Fledermaus 1 November
1910 **Die keusche Susanne** (Fritz Löhner-Beda) 1 act Kabarett Fledermaus 1 February
1910 **Die Klubbrüder** (Wilhelm Frieser) 1 act Wiener Colosseum 1 April
1910 **Vindobona, du herrliches Stadt** (Brammer, Grünwald) Venedig in Wien 22 July
1910 **Der fromme Silvanus** (Löhner-Beda) 1 act Kabarett Fledermaus 1 November
1911 **Rampsenit** (Löhner-Beda) 1 act Kabarett Fledermaus 1 January
1911 **Das goldene Strumpfband** (Brammer, Grünwald) 1 act Ronacher ?1 May
1911 **Eine fidele Nacht** (Löhner-Beda) 1 act Wiener Colosseum 1 September
1912 **Der Lockvogel** (Alexander Engel, Julius Horst) Walhalla Theater, Wiesbaden 11 January

1912 **Hoheit tanzt Walzer** (later *Hochzeitswalzer*) (Brammer, Grünwald) Raimundtheater 24 February
1913 **Die goldene Hanna** (Löhner-Beda) 1 act Apollotheater 4 January
1914 **Was tut man nicht alles aus Liebe** (Felix Dörmann) Ronacher 17 December
1915 **Botschafterin Leni** (Bernhard Buchbinder) Theater in der Josefstadt 19 February
1916 **Die schöne Komödiantin** (Eugen Burg, Louis Taufstein) 1 act Wintergarten, Berlin 13 January
1916 **Der Soldat der Marie** (Buchbinder, Jean Kren, Alfred Schönfeld) Neues Operetten-Theater, Berlin 2 September
1917 **Egon und seine Frauen** (Buchbinder, Kren) Thalia-Theater, Berlin 25 August
1917 **Bruder Leichtsinn** (Brammer, Grünwald) Wiener Bürgertheater 28 December
1919 **Der Künstlerpreis** (Rudolf Österreicher, Horst) Apollotheater 1 October
1919 **Was Mädchen träumen** (Leopold Jacobson, Robert Bodanzky) Raimundtheater 6 December
1919 **Wo Schwalben nisten**
1920 **Prinzessin Friedl** (Buchbinder, Kren) Neues Operetten Theater, Berlin 14 May
1920 **Zwölf Uhr Nachts!** (Dörmann, Hans Kottow) Raimundtheater 12 November
1920 **Baronesschen Sarah** (Neidhart) Komische Oper, Berlin ?25 December
1923 **Ein Jahr ohne Liebe** (Ludwig Hirschfeld, Alfred Deutsch-German) Thalia-Theater, Berlin 12 January
1925 **Sonja** (Rudolf Presber, Leo Walther Stein) Carltheater 6 March
1926 **Das Amorettenhaus** (Heinz von Waldberg, Max Steiner-Kaiser, Bruno Hardt-Warden) Carl-Schultze Theater, Hamburg January
1926 **Ich hab' dich Lieb...** (Willy Sterk) Raimundtheater 16 April
1926 **Ninon am Scheideweg** (Neidhart) Theater am Zoo, Berlin 27 December
1928 **La Barberina** Hamburg
1930 **Frühling in Wienerwald** (Löhner-Beda, Lunzer) Stadttheater 17 April
1931 **Bei der Wirtin Rosenrot** (Paul Knepler, Löhner-Beda) Theater des Westens, Berlin 14 March
1932 **Bravo Peggy!** (Wilhelm Lichtenberg, Armin Robinson, Harry Waldau) Operetten-Theater, Leipzig 27 March
1936 **Um ein bisschen Liebe** (Rudolf Lothar, Peter Herz) Stadttheater 5 June

ASHLEY, H[enry] J[effries] (d London, 18 November 1890).

A late arrival to the theatre, after nearly a decade working in an engineering office, Ashley played for several years as a comic actor in the British provinces before making his London début in 1860. In spite of limited singing ability, he found his way into the musical theatre (Ozokerit in *Aladdin II* tour, 1872 etc) and, for a decade, was one of the most prominent character men in British comic opera. He appeared in leading comedy rôles in an almost unbroken run of London productions between 1879 and 1890 including *Madame Favart* (Pontsablé), *Olivette* (Duc des Ifs), *Manola* (Brasiero), *Manteaux Noirs* (José), *La Mascotte* (Laurent), *Falka* (Tancred), *The Merry Duchess* (Brabazon Sikes), *Pocahontas* (Potts), *La Cosaque* (Primitif), *François les bas-bleus* (Pontcornet), *Dr D* (Doctor Dosemoffen), *Indiana* (Mulberry Mullitt then Matt o' the Mint on tour), *Paul Jones* (Bicoquet), *Marjorie* (Simon Striveling) and *Capitaine Thérèse* (Colonel Sombrero). He died during the run of this last piece, of the typhoid.

ASHMAN, Howard [Elliott] [GERSHMAN] (b Baltimore, Md, 17 May 1951; d New York, 14 March 1991).

Author, lyricist and director, Ashman began his career off-off-Broadway where he had two musicals produced in the late 1970s: *Dreamstuff*, a version of *The Tempest* mounted at the Workshop of the Players Art where he was at the time co-director, and a musicalization of Kurt Vonnegut's novel *God Bless You, Mr Rosewater*, which subsequently moved up from the WPA to off-Broadway's Entermedia Theater (49 performances). Although he had one play, *The Confirmation*, taken from its original small production to an abortive attempt at Broadway, he made most of his writing career on the musical side of the theatre. He authored a rewrite on the libretto of *The Vagabond King* (1977), contributed to the Manhattan Theatre Club's cabaret production *Real Life Funnies* (w Alan Menken) in the 1980–81 season, then scored an international hit with his spoof of the C-grade period horror movie, *Little Shop of Horrors*, which moved from its beginnings at the WPA (24 performances), where Ashman was sole director between 1977 and 1982, to a long run off-Broadway, productions around the world, and a would-be A-grade film version.

He contributed to the 1984 revue *Diamonds* and, in 1986, a musical based on the 1975 film satire of beauty contests, *Smile*, was produced on Broadway. Ashman supplied book and lyrics and also directed this, his one venture on Broadway, which was a 48-performance failure.

He and his *Little Shop of Horrors* partner, Alan Menken, subsequently wrote the songs for the Walt Disney film *The Little Mermaid*, on which he was also co-producer (w John Musker), and for its successor, *Beauty and the Beast*, before his premature death, aged 40.

1976 **Dreamstuff** (Marsha Malamet/Dennis Green) WPA Theater 2 April
1979 **God Bless You, Mr Rosewater** (Alan Menken/w Green) WPA Theater 17 May, Entermedia Theater 14 October
1982 **Little Shop of Horrors** (Menken) WPA Theater 6 May, Orpheum Theater 27 July
1986 **Smile** (Marvin Hamlisch) Lunt-Fontanne Theater 24 November

ASKEY, Arthur [BOWDEN, Arthur] (b Liverpool, 6 June 1900; d London, 16 November 1982).

'Big-hearted Arthur' Askey made his first theatrical appearances in concert party and pantomime before becoming popular as a radio comedian. He starred in the musical comedy *The Love Racket* which followed in the footsteps of Lupino Lane's cheerful series of musical shows at the Victoria Palace in 1943, took it to Australia (Tivoli, Melbourne 23 December 1949), and in the decade following this introduction to the musical stage, top-billed in London in *Follow the Girls* (1945), *The Kid From Stratford* (1948) and *Bet Your Life* (1952), playing the kind of free-wheeling star comedy rôles which had been the backbone of the dance-and-laughter musical comedies of the 1930s. With the passing of such shows, Askey's stage performances became largely limited to pantomime where he remained for many years one of Britain's outstanding exponents of the classic style of pantomime playing.

Autobiography: *Before Your Very Eyes* (Woburn Press, London, 1975)

ASPECTS OF LOVE Musical in 2 acts by Charles Hart and Don Black based on the novel of the same name by David Garnett. Music by Andrew Lloyd Webber. Prince of Wales Theatre, London, 17 April 1989.

Kept on the back burner as a potential subject for a musical play by composer Lloyd Webber and director Trevor Nunn for many years, David Garnett's *Aspects of Love* was developed as a medium-sized musical play in the wake of the composer's success with the extremely elaborate *The Phantom of the Opéra*. Charles Hart, the lyricist of *Phantom of the Opéra*, and Don Black, the composer's collaborator on his most intimate work to date, the song cycle 'Tell Me on a Sunday', supplied the text.

The very young Alex Dillingham (Michael Ball), entranced by the touring actress Rose Vibart (Anne Crumb), invites her to spend her weeks out at his wealthy uncle's unoccupied mansion in Pau. Uncle George (Kevin Colson) leaves his own little Parisian idyll with sculptress Giulietta (Kathleen Rowe McAllen) and descends on the intrusive couple with considerable charm. The tale moves on, and when Alex returns from the army, he finds that Rose has moved in with George. Dramatic recrimination gives way to a more comfortable situation as Rose weds George, becomes successful and brings a daughter, Jenny, into the family and the house at Pau. The growing Jenny falls in love with Alex, and the jealousy in the family shifts sides, but when George suffers a heart attack whilst spying on the young people and the widowed Rose pleads with Alex to stay by her, the young man realizes that he will be better off moving on with the uncomplicated Giulietta than remaining behind to be torn between Rose and Jenny.

Like all of the composer's works, *Aspects of Love* was composed through, and again like them, it held some individual numbers within that sung-through construction. The opening number, the tenor 'Love Changes Everything', which set the tone and theme of the show, proved to be the most popular piece. Launched as a single before the production of the show, it climbed to second place on the British hit parades, the most successful Lloyd Webber show song in hit-parade terms since *Evita*'s 'Don't Cry for Me, Argentina'. In the show, however, it was Rose's funeral evening cry of despair, 'Anything But Lonely', which proved the musical highlight, alongside Giulietta's drivingly sung and danced eulogy 'Give Me the Wine and the Dice', the broad duetting between Rose and Alex of 'Seeing is Believing' and the gentler strains of 'The Last Man You Remember' and the plangent Song of Childhood.

By the time that *Aspects of Love* made it to the stage, at London's Prince of Wales Theatre, it had lost a little of its intended intimacy. If the orchestral accompaniment was still smaller than in the town's vaster musicals, the cast had been increased in size, and the scenic concept used to cover the many shifts of locale included in the text was both mechanically complex and visually lavish. Nevertheless, the show maintained much of the more personal feeling of its small story and it became a particular favourite with those looking for relief from the current fashion for heavily spectacular or glitzy musical shows.

Twelve months after the Really Useful Company's London production had opened, the show was mounted on Broadway with Colson, Ball and Misses Crumb and McAllen repeating their original assignments. It was on a hiding to nothing. Resentment against Lloyd Webber's domination of the musical theatre, and an influential critic, with allegiances elsewhere, who had announced, well before opening, his dislike of the piece, helped ensure some gloatingly negative reviews, and the lack of spectacle and glitter discouraged word-of-mouth reports that might have reversed that decision. Some papers leapt hopefully into print insinuating early closure, but New York was able to find an audience for some 11 months (377 performances) as the show continued its London run through three years before taking to the road.

In 1991 a version more in keeping with the originally planned 'chamber' scale of the piece and played on one set was mounted in Canada with Keith Michell (George), Linda Balgord (Rose) and Ron Bohmer (Alex). This version was subsequently played in America and a similarly reduced-size production was staged in Australia, with Colson in his original rôle alongside Delia Hannah (Rose) and Peter Couzens (Alex) for a 16-week season in Sydney and a national tour. *Aspects of Love* went on to be seen in Japan (ad Keita Asari Aoyama Theatre 10 January 1992), Denmark (Aarhus Theatre 14 September 1992) and other venues, finding plenty of friends on the way, but never in any of them threatening to become the kind of blockbusting hit that its composer's earlier and more lavish works had.

USA: Broadhurst Theater 8 April 1990; Australia: Theatre Royal, Sydney 18 November 1992
Recording: original cast (Polydor)
Literature: Gänzl, K: *The Complete Aspects of Love* (Aurum, London, 1990)

ASTAIRE, Fred [AUSTERLITZ, Frederick] (b Omaha, Neb, 10 May 1900; d Los Angeles, 22 June 1987). Dancing star who moved from fame in the theatre to immortality on the screen.

Astaire and his sister, Adele (b Omaha, Neb, 10 September 1898; d Phoenix, 25 January 1981), worked as a dance team in vaudeville from 1906, before making their first appearances in the musical theatre as an item in the 1917 *Over the Top* and in the 1918 version of *The Passing Show*. They performed dance routines in supporting rôles in *Apple Blossoms* (1919) and *The Love Letter* (1921) with sufficient éclat to allow them to be effectively promoted to the top of the bill (although the romantic team garnered the plot) in *For Goodness' Sake* (1922) and, later the same year, in *The Bunch and Judy*, they were even given the principal places in the plot. The following year they repeated *For Goodness' Sake* in London, under the title *Stop Flirting*, with the same personal success they had won at home.

This success was thoroughly confirmed in *Lady, Be Good!* (New York 1924, London 1926), *Funny Face* (1927, New York and London) and the revue *The Band Wagon* (1931), but the musical comedy *Smiles*, in which they appeared in 1930, was a failure. After *The Band Wagon*, Adele retired to become the wife of Lord Charles Cavendish, and Fred continued his career alone. He starred opposite Claire Luce in *Gay Divorce* in New York (1932) in what would be his last Broadway appearance, and in London (1933), before entering the film world. There he became one of the greatest stars of the heyday of the Hollywood musical in a series of films from *Dancing Lady*

and *Flying Down to Rio* in 1933 through *The Gay Divorcee, Roberta, Top Hat, Follow the Fleet, Swing Time, Shall We Dance?, A Damsel in Distress, Carefree, The Story of Vernon and Irene Castle, Broadway Melody, You'll Never Get Rich, Holiday Inn, You Were Never Lovelier, Ziegfeld Follies, Blue Skies, Easter Parade* and *The Barkleys of Broadway* in the 1930s and 1940s, and such pieces as *The Band Wagon, Funny Face, Silk Stockings* in the 1950s up to his last musical film appearance in *Finian's Rainbow* (1968).

As a partnership, Adele and Fred showed an irresistible and apparently off-hand grace and stylishness in dance, which combined with attractive personalities and an understanding of comic timing to produce a performance whose technical difficulties were made to seem exceptional by being made to seem almost casually natural. Both possessed light, accurate singing voices and, above all, the ability to put across a song. In their days together, it was Adele who attracted most of the attention, being particularly praised for her comic gifts, the extent and nature of which can be seen by looking at the variety and style of her role of Susie in the post-production libretto of *Lady, Be Good!*. Fred was to come into his own in films, but there is no reason to suppose that he was any more effaced in the stage partnership with his sister than he was by his celluloid dance partners.

Astaire also ventured into songwriting, and one of his numbers 'I'm Building Up to an Awful Letdown' was heard in the London flop musical *Rise and Shine* and its touring derivative, *Darling You*.

Autobiography: *Steps in Time* (Harper, New York, 1959); Biographies: Green, S & Goldblatt, B: *Starring Fred Astaire* (Dodd Mead, New York, 1973), Croce, A: *The Fred Astaire and Ginger Rogers Book* (Outerbridge & Lazard, New York, 1972), Thompson, H: *Fred Astaire* (Falcon, New York, 1970), Thomas, B: *Astaire, the Man, the Dancer* (St Martin's Press, New York, 1984), Green, B: *Fred Astaire* (Baxter Books, New York, 1979), Mueller, J: *Astaire Dancing: The Musical Films* (Hamish Hamilton, London, 1986) etc

AS THE GIRLS GO Musical comedy in 2 acts by William Roos. Lyrics by Harold Adamson. Music by Jimmy McHugh. Winter Garden Theater, New York, 13 November 1948.

A spectacular Mike Todd production of a colourful extravaganza which looked four years into the future and fantasized on the election of a lady president of the United States of America. Lucille Thompson Wellington (Irene Rich) was the lady in question, which made her husband Waldo (Bobby Clark) the consort. Most of the consorting that he did was with a line of blossoming chorines. Clark's comedy, more redolent of the low, ad-libbing comic antics of turn-of-the-century musical theatre comedians than of the more orderly post-war years, was supported by a romantic threadlet of plot featuring presidential son Kenny (Bill Callahan) and his Kathy (Betty Jane Watson). The show's numbers were topped by the juvenile man's attractive '[I Got] Lucky in the Rain' and 'You Say the Nicest Things, Baby' and by some cheery pieces of comedy material for Clark, 'It Takes a Woman to Take a Man' and 'Father's Day'.

As the Girls Go stayed 420 performances on Broadway without turning itself into a financial success.

Plate 9. *The versatile* **Alice Atherton** *in two of her 'disguises' in* The Babes.

ATHERTON, Alice [HOGAN, Alice] (b Cincinnatti, ?1847; d New York, 4 February 1899). A versatile singing comedienne of the Victorian stage.

Although she was equally capable of taking dramatic and legitimate comedy parts and, indeed, was seen on Broadway in 1871 as Gavroche in *Les Misérables*, Alice Atherton made the bulk of her career in burlesque and musical farce. She appeared early on with Pauline Markham (Glowworm in *Chow Chow*, *Luna*, Mercury in *Ixon*), with Baker and Farron, and was a member of Lydia Thompson's famous troupe in America and, from 1874, in Britain (Twigletto in *Pippin*, Orion in *Paris*, Acrobrand in *The Forty Thieves*, O'Shacabac in *Bluebeard*, Hermance in *Oxygen*, Queen Ylang-Ylang in *Robinson Crusoe*, Queen Folichonne in *Piff-Paff*, Camille in *Mephisto* etc). She subsequently played in several early and incessantly touring musical-comedy companies: Samuel Colville's Folly Company, E E Rice's Surprise Party (Conrad in *The Corsair*, Prince Achmet in *Horrors*, Lady Macassar, then The Bad Man in *Babes in the Woods*, Hiawatha in *Hiawatha*, *Revels* etc) and the outfit led by her husband, Willie Edouin's Sparks (*Revels*, Ruby Chillington in *Dreams*).

She played opposite Edouin in Hoyt's *A Bunch of Keys* (1883) in America and in London before the pair won their biggest success together as the rambunctious twins in the burlesque *The Babes, or Whines from the Wood* (Tessie, 1884). Although Miss Atherton starred in the English version of the French comédie-vaudeville *Les 28 Jours de Clairette* (1892), she was more at home in the broad comedy of burlesque (Carrie in *Oliver Grumble*, Jane in *Jaunty Jane Shore*, title-rôles of *Vanderdecken* and *Airey-Annie*), Victorian musical playlets (*The Japs*, Charlie Cott in *Blackberries*, *Binks the Downy Photographer*, *On the March*) and such American farce musicals as *Hans the Boatman* (1891) and *The Marquis of Michigan* (1898), in which she starred in the last year of her career, playing opposite Sam Bernard, in the rôle of a professional strong-woman called Etna Vesuvius. It was in such pieces that, playing mostly with or for Edouin, she built herself a fine following on both sides of the Atlantic.

She carried with her for many years two songs, 'The Laughing Song' and Meyer Lutz's 'Two Eyes of Blue' which she interpolated into a number of her musical performances, and which became her 'trademark'.

ATTERIDGE, Harold R[ichard] (b Lake Forest, Ill, 9 July 1886; d Lynbrook, NY, 15 January 1938). Long-serving wordsmith for Broadway's Shubert production house.

A product of Chicago University at around the same time as the successful musical-comedy-writing team of Adams and Hough, the young Atteridge worked on several musicals for Chicago and interpolated the occasional song into Broadway shows ('The Dublin Rag' w Phil Schwartz in *Madame Sherry* etc) before he became, in the 1910s and 1920s, a regular house writer for the Shubert brothers. In that post, he turned out skeletons and sketches for their revues, and libretti, which could be freely embroidered upon by their stars, for such half-revue/half-musical shows as the made-over remnants of Edmund Eysler's Operette *Vera Violetta* (1911) or the home-made *The Whirl of Society* (1912), *From Broadway to Paris* (1912), *The Honeymoon Express* (1913) or *Dancing Around* (1914).

Amongst the revues and quasi-revues for which Atteridge supplied material over the years were included *The Passing Show* series, *The Whirl of the World* (1914), *Maid in America*, *A World of Pleasure* (1915), *The Midnight Rounders* (1920), *The Mimic World of 1921*, *Doing Our Bit*, *Make It Snappy* (1922), *Hitchy Koo of 1922*, *Topics of 1923*, the Mistinguett revue *Innocent Eyes* (1924), *Gay Paree* (1925), *The Great Temptations* (1926), *A Night in Spain* (1927), *Greenwich Village Follies of 1928*, and *Pleasure Bound* (1929). He also scored the occasional individual song success, as with the lyrics for 'By the Beautiful Sea' (w Harry Carroll).

For the musical comedy stage, he adapted Clyde Fitch's English version of the Horst and Engel comedy *Der blaue Maus* as *The Little Blue Devil* for Joe Weber, Harry Leon Wilson's famous *Ruggles of Red Gap* with a Sigmund Romberg score and Ralph Herz starring, Frances Goodrich and Albert Hackett's comedy success *Up Pops the Devil* as *Everybody's Welcome*, Mrs Gertrude Ranken Drew's *Billy* as *Listen, Dearie* (w Gertrude Purcell) and, in tandem with Rida Johnson Young, did over Beulah Marie Dix's and E G Sutherland's *The Road to Yesterday* as a libretto for Victor Herbert (*The Dream Girl*). He also adapted, often heavily, a number of Continental musicals for the American stage. His principal success, however, came with the loose-limbed stage musical vehicles he invented for Al Jolson, the star of the Winter Garden shows, whom he supplied with the bases for his series of Broadway appearances under the Shubert management.

1905 **A Winning Miss** (William F Peters) Garden Theater, Chicago
1908 **Happy Youngsters** (Peters) miniature musical comedy
1910 **The Girl in the Kimono** (Phil Schwartz/Helen Bagg) Ziegfeld Theater, Chicago 25 June
1911 **Vera Violetta** (*Vera Violetta*) reconstructed American version w Leonard Liebling (Winter Garden Theater)
1912 **Two Little Brides** (*Schneeglöckchen*) American version w James T Powers, Arthur Anderson (Casino Theater)
1913 **The Honeymoon Express** (Jean Schwartz/w Joseph W Herbert) Winter Garden Theater 6 February
1913 **The Man With Three Wives** (*Der Mann mit den drei Frauen*) American version w Paul Potter, Agnes Morgan (Weber & Fields Music Hall)
1913 **The Little Parisienne** revised *Madame Troubadour* w Herbert (tour)

1914 **The Belle from Bond Street** revised version of *The Girl from Kays* Shubert Theater 30 March

1915 **The Peasant Girl** (*Polenblut*) American lyrics w Herbert Reynolds (44th Street Theater)

1916 **Robinson Crusoe jr** (Romberg et al/w Edgar Smith) Winter Garden Theater 17 February

1918 **Sinbad** (Romberg et al) Winter Garden Theater 14 February

1919 **Monte Cristo jr** (Romberg, J Schwartz et al) Winter Garden Theater 12 February

1919 **The Little Blue Devil** (Harry Carroll) Central Theater 3 November

1919 **Ruggles of Red Gap** (Romberg) Fulton Theater 24 December

1920 **Cinderella on Broadway** (Bert Grant, Al Goodman) Winter Garden Theater 24 June

1921 **Bombo** (Romberg et al) Jolson Theater 6 October

1921 **The Last Waltz** (*Der letzte Walzer*) American version w Edward Delaney Dunn (Century Theater)

1922 **The Rose of Stamboul** (*Die Rose von Stambul*) American version (Century Theater)

1923 **The Dancing Girl** (Romberg) Shubert Theater, New Haven 16 January

1923 **The Courtesan** (J Schwartz, Romberg/w Harry Wagstaffe Gribble) Parson's Theater, Hartford, Conn 17 October

1924 **Marjorie** (Romberg, Stothart, Philip Culkin, Stephen Jones/Clifford Grey, Fred Thompson) 'additional dialogue' Shubert Theater 11 August

1924 **The Dream Girl** (Victor Herbert/w Rida Johnson Young) Ambassador Theater 20 August

1925 **Sky High** (*Der Tanz ins Glück*) American version adapted from British version (Shubert Theater)

1925 **Big Boy** (James F Hanley, Joseph Meyer/B G de Sylva) Winter Garden Theater 7 January

1927 **Listen, Dearie** (Charles Gilpin/w Gertrude Purcell) Chestnut Street Opera House, Philadelphia 18 April

1929 **Well, Well, Well** (later *Pleasure Bound*, revue) (Maurie Rubens, Muriel Pollock, Phil Baker, Arthur Schwartz/Max Lief, Nathaniel Lief/w Montague Glass, Jules Eckert Goodman) Chestnut Street Opera House, Philadelphia 7 January

1931 **Everybody's Welcome** (Sammy Fain) Shubert Theater 13 October

1934 **Thumbs Up!** (ex-*The Fatal Blonde*) (Hanley, Henry Sullivan et al/Ballard McDonald/w H I Phillips, Alan Baxter) St James Theater 27 December

AUBER, Daniel François Esprit (b Caen, 29 January 1782; d Paris, 13 May 1871).

One of the most prominent composers of the French opéra-comique of the first half of the 19th century, Auber was also one of the principal forebears of the various kinds of French opérette of the second part of that same century, and his works were often played alongside the early examples of modern comic opera and opéra-bouffe in the repertoires of the lighter (and sometimes not so light) operatic companies of the cross-over period in the 1860s and 1870s.

Although he had an outstanding international success with the serious grand opera *La Muette de Portici* (1828), many of Auber's most popular works were written in the opéra-comique spirit, mixing flagrantly comical scenes with the more romantic and even with the dramatic strains of opera. His musical illustration of the lively *Fra Diavolo* (1830), with its Eugène Scribe tale of wicked banditry and disguised lovemaking, stands at the head of his output, but such pieces as *Le Cheval de bronze* (1835), *Le Domino noir* (1837) and *Les Diamants de la couronne* (1841) all reached

out towards the comic operas of the later years of the century. In fact, several libretti originally set by Auber later became, with little alteration, the texts for Operetten. The most notable of these was *La Circassienne*, which subsequently became the book for von Suppé's *Fatinitza*, but the text for *Carlo Broschi* went into the making of Hermann Zumpe's successful Operette *Farinelli* and there were doubtless others hidden under the then nebulous and ubiquitous credit which admitted that a libretto was pilfered 'from the French'. The libretto used for his 1833 *Gustave III*, on the other hand, went on to be the basis for Verdi's *Un Ballo in maschera*.

Because of their great popularity on the English stage, a number of Auber's works also took the brunt of the burlesque tradition in Britain, where *La Muette de Portici* (known in its English version as *Masaniello*) became *Masaniello, or the Fish'oman of Naples* in Robert Brough's travesty (Olympic Theatre 1857) and *Masse-en-yell-oh* as parodied by Harry Paulton and Mostyn Tedde (Comedy Theatre 1886). *Fra Diavolo* was given a superior treatment by H J Byron as *Fra Diavolo, or the Beauty and the Brigands* (Strand Theatre 5 April 1858) and later as *Young Fra Diavolo, the Terror of Terracina* (Gaiety Theatre 18 November 1878), and the Gaiety (1875) and Imperial (1880) Theatres hosted Robert Reece's burlesque tale of *The Half-Crown Diamonds*.

L'AUBERGE DU TOHU-BOHU Opérette in 3 acts by Maurice Ordonneau. Music by Victor Roger. Théâtre des Folies-Dramatiques, Paris, 10 February 1897.

A farcical musical dealing with what happens when an inn-sign is shifted from its place and put over the door of a private home. The author of this prank is one Saturnin (Burguet) and his reasons are friendly but complex. His pal, Paul Blanchard (Jean Périer), is in love with Cécile Drémer (Mary Bréan), whose father (Bartel) is determined she shall wed the aristocratic Count Zarifouli (Landrin). Cécile and the said Count are to meet for the first time at the Auberge du cheval blanc, outside Paris. Saturnin's relations (Vavasseur, Virginie Rolland) have a house just opposite this inn, and they are away on holiday, so the boys decide to stage their own 'Auberge du cheval blanc'. Hence the shifted sign. The staff are played by Saturnin's friends: his circus girlfriend, Flora (Jane Pierny) and her troupe, and whilst one Bel Oeil (Simon-Max) disgustingly impersonates Zarifouli to papa Drémer, the troupe's strongman, Le Rougeaud (Gardel) and Flora impersonate the Drémers to the real Zarifouli. Then the owners of the house come home...

The never-still plot and action was decorated with a considerable score of light and bright music, of which Mlle Pierny and Périer won the largest share.

L'Auberge du Tohu-bohu gave the Folies-Dramatiques a long-running hit, totalling 231 performances over two seasons, and it was revived at the Théâtre de la Gaîté in 1901, by which time it had been played in virtually all the other main musical theatre centres.

Arthur Sturgess's London version of *The Topsy Turvy Hotel* had a score largely topped up with songs by Lionel Monckton (several), Harry Fragson and A Stanislas (one popular one, 'Toujours les blondes') and Napoleon Lambelet (one) and starred Maurice Farkoa (Paul Blanchard), Florence Collingbourne (Cécile), Violet Lloyd (Flora) and

John Le Hay (Lebeau), but even the addition of extra matinées and the young George Grossmith to the cast could not balance the books of William Greet's production beyond two months. For Broadway, Sturgess's libretto was given a local touch by Edgar Smith, and Aubrey Boucicault (Paul), Ethel Jackson (Cécile), Marie Dressler (Flora) and Edwin Foy (Lebeau) headed the cast of Charles Frohman's production. Miss Dressler and Foy let themselves loose on a kind of low comedy which was not precisely French vaudeville, she stuck in a song about 'The Gingerbread Doll' and he one of his own, 'I Happened to Be There', and Miss Jackson departed after three weeks, leaving them to run up a total of 96 performances on their own.

Juliette Méaly's company touring in Austria, Germany and Hungary presented L'Auberge du Tohu-bohu in those countries in 1901, with the star in the rôle of Flora. However, Vienna had already seen the piece, in a German version by Victor Léon, at the Theater in der Josefstadt two years earlier, with Adele Moraw (Florette), Karl Pfann (Blanchard), Ida Sachs (Cécile) and Gustav Maran (Graf Zarifuli), and Hungary had witnessed a vernacular production under the title Az óssze-vissza fogadó (ad Gyula Komor). The first German-language performances had been seen, however, even earlier – at Berlin's Thalia-Theater where the piece had appeared, hard on the heels of the original Paris production, in 1897.

Germany: Thalia-Theater *Tohu-bohu* 16 October 1897; Friedrich-Wilhemstädtisches Theater (Fr) 15 May 1901; Hungary: Budai Színkör *Össze-vissza fogadó* 16 July 1898, Magyar Színház (Fr) 20 April 1901; UK: Comedy Theatre *The Topsy Turvy Hotel* 21 September 1898; USA: Herald Square Theater *Hotel Topsy Turvy* 3 October 1898; Austria: Theater in der Josefstadt *Tohu-Bohu* 28 April 1899, Theater an der Wien (Fr) 23 April 1901

AUDRAN, Edmond (b Lyon, 11 April 1842; d Tierceville, Seine-et-Oise, 17 August 1901). One of the most successful composers of the international musical stage during the 19th-century heyday of the French opérette.

Edmond Audran was born into a musical family, the son of the Opéra-Comique tenor, Marius Audran, and with a brother who was, similarly, to become a professional tenor in Parisian opérette. He was given an early musical education, studying at the École Niedermeyer where one of his professors was the opérette composer Jules Duprato and, when his family moved to Marseille in 1861, he became maître de chapelle of the church of Saint-Joseph in that city.

During his early years in Marseille he composed some religious music, including a mass which was performed at Saint-Joseph and an oratorio, as well as a number of short opérettes, based on well-known texts which were produced at the local Grand Théâtre and Théâtre du Gymnase in the early 1860s. It was 15 years, however, after the first of these was seen on the stage before Audran saw a substantial stage composition of his mounted in the theatre. The celebrated librettist Henri Chivot, a friend of the family, offered him the book to Le Grand Mogol and the resultant piece, with Chivot's name splendidly attached to it alongside that of the neophyte 'local' composer, was produced at the Théâtre du Gymnase with the young Jane Hading in the starring rôle. It created considerable interest and, although it was not taken immediately to Paris, it won the young composer both further and foreign productions

(Milan, New York etc) and a commission for a new opérette from Louis Cantin, manager of the Théâtre des Bouffes-Parisiens.

Cantin's commission proved a good move. It brought forth the delightful Les Noces d'Olivette, a comic opera which turned out to be a splendid success for the adventurous manager in Paris and an international hit for the rapidly rising composer. However, the following year Audran and his librettists, Chivot and Duru, supplied Cantin with the even more successful La Mascotte, a piece which would establish itself as one of the classic opérettes of the period, and the vast and immediate success of the new composer was confirmed with a third consecutive hit, Gillette de Narbonne, as he launched forth on what was to be a stream of some 30 musical stage shows over a 20-year period.

More than a few of this perhaps rather over-full list of works proved less successful than the first fine trio of worldwide successes, but there were a good number which, if they did not reach quite the immense and widespread popularity of La Mascotte, did equal the record of the other two initial shows. A revised and enlarged version of Le Grand Mogol (1884) produced at Paris's Théâtre de la Gaîté established that piece in the general repertoire and won it a wide-ranging series of overseas productions, whilst the popularity of Audran's early works in Britain led the composer to follow the example set by Planquette and set an original English H B Farnie libretto, Indiana, specifically for British audiences. Like Audran's 1886 piece, Serment d'amour (The Bridal Trap, The Crowing Hen), Indiana was also played in America.

The charming tale of La Cigale et la fourmi (1886) gave the Audran/Chivot/Duru team another substantial international success, and the sweetly risqué Miss Helyett (1890) proved an immense hit in Paris prior to a career, in variously bleached versions, around the world, but whilst such other Audran pieces such as L'Oncle Célestin and L'Enlèvement de la Toledad did well in several countries, it was the 1896 opérette La Poupée which proved the most successful of Audran's later works. It scored outstanding successes in Britain and, most particularly, in Germany where it became the most widely played French opérette of all time. It also earned the composer a lawsuit when Henri Blondeau and Hector Monréal, authors of the text for Audran's unsuccessful Les Pommes d'or, sued him for plundering 'their' opérette for melodies to reuse in Miss Helyett and La Poupée.

With ten of his works played in Britain – one, La Toledad, in a music hall – 11 (if you count the less successful La Petite Fronde, Americanized and heavily botched as The Wedding Day, and Pervenche similarly treated as Fleur de lis) in America, eight (amongst which the otherwise only moderately popular Madame Suzette) in Germany and a full dozen, ranging from the most popular Az üdvöske (La Mascotte) to versions of La Duchesse de Ferrare (A Ferrarai hercegnő), Madame Suzette (Menyeckse kisasszony), La Dormeuse éveillée (Az ébren álmodó), Le Puits qui parle (A beszélő kut), Les Soeurs Gaudichard (Az ikrek) and La Fiancée des verts-poteaux (A kölcsönkért vőlegény), in Hungary, Audran in his lifetime won an international prominence and coverage equalled only by Offenbach and Lecocq amongst 19th-century French composers.

1862 **L'Ours et le pacha** (Eugène Scribe, J X B Saintine) 1 act Grand Théâtre, Marseille

1864 **La Chercheuse d'esprit** (Charles Favart) 1 act Théâtre du Gymnase, Marseille, Alcazar, Paris 1888

1866 **La Nivernaise** 1 act Théâtre du Gymnase, Marseille December

1868 **Le Petit Poucet** Marseille April

1877 **Le Grand Mogol** (Henri Chivot) Théâtre du Gymnase, Marseille 24 February

1879 **Les Noces d'Olivette** (Chivot, Alfred Duru) Théâtre des Bouffes-Parisiens 13 November

1880 **La Mascotte** (Chivot, Duru) Théâtre des Bouffes-Parisiens 29 December

1882 **Gillette de Narbonne** (Chivot, Duru) Théâtre des Bouffes-Parisiens 11 November

1883 **Les Pommes d'or** (Chivot, Duru, Hector Monréal, Henri Blondeau) Théâtre des Menus-Plaisirs 12 February

1883 **La Dormeuse éveillée** (Chivot, Duru) Théâtre des Bouffes-Parisiens 27 December

1884 **Le Grand Mogol** revised version (Chivot, Duru) Théâtre de la Gaîté 19 September

1885 **Pervenche** (Chivot, Duru) Théâtre des Bouffes-Parisiens 31 March

1886 **Serment d'amour** (Maurice Ordonneau) Théâtre des Nouveautés 19 February

1886 **Indiana** (H B Farnie) Avenue Theatre, London 11 October

1886 **La Cigale et la fourmi** (Chivot, Duru) Théâtre de la Gaîté 30 October

1887 **La Fiancée des verts-poteaux** (Ordonneau) Théâtre des Menus-Plaisirs 8 November

1888 **Le Puits qui parle** (Paul Burani, Alexandre Beaumont) Théâtre des Nouveautés 15 March

1888 **Miette** (Ordonneau) Théâtre de la Renaissance 24 September

1888 **La Petite Fronde** (Chivot, Duru) Théâtre des Folies-Dramatiques 16 November

1889 **La Fille à Cacolet** (Chivot, Duru) Théâtre des Variétés 10 July

1890 **L'Oeuf rouge** (William Busnach, Alfred Vanloo) Théâtre des Folies-Dramatiques 14 March

1890 **Miss Helyett** (Maxime Boucheron) Théâtre des Bouffes-Parisiens 12 November

1891 **L'Oncle Célestin** (Ordonneau, Henri Kéroul) Théâtre des Menus-Plaisirs 24 March

1892 **Article de Paris** (Boucheron) Théâtre des Menus-Plaisirs 17 March

1892 **Sainte-Freya** (Boucheron) Théâtre des Bouffes-Parisiens 4 November

1893 **Madame Suzette** (Ordonneau, André Sylvane) Théâtre des Bouffes-Parisiens 29 March

1893 **Mon Prince!** (Charles Clairville, Sylvane) Théâtre des Nouveautés 18 November

1894 **L'Enlèvement de la Toledad** (Fabrice Carré) Théâtre des Bouffes-Parisiens 17 November

1895 **La Duchesse de Ferrare** (Boucheron) Théâtre des Bouffes-Parisiens 25 January

1896 **La Reine des reines** (P-L Flers) Eldorado 14 October

1896 **La Poupée** (Maurice Ordonneau) Théâtre de la Gaîté 21 October

1896 **Monsieur Lohengrin** (F Carré) Théâtre des Bouffes-Parisiens 30 November

1897 **Les Petites Femmes** (Sylvane) Théâtre des Bouffes-Parisiens 11 October

1899 **Les Soeurs Gaudichard** (Ordonneau) Théâtre de la Gaîté 21 April

1901 **Le Curé Vincent** (Ordonneau) Théâtre de la Gaîté 25 October

AUF BEFEHL DER HERZOGIN (aka *Auf Befehl der Kaiserin*) Operetten-idyll aus alten, gemütlichen Tagen in 3 acts by Leopold Jacobson and Robert Bodanzky. Music

by Bruno Granichstädten. Theater an der Wien, Vienna, 20 March 1915.

Bodanzky and Jacobson made no pretence as to what they were trying to provide with their text for *Auf Befehl der Herzogin* (At the Countess's Orders) when they subtitled it 'an Operette-idyll from the good, old days'. But if the libretto to the piece rested on the good, old combination of love affairs and misunderstandings with a nice dash of period royalty thrown in, it gained more than a little individuality from a particularly well-drawn and sympathetic central character.

The Herzogin (Paula Zulka) discovers that her husband is being unfaithful to her and, hearing that Lintschi (Anny Rainer), the daughter of the old Spannbergerin (Mitzi Schütz), is being courted by a royal officer, hastily assumes that she has found her rival. When Lintschi is warned by the Morality Commissioner (Karl Tuschl) that the Herzogin has her eye on her visitor, she assumes that her Konrad (Hubert Marischka) is out of bounds to her and sadly agrees to the marriage set up by her mother with unhappy Toni (Ernst Tautenhayn), the son of mama's old sweetheart, the sausage-maker Weisskappel (Franz Glawatsch). The Herzogin orders this marriage to take place immediately but, when the Commissioner discovers his mistake, she leaves the palace and hastens in person to the inn with a wedding gift for the girl whom she has wronged. The gift is Konrad, who happily takes the delighted Toni's place as bridegroom.

Bruno Granichstädten's score followed its tale in good-old-Wienerische-days style, using none of the gently jazzy effects which became the composer's trademark. The first act ran through a selection of Vienna-accented (in speech and music) pieces including numbers for Lintschi, Konrad and Weisskappel, two duos for the lovers and a jolly one for the girl and Toni ('Süsses Fräulein Karolin') before the titular Herzogin put in her appearance at the top of the second act with the big number of the evening 'Wenn die Musik spielt'. Konrad and Lintschi's principal duo, 'Reich mir die Hand und sag' ade', and a jolly Viennese trio intervened before the Herzogin closed her appearance with a reprise which showed her determination to follow her husband's carefree footsteps ('Komm' die Herzogin will tanzen...'). The final act was Toni's and he brought the show to its musical end with a marriage song and a final jolly duo with the girl who will not, after all, be his bride ('Das hab' ich von meinem Papa').

Produced by Wilhelm Karczag at the Theater an der Wien, *Auf Befehl der Herzogin* followed behind the patriotic wartime Operette *Gold gab ich für Eisen* and proved (as was proved in other war-busy countries) that escapism goes down better than rousing sentiments in time of trouble. It was an immediate and sizeable success, the largest at the theatre for several years, and Karczag took the unusual step of running it on straight through the summer months when the theatre usually closed its doors. The show played at the Theater an der Wien until the end of October when, after seven months and 177 performances, it moved over to pass its 200th performance (12 November) in the repertoire at the Raimundtheater. In 1926 it posted up its 400th performance during a season at the Bürgertheater (16 January) with Franz Glawatsch and Selma Granichstädten in the leading röles.

A performance during the original run at the Theater an

Plate 10. **Amy Augarde** *was the most ubiquitous British musical character lady of her era – here she is as Bertha in* The Red Mill *alongside Ivy Tresmand, Little Tich and Ray Kay.*

der Wien was given over to the Hungarian war effort, and Hungary itself produced the piece before the year was out (ad Andor Gábor). In Berlin the *Herzogin* of the title was, not unreasonably, changed to a *Kaiserin* and the leading lady whose commands were so faithfully obeyed, although still not actually named as anything but 'Die Kaiserin' in the programme, was portrayed as the Austro-Hungarian empress, in a production which gave Granichstädten by far his greatest success in Germany. Given the war conditions, it was perhaps not surprising that *Auf Befehl der Herzogin* was not seen outside central Europe, but there it had a success that would undoubtedly, in other times, have travelled further.

Hungary; Király Szinház *A Czászárno* 18 December 1915; Germany: *Auf Befehl der Kaiserin* ?1915

AUGARDE, Amy [Louise]   (b London, 7 July 1868; d Reigate, 1 April 1959).

Amy Augarde's career spanned the development of the musical theatre from the comic opera and burlesque of Victorian times through Gaiety musical comedy and the Viennese, French and Broadway musicals of the 1920s to revue and the song-and-laughter shows of the 1930s in nearly half a century of active stage work which made up one of the most remarkable musical theatre lives of modern times.

Whilst in her teens, she joined the touring companies of Richard Barker (playing in the chorus of his *Manteaux Noirs* at fourteen as Louise Augarde) and of Richard D'Oyly Carte, and she made her West End début deputizing for Jessie Bond as Mad Margaret in *Ruddigore* at the Savoy. Her fine, full figure and fruity mezzo won her lead rôles in touring burlesque before she graduated ultimately to the Gaiety Theatre itself (*Little Jack Sheppard*, *The Shop Girl*). She created the title-rôle in the enormously successful touring musical *The New Barmaid* and, in her thirties, mixed leading rôles on tour (*Florodora*, *Campano*, *The New Barmaid*) with the occasional West End appearance, scoring a particular success as Madame Michu in George

Edwardes's production of *Les P'tites Michu* at Daly's Theatre.

This success was the forerunner of the second part of her career, as a singing character actress of great popularity. In her forties she became the ubiquitous choice as the older and usually comic lady in London musicals (*The Chocolate Soldier*, *The Red Mill*, *The Last Waltz*, *Catherine*), and continued to be a West End (*The Damask Rose*, *White Horse Inn*, *The Rose of Persia*) and provincial (*Hit the Deck*, *The Lilac Domino*) favourite into her sixties.

Her niece **Adrienne AUGARDE** (ċ Chicago, 17 March 1913), a deliciously pretty young performer, had a prominent career as a musical comedy ingénue, beginning as Dora in *The Toreador* and going on to appear in starring rôles in *The Duchess of Dantzic*, *Les P'tites Michu*, *Lady Madcap*, *See See* and *The New Aladdin* in London and on Broadway in *The Duchess of Dantzic*, *Peggy Machree*, *The Rose Maid* and *The Dollar Princess* before turning to vaudeville. She died, reportedly of appendicitis, whilst still in her twenties.

AU PAYS DU SOLEIL   Opérette-revue (opérette marseillaise) by Henri Alibert. Lyrics by René Sarvil. Music by Vincent Scotto. Moulin de la Chanson, Paris, 22 October 1932.

Au pays du soleil was the first of the series of merry, Marseille-flavoured musical plays with which Alibert, as author and performer, Sarvil and Scotto paralleled the success of Marcel Pagnol's famous Marseille plays in the 1930s. It told the story of an out-of-work marseillais lad called Titin (Alibert) whose would-be father-in-law won't let him marry his sweetheart, Miette (Jenny Hélia), and who then finds himself accused of a murder which has really been committed by a local smuggler. Proven innocence and happiness await at the final curtain.

The show's songs, catchily written in the simple, dancing and heavily accented style of their time and place, included several which became favourites, most particularly in the hands of the author-star: the waltzing 'À petits pas' (La Valse marseillaise), the fox-trotting duo 'Miette' for hero and heroine, the romantic slow-fox 'J'ai rêvé d'une fleur', the one-stepping 'Une rose (c'est bien peu de chose)' and the comical 'Un fondu, un momo (un jobastre, un fada)'.

The original production at Paris's Moulin de la Chanson was a great success and, while its successors in the same style and from (mostly) the same hands prospered in Paris, *Au pays du soleil* trod its way through the provinces of France until it was again seen in Paris, at the Théâtre de la Porte Saint-Martin (25 May 1951) with Rellys, the inheritor of the mantle of Alibert, and Mireille Ponsard taking the parts of Titin and his girl. In the same year Corsican tenor and filmstar Tino Rossi portrayed Titin on the screen in a version of *Au pays du soleil* co-written by Sarvil who also appeared in the film alongside Véra Norman, Jacqueline Pierreux, Milly Mathis and Berval. The hits of the original show were supplemented by favourite numbers from the subsequent *Arènes joyeuses* and *Un de la Canebière* and from the Scotto/Sarvil songbook ('Zou! un peu d'aioli', 'Adieu, Venise provençale', 'Le Plus Beau Tango du monde', 'Marseille mon pays').

In 1959 *Au pays du soleil* returned to the Paris stage again, when it was mounted at the Théâtre de l'Européen with Rellys, Sarvil and Mlle Ponsard still at the head of affairs and, although it seems to have been replaced as the favourite representative of its genre in the 1990s by *Un de la Canebière* and *Trois de la marine*, it still appears on French stages.

Film: 1951

Recording: Sarvil Company (Véga) etc

AU SOLEIL DU MEXIQUE

AU SOLEIL DU MEXIQUE Opérette à grand spectacle in 2 acts by Albert Willemetz and André Mouëzy-Éon. Music by Maurice Yvain. Théâtre du Châtelet, Paris, 18 December 1935.

Having killed a man in a brawl, the bullfighter Nino Chicuelo (André Baugé) flees Mexico with the apparent help of his old patron, Felipe Tampico, a two-faced fellow who is really after the boy's beloved Juanita (Fanély Revoil). Returning secretly to see Juanita, Nino cannot resist showing off his tauromachic skills at fiesta and he is only saved from arrest by the opportune arrival of wealthy, glamorous American Jessie Thompson (Danielle Brégis). Whilst Jessie whisks him amorously off to Waikiki on her yacht, Juanita heads for Guadaloupe and the safety of a convent, but all comes right in the final reel with the aid of a convenient revolution.

With 16 sets, ranging from the bull-ring to Waikiki, from La Maison de Danse to the Chapelle des Toréadors and the Caribbean convent; events including an eruption, an earthquake and a deluge; and such dances as a Grand Ballet espagnol, a Rumba Fluorescente and a Snake-Dance, Mouëzy-Éon's script for *Au soleil du Mexique* provided all the opportunities for a fine display of Châtelet spectacle. Illustrated by a suitable Yvain–Willemetz score and performed by a particularly strong cast, in which the star vocalists were supplemented by a good dose of comedy from favourite comedian Bach as Jérome Frascator, Jessie's film-star admirer, this exemplary opérette à grand spectacle made up into a fine success. It ran for 307 performances at the Châtelet and subsequently appeared on provincial stages for several decades.

Yvain's most open-stage piece to date, following his great successes with intimate musicals, *Au soleil du Mexique* prefigured not only his own ultimately even more popular *Chanson gitane*, but also the successful post-war *Belle of Cadix* type of opérette whose highly tuppence-coloured tales of love and revenge in sunny places were also in a direct line of descent from Mouëzy-Éon's libretto to *Au soleil du Mexique*.

AU TEMPS DES MERVEILLEUSES

AU TEMPS DES MERVEILLEUSES Opérette à grand spectacle in 2 acts by Albert Willemetz and André Mouëzy-Éon. Music by Henri Christiné and Tiarko Richepin. Théâtre du Châtelet, Paris, 22 December 1934.

Star baritone André Baugé topped the bill in Maurice Lehmann's spectacular production of *Au temps des merveilleuses* in the rôle of Roland des Essarts, an émigré plotting from the safety of Scotland against the French directoire. Leaving his beloved Scottish Lilian (Marcelle Denya) to go and sow trouble in France, he is pursued by a comical agent of the government, Pigeonneau (Bach), and then persuaded patriotically to fight for France in the Napoleonic wars. He passes heroically through Egypt, the ruins of Thebes and the tent of Bonaparte on his way to a happy ending and, of course, Lilian. The first act also arranged to allow the performers to visit a fête des tulipes, the old windmills of Holland and the Rivoli as well as the highlands of Scotland, and the second to display a panorama of the Palais-Royal stretching right to the back of the theatre's vast stage area, and a charge of live horses galloping against a travelator in the show's climax.

The extremely picturesque element of the show was complemented by a strong cast and a score (in which numbers were not individually credited to the two composers) which provided Baugé with the ringing 'Partir, c'est mourir un peu' and the romantic 'Dis-toi que je t'aime', Gilbert Moryn as a Scottish laird with a fine bass-baritone call for revenge, and the heroine who, with her soubrette (Monique Bert) and her father managed somehow to get into most of the second-act scenes, with a pair of love songs, 'Vers toi mon amour s'envole' and 'On dit que l'amour est roi'. Although neither Christiné nor Willemetz were as appreciably at home in the profitable world of the opérette à grand spectacle as in their winning and witty musical comedies, it was nevertheless a score which served its purpose for nearly a year's run at the Châtelet (342 performances) and the goodly afterlife which *Au temps des merveilleuses* later lived out in the French provinces.

AUTOLIEBCHEN

AUTOLIEBCHEN Posse in 3 acts by Jean Kren based on *Dix minutes d'auto* by Georges Berr and Pierre Decourcelle. Lyrics by Alfred Schönfeld. Music by Jean Gilbert. Thalia-Theater, Berlin, 16 March 1912.

Autoliebchen was the first of the series of hit musical comedies written by Jean Kren and composed by Jean Gilbert specifically for Berlin's Thalia-Theater, following the house's success with the composer's brought-in *Polnische Wirtschaft*, and it was, alone of all the series, not written to an original script by the prolific playwright and producer. The text of *Autoliebchen* was a version of the 1908 Paris comedy *Dix minutes d'auto* by Berr and Decourcelle (Théâtre des Nouveautés, 13 November) – the same Georges Berr whose work was currently being plundered with great success for Broadway musical comedy texts (*The Pink Lady*, *Oh! Oh! Delphine*).

George Triebler (Paul Bechert) is a travelling salesman for the Lindenschmidt wine firm, and to ease the strains of this occupation he has lined up a little female comfort for those evenings far from home in distant Budapest. She is called Prisca von Erdödy (Eugenie della Donna). But just when Triebler is all ready to settle down and get married to his hometown Fifi (Rosl Loibner), Prisca turns up, with her uncle Maurus Somossy (Emil Sondermann) close behind. Since George has cannily called himself 'Lindenschmidt' whilst on his boss's business, it is that boss's son – who also happens to be called George and is himself happily affianced – who collects the accusations. But Triebler has more problems to come. A year earlier, after a jolly carnival ball, dressed in a costume as the Trompeter von Säkkingen, he drove home a pretty masked lady and what happened between them .... Suffice it to say that when the story comes out, at just the wrong moment, George starts more and more to look like a veritable satyr. However, after an actful of farcical coming and going in the congenial atmosphere of the Zum kleinen Twostep ballroom, all comes to a comfortable ending. The

Plate 11. **Autoliebchen:** *The hit song of Jean Gilbert's internationally successful musical comedy – 'Das haben die Mädchen so gerne'.*

mysterious lady in the car was none other than Fifi, Lindenschmidt finds a new love in her sister Rely, Prisca gets the handsome Böttchermeister Max Rönnekamp, and Uncle Maurus the girls' mother, Aurelie Werkenthin (Johanna Junker-Schatz), with whom he has shared some of the evening's most comical moments.

The musical hit of the show was the march duet 'Das haben die Mädchen so gerne', a piece which became one of the most popular numbers of its era, but the evening was full of dance-based numbers – most notably variations on the two-step – from which two other duos 'Fräulein, könn'n Sie links 'rum tanzen' and the song of the 'Mädchen im Stübchen und im Salon' also became favourites.

Autoliebchen ran at the Thalia-Theater for nine months before being replaced by the next of the series, *Puppchen*, and promptly moved on to Vienna where it was played at the Apollotheater, billed as a 'vaudeville in one act', adapted by Carl Lindau into 'the dance-hall "Klein Paris" on carnival night'. Max Nekut was George and Irma Jarkowska played Fifi, with Relly Witzani (Prisca), Rosl Schlager (Rely), Alois Resni (Lindenschmidt), Eugen Günther as Lebrecht Döppchen (ex-Maurus) and Anna Selhofer as Irene (ex-Aurelie).

Budapest saw *Autotündér* (ad Gyula Komor) the following year, and London snapped up the show in the wake of the success of Gilbert's *The Girl in the Taxi* (*Die keusche Susanne*). Arthur Anderson and Hartley Carrick redid the book quite considerably, and Rutland Barrington, Thelma Raye and Bertram Wallis featured. *The Joy Ride Lady* didn't come up to her predecessor in popularity, but managed a fair run of 105 performances, broken by a shift to the

Garrick Theatre, before things German became undesirable in London's West End.

Austria: Apollotheater 1 December 1912; Hungary: Fővárosi Nyari Színház *Az autotündér* 13 June 1913; UK: New Theatre *Joy Ride Lady* 21 February 1914

LES AVENTURES DU ROI PAUSOLE Opérette in 3 acts by Albert Willemetz based on the book by Pierre Louÿs. Music by Arthur Honegger. Théâtre des Bouffes-Parisiens, Paris, 12 December 1930.

The first and most successful of the rare ventures of the composer Honegger into the light musical theatre, *Les Aventures du roi Pausole* was adapted by Willemetz from the magazine serial become novel (1901) of Pierre Louÿs as a slightly outrageous opéra-bouffe, and was produced by its librettist at the Théâtre des Bouffes-Parisiens of which he was, at the time, the director.

The folk of the Kingdom ruled by King Pausole (Dorville) live by amorality – both sexual and social. The King has an extensive harem, one wife for each night of the year, but his daughter Blanche Aline (Jacqueline Francell) has been brought up chastely, until the day she runs away with Mirabelle (Meg Lemonnier), the leading dancer of a troupe brought to entertain the royal family. The King sets out unenthusiastically after the two girls (for, yes, Mirabelle is actually a girl), accompanied by his chief Eunuch (René Koval) and the page, Giglio (Pasquali), and pursued by the Queen of the day, Diane de la Houppe (Germaine Duclos), determined not to miss out on her annual turn at a royal romp. Giglio, however, is the male triumphant. He disguises himself as a girl to join in the lovemaking of Mirabelle and Blanche Aline, then deputizes for the indisposed King so that Diane won't miss her long-awaited night, and ends up winning the hand of the Princess, granted by an exasperated monarch who will even go so far as to declare a republic just to be left in peace.

Honegger's score mixed some characteristic modern tones with elements of traditional opérette and opéra-bouffe in a score which produced some particularly creative ensembles, and a series of set piece solos and duos which did not, however, always follow the text into the zaniness of opéra-bouffe.

Les Aventures du roi Pausole was nothing if not risqué, even osé, with a kind of riskiness very different to that which the happy creatures of the jazz-age musical comedies – many written by Willemetz – had been naughtily parading across the Paris stage for a decade. It dangled deliciously on the verge of decadence, once again a different kind of decadence to that expressed in Louÿs's *La Femme et le pantin*, itself metamorphosed into Operetten of a very different flavour to this (*Frasquita* etc). But this flavour, this decadence proved a fine attraction to the Bouffes-Parisiens of 1930, and the show had a superb run of some 400 performances.

It was produced in Switzerland in the original French (Geneva, 1932), and reprised in Paris in 1937 (Bouffes-Parisiens) and again in 1947 at the tiny Théâtre des Capucines, before getting its first German-language production in Zürich (Stadttheater 1953 ad Hans Zimmermann). Following this it won productions in Hamburg and Munich, remaining thereafter on the fringe of the repertoire in both French and German versions. It was most recently revived at the Théâtre Municipal, Lausanne in 1990, and looks set for further showings in the jaded 'nineties, particularly given the fashion of the period for producing light musical theatre pieces by name composers in opera houses.

Germany: Staatsoper, Hamburg *Die Abenteuer des Königs Pausole* 1955

AXEL AN DER HIMMELSTÜR
Musical comedy in 3 acts (6 scenes) by Paul Morgan and Adolf Schütz. Lyrics by Hans Weigel. Music by Ralph Benatzky. Theater an der Wien, Vienna, 1 September 1936.

Artur Hellmer's first production after taking over the management at the Theater an der Wien in 1936, *Axel an der Himmelstür* was a piece set in that most favoured of contemporary Ruritanias, deepest Hollywood. It hinted that it was à clef and that its heroine was based on Greta Garbo, it suggested that it was a parody of all that went on in Hollywood but, like others of its kind, it simply used the extravagant personalities of Celluloid-city as the background for a colourful musical comedy. This one used some of the oldest bits of libretto in the book, from disguises to stolen jewels.

Zarah Leander played Gloria Mills, filmstar, and Max Hansen was Axel Swift, a reporter anxious to get near enough to interview her. He disguises himself as an elderly extra, gets invited to supper in her hotel room, comforts her when it turns out her fiancé, 'the Prince', is a confidence trickster, and then pretends to be an intruder when an English lady's jewels are stolen, so as not to compromise her by his presence. He ends up in prison and in court, before his friends clear up the fact that the old and young men are both he. Gloria (whose chauffeur stole the jewels, of course) has stopped being sorry about the 'Prince' by the final curtain. No one else apart from the two stars got much of a look in, but the other cast members included co-author Paul Morgan as producer Cecil McScott, Herbert Berghof as director Stuart Williams, Erich Dörner as hairdresser Theodor Herlinger, Heidemarie Hatheyer as Gloria's maid Dinah, and Lisi Klaast as Jessie Leyland.

Benatzky's score mixed the topical and the special material with straighter dance numbers of which the slow foxtrot 'Gebundene Hände' proved popular, alongside the tango song 'Mein schönes Fräulein, gute Nacht!' and the English waltz 'Eine Frau von heut'. The topical element was topped by an 'In Holly-Holly-Holly-Holly-Holly-wood' which crammed Douglas Fairbanks, Charlie Chaplin, Adolphe Menjou, Maurice Chevalier, Mickey Mouse, King Kong, Tarzan and Carl Laemmle into its lyrics, whilst 'Die allergrösste Zukunft hat die Liebe!' allowed the star to indulge in imitations of Jan Kiepura, Richard Tauber and Erna Sack. Miss Klaast and Dörner got a share (with Hansen) in a Tabu-foxtrot.

The two stars lit up the evening's entertainment splendidly and *Axel an der Himmelstür* went on to give the theatre its first decent run in four years with an unbroken 190 performances before contracts for real films inter-

vened and dragged first Leander (replaced by Lili Hatvany) and then Hansen away.

The book of the show was later used as the basis for the screenplay of the film *Liebespremiere* (1943) attached to a different score composed by Franz Grothe.

AYER, Nat[haniel] D[avis]   (b Boston, 30 September 1887; d Bath, England, 19 September 1952).

American-born pianist, vocalist and songwriter ('Oh! You Beautiful Doll', 'Ragtime Suffragette', 'King Chanticler', 'You're My Baby', 'At the Foxtrot Ball' etc) Ayer began his theatre career by contributing songs to such Broadway shows as *Miss Innocence* (1908, 'I'm Not That Kind of a Girl' w A Seymour Brown) *The Ziegfeld Follies of 1909, The Echo* (1910, 'Heigh Ho' w Brown), *A Winsome Widow* (1912, 'You're a Regular Girl' w Brown) and *The Wall Street Girl* (1912, 'I Should Have Been Born a Boy,' 'The Indian Rag' 'You're Some Girl' all w Brown) and was credited as co-composer of the musical farce *The Newlyweds and their Baby* (1909), a cartoon-based piece in which the critter in question was kidnapped and replaced by a dwarf for 42 performances.

It was in Britain, however, where he was one of the first American song-and-dancewriters to arrive as the new craze for American dances and dance-music was beginning, that he made the most prominent part of his career. There, after scoring a memorable early success with the songs for the London adaptation of the French revue *Les Fils Touffe sont à Paris* under the title *The Bing Boys Are Here* (1916, 'If You were the Only Girl in the World', 'Another Little Drink'), he became a regular contributor to revue (*The Bing Boys on Broadway, The Bing Girls Are There, Pell Mell, Look Who's Here, Cartoons*) and to musical comedy, writing a handful of London theatre scores of which the Leslie Henson vehicle *Yes, Uncle!* and *Baby Bunting*, in which American comedian Walter Catlett scored a striking West End success, were highly successful both at home and abroad.

Ayer also performed on the variety stage, scoring a personal success at the London Empire in 1915, in musical comedy, playing opposite Gertie Millar in his own *Houp-La!*, and in revue.

1909 **The Newlyweds and their Baby** (w John Bratton/Paul West, Seymour Brown/West, Aaron Hoffman) Majestic Theater, New York 22 March
1912 **Let George Do It** (West/Aaron Hoffman) West End Theater, New York 22 April
1916 **Houp-La!** (Fred Thompson, Hugh E Wright, Percy Greenbank) St Martin's Theatre 23 November
1916 **Oh! Caesar** (w Arthur Wood/Adrian Ross/A M Thompson, Max Pemberton) Edinburgh 23 December
1917 **Yes, Uncle!** (Austen Hurgon, George Arthurs, Clifford Grey) Prince of Wales Theatre 29 December
1917 **The Hula Girl** (w Phil Braham, Alfred Haines/George Reynolds, R Guy Keene) 1 act Hippodrome 18 December
1919 **Baby Bunting** (Worton David, Grey/F Thompson) Shaftesbury Theatre 25 September
1922 **The Smith Family** (Grey, Stanley Logan, Philip Page) Empire Theatre 6 September

B

BABES IN ARMS Musical in 2 acts by Richard Rodgers and Lorenz Hart. Lyrics by Lorenz Hart. Music by Richard Rodgers. Shubert Theater, New York, 14 April 1937.

The ultimate in what has become fondly known as the 'hey, let's put on a show' type of musical, *Babes in Arms* was made up of a featherweight book of which the backbone was the efforts of a group of teenagers, trying to prove their self-sufficiency and avoid being sent off to a work farm, to make themselves into a successful revue troupe, stiffened by some George Balanchine dances ('Johnny One Note', 'Peter's Journey'), and a score which contained more enduring songs per squarish page of music than any other of its time.

Amongst the young and mostly up-and-coming cast, Mitzi Green (already seen as a juvenile in movies) lit into 'The Lady is a Tramp', sighed extravagantly over a boy called Valentine in 'My Funny Valentine' and joined with Ray Heatherton in 'Where or When', 16-year-old neophyte Wynn Murray introduced the tale of 'Johnny One Note' and dove into the comical plaint of 'Way Out West', Rolly Pickert and Grace McDonald sparkled through 'I Wish I Were in Love Again' and the whole company, cast in rôles which were made to measure, joined together to celebrate being 'Babes in Arms'. The most to-be-familiar names amongst the cast, however, were the for the moment less-featured Alfred Drake, Dan Dailey, the Nicholas brothers and Robert Rounseville.

After a sticky start, Dwight Deere Wiman's Broadway production – at one stage the only musical playing on Broadway in an underpar season – became a splendid success, running 289 performances and largely recouping its costs. However, the show was not mounted outside America, possibly at least partly because of the success of Busby Berkeley's 1939 film version in which the young Judy Garland and Mickey Rooney headed a team of youngsters in memorably capturing the innocence of what little of the original piece remained. Of the show score, only the title song and 'Where or When' were sung in the film, alongside a series of old favourites which were used to make up the show-within-the-show. The songs of *Babes in Arms* found their screen afterlife elsewhere: 'The Lady Is a Tramp' made it to the movies in *Words and Music* (as did 'I Wish I Were in Love' and 'Johnny One Note') and in *Pal Joey* (sung by Jo Ann Greer), whilst 'My Funny Valentine', which also appeared in *Pal Joey* (sung by Trudy Ewen), was again heard in *Gentlemen Marry Brunettes*.

A revised version of *Babes in Arms* was mounted at the Goodspeed Opera House in 1979 (10 April, with two songs culled from *Too Many Girls* added to its score) and the popularity of both the favourite songs and of the film version, regularly re-seen via television, was responsible for three attempts (two of which made it to the stage) to mount further rewritten versions in Britain in the 1980s. The piece was seen again in New York when presented at the Tarrytown Music Hall (ad George Oppenheimer) in 1985 (26 June) without moving closer in.

UK: Theatre Royal, Plymouth 26 February 1985; Open Air Theatre, Regent's Park, London 3 August 1988
Recordings: selection (New World Records, Columbia)

BABES IN TOYLAND Musical extravaganza in a prologue and 3 acts by Glen MacDonough. Music by Victor Herbert. Grand Opera House, Chicago, 17 June 1903; Majestic Theater, New York, 13 October 1903.

Commissioned by producers Julian Mitchell and Fred Hamlin to follow up their 1902 success with the fairytale spectacular *The Wizard of Oz*, *Babes in Toyland* was constructed on similar lines to the earlier show. Glen MacDonough's libretto followed little Jane (Mabel Barrison) and Alan (top-billed William Norris) through the colourful realms of Toyland as they struggled, with the help of the familiar characters of children's storybooks, to outwit wicked, miserly Uncle Barnaby (George W Denham) and his allies, the Master Toymaker (Mark Smith) and Contrary Mary (Amy Ricard), and win their way to a happy ending. The production, like its predecessor, was staged with lavish scenic effects, from the prologue's shipwreck (paralleling *The Wizard of Oz*'s tornado) through all kinds of picturesque fairytale venues including a country fête in Contrary Mary's Garden, the Spider's Forest, the Floral Palace of the Moth Queen, Toyland's Christmas Tree Grove and the Master Toymaker's workshop and castle, to the final Palace of Toyland and its Court of Justice.

Alongside its spectacle, the other principal attraction of *Babes in Toyland* was its music. Herbert provided a score which was very much in advance of the one which the producers had cobbled together for *The Wizard of Oz*. It had plenty of very fine large-scale and orchestral numbers – notably the enduring 'March of the Toys' and its succeeding 'The Military Ball' – but also some charming and delicate musical moments ranging from the lovely trio 'Go to Sleep, Slumber Deep' (Alan, Jane, and a soprano fairy w chorus) and the sweet 'Never Mind, Bo Peep (we will find your sheep)' sung by Tom Tom (Bessie Wynn) and the widow Piper's other children to the culpable little shepherdess (Nella Webb), to the chirpily childish 'I Can't Do That Sum', added to the score after opening for Miss Barrison, and Tom Tom's dreamy hymn to 'Toyland'. There were occasional more obvious spots – if nothing quite as tacked-in as Lotta Faust singing 'Sammy' in *The Wizard of Oz* – notably when Contrary Mary sang fairly irrelevantly about 'Barney O'Flynn', but on the whole Herbert's score hit the medium line between cultured fairy play and pantomime jollity to perfection.

Babes in Toyland played a season of 192 performances at the Majestic Theater before going on the road and it established itself as an enduring favourite of its kind throughout America – sufficient of a favourite, indeed, that it became the subject of a Broadway lawsuit. This one, however, was settled with full logic. In the face of defence testimony from Mitchell, the Hamlin brothers, Ben Teal, MacDonough and others, one Mrs Riley who had claimed that she was the show's real author got short legal shrift.

In 1929 (Jolson Theater 23 December) the Shubert brothers brought the show back to Broadway for a Christmas season, and although it has not had a career outside America, versions of *Babes in Toyland* (sometimes textually quite remote from the original) have been played regularly throughout the country since the first production. It has also been filmed twice, once with a cast including Laurel and Hardy (1934) and once by Walt Disney (1961) in widely variant versions, and it was televised in 1955 and 1960.

Films: MGM 1934, Buena Vista 1961
Recordings: selections (Decca, Reader's Digest – part records)
  1961 film soundtrack (Buena Vista)

BABIL AND BIJOU, or The Lost Regalia Fantastic music drama in 18 scenes by Dion Boucicault. Lyrics by J R Planché. Music by Hervé, Frederic Clay, Jules Rivière et al. Theatre Royal, Covent Garden, London, 29 August 1872.

A hugely extravagant grand opéra-bouffe féerie created by the well-known playwright Dion Boucicault, in imitation of the then-popular French models, *Babil and Bijou* was produced at Covent Garden under the patronage of the wealthy Lord Londesborough. Boucicault announced that his piece would be the means of restoring the Covent Garden theatre to its place as Britain's national theatre, and gathered together such respected talents as Planché, the most celebrated author of extravaganza poetry, and the French composer Hervé, to contribute to the creation of the piece. However, his show turned out to be a vastly over-written piece of conservatively satirical pseudo-mythology whose principal attractions lay in its production values. It gained some popularity from its spectacular scenery, the presence of such favourite performers as comedian/director Lionel Brough, tenor Joseph Maas, Mrs Howard Paul and Mrs Billington in its cast, and, above all, from one enormous hit song, the juvenile boys' chorus 'Spring Gentle Spring' composed by Jules Rivière.

The show was kept on the stage for its announced and pre-planned season of 160 performances but, in spite of building attendances through the run as the entertainment was popularized with cuts, alterations and the addition of stand-up acts, *Babil and Bijou* lost Londesborough his entire £30,000 capitalization and ranked as one of the greatest financial disasters of all theatrical time. A substantially different show under the same title was staged at the Alhambra Theatre 8 April 1882. It was of a much more practical size and proved rather more successful.

Plate 12. **Babil and Bijou:** *A sketch-artist's impression of two scenes from the bank-breaking Dion Boucicault production at London's Theatre Royal, Covent Garden.*

BABIOLE Opérette villageoise in 3 acts by Clairville and Octave Gastineau. Music by Laurent de Rillé. Théâtre des Bouffes-Parisiens, Paris, 16 January 1878.

The most successful of de Rillé's mostly small opérettes, the pretty, rustic *Babiole* served for two seasons at the Théâtre des Bouffes-Parisiens under Charles Comte's management, before winning a series of overseas productions both in French (Maurice Grau's production with the show's original stars, Paola Marié and Mary Albert, in America) and in Robert Reece's English version (a touring version with Pattie Laverne starred in Britain followed by a production in Australia featuring Gracie Plaisted as 'the village madcap').

The lively if exasperating heroine of the piece ('la plus folle des jeunesses de ces pays') is the country lass Babiole (Paola Marié), who has decided that she is in love with fellow peasant Alain (Jeannin). She is not to be put off by the fact that Alain is already in love with the Bailli's daughter, Arabelle (Blanche Miroir) who is, in any case, promised to Carcassol (Minart) from the big city of Paris who has, in his turn, had a ding-dong in the past with the loose local miller's wife, Madeleine (Mary Albert), who was once Cascarinette of the Bal de Paphos. In order to win her lad, Babiole resorts to trickery, pseudo-sorcery and not a small touch of blackmail. She threatens to reveal the guilty secrets – and apparently there are plenty, even if not all that serious – of half the village, not forgetting the Bailli himself (Daubray), who has been apparently doing something reprehensible in the almond grove.

De Rillé's score was composed in a prettily old-fashioned style, with the ring of traditional country airs to its most attractive parts, notably Alain's longing for 'un p'tit ferme, un p'tit jardinet'. The heroine ranged through a leading lady's variety of numbers including a Rondeau de la sorcellerie and some Couplets de charme, whilst Madeleine joined her old lover in repeating the naughty Parisian dance of their premarital days together.

UK: Prince's Theatre, Manchester 10 March 1879; USA: Standard Theater (Fr) 21 October 1880; Australia: Bijou Theatre, Melbourne *Babiole, or the Village Madcap* 22 July 1887

BABOLIN Opérette in 3 acts by Paul Ferrier and Jules Prével. Music by Louis Varney. Théâtre des Nouveautés, Paris, 19 March 1884.

The singer Lorenzo (Louis Morlet), still dressed in his stage costume as the devil, gets embroiled in a country wedding whilst escaping from the angry Karamatoff (Berthelier), husband of his paramour, Bagatella (Mily-Meyer). Lorenzo persuades the bridegroom, Mélissen (Albert Brasseur), to quit his pretty Elverine (Mlle Vaillant-Couturier) and exchange places with him. However, he then discovers to his chagrin that his 'double' is on the receiving end of the attentions of Bagatella's mistress, the beautiful princess, Mirane (Juliette Darcourt), a royal who goes all weak at the sound of a fine singing voice. All was sorted out to a scoreful of waltzing melodies in Varney's happiest style for a good Parisian season of more than two months at the Théâtre des Nouveautés and a further 37 performances, after the summer break, at the Folies-Dramatiques.

Surprisingly, *Babolin*'s only production beyond France was in America where Francis Wilson starred as the little bridegroom in a version called *The Devil's Deputy* (Abbey's Theater 10 September 1894). For some reason – and it seems to have been financial – Wilson threw out Varney's score, and for reasons confirmedly financial he replaced

Sousa as a replacement composer. Edward Jakobowski ultimately supplied the music for a show which, in spite of a cast including Lulu Glaser, Adele Ritchie, Wilson, Rhys Thomas and J C Miron, rated only a 72-performance run. Cheever Goodwin's translation (which failed to credit the original authors, or even the fact that it was an adaptation) included nothing as eyebrow-raising as the French lyric in which the Princess confides 'tu perds ton charme en perdant ton organe' to her voiceless beloved.

BABY Musical in 2 acts by Sybille Pearson based on a story developed with Susan Yankowitz. Lyrics by Richard Maltby jr. Music by David Shire. Ethel Barrymore Theater, New York, 4 December 1983.

Baby looks at three couples and the effect that having, or in one case not having, a child has on them. It moves on from a dauntingly biological opening (with a lyric that rhymes 'spermatazoa' and slides depicting the mechanics of producing a child) through some warm and intimate scenes and songs as the rather too-young Lizzie (Liz Callaway) and Danny (Todd Graff), and the perhaps too-old Arlene (Beth Fowler) and Alan (James Congdon) head towards giving birth to their children and, at the same time, to a different kind of life and relationship for themselves. Pam (Catherine Cox) and Nick (Martin Vidnovic) have the disappointment of finding that physical problems make it unlikely they will ever conceive. They put themselves through all kinds of undignified, clinical efforts, but are strong and sane enough to come out at the end of it as close as ever.

The songs mixed the unashamedly sentimental ('Two People in Love', 'At Night She Comes Home to Me') with such friendly, comical moments as a display of the gruesome experience of a first-time-pregnant woman at the hands of those who have already had the experience of giving birth and love to talk about it in gory detail ('The Ladies Singing Their Song') and the perspicacious observation of the older father that children are 'Easier to Love' than an adult partner.

Baby achieved a run of 241 performances on Broadway and was subsequently played at Britain's provincial Manchester Library Theatre, with Susie Blake, Dilys Watling and Tim Flavin amongst its cast, at Sydney's small Q Theatre and Germany's equally intimate Giessen Kellertheater, establishing itself as an interesting and viable small-scale musical.

Australia: Q Theatre, Sydney 20 November 1987; UK: Forum Theater, Wythenshaw, Manchester 27 September 1990; Germany: Kellertheater, Giessen (Eng) May 1993
Recording: original cast (TER)

BABY BUNTING Musical play in 2 acts by Fred Thompson and Worton David founded on the play *Jane* by Harry Nicholls and William Lestocq. Lyrics by Clifford Grey. Music by Nat D Ayer. Shaftesbury Theatre, London, 25 September 1919.

This lively musical version of the highly successful 1890 farce *Jane* (Comedy Theatre, 18 December 196 performances) featured the American comedian Walter Catlett as the stock figure of the hero's haplessly 'helpful' best friend. Book-keeper William Pye (Catlett) tries to help his bachelor employer, Bunny Bunting (Ronald Squire), find a temporary wife to convince Samuel Giggleswick (Davy Burnaby), the visiting trustee of a wealthy Uncle, that the

Plate 13. **Baby Bunting**: *American comedian Walter Catlett (right) scored a lively hit in his one London appearance.*

injections of cash he is giving to the Bunting 'family' till are justified. Unfortunately, the rôle of wife gets double cast (Dorothy Brunton, Daisy Elliston) and confusion reigns for the entire second act.

The score included some attractive light-weight numbers to amusing lyrics – 'One Cannot Play Cricket in November', 'Married, But Haven't Got a Husband', 'What's the Matter With Fifty-Nine (if you feel like twenty-three)' – which illustrated the farcical action of the play happily. One of the biggest attractions of Grossmith and Laurillard's production, however, turned out to be Catlett, whose unfamiliar, laid-back American style of fun scored well with a London public saturated with the repetitive antics of local low comedians. He materially helped the show to a good London run of 213 performances.

A touring production followed, and a version of the show was mounted by J C Williamson Ltd in Australia, billed as 'Dorothy Brunton's Great London Success' with Miss Brunton repeating her original rôle to the Pye of Alfred Frith. She slipped 'The Japanese Sandman' into the remnants of the show's original score through seasons in Sydney and Melbourne (Her Majesty's Theatre 26 February 1921).

Australia: Criterion Theatre, Sydney 24 December 1920

BACALL, Lauren [PERSKE, Betty Joan] (b New York, 16 September 1924).

Famed for her more than 30 years of Hollywood films and her partnership with Humphrey Bogart, sandy-voiced Miss Bacall made her entry into the musical theatre in middle age to top-bill as the sabotaged star Margo Channing in the musical *Applause* (1970) in both New York and in London. She subsequently toured as Ruth Sherwood in *Wonderful Town* (1977) and made a second above-the-title Broadway appearance in another musicalized screenplay as a second strong woman, Tess Harding of *Woman of the Year*, in 1981.

Autobiography: *By Myself* (Knopf, New York, 1978)

BACH, Ernst (b Eger, Bohemia, 10 May 1876; d Munich, 1 November 1929).

An actor at the Vienna Volkstheater from 1899 and later at Berlin's Residenztheater and Lustspielhaus, Bach subsequently became director of Munich's Volkstheater (1917), a position he held up to his death in 1929.

Parallel to his performing and administrative work, he also led a highly successful career as a playwright and librettist, pairing with Franz Arnold on many popular pieces, both plays and musical comedies, during the years of the First World War and through the 1920s. Kollo's *Die Königin der Nacht* and Hirsch's *Der Fürst von Pappenheim* and *Dolly*, all widely played in Central Europe, were their most successful ventures on to the musical stage.

Several of their comedies were subsequently used as the basis for musicals: *Hurra! eine Junge* was used in London as the starting point for the highly successful musical comedy *Blue for a Boy*, after having already been a major success as a play under the title *It's a Boy!*, and another Leslie Henson piece, *Nice Goings On*, was also based on one of their plays. A second unidentified Bach/Arnold piece was the basis for the musical comedy *Oh, Letty*, whilst Jack Buchanan's *Toni* was a semi-remusicked version of their libretto to *Der Fürst von Pappenheim*. In Hungary *Ezüstpille* (ad Andor Gábor, music: Albert Szirmai, Vigszinház 9 May 1914), *Jó firma* (ad Jenő Molnár, arr Mihály Nádor Magyar Színház 5 June 1930) and *Strandszerelem* (ad Imre Harmath, Fővárosi Nyári Operettszinház 10 July 1929) all arose from Bach and Arnold originals.

1916 **Die Fahrt ins Glück** (Jean Gilbert/w Franz Arnold) Theater des Westens 2 September
1917 **Neptune auf Reisen** (Rudolf Nelson/w Arnold) Apollotheater January
1919 **Fräulein Puck** (Walter Kollo/w Arnold) Volkstheater, Munich 25 June
1921 **Die Königin der Nacht** (Kollo/w Arnold) Neues Operetten-Theater 2 September
1923 **Der Fürst von Pappenheim** (Hugo Hirsch/w Arnold) Deutsches Künstlertheater 16 February
1923 **Dolly** (Hirsch/Rudolf Bernauer/w Arnold) Deutsches Künstlertheater 16 October
1924 **Die vertauschte Frau** (Kollo/w Arnold) Operettenhaus am Schiffbauerdamm 22 December
1925 **Olly Polly** (Kollo/w Arnold) Neues Theater am Zoo 3 September
1928 **Arme Ritter** (Kollo/w Arnold) Volkstheater, Munich 22 September
1934 **Lieber, reich – aber glücklich** (Kollo/w Arnold) Johann Strauss-Theater, Vienna 11 May
1935 **Frauen haben das gerne** (Kollo/w Arnold) Residenzbühne 17 December

BAILEY, Pearl [Mae] (b Newport News, Va, 29 March 1918; d Philadelphia, 17 August 1990).

Originally a successful performer in vaudeville and in

cabaret, Pearl Bailey made her first appearance in a Broadway musical in 1946 in the rôle of the barmaid, Butterfly, in Harold Arlen's *St Louis Woman*, introducing 'Legalize My Name' and 'It's a Woman's Prerogative (to change her mind)'. In the 1950s she appeared in the musical *Arms and the Girl* (Connecticut, 'There Must Be Somethin' Better Than Love'), in the revue *Bless You All* (1950) and as Madame Fleur in the Caribbean whorehouse tale *House of Flowers* (1954), whilst also featuring in a number of musical films, including those of the stage shows *Carmen Jones* (as Frankie, performing 'Beat Out Dat Rhythm on a Drum') and *Porgy and Bess* (Maria, 1959), *Variety Girl* (1947), *Isn't It Romantic* and *St Louis Blues* (1958).

In the late 1960s she returned to the musical stage and played the rôle of Sally Adams in *Call Me Madam* in California and that of Dolly Levi in *Hello, Dolly!* both on Broadway (special Tony Award 1968) and around the country. She reprised this last rôle through America in 1975–6, making a second and final Broadway appearance as Mrs Levi at the Minskoff Theater 6 November 1975 for 42 performances.

Autobiography: *The Raw Pearl* (Harcourt Brace & World, New York, 1968), *Talking to Myself* (Harcourt Brace Jovanovich, New York, 1971)

DIE BAJADERE   Operette in 3 acts by Julius Brammer and Alfred Grünwald. Music by Emmerich Kálmán. Carltheater, Vienna, 23 December 1921.

Following on behind his wartime successes with *Die Csárdásfürstin* and *Die Faschingsfee* and the post-war *Das Hollandweibchen*, Kálmán scored yet another Vienna triumph with *Die Bajadere*, a romantic backstage Operette which contains some of the most beautiful of all his theatre music.

Brammer and Grünwald's libretto follows the efforts of the eastern Prince Radjami (Louis Treumann) to win the heart and hand of Odette Darimonde (Christl Mardayn), the prima donna of the Operette *La Bayadère*. This romance is counterpointed by the comical amours of the soubrette, Marietta (Luise Kartousch), and her two husbands, Napoléon (Ernst Tautenhayn) and Louis-Philippe (Eugen Strehn), each of whom she fancies only when she is not married to him. Radjami, obliged by his country's laws to take a wife in short time, has to hasten his wooing of the obdurate prima donna and he puts his faith in the power of a bunch of 'love roses'. Under the spell of the flowers, Odette finds herself accepting his invitation to a hurriedly arranged party, but when he attempts to top the evening with a wedding ceremony she awakens from her trance. It is three months and a further act of quiproquos before the two can bring down the curtain together.

Forgoing the more explicit, driving Hungarian rhythms and tones of *Die Csárdásfürstin* and the later *Gräfin Mariza*, Kálmán instead served the stars with some lush, heavily romantic melodies of which the tenor-baritone leading man's 'O Bajadere', in particular, rates as one of the composer's most memorable. He served the comedians equally well, with some sparky, vigorous modern dance tunes ('Fräulein, bitte woll'n sie Shimmy tanzen?', 'Schatzi, ich möchte einen Zobel von dir', 'Die kleine Bar dort am Boulevard') in a classically proportioned score in which romance and fun had equal and equally outstanding moments.

Die Bajadere was hugely successful in Vienna. Otto Storm and Raoul Aslan took over as Radjami, and Else Kochhann and Lya Beyer took turns as Odette, as its first run at the Carltheater stretched beyond 12 months and finally ended after 353 performances. It was brought back after *Die Brasilianerin* and *Madame Pompadour* had run their runs, and given a second season, passing its 400th performance, with Mardayn and Eric Deutsch-Haupt in the lead rôles, on 8 October 1923 and closing after its 406th. Berlin's Metropoltheater production, which ran concurrently with the Vienna one, starred Mizzi Günther as Odette. If it did not equal its Vienna counterpart in success, it nevertheless swept past its 100th (29 May) and 150th (19 August) nights before closing after 176 performances and giving over the stage to a revue.

In Budapest, Ernő Kulinyi's adaptation of *A bajadér* was, again, a major hit. Produced at the Király Színház, it boasted two of the town's favourite feminine stars at its billhead: Sári Fedák as Odette and the young Hanna Honthy as Marietta, and with Marton Rátkai – the Louis Treumann of Budapest – as the Prince, and Jenő Nador (Napoléon) and Arpád Latabár (Louis-Philippe) in comical support, the show ran straight through its 100th performance (17 February 1923) and on to the beginning of May.

Die Bajadere soon appeared in Madrid (15 November 1923), but France was a little slower to take up the piece which was not seen until Charles Montcharmont's combination of agency and theatre-management got the French version of Bertal and Maubon, already seen in Brussels, to the stage in Lyon in 1925. Maguy Warna and Berlin's Herr Leonard headed the romance, Gabrielle Ristori, Urban and Robert Hasti the fun, and Montcharmont found a willing taker for the piece in the brothers Isola, who chose to open their management of the Théâtre Mogador with his production. Maria Kousnetzoff and Leonard (replaced by Mlle Warna and Edmond Tirmont in a recasting which gave increasingly stronger vocal values to Radjami's rôle), Urban and Mlle Ristori played through a run of just under three months.

Die Bajadere, curiously, largely missed the English-speaking areas of the world. London, where *The Gipsy Princess* had disappointed, failed to take it up and, by the time it was produced in America, under the management of Abe Erlanger, it had been thoroughly transformed by William Le Baron and Buddy De Sylva into *The Yankee Princess*. Vivienne Segal starred as the lady in question through 80 performances. *Die Bajadere* later appeared in New York in another disguise when it was given in a Yiddish version, as *Parisian Love* (Schulman-Goldberg Theater).

Die Bajadere reappeared in Vienna in 1929 (28 November) for a four-week season at the Johann Strauss-Theater with Annie Ahlers, Walter Jankuhn, Tilly Maganja and with Tautenhayn in his original rôle but, in spite of its enormous initial success, a score of Kálmán's finest, and a comical plotline superior to almost any other in the Viennese musical theatre of its time, the piece has slipped behind the other principal Kálmán Operetten in the repertoire during the latter years of the century. The rather dangling third act of the romantic half of the plot seems to be the only possible explanation, apart from fashion or misfortune.

The title *Die Bajadere* was earlier used for an Operette by Fritz Bernhard, produced at the Neues Theater, Mainz 15 January 1911.

Germany: Metropoltheater 18 February 1922; USA: Knickerbocker Theater *The Yankee Princess* 2 October 1922; Hungary: Király Színház *A bajadér* 10 November 1922; France: Théâtre des Célestins, Lyon *La Bayadère* 4 March 1925, Théâtre Mogador, Paris 30 January 1926

Recordings: Complete in Russian (Melodiya), selection in Hungarian (Qualiton), selection in Italian (Fonit-Cetra)

BAKER STREET

BAKER STREET Musical in 2 acts by Jerome Coopersmith based on the Sherlock Holmes stories of Arthur Conan Doyle. Music and lyrics by Marian Grudeff and Raymond Jessel. Broadway Theater, New York, 16 February 1965.

Following the success of *Oliver!*, English classic literature – especially anything containing children – was ripe for the musicalizing and Arthur Conan Doyle's all-deducing Sherlock Holmes soon fell into the basket. The Americo-Canadian musical *Baker Street* used pieces of three Conan Doyle tales to manufacture a libretto in which Holmes (Fritz Weaver) and Watson (Peter Sallis) pursued a Moriarty (Martin Gabel) who is out to steal Queen Victoria's Diamond Jubilee presents. It also managed to involve the traditionally misogynistic detective with a beautiful American actress (Inga Swenson). The juvenile element was represented by the Baker Street Irregulars, a band of Holmes-supportive urchins led by one Wiggins (Teddy Green). The detective and his side-kick pursued Moriarty through Oliver Smith's depictions of London's underworld, docklands and streets, via a representation of the Diamond Jubilee Parade done by the Bill Baird Marionettes, to a boat moored on the Thames, before disposing of the Professor over the white cliffs of Dover (the Reichenbach Falls were a little far from W1) and returning to London to an ending which withheld itself (just?) from pairing Holmes off with the actress. If several of the numbers were reminiscent of earlier shows, the score threw up one piece, the actress's 'Letters', which pleased.

Lavishly mounted, expertly publicized (street signs around Broadway pointed to 'Baker Street'), and strongly patronized in the early part of its run, Alexander H Cohen's production of *Baker Street* transferred to the Martin Beck Theatre (3 November 1965) and ended its run there after 313 performances.

The show did not play London, but London witnessed its own *Sherlock Holmes* (Cambridge Theatre, 24 April 1989 Leslie Bricusse) a quarter of a century later. Holmes again chased Moriarty round the sights of London, again got entangled with a feminine protagonist, and the Baker Street Irregulars again did cockney-kiddie song and dance, and, whilst a non-musical Holmes piece with neither children nor women prospered down the road, it foundered quickly.

A successful German Sherlock Holmes musical, entitled *Ein Fall für Sherlock Holmes* (Gerd Natschinski/Jürgen Degenhardt) and produced at the Städtische Bühnen, Erfurt 10 April 1982, left Moriarty, children and amorous ladies aside and instead based itself on *The Hound of the Baskervilles*, but Germany had apparently already solved the problem of getting feminine interest into Doyle's tales: in 1907 the Munich Volkstheater produced a piece written by the young Julius Brammer and 'A C Wald'

(Alfred Grünwald), music by one George Criketown, entitled *Fräulein Sherlock Holmes* (31 August).

Recordings: *Baker Street* original cast (MGM), *Ein Fall für Sherlock Holmes* (Amiga), *Sherlock Holmes* (RCA)

BAKONYI, Károly

BAKONYI, Károly (b Nagyvárad, 29 July 1873; d Budapest, 25 October 1926). Librettist to several of Hungary's all-time musical theatre hits.

Trained in the law, Bakonyi worked as an adviser at the Ministry of Agriculture and came to the forefront as an operettic librettist when he collaborated with Ferenc Martos on the text for Jenő Huszka's highly successful *Bob herceg*, an operett which treated the British royal family to much the same kind of romantic high-jinks that Western European shows imposed on the monarchs of Central European states. He had a second and even greater success when he authored the libretto for the exquisite fairy-tale piece *János vitéz*, which, as set with songs by Kacsoh and Heltai, would become the most beloved work of the Hungarian musical theatre.

Kacsoh's subsequent *Rákóczi* was another, if less enduring, success, but Bakonyi found fame beyond the confines of Hungary when he collaborated with another neophyte stage composer, Imre (later Emmerich) Kálmán, on the military operett *Tatárjárás* (*Ein Herbstmanöver*, *Autumn Manouevres*, *The Gay Hussars*) and again on a second piece with a military turn, *Az obsitos* (*Soldier Boy*, *Gold gab' ich für Eisen* etc).

In a remarkable run of quality pieces, he paired with Buttykay on a version of the Cinderella tale, with Kálmán on *A kis király* (*Der kleine König*), once more with Huszka on the successful *Nemtudomka* (*Die Patronesse vom Nachtcafé*, Theater in der Josefstadt 15 May 1915), and, finally, teamed with one further rising composer, Albert Szirmai, with whom he turned out the highly successful *Mágnás Miska* (*Der Pusztakavalier*) and *Gróf Rinaldo* (*Rinaldo*).

In a limited (for the time) and remarkable career in which he helped launch some of the period's most successful local composers, and during which he never suffered a single flop, Bakonyi was responsible for a wide diversity of works – from the fantastical to the military vaudeville and the low comical – amongst which were the libretti to many of the most important Hungarian musicals of his era.

1902 **Bob herceg** (Jenő Huszka/Ferenc Martos) Népszinház 20 December
1904 **János vitéz** (Pongrác Kacsoh/Jenő Heltai) Király Színház 18 November
1907 **Rákóczi** (Kacsoh/Sándor Endrődi, Árpád Pásztor) 20 November Király Szinház
1908 **Tatárjárás** (Imre Kálmán/Andor Gábor) Vígszinház 22 February
1910 **Az obsitos** (Kálmán) Vígszinház 16 March
1910 **Hamupipőke** (Ákos Buttykay/Imre Farkas, Gábor) Magyar Királyi Operaház 26 October
1914 **A kis király** (Kálmán/w Martos) Népopera 17 January
1914 **Nemtudomka** (Huszka/Zsolt Harsányi) Király Színház 14 January
1916 **Mágnás Miska** (Albert Szirmai/w Gábor) Király Színház 12 February
1918 **Gróf Rinaldo** (Szirmai) Király Színház 7 November

BALALAIKA

BALALAIKA Musical play in 3 acts by Eric Maschwitz, a revised version of *The Gay Hussar*. Music by George Posford and Bernard Grün. Adelphi Theatre, London, 22 December 1936.

The show which was to become *Balalaika* was produced by Julian Wylie for Moss' Empires and Howard & Wyndham's Tours as part of their drive to supply product to fill their chain of provincial theatres. *The Gay Hussar* (2 October 1933, Manchester) was the work of the BBC's Eric Maschwitz and George Posford who had combined in 1931 on the radio musical *Good Night, Vienna*, and there were distinct similarities in the plot outlines of the two pieces, both of which dealt with aristocrats reduced by war or revolution, yet finding true love triumphant through misfortune. The principal protagonists here were the Czarist aristocrat Count Peter Karagin and the ballerina Lydia Marakova, daughter of a prominent revolutionary who attempts to murder Karagin's princely father in his box during the ballet. When the revolution succeeds, Peter flees to Paris where, working as a waiter in the café 'The Gay Hussar', he is ultimately reunited with Lydia when the murderous Marakov is sent to Paris as Ambassador under the new régime.

The Gay Hussar was sent out on the road playing a then very unusual schedule of multiple weeks in a venue, as the huge revolve which was the basis of the show's principal scenic effect, a ballet within a show, had to travel by road and the extensive get-in time meant Monday openings were out. As a result, the production proved not to be viable and *The Gay Hussar* was not persevered with. Following the huge success of Ivor Novello's Drury Lane piece, *Glamorous Night*, Maschwitz rewrote his piece on similar lines, took in new numbers both from Posford (most notably the show's hit, 'At the Balalaika') and from Bernard Grün, and had it staged as *Balalaika* at the Adelphi Theatre by Novello's director, Leontine Sagan, and choreographer, Joan Davis, with costumes by René Hubert who had, likewise, done the costumes for Novello's most recent piece. Muriel Angelus starred as the ballerina opposite Novello-esque French actor Roger Tréville, and Clifford Mollison and Betty Warren were the soubrets alongside Jerrold Robertshaw (Prince Karagin) and Eric Marshall (Colonel Balakirev).

The spectacular and successful production was soon transferred to His Majesty's Theatre and it fulfilled the bulk of its 570 performances there, returning to the Adelphi for the last months of its run as a twice-nightly show in a version somewhat shortened from its original three and a half hours. It was subsequently produced in Australia, with Robert Halliday, Margaret Adams and Marjorie Gordon starred for a fine three months at Melbourne's Her Majesty's Theatre and almost as long at Sydney's Theatre Royal (18 December 1937), and in Paris in a vast production by Maurice Lehmann at the Théâtre Mogador. There the show's musical content was increased by four additional numbers (two foxtrots, a valse russe and a valse viennoise) by Robert Stolz, a top-up which brought the original short and rather fragmentary score, lacking in obvious 'numbers', up to proportions regarded as more conventional opérette à grand spectacle ones by Continental audiences. Réda Caire and Jacqueline Francell starred and the celebrated Jean Périer was the Prince, but the lavishly mounted piece held up for only a few months. However, whilst Britain has forgotten *Balalaika*, an even further adapted version (add mus: Jack Ledru) has remained firmly, if marginally, in the French repertoire up to the present day.

The score again came under the hands of the 'improvers' when Hollywood took up *Balalaika* – the first British musical to become the object of a Hollywood film – and produced it in 1939 with a cast headed by Nelson Eddy, Ilona Massey and Walter Woolf King. This time it was Sigmund Romberg and others whose work was added, although 'At the Balalaika' remained the show's musical feature. The film was in all probability the spur to an American production at the St Louis Muny in 1941, with Nancy McCord and Arthur Kent starred, a revival in 1943 with Marthe Errolle and Bob Lawrence, and another production, with Irene Manning starred, at the Pittsburgh Light Opera in 1947.

Australia: Her Majesty's Theatre, Melbourne 4 September 1937; France: Théâtre Mogador 24 September 1938; USA: Municipal Opera, St Louis 25 August 1941; Film: 1939

Recordings: selection WRC (Australia), film soundtrack (Caliban), selections in French (TLP, Polydor)

BALANCHINE, George [BALANCHIVADZE, Gyorgi Melitonovitch] (b St Petersburg, Russia, 9 January 1904; d New York, 30 April 1983).

Originally a choreographer with the Diaghilev ballet companies, Balanchine made his entry into the lighter forms of theatre when he designed the dances for two London revues (*Wake Up and Dream* (1929) and *Cochran's 1930 Revue*) produced by C B Cochran, and the Divertissement Pastorale, Divertissement des Songes et des Heures, Grand Ballet des Nymphes, Divertissement des Mouches, and Bacchanale for the Isola brothers' starry revival of *Orphée aux enfers* at the Théâtre Mogador (1931), before returning to the ballet world to create works for Colonel de Basil's company. In 1934 he moved to America, where he founded the American Ballet School and the New York Ballet Company and, in 1936, made his first appearance as a choreographer on Broadway when he contributed the dances to the revived *Ziegfeld Follies*.

Balanchine entered the musical comedy world later the same year when he devised the dances for the heavily choreographic Rodgers and Hart musical *On Your Toes* ('Slaughter on Tenth Avenue', 'Princess Zenobia', 'On Your Toes'), and then went on to choreograph a series of mostly more conventional Broadway shows from *Babes in Arms* (1937) through the dance-angled *I Married an Angel*, *The Boys From Syracuse* (1938), *Keep off the Grass*, *Louisiana Purchase*, *Cabin in the Sky* (1940), *The Lady Comes Across*, *Rosalinda* (1942), Lerner and Loewe's *What's Up?* (1943), *Dream with Music*, *Song of Norway* (1944), *Mr Strauss Goes to Boston* (1945), a revival of *The Chocolate Soldier* (1947) and *Where's Charley?* (1948) to his final *Courtin' Time* (1951).

His work was also seen in the screen version of *On Your Toes* as well as in such less storylined movies as *The Goldwyn Follies* (1938) and *Star Spangled Rhythm* (1942).

Biography: Taper, B: *Balanchine* (Harper and Row, New York, 1963)

BALFE, Michael [William] (b Dublin, 15 May 1808; d Rowney Abbey, Hants, 20 October 1870).

One of the most popular composers of what was, at the time, called English opera, Balfe began his musical career as a violinist, playing in public from the age of seven. At the age of nine, he composed accompanying music for T H Bayley's *The Lover's Mistake*, by 16 he was conducting the orchestra at the Theatre Royal, Drury Lane, and at 19 he appeared on the Paris stage in the rôle of Rossini's Figaro.

Balfe's earliest operas were written in imitation of Italian models and staged in Italy, during his stay there between 1829–31, but he subsequently returned to Britain, where the rest of his works found a ready public, establishing him at the forefront of British theatrical composers. He had early successes with such pieces as *The Siege of Rochelle* and *The Maid of Artois*, set Scribe and de Leuven's text for *Le Puits d'amour* (UK: *Geraldine*) for production at Paris's Opéra-Comique in 1843, and later the same year had his most memorable success with the romantic opera *The Bohemian Girl* ('I Dreamt I Dwelt in Marble Halls').

The Enchantress (1845), *The Rose of Castille* (1857) and *Satanella* (1858) were others of his works which, with *The Bohemian Girl* and such pieces as Wallace's *Maritana* and Benedict's *The Lily of Killarney*, formed a solid part of the baggage of the English operatic companies of the middle years of the 19th century, travelling to English-language houses across the world in repertoires with translations of the most popular works of Bellini, Rossini and their Continental fellows and, often, a leavening of burlesques.

Sentimental, romantic dramas in their text, these pieces were set with music which was in no way as demanding as that of either the Italian classic operas, nor the more verismo pieces which would follow, and they would certainly have attracted the label 'light opera' in later days. It was a quality which undoubtedly added to their popularity, and only in the absence of an obvious comic element did these pieces differ from the light operatic pieces of the second half of the century.

In post-Hervé and Offenbach days, with the light musical theatre well established in fashion, pieces such as *The Bohemian Girl*, *The Rose of Castille* and the made-over *Letty, the Basketmaker* still remained in the repertoire alongside the newer style of musical play.

Biography: Barrett, W A: *Balfe: His Life and Works* (Remington & Co, London, 1882)

BALKANLIEBE (aka *Die Gräfin von Durazzo*) Operette in 2 acts by E Kahr and Bruno Hardt-Warden. Music by Rudolf Kattnigg. Neues Operetten-Theater, Leipzig, 22 December 1937.

Deposed Prince Marko Franjipan gallivants from the Illyrian countryside to the Hotel Excelsior in Venice, an evening on the Grand Canal and a winter sports venue in the Austrian alps on his way to regaining his throne from the Countess of Durazzo. On the way, he falls in love with her, but it turns out that the 'Countess' who has enraptured him is not the Countess at all but his affianced Zlata (Trude Colln), daughter of the helpful bandit Branko Juranitsch, who has captured the monarch and taken her place.

First mounted in Leipzig under the title *Die Gräfin von Durazzo*, this flashy, latter-day piece of Ruritanian romance, set with a lively if conventional score, has been one of the few German-language musicals since the 1930s to have gained any attention on home stages and to have won the honours of a commercial recording.

Recording: selection (Ariola-Eurodisc)

THE BALKAN PRINCESS Musical play in 3 acts by Frederick Lonsdale and Frank Curzon. Lyrics by Paul Rubens and Arthur Wimperis. Music by Paul Rubens.

Prince of Wales Theatre, London, 19 February 1910.

Following Lonsdale's trend-setting *King of Cadonia*, his second musical for producer Frank Curzon took the same Ruritanian themes of love and royal duty, which would later become internationally and exhaustingly popular, and this time reversed the sexes to allow producer's wife Isabel Jay to take the royal title-rôle. Her *King of Cadonia* co-star, Bertram Wallis, was the politically unstable Grand Duke whom she converts and weds. Princess Stephanie, refusing five potential husbands proposed by her ministers, goes out in disguise and catches the sixth and only other possible, Sergius, spreading revolution. She has him arrested, abdicates rather than be forced into marriage with any of the five, but is restored to the throne when the impressed Sergius abandons his anti-royalist stance to stand by her side. A comic sub-plot had two *Erminie*-type thieves (Lauri de Frece, Charles Brown) masquerading as an eligible duke and his servant, and the former becoming entangled with the 'widowed' palace charwoman (Mabel Sealby) whose husband (James Blakeley) is actually working at the restaurant where Sergius foments his revolution.

Paul Rubens's score was much less substantial than the Sidney Jones music for the earlier piece, giving the new musical a lighter flavour than *King of Cadonia*, and the comical characters' numbers came out better than some rather weak attempts at Daly's Theatre-style baritone and soprano material. However, *The Balkan Princess* proved distinctly popular, running for six months in London (176 performances) in the shadow of *The Arcadians*, *The Dollar Princess* and *Our Miss Gibbs*, before going on to an 111-performance run on Broadway, under the management of the Shubert brothers. Robert Warwick and Louise Gunning were the royal couple in New York, Percy Ames, Teddy Webb and May Boley headed the fun, and the piece was well-enough thought of to win a burlesque at Joe Weber's house as the 'canned comedy' *The Balky Princess* (Charles Brown, 17 April 1911), a piece which borrowed Rubens's tunes as its musical part.

Although it was scarcely an outstanding piece, something about *The Balkan Princess* pleased producers and the show proved remarkably tenacious. It was successfully produced in Australia, under the J C Williamson banner, with Florence Young and Frank Greene in the romantic rôles and Bert Gilbert, Lottie Sargent and W S Percy in charge of the comedy (and 'I Wonder Who's Kissing Her Now' squeezed into the score), it appeared in South Africa and on the Oriental circuits, and it even surfaced at Budapest's Király Színház (ad Andor Gábor) just weeks after the end of the London run. And to top it all, *The Balkan Princess* had a hardy touring life in Britain, a life which saw it still on the circuits 25 years after its first production.

Hungary: Király Színház *A balkani hercegnő* 23 September 1910; USA: Herald Square Theater 9 February 1911; Australia: Theatre Royal, Sydney 10 June 1911

BALL, Lucille [Désirée] (b Celoron, NY, 6 August 1911; d Los Angeles, 26 April 1989).

The redheaded comedienne and star of TV's long-popular *I Love Lucy* appeared only once on the musical stage when she took the star rôle in the 1960 musical *Wildcat* ('Hey, Look Me Over'). However, in her more natural habitat, on film, after early appearances in chorus, bit parts and increasing rôles in the early 1930s (*Roberta*, *Top Hat*, *Follow the Fleet*), Ball starred in the filmed versions of the stage musicals *Too Many Girls* (1940, Consuelo Casey), *Dubarry Was a Lady* (1943, May Daly), *Best Foot Forward* (1943, herself) and *Mame* (1970, Mame).

Miss Ball's daughter **Lucie [Désirée] ARNAZ** (b 17 July 1951) starred on Broadway in *They're Playing Our Song* (Sonia Walsk).

Biography: Gregory, J: *The Lucille Ball Story* (New American Library, New York, 1974), Sanders, C S & Gilbert, T: *Desilu* (W H Morrow, New York, 1993)

BALL, Michael (b Stratford-on-Avon, 27 June 1963).

After initial work in provincial theatres (*Sweet Charity*, *Godspell*), the strapping young tenor won the rôle of Frederic in a Manchester production of *The Pirates of Penzance*, from which he moved swiftly to London to create the rôle of Marius in the English version of *Les Misérables* ('Empty Chairs and Empty Tables').

He went on from there to succeed to the rôle of Raoul in London's *The Phantom of the Opéra* and subsequently created the part of Alex in *Aspects of Love*, introducing 'Love Changes Everything' which, in his version, reached number two on the British charts. He followed the London production by repeating his rôle on Broadway (1990).

In 1992 he represented Britain in the Eurovision Song contest in a career increasingly angled towards pop music.

THE BALLET GIRL Musical comedy in 2 acts by James T Tanner. Lyrics by Adrian Ross. Music by Carl Kiefert. Additional songs by Leslie Stuart and B Luard Selby. Grand Theatre, Wolverhampton, 15 March 1897.

This British musical, with its words prepared by the practised Gaiety Theatre team of Tanner and Ross and music by the West End's favourite orchestrator, Carl Kiefert, had the unusual distinction of being shown on Broadway without having been given a West End run. It moved on swiftly from its New York date, but had a successful touring career both in Britain and America. The British production introduced three songs by Leslie Stuart to leaven Kiefert's conventional score. The American score introduced several numbers by the show's producer, Edward E Rice.

USA: Manhattan Theater 21 December 1897

BALL IM SAVOY Operette in a Vorspiel and 3 acts by Alfred Grünwald and Fritz Löhner-Beda. Music by Pál Ábrahám. Grosses Schauspielhaus, Berlin, 23 December 1932.

The third of Ábrahám's successive trio of major hits, *Ball im Savoy* followed the example set by *Die Blume von Hawaii* by being first presented in Germany.

After the Japanese, Russian and South Pacific venues of the two earlier shows, the new piece went for its colourful location to the slightly more operettically conventional Venice, Nice and Paris, and its action and characters were correspondingly less extravagant. The ball of the title took place at the Savoy Hotel in Nice, where the Argentinian dancer Tangolita (Trude Berliner) sets out to rendezvous with her former lover, the Marquis Aristide de Faublas (Arthur Schröder) in spite of the fact he is on his honeymoon. With the help of the Turkish attaché, Mustapha Bey (Oszkár Dénes), Aristide sets himself up for a titillating night on the dance-floor, but Madelaine (Gitta Alpár), the Marquis's new wife, sees through the men's tricks and she turns up at the Savoy herself, setting the ball alight with scandal as she flirts outrageously with the young Célestin Formant (Victor de Kowa), leading her despairing husband to horrified thoughts of divorce. They are safely in Paris by the time he finds out that it was all a put-up job.

Like the locales and tale, the score for the piece was a little less exotic than before, but the mixture of traditional and modern which had made such an appeal in the earlier shows was the same. On the traditional side, Gitta Alpár triumphed with her soprano 'Toujours l'amour', whilst the modern side proved equally winning. Rózsi Bársony, cast in the rôle of Daisy Parker, a jazz composer, was glued into the proceedings rather as the Jim Boy of *Die Blume von Hawaii* had been, to allow for some of the lightly jazzy numbers in which Ábrahám specialized. Dénes delivered a 'Wenn wir Türken Küssen', there was a tango in praise of 'La Belle Tangolita' and the piece's strivings towards an international flavour brought forth a paso doble about 'Sevilla' and a slow-fox entitled 'O Mister Brown!'

A vast success in Berlin, the show hung on when 1933 struck, in spite of its composer's and its star's unwanted Jewishness, and at the same time it quickly moved out towards other productions. London, which had enjoyed *Viktória* but had not taken up *Die Blume von Hawaii*, was the first to mount its version. *Ball at the Savoy* (ad Oscar Hammerstein II) featured Dénes and Bársony in their original rôles alongside Maurice Evans and Natalie Hall as the spouses of the piece, Hammerstein directed, and the piece followed a successfully imported and luxuriantly staged version of *Wenn die kleinen Veilchen blühen* (*Wild Violets*) into the Theatre Royal, Drury Lane. In spite of the two clever Hungarians, it ran just half as long as the Stolz piece, folding in 148 performances as Drury Lane plunged into the tenuous position from which only Ivor Novello would eventually rescue it.

Hungary not unsurprisingly gave the piece (ad Jenő Heltai) a better reception. Hilda Harmath and Jenő Törzs appeared as the principals of the action, with Mária Lázár as the naughty dancer, but once again it was the sub-ordinate rôles with their jazzy melodies which drew the greatest applause: Gyula Kabos as Mustafa, and the ebullient Marika Rökk as Daisy. In Vienna, this prized pair of rôles were taken by Irén von Ziláhy and Curt Bois in Rudolf Beer's production at the old Johann Strauss-Theater, which was now called the Scala Theater. Egon von Jordan and Mary Losseff played the nominal leads and Hans Thimig was the young decoy. Rózsi Bársony arrived during the run to guest as Daisy, but the show's slightly disappointing run of under three months did not solve the failing theatre's problems.

If Vienna got Bársony, Australia got the other half of the family and the partnership when J C Williamson Ltd took husband Dénes to Sydney to play his original rôle alongside Mabel Gibson/Marie Bremner (Madelaine), Nellie Barnes (Daisy), Robert Coote (Célestin), James Raglan/Sydney Burchall (Aristide) and Cecil Kellaway through four weeks in Sydney and a bare month in Melbourne (5 October 1935).

Although *Ball im Savoy* disappointed in its English version, it nevertheless remained a favourite in Central Europe. It was revived at Budapest's Fővárosi Operettszinház 16 January 1948 and 23 April 1965, and in 1962 Marika Rökk once again took up the part she had played in the Hungarian première, 30 years earlier, in a revival at Vienna's Raimundtheater. The show had been made over by Hugo Wiener into two acts (still with the Venetian prologue), and the star was supported in the plotworthier rôles by Margit Bollmann, Spiro Makri and Franco Steinberg. Rökk was seen as Daisy as late as 1983 ('eine jazz-komponistin' can, after all, be any age) in a rare example of an artist appearing in one and the same rôle half a century on.

A 1936 film version featured Conrad Nagel and Marta Labarr, whilst a second, in 1954, featured Rudolf Prack and Eva Ingeborg Scholz in the leads, Bibi Johns as Daisy, Rudolf Platte as Mustafa and Nadja Tiller as Tangolita. It allowed a certain Herren Gietz and Gaze loose on the music, and director Paul Martin and Franz Tassié souped up a book which got Daisy rather more into the action than originally, as well as into an apropos of nothing 'Musik-Show' which also featured Caterina Valente, John Bubbles and the Three Peiheros.

UK: Theatre Royal, Drury Lane *Ball at the Savoy* 8 September 1933; Hungary: Magyar Színház *Bál a Savoyban* 23 December 1933; Austria: Scala Theater 25 December 1933; Australia: Theatre Royal, Sydney *Ball at the Savoy* 6 July 1935; Films: 1936, Central-Europa Film 1954

EINE BALLNACHT Operette in 3 acts by Leopold Jacobson and Robert Bodanzky. Music by Oscar Straus. Johann Strauss-Theater, Vienna, 11 October 1918.

There was little that was new in Jacobson and Bodanzky's libretto for Oscar Straus's 1918 Operette *Eine Ballnacht*. The ingénue was Countess Edith, niece to the old Graf Clemens Ortendorff, and destined in marriage for Count Harry, nephew to the equally aristocratic Fürst Gregor Gerolsheim, a young man whom she has never seen. The soubrette was the little shopgirl Riki Schöngruber who, although engaged to the commis Willi Höfer, goes to the ball of the title in Edith's place, and the usual ensuing complications and comicalities filled the remainder of the evening before everyone ended up happily in their arms of their predestined ones at the third-act curtain.

Straus provided a pretty score to this tale, made up of a vertebral number of waltzes, varied by polka, galop and other bouncy dance rhythms. Riki and Harry drew the prettiest waltz tune with their 'Wie nett war's, könnten Sie vergessen', but of the 3/4 melodies it was Willi's first act opener 'Ach! Was haben wir Frau'n für Sorgen' which was plugged most diligently through the evening. Riki had the most prominent moments of the score, sharing a dance duo with Clemens and a march duo and another waltz with Willi, whilst the ingénue rôle had its best moment in another dancing number (w Harry), 'Ich möchte mit Ihnen allein sein'.

The show won through by its tunes and by the manner of its telling rather than by any interesting elements in its tired tale, and it ran through a healthy season at Vienna's Johann Strauss-Theater. It did even better in Berlin, however. It was seen for more than 250 performances during the 1919–20 season under Heinz Saltenberg's management at the Wallner-Theater and the Komische Oper, with Kathe Dörsch starred as Riki, before going on to join *Ein Walzertraum* and *Der letzte Walzer* at the head of the list of Straus's most played works in Germany. In Hungary (ad Imre Harmath), the rôle of Riki fell to another outstanding young artist, the rising soubrette Hanna Honthy, in a satisfactory production at the Revü Színház.

Doubtless partly handicapped by its origins, at a time when German works were unwelcome outside Europe, *Eine Ballnacht* did not, however, go further and did not succeed in establishing itself in the revived repertoire.

Germany: Wallner-Theater 1919; Hungary: Revü Színház *A bálkirálynő* 29 January 1921

BANDITENSTREICHE Comic opera in 1 act by B Boutonnier. Music by Franz von Suppé. Carltheater, Vienna, 27 April 1867.

Suppé's short comic opera *Banditenstreiche*, produced at the Carltheater in 1867, was a disappointment. Its little tale of a swashbuckling bandit who helps a pair of young lovers to outwit the girl's ambitious father was illustrated by some fine Suppé music, but the piece did not win anything like the success of his *Das Pensionat*, *Die schöne Galathee*, *Flotte Bursche*, *Leichte Cavallerie* or *Zehn Mädchen und kein Mann*. It was put on the shelf whilst the Carltheater continued to play the older Suppé pieces or such favourites as *Mannschaft am Bord*, *Des Löwen Erwachen* or *Der Meisterschuss von Pottenstein*. In 1874, after Offenbach's *Die Banditen* had been seen in Vienna, an attempt was made to revive it, in a revised version (2 August), but the exercise lasted just 3 performances.

Two attempts have been subsequently made to build full-sized Suppé pasticcios around the *Banditenstreiche* text and score. The first, by that determined adaptor Gustave Quedtenfeldt and Otto Urak, was introduced at Nuremberg (25 February 1940) and the second by Ludwig Bender and Peter Waldenmaier 15 years later at Trier (28 April 1955).

BANÈS, Antoine [Anatole] (b Paris, 8 June 1856; d Paris, 10 January 1924).

Conservatoire-trained Banès made a career as a composer of light music whilst holding posts as an archivist at, and later administrator adjoint of, the Paris Opéra library (1911sq) and also working as a music critic for the *Nation* and, after the war, the *Figaro*. The most successful of his stage works – largely written in the earlier part of his career – was the internationally popular *Toto* (1892). Bilhaud and Barré's double-travesty musical comedy with its highly grateful star rôle ran an excellent 129 performances on its first Paris production and was subsequently played in Germany and Austria (*Tata-Toto*), Hungary (*Toto és Tata*), Britain, and at New York's Irving Place Theatre in its German translation as well as in a vernacular version on the regular Broadway stage.

Banès's subsequent works, although often written with proven authors, were reckoned by some to have owed a large part of their relative failure to unattractive libretti, but he scored a small success with the production of *Léda* at

73

the Monte-Carlo Opera House, under the management of Pierre Comte-Offenbach, and saw his *Le Roi frelon* win foreign productions at Budapest's Fővárosi Nyari Színház as *Korhelykirály* (20 September 1901 ad Emil Makai, Ferenc Molnár) and as *Pick und Pocket* in German (ad Hans Brennert, Erich Urban, add mus Bogumil Zepler) at the Belle Alliance Theater, Berlin (21 March 1903). His *Le Nouveau Regiment* was staged at Vienna's Theater in der Josefstadt (*Das neue Regiment* ad Heinrich Bolten-Bäckers, 12 October 1898) following its original Paris season and his *Le Bonhomme de neige* was dressed up as a Christmas pantomime for London audiences as *The Snowman* (Lyceum, 21 December 1899 additional music: Walter Slaughter).

His other works included two short pieces given at the Opéra Comique, an 'operatorio', *L'Arche de Noë*, staged at Marseille in 1911, a number of ballets and pantomimes for Parisian and provincial stages, and a one-act play *La Lyre brisée*, produced at Le Havre in 1878 (6 October).

1882 **Un do malade** (Pittaud de Forges, 'Laurencin') 1 act Eldorado 9 September

1883 **La Cadiguette** (Louis Péricaud, Lemoine) 1 act Eldorado 3 November

1884 **L'Escargot** (Paul Adely, Albert Barré) 1 act Eldorado 19 April

1884 **La Jarretière** (Adely, Barré) 1 act Eldorado 27 September

1885 **Au coq huppé** (Germain Villemer, Lucien Delormel) Eldorado 21 March

1887 **Les Délégués** (Émile Blavet, Fabrice Carré) Théâtre des Nouveautés 30 November

1892 **Toto** (Bilhaud, Barré) Théâtre des Menus-Plaisirs 10 June

1893 **Madame Rose** (Bilhaud, Barré) 1 act Opéra-Comique 25 September

1894 **Le Bonhomme de neige** (Henri Chivot, Alfred Vanloo) Théâtre des Bouffes-Parisiens 19 April

1895 **Le Roi frelon** (Barré) Théâtre des Folies-Dramatiques 11 April

1896 **Une nuit d'amour** (Maxime Boucheron, Barré) Théâtre des Bouffes-Parisiens 11 May

1897 **Le Nouveau Regiment** (aka *Mademoiselle Portez-Arme*) (Barré, E Martin, Henri Bernard) Olympia 12 March

1899 **La Pomme d'Adam** (Lucien Augé de Lassus) 1 act Casino, Trouville 25 August

1901 **La Soeur de Jocrisse** (Vanloo) 1 act Opéra-Comique 9 July

1909 **Léda** (Pierre Veber, Augé de Lassus) Théâtre de Monte-Carlo 17 April

1911 **Les Gabelous** (Barré) Théâtre des Variétés, Marseille 4 November

BANTOCK, [Ernest] Leedham [S] (b London, 1870; d Richmond, 15 October 1928).

A useful character man in George Edwardes's companies for 20 years, appearing in secondary roles in such London pieces as *A Gaiety Girl* (1893, Harry Fitzwarren, t/o Bobbie Rivers), *An Artist's Model* (1895, t/o James Cripps), *The Geisha* (1896, Arthur Cuddy), *San Toy* (1894, t/o The Emperor), *The School Girl* (1903, t/o Tubby Bedford), *A Country Girl* (1902, Douglas Verity), *The Cingalee* (1904, t/o Boobhamba) and *Lady Madcap* (1906, Col Layton) as well as in America and Australia (Hopkins in *In Town*, Bertie Boyd in *The Shop Girl*, Dawson in *Gentleman Joe*, Sir Lewis in *A Gaiety Girl*). Bantock also worked as both a director (notably for Marie Lloyd's only venture into the musical theatre, *The ABC* (1898)) and as an author, collaborating on the libretti for several success-

ful musical comedies composed by Howard Talbot, the most fruitful of which was George Edwardes's production of *The Girl Behind the Counter*. He also won an international hearing with the mini-musical *The White Chrysanthemum*, produced by Frank Curzon, and with *The Belle of Brittany*, mounted by Tom B Davis, both of which, like *The Girl Behind the Counter*, won good runs in town and country in Britain and several overseas productions.

Bantock's brother, **Granville BANTOCK** (b London, 7 August 1868; d London, 16 October 1946), celebrated and knighted in later life as a composer and conductor of serious music and an arts administrator, also worked in the light musical theatre in the early part of his career. He composed interpolated numbers for several West End shows (*Monte Carlo* 'Who'll Give a Penny to the Monkey' etc), wrote the bulk of the score for Marie Lloyd's touring vehicle *The ABC or Flossie the Frivolous* (w others/ 'Richard Henry' Grand Theatre, Wolverhampton 21 March 1898), and was musical director of George Edwardes's musical comedy company, touring America and Australia in 1894–5 with *A Gaiety Girl*, *The Shop Girl*, *In Town* and *Gentleman Joe*. He also co-authored a book describing this tour which remains an enjoyable record of life in the Victorian musical theatre (*Around the World with 'A Gaiety Girl'* w F Aflalo, John Macqueen, 1896).

Biography: Bantock, M: *Granville Bantock; A Personal Portrait* (Dent, London, 1972)

1905 **The White Chrysanthemum** (Howard Talbot/w Arthur Anderson) Criterion Theatre 31 August

1906 **The Girl Behind the Counter** (Talbot/w Anderson) Wyndham's Theatre 21 April

1907 **The Three Kisses** (Talbot/w Percy Greenbank) Apollo Theatre 21 August

1908 **The Belle of Brittany** (Talbot/w P J Barrow) Queen's Theatre 24 October

1909 **The Persian Princess** (Sidney Jones/Greenbank/w Barrow) Queen's Theatre 27 April

1917 **Physical Culture** (w Harold Simpson) 1 act Metropolitan 30 April

BARBE-BLEUE Opéra-bouffe in 3 acts by Henri Meilhac and Ludovic Halévy. Music by Jacques Offenbach. Théâtre des Variétés, Paris, 5 February 1866.

After their enormous success with *La Belle Hélène* at the Théâtre des Variétés, the Meilhac–Halévy–Offenbach team followed up with a burlesque of another favourite old tale, that of the gruesomely oversexed and apparently necrophiliac Chevalier Raoul, commonly known as Bluebeard, and his string of murdered wives. By the time Meilhac and Halévy had finished having their fun with Perrault's version of the bloody, revengeful tale, it had rather a different ring to it.

Bluebeard's last and avenging wife, the ladylike Fatima of the legend, became, in the burlesque, a bubbling country wench of burstingly obvious charms and indifferent morals called Boulotte (Hortense Schneider). She attracts the attentions of the many-wived local overlord, the Sire de Barbe-bleue (José Dupuis), when, against all justice, she wins the raffle for the virginal post of rosière and, unaware of the fate of her predecessors, she is delighted to find herself lined up for such an advantageous match. Boulotte, however, has to share Meilhac and Halévy's plotline with the area's obsessively jealous over-

overlord, King Bobèche (Kopp), a monarch who has the habit of executing courtiers who look too appreciatively at his Queen, Clémentine (Aline Duval), and with the complex family affairs of this curious royal family. The helpful courtier Count Oscar (Grenier) rediscovers Princess Hermia (Mlle Vernet), the baby daughter the royals exposed when they thought they had a son, living disguised as a florist in Boulotte's village, and her favourite shepherd Saphir (Paul Hittemans) turns out, in the best operettic tradition, to be the prince she is scheduled to marry. All would be well did not Bluebeard now decide that he prefers Hermia to Boulotte. He arranges with his alchemist, Popolani (Henri Couder), to dispose of Boulotte, and sets off to besiege the defenceless Bobèche (who has melted down all his guns to make statues) into giving him Hermia. But Nemesis is nigh. Popolani hasn't killed any of Bluebeard's previous wives, but kept them all stashed away, alive, for his own entertainment, and Count Oscar hasn't executed Clémentine's admirers either. They are all hidden in the royal basement. Boulotte leads the undead in the exposure of the nasty habits of the two potentates, and drags Blubeard home by the ear to live unhappily ever after.

Offenbach's score to the deliciously comical text of his collaborators was as sparkling as its predecessor. Barbe-bleue stalked the countryside declaring in the quickly famous Légende de Barbe-bleue: 'Je suis Barbe-bleue, ô gué, jamais veuf ne fut plus gai...', gaily condemned Boulotte to her death ('Le voilà donc, le tombeau'/'Vous avez vu ce monument') and threatened Bobèche tenoriously with his cannons ('J'ai pas bien loin dans la montagne'), but it was the prima donna who had the showiest rôle. She began as a saucy country lass ('Y'a des bergers dans le village') elected May Queen, got to play both a maiden under threat of murder ('Pierre, un beau jour, parvint') and a death scene ('Hola! Hola! ça me prend là!') in the second act, and invaded Bobèche's court disguised as a gipsy in the third ('Nous possédons'). The ingénue florist turned Princess was equipped with two numbers, her mother with one, and the piece also included a goodly amount of bristling choruses – notably a decidedly pointed one of fawning courtiers – to make up a score which bubbled with burlesque gaiety.

Barbe-bleue thoroughly confirmed the success of *La Belle Hélène* and ran through five solid months up to the summer recess. The week that it closed, the first of what were to be countless international productions throughout the next decade opened, at London's Olympic Theatre (ad H Bellingham) under the management and direction of Horace Wigan. Presented as an English-style burlesque, squashed up into a four-scene jollification of comedy under the title *Bluebeard Re-paired* and subtitled 'a worn out story done up a-new' it announced its score as 'the music composed by Offenbach, selected and arranged by J H Tully'. William Terrott in a Scots version of the title-rôle and Susan Galton as Mopsa (ex-Boulotte), with two future stars in Harriet Everard (Queen Greymare) and Nellie Farren (Robert) in supporting rôles, led the company through the month and a bit to the end of the season, playing *Bluebeard* as an after-piece to *The Lady of Lyons*.

Friedrich Strampfer and Vienna's Theater an der Wien followed with a rather less hacked-about *Blaubart* (ad Julius Hopp) a few months later, using many of the team that had won such a triumph with *Die schöne Helena* the previous year. Marie Geistinger and Albin Swoboda swapped the roles of Helen and Paris for those of Boulotte and Bluebeard in the same way that Schneider and Dupuis had done in Paris, Karl Blasel went from Menelaos to Bobèche, Carl Adolf Friese from Agamemnon to Oscar and Matthias Rott from Calchas to Popolani. The newly discovered voice of Jani Szika was put to use as Saphir. The success of the earlier piece was at least partly repeated and, although *Blaubart* would never equal the outstanding record of *Die schöne Helena* in the German language, the show was played in repertoire through the 1870s and was brought back at the Carltheater in 1887 with Geistinger starred alongside Alexander Guttmann (Bobèche), Adolf Brackl (Barbe-bleue) and Antonie Link (Hermia), in 1897–8, and again in 1902. Hopp's German version was readapted by Emil Pohl for Berlin's Friedrich-Wilhelm-städtisches Theater, which welcomed Josefine Gallmeyer as its original Boulotte.

Hungary, although a little slow off the mark, also reserved a fine welcome for *Kékszakállu herceg* when Endre Latabár's version was produced first at Kassa and then in Budapest – where the German version had already been seen – with Ilka Medgyaszay and Halmi (another pair who had introduced *La Belle Hélène* locally) starred. In 1873 a major new production with Lujza Blaha (Boulotte) and János Kápolnai (Barbe-bleue) was mounted in Budapest, and this star pair later played the piece at the Népszinház as it settled comfortably into the Hungarian Offenbach repertoire.

New York got its first *Barbe-bleue* in French, with Mlle Irma appearing as Boulotte to the Barbe-bleue of Aujac, and Marie Aimée made Boulotte a regular character in her repertoire during her years of touring America with French opéra-bouffe, but it was not until 1875 that Broadway got an English-language production of the piece, and then it was a decidedly hacked-about one. Alexander Henderson and Samuel Colville starred Julia Mathews in what they called *Boulotte* alongside Alfred Brennir, G H McDermott and Haydn Corri in a version which chopped around Offenbach's score and even popped in some bits of Strauss's *Indigo und die vierzig Räuber*. It was played for a fortnight on Broadway in repertoire with the more popular *Grande-Duchesse* and *Giroflé-Girofla*.

Australia did not get its first *Barbe-bleue* until 1872, when the Lyster & Cagli company introduced the piece in their Melbourne and Sydney seasons. Alice May (Boulotte), Richard Stewart (Bobèche), Armes Beaumont (Barbe-bleue) and T H Rainford (Popolani) featured amongst the cast of a production which was followed, in years to come, by many another as *Barbe-bleue* became, as elsewhere, a standard part of the revivable opéra-bouffe repertoire in Australia.

In Paris, *Barbe-bleue* was brought back in 1872 with Dupuis and Schneider, who had in between times given London their original characterizations in a visit to the St James's Theatre (28 June 1869), repeating their now famous rôles, whilst an 1888 revival gave Jeanne Granier the opportunity to play Boulotte on the same stage and opposite the same leading man as her illustrious predecessor, followed in 1904 by Anna Tariol-Baugé. The most recent Parisian production, in 1971 at the Théâtre de Paris, was of a foolishly revised version souped up to create a starring rôle where none was before, but *Barbe-bleue* has subsequently been seen in its original form outside Paris.

Apart from its home city, it was London, which actually gave the piece more hearings than either *Orphée aux enfers* or *La Belle Hélène*, which proved the most interested in *Barbe-bleue* in the decades after its production. After Schneider and Dupuis's visit in 1869, a new and more faithful English version of the show (ad Charles Lamb Kenney) was mounted at the Standard Theatre with Emily Soldene as a bosomy, mezzo-soprano Boulotte and Wilford Morgan as Bluebeard, and that version was taken up by John Hollingshead at the Gaiety, the following year, where Julia Mathews and E D Beverley starred. Miss Soldene, who had replaced composer Hervé as Chilpéric in his show's London production, later renounced the rôle of Boulotte and gave Australian audiences her interpretation of the title-rôle of *Barbe-bleue*. In the 1880s, the popular couple Florence St John and Claude Marius (Bobèche) found in the piece a vehicle for their highly effective talents and appeared in the show, with Henry Bracy as their Bluebeard, at both the Avenue Theatre (16 June 1883) and the Comedy (16 January 1885) before *Bluebeard* went into suspended animation. It was brought out in 1966 when the Sadler's Wells Opera Company continued its memorable series of Geoffrey Dunn translations, in a staging by Gillian Lynne which remained several seasons in the repertoire.

Germany has similarly shown an enduring fancy for *Blaubart* (aka *Ritter Blaubart*). A 1929 Metropoltheater production by Fritz Friedmann-Friedrich with Leo Slezak starred as the randy Ritter alongside the Boulotte of Käthe Dorsch was taken to Vienna in 1930 with Slezak, Grete Finkler, Fritz Imhoff (Bobèche) and Hanns Wilhelm (Popolani) featured, and in 1963 the Berlin Komische Oper mounted a highly successful production of a revised version (*Ritter Blaubart*), with Anny Schlemm as a bubbling Boulotte. This has led to regular further German stagings of an opéra-bouffe which, in spite of all its extravagant charms, remains today firmly in the shadow of *Orphée aux enfers* and *La Belle Hélène*.

The originally gory tale of an oriental wife-killer whose last spouse survives and proves his undoing is found in many cultures, but it has come down to the modern Western world through Perrault's *Histoires et contes du temps passé* (otherwise *Contes de ma mère l'Oye*) as originally translated into English by Robert Samber. It found its way on to the stage in many different versions from spectacular melodrama to musical extravaganza, of which Offenbach's has survived as by far the most memorable, but of which several others found success in their time. André Grétry's 1789 'heroic comic-opera' *[Raoul] Barbe-bleue* (lib: Jean-Michel Sedaine), played in German as *Raoul der Blaubart*, was an early success and it was followed by the first English-language stage musical versions: a 1791 pantomime at Covent Garden written by George Colman, and a 1798 Drury Lane 'musical dramatic romance' with music by Michael Kelly. Paris later welcomed a 16-scene féerie *Barbe-bleue* by Alphonse Keller at the Funambules in 1851 (23 August), and a verse piece, *Sept Femmes de Barbe-bleue*, in 1852, whilst another féerie of that same title by Anicet-Bourgeois and Masson was produced, at the Théâtre Beaumarchais, two seasons later (23 April 1854).

Bluebeard remained a favourite British pantomime topic for a century, whilst also coming into the hands of the burlesque makers. There was a *Bluebeard* parody as early as 1839, and later efforts included the 1853 *Hints to the Curious, or Bluebeard according to Act of Parliament* at the Strand Theatre, H J Byron's *Bluebeard from a new point of hue* (Adelphi Theatre 26 December 1860), a Crystal Palace piece (29 March 1869), *The Latest Edition of Bluebeard* (Alexandra Theatre May 1870), H B Farnie's celebrated burlesque *Bluebeard, or the Mormon, the Maiden and The Little Militaire* for Lydia Thompson, played by her throughout Britain and America, a *Bluebeard Retrimmed* (Royal Park Theatre May 1877), F C Burnand's Gaiety piece *Bluebeard, or the hazard of the dye* (12 March 1883) and J Pitt Hardacre's touring *Bluebeard-up-to-Date* (1893). In America, where the subject was long a favourite as a mid-19th-century circus production, Fred Eustis, Richard Maddern and Clay M Greene brought out a *Bluebeard jr* in Chicago (11 June 1889) and at New York's Niblo's Garden in the following year (13 January 1890).

The 20th century has rather seen the man with the overly replaceable wives go rather out of fashion, but in 1918 Béla Bartók turned out the most famous of operatic *Bluebeards* with *A kékszakállú herceg vára (Bluebeard's Castle)*, a one-act opera composed to a text by Béla Balázs and produced at Budapest's Opera House (24 May) prior to productions around the world. Another, full-length, operatic *Bluebeard* was composed by Emil Reznicek (*Ritter Blaubart* Darmstadt 29 January 1920).

UK: Olympic Theatre *Bluebeard Re-paired* 2 June 1866; Austria: Theater an der Wien *Blaubart* 21 September 1866; Germany: Friedrich-Wilhelmstädtisches Theater *Blaubart* 13 March 1867; Hungary: Kassa *A kékszakállu herceg* 7 November 1868, Budai Színkör *Blaubart* 15 June 1869, *Kékszakállu herceg* 29 May 1870; USA: Niblo's Garden 13 July 1868, revised version as *Boulotte* Wallack's Theater 19 August 1875; Australia: Princess Theatre, Melbourne 22 April 1872
Recording: complete (Bourg)

EL BARBERILLO DE LAVAPIÉS   Zarzuela in 3 acts by Luis Mariano de Larra. Music by Francisco Asenjo Barbieri. Teatro de la Zarzuela, Madrid, 18 December 1874.

One of the most successful zarzuelas of its period, *El barberillo de Lavapiés* had for its central character Lamparilla, the little Madrid barber of the title, a medical and general factotum related to the more famous Figaro or the Benjamin Partridge of German's *Tom Jones*. This little barber, however, gets mixed up in meaningful political doings: a plot against the Italianizing Prime Minister in favour of the more Spanish Count de Floridablanca. The Infanta herself supports the latter, and it is her lady-in-waiting, the Marquesita Estrella, who has to cross Madrid, through many a danger, as part of the plotting. Lamparilla's girlfriend, Paloma, volunteers him as escort. Jealousies, plots, disguises and another two acts of music intervene before the coup d'état is successfully accomplished.

El barberillo de Lavapiés was one of the few zarzuelas to be played outside Spanish-language territories and in any language but its own. It was seen in Germany under the title of *Lamparilla*, and heard in broadcast (ad Geoffrey Dunn) in Britain (BBC, 1954).

Recordings: complete (EMI, Alhambra/Columbia, Montilla/Zafiro)

BARBIERI, Francisco [de Asís Esteban] Asenjo (b Madrid, 3 August 1823; d Madrid, 17 February 1894).

Barbieri trained at Madrid Conservatoire from the age of 14 and worked at first as an orchestral and band clarinettist, an incidental pianist, occasionally as a vocalist, and in a variety of other musical and musical-theatre jobs before he succeeded in getting his first one-act zarzuela *Gloria y peluca* (9 March 1850) produced, at the age of 26. He had a considerable success with his first full-length piece, *Jugar con fuego* (6 October 1851), the following year, and thereafter turned out a steady stream of theatre pieces, establishing himself as one of the favourite zarzuela composers of his time. His most popular pieces included the 1854 *Los diamantes de la corona* (Teatro Circo 15 September), *Pan y toros* (1864), *El hombre es débil* (14 October 1871), *Robinson Crusoe* (Teatro Circo 18 March 1875) and, one of the most memorable of all Spanish musical theatre pieces, *El barberillo de Lavapiés* (Teatro de la Zarzuela 18 December 1874).

His other titles include *Tramoya* (1850), *Escenas de Chamberí* (1850), *La hechicera* (1852), *El Marqués de Caravaca* (1853), *Galanteos en Venecia* (1853), *Mis dos mujeres* (1855), *El Diablo en el poder* (1856), *Compromisos del nover* (1859), *De tejas arriba* (1866), *El pan de la boda* (1868), *Los holgazanes* (1871), *El tributo de las cien doncellas* (1872), *El proceso del can-can* (1873), *Los Comediantes de antaño* (1874), *Domador de pieras* (1874), *El Diablo cojuelo* (1878), *La guerra santa* (1879), *El señor Luis*, *El tumbón*, *Un dia de reinado*, *Don Simplicio Bobadilla*, *Gibraltar* and *El testamento azul*.

Outside his composing work, Barbieri also promoted concerts, did considerable work as a musical historian and, in later life, became a teacher at his local conservatoire.

Biography: Martinez Olmedilla, A: *El maestro Barbieri y su tiempo* (Imp. Sáez, Madrid, 1950)

BARDE, André [BOURDONNEAUX, André] (b Meudon, 17 July 1874; d 1945).

The determinedly bohemian Barde, described by Yvain as 'un des derniers poètes décadents de Montmartre', made his name in the years before the war principally as an author of witty small-house revues, most particularly in collaboration with Michel Carré on a series of pieces for such venues as La Cigale (*Pourquoi pas?*, *Midi à 14 heures* etc), the Théâtre des Capucines (*La Double Revue*, *Paris Sport* etc), the Théâtre Marigny (*Le Tour de Babel*) or the Scala. It was at the Capucines that he first entered the area of musical comedy when he provided the sexy, word-comical texts for Charles Cuvillier's highly successful *Son p'tit frère* and *Afgar, ou Les Loisirs andalous* and, although Barde continued to devote most of his theatre time to revue material, he and Cuvillier turned out not only further small-scale pieces but also a pair of successful larger opérettes: *La Reine s'amuse*, which made its way from Marseille to Paris before going on, like their earliest collaborations, to overseas productions, and *Flora Bella*, initially staged in a German version in Munich and later played both in a botched version on Broadway and in the original French in Lyon.

Whilst Cuvillier wandered the world with his musical plays, Barde retrenched into revue. He had some success with a *Carmen* burlesque, *Carminetta*, which went from Paris to a production by C B Cochran in London, but although he collaborated on another pair of pieces with Cuvillier, including yet another ancient-world burlesque in the medieval *Nonnette*, the brightest successes of his days as a witty young fellow were now a year or two behind him.

However, nearly 20 years after his first sparkling introduction to the musical theatre with *Son p'tit frère*, Barde's librettic career suddenly took off. Producer Gustave Quinson, looking for another Albert Willemetz to turn out texts for the new style of jazz-age musical comedy with which he was profitably filling his theatres, put Barde together with composer Maurice Yvain, recently triumphant with his first musical comedy, *Ta bouche*. The result was a second triumph, *Pas sur la bouche*, and Barde, whom the new style (which, give or take a dash of period burlesque, was pretty much an up-to-date version of his old style) fitted perfectly, was launched on a series of successes which lasted as long as the fashion for the combination of witty, slightly spicy texts and dancing music held sway in the French theatre. His collaboration with Yvain continued through a decade with *Bouche à bouche*, *Un bon garçon*, *Elle est à vous*, *Kadubec*, *Pépé*, *Encore cinquante centimes* (w Christiné), *Oh, Papa!* and *Vacances* in an almost unbroken run of success, as Barde simultaneously turned out hit shows with others of the top bracket of current French composers: *Comte Obligado* with Raoul Moretti, *Arthur* with Henri Christiné and – in what might have been a kind of a theatrical thank-you to an Hungarian stage which gobbled up his works gratefully – a remake of Lajos Lajtai's Hungarian hit *Öfelésege frakkja* (1931) as *Katinka*. He occasionally ventured into the city's more commodious theatres, but by and large his work prospered in the kind and size of houses where the words could be heard, and where they actually mattered.

Along with Willemetz, Barde led the French musical theatre through one of its brightest periods, carrying on the tradition for superior comic libretti which had illuminated the French musical theatre in the days of Nuitter, Tréfeu, Vanloo, Leterrier, Chivot, Duru, Meilhac and Halévy and their most talented contemporaries. The sexual emphasis of many of his libretti meant that few of his works were exported undamaged. However, not only Hungary, but also London, New York, Munich and Melbourne got a glimpse of the author's likeably louche humour and sophisticated style in close or distant adaptations of his works.

1907 **Son p'tit frère** (Charles Cuvillier) Théâtre des Capucines 10 April
1909 **Afgar, ou Les Loisirs andalous** (Cuvillier/w Michel Carré fils) Théâtre des Capucines 6 October
1910 **Les Muscadines** (Cuvillier) Théâtre des Capucines 28 April
1910 **L'Astronome et l'étoile** (Cuvillier/w Bertrand de St-Rémy) Buenos Aires July
1912 **Sappho** (Cuvillier/w Carré) Théâtre des Capucines 26 February
1912 **La Reine s'amuse** (Cuvillier) Théâtre des Variétés, Marseille 31 December
1913 **Flora Bella** (Cuvillier/ad Felix Dörmann) Theater am Gärtnerplatz, Munich 5 September
1917 **Carminetta** (Émile Lassailly/w Gustave Charpentier) Théâtre Michel 16 March

1917 **La République des vièrges** revised *Sappho* Théâtre Edouard VII 6 September

1917 **Judith Courtisane** (Cuvillier/w Régis Gignoux) Théâtre Michel 22 December

1918 **La Reine joyeuse** revised *La Reine s'amuse* Théâtre Apollo 1 November

1922 **Nonnette** (Cuvillier) Théâtre des Capucines 28 March

1923 **Benjamin** (René Mercier/w Benjamin Rabier, Paul Murio) Ba-ta-clan 11 April

1924 **Bob et moi** (Cuvillier/w Lucien Meyrargue) Théâtre Michel 6 April

1925 **Pas sur la bouche** (Maurice Yvain) Théâtre des Nouveautés 17 February

1925 **Bouche à bouche** (Yvain) Théâtre de l'Apollo 8 October

1926 **Un bon garçon** (Yvain) Théâtre des Nouveautés 13 November

1927 **Comte Obligado** (Raoul Moretti) Théâtre des Nouveautés 16 December

1928 **Déshabillez-vous** (René Mercier) Théâtre des Bouffes-Parisiens 22 December

1929 **Elle est à vous** (Yvain) Théâtre des Nouveautés 22 January

1929 **Arthur** (Christiné) Théâtre Daunou 4 September

1929 **Kadubec** (Yvain) Théâtre des Nouveautés 12 December

1930 **Pépé** (Yvain) Théâtre Daunou 25 October

1930 **La Femme de minuit** (Moretti) Théâtre des Nouveautés 11 December

1930 **Rosy** (Moretti) Théâtre des Folies-Wagram

1930 **Laïs, ou la courtisane amoureuse** revised *Son p'tit frère* (tour)

1931 **Encore cinquante centimes** (Christiné, Yvain) Théâtre des Nouveautés 17 September

1931 **La Scarabée bleu** (Jean Nouguès) Théâtre de la Gaîté-Lyrique 30 October

1933 **Le Garçon de chez Prunier** (Joseph Szulc/w Carré) Théâtre des Capucines 19 January

1933 **Oh, Papa!** (Yvain) Théâtre des Nouveautés 2 February

1933 **Katinka** (*Ofélésege frakkja*) French version w Pierre Varenne, Robert Delamare (Théâtre de l'Empire)

1933 **La Madone du promenoir** (Christiné) Concert-Mayol 3 November

1934 **Les Soeurs Hortensia** (Moretti) Théâtre des Nouveautés 11 April

1934 **Vacances** (Yvain/w Henri Duvernois) Théâtre des Nouveautés 20 December

1935 **Tonton** (Lajos Lajtai) Théâtre des Nouveautés 19 March

1935 **L'Auberge du Chat Coiffé** (Szulc/Alfred Lavauzelle) Théâtre Pigalle 18 December

1935 **Le Train de 8h47** (Cuvillier/George Courteline ad w Léo Marchis) Palais-Royal 22 December

1936 **La Poule** (Christiné, Lajtai/w Duvernois) Théâtre des Nouveautés 9 January

BARKER, Richard [WARTER, Henry de G] (b ?1834; d London, 1 August 1903).

At first an actor – and from the number of credits that have surfaced, apparently not a very prominent one – Barker was engaged as a lowish comedian by John Hollingshead for his initial Gaiety Theatre company and appeared on that theatre's opening night as Bertram in W S Gilbert's burlesque *Robert the Devil*. Whilst still performing, he began a parallel career as a stage director. In 1872 he appeared at the Opera Comique as The Sentry in *L'Oeil crevé* and as one of Offenbach's *The Blind Beggars* as well as directing the two pieces. Two years later his name appeared on the bill of the Criterion Theatre as having directed Gilbert's one-act piece *Topsyturveydom*.

He subsequently became a combination of company manager, stage director and confidante to Richard D'Oyly Carte in the early days of the producer's London career, and played a large part in getting Carte his freedom from his backers after the success of *HMS Pinafore*. He was even billed as lessee of the Opera Comique on the producer's behalf during the battle between Carte and the Comedy Opera Company. Over the years, thereafter, he worked both as a company manager and as a stage director for Carte.

In the 1880s and 1890s he had a busy career as a director, at first in Britain and later, increasingly, in America. He mounted John Hollingshead's revival of *Princess Toto* (1881) and his successful production of the comic opera *Dick*, Kate Santley's *The Merry Duchess* in both Britain and America, the spectacular *The Lady of the Locket*, and the original London production of *Ruddigore*. Some eyebrows were raised triangular when he was paid a vast £300 to stage the burlesque *Joan of Arc* in 1891 – it was an unprecedented amount to pay a man for the utilitarian task of arranging the actors on the stage.

Barker's Broadway assignments included many reproductions of Continental (*La Cigale*, *The Queen of Brilliants* etc) and British comic operas (*The Yeomen of the Guard*, *Erminie* revival, *The Chieftain* etc) as well as local pieces from both ends of the musical theatre scale – comic operas such as *The Wedding Day*, *The Jolly Musketeer*, *The Caliph*, *The Mandarin*, *Half a King*, *Fleur de Lis* or the Philadelphia *Princess Bonnie*, middle-brow extravaganzas like *Aladdin jr* and *Sinbad* and the lower brow farce-comedy style of show such as *A Stag Party*.

At the turn of the century he returned to Britain, notably to the Savoy Theatre, where, with Gilbert no longer in charge of directing his own works, he staged the post-Gilbertian *The Lucky Star*, *The Rose of Persia*, *The Emerald Isle* and *The Willow Pattern*.

Barker, along with such colleagues as Charles Harris and Gilbert himself, was instrumental in raising the function of the stage director a little above that of a man who grouped the largely static chorus of singers, platooned the chorus dancers around the stage and moved principals from left to right when they agreed to move. The latitude given to stars, particularly comedians, and the amount of gagging and ad-libbing permitted and even encouraged in most comic operas and musical comedies, still meant that even the physical staging of a show was very far from controlled by a director, but at this period a balance between organization and untrammelled performance was nearer to being established than at any time before.

BARNA, Izsó (b Budapest, 4 September 1859; d Budapest, 1940).

At first a conductor at Szeged and at other provincial Hungarian houses, Barna subsequently became musical director at Budapest's Városligeti Színház. He simultaneously led a busy career as a theatre composer, providing the incidental music for many plays, both Hungarian and adapted (Kotzebue's *Doktor Pipitér és szolgája Retipip*, Rónaszéki's *A Betörők*, Kövessy's *A Vigécek* and *A kaméliás férfi*, Mathias Feld's *Az északsarki utazók* and *A demokratos*, Georges Ohnet's *Sarah grófnő*, Soma Guthi's *A mádi zsidó*, *Az éjjeli ügyész* and *A mozgópostásné*, Paul Ferrier's *Az anyós*, the Jules Dornay/Xavier Montépin *Kintornás leány*, Jenő Faragó's *A lőcsei fehér asszony*, the

Gavault/Ordonneau *Kis városi botrány*, Ferenc Herczeg's *Avató játék* etc), and turning out scores for a long line of Possen, Singspiele and Operetten, as well as one short opera (*A szerzetes*), a number of spectaculars and revues. None of these works succeeded in winning productions beyond Hungary, but several, notably his version of the *Casanova* story, and Guthi's musical play *Smolen Toni* proved popular on home ground.

1885 **A szoknyás hadnagy** (*A Franciák Oroszországban*) (Géza Kyss) Győr, Budai Színkör 8 June 1888
1886 **Oh! Oszkár** (Béla Ujvári) Sopron November
1890 **Florinda kisasszony** (Albert Kövessy) Budai Színkör 2 August
1893 **A paradicsom** (Géza Gárdonyi) 1 act, Szeged 7 February, Budai Színkör 18 September 1894
1894 **Huszárosan** (Gusztáv Rónaszéki) Budai Színkör 31 August
1895 **A Méltóságos csizmadia** (Rónaszéki) Budai Színkör 22 June
1896 **Vasárnap délutan** (Rónaszéki) Budai Színkör 12 April
1899 **Midász király** (Ujvári) Népszinház 20 January
1899 **Singer-gyár** (Kövessy) Budai Színkör 21 July
1900 **Asszonyháború** (Károly Gerő) Népszinház 21 November
1901 **Budapest szépe** (Jenő Faragó, Géza Márkus) Budai Színkör 20 July
1902 **Egy görbe nap** (Bors Csicseri, Adolf Ágai, Tihamér Almási Balogh) Népszínház 8 February
1902 **Kin-Fu, vagy egy kínai ember** (Faragó, Márkus) Népszínház 31 May
1902 **Casanova** (Faragó) Népszínház 11 October
1903 **Senki** (Antal Nyárai, Miklós Balla) Népszínház 14 November
1904 **Rézi** (Alexander Engel, Julius Horst ad Árpád Abonyi, Faragó) Népszínház 16 September
1905 **Smolen Toni** (Soma Guthi) Fővárosi Nyári Színház 21 July
1906 **Vigyázz a csókra** Télikert 31 August
1907 **Berger Zsiga** (Ferenc Révész) Városligeti Nyári Színkör 29 May
1907 **A századik menasszony** (Géza Vágó, Adolf Mérei) Budai Színkör 7 June
1907 **A bús özvegy** (Faragó, Feld) Városligeti Nyári Színház 18 June
1910 **Világ vége** Városligeti Népszinház 16 April
1913 **A csodavászon** (Faragó) Népopera
1915 **Kávéházi Konrád** (Faragó/Soma Guthi) Budai Színkör 30 July
1916 **Négy a kislány** (Géza Vágó, Emil Tábori) Budai Színkör 11 August
1917 **Lavotta szerelme** (arr/Vágó) Városligeti Nyári Színház 13 April
1917 **Márványmenyasszony olajban** Kristálypalota 1 May
1918 **Jogot a nőknek** (Kövessy) Budapesti Színház 27 July
1923 **Mintha álom volna...** (Mihály Erdélyi, Ernő Kulinyi) Budai Színkör 1 September
1926 **Blaháné** (Ede Sas) Budapesti Színház 25 June

BARNABEE, Henry Clay (b Portsmouth, NH, 4 November 1833; d Jamaica Plains, Mass, 16 December 1917).

The original and only principal comedian of the famous Boston Ideal Comic Opera Company (the Bostonians), Barnabee appeared as Sir Joseph Porter in the group's first and acclaimed production of *HMS Pinafore* and, remaining with the company throughout its existence, made his career playing equivalent rôles in a whole range of comic operas, both imported and original, in a comic style which was rather better-mannered than that of some of his contemporaries, without being in any way less effective.

His most important creation was the all-consuming central comedy rôle of the Sheriff of Nottingham in De Koven's *Robin Hood* (1891), a rôle which became the keystone of a career which also included new rôles in such pieces as *Prince Ananias* (La Fontaine), *In Mexico* (Ezra Stebbins), *Maid Marian* (Sheriff of Nottingham), De Koven's *Don Quixote* (Quixote), *The Knickerbockers* (Governor William the Testy), *The Serenade* (Duke of Santa Cruz), *The Smugglers* (Don Brandieu), *The Viceroy* (title-rôle) and *The Ogalallas* (General Andover).

He was also seen in the wide repertoire of the Bostonians' company as the Mayor of Perth (*Rob Roy*), Major General Stanley (*Pirates of Penzance*), Lorenzo (*La Mascotte*), Abbé Bridaine (*Les Mousquetaires au couvent*), Bailie (*Les Cloches de Corneville*), John Wellington Wells (*The Sorcerer*), Lambertuccio (*Boccaccio*), Duc des Ifs (*Les Noces d'Olivette*), Bunthorne (*Patience*), Palsambleu (*François les bas-bleus*), Lord Allcash (*Fra Diavolo*), Izzet Pascha (*Fatinitza*), Lurcher (*Dorothy*), Midas (*Die schöne Galathee*), Bobèche (*Barbe-bleue*) and others such, as well as in a number of light operatic rôles.

He was over 70 when the Bostonians folded in 1905 and although he appeared at South Framingham later that year as the Hon. Jefferson Jackson Clover in the comic opera *Cloverdell*, he then put a virtual end to his career.

Autobiography: *My Wanderings* (Chapple Publishing Co, Boston, 1913)

BARNETT, Alice (b unknown; d London, 14 April 1901)

A grand-daughter of Henry Kemble, grand-niece of Sarah Siddons, and related by blood or marriage to many well-known theatricals including Sir Charles Santley, the exceedingly tall and imposing Alice Barnett originally trained only for the concert stage. She made her first appearance on the musical theatre stage as Little Buttercup in the 1879 tour of *HMS Pinafore*, and made her mark thereafter with D'Oyly Carte's companies, appearing as Little Buttercup in New York and Ruth (*Pirates of Penzance*) in London, before creating the rôles of Lady Jane in *Patience* ('Silvered is the Raven Hair') and, most famously, The Fairy Queen in *Iolanthe* (1882) introducing 'O Foolish Fay' and powering out her rage at being 'bearded by these puny mortals' in the first-act finale.

In a career interrupted by illness, which (helped by the fact that Gilbert wrote no rôle for her in *Princess Ida*) led her to give up her position at the Savoy Theatre in favour of Rosina Brandram, she appeared at London's Empire Theatre in *Pocahontas* (1884, Widow Thompson), spent a convalescent period in America (Buttercup, Lady McCassar in *Polly*, Arabella in *Billee Taylor*) and played with J C Williamson's Royal Comic Opera Company in Australia, where she was seen in the principal contralto rôles of the British comic opera repertoire and also appeared as Martha in the company's production of *Faust*.

From 1889 she appeared in Britain again, playing not only in comic opera – though she returned twice to Carte to play the Duchess of Plaza Toro (*The Gondoliers*) and created the rôle of Mistress Shelton in Cellier's *Doris* – but also in burlesque and in musical comedy. She toured in *In Town* and in *The Telephone Girl* (1897), briefly succeeded

Plate 14. **Barnum**: *Phineas Taylor Barnum (Mark Wynter) gets his showbiz career going exhibiting Joice Heth, 'the oldest woman in the world', in the biomusical's South African production.*

Lillie Belmore (one of the relations by marriage) as Ada Smith in *The Shop Girl* at the Gaiety Theatre, appeared grotesquely opposite the very small Little Tich in *Billy* (1898) and toured as Melanopis in *A Greek Slave* (1899). She also visited America once more and was seen being, as usual, a very tall, contralto heavy lady in *The Mandarin* (1896, Sing Lo).

BARNUM Musical in 2 acts by Mark Bramble. Lyrics by Michael Stewart. Music by Cy Coleman. St James Theater, New York, 30 April 1980.

A biomusical with a bit of a difference, this romanticized version of some events in the life of showman Phineas Taylor Barnum was told by a handful of principal performers and a relatively small team of singing-dancing-circus-feat-performing actors in a part-stylized, part-naturalistic production which gave the impression of playing out its tale in a circus ring.

P T Barnum (Jim Dale) has a great belief in the version of the old adage that you can fool almost all the people almost all the time. Therefore he is happier trying to make a career in showbusiness than in the more conventional kind of job his schoolmistress wife, Chairy (Glenn Close), would have him take. Barnum moves from promoting freak shows to promoting better freak shows and, in spite of setbacks, rises up the success ladder. When he moves into

classier areas and brings the soprano Jenny Lind (Marianne Tatum) to America, he finds himself caught up in an affair. But he breaks it off, returns repentant to Chairy and attempts to give up showmanship and lead a regular life. It proves impossible. When he is gypped of the political ambitions his wife has bred in him, and then widowed, he goes back into the show world, and Barnum and Bailey's circus is born.

The score for the show was highlighted by some of the most rousing march music to come out of the musical theatre in many years as the company demanded that everyone 'Come Follow the Band' and 'Join the Circus', alongside a series of songs for the central character which ranged from a pattering list of attractions in his Museum Song to a frenetic claim to be 'The Prince of Humbug' and a gentler duet with his wife on 'The Colors of my Life'. Amongst the supporting characters, Jenny Lind featured a set-piece 'Love Makes Such Fools of Us All', Tom Thumb (Leonard John Crofoot) danced to a bouncy assertion that 'Bigger Isn't Better', and Joice Heth (Terri White), who Barnum would have us believe was the 'oldest woman in the world', decided, looking at the modern state of things, 'Thank God I'm Old'.

The production featured a ring-master (William Witter) on a tall unicycle, rope-slides, stilt-walking, funambulism, plate-spinning, baton-twirling and all sorts of juggling and acrobatics, all slipped into and around the action of the piece in a whirl of action which took the story on from one scene to the next. One of the show's most successful numbers featured Miss White and the company describing the life in 'Black and White' which suits the hero so ill, in a performance half a minstrel show and half a blues recital.

A fine success on its original production, *Barnum* racked up 854 performances on Broadway, but it failed to take in the country with Stacy Keach in its central rôle. In London, however, it more than confirmed its New York success. Harold Fielding's production starred Michael Crawford as Barnum, supported by Deborah Grant (Chairy), Broadway's Witter repeating his one-wheeled Ringmaster, Sarah Payne (Jenny) and Jennie McGusty (Joice/Blues Singer) and, with the original Joe Layton staging enlivened with a few more circus tricks for the well-trained and dazzlingly febrile star, it ran at the London Palladium for 655 performances. After a lay-off for star recovery, the piece was mounted again, in Manchester, and returned for a second London run (14 March 1985, 383 performances) with Crawford now teamed with Eileen Battye, Michael Heath, Christina Collier and Sally Lavelle. In the latter stages of the re-run, the Tom Thumb spot was reorganized, with the balletic dance created for Crofoot being replaced by a highly acrobatic tumbling routine, and this production of the show was filmed for the BBC. An amateurish attempt to mount a third London season folded in disaster, but a 1991 British touring production, with Paul Nicholas in its central rôle and a much reduced star circus content, ventured into the West End for a Christmas season in 1992–3 (Dominion Theatre, 17 December), giving the piece a remarkable third West End showing in a decade.

Barnum spread itself to more parts of the globe than almost any other Broadway musical of the 1980s. France's Charles Level and Jacques Collard made the mistake of blowing the piece up and playing it in the Paris Cirque d'Hiver where, with Jean-Luc Moreau starred, it became an undersized circus rather than a multi-skilled small-cast musical, but in Germany a former circus man become very popular vocalist, Freddy Quinn, found the rôle of Barnum an ideal vehicle for his talents. Italy's Massimo Ranieri, Spain's Emilio Aragon and Australia's Reg Livermore (without most of the tricks) headed productions in their respective countries, Broadway take-over Mike Burstyn was Barnum in the Netherlands, whilst South Africa boasted the most athletic star of all in the person of British actor and popular vocalist Mark Wynter. Wynter later appeared in perhaps the most perilous version of the show, wire-walking his way to his wife in a *Barnum* played on the SS Norway, cruising in the Caribbean.

Phineas Taylor Barnum was earlier portrayed on the musical stage in a number of other musicals, often ephemerally, but more substantially by Thomas A Wise in the Jenny Lind biomusical *The Nightingale* (1927). An earlier musical based on his life was mounted in his former home town of Bridgeport, Connecticut, in 1962 (*Nobody But Barnum* Klein Memorial Theater, 30 November Albert Dickson, William Puva, Edward Marfiak, Steve Martin, Harry Ahlers).

UK: France: Cirque d'Hiver April 1981; UK: London Palladium 11 June 1981; Australia: Adelaide Festival Theatre 11 January 1982; Germany: Theater des Westens 27 March 1983
Recordings: original cast (CBS), London cast (Chrysalis), French cast (JMB), Australian cast (RCA), Italian cast (RGM), Spanish cast (Bat), Dutch cast (private) etc

BARON, [Louis] [BOUCHÈNE or BOUCHENEZ, Louis] (b Alençon, September 1838; d Asnières, 2 March 1920).

After teenage years as a shopboy in Paris, Baron – then calling himself 'Cléophas' – first appeared on stage in 1857 at the Théâtre de la Tour d'Auvergne, and worked at Limoges, Troyes, Toulouse and Rouen before making his first important Parisian appearances. He played in *Le Petit Poucet* at the Gaîté, and then, in 1866, joined the company at the Théâtre des Variétés, making his début there in *Le Photographe*. Although he briefly left the company to run the Théâtre de la Tour d'Auvergne after the Franco-Prussian war, he soon returned and he made the bulk of his very considerable career as a comic actor at the Variétés. Over half a century, he created rôles in plays, vaudevilles, revues and opérettes in standard 19th-century buffo-comic fashion ('the success of M Baron is principally based upon his gestures, that are often grotesque, and upon his scared look, as well as his walk, and finally his costumes, the exaggeration of which often goes beyond the range of comedy and borders on burlesque'). He became enormously popular in Paris and, it is said, the most highly paid comedian in the French theatre. When he joined Eugène Bertrand in the direction of the Variétés in 1886, it was reported that he was paid 6,000 francs a month and a percentage in the profits – nearly 20% more than even José Dupuis – and when Debruyère tried to lure him to quit the Variétés for the Gaîté he had to offer him 9,000 francs and 1% of the gross.

At the Variétés, Baron created rôles in a number of Offenbach pieces, notably as the chief of the Carabiniers in *Les Brigands* – in which the composer was forced to alter the accompaniment to the famous march of the Carabiniers so that the not very musical comedian could get and hold his notes – and as Baron Grog in *La Grande-Duchesse de Gérolstein*. He appeared in *La Boulangère a des écus* (Coquebert), *La Belle Hélène* (revival, Calchas), *Le Docteur Ox* (Niklausse), the second version of *La Périchole* (Panatellas), *La Vie parisienne* (revival, Bobinet), *Les Braconniers* (Camagnasse), *Le Permission de dix heures*, in Hervé's *Le Trône d'Écosse* (Baron des Trente-Six Tourelles) and Costé's little *Les Charbonniers* (Bidard) as well as such later pieces as *Mam'selle Gavroche* (1885, Baron de Boistêtu), *La Fille à Cacolet* (1889, Baron Cordesco), *Le Carillon* (1896, Margotin) and *Mademoiselle George* (1900, Marquis de Rochencourt).

Baron also starred alongside Anna Judic in the hit series of vaudeville-opérettes in which she featured in the 1870s and 1880s: *Le Grand Casimir* (Grand Duc), *Niniche* (Le Comte Corniski), *Lili* (Vicomte de Saint-Hypothèse), *La Roussotte* (Dubois-Toupet), *La Femme à Papa* (Baudin-Bridet), and, creating his most memorable rôle of all, as Célestin, the double-living composer of *Mam'zelle Nitouche*.

He appeared from time to time away from the Variétés, being seen at the Gaîté, the Folies-Dramatiques, the Palais-Royal and in the grandiose *La Poudre de Perlinpinpin* at the Châtelet, but he returned to his favourite theatre right up until his retirement in the early years of the new century.

His son (b 24 December 1870; d unknown), who

worked as **BARON fils**, played for many years in both musical and non-musical rôles in the Paris theatre, making early appearances in *Fleur de vertu* at the Bouffes-Parisiens (1894), at the Folies-Dramatiques in *La Falote*, *La Perle du Cantal* and *François les bas-bleus* (1895–6) and at the Athénée in *La Geisha* (Katana), *Le Cabinet Piperlin* and *Madame Putiphar* (1897–8), and later, after career largely in comedy at the Vaudeville, in such modern musical comedies as *Dédé* (1921, Leroydet), *J'adore ça* (1925, Monseigneur Spaghetto) and *Le Temps de s'aimer* (1926).

BARON TRENCK, der Pandur Operette in 3 acts by A M Willner and Robert Bodanzky. Music by Felix Albini. Stadttheater, Leipzig, 15 February 1908.

The libretto to Croatian composer Albini's most successful Operette, *Baron Trenck*, was written around a romanticized characterization of the scapegrace irregular army leader Franz von der Trenck (1711–1749) whose tale had – minus its less agreeable items of brutality, thievery and corruption – been famously metamorphosed into a lively romance by Hungarian author, Mór Jókai.

Baron Trenck, commander of the royal Pandur troops, rather too famous for his fire in battle and his amiability with the ladies, rescues the royal lady-in-waiting, Countess Lydia von Schwalbenau, from bandits. He gets little in the way of gratitude. The fascinating Lydia rides off on his horse, bearing with her a little rustic bride, on whom, before the interruption, he had been preparing to exercise his droit de seigneur. The two meet again, at Maria Theresia's little Favorita pleasure palace. The Empress has arranged for Lydia to wed the aged French ambassador, the Marquis de Bouillabaisse, and she will not respond to the lovestruck Trenck's urging to run away with him. The maddened Baron lets himself be put up as the prize in a royally organized lottery. Lydia takes a ticket, wins, and declares her love for Trenck in front of the scandalized court, only to be repudiated by the proud Pandur chief for as long as it takes to get from Act II to the brief Act III in which the natural operettic ending is tied.

The score of Albini's show was that of a big-sing Operette for the two leading players whose two principal long and large duets – the waltzing description of their amorous tastes in the first act ('Sei, wie er will, nur kein Kalfakter') and their second-act encounter ('Engel! Ich seh' dich endlich, endlich wieder') – provided the themes for thundering reprises in the big finales of the piece. The hero's marching entry-song ('So ist der Trenck!'), the heroine's introductory waltz ('Das ist zwar schrecklich') and a sextet Croatian March were the other principal numbers of a score which also included some soubret work for the little bride and her mate, and a comical number for Lydia's ageing maiden aunt and the royal major-domo.

First produced in Leipzig, *Baron Trenck* quickly found popularity and made its way around the world. Vienna saw it in Rainer Simons's production at the Volksoper, with Buers (Trenck), Frln Ritzinger (Lydia), Markowsky (Bouillabaisse), Fr von Kellersberg (Kornelia) and Fischer (Trautenbach); Budapest (ad Frigyes Hervey) saw it at the Városligeti Színkör and then, two years later, at the Budai Színkör, and it was translated into Croatian by Milan Smrekar for Albini's countrymen.

The English-language rights were taken up by F C Whitney, who mounted the piece in London in a version

(ad Frederick F Schrader) altered into two acts and equipped with some of the worst lyrics the London stage had heard in recent years. Walter Hyde and Caroline Hatchard did the big singing, Rutland Barrington, Marie George and Walter Passmore headed the lighter moments, and the piece was hailed as 'a great and undeniable success' by a critic who was pleased to find it 'more grandly operatic than is usual in a work of this class ... by no means all gaiety and jingle'. When it didn't go, Passmore was set to work up his rôle, new numbers for Barrington and Miss Hatchard were squeezed in, and the third act 'reconstructed', but it closed after 43 performances in the theatre Whitney had named after himself.

Whitney took his show to New York, and produced it at the Casino Theater. The book had been redone by Henry Blossom, and Albini's score had been further chopped up, pushed around and infiltrated by a trio, a chorus of 'Bold, Bad Bandits', and a waltz song for the heroine, all composed by Alfred Robyn. Fritz Sturmfels (Trenck), Blanche Duffield (Lydia), John Slavin (Nikola), Pacie Ripple and Joseph Herbert starred through 40 performances on Broadway.

Another Operette of the same title written by Franz Salcmhofcr and Otto Emmerich Groh was produced at the Vienna Bürgertheater 26 April 1935.

Austria: Volksoper (Kaiserjubiläums Stadttheater) 29 October 1909; Hungary: Városligeti Színkör *Trenk Baró* 1909; UK: Strand Theatre 22 April 1911; USA: Casino Theater 11 March 1912

BARRÉ, Albert (b Paris, 29 December 1854; d Paris, 31 May 1910).

The author of a goodly number of comedies and libretti for the French stage, Barré had his most considerable successes with the libretto for Antoine Banès's musical comedy *Toto* and with the 1904 vaudeville *Une nuit de noces* (w Kéroul). This latter piece was subsequently musicalized in Britain as *Telling the Tale* (Ambassador's Theatre 1918, Philip Braham/Sydney Blow, Douglas Hoare) and in America under the title of *Oh! I Say* (Casino Theater 1913, music: Jerome Kern). His *Le Portrait de ma tante* (w Kéroul) became the musical comedy *Léni néni* in Hungary (Zsigmond Vincze/Jenő Heltai, Magyar Színház 2 May 1914), whilst both the Berlin musical *Ihr sechs-Uhr Onkel* (Paul Lincke/Alfred Schönfeld/Jean Kren, Thalia Theater 15 August 1907) and Italy's *Supermoglie* (Checcacci, 1920) were credited as being based on unidentified Kéroul and Barré works.

1884 **L'Escargot** (Antoine Banès/w Paul Adely) 1 act Eldorado 19 April
1884 **La Jarretière** (Banès/w Adely) 1 act Eldorado 27 September
1892 **Toto** (Banès/w Bilhaud) Théâtre des Menus-Plaisirs 10 June
1893 **Madame Rose** (Banès/w Bilhaud) 1 act Opéra-Comique 25 September
1895 **Le Roi frelon** (Banès) Théâtre des Folies-Dramatiques 11 April
1896 **Une nuit d'amour** (Banès/w Maxime Boucheron) Théâtre des Bouffes-Parisiens 11 May
1897 **Le Nouveau Regiment** (aka *Mademoiselle Portez-Arme*) (Banès/w E Martin, Henri Bernard) Olympia 12 March
1907 **La Princesse Sans-Gêne** (Marius Baggcrs/w Henri Kéroul) Théâtre du Châtelet 16 November
1910 **La Vie joyeuse** (Henri Hirschmann/w Antony Mars) Théâtre Molière, Brussels 10 March

1911 **Les Gabelous** (Banès) Théâtre des Variétés, Marseille 4 November
1916 **Les Maris de Ginette** (Félix Fourdrain/w Kéroul) Théâtre Apollo 18 November

BARRIE, J[ames] M[atthew] (Sir) (b Kirriemuir, 9 May 1860; d London, 19 June 1937).

Although his theatrical fame is due wholly to his plays, the author of *Peter Pan* and *The Admirable Crichton* also made several sallies into the musical theatre. In 1893 he collaborated with Arthur Conan Doyle on an arch little musical comedy, *Jane Annie*, for the Savoy Theatre and, 22 years later, misled by his admiration for the French revue performer Gaby Deslys, he compiled the revusical *Rosy Rapture, the Pride of the Beauty Chorus*, with lyrics by E V Lucas and music by Jerome Kern and Herman Darewski, as a vehicle for her. He also ventured a 'revue in 3 scenes of yesterday, today and tomorrow' called *Josephine* (1906), played as part of a triple-bill at the Comedy Theatre, and a skit of his writing was interpolated into the second act of the Broadway version of *Das Puppenmädel* (*The Doll Girl*).

Both his musical book shows were quick failures, and Barrie has fared little better with the many musical versions made of his plays by other hands. *Peter Pan* has been given various degrees of music since John Crook's charming and long-used original score for the play itself, the most substantial being a 1950 Broadway remake of the play with a Leonard Bernstein/Trude Rittman score of 5 songs and incidental music (Imperial Theater 24 April) and an American musical comedy version (Moose Charlap, Jule Styne/Comden, Green Winter Garden 20 October 1954), tricked out with comical dancing Indians and peluche animals, and with a roughly filleted book made up from some portions of Barrie's text and some other material. *What Every Woman Knows* was made over twice under the title of *Maggie* (National Theater New York, 18 February 1953, William Roy/Hugh Thomas; Shaftesbury Theatre London, 12 October 1977, Michael Wild), *The Little Minister* became *Wild Grows the Heather* (London Hippodrome 3 May 1956, Jack Waller, Joseph Tunbridge), *The Admirable Crichton* was brutally reorganized as an *Our Man Crichton* (Shaftesbury Theatre, 22 December 1964) where the star was the soubrette, *A Kiss for Cinderella* became *The Penny Friend* off-Broadway in 1966 (William Roy again) and *Walker, London*, which Barrie had specifically refused to allow to be musicalized in 1925, was given songs in 1962 (Birmingham, 29 May).

The most successful musicalization of Barrie was practised on the most likely candidate, *Quality Street*, which was prettily remade as *Our Miss Phoebe* in London (Phoenix Theatre, 13 October 1950), and as the hugely successful *Drei alte Schachteln* (Walter Kollo/Hermann Haller, Ridcamus Theater am Nollendorfplatz, 6 October 1917) in Germany. This became, less successfully, *Miss Phoebe of Quality Street* in New York. The show was again and more discreetly adapted to music as *Phoebe* at the Pennsylvania's Buck's County Playhouse (23 August 1965).

A musical version of Barrie's other most probably adaptable piece, *Dear Brutus*, written by Julian Slade is, at time of writing, unproduced.

1893 **Jane Annie** (Ernest Ford/w Arthur Conan Doyle) Savoy Theatre 13 May
1915 **Rosy Rapture, The Pride of the Beauty Chorus** (Jerome Kern, Herman Darewski/E V Lucas) Duke of York's Theatre 22 March

Biography: Walbrook, H: *J M Barrie and the Theatre* (F V White, London, 1922), Hammerton, J A: *Barrie: the Story of a Genius* (Sampson Low, London, 1929), Darlington, W A: *J M Barrie* (Blackie, London, 1938), Mackail, D: *The Story of J M B* (Peter Davies, London, 1941), Birkin, A: *J M Barrie and the Lost Boys* (Constable, London, 1979) etc

BARRINGTON, Rutland [FLEET, George Rutland] (b Penge, 15 January 1853; d London, 31 May 1922). Musical comedian who made his first fame in the Savoy operas and his second in an equally long series of George Edwardes shows.

The young Barrington worked in the city before securing his first engagement as an actor with Henry Neville at the Olympic Theatre. He subsequently joined Mrs Howard Paul's entertainment and remained with her, on the road, until she disbanded her company to take up the rôle of Lady Sangazure in *The Sorcerer*. As the only star of D'Oyly Carte's cast, Mrs Paul was able to suggest that he hire her 24-year-old colleague as well, and Barrington thus successfully created the rôle of the curate, Dr Daly, in Gilbert and Sullivan's piece ('Time Was When Love and I Were Well Acquainted'). He remained with Carte to become the first Captain Corcoran in *HMS Pinafore* ('I Am the Captain of the Pinafore', 'Fair Moon, to Thee I Sing', 'Never Mind the Why and Wherefore') and, when it seemed that there would be no rôle for him in *The Pirates of Penzance*, he himself suggested that he be given the comparatively small part of the Police Sergeant ('When a Felon's Not Engaged in His Employment'), originally intended for Fred Clifton, who had played Bill Bobstay in *HMS Pinafore*.

Barrington continued as a backbone member of the D'Oyly Carte Company for more than a decade, creating Bunthorne (*Patience*), Lord Mountararat (*Iolanthe*, 'When Britain Really Ruled the Waves'), King Hildebrand (*Princess Ida*), Pooh Bah (*The Mikado*), Sir Despard (*Ruddigore*) and Giuseppe (*The Gondoliers*), before leaving the company to set up in management on his own account. When this venture bankrupted him, he ended up on the road with the operatic company run by one Mme Ilma Norina (otherwise Josephine Muntz, or Mrs Samuel Genese) performing a second-rate piece called *The Rose of Windsor*, and he was pleased to return to the Savoy where he appeared in such latter-day D'Oyly Carte productions as *The Nautch Girl* (1891, Punka, the Rajah), *The Vicar of Bray* (1892, Rev. William Barlow), *Haddon Hall* (1892, Rupert Vernon), *Jane Annie* (1893, Proctor), *Utopia Ltd* (1893, King Paramount) and, in his last return, *The Grand Duke* (1896, Ludwig).

In 1894 he again left the Savoy, this time to join George Edwardes's company at Daly's Theatre, replacing Harry Monkhouse in the senior comic rôle in *A Gaiety Girl*. He thus began another fruitful run of rôles, a run which saw the now stout and jowly Barrington introducing for Edwardes the character/comedy rôles of the Prince Regent/Nils Egilson in *His Excellency* (1895), Marcus Pomponius in *A Greek Slave* (1898, 'I Want to Be Popular'), the Mandarin, Yen How in *San Toy* (1899, 'Six Little Wives'), Quinton Raikes in *A Country Girl* (1902)

Plate 15. **Rutland Barrington**: *The famous Savoy comic had a second career as the star of several George Edwardes shows. Here he is seen as Marcus Pomponius, the dying-to-be-popular Roman potentate of* A Greek Slave.

and Boobhamba in *The Cingalee* (1904) as well as succeeding Monkhouse as Marquis Imari in *The Geisha*.

In his fifties Barrington continued his series of large comic creations in such pieces as *The White Chrysanthemum* (1905, Admiral Sir Horatio Armitage KCB) and as a ridiculous Pharoah in *Amasis* (1906, Amasis IX), and took comedy rôles in the new wave of Continental musicals – *The Girl in the Train* (*Die geschiedene Frau*), *The Joy-Ride Lady* (*Autoliebchen*), *Baron Trenck* – as well as repeating his Gilbert and Sullivan rôles in revival.

Barrington wrote the texts for several small operettas, including *Quid Pro Quo*, played as a forepiece to *Princess Toto* at the Opera Comique, and *A Knight Errant* (1895) played as a curtain-raiser to Gilbert's *His Excellency*. He also authored the childrens' musicals *The Water Babies* (1902) and *Little Black Sambo and Little White Barbara* (1904), played as Christmas entertainments at the Garrick Theatre.

1881 **Quid pro Quo** (Wilfred Bendall/w Cunningham Bridgman) 1 act Opera Comique 17 October
1890 **A Swarry Dansong** (Edward Solomon) 1 act Criterion Theatre 5 June
1891 **Incompatability of Temper** (Solomon) 1 act privately
1894 **A Knight Errant** (Alfred J Caldicott) 1 act Lyric Theatre 14 November
1895 **The Professor** (Solomon) 1 act St George's Hall 15 July
1902 **The Water Babies** (Frederick Rosse) Garrick Theatre 18 December
1904 **Little Black Sambo and Little White Barbara** (Bendall, Rosse) Garrick Theatre 21 December

1907 **His Escape** (H M Higgs) 1 act Coronet Theatre 15 July

Memoirs: *Rutland Barrington: A Record of 34 Years' Experience* (Richards, London, 1908), *More Rutland Barrington* (Richards, London, 1911)

BARRON, Muriel (b Glasgow, 12 April 1906; d unknown).

Soprano Muriel Barron joined the D'Oyly Carte Opera Company at the age of 22, and played minor rôles (Plaintiff, Giulia, Isabel etc) with them for several years. She covered the part of Shirley Sheridan in *The Cat and the Fiddle* in London before playing it on tour, toured as *The Dubarry* in 1934, and then joined the cast of *Glamorous Night* at Drury Lane, covering Mary Ellis and subsequently taking over her rôle after the London run. She appeared in the West End in Coward's *Operette*, and returned to Novello to once again succeed Mary Ellis, this time in the star rôle of *The Dancing Years*, when the piece was forced out of London by the war. When it returned to the West End for its principal run at the Adelphi Theatre in 1942, she retained the rôle of Maria Ziegler, and then continued on into the principal soprano rôle of Novello's next show, *Perchance to Dream*, in which she introduced 'Love is My Reason for Living'. She subsequently succeeded Phyllis Dare as Marta Karillos in *King's Rhapsody* (1950).

BÁRSONY, Rózsi (b Budapest, March 1909; d Vienna, March 1977).

A child actress, the blonde and beautiful Bársony joined the chorus at Budapest's Király Színház at the age of 16 and rose to principal parts as a soubrette in revue and operett. She made her first mark in *Éva grofnő* (1928) and *Eltörött a hegedüm* (Bözsi), starred with Ilona Titkos as the *Sisters* of Szirmai's successful operett, and made a hit in the soubrette rôle in *Viktória* (1930, Icike, introducing 'Mäusi'). She played in Eisemann's *Alvinci huszárok*, in *Az okos Mama* (Zizi), appeared as an American flapper in *Amerikai lányok* (1931) – a curious piece claiming to be American which credited Eliot and J C Nugent's *The Poor Nut* as its libretto and its songs to Messrs Cowan, C I May and Albert Gumble – and took the soubrette rôles in Szirmai's *A balerina* and the Leipzig première of Ábrahám's *Die Blume von Hawaii*.

She formed a partnership, both on-stage and off, with comedian Oszkár Dénes, and the two appeared together in the Viennese production of Ábrahám's *Die Blume von Hawaii* (1932, Bessy) before winning their biggest success when they created the soubret parts in the same composer's *Ball im Savoy* (1932) in Berlin. Bársony played Daisy Parker, 'eine jazz-komponistin'. They repeated these rôles in the London production of the show, and Bársony also took over her original rôle in Vienna.

She subsequently appeared in Budapest in such pieces as *Én és a kisöcsém* (1934) and *3:1 a szerelem javára* (1936, 'Nagysád jónapot'), in Vienna in *Märchen im Grand-Hotel* (1934, Mary-Lou), *Dschainah* (1935) and *Roxy und ihr Wunderteam* (1937) at the Theater an der Wien and in film (*Ball im Savoy*, *3:1 a szerelem javára*, *Viki*, *A harapos férj*, Ilonka in *Walzerkrieg* etc). She settled in Vienna after the war, and finished her career there, being seen at the Raimundtheater as Dodo in a revival of *Hochzeitsnacht im Paradies* as late as 1957.

BART, Lionel [BEGLEITER, Lionel] (b London, 1 August 1930). Songwriter who scored several sizeable successes on the British stage of the late 1950s and early 1960s.

Bart made his name in the mid-1950s as the writer of some of the earliest British rock-and-roll songs, notably for (and sometimes with) Tommy Steele ('Rock With the Caveman', 'Butterfingers', 'A Handful of Songs', 'Little White Bull'), Cliff Richard ('Living Doll') and, later, Anthony Newley ('Do You Mind').

His first experience of theatre work was in revue at the politically committed Unity Theatre where the musical *Wally Pone* (1958), a Soho gangster perversion of *Volpone* for which he contributed book, lyrics and music, was briefly staged, but the following year he found substantial success with his lyrics for the Bernard Miles/Laurie Johnson musical *Lock up Your Daughters* ('When Does the Ravishing Begin?', 'On a Sunny Sunday Morning', 'I'll Be There') and the songs for the East End musical *Fings Ain't Wot They Used t'Be* ('Fings Ain't Wot They Used t'Be'). He topped these successes with an international one with his 1960 musical adaptation of Dickens's *Oliver Twist*, *Oliver!*, which turned the evil Fagin of the novel into a lovable rogue to the accompaniment of a score of equally lovable songs ('Where Is Love?', 'Oom Pah Pah', 'It's a Fine Life', 'Food, Glorious, Food', 'You Got to Pick a Pocket or Two', 'Consider Yourself', 'I'd Do Anything'), yet which produced the most remarkable torch song of at least the decade in the powerful 'As Long as He Needs Me'. *Oliver!* established a long-run record for a musical in the West End (2,618 performances), and ran up a continuing and regular series of overseas productions and revivals, establishing itself as one of the great family musicals of the post-war era.

The spectacular *Blitz!* (1962), a wartime saga of Cohens and Kellys in an East End setting, and the splendidly gritty Liverpudlian saga of *Maggie May* (1964, 'It's Yourself I Want'), written to a libretto by Alun Owen, gave Bart further London successes, but a feeble burlesque of the Robin Hood legend, *Twang!!* (1965), was a violent failure. Bart ploughed his own fortune into keeping this sinking production alive and ended by ruining himself. In the period of financial and personal problems which followed, Bart's career foundered as an musical version of the celebrated film *La Strada* (1969) failed in one performance on Broadway, and other projects floated over the following 20 years, including an oft-announced musical on *The Hunchback of Notre Dame*, a new version of Offenbach's *La Vie parisienne*, and a well-publicized contribution to a musical on the life of Winston Churchill did not come to fruition.

Outside the theatre, Bart's most enduring composition was the theme song for the James Bond film 'From Russia With Love' (1963).

A musical compilation show based on his life was staged, under the title *Lionel*, at the New London Theatre in 1977.

1958 **Wally Pone** Unity Theatre 18 July
1959 **Fings Ain't Wot They Used t'Be** (Frank Norman) Theatre Royal, Stratford East 17 February, Garrick Theatre 11 February 1960
1959 **Lock Up Your Daughters** (Laurie Johnson/Bernard Miles) Mermaid Theatre 28 May
1960 **Oliver!** New Theatre 30 June

1962 **Blitz!** Adelphi Theatre 8 May
1964 **Maggie May** (Alun Owen) Adelphi Theatre 19 August
1965 **Twang!!** (w Harvey Orkin) Shaftesbury Theatre 20 December
1969 **La Strada** Lunt-Fontanne Theater, New York 14 December
1972 **The Londoners** (Stephen Lewis) Theatre Royal, Stratford East 27 March
1972 **Costapacket** (w Norman, Alan Klein) Theatre Royal, Stratford East 5 October

BARTHOLOMAE, Philip H (b Chicago, ?1880; d Winnetka, Ill, 5 January 1947). Playwright, librettist and producer who scored a handful of hits with musical versions of his plays in the 1910s and 1920s.

Son of a well-off family, and educated in Chicago and in Heidelberg, Bartholomae originally worked in his father's business before venturing fully into the theatre. He tried his hand from an early age at writing both plays and libretti, but made his first connection in the theatre when he promoted the vaudeville violinist, Saranoff. He placed the man on a bill with Sarah Bernhardt who subsequently performed a sketch Bartholomae had written. He had, however, to pay for his regular début as a dramatist. Unable to place the play *Over Night*, written whilst he was still an undergraduate at the van Rensellaer Polytechnic in Winnetka, he paid for the production himself. *Over Night* was picked up, taken to Broadway, and brought him an early success as a writer (Hackett Theater 2 January 1911, 162 performances). His first attempts at musical comedy, however, a series of shows with music by Silvio Hein, brought him less good fortune. He went into production under the banner of the Bartholomae-Miles Peebles Company and mounted his own production of his *When Dreams Come True*, with Joseph Santley starred, but the piece managed just eight weeks at Broadway's Lyric Theater. The pretty *Miss Daisy*, on which he also worked as director, did even less well and folded in 29 performances in New York. His next piece did not even make it as far as that.

Bartholomae had better luck, however, when he collaborated on a musical adaptation of *Over Night*, under the title *Very Good Eddie*, for Comstock and Marbury, and Miss Marbury subsequently joined with the Shuberts to produce his *Girl o' Mine* with rather less positive results (48 performances). However, two further partly self-made adaptations of his plays brought him two further successes. *Tangerine*, based on an apparently unproduced non-musical collaboration between Bartholomae and Lawrence Langner, was a long-running hit of the 1921–2 season, and *Kitty's Kisses*, a musical version of his 1912 play *Little Miss Brown*, followed its Broadway run by being recycled for use as the book to the show which was, in Britain, called Rodgers and Hart's *The Girl Friend*. A musical version of the successful comedy *Barnum Was Right*, by the same team of Conrad, Kahn and Bartholomae, which was announced at the same time did not apparently eventuate.

Bartholomae also contributed material to the Shubert revue *Over the Top* (1918) and to *The Greenwich Village Follies*.

He subsequently moved to the west coast and spent 15 years writing for the films before retiring in his early sixties.

1912 **Glorianna** (Silvio Hein/George V Hobart) Cort Theater, Chicago 12 October

1913 **When Dreams Come True** (Hein) Lyric Theater 18 August

1914 **The Model Maid** (Hein) Opera House, Providence 17 August

1914 **Miss Daisy** (revised *The Model Maid*) (Hein) Shubert Theater 9 September

1914 **At the Ball** (Hein/w Alice Gerstenberg) Van Curler Opera House, Schenectady 12 December

1915 **One of the Boys** (Hein) Palace Theater 24 May

1915 **Very Good Eddie** (Jerome Kern/Schuyler Greene/w Guy Bolton) Princess Theater 23 December

1918 **Girl o' Mine** (aka *Oh Mama!*) (Frank Tours, Augustus Barrett) Bijou Theater 28 January

1918 **The Victory Girl** (revised *Girl o' Mine*) (ad Alex Sullivan, Lynn Cowan) Syracuse 16 November

1921 **Tangerine** (Monte Carlo, Alma Sanders/Howard Johnson/w Bolton) Casino Theater 9 August

1926 **Kitty's Kisses** (Con Conrad, Gus Kahn/w Otto Harbach) Playhouse Theater 6 May

LA BASOCHE Opéra-comique in 3 acts by Albert Carré. Music by André Messager. Opéra-Comique, Paris, 30 May 1890.

'La Basoche' is a guild of law-students, two centuries old by the time of the piece, which has a legal 'King' and various other dignitaries at its head, and which has wide jurisdiction over the students. In the story, 17-year-old Princess Mary of England (Mlle Landouzy), wed by proxy to the King of France and on her way to meet her royal husband, takes a night out at a Paris inn. She sees student king Clément Marot (Soulacroix) in his 'royal' garb and assumes him to be her husband. The other half of the misunderstanding comes when Marot's wife, Colette (Mme Molé-Truffier), is taken to the real King of France as 'the Queen' and stoutly denies him in such a way that he suspects that his proxy, the Duc de Longueville (Lucien Fugère), has been carrying proxy too far. Mary finally makes it to court, and, not without a touch of regret, exchanges her teenaged 'King' for the real one.

Messager's score was an opéra-comique score par excellence, with some of its songs based on the words of the real poet, Marot, and with its lyrical music contrasted with a comical highlight in Lucien Fugère's self-contented 'Elle m'aime!' when the King's misunderstandings and accusations lead him to believe that Princess Mary prefers her ageing proxy to a royal husband.

Produced at the Opéra-Comique with considerable success, *La Basoche* was subsequently revived there in 1900 with Jean Périer as Marot (16 November), and again in 1919 (20 December), in 1931 and 1939, with Fugère hanging on long to his original rôle. It was also played at the Théâtre de la Gaîté in 1908 (30 May) with André Baugé and Edmée Favart featured, reprised at that house in 1927 with Ponzio and Louise Dhamarys, and again at the Théâtre de la Porte-Saint-Martin in 1934 under the management of Maurice Lehmann with Baugé paired this time with Yvonne Brothier. The show has subsequently remained more well-considered than performed, but in 1991 it was produced at the Théâtre Graslin, Nantes, with Piero Calissano and Sophie Fournier at the head of the cast and Vincent Le Texier in the rôle of the Duc, identified forever with Fugère.

Two different German versions of the show were produced, one in Hamburg and one in Berlin, and London and New York, similarly, mounted two different English-language versions. In Britain, Sir Augustus Harris and Eugene Oudin provided the text for D'Oyly Carte's production at his new Royal English Opera House (soon to be the Palace Theatre) with Ben Davies starred as a tenor Marot alongside Esther Palliser (Mary), Lucile Hill (Colette), David Bispham (Longueville) and W H Burgon (King), but a splendid critical reception was not followed by public interest and Carte was forced to announce that he would play *La Basoche* in rotation with Sullivan's *Ivanhoe* and with Bemberg's *Elaine* before the whole scheme collapsed.

America's version was made by Madeleine Lucette Ryley and produced, after its first Chicago performances (January 1893), at the Casino Theater with her husband, the popular comic opera comedian, J H Ryley, starred. It lasted just two weeks.

Germany: Stadttheater, Hamburg *Die zwei Könige* 19 October 1891, Friedrich-Wilhelmstädtisches Theater *Die Basoche* 29 October 1891; UK: Royal English Opera House 3 November 1891; USA: Casino Theater 27 February 1893

Recording: selection (EMI-Pathé)

BASTIA, Pascal [SIMONI, Pascal] (b Paris 11 September 1908).

One of the rare writers for the French musical theatre, since the days of Hervé, who has assured text, lyrics and music for his works, Bastia had successes with the musical plays *Dix-neuf ans* (1933) and *Le Groom s'en chargera* (1935), from which emerged his song 'Je tire ma révérence', an international hit as sung by Jean Sablon.

He also wrote the play *Ce monde n'est pas pour les anges* (1950), both texts and music for films, and pursued a wide variety of other literary and artistic activities. Some of his early work was signed with the fashionably foreign-sounding pseudonym Irving Paris.

Bastia's father, **Jean BASTIA** [Jean Michel Léon SIMONI b Bordeaux 29 June 1878; d 1940], actor (initially), journalist (Bordeaux, Poitiers, Reims, Geneva etc), playwright, revuist (*En Douce*, *Oh! Pardon* etc), songwriter and chansonner ('On n'est pas de bois' etc), with whom he collaborated on several of his earliest successes, also supplied lyrics to *Les Amants légitimes* (Théâtre de l'Étoile 8 December 1924 Fernand Malet/Marcel Ballot, Ambroise Janvier) – Yvette Guilbert's début on the musical comedy stage – and the texts to Chantrier's opérettes *Bébel et Quinquin* (Théâtre Michel 14 June 1924 w Paul Cloquelin), and the Mark Twain-based *Elle ou moi* (Théâtre Daunou 29 August 1925). He also joined Yves Mirande and Robert de Simone in adapting *Mercenary Mary* for the French stage. He founded Le Perchoir with Saint-Granier in 1916 and worked and performed there thereafter.

1927 **Ma femme** (w Pierre de Meure/Paul Briquet, Paul Gordeaux) Théâtre de la Potinière

1928 **Un joli monsieur** (as 'Irving Paris'/Jean Bastia, Paul Cloquelin) Nouveau Théâtre Comoedia

1933 **Dix-neuf ans** (w J Bastia) Théâtre Daunou 28 March

1935 **Le Groom s'en chargera** (w Jean Bastia, Georges de Wissant) Théâtre des Variétés 28 June

1941 **La Star et le champion** (w de Wissant) Casino de la Jetée, Nice

1945 **Mademoiselle Star** revised *La Star et le champion* Théâtre de l'Étoile

1947 **Quel beau voyage** Germany, then Casino Montparnasse, Paris September

1949 **Perdigal** Théâtre du Capitole, Toulouse

1949 **Priscilla** (aka *Le Chant du Far-West*) (Bastia) Grand Théâtre, Nancy

1951 **Ma Louisiane** (w Jean Suberville) Grand Théâtre, Nancy

1953 **Valets de Coeur** (Bastia) Théâtre Monceau

1957 **Nouvelle-Orléans** revised *Ma Louisiane* Théâtre de l'Étoile, Paris

1962 **Les Gardes françaises** (aka *Joli tambour*) Grand Théâtre, Reims 17 November

1985 **Vogue l'amour** (w Berjo) revised *Quel beau voyage* Le Havre 15 March

BA-TA-CLAN Chinoiserie musicale in 1 act by Ludovic Halévy. Music by Jacques Offenbach. Théâtre des Bouffes-Parisiens, Paris, 29 December 1855.

One of the zaniest of Offenbach's short opérettes, *Ba-ta-clan* has also remained steadily one of most appreciated, with regular performances both in French and in translation being given since the time of its first production up to the present day.

There is a lot of conspiratorial behaviour in Ché-i-no-or, the exceptionally curious oriental kingdom ruled over by Fé-ni-han (Pradeau). Ko-ko-ri-ko (Guyot) the captain of the guard, is secretly after the ruler's job, and two courtiers, who have been hiding under impossible Eastern names, but whose real names are Virginie (Marie Dalmont) and Alfred (Berthelier), are also plotting – but only to escape and get back to faraway France. In fact, Fé-ni-han is also a shipwrecked Frenchman, who has spent eight miserable years (mis)ruling this country without knowing a word of the local lingo. He means to force Alfred to take his place so that he can go home. All is solved when Ko-ko-ri-ko who, as his name implies, is also actually a Frenchman, sends a letter (the rules of the contemporary stage meant he couldn't speak, three actors was the limit) to say he will have the throne and they can all three go home.

The little score of *Ba-ta-clan* echoes the rebounding craziness of the story, with the voices and the orchestra behaving decidedly eccentrically as flights of gibberish Chinese mix with plumbingly deep Italian and sprays of occasionally illogical French in a merry burlesque of grand opera. There are also some more straightforward pieces for the three principals: Virginie's tale of her earlier life ('J'étais aimable, élégante'), her duo of reminiscences of Paris with Albert ('Te-souviens-tu de la maison dorée', La Ronde de Florette) and the monarch's ultimate revelation of his own history ('Je suis français').

The piece was introduced on the opening programme of Offenbach's 'winter' Bouffes-Parisiens, and it helped to set the new theatre off on very firm feet. In 1863 an enlarged version was mounted, but by that time *Ba-ta-clan* had begun its voyage to all corners of the world. Britain first heard the show in French, during a visit by the Bouffes-Parisiens company in 1857, but it was 8 years before an English language version by William Brough and Thomas German Reed was produced as *Ching Chow Hi, or a cracked piece of China* at the little Gallery of Illustration. Augusta Thompson, J A Shaw, R Wilkinson and Thomas Whiffen were the cast, and the piece did well enough for Reed to

Plate 16. **Ba-ta-clan**: *Jennifer McGregor (Fe-an-nich-ton) and Paul Ferris (Ke-ki-ka-ko) in the Australian Opera Company's production of 1984.*

revive it two seasons later. The same English version was later played in America, where Paul Juignet's Théâtre Français had given the original at Niblo's Saloon in 1864, by the Kelly and Leon Minstrels, who also later gave the piece its earliest Australian performances.

Vienna's Carl Treumann quickly had *Ba-ta-clan* adapted – the characters were, naturally, all Viennese rather than French in his version – and played as *Tschin-Tschin* at Johann Nestroy's Carltheater. Nestroy appeared as Tschin-Tschin, with Röhring, Swoboda and Frln Rudini in support. Treumann took the piece with him when he moved to his own little Theater am Franz-Josefs-Kai, where it was played with Wilhelm Knaack as Tschin-Tschin and Treumann himself as 'Peter Gix, steersman of a European frigate' (ie Alfred), Therese Schäfer as a Virginie who was now an odalisque and Grois as the ambitious 'ober-Bonze' in a cast which, unhampered by Parisian restrictions, now numbered no fewer than 11. Treumann's version was played in Budapest in 1862, but no Hungarian version seems to have resulted.

In France, *Ba-ta-clan* has appeared recently at Paris's Théâtre Déjazet (23 December 1987), whilst other productions have included one in 1982 by the Australian Opera Company (4 March, Sydney Opera House), where Offenbach's happy oddity shared a programme with Walton's *The Bear*, and another in 1983 by the Hamburg Staatsoper.

The opérette also gave its name to one of Paris's most celebrated cafés-concerts.

UK: St James's Theatre (Fr) 20 May 1857, Gallery of Illustration *Ching Chow Hi* 14 August 1865; Austria: Carltheater *Tschin-Tschin* 13 October 1860; Hungary: Budai Színkör *Tschin-Tschin* 11 April 1862; USA: Théâtre Français (Fr) 25 February 1864, Hooley's Opera House *Ching Chow High* 28 March 1870; Australia: Opera House, Sydney *Ching Chow Hi* 10 January 1880
Recordings: (Erato, Milan, Pluriel)

BATES, Thorpe [Thomas] (b London, 11 February 1883; d London, 23 May 1958).

Initially successful as a concert singer, Bates made his first theatre appearance starring opposite José Collins in *The Happy Day* (1916) at Daly's Theatre, where his dashing if slightly stiff demeanour and fine baritone won him an enthusiastic following. His popularity increased when he was again paired with Miss Collins to create the principal male singing rôle of Beppo in *The Maid of the Mountains* ('A Bachelor Gay Am I'). He switched to musical comedy to appear at the Gaiety in the 1920 revival of *The Shop Girl* (Bobbie Blake), but quickly returned to operetta for heroic rôles in *The Rebel Maid* (1921, Derek Lanscombe), in which he introduced the staunchly patriotic 'The Fishermen of England', *The Golden Moth* (1921, Captain Paul d'Artois), Broadway's version of *Die Bajadere* (*The Yankee Princess* 1922, Radjami), and the less than successful London productions of Lehár's *The Three Graces* (1925, Duke of Nancy) and *Frasquita* (1925, Armand), in which he was reunited with Miss Collins. For several seasons he took the rôle of Schober in productions of *Lilac Time* and it was in this part that he made his last West End appearance in 1930.

BATTLE, Hinton (b Neubräcke, Germany, 29 November 1956).

A member of the Dance Theater of Harlem, Battle made his Broadway début with a notable performance as a teenaged Scarecrow in *The Wiz* (1975). He subsequently played in the dance show, *Dancin'*, on Broadway and on the road and in the Broadway production of the Duke Ellington dance revue *Sophisticated Ladies* (1981, Tony Award, Featured Actor in a Musical), succeeded to the rôle of James Thunder Early in *Dreamgirls* (1984) and created the part of Uncle Dipsey in *The Tap Dance Kid* (1984, Tony Award, Featured Actor in a Musical).

He subsequently played in *Ain't Misbehavin'* in Las Vegas and in the out-of-town tryout of *Stardust*, and took a third Tony Award for his performance as John in the Broadway edition of *Miss Saigon* (1991).

BATTLING BUTLER Musical farce in 3 acts by Stanley Brightman and Austin Melford. Lyrics by Douglas Furber. Music by Philip Braham. Additional numbers by Donovan Parsons and Melville Gideon, and F W Thomas. New Oxford Theatre, London, 8 December 1922.

A musical seemingly inspired by F C Burnand's play *The Benicia Boy*, if, in fact, it was not the French comedy *Le Contrôleur des wagons-lits*, *Battling Butler* was used by Jack Buchanan to star himself as an errant husband who ends up having to take to the boxing-ring when his 'away weekend' excuse of being a boxer in training is rumbled by his forceful wife (Sydney Fairbrother). Fred Groves played the 'Battling' Butler of the title whom Alfred Butler has been pretending to be, Sylvia Leslie was the 'other' Mrs Butler (complications guaranteed here), and Peggy Kurton was Alfred's ingénue ward who accidentally gives the plot away, but still gets herself a Hugh (Fred Leslie).

Phil Braham's light-hearted and up-to-date score, including the pretty and popular 'Dancing Honeymoon' and the lovey-dovey 'Apples, Bananas and You' as well as a humorously plotful solo sung by poor Alfred as he prepares to face his doom in the boxing ring ('It's a Far, Far Better Thing'), aided a good comic script to a fine London success on its production at the Oxford Theatre. The show was still running strongly when C B Cochran wanted his theatre back, so Buchanan transferred *Battling Butler* to the Adelphi Theatre where it ran out the last part of its 238 performance London life.

A revamped, relocated (in New England) version (ad Ballard MacDonald) mounted by small-time touring producer George Choos under the title *Mr Battling Butler* ('a musical knockout in three rounds') did even better on Broadway. Braham's score was heavily invested with local songs mostly written by Choos's habitual supplier of numbers for his very small-town tours, Walter Rosemont, and Charles Ruggles, Walter Kent and Frances Halliday starred for a fine 312 performances before the show went out on the road with its title changed to that of its most popular song, *The Dancing Honeymoon*. America's version of the show also won a production in Australia where Dorothy Brunton and Charles Heslop top-billed alongside something billed as 'Millie the Mullet' through two and a half months in Melbourne and a month at Sydney's Grand Opera House (28 February 1925).

An MGM silent film of the piece was made in 1926 with Buster Keaton starred as Butler alongside heroine Sally O'Neil and Snitz Edwards.

USA: (aka *The Dancing Honeymoon*) Detroit 19 August 1923, Selwyn Theater *Mr Battling Butler* 8 October 1923; Australia: New Princess Theatre, Melbourne *Mr Battling Butler* 31 May 1924; Film: 1926

BAUER, Julius (b Raab Sziget, 15 October 1853; d Vienna, 11 June 1941).

A journalist on the *Wiener Extrablatter*, an author and librettist, and later a theatre director, Bauer made a fine start to his career as an operettic librettist when he collaborated with Hugo Wittmann on the book and lyrics for the younger Adolf Müller's successful Operette, *Der Hofnarr*. The pair subsequently provided Carl Millöcker with four libretti, including those for the memorable *Der arme Jonathan* and the internationally played *Das Sonntagskind* and *Die sieben Schwaben*, wrote *Fürstin Ninetta* for Johann Strauss and evolved the revusical *Adam und Eva*, played by Girardi and Marie Halton at the Carltheater.

Bauer subsequently wrote the texts for both *Der Juxheirat* and *Der Mann mit den drei Frauen* for Lehár with limited success, and *Heimliche Liebe* and *Der arme Millionär* for Paul Ottenheimer – and star Alexander Girardi – with considerably more, without a collaborator, but he rejoined Wittmann for a 1918 version of *Der Kongress tanzt*. His last musical theatre work was a Schubert pasticcio, arranged by Julius Bittner, a dozen years in the wake of *Das Dreimäderlhaus*.

1886 **Der Hofnarr** (Adolf Müller jr/w Hugo Wittmann) Theater an der Wien 20 November

1887 **Die sieben Schwaben** (Carl Millöcker/w Wittmann) Theater an der Wien 29 October

1890 **Der arme Jonathan** (Millöcker/w Wittmann) Theater an der Wien 4 January

1892 **Das Sonntagskind** (Millöcker/w Wittmann) Theater an der Wien 16 January

1893 **Fürstin Ninetta** (Johann Strauss/w Wittmann) Theater an der Wien 10 January

1894 **Der Probekuss** (Millöcker/w Wittmann) Theater an der Wien 22 December

1899 **Adam und Eva** (Carl Weinberger/w Wittmann) Carltheater 5 January

1904 **Der Juxheirat** (Franz Lehár) Theater an der Wien 22 December

1908 **Der Mann mit den drei Frauen** (Lehár) Theater an der Wien 21 January

1911 **Heimliche Liebe** (Paul Ottenheimer) Johann Strauss-Theater 13 October

1912 **Der arme Millionär** (Ottenheimer) Johann Strauss-Theater 17 October

1918 **Der Kongress tanzt** (Karl Lafite/w Wittmann) Rextheater 9 November

1928 **Der unsterbliche Franz** (Franz Schubert arr Julius Bittner/w Ernst Decsey, Bittner) Volksoper 24 April

BAUGÉ, André (b Toulouse, 6 January 1892; d Paris, 25 May 1966). The son of opérette prima donna Anna Tariol-Baugé, André Baugé became one of the most popular baritones of the French musical theatre in a career on stage, film and record reaching over 40 years.

After half a dozen years singing in the French provinces (initially as 'André Grillaud'), he made his Paris début in 1918 at the Théâtre des Variétés in the role of Lord Barsons in *La Dame de Monte-Carlo*. In the 1920s he spent a period at the Opéra-Comique where he was seen, amongst others, in the lead rôle of Messager's *La Basoche*, as Clavaroche in *Fortunio*, Jean in *Les Noces de Jeannette* and Florestan in *Véronique*, as well as as Escamillo, Alfio, Pelléas, Figaro and Lescaut. He left the Opéra-Comique temporarily to play in *Véronique* and *La Fille de Madame Angot* (1920) alongside Marguerite Carré, then definitively to create the leading rôle in the French version of *Monsieur Beaucaire* (1925, Beaucaire). He subsequently appeared in Tiarko Richepin's spectacular *Venise* (1927, Gianetto) in which he played alongside his mother, in France's baritonic version of Lehár's *Paganini* (1928, Paganini), and of Granichstädten's *Der Orlow* (1928, Alex), in *Vouvray* (1929) and as Robert Misson in *Robert le Pirate* (*New Moon*, 1929).

In the 1930s he starred in Goublier's less than successful *Billy-Bill*, *Le Clown amoureux* (1931, Jim), in the French productions of *Nina Rosa* (Jack) and *Valses de Vienne* (Strauss jr), in the title-rôle of Pierné's much-admired *Fragonard* (1934), in the Châtelet's spectacular *Au temps des merveilleuses* (1934, Marquis Roland des Essarts), *Au soleil du Mexique* (1935, Nino) and Romberg's *Le Chant du Tzigane* (1937, *Forbidden Melody*, Gregor). He also took the title-rôle in the opérette *Beaumarchais*, for which he had himself written the libretto to a pasticcio Rossini score, as well as performing regularly the rôles of the classic repertoire, notably Planquette's *Rip* and the Marquis in *Les Cloches de Corneville*. Although he retired in the mid-1940s he returned to the stage as late as 1958 when he appeared at the Théâtre du Châtelet as the elder Strauss in *Valses de Vienne*.

Baugé was, for a period, director of the Trianon-Lyrique, a well-meaning house producing a determined diet of opérette, and also played regularly in film.

1931 **Beaumarchais** (Gaetano Rossini arr Eugène Cools) Théâtre des Variétés, Marseille; Théâtre de la Porte-Saint-Martin 19 May 1932

LES BAVARDS Opérette in 1 act (later 2 acts) by Charles Nuitter based on the intermezzo *Los Habladores* attributed to Cervantes. Music by Jacques Offenbach. First produced as *Bavard et Bavarde* Théâtre du Kursaal, Bad Ems, 11 June 1862. Expanded version Théâtre des Bouffes-Parisiens, Paris, 20 February 1863.

The original one-act version of *Bavard et Bavarde*, a little rustic opérette based on the tiny 17th-century Spanish piece *Los Habladores* (1624), was produced at the spa-town of Bad Ems in the summer of 1862, and it had sufficient success there not only to be brought into Paris and the Théâtre des Bouffes-Parisiens, but also to undergo an expansion into a more substantial, two-act work on the way.

Spendthrift, chatterbox Roland is in love with Inès, the niece of Sarmiento, but when he tries to insinuate himself into their household he does so on a windstorm of words. Poor Sarmiento, already afflicted with a wife, Béatrix, who is a non-stop talker, suddenly has an idea. He sets Roland on to his wife, and the young man's verbosity quells even her. Roland's prize is a purse of money and the hand of Inès. Sarmiento's prize is a much quieter life in the future.

The score to *Les Bavards* is full of the humour of its characters, peaking in the second act in the tea-table scene which leads up to Roland's bravura gabble-victory over Béatrix, and a marvellous three-soprano trio for Béatrix, Inès and Roland (the 'boy' role is played en travesti).

The two-act *Les Bavards* was actually seen in Vienna before its first Parisian performance. In November 1862 a version written by Carl Treumann, under the title *Die Schwätzerin von Saragossa*, was mounted at his Theater am Franz-Josefs-Kai with Treumann playing a male Roland to the Beatrice of Anna Grobecker, the Sarmiento of Matthias Rott and the Inès of Anna Marek. Grois and Knaack supported as the Alcade and his scribe, and were supplied with a comical duet. When Paris saw the show, at the Bouffes-Parisiens with Delphine Ugalde (Roland), Lucille Tostée (Béatrix), Désiré (Cristoval), Mme Thompson (Inès), Pradeau (Sarmiento) and Édouard Georges (Torribio) featured, in the following February, it scored a splendid success, passing its hundredth night (29 February 1864) before giving way to the new *Les Georgiennes*. It was revived in 1866 (2 May), in April 1870 with Anna van

Plate 17.

Ghell featured and again in 1871, returned to Paris at the Menus-Plaisirs in 1890, and was played at the Opéra-Comique in 1924 (3 May) with Germaine Gallois as Roland and Nini Roussel as Inès.

The rest of Europe also took to *Die Schwätzerin von Saragossa*, as Treumann's version continued to be called in Austria and Germany, *A fecsegök* or *A Saragossai fecsegök* as Pál Tarnay's Hungarian version of the German version was variously called, and their Russian, Swedish, Croatian, Spanish, Italian and Norwegian equivalents. The show was seen again in Vienna when it was played on a double-bill with *La Chanson de Fortunio* for four performances at the Carltheater in 1896 with Sarolta von Rettich-Birk a memorable Beatrice and Julius Spielmann (Roland) and Betty Stojan as the lovers, and Berlin had another viewing in 1919 when the piece was played at the opera house (4 June). Apparently the only major European centre which somehow missed a vernacular *Les Bavards* was London. A brief French-language season from a visiting company at the Gaiety Theatre in 1871 seems to have been the city's only sighting of the show.

America first saw *Les Bavards* as *Der Schwätzer von Saragossa* with Hedwig L'Arronge in breeches in the now title-rôle of Roland, then in French from H L Bateman's company, with Lucille Tostée of the original Paris cast out-talking Mlle Duclos (Béatrice), Aline Lambèle as Inès and Duchesne as Sarmiento. She played the show in repertoire for two seasons at Pike's Opera House and at the Fifth Avenue Theater before returning to France. The show was later played in English as part of the repertoire of Alice

Oates's touring comic opera company and, subsequently, an American comic opera, *Castles in the Air*, which was based on *Les Bavards* (although professedly on its source) but swapped Offenbach's score for the music of Gustave Kerker (Broadway Theater 5 May 1890), was produced by De Wolf Hopper.

Vienna: Theater am Franz-Josefs-Kai *Die Schwätzerin von Saragossa* 20 November 1862; Germany: Frankfurt 30 September 1863, Friedrich-Wilhemstädtisches Theater, Berlin 9 November 1863; Hungary: Budai Népszinház *A fecsegök* 24 October 1863, Budai Színkör *A saragossai fecsegök* 3 May 1867; USA: Stadttheater *Der Schwätzer von Saragossa* 28 October 1867, Pike's Opera House (Fr) 9 October 1868, Park Theater 10 March 1873; UK: Gaiety Theatre (Fr) 1 July 1871

Recording: complete (Erato)

BAYARD, Jean-François [Alfred] (b Charolles, Seine-et-Loire, 17 March 1796; d Paris, 19 February 1853). An enormously prolific and successful French playwright who wrote, generally in collaboration, some two hundred colourful, popular-dramatic, romantic and comic plays which found repeated productions throughout Europe and beyond in the 19th century.

Bayard's style of play proved ideal fodder for the libretto-makers of the comic operas of later years, the example well set to them by no less a composer than Donizetti who made an enormous success of an opéra-comique written to Bayard and Jules Vernoy de Saint-George's *La Fille du régiment* (Opéra-Comique 2 February 1840). In an age where the authors of, in particular, German- and English-language libretti plagiarized freely from the French stage, and gave no credit (or at best a furry sort of 'taken from the French'), some of Bayard's works were too well-known not to be given credit but undoubtedly many other pieces, beyond those which acknowledged their sources, owed something to one or another of his plays.

The popular *Le Vicomte de Letorrières* (1841 w Philippe Dumanoir), a play adapted from a novel by Eugène Sue, underwent a whole series of European musicalizations, becoming *Der galante Vicomte* (aka *Der galante Abenteuer*) with music by Adolf Müller, at Vienna's Theater an der Wien (3 December 1877) with Frln Heisler starred as the Vicomte, and later making up with considerable success into *Az eleven ördög* (music: József Konti, Népszinház, 16 December 1885) in Hungary, and *Der Vielgeliebte* (Eduard Künneke/Rideamus, Herman Haller Theater am Nollendorfplatz, Berlin 1919) in Germany. An Hungarian musical comedy version appeared as *A primadonna* (Aladár Tombor/Albert Kövessy, Budai Színkör 1 July 1893), one German comic opera *Der Vicomte de Letorrières* by Bogumil Zepler and Emil Taubert was played at the Hamburg Stadttheater (4 February 1899) and later at Berlin's Neues Deutsches Theater (16 January 1903) and another (music: Gustav Hohmann) was premièred in April 1887. A vaudeville version, made by Carl Marg and decorated with a pasticcio score taken from Auber, Tolbecque, Caraffe, Labarre and Adolf Müller, was played at Vienna's Theater an der Wien, just two seasons after the play's original production, as *Die Gabe für sich einzunehmen, oder Arthur de Montpensier* (25 April 1843). A Spanish musical adaptation, *El Vizconde de Letorières* (Manuel Fernández Caballero/Garcia), was produced at Madrid's Teatro del Circo in 1858.

Of Bayard's other collaborations with Dumanoir, *La*

Vicomtesse Lolotte became the successful Hungarian *A titkos csók* (Szidor Bátor, Béla Hegyi Népszinház 7 December 1888), *Les Premières Armes de Richelieu* was made into *Az ötödik pont* (Dezső Megyeri Népszinház 16 December 1893) and into the British 'play with music' *The Dashing Little Duke* written by Seymour Hicks with songs by Frank Tours and Adrian Ross, and featuring Ellaline Terriss and Hicks, in turn, in its title-rôle (Hicks Theatre 17 February 1909), and *Le Capitaine Charlotte* was turned with international success into Richard Genée's Operette *Der Seekadett* as well as an Italian comic opera, *Il Capitano Carlotta*, composed by Raffaele Mazzoni (Città delle Pieve, 22 April 1891).

In Hungary there was further success for musical Bayard when his *Le Gamin de Paris* (w Émile-Louis Vanderburch) was made into *A suhanc* for *Az eleven ördög*'s composer Josef Konti (Népszinház 12 January 1888), whilst in Britain the musical version of the 1852 comédie-vaudeville *Un Fils de famille* (w de Biéville), produced as *The Dandy Fifth* (Clarence Corri/George R Sims Duke of York's Theatre, London 16 August 1898) proved a long-lived favourite which toured Britain for many years. In America, the same piece was decorated with a small handful of songs under the title *The Lancers*, whilst Spain got a musicalization as *El hijo de familia* (Gaztambide, Oudrid/Luis Olcona, Teatro del Circo, Madrid 24 December 1853) just a year and a bit after the play's first appearance on the French stage.

A musical version of the play *La Frontière de Savoie* (w Eugène Scribe, to whose niece Bayard was married) was mounted in Austria and Germany as *Der Cognac-König* (Franz Wagner/Victor Léon, Ludwig Held, 20 February 1897) whilst *Le Mari à la campagne* (w Jules de Vailly), originally written as a comédie à couplets, was more fully musicalized in Berlin in 1893 as *Der Leutnant zur See* (Louis Roth/E Schlack, L Herrmann Friedrich-Wilhelm-städtisches Theater 21 December). The most powerful of Bayard's musical theatre credits was, however, a rather nebulous one. The text of Suppé's *Boccaccio* was intermittently said to be adapted from a piece by Bayard, Adolphe de Leuven and Arthur de Beauplan, without any further precision being given.

Bayard's name was also attached as librettist (along with that of Scribe) to Hérold's 1832 one-act opéra-comique *Le Medecin sans medicine*, the full-length *Le Remplaçant* (1837) and Boulanger's one-act *Le Diable à l'école* (1842), as well as to other opéras-comiques in Boulanger's *Une Voix*, Montfort's *L'Ombre d'Argentine* (w de Biéville) and to a number of pieces designated opéra: Jakob Rosenhain's *Le Démon de la nuit* (w E Arago Paris Opéra 17 March 1851), Thys's *Alda* (1835) and Gastinel's one-act *Le Miroir* (1853).

LA BÉARNAISE Opérette in 3 acts by Eugène Leterrier and Albert Vanloo. Music by André Messager. Théâtre des Bouffes-Parisiens, Paris, 12 December 1885.

Produced by Delphine Ugalde as her initial production as manager at the Bouffes-Parisiens, *La Béarnaise* got off to a sticky start when the performer cast by Mme Ugalde for the show's large title-rôle proved unable to cope with Messager's music and had to be dropped during rehearsal. The young Messager was encouraged to play and sing his score over to the fearsome diva Jeanne Granier, but he got only part way through the first act before Mlle Granier stopped him and accepted the rôle. She learned it and rehearsed it in a week and scored a splendid success.

Young Captain Perpignac (Vauthier) has made himself rather unpopular at the French court with his good looks and flirtatious behaviour, and when he goes too far he finds himself royally transferred – to the court of the Duke of Parma – with an obligation to get himself thoroughly married. To give her beloved a chance to redeem himself, Jacquette (Mlle Granier) gets into masculine garb and takes Perpignac's place at the Italian court, carrying the pretence so far as to go through a marriage ceremony with the Countess Bianca (Mily-Meyer), before honour is restored and a more conventional marriage can take place. The principal comic rôles were those of the nosy Girafo (Gerpré), intent on tripping up the young soldier and, ultimately, thoroughly confounded, and the elderly, and thus also inevitably confounded, Chevalier Pomponio (Édouard Maugé).

The show's score went, in its largest part, to the star who had no less than six solos during the course of the evening: couplets as both Jacquette ('Eh, là! Papa tu me fais rire') and as Jacquet ('Pour mes tours et pour mes malices'), a drinking song and an attractive lullaby in the second act, as well as a chanson villageoise in the finale and half of a military duo sung with Perpignac. Bianca opened proceedings enjoying her widowhood to the strains of 'C'est si charmant le veuvage' and, later, after her marriage to Jacquet puzzled through the comical couplets 'Pour un détail', wondering why her new husband is so backward on fulfilling his marital obligations. Perpignac took his main musical moment in a madrigal.

La Béarnaise ran just under two months (64 performances) at the Bouffes-Parisiens, before beginning its foreign travels. The German-language theatre seems to have ignored it, but Budapest's ravenous Népszinház mounted a version (ad Béla J Fái, Lajos Evva) with Ilka Pálmay, Pál Vidor, Árpád Szathmári and Béla Szilágyi (15 performances), and both London and New York also took the show up. In Britain (ad Alfred Murray), Florence St John starred as Jacquette with the young Marie Tempest as her bride, G H Snazelle (Perpignac) and Edwin Lonnen heading the comedy, and the show played for a little over two months (75 performances). America's version (ad Cheever Goodwin), entitled *Jacquette*, with Mathilde Cottrelly in the title-rôle, Jefferson de Angelis as Girafo, Hubert Wilke (Perpignac) and Marion Manola (Bianca), flopped in just three weeks.

Hungary: Népszinház *A bearni leány* 26 February 1886; UK: Prince of Wales Theatre 4 October 1886; USA: Wallack's Theater *Jacquette* 13 June 1887

LE BEAU DUNOIS Opérette in 1 act by Henri Chivot and Alfred Duru. Music by Charles Lecocq. Théâtre des Variétés, Paris, 13 April 1870.

An opérette which verged merrily on the opéra-bouffe, *Le Beau Dunois* was set in the medieval times which the French burlesque writers had so successfully invested so many times before. In this episode, the gallant La Hire (Kopp) swears not to consummate his recent marriage to the lovely Loyse (Marie Aimée) until the English have been beaten back from Montargis. He gallops off to battle, leaving his new wife under the eye of the handsome young

Dunois (José Dupuis), and the inevitable happens. When La Hire comes glumly back, having lost his battle, he is not unhappy to lose his wife as well. Léonce (Caprican) and Lucy Abel (Odette) supported the more plotworthy folk.

The little score included a lilting laughing song, 'Avoir l'air de me dire en face', for Loyse, a mock-innocent waltz duo pastorale with the refrain 'O mon Lubin', a little drinking song for Dunois ('La vie à jeun est bien morose') and a basso-baritone scene for La Hire, handing over his wife, which led into a trio and chorale with a 'la faridondaine, la faridondon' refrain.

An agreeable success in Paris, the piece was subsequently played both in a German version in Vienna (ad Richard Genée) and in an Hungarian one (ad Endre Latabár) in Budapest.

Austria: Theater an der Wien *Der schöne Ritter Dunois* 17 September 1870; Hungary: Budai Színkör *A szép Dunois lovag* 21 April 1871

BEAUMARCHAIS   Opérette in 3 acts by André Baugé. Music taken from the works of Rossini arranged by Eugène Cools. Théâtre des Variétés, Marseille, 1931. Théâtre de la Porte-Saint-Martin, Paris, 19 May 1932.

Written by the popular baritone Baugé as a vehicle for himself, *Beaumarchais* allowed its star to perform the largest part of a score in which familiar melodies from *Il barbiere di Siviglia*, *Guglielmo Tell*, *Comte Ory* and *L'italiana in Algieri* were turned into such numbers as 'La beauté, chacun le sait bien', 'Les trois Colombes', 'Pour Madame de Pompadour' and 'Pleure, mon coeur'. *Beaumarchais* played a respectable Paris season, at the end of which Baugé returned to playing classic opérette with a revival of *Rip!*

Adaptations of the works of the real-life Pierre Augustin Caron de Beaumarchais (1732–1799), most particularly his *Le Barbier de Séville* (1775) and *Le Mariage de Figaro* (1784), seem to have been limited to the operatic (if comic operatic) stage, from Paisiello's first introduction of Figaro to the opera stage in 1782 through the celebrated works of Rossini and Mozart, to the comic hero's most recent appearance in William Hoffman and John Corigliano's Metropolitan Opera *The Ghosts of Versailles* (1991).

BEAUMONT, Alexandre   [BEAUME, Alexandre] (b 1827; d 1909).

The collaborator of Charles Nuitter in the adaptation of a number of popular operas including Weber's *Abu Hassan*, *Preciosa* and *Oberon*, Mozart's *Die Zauberflöte*, Verdi's *Macbeth*, Pedrotti's *Tutti in Maschera* and Ricci's *Il Marito e l'Amante* and *Crispino e la Comare* (*Le Docteur Crispin*), to the French stage, and also on several original operatic texts (Joncières' *Le Dernier Jour de Pompeii* etc), and a series of cantatas, Beaumont found one major success in the lighter musical theatre when, teamed again with Nuitter, he was responsible for the text to Lecocq's intricately plotted opérette *Le Coeur et la main*.

1855 **Une Nuit à Seville** (Frédéric Barbier/w Charles Nuitter) 1 act Théâtre Lyrique 14 September
1855 **Rose et Narcisse** (Barbier/w Nuitter) 1 act Théâtre Lyrique 21 November
1858 **Le Peau de l'ours** (Samuel David) 1 act Folies-Nouvelles 28 March
1863 **Un Othello** (Isidore Legouix/w Nuitter) 1 act Théâtre des Champs-Elysées 21 June

Plate 18. **Roma Beaumont** *played the child, Grete, to the Rudi of Ivor Novello in the Theatre Royal, Drury Lane production of* The Dancing Years.

1864 **Le Lion de Saint-Marc** (Legouix/w Nuitter) 1 act Théâtre Saint-Germain 24 November
1867 **Cardillac** (Lucien Dautresme/w Nuitter) Théâtre Lyrique 11 December
1868 **Le Vengeur** (Legouix/w Nuitter) Théâtre de l'Athénée 20 November
1874 **Les Dernières Grisettes** (Legouix/w Nuitter) Fantaisies-Parisiennes, Brussels 12 December
1875 **Amphytrion** (Paul Lacôme/w Nuitter) 1 act Salle Taitbout 5 April
1882 **Le Coeur et la main** (Charles Lecocq/w Nuitter) Théâtre des Nouveautés 14 October
1888 **La Volière** (Lecocq/w Nuitter) Théâtre des Nouveautés 1 February
1888 **Le Puits qui parle** (Edmond Audran/w Paul Burani) Théâtre des Nouveautés 15 March
1888 **La Demoiselle de Belleville** (*Die Jungfrau von Belleville*) French version w Nuitter (Théâtre des Folies-Dramatiques)
1890 **L'Égyptienne** (Lecocq/w Nuitter, Henri Chivot) Théâtre des Folies-Dramatiques 8 November
1898 **Le Soleil à minuit** (Albert Renaud/w Nuitter) Théâtre des Bouffes-Parisiens 14 October

Other titles attributed: *Le Clef d'argent* (Legouix), *Marion* (Boulanger)

BEAUMONT, Roma   (b London, 31 July 1914).

A child performer, then a chorister and supporting player (*Stand Up and Sing*, *Mr Whittington*) in London musicals, Miss Beaumont rose to principal rôles as the ingénue of touring productions of *For the Love of Mike*, *Tell Her the Truth* and *The Crest of the Wave*. This last engagement earned the very pretty and young-looking 24-year-old the important rôle of the child, Grete, in Novello's *The Dancing Years* (1939) at the Theatre Royal, Drury Lane ('Primrose'). She remained with this show through its very long-running success in London and the provinces, and then moved on to create the tripartite star rôle of Melinda/Melanie/Melody built to her measure in Novello's next musical, *Perchance to Dream* ('The Night That I Curtsied to the King'). She appeared as *Alice in Wonderland* and *Cinderella* in London seasons, before retiring from the stage as the wife of producer Alfred Black.

THE BEAUTY OF BATH

THE BEAUTY OF BATH Musical play in 2 acts by Seymour Hicks and Cosmo Hamilton. Lyrics by Charles H Taylor. Music by Herbert E Haines. Additional music by Frederic Norton and Jerome D Kern. Aldwych Theatre, London, 19 March 1906.

A successful musical play from the Charles Frohman/Seymour Hicks producing and writing team, *The Beauty of Bath* was based on the key scene from the favourite play *David Garrick* in which the hero attempts to disgust the heroine with his own bad behaviour so that, for her own good, she may be dissuaded from marrying him. The twist in this version of the tale was that the antics were intended to put the lass off the hero's double. Hicks and his wife, Ellaline Terriss, played the principal rôles – she as a nice young lady with a passion for an actor, he as the actor's double, who has fallen in love with her photograph and who takes on the task of disillusioning her – and the piece happily confirmed the team's success with *The Catch of the Season*. The physical likeness of the naval officer hero and the famous actor was achieved by the casting of Hicks's brother, Stanley Brett, in the look-alike rôle.

A strong book was supported by a colourful staging, in which a group of showgirls, playing the daughters of Sir Timothy Bun ('the Bath Buns'), provided a special attraction, and an enjoyable score in which the show's nominal composer, Herbert Haines, provided both the prettiest number – the title waltz – and the most amusing – an operatic burlesque duo for Sydney Fairbrother as a lugubriously lovelorn char and the juvenile Albert Valchera as her similarly smitten son. A liberal dose of interpolated numbers included the first songs written specifically for the London stage by 21-year-old Jerome D Kern, 'Mr Chamberlain' with a lyric by the equally new Pelham G Wodehouse, and 'The Frolic of the Breeze', as well as Frederic Norton's music-hally 'George's Little Love Affairs' and the initial stage success of 22-year-old Herman Darewski, 'My Little Hyacinth', which Miss Terriss made into the show's most popular number. It remained so in spite of the second act ball-scene of what had begun as a remarkably coherent musical play being filled up with extraneous songs, dances, impersonations and other items during the show's run.

Produced at the Aldwych Theatre, the show was transferred to Frohman's newly built Hicks Theatre in Shaftesbury Avenue as its opening attraction, and there it ran out its ten-month, 287-performance London run, prior to heading for the provinces. During the London run, a parallel version of the show played completely by children (including the show's star juvenile, Valchera, the young Ivy Sawyer and – in the chorus – Winifred Barnes) was mounted (11 February 1907) for a series of matinées.

THE BEAUTY PRIZE

THE BEAUTY PRIZE Musical comedy in 3 acts by George Grossmith and P G Wodehouse. Music by Jerome Kern. Winter Garden Theatre, London, 5 September 1923.

A mid-Atlantic collaboration between English producer/author Grossmith and the American-based Wodehouse and Kern, attempting to reproduce their Winter Garden Theatre success with *The Cabaret Girl*, *The Beauty Prize* was constructed round the stars of the earlier show: ingénue Dorothy Dickson, principal comedian Leslie Henson, Grossmith himself as dude comic, and Heather Thatcher, representing low comedy with glamour. The plot had Miss Dickson winning a newspaper beauty contest, for which the prize is the hand of Henson in marriage. Since she had the dashing Jack Hobbs already lined up, the exchange is rather improbable. By the end, Henson is more suitably paired off with Miss Thatcher, and Miss Dickson reconciled with her former fiancé.

The incidentals included a ship-board setting, a ballet based on the new craze for Mah Jong, a number in the jargon of Sinclair Lewis's fashionable book *Babbit* ('Meet Me Down on Main Street') performed by Henson and Grossmith, a song bemoaning the fact that 'You Can't Make Love By Wireless' and another for Henson about the 'Non-Stop Dancing' craze, but *The Beauty Prize* proved nowhere near as attractive as its predecessor and owed its six-month and 213-performance life largely to the reputations won over previous shows by its cast and theatre.

THE BEAUTY SPOT

THE BEAUTY SPOT Musical comedy in 3 acts by Joseph W Herbert. Music by Reginald De Koven. Herald Square Theater, New York, 10 April 1909.

Joseph Herbert's libretto to *The Beauty Spot* had already done duty as a play in South Africa and again, with music by Edward Jones attached, as a flop musical when produced in London by South Africa's Frank Wheeler (also director, choreographer, comic lead) and theatre-owner George Broadhurst (also additional numbers) under the title *The Prince of Borneo* (Strand Theatre 5 October 1899, 31 performances), before it was wedded in its third, American life to a standard Reginald De Koven score.

Popular comedian Jefferson de Angelis starred in the now leading rôle of General Samovar, with Viola Gillette as his ex-actress wife who once modelled, rather unclad, for the painting entitled 'The Beauty Spot' which she is now anxious to disown. The spot in question is, however, damning evidence. Alongside this saucy tale, the General's daughter, Nadine (Marguerite Clark), made her way to marrying artist Jacques (George MacFarlane) rather than the cousin (Frank Doane) to whom she has been engaged since birth and who has, in any case, wed a Bornean lady in the meanwhile.

New York did not object to the indelicacies of the birthmark plot as London had done with standard and sanctimonious vigour, and, although De Koven's score was no more notable than Jones's, the show did much better in its Broadway incarnation and totted up 137 performances before moving on.

The same title was later used for a musical play in two acts by Arthur Anderson, adapted from the French of P-L Flers, with lyrics by Anderson, Clifford Harris and 'Valentine' and music by James W Tate, which was produced at London's Gaiety Theatre, 22 December 1917. This 'beauty spot' was not a birthmark, but a landmark, and the plot of the show dealt with how naughty Napoléon Bramble (Arthur Whitby) enriched himself on the publication of a book of traveller's tales really written by a dead friend. The show was, however, heavily orientated by Parisian revueist P-L Flers towards the picturesque, and the production sculpted to feature the ill-fated French danseuse Régine Flory and her Polish dancing partner Jan Oyra. Their principal set piece 'Kadouja and the Spirit of Haschisch' depicted Flory as a victim of the drug as portrayed by her partner. Some light pieces by the show's nominal songwriters were supplemented by a couple of established American song hits, 'Poor Butterfly' taken from the previous year's New York Hippodrome *Big Show* and Harry Tierney's spelling song 'M.I.S.S.I.S.S.I.P.P.I'.

Producer Alfred Butt tried, with *The Beauty Spot*, to establish himself in power at the Gaiety Theatre, from where he had ousted the successful Grossmith and Laurillard management, but the public preferred to follow the old team to the Prince of Wales Theatre and Butt's attempt to make himself the new George Edwardes got off to a poor start when the show lasted only an unprofitable 152 performances. Mlle Flory salvaged the haschisch routine and took it back to Paris where she introduced it into the Casino de Paris reuve *Pa-ri-ki-ri* (1918).

THE BEAUTY STONE Romantic musical drama in 3 acts by Arthur Pinero and Joseph Comyns Carr. Music by Arthur Sullivan. Savoy Theatre, London, 28 May 1898.

Following the final termination of the Gilbert and Sullivan collaboration, Carte teamed his composer with a celebrated pair of writers in Pinero and Comyns Carr. In perhaps trying too hard to write in a style not comparable to that of Gilbert, and mindful of Sullivan's wish to try more serious subjects, the librettists supplied the composer with a sentimental medieval romance which was ill-fitted to the sort of musical treatment which the traditions of the Savoy Theatre encouraged.

Ruth Vincent played the cripple, Laine, who is given a beautifying talisman by the devil (Walter Passmore) which wins her the heart of the Flemish Lord, Philip of Mirlemont (George Devoll). When Mirlemont goes to war, his former mistress, Saïda (Pauline Joran), gets hold of the stone, and Laine returns to her former, twisted state, but Philip returns home blinded and, as the stone returns to the devil, to the arms of the woman whom he had known so beautiful. Henry Lytton and Rosina Brandram played Laine's parents – he, for a while, the rejuvenated holder of the stone and pursued by Saïda, Emmie Owen was given a rôle as 'crazy Jacqueline' which got her into boy's clothes and allowed her to nurture a passion for the devil, and a tiny rôle as an entrant in Philip's bride-seeking beauty contest was taken by chorister Ethel Jackson, the future *Merry Widow* of Broadway.

Sullivan's score included moments both gently appealing (Laine's prayer 'Dear Mother Mary') and showily dramatic (Saïda's powerful 'Mine, Mine At Last!') but, with lyrics which insisted on 'ye'-ing and 'thou'-ing throughout, *The Beauty Stone* was an awkwardly suboperatic piece which fitted together badly and it was shunted out of the Savoy after 50 performances.

Recording: complete (Pearl)

BEER, Gustav (b Vienna, 16 June 1888; d Nyack, NJ, 26 July 1983).

The son of composer Josef Beer (1851–1908), Gustav Beer was a regular purveyor of texts to the Viennese stage in the 1920s and early 1930s, collaborating with several of the most popular composers of the time – Eysler, Straus, Künneke, Reinhardt, Gilbert, Stolz – and with several successful librettists and lyricists, but without turning out any one major success. His first full-length piece *Die Millionengretl* had a 50-performance run at the Raimundtheater with Franz Glawatsch starred, but the subsequent *Die blonde Sphinx* played only three weeks at the same house. Of his other productions at the main musical houses, *Prinzessin Ti-Ti-Pa* lasted 53 performances with Josef König and Steffi Walidt featured in the lead rôles and with the ageing Mizzi Zwerenz as character lady, *Der Bauerngeneral* played less than two months, and *Die Dame mit dem Regenbogen* 74 performances. The most successful of this group of his works was the Suppé pasticcio *Die grosse Unbekannte* (Johann Strauss-Theater, 101 performances). He also contributed screenplays to Berlin's active UFA studios.

Beer joined the artistic exodus from Germany and Austria after 1933 and settled in America where, under the occasional nom de plume of Gustave W Wheatley, he was active in musical affairs and became President of American League of Authors and Composers from Austria (ALACA). He did not write for the American theatre but, with another expatriate, Alfred Grünwald, supplied the texts for Kálmán's posthumous *Arizona Lady*, mounted in Berne in 1954, and the Operette *Fiesta*, produced in Munich in 1955. An unspecified Beer play (w Hans Kottow) was musicalized for the Hungarian stage under the title *Krizsantém* (Jenő Nador/Ernő Kulinyi Városi Színház 19 December 1924).

1911 **Der Minenkönig** (Robert Stolz/w Ernst Marischka) 1 act Apollotheater 27 September (or 1 November)

1914 **Eine verschenkte Nacht** (Béla Laszky/w Fritz Lunzer) 1 act Deutsches Künstlertheater 1 February

1914 **Das Narrenhaus** (Hans Albert Cesek, Tivadar Pallós/w E Marischka) 1 act Hölle 1 February

1915 **Die Millionengretl** (Franz Schönbaumsfeld/w Alfred Deutsch-German) Raimundtheater 26 November

1920 **Rund um die Bühne** (Edmund Eysler/w Armin Friedmann) Apollotheater 1 March

1920 **Der König heiratet** (Eysler/w E Marischka) Künstlerbühne April

1922 **Der Glückstrompeter** (Heinrich Reinhardt/w Friedmann) Komödienhaus 7 December

1923 **Der Hampelmann** (Stolz/w Lunzer) Komödienhaus 9 November

1924 **Alles per Radio** (Fritz Lehner/w Karl Farkas) Ronacher 21 March

1924 **Puszipajtások** (Tivadar Pallós/w E Marischka ad Zsolt Harsányi) Lujza Blaha Színház, Budapest 9 October

1925 **Die blonde Sphinx** (Max Niederberger/Imre Földes ad) German version Wiener Bürgertheater 27 March

1925 **Die grosse Unbekannte** (Franz von Suppé arr Karl Pauspertl/w Julius Wilhelm) Johann Strauss-Theater 8 April

1928 **Prinzessin Ti-Ti-Pa** (Stolz/w Lunzer) Carltheater 15 May

1928 **Die singende Venus** (Eduard Künneke/w Lunzer) Schauspielhaus, Breslau 9 June

1930 **Durchlaucht Mizzi** (Eysler/w Lunzer) Neues Wiener Schauspielhaus 23 December

1931 **Der Bauerngeneral** (Straus/w Julius Brammer) Theater an der Wien 28 March

1933 **Die Dame mit dem Regenbogen** (Jean Gilbert/w Brammer) Theater an der Wien 25 August

1934 **Das ist der erste Liebe** (Eysler/w Hans Kottow) Volksoper 23 December

1954 **Arizona Lady** (Emmerich Kálmán/w Alfred Grünwald) Stadttheater, Berne 14 February

1955 **Fiesta** (Juan Cardona/w Grünwald) Theater am Gärtnerplatz, Munich 11 February

Other title attributed: *Das einzige Mittel*

THE BEGGAR'S OPERA Comic opera in 3 acts by John Gay. Music selected and arranged by Johann Christoph Pepusch. Lincoln's Inn Fields Theatre, London, 29 January 1728.

The most successful ballad opera of the 18th century, *The Beggar's Opera* has survived as virtually the only representative of its class and period to still win regular productions on the 20th-century stage.

Gay, an intermittent author and poet, disappointed by his expectations of royal patronage after many years spent being agreeable to those headed for power and position, is said to have taken his revenge in a piece in which the words and sentiments of 'fine gentlemen and ladies, satirists and philosophers' were put into the mouths of a crowd of Newgate-bait characters in a piece in which 'the scenes, characters and incidents are, in themselves, of the lowest and most disgusting kind'. In fact, whatever satire there was initially, the piece soon became simply a comical musical play about lust and greed amongst the picturesquely low-life folk of London, and it was as that rather than as a piece of any purposefully satirical character that it succeeded.

Refused by Colley Cibber at the Theatre Royal, Drury Lane, the show was taken up by Rich at the Lincoln's Inn Fields Theatre and set with a musical part, in an avowed burlesque of the Italian opera, compounded by the theatre's musical director, Dr Pepusch. Pepusch's 69 musical items were manufactured from a wide variety of popular music – from Ferrabosco and Rizzio to Handel's *Rinaldo* – and topped off by an original overture.

Mr Peachum (Mr Hippesley) is a thiefmaster and fence in London town, with an influence and connections which make him a powerful man. He and his wife (Mrs Martin) are horrified when their daughter Polly (Lavinia Fenton) secretly gets wed to the sexy thief-leader, Macheath (Tom Walker), and they devote themselves to getting their new son-in-law arrested and, if possible, hung. Macheath is betrayed to the law by the jealous whore Jenny Diver (Mrs Clarke) and imprisoned by Peachum's old pal, the jailor Lockit (Jack Hall), but he contrives to escape with the help of another of his feminine conquests, Lockit's daughter, Lucy (Mrs Eagleton). Recaptured, he seems bound for the gallows, but a last-minute pardon returns him to Polly, the only one of his apparently numerous 'wives' who had the acumen actually to get him before a clergyman.

The score of *The Beggar's Opera* was a chimeric thing which underwent constant change as eighteenth century artists and managements swapped it around and interpolated at will. The largest part of the original lyrics was the work of Gay, but it was said that other folk including

Plate 19. **The Beggar's Opera**: *The Peachum family – papa (H Peters), mama (Sofie Lis) and daughter Polly (Sheila Wolk) – in the Hessisches Staatstheater, Wiesbaden production of 1985.*

Swift ('When You Censure the Age'), Sir Charles Williams ('Virgins Are Like the Fair Flow'r'), Lord Chesterfield ('The Modes of the Town'), and the Master of the Rolls, Fortescue ('Gamesters and Lawyers Are Jugglers Alike') also made contributions. The highlight of an evening in which the principal characters were liberally supplied with vocal pieces was, however, Polly's little solo 'Oh, Ponder Well! Be Not Severe'.

The Beggar's Opera proved just the thing to appeal to those folk whom Gay intended to satirize, and it attracted enough fulminating from the righteous to boost its prospects even further. It became a huge hit and was played on 63 nights in its first season, returned in the fall, was played in 1729 with a cast of midgets, and brought back very frequently in the seasons that followed, entering the Theatre Royal, Haymarket, in 1728, and both the Theatre Royal, Drury Lane, and the Theatre Royal, Covent Garden, with Stoppelaer as Macheath, in 1732. In the same year, the famous Irish actress Peg Woffington, who had appeared as Macheath at the age of ten in a children's company, apparently succeeded in trebling the rôles of Macheath, Mrs Peachum and Diana Trapes, but the majority of leading men in the show were male and Charles Hulst, O'Keefe and Incledon were amongst the favoured Macheaths of the 18th-century stage.

The piece was played on English-speaking stages around the world throughout the 18th and 19th centuries, with Charles Santley, Sims Reeves and Mrs Howard Paul amongst the more memorable Macheaths of the 1800s, but William Harrison felt obliged to make a bowdlerized version of the show for his production in 1854. In 1870, a burlesque of what was itself in a large part a burlesque (*The Beggar's Uproar* by Hubert J Morice) was played at London's Surrey Theatre at the height of the burlesque fashion (7 May), and Gay's text was subsequently adapted into a whole series of 'revised versions'. The most successful of these was a 1920 revision, with a score arranged by Frederic Austin, which was produced at London's Lyric Theatre, Hammersmith (5 June), with Frederick Ranalow starred as Macheath, Austin as Peachum and Sylvia Nelis as Polly. It ran up a remarkable total of 1,463 performances, and re-established the show throughout the world, even though the production, with Percy Heming, Charles Magrath and Miss Nelis in its chief rôles, lasted only 37 performances when transferred to New York's Greenwich Village Theater (27 December 1920). The new wave of interest also won it a showing – in English – in France, when Wilfred Easton and Taylor Platt's company, headed by Andrew Shanks (Macheath) and Dorothy Gill (Lucy) went to play the piece at Paris's Théâtre Caumartin for a fortnight's season, and in other European venues.

Regularly produced in London's commercial theatre through the decades since, *The Beggar's Opera* was played in the West End in 1935, 1940 (w Michael Redgrave), 1941, 1948 (w Peter Pears), 1954, 1963, 1968, at the National Theatre in 1982 and the Royal Shakespeare Company in 1992–3. In New York it was repeated in 1928, 1957 and at the Billy Rose Theater in 1982 with Kevin Kline as Macheath. A film version was produced in 1952 with Laurence Olivier as Macheath, Dorothy Tutin and Adele Leigh respectively acting and singing the rôle of Polly and Stanley Holloway as Lockit, and it has been televised on several occasions.

Foreign-language versions of *The Beggar's Opera* have, by and large, preferred to build new scores and/or shows on to Gay's story rather than present the piece as written. Although the regular *Beggar's Opera* was not seen in Vienna until 1949, the Carltheater mounted a German version after the Lyric Hammersmith triumph, under the title *Der Liebling von London*, with text adapted by Felix Dörmann and the musical score arranged by Hans Ewald Heller (19 April 1924). It ran exactly a month, but it prompted another German-language adaptation, the much more successful Elisabeth Hauptmann, Bertolt Brecht/Kurt Weill *Der Dreigroschenoper*. Amongst later German versions there have been *Der Bettleropers* by Hans Magnus Enzensberger, music by Wolfgang Fortner and Volkmar Fritsche (Städtische Bühnen, Heidelberg 19 June 1966) and by Arim Tacke, music by Hans Hoffmann (Oldenberg 1988). Another adaptation of the story, this one in English, was made by John Latouche in the American musical comedy *The Beggar's Holiday* (26 December 1946), set with music by Duke Ellington.

Gay's musequel to *The Beggar's Opera*, a piece entitled *Polly*, was originally banned, apparently for being personally and offensively satirical, but when it was ultimately produced, 50 years on (Haymarket Theatre 19 June 1777), it proved to be neither, merely dull. It was a quick failure, as its predecessor continued to prosper. *Polly* was, nevertheless, revived several times in London, notably following

the success of the Lyric, Hammersmith version of *The Beggar's Opera* with one production, at the Kingsway Theatre (30 December 1922 ad Clifford Bax) running for 327 performances, at the height of the briefly reborn fashion for ballad opera.

USA: New York 3 December 1750; Australia: Albert Theatre, Hobart 30 March 1842; France: Théâtre Caumartin 22 November 1921; Austria: Johann Strauss-Theater 4 December 1949; Film: British Lion 1952

Recordings: complete versions (HMV, Argo, Desto, Decca etc), cast recordings (EMI, CBS, London etc)

Literature: Kidson, F: *The Beggar's Opera, its Predecessors and Successors* (Macmillan, New York, 1922); Schultz, W E: *The Beggar's Opera, its Content, History and Influence* (Yale University Press, 1923); Lewis, P: *John Gay: The Beggar's Opera* (Barnes & Noble, New York, 1973)

THE BEGUM Comic opera in 3 acts by Harry B Smith. Music by Reginald De Koven. Fifth Avenue Theater, New York, 21 November 1887.

The first work of both its to-be-celebrated librettist/lyricist and of the composer of *Robin Hood* to be played in New York, *The Begum* was produced by John McCaull with Mathilde Cottrelly starred in the title-rôle of the man-eating Begum of Oude and De Wolf Hopper as her husband, Howja-Dhu. Having tired of him, as of all her previous spouses, the Begum promotes him to the head of the army, declares war, and sits back to select her next consort whilst he gets himself killed. Since Hopper was the top-billed star of the show, it went without saying that Howja-Dhu survived this Machiavellic bit of queen-spidering and returned to claim his own.

The piece mixed elements of extravaganza and opéra-bouffe with the kind of low comedy which would become a favourite feature of early American comic operas and, contrastingly, a rather well-mannered score. It was cast up to the hilt, with its other Offenbachishly-named characters being played by Hubert Wilke (Klahm-Chowdee), Digby Bell (Myhnt-Julep), Edwin Hoff (Pooteh-Wehl), Jefferson de Angelis (Justt-Naut), Harry MacDonough (Asch-Kart), Laura Joyce Bell (Namouna) and Marion Manola (Aminah), but nevertheless played only three weeks on Broadway before going on to amortize its costs in other more profitable cities, including a fine run in De Koven's home town of Chicago.

LES BEIGNETS DU ROI Opérette in 3 acts by Albert Carré based on a vaudeville by Benjamin Antier. Music by Firmin Bernicat. Alcazar, Brussels, 10 February 1882. Revised version with additional music by André Messager as *Les Premières Armes de Louis XV* Théâtre des Menus-Plaisirs, Paris, 16 February 1888.

Hurriedly written and then rewritten by its highly-strung composer prior to its production in Belgium, *Les Beignets du Roi* scored a big success on its first appearance in Brussels.

The tale of the piece centred on the very young King Louis XV (Hélène Chevrier) and the complications ensuing on the awakening of his libido. Soubrette Antoinette (Mme Nadau) wins his favour by cooking his favourite beignets for him, and he then discovers that he would like more from her. However, the clever maid outwits him in the end, and gets him to decree that she may marry her Gaston de Norcy (Bréhy) rather than the lofty Duc de

Meillan (Mercier) decreed to her by her ambitious aunt (Mme Bouland). A more romantic romance, between Antoinette's school chum Atalante de Narbonne (Mme Désir) and Don Rodriguez (Lary), ran parallel to the lighter tale.

Antoinette's solo 'Le Roi m'a dit' was the saucily ingenuous hit of the score, whilst the King sang of how 'J'adore la crême au chocolat' and demanded 'Savez-vous faire une omelette?' before getting on to less culinary affairs, and there was a comic musical moment in the Trio des pendus in which Norcy, Rodriguez and the King all got ready to commit simultaneous suicide over unresolved love.

After the success of Bernicat's posthumous *François les bas-bleus*, the earlier piece was given a Paris staging with its finales revamped and several songs added by the young Messager (who had completed *François les bas-bleus*). The resultant piece played a barely satisfactory 44 times at the Menus-Plaisirs.

BEI KERZENLICHT Musical comedy by Siegfried Geyer and Karl Farkas. Music by Robert Katscher.

Siegfried Geyer's seven-handed comedy *Bei Kerzenlicht*, a dainty enough example of the most conventional master-and-man, mistress-and-maid identity swapping plot, had a fine international success. It was produced in London in Harry Graham's English version as *By Candlelight* (Prince of Wales Theatre, 18 September 1928) for a splendid run of 477 performances, and on Broadway in P G Wodehouse's version (30 September 1929, 128 performances) before Geyer adapted his play as a musical comedy, equipped with songs by Robert Katscher.

The small-scale musical play was – lacking all evidence to the contrary – seemingly first produced in Hungary (ad Armand Szantó, Mihály Szécsen) before being taken up by the Shuberts for Broadway. The little piece was then Shubertized, in line with the principle that bigger was better. Katscher's songs were thrown out, and the recently accidented Cole Porter hired to replace them. Rowland Leigh souped up the intimate play to conventional (over-) size and ladled glitzy chorines and additional settings into the action, and *You Never Know* (with a credit for 'additional numbers' given to Edwin Gilbert and Alex Fogerty ... and Robert Katscher) produced at the Shubert Theater, New Haven 3 March 1938. By the time it reached New York's Winter Garden Theater (21 September 1938), with Clifton Webb, Lupe Velez, Rex O'Malley and Libby Holman heading affairs, it was in a condition to play 78 performances. Porter's name has, however, given *You Never Know* an afterlife and it has been exhumed in various forms in American houses since his death and canonization. Vienna went back to the original Katscher version when the musical *Bei Kerzenlicht* was produced at the Wiener Künstlertheater in 1946 and again in 1956 when a production at the Theater in der Josefstadt (16 March) rang up an outstanding 143 consecutive nights at a theatre which rarely saw such runs.

A British attempt, some two decades on, to stage another remade version of *Bei Kerzenlicht*, written by Eric Maschwitz, also brought the piece back to more manageable size with eight principals, headed by Jacques Pills, Sally Ann Howes, Patricia Burke and Roger Dann, and a chorus of four. *Romance in Candlelight* (Piccadilly Theatre

15 September 1955) replaced Katscher's music with songs by Sam Coslow and closed in 53 performances.

Hungary: Royal Színház *Gyertyafénynél* 1 October 1937; Austria: Wiener Künstlertheater 22 May 1946
Recording: *Romance in Candlelight* selection (Columbia, EP)

BÉKEFFY, István (b Szeged, 31 August 1901; d Budapest, 9 June 1977).

A hugely prolific author of comedies, often written in collaboration with László Vadnai or Adorján Stella, of musical plays and adaptations, of novels, screenplays and lyrics, Békeffy wrote texts and/or lyrics for many musical plays, including a long series, many highly successful, in collaboration with Lajos Lajtai.

A number of his musical pieces were seen beyond Hungary in the 1930s, several in German versions – *A régi nyár* as *Sommer von einst*, *Sisters*, *Éjféli tango* as *Tango am Mitternacht*, *Esö után köpönyeg* as *Verzeih, das ich dich liebe* – whilst his *Öfelsége frakkja*, as adapted by André Barde, successfully became *Katinka* in France. He was still writing in his seventies, and his musical comedy *A Kutya* was played in German as *Der Hund, der Herr Bozzi hiess* (ad Géza Engel, Henriette Engel, Meiningen 29 September 1978) after his death.

1926 **Hol jártál az az éjszaka?** (w László Vadnai) Sziget Színpad 26 March
1927 **Mesék az irógépről** (Lajos Lajtai/w István Szomaházy) Városi Színház 8 October
1928 **A régi nyár** (Lajtai) Budai Színkör 15 June
1928 **Párizsi divat** (Lajtai) Városi Színház 22 December
1929 **Ez hát a szerelem** (*So This is Love*) Hungarian version (Fővárosi Operettszinház)
1930 **Sisters** (Lajtai) Király Színház 10 January
1930 **Lila test, sarga sapka** (Lajtai/w László Békeffy) Nyári Operettszinház 7 June
1930 **Az okos mama** (Lajtai) Király Színház 26 November
1931 **Egy kis csokor** (Dezső Losonczy) Andrássy uti Színház 3 January
1931 **Öfelsége frakkja** (Lajtai) Király Színház 19 September
1932 **Éjféli tangó** (Károly Komjáthy/w Vadnai) Király Színház 27 February
1932 **Régi orfeum** (Lajtai/w Jenő Faragó) Fővárosi Operettszinház 12 March
1932 **Amikor a kis lányból nagy lány lesz** (Lajtai) Budai Színkör 10 June
1932 **Egy asszony, aki tudja, mit akar** (*Eine Frau, die weiss, was sie will*) Hungarian lyrics w Tamás Emőd (Vigszinház)
1932 **A Rothschildok** (Lajtai/Ferenc Martos) Fővárosi Operettszinház 25 November
1932 **Bridge-Szalon** Andrássy uti Színház 27 November
1932 **Ecet és olaj** (*Essig und Öl*) Hungarian lyrics (Andrássy uti Színház)
1932 **Kadétszerelem** (Pál Gyöngy/w László Szilágyi) Fővárosi Operettszinház 23 December
1933 **Egy csók és más semmi** (Mihály Eisemann/Imre Halász) Magyar Színház 12 May
1934 **Öméltósága soförje** (Gyöngy) Király Színház 24 February
1934 **A cirkusz csillaga** (Eisemann, Komjáthy/László Bus Fekete) Vígszínház 22 June
1934 **Nápolyi kaland** (Lajtai/w Vadnai) Fővárosi Operettszinház 10 November
1935 **Történnek még csodák** (Pál Ábrahám/Halász) Magyar Színház 20 April
1936 **Esö után köpönyeg** (Michael Krasznay-Krausz/Mihály Szécsén) Andrássy uti Színház 6 November
1938 **Dinasztia** (Miklós Brodszky/w Imre Harmath/Pál Váli) Magyar Színház 16 April

1939 **Az Angol bank nem fizet** (Tamás Bródy/w Adorjan Stella) Pesti Színház 18 March

1939 **Pusztai szerenád** (Szabolcs Fényes/w Szilágyi) Fővárosi Operettszinház 29 September

1945 **Csárdáskirálynő** (*Die Csárdásfürstin*) new Hungarian adaptation (Fővárosi Operettszinház)

1946 **Florentin kalap** (*Un chapeau de paille d'Italie*) musical version w Tibor Polgár Fővárosi Operettszinház 19 April

1946 **Csicsónénak három lánya** (Komjáthy/w Dezső Kellér) Fővárosi Operettszinház 5 October

1947 **Rigó Jancsi** (Fényes/Sándor Lestyán ad) Fővárosi Operettszinház 9 May

1947 **Nincsenek véletlenek** (Bródy) Belvárosi Színház 25 July

1949 **VIII osztály** (Bródy) Fővárosi Operettszinház 4 February

1949 **Rip van Winkle** new Hungarian adaptation w Bródy, Fényes (Fővárosi Operettszinház)

1951 **Palotaszálló** (Bródy, János Kerekes/w Kellér, Tibor Mérei) Fővárosi Operettszinház 23 February

1952 **Luxemburg grófja** (*Der Graf von Luxemburg*) new Hungarian adaptation w Kellér (Fővárosi Operettszinház)

1954 **Szombat délutan** (Fényes) Fővárosi Vigszinház 19 February

1955 **Szerencsés flótás** (Fényes) Fővárosi kis Színpad 23 March

1971 **Mit vesztett el kisasszony?** (Fényes/w Iván Szenes) Fővárosi Operettszinház 26 February

1976 **A Kutya, akit Bozzi urnak hivtak** (Fényes/w György G Denes) 27 February

BELL, Digby V[alentine] (b Milwaukee, Wis, 1851; d New York, 20 June 1917). Tenor turned comedian who had a fine career on American musical stages.

Bell studied as a singer in Naples and made his first stage appearance in Malta as the Count in *La Sonnambula*. Returning to America, he first performed in concert at the Chickering Hall before making his début on the musical stage, in Montreal, as Beppo in *Fra Diavolo* (1877). He quickly found himself cast in comic rather than romantic rôles and, through a career of more than 30 years, he established himself as one of the most popular singing comedians in American musical theatre. One of his earliest New York engagements was in the British German Reed repertoire when, in spite of his young age, he appeared as Ebenezer Tare in *Ages Ago* and Joe Bumpus in *Charity Begins at Home* at the Bijou Theatre and, during the early 1880s, he also appeared on Broadway as Alfred Puddifoot in *Lawn Tennis* (subtitled 'an English comic opera'), as Grosvenor (*Patience*), Dr Daly (*The Sorcerer*), Samuel Nubbles in Edward Solomon's *Virginia*, King Charles in *Nell Gwynne* and Matt o'the Mill in *Indiana* as well as in American versions of the French *Les Noces d'Olivette* (Coquelicot), *Orphée aux enfers* (Jupiter), *Le Coeur et la main* (Don Gaétan), *La Princesse de Trébizonde* (Tremolini), *Madame Favart* (Charles) and the German *Nisida* (Zanina as Booma Poota), *The Passing Regiment* (van Tassel), *Der Feldprediger* (Piffkow), *Der Bettelstudent* (Ollendorf) and *Boccaccio* (Lotteringhi).

In 1887 he was seen at the Fifth Avenue Theater as Myhnt-Julep in McCaull's production of the Harry B Smith and Reginald De Koven musical *The Begum*, the following year as Toby in the American version of Czibulka's *Der Glücksritter* (*The May Queen*) and, in the succeeding seasons, mixed classic rôles (Koko, Major General Stanley, Baron Puck, Don Boléro d'Alcarazas) with native works, appearing with top billing in two McCaull productions written for him by Harry B Smith – *The Tar and the Tartar* (1891, Muley Hassan) and *Jupiter*

(1892, Jupiter) – and opposite Lillian Russell in both *Princess Nicotine* (1893, Don Pedro) and the Austro-British *The Queen of Brilliants*. He subsequently appeared largely in comedy, but played Adam Hogg in *The Chaperons* (1902), Sam Weller to DeWolf Hopper's Pickwick in the 1903 musical *Mr Pickwick* and appeared in Gilbert and Sullivan revivals well into his sixties.

He was married in 1882 to the singing character-lady **Laura Joyce BELL** (née MASKELL) (b London, ?1858; d New York, 29 May 1904) who, after an early career in London (*Loan of a Lover* at the Strand Theatre) moved to America and made her first appearances at Niblo's Garden, the Broadway Theater and in the title-rôle of the famous burlesque *Evangeline*. She appeared as a youngish Little Buttercup (1879), as Germaine to the Serpolette of Catherine Lewis (1879), played a season with J S Crossey's comic opera company (*First Life Guards in Brighton* 1880, *Madame Angot's Daughter* etc) and with Augustin Daly's company, and soon established herself as one of the best heavy singing ladies of her era. She appeared, often alongside her husband, in a long series of comic operas on Broadway, including *Zanina* (Zanina), *Hand and Heart* (Donna Scholastica), *La Princesse de Trébizonde* (Paola), *Orphée aux enfers* (Diana), *Bellman* (Tronda), *Boccaccio* (Peronella), *The Begum* (Namouna), *The May Queen* (Roxana), *Cinderella at School* (Merope Mallow), *Patience* (Lady Jane), *The Sorcerer* (Lady Sangazure), *Virginia* (Mrs Cowslip), *Indiana* (Lady Prue), *Der Bettelstudent* (Palmatica), *Nell Gwynne* (Lady Clare), *The Tar and the Tartar* (Alpaca) and *The Mikado* (Katisha).

BELL, Rose

Briefly one of the foremost players of opéra-bouffe in Britain at the height of the craze for such productions, Rose Bell first came to notice in America, when she toured – anglophone name and all – with Jacob Grau's company, sharing the leading rôles with no less a star than Marie Desclauzas. She won the New York Times' commendation as having 'the best French voice we have ever had in New York', dimmed a little by the subsequent comment '... she sings skilfully and with spirit, but she is not in the slightest degree funny'. She appeared in New York as Drogan (*Geneviève de Brabant*), Dindonette (*L'Oeil crevé*), Césarine (*Fleur de thé*), Gabrielle (*La Vie parisienne*) and Frédégonde (*Chilpéric*) between 1868 and 1869, and next surfaced in Britain, two seasons later, where she appeared at the Alhambra Theatre in a series of French and British musical productions, often in travesty rôles. At the height of her popularity, in the early 1870s, she was paired in three pieces with Kate Santley when she appeared as a soprano Paris (*La Belle Hélène*), Clorinde (*La Jolie Parfumeuse*) and in the title-rôle of *Don Juan*, and the two rival actresses developed fanatical followings which led to pitched fights and the law courts.

Bell created lead rôles in the English versions of *L'Oeil crevé* (Fleur-de-Noblesse), *The Wonderful Duck* (ie *Le Canard à trois becs*), *Le Voyage dans la lune* (Prince Caprice) and *Les Géorgiennes* (Lady Feroza), starred in the Offenbach pasticcio *The Bohemians* (1873), played Trainette in *Pom* in the provinces and also appeared at the Alhambra as Robin Wildfire in *Le Roi Carotte*, Algar in *The Demon's Bride* and, in what seems to have been her last

West End appearance, as Siebel in the 1880 production of *Mefistofele II* (*Le Petit Faust*).

BELLE, or The Ballad of Doctor Crippen
Music-hall musical in 2 acts by Wolf Mankowitz from a play by Beverley Cross. Lyrics and music by Monty Norman. Strand Theatre, London, 4 May 1961.

A lively, small-scale piece which told the story of poisoner Dr Crippen as performed by the members of the company of the Bedford Music Hall under the compèring of their chairman, Lasher (Jerry Desmonde). The title-character of *Belle* was the over-plumed, under-voiced music-hall singer (Rose Hill) to whom the meek Crippen (George Benson) had the misfortune to be married. He discovers love with his nurse, Ethel (Virginia Vernon), and events move on to their celebrated and deadly climax via a set of songs which either parodied or imitated turn-of-the-century styles. The most successful number was the 'Dit-Dit' song, in which the land-to-sea telegraph, which facilitated Crippen's and Ethel's high-seas capture, was sung of with much more amorous connotations. Other pieces, such as the heroine's tongue-in-cheek admission that 'I Can't Stop Singing' and her medical love duet with Crippen, gave enjoyable moments alongside some cornier numbers for the music-hall folk.

Belle chose its time poorly. The critical fashion was all for the low-life, Soho-style musical, and 'realism-in-musicals' was briefly as much the rage as 'politics-in-musicals' would become in the 1990s. And yet this piece encountered some opposition due to its 'tasteless' subject matter. That, added to the fact that out-of-town problems meant that *Belle* was still patchy on arrival, scuppered it in six weeks. A revival of a reconstruction of *Belle* by the Tavistock Repertory Company proved, 20 years later, that the show had deserved a better fate.

Recording: original cast (Decca)

LA BELLE ARABELLE
Opérette in 2 acts by Marc-Cab and Francis Blanche. Music by Guy Lafarge and Pierre Philippe. Théâtre de la Porte-Saint-Martin, Paris, 4 October 1956.

A made-to-order vehicle for the popular singing quartet Les Frères Jacques, *La Belle Arabelle* (the title was the name of the houseboat on which the four lived) featured the men as Arsène, André, Arthur and Alfred, four young fellows who go up and down the canals of France, earning their living by running a fair-booth. When they save a pretty amnesiac girl (Lucie Dolène) from drowning, complexities ensue, but it turns out she is a princess, her memory comes back, and she marries her Henri (Robert Piquet), whilst the boys go back to their barge and their 'guardian angel', Domino (Jeannette Batti). The show's score featured its quartet in 'La Colle au pinceau', 'J'emmène les gendarmes', 'Les Boît's à musique', 'Les Barons de Ballencourt' and a title-song in characteristic style.

La Belle Arabelle ran for 9 months at the large Théâtre de la Porte-Saint-Martin, and the show was later toured – without its stars – in a version which reduced the family to three brothers. It was most recently revived by the Opéra Royal de Wallonie in 1983 (Verviers, 11 November) with the harmony group Les Poivre et Sel featured as its jolly bargees.

Recording: original cast (Philips 45rpm)

LA BELLE DE CADIX
Opérette in 3 acts by Raymond Vincy and Marc-Cab. Lyrics by Maurice Vandair. Music by Francis Lopez. Casino-Montparnasse, Paris, 24 December 1945.

As much as one show can, *La Belle de Cadix* marked the same kind of a turning in the musical theatre in France as, around the same time, the production of *Oklahoma!* encouraged in America. It led the fashion definitively away from the light-footed and -hearted comedy musicals which had triumphed during the 1920s, but had now rather lost their zing, back to an up-to-date version of the colourful, romantic musical play with its standard operettic construction and cast.

The hero of the tale was celluloid star Carlos Médina (Luis Mariano) who goes to the Spanish hills to film scenes for his *La Belle de Cadix*. Local girl Maria-Luisa (France Aubert) is chosen to play his gipsy bride, but over-helpful Pépa (Jacquie Flynt) supplies a real gipsy king for the part of the screenic gipsy king and, thus, the two are married for real. Since Carlos is engaged to an American tobacco heiress (Simone Chobillon) and Maria-Luisa to a jealous and macho gipsy (Fabrézy), there is an actful of problems before they choose to stay married. Alongside the romantic tale ran the comical one of the little production assistant, Manillon (Roger Lacoste), who pretends to be the film's director in order to attract the girls, and who gets more than he bargained for in Pépa.

Vincy's well-proportioned book was illustrated by a set of songs which, first and foremost, gave the leading tenor an opportunity to shine. Mariano made himself a star with his performance of the tenor's long list of numbers and at the same time turned the show's title-song into an enormous hit. 'La Belle de Cadix' was followed up with his praises of 'Maria-Luisa', memories of 'Le Clocher du village', the celebration of 'La Fiesta bohémienne', a dejected farewell to Spain ('Une nuit à Grenade') and a duetting 'Rendez-vous sur la lune' which seemed to owe just a little to Rudolf Friml's 'Indian Love Call', all of which still left place for the heroine to wander through 'Les Sentiers de la montagne', Ramirès the gipsy to make another hit out of his scornful baritone piece on 'Le Coeur des femmes', and Manillon and Pépa to bounce through several happy soubret numbers.

Produced with all the colour that its settings allowed (designed by Mariano, a former art student), *La Belle de Cadix* which had been originally commissioned by Laurallier of the Casino Montparnasse for a 50-performance season over the Christmas period to replace a cancelled Edith Piaf show – emerged as a major hit. It celebrated the end of the war by playing two full seasons in Paris, and just two years later it was revived, in an enlarged version, by Maurice Lehmann at the Théâtre de l'Empire (17 December 1949) with Mariano paired with top soprano Lina Dachary. Thereafter *La Belle de Cadix* barely quitted the stages of France. It returned to Paris again in 1958 (Gaîté-Lyrique 20 November) with Antonio Rossano starred, in 1977 (Théâtre Mogador 5 February) with Miguel Cortez, in 1979 (Théâtre de la Renaissance) with Jose Villamor, who had played Ramirès in the previous production, and again in 1991 (Théâtre de la Renaissance, 17 February) with Cortez and Carlo di Angelo alternating

Plate 20. **La Belle Hélène**: *Whilst the heavy stuff is going on back at the palace, a burlesque Orestes just has a good time. Sadler's Wells Theatre, 1967.*

in Mariano's rôle. A film version was made in 1953 with Mariano starred alongside Carmen Sevilla, Jean Tissier, Pierjac, Claude Nicot and Claire Maurier.

Like the rest of the French musical plays of its time, *La Belle de Cadix* has, in spite of its home popularity, been rarely seen outside France, although Lopez has related that a contract for a Broadway production that was to have been signed between his publisher, Salabert, and the Shubert organization was abandoned when Salabert was killed in a plane crash on his way to America.

Film: 1953

Recordings: original cast (EMI-Pathé), selections (Odéon, CBS) etc

LA BELLE HÉLÈNE Opéra-bouffe in 3 acts by Henri Meilhac and Ludovic Halévy. Music by Jacques Offenbach. Théâtre des Variétés, Paris, 17 December 1864.

The fourth of Offenbach's great opéras-bouffes burlesqueing ancient historical legend or mythology (after *Orphée aux enfers*, *Geneviève de Brabant* and *Le Pont des soupirs*), *La Belle Hélène* was also his first written with the authorial team of Henri Meilhac and Ludovic Halévy, who would go on to supply him with the texts for many of his most famous works. It was also the first written expressly

for the leading lady, Hortense Schneider, who would become the darling of pre-war Paris in a series of similar rôles in Offenbach opéras-bouffes.

Being the most beautiful woman in the world can be a real burden. Especially when goddesses go round promising you to some exceptionally handsome shepherd (José Dupuis) as a prize in a contest, without stopping to think that you are already married to Ménélas, the King of Sparta (Kopp). There really isn't much the beautiful Helen (Mlle Schneider) can do, when fate, Venus and the augur Calchas (Grenier) conspire to send her husband off to Crete and then send her this dream of the handsome shepherd, who is actually Prince Paris of Troy in disguise and a very tangible dream. When the wretched husband objects noisily to being cuckolded, Venus revengefully sends a plague of immorality upon Greece, and Ménélas gets the blame. He sends for the grand priest of Cythera, who prescribes a pilgrimage to Venus' shrine for the almost-lapsed Queen, but when Helen is safely aboard the island-bound ship the priest throws off his disguise – it is Paris, he's got Helen in his hands for a whole sea voyage, and the Trojan War can now take place.

Offenbach's score was one of his gayest and most memorable. Paris's sweetly tenorizing tale of his Judgement ('Au mont Ida trois déesses'), Helen's celebration of

'Amour divins', her invocation of the interfering Venus ('Dis-moi, Vénus'), and the pair's waltzing attempts to convince themselves that their lovemaking is all a dream ('Oui! C'est un rêve') were the lyrical highlights of the evening. Then, in contrast, came the swingeing march ('Voici les rois de Grèce') which introduced individually the famous Kings of Greece from Agamemnon (Couder) to Achilles (Guyon) and the twin Ajaxes (Hamburger, Andof), the bouncing Patriotic Trio for Calchas, Agamemnon and Ménélas ('Lorsque la Grèce est un champ de carnage'), and a jolly lad-about-town number ('Au Cabaret du labyrinthe') for a monocled, travesty Orestes (Léa Silly), as well as such extravagant follies as the dazzling tyrolienne (in ancient Greece!) of the last act finale, sung by Paris in his disguise as the Grand Priest.

Cogniard's production of *La Belle Hélène* hit several sticky patches. A feud between the star and the second lady, Mlle Silly, was temporarily pasted over, but when the Judgement of Paris number, the tenor's best spot, went for nothing at dress rehearsal, Offenbach decided drastically to rewrite the number. Overnight, he composed three different settings of the verses. He summoned Dupuis the next morning, ordered him to choose the one he liked best, then set to orchestrate it whilst the tenor learned his new melody. As in so many other cases, the last-minute song proved one of the gems of the score.

The reviews of the show were mixed, but it got some splendid publicity from the indignant antics of the more rabid critics. One, who had reviled the authors for defiling the sacred works of classical antiquity, was taken down a peg by the revelation that he was unable to read a word of Greek. After a slow start, the show became first popular and then enormously popular. It ran right through the more than six months to the summer recess, and returned later in 1865 for further performances whilst the authors worked on its successor and the first burlesque, a glance at *La Belle Hélène dans son ménage* (G Rose/Mérenville), appeared at the Nouveautés (11 July 1867). At the same time *La Belle Hélène* began its dissemination through the world's theatres.

Friedrich Strampfer was first off the mark with his production (ad F Zell, Julius Hopp) at Vienna's Theater an der Wien, and he scored an unmitigated triumph. The young Marie Geistinger caused a sensation as the lightly clad schöne Helena, and, with Albin Swoboda as her Paris, Karl Blasel as Ménélas, and Carl Adolf Friese (Agamemnon), Matthias Rott (Calchas) and Frln Beyer (Orestes) in support, the Theater an der Wien company played the piece 65 times during its first nine months in the repertoire. The show was seen in Prague and in Berlin in German, with Geistinger repeating her Vienna rôle, but apparently in a different adaptation, written by Ernst Dohm, which inexplicably omitted the patriotic trio. In Vienna, Geistinger clocked up the show's 200th performance (to the Ménélas of Girardi) on 30 December 1875, but in Germany she and the show were greeted with some horrified comments from the press, the *Preussische Zeitung* railing hectically against 'this Jewish speculation on the spirit of modern society – a speculation which, in the most refined manner and with the aid of music, scoffs at, ridicules and caricatures whatever is regarded as high and sacred in domestic life'. It didn't hurt business.

The first English-language version was heard in London, when F C Burnand's much tampered-with *Helen, or Taken from the Greek* was mounted at the Adelphi Theatre with Miss Furtado as its Helen, Mrs Alfred Mellon playing Paris in travesty, and the comedians Paul Bedford (Calchas) and Johnnie Toole (Agamemnon) in support, but, after London had seen Schneider's performance of the original French show (St James's Theatre 13 July 1868), a more faithful version was made for British consumption by Charles Lamb Kenney. This one was produced at the Gaiety Theatre by John Hollingshead (18 July 1871) with Australia's Julia Mathews as its Helen and Constance Loseby another travesty Paris. With Annie Tremaine also playing in travesty as Orestes, the traditions of British burlesque were well maintained. Burnand had a second and more dignified try when he redid *La Belle Hélène* for the vast stage of the Alhambra and its star team of Kate Santley (Helen), Rose Bell (Paris) and Harry Paulton (Menelaos). The production ran an excellent 109 consecutive performances.

New York, curiously, had its first taste of *La Belle Hélène* in German when Hedwig L'Arronge-Sury appeared as die schöne Helena in a repertoire production at the Stadttheater. The city's German theatres regularly reproduced the piece in the years that followed even although, just a few months after that première, Lucille Tostée and her company had given New York a taste of the original piece in all its French glory. Without creating the sensation that Tostée's *Grande-Duchesse* had done, *La Belle Hélène* ran for a full month of consecutive performances, and both Tostée and Aimée played Helen liberally round the country during their American seasons for as long as opéra-bouffe was alive. The first American English version (ad Molyneux St John) was seemingly done by the ever enterprising Worrell sisters – Sophie was Helen, Irene was Paris and Jennie was Orestes – in 1868, but a more significant English-language version appeared in 1899 when the show was mounted at the Casino Theater with Lillian Russell starred as a well-rounded Helen for 52 performances.

The Scandanavian countries were amongst the first to stage their versions of *La Belle Hélène*, Italian and Spanish adaptations were swiftly mounted and, as always, Hungary was amongst the quickest to have a vernacular version of the show on the stage. Strangely, that version (ad Endre Latabár) was first mounted in Kassa, and *Szép Helena* was seen in Szeged (w Antónia Hetényi), Arad, Koloszvár, Miskolc, Nagyvárad and Debrecen (both these last two with the young Lujza Blaha as Helen) before playing Budapest for the first time, four years after the Zell/Hopp German version had already been seen there. Ilka Medgyaszay (Helen), Ferenc Halmi (Paris) and Ferenc Erczi (Ménélas) led the initial Várszinház production, which was overshadowed a dozen years later (7 October 1882) when the Népszinház took the show into its repertoire and mounted it with a big-gun cast: Ilka Pálmay (Helen), János Kápolnai (Paris), Vidor Kassai (Menelaos) and Elek Solymossy (Calchas).

Australia got its first *La Belle Hélène* in 1876, when Emilie Melville, Armes Beaumont (Paris), Jeannie Winston (Orestes), Henry Bracy (Ménélas) and George Leopold (Calchas) appeared at Sydney's Royal Victoria Theatre in an uncredited version. Soon after, Australians were able to see Emily Soldene's more Rubensesque Helen as Melville moved on to take her version of the piece to India and round the Pacific and adjacent oceans in her repertoire of opéras-bouffes and -comiques.

In France, *La Belle Hélène* established itself as one of the staples of the Offenbach repertoire. The Variétés remounted it in 1876 with Anna Judic as Helen and Dupuis in his original rôle, and again ten years later with the same pair still featured. Judic gave her last Parisian Helen in 1889 and was succeeded by Jeanne Granier (1890) and then by Juliette Simon-Girard (1899). The Opéra-Comique's Marguerite Carré appeared as Helen to the Paris of Fernand Francell and the Calchas of Max Dearly in 1919 (Gaîté-Lyrique 5 October), Géori Boué starred in a 1960 revival (Théâtre Mogador 25 February) and an undersized revival was mounted at the Bouffes-Parisiens in 1976 (24 September). Since then, more substantial revivals have played at the Opéra-Comique (25 April 1983, 21 September 1985) and at the Théâtre de Paris (13 November 1986) with multiple casts. In 1926 a sort of sequel, written by Fernand Nozière and set to music by Fernand Raphael, was mounted at Paris's Théâtre Daunou under the title of *Hélène*.

Elsewhere, the piece has also kept its popularity if, occasionally, lost its identity. Vienna was amongst the first to butcher the show when Gabor Steiner produced his own 'burlesque operette from the French' *Die schöne Helena von heute* (w Leopold Krenn, mus arr Ludwig Gothov-Grüneke) with Helene Ballot playing her namesake, as part of the 1911 and 1912 seasons at Ronacher. Max Reinhardt's physically spectacular version of a grossly rewritten version of the show produced at Berlin's Theater am Kurfürstendamm, in 1931, with opera star Jarmila Novotna starred as a Helen with a very much larger voice than Mlle Schneider would ever have dreamed of possessing (or Offenbach of hearing), Egon Fridell (Paris), Hans Moser, Theo Lingen, Friedl Schuster, Otto Wallburg and Max Pallenberg as Ménélas, favoured the visual side rather than the textual, and a subsequent remake of this version for London, 'adapted' by A P Herbert and (musically) E W Korngold to the extent of inventing a wholly new third act, won gasps of approval for Oliver Messel's extravagant settings and the two-thousand-ship beauty of its Helen (Evelyn Laye) as George Robey turned his hand to the comicalities of Ménélas. The 'authors' of this thoroughly raped *Helen* collected Offenbach's, Meilhac's and Halévy's royalties through 193 performances, and producer C B Cochran lost a small fortune.

Vienna proved particularly partial to the show. When memories of Geistinger's Helen (seen at the Carltheater again in 1887) had barely faded, Ilka Pálmay brought her Helen to the Theater an der Wien (1891) and was followed the next year by Minna Baviera and, as the show resurfaced regularly in the repertoire through the 1890s, by Julie Kopácsi-Karczag, Frln Frey, Annie Dirkens and others. During the pre-war years of the new century, both the two principal Viennese houses played the show in repertoire with Kopácsi-Karczag, Dirkens and Pálmay being joined by Betty Stojan, Frau Saville, Flora Siding, Dora Keplinger and Phila Wolff as the latest Helenas until a major revival was launched in 1911 (12 October) with Mizzi Günther playing Helen to the Ménélas of Louis Treumann and the Paris of Ludwig Herold. Later the same year (31 December) the show was seen at the Volksoper with Maria Jeritza in the starring rôle as another very

vocal Greek queen. The show reappeared regularly both during the war (Carltheater, Bürgertheater w Ida Russka) and after, proving itself the most enduring of Offenbach's pieces on the Viennese stage. It was most recently played in Vienna in 1990 at the Wiener Kammeroper with English soprano Gaynor Miles starred as a particularly glamorous and lightly clad Helena.

If, in Germany, the butchering begun by Reinhardt and his allies was followed up by more butchering, in London the wrongs of A P Herbert were righted, 30 years later, when the Sadler's Wells Opera Company produced a fine, funny and faithful new translation (ad Geoffrey Dunn 31 May 1963) with Joyce Blackham starred as a luscious Helen. The same company (English National Opera) revived that version in 1975, and the show was given a later staging by the ill-fated New Sadler's Wells company.

New York also went through a version of the souped-up Reinhardt/Korngold version under the title *Helen Goes to Troy* (24 April 1944), with Novotna repeating her heavyweight Helen 14 years on, and a programme which actually boasted 'Korngold ... has not only rearranged and reorchestrated the original Offenbach score, but also interpolated 14 newly adapted numbers, substituting [these] for some wilted music pieces of the original score'. Mr Korngold's Offenbach hash lasted 96 performances. *La Belle Hélène* survived this and other tasteless attacks (a *La Belle* perpetrated by one William Roy wilted before getting to Broadway) and it has made its way, as elsewhere, into American opera houses. It was played in 1976 at the New York City Opera with Karan Armstrong as Helen.

Austria: Theater an der Wien *Die schöne Helena* 17 March 1865; Germany: Friedrich-Wilhelmstädtisches Theater *Die schöne Helena* 13 May 1865; UK: Adelphi Theatre *Helen, or Taken from the Greek* 30 June 1866; Hungary: Kassa *Szép Helena* 7 March 1866, Budai Színkör (Ger) 6 May 1866, Várszinház *Szép Helena* 30 April 1870; USA: Chicago 1867, Stadttheater, New York *Die schöne Helena* 3 December 1867, New York Theater *Paris and Helen, or the Greek Elopement* 13 April 1868; Australia: Royal Victoria Theatre, Sydney 31 May 1876

Recordings: complete (Musidisc Festival, EMI-Pathé, EMI) cast recordings (Véga, Barclay), selections (EMI-Pathé, Philips etc), complete in Russian (Melodiya), complete in German (Philips), selection in English (HMV) etc

BELLE LURETTE Opéra-comique in 3 acts by Raoul Toché, Édouard Blau and Ernest Blum. Music by Jacques Offenbach. Théâtre de la Renaissance, Paris, 30 October 1880.

The last full-length opérette of Jacques Offenbach, its orchestration completed after the composer's death by Léo Delibes, *Belle Lurette* was produced posthumously at the Théâtre de la Renaissance in 1880, and had a respectable life, without establishing itself as part of the composer's revivable repertoire.

Belle Lurette (Jane Harding) is a little laundress, working in the establishment run by Marcelline (Mily-Meyer), courted by the jolly fellows of the area (Vauthier, Jannin, Alexandre), and putting her faith in the tarot cards which predict her a fine future. That future arrives in the person of Malicorne (Alfred Jolly) who picks the pretty laundress to be the bride of the Duke of Marly (Henri Cooper). When it turns out that she is to be a wife in name only to cover her husband's current affair, but yet ensure him his inheritance, she raises the roof. By the end she has won him properly, and Marcelline has pinned down Malicorne who turns out to be the fellow who helped himself to her virtue years before and then disappeared.

In a score which was heavily angled towards the heroine, the best-liked pieces were her countrified Ronde de Colette, a rhythmic Chanson du Jabot with which Alexandre, in the rôle of Belhomme, opened the evening's proceedings, and a parody of Strauss's 'Blue Danube' performed by Mily-Meyer and Jolly. An ensemble, 'Nous sommes les amoureux', and two further pieces for the heroine, the rondeau 'Chez la baronne' and a first-act romance ('Faut-il ainsi nous maudire'), were amongst the other attractive musical moments.

In spite of much applauded performances from Mily-Meyer and Mlle Hading, *Belle Lurette* lasted only a fair 82 performances in Paris. It was played by the Renaissance company in London, in its original French, and was later given in an English version (ad Frank Desprez, Alfred Murray, Henry S Leigh) for a respectable 83-performance run at the Avenue Theatre with Florence St John (Lurette), Lottie Venne (Marcelline), Claude Marius (Malicorne) and Henry Bracy (Marly) heading a strong cast. It was reprised in Paris in 1883 with Jeanne Granier in the title-rôle, appeared a couple of decades on in Austria (ad F Heidrich, F Maierfeld) with one Frln Kramm playing the title-rôle in the '1 Aufführung in deutscher Sprache' under August Lischke's direction at the Jantschtheater, and was subsequently played both in Hungary (ad Sándor Hevesi) and in Russia.

UK: Gaiety Theatre (Fr) 6 July 1881, Avenue Theatre *Lurette* 24 March 1883; Austria: Jantschtheater *Die schöne Lurette* 3 May 1900; Hungary: Király Színház *Szép Mosónő* 3 September 1904

THE BELLE OF BOHEMIA

THE BELLE OF BOHEMIA Musical farce in 2 acts by Harry B Smith. Music by Ludwig Englander. Additional music by Harry T MacConnell. Casino Theater, New York, 19 March 1900.

A musical with a two Dromios libretto and a serviceable score, *The Belle of Bohemia* was played at the Casino Theatre with star comic Sam Bernard and his brother Dick in the rôles of the swappable Adolf Klotz and Rudolph Dinkelhauser and a supporting cast including Trixie Friganza (Chloe), Virginia Earle (Katie), Irene Bentley (Geraldine McDuffy) and the two comedian brothers of British composer Teddy Solomon, Fred (Yellowplush) and Sol ('Arris).

Although *The Belle of Bohemia* lasted only 55 performances at the Casino Theater, it was shipped off to Britain, in the wake of the success there of *The Belle of New York*, with Richard Carle (Algy Cuffs) at the head of its cast supported by Miss Friganza, Marie George and Marie Dainton. It did not have the novelty attraction for Londoners that the earlier piece had done and, after a little over two months at the Apollo Theatre, Carle, Marie Dainton, and the Casino company moved on to play *The Belle of New York* and *The Casino Girl* in Budapest, Berlin and Vienna.

UK: Apollo Theatre 21 February 1901

THE BELLE OF BRITTANY

THE BELLE OF BRITTANY Musical play in 2 acts by Leedham Bantock and P J Barrow. Lyrics by Percy Greenbank. Music by Howard Talbot. Additional numbers by Marie Horne. Queen's Theatre, London, 24 October 1908.

A charming light musical show, written by the Bantock/Anderson team which had been responsible for the mini-musical *The White Chrysanthemum*, *The Belle of Brittany* mixed the style and story-telling of the old-fashioned opéra-comique, its marquises and country maidens, with some of the more contemporary traditions of turn-of-the-century musical comedy.

The story dealt with the hurdles that moneyless Marquis's son Raymond (Lawrence Rea) and miller's daughter Babette (Ruth Vincent) need to negotiate on the way to marriage. His father (George Graves) needs cash for his mortgage and wants his son to marry rich Denise (Lily Iris), her father (M R Morand) holds the mortgage but wants his daughter to marry the famous chef Baptiste Boubillion (Walter Passmore). The deux ex machina is old Jacques, the clarionet player (E W Royce), who gets hold of the important papers in the affair and ensures a happy ending.

Talbot's score was more than a mite conventional with its songs celebrating 'Daffodil Time in Brittany', 'The Kingdom of a Woman's Heart', 'A Little Café' and 'Little Country Mice' but it had its fine moments, as in Passmore's jolly description of himself as 'The King of the Kitchen' and some pretty soprano numbers for Miss Vincent. A certain delicacy in the show's writing and production meant that its success, though certain, was more limited than that of some more obvious pieces of the time, but Graves soon ensured that delicacy went out the window as he began to pad his part with the kind of stand-up comedy he had used in *The Merry Widow*. Miss Vincent and soubrette Maudi Darrell ('A Bit of the Very Best Brittany') were given extra numbers in some kind of compensation.

Tom Davis's production had a respectable run in London (147 performances) before Graves took it into the provinces, and the following year the Shuberts produced a version on Broadway. Christine Nielson and Frank Daniels starred as Babette and the Marquis, some Harold Atteridge/Harry Carroll numbers were inserted into Howard Talbot's score, and the piece ran through 72 performances.

The Belle of Brittany was also seen in Australia, where Winifred O'Connor (Babette), Tom Walls (Marquis), Percy Clifton (Poquelin), Gertrude Gilliam (Toinette) and Charlie Stone (Baptiste) took time out from the success of *The Arcadians* to play a satisfactory season.

USA: Daly's Theater 8 November 1909; Australia: Criterion Theatre, Sydney 25 February 1911

THE BELLE OF MAYFAIR

THE BELLE OF MAYFAIR Musical comedy in 2 acts by Basil Hood and Charles H E Brookfield (later billed as by Cosmo Hamilton and Brookfield). Music by Leslie Stuart. Vaudeville Theatre, London, 11 April 1906. New version 8 February 1907.

The Belle of Mayfair was originally conceived and carefully constructed by librettist Basil Hood as a modern society version of Shakespeare's *Romeo and Juliet* but, in the hands of producer Charles Frohman, it ultimately dissolved into an attractive but hardly unconventional Edwardian musical comedy of pretty girls, pretty dresses and very pretty songs tacked together with some light society chit-chat and various kinds of comedy, and Hood insisted that his name be withdrawn from the book credit.

Since the pretty girls involved were headed by Edna May, the darling of London since her success in *The Belle of New York*, and by the latest trans-Atlantic sensation, beauty-contest winner Camille Clifford, whose figure had won a crazed following in *The Prince of Pilsen* and *The Catch of the Season*, and since Leslie Stuart's score threw up such winning songs as 'Come to St George's', Miss May's Red Indian coon song (sic) 'In Montezuma' and several delightful ballads to what remained of Basil Hood's lyrics, any serious intent in the show's construction was not missed and *The Belle of Mayfair* became composer Stuart's biggest success after *Florodora*.

Miss May was Julia Chaldicott, daughter of nouveau-riche Sir John (Arthur Williams), and her Romeo was Raymond Finchley (Joe Farren Soutar) the son of the lofty Earl of Mount Highgate (Sam Walsh). There were more-or-less equivalents of the other characters: Paris became the Comte de Perrier (Charles Angelo), Friar Lawrence was Dr Marmaduke Lawrence, the Nurse became a cockney maid (Lillian Digges) and Mercutio was turned into Hugh Meredith, as played by Courtice Pounds, equipped with one of the evening's most attractive numbers, 'What the World Will Say'. The plot, however, had Raymond disguised as the leader of a Bashi-Bouzouk band, working his way into the second-act ball to elope with Julia and, since this was musical comedy, to the final consent of their parents. Louie Pounds, as an incidental fairy-godmother-ish person who didn't seem to have any parallel in Shakespeare, scored a particular success with Hood's pretty 'Said I To Myself' and a piece about how 'The Weeping Willow Wept'.

After its troubled life prior to opening, and a première where all the cheers went to the Poundses, *The Belle of Mayfair* continued to have a career that, if decidedly healthy (416 performances), was not unspotted with incidents. The most remarkable occurred several months into the run when Edna May walked out of the show. Irked by the amount of publicity accorded to Camille Clifford, she threw in the towel when that lady announced her engagement to the heir to Lord Aberdare and thus became the chief attraction of the evening to much of a curious public. There was further publicity when May's understudy, Ethel Newman, hopelessly sued the producers when she was not given the take-over, and more when 15-year-old Phyllis Dare was whisked from her convent school to be brought in as leading lady.

There were court proceedings in America too, when the Shuberts attempted to hijack the hit of the show 'Come to St George's' by including it, under a different title, in one of their new shows before *Florodora* producer Thomas Ryley, who had the Broadway rights to the new Stuart show, could get *The Belle of Mayfair* on to the stage. Ryley won his point and also success when *The Belle of Mayfair* proved that it did not need an Edna May or a Camille Clifford to ensure its popularity by sensational means, and it turned out one of the hits of the 1906/7 Broadway season with Christie MacDonald in its title-rôle. Van Rensslaer Wheeler was Raymond–Romeo, Irene Bentley took Louie Pounds's rôle, and the beauteous Valeska Suratt performed Miss Clifford's walk through 140 performances.

USA: Daly's Theater 3 December 1906; Australia: Theatre Royal, Melbourne 20 June 1908

THE BELLE OF NEW YORK Musical comedy in 2 acts by 'Hugh Morton' (C M S McLellan). Music by Gustave Kerker. Casino Theater, New York, 28 September 1897.

George Lederer's Casino Theater production of *The Belle of New York* featured pale, pretty Edna May as a Salvation Army lassie called Violet Gray and Harry Davenport as the debauched young man whose inheritance she threatens, in what was largely a rag-bag of comedy scenes and characters from the stockpot of the 19th-century American musical theatre, all illustrated by some bright if undistinguished songs by the prolific Gustave Kerker.

Harry Bronson (Davenport) is living the high life in New York on the contents of his wealthy, strictly moral father's wallet, and he finds its difficult to clean up his act when father Ichabod (Dan Daly) suddenly decides to come to town. Harry's intended bride, the gold-digging Cora Angélique (Helen Dupont) 'the queen of comic opera', the music hall's Kissy Fitzgarter (Mabel Howe), who also has claims on him, and his chef's daughter Fifi (Phyllis Rankin) don't help matters, but the most worries come from the polite but insane Karl von Pumpernick (J E Sullivan). Pumpernick is literally mad about Cora and he is pursuing this Mr Bronson who is threatening to wed her with a knife and harmful intent. Needless to say, he lights on the wrong Mr Bronson.

In spite of the fact that Ichabod turns out to be anything but overly strict, he disinherits worthless Harry in favour of Violet, his old business partner's daughter, and while she devotes herself to good works Harry has to go to work as a soda jerk. After a lively finale day out at Narragansett, when other incidental characters including Mamie Clancy (Paula Edwardes) and her boxer boyfriend, Blinky Bill (Frank Lawton) get to do a number or a speciality in the best tradition of the variety musical, the final curtain happily sees the two young people getting together as papa had planned all along.

A 56-performance failure on its New York production, *The Belle of New York* was almost closed after its second week when the authors sued producer Lederer for not paying them their royalties. Lederer retorted with a typical Broadway counter-suit saying that (for reasons ungiven) the authors owed him $30,000, and kept going. But if *The Belle of New York* had a sticky beginning, things looked up soon after. Its post-Broadway Boston engagement was a distinct success and Lederer's production was picked up and taken to London by Australian producer George Musgrove, desperate to fill a gap in the schedule at his ailing Shaftesbury Theatre. There, *The Belle of New York* took the public fancy by storm with its freshness and newness. If the lively Yankee characters and Kerker's tunes were old hat on Broadway they were, if anything, refreshing to a London accustomed to a beloved but fairly unvarying diet at the Gaiety and Daly's theatres. Gentle, cotton-wool-voiced Edna May became a star overnight, J E Sullivan's portrait of the 'polite lunatic' was copied everywhere, and the other comedians of the company, headed by Dan Daly and Frank Lawton, found themselves lionized as they had never been at home. The buxom, busy American chorus-line which flung itself energetically into its choreography instead of parading elegantly and dancing trippingly like a British chorus, also made a huge hit.

The Belle of New York was the overwhelming novelty of the 1898 London season and much of the 1899 one as well, remaining at the Shaftesbury for 697 performances, a record for an American musical in Britain that would stand for several decades. By the time it closed, its tunes, the best and/or best-liked of which were a lilting title waltz, Violet's 'They All Follow Me' and the attractive if unoriginal 'Teach Me How to Kiss' sung by Harry and Fifi, and its title had become sufficiently ingrained in the public consciousness to ensure it an extensive afterlife. *The Belle of New York* became a perennial touring show on the British and colonial circuits and returned for West End seasons in 1901, 1914, 1916, 1919 (additional songs by Herman Darewski), 1931, 1933, 1934 and in 1942 (ad Emile Littler) with Evelyn Laye as Violet, in ever changing textual and musical shape.

Musgrove, who had come to verbal blows with his partner J C Williamson over his productions at the Shaftesbury, made up and mounted the piece with Williamson in Australia with an imported company headed by Louise Hepner as Violet, former D'Oyly Carte man, Charles Kenningham, as Harry, Oscar Girard as Ichabod and Louise Royce (Cora). It proved a disappointment in a little more than a month in each of Melbourne and Sydney (Her Majesty's Theatre 6 May 1899), but Williamson – who blamed the flop on Musgrove for sending him doggy chorines from Britain – had the costumes and scenery on his hands, so it was brought out for further performances in 1902, 1903 and 1904 and eventually established itself as a familiar favourite.

The recent Continental successes won by the Gaiety and Daly's shows and by other British musicals encouraged European houses to pick up this latest London hit and *The Belle of New York* appeared throughout Europe around the turn of the century. The anglophile Gabor Steiner took up the piece for Vienna and produced its German version (ad Leopold Krenn, Carl Lindau) at his summer theatre, Venedig in Wien, with Frln Milton as Violet and director Karl Tuschl as Habakuk (ie Ichabod). The Narragansett entertainment became a 'grosses Casino-Fest' featuring a Festmarsch of 40 marchers, a valse d'ensemble by the ballet, a pas de deux by a gentleman billed as being from La Scala, Milan, and the ballerina étoile, an idyll waltz with song, and a 'can-can amusant' before the finale, which was composed, like the rest of this material, by Steiner's musical director Karl Kappeller, was reached. The piece had such success that Steiner played some performances at his winter house, Danzers Orpheum (18 November), and then brought it back to the Prater for a second summer season (31 May 1901). This time the rôle of Cora Angélique was played by one Frln Massari, later to be better known as Fritzi Massary. Simultaneously, *The Belle of New York* was given in English for a week at the Carltheater by the Casino Theater company which, with Richard Carle, Marie Dainton, Trixie Friganza and Lawton at its head, was touring Europe after the London failure of *The Belle of Bohemia*. Steiner's company finally played their hit show at the Theater an der Wien itself (15 March 1902).

Another German version (ad Benno Jacobson) was mounted at Berlin's Centraltheater, and in Hungary Emil Makai and Ernő Salgó's *New York szépe* was produced at

the Magyar Színház (1900), where it passed its hundredth performance 11 January 1902, and at the Budai Színkör (2 May 1903). The Casino Theater's touring English version was seen at the Vigszinház (21 May 1901), and the show returned to Budapest as late as 1934 in a revival at the Király Szinház (24 October). In Belgium (1903) the young Yvonne Printemps played Edna May's rôle, whilst Paris's P-L Flers, seeing the huge success that his Viennese counterpart, Steiner, was enjoying with his American musical in Vienna, mounted the show (ad Paul Gavault) at the Moulin-Rouge, hitherto devoted to music hall, with considerable extravagance. With Marie Marville and Ellen Baxone at the head of a whole line of glamour, it scored an enormous popular success and was both revived there (2 August 1911 with Frank Lawton in the cast and 'two hundred costumes') and restaged, first at the Théâtre des Variétés in 1915 with Jane Marnac, then at the Ba-ta-clan in 1918 and, again, in a rewritten version as *La Belle de mon coeur* (ad Henri Varna, Marc-Cab, René Richard) in 1953.

Broadway, which had rejected the show first time round, also got a revised version as *The Whirl of New York* (additional material by Al Goodman and Lew Pollock, Winter Garden Theater, 13 June 1921), and once again showed limited interest, but the potency of the show's title was demonstrated when it was attached to a Vera-Ellen/Fred Astaire film which had nothing to do with the stage piece.

The Belle of New York undoubtedly owed its survival to Musgrove's apparently irrational act in exporting the whole Casino company to London, but its wide and enduring popularity since has demonstrated that it clearly had more attractions to it than just a sexy chorus line, a couple of catchy songs, a bundle of interchangeable variety acts and some very low comedy.

UK: Shaftesbury Theatre 12 April 1898; Australia: Princess Theatre, Melbourne 1 April 1899; Hungary: Magyar Színház *New-York szépe* 30 January 1900, Vigszinház *The Belle of New York* 21 May 1901; Austria: Venedig in Wien *Die Schöne von New-York* 18 July 1900, Carltheater (Eng) 30 May 1901; Germany: Central-Theater *Die Schöne von New-York* 22 December 1900; France: Théâtre du Moulin-Rouge 29 May 1903, revised version as *Belle de mon coeur* Théâtre Mogador 28 February 1953
Recording: selection (EMI, 45EP)

LA BELLE POULE Opérette in 3 acts by Hector Crémieux and Albert de Saint-Albin. Music by Hervé. Théâtre des Folies-Dramatiques, Paris, 29 December 1875.

When Hortense Schneider – the greatest star of the Parisian musical stage – decided to leave the Théâtre des Variétés, she was courted by each and every house with a musical bent. After hearing the score of *La Belle Poule*, she chose to go to the Folies-Dramatiques.

La Belle Poule followed the love story of lusty village Poulette (Schneider) and the gentle Poulet (Simon-Max) through the usual kinds of operettic ups and downs. Poulet goes off to Paris to earn money so that he can wed his sweetheart the sooner, is temporarily supposed to be the illegitimate son of the Baron de Champignol (Ange Milher), and gets entangled with the sexy Foedora (Mlle Prelly) who, in her turn, temporarily abandons the wealthy Baron for his sake. Poulette turns out to be the long-lost Mlle Diane de Montfrison and is thus scheduled to be wed to the suitably lofty Chevalier d'Aigrefille (Eugène Didier). A cocky village rival, Jean Marcou (Luco), a motherly Marquise (Mlle Toudouze), and an eccentric Scotsman provided the comic diversions of the evening which, of course, ended up with all the right folk being paired with the right folk.

Hervé's score included a large number of winning opportunities for his star: a chanson Bordelaise ('Au cun d'un boï'), a military Chanson du dragon with a trumpeting refrain, a Péricholish letter song in which Poulette read out Poulet's farewell note, and some pretty couplets in which she pleaded with her rival 'C'est un joujou pour vous, madame, ne l'cassez pas, rendez-le moi'. The young Simon-Max, making his opérette début, had his finest moment in a gently comical tyrolienne ('Je souis un Prince de Tolède'), Foedora scored in a waltz song ('Dans votre empire'), whilst the Marquise de Montfrison went into musical raptures over her newly rediscovered rôle as a mother.

La Belle Poule was not a hit, and Schneider, flagrantly too old at 43 to be playing juvenile leads, was not a hit in it. The piece played just over a month before the diva and her producer called it a day. Nevertheless, *La Belle Poule* went on to be seen elsewhere. Marie Aimée played Poulette in the first performances in America and then toured the show in her repertoire, whilst Emily Soldene introduced *Poulet et Poulette* to Australia in her 1877 tour, appearing as Poulette to the Poulet of Charles J Campbell, and supported by a cast including Rose Stella (Foedora), Rosalie Durant (Marchioness), Edward Marshall (Baron) and John Wallace (Marcou). Her show was greeted as 'a very agreeable compilation (with) the advantage over many opérasbouffes of being coherent from first to last in its plotting and counter-plotting', but after three nights Soldene switched back to the hugely popular *La Fille de Madame Angot*, and *Poulet and Poulette* remained a very subsidiary item on her programmes.

USA: Eagle Theater 27 March 1877; Australia: Theatre Royal, Sydney *Poulet and Poulette* 6 October 1877; UK: Gaiety Theatre *Poulet et Poulette* 29 March 1878

BELLMAN Operette in 3 acts by Moritz West and Ludwig Held. Music by Franz von Suppé. Theater an der Wien, Vienna, 26 February 1887.

The script for Suppé's *Bellman* was written around the character of the historical Swedish poet Karl Michael Bellman (1740–1795) as portrayed in its original production by Josef Joseffy. His lady was the Gräfin Ulla (Regina Stein), mistress to the King Gustav III, and the comedy of the piece came from the herring-seller Niels Elvegaard (Siegmund Stelzer) and a pair of gunpowder-makers, Axel Junk and Claasen Steen (Franz Eppich, Carl Lindau). The ins and outs of the tale held nothing as dramatic as that other Gustavan tale *Un Ballo in maschera*, but it nevertheless provoked Suppé to some slightly more operatic music than was his wont.

Mounted at the Theater an der Wien by Camillo Walzel, *Bellman* proved a disappointment, and was played only 19 times. Nevertheless, its composer's reputation ensured it further showings, and an American production (ad Cheever Goodwin, William von Sachs) which featured Hubert Wilke in the title-rôle alongside De Wolf Hopper (Elvegaard), Jefferson de Angelis (Claasen), Laura Joyce

Bell (Tronda) and Marion Manola (Ulla) was played from late August 1887 to the end of the season on 8 October at Broadway's Wallack's Theater. A Budapest production (ad György Verő) confirmed Vienna's verdict (4 performances).

USA: Wallack's Theater 22 August 1887; Hungary: Népszinház 7 September 1887; Germany: ?1887

BELLS ARE RINGING Musical comedy in 2 acts by Adolph Green and Betty Comden. Music by Jule Styne. Shubert Theater, New York, 29 November 1956.

Memories of the heroines of those half-century-old musical comedies *Das Blitzmädel* and *La Demoiselle du téléphone*, as well as the more recent *The Five o'Clock Girl*, resurfaced in 1956 when Comden and Green turned out a new telephone-girl musical which was equipped with the latest up-to-date refinement: the answering service.

Ella Peterson (Judy Holliday) works at Susanswerphone, the answering service office run by Sue Summers (Jean Stapleton), but she doesn't have the same brisk, efficient style as her boss. Ella gets interested in her clients. She gets so interested that she develops a more-than-motherly feeling for Plaza 04433, otherwise playwright Jeffrey Moss (Sydney Chaplin). When things get troublesome for Jeff, she leaves her telephone and goes out into the world to help him. On her way through some of the more and less picturesque sights of New York (the underground railway provided the opportunity for one routine), she makes a few other 'helpful' calls to clients who might be useful to other clients. As a result of her interference, life takes a happy turn for them all and, needless to say, for Ella and Jeff. A subplot involved Sue with a little crook (Eddie Lawrence) using Susanswerphone as a cover for illegal betting, and a comical policeman (Frank Aletter) and his underling (Jack Weston) added to the fun as they tracked Ella through New York, convinced that her new-fangled firm is up to no good, only accidentally to catch the gambling gangsters at the final curtain.

The Comden/Green/Styne songs for the show included two which would become recital and recording standards: Ella's joyful thoughts of how she found Jeff 'Just in Time' and her gentle, dejected realization that she does not fit in with his brittle, campy friends or with the 'good fairy' image he has built up for her ('The Party's Over'). More tied to the script were two other enjoyable numbers for the heroine, 'It's a Perfect Relationship' in which she described the mother-and-son telephone relationship between herself and her client, and her lively, if temporary, farewell to her telephone when she realizes she cannot keep her sentiments out of her work ('I'm Goin' Back'). There were further comical moments for Sandor the bookie and Sue, and a revusical piece of special material party-chatter ('Drop That Name') in a score where the fun was never long away.

The Theatre Guild's Broadway production of *Bells Are Ringing* was a first-class hit. Miss Holliday – formerly a member of the nightclub group in which Comden and Green had performed – scored a personal success as the heroine of the evening and the show gambolled up a run of 924 performances on Broadway before taking to the road in 1959. By this time, London's Sandor Gorlinsky had taken up *Bells Are Ringing* and reproduced it in the vastness of the London Coliseum with Janet Blair (Ella), George

Gaynes (Jeff), Eddie Molloy (Sandor) and Jean St Clair (Sue) featured. A run of 270 performances left it rather short of those built up in smaller houses by such contemporary pieces as *Free as Air*, *Where's Charley?*, *Grab Me a Gondola* and *Expresso Bongo*, but the show found many takers.

There were further takers in Berlin, where the show was produced at the Titaniapalast (ad Ralf Wolter) in 1960, but not so many in Australia, where a Garnet Carroll production featuring Shani Wallis and Bruce Trent ran just over two unprofitable months in Melbourne. Although it has not been the subject of a first class revival, *Bells Are Ringing* has continued to win occasional productions in regional houses and, in the past few years, has been seen in both American and British out-of-town productions.

A film version, with Miss Holliday starred opposite Dean Martin, and Miss Stapleton repeating her original performance alongside Eddie Foy jr, retained almost half of the score, including 'Better Than a Dream' which had been added during the Broadway run, and added one additional number.

UK: London Coliseum 14 November 1957; Australia: Princess Theatre, Melbourne 5 April 1958; Germany: Titaniapalast *Ein Engel in der Leitung* 5 December 1960; Film: MGM 1960
Recordings: original cast (Columbia), film soundtrack (Capitol)

BELMORE, Bertha [née COUSINS] (b Manchester, 20 December 1882; d Barcelona, 14 December 1953). Britain's top musical character lady of the 1930s and 1940s.

After an early career as a song-and-dance girl in variety and a principal boy in pantomime, Bertha Belmore switched first to straight theatre, appearing with Ben Greet and on Broadway in *Julius Caesar* and, in later days, to the musical theatre and films, where she became the outstanding British 'dragon' lady of her time. She shared the first part of this career between Britain, where she played in *Irene* (1920, Mrs Cheston) and America, where she appeared in the *Ziegfeld Follies* and succeeded Edna May Oliver as Parthy Ann in *Show Boat*. She repeated her *Show Boat* rôle and played Mrs Medway in *Turned Up* in 1929 in Australia but, from 1933, she was for many years continuously present in London's West End playing comic heavies in such musicals as *Give Me a Ring* (Mrs Trellis), *Yes, Madam?* (Miss Peabody), *Please, Teacher!* (Miss Pink), *Big Business* (Emmeline Ray), *Virginia* (Minnie Fortescue), *Oh! You Letty* (Mrs Summers), *Bobby Get Your Gun* (Prunella Lockwood) and *Blue for a Boy* (Emily Bompard).

She returned to Broadway in Rodgers and Hart's *By Jupiter* (1942) as Pomposia, mother of the King of Pontus, performing the song and dance duo 'Life With Father' with Ray Bolger, and in *Rhapsody* (1944, Tina). Formidable of face ('she wasn't born, she was quarried') and of tone, she also appeared in characteristic rôles in several musical films, notably the filmed versions of *Over She Goes*, *Yes, Madam?* and *Please, Teacher*.

She was married to actor Herbert Belmore, and thus a member by marriage of a famous theatrical family which included Lillie Belmore (1871–1901), the original Ada Smith of *The Shop Girl*.

BENATZKY, Ralph [BENATZKY, Rudolph Josef František] (b Mährisch-Budwitz, 5 June 1884; d Zurich, 16 October 1957). Versatile composer of grand spectacle music and intimate musical comedies, remembered almost entirely for his songs for *Im weissen Rössl*.

Born in Moravia, the young Benatzky moved to Vienna when his schoolmaster father took up a post in the Austrian capital and he studied there, in Prague and in Munich, achieving a PhD degree in philology alongside his musical studies. He was in his mid-twenties before he opted seriously for a career in music, both as a songwriter and, from 1910, in the theatre, beginning as a conductor at the Kleines Theater in Munich.

From this time on, as he moved through musical direction posts in several cabaret-theatres, he supplemented his songwriting ('Ich muss wieder einmal in Grinzing sein', 'Draussen im Schönbrunner Parke', 'Ich weiss auf der Wieden ein kleines Hotel') with the composition of the scores and often the texts for a number of short cabaret musicals and Operetten, several of which (*Laridon*, *Kokettchens Mission*, *Das blonde Abenteuer*) were produced both in Germany and in Vienna, where Benatzky ultimately became musical director at the Kabarett Rideamus. The little vaudeville *Prinzchens Frühlingserwachen* was played by Fritzi Massary and Max Pallenberg at Vienna's Apollotheater, and one of these pieces was also adapted to the British variety stage as *The Frolics of Gabrielle* (Tivoli 25 March 1912, ad A Grey-Venne) following the success there of Reinhardt's similarly small-sized *Die süssen Grisetten*.

A full-length Operette, *Der lachende Dreibund*, was staged at Berlin's Theater am Nollendorfplatz in 1913, but Benatzky had his first significant success with the Operette *Liebe im Schnee* which was produced by Oscar Straus and staged by Miksa Preger at Vienna's Établissment Ronacher in 1916, with Mizzi Günther starred, before going on to other productions in other countries. *Liebe im Schnee* was followed by several other successes: *Yuschi tanzt*, which played a 109-performance run and a fortnight's revival at Vienna's Bürgertheater before productions in Germany and Hungary; *Apachen* (1920), first produced at the Apollotheater with Louis Treumann starred, which ended up in another celebrated variety theatre, the London Palladium; *Pipsi* (1921) which confirmed *Yuschi*'s run with 104 performances in its first run at the Wiener Bürgertheater before moving on to Budapest; and the 1922 *Ein Märchen aus Florenz* which played a hundred nights at Vienna's Johann Strauss-Theater (14 September 1923) and a run at Berlin's Deutsches Opernhaus with Richard Tauber as star.

Soon after this run of profitable Vienna productions, Benatzky moved to Berlin, where he became attached to the staff at the Grosses Schauspielhaus, providing music for their revues (*An alle*, *Für Dich*) and, after one further Viennese success with *Adieu Mimi*, which played a fine first run of 159 performances at the Johann Strauss-Theater in 1926, for a series of the extravagantly staged musical plays for which the Schauspielhaus became famous. His Johann Strauss pasticcio *Casanova* (1928) with its famous 'Nuns' Chorus' went on from Berlin to successes on other stages, but both it and a version of *Die drei Musketiere* (1929), for which he composed and arranged the score, were thoroughly eclipsed by Benatzky's most famous work, *Im weissen Rössl* (1930). A hit as oversized as its staging, *Im weissen Rössl* – for which Benatzky's basic score ('Es muss was Wunderbares sein', 'Im weissen Rössl am Wolfgangsee', 'Im Salzkammergut' etc) became encrusted with a whole variety of interpolations as time went on – moved on from the Grosses Schauspielhaus to an international career as *White Horse Inn*, *L'Auberge du cheval blanc*, *Fehér ló*, *Al cavallino bianco* and so forth, a career which made it one of the most popular musical plays the world had ever seen.

Parallel to his work in the world of the opérette à grand spectacle, Benatzky kept his hand in in the world of the small-sized musical comedy which had been his earliest area of work, and 1930 gave him a second international hit when he adapted the French comedy *Ma soeur et moi* (1928) to the musical stage as *Meine Schwester und ich*. Another musical comedy, *Cocktail*, did well in Berlin and was tried out without a tomorrow by the Shuberts in America, whilst *Zirkus Aimée* followed its German production with a Vienna one, as Benatzky continued a prolific output of Operette, revue (*Wien lacht wieder*, *Alles aus Liebe* etc), musical comedy and film scores from which the 1933 *Bezauberndes Fräulein*, a German musicalization of Paul Gavault's oft-adapted little comedy *La Petite Chocolatière*, proved the most individually successful in the theatre.

The composer won good notices for the 'taste and delicacy' with which his scores underlined the action and the mood of these light, comic pieces ('a rare combination of tickling comedy selvaged by a most personal fabric of melody and rhythm...I am at a loss whether to hand the palm to Benatzky the scribe or Benatzky the composer') and one of the foremost critics of the time asserted that '[he is] one of the small group of composers who have the stuff to step into the shoes of the old guard'. But at the height of this success came the rise of the Nazi party and Benatzky joined the general exodus of musical theatre talent in the months that followed, moving his centre of operations successively to Vienna, Paris and, with the dawning of war, to America and Hollywood.

Vienna's Theater an der Wien mounted his Hollywood tale of *Axel an der Himmelstür* with Zarah Leander and Max Hansen and some considerable success whilst, in a Paris still dazzled by the Théâtre Mogador's all-conquering production of *Im weissen Rössl*, he provided the music for another opérette à grand spectacle, *Deux sous de fleurs*, a period Scots piece produced by Léon Brigon at the Théâtre de l'Empire. Rita Georg, the prima donna of the Empire's previous success, *Katinka*, starred opposite tenor Charles Friant of the Opéra-Comique and the highly popular comedian Dranem, supported by 60 Max Rivers Girls, Dorothea Bachelor and the 12 Highland Queens, Major Simpson and his four bagpipers and Noni Prager, 'the marvellous skating dancer'. A probable success was aborted when the notorious Stavisky affair broke, for it was said that the fraudulent Russian had financed both of the Empire's shows.

Benatzky continued, as before, simultaneously to work on smaller-scale pieces, and, in the wake of *Meine Schwester und ich* and *Bezauberndes Fräulein*, he adapted a number of further French comedies as the kind of genuine musical comedy for which – rather than his large-stage work – he was known and appreciated: Tristan Bernard's *Le Petit Café* became *Das kleine Café*, de Flers and de Caillavet's *Le Roi* was turned into *Majestät-privat* and one of Armont and

Gerbidon's comedies became Benatzky's *Pariserinnin* in Vienna and *Párizsi nők* at Budapest's Belvárosi Színház. Following his departure for America, *Der Silberhof*, a musical adaptation of Charlotte Birch-Pfeiffer's celebrated play *Grille*, for which he wrote both text and music, was produced in Mainz.

Benatzky returned to Europe after the war, and spent his later years in Switzerland, continuing to write, rewrite and compose up to the last years of his life.

In the course of his highly active and varied career, Benatzky also wrote libretti for Karl Kaskel's opera *Die Schmieden von Kent* (Dresden 1916) and for Max Ast's one-act *Die Blinde* (Volksoper, Vienna, 12 March 1927 aka *Aria Appassionata*), and adapted *Porgy and Bess* into German.

In the cinematic world, he composed a replacement score for a film of Eysler's Operette *Der unsterbliche Lump*, as well as musically illustrating such other films of the early 1930s as *Die letzte Kompagnie*, *Arm wie eine Kirchenmaus*, *Chauffeur Antoinette* and *Ihre Durchlaucht, die Verkäuferin*. He adapted *Im weissen Rössl* for its 1935 film, re-adapted *La Petite Chocolatière* as a film under the title *Wer wagt gewinnt!*, and worked on both the script and the musical portion of the musical films *Die Puppenfee* ('Ich bin gut aufgelegt') and *Mädchenpensionnat*, and the scores of *Zu neuern Ufern* and *Der ganz grossen Torheiten*. His own *Meine Schwester und ich* (ad Friedrich Schröder) and *Bezauberndes Fräulein* (ad Georg Häntzschel) were both adapted to the screen by other hands in the 1950s.

1910 **Die Walzerkomtesse** (Ludwig Bruckner, Julius Friedrich) 1 act Kabarett Fledermaus, Vienna 1 October

1910 **Der Walzer von heute Nacht** (Adolf Klein) Walhalla-Theater, Wiesbaden 16 October

1911 **Laridon** 1 act Intimes-Theater, Hamburg 21 February, Kabarett Fledermaus, Vienna 1 March 1912

1911 **Cherchez la Femme** 1 act Künstlertheater, Munich 28 July

1911 **Kokettchens Mission** 1 act Künstlertheater, Munich; Kabarett Fledermaus, Vienna February 1912

1911 **Das blonde Abenteuer** 1 act Künstlertheater, Munich; Kabarett Fledermaus, Vienna February 1912

1913 **Der lachende Dreibund** (Leopold Jacobson) Theater am Nollendorfplatz, Berlin 31 October

1914 **Prinzchens Frühlingserwachen** 1 act Apollotheater, Berlin 16 March

1914 **Anno 14** (w Fritz Grünbaum) 1 act Kabarett Rideamus, Berlin 22 September

1914 **Das Scheckbuch des Teufels** 1 act Kabarett Rideamus, Berlin 18 November

1914 **General Wuitkoff** (Grünbaum) 1 act Budapester Orpheum 1 December

1915 **Fräulein Don Juan** (Paracelsus) 1 act Gartenbau 1 February

1916 **Du, goldige Frau** 1 act Budapester Orpheum 1 September

1916 **Liebe im Schnee** (w Willy Prager) Ronacher 2 December

1918 **Die tanzende Maske** (w Alexander Engel) Apollotheater 1 December

1919 **Liebesreigen** (w Karl Zimmer) Theater am Lietzenfee, Berlin 30 August

1919 **Die Verliebten** (Julius Wilhelm) Raimundtheater 29 March

1920 **Graf Cheveraux** (Fanfaron ie Armin Friedmann) 1 act Rolandbühne 1 March

1920 **Yuschi tanzt** (Jacobson, Robert Bodanzky) Wiener Bürgertheater 3 April

1920 **Bluffodont** 1 act Apollotheater 31 July

1920 **Apachen** (w Ignaz M Welleminsky) Apollotheater 20 December

1921 **Pipsi** (Julius Horst, Engel) Wiener Bürgertheater 30 December

1922 **Ein Märchen aus Florenz** (w Oscar Friedmann, Toni Schwanau) Johann Strauss-Theater 14 Sept 1923

1926 **Adieu Mimi** (Engel, Horst) Johann Strauss-Theater 9 June

1926 **Die Nacht von San Sebastian** (Hans Bachwitz) Operettenhaus am Dittrichring, Leipzig 23 December

1928 **Casanova** (Johann Strauss arr/Ernst Welisch, Rudolf Schanzer) Grosses Schauspielhaus, Berlin 1 September

1929 **Die drei Musketiere** (Schanzer, Welisch) Grosses Schauspielhaus, Berlin 28 September

1929 **Mit dir allein auf einer einsamen Insel** (w Arthur Rebner) Residenztheater, Dresden 31 December; Metropoltheater, Berlin August 1930

1930 **Meine Schwester und ich** (Robert Blum) Komödienhaus, Berlin 29 March

1930 **Im weissen Rössl** (w others/Robert Gilbert/Hans Müller) Grosses Schauspielhaus, Berlin 8 November

1930 **Cocktail** (Karl Vollmöller) Komödienhaus, Berlin 15 December

1931 **Morgen geht's uns gut** (Buchbinder ad Hans Müller) Lessingtheater, Berlin 31 December

1931 **Zur gold'nen Liebe** (w Max Wolff, Martin Zickel) Komische Oper, Berlin 16 October

1932 **Zirkus Aimée** (w Kurt Götz) Stadttheater, Basle 5 March

1932 **Flirt in Nizza** (w Robert Blum)

1933 **Bezauberndes Fräulein** Deutsches Volkstheater, Vienna 24 May

1933 **Deux sous de fleurs** (Saint-Granier/Paul Nivoix) Théâtre de l'Empire, Paris 6 October(?)

1934 **Das kleine Café** Deutsches Volkstheater, Vienna 20 April

1934 **Die Prinzessin auf der Leiter** revised *Meine Schwester und ich* Theater in Josefstadt 3 August

1934 **Büxl** Deutsches Volkstheater, Vienna 15 March

1935 **Der König mit dem Regenschirm** Theater in Josefstadt 18 April

1935 **The Flying Trapeze** (pasticcio w Mabel Wayne/Douglas Furber, Desmond Carter, Frank Eyton/Hans Müller ad Furber) Alhambra, London 4 May

1935 **Der reichste Mann der Welt** (Hans Müller)

1936 **Axel an der Himmelstür** (Paul Morgan, Adolf Schütz, Hans Weigel) Theater an der Wien 1 September

1936 **Egy lány, aki mindenkié** (*Wer gewinnt, Colette?*) (Tamas Emőd) Müvész Színház, Budapest 19 December

1937 **Pariserinnin** Theater in der Josefstadt 7 May, revised version Lucerne 22 December 1964

1937 **Herzen im Schee** (w H & Robert Gilbert, Armin Robinson) Volksoper 8 September

1937 **Majestät-privat** (ad w Karl von Hellmer) Theater an der Wien 18 December

1941 **Der Silberhof** Stadttheater, Mainz 4 November

1947 **Kleinstadtzauber**

1950 **Liebesschule** Göttingen 1 October

1951 **Mon Ami René** revised *Büxl* Karlsruhe 9 September

1953 **Don Juans Wiederkehr** revised *Liebesschule*

BENEŠ, Jára (b Prague, 5 June 1897; d Vienna, 10 April 1949).

Czech conductor and composer of popular dance music and songs who wrote more than 50 film scores (*Kein Wort von Liebe*, *Adresse unbekannte* etc) and also more than a dozen stage pieces. The most successful of these latter was the 1936 *Auf der grünen Wiese*, produced at Vienna's Volksoper and subsequently filmed. Beneš left Czechoslovakia when the Communist régime took over and his music was, in retaliation, banned there.

1935 **Der gütige Antonius** (Fritz Löhner-Beda, Hugo Wiener) Volksoper 23 December

1936 **Auf der grünen Wiese** (Löhner-Beda, Wiener) Volksoper 9 October

1938 **Gruss und Kuss aus der Wachau** (Löhner-Beda, Wiener, Kurt Breuer) Volksoper 17 February

1947 **Endstation** (Béla Szenes, Josef Petrak) Wiener Bürgertheater 20 May

1948 **Der gestohlene Walzer** (Fritz Eckhardt) Wiener Künstlertheater 5 March

1948 **Pfui Pepi** Wiener Künstlertheater

1949 **Sebastian, der Seitenspringer** (Peter Schwarz, Neumann) Theater 'Auges-Gottes' 16 January

1949 **Die kleine Schwindlerin** (A M Willner) Theater 'Auges-Gottes' 1 March

BENNETT, Michael [DI FIGLIA, Michael] (b Buffalo, 8 April 1943; d Tucson, 2 July 1987). Choreographer and director who developed and staged the record-breaking *A Chorus Line*.

After a short career as a chorus dancer on Broadway (*Subways Are For Sleeping*, *Here's Love*, *Bajour*), Bennett moved swiftly on to work as a choreographer and, having done the dances for two short-lived shows (*A Joyful Noise*, *Henry Sweet Henry*), had his first connection with success when he choreographed the musical play *Promises, Promises* (1968) with its lively office party scene, 'Turkey Lurkey Time'. The following year, he choreographed the more extravagant but less interesting *Coco*, before teaming with director Harold Prince on the highly successful production of *Company* ('Tick Tock') and then, with co-directorial billing, on *Follies* ('Mirror, Mirror', Tony Award). Brought in to doctor the musical *Seesaw* on the road – a function which he fulfilled on a number of shows without credit – he supervised revision to such an extent that he was ultimately billed as author of the piece's libretto as well as its director, and also as part of a complicated four-person choreography credit. The Tony Award for that choreography, however, was awarded to Bennett.

In the mid-1970s, Bennett was midwife to the creation of *A Chorus Line*, a musical built up on the tales of the professional and personal experiences of a group of dancers, and he subsequently directed (Tony Award) and choreographed (Tony Award w Bob Avian) the show which was to become not only one of the outstanding pieces of musical theatre of its era, but also one of the most successful and long-running. Although the Tony Awards for libretto and score which the show won went to its billed authors, Bennett was included in the citation when the piece was nominated as Pulitzer Prize winner of the 1975–6 season. To follow *A Chorus Line* was difficult, and the gentler tale of middle-aged romance in a *Ballroom* (1979, Tony Award w Avian, choreography) was not successful, but Bennett had a second major Broadway success with his staging of another showbusiness musical, *Dreamgirls*, in 1981. Signed to direct *Chess* for its London opening in 1986, Bennett cast the show, but was prevented by his final illness from fulfilling the contract.

He was for a period married to dancer Donna McKechnie (b Detroit, November 1944) who was his principal dancer in *Promises, Promises* and *Company* and who created the rôle of Cassie in *A Chorus Line* (Tony Award).

Biography: Mandelbaum, K: *A Chorus Line and the Musicals of Michael Bennett* (St Martins Press, New York, 1989), Kelly, K: *One Singular Sensation* (Doubleday, New York, 1990) etc

BENNETT, Robert Russell (b Kansas City, 15 June 1894; d New York, 18 August 1981).

Bennett began his musical life as an orchestral and dance band musician and subsequently worked for the publishing firm of Schirmer as a copyist and arranger. His earliest work as a musical-theatre arranger was on the songs for Herbert Stothart and Oscar Hammerstein II's 1922 musical comedy *Daffy Dill*, and other early assignments included full or part-orchestrations for Vincent Youmans and Stothart's *Mary Jane McKane*, Friml and Stothart's *Wildflower* and *Rose-Marie* and Jerome Kern's *Sitting Pretty*, *Sunny*, *Show Boat* and *Sweet Adeline*. Later credits included Gershwin's *Funny Face*, *Girl Crazy* and *Of Thee I Sing* (w Gershwin, William Daly), Cole Porter's *Anything Goes* (w Spialek) and *Kiss Me, Kate* and Irving Berlin's *Annie Get Your Gun* (w Lang, Royal) as Bennett established himself as the most important and successful orchestrator in the American musical theatre of his time.

Bennett was responsible for the orchestration of the music for *Oklahoma!*, which won him an Academy Award when the show was transferred to the screen, and subsequently for *Allegro*, *South Pacific*, *The King and I*, *Pipe Dream*, *Flower Drum Song* and *The Sound of Music*, thus creating the 'Rogers and Hammerstein sound' which became the standard Broadway musical sound of the 1950s and 1960s. He collaborated with Phil Lang on the orchestration of *My Fair Lady* and *Camelot*, and, over a period of some 50 years worked on the music of more than 200 American musical plays. Amongst his other postwar credits were numbered such shows as *Carmen Jones*, *Finian's Rainbow*, *By the Beautiful Sea*, *Bells Are Ringing*, *Redhead* and *New Girl in Town*.

Outside his theatre work, Bennett was also a composer of orchestral and chamber music and, in spite of his domination of and contribution to the Broadway orchestration scene, he was quoted as having more musical ambition in those fields than time or taste for the light musical theatre.

1933 **Hold Your Horses** (w others/Corey Ford, Russel Crouse) Winter Garden Theater 25 September
1944 **Rhapsody** (Fritz Kreisler arr/w John Latouche, Leonard Levison, Arnold Sundgaard) Century Theater 22 November

BENNETT, Wilda (b Asbury Park, NJ, 19 December 1894; d Winnemucca, Nev, 20 December 1967).

Through a decade, the young Wilda Bennett appeared on Broadway as a leading lady in Continental and American operettas, beginning with Victor Herbert's *The Only Girl* (Ruth Wilson) in 1914 and continuing through *The Riviera Girl* (*Die Csárdásfürstin* 1917, Sylva Varescu), Ivan Caryll's *The Girl Behind the Gun* (1918, Lucienne), and Victor Jacobi and Fritz Kreisler's *Apple Blossoms* (1919, Nancy). She took over the star rôle of Jean Gilbert's *The Lady in Ermine* (*Die Frau im Hermelin* 1922, Mariana) when Eleanor Painter walked out during rehearsals, and inherited the title-rôle of Fall's *Madame Pompadour* (1924), following the even noisier pre-Broadway sacking of Hope Hampton. In 1927 she made a final appearance on the metropolitan musical stage when she replaced Edna Leedom in the show which became *Lovely Lady* by the time it reached Broadway.

BERÉNY, Henrik [aka BERENY, Henri] (b Kassa, Hungary, 1 January 1871; d Budapest, 22 March 1932).

The young Berény orientated his music studies towards the violin and composition, taking lessons from, amongst others, Liszt in Hungary and the violinist Léonard in Paris. He composed his first stage work, the opera *Talmah* (1894), at the age of 23, and saw it played at the court theatre of Mannheim, at Baden and in Scandinavia. He subsequently made something of a speciality of writing scenarios and music for pantomimes (dance mime dramas), and won considerable success with such pieces as *Premier Carnaval*, *L'Homme aux poupées* and, most particularly, the melodramatic *La Main* performed to the best effect by his wife, Charlotte Wiehe. These pieces won multiple productions in Hamburg, Paris, Copenhagen, Stockholm, Berlin (Opera House), Budapest, New York (Vaudeville Theater, Savoy Theater, Garden Theater) and London (St George's Hall), and established the young composer's name. He had a similar success when he switched his activity to the rather more profitable and visible world of the regular musical theatre, winning widespread productions with the best of a small group of Operetten to which he composed the scores in the years before the Great War.

His first such piece, *Miss Chipp*, described as a romantic musical play, was produced in Paris in 1903, and was sufficiently well-liked to be played subsequently in his native Hungary (ad Géza Goda, Frigyes Hervay Vigszinház 11 May 1905), and, if *Der kleine Korsar* apparently went no further than its initial production in Stuttgart, his next two important works, premièred in Vienna and Berlin respectively, both won a degree of international success. *Lord Piccolo*, written to a libretto by Lindau and Schanzer, followed its run at the Johann Strauss-Theater with productions in Germany and Hungary and, most successfully, in a version by the Smith brothers, under the title *Little Boy Blue*, in America, whilst the vaudeville *Das Mädel von Montmartre*, adapted from the French comedy *La Dame de chez Maxim*, was played on Broadway by Richard Carle as *The Girl from Montmartre*. Another Operette, *Mein Mäderl*, was given 50 performances at the Raimundtheater with Betty Fischer, Anton Matscheg and Franz Glawatsch featured.

After the war, however, Berény worked again largely in the field in which he had begun, with such pieces as the 'musical legend' *A pupos Boldizsár* and the dance melodrama *Hasis* (Baden-Baden, 8 September 1923), and his last appearance in the musical theatre seems to have been with the score for the Parisian musical *Chou-Chou* in 1925.

1903 **Miss Chipp** (André de Lorde, Michel Carré) Théâtre des Bouffes-Parisiens, Paris 31 March
1904 **Der kleine Korsar** Stuttgart
1908 **Fastnacht in Nizza** (*Mardi Gras*) Hansa Theater, Hamburg 1 February
1910 **Lord Piccolo** (Carl Lindau, Rudolf Schanzer) Johann Strauss-Theater, Vienna 1 September
1911 **Das Mädel von Montmartre** (Schanzer) Neues Theater, Berlin 26 October
1913 **Mein Mäderl** (Eugen Burg, Lindau, Schanzer) Raimundtheater 21 January
1913 **Tubicám** Kisfáludy Szinház, Győr 28 November
1922 **A pupos Boldizsár** (Mihály Timár) Magyar Szinház, Budapest 15 September

1925 **Chou-Chou** (Raoul Praxy, Max Eddy) Théâtre Ba-ta-clan, Paris 28 February

BERKELEY, Busby [ENOS, William Berkeley] (b Los Angeles, 29 November 1895; d Palm Springs, Calif, 14 March 1976). Celebrated cinema choreographer who also worked for the stage.

After an early career as a performer, which included an appearance in the rôle of Madame Lucy on the initial national tour of *Irene*, Berkeley devoted himself to working as a choreographer. His first Broadway assignment, in 1925, was on the indifferent German musical *Holka Polka* (*Frühling im Herbst* aka *Spring in Autumn* and *Nobody's Girl*) with operatic tenor Orville Harrold, the original star of *Naughty Marietta*, and his soubrette daughter, Patti, a take-over as *Irene*, in the lead rôles, but Berkeley had much more success with the choreography for the Chicago musical *Castles in the Air*, the biggest hit the town had bred in its history. The following year he directed the dances for Friml's *The Wild Rose*, followed up by *Lady Do*, the Rodgers and Hart *A Connecticut Yankee* and Friml's musicalization of *The Squaw Man, The White Eagle*.

He returned to the stage briefly in Rodgers and Hart's *Present Arms*, performing 'You Took Advantage of Me', then provided the dances for a considerable series of musicals (*Good Boy, Rainbow, Hallo Daddy, Pleasure Bound*, Kálmán's *The Duchess of Chicago, A Night in Venice, Nina Rosa*) in the space of just two seasons whilst also setting himself up as a producer/director with a musical called *The Street Singer*. The all-round results were, at best, indifferent and Berkeley was represented on Broadway thereafter only by a handful of revues before he moved to Hollywood to make himself famous as the best marshaller of massed pretty girls in cinema history.

His cinema credits included film versions of the stage shows *Whoopee* (1930), *Flying High* (1931), *Wonder Bar* (1934), *Babes in Arms* (1939), *Strike Up the Band* (1940), *Lady, Be Good!* (1941), *Cabin in the Sky* (1943), *Girl Crazy* (1943), *Rose Marie* (1954) and *Jumbo* (1962) as well as the classics *42nd Street*, the *Gold Diggers* films, *Dames, Babes on Broadway* and many others, some of which he also directed.

He made an inauspicious attempt at a return to the theatre with the Jule Styne musical *Glad To See You* (1944) which closed on the road, but he returned to Broadway in 1971 to direct the revival of *No, No, Nanette* for which, after many vagaries, he was eventually credited as 'supervisor'.

Literature: Pike, B & Martin, D: *The Genius of Busby Berkeley* (Sherbourne Press, Los Angeles, 1974), Thomas, T & Terry, J: *The Busby Berkeley Book* (Graphic Society, New York, 1973)

BERLIN, Irving [BALINE, Israel] (b Temun, Russia, 11 May 1888; d New York, 22 September 1989). Celebrated Russian-born American songwriter who wrote intermittently for the musical theatre and revue.

Irving Berlin began the theatrical part of his career interpolating songs into Broadway musicals (*The Boys and Betty, The Girl and the Wizard, He Came from Milwaukee*) and revues, before gaining world-wide fame with the song 'Alexander's Ragtime Band' in 1911. He supplied further contributions to such pieces as Richard Carle's *Jumping Jupiter, The Never Homes, The Fascinating Widow, Gaby, My Best Girl, The Queen of the Movies*, and various Weber and Fields shows before turning out his first full Broadway score, for the Charles Dillingham revue *Watch Your Step* (1914). Subtitled 'a syncopated musical show', this very lightly-plotted entertainment featured the ragtime rhythms Berlin had been instrumental in giving a wider popularity in the 15 years since pieces like the Matthews and Bulger 'ragtime opera' *By the Sad Sea Waves* had purveyed ragtime more discretely on the musical stage or songwriters like Alfred Aarons had delivered ragtime songs on Broadway without raising too many ears.

Berlin subsequently provided the songs for another revue with a vestige of musical comedy libretto, *Stop! Look! Listen!* (1915), and for a series of large-scale revues including several editions of *The Ziegfeld Follies* and *The Music Box Revue*, staged at his own Music Box Theater, the highly successful *As Thousands Cheer*, and the army show *This is the Army*. Many of these shows produced extractable songs which became long-term favourites, including 'Oh, How I Hate To Get up in the Morning', 'A Pretty Girl Is Like a Melody', 'What'll I Do?', 'All Alone', 'Easter Parade' and 'You'd Be Surprised'.

Berlin contributed further interpolated numbers to the scores of *Step This Way, Jack o'Lantern, Rambler Rose, The Royal Vagabond* and placed one song, and then a second, in Ivan Caryll's musical *The Canary* (1917), but his first solo attempt at a book musical was an unusual one. Abandoning the more straightforward task of composing a piece which was to be called *Ring Around Rosie* to feature soubrette Queenie Smith, he opted instead to illustrate a low comedy vehicle for the Marx Brothers. *The Cocoanuts* (1925), as might have been expected, owed its success to the antics of its stars, and the 14 numbers which made up the musical part of the show ('The Monkey Doodle-Doo' etc) took a decidedly secondary place to the comedy. But the show was a fine success.

His next announced project, a musical with Frederick Lonsdale to be staged at London's Theatre Royal, Drury Lane, was said to have been abandoned when half-written on the excuse that the house was too big, and over the next two decades, Berlin provided songs for just two book musicals, both of which followed the fashion for anti-anyone-elected political musicals. *Face the Music* (1932), on which the songwriter also shared the book credit with Moss Hart, introduced 'Let's Have Another Cup of Coffee' and 'Soft Lights and Sweet Music' in the course of a book which decked some anti-police maunderings up with revusical glitter for 165 performances, and *Louisiana Purchase* (1940) mixed tarty ladies, young love and naughty politicians in a more traditional way, produced 'It's a Lovely Day Tomorrow' and 'Fools Fall in Love', and did more than twice as well (444 performances). Both shows served to emphasize Berlin's talents as a writer of individual songs rather than of show scores.

It was not until his 58th year that Berlin achieved an international hit with a book musical, when he replaced the late Jerome Kern as the composer of the Herbert and Dorothy Fields sharpshooting musical *Annie Get Your Gun*. *Annie Get Your Gun* proved not only to be a major theatre hit throughout the world, but also turned out a scoreful of songs, including 'There's No Business Like Show Business', 'Anything You Can Do (I can do better)', 'The Girl That I Marry', 'My Defences Are Down' and several more which became individually and widely popular. A second piece for *Annie Get Your Gun* star, Ethel Merman, written with Howard Lindsay and Russel Crouse, turned out a small masterpiece of vehicle writing in *Call Me Madam* ('You're Just in Love', 'It's a Lovely Day Today'), and won a second widespread success, but *Miss Liberty* (1949, 'Let's Take an Old-Fashioned Walk') and yet another political musical, *Mr President* (1962), were both failures.

Film versions of *The Cocoanuts*, *Annie Get Your Gun* and *Call Me Madam* were made, but Berlin also provided the scores or songs for numerous other movies from *Top Hat* ('Cheek to Cheek', 'Isn't it a Lovely Day?' etc), *Follow the Fleet* and *Alexander's Ragtime Band* to *Holiday Inn* ('White Christmas'), *Easter Parade*, *This is the Army* and *White Christmas*, introducing or re-introducing handfuls of popular songs on each occasion.

Berlin's chief fame remains as one of America's most productive and successful writers of all styles of popular songs from 'God Bless America' to 'Blue Skies' over nearly half a century of active writing, but his work for *Annie Get Your Gun*, *Call Me Madam* and the revue in its palmiest days also earned him a superior place in the history of the musical theatre.

1925 **The Cocoanuts** (George S Kaufman) Lyric Theater 8 December
1932 **Face the Music** (Moss Hart) New Amsterdam Theater 17 February
1940 **Louisiana Purchase** (Morrie Ryskind) Imperial Theater 28 May
1946 **Annie Get Your Gun** (Herbert Fields, Dorothy Fields) Imperial Theater 16 May
1949 **Miss Liberty** (Robert E Sherwood) Imperial Theater 15 July
1950 **Call Me Madam** (Howard Lindsay, Russel Crouse) Imperial Theater 12 October
1962 **Mr President** (Lindsay, Crouse) St James Theater 20 October

Biographies: Ewen, D: *The Story of Irving Berlin* (Holt, Rinehart & Winston, New York, 1950), Woolcott, A: *The Story of Irving Berlin* (Stein & Day, New York, 1974), Bergreen, L: *As Thousands Cheer* (Viking, New York, 1990) etc

BERNARD, Sam [BARNETT, Samuel] (b Birmingham, England, 3 June 1863; d New York, 18 May 1927). Dialect comedian who won durable fame in Broadway musicals.

Sam Bernard began his career in show business appearing at Henderson's Music Hall in Coney Island, before returning to his native Britain to play briefly in music halls there. After a number of years spent playing in vaudeville and in comedy (*The Corner Grocer*, *Lost in London* etc), where his speciality was a version of the heavily accented 'Dutch' low comedy character popular at the time, Bernard was taken on by Weber and Fields. He appeared at their theatre in burlesques of current theatrical hits such as *The Heart of Maryland* (*The Art of Maryland* also co-lib), *The Geisha* (*The Geezer*, Two Hi), *Secret Service* (*The Glad Hand*) and *La Poupée* (*Pousse Café*, Weishaben) and his success there was such that he was able to move on and up to star-billing as Hermann Engel in *The Marquis of Michigan* (1898) at the beginning of a series of comedy-centred musicals which established him as a Broadway favourite: *A Dangerous Maid* (an adaptation of the protean German *Posse Heisses Blut* 1898, Schmalz), the revusical *The Man in the Moon* (1899, Conan Doyle), *The Casino Girl* (1900, Khedive) and *The Belle of Bohemia* (1900, Adolf Klotz).

The leading comedy rôle of Leslie Stuart's London musical *The Silver Slipper* (Samuel Twanks) was remodelled to suit Bernard's dialect-comedy character for its Broadway production, but it was another British piece, *The Girl From Kays* (1903), which gave him his biggest success when he introduced to American audiences the likeably ghastly nouveau riche Yankee 'Piggy' Hoggenheimer ('I'm not rude, I'm rich'), so memorably created in London by Willie Edouin. During his career, Bernard returned three further times to Hoggenheimer, commissioning a new musical built around the character in 1906 (*The Rich Mr Hoggenheimer*), revising the original piece as *The Belle From Bond Street* (1914) with more success in America than in an abortive London season and, finally, a few months before his death, performing a new version of his musequel under the title *Piggy* at Broadway's Royale Theater.

In between Hoggenheimers, the little, balding comedian expertly continued to turn out German and Jewish low-comedy characters in musicals such as a remake of *A Dangerous Maid* as *The Rollicking Girl* (1905, Schmalz), *Nearly a Hero* (1908, Ludwig Knödler), *The Girl and the Wizard* (1909, Herman Scholz), *He Came from Milwaukee* (1910, Herman von Schellenvein) and *All For the Ladies/A Glimpse of the Great White Way* (1912–13, Leo von Labenheimer), and appeared as Ko-ko in the Casino Theater's all-star *Mikado* (1910) before spreading his comic talents into the field of revue in the Americo-Anglo-originally-French *As You Were* ('Who Ate Napoleons With Josephine When Bonaparte Was Away?') and *The Music Box Revue*s in the years following the war.

1896 **The Art of Maryland** (John Stromberg/Joseph W Herbert/w Ross, Fenton) Weber & Fields' Music Hall 5 September

BERNARD, Tristan [BERNARD, Paul] (b Besançon, 7 September 1866; d Paris, 7 December 1947).

Prolific and popular French playwright (*Triplepatte*, *Le Costaud des Épinettes*, *Le Petit Café*, *Le Sexe fort* etc) who ventured occasionally into the musical theatre, providing the text for Terrasse's successful opéra-bouffe *La Petite Femme de Loth* and the Garden of Eden tale which was the basis of Cuvillier's early *Avant hier matin*.

His 1911 play *Le Petit Café* was musicalized by Ralph Benatzky in Germany, Ivan Caryll and C M S McLellan in America, and also on home ground, whilst his *La Soeur* became, on the Broadway stage, the 1907 musical *The Hoyden* (Paul Rubens et al/Henry Blossom, John Golden, Cosmo Hamilton, 19 October) and another of his plays was the source for Budapest's *Finom família* (Béla Zerkovitz/Adolf Mérei, Royal Orfeum 31 January 1913).

1900 **La Petite Femme de Loth** (Claude Terrasse) Théâtre des Mathurins 10 October
1905 **Avant-hier matin** (Charles Cuvillier) 1 act Théâtre des Capucines 20 October
1912 **Miss Alice des P.T.T.** (Terrasse/Maurice Vaucaire) La Cigale 14 December
1938 **Le Flirt ambulant** (Henri Christiné/w Albert Willemetz) Théâtre Michel 13 January

BERNAUER, Rudolf (b Budapest, 20 January 1880; d London, 27 November 1953). Berlin producer and librettist of a number of successful Operetten and Possen for the Austrian and German stages.

Hungarian-born Bernauer studied in Berlin and he began his theatrical career there, as an actor at the Deutsches Theater, at the age of 20. The following year, together with Carl Meinhard, he initiated the satirical Bösen-Büben-Bälle. He subsequently abandoned acting to become regisseur at the Deutsches Theater (1906) and then, again in tandem with Meinhard, moved into theatre management on his own account. The pair began by promoting various small tours and sponsoring limited seasons in metropolitan houses, but they finally became full-scale lessees when they took on the Berliner Theater in 1908 (16 September). They operated the Berliner for 16 mostly successful years, nourishing it largely on a diet of old Possen and then, increasingly, of new musicals. They also expanded their management activities to take on, at various times, the Theater in der Königgratzer-Strasse (1911), the Komödienhaus (1913) and the Theater am Nollendorfplatz.

During his days at the the Deutsches Theater, Bernauer also began a career as a playwright, supplying, amongst his earliest efforts, the libretto which was to be blamed for the failure of Leo Fall's first major work, *Der Rebell*. However, he found his first, and one of his most considerable successes as a librettist soon after his move to the Berliner Theater when he collaborated with Leopold Jacobson on the adaptation of G B Shaw's *Arms and the Man* into the libretto to *Der tapfere Soldat* for Oscar Straus. Another adaptation, of Sardou's *Divorçons* as *Frau Lebedame* for the theatre at Prague, proved less successful, but a second piece for the same house, the olde-Englishe *Die keusche Barbara* (w Rudolf Schanzer), gave him another fair success and set in motion the career of its young composer, Oskar Nedbal.

The large part of Bernauer's writing was, however, done for his own theatre, where the team made up of himself, Schanzer, composer Walter Kollo and musical director/composer Willi Bredschneider turned out a series of hits in the years before and during the Great War. *Filmzauber* (1912), which capitalized on the new fashion for moving pictures, was exported to Britain and America as *The Girl on the Film*, whilst Bernauer and Schanzer's text of the highly successful *Wie einst im Mai*, attached to a new score by Sigmund Romberg, became a major success in America under the title *Maytime*. The war effectively put a stop to further exports, but the Berliner Theater throve on such Bernauer pieces as *Die tolle Komtess* (350 performances), *Blitzblaues Blut* (nearly 300), a revival of the team's 1910 *Bummelstudenten*, *Sterne, die wieder leuchtet* (seven months and an American production) and *Prinzessin Olala* (142 performances and revivals) and hits from other hands such as *Madame Pompadour* (1922) and *Mädi* (1923).

Hit by the rise of inflation and of some oversized gambling debts, Bernauer and Meinhard closed down their operation in 1925, and Bernauer thereafter had only a minor part to play in the Berlin musical theatre where he had so long been a dominant force. He turned to the cinema (*Ihre Majestät der Liebe*, *Der Frechdachs* etc), but, banned from working on stage or screen in 1933, he joined the general artistic exodus from Germany, and ended his days in England. His credits there included work on, and an appearance in, the screen version of *The Lilac Domino* (1937).

1903 **Schlumpeline Schlumebumbum** (Bogumil Zepler) Neues Kindertheater, Berlin 21 November
1905 **Der Rebell** (Leo Fall/w Ernst Welisch) Theater an der Wien 29 November
1906 **Der Fuss** (Fall) 1 act Stadttheater, Chemnitz 18 June
1907 **Frau Lebedame** (Anselm Götzel/w Alexander Pordes-Milo) Deutsches Theater, Prague 31 December
1908 **Der tapfere Soldat** (Oscar Straus/w Leopold Jacobson) Theater an der Wien 14 November
1910 **Die keusche Barbara** (Oskar Nedbal/w Jacobson) Theater Weinberge, Prague 14 September, Raimundtheater, Vienna 7 October 1911
1910 **Bummelstudenten** (Zepler, Willi Bredschneider, et al/ad w Rudolf Schanzer) Berliner Theater 31 December
1911 **Die grosse Rosinen** (Leon Jessel, Zepler, Bredschneider et al/w Schanzer) Berliner Theater 31 December
1912 **Der liebe Augustin** revised *Der Rebell* (Leo Fall/w Welisch) Neues Theater 3 February
1912 **Filmzauber** (Kollo, Bredschneider/w Schanzer) Berliner Theater 19 October
1913 **Wie einst im Mai** (Kollo, Bredschneider/w Schanzer) Berliner Theater 4 October
1914 **Jung England** (Leo Fall/w Welisch) Montis Operettentheater 14 February
1915 **Wenn zwei Hochzeit machen** (Kollo, Bredschneider/w Schanzer) Berliner Theater 23 October
1916 **Auf Flügeln des Gesanges** (Kollo, Bredschneider/w Schanzer) Berliner Theater 9 September
1917 **Die tolle Komtess** (Kollo/w Schanzer) Berliner Theater 21 February
1918 **Blitzblaues Blut** (Kollo/w Schanzer) Berliner Theater 9 February
1918 **Sterne, die wieder leuchtet** (Kollo/w Schanzer) Berliner Theater 6 November
1920 **Frau Ministerpräsident** (Fall/w Welisch) Residenztheater, Dresden 3 February
1921 **Prinzessin Olala** (Jean Gilbert/w Schanzer) Berliner Theater 17 September
1923 **Dolly** (Hugo Hirsch/Ernst Bach, Franz Arnold) Deutsches Künstlertheater 16 October
1924 **Geliebte seiner Hoheit** (Gilbert/w Rudolf Österreicher) Theater am Nollendorfplatz 24 September
1927 **Der Mikado** revised text w Rudolf Österreicher (Grosses Schauspielhaus)
1927 **The Birdseller** (*Der Vogelhändler*) English version w Harry S Pepper, Austin Melford (Palace Theatre, London)
1945 **Gay Rosalinda** (*Die Fledermaus*) English version w Melford, Sam Heppner (Palace Theatre, London)
Autobiography: *Das Theater meines Lebens* (Lothar Blanvalet, Berlin, 1955)

BERNICAT, Firmin (b Lyon, 1843; d Paris, March 1883).

Highly regarded throughout his career as a musician, Bernicat nevertheless found only journeyman work as an orchestrator and arranger in Parisian musical and theatrical circles for many years. He had some success with songs for the cafés-concerts ('La Ronde du Garde-Champêtre' etc) and apparently had an important hand in the orchestrations of some of Planquette's – and maybe other folks' – greatest successes, but although he supplied the music for a number of one-act opérettes played at such venues as the Café Tertulia, the Folies-Bergère and the Eldorado, he had to wait for his own confirmation as a composer in the regular theatre until 1882 when his full-length opérette *Les Beignets du roi* was produced at Brussels' Alcazar with considerable success.

Bernicat was in the middle of a second major work,

113

François les bas-bleus, when he died. Completed by Messager, *François les bas-bleus* was a great success at the Folies-Dramatiques, won foreign productions and regular revivals for over 50 years and led to Messager successfully revising *Les Beignets du Roi* for Paris under the title *Les Premières Armes de Louis XV* (1888, 45 performances). In Britain, a posthumous Bernicat pasticcio, with a libretto by actress–manageress Kate Santley, toured as *Vetah* for several seasons, and several of his short pieces were revived at the Moulin Rouge (*La Cornette* 27 March 1895, *On demande un Arlequin* 5 April 1896) and in other venues, ultimately giving the late composer more success in the years following his death than he had ever had in some dozen years of attempts during his lifetime.

1870 **Ali pot de rhum** (Gedhé [ie G. Delafontaine]) 1 act Alcazar 17 December

1872 **Monsieur et Madame Véronique** (Léon Quentin, Gedhé) 1 act Alcazar 15 July

1872 **Deux à deux** (Quentin) 1 act Café Tertulia 14 October

1873 **La Queue du Diable** (Quentin, Gedhé) 1 act Café Tertulia 15 February

1874 **Ah c't' Indien** (Gedhé) 1 act Folies-Bergère

1874 **Par la fenêtre** 1 act Folies-Bergère

1875 **Les Trois Grands Prix** (Alfred Delilia, Charles Lesenne) 1 act Salle Taitbout 28 March

1875 **Cabinet numéro six** (Th Massine) Théâtre des Bouffes-Parisiens 10 December

1876 **Les Deux Omar** (Gedhé, William Busnach) 1 act Fantaisies Oller 4 March

1876 **Le Voyage du petit marquis** (Louis Péricaud, Germain Villemer) 1 act Fantaisies Oller 5 October

1877 **La Jeunesse de Béranger** (Péricaud, Villemer) 1 act Eldorado 20 January

1877 **Le Pâte empoisonné** (Élie Frébault) 1 act Alcazar 22 September

1877 **Fou-yo-po** (Émile Max) 1 act Alcazar 10 October

1877/8 **La Cornette** (Péricaud, Villemer, Lucien Delormel) 1 act Eldorado

1878 **Le Moulin des amours** (Péricaud, Villemer) 1 act Eldorado 25 January

1878 **Une aventure de la clairon** (Péricaud, Villemer) 1 act Eldorado 23 November

1878 **Les Barbières de village** (Charles Blondelet, Félix Baumaine) 1 act Alcazar 28 November

1878 **Les Cadets de Gascoyne** (Georges Dorfeuil, Charles Mey) 1 act Alcazar 25 November

1878 **Une poule mouillée** (Auguste Jouhaud, Péricaud, Villemer) Concert du 19ème 21 December

1878 **Les Triomphes d'Arlequin** (Alexandre Guyon) 1 act Eldorado

1878 **On demande un Arlequin** (Péricaud, Delormel) 1 act Eldorado

1882 **Les Beignets du Roi** (Albert Carré, Paul Ferrier) Alcazar, Brussels 16 February

1882 **Les Premières [Armes] de Parny** (Péricaud, Delormel) Eldorado 20 June

1883 **François les bas-bleus** (w André Messager/Ernest Dubreuil, Eugeǹe Humbert, Paul Burani) Théâtre des Folies-Dramatiques 8 November

1886 **Vetah** (arr and add music Georges Jacobi, Frederick Bowyer/Kate Santley) Theatre Royal, Portsmouth 30 August

1888 **Les Premières Armes de Louis XV** revised *Les Beignets du roi* ad Messager Théâtre de Menus-Plaisirs 16 February

1892 **Le Forban** (Dorfeuil, Charles Mey) 1 act Gaîté-Montparnasse 23 April

Other titles attributed: *Un mari à l'essai, Deux coups de marteau*

BERNSTEIN, Leonard (b Lawrence, Mass, 25 August 1918; d New York, 14 October 1990). Internationally celebrated conductor and musician who supplied Broadway with several superior musical scores and at least one of its most outstanding shows of all time.

The young Leonard Bernstein had won recognition as a symphonic conductor before he entered the theatre as a composer in 1944 with the score for *Fancy Free* (18 April), a ballet choreographed by Jerome Robbins. The pair subsequently developed the theme of the ballet into the musical *On the Town* (1944, 'On the Town', 'Carried Away', 'New York, New York' etc), a light romantic comedy song-and-dance piece written in collaboration with Betty Comden and Adolph Green which had a fine success on Broadway, several overseas productions, and was later metamorphosed into a film.

Bernstein provided incidental music, including a half-dozen songs for a 1950 production of J M Barrie's fairy play *Peter Pan* (Imperial Theater 321 performances) and composed the songs and dance music for another highly successful musical comedy, on the standard Broadway format of the time – the musicalized version of the hit play *My Sister Eileen*, as *Wonderful Town* ('Ohio', 'A Little Bit in Love' etc) – before he produced a much more ambitious score for a short-lived first musical version of Voltaire's *Candide* (1956).

With the music for his next stage musical, *West Side Story* (1957), he took yet another path, combining the substance of the *Candide* score and the dance-orientation of *On the Town* with a driving and exciting contemporary quality to illustrate a modern New York version of the Romeo and Juliet story set amongst juvenile immigrant gangs. The worldwide success of *West Side Story* ('Tonight', 'Maria', 'A Boy Like That', 'America' etc) both on stage and screen established it as one of all-time greats of the musical theatre, but Bernstein preferred thereafter to concentrate on the other areas of his internationally successful musical life and wrote only one further stage musical, the unsuccessful *1600 Pennsylvania Avenue* (1976).

In 1973 a rewritten and more humorous version of *Candide* was produced. It moved on to Broadway success and the piece has, in a variety of different versions, been subsequently played in opera houses in America and Britain.

Apparently able to provide music to suit any style of text, Bernstein displayed his outstanding ability as a composer of class light theatre music most clearly in his two most enduring scores, *West Side Story* and *Candide*, whilst also providing for his shows orchestral and dance music which was of a substance and quality which has rarely been found in any area of the theatre.

Bernstein's other works for the theatre included the libretto and music for the one-act opera *Trouble in Tahiti* (19 April 1955), the incidental music for the play *The Lark* (1955) and the vocal music for *The Firstborn* (Coronet Theater 29 April 1958). He also composed the score for the film *On the Waterfront* and authored books on music, notably *The Joy of Music* (1959).

1944 **On the Town** (Adolph Green, Betty Comden) Adelphi Theater 28 December

1953 **Wonderful Town** (Comden, Green/Joseph Fields, Jerome Chodorov) Winter Garden Theater 25 February

1956 **Candide** (Richard Wilbur, John Latouche, Dorothy Parker/Lillian Hellman) Martin Beck Theater 1 December

1957 **West Side Story** (Stephen Sondheim/Arthur Laurents) Winter Garden Theater 26 September

1973 **Candide** (revised version w Hugh Wheeler, Sondheim) Chelsea Theater Center 18 December

1976 **1600 Pennsylvania Avenue** (Alan Jay Lerner) Mark Hellinger Theater 4 May

Biography: Ewen, D: *Leonard Bernstein* (Chilton, New York, 1960), Briggs, J: *Leonard Bernstein* (World, New York, 1961), Gruen, J: *The Private World of Leonard Bernstein* (Viking, New York, 1968), Peyser, J: *Leonard Bernstein* (Beech Tree Books, New York, 1987)

BERR, Georges (b Paris, 30 July 1867; d Paris, 25 July 1942).

A member of the company at the Comédie Française from the age of 19, and later a sociétaire and administrator, a professor at the Paris Conservatoire, and a theatrical director, Berr was also, over a period of more than 30 years, and in spite of being semi-blind and unable to read or write from his early forties onwards, a highly successful author of comedies for the Paris stage. He began his writing career with a plethora of little comedies and one-acters, monologues and even songs (which he signed by the pseudonym 'Colias') but also turned out some substantial plays (*Fiacre à l'heure, Plaisir d'amour*), pieces for the Grand-Guignol and even a ballet *Phébé* for the Opéra-Comique before going on to establish himself as one of the city's most prominent comic playwrights. He made only a brief skirmish into the musical theatre, in 1902, when he collaborated on the text for the successful Louis Varney opérette *La Princesse Bébé* and on that for the Châtelet spectacular *Les Aventures du Capitaine Corcoran*.

In the second decade of the 20th century, however, when the fashion for musical plays based on strong comedic libretti, usually taken from the French, became the prevailing style on the English-language stage, Berr's plays served as the bases for a whole series of extremely successful musical comedies. The composer Ivan Caryll was the instigator of the series, and made two major hits from Berr's works. The internationally successful *The Pink Lady* was based on *Le Satyre* (1907 w Marcel Guillemaud) and its successor *Oh! Oh! Delphine* on *La Grimpette* (1905 w Guillemaud) whilst *Un Coup de téléphone* (1912 w Paul Gavault) became, with more modest results, London's *The Kiss Call* (Gaiety Theatre 8 October 1919).

In Germany, *Dix minutes d'auto* (Théâtre des Nouveautés 13 November 1908 w Pierre Decourcelle) was turned into the Thalia-Theater's highly successful *Auto-liebchen* (1912), whilst a number of years later his 1928 piece *Ma soeur et moi* (w Louis Verneuil) was made into Ralph Benatzky's international hit *Meine Schwester und ich* (1930). In Italy, Berr maintained a credit on the Carlo Lombardo operetticization of *Changez la Dame*, and, back on the home front, his name appeared alongside that of Verneuil as the author of the Châtelet musical *Le Coffre-fort vivant* (1938), a version of the Frédéric Mauzens novel of the same title which Verneuil had earlier musicalized for Broadway as *The Canary* (music: Caryll).

1902 **La Princesse Bébé** (Louis Varney/w Pierre Decourcelle) Théâtre des Nouveautés 18 April

1902 **Les Aventures du Capitaine Corcoran** (Adrien Vély/w Paul Gavault) Théâtre du Châtelet 30 October

1926 **Qui êtes vous?** (Charles Cuvillier/w H Genty, Jouvault) Monte-Carlo 13 November

1938 **Le Coffre-fort vivant** ('Jean Sautreuil', Joseph Szulc/ Henri Wernert/w Verneuil) Théâtre du Châtelet 17 December

BERRY, W[illiam] H[enry] (b London, 23 March 1870; d London, 2 May 1951). Star comedian of 20 years of West End musicals.

'Bill' Berry paired a career in the city with amateur performances as a comic and concert entertainer for twelve years before George Edwardes was inspired to put him and his wife, Kitty Hanson, under contract. Under Edwardes's management he appeared at the Prince of Wales, the Gaiety and Daly's in a series of increasingly important comedy roles from *The Little Cherub* (1906, Shingle) through *See See* (1906, Cheoo), *Les Merveilleuses* (1906, St Amour/Tournesol), *The Merry Widow* (1907, Nitsch), *Havana* (1908, Reggie), *The Dollar Princess* (1909, Bulger), *A Waltz Dream* (1911, Lothar), *The Count of Luxemburg* (1911, Brissard), *Gipsy Love* (1912, Dragotin), *The Marriage Market* (1913, Blinker), *A Country Girl* (1914, Barry), and *Betty* (1915, Achille Jotte) before moving to a semi-permanent berth at the Adelphi Theatre. There for more than eight years and through several managements he remained installed as the theatre's accepted star and as a potent public draw for the musical comedy *Tina* (1915, van Damm), Friml's *High Jinks* (1916, Dr Thorne), the long-running Pinero musicals *The Boy* (1917, Meebles) and *Who's Hooper?* (1919, Valentine Hooper), *The Naughty Princess* (*La Reine s'amuse* 1920, King Michael), Novello's comic opera *The Golden Moth* (1921, Dipper Tigg), *The Island King* (1922, Hopkins) and *Head Over Heels* (1923, Alfred Wigg).

He continued as a great audience favourite through the 1920s, playing similar comedy rôles, most successfully as father Veidt in *Lilac Time* and Albert Chuff in *Princess Charming*, but less profitably in Lehár's *The Three Graces* (1924, Bouquet) and the American musical comedies *Poppy* (1924, Eustace McGargle, the rôle invented for W C Fields), *The Blue Kitten* (1925, Christopher Popp) and *The Girl from Cooks* (1927, Higgins), in Szirmai's *The Bamboula* (1925, Prince Robert) and the Anglo-American *Blue Eyes* (1928, Pilbeam) and *Merry, Merry* (1929, Jimmie Diggs). In the 1930s Berry appeared as Calchas in C B Cochran's all-star perversion of *La Belle Hélène* (*Helen!*) and repeated his earlier successes as Lothar and Veidt before abandoning the stage for film (*Mr Cinders, Funny Face* etc) and radio.

At his peak, during and after the war, the endearingly boggle-eyed and moon-faced Berry was the town's most popular musical comedian, but a sad lack of suitable rôles and strong shows in later years gave him little chance to maintain the position built on the splendid series of Edwardes productions in pre-war years, and in his best starring rôles at the Adelphi.

Autobiography: *Forty Years in the Limelight* (Hutchinson, London, 1939)

BERTÉ, Heinrich (b Galgócz, Hungary, 8 May 1857; d Voeslau nr Vienna, 24 August 1924). Austro-Hungarian composer who ultimately made his name as an arranger.

Berté and his brother Emil moved to Vienna as children, and 'Harry' was given a serious musical education both there and in Paris, where he studied under Delibes. Although the late-arriving composer's first staged work was an Operette, *Bureau Malicorne*, produced at the

Sommer Theater at Baden bei Wien, most of his earliest attempts at stage music were in the realm of ballet (*Die goldene Märchenwelt* Vienna Hofoper 2 April 1893, *Karnaval in Venedig* Munich 1901, *Automatenzauber* Orpheum 1901). His one-act comic opera *Die Schneeflocke* was produced in Prague in 1896, and subsequently both at Berlin's Neues Königliches Opernhaus and in Budapest (*Hophély* Magyár Királyi Operaház 4 March 1899), but his first major opportunity in the musical theatre did not come until 1904 when he had a full-length Operette, *Der neue Burgermeister*, accepted for production the Theater an der Wien.

Der neue Burgermeister played only seven performances, in spite of boasting the hugely popular Viennese star Alexander Girardi at the head of its cast but, in the following half-dozen years, Berté turned out a regular flow of such pieces, mostly for German regional theatres, with a respectable degree of success. Two, *Die Millionenbraut* and *Der schöne Gardist*, were brought to the Theater an der Wien for 26 and 32 performances respectively, and the latter was also produced at Budapest's Budai Színkör (*A szép gardista*), whilst his 1910 Hamburg piece, *Kreolenblut*, was played briefly on Broadway under the title *The Rose of Panama*, in Hungary as *Kreolvér* (1911) and in the French provinces as *Coeur de Créole* (1913). *Der Glücksnarr*, premièred at Vienna's Carltheater with Mizzi Zwerenz, Karl Blasel and Josef König featured, was less well-received and flopped in 20 performances.

A significant hit eluded Berté and, after this series of, at best, half-successes, further commissions did not eventuate. Deeply depressed, Berté turned to Emil, now an influential music publisher, for assistance, and it was the elder Berté who put forward his brother's name to his colleague Karczag at the Raimundtheater as a potential arranger/composer for the so-called Singspiel which was to become *Das Dreimäderlhaus*. This Schubert pasticcio became one of the most successful Viennese shows of all time, securing Berté financially as it was transformed into *Lilac Time*, *Blossom Time*, *Chanson d'amour*, *Harom a kislány* and so forth in various parts of the world and everywhere with huge success. Berté, however, never considered the piece as 'his' and, although he completed a second Schubert musical, he turned down the opportunity to work on the *Dreimäderlhaus* musequel, *Hannerl*, preferring to attempt once more to make the world appreciate his original writings.

Although one of his two subsequent shows, *Die drei Kavaliere*, was played in Hungary (*Harom a gavaller* Varszinház 25 April 1922) and published in France following its first showing in Hamburg, neither made any notable impact and, to his despair, *Das Dreimäderlhaus* remained his one claim to fame.

1887 **Bureau Malicorne** (F W Schmiedell) Baden bei Wien 22 February

1896 **Die Schneeflocke** (A M Willner) 1 act Prague 4 October

1904 **Der neue Burgermeister** (Ernst Gettke, Robert Pohl) Theater an der Wien 8 January

1904 **Die Millionenbraut** (Willner, E Limé) Theater am Gärtnerplatz, Munich 3 April, National-Theater, Berlin 2 December

1905 **Der Stadtregent** (Gettke, Pohl) Theater am Gärtnerplatz, Munich 1 April

1907 **Der schöne Gardist** (Alexander Landesberg, Willner) Neues Operetten-Theater, Breslau 12 October

1907 **Der kleine Chevalier** (Willner) 1 act Central-Theater, Dresden 30 November

1908 **Die Wunderquelle** (Wilhelm Sterk, Emmerich von Gatti) 1 act Hölle 1 November

1908 **Der Glücksnarr** (E Limé ad Landesberg, Willner) Carltheater 7 November

1909 **Der erste Kuss** Neues Operetten-Theater, Hamburg 14 November

1910 **Kreolenblut** (Ignaz Schnitzer, von Gatti) Neues Operetten-Theater, Hamburg 25 December

1914 **Der Märchenprinz** (Willner, Sterk) Schauburg, Hannover 28 February

1916 **Das Dreimäderlhaus** (Franz Schubert arr/Willner, Reichert) Raimundtheater 15 January

1917 **Tavasz es szerelem** (*Lenz und Liebe*) (Schubert arr/Bruno Hardt-Warden, Ignaz Welleminsky ad Jenő Heltai) Városi Színház, Budapest 15 September; Neues Operetten-Theater, Hamburg February 1918

1919 **Die drei Kavaliere** (Lothar Sachs, von Gatti) Neues Operetten-Theater, Hamburg 5 November

1920 **Kulissengeheimnisse** (Henri Cain, Édouard Adénis ad) Neues Operetten-Theater, Hamburg 28 January

Berté's nephew, the younger **Emil BERTÉ** (b Vienna, 6 December 1898; d Vienna, 17 January 1968), supplied the music for a handful of Operetten/Singspiele including yet another arrangement of Schubert, *Der Musikus von Lichtenthal*, and, most notably, the successful *Musik in Mai* produced at the Raimundtheater with Ernst Tautenhayn starred and subsequently played on Broadway as *Music in May* (ad Fanny Todd Mitchell, J Kiern Brennan, add mus Maurice Rubens, Casino Theater 1 April 1929).

1927 **Musik in Mai** (Heinz Merley, Kurt Breuer) Raimundtheater 13 May

1928 **Der Musikus von Lichtenthal** (Schubert arr/Breuer) Neue Wiener Bühne 30 March

1929 **Steppenkinder** (Hans Borutzky, Alfred Steinberg-Frank) Stadttheater, Augsburg 15 December

1930 **Das Kaiserliebchen** (Ernst Decsey, Steinberg-Frank, Max Blau) Wiener Stadttheater 4 January

1955 **Melodie aus Wien** Landestheater, Linz 22 October

BERTHELIER, [Jean-François Philbert] (b La Panissière, Loire, 14 December 1830; d Paris, September 1888). Comic actor and singer who was one of the major stars of the 19th-century French musical theatre.

The young Berthelier worked as a bookshop assistant in Lyon and as a commercial traveller in paintings before making his first stage appearances in 1849 as a tenor in the theatre at Poitiers. A couple of years later, he made his way to Paris and there established himself a small name as an actor and as a singer in cafés-concerts. It was at one of these latter, in Rue Madame, that Offenbach heard him singing Étienne Tréfeu's popular song 'Vive la France' and engaged him as a member of his initial company at the Bouffes-Parisiens. Berthelier's fame was made overnight when he introduced the rôle of Giraffier in *Les Deux Aveugles* (1855). He created rôles in *Une nuit blanche* (1855, Hercule), *Le Violoneux* (1855, Pierre), *Paimpol et Périnette* (1855, Paimpol) and *Ba-ta-clan* (1855, Ke-ki-ka-ko) during the Bouffes' first months, but later went on to stints at the Palais-Royal and at the Opéra-Comique (1856-62), taking part during the latter engagement in the premières of Gevaert's *Château Trompette* and of Offenbach's *Barkouf* (M Sainte-Foy). At the same time he continued a highly successful career as a chansonnier, now provided especially with songs made to his measure by such popular song-writers of the time as Gustave Nadaud, Edmond Lhuillier and Tréfeu ('Le Baptême du p'tit Énéniste', 'L'Invalide à la tête de bois' etc).

He subsequently created further and mostly more more substantial Offenbach rôles in the triple part of Myriame/Colin/Nicot in *Les Bergers* (1865), King Cacatois in *L'Île de Tulipatan* (1868), Casimir in *La Princesse de Trébizonde* (1869), Le Caporal in *Boule de Neige* (1871), Lastécouères in *Les Braconniers* (1873), the cretinous pupil in *Le Leçon de Chant* (1873), and Flammèche in *La Boulangère a des écus* (1875), introduced Lecocq's *Le Testament de M Crac* (1871, Isolin de Castafiol) and Hervé's *La Veuve du Malabar* (1873, Le Nabab Kéri-Kalé) as well as such less memorable opérettes as *Le Docteur Rose* (1872) and *Le Roi dort* (1876).

When the fashion and the wheel of success turned from Offenbach to Lecocq, Berthelier was on hand, as a member of the Théâtre de la Renaissance company, to partake of further major successes, starring in some of his best comedy rôles in Lecocq's *La Marjolaine* (1877, Palamède Van der Boom), *Kosiki* (1876, Xicoco), *Le Petit Duc* (1878, Frimousse), *La Petite Mademoiselle* (1879, Taboureau) and *La Camargo* (1878, Pont-Calé), and later, at the Nouveautés, in the two most important works of the second part of the composer's career, *Le Jour et la nuit* (1881, Don Brasiero de Tras os Montes) and *Le Coeur et la main* (1882, King of Aragon). He also appeared as Zappoli in the French Johann Strauss concoction *La Tzigane* (1877) at the Renaissance, and at the Nouveautés in *Le Voyage en Amérique* (Girandol), and *La Cantinière* (1880, Rastagnac), going on to a long, long list of further comic creations at that house, few of which, however, came up to the rôles with which he had been favoured at the height of Lecocq's success.

Amongst the shows in which he initiated parts in his later years were included *Le Droit d'aînesse* (1883, Tancrède), *Premier Baiser* (1883, Zug), *Le Roi de carreau* (1883, Tirechappe), *L'Oiseau bleu* (1884, Bricoli), *Babolin* (1884, Karamatoff), *La Nuit aux soufflets* (1884, Hercule III), *Le Château de Tire-Larigot* (1884, Marquis de Valpointu), *La Vie mondaine* (1885, Chiquito), *Serment d'amour* (1886, Gavuadan), *Adam et Ève* (1886, Adramalec), *Princesse Colombine* (1886, Seneschal), *Dix Jours aux Pyrénées* (1887, Chaudillac), *Le Bossu* (1888, Cocardasse) and, at the Gaîté, *Le Dragon de la reine* (1888). The now grossly overweight comedian died during the run of the last-named show.

Considered by some to be more of a vocalist than an actor – and his way with a comic song was apparently second to none – it was, nevertheless, in important comical rôles that he secured and kept, over more than 30 years, his prominent place in the Paris musical theatre.

Berthelier, the lover of the young Hortense Schneider in her early Paris days, was responsible for her introduction to Offenbach and the Bouffes-Parisiens, and, as such, was depicted on film in the Offenbach-loves-Hortense movie, *Valse de Paris*.

BERTRAND, Eugène

The manager of Paris's Théâtre des Variétés from 1869 until 1891, Bertrand came to Paris from Lille to take over the theatre which had been the birthplace in recent years of *La Belle Hélène*, *Barbe-bleue*, *La Grande-Duchesse de Gérolstein* and *La Périchole* from their now extremely wealthy producer, Hippolyte Cogniard. He carried on where his illustrious predecessor had left off, mounting Offenbach's *Les Brigands* and, after the end of the war, continued with new productions such as Hervé's *Le Trône d'Écosse*, Offenbach's *Les Braconniers*, the expanded *La Périchole* with Schneider, *Les Prés Saint Gervais* (1874), Serpette's *Le Manoir du Pic-Tordu*, Offenbach's *La Boulangère a des écus* (1875), Costé's *Le Dada* (1876), Offenbach's *Le Docteur Ox* and the winning little *Les Charbonniers* (1877) mixed with revivals of opéra-bouffe and vaudevilles, spectacles-coupés, comedies and revues.

In 1878 Bertrand began the triumphant series of vaudeville-opérettes in which Anna Judic starred and which would be the highlight of his management: *Niniche* (1878), *Le Grand Casimir* (1879), *La Femme à papa* (1879), *La Roussotte* (1881), *Lili* (1882), *Mam'zelle Nitouche* (1883) and *La Cosaque* (1884). When the vogue faded, the ageing Hervé, who had composed much of the music for the series, contributed a score to *Mam'selle Gavroche* (1885) in which Jeanne Granier attempted to take up where Judic had left off, before, in 1886, Bertrand took the actor, Louis Baron into partnership.

Plays, and revivals of musical pieces from *La Belle Hélène* and *Les Brigands* up to the Judic favourites, did rather better for the partners than the new musicals. The old formula proved it was run dry when a vaudeville from the Millaud, de Najac and Hervé team, *La Noce à Nini*, flopped (1887). Pieces like *La Japonaise* (1888) and *La Fille à Cacolet* (1889) did no better, and Bertrand's last days at the Variétés did not again bring the success he had known so richly in his Judic days.

BEST FOOT FORWARD Musical comedy in 2 acts by John Cecil Holm. Music and lyrics by Hugh Martin and Ralph Blane. Ethel Barrymore Theater, New York, 1 October 1941.

Another in the Broadway parade of college musicals, the wartime *Best Foot Forward*, with its young cast of under-draftable-age actors, joined *Good News* and *Leave it to Jane* on the successful list when its original production played 326 Broadway performances and put the phrase 'Buckle down, Winsocki' into the current parlance.

The college which welcomed the action of the piece was Pennsylvania's Winsocki, and this time, for change, there wasn't a football game in sight. It was prom time. Bud Hooper (Gil Stratton jr) is going steady with Helen Schlesinger (Maureen Cannon) but, as a josh, invites Hollywood starlet Gale Joy (Rosemary Lane) to be his date for the college prom. To his astonishment, she accepts, as her PR man (Marty May) thinks he can get press-inches out of the event. There turns out to be more event than he had suspected, when Helen launches her revenge and Gale's dress suffers embarrassingly. The status quo is re-established when the starlet goes back to her Hollywood heaven. June Allyson (Minerva Brooks) and Jack Jordan jr (Dutch Miller) were number two couple whilst Nancy Walker was Winsocki's eternal and eternally hopeful Blind Date. Choreography was by the young Gene Kelly.

Producers George Abbott and Richard Rodgers auditioned for songwriters to supply the songs for the show and chose the untried Hugh Martin and Ralph Blane, whose score hit the collegiate tone to a nicety and, with 'Buckle

Down, Winsocki', produced a lively cheerleading hit which was well supported by a second favourite in the comedienne's 'Just a Little Joint With a Jukebox'.

Best Foot Forward's style and subject matter probably accounted for the fact that it won no attention outside America, but at home it proved repeatedy popular. Hollywood took it up for a 1943 film in which Jordan and Misses Allyson and Walker and five of the show's songs repeated their Broadway assignment alongside Tommy Dix, Gloria deHaven and Lucille Ball (playing the film starlet as herself) and five new numbers to add to those kept from the show. It was broadcast on the Railroad Hour in 1949, and televised in 1954 with a cast headed by Jeannie Carson, Marilyn Maxwell, Robert Cummings and Jimmy Komack, in each case with a reduced score (and in each case without the little joint and its jukebox). A New York revival was mounted in 1963 (Stage 73 Theater 2 April) with Glenn Walken (Bud), Karin Wolfe (Helen), Paula Wayne (Gale), Grant Walden (Jack) and the young Liza Minnelli performing 'You Are Loving', one of three further additional numbers added to three from the film and rather more than half the original songs. The revival played for 224 performances.

Film: MGM 1943

Recording: 1963 revival (Cadence)

THE BEST LITTLE WHOREHOUSE IN TEXAS
Musical in 2 acts by Larry L King and Peter Masterson. Music and lyrics by Carol Hall. Actors' Studio, New York, 20 October 1977, Entermedia Theater 17 April 1978, 46th Street Theater 19 June 1978.

The story to the musical *The Best Little Whorehouse in Texas* sprang from an article about the real-life 'chicken ranch' brothel, written by journalist Larry L King, in *Playboy* magazine. Adapted into a stage show by King and Texan Peter Masterson, with a score by singer-songwriter Carol Hall, it was first produced at a workshop at the Actors Studio in November 1977 with Henderson Forsythe and Liz Kemp in the principal rôles. It was subsequently mounted at off-Broadway's Entermedia Theater the following year for a season of 50 performances before, with the backing of Universal Pictures, moving on to a long and successful career on Broadway.

Miss Mona (Carlin Glynn) runs a tidy little whorehouse – 'a l'il ole bitty pissant country place' – in the town of Gilbert, Texas, until the day that Melvin P Thorpe (Clinton Allmon), broadcaster, personality and power-crazed poseur, hones in on the 'Chicken Ranch' as the newest target upon which to display the extent of his influence and importance. When he shows up in Gilbert with his cameras, the primping intruder gets a dusty mouthful of a goodbye from sheriff Ed Earl Dodd (Henderson Forsythe), which is all relayed to the moral folk of Texas by the wonderful power of TV. Thorpe sets up a trap, and invades the Chicken Ranch with his crew on the night the Aggie football team and their sponsoring senator are celebrating their big game win in traditional fashion. Waving his evidence, he then proceeds to corner the Governor of Texas (Jay Garner), putting him in a position where, to save face, he has to voice shocked disapproval. It all gets far too big and high-up for little Gilbert and for Ed Earl. When orders come from as far above as the state government, the Chicken Ranch has to close. The girls and Miss

Mona leave their home to look for another as Melvin P Thorpe struts towards a civic honour under the arc-lights of glorious self-satisfaction and television.

King and Masterson's libretto crackled with hilariously unbelievable (to a non-Texan) technicolored Texan oaths and adjectives, which were reflected in the songs. The accompanying band opened proceedings with a country-and-folksy description of 'Twenty Fans', turning to keep everyone in the brothel cool, Miss Mona gave gentle encouragement to a shy new recruit ('Girl You're a Woman') and, at the end of the affair, glanced back at her own early days ('The Bus from Amarillo') as she set out to start over again, whilst Ed Earl mused over the 'Good Ol' Girl' who was almost his lover. A plain little waitress longed to be more daring in her dress and doings ('Doatsey Mae'), the Governor of Texas did his best to dance 'The Side Step' in double-talk and soft-shoe around the insistent Thorpe, and the footballers leaped into action in a virile Tommy Tune dance routine to the strains of 'The Aggie Song'.

The production was a splendid success on Broadway, running for 1,584 performances and returning swiftly for a repeat season at the Eugene O'Neill Theater in 1982 (31 May). Elsewhere, however, things went less well. In London, in spite of urgings that the show should go into the friendly, middle-sized Prince of Wales Theatre, Universal chose to mount *Best Little Whorehouse* in the vastness of the Theatre Royal, Drury Lane. Miss Glynn and Forsythe were joined by Fred Evans (Governor), Sheila Brand (Doatsey Mae) and Nigel Pegram (Thorpe) in a version which was never comfortably at home through 204 performances. In Australia television soap star Lorraine Bayly starred as Miss Mona alongside expatriate American Alfred Sandor, and once again the piece failed to catch in seasons in Sydney and Melbourne (Her Majesty's Theatre 7 February 1981).

In 1982 Universal turned out the film version. Dolly Parton was a swimmingly voluptuous Miss Mona who supplied a couple of additional numbers of her own to add to the remnants of the score, whilst Burt Reynolds played a matinée idol Ed Earl. It was all a long way from Texas, except in that it went thoroughly south.

Australia: Her Majesty's Theatre, Sydney 13 September 1980; UK: Theatre Royal, Drury Lane 26 February 1981; Film: Universal 1982

Recordings: original cast (MCA), film soundtrack (MCA)

DER BETTELSTUDENT
Operette in 4 acts by F Zell and Richard Genée based on *Fernande* by Victorien Sardou and *The Lady of Lyons* by Edward Bulwer-Lytton. Music by Karl Millöcker. Theater an der Wien, Vienna, 6 December 1882.

Millöcker's most successful Operette and, indeed, one of the very few 19th-century Viennese pieces which do not have the fashionable name of 'Strauss' attached to them which have survived on to the modern stage, *Der Bettelstudent* was one of the triumphs of the European musical theatre of its era, and was played regularly throughout the Continent for many years. Part of the show's attraction was that it was based on a particularly strong main plotline, one which borrowed elements from both Sardou's *Fernande* and Edward Bulwer-Lytton's celebrated *The Lady of Lyons* in its construction, but which has lasted

Plate 21. **Der Bettelstudent:** *The Countess Palmatica (Anny Schlemm) faces up to the inimical Colonel Ollendorf in the Vienna Volksoper's production of 1989.*

longer than either of those neverthless celebrated and once hugely popular models.

Colonel Ollendorf (Felix Schweighofer) of the ruling Saxon army has been rebuffed. He kissed the Polish Countess Laura Nowalska (Karoline Finaly) on the shoulder at last night's ball, and was slapped in the face for his pains. Now he is out for revenge. He has a handsome pair of beggar-students, Symon Rymanowicz (Alexander Girardi) and Jan Janicki (Josef Joseffy), released from jail, disguises them as the Count Wybicki and his secretary and lets them loose on the proud but poor Laura. She is soon captivated, and agrees to wed the apparently rich and powerful nobleman. Symon, too, has fallen genuinely in love and wants to expose the trickery rather than wed under false pretences, but Jan, who is an important official in the exiled Polish court's designs, begs him not to undo their incognitos until he has had time to bring his plots to fruition. Eventually, Laura goes to the altar unknowing, and Ollendorf has his revenge when he looses the inmates of the prison at the couple's wedding as the bridegroom's friends. Symon, however, has another rôle to play. Ollendorf, now aware that the rebel Poles are hiding the King's son somewhere, has bribed Jan to deliver him up. Jan encourages Symon to pretend to be the royal fugitive, and Symon's impersonation holds up events long enough for the rebels to storm Ollendorf's fortress and win the day. Symon and Laura are reunited, whilst Jan finds happiness with Laura's soubrette sister, Bronislawa (Frln Jona).

The hit of the score, unusually, turned out to be neither in the soprano nor the tenor numbers, nor in the soubrette's lively moments. It came from the rôle of Ollendorf, lugubriously describing to an unforgettable waltz melody the story of the fateful kiss ('Ach ich hab' sie ja nur auf der Schulter geküsst'). There were plenty of other outstanding moments for the other lead players, however – Symon's light tenor praise of Polish women ('Ich knüpfte manche zarte Bande') and his patriotic 'Ich hab' kein Geld, bin vogelfrei', the jolly masquerade of the two men ('Das ist der Fürst Wybicki mit seinem Sekretär') and two superb trios for Laura, Bronislawa and their mother, the exuberantly and indomitably aristocratic Countess Palmatica (Therese Schäfer, in one of the best older character rôles of the repertoire), out shopping ('Einkäufe

machen') or gluttonously preparing for the wedding ('Einen Mann hat sie gefunden').

Der Bettelstudent was produced by Franz Steiner at the Theater an der Wien and proved an immense success. By the time the 100th performance was passed on 3 September 1883, the company had visited the Carltheater to play their hit show, and the Theater an der Wien had hosted a performance by the Hungarian company from the Népszinház of their version of *A koldusdiák*. The 150th performance (5 September 1884) boasted a 'new overture' and by 1887 Siegmund Stelzer had taken possession of the rôle of Ollendorf alongside Ottilie Collin (Laura), Therese Biedermann (Bronislawa), Carl Streitmann (a rather more heroic Symon than the original) and Joseffy, as the piece continued as a fixed part of the theatre's repertoire through its 200th (March 1895) performance.

In Berlin, the Friedrich-Wilhelmstädtisches Theater's production proved a sensation, racing past its 200th performance in seven months (13 August 1883) and in Hungary (ad Lajos Evva, Béla J Fái) the reception won by *A koldusdiák* was equally as violent. The Népszinház's star, Lujza Blaha, was a travesti Symon with Aranka Hegyi as her Laura, János Kápolnai and Ilka Pálmay were the second pair, and Elek Solymossy (Ollendorf) and Anna Jenei (Palmatica) completed a star line-up with the biggest names Hungary had to offer. The production was played 93 times in repertoire, putting itself into the top ten musical pieces up to then played in the history of Budapest's most important musical theatre.

America heard its first *Bettelstudent* in German, but also with its star tenor rôle played in travesty. That star was one no less important than Hungary's, Marie Geistinger herself, playing alongside the Ollendorf of Carl Adolf Friese and the Laura of Emma Seebold. Ten days later, the first English version (ad Emil Schwab) opened in direct competition. W T Carleton was a male Symon to the Laura of Bertha Ricci and the Ollendorf of the English comic Fred Leslie, with German soubrette Mathilde Cottrelly as Bronislawa and Rose Leighton as Palmatica. The competition did no harm, for the English version racked up 110 performances whilst the original-language one popped in and out of the German houses' repertoires. *The Beggar Student* returned later in the year (6 October 1884) with Mark Smith (Symon), Digby Bell (Ollendorf), Lilly Post (Laura) and Cottrelly for a second season and it came back to Broadway again in 1913 (Casino Theater 22 March) with De Wolf Hopper playing Ollendorf, and yet again in 1930 (Heckscher Theater 17 November).

London's *The Beggar Student* (ad W Beatty-Kingston) was mounted on the splendid stage of the Alhambra with not the very best London cast. Fannie Leslie was a principal-boy style Symon, Savoy star Marion Hood was Laura, a capable comic in the person of Fred Mervin played Ollendorf, and Violet Melnotte, soon to be celebrated as a producer, took the small but featured rôle of Ensign von Richthofen. Fred Leslie took over his Broadway rôle during the run, and the show won through for a fine 112 performances. In 1886 it was back in London again for a nine weeks' season at the Comedy Theatre (13 December). This time Henry Bracy was a more suitable Symon with Mervin repeating his Ollendorf and Ada Lincoln as Laura. *The Beggar Student* was seen in London again in 1895 (Royalty Theatre 12 January), and it most recently reappeared in 1990 played by the semi-professional John Lewis group.

France, which had not welcomed much Viennese musical theatre with any enthusiasm, did not see *L'Étudiant pauvre* (ad E Hermil [ie Ange Milher], A J Numès) until 1889. Paris, happy in the wisdom that it was producing much of the best musical theatre the world had to offer at the time, sniffed at Millöcker's work as a pot-pourri of dance music and the show closed in 22 performances.

In Central Europe, after the first very fine flush, *Der Bettelstudent* held its place at the forefront of the repertoire. When the Theater an der Wien finally let the show loose from its repertoire after some 13 years, it began to appear in other Viennese houses. It was played at the Raimundtheater (8 May 1901) where it was reprised by Karczag in 1908 with Franz Glawatsch as Ollendorf, Marthe Winternitz-Dorda (Laura) and the evergreen Streitmann (Symon), again in 1916, in 1920 and in 1938 (ad Carl Hagemann) with Mizzi Günther as Palmatica, Fritz Imhoff (Ollendorf) and Hans Heinz Bollmann as Symon. It was introduced to the Jantschtheater in 1902 (17 October), the Johann Strauss-Theater in 1911, the Bürgertheater in 1917, and the Kaiser-Jubiläums Stadttheater (Volksoper) in 1909.

If there were one libretto of the Viennese Operette stage which ought – a travesty or so apart – to have remained safe from the 'improvers' of later ages, it would have seemed to be *Der Bettelstudent*. However, the lure for a publisher of a renewed copyright, the lure for a re-writer of royalties on the back of an out-of-copyright work, inevitably prove too much in Central Europe and, in consequence, in 1949 Herr Eugen Otto had a go at putting an old-fashioned Operette cliché or two into *Der Bettelstudent*'s text. In his tidily conventionalized version, amongst other alterations, Jan Janicki turns out to be – wait for it – the very Duke Adam Casimir that he has asked Symon to impersonate. Like so many similarly unfortunate (and similarly 're-copyrighted') remakes, it is this truly feeble one that holds the stage to this day in such venues as the Vienna Volksoper, who last remounted the work in 1983.

The original production of *Der Bettelstudent* was successful enough to provoke a number of spinoffs. On 25 March 1884 a humorous prologue to the piece, written by Wilhelm Henzen, illustrating the incident of the famous *Der Kuss auf der Schulter*, was mounted in Leipzig, whilst at Lübeck Franz Odemar's *Der Komponists Traum* (6 December) also used *Der Bettelstudent* as its subject matter.

Der Bettelstudent made its way to the screen for the first time in 1922, and further versions came in 1927 starring Harry Liedtke, in 1931 with Hans Heinz Bollmann, Jarmila Novotna and Hans Jaray, and in 1936 with Johannes Heesters, Marika Rökk and Fritz Kampers and the highlights of Millöcker's score complemented by two pastiches of his music done by Alois Melichar set to words by Franz Baumann. When it was re-released, the music of this version was credited to Peter Kreuder. The most recent film *Bettelstudent*, dating from 1956, credited its text to Fritz Böttger and its musical reorganization to Bruno Uher. Gerhard Riemann (Symon), Waltraut Haas (Laura) and Gustav Knuth (Ollendorf) featured and the Kessler twins somehow got into the film, if not the plot, as a pair of wandering dancers. An English-language film was brought out in 1932 with Lance Fairfax and Shirley Dale featured alongside comics Jerry Verno and Mark Daly, Frederick Lloyd and Jill Hands, and a 1957 East German *Mazurka der Liebe* also credited Zell and Genée's text as its source.

Several other musical pieces had been produced under the title *Der Bettelstudent* prior to this Operette, notably a 1781 Munich comic opera by Winter, and another by Buchweiser, mounted for the first time in 1793.

Germany: Friedrich-Wilhelmstädtisches Theater 24 January 1883; Hungary: Népszinház *A koldusdiák* 23 February 1883; USA: Thalia Theater (Ger) 19 October 1883, Casino Theater *The Beggar Student* 29 October 1883; UK: Alhambra Theatre *The Beggar Student* 12 April 1884; France: Théâtre des Menus-Plaisirs *L'Étudiant Pauvre* 18 January 1889; Australia: Opera House, Sydney 3 June 1889; Films: 1922, 1927, 1931, 1956, British Dominion Films (Eng) 1932

Recordings: complete (Amadeo, Eurodisc, EMI), selections (Telefunken, Eurodisc etc), selection in Hungarian (Qualiton)

THE BETTER 'OLE Fragment from France in 2 explosions, 7 splinters and a gas attack by Bruce Bairnsfather and Arthur Eliot. Lyrics by James Hurd. Music by Herman Darewski. Oxford Theatre, London, 4 August 1917.

During the later part of the First World War, London's musical theatre featured a third huge popular hit alongside the romantic spectaculars *Chu Chin Chow* and *The Maid of the Mountains*. *The Better 'Ole* had neither the staging splendours nor the musical values of this pair, but, from the sandbags decorating the theatre foyer to the positive picture, on stage, of the British at war, it was a piece and a production which had a huge appeal to returning servicemen and to their families.

The Better 'Ole (the title came from a cartoon of two soldiers sheltering from enemy fire in a crater ... 'If you know a better 'ole, go to it!') was in essence little more than a series of sketches, detailing the wartime adventures of 'Old Bill', the favourite cartoon character created by artist Bruce Bairnsfather. It painted a light-hearted but feeling portrait of the common man at war in confusing foreign parts as Old Bill (Arthur Bourchier) and his two pals Alf (Sinclair Cotter) and Bert (Tom Wootwell) gambolled through an evening of comedy and popular song, accidentally heroic adventures and girls, in a way which won the hearts of all. They gambolled for no less than 15 months, running up 811 performances on a heavy performance schedule, and the main run was followed by a quick revival.

Herman Darewski's catchy numbers 'My Word, Ain't We Carrying On?', 'From Someone in France to Someone in Somerset' and 'We Wish We Were in Blighty' were supplemented by the American hit 'What Do You Want to Make Those Eyes at Me For?' in a show which changed its elements freely. The most substantial alteration was not, however, a musical one. It came when producer C B Cochran, temporarily popped the whole one-act dramatic scena *Les Gosses dans les ruines* by Francisque Poulhot, in which the young Sybil Thorndike made an appearance, into the running-order of the show.

Following its London run, *The Better 'Ole* went on tour with enormous success, playing at one stage in three simultaneous companies in the English provinces and provoking copycat shows both in the theatre and the music-halls. In 1918 a (silent) film version was made with Charles Rock starred as Old Bill, whilst a second film, starring Syd

Chaplin, made in 1927 by Vitaphone, was equipped with a synchronized musical score.

In spite of the show's London success there was some considerable difficulty in setting up an American production. However, when the show was staged as a co-operative venture in Greenwich Village, with Charles Coburn starring as Old Bill, it quickly proved popular enough to warrant a transfer to the up-town Cort Theater, and subsequently to the Booth Theater for a fine run of 353 performances. Coburn was succeeded as Old Bill by De Wolf Hopper, and whilst Hopper took the show on to major tour dates, and companies covered America, he organized a condensed version of the show which he toured in American variety theatres. These tours met the same problem as was encountered by an Australian production, featuring Arnold Bell as Bill, Percy Cahill (Bert) and David Hallam (Alf). They arrived after the first film version and the Australian producers were obliged to advertise that 'this is the play, NOT the motion picture' through seasons at Melbourne's Tivoli and Sydney's newly reopened Tivoli (24 May 1919) for six weeks apiece.

USA: Greenwich Village Theater 19 October 1918, Cort Theater 18 November 1918; Australia: Tivoli Theatre, Melbourne 8 March 1919; Films: Welsh-Pearson 1918, Vitaphone 1927

BETTY Musical play in 3 acts by Frederick Lonsdale and Gladys Unger. Lyrics by Adrian Ross and Paul Rubens. Music by Paul Rubens. Additional numbers by Ernst Steffan and Merlin Morgan. Daly's Theatre, London, 24 April 1915.

Although the name of Paul Lincke was murmured in some quarters, the libretto of *Betty* was almost certainly intended by George Edwardes to be musically set by Victor Jacobi whose *Leányvásár* (*The Marriage Market*) had been such a success for him at Daly's Theatre. The intervention of the war forced Edwardes to change his plans and, in the place of a 'German' composer, Paul Rubens was ultimately given the assignment. When a journalist hinted that Rubens had merely put his name to a score written by Jacobi the composer took him to court, but withdrew his case after a recantation. The journalist had clearly not actually listened to the music, for the score of *Betty* was simply the best and brightest of Rubens and nothing like the altogether more substantial work of Jacobi.

The story of *Betty* had a reprobate young aristocrat wedding Betty, the kitchen maid, to spite his reprimanding father, but finding himself tricked when the father then settles the young man's allowance on the wife. Purse-strung, he is finally charmed into a happy ending by his wife of convenience. A new leading lady, 20-year-old soprano Winifred Barnes, was Betty, Donald Calthrop played her reticent lover, and G P Huntley as an aristocratic Lord Playne and Bill Berry as a comic couturier, Achille Jotte, shared the show's comedy. *Betty* proved a solid success at Daly's Theatre (391 performances) and subsequently made itself a remarkable touring life through more than a decade in the British provinces.

A New York production under the management of Charles Dillingham, with Joseph Santley and Ivy Sawyer as the couple, Raymond Hitchcock and Peter Page as the comedy, and veteran Joseph Herbert as the hero's father, did not take on in the same way and managed only 63 performances. This failure may have discouraged an Australian production, but Sydney and then Melbourne (Her Majesty's Theatre 7 February 1925) did finally see the show a decade on, with Edith Drayson and Maud Fane (who slipped Lehár's 'Gigolette' into the score) featured in the title-rôle in turn, alongside Harold Pearce (Beverly), Alfred Frith (Playne) and Cecil Kellaway (Jotte).

USA: Globe Theater 3 October 1916; Australia: Her Majesty's Theatre, Sydney 22 November 1924

BETTY IN MAYFAIR Musical play in 3 acts by J Hastings Turner adapted from his play *The Lilies of the Field*. Lyrics by Harry Graham. Music by H Fraser Simson. Adelphi Theatre, London, 11 November 1925.

A light musical play of some charm which starred Evelyn Laye as a modern miss who, having won her man (Arthur Margetson) whilst dressed in demure Victorian garb, keeps up the pretence of being an old-fashioned lass until honesty wins out and she confesses. Only then does she find he prefers her as a modern miss. Mary Leigh was the heroine's brighter sister, paired with Jack Hobbs in the livelier songs of Harold Fraser-Simson's pretty score ('The Days of Old', 'I Love You'), a score which was very largely made up of duets and other ensembles.

In a London season dominated by the advent of *No, No, Nanette* and *Rose Marie*, the comparatively quiet and old-fashioned *Betty in Mayfair* nevertheless found an audience and ran its way sweetly through six West End months (193 performances) before going out for a year of touring. An American production with Edna Best for star, announced by Lee Ephraim, did not eventuate.

BET YOUR LIFE Musical comedy in 2 acts by Alan Melville. Music by Kenneth Leslie-Smith and Charles Zwar. London Hippodrome, 18 February 1952.

Bet Your Life was a farcical comedy with songs, featuring favourite comic Arthur Askey as a jockey who is married to the daughter (Julie Wilson) of an anti-gambling crusader, and who dreams winning racing tips on his Corsican honeymoon. It was a libretto and a show which belonged to an earlier era, with its comedy tale reminiscent of the old Stanley Lupino and Lupino Lane shows, and a finale which brought the little hero on as the winner of the big race at Ascot, astride a real horse, much in the vein of *The Arcadians*.

The songs were a mixture of aggressive 'American' material for the American vocalist, Miss Wilson ('I Want a Great Big Hunk of a Man'), and more 'English' traditional for Sally Ann Howes as the juvenile love interest, paired here with Brian Reece (radio's famous PC 49) in the rôle of a racing journalist, as well as a little dash of the comic, and of the gipsyish, which the Corsican setting permitted.

Jack Hylton's production survived notices which found the show pejoratively old-fashioned and unsophisticated, and found an audience for four months at the Hippodrome, after which the piece was slimmed down, Miss Wilson replaced by Noele Gordon, and the schedule switched to a twice-nightly one which enabled *Bet Your Life* to run up a slightly flattering 362-performance total.

Recording: selection (Blue Pear)

BEYDTS, Louis (b Bordeaux, 29 June 1895; d Caudéran, 16 September 1953).

Beydts studied music in his native Bordeaux and, from

1924, in Paris, where his masters included Messager, the influence of whose refined musical style was evident in the composer's later works. He played in Parisian orchestral concerts and, simultaneously, wrote an amount of orchestral and vocal music which included a considerable number of incidental theatre scores, film music (*La Kermesse heroïque, Le Diable boîteux, Valse de Paris* etc), and several opérettes of which *Moineau* (1931) was the most substantial and the most successful. He also composed the music for Yvonne Printemps to sing in her husband's little opérabouffe *La S.A.D.M.P.* and *Le Voyage de Tschoung-Li*, as well as arranging her material for the little *Chagrin d'amour*.

Beydts was appointed Director of the Opéra-Comique in 1952 and held the post until his death the following year.

1931 **Moineau** (Henri Duvernois, Pierre Wolff/Guillot de Saxe) Théâtre Marigny 13 December
1931 **Les Canards mandarins** (Duvernois, Pascal Fortuny/de Saxe) Monte-Carlo
1931 **La S.A.D.M.P.** (Sacha Guitry) 1 act 3 November
1932 **Le voyage de Tschoung-Li** (Guitry) Théâtre de la Madeleine
1947 **L'aimable Sabine** (Léopold Marchand) Théâtre Marigny 25 April

BEZAUBERNDES FRÄULEIN Musical comedy (Lustspiel mit Musik) in 4 scenes, based on Paul Gavault's *La Petite Chocolatière*, by Ralph Benatzky. Music by Ralph Benatzky. Deutsches Volkstheater, Vienna 24 May 1933.

Benatzky followed his adaptation of the French comedy *Ma Soeur et moi* as the highly successful *Meine Schwester und ich* with another musicalization of a Parisian piece, Paul Gavault's hit comedy *La Petite Chocolatière* (1909). It was not exactly an original choice, for the play had already been turned into a musical in America as *Tantalising Tommy* (Hugo Felix/Adrian Ross, Michael Morton, Criterion Theater 1 October 1912), in Britain as *The Girl for the Boy* (Howard Carr, Bernard Rolt/Percy Greenbank/Austen Hurgon, George Arthurs, Duke of York's Theatre 23 September 1919) and in Italy as *La piccola cioccolataia* (Schinelli). However, Benatzky's version, a 12-handed, chorusless musical comedy, made in the manner of the best Parisian pieces of the 1920s, proved more successful than any of these.

Paul (Max Hansen), Felix (Hans Olden) and Felix's girlfriend, Rosette (Ingeborg Grahn), are spending the weekend at Paul's place in the country when a young woman turns up, victim of a motoring accident. Felix sees Paul's attraction to her, and sees also the chance of prying his friend free from the dreary idea of marrying Luise (Gusi Witt), the daughter of his employer (Alexander Fischer-Marich). His designs are confirmed when it turns out that Annette (Lizzi Waldmüller) is 'la petite chocolatière', the heiress to a cocoa fortune. Felix arranges things so that she is forced to stay the night and when, first, Luise and her papa and, then, Annette's father and fiancé (Otto Schmöle) turn up the next day, things get decidedly sticky. Back in town, Paul tries to patch things up with his boss, whilst Felix continues with his match-making tricks. When Paul, his future apparently in ruins, has got as far as thinking of jumping in the river, Annette appears on the scene, dressed in Salvation Army costume and, apparently, having renounced all worldly goods. Except Paul.

The score, slanted heavily in the direction of humour and of lively dance melodies, ranged from rumba to waltz, with Paul's 'Ach, Luise, kein Mädchen was ist diese?' and Felix's 'Hokuspokus fidibus' topping the list in musical popularity.

Bezauberndes Fräulein followed its Vienna season with another in Berlin, with Max Hansen and Lizzi Waldmüller repeating their Vienna rôles, later in 1933, and it was played in Italy the following year as *La Ragazza indiavolata* (Teatro Quirino, Rome 5 November 1934). It returned to Vienna in 1946 (Rex-Theater) and, amongst its other, intermittent but continuing productions, was recorded by German television in 1971.

Benatzky also wrote the screenplay for a filmed version of the same play, *Wer wagt gewinnt!* (1935), and *Bezauberndes Fräulein* was itself filmed in 1953 with his score adapted by Georg Hatzschel.

Germany: Deutsches Künstlertheater 1933; Film: 1953

LA BICHE AU BOIS

The fairytale 'La Biche au bois' written by the Countess d'Aulnoy (1649–1705) in the early 18th century and published as part of her *Fées à la mode*, became a favourite with producers of spectacular fantastical pieces in the 19th century. The most celebrated of these was the Parisian vaudeville-féerie written by the brothers Cogniard, Hippolyte and Théodore, first produced at the Théâtre de la Porte-Saint-Martin (29 March 1845), with the accompaniment of a pasticcio score by Pilati, and subsequently staged in various versions, mostly with made-up musical scores, throughout the 19th century.

The Cogniard version had the Princess Désirée, daughter of the King of the Island of Bells, transformed into a hind (biche) when a spell cast on her by the wicked fairy who wasn't invited to her christening is triggered off by her looking for the first time on the forbidden light of day. The Moorish Princess Aïka, jealous of the efforts of Prince Domino to free the enchanted Désirée from her feral shape, is the principal enemy of the pair as they struggle through the Kingdom of Fish, the Kingdom of Vegetables, the Siren Sea, the Depths of the Earth and other picturesque locations and ballets, until good triumphs over evil in a blaze of stage effects.

The loosely episodic fabric of this style of show provided the opportunity for the addition and substitution of scenes, songs and ballets as required to keep the piece both up-to-date and interesting to umpteenth-time visitors. However *La Biche au bois* was also given a significant musical working over when it was re-staged at the Théâtre de la Porte-Saint-Martin in 1867 with the young Hervé, who was cast in the rôle of Prince Souci, providing fresh music and arrangements to accompany the action (*La [Nouvelle] Biche au bois* add mus De Billemont, Artus 15 June). Later, the Théâtre du Châtelet, which became the principal home of *La Biche au bois* in the last decades of the century, was able to announce that 16 fresh scenes, from the hands of patented playwrights Ernest Blum and Raoul Toché, had been added to the original 14 for its 1896 edition of the show. The most appreciated of these turned out to be one slipped in to the Kingdom of the Vegetables portion of the plot, representing 'the amusing wedding scene of the dill-pickle and the tomato'.

English-language versions of *La Biche au bois* included *The Princess Changed into a Deer* produced by Alfred Bunn at the Theatre Royal, Drury Lane, in 1845 (and removed after one performance), Planché's successful extravaganza *The Prince of Happy Land, or The Fawn in the Forest* (Lyceum Theatre 26 December 1851) and F C Burnand's *The White Fawn*, illustrated with both music from Offenbach and Hervé and with music-hall songs, produced at Liverpool for Christmas 1867 and the following year at Holborn. In 1872 a grand opéra-bouffe féerie version, evidently based on the Cogniards' piece, with an original score commissioned from Georges Jacobi and Frederic Clay, was mounted at London's Alhambra Theatre (23 December) under the title – borrowed from a successful American extravaganza – of *[The] Black Crook*, and scored a considerable success.

Black Crook was the wicked fairy (Cornélie d'Anka) but it was the comical Dandelion (Harry Paulton) and soubrette Gabrielle (Kate Santley), the princess's helpmate, who had the best rôles (the princess, of course, being an animal for half the show). The much-photographed Branscombe sisters, a lightning caricaturist and all the famous forces of the Alhambra ballets also featured prominently through a fine run of 204 performances. A slightly slimmed version of the piece was revived at the same theatre in 1881 (3 December).

In America, *La Biche au bois* (which had nothing to do with the show presented as *The Black Crook*) was given as a spectacular *The White Fawn* in a version credited to James Mortimer – but seeming to owe a lot to both the Cogniards and Burnand – at Niblo's Garden, 17 January 1868 for 150 performances. Mark Smith (King Dingdong), Lizzie Wilmore (Finetta), Mena Montague (Aïka) and Lucy Egerton (Prince Leander) shared the centre of attention with a grand ballet of fireflies, a danse de poissons, a grand ballet of bells and a transformation scene which required 80 stagehands and 20 gasmen to operate it. The show progressed from Broadway to a superior 11 weeks in Boston and was a great success wherever it went thereafter.

Friedrich Strampfer at Vienna's Theater an der Wien also had a splendid success with the 'grosse Spektakel-Feerie mit Gesang, Tanz und Evolutionen in 4 akten und einem Vorspiel, in 13 Bildern' entitled *Prinzessin Hirschkuh* (11 June 1866). Matthias Rott (King Klingerlinging LXXVII), Carl Adolf Friese (Pelikan, ie Dandelion), Frln Lamberti (Aïka), Fr Berg (Furibunda), Carl Swoboda (Prince) and Frln Meyr (Giroflée, ie Gabrielle) led a cast who – doubtless not without reason – were billed smaller than the suppliers of costumes, scenery, props and the machinists, notably the gentleman who provided the 'Wasserwerke und elektrische Licht-Batterien' (already!). The largest type on the bill, however, was reserved for the BALLETS: the ballet of the fishes, the ballet of the vegetables, relating the tale of the love of a turnip for a carrot, the five-part grosses Tanz-Divertissement 'Les Amazones', and the dance of the sirens. *Prinzessin Hirschkuh* was played in Vienna 174 times in the 1860s and early 1870s.

BICKERSTAFF, Isaac [John] (b Ireland, 26 September 1733; d ?1812). One of the most successful and undoubtedly the best librettist for the 18th-century British musical stage.

Originally an officer in the army and then in the marines, Bickerstaff was, so it is said, drummed out of the service for persistent sodomy and shifted his activities instead to the theatre. There, he became one of the top stage writers of his time, writing and/or rewriting the texts for several plays (*The Plain-Dealer, The Absent Man, The Hypocrite, 'Tis Well It's No Worse* etc) and, most particularly, for a series of musical comedies which include most of those from that period which are still considered for occasional production in the 20th century.

The comic opera *Thomas and Sally*, the semi-pasticcio musical play *Love in a Village* ('The Miller of Dee') and *The Maid of the Mill*, a ballad opera based on Richardson's novel *Pamela*, were all considerable successes not only in Britain but throughout the English-speaking stages of the world, but it was *The Padlock*, a comic opera based on Cervantes' *El celoso extremeño*, which proved the most widely popular of Bickerstaff's pieces. It was played, with considerable success, all around the English-speaking world and even beyond, appearing, amongst other venues, in translation in Vienna (*Das Vorhängeschloss* with a fresh musical score by Carl Binder), and in Budapest (*A lakat*). It was most recently seen in London at the Old Vic in 1979.

Thomas and Sally was seen in London's West End as late as 1941 (New Theatre 1 July) and at New York's Little Theater in 1938 (4 January), versions of *Love in a Village* were reprised in London at the Everyman Theatre in 1923 and at the Lyric, Hammersmith in 1928 (mus arr Arthur Reynolds) where a revamped *Lionel and Clarissa*, also musically made over by Reynolds, had been previously seen in 1925 (28 October).

It has been suggested that the libretto to Mozart's *Die Entführung aus dem Serail* was descended from Bickerstaff's 1769 pasticcio comic opera *The Captive* (itself borrowed from Dryden), but the author, conversely, himself borrowed the text of Pergolesi's *La serva padrona* to make up the libretto for his *The Maid the Mistress/He Would If He Could*, and, in the style of the period, made use of such classic and Continental models as he pleased without always crediting his sources.

At the height of his success Bickerstaff's recurring habit got him into trouble again and this time the 37-year-old author was obliged to flee the country. In 1782 the *Biographica Dramatica* reported 'He is said to be still living abroad, to which *a deed without a name* has banished him, and where he exists poor and despised by all orders of people'. Unlike Oscar Wilde, a century later, he apparently lived some 30 years more, whether poor and despised is not known, but like Wilde he contributed no more to the British stage, which was much the poorer for his loss.

1760 **Thomas and Sally, or the Sailors Return** (Thomas Arne) Covent Garden 28 November
1762 **Love in a Village** (comp and arr Thomas Arne) Covent Garden 8 December
1765 **The Maid of the Mill** (Samuel Arnold et al) Covent Garden 31 January
1765 **Daphne and Amyntor** (various) Theatre Royal, Drury Lane 8 October
1767 **Love in the City** (Charles Dibdin et al) Covent Garden 21 February
1768 **Lionel and Clarissa** (C Dibdin) Covent Garden 28 February
1768 **The Padlock** (C Dibdin) Theatre Royal, Drury Lane 3 October

1768 **A Royal Garland** (Arnold) 1 act Covent Garden 10 October

1769 **The Ephesian Matron** (C Dibdin) 1 act Ranelagh House 12 May

1769 **The Captive** (C Dibdin) His Majesty's Theatre 21 June

1770 **The Maid the Mistress** (C Dibdin) Ranelagh House 28 May

1770 **A School for Fathers** revised *Lionel and Clarissa* Theatre Royal, Drury Lane 8 February

1770 **The Recruiting Sergeant** (C Dibdin) 1 act Ranelagh House 20 July

1770 **The Brick-dust Man and the Milk-Maid** (C Dibdin) Sadler's Wells Theatre 25 July

1771 **He Would If He Could, or An Old Fool Worse Than Any** (C Dibdin) revised *The Maid the Mistress* Theatre Royal, Drury Lane 12 April

1774 **The Romp** (pasticcio ad Bickerstaff, C Dibdin) revised *Love in the City* Crow Street Theatre, Dublin 23 March

1775 **The Sultan, or A Peep in the Seraglio** (various) Theatre Royal, Drury Lane 12 December

Biography: Tasch, P: *The Dramatic Cobbler* (Bucknell University Press, Lewisburg, Penn, 1972)

THE BICYCLE GIRL

The popularization of bicycling as a fashionable pastime in Victorian times resulted in musical comedy heroines being put in the saddle by various devices. The 'Girl' of Louis Harrison's American *The Bicycle Girl* (18 November 1895 Grand Opera House) portrayed by Nellie McHenry had her marital destiny decided by a cycle race, whilst her British counterpart ('a musical bicycle comedy' by Charles Osborne and E M Stuart. Music by Orlando Powell. Nottingham, 29 March 1897) got into gear herself and headed off the villain of the piece by *force de jarret*. A second British piece, *The Lady Cyclist* (which had lost a court contest for the more obvious title) swapped clothes with her lover on a cycling tour prefatory to some low comedy. All were opportunist pieces of little quality and faded away quickly, leaving the song 'Daisy Bell' as the most successful outcome of the bicycling craze. Many years later, Broadway's *The Girl Friend* went again to the bicycle – this time the seven-day cycle racing world – for its subject matter, but the libretto was not liked and the British version of the show junked the cycling tale and simply replaced it with the libretto of another show.

BIEDERMANN, Therese (b Vienna, 24 April 1863; d Vienna, 9 June 1942). Long-popular soubrette of the Viennese musical stage.

Therese Biedermann was on the stage from an early age, working as a child at the Theater in der Josefstadt, and then from 1882 in adult rôles in Operette at Mädling, at the Strampfertheater, at Brünn and from 1885 at the Landestheater in Graz. She had been there only one season when she was signed to join the company at the Theater an der Wien, beginning a career of nearly 20 years as one of the favourite soubrettes of the Vienna theatre.

She made her début at the Theater an der Wien as Ciboletta in the Viennese production of *Eine Nacht in Venedig*, appeared as Isabella in *Boccaccio* (1886), Leni in *Drei Paar Schuhe* and Bronislawa in *Der Bettelstudent* and went on to create and/or play, amongst other rôles, Lutte in Suppé's *Bellman* (1887), Hannele in *Die sieben Schwaben* (1887), Pitti-Sing in *Der Mikado* (1888), Christine in

Pagenstreiche (1888), Scrollina in *Capitän Fracassa* (1889), Lerina in *Das Orakel* (1889), a splendidly lively Molly to the Jonathan of Girardi in the highly successful *Der arme Jonathan* (1890), Orestes in *Die schöne Helena* (1891), Friquette in Lacôme's *Madame Bonbon* (ie *Madame Boniface*), Justine in *Fanchon's Leyer* (1892, *La Fille de Fanchon la vielleuse*), Paquerita in *Der Bajazzo* (1892), Anastasia Knapp in Strauss's *Fürstin Ninetta* (1893), Manotte Chicard in *Der Schwiegerpapa* (1893), another fine part as Nelly in *Der Obersteiger*, Susanne in *Husarenblut* (1894), Nitouche to Girardi's Célestin (*Mam'ze le Nitouche*) and Regerl to his Andredl (*Das verwunschene Schloss*), Annita in Strauss's *Jabuka* (1894) and Lisbeth in his revised *Simplicius*, Ludmilla Boroshazyi in *Kneisl & Co* (1894), Vreneli in Millöcker's *Der Probekuss* (1894), Ninetta in Dellinger's *Die Chansonette* (1895), Wan-Li in *Der goldene Kamerad* (1895), Jeanne in Strauss's *Waldmeister* (1895), Follette in *General Gogo* (1896), Polly in *Mister Menelaus* (1896), the travesty rôle of the boy, Beppo in *Der Schmetterling* (1896), Tilli in *Die Schwalben* (1897), Fritella in *Der verregnete Amor* (1897, *L'amour mouillé*), Susette in Strauss's *Die Göttin der Vernunft* (1897), Kitty Tortle in *Die Blumen-Mary* (1897), the dancer Feodora in *Der Opernball* (1898), Graf Nicki Sternfeld in the Hungarian operett *Die Küchen-Komtesse* alongside Ilka Pálmay (1898), Serpolette in a revival of *Die Glöcken von Corneville*, in *Die Gräfin Kuni* (1898), Madelon in *Der Blondin von Namur* (1898), Marianka Wondraschek in *Fräulein Hexe* (1898), Cascarette in *Katze und Maus* by Johann Strauss III (1898), Iris in *Die griechisches Sklave* (London's *A Greek Slave*), Madame Sillery in *Ihre Excellenz* (1899), the comical Pampeluna (ex-Carmenita) in *Ein durchgeganges Mädel* (1899, *A Runaway Girl*), the boy Heinrich in *Die Puppe* (1899, *La Poupée*), Yvette in *Fräulein Präsident* (1899) and Friquet in *La Chanson de Fortunio* before moving, at the turn of the century, to the opposition Carltheater.

The Carltheater served her up with the same mixture of repertoire rôles, new flops and also some rather more grateful new rôles for, after appearing as Fritz in *Die Diva* (1900), Aurore in *Die Primadonna*, Käthe in *Die drei Wünsche*, Marion in the Viennese version of *Les Saltimbanques* (*Circus Malicorne*), Sylvia in *Die Debutantin*, Molly Seamore in *Die Geisha* (1901), and giving a repeat of her Regerl, this time to the Andredl of Franz Glawatsch (1901), she introduced first the comical rôle of Dudley in the Viennese version of *San Toy* (1901) and then another showy rôle as the soubrette Fritzi in *Das süsse Mädel* (1901). She followed up as Régina in a revival of Offenbach's *La Princesse de Trébizonde* (1902), the gymnastic Jerry Bergauer in Reinhardt's *Der liebe Schatz* (1902) and, in her best Carltheater rôle to date as Mizzi in *Der Rastelbinder* (1902). She continued as Catherine in *Madame Sherry*, Roustanne in *Der Mameluck* (1903), Gusti Weinstein in *Das Marktkind* (1903), Charis in *Der Göttergatte* (1904), Franzi in *Das Veilchenmädel* (1904), Emma in *'s Zuckersgoscherl* (1904), Lona in *Der Schatzmeister* (1904), Rosette in the Hungarian operett *Der Schnurrbart* (1905), Sári in *Kaisermanöver* (1905) and Gilda in *Der Polizeichef* (1905) before moving on to a few performances on the variety stage and then, finally, putting an end to an enormously busy 20 years in the Viennese theatre in favour of spending more time as Frau von Singer.

BIG BEN   Light opera in 2 acts by A P Herbert. Music by Vivian Ellis. Adelphi Theatre, London, 17 July 1946.

Big Ben was an earnestly preachy piece in which MP Herbert let his politics get the better of his theatricality, and which was only lifted into some semblance of an entertainment by Vivian Ellis's delightful light music. In the same vein as Hugh McLellan's *Nelly Neil*, more than three decades before, Herbert presented a singing socialist heroine (Carole Lynne) and – what even the earlier show had balked at – had her straight-facedly voted into Parliament, asserting in the show's most plugged number that 'I Want to See the People Happy'. Needless to say, like Nellie, she paired off with a nice, rich and right-wing hero (Eric Palmer) at the final curtain, after having spent most of the act struggling in the house to beat an anti-drunkenness law which she judged unfair to the 'working' classes and getting sent to the Tower of London, in a moment of light relief, for contempt of parliament.

Herbert's libretto, which had actually been offered first to William Walton, before Ellis applied for and got the job of writing the music, had solely the merit of reuniting the men who would, soon after, in collaboration with the show's producer, C B Cochran, follow up *Big Ben*'s indifferent 172 performances with *Bless the Bride*.

Recording: original cast recordings on *Three by Vivian Ellis* (WRC)

BIG BOY

1) musical comedy in 2 acts by Harold Atteridge. Lyrics by B G De Sylva. Music by James F Hanley and Joseph Meyer. Winter Garden Theater, New York, 7 January 1925.

The Shuberts' Winter Garden extravaganza of 1925 starred Al Jolson, well into his second decade as a Broadway favourite, in a show where what plot there was had him as stable boy Gus, plotting against the plotters who are trying to stop him riding for the Bedford family (Maude Turner Gordon, Patti Harrold, Frank Beaston) in the Derby. Real horses galloped across the stage, and Gus, of course, won the race. In the meanwhile, however, he had got down to the real business of the evening and sung 'California, Here I Come', 'Keep Smiling at Trouble' and, briefly, 'If You Knew Susie'. The last named number didn't go for him, so he cut it out and left it for Eddie Cantor to turn into a hit.

Big Boy, however, didn't go as well as its predecessors and after less than two months it closed down when it was announced that the star was unwell. That common euphemism was given some credence when the show was re-opened the following season and ran through 120 further performances before being taken out to clean up on the road.

2) musical comedy in 2 acts by Douglas Furber, Fred Emney and Max Kester. Lyrics by Douglas Furber. Additional lyrics by Emney. Music by Carroll Gibbons. Saville Theatre, London, 12 September 1945.

A comedy musical designed to exploit the talents of hefty comedian Fred Emney (in the title-rôle) and his former Gaiety Theatre colleague, the acrobatic Richard Hearne, Britain's *Big Boy* was put together by Douglas Furber who had supplied much of the successful material performed by the pair with Leslie Henson at the Gaiety. It played 174 performances in London and toured, leaving as its principal legacy the soubriquet 'Mr Pastry' which Hearne carried with him the rest of his career.

BIG RIVER, the Adventures of Huckleberry Finn Musical in 2 acts adapted from the novel by Mark Twain by William Hauptmann. Music and lyrics by Roger Miller. Eugene O'Neill Theater, New York, 25 April 1985.

After many years of mostly unimpressive attempts, *Big River* finally got the Mark Twain Mississippi characters and one of their tales successfully on to the musical stage where, under the management of a consortium of producers, it won itself a Tony Award as the best musical of 1985 and a run of 1,005 performances through two and a half years on Broadway.

Huckleberry Finn (Daniel Jenkins) runs away from his drunken father (John Goodman) and sets off down the Mississippi River, in the company of the runaway slave Jim (Ron Richardson), on a raft. On the way they get joined by two confidence tricksters (Bob Gunton, René Auberjonois) in whose company Huck takes part in a phoney booth show, and in an attempt to blarney the recently bereaved Wilkes family out of their inheritance. When one of the family turns out to be a pretty girl (Patti Cohenour), Huck makes sure she gets the money back, but in the meantime his fine friends have cashed in by selling Jim as a slave. With the help of a real friend, Tom Sawyer (John Short), Jim is stolen back, and both he and Huck set off into the future.

The songs for *Big River*, the initial work of popular country singer-songwriter Roger Miller ('King of the Road', 'Little Green Apples' etc) for the musical theatre, caught the warmly unshowy nature of the tale and its people in such pieces as the attractive Huck–Jim duos 'Muddy Waters' and 'River in the Rain', the country comicalities of Tom's 'Hand for the Hog' and Papa Finn's bilious 'Guv'ment', and the Dixieland song of the showmen ('When the Sun Goes Down in the South'). The feminine element was given its moments in two goodbye songs for pretty Miss Wilkes, one bidding her father's corpse farewell ('You Oughta Be Here With Me') and the other saying goodbye to helpful Huck ('Leavin's Not the Only Way to Go'), and in a solo featured in the slave-sung 'The Crossing'.

Brought to Broadway after try-outs at the La Jolla Playhouse and the American Repertory Theatre, Cambridge, Mass, (17 February 1984, 28 performances) in an attractively unpretentious production, and with a minimum of ballyhoo (right behind a much ballyhooed and vastly glitzridden show which flopped smartly), *Big River* turned out, in a very soft season, to be a pleasant family-entertaining sleeper. From its fine run on Broadway it went on the road in America, and in 1989 was mounted by John Frost and Essington Entertainments in Australia (see page 126). Cameron Daddo (Huck), Drew Forsythe (King), John Bell (Duke) and Karen Knowles (Mary Jane) featured in a long and highly successful nationwide run.

Australia: Her Majesty's Theatre, Sydney 7 January 1989
Recordings: original cast (MCA), Australian cast (BRR)

BILLEE TAYLOR   Nautical comic opera in 2 acts by Henry Pottinger Stephens. Music by Edward Solomon. Imperial Theatre, London, 30 October 1880.

Plate 22. **Big River**: *John Bell, Cameron Daddo (Huckleberry Finn) and Drew Forsythe are the travellers on the Mississippi in Australia's version of the show.*

Billee Taylor was a genuine comic opera in a nautical vein which followed closely (in time) in the traces of *HMS Pinafore* without in any way imitating it. Stephens's book used as its inspiration the old ballad tale of Billee Taylor, which had already been used as the subject of a number of earlier stage musical shows including a burlesque at the Adelphi Theatre (J B Buckstone 9 November 1829), another in 1856 (12 May), Mowbray's *Soho Billy Taylor, or The Gay Young Fellow* (1 April 1861) and F C Burnand's *Military Billee Taylor, or The War in the Cariboo* (22 April 1869), in telling of the press-ganged sailor followed to sea by his lady love in man's attire.

In 'Pot' Stephens's version, however, the story was treated in a gently tongue-in-cheek fashion which took a different tone both from standard burlesque and from the witty and wordful style of W S Gilbert. Billee, 'a virtuous gardener' (Frederic Rivers), is a vain beauty who has attracted the attentions of Arabella Lane (Emma Chambers), the daughter of nouveau-riche Sir Mincing Lane (Arthur Williams), who leaves pints of ale in the garden shed to attempt to attract the object of her affections. Billee, however, plights himself to the poor but plucky charity girl Phoebe (Kathleen Corri) and, to prevent his marriage, aching Arabella allies herself with Crab (J A Arnold), a schoolmaster with a longing to be a genuine villain, and short-staffed Captain Flapper (Fleming Norton) of the *HMS Thunderball*, to get Billee carried off to sea. Phoebe and her chorus of charity-girlfriends promptly get into uniform and go after them, but Billee's

apparent virtues have won him quick promotion and, in his new position, he rather feels that a well-off wife would be an asset. Faithful Phoebe is rejected in favour of persistent Arabella. The hero's come-uppance is at hand, however, when it is revealed that the exploits for which he won his promotion were phoney. He is reduced to the ranks and his lieutenancy given instead to another fine sailor – Phoebe! Virtue is triumphant and the prig and the plotters get their desserts.

The score, the first full-scale work of 25-year-old Edward Solomon, musical director at the Globe Theatre, was in the happiest comic opera vein. He provided some very attractive ballads, but the show's most successful musical moments came in the comic pieces, notably 'All on Account of Eliza' in which the show's low comedian, Ben Barnacle (J D Stoyle), told of how he became a press-gang man because his sweetheart played him false. Another of the show's song successes was the Charity Girls' chorus 'We Stick to Our Letters', a success which owed not a little to the fact that the chorus in question had been cast with some exceedingly pretty girls, demure in their little grey dresses and brisk white mobs and aprons.

Following six months behind the London production of *The Pirates of Penzance*, and obliged to bear comparison with Gilbert and Sullivan's piece both in the press and with the public, *Billee Taylor* shared the honours evenly, winning some fine notices. D'Oyly Carte was quick to show an interest in what was clearly a piece of genuine competition for his show, but his interest was one of the elements which

Plate 23. **Billee Taylor:** *'We Stick to Our Letters' – the Charity Girls' chorus was one of the highlights of this long favourite nautical opéra-bouffe.*

onies as well as being seen in several European countries, notably in a tour organized by the composer and his paramour, soprano Lillian Russell, in 1884.

In 1881 New York's Rentz–Santley Company presented a burlesque of Stephens and Solomon's piece under the title of *Billy Taylor, or The Lass Who Stuck to the Sailor.*

USA: Standard Theater 19 February 1881; Australia: Princess Theatre, Melbourne 26 August 1882; France: Le Havre 1 February 1884

BILLY Musical in 2 acts by Ian La Fresnais and Dick Clement adapted from *Billy Liar* by Keith Waterhouse and Willis Hall. Lyrics by Don Black. Music by John Barry. Theatre Royal, Drury Lane, London, 1 May 1974.

'Billy Liar', the north country lad with the wishful imagination which he equates too closely with fact for the comfort of anyone around him, became a classic figure of English literature as Keith Waterhouse's original novel was translated first to the stage (1960 w Willis Hall), then to the screen with Tom Courtenay as *Billy Liar* (1963), and finally in 1974 to the musical stage.

Billy Fisher (Michael Crawford) day-dreams his way through life in Stradhoughton, Yorks, and lies his way out of each of the uncomfortable positions that real life puts in front of him. Current problems, apart from facing life in general, are that he has more or less proposed to both the primly devoted Barbara (Gay Soper) and rough-as-guts Rita (Elaine Paige), and that he has filched the stamp money from the firm of undertakers where he works. Both situations have come to a point when good friend Liz (Diana Quick) appears from the outside world, persuading him to come to London and do something instead of just talking about it. Billy gets as far as the train station, but in the end he turns back to the safety of Stradhoughton where his day-dreams can stay alive.

Billy's fantasies provided some colourful scenas amongst the daily grind of his little life of sad Yorkshire mishaps. He descended by parachute to review the all-girl army of his private country of Ambrosia, returned from the outside world as a Jack Buchanan top-hat and tails song-and-dance man to the acclaim of all Yorkshire, and pounded out a pop-star song as Billy Fisher, hitmaker ('The Lady from LA'), declaring with simple self-delusion 'Some of Us Belong to the Stars' until it was time to admit 'I Missed the Last Rainbow'.

The show's other musical moments included a duo for Barbara and Rita, both waiting with rather different attitudes for Billy to turn up for a double-date ('Any Minute Now'), a gently reminiscing number for Billy's old employer remembering that 'It Were All Green Hills (when I were a lad)' and a merry piece of family table-talk ('And') from which Billy escapes into dreamland.

Billy was a major hit, with Crawford's performance in the title-rôle, in his stage musical début, winning him a special place amongst the superlatives. H M Tennent Ltd and Peter Witt's production of the show played 904 performances to the large auditorium of the Theatre Royal, Drury Lane, with Roy Castle replacing Crawford in the last part of the run. In 1976 a German-language version (ad Werner Schneyder) was mounted at Vienna's Theater an der Wien, but a 1991 revival of *Billy* scheduled for London folded in the preparatory stages.

proved *Billee Taylor*'s undoing. The inexperienced management, which was already having problems coping with a potential hit show, quarrelled with the authors and, in the end, *Billee Taylor* was taken off after only three months at the Imperial Theatre. Carte promptly shipped director Charles Harris off to New York and, three weeks after the London closure, his production of *Billee Taylor* opened on Broadway where it fulfilled a good season of three and a half months at the Standard Theatre.

Other English-language stages soon snapped the piece up, and Australia saw its first *Billee Taylor* the next year. Top local tenor Armes Beaumont was Billie and Nellie Stewart played Phoebe, with Edwin Kelly as Sir Mincing Lane, H M Harwood as Ben and Emma Wangenheim as Arabella. The critic of the Melbourne *Argus* took violently against the show, which didn't help its prospects, but he was no longer around when it was revived by Williamson, Garner and Musgrove at the same house four years later with Julia Sidney playing Phoebe and the D'Oyly Carte's Alice Barnett as Eliza, and again in Sydney in 1886, each time with positive results.

Billee Taylor was also revived in both London (Gaiety 1882 twice, 1883, 1885, Crystal Palace 1886, Toole's Theatre 1886) and in New York (Niblo's Garden 1881, Booth's 1882, Bijou 1882, Fifth Avenue 1882, Casino 1885, American Theater 1898) and, although it never amassed a long metropolitan run, it was also played long and wide in the American country and in the British col-

Plate 24. **The Biograph Girl**: *'I Like to Be the Way I am in My Own Front Parlour ...'.* Mary Pickford (Sheila White) puts on an act for the press (Philip Griffith, Ron Berglas).

The title, *Billy*, was earlier used in Britain for a musical comedy by George Cooper and Adrian Ross, lyrics by Ross and music by F Osmond Carr (Tyne Theatre and Opera House, Newcastle 11 April 1898) conceived as a touring vehicle for the diminutive music-hall comic Little Tich who appeared as an impecunious wee nobleman battling against a horrid big businessman. With a cast featuring the young Evie Greene, exceedingly tall Alice Barnett and Joe Farren Soutar, it toured eight months.

In America, the same title was used for a musical by Stephen Glassman suggested by Herman Melville's *Billy Budd* (music and lyrics by Ron Dante and Gene Allen, Billy Rose Theater 22 March 1969).

Austria: Theater an der Wien 19 February 1976
Recording: original cast (CBS)

THE BIOGRAPH GIRL Musical comedy in 2 acts by Warner Brown. Lyrics by David Heneker and Warner Brown. Music by David Heneker. Phoenix Theatre, London, 19 November 1980.

A small-scale, revusical piece constructed around the myths and legends of the silent-movie days of Hollywood, *The Biograph Girl* featured a scoreful of deftly made songs and some comical and charming scenes in which the actors appeared as D W Griffith (Bruce Barry), Adolf Zukor (Ron Berglas), Mack Sennett (Guy Siner), Lillian Gish (Kate Revill), Mary Pickford (Sheila White) and other historical and semi-historical characters. Griffith apostrophized a world 'Beyond Babel' in rousing bass-baritone tones and scowled over the accolades which would come too late ('He Was One of the Pioneers'), Mary simpered to the press 'I Like To Be the Way I Am (in my own front parlour)' and joined with Lillian and Mack to wonder what would become of their work in the future ('Put It in the Tissue Paper').

In the giant shadow of *Evita*, *The Biograph Girl* had a short London career, but was subsequently played in New Zealand and Japan with great success as well as, in a much expanded version, in the British provinces.

Recording: original cast (TER)

BISSON, Alexandre [Charles Auguste] (b Briouze, Orne, 9 April 1848; d Paris, 27 January 1912).

The highly successful French playwright, author of such widely produced pieces as *115 Rue Pigalle*, *Le Député de Bombignac*, *Les Surprises du divorce* (w Antony Mars), *La Souricière* (w Albert Carré), *M. le Directeur* (UK: *The Chili Widow*), *Le Contrôlleur des wagons-lits*, *Le Coup de fouet*, *Un Mariage d'étoile*, *Feu Toupinel* and *La Femme X*, provided the libretti for several musical pieces, of which the musical comedy *Un Lycée de jeunes filles* (played in Hungary as *Szinitanoda* and in Germany as *Mädchenschule*) proved the most widely successful. Toulmouche's *La Veillée de noces*, produced in England as *The Wedding Eve*, and *Captain Thérèse*, written for the Carl Rosa Light Opera Company expressly to feature their contralto star, Agnes Huntington, also found some degree of success.

A number of Bisson's plays were used as the source for later musical comedies. On Broadway, *Le Péril jaune* (w Albert St Albin) became the Louis Hirsch/Channing Pollock and Rennold Wolf musical *The Grass Widows* (1917), *Les Surprises du divorce* was musicalized by Ephraim Zimbalist and Joseph Herbert as *Honeydew* (1920), whilst the Jerome Kern musical *The Night Boat* was based, without precise credit, on *Le Contrôlleur des wagons-lits*. The same play was musicalized in Italy in 1924 with a score by Romolo Alegiani as *Il Controllore dei vagoni letto*. Off-Broadway's Martinique Theatre hosted a version of *Le Véglione* (w Albert Carré) under the title *For the Love of Suzanne* (Deed Meyer/Bill Galarno) in October 1974 whilst in Czechoslovakia, Bisson's *Madame Durosel* (1890) was made into *Mama vom Ballett* (Bernard Grün/Rudolf Stadler, Ernst Stadler Deutsches Theater studio 20 February 1926).

Bisson also authored a two-volume *Petite Encyclopédie musicale* in collaboration with composer Théodore Lajarte.

1881 **Un Lycée de jeunes filles** (Louis Gregh) Théâtre Cluny 27 December
1882 **Ninetta** (Raoul Pugno/w Maurice Hennequin) Théâtre de la Renaissance 26 December
1885 **Le Moutier de Saint-Guignolet** (Frédéric Toulmouche/E Bureau, F Jattiot) Galeries St Hubert, Brussels, 5 May
1888 **La Veillée de noces** revised *Le Moutier de Saint-Guignolet* Théâtre des Menus-Plaisirs 27 November
1889 **Mam'zelle Pioupiou** (William Chaumet/w André Sylvane) Théâtre de la Porte-Saint-Martin 31 May
1890 **Captain Thérèse** (Robert Planquette/ad F C Burnand, Gilbert a' Beckett) Prince of Wales Theatre, London 5 July
1903 **La Petite Maison** (Chaumet/w Georges Docquois) Opéra-Comique 5 June
1909 **Chez la sonnambule** (Toulmouche) Théâtre Grévin 24 March

BITTER-SWEET Operette in 3 acts by Noël Coward. His Majesty's Theatre, London, 12 July 1929.

The most wholly successful stage musical written by the author of *Private Lives*, *Hay Fever* and so many brittle and witty revue songs and sketches was, perhaps surprisingly, an almost entirely sentimental operetta. Avowedly written under the influence of *Die Fledermaus*, it nevertheless replaced that piece's light comedy with a tale of romantic drama. Sarah Millick (Peggy Wood), a young English girl engaged to be married to man of her own class and mileu, runs away to Vienna with her romantic music teacher, Carl Linden (Georges Metaxa), only to discover there that woman cannot live on love alone. She ends up working in the second-rate café, where Carl conducts the band, as a dancing partner, but she soon finds that more than just dancing is expected of her. She refuses, and Carl is killed defending her honour against an amorous officer (Austin Trevor). Sari, as she is now called, goes on to become a successful singer and settles for a loveless but comfortable life as the wife of a kindly nobleman (Alan Napier).

Two scenes of English society life frame the sentimental and dramatic events of the lovers' life in Vienna which forms the centrepiece of the story in an effectively shaped libretto, accompanied by a rich operetta score which includes much of Coward's best stage music. The numbers range from the piece's key love song 'I'll See You Again' introduced in the opening act by the two lovers, to a beautiful harmonized sextet for six ageing society ladies ('Alas the Time is Past'), to the understated fun of a handful of Viennese 'Ladies of the Town' or a group of would-be aesthetes sporting their 'Green Carnation'. The show's third important rôle, that of the cabaret vocalist Manon, who enlivens the Viennese scenes with her jealousies and with a sparkling stand-up act, had the show's other most enduring number, the rueful 'If Love Were All'.

Evelyn Laye was originally offered the starring rôle of Sarah in the première production of *Bitter-Sweet*, but refused it because she felt Coward had been less than supportive during the time that Jessie Matthews was busy lifting her husband from her. Thus, it was the American actress Peggy Wood who ultimately created the rôle alongside Romanian Georges Metaxa, who had been playing in one of producer C B Cochran's London revues whilst a Europe-wide search for a romantic Continental hero had been pursued. Tiny revue artist and composer Ivy St Helier made the triumph of her career as Manon, a performance which was caught on film in the first and less wayward of two film versions.

Miss Laye subsequently played Sarah on Broadway and in London but, although the piece was produced in such diverse countries as Australia, with London vocalist Marjorie Hicklin as Sarah, Herbert Browne as Carl and Saffo Arnay as Manon, in France (where Jane Marnac produced and starred in 'The Time of Waltzes') and Hungary (where its title translated as 'Long Ago and Now'), it was, curiously, not taken into the international light opera repertoire and the first major revival (in an unfortunately cut version), with opera star Valerie Masterson as Sarah, was mounted only in 1988 (Sadler's Wells Theatre 23 February).

The first filmed version (ad Monckton Hoffe) starred Anna Neagle and Fernand Graavey and concentrated on the romantic action to the detriment – Miss St Helier's scene apart – of the score, but nevertheless created some fine, atmospheric moments. The second, with Jeanette MacDonald and Nelson Eddy, not surprisingly squeezed

Manon right out, ignored all but the central Viennese episode, cut all the bitter out of the bitter-sweet and invented several new songs to put alongside some of the real ones. They were sung, inevitably, by the two stars.

USA: Ziegfeld Theater 21 October 1929; Hungary: Király Színház *Régen és most* 6 December 1929; France: Théâtre Apollo *Au Temps des valses* 2 April 1930; Australia: Theatre Royal, Melbourne 26 March 1932; Films: British & Dominion 1933, MGM 1942

Recordings: complete (TER), selections (WRC, HMV, Columbia etc)

BLACK, Don [BLACKSTONE, Donald] (b London, 21 June 1936).

British lyricist who has scored major successes in theatre, film and popular song.

A member of the staff at *New Musical Express*, a sometime stand-up comedian, and a music business agent, Black was knocking 30 when he authored the first of a series of lyrics to popular songs, beginning with the English version of Udo Jürgens's Eurovision song 'Warum nur, warum?' as 'Walk Away' (1964). Numbers such as film themes 'Thunderball' (1965), 'Born Free' (1966 w John Barry, Academy Award) and 'To Sir with Love' followed, before he made his first venture into the musical theatre with the songs for a post-*Hair* musical about impotence called *Maybe That's Your Problem*. He had more success with the composer of that show, Walter Scharf, when they won an Academy award nomination for their song 'Ben' in 1972, and further film song successes with numbers for *Diamonds Are Forever* (w Barry, 1972), *The Man with the Golden Gun*, *The Pink Panther Strikes Again* and *True Grit* followed.

A second musical play, *Billy* ('Some of Us Belong to the Stars', 'I Missed the Last Rainbow', 'Any Minute Now') brought him a major stage success, but several other theatrical essays in the following decade, both in London and on Broadway, were less forthcoming. However, the song-cycle *Tell Me on a Sunday*, written with Andrew Lloyd Webber, produced first a hit song and, later, when the cycle was revised, extended and staged as one half of the entertainment *Song and Dance*, an international theatre success. The Broadway magic show *Merlin*, for which he supplied the songwords, also played through six months in New York.

A venture as a producer in association with Laurence Myers, on the production of his second (after the unfortunate *Bar Mitzvah Boy* a decade earlier) television-to-musical piece, a stage musical based on the Adam Faith series *Budgie*, folded quickly, but a second collaboration with Lloyd Webber (w Charles Hart) on *Aspects of Love* ('Anything But Lonely') gave him both another chart song ('Love Changes Everything') and another long-running West End success.

Black has served for some time as the chairman of the British Academy of Songwriters, Composers and Authors (BASCA).

1970 **Maybe That's Your Problem** (Walter Scharf/Lionel Chetwynd) Roundhouse 16 June
1974 **Billy** (John Barry/Ian Le Fresnais, Dick Clement) Theatre Royal, Drury Lane 1 May
1978 **Bar Mitzvah Boy** (Jule Styne/Jack Rosenthal) Her Majesty's Theatre 25 September
1980 **Tell Me on a Sunday** (Andrew Lloyd Webber) 1 act Royalty Theatre, January
1982 **The Little Prince and the Aviator** (John Barry/Hugh Wheeler) Alvin Theater, New York 1 January
1982 **Song and Dance** (including a revised version of *Tell Me on a Sunday*) (Palace Theatre)
1983 **Dear Anyone** (Geoff Stephens/Jack Rosenthal) Cambridge Theatre 9 September
1983 **Merlin** (Elmer Bernstein/Richard Levinson, William Link) Mark Hellinger Theater, New York 13 February
1988 **Budgie** (Mort Shuman/Keith Waterhouse, Willis Hall) Cambridge Theatre 18 October
1989 **Aspects of Love** (Lloyd Webber/w Charles Hart) Prince of Wales Theatre 17 April
1993 **Sunset Boulevard** (Lloyd Webber/w Christopher Hampton) Adelphi Theatre 12 July

THE BLACK CROOK

1) extravaganza by Charles M Barras. Music by Thomas Baker and others. Niblo's Garden, New York, 12 September 1866.

Often quoted as the first landmark in the history of the American musical theatre, this production, a spectacular built on the lines of the French grand opéra-bouffe féerie, was long alleged to have been created by the last-minute insertion into a fairytale piece destined for Niblo's Garden of the personnel and some of the repertoire of a stranded French ballet troupe, whose theatre had burned down. This myth has now been thoroughly exploded, and a contemporary source tells a different tale about the burning of the Academy of Music. Apparently *Black Crook* producers Henry Jarrett and Harry Palmer had turned down Niblo's Garden as a venue for their show as being too expensive and had, instead, booked into the cheaper and perhaps classier Academy of Music. When the Academy caught fire, they hastened back to manager William Wheatley at Niblo's before he could get wind of the disaster and thus hoist his prices, and hastily accepted his original offer. Thus, it seems, the whole of the already prepared production of *The Black Crook*, drama, dances and all, was transferred to Niblo's, and not just its ballet girls.

The extravaganza included a full score of songs and choruses by various writers, some new and some borrowed, a great deal of scenery and a goodly dose of the ballets and parades typical of the more grandiose French productions, all mixed in with scenes of fairytale drama and romance in a well-established mixture which created a highly attractive entertainment. Its priorities, however, were visible from its advertising: the splendid 'Tableaux, Costumes, Marches, Scenery' and the 'premium transformation' were splashed across announcements which did not mention the text or the music, and the 'Grand Parisienne Ballet Troupe' and the 'Garde Impériale' of marching girls were billed, whereas the names of the principal actors and singers were nowhere in sight.

Barras's tale was rather more Germanic than French, telling of the plots concocted by the vile Hertzog (C H Morton), under the spell of the diabolic Zamiel (E B Holmes), to deliver up a monthly ration of human souls to the powers below. Hertzog selects the artist, Rudolf (G C Boniface), whom he frees from the clutches of Count Wolfenstein (J W Blaisdell), as his victim of the night, but, as he leads him to his fate, the young man saves the life of a benighted dove. The dove is the disguised fairy, Stalacta (Annie Kemp Bowler), and in the course of the evening she outwits Hertzog and steers Rudolf to a happy ending

Plate 25. **The Black Crook**: *Kate Santley scored the hit of London's edition with her 'Nobody Knows As I Know', and Harry Paulton joined her to take the comic honours.*

with the fair Amina (Rose Morton). The comedy was provided by the dramatic folks' servants, with J G Burnett as von Puffengruntz producing the lowest of it, whilst the ballets performed the traditional spectacular march-patterns of 'amazons', and the mechanists turned one scene into another almost non-stop. The musical hit of the show was a soubrette number 'You Naughty, Naughty Men' as performed by Millie Cavendish in an incidental rôle.

The Black Crook provided New York with its most effective piece of grosse Spektakel-Feerie to date and roused an unparalleled interest as, with an ever fluid programme of components, it ran on Broadway for fifteen and a half months, closing 4 January 1868 after 475 performances. It was repeated thereafter, in often largely varying versions, both around the country and in return visits to the New York stage over a number of years.

The favoured story of the creation of *The Black Crook* was used as the background for the show *The Girl in Pink Tights* (Sigmund Romberg/Herbert Fields, Jerome Chodorov Mark Hellinger Theater 5 March 1954).

2) grand opéra-bouffe féerie in 4 acts by Harry and Joseph Paulton founded on *La Biche au bois*. Music by Georges Jacobi and Frederic Clay. Alhambra Theatre, London, 23 December 1872.

An early effort to reproduce in Britain the same kind of vast and spectacular grand opéra-bouffe féerie which was then popular in France, this version of the *La Biche au bois* legend owed nothing to its American homonym except its title. Lovely opéra-bouffe star Cornélie d'Anka starred as the vicious witch of the title out to thwart the enchanted Princess Désirée and her Prince, but the largest part of the evening's entertainment was, as in the American show, given over to its physical production, its ballets and the low comic element as personified by author Harry Paulton as a comic vizier and Kate Santley (who had appeared for a while as Stalacta in the American *Black Crook*) as the heroine's maid, in which rôle she delivered the show's stand-out song 'Nobody Knows As I Know' in the overtly roguish style she favoured. The production, staged for Christmas, played until the following August.

A simplified version with revised text and music was successfully produced at the same theatre in 1881.

[THE LATEST EDITION OF] BLACK-EYED SUSAN, or The Little Bill That was Taken Up Nautical burlesque in 5 scenes by F C Burnand. Music arranged by Mr Hermann. Royalty Theatre, London, 29 November 1866.

Douglas Jerrold's famous melodrama *Black-Eyed Susan, or All in the Downs* (Surrey Theatre, 8 June 1829) told the story of honest tar William, long at sea and now ready to quit the navy and return to his wife, the Susan of the title. But William's commander, Captain Crosstree, takes a fancy to Susan and, when he tries to lay hands on her, William knocks him down. For striking a superior officer, William is brought to court martial and, although everyone is on his side, the letter of the law condemns him to death. But the repentant Crosstree brings out William's discharge papers – on the fatal day, William was no longer a serviceman and thus falls not under service jurisidiction. He is free. The other characters included the villainous Uncle Doggrass, the owner of the cottage which houses long-alone Susan and William's old mother, Dame Hatley; his fellow smugglers,

Hatchett and Raker; and good little Gnatbrain and his sweetheart Dolly Mayflower.

It became the habit to introduce the occasional nautical song or dance into the course of Jerrold's drama – the St James's Theatre, for example, inserted the song 'All in the Downs' for Cecilia Ranoe in the minor rôle of Blue Peter, and a double hornpipe for Lydia Thompson (Dolly) and Charles Young (William) – but a number of genuine musical versions of the play also followed. Meyer Lutz composed the score for a light opera remake of *Black-Eyed Susan*, called *All in the Downs* (Gaiety Theatre 5 November 1881), and several burlesques were mounted, the notable one being Burnand's 1866 piece, one of the outstanding works of the British burlesque tradition. Other burlesques included *Ups and Downs of Deal, and Black-Eyed Susan* (Marylebone Theatre 1867), *Too Lovely Black-Eyed Susan* (1887) and *Blue-Eyed Susan* (F Osmond Carr/Henry Pettitt, George R Sims Prince of Wales Theatre 6 February 1892).

Burnand's burlesque was produced by Pattie Oliver at the Royalty Theatre, with Frederic Dewar as Captain Crosstree ('who would have had a very long part if he hadn't been cut down in the 3rd scene'), Nellie Bromley, the future creator of the Plaintiff in *Trial by Jury*, as Dolly Mayflower, Miss Oliver herself as Black-Eyed Susan ('who has accepted a Bill, which she hopes the public will endorse'), Rosina Ranoe and later Annie Collinson as William ('the Bill of the play'), John Russell as Doggrass and the acrobatic Edwin Danvers in a famous creation as William's mother. Charles Wyndham, later Sir Charles and a celebrated London manager, played the part of the smuggler, Hatchett. Needless to say, in the burlesque version, William's appearance before the court martial of a dazzling selection of colourful admirals for having murdered (in this version) Crosstree was aborted by the sudden revival of his supposed victim and all ended happily. Amongst his 'selected and arranged' score, which ranged from bits of Balfe to selections from street minstrelsy, Hermann included one number, the quintet 'Pretty See-usan, Don't Say No', which became a Victorian standard.

The burlesque ran for over 400 performances at the Royalty, creating an all-time record for a West End musical. It was played throughout the English-speaking theatre world, surfacing in Australia in 1867 and appearing on Broadway later the same year with Kate Ranoe (William), Mark Smith (Crosstree) and Mary Gannon (Susan) featured, and J C Williamson in the small rôle of Shaun O'Ploughshare. Broadway saw the piece again in 1869 in an 'americanized version' as *Black-Eyed Susing, or the Leetle Bill Which Was Taken Up* (Fifth Avenue Theater, 21 June), with Stuart Robson starring as Crosstree to the Susan of Mary Cary, and again in 1870 with Robson and Lina Edwin.

In London, it was revived first at the Royalty in 1870 as *Black-Eyed Susan (Encored)*, and yet again in an expanded shape and a spectacular production, with the favourite songs supplemented by new ones by Alfred Lee, the composer of 'Champagne Charlie', at the Alhambra under the management of William Holland (2 August 1884).

Australia: Haymarket Theatre, Melbourne 9 September 1867;

USA: Wallack's Theater *The Latest Edition of Black-Eyed Susan* 25 September 1867

THE BLACK PRINCE Opéra-bouffe in 3 acts by H B Farnie. Music taken from the works of Charles Lecocq and others. St James's Theatre, London, 24 October 1874.

Lecocq protested in print when this show was announced: 'This is the only information I have ever received of having composed a work under that title...'. In fact, in a period when Lecocq's name was a sure draw and his output limited, the London publishers J B Cramer and their in-house writer H B Farnie had taken it on themselves to compile this piece from a libretto carpentered together from three uncredited French plays (one of which was apparently Labiche and Delacour's *Le Voyage en Chine*) and music taken from some of the composer's one-act opérettes, topped up with pieces by Olivier Métra, Léon Roques and others. The programme admitted that 'the comedy is founded on a piece by MM Labiche and Delacour and the music has been selected from works of Lecocq unrepresented in England ...'

Following similar depredations practised by London managers on Hervé's *Les Chevaliers de la table ronde* and Offenbach's *Vert-Vert, The Black Prince*, in spite of a short run, focused attention on the unsatisfactory position in existence regarding authors' rights and copyright. In spite of a cast headed by Selina Dolaro, John Rouse and Nellie Bromley, and a featured spot for Mr E W Latham, 'the champion skater' in a Skaters' Fête scene in the Isle of Wight, *The Black Prince* was a salutory flop.

A BLACK SHEEP, and How It Came to Washington Musical comedy in 3 acts by Charles Hoyt. Music by Richard Stahl, Hoyt, William Devere, Otis Harlan, Conor and Kelly. [Music selected and arranged by Percy Gaunt.] Academy of Music, Buffalo, 10 September 1894. Hoyt's Theater, New York, 6 January 1896.

One of Hoyt's successful comedies with songs strewn about here and there, this one allowed its broadly comic story about likeable drunken layabout, 'Hot Stuff' Mudd (Otis Harlan), and an eccentric inheritance to run on to its predictable happy ending whilst most of the musical numbers were provided by the members of a variety troupe providentially visiting the scene of the second-act action. These ranged from Felix McGlennon's *Shop Girl* hit, 'Her Golden Hair Was Hanging Down Her Back' to a quadrille arranged on the melodies from *Ruddigore*.

Its lively, unselfconscious mixture of fun and music kept the young Julian Mitchell's staging on the road for a number of years, including a stay on Broadway for a good 144 performances.

BLAHA, Lujza [née Reindl-Várai, aka KÖLESI, Lujza, SOLDOSNÉ, Lujza] (b Rimaszombat (Gömör), 8 September 1850; d Budapest, 18 January 1926). The outstanding leading lady of the Hungarian stage during her lifetime, Blaha became, in a career of nearly half a century, a sufficiently great figure in Hungary to have one of the principal squares of Budapest named in her honour, and her 50th birthday made a national holiday.

Natural daughter of an actor and an actress, and herself an actress from her childhood, Blaha – at the time the wife of conductor János Blaha – made starring appearances as a teenager in comedy and opéra-bouffe in the Hungarian provinces, appearing at Nagyvárad as Offenbach's Hélène at the age of 18 and at Debrecen in the same rôle at 19. Widowed in 1870, she joined the company of the Nemzeti Színház in Pest in 1871, making her début in the musical comedy *Tündérlak Magyarországon* (Marcsa) and playing, during her four years there, in comedy and in a range of musical pieces including Auber's *Le Domino noir* (Angelo) and as Boulotte in *Barbe-bleue* (12 April 1873).

In 1875 she began both a four-year period as the wife of landowner Sándor Soldos (she was billed during this time as Soldosné), and a much longer association of some 26 years with the newly built Népszinház, the theatre which would quickly become the most important musical house in Budapest. Amongst the early musical pieces in which she played there were *Le Voyage de MM Dunanan* (Pamela), *La Rose de Saint-Flour*, *La Fille de Madame Angot* (Clairette), as the singing Rózsi Finum in the celebrated Hungarian play *A falu rossza*, *La Boulangère* (Margot), *Le Canard à trois becs* (Margit), *Die schöne Galathee* and *La Princesse de Trébizonde*. She made a fine success as Fanchette in Genée's *Der Seekadett*, starred in another breeches rôle in Lecocq's *Kosiki*, once more as Boulotte, took the title-rôle of *La Marjolaine* and then, having made an enormous hit in the play *A sárga csikó*, scored another when she succeeded to the rôle of Serpolette in *Les Cloches de Corneville*. She notched up a further pair of major successes when she appeared as Lecocq's *Le Petit Duc* and as Zsófi Török in the famous play *A piros bugyelláris* in successive productions. In 1879 she played the title-rôles of Lecocq's *La Camargo* and Offenbach's *Madame Favart*, and (now divorced, and once again Blaháné) the local version of Suppé's *Boccaccio* which gave her one of the biggest musical successes of her career.

In 1880 she played in an early Hungarian operett success, Ferenc Puks's *Titilla hadnagy* (Lieutenant Petit-trouvaille) but, with other members of the company taking more and more of the operettic rôles, the theatre's star now picked and chose her parts, many of which were in the non-musical area of the Népszinház repertoire. As she became, in real life, the Baroness Ödön Splényi, (without changing her stage name) she now went only for the best and most suitable musical parts, such as Bettina in *La Mascotte* (1881), a travesty Symon in *Der Bettelstudent* (1883), Hanka in the Hungarian play with music *A tót leány* and Molly in *Der arme Jonathan* (1890), whilst the theatre's newer musical stars, Aranka Hegyi and Ilka Pálmay, assured the casting of many of the other pieces. In 1883 the Népszinház company visited Vienna and Theater an der Wien audiences saw Blaha's versions of Serpolette, Symon and Bettina.

If her musical appearances were now less numerous, she did, however, take part in a number of the rising Hungarian-written and -composed operetts mounted at the Népszinház, starring as the Vicomte de Letorrières in József Konti's *Az eleven ördög* (1885), in *Királyfogás* (1886, Fjóra), as the titular 'gamin de Paris' in *A suhanc* (1888), in Sztojanovits's *Turandot* musical *Peking rózsája* (1888), Erkel's *A kassai diák* (1890), Szabados' Labiche musical *Az első és a második* (1892) and *Talmi hercegnő* (1898) among a wide-ranging straight and musical repertoire.

In her later career, she appeared only occasionally on the musical stage but, at the age of 58, she memorably created the title-rôle of Raoul Mader's musical version of Csiky's play *Nagymama* (Countess Szerémy), a rôle which she later repeated on film. In 1921 Budapest's 11-year-old Revü-Színház was renamed the Lujza Blaha Színház and was opened with a Lujza Blaha overture composed for the occasion by Izsó Barna. A second Budapest theatre bearing her name operated between 1954 and 1960.

Literature: Verő, G: *Lujza Blaha és a Népszinház* (Franklin-Társulat kiadása, Budapest, 1926); *Blaha Lujza naplója* [*The Diary of Lujza Blaha*] (Gondolat, Budapest, 1987)

BLANCHE, Ada [née ADAMS] (b London, 16 July 1862; d London, 1 January 1953).

A child of a theatrical family, Miss Blanche went on the stage at the Adelphi, under Chatterton, at the age of 14. She played juvenile rôles in plays, graduated to young adults, and made her first important musical appearance touring as Fiametta in *Boccaccio*. She toured with Lila Clay's company (Sophie Syntax in *Adamless Eden* etc), with the Holmes British Burlesque Company in America and, from 1886, worked at the Gaiety Theatre as a supporting player and understudy to Nellie Farren in burlesque (Boatswain in *Monte Cristo jr* 1886, Ernest in *Miss Esmeralda* 1887 etc) and played Farren's roles on tour. However, she found her most significant success as an outstanding and long-serving pantomime principal boy at the Theatre Royal, Drury Lane, on the road in the title-rôle of the long-touring English version of Serpette's *La Demoiselle du téléphone* (1897–1900) and, later, in character rôles. In the latter days of her career she created the heavy-lady comedy rôles of Mrs Smith in *The Arcadians* (1909), Mitsu in *The Mousmé* (1911), Mrs Baxter Browne in *The Pearl Girl* (1913) and Lady Elizabeth Weston in *The Rebel Maid* (1921), all under the management of her brother-in-law, Robert Courtneidge.

Of her three actress sisters, Addie Blanche also appeared successfully in Gaiety burlesque and was the mother of Marie Blanche who appeared prominently in the West-End musicals *Princess Caprice* (1912, Anna), *The Joy Ride Lady* (1914, Fifi), *High Jinks* (1916, Mrs Thorne), *Carminetta* (1917, Lady Susan), *Telling the Tale* (1918, Sidonie de Matisse), *His Little Widows* (1919, Blanche) and *Cherry* (1920, Cherry Burleigh). Another sister, Rosie Nott [Rosaline May ADAMS], was the first wife of Robert Courtneidge and the mother of Cicely Courtneidge, who was named after her actress grandmother, Cicely Nott [Sarah Ann ADAMS] (1832–1900).

LA BLANCHISSEUSE DE BERG-OP-ZOOM Opérette in 3 acts by Henri Chivot and Alfred Duru. Music by Léon Vasseur. Théâtre des Folies-Dramatiques, Paris, 27 January 1875.

Following his great success with *La Timbale d'argent* and a less happy experience with *La Famille Trouillat*, Vasseur submitted the pretty *La Blanchisseuse de Berg-op-Zoom* at the Folies-Dramatiques. Chivot and Duru's tale told of the forced marriage of van der Graff, the brewer, and Guillemine, the laundress, imposed on them when her father catches him climbing up to her bedroom window after dark. After a sticky start, the two young people discover, by the final curtain, that it was a good idea.

With Anna van Ghell in its title-rôle, supported by

Luco, Milher, Mario Widmer, Mlle Tassily and Vavasseur, the piece managed only some 50 performances in Paris, but was nevertheless picked up for production at Vienna's Theater an der Wien (ad and add mus Julius Hopp) later the same year. Lori Stubel was the waschermädchen of the title in a cast which included Jani Szika and top comics Alexander Girardi and Felix Schweighofer through 17 performances.

Austria: Theater an der Wien *Die Perle des Wäscherinnin* 14 November 1875

BLASEL, Karl (b Vienna, 16 October 1831; d Vienna, 16 June 1922).

Karl Blasel lived what was probably the most remarkable career in the history of the musical theatre. He created more than a hundred musical theatre rôles, and the Viennese versions of an uncountable number more, over a period of 80 years on the stage and some 60 spent at the two most important houses of the German-speaking musical theatre which, for a part of that time, also meant of the world.

Blasel began his career as a child, appearing at the Hofoper as one of the animals in *Der Zauberflöte*, and at the age of 18 he joined the chorus at the Laibacher Theater. By 1863, established as a comedian, he joined the company at the Theater an der Wien and there began a career that would eventually make him into the 'grand and great old man of Viennese comics'. He appeared early on as Menelaos, Bobèche and Le Menu (*Die Schäfer*), teamed with Matthias Rott as the gens d'armes of *Genoveva von Brabant*, and played Urban (*Das Donauweibchen*), Pagatl (*Prinzessin Hirschkuh*) and many other such rôles before he left the Theater an der Wien, in 1869, for the Carltheater.

There, in the 1870s and 1880s, he created the Viennese versions of more of Offenbach's principal comic rôles (Prince Paul, Cornarino, Ficus in *Tulipatan*, the dancemaster Baladon in *Kakadu*, Cabriolo, Kaschmyr in *Schneeball*, Jolicoeur in *Fleurette*, Vertpanné in *Tromb-al-ca-zar*, Persiflage in *Schönröschen*, Delicat to the Flammèche of Matras in *Margot die Millionenbäckerin* etc) and appeared in reprises of others of the composer's works (Bobinet, Fortunio, Jupiter, Mosthaber in *Hanni weint*, in travesty as Madame Madou in *Die Damen der Halle*, Popelinot in *Der Regimentszauberer* etc) as well as in other French opérettes (Cucurbitus in *Der Flötenspieler von Rom*, Alexibus XXIV in Delibes' *Confusius IX*, Anatol in *Hundert Jungfrauen*, Boléro in *Giroflé-Girofla*, Trenitz in *Madame Angots Tochter*, Baron de Cotignac in Coèdes's *Die schöne Bourbonnaise*, Montefiasco in *Graziella*, Bidard in *Der Kohlenhändler von Paris*, Briolet in *Jeanne, Jeannette, Jeanneton*, Beaupersil in *Niniche*, Job in *Papas Frau*, Picasso in *Der grosse Casimir*, Palamède in *La Marjolaine*, Merimac in *Olivette* etc) and as Passepartout in the Carltheater's long-running adaptation of Verne and d'Ennery's *Reise um die Erde in 80 Tagen*.

Blasel created and/or played the lead comedy rôles of a number of the earliest Viennese works of the modern tradition, including *Wein, Weib, Gesang* (Mehlthau), Suppé's short-lived *Isabella* (Don Marullo Cariazzo de los Crocodilos), *Der Herr von Papillon* (von Trommetron), Suppé's *Die Jungfrau von Dragant* (Ritter Mordigall) and Brandl's extremely popular *Des Löwen Erwachen* (Placide) and *Cassis Pascha*, Zaytz's *Mannschaft am Bord* (Jean), Con-

Plate 26. **Karl Blasel:** *Still near the beginning of his famously long career on the Viennese musical stage, Blasel appeared as King Bobèche in Offenbach's* Blaubart.

radin's *Flodoardo Wuprahall* (Schmafukerle), Suppé's *Die Frau Meisterin* (Longinus), *Leichte Kavallerie* (Bums) and *Zehn Mädchen und kein Mann* (Agamemnon). He also created the principal comedy rôles in Suppé's major Operetten – war-correspondent-by-accident Julian von Golz in *Fatinitza* (1876), Muzerelli in *Der Teufel auf Erden*, the goofy Lambertuccio in *Boccaccio* (1879), Don Pomponio di San Sebastian in *Donna Juanita* (1880), Baron Rompinelle, Governor of Martinique, in *Der Gaskogner* (1881) and Fanfani Pasha in *Die Afrikareise* (1883) – as well as in such other full-sized Viennese pieces as Strauss's *Prinz Methusalem* (Mandelbaum), *Die Mormonen* (the policechief), Zeller's *Die Carbonari* (1880, Conte Seneca da Ruffoli), *Der Kukuk* (Rastagnol) and Genée's *Nisida* (Don Leonida Palestro) and *Rosina* (Gaspard).

In 1883 Blasel returned to the Theater an der Wien company where, over the next two years, he was seen as Fanfani Pasha in *Die Afrikareise*, as Don Pomponio, Cabriolo, as the Chevalier des Martines in *Der Marquis von Rivoli*, Baron Forêt de Lorges in *Der schöne Nikolaus*, Heidekrug, Sparacani in Czibulka's *Pfingsten in Florenz*, Ben-Selim in *Zwillinge* and Griffardin in *Gillette de Narbonne* before, in 1886, he moved on again to take up the position of director of the Theater in der Josefstadt. Three years later, he took over control of the Carltheater where, during six years in command, he continued to perform in his old rôles (Bobinet in *Pariser Leben*, Cabriolo, Jupiter, Lambertuccio, Menelaos etc) whilst adding a whole list of new ones – Bob (otherwise Cadeau) in *Erminy*, Syfar in *Die Uhlanen*, Jérome Pasquille in *Die Kätzchen*, Pontarcy in *Das*

Fräulein von Telephone, Cyprian Boxtel in *Lachende Erben*, Kilian in *Edelweiss*, Prosper Giraud in *Le Pays d'or*, Wassermann in Jakobowski's *Die Brilliantenkönigin*, Porfirio Karka in *Die Königin von Gamara*, Marchese Tortoloni in *Lady Charlatan*, Birnhuber in *Coeur d'ange*, Toulouse in *Les Forains* (*Olympia*), Pan Gabriel Ostrogski in *Die Lachtaube*, Pinsonnet in *Le Voyage de Suzette*, Hadji-Chlasa Pascha in *Die Lieder des Mirza Schaffys* etc – in a programme of productions in which musical pieces were heavily featured.

Blasel gave up the management to Franz Jauner in 1895, but he stayed on briefly at the Carltheater as a performer (Tomasso Stirio in *Das Modell*, *Eine tolle Nacht*, Biseaux in *Der kleine Duckmauser* etc) before returning once more to the Theater an der Wien for a further long series of new rôles beginning with that of Baptiste in Verö's *Der Löwenjäger* (October 1896) and including the detective Niki in Millöcker's *Nordlicht*, Louis Brebillant in Weinberger's *Der Schmetterling*, Graf Wenzel von Dubrowa in *Die Schwalben* (1897), Pampinelli in *L'Amour mouillé* (*Das verregnete Amor*), Bonhomme in Strauss's *Die Göttin der Vernunft*, John James Pickleton, New Orleans umbrella merchant, in *Die Blumen-Mary* and Mats the Syndic in the German version of Gilbert's *His Excellency* (*Der Herr Gouverneur*, 1897). He had one of his best new rôles for some time as Beaubuisson in Heuberger's version of the farcical *Pink Dominos* tale, *Der Opernball* (1898), and introduced rôles in *Die Küchen-Komtesse* (Peter Knapp), *Der Dreibund* (Holger), *Der Blondin von Namur* (Duke of Melphi), *Fräulein Hexe* (Gottlieb Berger), Johann Strauss III's shortlived *Katze und Maus* (Gustav), *Ihre Excellenz* (Dupiton), *Gräfin Kuni*, *A Runaway Girl* (Jaromir Spindel) and *Fräulein Präsident* (Graf Chapuzot). On his seventieth birthday, he appeared as Menelaos to the schöne Helena of Julie Kopácsi-Karczag.

Another switch then took him back to the Carltheater once again to create – at what would have been a very late stage in anyone else's career – some of his most splendid rôles. He was cast as Graf Balduin in the Reinhardt hit *Das süsse Mädel* (1901) and Glöppler in Lehár's triumphant *Der Rastelbinder* (1902), introduced Vienna to old MacSherry in *Madame Sherry* (1903), created the bemused papa, Pieter te Bakkenskijl, in *Die geschiedene Frau* (1908), Hagen in Oscar Straus's burlesque of Wagner, *Die lustigen Nibelungen* (1904), Daszewski in *Die Schützenliesel* (1906) and Tobias Blank in *Künstlerblut* (1906), each of the last two alongside Girardi, as well as the comical King Joachim XIII in *Ein Walzertraum* (1907), and the old landowner Dragotin in *Zigeunerliebe* (1910). He was Pomarel, the husband of the lady who is supposed to be *Die keusche Susanne* (1911) and took the cameo part of lay brother Mattheus who unravels the plot of *Der liebe Augustin* (1912), whilst also repeating his Beaubuisson, Sindulfo (*Gasparone*), Izzet Pascha (*Fatinitza*), Don Pomponio and Lambertuccio and creating further rôles in *Das gewiss Etwas* (Philidore Taponet), *Das Baby* (Christian Schwabach), *Der liebe Schatz* (Tom Blackmayer), *Der Glücklichste* (Derim Khan), *Das Marktkind* (Sebastian Siebert), *Der Mameluck* (Kanno), *Der Göttergatte* (Maenandros), the highly successful *Das Veilchenmädel* (Graf Willy Sickendorff), *'s Zuckersgoscherl* (Kreuzschnabel), *Der Schätzmeister* (Clearing), *Der Schnurrbart* (Bela von Kozary), *Kaisermanöver* (Li-hu-Schwappl), *Der Polizeichef* (Spadillo), *Die Bonbonniere* (Max Wohlmann), *Krieg im*

Frieden (Henkel), *Der Elektriker* (Count Lamonde), *Hugdietrichs Brautfahrt* (King Ladislas), *Mutzi* (Dr Stroh), *Der selige Vincenz* (Kajak), *Der Rosenjungling*, *Der schwarze Tenor* (Leslo), *Johann der zweite* (Prosper), *Der Glücksnarr* (King Balduin), Oscar Straus's *Didi* (Belivon), *Das Puppenmädel* (Buffon), *Majestät Mimi* (Aladrio), *Alt-Wien* (Graf Leopold) and the Viennese version of *A kis gróf* (Susi, Dr Theophrastus Haring). In a special performance given to mark his 60 years in the business, he appeared as Choufleuri and as Fancourt Babberley in *Charley's Aunt* (1909) at the age of 78.

In 1913 he ceased to be a member of the Carltheater company, but he returned there as a guest to play in *Der erste Küss* (King Erwin XXX), Hopp's *Zwei Mann von Hess* and Ziehrer's *Fürst Casimir* (George Washington Didfeller). On 28 June 1920 he took part in the 500th performance of *Der Rastelbinder*, and he appeared in *Salon Pitzelberger* and in his rôles in *Der Rastelbinder* and *Die Schützenliesel*, which he had never relinquished, shortly before his death, at the age of 90.

His wife Johanna Blasel (1840–1910) played small rôles in plays and step-outs in musicals at the Carltheater from 1870, during her husband's time there, being occasionally featured (Javotte in *Angot*, Iwan in *Fatinitza*, Toinon in *Prinz Conti*), whilst their son Leopold Blasel (1866–1931) worked with his father in the management of his two theatres.

DIE BLAUE MAZUR Operette in 2 acts (3 scenes) by Leo Stein and Béla Jenbach. Music by Franz Lehár. Theater an der Wien, Vienna, 28 May 1920.

One of Lehár's last ventures into the lightly and sprightly comical musical play before setting off into the romantic unhappy-end pieces of his later years, *Die blaue Mazur* was written to a featherweight libretto. It told of how the heroine Blanka van Lossin (Betty Fischer), having wed the playboy aristocrat, Count Julian Olinski (Hubert Marischka), has to be convinced that he has left and will continue to leave his gallivanting past behind him. An unfortunate overheard comment about 'lost liberty' at the wedding reception leads to Olinski finding himself alone on his weddding night as Blanka flees to the home of old Baron von Reiger (Emil Guttmann) and his inseparable and aged bachelor friends (Josef Hauschultz, Karl Tuschl) until peace is made. The Theater an der Wien's leading romantic players were backed by their regular light comic partners, Ernst Tautenhayn as Adolar von Sprintz, a model young man with a double life, and Luise Kartousch as Gretl Aigner of the ballet who belongs to the half of that life that Adolar's uncle von Reiger knows nothing about.

Die blaue Mazur began as it went on, with one attractively dancing Lehár melody following another from the polonaise of the opening, through the mazurka and waltz rhythms of the principal pair's first duet ('Komm' ich sag' dir was in's Ohr'), the march septet which introduced the soubrets, Julian's waltz-song ('Ich darf nur Eine lieben'), and Blanka's leap back into mazurka strains for the first act finale. The second act opened with a gavotte trio, moved on to a madrigal quintet and wound up with Blanka in full waltz-time ('Lockend erwartet mich das Leben'), whilst the final scene began with two waltz duos and a third waltz for the soubrette before the two most popular pieces of the score, Blanka and Julian's title mazurka ('Tanzt der Pole die Mazur') and the polka duo for Adolar and Grete ('Mäderl, mein süsses Grederl') led up to the last finale with its all-round reassurances of Julian's intent to settle down.

Die blaue Mazur was a first-rate hit in Vienna. It zoomed past its 200th consecutive performance on 11 January 1921, and held the boards right through until 28 April. By the time it had played out a ration of matinées and odd performances in the Lehár season that ended 1922, it had totted up 333 performances at the Theater an der Wien. Elsewhere, however, it proved rather less of a favourite. Having been given in Berlin with Vera Schwarz starred in 1921, it went down as one of the less popular of Lehár's works in the German regions, and the Budapest production of *Kék mazur* (ad István Zágon) at the Király Színház went no further towards evoking the kind of enthusiasm that the Vienna one had. The show took its time to get to Britain, where a 1927 production by James White at Daly's Theatre (ad Monckton Hoffe, Harry Graham, add songs Herman Darewski), starring Gladys Moncrieff, lasted only 140 performances, and longer still to arrive in France (ad Marcel Dunan) where, with Pépa Bonafé as Blanche de Raisme and the rest of the cast and action similarly Gallicized, it had an unmemorable season under the management of Jean Casanova at the Ba-ta-clan two years later.

Germany: Metropoltheater 1921; Hungary: Király Színház *Kek mazur* 13 May 1921; UK: Daly's Theatre *The Blue Mazurka* 19 February 1927; France: Théâtre Ba-ta-clan *La Mazourka bleue* 8 February 1929

Recording: selection in Italian (EDM)

BLESS THE BRIDE

BLESS THE BRIDE Musical show in 2 acts by A P Herbert. Music by Vivian Ellis. Adelphi Theatre, London, 26 April 1947.

Following the failure of *Big Ben*, C B Cochran mounted a second and much more successful piece by the same team of Ellis and Herbert. Eschewing, this time, the political and the purposeful, *Bless the Bride* followed the tradition of the romantic comic opera in its period tale of Lucy Willow (Lizbeth Webb) who runs away with a romantic Frenchman (Georges Guétary) on her wedding day, loses him to the wars, and then finds him again just when she is about to marry her original unfortunate Englishman (Brian Reece). The heart of Herbert's charmingly unpretentious book came with the second-act antics of the bride's family, pursuing their improper daughter through devastatingly un-English France, and Ellis's score was in the happiest comic opera vein, ranging from the delicious waltz of the first act trio, 'I Was Never Kissed Before', the hero's ringing set-piece 'Ma Belle Marguerite' and his rhapsodic 'A Table for Two', to the jilted groom's touching if comic 'My Big Moment' and the humorous family ensemble 'The Englishman'. The most memorable moment of the score, however, came in the idyllic duo 'This is my Lovely Day' delivered by the beautiful young soprano and the darkly handsome Egypto-Frenchman, both of whom made themselves a name in their rôles.

Bless the Bride opened in London in the same week that the much-publicized *Oklahoma!* bowed at the Theatre Royal, Drury Lane, and the two, which shared a certain old-fashioned style and sentimentality but otherwise formed a lively contrast, remained, with *Annie Get Your Gun*, at the top of the town's musical entertainments for

Plate 27. **Bless the Bride**: *'I Was Never Kissed Before ...'. Jan Hartley-Morris (Lucy Willow) and Philip Creasy (Pierre) are overspied by the jealous Michelle Todd (Suzanne) (Northcott Theatre, Exeter).*

the next two years. After 886 performances Cochran decided to close *Bless the Bride* in order to free the Adelphi Theatre for his next Herbert/Ellis musical, *Tough at the Top*. It was a decision which proved a singular error of judgement, as there had been months or even years of life still in the earlier production and the new show failed.

Bless the Bride proved a great favourite on the provincial circuits for many years, and a top-class revival at Exeter's Northcott Theatre in 1985 with Jan Hartley-Morris in the rôle of Lucy prompted a London revival at Sadler's Wells Theatre in 1987 (11 August). Miss Hartley starred again, alongside Frenchman Bernard Alane, but the otherwise ill-cast and unfortunately cut version was not a success and a West End transfer did not eventuate.

Recordings: original cast (WRC, Columbia) selection (MFP) etc

BLITZ!

BLITZ! Musical play in 2 acts by Lionel Bart. Adelphi Theatre, London, 8 May 1962.

A panoramic spectacular of wartime London, Lionel Bart's successor to *Oliver!* lacked much of the heart of its famous predecessor, but had many more opportunities for stage display. A Cohens-and-Kellys tale of racial and family rivalry played out under Hitler's bombs on a huge and magnificent physical production, it nevertheless produced some attractive musical numbers ranging from the lively wartime pastiche 'Who's That Geezer Hitler?' to a pair of thoughtfully characterized pieces for the Jewish mother of the tale (Amelia Bayntun) ('Be What You Want To Be', 'So Tell Me') and a diffident little love song called 'I Want To Whisper Something' for the young man of the piece. The show's visual values accounted for much of the 16-month (568 performances) run which Donald Albery's production achieved.

A 1990 production by the National Youth Theatre, seen at the West End's Playhouse Theatre, prompted a further production by Theatre North which was subsequently toured through Britain in 1991.

Recording: original cast (HMV)

EIN BLITZMÄDEL Posse mit Gesang in 4 acts by Carl Costa. Music by Carl Millöcker. Theater an der Wien, Vienna, 4 February 1877.

One of the most successful musical comedies written by the team of Costa and Millöcker – the following year *Ihr Corporal* would bring them another long-lived success –, *Ein Blitzmädel* existed around its star part, a veritable rôle à tiroirs which, surprisingly enough, went not to a Gallmeyer or a Geistinger but to Fräulein C Bendel as her début rôle at the Theater an der Wien.

The star played Caroline, a telegraph operator who, in the course of her daily work, is required to send out a despatch by which she discovers that beastly Baron Istvan Inhass (Heinrich Thalboth) is plotting to get his protégé a job that she thinks her lawyer boyfriend, Rudolf Kern (Herr Eichheim), should have. To expose this nepotism, and to win her point and the job, she goes out into the world in a whole series of disguises – a marquise, a nun, a dancer, an anarchist – accompanied by her friend, the tenor singer Brüller (Felix Schweighofer, variously as an old marquis, a toreador, a student etc), gambolling through four acts of impersonations, antics, songs and dances from 'Im Telegrafenbureau' to 'Für den guten Zweck', 'Der Balletmeister und seine Nichte' and to 'Bruder Studio' until they have visited and enlightened all the functionaries who stand to lose by the Baron's plan. The result is, of course, a happy ending. Millöcker provided a waltzing score for the piece which was, nevertheless, largely secondary to the comical antics of the show's plot and action.

Produced in Vienna under the management of Maximilian Steiner, the show was played 45 times in two seasons, was quickly taken up on other German-language stages, and was seen again in Vienna for no fewer than 39 successive nights at the Theater in der Josefstadt in 1882–3 (9 December). The year after its Vienna opening, it was already on the programme of New York's Germania Theater with Julie Catenhausen in the principal female rôle, and that city got repeated revivals thereafter, notably at the Thalia Theater in 1885, the Amberg Theater (27 September 1890) with Paula Loewe starred, and again in the repertoire of the famous Viennese star Felix Schweighofer who played his original rôle of Brüller to the Caroline of Anna Leonardi in the 1899–1900 season. In 1909 the Irving Place Theater played it yet again (5 October), as *The Lightning Girl*, with Hedwig Richard starred.

An Hungarian version (ad Antal Bánfalvy) was first produced in 1884 and the original version reappeared yet again in Vienna at the Carltheater in May 1892 and, in 1916, at the Wiener Bürgertheater.

USA: Germania Theater 20 April 1878; Hungary: Budai Színkör *A tüzről pattant leány* 3 July 1884.

BLITZSTEIN, Marc (b Philadelphia, 2 March 1905; d Fort-de-France, Martinique, 22 January 1964). Striving composer who finally made his mark on the musical theatre with his one attempt at translation.

Blitzstein studied music in New York and Berlin and began his career as a composer writing contemporary music. He placed a short operetta, *Triple Sec*, in *The Garrick Gaieties* but, having failed to break through in either serious or light music, he decided to make his music an adjunct to left-wing political propaganda. The musical play *The Cradle Will Rock*, for which he wrote book, lyrics and music, won more attention for the politically based fuss which surrounded it than for its merits, and a 1937 radio musical *I've Got the Tune*, and a five-performance try-out *No For an Answer* followed in the same vein with conspicuous lack of success.

After the war, he composed the music for a 'socially conscious' ballet *The Guests*, and for a musical stage adaptation of Lillian Hellman's play *The Little Foxes*, called *Regina*, which played 56 performances on Broadway. The latter piece subsequently found itself an occasional home in variously hacked-about versions in opera houses. However, Blitzstein ultimately earned himself recognition in the theatre not as a composer but as an adapter, when he provided a new English-language libretto for *Die Dreigroschenoper* (Brandeis University Music Festival, Waltham, Mass 14 June 1952). During a long subsequent off-Broadway run, this version was ultimately responsible for arousing interest in Hauptmann, Brecht and Weill's piece in America.

Further attempts at a Broadway musical with *Reuben, Reuben*, which closed without reaching New York, and an adaptation of Sean O'Casey's *Juno and the Paycock*, under the title *Juno*, which folded in 16 performances, proved to have no more appeal than his earlier pieces. His final contribution to the New York stage was in the form of incidental songs to Hellman's play *Toys in the Attic* (Hudson Theater, 25 February 1960).

Blitzstein was murdered in Martinique in 1964. A compilation show of his work was staged at the Provincetown Playhouse under the title *Blitzstein!* in 1966 (30 November, 7 performances).

1938 **The Cradle Will Rock** Windsor Theater 3 January
1941 **No For an Answer** Mecca Temple 5 January
1949 **Regina** 46th Street Theater 31 October
1952 **The Threepenny Opera** (*Die Dreigroschenoper*) new English version (Brandeis University Music Festival)
1955 **Reuben, Reuben** Shubert Theater, Boston 10 October
1959 **Juno** (Joseph Stein) Winter Garden Theater 9 March

Biography: Gordon, E: *Mark the Music: The Life and Work of Marc Blitzstein* (St Martin's Press, New York, 1975)

BLONDEL Musical in 2 acts by Tim Rice. Music by Stephen Oliver. Old Vic, London, 9 November 1983; Aldwych Theatre, 20 January 1984.

Originally conceived by its author as a small-scale piece on the lines of *Joseph and the Amazing Technicolor Dreamcoat*, in the early days of his collaboration with Andrew Lloyd Webber, *Blondel* was finally written nearly a decade later and found itself, following Rice's spectacular run of West End success, mounted as a full-scale adult musical.

Blondel (Paul Nicholas) is a pop-bard with dreams of stardom. When King Richard (Stephen Tate) gets imprisoned, however, he follows the history books and hurries off to Europe with his backing group, the Blondettes, to set royalty right as to what his horrible understudy of a brother is doing to England. On his way, he is tracked by an assassin (Chris Langham) hired by Prince John (David Burt) to stop him. But Blondel gets to Richard, gets him out and home, and even gets his pop stardom thanks to a jolly number claiming 'I'm a Monarchist'.

Some of the most enjoyable parts of the score were the linking narratives, sung in cathedral harmonies by the harmony group Cantabile as they swung a Benedictus and hurried the tale along, whilst one lyric actually took the form of an acrostic on the name of Prime Minister Margaret Thatcher. Richard, in prison, bewailed his 'Saladin Days' as John, on the other edge of the Continent hissed ambitiously 'I Want To Be King', the hit man admitted 'I'm an A double S,A,S,I,N' and an intrusive creature called Fiona (Sharon Lee Hill), a loud-mouthed serf and Blondel's girlfriend, popped in and out of the mostly male show and sang a piece about 'Running Back for More'.

Blondel transferred from the Old Vic to the West End's Aldwych Theatre, but Cameron Mackintosh's production's run of 365 performances was a forced one and the show proved to have a limited future.

Blondel and/or King Richard have provided the substance for a number of other musical stage pieces, including the 18th-century comic opera *Richard Coeur de Lion* by Jean-Michel Sedaine and André Grétry (Théâtre Italien, Paris 21 October 1784), which was one of the successes of its time and is still occasionally played today. The Brough brothers brought out a *Richard Coeur de Lion, or The Knight of the Couchant Leopard* at the Theatre Royal, Drury Lane, in 1853 (mus arr J G Reed, 28 March), J Strachan's burlesque *Coeur de Lion (Revised and his enemies corrected)*, with music selected and arranged by John Fitzgerald, played at London's Strand Theatre in 1870, and the 1891 Germano-Hungarian operetta *Királyszöktetés (König und Spielmann)* (József Kerner/Hugo Stein ad Mór Fenyéri 11 August 1891) was mounted at Budapest's Budai Színkör. The King has also become an habitual part of the British pantomime of *The Babes in the Wood*, arriving as a deus ex machina to pardon Robin Hood, who has also got himself tacked into the current version of the tale of the Children in the Wood. Blondel only occasionally gets in as well.

BLOOD BROTHERS   Musical in 2 acts by Willy Russell. Liverpool Playhouse, 8 January 1983; Lyric Theatre, London, 11 April 1983.

A modern version of the *Corsican Brothers* story, set in Liverpool, *Blood Brothers* follows the tale of twin brothers separated at birth. One is brought up by a well-off family, the other by his impoverished mother. Without knowing their relationship, the two boys become friends, but when their different backgrounds and abilities lead them to civil position and prison respectively, in adult life, the tale ends in the tragedy that has been foretold.

Both funny and moving in its scenes of the childhood of Eddy (Andrew Wadsworth) and Mickey (George Costigan), the show focused principally on their mother, Mrs Johnstone, originally played by popular vocalist Barbara Dickson, to whose abilities most of the folk-strained songs

of the show were tailored. The songs, however, were secondary to the story in this musical and, apart from Eddy's gentle love song 'I'm Not Saying a Word' and his mother's final 'Tell Me It's Not True', were largely incidental. The play itself was a sinewy piece, most effective when concentrating on its people rather than on social generalizing, but in spite of outstanding performances from, in particular, the two 'boys', it failed to take on in London for more than an eight-month run. With the notice posted, however, the show suddenly became popular. It was too late to continue the run, but a second production, with boxing champion John Conteh clumsily cast as its narrator, was soon after sent on the road by Robert Fox with the avowed intent of bringing the show back to town.

This revival closed before reaching London but, after a wide range of provincial productions, as well as appearances in Germany (ad Jürgen Flügge, Hans Jorg Betschart) and in America, producer Bill Kenwright took a production starring popular singer Kiki Dee from the provincial circuits into London's Albery Theatre in 1988 (28 July). There the show finally achieved a lengthy metropolitan run, with Angela Richards, Stephanie Lawrence and Miss Dickson succeeding to the rôle of Mrs Johnstone as *Blood Brothers* continues, at the time of writing, into its fifth year, now at the Phoenix Theatre. Miss Lawrence led the cast of a company playing this production to America in 1993. A film version was announced but, in spite of author Russell's cinema success with *Educating Rita* and *Shirley Valentine*, it has yet to appear.

Following a Munich production of an altered version the English *Blood Brothers* was played in Germany in 1991 (English Theatre, Frankfurt 22 November 1991), followed in turn by a vernacular *Blutsbrüder* (Stadttheater, Heilbronn 11 April 1992) which followed more closely the original piece. Further translated versions have appeared in several other countries.

Germany: Schauburg Theater, Munich 7 April 1987; USA: Downtown Cabaret, Bridgeport, Conn 22 January 1988, Music Box Theater, New York 25 April 1993
Recordings: original cast (Legacy), 1988 revival cast (First Night), Japanese cast (Polydor), Dutch cast (Red Bullet)

BLOOMER GIRL   Musical in 2 acts by Sig Herzig and Fred Saidy based on a play by Lilith and Dan James. Lyrics by E Y Harburg. Music by Harold Arlen. Shubert Theater, New York, 5 October 1944.

Bloomer Girl arrived on Broadway hard in the wake of *Oklahoma!* and proved not only one of the quickest to attempt to imitate the successful formula of Rodgers and Hammerstein's show, but also, with its period American tale, its Agnes de Mille ballets and even two of the same featured players, one of the most closely imitative. It was also one of the longest-running.

Evelina (Celeste Holm) is a niece and disciple of 'Dolly' Bloomer (Margaret Douglass), a liberated lady who is into feminine suffrage and is also the popularizer of the 'liberating' knickerbocker dress. Unfortunately for family harmony, Evelina's father, Horatio Applegate (Matt Briggs) both manufactures hoop-skirts and unilaterally chooses his daughter's bridegroom, southerner Jeff Calhoun (David Brooks). If the 'bloomer girl' chooses dramatically to disparage her father's wares in public she

Plate 28. **Blood Brothers**: *Andrew Wadsworth (centre) and George Costigan (right) as the parted twins of the title in the musical play's original Liverpool production.*

is, on the other hand, attracted by her chosen swain, whom she on principle refuses to wed. Dolly and Evelina get into trouble for helping runaway slaves, then the Civil War happens and Jeff is on the other side, but all ends happily when Applegate and Dolly turn his factory to a touch of war-profiteering, making army uniforms (and bloomers), and when Jeff gets converted to the Union cause.

Arlen's score was not out of his top drawer, although Jeff's tuneful reactions to 'Evelina' and a pair of the negro-style pieces in which the composer specialized – 'The Eagle and Me' and 'I Got a Song' – assigned to the black slave characters of the cast, emerged from the score, and a duo for hero and heroine, 'Right as the Rain', also won some popularity. The principal ballet section was a Civil War Ballet, and there was also a staged production of *Uncle Tom's Cabin* to the music of 'Liza Crossing the Ice'. *Oklahoma!*'s Joan McCracken featured as principal dancer.

John C Wilson's production of *Bloomer Girl* played an excellent 654 performances on Broadway, but there the parallels with *Oklahoma!* ended for, although it was sub-sequently televised in 1956, with Barbara Cook and Keith Andes featured, and revived at the Goodspeed Opera House in 1981 (16 September), the show did not follow its predecessor into the theatres of other countries.

Recording: original cast (Decca)

BLOSSOM, Henry M[artyn jr] (b St Louis, Mo, 10 May 1866; d New York, 23 March 1919). Much-admired librettist and lyricist to the early 20th-century American stage.

The young Henry Blossom originally worked in his father's insurance firm but, after having had success in placing an early effort at a short story, he turned his ambi-tions and talents to the writing of a full-scale book. One of the works that followed was *Checkers*, a horse-racing novel which he subsequently dramatized and which was pro-duced with some success by Kirk La Shelle in 1903.

At this stage of his career, Blossom turned his hand to anything and everything in the way of writing, and his name turned up on a theatre bill, for what seems to be the first time, when a song, 'Dearie, my Sweet', which he had written with George A Spink, found its way into the score for George Edwardes's London musical *Three Little Maids*. It was a pointer and a beginning, and his next venture took him thoroughly in the way which he would follow, when he supplied the book and lyrics for the American musical comedy *The Yankee Consul*. The show had a splendid Chi-cago success, leading to the announcement that Blossom and composer Alfred Robyn had been signed to a five-year, five-show contract by producer Henry Savage, and it went on to garner fine New York reviews for having 'no horseplay, no local jibes, Rialtoisms or Tenderloin slang', to a grand run on Broadway, and to a long touring life.

The five shows with Robyn did not, however, eventuate. Blossom's next partner was no less a musician than Victor Herbert, and the first two texts with which he supplied the composer brought him two of his biggest successes: the Continental-style comic operetta *Mlle Modiste* (1905) and the low-comedy star-vehicle *The Red Mill* (1906) for Montgomery and Stone. Now at the top of his profession, and considered by many as the most literate and play-wrightly of librettists of his time, Blossom did not, however, wholly confirm his three big initial sucesses.

Of two vehicles for Elsie Janis, *The Slim Princess* proved superior to an adaptation of Tristan Bernard's *La Soeur* as *The Hoyden* without either being a genuine success, an adaptation of Maurice Ordonneau's *Un Voyage Cooks* as *The Man from Cook's* got drowned in variety acts on its way to the Broadway stage, whilst his one reunion with Robyn, another piece taken from the French (Hennequin and Mitchell's *Aimé des femmes*) and produced as *All for the Ladies*, not by Savage but by the Shuberts, had only a fair run in spite of top comic Sam Bernard at the peak of the bill. It was later chopped down to make a touring turn for the comedian.

Blossom's repeats with Herbert were more successful, for if *The Prima Donna* failed to come up to hopes, an adaptation of Frank Mandel's *Our Wives* as the libretto for *The Only Girl* gave him one more hit, and there was more than a little praise for both *The Princess Pat* and *Eileen* with their rather different Irish heroines. He was less lucky with two rewrites of Charles Hoyt's *A Texas Steer*, first as *A Trip to Washington* and then as *We Should Worry*, whilst, in another two-time try, his version of Frederick Jackson's *A Full House*, produced under the Klaw and Erlanger management as *She Took a Chance*, was withdrawn before Broadway and reset with a score by Victor Herbert as *The Velvet Lady*. Neither version, apparently, appealed to the mercurial Jackson who made his own unsuccessful musical version of his play for Britain as *The Purple Lady*. Blossom's last musical-theatre work, an adaptation of Walter Hackett and Roi Cooper Megrue's *It Pays to Advertise*, produced posthumously by the Selwyns, did not move on from its Boston tryout.

Amongst Blossom's other assignments, he provided what book there was to Ziegfeld's *The Century Girl* revue (1916), but he left it to other hands to musicalize his own successful stage play. *The Honey Girl* (aka *What's the Odds?*, Cohan and Harris Theater 3 May 1920), based on *Checkers*, with songs by Albert von Tilzer, had a libretto credited at various times to Edgar Allen Woolf and to Edward Clark.

1903 **The Yankee Consul** (Alfred G Robyn) Chicago; Broadway Theater 22 February 1904
1905 **Mlle Modiste** (Victor Herbert) Knickerbocker Theater 25 December
1906 **The Red Mill** (Herbert) Knickerbocker Theater 24 September
1907 **The Hoyden** (Paul Rubens, John Golden, Robert Hood Bowers et al/w Cosmo Hamilton et al) 19 October
1908 **The Prima Donna** (Herbert) Knickerbocker Theater 30 November
1911 **The Slim Princess** (Leslie Stuart/w George Ade) Globe Theater 2 January
1912 **Baron Trenck** American version of Frederick Schraeder's English version (Casino Theater)

1912 **The Man From Cook's** (Raymond Hubbell) New Amsterdam Theater 25 March
1912 **All For the Ladies** (Robyn) Lyric Theater 30 December
1913 **A Trip to Washington** (Ben Jerome) La Salle Theater, Chicago 24 August
1913 **A Glimpse of the Great White Way** (rewritten *All For the Ladies*) 44th Street Theater 27 October
1914 **The Only Girl** (Herbert) 39th Street Theater 2 November
1915 **The Princess Pat** (Herbert) Cort Theater 29 September
1917 **Eileen** (ex-*Hearts of Erin*) (Herbert) Shubert Theater 19 March
1917 **We Should Worry** (A Baldwin Sloane) Apollo Theater, Atlantic City 25 October
1918 **Follow the Girl** (Zoel Parenteau) 44th Street Theater 2 March
1918 **She Took a Chance** (ex-*The Bubble Girl*) (Uda Waldrop) Tremont Theater, Boston 22 October
1919 **The Velvet Lady** (revised *She Took a Chance* w music by Victor Herbert) New Amsterdam Theater 3 February
1919 **Among the Girls** (Hubbell/w Glen MacDonough/w Roi Cooper Megrue) Shubert Theater, New Haven 9 May; Park Square Theater, Boston 19 May

BLOSSOM TIME Musical in 3 acts by Dorothy Donnelly based on *Das Dreimäderlhaus* by A M Willner and Heinz Reichert. Music taken from Franz Schubert's works arranged by Sigmund Romberg. Ambassador Theater, New York, 29 December 1921.

Following the enormous Continental success of *Das Dreimäderlhaus*, the Shuberts produced their own version of the Franz Schubert biomusical. It followed the Viennese piece in many ways, but used new lyrics by Donnelly and some different musical arrangements of the Schubert raw material made by Romberg. For all that it was less artistically done than the Heinrich Berté version, it proved a huge Broadway success over 592 performances and toured apparently endlessly through America thereafter. The British version, *Lilac Time*, once again reorganized and rearranged, and once again less effective than Berté's effort, was another major hit which cornered the remaining English-language markets whilst *Blossom Time* satisfied its copyright owners by cleaning up long and large in America.

Another, English *Blossom Time*, written by Rodney Ackland with lyrics credited to Harry Purcell, John Drinkwater and G H Clutsam and a pasticcio Schubert score arranged by Clutsam, was produced at the Lyric Theatre, London 17 March 1942. Yet another version of the *Dreimäderlhaus* story and score, it was arranged to permit Richard Tauber to appear as the composer for 96 performances.

Recording: US version, selection (RCA Victor)

BLUEBELL IN FAIRYLAND Musical dream play in 2 acts by Seymour Hicks. Lyrics by Aubrey Hopwood and Charles H Taylor. Music by Walter Slaughter. Vaudeville Theatre, London, 18 December 1901.

One of the most successful of all Victorian and Edwardian children's fairy/fantasy plays, *Bluebell* had its little heroine transported to Fairyland to restore a good monarch to his throne. Its author, Hicks, in the dual rôle of the little crossing-sweeper Dicky (pre-Fairyland) and the Sleeping King (in the fairy scenes), starred with his wife, Ellaline Terriss, in the show's title-rôle, and their personal popularity helped to stretch the appeal of *Bluebell* well beyond the children for whom it was nominally intended.

In his habitual style, Hicks larded Slaughter's pretty score with popular music-hall style songs, mostly borrowed from the American repertoire, and Miss Terriss scored a notable success with William H Penn's 'The Honeysuckle and the Bee'.

Bluebell became a perennial British Christmas entertainment and returned to London both in 1905 (Aldwych Theatre 23 December) in a version announced as 'elaborated' and in 1916 in a major revival (106 performances) with its original stars and with some new songs by Herman Darewski. Regular London showings continued till 1937.

Australia: Theatre Royal, Sydney 14 December 1907

BLUE EYES Musical play in 2 acts by Guy Bolton and Graham John. Music by Jerome Kern. Additional numbers by Frank Tours. Piccadilly Theatre, London, 27 April 1928.

In the midst of the fun-and-dance shows of the late 1920s, *Blue Eyes*, a romantic costume musical about Bonnie Prince Charlie, sat oddly in London's West End. Guy Bolton and Graham John's very old-fashioned book had Evelyn Laye in the rôle of actress Nancy Ann Bellamy disguising herself as a boy to help her brother (George Vollaire) escape the clutches of the 'Butcher of Culloden' (Bertram Wallis). Bill Berry was the comic relief as a helpful actor who gave the reverse of the travesty coin by getting into disguise as a woman, as well as a humorous Scotsman, a French dancing master, and a flea-circus proprietor. The stiffly antique book, which nevertheless gave opportunity for lots of colourful military costumes and allowed Miss Laye to fight a dashing duel, was illustrated by an up-to-date Jerome Kern score in which the lilting 'Back to the Heather', sung by Vollaire and his partner (Sylvia Leslie) caught the ear. After Lee Ephraim's production of *Blue Eyes* had played out its life in 276 performances at the brand new Piccadilly Theatre and then at Daly's (playing simultaneously with the composer's *Show Boat* at the Theatre Royal, Drury Lane), one gently swinging number called 'Do I Do Wrong?', sung by baritone George Gwyther in the rôle of Nancy's noble lover, was rescued by Kern to be relyricked as 'You're Devastating' in *Roberta*.

Another musical under the same title had previously been produced on Broadway (Casino Theater 21 February 1921). Written by Leroy Clemens, Leon Gordon, Z Myers and Isidore Benjamin Kornblum, it was no period piece but an adaptation of a play called *Let Tommy Do It* starring comedian Lew Fields and with Mollie King in the title-rôle of a tiny tale of love and lies. It played 56 performances.

BLUE FOR A BOY, or What Shall We Do with the Body? Musical romp in 2 acts by Austin Melford adapted from *Hurra! eine Junge* by Franz Arnold and Ernst Bach. Lyrics by Harold Purcell. Music by Harry Parr Davies. His Majesty's Theatre, London, 30 November 1950.

This farce musical, built around the comic talents of Fred Emney, Richard Hearne and author Austin Melford, used the remnants of Bach and Arnold's story as previously made into the successful comedy *It's a Boy!* (Strand Theatre 1930, 366 performances), to supply as many opportunities for disguises, impersonations, and what were essentially variety turns, as it could be devised to hold. The vast Emney, with his cigar and monocle, bounced about in kiddie rompers pretending to be a baby, Bertha Belmore did an impression of a booming, over-dressed lady authoress, and Hearne impersonated the same lady who, when she finally turned up for real, was soubrette Eve Lister. It was Miss Lister who had the principal singing moments of the evening, sharing the title-song with Hermene French, and performing 'Lying Awake and Dreaming' and 'At Last It's Happened' alone.

Ultimately a series of sketches interspersed with songs, this jolly, unsophisticated combination of entertainments caught on where other such pieces had failed and Emile Littler's production remained for a year and a half (664 performances) at His Majesty's Theatre before going on the road.

THE BLUE KITTEN Musical comedy in 2 acts by Otto Harbach and William Cary Duncan based on *Le Chasseur de Chez Maxim* by Yves Mirande and Gustave Quinson. Music by Rudolf Friml. Selwyn Theater, New York, 13 January 1922.

Mirande (and Quinson)'s highly successful 1920 Palais-Royal comedy underwent certain modifications in the hands of Otto Harbach and William Cary Duncan before it was mounted on Broadway with the ageing Joseph Cawthorn starred as a now Dutch-accented former waiter called Theodore Vanderpop. Vanderpop has come into money, quit his job at Maxim's, and is now suffering the familiar torture of the nouveau riche – his former customers may recognize him. The torture gets excruciating when one of his daughter's suitors turns out to be a gay young blade who frequented the restaurant in his waitering days.

Friml decorated this formerly French tale with a determinedly up-to-date American score, topped by such sprightly numbers as 'Cutie' and 'The Blue Kitten Blues', but, although he revealed a steady hand with the dance-music style, the public apparently felt that it lay less well with him than the operettic manner of *Rose Marie*. Arthur Hammerstein's production of *The Blue Kitten*, which featured former Ziegfeld star Lillian Lorraine alongside Cawthorn at the top of the bill, played through 140 Broadway performances without making itself into a genuine success. When Hammerstein put it on the road with Richard Carle at its bill-head it turned out a quick flop.

Three years later, however, the show turned up at London's Gaiety Theatre. It had been adapted by Dion Titheradge, given extra lyrics by Greatrex Newman and extra songs by Howard Carr, Ivy St Helier and others, and Bill Berry starred as Christopher Popp alongside Ethel Levey, Roy Royston, Dorothy Brown and Bobby Howes, under the direction of Broadway's R H Burnside. Once again, the show ran precisely 140 performances.

UK: Gaiety Theatre 23 December 1925
Recording: selection on *Rudolf Friml in London* (WRC)

BLUE MONDAY Folk opera in 1 act by B G De Sylva. Music by George Gershwin. Globe Theater, New York, August 28 1922.

Gershwin's short, melodramatic folk opera ('Blue Monday Blues', 'Has Anyone Seen My Joe?', 'I'm Gonna See my Mother') was originally played as part of *George White's Scandals of 1922*, but it proved to be too startling

141

and downbeat for the tone of the revue and it was withdrawn after the first night. De Sylva's text was a little tale of jealousy in which Vi, egged on by the villainous Tom, shoots her boyfriend Joe whom she suspects of being unfaithful. The 'other woman' turns out, as in *Iolanthe*, to be, if not a fairy, at least his mother.

The show survived this single performance. It was reorganized and produced at Provincetown (2 June 1932), and again, under the title *135th Street*, at New York's Lincoln Center (20 May 1968) whilst continuing to be a source of fascination to lovers of Gershwin's music.

Germany: Opernstudio, Opernhaus Cologne 16 May 1985
Recordings: (Turnabout, Penzance)

THE BLUE MOON   Musical play in 3 acts by Harold Ellis. Lyrics by Percy Greenbank and Paul Rubens. Music by Howard Talbot and Paul Rubens. Northampton, 29 February 1904; Lyric Theatre, London, 28 August 1905.

A piece in the tradition of *The Geisha*, with a well-used story featuring an oriental singing girl (Florence Smithson), a British naval gentleman (Vernon Davidson) and much comedy (E Statham Staples, Alfred Clarke, Frank Couch), *The Blue Moon* was an early production effort by Gaiety stage-manager Pat Malone and ex-actor turned theatre manager, Robert Courtneidge. An attractive score and a standout performance by petite, dark, stratospherically soprano Miss Smithson in the heroine's rôle made the show a fine success on the road and Courtneidge brought it to town the following year.

Librettist Ellis having died meanwhile, Courtneidge had the show rewritten by his crony Alexander Thompson into something more in the popular musical comedy vein than the original light operatic one, and he cast star comics Willie Edouin (Moolraj the idolmaker, juggler and marriage-broker), Walter Passmore (low-comedy soldier) and Courtice Pounds (oversized and tenorious army Major) at the head of the bill. Miss Smithson was recalled at the last moment to replace a further star name, Ida Rene, and her singing of 'The Poplar and the Rainbow' and 'Little Blue Moon' did much to help the show to success. Elsewhere the comedy was rife, lurching from the topical ('A Good Time in Mars') to the burlesque ('Entertainments'), whilst soubrette Carrie Moore and ingénue Billie Burke were both featured in light numbers.

The Blue Moon did reasonably well in London (182 performances) and was duly sent on the road, with Miss Smithson still starring, in 1906, in three companies in 1907 and into 1908, as well as being taken up for America by the Shubert brothers. With the comic rôle of the private soldier, Charlie Taylor, hugely expanded for the benefit of James T Powers, Ethel Jackson featured in Miss Smithson's rôle, and Arthur Donaldson serenading 'Chandra-Nil, my lotus lily' (G A Spink) in one of the local additions to the score, it played 76 performances on Broadway.

The Blue Moon won more favour in Australia, where it was produced in 1907 by J C Williamson Ltd at Melbourne's Princess Theatre and Sydney's His Majesty's Theatre with Amy Murphy starred as Chandra Nil and Victor Gouriet and Edward Noble heading the English version of the comedy. The show also toured South Africa in 1908 under the management of Frank Wheeler, and was played in India and the East by the Fred Ellis Opera Company, but it remains significant largely in that it brought

together the producer, star and two of the writers who, four years later, would collaborate on the very much more memorable *The Arcadians*.

USA: Casino Theater 3 November 1906; Australia: Princess Theatre, Melbourne 25 June 1907

THE BLUE PARADISE   *see* EIN TAG IM PARADIES

BLUE ROSES   Musical play in 2 acts by Desmond Carter and Caswell Garth. Lyrics by Desmond Carter. Music by Vivian Ellis. Gaiety Theatre, London, 20 January 1931.

Producer Laddie Cliff's attempt to emulate the system initiated at the Gaiety Theatre by Hollingshead and Edwardes, and to create an alternative star team to hold the fort while he took his hit dance-and-laughter musicals on tour, included the production of two shows starring monocled provincial dude comic George Clarke. *Blue Roses*, which reached back in time for a plot which was a little too like the Gaiety's famous old *The Orchid*, boasted a pretty (if short) score, topped by the charming duo 'If I Had Three Wishes', originally performed by Vera Bryer and Roy Royston.

The enterprise proved to be a rather underpowered one and *Blue Roses* failed in 54 performances. However, it was later played successfully in Australia by Cliff's number-one team juvenile dance stars Madge Elliott and Cyril Ritchard in whose hands the piece might have done better in London. The Gaiety 'B' team was soon abandoned.

Australia: Her Majesty's Theatre, Sydney 13 February 1932

THE BLUE TRAIN   *see* MÄDI

BLUM, Ernest   (b Paris, 15 August 1836; d Paris, 18 September 1907).

After his début as a dramatist at the Théâtre des Variétés at the age of 18, Ernest Blum was for many years a supplier of all kinds of theatrical pieces – comedies, dramas, vaudevilles, spectacular féeries, revues and little and large opérettes – to the Paris stage, and a well-known figure in Paris theatre-café society. Albert Vanloo described him as 'un boulevardier impénitent' who, having eaten his supper, would pop into the Théâtre des Variétés for a look at the curtain-raiser. He did not stay for the main piece, as it was his invariable rule to be in bed by nine.

Amongst a plethora of revues and vaudevilles, often written in collaboration with Alexandre Flan, Siraudin and/or Clairville, Blum's earliest attempts in the musical theatre were in the shape of small opérettes and féeries (*L'Escarcelle d'or*, *Cendrillon*, *Le Voyage de Gulliver*), and his first significant success in the field came when he was already in his late thirties with his first full-sized piece, Offenbach's *La Jolie Parfumeuse*. He quickly followed it with an equally successful drama, *Rose Michel*. Blum collaborated on two further pieces with Offenbach (*Bagatelle*, *Belle Lurette*), had a hand in the making of the enormously successful vaudeville-opérette *Lili* (and also, apparently, without credit, of *Mam'zelle Nitouche* and a number of other shows) but, by this stage, he had already begun the partnership with Raoul Toché which was to lead them to a series of comedy successes including *Madame Mongodin* and *Monsieur Coulisset* (both hits at the Théâtre du Vaudeville and then on the international stage), the Palais-Royal comedies *Le Parfum* and *La Maison Tamponin*, as

Plate 29. **Blue Roses**: *George Clarke and the Gaiety chorus line up for a team photo.*

well as the enormously popular *Le Voyage en Suisse*, the pantomime played by the Hanlon Lees company in every corner of the globe in the later years of the 19th century.

The partnership provided the large-scale *Madame l'amiral* and *Les Aventures de Monsieur de Crac* (1886, 157 performances) to the Châtelet, but in general they did a little less well in the musical theatre. They nevertheless found success with the spectacular fantasy *Le Château de Tire-Larigot* and the tale of *Adam et Ève*, both written with the musical collaboration of Gaston Serpette.

After Toché's suicide, Blum worked mostly with Paul Ferrier and/or Pierre Decourcelle, turning out further Châtelet spectaculars, including *Le Petit Chaperon-rouge*, *Robinson Crusoe*, and, most notably, two colourful and successful hodge-podges, *Le Carnet du Diable* and *Le Royaume des femmes*, described as 'neither fairy play nor opérette, nor a spectacle nor vaudeville ... a popular, half-witty nothing full of fun, naughtiness, deviltry and go ... joyous, objectionable ...'.

Apart from *La Jolie Parfumeuse*, these two latter-day pieces proved internationally the most successful of Blum's musical theatre output. *Le Carnet du Diable* became *Cupido & Co* in Berlin and *Das Scheckbuch des Teufels* at Vienna's Danzers Orpheum whilst remusicked versions of his text for *Le Royaume des femmes* were produced as *Das Paradies der Frauen* and *Die verkehrte Welt* in Germany, as *Die verkehrte Welt* at Vienna's Venedig in Wien and as *Felfordult világ* in Hungary.

Several of Blum's most successful comic works later became the bases for musical plays. *La Maison Tamponin* (w Toché) became first *Prima Ballerina* (music: Carl Weinberger, Carltheater 23 November 1895, Thalia-Theater, Berlin 24 October 1896), and then *Auch so Eine!* (Theater in der Josefstadt 18 October 1901), *Madame Mongodin* (*Mrs Ponderbury's Past* in its English-language version) was the source for Richard Carle's American musical comedy *Mary's Lamb* (1908), whilst *Le Parfum* was succesfully made into *Im Pavillon* (Karl Kappeller/ad Lud-

wig Fischl, Alexander Landesberg) and played for 52 consecutive performances at Vienna's Theater in der Josefstadt (6 March 1896).

Alongside his theatrical career, Blum led a parallel career as a journalist (*Charivari*, *Rappel*, *Le Gaulois*), writing on topics from the comical to the stock market, and he also turned out a number of comic and biographical books.

1855 **Latrouillat et Truffaldini** (Hervé/w J Petit) Folies Nouvelles 10 May

1862 **Le Hussard persecuté** (Hervé) Délassements-Comiques 30 May

1862 **La Fanfare de Saint-Cloud** (Hervé/w Paul Siraudin) 1 act Délassements-Comiques 30 May

1864 **La Revue pour rire, ou Roland à Rongeveaux** (Hervé/w Clairville, Siraudin) Théâtre des Bouffes-Parisiens 27 December

1869 **L'Astronome du Pont-Neuf** (Emil Durand/w Jules Prével, Alexandre Flan) 1 act Théâtre des Variétés 18 February

1872 **L'Egyptienne réaliste** (Victor Chéri/w Clairville) 1 act Café Tertulia 20 January

1873 **La Jolie Parfumeuse** (Offenbach/w Hector Crémieux) Théâtre de la Renaissance 29 November

1874 **Bagatelle** (Offenbach/w Crémieux) 1 act Théâtre des Bouffes-Parisiens 21 May

1874 **La Famille Trouillat** (Léon Vasseur/w Crémieux) Théâtre de la Renaissance 10 September

1880 **Belle Lurette** (Offenbach/w Édouard Blau, Raoul Toché) Théâtre de la Renaissance 30 October

1882 **Lili** (Hervé/w Albert Millaud, Maurice Hennequin) Théâtre des Variétés 10 January

1884 **Le Diable au corps** (Romuald Marenco/w Toché) Théâtre des Bouffes-Parisiens 19 December

1884 **Le Château de Tire-Larigot** (Gaston Serpette/w Toché) Théâtre des Nouveautés 30 October

1885 **Mam'zelle Gavroche** (Hervé/w Edmond Gondinet, Albert de Saint-Albin) Théâtre des Variétés 24 January

1885 **Le Petit Chaperon-rouge** (Serpette/w Toché) Théâtre des Nouveautés 10 October

1886 **Adam et Ève** (Serpette/w Toché) Théâtre des Nouveautés 6 October

1889 **Le Royaume des femmes** (pasticcio/Cogniard ad w Toché) Théâtre des Nouveautés

1895 **Le Carnet du Diable** (Serpette/w Paul Ferrier) Théâtre des Variétés 23 October

1896 **Le Carillon** (Serpette/w Ferrier) Théâtre des Variétés 7 November

1896 **Le Royaume des femmes** new version (Serpette/ad w Ferrier) Eldorado 24 February

DIE BLUME VON HAWAII Operette in 3 acts by Alfred Grünwald and Fritz Löhner-Beda. Music by Pál Ábrahám. Neues Theater, Leipzig, 24 July 1931; Metropoltheater, Berlin, 29 August 1931.

Ábrahám's follow-up to his successful *Viktória (und ihr Husar)* swapped that show's Japanese, Russian and Hungarian settings for an equally colourful south seas venue and a final act in a cabaret in Monte Carlo. The principal pair of plot lines centred on the unsuccessful efforts of a local leader to bring the Princess Laya back to the South Pacific to reclaim her hereditary Hawaiian crown and thus thwart American efforts to annex the island, and on the love story between the Princess and her princely cousin, Lilo-Taro.

The show's deliciously eclectic score ranged from the Prince's full-blooded tenor serenades to 'Ein Paradies am Meerestrand' and to his 'Blume von Hawaii' and the Princess's showy 'Traumschöne Perle der Südsee' to some up-to-date 1930s dance rhythms in the soubret pair's 'Ich hab' ein Diwanpüppchen' and 'My Little Boy' and a series of jazzy numbers given to a Jolsonesque cabaret vocalist called Jim-Boy which sported suitably mid-Atlantic titles to go with their catchy tunes – 'My Golden Baby', 'Bin nur ein Jonny', 'Wir singen zur Jazzband im Folies-Bergère'. 'My Golden Baby' proved a sufficiently good imitation of its American models to become a song success in its English-language version.

First produced in Leipzig, the show moved briskly to Berlin where it opened at the Metropoltheater with Annie Ahlers starring as Princess Laya, Alfred Jerger as the tenor prince and Harald Paulsen, Serge Abranovic, Fritz Steiner and Claire Rommer in support. It quickly won success, with most of the loudest plaudits going to the musical score, and was soon reproduced in all the main Continental venues. In Hungary (ad Imre Földes) with Juci Lábass (Laya), Jenő Nador (Lilo-Taro) and Márton Rátkai wearing the black-face of Jim-Boy, it scored a similar success, while the Theater an der Wien's Vienna production played 150 times with Rita Georg and Otto Maran starring, and the Hungarian pair Oszkár Dénes and Rózsi Bársony featured as the jazzy Jim-Boy and the soubrette, Bessy.

A French production (ad Georges Delance) took place as part of a venture to start a new cheap-price musical theatre in Paris. Aimée Mortimer and Régine Marelli shared the rôle of Laya and tenors Max Moutia and Cyprien Delcros did the serenading as part of a project which never really got off the ground. When it sank it took *La Fleur d'Hawaï* with it.

Unlike Ábrahám's other two principal works, *Die Blume von Hawaii* did not travel to English-speaking climes, but it has remained highly popular on the Continent and it remains to this day a regularly played part of the repertoire in Operette houses. Two film versions have been produced under the title, the first by Richard Oswald (1933) starring Márta Eggerth as the Hawaiian princess and the second by

Geza von Cziffra (1953) with Maria Litto as a hopeful actress who stows away on a Hawaii-bound vessel in search of a rôle in a production of *Die Blume von Hawaii* and wins both tenor and triumph.

Hungary: Király Színház *Hawaii Rózsája* 28 January 1932; Austria: Theater an der Wien 19 August 1932; France: L'Alhambra *La Fleur d'Hawaï* 1933; Films: 1933, EOS-Films 1953

Recordings: selection (Philips, EMI Odeon, Eurodisc, Telefunken, Polydor etc), selection in Italian (EDM)

THE BLUSHING BRIDE Musical in 2 acts by Cyrus Wood based on a libretto by Edward Clark and the play *The Third Party* by Brandon and Arthur adapted by Mark Swan. Lyrics by Cyrus Wood. Music by Sigmund Romberg. Astor Theater, New York, 6 February 1922.

A love story set in a cabaret venue proved the opportunity for a musical comedy consisting of little more than a series of comical sketches, songs and speciality acts, pasted around the favourite touring musical-comedy stars Cecil Lean and Cleo Mayfield. He played Coley Collins, a professional gooseberry who dines with couples who should not be dining together alone, who chaperones his clients to the nightclub where the little Quaker girl Lulu Love (Miss Mayfield) looks after the hats and coats department. Comic Tom Lewis appeared as a plump little fellow taking a girl out to dinner and inevitably having his wife turn up. The Swanson sisters, Beatrice and Marcelle, put in an appearance and the vaudeville act, the Glorias, did their well-known routine of ice-skating without any ice. The basic score of the show was topped by 'Love's Highway', 'A Regular Girl' and a quartet about 'Springtime'.

Lee and J J Shubert's production started its life under the title of the original play *The Third Party*. It was next called *Lulu* and equipped with songs by perpetual loser and publicists' darling Gitz Rice (who never went anywhere without his wartime 'Lieutenant' glued to his name) before it came to the stage at Atlantic City (20 September 1920), still with Rice's songs, under the title *The Girl in the Private Room*, with the Swansons teamed with comic Fred Hillebrand and Queenie Smith featured in a toe dance. Title, score and most of the cast all went under the axe before, 17 months later, the piece reached New York equipped with its new accoutrements and enough appeal to last a more than respectable 144 nights on Broadway.

BOBADIL Comic opera in 2 acts by Walter Parke (also given as by L Travelli). Music by Luscombe Searelle. New Opera House, Sydney, 22 November 1884.

The expansive New Zealand-bred Searelle promised and got many international productions for his light operatic variant on the *Abu Hassan* legend following its initial production, in the repertoire seasons of the Majeroni–Wilson Opera Company, in Sydney and Melbourne. Charles Harding (Bobadil), Gracie Plaisted (Princess Zorayda) and Frances Saville (Lulu) headed the original cast, the composer conducted, and, beginning with an eight-weeks run in Sydney, the piece went on to a fine success in Adelaide, in Melbourne (Bijou Theatre 9 May 1885) and throughout Australia.

Bobadil was duly produced by its composer in New Zealand and South Africa, again with some 'success, but although its American production won fair notices (in spite of the fact that the scenery had allegedly not arrived) on its

Plate 30. **Die Blume von Hawaii**: *A little advertising shelters Bessie (Marianne Lang) and Buffy (Hans-Jörg Bock) from the tropical sun, but not from the lassie's papa (Theater Hof, 1986).*

Plate 31. Bob herceg: *Sári Fedák as Prince Bob of England and Gizella Ledofsky as his commoner beloved. They don't seem much more Victorian-Britain than the pretty folk pictured on the fairytale-ish music cover.*

début in Boston, the show had a truncated tour, stopping short of New York. It got just one copyright performance in Britain. A century later, however, it remains the only musical show to have come out of Australia and/or New Zealand to have been played in metropolitan productions in four continents.

USA: Columbia Theater, Boston 5 January 1903; UK: Bijou Theatre, Teddington 4 January 1903

BOB HERCEG Operett (daljáték) in three acts by Károly Bakonyi and Ferenc Martos. Music by Jenő Huszka. Népszinház, Budapest, 20 December 1902.

Jenő Huszka's *Bob herceg*, the most successful Hungarian musical play up to its time, is credited with marking the beginning of what would prove to be the richest period in the Hungarian musical theatre. It was equipped with a libretto by the two best and most successful of Hungary's contemporary musical theatre writers, who chose to set their piece in Great Britain, treating that country in the same sort of way that Western authors did when making operettas out of the things that they imagined might happen in Balkan and Central European kingdoms.

The action takes place in London. George (Sári Fedák), the son of the Queen of England (Sarolta Krecsányi), has the habit of going out into the city, disguised, under the name of 'Bob', as a poor, wandering student. On his ramblings, he meets and falls in love with a girl of the people, the baker's daughter Annie (Gisella Ledofszky). Annie has a suitor, the barber Plumpudding (Antal Nyárai), who is decidedly put out but, like the rest of the townsfolk, fall-to-your-knees stunned when Bob's real identity comes out

one day, in the middle of Bowie-Street (sic). His mother, who is intent that he should marry the Countess Victoria of Clarence (Margit Dóri), finds a son willing to give up his crown and the sword of Saint-George to marry as he will. When the Countess Victoria turns out to be dallying elsewhere, and is clearly only after the crown and not the heart of Prince 'Bob', it is one more step on the way to a happy ending. Géza Rásko played Lord Lancaster, the Captain of the Guard, Mihály Kovács was the Prince's faithful steward, Sir Pomponius, and the landlord of the pub was called Simson Pickwick.

Huszka's score featured some touches of 'Englishness', notably a Guards March chorusing about 'szép Albion' (fair Albion), in a piece whose score was severely devoted to its leading 'man', the heir to the throne of England, as played in travesty by megastar Fedák. She indulged in a drinking song ('Borba fojtom örömem'), a serenade ('Pöngeti, veri, billegeti a lantot ujjam'), a piece about Herkules and Omphale (Dal az Aranyszöke hajszálról, ie the song of the golden-blonde), an aubade (Hajnali dal), the lecke-kuplé (chastizing song) and the Dal az első csókról (Song of the first kiss).

The Népszinház's production of *Bob herceg* was a huge hit. It ran quickly to its 100th performance (8 April) and ended up playing a first run of 134 nights, outstripping every Operette, foreign or home-made, since *Rip*, 20 years earlier. It was quickly brought into the repertoire at the new Király Színház (12 May 1905), and won regular productions in Hungary thereafter (Városi Színház 20 November 1926, etc). It also visited Vienna, when a German-language version (ad Max Neal, Konrad Dreher) was mounted by Karczag and Wallner at the Theater an der

Wien. Gerda Walde played the travesty Prince, with Sarolta von Rettich-Birk as his mother, Ida Lorenz as Annie and Annie Wünsch as Countess Victoria, whilst the house's two actor-librettists, Bodanzky and Brammer, supported as Lord Southwell, royal master of Ceremonies, and Marshall Lord Bevis. *Prinz Bob* was, however, played only ten times. Henry Savage purchased the piece for America, but does not seem to have ever got it to the stage, and *Bob herceg* has remained a favourite only in its home country.

Austria: Theater an der Wien *Prinz Bob* (*Der Gassenkönig*) 23 September 1905
Recording: selection (Qualiton)

BOB'S YOUR UNCLE   Musical farce in 2 acts by Austin Melford. Lyrics by Frank Eyton. Music by Noel Gay. Saville Theatre, London, 5 May 1948.

Leslie Henson and Vera Pearce headed the romping through this latter-day musical farce which was one of the most successful examples of its kind in 1940s London. He played Uncle Bob Popejoy, she was the overaged and oversexed Mrs Edgoose, both tangled up in the wedding of Hector (Gordon Humphris) and June (Valerie Tandy), which old-flame Dick (Hamish Menzies) is trying to stop until he meets Sheila (Sheila Douglas-Pennant) in time for the final curtain.

The score provided some humorous numbers, notably Miss Pearce's ludicrously imaginative 'He Loves Me' and her duet with Henson 'Like Me a Little Bit More' as the show careered through a ten-month run (363 performances) and commensurate touring which marked one of the last successes for its comical kind of show before the onset of the new wave of romantic musicals.

BOCCACCIO   Operette in 3 acts by F Zell and Richard Genée. Music by Franz von Suppé. Carltheater, Vienna, 1 February 1879.

Franz von Suppé followed up his first great success with a full-length Operette, *Fatinitza*, with a second, three years later. *Boccaccio*'s neatly constructed text was allegedly borrowed from an unspecified theatre piece by Bayard, de Leuwen and de Beauplan, but, in any case, it used some plot motifs from one of the chapters of the real Boccaccio's famous work, the collection of often ribald tales known as *The Decameron*. It had, otherwise, little enough to do with the historical Italian author, Giovanni Boccaccio (1313–1375), for whom it was named – a trend which would long persist in the musical theatre – but at least his name supplied a nicely recognizable and slightly suggestive title.

Giovanni Boccaccio (Antonie Link) is a poet and novelist who takes the plots for his tales of duped husbands and faithless women from life and from his experience of it. This is an excellent excuse for making off with any available 14th-century Florentine wives (other people's) he can. The latest is Beatrice (Frln Bisca), wife of Scalza (Hildebrandt), the barber. However, Boccaccio is all swept away when he sees the unmarried Fiametta (Rosa Streitmann), the foster-daughter of the grocer Lambertuccio (Karl Blasel) and Peronella (Therese Schäfer), little knowing that she is really the farmed-out daughter of the Duke of Tuscany. Pietro, Prince of Palermo (Franz Tewele), a royal with an itch to be an author like Boccaccio, comes to Florence incognito in search of some 'real life', and the writer and his friends take him on a jaunt with Isabella (Regine Klein), the wife of the cooper, Lotteringhi (Franz Eppich), which ends up with the Prince hidden in a barrel to escape the jealous husband. Boccaccio himself, caught kissing Fiametta, persuades the foolish grocer that his olive

Plate 32. Boccaccio: *Whilst Boccaccio (Manfred Kusch) woos his Fiametta (Anne-Hagan Rentz), the comical action of the night pursues its merry way in a pretty production at the Landestheater, Schleswig-Holstein.*

tree has hallucinatory powers. But Fiametta now has to go home, to marry a royal husband. Fortunately the choice is none other than Pietro, who is able to hand her over to her slightly reformed Boccaccio. The final act, set in the Tuscan court, justified the poet's presence by positing that he had been hired to write and stage an entertainment for the royal betrothal. That entertainment, when given, took the form of a moral commedia dell'arte piece in which the principal comedians took part: Blasel as Pantalone, Eppich as Brighella, Hildebrandt as Narcissino, with the young Carl Streitmann as Arlecchino and Frln Pöth as Colombina.

Suppé's score was a worthy successor to that for *Fatinitza*, featuring such winning romantic numbers as Boccaccio and Fiametta's waltzing third-act 'Florenz hat schöne Frauen', their second-act duo 'Nur ein Wort' and the serenade 'Ein Stern zu sein', alongside a tunefully winsome yet amusing trio ('Wonnervolle Kunde, neu belebend') in which Fiametta, Isabella and Peronella read the love/sex-notes hurled at their feet, wrapped around stones by Boccaccio, Pietro and Leonetto, the march septet ('Ihr Toren, ihr wollt hassen mich') leading up to the conclusion of the show, and some substantial and substantially written finales. The comical highlight of the piece was the song of the cooper, banging away at his barrel-making to drown out his wife's nagging ('Tatäglich zankt mein Weib'), whilst the other cuckolded husbands also had their moments of fun, as in the opening act when Scalza and his friends serenade his wife to the plunking of his umbrella ('Holde Schöne'). The quality of the score for the second and, particularly, the third act – an act often used in Operette simply to briefly tie up the ends – helped to give *Boccaccio* an additional shapely strength.

Boccaccio was a splendid success at the Carltheater. It was played 32 times en suite before Antonie Link went into retirement and left her rôle to Regine Klein, and no fewer than 80 times by the end of the year. The 115th performance was played on 3 October 1881, by which time *Boccaccio* had become established as an international hit of some scope, but the Carltheater then curiously let the piece drop from its repertoire and thereafter it appeared there only intermittently (matinées in 1906 and 1922, 16 October 1923 w Erika Wagner and Christl Mardayn). The other Viennese theatres, however, snapped the show up and *Boccaccio* was mounted at the Theater an der Wien in 1882 (16 September) with Karoline Finaly in the title rôle, Alexander Girardi as Pietro, Carl Adolf Friese (Scalza), Josef Joseffy (Lotteringhi), Felix Schweighofer (Lambertuccio), Marie-Therese Massa (Beatrice) and with Fr Schäfer and Frln Streitmann in their original rôles. A new production was staged there in 1885, Julie Kronthal was Boccaccio in 1891 and the piece reappeared in 1901 and 1907. It also appeared at the Venedig in Wien summer theatre in 1899 (5 July), entered the Volksoper in 1908 (10 November) and played at the Johann Strauss-Theater in 1911, whilst Paula Zulka starred as Boccaccio at the Raimundtheater in 1915 (2 January).

Subsequent to this merry run of performances, *Boccaccio* began to suffer under the hands of the 'improvers' and, for a show which won such success on its initial productions and has ever since been quoted as one of the classic comic operas of its period, it has since been chopped-up, deconstructed and musically maltreated more often that would have been expected. A version which aimed to operaticize a show which was very far from being an opera, replacing dialogue with recitative and tacking in extraneous bits of Suppé music, was done by Artur Bodanzky and, after being seen at New York's Metropolitan Opera House in 1931, was staged at the Vienna Staatsoper, in each case with Maria Jeritza as Boccaccio. Another heavily remade version (ad Adolf Rott, Friedrich Shreyvogel, musical ad Anton Paulik, Rudolf Kattnigg) also gained currency and royalties for its remakers and publishers for a while, and the trend has continued in Vienna to the present day, where the most recent Volksoper production, whilst eschewing recitative, turned what remained of the piece (ad Torsten Fischer) from a comic opera into shapeless black-and-scowling melodrama, simply altering or cutting any portion of text or score which did not fit into the unimaginative 1960s-style 'concept' imposed by its director/adapter. Amongst the other unnecessary (although not unprecedented) alterations made, Boje Skovhus, who played the mangled rôle of Boccaccio, was not a mezzo-soprano.

Boccaccio followed up its original success in Vienna with another in Germany and a huge one in Budapest (ad Lajos Evva). Produced at the Népszinház with Lujza Blaha in the title rôle, and Elek Solymossy (Pietro), Mariska Komáromi (Fiametta), János Kápolnai (Lotteringhi), Zsófi Csatay (Isabella) and Emilia Sziklai (Beatrice) amongst the cast, it raced to its 50th performance (30 October 1880), was revived in 1882 (11 October), 1883 (11 September), 1887 (14 January) and 1889 (2 May w Aranka Hegyi), passed its hundredth performance on 9 May 1890, and was reprised again on 1 October 1904, running up a record which only *Les Cloches de Corneville*, *Der Zigeunerbaron* and *Rip van Winkle* amongst early musical plays equalled in the Hungarian capital. It found its way also into other houses, and in 1922 Juci Lábass starred in a revival at the Városi Színház.

Following its first German production, in Frankfurt, the original version was quickly seen in Prague (23 March 1880), Nuremberg (4 April 1880), Berlin and at New York's Thalia Theater where Mathilde Cottrelly donned the poet's breeches. The first English version appeared on Broadway only weeks after this, when Jeannie Winston appeared as Boccaccio at the Union Square Theater with Mahn's English Opera Company. She reprised the show the following year (Niblo's Garden 17 November 1881), by which time the Boston Ideal Company had another version, entitled *The Prince of Palermo, or the Students of Florence* (ad Dexter Smith), prominently displayed in their repertoire and Emilie Melville had appeared at San Francisco's Bush Theater and on the road in an Oscar Weil/G Heinrichs adaptation. In 1888 (Wallack's Theater 11 March) the piece got a high-class revival from the De Wolf Hopper company with the star as Lambertuccio to the Boccaccio of Marion Manola, the Scalza of Jeff de Angelis, the Lotteringhi of Digby Bell and the Peronella of Laura Joyce Bell. Broadway saw *Boccaccio* again (ad H B Smith) when Fritzi Scheff took on the rôle at the Broadway Theatre in 1905 (27 February) before Bodanzky and the Metropolitan Opera brought their operaticky version to the New York stage.

It was 1882 before London saw its first *Boccaccio* (ad H B

Farnie, Robert Reece) at the Comedy Theatre with Violet Cameron starred in the title-rôle alongside Alice Burville (Fiametta), J G Taylor (Pietro), Lionel Brough (Lambertuccio), W S Rising (Leonetto), Louis Kelleher (Lotteringhi), Kate Munroe (Isabella) and Rosa Carlingford (Peronella). It had, of course, been previously pillaged by the pasticcio-makers of London, and the Alhambra production of *Babil and Bijou*, running concurrently with Alexander Henderson's production, was using no less than five numbers lifted from Suppé's score. This preview didn't seem to harm the show's prospects, for the Comedy Theatre production ran for an excellent 129 straight performances before the theatre was shut for repairs, and it returned thereafter to carry on for nearly another month until the new *Rip van Winkle* was ready. It was brought back to the same house in 1885 (30 May) when Miss Cameron repeated her rôle opposite the young Marie Tempest (Fiametta) and Arthur Roberts (Lambertuccio) for a brief season.

Australia welcomed Emilie Melville and her version 'as sung more than 300 times by her in America' with Armes Beaumont (Pietro), Annie Leaf (Fiametta) and Mrs J H Fox (Isabella) in support, and this was followed into town by the Reece and Farnie version, played by Alfred Dunning's London Comic Opera Company with Kate Chard, and advertised as 'in no way similar' to the American *Boccaccio*! Australia thereafter saw the piece regularly for a number of years, played in various comic opera companies' repertoires.

As was so often the case, *Boccace* (ad Henri Chivot, Alfred Duru) reached Brussels in its French version (Galeries Saint-Hubert 3 February 1882) before moving into Paris. In the Folies-Dramatiques production Mlle Montbazon starred in the title-rôle to the Orlando (ex-Pietro) of Désiré, with Luco, Lepers and Maugé in the other male rôles and Berthe Thibault as Béatrice (ex-Fiametta) as the show added one more success to its international list. It was revived in Paris in 1896 with Anna Tariol-Baugé, in 1914 (Théâtre de la Gaîté-Lyrique) with Jane Alstein and again in 1921 with Marthe Chenal starred.

Boccaccio has continued to win revivals, if all too frequently in botched versions, in both opera and operetta houses in Europe, as well as being the subject of a justifiable quota of recordings. A film version which was produced in 1936 with Willi Fritsch playing *Boccaccio* seems, on the evidence of that casting, as if it probably didn't stick very close to the original.

The title was re-used for an American musical (Richard Peaslee/Kenneth Cavander) based on tales from *The Decameron* and played for seven performances at the Edison Theater in 1975 (24 November), whilst a number of other musical shows have been announced over the years as being 'based on a tale by Boccaccio'. At some periods, such an announcement would seem to have been nothing but a way of adding the respectability of a dead, foreign, classic (if sex-centred) author to a libretto which got closer to other parts of the body than to the knuckle. Others merely used a pale and proper outline of Boccacio's tales. The poet is credited, amongst others, as source on the highly successful French comic opera *Le Coeur et la main* (Lecocq/Charles Nuitter, Alexandre Beaumont, Théâtre des Nouveautés 19 October 1882), Lecocq's little

Gandolfo, in tandem with Shakespeare as the bases of the libretto to Audran's *Gillette de Narbonne*, and on a *Malbruck*, written by Angelo Nessi and composed by Ruggiero Leoncavallo (Teatro Nazionale, Rome 19 January 1910).

Germany: Viktoria Theater, Frankfurt 13 March 1879, Friedrich-Wilhelmstädtisches Theater 20 September 1879; Hungary: Népszinház 1 October 1879; USA: Thalia Theater 23 April 1880, Union Square Theater (Eng) 15 May 1880; France: Théâtre des Folies-Dramatiques 29 March 1882; UK: Comedy Theatre 22 April 1882; Australia: Opera House, Melbourne 2 September 1882; Film: Herbert Maisch 1936

Recordings: complete (EMI), selections (Philips, Eurodisc etc), selection in Hungarian (Qualiton, part record)

BOCK, Jerry [BOCK, Jerrold Lewis] (b New Haven, Conn, 23 November 1928). Composer of one of Broadway's greatest hits who closed up shop in his mid-forties.

Following music studies at the University of Wisconsin, Bock began his career as a composer writing material for college and camp shows, for radio, television and revue, making his first appearance on the Broadway stage when three numbers written in collaboration with Larry Holofcener were used in the revue *Catch a Star* in 1955. He subsequently contributed to the resuscitated *Ziegfeld Follies* (1957), but in between times had provided the score for his first Broadway musical, the Sammy Davis jr vehicle, *Mr Wonderful*. *Mr Wonderful* provided not only a certain Broadway success (383 performances) but also gave its songwriters two numbers – 'Too Close for Comfort' and the show's title-song – which proved hits both in the hands of the original artists and as recorded by Miss Peggy Lee.

Bock subsequently began a working partnership with lyricist Sheldon Harnick, from which the first musical theatre score to emerge was that for the short-lived prize-fighting musical *The Body Beautiful* (60 performances), but their second collaboration on *Fiorello!* ('Little Tin Box'), a biomusical of New York's former Mayor La Guardia, brought them a considerable hit, with a run of nearly 800 Broadway performances. A more conventional politics-and-prostitutes musical, *Tenderloin* (1960), from the same writing team, did a little less well, but the pair compounded their success with the smaller-scale *She Loves Me* (1963), an adaptation of an Hungarian play already played in English both on the stage and screen.

The year after *She Loves Me*, however, Bock and Harnick topped all their previous successes when they combined on the score for *Fiddler on the Roof* ('Matchmaker', 'Sunrise, Sunset', 'If I Were a Rich Man' etc). A record-breaking hit on Broadway, *Fiddler on the Roof* this time gave the composer a show success beyond America, as it established itself throughout the world as a classic of the modern musical theatre and a solid part of the basic repertoire wherever the musical theatre is performed.

Two further stage works, the three one-act plays of *The Apple Tree* (1966) and another Jewish saga of adversity, *The Rothschilds* (1970), both won good Broadway runs and further productions within America but, oddly, in view of the vast success of *Fiddler on the Roof* in other areas, they – like Bock's pre-*Fiddler on the Roof* shows – did not find the same acceptance elsewhere.

Amongst Bock's other works have been included the short film score *Wonders of Manhattan* (1956), the puppet musical *Man in the Moon* (1963) for Bill and Cora Baird's marionettes, incidental music for *Generation* (1965), and a television musical version of *The Canterville Ghost* (2 November 1966 w Harnick).

1956 **Mr Wonderful** (w Larry Holofcener, George Weiss/ Joseph Stein, Will Glickman) Broadway Theater 22 March
1958 **The Body Beautiful** (Sheldon Harnick/Stein, Glickman) Broadway Theater 23 January
1959 **Fiorello!** (Harnick/Jerome Weidman, George Abbott) Broadhurst Theater 23 November
1960 **Tenderloin** (Harnick/Abbott, Weidman) 46th Street Theater 17 October
1963 **She Loves Me** (Harnick/Joe Masteroff) Eugene O'Neill Theater 23 April
1964 **Fiddler on the Roof** (Harnick/Stein) Imperial Theater 22 September
1966 **The Apple Tree** (Harnick/w Harnick, Jerome Cooper-smith) Shubert Theater 16 October
1970 **The Rothschilds** (Harnick/Sherman Yellen) Lunt-Fontanne Theater 19 October

BODANZKY, Robert (b Vienna, 20 March 1879; d Berlin, 2 November 1923). One of the most successful librettists of the 20th-century Viennese stage.

At first an actor, Bodanzky was, like fellow librettist Julius Brammer, for a while a bit-part player at the Theater an der Wien where he appeared in 1904–5 in *Das Garnisonsmädel* (von Czapszynski), *Pufferl* (A Frenchman), *Prinz Bob* (Lord Southwell), *Vergeltsgott* (Police Commissioner), *Der Rebell* (Ein Chauffeur), *Die Fledermaus* (Marquis Carriconi), *Die Geisha* (Bronville), *Wiener Blut* (Graf Bitowsky) and the original production of *Die lustige Witwe* (Pritschitsch). It was at that same house that his first stage pieces were mounted: the little *Phryne* – later seen at Frankfurt's Intimes-Theater – in the studio theatre Hölle and the children's piece *Peter und Paul reisen ins Schlaraffenlund* as a Christmas entertainment in the main house for three successive years.

Pieces such as the joky little one-acter *Mitislaw der moderne*, the internationally played Felix Albini Operette *Baron Trenck* with its Croatian military-romantic libretto, and Ziehrer's *Liebeswalzer*, which played more than a hundred times at the Raimundtheater before, like *Baron Trenck*, going on to be seen on Broadway, established him within a couple of years as a top-flight librettist, and the vast success of his German-language adaptation of Kálmán's *Tátarjárás* (*Ein Herbstmanöver*) at the Theater an der Wien put the seal on his status. Thereafter, Bodanzky contributed to many of the most successful Operetten of his time, turning the libretto for the failed *Die Göttin der Vernunft* into the much more felicitous text to Lehár's *Der Graf von Luxemburg* and inventing the tempestuous *Zigeunerliebe*, *Eva* and *Endlich allein* for that same composer, the almost-féerique *Die schöne Risette* for Leo Fall, the long-running *Rund um die Liebe*, *Eine Ballnacht* and *Dorfmusikanten* for Oscar Straus, *Hanni geht tanzen*, *Wenn zwei sich lieben* (*Julicka* in Italy, *Lieutenant Gus* in America) and many others for Edmund Eysler, *Auf Befehl der Herzogin* for Bruno Granichstädten, *Marietta* for Walter Kollo and *Der Tanz ins Glück* and *Die Tanzgräfin* for Robert Stolz, as well as many other pieces which, if not the national and international hits that these were, did well enough in one or several productions: Reinhardt's *Prinzess Gretl* (156 performances at the Theater an der Wien), Benatzky's *Yuschi tanzt* (109 performances), Acher's *Was Mädchen träumen* (more than 100 performances), Straus's *Nachtfalter* (99 performances), *Die Liebe geht um!* (92 performances at the Raimundtheater and the Bürgertheater), Kálmán's *Der kleine König* (70 performances) and Eysler's *Das Zirkuskind* (77 performances), not to mention his German versions of the Hungarian hits *Szbill*, *Az ezüst sirály*, *Offenbach* and *Mágnás Miska*.

Bodanzky died at the age of 44, having contributed a remarkable amount – including a certain amount of originality in an era when that quality was not always present in operettic libretti – to the Viennese musical stage. However, of his many successful shows, only those with the name of Lehár attached to them – principally *Der Graf von Luxemburg* and *Zigeunerliebe* – have survived into the standard repertoire.

The libretto to the 1931 'Wiener Operette' *Mädel aus Wien* (Heinrich Strecker/Jo Gribitz, Fritz Gerold, Bürgertheater) was noted as being 'nach Bodanzky', and his name also appeared in a similar capacity on the bill for Stolz's *Hallo! Das ist die Liebe* (w Bruno Hardt-Warden ad Hugo Wiener) a remake of *Der Tanz ins Glück* produced at the Raimundtheater (4 January 1958).

1906 **Phryne** (Edmund Eysler/w Fritz Grünbaum) 1 act Hölle 6 October
1906 **Peter und Paul reisen ins Schlaraffenland** (Franz Lehár/w Grünbaum) Theater an der Wien 1 December
1907 **Ein Rendezvous** (Béla Laszky) 1 act Hölle 1 October
1907 **Mitislaw der Moderne** (Lehár/w Grünbaum) 1 act Hölle 5 January
1907 **Amor in Panoptikon** (Laszky) 1 act (puppet-musical) Hölle 1 November
1908 **Baron Trenck** (Felix Albini/w A M Willner) Stadttheater, Leipzig 15 February
1908 **Der Liebeswalzer** (Carl Michael Ziehrer/w Grünbaum) Raimundtheater 24 October
1908 **Loreley** (Laszky) 1 act Hölle 31 January
1909 **Ein Herbstmanöver** (*Tatárjárás*) German version (Theater an der Wien)
1909 **Die kleine Baroness** (Albini) 1 act Apollotheater 31 March
1909 **Der Graf von Luxemburg** (Franz Lehár/w Willner) Theater an der Wien 12 November
1910 **Zigeunerliebe** (Lehár/w Willner) Carltheater 8 January
1910 **Das Glücksmädel** (Robert Stolz/w Friedrich Thelen) Raimundtheater 28 October
1910 **Die schöne Risette** (Leo Fall/w Willner) Theater an der Wien 19 November
1911 **Das Zirkuskind** (Eysler/w Thelen) Raimundtheater 18 February
1911 **Eva** (Lehár/w Willner) Theater an der Wien 24 November
1911 **Casimirs Himmelfahrt** (Bruno Granichstädten/w Willner) Raimundtheater 25 December
1912 **Der kleine König** (*A kis király*) (Emmerich Kálmán/Károly Bakonyi, Ferenc Martos ad) Theater an der Wien 23 November
1913 **Prinzess Gretl** (Heinrich Reinhardt/w Willner) Theater an der Wien 31 January
1913 **Leute vom Stand** (Fall/w Grünbaum) 1 act Hölle 1 March
1914 **Endlich allein** (Lehár/w Willner) Theater an der Wien 30 January
1914 **Rund um die Liebe** (Oscar Straus/w Thelen) Johann Strauss-Theater 9 November
1915 **Auf Befehl des Herzogin** (Granichstädten/w Leopold Jacobson) Theater an der Wien 20 March
1915 **Wenn zwei sich lieben** (Eysler/w Willner) Theater an der Wien 29 October
1916 **Warum geht's denn jetzt?** (Eysler/w Jacobson) Bundestheater 5 July

1916 **Hanni geht tanzen** (Eysler) Apollotheater 7 November

1916 **Der Pusztakavalier** (*Mágnás Miska*) German version (Komische Oper, Berlin)

1917 **Nachtfalter** (Straus/w Jacobson) Ronacher 13 March

1918 **Walzerliebe** (Granichstädten/w Granichstädten) Apollotheater 16 February

1918 **Die Modebaronin** (Richard Goldberger/w Hans Sassmann) Konzerthaus 1 March

1918 **Eine Ballnacht** (Straus/w Jacobson) Johann Strauss-Theater 11 October

1919 **Sybill** [*Szibill*] German version (Stadttheater)

1919 **Der Liebesteufel** (Julius Bistron/w Jacobson) Komödienhaus 17 October

1919 **Dorfmusikanten** (Straus/w Jacobson) Theater an der Wien 29 November

1919 **Was Mädchen träumen** (Leo Ascher/w Jacobson) Raimundtheater 6 December

1920 **Yuschi tanzt** (Ralph Benatzky/w Jacobson) Wiener Bürgertheater 3 April

1920 **Liebesrausch** (*Az ezüst sirály*) German version (Carltheater)

1920 **Der Tanz ins Glück** (Robert Stolz/w Bruno Hardt-Warden) Raimundtheater 23 December

1921 **Die Tanzgräfin** (Stolz/w Jacobson) Wallner-Theater, Berlin 18 February

1921 **Indische Nächte** (Granichstädten/w Hardt-Warden) Apollotheater 25 November

1921 **Eine Sommernacht** (Stolz/w Hardt-Warden) Johann Strauss-Theater 23 December

1922 **Die Liebe geht um!** (Stolz/w Hardt-Warden) Raimundtheater 22 June

1922 **Offenbach** (aka *Der Meister von Montmartre*) German version w Hardt-Warden (Neues Wiener Stadttheater)

1923 **Marietta** (Walter Kollo/w Hardt-Warden, Willi Kollo) Metropoltheater, Berlin 22 December

THE BOHEMIAN GIRL
Opera in 4 acts by Alfred Bunn. Music by Michael Balfe. Theatre Royal, Drury Lane, London, 27 November 1843.

The most popular of the many so-called operatic works of the composer Balfe, *The Bohemian Girl* was part of a small group of English-language musical plays of the mid-19th century which became frequently played favourites. This group formed the backbone of the repertoires of the touring English opera companies which provided the basic musical theatre entertainment of British provincial and colonial towns for many years before the introduction of opéra-bouffe. Along with such pieces as *Maritana* and *The Lily of Killarney*, *The Bohemian Girl* was one of the most important pieces in a tradition which subsequently provided the bases for the romantic and sentimental portions of those comic operas (not always as comic, at least in part, as their description might hint) which were the principal fodder of the musical theatre of the third quarter of the 19th century.

The Bohemian Girl was a romantic tale of a girl, Arline, rescued from a stag by a noble Polish exile, Thaddeus, and carried off by his gipsy friends. Restored many years later to her family, she finally weds her rescuer in spite of the machinations of the gipsy queen. Balfe's attractive score, more in what would now be considered a light operatic vein, included the soprano 'I Dreamt That I Dwelt in Marble Halls', the most popular English show song of its time, as well as several other song hits, notably the lovely 'The Heart Bowed Down' and 'When Other Lips'.

The thousands of performances given *The Bohemian Girl*

around the world, in a multiplicity of languages, ensured that it would come into the hands of the burlesque writers. The best-known amongst such efforts included the brothers Brough's *Arline, or The Fortunes and Vicissitudes of a Bohemian Girl* (Haymarket Theatre 21 April 1851) with Priscilla Horton as Thaddeus, William Best and Henry Bellingham's *Arline, the Lost Child, or The Pole, the Policeman and the Polar Bear* (Sadler's Wells 23 July 1864), W S Gilbert's *The Merry Zingara!, or the Tipsy Gipsy and the Pipsy-wipsy!* (Royalty Theatre 21 March 1868) in which Pattie Oliver featured as a burlesque Arline, and H J Byron's *The Bohemian G'yurl and the Unapproachable Pole* (Opera Comique 31 January 1877) in England and New York's highly successful *The Bohea Man's Girl* (Olympic Theater 11 March 1845). Emma Taylor and Mary Taylor were duplicate Arlines and Charles Walcot played Floorstain in a version which made great play with the terms of the tea trade.

In 1934 an updated version of the show, re-set in America, was staged briefly at Broadway's Lyric Theater under the title *Gypsy Blonde* (F Gabrielson/K Jones 25 April).

USA: Park Theater 25 November 1844; Australia: Royal Victoria Theatre, Sydney 13 July 1846; Austria: Theater an der Wien *Die Zigeunerin* 22 July 1846; Germany: Hamburg *Die Zigeunerin* 17 December 1846; France: Rouen *La Bohémienne* 23 April 1862

Recording: selection (part record) (HMV) etc

BOHEMIOS
Zarzuela in 1 act by Guillermo Perrín and Miguel Palacios. Music by Amadeo Vives. Teatro de la Zarzuela, 24 March 1904.

An un-Spanish kind of zarzuela, with a libretto set in period Paris, *Bohemios* nevertheless found itself a fine degree of popularity in its own country. Perrín and Palacios turned out one of those familiar tales of genius starving in a Montmartre garret of which the composer Roberto and his poet pal Victor, writing The Great Opera, and the old singer Marcelo coaching his soprano daughter, Cossette, for fame, were the principals. A nice chap called Girard helps out, and when Cossette does her audition at the Opéra-Comique, accompanied by Roberto and singing his music, the garret goes out the window and wedding bells fly in.

BOHRMANN, Heinrich
(b Saarbrücken, 28 May 1838; d Vienna, 8 October 1908).

Playwright and librettist, Bohrmann wrote several comedies and Operetten for the Viennese stage in collaboration with 'J Riegen', otherwise Julius Nigri von Saint-Albino (1849–1895), whilst working variously as a theatre director at the Komische Oper in Pressburg, as the editor of Vienna's *Wiener Almanach* (1893–9) and subsequently of the fashion magazine *Im Boudoir* (1900–7).

The pair's two works for the Viennese theatre brought them one fine success – with a little help from a more professional rewriter in Richard Genée – with Strauss's *Das Spitzentuch der Königin*, and a more moderate result with Josef Bayer's *Der Chevalier von San Marco*, played first at the Carltheater and subsequently at New York's Thalia Theater (30 January 1882). The following year, the Thalia also mounted another Bohrmann–Riegen piece, set to music by the house's musical director, Engländer. *Der Prinz Gemahl* did well enough to be seen later outside New

York, and at Broadway's Wallack's Theater in an English translation. Bohrmann also authored an adaptation of Wilson Barret's *The Sign of the Cross* as 'an historical tableau of the time of the Emperor Nero in 5 acts and 9 scenes' with songs and music by William Rose and the text for Hugo Kobler's opera *Grüne Ostern* (Brunn 22 April 1899).

Riegen collaborated intermittently with other authors, including Richard Genée with whom he wrote the libretti for Czibulka's successful *Pfingsten in Florenz* and for Tomaschek's opera *Die Teufelsbrucke* (Pilsen, 1892), whilst Bohrmann also ventured some other pieces without his habitual partner. None, however, came up to their first musical piece as a team.

1880 **Das Spitzentuch der Königin** (Johann Strauss/w Riegen, Richard Genée) Theater an der Wien 1 October

1882 **Der Chevalier von San Marco** (Josef Bayer/w Riegen) Carltheater 7 November

1883 **Der Prinz Gemahl** (*The Prince Consort*) (Ludwig Engländer/ w Julius Hopp, Riegen) Thalia Theater, New York, 11 April

1886 **Der schöne Kurfürst** (Josef Hellmesberger/w Riegen) Theater am Gärtnerplatz, Munich 15 May

1891 **Der Gouverneur von Tours** (Carl Reinecke) Schwerin 20 November

1895 **Figaro bei Hof** (Alfred Müller-Norden/w Riegen) Centraltheater, Berlin 4 May

1897 **Ein Traum** (Max von Weinzierl/w Marko Bombelles) Raimundtheater 4 March

1901 **Djellah** (Rodolphe Weys) Lübeck April

BOLGER, Ray[mond Wallace] (b Dorchester, Mass, 10 January 1904; d Los Angeles, 15 January 1987).

A warmly funny dancing comedian, Bolger appeared on Broadway in *The Merry World* (1926), in a supporting rôle in the musical comedy *Heads Up!* (1929, Georgie) and in the revues *George White's Scandals* (1931) and *Life Begins at 8:40* (1934), before scoring a memorable success in the rôle of Phil Dolan III, the composer and teacher of popular music who gets mixed up with the ballet world in Rodgers and Hart's musical *On Your Toes* ('There's a Small Hotel', 'On Your Toes') in 1936.

Bolger subsequently appeared in further revues (*Keep Off the Grass*, *Three to Make Ready*) and introduced two further large leading rôles in musical comedies: as the henpecked Sapiens in Rodgers and Hart's *By Jupiter* (1942), and as the character called Charley Wykeham (who was actually a combination of the original Charley and the disguisable Lord Fancourt-Babberley) in the musical remake of *Charley's Aunt* called *Where's Charley?* (1948, 'Once in Love With Amy', Tony Award). He repeated his rôle in this last piece on film, having previously, in a dozen years in films, played in such pieces as *The Great Ziegfeld* (1936 as himself), *Rosalie* (1937), *Sweethearts* (1938), most memorably as the scarecrow in *The Wizard of Oz* (1939), *Sunny* (1941 as Bunny Billings), *The Harvey Girls* (1946), and *Look for the Silver Lining* (1949 as Jack Donahue).

He later appeared as Uncle Barnaby in the 1960 film version of *Babes in Toyland* and returned to the stage in two further musicals, *All American* (1962, Professor Fodroski) and *Come Summer* (1969, Phineas Sharp), in the later days of a career which frittered into nightclubs, concert and some television appearances and left the impression of having deserved more and, generally, better musical theatre rôles.

BOLTEN-BÄCKERS, Heinrich ('Heinz') [BOLTEN, Heinrich Eduard Hermann] (b Chemnitz, 10 April 1871; d Dresden, 30 January 1938). Author of the Berlin Apollotheater's series of turn-of-the-century Revue-operetten.

Born in Chemnitz but brought up in Dresden, Bolten became dramaturg at the Ostend Theater in his early twenties and it was there that his first pieces, *Berlin unter Wasser* and *Ein alter Spielmann*, were staged. He mixed theatrical occupations through the 1890s, adapting French operas (*L'Attaque du moulin*, *La Vivandière*), opérettes and vaudevilles for various German and Austrian theatres, writing German libretti for the operas of Urich (*Das Glockenspiel* 1895, *Der Lootse* Hamburg 26 September 1895), directing a touring theatre company, and working for a while at the Scala Theater in Cologne, before combining with his old colleague, Paul Lincke, formerly an orchestral player at the Ostend Theater and now reaching out as a composer, to write the short revue-Operette *Venus auf Erden* for the programe of Berlin's variety-based Apollotheater. Although he continued adaptation work in the straight theatre, providing German versions of the works of Pinero and other important writers, his musical theatre output thereafter was almost entirely devoted to supplying texts for Lincke, with whom he scored considerable successes with a series of further short spectaculars for the Apollotheater: *Frau Luna*, *Lysistrata* (Glühhwurmchen Idyll) and *Im Reiche des Indra*.

Bolten otherwise devoted himself to theatre management in Berlin, to high-profile activity in the German Authors and Composers' Association, and to ventures into early film production.

1895 **Die kleinen Schäfen** (*Les Petites Brebis*) German version (Theater in der Josefstadt)

1896 **Cousin-Cousine** German version (Thalia-Theater)

1897 **Der verregnete Amor** (aka *Der Liebesgott*) (*L'Amour mouillé*) German version (Theater an der Wien)

1897 **Venus auf Erden** (Lincke) Apollotheater, Berlin 11 May

1898 **Das neue Regiment** (*Le Nouveau Regiment*) German version (Theater in der Josefstadt)

1898 **Die kleinen Michus** (*Les P'tites Michu*) German version w Julius Freund (Metropoltheater, Berlin)

1899 **Brigitte** (*Véronique*) German version (Neues Königliches Operntheater, Berlin)

1899 **Die weisse Henne** (*La Poule blanche*) German version (Lustspieltheater)

1899 **Le Cabinet Piperlin** German version (Lustspieltheater)

1899 **Frau Luna** (Lincke) 1 act Apollotheater, Berlin 1 May

1899 **Im Reiche des Indra** (Lincke/w Leopold Ely) Apollotheater, Berlin 18 December

1900 **Fräulein Loreley** (Lincke) 1 act Apollotheater, Berlin 15 October

1902 **Lysistrata** (Lincke) Apollotheater, Berlin 1 April

1902 **Nakiris Hochzeit** (Lincke) Apollotheater, Berlin 6 November

1903 **Am Hochzeitsabend** (Lincke) 1 act Danzers Orpheum, Vienna 31 March

1905 **Prinzessin Rosine** (Lincke) Apollotheater, Berlin 18 November

1906 **Das blaue Bild** (Lincke) Apollotheater, Berlin 18 May

1906 **Kadettenstreiche** (Viktor Holländer) Eden-Theater, Aachen 19 July

1906 **Die schöne Vestalin** (*La Plus Belle*) German version (Apollotheater, Vienna)

1911 **Gri-gri** (Lincke/Jules Chancel ad) Metropltheater, Cologne 25 March

1913 **Rackerchen** (Theodore Blumer) Neues Luisen-Theater, Königsberg February

BOLTON, Guy [Reginald] (b Broxbourne, Herts, 23 November 1884; d London, 6 September 1979). Librettist to half a century of musical comedies on both sides of the Atlantic.

Born in Britain, of American parents, Bolton spent his earliest years working towards a career in architecture but, after the production of his first play in 1911, he orientated himself towards the theatre in preference. In a career that lasted 50 years, he worked, particularly in the earliest years, at an enormously high speed, turning out a number of plays and libretti every year and, in the three years surrounding his first contributions to the musical stage, he saw the plays *The Rule of Three* (Harris Theater 16 February 1914), *The Fallen Idol* (Comedy Theater 23 January 1915), a version of Jack London's *The Sea Wolf* (Hartford, Con 12 March 1915) and the 'social problem play' *Her Game* (Buffalo 21 June 1915) mounted, 'suggested' (w George Middleton) *Hit-the-Trail Holliday* (Astor Theater 13 September 1915) to George M Cohan who was listed as author, wrote the playlet *Children* (w Tom Carlton) for the Washington Square Players (20 March 1916) and *Happy Thought* (w Middleton, Cleveland 26 June 1916) as well as authoring his first musical comedy script and adapting three others.

If the original piece, *Ninety in the Shade*, a vehicle for comedy stars Marie Cahill and Richard Carle, set by Jerome Kern with dance melodies of the day, was a failure, the adaptations were, all three, successes. *Nobody Home*, a remake of the delightful and successful little London musical *Mr Popple of Ippleton*, with a replacement score by Kern, had a fair run of 135 performances at the intimate Princess Theater and the larger Maxine Elliott before touring. *Very Good Eddie*, a musical adaptation of the play *Over Night* done with its author, Philip Bartholomae, and Kern, followed in the same style of farcical comedy with song-and-dance and scored a splendid success (341 performances), whilst an adaptation of the richly dancing Hungarian musical play *Zsuzsi kisasszony* (Miss Susie) as *Miss Springtime* for Klaw and Erlanger welcomed even more customers in 224 performances at the rather larger New Amsterdam Theater.

After this felicitous beginning, Bolton carried on in both strains, collaborating with Kern on further farcical comedies with dancing songs, written somewhat in the style of the French vaudeville (if usually without some of its more comic complexities) and also adapting existing works, in an amazingly prolific schedule which ranged from further shows for the tiny Princess Theater to such pieces as the splashy Charles Dillingham revue *Miss 1917* (Kern, Victor Herbert/w P G Wodehouse Century Theater), not to mention a parallel if less substantial schedule of non-musical plays.

The Kern musicals proved, mostly, to be extremely successful. If *Have a Heart*, which followed the basics of a French vaudeville plot but reset the action in America, survived only 76 performances, *Oh, Boy!*, the next show in what was becoming regarded as a series at the Princess Theater, was a triumph. Like *Have a Heart*, it acknowledged no source for its libretto, but the elements of its plot were familiar ones of the Paris vaudeville and its British derivatives, bound together here in a briskly farcical piece which was one of Bolton's smartest achievements. *Oh, Lady! Lady!!*, written in a similar style, was a fair-to-middling success (219 performances), but an adaptation of George Ade's hit farce *The College Widow* as *Leave it to Jane* (an unrepresentative 176 performances) confirmed both the success of *Oh, Boy!* and the fact that there was plenty of subject and plot matter closer at hand than Paris. Five years and seven shows after the beginning of their collaboration, Bolton and Kern finally moved away from the vaudeville style and into a romantic dance-and-song musical built on more operettic libretto lines and triumphed all over again with the pretty, if textually loose, *Sally*.

In the meanwhile, Bolton had found mixed success elsewhere. Transplanting the very central European action and music of *Die Csárdásfürstin* into *The Riviera Girl* did not work (78 performances) and an attempt to americanize Josef Szulc's musical comedy *Loute* under one of the theoretically catchy but meaningless titles of the age, *See You Later*, foundered twice on the road. However a collaboration with the man who had been more influential than any other in bringing the French style to Broadway, *The Pink Lady*'s Ivan Caryll, gave him a fine success with the Klaw and Erlanger production *The Girl Behind the Gun* (160 performances). Transported to London as *Kissing Time*, this musical adaptation of the French vaudeville *Madame et son filleul* gave its author his first real West End hit (430 performances), following the disappointing London runs of *Very Good Eddie* and *Oh, Joy*.

A second collaboration with Caryll on another ex-French piece, Armont and Gerbidon's *Souris d'hotel*, was interrupted by the composer's death and the resultant *Little Miss Raffles/The Hotel Mouse* failed (88 performances), but a musical version of another play written by and with *Very Good Eddie*'s Philip Bartholomae produced another hit in the colourfully comical *Tangerine* (337 performances), a piece whose plot's trip to the Southern Seas happily brought back memories of turn-of-the-century native comic opera.

In 1924 George Grossmith, the London producer of *Kissing Time*, teamed Bolton with the young composer George Gershwin on a show for his Winter Garden Theatre. What value *Primrose* had was more in its performances and some of its songs than in its undoubtedly well-tailored libretto, but the collaboration thus cemented with Gershwin would soon bring forth riper fruit. Back on American stages, Bolton joined with Fred Thompson, another Grossmith man, to provide the libretti for Gershwin's dance-and-comedy shows *Lady, Be Good!* and *Tip-Toes* and with his long-time collaborator, P G Wodehouse, on probably his most successful single text, *Oh, Kay!*, which, although announced as a version of the Paris hit *La Présidente*, showed little signs of that 'source' by the time it reached its final form.

Trips into the field of the romantic biomusical with a Jenny Lind show called *The Nightingale*, written to feature his then wife Marguerite Namara as the famous singer, but ultimately and unsuccessfully played without her, into farce comedy with the Clark and McCullough vehicle *The Ramblers* and into the opérette à grand spectacle with the swashbuckling South American tale of *Rio Rita*, were mixed with more vaudevillesque musical comedy in the successful *The Five o'Clock Girl* (280 performances) and a share in the 1928 *She's My Baby* (the former sporting plotline flavours of *La Demoiselle du téléphone* and the latter of London's *Baby Bunting*, Germany's *Madame Sherry* and others), and another vehicle for *Sally's* dance star, Marilyn Miller, this time Ruritanianized as Princess *Rosalie*. He also took time to musicalize one of his own plays, *Polly With a Past* (w George Middleton), an exercise which gave him a rare and real flop in just two Broadway weeks.

The Broadway successes kept on coming: Ed Wynn's fairytale vehicle *Simple Simon*, another piece with Gershwin, *Girl Crazy*, and a first collaboration with Cole Porter on the famous libretto for *Anything Goes* which had to be rewritten by Lindsay and Crouse when current events were alleged to have rendered it distasteful. It was not rewritten by Bolton, because he had now shifted his headquarters to Britain where, during the 1930s, he turned out a series of musical shows which were amongst the most successful of their time. Britain was going through a fashion for the star-vehicle, comedy-based musical show and, for that reason, few pieces of the period survived beyond their original purposes, but the series of musical comedies which Bolton and his associates provided for the Gaiety Theatre company headed by Leslie Henson (*Seeing Stars*, *Swing Along*, *Going Greek*, *Running Riot*), the Flanagan and Allen *Give Me a Ring*, Jack Buchanan and Elsie Randolph's *This'll Make You Whistle* and Cicely Courtneidge and Bobby Howes's *Hide and Seek* were all fine of-the-moment successes which more than compensated for the occasional misfire such as the attempts to doctor the Australian musical presented as *At the Silver Swan* and Eric Maschwitz's embarrassing *Magyar Melody*.

Throughout the years, Bolton had followed the fashions in musical theatre with alacrity and efficiency, always a collaborator prized and much-liked for his inevitably swift and to-the-point work and his agreeable and 'English-gentleman' personality. From his wartime return to America, however, the writer – now in his mid-sixties – began to loose touch a little with the trends. His only subsequent musical successes were the lively and old-fashioned comedy musical *Follow the Girls* and its less long-lived successor *Ankles Aweigh*. Such other pieces as the weak Offenbach pasticcio biomusical *Music at Midnight* and the spectacle *Rainbow Square* were unfortunate episodes. His final work, at 80 years of age, was a share in the musicalization of his highly successful English version of Marcelle Maurette's French play *Anastasia*.

One of Bolton's other non-musical plays, *Who's Who?* (1934, w Wodehouse) was made into *Who's Who, Baby?* (Johnny Brandon/Gerald Frank, Players Theater 20 January 1968).

Bolton also wrote a number of film screenplays and novels including a piece detailing, with admitted fictional details and 'improvements' to the truth, his musical comedy life, under the title *Bring on the Girls*.

1915 **Ninety in the Shade** (Jerome Kern/Harry B Smith, Clare Kummer) Knickerbocker Theater 25 January

1915 **Nobody Home** (*Mr Popple of Ippleton*) American adaptation w new music by Jerome Kern (Princess Theater)

1915 **Very Good Eddie** (Kern/Schuyler Greene/w Philip Bartholomae) Princess Theater 23 December

1916 **Miss Springtime** (*Zsuzsi kisasszony*) English version (New Amsterdam Theater)

1917 **Have a Heart** (Kern/w P G Wodehouse) Liberty Theater 11 January

1917 **Oh, Boy!** (UK: *Oh, Joy!*) (Kern/w Wodehouse) Princess Theater 20 February

1917 **Leave it to Jane** (Kern/w Wodehouse) Longacre Theater 28 August

1917 **The Riviera Girl** (*Die Csárdásfürstin*) American version w Wodehouse (New Amsterdam Theater)

1918 **See You Later** (*Loute*) English version w additional music by Jean Schwartz/P G Wodehouse (Academy of Music, Baltimore)

1918 **Oh, Lady! Lady!!** (Kern/w Wodehouse) Princess Theater 31 January

1918 **The Girl Behind the Gun** (aka *Kissing Time*) (Ivan Caryll/w Wodehouse) New Amsterdam Theater 16 September

1918 **Oh, My Dear** (ex- *Ask Dad*) (Louis Hirsch/w Wodehouse) Princess Theater 26 November

1919 **The Rose of China** (Armand Vecsey/Wodehouse) Lyric Theater 25 November

1920 **Sally** (ex- *Sally of our Alley*) (Kern/Clifford Grey) New Amsterdam Theater 21 December

1921 **Tangerine** (Monte Carlo, Alma Sanders/w Bartholomae) Casino Theater 9 August

1921 **Little Miss Raffles** (Caryll/Grey) Stamford, Conn 1 December

1922 **The Hotel Mouse** (revised *Little Miss Raffles* w add mus by Vecsey) Shubert Theater 13 March

1922 **Daffy Dill** (Herbert Stothart/Oscar Hammerstein II/w Hammerstein) Apollo Theater 22 August

1924 **Sitting Pretty** (Kern/w Wodehouse) Fulton Theater 8 April

1924 **Primrose** (George Gershwin/Desmond Carter, Ira Gershwin/w George Grossmith jr) Winter Garden Theatre, London 11 September

1924 **Lady, Be Good!** (G Gershwin/I Gershwin/w Fred Thompson) Liberty Theater 1 December

1925 **Tip-Toes** (G Gershwin/I Gershwin/w Thompson) Liberty Theater 28 December

1925 **The Bamboula** (Albert Szirmai, Harry Rosenthal/Irving Caesar, Douglas Furber/w Harry M Vernon) His Majesty's Theatre, London 24 March

1926 **The Ramblers** (ex- *The Fly-By-Nights*) (Bert Kalmar, Harry Ruby/w Kalmar, Ruby) Lyric Theater 30 September

1926 **Oh, Kay!** (ex-*Cheerio!*) (G Gershwin/I Gershwin/w Wodehouse) Imperial Theater 8 November

1927 **The Nightingale** (Vecsey/w Wodehouse) Jolson Theater 3 January

1927 **Rio Rita** (Harry Tierney/Joseph McCarthy/w Thompson) Ziegfeld Theater 2 February

1927 **The Five o'Clock Girl** (Kalmar, Ruby/w Thompson) 44th Street Theater 10 October

1927 **She's My Baby** (Richard Rodgers/Lorenz Hart, Kalmar, Ruby/w Kalmar, Ruby) Globe Theater 3 January

1928 **Rosalie** (Gershwin, Sigmund Romberg/w William Anthony McGuire) New Amsterdam Theater 10 January

1928 **Blue Eyes** (Kern) Piccadilly Theatre, London 27 April

1929 **Polly** (Phil Charig/Irving Caesar/w Guy Middleton, Isobel Leighton) Lyric Theater 8 January

1929 **Top Speed** (Kalmar, Ruby) 46th Street Theater 25 December

1930 **Simple Simon** (Rodgers/Hart/w Ed Wynn) Ziegfeld Theater 18 February

1930 **Girl Crazy** (G Gershwin/I Gershwin/w John McGowan) Alvin Theater 14 October

1931 **Song of the Drum** (Vivan Ellis, Herman Finck/Desmond Carter/w Thompson) Theatre Royal, Drury Lane, London 9 January

1933 **Give Me a Ring** (Martin Broones) London Hippodrome 22 June

1934 **Anything Goes** (Cole Porter/w Wodehouse ad Russel Crouse, Howard Lindsay) Alvin Theater 21 November

1935 **Seeing Stars** (Broones/Graham John/w Thompson) Gaiety Theatre, London 31 October

1936 **At the Silver Swan** (Edmond Samuels, Percival Mackey/ Grey) Palace Theatre, London 19 February

1936 **Swing Along** (Broones/John/w Thompson, Douglas Furber) Gaiety Theatre, London 2 September

1936 **This'll Make You Whistle** (Maurice Sigler, Al Goodhart, Al Hoffman/w Thompson) Palace Theatre, London 14 September

1936 **Going Places** (Ellis/w Thompson) Savoy Theatre, London 8 October

1937 **Going Greek** (Sam Lerner, Goodhart, Hoffman) Gaiety Theatre, London 16 September

1937 **Hide and Seek** (Ellis, Lerner, Goodhart, Hoffman/w Thompson, Furber) London Hippodrome 14 October

1938 **The Fleet's Lit Up** (Ellis/w Thompson, Bert Lee) London Hippodrome 17 August

1938 **Running Riot** (Ellis/w Firth Shephard, Furber) Gaiety Theatre, London 31 August

1938 **Bobby Get Your Gun** (Jack Waller, Joe Tunbridge/Grey, Lee, Carter/w Lee, Thompson) Adelphi Theatre, London 7 October

1939 **Magyar Melody** revised *Paprika* (George Posford, Bernard Grün/Harold Purcell, Eric Maschwitz/w Thompson, Maschwitz) His Majesty's Theatre, London 20 January

1940 **Walk with Music** (ex- *Three after Three*) (Hoagy Carmichael/Johnny Mercer/w Parke Levy, Alan Lipscott) Ethel Barrymore Theater 4 June

1940 **Hold on to Your Hats** (Burton Lane/E Y Harburg/w Matt Brooks, Eddie Davis) Shubert Theater 11 September

1944 **Jackpot** (Vernon Duke, Howard Dietz) Alvin Theater 13 January

1944 **Follow the Girls** (Phil Charig/Milton Pascal, Dan Shapiro/w Davis, Thompson) Century Theater 8 April

1950 **Music at Midnight** (Offenbach arr Hans May/Purcell) His Majesty's Theatre, London 10 November

1951 **Rainbow Square** (Robert Stolz/w Purcell) Stoll Theatre, London 21 September

1955 **Ankles Aweigh** (Sammy Fain/Dan Shapiro/w Davis) Mark Hellinger Theater 18 April

1965 **Anya** (arr Rachmaninoff/George Forrest, Robert Wright/w George Abbott) Ziegfeld Theater 29 November

BOMBASTES FURIOSO Burlesque in 1 act by William Barnes Rhodes. Haymarket Theatre, London, 7 August 1810.

One of the most famous of pre-Victorian burlesques, this extravagant and grotesque mockery of the bombast of the dramatic stage, its writers and its performers, was a short play into which a half dozen musical pieces, set to the tunes of 'Tekeli', 'Hope Told a Flatt'ring Tale', 'Paddy's Wedding', 'O Lady Fair', 'My Lodging is on the Cold Ground' and 'Tural Lural Laddi', were inserted. It proved a popular part of playbills throughout Britain, remained on British-influenced stages for many decades and survived into occasional performances long after the fashions in burlesque had changed.

USA: Park Theater 15 October 1816; Australia: Emu Plains Theatre 16 May 1825

BOMBO Extravaganza in 2 acts by Harold Atteridge. Music by Sigmund Romberg. Jolson Theater, New York, 6 October 1921.

Built as a vehicle for Al Jolson at the peak of his pulling-power, *Bombo* justified its star's appearance in blackface by casting him as the negro servant to no less a gentleman than Christopher Columbus. Any pretence that the show was a musical play was fairly soon dissipated, and the words 'extravaganza' and 'revue' were used to describe a show which was, in fact, little more than a dressed-up concert for its star who took over the proceedings in the second act and delivered one number after another in his inimitable style. Amongst those numbers appeared, at various times, Buddy De Sylva and Louis Silvers's 'April Showers', the Gus Kahn/Dan Russo, Ernie Erdman 'Toot-toot-Tootsie' and, during the post-Broadway touring, Joseph Meyer and De Sylva's 'California, Here I Come'. Lost under this recital of minstrelsy were 20 pieces by Sigmund Romberg, several by Con Conrad and others by Cliff Friend.

Bombo served Broadway for 218 performances before Jolson took it on the road for two seasons.

BOND, Jessie [Charlotte] (b London, 11 January 1853; d Worthing, 17 June 1942).

Twenty-five-year-old Jessie Bond was heard by Richard D'Oyly Carte singing at a Royal Academy of Music concert and was hired to replace the ailing Mrs Howard Paul in extremis in the rôle of Hebe in the original production of *HMS Pinafore*. What had been written as a principal rôle was cut to virtually nothing due to the young singer's inability to cope with dialogue, but Miss Bond made sufficient of her opportunities to be taken to America to repeat her rôle and to be engaged for the next Carte production, *The Pirates of Penzance*. She remained a member of the D'Oyly Carte company through nine of the Gilbert and Sullivan comic operas, creating the rôles of Kate (*Pirates of Penzance*), Lady Angela (*Patience*), Iolanthe, Pitti Sing (*Mikado*), Melissa (*Princess Ida*), Mad Margaret (*Ruddigore*), Phoebe (*The Yeomen of the Guard*, a rôle written by Gilbert to allow her simply to be 'her own sweet self') and Tessa (*The Gondoliers*) as well as the more extravagantly comical Chinna Loofah in George Dance and Edward Solomon's *The Nautch Girl*.

She left the Savoy company to attempt to cash in on her fame by touring a Drawing Room Entertainment, but the enterprise was not a success, and she returned to the theatre. She subsequently appeared successfully in Continental and British comic opera – as Martha in Lacôme's *Ma mie Rosette*, as Molly opposite Harry Monkhouse in *Der arme Jonathan* and as the comical Susan Sinnett in *Wapping Old Stairs* as well as, less happily, in the fiasco *Miami* – and moved into the rising field of musical comedy to appear as the heroine of the Osmond Carr/Adrian Ross *Go Bang* (1894). She found herself quite eclipsed by dancing soubrette Letty Lind, and returned to Gilbert, declaring that 'never again will I appear as a lady in modern dress', to play the equivalent of her old Savoy rôles as Nanna in *His Excellency* (1895) before retiring from the stage.

MacGeorge, E: *Life and Reminiscences of Jessie Bond, the Old Savoyard* (John Lane, London, 1930)

UN BON GARÇON Opérette (comédie musicale) in 3 acts by André Barde. Music by Maurice Yvain. Théâtre des Nouveautés, Paris, 13 November 1926.

One of the succession of lively jazz-age musical comedies for which Barde turned out his usual spirited comic libretto and for which Yvain supplied another up-to-date and dancing score ('Je t'emmène à la campagne', 'Ce n'était pourtant pas difficile', 'Pour danser le Charleston', 'La Musique grisante'). The show's cast was headed by the comic Milton in the rôle of interfering Achille, who sets out to persuade an old lady friend of his called Madame Bouillon-Falloux (Mary Hett) that her daughter, Camille (Davia), should not, after all, marry her designated bridegroom, Lucien de Gravère (Robert Ancelin), who is already devoted to pretty Arlette Méryl (Pierette Madd). Urban (Pontavès), Gildès (Abbé Colignac) and Germain Champell (M de Gravère) completed the principal cast, under the direction of Régina Camier.

Léon Benoît-Deutsch's production of the show had a run of over a year in Paris before going on the French road and overseas.

Hungary produced *Un bon garçon* in a version by István Zágon which altered the title to *Csattan a csók* (literally 'Stunning Lips') in order to include the 'bouche' element of Yvain's earlier show-titles, whilst an American version (ad Gertrude Purcell, Max and Nathaniel Lief) changed the sex of the title-rôle (*Luckee Girl*) but also squeezed in so many interpolated songs by Maurie Rubens and others that there was little room left for the Paris score. Broadway audiences were adjudged more likely to prefer Werner Janssen and Mann Holiner's 'Come On and Let's Make Whoopee' to Yvain's classy dance melodies. Irene Dunne (Arlette), in her first Broadway lead rôle, had to give second best to the voluminous variety comic Billy House (Hercules), but this pair, Irving Fisher (Lucien), Frank Lalor (Pontavès), Doris Vinton (Camille) and the Four Diplomats got only 81 New York performances out of the resultant mish-mash. French-speaking theater-goers in New York had a chance to see the original *Un bon garçon* as played by a touring French musical comedy company with Hans Servatius and Jane de Poumcyrac featured during 1929.

Hungary: Magyar Színház *Csattan a csók* 7 October 1927; USA: Casino Theater *Luckee Girl* 15 September 1928, Jolson Theater (Fr) 18 March 1929

BONHEUR, Alice   (b Paris, 1874; d unknown).

Charming soprano whose long and truly international career mixed musical comedy engagements with appearances in variety and music hall in France, America and throughout Europe.

Pretty, vivacious Alice Bonheur – who had started her working days as a modiste's apprentice – began her life in the theatre playing at the Bodinière and at the Menus-Plaisirs in 1891 (*La Timbale d'argent* revival). She went on to create soubrette rôles in a half-dozen year series of opérettes, mostly at the Bouffes-Parisiens, a series amongst which the outstanding success was Messager's *Les P'tites Michu* (1897, Marie-Blanche), and which included *La Duchesse de Ferrare* (1895, Jeanne), *La Saint-Valentin*, *La Dot de Brigitte* (1895, Nicole), *Ninette* (1896, Diane), *La Reine des Reines* (Eldorado, 1896), *Les Petites Femmes* (1897, Bengaline), *La Dame de trèfle* (1898), *Le Soleil à minuit* (1898) and *Le Roi Dagobert* (1898).

She made a success in Paris and London in the little Théâtre des Capucines opérette *Chonchette* (1902), toured South America, appeared in the leading rôle of Henri Christiné's early *Service d'amour* at the Scala and in the title-rôle of the French version of Lionel Monckton's *A Country Girl* at L'Olympia (1903), and appeared at the

Boîte à Fursy in *Minne* (1905). She returned to the Capucines to play in Cuvillier's *Avant-hier matin* and to create the rôle of Glycère in Terrasse's whimsical *Paris, ou le bon juge* (1906), then swapped that tiny stage for the vastness of the Châtelet where she was seen in *La Princesse Sans-Gêne* (1907). She found her way back to the Capucines for *Le Coq de l'Inde* (1908), was seen at Vienna's Apollotheater in variety in 1909, created the French version of Franzi in the Parisian première of *Ein Walzertraum* (1910), then took another trip to the Argentine.

Back in Paris, she played in *Berlingot* at the Concert Mayol, in *La Fille de Madame Angot* and *La Fille du tambour-major* at the Gaîté, then toured to Egypt and through France before moving into a series of wartime revues in Paris. In 1918 she appeared at the Palais-Royal as Jacinthe in Cuvillier's *Mademoiselle 'Nom d'une pipe'* and in 1919 she played the more senior and less soubrette rôle of Mme Phidias in the Brussels production of *Phi-Phi*. She subsequently took over this rôle in the long-running Paris production, playing it for over two years at the Bouffes-Parisiens. She later graduated to older character and comic rôles appearing on the Parisian musical stage as late as *Vacances* (1934) and *L'Auberge du Chat Coiffé* (1935).

BONITA   Comic opera in a prologue and 2 acts by Wadham Peacock. Music by Harold Fraser-Simson. Queen's Theatre, London, 22 September 1911.

An ephemeral piece of South American romance-cum-adventure hokum which won notice in retrospect as the first composing venture of Fraser-Simson (his next would be *The Maid of the Mountains*) and as the one venture of the distinguished Shavian (etc) director, Granville Barker, on the musical stage. Barker's presence encouraged the critics to some nonsensically deep analyses of the work and its staging, but the director's attempts to teach motivation to the ladies and gentlemen of the *Bonita* chorus were not a success and the piece folded in 42 performances.

Bonita was also the primitive title of a Sigmund Romberg musical, an adaptation of Augutus Thomas's successful play *Arizona*, which went through several other titles (*Love Song*, *My Golden West*) before it finally reached Broadway as *The Love Call* (Majestic Theater, 24 October 1927).

LA BONNE D'ENFANT[S]   Opérette-bouffe in 1 act by Eugène Bercioux. Music by Jacques Offenbach. Théâtre des Bouffes-Parisiens, Paris, 14 October 1856.

The 'bonne d'enfants' of the title is Dorothée (Mlle Garnier), and the action of the piece is a not unfamiliar one, a little reminiscent of the famous old farce *The Area Belle*. Dorothée receives visits from two followers: the chimneyman, Gargaillou (Michel), and the sapeur, Mitouflard (Dubouchet). Gargaillou disguises himself in feminine garb when Mitouflard arrives and the comical situations fly until Dorothée gets rid of them both and goes off with the trumpeter, Brin d'Amour. In the meanwhile, the cast have tripped through half a dozen pretty burlesque numbers, including a jolly duet for Dorothée and her first-come pretender ('Je rôtis, je brûle') and another for the two fellows, drooling over the 'Superbe créature', and partaken of a strong representation of the military, as in Mitouflard's number about 'La Garnison de Charenton' and the Couplets 'De la trompette j'entends l'accent' with their ta-ra-ra refrain.

First seen on the bill at the Bouffes-Parisiens, *La Bonne d'enfant(s)* was introduced to London during Offenbach's 1857 season at the St James's Theatre, and to Vienna by the Bouffes-Parisiens company, with Lucille Tostée as Dorothée, in their summer season of 1862. It was subsequently seen in Vienna in its successful Hungarian version (ad Pál Tarnay) and in two different German adaptations, but does not seem to have found its way into an English version. In 1991 the piece was played in a programme at Metz (22 March) and subsequently seen, in the repertoire of the little Opéra de Guyenne, in the French provinces.

UK: St James's Theatre 26 May 1857; Austria: Theater am Franz-Josefs-Kai (Fr) 1 June 1862, Harmonietheater *A Dajka* (Hung) 27 May 1866 and *Die Kindsmädchen* 2 November 1867, Fürsttheater *Die Kindergärtnerin* 31 May 1884; Hungary: Budai Népszinház *A Dajka* 28 February 1863

BOOTH, Shirley [FORD, Thelma Booth] (b New York, 30 August 1898; d Chatham, Mass, 16 October 1992).

A warm, versatile actress who made a name as a quality player of both comedy and drama in the theatre (*Three Men on a Horse*, *The Philadelphia Story*, *My Sister Eileen*, *Goodbye, My Fancy*, *Come Back, Little Sheba*, *The Time of the Cuckoo* etc.) and on the screen large (*Come Back, Little Sheba*, Academy Award) and small (on the world's television sets as the lovable *Hazel*), Miss Booth made occasional ventures into the musical theatre, the earliest of which as the archetypal gossip columnist Louhedda Hopsons in the *HMS Pinafore* burlesque *Hollywood Pinafore* (1945).

In the 1950s she starred in three musicals, beginning with Arthur Schwartz's musical version of *A Tree Grows in Brooklyn* in which she played dear Aunt Cissy, dreaming of her long-lost love ('He Had Refinement') until disillusion sets in, and continuing in a similar character as lovable Lottie Gibson in the same composer's *By the Beautiful Sea* (1954). She then took the title-rôle in *Juno*, an attempt at musicalizing Sean O'Casey's classic drama *Juno and the Paycock* in which, in the classic dramatic rôle made famous by Sara Allgood, she introduced the 'Song of the Ma', 'Old Sayin's' and 'Where?' for 16 performances. She made a final musical appearance in 1970 as Mother Maria, the church-building Superior of the only marginally less short-lived *Look to the Lilies*.

BORDMAN, Gerald [Martin] (b Philadelphia, 18 September 1931).

After university studies in medieval English (Ph D) and a number of years running the family chemical business, Bordman retired and began what would be a series of definitive theatre reference works with the publication of *American Musical Theatre: A Chronicle* in 1978. The first and only systematic coverage of the history of the Broadway musical stage, it was particularly successful in that it avoided the overly 'patriotic' and/or proselytizing attitudes of some earlier works, and described the productions, imported and home-made, of the American musical stage in a popular academic style and from a factual 'eye-of-god' viewpoint.

He has subsequently authored the biographies of Jerome Kern (*Jerome Kern: His Life and Music*, 1980) and Vincent Youmans (*Days to Be Happy, Years to Be Sad*, 1982), monographs on *American Operetta* (1981), *American*

Musical Comedy (1982) and *American Musical Revue* (1985), and the *Oxford Companion to American Theatre* (1984), as well as producing several updated versions of *American Musical Theatre*.

BORDONI, Irene (b Corsica, ?16 January 1895; d New York, 19 March 1953). Broadway's French vedette of the 1920s.

The apparently Corsican Mlle Bordoni is said to have begun her stage career in France at the age of 13, playing at the Théâtre des Variétés, the Moulin-Rouge (*Par dessus le moulin*, 1908), the Capucines (Maggy in the revue *V'là la comète* 1910), the Scala and La Cigale before crossing the Atlantic. By these calculations, she was just 17 years of age when she first appeared on musical Broadway as a tiny and extremely (almost excessively) French soubrette in the 1912 revue *Broadway to Paris*. She returned to France where she appeared in revue at the Capucines (1913) and La Cigale (1913), impersonating Mistinguett, in the comedy *La Tontine* at the Antoine (1914) and in Rip's famous revue *1915* ('La Chanson du militaire') before recrossing the Atlantic.

Back in America Mlle Bordoni appeared in a supporting rôle in the 47 performances of the Elsie Janis show *Miss Information* (1915, Elaine), played at Fysher's cabaret mondaine, at the French theatre in a war drama, *Son homme*, featured in two editions of Raymond Hitchcock's *Hitchy-Koo*, and took a turn on the vaudeville stage before making a distinct mark in the multiple feminine lead in the Broadway version of the London version (where the rôle was taken by Alice Delysia) of Rip's Parisian revue *Plus ça change*, anglicized as *As You Were*.

She remained tiny and extremely French as, in the same manner as Anna Held before her and as Delysia in London, she made herself a subsequent career as the epitome of Broadway Frenchness, starring, under the management of her then husband E Ray Goetz, in a series of americanized Continental vehicles. These began with a version of the Armont/Gerbidon play *Jeunes Filles de palaces*, adapted as a song-studded *The French Doll* (1922, Georgine Mazulier) and included a version of Gábor Drégely's *A kisasszony férje* or *Der Gatte des Fräuleins* produced as *Little Miss Bluebeard* (1924, Colette) which she also played in London, a version of the French opérette *Pouche*, described as a romantic song-farce and entitled *A Naughty Cinderella* (1925, Germaine Leverrier), which allowed her to sing Paul Ruben's 'I Love the Moon', Henri Christiné's 'Do I Love You?', 'Mia luna' and 'That Means Nothing to Me' in place of the original score, the title-rôle in Sacha Guitry's *Mozart* (just before Yvonne Printemps arrived to give Broadway her version of her original rôle), and the 1928 *Paris* (Vivienne Rolland) in which she performed several made-to-measure Cole Porter songs ('Let's Do It', 'The Heaven Hop' etc) plus Walter Kollo's 'The Land of Going to Be' (Goetz) and Harry Warren's 'Wob-a-ly Walk'. She filmed a version of this last show in 1930.

The last of her vehicles, the 1931 *One More Night* (Herman Hupfeld/Russel Medcraft), an americanization of a Louis Verneuil piece (which would seem to have been *Ma Cousine de Varsovie*) in which she appeared as the Princess de Gouremnitza-Guvgulli (aka Colette) equipped with seven numbers which admitted only to being 'arranged by Russell Bennett', was produced by Galen Bogue. It did not

Plate 33. **Irene Bordoni:** *Broadway's Corsican-born epitome of Parisian-ness who had a fine hit introducing 'Let's Do It' in the show called, simply,* Paris.

make it to New York, but she returned to the Broadway musical stage in 1938 in *Great Lady* (Madame Colette) and, with rather more success, as Madame Bordelaise in *Lousiana Purchase* (1940). She later appeared in the Tchaikovsky pasticcio musical *The Lady from Paris* (1950) and in 1951 played for a while as Bloody Mary in the national tour of *South Pacific* in what is undoubtedly one of the rare times that the rôle has been played, physically (give or take a complexion), nearly as described in the text.

In 1953 she took part in the try-out of *Maggie*, but was dropped before Broadway and replaced by Odette Myrtil. It was her last stage appearance: two months later she was dead.

BOSTONIANS (The Boston Ideal Comic Opera Company).

Originally formed by theatrical and vocal agent Effie Ober in 1879 at the height of the *Pinafore* craze to give an 'ideal' production of that show, the Ideal Comic Opera Company, which its manager insisted be vocally impeccable, won an enormous success and, as a result, gradually developed into a light opera repertoire company touring America from its Boston base. The company, soon familiarly known as 'The Bostonians', quickly added such pieces as *The Sorcerer*, *The Pirates of Penzance*, a version of *Boccaccio* (*The Prince of Palermo*), *Les Cloches de Corneville*, *Les Noces d'Olivette*, *Fatinitza*, *The Bohemian Girl*, *La Mascotte*, *Zar und Zimmermann* and *Les Mousquetaires au couvent* to their repertoire, followed later by *Giroflé-Girofla*, *La Girouette*, *Barbe-bleue* and *François les bas-bleus* as well as the opéras-comiques *The Marriage of Figaro*, *Giralda*, *Fra*

Diavolo, *L'Elisir d'Amore* (as *Adina*), *La Reine Topaze* and *Martha*.

In 1887 the company's finances curled up and it collapsed, but it was reconstituted as 'The Bostonians' and, with several of its most famous members – comic Henry Clay Barnabee, tenor Tom Karl, baritone W H MacDonald – at the helm, began a second lease of life. If such old favourites as *Fatinitza* held their place in the repertoire, the new management also added a number of fresh pieces, ranging from *Mignon* to Offenbach's *Les Braconniers* and Cellier's *Dorothy* and a piece called *Pygmalion and Galatea* made up from Gilbert's play along with music from Suppé's *Operette* and other sources, but they also began a new policy of mounting original native works, and it was there that the group found their biggest hit since *HMS Pinafore*. Reginald De Koven and Harry B Smith supplied them with a short-lived *Don Quixote* and then with *Robin Hood*, the show which would become the classic American comic opera of its period. Later, having given an early opportunity to Victor Herbert with *Prince Ananais*, the company mothered another fine piece in his subsequent *The Serenade*. Amongst the other original works mounted were Oscar Weil's rewrite of *Le Voyage de Suzette* as *Suzette* and his apparently original *In Mexico*, Henry Waller's *The Ogalallas*, De Koven's *The Knickerbockers* and *Maid Marian*, Thomas P Thorne's *The Maid of Plymouth*, Jules Jordan's *Rip van Winkle* and Herbert's *The Viceroy*.

The company suffered badly when their soprano, Alice Nielsen, set up her own company and took several important members of the troupe with her, and within a half-dozen years both companies were gone. The Bostonians closed down in 1905, leaving behind a reputation and many memories of a first-class light opera company which had been responsible for producing two of the best local musical shows of the turn of the century.

BOUBLIL, Alain (b Tunis, 5 March 1941)

Originally an employee of Europe 1 radio, Boublil subsequently became a songwriter and music publisher and, under the influence of *Jesus Christ Superstar*, made an attempt at writing a piece of recorded musical theatre based on a similarly 'large' topic: *La Révolution française* (music: Claude-Michel Schönberg, Raymond Jeannot). The recording, labelled 'rock opéra', had a notable success, and the piece followed *Jesus Christ Superstar*'s example by being brought to the stage, at Paris's Palais des Sports.

Boublil's next venture followed the first in taking a vast subject as its bases. *La Révolution française* was succeeded by a recorded musical based on Victor Hugo's *Les Misérables*. Like the first show, this one moved from record to a stage presentation: a spectacular mounting by Robert Hossein at the Paris Palais des Sports.

A further record-to-stage venture followed, with the children's musical *Abbacadabra*, a fairytale piece which used the music of the pop group Abba as its score. Boublil subsequently worked on two further pieces in the same vein which remained records only (*La Fusée de Noë*, *Les Chevaliers des étoiles* w Jean-Pierre Bourtayre).

The great step in Boublil's career came, however, when Cameron Mackintosh, the London producer of *Abbacadabra*, then took up *Les Misérables*. Produced in London in a revised version, it established itself as one of the most outstanding and successful musicals of its era. Whilst *Les Misérables* ran on, in productions all around the world, Mackintosh produced a further Boublil/Schönberg musical, this time made for the British and American commercial theatre rather than for disc. *Miss Saigon*, an updated version of the *Madame Butterfly* tale set in the context of the Vietnam war, showed the altered position and aims of its author too clearly. But its clumsily shaped libretto and cold lyrics found partisans amongst those who admired its choice of the now fashionably expiatory Vietnam as a topic and, with all the power of the most successful and important producing house in the world behind it, the show went on to runs in London, New York and Tokyo, in the shadows of its overwhelmingly successful forebear.

1973 **La Révolution française** (Claude-Michel Schönberg, Raymond Jeannot/w Jean-Max Rivière) Palais des Sports
1980 **Les Misérables** (Schönberg/w Jean-Marc Natel) Palais des Sports 17 September
1983 **Abbacadabra** (Björn Ulvaeus, Benny Andersson/w Daniel Boublil ad David Wood) Lyric Theatre, Hammersmith, London 8 December
1985 **Les Misérables** revised English version ad Herbert Kretzmer Barbican Theatre, London 8 October
1989 **Miss Saigon** (Schönberg/w Richard Maltby jr) Theatre Royal, Drury Lane, London 20 September

BOUCHE À BOUCHE Comédie musicale in 2 acts by André Barde. Music by Maurice Yvain. Théâtre de l'Apollo, Paris, 7 October 1925.

The series of Maurice Yvain 'bouche' musicals, launched so successfully with *Ta bouche*, was continued, on a rather larger stage, in 1925 with *Bouche à bouche*. Thérèse Dornay played the demi-mondaine Natascha who, with the connivance of her miffed gentleman protector (Félix Oudart), mistakes the shy Bernard (Henri Defreyn) for a film star and sets her cap at him. When all the comical situations are done, Bernard is more suitably paired off with the old gentleman's ingénue daughter, Jenny (Maguy Warna). Milton headed the comedy as Boris, and Gabrielle Ristori supported in the role of Micheline.

Defreyn had the best musical moments of the piece in 'J'étais trop ému', 'Ça ne colle pas' and the waltzing title duet, shared with Mlle Warna, whilst Oudart delivered 'Où, quand et comment' and joined with Milton and Mlle Dornay in a set of comical couplets in praise of the petrol shares which were an essential part of the plot, 'Royal Dutch', in which Standard Oil and Shell were amongst those that got a plug. The comic highlight of the evening was the burlesque of an American film production which closed the second act.

Whilst not in the same enduring class as *Ta bouche* and *Pas sur la bouche*, *Bouche à bouche* produced plenty of attractive material and lasted several months in its rather less-than-intimate house.

BOUCHERON, Maxime (b Paris, 1846; d Paris, 9 November 1896). Librettist to 30 years of Parisian shows.

Originally a functionary at the Préfecture de la Seine, and later a journalist and theatrical columnist (*Le Triboulet*, *Le Figaro*), Boucheron made a notable entry into the musical theatre when he teamed with Paul Burani and composer Léon Vasseur on the eminently saucy 1878 opérette *Le Droit du seigneur* (229 performances and a revival in 1884). The same team reassembled for a second success with *Le Billet de logement* at the same theatre the following year, but a third volley, with *Le Petit Parisien* (70 performances) did less well. After some years away from the musical stage, Boucheron returned with another winsomely below-the-waistline libretto for *Miss Helyett* which, as musically illustrated by Audran, won him the biggest success of his writing career. Several other pieces written with Audran and, most particularly, the circus musical *Les Forains*, musically set by Louis Varney, had respectable careers before Boucheron's career ended with his premature death in 1896.

The Viennese Posse mit Gesang *Wolf und Lampel* (Julius Stern/Hoffmann/F Zell, Theater an der Wien 13 October 1888) was based on his successful vaudeville *Cocard et Bicoquet* (w Hippolyte Raymond, Théâtre de la Renaissance 22 February 1888).

1878 **Le Droit du seigneur** (Léon Vasseur/w Paul Burani) Théâtre des Fantaisies-Parisiennes 13 December
1879 **Le Billet de logement** (Vasseur/w Burani) Théâtre des Fantaisies-Parisiennes 15 November
1880 **Le Voyage en Amérique** (Hervé/w Hippolyte Raymond) Théâtre des Nouveautés 16 September
1882 **Le Petit Parisien** (Vasseur/w Burani) Théâtre des Folies-Dramatiques 16 January
1883 **Le Bouquet de violets** (André Martinet/w Georges Grisier) 1 act Casino d'Aulus 10 August
1883 **L'Ami d'Oscar** (Martinet) 1 act Casino d'Aulus 14 August
1890 **L'Entracte** (Martinet) 1 act Théâtre des Menus-Plaisirs 14 February
1890 **Miss Helyett** (Edmond Audran) Théâtre des Bouffes-Parisiens 12 November
1891 **Le Mitron** (Martinet/w Antony Mars) Théâtre des Folies Dramatiques 24 September
1892 **Article de Paris** (Audran) Théâtre des Menus-Plaisirs 17 March
1892 **Sainte-Freya** (Audran) Théâtre des Bouffes-Parisiens 4 November
1892 **Mariage galant** (Edmond Missa, Piétrapertosa/w François Oswald) Théâtre des Menus-Plaisirs 3 December
1894 **Les Forains** (Varney/w Mars) Théâtre des Bouffes-Parisiens 9 February
1895 **La Duchesse de Ferrare** (Audran) Théâtre des Bouffes-Parisiens 25 January
1896 **Une nuit d'amour** (Antoine Banès/w Albert Barré) Théâtre des Bouffes-Parisiens 11 May
1896 **Tante Agnès** (Frédéric Toulmouche) Olympia 27 October
1909 **Mam'zelle Gogo** (Émile Pessard/w Léon Xanrof) Théâtre Molière, Brussels February

BOUCICAULT, Dion [BOURSIQUOT, Dionysius Lardner] (b Dublin, 26 December 1820; d New York, 18 September 1890).

Although he authored a handful of small operettas and, on one occasion, a pantomime, the celebrated playwright and actor impinged rarely on the musical theatre. However, he transferred his theatrical belief that 'sensation' and spectacle was what the public wanted to the musical stage when he wrote and produced the vast, spectacular féerie *Babil and Bijou* at London's Covent Garden Theatre in 1872. The public enjoyed the elaborate, fantastical show, and Lord Londesborough who had backed it lost a fortune unheard of up to that time in a theatrical venture.

Boucicault adapted (w John Oxenford) his hit play *The Colleen Bawn* as the libretto for Julius Benedict's famous opera *The Lily of Killarney* ('The Moon Has Raised His Lamp Above', 'Eily Mavourneen') but, of his highly coloured plays, seemingly natural fodder for the musical stage, only *The Streets of New York* seems to have been thus adapted. A version by Edward Eliscu and Sol Kaplan was produced as *The Banker's Daughter* at off-Broadway's Jan Hus House in 1962 (21 January) and a second, by Barry Alan Grael with music by Richard B Chodosh, the following year at the Maidman Playhouse (29 October), whilst the British version of the same play was also adapted as a musical, *The Streets of London* (Gary Carpenter, Ian Barnett), produced at the Theatre Royal, Stratford East (18 March 1980) and subsequently played for three months at the West End's Her Majesty's Theatre (21 October 1980).

Boucicault's plays were also obvious meat for the burlesquers of his time, but once again he seems to have been strangely spared. *The Colleen Bawn* was the most thus favoured – H J Byron parodying it in his *Miss Eily O'Connor* (Drury Lane, 25 November 1961/Strand Theatre, 6 August 1862, music: James Tully) and William Brough and Andrew Halliday giving *The Colleen Bawn, Settled at Last* at the Lyceum (5 July 1872) – whilst his English version of Dumas's *Les Frères corses* (*The Corsican Brothers*) also found a large number of burlesque takers.

His son, actor **Aubrey BOUCICAULT** (b London, 23 June 1869; d New York, 10 July 1913), appeared on the New York musical stage in the leading rôle of Julian Edwards's comic opera *Madeleine* (1895), as Major Murgatroyd in *Patience* and alongside Eddie Foy in the Broadway version of *L'Auberge du Tohu-bohu* (1898, also add songs) as well as with Weber and Fields in *Higgledy-Piggledy* in a career largely devoted to non-musical theatre, whilst an elder son, **Dion G BOUCICAULT** (b New York, 23 May 1859; d Hurley, Bucks, 25 June 1929) produced a number of musical shows during a largely play-producing partnership with Robert Brough between 1886 and 1896 in Australia, and later directed several London musical shows (*Rosy Rapture*, *The Beloved Vagabond*). Daughter Nina Boucicault created the rôle of J M Barrie's *Peter Pan* (1904).

1844 **The Fox and the Goose, or the Widow's Husband** (Ambroise Thomas/w Benjamin Webster) 1 act Adelphi Theatre 2 October
1846 **The Wonderful Water Cure** (w Webster) Haymarket Theatre 15 July
1853 **The Sentinel** (Robert Stoepel) Strand Theatre 10 January
1872 **Babil and Bijou, or the Lost Regalia** (Hervé, Frederic Clay, Jules Rivière et al/J R Planché) Theatre Royal, Covent Garden 29 August

Autobiography: w Kenney, C L: *The Life and Career of Dion Boucicault* (New York, 1883), Biography: Walsh, T: *The Career of Dion Boucicault* (Dunlap Society, New York, 1915), Hogan, R: *Dion Boucicault* (Rayne, New York, 1969), Fawkes, R: *Dion Boucicault* (Quartet, London, 1979)

BOUFFAR, Zulma [BOUFFLAR, Zulma Madeleine] (b Nérac, 24 May 1841; d Pont-aux-Dames, 20 January 1909). One of the star prima donnas of the Offenbach age.

Zulma Bouffar made her first appearance on the stage at the age of six, at Marseille in *La Fille bien gardée*, and went on to appear as a vocalist at Lyon with some success. Owing to the French laws limiting child performers, her father then took her abroad, and the girl gave performances as a singer in a variety of venues in Belgium, Germany, Holland, Sweden and Denmark. After her father's death, the 13-year-old Zulma continued the life of a peripatetic entertainer, including in her repertoire songs from some of the new opérettes which were than becoming popular, notably the works of Offenbach and other material from the Bouffes-Parisiens repertoire.

She was seen by Offenbach in a performance in Liège or Homburg (reports differ), and the composer promptly brought her to his favourite watering place of Bad Ems where she made her début in 1864 in his opérette *Lischen et Fritzchen* (Lischen). She repeated the piece that season at the Bouffes-Parisiens with great success. At the same time she allegedly became the composer's mistress.

Over the next years Mlle Bouffar created a series of leading rôles on the Paris stage, the largest number in Offenbach opéras-bouffes where the music was made to measure for her highly agile soprano: the trousers rôle of Nani in *Les Géorgiennes* (1864), *Les Bergers* (1865, L'Intendant/Jeannet), Gabrielle in *La Vie parisienne* (when at Offenbach's insistence she was added to the slightly singing original cast at the Palais-Royal), and a run of travesti rôles in *Geneviève de Brabant* (1867, Drogan), *Le Château à Toto* (1868, Toto de la Roche), Delibes's *La Cour du Roi Pétaud* (1869, Prince Léo), *Les Brigands* (1869, Fragoletto) and *Le Roi Carotte* (1872, Robin Luron). In the shorter *Jeanne qui pleure et Jean qui rit* (Jean/Jeanne) she played both male and female rôles. She donned skirts for *Les Braconniers* (1873, Ginetta) and *Il Signor Fagotto* (Moschetta), but returned to breeches for her last Offenbach creation as Prince Caprice in *Le Voyage dans la lune* (1875).

Mlle Bouffar appeared in star rôles in Johann Strauss's *La Reine Indigo* (1875, Fantasca) and as the sexually mixed-up Kosiki in Lecocq's *Kosiki* (1876) and, at this time, so it is told, she was seriously considered by Bizet as a possible creator for the rôle of Carmen, but instead she rounded off the principal part of an outstanding career as a diva playing Princesse Arabelle in a Johann Strauss piece, which included some of the music from *Die Fledermaus*, entitled *La Tsigane*, in a revival of *Le Voyage dans la lune* at the Châtelet (1877), and as the legendary danseuse *La Camargo* in Lecocq's opérette of the same name (1878).

She played throughout Europe, notably in Belgium and in Russia, between her Paris engagements, and was still to be seen in the French capital in the 1880s, appearing in the 1880 production of *L'Arbre de Noël* at the Porte-Saint-Martin ('a little tired, a little heavier, a little older'), in *Mille et une nuits* at the Châtelet (1881) and in several other spectaculars where the demands were lesser than in less scenic works and where her looks, never dazzling and now quite simply ugly, were less important than her ever attractive personality. In later years, she attempted for a short and unsuccessful period the management of the Théâtre Ambigu (1891–3). She announced her retirement in 1902.

LA BOULANGÈRE A DES ÉCUS Opérette in 3 acts by Henri Meilhac and Ludovic Halévy. Music by Jacques Offenbach. Théâtre des Variétés, Paris, 19 October 1875.

La Boulangère a des écus brought the team of Meilhac, Halévy and Offenbach back together for the first time since *Les Brigands*, six years and a war earlier. More than that, the show was mounted by Eugène Bertrand at the Théâtre des Variétés, the site of the trio's earlier and greatest successes, and the titular rôle of the baker, Margot, was made to order for the star of those shows, Hortense Schneider, with fine parts also included for the other stars of the very starry Variétés company: Dupuis, Baron, Léonce, Pradeau, Berthelier and Paola Marié.

The handsome hairdresser Bernadille (Dupuis) has, through excess of gallantry, got himself mixed up in an abortive aristocratic conspiracy to murder the Regent and he is on the run, pursued by a droll pair of constables, Flammèche (Berthelier) and Délicat (Léonce). He runs to his sweetheart, the bar-keeper, Toinon (Mlle Marié), but, with his bloodhounding pursuers heading straight to this obvious hideout as well, ends up being hidden instead by her friend Margot, a baker who has become hugely rich by dabbling in stocks and shares. Coquebert (Baron), who has lost all his fortune on the same stock-market, and has now become Margot's adoring Switzer, muddies the pursuit by swapping places with the fugitive, but the Commissaire of police (Pradeau) is soon on the track. Complications ensue when Margot takes a shine to her friend's fellow, but in the end it is she who uses her money to bribe her way into the Regent's presence and charm him into pardoning Bernadille. The hairdresser and his Toinon head for the happily ever after, and Margot, equipped with a purchased title, makes do with the devotion of Coquebert.

La Boulangère had little of the bouffonerie of its authors' early days about it, even if the characters of the policemen and the foolish Switzer were supremely comical creations. It leaned heavily towards *La Fille de Madame Angot*, in particular, in some of its parts, but it was a fine and clever libretto which Offenbach decorated with some lively and attractive melodies ranging from the star's entrance number ('Lorsque j'étais fill' de boutique') to the jolly duo for Berthelier and Léonce, switching their disguises from charcoal-burners to flour-merchants ('Tout noir ... tout blanc'), to Toinon's pretty admission of love ('J'ai que je suis amoureuse'), her jealous scene with Bernadille when he puts in an appearance after a week away conspiring, and Bernadille's reflections on undeserving love.

All the plans for *La Boulangère* came to fruition, excepting one. Mlle Schneider, edging on the decline, compensated by throwing tantrums in rehearsal and finally got so impossible that Bertrand sacked her. Her replacement was his girlfriend, Marie Aimée, the pretty Fiorella of *Les Brigands*. A delightful artist, Aimée simply did not have the booming star presence the rôle of Margot had been written to provide for, and, when *La Boulangère* was produced, it proved to have a soft centre. It played just 47 times.

However, the following year Bertrand came up with an idea that nearly worked dazzlingly. He cast the celebrated star of the cafés-concerts, Mlle Thérésa, in a revival of *La Boulangère* (27 April), and that lady brought all the star presence needed to the rôle, successfully erasing the obvious fact that it had been written to the measure of Schneider. Offenbach did some considerable rewrites on, in particular, the second act, and brought it to a show-stopping climax with a finale in which Thérésa ('avec une verve, une vigeur, une *furia* dont il est impossible de se faire une idée') and Paola Marié joined in a patriotic 'marseillaise' ('Nous sommes ici trois cents femelles'). The third act, too, was improved and *La Boulangère* Mark 2 ran up to the summer break, and returned thereafter. Arnold Mortier reported 'Dupuis was encored, Berthelier and

Léonce were encored, Thérésa was encored in the famous finale of 300 women. Too many encores. You end up having the show twice in one evening. In a word, a hit. The Boulangère will carry on taking money.' It did, for a handy season of 61 nights, but too late to allow the piece to become established as it deserved.

In spite of its delayed and/or semi-success, the show was promptly picked up around the world. In Budapest (ad Jenő Rákosi), where Lujza Blaha played Margot and Emilia Sziklai was Toinon, *A talléros pekné* had a fine season of 28 performances. In Vienna the title became a little more explicit – the heroine was Margot, the millionaire baker of Paris as portrayed by Antonie Link and she was supported by Karoline Finaly (Toinon), Franz Eppich (Bernadille) and by Blasel, Matras and Ausim as the comical cops. In spite of her limited success in the rôle in Paris, Aimée put *La Boulangère* into her repertoire when she returned, shortly afterwards, to America, and she maintained it there for several seasons, without prompting anyone to essay an English version. However, an English version did emerge, eventually, in London when Alexander Henderson mounted H B Farnie's adaptation of *La Boulangère* with the characterful Madame Amadi (Margot), Tilly Wadman (Toinon), Frank Celli (Bernadille), Harry Paulton, Charles Ashford and George Temple as the policemen and the young Richard Mansfield as Coquebert. In typical Farnie fashion (or was this part of the French 'revisions'?), the principal page became the juvenile King of France in disguise, thus allowing a less spicy but boringly old-fashioned ending. The English *La Boulangère* ran 40 nights.

The title *La Boulangère a des écus* was previously used for a two-act vaudeville by Théaulon and a three-act piece of the same genre by Armand de Jallais, Henri Thiéry and Alphonse Vulpian (Délassements-Comiques 8 November 1856) as well as for Prémaray's five-act drama played at the Théâtre de la Porte-Saint-Martin in 1855.

Hungary: Népszinház *A talléros pékné* 22 February 1876; Austria: Carltheater *Margot, die Millionbäckerin von Paris (Margot, die reiche Bäckerin)* 17 February 1877; USA: Eagle Theater 26 February 1877; UK: Globe Theatre 16 April 1881

BOULE DE NEIGE Opérette in 3 acts by Charles Nuitter and Étienne Tréfeu. Music by Jacques Offenbach. Théâtre des Bouffes-Parisiens, Paris, 14 December 1871.

The 'boule de neige' of Nuitter and Tréfeu's libretto was a bear, and their tale told of how he was set up as the ruler over a revolting populace. The boyfriend of the bear's trainer, Olga, fleeing from one of the bear's sillier laws, takes refuge in a bearskin and by the time the evening is out he has deposed the animal. Equipped with a score which was largely second-hand – much of it being taken from Offenbach's failed *Barkouf* (Eugène Scribe, Hector Boisseaux Opéra-Comique 24 December 1860) – the show played only a fair run with Mme Peschard (Olga), Berthelier (Le Caporal) and Désiré (Balabrelock) in its featured rôles. It was subsequently taken up for a production in Vienna (ad Julius Hopp) where, after a première conducted by Offenbach himself, it played for a respectable 16 straight performances at the Carltheater with Frln Roeder (Olga), Josef Matras (Caporal) and Wilhelm Knaack (Balabrelock) starred, then five more in repertoire, before being brought back the following year four times more.

Austria: Carltheater *Schneeball* 3 February 1872

BOULLARD, Marius (b Ghent, 27 December 1842; d Paris, 22 October 1891).

As musical director at the Théâtre des Variétés, Boullard supplied the usual amount of 'composed and arranged' material to the Paris stage of the 1860s and 1870s. It was, however, only after he had left his post at the Variétés to Adolphe Lindheim that he found his principal successes. After supplying manager Bertrand with the score for the féerie *Le Roi dort*, he was again called upon, as a last minute replacement, to provide the score – composed and arranged – for the vaudeville-opérette *Niniche*. The huge international success of that show did not always carry his score with it, but Boullard's tactful arrangement of the show's music, to the measure of star Anna Judic, had done its share in launching *Niniche*'s original production. He later supplied part of the music for *La Roussotte*, another in the Variétés series of Judic vaudevilles, but Bertrand chose to go to the likes of Lecocq and Hervé for the rest of his shows, and the utilitarian Boullard rested on his rather unlikely laurels, as the composer of the oft-revived *Niniche*.

1863 **Nedel** (Mme Lionel de Chabrillan) 1 act Théâtre des Champs-Elysées 23 May
1863 **Militairement** (Mme Lionel de Chabrillan) 1 act Théâtre des Champs-Elysées 28 October
1866 **L'Île des Sirènes** (Xavier de Montépin, J Dornay) Théâtre des Nouveautés 27 November
1867 **Le Grillon** (Hector Girard) 1 act Théâtre des Nouveautés 9 March
1876 **Le Roi dort** (Eugène Labiche, Alfred Delacour) Théâtre des Variétés 30 March
1878 **Niniche** (Albert Millaud, Alfred Hennequin) Théâtre des Variétés 15 February
1881 **La Roussotte** (w Lecocq, Hervé/Meilhac, Halévy, Millaud) Théâtre des Variétés 25 January

BOURVIL [RAIMBOURG, André] (b Prétot-Vicquemare, 27 July 1917; d Paris, 23 September 1970). Star comedian of the postwar French stage and screen.

After early work as a comedian in cabaret and on radio, where he established a fine reputation playing and singing more often than not in a dumb peasant character, Bourvil moved out, after the war, into films and into the theatre. He made his first appearances in the musical theatre at the Alhambra in *La Bonne Hôtesse* (1946) and, promoted to top of the bill, in *Le Maharadjah* (1947) and moved on to the Théâtre de l'Étoile for *M'sieur Nanar* (1950). On the insistence of Georges Guétary, who was searching for a comedian with whom to establish a Crosby–Hope style of partnership, the slightly floundering actor was offered the comedy lead in the musical comedy *La Route fleurie* (1952) and it was his performance, alongside Guétary and another newcomer, Annie Cordy, in this long-running show which hoisted him to major stardom.

At intervals during a busy career in films, both comic and dramatic as well as musical (*Le Chanteur de Mexico*, *Sérénade au Texas* etc), he returned several times to the theatre, appearing again with Guétary in the highly successful *Pacifico* (1958, 'C'est du nanan', 'C'est pas si mal que ça chez nous', 'Bonne année'), in *La Bonne Planque*

(1963) with Pierette Bruno, and with Annie Cordy in the opérette à grand spectacle, *Ouah! Ouah!* (1965, 'Les Abeilles', 'Les Goths', 'Notre Jour J'), at the Alhambra.

A comedian of great drollery and warmth, his voice contained an irresistible laughter which survives on the musical comedy discs he made for Pathé-Marconi, including definitive performances of such classic opérettes as *Phi-Phi* (Phi-Phi) and *L'Auberge du Cheval Blanc* (Léopold).

Biographies: Lorcey, J: *Bourvil* (Pac, Paris, 1981), Berruer, P: *Bourvil du rire aux larmes* (Presses de la Cité, Paris)

THE BOY Musical comedy in 2 acts by Fred Thompson based on Arthur Pinero's play *The Magistrate*. Lyrics by Adrian Ross and Percy Greenbank. Music by Lionel Monckton and Howard Talbot. Adelphi Theatre, London, 14 September 1917.

The Boy (a title chosen for the musical by Pinero himself) was an expert adaptation of the playwright's famous play *The Magistrate*, telling of the legal gentleman who, after a jolly night on the town with his young stepson (whose mother has docked his real age to keep her own as minimal as possible, if not probable), ends up in court sentencing his own wife, who had been out protecting her guilty secret, for being nabbed in the very shady hotel he and the boy had themselves been visiting.

Aided materially by a lively score from Monckton and Talbot and a star performance of the first degree from Bill Berry as the guilty magistrate, Meebles, *The Boy* established itself as a major hit in London in the last part of the war. The song favourite of the piece was a lugubrious little ballad, 'I Want to Go to Bye-Byes', sung by the exhausted magistrate the morning after, but a pretty Make-Up duet for the equally ravaged Mrs Meebles (Maisie Gay) and her sister (Nellie Taylor) and a bristling 'The Game That Ends with a Kiss' for the soubrette (Billie Carleton, soon to be dead of a drug overdose) were other highlights. As the show ran on, the score was slimmed and the comedy increased but, as cast changes intervened, fresh songs (including Jerome Kern's 'Have a Heart') were introduced and by the time *The Boy* went on the road after a West End run of 801 performances it was musically as plump as ever.

The Messrs Shubert's production of the retitled *Good Morning Judge* (ex- *Kiss Me*) in America supplemented the score as well, notably with numbers by the young George Gershwin and Irving Caesar ('There's More to a Kiss Than XXX', 'I Am So Young and You Are So Beautiful' w Alfred Bryan) and Buddy De Sylva/Louis Silvers ('I'm the Boy [and I'm the girl]'). With George Hassell starring as the Judge of the title, but bereft of virtually all singing duties including 'I Want to Go to Bye-Byes', it did well both on Broadway (140 performances) and on the road. Australia's production of the English version, with Arthur Stigant (Meebles), Ethel Morrison (Mrs Meebles), Maud Fane (Joy), Lance Lister (Hughie) and Gladys Moncrieff (Diana) hopped successfully through four theatres in Melbourne and Sydney.

The Austrian musical *Das Baby* (Richard Heuberger/A M Willner, Heinrich von Waldberg, Carltheater 3 October 1902) was also based on *The Magistrate*.

USA: Shubert Theater *Good Morning Judge* 6 February 1919; Australia: Theatre Royal, Melbourne 23 October 1920

THE BOY FRIEND Musical comedy in 2 acts (originally 1 act) by Sandy Wilson. Players' Theatre, London, 14 April 1953; Wyndham's Theatre, 14 January 1954.

Originally commissioned as a short piece to make up one of the three halves (sic) of the programme at London's Players' club theatre, *The Boy Friend* was author-composer Wilson's first solo venture into the area of the musical play after successful work as a revue writer for the same kind of intimate theatre. Conceived and written as a small-scale 'new 1920s musical', *The Boy Friend* affectionately combined some of the favourite plot and style elements of the 1920s musical stage, whilst providing rôles for some of the principal members of the club.

Heiress Polly Browne (Anne Rogers) is the only girl at the Riviera finishing school run by Mme Dubonnet (Joan Sterndale Bennett) who doesn't have that sine qua non, a boy friend. Every prospective beau is suspected of being only after her attractive fortune until, with the Carnival Ball looming, she meets messenger boy Tony (Anthony Hayes). He thinks she's only a secretary and romance blossoms but, alas, before the big night, he vanishes, suspected of theft, and Polly's heart is cruelly chipped. But the truth comes out under the fairylights of the Ball: Tony is no messenger boy but a wealthy lordling in search of true love. And like Polly, he has found it. Maria Charles (Dulcie) and Ann Wakefield (Maisie) featured as the heroine's friends, Larry Drew was Bobby, the rich American won by Maisie, Fred Stone played Polly's father, Percival, whilst John Rutland was the hero's paternal English Lord and Violetta doubled as his wife and the French maid required to open the evening.

The show's score captured the feeling of the tale and the times prettily as the young pair dreamed of loving poverty in 'A Room in Bloomsbury' or promised that 'I Could Be Happy With You (if you could be happy with me)', Maisie bounced out her theory that there is 'Safety in Numbers' where men are concerned and swung into day-time dance with her Bobby in anticipation of the evening in 'Won't You Charleston With Me?'. Dulcie encouraged the sparkle in the eye of ageing Lord Brockhurst in 'It's Never Too Late to Fall in Love' whilst Madame Dubonnet swooned accusingly into 'Fancy Forgetting', suffered the 'You-Don't-Want-to-Play-With-Me Blues' as she tried to rekindle a wartime romance with Percival Browne, and consoled the heroine to the tale of 'Poor Little Pierrette'.

The Boy Friend's lovingly humorous re-creation of its period, avoiding all burlesque and forced extravagance, won it fine reviews and a fond public and the Players' Theatre remounted their show, tactfully lengthened into a full evening's entertainment, for a second season the following year, before taking it to the suburban Embassy Theatre for a Christmas season and, ultimately, to the West End's Wyndham's Theatre, with largely the same cast which had played the show from its beginning. *The Boy Friend* proved one of the phenomena of its period, playing for five years and 2,084 performances in London whilst overseas productions followed in procession.

Feuer and Martin's Broadway production, featuring the young Julie Andrews as Polly alongside John Hewer (Tony), Ann Wakefield (Maisie) and Dilys Laye (Dulcie), swapped the affectionate atmosphere of the original for a more burlesque style and larger production values all round, but still played 485 performances. New York got a

Plate 34. **The Boy Friend**: *'We're perfect young ladies ...' The girls of the original Players' Theatre company.*

chance to see a more sincere *Boy Friend* shortly afterwards when a revival mounted at off-Broadway's Cherry Lane Theater (25 January 1958) had a 763-performance run, and a Broadway reprise was given in 1970 (Ambassador Theater, 14 April, 119 performances).

Australia's *Boy Friend* began its career at the Elizabethan Theatre in Sydney for a five-week season with John Parker (Tony), Marie Tysoe (Polly) and Laurel Mather (Mme Dubonnet) featured. It soon moved on to the Comedy Theatre and to Melbourne (Her Majesty's Theatre 31 March 1956), as the show established itself around Australia in the same way that it had in the rest of the English-speaking world.

The Boy Friend was subsequently produced in Germany and Scandinavia, a Paris production was mounted by Simone Berriau with Valérie Saine (Polly), James Sparrow (Tony), Jean Moussy (Bobby) and Suzy Delair (Mme Dubonnet) featured, and the show kept up an almost permanent presence in the British provinces for many years, returning to London for a fresh run in 1967 (Comedy Theatre 29 November, 365 performances) with Cheryl Kennedy, Tony Adams and Marion Grimaldi, and again in 1984 (Albery Theatre 20 September, 156 performances) in a version gussied up with additional dance, and with Jane Wellman, Simon Green and Anna Quayle in the leading rôles. A film version, which used most of the score, and which featured Twiggy, Christopher Gable, Moyra Fraser and Tommy Tune, guyed the remnants of the piece, which were put into a framework which allowed the director to indulge in the extravagant spectacle the piece specifically denied and was not successful.

USA: Royale Theater 30 September 1954; Australia: Elizabethan Theatre, Sydney 30 January 1956; Germany: Nordmark Landestheater, Schleswig 29 January 1960, Theater in der Leopoldstrasse, Munich 20 August 1969; France: Théâtre Antoine 18 September 1965; Film: 1972 MGM

Recordings: original cast (HMV) American cast (RCA) American 1970 cast (Decca), Australian revival cast (Ace of Clubs), London 1968 cast (Par), London 1984 cast (TER) etc

THE BOYS AND BETTY   Musical comedy in 2 acts by George V Hobart based on *Le Papillon* by Robert Daunceny and René Peter. Music by Silvio Hein. Wallack's Theater, New York, 2 November 1908.

Betty was Betty Barbeau (Marie Cahill) and the boys were the students and boulevardiers of Paris who flock around to see her in George Hobart's tale of a runaway American wife who makes good as a florist in the French capital and then has to fight off the money-sticky fingers of her estranged husband (John Kellerd). Fortunately for her, he has compromised himself sufficiently with a dumb lady from the Folies-Bergère for her to win her freedom and the most handsome of her boys (Edgar Aitchison-Ely). The famous operettic basso, Eugene Cowles, featured in the rôle of a bluegrass Major.

Miss Cahill scored a fine success with 'Marie Cahill's Arab Love Song' ('Oh, wait for me in your home by the Pyramids, Love me all you can, I'll be your King and you'll be Queen of my caravan') in a score which took in such frenchified pieces as 'The Folies-Bergère', 'I Want to Go to Paris' and 'Girls, Girls, Girls', topped with contributions from a bundle of the sort of composers who contributed single numbers to such shows. Will Marion Cook provided 'Whoop 'er Up With a Whoop-la-la!' and London's Frederic Norton inserted 'A Little Farther' and 'Laura Lee' whilst a piece called 'She Was a Dear Little Girl' gave the young Irving Berlin his first single song credit in a Broadway show.

The Boys and Betty played 104 times on Broadway before Miss Cahill took husband Dan V Arthur's production around America.

THE BOYS FROM SYRACUSE   Musical comedy in 2 acts by George Abbott based on Shakespeare's *A Comedy of Errors*. Lyrics by Lorenz Hart. Music by Richard Rodgers. Alvin Theater, New York, 23 November 1938.

Richard Rodgers claimed on a number of occasions that he was particularly delighted with his idea of making a musical from a Shakespeare play because no one had ever done so before. Maybe nobody ever told him that he was wrong a number of times over, and his claim has been duly repeated as gospel down the years. The turning of *A Comedy of Errors* into a Rodgers and Hart musical (whoever's idea it was and no matter why) resulted very much from the fact that Hart's actor brother Teddy bore a strong resemblance to another comedian, Jimmy Savo, and Larry Hart had the idea that the two of them would make a fine pair of musical comedy Dromios. The songwriters brought their *On Your Toes* collaborator George Abbott in on the project and, although it had been intended that all three would collaborate on the libretto, Abbott apparently finished it so speedily that it ended up being a solo effort. He also volunteered to be not only the show's director, but also its producer.

If there were, thus, rather fewer people involved on the making of this musical play than was usual, there were correspondingly fewer problems too, and *The Boys from Syracuse* made its way to Broadway and a happy reception quite uneventfully. Rodgers and Hart had supplied a very uneven score, but one of which the best parts were headed straight for the standards list. Adriana (Muriel Angelus) introduced the lovely, dancing 'Falling in Love With Love', Luciana (Marcy Westcott) and Antipholus of Syracuse (Eddie Albert) amazed 'This Can't Be Love (because I feel so well)' and romanced through 'You Have Cast Your Shadow on the Sea', whilst the two girls teamed with Wynn Murray, in the comic rôle of Luce, in the trio 'Sing for Your Supper'.

The Boys from Syracuse ran for 235 performances on its initial run, but it was not picked up by overseas producers. It did, however, win a film version and in 1940 Universal Pictures issued a movie which starred Allan Jones, Joe Penner, Martha Raye and Rosemary Lane and which used a handful of numbers from the stage show plus two additional pieces ('The Greeks Have a Word for It', 'Who Are You?').

But that was not the end of the show's life. Unexpectedly, a small-scale revival, produced more than 20 years later at the off-Broadway Theater Four under the management of Richard York (15 April 1963) and featuring Stuart Damon, Ellen Hanley, Karen Morrow, Danny Carroll and Julienne Marie in its cast, caught on. It ran for 502 performances in its little theatre and, as a result, the piece finally ended up crossing the Atlantic. With the sort of perversity that can only come from dollar-blinded eyes, it was produced by Prince Littler in no less a venue than the huge Theatre Royal, Drury Lane. Bob Monkhouse, Denis Quilley, Lynn Kennington, Ronnie Corbett and Maggie Fitzgibbon headed the cast. The show survived this overblown treatment for less than three months, but it was nevertheless mounted at the Theatre Royal in Sydney, Australia, little more than a year later with a cast including Hazel Phillips, James Kenney, Lynne Cantlon, Alton Harvey and Nancye Hayes. It played ten weeks there but was not persevered with thereafter. Nearly 30 years later, however, London got a second and slimmer glimpse of the show when it was mounted for a season at the Open Air Theatre, Regent's Park (1991).

UK: Theatre Royal, Drury Lane 7 November 1963; Australia: Theatre Royal, Sydney 5 February 1966; Germany: Pforzheim 19 November 1972; Film: Universal 1940

Recordings: New York 1963 cast (Capitol), London cast (Decca), selection (Columbia)

LES BRACONNIERS   Opérette in 3 acts by Henri Chivot and Alfred Duru. Music by Jacques Offenbach. Théâtre des Variétés, Paris, 29 January 1873.

Chivot and Duru's libretto for Offenbach's opérette *Les Braconniers* was a perfect skein of comic opera disguises and mistaken identities, with things being not what they seemed more often than even W S Gilbert could have wished.

The poachers of the title, who are stripping the estates of horrid Count Lastécouères de Campistrous (Berthelier), are led by one Bibletto (Marie Heilbronn), who is actually not a Bibletto at all but a Bibletta. She is the child of one de Birague who, thanks to the result of a lawsuit half way through Act II, is proved to be the real heir to the Campistrous estates. However, before the jolly poacheress can rise to woman's estate and the hand of the usurper's nice son, Eléonore (Grenier), there are many comicalities to go through, the chief of which involve the rustic Marcassou (José Dupuis). On the night of his wedding to Ginetta (Zulma Bouffar) the poor multeteer is mistaken for the poacher chief, the next day he finds his wife denying him because she is sheltering Bibletta as her 'husband', and eventually he is even suspected of being the missing heiress. Léonce had an ubiquitous rôle as the helpful Bibès, turning up in a variety of disguises to urge the plot along, and Baron played Ginetta's barber uncle.

Offenbach's score was highlighted by Les Couplets du Bouton de rose, a serenade, and a Galop de la mule, but *Les Braconniers*, although having an honourable career in Paris, did not make the same effect as the great opérasbouffes that its composer had put out in the preceding years. The reputation and worldwide success of those earlier pieces, however, ensured that it got a viewing beyond France. Eugène Humbert mounted the piece with his Brussels Fantaisies-Parisiennes company, and that company introduced the show to London, just months after the Paris opening, alongside their memorable *La Fille de Madame Angot*, *Les Cent Vierges* and *La Belle Hélène* in a season at the St James's Theatre with Pauline Luigini, Alfred Jolly, Mario Widmer and Jeanne d'Albert featured. The 'scanty inspiration of the composer' was remarked on, and *Les Braconniers* was snuffed out by Lecocq's hugely admired piece.

Marie Geistinger and Maximilian Steiner mounted the piece in Vienna with the manageress preferring the soubrette rôle of Ginetta to that of Bibletto. That fell to Irma Nittinger, alongside Jani Szika (Marcassou), Martinelli (Lastécouères), Schreiber (Eléonore) and Carl Adolf Friese (Bibès), for the 22 times that *Die Wilderer* (ad Zell, Richard Genée) was played. An English version was produced in America by the famous light opera company The Bostonians. It proved a lesser favourite in their repertoire and was not played in any of their Broadway seasons.

UK: St James's Theatre (Fr) 26 July 1873; Austria: Theater an der Wien *Die Wilderer* 22 November 1873; USA: Portland, Maine *The Poachers* 14 October 1887

BRACY, Henry F   (b England; d Sydney, Australia, 31 January 1917).

During the late 1870s and the 1880s, Henry Bracy was one of the best and most successful comic opera tenors on the British stage. He created leading rôles in the English versions of *Les Mousquetaires au couvent* (Gontran), *La Mascotte* (Fritellini), *The Grand Mogol* (Mignapour), *Belle Lurette* (Marly) and *Babette* (Duc de la Roche Galante), as well as introducing the rôle of Hilarion in Gilbert and Sullivan's *Princess Ida* and tenor parts in two of the most successful English musicals of the time, Bucalossi's *Manteaux Noirs* (Don Luis) and *Erminie* (Eugène Marcel). He also appeared in the West End in *The Lady of the Locket*, *The Lily of Léoville*, as Grénicheux (*Les Cloches de Corneville*), Hector *(Madame Favart)*, Valentin (*Olivette*), Simon (*Der Bettelstudent*), Offenbach's Barbe-bleue and as Peter in Cellier's *The Sultan of Mocha*, whilst simul-

Plate 35. **Henry Bracy**: *Top tenor of the 19th-century stage on both sides of the world.*

taneously working as a stage director, latterly at the Avenue Theatre.

Bracy made some of his earliest important appearances on the stage in Australia, visiting there for the first time in 1873 and appearing, along with his wife, in *Lischen and Fritzchen* and in singing rôles in several plays (*Guy Mannering*, *The Merchant of Venice*, *The Wedding March*) before being engaged by operatic producer W S Lyster. With Lyster he performed in some of the first Offenbach and Lecocq performances in Australia (Menelaos in *La Belle Hélène*, Defendant in *Trial by Jury*, Piquillo in *La Périchole*, Boléro in *Giroflé-Girofla*, Ange Pitou in *La Fille de Madame Angot* etc) and appeared as Bras-de-Fer in the famous operatic pantomime *Fortunatus*. He appeared in Australia in *La Jolie Parfumeuse* (1876), as Eisenstein in *Die Fledermaus* (1877) with Fannie Simonsen, as Giletti to the *Madame l'Archiduc* of Catherine Lewis (1877), in *La Petite Mariée* (San Carlo) and *La Princesse de Trébizonde* and, in 1878, launched his own Bracy–Leopold company with former colleague George Leopold, producing, directing and touring such pieces as *The Bohemian Girl*, *La Fille de Madame Angot*, the pantomime *Egbert the Great*, and introducing *Les Cloches de Corneville* (Grénicheux) to Australia for the first time.

The Bracys then returned to Britain, where Henry established himself at the forefront of his profession, but they returned to the colony in 1889 to settle in St Kilda and Bracy formed his own English and Comic Opera Company, directing and starring in *The Old Guard*, *The Sultan of Mocha*, *The Beggar Student*, *Nemesis*, Lecocq's *Pepita* (*La Princesse des Canaries*), *The Bohemian Girl*, *Charity Begins at Home* etc. Renouncing the cares of management, he then settled in, first as principal tenor in the Williamson & Garner Royal Comic Opera Company

(*Dorothy*, *La Cigale*, Wilfred in *Marjorie*, *Iolanthe*, *The Mikado*, *Trial by Jury*, *The Vicar of Bray*, *The Mountebanks* etc) and then as house director for the same company. In this capacity, over perhaps the most prosperous decade of J C Williamson's musical comedy activities, he was responsible for staging the Australian productions of such pieces as *The Geisha*, *Florodora*, Sullivan's *The Rose of Persia*, *The Mountebanks*, *Mam'zelle Nitouche*, *Dorothy*, *La Poupée* and regular revivals of the Gilbert and Sullivan repertoire, whilst still appearing on stage in such rôles as Gaston in *La Belle Thérèse* (1895), Marmaduke in *Miss Decima* (1896), Simon in *The Beggar Student* (1897), Calino in *Nemesis* (1897), Peter in *The Sultan of Mocha*, Thaddeus in *The Bohemian Girl* etc. In 1903 he was briefly made General Manager of J C Williamson's production company and he continued a close association with Williamson and his company up until his death.

His wife, **Clara THOMPSON** (b London, 1846; d Los Angeles, 22 February 1941), sister to the more famous Lydia Thompson, also had a long and substantial career in comic opera and musical comedy, from the late 1860s when she appeared with Lydia's troupe of blondes in America (a trick bicycle speciality then Amber in *The Forty Thieves*, *Sinbad the Sailor* etc), and in London in burlesque and comedy with Pattie Oliver (Lady Anne in *The Rise and Fall of Richard III* etc). In the early 1870s she introduced Clairette (*La Fille de Madame Angot*), the twin title-rôle of *Giroflé-Girofla* (1875), *La Périchole* (1875) and other star opéra-bouffe rôles to Australia, appeared with Emilie Melville in *Fortunatus* (Little King Pippin), and starred as Rose Michon in *La Jolie Parfumeuse* (1876), Graziella in *La Petite Mariée*, Serpolette in *Les Cloches de Corneville*, Régina in *La Princess de Trébizonde*, *La Belle Hélène*, Fiorella in *Les Brigands*, *Maritana*, Prince Conti in *Les Prés Saint Gervais*, etc around Australia. She was less prominent than her husband when they returned to Britain, although she took over as Serpolette in London's *Les Cloches de Corneville*, but she found a second career when, on their return to Australia, she moved to more characterful rôles such as Mme Moutonnet (*La Belle Thérèse*, 1895), Mrs Merton (*The Vicar of Bray*), Mrs Bumpus (*Charity Begins at Home*), La Señora (*Miss Decima*, 1896), Duchess (*In Town*, 1896), Palmatica (*The Beggar Student*, 1897), Aunt Turlurette (*Nemesis*, 1897), Dame Durden (*Robin Hood*, 1899), Lady Constance (*The Geisha*, 1899) and the Gilbert and Sullivan heavy ladies. She was subsequently seen at the Lincoln Square Theatre in 1907 in the opera *Matilda*, made a very fine career as a character actress in America (*The Old Lady Shows Her Medals*, *Belinda* with Ethel Barrymore, *Humpty Dumpty* with Otis Skinner), and took part in early films for Kinemacolor and Biograph.

Two sons, Philip H Bracy (Grant in *The Medal and the Maid*, Régnier in *The Duchess of Dantzic* [UK and US], So-Long in *See See*), and Sydney Bracy (Merone in *The Toreador*, Lupin in *Amorelle (1810)*, Mustapha in *A Persian Princess*) both appeared in supporting rôles on the musical comedy stage in London. Sydney also took the rôles of Rudolph Schiller in the American production of *A Polish Wedding* (*Polnische Wirtschaft*), Guy of Gisborne in a 1912 revival of *Robin Hood* and Yussuf in Broadway's *Rose of Persia*, and appeared in Australia in Gilbert and Sullivan (Leonard in *Yeomen of the Guard* etc).

BRADFIELD, W[alter] Louis (b London, 13 June 1866; d Brighton, 12 August 1919). All-purpose Victorian musical leading man with an unusual ability to take either romantic or comic rôles.

Louis Bradfield began his career as a musical comedy star playing the Fred Leslie and Arthur Roberts low-comedy burlesque rôles in the touring companies of Auguste van Biene (Don Caesar, Servant, Captain Crosstree etc). He appeared in London for the first time when he succeeded Roberts in the star rôle of Captain Coddington in George Edwardes's production of *In Town* and he created his first metropolitan rôle, also for Edwardes, as Bobbie Rivers in *A Gaiety Girl* (1893). He played this part with the Gaiety company in Australia (where he also appeared in the title-rôle of *Gentleman Joe*) and in America and his versatility as a performer proved extremely useful when he was able to deputize during the tour not only for the lead comic but also, thanks to a handsome figure and a good baritone voice, for the principal singing hero as well.

This combination of talents won him a career-long run of rôles under Edwardes's management, as one of the few actors whom the producer could move back and forth between leading and featured rôles at Daly's Theatre and the Gaiety and the different styles of musical plays they housed in the heyday of his management (*An Artist's Model*, *My Girl*, *The Geisha*, *The Circus Girl*, *A Runaway Girl*, *San Toy*, *The Girl From Kays*, *The Cingalee*, *Les P'tites Michu*, *The Little Cherub*, *Les Merveilleuses*, *The Girls of Gottenberg*). He succeeded to the juvenile baritone rôle of Donegal in *Florodora* (1900) and the following year created the equivalent rôle of Berkeley Shallamar in *The Silver Slipper*, starred in the British production of *Madame Sherry* (1903) and scored a fine success as the fey, puckish Widgery Blake in *Butterflies* (1908). Latterly, he played for Edwardes and other managers in the provinces, appearing in the leading rôles of such pieces as *The Merry Widow* and *The Quaker Girl*. Only months before his death he was touring in the musical *Gay Trouville* alongside another ageing Daly's star, Hayden Coffin.

BRADLEY, Buddy [?EPPS, Clarence Bradley] (b ?Epps, Ala, 24 July 1908; d New York, 17 July 1972). American choreographer and teacher who made most of his career purveying American dance techniques in Britain.

The young Bradley appeared on the revue stage with Florence Mills, but he largely abandoned performing in favour of choreography and teaching in his early twenties. He provided tap and jazz dance routines for some of the era's favourite dance stars – Ruby Keeler, Eleanor Powell, Adele Astaire – under the management of producers George White, Earl Carroll and Florenz Ziegfeld before crossing to Britain in 1930 to do the dances for C B Cochran's production of the Rodgers and Hart revue *Evergreen*. He stayed in Britain, choreographing many pieces for the British stage during the period where dancing principals were the fashion, and including *Hold My Hand* (1931) with Jessie Matthews, *The Cat and the Fiddle* (1932), *Nice Goings On* (1933), *Mr Whittington* (1933, co-), *Lucky Break* (1934, co-), *Mother of Pearl* (1933), *Happy Week-End* (1934), London's *Anything Goes* (1935), *This'll Make You Whistle* (1935) with Jack Buchanan and Elsie Randolph, Emile Littler's ill-fated *Aloma and Nutane* (1938) and

Jessie Matthews' equally short-lived *I Can Take It* (1939), *Full Swing* (1943, co-), the Buchanan/Randolph *It's Time to Dance*, *Something in the Air* (1943) and *La-di-da-di-da* (1943, co-), as well as numerous revues.

He also occasionally took to the stage as a performer (*Cochran's 1931 Revue*, *It's Time to Dance*), and appeared in several films (*Evergreen*, *Gangway* etc).

He for many years ran the Buddy Bradley Studios of Dance in London, but ultimately returned to America in 1967.

Bradley varied his birthdate from 1908 to 1913, his place of birth from Alabama to Harrisburg, Penn, and his real name from Robert Bradley to Epps.

BRAHAM, David   [?ABRAHAM] (b London, ?1838; d New York, 11 April 1905).

Braham moved from London to America whilst in his teens and first worked as a violinist in Pony Moore's Minstrel company. He played in various pit orchestras, at one stage led a military band, and composed music-hall songs and theatre music, before becoming first an orchestral member and then musical director at, successively, Fox and Curran's Canterbury Concert (Music) Hall (1860), the American Theater, Wood's Theater, R W Butler's 444 Broadway and the Mechanics' Hall. He was musical director at the Theatre Comique from late 1865 with Josh Hart and later with Horace Lingard, making a first theatrical hit as a composer with his replacement score for the English burlesque *Pluto*. He accompanied the early opéra-bouffe performances of the Galton sisters in America, and headed the orchestras at the 8th Avenue Opera House, the Olympic, the Eagle and at the newly opened Union Square Theater (1871) before he joined Harrigan and Hart in a similar position (1873).

When the pair began to extend their comical sketches-with-songs into musical farces, Braham was given the job of composing such music as was required, to Harrigan's lyrics. He held his position with Harrigan and Hart, and, following Hart's departure, with Harrigan alone, through the entire length of their famous careers as theatrical entertainers and during that period he composed a number of enduring songs for their shows, including 'Whist! the Bogey Man!', 'The Mulligan Guards', 'The Babies on our Block', 'The Skids Are Out Tonight', 'Sallie Waters', 'The Little Widow Dunn', 'Paddy Duffy's Cart', 'Widow Nolan's Goat', 'Ebb and Flow', 'Maggie Murphy's Home', 'My Dad's Dinner Pail' etc.

During his years with Harrigan and Hart, he occasionally provided music for other projects including Maggie Mitchell's 1888 vehicle *Maggie the Midget*. After Harrigan's days were done Braham worked out his career at the Grand Opera House, and finally at Wallack's Theater where he was engaged up to his final illness.

Braham was related to the English singer-songwriter John Braham, and his brother Joseph Braham, also a musician, was the father of four further musicians and conductors: John (who conducted America's first *HMS Pinafore* in Boston), Harry (who was the first Mr Lillian Russell), Albert and William. David's own sons David jr and George worked as an actor and conductor respectively, whilst his daughter, Annie, became Mrs Edward Harrigan.

1868 **Pluto** (H B Farnie) Theatre Comique 1 February
1874 **The Donovans** Wallack's Theater 31 May

1874 **The Mulligan Guard** sketch (Harrigan) Theatre Comique 8 September
1877 **Old Lavender** (Harrigan) Theatre Comique 3 September (revised version 22 April 1878)
1877 **The Rising Star** (Harrigan) Theatre Comique 22 October
1877 **Sullivan's Christmas** (Harrigan) Theatre Comique 31 December
1878 **A Celebrated Hard Case** (Harrigan) Theatre Comique 18 March
1878 **The Mulligan Guards' Picnic** (Harrigan) Theatre Comique 23 September
1878 **The Lorgaire** (Harrigan) Theatre Comique 25 November
1879 **The Mulligan Guards Ball** (Harrigan) Theatre Comique 13 January
1879 **The Mulligan Guards Chowder** (Harrigan) Theatre Comique 11 August
1879 **The Mulligan Guards' Christmas** (Harrigan) Theatre Comique 17 November
1880 **The Mulligan Guards' Surprise** (Harrigan) Theatre Comique 16 February
1880 **The Mulligan Guards' Nominee** (Harrigan) Theatre Comique 22 November
1881 **The Mulligan' Silver Wedding** (Harrigan) Theatre Comique 21 February
1881 **The Major** (Harrigan) Theatre Comique 29 August
1882 **Squatter Sovereignty** (Harrigan) Theatre Comique 9 January
1882 **The Blackbird** (Harrigan) Theatre Comique 26 August
1882 **Mordecai Lyons** (Harrigan) Theatre Comique 26 October
1882 **McSorley's Inflation** (Harrigan) Theatre Comique 27 November
1883 **The Muddy Day** (Harrigan) Theatre Comique 2 April
1883 **Cordelia's Aspirations** (Harrigan) Theatre Comique 5 November
1884 **Dan's Tribulations** (Harrigan) Theatre Comique 7 April
1884 **Investigation** (Harrigan) Theatre Comique 1 September
1885 **McAllister's Legacy** (Harrigan) Park Theater 5 January
1885 **Are You Insured?** 14th Street Theater 11 May
1885 **The Grip** (Harrigan) Park Theater 30 November
1886 **The Leather Patch** (Harrigan) Park Theater 15 February
1886 **The O'Reagans** (Harrigan) Park Theater 11 October
1887 **McNooney's Visit** (Harrigan) Park Theater 31 January
1887 **Pete** (Harrigan) Park Theater 22 November
1888 **Waddy Googan** (Harrigan) Park Theater 3 September
1889 **4-11-44** (revised *McNooney's Visit*) (Harrigan) Park Theater 21 March
1889 **McKenna's Flirtation** (Edgar Selden) (Harrigan) Park Theater 2 September
1890 **Reilly and the Four Hundred** (Harrigan) Harrigans Theater 29 December
1891 **The Last of the Hogans** (Harrigan) Harrigans Theater 21 December
1893 **The Woolen Stocking** (Harrigan) Harrigans Theater 9 October
1894 **Notoriety** (Harrigan) Harrigans Theater 10 December
1896 **My Son Dan** (Harrigan)
1896 **Marty Malone** (Harrigan) Bijou Theater 31 August
1898 **The Finish of Mr Fresh** (anon) Star Theater 7 November

BRAHAM, Leonora   (b 3 February 1853; d London, 23 November 1931). Savoy Opera star soprano through much of Gilbert & Sullivan's best period.

At the age of 21, Leonora Braham joined Mr and Mrs German Reed's company at the St George's Hall, appearing there continuously in the juvenile soprano rôles of their highly popular four- or five-handed musical playlets for more than four years. Her first ventures into the regular theatre were in America where she starred in the New York productions of the British comic operas *Princess Toto*

(1879) and *Billee Taylor* (1880) and, on returning to Britain, she was hired by D'Oyly Carte to create the title-rôle in *Patience*, a part which had been rejected as too soubrette-y by his current prima donna, at the Opera Comique ('I Cannot Tell What This Love May Be'). For the next six years Miss Braham held the position of leading lady at the Savoy Theatre, through the creations of *Iolanthe* (Phyllis), *Princess Ida* (Ida, following Carte's quarrel with Lillian Russell), *The Mikado* (Yum Yum, introducing 'The Sun Whose Rays' and 'Three Little Maids') and *Ruddigore* (Rose Maybud) and the first revival of *The Sorcerer* (Aline).

In 1887–8 she and her then husband, Duncan Young, spent a season with Williamson, Garner and Musgrove's Royal Comic Opera Company in Australia (*Dorothy, Erminie, The Mikado* etc) but, on her return, she did not, in spite of her old position in the world of comic opera, succeed in finding appreciable work. She appeared in London only as a replacement in *Carina* (1888, t/o Zara) and in the short-lived *Gretna Green*, (1889/90 Ruth Ferris) and on tour in the title-rôle of *Nanon*, in Edward Jakobowski's *Paola* (1889, Paola) and the burlesque *Miss Esmeralda*. She went to South America with Edwin Cleary's comic opera company in 1890, then produced and starred in a tour of a small comic opera, *The Duke's Diversion*, on her own account in 1892 before again leaving Britain to spend two years touring British comic opera in South Africa. During this tour she also made a venture into heavier waters, and appeared as Santuzza in *Cavalleria Rusticana*.

Her only subsequent West End appearance of note was in the comedy rôle of Lady Barbara Cripps in George Edwardes's musical comedy *An Artist's Model* in 1895, although she continued to make provincial appearances around Britain (Julia Jellicoe in The *Grand Duke* and the Carte repertoire, Nora in *Shamus O'Brien*, Bathilde in *Olivette*, Madame Michu in *Les P'tites Michu*, Widow Melnotte in *Melnotte*) until after the turn of the century.

BRAHAM, Philip (b London, 18 June 1881; d London, 2 May 1934). British songwriter who was quick to catch the new dancing style in theatre music in the postwar years.

Educated at Charterhouse and Cambridge, Braham began a career in show business as a member of the March Hares concert party, for whom he also supplied performance material. His first regular theatre composition was the music-hall sketch *Alice Up-to-Date*, written with no less a librettist than Fred Thompson and actor-cum-writer Eric Blore and played at the London Pavilion, and in the early part of the war years he provided similar sketches and revues (*Sugar and Spice, Nurses, Brides* etc) for several London variety houses.

His first work on a major show was in supplying some songs for the musical comedy *Mr Manhattan*, of which Howard Talbot was the principal composer, and then on additional numbers for the revue *The Bing Boys Are Here*. In the next decade he composed or contributed to a huge number of West End revues, proving for some while the most successful of local composers in the face of the fashion for transatlantic songs (*Bubbly, Tails Up, Back to Blighty, See-Saw, Pot Luck, The Latest Craze, Jumble Sale, Rats, London Calling* w Noël Coward, *The Co-Optimists, Charlot's Revue, On With the Dance* w Coward, *Still Dancing, Charlot's Revue of 1928* etc). He contributed botching material for imported shows (two songs in *Dédé* etc), and

Plate 36. **Phil Braham**'s *'Dancing Honeymoon' proved a hit in both Britain and America as displayed in* Battling Butler. *France took the song, but not the show.*

also provided scores for a number of the song-and-dance musicals of the day. The farcical *The Officers' Mess* (200 performances) and the Jack Buchanan vehicle *Battling Butler* ('The Dancing Honeymoon'), subsequently played on Broadway with a largely different score, were his most successful book musicals in a career largely devoted to revue, before, in his last years, he became a musical director on early British sound films.

'Limehouse Blues' (w Douglas Furber) seen in *A to Z* and *Charlot's Revue* and used in the films of *The Ziegfeld Follies* and *Star*, remains Braham's most famous single number.

1913 **Alice Up-to-Date** (Eric Blore, Fred Thompson) 1 act London Pavilion 29 December

1914 **Violet and Pink** (Campbell) East Ham Palace 4 May, London Pavilion 11 May

1914 **Beauties** (Sydney Blow, Douglas Hoare) 1 act Victoria Palace 14 December

1916 **Mr Manhattan** (w Howard Talbot, Frank E Tours/C H Bovill, Fred Thompson) Prince of Wales Theatre 30 March

1916 **Back to Blighty** (w G H Clutsam, Herbert Haines/Blow, Hoare) Oxford Theatre September

1917 **The Hula Girl** (w Nat D Ayer, Alfred Haines/George Reynolds, R Guy Keene) 1 act Hippodrome 18 December

1918 **Telling the Tale** (Blow, Hoare) Ambassadors Theatre 31 August

1918 **The Officers' Mess** (Blow, Hoare) St Martins Theatre 7 November

1921 **Yes, Papa** (Eric Blore, Austin Melford) Coliseum, Cheltenham

1921 **Now and Then** (Reginald Arkell/J Hastings Turner) Vaudeville Theatre 17 September

1922 **Battling Butler** (Douglas Furber/Stanley Brightman, Austin Melford) New Oxford Theatre 9 December
1924 **Boodle** (w Max Darewski/Furber/Blow, Hoare) Empire Theatre 10 March
1925 **Up with the Lark** (Furber/Furber, Hartley Carrick) Adelphi Theatre 25 August

BRAMBLE, Mark (b Maryland, 7 December 1950).

Originally an employee in David Merrick's office, Bramble wrote one off-off-Broadway piece and collaborated with Michael Stewart on two musical adaptations – Werfel's *Jacobowsky und der Oberst* as *The Grand Tour*, and Maxwell Anderson's play *Elizabeth the Queen* as the off-Broadway *Elizabeth and Essex* – before finding international success with two consecutive stage musicals launched within four months of each other in 1980: the circus musical *Barnum* and the stage version of the famous musical film *42nd Street*.

A subsequent rewrite of the Rudolf Friml operetta *The Three Musketeers*, directed by its adapter as a swashbuckling action show, had less success (nine performances on Broadway), and the largest amount of the now London-based Bramble's work in the years that followed was as a director, notably of productions of *42nd Street* in Britain, Europe and Australia. He adapted and directed a British production of the French children's musical *Fat Pig* in 1987 and, in 1991, mounted the tryout of a new musical play based on Victor Hugo's *Notre Dame de Paris*.

1977 **T*ts D*amond** (Lee Pockriss/Steve Brown) The Loft January
1978 **Pal Joey** revised libretto w Jerome Chodorov (Athamson Theater, Los Angeles)
1979 **The Grand Tour** (Jerry Herman/w Michael Stewart) Palace Theater 11 January
1980 **Elizabeth and Essex** (Doug Katsaros/Richard Engquist/w Stewart) South Street Theater 24 February
1980 **Barnum** (Cy Coleman/Michael Stewart) St James Theater 30 April
1980 **42nd Street** (pasticcio/w Stewart) Winter Garden Theater 25 August
1983 **The Three Musketeers** revised libretto Hartman Theater, Stamford, Conn, 18 March, Broadway Theater, New York, 11 November 1984
1987 **Fat Pig** (*Le Cochon qui voulait maigrir*) English version (Henry Krieger/w Jenny Hawkesworth) Haymarket Theatre, Leicester 20 November
1991 **Notre Dame** (Callum McLeod/Paul Leigh) Old Fire Station, Oxford 25 June

BRAMMER, Julius (b Schraditz Mähren, 9 March 1877; d Juan-les-Pins, 18 March 1944). Top librettist of the heyday of the 20th-century Viennese stage.

For more than a decade a bit-part actor/singer at the Theater an der Wien, Brammer appeared fairly insignificantly in such rôles as an Innkeeper (*Die Dame aus Trouville*), Quendel (*Der Vogelhändler*), Probitt (*Der Toreador*), Ein Kellner (*Der Fremdenführer*), Schneider (*Wiener Frauen*), The Man with the monocle (*Der Lebemann*), Major Abatutta (*Bruder Straubinger*), Tabourin (*Die beiden Don Juans*), Heuven (*Der neue Burgermeister*), Baron Grenzenstein (*Der Generalkonsul*), Graf Montrigny (*Befehl des Kaisers*), Dr Runkel (*Der Herr Professor*), The Director of the New York Hotel Bristol (*Die Millionenbraut*), Lord Percy (*Wiener Blut*), von Abstorff (*Das Garnisonsmädel*), an Englishman (*Pufferl*), Lord Bevis (*Prince Bob*), Third Rat (*Der Rebell*), Kraps (*Peter

und Paul), Nowak (*Ein Herbstmanöver*), Cyprian Vollrath (*Der Mann mit den drei Frauen*), Hans (*Der schöne Gardist*), the dancemaster, Monsieur Deschamps (*Schneeglöckchen*), Graf Arrois (*Die schöne Risette*) and Lieutenant Rincke (*Ihr Adjutant*) between 1902 and 1911.

From 1907, in collaboration with Alfred Grünwald, he began writing libretti and lyrics for the musical theatre and, although a number of these works found their way to the stage in Germany and Austria, he did not give up his job as a performer until after Robert Winterberg's *Die Dame in Rot* had assured the pair of their future as stage writers.

Thereafter, Brammer and Grünwald became the most accomplished and successful team writing for the Austrian stage. In the years before the war, they had major Viennese hits with Ascher's *Hoheit tanzt Walzer* and Eysler's *Der lachende Ehemann*, and they scored one of the biggest successes of the war years with the outstanding *Die Rose von Stambul* as well as authoring the scripts for such other successes as *Die schöne Schwedin*, *Bruder Leichtsinn* and Leo Fall's *Fürstenliebe* (*Die Kaiserin*) and preparing the replacement libretto for Lehár's *Die Göttergatte* score as *Die ideale Gattin* (which they would later re-rewrite as *Die Tangokönigin*).

During the 1920s, the pair had virtual end-to-end hits with such internationally successful Operetten as *Der letzte Walzer*, *Die Bajadere*, the rather less popular *Die Perlen der Cleopatra*, *Gräfin Mariza*, *Die Zirkusprinzessin* and *Die gold'ne Meisterin*. Their final piece together, *Das Veilchen vom Montmartre*, gave them a further success, but Brammer's last Viennese collaborations with other partners, during the few years before the activities of the 1930s drove him from the country and out of the musical theatre, proved less fruitful.

1907 **Fräulein Sherlock Holmes** (Georges Criketown/w 'A G Wald' [ie Alfred Grünwald]) Volkstheater, Munich 31 August
1908 **Die grüne Redoute** (Leo Ascher/w Grünwald) 1 act Danzers Orpheum 26 March
1908 **Die lustigen Weiber von Wien** (Robert Stolz/w Grünwald) 1 act Colosseum 16 November
1908 **Die kleine Manicure** (Ascher /w Grünwald) 1 act Parisiana
1909 **Elektra** (Béla Laszky/w Grünwald) 1 act Kabarett Fledermaus 1 December
1910 **Georgette** (Laszky/w Grünwald) 1 act Kabarett Fledermaus 16 March
1910 **Vindobona, du herrliche Stadt** (Ascher/w Grünwald) Venedig in Wien 22 July
1911 **Das goldene Strumpfband** (Ascher/w Grünwald) 1 act Ronacher 1 May
1911 **Die Dame in Rot** (Robert Winterberg/w Grünwald) Theater des Westens, Berlin 16 September
1911 **Die Damenparadies** (Richard Fall/w Grünwald) 1 act Colosseum 1 November
1912 **Hoheit tanzt Walzer** (Ascher/w Grünwald) Raimundtheater 24 February
1912 **Eine vom Ballet** (Oscar Straus/w Grünwald) London Coliseum 3 June
1913 **Der lachende Ehemann** (Edmund Eysler/w Grünwald) Wiener Bürgertheater 19 March
1913 **Die ideale Gattin** (Franz Lehár/w Grünwald) Theater an der Wien 11 October
1915 **Die schöne Schwedin** (Winterberg/w Grünwald) Theater an der Wien 30 January
1915 **Die Kaiserin** (aka *Fürstenliebe*) (Fall/w Grünwald) Metropoltheater, Berlin 16 October

1916 **Die Rose von Stambul** (Fall/w Grünwald) Theater an der Wien 2 December

1917 **Bruder Leichtsinn** (Ascher/w Grünwald) Wiener Bürgertheater 18 December

1919 **Dichterliebe** (Felix Mendelssohn arr Ernst Stern/w Grünwald) Komische Oper, Berlin 20 December

1920 **Der letzte Walzer** (Straus/w Grünwald) Berliner Theater, Berlin 12 February

1921 **Die Tangokönigin** revised *Die ideale Gattin* w Grünwald Apollotheater 9 September

1921 **Die Bajadere** (Emmerich Kálmán/w Grünwald) Carltheater 23 December

1923 **Die Perlen der Cleopatra** (Straus/w Grünwald) Theater an der Wien 13 November

1924 **Gräfin Mariza** (Kálmán/w Grünwald) Theater an der Wien 28 February

1926 **Die Zirkusprinzessin** (Kálmán/w Grünwald) Theater an der Wien 26 March

1927 **Die gold'ne Meisterin** (Eysler/w Grünwald) Theater an der Wien 13 September

1928 **Die Herzogin von Chicago** (Kálmán/w Grünwald) Theater an der Wien 5 April

1930 **Das Veilchen vom Montmartre** (Kálmán/w Grünwald) Johann Strauss-Theater 21 March

1931 **Der Bauerngeneral** (Straus/w Gustav Beer) Theater an der Wien 28 March

1932 **Donauliebchen** (Eysler/w Emil Marboth) Wiener Bürgertheater 25 December

1933 **Die Dame mit dem Regenbogen** (Jean Gilbert/w Beer) Theater an der Wien 25 August

1952 **Bozena** (Straus/w Grünwald) Theater am Gärtnerplatz, Munich 16 May

BRANDL, Johann (b Kirchenbirk, Bohemia, 30 October 1835; d Vienna, 9 June 1913).

Conductor in several Viennese suburban theatres, then from 1865 to 1866 at the Theater in der Josefstadt, then a member of the music staff of the Carltheater between 1866 and 1882, Brandl composed a long list of musical accompaniments for Possen and other forms of more or less musical comedies played during his various tenures. These assignments included replacement scores for the German-language versions of the enormously successful French vaudevilles introduced by Anna Judic at the Paris Théâtre des Variétés (*Niniche, Papas Frau, Die Kosakin*), and for a range of other French vaudevilles and musical comedies (*Der Kukuk, Coco, Kleine Anzeigen* etc) as well as for shoals of local pieces by such prolific comic authors as O F Berg, Anton Langer and Julius Rosen.

Brandl botched to order for the Carltheater, interpolating more or less numbers into the French imports of the day (Costé's *Les Charbonniers*, Lecocq's *La Marjolaine* and *Hundert Jungfrauen*, Coèdes's *La Belle Bourbonnaise*, Offenbach's *La Jolie Parfumeuse* etc) when he was not replacing entire scores, but he also ventured as an author, writing or collaborating on the texts for several of his own pieces.

The Carltheater also produced Brandl's rather shorter list of original Operetten, including the highly successful and long-lived *Des Löwen Erwachen* (1872), a one-act piece which was regularly revived during the 19th century and played in 1893 at the Hofoper, the popular little *Cassis Pacha*, and two of his full-length pieces, *Die Mormonen* (1879, eight performances) and *Die drei Langhälse* (1880). The four-act Posse *Der Walzerkönig* (1885) was another success. His *Der liebe Augustin* was produced by Camillo

Walzel at the Theater an der Wien in 1887 for 27 performances.

1862 **Der Fremde** (Georg Szechenyi) Baden-bei-Wien July

186? **Die Freiwilligen in Mexico** (Julius Stern)

1865 **Tiktak** 1 act Pressburg August

1865 **Österreichs Rheinfahrt** (Carl Elmar) Theater in der Josefstadt 31 October

1865 **Die Universalerben** (Theodor Flamm) Theater in der Josefstadt 25 November

1865 **Diesseits und jenseits** (O F Berg) 1 act Theater in der Josefstadt 2 December

1865 **Ambo Solo** (Julius Rosen) Theater in der Josefstadt 9 December

1865 **Die Wiener auf der Alm** (Karl Bayer) 1 act Theater in der Josefstadt 16 December

1865 **Unterm Christbaum** (Elmar) 1 act Theater in der Josefstadt 16 December

1865 **Das alte und das neue Jahr** (Carl F Stix) 1 act Theater in der Josefstadt 31 December

1866 **20,000 Taler Reugeld** (Josef Doppler) 1 act Theater in der Josefstadt 8 January

1866 **Der erste Rausch** (Bayer) 1 act Theater in der Josefstadt 9 January

1866 **Ein Bauernball** (Elmar) 1 act Theater in der Josefstadt 27 January

1866 **Ein Narrenball** (Stix) 1 act Theater in der Josefstadt 27 January

1866 **Der Schuster-Michel** (Julius Findeisen) Theater in der Josefstadt 1 March

1866 **Alte Schulden** (Friedrich Kaiser) Theater in der Josefstadt 14 April

1866 **Eine Wiener Burgertochter** (J Seitz, Friedrich Schuster) Theater in der Josefstadt 28 April

1866 **Das Kreuz in der Klamm** (Kaiser) Thalia-Theater 12 August

1866 **Eine Promesse von Sothen** (Adolph L'Arronge) Carltheater 27 December

1866 **Meine Memoiren** (Berg) 1 act Carltheater 16 May

1867 **Die Schäferin** 1 act Harmonietheater 1 May

1867 **Eine Weinprobe** (Wilhelm Fellechner, Carl Heimerding) 1 act Carltheater 9 May

1867 **Eine neue Einrichtung** (Berg) 1 act Carltheater 16 May

1867 **Dreizehn** (Anton Langer) 1 act Carltheater 7 September

1867 **Füchsl auf der Pariser Ausstellung** Carltheater 23 October

1867 **Der kleine Beamte** (Berg) Theater in der Josefstadt 2 November

1867 **Der Direktor von Langenlois** (Berg) 1 act Carltheater 30 November

1867 **Landsturm und Zivilehe** (Langer, Julius Rosen) Carltheater 31 December

1868 **Die Pfarrerköchin** (Berg) Carltheater 20 April

1868 **Vom Schützentage** (Langer) 1 act Carltheater 21 July

1868 **Strizow in Wien** (Berg) 1 act Carltheater 15 September

1868 **Der Herr Landesgerichtsrat** (Berg) Carltheater 26 November

1868 **Wer ist tot?** 1 act Carltheater 12 December

1869 **Wort und Tat** (Rosen) Carltheater 5 January

1869 **Antikenschwindel** (Heinrich Wilcken) Carltheater 20 February

1869 **Der Hanswurst** (Rosen) 1 act Carltheater 20 February

1869 **Nur gemütlich** (Langer) 1 act Carltheater 16 December

1870 **Der Direktor von Langenlois** (Berg) 1 act Carltheater 8 January

1870 **Das Vergissmeinnicht** (Brandl) 1 act Carltheater 21 May

1870 **Brididi** (Henri de Rochefort) 1 act Carltheater 21 May

1870 **Im Redaktionsbureau** (Langer) 1 act Carltheater 21 May

1870 **Eine ländliche Verlobung** (Arthur Müller) 1 act Carltheater 24 September

1870 **Das Hasenschrecker** (Louis Grois) 1 act Carltheater 24 September

1870 **Zu Dreien** (Karl Grün) 1 act Carltheater 7 December

1871 **Zahnschmerzen** (Emil Pohl, Stix) 1 act Carltheater

1871 **Eine Vereinsschwester** (Langer) 1 act Carltheater 17 October

1871 **Pelikan der Zweite** (Labiche, Delacour ad) 1 act Carltheater 2 December

1872 **Raten und Renten** (Robert Jonas) 1 act Carltheater 6 April

1872 **Des Löwen erwachen** (Julius Rosen) 1 act Carltheater 26 April

1872 **Sein Salonstiefel** 1 act Carltheater 14 June

1872 **Vater Gorilla** (L'Arronge, Gustav von Moser) 1 act Carltheater 14 December

1873 **Der polnische Jude** (Erckmann-Chatrian ad) Carltheater August

1873 **Einst und jetzt** (Langer) 1 act Carltheater 2 December

1874 **Cassis Pascha** (*Un Turc pris dans une porte*) (Edouard Brisebarre, Eugène Riou ad) 1 act Carltheater 28 February

1874 **Die Bartolomäusnacht** (Aimé Wouwermans) 1 act Carltheater 29 April

1875 **Die Probirmamsell** (w Müller/Berg) Carltheater 6 November

1876 **Die Weiber, wie sie nicht sein sollen** (Berg) Carltheater 29 April

1876 **Vindobona** (Berg) Carltheater 7 October

1877 **O diese Weiber!** (Rosen) Carltheater 17 March

1877 **Ein vorsichtiger Mann** (Gustav Moser, E Jacobson) Carltheater 1 April

1877 **Die alte Jungfer** (Berg) Carltheater 14 April

1877 **Gevatter Neid** (Berg) Carltheater 14 November

1878 **S'Jungferngift** (Ludwig Anzengruber) Carltheater 21 April

1878 **Die verfallene Mauer** (Wilhelm Hess) 1 act Carltheater 21 September

1878 **Niniche** German version (replacement score) w Richard Genée (Carltheater)

1879 **Coco** German version with added music (Carltheater)

1879 **Der grosse Casimir** (*Le Grand Casimir*) German version (new part-score) Carltheater 15 April

1879 **Wildröschen** (Wilhelm Mannstädt, 'A Weller' [ie J A Müller]) Carltheater 4 July

1879 **Die Mormonen** (w Albert Klischnegg) Carltheater 22 November

1880 **Wiener Karrikaturen** (Berg) Carltheater 3 January

1880 **Papas Frau** (*La Femme à papa*) German version (replacement score) w Genée (Carltheater)

1880 **Die Theatergredl** (Berg) Carltheater 9 April

1880 **Der Kukuk** (*Le Coucou*) (Hippolyte Raymond, Alphonse Dumas ad) Carltheater 22 April

1880 **Kleine Anzeigen** (*Les Petites Correspondances*) German version with songs Carltheater 25 September

1880 **Die drei Langhälse** (Emil Pohl, Richard Genée) Carltheater 11 December

1881 **Die Statuten der Ehe** (Karl Morré) Carltheater 17 December

1882 **Die Töchter des Dionysus** (J S Müller) 1 act Carltheater 20 January

1882 **Hopfenraths Erben** (Wilcken ad Franz von Radler) Carltheater 11 February

1882 **Die Unzufriedenen** (Otto Weiss, Fedor Marmoth) Carltheater 18 March

1882 **Alois Blumauer** (Radler) Carltheater 30 December

1885 **Der Walzerkönig** (Mannstädt, Costa, Bruno Zappert) Carltheater 9 October

1887 **Der liebe Augustin** (Hugo Klein) Theater an der Wien 15 January

1891 **Die Kosakin** (*La Cosaque*) German version (replacement score) w Moritz West (Theater an der Wien)

1901 **Der Kellermeister** completed Ziehrer's score (Raimundtheater)

BRANDRAM, Rosina [MOULT, Rosina] (b London, 2 July 1845; d Southend-on-Sea, 28 February 1907). Long-serving Savoy Theatre heavy lady.

Encouraged on to the stage following some family financial problems, Miss Brandram, who had had a young gentlewoman's singing lessons with Sgr Nava in Italy in her early teens, but had, since the age of 17, been a safely married lady, joined the chorus of Richard D'Oyly Carte's Comedy Opera Company during its initial production of *The Sorcerer*, at the Opera Comique (1877). She played the rôle of Lady Sangazure on the show's first tour, succeeded Mrs Howard Paul in the same rôle at the Opera Comique, and thereafter remained in the employ of Carte and his successors for almost her entire career. She played the part of Little Buttercup in *HMS Pinafore* in loco Harriet Everard and created that of Kate in the American première of *The Pirates of Penzance* before succeeding Alice Barnett as Ruth in the same production and, later, at the Savoy as Lady Jane in *Patience*. She appeared with the other principal understudies in several of the D'Oyly Carte one-act curtain raisers, and also deputized for Jessie Bond in the rôle of Iolanthe before creating her first of Gilbert's 'dragon' ladies, rôles previously barred to her by her youth and by the presence of Misses Everard and Barnett, as Lady Blanche in *Princess Ida*.

Thereafter, Miss Brandram created all of the Savoy heavy ladies: Katisha (*Mikado*, 'Hearts Do Not Break', 'There Is Beauty in the Bellow of the Blast'), Dame Hannah (*Ruddigore*), Dame Carruthers (*The Yeomen of the Guard*, 'When Our Gallant Norman Foes'), the Duchess of Plaza Toro (*The Gondoliers*, 'On the Day That I Was Wedded'), Widow Jackson (*Captain Billy*), Mrs Merton (*The Vicar of Bray*), Lady Vernon (*Haddon Hall*), Miss Sims (*Jane Annie*), Lady Sophie (*Utopia Ltd*), the Marquise (*Mirette*), Inez de Roxas (*The Chieftain*), Baroness von Krakenfeld (*The Grand Duke*), Joan (*The Beauty Stone*), Dancing Sunbeam (*The Rose of Persia*), Wee Ping (*The Willow Plate*), the Countess of Newtown (*Emerald Isle*), Queen Elizabeth (*Merrie England* 'O Peaceful England') and Nell Reddish (*A Princess of Kensington*), taking time away from her base in the Strand only to appear for Gilbert as Dame Hecla Courtlandt in *His Excellency*.

When the comic opera company left the Savoy, Miss Brandram went with it and appeared with William Greet on tour in *Merrie England* and at the Savoy in the Christmas show *Little Hans Andersen* (1903), but when Greet moved into musical comedy there was no place nor part for her and, in the last performances of her career, she appeared instead as Ermerance in George Edwardes's very successful version of *Véronique*.

BRASSEUR, Jules [DUMONT, Jules Victor Alexandre] (b Paris, 1829; d Paris, 6 October 1890).

The comic actor Jules Brasseur made his début at the Théâtre de Belleville in 1847. He moved first to the Folies-Dramatiques and then, in 1852, to the Palais-Royal and, during 25 vastly popular and profitable years at that theatre created, amongst many others, the triple rôle of the Brazilian/Prosper/Frick in Offenbach's *La Vie parisienne* ('Je suis Brésilien'), Schnitzberg in Lecocq's *Le Myosotis* (1866), and Pitou in *Le Château à Toto* (1868). He later appeared with considerable success in a large number of the musical pieces which he produced during his period at the head of the Théâtre des Nouveautés (1878–1890), the house which he set up in replacement of the old Fantaisies-Parisiennes and which was the site of the productions of such pieces as Coèdes's *Fleur d'oranger* and *Les Deux Nababs*, Hervé's *Le Voyage en Amérique* (Barbazan), Lecocq's splendid *Le Jour et la Nuit* (Calabazas) and *Le Coeur et la main*, Chassaigne's *Le Droit d'aînesse*, de Lajarte's *Le Roi de carreau* (LaRoche Trumeau), Serpette's *Le Château de Tire-Larigot* (Chevalier de St-Roquet), *Adam et Ève* (Satan) and *La Lycéenne*, Planquette's *La Cantinière* (Babylas), Audran's *Serment d'amour* and *Les Puits qui parle* (Anastasius), Varney's *L'Amour mouillé* (Pampinelli) and *La Vénus d'Arles* (Le Baron), Jonas's *Premier Baiser* and Lacôme's *Les Saturnales*.

In 1884 he also took over for a time a share of the direction of the Théâtre des Folies-Dramatiques which he re-opened with the French première of Planquette's memorable *Rip*.

His son **Albert [Jules] BRASSEUR** (b Paris, 12 February 1862; d Maisons-Lafitte, 13 May 1932) made his first stage appearance alongside his father in *Fleur d'oranger* and subsequently – with a short pause for military service – created light comic singing rôles in many musical works at the Nouveautés (Pépinet in *La Cantinière*, Arthur in *Le Droit d'aînesse*, Mistigris in *Le Roi de carreau*, *Le Petit Chaperon rouge*, Beppo in *L'Oiseau bleu*, Mélissen in *Babolin*, Adrien Bézuchard in *Le Château de Tire-Larigot*, Grivolin in *Serment d'amour*, Adam in *Adam et Ève*, Bouvard in *La Lycéenne*, Cascarino in *L'Amour mouillé*, Eymeric de la Grande-Dèche in *La Vie mondaine*, Camusot in *La Vénus d'Arles*, Eusèbe in *Le Puits qui parle* etc). After his father's death, he moved to the Théâtre des Variétés (1890) where, over some 20 years, he played with great success in both musical and non-musical pieces, appearing in his father's rôle in *La Vie parisienne*, and in other classic comic rôles such as the title-rôle of *Chilpéric* (Variétés 1895 revival), Ménélas, the caissier in *Les Brigands*, Aristée/Pluton and later Styx, Frimousse, the Duke d'Enface of *L'Oeil crevé*, James (*Miss Helyett*), Grabuge the gendarme in *Geneviève de Brabent* and Valentin in *Le Petit Faust* as well as creating the rôles of Auguste in *Le Pompier de service* (1897), Robert Garnier in *Les Petites Barnett* (1898), Fassinet in *Mademoiselle George* (1900), Fontelin in *L'Age d'or* (1905), Coucy in *Le Sire de Vergy* and the title-rôle of *Monsieur de la Palisse*. He played at the Ambigu during the First World War in revivals of *Lili*, *La Roussotte* and *Mam'selle Nitouche*, but in the 1920s he appeared most frequently in comedy.

Brasseur also collaborated on the libretto of Planquette's unsuccessful *La Cremaillère*, and was associated with his father in the last years of his management of the Théâtre des Nouveautés.

BRATTON, John W (b Wilmington, Del, 21 January 1867; d Brooklyn, NY, 7 February 1947).

At first a performer, then a conductor in the musical theatre, Bratton later moved into the production of touring plays and musical comedies (*The Dingbat Family*, *Let George Do It* etc), in partnership with Johnny Leffler, whilst also composing more than a decadeful of songs, which were used both in his own productions and, interpolated into musical comedies on both sides of the Atlantic, in those of others. On several occasions he provided the whole, or a

large part of a musical comedy score, mostly for shows of a fairly loose musical construction.

Bratton had song successes with such numbers as 'Henrietta, Have You Met Her?' (w Walter Ford, *The Belle of Cairo*), the hugely popular 'In a Cosy Corner' (also known as 'My Cosy Corner Girl', w Chas Noel Douglas) sung in London in *The Earl and the Girl*, in New York in *The School Girl*, in Paris in the 1904 Moulin-Rouge revue and in Australia tacked into the musical comedy *The Rose of the Riviera*, 'He Was a Sailor' (*The Earl and the Girl*), 'My Little Hong Kong Baby' (w Paul West, sung by Adele Ritchie in Broadway's *A Chinese Honeymoon* and Ellaline Terriss in London's *The Cherry Girl*), 'A Picture No Artist Can Paint' (*Hodge, Podge & Co*), 'In Black and White' (*The School Girl*), 'Sue, Sue, I Love You', 'I'll Be Your Honey', 'Gladys O'Flynn' (*Buster Brown*), 'I'm On the Water Wagon Now' (w West, the hit of *The Office Boy*), 'Mender of Broken Dreams' (*Charlot's Revue*), 'The Sunshine of Paradise Alley' (w Ford), 'The Same Old Way', the children's classic 'The Teddy Bear's Picnic' (w Jimmy Kennedy) and 'Sweetheart, Let's Grow Old Together' (w Leo Edwardes).

Amongst the numerous other shows in which his songs were heard were *Fad and Folly* ('She Reads the New York Papers Every Day'), *Mrs Black Is Back* ('Can't You Guess?' w West), *The Rollicking Girl* ('The Girl I Left in Boston Town' w Douglas, Ernest Ball, 'Tricks' w West) and *The Gay White Way* ('Somebody's Been Around Here Since I've Been Gone' w West). His other titles included such pieces as 'The Amorous Esquimaux', 'There Are 57 Ways to Catch a Man' (*The Man from China*), 'I Want to Play Hamlet', 'He Ought to Have a Tablet in the Hall of Fame' 'Isabelle (a Girl who is One of the Boys)' and 'O'Dwyer Caught Cold'.

Although he moved out of the musical theatre after the first war, Bratton remained active as a lyricist until the last years of his life.

1900 **Hodge, Podge & Co** (Walter Ford/ad George Hobart) Madison Square Theater 23 October

1900 **Star and Garter** (Ford/J J McNally) Victoria Theater 26 November

1901 **The Liberty Belles** (w Aimé Lachaume, A Baldwin Sloane, Clifton Crawford, Alfred Aarons et al/Harry B Smith) Madison Square Theater 30 September

1904 **The Man From China** (Paul West) Chicago; Majestic Theater 2 May

1905 **Buster Brown** (West/Charles Newman, George Totten Smith) Majestic Theater 24 January

1905 **The Pearl and the Pumpkin** (West/West, W W Denslow) Broadway Theater 21 August

1909 **The Newlyweds and Their Baby** (w Nat D Ayer/West, A Seymour Brown/West, Aaron Hoffman) Majestic Theater 22 March

1912 **The Dingbat Family** (Mark Swan) Lyceum, Paterson, NJ 28 October

BRECHT, [Eugen] Bertolt [Friedrich] (b Augsburg, 10 February 1898; d East Berlin, 14 August 1956).

Better known for his non-musical plays (*Mutter Courage und ihr Kinder*, *Der gute Mensch von Setzuan*, *Der aufthaltsame Aufstieg des Arturo Ui* etc) and for his clamorous left-wing political stance, to the service of which his theatre works were often subjugated, Brecht also collaborated with composer Kurt Weill on several musical pieces, over a period of some three years, at the end of the 1920s. *Die*

Dreigroschenoper, his jolly adaptation of Elisabeth Hauptmann's German version of John Gay's *The Beggar's Opera*, proved an enduring entertainment, but the two authors' second piece for the musical theatre, the flung-together *Happy End*, was a quick failure. Weill and Brecht also collaborated on the operas *Aufstieg und Fall der Stadt Mahagonny* (1929) and *Der Jasager* (1930).

1928 **Die Dreigroschenoper** (Kurt Weill/w Elisabeth Hauptmann) Theater am Schiffbauerdamm 31 August

1929 **Happy End** (Weill/w Hauptmann) Theater am Schiffbauerdamm 2 September

BREDSCHNEIDER, Willi (b Arndorf, 31 January 1889; d Berlin, 16 January 1937).

Musical director at the Berliner Theater from the age of 20 (1909–16), Bredschneider wrote songs and stage music for a number of the theatre's productions, contributing to the extremely successful new version of the old Posse *Auf eigenen Füssen* which was played there as *Bummelstudenten* (1910), to its equally popular successor, *Grosse Rosinen*, and to two major international successes in *Wie einst im Mai* and *Filmzauber* amongst the successful run of musical comedies mounted at the Berliner Theater before and during the Great War.

He later worked as musical director at the Wallner-Theater and, as a composer, had success in both Germany and the Netherlands with one of the few musical shows for which he supplied the entire score, *Die beiden Nachtigallen*.

1910 **Bummelstudenten** (w Bogumil Zepler et al/ad Rudolf Bernauer, Rudolph Schanzer) Berliner Theater 31 December

1911 **Die grüne Neune** (Toni Impekoven) Lustspielhaus 22 March

1911 **Grosse Rosinen** (w Leon Jessel, Zepler et al/Bernauer, Schanzer) Berliner Theater 31 December

1912 **Filmzauber** (w Walter Kollo/Bernauer, Schanzer) Berliner Theater 19 October

1913 **Hochherrschaftliche Wohnungen** (Impekoven) Kömödienhaus 5 April

1913 **Wie einst im Mai** (w Kollo/Bernauer, Schanzer) Berliner Theater 4 October

1914 **Extrablätter** (w Kollo/Schanzer, Heinz Gordon) Berliner Theater 24 October

1915 **Wenn zwei Hochzeit machen** (w Kollo/Bernauer, Schanzer) Berliner Theater 23 October

1916 **Auf Flügeln des Gesanges** (w Kollo/Bernauer, Schanzer) Berliner Theater 9 September

1917 **Hampelmanns Geburtstag** (Impekoven) Schauspielhaus, Frankfurt-am-Main 17 March

1921 **Die beiden Nachtigallen** (Leo Walther Stein) Stadttheater, Halle am Saale 26 December

1927 **Mops der Spitzbube** (Karl Müller-Hoyer) Thalia Theater, Dresden 3 September

1929 **Das Wunderkind** (L W Stein, Rudolf Presber) Brussels

Other title attributed: *Ein Mädel mit Tempo*

BRETÓN [y Hernández], Tomás (b Salamanca, 29 December 1850; d Madrid, 2 December 1923).

One of the principal composers of the zarzuela in the three decades of its greatest prosperity, Tomás Bretón also worked, in parallel, as an operatic composer, going further than most of his compatriots towards establishing an exportable school of Spanish opera. His earliest operas, the one-act *Guzman el bueno* (1877) and *El campoñero de Begoña* (1878) made little mark, but the 1889 *Los amantes de Teruel* (1889) was a success which was played in Vienna

and Prague as well as in Spain and Argentina, and there was also some recognition for the Italian *Garin, l'eremita de Montserrat* (1892). *La Dolores* (Teatro Zarzuela, 16 March 1895) was the most successful of his operatic works, being internationally staged and regularly revived for many years, but his latter works – *Raquel* (1900), *Farinelli* (1902). *El cartamen de Cremona* (1906, one act), *Don Gil* (1914) and *Salamanca* (1916) – only the grandiose *Tabar* had anything like a success.

His most significant success in the zarzuela field also came, after 20 years of liberally supplying the lighter musical theatre with both full-length and short musical plays, in the early 1890s, with the one-act *La verbena de la paloma*, which has remained a staple in the zarzuela repertoire ever since. His other titles for the zarzuela stage include *El alma en un hijo* (1874), *Los dos caminos* (1874), *El viaje de Europa* (1874) *El 93* (1875) *El inválido* (1875) *Maria* (1875), *Un chaparron de maridos* (1876) *Vista y sentencia* (1876), *Cuidado con los estudiantes* (1877), *Los dos leones* (1877) *Huyendo de Elfas* (1877), *El bautizo de Popin* (1878), *Bonito pais* (1878), *El barberillo de Orán* (1879) *Corona contra corona* (1879), *Los amores de un principe* (1881), *Las senoritas de conil* (1881), *El grito en el cielo* (1886), *El domingo de ramos* (1895), *Las nieves* (1895), *Botin de guerra* (1896), *El guardia de corps* (1897), *El puente del Diabolo* (1898), *El reloj de curo* (1898), *El clavel rojo* (1899), *Ya se van los quintos madre* (1899), *La carñosa* (1899), *La Covadonga* (1901), *El caballo de señorita* (1901), *La bien planta* (1902), *La generosa* (1909), *Piel de oso* (1909), *Al alcance de la mano* (1911), *Las percheleras* (1911), *Los husares del Czar* (1914), *Las cortes de amor* (1916).

Biographies: Sanchez Salcedo, A: *Tomás Bretón: su vida y sua obra* (Imp. Clásica Española, Madrid, 1924); de Montillana, J: *Breton* (Salamanca, 1952)

BRIAN, Donald (b St Johns, Newfoundland, 17 February 1877; d Great Neck, NY, 22 December 1948). Bright-eyed and boyish star of more than 20 years of Broadway musicals.

Brian made his earliest professional appearances as a member of a glee club, and then played in the straight theatre before taking on his first singing rôles in touring productions of *Three Little Lambs* and *The Chaperons* (Tom Schuyler). He made his first Broadway musical appearance at the Winter Garden Theater, on the roof of the New York Theater, in a couple of slapdash pieces called *The Supper Club* (1901, Castor Beane) and *The Belle of Broadway* (1902, Tom Finch), then took over as Captain Donegal in *Florodora* when it played the same theatre, a performance which led to his succeeding Cyril Scott in the same rôle in the principal tour company. He followed up in Scott's rôle of Berkeley Shallamar in *The Silver Slipper*, and played alongside Chauncey Olcott in *Myles Aroon*, before coming to his first major Broadway creations: the juvenile lead rôles of Henry Hapgood in George M Cohan's *Little Johnny Jones* (1904) and of Tom Bennett in his *Forty-Five Minutes from Broadway* (1906).

Brian appeared again for Cohan in *Fifty Miles from Boston*, but then shot to the upper fame level in 1907 when cast as America's Danilo alongside Ethel Jackson in Henry Savage's production of *The Merry Widow*. Thereafter, for more than a decade, his remained a bankable top-of-the-bill name, and he appeared in the leading rôles of a run of imported musicals with unbroken success: as self-made

Freddy who is out to win *The Dollar Princess* (1909), the spy-master Marquis de Ravaillac in *The Siren* (1911), Jack Fleetwood, the backwoods hero of *The Marriage Market* (1913), Sandy Blair who sets out to rescue *The Girl from Utah* from the mormons (1914) and the Grand Duke who finds himself with a delightful if phoney wife in his arms in *Sybil* (1916). In each of these last four shows he co-starred with the beautiful Julia Sanderson. There was less success to be found in Victor Herbert's *Her Regiment* (1917, André de Courcy), but two other wartime musicals, the French comedy and Ivan Caryll music of *The Girl Behind the Gun* (1918, Robert Lambrissac), and the sentimentally winning *Buddies* (1919, Sonny) gave him further Broadway successes.

After a long and successful tour with this last piece, Brian reappeared on Broadway as Bumerli in a revival of *The Chocolate Soldier* (1921), but he walked out of the starring (and vocally demanding) rôle of Achmed Bey in *The Rose of Stambul* (1922) prior to the Broadway opening and, instead of appearing as the romantic poet of Fall's *Operette*, came back briefly to New York as the sweetly prosaic Albert Bennett of the Tierney/McCarthy *Up She Goes*. Alternating plays and musicals, he appeared on the road opposite Alice Delysia in *The Courtesan* (1923, The Vicomte), as Billy Early in *No, No, Nanette* (1925) and opposite his wife, Virginia O'Brien, as take-overs in the Chicago hit *Castles in the Air* (1926). He played opposite Edna Leedom in *Ain't Love Grand* (1927, Prince Paul de Morlaix) but was replaced by Guy Robertson before the troubled show reached Broadway as *Lovely Lady*.

In a career which mostly embraced light comedy plays thereafter he was seen on Broadway as a takeover in *Yes, Yes, Yvette*, as a rather older Danilo on the road (1930) and at Broadway's Erlanger Theater (1931 and 1932), as a replacement Bruno Mahler in *Music in the Air* and, finally, in his sixties, in *Very Warm for May* (1939, William Graham).

An occasional songwriter, Brian interpolated his 'Mendocino Stroll' in *The Marriage Market*.

BRIAN BORU Romantic opera in 3 acts by Stanislaus Stange. Music by Julian Edwards. Broadway Theater, New York, 16 December 1896.

A rare late 19th-century attempt to serve up some heroic/romantic Irish material instead of the cheerful Mulliganneries usually seen and heard in contemporary American theatres, accompanied by a score from the most strivingly substantial of the period's light musical theatre composers, *Brian Boru* was mounted by F C Whitney with a measure of success, which included 88 performances on Broadway.

Max Eugene featured as Ireland's champion, equipped with a bass-baritone 'For Ireland' and 'Sheathe the Sword' and faced with the attempts of the English Princess, Elfrida (Amanda Fabris), to woo him from his duty with repeated high Cs ('The Earth's Richest Dower'). The best of the soprano music, however, fell to Grace Golden, in the rôle of Boru's sister, Erina, alongside some stirring basso stuff for Bruce Paget as a Standard Bearer ('The Irish Patriot') and a selection of the regulation comic opera style of Irishisms as delivered by comedian Richard O'Carroll ('Paddy's Legs', 'Paddy and His Pig') and Amelia Summerville as 'Baby Malone, the Child of a

Giant' (trio: 'The Irish Cuckoo'). The English got little of a look-in with either fun or music in ex-Liverpudlian Stange's libretto and ended up confounded and defeated, a plot turn which, alone, sent *Brian Boru*'s audiences home in a happy frame of mind.

BRICUSSE, Leslie (b London, 29 January 1931). Songwriter who had early successes on the stage and the hit parades and later ones in films.

Bricusse first came to the fore as a writer with his Cambridge University shows, the revue *Out of the Blue* and the musical comedy *Lady at the Wheel* (1953 w Frederick Raphael). The musical was subsequently given a professional production (1958) with Maggie Fitzgibbon starred as a Monte Carlo rallyeuse who wins a nice Englishman (Peter Gilmore) rather than a beastly foreigner (Bernard Cribbins) ('Siesta', 'Pete Y'Know'). By this time, Bricusse had already appeared in London as a performer in *An Evening With Beatrice Lillie*, and as a replacement director on a money-no-object vanity production called *Jubilee Girl* (1956), whilst also making a name in films and as a songwriter ('Out of Town' w Robin Beaumont for Max Bygraves in *Charley Moon* (1956), 'Summer is a-comin' In' as sung by Kathie Kay (1958) etc).

He won an international stage and song success when he collaborated with Anthony Newley on *Stop the World – I Want to Get Off* ('What Kind of Fool Am I?', 'Once in a Lifetime', 'Typically English' etc), and scored further song hits when he supplied the lyrics to the musical *Pickwick* ('If I Ruled the World') and collaborated again with Newley on *The Roar of the Greasepaint – the Smell of the Crowd* ('Who Can I Turn To?', 'Nothing Can Stop Me Now', 'On a Wonderful Day Like Today'), but thereafter his success came in the film world rather than in the theatre as he turned out the theme songs for *Goldfinger* (w Newley, John Barry) and *You Only Live Twice* (w Barry), and the scores for the musical films *Doctor Doolittle* (1967 'Talk to the Animals' Academy Award), *Goodbye, Mr Chips* (1969), *Scrooge* (1970) and *Willie Wonka and the Chocolate Factory* (1971).

A third show with Newley, *The Good Old Bad Old Days* did not come up to the first, a show about King Henry VIII (*Kings and Clowns*) was a surprisingly unprofessionally written and produced London flop, and *The Travelling Music Show*, a pasticcio show set up around television personality Bruce Forsythe, was another quick failure. Musical versions of the play *Harvey* and of the British mystery classics of Conan Doyle (*Sherlock Holmes*) and Robert Louis Stevenson (*Jekyll and Hyde*), and expanded stage versions of the filmed *Goodbye, Mr Chips* and *Scrooge*, were subsequent projects which were seen briefly on the stage in Britain and America, whilst also Bricusse carried on with such assignments as *The Return of the Pink Panther* (1975), *Superman* (1978) and *Victor/Victoria* (1982) in the cinema, and the score for a 1976 ATV *Peter Pan* (w Newley).

1958 **Lady at the Wheel** (Robin Beaumont/Frederick Raphael, Lucienne Hill) Lyric Theatre, Hammersmith 23 January
1961 **Stop the World – I Want to Get Off** (Anthony Newley) Queen's Theatre 20 July
1963 **Pickwick** (Cyril Ornadel/Wolf Mankowitz) Saville Theatre 4 July
1964 **The Roar of the Greasepaint – the Smell of the Crowd** (Newley) Theatre Royal, Nottingham 3 August

Plate 37. **Brigadoon**: *A feller never knows what he'll find in the gloaming. Robin Nedwell (Jeff) found Leslie Mackie (Meg Brockie) in London's 1988 revival.*

BRIGADOON Musical play in 2 acts by Alan Jay Lerner. Music by Frederick Loewe. Ziegfeld Theater, New York, 13 March 1947.

The enduring hit of the 1947–8 Broadway season, *Brigadoon* launched the three-show-old partnership of Alan Jay Lerner and Frederick Loewe on what would be one of the remarkable musical theatre careers of the following decade and more. The most thoroughly romantic of the new swell of romantic Broadway musicals, *Brigadoon* dipped into the sweet waters of the well of the fantastical and the fairy for its subject matter and came out with a tale that succeeded in being wholly charming and not a whit saccharine. Nevertheless, the authors thought it best to pull that oft-used and theoretically disarming trick of pretending that their story was based on an old Continental legend.

Americans Tommy Albright (David Brooks) and Jeff Douglass (George Keane) are on a hunting trip in Scot-

land when they stumble on a little village that is not on the map. It is Brigadoon and, when the hunters arrive, the folk are preparing for the wedding of Jeannie MacLaren (Virginia Bosler) and Charlie Dalrymple (Lee Sullivan). Tommy is enchanted by Jeannie's sister Fiona (Marion Bell) whilst Charlie is pursued by the forward Meg Brockie (Pamela Britton), but they soon discover that Brigadoon is not what it seems. The town is under a spell, by which it appears on earth only one day in a century and, at the end of the day it will vanish into sleep for another hundred years. Disaster threatens when Jeannie's rejected suitor Harry (James Mitchell) tries to leave Brigadoon and send the town for ever into the darkness, but he is accidentally killed in his flight. The men leave before Brigadoon's day is done but, back in the loud shallows of New York, Tommy finds he cannot forget Fiona. He returns to Scotland and, in another miracle, Brigadoon awakes from its sleep, allowing Tommy to go to join the girl he loves.

The tale was illustrated with one of the most attractive sets of songs of its era, ranging from the charmingly tartan-tinted 'The Heather on the Hill', 'Waitin' for My Dearie' and the tenor's 'I'll Go Home With Bonnie Jean' and 'Come to Me, Bend to Me', to the romantic 'It's Almost Like Being in Love' and 'There, But for You, Go I' and the sparkling, but never brash, moments of man-hunting Meg Brockie's 'The Love of My Life' and 'My Mother's Wedding Day', supported by some fine ensembles and lashings of dance music to serve the large dance routines which were the fashion of the post-*Oklahoma!* period. The most effective of these was Agnes de Mille's depiction of the dusk-time chase of the villagers, through the rocks and trees, to prevent Harry's escape from Brigadoon, whilst the wedding of Jeannie and Charlie gave the opportunity for plenty of lively Scottish steps.

Brigadoon's dance-heavy layout, as well as the death of its 'baddie' and the man-hunts of Meg, prompted some comparisons with *Oklahoma!*, its Judd Fry and Ado Annie, but only on the first ground did this seem justified. After all, baddies had been dying in the musical theatre for many decades, and most opérette soubrettes had sex on the brain. In fact, *Brigadoon*'s fantasy-flavour, spiced with just a dash of the brashly modern in its New York scene, was very different from the tone of the Rodgers and Hammerstein show. What the two pieces did have in common was simply success and, as the show's songs worked their way swiftly into the standards list, Cheryl Crawford's production of *Brigadoon* ran on through a 581-performance stay on Broadway.

A reproduction under the management of Prince Littler at London's His Majesty's Theatre proved equally successful. Philip Hanna (Tommy), Patricia Hughes (Fiona), Hiram Sherman (Jeff) and Noele Gordon (Meg) headed a cast of characters of whom many, curiously, had their surnames altered, through a run of 685 performances. In Australia, Gwen Overton, Ken Cantril, Peter Turgeon and Olive Lucius were featured for nearly six months in Melbourne and something over four at Sydney's Theatre Royal (15 December 1951), confirming the appeal of the show for English-language audiences at both ends of the world.

A 1954 film version, which featured Gene Kelly and Cyd Charisse (sung by Carole Richards) as the principal lovers and Van Johnson as Jeff, cut the rôle of Meg down to almost nothing and eliminated her two comical songs, successfully remaking the piece as a virtually wholly romantic musical film which, nevertheless, retained a very large part of the rest of the show's score.

Brigadoon was slow to find itself major metropolitan revivals, although it was televised in 1968 with Sally Ann Howes and Robert Goulet featured, and reprised regularly at New York's City Center over the years. It returned to Broadway only in 1980 (Majestic Theater 16 October) with Martin Vidnovic, Meg Bussert, Elaine Hausman and Mark Zimmerman in the lead rôles, and with Olympic ice-skating star John Curry briefly seen as Harry, for 133 performances and was played again, in 1986, by the New York City Opera. In Britain, after several abortive announcements of a revival from Scotland over the years, a touring production sponsored by Ronnie Lee and with Robert Meadmore, Jacintha Mulcahy, Robin Nedwell and Leslie Mackie at the top of the bill was brought to the West End and played for 327 performances at the Victoria Palace in 1988–9 (25 October 1988).

Given the success of *My Fair Lady* in Central Europe, it was a little surprising that *Brigadoon* did not find itself a German-language production (ad Robert Gilbert) until 1980, but that production, at Karlsruhe, did not prove sufficient to encourage others and the show's career has been largely in the English-speaking theatre.

UK: His Majesty's Theatre 14 April 1949; Australia: Her Majesty's Theatre, Melbourne 17 March 1951; Germany: Badische Staatstheater, Karlsruhe 10 May 1980; Film: MGM 1954

Recordings: original cast (RCA), London revival cast (First Night), selection (Columbia)

LES BRIGANDS Opéra-bouffe in 3 acts by Henri Meilhac and Ludovic Halévy. Music by Jacques Offenbach. Théâtre des Variétés, Paris, 10 December 1869.

The fifth and last of the famous group of 1860s opérasbouffes written by the team of Meilhac, Halévy and Offenbach for the Théâtre des Variétés, now under the management of Eugène Bertrand, *Les Brigands* rendered nothing to its famous four predecessors (*La Belle Hélène*, *Barbe-bleue*, *La Grande-Duchesse de Gérolstein*, *La Périchole*) in burlesque gaiety and dazzling comic music. It did, however, have two distinct differences from them. The first was that it was not constructed with a starring feminine rôle for the overwhelming leading lady of the other four shows, Hortense Schneider. The second was that its Parisian career was impeded by the onset of the Franco-Prussian war, so that it did not succeed in establishing itself in quite the same way that its predecessors had.

The leading lady of *Les Brigands* was, in fact, a boy. Zulma Bouffar appeared in a rôle which can surely never have been intended, as has been suggested, for la Schneider, as Fragoletto, a young farmer who has turned brigand for the love of Fiorella (Marie Aimée), the daughter of the bandit chief Falsacappa (José Dupuis). All three become part of a conspiracy to trick three millions of money out of the Duchy of Mantua. The money is to be paid over to the representative of the government of Granada when that country's Princess arrives in Mantua to wed the Duke. The bandits waylay the Granadan embassy,

Fiorella takes the place of the Princess (Mlle Lucciani) with her father impersonating the lofty Gloria-Cassis (Gourdon) and Fragoletto as the Princess's pet page (Cooper), and they present themselves to Mantua (Lanjallay) only to find that there is no money. The Duke's unprepossessing cashier (Léonce) has spent his country's funds on wining and dining pretty ladies. Charles Blondelet played Campotasso, the Duke's first minister, and Kopp was the brigand Pietro, but the choice comical rôle went to Baron, cast as the chief of the local carabiniers, endlessly pursuing the brigand band and always, but always arriving on the scene just too late to effect a capture.

It was Baron and his clumsy band whose plodding chorus 'Nous sommes les carabiniers' became the catchphrase from Offenbach's score, but there were many and more melodious moments as well: Fragoletto's helterskelter saltarello description of how he has passed his initiation to the brigand band by robbing the Granadan envoy of 'Le Courrier du cabinet', Fiorella's lively boléro introduction as 'la fille du bandit' and her directions to the benighted Duke, lost in the mountains ('Après avoir pris à droite'), Falsacappa's ringing description of his qualifications in banditry ('Quel est celui qui par les plaines?') and the last act solos of the Duke, preparing to give up women for marriage ('Jadis régnait un prince'), and of the guilty cashier ('O mes amours, ô mes maitresses') were features of a score which also gave place to much more concerted music than had been the case in the earlier pieces. If that pleased the connoisseurs mightily, the theatre-going public were equally as happy with the comical carabiniers and the bristling burlesque bandits and their music.

Les Brigands ran through its first series of performances in December and January and returned to the Variétés stage for a second run in August. Almost immediately war was declared and soon the Variétés was closed. By the time *Les Brigands* returned to their theatre 12 months later (September 1871), in a slightly revised version, they had already been seen throughout the world.

Marie Geistinger and Maximilian Steiner mounted the piece (ad Richard Genée) at Vienna's Theater an der Wien where Jani Szika (Falsacappa), Karoline Finaly (Fragoletto) and Carl Adolf Friese (Antonio, the cashier) were, at various times, amongst the cast, and it was reprised over the next three seasons for a total of 72 performances without winning the same enormous fame as *Die Grossherzogin von Gerolstein* and *Die schöne Helena*. In Berlin a different adaptation, by Ernst Dohm, was used at the Friedrich-Wilhelmstädtisches Theater. The usually prompt Budapest, which saw *Die Banditen* soon after the German première, does not seem, however, to have got its Hungarian version (ad Ferenc Toldy) until 1871, and America, which was quickly introduced to *Les Brigands* in French by James Fisk's company at the Grand Opera House (Elise Persini as Fragoletto, Constant Gausins as Falsacappa and Céline Montaland as Fiorella) and later by original star Marie Aimée and by Paola Marié did not get a vernacular production until as late as 1883. New York did, however, earn a burlesque by the San Francisco Minstrels who — burlesquing a burlesque — had Rollin Howard apcaring as Fiorella Montaland de Silly in a piece which was as much a parody of opéra-bouffe in general as of *Les Brigands* (19 December 1870).

In Britain, however, an English *Falsacappa* (ad Henry S

Leigh) was produced in 1871 at the Globe Theatre with A
St Albyn (Falsacappa), Marguerite Debreux (Fragoletto),
Annetta Scasi (Fiorella) and Cornélie d'Anka in travesty as
the Prince of Boboli (ie the Duke), before the piece was
played in French at the St James's Theatre in 1873 (30
June). It was later given a second English-language run,
this time as *The Brigands* (13 September 1875) for two and
a half months back at the Globe Theatre, with Ada Ward,
Camille Dubois, Nellie Bromley, William Worboys and
Lin Rayne featured. One version which did not appear on
the stage at this time was one commissioned by the
publishers, Boosey and Co, from the young W S Gilbert.
However, once the author had become famous, this version was remembered by some astute person and, in 1889,
Broadway welcomed *The Brigands* by W S Gilbert and
Jacques Offenbach (Casino Theater 9 May). Fannie Rice
(Fragoletto), Lillian Russell (Fiorella) and Edwin Stevens
(Falsacappa) featured and the show proved a hit, passing
its hundredth performance on 31 August, taking a break
from 14 September and returning in the new year to run
again from 6 January to 23 February. When the ever-
opportunistic Horace Lingard mounted a touring production of this version in Britain and then brought it to
London, 'freshened' with a few textual alterations not to
mention such odd bits of extra music as conductor van
Biene's own 'Come Back to Me', the furious Gilbert sued.
Lingard moved quickly out of town.

Australia saw its first *The Brigands* in 1877, in a version
which admitted that it had been 'translated and partly
rewritten by Fred Lyster'. Local star tenor Armes
Beaumont was Falsacappa, with the British performers
Henry Bracy (Fragoletto) and his wife, Clara Thompson
(Fiorella), playing the lovers.

If the initial record won by *Les Brigands* in Paris was, due
to circumstances, rather disappointing, the show nevertheless succeeded in holding itself a place in the repertoire.
The Variétés reprised it in 1874, 1875, 1885 and in 1900
with Juliette Méaly as Fragoletto, Anna Tariol-Baugé as
Fiorella, Brasseur as Antonio, Amélie Dièterle as the
Duke, Guy as the brigand chief and Baron still in his
famous rôle of the chief carabinier. In 1921 it was revived
at the Gaîté-Lyrique with Jean Périer as the brigand chief,
and in 1931 it was taken into the repertoire at the Opéra-
Comique (13 June) where Louis Musy (Falsacappa),
Marcelle Denya (Fragoletto) and Emma Luart (Fiorella)
were joined by musical comedy star Dranem as Antonio.
The show was televised in 1970, and new productions
mounted in Geneva in 1986 and in Lyon in 1988.

Outside France, too, the show has made regular
reappearances, if not always in pristine condition.
Budapest saw Zsolt Harsányi's new Hungarian translation
in 1933 (1 April) whilst the Fővárosi Operettszinház played
A Banditák (ad Károly Kristóf) 2 March 1962, and several
German adaptations of varying honesty have appeared over
recent decades one of which, by Karl-Dietrich Gräwe and
Caspar Richter, was produced at the Berlin Opera in 1978
(4 February). The Gilbert *Brigands* was mounted at the
Edinburgh Festival in 1982. However, in spite of its persistence in the repertoire, *Les Brigands* remains in many
ways the forgotten member of the famous five pre-war
opéras-bouffes of the Variétés repertoire.

Austria: Theater an der Wien *Die Banditen* 12 March 1870;
   Germany: Friedrich-Wilhelmstädtisches Theater *Die Banditen*

24 September 1870; Hungary: (Ger) 13 October 1870, Budai
Színkör *A rablók* 24 June 1871; USA: Grand Opera House
(Fr) 14 November 1870, Casino Theater 9 May 1889; UK:
Globe Theatre *Falsacappa* 22 April 1871; Australia: Opera
House, Melbourne 7 August 1877

Recordings: complete (EMI, Lyon version), complete in German
   (RCA), selections (Milan, Decca) etc

BRIGHTMAN, Sarah   (b London, 14 August 1960).

As a member of the dance group Pan's People, Sarah
Brightman had an early success when she fronted the
group in the song 'I Fell in Love With a Starship Trooper'
(November 1978) which made its way into the British hit
parades.

She appeared on the London musical stage for the first
time in the original cast of *Cats* (Jemima) and moved from
there to succeed Bonnie Langford in the rôle of Kate in
the Theatre Royal, Drury Lane, revival of *The Pirates of
Penzance*. She withdrew from the cast on her marriage to
composer Andrew Lloyd Webber.

She was subsequently seen as Tara Treetops in the
musical version of the puzzle-book *Masquerade* at the
Young Vic and in the title-rôle of the Charles Strouse light
opera *The Nightingale* at the Lyric Theatre, Hammersmith,
before creating the rôle of Christine Daaé, the pursued
and pre-Raphaelite heroine of *The Phantom of the Opéra*, a
part composed for her by Lloyd Webber ('All I Ask of
You'). She repeated her rôle in *The Phantom of the Opéra* in
New York and Los Angeles and subsequently succeeded
to the part of Rose in Broadway's production of her, by
then, ex-husband's *Aspects of Love*, a rôle which she later
also took over in the London production.

During her marriage to Lloyd Webber, Miss Brightman
also created the written-to-measure soprano rôle in the
composer's *Requiem*, taking the duet 'Pie Jesu' into the top
ten, and recorded his song-cycle 'Tell Me on a Sunday' for
BBC television. She also appeared in series of concerts
entitled 'The Music of Andrew Lloyd Webber' in America
and Britain.

BRODSZKY, Miklós [aka Nikolaus or Nicholas
BRODSZKY] (b Odessa, Ukraine, 20 April 1905; d
Hollywood, 24 December 1958). Composer of several
musicals for the Hungarian and Austrian stage who made
his name further afield as the supplier of screen songs to
Mario Lanza.

Russian-born, but Hungarian-raised, Brodszky studied
music in Budapest and Rome and, at the age of 24, had a
great success with his first Operette, *Szökik az asszony* (A
runaway girl). Initially mounted at the Budai Színkör, the
show moved on to the Városi Színház where, with Hanna
Honthy starred, it ran up more than 150 performances by
the end of its first year, before going on to be played in
Berlin and in Innsbruck (30 January 1932) under the title
Die Flucht in die Ehe and in Vienna, as *Die entführte Frau*, by
a company from Olmütz (1930).

Brodszky confirmed that early success with his second
piece, *Az első tavasz* (the first spring), again starring the
very popular Hanna Honthy, whilst a third successful
piece, *Die verliebte Königin*, introduced by Gitta Alpár for a
two-month run in Vienna and later successfully played as *A
szerelmes királynő* in Budapest (Városi Színház 10 October
1936), encouraged London impresario C B Cochran to
take the composer to Britain. He announced a new musical

play to be written for Alpár to a text by James Bridie which never eventuated, but Brodszky did supply music for the 1937 Cochran revue *Home and Beauty* (Adelphi Theatre 128 performances) and later contributed to another London revue, *Big Top*.

Brodszky wrote liberally for the musical film, notably, in his early days, for such artists as Alpár, Franziska Gaal and for Richard Tauber, as well as for radio and recording, and if his years in Britain brought forth no stage scores, he continued to supply music to the screen. In 1949 he moved on to America where he provided, amongst others, songs for the films *The Toast of New Orleans* (1950, 'Be My Love'), *Because You're Mine* (1952, 'Because You're Mine'), and *Serenade* for Mario Lanza, for *The Flame and the Flesh* ('No One But You'), *Rich, Young and Pretty* ('Wonder Why'), *Love Me and Leave Me* ('I'll Never Stop Loving You') and *Meet Me in Las Vegas*, as well as additional material for the film version of *The Student Prince*, without again returning to the theatre.

1929 **Szökik az asszony** (Imre Harmath, Andor Kardos) Budai Színkör 14 June
1930 **Az első tavasz** (Harmath/Ernő Andai) Budai Színkör 16 April
1932 **Ezer jó** Royal Orfeum 12 June
1933 **A kék lámpás** (Harmath, László Szilágyi) Király Színház 3 March
1934 **Die verliebte Königin** (*A szerelmes királynő*) (Alfred Grünwald, Fritz Löhner-Beda) Scala Theater, Vienna 21 December
1935 **Mariora** (Harmath/László Bus Fekete)
1938 **Dinasztia** (Harmath, István Békeffy) Magyar Színház 16 April

BRÓDY, István (b Nagykároly 1 May 1882; d Budapest, 4 January 1941). Theatre manager, director and playwright, Bródy authored musical comedy texts for Lajtai, Rényi, and Ábrahám, as well as for his brother, **Miklós BRÓDY** (b 30 March 1877; d Kolozsvár, 17 December 1949). His musical play *Zenebona* was played in Vienna under the title *Spektakel*.

1903 **Bob Király** (Jenő Virányi/w Dezső Urai) Uj Színház 16 May
1903 **A.B.C.** (Miklós Bródy/w Ferenc Révész) Pest 26 November
1915 **Tiszavirág** (Aladár Rényi/w László Vajda) Király Színház 27 March
1916 **Csókvásár** (Pál Leitner) Revü Színház 1 June
1920 **Pünkösdi rózsa** (Imre Farkas) Revü Színház 3 January
1921 **Férjhez megy a feleségem** (Alfred Márkus, M Bródy) Eskütéri Színház 16 April
1923 **Asszonyok bolondja** (Lajos Lajtai) Budai Színkör 9 May
1925 **Leányálom** (Sándor Szlatinai/w Vajda) Városi Színház 14 November
1925 **Miami** (Viktor Jacobi arr/w Vajda) Fővárosi Operettszinház 27 November
1928 **Zenebona** (Pál Ábrahám/Imre Harmath/w László Lakatos) Fővárosi Operettszinház 2 March
1936 **Zöld béka** (Pál Gyöngy/Dezső Kellér) Kamara Színház 9 May

BRÓDY, Miksa (b Nagyvárad, 1875; d Budapest, 4 May 1924).

Journalist, theatre critic, playwright and librettist, Bródy provided the libretti for four of the most successful Hungarian operetts of the early 1910s: Vincze's *Tilos a csók* (*Das verbotene Kuss*), Jacobi's two international hits

Leányvásár (*The Marriage Market*) and *Szibill* and Kálmán's *Zsuzsi kisasszony* (*Miss Springtime*) in his only four ventures as a musical theatre author during that period. He also adapted Louis Ganne's French opérette *Hans le joueur de flûte* for the Hungarian stage with an efficacity which resulted in its becoming more popular in Hungary than in other areas beyond France. He subsequently adapted two Robert Stolz Operetten with considerable success, and authored one further original work, the text to the Buttykay operett *Olivia hercegnő*, which opened the Fővárosi Operettszinház in 1922.

1909 **Tilos a csók** (Zsigmond Vincze/w József Pásztor) Király Színház 8 October
1911 **Leányvásár** (Viktor Jacobi/w Ferenc Martos) Király Színház 14 November
1912 **Furulyás Jancsi** (*Hans le joueur de flûte*) Hungarian version (Népopera)
1913 **Szökik a nagysága** (?/w Martos) Budapesti Színház 22 March
1914 **Szibill** (Jacobi/w Martos) Király Színház 27 February
1915 **Zsuzsi kisasszony** (Imre Kálmán/w Martos) Vigszinház 27 February
1921 **Szerencsetánc** (*Der Tanz ins Glück*) Hungarian version (Városi Színház)
1921 **A kis grizett** (*Die Tanzgräfin*) Hungarian version (Vigszinház)
1922 **Olivia hercegnő** (Ákos Buttykay/w Imre Földes) Fővárosi Operettszinház 23 December

BROMME, Walter (b Berlin, 2 April 1884; d Berlin, 30 March 1943).

The son of a coal merchant, Bromme began his professional life working in his father's business before moving into the theatre in the dual capacity of theatre manager and composer of musical plays. In 1916 he joined Carl Wessel in the management of the former Deutsch-Amerikanisches Theater, now renamed the National-Theater, and mounted several musical comedies to which he had provided the cheerfully straightforward and often catchy songs, winning himself several popular successes. He occasionally provided his own lyrics, under the pseudonym of 'Walter Berg'.

He moved on to the Berliner Theater for the summer of 1919 and mounted his more ambitious *Die Dame im Frack*, with Käthe Dorsch in the starring rôle, for a run of two months, and continued thereafter to lease various Berlin houses for such pieces as *Eine Nacht im Paradies* (four months) and the most successful of his shows, *Mascottchen*, which had an eight-month run in Berlin and a season of 38 performances in Vienna (Carltheater 26 September 1924).

Schäm' dich Lotte played 121 Berlin performances, and *Donnerwetter – ganz famos* provoked one of the best critics of the time to comment of the 'workmanlike' composer 'he knows his business and sooner or later will write a show of real international calibre'. But he didn't.

1916 **Heiratsfieber** ('Walter Berg') Viktoria-Theater, Breslau 1 December
1917 **Studentenliebchen** (Theo Halton) National-Theater 15 January
1917 **Was junge Mädchen traumen** (Rudi Schwarz/Max Herbert) National-Theater
1917 **Das ist die Liebe** (Hugo Döblin) National-Theater 1 September

Plate 38.

1918 **Die ist richtig...!** (Will Steinberg/Arthur Lippschitz) National-Theater 16 January

1918 **Prinzenliebe** (Steinberg/Gerhard Schätzler-Perasini) National-Theater 7 September

1919 **Die Kinopuppe** (Leonhard Haskel) National-Theater 28 February

1919 **Die Dame im Frack** (Steinberg/Alexander Pordes-Milo) Berliner Theater 2 August

1920 **Eine Nacht im Paradies** (Steinberg/Georg Okonkowski) Theater am Nollendorfplatz 30 April

1921 **Mascottchen** (Steinberg/Okonkowski) Thalia-Theater 15 January

1921 **Schäm' dich, Lotte** (Steinberg/Okonkowski) Thalia-Theater 23 September

1922 **Madame Flirt** (Steinberg/Okonkowski) Berliner Theater 15 April

1923 **Schönste der Frauen** (Steinberg/Okonkowski) Metropoltheater May

1925 **Tausend süsse Beinchen** (Steinberg/Okonkowski) Metropoltheater 28 March

1925 **Messalinette** (Richard Bars, Pordes Milo) Berliner Theater 23 December

1926 **Donnerwetter – ganz famos** (Steinberg, Kessler) Berliner Theater 1 May

1926 **Miss Amerika** (Kurt Schwabach/Okonkowski, Steinberg) Berliner Theater 20 August

1927 **Heute Nacht ... eventuell** (Fritz Friedmann-Friedrich) Neues Theater am Zoo 25 December

1931 **Die Damenfriseur** (Robert Blum) Thalia-Theater 18 September

1933 **Marie-Louise** (H H Hermann) Metropoltheater 7 October

1934 **Spiel nicht mit der Liebe** (Richard Kessler) Komische Oper 4 October

1936 **Ball am Bord** (Kessler) Städtische Bühnen, Chemnitz 26 January

BRONHILL, June [GOUGH, June Mary] (b Broken Hill, Australia, 26 June 1929).

As a member of the Sadler's Wells Opera Company during the 1950s and 1960s, soprano June Bronhill (the name, like that of her compatriot Melba, was based on her home town) appeared in the light soprano repertoire, most notably as Eurydice in the company's celebrated production of *Orpheus in the Underworld*.

She made her first appearance on the London musical stage in the rôle of Elizabeth Barrett Browning in *Robert and Elizabeth*, a rôle written to the measure of her uniquely fluid, high and staunch soprano with the type of demanding tessitura rarely seen in the musical theatre ('Woman and Man', 'I Know Now', Soliloquy etc). She repeated that part in Australia where she was also seen as Maria in *The Sound of Music*. She later toured Britain as *The Merry Widow*, but returned only once to the West End, in later years, to play the Mother Superior in the 1981 revival of *The Sound of Music*.

In Australia, however, where she returned latterly to live, she continued to appear both in concert and on the stage appearing as the *Merry Widow* as late as 1983 and, no longer the tiny svelte performer of earlier days, in pieces ranging from *Women Behind Bars* (in the rôle created by female impersonator Divine) to Little Miss Splendid in the *Mr Men* children's musical to *A Little Night Music* (1978), Mrs Pearce in *My Fair Lady* (1988), Katisha in *The Mikado*, Ruth in *The Pirates of Penzance* (1984) and Miss Jones in *How to Succeed in Business* (1993).

During the 1960s she recorded a series of light operas and musicals which remain the standard English recordings of such pieces as *Tom Jones, Merrie England, The Arcadians, The Merry Widow, The Count of Luxemburg, Lilac Time, The King and I* et al.

Autobiography: *The Merry Bronhill* (Methuen, London, 1987)

BROONES, Martin (b New York, 10 June 1892; d Beverly Hills, Calif, 10 August 1971).

After almost a decade contributing music to several revues (*Park Theater Revue, Hassard Short's Ritz Revue* etc) and plays, Broones provided the full score for the 1927 revue *Rufus Le Maire's Affairs*, featuring his wife Charlotte Greenwood ('I Can't Get Over a Girl Like You [loving a boy like me]') on Broadway, and later toured widely with Sophie Tucker. He subsequently became musical supervisor at MGM in the earliest years of sound cinema and worked in Hollywood for four years. In 1933 he returned to the musical theatre and provided the scores for four successful London musical comedy shows, the Flanagan and Allen vehicle *Give Me a Ring*, a remusicked version of the French hit *Toi c'est moi* featuring Miss Greenwood in the starring rôle, and two pieces for producer Firth Shephard which set in motion the Leslie Henson series of comedy shows at the Gaiety Theatre.

1933 **Give Me a Ring** (R P Weston, Bert Lee, Guy Bolton) London Hippodrome 22 June

1935 **The Gay Deceivers** (*Toi c'est moi*) new score for English version (Gaiety Theatre)

1935 **Seeing Stars** (Graham John/Bolton, Fred Thompson) Gaiety Theatre 31 October

1936 **Swing Along** (John, Douglas Furber/Bolton, Thompson) Gaiety Theatre 2 September

BROUGH, Lionel (b Pontypool, 10 March 1836; d Lambeth, London, 8 November 1909). Much-loved comedian of the musical and straight stages of Victorian London.

The son of Barnabas Brough, at one time a writer for the stage under the pseudonym of 'Barnard de Burgh', and the brother of top burlesque and extravaganza writers William Brough and Robert Brough, the young Lionel (fondly known as 'Lal') began his working life in a lowly job in the offices of the *Illustrated London News*. He rose to an assistant publisher's position on the *Daily Telegraph* and was responsible there for organizing the first street paper-sellers, a troupe of 240 boys.

During this time he confined his theatrical ambitions and stage appearances largely to the amateur theatre, but he appeared with Vestris and Charles Mathews at the Lyceum in 1854 in his brother William's burlesque *Prince Prettypet and the Butterfly* and a comedy, and ventured again in 1858 under the nom de théâtre 'Lionel Porter' in a drama by Edmund Falconer. He returned to the newspaper world as a sub-editor on the *Morning Star*, but in 1864 he threw in journalism and joined Alexander Henderson's company at the Prince of Wales' Theatre, Liverpool.

He made himself a fine name in Liverpool and, after three years, moved to London and an engagement at the Queen's Theatre. He quickly became very prominent in the West End as a comedian in comedy and burlesque, appearing, amongst many other burlesques, in the title-rôle of the Crystal Palace *Blubeard* to the Sister Ann of Edward Terry, in Reece's *The Stranger Stranger Than Ever*, W S Gilbert's *La Vivandière* (Count Roberto) and Burnand's *Fowl Play* (Joseph Wylie) at the Queen's, as John Smith opposite the Pocohantas of Mrs John Wood in *La Belle Sauvage* and as Bunn to her Jenny Leatherlungs in *Jenny Lind at Last* at the St James's, as Patent Leatherby in the Gaiety's *Guy Fawkes*, and in the title-rôle of *Bluebeard*, as Jim Cocks in *Robinson Crusoe*, King Gramerci XXXVII in *Piff Paff* and Don José in *Carmen, or Sold for a Song*, all with Lydia Thompson's company.

He starred in and directed the vast stage musical *Babil and Bijou* (1872) for Dion Boucicault at the Theatre Royal, Covent Garden, and the coming of opéra-bouffe and -comique saw him extend his talents to such roles as Baron Gondremarck in *La Vie parisienne*, Baron Palamède in *La Marjolaine*, Valentin in *Le Petit Faust*, Laurent XVII in *La Mascotte*, Lambertuccio in *Boccaccio*, The Beadle in *Nell Gwynne* and Nick Vedder in *Rip van Winkle*, occasionally staging the shows as well as performing, and winning himself a place as one of the town's favourite musical comedians.

During the 1870s and 1880s he mixed appearances on the musical stage with classic comedy (Tony Lumpkin being one of his notable successes) and Shakespeare, played with Willie Edouin's troupe (Bill Booty in *The Babes*, *The Japs* etc), visited America with Violet Cameron's company (1885, title-rôle in *The Commodore*, Sir Richard Varney in *Kenilworth*) and toured comedy in South Africa (1889), and in the 1890s he was still appearing in fine West End rôles, playing Matt in *La Cigale*, creating Pietro in *The Mountebanks* and Mr McGuire in *Haste to the Wedding* for W S Gilbert and, in his early sixties, starring with Kate Cutler as Dominie Crockett in *Little Miss Nobody*.

Regarded as one of the great all-round performers of his era, Brough was beloved by actors, critics and audiences. When he appeared in a miserable piece called *Mignonette* which had the audience hooting at its ineptitudes, he was spared, and a voice from the gods said it all: 'we're sorry for you, Lal Brough!'

BROUGH, [Lionel] Robert (b 1857; d Sydney, Australia, 20 April 1906). The son of burlesque writer Robert Brough, the younger Robert made an early start as an actor, performing comic rôles in the British provinces before succeeding to the rôle of Dick Deadeye in D'Oyly Carte's second touring company of *HMS Pinafore* (1879). In 1881 he appeared as Zapeter in *Princess Toto* and in the operetta *Lovers' Knots* at the Opera Comique, in 1882 as King John in the burlesque *Little Robin Hood* at the Gaiety, in 1883 in the principal comedy rôle of the Doge in *Estrella* (Manchester/Gaiety) and in 1884 took over as the Emperor of Morocco in Jakobowski's *Dick* and appeared as Corporal O'Flanagan in the short run of Solomon's *Pocahontas* (Empire), a piece which he also co-directed.

In 1885 he and his wife, the contralto **Florence TREVALLYAN** [Florence Trevallyan MAJOR b London, ?1857; d London, 7 January 1932], who had played with Kate Santley in *Orpheus in the Underworld*, *Princess Toto* and *La Fille de Madame Angot* on the road (1877) and *La Marjolaine* (1877, Karl) in town, toured for D'Oyly Carte as Little Buttercup and Mrs Partlett (1878–9) and with Alfred Heming in burlesque (Zuniga in *Cruel Carmen* etc) and comedy, and appeared in London in the comic operas *Manteaux Noirs* (1882, Clorinda) and *Estrella* (1883, Brigetta), joined Williamson, Garner and Musgrove's company in Australia. They appeared together in *Iolanthe* (Lord Chancellor, Fairy Queen) and *Falka* (Tancred, Alexina) and Brough repeated his Zapeter in Australia's *Princess Toto*, but they soon seceded from the company and Brough went into a management partnership with Dion Boucicault jr.

Amongst their early productions were *Young Fra Diavolo* (with Brough as Beppo), *Little Jack Sheppard* (Jonathan Wild), *Dick* (director, Alderman Fitzwarren) and *The Forty Thieves* (Ali Baba) but, under the influence of the determined Florence, who pronounced a distaste for and an unease in musical theatre, the firm then abandoned musicals in favour of straight theatre. Brough and Boucicault managed the Criterion, Sydney and the Bijou, Melbourne, operating successfully together for a decade and when Boucicault returned to Britain, Brough continued alone until 1902, producing what were regarded as the best quality theatrical entertainments in Australia, until shortly before his death when he gave up management and returned to performing for other firms.

After his death Florence remarried and, her Australian popularity having faded, returned to Britain.

BROUGH, William (b London, 28 April 1826; d Haverstock Hill, 15 March 1870). The son of Barnabas Brough and the elder brother of actor Lionel, William Brough paired with his other brother, **Robert B[arnabas] BROUGH** (b London, 10 April 1828; d Manchester, 26 June 1860), to establish a great reputation as one of the most successful purveyors of fine and fanciful extravaganza and burlesque to the English-speaking stages of the 1850s.

The 'Brothers Brough' made their first appearance on a playbill when their burlesque of Shakespeare's *The Tempest, The Enchanted Isle*, was produced at the Empire Theatre in Liverpool in early 1848, under the management of W R Copeland. The production was seen by Benjamin Webster, manager of London's Adelphi Theatre, and in consequence *The Enchanted Isle* was given a Christmas season in London the same year. It proved an enormous success, and was revived the following year at Webster's Haymarket Theatre with Priscilla Horton as Ariel and Buckstone as Caliban, in 1850, and again in 1860. The Haymarket, too, had a Brough Brothers extravaganza for the Christmas season of 1848–9, and this version of the *Prince Camaralzaman* tale from *The Arabian Nights* proved even more successful than their first piece, being played throughout the country and becoming a regular basis for pantomime performances in the years that followed. Buckstone and Miss Horton starred again in the 1850 *The Arabian Nights* alongside the vocalist Annie Romer who, the following year, became Mrs William Brough.

The partnership between William and Robert lasted for over five years, during which time the brothers regularly supplied the Easter and Christmas extravaganzas for Webster's two theatres, before the pair split, to write individually. William spread his talents amongst comedies, burlesques for the Lyceum Theatre, musical and non-musical playlets and sketches for the earliest entertainments for Mr and Mrs German Reed (the former Miss Horton) at what was to become their famous Gallery of Illustration (*A Visit to Holly Lodge After the Ball, The Enraged Musician* (both w R Brough), *A Month from Home, My Unfinished Opera, Our Home Circuit, Seaside Studies, An Illustration on Discords, The Rival Composers, The Bard and his Birthday, A Peculiar Family*) and even turned his hand to the writing of burlesque material for the Christy Minstrels (*La Sonnambula* etc).

In the burlesque field, he had a particular success with his parody of Byron's *The Corsair* as *Conrad and Medora* (USA: *Conrad the Corsair*) and, an even greater one with the burlesque of Shakespeare's *A Winter's Tale* as *Perdita, or the Royal Milkmaid*, produced by Charles Dillon at the Lyceum with Marie Wilton, Miss Woolgar and the young J L Toole amongst the cast. In the fashion of the day, these pieces were equipped with pasticcio scores of a wide range in musical styles. His burlesque of *Ernani*, for example, used tunes from 'Pop Goes the Weasel' to 'Suoni la tromba' as the melodies for the author's comic lyrics. Amongst his later works, the fairy extravaganza *Prince Amabel* and the historical burlesque *The Field of the Cloth of Gold*, both regularly reprised after their initial productions, became long-lived favourites, the latter eventually proving the most internationally popular of all Brough's works. Within months of its first staging, whilst it continued its remarkable Easter-to-Easter run in London, it had gone round the English-speaking theatre world. In February of 1869 whilst it played at the Strand in London and at Wood's Museum in New York, it was to be seen in two rival productions at Chicago's Crosby's Opera House and McVicker's Theatre, opening at both houses in the same week that Melbourne's Duke of Edinburgh's Theatre put up Australia's first production.

Brough also had success in the area of imported opérabouffe, for his adaptation of Offenbach's *Ba-ta-clan* as *Ching-Chow-Hi* became the standard English version of the piece throughout the English-speaking theatre, and it would undoubtedly have been prelude to many more versions of French pieces, had not his death intervened in his early forties.

His 1864 farce *The Area Belle* (w Andrew Halliday) was made into the operetta *Penelope* by George P Hawtrey with music by Edward Solomon (Comedy Theatre 9 May 1889).

Robert Brough also turned out several years' worth of further burlesque pieces, including *Mephistophiles, or An Ambassador from Below* (w Henry Sutherland Edwards, Haymarket Theatre, 14 May 1852), *The Overland Journey to Constantinople as Undertaken by Lord Bateman, with Interesting Particulars of the Fair Sophia* (Adelphi Theatre, 17 April 1854), *Medea, or The Best of Mothers With a Brute of a Husband, or A Libel on a Lady of Colchis* (Olympic Theatre, 14 July 1856), *Masaniello, or the Fish'oman of Naples* (Olympic Theatre, 2 July 1857), *The Siege of Troy* (Theatre Royal, Lyceum, 27 December 1858), and *Alfred the Great, or The Minstrel King* (Olympic Theatre, 26 December 1859).

1848 **The Enchanted Isle, or Raising the Wind on the Most Approved Principles** (pasticcio/w Robert Brough) Liverpool Amphitheatre, Adelphi Theatre, London, 20 November

1848 **Camaralzaman and Badoura, or The Peri Who Loved a Prince** (pasticcio/w R Brough) Haymarket Theatre 26 December

1849 **The Sphinx** (pasticcio/w R Brough) Haymarket Theatre 9 April

1849 **Frankenstein, or The Model Man** (pasticcio/w R Brough) Adelphi Theatre 26 December

1849 **The Ninth Statue, or The Jewels and the Gem** (pasticcio/w R Brough) Haymarket Theatre 26 December

1850 **The Last Edition of Ivanhoe, with all the newest improvements** (pasticcio/w R Brough) Haymarket Theatre, 1 April

1850 **The Second Calendar, or The Queen of Beauty who had the Fight with the Genie** (aka *The Arabian Nights*) (pasticcio/w R Brough) Haymarket Theatre 26 December

1851 **Arline, or The Fortunes and Vicissitudes of a Bohemian Girl** (pasticcio/w R Brough) Haymarket Theatre 21 April

1851 **The Princess Radiant, or The Story of the Mayflower** (pasticcio/w R Brough) Haymarket Theatre 26 December

1851 **Little Red Riding Hood** (pasticcio/w R Brough) Adelphi Theatre 26 December

1852 **O Gemini, or Brothers of Course** (pasticcio/w R Brough) Adelphi Theatre 12 April

1853 **Richard Coeur de Lion, or The Knight of the Couchant Leopard** (pasticcio arr J G Reed/w R Brough) Theatre Royal, Drury Lane 28 March

1854 **Prince Prettypet and the Butterfly** (pasticcio) Theatre Royal, Lyceum 26 December

1856 **Perdita, or The Royal Milkmaid** Theatre Royal, Lyceum 15 September

1856 **Conrad and Medora** (pasticcio) Theatre Royal, Lyceum 26 December

1857 **Lallah Rookh and the Peri, the Princess and the Troubadour** (pasticcio) Theatre Royal, Lyceum 24 December

1858 **The Caliph of Baghdad** (pasticcio) Adelphi Theatre 5 April

1859 **Dinorah Under Difficulties** (pasticcio) Adelphi Theatre 7 November

1860 **The Forty Thieves** (pasticcio arr J Barnard/with others) Theatre Royal, Lyceum 7 March

1860 **The Sylphide!** (pasticcio arr W H Montgomery) Royal Princess's Theatre 9 April

1860 **Endymion, or the Naughty Boy who Cried for the Moon** (pasticcio) St James's Theatre 26 December

1861 **Perseus and Andromeda, or The Maid and the Monster** (pasticcio) St James's Theatre 26 December

1862 **A Shilling Day at the Great Exhibition** (pasticcio/w Andrew Halliday) Adelphi Theatre 9 June

1862 **Prince Amabel, or the Fairy Roses** (aka *Turko the Terrible*) (pasticcio) St James's Theatre 5 May

1862 **The Colleen Bawn Settled at Last** (pasticcio/w Andrew Halliday) Lyceum Theatre 5 July

1862 **Rasselas, Prince of Abyssinia, or The Happy Valley** (pasticcio) Haymarket Theatre 26 December

1863 **The Great Sensation Trial, or Circumstantial Effie-Deans** (pasticcio) St James's Theatre 6 April

1863 **King Arthur, or the Days and Knights of the Round Table** (pasticcio) Haymarket Theatre 26 December

1864 **Hercules and Omphale, or The Power of Love** (pasticcio arr Ferdinand Wallerstein) St James's Theatre 26 December

1865 **Ernani, or The Horn of a Dilemma** (pasticcio arr B Issacson) Alexandra Theatre 20 May

1865 **Ching Chow Hi, or a Cracked Piece of China** (*Ba-ta-clan*) English version w Thomas German Reed (Gallery of Illustration)

1866 **Papillionetta, or The Prince, the Butterfly and the Beetle** (pasticcio) Prince of Wales Theatre, Liverpool, Sadler's Wells Theatre 2 June

1867 **Pygmalion, or the Statue Fair** (pasticcio) Strand Theatre 22 April

1868 **The Field of the Cloth of Gold** (pasticcio) Strand Theatre 11 April

1868 **The Gnome King, or The Fairy of the Silver Mine** (pasticcio) Queen's Theatre 26 December

1869 **Joan of Arc** (pasticcio) Strand Theatre 29 March

1869 **The Flying Dutchman, or The Demon Seaman and the Lass that Loved a Sailor** (pasticcio arr Hermann) Royalty Theatre 2 December

BROUGHTON, Phyllis (b London, 17 March 1862; d London, 21 July 1926).

Phyllis Broughton made her first stage appearance at the age of 14 as a dancer at the Canterbury Music Hall, and she and her sister Emma were soon hired by John Hollingshead for the Gaiety Theatre. They played there principally in burlesque and Phyllis graduated to such leading rôles as Sir Ralph Mont-Faucon in *Little Robin Hood* (1882), Henry in *Valentine and Orson* (1883), Ferdinand in *Ariel* (1883), Maimoune in *Camaralzaman*, Mary Kenyon in *Called There and Back*, Ophelia in *Very Little Hamlet* (1884) and Olinska in *Mazeppa* (1885), before leaving the Gaiety to join the burlesque (Sir Walter Raleigh in *Kenilworth*, Onduletta in *Lurline* etc) and comic opera company at the Avenue Theatre under the direction of Claude Marius.

She created and played a series of soubrette rôles with the Carl Rosa Light Opera Company at the Prince of Wales (Lady Prue in *Indiana*, *Madame Favart*, Follow-the-Drum in *The Old Guard*, Chopinette in *Paul Jones*, Cicely in *Marjorie*, Marcelline in *Captain Thérèse*), appeared as Virginia Squeeze in the pantomime *The Swiss Express*, in the musical playlet *A Pantomime Rehearsal* (t/o Lily Eaton-Belgrave) and in burlesque (Catherine of Rochelle in *Joan of Arc*, t/o Dolly in *Blue-Eyed Susan*) before moving into the latest style of entertainments in the very first of George Edwardes's modern-dress musical comedies.

She was cast in the travesty rôle of the teenaged Lord

Clanside in *In Town*, but then succeeded Lottie Venne as Lady Virginia Forrest in *A Gaiety Girl*, the first of a series of rôles as smart middle-aged ladies which was pursued with Arthur Roberts in *Gentleman Joe* (1895, t/o Mrs Ralli Carr), *Biarritz* (1896, Tessie Carew) *Dandy Dan the Lifeguardsman* (1897, t/o Lady Catherine Wheeler) and *HMS Irresponsible* (1901, t/o Victoria Chaffers). Appearing less frequently in her forties and fifties, she was seen in *The Earl and the Girl* (1903 and 1914, Virginia Bliss) and *The Dairymaids* (1906, 1908, Lady Brudenell) as well as in a small number of non-musical plays.

An attractive and spirited performer, Broughton was notably popular with both public and professionals through some 20 years of regular London performances. She was on several occasions called in to replace an insufficient or ailing leading lady and was a favourite (ie supportive and uncomplaining) partner of the notoriously unreliable Roberts. She also spent a certain amount of time at the centre of some nice publicity-worthy scandal, and won £2,500 and costs from Lord Dangan in 1889 in a breach of promise suit.

Miss Broughton was the daughter of Emily Jecks, and thus the niece of another top-class musical actress, Harriet Coveney (1827–1892) and cousin to Clara Jecks.

BROWN, Georgia [KLOT, Lily] (b London, 21 October 1933; d London, 6 June 1992).

Georgia Brown first came to notice on the musical stage when she appeared at London's Royal Court Theatre in the rôle of Lucy Lockit in *The Threepenny Opera* (1955) before repeating the part in the rather more successful off-Broadway production in New York. She returned to the Royal Court in the short-lived *The Lily-White Boys* (1960) and, later the same year, created her most memorable rôle as Nancy in *Oliver!* (1960), introducing 'As Long as He Needs Me', 'Oom Pah Pah' and 'It's a Fine Life'. She again visited America to repeat her rôle in the 1962 Broadway production.

London saw her once more when she succeeded to the title-rôle of Bart's later musical *Maggie May*, but her career as a vocalist brought her back to the theatre only intermittently thereafter. She took over in the compilation show *Side By Side By Sondheim*, played the title-rôle in *Carmelina*, Broadway's musical version of *Buona Sera, Mrs Campbell*, appeared as the slightly ageing star, Dorothy Brock, in London's edition of *42nd Street* and starred in the short-lived Gilbert Bécaud musical play, *Roza*, in America, without finding another new vehicle of the importance of *Oliver!*

BROWN, Lew [BROWNSTEIN, Louis] (b Odessa, Ukraine, 10 December 1893; d New York, 5 February 1958). One unit of the songwriting trio of De Sylva, Brown and Henderson.

Having moved to America when Louis was still a child, the Brownstein family continued from their original stop in New Haven to New York where the young Louis attended high school. After a variety of post-school jobs, he tried his hand at writing song lyrics and took his first serious steps in the music business when in 1912 he began a working relationship with Albert von Tilzer, the established composer of numbers like 'Take Me Out to the Ball Game' and 'Put Your Arms Around Me, Honey'.

Together, the pair had some fine song successes over a period of eight years – 'I'm the Lonesomest Gal in Town' (1912), 'Give Me the Moonlight, Give Me the Girl' (*Hullo, America*, UK 1917), 'I May Be Gone For a Long, Long Time' (*Hitchy Koo of 1917*), 'Oh, By Jingo, Oh By Gee!' (*Linger Longer Letty* 1919), 'Chili Bean' (*Pot Luck*, UK), 'My Gee-Gee from the Fiji Isles', 'I Used to Love You', 'Dapper Dan' (*A to Z*, UK) before Brown was introduced to musician Ray Henderson.

The first Brown/Henderson effort was a song called 'Georgette', sung with success in the 1922 *Greenwich Village Follies*, and the two continued a non-exclusive collaboration ('Why Did I Kiss That Girl?', 'Don't Bring Lulu' w Billy Rose, 'If You Hadn't Gone Away' w Rose) whilst Brown continued to turn out songs with a variety of other composers: 'Red Moon' (w Travers, Max Kortlander, de Martini), 'Last Night on the Back Porch' (w Carl Schraubstader), 'When It's Night Time in Italy, It's Wednesday Over Here' (w James Kendis), 'Shine' (w Cecil Mack, Ford Dabney), 'Where The Lazy Daisies Grow' and 'Then I'll Be Happy' (w Cliff Friend), 'Collegiate' (w Moe Jaffe, Nathan J Bonx), 'I'd Climb the Highest Mountain' (w Sidney Clare).

The songwriting team that was to become famous to a generation as 'De Sylva-Brown-n-Henderson' came together for the first time on Broadway with a contribution to Al Jolson's *Big Boy* (1925), and success came with their score for the 1926 edition of the revue *George White's Scandals*. The lasting hit of the 1925 *Scandals*, for which they had also written the main score, had been Irving Berlin's interpolated 'All Alone', but in the 1926 show the hits were their own. A Blues section which included several famous old blues numbers, Gershwin's 'Rhapsody in Blue' and bits of Schubert and Schumann, was topped off by De Sylva, Brown and Henderson's new 'The Birth of the Blues', whilst Ann Pennington danced frenetically to the rhythms of their Charlestonny new dance, 'The Black Bottom'.

Brown's first full Broadway musical comedy score was written not with these partners, but with his early songwriting associate, Cliff Friend. *Piggy* was comedian Sam Bernard's third variation on the antics of his favourite character, Mr Hoggenheimer of Park Lane, as originally played by him in the British musical *The Girl From Kays*, and it was lively enough to last out 11 weeks. Major success came, however, with the trio's first book musical score, their set of songs for the college musical *Good News* ('The Best Things in Life Are Free', 'The Varsity Drag') and, over the next four years, whilst continuing to supply the *George White Scandals* with annual material, they turned out four further pieces in the same vein. They were four pieces of variable value, but each one was popular through a good Broadway run and most were exported (with uneven results) to London and to Australia and even, on one occasion, to France. *Manhattan Mary*, a vehicle for Ed Wynn, was short on song hits but long on personality; *Hold Everything!* invaded the world of boxing, introduced 'You're the Cream in My Coffee', and made a star of Bert Lahr; *Follow Thru* turned to golf and produced 'Button Up Your Overcoat'; and *Flying High* gave Lahr the opportunity to take to the skies, if without any staying-powerful songs.

The hottest songwriting team on contemporary Broadway was, naturally, courted by Hollywood, and they had some outstanding film success with songs for pieces such as *The Singing Fool* (1928, 'Sonny Boy') and *Sunny Side Up* (1929, 'If I Had a Talking Picture of You', 'Sunny Side Up'), but the combination broke up when De Sylva moved on to an executive position in the film industry, and Brown and Henderson returned to Broadway. They turned out a score for the *Scandals of 1931* in which 'Life Is Just a Bowl of Cherries' was the take-away tune, but they did not succeed in producing anything of the same kind of lasting value for either of the two subsequent revusical shows to which they contributed the songs. *Hot-Cha*, even with Bert Lahr, was a 15-week semi-flop, and *Strike me Pink*, which the pair produced themselves, had Jimmy Durante and a lot of limp material.

Brown teamed with Harry Akst on an unimpressive 1935 revue, *Calling All Stars*, before going back to Hollywood to become a director, producer and sometime writer in films, returning to the theatre just once more as producer-director-librettist-lyricist-part composer of a curiously flimsy piece called *Yokel Boy*. It had a six-months' run and added 'Comes Love' and a version of the interpolated 'Beer Barrel Polka' (Wladimir Timm, Jaromir Vejvoda) to Brown's list of successful song credits, a list which was occasionally added to in the following years by such pieces as the 1943 song 'Madame, I Like Your Crêpes Suzette' (w Burton Lane, Ralph Freed) written for De Sylva's film version of *Du Barry Was a Lady*.

Brown was portayed by Ernest Borgnine in a De Sylva-Brown-n-Henderson film biomusical called *The Best Things in Life Are Free*.

1927 **Piggy** (Cliff Friend/Daniel Kusell, Alfred Jackson) Royale Theater 22 October

1927 **Good News** (Ray Henderson/w B G De Sylva/Laurence Schwab, De Sylva) 46th Street Theater 6 September

1927 **Manhattan Mary** (Henderson/w De Sylva) Apollo Theater 26 September

1928 **Hold Everything!** (Henderson/w De Sylva/Jack McGowan, De Sylva) Broadhurst Theater 10 October

1929 **Follow Thru** (Henderson/w De Sylva/Schwab, De Sylva) 46th Street Theater 9 Janaury

1930 **Flying High** (Henderson/w De Sylva/McGowan) Apollo Theater 3 March

1932 **Hot-Cha!** (Henderson/w H S Kraft, Mark Hellinger) Ziegfeld Theater 8 March

1933 **Strike Me Pink** (Henderson/Mc Gowan, Mack Gordon) Majestic Theater 4 March

1939 **Yokel Boy** (Sam H Stept/Charles Tobias) Majestic Theater 6 July

BROWN[E], Louise (b Madison, Wis).

A durable dancing ingénue of indeterminate age who was advertised as 'the spinning top' because of her pirouetting propensities, Louise Brown(e) first came to notice in her native America when she succeeded to the rôle of Sally in the musical *Sally, Irene and Mary* (1925), and was cast in the starring rôle of Suzanne Trentoni created on the straight stage by Ethel Barrymore in the musical *Captain Jinks*. This plum part had been announced as a vehicle for Marilyn Miller, several years earlier, but the show had not materialized and, when it finally did – with different writers and sponsors attached – Miss Browne got the job instead. It won her a two-year contract with Miss Miller's chief sponsor Florenz Ziegfeld, who featured her in his revue *No Foolin'* the following year.

Louise Browne visited Britain to star as Kitty Brown in *The Girl Friend* (ie *Kitty's Kisses*, 1927), appeared on

Broadway as the heroine of *Rainbow* (Virginia Brown), *Lady Fingers* (Hope Quayle) and *Woof Woof* (Susie Yates), and then returned to London to star in *Heads Up* (1930, Mary Trumbell), and in Adele Astaire's rôle of Pat in *The One Girl* (1932). Thereafter she made her career in Britain, playing in the revues *Yours Sincerely* and *After Dark*, briefly in the Hungarian musical *Happy Weekend* (*Zackbamackska* 1934, Polly Petworthy), touring in *Gay Divorce* (1934) and creating the rôle of April in *Jill Darling*, in which she introduced 'I'm on a See-Saw' (w John Mills) to London audiences.

She then renewed a partnership with light comedian-dancer Roy Royston, pairing in a series of dancing-ingénue leads, constructed on the Cyril Ritchard–Madge Elliott plan, in a run of successful comic musicals at the Gaiety Theatre: *Seeing Stars* (1935, Princess Valerie), *Swing Along* (1936, Lili Breval), *Going Greek* (1937, Iris Carew) and *Running Riot* (1938, Betty Browne). When the war intervened, Miss Browne and her ubiquitous stage mother vanished from the London theatre scene and, apparently, all others.

BRUDER LEICHTSINN Operette in a Vorspiel and 2 acts by Julius Brammer and Alfred Grünwald. Music by Leo Ascher. Wiener Bürgertheater, Vienna, 28 December 1917.

Bruder Leichtsinn (Otto Storm) is not a person but a personification. He is irresponsibility, negligence, thoughtlessness and, like all virtues and vices, he has his favourites amongst human beings. One of these was the well-known singer, Adele Garnier (Ida Russka), who gave up the love of a good man for a carnival night fling with Graf Fabrice Dunoir (Karl Streitmann) of which was born their daughter, Musotte (Frln Russka again). Leichtsinn watches over 'his' child, as she leads a lively, heedless life with her friends in a private school in Brussels, and falls in love with an anonymous person who writes her the most charming letters. Dunoir comes to adopt her, but it is again carnival night and Leichtsinn takes everyone on the town. Whilst Musotte's schoolfriend, Nelly (Mimi Kott), nets her lawyer (Carlo Böhm), and papa Karl Pampinger (Josef Joseffy) is caught by his wife (Viktoria Pohl-Meiser) flirting with the apparently respectable school-headmistress (Emmy Stein), Musotte's father allows her, as he had promised her mother, to make her free choice of husband. She chooses the anonymous letter-writer. Leichtsinn looks after his own: the writer is the mulatto engineer Jimmy Wells (Ludwig Herold), who wrote to the girl because he speaks so poorly ... but he loves her.

Ascher's score featured several winning waltzes: the duet between Leichtsinn and Adele in the Vorspiel ('Wer den Leichtsinn liebt'), Musotte's letter song, 'Mein reizendes Fräulein', the carnival night duet between Leichtsinn and Dunoir ('Das Küssen und Kosen und Lieben') and a waltz-ensemble ('Lockend klingt mein Walzermärchen'), set alongside a group of marches and a dance duo for Pampinger and the schoolmistress which started out in tango time ('Den Tango den tanz' ich so fesch').

The show ran for a good 176 performances in wartime Vienna, was subsequently seen in Germany, and scored a particularly fine success in Hungary under the title of *Heje-huja báró* (ad Imre Harmath, Adorjan Ötvös) with an initial run of over a hundred performances.

Germany: ?1918; Hungary: Margitszigeti Színkör *Hejehuja báró* 15 June 1918

BRUDER STRAUBINGER Operette in 3 acts by Moritz West and Ignaz Schnitzer. Music by Edmund Eysler. Theater an der Wien, Vienna, 20 February 1903.

At a time when the Viennese musical theatre was desperately in need of new, and preferably modern, musical blood to replace the departed composing stars of the 19th century, the chief sources of hope seemed to come from Carl Michael Ziehrer's *Die Landstreicher*, Heinrich Reinhardt's *Das süsse Mädel* and the young Franz Lehár's *Der Rastelbinder*, until Karczag and Wallner of the Theater an der Wien mounted the old-Austria piece *Bruder Straubinger*, the maiden work of another young composer, Edmund Eysler.

West and Schnitzer had put together a splendid rôle for the theatre's star, Alexander Girardi, as 'brother' Straubinger who, when his identity papers are stolen by Bonifaz, an army deserter (Arthur Strasser), is obliged to make do with those of his grandfather – which make him 114 years old. Disguised as an army veteran, he gets a 1,000 gulden-a-month pension out of the Landgraf Philipp (Karl Meister), but sees his sweetheart, Marie (Lina Abarbanell), who works for the showman Schwudler (Siegmund Natzler) as a wild-woman exhibit called Oculi, first pursued by the Landgraf and then, when the Landgräfin Lola (Mary Hagen) spots it, about to be forcibly engaged to the phoney Straubinger. The young pair convince the Landgräfin that the 'old' husband is a preferable match and, in the end, the papers are restored, the 'old' man can become young again, and the naughty Landgraf returns, chastened, to his wife.

Eysler's score, partly manufactured from pieces left over from his first attempt to write a show to Schnitzer's Strauss-rejected *Der Schelm von Bergen* libretto (as *Der Hexenspiegel*), was full of waltzing and marching melody, topped by one of the biggest show-song hits in years: Girardi's 'Küssen ist keine Sünd' a catchy waltz-song in which the elderly veteran expounds on the virtues of kissing. The star also had a lively entrance number, the bouncing, waltzing 'Gott grüss' dich, Bruder Straubinger', as did both the Landgraf (the more lyrical waltz 'Es kommt mit leisem Kosen') and Oculi with her wildly jaunty 3/4 showpiece (to D in alt), 'Ja, so singt sie'. She later joined Straubinger happily in a winning march-time Trommel-Duett ('Er ist ganz in mich verschossen'). There were also two comical numbers for Schwudler, a delicious swinging waltz for Lola ('Bald ist die Wilddiebe hier'), a drinking song for the aristocratic pair and ensembles, ranging from the softly surging trio 'Vierblättriges Klee' to a brisk march quartet in the final act. A large part of the score became popular without any other single number equalling the phenomenal and enduring favour given to 'Küssen ist keine Sünd'.

The show was a singular hit, but Karczag was obliged by treaty to mount Planquette's *Mam'selle Quat' Sous* (*Die beiden Don Juans*) and so, after little more than a month, *Bruder Straubinger* was replaced. After two weeks, however, with the contractual obligation out of the way, the French piece was whisked off, and Girardi got back into his veteran's outfit until the end of the season (65 performances). When the theatre reopened after the summer break, *Bruder Straubinger* reopened with it, and it played on to its 109th performance. It passed its 125th in repertoire on 2 February 1905 before going on to be seen at the Raimundtheater between 1909 and 1911 in Girardi's seasons there (200th performance 14 February 1911), and at the Johann Strauss-Theater in 1913 (11 April). A new production was mounted at the Wiener Bürgertheater in 1929, and the show returned to the Theater an der Wien in 1934 for special performances to mark Esyler's 60th birthday. On this occasion, Hubert Marischka played the Girardi rôle, with Mimi Shorp as Oculi and Fritz Steiner as Schwudler. On 8 March of that year it notched up its 300th performance.

Although the show was apparently 'translated into 16 languages', its greatest popularity was very largely centred in middle Europe. It became the most popular of all of Eysler's popular works in Germany and played a good initial 36 performances (ad Jenő Faragó) at Budapest's Népszinház in its initial production there. However, in a period where Viennese Operette had not yet begun to export in the way that it would do in a couple of years' time, post-*Die lustige Witwe*, it did not appear on the vernacular stages of London, Paris or New York. Australia got just a fragment, the hit song, when soubrette Carrie Moore interpolated 'Kissing is No Sin' into a musical farcical comedy called *Much Married* which was played at Melbourne's Bijou Theatre in 1913 (5 July).

A film version was produced in 1950 under the title of the show's still famous song.

Germany: Centraltheater 26 September 1903; Hungary: Népszinház *Vándorlegény* 30 October 1903; Film: *Küssen ist keine Sünd* 1950

BRÜDERLEIN FEIN

Altwiener Singspiel in 1 act by Julius Wilhelm. Music by Leo Fall. Bernhard Rose-Theater, Berlin, 31 December 1908.

A little three-handed, one-act piece, containing seven musical numbers, *Brüderlein fein* followed the old musician Josef Drechsler and his wife, Tony, on a sentimental journey of remembrances on the occasion of their 40th wedding anniversary. A musical clock rings out with the little melody 'Brüderlein fein' and Drechsler remembers the time when he composed the tune, for a production of Raimund's *Der Jugend*, and the day of their wedding. The third character of the piece was the old housekeeper, Gertrud, who also played the hero of *Der Jugend* in the dream sequence. The principal numbers of the score were the waltz duo 'Nicht zu schnell und nicht zu langsam' for Drechsler and Tony, their pseudo-waltz 'Unter dem blühenden Lindenbaum' and Gertrud's Lied der Jugend.

First played at Berlin's Rose-Theater and subsequently at the Theater an der Wien's studio theatre, Hölle, *Brüderlein fein* won all hearts, and proved to be one of the best-liked and most often reprised of smaller works in a period where such shows were much less seen than they had been in earlier years. It was reprised in Vienna, at the Johann Strauss-Theater in 1913 as a forepiece in a 'Girardi zyklus', and again in 1920 in a spectacle-coupé with Reinhardt's *Die süssen Grisetten*, and at the Theater an der Wien in 1919, whilst winning performances in similar situations in Germany and Hungary.

In London, during the short-lived fashion for playing one-act Operetten in variety houses, *Darby and Joan* (ad Arthur Anderson) was played on the bill at the London Coliseum.

Austria: Hölle 1 December 1909; Hungary: Urania Színház *Édes öregem* 24 November 1910; UK: London Coliseum *Darby and Joan* 11 December 1912

BRUMMELL

Opérette in a prologue and 3 acts by Rip and Robert Dieudonné. Lyrics by Rip. Music by Reynaldo Hahn. Théâtre des Folies-Wagram, Paris, 17 January 1931.

Although the real 'Beau Brummell' – George Bryan Brummell (1778–1840) – was a close friend of George IV of England and a man whose career knew some dramatic highs and (mostly) lows, his name has become simply synonomous in modern times with the idea of the rarefied dandy. Rip's opérette presented Pizani as the Beau, an elegant gentleman in prey to a passion for his little washerwoman and childhood friend Peggy (Sim-Viva). He rusticates himself in private misery, only to be followed to his retreat by half of fashionable Bath, headed by the amorous Lady Eversharp (Marguerite Deval) and the Prince of Wales (Henri Jullien), all, following the maker of their fashions, dressed in peasant garb. Ultimately Brummell lets Peggy go to a more suitable lover and puts on again the motley of his courtly calling. Producer/director Edmond Roze appeared himself in the supporting rôle of Helliot.

Reynaldo Hahn's score contained some typically pretty pieces, including Peggy's solo 'Entre les deux mon coeur balance' and the hero's Chanson pastorale. There was a song in praise of 'le knock-out' from boxing-mad Jim, who also headed the search for Brummell declaring that the best method was simply 'Cherchez la femme', whilst rustic Dick longed in song to be one of 'les Dandys de Brummell ... aussi pauvres que des cigales, mais riches de l'or d'Israël'. The best part of the score, however, fell to Mlle Deval, whether joining in a hunting chorus and delivering her Couplets de l'equitation ('A dada'), heading some aristocratic 'Bergers Watteau', consoling Brummell in her Air Galant or, in a paroxysm of Rip lyrics redolent of the Lady Parvula of *Valmouth*, musing on the attractions of a rough man: 'lorsque cet éffronté a soudain éructé une phrase méchante ... il m'enchante, lorsque ce parvenu pose sur un sein nu son oeil de cannibale ... il m'emballe, quand cet ex-épicier, après un mot grossier, parle de savoir-vivre ... il m'enivre, quand ce vil clabaudeur raconte sans pudeur ses amours qu'il méprise, il me grise ...'

Brummell did not find the same kind of prosperity as its partner-in-pastels, *Ciboulette*, and won only a fair run. This French opérette, however, presented Brummell altogether more successfully than two British musicals of the 1930s, *Beau Brummell* (Saville Theatre, 1933) with Harry Welchman as Brummell and *By Appointment* (New Theatre, 1934) where the dandy was played by Gavin Gordon, both of which were quick flops. An American musical *Beau Brummell*, written by Gladys Unger, lyrics by Edward Eliscu and Raymond Egan, and with music by Harry Tierney, was tried out at St Louis's Municipal Light Opera in 1933 (7 August) with Leonard Ceeley as the Beau and Nancy McCord (Marianne) Allan Jones (Reginald), Doris Patston (Kathleen) and George Hassell (Prince of Wales) in the other principal rôles, the whole 'under the personal direction of J J Shubert'. It went no further.

BRUNTON, Dorothy (b Melbourne, Australia, 14 October 1893; d Sydney, 5 June 1977).

Dorothy Brunton was the daughter of one of Australia's foremost scenic artists, the English-born John Brunton (d Sydney, 21 October 1909), who had been brought from Liverpool by the Williamson, Garner and Musgrove combine, and who spent the remainder of his career working in Australia, latterly for 15 years with Bland Holt.

'Dot' made her first appearance on the musical stage under Williamson's banner in a small rôle in *The Balkan Princess* (1911) and subsequently covered lead rôles in *The Girl in the Taxi* and several other musicals, before playing five years of soubrette and, later, lead rôles for the Williamson organization in such pieces as *Nightbirds*, *The Cingalee* (Peggy), *The Merry Widow* (Fifi), *Autumn Manoeuvres* (June), *Gipsy Love* (Jolan), *The Girl in the Taxi* (Jacqueline), *The Girl on the Film* (Freddy), *Dorothy* (Phyllis), *Princess Caprice* (Clementine), *The Belle of New York* (Fifi/Violet), *High Jinks* (Sylvia), *So Long, Letty* (Letty), *Tonight's the Night* (June), *A Waltz Dream* (Franzi), *Canary Cottage* (Trixie) and *Three Twins* (Kate). In the process, she became one of Australia's favourite musical comedy performers of the wartime years.

A venture to Britain saw her playing good rôles in Isidore Witmark's *Shanghai* at the Theatre Royal, Drury Lane (1918), *Soldier Boy* (1919) and, more successfully, with Walter Catlett in *Baby Bunting* (1919, Janet Chester) before she returned to Australia for a further run of lead rôles in the Australian productions of such pieces as *Yes, Uncle!* (Mabel), *Baby Bunting, Going Up, Oh, Lady! Lady!!, Battling Butler* (Mrs Butler), *The Rise of Rosie O'Reilly* (Rosie), the Australian musical version of *Tons of Money* (Louise Allington) and *Little Jessie James* (Jessie) whilst repeating her most successful rôles of earlier years, notably the musical comedy rôles of *High Jinks* and *So Long, Letty*.

A second London venture brought only the Harry Welchman turkey *The White Camellia* (1928, Fleurette Chamier), and she returned definitively to Australia where she starred in *Dearest Enemy* (Betsy), *Florodora* (Dolorcs), *The Merry Widow* (Hanna) and *The Duchess of Dantzic* (Catherine) in the later part of a prominent career before retiring to marriage.

BRUYAS, Florian (d 1974).

A former member of the French senate and administrator of the Conservatoire of Music at Lyon, Bruyas was the author of the only systematic and detailed chronicle of the history of the musical theatre in France (*Histoire de l'opérette en France 1855–1965* Emmanuel Vitte, Lyon 1974). He died shortly after the publication of his work, before he was able to introduce the additions, revisions and corrections he had subsequently gathered, but his book remains, in spite of this, one of the principal vertebrae in the backbone of scholarly world musical theatre literature.

BRYAN, Dora [BROADBENT, Dora] (b Southport, Lancs, 7 February 1924).

Singing comedienne Dora Bryan appeared in several successful London revues (*The Lyric Revue, The Globe Revue, At the Lyric* etc) and in a number of non-musical films (*The Fallen Idol, The Cure for Love, The Blue Lamp* etc)

before making a personal hit in her first appearance in a book musical as the heart-of-gold Lily in *The Water Gipsies* (1955, 'Why Did They Call Me Lily?', 'It Would Cramp My Style'). In a career mixing comedy and film (*A Taste of Honey*) with occasional musical appearances, she subsequently took the rôle of Lorelei Lee in the London production of *Gentlemen Prefer Blondes* (1962) and succeeded Mary Martin as Dolly Levi in *Hello, Dolly!* with considerable success, taking the piece on tour after her London run was over. After many years away from the musical stage, she returned in 1986 to play alongside Cyd Charisse in a revival of *Charlie Girl* (Kay Connor), reprised her *Hello, Dolly!* on the road, and top-billed in a very personal revusical production of *70 Girls 70* at the Chichester Festival in 1990, in the West End the following year, and subsequently on tour around Britain.

Autobiography: *According to Dora* (Aurum Press, London, 1986)

BRYNNER, Yul [KHANO, Taidje] (b Sakhalin, 11 July 1911; d New York, 10 October 1985).

Born in Russia, and brought up in China and France, Brynner began his career as an actor in America where, in 1945, he made his Broadway musical début alongside Mary Martin in the Chinese-set musical *Lute Song* (1946, Tsai-Yong), a rôle he subsequently repeated in the show's London production (1948). In 1951 he starred opposite Gertrude Lawrence as the King of Siam in *The King and I* ('A Puzzlement', 'Shall We Dance?'), a rôle which he repeated opposite Deborah Kerr on film, and with which he became thoroughly identified through repeated reappearances on stage in America and in Britain. Brynner was seen on Broadway as the King more than 30 years after his creation of the rôle, shortly before his final illness. He appeared in only one further musical rôle, as Odysseus in the short-lived *Home Sweet Homer* (1975).

BUB ODER MÄDEL? Operette in 2 acts by Felix Dörmann and Adolf Altmann. Music by Bruno Granichstädten. Johann Strauss-Theater, Vienna, 13 November 1908.

Fürst Fritz Ragan (Louis Treumann) has lived a wild-oat-flinging life on the expectation of inheriting the fortune of his childless uncle, Fürst Johann Georg Ragan (Karl Mauth), and has even lined himself up a sweetheart without a gulden to her name (Mizzi Freihardt). Uncle Johann thinks it time to bring to boy to heel, and he announces that his own wife is about to give birth to an heir. Fritz has to take a pull in his high living and is obliged to go looking for a rich wife in Lady Brighton's 'Amerikanisches-Millionmädchen-Heiratschule'. Of course, in the end there is no baby and the chastened Fritz is able to marry where his heart is.

If the story was barely new, it was told in a lively style and tricked out with up-to-date references, comical debt-collectors and picturesque rich Americans, including the pretty pensionnaires of the millionaire-girls's Marriage-School, and it was illustrated by Granichstädten with a score in his catchy, bordering-on-the-jazzy style.

Leopold Müller's production at the Johann Strauss-Theater ran for 86 straight performances, followed by a further handful in repertoire which brought its total to 101 nights by 26 March 1909, but, although the show went on to productions in Germany and in Hungary (ad Adolf Merei), its most considerable success came in America.

Plate 39. **Yul Brynner**: *'Long live the king ...'. Brynner in his one, unforgettable rôle.*

Louis Werba and Mark A Luescher's Broadway production (ad H B Smith, Raymond W Peck, R B Smith) featured J Humbird Duffey as the extravagant Duke of Barchester and Adrienne Augarde as his housekeeper's daughter, Daphne, whilst a comical quartet of the Duke's creditors brought together the comedians Ed Gallagher (Dennis) and Al Shean (Schmuke) for the first time. Adaptors Harry and Robert Bache Smith were advertised as 'authors of *The Spring Maid*', the producers' biggest and recent hit, and 'The Rose Waltz' and 'The Moon Song' as 'the whistling successes of the Continent'. Well mounted and managed, almost unbotched (a couple of minor bits by Robert Hood Bowers), the show proved a worthy successor to the earlier hit, playing for 176 performances on Broadway and touring vigorously.

Germany: ?1909; Hungary: Várszinház *Fiu vagy leány* 20 October 1910; USA: Globe Theater *The Rose Maid* 22 April 1912

BUCALOSSI, Procida (b Italy, ?1838; d Godstone, Surrey, 10 May 1918).

The composer of a number of comic operas for the British stage, Italian-born Bucalossi scored an international hit with his *(Les) Manteaux Noirs*, a version of Scribe's *Giralda*, set previously as an opéra-comique by Adolphe Adam, and rewritten by Harry Paulton for the English stage. None of his other works found anything like the same success, but Bucalossi was well enough considered as a musician in Victorian London to be invited to submit the music for one act of the vast Alhambra spectacle *Rothomago* along with Frederic Clay, Georges Jacobi and Gaston Serpette.

A regular contributor of songs and dance music to the West-End musical theatre (*La Poule aux oeufs d'or*, the Drury Lane pantomime *Beauty and the Beast* etc), Bucalossi also worked as a conductor at several London theatres, including a period at the Theatre Royal, Drury Lane, but he made his principal mark as a writer of ballads (originally as 'Charles Valentine') and as a prolific and extremely popular arranger and composer of dance music.

His sons **[Procida] Ernest [Luigi] BUCALOSSI** (b London, 1863; d Ottershaw, Surrey, 15 April 1933) and **Brigata [Procida Leonardo] BUCALOSSI** (b London, 1862; d London, 21 December, 1924) were both active in the musical theatre. Ernest worked at first as a performer with D'Oyly Carte's companies (as Ernest Elton) and later as a musical director and composer (*A Shower of Blacks* (1887), *Binks, the Downy Photographer* (1893), *En Route* (1896), *The Maid and the Motor Man*, *Robin Hood* burlesque (1907), *A Wife for a Song* (1 act, 1910) etc.) and Brigata as a performer, a not very successful producer, sometime composer (*A Capital Joke* (1889), *The Prancing Girl* (1891)) and, most particularly, a conductor, a position which, like his father, he held for a period at the Theatre Royal, Drury Lane.

1865 **Love Wins the Way** (Finlay Finlayson) 1 act Gallery of Illustration 24 October
1876 **Pom** (Bucalossi) Royalty Theatre 25 March
1876 **Coming Events** (Bucalossi) 1 act Royalty Theatre 22 April
1879 **Rothomago** (w Edward Solomon, Gaston Serpette, Frederic Clay/H B Farnie) Alhambra Theatre 22 December
1881 **The Stores** (Edward Rose, Augustus Harris) 1 act Theatre Royal, Drury Lane 14 March
1882 **(Les) Manteaux Noirs** (Harry Paulton, Walter Parke) Avenue Theatre 3 June
1884 **Lallah Rookh** (Horace Lennard) Novelty Theatre 1 May
1889 **Delia** (Frank Desprez) Bristol 11 March
1892 **Brother George** (Desprez) Portsmouth 16 May
1894 **Massaroni** (F Leslie Moreton, Arthur Rousbey) Leinster Hall, Dublin 23 January
1896 **En Route** (ex-*Bombay to Henley*) (w Ernest Bucalossi/Parke, Cecil Maxwell) Parkhurst Theatre 21 September

THE BUCCANEER Musical play in 2 acts by Sandy Wilson. New Watergate Theatre, London, 8 September 1953; Lyric Theatre, Hammersmith, 8 September 1955.

Wilson's successor to *The Boy Friend*, deliberately written in a different though equally light vein, *The Buccaneer* told the tiny tale of the attempt to save a comic paper embodying the virtues of old Britain. At first mounted, like

The Boy Friend, in a club venue, it was later given a more substantial production by H M Tennent Ltd in which Kenneth Williams repeated his singular performance as a precocious child, with some success.

Recording: London cast (HMV, AEI) etc

BUCHANAN, Jack (b Helensburgh, Scotland, 2 April 1891; d London, 20 October 1957). Dance and comedy star of the London theatre between the wars.

Buchanan made his first London appearance as a slim, dapper, dancing juvenile man at the age of 21, in the small rôle of the dancing-master Deschamps in the Austro-American musical *The Grass Widows* (1912), and he subsequently mixed revue engagements – notably a personal success in Charlot's *Bubbly* in 1917 – with a tour in George Grossmith's rôle of Dudley Mitten in *Tonight's the Night* and short periods in London's *Wild Geese* (1920, Bill Malcolm) and *Faust on Toast* (1921, Faust). His first book musical success came when he starred as the titular Mr Alfred Butler in the six-month run of his own production, *Battling Butler* (1922), and he followed this by appearing as the eponymous *Toni* in Grossmith and Malone's touring adaptation of the Berlin musical *Der Fürst von Pappenheim*, leaving the show on the road to go to America for André Charlot.

After scoring a fine Broadway success in *Charlot's Revue* (1924), he returned to Britain to take up the part of *Toni* for a London season and followed this with 20 further years of starring rôles in musical comedy, interspersed with both musical and light comedy films. He began his stage series with his own production of the circus musical *Boodle* (1925, Algernon Kenilworth) and followed up with a good run as the hero of *Sunny* (1926, Jim Deming) before, in 1928, beginning his celebrated top-of-the-bill partnership with dancing comedienne Elsie Randolph.

Miss Randolph, who had been seen in minor rôles in *Battling Butler* and *Toni* and better ones in *Boodle*, where she still gave second best to June, and *Sunny* became a wisecracking foil to Buchanan's suave light comedy and a superb dancing partner in a stage relationship which, like that of the Astaires, was a humorous one rather than a romantic one. In *That's a Good Girl* (1928, Bill Barrow), produced, directed and choreographed (w Anton Dolin) by Buchanan – they blended the lightest of comedy, dance and song to a nicety and to the taste of the age for 363 London performances, a tour and a film. As producer, Buchanan did better here than with *Lady Mary* (w Lee Ephraim) which he mounted in the same year, but in which he did not appear. Thereafter, his producing ventures were limited to shows in which his own attractive name topped the bill.

Buchanan filmed *Paris* (1930) in Hollywood, then returned to Britain for a new stage show, *Stand up and Sing* (1931, Rockingham Smith), in which he added a co-author's credit to his previous multiple functions. This piece happily repeated the West End success of the previous musical, as did the delightful *Mr Whittington* (1933–4, Dick Whittington) in which the favourite pair appeared for Moss' Empires through a tour and nearly 300 London performances. After a mistaken venture into the Eric Charell flop *The Flying Trapeze* (1935, René), a spectacular circus piece based on a pot-pourri of music by Ralph Benatzky, he returned to Miss Randolph, his

Plate 40. **Jack Buchanan** and **Elsie Randolph**: *Britain's favourite pair of dance-and-laughter merchants.*

accepted matinée idol style and to the way of success in his own production of *This'll Make You Whistle* (1935–6, Bill Hopping) and its subsequent film. The pair appeared happily together one last time, after a collaboration of more than 15 years, in *It's Time to Dance* (1943, Willmot Brown).

In between, Buchanan had made one of his periodic trips to New York, this time for his first Broadway book musical, *Between the Devil* (1937, Peter Anthony), filmed *The Gang's All Here* (1939) and produced and directed an unfortunate Chopin pot-pourri called *Waltz Without End* (Cambridge Theatre, 1942), but thereafter his theatrical activities became more sporadic. In 1947 he produced *Good Night Vienna*, which he had filmed so successfully more than a decade previously, as a tour with Bernard Delfont, he appeared in the revue *Fine Feathers* and, at 60 years of age, took over the suave, young lead rôle of *King's Rhapsody* following Ivor Novello's death. The Hollywood film of *The Bandwagon* (1953) showed that he was no longer either young or suave and, although he still evinced producing interest in the 1950s, that side of his career also ended on a gentle fade.

Biography: Marshall, M: *Top Hat and Tails* (Elm Tree, London, 1978)

BUCHBINDER, Bernhard [KLINGER, Gustav] (b Pest, 7 July ?1854; d Vienna ?24 June 1922).

At first a journalist on the *Neues Pester Journal* in his native Budapest, Klinger-Buchbinder (whose date of birth is given variously as anything between 1849 and 1854, on the 6th, 7th or 8th of July) first found success as the author of back stairs novels, and it was not until, already well into his thirties, when he quit Hungary for Austria and fiction for a career in the theatre, that he entered the most successful phase of his writing life.

His first substantial attempts in the musical theatre were in a collaboration with conductor/composer Rudolf Raimann on a piece played at Munich and with the Operette *Colombine* 'based on an idea by Julius Riegen' and set to music by Hans von Zois. Produced at Graz, this latter was sufficiently successful to be subsequently taken up by Fritz Steiner for the Carltheater (15 March 1889) where it was directed by Carl Adolf Friese and played by a cast including Wilhelm Knaack and Emma Seebold. Buchbinder had, by then, already broken into the metropolitan theatre with his adaptation of Scribe's *Ne touchez pas à la reine* as the text to Alfred Zamara's *Der Sänger von Palermo*, produced at the same theatre with the same director and stars the previous year, but neither piece stayed long in the repertoire, and the author turned to operatic ventures with Raoul Mader's Spieloper *Die Flüchtlinge*, produced at the Hofoper (19 February 1891), and Robert Fuchs' *Die Teufelsglocke*, played at Leipzig in 1893, and to plays, both adapted from the Hungarian and original, before finally venturing into the world of the musical comedy.

A collaboration with top-flight Operette writer A M Willner produced three libretti, including that of *Die Göttin der Vernunft* for Johann Strauss, of which *Der Schmetterling* (57 performances) was the most successful, but real success finally came when he returned to collaborate with his earliest partner, Rudolf Raimann, now musical director at the Theater in der Josefstadt. Together, the two men produced the highly successful Posse *Das Waschermädl* as a vehicle for the wife of the theatre's manager, Josef Jarno, the star soubrette Hansi Niese (38 performances, *A szoknyáshős* 15 June 1906 in Hungary), and they followed up with a series of like collaborations, notably *Der Schusterbub* (53 performances) and the oft-revived *Er und sein Schwester* (80 performances), in which Niese starred alongside Alexander Girardi in Vienna and which was a major hit in Budapest as *A postás fiú és a huga* (6 June 1902 Magyar Színház). However, Buchbinder's most enduring success came with another vehicle for Niese, a romantic musical comedy written in collaboration with composer Georg Jarno, the star's brother-in-law. The countrified tale of *Die Förster-Christl* and her attractions for the Austrian emperor was one of the most popular pieces of its era – an era which was under the sway of the very differently spiced *Die lustige Witwe*, produced little more than a year earlier – and, after a fine first run, remained in the repertoire for many decades thereafter.

Buchbinder collaborated with Jarno (*Das Musikantenmädel*, *Die Marinen-Gustl*), Zerkovitz (*Die Wundermühle*) and Leo Ascher (*Botschafterin Leni*) on further pieces for the Josefstadter Theater and Niese, most of which were subsequently played in Germany and in Hungary (*A Muzikusleány* 4 April 1911, *Tengerész Kató* 21 September 1912, *Kotnyeles naccsága* 4 April 1915), before moving on to

centre his activity on Berlin, where Girardi had had a considerable success with his Posse *Immer oben auf* in the years before and during the First World War. There, he had the second of his most important musical comedy successes when he collaborated with the tried producer/author team of Jean Kren and Alfred Schönfeld on the book and lyrics for Ascher's *Der Soldat der Marie*. This was the first of six mostly successful musical plays written for the Berlin theatre over the next few years to scores variously by Jean Gilbert, Robert Winterberg and Ascher. Gilbert's *Das Vagabundenmädel* ran for nearly 200 performances at the Thalia-Theater and was played in Hungary as *Csavargolány* (Budapesti Színház 22 November 1918), Ascher's *Egon und seine Frauen* played seven months at the Thalia and *Jungfer Sonnenschein* was seen 140 times at the same house after a season at the Carltheater in Vienna. At the Neues Operettenhaus, *Die Dame von Zirkus* passed the 200-performance mark in its first run and was revived soon after and *Prinzessin Friedl* held the stage for three months, whilst *Graf Habenichts* was played successfully at the Wallner-Theater.

Buchbinder died in 1922 (on a date almost as ill agreed-upon as that of his birth) after a career of nearly 20 successful years in the theatre during which his pieces had been widely and successfully played in Austria, Germany and Hungary. Posthumously, his *Nachtfalter* (1926) was produced in Bozen, his version of the Hans Müller Posse mit Gesang *Morgen geht's uns gut*, with music by Ralph Benatzky, was produced at the Raimundtheater (31 August 1929), and his name appeared as the author of the screenplay to the musical film *Versuchen sie meine Schwester?*.

His libretto (w Willner) for *Die Göttin der Vernunft* was later made over to become the text for the rather more successful *Der Graf von Luxemburg*.

1887 **Studenten am Rhein** (Josef Goldstein) 1 act Pest 8 January
1887 **Das Ellishorn** (Rudolf Raimann/w Philippi) Theater am Gärtnerplatz, Munich 7 May
1887 **Colombine** (Hans von Zois) Graz, 12 November; Carltheater, Vienna 15 March 1889
1888 **Der Sänger von Palermo** (Alfred Zamara/Scribe ad) Carltheater 14 February
1890 **Held Marko** (*Der Mameluck Napoleons*) (Emil Rosé) St Petersburg December
1891 **Die Flüchtlinge** (Raoul Mader) Hofoper 19 February
1893 **Das Wiener Volkslied** (Karl Kleiber) Theater in der Josefstadt 21 October
1894 **Heirat auf Probe** (Leopold Kuhn/C Görss/Karl Gerő ad w Ferenc Rajna) Theater an der Wien 7 April
1895 **Der Heirathsschwindler** (Max von Weinzierl) Raimundtheater 5 October
1896 **Ein kecker Schnabel** (Leopold Natzler) Raimundtheater 14 November
1896 **Der Schmetterling** (Carl Weinberger/w A M Willner) Theater an der Wien 30 November
1897 **Die Göttin der Vernunft** (Johann Strauss/w Willner) Theater an der Wien 13 March
1897 **Verlogenes Volk** (von Weinzierl) Raimundtheater 18 November
1898 **Die Küchenkomtesse** (*A kuktakisasszony*) German version w add music by Raimann (Theater an der Wien)
1898 **Fraulein Hexe** (Josef Bayer/w Willner) Theater an der Wien 19 November
1900 **Die Diva** (Weinberger/w Josef Wattke) Carltheater 12 October
1901 **Der dritte Eskadron** Theater an der Wien 2 November

1902 **Der Spatz** (Weinberger) Deutsches Volkstheater 14 January

1902 **Er und seine Schwester** (Raimann) Theater in der Josefstadt 11 April

1903 **Der Musikant und sein Weib** (Raimann) Theater an der Wien 12 April

1903 **Der Glücklichste** (Hans Cesek) Carltheater 25 April

1903 **48 Stunden Urlaub** (Ludwig Gothov-Grüneke) Raimundtheater 7 November

1903 **Der Mameluck** revised *Held Marko* (Ludwig Schytte/w Mór Jókai) Carltheater 22 December

1905 **Das Wäschermädl** (Raimann) Theater in der Josefstadt 31 March

1906 **Der Schusterbub** (Raimann) Theater in der Josefstadt 16 January

1907 **Sie und ihr Mann** (Raimann) Raimundtheater 5 April

1907 **Der Eintagskönig** (Raimann/w Hans Liebstöckl) Lustspieltheater 15 May

1907 **Die Förster-Christl** (Jarno) Theater in der Josefstadt 17 December

1908 **Immer oben auf** (Paul Lincke/Alfred Schönfeld/w Jean Kren) Thalia-Theater, Berlin 22 January

1909 **Paula macht alles** (Raimann) Theater in der Josefstadt 23 March

1909 **Der Weiberfeind** (Alfred Rieger) Bellevue Theater, Stettin 10 December

1910 **Das Musikantenmädel** (Jarno) Theater in Josefstadt 18 February

1911 **Die Frau Gretl** (Raimann) Theater in der Josefstadt 7 April

1911 **Das neue Mädchen** (Richard Fronz) Bürgertheater 2 September

1912 **Die Marinen-Gustl** (Jarno) Theater in der Josefstadt 22 March

1912 **Unser Stammhalter** (Raimann) Lustspieltheater 15 November

1914 **Die Wundermühle** (Béla Zerkovitz) Theater in der Josefstadt 24 March

1915 **Botschafterin Leni** (Leo Ascher) Theater in der Josefstadt 19 February

1916 **Der Soldat der Marie** (Ascher/Schönfeld/w Kren) Neues Operettentheater, Berlin 2 September

1916 **Das Vagabundenmädel** (Jean Gilbert/Schönfeld/w Kren) Thalia-Theater, Berlin 2 December

1917 **Egon und seine Frauen** (Ascher/w Kren) Thalia-Theater, Berlin 25 August

1918 **Jungfer Sonnenschein** (Jarno) Volksoper, Hamburg 16 February; Carltheater 18 May

1918 **Graf Habenichts** (Robert Winterberg/w Kren) Wallner-Theater, Berlin 4 September

1919 **Die Dame von Zirkus** (Winterberg/w Kren) Neues Operettentheater, Berlin 31 May

1920 **Prinzessin Friedl** (Ascher/w Kren) Neues Operettentheater, Berlin 14 May

1926 **Der Nachtfalter** (Weinberger/w Mathilde Schurz) Bozen March

BUCKLEY, Betty (b Big Springs, Tex, 3 July 1947).

After early performances in her native Texas, Betty Buckley was first seen on Broadway when she created the rôle of Martha Jefferson in *1776* (1969), introducing 'He Plays the Violin'. She followed this up by appearing as Fran Kubelik in London's production of *Promises, Promises* later the same year, and was next seen in New York in the short-lived off-Broadway piece *The Ballad of Johnny Pot* (1971). She later succeeded to the rôle of Catherine in *Pippin* in a career which moved on to embrace film (*Carrie, Tender Mercies*) and television (*Eight is Enough*) as well as musical theatre (*I'm Getting My Act Together and Taking it*

on the Road) and cabaret, and returned to Broadway to appear as Grizabella in the American production of *Cats* (1982).

She subsequently created the rôle of Drood in the musicalization of *The Mystery of Edwin Drood* (1986), replaced Bernadette Peters in Broadway's version of *Song and Dance*, took the rôle of Carrie's mother, Margaret White, created in Britain by Barbara Cook, in the Broadway version of the musical based on the film, *Carrie*, and in 1990 appeared in Washington top-billed in a compilation musical called *Stardust*.

BUDAY, Dénes (b Budapest, 8 October 1890; d Budapest, 19 October 1963).

Composer and conductor Buday won his early success as a writer of vocal music, and made his first venture on to the musical stage in Vienna with a one-act opera, *Loreley*, before finding his way into the lighter musical theatre. He had his first big success with the operett *Csárdás*, produced at the Budai Színkör with Hanna Honthy starred, and subsequently had a second hit with the same star in the 1941 *Fityfiritty*. His preferred musical mixture of native Hungarian operett elements and modern dance rhythms was also employed in film in Hungary and in Germany.

1916 **Fogadjunk!** (Imre Harmath) Budai Színkör 21 July

1921 **Matyas király** (w Frigyes Fridl/Andor Zsoldos) Magyar Királyi Operaház 18 September

1923 **A kék postakocsi** (Szilágyi) Várszinház 22 December

1926 **Ki a Tisza vizét issza** (Harmath) Kisfaludy Színház 3 September

1927 **Diákszerelem** (Ernő Andai/Ernő Innocent Vincze) Kisfaludy Színház May

1929 **Erdélyi diákok** (Andai/Innocent Vincze) Budai Színkör 31 August

1936 **Csárdás** (László Szilágyi) Budai Színkör 16 June

1936 **Szakitani nehéz dolog** (Mihály Szécsen/Kálmán Csántho) Magyar Színház 12 December

1940 **Három huszár** (Szilágyi, Gyula Halász) Fővárosi Operettszinház 12 April

1941 **Fityfiritty** (Rudolf Halász) Fővárosi Operettszinház 8 March

1941 **Csodatükör** (József Babay) Fővárosi Operettszinház 7 October

1943 **Egy boldog pesti nyár** (w Mihály Eisemann, Szabolcs Fenyes/Szilágyi, Attila Orbók) Fővárosi Operettszinház 14 April

1943 **A tábornokné** (Miklós Tóth, Kálmán Vándor) Magyar Színház 24 April

1956 **Három szegény szabólegény** (Babay) Petőfi Színház 20 January

BUDDIES Comedy of quaint Brittany in 2 acts and an epilogue by George V Hobart. Music and lyrics by B C Hilliam. Selwyn Theater, New York, 27 October 1919.

The post-wartime *Buddies* set a familiar little love story in the battered fields of Brittany to the accompaniment of a ration of love-songs, a few numbers coloured with the kind of common-man-at-war sentiments which had so successfully been used in the recent *The Better 'Ole*, and some unashamedly sentimental recreations of the kind of moments in wartime France that the returned soldiers were happy to remember.

When Babe (Roland Young), Sonny (Donald Brian) and their American army pals are billeted in the French farmhouse of Madame Benoît (Camille Dalberg), Babe takes the opportunity to fall in love with young Julie Benoît

(Peggy Wood). But he is too shy to express his feelings and Julie, hoping to make him speak, flirts instead with Sonny. It is an old trick, but it works. The score by B C Hilliam (subsequently Mr Flotsam of the British variety act 'Flotsam and Jetsam') featured such longing titles as 'Hello, Home', 'My Buddies', 'The Homes They Hold So Dear', 'To Be Together is the Thing' as well as the good old-fashioned 'Fairy Tales' (known as The Cinderella Song), the half-hesitant 'Darling, I ...' and the praises of 'My Indispensable Girl'. The interpolations included a Cole Porter/Melville Gideon piece called 'I Never Realized'. The evening's top musical moment came, however, in the piece known as The Italie Marching Song: 'Oh! Tell Me Where My Buddie (sic) Is'.

Arch Selwyn's production of *Buddies* – originally subtitled 'a comedy of quaint Brittany', but later just 'a merry musical play' – had a grand success and a 265-performance run on Broadway before going on the road. It provoked a follow-up from author Hobart in the sentimental melodrama *Sonny* (Cort Theater 16 February 1921, 80 performances) which was, in fact, not about the character of the previous piece, but simply another wartime tale musicked this time by Raymond Hubbell. It also encouraged Hilliam to a second musical, *Princess Virtue* (Central Theater 4 May 1921), which did not repeat the success of *Buddies*. It flopped in two weeks. A later musical show, featuring Bill 'Bojangles' Robinson and Adelaide Hall in another World War I jaunt, called itself *Brown Buddies* (Liberty Theater, 7 October 1930) through 111 performances.

A BUNCH OF KEYS

Musical comedy in 3 acts by Charles Hoyt. San Francisco Opera House, New York, 26 March 1883.

An 'original operatic absurdity', otherwise a farce comedy, combining the most obvious of low comedy mixed with broad songs and dances, *A Bunch of Keys* was commissioned from the then unknown Charles Hoyt by actor-manager Willie Edouin as a vehicle for himself, his wife Alice Atherton, and his troupe. Hoyt turned out the umpteenth piece of recent decades which used a musical comedy will as its centrepiece, but managed to imbue the tale with enough differences and, above all, enough exuberantly popular humour to make it a long-touring favourite.

Edouin played Littleton Snaggs, a lawyer, who is responsible for disposing of an unprofitable hotel which has been left to whichever of the three Keys sisters is adjudged the plainest. Although their gentleman friends are willing to accept the stigma for what they think will be the profit, the girls are not. Before a happy ending was reached, with faces literally saved all round, Miss Atherton as Teddy Keys and the rest of the company had entertained with a barrage of movable song and dance numbers, gathered from hither and yon. The young James T Powers played the hotel's bellboy in a flurry of acrobatics and physical comedy.

In the wake of the success of *Fun on the Bristol* and of *My Sweetheart*, similar loose-limbed pieces crowded into the British provinces in the 1880s, but Edouin ventured a version of *A Bunch of Keys* (ad George Lash Gordon) in the sophisticated purlieus of London. There, in spite of a cast including himself and his wife, Powers, and worthy locals

Hetty Chapman and Irene Verona (both future 'heavies') as the other two sisters, it was greeted as 'pitiful trash' and bundled quickly out of town. Australia got a glimpse of the piece in 1897 when Harry Rickards toured it in secondary and variety-orientated houses.

UK: Avenue Theatre 25 August 1883; Australia: Opera House, Brisbane 18 September 1897

BUONA NOTTE, BETTINA

Musical comedy in 2 acts by Pietro Garinei and Sandro Giovannini. Music by Gorni Kramer. Teatro Lirico, Milan, 14 November 1956.

An Italian musical play avowedly suggested by Françoise Sagan's success with her novel, *Bonjour tristesse*, *Buona Notte, Bettina* featured Walter Chiari and Delia Scala in a tale of what happens when a demure young lady writes a risqué novel. Following its success on home ground, the piece was seen in several Eastern European countries (Poland, Eastern Germany, Hungary, Czechoslovakia), in Spain as *Buenas nochas Bettina* (Teatro de la Commedia 31 December 1958), Portugal, South America and in Britain (ad Ted Willis, Ken Ferrey, Eric Shaw, Sonny Miller) where Jack Hylton mounted the show as *When in Rome ...* with Dickie Henderson and June Laverick in the leading rôles (298 performances).

UK: Adelphi Theatre *When in Rome ...* 26 December 1959; Germany: Rostock *Gute Nacht Bettina* 13 February 1966; Hungary: Fővárosi Operettszinház *Tigris a garázsban* 21 October 1966

Recordings: original cast (Carisch), *When in Rome* (Oriole) 45 rpm

BURANI, Paul

[ROUCOUX, Urbain] (b Paris, 26 March 1845; d Paris, 9 October 1901). Prolific, all-purpose Parisian author whose successes included several in the musical theatre.

At first a public functionary, then a part-time actor, Burani made himself a name as a popular singer-song-writer, performing his own compositions in the cafés-concerts ('Les Pompiers de Nanterre', 'Le Sire de Fish-Tong-Kang', 'Pour vingt-cinq francs' etc) whilst continuing to hold down his day job in a government office. He wrote lavishly for both magazines and newspapers (*Gil Blas*, *L'Evènement*, *L'Estaffette* etc), authored tales (*Contes de la Chambrée*) and novels, and at one stage founded his own satirical journal which in its short life earned him three months in prison for 'intemperance of language'. He was also prominent in the Parisian theatre for a period of 20 years as the eclectic author of everything from revues (with composers of the quality of Varney, Vasseur and Hervé) to melodramas (*Le Metropolitain de Londres* etc) and from vaudevilles to libretti and lyrics for opérette – ultimately making it to the Opéra-Comique with the text to Chabrier's *Le Roi malgré lui* (w Emile de Najac, 18 May 1887) – as well as a barrage of military, fairy and modern spectaculars (*Coco Fêlé*, *Orient-Express* etc).

Amongst his early works, Burani had long-running opérette successes with two pieces written with Maxime Boucheron and composed by Léon Vasseur (*Le Droit du seigneur*, *Le Billet de logement*), provided the text for *La Cantinière* to Planquette and scored a considerable hit with Bernicat's internationally played *François les bas-bleus* (*Victor the Bluestocking*, *Fanchon*, *Die Strassensängerin*, *Kék Féri*, *Fantine* etc). He subsequently wrote two further pieces with the young composer who had finished the uncompleted score for Bernicat's posthumous piece, André

Messager, in *La Fauvette du Temple* and *Le Bourgeois de Calais*. He adapted Dumas's *Le Mariage au tambour* (*Die Marketenderin, Esketés dobszóval*) to the spectacular musical stage, provided Audran with the text for his *Le Puits qui parle* (*A beszélő kut* in Hungary) and had a further success with the text to Planquette's *Le Talisman* (*The Talisman, A varázgyürü*).

The most celebrated of his vaudevilles, *Le Cabinet Piperlin* (w Hippolyte Raymond), originally written to be played as a musical comedy but ultimately presented without music, was later played as a musical both in France (*Le Cabinet Piperlin*) and in England (*The Antelope*, Waldorf Theatre 28 November 1908). He was also credited, with Maurice Ordonneau, as the author of the original of Ordonneau's subsequent text for the highly successful *Madame Sherry*.

1873 **Pomponne et Fridolin** (w Carlo Wansinck, Émile Clerc) Ba-ta-clan 3 September

1875 **Le Neveu du Colonel** (Wenzel/w Wansinck) 1 act Alcazar 30 September

1875 **Absalon** (Campésiano/w Alfred Pouillon) 1 act Folies-Bergère 13 November, Alcazar 25 May 1876

1876 **Les Oeufs de Pâques** (J Müller) 1 act Scala 10 April

1877 **La Goguette** (Antonin Louis/w Hippolyte Raymond) Théâtre de l'Athénée 13 April

1878 **Le Droit du seigneur** (Léon Vasseur/w Maxime Boucheron) Fantaisies-Parisiennes 13 December

1879 **Mon gendre tout est rompu** (Auguste Coèdes/w William Busnach) 1 act Casino de Dieppe 22 August

1879 **Le Billet de logement** (Vasseur/w Boucheron) Théâtre des Fantaisies-Parisiennes 15 November

1880 **Madame Grégoire** (Édouard Okolowicz et al/w Maurice Ordonneau) Théâtre des Arts May

1880 **La Cantinière** (Robert Planquette/w Félix Ribeyre) Théâtre des Nouveautés 26 October

1881 **La Reine des Halles** (Louis Varney/w Alfred Delacour, Victor Bernard) Comédie Parisienne 4 April

1882 **Le Petit Parisien** (Vasseur/w Boucheron) Théâtre des Folies-Dramatiques 16 February

1882 **Un carnaval** (Campésiano/w Pouillon) 1 act St Germain-en-Laye 6 May

1882 **La Barbière improvisée** (Joseph O'Kelly/w Jules Montini) 1 act Salle Herz 10 December, Théâtre des Bouffes-Parisiens 1 May 1884

1882 **La 1002ème Nuit** (Lucien Poujade/w P Richard) Reims 27 December; Théâtre du Château d'Eau 8 July 1885

1883 **François les bas-bleus** (Firmin Bernicat, André Messager/w Ernest Dubreuil, Eugène Humbert) Théâtre des Folies-Dramatiques 8 November

1883 **Fanfreluche** (revised *La Nuit de Saint-Germain*) (Gaston Serpette/Gaston Hirsch, Raoul de Saint-Arroman ad) Théâtre de la Renaissance 16 December

1885 **Le Mariage au tambour** (Vasseur) Théâtre du Châtelet 4 April

1885 **La Fauvette du Temple** (Messager/w Humbert) Théâtre des Folies-Dramatiques 17 November

1885 **La Cremaillère** (Planquette/w Albert Brasseur) Théâtre des Nouveautés 29 November

1887 **Ninon** (Vasseur/w Émile Blavet, Emil André) Théâtre des Nouveautés 23 March

1887 **Le Bourgeois de Calais** (Messager) Théâtre des Folies-Dramatiques 6 April

1888 **Le Puits qui parle** (Edmond Audran/w Alexandre Beaumont) Théâtre des Nouveautés 15 March

1888 **La Belle Sophie** (Edmond Missa/w Eugène Adenis) Théâtre des Menus-Plaisirs 11 April

1889 **Le Prince Soleil** (Vasseur/w Hippolyte Raymond) Théâtre du Châtelet 11 July

1891 **Compère Guilleri** (Henri Perry/w Jean Cavalier) Théâtre des Menus-Plaisirs 18 September

1892 **Le Commandant Laripète** (Vasseur/w Armand Silvestre, Albin Valabrègue) Palais-Royal 3 March

1893 **Le Talisman** (Planquette/w Adolphe d'Ennery) Théâtre de la Gaîté 20 January

1893 **Jean Raisin** (Marius Carman) Théâtre des Folies-Dramatiques 30 March

1894 **L'Élève de Conservatoire** (Léopold de Wenzel/w Henri Kéroul) Théâtre des Menus-Plaisirs 29 November

1895 **Les Vingt-huit jours de Champignolette** (Planquette) Théâtre de la République 17 September

1896 **Rivoli** (André Wormser/w Michel Carré) Théâtre des Folies-Dramatiques 30 October

1897 **Le Cabinet Piperlin** (Hervé/w Raymond) Théâtre de l'Athénée Comique 17 September

1902 **La Bouquetière du Château d'Eau** (Constantin Lubomirski) Théâtre du Château d'Eau 10 January

1902 **Madame Sherry** (Hugo Felix/w M Ordonneau ad Benno Jacobson) Centraltheater, Berlin 1 November

Other title attributed: *La Fée aux perles* (Olivier Métra/w d'Ennery, ?1880)

BURKE, Billie [BURKE, Mary William Ethelbert Appleton] (b Washington, 7 August 1885; d Los Angeles, 14 May 1970).

Born into a circus family, Billie Burke played in British pantomime and variety before she made her first musical comedy appearance, at the age of 17, playing an American girl in George Edwardes and Charles Frohman's London production of *The School Girl*, and performing Leslie Stuart's 'My Little Canoe'. She took over the soubrette rôle in Edwardes's *The Duchess of Dantzic* (1903) and toured in the juvenile part of the same piece, played a supporting rôle in Robert Courtneidge's London production of *The Blue Moon* and appeared in both revue and variety before succeeding to the much squabbled-over lead rôle of *The Belle of Mayfair* for its last performances.

She made the largest part of her subsequent career in non-musical theatre and film and in the real-life rôle of Mrs Florenz Ziegfeld jr, but she returned to the musical stage just once in the title-rôle of Annabelle Leigh (whom she had portrayed in the 1919 film of the play *Good Gracious Annabelle*, on which the show was based) in Ziegfeld's musical *Annie Dear* (1924). On film, during a long and successful career as an often feather-headed character lady, she memorably devoted the remnants of her pretty voice to the rôle of the good witch, Glinda, in *The Wizard of Oz* (1939). She also appeared in the 1940 film of *Irene* as Mrs Vincent, in *The Barkleys of Broadway* (1949, Millie Belney), and was herself portrayed on film, in her lifetime, by Myrna Loy in *The Great Ziegfeld* (1936).

Memoirs: *With a Feather on My Nose* (Appleton-Century-Crofts, New York, 1949), *With Powder on My Nose* (Coward, McCann, New York, 1959)

BURKE, Marie [née HOLT, Marie Rosa] (b London, 18 October 1894; d London, 21 March 1988).

Trained as a vocalist in Italy, Marie Burke (the 'Burke' came from her early but brief marriage to a fellow student, operatic tenor Tom Burke) began her career in opera, appearing as Musetta at Verona and as Nedda and Micaëla in a small Milan theatre. She gave several concerts in Italy before returning to Britain in 1917 and made her first stage appearance there in London as Isilda in C B

Cochran's production of *Afgar* (1919). She subsequently played in *Make it Snappy* and *The Lady in Ermine* (Sophie Lavalle, then Mariana) in America before touring in a concert party in Britain and then going first to South Africa, and then to Australia, as a vocalist in a variety combination with Arthur Klein. During her stay in Australia, the Williamson & Tait organization hired her for their musical comedy company, and she spent the next three and a half years in Australia appearing in starring rôles in the highly successful local productions of *Wildflower* (Nina) and *Katja the Dancer* (Katja), in *The Cousin from Nowhere* (Julia, replacement) and *Frasquita* (Frasquita).

On returning to London, she was cast as Julie in London's *Show Boat* and she followed up as a series of titled and often exotic ladies in the appalling *Open Your Eyes* (Countess Zanini), the unsuccessful *The Student Prince* (Margaret), Drury Lane's *The Song of the Drum* (Countess Olga von Haultstein) and the long-running London version of *Walzer aus Wien* (another Countess Olga). She joined Bobby Howes at the Saville Theatre as the vamp of *He Wanted Adventure* (1933, Ziska) and the following year repeated her *Walzer aus Wien* rôle in New York.

She subsequently appeared largely in non-musical theatre, whilst continuing to sing in variety and concert and as a popular principal boy in pantomime, making late musical theatre appearances in her sixties in *King's Rhapsody* and *Happy Holiday* (1954, Hon Fiona McLeod).

Her husband, Burke, after a dazzling opera debut alongside Melba at Covent Garden in 1919, soon found himself 'relegated' to musical comedy, variety, revue, concert and concert party work. He was seen in the musical theatre in Broadway's *The Dancing Girl* (1923, Rudolpho), *The Mikado* (1925, Nanki Poo), *HMS Pinafore* (1926, Ralph) and the 15-performance *The Lace Petticoat* (1927, Paul Joscelyn) and in London in *Dear Love* (1929, Pierre) and the flop *The Gay Masqueraders* (1935, Carol).

Their daughter **Patricia BURKE** (b Milan, 23 April 1917), after an early career in straight theatre (and one musical appearance in *Nymph Errant*, aged 16), worked through supporting rôles in the foolish *Take it Easy* (1937, Ruth Marsden), the Cicely Courtneidge/Bobby Howes *Hide and Seek* (1937, Rene), *Sitting Pretty* (1939, Mary Pugh) and several revues, and became a musical leading lady in the stage and film versions of the topical wartime musical *The Lisbon Story* (1943, Gabrielle). Thereafter she returned largely to the straight theatre, appearing only briefly in *Romance In Candlelight* (1955), *Belle* (1961) and in succession to Hy Hazell in *Charlie Girl* on the musical stage.

BURKHARD, Paul (b Zurich, 21 December 1911; d Zell-im-Tösstal, 6 September 1977). Modest Swiss composer who notched up a show and song hit when one of his little pieces was glitzed up into a revusical entertainment.

Burkhard studied at the Zurich Conservatoire and subsequently worked as a répétiteur and then conductor at the Berne Stadttheater (1932–5) and at the Zurich Schauspielhaus (1939–45) before becoming the musical director of the Beromünster radio orchestra (1945–57). After a local success with his first piece, *Hopsa* (text and music), a Swiss Operette with a trendy American setting, he composed two further theatre scores before he turned out the

songs for the small-scale Lokalstuck *Der schwarze Hecht*, produced at Zurich's Schauspielhaus in 1939. A decade later, Erik Charell partly rewrote, and gave a very much larger and thoroughly extravagant staging to the little piece in a production in Munich, and this Revue-operette version, under the title *Feuerwerk*, gave Burkhard and the song 'O, mein Papa' an international success. As a result, *Hopsa* was given the same Revue-operette treatment (ad Armin Robinson, Robert Gilbert, Paul Baudisch) but without the same kind of results.

Burkhard subsequently had a number of further musical plays produced in Switzerland, including the locally flavoured *Die kleine Niederdorf-Oper* and an adaptation of Oscar Wilde's *The Importance of Being Ernest* (*Bunbury*). He also provided incidental music for Friedrich Dürrenmatt's *Frank V, Oper einer Privatbank* (Munich 1960), and created the scores for a number of children's pieces, notably the Christmas opera *Ein Stern geht auf aus Jakob* (Hamburg, 6 December 1970).

1935 **Hopsa** Stadttheater, Zurich 30 November
1936 **Dreimal Georges** (Rudolph Schanzer, Ernst Welisch) Stadttheater, Zurich 3 October
1938 **Die Frauen von Coraya** (aka *Der Paradies der Frauen*) (Eduard Rogati) Stadttheater, Stettin 19 February
1939 **Der schwarze Hecht** (Jürg Amstein) Schauspielhaus, Zurich 1 April
1942 **Casanova in der Schweiz** (Richard Schweizer) Stadttheater, Zurich
1947 **Tic-Tac** (Guy de Pourtalés ad Fridolin Tschudi, Fritz Schulz)
1948 **Weh, dem, der liebt** (K Nachmann)
1949 **Das kleinen Märchentheater** (Tschudi)
1950 **[Das] Feuerwerk** revised *Der schwarze Hecht* (Amstein, Robert Gilbert/Erik Charell, Amstein) Bayerisches Staatsoper, Munich 16 May
1951 **Die kleine Niederdorf-Oper** (Walter Lesch) Schauspielhaus, Zurich 31 December
1956 **Spiegel, das Kätzchen** (G Keller) Theater am Gärtnerplatz, Munich 20 November
1957 **Hopsa** (revised version ad Armin Robinson, Paul Baudisch, Robert Gilbert) Wiesbaden 12 October
1957 **Die Pariserin** (Henri Becque ad N O Scarpi, Tschudi) Schauspielhaus, Zurich 31 December
1960 **Hez? Zitterbein möcht Königin sein** (Margit Bragger) Stadttheater, Berne 4 December
1961 **Barbasuk**
1962 **Die Dame mit der Brille** (Karl Suter, Robert Gilbert) Schauspielhaus, Zurich 31 December
1964 **Die Schneekönigin** Zurich
1965 **Bunbury** (Hans Weigel) Stadttheater, Basle 7 October 1965
1977 **Regenbogen** (Michael Longard) Stattheater, Basle 30 November

BURNABY, G Davy (b Buckland, Herts, 7 April 1881; d Angmering, 17 April 1949). Big Davy Burnaby led a long career as a comedian in plays, concert parties, revue and, most particularly, as a regular comic presence in the postwar West End musical theatre.

During his early career, he toured in George Grossmith's rôle in *The Orchid*, and he first played on the West End musical stage when he succeeded to the part of Viscount Gushington in *The Girl Behind the Counter* and appeared in the light comedy rôle of the Comte de Casserole in *The Belle of Brittany* (1908). He took part in George Grossmith's revue, *Hullo ... London!* at the Empire

Theatre in 1910 but it was from 1914, when he appeared in both America and in Britain in a comedy rôle in the same Grossmith's *Tonight's the Night* (Robin Carraway), that he began the series of musical rôles which would make him a West End favourite: *The Only Girl* (John Ayre), *Theodore & Co* (Duke of Shetland), *Yes, Uncle!* (Brabazon Hollybone), *Baby Bunting* (Samuel Gigglewick), *The Little Whopper* (Butts), *Oh! Julie* (General Zonzo) and *A Night Out* (Matthieu).

From 1921 he spent nearly a decade as a basic member of *The Co-Optimists* concert party, before returning bulkily to the musical stage in *Waltzes from Vienna* (Ebeseder). In 1942 he made a last stage musical appearance as General Malona in the revival of *The Maid of the Mountains*. Burnaby also appeared in many comedy films including *Three Men in a Boat* (1933), *Are You a Mason?* (1934) and *Feather Your Nest* (1937) as well as the filmed *The Co-Optimists* (1929).

The author of numerous song lyrics, including the wartime hit 'Lords of the Air' (w Michael North), he also wrote the libretto and some of the lyrics for the successful touring comic opera *The Maid of the East* (1919).

1919 **The Maid of the East** (William Neale/w Edward Lauri) Tyne Theatre, Newcastle 10 February

BURNAND, F[rancis] C[owley] (Sir) (b Ramsgate, 29 November 1836; d Ramsgate, 21 April 1917). Bulwark of the Victorian burlesque tradition.

Educated at Eton and at Cambridge, Burnand was instrumental in the founding of the Cambridge University Dramatic Society (ADC), where some of his earliest efforts as a dramatist were played. Three of these, the burlesques *Villikins and His Dinah* (1855), *Lord Lovel* (1856) and *Alonzo the Brave* (1857), were subsequently played in the British provinces and *Villikins* even appeared in India before the young writer succeeded in placing his first piece on the West End stage. The burlesque *Dido* (1860) was mounted by Chatterton at the St James's Theatre with Charles Young playing the travestied Queen of Carthage, and it proved a great success, running for some 60 nights in London and being swiftly seen throughout the colonies, with Young appearing in his original rôle (Theatre Royal, Melbourne 2 September 1861).

In the years that followed, Burnand began writing material for the popular comic papers of the time, notably *Fun* and *Punch*, while supplying Easter and Christmas burlesques and plays to a remarkable number of London theatres. In 1863 he achieved one of the most outstanding burlesque successes of the period with the classical extravaganza *Ixion, or the Man at the Wheel*, first produced by Mrs Charles Selby at the Royalty and played regularly in English-speaking theatres for more than a decade thereafter.

In 1865, when French opéra-bouffe, headed by the works of Offenbach, held sway as the most advanced form of musical theatre, Burnand combined with composer Frank Musgrave, musical director at the Strand Theatre, to produce the first British efforts in that field with the original operatic burlesques *Windsor Castle* and *L'Africaine*, both successfully produced under the management of the Swanborough family. Arguably the first British opéras-bouffes – with original book, lyrics and music – they gave

credibility to Burnand's later claim to have been the originator of the contemporary British musical.

The following year he was responsible for the fairly rough first English adaptation of Offenbach's *La Belle Hélène* as *Helen, or Taken from the Greek*, and also for the most successful burlesque of the age, the famous travesty of Douglas Jerrold's nautical drama *Black-Eyed Susan* which played for the unprecedented total of 400 nights in its first run. Equally successful was another adaptation, a one-act operetta version of Maddison Morton's famous farce *Box and Cox*, set to music by Arthur Sullivan to be played by an amateur group of which Burnand's friend Quintin Twiss was a leading light. Staged professionally at the German Reed's Gallery of Illustration, *Cox and Box* gave that establishment the biggest success of its long and admired career and it has remained one of the few short Victorian operettas – and the only example of Burnand's work – to have survived into the modern repertoire.

Burnand ventured in all directions. He was credited as the composer of one of the songs ('Little Wilhelmina') used in the score arranged by W C Levey for his little Drury Lane piece, *The Girls of the Period*, and he went against the accepted tradition when he produced what was another novelty in the musical theatre: a burlesque written not in rhyming couplets, but in prose. *The Military Bill Taylor* was sniffed at as 'a most eccentric piece ... a farcical extravaganza in prose, interspersed with songs and music after the fashion of burlesque, and aiming at nothing higher than the creation of a passing laugh out of the most incongruous materials'. Originality paid, on this occasion, as *Bill Taylor* ran more than a hundred nights at the Royalty (100th performance 17 August) without yet encouraging the burlesque to forsake its couplets and take up rhymeless dialogue.

A further collaboration with Sullivan produced the full-length musical *The Contrabandista*, but when Sullivan turned to W S Gilbert as a permanent partner, Burnand took the 'desertion' badly and he missed no opportunity thereafter to snipe bitterly at Gilbert and his work, principally through the pages of *Punch* where he became increasingly important and influential, ultimately taking up the post of editor in 1880 and maintaining it for 25 years.

His considerable dramatic output continued, alongside a great bulk of other writing, until the mid-1890s. It consisted principally of pasticcio burlesques, notably a series for the Gaiety Theatre, as well as some further short pieces for the German Reeds, but his most important single success came with the play *The Colonel*, a piece loosely adapted from the French comedy *Le Mari de campagne*, and twitting the aesthetic craze. It is said that Burnand hurried his play to the stage to try to deflate the effect of Gilbert's forthcoming *Patience* after an unguarded conversation with Freddie Clay had enlightened him to his 'rival's' new theme.

Burnand was also responsible for English adaptations of a number of successful Continental musicals, including Strauss's *Indigo und die vierzig Räuber*, *La Vie parisienne*, *La Cigale et la fourmi*, *Miss Helyett*, *Le Coeur et la main* and the vaudeville *La Demoiselle du téléphone*, but in later years he contributed only the burlesque *Tra-la-la-Tosca* and the comic opera *His Majesty*, with a score by Sir Alick MacKenzie, to the original musical theatre.

In company with Henry Byron and Robert Reece,

Plate 41. **F C Burnand** and **H J Byron**: *Victorian Britain's barons of burlesque.*

Burnand dominated a whole era and area of light musical theatre in Britain. These three writers and their less prolific and/or successful fellows took the burlesque and extravaganza tradition which had been crystallized by Planché and continued by the Broughs, the a' Becketts and Talfourd, and broadened it into a much more vigorous type of entertainment. The emphasis on punning and other forms of word-play became much heavier and sometimes excessive, the stories eventually less and less related to the topic which they nominally burlesqued, and the music less often from opera, opéra-bouffe or the traditional song but rather from the music hall or the street organ. Burnand's facility enabled him to turn out a great number of such works and his credit lies in the fact that, while burlesque was beginning to droop from its most literary and literate state, he produced, in *Ixion* and *Black-Eyed Susan*, two of the most popular and long-lasting examples of the genre.

In collaboration with William Brough, Burnand authored *Beeton's Book of Burlesques* (London, 1865).

1854 **Villikins and his Dinah** (pasticcio)
1856 **Lord Lovel** (pasticcio)
1857 **Alonzo the Brave** (pasticcio)
1860 **Dido** (pasticcio/arr Hayward) St James's Theatre 23 March
1860 **Light and Shade** Hanover Square Rooms 21 December
1861 **The King of the Merrows, or the Prince and the Piper** (pasticcio) Olympic Theatre 26 December
1862 **Fair Rosamond** (pasticcio) Olympic Theatre 21 April
1862 **Robin Hood, or the Forester's Fate** (pasticcio arr J H Tully) Olympic Theatre 26 December
1863 **Acis and Galatea** (pasticcio) Olympic Theatre 6 April

1863 **Ixion, or the Man at the Wheel** (pasticcio) Royalty Theatre 28 September
1863 **Patient Penelope, or the Return of Ulysses** (pasticcio) Strand Theatre 25 November
1864 **Venus and Adonis** (pasticcio) Haymarket Theatre 29 March
1864 **Rumpelstiltskin, or the Woman at the Wheel** (pasticcio) Royalty Theatre 30 March
1864 **Faust and Marguerite** (pasticcio arr Ferdinand Wallerstein) St James's Theatre 9 July
1864 **Snowdrop, or the Seven Mannikins and the Magic Mirror** (or The Seven Elves, the Magic Mirror and the Fatal Sewing Machine) (pasticcio) Royalty Theatre 21 November
1864 **Cupid and Psyche, or as Beautiful as a Butterfly** (pasticcio) Olympic Theatre 26 December
1865 **Pirithous, the Son of Ixion** (pasticcio) Royalty Theatre 13 April
1865 **Ulysses, or the Iron Clad Warrior and the Little Tug of War** (pasticcio) St James's Theatre 17 April
1865 **Windsor Castle** (Frank Musgrave) Strand Theatre 5 June
1865 **The Widow Dido in a New Dress** (revised *Dido*) (pasticcio) Royalty Theatre 8 November
1865 **L'Africaine** (Musgrave) Strand Theatre 18 November
1866 **Paris, or Vive Lemprière** (pasticcio arr Musgrave) Strand Theatre 2 April
1866 **Bobadil el chico, or The Moor the Merrier** (pasticcio arr Tully) Astleys Theatre 2 April
1866 **A Yachting Cruise** 1 act Gallery of Illustration 2 April
1866 **Sappho, or Look Before You Leap** (pasticcio) Standard Theatre 11 June
1866 **Helen, or Taken From the Greek** (*La Belle Hélène*) English version (Adelphi Theatre)
1866 **Der Freischutz, or A Good Cast for a Piece** (pasticcio

arr Musgrave) Strand Theatre 8 October

1866 **Anthony and Cleopatra** (pasticcio) Haymarket Theatre 21 November

1866 **The Latest Edition of Black-Eyed Susan, or The Little Bill That Was Taken Up** (pasticcio arr Hermann) Royalty Theatre 29 November

1866 **Guy Fawkes, or The Ugly Mug and the Couple of Spoons** (pasticcio) Strand Theatre 26 December

1867 **Cox and Box** (Arthur Sullivan) 1 act Adelphi Theatre 11 May

1867 **Mary Turner, or The Wicious Willain and Wictorious Wirtue** (pasticcio) Holborn Theatre 26 October

1867 **The Contrabandista, or The Law of the Ladrones** (Sullivan) St George's Opera House 18 November

1868 **Hit and Miss, or All My Eye and Betty Martin** (*L'Oeil crevé*) English version (Olympic Theatre)

1868 **The White Fawn** (pasticcio arr Charles Hall) Holborn Theatre 13 April

1868 **Fowl Play, or A Story of Chikkin Hazzard** (pasticcio arr W H Montgomery) Queen's Theatre 20 June

1868 **Enquire Within** (Thomas German Reed) 1 act Gallery of Illustration 2 August

1868 **The Rise and Fall of Richard III, or A New Front to an Old Dicky** (pasticcio arr Hermann) Royalty Theatre 24 September

1868 **The Frightful Hair** (pasticcio) Haymarket Theatre 26 December

1869 **Claud du Val, or The Highwayman for the Ladies** (pasticcio arr Hermann) Royalty Theatre 23 January

1869 **The Girls of the Period** (pasticcio arr William C Levey) Theatre Royal, Drury Lane 25 February

1869 **The Military Bill Taylor, or The War in the Cariboo!** (pasticcio arr Hermann) Royalty Theatre 22 April

1869 **Very Little Faust and More Mephistopheles** (pasticcio) Charing Cross Theatre 18 August

1869 **The Beast and the Beauty, or No Rose Without a Thorn** (pasticcio arr Hermann) Royalty Theatre 4 October

1870 **Beggar my Neighbour (A Blind Man's Buff)** (*Les Deux Aveugles*) English version (Gallery of Illustration)

1870 **Sir George and a Dragon, or We Are Seven** (pasticcio arr John Fitzgerald) Strand Theatre 31 March

1870 **F M Julius Caesar, or The Irregular Rum-Un** (pasticcio) Royalty Theatre 7 September

1870 **E-liz-a-beth, or The Don, the Duck, the Drake and the Invisible Armarda** (pasticcio) Vaudeville Theatre 17 November

1870 **The White Cat** (pasticcio) Globe Theatre 26 December

1871 **All About the Battle of Dorking** (pasticcio/w Arthur Sketchley) Alhambra Theatre 7 August

1871 **Arion** (pasticcio) Strand Theatre 20 December

1871 **My Poll and Partner Joe** (pasticcio) St James's Theatre 6 May

1872 **La Vie parisienne** English version (Holborn Theatre)

1872 **King Kokatoo** (*L'Île de Tulipatan*) English version (Leeds)

1872 **My Aunt's Secret** (James L Molloy) 1 act Gallery of Illustration 13 March

1872 **Very Catching** (Molloy) 1 act Gallery of Illustration 18 November

1873 **Little Chang** (pasticcio) Newcastle-upon-Tyne 6 May

1873 **Mildred's Well** (Thomas German Reed) 1 act Gallery of Illustration 6 May

1873 **Kissi-Kissi** (*L'Île de Tulipatan*) English version (Opera Comique)

1873 **Our Own Anthony and Cleopatra** (pasticcio) Gaiety Theatre 8 September

1873 **La Belle Hélène** new English version (Alhambra Theatre)

1873 **Little Tom Tug, or The Fresh-Waterman** Opera Comique (pasticcio arr Frederic Stanislaus) 12 November

1874 **The Great Metropolis** (*Le Voyage de MM Dunanan père et fils*) English version with pasticcio score (Gaiety Theatre)

1874 **He's Coming (via Slumborough, Snoozleton and Snoreham)** (German Reed) 1 act St Georges Hall 12 May

1874 **Here's Another Guy Mannering** (pasticcio) Vaudeville Theatre 23 May

1874 **Too Many By One** (Frederic H Cowen) 1 act St George's Hall 26 June

1874 **Ixion Rewheeled** (revised *Ixion*, pasticcio arr W C Levey) Opera Comique 21 November

1875 **A Tale of Old China** (Molloy) 1 act St George's Hall 19 April

1876 **Matched and Mated** (German Reed) 1 act St George's Hall 6 November

1877 **Our Babes in the Wood** (pasticcio) Gaiety Theatre 2 April

1877 **Number 204** (German Reed) 1 act St George's Hall 7 May

1877 **King Indigo** (*Indigo und die vierzig Räuber*) English version (Alhambra Theatre)

1877 **The Red Rover, or I Believe You, My Buoy** (pasticcio arr Fitzgerald) Strand Theatre 26 December

1878 **Answer Paid** (Walter Austin) 1 act St George's Hall 4 February

1878 **Dora and Diplunacy, or A Woman of Uncommon Scents** (pasticcio arr Fitzgerald) Strand Theatre 14 February

1878 **A Tremendous Mystery** (King Hall) 1 act St George's Hall 5 November

1878 **Overproof, or What Was Found in a Celebrated Case** (pasticcio arr W F Glover) Royalty Theatre 6 November

1879 **The Hunchback Back Again, or Peculiar Julia** (pasticcio arr Karl Meyder) Olympic Theatre 23 December

1879 **Robbing Roy, or Scotched and Kilt** (pasticcio arr Lutz/w Henry Pottinger Stephens) Gaiety Theatre 11 November

1879 **Balloonacy** (pasticcio arr Edward Solomon/w Stephens) Royalty Theatre 1 December

1880 **The Corsican Brothers and Co Ltd** (pasticcio/w Pottinger Stephens) Gaiety Theatre 25 October

1881 **Whittington and his Cat** (pasticcio) Gaiety Theatre 15 October

1883 **Bluebeard, or the Hazard of the Dye** (pasticcio, Gaiety Theatre 12 March

1883 **Ariel** (pasticcio) Gaiety Theatre 8 October

1884 **Camaralzaman** (pasticcio) Gaiety Theatre 31 January

1884 **Paw Claudian** (pasticcio) Gaiety Theatre 14 February

1885 **The O'Dora, or A Wrong Accent** (pasticcio arr John Fitzgerald) Toole's Theatre 13 July

1885 **Mazeppa, or Bound – to Win** (pasticcio arr Lutz) Gaiety Theatre 12 March

1886 **Faust and Loose, or Brocken Vows** (pasticcio arr Fitzgerald) Toole's Theatre 4 February

1888 **Airey Annie** (pasticcio) Strand Theatre 4 April

1889 **Pickwick** (Solomon) 1 act Comedy Theatre 7 February

1890 **Tra-la-la Tosca** (Florian Pascal) Royalty Theatre 9 January

1890 **Domestic Economy** (Solomon) 1 act Comedy Theatre 7 April

1890 **Captain Thérèse** English version Prince of Wales Theatre 25 August

1890 **The Tiger** (Edward Solomon) 1 act St James Theatre 3 May

1890 **La Cigale** (*La Cigale et la fourmi*) English version (Lyric Theatre)

1891 **Miss Decima** (*Miss Helyett*) English version (Criterion Theatre)

1892 **Incognita** (*Le Coeur et la main*) English version (Lyric Theatre)

1893 **Sandford and Merton** (Solomon) 1 act Vaudeville Theatre 20 December

1894 **The Chieftain** (revised *La Contrabandista*) Savoy Theatre 12 December

1896 **The Telephone Girl** (*La Demoiselle du téléphone*) English version w Augustus Harris, Arthur Sturgess (Grand Theatre, Wolverhampton)

1897 **His Majesty** (Alexander McKenzie/R C Lehmann) Savoy Theatre 20 February

Autobiography: *Records and Reminiscences* (Methuen, London, 1904) (2 vols)

BURNETT, Carol [Creighton] (b San Antonio, Tex, 26 April 1933).

A ratchet-voiced comedienne who first made her name performing in nightclubs and on television, Miss Burnett won herself the public ear when she performed 'I Made a Fool of Myself over John Foster Dulles' on television's Jack Parr Show. In consequence, she made her musical comedy début in a starring rôle, as the lusty Princess Winnifred (she of the pea) in the fairytale burlesque *Once Upon a Mattress* (1959), which moved from off-Broadway to on-Broadway and won both itself and her a fine success.

After several years of further and ever increasing television success (including TV versions of *Once Upon a Mattress* and *Calamity Jane*), a memorable appearance with Julie Andrews in concert at Carnegie Hall (1962), and a detour to the film world for *Who's Been Sleeping in My Bed?* (1963), she returned to the musical stage as Hope Springfield, the accidental movie star of *Fade Out – Fade In* (1964). This show had a bumpy time on Broadway (a number of the bumps raised by the star herself, who was unhappy with her material) and in spite of being withdrawn, revamped and restaged, it failed to gel.

From 1967 to 1978 she starred in *The Carol Burnett Show* on CBS-TV but, although she performed in any number of specials and concerts and several films, her theatre appearances were few. She repeated her teaming with Julie Andrews at the Lincoln Center (1971) and paired with Rock Hudson in a regional *I Do! I Do!* but latterly her nearest approaches to a return to the musical theatre were in the film of *Annie* (1982, Miss Hannigan) and the concert version of *Follies* (1985, Carlotta Campion).

BURNS, David (b New York, 22 June 1902; d Philadelphia, 12 March 1971).

A plumpish, pugnacious comedian, much in demand in his early days as a gangster-type, Burns made his first Broadway musical appearance in Irving Berlin's *Face the Music* (1932, Louie), but spent much of the next six years in London where he appeared as Constantine in Cole Porter's *Nymph Errant* (1933) and as various gangsters in the British musical comedies *Big Business* (1937, Spike Morgan), *Hide and Seek* (1937, Bennie) and *Bobby Get Your Gun* (1938, Flash Tomkins).

Back home, he succeeded to the part of Ludlow Lowell in *Pal Joey* (1941) and later to that of Ali Hakim in *Oklahoma!* (1946), and appeared in character roles in *My Dear Public* (1943, Walters), as another gangster in *Billion Dollar Baby* (1945, Dapper Welch), in *Heaven on Earth* (1948, H H Hutton) and *Out of This World* (1950, Niki Skolianos). His greatest successes, however, came in his fifties and sixties when, apart from playing his last musical hoodlum rôle in *Do Re Mi* (1960, Brains Berman), he created a trio of top-class crusty senior roles as Mayor Shinn in *The Music Man* (1957), Senex in *A Funny Thing Happened on the Way to the Forum* (1962, Tony Award) and Horace Vandergelder in *Hello, Dolly!* (1964). His final musical rôle on Broadway was as the foolish old Colonel Purdy in the brief run of a musicalized version of *Teahouse of the August Moon* as *Lovely Ladies, Kind Gentleman* (1970), as he died after collapsing onstage at Philadelphia's Forrest Theater, during the road tryout of *70 Girls 70*, the following year.

BURNSIDE, R[obert] H[ubber Thorne] (b Glasgow, Scotland, 13 August 1870; d Metuchen, NJ, 14 September 1952). Stage director and librettist for a series of Broadway extravaganzas and musical comedies.

Burnside was born into the theatre, as the son of the manager of Glasgow's Gaiety Theatre, and he worked from an early age in various backstage capacities in the London theatre, including a period at the Savoy, where he ultimately became an assistant to director Richard Barker. He moved to America in 1894 and there, from the burlesque *Thrilby* (1895) through nearly half a century of productions, he made an extensive career as a director of musicals and, most notably, of the grandiose spectacles staged on one of the world's largest stages at the New York Hippodrome. Amongst the book musicals which he staged were included, in the wake of his Savoy experience, the American productions of *The Emerald Isle* for 'the Jefferson de Angelis Opera Company under the management of R H Burnside' and *The Earl and the Girl*, the successful early American musical *Fantana* (1905), and the series of musicals produced at the Globe Theater for the Montgomery and Stone comedy team and, after Montgomery's death, for Stone alone (*The Lady of the Slipper, Chin-Chin, Jack o'Lantern, Tip Top, Stepping Stones, Three Cheers*).

In the 1920s he directed Broadway's version of *Madame Pompadour*, Jerome Kern's *The City Chap* and *Criss-Cross* and Youmans' *Great Day!* and visited London to stage Friml's *The Blue Kitten* and his own short-lived paste-up piece, *The Girl from Cooks*, at the Gaiety Theatre, a production which ended in fiasco with cast and landlords fighting over the costumes to replace monies owed.

In 1903 Burnside began a parallel career as a librettist and lyricist and, alone or in collaboration, he turned out regular texts for musical comedies as well as the structures and such words and/or lyrics as were needed for the Hippodrome extravaganzas (*Hip Hip Hooray, Happy Days, Good Times, Better Times*), over a period of some 25 years. A number of his early pieces were written with composer Gustave Kerker, but his most successful musical plays were the pieces to which he and Anne Caldwell wrote the libretti (and Ivan Caryll the music) for Montgomery and/or Stone.

In his seventies he was still active as a director, mounting a cowboy spectacular for the World's Fair in New York and staging productions of the Gilbert and Sullivan canon. In 1944 he directed the revival of De Koven's *Robin Hood* at Broadway's Adelphi Theater.

1903 **Sergeant Kitty** (A Baldwin Sloane) Daly's Theater 18 January 1904
1904 **Burning to Sing, or Singing to Burn** (Gustave Kerker) 1 act Lyric Theater 10 May (Lambs' Club Gambol)
1905 **The Tourists** (Kerker) Daly's Theater 25 August 1906
1906 **The Girl From Vienna** (Kerker) Casino Theater 16 February
1906 **My Lady's Maid** (*Lady Madcap*) American version (Casino Theater)
1907 **Fascinating Flora** (Kerker/w Joseph W Herbert) Casino Theater 20 May

1908 **The Pied Piper** (Manuel Klein/w Austen Strong) Majestic Theater 3 December

1911 **The Girl I Love** (John S Zamecnik, H L Sandford/w Clarence Vincent Kerr) La Salle Theater, Chicago 5 February

1911 **The Three Romeos** (Raymond Hubbell) Globe Theater 13 November

1914 **The Dancing Duchess** (Milton Lusk/w Kerr) Casino Theater 19 August

1914 **Chin-Chin** (Ivan Caryll/w Anne Caldwell) Globe Theater 20 October

1917 **Jack o'Lantern** (Caryll/w Caldwell) Globe Theater 16 October

1919 **Miss Millions** (Hubbell) Punch & Judy Theater 9 December

1920 **Tip Top** (Caryll/w Caldwell) Globe Theater 5 October

1923 **Stepping Stones** (Kern/w Caldwell) Globe Theater 6 November

1927 **The Girl From Cook's** (Hubbell, Jean Gilbert/ad w Greatrex Newman) Gaiety Theatre, London 1 November

1928 **Three Cheers** (Hubbell et al/w Caldwell) Globe Theater 15 October

BURROWS, Abe [BOROWITZ, Abram Solman] (b New York, 18 December 1910; d New York, 17 May 1985).

Originally an accountant, later a commercial broker, and also a performer, Burrows supplied his earliest writings to radio and from 1939, from a Hollywood base, to film, whilst establishing himself in the late 1940s as a chat-show personality with his own shows on CBS. He entered the musical theatre when he was brought in to collaborate on the until then unsatisfactory adaptation of Damon Runyon's stories as the libretto for *Guys and Dolls* (Tony Award), and thereafter worked on a number of further musical plays, both as author and/or director, and also on a several occasions (without credit) as a play doctor.

Burrows took an unadvertised hand in the turning of Molnár's *A jő tunder* into a conventional musical play as *Make a Wish* (102 performances) and joined Charles O'Neal to adapt his book *Three Wishes for Jamie* to the musical stage (94 performances, also director), but had much more success with the original libretto to *Can-Can* (also director) and the adaptation of the screenplay *Ninotchka* as the basis for another Cole Porter musical, *Silk Stockings*. He collaborated with *Pajama Game* author Richard Bissell and his wife on a musical about the making of that musical which, as *Say, Darling* (also directed), gave him a further success, but found that musicalizing Jane Austen's *Pride and Prejudice* as *First Impressions* was less profitable (84 performances, also director).

A reunion with Frank Loesser, a decade after *Guys and Dolls*, on an adaptation of the book *How to Succeed in Business Without Really Trying* (also directed) gave the pair a second major hit, and a second Tony Award, but it was to be Burrows's last. He worked (as did several other writers, in turn), on the continuing but fruitless attempts to make a musical play out of *Breakfast at Tiffany's*, contributed to the 1976 efforts to revive the *Hellzapoppin* formula, without the results being seen on Broadway, and directed a brief revival of *Can-Can* in 1981.

His other directing assignments included *Two on the Aisle*, *Happy Hunting* and *What Makes Sammy Run*.

1950 **Guys and Dolls** (Frank Loesser/w Jo Swerling) 46th Street Theater 24 November

1951 **Make a Wish** (Hugh Martin/w Preston Sturges) Winter Garden Theater 18 April

1952 **Three Wishes for Jamie** (Ralph Blane/w Charles O'Neal) Mark Hellinger Theater 21 March

1953 **Can-Can** (Cole Porter) Shubert Theater 7 May

1955 **Silk Stockings** (Porter/w George S Kaufman, Leueen McGrath) Imperial Theater 24 February

1958 **Say, Darling** (Jule Styne/Adolph Green, Betty Comden/w Richard & Marian Bissell) ANTA Theater 3 April

1959 **First Impressions** (Robert Goldman, Glenn Paxton, George Weiss) Alvin Theater 19 March

1961 **How to Succeed in Business Without Really Trying** (Loesser/w Jack Weinstock, Willie Gilbert) 46th Street Theater 14 October

1966 **Breakfast at Tiffany's** (Bob Merrill/w others) Majestic Theater 14 December

Autobiography: *Honest, Abe (is there really no business like show-business?)* (Little, Brown, Boston, 1980)

BURVILLE, Alice

A favourite soprano of the 1870s and early 1880s, Alice Burville rose from the tiny rôle of a Maid of Honour in the West End production of *La Branche cassée* (1874) to take the leading ingénue roles in the London presentations of *Dagobert* (1875, Princess Fleur d'amour), *Fleur de thé* (1875, Fleur de thé), *The Duke's Daughter* (*La Timbale d'argent*, 1876, Malvina), *La Chanson de Fortunio* (1876, Laurette) and *Le Petit Duc* (1878, Duchesse). She also took over as Rosalinde in London's first *Die Fledermaus* (1877) and as Josephine in the original production of *HMS Pinafore* and played the title-rôle in a West End revival of *Geneviève de Brabant*.

She visted America in 1877 with Lydia Thompson's troupe playing Polly Hopkins in *Robinson Crusoe*, Suzel in *Oxygen*, Joconde in *Piff-Paff*, Fatima in *Bluebeard* etc, and also appeared there several years later in more conventional comic opera, when her credits included Arabella in *Billee Taylor* (1881) and Lady Angela in Broadway's *Patience* (1881-2). She returned home to appear as Fiametta in the British production of *Boccaccio* (1882), but this was her last major London rôle, her work thereafter being largely in the provinces where she appeared in the title-rôle of *Merry Mignon*, composed by her husband, John Crook, and took the lead in the provincial musical *The Bachelors* (1885).

BUSNACH, [Bertrand] William (b Paris, 7 March 1832; d Paris 21 January 1907).

The descendant of an Algerian Jewish family (original name Abou-Djenach), the eccentric Busnach made himself a small fortune in Paris as an exchange agent before turning his attentions to the theatre. In the years that followed, he became a prodigiously prolific author of theatrical pieces, from vaudevilles and comedies to sketches and opérettes, from the heaviest of dramas to the most spectacular of spectaculars. Always writing, always with pieces of some kind playing in several theatres, always with ten others in preparation with a variety of collaborators, he lived in a perpetual personal muddle, but always with his fingers on everybody's doings, and at the middle of a spider's-web of connections.

His earliest contribution to the musical stage was in the way of a veritable shower of the little one-act opérettes which were liberally used and used up in spectacles coupés, as forepieces or as occasional pieces in the French theatre of the 1860s. None of these pieces proved particularly durable, but Busnach made a more important contribution to the Parisian musical stage when he turned manager and, during some two years of struggle at the head of what he and his financially supportive colleague Léon Sari called the Théâtre de l'Athénée, gave the first significant opportunities to the young Charles Lecocq by producing his *L'Amour et son carquois* and *Fleur de thé*.

As an author, he got very rarely near the standard of those pieces, but he did supply Offenbach – with whom he had been associated as early as 1855 as co-scenarist on the pantomime *Polichinelle dans le monde* – with the text of his charming little *Pomme d'api*, and collaborated on the texts for Litolff's *Héloïse et Abélard* and Lecocq's *Kosiki* and *Ali Baba*. With one or two of his other hats on, he also adapted Zola's *Nana*, *L'Assommoir*, *Germinal* and *Pot-Bouille* to the stage, as well as co-authoring *Le Remplaçant* with Georges Duval, and teaming with Clairville on the Châtelet féerie *La Belle au bois dormant*.

Busnach's output also included a number of unsuccessful novels and a newspaper, *La Gazette des Parisiennes*, which appeared in 1866 for one issue. He died at the age of 74 shortly after a surprise marriage to a young woman in her twenties.

1861 **Les Brioches du Doge** (F Demarquette/w Hector Crémieux) 1 act Théâtre des Bouffes-Parisiens 19 August
1864 **Les Virtuoses du pavé** (Auguste Leveillé/w Édouard Cadol) Théâtre des Folies-Marigny 19 April
1864 **Les Petits du premier** (Émile Albert/w Brunswick) 1 act Théâtre Saint-Germain 3 December
1865 **Les Gammes d'Oscar** (Georges Douay) Théâtre des Folies-Marigny 20 May
1866 **Robinson Crusoé** (Jules Pillevesse) 1 act Fantaisies-Parisiennes 21 February
1866 **Le Myosotis** (Charles Lecocq/w Cham) 1 act Palais-Royal 2 May
1866 **Le Don Juan des Fantaisies** (w Alexandre Flan) 1 act Fantaisies-Parisiennes 19 June
1866 **Quai Malaquais** (A de Roubin/w Élie Frébault) 1 act Folies-Marigny 6 July
1866 **La Vipérine** (Jean-Jacques de Billemont/w Jules Prével) 1 act Théâtre des Folies-Marigny 19 October
1867 **Marlborough s' en va-t-en guerre** (Georges Bizet, Émile Jonas, Isidore Legouix, Léo Delibes/w Paul Siraudin) Théâtre de l'Athénée 15 December
1868 **La Pénitente** (Comtesse de Grandval/w Henri Meilhac) 1 act Opéra-Comique 13 May
1868 **Les Jumeaux de Bergame** (Lecocq) 1 act Théâtre de l'Athénée 20 November
1869 **L'Ours et l'amateur de jardins** (Legouix/w Marquet) 1 act Théâtre des Bouffes-Parisiens 1 September
1871 **Le Phoque à ventre blanc** (Georges Donay) 1 act Alcazar 17 July
1872 **Les Visitandines** 1 act Folies-Bergère 5 March
1872 **Héloïse et Abélard** (Henri Litolff/w Clairville) Théâtre des Folies-Dramatiques 19 October
1872 **Sol-si-ré-pif-pan** (Henri Vincent) 1 act Théâtre du Château d'Eau 16 November
1873 **Mariée depuis midi** (Georges Jacobi/w Armand Liorat) 1 act Théâtre du Gymnase, Marseille 20 August, Théâtre des Bouffes-Parisiens 6 March 1874
1873 **Pomme d'api** (Jacques Offenbach/w Ludovic Halévy) 1 act Théâtre de la Renaissance 4 September
1873 **La Liqueur d'or** (Laurent de Rillé/w Armand Liorat) Théâtre des Menus-Plaisirs 11 December

1874 **La Belle au bois dormant** (Litolff/w Clairville) Théâtre du Châtelet 4 April
1874 **Charbonnier est maître chez lui** (Édouard Clairville fils/w Clairville) 1 act Théâtre du Château d'Eau 29 November
1876 **Les Deux Omar** (Firmin Bernicat/w Gedhé [G Delafontaine]) 1 act Fantaisies-Oller 4 April
1876 **Kosiki** (Lecocq/w Liorat) Théâtre de la Renaissance 18 October
1877 **L'Oppoponax** (Léon Vasseur/w Charles Nuitter) 1 act Théâtre des Bouffes-Parisiens 2 May
1879 **Mon gendre, tout est rompu** (Auguste Coèdes/w Paul Burani) Casino de Dieppe 22 August
1880 **La Princesse Marmotte** (de Rillé/w Clairville, Octave Gastineau) Galeries St Hubert, Brussels 24 January
1882 **La Petite Reinette** (Louis Varney/w Clairville) Galeries Saint-Hubert, Brussels 11 October
1886 **Madame Cartouche** (Vasseur/w Pierre Decourcelle) Théâtre des Folies-Dramatiques 19 October
1886 **Le Signal** (Paul Puget/w Ernest Dubreuil) 1 act Opéra-Comique 17 November
1887 **Le Chevalier timide** (Edmond Missa) 1 act Théâtre des Menus-Plaisirs 1 September
1887 **Ali Baba** (Lecocq/w Albert Vanloo) Alhambra, Brussels 11 November
1890 **L'Oeuf rouge** (Edmond Audran/w Vanloo) Théâtre des Folies-Dramatiques 14 March
1891 **La Fille de Fanchon la vielleuse** (Varney/w Liorat, Albert Fonteny) Théâtre des Folies-Dramatiques 3 November
1893 **Cliquette** (Varney) Théâtre des Folies-Dramatiques 11 July
1896 **Le Lézard** (Frédéric Toulmouche/w Liorat) 1 act Scala 29 August
1906 **Le Rat** (Raidich/w Clairville) 1 act Théâtre Grévin 14 January

BUTT, Alfred [Sir] (b London, 20 March 1878; d Newmarket, 8 December 1962). Theatrical businessman and politican who juggled several London theatres to varying degrees of profit.

Having begun his working life as a clerk in the accounts office at Harrods department store, Butt moved on to become secretary at the Palace Theatre (1898) and eventually rose through the positions of assistant manager and manager to become managing director and chairman of the theatre. At various times thereafter he also gathered under his aegis the management of the Empire Theatre (1914–28), the Theatre Royal, Drury Lane (1925–31) and, after squeezing out the successors of George Edwardes from the Gaiety board, for a while took over the management of both the Gaiety and the Adelphi Theatres (1916–19). He was also responsible for the construction and management of the Victoria Palace (1911–30) and Paris's Théâtre Mogador (1919), the latter built allegedly out of admiration for the singer Régine Flory but disposed of after the opening show failed. He also controlled the Dominion Theatre, the Queen's, the Globe and a number of provincial houses for longer or shorter periods.

Under Butt's management, the Palace and Victoria Palace were largely given up to variety and revue, the former hosting only Seymour Hicks's *Cash on Delivery*, Lily Elsie's return to the stage in *Pamela* (1917) and the brief British production of *Very Good Eddie* until Jack Waller took the house to produce *No, No, Nanette*. The Adelphi Theatre, however, prospered as a musical house with its series of Pinero musicals starring Bill Berry (*The Boy, Who's Hooper?* etc), and the Theatre Royal, Drury Lane, did splendidly with its run of large-scale American operettas (*Rose Marie, The Desert Song, Show Boat, The New Moon, The Three Musketeers* etc). Butt failed, however, to find the measure of the smaller Gaiety Theatre, with its special traditions in the world of the musical comedy, and his ventures there (*The Beauty Spot, The Kiss Call*) foundered so badly that he had to dispose of his interests in both the Gaiety and the Adelphi after less than three years in control.

Amongst the other imported shows produced wholly or partly under his managements were the three Adele and Fred Astaire vehicles *Stop Flirting* (w Aarons, Malone and Grossmith) (1923), *Lady, Be Good!* (1926) and *Funny Face* (1928), the De Sylva, Schwab and Gensler *Queen High* (1926), Ábrahám's *Viktória* (1931) and the less successful *The Red Mill*, produced at the Empire in 1919. After almost two decades of holding the strings of much of London's theatreland, Butt sold out his theatrical holdings to Stoll Moss in 1930 and resigned from Drury Lane the following year, his final production there being the musical spectacular *The Song of the Drum*.

An expert manipulator of companies and shareholdings, Butt was a theatrical landlord to whom shows were product, and he had most of his principal successes with proven, imported material or with established formulae like the Berry series of musicals, and showed little or none of the ability of some of his less expansive contemporaries, the producers, for introducing and/or creating new shows.

Butt was knighted for his wartime services in connection with food rationing in 1918, became a Unionist member of Parliament in 1922 (until 1936), and was created a baronet in 1929.

BUTTERFLIES   Musical play in 3 acts founded on *The Palace of Puck* by William J Locke. Lyrics by T H Read and Arthur Anderson. Music by J A Robertson. Apollo Theatre, London, 12 May 1908.

Butterflies was created as a made-for-the-provinces vehicle for actress-manager Ada Reeve, cast here as Rhodanthe, a warm and wise woman of the world, mixed up in a series of events which resembled an earlier and much politer version of *The Rocky Horror Show*. The characters of the piece included two former Daly's Theatre favourites, Hayden Coffin as the star's dashing love interest and W Louis Bradfield as the whimsical Puck, in whose home the events of the piece take place. Under his influence, the collection of folk who have apparently wandered into 'the palace of Puck' have their eyes opened, their uneasy souls calmed and are sent forth in the morning, knowing themselves a little better than before, to find their own road to happiness.

Some pretty songs ('Morals', 'Three Blind Mice', 'The Girl with the Clocks') by Australian musical director J A Robertson, some of which featured lyrics by Percy French, plus Coffin's inevitable interpolations, provided a pleasant musical side to the entertainment, but it was the show's solid basis in its original play which won it a shift to a London theatre and an unexpected 217-performance London run. Following the London season, Miss Reeve took *Butterflies* to Glasgow for Christmas, publicizing her show with papier maché butterflies stuck to a burr which

Scotland's children obliged by sticking on everyone in sight. It later went on the road for which it had originally been intended.

Butterflies gave a first opportunity to dancer Phyllis Monkman, taken from the chorus to be featured in 'La Naissance du papillon' when the incumbent of the rôle refused to wear the scanty dress provided.

BUTTERWORTH, Clara

The young vocalist Clara Butterworth made her first West End appearances as the Indian Princess in the 1914 revival of *The Country Girl* and as the heroine of *Young England* (1916) at Daly's Theatre. She found celebrity when she starred in the leading rôle of Georgine in the long run of *The Lilac Domino* (1919) and confirmed her status when she created the rôle of Lady Mary Trefusis in the light opera *The Rebel Maid* (1921) composed by her husband, Montague Phillips, and appeared as Lilli Veidt in a second long-running hit, the London production of *Lilac Time*. She was also seen in one quick flop, London's version of The Dutch musical *Medorah* (1920, t/o Medorah).

BUTTYKAY, Ákos [GÁLSZÉCSY ÉS BUTYKAI, Ákos] (b Halmi, 22 July 1871; d Debrecen, 26 October 1935). Composer of several superior operetts for European stages.

Buttykay studied both law and music in Budapest, before going to Weimar for a year to further his studies in piano and composition. He continued studying at the Budapest Zeneakadémia whilst making his first attempts both as a theatre composer, with the ballet *A bűbájos malom*, and in the orchestral field. His first symphony, a piece of serious intent, was played with some success before, to general surprise, he produced his first operett *A bolygó görög* (the wandering Greek). A piece written in a light operatic vein, it was produced at the Király Színház in 1905 with considerable success, leading to a revival as early as 1909. He had further theatre successes with his music to the Singspiel *A harang* (w Kacsoh) and with *Csibészkirály*, a piece which would turn up, curiously, nearly a decade later in America under the title *Pom-Pom*, stripped of Buttykay's score (Hugo Felix/Anne Caldwell Cohan Theater, 28 February 1916). He composed the incidental music for Imre Madách's drama *Az ember tragédiája* (1918), but his one genuine international triumph in the musical theatre came with *Az ezüst sirály* (the silver seagull) an operett in which his wife, singing star Emmi Kosáry, and Ernő Király played the leading rôles first in Budapest and then for a run of over 200 performances at Vienna's Carltheater (*Liebesrausch* ad Robert Bodanzky) in 1920–1. The show had a similar success in Germany and was apparently given a performance German in New York (2 October 1923).

In 1922 his *Olivia hercegnő*, with Kosáry and Király again starred, was selected to open the new Fővárosi Operettszínház, and in the same year he ended a career of 15 years as a piano professor at the Zeneakadémia. Thereafter, although he turned out several more stage pieces, including a revised version of his old collaborator Kacsoh's famous *János vitéz* in 1931, he devoted his writing largely to orchestral and concert works ('Magyar rapszódia'), chamber and piano music.

1905 **A bolygó görög** (Árpád Pásztor) Király Színház 19 October
1907 **A harang** (w Pongrác Kacsoh/Pásztor) Király Színház 1 February
1907 **Csibészkirály** (Lajos Széll) Király Színház 21 February
1912 **Hamupipőke** (Károly Bakonyi, Imre Farkas, Andor Gábor) Magyar Királyi Operaház 26 October
1920 **Az ezüst sirály** (Imre Földes) Városi Színház 6 February
1922 **Olivia hercegnő** (Földes) Fővárosi Operettszinház 23 December
1925 **A császárnő apródja** (Jenő Faragó, Imre Harmath) Király Színház 24 March

BYE BYE BIRDIE Musical in 2 acts by Michael Stewart. Lyrics by Lee Adams. Music by Charles Strouse. Martin Beck Theater, New York, 14 April 1960.

With 'college' musicals a thing of the past, *Bye Bye Birdie* – the first American musical comedy to take the new trends in 'pop' music for its subject – brought their 1960s equivalent to Broadway in the same welter of innocent good humour and catchy songs heretofore provided by such pieces as *Leave it to Jane* or *Good News*.

Conrad Birdie (Dick Gautier) has hit pop-star success, and the bank-account of his manager, Albert Peterson (Dick van Dyke), should be just about to start heading happily for the black, but nothing is going right. Albert's faithful secretary-and-girlfriend, Rosie (Chita Rivera), is resigning until he gets a proper job, and Conrad is about to be drafted. Albert lines up one last promotion: Conrad will kiss goodbye to lucky 15-year-old fan Kim McAfee (Susan Watson), to the accompaniment of a special new song, on national TV. Disaster strikes in every possible form. Kim's steady, Hugo (Michael J Pollard), knocks Conrad out in front of NBC's cameras, the star runs off into what passes for nightlife in Sweet Apple, Ohio, and gets arrested for consorting threateningly with an under-aged girl, and on top of all that, Albert's mother (Kay Medford) gets in on the act as only a Broadway musical mother can. At the end of it all, Albert is happy to throw in the pop-music business and head quietly off with Rosie to a small-town teaching job.

The songs of the show included a package of winners: Albert's bright advice to 'Put on a Happy Face' to the teeny-fans who are losing their idol to the army, their chorused insistence that 'We Love You, Conrad', the pop-singer's frantic realization that he's got 'A Lot of Livin' to Do' before getting incarcerated in the army, his plastic confession to his public that all you need to do in life to be him is to be 'Honestly Sincere', the plaint of the parents of Sweet Apple over the problems with modern 'Kids', and those kids tying up the town's telephone system with their delightfully-staged 'Telephone Hour'. There were two dance routines inserted, in the manner of the time, featuring Rosie, the first as she furiously goes through a list of ways 'How to Kill a Man' who lets his mother tell him what to do, the other an incidental irruption into a Shriners' meeting during her night on the town after the disaster.

Edward Padula's production of the show was a 607-performance hit on Broadway, and *Bye Bye Birdie* headed out into the country and across the Atlantic where H M Tennent Ltd mounted a reproduced London version with Peter Marshall (Albert), Marty Wilde (Conrad), Sylvia Tysick (Kim) and Angela Baddeley (Mrs Peterson) featured alongside Miss Rivera. London had already had its first musical about the pop world in the very differently coloured *Expresso Bongo* and it did not reserve the same welcome for *Bye Bye Birdie* that Broadway had. The run was stretched to 268 performances, but the show did not establish itself in the revivable repertoire in Britain in the same way that it did in America. An Australian production, with Frank Buxton and Patricia Finlay featured, played four months in Melbourne and subsequently at Sydney's Her Majesty's Theatre (21 October 1961).

A film version was produced in 1963 which retained van Dyke and much of the score (although reallocating numbers), added a zingy title-song and featured Ann-Margret (Kim), Janet Leigh (Rosie), Maureen Stapleton (Mrs Peterson), Jesse Pearson (Conrad) and pop vocalist Bobby Rydell as a pumped-up Hugo.

An attempt to *Bring Back Birdie*, written by the same authors and produced at the Martin Beck Theater (5 March 1981) with Donald O'Connor, Maria Karnilova, Maurice Hines and Miss Rivera played just four performances, but the original show, 30 years on become as delightful a period piece as the shows of the *Good News* era, continued its healthy life, going on the road in a major revival in 1991 with Tommy Tune and Anne Reinking in the leading rôles. Two additional songs by Adams and Strouse ('A Giant Step', 'He's Mine') were added to the score for this production.

UK: Her Majesty's Theatre 15 June 1961; Australia: Her Majesty's Theatre, Melbourne, 4 March 1961; Film: Columbia 1963
Recordings: original cast (Columbia), London cast (Philips), film soundtrack (RCA Victor) etc

BY JUPITER Musical in 2 acts by Richard Rodgers and Lorenz Hart based on *The Warrior's Husband* by Julian Thompson. Lyrics by Lorenz Hart. Music by Richard Rodgers. Shubert Theater, New York, 3 June 1942.

The Warrior's Husband (1932), originally produced on Broadway with Katharine Hepburn in its starring rôle as the warrior queen, Hippolyta, was musicalized by Rodgers and Hart very largely in a clinic where Hart was drying out after one of his more excessive bouts with alcohol. Its theme of the subjugation of a powerful woman by an inferior man by his use of the appendages of his sex was a well-worn one on the musical stage, but it was stated here with rather more aplomb than usual and prettily dressed up in the usually infallible garb of Ancient Greece.

Hippolyta (Benuta Venay), Queen of the Amazons, and her army of female warriors rule and protect their country whilst the Consort, Sapiens (Ray Bolger), and the other husbands stay at home. This situation is not, you understand, because the women are in any way meritorious, but because Hippolyta has this magic girdle which ensures her superiority. The Greeks, led by Theseus (Ronald Graham) and Hercules (Ralph Dumke), apparently find this arrangement some kind of a challenge and they invade Pontus to steal the girdle and ensure masculine superiority. They get beaten in the field, but their irresistible anatomy wins the day. The feeble Sapiens becomes King and, since Hippolyta has a husband in this version, Theseus is unhistorically paired off with her sister, Antiope (Constance Moore).

The score of *By Jupiter* did not produce any Rodgers and Hart standards, but several of the pieces worked well in the theatre: the comical 'Everything I've Got' for Hippolyta and Sapiens, the pretty ballad 'Nobody's Heart',

Bolger's comical turn 'Now That I've Got My Strength' and, most particularly, his dance routine to the otherwise not first-class 'Life With Father' with boot-faced character actress Bertha Belmore, cast (as she had been in the 1932 play) as the King's mother, Pomposia.

By Jupiter, produced by Rodgers himself and Dwight Deere Wiman, ran for 427 performances on Broadway, closing when Bolger withdrew to go and do some troop entertaining and it was not considered practical to replace him. It was picked up for Britain by Jack Waller and produced at Manchester with Bobby Howes topbilled as Sapiens alongside Marjorie Brooks (Hippolyta), Adele Dixon (Antiope), Chic Elliott (Pomposia) and Bruce Trent (Theseus) with one Hyacinth Hazell in the rôle of Penelope. It closed on the road to London.

In New York, however, the piece was brought back to the Theatre Four in 1967, following the successful revival there of *The Boys From Syracuse* (1963), with a cast headed by Bob Dishy (Sapiens), Jackie Alloway (Hippolyta), Robert R Kaye (Theseus), Sheila Sullivan (Antiope) and Irene Byatt (Pomposia). It did not do as well as its predecessor and closed after 118 performances.

UK: Prince's Theatre, Manchester 25 July 1944
Recording: off-Broadway revival cast (RCA) etc

BYNG, George W[ilfred Bulkeley] (b ?Dublin, 1861; d London, 1932). Longtime conductor and journeyman composer for the British stage.

Trained at the Royal Academy of Music in Dublin, Byng was, from the age of 11, a member of the orchestra at the local Theatre Royal, latterly under the baton of Frederic Stanislaus with whom he was subsequently engaged at Manchester. He worked as an orchestral player and then a conductor in a whole series of London theatres, being first violin at London's Gaiety Theatre, musical director at the Royalty with Arthur Roberts in 1889–90 (*The New Corsican Brothers*, *Tra-la-la Tosca*) and subsequently on tour with the comedian in *Guy Fawkes Esq* (for which he also provided the score) and *In Town*. He accompanied the Gaiety burlesque company which played *Faust up-to-Date* and *Carmen up-to-Data* around the European capitals, and he returned to London to conduct Willie Edouin's season at the Strand (1893), and again for *On the March* and Roberts's *The White Silk Dress* at the Prince of Wales (1896–7). He then spent a long period as musical director in succession to Georges Jacobi at the Alhambra (1897–1910).

Byng turned out scenic music as required over the years and, for the Alhambra, the large amount of dance music featured on their programmes including the ballets *Jack Ashore*, *The Gay City*, *The Red Shoes* and *Gretna Green*, but he also scored all or part of several musical comedies, including Roberts's highly successful touring vehicle *HMS Irresponsible*. He revised Audran's *La Poupée* (originally intended to be a Roberts vehicle) for Henry Lowenfeld's vastly successful London production and, in contrast, supplied the music for *The Showman's Sweetheart*, a touring vehicle for Minnie Palmer, and 11 numbers for what was virtually a new score for the touring show *A Trip to Chicago*.

1890 **Guy Fawkes Esq** ('Doss Chidderdoss'/Fred Leslie, Herbert Clark) Nottingham 7 April

1894 **The House of Lords** (w Ernest Ford/Harry Greenbank) 1 act Lyric Theatre 6 July
1896 **The White Silk Dress** (w Alick McLean, Reginald Somerville/H J W Dam) Prince of Wales Theatre 3 October
1898 **The Showman's Sweetheart** (Guy Eden, Arthur Law/Law) Queen's Theatre, Crouch End 29 August
1898 **A Trip to Chicago** replacement songs w E Boyd Jones (tour)
1899 **The Mysterious Musician** (Eden) 1 act Terry's Theatre 27 June
1900 **Punch and Judy** (w Arthur Meredyth/Law) Theatre Royal, Croydon 25 June
1900 **HMS Irresponsible** (J F Cornish) Royalty Theatre, Chester 2 August, Royal Strand Theatre 27 May 1901
1902 **The Variety Girl** (Albert E Ellis/Chris Davis) Opera House, Cork 1 September
1904 **The Duchess of Sillie-Crankie** (Herbert Fordwych, Arthur Wimperis/Fordwych) Terry's Theatre

BYRON, H[enry] J[ames] (b Manchester, 8 January 1835; d Clapham Park, London, 11 April 1884). Victorian man of the theatre whose burlesques were the backbone of the British tradition.

Born in Manchester, the son of the British consul at Port au Prince, Byron worked at first as a doctor's clerk and then studied for the law before turning definitively to the theatre. There he became one of the most notable figures of his time, both as a prolific writer of more than a hundred successful plays (the record-breaking *Our Boys*, *Uncle Dick's Darling*, *A Lancashire Lass*, *Tottles*, *Wait and Hope*, *Dearer Than Life* etc) and musical shows and, most particularly, as the supreme exponent of the punning burlesque and extravaganza. He also operated as a producer, being for a time the partner of Lady Bancroft (Marie Wilton) at the famous Prince of Wales Theatre, as well as an occasional performer.

Amongst Byron's early works, the burlesque of *La gazza ladra*, *The Maid and the Magpie*, in which Marie Wilton won outstanding praise as a burlesque boy, and the *Aladdin* which introduced the character of Widow Twankay into the story for the first time, were the most memorable pieces, but others burlesques such as *Cinderella* (introducing the character of 'Buttons' which would become a British pantomime favourite), *Fra Diavolo*, *The Lady of Lyons*, *The Pilgrim of Love*, *The Miller and his Men*, *Mazeppa* and *Miss Eily O'Connor* all won more than one London run as well as long provincial lives and a wide dissemination to the English-speaking stages of America and the colonies.

His Arabian Nights and fairytale burlesques became used and re-used as some of the most favoured pantomime openings (followed by the ever-reducing harlequinade), his *1863* was an early English-language example of the genuine, Parisian-style 'review' of the year's events before the 'revue' genre degenerated into a virtual variety show, his adaptation of *La Fille de Madame Angot* for the English stage proved the best of the series of such versions and helped lead the show to triumph on English-language stages, whilst his burlesques for the Gaiety Theatre provided the famous team of players there with the material they required to make and hold their fame. Oddly, however, in spite of his great straight play successes, Byron never authored an original libretto to a legitimate musical play, his only venture in that area being on the Alhambra's romantic spectacular *The Demon's Bride* in which the book was commissioned from France's Leterrier and Vanloo and Byron's job was merely to 'adapt' it to the Alhambra's purposes.

1857 **Richard the Lionheart** (pasticcio) Strand Theatre 23 November

1858 **The Lady of Lyons, or Twopenny Pride and Pen-nytence** (pasticcio) Strand Theatre 1 February

1858 **Fra Diavolo, or Beauty and the Brigands** (pasticcio) Strand Theatre 5 April

1858 **The Bride of Abydos, or The Prince, the Pirate and the Pearl** (pasticcio) Strand Theatre 31 May

1858 **The Latest Edition of the Lady of Lyons** (revised *The Lady of Lyons*) (pasticcio) Strand Theatre

1858 **The Maid and the Magpie** (pasticcio) Strand Theatre 11 October

1858 **Mazeppa** (pasticcio) Olympic Theatre 27 December

1859 **The Very Latest Edition of the Lady of Lyons** (pasticcio) Strand Theatre 11 July

1859 **The Babes in the Wood and the Good Little Fairy Birds** (pasticcio) Adelphi Theatre 18 July

1859 **The Nymph of the Lurleyburg, or The Knight and the Naiads** (pasticcio) Adelphi Theatre 26 December

1859 **Jack the Giant Killer, or Harlequin, King Arthur and ye Knights of ye Round Table** (pasticcio) Princess's Theatre 26 December

1860 **The Forty Thieves** (pasticcio/w Planché, W & R Brough, Halliday, Buckingham, Kennedy) Lyceum Theatre 7 March

1860 **The Pilgrim of Love** (pasticcio) Haymarket Theatre 9 April

1860 **The Miller and his Men** (pasticcio/w Francis Talfourd) Strand Theatre 9 April

1860 **Cinderella, or The Prince, the Lackey and the Little Glass Slipper** (pasticcio) Strand Theatre 26 December

1860 **Bluebeard from a New Point of Hue** (pasticcio) Adelphi Theatre 26 December

1861 **Aladdin, or the Wonderful Scamp** (pasticcio) Strand Theatre 1 April

1861 **Esmeralda, or the Sensation Goat** (pasticcio) Strand Theatre 28 September

1861 **Miss Eily O'Connor** (pasticcio) Theatre Royal, Drury Lane 25 November

1861 **The Rival Othellos** (pasticcio) Strand Theatre 28 November

1861 **Puss in a New Pair of Boots** (pasticcio arr Frank Musgrave) Strand Theatre 26 December

1862 **The Sensation Fork, or The Maiden, the Maniac and the Midnight Murderer** (pasticcio) Her Majesty's Concert Room 19 May

1862 **The Rosebud of Stinging-Nettle Farm, or The Villainous Squire and the Virtuous Visitor** (pasticcio) Crystal Palace 21 July

1862 **Goldenhair the Good** (pasticcio) St James's Theatre 26 December

1862 **Ivanhoe According to the Spirit of the Times** (pasticcio arr Musgrave) Strand Theatre 26 December

1863 **Beautiful Haidee, or The Sea Nymphs and the Sallee Rovers** (pasticcio) Princess's Theatre 6 April

1863 **Ali Baba and the Thirty-Nine Thieves** (pasticcio) Strand Theatre 6 April

1863 **Ill-Treated Trovatore** (pasticcio) Adelphi Theatre 21 May

1863 **The Motto 'I Am All There'** (pasticcio) Strand Theatre 16 July

1863 **Lady Belle Belle, or Fortunio and his Seven Magic Men** (pasticcio) Adelphi Theatre 26 December

1863 **1863, or The Sensations of the Past Season** (pasticcio) St James's Theatre 26 December

1863 **Orpheus and Eurydice, or The Young Gentleman who Charmed the Rocks** (pasticcio) Strand Theatre 26 December

1864 **Mazourka, or The Stick, the Pole and the Tartar** (aka *Tiddeliwinki*) (pasticcio) Strand Theatre 27 April

1864 **Princess Springtime** (pasticcio) Haymarket Theatre 26 December

1864 **The Grin Bushes, or Mrs Brown of the Missis Sippi** (pasticcio) Strand Theatre 26 December

1864 **The Lion and the Unicorn** (pasticcio) His Majesty's Theatre 26 December

1865 **Pan, or The Loves of Echo and Narcissus** (pasticcio) Adelphi Theatre 10 April

1865 **La! Sonnambula, or The Supper, the Sleeper and the Merry Swiss Boy** (pasticcio) Prince of Wales Theatre 15 April

1865 **Lucia di Lammermoor, or the Luckless Laird, the Lovely Lady and the Little Lover** (pasticcio) Prince of Wales Theatre 25 September

1865 **Little Don Giovanni, or Leporello and the Stone Statue** (pasticcio) Prince of Wales Theatre 26 December

1866 **Der Freischutz, or The Bill, the Belle and the Bullet** (pasticcio) Prince of Wales's Theatre 10 September

1866 **Pandora's Box, or The Young Spark and the Old Flame** (pasticcio) Princess's Theatre 26 December

1867 **William Tell with a Vengeance, or The Pet, the Patriot and the Pippin** (pasticcio) Strand Theatre 5 October

1868 **Lucrezia Borgia M D, or The Grande Doctress** (pasticcio arr J T Haines) Theatre Royal, Holborn 28 October

1869 **The Corsican Brothers, or The Troublesome Twins** (pasticcio) Globe Theatre 17 May

1869 **Lord Bateman, or The Proud Young Porter and the Fair Sophia** (pasticcio arr George Richardson) Globe Theatre 26 December

1870 **Robert Macaire, or The Roadside Inn Turned Innside out** (pasticcio) Globe Theatre 16 April

1870 **The Enchanted Wood, or The Three Transformed** (pasticcio) Princes Adelphi Theatre 4 May

1871 **The Orange Tree and the Humble Bee, or The Little Princess who was Lost at Sea** (pasticcio) Vaudeville Theatre 13 May

1871 **Giselle, or The Sirens of the Lotus Lake** (arr G Barnard) Olympic Theatre 22 July

1871 **Camaralzaman and the Fair Badoura, or The Bad Djinn and the Good Spirit** Vaudeville Theatre 22 November

1872 **The Lady of the Lane** (arr John Fitzgerald) (pasticcio) Strand Theatre 31 October

1873 **La Fille de Madame Angot** English version (Philharmonic Theatre)

1873 **Don Juan** (arr Georges Jacobi) Alhambra Theatre 22 December

1874 **Guy Fawkes** (arr Meyer Lutz) Gaiety Theatre 14 January

1874 **Normandy Pippins** (pasticcio arr Frederick Stanislaus) 1 act Criterion Theatre 18 April

1874 **La Jolie Parfumeuse** English version (Alhambra Theatre)

1874 **The Demon's Bride** (Georges Jacobi/Eugène Leterrier, Albert Vanloo ad) Alhambra Theatre 7 September

1876 **Little Don Caesar de Bazan, or Maritana and the Merry Monarch** (pasticcio arr Meyer Lutz) Gaiety Theatre 26 August

1877 **The Bohemian G'yurl and the Unapproachable Pole** (pasticcio arr Lutz) Gaiety Theatre 31 January

1877 **Little Doctor Faust, the Gaiety not the Goethe Version** (pasticcio arr Lutz) Gaiety Theatre 13 July

1878 **The Forty Thieves** (pasticcio arr Lutz/w Gilbert, Burnand, Reece) Gaiety Theatre 13 February

1878 **Il Sonnambulo, and Lively Little Alessio** (pasticcio arr Lutz) Gaiety Theatre 6 April

1878 **Young Fra Diavolo, the Terror of Terracina** (pasticcio arr Lutz) Gaiety Theatre 17 November

1879 **Pretty Esmeralda, and Captain Phoebus of Ours** (pasticcio arr Lutz) Gaiety Theatre 2 April

1879 **Handsome Hernani, or The Fatal Penny Whistle** (pasticcio arr Lutz) Gaiety Theatre 30 August

1879 **Gulliver** Gaiety Theatre (pasticcio arr Lutz) 26 December

1880 **Il Trovatore, or Larks with a Libretto** (pasticcio arr Lutz) Olympic Theatre 26 April

1881 **Pluto, or Little Orpheus and his Lute** (pasticcio arr Michael Connelly) Royalty Theatre 26 December

1882 **The Villainous Squire and the Village Rose** revised *The Rosebud of Stinging Nettle Farm* Toole's Theatre 5 June

1882 **Frolique** (w H B Farnie) (pasticcio) Strand Theatre 18 November

Literature: ed. Wise, J: *Plays by H J Byron* (Cambridge University Press, Cambridge 1984)

BY THE BEAUTIFUL SEA   Musical in 2 acts by Herbert and Dorothy Fields. Lyrics by Dorothy Fields. Music by Arthur Schwartz. Majestic Theater, New York, 8 April 1954.

Following the pretty period musical *A Tree Grows in Brooklyn* in 1951, lyricist Dorothy Fields, composer Arthur Schwartz and star Shirley Booth came together a second time on a show with a similarly winning and unextravagant flavour in *By the Beautiful Sea*, a piece built up around the character of real-life performer Lottie Gilson, otherwise known as 'The Little Magnet'.

Miss Booth played Lottie Gibson, a vaudeville per-former, who spends her off-season at her boarding house in Coney Island. There she leads to the good her love for the impecunious Shakespearian actor Dennis Emery (Wilbur Evans). The main hurdles which have to be got over are money, and his daughter by an earlier marriage, the 17-year-old child actress Betsy Busch (Carol Leigh) who has become jealously possessive of her re-found father and resents Lottie's vaudeville connections. She is finally won over when Lottie gets her out of her imper-sonation of a 13-year-old, into a pretty frock and the arms of a handsome waiter (Richard France). Schwartz and Fields's songs included the heroine's rueful admission that 'I'd Rather Wake Up By Myself' than with any man but Dennis, and his quiet thoughts that he has been 'Alone Too Long', alongside a lively opening title chorus and a speciality spot in which Lottie performed her act-as-known.

Robert Fryer and Lawrence Carr's production ran through an insufficient 270 performances on Broadway before the show was put away. Thirty years later, Schwartz worked on a fresh version of the text, reset in Blackpool as a vehicle for British stars Dora Bryan and Bonnie Lang-ford, with a score made up of Schwartz standards and some new material, but the project did not come to fruition.

Recording: original cast (Capitol)

C

CAB, Marc *see* MARC-CAB

CABALLERO, Manuel Fernández (b Murcia, 14 March 1835; d Madrid, 26 January 1906).

A musician and conductor in various Madrid theatres during the 1850s and 1860s (Teatro Real, Teatro de Variedades, Teatro Lírico, Teatro Lope de Vega, Teatro Español), Caballero provided the usual string of musical pieces needed as incidental music by his theatres whilst also turning out the scores for a number of original zarzuelas. He subsequently went to South America with a zarzuela company and, on his return, set himself to composition with such a will that in the next years (latterly, blind and composing by dictation) he turned out a huge number of stage musical pieces, apparently bringing his total to well over 200.

Amongst the most successful of his pieces were *El salto del pasiego* (lib: Luis de Eguilaz, Teatro Zarzuela 17 March 1878), *El duo de la Africana* (lib: Miguel Echegaray, Teatro Apolo 13 May 1893), *La viejecita* (w Hermosa, lib: Miguel Echegaray, 1 act Teatro Zarzuela 4 April 1897), *Gigantes y cabezudos* (lib: Miguel Echegaray, 1 act Teatro Zarzuela 29 November 1898) and *Los sobrinos del Capitan Grant* (lib: Miguel Ramos Carrión, Teatro Circo de Rivas 1877), a musicalization of Jules Verne's tale. He also composed an *El Vizconde de Letorières* Teatro del Circo, 1858) on Bayard and Dumanoir's much-musicalized play *Le Vicomte de Letorrières*, *El prima dia feliz* (Teatro Zarzuela 30 January 1872) using the text of Auber's opera *Le Premier Jour de bonheur* (played in Madrid in 1870), and a version of the *1001 Nights* (*Las mil y una noches*, 1882 w Rubio).

His other titles includes *Tres madres para una hija* (1854), *La vergonzosa en palacio* (1855), *Mentir a tiempo* (1856), *Juan Lanas* (1856), *La jardinera* (1857), *Un cocinero* (1858), *Frasquito* (1859), *Los dos primos* (1860), *El loco de la guardia* (1861), *Equilibrios do amor* (1862, w Cristóbal Oudrid y Segura), *Los dos mellinos* (1862), *Los suicios* (1862), *Luz y sombra* (1867), *El atrevido en la corte* (1872), *La gallina ciega* (1873), *Las hijas de Fulano* (1874), *El velo de encaje* (1874), *Este joven ne conviene* (1875 w Casares), *La clave* (1875), *Las nuevas de la noche* (1875 w Casares), *Entre el alcade y el rey* (1875 w Emilio Arrieta), *La marsellesa* (1876), *El siglio que viene* (1876), *Las dos princesas* (1878), *El lucero del alba* (1879), *El cepillo de las animas* (1879), *El corpus de sangue* (1879), *Amor que empieya y amor que acaba* (1879), *Las hazanas de Hercules* (1880), *Al polo* (1880 w Joaquin Espin), *El sacristan de San Justo* (1880 w Nieto), *Mantos y capos* (1881 w Nieto), *De Verano* (1881 w Angelo Rubio), *La farsanta* (1881 w Rubio), *El gran Tamerlano di Persia* (1882 w Nieto), *La nina bonita* (1882), *El Capitan Cestellas* (1883 w A Almagro), *Trabajo perdito* (1884), *Los bandos de Villa-frita* (1884), *El guerillero* (1885 w Ruperto Chapí, Arrieta), *La mejor receta* (1885), *Una noche en Loreto* (1885)

Locos de amor (1886), *Cielon XXII* (1886), *Las mujeres que matan* (1887), *Bazar* (1887) *Château Margaux* (1887), *Aguas azotados* (1888), *El golpe de gracia* (1888), *Olé Sevila* (1889), *Los Zangolatinos* (1889), *A ti suspiramos* (1889, w Hermosa), *España* (1890), *La choza del Diablo* (1891), *El fantasma de fuego* (1891), *Los aparecidos* (1892), *La triple alizanza* (1893), *Los dineros del sacristan* (1894), *Campañero e sacristan* (1894, w Hermosa), *Los africanistas* (1894), *El cabo primero* (1895), *El rueda de la fortuna* (1896), *Tortilla al ron* (1896 w Hermosa), *El Saboyano* (1896), *El padrino del nene* (1896), *L'espulsion de los Judios* 1493 (1896, w Hermosa), *El Señor Joaquim* (1898), *Aun hay patria, Veremundo!* (1898, w Hermosa), *La magia negra* (1898, w Valverde jr), *La virgen del puerto* (1899, w Mario Caballero), *Citrato? Der ver sera* (1899, w Valverde jr), *El traje de luzes* (1899 w Hermosa), *El rey de los aires* (1900), *Los estudiantes* (1900), *La tribu savage* (1901, w Hermosa), *La barcarola* (1901 w Lapuerta), *La diligencia* (1901), *El favorito del duque* (1902), *La trapera* (1902, w Hermosa), *La manta zamorana* (1902), *Sena Justa* (1902), *El dios grande* (1903, w Mario Caballero), *La inclusera* (1903, w Valverde jr), *Rusia y Japan* (1905, w Hermosa), *Los huertanos* (1905, w Hermosa), *Aires nacionales* (w Calleja), *La reina topacio*, *La cacharvera* etc.

CABARET Musical in 2 acts by Joe Masteroff based on the play *I Am a Camera* by John van Druten and the stories of Christopher Isherwood. Lyrics by Fred Ebb. Music by John Kander. Broadhurst Theater, New York, 20 November 1966.

The libretto of the musical *Cabaret* was based on Christopher Isherwood's lightly autobiographical short stories about life in Berlin in the years under the rule of the Nazi party, and on the play drawn by John van Druten from them and produced, with considerable success, as *I Am a Camera* (Empire Theater, New York, 28 November 1951). The musical's action was set up in the 'framework' manner, so successfully used on *Man of La Mancha* the previous season, with the principal tale of the piece loosely (though not wholly) inset into the entertainment and goings-on in a strivingly decadent Berlin cabaret house, and introduced by a leering, epicene Master of Ceremonics (Joel Grey).

Sally Bowles (Jill Haworth), a little middle-class lass from Chelsea, London, is working as a singer at Berlin's Kit-Kat Club and doing her not very good best to live the thrillingly decadent life which the city is supposed to offer. Into her orbit comes Cliff Bradshaw (Bert Convy), a young American writer, and Sally soon moves determinedly in to join him in his room in the boarding house run by Fräulein Schneider (Lotte Lenya). Their fellow lodgers include the cheerful whore, Fräulein Kost (Peg Murray), and the gentle, greying fruiterer Herr Schultz (Jack Gilford). As the

Plate 42. Cabaret: *Joel Grey repeats his original rôle as the master of ceremonies at the St Louis Muny.*

clouds gather, Sally, now pregnant by Cliff, is still determined to show the world what a good time she is having and she will not or cannot hear the noises of Nazism around her. But the others can.

Schultz courts Frln Schneider with old-world courtesy and they become engaged, but the fruiterer is Jewish and, when some Nazi sympathizers break up their engagement party, the old maid is obliged to let her dream of a marriage go. Cliff finds he has been almost unwittingly couriering Nazi funds for one of his language pupils and he is beaten up when he refuses to continue to do so. It is time to leave Berlin. But poor, self-deluded Sally cannot let the party end. She has her child aborted and, all responsibility gone, she watches Cliff take the train for Paris alone. Back in the cabaret, the Emcee introduces the same show as before, but it is harsher, and soon it will be dark.

Ebb and Kander's songs were shared between material for the cabaret scenes and numbers set into the two romances of the text. Amongst the cabaret songs, Sally fluted out a plea 'Don't Tell Mama' and insisted that life is a 'Cabaret' where you must live for the day, whilst the Emcee welcomed the audience with a polyglot 'Willkommen', tried to make a little jolly troilism suitably decadent in 'Two Ladies', danced with a gorilla to explain that 'If You Could See Her Through My Eyes' she wouldn't look Jewish at all, led a number in praise of cash ('The Money Song') and, in a different vein, the hope of the youthful Hitlerians that 'Tomorrow Belongs to Me'. The rôle of Fräulein Schneider was enriched with her thrill over a gift of a pineapple ('It Couldn't Please Me More') and of being 'Married', and with the pragmatic 'So What?' and 'What Would You Do?', explaining the logic of her decision to let married happiness go in the face of trouble, whilst Cliff wallowed in the surprise of his 'Perfectly Marvelous' affair with Sally in 'Why Should I Wake Up?'.

Harold Prince's production (Tony Award) played 1,166 performances on Broadway, and the show went on to a first national tour, with Signe Hasso (Schneider), Robert Salvio

(Emcee), Gene Rupert (Cliff) and Melissa Hart (Sally) featured, followed by further productions throughout America and beyond. In London, Richard Pilbrow joined with Prince to present a reproduction of the show with Lila Kedrova (Schneider), Kevin Colson (Cliff), Peter Sallis (Schultz), Barry Dennen (Emcee) and with Judi Dench (later Elizabeth Seal) as Sally, which played through 336 performances. In Vienna (ad Robert Gilbert), the Theater an der Wien's production effectively cast the rôle of the Emcee with a woman, Blanche Aubry, alongside Lya Dulizkaya (Schneider), Violetta Ferrari (Sally), Klaus Wildbolz (Cliff) and Harry Fuss (Schultz) for a season of 59 performances. But Australia's J C Williamson Ltd, having announced a production for Sydney's Theatre Royal in 1971, then cancelled it. Four weeks of *1776* and the British comedy *Move Over Mrs Markham* were hustled in instead. *Cabaret* got its first Australian performance 'by arrangement with J. C. Williamson' in the less upmarket but maybe more suitably atmospheric Doncaster Theatre Restaurant.

The show had had a good and widely enough spread life, if not an outstanding one, and that might pretty well have been it. But a 1972 film version of *Cabaret* gave the show a second and even more popular lease of life. The screenplay kept, though slightly altered, the Cliff/Sally story, but cut the Schneider/Schultz plot and replaced it by another love story, for younger and more beautiful people, culled from elsewhere in Isherwood's tales. The score, deprived of Frln Schneider's characterful numbers, more than compensated with a new solo for Sally in the trumpetingly desperate 'Maybe This Time', a raunchier 'Mein Herr' to replace the nearly-naughty 'Don't Tell Mama', and a new money number, 'Money, Money, Money', like the two other added pieces featuring the film's star, Liza Minnelli, in the rôle of Sally. Grey repeated his stage Emcee, at the head of Bob Fosse's cabaret entertainment, whilst Marisa Berenson and Fritz Wepper were the personable pair with problems of Jewishness and Helmut Griem appeared as a representative of cultured decadence, a beautiful, blue-eyed Baron who has affairs with both Sally and Brian (ex-Cliff).

The enormous success of the film – one of the very few films of a popular musical play to actually outrank its original stage show – led not only to a worldwide fame for the piece, and to many further productions in a multiplicity of areas and languages, but also to a considerable alteration in the nature of the show and, in particular, of the rôle of Sally Bowles. The stinging vocalizing of Miss Minnelli was remembered by future inhabitants of the rôle rather than the vulnerable character that went with it and, as a result, a typically mounted French production which toured Europe from 1986 introduced a brazen-voiced vamp of a Sally (Ute Lemper) who was about as far from the silly, sympathetic and real little creature of the original show as could be. As directors revel in the show's 'decadence' in much the same way that the section of Berlin folk portrayed in the piece did in the 1930s, rare now is the production, amongst the many annual ones mounted worldwide, in theatres large and small, which features a Sally Bowles rather than a Liza Minnelli-Bowles.

In the second, post-film life of *Cabaret*, Australia finally got its first-class production, 13 years after the stillborn one. New York witnessed a revival in 1987 (22 October,

Imperial Theater) with Grey repeating his original rôle alongside Regina Resnik (Schneider), Alyson Reed (Sally), Gregg Edelmann (Cliff) and Werner Klemperer (Schultz) for a run of 254 performances, whilst a London repeat, which inserted the successful new numbers from the film-score into the stage script, featuring Vivienne Martin (Schneider), Kelly Hunter (Sally), Wayne Sleep (Emcee), Peter Land (Cliff) and Oscar Quitak (Schultz) was mounted at the Strand Theatre in 1986 (17 July) and ran through 322 performances. However *Cabaret* has found its home very largely in regional theatres where it has become one of the favourite items of the modern musical repertoire.

UK: Palace Theatre 28 February 1968; Austria: Theater an der Wien 14 November 1970; Australia: Doncaster Theatre Restaurant, ?1972; France: Théâtre du 8ème, Lyon 13 May 1986; Germany; Schauspielhaus, Düsseldorf 6 December 1986; Film: Allied Artists 1972
Recordings: original cast (Columbia), London cast (CBS), Austrian cast (Preiser), film soundtrack (ABC) etc

THE CABARET GIRL Musical comedy in 3 acts by George Grossmith and P G Wodehouse. Music by Jerome Kern. Winter Garden Theatre, London, 19 September 1922.

When the box-office for the happily successful *Sally* at George Grossmith's Winter Garden Theatre base finally faded away, almost overnight, the producer-performer decided to order his own musical play from that show's composer, Jerome Kern, as a hurried replacement. Using the in-topic of the newly popular style of entertainment called cabaret as a keystone, Grossmith and P G Wodehouse cobbled together a standard the-showgirl-and-the-aristocrat libretto whilst heading across the ocean to America and a meeting with the composer. They spent a week with him lyricking his tunes whilst he composed the melodies to the action numbers and finales supplied from their text, and, less than a fortnight later, the two Englishmen were able to get back on their ship and head home with a rehearsal script for *The Cabaret Girl*.

Sally star Dorothy Dickson was Marilynn Morgan (an open reference to original *Sally* star Marilynn Miller) who, in the course of the evening's little bit of action, gets herself both a job with the fictional equivalent of London's Hotel Metropole late-night cabaret and a handsome young aristocrat (Geoffrey Gwyther) in pretty much the same way as Broadway's musical heroines who had been crowding out the star dressing rooms of the Ziegfeld Follies and the homes of the upper 400 for the past few years. Grossmith paired with Leslie Henson (who was out ill for much of the run) as Messrs Gravvins and Gripps, the producers of the cabaret (and both 'Gr' for Grossmith) who meddle in everything going, permitting them to comick their way through the largest portion of the entertainment. They were equipped with a number 'Mr Gravvins, Mr Gripps' which borrowed happily from the *Ziegfeld Follies'* celebrated Gallagher and Shean song. It proved one of the most popular numbers of the show alongside two solos for Miss Dickson – 'Ka-lu-a', brought in from Kern's earlier *Good Morning, Dearie*, and 'Shimmy with Me', and a happy duo with Grossmith, 'Dancing Time'.

Pretty costumes and songs, the Winter Garden favourites and the theatre's reputation for lively entertain-

THE CABARET GIRL

JEROME KERN.

CHAPPELL

Plate 43. **The Cabaret Girl**: *The entertainment catchword of the moment went into the title of this piece, and its heroine's ambitions were a place in the cast of the Midnight Follies instead of the usual Ziegfeld variety.*

ment did more to help *The Cabaret Girl* to a fine run of 361 performances in London than any integral merits. However, set up by that run, it toured into 1925 and was given an Australian production, with Madge Elliott top-billing as the now renamed Flick Morgan and Alfred Frith and Cyril Ritchard heading the comedy, through two months in Melbourne (Her Majesty's Theatre 8 March 1924) and a little more in Sydney. The show was never, however, transported to America.

Australia: Her Majesty's Theatre, Sydney 25 August 1923
Recording: selection on *Jerome Kern in London* (WRC)

LE CABINET PIPERLIN Opérette in 3 acts by Hippolyte Raymond and Paul Burani. Music by Hervé. Théâtre de l'Athénée-Comique, Paris, 17 September 1897.

The agency of the title of *Le Cabinet Piperlin* was one which offered gentlemen insurance against the infidelity of their wives and, in this tale, it is threatened with bankruptcy because of the widely spread-about attractions of one young gentleman. The head of the agency can only set Colombe, his own very pretty wife, out to distract the young man in question from his expensive depredations.

Hervé had written a full musical score for the original production of *Le Cabinet Piperlin* at the Théâtre de l'Athénée in 1878, but the theatre's director, alarmed at the size of the musical content for what was intended to be a simple vaudeville à couplets, refused to use it in its entirety. Hervé withdrew the whole music and the piece was ultimately played, with great and international success, as a comedy without music. After the composer's death, his son, the actor and director Gardel, discovered the widowed score amongst his father's effects and the 20-

year-old opérette-cum-vaudeville was dusted off, its 22 musical pieces arranged by Hervé junior, and *Le Cabinet Piperlin* presented as a musical by Maurice Charlot at the Athénée-Comique. Guyon fils played Piperlin, with Augustine Leriche as Colombe, Vallières (Dardinel), Jannin (Vétiver), Baron fils (Roussignac) and Jeanne Petit (Zenaïde) through a run of 70 nights, prior to the show being mounted in both Budapest (ad Viktor Rákosi, Emil Makai) and in Vienna (ad Heinrich Bolten-Bäckers).

The original vaudeville was also used as the basis for the unsuccessful Adrian Ross/Hugo Felix musical *The Antelope* (Waldorf Theatre, London, 28 November 1908).

Hungary: Magyar Színház *B.A.L.E.K.* 3 December 1898, Austria: Lustspieltheater 25 December 1899

CABIN IN THE SKY Musical fantasy in 2 acts by Lynn Root. Lyrics by John Latouche. Music Vernon Duke. Martin Beck Theater, New York, 25 October 1940.

God has decided that Little Joe (Dooley Wilson), the no-good husband of the devout Petunia Jackson (Ethel Waters), has had his time on earth, but he listens to Petunia's pleas and allows the fellow six months in which to shape up. The Lord's General (Todd Duncan) is sent down from heaven to help the sinner on the path to repentance and improvement. However, there is competition for the body and soul of Little Joe in the shape of the infernal Lucifer (Rex Ingram) and it is he who wins. The man quarrels with his wife and shoots her dead. But foolishly faithful Petunia has the last word. At the gates of Saint Peter, she persuades the powers that be to find a place in heaven for her errant husband.

The sentimental fantasy of the book was accompanied by a score which was highlighted by Miss Waters's 'Taking a Chance on Love', a happy title duo for the Jacksons and 'Honey in the Honeycomb' delivered by co-choreographer Katherine Dunham as the slinky Georgia Brown, through a Broadway run of 156 performances. A film version of the tale made in 1943 with Miss Waters starred alongside Ingram, Eddie 'Rochester' Anderson and Lena Horne retained just those three numbers, complementing them with three pieces by Harold Arlen, two by Duke Ellington and one by Cecil Mack, Lew Brown and Ford Dabney.

The show was revived at off-Broadway's Greenwich Mews Theater in 1964 (21 January) with Rosetta LeNoire, Tony Middleton, Bernard Johnson and Ketty Lester featured in a version for which Duke extended his original score (46 performances).

Film: MGM 1943

Recordings: 1964 revival cast (Capitol), film soundtrack (Hollywood soundstage)

CAESAR, Irving [CAESAR, Isidor] (b New York, 4 July 1895). *No, No, Nanette* lyricist who never found another book musical hit.

After an early working life including stints as a stenographer and a press representative, Caesar toured as a performer in vaudeville before beginning to write song lyrics. His first major hit came when he wrote the words for George Gershwin's 'Swanee' (1918), introduced into the show *Sinbad* by Al Jolson, and he thereafter contributed a few lyrics to Ivan Caryll's *Kissing Time* (1918), more to the disastrous *Lady Kitty Inc* (1920) and to F C Coppicus's short-lived production of the American version of Hugo

Hirsch's *Die tolle Lola* (1921, *Lola in Love*) as well as to a number of revues, notably several editions of *The Greenwich Village Follies*.

He came securely into the musical theatre in 1923 when he took an 'additional lyrics' credit alongside Otto Harbach, Frank Mandel and Vincent Youmans on the score for *No, No, Nanette*. In spite of that credit, however, Caesar's portion of the words included those for most of the show's highlight songs: 'Tea for Two', 'I Want to Be Happy', 'Too Many Rings Around Rosie', 'You Can Dance With Any Girl At All' and the 'Where Has My Hubby Gone Blues'.

Caesar contributed some additional material to a second international hit in *Mercenary Mary* and worked on the naïvely appealing *Honeymoon Lane* with and for Eddie Dowling, but none of the other original stage musicals with which he was subsequently involved as lyricist, and occasionally as a librettist, as a re-rewriter with or without credit, or even as a composer, brought him anything like the same success. *Yes, Yes, Yvette* (in which he placed his song 'I'm a Little Bit Fonder of You') did not live up to its predecessor, Romberg's *Nina Rosa* found its major success when its lyrics were rewritten in French, Caesar's adaptation of Robert Katscher's Continental hit revusical comedy *Die Wunder-Bar*, which had run over 200 performances at the Savoy in London, into a vehicle for Al Jolson, was not a hit in New York, and it was Harry Graham's London translation of *White Horse Inn* (*Im weissen Rössl*) which became the standard English-language one rather than Caesar's edition, written for the vastly spectacular Center Theater production in New York. His final Broadway appearance was as producer, librettist, co-lyricist and composer of the unsuccessful *My Dear Public* (1943).

Caesar wrote elsewhere for revue and films, and his song successes included several in the 'Swanee' vein ('My Mammy', with music by Walter Donaldson, 'Yankee Doodle Blues', 'Is it True What They Say about Dixie?', 'Dixie Rose'), 'That Funny Melody', Joseph Meyer and Roger Wolfe Kahn's 'Crazy Rhythm' (*Here's Howe*), and Youmans's 'Sometimes I'm Happy', interpolated into the show *Hit the Deck*, all of which later appeared in various compilation shows.

1920 **Lady Kitty Inc** (Paul Lannin/w Melville Alexander/ Edward A Paulton) Ford's Opera House, Baltimore 16 February

1922 **Lola in Love** (*Die tolle Lola*) English version (Scranton, Pa)

1923 **No, No, Nanette** (Vincent Youmans/w Otto Harbach/ Frank Mandel, Harbach) Garrick Theater, Detroit 23 April;, Palace Theatre, London 11 March 1925

1924 **In Dutch** (Joseph Meyer, Alfred Newman, William Daly/w William Cary Duncan) Newark, NJ, 22 September

1924 **Betty Lee** (Louis Hirsch, Con Conrad/w Harbach/Harbach) 44th Street Theater 25 December

1925 **The Bamboula** (Albert Szirmai/w Douglas Furber/Guy Bolton, Harry Vernon) His Majesty's Theatre, London 24 March

1926 **Sweetheart Time** (Meyer, Walter Donaldson/Harry B Smith) Imperial Theater 19 January

1926 **Honeymoon Lane** (James T Hanley/w Eddie Dowling) Knickerbocker Theater 20 September

1926 **Betsy** (Hart, Rodgers/ w David Freeman) New Amsterdam Theater 28 December

1927 **Talk About Girls** (ex-*Suzanne*) (Stephen Jones, Harold Orlob/J H Booth, William Cary Duncan) Waldorf Theater 14 June

1927 **Yes, Yes, Yvette** (Phil Charig, Ben Jerome) Harris Theater 3 October

1928 **Here's Howe** (Roger Wolfe Kahn, Meyer) Broadhurst Theater 1 May

1929 **Polly** (Charig/w Guy Bolton, Arthur Hammerstein) Lyric Theater 8 January

1930 **Ripples** (Oscar Levant, Szirmai et al/w Graham John/William Anthony McGuire) New Amsterdam Theater 11 February

1930 **Nina Rosa** (Romberg/Harbach) Majestic Theater 20 September

1931 **[The] Wonder Bar** (*Die Wunder-Bar*) revised English version w Aben Kandel (Nora Bayes Theater)

1933 **Melody** (Romberg/Edward Childs Carpenter) Casino Theater 14 February

1936 **White Horse Inn** (*Im weissen Rössl*) English lyrics (Center Theatre)

1943 **My Dear Public** (Gerald Marks/w Sam Lerner) 46th Street Theater 9 September

LA CAGE AUX FOLLES Musical in 2 acts by Harvey Fierstein based on the play of the same name by Jean Poiret. Music and lyrics by Jerry Herman. Palace Theater, New York, 21 August 1983.

Jean Poiret's play, first produced at Paris's Palais-Royal in 1973, had a seven-year run (2,467 performances) there prior to being made into an equally successful film and then, after many and lavishly reported problems, writings and re-writings, into a musical.

Georges (Gene Barry) and Albin (George Hearn) run a night-club, 'La Cage aux Folles', at Saint-Tropez, where the feature is a travesty floor show with Albin, otherwise Zaza, as the glittering star. Albin's tantrums apart, theirs is a loving ménage, and it is even blessed with a son, Jean-Michel (John Weiner), the result of a small aberration of Georges's with a chorus girl a couple of decades previously. However, that son has now got to the age where he wishes to marry. He wishes to marry a girl, and he has to introduce Anne Dindon (Leslie Stevens) and her parents to his parents, about whom he has lied a little. Lying was necessary, as Anne's father (Jay Garner) is a local politician of a staunchly reactionary breed who is not likely to appreciate that his future son-in-law's mother is a man. Albin is to be demoted to Uncle Al for the night but, when Jean-Michel's real mother refuses to appear, he descends on the party as a boundingly impressive maman. A series of farcical events leads up to his exposure, Jean-Michel and Anne join Georges in standing by him, and, with the press awaiting gloatingly at the door to record his connection with the kind of people he has always condemned, deputé Dindon can only give in.

Herman's songs ranged from a veritable blowtorch-song for the 'betrayed' Albin, 'I Am What I Am', a number which soon made its way out of the show and into a hundred club acts and cabaret performances, to the gentle, loving strains of Georges's chanson 'Song on the Sand', the lilting 'With Anne on my Arm' for Jean-Michel (and later for Georges and Albin) and a singalong 'The Best of Times', headed by Albin and restaurateuse Jacqueline (Elizabeth Parrish), in a colourful score which illustrated its tale happily and effectively.

Allan Carr's Broadway production, directed by Arthur Laurents and choreographed by Scott Salmon, played through a successful 1,761 performances, and the show was subsequently taken up by overseas producers in a way

that few Broadway musicals of the past decades had been. However neither a production at London's Palladium, with Dennis Quilley and Hearn featured (301 performances), nor one in Australia, starring Keith Michell and Jon Ewing, turned out a success. A German adaptation (ad Erika Gesell, Christian Severin) mounted at the Theater des Westens with Gunter König and Helmut Baumann in the lead rôles, was followed by a remarkable small-theatre Austrian première at the Sommerfestspiele in Amstetten, with Joachim Kemmer and Wolf-Dietrich Berg playing Albin and Georges in a production which reproduced the atmosphere and choreography of the 'Cage aux Folles' much more excitingly than the vastness of stages such as the Palladium.

This resulted in the show spreading itself widely through German and Austrian provincial theatres, its prospects not hindered by the odd Intendant who welcomed the opportunity to pop into skirts in a way become more popular in the 1980s and 1990s than at any time since the Victorian era. *La Cage aux Folles* (sometimes literally translated as *Ein Käfig voller Narren*) was taken up from Amstetten to be mounted at the Vienna Volksoper in 1991 without equal felicity, but the ever-enterprising Budapest Fővárosi Operettszinház added the piece to its repertoire in 1991 with Sándor Németh (Georges) and Péter Haumann (Albin) initiating the lead rôles happily and Rome's Teatro Sistina welcomed an Italian version (9 October 1991) as *La Cage aux Folles* established itself as the most popular Broadway musical of its era on Central European stages.

Australia: Her Majesty's Theatre, Sydney, 2 March 1985; Germany: Theater des Westens *Ein Käfig voller Närren* 27 October 1985; UK: London Palladium 7 May 1986; Austria: Theater Amstetten *Ein Käfig voller Närren* 3 August 1989; Hungary: Fővárosi Operettszinház *Örult nők kektrece* 20 September 1991

Recordings: original cast (RCA), Australian cast (RCA), German cast (Polydor), Colombian cast (Talete) Italian cast (Carisch) etc

CAGE ME A PEACOCK Musical in 2 acts by Noel Langley based on his novel of the same name. Additional lyrics by Adam Leslie. Music by Eve Lynd. Strand Theatre, London, 18 June 1948.

A spicily comical little musical based on the South African novelist's saucy retelling of the Rape of Lucrezia legend. If the stage version needfully softened down the multiplicity of sexual variations explicitly implicit in the book, it still made for an enjoyable evening and a ten-month run in London's West End. Bill O'Connor was the organizing Mercury, Yolande Donlan the nymphet who becomes Lucrezia, Simon Lack played Tarquinius, and Roy Dean the shyly and bisexually obliging Casso.

With the 337 performances of *Cage Me a Peacock*, Eve Lynd notched herself up a spot as the first woman composer to have a musical staged in the West End since Liza Lehmann, nearly half a century earlier, supplying a set of songs for the show which included a successful single ('Time Alone Will Tell') and which, nearly half a century on, still allow her to hold the London long-run record for a musical composed by a woman.

During his time in Hollywood as a highly successful screenwriter (*The Wizard of Oz* etc), Langley had previously had his piece played in a musicalized version at

Los Angeles' Pelican Theater (23 April 1942) with a score by Bud McCreery.

CAGLIOSTRO IN WIEN Operette in 3 acts by F Zell and Richard Genée. Music by Johann Strauss. Theater an der Wien, Vienna, 27 February 1875.

Strauss's next Operette after *Die Fledermaus* did not come up to the expectations aroused by the success of its predecessor. *Cagliostro in Wien* centred itself, in name at least, on a colourful historical character, the 18th-century Italian adventurer and quack alchemist, Count Alexander Cagliostro (otherwise Joseph Balsamo). Apparently, in real life, a master impostor and involved in the affair of Marie-Antoinette's diamond necklace, here he was transported into a Viennese setting and a rather less lively adventure.

In the first act, set in a festival marking Vienna's hundred years of freedom from Turkish oppression in 1783, the charlatan Alessandro Cagliostro (Carl Adolf Friese), his wife Lorenza Feliciani (Marie Geistinger) and his servant, Blasoni (Alexander Girardi) come to dazzle the profitable people of Vienna with their tricks. During the festivities Lorenza attracts the attentions of the young Hungarian officer, Graf Stefan Fodor (Jani Szika), whilst his friend, the Rittmeister Baron Lieven (Eichheim), romances pretty Emilie (Karoline Finaly), niece of the wealthy widow, Frau Adami (Henriette Wieser). When Cagliostro tries to set up a big coup, Lorenza – her sensitivities awakened by her honest young admirer – refuses to help. Cagliostro agrees to divorce her, for a consideration, and sets his sights and talents on the winning of the heiress, Emilie. However, when Cagliostro attempts to drug Lieven whilst his marriage ceremony with Emilie goes ahead, Blasoni also proves faithless and, his plan in tatters, the alchemist flees from the law, leaving the young folk, and Fodor and Lorenza, together for a happy ending.

The opportunities of Strauss's score were given mainly to the leading lady. Lorenza had two fine numbers in the opening act: a gipsyish Zigeunerkind piece ('Wie glänzt dein Haar'), immediately followed by a Strofenlied ('Ja Cagliostro heisst der Mann') as well as a healthy share in the big first-act finale, working up her 'Beim Dudeln war'n Weana' through some high tessitura vocalizing and even a bit of yodelling to the climax of the act. The second act 'Mag alle Welt auch preisen der Alchimie' and the third-act waltz 'O süsses Wörtchen' gave her further opportunities. Cagliostro himself had little in the way of music, finding his best moment in a magic mirror trio with Emilie and her mother who, in her turn, had a second-act romanze ('Bald sind die Künzeln alle Weg') and got involved in some delightful cod wooing with Blasoni in the waltzing 'Ihnen fliegendurchs Leben an Ihnen Seite'. Fodor made the most of an entry song on horseback and joined Lorenza in the big duet of the evening, the hard and high 'Belieben sie mich zu anhören'.

Cagliostro was played 35 times en suite at the Theater an der Wien, and 14 more during the season, then left the repertoire. It was played at Berlin's Friedrich-Wilhelmstädtisches Theater the same year, and in its German version in both Budapest and Prague, but it proved one of the least liked of Strauss's stage works and seems to have gone little further. France merely got some bits of its score – mostly Lorenza's biggest and showiest bits – pasted together with some of *Die Fledermaus* and some freshly written bits to make up the music for the Parisian Strauss show *La Tzigane*.

The name of Strauss, however, persuaded people to persist with the piece. In 1881 the Theater an der Wien brought *Cagliostro* back in a new production which was played just seven times, the Wiener Bürgertheater mounted a new version by Ludwig Herzer, with the music re-arranged by Erich Wolfgang Korngold, which featured Jacob Feldhammer as Cagliostro, Ida Russka as Lorenza Feliciana and Mizzi Zwerenz as 'the rich hostess of the 'Blauen Insel' inn' and lasted all of 17 performances, and there were other periodic and mostly hacked-about revivals in Germany, including a version by the indefatigable rewriter Gustav Quedtenfeldt (w Karl Tutein) under the title of *Verzaubertes Wien* (Danzig, 3 May 1941). However, in spite of the name of Strauss on the billhead, the piece resolutely refused to go, no more so that when a mannered, poppy version, which was scarcely a version, was mounted at Vienna's Ronacher in 1986 (22 May).

The name of Cagliostro had become, in the 19th century, synonomous with the archetypical charlatan, and the adventures attached to his name had little or nothing to do with his real life. But it seems that Eugène Scribe and Vernoy de Saint-Georges stayed rather closer to history – or at least to the accepted tales – than the Viennese librettists were to do in a *Cagliostro* set as an opéra-comique by Adolphe Adam and mounted at Paris's Opéra-Comique in 1844 (10 February).

Germany: Friedrich-Wilhelmstädtisches Theater 18 September 1875; Hungary: Deutschige Theater in der Wollgasse May 1876

CAHILL, Marie (b Brooklyn, NY, 7 February ?1870; d New York, 23 August 1933). Cheerful comic star of the early 20th-century American stage.

After early beginnings playing in stock, Miss Cahill's young career embraced farce-musical in New York (Hoyt's *A Tin Soldier*, McKenna's *Flirtation* with Harrigan and Hart), an appearance at the Paris Théâtre de la Gaîté, entertaining as a guest act in the musical comedy *Morocco Bound* at London's Shaftesbury Theatre, and touring burlesque around America (Blanche Calvé Santootsie in *Excelsior Jr*, Lyric Theater, New York, 1895) before she established herself as a successful musical comedienne and, ultimately, a star on Broadway.

She appeared in a comic song-and-dance rôle in Victor Herbert's *The Gold Bug* (1896, Lady Patty Larceny), paired with Sadie Kirby as one of the music-hall Gelatine Sisters in the Broadway staging of the British musical *Monte Carlo*, played a baddie alongside Raymond Hitchcock in *Three Little Lambs* (1899, Phyllis Argyle), took to vaudeville burlesque with the Agoust family jugglers in *Star and Garter* (1900, Mme Piquet) and interpolated much the same kind of comedy and the song 'Nancy Brown', with considerable benefit to the show's receipts, into Harry B Smith's rather more structured *The Wild Rose* (1902, Vera von Lahn).

Miss Cahill appeared as Aramantha Dedincourt in *The Chaperons* (1902) and then moved firmly on to stardom in the title-rôle of *Sally in Our Alley* (1902), in which she made a particular hit with the song 'Under the Bamboo Tree'. She repeated this success the following year in a show named for her earlier hit number, *Nancy Brown*

('Congo Love Song'). However, her penchant for giving her own performance and her own songs in no matter what book-musical context resulted in a showdown with Victor Herbert and her removal from the star comedy rôle of his *It Happened in Nordland* (1904, Katherine Peepfogle). Thereafter she stuck starrily to such less musically structured shows as *Moonshine* (1905, Molly Moonshine, 'I'm a' Lookin'"), an adaptation of the play *My Wife's Husband* as *Marrying Mary* (1906, Mary Montgomery, 'I Love the Last One Best of All'), *The Boys and Betty* (1908, Betty Barbeau) and *Judy Forgot* (1910, Judy Evans) under the management of her husband, *Nancy Brown* producer Daniel V Arthur, whilst being served as to her songs principally by Silvio Hein, Cole and Johnson, and Benjamin Hapgood Burt.

In 1912 Miss Cahill appeared as Little Buttercup in a starry New York *HMS Pinafore* and as Celeste Deremy in an americanized version of Heuberger's successful Viennese Operette *Der Opernball*, in 1915 she starred opposite Richard Carle in the maiden Guy Bolton/Jerome Kern musical, *Ninety in the Shade*, and in 1919 she decorated George Hobart and Herbert Hall Winslow's *Just Around the Corner* with several songs. In 1930 she and Carle took their last Broadway bows together in *The New Yorkers* (Gloria Wentworth).

A strong, healthy little comedienne of buxom proportions and a very positive personality, she won most of her success by simply playing and singing herself, but she proved equally, in several shows, that she was capable of acting a rôle as well as simply being a star.

CAHN, Sammy [COHEN, Samuel] (b New York, 18 June 1913; d New York, 16 January 1993). Top filmland songwriter whose stage career was less productive.

Originally a violinist, the young Cahn joined Saul Chaplin in organizing a dance band, and he moved into songwriting when the theme song they wrote for themselves, 'Rhythm is My Business', found success above and beyond its original use. Thereafter, Cahn turned out the lyrics for a large number of popular songs ('Three Coins in a Fountain', 'Thoroughly Modern Millie', 'The Tender Trap', 'High Hopes', 'Love and Marriage', 'My Kind of Town', 'It's Been a Long, Long Time', 'Five Minutes More', 'Call Me Irresponsible', 'The Second Time Around', 'The Things We Did Last Summer', 'All the Way' etc), including many for the motion picture world which rewarded him with four Academy Awards. He also made several incursions into the musical theatre, the first and the last of which in person. He was seen deputizing for the show's star comedian in the bootless Philadelphia tryout of his earliest stage musical, *Glad To See You*, and in his elder years appeared performing his own works with a small supporting group variously as *Words and Music* and *Sammy Cahn's Songbook* in New York and London. Only *High Button Shoes* of the book musicals to which he contributed, however, proved a genuine success.

Cahn also combined with James van Heusen on a television musical version of Thornton Wilder's play *Our Town*.

1944 **Glad To See You** (Jule Styne/Fred Thompson, Eddie Davis) Shubert Theater, Philadelphia 13 November
1947 **High Button Shoes** (Styne/Stephen Longstreet) New Century Theater 9 October
1964 **Les Poupées de Paris** (James van Husen) puppet-show World's Fair 22 April
1965 **Skyscraper** (van Husen/Peter Stone) Lunt-Fontanne Theater 13 November
1966 **Walking Happy** (van Husen/Roger O Hirson, Ketti Frings) Lunt-Fontanne Theater 26 November
1970 **Look to the Lilies** (Styne/Leonard Spiegelglass) Lunt-Fontanne Theater 29 March
1980 **An April Song** (Mitch Leigh/Albert Marre) John Drew Theater of Guild Hall 25 August

Autobiography: *I Should Care* (Arbor House, New York, 1974)

CAILLAVET, G[aston] A[rman] de (b Paris, 15 March 1870; d Essendièras, 15 January 1915).

The author of a richly successful list of plays and libretti, de Caillavet and the partner de plume of most of his career, Robert de Flers, were regarded as the most cultured and spirituel of humorists and theatrical authors of their time. The heart of their musical theatre work consisted basically of four much-admired opéras-bouffes, set to music by Claude Terrasse (*Les Travaux d'Hercule, Le Sire de Vergy, M de la Palisse, Paris,ou le bon juge*), in which they tickled Grecian and Gallic antiquity with the same kind of verve that Crémieux, Tréfeu, Meilhac and Halévy had done in Offenbachian days. They also supplied the text for a much-liked little Terrasse opérette, *Chonchette*, and libretti for two pieces for André Messager: a light operatic adaptation of de Musset's *Le Chandelier* entitled *Fortunio*, and a dramatization of a piece by Charles Nodier as the text to the légende lyrique *Béatrice* (Théâtre de Monte Carlo, 21 March 1914). Both of these, although distinctly different in tone, were played at the Opéra-Comique. Their last works for the musical stage, before de Caillavet's premature death, were the enormously successful French adaptations of *Die lustige Witwe* and *Der Graf von Luxemburg*.

The plays of de Caillavet and de Flers were subsequently used as the bases for a number of musical comedies: their 1906 comedy *Miquette et sa mère* (1906) was the source for Fall's *Das Puppenmädel, Le Roi* (1908), which had already been illustrated with some music by Emmanuel Arène on its original production, was made into a full scale musical comedy by Ralph Benatzky under the title *Majestät-privat* (Theater an der Wien 18 December 1937), an Italian musical, *Primarosa*, was taken from their *Primerose* (1911), whilst *La Belle Aventure* (1914) became the source for *In der Johannisnacht* (Jean Gilbert/Robert Gilbert, Thalia Theater, Hamburg 1 July 1926).

1901 **Les Travaux d'Hercule** (Claude Terrasse/w Robert de Flers) Théâtre des Bouffes-Parisiens 7 March
1902 **Chonchette** (Terrasse/w de Flers) 1 act Théâtre des Capucines 11 April
1903 **Le Sire de Vergy** (Terrasse/w de Flers) Théâtre des Variétés 16 April
1904 **M de la Palisse** (Terrasse/w de Flers) Théâtre des Variétés 2 November
1906 **Paris, ou le bon juge** (Terrasse/w de Flers) Théâtre des Capucines 18 March
1907 **Fortunio** (André Messager/w de Flers) Opéra-Comique 5 June
1908 **La Veuve joyeuse** (*Die lustige Witwe*) French version w de Flers (Théâtre Apollo)
1911 **Le Comte de Luxembourg** (*Der Graf von Luxemburg*) French version w de Flers (Théâtre Apollo)

Plate 44. **Cairo**: *The famous bacchanale finale of Act II, choreographed by Fokine for America ... and redone by Espinosa for London.*

CAIRO Mosaic in music and mime in 3 acts and 11 scenes by Oscar Asche. Music by Percy Fletcher. Century Theater, New York, as *Mecca*, 4 October 1920.

Oscar Asche's successor to *Chu Chin Chow* did not, as might have been expected, make its first appearance on the stage of Her Majesty's Theatre, London, but that was only because there was no question of closing the lucrative *Chu Chin Chow*, which was running on strongly there towards its record-breaking total of performances. Instead, it was *Chu Chin Chow*'s American producers, F Ray Comstock and Morris Gest, who mounted *Mecca*, and Lionel Braham, Gladys Hanson and John Doran who introduced the rôles that Asche had written for himself, his wife Lily Brayton and *Chu Chin Chow*'s most valuable star, Courtice Pounds, at Broadway's Century Theater. These rôles were, not unnaturally, written to be as like to those of the previous hit as was possible in an original tale which, even more than its predecessor, seemed to owe a good deal to Eddie Knoblock's *Kismet*.

Charlatan Ali Shar (Braham), his pretty daughter Zummurud (soprano Hannah Toback) and his clown (Doran) come to Cairo and get mixed up in the power struggle between the young Sultan (Orville R Caldwell) and the evil Nur al-Din (Herbert Grimwood) when the Sultan falls in love with and weds Zummurud. The Lily Brayton rôle, like that in *Chu Chin Chow*, was one of a dramatically vengeful non-singing lady. Hanson played the Princess Shazarad, who seeks out and revenges herself on the murderer of her son, who is, of course, the wicked Wazir. Similarly, another wily easterner part, a Chinese spy called Wei San Wei, was provided for Frank Cochrane (and played on Broadway by Thomas Leary) paired with a

comic-feminine counterpart, Wei Wa Shi, as played by tiny Ida Mülle.

The other parallel between *Mecca* and *Chu Chin Chow* was in its production values. If the earlier show had been spectacular, the new one was super-spectacular. Asche, unable to direct it himself because of his rôle in *Chu Chin Chow*, gave way to his faithful lieutenant E Lyall Swete who had staged Broadway's *Chu Chin Chow*. London's Joseph and Phil Harker were again hired to do the scenery, top British designer Percy Anderson was teamed with Alice O'Neil and Leon Bakst for the costumes, and ballet choreographer Michel Fokine set to create the vast, spectacular dance routines. The result was stunning, and hailed all round as the most vivid piece of spectacular entertainment ever seen on the Broadway stage, with Fokine's second-act closer, a balletic bacchanale of semi-(for the time)-naked easterners, proving the gasp-worthy highlight of the night.

Mecca played 130 nights on Broadway, and the following year duly followed *Chu Chin Chow* onto the London stage. Asche, Miss Brayton, Pounds and Cochrane all took up 'their' parts, Fedora Rozelli was the soprano, Gracie Leigh the comedienne, and the dances were redone by Espinosa. But the title was different. In spite of the fact that the word *Mecca* had been used as a brand-name for everything from cafés to constipation cures, someone was able to convince the Lord Chamberlain that it would be indecent to call a musical play by the name of the holy city of Islam. So *Mecca* became *Cairo*. Once again, the show's production won wild reactions, rather masking the fact that Asche's dialogue and lyrics were pretty creaky stuff and that Fletcher had not succeeded in turning out anything to equal the favourite songs of *Chu Chin Chow*. *Cairo* played 287 times in London, and Asche then sold off his scenery and costumes to Australia's J C Williamson Ltd and set off to the southern hemisphere to play what would be the last performances of his show. He presented *Cairo* for eight weeks in Sydney and then for a further seven weeks in Melbourne (Her Majesty's Theatre 23 December 1922) before switching to *Julius Caesar* and *Chu Chin Chow* for the last five weeks of his engagement.

UK: His Majesty's Theatre 15 October 1921; Australia: Her Majesty's Theatre, Sydney 16 September 1922

CALDWELL, Anne (b Boston, 30 August 1867; d Beverly Hills, Calif, 22 October 1936).

After an early career as a performer and a brief attempt at composing, during which she and her husband, James O'Dea (b Hamilton, Ont, 25 December 1871; d Rockville Center, NY, 12 April 1914), had songs included in the English import *Sergeant Brue* (1905, 'Every Saturday Afternoon'), the Casino Theater's *The Social Whirl* (1906) and Sam and Lee Shubert's juvenile show *The Top of the World* (1907), Caldwell made a successful career as a prolific Broadway librettist and lyricist, without ever being responsible for the book of an enduring success or of more than a tiny handful of lyrics for songs which would become standards.

Her first musical comedy venture, following several attempts at playwriting (*A Model Girl, The Nest Egg, Uncle Sam*), was as co-librettist on *The Lady of the Slipper*, a starry Charles Dillingham variation on the Cinderella tale, with a score by Victor Herbert, which featured Elsie Janis and Montgomery and Stone at the head of its bill for a good run. Caldwell continued the association with Dillingham, Montgomery and Stone by supplying the lyrics and a share of the libretto for their next, and last, show, the Aladdin variant *Chin-Chin* and, after Montgomery's death, wrote all of Stone's subsequent star vehicles (*Jack o'Lantern, Tip Top, Stepping Stones, Criss Cross, Three Cheers*), first with Ivan Caryll ('Wait Till the Cows Come Home'), then with Jerome Kern and, lastly, with Raymond Hubbell.

During the production of *Go To It!*, an unfortunate musical adaptation of the old Hoyt comedy *A Milk White Flag*, at the Princess Theatre, Caldwell encountered the composer of that theatre's previous successes, Jerome Kern, and the two subsequently came together as author and composer of Dillingham's production *She's a Good Fellow*. This had a sufficient success for them to continue the collaboration over a series of shows which combined American variations on Continental and British farce plots with the kind of song-writers' scores currently popular and, often, also with a dose of star turns and even palpable variety acts. If the Caldwell/Kern shows are, in consequence, not remembered as the most replayable of the celebrated composer's stage pieces, they nevertheless included several reasonably long-running successes and some songs, to Caldwell's lyrics, which rate comparison with his more famous pieces ('The First Rose of Summer', 'Left All Alone Again Blues', 'Whose Baby Are You?', 'Ka-lu-a', 'Once in a Blue Moon').

In between these two major portions of her career, Caldwell authored a musical, *The Model Maid*, which served to launch swimming star Annette Kellerman as a musical comedy player and collaborated on several shows with composer Hugo Felix, who was staunchly attempting to repeat his early success with *Madame Sherry*. The pair did reasonably well both with a rehashed version of the Lajos Széll/Ákos Buttykay Hungarian hit *Csibészkirály*, here called *Pom-Pom*, and a happily-touring piece called *The Sweetheart Shop*, without pulling out a real hit. She also combined with Vincent Youmans on the numbers for *Oh, Please!*, which produced the song 'I Know That You Know', and had a latter-day success with the musical *Take the Air* which mixed a female air-pilot, some smugglers and the requisite amount of singing and dancing for a run of over 200 Broadway performances.

A plump and agreeable person with a tidy and efficient pen rather than any inspired touches, Caldwell proved her ability regularly to turn out material suitable to star performers such as Montgomery and Stone, on the one hand, and libretti in the popular light farcical style on the other, as well as composing unfussy, well-measured lyrics which satisfied such major figures as Dillingham, Caryll and Kern into repeated collaborations.

1907 **The Top of the World** (Manuel Klein/w James O'Dea/Mark Swan) Majestic Theater 19 October
1912 **The Lady of the Slipper** (Victor Herbert/O'Dea/w Lawrence McCarthy) Globe Theater 28 October
1914 **When Claudia Smiles** (Jean Schwartz) 39th Street Theater 2 February
1914 **Chin-Chin** (Ivan Caryll/w R H Burnside) Globe Theater 20 October
1915 **The Model Maid** (Raymond Hubbell) Atlantic City 26 January
1916 **Pom-Pom** (Hugo Felix) Cohan Theater 28 February
1916 **Go To It!** (A Baldwin Sloane/w John Golden, John Hazzard) Princess Theater 24 October
1917 **Jack o' Lantern** (Caryll/w Burnside) Globe Theater 16 October
1918 **The Canary** (Caryll/Louis Verneuil ad H B Smith) Globe Theater 4 November
1919 **She's a Good Fellow** (ex-*A New Girl*) (Jerome Kern) Globe Theater 5 May
1919 **The Lady in Red** (*Die Dame in Rot*) American version (Lyric Theater)
1920 **The Night Boat** (Kern) Liberty Theater 2 February
1920 **The Sweetheart Shop** (Felix) Knickerbocker Theater 31 August
1920 **Tip Top** (Caryll/w Burnside) Globe Theater 5 October
1921 **Good Morning, Dearie** (Kern) Globe Theater 1 November
1922 **The Bunch and Judy** (Kern) Globe Theater 28 November
1923 **Stepping Stones** (Kern) Globe Theater 6 November
1924 **Peg o' My Dreams** (Felix) Jolson Theater 5 May
1924 **The Magnolia Lady** (Harold Levey) Shubert Theater 25 November
1925 **The City Chap** (Kern/James Montgomery) Liberty Theater 26 October
1926 **Criss Cross** (Kern/w Otto Harbach) Globe Theater 12 October
1926 **Oh, Please!** (Vincent Youmans/w Harbach) Fulton Theater 17 December
1927 **Yours Truly** (Hubbell) Shubert Theater 25 January
1927 **Take the Air** (Dave Stamper/Gene Buck) Waldorf Theater 22 November
1928 **Three Cheers** (Hubbell/w Burnside) Globe Theater 15 October

CALL ME MADAM Musical comedy in 2 acts by Howard Lindsay and Russel Crouse. Lyrics and music by Irving Berlin. Imperial Theater, New York, 12 October 1950.

Irving Berlin's second vehicle, after the hugely successful *Annie Get Your Gun*, for star vocalist Ethel Merman cast her, much in the fashion that English comedienne Cicely Courtneidge had been cast a few years earlier in *Her Excellency*, as an interfering Ambassadress in foreign parts. Lindsay and Crouse's romantic-comic and wholly unsatirical tale presented the star as Mrs Sally Adams (a character said to be modelled on the real-life Pearl Mesta, rather than Miss Courtneidge), a famed and beloved Washington hostess to the powerful, who is sent as United States representative to the tiny and unprofitable duchy of Lichtenburg. Sally is very taken with local politician Cosmo Constantine (Paul Lukas) and she promptly starts to break the laws of diplomacy by using her position and her personal millions to get him the job of Prime Minister. Ambassadoring takes second place to romancing, and Sally's assistant Kenneth (Russel Nype) is not slow to follow his chief's example, taking a reciprocial fancy to the local Princess Maria (Galina Talva). As Prime Minister, Cosmo proudly refuses the millions of aid Sally has organized from America, and she is soon recalled for having trampled over diplomatic rules but, at the curtain fall, it is clear that she will soon be on her way back to Lichtenburg as Mrs Cosmo Prime Minister.

Berlin equipped his star with a swingeingly joyous set of numbers, declaring herself 'The Hostess With the Mostes'', leading the 'Washington Square Dance', expansively wooing Cosmo with the offer 'Can You Use Any Money Today?' and with the blunt information that 'The Best Thing for You Would Be Me', but scoring her best and most memorable moment, in countermelody, with her prognosis to the off-his-oats Kenneth, 'You're Just in Love'. The rest of the cast were well-equipped musically, too, with Kenneth and Maria joining sweetly in 'It's a Lovely Day Today', Cosmo welcoming everyone to 'Lichtenburg' and expressing his determination never to make a money match ('Marrying for Love'), and a comical bunch of visiting American politicians going into a stand-up routine insisting how 'They Like Ike'.

Leyland Hayward's production of *Call Me Madam* had a fine 644-performance run on Broadway, and sent out its national touring company with Elaine Stritch and Kent Smith at its head early in 1952. Shortly before this, Jack Hylton opened *Call Me Madam* at the London Coliseum where, with Billie Worth and Anton Walbrook at the head of proceedings and Jeff Warren and Shani Wallis as the juvenile pair, it scored another fine success through 485 performances before going on the British road. The following year Australia saw the show, with local *Annie Get Your Gun* star Evie Hayes following Miss Merman's path to the rôle of Sally alongside René Paul (Cosmo) and Sid Lawson (Kenneth) through four and a half Melbourne months and a similar period at Sydney's Theatre Royal (30 January 1954).

A 1953 film version, pairing Miss Merman with George Sanders and featuring Vera-Ellen and Donald O'Connor as the younger pair, retained much of the original score, but added one song culled from the 1940 *Louisiana Purchase* (which had not been used in its own film version) and, for some reason, replaced 'The Washington Square Dance' with an even earlier 'International Rag'.

Call Me Madam has been intermittently played in the decades since its first productions, and it won a full-scale London revival when a provincial production featuring TV soap-star Noele Gordon was transferred to the Victoria Palace in 1983 (14 March) for 72 performances.

UK: London Coliseum 15 March 1952; Australia: Her Majesty's Theatre, Melbourne 5 September 1953; Film: 1953 Twentieth Century-Fox

Recordings: original cast star (Decca), members of original cast (RCA), London cast (Columbia), Danish cast (Decca), film soundtrack (Decca)

LA CAMARGO Opéra-comique in 3 acts by Albert Vanloo and Eugène Leterrier. Music by Charles Lecocq. Théâtre de la Renaissance, Paris, 20 November 1878.

Charles Lecocq and producer Victor Koning followed up their great hit *Le Petit Duc* with another, if less durable, success in an opérette featuring as its heroine *La Camargo*, otherwise the historical 18th-century Belgian ballet dancer Marie-Anne de Cupis de Camargo. Mlle de Camargo (already the subject of a *La Camargo* by Dupuety and Fontan) underwent the usual kind of operetticization, lending her name to a character and an adventure that doubtless had little to do with her, as authors Vanloo and Leterrier cooked her into a tale with the equally historical, if (apparently deservedly) short-lived, French brigand Louis Mandrin.

Zulma Bouffar played the danseuse and Vauthier the brigand who, having fallen for her charms, first wins his way to her side backstage at the Opéra, disguised as nobleman, then by having her kidnapped and brought to his castle, and finally by getting himself hired as a detective under the orders of her accepted 'protector', the police chief Marquis de Pontcalé (Berthelier), with the mission to track himself down. Ultimately, Camargo – herself disguised as a little street singer – outwits Mandrin but, having had her revenge upon him for his deceits, helps him escape arrest at the final curtain.

Into the tale of Mandrin's pursuit of the dancer and Pontcalé's pursuit of the brigand, the authors wove a set of delicious rôles for the principal members of the Théâtre de la Renaissance company. Mily-Meyer, who had shot to the fore as la Petite Duchesse in the previous opérette, was the sparky little Colombe, daughter of Pontcalé's draper (Pacra) and affianced to the draper's son, Saturnin (Lary). Saturnin discovers womanhood in the person of Camargo and wants to postpone his wedding until he has had a chance to experience a worldly love affair, but after a couple of acts fetching and carrying for the star for no return, he is happy to settle down back in Lyon with Colombe. Marie Desclauzas followed up her Diane de Château-Lansac with a very different creation, the lavish créole 'Juana, princesse de Rio-Negro, from Santo Domingo, Antilllllllles!'. Persuaded she has been ravished by Mandrin during a robbery, she decides to make it her mission in life to reform the bandit, and goes round indemnifying all his victims until she discovers, disappointedly, that she wasn't ravished at all.

Lecocq's score was a typically tuneful one, with the heroine of the piece getting the most frequent opportunities, beginning with an entrance number ('Partout on me fête') and a rondo in the opening act, going on to a pretty plea ('Laissez-moi, monsieur le voleur'), a full ballet-pastorale ('Voici d'abord une bergère') rippling up to high C, and a duo ('Ce serait une vie heureuse') and couplets with Mandrin in the second, as well as a duo with Pontcalé and two pieces in her street-singer disguise (Duetto de Javotte et Margotte, Chanson de la marmotte en vie) in the last. Mily-Meyer had a pair of spunky little numbers, Pontcalé boasted about his talent for detective work in the Couplets de l'oeil and paired with his phoney 'assistant' to sing about 'La police, la justice', whilst Juana related her adventure ('Je dormais, tout dans le nature'), Saturnin pleaded his ignorance of sex in a sweet romance, and Mandrin and his bandits joined in some lively moments. The vocal balance in these was helped by the fact that two of the bandits were played by two of the prettiest young ladies of the company (Léa d'Asco, Mlle Piccolo) in travesty.

La Camargo was pronounced a success and held the stage for three months at the Renaissance. It was later remounted there (14 November 1881) with Hélène Chevrier in the title-rôle alongside Alfred Jolly (Pontcalé), Desclauzas, Vauthier, Mily-Meyer and Jannin (Saturnin). Then, rather curiously, it simply faded from the repertoire.

Outside France, things went little better. The piece was played in the repertoire of Maurice Grau's opéra-bouffe company in America with Paola Marié playing the dancer and Jouard the bandit alongside Mme Angèle (Juana), Mlle Grégoire (Colombe) and Mézières (Pontcalé), it was seen just six times in a German version at Austria's Theater an der Wien in 1879, and only in Budapest (ad Béla J Fái) did it become a genuine success when Lujza Blaha took up the all-singing, all-dancing, all-comedy prima donna rôle for a season of 25 performances.

Hungary: Népszinház *Kamargo* 28 March 1879; Austria: Theater an der Wien 9 December 1879; USA: Academy of Music 21 May 1880; Germany: Aachen 19 June 1880

Recordings: complete (Rare Recorded Editions)

CAMELOT

CAMELOT Musical in 2 acts by Alan Jay Lerner based on *The Once and Future King* by T H White. Music by Frederick Loewe. Majestic Theater, New York, 3 December 1960.

Camelot had the impossibly difficult task of following behind *My Fair Lady* in the opus of Lerner and Loewe, and it emerged from the trial with very considerable credit, in the face of much adversity.

Based on T H White's whimsical retelling of the Arthurian legend, the show presented a boyish and immature Arthur (Richard Burton) and a skittishly innocent Guenevere (Julie Andrews) brought together to grow into their positions as King and Queen, the patrons of the famous Round Table, and the representatives of all that is good and orderly in the world. Arthur's old tutor and protector, the magician Merlyn (David Hurst), is lured away by the spirit Nimüe, leaving the young man with only his own resources on which to rely in creating the best of all possible worlds. However, for all his goodness and all his efforts, he sees his queen falling helplessly in love with his best friend, Lancelot du Lac (Robert Goulet), and is eventually undone by the evil Morgan Le Fey (M'el Dowd) and her vicious son, Mordred (Roddy McDowall). Camelot and the ideals for which it stood were too good to last. Robert Coote appeared as a comical knight, Sir Pellinore, passing through the evening's action in his pursuit of the Questing Beast.

The score of the show brought forth several sentimental pieces which became favourites: Lancelot's ringing 'If Ever I Would Leave You', Guenevere's gentle 'I Loved You Once in Silence' and the King's ruminatings on 'How to Handle a Woman' whose lyric resulted in the axiom that loving is the best method. The romantic portions were contrasted by some more sprightly moments – Guenevere's disappointed prayer to her patron Saint over having never experienced any of the storybook excitements which a princess should have as part of 'The Simple Joys of Maidenhood', or the catalogue of ghastly fates she encourages her followers to propose for the irritatingly virtuous Lancelot in 'Take Me to the Fair' - and by some warmly picturesque ones, such as the description of 'Camelot', and some, such as Mordred's attack on 'The Seven Deadly Virtues', more hectic.

Staged with spectacular period lavishness, *Camelot* was an indubitable success, winning a little extra glamour from the well-publicized approval of President John Kennedy (who was said, by those who did not favour him, to compare himself and his America with Arthur and Camelot) and ran for 873 performances on Broadway. William Squire and Kathryn Grayson headed out the first American national tour, whilst J C Williamson Ltd mounted an Australian production in 1963 with Paul Daneman and Jacquelyn McKeever starred and designed even more luxuriantly than the original by John Truscott. It played at Her Majesty's, Melbourne (22 February 1964) for more than seven months and at Sydney's Her Majesty's thereafter (17 October 1964). As a result of this production's success, Truscott was retained to design Jack Hylton's London production, mounted with truly extravagant spectacle on the stage of the Theatre Royal, Drury Lane. Laurence Harvey and Elizabeth Larner appeared in the starring rôles with Barry Kent (Lancelot), Nicky Henson (Mordred) and Miles Malleson (Merlyn) in support through a run of 518 performances.

In 1967 a film version (again designed by Truscott) was made, with Richard Harris and Vanessa Redgrave starred, and a dubbed Franco Nero as Lancelot, and Harris later took up the rôle of King Arthur on the stage, touring it for many years through America, and playing it, in the wake of a revival with Burton and Christine Ebersole starred (New York State Theater 8 July 1980), on Broadway (Winter Garden Theater 15 November 1981), and in a sadly truncated and dilapidated state, in London (Apollo Victoria Theater 12 November 1982) and Australia (Sydney Entertainment Centre 24 September 1984). In 1992 Goulet – now graduated from Lancelot to Arthur – headed out a further touring company as *Camelot* began to show signs of making up ground even on *My Fair Lady* in the enduring popularity stakes.

A German-language version (ad Marcel Valmy) was seen for the first time in 1981.

Australia: Her Majesty's Theatre, Adelaide 30 November 1963; UK: Theatre Royal, Drury Lane 19 August 1964; Germany: Badische Staatstheater, Karlsruhe 3 October 1981; Film: 1967 Warner Brothers

Recordings: original cast (Columbia), London cast (HMV), film soundtrack (Warner Bros), London 1982 cast (TER)

CAMERON, Violet [THOMPSON, Violet Lydia] (b London, 7 December 1862; d Worthing, 25 October 1919). Top London musical star of the mid-Victorian era.

A niece, by a network of second marriages, of Lydia Thompson, and a cousin of the successful musical-comedy performers Violet and Florence Lloyd and of actress Zeffie Tilbury, Miss Cameron made her first appearances on the stage as a child performer, playing in burlesque and plays and, under a three-year contract, in children's rôles at Drury Lane. She is said to have sung Siebel in *Faust* at the age of twelve.

She toured with her uncle-in-law, Alexander Henderson, and appeared with Lydia Thompson in *Bluebeard* (Sister Ann), *Piff-Paff* (Joconde), *Robinson Crusoe* (Polly Hopkins) and *Oxygen* (Suzel) at the Folly Theatre, shifting into the French opéras-bouffes Henderson then staged (Pearline in *The Sea Nymph*, Antoinette in *La Créole*, Alexandrivoire in *L'Oeil crevé*) before being cast, as the company ingénue, in the juvenile rôle of their next production, *Les Cloches de Corneville*. The huge London success of that piece, and her winning performance as Germaine, made Violet a star, and she moved on to play in the rising Henderson's Strand Theatre productions in leading rôles in *Nemesis*, *Madame Favart* (Suzanne), *The Naval Cadet* (Inez Maria Estrella) and *Olivette* (Bathilde) whilst at the same time hitting the scandalous headlines by her alleged affair with the criminal Lefroy.

She made a second major hit when she starred as Bettina in *La Mascotte*, a third when she introduced London to the title-rôle of *Boccaccio*, and more as the original Gretchen to the *Rip van Winkle* of Fred Leslie and in the title-rôle of *Falka* in a four-year period in the early 1880s which were the remarkable peak of her career. She subsequently appeared in comic opera (*The Lady of the Locket*), burlesque (*The Vicar of Wideawakefield*, *Kenilworth*, *Lurline*) and was launched on a Broadway season in a version of *La Créole* entitled *The Commodore* and the burlesque *Kenilworth* financed by Hugh Cecil Lowther, otherwise Lord Lonsdale, with whom her name was scandalously linked, without the same success. A seven-month New York booking was cut to seven weeks, and Violet returned home suing her jealous husband (apparently responsible for breaking the scandal) for divorce on grounds of cruelty and slander.

Back in London, she starred in Lydia Thompson's production of *The Sultan of Mocha* (1887, Dolly) and succeeded to the rôle of Fraisette in *The Old Guard* whilst tales of her divorce (Lonsdale was co-respondent) filled the papers, and then took over as Faust in George Edwardes's *Faust up-to-Date* and as *Captain Thérèse*, in place of the insufficient Attalie Claire, with the Carl Rosa Company. She remained at the Prince of Wales Theatre to play Prince Giglio in *The Rose and the Ring* and Alan a Dale in the American comic opera *Robin Hood* (retitled *Maid Marian*), then moved to the Shaftesbury to appear as Adeline Dupret in the short-lived *La Rosière* and as Ethel Sportington in the musical comedy *Morocco Bound* (1893).

She starred in the title-rôle of the unfortunate light-operatic version of *The Green Bushes* known as *Miami*, and then took her distance from the musical stage, appearing for a while in variety and music halls before retiring. She returned to appear in revue at the Crystal Palace, as principal boy in the 1900 Drury Lane pantomime and, one last time, to play a Mother Superior with a wimple and a specially written song in Leslie Stuart's *The School Girl* in 1903.

Plate 45. **Violet Cameron**: *One of the most successful stars of London's Victorian musical stage.*

Her son, actor Cecil Cameron, married May Leslie Stuart, daughter of the composer, whilst her daughter, Doris Cameron, wed D'Oyly Carte vocalist Frederick Hobbs.

LE CANARD À TROIS BECS Opéra-bouffe in 3 acts by Jules Moinaux. Music by Emil Jonas. Théâtre des Folies-Dramatiques, Paris, 6 February 1869.

The most successful of Jonas's works for the theatre, *Le Canard à trois becs* was a piece in the extravagantly bouffe style of the 1860s. The three-beaked duck of the title is the mascot of the city of Ostend, and it is said that Flanders will be protected from the marauding armies of Spain as long as it survives. Three randy young Spaniards, Pasmotto (Mendasti), Spaniello (Marcel) and Chutentos (Speck), steal the bird, raising sufficient alarm for the burgomaster (Girardot), the entire city guard and the sea captain van Ostebal (Ange Milher), who has never yet been to sea, to set off unwillingly to protect their city. The trio's only objective is, theoretically, achieved – to get van Ostebal out of the way so they can chat up his daughter Madeleine (Mlle Massue), wife Marguerite (Mlle Lovato) and maid, Barbe (Mlle Daroux). But van Ostebal doesn't go: he chases the crooks on home ground. However, he gets slightly detracked, and whilst he stalks the inoffensive secretary (Chaudesaigue) of the burgomaster as a dangerous insurgent, and his maiden-lady sister, Sophronie (Adèle Cuinet) stalks Spaniello with amorous intent, the infidelties are all happily arranged. So is the duck, which ends up on the finale table.

The fellows, together and separately, had the jolliest time of the musical part of the evening. They launched a martial trio declaring 'Les Castiliens sont tous des frères', a tyrolienne trio with Spaniello yodelling happily away on the top line, and a piece describing 'la théorie de la sérénade' – 'pour composer une sérénade vous prenez le mot manola, vous y joignez celui d'alcade, grille, resille, et puis alza...' – and went through a comical ensemble in the final act, trying to hide the wretched duck ('Le canard l'a bien passée'). Spaniello also had his romantic moments, waylaying his prey in a first-act waltz duo, wooing her in the waltz Couplets de la fascination, and going solo in his Rondeau de la voyage. Van Ostebal blustered out his claims to fame ('Van Ostebal est un marin, un malin...') and made love to his wife in a fashion which compared poorly with what Spaniello had been offering shortly before, Sophronie gave out her Couplets de la rosière, Marguerite her Couplets de la cocotte and the chorus had its moment in a Patrol Chorus with a 'ra fla rra rra rra' refrain.

Le Canard à trois becs was well received in Paris, and, without quite placing itself in the very top row of revivable pieces after its fine first run, was nevertheless brought back at the Théâtre de la Renaissance in 1881 and again at the Bouffes-Parisiens in 1888. It was also widely seen through other theatrical centres, being played at Vienna's Carltheater for five performances in the repertoire of Eugène Meynadier's company, with Mme Matz-Ferrare and Christian featured, and later the same year in a German version at the Strampfertheater. London too got its first glimpse of the piece in the original French, sharing the Folies-Dramatiques company's bill with the second act of *Chilpéric*. It was hailed as 'one of the drollest specimens of the opéra-bouffe we have seen', and was duly mounted the following year in English (ad Charles Lamb Kenney) with Nita de Castro, Rose Bell, Harriet Coveney, George Honey, Edward Perrini and Charles Odell in the cast. The programme was filled out with Offenbach's *L'Île de Tulipatan* and the bill ran a good two months. America, on the other hand, saw the show in French, with a cast headed by Coralie Geoffroy, but did not pursue it into English.

In Hungary, *A háromcsórű kacsa* (ad Endre Latabár, Gábor Beödy Balogh) did exceedingly well. First mounted at the Budai Színkör with Elek Solymossy as van Ostebal, it was subsequently taken up by the Népszinház where, after a first production in 1876 with Lujza Blaha in the rôle of Margit, it was revived in 1882 (15 September) and again in 1888 (31 May) with Aranka Hegyi (Margit), Izsó Gyöngyi (van Ostebal), Sándor Dardai (Spaniello) and Vidor Kassai (van Bontrouche). The end of the 1880s more or less marked the end of the show's career, but

during its two decades – the palmy days of the opéra-bouffe – it had held its place amongst the most popular pieces of its kind.

Austria: Carltheater (Fr) 17 July 1871, Strampfertheater *Die Ente mit den drei Schnabeln* 18 November 1871; UK: Globe Theatre (Fr) 13 July 1872, Opera Comique *The Wonderful Duck* 31 May 1873; Hungary: Budai Színkör *A háromcsórű kacsa* 12 September 1872; USA: Lyceum Theater (Fr) 16 October 1875

THE CANARY *see* LE COFFRE-FORT VIVANT

CAN-CAN Musical in 2 acts by Abe Burrows. Music and lyrics by Cole Porter. Shubert Theater, New York, 7 May 1953.

A jolly piece of Parisian ooh-la-la built around a classic set of comic and romantic characters, and illustrated with a scoreful of American-in-Paris numbers which turned out a good percentage of durable favourites, *Can-Can* gave songwriter Cole Porter his second longest Broadway run without establishing itself internationally in the same way that the top-ranking *Kiss Me, Kate* had done.

The girls who dance the can-can at Montmartre's Bal du Paradis, run by la Môme Pistache (Lilo), are regularly arrested and regularly acquitted on morals charges, until the day a serious-minded new judge, Aristide Forestier (Peter Cookson), decides that the law is being made light of. He goes to Montmartre to see the law-breaking for himself and instead falls for Pistache. When he tries, with the utmost correctitude, to advise her, he gets caught and summarily debarred. Indignant at the injustice, he joins Pistache in the opening of a new venue with the plan that they will be arrested and brought to trial, thus allowing him to have, in open court, the say he has been denied by his peers. After a vicissitude or two, the pair stand up in court together to show the world that obscenity is in the eye of the beholder. The romantic plot was contrasted with a comic one which involved the dancer Claudine (Gwen Verdon) with a penniless bad artist called Boris (Hans Conried) and a randy art critic, Hilaire Jussac (Erik Rhodes).

The songs of *Can-Can* included Pistache's romantic 'I Love Paris' and 'C'est magnifique', the more pointed 'Never Give Anything Away (that you can sell)' and 'Live and Let Live', and a moving little number called 'Allez-vous en', whilst Aristide sang passively to a passing poule that 'It's All Right With Me' and the comical characters played up such pieces as the topico-comical 'Come Along With Me' and 'Never Be an Artist'. One of the highlights of the show was the Garden of Eden Ballet, staged as part of the entertainment at the Quat'z arts ball which closed the first act, and which put Gwen Verdon, dancing the central part, into prominence. Miss Verdon's threatening to steal the show resulted in her rôle being severely cut before opening, but she went ahead and stole it anyhow.

Cy Feuer and Ernest Martin's production of *Can-Can* ran for 892 performances on Broadway, during which time Prince Littler and Rodgers and Hammerstein (as Williamson Music Ltd) reproduced the show on the huge stage of the London Coliseum with Irene Hilda (Pistache), Gillian Lynne (Claudine), Edmund Hockridge (Aristide), Alfred Marks (Boris) and George Gee (Jussac) featured. London's version played 394 performances. Following the

Broadway run, the show went on the road in America with Rita Dimitri, Ronnie Cunningham and John Tyers in the leading rôles, whilst in Australia Sheila Arnaud (Pistache), William Newman, Eric Reiman and Eleanor Trieber featured in a good run at Melbourne's Her Majesty's Theatre and Sydney's Empire (12 May 1956).

A film, made under the same title, used Frank Sinatra, Shirley Maclaine, Louis Jourdan and Maurice Chevalier and eight of the show's musical pieces (plus three others from other Porter shows) attached to a different story which tried a little too hard to be another *Gigi*.

The huge success of *Kiss Me, Kate* in German-language theatres helped to win *Can-Can* (ad Robert Gilbert) a number of productions in Austria and Germany. In 1965 the first of these was seen in Stuttgart, and the show was subsequently seen in Rostock (1 June 1968) and at Vienna's Theater an der Wien, where it played a season of 52 performances the same year. Back home, *Can-Can* reappeared in a short-lived 1981 production featuring Zizi Jeanmaire in the rôle of Pistache (Minskoff Theater 30 April, 5 performances) whilst in 1988 London hosted a heavily revised version (ad Julian More Strand Theatre 28 October 1988) with an international star cast including America's Donna McKechnie (Pistache), France's Bernard Alane (Aristide), Britain's Janie Dee (Claudine) and Ireland's Milo O'Shea (Jussac) and the score expanded with a songbookful of Porter numbers belonging to other shows through 102 performances.

The tale of the the can-can, its banning, and the bringing of its exponents before the law courts had been used nearly a century earlier as the subject of the Hungarian operett *Cancan a törvényszék előtt* (the can-can before the tribunal) written by István Friebeisz Rajkai, composed by Jakab Jakóbi, and produced at the Budai Népszínház 17 April 1864 and at Vienna's Theater an der Wien (*Der Cancan vor Gericht*) 22 June 1865. This later became the source for the comic dance piece *Farsangi kaland* (Népszínház 8 March 1878), and was also reorganized as a Spanish zarzuela by Francisco Asenjo Barbieri (*El proceso del can-can*, 1873).

UK: London Coliseum 14 October 1954; Australia: Her Majesty's Theatre, Melbourne 29 October 1955; Germany: Staatstheater, Stuttgart 28 August 1965; Austria: Theater an der Wien 2 March 1968; Film: 1960 Twentieth Century Fox
Recordings: original cast (Capitol), London cast (Parlophone), film soundtrack (Capitol), London 1988 version (Virgin), Mexican cast (RCA), etc

LA CANCIÓN DEL OLVIDO   Zarzuela in 1 act and 4 scenes by Federico Romero and Guillermo Fernández Shaw. Music by José Serrano. Teatro Lírico, Valencia 17 November 1916.

One of the most popular 'genero chico' pieces amongst those zarzuelas which use traditional international operetta plot and character elements rather than the Spanish 'slice-of-life' as their material. *La canción del olvido* is set in turn-of-the-18th century Naples, and its heroine is a Roman princess, Rosina. Rosina has fallen in love with a swash-unbuckling army captain called Leonello and has followed him to the Neapolitan countryside where she finds that he is busy setting his sights at the courtesan Flora Goldoni. In good operettic style, Rosina gets herself a bundle of disguises and a tenor helpmate, the troubadour Toribio,

and by the end of the fourth scene she has won her soldier. The principal pieces of Serrano's score were Leonello's womanizing 'Junto al puente de la Peña' and the 'song of oblivion' of the title ('Marinella, Marinella').

Recordings: Alhambra, Zafiro, Columbia, Hispavox

CANDIDE   Comic operetta in 2 acts by Lillian Hellman based on the satire by Voltaire. Lyrics by Richard Wilbur. Additional lyrics by John Latouche and Dorothy Parker. Music by Leonard Bernstein. Martin Beck Theater 1 December 1956. Revised version by Hugh Wheeler with additional lyrics by Stephen Sondheim, Chelsea Theater Centre, 19 December 1973; Broadway Theater, 8 March 1974.

Voltaire's extravagant, satiric saga, with its mockery of 'the best of all possible worlds' and the innocent hero who believes in such a thing, was at first made into a comic operetta by playwright Lillian Hellman with lyrics largely by Richard Wilbur set to music by Leonard Bernstein. The resultant piece was produced by Ethel Linder Reiner and Lester Osterman jr at New York's Martin Beck Theater with Robert Rounseville (Candide), Barbara Cook (Cunégonde), Max Adrian (Pangloss) and Irra Petina (Old Lady) featured, but failed in 73 performances. A London version mounted in 1959, under the management of Linnit and Dunfee, with Denis Quilley, Mary Costa, Laurence Naismith and Edith Coates in the principal rôles fared even less well and closed after 60 performances.

In 1974, a rewritten version by Hugh Wheeler, which emphasized the comic extravagances of the text and made its black points through humour rather than a less attractive dogmatism, was produced by Harold Prince and the Chelsea Theater Center in Brooklyn, New York. The musical score had been altered along with the text, and additional lyrics supplied by Stephen Sondheim. Prince mounted the now highly colourful show on a set consisting of multiple acting areas, arranged around the audience, and this time the reaction was positive. This production of *Candide* moved to the Broadway Theater, which was suitably reconstructed to allow the same style of presentation, and it remained there for 740 performances, establishing the show and its new version as one of the most interesting and intelligent of its time.

At the Castle Thunder-ten-Tronck, Westphalia, the philosopher Dr Pangloss (Lewis J Stadlen) teaches the baronial family's daughter Cunégonde (Maureen Brennan), son Maximilian (Sam Freed) and bastard nephew Candide (Mark Baker) his optimistic creed that all is for the best in the best of all possible worlds. He teaches rather more physical things to the maidservant Paquette (Deborah St Darr). The world soon begins to test this maxim to the full. First Candide is expelled from the castle for experimenting with his cousin in the garden, then Westphalia is invaded, Cunégonde raped 98 times and Candide carried off by Bulgarians, strolling players and then merrily flagellated by the Inquisition, before he meets up with his beloved Cunégonde again. Cunégonde has put her 98 experiences to good use by becoming a fashionable courtesan, but Candide accidentally kills her two protectors and, helped and hindered by an Old Lady (June Gable) with an alarmingly physical history, they head off to find a piece of the world in which they can peaceably appreciate Pangloss's words of wisdom together. From

Cadiz to Cartagena, from a monastery to El Dorado, via piratical attacks, repeated ravishment all round, and separations and encounters not only with each other but with Maxmilian and Paquette (who apparently escaped the massacre at Thunder-ten-Tronck after all) and the Old Lady, they arrive by separate paths – she as an odalisque, he with the gold of El Dorado to buy her release – in Turkestan. There, their optimism and philosophy still intact in spite of all, they find the Wisest Man in the World, who seems to be Pangloss but who has changed his dicta. He is now keen on the work ethic, so Candide and Cunégonde, being of the dutiful kind, settle down blissfully on a little farm with a cow. It promptly drops dead. The world is just as good as it ever was.

The score of *Candide* was one which thoroughly merited the description of comic operetta although, by this stage, opéra-bouffe might have been nearer the point. It included ensemble and orchestral music of a quality and adventurousness rarely seen on the postwar musical stage, as well as some magnificently funny solo set pieces of which Cunégonde's extravagantly coloratura burlesque of the operatic jewel song, 'Glitter and Be Gay', proved the take-out tune. Elsewhere, the score ranged from the opening, innocent conviction of the young folk that 'Life is Happiness Indeed' and their discovery of sex in 'Oh Happy We' to a bouncing celebration of the Inquisition's 'Auto da fé' and the Old Lady's encouraging description of her sliced-up charms in 'I am Easily Assimilated'. The nasty Governor of Cartagena (doubled in this version by the actor playing Pangloss) serenaded a befrocked Maximilian ('My Love') and led a lively 'Bon Voyage' as he sent Candide and his friends off to sea in a leaky boat, whilst a moment of peaceful contrast amid the hurly-burly and horrors came in a sweet duet for two El Doradian sheep. Several numbers from the original version (Candide's Lament, 'Quiet', the waltz 'What's the Use?' etc) were omitted or revamped in the revised *Candide*, and three new numbers inserted.

The new *Candide* made its way slowly around the world. It was produced in Vienna in 1976, in a version by Marcel Prawy based closely on the Chelsea Theater Centre text, under the direction of Larry Fuller, with Heinz Marecek (Pangloss), Heinz Ehrenfreund (Candide), Melanie Holliday (Cunégonde) and Blanche Aubry (Old Lady), and mounted at Birmingham Repertory Theatre in England in a production which was then played at the Edinburgh Festival of 1981 with Nickolas Grace (Pangloss), Rosemary Ashe (Cunégonde), Mark Wynter (Maximilian), Nichola McAuliffe (Old Lady) and William Relton (Candide), but an Australian production mounted at Sydney's Seymour Centre, prior to a Melbourne season at the Comedy Theatre (19 July 1982), confused camp with bouffe in its staging, and failed to take.

In 1982 an attempt was made, at the New York City Opera, to reshape the show yet again, reusing parts of the original score which had been abandoned, but that version was itself abandoned after that production, and yet another remake practised on the show for a Scottish Opera production, subsequently played at London's Old Vic (6 December 1988 ad John Wells, 34 performances), which attempted to soften the comical opéra-bouffe aspect and replace it with more of the black moralizing of the first *Candide*. Grace, Marilyn Hill Smith (Cunégonde), Mark

Baker (Candide) and Ann Howard/Patricia Routledge (Old Lady) featured in a *Candide* which had lost more than a little of the cutting edge and wisdom which, as authors like Gay and the best librettists of Offenbach have shown, is rarely so effectively displayed as in the bouffe idiom.

A second German adaptation (ad Johannes Felsenstein) was produced in Germany in 1989, whilst in English-speaking countries the show made its way resolutely into the opera houses which can afford to give its orchestral textures the values needed if not always the vital comedy and the most suitable weight of voices.

UK: Saville Theatre 30 April 1959; Austria: Stadthalle, Vienna 5 August 1976; Australia: York Theatre, Seymour Centre, Sydney 20 April 1982; Germany: Wuppertaler Bühne 14 May 1989

Recordings: original cast (Columbia), 1973 revival cast (Columbia), New York City Opera cast (New World), Scottish Opera cast (TER), studio cast w Bernstein (Deutsche Grammaphon) etc

CANTERBURY TALES Musical in 2 acts by Martin Starkie and Nevill Coghill. Lyrics by Nevill Coghill. Music by Richard Hill and John Hawkins. Phoenix Theatre, London, 21 March 1968.

The first version of what would become the musical *Canterbury Tales* was a play put together from Professor Coghill's modern English version of Chaucer's medieval poem by actor and broadcaster Starkie, and was played by the John Ford Society of Exeter College at the Oxford Playhouse (26 October 1964) as part of the College's 650th anniversary celebrations. Separately and simultaneously, composers John Hawkins and Richard Hill produced a concept recording, *Canterbury Pilgrims*, which utilized some of Coghill's translation. When they applied for the requisite permissions, the two projects became one and the musical comedy which was called *Canterbury Tales* resulted.

The piece, like the poem, framed the famous tales in the situation of a pilgrimage to Canterbury and, initially, the authors selected four of those tales for inclusion: The Miller's Tale, The Reeve's Tale, The Merchant's Tale and The Wife of Bath's Tale. The songs were little and, in the main, bouncy, illustrating the simplicity of the tales in an uncomplicated way. The juvenile hero of the Miller's Tale (Nicky Henson) gave forth with a version of a medieval lyric which crowed 'I Have a Noble Cock', the much-married Wife of Bath (Jessie Evans) rousted her way through 'Come Along and Marry Me, Honey' and the Prioress (Pamela Charles) provided the legitimate soprano moments in the April Song and in the thanksgiving closer to an evening of unmitigated if harmless sexual entertainment, 'Love Will Conquer All'. Kenneth J Warren (Miller) and Wilfred Brambell (Reeve) played various foolish and lecherous old men, Billy Boyle (Clerk of Oxenford) became the young Knight of the Wife of Bath's tale, whilst Gay Soper was all the ingénues.

Starkie's production of *Canterbury Tales* hit London at just the right moment. The restrictions on things sexual in the theatre were in an advanced state of erosion and the stage censor was soon to be abolished. Also, with the label of 'classic' hung on it (much in the same way that softish-porn films so often insist they are based on de Maupassant stories), it was both rude and all-right at the same time. Chaucer was on the curriculum, and this was a family show even if it did show one chap getting a red-hot poker up his backside, and included voyeurism, rape, cuckoldry and various other things that could be called 'bawdy', because they belonged safely to a literary and long past age, rather than 'censorable'. It also hit just the right tone and level and, as a result, became a singular hit. *Canterbury Tales* played 2,080 West End performances in a run of some five years, briefly attempting the original idea of introducing new tales from time to time with versions of the Nunne Priest's Tale and the Pardoner's Tale, before going out to multiple productions in provincial theatres. In the meantime, it had travelled round the world from Scandinavia to South Africa, from Germany (ad Robert Gilbert) and Hungary (ad Márton Mesterházi) to America and Australia.

The American version, made up of four tales rather than the five which the English one had become with the addition of the Nunne Priest's Tale to the original quartet, added instead one extra number for Hermione Baddeley as the Wife of Bath. Reid Shelton (Knight), Ed Evanko (Squire), George Rose (Reeve), Martyn Green (Chaucer) and Sandy Duncan (all the ingénues) featured in a production which played only 122 performances. In Australia, however, with Johnny Lockwood and Evelyn Page top-billed, the show was a major success. An initial two and a half months at Sydney's Theatre Royal was followed by a Melbourne season (Comedy Theatre 16 August 1969) before the show went round the country twice, returning for two further Sydney months the following year (24 April 1970). As a result, it was Australia that was later chosen to launch a sequel, *More Canterbury Tales* (Her Majesty's Theatre, Melbourne 23 October 1976). It went the way of all musequels and quicker than most.

Revivals in both London (Shaftesbury Theatre 24 April 1979) and New York (Rialto Theater 12 February 1980) suffered the same fate: if *Canterbury Tales* had timed its first entrance exceedingly well, it was clearly seen to be not a piece for the I've-seen-it-all-hang-out-before 1980s.

The era spawned several other at least partly musical *Canterbury Tales* shows, anxious to capitalize on Chaucer's permissible permissiveness. An American *Get Thee to Canterbury* (Paul Hoffert/Jan Steen, David Secter) followed hot behind the London show (Sheridan Square Playhouse 25 January 1969, 20 performances), and the 1960s lasted long enough (or arrived late enough) in Switzerland for a new *Canterbury Tales* musical to be mounted in St Gallen in 1991 (Roman Rutihauser/Liana Ruckstuhl 31 December).

USA: Eugene O'Neill Theater 3 February 1969; Australia: Theatre Royal, Sydney 17 May 1969; Hungary: József Attila Színház 21 February 1970; Germany: Theater im Goetheplatz, Bremen September 1970
Recordings: original cast (Decca), American cast (Capitol) etc

CANTIN, Louis (b Avignon, 1822; d Antibes, 11 April 1893).

For 15 years, at the height of the French domination of the world's musical stages, producer Louis Cantin controlled an important part of the Paris musical theatre.

The young man started his career in the theatre as an orchestral viola player, but his career as a musician was ruined when he damaged a finger in a game of *toupie hollandaise* and he had, ultimately, to have it amputated. For a while he worked as a clerk, but he rose through the theatre hierarchy to take a financial interest in the Théâtre des Folies-Dramatiques and, when the lease of the then unfortunate house came up for sale, he managed to get together enough money to take the building on. If things were difficult at first, and even at periods during his later occupancy, he nevertheless brought to the stage of his theatre the two greatest and most successful opérettes of the era. The first was *La Fille de Madame Angot* (1872), picked up from Brussels's Théâtre des Fantaisies-Parisiennes, and then, after a run of mostly less successful works of which Lacôme's *Jeanne, Jeannette et Jeanneton* (1876) was the most durable, he topped even that first triumph with the commissioning and production of the first full-sized work by the young Robert Planquette, *Les Cloches de Corneville* (1877).

Having lifted the Folies-Dramatiques into an eminent position alongside the Théâtre des Variétés, the Théâtre de la Renaissance and the Théâtre des Bouffes-Parisiens as one of the principal musical houses of the town, Cantin sold out while *Les Cloches de Corneville* was still profitably running and instead took over the control of the Bouffes-Parisiens from Charles Comte, in September 1879. Before long, he achieved a high rate of success in his new theatre, commissioning and producing, notably, the first metropolitan works of two further young composers destined for stardom in Edmond Audran (*Les Noces d'Olivette*, 1879) and Louis Varney (*Les Mousquetaires au couvent*, 1880).

Although works by other composers including Serpette, Hervé and Lacôme were presented at the Bouffes, Audran became virtually Cantin's house composer and, as a result, the theatre became the launching pad for his enormously successful *La Mascotte* (1880) and *Gillette de Narbonne* (1882).

Although he had swiftly brought the Bouffes to the undisputed head of the opérette world, a series of failures in 1883–4, beginning with Audran's first flop *La Dormeuse éveillée*, and proceeding with Leopold Wenzel's *Le Chevalier Mignon* and Raoul Marenco's *Le Diable au corps*, discouraged Cantin to such a degree that he decided, in January 1885, to give up the management of the theatre and, although he thereafter dabbled in theatrical ventures, his influential and outstanding days were at an end.

Enormously rich from his theatrical successes (and his canny and timely withdrawals), Cantin lived out his days in splendour between his mansion on the Boulevard Péreire, later the home of Sarah Bernhardt, a country estate at St Mandé and a villa at Cap d'Antibes, declaring that the loss of his finger was, in fact, the origin of his fortune.

LA CANTINIÈRE Opérette in 3 acts by Paul Burani and Félix Ribeyre. Music by Robert Planquette. Théâtre des Nouveautés, Paris, 26 October 1880.

A vaudevillesque piece in the popular military mode, *La Cantinière* featured Léa Silly, years previously the original Orestes of Offenbach's *La Belle Hélène*, in its title-rôle as Victoire, the wife of Babylas (Jules Brasseur), the pair being the happy purveyors of nourishment to the 36th cavalry regiment. Berthelier featured as the vain, womanizing Adjutant Rastagnac, Albert Brasseur as Pépinet, the volunteer son of a provincial merchant family who calls himself the Vicomte de Bellechasse, and Mlle Gilberte as Nichette, a potential rival cantinière, in a series of amorous and professional complications accompanied by a Planquette score which was topped by Berthelier's vigorous Chanson de l'Adjutant: 'Je le coupe en deux, en trois, en quatre'.

La Cantinière played for a little short of two months at the Nouveautés before giving way to the Christmas revue, but it was brought back for a second season in 1885 (4 April), and remounted both at the Folies-Dramatiques in 1887 and again at the Théâtre des Menus-Plaisirs in 1897.

CANTOR, Eddie [ITZKOWITZ, Isidore] (b New York, 31 January 1892; d Hollywood, Calif, 10 October 1964). A frenetic, jigging little singing comedian who became a blackface star in the *Ziegfeld Follies*.

After a number of years working a blackface act in vaudeville (including an appearance in the London revue *Not Likely*), Cantor made his entry on to the musical comedy stage when he was cast as the 'effeminate negro', Sam Beverley Moon, in Oliver Morosco's west-coast production of *Canary Cottage* (1916). He did not go on with the show to New York, where his rôle became Sam Abstestos Hicks and was played by Hugh Cameron, for he had already moved on to Ziegfeld and the shows which would make him famous. After half a dozen years in revue (*Midnight Follies*, four editions of the *Ziegfeld Follies*, *Make it Snappy*), he made the first of what would be handful of starring appearances in book musicals on Broadway. Ziegfeld's production of *Kid Boots* (1923) featured him as a golf caddy-master and allowed him to sing 'Dinah', 'Alabammy Bound' and 'If You Knew Susie' alongside the show's regular score, and *Whoopee* (1928) had him as the hypochondriac 'nervous wreck' of the original play's title, performing 'Makin' Whoopee' through a successful Broadway season. Cantor subsequently filmed both shows – *Kid Boots* as a silent film in 1926 and *Whoopee*, with sound, in 1930.

After a long career in Hollywood (*The Kid from Spain*, *Roman Scandals*, *Kid Millions*, *Strike Me Pink* etc) and on radio, he appeared once more in a Broadway musical, in 1941, as the star of the musical version of *Three Men on a Horse*, *Banjo Eyes*, singing 'We're Having a Baby' and a blackface pot-pourri of his past hits.

Cantor's voice was heard in the film *The Eddie Cantor Story* (1953) in which he was impersonated by Keefe Brasselle.

Autobiography: *My Life is in Your Hands* (Harper, New York, 1927), *Take My Life* (Doubleday, New York, 1957); *The Way I See It* (Prentice-Hall, New Jersey, 1959)

LE CAPITAINE FRACASSE

Théophile Gautier's 1863 novel of the Baron-turned-actor has, in theory, proved a regular basis for musical theatre pieces. However, *Capitän Fracassa*, the comic Operette in three acts 'taken from a French original' by Richard Genée and F Zell, with music by Rudolf Dellinger, produced at Hamburg (2 March 1889) and subsequently at the Theater an der Wien (21 September 1889, 17 performances), apparently shared little with the work but its title. The tale of the German work is a Venetian one of stolen jewels and a romance between the disguised Count Oberto and the Princess Blanche de Coligny, and Fracasse was a comical and apparently almost plot-incidental character, played in the Viennese version by Alexander Girardi. John McCaull mounted the piece in America in 1890 (ad H B Smith) as a vehicle for DeWolf Hopper (Fracasse) and Jeff de Angelis (Momo), but without success.

A 1909 Italian comic opera in three acts by Guglielmo Emmanuel, O Magici and Mario Costa (Teatro Alfieri, Turin 14 December), which clearly credited the novel as its source, had a more widespread success. After being presented in its country of origin with Emma Vecla (Isabella) and Riccardo Tegani (di Sicognac) starred, it was seen at the Vienna Volksoper (26 January 1911) and was purchased by George Edwardes for Britain, without, however, coming to production before the producer's death intervened. An earlier Italian *Captain Fracasse*, written by Luigi Campesi and composed by Giovanni Valente, had been produced before either of the better-known pieces, at Naples's Teatro della Varieta in 1881 (3 January).

A French *Capitaine Fracasse*, with a score by Émile Pessard, was produced in Paris in 1878 (lib: Catulle Mendès, Théâtre Lyrique 2 July) with Melchissdec and Pauline Luigini starred, whilst a 'comédie musicale' under the same title, by Jean-Marie Lecocq and Louis Dunoyer de Segonzac, was played at the Théâtre de la Renaissance in 1986 (25 June).

EL CAPITAN Comic opera in 3 acts by Charles Klein. Lyrics by Thomas Frost. Music by John Philip Sousa. Broadway Theater, New York, 20 April 1896.

One of the earliest successful comic operas to come out of America, *El Capitan* was also the one successful attempt by 'March King' John Philip Sousa to provide an enduring musical score for the theatre. His success was largely helped by Charles Klein's supply of a libretto which, if it was made in the familiar mould of Continental comic opera texts, with a web of well-used plot elements, was nevertheless a shapely, coherent and funny piece of its kind.

The Viceroy of Peru, Cazzaro, has been deposed, and Don Errico Medigua (De Wolf Hopper) sent out to replace him. Cazzaro has, however, not taken his dismissal lightly and is plotting, with a band of bravos and some of the local populace, to regain his position by force. To this end he has hired the famous Spanish mercenary, el Capitan, who is on his way to Peru. But Don Medigua has disovered all this plottery whilst still on the high seas to Peru, and knowing el Capitan to have been killed in a shipboard brawl, he hides from the Peruvian populace until the moment is ripe to emerge, himself, in personation of the man whose reputation he has meanwhile taken great care to build up to a ferocious height. The phoney 'El Capitan' leads the rebel army round in swashbuckling circles until they are too exhausted to face the Spanish troops, then promptly defeats himself in battle and, with his viceregal hat once more in place, takes up the throne in time for the curtain.

Alice Hosmer played Medigua's wife, Princess Marghanza, distraught at being exiled from the social delights of the metropolis, Bertha Walzinger his daughter, Isabel, who conducts an incidental romance with one Count Hernando Verrada (Edmund Stanley) to provide the opportunity for some sentimental music, Edna Wallace Hopper was the tempestuous Estrelda, daughter to Cazzaro, and determined to hook herself the famous war-leader as a husband, whilst librettist Klein himself appeared as the bewildered Chamberlain, Pozzo, kidnapped by the enemy in mistake for his employer.

Sousa's comic-operatic score, an amount of it re-used from those of his previous shows which had not made it to New York, included some fine concerted music, and a regular layout of numbers from the romancing of the juveniles ('Sweetheart, I'm Waiting'), to the comical 'A Typical Tune of Zanzibar' and the marching strains of el Capitan's entrance song, both sung by the disguised Medigua.

After *El Capitan*'s first Broadway run of 112 performances, Hopper took his show to the country, returning for repeat seasons in New York both in 1897 (Broadway Theater 22 February) and 1898 (Fifth Avenue Theater 21 February) before taking the company across to London to play their show at the Lyric and Comedy Theatres with Miss Hosmer, Jessie Mackaye, Nella Berger, Harold Blake and Henry Norman in support of the star. *El Capitan* was well received in London, and it ran for some five months, after which Hopper tried his subsequent *The Charlatan* (*Mystical Miss*). It, too, did better in London than on Broadway, before the star announced that he had to go home and tour.

Hopper kept *El Capitan* to hand for a number of years, and it now shares with *Robin Hood* the distinction of representing 19th-century American comic opera to end-of-20th-century folk, a fact which has earned it a number of interested revivals, notably one at the Goodspeed Opera House in 1973 (11 June) with John Cullum featured in Hopper's rôle.

UK: Lyric Theatre 10 July 1899
Recording: Minnesota Opera Co (3 records)

LE CAPITOLE Opéra-bouffe in 3 acts by Paul Ferrier and Charles Clairville. Music by Gaston Serpette. Théâtre des Nouveautés, Paris, 5 December 1895.

In between the famous Ancient Greek Parisianisms of *La Belle Hélène* and those of *Son p'tit frère* and *Phi-Phi*, there were plenty of other pieces which garbed what were in essence boulevard comedies in the trappings of classical times with less, but not negligible, success. One of these was *Le Capitole*.

The central figure of the piece is Métella (Jane Pierny), nubile wife of the pompous and elderly consul, Cornélius Major (Germain), and a descendant of the famously raped Lucretia. Cornélius is careless enough to send his wife the tidings of his victory over the Ligurians by his unnecessarily handsome lieutenant, Narcisse (Abel Tarride), and the action leaps into forward gear. Unlike her ancestress, Métella initially keeps her virtue, but not the semblance of it. Her husband prefers to pretend ignorance as he is expecting to be awarded a Triumph, and cannot risk the ridicule of having been cuckolded. However, before the three acts of the evening are done, ridicule has well and truly arrived along with all the other elements of a bedroom farce which ends in classic style with the old husband thoroughly bamboozled and the young wife making the most of his lieutenant.

Serpette decorated the tale with a score which was rated one of his most light-hearted and melodious, and *Le Capitole* played seasons in Paris in 1895–6 and again later in 1896, whilst going on to further productions in Ger-

many (ad Wilhelm Mannstädt) and in two different versions in Hungary (ad Gyula Komor, ad Dezső Bálint).

Germany: Theater am Alexanderplatz *Metella* 4 October 1897; Hungary; Budai Színkör *Az erenyes Metella* 26 September 1896, Népszinház *A konzul felesége* 20 May 1904

CAPTAIN THÉRÈSE Comic opera in 3 acts by Alexandre Bisson and F C Burnand. Lyrics by F C Burnand and Gilbert a' Beckett. Music by Robert Planquette. Prince of Wales Theatre, London, 25 August 1890.

The fifth Planquette opérette made, or seriously remade, specifically for the London stage, *Captain Thérèse* was also specifically made as a starring vehicle for the American contralto Agnes Huntington, who had made a great hit in the title-rôle of the Carl Rosa Light Opera Company's Planquette piece *Paul Jones*. Alexandre Bisson evolved a tale which allowed the statuesque Miss Huntington to get into men's clothes again as quickly and as long as possible, his work was translated by F C Burnand, set by Planquette and handed over to the Carl Rosa Company.

Unfortunately, by that time, Miss Huntington had walked out on Rosa and gone home to earn better money than was available in England and to marry a millionaire socialite. The rôle of *Captain Thérèse*, who gets into soldier's uniform for the usual operettic reasons, was played by Canadian vocalist Attalie Claire, soon replaced by Violet Cameron, the Vicomte Tancrède de la Touche was Hayden Coffin, singing of 'A Soldier's Life', Joseph Tapley played the tenor hero Philip de Bellegarde, Phyllis Broughton the soubrette, and Madame Amadi a nun, in a line-up which was more than a touch more-of-the-sameish. London's *Captain Thérèse* played 40 times, and the show was subsequently seen on Broadway with Miss Huntington in the rôle written for her (11 performances), in Paris with Yvonne Kerlord (Thérèse), Vauthier (Sombrero), Paul Fugère (Duvet) and Lucien Noël (Bellegarde) starred (26 performances), and in Budapest (ad Béla J Fái, Jenő Farágo) for eight performances, without achieving a proper success anywhere.

USA: Union Square Theater 15 February 1892; France: Théâtre de la Gaîté 1 April 1901; Hungary: Népszinház *Teréz kapitány* 15 November 1901

THE CARD Musical in 2 acts by Keith Waterhouse and Willis Hall based on the novel by Arnold Bennett. Music and lyrics by Tony Hatch and Jackie Trent. Queen's Theatre, London, 24 July 1973.

Arnold Bennett's novel of the English provinces was made up into a musical play in the *Half a Sixpence* vein by the authors of *Billy Liar*, Waterhouse and Hall, and the husband and wife songwriting team Tony Hatch and Jackie Trent ('Downtown', 'I Couldn't Live Without Your Love', 'Where Are You Now?' etc).

Denry Machin, the tart little hero of this 'how-to-succeed-in-business-politics-and-love-by-trying-exceedingly-hard' tale was played by Jim Dale, one time pop singer and *Carry On* film star turned respectable actor. Millicent Martin (Ruth) and Eleanor Bron (Countess of Chell) were the women he used to help his rise, Joan Hickson was his mother, and John Savident the hated employer whom he was to rise above. When he gets to the top, however, Denry sees clearly enough to turn for love to the faithful Nellie (Marti Webb) who has slogged for him

Plate 46. **Careless Rapture**: *Ivor Novello and Dorothy Dickson climbed every mountain in China in one of the scenic moments of the author's second Drury Lane musical spectacular.*

since the beginning. The mostly up-beat score included a lively retailing of the capitalist system in 'That's the Way the Money Goes' and a pretty ballad for Nellie, 'I Could Be the One', alongside its most popular number, the duet 'Opposite Your Smile'.

One hundred and thirty performances in the West End, under the management of the young Cameron Mackintosh and Jimmy Wax, did not seen enough to establish *The Card* as a revivable prospect, but the piece did win a production in Germany with the rather literally translated title of *Das As* in 1979, and in 1992, after Mackintosh had risen to be the world's most successful producer of musicals, he sponsored a revival of a rewritten version of *The Card* at Newbury's Water Mill Theatre.

Germany: Staatsoperette, Dresden *Das As* 22 June 1979
Recording: original cast (Pye)

CARELESS RAPTURE Musical play in 3 acts by Ivor Novello. Lyrics by Christopher Hassall. Theatre Royal, Drury Lane, London, 11 September 1936.

After the truncated success of *Glamorous Night* at the

Theatre Royal, Drury Lane, the board of that theatre turned down Novello's next piece and instead mounted a pantomime and a disastrous failure in the mish-mash musical *Rise and Shine*. They were quickly back at Novello's door, and *Careless Rapture* went into the theatre for which it had been designed after all. Its author starred as the sculptural Michael, bastard brother of Sir Rodney Alderney (Ivan Samson) and in love with the same woman, musical comedy star Penelope Lee (Dorothy Dickson). He follows her from a beauty parlour run by Zena Dare, to a singing lesson with Olive Gilbert, to the theatre, for an extract of the operetta *The Rose Girl*, and then whisks her off to Hampstead Heath for a jolly time amongst a carnival of scenery. When Sir Rodney takes her as far away as China in search of special effects, Michael follows, and, after time out for a rehearsal by the local operatic society, an earthquake and an attack by Chinese bandits (the chief of which was also played by Novello) he finally gets the girl in time for the final curtain.

If the tale was fairly preposterous, the settings were gorgeous, the dance opportunities for Miss Dickson and Walter Crisham legion, the earthquake equally as good as

223

the shipwreck of the previous show, and Miss Dickson's 'Music in May', Miss Gilbert's deeply intoned 'Why Is There Ever Goodbye?' and the duo 'Love Made the Song', sung by the leading lights of the Chinese operatic society, just a notch below the *Glamorous Night* songs, which had been written for an altogether more substantial and rangy leading lady's voice.

Novello's popularity and the spectacle helped *Careless Rapture* to 296 performances at Drury Lane and a tour in 1937–8, with Barry Sinclair and Ivy Tresmand featured, before it was replaced by *Crest of the Wave*, the next in the Novello series of romantic spectaculars.

Recording: original cast (HMV, EMI), selection (EMI, WRC)

CARIOU, Len [CARIOU, Leonard] (b St Boniface, Manitoba, 30 September 1939). Broadway leading man of the 1970s.

Cariou began his career as a chorus singer in his native Canada, but made his Broadway début in classic drama, returning to the musical theatre in 1970 to play the love interest to topbilled Lauren Bacall in *Applause* (Bill). He made intermittent essays in musical rôles over the next 20 years, creating the rôle of Fredrik Egermann, the central character of *A Little Night Music* (1973), and the title-rôle of *Sweeney Todd* (1979) as well as appearing briefly as Teddy Roosevelt in Broadway's *Teddy and Alice* and as Florenz Ziegfeld in the London extravaganza loosely based on the famous producer's life (*Ziegfeld*, 1988).

He repeated his *A Little Night Music* rôle in the cinema version of the show.

CARLE, Richard [CARLETON, Charles Nicholas] (b Somerville, Mass, 7 July 1871; d Hollywood, 28 June 1941). Long-popular comedy star of the American musical theatre.

Carle began his stage career playing supporting comedy rôles in mostly musical theatre – the musical farce-comedies *A Mad Bargain* (Worthington) and *A Country Sport* (Washington Strutt), the burlesque *Excelsior Jr* (1895, De Reske) and in the British variety musical *The Lady Slavey* (Lavender), as an effete and awkward English Lord – before rising to the top of the bill in the revusical *A Round of Pleasure*, a return season of *The Lady Slavey* and in the star comedy rôle of the beleaguered soothsayer, Heliodorus, in the Broadway production of Sidney Jones's *A Greek Slave*. At the same time, he worked rather less prominently as a librettist and lyricist, supplying lyrics to such pieces as the play (with a song) *The Girl from Maxim's*, *The Rogers Brothers in Wall Street* and *The Rogers Brothers in Central Park* and authoring a little piece played at Koster and Bial's Music Hall. Ultimately, he took the chief comic part in the musical comedy *Mam'selle 'Awkins* (1900, Jonathan) for which he had himself written the straightforward and lightly blue libretto.

In the uninfectious rash of American musical comedies which briefly swept London after the success there of *The Belle of New York*, Carle starred with the Casino Theater company in *An American Beauty* (1900, Bayley Bangle), *The Casino Girl* (1900, J Offenbach Gaggs) and *The Belle of Bohemia* (1901, Algy Cuffs) and simultaneously worked with the British composer Walter Slaughter on a musical, *Little Miss Modesty*, which ultimately remained unstaged.

Plate 47. **Richard Carle***'s musical version of the French play* Madame Mongodin *proved a fine touring vehicle for comic Harry Conor as the show's hagridden 'hero'.*

When London proved no real taker for the Casino shows, he joined the company on a tour of the Continent, appearing in Austria, Germany and Hungary as Ichabod Bronson in *The Belle of New York* and in *The Casino Girl*.

He returned to America to star in another British musical, the George Dance/Ivan Caryll *The Ladies' Paradise*, which his *Mam'selle 'Awkins* collaborator, producer Alfred Aarons, staged lavishly and disastrously at no less a venue than the Metropolitan Opera House then, with $3,000 owing to him in unpaid salary, moved on to Chicago, then flourishing as a source of new musical theatre, to appear in and collaborate in the writing and composing of a number of new works which featured the kind of put-upon, awkward star-comic characters and out-front, rudish humour in which he specialized.

He toured in the established Chicago favourite *The Burgomaster* (Peter Stuyvesant) and in the new *The Explorers* (1902, Bonaparte Hunter) and *The Storks* (1902, Mlzadoc), before launching himself on a trio of writing-playing-producing successes which confirmed their author-star as a nation-wide favourite. *The Tenderfoot* (1903, Professor Zachary Pettibone LLD BA), *The Maid and the Mummy* (1904, Washington Stubbs) and *The Mayor of Tokio* (1905, Marcus Orlando Kidder) all started out from Chicago and took in New York seasons as part of long and lucrative touring lives. At the same time he contributed to what was announced as Chicago's first local, topical revue, the 1905 *All Around Chicago*, mounted by William Brady at McVickers Theater. He topped off this run of acting and writing successes, however, with a small triumph in his 1906 production of a written-over version of the London Gaiety

Theatre hit *The Spring Chicken*. Equipped with an americanized text decorated with several of his own songs, he starred in the little-man rôle of Girdle created by Edmund Payne in Britain under the billing 'Richard Carle presents himself and his songs in George Edwardes success of two London seasons...'. Whilst he toured *The Spring Chicken*, his latest piece of authorship, *The Hurdy Gurdy Girl*, set out from Boston under the management of Charles Marks without him, and with Annie Yeamans and John E Hazzard starring.

His success with *The Spring Chicken*, a piece based on French comedy, prompted him to himself adapt a French comedy, *Madame Mongodin* (better known to English audiences as *Mrs Ponderbury's Past*), to the musical stage. *Mary's Lamb* (1908) provided him with a vehicle which, when his 1909 show *The Boy and the Girl* flopped quickly, lasted him for two years of highly successful touring in the meek and mild rôle of 'Leander Lamb, a martyr'. Returning to Chicago, he appeared in Charles Dillingham's production of Deems Taylor's *The Echo*, but preferred to go on the road with one of his own creations, *Jumping Jupiter* (1910), when the earlier piece went towards New York. Both shows failed, but another French farce/Viennese Operette adaptation, *The Girl From Montmartre*, taken by Harry B Smith from a text based on Feydeau's *La Dame de Chez Maxim* and featuring Carle (Dr Petypon) opposite another drawing name in Hattie Williams, did better. A second show with the same team, an americanized version of Leo Fall's charming *Das Puppenmädel* – originally the French comedy *Miquette et sa mère* – peppered with homemade songs and entitled *The Doll Girl* (Marquis de Tourelle) also did well.

The peak of his popular success having now passed, and his producing operation Carle-Marks Inc gone into bankruptcy (with a name like that, what did he expect?), Carle subsequently mixed musical stage appearances with revue, vaudeville and character rôles in films, appearing on the road in the try-out of *The Blue Kitten* (1922), as Chauncey Cheesboro in Chicago's *Molly Darling* (1922), in *Some Colonel* (1922), and on Broadway in character rôles in *Ninety in the Shade* (1915, Willoughby Parker) and *Adrienne* (1923, John Grey), in *Happy Days* (1928) and, paired with Marie Cahill, in *The New Yorkers* (1930, Windham Wentworth).

Late in life, Carle, who had performed in films from the 1920s (*Madame X* etc), made a fine second career as a cinematic character actor, being seen, amongst others, in such screen pieces as *Anything Goes* (1936, Bishop Dobson), *The Merry Widow* (1934, an attorney), *One Hour with You* (1932, a detective), *San Francisco* (1936) and *One Night in the Tropics*.

1899 **The Rogers Brother in Wall Street** (Maurice Levi/J J McNally) Victoria Theater 18 September
1899 **Sir Andy de Boojjack** Koster and Bial's Music Hall 17 October
1900 **Mam'selle 'Awkins** (Alfred Aarons, Herman Perlet) Victoria Theater 26 February
1901 **My Antoinette** (revised *The Ladies' Paradise*) with add mus by Aarons (tour)
1902 **The Storks** (Frederic Chapin/w Guy F Steeley) Dearborn Theater, Chicago 18 May
1903 **The Tenderfoot** (Harry L Heartz) Dearborn Theater, Chicago 12 April; New York Theater, New York 22 February 1904

1904 **The Maid and the Mummy** (Robert Hood Bowers) Garrick Theater, Chicago May; New York Theater, New York 25 July
1905 **The Mayor of Tokio** (William Frederick Peters) Studebaker Theater, Chicago 12 June; New York Theater, New York 4 December
1906 **The Spring Chicken** American adaptation and additional songs (Daly's Theater)
1907 **The Hurdy Gurdy Girl** (Heartz) Tremont Theater, Boston 3 June; Wallack's Theater, New York 23 September
1908 **Mary's Lamb** (Carle) New York Theater 25 May
1909 **The Boy and the Girl** (w M E Rourke/Heartz) Chicago; New Amsterdam Theater, New York 31 May
1910 **Jumping Jupiter** (w others/w Sydney Rosenfeld) Chicago; Criterion Theater, New York 6 March 1911

CARLETON, William T[urnham] *see* CELLI, FRANK

CARMEN JONES Musical play in 2 acts by Oscar Hammerstein II based on Meilhac and Halévy's adaptation of Prosper Merimée's *Carmen*. Music by Georges Bizet. Broadway Theater, New York, 2 December 1943.

An americanization of the *Carmen* tale and of Bizet's opera, written by Oscar Hammerstein II, *Carmen Jones* featured a Carmen who works in a parachute factory in the southern United States, a G I Joe (ie Don Jose) with a girlfriend called Cindy Lou, and an Escamillo who was no longer a bullfighter, but a boxer called Husky Miller. If the characters' names sounded like something out of a Weber and Fields burlesque, the show nevertheless followed the same tragic lines as the opera and had nothing of the burlesque to it, beyond the fact that many of the lyrics that were fitted to re-orchestrated versions of Bizet's melodies were written in a coon-songish 'Dis' and 'Dat' and 'Dere' lingo. The Flower Song became 'Dis Flower', the Card Song was 'Dat Ol' Boy', the Habanera was 'Dat's Love', the smugglers' quintet became 'Whizzin' Away Along de Track' and, in the highspot of the evening, the Chanson Bohémienne was turned into 'Beat Out Dat Rhythm on a Drum'.

Billy Rose's original production had its lead rôles double cast, with Muriel Smith and Muriel Rahn alternating as Carmen Jones, Luther Saxon and Napoleon Reed sharing Joe, and Carlotta Franzell and Elton J Warren taking turns at Cindy Lou. Glenn Bryant did Husky Miller every night. The show had a successful 502-performance run on Broadway and was subsequently toured and then filmed with Dorothy Dandridge (sung by Marilyn Horne), Harry Belafonte (sung by LeVern Hutcheson) and Joe Adams (sung by Marvin Hayes) in the principal rôles.

It took some time for the piece to travel. *Carmen Jones* was first played in Britain at the Crucible Theatre, Sheffield, in 1986 with Laverne Williams and Lynne Kieran sharing the title rôle, and it reached in London in 1991 when it was mounted for what turned out to be an extended run at the Old Vic with Sharon Benson and Wilhelminia Fernandez alternating, whilst a production by the New York Harlem Ensemble was toured through European one-night stands in 1987.

The story or, more particularly, Bizet's opéra-comique of *Carmen*, has been re-used in many ways on the stage since it first appeared at Paris's Opéra-Comique in 1875. In Victorian times, when it verged on the repertoire of the light opera companies, it underwent many burlesque versions, notably in Robert Reece's pasticcio *Carmen, or Sold for a Song* played with wide success by Lydia Thompson in America and in Britain with Lionel Brough as Don José and John Howson as Escamillo, J Wilton Jones's *Cruel Carmen* (1880), the Frank Green/Frank Musgrave *Carmen, or Soldiers and Seville-ians* played by Selina Dolaro on Broadway (1880), Alfred Murray's *Little Carmen* (Globe Theatre, 7 February 1884) which introduced Edward Jakobowski's music to the West End, and, most successfully of all, the Gaiety Theatre's *Carmen Up-to-Data*.

In 1917 André Barde and Charles Carpentier authored a tongue-in-cheek musequel to the tale told by Merimée, Meilhac and Halévy in a piece called *Carminetta* (mus: Émile Lassailly, Théâtre Michel, Paris 16 March) which later had some success when produced by C B Cochran in Britain.

The most successful of modern *Carmen* variations have been the operatic *La Tragédie de Carmen* as remodelled by Peter Brook for presentations in France and America (ad Sheldon Harnick), and the small-scale Anglo-Viennese musical *Carmen Negra* (arr Callum McLeod/Stewart Trotter) which resets the piece in a South American republic with an Escamillo who is the captain of his country's World Cup football team. The Toreador's Song became 'Santa Maria's Going to Win the Cup'. Produced at Vienna's Kammeroper in 1988, with Lynne Kieran (Carmen) and Michael Heath (José) starred, the piece caused a sensation and was played for three successive seasons before being recorded for television. It was followed on the European touring circuits, whilst *Carmen Jones* extended its run at London's Old Vic into its second year, by another remake entitled *Rocky Carmen* with a pop star Esca Millo, which, undoubtedly will not be the last perversion of Merimée and/or Bizet to find its way to the world's stages.

UK: Crucible Theatre, Sheffield 14 March 1986, Old Vic 8 April 1991; France: tour 1987; Film: 1954 Twentieth Century Fox
Recordings: original cast (Decca), soundtrack (RCA), studio cast w Grace Bumbry (Heliodor), British cast (EMI)

CARMEN UP-TO-DATA
Burlesque in 2 acts by George Sims and Henry Pettitt. Music by W Meyer Lutz. Gaiety Theatre, London, 4 October 1890.

Sims and Pettitt prepared their burlesque version of *Carmen* to follow the enormous success of their *Faust Up-to-Date* and, even though their new show did not benefit from the support of the Gaiety's star team of Nellie Farren and Fred Leslie, who had gone touring with the last Gaiety piece, they scored another grand hit.

Florence St John, London's queen of comic opera and quite capable of singing Bizet's original operatic version, was their Carmen, opposite Edwin Lonnen as an Irish masher of a Don Jose. Escamillo (Jenny Dawson/Alma Stanley) was played as a principal boy in tights and Michaela (Maria Jones) became a bulgingly healthy country wench. The part of Zuniga was made into a principal comic rôle for Arthur Williams as 'The Villain of the Day'. Lutz's score ranged from the genuine romance of 'One Who is Life to Me' to the saucy 'Ask Me to Marry' for the star, Escamillo demonstrated 'The Swagger' and José sang about 'The Jolly Boys' Club', whilst Letty Lind did farmyard imitations and danced a hornpipe. However, the song hit of the show fell to Lonnen. Since the comedian had made himself famous with his series of Irish

songs in previous burlesques, the authors had justified this show's interpolation by actually making José Irish, but Lonnen asked for a version of the Dave Braham song 'Whist! the Bogie Man' which was the rage of the minstrel world, and Lutz, Sims and Pettitt put together a colourable imitation called 'Hush, the Bogie' which, performed in the semi-dark to a bouche fermée chorus, became the rage of the whole country.

The show underwent many changes through its 248 London performances, often due to cast changes – at one time Escamillo stopped being a 'boy' and was sung by very legit vocalists W H Brockbank and Frank Celli – before heading off to the country where it toured solidly for three years before living out many more years on the minor circuits. George Musgrove took the Gaiety company to Australia in 1892, with Marion Hood starring alongside Lonnen and Robert Courtneidge as Zuniga, and two companies took productions to the Continent. Josephine Findlay and Walter Passmore starred in Berlin, Bremen, Hamburg and Brussels (*Carmen fin de siècle*), whilst Percy Hutchinson's Royal English Burlesque Company with Fanny Wentworth (Carmen), Fred Wright (Jose), Grace Huntley (Escamillo) and James Stevenson (Zuniga) played *Carmen von heute* in Vienna, Bucharest and Budapest.

Germany: Reichsallen Theater 14 April 1892; Australia: Theatre Royal, Adelaide 16 July 1892; Austria: Carltheater September 1892; Hungary: Városligeti Színkör 19 September 1892

LE CARNET DU DIABLE
Opérette fantaisie in 3 acts by Ernest Blum and Paul Ferrier. Music by Gaston Serpette. Théâtre des Variétés, Paris, 23 October 1895.

A féerie à grand spectacle, lavishly staged by Fernand Samuel, *Le Carnet du diable* was hailed as 'an impudently smutty piece ... a spicy compound into which the authors have thrown an unusual dash of originality and the composer a sprinkling of tuneful grace' as it established itself as one of the favourites of its kind throughout Europe.

Satanella (Mlle Théry) complains to her uncle, the King of the Underworld (Édouard Georges), about the philanderings of her husband Belphegor (Baron) and Satan inflicts upon the errant little devil a year's celibacy. He may lust but not assuage that lust: his cheque book on the bank of love is withdrawn. But Belphegor finds a way out: he makes a deal with the luckless student Arsène Marjavel (Albert Brasseur) by which he will give the boy good luck in exchange for his *carnet de banque*. Belphegor rushes off to spend, spend, spend his new supply of sex-cheques, while Arsène, who has been previously miserably cut out by his cousin Casimir (Schutz) with the gorgeous Peruvian belle Mimosa (Juliette Méaly), now not only wins but weds her. Alas! come the wedding night, his bargain with the devil catches up with him. He has no *carnet* and cannot call on his 'account' with Baron Cupido's bank. The bride will stay undeflowered. Fortunately Venus (Mlle de Gaby) responds to Mimosa's indignant pleas and a new cheque book is issued in time for a consummation and a pictorial apotheosis. One of the sub-plots was a comical romance between Mimosa's impossibly wealthy papa, General Ruy del Rio Secco (A Simon), and a bar wench, Jacqueline, as played by Ève Lavallière.

The scenes ranged from views of Hell and Paris to the comical banking establishment run by the Baron Cupido (Lassouche), there were ballets, tableaux vivants, pantomime and burlesque dance (Lavallière impersonating Cléo de Mérode), and there were also the titillating moments so beloved of the Paris spectacular: the wedding night undressing of the bride, the appearance of Venus in all her heroic nudity, and the usual bevy of scantily clad chorines.

Le Carnet du diable proved a fine success a the Variétés, and it was tarted up and trotted out for further runs, the first just two seasons on (18 September 1897, 40 performances), the next 'enlarged and revised' in 1899, and again in 1900. In the meantime, it made the tour of Central Europe, being mounted in Berlin under the title of *Cupido & Co* (add material by Maurice Rappaport and Hermann Haller) and in Vienna as the 'phantastiche Burleske' *Das Scheckbuch des Teufels* (ad Carl Lindau and F Antony, add mus Maximilian Steiner). The subject matter proved just too much for the English-speaking countries.

Germany: Belle-Alliance Theater *Cupido & Co* 23 December 1902; Austria: Danzers Orpheum *Das Scheckbuch des Teufels* 21 December 1906

CARNEVAL IN ROM Comic opera in 3 acts by Josef Braun based on *Piccolino* by Victorien Sardou. Music by Johann Strauss. Theater an der Wien, Vienna, 1 March 1873.

The second Operette composed by Johann Strauss was founded on a solid piece of French theatre in Victorien Sardou's sentimental comedy *Piccolino* (Gymnase, 18 July 1861), a piece which had already served as the basis for an operatic version by Mme de Grandval (Théâtre des Italiens, 5 January 1869) and was to become, three years later, the libretto (w Charles Nuitter) to Ernest Guiraud's three-act opéra-comique *Piccolino*, mounted with success at the Paris Opéra-Comique (11 April 1876). In fact, *Piccolino*, which was subsequently played a number of times in Britain, in Budapest, in Latin America and Scandinavia, ultimately had wider success than Strauss's work but, without the saleable name of the waltz king attached to it, it has faded away in the 20th century.

Marie Geistinger starred in *Carneval in Rom* as the little peasant girl, Marie, who has passed an idyllic time in her Swiss mountain village with the visiting painter Arthur Bryk (Albin Swoboda). But Bryk has gone on to Rome, leaving her with only her portrait and the hope he will return, as he has promised. Instead, two other painters, Benvenuti Rafaeli (Jani Szika) and Robert Hesse (Schreiber), turn up. Rafaeli is a wealthy amateur of no talent, and he buys Bryk's painting of Marie to sell as his own work. She uses the money to go to Rome in search of Arthur. Bryk is on the brink of an adventure with the coquettish Countess Falconi (Caroline Charles-Hirsch), wife of the elderly Count (Carl Adolf Friese), but Marie, who has made her trip disguised as a boy, gets herself taken into Arthur's house as a pupil and succeeds in spoiling each opportunity for a rendezvous between the Countess and the painter. When Rafaeli turns up with Arthur's painting of Marie, realization blooms in the man's brain, and, as Rome celebrates Carnival, he finally comes back together with his little Swiss maid. The final carnival scene gave the opportunity to feature a 12-handed Ländler, a pas de trois 'Fête du carnaval', a 30-dancer Intermezzo, a ballet of clowns and flowers (with specially credited 'living

flowers'), and a grand dance finale. The other specially credited item was a so-called 'Velocipedes-Wagen'.

Strauss's score of 16 musical pieces gave the showiest moments, as might have been expected, to Charles-Hirsch, the creator of *Die Fledermaus*'s Adele and a Hofoper Queen of the Night, in the rôle of the sophisticated soprano Gräfin Falconi. She featured a coloratura aria 'Kann er nicht liebenswürd'ger sein' and duos with Bryk ('Was auch immer gesche') and her husband ('Nich länger duld' ich dieses Treiben'). But Marie was the prima donna rôle, and it was not neglected. If her opportunities were less showy, pieces such as the little love song 'Nur in Liebe kan ich leben', the dancing 'Wer bleibt auf seinem Platze lang' and her duos with Bryk in the second and third acts assured Geistinger's place at the top of the bill. The Count contributed a waltz song ('So ein arme, arme Ehemann'), Bryk an aria, auctioning off, in disguise as a 'fromme Pilgermann', goods pretending to come from the holy land ('Dies Paar Pantoffel') and the second act wound up to a jolly choral tarantella as the carnival took over.

Carneval in Rom proved, by and large, a success. It was played 54 times during its first year at the Theater an der Wien, reappeared again in 1874, in 1880 for another 20 performances, and was brought back in a new production in 1894 (28 April) with Carl Streitmann (Bryk), Josef Joseffy (Hesse), Lilli Lejo (Marie) and Karl Wallner (Falconi) for seven performances. Productions were mounted in the other German-speaking countries and in 1881 Marie Geistinger included the piece in the repertoire for her American season, appearing in a production with Adolfi, Fritsch, Max Lube and Emma Seebold at the German-speaking Thalia Theater in New York. However, the only English-language production seems to have been one mounted at San Francisco's Bush Street Theater in 1880, with Emilie Melville in the rôle of Marie.

Strauss's fame guaranteed *Carneval in Rom* the occasional revival – it was seen at the Carltheater for a handful of performances with Ottilie Collin, Felix and Sigmund Natzler in 1898 (4 October), at the Volksoper, and in the inevitable remakes, first as *Der blaue Held* (lib: Ferdinand Stollberg) in 1912 (Theater an der Wien, 18 October), and subsequently, under its original title, for a production at Dortmund (Eugen Rex/Franz Marszalek, Stadttheater, 30 November 1937).

Germany; Friedrich-Wilhelmstädtisches Theater 25 April 1874; USA: Bush Street Theater, San Francisco 1880, Thalia Theater, New York (Ger) 1 April 1881
Recording: 1937 version (RCA)

CARNIVAL Musical in 2 acts by Michael Stewart based on the screenplay *Lili* by Helen Deutsch and the story by Paul Gallico. Music and lyrics by Bob Merrill. Imperial Theater, New York, 13 April 1961.

At first a story by Paul Gallico, *Lili* became a successful Hollywood film in 1953, with Leslie Caron featured in its title-rôle and Mel Ferrer as leading man, before being made up into a musical play. Screenwriter Ms Deutsch and Bronislaw Kaper supplied a hit song, 'Hi Lili, Hi Lo', as an accompaniment to the film, but it was another prolific writer of song hits, Bob Merrill, who joined with librettist Michael Stewart to provide the score for *Carnival*.

The orphaned Lili (Anna Maria Alberghetti) finds work in Schlegel's 'Grand Imperial Cirque de Paris' but, although she attracts the flamboyant eye of magician Marco the Magnificent (James Mitchell) and the unconfident heart of the crippled ex-dancer Paul Berthalet (Jerry Orbach), it seems that she will not be able to hold a place in the company. Then she meets four little puppets, created by Paul. They can speak to her, as Paul cannot, and she makes a bubbling front-lady in a team with them, a performance which ensures her popularity and her job. She is still dazzled by Marco, however, and it is only when she is contemplating running away with the magician that she realizes that the love the puppets have shown her comes, in reality, from their master.

Merrill produced a number which topped even 'Hi Lili, Hi Lo' in the carouselling theme to the show, 'Love Makes the World Go Round', at the front of a score which went from lively, circussy pieces ('Direct from Vienna', 'The Sword, the Rose and the Cape'), to charming songs for Lili solo ('Yes, My Heart') and with the puppets ('Yum Ticky, Ticky, Tum, Tum'), and the more deeply felt moments of Paul's 'I've Got to Find a Reason (for living on this earth)' and 'Everybody Likes You'. It even touched zany comedy as the faithless Marco plunged swords into the box containing his assistant and girlfriend, Rosalie (Kaye Ballard), as he assured her that 'It Was Always You'. Director/choreographer Gower Champion provided one of the memorable moments of the evening in his setting of the opening of the show, depicting the mounting of the circustents and the gradual winding up of the personnel until they leaped into life as the rather too-grandly named Grand Imperial Cirque de Paris.

David Merrick's Broadway production of *Carnival* ran through 719 performances, but the show was on the road, with Susan Watson and Ed Ames featured, well before the New York run was finished. H M Tennent Ltd mounted a London reproduction in 1963 with Sally Logan, Michael Maurel, Mitchell and Shirley Sands featured, but it proved peculiarly ill-cast and folded in just 34 performances. An Australian production by J C Williamson Ltd with Patricia Moore starred, supported by Kevin Colson and Jill Perryman, was also a failure. In Raymondo de Larrain's French production (ad Jean Cosmos, Paul Misraki) Christine Delaroche played the rôle of *Mouche* alongside Jean-Claude Drouot and Magali Noël, whilst a German-language adaptation (ad Robert Gilbert) was mounted in 1962 at the Stadttheater, Zurich.

UK; Australia: Her Majesty's Theatre, Melbourne 19 October 1962; Lyric Theatre 8 February 1963; France; *Mouche*
Recordings: original cast (MGM), London cast (HMV), French cast (Barclay EP)

CAROUSEL Musical play in 2 acts by Oscar Hammerstein II based on *Liliom* by Ferenc Molnár. Music by Richard Rodgers. Majestic Theater, New York, 19 April 1945.

Ferenc Molnár's 1909 play, *Liliom, egy csirkefogó élete és halála* (Liliom, the life and death of a vagrant), followed its enormous success in Budapest by slowly making its way around the world – to Berlin's Lessing-Theater (1914), to London's Kingsway Theatre (as *The Daisy*, 1920), to Bucharest (1922), Paris (1923), Shanghai (1925) and to Hamburg's Thalia-Theater (1925) where the title-rôle, created by Gyula Hegedűs, was played by Max Pallenberg. Broadway saw it under the aegis of the Theatre Guild in 1921 (ad Benjamin Glazer 20 May) with Joseph Schildkraut and Eva Le Gallienne, and it was that production which was to lead to the play ultimately being made into a musical.

The Theatre Guild had produced the first collaboration between Oscar Hammerstein II and Richard Rodgers, *Oklahoma!*, with outstanding success, and in looking for a follow-up, the Guild's Terry Helburn suggested a musicalized *Liliom*. It seemed a sane idea: like *Oklahoma!* the piece was rural, innocent yet dramatic-with-a-death, and there was no need for it to be set in its original Hungary, nor to maintain the bitter and unhopeful ending in which the deceased Liliom, allowed briefly back on earth, succeeds for a second time in messing up the lives of those he loves. Its principal difference from the prosaic *Oklahoma!* was its introduction of the fantastical elements in the show's heavenly scene. Molnár, who was said to have refused Puccini permission to make the piece into an opera, permitted the authors of *Oklahoma!* to make it into a musical.

Carousel was set in New England. The sexy fairground barker Billy Bigelow (John Raitt) is sacked by his jealous employer (Jean Casto) for dallying with mill-girl, Julie Jordan (Jan Clayton). Julie loses her job too, and the pair of them settle down together and go through the problems of making ends meet. When they don't, Billy becomes sullen, rough and withdrawn, and he is finally drawn to easy, dishonest means of supplying for himself, Julie and their unborn child. He takes part in a robbery and is killed. But, 16 years on, he is allowed by the representatives of the powers on high to come down from Heaven to speak with the daughter he never met. He blows it, just as he blew the rest of his life, but as he returns to Heaven the child is led into her growing-up years on a message of sweetness and hope. The fantasy characters of the musical – the guardians of Heaven – were originally written as a church-minister-like gentleman and his wife representing Mr and Mrs God, but in the final version they were replaced by the Starkeeper, a jot further down the heavenly line of command, and a little more conducive to a touch of wryness in his character.

The score of *Carousel*, which began with the whirling tones of the fairground's Carousel Waltz where a potpourri overture would have been more normal, included a long list of numbers which became favourites: another, and equally as pretty, piece in the oblique 'People Will Say We're in Love' line of love song which pretended 'If I Loved You', the rumbustiously joyful 'June is Bustin' Out All Over', the sweet dream of the future of the number two couple, best-friend Carrie Pipperidge (Jean Darling) and her comfy salt, Enoch Snow (Eric Mattson), 'When the Children Are Asleep', and Julie's lovely love song 'What's the Use of Wond'rin'?' The most substantial musical piece, which filled out and softened down the inherently unattractive character of swaggering, shallow Billy, was his lengthy baritone soliloquy on learning of his impending fatherhood – half proud, half worried, and only a little tough. The most durable number, however, eventually turned out to be the hope-filled anthem sung by Nettie Fowler (Christine Johnson), 'You'll Never Walk Alone', the first of what would be a series of big, soaring songs for robustly voiced (mezzo)-sopranos in Rodgers and Hammerstein's musicals. For some unknown reason, this piece with its gospel message 'you'll never walk alone while you walk with God' and its distinctly tricky tessitura, became the hymn of the supporters of British football teams, ensuring itself a roaring (if vocally truncated) performance by a cast of 50,000 all around the United Kingdom most Saturdays of every year.

Apparently Molnár who, having begun his career translating Operetten for the Hungarian stage, was no novice in the musical theatre, approved the sweetened ending and the softened characterizations, and the public soon proved that he was right to do so. The Theatre Guild's production of *Carousel* ran for 890 performances on Broadway, toured for two seasons, and the show was mounted at London's Theatre Royal, Drury Lane, in the footsteps of *Oklahoma!*, which was shunted out to finish its run at the unloved Stoll Theatre in order to let its successor in. Stephen Douglass (Billy), Iva Withers (Julie), Mattson, Margot Moser (Carrie) and Marion Ross (Nettie) featured in the cast of Prince Littler's production and, if its run fell somewhat short of that of the blither *Oklahoma!*, its 566 performances more than confirmed the earlier hit.

However, the darkish-coloured *Carousel* did not find general acceptance easy. J C Williamson Ltd in Australia rejected it as gloomy, and even the success of the well-cast and sung, if further softened, film version with Gordon Macrae and Shirley Jones in the leading rôles did not help the piece to other stages. Australia finally saw *Carousel* nearly 20 years on when, after the success of *The Sound of Music*, Garnet Carroll followed up by producing the older Rodgers and Hammerstein show. The results were not comparable.

The show was played by an American company at the Brussels Worlds Fair in 1958, it was seen again in New York in a Music Theater of Lincoln Center production in 1965 (10 August) with Raitt starring opposite Eileen Christy, and was televised in America in 1967, but it did not, by and large, receive the follow-up attention that the other Rodgers and Hammerstein hits did. In the 1980s, with the rise of director power in the theatre, the show won some regional productions under the aegis of directors who found its source and those very 'serious' elements which had earlier hampered its wider acceptance, preferable to the 'frivolity' of other musical shows. It rode into a major 'operatic' recording and a production at Britain's National Theatre (10 December 1992) on the crest of such sentiments and although, rising half a century from its first production, *Carousel* still awaits a major commercial revival, posh credits such as these must inevitably earn it one soon.

UK: Theatre Royal, Drury Lane 7 June 1950; Australia: Princess Theatre, Melbourne 6 June 1964; Film: 1956 Twentieth Century Fox
Recordings: original cast (Decca), London cast (Columbia), film soundtrack (Capitol), television cast (Columbia), 1965 revival (RCA) etc

CARR, F[rank] Osmond (b nr Bradford, Yorks, 23 April 1858; d Uxbridge, Mddx, 29 August 1916). Composer for several of the earliest Victorian 'musical comedies'.

A Mus Doc and MA graduate, Carr made a first pseudonymous step into the musical theatre along with a fellow Cambridge University man, Arthur Ropes, when four matinée performances of their burlesque *Faddimir* were given in London in 1889. *Faddimir*'s quality won both lyricist Ropes (later Britain's busiest lyricist as 'Adrian Ross') and 'Oscar Neville' (Carr) immediate notice from George Edwardes and, within months, the composer had a song being sung by Nellie Farren in *Ruy Blas and the Blasé Roué* at the Gaiety Theatre as Edwardes commissioned Carr and Ross to write, first, the songs for a burlesque of *Joan of Arc*, and soon after the score for *In Town* (1892), the piece with which he initiated his famous series of modern-dress musical shows.

The collaborators also provided the songs for the even more successful *Morocco Bound* (1893), a piece which crystallized the half-book/half-music-hall 'variety musical' form, and for the musical comedy *Go-Bang*, both for producer Fred Harris, before Edwardes reclaimed Carr to collaborate with W S Gilbert (then divorced from Arthur Sullivan) on the author's clever *His Excellency*. The composer took the stride from the music-hall strains of *Morocco Bound*'s hit 'Marguerite of Monte Carlo' to Gilbertian comic opera skilfully and, in spite of the inevitable comparisons with Sullivan, produced a sufficiently successful score to allow the show a good London run and several overseas productions.

When 1896 vehicles for Little Tich (*Lord Tom Noddy*) and *In Town* star Arthur Roberts (*Biarritz*, libretto by Jerome K Jerome), both flopped, and a final London attempt with *The Maid of Athens* (1897), which he was obliged to produce himself, was a total write-off, the composer who for two or three years had been the toast of the town was suddenly done. The half-dozen musicals he wrote in the next decade were played only in the provinces.

A more than competent all-round musician, Carr was pushed into perhaps excessive limelight by the two great novelty hits for which he composed the music, but he proved in *His Excellency* that he was capable of substantial music on a level just below the top.

1889 **Faddimir, or the Triumph of Orthodoxy** (Adrian Ross) Vaudeville Theatre 29 April
1891 **Joan of Arc** (Ross, John L Shine) Opera Comique 17 January
1892 **Blue-Eyed Susan** (Henry Pettitt, George Sims) Prince of Wales Theatre 6 February
1892 **In Town** (Ross, James Leader [ie James T Tanner]) Prince of Wales Theatre 15 October
1893 **Morocco Bound** (Ross/Arthur Branscombe) Shaftesbury Theatre 13 April
1894 **Go-Bang** (Ross) Trafalgar Square Theatre 10 March
1894 **His Excellency** (W S Gilbert) Lyric Theatre 27 October
1895 **Bobbo** (Ross, Tanner) 1 act Prince's Theatre, Manchester 12 September
1896 **Lord Tom Noddy** (George Dance) Bradford 6 April; Garrick Theatre 15 September
1896 **Biarritz** (Ross/Jerome K Jerome) Prince of Wales Theatre 11 April
1897 **The Maid of Athens** (Charles Edmund Pearson, H Chance Newton) Opera Comique 3 June
1898 **Billy** (G Cooper, Ross) Newcastle 11 April
1898 **The Celestials** (C H Abbott, John D Houghton) Blackpool 1 August
1901 **The Southern Belle** (anon) Southend-on-Sea 7 March
1903 **The Rose of the Riviera** (Reginald Bacchus, George Sheldon) Brighton 25 May

1904 **Miss Mischief** (Bacchus) West London Theatre 30 October
1906 **The Scottish Bluebells** (David James) Edinburgh 31 March

CARRÉ, Albert (b Strasbourg, 22 June 1852; d Paris, 12 December 1938).

A nephew of the elder Michel Carré, and cousin to Michel fils, Albert Carré began in the theatre as an actor and occasional librettist before moving on to start his principal career, as a theatre manager, at Nancy in 1884. He subsequently shifted his activities to Paris where he spent periods in charge, successively, of the Théâtre du Vaudeville, the Gymnase, in succession to Léon Carvalho at the Opéra-Comique (1898–1913 and 1918–1925) and at the Comédie-Française (1914–18). Under his management, the Opéra-Comique knew some of its finest hours as he produced, amongst other pieces, Reynaldo Hahn's *Île de Rêve*, d'Indy's *Fervaal*, *La Bohème*, Massenet's *Cendrillon*, *Griseldis* and *Le Jongleur de Notre Dame*, Charpentier's *Louise*, Camille Erlanger's *Le Juif polonais*, *Hansel und Gretel*, Debussy's *Pelléas et Mélisande*, *La Tosca*, Leroux's *La Reine Fiamette*, Dukas's *Ariane et Barbe-Bleue*, Messager's *Fortunio*, Ravel's *L'Heure espagnole*, *La Lepreuse* and de Falla's *La vida breve*. After a period at the Comédie-Française and another as a Colonel in the army, he returned to the Opéra-Comique for a further seven years. The end of his life was less fortunate, and he died in want in 1938.

Over the years, Carré also wrote a number of plays (*La Bosse du vol*, *Le Docteur Jojo*, *La Souricière* etc) and several libretti for the musical theatre, including the book to *Les Beignets du roi* composed by Firmin Bernicat for Brussels and later produced in a revised version in Paris, the text of Messager's successful light opera, *La Basoche*, which he himself mounted at the Opéra-Comique, and the féerie *La Montagne enchantée* (1897 w Emile Moreau) produced at the Théâtre de la Porte-Saint-Martin, and equipped with incidental music by two of his Opéra-Comique regulars, Messager and Xavier Leroux.

In 1897 a musical piece called *The Kangaroo Girl* (ad Hamilton Aidé), based on *Le Docteur Jojo*, was toured in the British provinces, and his play *Le Véglione* (w Alexandre Bisson) was adapted as *For the Love of Suzanne* at off-Broadway's Martinique Theatre in 1974.

His two-time wife, **Marguerite CARRÉ** (née Giraud, b Cabourg, 16 August 1880; d Paris, December 1947), was the daughter of the manager of the theatre at Nantes. She was hired by Carré for the Opéra-Comique in 1902 and, under his nurturing and – it is said – in proportion to the increase in his passion, rose from small rôles to be prima donna at the Salle Favart. There she appeared as Mimi, Butterfly, Snegourotchka, Mélisande and Pamina, and created lead rôles in such pieces as Terrasse's *Le Mariage de Telemaque*, Leroux's *Le Carillioneur*, Albéniz's *Pepita Jimenez*, Noguès' *Chiquito le joueur de pelote*, Hué's *Titania*, *Fortunio* (Jacqueline), *La Lepreuse* and *La Fille de Roland*. After the First World War she temporarily left the Opéra-Comique and went to star at the Gaîté-Lyrique, appearing in *La Belle Hélène*, *Les Travaux d'Hercule*, *La Petite Femme de Loth*, as Lange in *La Fille de Madame Angot*, as O Mimosa San in *The Geisha* and regularly in a made-to-order mini-musical, *Manon en voyage*. She left for a second time in

1924, divorcing Carré at the same time, but returned both to husband and to the Salle Favart in 1929.

1876 **Les Amants d'Amanda** (Victor Robillard) Théâtre des Ambassadeurs 20 August
1880 **Maître Pierrot** (Félix Pardon) 1 act Contrexéville 9 August
1882 **Les Beignets du roi** (Firmin Bernicat/Benjamin Antier ad) Alcazar, Brussels 10 February
1883 **L'Amour en livrée** (Georges Street/w Paul Meyan) 1 act Eldorado 10 March
1884 **Le Panache blanc** (Philippe Flon/w A Audibert) 1 act Théâtre de la Monnaie, Brussels 15 February
1888 **Les Premières Armes de Louis XV** revised version of *Les Beignets du roi* Théâtre des Menus-Plaisirs 16 February
1890 **La Basoche** (André Messager) Opéra-Comique 30 May
1891 **Deux Reservistes** (Street/w Meyan) 1 act Casino de Paris 22 October
1895 **Le Roi Frelon** (Antoine Banès) Théâtre des Folies-Dramatiques 11 April
1924 **Faust en menage** (Claude Terrasse, Régine Flory et al) Théâtre de la Potinière 5 January
1927 **Frétillon** (Terrasse) Théâtre Municipal de Strasbourg 5 March
1932 **Le Roi bossu** (Elsa Barraine) 1 act Opéra-Comique 17 March

Autobiography: *Souvenirs de Théâtre* (Plon, Paris, 1950)

CARRÉ, Fabrice [LABROUSSE, Fabrice] (b Paris, 9 July 1856; d Paris, October 1921).

The author of a number of plays, in collaboration with such authors as Bisson, Bilhaud (*Ma Bru*), Paul Ferrier and Émile Blavet, Fabrice Carré nevertheless had his most successful moments in the musical theatre, particularly with the libretti for the joyously comical vaudeville-opérette *Josephine vendue par ses soeurs* (1886 w Ferrier) and the similarly imaginative and happily flavoured *L'Enlèvement de la Toledad* (1894). His *Mam'zelle Carabin*, musically set by Pessard, gave him a third musical theatre success both in France and abroad.

1883 **Mademoiselle Irma** (Victor Roger) 1 act Casino de Trouville 18 August
1886 **Josephine vendue par ses soeurs** (Roger/w Paul Ferrier) Théâtre des Bouffes-Parisiens 20 March
1887 **Les Délégués** (Antoine Banès/w Émile Blavet) Théâtre de la Renaissance 30 November
1889 **Le Retour d'Ulysse** (Raoul Pugno) Théâtre des Bouffes-Parisiens 1 February
1890 **La Vocation de Marius** (Pugno/w A Debelly) Théâtre des Nouveautés 29 March
1892 **La Femme de Narcisse** (Varney) Théâtre de la Renaissance 14 April
1893 **Mam'zelle Carabin** (Émile Pessard) Théâtre des Bouffes-Parisiens 3 September
1894 **L'Enlèvement de la Toledad** (Edmond Audran) Théâtre des Bouffes-Parisiens 17 October
1896 **Monsieur Lohengrin** (Audran) Théâtre des Bouffes-Parisiens 30 November
1898 **La Petite Tache** (Roger) Théâtre des Bouffes-Parisiens 26 March

CARRÉ, Michel [Antoine] (b Paris, 7 February 1865; d Paris, 11 August 1945).

Michel Carré (fils) was the son of **Michel [Florentin] CARRÉ** (b Besançon, 21 October 1819; d Argenteuil 27 June, 1872), the celebrated French operatic librettist of *Faust*, *Le Pardon de Ploermel*, *Les Pêcheurs de perles*, *Mireille*, *Mignon*, *Roméo et Juliette*, *Hamlet*, *Paul et Virginie*, and *Les Contes d'Hoffmann*. However, although he worked with Gounod, Meyerbeer, Saint-Saëns, Ambroise Thomas, Bizet and Félicien David on serious works, the elder Carré also collaborated in a lighter vein with Massé on his two most successful pieces, *Galathée* (the source for Suppé's *Die schöne Galathee*) and *Les Noces de Jeannette*, with composers such as Aimé Maillart, Jules Duprato, Erlanger and Théophile Semet, with Offenbach on the short and very sweet *Le Mariage aux lanternes*, and, in another different vein, on the great, extravagant Jules Verne spectaculars.

Carré fils, having switched from painting to writing before his twentieth birthday, quickly became a prolific playwright, revuist, and librettist for the musical stage. In his later days he also worked as a screenwriter and film director but, unlike his father, his operatic work was limited, including only two works composed by the Belgian composer Van den Eeden (*Numance* (1898) and *Rhéna* (1912)), three borderline pieces by Missa: the 1894 *Dinah* (w Paul de Choudens, based on Shakespeare's *Cymbeline*), *Muguette* and the one-act drame lyrique, *Maguelone* (1903), and the 1929 *Le Peau de chagrin* (Charles Levadé/w Pierre Decourcelle).

In the light musical theatre he worked early on with composer Gabriel Pierné on the spectacular *Bouton d'or*, and also on one piece with the ageing Lecocq, but he had his first significant success with the scenario for André Wormser's wordless pantomime *L'Enfant prodigue* (Théâtre des Bouffes-Parisiens, 1890), which pleased Paris, Vienna and London mightily through good runs and revived interest in a once popular genre which had, by then, somewhat faded. The only one of his book musicals which achieved a notable success was the saucy *Afgar, ou les loisirs andalous*, on which he collaborated with his habitual revue-writing partner André Barde and composer Charles Cuvillier, but, in a wide-ranging career stretching over nearly half a century, he had the unusual distinction of working in traditions as wide apart as the opérettes of Lecocq and the cinema where he had the distinction of making the first full-length French movie with his 1907 screen version of *L'Enfant prodigue*.

1887 **Adèle de Ponthieu** (André Wormser) Aix-les-Bains 10 September
1890 **Friquette et Blaisot** (Alfred Millet/w Charles Narrey) 1 act Casino, Cabourg 13 January; Théâtre des Bouffes-Parisiens 13 January 1890
1890 **Hilda** (Millet/w Narrey) 1 act Opéra-Comique 5 January
1893 **Bouton d'or** (Gabriel Pierné) Nouveau-Theatre 4 January
1894 **Nos bons chasseurs** (Charles Lecocq/w Paul Bilhaud) Casino de Paris 10 April
1895 **Le Dragon vert** (Wormser) Nouveau Théâtre 21 February
1895 **Pris au piège** (André Gedalge) 1 act Opéra-Comique 7 June
1896 **Rivoli** (Wormser/w Paul Burani) Théâtre des Folies-Dramatiques 30 October
1899 **Le Quart d'heure de Rabelais** (Petras Martin/w Henri Rémond) Théâtre de l'Application 17 May
1902 **Miss Bouton d'or** (Louis Ganne) Olympia 14 October
1903 **Miss Chipp** (Henri Bereny/w André de Lorde) Théâtre des Bouffes-Parisiens 31 March
1903 **Muguette** (Edmond Missa/w Georges Hartmann) Opéra-Comique 18 March
1906 **Miss Fauvette** (Ludo Ratz) Little-Palace 29 January
1906 **La Clé du Paradis** (Rodolphe Berger) Théâtre des Mathurins 3 December

1909 **Afgar, ou Les Loisirs andalous** (w Barde/Cuvillier) Théâtre Scala 2 April
1909 **Le Premier Pas** (Georges Menier) 1 act Théâtre Michel
1911 **Marmaid** (Alexandre Duval) Comédie-Royale 22 March
1912 **Sappho** (Cuvillier/w Barde) Théâtre des Capucines 26 February
1918 **La Fausse Ingénue** (Cuvillier) Théâtre Fémina 17 March
1920 **L'Amour qui rôde** (Vincent Scotto/w Albert Acremant) Eldorado 2 May
1920 **La Mousmé** (Marius Lambert/w Acremant) Théâtre Michel 10 July
1921 **Le Coq a chanté** (Jean Rioux) Marseille 4 May, Théâtre de la Gaîté-Lyrique 6 September
1922 **Pan-Pan** (Scotto/w Acremant) Ba-ta-clan 19 April
1922 **Le Fakir de Benarès** (Léo Manuel) Théâtre Mogador 21 April
1926 **Les Rendez-vous clandestins** (Léo Pouget/w Yoris d'Hansewick) La Cigale 26 April
1929 **Mariska** (Mario Cazès/w Sibre, Goudard) Trianon-Lyrique 22 December
1931 **Vieux garçons** (Louis Urgel) 1 act Théâtre de la Gaîté-Lyrique 21 February
1932 **Sylvette** (Henri Février, Marc Delmer/Claude Roland/w René Peter) Trianon-Lyrique 12 February
1933 **Le Garçon de Chez Prunier** (Joseph Szulc/w Barde) Théâtre des Capucines 19 January

CARROLL, Earl (b Pittsburgh, Pa, ?21 September 1892; d Mt Carmel, Pa, 17 June 1948).

Carroll worked hopefully in and around the theatre and the songwriting world from an early age before finding himself a position in a New York music publishing house in 1912. He began supplying lyrics (sometimes as 'Carl Earl') to the popular tunesmiths of the time and, over the next few years, he provided the songwords and even some tunes for a number of musical plays, notably in collaboration with west-coast producer and writer Oliver Morosco. Together they scored a double success in the early war years with *So Long, Letty* and *Canary Cottage*, both of which shows followed up their careers on the west coast, on Broadway, and round America with successful productions in Australia.

Carroll turned to management in 1919, and became celebrated as the guiding spirit behind a series of girlie revues produced over 17 years as the *Earl Carroll Vanities* (13 episodes) and, occasionally, the *Earl Carroll Sketch Book* (two). He ventured barely into the book musical, sponsoring *How's the King* (1925), the publicity musical *The Florida Girl* (1925), a piece backed by and vaunting the wares of a property company, the revusical *Murder at the Vanities* (1933) and the society piece *Just Because*, mounted on $75,000 gathered from its writer's wealthy friends. A second vanity production, *Fioretta*, to which he also put his name as a co-writer, lost $350,000 for its wealthy sponsoress and ended with one of the writers committing suicide.

He built the Earl Carroll Theater in New York in 1922, and a second house under the same name in 1931. He was killed in an airplane crash in 1948.

A fictionalized biography concentrates on depicting Carroll as what it hopefully calls 'the most notorious connoisseur of female flesh in show business'.

1914 **The Pretty Mrs Smith** (Alfred Robyn/Elmer B Harris, Oliver Morosco) Burbank Theater, Los Angeles 25 January; Casino Theater, New York, 21 September
1915 **So Long, Letty** (Harris, Morosco) Morosco Theater, Los

Angeles 3 July; Shubert Theater, New York 23 October 1916

1916 **Canary Cottage** (Harris, Morosco) Empress Theater, San Diego, 18 March; Morosco Theater, New York 5 February 1917

1917 **The Love Mill** (Alfred Francis) Baltimore 12 February; 48th Street Theater, New York 7 February 1918

1929 **Fioretta** (George Bagby, 'G Romilli'/w Charlton Andrews) Earl Carroll Theater 5 February

Biography: Murray, K: *The Body Merchant* (Ward Ritchie, Pasadena, 1976)

CARTE, Richard D'Oyly (b London, 3 May 1844; d London, 3 April 1901). Godfather to the Savoy operas.

In his earliest days in the theatre, Richard D'Oyly Carte worked as a theatrical and concert agent, a tentative composer, and then as business and company manager for several musical shows. It was while he was engaged as manager for Selina Dolaro's season at the Royalty Theatre in 1875 that the search for a forepiece to share the bill with the diva's version of Offenbach's *La Périchole* led to his being instrumental in bringing composer Arthur Sullivan and librettist W S Gilbert back together. Their one-act cantata *Trial by Jury*, composed specifically to fill the empty spot, not only fitted the bill perfectly but also proved the highlight of the season and ensured its success. In 1876 Carte took out two opéra-bouffe tours, playing *La Fille de Madame Angot*, *La Grande-Duchesse de Gérolstein*, *Trial by Jury* and his own short *Happy Hampstead*, before returning to the Royalty in 1877 as manager for Kate Santley and her productions of *Orphée aux enfers* and *La Marjolaine*.

In late 1876 it had been announced that Fred Sullivan, brother of Arthur and already the producer of a provincial season of *The Contrabandista*, was to take the Globe Theatre to produce a new and full-length work by Gilbert and Sullivan. But Fred Sullivan died in January 1877 and, after dispensing some considerable efforts in raising the necessary capital and putting together 'The Comedy Opera Company', it was Carte who instead opened Gilbert and Sullivan's first full-sized comic opera, *The Sorcerer*, at the Opera Comique in November 1877, as manager for his syndicate. The show won sufficient success for the team to venture a second similar piece and, when *HMS Pinafore* turned out to be an enormous hit, Carte declared himself independent of his backers. With Gilbert and Sullivan supporting him, he faced out their clumsy (if, apparently, at least partly justified) counter-attacks and won himself the position of producer and rights-holder to *HMS Pinafore*. Thereafter, Carte produced all of the celebrated Gilbert/Sullivan comic operas, at first at the Opera Comique and subsequently at the Savoy Theatre, built (like its contiguous hotel) on the profits from *HMS Pinafore* and *The Pirates of Penzance*.

From *The Pirates of Penzance* in 1880 to *The Gondoliers* in 1889 the team had a run of almost unbroken success, unparalleled in the then history of the British musical theatre. Carte ran Gilbert and Sullivan's shows end-to-end at the Savoy, operated multiple repertoire companies playing them around Britain and occasionally on the Continent, and had a hand in most of their principal American productions, leading an intermittent but forceful fight against the copyright incoherencies and piracies of the time. He also kept a close watch on other potentially winning writers, and was instrumental in staging some of the best of the other British pieces of the time (*Rip van Winkle*, *Manteaux Noirs*, *Billee Taylor* etc) in America and/or on the road.

When Gilbert and Sullivan split, Carte continued to run comic opera at the Savoy, producing Edward Solomon's *The Nautch Girl* and *The Vicar of Bray*, Sullivan's *Haddon Hall*, and the unfortunate *Jane Annie* before his writers came back together to supply him, less happily than before, with *Utopia (Limited)* and *The Grand Duke*.

At this same time, he built and opened the Royal English Opera House in Cambridge Circus, initiating it with Sullivan's *Ivanhoe* and following up with Messager's *La Basoche* and Bemberg's *Elaine* before getting out of what had from the start proven an unprofitable venture. His theatre became the Palace Music Hall, and then the Palace Theatre.

With no further new Gilbert and Sullivan musicals to fill the Savoy, Carte instead produced Messager's *Mirette*, a rewrite of Sullivan's early *The Contrabandista* as *The Chieftain*, McKenzie's *His Majesty*, a new version of *La Grande-Duchesse de Gérolstein*, Sullivan's *The Beauty Stone*, a remusicked version of *L'Étoile* as *The Lucky Star* and a series of revivals of Gilbert and Sullivan favourites before finding his most successful new piece in several years with the pairing of Sullivan and Basil Hood on *The Rose of Persia*. It was to be his last, for shortly before the production of the first piece by the two writers who seemed as if they might provide him with comic operas for years to come, Carte died.

His wife, Helen (née Black, aka Lenoir) continued to run the operation for some time, but the profitability of comic opera had been severely dampened by the vogue for musical comedy and she soon had to give in. During the run of *The Emerald Isle*, she ceded the Savoy Theatre and its company to William Greet.

The D'Oyly Carte company continued at first with comic opera. Greet produced *Ib and Little Christina*, *The Willow Pattern*, *Merrie England* and *A Princess of Kensington* before briefly, and at first not unsuccessfully, switching the company to the more profitable field of musical comedy with *The Earl and the Girl*. Ultimately, however, it was the Gilbert and Sullivan repertoire to which they returned, and the company which bore Carte's name continued to purvey the 'Savoy operas' to Britain and the rest of the world until financial considerations forced its closure in 1982. However, on the death of Bridget D'Oyly Carte, grand-daughter of Richard, a substantial legacy from her personal fortune enabled a new D'Oyly Carte Opera Company to be set up. That company began operations in 1988 with productions of *Iolanthe* and *The Yeomen of the Guard* and continues to run seasons in London and the British provinces, though no longer on the full-time basis and with an ad hoc, rather than a permanent, company.

1868 **Dr Ambrosias, His Secret** (T H Bayley) St George's Hall 8 August

1871 **Marie** 1 act Opera Comique 26 August

1876 **Happy Hampstead** (Frank Desprez) Alexandra Theatre, Liverpool 3 July, Royalty Theatre, London 13 January 1877

CARTER, [Herbert] Desmond (b Bristol, 15 June 1895; d London, 3 February 1939). Ubiquitous West End lyricist of the 1920s and 1930s.

Carter worked as an insurance clerk before finding his

way into the worlds of songwriting and the musical theatre. His earliest theatrical experiences were gained in the provinces, where he contributed his first songwords to a pair of regional children's productions, but he moved swiftly on to another level when he was given his first London break on the George Grossmith production of *Primrose* at the Winter Garden Theatre. His words were set to the music of the young George Gershwin.

Thereafter, Carter quickly became one of the town's busiest lyric-writers, contributing over the 15 years of his career to such revues as *Shake Your Feet*, *Cochran's Revue of 1930* ('Wind in the Willows'), *The Chelsea Follies*, *Fanfare*, *Rhyme and Rhythm*, *Follow the Sun*, *Transatlantic Rhythm*, *And on We Go*, and posthumously *Rise Above It*, supplying additional or alternative lyrics for both imported and new shows (*Merely Molly*, *So Long, Letty*, *The Millionaire Kid*, *A Connecticut Yankee at the Court of King Arthur*, *Love Laughs*, *Follow Through*, the revival of *Tonight's the Night*, *Tell Me More*, *Lady, Be Good!*, *Sunny*, *Funny Face*, *Lido Lady* etc), and having a major lyricist's credit on more than 30 shows, including many of the dance-comedy hits of the era (*Lady Luck*, *That's a Good Girl*, *So This Is Love*, *Love Lies*, *The Love Race*, *Jill Darling*, *Sporting Love*, *Over She Goes*). He also had a hand in the more operettic adaptations of *Walzer aus Wien*, *Die Dubarry* and *Wenn die kleinen Veilchen blühen* and contributed to such novelties as the dance play *Ballerina*.

1922 **The Rose and the Ring** (Robert Cox/Harris Deane) Liverpool Playhouse December; Wyndham's Theatre, London 19 December

1923 **The Magic Sword** (Cox/Deane) Liverpool Playhouse 22 December

1924 **Primrose** (George Gershwin/w Ira Gershwin/George Grossmith, Guy Bolton) Winter Garden Theatre 11 September

1925 **Dear Little Billie** (H B Hedley, Jack Strachey/Firth Shephard) Shaftesbury Theatre 25 August

1926 **Just a Kiss** (*Pas sur la bouche*) English lyrics w Graham John, Vivian Ellis (Shaftesbury Theatre)

1926 **My Son John** (*Riquette*) revised English lyrics w Harry Graham (Shaftesbury Theatre)

1927 **Lady Luck** (Hedley, Strachey/Shephard) Carlton Theatre 27 April

1920 **That's a Good Girl** (Phil Charig, Joseph Meyer/w Furber, I Gershwin/Furber) London Hippodrome 5 June

1928 **The Yellow Mask** (Vernon Duke/Edgar Wallace) Carlton Theatre 8 February

1928 **So This is Love** ('Hal Brody'/Stanley Lupino, Arthur Rigby) Winter Garden Theatre 25 April

1929 **Love Lies** ('Hal Brody'/Lupino, Rigby) Gaiety Theatre 20 March

1930 **Darling, I Love You** (Hedley, Harry Acres/Stanley Brightman, Rigby) Gaiety Theatre 22 January

1930 **Here Comes the Bride** (Arthur Schwartz/w Howard Dietz/R P Weston, Bert Lee) Piccadilly Theatre 20 February

1930 **The Love Race** (John Clarke/Lupino) Gaiety Theatre 25 June

1930 **Little Tommy Tucker** (Vivian Ellis) Daly's Theatre 19 November

1931 **Song of the Drum** (Ellis, Finck/Fred Thompson, Bolton) Theatre Royal, Drury Lane 9 January

1931 **Blue Roses** (Ellis/w Caswell Garth) Gaiety Theatre 20 January

1931 **My Sister and I** (*Meine Schwester und ich*) (aka *Meet my Sister*) English lyrics w Frank Eyton (Shaftesbury Theatre)

1931 **Waltzes from Vienna** (*Walzer aus Wien*) English version w Garth (London Coliseum)

1931 **Hold My Hand** (Noel Gay/Lupino) Gaiety Theatre 23 December

1932 **The Dubarry** (*Die Dubarry*) English version w Rowland Leigh (His Majesty's Theatre)

1932 **Wild Violets** (*Wenn die kleinen Veilchen blühen*) English version w Hassard Short, Reginald Purdell (Theatre Royal, Drury Lane)

1932 **The Compulsory Wife** (Strachey/w Collie Knox, Strachey/C Bailey Hick) tour

1933 **That's a Pretty Thing** (aka *Paste*) (Gay/Lupino) Daly's Theatre 22 November

1933 **Jill Darling** (Ellis/w Marriot Edgar) Alhambra Theatre, Glasgow 23 December; Saville Theatre 19 December 1934

1934 **Sporting Love** (Billy Mayerl/w Eyton/Lupino) Gaiety Theatre 31 March

1935 **The Flying Trapeze** (Ralph Benatzky arr Mabel Wayne/w Douglas Furber, Eyton/Furber) Alhambra Theatre 4 May

1935 **A Kingdom for a Cow** (*Die Kuhhandel*) English lyrics (Savoy Theatre)

1936 **Rise and Shine** (aka *Darling You*) (Robert Stolz et al/w Graham et al/ad w Graham, then Con West, Geoffrey Orme) Theatre Royal, Drury Lane 7 May

1936 **Over She Goes** (Mayerl/w Eyton/Lupino) Saville Theatre 23 September

1937 **Big Business** (Jack Waller, Joseph Tunbridge/w Lee/w Lee, K R G Browne) London Hippodrome 18 February

1937 **Crazy Days** (Mayerl/w Eyton/Lupino) Shaftesbury Theatre 14 September

1938 **Bobby Get Your Gun** (Waller, Tunbridge/w Clifford Grey, Lee/Thompson, Bolton, Lee) Adelphi Theatre 7 October

CARYLL, Ivan [TILKIN, Félix] (b Liège, Belgium, ?1860; d New York, 29 November 1921). Principal composer and conductor for the heyday of the Gaiety musical comedy who encouraged the development of a more book-orientated type of comedy musical in a second career in America.

Born in Belgium and educated at the Paris Conservatoire, Ivan Caryll settled in Britain in the mid-1880s and made the bulk of his career there, becoming, in tandem with Lionel Monckton, the composer for the internationally famous series of musical comedies created at the Gaiety Theatre under the management of George Edwardes in the 1890s and 1900s.

His earliest days in London were spent largely in musical hack work and in teaching. However, he got a serious opportunity as a composer in 1886 while he was working at the Comedy Theatre on the extremely successful comic opera, *Erminie*. That show's producer, Violet Melnotte looking for a follow-up to her hit, decided to produce his French opéra-comique *The Lily of Léoville*, a piece written during Caryll's Parisian days in collaboration with French librettist Félix Rémo. Although *The Lily of Léoville* was a failure, the music gained some fair notice and a German version was subsequently produced in Hamburg (*Das Andreasnacht*, Carl-Schultze Theater 6 December 1890, ad Friedrich Wilhelm Wulff, W Behre). It was to be several years before Caryll gained a second chance at a full score.

In the meanwhile, he made contact with some of the town's other important producers, supplying, amongst other journeyman work, four pieces to be interpolated into the score of George Edwardes's Gaiety burlesque *Monte Cristo Jr* (1886) and a series of numbers to flesh out the compilation of Firmin Bernicat music which Kate

Santley assembled for the score of her touring vehicle *Vetah*.

It was however as a conductor that Caryll made his first noticeable mark. When Henry J Leslie bought the Gaiety theatre production of *Dorothy* from Edwardes and transferred it to the Prince of Wales Theatre, Gaiety musical director Meyer Lutz remained at his own theatre, and Caryll was appointed conductor for the revamped show which was to become the musical theatre hit of the era. He remained Leslie's musical director through the whole four years and three shows of the producer's dramatic career, shifting with him to his new Lyric Theatre on Shaftesbury Avenue where *Doris* and *The Red Hussar* were produced and remaining there, when Leslie's operation exploded, as musical director for the theatre's new manager, Horace Sedger.

Under Leslie, Caryll fulfilled the musical director's normal function of supplying incidental music as necessary, and he composed several curtain-raisers to order, but when Sedger's first attraction, Audran's *La Cigale et la fourmi*, was extensively revamped to suit what the producer considered British tastes, that revamping included the rejection of some of Audran's score, and Caryll was called upon to supply alternative music. He finally contributed nearly a third of the score, including two principal songs for the leading man and a full-scale finale. His work on this highly successful production brought him commissions to work over Audran's *Miss Helyett* (1891) and Lacôme's *Ma mie Rosette* (1892) for their London productions and, following the death of Alfred Cellier, to complete the arrangement of *The Mountebanks* (1892) for production at the Lyric.

Finally, Sedger entrusted Caryll with the composition of his first full score since *The Lily of Léoville*. The manager had used a sexy little American performer called May Yohé in his production of Albéniz's *The Magic Opal* and he now (convinced by a large cash injection from the lady and her lordly backer) decided to have a piece written specially for her. The result was a latter-day burlesque called *Little Christopher Columbus* for which Caryll, handicapped by a star with a range of about an octave, composed a set of songs which finally put him on the road to success as a theatre writer. From a delightful light score which danced neatly between the comic opera style of *Dorothy* and *La Cigale* and a refined kind of music-hall writing, Miss Yohé's coon song 'Oh Honey, My Honey' and the ballad 'Lazily, Drowsily' both became enormous hits, and both the ballads and the comedy numbers showed that the well-educated and versatile Caryll was an ideal composer for that new type of musical theatre, part comic opera and part burlesque, which was now becoming popular.

The ever-watchful George Edwardes was quick to realise this and, at the end of the run of *Little Christopher Columbus*, Caryll made the move from the Lyric to the Gaiety. The success of *Little Christopher* was soon confirmed when Caryll provided the score to Edwardes's landmark production of *The Shop Girl* ('Love on the Japanese Plan', 'Over the Hills') and he promptly settled in as composer-in-residence and musical director at the Gaiety Theatre. He remained there for 15 years, baton in hand, supplying music for all the great hits of that theatre's most prosperous period from *The Shop Girl* (1894) through to *Our Miss Gibbs* (1909). Under Edwardes's aegis, a writing partnership with Lionel Monckton evolved, beginning with Monckton as a subsidiary 'additional songs' partner, but later on equal terms, with both partners turning out much of the best of the light theatre music on the London stage in its most successful Victorian and Edwardian years.

After his move to the Gaiety, Caryll continued to work for Sedger. An attempted follow-up for May Yohé called *Dandy Dick Whittington* failed under the double handicap of an old pantomime book and the lady's cavalier attitudes to work, but when Sedger brought the touring musical *The Gay Parisienne* to town, and had it equipped with a particularly catchy replacement Caryll score, it proved a mighty success, both at home and overseas. The Caryll version continued to tour for several decades. Amongst other 'outside' work, he provided a new score for Vanloo and Leterrier's *L'Étoile* for D'Oyly Carte, composed the music for George Dance's unhappy *A Ladies' Paradise* and provided additional songs for two of the biggest hits of the era, *Florodora* and *A Chinese Honeymoon*. The soon faded Miss Yohé gave him an additional Broadway showing by introducing his 'Down by the River' and 'Kiss Me to Sleep' into Broadway's *The Giddy Throng* (1900).

As Edwardes spread his production arm further afield, Caryll was given the opportunity to vary his style from the regular Gaiety formula, and the early years of the new century saw him turn out some of his best work both in the musical comedy manner with the charming *The Girl from Kays* and in the light opera vein with *The Duchess of Dantzic*, a piece written in his Prince of Wales Theatre days and originally intended as a vehicle for Florence St John. Evie Greene played the titular Madame Sans-Gêne, equipped with a score which echoed the most attractive tones of French opéra-comique. *The Earl and the Girl*, written with Seymour Hicks and staged by William Greet with the remnants of the D'Oyly Carte Opera Company, was another notable Caryll success in this period. At Christmas 1903, Caryll had the until recently unparalleled distinction of having five musicals running at the same time in the West End of London (*The Girl from Kays*, *The Duchess of Dantzic*, *The Orchid*, *The Earl and the Girl*, *The Cherry Girl*).

In 1910, with *Our Miss Gibbs* still giving him one of the greatest successes of his career, Caryll decided to leave both the Gaiety and Britain and head for New York. Still only 50 years old, he had plenty left to give, but the feeling at the Gaiety was changing and Edwardes, as he had always done, was looking for new ways and new faces to keep the old theatre ahead of the times. Caryll had worked with the American librettist C M S (Hugh) McLellan on a piece called *Nelly Neil* in an ill-judged attempt to provide Edna May with a West-End successor to *The Belle of New York*, and the pair joined forces again in New York with a series of musicals based, like *The Girl from Kays*, on French plays, a series which attempted, with some success, to rival the fashion for Viennese operetta. Caryll, whose talent was a chameleon one, made the transition with aplomb and his second Broadway venture, *The Pink Lady*, in particular, proved as great a success as his English shows. While everything that was singable in Vienna was making its way to America, *The Pink Lady* (adapted from the farce *Le Satyre*) actually made the reverse trip to play London, Paris and Budapest. Its most famous tune, the Pink Lady Waltz ('My Beautiful Lady'), which remains one of Caryll's best known numbers, resurfaced in 1988 in the score of the

London Palladium extravaganza, *Ziegfeld*. A musical version of the Paris farce *La Grimpette* under the title *Oh! Oh! Delphine* was another delightful and happily exported triumph, and a third piece built on the same strong-booked principle, *The Little Café*, if not quite such a hit as the previous two, nevertheless did well.

Caryll's subsequent Broadway shows included three successful fairytale-style musical comedies written to feature comedian Fred Stone, both with his partner, Dave Montgomery (*Chin-Chin*) and, following Montgomery's death, alone (*Jack o'Lantern*, 'Wait Till the Cows Come Home', *Tip Top*). At the same time, George Grossmith picked up his latest French-based musical comedy, *The Girl Behind the Gun*, and transferred it to London under the title *Kissing Time* to open the new Winter Garden Theatre. It was a great success, and Caryll returned to London for one last Gaiety musical, a version of the Paris farce *Un coup de téléphone* called *The Kiss Call* (1919).

His final shows did a little less well. Both were musical comedies – one adapted from Adolf Philipp's touring musical *Mimi* as *Kissing Time* (borrowing the title of the London version of *The Girl Behind the Gun*), the other a version of the international comedy hit *Le Souris d'hôtel*, played as *Little Miss Raffles* and then as *The Hotel Mouse* – and both were produced on Broadway, the latter posthumously, with only relative success.

During his whole career in both England and America, Caryll maintained close links with the European, and particularly the Parisian theatre and, indeed, kept a richly appointed home in France to which he repaired regularly with his current wife and children. He continued to write songs and incidental music for Parisian comedies – notably *La Marraine de Charley*, the French version of the English farce *Charley's Aunt* ('La Canotière d'Oxford', 'Le Chanson des Houblons' and a version of 'Honey, My Honey') – and five of his English-language musicals (*Le Toréador, La Demoiselle de magasin, Les Jolies Filles de Gottenberg, La Dame en Rose, Hello!! Charley* otherwise *The Earl and the Girl*) received Paris productions in a period when the products of the English stage were largely shunned by the French.

Although these imports gained some considerable success, the musical *S.A.R.* (1908), a version of the hit play *Le Prince Consort* written specifically for Paris, was probably the best received of his works in France. Caryll also composed one score, for the spectacular *Die Reise in Cuba*, specifically for Gabor Steiner's Venedig in Wien pleasure-garden theatre in Vienna, another city which had welcomed versions of his British musicals (*Die Ladenmamsell, Das Cirkusmädel, Der Toreador, Ein durchgeganges Mädel, Miss Gibbs, Der Laufbursche, Die verhexte Wien[erstadt]* ad from *The New Aladdin*).

Caryll's career encompassed three eras of musical theatre and he seemed to be equally happy in each of them. If his greatest successes were made in the light musical comedy area, epitomized by the Gaiety Theatre shows in which he made his name, he proved with scores as divergent as the classic operetta *The Duchess of Dantzic* and *S.A.R.* on the one hand and the post-war *The Girl Behind the Gun*, with its modern fox-trot and one-step rhythms, on the other, that he was a theatre composer who, unlike his contemporaries Lionel Monckton and Sidney Jones, could and would move with times and musical styles. His scores for *The Pink Lady* and *Oh! Oh! Delphine*, a pair of shows which marked a turning towards a more intimate, book-based kind of musical play on the Broadway stage, contain numbers which equal the best that both the Viennese waltz-masters and the new wave of American dance-song-writers were writing in the years around the First World War. A true theatre composer of his time, he was equally as capable of turning out a complicated finale or concerted number as he was a catchy point number or comedy song but, largely because so much of his work was written for a kind of show which was by its nature ephemeral, few of his songs have survived as standards.

Caryll was married for a period to the American vocalist Geraldine Ulmar and also to another performer, Maud Hill (Maud Plantaganet in *The Shop Girl* etc). His daughter Primrose Caryll was seen as a musical comedy performer on the American stage in a modest career which included an appearance in her father's *Kissing Time*, whilst his son Felix Caryll took minor rôles in several London musicals.

1886 **The Lily of Léoville** (Félix Rémo ad Alfred Murray) Comedy Theatre 10 May

1887 **Jubilation** ('Richard Henry') 1 act Prince of Wales Theatre 14 May

1888 **Warranted Burglar Proof** (w Henry, Leslie/B C Stephenson) 1 act Prince of Wales Theatre 31 March

1889 **Love's Trickery** (Cunningham Bridgman) 1 act Lyric Theatre 31 August

1890 **La Cigale** (*La Cigale et la fourmi*) additional music for English version w F C Burnand (Lyric Theatre)

1890 **The Sentry** 1 act (Rémo, T Murray Watson) Lyric Theatre 5 April

1891 **Miss Decima** (*Miss Helyett*) additional music for revised English version w F C Burnand (Criterion Theatre)

1891 **Love and Law** (Frank Latimer) 1 act Lyric Theatre 4 March

1892 **Ma mie Rosette** revised English version w George Dance (Globe Theatre)

1892 **Opposition** ('Richard Henry') 1 act Lyric Theatre 28 June

1893 **Little Christopher Columbus** (USA: *Little Christopher*) (George R Sims) Lyric Theatre 10 October

1894 **The Shop Girl** (w Lionel Monckton/Adrian Ross, H J W Dam/Dam) Gaiety Theatre 24 November

1894 **The Yaller Girl** (Sims) 1 act Moore and Burgess Minstrels 31 December

1895 **Dandy Dick Whittington** (aka *The Circus Boy*) (George Sims) Avenue Theatre 2 March

1895 **Uncle Tom's Cabin** (Sims) tableaux vivants

1896 **The Gay Parisienne** (USA: *The Girl from Paris*) (w others/George Dance) Duke of York's Theatre 4 April

1896 **The Circus Girl** (w Monckton/Harry Greenbank, Ross/Walter Palings, James T Tanner) Gaiety Theatre 5 December

1897 **La Beigneuse** (George Sims) 1 act Palace Theatre

1898 **A Runaway Girl** (w Monckton/H Greenbank, Aubrey Hopwood/Seymour Hicks, Harry Nicholls) Gaiety Theatre 21 May

1899 **The Lucky Star** (*L'Étoile*) new score for English version w Charles H E Brookfield Savoy Theatre 7 January

1900 **The Messenger Boy** (w Monckton/Ross, Percy Greenbank/Murray, Tanner) Gaiety Theatre 3 February

1901 **Die Reise nach Cuba** (Leopold Krenn, Carl Lindau) Venedig in Wien, Vienna 3 August

1901 **The Ladies' Paradise** (George Dance) Theatre Royal, Hanley 11 March

1901 **The Toreador** (w Monckton/P Greenbank, Ross/Nicholls, Tanner) Gaiety Theatre 17 June

1902 **The Girl from Kays** (w Cecil Cook/Owen Hall) Apollo Theatre 15 November

1903 **The Duchess of Dantzic** (Henry Hamilton) Lyric Theatre 17 October

1903 **The Orchid** (w Monckton/Ross, P Greenbank/Tanner) Gaiety Theatre 28 October

1903 **The Earl and the Girl** (P Greenbank/Hicks) Adelphi Theatre 10 December

1903 **The Cherry Girl** (Hopwood/Hicks) Vaudeville Theatre 21 December

1905 **The Spring Chicken** (Ross, Greenbank/Grossmith) Gaiety Theatre 30 May

1906 **The Little Cherub** (aka *The Girl on the Stage*) (Ross/Owen Hall) Prince of Wales Theatre 13 January

1906 **The New Aladdin** (W H Risque, Ross, Greenbank et al/Tanner) Gaiety Theatre 29 September

1907 **Nelly Neil** (C M S McLellan) Aldwych Theatre 10 January

1907 **The Girls of Gottenberg** (Ross et al/Grossmith, L E Berman) Gaiety Theatre 15 May

1908 **Son Altesse Royale (S.A.R.)** (Léon Xanrof, Jules Chancel) Théâtre des Bouffes-Parisiens, Paris 11 November

1909 **Our Miss Gibbs** (Ross, P Greenbank/Tanner et al) Gaiety Theatre 23 January

1911 **Marriage à la Carte** (McLellan) Casino Theater, New York 2 January

1911 **The Pink Lady** (McLellan) New Amsterdam Theater, New York 13 March

1912 **Oh! Oh! Delphine** (McLellan) Knickerbocker Theater, New York 30 September

1913 **The Little Café** (McLellan) New Amsterdam Theater, New York 10 November

1914 **The Belle of Bond Street** revised *The Girl from Kays* Shubert Theater, New York 30 March

1914 **Chin-Chin** (Anne Caldwell, James O'Dea/Caldwell, R H Burnside) Globe Theater, New York 20 October

1914 **Papa's Darling** (H B Smith) New Amsterdam Theater, New York 2 November

1917 **Jack o'Lantern** (Caldwell, Burnside) Globe Theater, New York 16 October

1918 **The Girl Behind the Gun** (aka *Kissing Time*) (Guy Bolton, P G Wodehouse) New Amsterdam Theater, New York 16 September

1918 **The Canary** (H B Smith, Wodehouse, Caldwell) Globe Theater, New York 4 November

1919 **The Kiss Call** (P Greenbank, Ross, Clifford Grey/Fred Thompson) Gaiety Theatre 8 October

1920 **Tip-Top** (Caldwell, Burnside) Globe Theater, New York 5 October

1920 **Kissing Time** (Philander Johnson, Grey, Irving Caesar/George Hobart) Lyric Theater, New York 11 October

1921 **Little Miss Raffles** (Grey/Guy Bolton) Stamford, Conn 1 December

1922 **The Hotel Mouse** revised *Little Miss Raffles* w Armand Vecsey Shubert Theater, New York 13 March

CASANOVA, Giovanni Jacopo de Seingalt (b Venice, 1725 ; d Bohemia, 4 June 1798).

The name of Giovanni Jacopo Casanova has, thanks to a 12-volume set of memoirs that are probably as about as genuine as those of Frank Harris, joined that of Don Juan as synonymous with the notion of the dashing, Mediterranean-macho sex maniac. However, on those allegedly rare occasions when he was not out putting it about, the real Casanova was apparently a highly skilled adventurer and intriguer who made himself a profitable place in Venice, Paris, St Petersburg, Constantinople, Madrid and in various other cities where royalty and public figures were ready to be attracted by his charms and to find useful

his spying talents. His name has been attached, over the years, to a whole series of theatrical pieces, some concentrating more on the spying and the royal connections, others on the more trouserless moments, and most getting happily fictional in both directions.

The best-known of the *Casanova* musical shows is undoubtedly the spectacular Operette in seven scenes by Rudolph Schanzer and Ernst Welisch, illustrated with music from the works of Johann Strauss arranged by Ralph Benatzky, and produced at Berlin's Grosses Schauspielhaus in 1928 (1 September). Michael Bohnen played a Casanova who wooed the dancer Barberina (Anny Ahlers) in scene one, the Countess Dohna (Emmy Sturm) in scene two, carried off the virginal Laura (Anni Frind) from her convent in scene three on behalf of his friend Hohenfels, waltzed with the Empress of Austria in scene four, and returned to Venice, his exile rescinded, in scene seven in time for Carnival, which allowed the theatre's designer, Ernst Stern, to go to town with a revolving stage depicting great chunks of the Grand Canal. The vastly extravagant Erik Charell staging and a well-arranged score, which made one piece of reprocessed Strauss into a hit as the Nuns' Chorus, helped the show to a fine success and productions on the equally spectacle-filled stage of the London Coliseum (24 May 1932) and of Vienna's Volksoper (10 October 1935).

Another, earlier German *Casanova*, an Operette in 3 acts by Jacques Glück and Wilhelm Steinberger, with music by Paul Lincke, with a text based on just one of its hero's amorous adventures, was first produced in Chemnitz (5 November 1913), and later seen in Budapest (ad Emil Balassa) as *A szerelem királya* ('the king of love' Revü Színház 16 October 1920). By that time Hungary, however, had already had its own, highly successful *Casanova* in the grand Operette in 3 acts by Jenő Faragó, music by Izsó Barna, first produced at the Népszinház 11 October 1902 for a splendid run of 56 performances, and revived on a number of occasions thereafter.

A further German *Casanova*, a musical by Helmut Bez and Jürgen Degenhardt, composed by Gerd Natschinksi, which gallivanted through as many traditional Operette venues, from Warsaw to London, and ladies as could be fitted in to two acts, was produced in Berlin in 1976 (Metropoltheater, 10 September), whilst the 1942 Paul Burkhard comic opera *Casanova in Schweiz* apparently took the much-librettoed hero to its composer's native Switzerland.

The German fascination with the gentleman also reached into more operatic spheres, when Lortzing composed a successful *Casanova* (Leipzig, 1841) based on a French vaudeville, *Casanova au Fort Saint-André*, (the fellow really got around) followed by a 16-scene spectacular by Ernst Ritterfeld, music by Robert Leonard, mounted at the Centraltheater, Hamburg 25 October 1898, another opera by B Pulvermacher (Liegnitz 21 November 1890) and yet another by Arthur Kusterer (Karlsruhe 22 September 1922). The Polish composer Rózycki followed the example in 1923 (Warsaw, 3 May), imitated by Volkmar Andreae whose *Der Abenteuer des Casanova* was produced in Dresden in 1924 (17 June).

The rest of the world has shown less interest than Germany in the gallivanting Giacomo, although it was announced in 1931, in the wake of Benatzky's piece, that

Rudolf Friml and Bernard Bercovici were preparing a *Casanova* (which had started out to be a *Don Juan*) for the benefit of Dennis King, just at the same time that another musical on the same subject was also announced. Neither happened. A British provincial *Casanova* (Norton York/Ivor Burgoyne 11 April 1972) which managed to swish him past Madame de Pompadour, Catherine the Great, David Garrick, the Duke of Bedford and others, folded out of town.

THE CASINO GIRL Musical farce in 3 acts (later 2) by Harry B Smith. Music by Ludwig Englander. Casino Theater, New York, 19 March 1900.

The Casino Girl was one of the most successful examples of turn-of-the-century American musical comedy. Built on the Gaiety Theatre principle, it used that house's standard combination of exotic settings, pretty girls (Mabelle Gilman in the title rôle, Virginia Earle in breeches, and all the Casino chorus, mostly hired for looks rather than talent), much comedy (principally from Sam Bernard) and some light-hearted and topical songs from a variety of composers (the playbill credited 'interpolated numbers by John Philip Sousa, Harry T MacConnell, Reginald De Koven, Arthur Nevin, Will Marion Cook and Fred Solomon') including such jolly titles as 'Isabella's Umbrella', 'A Lesson in Acting', 'American Heiresses' and 'De Voodoo Man', to make up a piece which would be the Casino Theater's own answer to the enormously popular products of the London stage, and it fulfilled that function more than adequately.

The songs and comedy were set into a story which had Casino chorus girl, Laura Lee (Mabelle Gilman), pursued to Cairo by an amorous English earl called Percy Harold Ethelbert Frederick Cholmondley (Virginia Earle), and the other characters included such standard favourites as the amorous Pilsener Pasha, khedive of Egypt (Bernard) with 'Only a Hundred Wives' and a Dutch accent, a soubrette called Dolly Twinkle to sing about 'The Automobile Girl', girls rejoicing in the names of Lotta Rocks (Irene Bentley) and Roxy Rocks (Ella Snyder) and a pair of comic thieves, Fromage (Albert Hart) and Potage (Louis Wesley), blatantly borrowed from *Erminie*, the former of whom pretends to be 'The Diamond Dude'. One of the novelty numbers, in a second act made up largely of speciality acts, and constantly done over during the show's run, was an 'Electric ballet', danced on a darkened stage with red and/or white lights variously illuminated in the dancers' cleavage, under their hats or around their hips, and finally lighting up a large butterfly on each hat, so that only the butterflies were seen exiting.

In between the three seasons of the various versions of the show which made up *The Casino Girl's* Broadway life – 91 initial performances plus 40 more in R B Smith's revised version (6 August 1900), then 32 more the following season from 8 April 1901 in its 'anglicized' version at the Knickerbocker – producer George Lederer took an American cast including Richard Carle (yankee impresario J Offenbach Gaggs), James E Sullivan (Pasha), Miss Gilman (Laura) and Marie George (Dolly) to Britain. There, with the English earl turned into an American dude called Percy Harold Ethelbert van Stuyvesant and no longer played in travesty, it more than confirmed its original success with a fine run of 196 performances at the Shaftesbury Theatre, the only trans-Atlantic musical to find

success in London in the wake of *The Belle of New York*. It also became one of the few Broadway shows of its era to travel even further, when, as well as being seen under J C Williamson's management in Australia in 1901, where George Lauri (Pilsener), Carrie Moore (Laura), Charles Kenningham (Percy), Hugh J Ward (Gaggs) and Grace Palotta (Roxana) headed the cast, it was also taken to the Continent in the repertoire of the Casino company. Ultimately, it was even made over into an Hungarian version (ad Jenő Heltai), which was briefly played at Budapest's Népszinház in 1902.

UK: Shaftesbury Theatre 11 July 1900; Australia: Her Majesty's Theatre, Sydney, 6 July 1901; Hungary: *Az aranyos* Népszinház 28 February 1902

CASSIDY, Jack (b Richmond Hill, NY, 5 March 1927; d Los Angeles, 12 December 1976).

Cassidy first appeared on Broadway in 1943 in *Something for the Boys*, and played in the chorus of the musicals *Sadie Thompson* (1944), *Marinka* (1945), *The Firebrand of Florence* (1945), the road-folding *Spring in Brazil* (1945, Pancho), *The Red Mill* (1945 revival), *Around the World in 80 Days* (1946) and *Music in My Heart* (1947), in the revues *Inside USA*, *Small Wonder* and *Alive and Kicking*, and regionally as Rocky Barton in *Billion Dollar Baby* (1949), before succeeding to a minor part in Broadway's *South Pacific* (1952 t/o Richard West). He had his first leading rôle on Broadway when he played the dreamboat Chick Miller in *Wish You Were Here*, introducing the show's title song, and followed up as Johnny O'Sullivan in *Sandhog* before taking *Oklahoma!* (Curly) to Paris and Rome in a State Department sponsored tour in 1955.

He starred opposite Carol Lawrence in the short-lived *Shangri-La* (1956, Charles Mallinson) on Broadway, took *Wonderful Town* overseas, appeared as Macheath in *The Beggar's Opera* at the City Center (1957), and appeared regionally in *Half in Earnest* (1957, Jack), *The Vagabond King* and *Gypsy*, but he was not seen on Broadway again until 1963 when he successfully created the rôle of the slickly unpleasant Kodaly in *She Loves Me*. He followed up as the filmstar Byron Prong in *Fade Out – Fade In* but, of his following Broadway shows, *Pleasures and Palaces* (1965, replacing Alfred Marks as Potemkin) folded on the road, and *It's a Bird ... its a Plane ... it's Superman* (1966, Max Mencken) and *Maggie Flynn* (1968, Phineas) were short-lived.

His sometime wife, **Shirley [Mae] JONES** (b Smithton, Pa, 31 March 1934), best known for her memorable film interpretations of Laurey in *Oklahoma!*, Julie Jordan in *Carousel* and Marian the librarian in *The Music Man*, appeared on Broadway opposite Cassidy in *Maggie Flynn* and regionally in *Bitter-Sweet* and other musical shows. His sons, David Cassidy (b 12 April 1950) and Patrick Cassidy, both made a youthful impact in television and popular music. David was seen in the musical theatre in *The Fig Leaves are Falling* (1969, Billy) and *Joseph and the Amazing Technicolor Dreamcoat* (t/o Joseph, 1983) whilst Patrick appeared on Broadway in the rôle of Frederic in *The Pirates of Penzance* in 1982 and in *Leader of the Pack* (1985, Jeff Barry).

CASTLE, Vernon [BLYTH, Vernon] (b Norwich, 2 May 1887; d Houston, Tex, 15 February 1918).

The young singing, dancing English actor played, from

the age of 19, in a series of shows for producer/comedian Lew Fields, appearing on Broadway between 1906 and 1911 as A Contractor in the burlesque *The Great Decide*, the Hon Aubrey Battersea in *The Girl Behind the Counter*, Souseberry Lushmore in *The Midnight Sons*, Hon Algy Clymber in *Old Dutch*, Oxford Tighe in *The Summer Widowers* and Zowie in *The Hen Pecks* as well as in the revues *About Town* and *The Mimic World*, mostly in the kind of dude rôles which his relative-by-marriage, George Grossmith, had made so popular, alongside the low comedy of Fields. In 1911 French producer Jacques Charles hired Castle to repeat the comedy barbershop routine which he performed in *The Hen Pecks* at the Paris Olympia and agreed to take his girlfriend, Irene Foote, as a chorine and a possible dance-partner for the comic if the pair were able to put together a dancing act.

Before the two arrived in Paris, the future **Irene CASTLE** (b New Rochelle, NY, 7 April 1893; d Eureka Springs, Ark, 25 January 1969), who had been a dancer in Castle's last shows with Fields, had persuaded Vernon to renounce the inelegance of the low comedy for which he had been hired and to develop the dance act Charles had suggested. Thus, they simply failed to turn up for the show in which Vernon should have played his barber sketch, and when they did they arrive in Paris, they were put into the bill at the Olympia without attracting notice. Charles subsequently loaned the unprofitable pair to the Café de Paris, whose management was in search of a new attraction, and suddenly they became the rage of the town with their elegant performance of the foxtrot and the one-step. Breaking their contract with the Olympia, they moved full-time to the Café de Paris where their success continued unabated until they decided to return to America. They had profited from their Paris stay not only financially but also professionally: they had picked up both the tango and the maxixe from South American teachers in Paris and Irene had equipped herself with a wardrobe to make both male and female eyes fall from their sockets. These were the elements which would make their success on their return home.

That return did not begin easily. The couple were first engaged to appear with Montgomery and Stone in *The Lady of the Slipper* (1912) but Irene's insistence on wearing a particularly revealing dress from her new wardrobe in what was essentially a family show led to a battle with producer Dillingham. This time Mrs Castle did not get her own way and she left the cast before opening. Her husband followed her soon after. Broadway's first opportunity to see the Castles together came in the American version of the Gaiety musical *The Sunshine Girl* (1913), but once again Irene lost out, and Vernon introduced the tango with the show's star, Julia Sanderson. *The Sunshine Girl* and its tango put an end to Castle's career in musical comedy. Thereafter, he and Irene continued their career as exhibition dancers, making themselves the best-known purveyors of dances to the ballrooms of the world. They appeared as themselves in the Irving Berlin revue *Watch Your Step* in a final Broadway appearance, and made some short films and one feature, *The Whirl of Life*, for the cinema, but their career came to an untimely end when Castle was killed in a wartime air crash in Texas at the age of 31. Irene subsequently made film appearances as an actress.

In 1939 a romanticized version of the Castles' career was filmed, as *The Story of Vernon and Irene Castle*, with Fred Astaire and Ginger Rogers appearing as the dancing pair. One dance routine, which had been preserved on a Parisian film, was precisely recreated under Mrs Castle's direction to such effect that the Castles' reputation has moved into the future boosted by the talents of Astaire and Rogers. In fact, they were technically much less adept than their film equivalents: an elegant English light comedian and a well-trained American chorus dancer whose combined skills, appearance, and decisive opportunism in creating dance crazes on both sides of the Atlantic in what was a very short career, made them into household names – names given a renewing boost 20 years later by the talents of Astaire and Rogers.

Castle's sister, **Coralie BLYTHE** (1880–1928), was a successful musical comedy soubrette in London, appearing for George Edwardes for a number of years at the Gaiety and Daly's, understudying the Edwardes stars, and creating supporting rôles in a number of London musicals including *The Silver Slipper* (Wrenne), *Mr Popple of Ippleton* (Louise), *The Girl Behind the Counter* (Susie), *The Three Kisses* (Ethel Trevor) and *The Dashing Little Duke* (Césarine). She also played briefly in America in the tryout of *The White Chrysanthemum* (t/o Sybil). She was the wife of Lawrence Grossmith (1877–1944).

Biography: Castle, I: *Castles in the Air* (Doubleday, New York, 1958)

CASTLES IN THE AIR Comic opera (musical comedy) in 3 acts by Raymond W Peck. Music by Percy Wenrich. Olympic Theater, Chicago, 22 November 1925; Selwyn Theater, New York, 6 September 1926.

This sole successful attempt by songwriter Percy Wenrich ('On Moonlight Bay', 'When You Wore a Tulip') at a stage musical had a plot which mixed a touch of *She Stoops to Conquer* with a disguised Prince, high society and a trip to Latvia, as well as a light if unexceptional score ('Land of Romance', 'The Rainbow of Your Smile', 'I Would Like to Fondle You'). Stanley Forde played the central rôle of Philip Rodman, a comical yankee millionaire who helps the Prince (Irving Beebe) from his disguise as an American student called John Brown back to his throne with pretty Evelyn Devine (Vivienne Segal) at his side.

John Meehan and James W Elliott's production of the piece, which had gone through the titles of *Romance Land* and *The Land of Romance* before settling on the slightly less obvious *Castles in the Air*, opened in Chicago, where it was acclaimed as the biggest musical hit the city had yet seen. London's C B Cochran – doubtless remembering how Jack Waller had found *No, No, Nanette* in Chicago – snapped up the English rights, as the show ran on for an amazing 37 weeks before a second company was sent out to tour, the A team headed for Broadway, and Donald Brian and Virginia O'Brien took over in the continuing run in Chicago. Without finding quite the mode that it had in Chicago, the piece lasted 160 performances on Broadway, with Forde, Miss Segal and J Harold Murray starred, but the happy adventure ended in court when the two producers stopped seeing eye to eye. Elsewhere, happiness didn't get a look in. Cochran's London production with Helen Gilliland and Allen Kearns starred lasted only 28 performances, whilst an Australian J C Williamson Ltd mounting with Roy Russell and Rowena Ronalds in its leading rôles did not create enough interest to make the usually automatic move from Sydney to Melbourne worthwhile.

The same title had been previously used on Broadway for a comic opera by Charles A Byrne based on Cervantes's *Los dos habladores* with music by Gustave Kerker (Broadway Theater 5 May 1890). A vehicle for the comedy of the newly risen star De Wolf Hopper, whose rôle as a jolly judge called Filacoudre didn't have much to do with a plot which was based on the same original as Offenbach's *Les Bavards*, it featured Marion Manola in breeches as the young man who out-talks the garrulous wife (Rose Leighton) of the father (Thomas Q Seabrooke) of his beloved (Della Fox), amongst a host of comic incidentals, for a run of 105 nights.

London, too, had seen a previous *Castles in the Air*, a version of Bolten-Bäckers and Lincke's Berlin musical *Frau Luna*, played at the Scala Theatre in 1911 in a double-bill with a demonstration of Kinemacolour.

UK: Shaftesbury Theatre 20 June 1927; Australia: Her Majesty's Theatre, Sydney 15 October 1927

THE CAT AND THE FIDDLE Musical love story in 2 acts by Otto Harbach. Music by Jerome Kern. Globe Theater, New York, 15 October 1931.

When Jerome Kern deliberately turned to writing what he hoped would be a more substantial style of musical play, he did not follow up the American period operetta line which he had exploited so well in *Show Boat*. Both *The Cat and the Fiddle* and its successor, *Music in the Air*, looked back to the European continent for their settings and subject matter and, in spite of their texts being written by Otto Harbach and Oscar Hammerstein respectively, the result was that he was served up two of the weakest and most hyper-conventional libretti of his career. *The Cat and the Fiddle*, which presented the same confrontation as had been seen a dozen years earlier on Broadway in a little French one-acter called *La Musique adoucit les coeurs* (André Mauprey, Théâtre Parisien 15 December 1919), had the advantage over its fellow piece of being the more contemporary in flavour and in involving some lively American-in-Brussels scenes and songs.

The young American musician Shirley Sheridan (Bettina Hall) meets the romantic Roumanian composer Victor Florescu (Georges Metaxa) on the quais of Brussels. Romance blossoms, but they lose touch when a letter goes astray, and meet again only when Shirley is approached by Clément Daudet (José Ruben) to interpolate some of her light, jazzy songs into an overly-romantic musical scena in a revue. *The Passionate Pilgrim* is Victor's seriously-conceived and -composed unhappy-ending work. Shirley loosens up his conservatoire tones and changes his ending, but although the show is a success, the lies of the jealous Odette (Odette Myrtil) hold off a romantic reconciliation until the final curtain. Doris Carson (Angie) and Eddie Foy jr (Alexander) provided the light comedy as Shirley's dancing brother and sister-in-law, whilst the Metropolitan Opera's George Meader made a special hit as a street singer, Pompineau, and the Albertina Rasch dancers added to the spectacle of this show about the writing of a show.

The song success of *The Cat and the Fiddle* was the jaunty little 'She Didn't Say "Yes"', represented as a specimen of Shirley's work and sung in the show first by the streetsinger and later, in meaningful context, by Shirley. Pompineau also delivered the serenade 'The Night Was Made for Love' and 'I Watch the Love Parade', whilst Victor sang his newly composed songs 'The Breeze Kissed Your Hair' and 'A New Love Is Old', Shirley delivered a more romantic effort of her own, 'Try to Forget', and Odette led the representation of an excerpt from *The Passionate Pilgrim* in a score where a large part of the music was simply tacked into the script as being 'numbers' written as such.

Max Gordon's production of *The Cat and the Fiddle* played for a slightly forced 395 performances on Broadway in the early days of the Depression, with salary cuts and even a shift in theatre included as Gordon worked to keep the show alive until it was time to take it touring. C B Cochran mounted a London edition at the Palace Theatre with his *Bitter-Sweet* star, Peggy Wood, as Shirley and Francis Lederer as Victor. The old romantic musical comedy star Henri Leoni played Pompineau, and Alice Delysia appeared as what had been Odette but was now Alice. The show ran 226 performances, which was not enough to help Cochran out of the financial hole dug for him by *Helen!* in the same season, and had a short tour.

A film version, with a screenplay by Sam and Bella Spewack, dug frantically into the book of operettic conventions and came up with an altered plot which had Shirley (Jeanette MacDonald) going on for the Odette character – now played by a real diva in Vivienne Segal – when she walks out on the show. Joseph Cawthorn supplied the intentional comedy and Ramon Novarro was romance.

An earlier musical with the same title was played on the American touring circuits in 1907. A soi-disant spectacular musical dramatic fantasy of a kind not meant for Broadway consumption, it nevertheless put in a brief New York appearance at the West End Theater (16 December 1907). London followed its *The Cat and the Fiddle* not with another but with a *Hi Diddle Diddle*, a revue mounted at the Comedy Theatre (3 October 1934) with June and Douglas Byng.

UK: Palace Theatre 4 March 1932; Film: 1934
Recording: selection (part record) (RCA, Fontana)

THE CATCH OF THE SEASON Musical comedy in 2 acts by Seymour Hicks and Cosmo Hamilton. Lyrics by Charles H Taylor. Music by Herbert Haines and Evelyn Baker. Vaudeville Theatre, London, 9 September 1904.

Seymour Hicks's musical, a straightforward, modern version of the *Cinderella* tale, was written as a vehicle for himself and his wife, Ellaline Terriss. When Mrs Hicks got pregnant, the production looked in danger, but Charles Frohman decided to continue, and brought in the young Zena Dare to create the central rôle of Angela Crystal opposite the Duke of St Jermyns of Hicks. Hicks got his share of the action by using the Fairy-Godmotherless version of the old tale in which the disguised Prince and Cinderella meet long before the ball. Statuesque Ethel Matthews and Hilda Jacobson featured as the very un-ugly sisters, whilst Sam Sothern appeared as the Dandini-equivalent Lord Dundreary, doing an impersonation of the famous performance given by his father in *Our American*

Cousin. Juvenile Albert Valcherra was the page-boy, Bucket, sighing comically over the heroine, whilst Shakespearian actress Rosina Filippi played Lady Caterham, the wealthy aunt who turns up in time to replace the fairy element and transform Angela into 'Molly O'Halloran from County Clare' in time for the ball. A topical element was introduced with the character of Mr William Gibson (Compton Coutts) who paraded his very tall daughters, the Gibson Girls, across the stage, dressed in specially created 'emotionalized costumes' designed by Lady Duff Cooper. The Gibson Girls became a feature of the show, none more so than Camille Clifford, swiped from the cast of the American show *The Prince of Pilsen* to display her allegedly 11-inch waist, blossoming bosom, amazing posture and inexistent singing voice before a gasping public as Sylvia Gibson.

Herbert Haines and Evelyn Baker's first West End score accompanied the performance well. Hicks sang briskly of 'The Church Parade', Miss Dare got Irish as 'Molly O'Halloran', and the Hon Honoria Bedford (Miss Jacobson) sang to her 'Cigarette' and enumerated the adventures that went with each of the 'Charms on my Chain'. In Hicks's favourite fashion, however, the score soon became dotted with interpolations, as *The Catch of the Season* ran on and on, making itself into one of the favourite actor's greatest successes. There was time for Mrs Hicks to have her baby, return to take up the rôle intended for her, and still be succeeded by sister-in-law Maie Ash, Alice Russon, Zena Dare's younger sister, Phyllis, and little Madge Crichton before the show got to its 621st and last London performance. The Gibson Girls turned over as quickly as the song content, and at least one got herself a genuine Earl.

Whilst London's production ran on, Frohman opened the show on Broadway, with Edna May as Angela to the Duke of Joe Farren Soutar, Fred Kaye playing the Dandini rôle, now no longer a burlesque and christened Lord Baghdad Monteagle, former Gaiety girl Margaret Fraser (Honoria) and Fred Wright jr (Gibson). The inimitable Sylvia Gibson had disappeared, and in her place was a barrage of new songs from the pens of Jerome D Kern, musical director William T Francis and Luke Forwood ('My Little Buttercup'). The resultant piece ran for 93 performances.

The Catch of the Season continued to tour in Britain until 1908, but it also surfaced at Budapest's Népszinház in 1907 (ad Jeňo Heltai), in Australia, where Fanny Dango played Angela to the Duke of Andrew Higginson and her real-life sister, Lydia Flopp, appeared as Sophia, and, several years later, in Vienna (ad Fritz Lunzer, Karl Tuschl) at the Venedig in Wien summer theatre and later as a Christmas entertainment at the Theater an der Wien. Tuschl himself played Gibson, with Paul Guttmann doing Lord Dundreary and Clara Karry and Max Willenz heading the romance. The score had by now undergone a further facelift, and one Captain Rushpool (Bernhard Bötel) enlivened Act 1 with musical director Otto Stransky's 'Küss, mein Mädel, mich ein letztes Mal', Guttmann led a tango quartet in the second act, and there was a 'grotesque dance trio' for Tuschl, Guttmann and Karl Matuna, as the heroine's father, which demanded 'Kennen Sie schon den neusten Tanz?'.

The Catch of the Season returned to London in a wartime revival (Prince's Theatre 17 February 1917) with Hicks starring alongside Isobel Elsom for a season of 84 performances.

USA: Daly's Theater 28 August 1905; Hungary: Népszinház *A balkirálynő* 16 November 1907; Australia: Her Majesty's Theatre, Sydney 18 December 1909; Austria: Venedig in Wien *Die Ballkönigin* 15 July 1913, Theater an der Wien 25 December 1913

CATLETT, Walter (b San Francisco, 4 February 1889; d Los Angeles, 4 November 1960).

Walter Catlett spent his earliest years in the theatre playing in stock in California, and appeared on the New York stage for the first time in the juvenile comedy rôle of Artie, Earl of Somerset, in a revival of *The Prince of Pilsen*. Half a dozen years of variegated touring intervened before he returned to Broadway, this time as the comical Harry Miller in the west-coast musical *So Long, Letty*, and after a second and less forthcoming west-coast musical, *Look Pleasant*, and a stint in the *Ziegfeld Follies of 1917*, a series of further good musical comedy rôles followed. He was seen in New York in *Follow the Girl* (1918, Buck Sweeney), and *Little Simplicity* (1918, Prof Erasmus Duckworth), and made a very successful London début as the hero's flip, jokey sidekick in *Baby Bunting* (1919) before scoring his biggest success to date in the rôle of the wisecracking Otis Hooper (of the Anglo-American Vaudeville Agency, Squantumville, Maine) in *Sally* (1920) at New York's New Amsterdam Theater ('The Church 'round the corner', 'On with the Dance', 'The Lorelei').

Another Jerome Kern musical, *Dear Sir* (1924, André Bloxom), briefly gave him another brash comedy part as a phoney millionaire, but his second great new rôle came later the same year when he created the part of the slick-pattering lawyer, 'Watty' Watkins in *Lady, Be Good!*, alongside Adele and Fred Astaire, introducing the show's title number.

The west-coast musical productions of *Patsy* (1926) and *Honey Girl* (1926) and New York's *Lucky* (1927, Charley Simpson) were less forthcoming and *Here's Howe* (1928, t/o Basil Carroway) and *Treasure Girl* (1928, Larry Hopkins) closed out Catlett's Broadway career on a note somewhat lower than the days of *Sally* and *Lady, Be Good!*. It closed, however, simply because he moved on towards Hollywood and a three-decade film career as a character performer (*Rain, Mr Deeds Goes to Town, On the Avenue, Bringing up Baby, Yankee Doodle Dandy, Look for the Silver Lining, Here Comes the Groom, Friendly Persuasion* etc) highlighted for many by his loan of his voice to Mr J Worthington Foulfellow in Walt Disney's cartoon *Pinocchio*.

CATS Musical in 2 acts based on T S Eliot's *Old Possum's Book of Practical Cats*. Music by Andrew Lloyd Webber. New London Theatre, London, 11 May 1981.

The most popularly successful musical of the 1980s and, depending on which way you count your statistics, possibly of all time, *Cats* is, in any case, one of the most remarkable phenomena in the history of the musical theatre.

The show had its origins in the settings of some of T S Eliot's poems from *Old Possum's Book of Practical Cats* (1939) made by composer Lloyd Webber and originally performed privately at his Sydmonton Festival. They were well enough received for the composer to consider taking

Plate 48a. **Cats**: *A litter of Japanese cats surround Old Deuteronomy.*

Plate 48b. *A very original Cat: Susan Jane Tanner as that fluffy heroine of transpontine melodrama, the Lady Griddlebone.*

them further, and it was variously envisaged that they might make up a song-cycle, a television programme, or even half of a two-part stage show, sharing a programme with a staged version of his orchestral piece 'Variations on a Theme of Paganini'. Ultimately, however, it was resolved to make *Cats* into a full evening's entertainment on its own.

Lloyd Webber and young producer Cameron Mackintosh assembled a team headed by director Trevor Nunn and choreographer Gillian Lynne, who had worked together on two productions with a dance content at the Royal Shakespeare Company, and the selection of songs and personalities that made up *Cats* were arranged on to a slim, meticulously worked-out framework of character and motivation in which the climax of affairs was the Jellicle Ball, and the opportunity given there to one cat to have an additional life. With the co-operation of Valerie Eliot, the poet's widow, the team was able to make use of a range of various published and unpublished Eliot pieces and it was from these that the character of Grizabella, the glamour cat, who had not made her way into *Old Possum's Book*, was reconstructed, to be literally given a second chance. For at the end of the evening, with its presentation of a bounding gallery of feline characters, it was the tarty, bedraggled Grizabella who became the heroine of the tale as she ascended radiantly from her rubbish-tip on an old car-tyre, transported towards a rebirth and the Heaviside Layer.

The most unusual element of the show's concept was that it was planned as a dance show, choreographed from beginning to end in a fashion unprecedented in a West End musical, and with all its rôles barring two – the venerable Old Deuteronomy and Grizabella – played by skilled dancers. That concept was given extra breadth when it was decided to mount the show in the unloved New London Theatre, Sean Kenny's 'theatre of the future' which had for seven years floundered along, seeming to have no future. The large revolve built into the three-sided auditorium floor became the playground for *Cats*. However, the unusual show soon hit unusual problems and, given the pressures put on artists rehearsing a dance piece longer than most full-length ballets, injuries were legion. The most devastating was that to Royal Shakespeare Company star Judi Dench and, late in rehearsals, she had to be replaced. The dance element of her rôle was taken by another company member, her part as Grizabella was taken up by *Evita* star, Elaine Paige.

In spite of its special form and a 'plotline' which was – by the time the show came to the stage – not at all evident, *Cats* was an instant success. Its cavalcade of scrambling, dancing creatures immediately took hold of the audience as they leaped from the giant, revolving rubbish heap that was the setting for the entertainment, around the auditorium and back, to begin the series of items that make up the evening: the plump and comical Gumbie Cat (Myra Sands), the pop-pussy Rum-Tum-Tugger (Paul Nicholas), Bustopher Jones (Brian Blessed), the cat of the gentlemen's clubs, in his white spats, the kitten-burglars Mungojerrie (John Thornton) and Rumpleteazer (Bonnie Langford), Gus, the Theatre Cat (Stephen Tate) with his grand tale of the terrible Growltiger (Tate) and his lady Griddlebone (Susan Jane Tanner), Skimbleshanks, the Railway Cat (Kenn Wells), the magical Mister Mistoffelees (Wayne Sleep), and the mysterious Macavity (Thornton), his tale walloped out by a pair of vamp-cats (Geraldine Gardner, Sharon Lee Hill), all danced and sang through their poem-numbers, until the final ball scene when Grizabella (Miss Paige) got her apotheosis.

Although there was an attempt to launch a couple of numbers pre-production, the songs of the show were not the kind to become popular singles, with one exception. Grizabella's despairingly hopeful 'Memory', put together from an existing Lloyd Webber melody and a lyric made up by Nunn from fragments and suggestions of Eliot and powered forth achingly by Miss Paige, became a highlight of the show, and a major hit outside it.

There were problems in reproducing the original production of *Cats* in other theatres without tearing auditoria to pieces and, as further productions followed, an alternative version of the London staging adapted to a semi-proscenium or proscenium theatre was evolved. Broadway's version of the show also included some alterations in the score – replacing the original 'Billy McCaw' ballad in the pirate scene with a burlesque Italianate aria, and rearranging Mungojerrie and Rumpleteazer's music – and these were mostly maintained in subsequent productions.

The Broadway production opened little more than a year after London's, with Betty Buckley (Grizabella), Stephen Hanan (Gus), Ken Page (Deuteronomy), Harry Groener (Munkustrap), Bonnie Simmons (Griddlebone) and Terence V Mann (Rum Tum Tugger) amongst the cast. The show received much the same reception as in Britain, and found much the same long-lived success. T S Eliot won a posthumous Tony Award for his 'libretto' to put with the one he had won, living, for *The Cocktail Party*, and the Nobel Prize he had picked up in 1948. At the time of writing, *Cats* is in its 13th year at the New London Theatre, the longest running musical in the history of the West End theatre, and in its eleventh at Broadway's Winter Garden Theater, whilst its kittens, in all sorts of languages (but always in the original production, give or take a permitted variation) can be seen all over the world from Zurich to Mexico City.

A Los Angeles company, an American touring company, reproductions in Canada, Australia, Vienna, Budapest (ad József Romhányi, in repertoire), in a specially built theatre in Tokyo, in Norway and in Finland led the introduction of *Cats* to the rest of the world. Miss Lynne went to Hamburg to stage the German production and, in 1989, to Paris to mount the first production of a British musical there since *Jesus Christ Superstar*, whilst in Britain a first provincial company went out whilst the show still held the stage in London, an unusual exercise in postwar Britain. In London, the *Cats* advertising changed from 'the longer you wait, the longer you'll wait' to the curiously imprecise 'now and forever'. Forever is, of course, quite a long time, but *Cats* is getting closer to it than any major-house musical before it.

USA: Winter Garden Theater 7 October 1982; Hungary: Madach Színház *Macskak* 25 March 1983; Austria: Theater an der Wien 24 September 1983; Australia: Theatre Royal, Sydney 27 July 1985; Germany: Operettenhaus, Hamburg 18 April 1986; France: Théâtre de Paris 23 February 1989

Recordings: original cast (Polydor), Broadway cast (Geffen), Hungarian cast (Favorit), Austrian cast (Polydor), Japanese cast (Canyon), Australian cast (EMI), German cast (Polydor), Dutch cast (Mercury), Mexican cast (Polydor) etc.

CATTARINA, or Friends at Court

Comic opera in 2 acts by Robert Reece. Music by Frederic Clay. Prince's Theatre, Manchester, 17 August 1874; Charing Cross Theatre, London, 15 May 1875.

One of the earliest British musical plays of the modern age, *Cattarina* was commissioned by the performer/producer Kate Santley who played it successfully on tour and for a fine 75 performances in London. A Ruritanian setting and a half-burlesque, half-opéra-comique libretto of peasants, princes, disguises, usurpers and topical jibes held up a charming score from which Miss Santley turned the roguish 'It Is So Like the Men' into a popular hit. Touted before production as Britain's answer to *La Fille de Madame Angot*, it did not come anywhere near the level of Lecocq's piece, but it nevertheless provided a stone in the path leading to *The Sorcerer* and *HMS Pinafore*, which did.

CAWTHORN, Joseph

(b New York, 29 March 1867; d Beverly Hills, Calif, 21 January 1949). Favourite 'Dutch' comedian of a quarter-of-a-century of American musicals.

Cawthorn started his stage life as a child in music hall and worked in both America and Britain in minstrel shows, pantomime and vaudeville before moving into the theatre, first in plays and then in musicals, where he made a speciality of the 'Dutch' dialect comedy rôles which were widely and extravagantly popular at the time.

He toured in *Excelsior Jr* with the equally up-and-coming Marie Cahill before playing 'Dutch' rôles in *Nature* (1897, Hans Schultz) and in *Miss Philadelphia* (1897, William Penn jr), which led to his engagement for the comic tenor rôle of Boris in Alice Nielsen's production of the Victor Herbert comic opera *The Fortune Teller* (1898). He then moved on to the Casino Theater to match the Dutch humour of his Siegfried Götterdammerung with the Turkish-Irishisms of Thomas Q Seabrooke and the lugubrious comicalities of Dan Daly in *The Rounders* (1899) before returning to Miss Nielsen for both Herbert's *The Singing Girl* (1899, Aufpassen) and a trip to London for a season of a revised version of *The Fortune Teller* in 1901.

He appeared at the New Amsterdam Theatre in 1903–4 in the title-rôle of an americanized version of the Drury Lane pantomime *Mother Goose* and returned to the Dutch dialect to recreate the most famous of all dialect characters, J K Emmet's Fritz, in a new Fritz show called *Fritz in Tammany Hall* in 1905 and to play in John Philip Sousa's *The Free Lance* (1906, Siegmund Lump). He was tacked into the plot and cast of the Elsie Janis vehicle, *The Hoyden*, after that show's Broadway run, as Baron Hugo Weybach and carried on in similarly accented rôles in the cartoon musical *Little Nemo* (1908, Dr Pill), *Girlies* (1910, Dr Oscar Spiel), and Leslie Stuart's *The Slim Princess* (1911, Louis von Schloppenhauer), again alongside Miss Janis.

In 1913–14 he had a considerable success, playing now opposite Julia Sanderson, in two musicals imported from London's Gaiety Theatre: *The Sunshine Girl*, in which he played a revised version of Teddy Payne's Floot, christened Schlump to allow him to indulge his favourite accent, and *The Girl from Utah* where Payne's Trimmit became re-nationalized as Trimpel. He took the comic lead of Otto Spreckles when Miss Sanderson played the title-rôle in Victor Jacobi's Hungarian operett *Sybil* (1916) and paired with her yet again in Jacobi's Broadway piece *Rambler Rose* (1917, Joseph Guppy) and in Ivan Caryll's French farce musical *The Canary* (1918, Timothy).

Like the last two shows, another Jacobi musical, *The Half Moon* (1920), cast Cawthorn in a non-Germanic rôle as the Hon Hudson Hobson, but he was back to being Otto in *The Bunch and Judy* before a broken knee-cap forced him to renounce the rôle during the show's pre-Broadway run. He returned to town star-billed in Rudolf Friml's *The Blue Kitten* (1922, Theodore Vanderpop) and made his farewell to Broadway as the lovable and duly-accented father of Marilyn Miller in Kern's *Sunny* (1925, Siegfried Peters) before beginning a successful and prolific career as a character actor in films. His celluloid credits ran from *The Taming of the Shrew* and *White Zombie* to musical pieces such as *Street Girl*, *Good News*, *Love Me Tonight* (Doctor with a song with Jeanette Mac-

Plate 49. **Joseph Cawthorn** *teamed with Julia Sanderson and Donald Brian in a famous combination for Broadway's* The Girl from Utah.

Donald), *Twenty Million Sweethearts*, *Music in the Air*, *Sweet Music*, *Sweet Adeline*, *Gold Diggers of 1935*, *Harmony Lane*, *Go Into Your Dance*, *Naughty Marietta* (Herr Schumann), *The Great Ziegfeld* (Dr Florenz Ziegfeld sr), *Scatterbrain* and *Lillian Russell*.

Cawthorn also turned his hand to occasional songwriting and provided himself with such numbers as 'My Father's Wooden Leg' (*The Hoyden* w Harry Dillon) 'I Can Dance with Anyone But My Wife' (*Sybil* w John Golden) and 'You Can't Play Every Instrument in the Band' (*The Sunshine Girl* w Golden) to perform in his stage musical appearances.

CELLI, Frank H [STANDING, Francis] (b 1841; d London, 27 December 1904). A fine-voiced baritone singer, who took leading rôles in Victorian musicals on both sides of the Atlantic.

Celli was educated for the civil service, but went on the stage at the age of 20 and spent his early career in a mixture of opera, concerts and opéra-bouffe, appearing on the London stage for the first time as Matt o' the Mint in *The Beggar's Opera* at the Marylebone Theatre. He played in the provinces in a number of dramatic rôles (usually with

a song or two), and in the West End during the 1870s in such rôles as Prince Jonquil in *The Black Crook*, Cornarino in *The Bridge of Sighs*, as Fridolin in *Le Roi Carotte* and Belamy in *The Dragoons* (*Les Dragons de Villars*). He also appeared, between musical theatre engagements, in oratorio and with both the Mapleson and Carl Rosa Opera Companies.

In 1880 he was London's Brissac in *Les Mousquetaires*, the following year appeared as the Marquis in *Les Cloches de Corneville*, Armand in *La Belle Normande*, as Bernadille in *La Boulangère* and in the title-rôle of Edward Solomon's *Claude Duval*. In 1884 he took the lead rôle of John Smith in the same composer's short-lived *Pocahontas*, and in 1885 made his début on Broadway playing Fra Bombardo in the Casino Theater production of *Amorita* (*Pfingsten in Florenz*).

In 1889 he played the rôle of Ralf of Chestermere in the tryout of *Marjorie*, only to be succeeded by his former understudy, Hayden Coffin, when the show was mounted in the evening bill, and the following year he went to the Gaiety Theatre to succeed to the rôle of Escamillo in *Carmen Up-to-Data* which had originally been played by a girl in travesty. He later appeared in the short-lived light opera *The Bric-à-Brac Will*, and in 1898 took part in a revival of *La Poupée* and appeared as Brother Tamarind in *A Runaway Girl* on Broadway. In his last West End appearance, in a rôle as far away from opera as could be imagined, he played the comical Spoofah Bey in the variety musical *Morocco Bound*, and he was seen on the road as late as 1902, starring with Mlle Mars and Wilfred Shine in the 'musical stage society play' *Nana*.

Celli twice left the stage for a comfortable retirement, but was obliged to return the first time when he lost his savings on speculations. On the second occasion, he reconverted as a singing teacher, and was engaged at the Guildhall at his death.

Celli was married to Susan Pyne, sister of Louisa Pyne of the Pyne–Harrison Opera Company, and his brothers were the actor Herbert Standing (1846–1923) and the prominent Broadway musical theatre vocalist William T Carleton, whose son, William P Carleton, also performed on the musical stage in America.

William T[urnham] CARLETON [STANDING, William] (b England, ?1849; d Flushing, NY, 25 September 1922) had a career every bit as fruitful as his brother, but mostly on the left-hand side of the Atlantic. After early experience in opéra-bouffe in Britain, he played for nearly a decade in the Clara Kellogg and C D Hess English opera companies in the American 1870s (Raoul in *Les Huguenots*, Danny Mann in *The Bohemian Girl*, Dutchman in *The Flying Dutchman*, Escamillo in *Carmen*, *Martha*, *Maritana*, *Rigoletto*, Valentine in *Faust*, *Mignon*, *Il Trovatore*, *Star of the North*, *Aida* etc) before switching to the comic-opera stage where he made his mark alongside Dolaro in *Olivette* (1881, Valentine). He quickly became one of Broadway's top baritones, appearing in the first half of the 1880s in *The Snake Charmer*, *Patience* (Calverley), *Claude Duval* (Duval), *La Mascotte* (Pippo), *The Merry War* (Umberto), *Manteaux Noirs* (Don Luis), *Rip van Winkle* (Rip), *Iolanthe* (Strephon), *The Queen's Lace Handkerchief* (Cervantes), *The Beggar Student* (Symon), *Nanon* (D'Aubigné) and *The Drum Major's Daughter* (Robert) before leaving the baritone slot in *Amorita* to Celli and setting up his own comic opera company. He toured for a number of years with a repertoire including *The Merry War*, *La Mascotte*, *Fra Diavolo*, *Nanon*, *The Mikado*, *The Queen's Lace Handkerchief*, *The Brigands* et al, starred in a short-lived attempt to mount *Erminie*'s successor, *Mynheer Jan* (1888) in America, and later returned to Broadway to play Vincent Knapps to the *La Cigale* of Lillian Russell, Pietro in her *The Mountebanks* and Mourzouk in her *Giroflé-Girofla* (1892), Grosvenor to the Bunthorne of Dixey in *Patience* (1896), the Marquis in a revival of *Erminie* (1899) and Dakota Dick in *Three Little Lambs* (1899). In 1901 he apparently played not only Gilfain but also the young hero, Frank Abercoed, during the run of *Florodora* before returning to the right age group as the Lord Lieutenant in *The Emerald Isle* (1902) and as Sir Peter Teazle in Lillian Russell's *Lady Teazle* (1904), in a career now more angled towards non-musical rôles. However he was seen on the musical stage in *The Prince of Bohemia* (Ashby Tritton) in 1910 and again as late as 1919 when he took over from De Wolf Hopper in *Everything* at the Hippodrome.

William P[ropert] CARLETON had a decade in the limelight as a Broadway juvenile, being seen in *The Cherry Pickers* (1896), *The Belle of New York* (1900, Harry Bronson), *The Cadet Girl* (1900, Lucien), *The Prima Donna* (1901, Abdallah), *Winsome Winnie* (1903, Desmond), *The Tattooed Man* (1907, Abdalah), *Mam'selle Sallie/A Knight for a Day* (1907, Marco Bozzaris), *The Yankee Girl* (1909), *The Wall Street Girl* (1912, Dexter Barton), and *Broadway and Buttermilk* (1916, Tom Burrowes) as well as a series of plays.

Celli's sister, Ellen Standing (d 1906), was also a performer in such musicals as *The Shop Girl*, *Little Miss Nobody* and *A Chinese Honeymoon*. His own daughter was an actress under the name Faith Celli (1888–1942), whilst his nephew (Sir) Guy Standing married the American musical comedy actress Isabelle Urquhart and, by a second marriage, was the father of actress Kay Hammond. Miss Hammond's son returned to the name his great-grand-uncles had shunned and had a fine stage career as John Standing (né Leon, b 16 August 1934). He appeared in the musical theatre as Clive Popkiss in *Popkiss* (1972).

Celli also ventured as an author, penning the provincial musical play *Stirring Times* (1897).

CELLIER Alfred (b London, 1 December 1844; d London, 28 December 1891). Composer of London's longest-running musical of the 19th century.

The son of an East London schoolteacher of French descent, and a schoolmate of Sullivan at the Chapel Royal, Cellier began his musical career as a boy chorister. He continued as a church and concert organist and, for a period, as director of the Belfast Philharmonic, but he ended up by following the same path as his more famous contemporary, as a theatre conductor and composer. His first one-act operetta, *Charity Begins at Home* (1872), was very successfully staged by Thomas German Reed, who had produced Sullivan's early works, as part of the entertainment at his Gallery of Illustration. It proved popular enough to be regularly revived in Britain, played for a season on Broadway, mounted several times in Australia, and established itself alongside *Cox and Box* and *Ages Ago* amongst the most durable items of the German Reeds' repertoire.

After a period as musical director at London's Court Theatre, during which time he illustrated several of their musical pieces, such as a'Beckett's burlesque *Christabel* (1872), with scores 'arranged, with original scraps by ...', Cellier took up a similar post under Charles Calvert at the Prince's Theatre in Manchester. There he supplied incidental scores for productions ranging from Calvert's large-scale *Henry IV* to the annual Christmas pantomime. He took out a Frederic Sullivan tour of *The Contrabandista* in 1874 and, later the same year, had his first full-length comic opera *The Sultan of Mocha*, written to a libretto by an anonymous local gentleman, produced at the Prince's. *The Sultan of Mocha* was received with great delight and was played in Manchester for several seasons before being taken to London in 1876 where it proved itself to be one of the most notable British-written works of that new era of musical theatre which had not long since been set in motion by the French composers of opéra-bouffe.

Manchester produced Cellier's next three full-length works, *Tower of London*, *Nell Gwynne* and *Belladonna*, without comparable success, as well as an *Aladdin* (1875) written to a text by Alfred Thompson and starring Mrs

John Wood, but in the meanwhile the composer had left the midlands and returned to London, where he busied himself providing music for a range of theatres, writing genteel operetta for Reed's Gallery of Illustration, pantomime music for Covent Garden (1878), or incidental music for pieces such as George Lash Gordon's *Millions in It* (1877) and Ross Neil's fairy play *Elfinella* (1878), as the commission demanded. In 1877, he succeeded George Allen as the conductor of the Comedy Opera Company's production of Gilbert and Sullivan's comic opera *The Sorcerer* at the Opera Comique, and he subsequently took musical charge of Richard D'Oyly Carte's productions in Britain, America and Australia on a number of occasions. He conducted the original London productions of *HMS Pinafore* and *Ivanhoe*, the New York *Billee Taylor*, and also supplied a series of highly successful and long-running one-act forepieces for the Savoy operas, before his brother, **François CELLIER** (b London, 1849; d London, 5 January 1914), definitively took over the position of company musical director, a post which he retained until Carte's death in 1901.

Alfred continued throughout to turn out a steady stream of vocal and theatre music. His connection with Blanche Roosevelt, a one-time Josephine from London's *HMS Pinafore*, led to her 'Blanche Roosevelt English Opera Company', which had played *The Sultan of Mocha* in America, producing the première of a musical based on Longfellow's *The Masque of Pandora* at Boston. With Ms Roosevelt starring alongside Hugh Talbot, Charlotte Hutchings, Joseph Greenfelder and W S Daboll, it was a two-week failure. Cellier, however, stayed on for a time in America, and conducted for the Comley–Barton Company's more successful production of *Olivette*.

Back in Britain, he provided a full score of incidental music for the Kendals' 1885 production of *As You Like It* at the St James's Theatre, but his major success as a composer came in 1886 when George Edwardes, to whose burlesque *Little Jack Sheppard* he had contributed several pieces, produced his comedy opera *Dorothy* at the Gaiety Theatre. A musical revision of the Manchester *Nell Gwynne* score attached to a new libretto by *Charity Begins at Home* librettist, Charlie Stephenson, *Dorothy* was produced whilst the delicately-constitutioned Cellier was in Australia, getting a change of air, conducting a comic opera season for the management of Williamson, Garner and Musgrove, and winning himself a certain social success.

Dorothy proved to be a phenomenon. It gave Cellier the biggest song hit of the time in the baritone serenade, 'Queen of My Heart', and it ultimately became the longest-running musical show of its era in the London theatre. This overwhelming success resulted in a new West End run for *The Sultan of Mocha*, a production for a Stephenson remodel of *Tower of London* as *Doris* (1889) and a pairing with W S Gilbert for *The Mountebanks* (1892), a work which was completed by Ivan Caryll when Cellier died before finishing his score. *Doris*, which turned out a tenor bon-bon in 'I've Sought the Brake and Bracken', and *The Mountebanks* both had good London runs and the latter piece, if not quite at the level of the best of Gilbert and Sullivan's collaborations, was exported with some success.

Some time after his death, some of his music was used as additional material in Frederick Rosse's score for the Rutland Barrington children's musical *The Water Babies* produced at the Garrick Theatre in 1902 (18 December) and revived there again the following Christmas.

Elegant and infallibly musical, Cellier's work has a refinement and a pretty, somewhat dignified melodiousness, not altogether compatible with his voluble, bohemian character, and lacking only the sense of humour and burlesque gaiety of which Sullivan was capable. This fact renders most unlikely his alleged claim, reported in one Australian paper during his stay there, that during his time as musical director with Carte's company he had been the uncredited composer of *The Pirates of Penzance*'s 'Poor Wandering One'.

1872 **Charity Begins at Home** (B C Stephenson) 1 act Gallery of Illustration 7 February
1873 **Dora's Dream** (Arthur Cecil) 1 act Gallery of Illustration 3 July
1874 **Topsyturveydom** (W S Gilbert) 1 act Criterion Theatre 21 March
1874 **The Sultan of Mocha** (?Albert Jarret) Prince's Theatre, Manchester 16 November
1875 **Tower of London** (anon) Prince's Theatre, Manchester 4 October
1876 **Nell Gwynne** (H B Farnie) Prince's Theatre, Manchester 17 October
1877 **Two Foster Brothers** (Gilbert a' Beckett) 1 act St George's Hall 12 March
1878 **The Spectre Knight** (James Albery) 1 act Opera Comique 9 February
1878 **Belladonna** (Alfred Thompson) Prince's Theatre, Manchester 27 April
1878 **After All** (Frank Desprez) 1 act Opera Comique 23 December
1880 **In the Sulks** (Desprez) 1 act Opera Comique 21 February
1881 **The Masque of Pandora** (Stephenson) Boston Theater, Boston 10 January
1883 **Too Soon** (Charles Barnard) 1 act Madison Square Theater, New York 18 February
1886 **The Carp** (Desprez) 1 act Savoy Theatre 13 February
1886 **Dorothy** (Stephenson) Gaiety Theatre 25 September
1888 **Mrs Jarramie's Genie** (w François Cellier/Desprez) 1 act Savoy Theatre 14 February
1889 **Doris** (Stephenson) Lyric Theatre 20 April
1892 **The Mountebanks** (Gilbert) completed by Ivan Caryll Lyric Theatre 4 January

LES CENT VIERGES Opérette in 3 acts by Clairville, Henri Chivot and Alfred Duru. Music by Charles Lecocq. Théâtre des Fantaisies-Parisiennes, Brussels, 16 March 1872; Théâtre des Variétés, Paris, 13 May 1872.

Paris proved slow to give Lecocq another opportunity after his success with *Fleur de thé*, Belgium seemed a propitious place to be during the Franco-Prussian war and the days of the commune, and Brussels boasted one of the most go-ahead producers around at the time in the person of the enthusiastic Eugène Humbert. These circumstances combined to make Humbert's Théâtre des Fantaisies-Parisiennes the launching pad for the composer's second major work, the delightfully ridiculous and thumpingly saucy *Les Cent Vierges*.

An English colony in the south seas, under the governorship of Sir Jonathan Plupersonn (Alfred Jolly), has been established with a wholly male population. To relieve the situation thus provoked, the government is sending out a shipload of a hundred girls ('vierges'). Unfortunately, the ship gets lost, and the deprived colonists are left to their own resources a bit longer whilst a second load of potential brides is recruited. Pretty French honeymooner Gabrielle (Mlle Gentien) and her bosomy pal Eglantine (Mme Delorme), sightseeing at London docks, get uncomprehendingly included in the hundred and end up heading for the Green Islands, with their husbands, Duc Anatole de Quillembois (Mario Widmer) and Poulardot (Charlier), following in horrified pursuit. By the time the bride-ship gets to its destination, however, all but 14 girls have jumped ship, and Plupersonn decides that they (plus the two extras caught prowling about, who are the two husbands in disguise) will have to be distributed by lottery. The drooling governor and his secretary, Brididick (Nardin), draw the two phoney virgins, and the situation winds up to a farcical series of events which are only defused when the original ship arrives with a chorus of girls for all.

The showpiece of Lecocq's score was Gabrielle's second-act waltz song of homesickness, 'O Paris, gai séjour', but the prima donna was well supplied with other numbers, from her opening admission 'J'ai la tête romanesque' to her final extravagant burlesque of passion as she seduces the jelly-kneed governor to give her husband time to lead the revolt of the womanless islanders ('Je t'aime! Je t'aime!'). Anatole, at first romantic, then plotting in quartet with his wife and the Poulardots, had his best moments in his guise as Éméraldine, getting into the character with 'J'ai pour mari Barbarini' and following up in the comical quartet with his 'mother' (Poulardot) and their 'husbands', 'A table, chassons l'humeur noire', where Anatole tries to delay the end of their dinner, and what must inevitably follow, with a comical song ('Un vieux et riche Céladon').

Les Cent Vierges was a ringing hit in Brussels and, less than two months from opening night, Eugène Bertrand produced a Paris edition for his Théâtre des Variétés. Anna van Ghell (Gabrielle), Gabrielle Gauthier (Eglantine), Berthelier (Anatole), Paul Hittemans (Poulardot), Kopp (Plupersonn) and Léonce (Brididick) headed the top class cast, and the piece made it past its 100th performance before being taken up by the stages of the world. The original French version was seen in St Petersburg and in New York, where Marie Aimée's company, with the prima donna as Gabrielle alongside Juteau, Duchesne, Lecuyer and Mlle Bonelli, played the first of several seasons of Les Cent Vierges in repertoire, whilst the first foreign-language versions were mounted in Berlin and in Madrid.

As was regularly the case at the time, the Spanish only actually borrowed the libretto of the show and reused it with local music. El Tributo de la cien donzellas, a 3-act zarzuela by Santisteban, with music by Francisco Asenjo Barbieri, was produced at the Teatro Zarzuela 7 November 1872.

Franz Jauner at the Vienna Carltheater produced Hundert Jungfrauen soon after, with Hermine Meyerhoff (Gabrielle), Karl Blasel (Anatole), Josef Matras (Rumpelmeier, ex-Poulardot), Franz Eppich (Plupersonn), Lori Stubel (Eglantine) and Lecocq's score titivated by Johann Brandl with a sailor song and chorus in Act I, a song for Antonie Link in the travesty character of a sea-cadet in Act II, and a quartet in Act III. The show played 24 times straight off and another 15 during the season, was

brought back four times more the following year and thrice in 1875. It popped up again in the repertoire in 1878–9 with Carl Streitmann as Brididick (28 December, 5 performances), and was revived yet again in 1900 (17 March).

The first English-language performances of the show seem to have been given in Australia, closely followed by Britain, by then anxious for more Lecocq in the wake of the huge success of La Fille de Madame Angot. There had been a brief sighting of Les Cent Vierges during a London visit by the Brussels company in 1873, with most of the original cast and Pauline Luigini as Gabrielle, but it had suffered 'violent attacks on its immorality' and had had to be taken off. However, this did not stop Mrs Sara Lane putting out a version by the Australian writer William M Akhurst, a version already seen in his home country a few months earlier, under the title To the Green Isles Direct, at the Britannia Theatre, Holborn. In September a second, 'freely adapted' English version was produced by Mr and Mrs A D McNeil at Edinburgh's Royal Princess's Theatre (Green Isle of the Sea, 21 September) and Mrs Liston's company took another version (ad John Grantham, Theatre Royal, Brighton 19 October 1874) of the show to the country, whilst John Hollingshead produced yet another, by Robert Reece, which was staged under the slightly more titillating title of The Island of Bachelors, but which got rid of much of what The Era described as that 'perilous stuff' without altering the basic plot too much. Constance Loseby and Nellie Farren were the girls, Arthur Cecil and J G Taylor their husbands, and Charles Lyall the Governor through two months of performances.

In America, the show had a rather unusual English-language production, with the multiple disguises of the plot getting a confusing fillip when Reece's The Island of Bachelors was performed by Kelly and Leon's Minstrels. Leon, as ever, took the prima donna rôle of Gabrielle, so that while the men of the plot were disguised as women, the leading lady was, in fact, played by a man.

In Paris, Les Cent Vierges had a major revival at the Folies-Dramatiques in 1875 with Mlle Prelly, Simon-Max, Luco, Milher and Mlle Toudouze featured, and it was reprised again at the Bouffes-Parisiens in 1885 with Charles Lamy, Mlle Edeliny, Édouard Maugé, Mesmaker and Mlle Keller, but when the show was reproduced at the Théâtre Apollo during the Second World War (15 September 1942), all the British content had, by order, to be removed, and in consequence Albert Willemetz and André Mouëzy-Éon were set to rewrite the piece with no reference to beastly Britons. The music remained untouched, but was occasionally resituated in a libretto which kept the bones of the original, but which now set the first part in France and gallicized the Governor as Duflacnard and his assistant as Clopinette. It also introduced a very funny new character called Marcel, pursuing the wedded but unbedded Gabrielle from Paris to the Green Isles in a barrage of disguises and ultimately winning her whilst her rakish and unsuitable husband returns to his life amongst the girls of the Bal Mabille. Germaine Roger (Gabrielle), Duvaleix (Poulardot), Urban (Duflacnard), Milton (Anatole) and René Lenoty (Marcel) headed the cast. This skilful adaptation – which had the rare quality of actually heightening the comedy of its original – was subsequently staged by Mlle Roger during her management of the Gaîté-Lyrique (1946) with Madeleine

Vernon, Pasquali, Léo Bardollet, Robert Destain and Jane Montange, and it has become the standard version of the piece still played in France.

Germany: Friedrich-Wilhelmstädtisches Theater *Hundert Jungfrauen* 5 December 1872; USA: Olympic Theater (Fr) 23 December 1872, Kelly and Leon's Music Hall *The Island of Bachelors* 17 July 1876; Austria: Carltheater *Hundert Jungfrauen* 15 March 1873; UK: St James's Theatre (Fr) 20 June 1873, Britannia Theatre *To the Green Isles Direct* 25 May 1874, Gaiety Theatre *The Island of Bachelors* 14 September 1874; Australia; Opera House, Melbourne 27 February 1874; Hungary; Budai Színkör *Szaz Szüz (A zöld Sziget)* 1 July 1874

CHABRIER, [Alexis] Emmanuel (b Ambert, 18 January 1841; d Paris, 13 September 1894).

The youthful Chabrier, who had gone through a couple of years of musical training following his general education, made a couple of half-hearted efforts at writing an opérette to words by the poet Rimbaud (*Fisch-ton-Kan* (1863), *Vaucochard et fils 1er* (1864)) and also tried his hand at an opera. However, in spite of a life which, away from his day job with the Ministry of the Interior, was led largely in artistic circles, it was a good number of years before he finally composed a piece which was produced on the commercial stage.

It was those artistic contacts which gave him the opportunity. A meeting with librettist Albert Vanloo, already a force in the musical theatre, persuaded the author and his partner, Eugène Leterrier, to entrust their next libretto to Chabrier and, with their name attached to it, the piece was accepted by Charles Comte for the Théâtre des Bouffes-Parisiens. *L'Étoile* had only a short run and the composer, disappointed, turned away from the genre, contributing only one further piece, a one-act opérette, *Une éducation manquée*, again to a text by Vanloo and Leterrier, for private performance, in a successful subsequent career as a composer of which the theatrical highlight was the production of the opera *Le Roi malgré lui* (1887).

In spite of the limited attention paid to his pieces at the time of their production, Chabrier's works and, in particular, *L'Étoile* have become favourites with a group of enthusiasts and they have won a number of recordings and productions in recent years.

1877 **L'Étoile** (Albert Vanloo, Eugène Leterrier) Théâtre des Bouffes-Parisiens 28 November
1879 **Une éducation manquée** (Vanloo, Leterrier) 1 act Cercle Internationale de la Presse 1 May

Biography: Myers, R: *Emmanuel Chabrier and his Circle* (Dent, London, 1969)

CHAMPION, Gower (b Geneva, Ill, 22 June 1920; d New York, 25 August 1980). Choreographer and director for several sizeable Broadway successes.

Champion began his career as a dancer, appearing (temporarily as 'Christopher Gower') in the theatre in such pieces as *The Streets of Paris* (1939), *The Lady Comes Across* and *Count Me In* (1942), in television and in films, both solo (*Till the Clouds Roll By*) and in a partnership with his then wife, Marge Champion [née BELCHER, Marjorie Celeste, aka Marjorie Bell] (b Los Angeles, 2 September 1921) (*Mr Music*, *Show Boat*, *Lovely to Look At*, *Give a Girl a Break*, *Jupiter's Darling*, *Three for the Show*) up to the mid-1950s. By this time he had already begun a career as a choreographer and director with the revues *Small Wonder*,

Lend an Ear and *Three For Tonight*, which top-billed the Champions themselves, and had choreographed his first Broadway book musical, the Hugh Martin/Preston Sturges *Make a Wish* (1951) at the Winter Garden Theater.

Champion directed several pieces, including the George M Cohan musical *Forty-Five Minutes From Broadway*, for television, but significant theatre success first came his way in 1960, when he directed and choreographed the youth-orientated first musical of Michael Stewart, Lee Adams and Charles Strouse, *Bye Bye Birdie*. This bright-eyed tale of kids, parents and pop music had some memorable staging moments ranging from a tangle of teenage telephone calls to Chita Rivera's irrelevant but exciting performance of a madcap dance routine in a Shriners' meeting (Tony Awards, direction, choreography).

Champion confirmed his *Bye Bye Birdie* success the next year in Stewart's charming adaptation of the film *Lili* into the long-running *Carnival*, and director and author hit the very biggest time with their third effort together, *Hello, Dolly!* (1964, Tony Awards direction, choreography), in which Champion's staging of the show's title number, with its dancing waiters and extended use of the stage, won particular praise. In 1966 he showed that he was capable of ingenuity without mass spectacle or dancing stars when he directed Robert Preston and Mary Martin in the two-handed *I Do! I Do!* for *Hello, Dolly!* producer David Merrick, for whom he also staged the *The Happy Time* (1968), *Sugar* (1972) and *A Broadway Musical* (1978). A further piece from this period, *Prettybelle* (1971), closed out of town.

A colourful rewrite of the old hit musical *Irene*, staged with infectious life and period style, had more luck and more staying power than the inherently downbeat Michael Stewart/Jerry Herman successor to *Hello, Dolly!*, the filmland tale of *Mack and Mabel*. However Champion's last work, the direction and choreography for the stage version of the movie musical *42nd Street* (1980), gave him one more international hit. But the Tony Awards which he was given for both his direction and choreography of the show came posthumously for Champion who died on the day that *42nd Street* opened on Broadway.

CHANCEL, Jules (b Marseille, 1867; d unknown)

Journalist (*Écho de Paris*, *Le Gaulois*, *l'Illustration*, *Figaro*, *Charivari* and various provincial papers) and intermittent playwright (*Maîtresse femme*, *Cercle vicieux*, *L'Erreur*, *Son professeur*, the Eldorado saynète *Grandeur et servitude*, *L'Auréole* etc), Chancel had his biggest success, in tandem with Léon Xanrof, as the author of the play *Le Prince Consort*. The pair later adapted their play as a libretto for Ivan Caryll under the title *S.A.R.* (Son Altesse Royale). They were also responsible for the French version of the libretto of *Ein Walzertraum*, a piece which, for all its acknowledgement of a Germanic source, had a principal tale very close to that of *Le Prince Consort*.

Chancel was also credited (w Henriot) as the author of the unnamed play from which Paul Lincke's successful Operette *Gri-Gri* was taken, and of the piece's French version.

1908 **S.A.R.** (Ivan Caryll/w Léon Xanrof) Théâtre des Bouffes-Parisiens 11 November

1910 **Rêve de Valse** (*Ein Walzertraum*) French version w Xanrof (Théâtre Apollo)

1924 **Gri-Gri** French version w Henriot (Gaîté-Rochechouart)

CHANNING, Carol [Elaine] (b Seattle, Washington, 31 January 1921).

A hugely blonde and pop-eyed musical comedienne, Carol Channing appeared in a minor capacity in *No for an Answer* (1941) and *Let's Face It!* (1942), before coming properly to the fore for the first time when she was featured by Gower Champion in the 1948 revue *Lend Me An Ear* with its musical comedy burlesque 'The Gladiola Girl'. This performance helped win her the starring rôle of Lorelei Lee in the stage musical version of *Gentlemen Prefer Blondes* (1949), in which she created 'A Little Girl From Little Rock' and 'Diamonds Are a Girl's Best Friend'.

Miss Channing subsequently replaced Rosalind Russell as Ruth Sherwood in Broadway's *Wonderful Town*, toured in the same rôle (1955) and appeared in the title-rôles of the short-lived musical *The Vamp* (1955, Flora Weems), which cast her as another husky, wide-eyed girl-on-the-make, and the showcase revue *Show Girl* (1961), before making her greatest success with an acclaimed performance as the eponymous heroine of *Hello, Dolly!* (1964), introducing the celebrated title song, 'Goodbye, Dearie' and 'Before the Parade Passes By'. She played this rôle for eighteen months on Broadway and subsequently on tour in America as well as in an unfortunate 1979 revival at London's Theatre Royal, Drury Lane. This broadened and coarsened latter-day version of *Hello, Dolly!* had been preceded by an attempt to bring Lorelei Lee back to Broadway, 25 years after her creation, in a version of *Gentlemen Prefer Blondes*, retitled *Lorelei* (1974), with only a limited success.

Miss Channing also appeared in her own revue (*Carol Channing with Ten Stout-Hearted Men*, 1970) in Canada, America and in Britain, and in a tryout of the Jerry Herman compilation show *Jerry's Girls*, and contributed to the memorable fun of the musical film *Thoroughly Modern Millie* as a daft champagne-blonde with aeronautic tendencies.

LA CHANSON DE FORTUNIO Opéra-comique in 1 act by Hector Crémieux and Ludovic Halévy. Music by Jacques Offenbach. Théâtre des Bouffes-Parisiens, Paris, 5 January 1861.

The little opéra-comique *La Chanson de Fortunio* was a descendant of de Musset's famous four-act comedy *Le Chandelier*, the principle of which was that if a married woman has an obviously sighing would-be lover around her, a jealous husband will be so busy keeping his eye on the foolish fellow that he will miss detecting his wife's real liaison. *Le Chandelier* was played, until censorship struck it, for a number of years at the Comédie-Française and, during that time, the young Offenbach supplied the music for the song in which the amorous lawyer's clerk Fortunio expresses his adoration of his master's wife.

Crémieux and Halévy's pocket-sized piece on the same theme took for its central character the same Fortunio (Désiré), older, now himself a laywer, and married to a young wife, Laurette (Mlle Chabert), who is sighed after by the young clerk, Valentin (Julia Pfotzer). The lawyer's clerks dig up the famous song which did the trick for Fortunio and use it to conquer their girlfriends whilst

Valentin makes sufficient progress with Laurette, in spite of her husband's suspicions, to leave him some hope at the final curtain. The chief clerk, Friquet, was played by the lanky Bache, the others by girls.

The song, a version of Offenbach's old number, was made over by its composer to suit the light operatic talents of Mlle Pfotzer rather than the barely-singing performance of the Comédie-Française's Daubray, and became the centrepiece of the entertainment, as sung by Valentin as the climax of the show. Valentin, equipped with a drinking song – about water – and his admission of love ('Je t'aime'), Friquet ('C'est moi qui suis le petit clerc') and the other little clerks had the bulk of the show's music, with Laurette having her moment chiding her husband for his jealousy in 'Prenez garde à vous!'

First produced by Offenbach at the Bouffes-Parisiens, *La Chanson de Fortunio* was both highly admired and hugely enjoyed, and it became one of the staples of the Offenbach repertoire of one-act opérettes, regularly revived over the years in spectacles coupés. It also found great popularity outside France, most particularly in the German language. Carl Treumann mounted the piece (ad Ferdinand Gumbert) at his Theater am Franz-Josefs-Kai in 1861, with himself in the rôle of Fortunio alongside Anna Grobecker (Friquet), Anna Marek (Valentin) and Therese Schäfer (Laurette). This version, which apparently gave the 'adventure' to Friquet and introduced Babette the cook (Babet, a grisette, in the original French version), played by Elise Zöllner, as the second boy's love interest, was a great success. Not counting the performances of the original piece given at Treumann's theatre by the Bouffes company, with Désiré and Mlle Pfotzer in their original rôles, in 1862, *Meister Fortunio* was played no less than 75 times in the repertoire of the Kaitheater, the highest total achieved by any work in the little house's existence. When Treumann returned to the Carltheater, *Meister Fortunio* was played there regularly, Schäfer moving on to play Babette, whilst Karl Blasel (Fortunio) and Hermine Meyerhoff (Laurette) played alongside Grobecker in one of her happiest, remade-to-measure trouser rôles. The show was revived at regular intervals in later Viennese years.

Berlin followed with another German version (ad Georg Ernst) whilst, a few months after the Bouffes company had introduced the show to Budapest on their 1861 tour, the Nemzeti Színház brought out an Hungarian version (ad Lajos Csepregi) with Kálmán Szerdahelyi, Vilma Bognar and Ilka Markovits featured, which was to have a similarly long and often reprised career. In America, the piece was first played in the German/Treumann adaptation with Klotz as Fortunio, Hedwig l'Arronge as Valentin and Eugenie Schmitz as Friquet, then, in the original French version, by Bateman's opéra-bouffe company with Irma (Valentin), Francis (Fortunio), Aline Lambèle (Laurette) and Leduc (Friquet) on a double-bill with *Les Bavards*. It remained a regular item on the German theatre's bills for a decade, but this did not apparently encourage anyone to try an English version in New York until 1900.

The first English adaptation seems to have been that produced at London's Gaiety Theatre, already the scene of a visiting French performance in 1871, in 1876 (ad uncredited) as part of Johnnie Toole's season. W H Leigh was Fortunio, Alice Burville played Lauretta and Miss Stembridge, Valentine, but the piece never caught on in the English-language theatre in the same way that it had in German and French. It did, however, reappear in the repertoire of the Welsh National Opera in 1979.

Le Chandelier itself was subsequently adapted as an opéra-comique by Gaston de Caillavet and Robert de Flers, set to music by André Messager, and produced at the Opéra-Comique 5 June 1907 as *Fortunio* with a considerable success which has led to its survival in the occasional repertoire up to the present day.

Austria; Theater am Franz-Josefs-Kai *Meister Fortunio und sein Liebeslied* 25 April 1861; Germany: Friedrich-Wilhelmstädtisches Theater 21 August 1861; Hungary: Nemzeti Színház (Fr) 13 July 1861, Nemzeti Szinház *Fortunio (báj)dala* 21 January 1862; USA: Stadttheater *Fortunioslied* 14 September 1867, Pike's Opera House (Fr) 21 December 1868, American Theater *The Magic Melody* 22 January 1900; UK: Gaiety Theatre (Fr) 1 July 1871, *The Song of Fortunio* 3 January 1876

Recording: (Bourg)

CHANSON GITANE
Opérette in 2 acts by André Mouëzy-Éon and Louis Poterat. Music by Maurice Yvain. Théâtre de la Gaîté-Lyrique, Paris, 13 December 1946.

Following the immense success of Lopez's *La Belle de Cadix*, Maurice Yvain, whose greatest stage successes had been with the jazzy musical comedies of the 1920s, collaborated musically on a romantic opérette in the style of the new hit. *Chanson gitane*, lavishly produced at the Gaîté-Lyrique, told the familiar story of Count Hubert des Gemmeries (André Dassary) and the gipsy girl, Mitidika (Mag Walter), whom he marries but for whom he cannot find acceptance in society. She goes back to her people, followed by an accusation of the theft of the diamonds of the Duchesse de Berry, but ultimately the pair come together again to live their lives far away from the prejudices of his people and hers.

Yvain's score had a ready-made hit in the gipsy girl's song 'Sur la route qui va', already popularized in the cinema, but it also included a number of delightful new pieces ranging from the hero's ardent solos ('L'Amour qu'un jour tu m'as donné') and some coloratura for the soprano (Rita Mazzoni) cast as the Duchesse de Berry, to the rhythmic 'Au pas d'un petit poney' and a splendid danced 'Aragonesa' for the heroine and soubrette.

A ten-month run at the Gaîté-Lyrique was followed by Parisian revivals in 1950 and 1954 and provincial productions have continued at regular intervals since, as *Chanson gitane* established itself alongside the very different *Ta bouche* and *Pas sur la bouche* as one of the core items of the composer's stage work.

Recording: selection (Pathé-EMI)

LE CHANTEUR DE MEXICO
Opérette à grand spectacle in 2 acts by Félix Gandéra and Raymond Vincy. Lyrics by Henri Wernert and Raymond Vincy. Music by Francis Lopez. Théâtre du Châtelet, Paris, 15 December 1951.

Le Chanteur de Mexico followed behind *La Belle de Cadix* and *Andalousie* in the continuing series of Raymond Vincy/Francis Lopez opérettes, as a vehicle, and an ever more lavish one – mounted this time on the stage of the huge Théâtre du Châtelet – for star tenor Luis Mariano.

Mariano played Vincent Etchebar, a striving singer from Saint Jean-de-Luz who, with his pal Bilou (Pierjac) in tow, goes up to Paris to try his luck in the big city. They fall in with pretty Cri-Cri (Lilo), and before long Vincent wins a competition and, without knowing it, the heart of Cri-Cri. When the opérette singer Eva (Jacqueline Chambard) needs someone to replace her tenor, Miguelito, who is refusing to go on tour to Mexico, Vincent gets the job. When he arrives in South America, he gets mixed up with the rebel Zapata (Robert Jysor) and the whip-cracking Tornada (Monique Bert) – both of whom are after the real Miguelito – and events both hair-raising and amorous make up the action of the second act before the happy ending arrives with its ritual pairing-off.

The songs of *Le Chanteur de Mexico* were in the already recognizable vein, and existed very largely for the benefit of Vincent/Mariano. He yodelled out the praises of 'Mexico' and 'El Tequila', crooned to the 'Rossignol de mes amours' and his 'Maïtechu', got misty over his home-town in 'Il est un coin de France' whilst nevertheless insisting that 'Je me souviendrai d'Acapulco' and, from way above the city – in one of the evening's most appreciated stage pictures – commented on what it was like 'Quand on voit Paris d'en haut'. The other principals got the odd look in, Cri-Cri coming out the best with her 'Ça me fait quelqu'chose', Eva waltzingly admitting that she is 'Capricieuse' and Zapata pounding out the regulation baritone number which had become a feature of the Vincy/Lopez shows since *La Belle de Cadix*'s 'Le Coeur des femmes'.

Le Chanteur de Mexico was all it was designed to be: a first-rate vehicle for Mariano and a splendid stage spectacle, and if it was a little less fresh and attractive than the two preceding vehicles, the public enjoyed it just as much. They filled its vast theatre for a year for Mariano and then a second year for his successor, Rudi Hirigoyen – no taller than Mariano, but equipped with a popular tenor voice which did masculine miracles with the music. By the time the show finished its first Paris run, it had clocked up 905 performances.

In 1956 Mariano teamed with Bourvil (Bilou) and Annie Cordy (Cri-Cri) to put *Le Chanteur de Mexico* on film in what proved, in spite of some rather lopsided cutting of the original story-line, to be one of the most popular French musical films of its time. As for the show, there can scarcely have been a year in the 40 since its first performances where it has not toured or played at least one provincial French house, remaining one of the most frequently played of all Lopez's popular early works.

Film: 1956

Recordings: complete (Festival), selections (Odéon etc)

CHAPÍ [y Llorente] Ruperto
(b Villena, Alicante, 27 March 1851; d Madrid, 25 March 1909).

Chapí studied at the Madrid Conservatoire and worked as a musician in theatre orchestras and then as a military bandmaster whilst taking his first steps as a composer. He followed further studies in Rome during his twenties, and made an attempt at operatic composition – several of his operatic pieces being produced in Madrid (*Las naves de Cortes*, *La hija de Jefté*, *Roger de Flor*, *La muerte de Garcélaso*) – but in the 1880s returned to the light musical theatre where, nearly a decade after the production of his first zarzuela, he found an initial success with *La tempestad* (lib: M Ramos Carrión, Teatro de Jovellanos 2 March 1882), a three-act musical version of Erckmann-Chatrian's *Le Juif polonais*.

Amongst the list of more than 150 full-length and,

mostly, short zarzuelas that he subsequently composed, the three-act *La bruja* (lib: Carrión Teatro Zarzuela 10 December 1887), the shorter *Los tentaciones de San Antonio* (lib: A Ruesga, V Prieto, Teatro Felipe 20 August 1890), which was played in Italian in both Italy and Vienna, *El rey que rabió* (lib: Carrión, Vital Aza Teatro Zarzuela 20 April 1891), produced in Hungary as *Az unatkozó kiraály* (Népszinház 10 December 1898), and *La revoltosa* (lib: José Lopez Silva, Fernández Shaw, Teatro Apolo 25 November 1897) proved some of the most successful at home and, occasionally, abroad.

Chapí also continued to write operatic scores, his three-act opera, *Circe*, being mounted as the opening attraction at Madrid's Teatro Lirico in 1902, followed by a *Don Juan de Austria* and his final work *Margarita la Tornera*, and also devoted himself to the foundation and running of the Spanish performing rights society.

Chapí's other works included *Abel y Cain* (1873) *La calandria* (1880), *Los dos huérfanos* (1880), *Musica clasica* (1880), *La calle de cassetas* (1880), *Nada entre dos platos* (1881), *La Flor de lis* (1884), *El milagro de la Virgen* (1884), *El Guerrillero* (1885 w Arrieta, Manuel Fernández Caballero), *El Pais de Abaniro* (1885), *Término medio* (1885), *Los quintos de mi pueblo* (1885), *¡Ya pican!*, *¡Ya pican!* (1885), *El domingo gordo* (1886), *El figón de las desdichas* (1887), *Playeras* (1887), *Los lobos marinos* (1887), *El fantasma de los aires* (1887), *Ortografia* (1888), *El Cocodrillo* (1889), *A casarse tocan* (1889), *Las hijas del Zebedeo* (1889), *Nocturno* (1890), *Todo por ella* (1890), *La leyenda del rey monje* (1890), *¡Las doce y media y serena!* (1890), *Los nuestros* (1890), *Los alojados* (1891), *El mismo Demorio* (1891), *Los trabajadores* (1891), *La bala del rifle* (1892), *El organista* (1892), *Las campanadas* (1892), *El reclamo* (1893), *Los gendarmes* (1893), *Via libre* (1893), *El Duque de Gandia* (w A Llanos 1894), *La Czarina* (1894), *El moro muza* (1894), *El tambor de Granaderos* (1894), *El cura del regimento* (1895), *Mujer e reina* (1895), *El cortejo de la Irene* (1896), *El Señor Corregidor* (1896), *La gitanilla* (1896), *El bajo de arriba* (1896), *Los golfos* (1896), *El niño del estanguero* (1897), *El segundo de legeros* (1898), *Pepe Galardo* (1898), *La chavala* (1898), *Curro Vargas* (1898), *Los hijos del batallón* (1898), *La afrancesada* (1899), *El fonografo ambulante* (1899), *La cara de Dios* (1899), *La seña Frascita* (1899), *Los buenos mozos* (1899), *La cortijera* (1900), *Maria de los Angeles* (1900), *El gatito negro* (1900), *Mississippi* (1900), *El estreno* (1900), *El barquillero* (1900), *Blasones y talegas* (1901), *¿Quo vadis?* (1901), *El sombrero de plumas* (1902), *El puñao de rosas* (1902), *Plus ultra* (1902), *La venta de Don Quijote* (1902), *El tio Juan* (1902), *El rey mago* (1903), *El equipage del Rey José* (1903), *La chica del maestro* (1903), *La cuna* (1904), *La tragedia de Pierrot* (1904), *La guardia de honor* (1905), *Miss Full* (1905), *El seductor* (1905), *La leyenda dorada* (1905), *El hijo de Doña Uraca* (1905), *El amor en sol-fa* (1905 w J Serrano), *El alma del pueblo* (1905), *La sobresaliente* (1905), *La reina* (1905), *La cortijera* (1906), *La joroba* (1906), *El maldito dinera* (1906), *El Triunfo de Venus* (1906), *La pesadilla* (1906), *El rey del petróleo* (1906), *La fragua de Vulcano* (1906), *La patria chica* (1907), *El pino del norte* (1907), *Ninon* (1907), *Los veteranos* (1907), *La carabina de Ambrosio* (1908), *El merendo de la alegria* (1908), *La Doña roja* (1908), *Las mil maravillas* (1908), *Las Madrileñas* (1908), *Las calderas de Pedro Bolero* (1908), *Aqui hace farta un hombre* (1909), *Los majos de plante* (1909), *El diablo con faldas* (1909), *La magia de la vida* (1910), *Entre rocas* (1910), *Los mostenses*, *Las peluconas*, *Los guerrilleros*, *La bravias* etc.

Biographies: Salcedo, A S: *Ruperto Chapí, su vida y sus obras* (Cordoba, 1929), Aguilar Gómez, J: *Ruperto Chapí y su obra lirica* (Excma, Alicante, 1973), Sagardia, A: *Ruperto Chapí* (Espasa-Calpé, Madrid, 1979)

LES CHARBONNIERS Opérette in 1 act by Philippe Gille. Music by Jules Costé. Théâtre des Variétés, Paris, 4 April 1877.

Les Charbonniers is a little piece about a pair of coal merchants – Thérèse Valbrezègue (Anna Judic) and Pierre Cargouniol (José Dupuis) – with a quarrel. They take their grievances before the local under-secretary to the comissioner of police (Baron) and, by the time they are through putting their points of view, come to have more than a little liking for each other. Léonce made up the cast as Tardivel, an interrupting running joke of a fellow with a need for a passport.

Decorated with a pretty score by Jules Costé, which comprised a trio, a duo, a Chanson du Coucou ('Deux paysans, hors du village'), some Couplets ('Ah! mais, monsieur! Ne me chatouillez pas comme ça!') for Judic and an air for Dupuis ('Mais regardez-moi ces bras la!'), *Les Charbonniers*, initially played on a double bill with Edmond Gondinet's vaudeville *Professor pour dames*, gave all concerned a welcome success. So great a hit did it prove that manager Bertrand – allegedly in gratitude, but with a weather eye to publicity – opened his second gallery free to the coal-merchants of Paris, on the condition that they came, black-faced, from their work. The little piece proved to be remarkably durable, and it was played in several other countries and languages over the 25 years following its first appearance, as well as being revived on several occasions in Paris.

The opérette remained for many years a supporting item in the repertoire of the busily travelling Judic. Vienna first saw a performance in French during her visit to the Theater an der Wien in 1883, and then another, played in a spectacle coupé with *Le Fiacre 117*. When the star returned to the Carltheater in 1889 (4 May), on the same tour in which she introduced *Les Charbonniers* in London, she played the piece again, and in 1892 she brought it back for a third time. The Carltheater had, however, long since introduced a German-language version, with musical interpolations by Brandl, which was played by Hermine Meyerhoff, Karl Blasel, Franz Eppich and Hildebrandt for 30 performances over a 12-month period immediately following the Paris production. The German version appeared again as late as 1901 (30 October), when it replaced a version of *Trial by Jury* as a forepiece to a ballet at Danzers Orpheum.

Budapest's Népszinház mounted an Hungarian version (ad Jenő Rákosi) on a double bill with Offenbach's *Ancsi sir, Jancsi nevet* (*Jeanne qui pleure et Jean qui rit*) in 1878 and that version was revived frequently (Vígszinház, 5 November 1901 etc).

The show's text was used as the bases for several other pieces, notably the little London musical *A Shower of Blacks* (ad Walter Parke, Arthur Shirley, music: Ernest Bucalossi Terry's Theatre 26 December 1887) and a Lewis Clifton/J W Houghton piece called *Cuckoo*. A later London adaptation of the piece, played as *The Judgement of Paris*, which retained Costé's music, was mounted as a forepiece at the Lyric Theatre in 1897 with Marie Elba, Homer Lind and A S Winckworth in the cast, whilst a fresh Hungarian version, *Szenesek, ha szerelmesek*, was seen at Budapest's Vigszinház as late as 15 June 1940.

Hungary: Népszinház *Szenes legeny, szenes lány* 18 January 1878; Austria: Carltheater *Der Kohlenhändler von Paris* 1 February 1878; Theater an der Wien (Fr) 18 November 1883; UK: Gaiety Theatre (Fr) 8 June 1889; Lyric Theatre *The Judgement of Paris* 30 October 1897

CHARELL, Erik [LÖWENBERG, Erich K] (b Breslau, Germany, 9 April 1895; d Zug, 15 July 1974).

A dancer, turned choreographer, turned director, Charell made his name as a stager of the entertainments at the Grosses Schauspielhaus, Berlin, from 1924. The earliest of these were revues (*An Alle* 1924, *Für dich* 1925 etc), highly coloured pieces, relying on much in the way of spectacular scenery and special effects, many and glittering costumes, and much gymnastic and regimented mass dancing, and Charell carried these revusical techniques over into large-scale productions of musical plays, such as the theatre's home-made versions of the grandiose *Casanova* (1928) and *The Three Musketeers* (1929), and the Berlin production of Fall's *Madame Pompadour* with Fritzi Massary and Max Pallenberg. He was altogether less happy with his gimmicky productions of such classics as *The Mikado* and *Die lustige Witwe*, both of which were transported out of their era and setting to allow for glitzy scenic display and a mass of dancing, with texts lazily rewritten when they refused to be forced into his 'concept'. Both these productions were lambasted, and the disaster of the jazzed-up *Die lustige Witwe* production led Massary, the queen of the Berlin musical stage, to quit the musical theatre.

In 1930 Charell had his most memorable success when he staged the Grosses Schauspielhaus's world première of *Im weissen Rössl*. Put into the Austrian mountains, miles from the nearest spangle and shimmy-step, he created a genuine piece of large-stage theatrical spectacle around the famous old play and the songs supplied by house composer Benatzky and others, contributing sufficiently to later be given an intermittent author's credit. He was also billed as author of the Grosses Schauspielhaus's 1926 show *Von Mund zu Mund* (1 September, music: Herman Darewski). He followed up his biggest stage triumph with a second major success, this time in the film world, when he directed the spectacular movie *Der Kongress tanzt* in 1931.

Charell subsequently directed *White Horse Inn* and *Casanova* in Britain and *L'Auberge du Cheval Blanc* in Paris with equivalent success, but he was shorn of his job in Berlin by the Nazi régime and encouraged to leave Germany. An attempt to create a new Benatzky pasticcio spectacular on a circus theme in London (*The Flying Trapeze*, Alhambra Theatre 1935) was an expensive failure and an attempt at *Swingin' the Dream* (1939) for Broadway was a 13-performance flop, but a decade later, having now returned to peacetime Germany, he put the circus idea to good use when he took the tiny Swiss musical *Der schwarze Hecht* and, giving it a rewrite and a whooped-up staging full of tricks and effects, turned it into the highly successful *Feuerwerk* (1950).

CHARIG, Phil[ip] (b New York, 31 August 1902; d New York, 21 July 1960).

Songwriter Charig showed up on Broadway for the first time in 1926, when his 'Sunny Disposish' (lyric: Ira Gershwin) earned him notice alongside the Gershwin brothers' material in the revue *Americana* at the Belmont Theater. This success set him off on a short-lived flush of theatre composing, beginning with the Chicago revue *Allez-Oop* (1927 w Leo Robin) and two book musicals for Broadway: *Yes, Yes, Yvette* and *Just Fancy* ('You Came Along' w Joseph Meyer, Robin).

Under the aegis of the publishers Chappell, he was paired with the young British composer Vivian Ellis on the score for a British touring musical based on *Peg o' My Heart*, contributed additional numbers to the score put together by 'Doc' Szirmai, at that time based in Britain, for the not unsuccessful *Lady Mary* ('You Came Along', 'I've Got a Feeling for Somebody'), and was set to work to supply a score for the Jack Buchanan/Elsie Randolph vehicle *That's a Good Girl*. 'Fancy Our Meeting', 'The One I'm Looking For', 'Sweet So-and-So' and the rest of that show's songs were all improbably credited to a five-sided combine of musicians and lyricists, but the result was sufficiently accommodating for Buchanan to order a second score from Charig (paired this time with Ellis) for *Stand Up and Sing*, two years later ('There's Always Tomorrow', 'It's Not You', 'Stand up and Sing').

Helped by the frenzied fashion for American music and composers in Britain at the time, Charig was also allotted the score for Weston and Lee's *Lucky Girl*, and, in between times, he supplied the American stage with scores for ephemeral musicalizations of Bolton and Middleton's *Polly with a Past* (*Polly*) and Rudolf Lothar's *The Phantom Ship* (*The Pajama Lady*) but, after some four or five years had passed without another 'Sunny Disposish' appearing, his services became less in demand. Following a short-lived musical called *Nikki*, which had the peculiarity of starring filmland's Fay Wray and Douglas Montgomery and featuring the young Archie Leach (later Cary Grant), he vanished from the Broadway and West End lists for over a decade.

He returned with the score for the lively, loose-limbed wartime show *Follow the Girls* which, without including anything outstanding in the way of music and producing only one number, the suggestive 'I Wanna Get Married', which garnered its composer notice, gave him a sizeable success in New York and in London. In 1955 his name was attached with those of Sammy Fain, Jerry Bock and Neil Simon to a quickly gone revue, *Catch a Star!*, at Broadway's Plymouth Theater, a piece which marked Charig's exit from the musical theatre, 30 years after his first appearance.

1927 **Yes, Yes, Yvette** (w Ben Jerome/Irving Caesar/James Montgomery) Harris Theater 3 October
1927 **Just Fancy** (w Joseph Meyer/Leo Robin/Joseph Santley, Gertrude Purcell) Casino Theater 11 October
1927 **Peg o' Mine** (w Vivian Ellis/Desmond Carter/Fred Jackson) Sunderland, England 31 October
1928 **That's a Good Girl** (w Meyer/Douglas Furber, Carter, Ira Gershwin) London Hippodrome 5 June
1928 **Lucky Girl** (Furber/R P Weston, Bert Lee) Shaftesbury Theatre, London 14 November
1929 **Polly** (w Herbert Stothart/Caesar/Guy Bolton, George Middleton, Isobel Leighton) Lyric Theater 8 January

1930 **The Pajama Lady** (w Richard Myers/R B Smith, John Mercer/H B Smith, George Lederer) National Theater, Washington 6 October

1931 **Stand Up and Sing** (w Ellis/Furber, Jack Buchanan) London Hippodrome 5 March

1931 **Nikki** (James Dyrenforth/John Monk Saunders) Martin Beck Theater 29 September

1944 **Follow the Girls** (Dan Shapiro, Milton Pascal/Guy Bolton, Fred Thompson) Century Theater 8 April

CHARITY BEGINS AT HOME   Operetta in 1 act by B C Stephenson. Music by Alfred Cellier. Gallery of Illustration, London, 7 February 1872.

An early collaboration by the authors of *Dorothy*, this little piece – the first from the pen of composer Cellier – was written for the German Reed family's drawing-room entertainment at the Gallery of Illustration. Stephenson's book, supported by a small and sparkling score, dealt with the efforts of a tiny village school threatened with closure to come up to the inspector's demands, and allowed the performers – Mrs Reed, Alfred Reed, Corney Grain and Fanny Holland – to disguise themselves as school pupils for some comical scenes and songs with the Inspector (Arthur Cecil). Along with *Cox and Box* and *Ages Ago* it proved to be the most enduringly successful of all the many German Reed productions, was regularly revived over the next 30 years (St George's Hall 1874, 1876, 1877, 1878, 1879, 1892, 1902) and became a popular choice as a fore-piece and a benefit item in the Victorian theatre.

John McCaull and Charles E Ford programmed *Charity Begins at Home* (with *Ages Ago*) as the opening attraction for their Bijou Theater and, with a cast including Digby Bell and Carrie Burton, the little piece played for nearly two months on Broadway, before being taken up in other English-speaking theatres throughout the world.

USA: Bijou Theater 31 March 1880; Australia: Princess Theatre, Melbourne 5 February 1887

CHARLIE GIRL   Musical comedy in 2 acts by Hugh and Margaret Williams and Ray Cooney. Music and lyrics by David Heneker and John Taylor. Adelphi Theatre, London, 15 December 1965.

An up-to-date version of the *Cinderella* story, at one stage angled towards being a comedy vehicle for Cicely Courtneidge, *Charlie Girl* was ultimately produced in London under the management of Harold Fielding with the former film star and musical comedy ingénue Anna Neagle top-billed alongside popular singer Joe Brown. She was Lady Hadwell, the impoverished owner of Hadwell Hall and the mother of three daughters – two suitably ladylike, and the third a scruffy tomboy (Christine Holmes). He was the 'Buttons' of the affair, the estate handyman, Joe, with an easygoing manner and a heart full of love for the youngest daughter, Charlie. Prince Charming arrives on the scene in the person of Jack Connor (Stuart Damon), the dreamboat son of Lady Hadwell's old chorus-line buddy, Kay (Hy Hazell), who married American and very, very rich, but Cinderella and the Prince do not get together in this version. Joe wins the pools, saves the stately home, and ends up with his Charlie, whilst Jack contents himself with the obvious possibilities of her elder sister. In a flashback to the earliest days of modern musical comedy and the famous rôle of Roberts in *The Lady Slavey*, Derek Nimmo appeared as a pools man who agrees to

stand in as a butler to impress the visitors and thereafter contributes most of the evening's comedy.

The show's score mixed the tones of the modern popular music world in Charlie's 'Like Love' and 'Bells Will Ring' with Joe's cockney praises of 'Charlie Girl' and the old-time music-hall 'Fish and Chips' and some more gracious material for Miss Neagle who closed the first act, setting off for the ball on the arms of the male chorus, with a smiling admission that 'I Was Young (when this last happened to me)'. Jack admired his perfect profile to 'What's the Magic?' and suffered horrors at an apparent rejection ('That's It?'), the two old girlfriends plotted a marriage between their off-spring in 'Let's Do a Deal' and Kay walloped out her enjoyment of 'The Party of a Lifetime', whilst, instead of singing, Nimmo went through a routine in which he displayed his double-jointed toes to the audience at length.

Charlie Girl, almost universally damned by the critics, proved to be a combination of elements which throughly appealed to the public. It ran for five and a half years (2,202 performance) in the West End, with Miss Neagle and Nimmo holding their rôles throughout, and put itself into the top league of London long runs before heading on to Australia. There, with Miss Neagle and Nimmo starring alongside local pop star Johnny Farnham, it proved a surprise hit all over again. Business was so great on the first stop of what was supposed to be a tour, that the entire Australian season was spent in Melbourne with only time for a quick stop in Auckland, New Zealand, on the way home.

The show was not toured in Britain, but 20 years on Fielding revived it, in a revised version, at London's Victoria Palace (19 June 1986) with Cyd Charisse in Miss Neagle's rôle alongside Paul Nicholas, Lisa Hull, Dora Bryan, Mark Wynter and Nicholas Parsons. After a 246-performance run in town, the show finally went to the British provinces, with Nicholas and Bonnie Langford paired alongside former ballerina Doreen Wells, in what had now become a dance rôle, as Lady Hadwell.

Australia: Her Majesty's Theatre, Melbourne 25 September 1971
Recordings: original cast (CBS), Australian cast (HMV), London revival cast (First Night) etc

CHARLOT, André   (b Paris, 26 July 1882; d Woodland, Calif, 20 May 1956).

André Charlot was one of the earliest producers to introduce the modern style of variety-based revue to pre-war London, and subsequently, with C B Cochran, the most successful purveyor of this kind of entertainment in Britain. He first appeared on the London scene with the George Grossmith/Melville Gideon revue *Kill That Fly!* at the Alhambra in 1912, eight months after the earliest important such entertainment *Everybody's Doing It* had been produced at the Empire and two before *Hullo, Ragtime* made its appearance at the Hippodrome.

Between the wars he kept up a steady stream of revue productions in London, took both his 1924 and 1925 productions to New York, and, at the same time, intermittently and rarely successfully tried his hand at book musicals. The first of these, *Flora* (1918), lasted two months, in spite of having Gertie Millar in the title-rôle, a London production of Jerome Kern's *Very Good Eddie* (1918) vanished in 46 performances, and the loose-limbed musical farce *The Officers' Mess* (1918) proved the best of the group with a total of 200 performances in two theatres. An unrecognizably adapted version of Charles Cuvillier's *Son p'tit frère* played 112 performances at the Comedy Theatre under the title *Wild Geese*, but *Now and Then* (1921), virtually a revue, failed in two months and a badly mangled version of Willemetz and Christiné's delicious *Dédé* (1922) survived only 46 performances at the Garrick before being tricked out revusically and sent on the road as *The Talk of the Town* in an effort to recoup.

It was 1930 before Charlot looked at a libretto again and that was for a show part musical play and part cabaret, Robert Katscher's novel Revue-Operette *Die Wunder Bar*. Its 200-performance run may have been responsible for his venturing to Vienna to produce Miklós Brodszky's *Die verliebte Königin* at the Johann Strauss-Theater, and his staging of another Continental piece, Hans May's *Dancing City* (*Der tanzende Stadt*) at the London Coliseum in 1935. This vast operetta spectacular, with Lea Seidl and Franco Foresta starred, proved a total flop and was the last book musical Charlot produced.

CHARNIN, Martin [Jay] (b New York, 24 November 1934).

Charnin originally ran parallel writing and performing careers and, within weeks of his first lyrics being professionally performed in the off-Broadway revue *Kaleidoscope* (1957), he appeared on Broadway in the original cast of *West Side Story* (Big Deal). He wrote material for several more off-Broadway revues – *Fallout* (1959), *Pieces of Eight* (1959), *The Little Revue* (1960), *Seven Come Eleven* (1961) – before working on his first book musical, the short-lived *Hot Spot*, in 1963. His next two musicals failed to make it to Broadway, and Lionel Bart's *La Strada*, for which he supplied 'additional material' with Elliott Lawrence, was a one-performance flop. It was 1970 before he tasted success, in a collaboration with Richard Rodgers on the Danny Kaye musical *Two by Two*, but the musicalized cartoon strip *Annie* (1977, 'Tomorrow', 'Easy Street', 'You're Never Fully Dressed Without a Smile') more than made up for previous disappointments, giving its lyricist his one, but very considerable international theatre success to date.

Charnin has produced and directed for television (notably several compilation shows related to musical theatre), for the straight theatre and for the night-club circuits where he has performed his own 'An Evening With Martin Charnin', and during the 1980s conceived and mounted the cabaret revue *Upstairs at O'Neals* (1982) and *The No Frills Revue* (1987).

His most successful non-theatre song to date has been 'The Best Thing You've Ever Done', introduced by Barbra Streisand.

1963 **Hot Spot** (Mary Rodgers/Jack Weinstock, Willie Gilbert) Majestic Theater 19 April
1963 **Zenda** (Vernon Duke/w Leonard Adelson, Sid Kuller/Everett Freeman) Curran Theater, San Francisco 5 August
1967 **Mata Hari** (Edward Thomas/Jerome Coopersmith) National Theater, Washington DC 18 November
1968 **Ballad for a Firing Squad** revised *Mata Hari* Theater de Lys 11 December
1970 **Two by Two** (Richard Rodgers/Peter Stone) Imperial Theater 10 November

1977 **Annie** (Charles Strouse/Thomas Meehan) Alvin Theater 21 April
1979 **I Remember Mama** (Richard Rodgers/w Raymond Jessel/Meehan) Majestic Theater 31 May
1981 **The First** (Bob Brush/w Joe Siegel) Martin Beck Theater 17 November
1990 **Annie II** (Strouse/Meehan) Kennedy Center, Washington 4 January
1992 **Annie Warbucks** revised *Annie II* Marriot's Lincolnshire Theater, Chicago 9 February

CHASSAIGNE, Francis (b 1848; d Paris, December 1922). French composer of two major English-language hits.

Chassaigne studied in Brussels and began his composing life by writing popular songs (Thérésa's 'Jeanne la sabotière' etc) and a long list of small theatrical pieces for production in the Eldorado and other Parisian cafés-concerts. In 1883, Brasseur gave him his chance to compose a full-length work for the Théâtre des Nouveautés to a libretto signed by no less experts than Leterrier and Vanloo, but in spite of all the care and casting lavished on it *Le Droit d'aînesse* was only a semi-success in Paris. Elsewhere, however, it was a very different case for, under the title of *Falka*, H B Farnie's English version of *Le Droit d'aînesse* triumphed hugely in Britain, America, Australia and South Africa, toured for decades throughout the English-speaking world, and was even used as the base for another British comic opera-burlesque, *Brother Pelican*.

A similar, if less extravagant, reaction greeted his only other full-length work for the Paris stage, *Les Noces improvisées* (1886) which, after only a fair run at the Théâtre des Bouffes-Parisiens, once again found markedly more favour on foreign shores, and most notably in America, under the title, in Alfred Murray's English translation, of *Nadgy*. That outstanding New York success was undoubtedly the reason for the production, two seasons later, of a full-length piece called *The Brazilian*, music announced as by Chassaigne, at the same Casino Theater (2 June 1890). Since Chassaigne composed only two full-length opérettes, the genesis of *The Brazilian* remains a mystery, but it seems that its score may have been compiled from music taken from the composer's other, smaller works by the Casino Theater's Gustave Kerker, who included its 'composition' amongst his credits, in the same fashion that he claimed his remake of Lecocq's *Fleur de thé* as *The Pearl of Pekin*. *The Brazilian* did not succeed in giving the French composer a third, if less legitimate, success.

1868 **À qui la faute** (Louis de Romain) 1 act Alcazar
1869 **Matou dix-sept** (Romain) 1 act Eldorado 15 November
1872 **Un coq en jupon** (Lucien Delormel, Germain Villemer) 1 act Eldorado 4 July
1872 **La Bergère de Bougival** (Delormel, Villemer) 1 act Eldorado 20 July
1873 **Un double clé** (Jules de Rieux) 1 act Eldorado 1 February
1873 **Les Horreurs de carnaval** (Auguste Jouhaud) 1 act Eldorado 27 February
1873 **Monsieur Auguste** (de Rieux) 1 act Eldorado 3 May
1873 **L'Héritage de Madame Angot** (de Rieux, Villemer) 1 act Eldorado 24 October
1874 **Une nuit de Mardi Gras** (Jouhaud, Villemer) 1 act Eldorado 27 January
1874 **Le Professeur de tyrolienne** (Villemer, Delormel) 1 act 21 March

CHÂTEAU DE TIRE-LARIGOT

1874 **Une table de café** (de Rieux, Alexandre Guyon) 1 act Eldorado 25 July
1875 **Les Tyroliens de Pontoise** 1 act Eldorado 17 November
1876 **Deux mauvaises bonnes** (Delormel, Louis Péricaud) 1 act Eldorado 11 November
1877 **À l'américaine** (Alphonse Siégel) 1 act Eldorado 10 November
1877 **Trois têtes dans un bonnet** (Jouhaud, Péricaud, Villemer) 1 act Concert du 19ème 6 March
1877 **Les Enfants de la balle** (Delormel, Péricaud) 1 act Eldorado 24 March
1877 **La Famille de Paméla** (Delormel, Péricaud) 1 act Eldorado 11 August
1878 **La Tache de sang** (Gaston Marot) 1 act Eldorado 12 January
1878 **Actéon et la centaure Chiron** (de Leuven) 1 act Palais-Royal 28 January
1878 **Un vieux rat** (Louis de Gabillaud) 1 act Concert Européen 24 May
1878 **Une servante qui jure** (Charles Blondelet, Félix Beaumaine) 1 act Eldorado
1878 **Les Frères Paléale** (Siègel) 1 act Eldorado 24 September
1879 **La Demoiselle de compagnie** (Péricaud, Delormel) 1 act Eldorado 20 March
1879 **Claude l'ivrogne** (A A Charles) 1 act Eldorado 22 April
1879 **Un Concièrgicide** ('Hermil' [ic Ange Milher], Numès) 1 act Eldorado 23 August
1881 **Zizi** (A Philibert, Siégel) 1 act Eldorado
1883 **Le Droit d'aînesse** (Eugène Leterrier, Albert Vanloo) Théâtre des Nouveatés 27 January
1886 **Les Noces improvisées** (Armand Liorat, Albert Fonteney) Théâtre des Bouffes-Parisiens 13 February
1890 **The Brazilian** (arr Gustave Kerker/Max Pemberton, Edgar Smith) Casino Theater, New York 2 June

Other title attributed: *Tog* (Hermil, Numès)

LE CHÂTEAU DE TIRE-LARIGOT Opérette fantastique in 3 acts by Ernest Blum and Raoul Toché. Music by Gaston Serpette. Théâtre des Nouveautés, Paris, 30 October 1884.

The spirit Alcofribas (Lauret) has been condemned by the Devil to rebuild the Château de Tire-Larigot, but he cannot, for the château is doomed to stay a ruin until the honour of the last member of the Valpointu family has been revenged upon those Saint-Roquets who did them wrong. Since there are now no Valpointus left, the old Marquis (Berthelier) comes down from his picture frame, and tries to seduce the new wife (Jeanne Andrée) of the very distant last descendant of his enemy, Saint-Roquet (Brasseur). But the old Saint-Roquet also turns from paint to flesh, and a three-act battle for the virtue of the lady, with many a disguise and picturesque location, ensues.

Illustrated with a score by Serpette, who was becoming the most attractive Parisian composer of such fantastical pieces, *Le Château de Tire-Larigot* played for over a hundred performances in its first run, was briefly revived the following year, and found its way onto the programme of Budapest's Népszinház (ad Viktor Rákosi) the year after that.

Hungary: Népszinház *As összedült kastély* 23 January 1886

LA CHATTE METAMORPHOSÉE EN FEMME Opérette in 1 act by Eugene Scribe and Mélesville, based on the vaudeville by the same authors and the fable by

La Fontaine. Music by Jacques Offenbach. Théâtre des Bouffes-Parisiens, Paris, 19 April 1858.

A rare venture by the aged Scribe into the modern musical theatre, the remake of his little play of 'the cat changed into a woman' made up into a distinctly successful short opérette which was played around the world for several decades.

Set (for some reason) in Biberach in Swabia, the piece had for its central character a distressed fellow called Guido (Tayau), a Trieste businessman who has fallen on hard times. To make ends meet, he is obliged to get rid of everything he owns, even his cat which he adores with an almost unnatural passion. The charlatan Dig-Dig (Désiré) comes to his house and offers a little metempsychosis: he will transfer the soul of the cat into the body of a young woman. Suddenly the cat-like Minette (Lise Tautin) is there, and Guido is delighted to say the least, then distraught when he finds that his housekeeper Marianne (Marguerite Macé) has sold 'the cat' to the governor's wife. Of course, it is all a trick. Dig-Dig is Guido's wealthy uncle's intendant in disguise and Minette is the cousin whom Guido has always refused to marry. The outcome is satisfactory all round. The governor's wife can have the real cat, and Minette will be Guido's wife.

The score gave Minette some delightful feline moments, including a trilly Air to Brahma and a miaou song, as well as a big love duo and an eating trio; Marianne had a introductory song ('Le Ciel a voulu dans sa sagesse') with which to set things going; and Dig-Dig and Guido joined in a comical invocation to the forces of metempsychosis.

After its first performances at the Bouffes-Parisiens, *La Chatte metamorphosée en femme* was maintained in the theatre's repertoire and it was also played by the Bouffes company during their foreign tours. This led to several local adaptations appearing in its wake, the first of which was that played in Budapest, at the Nemzeti Színház (ad Endre Latabár, Kálmán Szerdahelyi), two seasons after the French company's visit. Carl Treumann included *Die verwandelte Katze* in the repertoire at his little Viennese Kaitheater, and the libretto pleased sufficiently for Julius Hopp to turn out a version (presumably of the original vaudeville) with his own music attached (Theater an der Wien 1865), and for Theodor Hauptner to venture his own *Die entzauberte Katz*, seen both in German and Hungarian versions. An English remake, adapted by hands unidentified, was first seen at the Theatre Royal, Drury Lane in 1863, and was later produced by the German Reeds at their Gallery of Illustration and at the St George's Hall, where it shared the bill with the first production of Sullivan's *The Contrabandista*.

Intermittently played in the 20th century, *La Chatte metamorphosée en femme* was again seen in 1986 on the programme of the Carpentras Offenbach Festival.

USA: Théâtre Français (Fr) 21 November 1859; Hungary: Budai Népszinház 12 July 1861, Nemzeti Színház *Az átváltozott macska* 12 October 1863; Austria: Theater am Franz-Josefs-Kai *Die verwandelte Katze* 25 September 1862; UK: Theatre Royal, Drury Lane 23 June 1863; Australia: Opera House, Sydney 6 September 1879

CHAUMONT, Céline (b Paris, 1848; d Paris, 4 February 1926).

After a good half-dozen years in the theatre, Mlle

254

Chaumont made a memorable début on the musical stage, at the age of 21, in the leading feminine rôle of Régina in Offenbach's *La Princesse de Trébizonde* (1869) at the Théâtre des Bouffes-Parisiens. In spite of limited vocal means, she scored a considerable personal success through her charm, excellent diction and her undoubted ability as an actress with a particular way with a double entendre ('with no more voice than a cat when you squeeze her tail, she contrives by artful singing to put more expression into the music than could be imagined ...'). She subsequently starred in Hervé's *Le Trône d'Écosse* (1871, Flora), caused a sensation as the undone heroine of the exceedingly near-the-knuckle tale of Serpette's *La Cruche cassée* (1875, Colette) and created the feminine leading rôle of Lecocq's *Le Grand Casimir* (1879, Angelina, and revival 1884). She visited London in 1872 to play *La Princesse de Trébizonde* at the St James's Theatre, but the largest part of her subsequent career was spent making a highly successful place for herself in the non-musical theatre where she created, amongst others, the rôle of Cyprienne in Sardou's famous *Divorçons*.

She later took over the management of the Palais-Royal for a period, and subsequently moved into teaching drama.

CHEIREL, Jeanne [LERICHE, Jeanne] (b Paris, 18 March 1868; d Paris, 26 October 1934).

A niece of the actress and singer Augustine Leriche (thus the anagrammatic stage name) who had appeared in many vaudevilles and opérettes during a long and highly successful career (*La Femme à papa*, *Rip*, *La Fiancée en loterie*, *La Geisha*, *L'Amour mouillée* etc), the young Jeanne began her stage career as an straight actress, working for Victor Koning at the Gymnase (*Frou-Frou*, *Sapho*, *L'Abbé Constantin* etc). She moved, in succession, to the Variétés, the Porte-Saint-Martin (*Le Crocodile*) and, in 1890, the Palais-Royal (*Le Paradis*, *Un fil á la patte*, *Coralie et Cie* etc). Although she had previously performed as a vocalist at the Scala café-concert, she did not make her first appearance on the musical stage until some time later, when she created the rôle of the prudish Marquise, Edith de Chatellerault, in the enormously successful *Les Fêtards* (1897) at the Palais-Royal.

A career of more than 20 years as a 'solide et sûre' leading actress on the Paris stage prefaced a memorable return to the musical theatre, in her fifties, as the conniving 'Countess' in the jazz-age musical comedy *Ta bouche* (1922, 'Des terres et des coupons') and, thereafter, she became the model of the musical middle-aged character lady of charm, using her agreeable light baritone singing voice in specially written rôles and numbers in a series of similarly styled musical comedies: Hortense in *Madame* (1923), La Baronne Sakrinkolovitz in *Gosse de riche* (1924, 'Combine', 'Avez-vous compris?', 'Quand on est des gens du monde'), as a memorable Mlle Poumaillac in *Pas sur la bouche* (1925, 'Quand on n'a pas ce qu'on aime', 'O Sam!') in which she actually got the ingénue's man in the final reel, as Hélène in Reynaldo Hahn's *Le Temps d'aimer* (1926) at the Michodière, and in Marcel Lattès's richly cast *Le Diable à Paris* (1927) alongside Dranem, Raimu, Edmée Favart and Juliette Simon-Girard.

In her later days she also made a fine name on the cinema screen.

Plate 50. **Jeanne Cheirel**: *A juvenile leading lady who became a character lady par excellence in the Parisian jazz-age theatre.*

LA CHERCHEUSE D'ESPRIT Opéra-comique in 1 act by Charles S Favart. Music taken from various sources. Théâtre de la Foire Saint Germain, Paris, 20 February 1741.

A sweetly rustic piece, in which Madame Justine Favart starred as a simple girl whose mother insists she lacks 'esprit', but who nevertheless ends up marrying the young man she likes instead of being stuck – as mama had intended – with his widowed father. Enormously popular on its production, it was played for more than 200 successive nights, a vast run for the period, and was frequently revived both in France and abroad, proving one of the most successful of such entertainments to come from the French stage. No one is credited with the compilation of the 70 musical fragments taken from popular melodies ('Tes beaux yeux, ma Nicole', 'L'Autre Jour Colin', 'Attendez-moi sous l'orme', 'Diversité flatte le goût' etc) which made up the show's original musical illustration, but there have been a number of subsequent attempts to rearrange or replace the pasticcio score, notably by Jules François Pillevesse (Théâtre du Vaudeville 2 June 1863) and by the young Edmond Audran (1864 Gymnase, Marseille and later in Paris, Alcazar 1888).

In Offenbach's *Madame Favart*, the actress's off-stage performance of *La Chercheuse d'esprit* is the key to the happy ending of the plot.

UK: Little Haymarket Theatre 28 November 1749; Germany: Munich 1749

THE CHERRY GIRL Musical play in 2 acts by Seymour Hicks. Lyrics by Aubrey Hopwood. Music by Ivan Caryll. Vaudeville Theatre, London, 21 December 1903.

Following the success of *Bluebell in Fairyland*, Charles Frohman and Seymour Hicks attempted to repeat the show's pattern with another seasonal fairy-play-cum-musical-comedy. This time Ellaline Terriss played Pansy, a little girl in a London attic, who changes places with the Queen of the Pierrots and gets into all sorts of adventures with the nice white pierrot (Seymour Hicks) and the nasty black one (Stanley Brett). Thanks to an opportunely introduced magic talisman, everyone zoomed off to 18th-century England in the second half. The Ivan Caryll score was supplemented by a veritable mass of popular American songs ('Little Yellow Bird', 'Rip van Winkle Was a Lucky Man', 'My Little Hong Kong Baby', 'Dixieland Cakewalk'), in the 'borrowing' style Hicks favoured, mostly for the benefit of himself and his wife, whilst tenor Courtice Pounds got to serenade 'Fascinating Frou-Frou of the Frill' and joined Murray Hill to sing of 'When the Stars Are Shining in the Sky'. Pounds, however, got into trouble when it was decided that one of his comedy lines insinuated that the makers of the beef extract Bovril used horsemeat for their product. Bovril attacked Frohman, and the line had to be tactfully altered.

Staged with the same fairytale glamour as *Bluebell*, and largely featuring children and dancing alongside its singalong songs, *The Cherry Girl* was a distinct success in 215 London performances and a tour, without winning the repeat productions the earlier show had done.

CHESS Musical in 2 acts by Tim Rice. Music by Björn Ulvaeus and Benny Andersson. Prince Edward Theatre, London, 14 May 1986.

A collaboration between British librettist and lyricist Rice and the two male members of the famous Swedish popular singing group Abba, *Chess* was founded on an idea which Rice and Andrew Lloyd Webber had long juggled about as a possible topic for a musical, in the wake of the mediatization of the game of chess in the Bobby Fischer years. Originally written and produced, *Jesus Christ Superstar*-style, as a concept recording, and subsequently performed in concert in Europe in 1984, the sung-through *Chess* was ultimately brought to the stage in London in 1986, under the management of Robert Fox. Its production encountered a major setback when director/choreographer Michael Bennett fell terminally ill after the casting and designing had been done, and Trevor Nunn (director) and Molly Molloy (choreography) were brought in to replace him through an expensively extended rehearsal period, in which they attempted to fit a dif-

ferently felt production into the already established settings and casting.

The World Chess Championship is being played at the picturebook Tyrolean town of Merano, between the American Frederick Trumper (Murray Head), and the Russian Anatoly Sergeievsky (Tommy Korberg). The temperamental, loud-mouthed Trumper is accompanied by his manager and girlfriend, Hungarian-American Florence Vassy (Elaine Paige), whilst Sergeievsky is surrounded by a vast back-up team, headed by the finagling Molokov (John Turner), determined that he shall not lose national prestige by a defeat. The whole event, under the management of a theoretically impartial Arbiter (Tom Jobe), is surrounded by considerations of merchandizing, profit-making and national propaganda poorly masked under a domino of sport. A sympathy springs up between the Russian and Florence, the edgy Trumper loses his temper, his confidence and the match, and the previously forbearing Florence walks out on him to join Sergeievsky who celebrates his win by defecting. A year later, he defends his title in Bangkok against a new Molokov-supported Soviet. Molokov plots with American TV-man Walter de Courcey (Kevin Colson) to exchange Florence's long imprisoned father for a chess-table triumph for his man, and Sergeievsky's abandoned wife, Svetlana (Siobhan McCarthy), is brought from Russia in an attempt to destabilize the champion. With unexpected support from Trumper, Sergeievsky keeps his concentration and wins, but then returns to Russia. Perhaps to ensure the liberty of Florence's father – if he is still really alive.

Chess won itself a place in the hit parades before the opening of the show when the mistress/wife duet 'I Know Him So Well' as sung by Miss Paige and Barbara Dickson topped the charts, and Murray Head's performance of the atmospheric 'One Night in Bangkok' followed it, becoming a hit throughout Europe, but the stage production threw several other numbers of a score, which was as rich in outstanding numbers as any other of the past 20 years, into relief: the Russian's determined 'Who Needs a Dream?' and his soaring pop tenor Anthem ('My Land'), the American's flaming tantrum of self-justification 'Pity the Child' with its scalding use of the high tenor register, Florence's gentle 'Heaven Help My Heart', her heated 'Nobody's on Nobody's Side' and the pair of duets with Sergeievsky, the awkward getting to know each other of the Mountain Duet and 'You and I'. A comical moment was provided by two English Embassy officials, prissily processing the defector's papers (Embassy Lament) and another by Molokov and his men ('The Soviet Machine'), whilst the Endgame section of the score, with Sergeievsky striving to win his match as distractions pound at him from all sides, was a fine and theatrically effective moment of concerted music.

The production at the Prince Edward Theatre showed little sign of any of the earlier problems except in the 'One Night in Bangkok' number which there had been insufficient time to choreograph into a proper dance routine as originally intended. On a stage dominated by banks of television screens, and a vast floor of chessboard squares from which arose a dazzling mountainside scene, the drama of the piece and its music powered through to enormous effect. *Chess* played for three years (1209 performances) in London.

Curiously, one person was not happy with *Chess*, and

that was director Nunn. He shunned his production throughout its run and, when the time came for the show to be produced on Broadway, he rejected the London staging and devised a different production. In the decades-old tradition of the Shubert producing firm, *Chess* was botched. The piece was reshaped, bits of dialogue tacked in, music cut and other music – at least by the show's original writers and not, as in the old days, from outside songwriters – put to replace it. The alterations proved ill-judged (the unsympathetic portrait of the show's American character even brought forth touchy mumblings of anti-Americanism!), the new *Chess* (ad Richard Nelson), with David James Carroll, Philip Casnoff and Judy Kuhn in its central rôles, was unhappily received and folded in 68 performances.

If the alterations made for this production were largely abandoned thereafter, the show seemed nevertheless fated to be one of those which are eternally fiddled with by foreign hands. Some of the alterations were claimed to be justified by the changed political situation and the fall of the communist world – for events had made *Chess* a period piece rather more swiftly than had seemed likely. Rather more of them were simply the efforts of other directors to produce a *Chess* in line with their own imagination: a rare opportunity in the modern musical theatre where breath-for-breath reproductions of major musicals have become the rule. Both on tour and regionally in America, where, in spite of its short Broadway life *Chess* had won many friends, on tour in Britain and in Australia, later productions were mounted under the command of directors given an apparently free hand, even to the extent of altering the text and score to fit their concepts. Australia's version, which cast the piece curiously young and set the entire tale and its romance in one brief championship in Bangkok, rather unbalanced affairs by bolstering the part of the Russian wife with an extraneous (ex-Broadway version) number in a lively, colourful production which lost the moody drama of the original and failed to find an audience for more than six months.

In 1992, whilst a production in New Zealand which featured Head and Korberg in their original rôles went stirringly through a four-city tour of longer seasons than was normal in that lightly populated land, *Chess* made a discreet return to New York. This time it was played off-Broadway (Master Theater 1 February, 83 performances), with a reduced cast. Later the same year, as English-language productions continued, the piece made its first stage appearance in Europe when an Hungarian version was produced at Budapest's Rock Szinház, whilst a German-language version was mounted at St Pölten in Austria in early 1993.

USA: Imperial Theater 28 April 1988; Australia: Theatre Royal, Sydney 3 February 1990; Hungary: Rock Színház/Arizona 29 May 1992; Austria: Stadttheater, St Pölten 13 March 1993
Recordings: concept recording (RCA), American cast (RCA)

CHEVALIER, Maurice [Auguste] (b nr Paris, 12 September 1888; d Paris, 1 January 1972). Parisian music-hall star who became Hollywood's singing very-Frenchman.

After an early career spent performing in cafés and suburban music halls, Chevalier scored his first significant success at Marseille and, soon after, he made his earliest Paris stage appearances featuring in a minor capacity in revue at the Folies-Bergère under such stars as Mistinguett and Morton. During the war years he established himself alongside Mistinguett at the head of the Folies bill, and in 1921 made his initial appearance on the musical-comedy stage, starring as Robert Dauvergne, the irresponsible and louche best friend of the hero of *Dédé*, the show with which Albert Willemetz and Henri Christiné followed up their enormous hit, *Phi-Phi*.

Although his rôle was not the title one, it was made up to give the top-billed star an infinity of chances for applause, and his songs, the gently loping 'Dans la vie faut pas s'en faire' and the sexually generous 'Je m'donne' became popular hits in a hit show. Announced by Cochran for a London version of the show and by Dillingham for a Broadway one, he did neither, but instead followed up the next year in Paris in another successful jazz-age musical comedy, Maurice Yvain's *Là-haut*, in which he played the recently deceased Evariste, returning to earth and his lady under the eye of a guardian angel. Again he had songs made to measure ('Si vous n'aimez pas ça n'en degoutez pas les autres', 'C'est Paris'), but he also had a co-star in the brilliant comedian Dranem who, as the angel, managed to pretty well wipe him off the stage. Chevalier walked out of the show, and ended his musical theatre career.

Thereafter came the straw hat and the 1930s Hollywood films (*The Love Parade, One Hour With You, Love Me Tonight, Folies-Bergère* etc) including one or two tenuously based on stage musical shows (*The Smiling Lieutenant, The Merry Widow* with Jeanette MacDonald), until his popularity abruptly faded and he returned to France and the variety stage. A mixture of music hall and movies filled most of the 1950s and 1960s, musically marked by appearances in his seventies in the films *Gigi* (1958 Honorine, 'I'm Glad I'm Not Young Any More', 'Thank Heaven for Little Girls'), *Can-Can* (1959) and the non-musical digest of *Fanny* (1961).

Memoirs: *C'est l'amour* (Julliard, Paris, 1960) in English as *With Love* (Little, Brown, Boston, 1960), *Môme à cheveux blancs* (Presses de la Cité, Paris, 1969) in English as *I Remember It Well* (Macmillan, New York, 1970), *Maurice Chevalier's Own Story* (Nash & Grayson, London, 1930), *The Man in the Straw Hat* (Cromwell, New York, 1949), etc, Biographies: Rivollet, A: *Maurice Chevalier: De Ménilmont au Casino de Paris* (Grasset, Paris, 1927), Willemetz, A: *Maurice Chevalier* (René Kistler, Paris, 1954), Harding, J: *Maurice Chevalier* (Secker & Warburg, London, 1982), Boyer, W: *The Romantic Life of Maurice Chevalier* (Hutchinson, London, 1937), Bret, D: *Maurice Chevalier: Up on Top of a Rainbow* (Robson, London, 1992) Behr, E: *The Good Frenchman: The True Story of the Life and Times of Maurice Chevalier* (Villard Books, New York, 1993) etc

CHICAGO Musical vaudeville in 2 acts by Fred Ebb and Bob Fosse based on the play by Maurine Dallas Watkins. Lyrics by Fred Ebb. Music by John Kander. 46th Street Theater, New York, 3 June 1975.

Miss Watkins's 'satirical comedy' *Chicago* was a 182-performance success when mounted on Broadway in 1926 (30 December) by Sam H Harris, with Francine Larrimore in the rôle of the murderess Roxie Hart, freed to spend her life touring as an attraction in vaudeville thanks to the efforts of a three-faced, money-grubbing lawyer and a manipulable press.

The 1975 musical based on the play followed its outlines

fairly securely. It played up the show-business side of the story and eliminated some of the newspaper-world portion of the original, cutting one of the play's principal characters, a newspaperman, and building up the rôle of Velma Kelly, a rival murderess with showbusiness ambitions, from almost nothing to a major part.

When the furniture salesman whom Mrs Roxie Hart (Gwen Verdon) has been screwing on the side decides to call it a day, she shoots him and, to her amazement and horror, is arrested. In the prison run by Mama Morton (Mary McCarty) she soon discovers the one thing a murderess needs is lawyer Billy Flynn (Jerry Orbach) who has never yet lost a case for a female client. Under his tutelage, a sensational, if fiction-studded, interview with newspaper sob-sister Mary Sunshine (M O'Haughey) gets her on the front-pages. She's news, and she takes to it like a lemming, squeezing out the up-to-then newsworthy Velma Kelly (Chita Rivera) with her tales, and getting herself the prime trial date Velma had counted on. Tutored by Flynn, she gives a fine performance on the big day, only to find, as she is acquitted, that there has been a sensational multiple murder in a nearby court and she is yesterday's news. The front-page photos are a thing of the past. There is nothing left in life except to hit the lesser vaudeville circuits in that slightly notorious double act with Velma Kelly.

The score of *Chicago* included many suitably showbizzy numbers which became popular both in the show and, particularly with theatre folk, outside it: Velma's slinky introduction to the age of jazz, sex and liquor, 'All That Jazz', the mercenary Billy's twinkle-toothed creed 'All I Care About (is love)' and his belief that 'Razzle Dazzle' is all you need in life, dumbcluck Amos Hart's identification of himself as 'Mr Cellophane', and the sextet of murderesses relating the circumstances of the crimes they didn't commit in the 'Cell Block Tango'. Velma and Mama Morton duetted sourly about whatever happened to the 'Class' they so clearly lack, Mary Sunshine – played by a falsetto male – touched on the coloratura as she twittered out her belief that 'There's a Little Bit of Good in Everyone', whilst Roxie cooed out the praises of her 'Funny Honey' husband who she thinks is going to take the rap for her, and finished each half in tandem with Velma, giving out with the realization that '(I am) My Own Best Friend' and a vaudevillesque hymn to 'Nowadays'.

The story was played like a succession of vaudeville acts on a black-hole of a stage, with the accompanying jazz-band, perched above the action, under the leadership of a conductor who also announced the 'turns'. This style of presentation gave the opportunity for a number of director/choreographer Bob Fosse's characteristic dance pieces of which Billy's entrance, in a shower of pink feather fans, was the most amusing, and everything that was danced by Misses Verdon and Rivera memorable.

Chicago played 898 performances on Broadway before going into a series of overseas productions. A German production (ad Erika Gesell, Helmut Baumann) was mounted in Hamburg in 1977, whilst in Britain a production originating at the Crucible Theatre in Sheffield was transferred to London's Cambridge Theatre, with Antonia Ellis, Jenny Logan and Ben Cross featured, for 590 performances. This success sparked a number of further provincial productions in Britain before, in 1981,

Plate 51. **Chilpéric**: *The Spaniards arrive and the big trouble of the evening's entertainment begins.*

Australia's Sydney Theatre Company produced *Chicago* with Nancye Hayes, Geraldine Turner and Terence O'Donovan featured. It proved highly successful and the show was brought back for several further Australian seasons.

Germany: Thalia Theater, Hamburg 21 May 1977; UK: Cambridge Theatre 10 April 1979; Australia: Sydney Opera House/Drama Theatre 6 June 1981
Recordings: original cast (Arista), Australian cast (Polydor)

CHILPÉRIC Opéra-bouffe in 2 (later 3) acts by Hervé. Théâtre des Folies-Dramatiques, Paris, 24 October 1868.

One of the most successful of the handful of extravagantly humorous full-length opéras-bouffes written and composed by the playwright/composer Hervé, *Chilpéric* went even further in its almost surreal burlesque humour than Meilhac and Halévy had done with their recent texts for Offenbach's *La Belle Hélène*, *Barbe-bleue* or *La Grande-Duchesse de Gérolstein*. Hervé went back to the medieval era, so successfully used by Offenbach and Tréfeu in *Geneviève de Brabant*, for his subject matter, and he alighted on the Merovingian King Chilpéric I of Neustria and Soissons, whose life and career were decorated with murderous women. His second wife, Galswinthe, was murdered by Frédégonde, who became his third wife, and who subsequently came to clutches with Galswinthe's sister, Brunehaut. All these dangerous ladies turned up in Hervé's opéra-bouffe.

Frédégonde (Blanche d'Antigny, a late replacement for *Oeil crevé* star Julia Baron) starts the evening as an innocent little shepherdess, but she is spotted during a hunt by the randy king (Hervé) and whisked off to court to be royal laundress etcetera. No one is very pleased, not Frédégonde's peasant swain, Landry, nor Chilpéric's brother Sigebert (Berret), nor his brother's Spanish wife Brunehaut (Caroline Jullien), who had lined up her sister Galswinthe (Mlle Berthal) as a wife for the King, intending then to assassinate the royal couple and claim the throne herself by kinship. Since this Spanish marriage brings advantages of state, however, it is still on, and Chilpéric has eventually to get rid of Frédégonde, who has shown remarkable powers of adaptation in her swift transformation from shepherdess to royal plaything. She doesn't let herself be evicted quietly. Now the murdering starts. Brunehaut has seduced Landry and persuaded him to kill Frédégonde, Frédégonde has attracted the court chamberlain, Le Grand Légendaire, and has asked him nicely to strangle Galswinthe on her wedding night, whilst Chilpéric has become deeply suspicious of Brunehaut's machinations and ordered the court doctor (Milher) to slip her something poisonous. Everything comes to a peak in the nuptial chamber on the royal wedding night, when the King has slipped out to defend his city against an irritatingly untimely attack by his disloyal brother. The three would-be murderers attack, the three women fight back, and in the dark it all gets very confused before someone presses a button which sends the whole lot and the bed straight down to the dungeons. Chilpéric wins his little battle, and sorts everyone out in time for a jolly finale with no deaths and only a little bit of stripping and whipping.

Hervé's lively score was as full of fun as his libretto, with Frédégonde being particularly well provided with an introductory waltz ('Voyez cette figure'), some pyrotechnic musical tantrums on her dismissal from court, and a lament in burlesque of the grand operatic ('Nuit fortunée'), whilst Chilpéric scored with his entrance number, the nonsensical Chanson du jambon, sung perched unhappily on the back of a real, live horse like the ones they use at the Opéra, and with his second-act butterfly song ('Petit papillon, bleu volage'). Galswinthe's bolero ('À la Sierra Morena') added a touch of the Spanish, whilst a basso druid (Varlet) opened proceedings Norma-like, invoking 'Prêtres D'Ésus'.

The Folies-Dramatiques production was a fine success, running for more than a hundred nights, and Chilpéric was soon gratified by Christmas-tide burlesques of its burlesque. Herve's music was borrowed to decorate the Eldorado's Chilméric (10 December 1868), whilst the Alcazar made a double shot, combining both the season's big hits in the title of its revue Chilpéricholle (31 December 1868). At the same time the show began to be seen in other countries. America was apparently the first, getting a taste of the original French version when Joseph Grau's opéra-bouffe troupe introduced the show with Carrier (Chilpéric), Rose Bell (Frédégonde), Marie Desclauzas (Galswinthe) and Mlle Rizarelli playing Landry in travesty. The current craze for French opéra-bouffe meant it had much competition and, since Grau held the season's megahit Geneviève de Brabant in his repertoire, Chilpéric was played only irregularly, though not without success, as a supporting piece to Offenbach and Tréfeu's hit. An English-language version was seen later, in 1874, when Emily Soldene visited America and took the rôle of the comical king herself alongside Agnes Lyndhurst and Lizzie Robson.

Soldene had already appeared as Chilpéric in London, when she had deputized for the composer-star in Richard Mansell's production (ad Mansell, Robert Reece, F A Marshall) at the Lyceum. London's Chilpéric was probably the most successful staging of the show anywhere. Hervé repeated his Paris performance alongside soprano Emily Muir (Frédégonde) and the young Selina Dolaro (Galswinthe), and the show caused a real sensation, giving a huge boost to the budding craze for opéra-bouffe in Britain. It ran from 22 January to 9 April, being taken off only to allow the composer's Le Petit Faust to be seen. The

following year Soldene brought it back (Philharmonic Theatre 9 October), playing her version concurrently with another production by J E Mallandaine at the Royalty Theatre (28 September). In 1872 the Folies-Dramatiques company visited London to play the show in French (Globe Theatre 3 June) and in 1875 (10 May) the Alhambra gave Chilpéric an extravagant new mounting with Charles Lyall (Chilpéric), Lennox Grey (Frédégonde), Kate Munroe (Galswinthe), Adelaide Newton (Landry), Harry Paulton (Dr Ricin) and Emma Chambers (Bruneheaut) featured, a production which ran for three months. A fresh English version (ad Henry Hersee, H B Farnie) was produced at the new Empire Theatre in 1884 (17 April) with Herbert Standing, Camille d'Arville and Madge Shirley in the leading rôles, capping a career for Chilpéric which was only bested by a handful of opéras-bouffes in London.

Australia followed quickly where London led – although W S Lyster felt obliged to add a subtitle 'the King of the Gauls' to help antipodeans bemused by the show's name – and later got a second dose of Chilpéric when Soldene played what was announced as 'her original rôle' during her Australian seasons.

In 1895 the Théâtre de Variétés mounted a new production of Chilpéric, its libretto reorganized into three acts by Paul Ferrier, with a cast headed by Albert Brasseur (Chilpéric), Marguerite Ugalde (Frédégonde) and Marcelle Lender (Galswinthe), Baron as the doctor and Vauthier as Siegebert, and the piece found a renewed popularity which led it, this time, to find its way into the German language. Eduard Jacobson and Wilhelm Mannstädt's König Chilperich was seen at Berlin's Theater Unter den Linden later the same year, with Alexander Klein and Frln Fischer in the lead rôles, and with sufficient success for it to be brought back again in the new year. The Vienna Carltheater staged the same version 11 months later with Julius Spielmann playing Chilpéric, Betty Stojan as Frédégonde and Ernst Tautenhayn as Landry. It was played some 25 times.

The passing out of favour – and of comprehension – of the more extreme style of burlesque in the 20th century has led Chilpéric to disappear from the repertoire since.

USA: Théâtre Français (Fr) 1 June 1869, Lyceum Theater (Eng) 9 December 1874; UK: Lyceum Theatre 22 January 1870; Australia: Prince of Wales Theatre, Melbourne Chilperic, the King of the Gauls 25 July 1874; Germany: Theater Unter den Linden König Chilperich 21 December 1895; Austria: Carltheater König Chilperich 28 November 1896

CHIN-CHIN, or a Modern Aladdin Musical fantasy in 3 acts by Anne Caldwell and R H Burnside. Lyrics by Anne Caldwell et al. Music by Ivan Caryll. Globe Theater, New York, 20 October 1914.

An updated version of the Aladdin story, rewritten to feature the comedians Montgomery and Stone, Chin-Chin cast its stars as twin slaves of the lamp, Chin Hop Hi (Stone) and Chin Hop Lo (Montgomery) who managed the evening's affairs rather like a couple of French revue compères. The action zipped from one location to another as they tried to stop the nasty Abanazar (Charles T Aldrich) from robbing Aladdin (Douglas Stevenson) of the lamp, or helped the boy win the hand of Violet Bond (Helen Falconer), daughter of the ridiculously rich Cornelius Bond

Plate 52. **A Chinese Honeymoon**: *The plot, in easy stages.*

(R E Graham), who is himself eager to lay hands on the magic lamp. When he wasn't being a genie, Stone appeared as Paderewski, a ventriloquist, Madame Falloffski and a gendarme, whilst Montgomery impersonated the Widow, a coolie, a clown and a second gendarme.

The stars introduced themselves singing about 'A Chinese Honeymoon' (lyric: Bryant, Williams), and Stone followed the then fashion for all that swung by launching into 'Ragtime Temple Bells' (lyric: James O'Dea), whilst Aladdin and his Violet shared some romantic moments ('Love Moon', 'The Mulberry Tree') and the hero scored a success with his farewell to youthful excesses in 'Goodbye Girls, I'm Through' (lyric: John Golden). Some lyric soprano pieces were inserted for a creature called the Goddess of the Lamp, as played by Belle Story, waltzing about 'Violet' (the colour, not the girl) and the 'Grey Dove', and getting sentimental in the final 'In January, You Love Mary'. A toys' chorus, a piece about 'Shopping in the Orient' and a ballet divertissement, 'Will o'the Wisp', were amongst the other items on the evening's bill.

Chin-Chin was a splendid success, and served its fun-making stars for 295 performances on Broadway before they took it to the country. A production announced by Alfred Butt for London's Palace Theatre in 1915 did not in the end take place.

A CHINESE HONEYMOON Musical comedy in 2 acts by George Dance. Music by Howard Talbot. Theatre Royal, Hanley, 16 October 1899; Royal Strand Theatre, London, 5 October 1901.

One of the many landmark musicals which started small, *A Chinese Honeymoon* – thrown together in four weeks by its authors – was first staged at Hanley, in the British potteries country, under the management of touring producer, H Cecil Beryl. It was sent out for an eight-week tour which was scheduled to end in time for the artists to take up their pantomime engagements, but it did well enough in this first little tour for Beryl to send it out again, in the new year, to another nine dates. Then, the show having more than served the purpose for which it had been made, he handed it back to author Dance who put it out himself for 32 weeks more, and announced fresh tours to come. But Frank Curzon now surfaced with a proposal for a London run, so Dance offered his touring scenery, costumes and rights to producer Milton Bode. Bode said 'no, thanks' and Dance thus retained what would become some of the most valuable touring rights in the pre-war theatre. Before taking *A Chinese Honeymoon* to London, Frank Curzon ordered some rewrites, in particular the expansion of the rôle of the little waitress Fi-fi as a vehicle for tiny comedienne Louie Freear, and some extra songs. The alterations were duly made and the resultant show was produced at the unfashionable Royal Strand Theatre. It stayed there for 1,075 performances, becoming the first musical play in theatre history to top 1,000 consecutive metropolitan performances.

British visitor Tom Hatherton (Stephen Adeson/Leslie Stiles) falls in love with a little Chinese girl and he stays in China to woo her, spending his other hours in the company

of the devoted little waitress Fi-fi (Miss Freear). Unfortunately, Tom's beloved is none other than Soo-Soo (Violet Dene/Beatrice Edwards), daughter of the Emperor Hang-Chow (W T Thompson/Picton Roxburgh) and thoroughly out of his reach. Hang Chow is himself looking for a new wife, and has sent Admiral Hi Lung (Herbert Bouchier/Percy Clifton) around the world with a photograph to find him one, without revealing his rank. Hi Lung has no luck. Now arrive honeymooning Mr Pineapple (Lionel Rignold) and his jealous new little bride (Florence Wilton/Marie Dainton). They have a tiff and on the rebound Mr Pineapple goes and kisses the disguised Soo Soo. Since she is royal, the law of the land means he must marry her, so poor Pineapple is carried off to be wed all over again, whilst Mrs Pineapple is rounded up as a candidate for the Emperor's hand. Pineapple's life is made even more difficult by the fact that the wireless Hang Chow has engaged an official mother-in-law from Britain. Mrs Brown (Marie Daltra/Mary Ann Victor) turns out to be Pineapple's old housekeeper, who was furiously slighted at his wedding another. When Soo-Soo, who loves Tom, takes a sleeping drug to feign death and escape from the palace, Pineapple is ordered to commit suttee, and things get very hot indeed before the ultimate deus ex machina, the British Consul, turns up and sets his subjects to rights. Mrs Brown becomes Empress Hang Chow and poor Fi-fi is left to waitress alone.

The show's songs became quickly popular, most especially the three music-hally ones sung by Louie Freear who, herself, became a star overnight. She described her musical family in 'Martha Spanks the Grand Pianner', insisted

'I Want to Be a Lidy' and told about her piano teacher's habits in Ernest Woodville's 'The Twiddley Bits'. Mrs Pineapple's up-to-date piece about 'The à la Girl', Tom and Soo Soo's romancing to the strains of 'Roses Red and White', the Pineapples' title sextet with their omnipresent bridesmaids and a set of topical tunes were mixed with pretty ballads in a score which left place for what would be a cavalcade of subsequent interpolations.

Whilst the London production ran on and on, Dance kept *A Chinese Honeymoon* on the road, and the overseas productions followed – everywhere with success. George Walton had been the quickest off the mark, opening the show at Cape Town's Theatre Royal on 14 February 1901, before it had even been scheduled for the West End, and he was followed by the young American team, the Shubert brothers, making their début as Broadway producers in partnership with Messrs Nixon and Zimmerman. Their production featured Thomas Q Seabrooke and Adele Ritchie as the Pineapples, Van Rensselaer Wheeler (Tom), Katie Barry (Fi-fi), Amelia Stone (Soo Soo), William Pruette (Hi Lung) and some interpolated numbers through a splendid 356 New York performances, before going out to confirm the way the brothers were about to continue with further success on the road.

George Musgrove produced *A Chinese Honeymoon* in Australia, with Edward Lauri and Cissie Neil as the Pineapples, former star tenor Henry Hallam as the Emperor, Josephine Stanton as Soo Soo and May Beatty as Fi-fi, and once again the show was a major hit. Its 165-performance run in Melbourne established a record for that city before Musgrove took the show on round Australia and New Zealand. Maurice Bandmann toured *A Chinese Honeymoon* in the Mediterranean countries, Henry Dallas's Company took it to the Orient, playing to English audiences from Hong Kong to Shanghai, and by 1903 there were five companies playing the show in Britain and four more in Canada and America. One of two German versions (ad C M Roehr, Richard Wilde) was produced by Jose Ferenczy in Berlin as *Chinesiche Flitterwochen* with Schulz as August Timpe and Frln Heinrich as his Marie, whilst Hungary saw *Kínai mézeshetek* (ad Jenő Faragó, Béla J Fái) for 25 performances in repertoire at the Népszinház with Klara Küry starred.

In Britain, provincial tours went out end-to-end for many years and in 1915 *A Chinese Honeymoon* was given a wartime revival in London, in which Arthur Wellesley and Marie George played the Pineapples and Maria Daltra took up her old rôle of Mrs Brown for a 36-performance season.

It was suggested at one time that Dance had pilfered the libretto for *A Chinese Honeymoon* from the early Lecocq success *Fleur de thé*, but although one plotline indeed followed more or less the same course, the show was no more nor less derivative than most others, and their Eastern setting – not precisely a novelty – was the two shows' most similar element.

USA: Casino Theater 2 June 1902; Australia: Princess Theatre, Melbourne 30 June 1902; Germany: Centralhallen Theater, Hamburg *Ein Honigmond in China* 12 February 1903, Centraltheater, Berlin *Chinesische Flitterwochen* 25 April 1903; Hungary: Népszinház *Kínai mézeshetek* 21 April 1903

CHIVOT, [Charles] Henri (b Paris, 13 November 1830; d Vésinet, 18 September 1897). Star librettist of the peak years of French opérette.

A clerk in a lawyer's office at seventeen, later in the offices of the PLM, and subsequently, for 30 years, a chef de bureau in the direction générale, Henri Chivot made his earliest excursion into the theatre in 1855, when he placed a play at the Palais-Royal. His first ventures in the field of musical theatre were in opera and opéra-comique, a decade on, when he was responsible for the texts for such pieces as Savary's one-act *Un rêve* (1865), for von Flotow's *Zilda* (w J H Vernoy de St-Georges) and Frédéric Barbier's *Le Soldat malgré lui* (1868), but it was as the author of some of the outstanding libretti written for the French light musical stage, at the height of its 19th-century success, that he found his fame.

Chivot teamed, from early on, with Alfred Duru, and the two continued an almost exclusive writing partnership for nearly a quarter of a century, until Duru's death in 1889. The pair did well with their first major opéra-bouffe text, a burlesque of the Arthurian legend which was set by Hervé as *Les Chevaliers de la table ronde*. It had a good Parisian run, followed by a season in a badly botched version in London (*Melusine, the Enchantress*, Holborn Amphitheatre ad G M Layton, 24 September 1874). They confirmed this début with their first collaboration with the young Charles Lecocq on the oriental comic opera *Fleur de thé*. The saucy *Fleur de thé* went on to a fine international career and its libretto was, thereafter, borrowed from – sometimes more, sometimes less – for several other musical plays around the world. However, the pair's next collaboration with Lecocq, the vaudevillesque *Le Carnaval d'un merle blanc*, a piece long held in the repertoire in Paris after its original season,

was borrowed from even more successfully. Britain's master-thief, H B Farnie, adapted the libretto into English and, attaching it to a pasticcio score of Lecocq, Serpette, Offenbach, Hervé and anything else available, presented the result as *Loo and the Party Who Took Miss* at London's Strand Theatre (28 September 1874). A remarkable first run of 163 performances was prelude to several West End revivals.

The authors had another, and even more considerable, hit in collaboration with Lecocq when they turned out the deliciously comical libretto for his *Les Cent Vierges*, but the composer found different collaborators after his important success with *La Fille de Madame Angot* and the only time that the trio again came together during the next decade was on the Parisian flop (but Hungarian hit), *Le Pompon*. Instead, Chivot and Duru supplied Offenbach, with whom they had already had a success with the comical one-acter *L'Île de Tulipatan* some years previously, with the texts for the two most successful works of the later years of his career: the splendidly constructed libretto to the comic opera *Madame Favart*, and the joyous tale of *La Fille du tambour-major*.

Around the same period, Chivot gave an Oriental libretto, which he had written without Duru's collaboration, to the aspiring composer son of a family friend, Opéra-Comique tenor Marius Audran. Edmond Audran's *Le Grand Mogol* was a hit in Marseille, and set the young composer off on what was to be an outstanding career in the musical theatre. He was more than a little helped on his way by the series of splendid libretti provided to him by Chivot and Duru: the complex tale of *Les Noces d'Olivette*, the international favourite *La Mascotte*, and the allegedly Shakespearian-based *Gillette de Narbonne*.

A revised version of *Le Grand Mogol* (this time done with Duru) and the cautionary Belgian tale of *La Cigale et la fourmi* brought the pair further international successes with Audran, a reunion with Lecocq brought forth the widely played *La Princesse des Canaries*, and the authors also combined with Robert Planquette on the seafaring tale of *Surcouf*, later to become – with the indefatigable Farnie's aid – a major success in the English-language theatre, as *Paul Jones*, and, in what was to be the last of their works together, with Léon Vasseur on the spectacular and widely produced *Le Voyage de Suzette*.

After Duru's death, Chivot collaborated in the writing of other and even more spectacular pieces (*Le Pays de l'or*, *Le Bonhomme de neige*), but the great success of earlier days did not repeat itself. He did, however, apparently have an uncredited hand in several profitable pieces, including Victor de Cottens and Paul Gavault's four-act 'opérette-vaudeville' *Le Papa de Francine*.

Even apart from the fruitful depredations of Mr Farnie, a number of Chivot and Duru's libretti were re-used – detached from their original scores – outside France, although not always with credit. America's most frequent plagiarist of the same period, J Cheever Goodwin, made the libretto for their Audran opérette *Pervenche* into the text for his American musical *Fleur-de-Lis* (mus: William Furst, 1895), whilst *La Petite Fronde*, in the hands of Stanislaus Stange, became the book for Julian Edwards's *The Wedding Day* (1897). Oscar Weil's *Suzette*, produced by the Bostonians at Herrmann's Theater in 1891 (11 October) was apparently a remusicked version of *Le Voyage de*

Suzette, whilst the Broadway musical *The Prima Donna* (Aimé Lachaume/Harry B Smith, Herald Square Theater 14 April 1901) did not dispose of any French music, but was simply based on Chivot and Duru's 1880 vaudeville *Le Siège de Grenade*.

In Vienna, another of their successful vaudevilles, *Les Noces d'un reserviste*, became *Die Hochzeit des Reservisten* as adapted by Zell, Hofmann and Fuchs and set to music by Julius Stern (Theater an der Wien 26 December 1888), and the vaudeville *L'Oncle Bidochon* (Théâtre Cluny 2 March 1894 w Vanloo, Roussel) became the Berlin Schwank *Frau Lohengrin* (ad Eduard Jacobson, Wilhelm Mannstädt, ly: G Görss, mus: Gustave Steffens, Adolf-Ernst-Theater, 21 December 1895). Berlin also gave a *Kam' rad Lehmann* (Jean Kren, Leopold Ely, mus: Julius Einödshofer, Julius Stern, Belle-Alliance Theater 7 May 1904) which was billed as taken from an unspecified Chivot/Duru work

1865 **Un rêve** (Edmond Savary/w Alfred Duru) 1 act Théâtre Lyrique 13 October

1866 **Les Chevaliers de la table ronde** (Hervé/w Duru) Théâtre des Bouffes-Parisiens 27 December

1867 **Les Defauts de Jacotte** (Victor Robillard/w Duru) 1 act Fantaisies-Parisiennes 27 April

1868 **Fleur de thé** (Charles Lecocq/w Duru) Théâtre de l'Athénée 11 April

1868 **L'Île de Tulipatan** (Jacques Offenbach/w Duru) 1 act Théâtre des Bouffes-Parisiens 30 September

1868 **Le Soldat malgré lui** (Frédéric Barbier/w Duru) Fantaisies-Parisiennes 17 October

1868 **Le Carnaval d'un merle blanc** (Lecocq/w Duru) Palais-Royal 30 December

1869 **Gandolfo** (Lecocq/w Duru) 1 act Théâtre des Bouffes-Parisiens 16 January

1869 **Le Docteur Purgandi** (Robillard/w Duru) 1 act Folies-Bergères 2 May

1869 **Le Rajah de Mysore** (Lecocq/w Duru) 1 act Théâtre des Bouffes-Parisiens 21 September

1870 **Le Beau Dunois** (Lecocq/w Duru) Théâtre des Variétés 13 April

1872 **Les Cent Vierges** (Lecocq/w Clairville, Duru) Théâtre des Folies-Parisiennes, Brussels 16 March

1873 **Les Braconniers** (Offenbach/w Duru) Théâtre des Variétés 29 January

1873 **Les Pommes d'or** (Audran/w Duru, Henri Blondeau, Hector Monréal) Théâtre du Château d'Eau 8 February

1875 **La Blanchisseuse de Berg-op-Zoom** (Léon Vasseur/w Duru) Théâtre des Folies-Dramatiques 27 January

1875 **Le Pompon** (Lecocq/w Duru) Théâtre des Folies-Dramatiques 10 November

1877 **Le Grand Mogol** (Edmond Audran) Théâtre de la Gymnase, Marseille 24 February

1878 **Madame Favart** (Offenbach/w Duru) Théâtre des Folies-Dramatiques 28 December

1879 **Les Noces d'Olivette** (Audran/w Duru) Théâtre des Bouffes-Parisiens 13 November

1879 **La Fille du tambour-major** (Offenbach/w Duru) Théâtre des Folies-Dramatiques 13 December

1880 **La Mère des compagnons** (Hervé/w Duru) Théâtre des Folies-Dramatiques 15 December

1880 **La Mascotte** (Audran/w Duru) Théâtre des Bouffes-Parisiens 28 December

1882 **Boccace** French version w Duru, Gustave Layge (Galeries St Hubert, Brussels, Théâtre des Folies-Dramatiques, Paris)

1882 **Gillette de Narbonne** (Audran/w Duru) Théâtre des Bouffes-Parisiens 11 November

1883 **La Princesse des Canaries** (Lecocq/w Duru) Théâtre des Folies-Dramatiques 9 February

1883 **La Dormeuse éveillée** (Audran/w Duru) Théâtre des Bouffes-Parisiens 27 December

1884 **Le Grand Mogol** (revised version w Duru) Théâtre de la Gaîté)

1884 **L'Oiseau bleu** (Lecocq/w Duru) Théâtre des Nouveautés 16 January

1885 **Pervenche** (Audran/w Duru) Théâtre des Bouffes-Parisiens 31 March

1886 **La Cigale et la fourmi** (Audran/w Duru) Théâtre de la Gaîté 30 October

1887 **Surcouf** (Robert Planquette/w Duru) Théâtre des Folies-Dramatiques 6 October

1888 **La Petite Fronde** (Audran/w Duru) Théâtre des Folies-Dramatiques 16 November

1889 **La Fille à Cacolet** (Audran/w Duru) Théâtre des Variétés 10 July

1890 **Le Voyage de Suzette** (Léon Vasseur/w Duru) Théâtre de la Gaîté 20 January

1890 **L'Egyptienne** (Lecocq/w Charles Nuitter, Alexandre Beaumont) Théâtre des Folies-Dramatiques 8 November

1892 **Le Pays de l'or** (Léon Vasseur/w Vanloo) Théâtre de la Gaîté 26 January

1893 **Bicyclistes en voyage** (pasticcio ad Marius Carman/w Blondeau) Théâtre de la Gaîté 5 October

1894 **Le Bonhomme de neige** (Antoine Banès/w Vanloo) Théâtre des Bouffes-Parisiens 19 April

1897 **La Souris blanche** (Vasseur, de Thuisy/w Duru) Théâtre Déjazet 9 November

1898 **Le Maréchal Chaudron** (Lacôme/w George Rolle, 'J Gascogne' E Ratoin) Théâtre de la Gaîte 27 April

THE CHOCOLATE SOLDIER *see* DER TAPFERE SOLDAT

CHODOROV, Jerome (b New York, 10 August 1911).

Originally a journalist, Chodorov subsequently worked as a screenwriter in Hollywood before joining Joseph Fields to write for the stage. The pair had a considerable success with the plays *My Sister Eileen* (1940) and *Junior Miss* (1941). Chodorov supplied some sketches to revue in the 1940s, and made his first full-scale venture with a revue called *Pretty Penny* which was produced at the Bucks County Playhouse, with a consort of biggish names involved, in the summer of 1949. It did not go any further, but his first attempt at a book musical, a version of *My Sister Eileen*, was on a different level. Set with a score by Comden, Green and Bernstein, *Wonderful Town* was a major success.

Neither *The Girl in Pink Tights* (115 performances), a piece using the staging of the 1866 opéra-bouffe féerie *The Black Crook* as its background, nor the comical *I Had a Ball* (199 performances) with Buddy Hackett starred, achieved the same kind of success as *Wonderful Town*, and Chodorov's musical theatre work was subsequently limited largely to revisions and adaptations both credited (*The Great Waltz*, *The Student Prince*, *Pal Joey*) and, as a script doctor, uncredited. In 1967 he authored the libretto for a biomusical of Dumas father and son, set to a Saint-Saëns pasticcio and staged on the West Coast, and a television musical *Olympus 7-0000* with a score by Richard Adler.

1953 **Wonderful Town** (Leonard Bernstein/Betty Comden, Adolph Green/w Joseph Fields) Winter Garden Theater 25 February

1954 **The Girl in Pink Tights** (Sigmund Romberg/Leo Robin/w J Fields) Mark Hellinger Theater 5 March

1964 **I Had a Ball** (Jack Lawrence, Stan Freeman) Martin Beck Theater 15 December
1965 **The Great Waltz** (Johann Strauss arr Robert Wright, George Forrest) San Francisco 14 September
1966 **The Student Prince** revised libretto (Los Angeles Civic Light Opera)
1967 **Dumas and Son** (Camille Saint-Saëns arr Wright, Forrest) Dorothy Chandler Pavilion, Los Angeles 1 August
1978 **Pal Joey** revised libretto w Mark Bramble (Ahmanson Theater, Los Angeles)

CHONCHETTE   Opérette in 1 act by Robert de Flers and Gaston de Caillavet. Music by Claude Terrasse. Théâtre des Capucines, Paris, 11 April 1902.

The Chonchette (Alice Bonheur) of the title is a pretty laundress who is hesitating between marriage to her Charles (Le Gallo) or venturing on to the stage. Max Dearly played the old actor, Saint-Guillaume, from whom the heroine has been taking acting lessons, whilst the comical figures of the Baron and the Vicomte completed the cast of the five-handed, eight-number little show which became a hit for manager Mortier at the tiny Théâtre des Capucines. The Capucines company played the show in a bill with Berény's mimodramas *La Main* and *L'homme aux poupées* at London's St George's Hall with Marie-Louise Faury deputizing for Mlle Bonheur, and the piece was subsequently played in Vienna, with Mimi Marlow as Chonchette, and for 14 performances at the Théâtre Parisien in New York with Robert Casadesus as Saint-Guillaume and Lucienne Debrennes as Chonchette. For many years after its production *Chonchette* was fondly remembered and occasionally restaged by those with a taste for the charming and classy in the musical theatre.

UK: St George's Hall July 1902; Austria: Venedig in Wien (Parisiana) 1909; USA: Théâtre Parisien 19 November 1919

CHOPIN, Frédéric   [Fryderyk Franciszek] (b Zelazowa Wola, Poland, 22 February 1810; d Paris, 17 October 1849).

The musical-playmakers of the post-*Dreimäderlhaus* era decided that the Polish composer's celebrity-cluttered romantic life was ideal material for the same treatment suffered by Schubert, and Chopin became the subject of two musically fabricated Operetten in the 1920s. In Germany, *Chopin*, a Singspiel by Rudolf Presber and Leo Walther Stein, with Chopin's music arranged by Harry Schreyer (Staatstheater Bemberg, 1924), had a discreet life, but an Hungarian musical play made on the same lines by Jenő Faragó (who had already 'done' Offenbach with considerable success) and István Bertha and produced at Budapest's Király Színház under the same title (4 December 1926), with Juci Labáss top-billed as Aurora and Jenő Nador as Chopin proved a considerable success. It was later metamorphosed into a Broadway piece which was eventually called *White Lilacs* (previously *Chopin*, then *The Charmer*, 10 September 1928) credited to Harry B Smith and Hungarian musical director Károly Hájos, and produced by the Shuberts, with Guy Robertson starring as the composer and Odette Myrtil as George Sand. In London, G H Clutsam, responsible for Britain's version of *Dreimäderlhaus* (*Lilac Time*), combined with fading producer Robert Courtneidge on a Chopin follow-up. Their *The Damask Rose* (Golders Green 17 June 1929, Savoy Theatre, 26 March 1930) did not, however, go for a

Fred-loves-George libretto, but instead involved Walter Passmore, Amy Augarde, Nancie Lovat and friends in a Russian tale. It was a quick flop.

Another *Chopin*, billed as an opera in four acts with music arranged by Giacomo Orefice to a biomusical text by Angelo Orvieto was produced in Milan in 1901 (Teatro Lirico, 25 November), and a German one written by Eduard Rogati and Hans Sichert with the music adapted by Walter Keyl, appeared at the Stadttheater, Fürth, 8 April 1939. Britain's Eric Maschwitz and Bernard Grün jumped on the Chopin-wagon the following year with a London piece called *Waltz Without End* (Cambridge Theatre, 29 September 1942), and Broadway took a second swing at the composer's music in *Polonaise* (Alvin Theater 6 October 1945, mus ad Bronislaw Kaper/John Latouche/Gottfried Reinhardt, Anthony Veiller) but this time without attaching anything of his life story – genuine or fictional – to it.

Chopin's piano fantaisie-impromptu, made up into the song 'I'm Always Chasing Rainbows' by Harry Carroll and Joseph McCarthy, appeared in the Broadway musical *Oh, Look!* (Vanderbilt Theater 7 March 1918) and later in the 1973 revival of *Irene* as well as in the films *The Ziegfeld Girl* and *The Dolly Sisters*, whilst the second melody of the 'Minute Waltz' was used as the tune to the original *Irene*'s 'Castle of my Dreams'.

A CHORUS LINE   Musical by James Kirkwood and Nicholas Dante. Lyrics by Edward Kleban. Music by Marvin Hamlisch. Public (Newman) Theater, New York, 15 April 1975; Shubert Theater, New York, 25 July 1975.

A backstage musical with a singular difference, *A Chorus Line* became the longest-running musical in Broadway's history when it played for some 15 years and 6,137 performances at the Shubert Theater between 1975 and 1990.

A Chorus Line was evolved from the life stories and theatrical experiences of a group of Broadway chorus dancers, and it was put together, through a series of taping sessions and performance workshops, under the aegis of director-choreographer Michael Bennett, who had previously been involved in two other musicals constructed on similar lines, if by more conventional writing methods. The 1970 *Company* and the 1971 *Follies* had both been built on a semi-revusical format, in which a group of people were brought together on stage, in those two previous instances for a party, before the loosely structured entertainment turned aside to look at various members of the group, their personality and/or their problems, in more or less detail, in scene or in song. *A Chorus Line* differed in that its characters were gathered together for a more rigorous purpose – to dance an audition for a job – and had their personalities and problems, as well as their dance talents, put on show for a purpose – to win one of the places available in the chorus line. Unlike its predecessors, it also built to a firm finish, with the selection of the artists chosen for the job, resolving the evening's action in a way that neither of the earlier shows did. However, within that more positive framework it still retained what was largely an at least seemingly randomly ordered series of 'spots' for the artists involved.

The action takes place in an unoccupied theatre, where the final recalls for the small chorus of an unnamed show are taking place. The dancers perform an encapsulated version of the set routines, and a first cut is made. Those 17 performers who have been asked to remain for a further round of auditioning are not, however, asked to dance again. They are asked to talk. The show's choreographer, Zach (Robert LuPone), tries to bring each one out to tell his or her story in front of the others. Their problems, past and present, and their preoccupations pour out in a series of songs and speeches, some accompanied by dance, and the series is only interrupted when one dancer, Paul (Sammy Williams), finds the strains of baring his life story too much, and breaks down. When the dancing is resumed, it is Paul, physically fragile as well, who is again the casualty, and when he has been taken off to be cared for, the dancers resume their work aware, all over again, that it could have been any one of them carried, crippled, from the stage: their livelihood and their careers hang on such tenuous things. At last, the choreographer makes his choice from amongst the auditionees, and the action ends as the dancers are seen performing the routine they earlier rehearsed, dressed in the sparkles and spangles of that kind of showbiz.

The songs which accompanied the action were largely built around one or other of the artists and her or his tale, with only such pieces as the opening audition dance, the show number 'One', and the expression of the dancers' feelings about their work headed by Diana Morales (Priscilla Lopez) in 'What I Did for Love' standing outside the 'revusical' section. Three girls (Carole Bishop, Kay Cole, Nancy Lane), come to dancing originally as the escape from unlovely homes, entwined their voices to sing of how everything was beautiful 'At the Ballet', the lively Mike (Wayne Cilento) tapped himself catatonic describing his start in dance after seeing his sister's efforts ('I Can Do That'), Kristine (Renée Baughman) with the support of her husband, Al (Don Percassi), verged on hysteria as she pointed out the bête noire in her abilities – her inability to 'Sing', and Diana Morales related the sour tale of an unsympathetic drama teacher who could have put her off theatre for life ('Nothing'). Talented Val (Pam Blair) told of how her looks stopped her getting jobs ('Dance: Ten, Looks: Three') until she indulged in a touch of plastic surgery to her 'tits and ass', the pains and joys of puberty burst forth in the ensemble 'Hello Twelve', and Cassie (Donna McKechnie), Zach's ex-mistress and a failed actress now returning to her first and loved métier as a dancer, gave her all to 'The Music and the Mirror'.

A Chorus Line, with a cast including a number of the dancers who had taken part in the taping sessions which had provided much of the raw material for the libretto (though not, necessarily, always playing 'themselves'), was first mounted as part of the season of the New York Shakespeare Festival. Word flew round theatre circles from the first preview performance, and the show was a packed-out hit in its little house as it was honed into its final form. The most significant 'plot' alteration at this time concerned the character of Cassie, which had become the most important of the female rôles. Originally, this dancer who had gone on from chorus work to featured rôles was portrayed, realistically, as unable to restrict herself in her performance style to playing identically to seven other choristers, and she was – undoubtedly logically – not chosen for the final line. But audiences apparently found it

unacceptable that the girl, willing and eager to take a job for which she was perhaps over-qualified, just to get back to work, should be rejected. Sentiment and audience-pleasing won out, and Cassie became part of the final selection.

The show moved briskly to Broadway, and met there with the same kind of triumph it had found in its festival performances as well as a bundle of Tony Awards, as its favourite extractable numbers, notably 'What I Did For Love' and 'One', caught on as popular song favourites outside the theatre. Whilst the show passed its 15 memorable years at the Shubert Theater, a series of re-productions followed, the earliest being an American touring company which began its career in San Francisco in May 1976, and a Canadian production which opened in Toronto at the same time. It was this latter company which introduced the show to London. Ever since the show's opening on Broadway, word had been carefully passed round in British theatre circles that it could not and would not be staged in London – Britain lacked dancers with the abilities to take the rôles. Thus, the ground was neatly laid for the 'Canadian' company (dubbed 'international,' although it played only London beyond the American continent) to introduce *A Chorus Line* to Britain.

When, after six months, this competent but rather unexciting company was obliged to move on, the show was recast with British performers. If the quality of the performances was in no way technically reduced (a number of the artists would go on to create or play rôles in London's *Cats*), the knockers were proved unexpectedly right in one area. Most of the young Britons imitating the very real and wholly American 'Broadway gipsies' of the show were unconvincing dramatically. Whereas the chorus artists in the American companies had, more or less, to play themselves, the British – bred in a different theatrical environment – were being required to play rôles ultimately foreign to them. Britain's replacement-cast *A Chorus Line* also suffered some distasteful publicity with the dismissal in rehearsal of Tony-Award-winning actress and dancer Elizabeth Seal (Cassie) in a dramatic and much-reported case which outdid anything in the show's own action. The episode left a sour taste in British theatre circles, and was responsible for British Equity forcing a revision in casting-and-firing legislation. In some strange undefinable way, *A Chorus Line* did not ever catch the imagination of the theatre-going public in Britain in the same way it had in America, yet it totalled 903 performances in more than two years at the Theatre Royal, Drury Lane, and was later toured.

Australia's production of *A Chorus Line*, its cast headed by Ross Coleman (Paul), Peta Toppano (Diana), Cheryl Clark (Cassie), Scott Pearson (Zach) and Pamela Gibbons (Sheila), was, conversely, greeted with great enthusiasm, but the show was seen only rarely in translated versions, and when it was introduced to France and other Continental countries, more than a decade after its Broadway début, it was by American touring performers and not in a local adaptation. A German-language version (ad Michael Kunze) was produced at Vienna's Theater an der Wien in 1987, but proved as much of a disappointment as the tour, and an Italian adaptation (ad Gerolamo Alchieri, Michele Renzullo) was mounted at the Todi Festival in 1990 (5 September) and played for a season in Milan.

A film version, produced by Feuer and Martin and directed by Richard Attenborough in 1985, updated the piece, opened it out to go beyond the confines of the audition stage which was the sole set of the stage show, and introduced several new musical pieces, at the expense of some of the original music. Alyson Reed, Michael Douglas, Cameron English, Yamil Borges, Vicki Frederick, Charles McGowan and Audrey Landers were amongst those featured. The film provoked a certain amount of discussion, and won some partisans, but was ultimately not a success.

A Chorus Line was the outstanding phenomenon of the Broadway musical theatre in the 1970s and, if it left fewer re-usable parts in the way of extractable numbers than other shows of its period, and if it exported less well than some less special shows of its era, its original New York production remains a landmark in the history of the musical stage.

UK: Theatre Royal, Drury Lane 22 July 1976; Australia: Her Majesty's Theatre, Sydney, 21 May 1977; Austria: Raimundtheater 16 October 1987; France: Théâtre du Châtelet 16 December 1987; Film: Embassy Films 1985
Recordings: original cast (Columbia), Norwegian cast (NorDisc), Austrian cast (Polydor), Italian cast (Carisch), film soundtrack (PolyGram) etc
Literature: Mandelbaum, K: *A Chorus Line and the Musicals of Michael Bennett* (St Martins Press, New York, 1989); Flinn, D M: *What They Did For Love* (Bantam, New York, 1989); Viagas, R, Walsh, T, Lee, B: *On The Line* (Morrow, New York, 1990).

CHRISTINÉ, Henri [Marius] (b Geneva, 27 December 1867; d Nice, 12 November 1941). The first and one of the foremost composers of the postwar age of French musical comedy.

Swiss-born, of French parents, the young Christiné began his working life as a schoolteacher in his native Geneva. His career orientation was changed when he married a café-concert singer and abandoned Switzerland for the southern part of France. The couple made their headquarters in Nice, and there Christiné began to turn out songs, at first for the use of his wife and then, with considerable success, for the established stars of the music halls of the time. From a prodigious output, such pieces as 'La Petite Tonkinoise', 'La Légende des flots bleus', 'Je sais que vous êtes jolie', 'Elle est épatante, cette petite femme-là', 'Reviens', 'Le Long du Missouri' and 'La Dame du Métro', for which Christiné supplied words and/or music, numbered amongst a long line of successes which resulted in his setting up his own music publishing company.

He made his earliest entry into the world of the musical theatre with the two-act *Service d'amour*, advertised as a 'pièce à grand spectacle' and produced at the Scala with Alice Bonheur, Claudius, Sulbac and Girault featured, on a bill with the pantomime *La Chula*, Jane Thylda and Mayol. He subsequently provided the music for several other pieces for the same house, without detracting from his principal career as a songwriter. It was ten years from the last of these early theatrical ventures, in the last days of the war, that he was asked to supply the score for a little classical burlesque intended for Gustave Quinson's tiny new underground Théâtre de l'Abri. Circumstances led *Phi-Phi* ('Les petits païens', 'Ah! tais-toi!', 'Ah, cher monsieur, excusez-moi', 'Bien chapeautée' etc), with its daz-

zling musical combination of the chanson and up-to-date opérette and dance strains, of sprightly song and splendidly written ensemble-work, to be mounted at the Théâtre des Bouffes-Parisiens instead. It proved both an enormous success and the impetus and model for a whole era of jazz-age musical comedies which dominated the French musical stage through the 1920s and into the 1930s.

Christiné held his place at the head of the new genre he had been instrumental in propelling to popularity, turning out the scores for a series of successful musicals, headed by *Dédé* ('Je m'donne', 'Dans la vie faut pas s'en faire', 'Si j'avais su') and followed by such pieces as *Madame*, *J'aime*, *Arthur* and *Encore cinquante centimes*, until the tales and tunes of sophisticated musical comedy began to become repetitive and the vogue for things more spectacular and less witty arrived in the 1930s. When that happened, Christiné switched styles, and he composed some of his last theatre music for the large-scale romantic costume musicals *Au temps des merveilleuses* and *Yana* at the Théâtre du Châtelet.

In 1934 a musicalized version of Francis de Croisset's successful play *Le Bonheur, mesdames!* was produced equipped with a pasticcio score of Christiné music.

If the brightly melodious and modern musical comedies which Christiné and his authors turned out for the delight of post-war Paris won him a place second to none in the French musical theatre of his time, his works – in spite of a quality evidently superior to most of what was being contemporaneously produced in other centres – exported poorly. England did unspeakable things to the libretto of *Phi-Phi* and barely better to *Dédé*, apparently on the same sort of moral grounds that had led to the French opéras-bouffes being bowdlerized on the insular side of the English Channel half a century earlier, but Britain's producers also ripped the scores to pieces, larded them with sub-standard interpolations, and, not surprisingly, ended up with a pair of flops. America, after an abortive attempt with another botched version of *Phi-Phi* which closed out of town, and Charles Dillingham's failure to come up with his announced production of *Dédé*, ignored the genre and concentrated on home-composed musical comedies and imported romantic Operetten.

If the libretti of the French shows were more than the dainty non-Gallic theatres could take, versions of Christiné's songs, nevertheless, proved popular as interpolations into such Broadway shows as *A Naughty Cinderella* ('Do I Love You?', ie 'L'Homme du dancing'), *The Better 'Ole* ('It's Our Wedding Day' ie 'Je sais que tu es gentil'), *The Doll Girl* ('That's Love With a Capital "L"' ie 'Je sais que tu es gentil' again), *Ninety in the Shade* ('My Mindanao Chocolate Soldier'), *The Echo* (French Fandango), and *The Lady in Red* ('Lulu Lavinia').

Only Hungary, which welcomed *Mercenary Mary* with acclaim whilst wholly bypassing the contemporary works of such as Gershwin, Porter and Kern, showed a boundless enthusiasm for the shows of Christiné and of his Parisian contemporaries. *Fi-Fi* (Lujza Blaha Színház 7 December 1921), *Szeretlek* (*J'aime*, Király Színház 26 May 1928), *A Csodadoktor* (*Encore cinquante centimes*, Magyar Színház 12 May 1934), *Békebeli boldogság* (*Le Bonheur, mesdames!* Andrássy uti Színház 20 September 1934) and *Leányálom* (*La Madone du promenoir*, Andrássy uti Színház 4 January 1935) all got showings in Budapest.

1903 **Service d'Amour** (Maurice Dumas) Scala 27 February
1904 **Mam'selle Chichi** (Charles Esquès) Scala 2 July
1907 **Les Vierges du harem** Scala 26 February
1908 **Cinq minutes d'amour** (Esquès) Scala 29 February
1918 **Phi-Phi** (Albert Willemetz, Fabien Sollar) Théâtre des Bouffes-Parisiens 13 November
1921 **Dédé** (Willemetz) Théâtre des Bouffes-Parisiens 10 November
1923 **Madame** (Willemetz) Théâtre Daunou 14 December
1925 **J'adore ça** (Willemetz, Saint-Granier) Théâtre Daunou 14 March
1925 **P.L.M.** (Rip) Théâtre des Bouffes-Parisiens 21 April
1926 **J'aime** (Willemetz, Saint-Granier) Théâtre des Bouffes-Parisiens 22 December
1929 **Arthur** (André Barde) Théâtre Daunou 4 September
1931 **Encore cinquante centimes** (w Maurice Yvain/Barde) Théâtre des Nouveautés 17 September
1933 **La Madone du promenoir** (Barde) Concert-Mayol 3 November
1934 **Le Bonheur, mesdames!** (de Croisset, ad Willemetz, Fred de Grésac) Théâtre des Bouffes-Parisiens 6 January
1934 **Au temps des merveilleuses** (w Tiarko Richepin/Willemetz, André Mouëzy-Éon) Théâtre du Châtelet 25 December

1936 **La Poule** (w Lajos Lajtai/Henri Duvernois/ad Barde) Théâtre des Nouveautés 9 January
1936 **Yana** (w Richepin/Willemetz, Mouëzy-Éon, Henri Wernert) Théâtre du Châtelet 24 December
1938 **Le Flirt ambulant** (Tristan Bernard, Willemetz) Théâtre Michel 13 January

CHRYSANTHEMUM Melodrama in ragtime in 2 acts by Neville Phillips and Robin Chancellor. Music by Robb Stewart. New Lindsay Theatre Club, London, 14 March 1956; Prince of Wales Theatre, 13 November 1958.

Another product of the adventurous club theatres of the British 1950s, *Chrysanthemum* did for the 1910s what *The Boy Friend* did for the 1920s and *Grease* for the 1950s, with just a touch more of the burlesque in its make-up. If it did not have the success in establishing itself that those other two blockbusters did, that seems to have been due as much to bad luck and its authors' naïvety as anything else. Moved from its club venue to the West End, with Pat Kirkwood and her then husband, Hubert Gregg, top-billed, Sandor Gorlinsky's production suffered a series of vicissitudes

Plate 53. **Chrysanthemum**: *Chrysanthemum Brown (Pat Kirkwood) comes home with the milk too many years after she went out for it for her father (Raymond Newell) not to have a few questions to ask.*

267

which, after a change of theatre, resulted in a closure after 148 performances.

Chrysanthemum Brown (Valerie Tandy/Pat Kirkwood), who vanished from her London home whilst going out for the milk, returns home in prosperous state years later, refusing to say where she has been. In fact, she was kidnapped by the horrid Ma Carroty and white-slaved to Buenos Aires and a fate not quite as bad as death. Ma Carroty is still at it, and her next victim is the beloved of our heroine's brother Bob (Donald Scott/Roger Gage), ingénue Mary-Ann Blessington-Briggs (Patricia Moore). But the villainess has not counted with Chrysanthemum who, disguised as a Chinese cabaret vocalist, eases her way into Ma Carroty's lair at the gruesome transpontine Skull and Chopsticks, leads the rescue, proves that her virtue survived in Argentina, wins the heart and hand of Mary-Ann's brother, John (Colin Croft/Gregg), and exposes the *real* identity of the evening's criminal . . .

From a score bristling with gentle parodies and witty lyrics, the pretty waltz song 'Love Is a Game' proved the favourite. The young lovers gave forth with a version of the pre-war weather duet ('Thanks to the Weather') and the disguised Chrysanthemum pounded out a 'Shanghai Lil', but the best material, added to beef up the leading man's part for Gregg when the show transferred to the West End, came in a couple of wordfully witty numbers in which he lectured his little sister on the perils of walking in the park ('Watch Your Step') and frantically phoned Scotland Yard after her disappearance, only to get a series of wrong numbers. When *Chrysanthemum* was later mounted in America, with Patrice Munsel starred in the title-rôle, some further material was added which gave an extra comic flavour to the already vast rôle à tiroirs of Chrysanthemum. She avoided her father's queries over her disappearance in a catalogue of improbabilities 'Don't Ask Me That', and, in mid-rescue, took time out to relate the awful tale of her adventure to Mary-Ann, lying trussed up in Ma Carroty's den and wanting only to be set free.

This American production provoked interest from Gower Champion and also from Hollywood, but any prospects of a film died in 1967 when America's very own version of *Chrysanthemum*, *Thoroughly Modern Millie*, hit the screens. Protected by the expensive American legal system from three penniless young Britons who had no doubt at all that they had been plagiarized, *Thoroughly Modern Millie* went on to classic status, whilst *Chrysanthemum* was relegated to an occasional production in provincial and amateur theatres.

USA: Royal Ponciana Playhouse, Palm Beach 22 January 1962
Recording: original cast (Nixa, AEI)

CHU CHIN CHOW Musical tale of the east in 3 acts by Oscar Asche. Music by Frederic Norton. His Majesty's Theatre, London, 31 August 1916.

Chu Chin Chow was a version of the Arabian Nights Ali Baba and the 40 thieves tale, put together by actor, director and sometime playwright Asche as a vehicle for himself and his wife, actress Lily Brayton, and produced in wartime London in the theatre which normally housed the respected productions of Beerbohm Tree. Staged with a sumptuous extravagance, it proved to be one of the phenomena of the British stage of the early part of the century. The show's initial London run of 2,235 per-

formances set a London long-run record for a musical which survived for some forty years, and *Chu Chin Chow* went on to be an international hit in English-speaking theatres.

The robber chief Abu Hasan (Asche) is preparing to pull a coup in the home of the rich merchant Kasim Baba (Frank Cochrane), and his beautiful captive, Zahrat al-Kulub (Lily Brayton), has been introduced into the house, in the guise of a slave girl, to spy out the land. Ali Baba (Courtice Pounds), Kasim's poor, layabout brother, accidentally discovers Hasan's lair and the riches hidden there and, when the greedy Kasim goes to steal what he can from the hoard, he is captured and killed. Hasan plans to launch his attack on the late merchant's household on the occasion of the wedding of Ali's son Nur al-Huda (J V Bryant) and the slave girl Marjanah (Violet Essex), but Zahrat foils his plan and wins her revenge, disposing of Hasan's men with the traditional boiling oil before stabbing the robber to death. Ali ends the evening in the well-padded arms of his brother's widow, Alcolom (Aileen D'Orme).

Norton provided a score which included two numbers which became standards: Pounds and Miss D'Orme billed and cooed with comical, middle-aged passion to the strains of 'Any Time's Kissing Time', whilst the Cobbler hired to sew the pieces of Kasim's quartered body back together for burial sang of his trade in the bass-baritone Cobbler's Song ('I sit and cobble at slippers and shoon...'), a number which became a drawing-room and concert standard for half a century of low-voiced vocalists. Ali's comical 'When a Pullet is Plump (she's tender)', Nur al-Huda's serenade 'Corraline', the staunch march for the 40 thieves ('We Are the Robbers of the Wood') and Hasan's disguised declaration 'I Am Chu Chin Chow of China' were other favourite moments of a score which also included a lot of incidental music to serve the show's many scene changes (originally 15, later several more), parades and dances. Amongst the several songs and scenes which were inserted during the show's run, Miss D'Orme's lovely, plaintive 'I Long for the Sun' was the most successful.

The well-rounded soprano won her extra number through being one of the hits of the show, alongside Pounds – the keystone and real star of the evening – and the magnificent production values (scenery by Joseph and Phil Harker, costumes by Percy Anderson, director Asche, dances by Espinosa) whilst Asche and Miss Brayton provided the dramatic backbone to the entertainment with strong, melodramatic performances which complemented the comical ones ideally. The show was indeed 'a beauty show – of scene and person, of dress and undress', but it also had a fine strong story, familiar and happy characters and characterizations, and attractive songs which helped to ensure its survival after that first lavish production.

Grossmith and Laurillard took the show to the provinces with a cast headed by Bobbie Comber (Ali), Henry Latimer (Hasan) and Madge McIntosh (Zahrat), and *Chu Chin Chow* kept up a provincial presence in Britain for many years until, in 1940 (3 July), it was brought back to London for a second wartime run with the famous melodrama villain Lyn Harding as Hasan, Rosalinde Fuller as Zahrat, Jerry Verno as Ali, Kay Bourne as Alcolom, Dennis Noble as Nur al-Huda and with Sydney Fairbrother repeating her original rôle as Ali's shrewish and ill-fated wife, Mahbubah. Chased from London by the bombs after 80 performances, it returned, partly recast, the following year for another 158 nights. In 1953 *Chu Chin Chow* was given as an ice production at London's Empire Pool, Wembley.

Elliott, Comstock and Gest produced *Chu Chin Chow* in New York the year after its London opening. Tyrone Power (Hasan), Henry E Dixey (Ali), Florence Reed (Zahrat), Kate Condon (Alcolom) and Tessa Kosta (Marjanah) featured, the London designs were repeated, and Alexis Kosloff arranged new parades and dances for what looked like being another successful production. However, management went awry and, after a transfer, less than three months into the run, to the Century Theater, the expensively staged show closed after 208 performances, still in the red. It was left to a highly successful post-New York tour to recoup and add considerable profits to the producers' outlay.

Asche himself later took *Chu Chin Chow* to his native Australia, but only after Hugh D Mackintosh had already mounted a version there, with ex-Savoy star C H Workman (Ali), Vera Pearce (a Zahrat who sang better than any other female member of the cast!), Louie Pounds (Alcolom) and Maggie Moore (Mahbubah) amongst the cast and London's Frank Cochrane restaging Asche's direction. Ward's version played nearly three months in Melbourne before moving on to Sydney's Grand Opera House (26 March 1921).

Herbert Wilcox made a silent film version of *Chu Chin Chow* in 1923, but, after the coming of sound, a second version was made with George Robey starred as Ali Baba and Thelma Tuson as a richy funny Alcolom. Anna May Wong played the melodrama of Zahrat with conviction, whilst Fritz Kortner gave a burlesque stage performance as Hasan in what was, otherwise, one of the better filmed musicals of its time. Sydney Fairbrother again played her original rôle.

USA: Manhattan Opera House 22 October 1917; Australia: Tivoli, Melbourne 11 December 1920; Belgium: (in French) Casino, Brussels 1930; Films: Graham–Wilcox Films 1923 (silent), Gainsborough Films 1934
Recordings: selections (MFP, HMV)

CHUECA, Federico (b Madrid, 5 May 1848; d Madrid, 20 June 1908).

Originally set for a career in medicine, Chueca came gradually to music as a player, a conductor and at last as a composer. The final impetus for a change of career was given when a set of waltzes he had composed was included, with great success, in the schedules of the Sociedád de Conciertos. His earliest works for the theatre were composed in collaboration with Joaquín Valverde, who expanded Chueca's melodies into harmonized and orchestrated numbers as the musical illustration to a series of short zarzuelas which included several that became highly popular in their country of origin. They also provided the music for what became the most internationally successful of all Spanish pieces, *La gran via*.

The other Chueca/Valverde pieces include *Las ferias* (1878), *La canción de la Lola* (1880), *Fiesta nacional* (1882), *Luces y sobras* (1882), *De la noche a la mañana* (1883), *Caramelo* (1884), *Vivitos y coleando* (1884), *Cadiz* (1886),

Un año pasado por agua (1889), *Le magasin de musique* (1889), *De Madrid á Paris* (1889), *La Casa del Oso* (1891), *Mayas y toreros* (1901) and *El bateo* (1901) whilst the further list of Chueca's other collaborations and single-handed compositions for the stage include *¡Hoy sale, hoy!* (1884 w Francesco Asenjo Barbieri), *El ultimo chulo* (1889), *El chaleco blanco* (1890), *El arca de Noé* (1890, aka *Fotografías animadas*), *El tendero de comestibles* (1891), *Los descamidados* (1893), *El coche correo* (1895), *Las zapatillas* (1895), *Los arrastraos* (1896, aka *El capote de paseo*), *Agua, azucarillos y aguardiente* (1897), *El manton de Manila* (1898), *La alegría de la huerta* (1900), *La corrida de toros* (1903), *La borracha* (1904), *El estudiante* (1907 w L Fontanals), *Las mocitas del barrio* (1909), *La Plaza de Anton Martin*, *Turcos y rusos* and *Locuros madrileñas*.

LA CHULAPONA Zarzuela in 3 acts by Federico Romero and Guillermo Fernández Shaw. Music by Federico Moreno Torroba. Teatro Calderón, Madrid, 31 March 1934.

La Chulapona was amongst the most popular of the latter-day Spanish musical plays, and it has remained in the zarzuela repertoire in the more than a half-century since its initial production, being the subject of a major Madrid revival as recently as 1988.

In the tradition of the classic zarzuela, *La Chulapona* is set in the suburbs of Madrid and deals with the everyday (love) lives of the people who live there. The principals are two laundry-workers, Manuela (Selica Pérez Carpio) and Rosario (Felisia Herrero), and José Maria (Vicente Simón), the boyfriend of the former. The jealous Rosario – the chulapona, or come-hitherish girl of the title – briefly seduces José Maria away from her friend, but the boy soon returns repentant and is reconciled with the girl he really loves. There is, however, no happy ending. Rosario is pregnant, and rather than let the child be born fatherless, Manuela gives up her man and her dream of happiness.

Moreno Torroba's score was full of dancing rhythms, ranging from mazurka and schottische (chotis) to paso doble, a jaunty guajira and habanera, but those apparently light-hearted rhythms never got in the way of the romantic/dramatic nature of the show's main story, and some impressive pieces – both solo and ensemble – were the result. If the Act I duo between José-Maria and Rosario ('Es pañuelito blanco') proved the musical highlight of the evening, the soprano/chorus mazurka of the opening scene ('Yo que con las demas'), the tenor romanza of the second and the soaring final showdown rendered it nothing in effectiveness in a piece which had something of the air of a lilting Spanish *Cavalleria rusticana* to it.

An English-language version of the piece (ad Mary Lynn Whitman) was played in New York in 1959, but elsewhere beyond Spain the show has been seen largely in touring Spanish zarzuela companies.

USA: Greenwich Mews Theatre *Ole!* 18 March 1959; France: Opéra-Comique 19 May 1989
Recording: selection (Columbia/Zacosa)

CIAO, RUDY Commedia musicale in 2 acts by Luigi Magni, Piero Garinei and Sandro Giovannini. Lyrics by Garinei and Giovannini. Music by Armando Trovaioli. Teatro Sistina, Rome, 7 January 1966.

This Italian biomusical on filmstar Rudolph Valentino starred Marcello Mastroianni, the star of, amongst others, Fellini's film $8\frac{1}{2}$ (1963), alongside a cast of no fewer than 13 feminine partners including Ilaria Occhini and Olga Villi as his two wives and Raffaela Cara as the dancer Bonita. Mastroianni sang of 'Il mio nome' and demanded 'Questa si chiama amore?' and joined in an ensemble with the women on 'Piaceva alle donne', which more or less summed up the subject of the work.

After a run of a hundred performances at the Teatro Sistina, the show lost its élan when Mastroianni's other prospects resulted in his departure, but *Ciao, Rudy* was subsequently remounted by Leo Wächter in 1972, with Alberto Lionello and nine feminine partners (including Paola Borboni, Guisi Raspani Dandolo and Simona Sorlisi from the original team). The show's principle was later borrowed for a Broadway piece based on the Mastroianni film $8\frac{1}{2}$ and called *Nine*.

Recordings: original cast (RCA), revival cast (RCA)

CIBOULETTE Opérette in 3 acts by Robert de Flers and Francis de Croisset. Music by Reynaldo Hahn. Théâtre des Variétés, Paris, 7 April 1923.

The most successful stage musical work of Reynaldo Hahn, *Ciboulette* was written to a text by two of the most admired French playwrights of its time, de Flers and – in succession to his longtime partner de Caillavet – Francis de Croisset. It was no longer a burlesque text, like the ones de Flers and de Caillavet had written for Terrasse with such success, but a piece of prettily pastel-coloured romance, with some gentle humour and a certain charm, which Hahn illustrated with a score written in a similar vein.

Rodolphe Duparquet (Jean Périer), comptroller of the Les Halles markets, watches sadly as the actress Zénobie (Jeanne Perriat) plays fast and loose with the affections of the naïve young Vicomte Antonin de Mourmelon (Henri Defreyn) and, finally, he reveals her duplicity to the young man. Antonin has lost a mistress but found a friend, and soon he finds another in the person of Ciboulette (Edmée Favart), a little farm-girl who comes into town to sell her goods at Les Halles. Ciboulette has been told that she will find her destined husband under a cabbage, win him away from a woman who will go white-haired in an instant, and that she will receive notice of his death in a tambourine. When Antonin emerges from the back of her vegetable cart, the first condition is fulfilled, when Ciboulette tips a bag of flour over Zénobie's head, the second comes true, and, in the third act, when Ciboulette has gone on to become a famous prima donna, like all the best operettic vegetable-sellers, she gets the letter – which the suicidal Antonin had entrusted to a butler for later delivery – after their reunion has been happily effected.

Hahn equipped his Ciboulette with several sweet and sprightly soprano numbers ('Dans un' charrett'', 'Moi, je m'appelle Ciboulette', 'C'est sa banlieu', the Chanson de la Route) as well as a prima donna number for the last act ('Amour qui meurs, amour qui passes!'), and she joined prettily in duet 'Comme frère et soeur' with her new-found friend, but the highlight of the show was Duparquet's number 'C'est tout ce qui me reste d'elle'. When the tearful Ciboulette comes to dampen his shoulder after giving the insufficiently backboned Antonin his marching orders,

Duparquet tells her his own sad story of love. His christian name gives it away – he is the Rodolphe of Murger and Puccini, and his love story is the tale of his little, lost Mimi. All that he has left is a tiny handkerchief that was hers, which he keeps in his coat pocket, next his heart. Daringly ingenuous and sentimental, Duparquet's scene and song triumphed by the quality of their writing, and they added an extra dimension to an otherwise conventional, if skilfully made, opérette with which Hahn and his librettists had the curious idea to challenge the fashionable musical comedies of the 1920s.

Ciboulette was a decided success in Paris, and it was reprised on several occasions: at the Théâtre Marigny in 1926 (2 October) with Mlle Favart, Defreyn and with André Baugé as Duparquet, again at the Gaîté-Lyrique in 1931 with Nini Roussel starred, and in 1935 (20 January) with Renée Camia, André Noël and Aquistapace. In the same year, a film version was produced by Claude Autant-Lara with Simone Berriau, Dranem and Robert Burnier featured. However, although the piece proved both popular and well-regarded in France, it attracted no buyers elsewhere. Hassard Short announced a production for Broadway which never eventuated, and the other main centres showed no interest. Yet the piece continued to hold its place in the French repertoire, returning to Paris in 1953 (13 March) at no less a venue than the Opéra-Comique with Géori Boué, Raymond Amade and Roger Bourdin featured, and again in 1975 (25 October) with Nicole Broissin, André Battedou and Henri Gui. It has also continued to be played regularly in provincial houses without showing any signs of being considered old or, by modern standards, saccharine.

Recordings: complete (EMI) selections (EMI, Decca, Ducretet Thomson) etc

LA CIGALE ET LA FOURMI Opérette in 3 acts by Henri Chivot and Alfred Duru. Music by Edmond Audran. Théâtre de la Gaîté, Paris, 30 October 1886.

The almost tragic tale of 'the grasshopper and the ant', as retold by Chivot and Duru, provided Edmond Audran with the basics for a highly successful opérette which brought to a peak the mostly fine run of success that had followed the great triumphs of the composer's earliest years in the theatre.

The busily home-proud ant is Charlotte (Mlle Thuillier-Leloir) who lives in her native village with her country husband, Guillaume (Émile Petit); the grasshopper is her fun-loving and irresponsible foster-sister, Thérèse (Jeanne Granier), who uses her charms on her Uncle Mathias (Scipion) to such effect that he sets her up in a flower-stall in a hotel in the big city of Bruges. She soon catches a number of eyes. The Chevalier Franz de Bernheim (Mauguière), needing a cover for his affair with the married Duchesse de Fayensberg (Mlle Fassy), uses Thérèse, and soon falls in love with her, at the same time that the starry-eyed Duc de Fayensberg (Raiter) is promoting her on a career which quickly makes her the reigning prima donna of the town. When Thérèse discovers the truth about Franz's first approaches to her, she causes a public scandal by singing a song which thinly veils the truth at Fayensberg's society ball, and flees the city. She wanders the land, working as a street singer, until she finally comes to the warm home that Charlotte has built for her family. There she is nursed back to health, and there Franz comes at last to find her.

The prima donna's rôle was well supplied with songs: the happy, country Chanson de la cigale, the rustic number in which the flower-girl's talents are displayed to Fayensberg ('Un jour, Margot'), the popular gavotte 'Ma mère, j'entends le violon' which the fashionable diva sings at a fair for the benefit of a beggar, her plea to Franz for honesty ('Franz, je vous ai donné ma vie'), the fatal fable ('C'est l'histoire d'un cigale'), and the dramatic 'Je suis sans pain et sans asile'. Charlotte had a contrasting Chanson de la fourmi, and joined happily with Thérèse in memories of childhood Christmases, whilst there was a touch of gentle comedy in the number for Vincent, the lovesick peasant boy who follows Thérèse to Bruges and takes a job as prompt at the theatre where she is starring, just to be near her ('Je souffle! Metier peu folâtre').

Debruyère's production at the Gaîté was mounted in a style suitable to its large stage, with a ballet of the Judgement of Paris inserted into the second-act ball scene, and it did extremely well, playing for 140 performances before the producer replaced it temporarily with a revival of Orphée, bringing the show back after the summer break for a further series of performances. It was later restaged in 1904 (10 November), with Juliette Simon-Girard starred alongside Dalcourt (Franz), Mlle Leclerc (Charlotte), Regnard (Duc) and Emil Soums (Vincent), again in 1915 at the Trianon-Lyrique (26 October) and once more at the Théâtre des Gobelins in 1921 with Rosalia Lambrechts in the central rôle.

In the meanwhile, however, the piece had had a remarkable career further afield. If the German and the Hungarian theatres, which played many of Audran's lesser works, oddly did not pick up on La Cigale, London's Horace Sedger did. He had the piece adapted by oldtimers F C Burnand and Gilbert a' Beckett and had Ivan Caryll revamp the score in order to make the huge title-rôle, thus made for the benefit of Granier, less overwhelming, by adding solos for Franz and replacing a number of other songs. The resultant show, with Geraldine Ulmar as Marton (as the heroine was now called), an American tenor who went to considerable trouble to prove he had the right to call himself the Chevalier Scovel as Franz, Lionel Brough as Mathias and Lila Clay and her 15-woman orchestra featured on stage, was a major success ('a more exquisite comic opera ... has not been seen in London for many years'). La Cigale played a remarkable 423 times at the Lyric Theatre before going on the road (although Sedger's dubious management meant that at the end of it the books showed the production £2,380 in the red), whilst a Broadway production, starring Lillian Russell (Marton) and Viennese star Carl Streitmann (Franz) and directed by Richard Barker, was running through its 112 performances at the Casino Theater. Australia saw the show in J C Williamson's production with Charles Ryley (Franz), Howard Vernon (Duc), Flora Graupner (Charlotte) and Marie Halton (Marton) the following year. Miss Halton's sudden departure cut what looked like being an exceptional first run, but the piece was remounted for several consecutive Australian seasons, and it continued to tour English-language theatres all around the world for a number of years, making itself one of the few European musicals to have found a wider appreciation outside the old Continent than at home.

UK: Lyric Theatre La Cigale 9 October 1890; USA: Casino Theater La Cigale 26 October 1891; Australia: Princess Theatre, Melbourne La Cigale 12 February 1892

CIN-CI-LÀ Operetta in 3 acts by Carlo Lombardo. Music by Virgilio Ranzato. Teatro dal Verme, Milan, 18 December 1925.

One of the most popular Italian operettas of its period, Cin-ci-là was set to a libretto which had an aura of the previous century about it. The tale was set in China, and its principals were a sexually unenlightened Prince and Princess who, having been wed, apparently expect their heir to arrive by the next stork. When Papa's little Parisian friend, Cin-ci-là, arrives in town, with her boyfriend Petit-Gris, the lessons on lovemaking are in good hands.

The score to the piece didn't have much of the previous century about it. It boasted what it called (but which didn't sound much like) a blues and also a reasonably perfunctory chorus foxtrot, but was at its happiest when relaxing into less determinedly modern rhythms. Cin-ci-là and Petit-Gris came out best with a couple of light-hearted dance-y pieces, a 'Boxe d'amore' which mixed intermittently Chinesey tones with a refrain about 'Picca-dilly-dilly-dilly' and a hip-cocking little 'Oh, Cin-ci-là', and the Parisian lady flaunted herself in 'Rose! Rose!' to a bouncy music-hally melody which sounded for all the (rest of the) world like 'Margie'. The little bride and groom had their happiest moments when least strenuous in a loping duo 'La Favola delle tortore'.

Still performed, 60-something years later, in the repertoire of Italian operetta companies, Cin-ci-là has also been played in a German version (ad Rolf Sievers, Will Kaufmann, Rudolf Perak) – one of the few operettas of its class to win a production beyond Italy.

Germany: Centraltheater, Dresden Chinchilla 3 November 1937
Recordings: selection (Oxford), part-record (EDF, Cetra) etc

CINDERELLA

The tale of Cinderella, otherwise known as Cendrillon, Aschenbrödl or Aschenputtl, Cenerentola, Hamupipőke, Popelka or by various other nationally different names, has come down to modern days from the French tales of Perrault. The now standard version of the story of the unloved stepdaughter, whose fairy godmother sent her to the Prince's ball in a magic coach and gown with glass slippers and a time limit, and who was subsequently tracked down by the love-struck royal thanks to having such abnormally tiny feet that no other fitted the shoe she had lost in her midnight flight, has been played on the stage for two centuries. It has gone through all kinds of transformations, modernizations and alterations, it has been played as an opera, an opérette, a burlesque, updated as a musical comedy, and undergone all kinds of rather undignified treatment as a British seasonal pantomime, it has often (away from the pantomime world) seen its magical element and the fairy godmother dispensed with, but always, at the end of the affair, the penniless, smut-faced lass gets the prince.

Quite when this winsome creature first made her stage appearance is not certainly known, but a one-act Cendrillon by Jean-Louis Laruette and Louis Anseaume was produced at the Paris Opéra-Comique on 20 February 1759. Britain first saw the lady of the glass slipper at the Theatre Royal, Drury Lane in January 1804, when a piece entitled *Cinderella, or the Glass Slipper*, written by a Mr James and with music composed by Michael Kelly, featured Miss Decamp as its heroine for a fine 51 performances. A highly successful operatic version by Nicolas Isouard was produced at the Opéra-Comique in 1810 (22 February), but it was supplanted just a few years later by Rossini's work *La Cenerentola, ossia La bonta in trionfono* (Rome, 25 January 1817). Several other operatic *Cinderellas* followed, and the fact that Rossini had largely cornered the field did not prevent composers of the quality of Massenet (Opéra-Comique, 24 May 1899) and Wolf-Ferrari (Venice, 22 February 1900) from joining the ranks of *Cinderella* composers. An English-language opera by John Farmer and Henry S Leigh was premièred at Harrow (or, according to some sources, Oxford) in 1882.

Parallel to this operatic career, Cinderella became a favourite as a burlesque and pantomime heroine. The first English *Cinderella* burlesque seems to have been that produced at the Lyceum in 1845, authored by Albert Smith and Mr Kenny, but it was H J Byron's 1860 piece, *Cinderella, or the Lover, the Lackey and the Little Glass Slipper* (Strand Theatre 26 December), which introduced the character of Buttons, the amorous pageboy, for the first time, which gave *Cinderella* its shape for the future, as it went on to be played over and over again in all corners of the English-speaking world both as an extravaganza and as a pantomime opening. The British stage days of such pieces as *Cinderella, or Harlequin and the Magic Pumpkin and the Great Fairy of the Little Glass Slipper* – which opened in the Hobgoblins' Hermitage, progressed to the Butterfly Haunt in the Dell of Delight for a Grand Pas de Papillons, and then to the Enchanted Fountain, before getting around to the Baron Pumpolino, and his daughters Clotilda, Thisbe and Cinderella – were numbered. Byron had, to a large degree, put definitive order into the tale.

He did not, however, stem the flow of *Cinderella* shows. In 1870 Henry Lemon wrote a *Cinderella* for the Crystal Palace Theatre (18 April), Frank Green authored a piece mounted in 1871, the same year in which Alfred Thompson and Émile Jonas's *Cinderella the Younger*, a full-scale opéra-bouffe with an original score, was produced at the Gaiety Theatre, prior to an international career as *Javotte*. In 1883 (8 September) the Gaiety Theatre produced an *Our Cinderella* written by Robert Reece, and the same theatre was the venue for *Cinder-Ellen Up Too Late* (24 December 1891), originally prepared and produced during the Gaiety's Australian tour to star Ellen (Nellie) Farren. The most recent British burlesque came in 1962 (17 December) with the production of Ned Sherrin and Caryl Brahms's part-pasticcio *Cindy-Ella, or I Gotta Shoe*.

In a period where pantomimes gave up pasticcio scores for original music, a number of well-known British composers provided scores to the story. In 1889 John Crook put music to J Hickory Wood's version, in 1908 Alfred and Herbert Haines supplied a new score for the Adelphi Theatre's *Cinderella*, and J M Glover put Drury Lane's 1919 pantomime version to music. In 1966 the Shadows pop group provided original music for the London Palladium's production, whilst a television musical score written by Rodgers and Hammerstein was brought to the stage by Harold Fielding in 1958 with Tommy Steele starred as Buttons.

On the Continental stage, in the shadow of Rossini and Massenet, operettic-cum-féerie versions of the tale were composed in France by Victor Chéri (*Cendrillon, ou la pantoufle merveilleuse*, Clairville, Blum, Monnier Théâtre du Châtelet 4 June 1866), de Groot and others, and in Italy by Ottorino Piccini (December 1922 Empoli) whilst Victor Roger and Gaston Serpette supplied the score for a *Cendrillonette*, written by Paul Ferrier and produced at the Bouffes-Parisiens on 24 January 1890. Another *Cendrillonette* appeared in Paris on 20 December 1913. Several famous names tackled the subject in Austria: amongst a rash of *Aschenbrödl*s (Fred Langer, Leo Blech etc), the burlesque *Die Maxen sind Pfutsch, oder Das Aschenbrödel* was written by Johann Nestroy with music Adolf Müller, whilst Johann Strauss's *Aschenbrödl* ballet preceded by several years another written by Sidney Jones for London.

In Hungary two highly ranked composers in Ákos Buttykay and Ede Poldini produced versions of *Hamupipőke*, whilst a spectacular by Leo Vécsey and Gyula Selley gave the heroine an 'aranycipő' or a golden slipper, rather than the usual glass one. Amongst the many other central European variants and versions of the tale, from the most traditional to the modernized, Czechoslovakia added another up-to-date Cinderella with Lubomir Veteka and Frantiček Aacharnik's *Aschenbrödl Cindy* (Janáček Theater, Brno 12 October 1979).

America, which had welcomed Byron's burlesque, also followed up with several burlesques, extravaganzas and musical shows on the Cinderella theme or with her decorating their titles, including Woolson Morse's burlesque *Cinderella at School* (1881), Alfred Thompson and Harry B Smith's *The Crystal Slipper* (Chicago 26 November 1887), the 1904 Boston piece *Cinderella and the Prince* (R A Barnet/Louis F Gottschalk), Chicago's 1908 *A Stubborn Cinderella* which wasn't actually about the lady at all, and, most substantially, the 1912 Victor Herbert musical *The Lady of the Slipper*, mounted on Broadway with Elsie Janis as its Cinderella and Montgomery and Stone as its comedy. There were also a revusical *Cinderella on Broadway*, a jazz-age *Cinders* (Dresden Theatre, 3 April 1923) and a modernish *If the Shoe Fits* (Century Theatre, 5 December 1946).

Apart from the long list of children's pieces which have descended from the tale of Cinderella, there have also been a rash of musical plays which have used the story as their source. The 1904 hit *The Catch of the Season*, the 1929 *Mr Cinders*, which reversed the sexes of the tale, and the 1965 *Charlie Girl*, all produced in Britain, were all long-running hits, whilst America went through a whole period of 'Cinderella' heroines in the 1910s and 1920s, musical comedy heroines whose rise from poverty to Princes (or at least rich commoners) mostly had little enough in common with the rest of Perrault's smut-nosed heroine's activities. So popular did these tales become that the period 1921 to 1924, following the hits of *Sally, Irene*, and *Mary*, became known as 'the Cinderella era' on Broadway.

Of the genuine *Cinderellas*, it is Rossini's opera (without fairy godmother) which has survived to the present day, rather than any of her lighter sisters, but Jonas's *Cinderella the Younger* (also without fairy godmother), which had a fine career in its time, remains probably the most solidly amusing and attractive of the non-pantomime pieces.

CINDERELLA THE YOUNGER Opéra-burlesque (musical extravaganza) in 3 acts by Alfred Thompson. Music by Émile Jonas. Gaiety Theatre, London, 23 September 1871.

One of the first British musical plays of the modern era, *Cinderella the Younger* was the follow-up to the Gaiety Theatre's first successful burlesque operetta, *Aladdin II*, and, as on that occasion, Hollingshead entrusted the score to a proven composer of French opéra-bouffe in the person of Émile Jonas of *Le Canard à trois becs* fame. Alfred Thompson, author, director and costume designer of the previous piece, supplied a happily bouffe version of the famous tale as a libretto.

Javotte (Julia Mathews) lives in the town of Pumpernickel with her two horrible sisters Pamela (Annie Tremaine) and Bellezza (Constance Loseby), her existence made bearable only by the kindness of her godfather, the nightwatchman Peter (John Furneaux Cook) and by the visits of the royal dancing master (Mlle Clary), who has taken a fancy to her. He is, of course, not a dancing master at all, but the Grand Duke Max out in disguise, but before Javotte goes to the ball and becomes Grand Duchess of Pumpernickel there are several scenes of howling comedy, featuring two rogues called Dodgerowski (J D Stoyle) and Prigowitz (J G Taylor) to be negotiated. The pair invade the ugly sisters' boudoir dressed as hairdressers, and woo them in order to rob them, and they turn up again at the Duke's ball, this time disguised as policemen, but with larcenous intent.

Jonas's music was decidedly attractive, with the heroine's 'Take Back the Ring You Gave Me' and 'It Isn't Much Sleep That I Get', a jolly Policeman's song for John Maclean as von Tickelsbach, one of whose many posts (and he has to remember which he is in) is Chief of Police, a Brindisi for the Duke, and a gendarmes' chorus for the line of travesty chorus girls proving to be amongst the happiest musical moments.

Cinderella the Younger played only 24 performances at the Gaiety, but it was later given in Paris as *Javotte* with Dephine Ugalde as Javotte alongside Marius Audran (father of the composer), Aujac, Peters, Solon and Mlle Douan, as well as in Vienna, and in Budapest during the early 1870s. It was revived by Strampfer, in 1882, at the Carltheater (16 September) with Jenny Stubel as Javotte and Karl Drucker and Steinberger as the thieves, and again at Budapest's Várszinház in 1884 (16 December), making it the most travelled and translated of Britain's pre-*HMS Pinafore* modern musical theatre products.

France: Théâtre de l'Athénée *Javotte* 22 December 1871; Austria: Strampfertheater *Javotte, das neue Aschenbrödl* 8 November 1872; Hungary: Budai Színkör *Javotte* 23 August 1873

CINDER-ELLEN UP TOO LATE Burlesque in 3 (later 2) acts by 'A C Torr' (Fred Leslie) and W T Vincent. Music by Meyer Lutz. Princess Theatre, Melbourne, 22 August 1891; Gaiety Theatre, London, 24 December 1891.

Although *Cinder-Ellen Up Too Late* still – a century on – holds the record as the longest-running West End musical to have been first produced in Australia, the record is a rather phoney one. The show did, indeed, see the stage for the first time at Melbourne's Princess Theatre, but – apart from a small musical contribution to the score by locals J A Robertson and Bert Royle, and the fact that the sets and costumes were locally made – the show was an entirely 'away-from-home' British production.

George Edwardes's Gaiety Theatre company, complete with its biggest stars, Nellie Farren and Fred Leslie, was touring in Australia and, as the tour drew on, they began to prepare the new show which they would open at their home base for Christmas. *Cinder-Ellen*, mostly written by Leslie, featured his co-star as Cinderella (complete with the pun on her real christian name, Ellen) whilst he – to the audience's amazement – was listed simply as a 'Servant'. But he still had the largest and most comical rôle in the show.

Cinder-Ellen was not the best of the Gaiety new burlesques, but it was severely handicapped, on its London production, by being deprived of Nellie Farren, ill and effectively at the end of her career. After an indifferent opening, with Leslie paired with Katie James in replacement, the show was rearranged, remade, recast, the best of the songs (the Australian 'Bright Little Glass', borrowed from John Sheridan's *Bridget O'Brien Esq*, debutante Lionel Monckton's 'What Will You Have to Drink?', 'Teaching McFadyen to Dance') supported with some new ones and, finally and effectively, enlivened by the interpolation into the evening of the music hall's Lottie Collins, performing her adored 'Ta-ra-ra-boom-de-ay'.

It was Miss Collins who really turned the tide, and ultimately *Cinder-Ellen* took off. It ran through six months at the Gaiety, a major tour, and then a return to the Gaiety, with Letty Lind now playing Cinder-Ellen ('I'm in Love With the Man in the Moon') in a piece which had been so altered since Melbourne as to be barely recognizable. Then Fred Leslie died. Deprived of both its stars, *Cinder-Ellen* closed in ten days. The days of the 'new burlesque' were all but over.

THE CINGALEE, or Sunny Ceylon Musical play in 2 acts by James Tanner. Lyrics by Adrian Ross and Percy Greenbank. Music by Lionel Monckton. Additional dialogue, music and lyrics by Paul Rubens. Daly's Theatre, London, 5 March 1904.

By the time of the production of *The Cingalee*, George Edwardes's run of musical plays at the Daly's Theatre was nigh on a decade old. It had produced such classics of the musical theatre as *The Geisha* and *San Toy* in a run of unbroken success, even when the producer had switched to a combination of writers – Monckton and Tanner – which more resembled his 'Gaiety team' than the Jones–Hall combination of the theatre's greatest days. After the new pair had triumphed with *A Country Girl*, they followed up with *The Cingalee*.

It was not in the same class. Its plot was very *Florodora-cum-Nautch Girl* with its little Sinhalese tea-picker, Nanoya (Sybil Arundale), in love with her boss, Harry Vereker (Hayden Coffin), who is not really her boss because she is, in deeply hidden reality, the legal owner of the plantation. Nanoya has gone into hiding, to avoid consummating a marriage contracted in childhood with the potentate Boobhamba (Rutland Barrington). The crooked lawyer Chambuddy Ram (Huntley Wright) is ordered to find her, and also to recover a famous black pearl which has been stolen, and which turns up in the possession of comedienne Peggy Sabine (Gracie Leigh). After a few quiproquos, all comes right when Boobhamba decides he'd rather wed someone else.

The Cingalee was rather like a pale remake of the earlier Daly's hits, with Coffin yet again a high-collared hero, Wright as yet another wily Easterner, Barrington yet another Pasha, and a score which was not in any way up to those for *The Geisha* or *Florodora*. There were romantic pieces ('Pearl of Sweet Ceylon', 'Sloe Eyes', 'My Cinnamon Tree') for Coffin, Miss Arundale and for Isabel Jay as Lady Patricia Vane, and comical ones for Wright and Miss Leigh ('The Wonderful English Pot', 'Monkeys', 'Gollywogs'), mostly written by Paul Rubens. There were also £14,000 worth of production values, many picturesque dances and, before long, plenty of alterations including the heavy write-up of a best-friend rôle to allow W Louis Bradfield to add some extra attractions to the show.

Oddly enough, it didn't seem to need it. *The Cingalee* ran for 365 performances at Daly's before going out to a considerable life on the road, but some of the profits went west when one of those unproduced authors who seemed to cling to Edwardes's heels claimed that the libretto had been plagiarized from his unseen masterwork and, in one of the British courts' more ludicrous decisions, won £2000 damages from a judge with no understanding of things theatrical. More than half a century later *The Cingalee* improbably resurfaced in London when Harold Fielding produced a potted version of the show as part of the entertainment at his Fielding's Music Hall.

John C Duff took the show to America and produced it with Melville Stewart (Harry), Genevieve Finlay (Nanoya), Hallen Mostyn (Boobhamba), William Norris (Ram) and complete lack of success (33 performances), whilst J C Williamson introduced it to Australia in 1905, with Margaret Thomas (Nanoya), Alexia Bassian (Peggy), George Lauri (Ram) and Haigh Jackson (Harry). He, too, apparently found some staying power in it, for he played it in his company's repertoire as late as 1912, with Miss Arundale repeating her original rôle on the other side of the world.

USA: Daly's Theater 24 October 1904; Australia: Her Majesty's Theatre, Sydney 6 May 1905

THE CIRCUS GIRL   Musical play in 2 acts by James T Tanner and 'Walter Palings' (Walter Pallant). Lyrics by Harry Greenbank and Adrian Ross. Music by Ivan Caryll. Additional music by Lionel Monckton. Gaiety Theatre, London, 5 December 1896.

One of the most thoroughly popular of the Gaiety Theatre series of musical comedies, both at home and abroad, *The Circus Girl* was conceived after George Edwardes had seen a Viennese production of the hugely successful Julius Freund/Wilhelm Mannstädt Posse *Eine tolle Nacht*, and been taken with a scene in which the action took place in a circus ring, viewed from backstage. He bought the rights to the piece, then had his house author, James T Tanner, write a musical around that one situation. Walter Pallant, chairman of the Gaiety Theatre's board of directors, also contributed sufficiently to get a co-author's credit.

The good old plot (if that was not too much of a name for it) placed a bunch of English folk in Paris, mixed them up with the personnel of a touring circus company, and let the obvious happen. Ellaline Terriss was Dora Wemys, the intended wife of the Hon Reginald Gower (Lionel Mackinder), but deeply taken with Dick Capel (Seymour Hicks) who she thinks is a circus artist. Reggie, in his turn, is (at least initially) keen on the Circus Girl, La Favorita (Ethel Haydon). Harry Monkhouse was Sir Titus, Dora's papa, on the loose in naughty Paris and eventually shot out of the circus cannon, Maurice Farkoa was a philandering Frenchman, Arthur Williams played the circus ringmaster, Drivelli, and Connie Ediss his plumply jealous wife, whilst little Teddy Payne was the bartender, Biggs, who has to fight the circus strongman, Toothick Pasha (Arthur Hope), to win his Lucille (Katie Seymour). Tanner took his characters through the streets of Paris, via the circus ring, to a police comissariat and finally, with all the pairs paired up as intended, to an Artists' Ball.

The songs of the show were in the already established Gaiety mould. Ellaline Terriss scored the hit of the night with the plain little ditty called 'A Simple Little String', Connie Ediss, left astray at the costume ball, snorted furiously that it wasn't 'The Way to Treat a Lady' with many a topical reference, Payne and Seymour went through two of their comical dance-and-song duos ('Professions', 'Clowns') with pantomime, impersonations and eccentricities, whilst Hicks and Miss Terriss also had a routine called 'In the Ring' into which they were able to squeeze a display of the variety of their talents. Farkoa did his matinée idol bit, singing of 'Wine, Women and Song' with a toss of his blonded forelock, and Payne described his barman's calling and the therapeutic values of various drinks.

The Circus Girl was a great hit at the Gaiety. It ran for 497 performances in London before going out for an extended touring life in the British provinces and to productions in almost every outpost of Empire.

Augustin Daly took up the show for Broadway, and produced it at his own theatre with a cast which featured Virginia Earle (Dora), Herbert Gresham (Titus), former opéra-bouffe star Catherine Lewis as Mme Drivelli and James T Powers as Biggs, alongside a supporting cast made up from members of his much admired repertory company. Once again a fine success, it ran through 172 performances, with a summer break in the middle, and returned the following season for another 40 nights.

Budapest saw the show in 1901 when it was produced at the Népszinház (ad Jenő Faragó, Béla J Fái) for 26 performances, Vienna shortly after, when Gabor Steiner introduced it at his Danzers Orpheum (ad Leopold Krenn, Carl Lindau) with Karl Tuschl as Bix of the Café Régence, Frln Grabitz as Dora, the young Frln Massari (sic) in the rôle of La Favorita, and an Artists' Ball full of 'Ballet-Evolutionen'. It played 50 performances before Steiner took it across for a handful of performances in a summer guest season at the Theater an der Wien.

Australia's version of the show, mounted by J C Williamson, included George Lauri (Biggs), Carrie Moore (Dora), Florence Young (La Favorita) and Harold Thorley (Dick) in its cast through a good series of performances in repertoire.

USA: Daly's Theater 23 April 1897; Hungary: Népszinház *Czirkusz-élet* 20 March 1901; Austria: Danzers Orpheum *Das Cirkusmädel* 31 January 1902; Australia: Her Majesty's Theatre, Melbourne 19 July 1902

CITY OF ANGELS   Musical in 2 acts by Larry Gelbart. Lyrics by David Zippel. Music by Cy Coleman. Virginia Theater, New York, 11 December 1989.

Author Stine (Gregg Edelman) has been hired by Hollywood to turn his detective novel, *City of Angels*, with its mumblingly macho private-eye hero, Stone (James Naughton), into a screenplay. The scenes of the screenplay, shown on the stage in black and white, are interspersed with scenes (in colour) showing Stine's comical struggle to keep together what he regards as the 'integrity' of his work, in face of the cuts and changes made by commercially-(if at all)-minded producer-director, Buddy Fidler (Rene Auberjonois) and, equally unsuccessfully, to keep his pants on during the absence of his wife (Kay McClelland). Randy Graff played Donna, Buddy's secretary, who messes up his happy home by helping him get them off, and also played the rôle of Ollie, secretary to Stone, in the film tale.

That tale put Stone into a complex and murderous high-society mystery which involved the glamorous and (so it eventuates) dangerous Alaura Kingsley (Dee Hoty), her iron-lungbound, mega-millionaire husband (Keith Perry), nymphet step-daughter Mallory (Rachel York) and stepson, Peter (Doug Tompos), in an airport-paperback saga of bullets and bedrooms. Fidler ensures that any attempts to water the sex'n'violence of the script down with such dreary nonsense as social significance, as represented by the character of a racist Hispanic cop (Shawn Elliott), are quickly bundled out, and that the character with whom he identifies (also played by Auberjonois) is given an improved fate. In the end, both Stone and Stine rebel when the screenplay becomes an unrecognizable mess, and when a posy popular vocalist is cast to play the detective in the film.

If Coleman's score did not bring out any numbers in the hit-parade-extractable vein of his early shows, it nevertheless included plenty of enjoyable moments which made their point in context. Stine and Stone assured each other liltingly that 'I'm Nothing Without You', Donna did herself down craftily as a bad-luck-with-men girl in 'You Can Always Count on Me', the irritating Fidler gave his credo in 'The Buddy System' and Alaura and Stone swapped Hollywood come-on clichés in 'The Tennis Song'. Miss McClelland expended one of the most beautiful voices heard on Broadway in many seasons on the rueful, wifely 'It Needs Work' and, in her alter ego as Stone's fallen and temporarily lost love in the movie scenes, the cabaret song 'With Every Breath I Take'.

City of Angels bucked the once upon a time normal out-of-town tryout system, saving its cartel of producers (Nick Vanoff, Roger Berlind, Jujamcyn Theaters, Suntory International Corp, Shubert Organisation) something like a million dollars in production expenses by opening almost cold on Broadway, having run itself in only in a series of previews at the Virginia Theater. The risk proved, in the event, not to be one, and the show was frozen at an early date prior to opening to fine reviews and a solid success.

The show, with its wittily written, niftily constructed

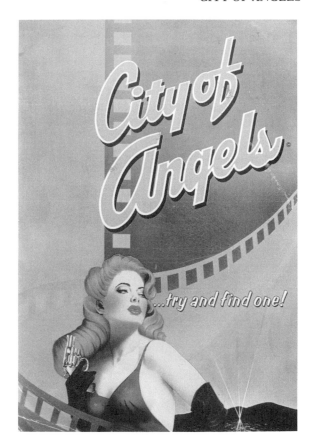

Plate 54.

book, studded with swarms of pithy one-liners and dazzlingly, but unobtrusively, directed by Australian director Michael Blakemore, showed that – in spite of much recent evidence to the contrary – intelligent life still existed in the world of the musical comedy libretto. Coming at the end of the most unproductive Broadway decade for a century, it was doubly welcome. Those virtues were recognized by Tony Awards for best musical, book and score as well as for McNaughton and Miss Graff. However, the show's very intelligence and its demands on audiences – who needed to pay attention to the show's lines and sometimes even its lyrics at peril of getting confused in the switches between reality and filmland – meant that, like other, earlier shows which shared its qualities, it found strong favour amongst practised playgoers, but rather less amongst that part of the public to whom the word 'musical' was simply synonymous with revusical glitz.

Edelmann was succeeded by Michael Rupert and McNaughton by Tom Wopat as Broadway's production ran on for two years and 878 performances, whilst a touring company, headed by Barry Williams, took the show to other areas of the country. Following the New York closure, *City of Angels* was introduced to London with Roger Allam (Stone), Martin Smith (Stine), Susannah Fellowes (Alaura) and Haydn Gwynne (Donna) featured. It found itself on the end of some of the best reviews won by a new musical in very many years.

However, the wider popularity won by 'easier' shows – whether more romantic or spectacular or cabarettish – has so far been denied it and, at the time of writing, *City of Angels* has not been seen further afield.

UK: Prince of Wales Theatre 30 March 1993
Recordings: original cast (Columbia), London cast (First Night)

CLAIRE, Ina [FAGAN, Inez] (b Washington, DC, 15 October 1892; d San Francisco, 21 February 1985).

Ultimately best known as a light comedienne of considerable style, Ina Claire began her career as an impersonator in vaudeville before appearing in leading ingénue rôles in several musicals, prior to the First World War. Her first such part was alongside comedian Richard Carle in his own *Jumping Jupiter* (1911, Molly) and she followed this, later in the same year, with the title-rôle, created in London by Gertie Millar, in the American production of Lionel Monckton's *The Quaker Girl*, playing opposite Clifton Crawford at Broadway's Park Theater for an extended run.

In 1913 she joined Al Jolson and Gaby Deslys in the cast of *Honeymoon Express* in replacement for Fannie Brice (Marcelle), before travelling to London to create the title-rôle in Sidney Jones's *The Girl from Utah* (Una Trance), under the management of George Edwardes at the Adelphi Theatre. She appeared at the same venue in the ingénue rôle of Sam Bernard's imported production of *The Belle of Bond Street* before returning to America and another short-lived musical, the variety-based *Lady Luxury* (1914) at the Casino Theater.

Thereafter she appeared in vaudeville, in two editions of the *Ziegfeld Follies*, and increasingly in straight theatre and, from 1915, in films, where she repeated such of her stage successes as *Polly with a Past* and *The Awful Truth*, without returning to the musical theatre.

CLAIRVILLE [NICOLAIE, Louis François] (b Lyon, 28 January 1811; d Paris, 7 February 1879).

The celebrated vaudevilliste known simply as Clairville was born into a family of actors and himself took to the stage at the age of ten. He continued to perform for a number of years, and later to direct as well, but, beginning by turning his hand to the writing of additional lyrics and bits of dialogue 'as required' as a sideline, he soon found his real niche, as an author. He is said to have been the writer of some 400 (some reports say 600) theatrical pieces: opérettes and musical comedies, comedies, sketches, revues, dramas and, above all, a long series of fairy spectaculars – the French equivalents of the British Victorian pantomime – with their good and bad sprites, their princes and princesses, and their trips through all the delights of the scenic artists', the machinists' and the dance-master's repertoires. Shows such as *Rothomago* (w Adolphe d'Ennery, A Monnier), *Les Sept Châteaux du Diable* (w d'Ennery), *Les Voyages de Gulliver* (w Monnier, Ernest Blum), *La Belle au bois dormant* (w William Busnach), *Les Bibelots du Diable* (w Cogniard brothers), *Le Puits qui chante* (w Eugène Grangé), *La Poule aux oeufs d'or* (w d'Ennery), *Cendrillon* (w Monnier, Ernest Blum), *Peau d'âne* (w Émile Vanderburch, 'Laurencin'), *La Queue de chat* and *La Patte à Coco* (both w Gaston Marot), *Les Contes de ma mère l'oye* (w Jules Cordier), *Pif-Paf* (w Monréal, Blondeau), and Thérésa's vehicles *La Cocotte aux oeufs d'or* and *La Reine Carotte*, the fore-runners or bastard-cousins of the grands

opéras-bouffes féeries, were – give or take a pasticcio score – all but musicals, and some of Clairville's later spectaculars, such as *Peau d'âne*, with its full score of original music, virtually crept over the difficult line between the genres.

A number of the Clairville féeries were taken up by overseas producers. *Rothomago*, illustrated with an original score, became a success as a grand opéra-bouffe féerie at London's vast Alhambra Theatre, where a pasticcio version of *La Poule aux oeufs d'or* also got a showing, whilst *Peau d'âne*, Germanized as *Die Eselshaut*, turned up as a musical spectacular in Austria, credited to Therese Megerle and composer Adolf Müller, and *Die Tochter der Teufels*, a 'grand phantastische Zauberposse mit Gesang und Tanze' adapted by Emmerich von Bukovics, and with music credited to Lecocq and Karl Alexander Raida, was played at Berlin's Viktoria Theater. Like many other such productions throughout central Europe, it did not credit the original French authors.

Clairville's earliest ventures into genuine opérette and opéra-comique included the libretto to Hervé's first full-length work, the revusical *Les Folies dramatiques* (1853), the text for Adolphe Adam's *Le Muletier de Tolède*, later re-used with slightly more success by Michael Balfe as the book of his *The Rose of Castille* (1857), and that for Offenbach's little *Daphnis et Chloë*, but he moved thoroughly into the contemporary musical theatre when he co-authored the text for Lecocq's *Les Cent Vierges* with the young team of Chivot and Duru.

In the years that followed, his name was attached as co-author (although, in each case, it was apparently he who did the actual writing of both book and lyrics) to the two greatest international hits of the musical theatre of the era: *La Fille de Madame Angot* and *Les Cloches de Corneville*. There were other fine, and notably finely written, successes too – Lacôme's *Jeanne, Jeannette et Jeanneton*, Litolff's *Heloïse et Abélard* – and Clairville was still at the peak of his powers when he died at the age of 68, leaving behind him a bundle of work which kept the Paris theatre in Clairville premières for several further years. His outline for *Le Chevalier Mignon*, unwritten at his death, and written up by his nephew, Charles, and set by Leopold Wenzel, was an uncharacteristic full-scale flop, but it was 14 years after his death that the last 'new' Clairville musical made its début with Varney's setting of *Cliquette* (1893).

A number of his pieces, again often uncredited, later served as the bases for musical plays by others. *Coco*, a 'grand vaudeville in 5 acts' (w Eugène Grangé, Alfred Delacour, Théâtre des Nouveautés June 1878) played at the Budapest Népszinház with its original music by Coedès and others in May 1879, at the Vienna Carltheater (22 March 1879) with music by Brandl attached, and in Ghent in an adaptation by one Wytink (*Koko*) with music by Franz Herzeele in 1885 (November) was one of the most successful, but the earliest seems to have been whatever served as the basis for the one-act operette *Die kleinen Leiden des menschlichen Lebens* ('nach Clairville') produced at Vienna's Hoftheater as early as 1846. In London, his libretto to de Billemont's *Le Grand Duc de Matapa* (w Octave Gastineau) served as the bases for Lydia Thompson's 1876 extravaganza *Piff-Paff, or The Magic Armoury* (Criterion Theatre 31 January) a piece which, in its turn, was readapted as the comic opera *Glamour* by William Hutchison (1886).

Clairville's son, Édouard, billed as Clairville fils, composed the scores to several small opérettes, some with texts by his father.

1848 **La Tireuse de cartes** (pasticcio/w 'Jules Cordier') Théâtre des Variétés 9 January

1849 **Le Moulin joli** (Alphonse Varney) 1 act Théâtre de la Gaîté 18 September

1852 **Les Néréïdes et les cyclopes** (pasticcio/w Lambert Thibout) Théâtre du Vaudeville 26 June

1853 **Les Folies dramatiques** (Hervé/ w Philippe Dumanoir) Tuileries 1 March, Palais-Royal 2 March

1853 **Les Trois Gamins** (pasticcio/w Louis Vanderburch) Théâtre des Variétés 22 November

1854 **Les Étoiles** (Auguste Pilati) Théâtre Lyrique 6 February

1854 **Le Muletier de Tolède** (Adolphe Adam/w Adolphe d'Ennery) Théâtre Lyrique 16 December

1858 **La Chaise à porteurs** (Victor Massé/w Dumanoir) 1 act Opéra-Comique 28 April

1858 **L'Agneau de Chloë** (Édouard Montaubry) 1 act Théâtre Lyrique 9 June

1860 **La Belle Nini** (Hervé/w Dumanoir) Palais-Royal 28 January

1860 **Daphnis et Chloë** (Jacques Offenbach/w 'Cordier') 1 act Théâtre des Bouffes-Parisiens 27 March

1860 **La Fille du Diable** (Julien Nargéot/w Paul Siraudin, Thibout) Théâtre des Variétés 9 June

1861 **Panne-aux-airs** (Frédéric Barbier) Théâtre Déjazet 30 March

1861 **Ya-Mein-Herr** (comp and arr Victor Chéri/w Alfred Delacour, Thibout) Théâtre des Variétés 6 April

1861 **Les Danses nationales de la France** (Chéri/w Delacour, Thibout) Théâtre des Variétés 19 August

1864 **La Liberté des théâtres** (Hervé) Théâtre des Variétés 10 August

1864 **La Revue pour rire/Roland à Rongeveaux** (Hervé/w Siraudin, Ernest Blum) 1 act Théâtre des Bouffes-Parisiens 27 December

1865 **Les Chevrons de Jeanne** (L Giunti-Bellini) 1 act Folies-Marigny 2 October

1868 **Roger Bontemps** (Jean-Jacques de Billemont/w Bernard Lopez) Théâtre des Fantaisies-Parisiennes, Brussels 18 March

1868 **Le Grand Duc de Matapa** (de Billemont/w Octave Gastineau) Théâtre des Menus-Plaisirs 16 November

1870 **Deucalion et Pyrrhe** (Eugène Diache/w Adolphe Guénée) 1 act Théâtre des Variétés 26 March

1872 **Les Coulisses de la scène** (Félix Parent, J-E Cohen/ Victor Koning, Victor Bernard) Théâtre des Menus-Plaisirs 13 January

1872 **L'Égyptienne réaliste** (Chéri/w Blum) 1 act Cafe Tertulia 20 January

1872 **Les Cent Vierges** (Charles Lecocq/w Henri Chivot, Alfred Duru) Théâtre des Fantaisies-Parisiennes, Brussels 16 March

1872 **Les Griffes du diable** (Auguste Coèdes/w Charles Gabet) Théâtre des Menus-Plaisirs 18 April

1872 **Heloïse et Abélard** (Henri Litolff/w William Busnach) Théâtre des Folies-Dramatiques 19 October

1872 **La Fille de Madame Angot** (Lecocq/w Koning, Siraudin) Théâtre des Fantaisies-Parisennes, Brussels 4 December; Théâtre des Folies-Dramatiques, Paris 21 February 1873

1872 **La Cocotte aux oeufs d'or** (Coèdes/w Grangé, Koning) Théâtre des Ménus Plaisirs 31 December

1874 **La Resurrection de la Mère Angot** (Lecocq) 1 act Théâtre des Folies-Dramatique 24 February

1874 **Le Treizième Coup de minuit** (de Billemont/w Gaston Marot) Théâtre du Château d'Eau 1 September

1874 **La Belle au bois dormant** (Litolff/w Busnach) Théâtre du Châtelet 4 April

1874 **Charbonnier est maître chez lui** (Édouard Clairville fils/w Busnach) 1 act Théâtre du Château d'Eau 29 November

1875 **Madame la Baronne** (Clairville fils) 1 act Théâtre du Tivoli 31 July

1876 **Jeanne, Jeannette et Jeanneton** (Paul Lacôme/w Delacour) Théâtre des Folies-Dramatiques 27 October

1877 **Les Cloches de Corneville** (Robert Planquette/w Gabet) Théâtre des Folies-Dramatiques 19 April

1878 **Babiole** (Laurent de Rillé/w Gastineau) Théâtre des Bouffes-Parisiens 16 January

1878 **Le Troisième Mari** 1 act (Clairville fils) Théâtre des Folies-Dramatiques 10 April

1878 **Le Cabaret du pot cassé** (Pauline Thys/w Thiboust) Fantaisies-Parisiennes, Brussels October

1879 **Panurge** (Hervé/w Gastineau) Théâtre des Bouffes-Parisiens 10 September

1879 **L'Education mutuelle** (Clairville fils) 1 act Théâtre des Bouffes-Parisiens 13 September

1879 **Pâques fleuries** (Lacôme/w Delacour) Théâtre des Folies-Dramatiques 21 October

1880 **La Princesse Marmotte** (de Rillé/w Busnach, Gastineau) Galeries St Hubert, Brussels 18 January

1881 **Les Deux Roses** (Hervé/w Bernard, Grangé) Théâtre des Folies-Dramatiques 20 October

1882 **La Petite Reinette** (Varney/w Busnach) Galeries St Hubert, Brussels 11 October

1893 **Cliquette** (Varney/w Busnach) Théâtre des Folies-Dramatiques 11 July

CLAIRVILLE, Charles [Victor Nicolaï] (b Paris, 27 November 1855; d Paris, 1918).

A nephew of the famous Clairville, Charles worked for much of his life as a civil servant whilst also operating as a journalist on the side and, simultaneously, authoring a large number of mostly very lightweight comedies, libretti, féeries, revues and monologues for the Paris stage. His very first full-scale opérette, *Madame Boniface*, remained his most substantial and successful, but a number of his other opérettes and vaudeville-opérettes were played beyond France after hometown successes – *Le Fétiche* (*A babona* in Hungary), *Le Brillant Achille* (*Die eiserne Jungfrau* in Austria and Germany), *Patart, Patart et Cie* (*Kneisl & Co* in Vienna), *Le Capitole* (*Az erenyes Metella* in Hungary, *Metella* in Germany), *Ninette* – without his managing to find a really first-class musical theatre hit.

1880 **Pierrot jaloux** (Lucien Roulland) 1 act Deauville 1 August

1883 **Madame Boniface** (Paul Lacôme/w Ernest Depré) Théâtre des Bouffes-Parisiens 20 October

1884 **Le Chevalier Mignon** (Leopold Wenzel/from Clairville w Depré) Théâtre des Bouffes-Parisiens 23 October

1885 **Le Baron Frick** (various/w Depré) Cercle Artistique et Littéraire December

1888 **Le Valet de coeur** (Raoul Pugno/w Paul Ferrier) Théâtre des Bouffes-Parisiens 19 April

1889 **Riquet à la houppe** (Louis Varney/w Ferrier) Théâtre des Folies-Dramatiques 20 April

1890 **Le Fétiche** (Victor Roger/w Ferrier) Théâtre des Menus-Plaisirs 13 March

1891 **La Famille Vénus** (Léon Vasseur/w R Bénédite, Depré) Théâtre de la Renaissance 2 May

1891 **Mademoiselle Asmodée** (Paul Lacôme, Roger/w Ferrier) Théâtre de la Renaissance 23 November

1892 **Le Brillant Achille** (Varney/w Fernand Beissier) Théâtre de la Renaissance 21 October

1892 **Nini Fauvette** (Edmond Missa/w André Sylvane) Théâtre des Nouveautés 16 January

1893 **Patart, Patart et Cie** (Louis Gregh/w Sylvane) Théâtre des Folies-Dramatiques 9 October

1893 **Mon Prince!** (Edmond Audran/w Sylvane) Théâtre des Nouveautés 18 November

1893 **Miss Dollar** (André Messager/w Albert Vallin) Nouveau Théâtre 22 December

1895 **Chiquita** (Gaston Serpette) 1 act Théâtre des Nouveautés 4 February

1895 **Le Capitole** (Serpette/w Ferrier) Théâtre des Nouveautés 5 December

1896 **Ninette** (Lecocq/w Charles Hubert, Christian de Trogoff) Théâtre des Bouffes-Parisiens 28 February

1898 **La Dame de trèfle** (Emile Pessard/w Maurice Froyez) Théâtre des Bouffes-Parisiens 13 May

1898 **Gueule d'or** (Charles Raiter/w Benjamin Lebreton) Bobino 12 August

1898 **La Geisha** French version w Jacques Lemaire, Antony Mars (Théâtre de l'Athénée)

1899 **Une excellente affaire** (Vasseur, de Thuisy/w Henri Bocage, C Worms) Théâtre des Folies-Dramatiques 18 February

1902 **Le Minotaure** (Paul Marcelles/w Adrien Vély) Galeries Saint-Hubert, Brussels November

1903 **Le Sire de Montgicourd** (Porinelly/w d'Arbois, Mirabaud)

1904 **Voluptata** (Marcelles/w P-L Flers) Moulin Rouge 20 January

1904 **La Môme Phémie** (Le Barré) 1 act La Cigale 31 May

1904 **Frou-frous et culottes rouges** (w Paul Blouet)

1906 **Descends, donc, de ton cadre** (Marcelles/w Gaston Guérin) 1 act Boîte à Fursy 1 March

1906 **Le Rat** (Raidich/w William Busnach) 1 act Théâtre Grévin 14 January

1907 **Eglé, ou L'enfant de la vache** (Claude Terrasse/w Emile Moreau, Depré) Moulin Rouge 7 May

1914 **Mam'zelle Caprice** (Albert Chantrier) Nouvelle Cirque 20 March

CLARK, Bobby [CLARK, Robert Edwin] (b Springfield, Ohio, 16 June 1888; d New York, 12 February 1960). A low comedian of the old school, smart-assed but likeable, 'baggy top-coat, cigar smoked both ends, recklessly swinging his fat stick' and sporting a pair of spectacles drawn onto his face, Bobby Clark was considered by many to be quite simply the funniest man on Broadway, through 30 years of musicals and revues.

The young Clark established a partnership with fellow comedian Paul McCullough (1883–1936) in 1905, and together they built a successful career in minstrelsy, vaudeville and ultimately in revue and the musical theatre. They appeared in London in the revue *Chuckles of 1922* and on Broadway in two editions of the *Music Box Revue* before going into their first book musical, Lyle Andrews's production of a musical, based on an Edward Laska play, which went from being called *We've Got to Have Money* to *The Fly-by-Nights* to *The Ramblers*. When it got to town, with Clark starred as a spiritualistic medium, Professor Cunningham, alongside the servant, Sparrow, of McCullough, it proved a jolly Broadway success. It played for 290 performances, a run for which the two comedians took a large share of the credit. In between variety and film engagements, they subsequently appeared together in *Strike Up the Band*, *Here Goes the Bride*, *Walk a Little Faster* and *Thumbs Up* before McCullough's suicide in 1936.

Clark then continued his career alone, playing in the *Ziegfeld Follies of 1936*, *The Streets of Paris*, and the revusical *Star and Garter*, appearing top-billed as the happily crooked Joe Bascom of *Mexican Hayride*, as the star of a revival of *Sweethearts* (1947), as Waldo Wellington, husband to America's first woman President, in *As the Girls Go* (1948) on Broadway and, in Los Angeles, alongside Mitzi Gaynor in *Jollyanna* (1952), a rewrite of the Broadway failure *Flahooley*.

He later turned his hand to directing, but continued to perform away from Broadway and, in 1956, toured as Applegate in *Damn Yankees* in his final appearance on the musical stage.

CLARY, Mlle

One Mlle Clary (née Poirel-Tardieu) went to Britain as a member of Humbert's Théâtre des Fantaisies-Parisiennes company which played at the Gaiety Theatre in 1871 (Hélène in *La Belle Hélène* etc) and stayed on, pleading in court, when Humbert tried to force her to return to continue her contract in Belgium, that she suffered too heavily from sea-sickness to make the crossing. Her court performance must have been convincing, for she remained in Britain where she created the rôles of the Grand Duke in Jonas's *Cinderella the Younger* (1871) and Sparkeion in Sullivan and Gilbert's *Thespis*, and played Naphtha in a revival of Hervé's *Aladdin II*, all at the Gaiety, as well playing as Alexandrivoire in London's *L'Oeil crevé* (1872), Mephisto in *Le Petit Faust* at Holborn, and in the Offenbach pasticcio *The Bohemians* (1873) at the Opera-Comique. She then vanished from theatrical annals.

In 1879 another Mlle Clary, this one admitting to the prénom of Élise, wholly untrained and 17 years of age, was taken on by Louis Cantin and given the starring ingénue rôle of Audran's *Les Noces d'Olivette*. She scored a considerable personal success in that considerable success, and she subsequently created two further important rôles in Parisian opérettes: the soubrette part of Louise in *Les Mousquetaires au couvent* ('Mon Père, je m'accuse') and the bright little gardener girl, Joséfa, in Lecocq's *Le Coeur et la main*. Then she, too, disappeared.

There was even a third and later Mlle Clary on the Paris stage, but she achieved nothing to rate with her homonyms before she vanished from view.

CLAY, Frederic (b Paris, 3 August 1839; d Marlow, Bucks, 24 November 1889). The first significant composer of the modern era of British musical theatre.

The son of James Taylor, MP for Hull over a period of nearly 20 years but more celebrated for his skill as a whist player, young Clay studied music in Leipzig but began his working life as a civil servant, in the Treasury Department. He subsequently became secretary to a series of cabinet ministers and was employed on several occasions to carry out confidential missions on behalf of Mr Gladstone himself.

His first efforts to compose for the stage (*Out of Sight*, *The Pirates' Home*, both w B C Stephenson) were performed by amateurs, but he moved into the professional field when he composed the incidental music for Tom Taylor's play *Court and Cottage* (Covent Garden Theatre, 1862). An inheritance of £6,000 allowed him to give up his secretarial duties and to devote himself full-time to a musical career, the first fruits of which were three short operettas written to texts by three highly successful librettists, the celebrated modern playwright Tom Robertson, Charlie Stephenson and W S Gilbert.

The last of these, *Ages Ago*, made an enormous success at the German Reeds' Gallery of Illustration, and Clay subsequently wrote three further works with Gilbert, another one-acter for the Reeds and Gilbert's first two full-length comic operas, *The Gentleman in Black* (the first genuine British musical play of the modern era) and *Princess Toto*, each of which found a certain success if not a long West End run.

Clay was well-enough established, by 1872, as Britain's foremost light theatre composer, to be teamed with the Continental musicians Hervé, Rivière, de Billemont and Jacobi on the scores for the year's two grands opéras-bouffes féeries, *Babil and Bijou* (River of Life March, 'Wanda, Pure Spirit of the Waters') and *The Black Crook*. He more than held his musical own, and his 'Nobody Knows as I Know', as sung by Kate Santley, was the song hit of the second show.

Miss Santley then commissioned Clay to write an opéra-bouffe for her, and the resultant *Cattarina* was successfully toured (with Clay conducting) and played in London. It did not challenge the best French models of the period either in style or in stamina, but a second venture with Miss Santley proved finer fare. W S Gilbert proved a more effective librettist than Robert Reece, and *Princess Toto* was successful enough to not only be brought to London (where a disagreement between Gilbert and the producer/star seems to have cut its life short) but to be played in both America and Australia, and to be later revived.

Santley's *Black Crook* co-star and author, Harry Paulton, also called upon Clay and his music again when he wrote himself another Alhambra vehicle, *Don Quixote*, but the most successful of Clay's theatre pieces was undoubtedly a third piece for Miss Santley, his 1883 collaboration with George Sims on the racing musical *The Merry Duchess*. The fair producer starred in the piece in London for 177 performances, before it was sent on tour and played, like *Princess Toto*, in America and Australia, with a little more success than the earlier show.

A second collaboration with Sims produced a fine fairytale piece, *The Golden Ring*, for the Alhambra at the end of the year but, walking home from the theatre with his colleague one evening soon after the opening, Clay suffered a stroke. Although he gradually recovered, he was unable to write any further music and, shortly after his fiftieth birthday, he died. His brother Cecil, a barrister, husband of Rosina Vokes, and the author of the remarkably successful musical playlet *A Pantomime Rehearsal* (music: Edward Jones, Terry's Theatre 6 June 1891, Theatre Royal, Sydney 25 July 1903 etc) later used some of Frederic's trunk music as part of the score of a musical version of the Vokes Family's *In Camp* entitled *On the March* (1896).

Apart from his theatre work, which included such items as a song and incidental music for the play *Monsieur Jacques* (1876, Gaiety Theatre) and for the 1881 production of Pinero's *The Squire*, Clay also composed a number of successful single songs including 'The Sands of Dee' (to Charles Kingsley's poem), 'She Wandered Down the Mountainside', ''Tis Better Not to Know' and, particularly, 'I'll Sing Thee Songs of Araby', written as part of a cantata, *Lallah Rookh*, performed at the Brighton Festival

in 1877. Another cantata *Sardanapalus* was produced at the Leeds Festival of 1882.

Until the advent of Arthur Sullivan, whom he is said to have introduced to Gilbert at the Gallery of Illustration, Clay held pride of place amongst British theatre composers but, like all his contemporaries bar Sullivan, nothing of his work has survived into the modern repertoire.

1865 **Constance** (Tom Robertson) 1 act Royal English Opera, Covent Garden 23 January
1868 **The Bold Recruit** (B C Stephenson) 1 act Theatre Royal, Canterbury 4 August, Gallery of Illustration 19 July 1870
1869 **Ages Ago** (W S Gilbert) 1 act Gallery of Illustration 22 November
1870 **The Gentleman in Black** (Gilbert) Charing Cross Theatre 26 May
1872 **Happy Arcadia** (Gilbert) 1 act Gallery of Illustration 28 October
1872 **Babil and Bijou** (w Hervé, Jules Rivière, Jean-Jacques de Billemont/J R Planché/Dion Boucicault) Covent Garden Theatre 29 August
1872 **Ali Baba à la Mode** (w J E Mallandaine, George Richardson, George Grossmith & pasticcio/Robert Reece) Gaiety Theatre 14 September
1872 **[The] Black Crook** (w Georges Jacobi/Harry Paulton, Joseph Paulton) Alhambra Theatre 23 December
1873 **Oriana** (James Albery) Globe Theatre 16 February
1874 **Cattarina** (Robert Reece) Prince's Theatre, Manchester 17 August, Charing Cross Theatre 15 May 1875
1876 **Don Quixote** (H Paulton, Alfred Maltby) Alhambra Theatre 25 September
1876 **Princess Toto** (Gilbert) Theatre Royal, Nottingham 26 June, Strand Theatre 2 October
1883 **The Merry Duchess** (George R Sims) Royalty Theatre 23 April
1883 **The Golden Ring** (Sims) Alhambra Theatre 3 December

CLAY, Lila [HUTTON, Lila Constance] (b Camden Town, London; d London, 28 July 1899). Musician and guiding light of the feminine musical theatre activities which appeared intermittently in Victorian London.

Miss Clay worked as a piano demonstrator at a Baker Street showroom until she got together the money and personnel to produce a Ladies' Minstrels Show, including an all-women operetta, *A Dress Rehearsal* (1879), written for her by George Sims and Louis Diehl. Thereafter she worked cheerfully in the the theatre as a pianist and, when she could gather some backers, at the head of her Lady Minstrels. She found success when she and the Minstrels – a company including such popular performers as Emily Cross (the original London Ruth in *The Pirates of Penzance*), Emma D'Auban, Alice Aynsley Cook and soprano Edith Vane – appeared at the Opera Comique, with Lila conducting a programme consisting of half a minstrel show, under the title *Something New*, and an all-women operetta – at first *On Condition*, then *An Adamless Eden* (1882). She quarrelled with her American backer, 'Colonel' R B Caverley, when he tried to get heavily commercial and laid his hands hard on the rights of the very successful *Adamless Eden*, and she ended up taking her ladies off on tour with another operetta, *Posterity* (1884), and then to America.

She had a second West End success in 1892, when she was hired to lead an on-stage ladies' orchestra in *La Cigale* at the Lyric Theatre (for which she also wrote a little music), but an attempt to bring back the Lady Minstrels in 1896 in collaboration with Caverley fizzled out expensively.

'Featherbrained always and foolish often', Sims described her, yet 'to talk with her was always an exhilarating experience', the ever-cheerful Lila drifted happily through her off-and-on musical and theatrical life until an early death.

CLAYTON, Herbert (b London, 1 December 1876; d London, 16 February 1931). Baritone-turned-producer and librettist, who pulled off one of the more unexpected coups of the 1920s by introducing *No, No, Nanette* to Britain.

In his early years a member of the Musketeers concert party, with George Ridgewell and Leslie Stiles (himself later a West End leading man of musicals), the tall, handsome Clayton joined the chorus at the Gaiety Theatre for *The Circus Girl* (1896) and then went on tour playing the small rôle of the Turk in the same show. In 1901 he had his one significant London rôle under George Edwardes's management as Carajola, the real toreador, in *The Toreador* but, after several more years of touring in Edwardes's companies (*San Toy, A Greek Slave, The Duchess of Dantzic, The Count of Luxembourg*) he returned to London to create the part of the handsomely rejected Captain Papp in Frank Curzon's production of *Miss Hook of Holland* (1907, 'Soldiers of the Netherlands'). The following year he co-starred with *Hook* star, G P Huntley, in an unsuccessful musical, *The Hon'ble Phil* (1908), which the two of them had written, and then visited America to play the character rôle of Abdallah (created at the Savoy by his old colleague Ridgewell) in Sullivan's *The Rose of Persia*. He then continued on to Australia, where he starred for J C Williamson in *King of Cadonia* (Alexis), *A Country Girl* (Challoner) and *The Dollar Princess* (Fredy).

On his return to Britain, Clayton turned to producing and/or writing and directing, at first with small-scale revues on the minor British touring circuits. He supplied text and direction for a No 3-houses piece called *Sunshine and Laughter*, produced by first time producer-cum-composer Jack Waller and, as a result, the two ventured into partnership together, at first writing musical shows produced in music halls by Tom Walls, then, from 1924 onwards, sponsoring similar pieces themselves. Intending to branch out into top-line producing, the pair ventured to America in that same year and bought up the rights to several musical comedies. Their shopping-basket included *Canary Cottage, The Kiss Burglar, So Long, Letty* and a piece then playing in Chicago called *No, No, Nanette*. Later, when other British managements began chasing the now enormously successful *Nanette*, they found that its British rights were already the property of two men who had never staged a London show. When they did stage it, as their first London venture, it launched them straight to the top of the West End world.

They followed up with further imports of plays and musicals including the highly successful *Mercenary Mary* (1925), *Hit the Deck* (1927), what passed as *The Girl Friend* (1927), *Good News* (1928), *Merry, Merry* (1929) and *Hold Everything!* (1929), as well as producing a piece of their own, *Virginia*, which, given the temperature of the times, they pretended was not their own, but an American piece until after the notices had come in. *Virginia* gave them a good run and a hit song, 'Roll Away Clouds'. The losses incurred on *Good News* and *Hold Everything!* (and the large percentages required by trans-Atlantic writers and producers) then encouraged them to renounce imports and to construct another major musical of their own. The result was *Dear Love*, a romantic piece starring opera singer Tom Burke, which won fine notices, was snapped up by the Shuberts and which closed after five months. The Shuberts' production was gradually metamorphosed into a revue in which little (if anything) of *Dear Love* remained by the time Broadway was reached.

The partners did better with a spectacular piece called *Silver Wings*, produced at the vast new Dominion Theatre, but Clayton and Waller then went their separate ways, and Clayton combined with touring manager Robert MacDonald on a revival of *The Maid of the Mountains* (1930) and the production of the Vivian Ellis musical *Little Tommy Tucker* at Daly's Theatre (1930) before his premature death in 1931.

1908 **The Hon'ble Phil** (Harold Samuel/Harold Lawson/w G P Huntley) Hicks Theatre 3 October
1923 **Our Liz** (Jack Waller, Pat Thayer/w Con West) Hippodrome, Southampton 13 August
1923 **Suzanne** (Waller, Haydn Wood/w West) Palace Theatre, Plymouth 31 December
1924 **Tilly** (Wood, Waller/Bert Lee, R P Weston/w West) Empire Theatre, Leeds 21 July
1928 **Virginia** (Waller, Joseph A Tunbridge/w Weston, Lee, Douglas Furber) Palace Theatre 24 October
1929 **Dear Love** (Waller, Tunbridge, Wood/w Lauri Wylie, Dion Titheradge) Palace Theatre 14 November

CLÉRICE, Justin (b Buenos Aires, 16 October 1863; d Toulouse, 9 September 1908). A popular French composer who turned out a stream of musical stage pieces, and who saw his works produced in several European countries without achieving any one major success.

Born of a French father, whose profession as a carriage-maker had taken him to the Argentine, the young Clérice followed his pianist sister into musical pastimes and, at 15, wrote and conducted an amateur opérette in Buenos Aires. After his father's death, his mother brought her family back to Paris where the teenaged Justin and his brother, Charles, got their first jobs in the musical world – designing music covers: Charles (later a successful designer) the drawings, Justin the letters. Playing the piano in cabaret to earn a living, he attended the Paris Conservatoire, where he studied with Pessard and Delibes, and began writing theatrical pieces. He won his first production at Lisbon, where his *O Moliero d'Alcala* had more than a little success, but, in spite of this, he found that doors were not so easy to open in Paris and he was unable to place any of his writings there until his friend, the actor Volny, persuaded producer/composer Oscar de Lagoanère to give the young composer an opportunity.

Thus, Clérice made his Paris début at the Bouffes-Parisiens as the composer of a one-act opérette, *Figarella*, followed soon after by a second, again at the Bouffes, but, in spite of placing a ballet *Au pays noir* (1891) at the Théâtre Royale in Antwerp, his theatrical career did not take off. During this period, however, he made himself a place within a section of elegant Parisian society and turned out several successful songs ('Pour elle', 'Deux sous

Plate 55. **Justin Clérice**

d'amour') in collaboration with lyricists including Maurice de Féraudy and Miguel Zamacoïs for artists such as Paulette Darty and Lyse Berty.

When he finally achieved a Paris production of a full-length work with the attractive *Le Troisième Hussards*, it was to find disappointment and a run of less than a month, and, although he did altogether better with the score for Fernand Beissier's pantomime *Léda* (1896), produced at the Concert Européen, his next substantial opportunity came in London where Henry Lowenfeld staked the profits he had made on *La Poupée* on staging a new Clérice piece, *La Petite Vénus*, written with Maurice Ordonneau and translated as *The Royal Star*. He followed this with an English version of *O Moliero d'Alcala* (*The Coquette*, 11 February 1899). The first ran three months, but the latter folded in five stormy weeks and resulted in the beer-tycoon producer bowing out of the theatre for good.

In the early years of the 20th century Clérice continued to write in all musical spheres in search of significant success: an épopée militaire called *Vercingetorix*; the ballet *Une fête à Rome* (1900) for the Hippodrome, *Paris-fêtard* for the Olympia, and the long-running spectacular dance piece, *Timbre d'or*, for the Folies-Bergère; incidental music for the Comédie-Française's production of Francis de Croisset's *Chérubin*, small opérettes, of which *Minne* was the best received, a three-act piece called *Au temps jadis* which was christened a ballet-opéra (Monte Carlo 1904), and a series of full-length stage pieces each of which achieved some measure of success without winning major acclaim or a place in the repertoire.

In spite of the fact that Clérice's works broke no records

in Paris, they were nevertheless welcomed in other countries. Hungary hosted productions of *Les Petites Vestales* (*A vesztaszüzek* Magyar Színház 11 October 1901), *Le Voyage de la mariée* (*A ferjhezment kisasszony* Magyar Színház 16 September 1905), *Ordre de l'Empereur* (*Liliom kisasszony* Király Színház 5 October 1905), and *Les Filles Jackson* (*Cserelányok* Király Színház 28 February 1906), both the last-named piece (*Die Tochter Jackson und Cie*) and *Die kleinen vestalinnen* (Munich 1902) were played in Germany whilst *Ordre de l'Empereur* was seen at Vienna's Theater an der Wien (*Auf Befehl des Kaisers* 16 April 1904).

Les Filles Jackson was Clérice's last major work played in Paris, although he contributed to revues at such venues as the Parisiana (*Les Plaques de l'Année*, *Vive la Parisienne!*, *Paris s'amuse*) and had the one-act *Oeil de gazelle*, which presented the peculiarity of including the tango in its score, staged in Monaco. His opéra-comique *Les Bohémiens*, *L'amour aux castagnettes*, and another military piece written in collaboration with the specialist of the genre, Antony Mars, were all unproduced when he died in 1908 at the age of 44, with the unusual record, for an admittedly second-string composer, of having had his works produced in Portugal, France, Britain, Belgium, Germany, Austria and Hungary.

1887 **O Moliero d'Alcala** (Eduardo Garrido, Armand Lafrique) Theatro Trinidade, Lisbon 10 April
1889 **Figarella** (Charles Grandmougin, Jules Méry) 1 act Théâtre des Bouffes-Parisiens 3 June
1889 **Monsieur Huchot** (Jacques Téresand) 1 act Théâtre des Bouffes-Parisiens 3 October
1892 **Pierrot remouleur** 1 act Hotel Continental 30 April
1894 **Le Troisième Hussards** (Antony Mars, Maurice Hennequin) Théâtre de la Gaîté 14 March
1895 **Phrynette** (Fernand Beissier) 1 act Parisiana 29 January)
1896 **Hardi les Bleus** (Léon Garnier, A L'Hoste) Ba-ta-clan 24 October
1896 **Pavie** (Garnier, J Joubert) Casino Municipale, Nice; Ba-ta-clan 28 January 1897
1897 **La Vie du soldat** 1 act Parisiana 17 April
1897 **Oncle Jean** (de Méria) 1 act Dunkirk 4 December
1898 **Le Roi Carnaval** (Lucien Puech, Bannel) 1 act Parisiana 1 February
1898 **The Royal Star** (*La Petite Vénus*) (Maurice Ordonneau ad Francis Richardson) Prince of Wales Theatre, London 16 September
1900 **Les Petites Vestales** (w Frédéric Le Rey/Ernest Depré, Arthur Bernède) Théâtre de la Renaissance 22 November
1900 **Ordre de l'Empereur** (Paul Ferrier) Théâtre des Bouffes-Parisiens 4 March
1902 **L'Agence Léa** (w Rodolphe Berger, Edouard Mathé/Miguel Zamacoïs) Théâtre des Capucines 31 January
1904 **Le Béguin de Messaline** (Maurice de Féraudy, Jean Kolb) La Cigale 30 January
1904 **Une journée à Paris** (Germain, Paul Moncousin) 1 act Théâtre de la Gaîté 1 December
1904 **Les Robinsonnes** (P Delay) 1 act Eldorado 8 September
1904 **Otéro chez elle** (Germain, Moncousin) 1 act Théâtre des Mathurins 10 October
1904 **Le Voyage de la mariée** (w Edmond Diet/Paul Ferrier, Ordonneau) Galeries St-Hubert, Brussels 9 December
1905 **Minne** (Willy) 1 act Boîte à Fursy 6 February
1905 **Paris s'amuse** (Eugène Joullot) Parisiana March
1905 **Au temps jadis** (Maurice Vaucaire) Monte Carlo 16 April
1905 **Les Filles Jackson et Cie** (Ordonneau) Théâtre des Bouffes-Parisiens 29 November
1906 **Paris fêtard** (Ernest Grenet-Dancourt, Georges Nanteuil) 1 act Olympia 3 February

Plate 56. **Laddie Cliff** *as Albert 'Skinney' Skinner and Vera Bryer as Jane give choreographic illustration to the lyric 'Dance the Polka Again' in* The Millionaire Kid.

1907 **Vive la Parisienne!** (w Charles Borel-Clerc, Émile Bonnamy et al/Maurice Froyez) Parisiana 16 January
1908 **Oeil de Gazelle** (Paul Ferrier) 1 act Monte Carlo February
1909 **Le Baiser de Ninon** (Moncousin) 1 act Saint-Cloud September

CLIFF, Laddie [PERRY, Clifford Albyn] (b Bristol, 3 September 1891; d Montana, Switzerland, 8 December 1937). Bespectacled comedian and dancer who successfully turned producer in the dance-and-laughter era of the British musical theatre.

Cliff began his performing career playing in concert parties, music hall and pantomime, at first in Britain, then in Australia (1906) and subsequently, between 1907 and 1916, in America, where he was introduced to the musical theatre in the little *Gaby* (1911) and a production of *Tonight's the Night* in Chicago, appearing in the rôle of Henry originated by Lauri de Frece and played in London by the young Leslie Henson.

He returned to Britain the following year and played in the revue *The Bing Girls Are There* at the Alhambra, and landed his first West End musical comedy rôle in Bernard Hishin's London production of *His Little Widows* (1919, Pete Lloyd), supporting Gene Gerrard and dance-and-duetting 'I Don't Believe You' with Joan Hay. His dancing talents won him choreographic assignments on Charlot's *The Wild Geese* and the revue *Pins and Needles*, his comic abilities a place in the cast of the revue *Jigsaw* performing 'Swanee', and the combination of all his talents found him a prominent place in the celebrated concert-party The Co-Optimists.

He appeared in revue and also in several musicals over the following years, replacing Joe Coyne in *Katinka* (1923, t/o Hopper), succeeding Lupino Lane in the cast of *Brighter London* and taking part in Charlot's *Leap Year* and 1925 revue, as well as choreographing George Grossmith and Pat Malone's production of Gershwin's *Primrose* (1924), before turning his attentions to producing.

Cliff's first production, in conjunction with Firth Shephard, was the musical comedy *Dear Little Billie* (1925, Sir Frederick Fotheringay), written by Shephard, composed by H B Hedley and Jack Strachey, directed by Cliff and featuring his fellow Co-Optimist and wife, Phyllis Monkman, Robert Michaelis, Vera Robson and Cliff himself in the lead rôles. It had a fair tour and 86 performances in London. The following year he took a reef in his producing activities and performed in *Tip-Toes* (1926, Al Kaye) at the Winter Garden, but in 1927 he took a lease on the newly built Carlton Theatre and, in partnership with Edward O'Brien, opened it with another Shephard/Hedley and Strachey musical, a new version of *His Little Widows* called *Lady Luck* (1927, Biff Morton). This time he and Miss Monkman were joined at the head of the cast by Leslie Henson and the Australian song and dance pair, Madge Elliott and Cyril Ritchard, Felix Edwardes and Max Rivers were hired to direct and choreograph, and the result was a run of nearly ten months.

Edgar Wallace's musical comedy drama *The Yellow Mask* (music: Vernon Duke), which followed *Lady Luck* into the Carlton, found Cliff producing in partnership with provincial panto giant Julian Wylie and Bobby Howes making his star début. It provided another success, although one which had to be moved twice owing to theatre problems and it ended up as a then rare example of a musical played in the variety hallows of the London Palladium.

In 1928 he produced *So This is Love*, a dance-and-laughter musical in which he successfully featured himself (as Hap J Hazzard) and Stanley Lupino alongside Ritchard and Miss Elliott at the Winter Garden. This piece established a comedy-with-choreography formula which was then most successfully followed up in *Love Lies* (1929, Rolly Ryder), *The Love Race* (1930, Bobby Mostyne) and *The Millionaire Kid* (1931, Albert Skinner), with Lupino and Cliff supplying the fun, Ritchard and Elliott the graceful dancing and romance, and Cliff teaming up with a soubrette (such as Vera Bryer) for the more light-hearted dance pieces.

Whilst this run of productions played London and the provinces, Cliff continued further enterprises. He presented Phyllis Monkman in *So Long, Letty* in the provinces, stepped unconvincingly into unfamiliar territory with the production of Lehár's *Frederica*, starring Joseph Hislop and Lea Seidl, at the Palace, and attempted twice, with limited success, to set up a 'B team' headed by the monocled provincial comedian George Clarke, to hold the fort in town while his 'A' team toured their London hits. *Darling, I Love You* (1929) and *Blue Roses* (1931) proved much less effective than the 'A' shows.

Ritchard and Miss Elliott moved on to America and Australia, but the Lupino/Cliff partnership continued and, after a short break filled with revue and concert party activities, they came back to the Gaiety Theatre in 1934 for ten months of *Sporting Love* (Peter Brace). Lupino was absent for the three months of *Love Laughs* – (1935, Gus Burns), but he returned to join Cliff for another big success in *Over She Goes* (1936, Billy Bowler) and for *Crazy Days* (1937, James J Hooker). For this last occasion it was Cliff who was missing from the team. Taken ill during the try-out, he had to be replaced and, a fortnight after the show's failure in London, he died.

In his later years, Cliff appeared in a number of films and, of his productions, *Love Lies*, *The Love Race*, *Sporting Love* and *Over She Goes* were all made up into films. In the two earlier pieces Cliff's stage rôles were taken by Jack Hobbs, but in the last two he himself appeared to put his partnership with Lupino on celluloid.

CLIFFORD, Camille [CLIFFORD, Camilla Antoinette].

Danish-born and American-bred showgirl and beauty contest winner, who became a short-lived sensation on the British musical stage.

Miss Clifford had appeared only in the chorus of the Herald Square Theater's musical comedy *The Defender* (1902) and *The Prince of Pilsen* (1903) when she went to Britain, in 1904, as part of the American company which played the latter show at London's Shaftesbury Theatre. Her wordless but well-staged appearance as 'the Gibson Girl' made her the fashion of the season, and she stayed in Britain to make the most of the unexpected stardom conferred on her by her reputed 11-inch waist and adjacent measurements.

A rôle was written into the London hit *The Catch of the Season* in which she spoke and voicelessly made her way through a number called 'The Gibson Girl', and a spot was organized for her in which to strut her stuff in a new

musical, *The Belle of Mayfair*. She proved so popular that she was again given a song, 'Why Do They Call Me a Gibson Girl?', and billing of a size which provoked the walk-out of the show's nominal star, Edna May. Miss Clifford was able to enjoy her fame for the rest of the run, after which it was put to rest in a marriage with the Hon Henry Lyndhurst Bruce (1906) and retirement from the stage.

After her husband's death in 1914, she returned briefly to the stage, appearing in 1916 in a music-hall scena, *The Girl of the Future*, before remarrying and once again demurely quitting the boards.

CLIVIA

Operette in 3 acts by Charles Amberg and F Maregg (ie Franz Massarek). Music by Nico Dostal. Theater am Nollendorfplatz, Berlin, 23 December 1933.

A local-colourful German Operette which moved into the topical Ruritania of America's filmland for its story, *Clivia* had a heroine (Lillie Claus) who was the 1930s equivalent of an operettic fairy princess – a film star. Sent out to Boliguay, South America, to work on a movie, Clivia Gray gets mixed up with a hugely complex and intermittently political plot featuring one Juan (Walter Jankuhn), who is really the President of Boliguay in disguise; his sister, Jola (Lill Sweet), a kind of Boliguayan Amazon, who heads a troupe of feminine border guards; a comical German tourist called Kasulke (Egon Brosig) who invents things; a comical American reporter called Lelio (Erik Ode) who is destined to pair off with Jola; and a Chicago financier called Potterton, who is using the filming as a front and is really bent on fomenting revolution. When Juan is finally convinced that Clivia is not part of the by then failed plot, she can become Mrs President.

Dostal's score illustrated the rather garish combination of jolly improbabilities and screenish romance aptly, featuring several showy numbers for its leading lady, notably the umpteenth 'Ich bin verliebt' of Operette history, and some romantic baritone work for the President, but the most enjoyable musical moment came in a little tarantella for the light-hearted Lelio, singing of what goes on 'Am Manzanares'.

Clivia did well enough at Jankuhn's Theater am Nollendorfplatz to earn a return season (17 September 1937) with Lillie Claus (Frau Dostal) again featured in the title-rôle. It was subsequently played widely in German houses, introduced in Poland, Luxemburg, Switzerland, Finland and Yugoslavia, filmed for television with Claude Farell and the voice of Anneliese Rothenberger featured, and has held a place on the fringes of the German-language repertoire since. In the 1960s it was seen in Belgium and in France in a French-language version.

France: Grand Théâtre, Bordeaux 25 January 1966; TV film: Central-Europa/Prisma 1952

Recordings: selections (RCA), part-record (Eurodisc, EMI Electrola, Telefunken) etc

LES CLOCHES DE CORNEVILLE

Opéra-comique in 3 acts by Clairville and Charles Gabet. Music by Robert Planquette. Théâtre des Folies-Dramatiques, Paris, 19 April 1877.

Les Cloches de Corneville was the first full-length opéra-comique to be written by 24-year-old composer Robert Planquette, whose career to that time had been limited largely to the world of the café-concert, where he had, in his teens, made his mark with the march 'Sambre et

Meuse' and with various songs and scenas for Anna Judic and others.

The libretto to *Les Cloches de Corneville*, written very much in the old opéra-comique style with its marquises and maidens and missing heirs, was basically the work of one Charles Gabet, a police inspector with theatrical aspirations and a few mediocre play credits, remade with considerable assistance from and lyrics by Clairville, the co-author of *La Fille de Madame Angot*. The authors had originally offered their piece to Hervé, but the inventor of the opéra-bouffe found the text lacking in the kind of comic extravagance in which he specialized and, when he came up with some outrageously crazy suggestions for changes to the script, they preferred to look elsewhere for music. History (which is, in any case, a bit self-contradictory on the making of *Les Cloches de Corneville*) does not relate how and why they found their way to Planquette.

The completed show failed to find a buyer. Its libretto was too old-fashioned, it was too reminscent of too many other pieces – even Clairville's *Angot* success did not find it a home. Planquette's music, however, did find one: on musical plate stands. Thus, nearly a century before *Jesus Christ Superstar* and its pre-production recording, the melodies of *Les Cloches de Corneville* were apparently purveyed to the public (or that part of it which bought musical plate-stands) prior to the show's staging.

It was Louis Cantin, the most adventurous and outstanding Parisian impresario of his time, who finally took up *Les Cloches de Corneville* and, four years after its completion, produced it at the Folies-Dramatiques. If it won some sneeringly snooty comments from the critics over what one of them pleased to dub its 'musiquette' and accusations of being stained with the simplicity of the café-concert, it also won a warm reception from the public.

Miserly old Gaspard (Ange Milher) is the steward of Corneville castle, the lords of which fled the troubled region many years previously along with the Comte de Lucenay who, at the same time, left his young daughter, Germaine (Marie Gélabert) in the trusty's care. Through the years, Gaspard has cared for the castle estates, piling up the revenues, which he has come now to regard as virtually his own, and weaving a myth that the castle is haunted to keep the local peasants away. When a new magistrate (Luco) comes to town and talks of reopening the castle, Gaspard decides to win him over by giving him Germaine as a wife. But Germaine has already promised to wed no-one but the layabout Jean Grénicheux (Simon-Max), who saved her from drowning, and Grénicheux, previously promised to Gaspard's maid, Serpolette (Juliette Simon-Girard), is delighted at the profit to be made by such a marriage.

A mysterious young man, who is none other than Henri, the long absent heir to the Marquisate of Corneville (Ernest Voix), turns up in town and hires himself three servants at the hiring fair – they are Grénicheux and Serpolette, who are thus protected from the furious Gaspard, and Germaine, safe, for the period of her hiring, from marriage to the magistrate. Henri announces his identity and the fact that it was he, not his new servant, who saved Germaine from the sea, and the merry band head off to take over Henri's ancestral castle. There they discover both Gaspard's hoard and the papers proving that he houses the heiress of Lucenay. The old man comes to

gloat over his gold, and he is frightened out of his wits when Henri and his friends appear, ghostlike, in the armour of the Marquis's ancestors. In the final act Gaspard recovers his reason and his honesty and all is confessed. Henri will wed Germaine, Serpolette, who for an act supposed herself to be Mlle de Lucenay, takes Grénicheux ... as her servant, and the magistrate sagely forgets about the foolishness of taking a young wife.

If the libretto was perhaps not the most original, it did have the great advantage of containing a series of splendid characters and acting rôles, and Cantin's casting emphasized this advantage. The comedian Milher, as Gaspard, with his two big central comic yet dramatic scenes: his second-act confrontation with the 'ghosts' and his third-act mad scene and confession, proved adept at both the comedy and the pathos. The young Simon-Max mixed comedy and tenorizing as the cocky Grénicheux in a way which was to characterize an exceptional career, whilst the two girls' rôles were cast with fresh-voiced teenagers: Marie Gélabert, straight out of the Conservatoire, who had originally refused the part of Germaine to get married but returned at the last moment when Berthe Stuart, the singer cast instead, fell ill, and Juliette Girard (Serpolette). Both were to become enduring stars.

The trump card of *Les Cloches de Corneville* was, however, its musical score. From end to end, it was a veritable parade of hits, highlighted by Grénicheux's lilting carol to the sea, 'Va, petit mousse' and his sweetly sung pack of lies 'Je regardais en air', telling how he saved the drowning girl, Germaine's famous telling of the legend of the bells with its digue-digue-don refrain, Serpolette's vigorous 'Chanson du cidre de Normandie', Henri's waltz rondeau 'J'ai fait trois fois le tour du monde' and the soaring, powerful entrance of his ghostly troupe 'Sous les armures de leur taille' which climaxed the first act. There were also some splendid ensembles, topped by the comical trio 'Fermons les yeux'.

Les Cloches de Corneville played for two months and then closed whilst other shows necessarily passed across the Folies-Dramatiques stage. But it was only a temporary closure, and six weeks later the show was back, to begin a non-stop run of nearly 18 months – a dazzling record for the times. Perhaps it could have run even longer, but Cantin left the Folies-Dramatiques to take up the management of the Bouffes-Parisiens, and his successor Blandin, only able to take an inherited triumph for so long, removed *Les Cloches* on Christmas day, after its 580th performance, in order to introduce a triumph of his own: Offenbach's most successful later show, *Madame Favart*. Offenbach's work was, in its turn, removed before its time to allow what was to be the first of many reprises of *Les Cloches de Corneville* at the Folies-Dramatiques, prior to its emigration on to other metropolitan stages. By that time it had largely passed its thousandth Parisian performance. In 1892 the Gaîté presented the show with a particularly fine cast headed again by Mlle Gélabert, by the actor Paulin Ménier as Gaspard, the star baritone, Louis Morlet, as Henri and Paul Fugère as a comical Grénicheux, and the piece was repeated frequently there over the next 65 years. Juliette Simon-Girard (she had married her co-star, Simon-Max) repeated her original rôle at the Théâtre de la Porte-Saint-Martin in 1908, and André Bauge (Théâtre Mogador 1940) and Michel Dens (Gaîté-Lyrique 1953, 1958) were both seen as the Marquis in later revivals. The last major Parisian revival was at the Théâtre de la Porte-Saint-Martin in 1968.

The career of *Les Cloches de Corneville* outside France was equally spectacular. Whilst the piece was still playing its first months at the Folies-Dramatiques, it appeared in Madrid and in Brussels and, in its first English-language production, was played at New York's Fifth Avenue Theater by the touring C D Hess Opera Company with Zelda Seguin (Germaine) and Emilie Melville (Serpolette) starring. Within the next few years, New York would hear the French *Cloches* from Mlle Aimée and Paola Marié and English ones from Catherine Lewis and Laura Joyce, from the Boston Ideals and Emma Abbott's Opera Company, as the piece became an obligatory part of the baggage of every touring comic opera company. It appeared on Broadway in repertoire in 1898 with Frank Moulan as the old Bailli and again as late as 1931.

If the repertoire system then in vogue for opéra-bouffe and opéra-comique productions in America did not allow *Les Cloches de Corneville* to set up any kind of a Broadway run, the same was not the case in Britain where such shows played straight seasons. Until the arrival of Planquette's piece, however, none had ever played as long a run as *Les Cloches de Corneville*. The story is told that publisher, Joseph Williams, arrived late at, and then walked out of the Paris production straight after the first number he heard. That number was the Legend of the Bells, and he walked out in order to buy the British rights. Those rights he sublet, a little curiously, to producer Alexander Henderson who staged the piece (ad H B Farnie, Robert Reece) at the second-rate Folly Theatre with his resident stars American soprano Kate Munroe (Serpolette), very young Violet Cameron (Germaine) and Australian baritone John Howson (Henri), all of whom had recently appeared in his potted version of Offenbach's *La Créole*. Gaspard was played by the New Zealand-Irish actor Shiel Barry. The show was a sensational success and, come summer, Henderson closed down briefly to effect a transfer to the better Globe Theatre where *Les Cloches de Corneville* remained past its second anniversary, closing after 704 performances largely to permit the now hugely successful Henderson to produce Genée's *Der Seekadet*. That piece was quickly gone and, less than three months after closing, *Les Cloches de Corneville* was back in the West End for another four and a half months. Following not-very-successful productions of *La Famille Trouillat* and *La Boulangère*, it returned again the next year for three further months, breaking every London long run record and comprehensively outrunning its famous contemporary, *HMS Pinafore*, housed similarly in an unfashionable theatre. Shiel Barry is said to have played Gaspard for every one of the London performances and thereafter he made a career of the rôle in the endless tours which swarmed through Britain for decades. The show's last London appearance was in 1931.

Meanwhile, *Les Cloches de Corneville* had caused an equal sensation in the other main European musical capitals. In Budapest (ad Jenő Rakosi), with young Ilka Pálmay as Serpolette, it proved to be the most successful musical piece in the glorious history of the Népszinház. At Vienna's Theater an der Wien, where Albin Swoboda (Henri), Felix Schweighofer (Gaspard), Hermine Meyerhoff (Haiderose,

ie Serpolette), Sophie König (Germaine) and Alexander Girardi (Grénicheux) starred in Maximilian Steiner's production, it won more success than the year's two other major works, Millöcker's *Das verwunschene Schloss* and Strauss's *Blindekuh*. It was retained in the repertoire until 1883 (100th performance 26 November 1882), and thereafter played both there (in repertoire 1898–1902 w Therese Biedermann as Serpolette, 1922) and at several other Viennese theatres (Carltheater 30 November 1883, Jantschtheater 30 November 1901; Kaiser-Jubiläums-Stadttheater 29 January 1908; Raimundtheater 1909 w Gerda Walde as Haiderose, Franz Gross as Gaspard; Bürgertheater 1917–20 w Grete Holm as Haiderose).

Ernst Dohm's German version was mounted in Berlin, and the show was also played in Czech, Polish, Italian, Swedish, Slovenian, Lettish, Estonian, Norwegian, Finnish, Lithuanian and Croatian, remaining a prominent part of the European repertoire for more than half a century.

The British colonies were no different to the rest of the world. *Les Cloches de Corneville* triumphed on the Pacific and oriental circuits just as it had everywhere else. The first Australian production was staged by Henry Bracy, with himself in the rôle of Grénicheux and his wife, Clara Thompson as Serpolette, and the show was repeated by most comic opera combinations which played in the colony thereafter. Pattie Laverne was a popular Serpolette, Emilie Melville played the same rôle to the Germaine of Nellie Stewart, and Australia and New Zealand also saw performances from the inveterately touring juvenile troupe, Pollard's Lilliputians, as well as Kelly and Leon's Minstrels' production of the show in which Kelly appeared as Gaspard and Leon as Serpolette. Kelly, however, later went on to play the miser alongside more conventional soubrettes when, for many years, he appeared as Gaspard for the Royal Comic Opera Company and other companies throughout Australia and New Zealand.

Les Cloches de Corneville shares with Lecocq's *La Fille de Madame Angot* the distinction of being the most internationally successful product of the French post-opéra-bouffe musical theatre. In the last two decades of the 19th century, these two pieces were revived regularly in the main centres and played almost unbrokenly on the touring circuits, even after the advent of the George Edwardesian musical comedy and the decline in interest in the French style of opéra-comique. In the early part of the 20th century, the show was almost permanently on display in France. However, whilst a limited selection of the works of the more marketable names in light musical theatre – Offenbach, Strauss and Lehár – have found a way to remain in the repertoire of some modern houses, *Les Cloches de Corneville* has now virtually ceased to be played outside France. In France it continues to hold its place in the repertoire, and it remains one of the outstanding musical theatre classics of the 19th century.

USA: Fifth Avenue Theater *The Chimes of Normandy* 22 October 1877; UK: Folly Theatre 28 February 1878; Hungary: Népszinház *Kornevilli harangok* 23 March 1878; Germany: Friedrich-Wilhelmstädtisches Theater *Die Glocken von Corneville* 27 March 1878; Austria: Theater an der Wien *Die Glocken von Corneville* 29 September 1878; Australia: Academy of Music, Melbourne 23 November 1878

Recordings: complete (EMI, Decca), selections (EMI-Pathé, Philips, Véga etc)

CLOCLO Operette in 3 acts by Béla Jenbach taken from the play *Der Schrei nach dem Kind* by Alexander Engel and Julius Horst. Music by Franz Lehár. Wiener Bürgertheater, Vienna, 8 March 1924.

Luise Kartousch starred as Parisian revue star, Cloclo Mustache, whom the evening followed through the ups and downs of her love affairs with her beloved, but distressingly poor, Maxime de la Vallé (Robert Nästlberger) and the wealthy and distinctly married Severin Cornichon (Ernst Tautenhayn), Mayor of Perpignan. Maxime, of course, wins in the end but Severin is a good egg and, having stuck by his little friend through some troubles with the law, and even blushed silently as his own wife, Melousine (Gisela Werbezirk), believing Cloclo to be Severin's wild-oat daughter, has taken the girl under her wing, he sticks by her when she becomes a married woman.

Lehár's score, with tinges of modern dance now appearing alongside the basic waltzes and marches, and much third-act champagne, was the last in which he employed his gay, pre-war *Die lustige Witwe* style before moving on to the lusher, romantic unhappy-ending mode of his later works. The bulk of the opportunities fell to the heroine. She made her entrance claiming 'Ich suche einen Mann', cooed with Maxime 'Wenn eine schöne Frau besiehlt' and, having told Severin 'Geh schön nach Haus zu deiner Frau', joined with him to dance to the strains of the 'Tonga Bay', which she insisted was 'erotisch ... schick und modern'. The most enjoyable moment, however, came when provincially correct Melousine sang topically about her intention to throw over respectability and follow the ideas recently popularized in the scandalous novel, 'La Garçonne'.

Cloclo was not a triumph. It played to 31 May, visited Berlin, where Gisela Werbezirk repeated her show-stealing performance, and was revived at the Johann Strauss-Theater on 4 September 1925 with Gisela Kolbe (Cloclo) and Max Brod (Severin) for a further two-month season during which it passed its hundredth Viennese performance (17 September). In the meanwhile, Budapest had seen an Hungarian version (ad Zsolt Harsányi), rebaptized *Apukam*!

A London version (ad Douglas Furber, Harry Graham) with Cicely Debenham (Cloclo), Claude Bailey (Maxime), A W Baskcomb (Severin) and Sidney Fairbrother (Melusine) in the lead rôles interpolated four songs by Max Darewksi and one by Harry Rosenthal (including the whole third-act music) and played 95 performances at the Shaftesbury and Adelphi Theatres.

Another Operette with the same title, with a score by Ferdinand Pagin and a text by Leo Stein and Alexander Landesberg, was produced at Danzers Orpheum, Vienna 23 December 1902 with Fritzi Massary as the titular Clotilde (31 performances), and yet another in Paris (Albert Valsien/Francis Kams/Jean Guitton, Eldorado 3 September 1920).

UK: Shaftesbury Theatre 3 August 1925; Hungary: Fővárosi Operettszinház *Apukam*! 15 April 1924; Germany: Berliner Theater 8 November 1924

Recording: selection in Italian (EDM)

LA COCARDE DE MIMI-PINSON Opérette in 3 acts by Maurice Ordonneau and Francis Gally. Music by

Plate 57. Cloclo: *Maria Rolle was Lehár's little heroine – seen here with Günter Fritzsche as Chablis–in the Dresden Staatsoperette's 1971 production.*

Henri Goublier fils. Théâtre de l'Apollo, Paris, 25 November 1915.

A little patriotic musical play, which scored a hit in Paris in the early days of the Great War, *La Cocarde de Mimi-Pinson* was set in the couture house Robichon-Frivolet and its heroine was Marie-Louise (Jenny Syril), the seamstress who sews a little medallion and a cocarde of ribbons inside the jacket of Jean Robichon (Albert Beauval), the son of her employer (Héraut), to keep him from harm at the front. The charm works, and Marie-Louise wins the wounded, but safe, Jean from Mme Frivolet (Valentine Rauly) in the final act. That finale also paired soubrette Zoë Crochu (Mary Richard) and comic La Mazette (A Massart), and the cook Sophie (Madeleine Guitty) and Jean's batman Bouriche (Carlos Avril), in time for a parade of soldiers headed by a lieutenant bearing a tricolore, and a patriotic chorus. Goublier's largely red-white-and-blue score included several pretty numbers for the heroine (Légende des petits rubans, Rondo de la cocarde etc), some lively pieces for soubrette Zoë, who led a nurses' march in the second act, and a delightfully comical duo for Bouriche and Sophie dreaming of their future together running a little bar ('Un petit comptoir en étain').

The show had a first run of 130 performances, a fine wartime career, and was remounted in Paris, at the Ba-ta-clan in 1920 with Zabeth Capazza featured and, later, at the Gaîté-Lyrique (20 April 1936). On this last occasion, with the topical and patriotic element no longer apt, the piece was shifted 300 years back, to a more picturesque costume era, whilst maintaining the score, which had won much popularity in its time, as it was. Sylvane Pressac (Marie-Louise), Monette Dinay (Zoë), Jeanne Perriat (Frivolet), Christiane d'Or (Sophie), Robert Allard (Bouriche) and Le Clezio (Jean) headed the cast through a brief run.

Recording: two record set (Decca)

COCÉA, Alice [Sophie] (b Sinaia, Romania, 1899; d France, June 1970).

Born in Romania, but brought to France in her early teens, Mlle Cocéa made her first appearances on the professional stage whilst still a student, but she began her Parisian career in 1917 when she took part in a revival of Guitry's *Le Scandale de Monte-Carlo* at the Théâtre des Bouffes-Parisiens. She followed up in *Psyché* and *La Petite Reine* (1917) at the Gymnase and then appeared, singing American ragtime tunes and impersonating Cleopatra in a Shakespearian burlesque, in the opening revue (*Une revue*) at Gustave Quinson's tiny wartime Théâtre de l'Abri. Quinson next cast her in the ingénue rôle of a little musical comedy intended to follow the revue, but circumstances resulted in *Phi-Phi* being moved to his Théâtre des Bouffes-Parisiens and there both the show and its 19-year-old leading lady made a sensation. As Aspasie, the wide-eyed courtesan of this long-running Greek historiette, she introduced 'Bien chapeautée', 'Mon cher Monsieur, excusez-moi' and 'Je connais toutes les historiettes', before moving on to star in *Phi-Phi*'s successor, *Dédé*, as the amorous shoe-shop vendeuse, Denise. There, she made a further hit performing 'Et voilà comme' and duets with Maurice Chevalier ('Si j'avais su') and Urban ('Tous les chemins mènent à l'amour').

Mlle Cocéa appeared thereafter in starring rôles in several further musical pieces: alongside Henri Defreyn in the one-act *Ne m'épousez pas!* (1922), opposite Dranem in Raoul Moretti's *En chemyse* (1924), in the title-rôle of Yvain's *Gosse de riche* (1924), and with Defreyn and Marguerite Deval in *A Paris tous les deux* (1926) before heading definitively for the non-musical theatre and the cinema and returning to the musical stage only in 1935 to play in *Trente et quarante*.

En route, she became la Comtesse Stanislas de la Rochefoucauld, with, as one French commentator remarked, 'grand profit pour sa carrière'.

COCHRAN, C[harles] B[lake] (Sir) (b Sussex, 25 September 1872; d London, 31 January 1951). C B Cochran entered the theatre as a highly successful producer of revue and, like Britain's other most-publicized revue producer, André Charlot, often found that book musical successes were harder to come by.

His first attempt at a musical play was *Houp-La!* (1916), with a score by revue composer Nat D Ayer and with Gertie Millar starring, and it was a whole-hearted failure. However, the revusical wartime saga of Bruce Bairnsfather's Old Bill, staged at the Oxford Theatre as *The Better 'Ole* (1917), proved a long-running success and versions of two French pieces, Émile Lassailly's burlesque opérette *Carminetta* (1917) and Charles Cuvillier's colourful *Afgar* (1919), also had good runs. There was less success for the pageant *Jolly Jack Tar* (1918), the home-made

musicals *Pretty Peggy* and *Cherry* (1920) and Marcel Lattès's *Maggie* (1919). Amongst a continuing barrage of revues, he returned to French sources and brought a badly mangled version of Christiné's *Phi-Phi* to the London Pavilion and failure, from America he took George M Cohan's *Little Nellie Kelly* (1923) to the New Oxford for a good run, and he produced a musical version of the old farce *Turned Up* (1926) at the same venue with less, but not negligible, results.

In 1929 Cochran produced the first musical by Noël Coward, with whom he had worked over the years on revues. *Bitter-Sweet* was a splendid success, and Cochran subsequently produced Coward's *Conversation Piece* (1934). Otherwise, he preferred to look for patented overseas successes to bring to London and in the 1930s he introduced London to Kern's *The Cat and the Fiddle* (1932) and *Music in the Air* (1933), Porter's *Anything Goes* (1935), Oscar Straus's *Eine Frau, die weiss, was sie will* (*Mother of Pearl*) as a vehicle for Alice Delysia, Lehár's *Paganini* (1937) with Richard Tauber and Evelyn Laye, and a spectacular revival of another tastelessly mangled classic, Offenbach's *La Belle Hélène* (*Helen!*). Porter's piece was the most successful of the group, running over six months, and of the others only *Paganini* was an outright failure, although the very lushly staged *Helen!* lost large amounts of money for its producer. The only musical initiated by Cochran during the 1930s, Porter's *Nymph Errant*, failed to come up to expectations.

After nearly a decade without producing a musical and several years without producing anything, Cochran put an effective coda to his career, in his seventies, by producing three works by Vivian Ellis and A P Herbert. If *Big Ben* (1946) and *Tough at the Top* (1949) were not very impressive stayers, the second of the trio, *Bless the Bride* (1947), in contrast, gave him the longest-running musical theatre success of his busy and colourful career as a showman producer. When the total of his career as a producer of musical plays was summarized, Cochran was able to take the credit for the creation of a quartet of fine and successful musicals: *Bless the Bride*, *The Better 'Ole*, *Bitter-Sweet* and *Conversation Piece*. One per decade of his life in the musical theatre.

Memoirs: *Secrets of a Showman* (Heinemann, London, 1925); *I Had Almost Forgotten* (Hutchinson, London, 1932); *Cock-a-Doodle-Doo* (Dent, London, 1941); *A Showman Looks On* (Dent, London, 1945); Biography: Cleugh, J: *Charles Blake Cochran: Lord Bountiful* (Pallas, London, 1946), Graves, C: *The Cochran Story* (W H Allen, London, 1951); Heppner, S: *Cockie* (Frewin, London, 1969); Harding, J: *Cochran* (Methuen, London, 1988)

COCO Musical in 2 acts by Alan Jay Lerner. Music by André Previn. Mark Hellinger Theater, New York, 18 December 1969.

A slightly biomusical on the life of Parisian couturière, Coco Chanel, the famed popularizer of the 'little black dress' and the godmother of the Chanel No 5 perfume, *Coco* presented the ageing and long-retired Mlle Chanel (Katharine Hepburn) making a return to the scene of her fame. Her lawyer, Greff (George Rose), unconvinced that she can re-make herself a place in the modern fashion world, hires the fussy, limp-wristed Sebastian (René Auberjonois), boyfriend of a leading fashion critic, as her assistant. When she sees the gussied-up dresses he is

287

intending to produce under her name, Chanel tears and snips the excrescences from every one, bringing back some of the simplicity that was her trademark. Paris and Sebastian's pal hate what she has done, but the American mass-market chains love it. Orbachs, Bloomingdales, Best and Saks provide a happy ending. A juvenile love story between Noelle (Gale Dixon) and Georges (David Holliday) was worked into the main plot.

The short score included six numbers for the star, refusing to knuckle under to the fact that 'The World Belongs to the Young' and ending up 'Always Mademoiselle', Noelle sang the healing virtues of 'A Brand New Dress' and Sebastian revelled in the 'Fiasco' of the dress show. The many gowns for the show were designed by *My Fair Lady* couturier Cecil Beaton.

Freddie Brisson's production of *Coco* owed its 333 Broadway performances principally to the musical comedy début of Miss Hepburn (replaced for the last performances by Danielle Darrieux), but they were insufficient to balance the books.

The same title was also used, some years earlier, for the internationally successful spectacular musical comedy written by Clairville, Eugène Grangé and Alfred Delacour, and played throughout Europe with a score, variously, by Auguste Coèdes and others (Théâtre des Nouveautés, Paris 12 June 1878, Budapest Népszinház 16 May 1879, Karl Alexander Raida (Germany), Johann Brandl (Carltheater, Vienna 22 March 1879) or Franz Herzeele (Ghent November 1885) attached.

Recording: original cast (Paramount)

THE COCOANUTS Musical comedy in 2 acts by George S Kaufman. Music and lyrics by Irving Berlin. Lyric Theater, New York, 8 December 1925.

A comedy-musical vehicle for the famous vaudeville team the Marx Brothers, *The Cocoanuts* had a tiny, hoary main plot about stolen jewels. The jewels belong to rich Mrs Potter (Margaret Dumont), the thieves are Harvey Yates (Henry Whittemore) and Penelope Martyn (Janet Velie), but the suspect is the impecunious Robert Adams (Jack Barker), the beloved of Mrs Potter's niece Polly (Mabel Withee). That plot, however, was an incidental in a show where the antics of the very dubious, octopus-like Henry W Schlemmer, Florida developer and hotelier (Groucho Marx) and his confederates Willie the Wop (Chico Marx), Silent Sam (Harpo Marx) and Jamison (Zeppo Marx) – occasionally mixed up in the plotline, but more often wildly and zanily doing their own thing – were the thing. The ribbing of the Florida developers was undoubtedly an answer to an earlier musical show of the same year, Earl Carroll's *Florida Girl* (aka *Oh, You!*), backed by the Coral Gables Development Company and unashamedly touting its wares. Irving Berlin's songs, also rather incidental to most of the comedy, ranged from the opening desciption of 'Florida by the Sea' to dances relatively normal (tango, 'They're Blaming the Charleston') or zoological and abnormal ('The Monkey Doodle-Doo'), numbers such as 'A Little Bungalow' and 'Lucky Boy', and an excerpt from *Carmen* reset as 'The Tale of the Shirt'.

Sam H Harris's production of *The Cocoanuts* served its purpose splendidly, and the Marx Brothers played 377 performances of an ever-changing show which was accounted 'one of the season's outstanding successes'. The brothers subsequently put a version of their show on film. Oscar Shaw and Mary Eaton joined Miss Dumont in a version which used only three of the show's songs ('Florida by the Sea', 'The Monkey Doodle-Doo' and the travestied *Carmen*) plus one new number ('When My Dreams Come True').

An attempt to mount *The Cocoanuts* in London, without the Marx Brothers, but with British provincial comic Fred Duprez (Julius Slimmer) and Madeleine Seymour (Mrs Potter) in the featured rôles, lasted only 16 performances. In America, similarly, the piece was too attached to the image of its famous creators to be considered revivable, but Washington's Arena Stage mounted a production on the occasion of Irving Berlin's hundredth birthday (11 May 1988) with Stephen Mellor as Schlemmer and Halo Wines as Mrs Potter.

UK: Garrick Theatre 20 March 1928; Film: Paramount 1929
Recording: film soundtrack (Soundtrak)

COE, Peter (b London, 18 April 1929; d nr Byfleet, 25 May 1987). Refreshingly unmannered British director whose ventures into the musical theatre turned out both some important new works in the early years of his career, and some fine stagings of imported pieces in his later days.

After early work in provincial repertory theatres, Coe was appointed director at the newly built Mermaid Theatre in 1959. In its first season he directed his first musical piece with the production of Bernard Miles's adaptation of Henry Fielding, *Lock Up Your Daughters*. Owing to the restrictions of the Mermaid stage space, Coe and designer Sean Kenny evolved a multiple-area series of skeletal constructions to represent the various scenes of the action, a technique not then common in the musical theatre. The style was refined and enlarged for Coe's next musical play, the original production of *Oliver!*. Both production and setting have been reproduced many times since in Britain, America and elsewhere.

Amongst a subsequent series of mostly play productions, Coe directed *Pickwick*, the inevitable follow-up to *Oliver!*, in Britain (1963) and America, the Dumas burlesque *The Four Musketeers* (1967), *Kiss Me, Kate* for the Sadler's Wells Opera Company (the first modern musical to be played there), his own attempt at a post-censorship show, *Decameron '73* (1973) and, in contrast, the Moral Rearmament musical *Ride, Ride* (1976).

He spent a period in Canada running the Citadel Theater (1978–81) and another in America as Artistic Director of the American Shakespeare Theatre in Stratford, Connecticut (1981–2), before returning to Britain where he directed Michael Crawford in *Flowers for Algernon* and staged Harold Fielding's British productions of the Broadway musicals *On the Twentieth Century* and *Barnum*. He was killed in a road accident in 1987 at the age of 58.

COÈDES, Auguste (b Paris, 11 December 1840; d Passy, 13 July 1884). A composer of songs and piano music, prompter at the Opéra and later chef de chant at the Théâtre Lyrique, who provided scores for a variety of Parisian musicals shows in the 1870s.

After beginning his working life as an employee of the post-office, Coèdes turned to music and at first made his living as a pianist and accompanist with touring productions. One of these was an opérette company travelling in the Argentine, where he remained for three years whilst France was involved in the Franco-Prussian war. On his return, he won the prompter's post at the Opéra and became a well-known figure in Parisian musical circles, prized as a lively companion and an excellent pianist and vocalist. His early theatrical compositions included ballet music for the Folies-Bergère (*Les Folies amoureuses*) and some music for the féerie spectacular *La Cocotte aux oeufs d'or* but in 1874, following the success of the opérette *La Belle Bourbonnaise*, produced by Louis Cantin at the Folies-Dramatiques with Marie Desclauzas in the title-rôle and later seen at Vienna's Carltheater and Berlin's Friedrich-Wilhelmstädtisches Theater (*Die schöne Bourbonnaise*), he gave up his employment at the Opéra to concentrate on composing for the theatre.

Thereafter he had little luck, whether under the management of Cantin or with Brasseur at the Nouveautés where his *Fleur d'oranger* was chosen as the first opérette to play the new theatre, until his last opérette, *La Girouette*, in 1880. After a good Paris run, it was produced by Augustin Daly in America as *The Weathercock* (1882) and in Britain with the young Robert Courtneidge starred (1889, Portsmouth/Avenue Theatre). His final stage work seems to have been the score for the Théâtre des Nouveautés revue *Les Parfums de Paris* (1880), which toplined Hortense Schneider, Brasseur and Berthelier. Thereafter he sank into insanity and died at the age of 43.

Coèdes also supplied some of the music which accompanied the vaudeville *Coco* (w Adolphe Lindheim et al), first produced in Paris (Théâtre des Nouveautés 12 June 1878), then in Budapest (Népszinház 16 May 1879) and expanded into a fuller-scale musical comedy, with additional music by Karl Alexander Raida in Germany, by Johann Brandl in Austria (Carltheater 22 March 1879), and by Franz Herzeele in Belgium (Ghent November 1885).

1872 **Les Griffes du Diable** (Clairville, Charles Gabet) Théâtre des Menus-Plaisirs 18 April
1872 **Le Bouquet de Lise** (Ernest Gerny, Eugène Sari) 1 act Folies-Bergère 20 April
1872 **La Cocotte aux oeufs d'or** (w Hervé, G Raspail/Clairville, Eugène Grangé, Victor Koning) Théâtre des Menus-Plaisirs 31 December
1873 **Il y a un trou** (Pagès de Noyez) Fantaisies-Pigalle 15 March
1873 **Une drôle de soirée** (Élie Berthet) 1 act Théâtre de l'Odéon 3 April
1874 **La Belle Bourbonnaise** (Ernest Dubreuil, Henri Chabrillat) Théâtre des Folies-Dramatiques 11 April
1875 **Claire de lune** (Dubreuil, Henri Bocage) Théâtre des Folies-Dramatiques 11 March
1876 **Fleur de baiser** (Alexandre) Théâtre des Folies-Dramatiques 24 February
1876 **Les Mirlitons** (Alfred Duru, Chabrillat, Bocage, Ernest Blum) Théâtre des Folies-Dramatiques 19 April
1877 **L'Éducation d'Achille** Cercle Artistique et Littéraire 28 February
1877 **Le Chevalier de Lastignac** (Bias) Casino Théâtre, Dieppe 14 August
1878 **Le Chat botté** (w Gaston Serpette, Bourdeau/Étienne Tréfeu, Blum) Théâtre de la Gaîté 18 May
1878 **Fleur d'oranger** (Alfred Hennequin, Victor Bernard) Théâtre des Nouveautés 7 December

1879 **Mon gendre, tout est rompu** (Paul Burani, William Busnach) 1 act Casino de Dieppe 22 August
1879 **Les Deux Nababs** (Hippolyte Raymond, Alphonse Dumas) Théâtre des Nouveautés 21 January
1880 **La Girouette** (Bocage, Emil Hemery) Théâtre des Fantaisies-Parisiennes 3 March

LE COEUR ET LA MAIN Opérette in 3 acts by Charles Nuitter and Alexandre Beaumont. Music by Charles Lecocq. Théâtre des Nouveautés, Paris, 19 October 1882.

After his split with Victor Koning of the Théâtre de la Renaissance, Lecocq struck up a new alliance with manager Brasseur at the Théâtre des Nouveautés and, showing in no mean way that he was far from being finished, as Koning had apparently feared, the composer went on to produce two of his finest works for that house. The first was *Le Jour et la nuit*, the second *Le Coeur et la main*, the libretto of which was said to be based on an unspecified tale of Boccaccio.

Princess Micaëla of Aragon (Mlle Vaillant-Couturier) is to be wed, sight unseen, to Prince Gaétan, Duke of Madeira (Vauthier), but, unlike most of her musical theatre sisters, she is happy enough to accept what is a normal enough occurrence in royal families. It is the Prince who balks. He slips his royal guard on the way to Aragon, and climbs over a wall into a garden where he quickly sets himself to chatting up the pretty girl gardener. There is nothing he can do about the marriage – state affairs are, after all, state affairs – but he sulks his way through the ceremony and won't even look at his bride. The King (Berthelier) and the duenna, Doña Scholastica (Mlle Felcourt), put guards on all the corridors surrounding the nuptial chamber to make sure he doesn't shirk his wedding-night duty, but Gaétan spends the night with the gardener-girl before going off to the army the next morning. On manoeuvres, the gardener-girl keeps coming to visit him, in various disguises, and he is very put out when the King congratulates him on his husbandly success: the Princess is pregnant. But Gaétan hasn't been cuckolded, the gardener-girl is, after all, Micaëla. Élise Clary played Joséfa, the real gardener-girl, and Montaubry her soldier lover, Morales, who joined her to provide the soubret entertainment and plenty more complexities, whilst Scipion appeared as the comical Don Mosquitos.

The most popular parts of the score of *Le Coeur et la main* were Micaëla's set-piece bolero 'Un soir José, le capitaine', delivered as an entertainment for Gaétan as they make merry over supper on the wedding night, and Gaétan's Chanson du Casque, also delivered as an item, at the post-wedding ball. The King had his comical moments ('Vlan! j'ai perdu mon gendre'), Morales a lively drinking song ('Au soldat après la parade') and Micaëla a pretty rondeau (À l'ombre des charmilles'). Josefa and Morales peeped longingly at the empty royal bedroom in 'C'est là leur chambre nuptiale' before making use of it, whilst the Prince went into shock at the thought that his unseen wife has been unfaithful ('Quand ça tombe sur un confrère') to good comical effect, in a charming score which joined with a particularly sparkily written text to good effect.

Brasseur's production of *Le Coeur et la main* played a fine 128 performances on its first run and was brought back in the following season (2 May 1883) for another 54 performances. By this time, the first foreign productions had already got under way. In Budapest, where the piece (ad Lajos Evva, Béla J Fái) was, not unreasonably, titled *A kertészleány* (the gardener-girl), Ilka Pálmay scored a great hit as Micaëla to the Gaston (sic) of Pál Vidor and the King of Elek Solymossy for a fine run of 40 nights, and the show was revived in 1889 (25 October). The Népszinház company also played the piece in Vienna, which seems to have been the only occasion on which that city saw *Le Coeur et la main*.

The first English-language production came in America, where the show was the subject of a race and a subsequent court case over rights between John McCaull and James Duff. McCaull mounted *Heart and Hand* with John Howson as the King, Marianne Conway (Micaëla) and Laura Joyce (Scholastica), whilst the opposition put out *Micaëla*, 11 days later, with J H Ryley, Marie Conron and Wallace McCreery as Morales. The conflict did no one any good and McCaull withdrew his piece after three weeks with Duff close behind. A third English-language version was played, nearly a decade later, in Britain. Horace Sedger's production of *Incognita* (ad F C Burnand, Harry Greenbank) was heavily botched by numbers by 'Yvolde', Herbert Bunning and Hamilton Clark, and it featured a lady who called herself Sedohr Rhodes (Micaëla), Wallace Brownlow (Gaétan), Harry Monkhouse as a King who got disguised as a gipsy girl in the third act, Aida Jenoure (Josefa) and John Child (Morales O'Donoghue) in a version in which the carefully constructed bedroom farceries of the original were replaced by elderly burlesque and grotesque comedy. It played a fair 103 performances without *Le Coeur et la main* being given a real chance. It was, perhaps, no coincidence that the only foreign country to make a success of the show was Hungary, where the text had been intelligently treated.

Hungary: Népszinház *A kertészleány* 16 December 1882; USA: Bijou Theater *Hand and Heart* 15 February 1883, Standard Theater *Micaëla* 26 February 1883; Austria: Theater an der Wien *A kertészleány* 15 June 1883; UK: Lyric Theatre *Incognita* 6 October 1892

Recording: complete (Gaieté-Lyrique)

COFFIN, [Charles] Hayden (b Manchester, 22 April 1862; d London, 8 December 1935). Identikit baritone leading man of the Victorian and Edwardian eras.

English-born of American parents, the baritone Coffin, blessed with a fine masculine face and figure and a strong, ringing singing voice, made a mark in his very first professional stage appearances, taking over from Frank Celli as John Smith in *Pocahontas* (1885), playing Cosmo, the Venetian hero of *The Lady of the Locket* (1885), Boleslas in *Falka* (1885) and the hero of Ivan Caryll's first opérette, *The Lily of Léoville* (Coriolon, 1886). However, he was moved into star class by his performance of the serenade 'Queen of My Heart' in the rôle of Harry Sherwood in Cellier's very long-running *Dorothy* at the Gaiety Theatre in 1886.

He partnered his co-star, Marie Tempest, in the successors to *Dorothy* – *Doris* (1889) and *The Red Hussar* (1889) – appeared for the Carl Rosa company in *Marjorie* (1890, Ralf) and *Captain Thérèse* (1890, Tancrède de la Touche), sang 'O Promise Me' in the rôle of Robin Hood in the British production of De Koven's comic opera (rechristened *Maid Marian*, 1891), played Vincent and

Plate 58. **Hayden Coffin** *in one of his most enduring rôles, as Edward German's singing Tom Jones.*

then took over the rôle of Franz de Bernheim from the insufficient 'Chevalier Scovel' in *La Cigale* (1891). He starred opposite Decima Moore in *Miss Decima* (*Miss Helyett*, 1891, Peter Paul Rolleston), and established himself as London's preferred baritone hero before making a trip to America to play the romantic lead in Maurice Barrymore's unfortunate *The Robber of the Rhine* (1892, Waldemar).

He subsequently joined Lillian Russell in a 1892–3 New York season of *La Cigale* (Franz), *The Mountebanks* (Alfredo) and *Giroflé-Girofla* (Marasquin), before returning to Britain. There he found his niche, becoming one of the four stars of George Edwardes's famous Daly's Theatre company, alongside Miss Tempest, Letty Lind and comic Huntley Wright. Over the next decade, he created the romantic leads in *A Gaiety Girl* (1893, Charlie Goldfield, 'Tommy Atkins', 'Sunshine Above') at the Prince of Wales and Daly's, and in *An Artist's Model* (1895, Rudolph), *The Geisha* (1896, Reginald Fairfax, 'Star of my Soul', 'Jack's the Boy'), *A Greek Slave* (1898, Diomed, 'Freedom'), *San Toy* (1899, Bobbie Preston, 'Love Has Come From Lotus Land'), *A Country Girl* (1902, Geoffrey Challoner, 'In the King's Name ... Stand!') and *The Cingalee* (1903, Harry Vereker) at Daly's, before moving on to other theatres and further starring rôles in such pieces as *Véronique* (1904, Florestan), *The Girl Behind the Counter*

(1906), the title-rôle in Edward German's *Tom Jones* (1907), *Butterflies* (1908, Max), *The Dashing Little Duke* (1909, Chevalier de Matignon), *Two Merry Monarchs* (1910, Prince Charmis) and *The Quaker Girl* (1910, Captain Charteris).

After the First World War, with dance music taking over musical theatre, Coffin, who had personified the virile musical theatre hero to London audiences for more than a quarter of a century, diversified into straight theatre and films, performing into his seventies with only occasional musical appearances in such staunchly old-fashioned pieces as *Young England* (1916, John Oxenham), *Valentine* (1918, Gaston Dulacq), the touring *Gay Trouville* (1919, Raphael Correze), *The Rebel Maid* (1921, Lord Milverton) and *The Damask Rose*. Amongst his last engagements were several seasons in the rôle of the Mad Hatter in the musical version of *Alice in Wonderland*, touring productions of *Monsieur Beaucaire* and *The School for Scandal*, and a number of film rôles.

Autobiography: *Hayden Coffin's Book* (Alston Rivers, London, 1930)

LE COFFRE-FORT VIVANT Opérette à grand spectacle in 2 acts and 20 scenes by Georges Berr and Louis Verneuil based on the novel by Frédéric Mauzens. Lyrics by Henri Wernert. Music by Joseph Szulc and 'Jean Sautreuil'. Théâtre du Châtelet, Paris, 17 December 1938.

An opérette à grand spectacle staged with suitable splendour by Maurice Lehmann on the great Châtelet stage, *Le Coffre-fort vivant* (the living safe) followed the fortunes of a jewel of great price – from the lid of the very first and diamond-studded tobacco case – which is accidentally swallowed by shop-boy Mathias (Bach). Pursued by gangsters (Dinan, Robert Allard), the vendor (Jean Coizeau), the would-be buyer (Edmond Castel), a hospital nurse (Monette Dinay) and the piece's singing hero (Robert Burnier), Mathias gallops from Martinique to Mexico to Hollywood, his flight illustrated by La Macouba (grand ballet antillaise), a Hollywood Romantique routine, a parachute scene and a series of tableaux and specialities, until the diamond reappears in the course of nature.

In fact, this libretto had been a round for more than 20 years. The rights had originally been secured by composer Ivan Caryll who had a scenario prepared by Verneuil (in French) written up by Harry B Smith (in English) and the resultant musical produced on Broadway by Charles Dillingham as *The Canary* (Globe Theater 4 November 1918) with Julia Sanderson (Julie) and Joseph Cawthorn (Timothy) top-billed and one Wilmer Bentley (brother-in-law to the adapter) in a minor rôle. The 'canary' of the title was the name of the diamond. A 152-performance run in New York was followed by a good American touring life.

Second time around, the musical part to the libretto was composed by Joseph Szulc and 'Jean Sautreuil', a pseudonym which for some unfathomable reason covered the identity of Maurice Yvain who had written the Châtelet's previous show without need of such disguise. Aided by Lehmann's lavish production, the star comedian-and-matinée idol tandem of Bach and Burnier, and an attractive if not memorable score, *Le Coffre-fort vivant* played six months at the Châtelet before being withdrawn

for the summer. When the summer of 1939 was over, the theatre remained closed.

COGNIARD, [Charles] Théodore (b Paris, 30 April 1806; d Versailles, 13 May 1872)
COGNIARD, [Jean] Hippolyte (b Paris, 29 November 1807; d Paris, 6 February 1882).

The Cogniard brothers, celebrated Parisian theatre directors and authors in the middle years of the 19th century, were a pair of orphans who studied medicine before directing their intentions towards the theatre. Their first piece as authors, the 'episode de la guerre d'Alger' *La Cocarde tricolore*, was produced at the Folies-Dramatiques in 1831. It scored a considerable success, running for more than 200 nights, and the brothers followed it up with a bevy of spectaculars, dramas, vaudevilles and libretti, establishing themselves at the forefront of the brigade of purveyors of large-scale entertainments with such pieces as *Le Royaume des femmes* (1833, by Hippolyte Cogniard and Desnoyers), *La Fille de l'air* (Théâtre des Folies-Dramatiques 3 August 1837), *Le Naufrage de la Méduse* (Théâtre de la Renaissance 31 May 1839, music by Flotow, Grisar, Pilati et al), *Pied de mouton* (Théâtre de la Porte-Saint-Martin 8 September 1860, w Hector Crémieux), *Les Mille et une nuits* (Théâtre de la Porte-Saint-Martin 24 January 1843), *La Biche au bois* (Théâtre de la Porte-Saint-Martin 29 March 1845), *La Chatte blanche* (Cirque Nationale, 14 August 1852) and *La Poudre de Perlinpinpin* (Cirque Nationale, 24 December 1853).

Over the years – either together or singly – they directed a series of Paris theatres, notably the Folies-Dramatiques (together), the Théâtre du Vaudeville (Hippolyte) and, most memorably, the Théâtre des Variétés (Hippolyte) during the period of the production of Offenbach's famous opéras-bouffes: *La Belle Hélène*, *Barbe-bleue* and *La Grande-Duchesse de Gérolstein*.

A number of their féeries and spectaculars were reprised for decades in Paris's larger houses, and several were given a full and fresh score of music, turning them into legitimate opérettes or, more often, grands opéras-bouffes féeries. *La Biche au bois* was remade several times, in several countries, with scores by various hands including those of Hervé, *La Cocarde tricolore* was made into an opérette by Maurice Ordonneau with music by Robert Planquette (1892) whilst *Le Naufrage de la Méduse* was remusicked by Friedrich von Flotow for the German stage under the title of *Die Matrosen* (Hamburg, 23 December 1845). *Le Royaume des femmes*, banned at one stage, went through a whole series of remakes in France, being rewritten by Blum and Desnoyers in 1862 (as *La Reine Crinoline*), by Blum and Cogniard for the Variétés (1866), by Blum and Toché for the Nouveautés during the Exhibition of 1889, and again by Blum and Ferrier, to a score by Serpette, in 1896 for the Eldorado, but it also became *Die Fraueninsel* (*Die verkehrte Welt*) with a score by Carl Millöcker at the Deutsches-Theater, Pest in 1868 February) and two different *Die vekehrte Welt*s in Berlin (adapted from the two last French versions), as well as in Vienna, and in Budapest. *La Fille de l'air*, already Lisbonicized as *A filha de ar* (Joaquim Casimiro Lisbon Gymnase 17 June 1856) was later remade by Armand Liorat and composer Paul Lacôme for a Parisian production. The text for the Louis Varney opérette *Coquelicot* (Théâtre des Bouffes-

Parisiens 2 March 1882) was based on the brothers' vaudeville of the same title (Théâtre des Folies-Dramatiques 14 January 1836) by librettist Armand Silvestre, and many other pieces, credited and uncredited, and not always oversized, also looked back to the kings of the Paris spectacular theatre for their inspiration.

The Cogniards were not, however, as authors wedded only to the vaster forms of popular entertainment. Their names also appeared on bills at the Opéra-Comique (*Le Souper du mari*, music: Despréaux 14 January 1833 w Desnoyers etc) and at the Théâtre Lyrique (*La Fée Carabosse* music: Victor Massé 28 February 1859 w Lockroy etc) as part of a musical theatre career of the widest and most brilliant kind.

COHAN, George M[ichael]   (b Providence, RI, 3 July 1878; d New York, 5 November 1942). The much-loved 'Yankee-doodle-boy' of the American musical stage, Cohan – as author, performer and producer – was responsible for many of the best examples of a bristling, positive and tuneful brand of genuine musical comedy which took the old farce-comedy style of show into the 20th century.

Born into a family of vaudeville artists, Cohan began his performing life at an early age, appearing with his parents, Jerry (né Jeremiah Joseph Keohane) and Helen Cohan, and his sister, Josephine Cohan, as a member of the highly successful family act, The Four Cohans. In his early twenties he developed one of the sketches from the act into a song-and-dance show, on the broad lines of the popular 19th-century musical farcical comedies, writing the text and composing the songs, and staging it himself, under the management of Louis Behman, as *The Governor's Son* (1901). The Four Cohans and George's wife, Ethel Levey, had leading roles in this rather confusing traditional mishmash of mistaken identity, disguise and detecting, broadly played and perforated by lively, raw songs and, although it lasted only a few weeks at New York's Savoy Theater, it provided the family with an ever-developing vehicle for two full seasons of touring.

The success of *The Governor's Son* encouraged Cohan to follow it with another piece on the same lines, *Running For Office* (1903), and then with a more substantial musical play, *Little Johnny Jones* (1904). This one was a zippy, vigorous piece of up-to-date crooks-and-heroes stuff, with Cohan starring as its brash, cheeky all-American-boy hero, outwitting the baddies and rescuing his girl (Miss Levey) from the dens of Chinatown, and it included such songs as 'The Yankee Doodle Boy', 'Give My Regards to Broadway' and 'Life's a Funny Proposition After All'. Staged with enormous vigour and enthusiasm *Little Johnny Jones* was a fine success and, in spite of critical disdain, paid three visits to New York in its first year of touring.

From there on, Cohan continued regularly to turn out pieces in the same spirit and style. In 1906 he provided himself and Miss Levey with a new vehicle in *George Washington Jr* ('You're a Grand Old Flag', 'I Was Born in Virginia') and penned and, on commission from Abe Erlanger, directed *Forty-Five Minutes from Broadway* in which Donald Brian, the juvenile lead man from *Little Johnny Jones,* was starred with comedienne Fay Templeton and Victor Moore. The score included 'Mary's Grand Old Name', 'So Long, Mary' and a happy, catchy title number to add to Cohan's growing list of popular favourites.

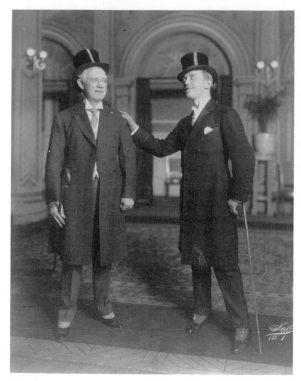

Plate 59. **George M Cohan** *and father Jerry.*

At this stage, he decided to add the duties of producer to his other functions and, in partnership with Sam Harris, the producer of *Little Johnny Jones* and *George Washington Jr*, he began a busy production schedule which, in the years that followed, included all the future Cohan musicals, both those with and those without the author starred, and the parallel list of successful straight plays which he also wrote (*Get-Rich-Quick Wallingford*, *Broadway Jones* etc). The partnership also mounted pieces by other writers, including the musicals *The Red Widow* (Chas Gebest/Channing Pollock, Rennold Wolf) and *The Beauty Shop* (Gebest) both starring Raymond Hitchcock, and the extremely successful *Going Up* (Louis Hirsch/James Montgomery) as well as such occasional imports as Jean Gilbert's *Polnische Wirtschaft* (*The Polish Wedding*). In 1910 Cohan and Harris, already proprietors of Broadway's Gaiety Theater, built the 1,000-seater George M Cohan Theater on Broadway and 43rd Street and, when it moved out of their hands and into the control of Abe Erlanger, they instead took command of the Astor and the Grand Opera House.

The series of Cohan musicals continued for a half-dozen years, with Cohan writing, composing, directing and starring in an expanded version of *Running for Office*, in *The Honeymooners* (1907), *The Yankee Prince* (1908), *The Little Millionaire* (1911), which marked his parents' last appearance as performers, and a new version of *Forty-Five Minutes From Broadway* (1912), whilst his other pieces were left in the hands of other performers. *The Talk of New York* (1907) reused the character of Kid Burns, created by Victor Moore in *Forty-Five Minutes From Broadway*, *Fifty Miles From Boston* (1908) introduced the song 'Harrigan' and had the young Edna Wallace Hopper as its heroine, *The American Idea* (1908) counted Trixie Friganza amongst its cast, and *The*

Man Who Owns Broadway (1909) toplined Raymond Hitchcock in his first star rôle for Cohan and Harris.

From 1914 Cohan spent a time in and on revue (*Hello, Broadway!*, *The Cohan Revue*) before he and Harris produced their last show, Cohan's burlesqued comic opera *The Royal Vagabond*, together in 1919. From then, Cohan went out on his own, producing *Mary* (1920), the latest work of *Going Up* composer Louis Hirsch, with great success, and the same composer's *The O'Brien Girl* (1921) with only a little less, before turning out the first real 'Cohan musical' for a number of years in *Little Nellie Kelly* (1922). A jaunty piece well in the tradition of the currently fashionable Cinderella genre best exemplified by *Irene* and *Sally*, with a song hit something like those of earlier shows in 'Nellie Kelly I Love You', *Little Nellie Kelly* gave him another splendid success all around America. It also became the first and only Cohan musical to play in Britain when C B Cochran transported it to the New Oxford Theatre for a fine seven-and-a-half-month run.

The Rise of Rosie O'Reilly, the following year, repeated the formula with sufficient success in both America and also in Australia where *Little Nellie Kelly* had similarly prospered. In 1927 Cohan returned to the musical stage to appear for the last time in one of his own works, *The Merry Malones*. Although the piece was well and truly in what had now become the old-fashioned musical comedy format, a sparky remake of everything Cohan had written before in the way of scenes and songs, under the flourishing and different conditions of the 1920s American stage it had a much longer run at the new Erlanger Theatre than had had his earlier, more genuinely and youthfully zippy shows.

Billie, a musicalization of his play *Broadway Jones*, closed out the canon of Cohan musicals and, thereafter, Cohan concentrated on writing, performing and producing for the straight theatre, returning only once to the song-and-dance stage, in 1937, to play the role of Franklin D Roosevelt in Rodgers and Hart's *I'd Rather Be Right* for his old partner, Sam Harris.

Cohan's down-to-earth farcical and sentimental plays, his simple, catchy songs full of obvious and chauvinistic sentiments irresistibly displayed, his colourful, unflaggingly energetic staging, and his brash, breezy star performances all combined to keep alive and give a joyful fillip to the continuing tradition of popular American musical comedy as established by Hoyt and Harrigan.

His life was used as the basis for the musical *George M* (1968) which featured many of his best-known songs as its score, as did a 1942 film, *Yankee Doodle Dandy*, in which James Cagney portrayed Cohan.

1901 **The Governor's Son** Savoy Theater 25 February
1903 **Running for Office** 14th Street Theater 27 April
1904 **Little Johnny Jones** Liberty Theater 7 November
1906 **Forty-Five Minutes From Broadway** New Amsterdam Theater 1 January
1906 **George Washington Jr** Herald Square Theater 12 February
1907 **The Honeymooners** New Amsterdam Theater 3 June
1907 **The Talk of New York** Knickerbocker Theater 3 December
1908 **Fifty Miles From Boston** Garrick Theater 3 February
1908 **The Yankee Prince** Knickerbocker Theater 20 April
1908 **The American Idea** New York Theater 5 October
1909 **The Man Who Owns Broadway** New York Theater 11 October

1911 **The Little Millionaire** Cohan Theater 25 September
1918 **The Voice of McConnell** Manhattan Opera House 25 December
1919 **The Royal Vagabond** (ex-*Cherry Blossoms*) revised libretto Cohan and Harris Theater 17 February
1922 **Little Nellie Kelly** Liberty Theater 13 November
1923 **The Rise of Rosie O'Reilly** Liberty Theater 25 December
1927 **The Merry Malones** Erlanger Theater 26 September
1928 **Billie** Erlanger Theater 1 October

Autobiography: *Twenty Years of Broadway, and the Years it Took to Get There* (Harper, New York, 1925), Biography: McCabe, J: *George M Cohan, the Man Who Owned Broadway* (Doubleday, Garden City, 1973), Morehouse, W: *George M Cohan, Prince of the American Theater* (Lippincott, Philadelphia, 1943)

COLE, Bob [COLE, Robert Allen] (b Athens, Ga, 1 July 1869; d Catskill, 2 August 1911). A slickly elegant song and dance man who doubled as a composer of songs for turn-of-the-century American shows.

Cole began his career as a performer working in a series of different musical acts and touring shows before joining Sam Jack's Creoles and then, in 1894, forming his own All-Star Stock Company, a touring group made up entirely of black performers. After the quick demise of that unprofitable venture, he joined the established Black Patti Company (1896), but soon left them to form another outfit of his own. This new group presented the musical comedy show *A Trip to Coontown*, which Cole had written with fellow performer Billy Johnson, and in which he starred in a 'little tramp' character which he had developed. At the same time, Cole and Billy Johnson also began to provide numbers to the scores of such variety musical shows as *A Reign of Error* (1899), *The Supper Club* (1901), *Champagne Charlie* (1901), *The Hall of Fame* (1902) and *Huck Finn* (1902) and others of their songs were from time to time borrowed to serve as part of the patchwork scores of various old'n'new pasticcio shows.

When Johnson's drinking habits turned him into an unreliable partner, Cole split away and formed a new partnership with another Johnson – J Rosamund Johnson. This duo went successfully into vaudeville as an act, performing much of their own material, but they also supplied numbers not only to the narrow world of specifically black shows and the rather wider one of vaudeville, but also to such mainstream Broadway artists as May Irwin, who made something of a speciality of belting out what were known as coon songs. Amongst the shows in which Cole and the second of his Johnsons placed numbers were *The Little Duchess* (1900), *The Rogers Brothers in Central Park* (1900), *Sally in Our Alley* (1902, 'Under the Bamboo Tree'), *The Sleeping Beauty and the Beast* (1902), *The Girl from Dixie* (1903, six songs), *Mr Bluebeard* (1903), *Nancy Brown* (1903, eight songs), *Mother Goose* (1903), *In Dahomey* (1903, 'My Castle on the Nile'), *An English Daisy* (1904) and *Moonshine* (1905, 'The Conjure Man'). They also wrote much of the music for the musical comedy *The Belle of Bridgeport* (1900), the made-over British pantomime *Humpty Dumpty* (1904) and the 20-performance run of *In Newport* (1904).

In 1906 the partners performed around America in their own novelty *He Handed Me a Lemon*, in 1907 they brought their full-length touring musical, *The Shoofly Regiment*, to

Broadway (15 performances), and two years later they followed up with a second such piece, *The Red Moon* ('Love Me, Baby Mine'), produced by A L Wilbur (32 performances). Both these shows, however, proved seriously unprofitable, and Cole found himself back performing in vaudeville. Soon after, however, badly affected by paresis, the incurably ill Cole drowned himself.

1897 **A Trip to Coontown** (Billy Johnson) South Amboy, NJ, 27 September Third Avenue Theater 4 April 1898

1898 **Kings of Koondom** (B Johnson) Koster and Bial's Music Hall August

1900 **The Belle of Bridgeport** (J Rosamund Johnson et al/w James W Johnson et al/Glen MacDonough) Bijou Theater 29 October

1904 **Humpty Dumpty** (w Fred Solomon, J R Johnson/Wood, Collins ad J J McNally) New Amsterdam Theater 14 November

1904 **In Newport** (J R Johnson/J W Johnson) Liberty Theater 26 December

1905 **The Shoofly Regiment** (J R Johnson/J W Johnson et al) Bijou Theater 6 August 1907

1909 **The Red Moon** (w J R Johnson) Majestic Theater 3 May

COLE, Jack (b New Brunswick, NJ, 27 April 1914; d Los Angeles, 16 February 1974). Much admired but un-Tony-ed Broadway choreographer of the postwar decades with a flair for the exotic.

Originally a dancer, during which career he appeared in several musicals and revues (*Caviar*, *Thumbs Up!*, Raki in *Venus in Silk*, *May Wine*, *Ziegfeld Follies*, *Alive and Kicking*), Cole made his Broadway début as a choreographer on *Something for the Boys* in 1942. He then worked on the shortlived *Allah Be Praised!* and *Magdalena* before creating the famous dances for *Kismet* (1953, Dance of the Ababu Princesses), dances which were reproduced both in London and, largely, in the subsequent film version. He choreographed *Jamaica* for Broadway, *Candide* for London, and both directed and choreographed *Donnybrook* (1962) and *Kean* (1962), before staging the dances for two further hits, *A Funny Thing Happened on the Way to the Forum* (1962) and *Man of La Mancha* (1965), as well as the unsuccessful *Foxy*, *Zenda* (1963), *Royal Flush* (1964, also director), *Chu-Chem* (1966, also Lord Hoo Hah) and *Mata Hari* (1967).

Cole's stage career was paired with an equally effective one in the cinema where he choreographed a number of musical and part-musical films from *Cover Girl* in 1944, through such pieces as *The Jolson Story* (1946), *The Merry Widow* (1952), *Gentlemen Prefer Blondes* (1953) and *Kismet* (1955) up to *Let's Make Love* in 1960.

Wayne Cilento appeared as Cole in a musical piece based on his works.

Biography: Loney, G: *Unsung Genius: The Passion of Jack Cole* (Franklin Watts, New York, 1984)

COLEMAN, Cy [KAUFMAN, Seymour] (b New York, 14 June 1929). The most evidently versatile of Broadway composers working between the 1960s and the 1990s, Coleman turned out a three-decade series of hit shows which included both a number of song standards and some of the most genuinely comic musical stage-writing of the post-war era.

Educated classically, Coleman made a fast start in the musical world, performing as a pianist in venues including the Steinway and Carnegie Halls from the age of six. He

Plate 60. **Cy Coleman**

moved on into the world of jazz and, in his twenties, played with his own trio in New York nightclubs whilst at the same time beginning a career as a songwriter. In the late 1950s he was responsible for several song hits ('Witchcraft' 1957 w Carolyn Leigh, 'The Best Is Yet to Come' 1959) and contributions to revues such as *John Murray Anderson's Almanac* ('Tin Pan Alley'), *Ziegfeld Follies of 1956* ('The Lady is Indisposed') and *Demi-Dozen* ('You Fascinate Me So'), before he completed his first musical comedy score, *Wildcat* (1960), an unpretentious Broadwayish star vehicle for television star Lucille Ball. *Wildcat* gave him his biggest song hit to date in the star's infectious invitation, 'Hey, Look Me Over'.

A musicalization of Patrick Dennis's *Little Me* (1962) to a libretto by Neil Simon produced a very funny burlesque of the celebrity biography with astutely witty musical illustrations ('The Other Side of the Tracks', 'Real Live Girl', 'I've Got Your Number') which showed up a rare talent for musical humour and parody, whilst *Sweet Charity*

(1966, 'Big Spender'), a brassy Tin-Pan-Alley show with a big-hearted heroine, gave him an international show hit and a parallel song hit. *Seesaw* (1973), another tale of a klutzy girl who scares away a conventional man, brought forward some further fine songs ('Nobody Does it Like Me', 'It's Not Where You Start') whilst *I Love My Wife* (1977), a small-scale and long-running comedy with songs, went on from Broadway to success in several other countries.

On the Twentieth Century (1978), a dazzling operetta burlesque, brought its composer a belated first Tony Award, whilst *Barnum* (1980, 'Come Follow the Band', 'The Colors of My Life', also co-producer), a surprisingly affecting piece of spectacular razzmatazz based on the character of the famous showman, went on from major success on Broadway and in London to be played in more countries throughout the world than any other Coleman work, and than almost any other Broadway show of its period.

After several false starts during the 1980s, Coleman returned to the top of the heap in 1990 with a third sizzling burlesque in the highly successful parody of the gumshoe cinema *City of Angels* (Tony Award), and he followed this in the next season with another 'best musical' award for a very different type of show in the glittery *The Will Rogers Follies*.

Coleman has also worked in both television (Shirley Maclaine's *If They Could See Me Now* and *Gypsy in My Soul* etc), and in film where, beyond the cinematic version of *Sweet Charity*, he supplied scores for such films as *Father Goose*, *The Art of Love*, *The Troublemaker*, *Power*, *Garbo Talks* and *Family Business*. He has also continued a performing and recording career as a pianist.

1960 **Wildcat** (Carolyn Leigh/N Richard Nash) Alvin Theater 16 December
1962 **Little Me** (Leigh/Neil Simon) Lunt-Fontanne Theater 17 November
1966 **Sweet Charity** (Dorothy Fields/Simon) Palace Theater 29 January
1973 **Seesaw** (Fields/Michael Stewart ad Michael Bennett) Uris Theater 18 March
1977 **I Love My Wife** (Stewart) Ethel Barrymore Theater 17 April
1978 **On the Twentieth Century** (Adolph Green, Betty Comden) St James Theater 19 February
1979 **Home Again, Home Again** (Barbara Fried/Russell Baker) American Shakespeare Theater, Stratford 12 March
1980 **Barnum** (Stewart/Mark Bramble) St James Theater 30 April
1988 **Let 'em Rot** (w A E Hotchner/Hotchner) Coconut Grove Playhouse, Florida 16 February
1989 **Welcome to the Club** (revised *Let 'em Rot*) Music Box Theater 13 April
1989 **City of Angels** (David Zippel/Larry Gelbart) Virginia Theater 11 December
1991 **The Will Rogers Follies** (Green, Comden/Peter Stone) Palace Theater 1 June

COLETTE, [Gabrielle Sidonie Claudine] (b Saint-Sauveur-en-Puisaye, 28 January 1873; d Paris, 3 August 1954).

A music-hall artist of limited talent, Colette caused a brief scandal when she appeared at the Moulin-Rouge with the Marquise de Belbeuf in an overtly lesbian pantomime which was quickly withdrawn from the bill. She had considerably more success as a writer, becoming a much admired figure in French arts and letters, and the second woman to be awarded the Légion d'honneur. Several of her celebrated novels and novellas were subsequently adapted to the stage (w Léopold Marchand), occasionally with musical trimmings. A musical based on her *Claudine* tales, with music by Rodolphe Berger, was played at the Moulin-Rouge (13 November 1910) with Polaire, Marise Fairy and Claudius heading the cast, whilst the much-loved Hollywood film based on her tale of *Gigi* (Frederick Loewe/Alan Jay Lerner) was subsequently adapted, with limited success, for the stage.

There have also been several unsuccessful attempts to put the lady herself on the stage. In America, Diana Rigg was featured as Colette in a new and Broadway-bound version of a 1970 off-Broadway *Colette* (played at the Ellen Stewart Theater 6 May, with Zoë Caldwell as its heroine), with songs by Tom Jones and Harvey Schmidt, which folded on the road (Seattle, 9 February 1982). It subsequently became *Colette Collage* (York Players 31 March 1983) in a third metamorphosis. In Britain, Fenella Fielding was seen in the first version of the Schmidt/Jones piece, out of town, and Cleo Laine appeared in the title-rôle of a *Colette* (John Dankworth) brought from the provinces to the Comedy Theatre in 1979 (24 September, 47 performances).

COLLIN, Ottilie [née MÜLLER] (b Vienna, 19 May 1863; d Vienna, 29 February 1960). Viennese soprano who created important rôles in a number of classic 19th-century Operetten.

Ottilie Collin made her stage début at Graz and appeared at Teplitz, in the title-rôle of Suppé's *Die schöne Galathee*, at 18 years of age. In 1883 she was engaged at Berlin's Friedrich-Wilhelmstädtisches-Theater and, in her two seasons there, she created, amongst others, the principal soprano part of Annina in Johann Strauss's *Eine Nacht in Venedig*. Impressed by her performance, the composer had her taken to Vienna to repeat the rôle in the revised version of the show staged there, and she remained in Austria to create, with even more sensational success, the rôle of Sáffi in his *Der Zigeunerbaron* (1885, 'Habet acht!', 'Wer uns getraut?').

In a period of seven years as a principal soprano at the Theater an der Wien she created the rôles of Rita in Czibulka's *Pfingsten in Florenz* (1884), Georgine von Callac in *Zwillinge* (1885), Minna Heidekrug in *Der Feldprediger* (1884), Gilda in *Der Viceadmiral* (1886), Poldi in *Der Botschafter* (1886), Fellsa d'Amores in *Der Hofnarr* (1886), Christell Eimen in Brandl's *Der liebe Augustin*, Tilly in Strauss's *Simplicius* (1887), Yum Yum in the Viennese version of *Der Mikado* (1888), Syuda in *Die indische Witwe* (1889), Lisa in *Der Schlosserkönig* (1889), Pythia in *Das Orakel* (1889), Harriet in *Der arme Jonathan* (1890) and Princess Marie in *Der Vogelhändler* (1891, 'Fröhlich Pfalz', 'Als geblüht der Kirschenbaum'), as well as appearing in such parts as Raphaël (*La Princesse de Trébizonde*), Laura (*Der Bettelstudent*), Fiametta (*Boccaccio*), Adele (*Die Fledermaus*), Kätchen (*Die sieben Schwaben*) and Else (*Der lustige Krieg*), before returning to Berlin and the post of prima donna at the Friedrich-Wilhelmstädtisches Theater.

She remained in Berlin until 1896, after which she

limited her activities to intermittent guest appearances, playing at Munich, at the Vienna Carltheater in *Carneval in Rom*, *Der lustige Krieg* (Violetta) and as Lili in Ferron's *Das Krokodil* (1898) and returning to the Theater an der Wien as late as 1901 to repeat her Sáffi in the last stages of a famous career.

COLLINS, José (b London, 23 May 1887; d London, 6 December 1958). Dark and dashing British vocalist who found fame as the heroine of *The Maid of the Mountains*.

Daughter of the music-hall star Lottie Collins [Charlotte Louise COLLINS] (1865–1910), the famous performer of 'Ta-ra-ra-boom-de-ay' and a sometime member of the Gaiety Theatre company, José Collins also made her earliest appearance on the stage in the music halls. She then toured in Britain in *A Chinese Honeymoon*, made her West End début in the short-lived *The Antelope* (1908, Iris Fenton), and played in several other musicals in the British provinces before making a firm mark on the musical stage during a period of some five years spent in America.

She appeared on Broadway in local versions of a run of Continental Operetten: Eysler's revusical *Vera Violetta* (1911, Mme von Grünberg), *Die Fledermaus* (*The Merry Countess*, 1912, Rosalinde), *Endlich Allein* (*Alone at Last*, 1915, Tilly Dachau) and Rényi's *A kis gróf* (Suzi, 1914, Suzi), played in revue (Angela to the Gus of Jolson in *The Whirl of Society*, *The Passing Show of 1914*) and in vaudeville before returning to Britain, under contract to the struggling Daly's Theatre. She made her first appearance there as Camille Joyeuse in *The Happy Day* (1916), but it was her second show for Daly's, the record-breaking *The Maid of the Mountains* ('Love Will Find a Way', 'Farewell', 'A Paradise for Two' etc), in which she created the rôle of the gipsyish heroine, Teresa, which launched her as a major star.

In five years at Daly's, as she followed Teresa with another gipsyish rôle in *A Southern Maid* (1920, Dolores) and with the very vocal Hungarian prima donna of Jacobi's *Sybil* (1921), José Collins was instrumental in building a following for the once famous house which helped restore it to prosperity, before its sale to tycoon Jimmy White encouraged manager Robert Evett and his star to decamp and set up their own productions at another once famous house, the Gaiety. Miss Collins subsequently starred in English versions of *Die letzte Walzer* (*The Last Waltz*, 1922, Vera Lisaweta) and *Frasquita* (1925, Frasquita) and in the title-rôles of remade-to-measure vehicles such as *Catherine* (*Die Siegerin*, 1923) and *Our Nell* (1924, ex-*Our Peg*), but without ever recreating the wild euphoria of the Daly's years in which she had been one of the British theatre's brightest stars.

In 1926 she toured for White in the rôle of Maia in *A Greek Slave*, which closed prior to London, and thereafter she abandoned the musical theatre, appearing in revue, variety and the occasional straight play in the last years of her career.

Her sister, who worked as Lucia Lottie Collins (whilst denying that she was seeking to be compared with or capitalize on the fame of her mother), appeared in variety and music hall.

Autobiography: *The Maid of the Mountains: Her Story* (Hutchinson & Co, London, 1932)

COLLITS' INN Musical romance in 3 acts by T Stuart Gurr. Lyrics by Gurr and Varney Monk. Music by Mrs Monk. Princess Theatre, Melbourne, 23 December 1933.

Collits' Inn was probably the most successful attempt made, during the 1930s, to create a native Australian musical play as a vehicle for the country's biggest ever stay-at-home musical theatre star, Gladys Moncrieff. The historic Collits' Inn is an olden days pub in the Blue Mountains and, in the story set around it, Miss Moncrieff played the owner's daughter, Mary, sought in wedlock by both the bushranger Robert Keane (Claude Flemming) and John Lake (Robert Chisholm), the army officer in charge of the local road-making. Comedian George Wallace decorated the piece with ad libs in Victorian manner as Dandy Dick, the pub's roustabout. Mrs Monk's music included a 'Stay While the Stars Are Shining' for her soprano star and a military 'The Red Coat' for her hero as well as a picturesque aboriginal corroboree which proved the production highlight of the evening.

First produced by amateurs, the show was subsequently mounted professionally by film-maker Frank Thring (Eftee Attractions), with the idea that, after establishing itself in the theatre, it would then make a movie. A fine run of over a hundred performances in Melbourne was followed by a Sydney season at the New Tivoli Theatre (21 June 1934) and a return to Melbourne, and, although the intended film never got past the stage of a few tests, the popularity of *Collits' Inn* prompted Thring to a second attempt at a stage musical. Mrs Monk's *The Cedar Tree* (Princess Theatre, Melbourne 22 December 1934), did not, however, find the same success, and there proved to be limited audiences for his productions of two London musicals with Australian or New Zealand input, *The Beloved Vagabond* (Princess Theatre 14 April 1934) and *Jolly Roger* (Princess Theatre 3 November 1934). Before a fifth attempt – a version of *Robbery Under Arms* from *The Beloved Vagabond*'s Dudley Glass – was completed Thring died, leaving *Collits' Inn* as the most successful of his series.

Recording: selection (RZ)

COLORADO Opérette à grand spectacle in 2 acts by Claude Dufresne. Lyrics by Jacques Larue. Music by Jacques-Henry Rys. Théâtre de la Gaîté-Lyrique, Paris, 16 December 1950.

Where America had *Oklahoma!*, France had *Colorado* (without the exclamation mark), a song and scenery show produced by Germaine Roger-Montjoye at the Gaîté-Lyrique. The libretto pitched Jim Bullit (Armand Mestral, bass and dressed in black) the powerful goldfields land-owner and boss of its lucrative saloon, against the young, aspiring golddigger Ricardo Diaz (Lou Pizzara, tenor and dressed in white), the beautiful Katharina Sanders (Claude Chenard, soprano), come west in 1877 to lay her hands on some of the land to which her late father had laid claim, and the little saloon pianist Pancho (Maurice Baquet). A Christmas scenario with a children's ballet, a Fête des Étoiles with a 'Ballet des Nationalités', another routine called Gold-Fever, a tap dance en pointe and a masked ball with a Ballet des Valses Romantiques were amongst the visual attractions, whilst a lively march in praise of 'Colorado' and Ricardo's hymn to 'Katharina' were the most popular portions of a score which also included a foxtrot ('Je suis Inca'), a blues ('Crois à ta chance') and a negro lullaby.

The show had a considerable success, playing through 11 months, during which time the baritone Michel Dens alternated with Pizzara in the hero's rôle. After a solid provincial career, it returned to the Gaîté for a second run in 1959 (12 February) with Mestral and Baquet repeating alongside Bernard Alvi (Ricardo) and Andrée Grandjean (Katharina), prior to further touring and repertory productions.

COLSON, Kevin [William] (b Sydney, Australia, 28 August 1938). Australian actor and vocalist who has had two careers in the musical theatre.

Tall, rich-voiced Colson had his earliest successes in the musical theatre as a young leading man, taking top rôles in the Australian productions of *Irma la Douce* (1961, Nestor), *Carnival* (1962, Paul) and *Sail Away* (1963, John van Mier) before moving on to London where he succeeded Keith Michell in the co-starring rôle of *Robert and Elizabeth* and played the parts of Cliff in London's edition of *Cabaret* (1968) and Charles Darnay to the Carton of Edward Woodward in *Two Cities* (1969), both at the Palace Theatre.

He then moved out of the theatre and into the world of business, returning only at the end of this career to once more appear on the musical stage. This second stage-life began when he played the rôle of Ben in the British première of *Follies* (1985) at Manchester, after which he created the rôle of Walter de Courcey in *Chess*, subsequently playing Molokov in the same production, before going on to introduce the part of George in *Aspects of Love* at the Prince of Wales Theatre. He went on to play the same rôle in the show's productions in New York and in Australia.

COMDEN, Betty [COHEN, Elizabeth] (b New York, 3 May 1915). A half, to the other-half of Adolph Green, of the most durable lyric and book-writing pairing in musical theatre history.

Having begun in the music business as a performer in a night club act The Revuers, Miss Comden there established a lyric-writing partnership with fellow performer, Green, which began with their devising cabaret material, both for themselves and for others. The group appeared in and they supplied three songs ('We Had a Show', 'Variety' 'The Baroness Bazooka') for the aborted production of *Three after Three* (New Haven, 24 November 1939), but Comden and Green blossomed as writers when they supplied both text and lyrics for a first full Broadway musical, the free-wheeling and sparkling *On the Town* (1944). That show's success set the partnership into a Broadway orbit in which their lyrics to Leonard Bernstein's music in *Wonderful Town* (1953, 'Ohio'), the book and lyrics of *Bells Are Ringing* (1956, 'Just in Time', 'The Party's Over'), a musical written to feature Judy Holliday who had been a member of their act, the adaptation of *All About Eve* as *Applause* (1970, 'Applause') and the libretto and lyrics to the opéra-bouffe version of *On the Twentieth Century* (1978) have brought them notable successes around the world.

Several other shows to which they contributed more or less of the sung and/or spoken portion – *Do Re Mi* (400 performances, 'Make Someone Happy'), *Say, Darling* (332 performances), *Hallelujah, Baby!* (293 performances) and a musical comedy version of Barrie's *Peter Pan* – also had good Broadway runs and, in the case of the last named, a number of subsequent productions. In 1991, after a rather discreet decade which brought no new Broadway success, the pair returned as the lyricists of the Tony Award-winning *The Will Rogers Follies* in 1991.

Other stage credits have included the sketches and lyrics for the 1951 revue *Two on the Aisle*, material for several other revues and compilation shows, and additional material for the transformation of Jule Styne's *Gentlemen Prefer Blondes* into *Lorelei*.

A considerable period of the pair's early writing career was spent in Hollywood, where they provided scripts and/or songs for many musical films, including *Good News* (1947), *The Barkleys of Broadway* (1949), the screen adaptation of *On the Town* (1949) and *The Band Wagon* (1954), and screenplays for comedies (*Auntie Mame* etc). Their best-known original film screenplay was that for the movie musical classic *Singin' in the Rain* which they subsequently adapted in an unfortunate Broadway stage version. A different adaptation of their tale, written by actor-author Tommy Steele for the British stage, was, however, mounted in several other countries with very much happier results.

Miss Comden has continued to make infrequent stage appearances since featuring in the original cast of *On the Town*, appearing with Green in the revue *A Party with Comden and Green* (1958, 1977) and in concert in *Follies* as well as playing, in extremis, in the comedy rôle of Letitia Primrose in *On the Twentieth Century*. She has also appeared on the non-musical stage.

1944 **On the Town** (Leonard Bernstein/w Adolph Green) Adelphi Theater 28 December
1945 **Billion Dollar Baby** (Morton Gould/w Green) Alvin Theater 21 December
1947 **Bonanza Bound** (Saul Chaplin/w Green) Shubert Theater, Philadelphia 26 December
1953 **Wonderful Town** (Bernstein/w Green/Jerome Chodorov, Joseph Fields) Winter Garden Theater 25 February
1954 **Peter Pan** (Jule Styne, Mark Charlap/w Green, Carolyn Leigh/J M Barrie ad) Winter Garden Theater 20 October
1956 **Bells Are Ringing** (Styne) Shubert Theater 29 November
1958 **Say, Darling** (Styne/w Green/Richard Bissell, Marion Bissell) ANTA Theater 3 April
1960 **Do Re Mi** (Styne/w Green/Garson Kanin) St James Theater 26 December
1961 **Subways Are for Sleeping** (Styne/w Green) St James Theater 27 December
1964 **Fade Out – Fade In** (Styne/w Green) Mark Hellinger Theater 26 May
1967 **Hallelujah Baby** (Styne/w Green) Martin Beck Theater 26 April
1970 **Applause** (Charles Strouse/Lee Adams) Palace Theater 30 March
1974 **Lorelei** revised *Gentlemen Prefer Blondes* (Palace Theater)
1978 **On the Twentieth Century** (Cy Coleman/w Green) St James Theater 19 February
1982 **A Doll's Life** (Larry Grossman/w Green) Mark Hellinger Theater 23 September
1985 **Singin' in the Rain** (pasticcio) Gershwin Theater 2 July
1991 **The Will Rogers Follies** (Coleman/w Green/Peter Stone) Palace Theater 1 May

COME SPY WITH ME   Comedy musical in 2 acts by Bryan Blackburn. Whitehall Theatre, London, 31 May 1966.

A vehicle for travesty artist Danny La Rue which took a few swipes at such glamorous-spy television series of the era as *The Man from Uncle* and *The Avengers* whilst accomplishing its principal aim of getting La Rue into as many frocks and fixes as possible in the space of two acts. Agent Danny Rhodes (La Rue) is on the trail of beastly Dr Sigmund Fink (Barrie Gosney), vampish Tamara Flesch (Valerie Walsh), 'Greensleeves' (Riggs O'Hara) and Momma (Rose Hill), trying to stop them getting their hands on a vital virility drug. Since Fink knows who he is, Danny gets into a frock – that is to say, several frocks – as an Irish nurse, a diplomatic lady, a cabaret singer, and as each of the other principal ladies. The most up-front of these was the little lift operator, Mavis Apple (Barbara Windsor), the unwitting possessor of the vile phial who, alas, swallows its contents.

It was Mavis who had the best 'number' of the show, a telephone distress monologue, calling for help from the den of iniquity that is the gang's base, only to butt against wrong numbers and officious operators, but Danny's ally, the smoother than shaving-soap Agent VO8 (Garry Miller), had some croony moments and the baddies got to sing a number about the welfare state. A mixture of burlesque and British films, directed by Ned Sherrin, with a much-appreciated star performance at its centre, Peter Bridge and Brian Rix's production of *Come Spy with Me* spent a jolly 468 performances in the West End.

A French musical, *SO6*, which featured comedian Roger Nicolas in a similar parody of telly-spyland, was mounted in Paris the following year.

Recording: original cast (Decca)

COMPANY   Musical in 2 acts by George Furth. Music and lyrics by Stephen Sondheim. Alvin Theater, New York, 26 April 1970.

An unusual piece for its time, the entertainment *Company* did not have a conventional, forward-going plotline, but was made up of a series of revusical character sketches, comical scenes and songs linked together by the character of bachelor Robert (Dean Jones), a friend of all the 'lurrrvly' New York married couples who made up most of the rest of the cast. Their main aim in life is quickly seen to be that of getting poor Robert as married as they as quickly as possible.

The show opens with everyone gathering to celebrate Robert's birthday, before it side-steps into a series of flash-around scenes showing him visiting each couple: niggling, bourgeois Sarah (Barbara Barrie) and Harry (Charles Kimborough), adoring Peter (John Cunningham) and Susan (Merle Louise) who are getting fashionably divorced but not separated, effortfully trendy David (George Coe) and his tactfully conservative Jenny (Teri Ralston), likeable Paul (Steve Elmore) and his temporarily frenetic Amy (Beth Howland), who are finally getting married after years of living together, and patiently adult Larry (Charles Braswell) and the smart, loud-mouthed Joanne (Elaine Stritch) he's got himself stuck with. His encounters with this parade of often irritatingly trivial and foolish folk were interspersed with some different kinds of encounters. Air-hostess April (Susan Browning), kooky Marta (Pamela Myers) and danc-

ing Kathy (Donna McKechnie) roll in and out of his bed but, in spite of them, and in spite of the efforts of all those friends, Robert emerges at the end of the entertainment 35 years old and still his own man. But, given the pressures, you can't help wondering for how long.

The songs of the show illustrated its characters and its topics wittily and incisively. Harry and Sarah's bickering lies were accompanied by the assertion that 'It's the Little Things You Do Together' which make a marriage work, Robert tried to make flattering post-coital conversation as April clambered out of bed to catch her plane to 'Barcelona', drink-sodden Joanne got waspish about the serious middle class to which she belongs as represented by 'The Ladies Who Lunch', whilst the whole brigade patted themselves on the back in harmonized unison at being such good friends to 'Poor Baby' Robert in 'What Would We Do Without You?' and 'Side by Side by Side'.

In a score which rendered up many durable concert and nightclub favourites, probably the most enjoyable pieces were two which did not extract so easily from the show: Amy's gallopingly frantic list of last-minute reasons why she is not 'Getting Married Today', counterpointed by the happy premarital crooning of her husband-to-inevitably-be and the dour soprano comments of a church chorister, and the trio for Marta, April and Kathy, boop-be-dooping exasperatedly and in thoroughly up-to-date style through the assertion that 'You Could Drive a Person Crazy' with marital half-promises. Robert himself got to let loose in the last stages of the show with a piece which was in a different vein to the rest of the evening's crisp, dry and/or slightly satirical material: a striving, sentimental hymn to 'Being Alive' which quickly found its way into the repertoire of half a hundred male torch singers and was for many years thereafter torn to a tatter twenty times a day in musical comedy auditions.

Harold Prince's Broadway production of *Company* proved a fine success, running through 705 performances whilst, a year into the run, a company took the show on the road with George Chakiris (Robert) at its head. Both were still in action when Prince and Richard Pilbrow mounted a London production at Her Majesty's Theatre. Larry Kert, who had replaced Jones as Robert a few weeks after the show had opened, and several of the original cast (Misses Howland, McKechnie, Ralston, Elmore) took part at the head of an all-American cast, but the show found more acceptance amongst theatre professionals than with the general public in a run of what was considered a disappointing 344 performances. Its appeal to theatre folk (not unconnected with the fact that each actor had a rôle and a scene), its well-known songs and its economic, chorusless construction all combined, however, to ensure it a steady run of subsequent provincial productions, both in America and in Britain, as well as occasional showings elsewhere.

A production in Germany followed close on behind the original staging, in 1973, but an Australian professional production did not emerge until 1986 when the piece was mounted for a season with a cast including many of Australia's best musical theatre performers at the Sydney Opera House's Drama Theatre.

UK: Her Majesty's Theatre 8 January 1972; Germany: Düsseldorf 1973; Australia: Drama Theatre (Opera House), Sydney 9 January 1986
Recording: original cast (Columbia); London cast (CBS)

COMSTOCK F Ray (b Buffalo, NY, 1880; d Boston, 15 October 1949). A Broadway producer who mounted both small-house musicals and vast spectaculars in a widely varying career, Comstock is largely remembered (when he is remembered) for his productions at the little Princess Theater, in the 1910s.

After beginnings as a theatre usher and box-office manager, the young Comstock made his début as a producer of musical comedy in 1904 with a touring production of the Chicago show *The Runaways* which had been taken to Broadway the previous year by another young producer, Sam Shubert. He moved on to Broadway for the first time, in collaboration with director-author R H Burnside, with *Fascinating Flora* (1907), a run-of-the-mill musical comedy which nevertheless rated a useful 113 performances in New York before going on the road. Comstock subsequently interested himself for a while in the black musical comedies which were threatening to turn profitable in the years prior to the war, and he mounted two of the better-liked ones, *Bandana Land* (1908) and *Mr Lode of Koal* (1909), just as the thin vein was running unprofitably out. He then joined with Morris Gest to mount the Broadway production of Joseph Herbert's much-rewritten *The Beauty Spot* (1909) for a good 137 performances in New York, and the pair later had a 'by arrangement' credit on the Shubert production of *The Peasant Girl* (1914–15).

Comstock struck a more productive line when he teamed, variously, with agent Elisabeth Marbury, with Gest and with William Elliott on a series of musical plays mounted at the small Princess Theater. Beginning with an adaptation of the successful London musical comedy *Mr Popple of Ippleton* (*Nobody Home*) in 1915, he co-mounted *Very Good Eddie* (1915), *Go To It* (1916), *Oh, Boy!* (1917), *Oh, Lady! Lady!!* (1918) and *Oh, My Dear!* (1918) in the little house, whilst also staging *Oh! Look* (1918) at the Vanderbilt and *Leave it to Jane* – squeezed out of the Princess by the success of *Oh, Boy!* – and the musical comedy *Kitty Darling* (1917, w Gest, Elliott) in larger houses.

From the small-scale Princess Theater-style pieces, Comstock went to the other end of the scale when, in the continuing partnership with Morris Gest, he mounted the Broadway productions of the London hits *Chu Chin Chow* (1917 w Elliott) and *The Maid of the Mountains* (1918 w Elliott), the risqué spectacular *Aphrodite* (1919), C B Cochran's London version of the equally sexy *Afgar* (1920) and *Chu Chin Chow*'s successor, *Mecca* (1920). Amongst a heavy schedule of plays and imported companies they also sponsored such pieces as the Russian revue *Chauve-Souris* and the extravagant *The Miracle*. Comstock also, however, suffered a number of failures, including Kern's *Zip Goes a Million*, an americanized and botched *Phi-Phi* and Armand Vecsey's *The Rose of China*, and he went from having 11 shows on Broadway and/or announced, and nine touring, at the beginning of 1920, to a virtual wipe-out of his musical comedy activities a year later. He retired from the theatre in 1929.

COMTE OBLIGADO Opérette in 3 acts by André Barde. Music by Raoul Moretti. Théâtre des Nouveautés, Paris, 16 December 1927.

The 'Comte Obligado' is not a real count, he is Antoine (Milton), the little lift-boy (the 'boy' has nothing to do with age) in the Paris couture house Maison Amandine, who has inherited a magnificent fortune. Alas, for all his dreamy plans, by the time the government has thievingly helped itself to 90 per cent of his windfall, there is just enough left for him to blow on one wild spree. And so 'Comte Obligado' goes out into the world where, taken under the wing of the wealthy and social Madame de Miranda (Marthe Ferrare) who is under the impression that he is a fabulously rich Algerian, he is made a fuss of by all until the truth comes out. Dropped by his fair-weather leeches, the sad lad flings the last of his disappointing money on a horse. It wins him a second, untaxed fortune. Which goes to show that, in France, the government prefers you to win your money gambling than from the life's work of your family.

Milton, equipped with a delightful rôle, also had two song hits in Raoul Moretti's score with 'La Caravane' (otherwise 'La Fille du bédouin') and 'Les Artichauts', whilst the incidental but necessary juvenile couple, played by Davia and Robert Darthez, took the central part of the score with her solo 'Si Maman le veut' and their duos 'Ça fait passer un moment' and 'Un petit bout de femme'. The dandy Urban tangoed to 'Mio padre' and sang of 'Le Petit Oiseau des îles' and Mlle Ferrare ventured 'Yoo-oo, ma Caroline' in the other principal parts of a musical accompaniment which helped *Comte Obligado* to a fine success.

The piece which, in the modern musical comedy vein, featured a cast of 13 and no chorus, was played for many years throughout the French provinces and, in 1935, Milton starred in a filmed version. New York also got a quick glimpse of *Comte Obligado* when a touring French musical comedy company, with Servatius in the comic lead, included the show in its season on Broadway in 1929.

USA: Jolson Theater 11 March 1929; Film: Léon Mathot 1935

A CONNECTICUT YANKEE Musical in a prologue and 2 acts by Herbert Fields adapted from Mark Twain's *A Connecticut Yankee in King Arthur's Court*. Lyrics by Lorenz Hart. Music by Richard Rodgers. Vanderbilt Theater, New York, 3 November 1927.

Twain's satirical fantasy novel *A Connecticut Yankee in King Arthur's Court* (1889) was made into a slightly less satirical silent film by Harry Myers in 1920, and a sight of that film encouraged Fields, Rodgers and Hart to option the novel as material for a musical. It was 1927 before the piece finally got written, and, when it did, it was both updated and sweetened-up with some good old-fashioned anachronism-jokes and situations to make it into a lively, traditional musical comedy book.

The prologue introduced Martin (William Gaxton), on the eve of his wedding, paying more attention to pretty Alice Carter (Constance Carpenter) than to his fiancée, Fay Morgan (Nana Bryant), until the exasperated lass understandably whacks him over the head with a bottle of champagne. Martin goes down ... and back. When he wakes up, he is in King Arthur's Court. Fay, naturally, is Morgan le Fey, Alice is the delicious Alisande la Carteloise, friend Lawrence Lake (William Rosell) has become Lancelot du Lac, Gerald Lake (Jack Thompson) is Galahad, alongside Merlin (William Norris), Arthur (Paul Everton) and so forth. Rescued from an inexplicable

299

stranger's fate by a convenient prediction of an eclipse, Martin then proceeds to modernize Camelot with 20th-century 'improvements' in precisely the same way that comic opera comedians of the 19th century regularly 'improved' foreign lands by introducing English (or American) habits and institutions. But Morgan le Fey is on the warpath, and when Martin truly wakes up, he is determined to swap the modern Fay for Alice.

The score of *A Connecticut Yankee* brought out a pair of hit numbers, one new, one borrowed. The new one was the demi-period duet for Martin and Alisande, 'Thou Swell', the borrowed one was 'My Heart Stood Still', originally used in Rodgers and Hart's London revue *One Dam Thing After Another* earlier the same year and, according to Rodgers, stuck hastily into this show in order to stop insufficiently voiced comedienne Beatrice Lillie claiming it for another of their shows. As sung by the star pair, it gave them a second hit. Stanley Green has pointed out that the entire chorus lyric of this unstaccato song holds only six bisyllabic words, all the rest are, unusually, monosyllables. Galahad and his Evelyn (June Cochrane) were the number two pair, singing about being 'On a Desert Island with Thee'.

Lew Fields and Lyle Andrews's production of *A Connecticut Yankee* had a fine Broadway run of 418 performances, the longest metropolitan life of any of the Rodgers–Hart musicals of that period, and the show was taken up by 'British Amalgamated Theatres Ltd' to be produced at London's Daly's Theatre. Miss Carpenter repeated her original rôle opposite Harry Fox, with Billy Holland and Gladys Cruickshank in support and J G Taylor as Merlin. For Britishers, who were apparently presumed not to know what Connecticut was, it was retitled *A Yankee in King Arthur's Court*, and Vivian Ellis and Desmond Carter had two songs interpolated into the score – one, 'I Don't Know How', to replace the hit number that England had already heard. The show lasted only 43 performances at a theatre that had given a much warmer welcome to the same songwriters' *Peggy-Ann*, before it was bundled briefly on the road in the new year.

In 1943 Rodgers himself sponsored a Broadway revival (Martin Beck Theater 17 November 1943) in an effort to give the sinking Hart an interest and a job. The text was partly rewritten to put it into a 1943 wartime setting and five pieces of the original score topped up with a half dozen new ones. Vivienne Segal, as Morgan le Fey, reaped the best of what would be Hart's last songs, relating how she had disposed of each of her husbands 'To Keep My Love Alive'. Dick Foran and Julie Warren played the number one couple, and Vera-Ellen and Chester Stratton the second, through 135 performances. This version of the show was televised in America in 1955.

UK: Daly's Theatre 10 October 1929
Recording: selection from 1943 cast (Decca, AEI)

CONRAD, Con [DOBER, Conrad K] (b New York, 18 June 1891; d Van Nuys, Calif, 28 September 1938). At first a pianist in film houses and a performer in vaudeville, Conrad turned out a bundle of popular songs in the 1920s, and also contributed to a small group of mostly successful musical plays.

A long list of single songs – 'Singin' the Blues (till my daddy comes home)', 'Palesteena' (both w J Russell Robin-

son), 'Ma! He's Making Eyes at Me' (w Sidney Clare), 'Barney Google' (w Billy Rose), 'Lonesome and Sorry' (w Benny Davis), 'Let's all go to Mary's House' (w Harry Woods), 'Margie' (w Robinson, Davis), 'Goodnight' (w Harry Woods, Irving Bibo), 'A Prisoner of Love' (w Leo Robin), 'Memory Lane' (w B G de Sylva, Lary Spier), 'You've Got to See Mamma Every Night (or you can't see mamma at all)' – and, following his move to Hollywood in 1929, of music for such films as *Fox Movietone Follies of 1929* ('The Breakaway', 'That's You Baby', 'Walking with Susie'), and most notably for *The Gay Divorcee* ('The Continental', winner of the initial Academy Award in 1934, 'A Needle in a Haystack' w Herbert Magidson) make up much of Con Conrad's credits, but he also contributed for several years to the Broadway musical theatre. Amongst his stage work were included revue songs (*Greenwich Village Follies of 1923* w Louis Hirsch, *Americana* w others, *Broadway Brevities*, interpolated numbers in such shows as *Bombo* (1921, four, including Jolson's 'Morning Will Come'), *Big Boy* (1925) and *Take the Air* (1927) and, most substantially, a handful of musical comedy scores.

Although each of the four Broadway musicals on which Conrad worked between 1924–6 had a good run in America, it was in Britain and in Hungary that *Mercenary Mary* ('Honey, I'm in Love with You') proved a long-running hit, whilst his songs for the comical *Kitty's Kisses* got a longer showing when some of that show's music was amalgamated with some pieces by Rodgers and Hart to make up the score of what London called *The Girl Friend*. His *Betty Lee* followed its American run by being produced by Hugh J Ward in Australia (Princess Theatre, Melbourne 12 June 1926) alongside the local production of *Mercenary Mary*. He also supplied the handful of numbers which illustrated the Shuberts' musical play based on Jack Lait's *Gus the Bus* cartoon.

Conrad also briefly turned producer and mounted the 1928 *Keep Shufflin'* on Broadway.

1924 **Moonlight** (w William B Friedlander/William Le Baron) Longacre Theater 30 January
1924 **My Boy Friend** (aka *Gus the Bus*) (Jack Lait) Parsons Theater, Hartford, Conn 1 December
1924 **Betty Lee** (w Louis Hirsch/Irving Caesar, Otto Harbach/Paul Armstrong, Rex Beach) 44th Street Theater 25 December
1925 **The Comic Supplement** (w Henry Souvaine/J P McEvoy/McEvoy, Augustin Duncan) National Theater, Washington 20 January
1925 **Mercenary Mary** (w Friedlander/Caesar/Isabel Leighton) Longacre Theater 13 April
1926 **Kitty's Kisses** (Gus Kahn/Harbach, Philip Bartholomae) Playhouse Theater 6 May

THE CONSUL Musical drama in 3 acts by Gian-Carlo Menotti. Barrymore Theater, New York, 15 March 1950.

Although uncompromisingly dramatic and operatic in its content, *The Consul*, like many of Gian-Carlo Menotti's other works, attempted to straddle the line between the commercial theatre and the opera house. The show dealt with the plight of Magda Sorel (Patricia Neway), the wife of a conspirator in an iron curtain country, who tries unavailingly to get through the bureaucratic barriers of a consular office to join her escaped husband (Cornell MacNeil) abroad, but ultimately ends in a despairing suicide. The drama's musical centrepiece was Magda's aria

'To This We've Come (that men withhold the world from men)'. Gloria Lane played the important rôle of the Consulate secretary and Marie Powers, star of Menotti's *The Medium*, had top billing in the supporting rôle of Magda's mother.

Produced on Broadway under the management of Chandler Cowles and Efram Zimbalist jr, and directed by an author-composer who was outspokenly critical of the manner in which a director and/or producer could distortionately come between the writer and the audience in commercial theatre, the piece was much admired and succeeded in playing through a run of 269 performances. It was subsequently staged in London both commercially with Misses Neway and Lane (Cambridge Theatre, 1951) and then at Sadler's Wells Opera (11 November 1954) with Amy Shuard as Magda and Anna Pollak as the Secretary, produced in Australia with Marie Collier as Magda in 1953 as part of an operatic season, and televised by American PBS in 1978. Since its initial performances, it has, however, gravitated naturally towards a small niche in the opera house repertoire rather than on the commercial stage which, particularly given Menotti's dicta, seemed an unlikely place for it anyway.

UK: Cambridge Theatre 7 February 1951; Germany: Hamburg 1951; Austria: 1951; Australia: Melbourne Opera Group 1953
Recording: original cast (Decca); TV film (Mercury).

THE CONTRABANDISTA or The Law of the Ladrones

Comic opera in 2 acts by F C Burnand. Music by Arthur Sullivan. St George's Opera House, London, 18 December 1867.

F C Burnand's claim to have been at least the co-instigator of the modern English-language musical theatre is confirmed not merely by the fact that he wrote the texts for the first two British opéras-bouffes (*Windsor Castle*, *L'Africaine*) with original musical scores, but also by his authorship of the first genuine comic opera of the era. *The Contrabandista*, mounted by Gallery of Illustration manager Thomas German Reed in his first attempt at staging a full-length show in a proper theatre, showed that its author had a good knowledge of the most recent (and the not so recent) French musical stage, but the piece was none the worse for being derivative.

Since there has been a dead-heat in the voting for the new leader of the Ladrones, it is decreed, by brigand law, that the new chief of the band shall be the first stranger who wanders into their territory. A little British photographer, Peter Adolphus Grigg (J A Shaw), is captured, invested with burlesque pomp, and given in marriage to the fierce chieftainess, Inez de Roxas (Lucy Franklein). But the defeated candidates cheat. Sancho (Mr Neilson) overhears San Jose (Thomas Aynsley Cook) plotting murderously with Inez, and resolves to turn traitor. Things get sticky for Grigg and Rita (Arabella Smythe), a hostage who sings the soprano line, until the cavalry arrive, headed by Rita's boyfriend Vasquez (Edward Hargrave).

Grigg had the best rôle and the best song of the young Arthur Sullivan's score, the bouncy 'From Rock to Rock', whilst Miss Franklein had some splendidly rumbling contralto writing in her rôle and there were some fine ensemble pieces as well. Played on a bill with Offenbach's *Ba-ta-clan* and *La Chatte metamorphosée en femme*, and later with Auber's *L'Ambassadrice*, the show was seen an excellent 72

times. It was played in the English provinces under the management of Sullivan's brother, Frederic (1874, with Alfred Cellier conducting), and on a number of occasions on tour in America, after *HMS Pinafore* had made Sullivan's name saleable. The conductor of one of these tours was John Philip Sousa, who subsequently took the libretto of *The Contrabandista* as the basis for a score of his own called *The Smugglers* (Washington, DC, 25 March 1882). He was, in fact, not the only one to do so, for a piece produced, and allegedly written, by Horace Lingard under the title *I Ladroni*, billed on its San Francisco première as 'an entirely new and comic opera' turned out to be a variation – to put it politely – on *The Contrabandista*. Signor Operti (he of the 'composed and arranged' of Broadway's *The Black Crook* revival) was credited with selection, arrangement and composition of the music, and Lingard starred as Mr Triptollinmoss Figg, performing 'From Rock to Rock' in an evening that included several other pieces of recognizable Sullivan and a goodly amount of made-over Burnand.

In 1894, Richard D'Oyly Carte, in need of a new entertainment, had the authors revise *The Contrabandista* for the Savoy Theatre (12 December). Lengthened, broadened, retitled *The Chieftain* and cast with Walter Passmore (Grigg), Courtice Pounds (Vasquez), Florence St John (Rita), Rosina Brandram (Inez), M R Morand (Jose), Richard Temple (Sancho) and Florence Perry in the new rôle of Mrs Dolly Grigg, it was a 97-performance disappointment. A production of *The Chieftain* by A H Canby at New York's Abbey Theater (9 September 1895) with Christie MacDonald as Dolly, Lulu Glaser as Rita and Francis Wilson as Grigg played 54 times.

The title *Los Contrabandistas* was earlier used for a one-act Parisian opérette by Émile Thierry and Julien Nargeot produced at the Théâtre ds Champs-Elysées, 28 May 1861.

Recording: amateur version with rewritten lyrics (Rare Recorded Editions)

CONVERSATION PIECE

Romantic comedy with music in 3 acts by Noël Coward. His Majesty's Theatre, London, 16 February 1934.

Written by Coward as a vehicle for the French actress and vocalist Yvonne Printemps, who spoke no English, *Conversation Piece* told the tale of a young French singer, Melanie (Mlle Printemps), who is taken to Brighton and richly set up for the season under the management of the impoverished Paul, Duc de Chaucigny-Varennes (Coward), with the object of winning her a rich husband who will support them both. The girl's charms are sufficient to enchant the young Marquis of Sheere (Louis Hayward) to an offer of marriage, his father, Lord Beneden (Athole Stewart), to a more equivocal offer of 'protection', and to win an approach from a representative of the Prince Regent himself, but Melanie does not play the game. She has fallen in love with Paul and when, with the help of his old and amorous friend Lady Julia Charteris (Irene Browne), he sets up a party to help her progress, she ruins everything by inviting the courtesans of Brighton (Heather Thatcher, Moya Nugent, Betty Shale). The furious Paul is about to find financial salvation with Julia when he realizes, in time for the final curtain, where his heart truly lies.

Like the script, the score was written to measure for the star, who had the only solos of the evening, the most enduring of which was the lovely waltz 'I'll Follow My Secret Heart'. The supporting cast got the comical moments with the gentlemen's description of 'Regency Rakes' and the professional ladies complaining that 'There's Always Something Fishy about the French'.

Coward stepped in, in rehearsals, to replace the actor Romney Brent who had been cast as Paul, and his presence on the bill undoubtedly added to the appeal of a piece which, at moments enchanting, was at others very talky and at others, for the benefit of the star, even lapsed into French. When he withdrew, to be replaced by the rather more apt Pierre Fresnay (Mlle Printemps' long-time partner à la ville), the Parisian star's name proved to be insufficient to support the box-office and Coward was obliged to return. C B Cochran's production of *Conversation Piece* ran for a semi-satisfactory 177 performances before Archie Selwyn and Harold Franklin joined the producer in taking it across the Atlantic for a Broadway season. Mlle Printemps and Fresnay scored personal hits at the head of a British cast mostly taken from the originals, but 55 performances was the limit of its run.

Conversation Piece was played for 8 performances at the New York Barbizon-Plaza (18 November 1957) with a cast headed by René Paul and Joan Copeland, but has not received a major revival.

USA: 44th Street Theater 23 October 1934
Recording: complete with dialogue (Columbia), original cast excerpts (HMV)

COOK, Barbara [Nell] (b Atlanta, Ga, 25 October 1927). Classy young Broadway soprano who transformed into a cabaret vocalist and character lady.

Barbara Cook first appeared on Broadway in the juvenile soprano rôle of Sandy in *Flahooley* (1951) and subsequently played Ado Annie in *Oklahoma!* (1953) and Carrie in *Carousel* (1954) at the City Center and appeared as Jane in the 1954 TV version of *Babes in Toyland*. She created the rôles of Hilda Miller in *Plain and Fancy* (1955) and of Cunégonde in the original version of Leonard Bernstein's *Candide* (1956), introducing the vocally taxing burlesque jewel song, 'Glitter and Be Gay', starred in revivals of *Carousel* (1957, Julie) and *The King and I* (1960, Anna), and in 1957 created her most memorable rôle as Marian, the librarian, in *The Music Man* ('Goodnight My Someone', 'Till There Was You').

She subsequently appeared as Liesl Brandel in *The Gay Life* (1961), Amelia Balash in *She Loves Me* (1963, 'Ice Cream'), Carol Deems in *Something More!* (1964) and as Dolly Talbo in *The Grass Harp* (1971) on Broadway, played in *Funny Girl*, *The Boy Friend* and *The Unsinkable Molly Brown* outside New York, and Evelina in a television *Bloomer Girl*. She then quit the heroine's roles her exceptional soprano and attractive looks had kept her in for so long and orientated herself towards the nightclub and cabaret world.

Her solo theatre-concert performances and a TV/recording portrayal of Sally in *Follies* in the late 1980s won her a strong, particular following and signalled the beginning of a second theatre career as a character performer, a career begun less fortunately than the first with the leading rôle in the try-out of the flop musical *Carrie* at Stratford-on-Avon.

COOK, J[ohn] Furneaux (b London, 1839; d London, 19 January 1903). One of the most substantial singing character men of the 19th-century British musical stage.

Young Cook sang in glee clubs as a boy, appeared as a child actor in *The Tempest* and *King John* at the Princess's Theatre, but renounced singing when his voice broke and became an engraver until his brother-in-law, the composer and conductor Meyer Lutz, directed him towards the lyric stage. He toured, with his brother T Aynsley, for several seasons in Henri Corri's operatic company and then in the Charles Durand Opera Company before appearing at the Gaiety Theatre in April 1871 as Corbillon in the Offenbach pasticcio *Malala*, Lord Lyndham in *Peter the Shipwright* (*Zar und Zimmermann*) and in Balfe's *Letty, the Basketmaker*. He had his first original musical rôle later that year when he created the part of the godfatherly Peter, the Watchman in Jonas's *Cinderella the Younger* (1871) and, although he spent another period touring with Durand, the bulk of his long subsequent career was played in baritone rôles in the musical theatre.

He created the rôles of the Sultan in *The Sultan of Mocha* (1874 and 1881), Baron de Montmorency in *The Tower of London* (1875), Weasel in *Nell Gwynne* (1876) and the Magistrate in Solomon's little *Contempt of Court* (1877), played Larivaudière in *La Fille de Madame Angot* (Alhambra revival), and toured for D'Oyly Carte in *The Sorcerer* (1878). He also appeared as Prince Casimir in the Alhambra's *La Princesse de Trébizonde* revival and created the part of Sir Ralph Ashton in *The Lancashire Witches* (1879) in Manchester and that of Samuel in *Pirates of Penzance* (1879) in New York. He later toured as the Sergeant of Police in the same piece, took over as Sir Mincing Lane in the original production of *Billee Taylor* (1880), created Sergeant Crowe in *The King's Dragoons* (1880) and toured both with Alice Barth's company (*Widows Bewitched* etc) and with Carte as Corcoran and Marmaduke.

He appeared in London as Batifol in *La Belle Normande* (1881), the Lord Mayor in *The Grand Mogol* (1881), Gnatbrain in Lutz's *All in the Downs* (1881) and Mr Dunn in his *Knight of the Garter* (1882), Farmer Bowman in *The Merry Duchess* (1883), and in *Cox and Box* at the Court Theatre (1883) before rejoining D'Oyly Carte's tours (1884–5) as Pooh Bah, Mountararat, Dick Deadeye and the Sergeant of Police. In 1886 he created the rôle of the heroine's father, Squire Bantam, in *Dorothy* (singing again some of the music he had performed in its earlier existence as *Nell Gwynne*), and he repeated that part later in the 1892 revival and again at his Gaiety Theatre benefit in 1897.

Cook followed this long-running success with its successor, playing Alderman Shelton in *Doris* (1889), then created the rôles of Elvino di Pasto in W S Gilbert and Alfred Cellier's *The Mountebanks* (1892), Bullion in Goring Thomas's *The Golden Web* (1892), the comical heavy, Silas Block in the latter-day burlesque *Little Christopher Columbus* (1893), and Major Penyon in the farcical musical comedy *The White Silk Dress* (1896). He toured as John Mayfield in the comic opera *Kitty* and as the Christian and chorusmaster in Wilson Barret's famous *The Sign of the Cross*, but soon after these last performances his eyesight began to fail, and he was obliged to give up the stage.

Totally blind for the last three years of his life, he died at the age of 63.

Thomas Aynsley COOK (b London, July 1831; d Liverpool, 16 February 1894), the elder brother of Furneaux Cook, worked as a boy soprano at the Temple before attending Wurzburg Conservatoire and making his first almost adult appearance as a teenage Commendatore in *Don Giovanni*. On his return to Britain, he worked for many years with English opera companies (National English Opera Co, Pyne-Harrison, English Opera Co, Parepa-Rosa Co, Henri Corri's Co etc) playing basso rôles in both Britain and America in the late 1850s and early 1860s, yet was still apt to appear on the bill with Bryant's Ministrels (New York 1860) or at the Broadway Musical Hall, where he played alongside another young performer with a future, Tony Pastor.

At the coming of opéra-bouffe he made an immediate impact when he appeared as Britain's first General Boum in *La Grande-Duchesse*, and thereafter his career included long periods of musical theatre appearances amongst which were included the rôles of the Commandant in Clay's first professional musical, *Constance* (1865), San Jose in Sullivan's first full-length work *The Contrabandista* (1867), several seasons at the Gaiety Theatre playing in such pieces as Adam's *Dolly* (*La Poupée de Nuremberg*), *Barbe-bleue*, as Matt o' the Mint in *The Beggar's Opera*, *The Quaker*, Donizetti's *Betly*, Daniel in *Zampa*, *Fra Diavolo*, Sackatoo in the Offenbach pasticcio *Malala*, Von Bett in *Peter the Shipwright* (*Zar und Zimmermann*) and Don Jose in *Maritana*. He also appeared in burlesque and in such pantomime rôles as Baron Sponsorwitz in *The Sleeping Beauty* (Covent Garden).

An original member, with his wife (Mrs Aynsley Cook, née Payne 1832–1880, a member of the famous pantomime family), of the Parepa-Rosa Opera Company, he returned regularly to that company whilst still building a list of musical theatre credits to rival that of his brother: General Kantschukoff in London's *Fatinitza*, Cocorico (ex-Sifroy) in *Geneviève de Brabant*, the Viceroy in *La Périchole* with Soldene (1878), King Gros-Minet in *La Poule aux oeufs d'or* (1878) at the Alhambra – performing two duets by Gevaert with Soldene who here played his daughter – Dick Deadeye on tour with Blanche Roosevelt (1879), The Marquis in *The King's Dragoons* (1880), King James in *The Lancashire Witches* (1881), Monthabor in *La Fille du tambour-major* (1881), Sir Temple Griffin in Solomon's *Lord Bateman*, Schnapps in *The Beggar Student* (1883), Count Pomposo di Vesuvio in *Estrella* (1883), Arimanes in *The Golden Ring* (1883), Captain Santiago in *La Seranata* (1888) and Dr Manacle in Goring Thomas's *The Golden Web* (1893). He was taken ill in Liverpool whilst touring with Rosa and died there at the age of 62.

His daughter, Annie, a contralto with the Carl Rosa opera company, became Mrs Eugene Goosens.

Alice Aynsley COOK (b London, ?1850; d London, 7 April 1938), the Cooks' sister, began her career in burlesque at the Gaiety Theatre, appearing as Isoline in *Geneviève de Brabant*, Hassarac in *Ali Baba à la Mode* (1872), Zerlina in *Don Giovanni*, in *Martha*, and in the little operetta *Fleurette* (1873) before going on tour as Mme Lange in Fred Wright's tour of *La Fille de Madame Angot* (1874). She returned to the Gaiety to play Fanny in *The Island of Bachelors* (1874), and went on to create or play a series of mezzo-soprano rôles in British musical plays: Meg in *Tower of London* (1875), Lady Clare in *Nell Gwynne* (1876), Frank Musgrave's little *Prisoners at the Bar* (1878), Widow Nutter in *The Lancashire Witches* (1879), the title-rôle of the touring burlesque *Cruel Carmen* with the Walton family (1880), Dorothy in Crook's *The King's Dragoons* revival (1881), Dolly Mayflower in Lutz's *All in the Downs* (1881), Felix in *On Condition* with Lila Clay's all-woman company and Miss Newton in Lutz's *The Knight of the Garter* (1882) as well as appearing in the non-musical theatre.

She played as Ruth, Lady Sangazure, Little Buttercup, Lady Jane and Katisha in D'Oyly Carte's touring companies (1884–5), toured with the Vokes family (1886–8 *In Camp, Fun in a Fog* etc) and in the title-rôle of the extravaganza *Randolph the Reckless* (1889), visited South America in 1891 for Edwin Cleary with a repertoire including *Billee Taylor*, *Erminie*, *Dorothy* and the Gilbert and Sullivan canon, and later South Africa for the Edwardes-Wheeler Company in *A Gaiety Girl* (Lady Virginia), *In Town* (Duchess) and *Morocco Bound* (Countess). She was again seen on the British stage, now as a 'heavy lady', as Lady Joan Saxmundham in Arthur Roberts's burlesque *Claude Du-val* (1894), on tour for Edwardes as Dame Hecla Courtlandt in *His Excellency* and then in *The Telephone Girl*, as Miss Seraphine Plummer in *Regina BA* (1897), Mrs Amelia Rourke in *That Terrible Turk* (1898), Mlle Tournesol in *Milord Sir Smith* (1898), Mrs Miranda Q Strongmynde in *The American Heiress* (1899), Countess Nitsky in *The Prince of Borneo* (1899), Sarah Slade in *The Gay Cadets* (1901), Mrs Bumble in *The Golddiggers* (1902), Lady Bingo Barr in *Bill Adams* (1903) and as Mrs Marjorie Buttery in Ada Reeve's *Moll, the Rogue* (1905) towards the end of a career of more than 30 years as a musical-theatre character lady.

COOK, Will Marion (b Washington, DC, 27 January 1869; d New York, 19 July 1944). The composer of much music for black theatre shows and performers in an era when there seemed briefly to be commercial possibilities in such entertainments.

The son of a well-off and educated family, Cook studied music at Oberlin College from the age of 13 and, later, in Europe with the aim of a career as a concert violinist. When that career proved unattainable, he instead began composing black-accented songs – often, but not always, with lyrics littered with 'dis' and 'dat' and 'dem's – for the popular stage. He had a small success with his first full stage piece, the 45-minute *Clorindy, or the Origin of the Cakewalk* ('Who Dat Say Chicken in Dis Crowd?', 'Darktown is Out Tonight', 'Jump Back, Honey'), which had a good summer run when produced as a post-show entertainment on the stage of the Roof Garden of New York's Casino Theater. It failed, however, when put on the road as a regulation-sized musical. He thereafter placed songs in several Broadway shows (*The Casino Girl*, *The Wild Rose*) and provided Ernest Hogan with the songs for his *Jes' Lak White Fo'ks* (1899) before composing and putting together the basic score – much interpolated into – for the full-length Williams and Walker musical comedy *In Dahomey* ('Brown-Skin Baby Mine', 'Molly Green', 'Leader of the Colored Aristocracy', 'On Emancipation Day'). After an indifferent New York run (53 performances), *In Dahomey* established itself as a favourite in

London where its unfamiliar fun, its general novelty and its high spirits took it to a run of 251 performances.

Broadway success, however, eluded Cook, and his co-written and composed *The Southerners*, which won a little notoriety for mixing black and white performers (although this was, in fact, not novel), and two further Williams and Walker pieces, *Abyssinia* (31 performances) and *Bandana Land* (89 performances), all had rather longer lives out of town than in New York. His Broadway career was largely limited to supplying the occasional interpolated number, as in earlier years, to such shows as *The New Yorkers* and *The Boys and Betty* ('Whoop her up with a whoop-la-la!'). He also got a brief showing on the Viennese stage when one of his songs, relyricked by Max Baer as 'Liebesabenteuer', was interpolated into the Theater an der Wien's production of the Gaiety Theatre musical *Der Toreador* for Carlo Böhm (1903).

Cook was involved, in one capacity or another, with a number of specifically black musical plays in the 1910s, composing the basic scores for the Negro Players' *The Traitor* and Miller and Lyles's *Darkydom*, but his career was hampered by a bitterly unstable temperament and an inability to accept the limitations of his life in music after the extravagant hopes and overdone publicity of his early years.

1898 **Clorindy, or the Origin of the Cakewalk** (Paul Laurence Dunbar) 1 act Casino Roof Garden 5 July
1899 **Jes' Lak White Fo'ks** (Dunbar/Cook) 1 act Cherry Blossom Theater
1903 **In Dahomey** (w others/Alex Rogers, Dunbar/Jesse A Shipp) New York Theater 18 February
1904 **The Southerners** ('Will Mercer', Richard Grant) New York Theater 23 May
1906 **Abyssinia** (w Will Vodery, Bert Williams et al/Earl C Jones/Shipp, Rogers) Majestic Theater 20 February
1908 **Bandana Land** (w others/Alex Rogers/Shipp, Rogers) Majestic Theater 3 February
1913 **The Traitor** (w others) Lafayette Theater March
1915 **Darkydom** (w others) Lafayette Theater 23 October

COOPER [VANDERJUICH, Henri] (b Brussels, 1845; d Paris, 7 December 1914). An always young-looking tenor and light comedy actor, long a feature of 19th-century Parisian musical shows.

Cooper (he was always billed just as 'Cooper') made his first appearance in Paris at the Théâtre des Bouffes-Parisiens in *La Bonne aux camélias* before joining the company at the Théâtre des Variétés where he remained for the bulk of the next 25 years. His attractive tenor was put to early use there, and he won quick notice when he created the rôle of the pretty page Adolphe de Valladolid in *Les Brigands* (1869). He subsequently created a number of other Offenbach parts including Frontignac (*La Créole*), Frantz (*Le Docteur Ox*) and le Duc de Marly in *Belle Lurette*, (Théâtre de la Renaissance) but his biggest personal successes came in Hervé's *Mam'zelle Nitouche* (1883) in which he created the romantic-comic tenor rôle of Champlâtreux opposite Anna Judic, in the comedy *Ma Cousine* and, on a 'loan' to the Théâtre de la Gaîté, when he played Prince Mignapour in the first metropolitan production of Audran's *Le Grand Mogol* (1884). He also toured with Judic's company to America in 1885.

Cooper created many other rôles in both plays (notably *Le Crocodile*) and opérettes (*Mam'zelle Crénom, Le Valet de Coeur, La Fille à Cacolet* etc), and also appeared in revivals of the classic opéra-bouffe, opérette and féerie repertoire (Ange Pitou, Gardefeu, San Carlo in *La Petite Mariée*, Blaisient in *Rothamago* etc), scoring one of his biggest successes as Faust in Hervé's *Le Petit Faust* in the big 1882 revival at the Théâtre de la Porte-Saint-Martin, and re-appearing in the same rôle again in 1891 at the Variétés and, long after the end of his contract there in 1893, in 1908 at the Folies-Dramatiques.

In the later part of his career he began performing early 19th-century songs in the cafés-concerts, but in the theatre he inclined more to non-musical comedy, touring Russia with the Théâtre Michel and spending a number of years as a member of the company at the Palais-Royal.

CORDY, Annie [COOREMAN, Annie] (b Scharebeck, Belgium, ?1928). France's most outstanding musical comedy soubrette for some 40 years, in a career handicapped – in that field at least – by the paucity of new material in post-war France.

Mlle Cordy came to Paris in the early 1950s, soon after beginning a singing career in her native Belgium, and was appearing in variety at the Bobino when she was selected to play the comedy soubrette rôle in Raymond Vincy and Francis Lopez's small-scale musical *La Route fleurie* alongside Georges Guétary, Claude Arvelle and another variety performer, Bourvil. The long run of *La Route fleurie* established her as a comedy and singing star and, thereafter, she led a crammed career of stage, film and variety work for some 40 continuing years. Following *La Route fleurie*, she appeared with Luis Mariano in the film of the Vincy/Lopez *Le Chanteur de Mexico* and, on the stage, was starred above the title as *Tête de linotte* and again opposite Mariano in *Visa pour l'amour* (1961), both for long runs.

She paired with Bourvil for the musical comedy *Ouah! Ouah!*, with comedian Darry Cowl in *Pic et Pioche* (1967) and starred in a third musical comedy, *Indien vaut mieux que tu l'aura*, before taking the title-rôle in the French production of *Hello, Dolly!* (1972). Her latest stage musical appearances have been as the star of *Nini la chance* (1980) and *Envoyez la musique* (1982) in a career now largely devoted to television (sit-com, drama and variety) and some major character rôles on film.

THE CORSAIR Burlesque in 2 acts by Edward E Rice. Music by John Braham. Bijou Theater, New York, 18 October 1887.

Byron's celebrated romantic poem *The Corsair* fell under the pens of the burlesquers on several occasions, and the results included William Brough's London success *Conrad and Medora* (Lyceum 1856) played in America by Mrs John Wood as *The Corsair* later the same year and James Barnes's American *Chow Chow, or a Tale of Pekin* (Wood's Museum, 9 September 1872). Then, in 1887, Edward Rice decided to give *The Corsair* the same treatment he had so effectively given to Longfellow's *Evangeline*. A spectacular staging, Amelia Summerville in tights as the titular Conrad, and such incidentals as an apparently dancing mule (paralleling the heifer of the earlier show) helped Miles and Barton's production of the burlesque to 180 Broadway performances prior to a long life on the road and even some across the seas. Rice toured a company to Australia in 1891–2 which included *The Corsair* with

Virginia Earle and local contralto Fanny Liddiard featured amongst its repertoire. The show was, in fact, so successful in America that it inspired Lew Dockstader's minstrel company to burlesque the burlesque with a piece called *The Coarse Hair*.

Byron's work was also the basis for several serious operas, an English one played at the Crystal Palace (1 April 1873) and two Italian, Verdi's 1848 *Il corsaro* (Trieste, 25 October) and Alessandro Marracino's *Corrado* (Theatro Adriano, Rome 21 May 1900).

Byron's other Turkish verse work, *The Bride of Abydos*, also fell into the hands of the extremes of the musical theatre, making up both into an opera (*La Fiancée d'Abydos*, Adrien Barthe/Jules Adénis, Théâtre Lyrique, Paris 30 December 1865) and, more famously, into another highly successful burlesque, *The Bride of Abydos, or the Prince, the Pirate and the Pearl*, by H J Byron produced at London's Strand Theatre (31 May 1858) with Pattie Oliver in the title-rôle.

Australia: Opera House, Melbourne 3 October 1891

CORT, John L (b Newark, NJ, 1860; d Stamford, Conn, 17 November 1929). Theatre-owner and producer of mostly unsuccessful or undistinguished musicals, Cort nevertheless kept up a presence on Broadway for over 20 years.

Originally a performer in vaudeville, Cort switched instead to speculating on theatre-building, and he built up a successful chain of vaudeville houses before overstretching himself and losing the lot. He began over again, and soon built up a new series of playhouses throughout America, beginning with the Cort Theater in Chicago (1908) and including Broadway's Cort Theater (1912, opened memorably with *Peg 'o My Heart*) and similarly named houses in Boston, in Jamaica, Long Island, in the Bronx (later the Windsor Theater), Atlantic City and elsewhere. At the same time he launched a heavy schedule of productions, a large number of them musicals, too many of which were distinctly not number-one entertainments, frequently when from the pen of his son, Harry L[insley] Cort (b Seattle, 1893; d New York, 6 May 1937), who had himself attempted a career as a producer in Chicago. Another son, Edward, a theatre manager in Long Island, also occasionally picked up a pen.

Cort allied himself, in turn, with Klaw and Erlanger's theatrical combine and, when they seemed to be encroaching on his preserves, with the Shuberts, whom he, in turn renounced to return to the Klaw and Erlanger umbrella, successfully keeping himself afloat in a competitive business for some two decades.

Cort's productions included *The Alaskan* (1907), *The Rose of Panama* (*Kreolenblut*), Gustav Luders's *The Gipsy*, Frank Mandel's early effort *Miss Princess* (1912), Sousa's *The American Maid* (1913), *What's Going On?*, the Chicago hit *A Modern Eve* (a largely remusicked *Die moderne Eva*), Victor Herbert's attractive *The Princess Pat* (1915), Cuvillier's much botched *Flora Bella*, *Molly O* (1916), the successful *Flo-Flo* (1917), Friml's *Glorianna*, *Fiddlers Three* (1918), the flyweight but successful *Listen Lester* (1918) and *Just a Minute* (1919) both co-written by Harry, *Roly Boly Eyes* (1919), Harry's *Jim Jam Jems* (1920), *Go-Go*, Harry's *Sharlee* (1923), *Suzanne* and Harry's *China Rose* (w Charles Dillingham, Martin Beck 1925). He also sup-

ported *Shuffle Along* (1921) as part of the Nikko Producing Company.

LA COSAQUE Comédie-vaudeville in 3 acts by Henri Meilhac and Albert Millaud. Music by Hervé. Théâtre des Variétés, Paris, 1 February 1884.

La Cosaque was the last of that series of vaudevilles, of which *Niniche*, *Lili* and *Mam'zelle Nitouche* had been the enduring triumphs, mounted by Eugène Bertrand at the Variétés with Anna Judic as their overwhelming star. Tasting just a little of being one dip too many into the same well, it was unable to top its predecessors and ran for only 70 performances at the Variétés in comparison with the several hundred nights of even the least popular of the others.

Princess Anna Semionowna Makinskoff (Judic) has come of age, and gone exorbitantly extravagant with the family fortunes, so her family have decided to lock her up until she can be safely married off to her cousin Féodor (Lassouche). Anna swaps clothes with a maidservant, hitch-hikes a ride to Paris with the lace salesman, Jules Primitif (José Dupuis), and ends up with a job in the shop where he works. When she is about to be sacked she promptly buys the business, and when she is ordered by the Czar, no less, to wed within 24 hours, she proposes to Jules. He, refusing to wed the multi-millionairess simply to spite her family, finally does so for better reasons. Christian (Prince Grégoire) and Roux (Prince Cyrille) were the other Russian aristocrats.

The score was almost entirely for the benefit of Judic who had nine numbers including la Légende de Marfa ('La Cosaque, la voilà!'), the rondeau 'Je suis une femme accomplie', the Couplets de la Patte and the Couplets de l'enlèvement' (all in Act 1), the Couplets des parapluies and a Chanson des Joncs in the second, the Couplets du Coiffeur and her final declaration ('Tu ne comprends donc rien') in the last. Dupuis had two numbers, but the original Paris of *La Belle Hélène* now ventured no higher than an F natural.

Judic played *La Cosaque* in her repertoire in London after its closure in Paris, and the following year repeated it at Broadway's Star Theater, but London had already seen the piece, little more than two months after its Paris opening, when the irrepressible Kate Santley played an English version at the Royalty Theatre. Claude Marius (Prince Gregoire), Henry Ashley (Jules), Miss Amalia (Mme Dupontin) and Sidney Harcourt (Prince Feodor) supported the star for 41 performances, tactfully closing the week before Judic arrived in town. In Vienna, the Hervé score was replaced, as in the other Judic vaudevilles, by one by Johann Brandl when *Die Kosakin* (ad Moritz West) was produced for 27 performancess at the Theater an der Wien. Ilka Pálmay was Anna, Girardi played Casimir (ex-Jules) and Carl Lindau (Prince Cyril), Siegmund Stelzer (Prince Gregor) and Herr Stillfried (Prince Feodor) were the aristocrats.

UK: Royalty Theatre *La Cosaque* 12 April 1884; Gaiety Theatre (Fr) 18 June 1884; USA: Star Theater (Fr) 4 March 1885; Austria: Theater an der Wien *Die Kosakin* 31 October 1891

COSCOLETTO, or Le Lazzarone Opéra-comique in 2 acts by Charles Nuitter and Étienne Tréfeu. Music by Jacques Offenbach. Bad Ems, 24 July 1865.

A tiny tale about a little 'bandit', a flowergirl and a married macaroni cook, some amorous entanglements and a touch of food-poisoning, all set in Neapolitan banditland, *Coscoletto* was not one of Offenbach's more popular works, but following its initial showing at Bad Ems where Madame Albrecht appeared in the travesty rôle of the brigand it proved of sufficient interest to win several other productions.

It was seen at Vienna's Theater an der Wien (ad Julius Hopp) with no less a star than Marie Geistinger as the brigand of the title, and the famous comics Knaack (Arsenico), Swoboda (Policarpo) and Rott (Frangipani) in support, sharing a bill with Therese Braunecker-Schäfer's imitation of *Die falsche Carlotta Patti* for 28 nights. In Hungary, one Hungarian version was played at the Budai Népszinház with János Timar, István Szentgyörgi and Vidor Kassai in 1868, whilst another was mounted three years later at the Budai Színkör. *Coscoletto* was not taken up for a Paris production and, unlike most of Offenbach's works, was not purchased for publication either, but it nevertheless put in a reappearance in 1992 in Nuremberg (Opera, July) in what may have been its first German staging – 127 years after its birth.

Austria: Theater an der Wien 5 January 1866; Hungary: Budai Népszinház *A Makaróniárus* 1868, Budai Színkör *Coscoletto, a Nápolyi lazzaroni* 7 June 1871

COSTA, Karl [KOSTIA, Karl] (b Vienna, 2 February 1832; d Vienna, 11 October 1907). Prolific and successful author of a long list of musical comedies and plays with more or less music, for the Viennese stage.

Costa began his professional life as a lottery official and subsequently worked as secretary to the playwright Anton Langer. This proximity encouraged him to write himself, and he became a regular supplier of Volksstücke, Possen, of Operette and all kinds of musical comedy texts to the Viennese stage. Of the Operetten, his first, the book for Suppé's *Leichte Kavallerie*, remained his most successful, but his other most significant hits were made in a series of Possen written with Karl Millöcker and including *Ein Kassastuck* (1877), *Ein Blitzmädel* (1877) and the long-lived *Ihr Corporal* (1878). He had another fine success with the Posse *Der Walzerkönig*, set to music by Brandl.

Costa was for a while director of the Theater in der Josefstadt.

His highly successful Volksstuck *Bruder Martin* was subsequently made into a full-scale musical by Wilhelm Sterk and composer Leon Jessel under the title *Die goldene Mühle* (Volksoper 2 March 1937, Johann Strauss-Theater 21 April 1937).

1866 **Leichte Kavallerie** (Franz von Suppé) Carltheater 21 March
1866 **Die Hexe von Boissy** (Giovanni von Zaytz) Carltheater 24 April
1866 **Die Freigeister** (Suppé) Carltheater 23 October
1866 **Der Hausdoktor** (Karl Kleiber) 1 act Fürsts Singspielhalle 10 November
1868 **Die Frau Meisterin** (aka *Die verwandelten Weiber*) (Suppé) Carltheater 20 January
1868 **Wiener Zugstücke** (Anton Storch) Theater in der Josefstadt 26 April
1868 **Ihr Seliger** (Storch) Theater in der Josefstadt 30 December

1870 **Eine Frau nach der Mode** (Franz Roth) Theater in der Josefstadt 7 September
1870 **Die Jungfrau von Dragant** (Suppé/w Moritz A Grandjean) Carltheater 30 November
1870 **Wir Demokraten** (Franz Roth) Theater in der Josefstadt 25 December
1871 **Der Prinz von der Nädel** (F Roth) Theater in der Josefstadt 6 January
1871 **Der blinde Harfenist** (Kleiber) Theater in der Josefstadt 21 October
1872 **Das Orakel zu Delphi** (Carl Michael Ziehrer) Linz 21 September
1874 **Der Registrator auf Reisen** (Carl Ferdinand Conradin/w Moser, Adolf L'Arronge)
1874 **Stunden der Täuschung** (Conradin) Carltheater 13 June
1875 **Ein Kreuzer** (Kleiber) Theater in der Josefstadt 30 January
1876 **Fliegende Blätter** (Richard Genée) 1 act Theater an der Wien
1875 **Ein alter Junggeselle** (F Roth) Theater in der Josefstadt 6 March
1876 **Luftschlösser** (Genée/Wilhelm Mannstädt, A Weller [ie Johann Müller] ad) Theater an der Wien 11 July
1876 **Die Hölle im Hause** (pasticcio) Theater an der Wien 29 September
1877 **Ein Blitzmädel** (Karl Millöcker) Theater an der Wien 4 February
1877 **Ein Kassastuck** (Millöcker) Theater an der Wien 21 October
1878 **Ihr Corporal** (Millöcker) Theater an der Wien 19 January
1879 **Alexander der Grosse** (Ziehrer) Marburg January
1879 **Himmelschlüssel** (Millöcker) Theater an der Wien 15 March
1882 **Der Mann im Monde** (Millöcker/w Jacobson) Theater an der Wien 16 February
1882 **Der Putzgredl** (pasticcio) Theater in der Josefstadt 8 October
1884 **Der Erbe des Wucherers** (Eugen Schreiber) Theater in der Josefstadt 27 September
1884 **Ein Medium** (Ernst Reiterer) Theater in der Josefstadt 13 April
1884 **Abrakadabra, oder Über Land und Meer** (Schreiber) Theater in der Josefstadt 25 December
1885 **Ihr Reservist** (Pohl) Theater in der Josefstadt 22 April
1885 **Der Walzerkönig** (Johann Brandl/w Bruno Zappert/w Wilhelm Mannstädt) Carltheater 9 October
1890 **Die Hochzeit von Leni** (Louis Roth) Carltheater 14 February
1890 **Zur fesche Wienerin** (Kleiber) Theater in der Josefstadt 19 April
1890 **Der Gimpel** Austrian version (Carltheater)
1891 **Haben's kein Türken g'sehn?** (Adolf Gisser) Fürsttheater 15 September
1892 **Der Freiwillige** (F Sonkup/w Richard Genée) Prague 29 June
1894 **Der Komet** (Karl Kratzl) 1 act Ronacher
1894 **Der Bajazzo in der Heimat** (Eduard Kremser, pasticcio/w Benjamin Schier) Theater in der Josefstadt 7 March
1894 **Bruder Martin** (Max von Weinzierl) Raimundtheater 5 December
1896 **Der Schönheitspreis** (von Weinzierl) Raimundtheater 7 March
1896 **Wiener Edelknaben** (F Roth) Deutsches Volkstheater 8 September
1897 **Die Goldtante** (Leo Held) Theater an der Wien 6 November
1897 **Glücksnarren** (von Weinzierl) Raimundtheater 8 April
1898 **Die Fechtbrüder** (von Weinzierl) Raimundtheater 29 November
1905 **Onkel Sonders** (F K Holtzer) Raimundtheater December

COSTA, [Pasquale] Mario (b Taranto, 24 July 1858; d Monte Carlo, 27 September 1933).

Originally a writer of Neapolitan songs, Costa came to the theatre for the first time with the score for the 1893 pantomime *L'Histoire d'un pierrot* (Théâtre Déjazet 14 January 7 performances). He had a success with his light operatic version of Theophile Gautier's *Le Capitaine Fracasse*, and another with his 1922 operetta, *Scugnizza* (w Carlo Lombardo), a piece which remained one of the principal items of the Italian operetta repertoire for many years. Lombardo also compiled a pasticcio operetta, *Il re di chez Maxim* (lyrics: Arturo Franci) based on Costa's music which found a certain success (Teatro Fossati, Milan 10 May 1919).

1909 **Il Capitan Fracassa** (O Magici, Guglielmo Emmanuel) Teatro Alfieri, Turin 14 December
1921 **Posillipo** (Di Giacomo, Murolo, A Campanile) Teatro Eliseo 8 November
1922 **Scugnizza** (w Carlo Lombardo) Teatro Alfieri, Turin 16 December
1925 **Il re delle api** Teatro Lirico, Milan 11 February
1925 **Mimi Pompom** (G Adami) Teatro Lirico, Milan 23 October

COTTENS, Victor de (b Eaux-Vives, 21 August 1862; d Vichy, 26 February 1956).

The French-born, Algerian-educated playwright, revue author and vaudevillist de Cottens worked as a journalist before making his way into the theatre as an author of comedies, vaudevilles, a long list of revues and a regular supply of opérette libretti. He had several successes in the musical theatre with libretti set by Louis Varney, the most important of which was the first, *Le Papa de Francine*. He collaborated on a number of spectacular pieces for the great Châtelet stage and, latterly, adapted several English-language successes to the French stage. He also moved into management, directing successively the Théâtre du Vaudeville, the Folies-Wagram, the Olympia and the Théâtre Marigny before ultimately retiring to Vichy where he set up a casino.

1891 **Mam'zelle Coquelicot** (Monteux-Brissac/w Paul Ginisty) 1 act La Cigale 30 October
1896 **Le Papa de Francine** (Louis Varney/w Paul Gavault) Théâtre Cluny 5 November
1896 **Napoléon malgré lui** (w Gavault) 1 act Le Fourmi 3 April
1897 **Le Pompier de service** (Varney/w Gavault) Théâtre des Variétés 18 February
1898 **Les Demoiselles de Saint-Cyriens** (Varney/w Gavault) Théâtre Cluny 28 January
1899 **Robinson n'a pas cru Zoë** (Harry Fragson, Victor Maurel/w Robert Charvay) Boîte à Fursy 23 December
1900 **Le Fiancé de Thylda** (Varney/w Charvay) Théâtre Cluny 26 January
1900 **Frégolinette** (Varney) 1 act Théâtre des Mathurins 25 April
1900 **Mademoiselle George** (Varney/w Pierre Veber) Théâtre des Variétés 1 December
1902 **Le Voyage avant le noce** (Varney/w Charvay) Trianon-Lyrique 19 December
1904 **A Country Girl** French version w Fordyce (L'Olympia)
1905 **Les Quatre cent coups du Diable** (Marius Baggers/w Victor Darlay) Théâtre du Châtelet 23 December
1906 **Pif-Paf-Pouf! ou un voyage endiablé** (Baggers/w Darlay) Théâtre du Châtelet 6 December
1907 **Le Prince de Pilsen** (*The Prince of Pilsen*) French version (L'Olympia)

1908 **Son Altesse l'amour** (Maurice Jacobi/w P Veber) Moulin-Rouge 25 March
1915 **La Chasse aux Boches** (F Perpignan/Leroux) 1 act Folies-Bergère 9 April

Autobiography: *Paris dont je revais* (Vichy, 1948)

COTTRELLY, Mathilde [MEYER, Mathilde] (b Hamburg, 1851; d White Plains, NY, 15 January 1933). German actress and theatre administrator who made a prominent career in New York's German and English-language theatres.

Born into a professional musical family, Mathilde Meyer began working in the theatre as a child ('die kleine Meyer') and appeared in plays and in musical theatre in Germany, becoming popular as a soubrette at Berlin's Wallner Theater prior to marrying and retiring at the age of 15. Widowed at eighteen, she returned to the stage, playing in drama in Germany and in Russia, before moving to America in 1875.

She performed in New York first in German language theatre, where she was acclaimed as 'a genuine comic singing actress', appearing at the Germania Theater in a series of plays and musical comedies (*Lockere Zeisige, Comtesse Helene, Ziegenlieschen, Das Mädel ohne Geld, Luftschlösser, In Freud' und Leid, Die Reise durch New York in 80 Stunden, Ein vorsichtige Mann, Drei Paar Schuhe, Verfehlter Beruf, Geldfieber*), and then at the Thalia (ex-Bowery Theater) which she opened as a German house in conjunction with Gustav Amberg and Wilhelm Kramer in 1879, and at San Francisco's Tivoli Theater. She appeared in *Die Fledermaus* (Adele) *Die Lachtaube* (Pauline), *Flotte Bursche* (Frincke), *Drei Paar Schuhe* (Irma), *Orpheus in der Unterwelt*, in the title-rôles of *Boccaccio, Giroflé-Girofla* and *Nisida*, made an enormous hit as Fanchette Michel in Genée's *Der Seekadett*, played Wladimir in *Fatinitza* in German and in English and both repeated her Adele to Geistinger's Rosalinde and played Isabella to the German star's Boccaccio during the 1880-1 season, before joining John McCaull's comic opera company.

She appeared with McCaull in English-language versions of a string of international comic operas including *The Queen's Lace Handkerchief* (*Das Spitzentuch der Königin*, Donna Irene), *Prince Methusalem* (Methusalem), *The Merry War* (*Der lustige Krieg*, Else), *Falka* (*Le Droit d'aînesse*, Edwige), Planquette's *Nell Gwynne* (Nell), *Die Fledermaus* (Adele), Millöcker's *The Black Hussar* (*Der Feldprediger*, Barbara), *Chatter* (Lotti, which she also played as *Die Näherin* in German) *The Seven Swabians, Apajune the Water-sprite* (Heloise) and *Der Bettelstudent* (Bronislawa), Dellinger's *Don Caesar* and *Lorraine, The Crowing Hen* (*Serment d'amour*, the Marquise), *Josephine vendue par ses soeurs* (Benjamine), von Suppé's *Clover* (*Die Jagd nach dem Glück*, Petronella) and Messager's *Jacquette* (*La Béarnaise*, Jacquette), as well as creating the title-rôle of De Koven's *The Begum* (1887) and that of Polyxena in another American comic opera, Sydney Rosenfeld's version of *The Lady or the Tiger*.

She moved, with age, from soubrette rôles into a mixture of comic and character rôles and at the same time acted for some nine years as a silent partner in McCaull's management, dealing with both the financial and artistic sides of affairs with some skill, although apparently not sufficient for the organization and her investment in it ultimately to make good. She still made occasional appearances in the German (*Die Näherin*, Elizabeth in a *Tannhäuser-Parodie*, Gabrielle in *Pariser Leben*) and English musical theatre (*1999* at the Casino, *The Robber Baron* in 1901 at the Terrace Garden), but in later years, her stage appearances were largely in non-musical rôles. Her still obvious Continental accent led her to be cast frequently in Jewish parts, and among her creations were those of Mrs Isaac Cohen in *Abie's Irish Rose*, Emilia Müller in *The Bubble*, the dowager Frau Rothschild in the American version of the play *The Five Frankfurters*, and the later *Potash and Perlmutter* plays. As late as 1912, however, she was featured in the American production of the musical *A Polish Wedding* (*Polnische Wirtschaft*, Gabrielle).

A COUNTRY GIRL   Musical play in 2 acts by James T Tanner. Lyrics by Adrian Ross. Additional lyrics by Percy Greenbank. Music by Lionel Monckton. Additional songs by Paul Rubens. Daly's Theatre, London, 18 January 1902.

After the vastly successful orientalisms of Sidney Jones's *The Geisha* and *San Toy*, George Edwardes made a purposeful change of policy at his thriving Daly's Theatre. The new show was not written by the old Daly's team of Jones, Hall and the late Harry Greenbank, but by what had been essentially, to that time, part of his Gaiety Theatre team, a team used to producing entertainment of a much more frothy and insubstantial nature. Lionel Monckton and James Tanner, with the Daly's team of stars to serve, wrote a modern-dress piece set wholly in England, but one which featured a tale and a score made well to the measure of the Daly's audiences.

Geoffrey Challoner (Hayden Coffin), the impoverished squire of a Devonshire village, has let his manor to wealthy Sir Joseph Verity (Fred Kaye) and gone off, with his faithful servant Barry (Huntley Wright), to seek his fortune. When he returns, he has with him a Rajah (Rutland Barrington) who is no Rajah at all but an Englishman who fictitiously fell off an Alp, years ago, to escape an encumbering wife, and the Indian Princess Mehelaneh (Maggie May). The Princess is anxious to give herself and her vast fortune to Geoffrey, and Barry actively promotes the match, but Geoffrey's heart is true to his home-town Marjorie Joy (Lillian Eldée). While he has been away, Marjorie Joy has become a famous singer, but she returns home and puts on her old sunfrock and bonnet and pretends to be still the little village girl. Misunderstandings – notably a chaste kiss between Geoffrey and the village flirt, his old friend Nan (Evie Greene) – intervene before the lovers are reunited, in the midst of a series of comical scenes, at a ball in a London mansion. Ethel Irving played Barry's sweetheart Sophie, become Madame Sophie and a couturière, and Beryl Faber was the formidable Mrs Quinton Raikes, past and present wife to the phoney Rajah.

Monckton's score included some pieces in his happiest vein, notably Nan's lilting little song 'Try Again, Johnny' and her cautionary tale of 'Molly the Marchioness', the Princess's lovely soprano description of her home 'Under the Deodar', and a jolly seafaring piece for Barry, 'Yo Ho, Little Girls, Yo Ho!'. Paul Rubens, supplying additional numbers in the same way that Monckton had served Sidney Jones in the earlier shows, turned out one of the show's most popular numbers in 'Two Little Chicks' for Wright

and Miss Irving, and the Geoffrey/Marjorie duet 'Coo', the exemplary banality of which did nothing to stop it becoming popular. Coffin had his best moment in the virile 'In the King's Name – Stand!' and Barrington a topical patter waltz, no less, called 'Peace, Peace'.

The show was a hit of the proportions of its great predecessors at Daly's Theatre. It played there for two years and 729 performances, and was on the road for the first of what would be many years of touring within a matter of months. J C Duff opened his production at the New York Daly's Theater immediately after, with Melville Stewart (Geoffrey), Hallen Mostyn (Rajah), William Norris (Barry), Helen Marvin (Nan), Grace Freeman (Marjorie), Minnie Ashley (Sophie) and Genevieve Finlay (Princess) featured, and he too had a fine success with 115 metropolitan performances followed by a substantial tour, before Stewart eventually brought the show back to Broadway (29 May 1911), still starring alongside Misses Freeman and Finlay, nine years on.

In 1903 four companies were touring in Britain, variously under the banners of Edwardes, George Dance and Charles Macdona, Edwardes's South African Wheeler–Edwardes company had the show featured in its repertoire, and Australians got their first sight of it in J C Williamson's production with Florence Young (Marjorie), George Lauri (Barry), Harold Thorley (Geoffrey) and Evelyn Scott (Nan) featured. The following year, as no less than five *Country Girl* companies did the rounds on the British circuits, the show was given an unaccustomed production in France. The brothers Isola mounted a French version (ad Victor de Cottens, Fordyce) at L'Olympia, during their four-show flirtation with foreign musicals there, with a cast headed by Max Dearly, Alice Bonheur and Mariette Sully.

A Country Girl returned to London in 1914 under the management of Edwardes (Daly's Theatre 28 October) with Robert Michaelis (Geoffrey), Gertie Millar (Nan), W H Berry (Barry) and Nellie Taylor (Marjorie) heading its cast for a good 173 stopgap performances. The indefatigable touring manager J Bannister Howard brought the piece back again in 1931 (Daly's Theatre 29 September, 56 performances), as part of his series of seasons of old favourites, with Dorothy Ward featured as Nan.

USA: Daly's Theater 22 September 1902; Australia: Her Majesty's Theatre, Sydney 7 November 1903; France: L'Olympia October 1904

COUPS DE ROULIS   Opérette in 3 acts by Albert Willemetz based on the novel of the same title by 'Maurice Larrouy' (René Milan). Music by André Messager. Théâtre Marigny, Paris, 29 September 1928.

With the coming of the jazz-age musical comedy in the years following the First World War, the much-admired composer of *Les P'tites Michu* and *Véronique*, by then well into his sixties, proved himself game to switch genres and attempt to compete with the new wave of musical theatre composers on their own ground. In such pieces as *La Petite Fontionnaire* (1921) and *Passionnément* (1926) he adapted with increasing success to the light comedy, rhythmic dance melodies and small orchestra and chorus the new style imposed. *Coups de roulis*, written to a libretto by the new movement's first and most celebrated librettist, Willemetz, was the next and last of his efforts in the style. Its story, in line with its title, took place largely at sea, where a pompous politician, Puy Pradal (Raimu), and his pretty daughter, Béatrice (Marcelle Denya), on a fact-finding mission aboard the warship 'Montesquieu', get involved, respectively, with an ambitious Egyptian actress called Sola Myrrhis (Maguy Warna) and with not one but two of the ship's officers, Captain Gerville (Pierre Magnier) and Ensign Kermao (Robert Burnier), as the ship trots back and forth between France and Egypt.

The hit of the show's score was the march 'En amour, il n'est pas de grade' with which the favoured suitor (Burnier) brought the first-act finale to a climax, but both the Opéra-Comique's Mlle Denya ('Tous les deux me plaisent', 'C'est charmant, très parisien', 'Coups de roulis', 'Les hommes sont tous les mêmes') and Mlle Warna were well equipped, and Burnier's couplets 'Ce n'est pas la première fois' again showed Messager's decided facility with the new mode of light music. The more lyrical moments were accompanied by a brochette of lively comedy numbers for Raimu describing how one can make a contribution to the country's good 'Avec la danse' or for Gustave Nelson, as a common sailor, singing about sea-legs.

Messager died during the show's run, but *Coups de roulis* was a splendid success both in Paris, where it was revived in 1934 (Gaîté-Lyrique, 30 October), and in the provinces where it still appears from time to time, 60 and more years after its first production.

Recording: complete (Gaîté-Lyrique); Film: Jean de la Cour 1932

LA COUR DU ROI PÉTAUD Opéra-comique in 3 acts by Adolphe Jaime and Philippe Gille. Music by Léo Delibes. Théâtre des Variétés, Paris, 24 April 1869.

La Cour du Roi Pétaud was Delibes' one full-length opérette, written after a goodly number of short pieces, and before he moved on to make his name in the world of opera with *Le Roi l'a dit*, *Jean de Nivelle* and *Lakmé*. The plot had the heroine, the daughter of the titular King Pétaud, turned into a goose, which therefore meant that her neighbouring Prince was obliged to court her in the guise of an Arcadian gooseherd. Marie Aimée (Princess Girandole) and Zulma Bouffar (Prince Léo) were the lovers of the original cast, with Grenier, Léonce and Christian holding up the comedy of a piece, the success of whose score was an undeniable encouragement to its composer to continue to more ambitious works.

The show had a wide international distribution, if without any particularly dazzling results. In H B Farnie's London version Selina Dolaro was the goose and Emily Soldene her Prince for a good ten weeks at the Philharmonic Theatre, whilst in Austria (ad Julius Hopp) the piece became *Confusius IX* with Lori Stubel (Leo), Hermine Meyerhoff (Girandole), Josef Matras (Confusius), Karl Blasel (Alexibus) and Wilhelm Knaack (Wetterhahn) heading the cast through 17 performances to the end of 1872, and four more later in repertoire (1873, 1874). Emil Follinusz's Hungarian version used versions of both French and German titles for its productions at the Budai Színkör and the Népszinház (23 February 1877).

Austria: Carltheater *Confusius IX* 11 December 1872; UK: Philharmonic, Islington *Fleur de Lys* 9 April 1873; Hungary: Budai Színkör *Petó király udvara* (*Confucius*) 25 July 1874

COURTNEIDGE, Cicely [Esmeralda] (Dame) (b Sydney, Australia, 1 April 1893; d London, 26 April 1980). Britain's favourite funny, singing auntie of the wartime years.

Born in Australia during her father's tour there with the Gaiety Company, Cicely Esmeralda was named for one theatrical grandmother (Cicely Nott) and for the show playing that night – the burlesque *Miss Esmeralda*. She made her earliest appearances on the musical stage under her father's management, taking a tiny rôle in *Tom Jones* (1907, Rosie Pippin) and covering both Phyllis Dare and May Kinder in *The Arcadians* (1909) before taking over briefly and then being given the soubrette rôle in *The Mousmé* (1911, Miyo ko San) at the age of 18. She had an irrelevant rôle with a number in Courtneidge's version of *Der liebe Augustin* (*Princess Caprice*, 1912, Clementine) and in *The Pearl Girl* (1913, Betty Biddulph) she was paired in a light comedy rôle with the young Jack Hulbert, who was soon to become her husband and long-time professional partner.

She won top-billing as the juvenile of *The Cinema Star* (1914, Phyllis), romancing Harry Welchman, played Eileen in a revival of *The Arcadians* (1915), but went down with the disastrous *The Light Blues* (1916, Cynthia Petrie) and her father's poleaxed finances and ended up touring in his very much less grand *Oh, Caesar!* (1916, Margaret Potts). With Courtneidge no longer significantly active, she found work and especially good work hard to come by and, over the next decade, was seen in the London theatre only in a handful of revues, as she turned from soubrette into comedienne. Her only musical theatre performance in the 20 years following *Oh Caesar!* was an appearance at the Gaiety in Rodgers and Hart's *Lido Lady* (1926, Peggy Bassett), alongside Phyllis Dare, this time under the management not of her father, but of her husband.

In the later 1920s and the 1930s, Hulbert established himself as a producer and the couple starred themselves not only in *Lido Lady* but in several successful revues (*By the Way*, *Clowns in Clover*, *The House That Jack Built*, *Folly to be Wise*), before Hulbert's venture collapsed. They then turned to films and, although performing mostly separately in pieces such as *Jack's the Boy* (him) or *Aunt Sally* and *Soldiers of the King* (her), confirmed themselves in the public's mind as a beloved comic couple to bouncing box-offices.

Miss Courtneidge returned to the stage to star opposite Bobby Howes in *Hide and Seek* (1937, Sally), and serious success struck next time up, when she and Hulbert paired in the comical spy musical *Under Your Hat* (1938, Kay Porter) which totted up over 500 London performances in a run diced by wartime circumstances. The great success of *Under Your Hat* set in motion a thereafter unbroken series of similar shows which continued with *Full Swing* (1942, Kay Porter again) and *Something in the Air* (1943, Terry Porter) through more than four years in the West End.

With Hulbert concentrating largely on directing, the on-stage partnership was split for *Under the Counter* (1945, Jo Fox) in which Courtneidge scored one of her biggest successes in both Britain and Australia. However, she felt herself criticked out of New York by a kind of general anti-British feeling which was not again to raise its curious head until the late 1980s. She followed up her Australian

COURTNEIDGE, Robert

Plate 61. **Cicely Courtneidge** *and husband Jack Hulbert.*

venture with two further London musicals in which she capitalized on her now-established public character of the zany English grandeish dame with a twinkle in her eye and unending vitality – *Her Excellency* (1949, Lady Frances Maxwell) and *Gay's the Word* (1951, Gay Daventry, 'Vitality'), but, after a less than triumphant return to revue in *Over the Moon* (1953) and a musical which didn't make town (*Starmaker* 1956, Susie Green), she played thereafter largely in comedy (*The Bride and the Bachelor, The Bride Comes Back* etc) and in films (*The L-Shaped Room, Those Magnificent Men in their Flying Machines* etc).

She missed the chance of one last long West End run when she turned down the star rôle of *Charlie Girl* to take on that of Madame Arcati in the short-lived London production of *High Spirits* (1964), leaving the run and the money to Anna Neagle, and she only returned to the musical stage thereafter at an advanced age, in tandem with Hulbert, in a compilation show based on their lives (*Once More with Music*, Guildford 1976).

Autobiography: *Cicely* (Hutchinson, London, 1953), Hulbert, J: *The Little Woman's Always Right* (W H Allen, London, 1975)

COURTNEIDGE, Robert (b Glasgow, 29 June 1859; d Brighton, 6 April 1939). Producer for the British stage whose up-and-down career was highlighted by his introduction of *Tom Jones* and *The Arcadians*.

Courtneidge began his theatrical career as an amateur actor in his native Scotland before winning supporting rôles at the Prince's Theatre, Manchester, then with the Charles Dillon and Barry Sullivan companies, and – in the musical theatre – both in companies touring the Gaiety Theatre musicals and with Kate Santley in her *Vetah* (1886, Hamet Abdulerim Abensellan). In 1892 he toured to Australia, playing comic rôles in the Gaiety company's *Carmen Up-to-Data* (Zuniga), *Faust Up-to-Date* (Valentine), *Miss Esmeralda* (Gringoire) and *Joan of Arc* (Jacques) and stayed to appear (1893–4) with Williamson, Garner and Musgrove in *La Mascotte* (Rocco), *Paul Jones* (Petit-Pierre) and opposite Ethel Haydon in pantomime. His other rôles as a musical performer included Pepin in the

British production of Coèdes's *Girouette* (1889) and Major Styx in the Scots musical *Pim Pom*.

In 1896 Courtneidge became manager of the Prince's Theatre (Manchester) and, as such, a prominent member of the Provincial Managers' Association. In 1898, in a quest for material to fill their houses, the PMA ventured into production, with Courtneidge as their executive. The extensive success of the George Dance/Carl Kiefert musical *The Gay Grisette*, which Courtneidge produced and directed for them, led him to a directing assignment for George Edwardes on the original production of Ivan Caryll's *Madame Sans-Gêne* operetta, *The Duchess of Dantzic* (conducted by Kiefert), and then to an extended career as a producer-director. He began, following his resignation from his Manchester post in 1904, with the production (w Arthur Hart and Pat Malone) of *The Blue Moon* at Northampton.

Courtneidge mounted a revised version of this piece, starring the young Florence Smithson, in London the next year and, following a successful season, it was picked up by the Shuberts for New York. He followed up with the farcical and highly successful *The Dairymaids* (1906), Edward German's beautifully crafted *Tom Jones* (1907) and, in 1909, mounted his biggest hit, Lionel Monckton and Howard Talbot's *The Arcadians* (1909).

The Mousmé, the successor to *The Arcadians*, proved a very expensive semi-failure for its producer, so far used to nothing but success, but versions of Fall's *Der liebe Augustin* staged as *Princess Caprice* (1912) and Ivan Caryll's American musical comedy *Oh! Oh! Delphine* (1913) did altogether better. The home-made musical comedy *The Pearl Girl* was something of a disappointment, but just when it seemed that Courtneidge might have another genuine hit on his hands with *The Cinema Star*, the war intervened, and this German musical comedy, a version of Jean Gilbert's *Die Kino-Königin*, was forced to close its London run.

From there on things went badly for Courtneidge. The very appreciable but indifferently cast *My Lady Frayle* failed to take on, a trivial piece called *The Light Blues* (which counted the young Noël Coward in its cast) was a full-scale flop, and the rather stiff-necked patriotic operetta *Young England* went nowhere towards recouping anything lost. The producer turned his attentions, instead, to the provinces and to less expensive productions and put out *Oh, Caesar!* (an early appearance for the young Evelyn Laye) and the music-hally *Petticoat Fair, Fancy Fair* and *Too Many Girls*, extravaganzas which played theatres and variety houses indifferently. As a director he fared better, with his staging of the long-running hit *The Boy* for Alfred Butt at the Adelphi Theatre.

In 1920 Courtneidge again ventured into the West End with a share (w MacDonald and Young) of Cuvillier's short-lived *The Sunshine of the World*, and attempted slightly stiffer stuff with the production of the comic opera *The Rebel Maid*, but monetary considerations soon forced him back into the provinces where the old-fashioned *Gabrielle* (1921) proved a continuous money-spinner for several years and *The Little Duchess* something less of one.

He returned to London several more times with plays, but on only two further occasions with musicals, as director of Lehár's *The Blue Mazurka* (1927) for James White at Daly's and as producer-director of an unimpressive

310

Chopin pot-pourri called *The Damask Rose* (1930). He made one final provincial venture with the musical *Lavender*, but none of these proved a hit and he never again reached the heights of his earliest days as a producer and of *The Arcadians*.

Courtneidge was regularly credited with co-authoring status on a number of his shows, although it is doubtful whether his input as a writer was much greater than needed to allow him to claim a continuing interest in the copyright and royalties of the pieces in question. His name appears on some material for *The Dairymaids*, *Tom Jones*, *The Arcadians*, *The Mousmé*, *Too Many Girls*, *Gabrielle*, *The Little Duchess*, *The Damask Rose*, *Lavender*, and as the sole author of *Petticoat Fair* and *Fancy Fair*, as well as on the libretto of *The Babes and the Baron*, a revamped version of a Princes' Manchester pantomime played for a short run in New York.

A seriously professed socialist, Courtneidge was known for giving opportunities to brothers in conviction – most notably the left-wing journalist turned highly effective librettist, Alexander M Thompson – and he is said to have given a practical turn to his beliefs by becoming the first producer to pay chorus members for rehearsals and to give his casts holidays with pay. However, he showed less consideration for his suppliers: he was bankrupted several times, leaving them to whistle for their money whilst he started up operations once again with a clean slate.

Autobiography: *I Was an Actor Once* (Hutchinson, London, 1930)

COUSIN BOBBY Operette in 3 acts by Benno Jacobson and Franz Wagner. Music from the works of Karl Millöcker adapted by L Sänger. Theater des Westens, Berlin, 29 December 1906.

'Cousin' Bobby is nobody's cousin. He is a variety-theatre impresario who, in a tale which seems to contain more mistaken identities than virtually any other similar piece, gets mistaken for one Agamemnon Mogulopulous, the wealthy nephew of penniless Swiss hotel owner Nero Sanstleben, who is looking to his unknown relative for financial help. When the real Agamemnon turns up, he is mistaken for the new barman. The ladies in the piece were Nero's daughter Herta, his sister and Agamemnon's mother, Lydia, and variety singer, Marietta Leona, as well as the four Mogulopulous daughters and Bobby's four little chorus-girls who are, en masse, mistaken for each other.

The music of the show was put together from the late Karl Millöcker's trunk, and the resultant show was successful enough in Berlin to be taken up in Hungary (ad Emil Taburi) and to be optioned and announced for Broadway's 1909–10 season, though apparently without production.

Hungary: Budai Színkör *A komédiások* 28 April 1908

COUSIN-COUSINE Opérette in 3 acts by Maurice Ordonneau and Henri Kéroul. Music by Gaston Serpette. Théâtre des Folies-Dramatiques, Paris, 23 December 1893.

The part of the show which dealt with the cousin-cousine relationship showed two cousins (male and female, as per the show's title), from two non-speaking parts of a family, falling in love. Thérèse Courtalin (Aline Vauthier) pretends to be her schoolfriend, Henriette de Roche-fontaine (Mlle de Berio), so that the course of love with Edgard de Pommerol (Perrin) can run smoothly. Henriette (pretending to be Thérèse) runs a similar course with Gaston Jolivet (Lamy). The other part of the show dealt with the eccentric lawyer, Patenôtre (Guy), whose passion for choral music intrudes into his daily life to such an extent that his office workers, organized into an orphéon, make up a permanent chorus (Greek variety) for the play. Patenôtre is 'visiting' the housemistress (Louise Balthy) of the girls' school when fire breaks out and he is forced to escape in feminine garb. The two young lovers turn up with fire hoses and encounter their sweethearts, apparently sporting each other's names, and it takes another act of comedy, including regular appearances by Patenôtre's ever-interrupting choristers, before things come to their natural operettic end.

Played for 90 highly successful nights in its first run at the Folies-Dramatiques, *Cousin-Cousine* did not reach the stages of Britain, America or Austria, but it was seen in several other countries and languages. It was mounted in Australia, with Florence Young taking the title-rôle of what had become (for the ungendered English) *La Belle Thérèse* alongside Henry Bracy (Gaston), Courtice Pounds (Louis Pomerol), Clara Thompson (Mme Moutonnet) and Howard Vernon (Bellefontaine), in Germany (ad Heinrich Bolten-Bäckers), and in Hungary (ad Gyula Komor), where the unloved title was changed to the distinctly more commercial 'Fire at a girls' school'.

Australia: Princess Theatre, Melbourne *La Belle Thérèse* 7 December 1895; Germany: Thalia-Theater 18 September 1896; Hungary: Budai Színkör *Tüz a leánygimnaziumban* 15 August 1902

COWARD, Noël [Peirce] (b Teddington, Mddx, 16 December 1899; d Blue Harbour, Jamaica, 26 March 1973)

Dramatist, revue-writer, lyricist, performer and personality, Noël Coward made himself a special place in the theatre of his age whilst finding only one genuine success as a composer and author for the book musical stage.

Coward began his connection with the theatre as a child actor in plays and musical comedies, but before long began writing and composing songs – of which 'Forbidden Fruit' (1915) is the earliest surviving example – and plays, of which *I'll Leave it to You* (1920) was the first to be staged. His earliest contributions to the musical theatre as a writer were in the form of pieces of revue material for André Charlot and for the Co-Optimists concert party, and in 1923 he collaborated with Ronald Jeans on the writing of Charlot's successful revue, *London Calling*, in which he also performed. His career as a playwright began to blossom soon after, and he successfully mixed a run of his own individual kind of brittle, personal comedies and slightly daring dramas with further revues (*On with the Dance*, *This Year of Grace*) until, according to his own tale, a hearing of *Die Fledermaus* tempted him into trying his hand at a musical play.

The result was *Bitter-Sweet* (1929), a lushly sentimental period piece which he called an 'operette' and which, in the midst of the current craze for dance-and-laughter musical shows and revues, seemed an unlikely winner. However, the show, with its hit songs 'I'll See You Again' and 'If Love Were All', became the first British romantic musical to triumph in London since the war, running for nearly two years before going on to Broadway, to Paris, to Budapest and on to film. Its success encouraged Coward to continue in the same vein and, in the 1930s and 1940s, while he turned out the most famous of his comic plays (*Private Lives, Present Laughter, Blithe Spirit*) and further bright and witty revues (*Words and Music, Set to Music, Sigh No More*), he persisted in following the romantic operetta trail with his musical stage pieces.

Conversation Piece (1934), which he wrote for and played with French actress Yvonne Printemps, and which produced perhaps his most famous lyrical song, 'I'll Follow My Secret Heart', won some success, but *Operette* (1938, 133 performances) and *Pacific 1860* (1946, 129 performances) were both failures in spite, in the latter case, of containing some of his best music. An attempt to be more modern, with a *Wunder-Bar*-ish crooks-and-cabaret musical called *Ace of Clubs* (1950) misfired uncomfortably, and he returned to period operetta with a not very successful adaptation of Oscar Wilde's *Lady Windermere's Fan* as *After the Ball* (1954). The 1961 musical *Sail Away* ('Why Do the Wrong People Travel?', 'The Customer's Always Right') had its lead soprano and her love story cut out during pre-Broadway try-outs and thus, almost accidentally, Coward ended up writing the show which, of all his musical stage pieces, was nearest in tone to his revues. It was also the nearest since *Conversation Piece* to being a success. A final musical theatre score, in the wake of *My Fair Lady*, for an adaptation of Terence Rattigan's *The Prince and the Showgirl* as the uncomfortably imitative *The Girl Who Came to Supper* was both uncharacteristic and a quick failure.

Alongside his conventional musicals, Coward also wrote songs which were utilized in several of the plays which made up the various evenings of the collection of one-act pieces called *Tonight at 8.30* ('Has Anybody Seen Our Ship?', 'We Were Dancing'), and in the patriotic play *Cavalcade* ('Twentieth Century Blues').

Coward's many-faceted career as a writer and performer, which included books of autobiography, poetry, short stories and novels as well as stage works, was extended in his later years by a series of very successful cabaret performances of largely his own material in which many songs which might otherwise have gone down with failed shows were given a second life. He turned down the offer to star as the Emperor of China in the London production of Cole Porter's *Aladdin* (1959) and in 1967 he made his nearest approach to a reappearance on the musical stage since *Conversation Piece* when he appeared on television as Caesar in the Richard Rodgers/Peter Stone musical adaptation of *Androcles and the Lion*.

Largely self-taught as a composer, Coward relied on more traditionally educated musicians to notate and fill out his musical lines, but his melodic invention and the immaculate blending of his words and music made his songs extremely effective. He used the traditional elements of the light musical theatre as his bases and succeeded in producing some outstanding lyrical pieces (the waltzes 'I'll See You Again', 'I'll Follow My Secret Heart' and *Pacific 1860*'s 'This is a Changing World', 'This is a Night for Lovers'), such sympathetic words-and-music pieces as 'If Love Were All', and a whole series of those brisk and brittle comedy songs, overflowing with genuinely clever and sometimes wicked words, rhymes and ideas ('Green

Carnations', 'His Excellency Regrets', 'Alice is at it Again', 'There's Always Something Fishy About the French', 'The Stately Homes of England', 'Three Juvenile Delinquents', 'The Customer's Always Right', 'The Bronxville Darby and Joan', 'Josephine') which became his trademark and which, like his plays, have survived individually more strongly than any of his stage musicals.

1929 **Bitter-Sweet** His Majesty's Theatre 12 July
1934 **Conversation Piece** His Majesty's Theatre 16 February
1938 **Operette** His Majesty's Theatre 17 February
1946 **Pacific 1860** Theatre Royal, Drury Lane 19 December
1950 **Ace of Clubs** Cambridge Theatre 7 July
1954 **After the Ball** Globe Theatre 10 June
1961 **Sail Away** Broadhurst Theater, New York 3 October
1963 **The Girl Who Came to Supper** (Harry Kurnitz) Broadway Theater, New York 8 December

Autobiography: Coward, N ed Morley, S: *Autobiography (Present Indicative, Future Indefinite, Past Conditional)* (Methuen, London, 1986), Coward, N ed Payn, G and Morley, S: *The Coward Diaries* (Macmillan, London, 1982); Biography: Lesley, C: *The Life of Noël Coward* (Jonathan Cape, London, 1976), Morley, S: *A Talent to Amuse* (Heinemann, London, 1969), Castle, C: *Noël* (Abacus, London, 1972). Mander, R, Mitchenson, J: *Theatrical Companion to Noël Coward* (Rockliff, London, 1957) etc.

COWLES, Eugene [Chase] (b Stanstead, Quebec, Canada, 1860; d Boston, 22 September 1948). The possessor of an impressive bass voice, Cowles played two decades of priests, fathers and such other rôles as basses of all ages are traditionally doomed to, on the turn-of-the-century Broadway stage.

Originally a bank clerk in Chicago and a local church and concert singer, he joined the Boston Ideal Opera Company (The Bostonians) in 1888. He remained an important member of the group for eight years, creating the rôle of Will Scarlett in *Robin Hood* as well as often written-to-measure bass parts in such other early American pieces as De Koven's *The Knickerbockers* (1893, Anthony von Corlear), Victor Herbert's *Prince Ananias* (1894, George La Grabbe), *The Maid of Plymouth* (1894, Miles Standish), *The Ogallallas* (1894, Cardenas), *A Wartime Wedding* (1896, Felipe), and *The Serenade* (1896, Romero), and he appeared in the part of Squire Bantam (*Dorothy*) and in other like rôles in the company's wide-ranging repertoire.

When Alice Nielsen split from the group to form her own company, Cowles went with her, and he appeared in America and Britain as Sandor in her production of Victor Herbert's *The Fortune Teller*, in which he created the celebrated Gypsy Love Song ('Slumber On, My Little Gypsy Sweetheart'), and then as Duke Rodolph in *The Singing Girl* (1899, 'The Wonderful Magician'). He later played on Broadway alongside Fritzi Scheff as Mondragon in Herbert's *Babette* (1903), with Marie Cahill as Henry Clay Kulpepper in the musical comedy *Marrying Mary* (1906), in James Hackett's Chicago production of *The Alcayde* (1906), as a bluegrass Colonel in *The Boys and Betty* (1908), General Petipons in Herbert's *The Rose of Algeria* (1909), in the short-lived *Sweet Sixteen* (1910) and on the road in *The Tik-Tok Man of Oz* (1913, Ruggedo). He also played in a number of Gilbert and Sullivan productions, and, at the age of almost 60, was still to be seen, on the road, playing in *Chu Chin Chow*.

COX AND BOX, or The Long Lost Brothers Musical triumviretta in 1 act adapted from J Maddison Morton's farce *Box and Cox* by F C Burnand. Music by Arthur Sullivan. Adelphi Theatre, London, 11 May 1867.

One of the most successful of the short musical plays written in Britain in the wake of the works of Offenbach, *Cox and Box* was apparently the result of Sullivan's attempting to produce something on the lines of Offenbach's widely-played hit *Les Deux Aveugles*. Burnand adapted the script from Maddison Morton's frequently performed comedietta, and the first performances of the little three-handed comedy musical were given in private by the society amateur group, the Moray Minstrels, before *Cox and Box* got its first public performance at a benefit concert at the Adelphi Theatre.

Mr Bouncer (Arthur Cecil) has rented the same room both to the hatter Mr Cox (Quintin Twiss) and the printer Mr Box (George du Maurier), since one works at night and the other in the day. Inevitably, one day, the two coincide and, after the hard words have flown, find they have a common interest in one Mrs Penelope Ann Wiggins. Their interest is to avoid her and, at first, each tries to force the other to take the lady until news comes that she has drowned and left her fortune to her intended. Then both are less anxious to disclaim her. But Penelope Ann has not drowned. She is heading for London to find Box and/or Cox with the news that she has married Knox. Cox and Box delightedly discover that they are, by the laws of the dramatic theatre, indubitably long lost brothers and they decide to share the wretched Bouncer's room. The songs of the piece included a 'Rataplan' piece for Bouncer, reminiscing interminably over his days in the military, a Lullaby for the snoozy Box, and a serenade, 'The Buttercup', to help pass the time.

After its Adelphi Theatre performances, *Cox and Box* was put on the programme at the German Reeds' Gallery of Illustration with Reed (Cox), Cecil (Box) and J Seymour (Bouncer) in the cast. It was played on a double-bill with W S Gilbert's *No Cards* and, later, with *Ages Ago*, for an entire year. In contrast, it was also played as part of the programme at the vast Alhambra Theatre with the composer's brother, Fred, playing Cox, and later on several occasions at the Court Theatre. It was ultimately taken into the repertoire of the D'Oyly Carte companies and played at the Savoy as a forepiece to *The Chieftain*, becoming – in spite of not being written by Gilbert – accepted as part of the Savoy canon.

The piece won other English-language performances following its London success, being first mounted in Australia as part of a 'Gallery of Illustration' programme given by Alice May with Edward Farley (Cox) and Howard Vernon (Box) featured. Offenbach's *The Rose of the Auvergne* and a local extravaganza *The Belle of Woolloomooloo* made up the programme. It was apparently played for the first time in America in 1875 and Broadway's Standard Theatre hosted it as a forepiece to *Pinafore* in 1879 as played by Thomas Whiffen (Box), Hart Conway (Cox) and Charles Makin (Bouncer). Both countries, and other English-speaking stages, later saw *Cox and Box* played as a forepiece with the Gilbert and Sullivan repertoire.

Australia: Masonic Hall, Sydney 26 December 1872; US: 13 August 1875, Standard Theater, New York 14 April 1879
Recordings: complete (Decca), selections (BASF, PRT etc)

COYNE, Joseph [E] (b New York, 27 March 1867; d Virginia Water, Surrey, 17 February 1941). Light comedy actor-who-sings who moved from silly-ass rôles in his native America to stardom as Britain's Danilo in *The Merry Widow*.

Coyne first appeared on the New York stage at Niblo's Gardens in the Kiralfy Brothers' dance-and-drama spectacular *Excelsior* at the age of 13, but he spent most of his earliest years touring in vaudeville as half of the act 'Coyne and Evans'. He played in the variety farce-comedies *The District Attorney* (1895, Corrigan) *The Good Mr Best* (1897, Marmaduke Mush), *The Girl in the Barracks* (1899, Paul Roland), as Willett Work in *Star and Garter* (1900), a vaudeville farce constructed largely to feature the Agoust family of jugglers, and in *The Night of the Fourth* (1901, Keenan Swift), each of which passed a brief period in New York, and he made his first appearance in a regular musical as Bertie Tappertwit (the name of the character speaks for itself) in Charles Frohman's London production of *The Girl from Up There*, a piece basically constructed as a vehicle for *Belle of New York* star Edna May.

Returning to America, he got his Broadway break in the George Grossmith rôle of Archie in the Gaiety musical *The Toreador*, and he followed up with a range of more or less goofy gentlemen in *The Rogers Brothers in London* (1903), *In Newport* (1904, Percy van Alstyne), *The Rollicking Girl* (1905, Panagl), *The Social Whirl* (1906, Artie Endicott) and the American version of *Lady Madcap*'s Trooper Brown (*My Lady's Maid*), originated by G P Huntley, before returning to London for Frohman, this time to play leading man to Edna May in a palpable, but weak, attempt to clone *The Belle of New York* called *Nelly Neil*. His personal success in the rôle of the loose-limbed, comic-aristocratic Billy Ricketts sparked something in the mind of rival producer George Edwardes and Coyne found himself offered a rôle rather different to the upper-class dopes he had been accustomed to playing – the romantic lead of Count Danilo Danilowitsch in Edwardes's English-language version of Lehár's *Die lustige Witwe*.

Coyne's success in *The Merry Widow* made him an enormous London star and led him into a whole series of major light comic-romantic leading rôles for Edwardes, first opposite his *Merry Widow* co-star Lily Elsie in *The Dollar Princess* (1909, Harry Condor), then with Gertie Millar in *The Quaker Girl* (1910, Tony Chute) and *The Dancing Mistress* (1912, Teddy Cavanaugh), and with Ina Claire in *The Girl from Utah* (1913, Sandy Blair). During the war he appeared in several plays, in London's production of Irving Berlin's revues *Watch Your Step* and *Follow the Crowd*, and in the local revue *The Bing Girls Are There*, but he returned to the musical theatre to play opposite Winifred Barnes in the Grossmith and Laurillard version of the Belgian musical *Arlette* (1917, Prince Paul) and to star, successively, in the Gaiety Theatre's long-running production of the American musical *Going Up* (1918, Robert Street), in Charlot's version of the French musical comedy *Dédé* (1922, André La Huchette), and in the London production of Friml's *Katinka* (1923, Thaddeus T Hopper).

He had another huge success when, knocking sixty, he was cast in the rôle of Jimmy Smith in Clayton and Waller's triumphant British production of *No, No, Nanette* (1925), followed by the London version of *Queen High* (1926, T Boggs Johns), but his last appearances in a musical – in the disastrous *Open Your Eyes* (1929) and in the unsuccessful London version of Benatzky's *Meine Schwester und ich* (*Meet My Sister*, Filosel, 1931) – were less memorable.

CRAWFORD, Cheryl (b Akron, Ohio, 24 September 1902; d New York, 7 October 1986).

Cheryl Crawford worked as a secretary with the Theatre Guild, as an actress and as a casting director before being instrumental in the founding of the Group Theatre (1931) where she directed several productions. She moved into management in 1938, and produced her first musical piece in 1942 with a revival of *Porgy and Bess*. In a wide-ranging theatrical career thereafter, during which she collaborated on the establishment of the American Repertory Theater (1946) and the Actors' Studio (1946), she produced, amongst a series of mostly less than successful plays, several distinctly successful Broadway musicals – *One Touch of Venus* (1943), *Brigadoon* (1947) and *Paint Your Wagon* (1951). She also mounted several less successful ones – *Love Life* (1948), *Regina* (1949), *Flahooley* (1951), *Jennie* (1963), *Celebration* (1969), the off-Broadway *Colette* (1970), and *Reuben Reuben* (1955) which died prior to New York – but it was notable that, in spite of her many efforts towards the avant-garde in the theatre, her biggest producing successes came with the most traditional of musical plays.

The Cheryl Crawford Theater at the West Side Arts Center is named for her.

Autobiography: *One Naked Individual* (Bobbs-Merrill, Indianapolis, 1977)

CRAWFORD, Clifton (b ?Glasgow, [?Australia], 1875; d London, 3 June 1920). A popular light comedy-with-dance player for some 20 years of Broadway musicals.

Originally a golfer and golf coach in Scotland, the 21-year-old Crawford moved to the green fields of Boston to pursue his calling. He was heard entertaining his wealthy clients at the Boston Golf Club by R A Barnet of the Boston Cadets musical company and, before long, he had exchanged his niblick for a stick of grease paint.

Crawford was first seen on Broadway in his mid-twenties when he appeared in such musical shows as A H Chamberlyn's ex-Cadets production of *Milady and the Musketeers* (1901, Arra-Miss), *Foxy Grandpa* (1902), *Mother Goose* (1903) and *Seeing New York* (1906). He soon slipped into light-handed leading-man rôles, and appeared as Tom Stanhope in the successful *Three Twins* (1908), opposite Ina Claire in the rôle created by Joe Coyne in *The Quaker Girl* (1910, Tony Chute), as the juvenile leading man of his own musical, *My Best Girl* (1912, Richard Vanderfleet), and paired with Emma Trentini in Friml's *The Ballet Girl* (1914), a version of Nedbal's *Polenblut* which reached Broadway as *The Peasant Girl* (1915). He played in the Winter Garden show *A World of Pleasure* (1915), in the revamped Hungarian operett *Her Soldier Boy* (1916, Teddy McLane) and, billed above the title alongside Marilyn Miller, in *Fancy Free* (1918, Albert van Wyck). In 1914 he took time out from Broadway to visit London, where he starred in the Gaiety Theatre's revusical comedy, *After the Girl* (Freddy Charlston).

Crawford also worked, from his golfing days, as a songwriter and he scored a major song hit with the number

'Nancy Brown' as sung by Marie Cahill in *The Wild Rose*. He interpolated songs into a number of other productions, including several in which he appeared – *The Liberty Belles* ('De Trop', 'Starlight'), *Her Soldier Boy*, *The Quaker Girl* ('I Want to Tell You Something'), *Fancy Free* ('Eve'), *The Canary* ('This is the Time'), London's *My Darling* ('The Shady Side of Bond Street') and the original production of the play *My Lady Friends* ('I Want to Spread a Little Sunshine') which would later be the basis for *No, No, Nanette*. He had less luck with his attempts to compose a Broadway musical. Neither *Captain Careless*, played around the country by B C Whitney for two seasons, nor *I Love a Lassie*, announced by its librettist-lyricist-producer-star for Broadway but a casualty at Providence, Rhode Island, after a fortnight's life, made it to New York, whilst *My Best Girl*, which did, had only a limited stay.

Crawford was killed when he fell from a window in a London hotel at the age of 45.

1901 **Liberty Bells** (w others/H B Smith) Madison Square Theater 30 September
1906 **Seeing New York** (A Baldwin Sloane/Joseph Hart/w Hart) New York Theater Roof 5 June
1906 **Captain Careless** (w Bob Adams/Robert M Baker, Hal Stephens) Detroit 11 September
1912 **My Best Girl** (w Augustus Barratt/Rennold Wolf, Channing Pollock) Park Theater 12 September
1919 **I Love a Lassie** (Jerome K Jerome ad Erwin Connelly) Shubert Theater, New Haven 15 May

CRAWFORD, Michael [DUMBLE-SMITH, Michael] (b Salisbury, 19 January 1942). One of Britain's most popular comedy actors, who found a singing voice and an even larger, international fame in the musical theatre.

First seen on the musical stage as a boy soprano in Benjamin Britten's *Noye's Fludde* and *Let's Make an Opera*, Crawford had early successes on the stage in the *Black Comedy/White Lies* double-bill of plays and the farce *No Sex, Please, We're British* and in such films as *The Knack* and *The Jokers*, before tackling his first musical rôles as Hero in the screen's *A Funny Thing Happened on the Way to the Forum* (1966) and Barnaby in the film version of *Hello, Dolly!* (1969).

He became one of the best known and most loved of all British performers through his television characterization of the gormless, accident-prone Frank Spencer in the long-running series *Some Mothers Do Have 'Em*, and he paralleled his television career by taking four major musical theatre rôles over a period of some 15 years with a success which ultimately redirected his career towards the musical stage.

In 1974 he scored a first-class hit when he starred in his first stage musical as the forever fibbing Billy Fisher in *Billy* ('Some of Us Belong to the Stars') at the Theatre Royal, Drury Lane, but his second musical venture, as the mentally retarded hero of *Flowers for Algernon* (1979), was, in spite of undeniable qualities, short-lived. In 1981 he returned to the musical stage to play the title-rôle (with additional tricks) in the London production of the Broadway musical *Barnum*, scoring a second major hit and following the exhausting first run of the show with a return run and a television film of the show in 1985. At the end of that run he joined the cast of *The Phantom of the Opéra*, creating the rôle of the Phantom ('Music of the Night') in London, New York and Los Angeles in the third outstand-

Plate 62. **Michael Crawford** – *before he disappeared behind a mask – as London's P T Barnum.*

ing hit of a musical theatre career where the three rôles had filled more than ten years of his working life.

More recently, he has appeared throughout the world as the featured performer of the concert 'The Music of Andrew Lloyd Webber'.

CRÉMIEUX, Hector [Jonathan] (b Paris, 10 November 1828; d Paris, 30 September 1892). One of the most brilliant authors of opéra-bouffe texts in the palmiest days of the genre.

The young Crémieux studied law and subsequently entered on a career in the state service where he came under the eye of the theatrically-inclined and highly influential Duc de Morny. Under Morny's encouragement he progressed from his earliest attempt, in collaboration with his brother, at writing for the dramatic stage (*Fiesque*, 1850), to a series of féeries (the internationally successful *Pied de Mouton*, *Aladin, ou la lampe merveilleuse* etc), comedies (*L'Abbé Constantin* w Decourcelle), vaudevilles and short opérettes, making himself a reputation as one of the most outstanding exponents of the witty, cockeyed opéra-bouffe style. His burlesque talents were demonstrated in his collaborations with Halévy on the libretti for Offenbach's *Orphée aux enfers* and *Le Pont des soupirs* and with Adolphe Jaime on *Le Petit Faust*, *Les Turcs* and *Le Trône d'Écosse* for the most marvellously cockeyed composer of them all, Hervé, whilst on the smaller scale he also authored or co-authored the texts for some of the most internationally successful short musicals pieces of the 1850s and 1860s including such opérettes as Offenbach's *Une Demoiselle en loterie*, *La Chanson de Fortunio* and *Monsieur Choufleuri* and Henri Caspers' *Ma tante dort*.

Crémieux continued to be successful when opéra-bouffe gave way to the more measured opéra-comique style in the post-war era, having his biggest success of this period, once more, in collaboration with Offenbach and with Ernest Blum on the vaudevillesque tale of *La Jolie Parfumeuse*.

In 1887 he retired and took up a post as secretary general of the Société des dépôts. The society failed, Crémieux got into personal financial difficulties and, ill himself, suffered the deaths of his wife and his brother in quick succession before putting a bullet through his own head at the age of 63.

1856 **Elodie, ou le forfait nocturne** (Léopold Amat, Jacques Offenbach) 1 act Théâtre des Bouffes-Parisiens 19 January

1856 **Le Financier et le savetier** (Offenbach/w Edmond About) 1 act Théâtre des Bouffes-Parisiens 23 September

1857 **Une Demoiselle en loterie** (Offenbach/w Adolphe Jaime) 1 act Théâtre des Bouffes-Parisiens 27 July

1858 **Orphée aux enfers** (Offenbach/w Ludovic Halévy) Théâtre des Bouffes-Parisiens 21 October

1860 **Ma tante dort** (Henri Caspers/w About) 1 act Theatre Lyrique 21 January

1861 **La Chanson de Fortunio** (Offenbach/w Halévy) 1 act Théâtre des Bouffes-Parisiens 5 January

1861 **Le Pont des soupirs** (Offenbach/w Halévy) Théâtre des Bouffes-Parisiens 23 March

1861 **Monsieur Choufleuri restera chez lui le ...** (Offenbach/w 'Saint-Rémy', Halévy) privately 31 May, Théâtre des Bouffes-Parisiens 14 September

1861 **La Baronne de San Francisco** (Caspers/w Halévy) Théâtre des Bouffes-Parisiens 27 November

1861 **Le Roman comique** (Offenbach/w Halévy) Théâtre des Bouffes-Parisiens 10 December

1861 **Les Deux Buveurs** (Léo Delibes/w Halévy) 1 act Théâtre des Bouffes-Parisiens January

1861 **Les Eaux d'Ems** (Delibes/w Halévy) 1 act Kursaal, Bad Ems; Théâtre des Bouffes-Parisiens 9 April 1863

1862 **Un fin de bail** (Adolphe Varney/w Halévy) 1 act Théâtre des Bouffes-Parisiens 29 January

1862 **Mon ami Pierrot** (Delibes/w Halévy) 1 act Kursaal, Bad Ems July

1862 **Jacqueline** (Offenbach/w Halévy) 1 act Théâtre des Bouffes-Parisiens 14 October

1865 **Les Bergers** (Offenbach/w Philippe Gille) Théâtre des Bouffes-Parisiens 11 December

1867 **Robinson Crusoe** (Offenbach/w Eugène Cormon) Opéra-Comique 23 November

1869 **Le Petit Faust** (Hervé/w Jaime) Théâtre des Folies-Dramatiques 28 April

1869 **Les Turcs** (Hervé/w Jaime) Théâtre des Folies-Dramatiques 22 December

1871 **Le Trône d'Écosse** (Hervé/w Jaime) Théâtre des Variétés 17 November

1873 **La Veuve du Malabar** (Hervé/w Alfred Delacour) Théâtre des Variétés 26 April

1873 **La Jolie Parfumeuse** (Offenbach/w Ernest Blum) Théâtre de la Renaissance 29 November

1874 **Bagatelle** (Offenbach/w Blum) 1 act Théâtre des Bouffes-Parisiens 21 May

1874 **La Famille Trouillat** (Léon Vasseur/w Blum) Théâtre de la Renaissance 10 September

1875 **Geneviève de Brabant** (enlarged and revised version of Étienne Tréfeu's original) Théâtre de la Gaîté 25 February

1875 **Le Manoir du Pic-Tordu** (Gaston Serpette/w Alfred de Saint-Albin) Théâtre des Variétés 28 May

1875 **La Belle Poule** (Hervé/w Saint-Albin) Théâtre des Folies-Dramatiques 30 December

1877 **La Foire Saint-Laurent** (Offenbach/w Saint-Albin)
Théâtre des Folies-Dramatiques 10 February
1881 **L'Oeil crevé** revised version (Théâtre de la Renaissance)

LA CRÉOLE Opérette in 3 acts by Albert Millaud. Music by Jacques Offenbach. Théâtre des Bouffes-Parisiens, Paris, 3 November 1875.

There was very little that was different in the plot of *La Créole* except for the colour of its prima donna. Having to stain herself each night with réglisse for the show's title-rôle may indeed have hastened Mlle Judic's departure from the Bouffes for the Variétés.

Commander Feuilles-Mortes (Daubray) wants his ward, Antoinette (Mlle Luce), to marry his nephew, René (Anna van Ghell). This is unfortunate, for it is René's friend Frontignac (Cooper) who is in love with Antoinette, whilst René has set his heart on the dusky Guadaloupean Dora (Anna Judic). Dora goes after an important letter so that all the right pairings can come about with the help of a little bribery.

Judic was given some compensation for having to spend extra time making-up by having the first act off. Baritone Lucien Fugère, in the supporting rôle of Saint-Chamas, set affairs moving and, thereafter, soprano Anna van Ghell in the breeches rôle of René got the largest part of the music, with the Commandant popping in a little Romance by way of musico-comic relief. When Dora did appear, brought back to France aboard the Commander's ship once all the exposition had been done, she more than made up for lost time, delivering a romance of her own ('Il vous souvient de moi, j'éspère'), the couplets 'Si vous croyez que ça m'amuse', a chanson créole in the second-act finale ('Oui, c'est René que j'aime') and a lively Chanson des dames de Bordeaux ('C'est dans la ville de Bordeaux') in the final act. The jeune première had a pretty little villanelle ('Je croyais que tu m'aimais').

La Créole was not a particular success. It managed only to pass its 60th night before being withdrawn. However, Offenbach's name on the score guaranteed it productions elsewhere. In London, the piece was produced in a slimmed-down version (ad H B Farnie, Robert Reece) on a bill with two short pieces, Hervé's *Up the River* and Lecocq's *The Sea Nymphs* (*Ondines au champagne*). Kate Munroe starred as the Créole with a cast including Nellie Bromley (René), Violet Cameron (Antoinette) and John Howson (Commodore). It held its place in the bill when Lecocq's piece was replaced by a potted version of *L'Oeil crevé*, and closed after a fine season of three months. A decade later, Miss Cameron chose the piece as a vehicle for a season her friend, Lord Lonsdale, sponsored for her in America. Played as *The Commodore*, it was given one trial performance at the Avenue Theatre before the company set out. The liaison between producer and star was turned into a juicy scandal in New York, and, in the flurry, their show lasted only a handful of nights longer than it had in London.

Maximilian Steiner's production of *Die Creolin* at Vienna's Theater an der Wien (ad Julius Hopp) boasted no less a star than Marie Geistinger in the rôle of Dora, alongside Felix Schweighofer (de Feuillemorte), Jani Szika (Frontignac), Bertha Steinher (Antoinette), Frln Wieser (René) and Alexander Girardi as the 'first notary', but it was played just 27 times, and the piece never took on in German-langauge theatres.

It must have seemed a bright idea to dig up *La Créole* when a Parisian musical theatre piece was being discussed for coloured American variety star Josephine Baker. Albert Willemetz and Georges Delance did a heavy remake on the libretto and its score – one which allowed a new character called Cartahut (Dréan) to open the evening on its highest note with 'Les Dames de Bordeaux' and brought Dora on straight afterwards with the Chanson Créole. No waiting till the second act in 1934 – get the star on. For, after all, she didn't have Judic's problem with making-up. The new version of *La Créole* was produced at the Théâtre Marigny (15 December) with René-Charle (René), Rose Carday (Antoinette) and Urban (Commandant) supporting and with Carmen Lahez as a new comical character called Crème-Fouettée. It turned out to be not such a very bright idea. The lithe Mlle Baker showed up with much less voice even than Mlle Judic (she also wore much less clothing), but the production nevertheless found both a special audience and a new hearing for Offenbach's music.

Austria: Theater an der Wien *Die Creolin* 8 January 1876; Germany: Wallner Theater *Die Creolin* 4 June 1876; UK: Folly Theatre *La Créole* 15 September 1877, Avenue Theatre *The Commodore* 10 May 1886; USA: Casino Theater *The Commodore* 4 October 1886

Recording: 1934 version, complete (Bourg)

CROFT, Anne (b Skirlaugh, Hull, 17 August 1896; d London, 23 March 1959). Vocalist and producer for the London and provincial musical stage.

Anne Croft appeared in London as a young soprano in leading juvenile rôles in *The Cinema Star* (1914, t/o Phyllis) and *My Lady Frayle* (1915, Virginia) and after a long period playing in revue and pantomime, appeared in the title-rôle of Steven Jones's *Poppy* (1924), as Riquette in the pre-London tour of Oscar Straus' *Riquette* and in its later London incarnation as *My Son John* (1926, Sandy Fayre). She then starred in *The Girl Friend* (Kitty), *Hit the Deck* (Looloo) and *The Five o'Clock Girl* (Patricia) in Australia in 1928–9, before returning to London, where she took the soprano rôle in the arioso musical *Dear Love* (1929, Suzanne) and played José Collins's famous rôle of Teresa in a revival of *The Maid of the Mountains* (1930). She toured in two Continental West-End failures, Benatzky's *Meet My Sister* (*Meine Schwester und Ich*, 1931, Dorine) and Eisemann's *Happy Week-End* (*Zsákbamacska*, 1934, Polly Petworthy), but had more success when she moved into management on her own behalf to star in several tours of *The Chocolate Soldier* and two new musicals, the comedy opera *Prudence* (1932, Prudence) and the colourful *Tulip Time* (1935, Angela), which she brought to London's large Alhambra Theatre for a heavy schedule of profitable performances.

She was married to actor Reginald Sharland, who appeared with her in her Australian shows, and her son David [John] Croft (b Sandbanks, Dorset, 7 September 1922), better known as a television writer and producer, wrote lyrics for the musical plays *Star Maker* (1956), *The Pied Piper* (1958) and *Ann Veronica* (1969), which he also directed. A second son, Peter Croft, also appeared on the musical stage.

CROISSET, Francis de [WIENER, Franz] (b Brussels, 28 January 1877; d Neuilly, 8 November 1937).

A scion of a Belgian family more used to producing painters and sculptors than writers, de Croisset studied law before turning to the writing of verse, journalism and to some light-handed theatrical pieces, tinted occasionally with a saleable colouring of scandalousness. Following the death of Gaston de Caillavet, de Croisset joined his former partner, Robert de Flers, to write a number of plays and also the book and lyrics of *Ciboulette*, a sweetly genteel tale which made up into a popular and often-played opérette. In a career largely devoted to the non-musical theatre, and a life centred on travel – usually to India and the east, where he ultimately converted to Buddhism – he also collaborated on the libretto for Massenet's 1905 opera *Chérubin*, and on the 1934 musical version of his first major play success, *Le Bonheur, mesdames!* Adapted to the musical stage with the addition of a pasticcio score of pre-war Christiné songs, it followed its Parisian run by being seen in Hungary under the title *Bekbéli boldogsag*.

His highly successful play, *La Passerelle* (w Fred de Grésac), was subsequently made into the Broadway musical *Orange Blossoms* (1922), whilst his 1907 *Paris–New York* (w Emmanuel Arène) was musicalized in 1919 by Jean Bénédict and played at the Trianon-Lyrique.

1923 **Ciboulette** (Reynaldo Hahn/w Robert de Flers) Théâtre des Variétés 7 April
1927 **Le Diable à Paris** (Marcel Lattès/w de Flers) Théâtre Marigny November
1934 **Le Bonheur, mesdames!** (Henri Christiné arr/w Albert Willemetz, Fred de Grésac) Théâtre des Bouffes-Parisiens 6 January

Memoirs: *La Vie parisienne au théâtre* (Grasset, Paris, 1929)

CROOK, John [Francis] (b London, ?1847; d London, 10 November 1922). Longtime conductor for the London and provincial musical stage who, late in his career, found major success as a songwriter for touring musical comedy.

One of the succession of fine conductor/composers who took musical control of the Manchester Prince's Theatre and Theatre Royal in their heyday in the 1870s and 1880s, Crook was known, along with Alfred Cellier and Frederic Stanislaus, as one of the 'Manchester three'. Originally an organist in Norwich, he became a conductor with the Henri Corri Opera Company and took over at Manchester in succession to Stanislaus. Like his two predecessors, he successfully composed a full-scale comic opera for production at Captain Bainbridge's theatres and although, like Stanislaus's *The Lancashire Witches* the previous year, *The King's Dragoons* did not reach London, it found success elsewhere in the British provinces and as far afield as Australia and New Zealand at a time when such original works were only beginning to flow from British pens.

From his Manchester base Crook supplied the songs for two long-lived touring shows, the burlesque comic opera *Merry Mignon* and the musical comedy *Larks*, before he caught the attention of the influential librettist and director, H B Farnie, who took him to London with the comic opera *Indiana*, which had been produced at Manchester's Comedy Theatre, to oversee the musical side of his new collaborations with Audran and Planquette.

Crook conducted *Indiana* at the Avenue Theatre, interpolating music of his own into Audran's score in the time-honoured fashion, and simultaneously organized the musical side of the remaking of Planquette's *Les Voltigeurs de la 32ème* into *The Old Guard* (1887), one of the most durable touring comic operas of the period, of Chassaigne's *Les Noces improvisées* as *Nadgy* (1888) and of Wenzel's *Les Dragons de la reine* as *The Young Recruit* (1892). Largely uncredited, he also composed such music as was necessary to the rewriting of the pieces. When the French connection faded out, the Avenue Theatre returned to burlesque and Crook composed original scores for the old favourite *The Field of the Cloth of Gold* and the Arthur Roberts vehicle *Lancelot the Lovely* while maintaining his place in the pit for both shows and also for the Tito Mattei comic opera *La Prima Donna* which followed.

He subsequently moved to the Prince of Wales Theatre to conduct the Carl Rosa Light Opera Company's *Captain Thérèse* and the mime *L'Enfant prodigue*, and worked regularly as a conductor in London thereafter, leading the orchestras at the Theatre Royal, Drury Lane, the Adelphi (1895–8), the Lyceum, the Duke of York's and the Vaudeville (1901) before going to Australia to conduct *The Scarlet Feather* for George Musgrove.

He continued throughout as a prolific songwriter both for the theatre and the music hall, supplying songs for many stand-up stars – most famously 'The Coster's Serenade' for Albert Chevalier – and as interpolated numbers for various musicals. He also composed and compiled the songs for several of the earliest and the most outstanding touring musical comedies of the turn of the century. His score for the Methusalemic variety musical *The Lady Slavey* became encrusted with interpolations over 20 years of constant touring, but the success of the songs which he wrote for *The New Barmaid* was such that the bulk of the score remained as written over its 20-year run around the British provinces and colonies.

Capable of writing a score in the classic vein, as he had proven with his very first stage piece, Crook found himself instead one of the most successful composers of popular burlesque and musical comedy songs of his time, a talent witnessed by his large contribution to these two most successful variety musicals of all time. When that particular craze had passed, however, he continued his conducting career in Britain and in Australia, and turned his hand to a different kind of theatre music, composing the original, and for a long time standard, incidental music for Barrie's *Peter Pan* and, alongside songs by Darewski and Kern, for the same author's musical comedy *Rosy Rapture*.

1880 **Sage and Onions** (Alfred Maltby) 1 act Prince's Theatre, Manchester 12 April
1880 **The King's Dragoons** (J Wilton Jones) Theatre Royal, Manchester 1 November
1881 **Young Dick Whittington, or Here's the Cat** (Jones) Leicester 18 April
1882 **Merry Mignon, or The Beauty and the Bard** (Jones) Royal Court Theatre, Liverpool 24 April
1883 **Tit Bits** (George Lash Gordon, Fred Stimson) Winter Gardens, Blackpool 25 May
1886 **Larks** (w Meyer Lutz, Frederic Stanislaus, Barrett, Alfred Lee/Jones) Winter Gardens, Southport 22 February
1886 **Robinson Crusoe** (H B Farnie, Robert Reece) Avenue Theatre 23 December
1888 **Quits** (B T Hughes) 1 act Avenue Theatre 1 October
1889 **Lancelot the Lovely** ('Richard Henry') Avenue Theatre 22 April

1889 **The Houseboat** (H W Williamson) 1 act Avenue Theatre 6 May

1889 **The Field of the Cloth of Gold** (new score/William Brough) Avenue Theatre 24 December

1890 **Venus** (new score/William Yardley, Edward Rose, Augustus Harris) Prince of Wales Theatre, Liverpool 24 March

1893 **A Modern Don Quixote** (George Dance) Theatre Royal, Nottingham 17 July

1893 **The Lady Slavey** (Dance) Theatre Royal, Northampton 4 September

1893 **Helen of Troy Up-to-Date or The Statue Shop** (Jones) 1 act Pier Theatre, Folkestone 23 May

1894 **Jaunty Jane Shore** ('Richard Henry') Strand Theatre 2 April

1894 **King Kodak** (w Walter Slaughter, Edward Solomon, Alfred Plumpton, Milton Wellings, Herman Finck, Lionel Monckton/Arthur Branscombe) Terry's Theatre 30 April

1894 **Claud Du-val** (w Monckton/Frederick Boyer, Arthur Roberts) Prince's Theatre, Bristol 23 July; Prince of Wales Theatre 25 September

1894 **All My Eye-Van-Hoe** (w Howard Talbot, Solomon et al/Philip Hayman) Trafalgar Square Theatre, 31 October

1894 **The County Councillor** (Harry Graham) touring production

1894 **Giddy Miss Carmen** (w Lutz, Sidney Jones et al/Sidney Lester) Brighton Aquarium 27 August

1895 **One of the Girls** (w Lutz, Jones/Herbert Darnley, J J Dallas) Grand Theatre, Birmingham 9 March

1895 **Qwong Hi** (Fenton Mackay) 1 act Prince's Theatre, Bristol 1 April

1895 **On the March** (w Solomon, Frederic Clay/Yardley, B C Stephenson, Cecil Clay) Prince of Wales Theatre 22 June

1895 **The New Barmaid** (Frederick Bowyer, W E Sprange) Opera House, Southport 1 July

1895 **Newmarket** (w J M Capel, Plumpton et al/Mrs Frank Taylor, Ernest Boyd-Jones) Opera Comique 22 August

1896 **The Transferred Ghost** (Neville Lynn) 1 act Garrick Theatre 19 November

1897 **Breaking it Off** (Neville Doone, Horace Newte) 1 act Empire, Southend 21 March

1898 **Black and White** (Mark Melford, W Sapte) Prince of Wales Theatre, Southampton 3 January

1898 **Oh! What a Night** (*Eine tolle Nacht*) new score to English version by William Terriss, Clement Scott (Opera House, Wakefield)

1902 **Nana** (w Herbert Simpson, Henry May/Brian Daly) Grand Theatre, Birmingham 5 May

1911 **A Little Japanese Girl** (Loie Fuller) 1 act London Coliseum

1915 **Rosy Rapture, the Pride of the Beauty Chorus** (w Herman Darewski, Jerome Kern/E V Lucas [as F W Mark]/J M Barrie) Duke of York's Theatre 22 March

CROQUEFER, ou Le Dernier des Paladins Opérette-bouffe in 1 act by Adolphe Jaime and Étienne Tréfeu. Music by Jacques Offenbach. Théâtre des Bouffes-Parisiens, Paris, 12 February 1857.

An extravagant bouffonnerie, in the line of the composer's *Ba-ta-clan*, *Croquefer* brought to the stage the inherited battle between two curious medieval knights. The crazy Croquefer (Pradeau) and his servant Boutefeu (Léonce) are defending the one remaining tower of Croquefer's castle against the remnants of Mousse-à-Mort (Michel) who has lost not only a leg, an arm and an eye but, since theatrical restrictions allowed at the time only four speaking characters, his tongue. Croquefer has his rival's daughter Fleur de Soufre (Mlle Maréchal) cap-

tive, and thinks of marrying her, but (just when the two knights have finally got round to coming together on horse-back in combat) she discovers some Borgia poison in the wine cellar and spikes everyone's drinks long enough for them to sing an operatic-tragic burlesque quintet. Finally the maiden weds Croquefer's physically perfect nephew, Ramasse-ta-tête (Tayau), instead and the feud and the opérette are declared over.

The seven musical pieces of the score included a regretful ballad for Croquefer ('Mon château, qu'il était chic'), a duet for the two young folk ('Comment, c'est vous, un gentilhomme?') which ended up in typically loony fashion with couplets in praise of the Paris Opéra, and a drinking song ('A vos santés, je bois') for the poisoned wine.

The Bouffes-Parisiens company took *Croquefer* in its repertoire to Britain and to Austria, and it was later played in German at the Theater an der Wien, and in Hungarian (ad Pál Tarnay) in Budapest. Robert Reece proved himself game to translate its surreal incongruities into English, and Thomas German Reed played *The Last of the Paladins* on the programme at his Gallery of Illustration without it finding further takers.

UK: St James's Theatre (Fr) 1 July 1857, Gallery of Illustration *The Last of the Paladins* 28 December 1868; Austria: Theater am Franz-Josefs-Kai (Fr) 1 June 1862, Theater an der Wien *Ritter Eisenfrass, der letzte der Paladine* 1 October 1864; Hungary: Budai Népszinház *A vasgyúró* 25 February 1864
Recording: complete (Bourg)

CROUSE, Russel [McKinley] (b Findlay, Ohio, 20 February 1893; d New York, 3 April 1966).

After an initial career as a newspaperman, Crouse made his first venture into the musical theatre in collaboration with Morrie Ryskind, Oscar Hammerstein and composer Lewis Gensler on the gangstery musical *The Gang's All Here* in 1931. In spite of this show's quick failure, Crouse then gave up his journalistic job and became a publicist for the Theater Guild, with the intention of devoting himself to writing for the stage. After an involvement in a Shubert spectacular called *Hold your Horses*, he found his first success when he was brought in, in an emergency, to help director Howard Lindsay revamp the libretto for Vinton Freedley's production of the Cole Porter musical, *Anything Goes*.

Following the wide and long success of *Anything Goes*, Crouse wrote a series of both plays and musical libretti in collaboration with Lindsay. The plays included the enormously successful *Life with Father* and *State of the Union*, the musicals began with an attempt to repeat the success of *Anything Goes* with Porter and the earlier show's star, Ethel Merman, in *Red, Hot and Blue*. After a long interval away from the musical stage, the team – this time with Irving Berlin as songwriter – gave Miss Merman another swingeing, made-to-measure rôle, 14 years after the first, as the Washington matron let loose in Ruritanian politics in *Call Me Madam*, but their greatest success came with the libretto which they provided for another lady star, Mary Martin, as the nun-turned-nanny heroine of the last of the Rodgers and Hammerstein musicals, *The Sound of Music* (1959). This show achieved the kind of enduring success won by few, equalling and even passing its authors' earlier triumph with *Life With Father* in its international longevity.

Alongside their trio of major musical hits, Crouse and

Lindsay also teamed with Harold Arlen on the Ed Wynn musical *Hooray for What?*, authored a fourth Merman musical, *Happy Hunting*, and a second Irving Berlin one, *Mr President*, with rather less success. In 1956 a musical version of their play *Strip for Action* folded on the road.

1931 **The Gang's All Here** (Lewis Gensler/w Morrie Ryskind/Oscar Hammerstein II) Imperial Theater 18 February
1933 **Hold Your Horses** (Robert Russell Bennett et al/w Corey Ford) Winter Garden Theater 25 September
1934 **Anything Goes** (Cole Porter/w Lindsay, Bolton, Wodehouse) Alvin Theater 21 November
1936 **Red, Hot and Blue** (Porter/w Lindsay) Alvin Theater 29 October
1937 **Hooray for What?** (Harold Arlen/E Y Harburg/w Lindsay) Winter Garden Theater 1 December
1950 **Call Me Madam** (Irving Berlin/w Lindsay) Imperial Theater 12 October
1956 **Strip for Action** (Jimmy McHugh/Harold Adamson/w Lindsay) Shubert Theater, New Haven 17 March
1956 **Happy Hunting** (Matt Dubey, Harold Karr/w Lindsay) Majestic Theater 6 December
1959 **The Sound of Music** (Richard Rodgers/Oscar Hammerstein/w Lindsay) Lunt-Fontanne Theater 16 November
1962 **Mr President** (Berlin/w Lindsay) St James Theater 20 October

Biography: Skinner, C Otis: *Life With Lindsay and Crouse* (Houghton, Mifflin Co, Boston, 1976)

CRYER, Gretchen (b Dunreith, Ind, 17 October 1935).

Playwright and performer in both musical (*Little Me*, *110 in the Shade*, *1776*) and straight theatre, Cryer collaborated with composer Nancy Ford on a series of small-scale musical plays for off-Broadway venues.

They had some success with their *Now is the Time for All Good Men*, a piece about an imprisoned draft-dodger who can't get over his past (112 performances, also cast member) in 1967, and with *The Last Sweet Days of Isaac*, a three-handed piece which went on from its New York production to be seen in York and, briefly, in London, but they scored a substantial hit with their tale of a 1970s woman with a band and man problems, *I'm Getting My Act Together and Taking it on the Road*, in which Cryer took the central rôle in the earliest part of the long run.

Cryer and Ford have performed their songs both in concert and on record, and a revue of their songs, *Hang on to the Good Times* (Cryer, Ford w Richard Maltby jr), which included material from *Shelter* and *I'm Getting My Act Together*, was mounted at the Manhattan Theatre Club in 1985.

1965 **Booth is Back in Town** (Arthur Rubinstein/Austin Pendelton) Forum, Lincoln Center, workshop
1967 **Now is the Time for All Good Men** (aka *Grass Roots*) (Nancy Ford) Theater de Lys 26 September
1970 **The Last Sweet Days of Isaac** (Ford) Eastside Playhouse 26 January
1971 **The Wedding of Iphigenia/Iphigenia in Concert** (Peter Link/w Doug Dyer, Link) Public Theater 16 December
1973 **Shelter** (Ford) John Golden Theater 6 February
1978 **I'm Getting My Act Together and Taking it on the Road** (Ford) Public Theater 14 June, Circle in the Square 16 December

DIE CSÁRDÁSFÜRSTIN Operette in 3 acts by Leo Stein and Béla Jenbach. Music by Emmerich Kálmán. Johann Strauss-Theater, Vienna, 17 November 1915.

One of the most successful, and certainly the most widely enduring of Kálmán's Operetten, *Die Csárdásfürstin* was nevertheless composed to a very conventional libretto detailing the umpteenth operettic romance between an aristocrat and a cabaret singer. The singer is the Hungarian Sylva Varescu (Mizzi Günther), the aristocrat is Edwin Ronald (Karl Bachmann), the son of the Viennese Fürst Leopold Maria von und zu Lippert-Weylersheim (Max Brod). He promises to wed her, and goes through a form of betrothal, but his family announces his engagement to their niece, the Countess Stasi (Susanne Bachrich). Sylva turns up at a ball at Edwin's home on the arm of Graf Boni Káncsiánu (Josef König), who has pretended to be her husband for the occasion, and Edwin makes a public stand, refusing the alliance with Stasi as Sylva reveals herself as no countess but a common cabaret singer. Ultimately Edwin's father cannot object to his son's choice, for the ageing good-time aristocrat Feri von Kerekes (Antal Nyárai) recognizes in the venerable Fürst's wife a chorus girl with whom he had had a fling many years ago. Boni pairs off with Stasi in the all-round happy ending.

The score of the piece was in Kálmán's happiest Austro-Hungarian vein, with Boni and Feri's little march-time memories of 'Die Mädis, die Mädis, die Mädis vom Chantant', the pretty Schwalbenduett ('Machen wir's den Schwalben nach') between Edwin and Stasi, and Boni and Stasi's song and dance 'Mädel guck!' contrasting with the more thoroughly lyrical moments of Edwin and Sylva's waltz duets, 'Tausend kleine Engel singen', 'Mädel gibt es wunderfeine' and 'Weisst du es noch?'. Sylva's cabaret showpiece 'Heia, heia, in den Bergen ist mein Heimatland' and Boni's laughingly rueful 'Doch ganz ohne Weiber geht die Chose nicht' were other successful moments.

Erich Müller's production of *Die Csárdásfürstin* was a great wartime hit in Vienna, running through the whole of 1916 and, as Cordy Millowitsch and Irene Fidler succeeded Frln Günther in the title-rôle, into 1917, closing in May after a first run of 533 performances. It was kept in the repertoire of the Johann Strauss-Theater for a decade thereafter. In Hungary *Csárdáskirálynő* (ad Andor Gábor) scored a similarly great hit at the Király Színház, with Emmi Kosáry and Ernő Király as its romantic leads and Ida Szentgyörgi and Márton Rátkai as the second pair, running for nearly 200 performances in its first series, passing the 200th performance on 15 May 1917 and the 300th on 29 January 1918, and being given a major revival at the same house in 1927 (16 April). The show also quickly established itself as the most popular of Kálmán's works in Germany.

The English-language versions of the piece did rather less well. In Klaw and Erlanger's American production (ad Guy Bolton, P G Wodehouse) the Hungarian vocalist of the original became *The Riviera Girl*, a vaudeville singer as played by Wilda Bennett, and the show's score was gratified with the addition of such local lollipops as Juliette Day and Sam Hardy's un-Hungarian suggestion '(Let's Build a little) Bungalow in Quogue'. The show lasted 78 performances on Broadway. London's less tastelessly tinkered-with version made its heroine, less improbably, into *The Gipsy Princess* (ad Arthur Miller, Arthur Stanley) and pro-

Plate 63. *Hans-Joachim Müller gets the kind of attention he is used to from the Mädis vom Chantant in the 1985 Lübeck Bühnen der Hansestadt production of* **Die Csárdásfürstin.**

ducers Claude B Yearsley and Walter de Groot imported a real Hungarian prima donna, Sári Petráss, for the starring rôle alongside Germany's M de Jari (Edwin), Phyllis Titmuss (Stasi), Billy Leonard (Boniface), Mark Lester (Feri) and three speciality dancers. They got 204 performances out of runs at the Prince of Wales and the Strand Theatres before the show went into the provinces where it was played more and longer than most other shows that had only managed a choppy 200-odd performance life in town. It was seen again, in a brief wartime revival, at the Saville Theatre (14 June 1944) in a scaled-down 'modern version' by Miller, and it was not until 1981, when a new adaptation by Nigel Douglas was played at Sadler's Wells Theatre (1 August), with Douglas himself playing Feri alongside Marilyn Hill Smith (Sylva) and Tudor Davies (Boni), that London got to see a faithful English *Csárdásfürstin.*

A late first Australian production appeared in 1936, with Maria Elsner as *The Gipsy Princess*, London's Dunstan Hart as Edwin and Charles Heslop and Cecil Kellaway heading the roués in Sydney, and Gladys Moncrieff teaming with Heslop and Don Nicol in Melbourne (Her Majesty's Theatre 17 October 1936). Like its English counterpart it did only fairly, but it was given a fresh showing in the 1980s when the new version of the show – still insisting that its title-heroine was *The Gipsy Princess* – was played in the repertoire of the Australian Opera Company.

Die Csárdásfürstin was very slow to get to France, and it was not until 1930 that *Princesse Czardas* (ad André Mauprey, René Peter, Henri Falk) was mounted at the Trianon-Lyrique with Louise Balazy, Léon Marcel, Paul Darnois, Charles Darthez and Reine Prévost featured. The production was successful enough for the show to be restaged the following year at the much larger Gaîté-Lyrique (7 August 1931) with Maya Silva, Gilbert Nabos

and Lamy, and, as it had eventually done in most other countries, it proved to be the most popular of Kálmán's shows with French audiences. It was seen again in Paris in 1950 with Marta Eggerth and Jan Kiepura featured in the leading rôles and, in France, as in Austria, Germany and Hungary, it has remained part of the standard repertoire, one of the few Viennese Operetten regularly produced in provincial French houses to the present day.

A major revival was seen in Berlin, at the Admiralspalast, in 1931, whilst a largely rewritten script was manufactured in Hungary to make a star rôle out of the part of Edwin's mother as a vehicle for the country's greatest but ageing operett star, Hanna Honthy. In Vienna, the most recent production has been that played at the Volksoper (23 October 1982) in another altered version by Robert Herzl which includes an interpolated song, 'Heute Nacht hab' ich geträumt von dir', for the previously songless Edwin.

Germany: Neues Operetten-Theater, Hamburg 16 September 1916; Hungary: Király Színház *Csárdáskirálynő* 3 November 1916; USA: New Amsterdam Theater *The Riviera Girl* 24 September 1917; UK: Prince of Wales Theatre, London *The Gipsy Princess* 20 May 1921; France: Théâtre du Trianon-Lyrique *Princesse Czardas* 12 March 1930; Australia: Theatre Royal, Sydney *The Gipsy Princess* 4 July 1936

Recordings: complete (EMI, Eurodisc, Denon), complete in French (Chant du Monde), complete in Hungarian (revised version, Qualiton), selections (Eurodisc, CBS, Saga etc), selection in Italian (EDM) etc.

CULLUM, John (b Knoxville, Tenn, 2 March 1930). One of Broadway's finest singing actors of the postwar era.

Cullum first appeared musically on Broadway in the rôle of Sir Dinadan in *Camelot* (1960) but, apart from a brief spell in the road-closed *We Take the Town* (1962, Johnny Sykes), in a cast which ranged from Robert Preston to Romney Brent and the infant Pia Zadora, straight theatre work, including a Laertes to Richard Burton's *Hamlet*, kept him away from the musical theatre until 1965. In that year he succeeded Louis Jordan in the rôle of Dr Mark Bruckner in *On a Clear Day You Can See Forever* during the show's try-out, creating the show's title-song and 'Come Back To Me' in its Broadway production. He subsequently succeeded Richard Kiley and José Ferrer in the title-rôle of *Man of La Mancha* (1967), appeared as the Captain in the 1967 television musicalization of *Androcles and the Lion*, took over the role of Edward Rutledge, which he later played also in the film version, in *1776* in the New York production (1971), and created the rôle of Christopher Columbus in Meredith Willson's *1491* at the Los Angeles Civic Light Opera.

He appeared at Jones Beach as the King (*The King and I*, 1972) and Billy Bigelow (*Carousel*, 1973) and in Washington as Don Medigua in a revival of *El Capitan*, and in 1975 he starred as Civil War protester Charlie Anderson in the long-running stage musical version of *Shenandoah* at New York's Alvin Theatre. In 1978 he turned in a virtuoso comedy-and-singing performance as the flamboyantly baritone Oscar Jaffee in the operetta burlesque *On the Twentieth Century*, which, like the *Shenandoah* performance, earned him a Tony Award as Best Actor in a Musical. He returned briefly to Broadway in a touring revival of *Shenandoah* in 1989, and in 1990 succeeded Kevin Colson in the rôle of George in *Aspects of Love*.

CURLEY McDIMPLE   Musical in 2 acts by Mary Boylan and Robert Dahdah. Music and lyrics by Robert Dahdah. Bert Wheeler Theater, New York, 22 November 1967.

An off-Broadway burlesque of Hollywood tot-stars of the 1930s, with special reference to Shirley Temple. Eight-year-old Bayn Johnson as Curley McDimple headed a cast of seven, including Bernadette Peters (Alice) and Paul Cahill (Jimmy), equipped with a list of songs with titles like 'Dancing in the Rain', 'Love is the Loveliest Love Song', 'Hi de Hi de hi, hi de hi de ho', 'Swing-a-ding-a-ling', 'I've Got a Little Secret' and, of course, 'Curley McDimple' and lashings of tot-n-tap-dancing, through a fine run of 931 performances. During those performances, an additional rôle was added for Butterfly McQueen – the maidservant of the cinema's *Gone with the Wind*.

Recording: 2 songs 45rpm (Capitol)

CURZON, Frank   (Sir) [DEELEY, Francis Arthur] (b Wavertree, Liverpool, 17 September 1868; d London, 2 July 1927).

The young Curzon left his father's oil business to become an actor and, after a couple of tentative tries at management at the Marina Theatre, Lowestoft, and with the play *Tom, Dick and Harry* in London in the early 1890s, and later with several years of touring productions, he finally found success, in partnership with Charles Hawtrey, with his presentations of the plays *A Message From Mars* and *Lord and Lady Algy*.

In 1900 he took a lease on the Prince of Wales Theatre and presented Marie Tempest as *English Nell*, and the following year he expanded to take in the Royal Strand Theatre as well. He hit the jackpot when he purchased the London rights to the touring musical comedy *A Chinese Honeymoon* from author George Dance and took it to London and this unfashionably half-West and half-East End theatre. *A Chinese Honeymoon* became the first musical in theatre history to run over a thousand consecutive metropolitan performances, making Curzon's fortune, and allowing him to stretch further afield with his future projects in both the musical and straight theatre. He soon became long-term manager of the Prince of Wales Theatre (1901) and at various other times was installed at the Avenue, Comedy, Wyndham's and Criterion Theatres as well.

As a musical comedy producer, he followed up *A Chinese Honeymoon* at the Strand with *Sergeant Brue* (1904) and *Miss Wingrove* (1905), then staged *The White Chrysanthemum* (1905, Criterion), *The Girl Behind the Counter* (1906) and *Captain Kidd* (1910, Wyndhams), *The Three Kisses* (1907, Apollo) and, after housing several of George Edwardes's musical comedy successes at the Prince of Wales, ran up a series of new musicals of his own there: *Miss Hook of Holland* (1907), *My Mimosa Maid* (1908), Frederick Lonsdale and Sidney Jones's substantial and successful *King of Cadonia* (1908), *Dear Little Denmark* (1909) and *The Balkan Princess* (1910). Each of these Prince of Wales shows starred his wife, former D'Oyly Carte Opera Company soprano Isabel Jay. After his lease on the Prince of Wales Theatre ended in 1915 he ceased to produce musicals, but remained in the public eye, taking the honours in the 1927 Derby shortly before his death.

CUSHING, Catherine Chisholm   (b Mount Perry, Ohio, 15 April 1874; d New York, 19 October 1952).

Sometime editor of *Harper's Bazaar*, Miss Cushing was also the author of a number of successful plays including *Kitty McKay* (1913) and a stage version of *Pollyanna* (1916) as well as vehicles for May Irwin and Billie Burke. She had a less full life in the musical theatre, but she authored a number of adaptations, including two of her own works, for the musical stage in a period of a half-dozen years.

Her first original Broadway musical, *Glorianna*, set with a score by Rudolf Friml, was based on her own play *Widow by Proxy* (1913), and her second, the much-praised *Lassie*, with a score by Hugo Felix, on her *Kitty McKay*. The third, *Marjolaine*, was a version of Louis Napoleon Parker's equally romantically centred piece, *Pomander Walk*, and her fourth a musical version of *Uncle Tom's Cabin* which was constructed to allow the variety act The Duncan Sisters to play practically the whole famous tale by themselves, in the characters of *Topsy and Eva*.

Glorianna had only a fair Broadway run, but proved a much stronger prospect when played in Chicago and on the road by Fritzi Scheff and held a place on the touring circuits for an extended period. *Lassie*, which was touted as one of the best musical plays for years after a hugely popular run-in to Broadway, proved to be more the critic's choice than the public's and, though the producers Paul Salvain and Gil Boag pushed its run to 149 performances at the Nora Bayes Roof-Garden Theater and then in a transfer in an effort to get New Yorkers to agree with the press and patrons of other towns, the piece did not fulfil the more extravagant hopes it had aroused. *Marjolaine* played 136 performances on Broadway and had a brief London production, but whilst the Duncan sisters imitated Topsy and Eva for only 159 New York performances, and a short London season dogged by illness, during which one of the sisters was temporarily replaced by Gracie Fields, their show had an exceptionally long and profitable road life.

The author's only effort at a wholly original musical libretto was the 1922 piece *Bibi of the Boulevards* which, attached to a score by Friml, failed on the road, a rare occurrence in a career which seemed otherwise to have a subscription to at least semi-success.

1918 **Glorianna** (Rudolf Friml) Liberty Theater 28 October
1920 **Lassie** (Hugo Felix) Nora Bayes Theater 6 April
1922 **Marjolaine** (Felix/Brian Hooker) Broadhurst Theater 24 January
1922 **Bibi of the Boulevards** (Friml) Majestic Theater, Providence 12 February
1923 **Topsy and Eva** (Rosetta Duncan, Vivian Duncan) Chicago; Harris Theater, New York 23 December 1924

CUTLER, Kate   (b London, 14 August 1870; d London, 14 May 1955). A, and for many, the favourite ingénue of the early musical comedy days in London.

Kate Cutler made her début as Inez in the English version of Lecocq's *La Princesse des Canaries* (*Pepita*), aged 17, and she appeared with the Carl Rosa Light Opera Company as Malaguena in *Paul Jones* (1889) before beginning a steady rise to an outstanding career as a leading lady in musical comedy.

She joined the company of George Edwardes's *In Town* as take-over to the lesser rôle of Lady Gwendoline, but succeeded Florence St John in the star part, then, in *A*

Plate 64. **Kate Cutler** *as Suzette in* The French Maid.

Gaiety Girl, moved up once again from a smaller part to replace Decima Moore as the singing ingénue of the piece. She succeeded Ada Reeve in the title-rôle of *The Shop Girl* (1894) and Isa Bowman as the juvenile lady of *All Abroad* (1895, Connie) and created her own first musical comedy lead rôle as the ingénue heroine of the Arthur Roberts show *Gentleman Joe* (1895, Mabel Kavanagh). She appeared as Trilby in *A Model Trilby* (1895), created the juvenile lead of *My Girl* (1896, May Mildreth) out of town (Ellaline Terriss took over for the London run), and then began a run of London lead rôles through *Monte Carlo* (1896, Dorothy Travers), the long-running *The French Maid* (1897, Suzette), *Little Miss Nobody* (1898, Elsie Crockett) and *L'Amour mouillé* (1899, Catarina), culminating in the ingénue rôle of Angela in the original production of *Florodora*, introducing 'The Fellow Who Might', a performance which took her firmly to the head of the ingénue field.

She took on the task of starring opposite Arthur Roberts again in a London season of his *HMS Irresponsible* (Victoria Chaffers), took over the soprano lead in *A Chinese Honeymoon* (1901, Soo Soo) when that piece began to be cast up once success became evident, and created one of her most appealing rôles as Nora, the befuddled young bride of *The Girl from Kays* (1902, 'Papa') opposite Willie Edouin. *The Lovebirds* (1904, Grace Rockingham) gave her a rare experience of failure, quickly remedied by a delightful star rôle as the Baroness Papouche in Edwardes's Gaiety Theatre musical *The Spring Chicken* (1905), before she abandoned the musical stage to begin a second out-

standing career as a straight actress. She made brief returns to the musical stage as gracious older ladies in *That's a Good Girl* (1928, Helen, also on film), *Dear Love* (1929, Mrs Gerard) and *Command Performance* (1933, Queen of Vassau).

Unfailingly graceful, ladylike and charming ('she always looks as if she has a sprig of lilac under her nose') and the possessor of a pretty light soprano, Miss Cutler was, as a genuine and durable ingénue, the ideal partner for some of the more rumbustious comedy actors of her time.

She was married to director and choreographer Sidney Ellison, the stager of *Florodora*.

CUVILLIER, Charles [Louis Paul] (b Paris, 24 April 1877; d Paris, 14 February 1955). French tunesmith whose simple, often rather un-French, music illustrated several successful shows during the interregnum between the old days of the opérette and the arrival of the jazz-age musical comedy.

After some early efforts composing ballet and incidental music, the Conservatoire-trained Cuvillier made his first entry into the light musical theatre in his late twenties with the opérette *Avant-hier matin*, produced at the little Théâtre des Capucines in 1905. This tiny three-handed piece about Adam and Eve in the Garden of Eden – written by the up-and-coming playwright Tristan Bernard and played only with piano accompaniment – won its composer a certain success. That success was compounded 18 months later by two rather larger-scale works seen on the same stage: *Son p'tit frère*, a comical piece of sexy classical antiquity, and *Afgar, ou Les Loisirs andalous* which also delved into exotic places – an eastern harem – for the amorous high-jinks of its subject matter. Both pieces had libretti by André Barde, later to be one of the mainstays of post-war musical comedy in France, and they anticipated the more famous *Phi-Phi* and its successors in that genre both in their intimate comedy style and their light and lively music.

Cuvillier supplied other small-scale pieces to the Paris stage, but also had an opérette produced in Buenos Aires and another piece, a fresh scoring of the old Charles Favart opéra-comique *Les Trois Sultanes*, staged at the Opéra in Monaco. Neither of these works progressed to a Paris production, and neither did a third 'foreign' Cuvillier piece, first seen in Germany. The composer's first full-scale, large-stage opérette and his biggest single theatrical success was never seen in France. The 1912 *Der lila Domino* was produced first in Leipzig and there picked up for America where its Harry and Robert Smith version lasted only three weeks on Broadway. However, in spite of this unequivocal failure, Joseph L Sacks staged this version at London's Empire Theatre where, further adapted by Adair Fitzgerald and Howard Carr, it won an enormous success.

In the wake of this trans-Channel triumph, Cuvillier became all the rage in London, where Cochran's production of his ten-year-old *Afgar*, starring Alice Delysia, at the London Pavilion confirmed him in public favour. A fairly unrecognizable version of *Son p'tit frère* as *The Wild Geese* and a made-for-England musical, *The Sunshine of the World*, fared less well, but a collaboration with Harry Vernon and Clifford Grey on the revue *Johnny Jones* for George Robey and an adaptation of his *La Reine s'amuse*, produced by Grossmith and Laurillard at the Adelphi

Theatre as *The Naughty Princess* both brought excellent runs. *La Reine s'amuse*, produced originally at Marseille, finally gave Cuvillier full-sized success in France, as well as providing him with the biggest song hit of his career in the waltz 'Ah! la troublante volupté'.

Flora Bella, another piece produced first in Germany, and later played in the French provinces, was seen for a reasonable run on Broadway, although in a badly botched form, in 1916. However, in spite of the fact that such of his pieces were staged outside France in large auditoriums like London's Empire Theatre and Broadway's New York Theater, Cuvillier continued during and after the war to work at home on the smaller scale which he had been instrumental in making popular. Allied mostly with Barde, he composed the music for several other agreeable and successful musical comedies both for small, and occasionally larger, Paris stages without again reaching out to the international scene, in spite of the fact that, as late as 1926, he was announced in the trade papers as preparing an operetta, *Incognito*, in collaboration with Peter Garland and a musical comedy, *Ça ira*, with American intentions.

1905 **Avant-hier matin** (Tristan Bernard) Théâtre des Capucines 20 October
1906 **La Carte forcée** (Hugues Delorme) 1 act Palais-Royal 4 October
1907 **Le Flirt de Colombine** (Jacques Redelsperger) Nice, 30 January, Théâtre des Capucines 3 February
1907 **Son p'tit frère** (André Barde) Théâtre des Capucines 10 April
1908 **Les Rendez-vous strasbourgeois** (Romain Coolus) 1 act Comédie-Royale 12 February
1909 **Afgar, ou Les Loisirs andalous** (Barde, Michel Carré fils) Théâtre des Capucines 10 April
1909 **Mam'selle Main-leste** (Miguel Zamacoïs) Scala 1 December
1910 **Les Muscadines** (Barde) Théâtre des Capucines 28 April
1911 **L'Astronome et l'étoile** (Barde, Bertrand St Rémy) Buenos Aires July
1912 **Les Trois Sultanes** (Charles Favart) Monaco January
1912 **Der lila Domino** (Emmerich von Gatti, Béla Jenbach) Stadttheater, Leipzig 3 February
1912 **Sappho** (Barde, Carré) Théâtre des Capucines 27 February
1912 **L'Initiatrice** (Robert Dieudonné, Delorme) Concert Mayol 6 November
1912 **La Reine s'amuse** (Barde) Théâtre des Variétés, Marseille 31 December; Olympia, Paris 6 February 1913
1913 **Les Adam** revised *Avant-hier matin* Automobile Club 20 February
1913 **Flora Bella** (Barde ad Felix Dörmann) Theater am Gärtnerplatz, Munich 5 September
1917 **La République des vierges** revised *Sappho* Théâtre Édouard VII 6 September
1917 **Judith Courtisane** (Régis Gignoux, Barde) Théâtre Michel 22 December
1918 **La Reine joyeuse** revised *La Reine s'amuse* Théâtre Apollo 1 November
1918 **La Fausse Ingénue** revised *Les Muscadines* (Carré) Théâtre Fémina 17 March
1918 **Mademoiselle 'Nom d'une pipe'** (Georges Duval) Palais-Royal 16 July
1920 **The Sunshine of the World** (Gladys Unger, James Heard) Empire Theatre, London 18 February
1920 **Phryné** (Redelsperger)
1922 **Nonnette** (Barde) Théâtre des Capucines 28 March
1922 **Par amour** (Maurice Magre) Théâtre Fémina 28 October

1922 **Annabella** (Magre) Théâtre Fémina 8 November
1924 **Bob et moi** (Barde, Lucien Meyrargue) Théâtre Michel 6 April
1926 **Qui êtes vous?** (H Genty, Jouvault, Georges Berr) Monte-Carlo 13 November
1929 **Boulard et ses filles** (Louis Verneuil, Saint-Granier, Jean le Seyeux) Théâtre Marigny 8 November
1930 **Laïs, ou la courtisane amoureuse** revised *Son p'tit frère* (Barde)
1935 **Le Train de 8h 47** (Georges Courteline ad Léo Marchis, Barde) Palais-Royal 22 December

CYRANO DE BERGERAC

Like several other famous and obvious subjects which or who have been regularly musicalized over the years, Edmond Rostand's tale of the man with the nose and the dose of self-abnegation, *Cyrano de Bergerac*, has repeatedly proved unattractive as a musical theatre prospect.

In 1899 Victor Herbert set a book by Stuart Reed and lyrics by Harry B Smith as a *Cyrano de Bergerac* which was produced by Francis Wilson at the Knickerbocker Theater (18 September) with himself as Cyrano to the Roxane of Lulu Glaser. Since Wilson was star and producer, this version rather shirked the original ending, leaving at least the possibility at the final curtain that Cyrano will get the girl after all. But no one cared very much. Herbert's musical lasted 28 nights on Broadway and even proved a dog on the touring circuits.

Walter Damrosch composed an operatic *Cyrano* which was mounted forgettably at the Metropolitan Opera House (17 February 1915) before, in 1932, the Shuberts tried another musical piece on the same subject, mounted at the St Louis Municipal Light Opera (Charles O Houston, Samuel D Pockrass) under the title *Roxane*. Then, after taking it no further than this tryout first time around, they brought it out again seven years later in a revised version with new music by Vernon Duke as, variously, *The White Plume* and *The Vagabond Hero* (Washington 26 December 1939). It still stayed staunchly away from Broadway. A further variant on the theme, a Wright and Forrest *A Song for Cyrano* with a libretto by its Cyrano, José Ferrer, played a regional summer season in 1972.

In 1973, however, a *Cyrano* did make it to town, with Christopher Plummer starred as the gloomed Gascon and Leigh Beery as his Roxane (Michael J Lewis/Anthony Burgess, Broadway Theater 13 May). It ran just 49 performances. However it resurfaced for another showing in another language when it was mounted in Karlsruhe, Germany in 1986 (25 October).

Music-hall managers and stars Weber and Fields had, perhaps, more success than any of these serious and semi-serious Cyranos when they presented their musical burlesque of the original Rostand play. Staged as *Cyranose de Bric-a-Brac* (3 November 1898) it featured the low comical Lew Fields as a Dutch-accented Gascon.

Away from America there has been less interest in making music with de Bergerac, but slightly more in the way of positive results. Lecocq's *Ninette*, even though its title might not have suggested the fact, began its pre-production life as a serious variant on the Cyrano tale, intended for the Opéra-Comique. Cyrano himself, as portrayed by Albert Piccaluga, was still in the story when *Ninette* appeared at the Bouffes-Parisiennes (28 February 1896) but he had been displaced in so far as the title was concerned by the historical Ninon de l'Enclos. Clairville's libretto had her measuring wits with the nasal Gascon and coming out the better. She did it for 107 Parisian nights.

Henri Cain prepared another French text which, adapted into Italian, was made into an opera, *Cyrano*, by Franco Alfano. It went on from Rome's Teatro Reale (22 January 1936) to further performances in Buenos Aires and at Paris's Opéra-Comique. Central Europe had a go at Rostand too. A *Cyrano de Bergerac* (Paraschkev Hadijev/ Banko Banev) was produced in Bulgaria in 1912 and in 1977 a Czech rock opera (*Cyrano aus der Vorstadt*, Marian Varga/Kamil Peteraj, Jan Štrasser, Alta Vášova) presented a *Your Own Thing* type of Cyrano with the hero as a member of a pop-band, Roxane as the vocalist, and Christian the front singer for whom Cyrano writes the songs. The 'Cyrano' connection was a meagre one, which may have helped the piece to its success in Bratislava.

London has remained without a musical *Cyrano*, but not for lack of trying. Producers' desks have received a number of variations on his theme over the years, but only once has anyone seen almost fit to put one on the stage. Written, composed and co-produced (w Harry Lowe) by American tenor Lyn (Leonard) Ceeley, who starred himself as Cyrano to the Roxane of soprano Lorraine Bridges, it was ultimately entitled not *Cyrano*, as its original advertisements had billed it, but *Gardenia Lady* (Leeds, 11 August 1947) and Mr Ceeley switched to playing René the Lionheart of Bordeaux instead of Cyrano de Bergerac at the last minute. Nell Gwynn and King Charles also got into the evening's action. The owner of the programme I have wrote across it in purple ink 'It stank!'.

1992 saw yet another, Dutch *Cyrano* (Ad van Dijk/Koen van Dijk Stadsschouwburg, Amsterdam 17 September) join the list. Bill van Dijk (Cyrano), Ryan van Akker (Roxane) and Danny de Munk (Christian) featured in a production mounted on a scale in keeping with its international ambitions, and the show was subsequently announced for an American production.

Recordings: 1973 original cast (AM), 1992 Dutch cast (Indisc)

CZIBULKA, Alfons (b Szepesváralj [ie Spiská Nová Ves], 14 May 1842; d Vienna, 27 October 1894). Hungarian-born composer whose earliest theatre works marked him out as one of the hopes of the Viennese Operette.

Czibulka made his earliest mark in the music world as a teenaged concert pianist, but he subsequently worked in Linz, Innsbruck, Trieste, at Pest's Nemzeti Színház, and mostly in Vienna, as a conductor and a military bandmaster. He also composed a considerable amount of dance music, both original and in the form of arrangements of theatre melodies by other composers, amongst which his pot-pourris of the works of Sullivan proved popular. In the last decade of his life he also turned out the scores for several Operetten produced variously in Germany and at Vienna's Theater an der Wien and Carltheater, where he was for a period musical director. He subsequently became a military bandmaster with an Austro-Hungarian Infantry Regiment.

His two most successful Operetten, the (virtually) initial *Pfingsten in Florenz* and *Der Glücksritter*, produced in Vienna, were both played subsequently in Hungary (*Pünkösd Flórenzben*, *A szerencselovag*), in Germany, and were also seen in English-language versions on Broadway, under the titles of *Amorita* and *The May Queen* (1889), respectively. His later works were less successful, and his death in his early fifties intervened before the promise of his first works was thoroughly fulfilled.

1860 'S Lorle (*Ein Berliner im Schwarzwalde*) Pressburg 30 July
1884 **Pfingsten in Florenz** (Richard Genée, Julius Riegen) Theater an der Wien 20 December
1885 **Der Jagdjunker der Kaiserin** (Genée, F Zell) Walhalla Theater, Berlin 3 December; revised version Carltheater 20 March 1886
1887 **Der Glücksritter** (Genée, Wilhelm Mannstädt, Bruno Zappert) Carltheater 22 December
1888 **Gil Blas von Santillana** (Zell, Moritz West) Carl-Schultze-Theater, Hamburg 23 November
1892 **Der Bajazzo** (Victor Léon, Heinz von Waldberg) Theater an der Wien 7 December
1893 **Monsieur Hannibal** (Mannstädt, Karl Dreher) Theater im Gärtnerplatz, Munich 5 September

D

THE DAIRYMAIDS   Farcical musical play in 2 acts by Alexander M Thompson and Robert Courtneidge. Lyrics by Paul Rubens and Arthur Wimperis. Music by Paul Rubens and Frank Tours. Apollo Theatre, London, 14 April 1906.

Robert Courtneidge's second West-End venture was a largely low comical musical in which a couple of sailors win a couple of upper-class lasses who are playing at being dairymaids on a model farm. In the final act the girls (Carrie Moore, Agnes Fraser) were back at school, which allowed the boys (former Savoy comic Walter Passmore, Horace Land and acrobatic newcomer Dan Rolyat as their servant) to get dressed up as schoolgirls to follow them. Courtneidge's *Blue Moon* star Florence Smithson was pasted in to the story as a more demure love interest and was allotted the least flimsy of the songs, whilst longtime favourite Phyllis Broughton played the aristocratic mistress of the farm.

The show proved highly successful, partly due to its fine cast and partly to a novel item in the shape of a gymnasium routine in which Carrie Moore and four little chorines wielded tiny dumbbells to the strains of the show's hit song, 'The Sandow Girl'. A catty number called 'Dover Street' for Passmore and the tale of 'The Sea Serpent' as comically put over by Rolyat and the girls proved other popular moments of musical fun. The show ran eight months before coming off to allow the cast to go to their pantomime engagements, but it was subsequently toured, with Phyllis Dare featured and equipped with some newly tailored Rubens songs, and later revived ('several new numbers ... more or less rewritten') in London in 1908 (Queen's Theatre 5 May) with Rolyat and Misses Smithson and Broughton repeating alongside Miss Dare, and again in 1915 (Aldwych Theatre 22 May) in an 18-performance season by touring manager J Bannister Howard.

Charles Frohman mounted *The Dairymaids* on Broadway, with Huntley Wright in the rôle created by Rolyat and Julia Sanderson heading the Sandow girls for a run of 86 performances, Australia got a J C Williamson production, with London's Fanny Dango at the head of the dumbbells, and gave it a fine welcome, and Frank Wheeler took the show around South African cities in his repertoire from 1907 onwards, whilst three companies continued through the British provinces in 1908.

USA: Criterion Theater 26 August 1907; Australia: Her Majesty's Theatre, Melbourne 7 September 1907

DALE, Jim   [SMITH, James] (b Rothwell, Northants, 15 August 1935).

After early work as a variety comedian, Dale began a stage career in his late twenties. He shot quickly up through six years of theatre and film work, ranging from Shakespearian rôles (Autolycus, Bottom, Gobbo, Petruchio) and a notable Scapino (Young Vic, 1970) to the gormless young men of the *Carry On* film series, before he made his musical theatre début in the title-rôle of Denry Machin in the musical version of Arnold Bennett's *The Card* (1973).

He later moved to America and there created the athletic title-rôle in the musical *Barnum* (1980, Tony Award, 'The Colors of my Life', 'The Prince of Humbug'). He made another musical theatre appearance when he succeeded Robert Lindsay as Bill Snibson in Broadway's *Me and My Girl*, later taking the piece on tour.

DALY, [John] Augustin   (b Plymouth, NC, 20 July 1838; d Paris, 7 June 1899).

One of the most celebrated drama producers of the American theatre during the last 30 years of the 19th century, Daly – who expected full training and unquestioned versatility from his contract actors – on several occasions staged musical pieces as part of his programme at the New York theatre named for him (1879 ssq). Although star specialist musical players were brought in for some pieces, the result was that a performer such as the rising Ada Rehan appeared in supporting rôles in musical shows between her dramatic performances.

In the earlier part of his career Daly was responsible for the New York staging of Offenbach's *Le Roi Carotte*, produced with an outstanding cast headed by John Brougham, Mrs John Wood, Emma Howson and Rose Hersee, but his Daly's Theater productions tended to be taken from amongst London's most surefire hits (*A Gaiety Girl, The Geisha, The Circus Girl, A Runaway Girl*).

In London's Leicester Square, he built what was originally to have been the Agnes Huntington Theatre, in collaboration with George Edwardes, with a view to the house being shared between Daly's drama performances and Edwardes's musical ones. However, Daly soon gave up his British trips and, in consequence, the theatre, which had ultimately been named after him rather than the elusive Miss Huntington, became the base for the important and influential series of musical plays, headed by *The Geisha*, which Edwardes produced there. The theatre, with his name always attached, was later the home of many musical hits, notably the wartime *The Maid of the Mountains*, but it was destroyed in 1937 to allow the building of a cinema.

Biography: Daly, J F: *The Life of Augustin Daly* (Macmillan, New York, 1917)

DALY, Dan   (b Boston, ?1858; d New York, 26 March 1904). A gangling, deadpan comic who became a star in turn-of-the-century Broadway musicals.

Daly began his career as an acrobat in circuses and variety, playing in a team with his brothers in a piece called

Vacation, before moving on to the first stages of a theatre career which would bring him a decade of success in musicals. He appeared in 1879 in the extravaganza *The Crystal Slipper* and later in the farcical, circussy *Upside Down*, in a small rôle in *The City Directory* (1891) and in larger ones in the variety musical *About Town* (1894, Rube Hayes), George Lederer's slightly more vertebrate *The Twentieth Century Girl* (1895) and the Casino revue *The Merry World*, before winning a leading part in a short-lived Broadway version of *Niniche* called *The Merry Countess* (1895, Vicomte de Beaupersil).

He rose to the leading comic rôle of the bailiff-turned-butler, Roberts, in the American rewrite of *The Lady Slavey* (1896) and made his most famous creation as Ichabod Bronson, the two-faced President of the Young Men's Rescue League and Anti-Cigarette Society of Cohoes, in the Casino Theater's *The Belle of New York*, first in New York, and then in London, where his mixture of lugubrious comedy and acrobatic dancing was found highly original and hugely enjoyable.

He followed up playing the goofy Duke of Paty de Clam in another Casino show, *The Rounders* (a version of the Paris hit *Les Fêtards*), and Baron Chartreuse in another, and less successful, Continental adaptation, *The Cadet Girl*, at the Herald Square Theater before he appeared in *The Girl From Up There*, a calculated but barely successful attempt to create another international success like *The Belle of New York* and featuring a number of the earlier show's stars, headed by *The Belle of New York*, Edna May, herself. He subsequently had top-billing as a penniless American in Paris, Upson Downes, in the Herald Square's *The New Yorkers* (1901) and in the title-rôle of an attempt to make a musical out of George Hobart's tale of *John Henry* (1905).

This show proved to be his last musical comedy appearance, as he thereafter appeared only in variety, where he could earn the $1,000 per week which a book show could not come up with, before a premature death at the age of 40, one week after the passing of his wife.

DAM, H[enry] J W (b California, 1859; d Havana, Cuba, 26 April 1906).

For reasons which are now lost in time, George Edwardes commissioned the libretto of his initial Gaiety Theatre musical comedy not from one of his usual writers, nor from the men who had just given him such a success with *A Gaiety Girl*, but from the little-known journalist and playwright H J W Dam, formerly of San Francisco and New York but now based in London and working on the *Star* newspaper. Dam's principal credits to that time had been the plays *The Silver Shell* and *Diamond Deane* and the re-adaptation of Brandon Thomas's adaptation of the text to Edward Jakobowski's *The Queen of Brilliants* (*Die Brillantenkönigin*) for Abbey and Grau's American production.

For *The Shop Girl*, Dam accomplished a fair imitation of the style of Owen Hall's *A Gaiety Girl* book and also provided the lyrics to some of the show's songs, but in spite of the success of the new musical comedy he did not work again at the Gaiety. In a discreet career, he provided a farcical book for Arthur Roberts's semi-successful *The White Silk Dress* and adapted Clérice's Portuguese hit *O Moliero d'Alcala* for Henry Lowenfeld, without confirming

his undoubtedly sucessful entry into the musical theatre with *The Shop Girl*.

1894 **The Queen of Brilliants** (*Die Brillantenkönigin*) American adaptation of English version (Abbey's Theater, New York)
1894 **The Shop Girl** (Ivan Caryll/w Adrian Ross) Gaiety Theatre 23 November
1896 **The White Silk Dress** (Alick McLean, Reginald Somerville, George Byng) Prince of Wales Theatre 3 October
1899 **The Coquette** (*O Moliero d'Alcala*) English version (Prince of Wales Theatre)

LA DAME EN DÉCOLLETÉ Opérette in 2 acts by Yves Mirande and Lucien Boyer. Music by Maurice Yvain. Théâtre des Bouffes-Parisiens, Paris, 22 December 1923.

Following his great successes with *Ta bouche*, *Là-haut* et al, Yvain attempted, in *La Dame en décolleté*, to compose a score which included a little more than the series of bright, jazzy melodies which had helped make the earlier pieces such favourites. Edmond Tirmont (Georges du Vélin) and Marthe Davelli (Lucette de Verneuil), both pensionnaires of the Opéra-Comique, took the romantic rôles of a couple of fêtards preparing to renounce their naughty ways for true love and marriage, alongside the comedian Dranem, in the rôle of the clerk, Girodot, who loses the remnants of the bride's inheritance at baccarat and sets in train the events which hold up the wedding until the end of the evening. In spite of some lovely lyrical moments, it was Dranem who scored the song hit of the evening with his comical 'Je n'ai pas pu'. The Paris public soon made it clear that they preferred the mixture as before and Yvain's other musical of the season, the lively and less substantial *Gosse de riche*, had a longer life than the two months *La Dame en décolleté* spent in Paris before it began a rather more substantial provincial life.

DIE DAME IN ROT Operette in 3 acts by Julius Brammer and Alfred Grünwald. Music by Robert Winterberg. Theater des Westens, Berlin, 16 September 1911.

Brammer and Grünwald's libretto for the Operette *Die Dame in Rot* went near to taking on *Bob herceg* for the most amusing (from a British point of view) attempt at a British-Ruritanian tale. The first act took place in the London Royal Academy, the director of which is called Lolipop, Marie Ottman played the lovely Miss Pearly Queensland, cousin to Lord Snobly Middletown, and other characters rejoiced in the names of Lord Wonderfull, Kitty Weed and Lord Fred of Cookstown.

In fact the tale could have been set anywhere, for it dealt simply with a *Miss Helyett/The Beauty Spot* type of a scandal. The artist Felix Werndorff glimpsed the lovely socialite Miss Queensland skinny-dipping and went home and painted the scene. When the painting was exhibited at the Royal Academy the unwitting model was recognized and gossip ran rife. Her bethrothal to Lord Snobly is broken off, the picture is slashed, and at the final curtain Pearly is, naturally, ready to become Mrs Artist.

Susanne Bachrich (Kitty), Albert Kutzner, Gustav Matzner and Franz Gross (as a Japanese count called Dr Graf Ikamo Hitamaro) supported the star through an encouraging run at the Theater des Westens, after which *Die Dame in Rot* went on from Berlin to the German provinces, but apparently not to Vienna. This omission didn't stop it, of course, from finding its way to Budapest in 1915 (ad Zsolt Harsányi) and, with the rage for Continental Operette still burning beyond the Atlantic, to America. It got off to a first start there in 1915, under the management of E C Herndon and music publisher Louis Dreyfus, produced at Atlantic City with Dreyfus's wife, Valli Valli, in the starring rôle of Sylvia Stafford and Glenn Hall as the artist, in an Anne Caldwell version which swapped the comical demi-Australian names for staunchly suitable ones. The show was gratified with excellent notices as it ran through Toronto, Philadelphia and Chicago, but the producing partners fell out when their show proved a big Chicago hit, and *The Lady in Red* ended up being taken off.

Four years later, however, the orphaned show resurfaced and, after passing through several hands, was put out again under the management of John P Slocum. Slocum apparently got rid of much of the score, trying to ensure success by pumping up the remnants of the original music with songs from a veritable hit parade of the world's best show composers: Walter Donaldson (China Dragon Blues, 'Play Me That Tune'), Henri Christiné ('Lulu Lavinia'), Leo Fall ('Visions of the Fireside'), George Gershwin ('Something about Love'), Jean Gilbert ('Mr Love Will Catch You Yet'), and Jerome Kern ('Where is the Girl for Me?'), as well as the more modest English music-hall songwriters George Arthurs and Worton David ('Cupid Never Wrote the Alphabet') and Otto Motzan. Adele Rowland was *The Lady in Red* this time, once again the pre-Broadway reviews were fine, but when the show finally reached New York 48 performances proved to be its metropolitan lot.

USA: Atlantic City 19 April 1915, Lyric Theater, New York *The Lady in Red* 12 May 1919; Hungary: Fővárósi Nyari Színház *A pirosruhás hölgy* 3 July 1915

DAMES AT SEA

DAMES AT SEA New 30s musical in 2 acts by Robin Miller and George Haimsohn. Music by Jim Wise. Bouwerie Lane Theater, New York, 20 December 1968.

A very small-scale, six-handed burlesque musical which, with a delightful cheek, took up the challenge of giving its own affectionate version of the movie musicals of the 1930s with their vast casts and spectacular productions. Little Ruby from Centerville, USA, finds fame, fortune and the juvenile man amongst a bevy of showbiz and Hollywood clichés and a scoreful of tongue-in-cheek songs which range from a one-handed, tap-danced, ticker-tape-draped paean to 'Wall Street', a torch-song of desperate proportions to 'That Mister Man of Mine' and a swoopingly comical do-you-remembering Beguine, to the little heroine's breathless longing for 'The Sailor of My Dreams' and her super-dejected admission that it is 'Raining in My Heart'.

Originally staged in a one-act version in a Greenwich Village café in 1966 under the title *Golddiggers Afloat*, the piece was subsequently upped to two acts and produced at off-Broadway's Bouwerie Lane Theater with Bernadette Peters (Ruby) and David Christmas (Dick) repeating their recreations of the Keeler and Powell-types which the names of their characters indicated. It ran there for 575 performances, played London briefly with Sheila White featured as Ruby, and was seen in a Harry Miller production at the Playbox Theatres in Sydney and Melbourne (11 March 1970) with Nancye Hayes featured. A production from Sarasota, Florida was brought to New York for a second round in 1985 and played at off-Broadway's Lamb's Theater (12 June) for 278 performances with Donna Kane (Ruby) and George Dvorsky (Dick) in the widest-eyed rôles. It was also televised in 1971 with Ann-Margret, Ann Miller and Dick Shawn amongst the cast.

Thanks to its charms and its economical size, *Dames at Sea* has become a perennially favoured show with provincial and touring companies with limited resources.

UK: Duchess Theatre 27 August 1969; Australia: Playbox Theatre, Sydney 10 September 1969
Recordings: Off-Broadway cast (Columbia); London cast (CBS); UK tour cast (TER); TV cast (private label).

DAMN YANKEES

DAMN YANKEES Musical in 2 acts by George Abbott and Douglass Wallop based on Wallop's novel *The Year the Yankees Lost the Pennant*. Music and lyrics by Richard Adler and Jerry Ross. 46th Street Theater, New York, 5 May 1955.

The initial success scored by the Adler/Ross team with *The Pajama Game* was followed by a second hit, again shared with author Abbott (this time also director) and choreographer Bob Fosse, in this everyday American version of the Faust legend in which – with more than a reminiscent touch of the Vebers' 1926 French show *L'Homme qui vendit son âme au Diable* – Joe Hardy (Stephen Douglass) sells his soul to the devil (Ray Walton) in order to see his favourite team win baseball's top honours. Metamorphosed from paunchy middle-age into the exciting, home-run-hitting 'Shoeless Joe from Hannibal, Mo', Joe finds that glory and the pennant are not everything in the face of separation from his wife (Shannon Bolin), a nosily investigative reporter (Rae Allen) determined to question his origins, and the prospect of eternal hellfire.

The show was a splendid mixture of a warm and funny libretto and a fine popular score, from which the baseball players' ingenuous barbershop assertion that all you need to win a game is 'Heart', and 'Whatever Lola Wants', the self-confidently sexy tango sung by the devil's mantrap assistant (Gwen Verdon), both became standards. *Damn Yankees* was shot through with an appealingly human (when it wasn't superhuman) quality, which had been much less evident in the team's earlier show, and which helped assure it a grand run of 1,019 performances on Broadway followed by a long touring life.

Walston had a fine rôle as the plausibly devilish Appleby, thwarted of his rightful prey, but Gwen Verdon as the luscious Lola, who changes sides at the vital moment, was lifted into the star category by her performance, a performance highlighted by her hit song and by Fosse's comedy mambo 'Who's Got the Pain?'.

A fine London season starred Ivor Emmanuel, Elizabeth Seal (a quick replacement for Belita) and Bill Kerr for 258 performances at the vast London Coliseum, whilst Australia saw Barbara Newman (Lola), Alton Harvey (Appleby) and Warren Brown (Joe) featured through three and a half months in Melbourne prior to a season at the Sydney's Empire Theatre (17 June 1958).

Damn Yankees was subsequently made into a film in which Miss Verdon and Walton starred with Hollywood's Tab Hunter as Joe whilst a television version was broadcast in 1967 with Phil Silvers and Lee Remick in the principal rôles.

In the 1970s the show was given a German production, happily localized by Franklin Fanning so that it referred to the football team of the city which produced it instead of the (to non-Americans) incomprehensible game of baseball.

UK: London Coliseum 28 March 1957; Australia: Her Majesty's Theatre, Melbourne 1 February 1958; Germany: Oberhausen *Damn Yankees, oder Das Jahr in dem rot-weiss Oberhausen Deutscher Meister wird* 19 May 1979

Recording: Original cast (RCA Victor), film soundtrack (RCA)

DANCE, George (Sir) (b Nottingham, ?1865; d London, 22 October 1932). Versatile librettist and lyricist who wrote the texts for several major hits in the Victorian musical theatre before moving on to a highly successful career as a touring manager.

Dance worked for three years in his father's business before becoming a journalist and theatrical correspondent in his native Nottingham, but he had already, from his teens, tried his hand at writing music-hall and drawing-room comedy songs, and had won some considerable success ('Girls are the Ruin of Man', 'His Lordship Winked at the Counsel', 'English as She is Spoke' for Charles Coburn, Alice Atherton's 'Laughing Song'). He entered the musical theatre in 1886, when he compiled an unsolicited but made-to-measure burlesque of *Oliver Cromwell*, equipped with a mixture of old and new music, for the touring company of Willie Edouin and his wife Alice Atherton. Edouin accepted the piece by return mail and *Oliver Grumble* proved happy enough in the provinces to be given a short London season, getting bumped from Edouin's touring baggage only because the Mark Melford comedy *Turned Up*, produced by the company in the same season, proved a major hit.

It was, however, five years before Dance was heard of again in the musical theatre, and this time under very different circumstances – as the author of a comic opera destined for the Savoy Theatre in the interregnum occasioned by the break-up between Carte and Gilbert. *The Nautch Girl*, set to music by Edward Solomon, proved an excellent piece, witty and funny and in no way inferior to the Savoy's recent productions. It played for 200 nights at the Savoy, went on tour and even to the Orient, but the collaboration with Solomon and Carte was not pursued and Dance's next assignments were again in different areas.

He adapted Paul Lacôme's *Ma mie Rosette* from five acts into two for the London stage, where it ran longer than the original piece had done in Paris, and composed another burlesque, this time for Arthur Roberts (*A Modern Don Quixote*), which was subsequently judged worthy of not one but two London showings. It was, however, another show designed for the provinces which proved his first really big hit. *The Lady Slavey*, the archetypical example of the vastly popular 'variety musical' – all story in the first act, and frittering away into a series of 'turns' in the second, with the story returning to have its ends tied up only in the last minutes – had a London run and, indeed, productions on Broadway and in many other venues around the English-speaking world, but it was the touring show par excellence and held a sometimes multiple place on the roads of Britain for some 20 years.

The Gay Parisienne, which came along the following year, was more vertebrate, more successful in the metropolites (US: *The Girl from Paris*) and almost as successful on the road as *The Lady Slavey*, touring ceaselessly for more than a decade. However, a rather tasteless vehicle for the dwarfish variety star Little Tich, *Lord Tom Noddy*, provoked some very off-colour reactions and did not catch on.

With *The New Mephisto* and *The Gay Grisette*, Dance proved yet again that he had British provincial tastes taped to a nicety, and both pieces toured almost continuously for many years whilst avoiding the West End, but a third piece similarly tailored for the provinces, *A Chinese Honeymoon*, was taken out of the touring circuits and moved into town by Frank Curzon. Suitably polished up for metropolitan consumption, *A Chinese Honeymoon* proved the biggest hit in musical theatre history. It became the first musical ever to run one thousand consecutive performances in London (or any other theatrical centre), was played worldwide, and toured incessantly for years and years.

Dance's only two subsequent pieces were not successful, and a last work called *Mlle Paris* never made it to the stage, but his principal activity by this time was management. Again avoiding the West End, and preferring tried to new material, he concentrated over many years on sending out long-running touring companies of established West End musical hits, notably the number one and number two companies of the big musical successes produced by George Edwardes at the Gaiety, Daly's and the Adelphi Theatres. His intelligently managed touring operations and his phenomenal authorial success meant that, in spite of a large amount of practical philanthropy (a £30,000 gift to the Old Vic fund earned him a knighthood in 1923), he has been one of the very few theatrical producers to leave a considerable fortune at his death.

A genuine man of the theatre, Dance was involved in all areas of British theatre life and management. He was for a time the proprietor of the Theatre Royal, Richmond, and took over briefly as managing director of the Gaiety Theatre after George Edwardes's death, before throwing in his hand in the face of the power politics and property-grabbing going on in the theatre at that time.

1886 **Oliver Grumble** (pasticcio) Novelty Theatre 25 March
1891 **The Nautch Girl** (Edward Solomon/w Frank Desprez) Savoy Theatre 30 June
1892 **Ma mie Rosette** English adaptation w Ivan Caryll (Globe Theatre)
1893 **The Lady Slavey** (John Crook) Theatre Royal, Northampton 4 September; Avenue Theatre, London 20 October 1894
1893 **A Modern Don Quixote** (Crook) Strand Theatre 25 September
1894 **The Gay Parisienne** (Ernest Vousden, later Caryll et al) Theatre Royal, Northampton 1 October; Duke of York's Theatre, London 4 April 1896
1896 **Lord Tom Noddy** (F Osmond Carr) Garrick Theatre 15 September
1897 **The New Mephisto** (Vousden) Grand Theatre, Leeds 29 March
1898 **The Gay Grisette** (Carl Kiefert) Theatre Royal, Bradford 1 August
1899 **A Chinese Honeymoon** (Howard Talbot) Theatre Royal, Hanley 16 October; Royal Strand Theatre, London 5 October 1901
1901 **The Ladies' Paradise** (Caryll) Theatre Royal, Hanley 11 March
1902 **The West End** (Edward Jones/Ernest Boyd-Jones/w George Arliss) Theatre Royal, Norwich 29 September

THE DANCING MISTRESS Musical play in 3 acts by James T Tanner. Lyrics by Adrian Ross and Percy Greenbank. Music by Lionel Monckton. Adelphi Theatre, London, 19 October 1912.

George Edwardes re-teamed his *Quaker Girl* authors and stars for this follow-up to the earlier hit at the Adelphi Theatre. Gertie Millar appeared as a dance teacher at a ladies' finishing school, Joe Coyne as an aviator, Gracie Leigh as the school's Scottish tuck-shop lady and Mlle Caumont as a vast French mistress, in a plot which took them picturesquely from Brighton to Oberwald and a hotel in London. Other favourite features included a chorus of schoolgirls, some skating and skiing (providing Miss Leigh with the opportunity for a comic routine with her equipment) and a jolly dance to 'The Porcupine Patrol'. Georges Carvey followed *The Quaker Girl*'s 'Come to the Ball' with another charming waltz, 'When You Are in Love', and Miss Millar sang happily through 'Dance, Little Snowflake' for a satisfactory 242-performance run without the piece ever looking like becoming another *Quaker Girl*.

An Australian production featured Maggie Dickinson in the rôle made for Miss Millar and Leslie Holland as the aviator, supported by soprano Ethel Cadman, the veteran Maggie Moore as the Frenchwoman and Minnie Love the Scots one for a fairly brief run in repertoire in Sydney and Melbourne (16 October 1913).

Australia: Criterion Theatre, Sydney 2 August 1913

THE DANCING YEARS Musical play in 3 acts by Ivor Novello. Lyrics by Christopher Hassall. Theatre Royal, Drury Lane, London, 23 March 1939.

The most successful of Ivor Novello's series of spectacular musical plays, *The Dancing Years* was produced at the Theatre Royal, Drury Lane not long before the outbreak of war, and told a story which was actually relevant to and inspired by the conflict. The suppression of the music of Jewish composers in Germany (much on the lines of the suppression of German music in Britain in the First World War) was the spur to a Ruritanian musical with a bitter twist to it.

Rudi Kleber (Novello) is brought from suburban obscurity to fame as a composer of operettic music by the prima donna Maria Ziegler (Mary Ellis) but, although they live happily together, he cannot ask her to marry him because of a promise given to a child friend (Roma Beaumont) of his early days. In the misunderstandings that result, Maria marries her old admirer, Prince Metterling (Anthony Nicholls), and the lovers are foolishly parted for ever, but when the war comes the Princess is able to use her social position to save the arrested, Jewish Rudi.

Novello starred in his usual non-singing capacity opposite Mary Ellis, the leading lady of his *Glamorous Night*, who introduced several songs which were to become Novello standards – the showy 'Waltz of My Heart', the gentle 'My Dearest Dear' and the first act's enduring closer 'I Can Give You the Starlight'. As was Novello's habit, the first two of these were presented as songs written by the composer within the show, as were the soprano/contralto duet 'The Wings of Sleep' introduced by Ellis and Olive Gilbert, and the long musical section representing Rudi's Operette, *Lorelei*, which included the soaring tenor melody 'My Life Belongs to You'. Miss Beaumont,

Plate 65. **The Dancing Years**: *Rudi Kleber (Ivor Novello) is taken by the Nazis.*

as the young Grete, danced and sang a parody of a turn-of-the-century musical comedy song called 'Primrose' and Freddie Carpenter choreographed the lovely 'Leap Year Waltz' into one of the highlights of the show.

After opening to a fine reception at the Theatre Royal, Drury Lane, *The Dancing Years* became an early casualty of the war. It was closed down by enemy action and, when it became safe to re-open, it found its theatre unavailable through having been taken over as the headquarters of the troops' entertainment unit, ENSA. Producer Tom Arnold, however, was an old habitué of the road, and he remounted *The Dancing Years* in Manchester (16 September 1940) with Muriel Barron replacing Miss Ellis and sent it out on a very extended tour. Its success on the road was so great that, in March 1942, he took the continuing production (with most of its original company still intact) back into the West End and there, at the Adelphi Theatre, the show was able to compile the sort of West End run it had been promised before the interruption (969 further performances). At the end of the run, the company went back on the road and *The Dancing Years* was to be found travelling through Britain almost unbrokenly over the next five years.

After it had been staged in Australia (the only one of Novello's shows so to be) by J C Williamson Ltd with Max Oldaker, Tara Barry and Elizabeth Gaye featured, given an American première in St Louis with Wilma Spence, Eduard Franz and Marjorie Bell in the leading rôles, revived in London in 1947 starring Jessica James and Barry Sinclair, and filmed with Giselle Préville and Dennis Price in 1950, Arnold brought the show back to London once more in 1954 in an on-ice version. In his will the author-composer left the rights of *The Dancing Years* to Arnold's young son who saw it return to London yet again in 1968 with June Bronhill as Maria (Saville Theatre 6 June) but who has since been less keen to allow it to be produced again in the West End in spite of continuing provincial performances, sometimes in a version which removes the final Nazi episode.

Australia: Her Majesty's Theatre, Melbourne 29 June 1946; USA: Municipal Opera, St Louis 5 June 1947; Film: Associated British 1950

Recordings: original cast (HMV), 1968 revival cast (RCA), selection (Columbia)

DANDY DAN, THE LIFEGUARDSMAN Musical comedy in 2 acts by Basil Hood. Music by Walter Slaughter. Belfast, 23 August 1897; Lyric Theatre, London, 4 December 1897.

Following the grand success of his impersonation of the cabby *Gentleman Joe*, comedian Arthur Roberts commissioned a second vehicle from that show's authors, Basil Hood and Walter Slaughter. The character they created for him this time, a soldier with a 'mash' on a pretty nursemaid, provided the irresponsible comedian with all the opportunities for broad comedy and quick-change impressions expected of him by his public, the latitude for unscripted deviations that he required, as well as some bright and brittle-lyricked songs in the same mould as the *Gentleman Joe* ones ('Dandy Dan, the Lifeguardsman', 'The Magic of My Eye', 'My Little Game'). Phyllis Broughton and Bill Denny headed the support, with little Isa Bowman as the nursemaid and George A Highland, later one of Australia's most prominent directors of musicals, in a small rôle.

Dandy Dan had a run of 166 London performances, latterly in a 'second edition', with a burlesque on the current theatrical scene entitled *Much Ado About Something, or Beerbohm Tree-lawney of the Wells* inserted as an extra plaything for the star, before Roberts took it on a profitable tour.

THE DANDY FIFTH English military comic opera in 3 acts by George R Sims based on *The Queen's Shilling* by G W Godfrey, being an adaptation of *Un Fils de famille* by Jean-François Bayard and de Biéville [ie E Desnoyers]. Music by Clarence C Corri. Prince of Wales Theatre, Birmingham, 11 April 1898; Duke of York's Theatre, London, 16 August 1898.

A latter-day military comic opera of the kind very popular in Britain 20 and more years earlier (and interminably popular in France), *The Dandy Fifth* was adapted from a half-century-old original, the very popular *Un Fils de famille* (Théâtre du Gymnase, Paris 25 November 1852), played in London as *The Queen's Shilling* in 1879. It was expressly designed by Sims for the provincial audiences he had previously proved he understood so well. The story, which centred on the efforts of a private soldier, Dick Darville (Arthur Appleby/H Scott Russell) to win Kate (Ruth Davenport), the daughter of his General, in spite of the rivalry of Colonel Slasherton (Leonard Calvert/Cecil Morton York), was filled with plenty of boisterous good fun and simple heroics and illustrated with songs by Clarence Corri, musical director at the Manchester Theatre Royal and a member of a famous musico-theatrical family. Several of these songs, such as the endearing 'The Sprig o' Horringe Blossom' and the patriotic 'Toast of the Dandy Fifth' were successful both in and out of the show, but the hit of the evening was 'Tommy's Tourna-

ment' a tambour-thumping piece with its cheerworthy cap line 'a little British army goes a **** long way'.

The Dandy Fifth toured in Britain for more than a decade, taking in an eight-week London season, but mostly sticking to the provinces where its unsophisticated good humour and sentiment and easily digestible score made it a long-term favourite.

Un Fils de famille was musicalized as *El hijo de familia* in Spain (Gaztambide, Oudrid/Luis Olcona, Teatro del Circo 24 December 1853) and played in America in a version with songs under the title *The Lancers*.

DANIELS, Frank [Albert] (b Dayton, Ohio, 1860; d West Palm Beach, Fla, 12 January 1935). Impish little comic who had a fine career as a top-billed star in the musical theatre.

After an apprenticeship as a wood-engraver in Boston, Daniels began a stage career at 19 playing rather more-than-teenaged rôles in comic opera (Bailie in *Cloches de Corneville*, Judge in *Trial by Jury*, Dick Deadeye). He toured in farce with Charles Atkinson, and played the rôle of the jailor Enterich in a Boston production of *Der Bettelstudent*, but he found his first significant successes in musical farce-comedy, playing broadly comical rôles in William Gill's *The Electric Spark* in America and England (1883), and in Charles Hoyt's *The Rag Baby* (1884, Old Sport) and *Little Puck* (1888, Giltedge) for long periods on the American tour circuits.

Daniels appeared in a character part in the Philadelphia musical *Princess Bonnie* (Shrimps), but found himself with a genuine musical-comedy star part for the first time when he was cast in the grotesque title-rôle of Kibosh, in Victor Herbert's colourful burlesque-comic opera *The Wizard of the Nile* (1895). Herbert and *Wizard of the Nile* librettist Harry B Smith created a second comic opera, *The Idol's Eye* (1897), to feature the new comedy star, and Kirk La Shelle and Frederick Ranken joined with the composer in a third vehicle made on the same lines, *The Ameer* (1899, Iffie Khan).

In 1902 he starred as 'My Man Blossoms' in *Miss Simplicity* at the Casino Theater, and the following year as the little jockey-in-spite-of-himself in Charles Dillingham's production of *The Office Boy* (*Le Jockey malgré lui*, 1903, Noah Littler) as made over for America by Smith and Ludwig Englander, at the Victoria, providing himself in each case with a vehicle in which to tour for the rest of each of the years in question. In 1905 he took up the rather less broadly out-front rôle of *Sergeant Brue*, created by Owen Hall for Willie Edouin in London, and successfully played it at the Criterion Theater.

In 1907 Dillingham starred him in *The Tattooed Man*, another Herbert/Smith piece, suggested by the hit song of *The Idol's Eye*, which once again cast him as a broadly-painted and -played Easterner, here called Omar Khayyam jr, for a successful New York season and a long tour, and in the following years he stayed on the road for a good stretch playing G P Huntley's rôle of the bumbling Mr Hook in *Miss Hook of Holland*, the comical Marquis de St Gautier, created by George Graves, in another British import, *The Belle of Brittany*, and in Frank Lalor's rôle of the naughty Dondidier in Ivan Caryll's New York's hit *The Pink Lady*. He returned to Broadway for a stint at Weber and Fields's establishment (*Roly Poly*, *Without the Law*) at the end of 1912 in his last New York engagement before retiring from the stage.

D'ANKA Cornélie Attractive, blonde and bordering-on-the-plump star of the opéra-bouffe era in Britain.

After making her début on the London stage as the Prince of Boboli in *Falsacappa* (April 1871), Mlle d'Anka appeared at the Court and Gaiety Theatres as Richard Coeur de Lion in the burlesque *Isaac of York* (1872), and at the Alhambra in the thoroughly soprano rôles of Princess Cunégonde in *Le Roi Carotte*, the title-rôle of *The Black Crook* (1872), Offenbach's Eurydice (*Orphée aux enfers*, 1877) and in the title-rôle of *Grande-Duchesse de Gérolstein* (1878). Her most celebrated rôle, however, was that of Mlle Lange in *La Fille de Madame Angot* in which she appeared with the Gaiety Company at the Globe (1874), at the Opera Comique (1875), at the Alhambra (1878), at the Connaught (1879) and at the Theatre Royal, Drury Lane (1880).

In the mid-1880s she was still active, if plumper, touring in the title-rôle of *Estrella* and as the Grande-Duchesse, and appearing as Zoë in Violet Cameron's production of *The Commodore* (*La Créole*). Then, like so many of her contemporaries, she disappeared from theatrical annals, hopefully to a happy-ever-after.

LA DANSEUSE AUX ÉTOILES Opérette à grand spectacle in 2 acts by Henri Varna and Guy des Cars based on the novel *La Demoiselle de l'Opéra* by des Cars. Music by Vincent Scotto. Théâtre Mogador, Paris, 18 February 1950.

Henri Varna built a spectacular show around Guy des Cars' romantic *histoire d'amour* between the celebrated ballerina Adéline Piedplus (Marta Labarr) and the handsome Lieutenant Ludovic de Chanalèze (Jean Chesnel). He purposefully reduced the tale from the novel's lifelong timespan to just a few years, to allow the protagonists to remain young and attractive throughout the evening, and set it in a succession of stage pictures of the Paris of the 1870s, ranging from a tableau-vivant of Dégas' 'Les danseuses à la barre' through the coulisses of the Paris Opéra, the city's cafés and 'le bal de la Closerie des Lilas' to the gardens of the Élysée and a full-scale ballet, the whole set to the accompaniment of a Vincent Scotto score in which dance music predominated. *La Danseuse aux étoiles* was played through a run of more than a year and a half, with Tessa Beaumont succeeding Mlle Labarr in the starring rôle.

DAPHNIS ET CHLOË Opérette (musical-parody idyll) in 1 act by Clairville and Jules Cordier. Music by Jacques Offenbach. Théâtre des Bouffes-Parisiens, Paris, 27 March 1860.

A little parody of the pastoral in general, and the pastorale of the same name by Longus in particular, *Daphnis and Chloë* was a version of an 1849 playlet (Théâtre du Vaudeville) supplied to Offenbach by the prolific Clairville and, under the pseudonym of 'Cordier', which had served him for occasional writings since 1840, by Monsieur Éléonor Tenaille de Vaulabelle.

The lubricious Pan (Désiré) has his eyes on the innocent nymph, Choë (Mlle Chabert), and he takes the place of his own statue to fool the girl into giving him a kiss. But Chloë

Plate 66. **Daphnis und Chloë**: *Dirk Lohr as Daphnis and Carmen Weber as Chloë in the Dresden Staatsoperette's production of the enlarged version of Offenbach's little opérette.*

is in love with the beauteous and exceedingly coveted shepherd Daphnis (Juliette Beau) and he – though he knows not what the emotions that stir in him are – returns her feelings. The jealous Calisto (Marie Cico) and her accompanying bacchantes try to make Daphnis forget Chloë with the help of a little Lethe water, whilst Pan takes on the job of instructing the naïve hamadryed in the workings of that thing called love. His lessons are helpful enough that, when he is laid low by an accidental draught of Lethe water, Chloë can pass on what she has learned to Daphnis. It is all that is needed for a happy ending.

The tiny tale was accompanied by a score of nine numbers, beginning with a Bacchic ode of embarrassment as each bacchante sees her manoeuvrings to meet Daphnis alone stymied by her sisters, and including a pastorale for Daphnis, and duos for Chloë with both her lover and the lecher.

Following its Paris production, *Daphnis and Chloë* was seen in Berlin and then in Vienna, where, played as one of the earliest productions at Karl Treumann's Theater am Franz-Josefs-Kai during a guest season by Johann Nestroy, it became highly popular. What seems to have been Wilhelm Friedrich's version (sometimes attributed to Treumann or to Nestroy, and uncredited on the playbills) turned the little piece into a virtual stand-up vehicle for Nestroy in the rôle of Pan, a rôle rewritten in a satirical style to parallel his success as Jupiter in *Orpheus in der Unterwelt*. Anna Grobecker and Anna Marek were the overwhelmed pair of Arcadians, and Anna Müller appeared as Calisto. The original version was played at the

Carltheater the following year (6 July) and further adaptations were later played at the Variététheater (1870) and at the Komische Oper (1874). *Daphnis und Chloë* is still intermittently played in German-language theatres, although the 'versions' have crept even further from the original, and the score has been puffed-up with music taken from other sources.

Another, full-length opérette by the same title, written by André Mouëzy-Éon and Félix Gandera, composed by Henri Moreau-Febvre and subtitled 'la leçon d'amour', was produced at the Théâtre Edouard VII, Paris, in 1918 with Marguerite Deval and Henri Defreyn starred.

Germany: Friedrich-Wilhelmstädtisches Theater 23 December 1860; Austria: Theater am Franz-Josefs-Kai 2 March 1861; Hungary: Budai Színkör (Ger) 22 April 1862, Budai Népszinház 11 June 1862

DARE, Phyllis [DONES, Phyllis Haddie] (b London, 15 August 1890; d Brighton, 27 April 1975). One of the most enduring ingénues of the London musical theatre, occasionally in vocally demanding rôles.

Phyllis Dare made her first stage appearances, with her elder sister, Zena, as a child, playing regularly in pantomime and, at the age of 11, appearing alongside Seymour Hicks and Ellaline Terriss in *Bluebell in Fairyland* at the Vaudeville Theatre. She was still only 15 years old when Hicks called on her to take over as the fifth in a succession of leading ladies who played the Cinderella rôle of Angela in *The Catch of the Season*, a rôle which had originally been created by her sister. Although she returned to her schooling when her stint at the Vaudeville was over, she was soon back on the stage, in newsworthy circumstances. When Edna May flounced out of Leslie Stuart's *The Belle of Mayfair* (1906), producer Stephano Gatti called on Phyllis to take over the show's very large made-for-May rôle and, while lawsuits lurched around on all sides, the young star confirmed herself as one of the town's favourite ingénues.

She subsequently played the star juvenile parts of Robert Courtneidge's long-running successes *The Dairymaids* (1907, Peggy) and *The Arcadians* (1909), introducing 'The Girl with the Brogue' in her rôle as Irish Eileen, and made a notable success of the rôle of the tempting Gonda van der Loo in the English version of Leo Fall's *Die geschiedene Frau* (*The Girl in the Train*, 1910) for George Edwardes. Edwardes subsequently starred her in *Peggy* (1910, Peggy), in Gertie Millar's rôle of Prudence in the Paris season of *The Quaker Girl*, in *The Sunshine Girl* (1912, Delia Dale), in succession to Miss Millar in *The Dancing Mistress* (1913, Nancy Joyce) and in tandem with Ina Claire in *The Girl From Utah* (1914, Dora Manners).

She continued to tot up the juvenile star rôles for more than another decade, appearing in the revival of *Miss Hook of Holland* (1914, Sally Hook), in the title-rôle of *Tina* (1915, 'The Violin Song'), *Kissing Time* (1919, Lucienne), as Mariana in the English version of Gilbert's *Die Frau im Hermelin* (1922, *The Lady of the Rose*), in what was effectively her own production of *The Street Singer* (1924, Yvette), *Lido Lady* (1926, Fay Blake, provoking some harsh words from Richard Rodgers about being landed with a 40-year-old ingénue) and *The Yellow Mask* (1928, Mary Bannister) before turning to straight theatre.

She subsequently toured in the very vocal rôle of Frieda in Jerome Kern's *Music in the Air* (1934) and made a late

Plate 67. 'Bring me a rose ...'. **Phyllis Dare** *and Alfred Lester in a racecourse scene from* The Arcadians.

and last return to the musical stage to play the lightly musicked part of Marta Karillos, the King's mistress, opposite Ivor Novello, in his *King's Rhapsody* (1949) ('The Mayor of Perpignan').

Her sister, **Zena DARE** [Zena DONES] (b London, 4 February 1887; d London, 11 March 1975) made an equally early start in musical comedy, starring in Seymour Hicks' touring musical *An English Daisy* (1902, Daisy Maitland) at 15 and creating the juvenile lead of *Sergeant Brue* (Aurora Brue) in London two years later. When Ellaline Terriss was unable to play the star rôle of the new Hicks musical, *The Catch of the Season*, she created this latest and long-running Cinderella part opposite Hicks and played it until Miss Terriss was able to return from giving birth and take over.

Zena next succeeded Adrienne Augarde in the title-rôle of *Lady Madcap*, under the management of George Edwardes, and appeared for him again in *The Little Cherub* (1906, Lady Isobel Congress) the following year, before returning to Hicks to succeed Miss Terriss in the star rôle of *The Beauty of Bath* (1906, Betty Silverthorne). In *The Gay Gordons* (1907, Victoria Siddons) she played second lead alongside Miss Terriss, taking over the star part when the show moved out of town. She appeared in musical pieces in several music halls, as the fashion for one-act shows in variety caught on, and toured in Miss Terriss's breeches rôle of *The Dashing Little Duke* before retiring to marriage.

When she returned to the stage, 15 years later, it was to play in often dramatic rôles in straight theatre (including a fondly remembered Mrs Darling in *Peter Pan*) until Ivor Novello induced her back to the musical stage with a non-singing rôle in *Careless Rapture* (1936). She subsequently succeeded Margaret Rutherford as Lady Charlotte Fayre in Novello's *Perchance to Dream* and appeared with her sister, for the first time since their childhood, when cast in the strong acting rôle of the conniving Queen Elana in *King's Rhapsody* (1949). She was over 70 when she appeared at the Theatre Royal, Drury Lane, as Mrs Higgins in the first London production of *My Fair Lady*, a rôle which she then retained for seven years in London and on the road.

Autobiography: *From School to Stage* (Collier and Co, London, 1907), *Phyllis Dare, by Herself* (1921)

DAREWSKI, Herman (b Minsk, Russia, 17 April 1883; d Kennington, London, 2 June 1947). Songwriter and music publisher whose song successes were contrasted with some flamboyant business failures.

Born in Russia, brought up in Britain, Darewski studied music in Vienna and then returned to Britain where he became a conductor at the spa town of Bridlington, then at Blackpool, a member of the staff of Francis, Day & Hunter music publishers, and an adept writer of popular songs and interpolated numbers for musical comedy. His first song success came with 'My Little Hyacinth', interpolated into *The Beauty of Bath* (1906) by Ellaline Terriss, and he had a further success with 'I Used to Sigh for the Silvery Moon' as interpolated into Charles Dillingham's Broadway production of *The Candy Shop* (1909). He also provided the tune to Elsie Janis's lyrics for 'For I Love Only You' (*The Slim Princess*, 1911). He subsequently established his own Herman Darewski Music Publishing Company Ltd which, apart from publishing his own works, also put out such popular numbers as 'Any Old Iron', 'Sussex by the Sea', 'Arizona', 'I Know Where the Flies Go in Wintertime', 'Ours is a Nice House Ours Is' and ensured the British distribution of many American hits.

His first musical theatre scores, mostly in collaboration with other writers, were written for revue, beginning with such shows as *Mind Your Backs* (Hackney Empire, 1913), and Austen Hurgon's 1914 Coliseum piece *Happy Days* (1914) and including de Courville's Hippodrome shows *Business As Usual* ('When We've Wound Up the Watch on the Rhine'), *Push and Go* (1915, w Jean Schwartz et al) and *Joyland* (1915), and his Comedy Theatre *Shell Out* (1915). In between the revue songs, he found time to contribute more or less music to a number of musical plays, of which the first was J M Barrie's vehicle for Gaby Deslys, *Rosy Rapture* (1915), a revusical affair in which his songs (including 'Which Switch is the Switch, Miss, for Ipswich?') supplemented half a score by Jerome Kern.

Darewski contributed numbers to such pieces as Émile Lassailly's *Carminetta* and revivals of *Bluebell in Fairyland* and *The Catch of the Season*, but had his biggest success when he supplied the bulk of the songs for the enormously successful C B Cochran wartime musical *The Better 'Ole* (1917). The unfortunate Gertie Millar vehicle *Flora* (1918) gave him only a brief exposure, but his re-musicked version of the Rip revue *Plus ça change* for Cochran and Alice Delysia as *As You Were* ('If You Could Care For Me') was another hit, whilst his 'The Shimmy Shake' and 'Le Petit Nid' ('In That Little Home That's Built For Two') gave

him a wider audience when they were heard in the Parisian version of Ivan Caryll's *The Earl and the Girl*, *Hello!! Charley* (1919).

At this time, often three or four West End revues and/or musicals at one time bore Darewski's name, in a larger or smaller capacity, on their bill. However, none of the musical comedies for which he provided the major part of the score (*Jolly Jack Tar*, *The Eclipse*, *Oh! Julie*) proved particularly successful, with the exception of a Gaiety Theatre revival of *The Shop Girl* (1920) for which the original Ivan Caryll score was topped up with eight new Darewski songs ('The Guards' Brigade'), and, by the early 1920s, his name was much less frequently seen.

In 1920 Darewski (who had bought up the old music publishers Charles Sheard in 1918) purchased the famous publishing house of Metzler, but in 1922 he encountered financial problems and was obliged to sell his publishing interests in bankruptcy. From the 1920s he operated once more as a musical director at various seaside resorts and at the head of his own band, whilst still providing the odd song to such musicals as *The Blue Mazurka* and *Up with the Lark*, but without regaining the profile he had had in the 1910s.

1914 **The Chorus Girl** (Harry Grattan) 1 act London Palladium 20 July
1914 **Going, Going, Gone** 1 act Chelsea Palace
1915 **Rosy Rapture, the Pride of the Beauty Chorus** (w Jerome Kern/F W Mark/J M Barrie) Duke of York's Theatre 22 March
1917 **The Better 'Ole** (James Heard/Bruce Bairnsfather, Arthur Eliot) Oxford Theatre 4 August
1918 **Flora** (w Melville Gideon/Harry Grattan, Heard) Prince of Wales Theatre 12 March
1918 **Jolly Jack Tar** (Heard, Davy Burnaby, J P Harrington/Seymour Hicks, Arthur Shirley) Prince's Theatre 29 November
1919 **A Good-Looking Lass** (Leon Pollack, Lauri Wylie) 1 act Chelsea Palace 11 August
1919 **The Eclipse** (w Gideon, Cole Porter/Adrian Ross/Fred Thompson, E Phillips Oppenheim) Garrick Theatre 12 November
1920 **Oh! Julie** (w H Sullivan Brooke/Harold Simpson/Firth Shephard, Lee Banson) Shaftesbury Theatre 22 June
1922 **Listening In** (Worton David, Will Hay) Apollo Theatre 31 July

Autobiography: *Musical Memories* (Jarrold, London, 1937)

Darewski's brother, Julius Darewski, was a very prominent London theatrical and musical agent and occasional producer, whilst another (disowned) brother, operating under the name **Ernest C ROLLS** [DAREWSKI, Josef Adolf], produced musical comedy and revue in both Britain and in Australia with more side than skill. He was sued for theatrical dishonesty before he was 21, bankrupted in 1921 after losing £16,000 on the musical *Oh! Julie* and £12,000 on the revue *Laughing Eyes*, and his mismanagement of Australia's J C Williamson Ltd almost led that famous firm to disaster. After directing some extravagant productions of a series of mostly American musicals on the Australian stage (*Sunny*, *Good News* etc) he went into management there himself, mounting Australia's *Whoopee* (1929) and the flop local *Funny Face* (1931), and, in the wake of Frank Thring's new Australian musical productions, even producing an original piece, *Flame of Desire* (Apollo Theatre, Melbourne 19 October 1935), for which he took a half book-credit with J L Gray (mus: Jack O'Hagan) and imported Ethelind Terry to star. He sacked her, and the show went down the drain anyway. He then won the job at Williamson's by engineering a financial takeover of the firm by New Zealand department store magnate John McKenzie who then put him in charge. His production of *I Married an Angel* was Williamson's all-time top money-loser and he was quickly given the boot when his second year's contract expired. Rolls' family did not disown him for his failures, nor for his flash manners and flashy productions (all well-established family failings). They disowned him when he was convicted of exposing himself in a rather different kind of 'flash'.

A further brother, **Max DAREWSKI** (b Manchester, 3 November 1894; d London, 25 September 1929), also composed for the musical theatre. At first, Max was celebrated as an infant prodigy at the piano, touring through Europe (under the not always appreciated 'management' of brother Herman) and appearing before crowned heads in the best prodigy fashion. He also conducted his own and other music, in novelty circumstances, before the age of ten. Amongst a proliferation of piano compositions, he composed music for a number of revues, including *Oh! Molly* (1912) and *Venus Limited* produced by brother Rolls, at the Pavilion and the Finsbury Park Empire respectively, but without being connected with anything very successful. He also got a tiny Broadway showing when he shared a credit on the title song for the 1916 musical *Go to It*.

He provided the score for Alfred Butt's musical comedy vehicle for Gaby Deslys, *Suzette* (1917), which, with a London run of 255 performances – not really due to its songs – proved his longest-lived piece. His only other full score was for the touring musical *Mamzelle Kiki* (1924), but he shared the composition of the Gaiety musical *His Girl* (1923) and the Jack Buchanan musical *Boodle* (1925) and had songs interpolated into various other musicals including the London versions of *Der Orlow* (*Hearts and Diamonds*), for which he was also musical director, Lehár's *Cloclo*, and revivals of *Tonight's the Night* and *The Maid of the Mountains*. Maurice Chevalier made a success of his 'One Hour of Flirt with You' (1917) under the less curious title of 'J'aime les fleurs' in the Casino de Paris revue *Pa-ri-ki-ri*. In what seemed to be the family tradition, he was glaringly bankrupted in 1924.

1917 **Seeing Life** (Arthurs) 1 act Oxford Music Hall 15 January
1917 **Suzette** (Austen Hurgon, George Arthurs) Globe Theatre 29 March
1922 **His Girl** (w Ernest Longstaffe/Austen Hurgon, F. W. Thomas, Claude E Burton, Arthur Anderson) Gaiety Theatre 1 April
1924 **Mamzelle Kiki** (Douglas Hoare, Graham John, Sydney Blow) Portsmouth 25 August
1925 **Boodle** (w Phil Braham/Hoare, Blow, Douglas Furber) Empire Theatre 10 March

D'ARVILLE, Camille [DYKSTRA, Neeltye] (b Overijssel, Netherlands, 21 June 1863; d San Francisco, 10 September 1932). Biggish blonde Dutch soprano who had a long career as a leading lady on both sides of the Atlantic.

Having studied music in Amsterdam and in Vienna, where she made her first stage appearance, D'Arville went to Britain in 1882 for an engagement which turned out to

be non-existent. She remained there and made some appearances in music halls before landing the title-rôle in Harry Paulton's comic opera, *Cymbia* (1883). She then succeeded to the lead juvenile rôle of Katrina in *Rip van Winkle* at the Comedy Theatre (1883), played Gabrielle in the H B Farnie version of *La Vie parisienne*, Frédégonde in a revival of *Chilpéric* and starred in *Falka* on tour before going back to Holland to appear in the Dutch production of *Rip!* On her return to Britain, she toured with her original 'discoverer', Harry Paulton, in *Erminie*, played the leading rôle in Paulton's next work *Mynheer Jan* (1887, Katrina) and then travelled to America with him to appear there in *The Queen's Mate* (*La Princesse des Canaries*, 1888, Anita). She took leading rôles in the British versions of the French *Babette* (1888, Babette) and *Surcouf* (*Paul Jones* 1889, Yvonne) and in the British musicals *Carina* (1888, Carina) and *Marjorie* (1890, Majorie) and succeeded Marion Hood as leading lady to Nellie Farren in the Gaiety tour of *Monte Cristo Jr* (1889, Mercedes), but then returned to America, where she was to spend most of the remainder of her career.

After appearances at the Casino Theater as Lange in *La Fille de Madame Angot* and in versions of *La Grande-Duchesse* and *Der arme Jonathan*, she joined the Boston Ideal Opera Company and, as their prima donna, played the classic comic opera repertoire, including many performances of *Robin Hood* (Maid Marian), *The Bohemian Girl* (Arline) and *La Mascotte* (Bettina), and created the rôles of Katrina in *The Knickerbockers* and Edith in *The Ogallallas*. She next appeared in the title-rôle of *Prince Kam* (1894) and in a star rôle, created especially for her, in Julian Edwards's *Madeleine* (1895, Madeleine), starred in *A Daughter of the Revolution* (1895, Marion Dunbar), Oscar Hammerstein's *Santa Maria* (1896), *Kismet* (1897, Kismet), on the road with the Camille D'Arville Comic Opera Company as *Peg Woffington* in a specially comissioned Victor Herbert/Harry Smith vehicle, and spelled Hilda Clark as Lady Constance in *The Highwayman* (1898) before retiring to married life. She returned to the stage a few years later and was seen in 1906–7 in another Edwards musical, *The Belle of London Town*, before taking a more definite farewell of the stage.

THE DASHING LITTLE DUKE Play with music in 3 acts by Seymour Hicks based on the play *A Court Scandal*, itself an adaptation of *Les Premières Armes de Richelieu* by Jean-François Bayard and Philippe Dumanoir. Lyrics by Adrian Ross. Music by Frank Tours. Hicks Theatre, London, 17 February 1909.

The Dashing Little Duke was written by Hicks as a vehicle for his wife, Ellaline Terriss, at a time when travesty playing was, apart from pantomime, largely a thing of the past. As an underaged husband separated from his wife by courtly machinations (unlike the better-known couple of *Le Petit Duc*, this wife is wholly adult), Miss Terriss had the lightest and most musical comedy part of a score in which supporting performers such as American soprano Elizabeth Firth (Britain's Valencienne in *The Merry Widow*), and top vocalists Courtice Pounds and Hayden Coffin were given the more musically substantial songs. When Miss Terriss, nevertheless, found the rôle rather heavy, Hicks (who had played the part of the little duke in the source play, *A Court Scandal*) stepped in to play matinées for her in what must be the only example of a husband and wife sharing a star rôle in a major musical.

The show did not catch on as well as its star's importance might have suggested it would, and Hicks reorganized it, making it more of a standard musical comedy by working up the incidental soubrette rôle, with the addition of three Jerome Kern songs, for American musical comedy star Julia Sanderson. Efforts were in vain and *The Dashing Little Duke* closed after 101 performances with a large deficit which was not recouped on a tour where the rôle of the Duke was taken by Zena Dare.

Another musical, the Hungarian *Az ötödik pont* (the fifth point) by Desző Megyeri (Népszinház, 16 December 1893), was based on the same play.

DASSARY, André [DEYHRASSARY, André] (b Biarritz, 10 September 1912; d Biarritz, July 1987). Flowing-voiced tenor who made a highly successful career as a stage performer and as a recording artist with a repertoire ranging from popular songs to light opera.

Having at first worked successfully as a masseur, notably with the French team at the World University Games of 1937, Dassary began a singing career as vocalist with the orchestra of Ray Ventura. In 1941 he had his first stage success in the leading rôle of the opérette à grand spectacle *L'Auberge qui chante*, at the Théâtre Mogador. He subsequently starred in *Valses de France* (1942, Victor Capoul) at the Châtelet, in *L'Ingénue de Londres* (1946), and had his biggest stage success when he created the star tenor rôle of Hubert in Maurice Yvain's long-running romantic opérette *Chanson gitane* (1946) at the Gaîté-Lyrique.

He followed up with the less successful *Symphonie portugaise* (1949), but scored two further successes as the tenor star of Francis Lopez's *Toison d'or* (1954) and the Lehár pasticcio *Rose de Noel* (1958). Thereafter, he was seen, like opérette in general, largely outside Paris whilst remaining widely heard on radio and television. He also appeared in several musical films (*Feux de joie*, *Tourbillon de Paris*, *Paris chante toujours* etc) and recorded a variety of musical comedy and opérette music ranging from *Le Pays de sourire* and *Frasquita* to French versions of *The Desert Song* and *Rose Marie*.

D'AUBAN, [Frederick] John (b ?1842; d London, 15 April 1922).

The son of C J D'Auban (b ?1799; d 29 May 1866), a well-known 'professor of dancing,' Johnnie D'Auban was, like the rest of his family, trained into the family act, the D'Aubans and the Wardes (the Wardes being another dance family, with whom they were closely and maritally linked), from an early age. He worked largely in music halls, making a sensation with his adeptness on the star-trap, appeared on the Paris stage and also played at the Alhambra under John Hollingshead (1865). In 1868, Johnnie and John Warde, billed as 'a pair of accomplished pantomimists and comic dancers ... from the Théâtre de la Porte-Saint-Martin', were engaged by Hollingshead for the first programme at the new Gaiety Theatre as 'principal grotesque dancers and pantomimists'. The pair appeared on the opening programme in Gilbert's burlesque *Robert the Devil* as 'two mysterious fiddlers'.

D'Auban continued to perform for some years, appear-

ing at the Alhambra in the comic ballet *All's Well That Ends Well*, in pantomimes, and in various productions at the Gaiety where he was, for a period, dance master, but he made an increasing career as a choreographer, establishing himself over some 30 years as one of the foremost dance designers in the musical theatre. He was associated with D'Oyly Carte throughout virtually the impresario's entire career, from *The Sorcerer* to *The Grand Duke* and *The Emerald Isle*, as well as with the Gaiety Theatre's famous series of new burlesques, and each of these areas brought forth one of his two most famous single routines: the comic dance for Emma Howson, George Grossmith and Richard Temple to the trio 'Never Mind the Why and Wherefore' in the original production of *HMS Pinafore*, and the celebrated pas-de-quatre (barn-dance) introduced into the Gaiety burlesque *Faust Up-to-Date*.

Amongst the original musical shows which D'Auban choreographed for the British stage (in an era when the dances were not always formally credited on theatre programmes) were *Cattarina* (1874), *Princess Toto* (1876), *The Sorcerer* (1877), *HMS Pinafore* (1878), *Gulliver* (1879), *Bil-lee Taylor* (1880, also played Jumbo, the black cook, featured dancer), *Patience* (1881), *Claude Duval* (1881), *All in the Downs* (1881), *Rip van Winkle* (1882), *Iolanthe* (1882), Lila Clay's *An Adamless Eden* and *On Condition* (1882), *Falka* (1883), *The Mikado* (1885), *Vetah* (1886), *Ruddigore* (1887), *Miss Esmeralda* (1887), *Frankenstein* (1887), *The Yeomen of the Guard* (1888), *Faust Up-to-Date* (1888), *Ruy Blas and the Blasé Roué* (1889), *The Red Hussar* (1889), *Paul Jones* (1889), *Carmen Up-to-Data* (1890), *The Rose and the Ring* (1890), *The Nautch Girl* (1891), *The Mountebanks* (1892), *Haddon Hall* (1892), *Jane Annie* (1893), *Utopia (Limited)* (1893), *Little Christopher Columbus* (1893), *King Kodak* (1894), *The Queen of Brilliants* (1894), *His Excellency* (1894), *The Chieftain* (1894), *An Artist's Model* (1895), *The New Barmaid* (1896 w Will Bishop), *The Grand Duke* (1896), *Man About Town* (1897), *His Majesty* (1897), *The Yashmak* (1897), *Regina BA* (1897 w John Tiller), *The Beauty Stone* (1898), *Little Miss Nobody* (1898), *The Gay Pretenders* (1900) and *The Emerald Isle* (1901).

His wife, Emma D'Auban (b ?; d Staines, 13 October 1910) performed both with John and with the family act, and took occasional principal dancing rôles in musicals, creating the part of the ballet girl, Nellie Bly, in Edward Solomon's *The Vicar of Bray* and appearing with John in a featured spot in *The Golden Web* (1893).

His son, Ernest D'Auban (b 1873; d 3 February 1941) who worked as a director and choreographer, notably for many years at the Theatre Royal, Drury Lane (whose pantomimes he also reproduced on Broadway), and daughter, Mariette D'Auban, dancer and choreographer, who worked on such shows as *Mignonette* (1889), *Cinder-Ellen Up Too Late* (1891), *In Town* (1892), *Morocco Bound* (1893), *The Lady Slavey* (1894), *Don Juan* (1893 w Warde) and *Go-Bang* (1894), were also involved in the family trade.

DAVIES, Harry Parr (b Briton Ferry, Wales, 24 May 1914; d London, 14 October 1955). Composer of a range of popular numbers from character songs to ballads in a short career on the British stage and screen.

Accompanist to Gracie Fields from the age of 18, Davies simultaneously supplied the singer with several successful numbers, including 'The Fairy on the Christmas Tree', 'The Sweetest Song in the World' (from the film *We're Going to Be Rich*, 1938), and her famous 'Wish Me Luck as You Wave Me Goodbye' (w Phil Park, in the film *Shipyard Sally*, 1939), as well as penning a number of cinema songs for George Formby ('In My Little Snapshot Album' w Will Haines, Jimmy Harper in *I See Ice*, 1938, the title song of his 1938 film *It's in the Air*).

He made his first appearance in the West End as the composer of George Black's long-running Hippodrome revue *Black Velvet*, and followed that with scores or songs for a series of other revues: *Haw Haw, Come Out to Play, Top of the World, Gangway* ('My Paradise' for Ann Ziegler and Webster Booth), *Happidrome, Big Top, Best Bib and Tucker, Fine Feathers, The Shephard Show*, and the Coronation revue *Glorious Days* (1952) at the Palace Theatre.

His first musical comedy score was that for Cicely Courtneidge's successful *Full Swing*, but he scored a major success with the wartime Hippodrome musical play *The Lisbon Story* in which a quartet, incidental to the spy drama, performed his most famous show song, 'Pedro the Fisherman', as a scene-change cover and the romantic heroine sang 'Never Say Goodbye'. There was further success for him in another Cicely Courtneidge vehicle, *Her Excellency*, and in the charming pastel adaptation of J M Barrie's *Quality Street* as *Dear Miss Phoebe* ('I Leave My Heart in an English Garden'), but statistically the longest run of all his pieces was won by the farcical musical *Blue for a Boy* in which Fred Emney starred for over 600 West End performances. It was also his last, for the young composer died in 1955 at the age of 41.

1942 **Full Swing** (w George Posford/Arthur Macrae, Archie Menzies, Jack Hulbert) Palace Theatre 16 April
1943 **The Lisbon Story** (Harold Purcell) London Hippodrome 17 June
1943 **The Knight Was Bold** (Barbara Gordon, Basil Thomas/Emile Littler) Piccadilly Theatre 1 July
1944 **Jenny Jones** (Purcell/Ronald Gow) London Hippodrome 2 October
1949 **Her Excellency** (w Manning Sherwin/Purcell, Max Kester/Purcell, Kester, Menzies) London Hippodrome 22 June
1950 **Dear Miss Phoebe** (Christopher Hassall) Phoenix Theatre 13 October
1950 **Blue for a Boy** (Purcell/Austin Melford) His Majesty's Theatre 30 November

DAVIS, Jessie Bartlett [née BARTLETT] (b nr Morris, Ill, September 1859; d Chicago, 14 May 1905). Biggish, blondish and beautiful young contralto who won fame as a member of the Boston Ideal Comic Opera Company.

After beginning her career, in Chicago, as a concert and church singer, and making an early stage appearance as Little Buttercup with the Church Choir *HMS Pinafore* company, Miss Davis toured in operatic companies and, on one occasion, sang Siebel to the Marguerite of Adelina Patti. After studying in Paris, she returned to the American stage and appeared with W T Carleton's company as a travesty Griolet (*La Fille du tambour-major*) and as Else (*Der lustige Krieg*), as Pygmalion in Massé's *Galathée*, and with the touring American Opera Company.

In 1889, she joined the recently reformed Boston Ideal Comic Opera Company as a replacement for the equally statuesque Agnes Huntington and, over the following

years, appeared with the Bostonians in *Pygmalion and Galatea* (Cynisca), *Fatinitza* (Wladimir), in Indian rôles in both *The Ogallallas* and *The Maid of Plymouth*, in *Prince Ananias* (Idalia), *In Mexico* (Theresa), *The Bohemian Girl* (Gipsy Queen), *The Serenade* (Dolores), *Rip van Winkle, The Knickerbockers* (Priscilla), Oscar Weil's *Suzette* (Marchioness of Tollebrauche), *Don Quixote* (Dorothea), *Martha, Il Trovatore* (Azucena), as *Carmen* and, most famously, in the breeches rôle of Alan-a-Dale in *Robin Hood* in which part she became associated with the celebrated Clement Scott/De Koven solo 'O Promise Me', apparently introduced by Hayden Coffin in the show's London version.

She left the company for the lucrative land of vaudeville shortly before the Bostonians collapsed, but was seen once more on Broadway, now alarmingly under-voiced, in the brief rôle of the cadet Delaunay in the 1903 revival of *Erminie* before a premature death.

Her sister, character actress and vocalist **Josephine Bartlett**, was also a popular member of the Bostonians, being particularly noted for her Dame Durden in *Robin Hood*. She also created the rôle of Mme Cécile in Victor Herbert's *Mlle Modiste* (1905).

DAVIS, Owen (b Portland, Maine, 29 January 1874; d New York, 14 October 1956).

The Harvard-educated Davis made himself a highly lucrative career as the author of sentimental melodramas (*Nellie, the Beautiful Cloak Model* etc) – pieces which included the occasional musical number, to which Davis was happy to provide such lyrics as were required – before the market for such shows was killed by the rise of the movies. He moved on to try his talents in the profitable purlieus of Broadway and there made his mark with a number of successful comedies and with some more serious pieces, one of which (*Icebound*) won him a Pulitzer Prize (1923).

His few purpose-built musicals did not range as widely in value as his plays. In fact, they were flops. His earliest such pieces were touring musicals played on far from the best circuits, and the first effort of his second career saw the Broadway-bound Shubert production of his *Page Mr Cupid*, with Ernest Truex starred, fold on the road. However, he had a major musical theatre success, at one step removed, when his play *The Nervous Wreck* (1922) was used as the source for the hit musical *Whoopee* (New Amsterdam Theater, 4 December 1928) with Eddie Cantor in its leading rôle. As a result of this hit, the next musical theatre months brought further Davis adaptations. His *Easy Come, Easy Go* (1925) was turned into *Lady Fingers* (Vanderbilt Theater, 31 January 1929) for Eddie Buzzell (132 performances) and he adapted his own *Shotgun Wedding* as the text for the Rodgers and Hart musical *Spring is Here* (104 performances).

A second collaboration with Rodgers and Hart, and with producers Aarons and Freedley, on a piece called *Me for You*, folded up after a fortnight's try-out and was transformed by other hands into *Heads Up!* (1929), whilst a final return to the musical theatre, eight years later, brought another failure with the 60 performance run of *Virginia*.

1901 **Circus Day** (George E Nichols) Metropolis Theater 30 September
1905 **How Baxter Butted In** (various) Murray Hill Theater 13 November

1907 **Cupid at Vassar** (A Baldwin Sloane/w George Totten Smith) Waterbury, Conn 23 August

1920 **Page Mr Cupid** (Jean Schwartz/Blanche Merrill) Crescent Theater, Brooklyn 17 May

1929 **Spring is Here** (Richard Rodgers/Lorenz Hart) Alvin Theater 11 March

1929 **Me for You** (Rodgers/Hart) Shubert Theater, Detroit 15 September

1937 **Virginia** (Arthur Schwartz/Albert Stillman/w Laurence Stallings) Center Theater 2 September

Autobiography: *I'd Like To Do it Again* (Farrar & Rinehart, New York, 1931), *My First Fifty Years in the Theater* (Walter H Baker, Boston, 1950)

DAVIS, Sammy, jr

DAVIS, Sammy, jr (b New York, 8 December 1925; d Los Angeles, 16 May 1990). Charismatic little song-and-dance man who made occasional stage musical appearances.

Davis began his career as a juvenile dancer and impressionist in a variety act with his father, Sammy Davis, and his uncle, Will Mastin, before embracing stage and film acting. His first appearance on the musical stage was in *Mr Wonderful* (1956, Charlie Welch) in which he appeared alongside his father and uncle as a rising young nightclub performer who bore more than a passing resemblance to himself. His performance helped both the song 'Too Close for Comfort' and *Mr Wonderful* to different degrees of success.

In a career mixing nightclub performing, variety, recording, stage and film, Davis appeared as Sportin' Life in the movie version of *Porgy and Bess* (1959), returned to the stage as the hero of a musical version of Clifford Odets's boxing play *Golden Boy* (1964), which he played in both America and Britain, appeared as the Street Singer in the 1963 film of *Die Dreigroschenoper* and as Big Daddy in Hollywood's version of *Sweet Charity* (1968). He also appeared several times on the stage in the very central rôle of Littlechap in the musical *Stop the World ... I Want to Get Off* (State Theater 1978 etc), the principal work of songwriters Anthony Newley and Leslie Bricusse, whose torchy, self-interrogating ballads were latterly a basic part of his act.

Autobiography: w Boyar, J & B: *Yes, I Can* (Farrar, Strauss & Giroux, New York, 1966), *Hollywood in a Suitcase* (Morrow, New York, 1980), *Why Me?* (Farrar, Strauss & Giroux, New York, 1989)

DAVIS, Thomas B[uffen]

DAVIS, Thomas B[uffen] (b London, 27 March 1867; d Tunbridge Wells, 14 December 1931).

Tom Davis, a former solicitor who had spent some years finding himself a place in the theatre, entered West End management when he picked up the rights to the musical *Little Miss Nobody*, which the actor Yorke Stephens had staged at the Cheltenham Opera House for one shop-window performance. He brought *Little Miss Nobody* to London in a season when the town was quite buzzing with outstanding new pieces and, cleverly cast and carefully staged, at a time when it was more usual to fix up a show after it had opened rather than before, he succeeded, against all expectations, in coming out with a hit.

Davis secured a long lease on the Lyric Theatre, where *Little Miss Nobody* was playing, and he followed that show first with an English version of Varney's *L'Amour mouillé* and, when that failed to take, with a season by De Wolf

Hopper and his American company in *El Capitan*, while he prepared what was to be his big play for success, the first musical by top songwriter Leslie Stuart and librettist-of-the-hour Owen Hall. When *Florodora* was produced, in November 1899, Davis found himself with a bigger hit on his hands than anyone could have envisaged. A year and a half's run at the Lyric was only the very beginning of a fabulous national and international career for the show.

Stuart and Hall's follow-up, *The Silver Slipper*, had a good if not outstanding run, but Davis's attempt to take on the reconstructed Adelphi Theatre, renamed the New Century, with an American musical comedy, *The Whirl of the Town*, foundered and a re-pairing of Hall and his *Geisha* partner, Sidney Jones, produced an unexpected flop in *The Medal and the Maid* (1903).

Davis was forced to give up the Lyric Theatre and, when he returned to town the following year with *Mr Popple of Ippleton*, he took a lease on the next-door Apollo Theatre instead. Both *Mr Popple* and the subsequent *The Belle of Brittany* (1908) did well enough, but an English version of *Le Sire de Vergy* (1905) and Sidney Jones's *A Persian Princess* (1909) were disasters, and another severe failure with the Austro-American musical *The Grass Widows* (1912) ended Davis's series of musical productions damply.

The Apollo Theatre nevertheless flourished as a musical house under Davis's leasehold, and for an extended period housed H G Pelissier's *Follies*, the pierrot show-cum-revue which Davis had been instrumental in bringing to London. After his peak period was past, he long retained an interest in the theatre in Birmingham, where he was responsible for the construction of the city's Theatre Royal.

DAWN, Hazel

DAWN, Hazel [LA TOUT, Hazel Dawn] (b Ogden, Utah, 23 March 1891; d New York, 28 August 1988). An extremely attractive girl from Utah who launched her career in musical theatre before going on to further success as an actress.

At the age of 18, Hazel Dawn, who had prepared herself for a musical career by studying voice and violin on the Continent and at London's Royal College of Music, made her musical comedy début in a tiny featured rôle in Frank Curzon's production of *Dear Little Denmark* at London's Prince of Wales Theatre. She segued into another bit part in the same management's *The Balkan Princess* and then into another, in George Edwardes's production of *The Dollar Princess*. However, she had to return to America to win her big break. In 1911 she was cast in the leading rôle of the Broadway production of Ivan Caryll's *The Pink Lady*, an enormous success which established her as a star and allowed her to return to Britain in that capacity for a season of *The Pink Lady* at the Globe Theatre, blondely performing the famous Pink Lady waltz song, 'My Beautiful Lady', and accompanying herself on the violin.

She followed up as another French demi-mondaine, Gaby Gaufrette – Queen of the Night Restaurants, in Caryll's musical version of Tristan Bernard's *The Little Café* (1913), equipped with another winning waltz-song ('Just Because It's You') and then, less successfully, as the daughter of an English lord who is *The Débutante* of the title in Victor Herbert and Harry B Smith's 1914 musical. After this production she abandoned the musical theatre for Ziegfeld revue (*The Century Girl*), film (a detective disguised as a nurse in *The Lone Wolf, Under Cover* etc) and the straight theatre (*Getting Gertie's Garter, Up in Mabel's Room*) before settling down, in 1931, to more than a half-century of retirement which included a stint as a caster for J Walter Thompson.

Miss Dawn's sister, Margaret Romaine, followed the same studies in Europe, sang at the Opéra-Comique, and returned to America to take a leading rôle in the Broadway musical *The Midnight Girl*, and her daughter, who billed herself as Hazel Dawn jr, also had a small and rather unprepossessing career in musicals (Susan van Tuyl in *My Romance* etc).

DAY, Edith (b Minneapolis, Minn, 10 April 1896; d London, 2 May 1971). Pretty, sweet-voiced ingénue who starred in some of the biggest musical hits of the American and British stage during the 1910s and 1920s.

Edith Day first appeared on the New York stage in support of Mitzi in the Hungaro-American musical *Pom-Pom* at the Casino Theatre in 1916 (Evelyn). She subsequently played a supporting rôle in the Anna Held vehicle *Follow Me* (1916, Denise) and toured as the principal ingénue in *His Little Widows* before landing her first Broadway lead rôle as Grace Douglas in George M Cohan and Sam Harris's highly successful production of *Going Up* at the Liberty Theatre (1917), singing and dancing the show's hit number, 'The Tickle Toe'. This success was followed by an even greater one, when she created the rôle of Irene O'Dare in Carle Carleton's production of *Irene*, introducing 'Alice Blue Gown', opposite Walter Regan at New York's Vanderbilt Theatre and (having briefly become Mrs Carle Carleton), opposite her next (and equally brief) husband, Pat Somerset, at the Empire Theatre, London. During her days with Carleton, the producer also attempted to launch her as a film actress in Crest Pictures's *The Grain of Dust* (1918), but the success the little dark actress had won on the stage was not repeated on the screen.

An attempt to follow up the memorable hit of *Irene* with a weak British imitation of the show called *Jenny* (1922) at the same London theatre was a flop and Miss Day returned to America where she added to her tally of successes when she created the musical version of the famous Kitty of *The Marriage of Kitty* in Victor Herbert's musical of the play entitled *Orange Blossoms* (1922, 'A Kiss in the Dark'). She made yet another musical comedy hit when she starred as Nina Benedetto, the heroine of the Vincent Youmans musical *Wildflower* (1923, 'Bambalina'), before again visiting Britain to play the title-rôle, created in New York by Mary Ellis, in the triumphant London version of *Rose Marie* (1925) at the Theatre Royal, Drury Lane.

She followed up with equal success, at the same theatre, as Margot Bonvalet in *The Desert Song* (1927) and as Magnolia Hawkes in *Show Boat* (1928), establishing herself over a period of some four years as one of London's top singing heroines, but the failures of *Rio Rita* (1930, Rita) at the Prince Edward Theatre, of Friml's *Luana* (1932, Luana), which failed to reach London, and of *Sunny River* (1934, Lolita) at the Piccadilly Theatre were relieved only by repeat appearances as Rose Marie and Margot before her ingénue career was done.

In 1962 Noël Coward, hearing that she was in money difficulties, persuaded producer Harold Fielding to offer

Plate 68. **Edith Day** *and Sydney Arnold as Noël Coward's Mr and Mrs Sweeney, the dear old couple who hate one another, in* Sail Away.

her the rôle of Mrs Sweeney in *Sail Away*. She paired with Sydney Arnold in one of the show's high points as the dear old couple who hate one another in 'Bronxville Darby and Joan'.

A DAY IN HOLLYWOOD, A NIGHT IN THE UKRAINE Musical double feature by Dick Vosburgh. Music by Frank Lazarus. New End Theatre, London, 15 January 1979; May Fair Theatre, 26 March 1979.

The work of American comedy writer Vosburgh and South African musician/performer Lazarus, *A Day in Hollywood, A Night in the Ukraine* was first produced at North London's New End Theatre, a tiny fringe-theatre venue transformed from a morgue. Its Hollywood part featured a number of revusical items, old and new, on movie-mag topics ('I Love a Film Cliché', 'Movie Fan's Love Song', 'All God's Chillun Got Movie Shows', 'Goldwyn and Warner and Mayer and Zanuck and Zukor and Cohn') as performed by a group of six cinema ushers, whilst the second part had the same artists giving a performance of a little musical comedy based on Chekhov's *The Bear*, played in the style of a Marx brothers film. Lazarus gave an uncanny impersonation of Chico, whilst Sheila Steafel, mutely plucking unheard music from the spokes of a bicycle wheel, was an unforgettable Harpo.

Under the management of Helen Montagu, the little show transferred to the larger May Fair Theatre, where it found an audience for 168 performances, but a Broadway production of a truly coloured-up version, mounted by Alexander H Cohen, did very much better. The cheerful end-of-the-pier material of the first half was cut away and replaced by American material old (a Richard Whiting songbook) and new to newish (three Jerry Herman songs including the wonderfully woeful saga 'The Best in the World') and some glittering choreography by Tommy Tune, and the resultant entertainment garnered a handful of Broadway awards and a long run (588 performances).

An updated version of *A Night in the Ukraine* was produced in Washington, DC in 1991 (23 October).

USA: John Golden Theater 1 May 1980

DE ANGELIS, [Thomas] Jefferson (b San Francisco, 30 November 1859; d Orange, NJ, 20 March 1933). For more than 30 years one of the classiest comic actors in the Broadway musical theatre, de Angelis introduced comedy rôles in many of the earliest American comic operas and musical comedies of the modern era.

After youthful experience in vaudeville, the 21-year-old son of theatrical parents put together a dramatic company with which he took to the roads not only of America but of Australia and the Orient, for some four years. He began by purveying a 'protean drama' *One Word* in which, teamed with his sister Sally de Angelis, he appeared as old Karl Hoffnung, a German musician, as his son Karl, as Max, a stockbroker, and as Schnitzberg, a grocer, giving songs and banjo solos in between the moments of drama and sentiment and costume-change. He later included versions of the Gilbert and Sullivan musicals and several French musical shows amongst his presentations. After returning home and recovering from these efforts, he found himself a more probable niche as an actor in musical farce-comedy and he made his first Broadway appearance as Herman Zwugg in *A Bottle of Ink* in 1885.

He now recognized that low comedy rather than high drama was his forte, and joined the McCaull Opera Company, appearing in good comedy rôles in the comic opera seasons of 1887–9 at Wallack's Theater, other New York venues and also on the road. Amongst the rôles which he played for McCaull were Girafo in *Jacquette* (*La Béarnaise*), Cyprian in *Prinz Methusalem*, D'Effiat in Dellinger's *Lorraine*, Sir Mulberry Mullitt in Audran's *Indiana*, Scalza in *Boccaccio*, Clausen in Suppé's *Bellman* and Don Cristoval in the same composer's *Clover* (*Die Jagd nach dem Glück*), Giles in Czibulka's *The May Queen* (*Der Glücksritter*) and Momo in the unsuccessful production of Dellinger's *Capitän Fracasse*, as well as comedy parts in *Ruddigore*, *Falka*, *Der Bettelstudent*, *Princess Ida*, *The Mikado* and in two new native pieces, *The Lady or the Tiger* (Menander) and *The Begum* (Jhustt-Naut).

During 1890 he appeared at the Casino Theater opposite Lillian Russell and Fanny Rice in the title-rôle of Millöcker's *Der arme Jonathan*, and over the next five years was featured at that theatre in another series of principal comic rôles in imported comic operas: Hellmesberger's *Apollo* (Adrastas), *La Grande-Duchesse* (Puck), *Indigo* (Ali Baba), *The Tyrolean* (*Der Vogelhändler*, Tipple), *Oncle Célestin* (Pontaillac), Millöcker's *The Child of Fortune* (*Das Sonntagskind*, Tristan) and *The Vice Admiral* (Punto) and *The Little Trooper* (*Les 28 Jours de Clairette*, Gibard), before moving on to yet another series of musical shows, this time American-made works.

He supported Lillian Russell in De Koven's *The Tzigane* (1895, Vasili), got above the title for the first time in William Furst's *Fleur-de-Lis* (1895, Comte des Escarbilles)

and then starred in Ludwig Englander's *The Caliph* (1896, Hardluck XIII) and in three Julian Edwards musicals, *Brian Boru* (1895, Pat O'Hara), *The Wedding Day* (1897, Polycop) and *The Jolly Musketeer* (1898, Comte de Beaupret), the last of which provided him with rather longer employment than the others, through two years of touring. *A Royal Rogue* (1900, Baptiste Ballou), which starred him alongside Josephine Hall, was a quick failure, but he was well provided with the rôle of Professor Bunn in Edward German's *The Emerald Isle* in New York and on the road and followed this up with another English musical, appearing around America as Sammy Gigg (played by Francis Wilson on Broadway) in *The Toreador*, under his own management.

His biggest success as a musical comedy star came with the Robert Smith/Raymond Hubbell *Fantana* (1905, Hawkins), a success which was not repeated with Edwards's *The Girl and the Governor* (1906–7), but he returned more happily in *The Beauty Spot* (1909) playing a comedy character called General Samovar, dreamed up by his fellow comedian-cum-writer Joseph Herbert and set to music by De Koven. In 1910 he appeared as the Mikado in the starry *Mikado* at the Casino and the following year toured for H H Frazee and George Lederer in his own musical *The Ladies' Lion*, but the best moments of his career had now passed, and passed without him having really found the one outstanding rôle with which he could be identified.

Over the next dozen years he continued to work in the musical theatre, playing New York and/or the road in such pieces as *The Pearl Maiden* (1912, Pinkerton Kerr), *Madame Moselle* (1914), the short-lived Fritzi Scheff vehicle *Husbands Guaranteed* (1916), revivals of De Koven's *Rob Roy* and *The Highwayman* and of the veteran farce-comedy *A Trip to Chinatown*, and alongside Gertrude Lawrence in the unsuccessful *Rock-a-Bye Baby* (1919). He even appeared as Bumerli in *The Chocolate Soldier* when over 60 years of age. His final appearance in the Broadway musical theatre was as Nitsch in a revival of *The Merry Widow* (1921/2).

In 1915 de Angelis made a new attempt at being a manager when he set up a summer stock company to play comic opera at Lancaster, Pennyslvania. When the local sponsor failed to come up with the first week's wages, he was obliged to produce $1,000 from his own pocket before shutting down the company.

Autobiography: w Harlow, A: *Vagabond Trouper* (Harcourt, Brace, New York, 1931)

DEAREST ENEMY American musical comedy in 2 acts by Herbert Fields. Lyrics by Lorenz Hart. Music by Richard Rodgers. Knickerbocker Theater, New York, 18 September 1925.

Following Broadway's discovery of Rodgers and Hart's work in *The Garrick Gaieties*, the writers were able at last to get a production for the musical play which they had been auditioning around town for the past year. *Dearest Enemy*, set in the American revolution, had its heroine Betsy Burke (Helen Ford) and her female friends waylaying the British, and notably the gallant Captain Sir John Copeland (Charles Purcell), with their charms long enough to allow a cornered detachment of American troops to make their escape and assemble for battle. Betsy and Sir John fall in love, but the girl nevertheless carries out her part in the plan which results in an American victory in which John is taken captive. General Washington is the deus ex machina who brings the happy ending in the last scene.

The highlight of the show's score was Purcell and Miss Ford's performance of the love duet which climaxed the first act, 'Here in My Arms'. Flavia Arcaro as Mrs Murray led the girls of the piece in both lamenting ('Heigh-ho, lackaday') and appreciating ('War is War') the state of war, and performed two pieces in the entertainment designed to keep the British soldiers from thoughts of leaving her house ('The Hermits', 'Full Blown Roses', 'Where the Hudson River Flows'). The two lovers joined in two further duets, 'Bye and Bye' and 'Here's a Kiss', (both of which had been picked by the out-of-town critics as hit material above 'Here In My Arms'), alongside Betsy's admission of her love, 'I'd Like to Hide It'. Mrs Murray's daughter Jane (Helen Spring) and her officer, Captain Harry Tryon (John Seymour) provided the traditional soubret moments ('I Beg Your Pardon', 'Sweet Peter').

In spite of the concurrence of *The Vagabond King, Sunny* and *No, No, Nanette*, all of which opened in New York at around the same time as *Dearest Enemy*, and in spite of predictions that the piece would prove too serious in its subject-matter for popular consumption, George Ford's production had a fine 36-week, 286-performance run at the Knickerbocker Theater, setting the Broadway foundation-stone for the long and memorable career of the Rodgers and Hart partnership. It subsequently went on the road in America, but found its only taker outside its homeland in a J C Williamson Ltd Australian production. Dot Brunton (Betsy), Maidie Hope (Mrs Murray) and Sydney Burchall (John) starred in a version peppered with interpolated songs for a disappointing month and a half in Melbourne (Theatre Royal, 12 September 1931) and less than a month in Sydney.

A proposed 1931 Broadway revival, under Ford's management, was called off before making it to the stage, but the show was seen again when it was revived at the Goodspeed Opera House in 1976.

Australia: Her Majesty's Theatre, Sydney 7 March 1931
Recording: studio cast (Beginners Records)

DEARLY, Max [ROLLAND, Lucien Paul Marie Joseph] (b Paris, 22 November 1874; d Neuilly, 2 June 1943). Long-time star of the French musical, comic and variety stages, who also worked as a director and a writer.

After ten years performing in the French provinces, Dearly moved to Paris and settled in at the Scala café-concert where, between 1898–1900, he wrote and performed a series of comic songs which won him considerable popularity. He joined the company of the Théâtre des Variétés in 1901, and soon established himself there as a Parisian favourite in comedy rôles. In his first years at the Variétés he appeared as Mercury in *Orphée aux enfers*, in the première of Terrasse's *Le Sire de Vergy* where he later graduated to the title-rôle, as St Guillaume in *Chonchette*, as Tourillon in the first regular performance of a French version of *Die Fledermaus*, in such classics as *La Vie parisienne, Le Petit Duc* and *L'Oeil crevé*, in the French version of *The Country Girl*, and as Radaboum in the première of *Le Paradis de Mahomet*, the last work of Planquette.

In the years that followed, he appeared in a rich list of

plays and musical pieces both at the Variétés and at other Parisian theatres, as well as playing in the music halls where he was responsible for writing and creating 'La Danse apache', the treat-'em-rough athletic dance routine, performed to Offenbach's *Papillon* music, which became for a while the sort-of-sadistic sensation of Paris (Moulin-Rouge, 1908) and later the rest of the world. With few original native pieces of distinction giving him the kind of opportunities he might capitalize on (*La Reine s'amuse, Boulard et ses filles* etc), Dearly appeared largely in the classic musical repertoire – Golo in *Geneviève de Brabant*, Bobinet then Gondremarck in *La Vie parisienne*, Trenitz in *La Fille de Madame Angot*, Calchas in *La Belle Hélène* – as well as in French versions of foreign works – Imari in *The Geisha*, Simplicitas in *The Arcadians*, Baron des Aubrais in *La Chaste Suzanne* (*Die keusche Susanne*) – and, working in an individual style which mixed a relaxed kind of comedy with a sufficient singing voice, established himself as one of the great performers of the French musical theatre of his era.

First seen in Britain in a visit to the St George's Hall with the Théâtre des Capucines company and *Chonchette* early in his career, he later worked there in variety and in 1915 appeared for a time at the Winter Garden Theatre under the management of Grossmith and Laurillard in the rôle of Pedro, created by Maurice Farkoa, in the London production of *Tonight's the Night*.

Dearly had a hand in the adaptation of *The Arcadians* for its French performance and in the libretto for the 1931 musical *Billy-Bill* (Scala 1931), and also worked in later years as a director, staging the first French production of Messager's *Monsieur Beaucaire* at the Théâtre Marigny, a lavish *La Vie parisienne* (1931, also played Gondremarck) and the vast and starry *Orphée aux enfers* (1931, also played Jupiter) at the Mogador.

DEAR MISS PHOEBE Musical play in 2 acts by Christopher Hassall, adapted from J M Barrie's play *Quality Street*. Music by Harry Parr Davies. Phoenix Theatre, London, 13 October 1950.

A tasteful musical adaptation of Barrie's hit play of 1902 in which the dowdied Phoebe Throssel (Carole Raye) poses as her own bright, young niece to win back the love of Valentine Brown (Peter Graves) whom she lost to the Napoleonic wars. A chastely English score ('Whisper While You Waltz', 'Living a Dream', 'Spring will Sing a Song for You') turned up one enduring number in the all but patriotic duet 'I Leave My Heart in an English Garden'. Eight months in London prefaced a tidy tour.

An earlier *Quality Street* musical, *Drei alte Schachteln* (Walter Kollo/Rideamus/Herman Haller) was a considerable success in Germany, but a brisk Broadway flop (*Phoebe of Quality Street*, Shubert Theater, 9 May 1921).

DEAR WORLD Musical in 2 acts by Jerome Lawrence and Robert E Lee based on *The Madwoman of Chaillot* by Jean Giraudoux. Mark Hellinger Theater, New York, 6 February 1969.

Following the success of *Mame*, authors Lawrence and Lee, composer Jerry Herman and star Angela Lansbury came together in a second musical which allowed the star to portray a flamboyantly eccentric woman of a certain age. The rôle of Giraudoux's Countess Aurelia – the Madwoman of Chaillot who pits herself against the horrid

Plate 69. **Dédé**: *James Sparrow (Dédé) and the vendeuses of his Parisian love-nest shoe-shop ... a staff borrowed from a nightclub chorus!*

Developers to save her 'Dear World' from pollution and destruction – gave the star at least as many splendid opportunities as its predecessor, if in a very different style. However, *Dear World*'s more sophisticated tone and delightful, though less obvious, score (including a loopy tea party scene which remains one of Herman's finest pieces of writing) did not have the same general appeal as the earlier show and Alexander H Cohen's Broadway production won only a disappointing 132-performance run.

Recording: original cast (Columbia)

DÉDÉ Opérette in 3 acts by Albert Willemetz. Music by Henri Christiné. Théâtre des Bouffes-Parisiens, Paris, 10 November 1921.

After Willemetz and Christiné had sent the new jazz-age comédie musicale into orbit with the incomparable *Phi-Phi*, it remained to be seen with what they would follow their hit of an era. In fact, they followed it with another hit, one which stuck to the smallish-scale musical comedy lines they had established (there were now six chorus girls and even some chorus men, which there had not been in the previous piece) but which, otherwise, was completely different in its text and style.

Dédé (which traded on the connection with *Phi-Phi* in its title, at least) was an up-to-date story of jazz-age naughtiness, set in a modern shoe shop, where the owner, Dédé de la Huchette (Urban), is trying to set up an affair with Odette (Maguy Warna), an apparently married woman he has met at a tango-tea. Dédé is adored by his head assistant, Denise (Alice Cocéa), who is, in turn, sighed after demonstratively by her last employer, the lawyer Leroydet (Baron fils), and everybody, at some stage during the proceedings, gets a cheerfully useless helping hand from Dédé's irritating, penniless, self-confident old chum, Robert (Maurice Chevalier). The comedy, full of extremely funny and almost inevitably sex-based situations, zipped along cheerfully in the hands of such experienced performers as Urban, *Phi-Phi* star Mlle Cocéa, and of the music-hall's Chevalier, making his musical theatre début as the blandly laid-back Robert.

Christiné's score was full of catchy, lilting songs. Chevalier had all the cream, expressing his shruglful philosophy in 'Dans la vie faut pas s'en faire', singing cheerfully

about his sexual laissez-aller in 'Je m'donne' and joining Mlle Cocéa for the lazily bouncing 'Si j'avais su'. All three songs became hits. There were, however, plenty of good things for all in the score of *Dédé*, not only in the way of solos but also in some highly comical ensembles, as exemplified by the second-act finale in which Dédé and Robert invent a play within a play to give the opportunity for the compromised Odette to escape unseen from her shoe-shop rendez-vous ('Une femme de monde trompait son mari').

Dédé had a highly successful first run of seven months, returning, after the summer had been filled with a *Phi-Phi* revival, in the autumn for the second half of its run through nearly six months more. It was revived in Paris in 1927, filmed in 1934 with a cast headed by Albert Préjean, Danielle Darrieux, Mireille Perrey, Baron fils and Claude Dauphin, played regularly throughout France in tours and provincial productions, revived again in 1973 (Théâtre des Nouveautés) with the popular singer Antoine in Chevalier's rôle and the English actor James Sparrow as Dédé, and brought back to the Paris stage yet again in 1981 (Théâtre de la Renaissance) whilst keeping up a regular presence in the French provinces culminating in a major revival at Lyon's Théâtre des Célestins with Sparrow and Jean-Paul Lucet in 1992 (27 November).

The Paris success encouraged both Charles Cochran in London and Charles Dillingham on Broadway to go after the show and its star, and negotiations got far enough for each of them to announce a forthcoming production with Chevalier starring, but neither happened. America did not see *Dédé* at all, whilst London got a damaged version (ad Ronald Jeans) produced by André Charlot and Paul Murray, starring Guy Le Feuvre (Robert), Joe Coyne (Dédé) and the young Gertrude Lawrence (Denise). Coyne was top-billed, and thus got 'Si j'avais su' and 'Dans la vie faut pa s'en faire' ('Trouble Never Troubles Me') as well as a couple of Phil Braham extras ('There's a Proper Time', 'Collecting Girls'). This *Dédé* survived only 46 performances, before it was frilled up with extraneous revusical material and sent on the road under the title *The Talk of the Town*.

UK: Garrick Theatre 17 October 1922; Film: René Guissart 1934

Recordings: complete with dialogue (Decca), 1973 revival cast (RCA)

DE FRECE, Lauri [DE FRECE, Maurice] (b Liverpool, 1880; d Deauville, 25 August 1921). Favourite British musical theatre comedian of the early part of the 20th century, whose career was cut short by a premature death.

The son of Henry De Frece (b 1835; d 28 January 1931), and the grandson of Isaac De Frece (d 6 August 1902), Liverpool theatre and music-hall proprietors for over half a century, little Lauri de Frece began a career as a musical comedian in his early twenties. He toured for a considerable time with George Dance's travelling versions of George Edwardes's musicals, notably as Chambuddy Ram in *The Cingalee*, and in the South African musical comedy company of Sass & Nelson, and had his first London success as Sebak, the comical keeper of the crocodiles, in Philip Michael Faraday and Frederick Fenn's comic opera *Amasis* (1906). He followed this with further personal successes as the chauffeur, Yarker, in Ada Reeve's production of *Butterflies* (1908) and as Blatz in Frank Curzon's production of *The Balkan Princess* (1910). He joined George Edwardes to tour as Van Eyck in *The Girl on the Train*, then moved to town and Daly's Theatre to replace W H Berry in *The Count of Luxemburg* (1911, Brissard) and to appear as Kajetan in *Gipsy Love* (1912).

He played older rôles in the tour of *Gipsy Love* (Dragotin) and in Robert Courtneidge's productions of *The Pearl Girl* (1913, Jecks) and *The Cinema Star* (1914, Josiah), then joined Grossmith and Laurillard for their American production of *Tonight's the Night* (1914, Henry). The rising Leslie Henson took the rôle of Henry for London, and de Frece moved back to Daly's to succeed Berry again, this time in *Betty* (Achille Jotte), before, the following Christmas, he finally found his best own part since *Amasis* when he created the comedy rôle of little wife-fleeing Antonio in *The Maid of the Mountains* (1917), pairing memorably with Mabel Sealby in 'Husbands and Wives' and holding a comical conversation with a lobster in the same manner that he had chatted to *Amasis*'s crocodile a decade earlier. He played this rôle for the three and a half years of the show's run, but was stricken with peritonitis whilst sailing on Solly Joel's yacht, 18 months later, and died not long after his fortieth birthday.

His wife, **Fay Compton** (b 18 September 1894; d 12 December 1978) (formerly the wife of *Follies* impresario, H G Pelissier, and later of two others) also appeared in *The Pearl Girl*, *The Cinema Star* and *Tonight's the Night* (USA) and played in the London version of Victor Herbert's *The Only Girl* before beginning a career in the straight theatre which made her a major star in pieces ranging from *Hamlet* (Ophelia to Gielgud's Hamlet) and *Blithe Spirit* (Ruth) to *The Little Foxes* (Regina) and *Autumn Crocus* (Fanny Grey). She appeared regularly as a pantomime principal boy, but in 1943 she returned briefly to the musical stage to play Ivan Caryll's *The Duchess of Dantzic* on tour for Bernard Delfont.

A brother, [Sir] Walter De Frece (b Liverpool, 7 October 1870; d 7 January 1935), continued the family interest in theatre property, controlling a wide circuit of Hippodromes throughout the country and running the De Frece Circuit of vaudeville entertainments whilst also acting as a Member of Parliament. He was married to the music-hall vocalist and male impersonator Vesta Tilley (b Worcester, 13 May 1864; d Monte Carlo, 16 September 1952) who made occasional appearances on the musical stage, notably as *Randolph the Reckless* in Victor Stephens's touring extravaganza (1891), in the burlesque *Cartouche & Co* (1892) and, briefly and unsuitably, on Broadway in the title-rôle of the comedy opera *My Lady Molly* (1904).

DEFREYN, Henri Charming, light comedy leading man, with more of a tenorish baritone singing voice than most such, who found his most famous rôle as France's first Danilo in *La Veuve joyeuse*.

Defreyn made his first appearance on the stage in his native Brussels, in the première of the aged Lecocq's opérette *Yetta* (1903), and he moved swiftly to Paris where his elegant stage presence and pleasant light baritone won him rôles at the Bouffes-Parisiens (*La Fille de la mère Michel*, 1903), at the Boîte à Fursy (*Le Chien d'Alcibiade*, *Le Retour du quincaillaire*, 1905) and at the Théâtre des

Variétés, where he took the juvenile leading rôle of the Prince in Planquette's last work, *Le Paradis de Mahomet* (1906), playing opposite Juliette Méaly and alongside Max Dearly, Baron and Amélie Diéterle.

The following year, he was the hero of Cuvillier's *Son p'tit frère* (Agathos) at the Capucines, playing for the first time opposite Marguerite Deval, with whom he paired effectively for a second time in Ivan Caryll's French musical *S.A.R.* (1908) and, again, as the sexually frustrated hero of Cuvillier's *Afgar* (1909). He also appeared in a further Cuvillier work, *Rendezvous strasbourgeois* (1908, Muller) with Anna Tariol-Baugé at the Comédie-Royale and introduced Belgium to the distinctly successful Greek fun of *Son p'tit frère*.

His most important opportunity to date came when he created the rôle of Danilo in the French version of *Die lustige Witwe* (*La Veuve joyeuse*) at the Apollo in 1909 and, in the some five years which followed, he remained at that theatre playing a mixture of Viennese imports and largely new French works, peppered with repeated repeat seasons of *La Veuve joyeuse*. Amongst the translated rôles which he created for the French stage at this time were *Rêve de valse* (*Ein Walzertraum*, Niki), *La Divorcée* (*Die geschiedene Frau*, Karl von Lysseveghe), *Le Comte de Luxembourg* (René), *Le Soldat de Chocolat* (*Der tapfere Soldat*, Bumerli) and *La Chaste Suzanne* (*Die keusche Susanne*, Hubert), whilst the mostly less impressive list of creations included Baron Placide in Terrasse's *Monsieur de la Palisse* (1913), de Tiercé in the same composer's *Les Transatlantiques* (1911), Hirchmann's *Les Petites Étoiles* (1912), Lattès' *La Jeunesse dorée* (1913, Lord Sweet), Ganne's *Cocorico* (1913, Chamaillac) and the first Paris performances of his *Hans, le joueuer de flûte* (1910, Yoris) and of Xavier Leroux's *La Fille de Figaro* (1914, Sanchez). The occasional classic revival gave him the opportunity to be seen in such a rôle as Pippo in *La Mascotte*.

Defreyn visited London to play in the tryout of *Véronique* at the Adelphi Theatre (1915) and, back at home, appeared in revivals of *La Fauvette du Temple* (Gaîté, 1914, Joseph) and *Son p'tit frère* and in such new pieces as *Le Poilu* (1916, Robert Valdier) at the Palais-Royal opposite the young Yvonne Printemps, *La Petite Dactylo* and Cuvillier's *La Fausse ingénue* (1918, Clerambault), mixing musical comedy with revue and comedy before joining the company at the Théâtre Edouard VII for four years (*Daphnis et Chloë*, *Rapatipatoum* etc). At the end of this engagement he moved on to star in further musicals – the Franco-British *Nelly* (1921, Roger d'Herblay), the Franco-American *La Dame en rose* (1921, Garidel), Messager's *La Petite Fonctionnaire* (1921, Le Vicomte), and repeats of his Apollo triumphs – before, his voice now having strengthened notably from the light, pleasant instrument of his earlier days, he at last created his most enduring rôle in a native work when he played Antonin, the lightly comical hero of Reynaldo Hahn's *Ciboulette*, alongside Edmée Favart in the piece's initial production (1923).

Defreyn switched eras with ease, leaving behind the old style of opérette to star in a number of postwar French jazz-age musical comedies including Szulc's *Flup..!* (1922, Duc Raymond de Florigny), Yvain's *Gosse de riche* (1924, André Sartène), *Les Amants légitimes* (1924) alongside Yvette Guilbert, *Bouche à bouche* (1925, Anatole), *Pouche* (1925, Bridier) and the Elys/Ménier *À Paris tous les deux*

(1926), and appeared still, periodically, as Danilo, 15 years after his original performances, but always with considerable success. In the late 1920s and the 1930s he was still elegantly in evidence in the French musical theatre, appearing in a whole variety of pieces ranging from Reynaldo Hahn's *Le Temps d'aimer* (1926, François Bucaille), a version of *Puss in Boots* called *Carabas et Cie*, and a pair of successful little Victor Alix musical comedies (Gaspard de Phalines in *Les Bleus de l'amour*, Julien de Château-Fronsac in *Mon amant!*) to the dashing central characters of the musical comedy *Le Groom s'en chargera* (1934, Jules Audincourt) produced at the Variétés, where he had first starred nearly 30 years earlier, and of George van Parys's *Ma petite amie* (1937), mounted at the Bouffes-Parisiens where he had made his first Paris appearance even longer ago.

DE GRÉSAC, Fred[érique Rosine] (b France, 1866; d Hollywood, 20 February 1943).

An enterprising journalist, author, playwright and social personality in turn-of-the-century Paris, Mme de Grésac won herself a certain notoriety during the Dreyfus case. Journalists having been forbidden to cover the case, the authorities were unable to discover how news was getting from the purposely out-of-town venue of the trial back to the *Figaro*. No one suspected the handsome, well-dressed society woman who made her way, each evening, back to the capital with all the news a paper could want.

In less exciting times and circumstances, Mme de Grésac was also the author of a number of plays, ranging from drawing room comedy to melodrama, and she had her biggest stage success, in collaboration with Francis de Croisset, with the play *La Passerelle* (*The Marriage of Kitty*), first produced in Paris in 1902. Another play, *La Troisième Lune* (1904, w Paul Ferrier) also found success and introduced its authoress to the musical theatre when it was adapted as a musical by Charles Brookfield, with music by Sidney Jones, and produced at London's Prince of Wales Theatre under the management of George Edwardes as *See See* (20 June 1906).

She subsequently moved, with her husband, the celebrated operatic baritone Victor Maurel, to the United States and there she wrote the libretti for several musicals, teamed with such seasoned practicioners as Victor Herbert and Harry B Smith, the most successful of which were Kitty Gordon's vehicle, *The Enchantress* ('I Want to Be a Primadonna', 'The Land of My Own Romance'), and the cute if confused bit of Ruritanian nonsense that was *Sweethearts*. She had a 'sleeper' success with the Silvio Hein musical *Flo-Flo*, provided the text for a 'scandalous' little vaudeville-circuits show called *The Bride Shop* whose scandal came largely from its inclusion of a fashion parade of feminine underwear, and in 1922 had her second Parisian play musicalized. *Orange Blossoms* (1922), produced by Edward Royce for a Broadway run of 95 performances, was a musical version of *La Passerelle*.

Her work was seen once more on the London stage when she was commissioned by José Collins and Robert Evett at London's Gaiety Theatre to provide a vehicle for the singer, based on the Continental hit *Die Siegerin*, in the character of Catherine the Great. As *Catherine* the piece ran 217 performances. And a decade further on she had one further Parisian credit, on the libretto of a pasticcio

Plate 70. **Fréderique de Grésac** – *better known as Fred* – *the author of libretti for the Paris and Broadway stages.*

343

musicalization of her old collaborator de Croisset's hit play *Le Bonheur, mesdames!*.

Mme de Grésac later moved to Hollywood where she became a successful author of film scenarios for such performers as Rudolph Valentino, Douglas Fairbanks and Lilian Gish. She died in Hollywood at the reported age of 75.

1911 **The Enchantress** (Victor Herbert/w Harry B Smith) New York Theater 19 October

1911 **The Wedding Trip** (Reginald De Koven/w H B Smith) Knickerbocker Theater 25 December

1913 **The Purple Road** (*Napoleon und die Frauen*) American version w William Cary Duncan (Liberty Theater)

1913 **Sweethearts** (Herbert/Robert B Smith/w Harry B Smith) New Amsterdam Theater 8 October

1917 **Flo-Flo** (Silvio Hein/Edward A Paulton) Cort Theater 20 December

1918 **The Bride Shop** (Hein, Walter Rosemont)

1922 **Orange Blossoms** (Herbert/B G De Sylva) Fulton Theater 19 September

1923 **Catherine** (*Die Siegerin*) English version w Reginald Arkell, Louis N Parker (Gaiety Theatre, London)

1934 **Le Bonheur, mesdames!** (Henri Christiné arr/w Francis de Croisset, Albert Willemetz) Théâtre des Bouffes-Parisiens 6 January

DE KOVEN [Henry Louis] Reginald (b Middleton, Conn, 3 April 1861; d Chicago, 15 January 1920). A prolific composer of comic opera for the American musical stage of the 1890s and 1900s, De Koven scored one enduring hit with his *Robin Hood* amongst a long series of often tidily attractive, if inherently old-fashioned, theatre scores.

At the age of 13, De Koven went to England, where he was educated at Oxford, then moved on to further studies in Germany, Austria (where he is said to have been musically coached by Genée and Suppé), and in France (where he took lessons with Delibes). He went into business on his return to America but, having made an advantageous marriage, soon retired from his desk to devote himself to composing music.

His first attempt at a comic opera, *The Begum*, written in conjunction with another neophyte, librettist Harry B Smith, was produced by John McCaull at New York's Fifth Avenue Theater with a fine cast including De Wolf Hopper, Mathilde Cottrelly, Jeff de Angelis and Hubert Wilke. It lasted only three weeks before being sent out of town, but in Chicago, where the De Kovens were socially important, it did rather better. *The Begum* was followed by a version of the *Don Quixote* tale, mounted by the enterprising light opera company, the Bostonians, with Henry Clay Barnabee as the Don. It was played fairly discreetly in their repertoire for only one season, but the company put their faith in De Koven and Smith a second time and came up very much more happily with a piece based on another famous character of literature and stage, *Robin Hood*. *Robin Hood*, with its neat, four-square comic-opera score and a traditional emphasis on low comedy in its book, was a major hit, proving one of the most successful home-made pieces to yet be played on the American musical stage and providing the cornerstone to its composer's career.

The writers of *Robin Hood* easily found takers for a run of further pieces in a similar style, but the results were uneven. *The Fencing Master* was produced, with Marie

Plate 71. **Reginald De Koven**: *The man who set* Robin Hood *to music.*

Tempest and Hubert Wilke starred, at the Casino Theater and won a fine run of more than three months, whilst the Bostonians brought out *The Knickerbockers*, a 'real New York operetta' with Camille D'Arville, Edwin Hoff, Barnabee and Jessie Bartlett Davis featured, and drew a very quick blank. Miss Tempest joined the composer again for *The Algerian*, and won another good run, but Smith was again on hand to provide the text for De Koven's second major success, a piece for which he brought to the American musical stage another British folk hero, *Rob Roy*. William Pruette starred in the title-rôle of a piece which was in no way inferior to *Robin Hood*, boasted some splendid songs, and won a first run of 168 performances, quickly brought up to the excellent total of some 200 nights by a return engagement.

Rob Roy was to remain De Koven's longest-running Broadway show, just as *Robin Hood* would remain his most popular and long-lived. Thereafter, his rather backward-looking light opera scores began to sound too much alike as well as being too little in tune with a public taste which was running more towards dance music and simple-rhythmed modern songs as its theatrical diet. In the following seasons, both *La Tzigane* (36 performances) with

Lillian Russell, Wilke and De Angelis and *The Mandarin* (40 performances) with Bertha Waltzinger and George Honey could muster only a little more than a month in New York, whilst *The Paris Doll* did not even make it to town. *The Highwayman*, produced by Andrew A McCormick, with Jerome Sykes in the chief comic rôle of Foxy Quiller, did altogether better, running up 126 Broadway performances, but when Sykes headed the production of *The Three Dragoons* the following season the result was mediocre (48 performances).

De Koven contributed to the music for a multiple-authored spectacular, *The Man in the Moon* (192 performances), and was called in by Florenz Ziegfeld to 'improve' the scores for Broadway versions of *La Femme à Papa* (combined with bits of *Mam'zelle Nitouche*) and its fellow vaudeville-opérette, *Niniche*, to serve as a vehicles for Anna Held, whilst Klaw and Erlanger, in their turn, commissioned the music for a sequel to *The Highwayman* for Sykes. *Foxy Quiller* lasted 50 Broadway performances, which was marginally less than another attempt at a musequel: a *Robin Hood* follow-up produced by the Bostonians under the title of *Maid Marian*.

The Jersey Lily played just 24 performances in New York, in spite of Blanche Ring's performance of the interpolated hit 'Bedelia', and Ziegfeld's production of the Ruritanian bandit piece *The Red Feather* with Grace van Studdiford starred played only 60 New York nights in spite of being housed in the brand new Lyric Theater, where De Koven had announced the foundation of his American School of Opera. The School lasted longer in Manhattan than *The Red Feather*, but not very much longer, and the operetta had a vigorous afterlife on the road. In the meanwhile, the Lyric had housed the composer's more successful venture into the whimsical fairy-tale world of *Happyland* with De Wolf Hopper (82 performances). Another Ruritanian piece, *The Student King*, with Lina Abarbanell starred, was done with in 40 Broadway performances, whilst a piece called *The Golden Butterfly*, written for neophyte producer-star Grace von Studdiford, did little better (48 performances), and the success obtained by the low-comical *The Beauty Spot* (137 performances) could not, in all fairness, have been said to owe much to its score.

Two further quick flops put an end to a career of a quarter of a century composing for the Broadway theatre. De Koven retired to journalism, writing music criticism for the *New York Herald*, and then to Chicago and, in his last years, turned out the scores for two light operas, *The Canterbury Pilgrims* (8 March 1917) and a *Rip van Winkle* (Chicago, 2 January 1920), produced just a few days before his death. His final attempt at a light musical piece, a semi-period piece called *Yesterday*, which transported its contemporary hero back to 1867 Paris to impersonate a Grand Duke, rehearsed ten weeks and died in two when the Shuberts cancelled its scheduled opening at Broadway's Broadhurst Theater and folded it away in Washington.

De Koven's career in the musical theatre was one which was regarded in very different ways by different of his contemporaries. To those critics, in particular, who had little time for the freer rhythms and looser, less academic harmonies of musical comedy, his traditional comic operas represented a step in the right direction, and he often won fine notices as a result. To others, he and his music were fossilized and dull, and his successes were attributed more

to the antics of the comedians than to the show's scores. There is also probably something in his own claim that his social and financial position, not to speak of his Oxfordized-manner and eyeglass, won him if not enemies at least happy detractors amongst those in and, more especially, those around the theatre. Looking back at his music, a century later, it is true that there is much in it that is academic and somewhat lifeless, but there are also a number of pages which are comic-operatic writing of a very attractive kind.

1887 **The Begum** (H B Smith) Fifth Avenue Theater 21 November
1889 **Don Quixote** (H B Smith) Boston Theater 18 November
1890 **Robin Hood** (H B Smith) Opera House, Chicago 9 June; Standard Theater, New York 28 September 1891
1892 **The Fencing Master** (H B Smith) Boston; Casino Theater, New York 14 November
1893 **The Knickerbockers** (H B Smith) Boston January; Garden Theater, New York 29 May 1893
1893 **The Algerian** (H B Smith) Garden Theater 26 October
1894 **Rob Roy** (H B Smith) Herald Square Theater 29 October
1895 **The Tzigane** (H B Smith) Abbey's Theater 16 May
1896 **The Mandarin** (H B Smith) Herald Square Theater 2 November
1897 **The Paris Doll** (H B Smith) Hartford, Conn, 14 September
1897 **The Highwayman** (H B Smith) Broadway Theater 13 December
1899 **The Three Dragoons** (H B Smith) Broadway Theater 30 January
1899 **The Man in the Moon** (w Ludwig Englander, Gustave Kerker/Louis Harrison, Stanislaus Stange) New York Theater 24 April
1899 **Papa's Wife** (*La Femme à Papa*) new score (Manhattan Theater)
1900 **Foxy Quiller** (H B Smith) Broadway Theater 5 November
1901 **The Little Duchess** (*Niniche*) new score (Casino Theater)
1902 **Maid Marian** (H B Smith) Garden Theater 27 January
1903 **The Jersey Lily** (George Hobart) Victoria Theater 14 September
1903 **The Red Feather** (Charles Emerson Cook/Charles Klein) Lyric Theater 9 November
1905 **Happyland** (Frederick Ranken) Lyric Theater 2 October
1906 **The Student King** (Stange, Ranken) Garden Theater 25 December
1907 **The Girls of Holland** (ex- *The Snowman*) (Stange) Lyric Theater 18 November
1908 **The Golden Butterfly** (H B Smith) Broadway Theater 12 October
1909 **The Beauty Spot** (Joseph Herbert) Herald Square Theater 10 April
1911 **The Wedding Trip** (H B Smith, Fred de Grésac) Knickerbocker Theater 25 December
1913 **Her Little Highness** (ex- *Queen Anna*) (Channing Pollock, Rennold Wolf) Liberty Theater 13 October
1919 **Yesterday** (Glen MacDonough) Playhouse, Wilmington 10 March

Biography: De Koven, Anna: *A Musician and His Wife* (Harper, New York, 1926)

DELACOUR, Alfred [LARTIGUE, Alfred Charlemagne] (b Bordeaux, ?1815; d Paris, 1883).

Originally a doctor, pharmacist and medical author, Delacour switched careers in 1847 and, although he continued to manufacture a pill which he had patented which apparently had vaunted effects on gout and rheumatism, he became instead the author of a long list of some 130 dramas and comedies, many written in association with such top-flight authors as Eugène Labiche, Clairville, Eugène Grangé, Marc-Michel and Maurice Hennequin, and dramas. The most widely successful of these were, on the humorous hand, the famous farces *Les Dominos roses* (w Alfred Hennequin) and *La Cagnotte* (w Labiche), and, on the dramatic, the equally famous *Le Courrier de Lyon* (w Paul Siraudin, Eugène Moreau). Delacour also collaborated on the texts of a wide-ranging set of musical theatre pieces including Offenbach's successful one-act opérette *Un mari à la porte*, a burlesque of Wagner's opera *Tannhäuser*, the internationally successful opéra-comique *Le Voyage en Chine*, and Paul Lacôme's most enduring opérette, the delightful *Jeanne, Jeannette et Jeanneton*.

In 1877 he joined with Victor Wilder to create two pieces with music by Johann Strauss but neither proved an enduring success. The pair fabricated a new libretto to some of the score of Strauss's *Die Fledermaus* for Paris (the original French basis to the Viennese work having been used without authority) and supplied Vienna with the libretto to *Prinz Methusalem*. Written in French by Delacour and Wilder, and adapted into German before being set by the composer, the show lasted longer than *La Tzigane* but nevertheless won only limited success.

Les Dominos roses was adapted into a musical in Britain and America as *Tonight's the Night*, in Hungary as *Három légyott* (Népszinház 22 October 1897) and, most successfully, in Austria as *Der Opernball*. *La Cagnotte* became the Posse mit Gesang *Vergnügungszügfer* (Karl Stix/C F Stenzl) produced at the Carltheater in 1870, *Die Sparbüchse* (Ludwig Kusche/Charles Regnier, Saarbrücken Stadttheater 31 December 1953) and, in France, *La Cagnotte* (Jack Ledru/Guy Lafarge) produced at Lille in 1983. It was also apparently plundered, without credit, for a shabby British musical called *Instant Marriage*.

1851 **Le Coup de pied retrospectif** (w Adolphe Guénée) 1 act Délassements-Comiques 24 December

1852 **Paris qui dort** (Julien Nargéot/w Lambert Thiboust) Théâtre des Variétés 21 February

1859 **Un mari à la porte** (Jacques Offenbach/Léon Morand) 1 act Théâtre des Bouffes-Parisiens 22 June

1861 **Ya-Mein-Herr** (Victor Chéri et al/w Clairville, Thiboust) Théâtre des Variétés 6 April

1861 **Les Danses nationales de la France** (Chéri/w Clairville, Thiboust) Théâtre des Variétés 19 August

1865 **Le Voyage en Chine** (François Bazin/w Eugène Labiche) Opéra-Comique 9 December

1867 **Le Fils du brigadier, ou Le Cheval de l'adjoint** (Victor Massé/w Labiche) Opéra-Comique 25 February

1868 **Le Corricolo** (Fernand Poïse/w Labiche) Opéra-Comique 27 November

1873 **La Veuve du Malabar** (Hervé/w Hector Crémieux) Theatre des Variétés 26 April

1876 **Fatinitza** French version w Victor Wilder (Théâtre des Nouveautés)

1876 **Le Roi dort** (Marius Boullard/w Labiche) Théâtre des Variétés 31 March

1876 **Jeanne, Jeannette et Jeanneton** (Paul Lacôme/w Clairville) Théâtre des Folies-Dramatiques 27 October

1877 **Prinz Methusalem** (Johann Strauss/w Wilder tr Karl Treumann) Carltheater, Vienna 3 January

1877 **La Tzigane** (*Die Fledermaus* etc) new libretto w Victor Wilder, Théâtre de la Reniassance 30 October

1878 **Coco** (Auguste Coèdes/w Clairville, Eugène Grangé) Théâtre des Nouveautés 12 June

1879 **Pâques fleuries** (Lacôme/w Clairville) Theatre des Folies-Dramatiques 21 October

1881 **La Reine des Halles** (Louis Varney/w Victor Bernard, Paul Burani) Comédie-Parisienne 4 April

1882 **La Nuit de Saint-Jean** (Lacôme/J de Lau-Lusignan) 1 act Opéra-Comique 18 November

DELFONT, Bernard (Lord) [WINOGRADSKY, Boris] (b Tokmak, Russia 5 September 1909).

At first a dancer, with his brother Louis (later Lord Lew Grade), and then a theatrical agent, Delfont began as a producer touring plays and mounting revivals of such musicals as *The Duchess of Dantzic* (1943, w Tom Arnold) and *The Count of Luxemburg* (1943, w Joseph Fenstone), and of *Rose Marie* (Stoll Theatre, 1942) and *The Student Prince* (Stoll Theatre, 1944), on the road and in London. His first original production was the Richard Tauber musical *Old Chelsea*, his first West End importation the Broadway *Something for the Boys* (1944), and he subsequently mounted the Fred Emney vehicle, *Big Boy* (1945), *Under the Counter* (w Arnold, Lee Ephraim), a version of *Die Fledermaus* retitled *Gay Rosalinda*, *The Birdseller* (*Der Vogelhändler* w Arnold, Littler), with Tauber as conductor, Britain's first stage production of *The Wizard of Oz* (1946), the long-running *Bob's Your Uncle* (1948) and the short-lived *Hat in the Air* (*Roundabout*) in London, whilst touring such pieces as *Good Night, Vienna* (w Jack Buchanan), *Bless the Bride* and *The Chocolate Soldier*.

After a period during which he was principally involved with a series of French revues at the London Hippodrome and the Prince of Wales Theatre, he ventured back into the musical theatre, and over two decades racked up a good percentage of successes as he produced, or had an interest in the production of such pieces as the Cicely Courtneidge musical *Starmaker* (1955), the London production of *Where's Charley?* (1957), *Stop the World – I Want to Get Off* (1961), *Pickwick* (1963 w Arnold), *Maggie May* (1964), *Little Me* (1964), *Our Man Crichton* (1964 w Arnold, Arthur Lewis), *The Roar of the Greasepaint ... the Smell of the Crowd* (1964), *Twang!!* (1965 w John Bryan), *When You're Young* (aka *Smilin' Through* 1966), *The Matchgirls* (1966 w Geoffrey Russell), *Funny Girl* (1966), *Joey, Joey* (1966), *Queenie* (1967), *Sweet Charity* (1967 w Harold Fielding), *The Four Musketeers* (1967), *Golden Boy* (1968), *You're a Good Man, Charlie Brown* (1969 w Fielding), *Mame* (1969 w Fielding), *Your Own Thing* (1969), *Promises, Promises* (1969 w David Merrick, H M Tennent), *The Great Waltz* (1970 w Fielding), *Applause* (1972), *The Good Old Bad Old Days* (1972), *The Threepenny Opera* (1972 w Michael White), *The Good Companions* (1974 w Richard Mills, Richard Pilbrow), *A Little Night Music* (1975 w Pilbrow), *Mardi Gras* (1976), *The Best Little Whorehouse in Texas* (1981), *Underneath the Arches* (1982) and the *Little Me* revival of 1984.

Alongside his musical theatre activities, Delfont continued a parallel production schedule of plays, revues and, most particularly, of summer season variety shows throughout Britain. He was knighted in 1974 and made a peer in 1976 for his contribution to entertainment and to charity, and has continued into the 1990s as President of the First Leisure Corporation and as a member of the board of Delfont Mackintosh Theatres controlling London's Prince of Wales and Prince Edward Theatres.

Autobiography: *East End, West End* (Macmillan, London, 1990)

DELIBES, [Clément Philibert] Léo (b St Germain du Val, 21 February 1836; d Paris, 16 January 1891).

Before going on to write the works which ensured his international fame – the ballets *Coppélia* (1870), *La Source* (1866, w Minkus) and *Sylvia*, and the opéras-comiques *Lakmé, Le Roi l'a dit* (1873) and *Jean de Nivelle* – the young Léo Delibes contributed scores through more than a decade to the musical theatres of Paris, producing a series of one-act opéras-bouffes and opérettes in the manner of, and for the use of, the composer/theatre-managers Hervé, Offenbach and others.

It was Hervé who gave the teenaged composer his first opportunity, when he mounted and played in Delibes' little burlesque *Deux sous de charbon* at his Folies-Nouvelles, but his second piece, the low comic *Les Deux Vieilles Gardes*, produced by Offenbach, was much more successful and, like the subsequent bouffonnerie *L'Omelette à la Follembuche*, it was included as part of the Bouffes-Parisiens international touring repertoire in the early 1860s. *Six Demoiselles à marier*, which also found its way into theatres beyond France, was seen at Vienna's Theater an der Wien (13 October 1860) in a version musically adapted by Adolf Müller, with sufficient impact for its libretto to be later reused to make up the text for Suppé's more celebrated *Zehn Mädchen und kein Mann*. *Le Serpent à plumes* and, in particular, his last short work, the delightful five-handed *L'Écossais de Chatou* also found success, the latter being played in Austria as *Ein Schotte* (Theater an der Wien 20 November 1880) and in Hungary as *A chatoui skótok* (ad Ferenc Reiner). In 1869 Delibes produced the score to his one full-length opéra-bouffe, the successful *La Cour du Roi Pétaud* before moving on into loftier spheres.

1856 **Deux sous de charbon** (Jules Moinaux) 1 act Folies-Nouvelles 9 February

1856 **Les Deux Vieilles Gardes** (Villeneuve, H Lemonnier) 1 act Théâtre des Bouffes-Parisiens 8 August

1856 **Six demoiselles à marier** (Adolphe Choler, Adolphe Jaime) 1 act Théâtre des Bouffes-Parisiens 12 November

1857 **Maître Griffard** (Eugène Mestépès, [Jaime]) 1 act Théâtre Lyrique 3 October

1859 **L'Omelette à la Follembuche** (Eugène Labiche, Marc-Michel) 1 act Théâtre des Bouffes-Parisiens 8 June

1860 **Monsieur de Bonne-Étoile** (Philippe Gille, [Jaime]) 1 act Théâtre des Bouffes-Parisiens 4 February

1861 **Les Musiciens de l'orchestre** (w Aristide Hignard, Erlanger/Bourdois) Théâtre des Bouffes-Parisiens 25 January

1861 **Les Deux Buveurs** (Hector Crémieux, Ludovic Halévy) 1 act Théâtre des Bouffes-Parisiens January

1861 **Les Eaux d'Ems** (Crémieux, Halévy) 1 act Kursaal, Bad Ems; Théâtre des Bouffes-Parisiens 9 April 1863

1862 **L'Homme entre deux âges** (w H Cartier/Émile Abraham) 1 act Théâtre des Bouffes-Parisiens 6 May

1862 **Mon ami Pierrot** (Crémieux, Halévy) 1 act Kursaal, Bad Ems July

1863 **Le Jardinier et son seigneur** (Théodore Barrière, Michel Carré) 1 act Théâtre Lyrique 1 May

1864 **La Tradition** (Henri d'Erville) 1 act Théâtre des Bouffes-Parisiens 5 January

1864 **Le Serpent à plumes** (Gille, Cham) 1 act Théâtre des Bouffes-Parisiens 16 December

1865 **Le Boeuf Apis** (Gille, Eugène Furpille) Théâtre des Bouffes-Parisiens 15 April

1867 **Marlborough s'en va-t-en guerre** (w Georges Bizet, Emil Jonas, Isidore Legouix/William Busnach, Paul Siraudin) Théâtre de l'Athénée 15 December

1869 **L'Écossais de Chatou** (Jaime, Gille) 1 act Théâtre des Bouffes-Parisiens 16 January

1869 **La Cour du Roi Pétaud** (Jaime, Gille) Théâtre des Variétés 26 April

Biography: de Curzon, H: *Léo Delibes, sa vie et ses oeuvres* (Legouix, Paris, 1926)

DELLINGER, Rudolf (b Kraslice, 8 July 1857; d nr Dresden, 24 September 1910). Composer of Germany's first real Operette hit and of several other pieces popular in that country in their time.

The son of a musical instrument-maker, Dellinger was trained at the Prague Conservatorium, and became first an orchestral clarinettist and subsequently a conductor at the Stadttheater in Brno. He moved on to similar posts at the Carl-Schultze Theater in Hamburg and, ultimately, at the Residenztheater, Dresden. His first Operette, *Don Cesar*, a piece based on the same French original as the successful English *Maritana*, was produced at Hamburg during his tenancy there and it met with enormous success. It was subsequently produced at Budapest's Népszinház, the Vienna Carltheater and Berlin's Walhalla-Theater later in the same year, and by John McCaull in New York the following with sufficient success for the American management to option Dellinger's next work sight unseen. Thus *Lorraine*, another period French piece, although a comparative failure in Hamburg and Leipzig, nevertheless won a brief production at New York's Star Theater (ad William J Henderson) with a cast including De Wolf Hopper, Emily Soldene and John Perugini.

Dellinger had two further works produced at Hamburg during his ten-year period at the theatre's musical helm, a musicalization of Dumas's *Les Demoiselles de Saint-Cyr* and a *Kapitän Fracassa*, a further French-based piece, with a text by Zell and Genée, which found sufficient success to warrant a production at Vienna's Theater an der Wien (17 performances) and another by McCaull in America. Then, in 1893, he shifted to Dresden. Of his three final works, all produced at Dresden, *Die Chansonette* – in which he finally abandoned his period French settings for a modern Italian one – was subsequently seen for an appreciable 43 performances at the Theater an der Wien (16 February 1895), at Berlin's Theater Unter den Linden (22 August 1895) and had a highly healthy career in the German provinces, whilst the 1901 *Jadwiga* also found some success, without braving the metropolites. None, however, came up to the level of popularity he had won with his first and most successful piece, which continued to be revived in both town and country for many years.

1885 **Don Cesar** (Oscar Walther) Carl-Schultze Theater, Hamburg 28 March

1886 **Lorraine** (Walther) Carl-Schultze Theater, Hamburg 2 October

1889 **Kapitän Fracassa** (Richard Genée, F Zell) Carl-Schultze Theater, Hamburg 2 March

1891 **[Das Fräulein von] Saint-Cyr** (Walther) Carl-Schultze Theater, Hamburg 10 January

1895 **Die Chansonette** (Victor Léon, Heinrich von Waldberg) Residenztheater, Dresden 16 September

1901 **Jadwiga** (Paul Hirschberger, Robert Pohl) Residenz-theater, Dresden 5 October

1910 **Der letzte Jonas** (Wilhelm Ascher, R Pohl) Residenz-theater, Dresden 2 April

DELYSIA, Alice [LAPIZE, Élise] (b Paris, 3 March 1889; d Brighton, 9 February 1979). Parisian showgirl-turned-diseuse who made herself a French niche on the British stage.

Delysia made her first appearances on stage in the chorus of the Paris production of *The Belle of New York*, in revue at the Théâtre des Variétés, in opérette at the Gaîté-Lyrique, and (billed as Elise Delisia) as one of the eight French lovelies chosen to go to New York to appear in the Broadway production of *The Catch of the Season* in 1905. She got her first opportunity to show off her ample charms in a principal rôle as the jealous actress, Diane, in the French production of Lionel Monckton's *The Quaker Girl* at the Olympia (1912), and subsequently appeared prominently both in revue, and as Séraphine in Cuvillier's *La Reine s'amuse* (1913), before she visited London to play in the comedy *L'Ingénue*. She remained in Britain to appear with great success in several revues for C B Cochran (*Odds and Ends*, *More*, *Pell-Mell*) and then in the lead rôles of his London productions of the French musicals *Carminetta* (1917) and *Afgar, ou les loisirs andalous* (1919) and of Rip's revue *Plus ça change* (*As You Were*).

She visited America to repeat her 'slightly scandalous' *Afgar* rôle in 1920, and again to tour with Donald Brian in a musical play called *The Courtesan* (1923, Marie Pélissier), and on returning to London, starred in a solid series of West End revues, musicals and plays which included *Princess Charming* (1926, Wanda Navaro), *The Cat and the Fiddle* (1932, Alice ex-Odette), and, in perhaps her most successful performance of all, as Josephine Pavani, singing 'Every Woman Thinks She Wants to Wander' in Oscar Straus's *Mother of Pearl* (*Eine Frau, die weiss, was sie will*, London 1933, Australia 1934). She also appeared in London in the semi-Australian musical *At the Silver Swan* (1936, Alice Brevanne), but her subsequent career was devoted to straight theatre, and to music hall and concert appearances.

DE MILLE, Agnes [George] (b New York, 1905). Choreographer whose balletic scenas in *Oklahoma!* led to a rash of similar dance-pieces on the postwar Broadway stage.

A member of a well-known American theatre family, dancer and choreographer Agnes de Mille ran her own troupe from an early age. She made her first foray into the musical theatre under the aegis of C B Cochran, in London, when she arranged the original set of dances for his production of the Cole Porter musical *Nymph Errant* (1933) and devised the ballet *Three Virgins and a Devil* for the revue *Why Not Tonight?* (1934). Returning to America, she choreographed a ballet scene for the Ed Wynn musical *Hooray for What!* (1937) and also worked on the short-lived *Swingin' the Dream*. Whilst continuing to perform herself, she worked extensively with New York's Ballet Theater (*Black Ritual*, *Drums Sound in Hackensack*) and choreographed *Rodeo* for de Basil's Ballet Russe de Monte Carlo, before returning to the musical theatre to stage the dances for the new musical *Oklahoma!* (1943). The show itself

proved a sensational success, and Miss de Mille's contribution, notably the dream sequence ballet 'Laurey Makes Up Her Mind', conceived with a balletic artistry and performed by a body of dancers of high technical skills, won strong admiration amongst the general admiration for the show as a whole.

Oklahoma! made its choreographer the dance director of the moment, and Miss de Mille and her ballet scenas (not to mention imitations of them by other folk) appeared in many major musicals over the following seasons. She worked on two subsequent Rodgers and Hammerstein musicals, *Carousel* (Carousel Waltz) and *Allegro* (also director), on *One Touch of Venus* ('Venus in Ozone Heights', 'Forty Minutes for Lunch'), the patent attempt to photocopy *Oklahoma!* which was *Bloomer Girl* (Civil War Ballet), and with particular success on *Brigadoon* with its choreographed chase episode, its Scottish wedding scena and lengthy funeral dance sequence. She also choreographed a second Loewe and Lerner musical in *Paint Your Wagon* (1951).

Whilst continuing to work in the ballet and American dance fields, Miss de Mille also lined up musical theatre choreographic credits on such pieces as *Gentlemen Prefer Blondes* (1949), *The Girl in Pink Tights* (1954), *Goldilocks* (1958), *Juno* (1959), *Kwamina* (1961) and *110 in the Shade* (1963), and directorial credits on *Out of This World* (1950) and *Come Summer* (1969).

Although ballet, of varying degrees of expertise, had been widely used in the musical theatre since its earliest days, and the so-called 'integration' of dance into the story fabric of a show had been both intermittently deemed desirable and practised on numberless occasions during the previous centuries, the acclaim won by Miss de Mille's ballets for *Oklahoma!* precipitated a new fashion for balletic dancing in musical comedy, as opposed to the drills, chorus unison dance, speciality solos and/or ballroom dance, all of which had been popular in the preceding decades of often dance-heavy productions. For a number of years after *Oklahoma!* no musical play of any pretension was deemed complete without its ballet or dance drama scena, and the trend had an undoubted effect on the formation of American musical theatre dance and dancers of those most productive Broadway decades which followed.

Miss de Mille's father, William C de Mille, and her uncle, Cecil B de Mille, whose name became a byword in the movie world as the purveyor of extravagant filmed spectacle, both authored musical comedies in the early part of their careers (*The Antique Girl*, *At the Barracks*).

Autobiography: *Dance to the Piper* (Little, Brown, Boston, 1952), *And Promenade Home* (Little, Brown, Boston, 1958), *Speak to Me, Dance with Me* (Little, Brown, Boston, 1973)

LA DEMOISELLE DU TÉLÉPHONE Vaudeville-opérette in 3 acts by Maurice Desvallières and Antony Mars [and André Sylvane, uncredited]. Music by Gaston Serpette. Théâtre des Nouveautés, Paris, 2 May 1891.

Agathe Liseron (Mily-Meyer), the heroine of Desvallières and Mars's highly successful vaudeville, is a telephone operator who is able, through her professional talents, to keep an ear on her chap and on his conversations when he seems to be dallying with a lady of the stage called Olympia (Jane Pierney). The complications develop in lively style as she sets out to discredit her rival, with a boxful of disguises close to hand, and a song ever at the ready even if it isn't really necessary. Colombey (Pontarcy), Germain (Pichard), Guy (Sigismond) and Abel Tarride (Blackson) headed the male team of Paris's Théâtre des Nouveautés company through what looked rather like a close cousin to Vienna's hit musical comedy *Ein Blitzmädel* of 14 years earlier.

A first Parisian run of 116 performances set the comedy musical off round the world. German versions were played in Berlin and at Vienna's Carltheater (ad Hermann Herschl, add song by E Kornau, J Löti) where Karl Blasel (Pontarcy), Wilhelm Knaack (Richard), Paula Delma (Agathe) and Frln Andrée (Olympia) appeared in six performances. In England, adapted by Sir Augustus Harris, F C Burnand, Arthur Sturgess and (musically) by James Glover, *The Telephone Girl* was a big success on the road, touring provincial and suburban theatres, with Ada Blanche starring as Lottie (ex-Agathe), for several years without tackling the West End. Broadway's Casino Theater version threw out the Serpette score and, as was the habit at the time, replaced it with some Gustave Kerker material for Clara Lipman, Louis Mann and Eleanor Elton. It also added some lower comedy than the original authors had planned, and the resultant show, also called *The Telephone Girl*, racked up 104 performances, before setting off for a good life on the touring circuits.

Germany: Wallner Theater *Telephone-Amt 7* 8 October 1891; Austria: Carltheater *Das Fräulein vom Telephon* 28 February 1892; UK: Grand Theatre, Wolverhampton *The Telephone Girl* 25 May 1896; USA: Casino Theater *The Telephone Girl* 28 September 1897

UNE DEMOISELLE EN LOTERIE Opérette-bouffe in 1 act by Adolphe Jaime and Hector Crémieux. Music by Jacques Offenbach. Théâtre des Bouffes-Parisiens, Paris, 27 July 1857.

One of the number of little Offenbach works of the 1850s which found more favour in its German-language versions than its original. The demoiselle who puts herself up for lottery is the footloose Aspasie (Lise Tautin), who counts on this game to collect a neat dowry to take to the winner. The lottery attracts the cousin, Agénor Pigeonneau (Désiré), who has helped himself to what should have been Aspasie's inheritance, and in the end, after some jolly and often vocally extravagant opéra-bouffe music, she ties him up as a comfortable husband.

After its Paris première, the Bouffes-Parisiens company, headed by Mlle Tautin, introduced the piece first to Vienna's Theater am Franz-Josefs-Kai and then to Budapest before it went on to be played at the Theater an der Wien and at Budapest's Budai Színkör in a German version by F Zell.

Austria: Theater am Franz-Josefs-Kai (Fr) 10 June 1861, Theater an der Wien *Eine Künstreiterin* (*Eine weibliche Haupttreffer*) 15 February 1864; Hungary: Budai Népszinház (Fr) 13 July 1861, Budai Színkör *Eine Künstreiterin* 28 April 1864

DENNY, W[illiam] H[enry] [LEIGH-DUNMORE, William Henry] (b Balsall Heath, Birmingham, 22 October 1853; d London, 31 August 1915).

Denny began in the adult theatre at 17 and appeared in London for the first time with Phelps's company playing small rôles in Shakespeare and classic plays. He was seen

at the Gaiety in comedy and burlesque, toured America with Lydia Thompson (as 'W H Leigh') in *Piff Paff* (Generalissimo) etc, and appeared in several New York and London theatres in drama and comedy before, in 1888, he joined D'Oyly Carte's company at the Savoy Theatre. He replaced Rutland Barrington, who had gone into management on his own account, and thus created the rôle of the lugubrious jailer Shadbolt in *The Yeomen of the Guard*. When the chastened and poorer Barrington returned, Denny remained with the company to create further Savoy Theatre lead comic rôles in *The Gondoliers* (Grand Inquisitor), *The Nautch Girl* (Bumbo, the idol), *Haddon Hall* (The McCrankie) and *Utopia Ltd* (Scaphio).

He then moved on to work with Arthur Roberts, succeeding Eric Thorne as Sir Philip Saxmundham in the burlesque *Claude Du-Val* (1894), appeared in Jakobowski's Broadway-bound comic opera *The Queen of Brilliants* with Lillian Russell at the Lyceum and toured for Morell and Mouillot in *Don Juan* (Rodrigo). He rejoined Roberts to play the comical nouveau riche Pilkington Jones in *Gentleman Joe* (1895), to appear as the star's policeman rival-in-love in *Dandy Dan the Lifeguardsman* (1897) and to play Bob Chaffers in the loose-limbed *HMS Irresponsible* (1900–1).

In 1902 he appeared in the British touring musical *The Gay Cadets* before working out the latter end of his multi-coloured career in Shakespeare in Australia (Malvolio, Bottom), musical comedy in America (Mr Hazell in *The Earl and the Girl* (1906), Baron Lecocq in *The Beauty Spot* (1909), Herr Starke in *The Gay Hussars* (1910) etc), and on the music halls in Britain.

DENS, Michel [MARCEL, Maurice] (b Roubaix, 22 June 1912).

After an early career in the French provinces, where he mixed operatic and opérette rôles in several of the larger theatres, Dens played for the first time at the Opéra-Comique in 1947, beginning his tenancy there as Albert in *Werther*. He appeared in the same year at the Paris Opéra in the title-rôle of *Rigoletto*. In the 1950s he was seen in a long series of opérettes at the Théâtre de la Gaîté-Lyrique, playing both the classic baritone rôles (Marquis de Corneville, Brissac etc) and several generally accepted tenor rôles, notably Sou Chong in *Le Pays de sourire*, and taking part in several more recent French works (Ricardo in *Colorado*, *Romance au Portugal*, Karl in *Le Moulin sans souci*). At this period he also recorded for Pathé-Marconi the leading baritone (and some tenor) rôles in the majority of the famous series of classic opérette recordings which have remained standard reference in the genre ever since. He has continued to perform through into his late seventies, appearing in 1988 as Ménélas (*La Belle Hélène*) and in Jean Perier's high-baritone title-rôle in *Hans, le joueur de flûte* in the provinces.

DESCLAUZAS, Marie [ARMAND, Malvina Ernestine] (b Paris, 1840; d Neuilly, 9 March 1912). Buxom and eventually hefty star of the opérette stage who became the most admired musical character comedienne of her era.

Marie Desclauzas began her stage career as a child, touring and, in her mid-teens, appearing in Paris at the

Ambigu and the Cirque under Hostein in dramas and in féeries where her attractively rounded figure earned her a series of leggy travesty rôles. She then turned to opéra-bouffe and made herself a solid career as leading lady. This included a starring season under the management of Jacob Grau and James Fisk in 1868–9 in America, where she appeared as Geneviève de Brabant and Drogan, Boulotte, Fleur de Noblesse (*L'Oeil crevé*), Piquillo (*La Périchole*), Césarine (*Fleur de thé*), Galswinthe and in *La Vie parisienne*, before she became prima donna of the fine company at the Brussels Théâtre des Fantaisies-Parisiennes.

When that theatre's director, Eugène Humbert, produced the latest opéra-comique by the young Charles Lecocq, whose *Les Cent Vierges* had done so well for them earlier in the year, 32-year-old Desclauzas was duly given the leading rôle. She made such a success as Madame Lange, the luscious, plotting merveilleuse of *La Fille de Madame Angot* that, when the piece was taken to Paris and scheduled to be recast with metropolitan performers, Lecocq himself insisted that the Belgian creatrice of Lange be retained. Humbert released his star to the management of the Folies-Dramatiques and Desclauzas triumphed all over again in the capital. After a long stretch as Lange, she appeared as Manon in Auguste Coèdes's *La Belle Bourbonnaise* and as La Belle Cousine in Hervé's *Alice de Nevers*, but her now rather considerable bulk, especially when not hidden under the useful lines of *Angot*'s empire gowns, barred her from most leading rôles and she tactfully changed direction, at 35, to make a speciality of character rôles which required a strong singing voice and a powerful personality rather than a shapely leg.

In the 20 years that followed she created rôles of this kind in a whole line of opérettes and plays, many at the Théâtre de la Renaissance and for Lecocq, and many written especially to suit her comic talents. These included *Le Roi d'Yvetot* (1876), *Le Petit Duc* (1878, the Directrice of the Académie pour Demoiselles Nobles), *La Camargo* (1878, Donna Juana de Rio-Negra), *La Petite Mademoiselle* (1879, Madelon), *La Jolie Persane* (1879, Babouche), *Les Voltigeurs de la 32ème* (1880, Dorothée), *Janot* (1881, Alexina), *Mademoiselle Moucheron* (1881, Mme Boulinard), *Madame la Diable* (1882), *La Bonne Aventure* (1882, Beppa), *Ninette* (1882, Countess Kouci-Kouca), *Les Trois Devins* (1884, Christine), *Les Petits Mousquetaires* (1885, Armide de Tréville), *Il était une fois* (1886, La Reine Virginie), *L'Amour mouillé* (1887, Catarina), *Le Petit Moujik* (1896, Mme Picou) and *Les Fêtards* (1896, Madame Maréchale). She also appeared in such rôles as Aurore (*Giroflé-Girofla*), Lucrézia (*La Petite Mariée*), Marcelline (*Belle Lurette*) and Fanfreluche (*La Poule aux oeufs d'or*) and took time off to appear, with equal success, in comedy for Koning at the Gymnase (Mme Baudoin in *Les Amants légitimes*, Déborah in *L'Homme à l'oreille cassée* etc) and elsewhere.

Her most famous creations were the irresistibly comical rôle of the Directrice in *Le Petit Duc*, a part to which she returned again and again over a period of 20 years, and the vast, blowsy wardrobe mistress of the farcical *Les Fêtards*, with her memories of her days as a tight-waisted circus rider and her royal romance, but such was the artist's emprise over this kind of rôle that, for decades thereafter, such character parts, in old and new opérettes, were known in France as 'les rôles de Desclauzas'.

THE DESERT SONG

THE DESERT SONG   Musical play in 3 acts by Otto Harbach, Oscar Hammerstein II and Frank Mandel. Lyrics by Otto Harbach and Oscar Hammerstein II. Music by Sigmund Romberg. Casino Theater, New York, 30 November 1926.

The most internationally successful and the most enduring of Sigmund Romberg's long line of romantic operettas, *The Desert Song* was allegedly based on the doings of a genuine Berber chieftain (it was the Arab's chief qualification for a *New York Times* obituary), but its tale of romance and disguise, mixed with the standard amount of parallel comic action, as put together by Hammerstein, Harbach and Mandel ran smoothly in the regulation comic opera groove and, if anything, seemed to owe more of its colour and incidents to the recent Hollywood success *The Sheik* (1922) than to Morocco's publicity-hungry desert murderers.

The anti-French Arab guerillas of the North African deserts who have been raiding and pressuring the colonial government, as represented by army chief Captain Paul Fontaine (Glen Dale) and the new Governor, General Birabeau (Edmund Elton), are led to damaging effect by a mysterious person known as the Red Shadow. In fact, the Red Shadow is none other than the Governor's son, Pierre (Robert Halliday), who pretends to be a weak-witted fool at home whilst sneaking out to put on Arab garb and lead the locals' attacks on his father's forces. His gormless act means that he has little chance of winning the lovely Margot Bonvalet (Vivienne Segal) from Fontaine, so he gets into his costume and carries her romantically off into the desert. When General Birabeau comes to free her, Pierre is unable to draw his sword against his father and forfeits his leadership of the Arab band. Later, when Fontaine has set forth to take the Red Shadow, dead or alive, the jealous Arab dancing girl, Azuri (Pearl Regay), reveals to the General that he has put a price on the head of his own son. But the ending is happier than *Il Trovatore*: Pierre produces the Red Shadow's costume and announces that he has killed the rebel. Only his father need know the truth. The comic element was provided by Bennie Kidd (Eddie Buzzell), a society columnist deputizing uncomfortably as a war correspondent, and his desperately devoted secretary, Susan (Nellie Breen).

Romberg's score contained several songs which were to become romantic standards – the hero's waltzing invitation to Valentino-style desert bliss in 'The Desert Song' ('Blue heaven, and you and I ...'), Margot's soprano dreams of Elinor-Glynnish 'Romance', the driving chorus of 'The Riff Song' and the Red Shadow's ballad, 'One Alone', which was one part of an 'Eastern and Western Love' section which also included the lovely 'Let Love Go' and 'One Flower Grows Alone in Your Garden'. A pretty 'Why Did We Marry Soldiers?' and French Marching Song for the ladies' chorus, a lightly humorous demonstration of tough seduction techniques ('I Want a Kiss'), and the heroine's showpiece Sabre Song were amongst other highspots of a score in which the straight comedy numbers – Bennie's musings over the feminine quality known as 'It', his fears, under pressure from a saucy Spaniard (Margaret Irving), that he will soon be 'One Good Man Gone Wrong', and Susan's 'I'll Be a Buoyant Girl' – were slightly submerged.

The libretto of *The Desert Song* was, give or take a sag in the last stages of the second act, very much better made than those for most contemporary musical romances, and the show's emphasis on the sentimental and seductive side of its content, richly illustrated musically, proved to be well in the line of current taste. Schwab and Mandel's production of *The Desert Song* (prematurely entitled *Lady Fair* on its initial showing at Poli's Theater in Washington) was a great Broadway hit through a run of 471 performances, as the preface to a very long career.

The Theatre Royal, Drury Lane production, in London, with Harry Welchman (Pierre) and Edith Day (Margot) starred, Maria Minetti as Clementine and Clarice Hardwicke as Susan, echoed the popularity of the Broadway edition with a splendid run of 432 performances, and the show was soon on the road for what would be the first of a seemingly interminable number of tours in both countries. In Australia, too, where Lance Fairfax introduced the exploits of the Red Shadow alongside Virginia Perry (Margot), Herbert Mundin (Benny), Peter Gawthorne (Birabeau) and Stephanie d'Este (Azuri) in J C Williamson Ltd's production, the piece was a huge hit. It ran some 220 performances in its initial season in Melbourne, and, with Marie Bremner succeeding to the rôle of Margot, some five months in Sydney (Her Majesty's Theatre 30 March 1929), becoming a perennial and oft-reproduced favourite with which its star (and his entrance on horseback) was identified ever after.

Whilst, in America, *The Desert Song* returned only once, and briefly, to Broadway (Uris Theater 5 September 1973) as well as to the repertoire of the New York City Opera, in Britain a number of further metropolitan appearances followed the first. Alec Fraser and Sylvia Welling starred in a 1931 reprise (Alhambra Theatre 8 June), the original stars returned to the London Coliseum in 1936 (24 September), and Bruce Carfax and Doris Francis featured in a 1939 revival at the Garrick Theatre (29 June). Welchman made a third London appearance as the Red Shadow, this time paired with Eleanor Fayre, at the Palace Theatre in 1943 (16 January) and in 1967 provincial favourite John Hanson braved London, paired with soprano Patricia Michael, for a 383-performance run at the Palace Theatre.

Unlike its near contemporary *Rose Marie*, *The Desert Song* did not make major inroads into Europe, with one exception: France. After the serious success of *Rose-Marie*, the Isola Brothers had followed up with *Hallelujah!* (ie *Hit the Deck*) with much more mitigated results. They hastened to mount another American romantic piece and *Le Chant du désert* (ad Roger Ferréol, Saint-Granier) produced as an 'opérette à grand spectacle en 2 parties et huit tableaux' served their purpose well. Robert Couzinou (Pierre) played l'Ombre Rouge, Marcelle Denya was Jenny (ex-Margot) singing 'Rêver', whilst the comic Dorville was Onésime (ex-Bennie) in his quest for 'Ça!'. The production had a seven-month career, but did not come near challenging the remarkable success of Friml's piece in France.

The Desert Song made its way briskly on to film, with John Boles appearing as the Red Shadow to the Margot of Carlotta King and Myrna Loy (Azuri), Edward Martindel (Birabeau), Louise Fazenda (Susan) and Johnnie Arthur (Bennie) featured, in the first of three Warner Brothers films (1929). Dennis Morgan and Irene Manning paired for a second version in 1943, and a third, a decade later, featured Gordon Macrae and Kathryn Grayson. A tele-

vision broadcast of 1955 gave Nelson Eddy an airing as the Red Shadow.

Seventy-five years on, *The Desert Song* remains in the repertoire in English-speaking countries and, beyond American shores, it shares with *Rose Marie* the representation of its era of American romantic musicals.

UK: Theatre Royal, Drury Lane 7 April 1927; Australia: Her Majesty's Theatre, Melbourne 15 September 1928; France: Théâtre Mogador *Le Chant du désert* June 1930; Films: Warner Brothers 1929, 1943 and 1953
Recordings: selections (HMV, Capitol, RCA, Columbia, etc)

DÉSHABILLEZ-VOUS Comédie musicale in 3 acts by André Barde. Music by René Mercier. Théâtre des Bouffes-Parisiens, Paris, 22 December 1928.

Titles had got a good deal saucier in jazz-age musical comedy since the relatively harmless *Ta bouche*. With Mireille Perrey going on about 'Nuits d'Argentine', Jacqueline Francell insisting 'L'Amour ça n'a l'air de rien', Edmond Roze juxtaposing 'Trop petit, trop grand' and Jeanne Perriat and Robert Ancelin detailing what happens 'Dans un chemin de fer' this one more or less earned its titular command to 'get 'em off' in a four-month run, without succeeding in going very much further.

DÉSIRÉ [COURTECUISSE, Amable Désiré] (b Lille, 1822; d Asnières, September 1873).

In 1847 the young comedian known as Désiré asked Hervé for a two-handed musical sketch to play at his benefit and, because Désiré was short and plump and Hervé tall and gangling, the author selected the subject of Don Quixote. He wrote a zany burlesque of Cervantes for the two of them to play together, and illustrated it with original music rather than the borrowed tunes usual in such pieces. The two performers made a great success of their saynète and it was subsequently taken up by Adolphe Adam and played at his Théâtre Lyrique in 1848. *Don Quichotte et Sancho Pança* is quoted in most histories which like to try to put a finger on the first this and the first that as being the first opérette of the modern era.

Désiré subsequently became a star comedian in opéra-bouffe at Hervé's Folies-Nouvelles and Offenbach's Bouffes-Parisiens and he created comic rôles in many of Offenbach's works, large and small, decorating them with the improvisations which were his trademark. Amongst the rôles he introduced were Dig-Dig in *La Chatte metamorphosée en femme*, Pan in *Daphnis and Chloë*, Fortunio in *La Chanson de Fortunio*, M Choufleuri in *M Choufleuri restera chez lui le ...*, Cristoval in *Les Bavards*, Bertolucci in *Il Signor Fagotto*, Cabochon in *Jeanne qui pleure et Jean qui rit*, Fritzchen in *Lischen et Fritzchen*, the title-rôle in *Vent du soir*, Pigeonneau in *Une Demoiselle en loterie*, Mardi Gras in *Le Carnaval des revues*, Madame Madou in *Mesdames de la Halle*, Jol-Hiddin in *Les Géorgiennes*, Dunanan père in *Le Voyage de MM Dunanan*, Veautendon in *Les Bergers*, Raphael in *La Diva*, Balabrelock in *Boule de neige* and, above all, the original Jupiter of *Orphée aux enfers* (1858), the Cornarino Cornarini of *Le Pont des soupirs* (1861) and the Cabriolo of *La Princesse de Trébizonde* (1869). He also played Golo in the revised version of *Geneviève de Brabant* at the Bouffes-Parisiens in 1859.

Amongst the rôles which he created in works by other writers were the Marquis de Criquebouef in Delibes'

L'Omelette à la Follembuche and Ducornet in his *L'Ecossais de Châtou* and, having moved on in turn to the Variétés, the Palais-Royal and the short-lived Athénée, the rôle of the tubby mandarin Tien-Tien (paired with the skinny Léonce as Ka-o-lin) in Lecocq's first major work, *Fleur de thé* (1868). He also played in Lecocq's *L'Amour et son carquois*, created Madopolam in his *Le Rajah de Mysore*, and Chicorat in his *Le Testament de M Crac* (1871), and introduced the principal comic rôle of the judge, Raab, in Vasseur's hugely successful *La Timbale d'argent*. In 1872 he appeared at the Bouffes-Parisiens in *Le Docteur Rose* and in 1873 alongside Judic in Vasseur's *La Petite Reine* in some of his last new rôles before his death later that same year.

The same name was later assumed by another French musical comedy actor, who appeared from the 1880s in such pieces as *Jeanne, Jeannette et Jeanneton*, *Ali Baba*, *Miss Helyett*, *Le Cadeau de noces*, *Le Roi Dagobert*, *La Fille de Madame Angot* (Larivaudière in the Opéra-Comique performance), *La Divorcée*, *Les Transatlantiques*, *Les Cloches de Corneville* (Bailli), *Les 28 Jours de Clairette* (Capitaine), *Madame Boniface* (Jacquot), *Mam'zelle Nitouche* (Chateau-Gibus), *Rip* (Nick Vedder) etc.

DESLYS, Gaby [CAIRE, Marie-Élise Gabrielle] (b Marseille, 4 November 1881; d Paris, 11 February 1920). Little, blonde, extravagantly-half-dressed Marseillaise dancer who made herself a reputation in variety and theatre around the world.

Mlle Deslys made her first Parisian appearances in revue at the Théâtre des Mathurins, and quickly became a fashionable beauty of the early years of the new century, famous for her fabulous dresses and head-dresses and also for her determinedly publicized liaison with the King of Portugal. A professional liaison with dancer Harry Pilcer was more durable and almost as famous, whilst the adoration of author J M Barrie resulted in her appearing on the London stage, with decidedly fractured English, as the star of a curious concoction called *Rosy Rapture, the Pride of the Beauty Chorus* (1915).

Although Mlle Deslys's career was made largely and extremely successfully in revue, she was seen in several theoretically more vertebrate pieces. In 1906 George Edwardes interpolated her into *The New Aladdin* at the Gaiety Theatre with a couple of songs and some success, and in 1910 she appeared at Vienna's Apollotheater in the 3-scene vaudeville *Susettes Launen* (Albert Chantrier/Gabriel Timmony). In 1911 she featured in what had started out at that same Apollotheater as Eysler's short Operette *Vera Violetta*, in its Broadway metamorphosis into a virtual variety programme, cast as Mme Adele de la Cloche, and performing the 'Gaby Glide' with Pilcer as her partner. In 1912 she returned to Vienna with Pilcer to play the sketches *Eine Woche in Trouville* and *Mam'selle Chic* and she repeated at London's Palace with *Mam'selle Chic, or A Day in Trouville* (26 August).

In 1913 she featured in Broadway's 'spectacular farce with music' *The Honeymoon Express* (Yvonne Dubonnet). She was seen on the London stage again in the brief 1914 *The Belle from Bond Street* and finally, in 1917, in the musical comedy *Suzette* performing a kind of apache dance-scena called 'The Cat and the Canary', with Pilcer, and a murder mime called *La Fourchette*. Her final Broadway appearance was in another piece more revue than book

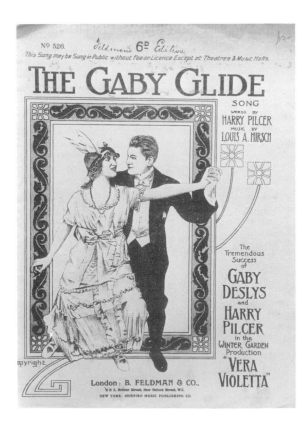

Plate 72. **Gaby Deslys:** *Famous for her millinery, and famed in song. The 'Gaby Glide' was one of the many numbers which crowded out Eysler's score in the Shubert production of* Vera Violetta.

musical, Irving Berlin's *Stop! Look! Listen!*, in 1915–16. Australia, unable, apparently, to afford Gaby, decided to make do with what it clearly considered the important part of her act. Harry Rickards advertised 'the Gaby Deslys costume' and the 'Gaby Deslys Parade' as part of his 1914 show at Melbourne's Tivoli.

Mlle Deslys also appeared on film, playing in such pieces as *Infatuation* in which the public was warned that she displayed 'the wiles, the charm, the gowns of the woman who causes the overthrow of a monarchy' and *The God of Luck*. Soon, however, she burnt herself out and she died of a 'respiratory ailment' following a sore throat and a bout of 'flu, at the age of 37.

An Operette entitled *Gaby Deslys*, with a score by Bernhard Grün was produced in central Europe in 1935.

Biography: Gardner, J: *Gaby Deslys: A Fatal Attraction* (Sidgwick & Jackson, London, 1986)

DESPREZ, Frank (b Bristol, 10 February 1853; d London, 22 November 1916).

After having spent some youthful time, far from his native Bristol, as a cowboy in Texas, Desprez returned to Britain in 1875. He began his career as a theatrical writer unpromisingly, supplying prima donna Selina Dolaro with a mutilated version of *La Fille de Madame Angot* which all but eliminated the co-starring rôle of Clairette and expanded that of Mlle Lange (who doesn't appear till Act II) for his employer and, when this piece went on the road, he also authored a little forepiece for it. *Happy Hampstead* was set to music by Dolaro's manager, Richard D'Oyly Carte.

Desprez subsequently became one of Carte's closest friends and worked with him for many years as secretary whilst, at the same time, writing the texts for the little operettas which preceded the Gilbert and Sullivan shows on the bills at the Opera Comique and the Savoy. Virtually all of these had very long runs, in tandem with and sometimes beyond the runs of the principal pieces, and they were played throughout the country as forepieces, benefit and short-programme items, much as the short works of Offenbach and his contemporaries had been in France a decade and more earlier. Working with composers such as Cellier and Solomon, Desprez established himself as the best-displayed practitioner of the one-act form in Britain.

Perhaps his most played work, however, was the two-act musical comedy *Tita in Thibet*, written for Kate Santley, which later became a staple in the touring baggage of the Majilton company by whom it was played more than a thousand times in the provinces. Undoubtedly his best work was his lyrical contribution to the Savoy Theatre's *The Nautch Girl*, the show which deputized more than adequately for the Gilbert and Sullivan series during the quarrel between the two famous writers.

In 1884 Desprez began writing for *The Era*, London's foremost theatre paper, and he became its editor in 1893, a position he held until illness forced him to retire in 1913.

1875 **La Fille de Madame Angot** English version (Royalty Theatre)

1876 **Happy Hampstead** (Richard D'Oyly Carte) 1 act Alexandra Theatre, Liverpool 3 July

1878 **After All** (Alfred Cellier) 1 act Opera Comique 23 December

1879 **Tita in Thibet** (aka *Brum, a Birmingham Merchant*) Royalty Theatre 1 January

1880 **In the Sulks** (A Cellier) 1 act Opera Comique 21 February

1881 **Quite an Adventure** (Edward Solomon) 1 act Olympic Theatre 7 September

1881 **Mock Turtles** (Eaton Fanning) 1 act Savoy Theatre 15 October

1883 **Lurette** (*Belle Lurette*) English version w Alfred Murray, H S Leigh (Avenue Theatre)

1883 **A Private Wire** (Percy Reeve/w Arnold Felix) 1 act Savoy Theatre 31 March

1886 **The Carp** (A Cellier) 1 act Savoy Theatre 13 February

1888 **Mrs Jarramie's Genie** (A Cellier, François Cellier) 1 act Savoy Theatre 14 February

1889 **Delia** (Procida Bucalossi) Bristol 11 March (as 'F Soulbieu')

1891 **The Nautch Girl** (Solomon/w George Dance/Dance) Savoy Theatre 30 June

1892 **Brother George** (Bucalossi) Portsmouth 16 May

DESTRY RIDES AGAIN Musical in 2 acts by Leonard Gershe based on the story by Max Brand. Music and lyrics by Harold Rome. Imperial Theater, New York, 23 April 1959.

A musical theatre version of the story which had previously been made successfully into a film several times over, most memorably in 1939 with James Stewart and Marlene Dietrich and Friedrich Holländer's well remembered song 'See What the Boys in the Back Room will Have', but also with such western heroes as Tom Mix and Audie Murphy.

This time Andy Griffith was Tom Destry, son of a famous lawman, summoned to be deputy sheriff of outback Bottleneck by Wash (Jack Prince), the theoretically innocuous town drunk promoted to puppet sheriff by the real boss of the town, gambler Kent (Scott Brady). Destry sets to his job without the use of a gun, escapes the wiles of Kent's moll, the dance-hall girl, Frenchy (Dolores Gray), set on him by the gambler, and arrests Kent's crony, Gyp Watson (Marc Breaux), the killer of the last sheriff. Things get rough when Kent's gang set out to break Watson from jail, and finally the peace-loving sheriff is forced to put on his guns. A virtuoso display of gunfire ensures him victory and the love of a reformed Frenchy. The spare and straight dramatic-comic story was musical-comedied-up by the addition of a conventional set of stage prostitutes and their madam.

Rome supplied some nicely gentle comic moments for his hero, realizing that he will remember 'Tomorrow Morning' all sorts of clever things with which he could have defended himself against his tormentors today; enumerating the consistently ghastly fate of the famous gunmen of history ('Ballad of the Gun'); or explaining opaquely 'Only Time Will Tell', to hide the fact that he has been to fetch a Federal judge to head the murderer's trial and put it out of Kent's crooked reach. Frenchy had her best moment heading the mock-trial 'Are You Ready, Gyp Watson?', topped off by a fine and funny male chorale tipping the verdict of 'Not Guilty', whilst the dried-out sheriff of Bottleneck leaped about to a lively 'Hoop-de-Dingle'. Breaux joined with Swen Swenson and George Reeder in the show's dance highlight, a dazzling Michael Kidd number danced with bullwhips, which proved to be the most remembered moment of the production.

Hampered by trade-union demands, David Merrick's production had an insufficient 472-performance run on Broadway, and *Destry Rides Again* did not progress further afield until 1982 when director Robert Walker produced a slimmed-down version of the show on the London fringe. A cast of 17 actor-musicians, headed by Alfred Molina (Destry) and Jill Gascoine (Frenchy), played, sang and acted their way with acrobatic vigour through a *Destry* from which the prostitutes and their numbers had been cut, in which the famous fight between Frenchy and Mrs Callahan, played on screen by Dietrich and Una Merkel, was brought up, and which no longer in any way resembled a conventional musical comedy. The production won the show many London friends and fans without progressing to a West End house.

UK: Donmar Warehouse 30 September 1982
Recordings: original cast (Decca), London version (TER)

DESVALLIÈRES, [George Ernest] Maurice (b Paris, 3 October 1857; d Paris, 23 March 1926).

The grandson of author and playwright Ernest Legouvé, and himself the author of a long list of vaudevilles and comedies, Desvallières had his most important successes with the comedies *L'Hôtel du libre échange* (*Hotel Paradiso* or *A Night Out*, w Georges Feydeau), *Fils à papa* (w Antony Mars) and *Champignol malgré lui* (*The Other Fellow*, w Feydeau). He also contributed to six original musical pieces, of which *La Demoiselle du téléphone* (played in Britain, America and Australia as *The Telephone Girl*, in Austria as *Das Fräulein vom Telephon*, in Germany as *Telephone-Amt*), *Mam'zelle Quat' Sous* (produced in Austria as *Die beiden Don Juans* with Girardi, and in Hungary as *A garasos kisasszony*) and the highly comical Mormon tale of *Les Douze Femmes de Japhet* (*Japhet und seine zwölf Frauen*, *Jafet 12 feleség*) were the most successful. His most enduring musical theatre work, however, came in two adaptations from the German musical stage, *Die Dollarprinzessin* and *Die keusche Susanne*, this latter a musicalization of his own *Fils à papa*, both of which won long and continuing lives in their French versions.

L'Hôtel du libre échange has been made into a musical comedy as *A Night Out* (Winter Garden, London 19 September 1920) and with much less success as *Hotel Passionato* (Philip Springer/Joan Javits/Jerome J Schwartz, East 74th Street Theater 1965), whilst the Hungarian musical play *A kölcsönkért feleség* (Fővárosi Nyári Színház 27 July 1921), adapted by Géza Vágo and musically set by Andor Szoldos to lyrics by Mihály Szántó was based on Desvallières's play *Prête-moi ta femme* (Palais-Royal 10 September 1883).

1890 **Mademoiselle Nou Nou** (w Georges Feydeau) 1 act Brussels 25 April
1890 **Les Douze Femmes de Japhet** (Victor Roger/w Antony Mars) Théâtre de la Renaissance 16 December
1891 **La Demoiselle du téléphone** (Gaston Serpette/w Mars) Théâtre des Nouveautés 2 May
1897 **Mam'zelle Quat' Sous** (Robert Planquette/w Mars) Théâtre de la Gaîté 5 November
1905 **L'Age d'or** (Louis Varney/w Feydeau) Théâtre des Variétés 1 May
1908 **Mam'zelle Trompette** (Hirlemann/w Paul Moncousin) Théâtre des Folies-Dramatiques 15 September
1911 **La Princesse Dollar** (*Die Dollarprinzessin*) French version w Mars (Théâtre Apollo)
1913 **La Chaste Suzanne** (*Die keusche Susanne*) French version w Mars (Théâtre Apollo)
1920 **La Princesse Carnaval** (Henri Hirschmann/w Moncousin) Théâtre Apollo 24 January

DE SYLVA B G [DE SYLVA, George Gard] ('Buddy') (b New York, 27 January 1895; d Los Angeles, 11 July 1950). Lyricist whose greatest success on the musical stage came as one head of the songwriting team De Sylva, Brown and Henderson.

The son of a vaudeville artist, De Sylva began writing song lyrics while at college getting the kind of education which would mean he wouldn't have to go into show business. Al Jolson took kindly to his work and used several of his lyrics, resulting in the young writer's first hits when 'I'll Say She Does' (music: Gus Kahn) and 'Chloe' (music credited to Jolson) emerged from the half-dozen of his numbers used at various times in Jolson's Winter Garden show *Sinbad* (1918). *I'll Say She Does* later became the title of one of De Sylva's first musical comedy ventures, when he supplied the songs for a musical version of Avery Hopwood's *Our Little Wife* which was initially produced under that fashionably meaningless title-phrase. After a tryout in stock it was revamped and remounted by producer A H Woods as *Dodo*, but it still failed to find its way to Broadway.

De Sylva had, by this stage, moved to New York and taken a job with the music publishers, Remick, as a result of which he was allotted the writing of part of the lyrics for George Gershwin's 1919 musical comedy début, *La La Lucille*. He also supplied the words to the songs for Jerome Kern's *Zip Goes a Million* and although that show, like *Dodo*, folded pre-Broadway, one song from its score later found itself a home in the score of Kern's *Sally*. 'Look For the Silver Lining' turned out to be De Sylva's biggest hit to date. He provided the lyrics for two more numbers for Jolson to use in *Bombo* (1921), and the results were 'April Showers' (music: Louis Silvers) and 'California, Here I Come' (music: Joseph Meyer), both of which the star plugged happily into the standard class.

Subsequent theatre assignments included a collaboration with Victor Herbert on *Orange Blossoms*, the adaptation of Kálmán's European hit *Die Csárdásfürstin* as *The Yankee Princess*, two further book shows and three editions of *George White's Scandals* with Gershwin ('Stairway to Paradise', 'Somebody Loves Me') and one with Joseph Meyer, which included yet another song hit, 'If You Knew Susie', for Al Jolson. Two successful Broadway collaborations with composer Lewis Gensler (*Captain Jinks*, *Queen High*) kept him to the musical comedy forefront thereafter, whilst an even more fruitful collaboration was being born in the revue world. For the 1925 and 1926 editions of *George White's Scandals*, De Sylva joined up with lyricist Lew Brown and composer Ray Henderson, each, like himself, the writer of recognized song hits, and after having produced 'The Birth of the Blues', 'The Girl is You and the Boy is Me', 'Lucky Day' and the 'Black Bottom' for the 1926 show, the trio continued into the musical theatre together, scoring a major hit with their first effort as a team, the ultimate college musical *Good News* (1926).

They followed up this winner with an Ed Wynn vehicle for George White, *Manhattan Mary*, the boxing musical *Hold Everything!* ('You're the Cream in My Coffee') which hoisted Bert Lahr to stardom, *Follow Thru* which dealt with golf and contained 'Button Up Your Overcoat' and (after boxing and golf) an aeronautics musical, *Flying High*, whilst at the same time putting a first foot into the cinematic world. Their first screen ventures included the scores for Al Jolson's *The Singing Fool* ('Sonny Boy') and for *Sunny Side Up* which, apart from its title song, also produced 'If I Had a Talking Picture of You' to add to their list of hits.

De Sylva broke up the team to move on to a further career as a producer of films and, subsequently, of Broadway shows. He teamed with Laurence Schwab, the producer of *Good News* and *Follow Thru*, with whom he had also worked as a co-librettist, to stage *Take a Chance* ('Eadie Was a Lady') with Ethel Merman and Jack Haley topping the bill, then doubled book writing and producing on another and more successful show which also starred Miss Merman when he presented the Cole Porter musical *Dubarry Was a Lady* (1939). He was also involved as co-producer on two other successful musicals in the following year – Irving Berlin's *Louisiana Purchase* and Porter's *Panama Hattie*.

After the split with Brown and Henderson and *Take a Chance*, De Sylva did little more in the way of songwriting, confining his later writing to libretti.

A 1956 Hollywood biopic on the team, *The Best Things in Life Are Free*, had De Sylva portrayed by the robust singing actor Gordon McRae.

1919 **La La Lucille** (George Gershwin/w Arthur Jackson) Henry Miller Theater 26 May

1919 **I'll Say She Does** (Avery Hopwood) Garrick Theater, Washington DC 10 August

1919 **Zip Goes a Million** (Jerome Kern/Guy Bolton) Worcester Theater, Worcester, Mass 8 December

1920 **Dodo** revised *I'll Say She Does* Poli's Theater, Washington 25 April

1920 **Orange Blossoms** (Victor Herbert/Fred de Grésac) Fulton Theater 19 September

1922 **The Yankee Princess** (*Die Csárdásfürstin*) American version w William Le Baron (Knickerbocker Theater)

1922 **Blue Monday** (Gershwin) 1 act (in *George White's Scandals of 1922*) Globe Theater 28 August

1924 **Sweet Little Devil** (ex-*A Perfect Lady*) (Gershwin/Frank Mandel, Laurence Schwab) Astor Theater 21 January

1925 **Big Boy** (Joseph Meyer, James Hanley/Harold Atteridge) Winter Garden Theater 7 January

1925 **Tell Me More!** (Gershwin/w Ira Gershwin/Fred Thompson, William K Wells) Gaiety Theater 13 April

1925 **Captain Jinks** (Lewis E Gensler, Stephen Jones/Mandel, Schwab) Martin Beck Theater 8 September

1926 **Queen High** (Gensler/w Schwab) Ambassador Theater 8 September

1927 **Good News** (Henderson/w Brown/w Schwab) 46th Street Theater 6 September

1927 **Manhattan Mary** (Henderson/w Brown/w George White) Apollo Theater 26 September

1928 **Hold Everything!** (Henderson/w Brown/w Jack McGowan) Broadhurst Theater 10 October

1929 **Follow Thru** (Henderson/w Brown/w Schwab) 46th Street Theater 9 January

1930 **Flying High** (Henderson/w Brown/McGowan) Apollo Theater 3 March

1932 **Humpty Dumpty** (Nacio Herb Brown, Richard Whiting/Schwab) Pittsburgh, 12 September

1932 **Take a Chance** revised *Humpty Dumpty* (Brown, Whiting, Vincent Youmans/Schwab) Apollo Theater 26 November

1939 **Dubarry Was a Lady** (Porter/w Herbert Fields) 46th Street Theater 6 December

1940 **Panama Hattie** (Porter/w Herbert Fields) 46th Street Theater 30 October

LES DEUX ARLEQUINS Opérette in 1 act by Eugène Mestépès. Music by Émile Jonas. Fantaisies-Parisiennes, Paris, 29 December 1865.

A little saynète for two, in which Harlequin (Bonnet), wishing to test his Colombine's fidelity after a long trip away, brings news of his own death. She (G Fontanel) sees through the trick, says she has found another harlequin, and then impersonates the 'rival'.

One of the most successful of Jonas's short pieces, it was played throughout Europe following its Paris première, notably on the opening programme of the London Gaiety Theatre (ad Gilbert a' Beckett) when the two harlequins were played by Charles Lyall and Constance Loseby.

Austria: Theater an der Wien *Die beiden Harlekine* 26 January 1867; UK: Gaiety Theatre *The Two Harlequins* 21 December

LES DEUX AVEUGLES Bouffonnerie musicale in 1 act by Jules Moinaux. Music by Jacques Offenbach. Théâtre des Bouffes-Parisiens, Paris, 5 July 1855.

A two-handed comic sketch in which two phoney blind beggars squabble for the best begging-patch, indulging first in a musical battle in which Giraffier (Berthelier) accompanies himself on a mandolin and Patachon (Pradeau) blasts away on a trombone, and then in a game of cards which shows up the falsity of their pretence at blindness.

Produced as the opening attraction at Offenbach's summer Théâtre des Bouffes-Parisiens, Moinaux's little comedy became the theatrical must of the season and helped materially to launch Offenbach both as a composer and as a theatre manager. It was played frequently thereafter, throughout France, reaching the Opéra-Comique in 1858, and also helped to set in motion the passion, soon to become overwhelming, for Offenbach's works in the other parts of the world. It was the first Offenbach piece played in Berlin, in Vienna (initially by Levassor, in French, later in a German-language version) and in Antwerp and it was featured in London in the repertoire of the Bouffes-Parisiens company on their first season there. Thereafter English translations, in particular, proliferated (*Going Blind*, *Beggar My Neighbour*, *A Mere Blind*, *The Blind Beggars*, *Two Blinds* etc) as the piece was played over and over again as a favourite part of 19th-century multiple-part bills and even, as in Australia's first performances by the Harry Rickards company, as part of a virtual variety bill.

Germany: Krolls Theater 10 March 1856; Austria: Carltheater (Fr) 19 April 1856, Theater am Franz-Josefs-Kai *Zwei arme Blinde* 26 May 1863; UK: Hanover Square Rooms (Fr) 27 July 1856, Gallery of Illustration *Beggar My Neighbour* 29 March 1870 etc; USA: Metropolitan Music Hall 31 August 1857, Wallack's Theater *Going Blind* 31 October 1858; Hungary: Budai Színkör *Die beiden Blinde* 15 June 1865; Australia: School of Arts, Sydney *The Blind Beggars* 9 September 1873

Recording: complete (Bourg)

DEVAL, Marguerite [BRULFER DE VALCOURT, Marguerite] (b Strasbourg, 19 September 1868; d Paris, 18 December 1955). Extremely popular and long-admired soubrette turned comedienne, with a career of more than 60 successful years on the Paris stage.

Marguerite Deval began her Parisian career in 1884 as a little round-faced, curly-headed soubrette in the very short

Plate 73. **Marguerite Deval:** *One of Paris's favourite musical comediennes and meneuses de revue for several decades.*

runs of Wenzel's *Le Chevalier Mignon* (Louise) and Marenco's *Le Diable à corps* (Bertha) at the Bouffes-Parisiens, and she moved on, through a lively career as a leading actress, to the rôle of an aged concierge in a post-(Second) war musical comedy. In spite of being involved in the creation of few musical shows which have remained in even the marginal repertoire, she nevertheless introduced several pieces which were highly successful in their time, running the gamut of styles from 1880s opéra-comique and opérette in her young days, through starring rôles in many a Parisian revue, to the often intimate song-and-dance musical comedies of the years between the wars, in which she found herself particularly at home. She scored most of her biggest successes in the smaller theatres, where finesse rather than flash paid.

In the earliest category were included, apart from the classic juvenile rôles, creations in Serpette's *Adam et Ève* (1886, Suzanne), Lacôme's *La Fille de l'air* (1890) and three Audran opérettes, *Article de Paris* (1892, Rose), *Mon Prince!* (1893, soubrette Rita with three numbers) and *Monsieur Lohengrin* (Une Dame), and the rather different styles of Terrasse, for whom she created the leading rôles of *La Petite Femme de Loth* (1900) and *Péché Veniel*, of Ivan Caryll, whose *S.A.R.* (1908) gave her a magnificent rôle as the plotful Queen Mother, Xénofa, of Rodolphe Berger and P-L Flers for whom she created the title-rôle of *Mes-*

salinette, ou le tour du demi-monde en 80 nuits (1902) and, most particularly, of Cuvillier in whose *Son p'tit frère* (1907, Laïs) and *Afgar* (1909, Zaydée) she created the starring rôles, pairing in both pieces with the actor/singer Henri Defreyn, with whom she formed a winning duo on many occasions.

She had another outstanding success in Rip's celebrated revue *1915*, and passed from further opérettes – (*La Folle Nuit* (1917), *La Petite Femme de Loth* revival (1918), *Daphnis et Chloë* (1918) etc) to post-war musical comedy in *Mon Vieux, Ri-Ri*, Willemetz and Richepin's *Rapatipatoum*, in a pairing with Dranem at the head of the comedy of Christiné's *P.L.M.*, *À Paris tous les deux*, *Le Renard chez les poules*, Georges Auric's *Sans façon*, *Zou* (1930, as the meddling mother, Léa de Bourges), *Rosy* (1930), *Brummel* (1931, Lady Eversharp) and Victor Alix's *Mon Amant! ...* (1932, Baronne de Mazelles) in which she played yet again in tandem with Defreyn. She was 77 years of age when she appeared at the Théâtre des Capucines, which had seen some of her best musical moments prior to the first war, as the old concierge of Josef Szulc's *Pantoufle* in 1945.

DIBDIN, Charles (b Southampton, 4 March 1745; d London, 25 July 1814).

One of the most important writers for the English-language musical theatre of the 18th century, Charles Dibdin made a career not only as a composer and author, but also as an actor and singer. He worked as a vocalist at the Covent Garden Theatre from the age of 15, and later as a principal in productions both there and at Drury Lane. He also performed many of his own songs, both in and out of a musical-play context. He found quick success as a theatrical songwriter when he allied himself with the cleverest musical stage author of the age, Isaac Bickerstaff, winning a major success with his songs for the 1768 piece *Lionel and Clarissa* and *The Padlock*, in the second of which he also appeared (after the sacking of the original actor in rehearsal) in the prime comic rôle of the black servant, Mungo.

From an early age Dibdin also worked steadily as a dramatic author, at first mostly adapting and/or adding original songs to versions of other, largely foreign, works such as *La serva padrona* (as *The Maid and the Mistress*), Duni's *La Fée Urgèle* (*A Christmas Tale*), Philidor's *Blaise le Savetier* (*The Cobbler*) and *Le Déserteur* and Grétry's *Les Deux Avares*, and then, more effectively, moving into a field of original ballad opera where his contribution was highlighted by such enduring works as *The Waterman* and *The Quaker*. In later days, he worked as a solo recitalist, managed a small theatre, and ultimately retired from the theatrical scene at the age of 60.

The author or adapter of over a hundred stage works, he was one of the few composers of 18th-century popular light theatre music whose shows survived beyond the coming of the opéra-bouffe and the profound change in musical theatre which operated in Britain in the 1860s, and some of his pieces such as *The Padlock* and *Lionel and Clarissa* even survived into productions in the 20th century, alongside his most successful single song 'Tom Bowling'.

Dibdin's illegitimate sons, Charles [Isaac Mungo] Dibdin (1768–1833) and Thomas [John] Dibdin (1771–1841), also had careers in the theatre.

1764 **The Shepherd's Artifice** (Dibdin) Theatre Royal, Covent Garden 21 May

1767 **Love in the City** (w pasticcio/Isaac Bickerstaff) Theatre Royal, Covent Garden 21 February

1768 **Lionel and Clarissa** (Bickerstaff) Theatre Royal, Covent Garden 25 February

1769 **The Padlock** (Bickerstaff) Theatre Royal, Drury Lane 3 October

1769 **Damon and Phillida** (Colley Cibber ad Dibdin) Theatre Royal, Drury Lane 21 February

1769 **The Ephesian Matron** (Bickerstaff) 1 act Ranelagh House 12 May

1769 **The Captive** (Bickerstaff) Theatre Royal, Haymarket 21 June

1769 **Amphytrion** (Hawksworth) Theatre Royal, Drury Lane 23 November

1770 **The Brick-Dust Man and the Milk-Maid** (Bickerstaff) 1 act Sadler's Wells Theatre 25 July

1770 **The Maid the Mistress** (*La serva padrona*) new music for English version by Bickerstaff Ranelagh House 28 May

1770 **The Recruiting Sergeant** (Bickerstaff) Ranelagh House 20 July

1771 **He Would If He Could** revised *The Maid the Mistress* 1 act Theatre Royal, Drury Lane 12 April

1773 **The Wedding Ring** (*Il filosofo di campagno*) (Dibdin) Theatre Royal, Drury Lane 1 February

1773 **The Deserter** (*Le Déserteur*) English version w additional new songs Theatre Royal, Drury Lane 2 November

1773 **A Christmas Tale** (*La Fée Urgèle*) new English version w new songs Theatre Royal, Drury Lane 27 December

1774 **The Romp** revised *Love in the City* Crow Street Theatre, Dublin 23 March; Theatre Royal, Covent Garden, London 18 March 1778

1774 **The Waterman, or The First of August** (Dibdin) His Majesty's Theatre 8 August

1774 **The Cobbler, or A Wife of Ten Thousand** (*Blaise le Savetier*) English version w new music Theatre Royal, Drury Lane 9 December

1775 **The Two Misers** (*Les Deux Avares*) (w pasticcio/Kane O'Hara) Theatre Royal, Covent Garden 21 January

1775 **The Quaker** (Dibdin) Theatre Royal, Drury Lane 3 May

1775 **The Sultan, or A Peep into the Seraglio** (Bickerstaff) Theatre Royal, Drury Lane 12 December

1776 **The Blackamoor wash'd white** (Henry Bate Dudley) Theatre Royal, Drury Lane 26 June

1776 **The Metamorphosis** (Dibdin) Haymarket Theatre 26 August

1776 **The Seraglio** (w Edward Thompson) Theatre Royal, Covent Garden 14 November

1777 **All is Not Gold That Glitters** (Dibdin) Theatre Royal, Covent Garden nd

1778 **Poor Vulcan** (w Arne, Arnold/Dibdin) Theatre Royal, Covent Garden 4 February

1778 **The Gipsies** (Arnold) His Majesty's Theatre 3 August

1778 **The Wives Revenged** (Sedaine ad Dibdin) 1 act Theatre Royal, Covent Garden 18 September

1778 **Rose and Collin** (Sedaine ad Dibdin) 1 act Theatre Royal, Covent Garden 18 September

1778 **Annette and Lubin** English version Theatre Royal, Covent Garden 2 October

1779 **The Touchstone** (w Hannah Cowley) Theatre Royal, Covent Garden 4 January

1779 **The Chelsea Pensioner** (Dibdin) Theatre Royal, Covent Garden 6 May

1780 **The Shepherdess of the Alps** (*La Bergère des alpes*) Theatre Royal, Covent Garden 18 January

1780 **The Islanders** (Saint-Foix ad) Theatre Royal, Covent Garden 25 November

1781 **The Marriage Act** revised *The Islanders* Theatre Royal, Covent Garden 17 September

1781 **Jupiter and Alcmena** Theatre Royal, Covent Garden 27 October

1782 **None Are So Blind As Those Who Won't See** (Arnold) Theatre Royal, Haymarket 2 July

1785 **Liberty Hall, or The Test of Good Behaviour** (Dibdin) Theatre Royal, Drury Lane 8 February

1785 **A Match for a Widow** (Joseph Atkinson) Theatre Royal, Dublin

1787 **Harvest Home** (Dibdin) Theatre Royal, Haymarket 16 May

1789 **The Fortune Hunters, or You May Say That** Sadler's Wells Theatre 13 April

1798 **Hannah Hewitt, or The Female Crusoe** 1 act Theatre Royal, Drury Lane 7 May

1806 **The Broken Gold** Theatre Royal, Covent Garden 8 February

Other titles credited: *The Widow of Abingdon, The Razor-Grinder, An Old Woman of Eighty, She's Mad for a Husband, The Mad Doctor, The Impostor* etc

Autobiographies: *The Musical Tour of Mr Dibdin* (Sheffield, 1788), *The Professional Life of Mr Dibdin* (London, 1803); Biographies: Kitchener, W: *A Brief Memoir of Charles Dibdin* (London, 1884), Thorn, H: *Charles Dibdin* (London, 1888) etc

DICK Comic opera in 2 acts by Alfred Murray. Music by Edward Jakobowski. Globe Theatre, London, 17 April 1884.

A comic-opera variation on the familiar *Dick Whittington* story, this piece had Dick outwitting the Emperor of Morocco to win the hand of Alice Fitzwarren in a plot in which the key cat-eats-rats part of the tale was almost incidentally popped into the final act to round off what was basically a good deal of topical and Oriental high-jinks. A commission from the Gaiety Theatre's John Hollingshead to the up-and-coming author and composer, it was played at three London theatres (Globe, Gaiety, Empire) for a total of over a hundred performances with Camille Dubois (later Fannie Leslie) and soprano Ethel Pierson as hero and heroine and co-producer and comic John Shine as Fitzwarren. It was also subsequently played both in Australia, by the Brough and Boucicault management with Fanny Robina featured as Dick, and on the Eastern circuits.

Other stage musical variants of the *Dick Whittington* tale have included the London opéras-bouffes *Whittington* (Jacques Offenbach/H B Farnie, Alhambra 26 December 1874) and *Dandy Dick Whittington* (Ivan Caryll/George Sims Avenue Theatre 2 March 1895), and the 19th-century burlesques *Whittington Junior and His Sensation Cat* (Robert Reece, Royalty 1870), *Young Dick Whittington or Here's the Cat* (J Wilton Jones, Leicester, 1881) and *Whittington and His Cat* (F C Burnand, Gaiety Theatre, 1881) as well, in more recent days, as a long run of pantomimes, in which form the tale has found its most enduring exposition.

A 1920s Jack Buchanan–Elsie Randolph show, *Mr Whittington*, showed even less care for the old tale than *Dick* had done, and limited itself to the basic 'turn again' theme. It didn't even have a cat in the cast.

Australia: Melbourne Opera House 6 August 1887

DICKENS, Charles [John Huffham] (b Portsea, 7 February 1812; d Gadshill, 9 June 1870).

The popular novelist Charles Dickens made one venture into the musical theatre in his lifetime, when he combined with the composer John Hullah on an operetta, *The Village Coquettes*, produced at the St James's Theatre 6 December 1836. However, he won a much wider theatrical representation after his death, when many of his works were adapted for the stage, both straight and musical.

The composer Karl Goldmark made a highly successful opera, *Das Heimchen am Herd* (Hofoperntheater, Vienna 21 March 1896), from the novel *The Cricket on the Hearth*, a work which was also set to music by Zandonai (Turin 28 November 1908) and by Alexander Mackenzie (London 6 June 1914), whilst Eric Coates made a three-act opera, *Pickwick*, from *The Pickwick Papers*, but the majority of Dickens adaptations were in a lighter musical vein.

The Pickwick tales were used again in the 19th century as the bases for Edward Solomon's one-act London operetta *Pickwick*, and for Charles and Manuel Klein's full-length *Mr Pickwick*, produced at Broadway's Herald Square Theater in 1903 with De Wolf Hopper starred as Pickwick, whilst the other most-used Dickens piece of earlier years, *Barnaby Rudge*, was put to use (mixed with other elements) in making up the American comic opera *Dolly Varden* (Herald Square Theater 7 January 1902). A British piece on the same bases, *Dolly Varden, or the Riots of '80* (Brighton Aquarium, E Cympson) was produced in 1889 and a third *Dolly Varden* made regular appearances in the repertoire of the juvenile operetta companies. In Hungary, Iszó Barna wrote a musical score for a version of *A Christmas Carol* entitled *Karácsony* (Népszinház 13 December 1901) which was not strictly a musical but a seasonal spectacular.

It was the production of the enormously successful British musical comedy version of *Oliver Twist* as *Oliver!* (1960) which opened the floodgates for singing-and-dancing Dickens adaptations, mostly on the English-language stage. In its wake, *The Pickwick Papers* was given another musicalization as a long-running vehicle for then substantial Welsh star Harry Secombe (*Pickwick*, Saville Theatre 4 July 1963), and yet another, as *Herr Pickwick*, in Prague (Petr Zdenk/Ivo Fischer 1970). *David Copperfield* became, more snappily (but without an exclamation point), *Copperfield* (Joel Hirschorn, Al Kasha Anta Theater 16 April 1981) for 13 performances on Broadway, and *A Tale of Two Cities*, with its title similarly circumcised to *Two Cities* (Jeff Wayne/Jerry Wayne/Constance Cox Palace Theatre 27 February 1969), played 44 uncomfortable nights on the London stage. *A Christmas Carol* got a number of goings over as a festive entertainment, plus more full-sized American remakes as *Comin' Uptown* (Garry Sherman/Peter Udell/Philip Rose, Udell Winter Garden Theater 20 December 1979) and *Penny for Penny* (Michel Legrand/Sheldon Harnick) with Richard Kiley as Ebenezer Scrooge, and a British one as *Scrooge* (Leslie Bricusse, 1992). Two attempts at versions of *Great Expectations* (*My Gentleman Pip*, Harrogate 3 December 1968; *Great Expectations* Guildford 24 December 1975 with John Mills as Joe Gargery) and a *Hard Times* (Coventry, 6 November 1973) were seen in the British provinces.

If *Nicholas Nickleby* itself escaped being made into *Nicholas!*, its most eligible characters, the theatrical Crummles family, were used for a range of shows including William Mitchell's 19th-century American burlesque *The Savage and the Maiden* and two small-scale modern English pieces, *Step Into the Limelight* (Bristol, 15 January 1962)

Plate 74. **Dorothy Dickson** *takes a singing lesson from Olive Gilbert in* Careless Rapture.

and *Nickleby and Me* (Ron Grainer/Caryl Brahms, Ned Sherrin Stratford East, 16 December 1975). The same period also brought forward several singing-Dickens films, including musical versions of *A Christmas Carol* and *The Old Curiosity Shop* (*Quilp*), and a television musical of *The Cricket on the Hearth* (Maury Laws/Jules Bass/Romeo Muller, Arthur Rankin 18 December 1967).

The most recent musicalized Dickens to deck the Broadway and London stage has been the music-hally retelling, with alternative endings, of the melodramatic incidents of his uncompleted *The Mystery of Edwin Drood* (Imperial Theater 2 December 1985).

DICKSON, Dorothy (b Kansas City, 26 July 1898). American dancing ingénue of the 1920s who scored several successes in such rôles on the London stage before becoming Ivor Novello's leading lady for two shows.

Dorothy Dickson began her performing career in a ballroom dance team with her husband, Carl Hyson [né Heisen] and was moved into the theatre when Ray Comstock spotted them performing in a Kansas City hotel. She made her first stage appearances paired with Hyson as a featured dance duo in the original production of *Oh, Boy!* and in the *Ziegfeld Follies of 1917*, played the Coconut Grove and then quickly moved up the ladder to play the ingénue rôle in Frank Tours's musical *Girl o'Mine* (1918, Betty) at the Bijou Theater. A few weeks after that show's quick passing, she was popped hurriedly into a featured dancing rôle in Jerome Kern's *Rock-a-Bye Baby* (Dorothy Manners) and when that show, too, vanished swiftly, she moved on to a third Broadway engagement within six months, back in the *Ziegfeld Follies*. In 1919 she took a dancing rôle in George M Cohan's parody comic opera *The Royal Vagabond* (Carlotta) and the following year appeared with Hyson in a spot in *Lassie* at the Nora Bayes Theater (Lady Gwendolyn Spencer-Hill).

In 1921 the pair were seen in London in C B Cochran's revue *London, Paris and New York* and, as a result, Miss Dickson was offered the title-rôle in George Grossmith and Pat Malone's London production of *Sally*. The success of *Sally* established her as a West End star and, settling in Britain, she appeared in the years that followed in 'Marilynn Miller' rôles in two other Kern musicals *The*

Cabaret Girl (1922, Marilynn Morgan) and *The Beauty Prize* (1923, Carol Stuart), as well as in the title-rôle of the British musical *Patricia*, in Charlot's revue, as Peter Pan in a revival of Barrie's play, and in three made-for-Broadway pieces, *Tip-Toes* (1926, Tip-Toes Kaye), *Peggy-Ann* (1927, Peggy-Ann) and, in succession to Mamie Watts, in *Hold Everything!* (1929, t/o Sue O'Keefe).

After playing in the London productions of the Continental musicals *The Wonder Bar* (1930, Liane) and *Casanova* (1932, Princess Potomska), she appeared for a while in revue and in straight theatre, but she returned to the musical stage in 1936 to play opposite Ivor Novello in his grandiose *Careless Rapture* (Penelope Lee) and *The Crest of the Wave* (1937, Honey Wortle) at the Theatre Royal, Drury Lane. Her later work was limited to revue, plays and variety.

DIETZ, Howard (b New York, 8 September 1896; d New York, 30 July 1983). The lyricist of many enduring songs and popular revues, who did not ever approach finding a real success in the field of the book musical.

Dietz began writing light verse at college, where he numbered Hammerstein and Lorenz Hart amongst his contemporaries and, after working in both journalism and advertising, had an early song success with 'Alibi Baby' (music: Stephen Jones) in the musical comedy *Poppy* (1923). He was thrown in at the deep end when asked by Jerome Kern to write the lyrics for the musical comedy *Dear Sir*, but the show failed and, in the years that followed, whilst Dietz concentrated on the first part of his 30-year Hollywood stint as head of publicity at MGM, his theatre-lyrical output was largely angled towards revue.

One of these revues was *The Little Show*, in which he paired with composer Arthur Schwartz, and the pairing turned out to be a durable one. In the decade 1927–37, Broadway welcomed a wave of Dietz/Schwartz revues and a long list of popular songs ('I Guess I'll Have to Change My Plan', 'Something to Remember You By', 'Dancing in the Dark', 'A Shine on Your Shoes' etc), but the only musical comedy scores which the team produced were a tacked-together affair made up for the British show *Here Comes the Bride* and Broadway's *Revenge with Music* and *Between the Devil*. The first of the three was produced by Julian Wylie at the Blackpool Opera House in 1929, played at the Piccadilly and Lyceum, Theatres in London for 175 performances in early 1930 and produced one memorable song, 'High and Low'. The second, a piece based on the Spanish 'Three-cornered Hat' tale, which Dietz also directed, had a shorter life but left a richer legacy ('You and the Night and the Music', 'If There is Someone Lovelier Than You', 158 performances), as did the third, the farcical *Between the Devil* ('I See Your Face Before Me', 'By Myself', 93 performances.)

It was 1944 before, after a false start with the quickly closing *Dancing in the Streets*, Dietz returned to Broadway with two further shows written in collaboration with composer Vernon Duke. Neither proved successful, and it was 15 years more before he and Schwartz made their only further attempts together at a book musical for Broadway, first with the old-fashioned *The Gay Life* (1961, 113 performances) and then with an unfortunate period vehicle for Mary Martin, *Jennie* (1963, 82 performances).

Dietz was married to designer Lucinda Ballard (b

1906) (*Annie Get Your Gun*, *Silk Stockings* *The Sound of Music* etc.).

1924 **Dear Sir** (Jerome Kern/Edgar Selwyn) Times Square Theater 23 September
1929 **Here Comes the Bride** (Arthur Schwartz/w Desmond Carter/R P Weston, Bert Lee) Blackpool Opera House 7 October; Piccadilly Theatre, London 20 February 1930
1934 **Revenge With Music** (Schwartz) New Amsterdam Theater 28 November
1937 **Between the Devil** (Schwartz) Imperial Theater 22 December
1943 **Dancing in the Streets** (Vernon Duke/w John Cecil Holm) Boston 23 March
1944 **Jackpot** (Duke/w Guy Bolton, Sidney Sheldon, Ben Roberts) Alvin Theater 13 January
1944 **Sadie Thompson** (Duke/w Rouben Mamoulian) Alvin Theater 16 November
1961 **The Gay Life** (Schwartz/Fay and Michael Kanin) Shubert Theater 18 November
1963 **Jennie** (Schwartz/Arnold Schulman) Majestic Theater 17 October

Autobiography: *Dancing in the Dark* (Quadrangle, New York, 1974)

DILLINGHAM, Charles [Bancroft] (b Hartford, Conn, 30 May 1868; d New York, 30 August 1934). Top-flight Broadway producer of the first decades of the 20th century.

The young Dillingham's early working life was spent in the newspaper world, latterly as a dramatic critic and an editor at the *New York Evening Sun*, but in 1898 he wrote and produced a play of his own and, although it was a failure, he soon found himself a live-in part of the American theatre world. He took a job on the staff of producer Charles Frohman, but this proved to be only an interim position but, within two years, he had set himself firmly on the way to a secure career as a producer with a regular and often ambitious programme of plays.

He produced his first musical, an adaptation of the French opérette *Le Jockey malgré lui*, with its score torn out and replaced by some Ludwig Englander music, in 1903, under the title *The Office Boy*. Frank Daniels was its star and Louise Gunning and Eva Tanguay sang most of its songs through two Broadway months. Thereafter, for some 30 years, Dillingham staged a regular list of musicals, largely home-made, turning only very occasionally, and usually with fine taste, to European stages for proven material which (with one notable exception) he treated better than he had *Le Jockey malgré lui* – the jolly *Sergeant Brue* for Daniels (1905), the international hit *The Girl on the Train* (1910, *Die geschiedene Frau*), London's *Betty* (1916), *One Kiss* (a sad, sanitized version of the French *Ta bouche*, 1923) and Leo Fall's splendid *Madame Pompadour* (1924).

His earliest efforts as a producer included a series of Victor Herbert musicals, beginning with the underfortunate Fritzi Scheff vehicle *Babette* (1903), continuing with *Miss Dolly Dollars* (1906) and, with very much more success, a second piece for Miss Scheff, *Mlle Modiste* (1905), the Montgomery and Stone comedy musical *The Red Mill* (1906) and another Daniels vehicle, *The Tattooed Man* (1907). The association between Herbert and Dillingham continued through the years, sometimes with more and sometimes with less success. *La Prima Donna*

(1908) for Scheff was not a winner, but *The Lady of the Slipper* (1913) for Montgomery and Stone very definitely was, and the association ended only after 14 years of collaboration with the revues *The Century Girl* (1916) and *Miss 1917*, co-productions between Dillingham and Ziegfeld.

The association with Montgomery and Stone, however, continued beyond that, and with considerable success. *The Red Mill*, *The Old Town* (1910) and *The Lady of the Slipper* were followed by *Chin-Chin* (1914) and, after Montgomery's death, Dillingham produced for Stone, alone, *Jack o'Lantern* (1917), *Tip Top* (1920), *Stepping Stones* (1923), *Criss Cross* (1926) and *Ripples* (1930), this last being Dillingham's final musical comedy production.

Two Ludwig Englander musicals, the olde Englishe *A Madcap Princess* (1904) and the musicalization of *She Stoops to Conquer* as *The Two Roses* (1904) for Miss Scheff, a concoction made over from Tristan Bernard's *La Soeur* by many hands into something called *The Hoyden* and Gustave Luders's *The Fair Co-Ed*, both constructed to feature the young impressionist Elsie Janis, were also amongst the other productions of Dillingham's earlier years, at the end of which he had done sufficiently well to sponsor the building of the new Globe Theater on Broadway and 46th Street.

The Old Town was the opening attraction, and Dillingham continued there with *The Echo* (a quick failure) and *The Girl on the Train*, which also surprisingly failed to run. Leslie Stuart's made-for-Broadway musical *The Slim Princess* with Elsie Janis in the title-rôle did only a little better, and it wasn't until Eddie Foy arrived at the beginning of 1912 with *Over the River* that Dillingham (in association with Ziegfeld) had something that looked like a success back in his theatre.

There was no doubt, however, about the success of the Irving Berlin revue *Watch Your Step* which, with *Chin-Chin*, made 1914 a bonanza year for their producer, and thereafter Dillingham turned much of his attention to revue productions. The following year he took over the management of the vast New York Hippodrome from the Shuberts and, beginning with *Hip! Hip! Hooray!* (1915), produced, over the next seven years, a series of extravagant and generally successful super-sized spectacles.

On the musical comedy front, Dillingham continued to place his faith in the attractions of the multi-talented Elsie Janis (*Miss Information*, 1915) and the music of Ivan Caryll, who had served him so well with his scores for the Fred Stone shows (*The Canary*, 1918), but he also produced a series of musical comedies with scores by Jerome Kern, beginning with *Miss Information* and continuing through the *Miss 1917* revue (w Herbert), *She's a Good Fellow* (1919), *The Night Boat* (1920), *Good Morning, Dearie* (1921), *The Bunch and Judy* (1922), *The City Chap* (1925) and *Lucky* (1927), with varying results, until a memorable success was reached with *Sunny* in 1925.

The operetta *Apple Blossoms* (1919), with a score by Victor Jacobi and Fritz Kreisler, was a splendid success at the Globe, but *The Girl From Home* (1920), a musical version of *The Dictator* brought in from Chicago, gave him the quickest failure of his career when squabbles amongst author, star and producer forced him to close after just three weeks on Broadway. It was left to Fred Stone and *Tip Top* to keep the Dillingham production schedule bubbling

along profitably in 1920. When Jacobi supplied Dillingham with a second score, for *The Half Moon* (1920), and a third, *The Love Letter* (1921), fortune failed to smile as it had the first time.

Dillingham shared billing with John Cort and Martin Beck to produce one last work by the composer A Baldwin Sloane, who had been one of the earliest American writers to point his nose in musical comedy three decades previously, but *China Rose* did less well than Dillingham's solo productions of the inevitable Elsie Janis revue, *Puzzles of 1925*, and of *Sunny* which brought 1925 to a successful finish for him. The failure of Vincent Youmans's *Oh Please!* (1926) and of Rodgers and Hart's *She's My Baby* (1928) were unpleasant surprises, and the variety musical *Sidewalks of New York* (1927) and *Three Cheers* (1928), intended for Fred Stone who had to drop out in favour of Will Rogers, did a little to even the balance.

Whatever balance there might have been, however, went wholly awry when the Depression struck. Dillingham was ruined, and although his name appeared as producer of the revue *New Faces* in 1934, it was only as a mark of esteem to a hugely liked man from the fellow producers who backed the show and pinned his name to the masthead. Shortly after, Dillingham died.

An endlessly enthusiastic and gentlemanly producer with a lavish yet tasteful production style, his long list of musical productions glittered with the great names of the period, but all too often with the wrong shows. He produced nine musicals with scores by Jerome Kern, yet amongst all the flops and semi-successes he got only *Sunny* and, to a lesser degree, *The Night Boat* and *Good Morning, Dearie* of the real money-makers. He produced no less than nine Victor Herbert-pieces and, though he got *The Red Mill* and *Mlle Modiste*, he missed *Naughty Marietta* and *Sweethearts*. After *Watch Your Step* and *Stop! Look! Listen!* (1915) he got nothing else from Berlin, and the Youmans, Rodgers and Hart and Leslie Stuart pieces he produced were nowhere near their best. Similarly, having secured the American rights to such internationally successful foreign shows as *Die geschiedene Frau* and *Ta bouche*, he found them drawing a blank on Broadway. Yet he was not only a successful theatrical businessman, but one of the most respected, trusted and liked men on Broadway.

Dillingham was briefly married to actress and vocalist Jennie Yeamans (1862–1906).

DIRKENS, Annie [HAMMERSTEIN, Baroness Anna von] (b Berlin, 25 September 1869; d Vienna, 11 November 1942). Star soubrette of the Viennese stage for 20 years up to the First World War.

German-born daughter of a railway official of British origin, Annie Dirkens trained in Berlin and Dresden and appeared at Berlin's Viktoria-Theater at 19 years of age as a soubrette. She subsequently played at the Adolf-Ernst Theater, at Hamburg's Carl-Schultze Theater and at the Leipzig Stadttheater before being engaged, in 1895, at the Theater an der Wien. There, after making her début as Zeller's Brief-Christl, she created a two-year series of Operette rôles, including Catherine Molton (*Der goldene Kamerad*), Pauline (Johann Strauss's *Waldmeister*, 1895), Tessa (*Mister Menelaus*), the title-rôle of the marvellous 'boy' violinist Paola/Paolo in von Taund's *Der Wunderknabe*, the trouser-rôle of Gaston Dulac in the German-language version of Verő's *Der Löwenjäger* (1896) and Comtesse Mathilde Nevers in Strauss's *Die Göttin der Vernunft* (1897). During the same period she visited London with the Saxe-Coburg company and appeared briefly in the British version of *Der Wunderknabe* (*The Little Genius*).

Mixing straight and musical shows, she played for a period at the Theater in der Josefstadt, scoring a major hit in the German version of *Les Fêtards* (*Wie man Männer fesselt*) in both Vienna and Berlin, and made her début at the Carltheater, star-billed, as Adrienne in Weinberger's *Die Diva* (1900). She appeared there again the following year in the title-rôle of *Die Primadonna* (Nina Traquet), starred at the Berliner Theater in *Der jüngste Leutnant* etc and took the title-rôle in the French spectacular *Die Ringstrassen-Prinzessin* (*Messalinette*, 1905) at Danzers Orpheum, before, in 1906, travelling to America where she repeated her *Fêtards* rôle at the Irving Place Theater.

Subsequent Viennese musical appearances included Minna in *Miss Hook of Holland* (1907), her most memorable creation as the free-loving actress Gonda van der Loo in *Die geschiedene Frau* (1908), a season at the Établissement Ronacher in Ziehrer's *In 50 Jahren*, then as Ella (ex-Eileen) in *Die Arkadier* (1911), and the title-rôle of the irresistible Alma in *Alma, wo wohnst du?* at the Lustspieltheater (1911).

A field sister in the ambulance corps during the First World War, she had the misfortune to have her own husband, the Baron von Hammerstein, brought, dying, into her care. When she returned to the theatre after the war, she found that her best days were past. She appeared at the Bürgertheater in Hugo Hirsch's *Die Scheidungsreise* (1921), but played largely in non-musical theatre before her career faded out. In her elder days she ran a tobacco kiosk near the Vienna Burgtheater.

LA DIVA Opéra-bouffe in 3 acts by Henri Meilhac and Ludovic Halévy. Music by Jacques Offenbach. Théâtre des Bouffes-Parisiens, Paris, 22 March 1869.

A piece written and composed specially for the great opéra-bouffe star, Hortense Schneider, which, for all that there were apparently striking similarities with an earlier work, *Adélaïde, ou Dix ans de la vie d'une artiste*, was touted as being all but an autobiomusical. Schneider played a Parisian shopgirl who, when her intended turns up late for her wedding, chucks him and her shopworking life and goes off to become a star. She shoots to the top, and soon has marquises and dukes chasing after her in all too predictable a fashion. Désiré headed the male cast in the rôle of Raphaël.

In spite of an attractive score, in which the simple duo 'Tu la connais, ma douce maîtresse, la blonde Lischen' proved both the most reminiscent and the most popular, and in spite of Schneider at the head of affairs, the piece was apparently found to be in less than the best taste, and it was a round flop. However, such failure in Paris did not stop even this least successful of Offenbach works from being given further showings, albeit in a heavily worked-over state. The piece produced at the Theater an der Wien by Marie Geistinger and Maximilian Steiner, under the title *Die Theaterprinzessin* (ad F Zell, Richard Genée), was advertised as a 'musikalische Burleske' which made 'partial use' of the plot of *La Diva*. Geistinger starred as house-

maid Susi Apfelwein who, five years later, is seen in a new metamorphosis as the Viennese Operette prima donna Adele Cliquot. She played her for 23 performances. The following year this version was played in Hungary, and the show was subsequently seen in Germany, but without establishing itself in any of these areas as a repeatable part of the Offenbach canon.

The show's slightly self-congratulatory title was also used for a German Operette. Weinberger's *Die Diva*, produced at Vienna's Carltheater with Annie Dirkens starred, did no better than Offenbach's works, and pieces called *The Primadonna* have found a similar fate in both Britain and America.

Austria: Theater an der Wien *Die Theaterprinzessin* 21 December 1872; Hungary: *Adel, vagy szinpad a szinpadon* 1873; Germany: Wallnertheater *Die Theaterprinzessin* 1875

DIVORCE ME, DARLING! Musical comedy of the 1930s in 2 acts by Sandy Wilson. Players' Theatre, London, 15 December 1964; Globe Theatre, 1 February 1965.

A sequel to Wilson's blockbusting *The Boy Friend*, *Divorce Me, Darling!* followed the characters of the first show beyond marriage and towards some tiny threatenings of divorce. Polly (Patricia Michael) flirts a little with Bobby (Cy Young), whose sister (Irlin Hall) turns up equipped with a stout pair of lungs and a song called 'Here Am I, But Where's the Guy?'. Mme Dubonnet (Joan Sterndale Bennett) has become a cabaret artiste ('Blondes for Danger') and an even older Lord Brockhurst is still 'On the Loose' chasing nubile girlies. Several *Boy Friend* artists played 'themselves' again (Maria Charles, Geoffrey Hibberd, Violetta) in a charming not-so-small piece whose 87 performances in the West End did not reflect the extent of its attractions.

A production at the Texas Theatre Under the Stars in 1984 paired *Divorce Me, Darling!* in an evening's entertainment with the original short version of *The Boy Friend*.

(See also page 362.)

USA: Theatre Under the Stars, Houston, Texas 14 July 1984
Recording: original cast (Decca)

DIXEY, Henry E [DIXON, Henry] (b Boston, 6 January 1859; d Atlantic City, 25 February 1943). Musical burlesque and comedy star, who won enduring fame in the long-running *Adonis*.

Dixey began his career as a boy actor in Boston and is alleged to have made his début as half-a-cow in a revival of *Evangeline*. He made his early Broadway appearances in minor comic rôles in *The Babes in the Wood* at the Union Square and as the harem-keeper, Mustapha, in *Fatinitza* at Booth's Theatre in 1880, during a period as a chorister and bit-part player with the Boston Ideal Comic Opera Company. He next played supporting rôles in the burlesques *Evangeline*, *The Corsair*, *Robinson Crusoe* and *Hiawatha* and the entertainments *Revels* and *Horrors* with Edward Rice's Surprise Party company of musical farce-comedians, and his first major musical theatre engagements came in 1883 when he was seen at the Fifth Avenue Theatre playing J H Ryley's rôle of the Lord Chancellor opposite the original American *Iolanthe*, Marie Jansen, and, paired with the same star, as the comical monarch, Laurent XVII, in *La Mascotte*.

Plate 75. **Divorce Me, Darling!**: *Anna Sharkey (left) and Patricia Michael (centre) forget themselves momentarily to look amazed-horrified at the goings-on between Fred Stone and Joan Heal.*

He appeared thereafter in further leading musico-comic rôles as Sir Joseph Porter, Sir Mincing Lane in *Billee Taylor*, Peter Papyrus in *The New Evangeline*, partnering Louise Lester as the comical horse-dopers of the English musical *The Merry Duchess*, as Frippaponne in Rice's *Captain Hélène of the Guards* and as John Wellington Wells in *The Sorcerer*, but in 1884 his long-time employer, Edward Rice, provided him with the plum part needed to turn a lead comedy actor into a popular star when he produced the burlesque *Adonis* at the Bijou Theatre with Dixey in the leggy title rôle.

Adonis, a sort of *Die schöne Galathee* with the sexes reversed and decorated with a movable set of songs ('It's English, You Know', 'I'm Nobody from Nowhere', 'The Wall Street Broker') and burlesque scenes, had a record-breaking 19-month run on Broadway, returned regularly over the next decade, and played a summer season at London's Gaiety Theatre, in each case with Dixey in the rôle which had made him famous. His appearances thereafter ranged from classic comedy to a variety of star vehicles, most of which were musical, including a revusical piece called *The Seven Ages* (1889), a spectacular burlesque *Rip van Winkle* in Chicago (1890), revivals of *Patience*,

Iolanthe, *La Mascotte* and *The Sorcerer*, under his own management, and all-star Gilbert and Sullivan at the Herald Square Theatre in 1896 in which he was seen as Sir Joseph Porter and Bunthorne.

Dixey appeared in the revusical *In Gayest Manhattan* at Koster & Bials in 1897, paired with Francis Wilson as Ravannes in a revival of *Erminie*, the show which (depending how you count) had deprived *Adonis* of its long-run records, and in 1900 had his first modern musical comedy rôle when he took a turn as Peter Stuyvesant in Luders and Pixley's long-touring *The Burgomaster*.

He visited London in 1901 and appeared at the Adelphi Theatre in a version of the New York revue *The Whirl of the Town*, but on his return to America appeared almost entirely in plays (including Barrie's *Little Mary*) and vaudeville, returning to the musical stage only in 1917 to play Courtice Pounds's rôle of Ali Baba in the spectacular Broadway production of *Chu Chin Chow*. He later played alongside Fay Marbe and Vivienne Segal in the out-of-town tryout of Ivan Caryll's *Little Miss Raffles* (1921) and made his final appearance on the musical stage in 1928 when he replaced George M Cohan in Cohan's own *The Merry Malones*.

Dixey produced several pieces, in alliance with Rice and with the firm of Miles and Barton (*The Corsair*), and made sufficient contribution to the text of *Adonis* to be sometimes credited as its co-author.

He died after being knocked down by a bus in Atlantic City at the age of 84.

LE DOCTEUR OX   Opérette in 3 acts by Philippe Gille and Arnold Mortier, adapted from the novel by Jules Verne. Music by Jacques Offenbach. Théâtre des Variétés, Paris, 26 January 1877.

Mortier and Gille's musical version of Verne's story followed the career of Doctor Ox (José Dupuis) and his attempts to rouse the very underpaced village of Quiquendonne to vigour and intellectual excellence by spraying its inhabitants with oxygen. It did not follow the original novel, however, when it introduced a couple of opéra-bouffe love stories for the benefit of the Théatre des Variétés' leading ladies. Anna Judic played an amorous gipsy princess, Prascovia, who is rebuffed by the scientific doctor and thereafter determines to wreck his plans, whilst Mlle Beaumaine played Suzel, the daughter of the burgomaster van Tricasse (Pradeau), who awakens peculiar feelings of friendship in Ox. Léonce appeared as Ygène, the Doctor's familiar (Ox + Ygène = oxygène), Baron was burgomaster Niklausse van Tricasse, Guyon was the local fire-commissioner and Cooper appeared as his son, Franz.

The show was decorated with a typical Offenbach score in which Judic's couplets 'Tout s'eveille dans la nature' with its roucouling runs, her marche bohémienne ('Pour l'enfant de Bohème'), her Légende de la Guzla (apparently a musical instrument) and her dialect Duo flamand with the Doctor ('Changeons de langue') proved the star highlights, alongside an entrance number for Dupuis and some last-act couplets for the number two couple, Cooper and Mlle Beaumaine.

Le Docteur Ox was produced with all the lavishness and the starry casting the Variétés had at its disposal at the time but, in spite of a warm initial reception, it failed to draw for long. It managed only a disappointing 42 performances in Paris, but even that was more than Franz's Steiner's Vienna production (ad uncredited) which featured Hubert Wilke as Ox, Karoline Finaly as Prascovia, Girardi as Ygène and Wilhelm Knaack as the Burgomaster. It failed wholly to take and was played just ten times.

Docteur Ox itself may have had a limited career, but it spawned an exceedingly long-lived British burlesque, *Oxygen* (arr John Fitzergald/Robert Reece, H B Farnie 31 March 1877), based on a mixture of Verne's story and Offenbach's opérette, which was played by Lydia Thompson and her company in both Britain and America.

A revised version of the original work was produced in Cologne in 1978 (19 September).

Austria: Theater an der Wien *Doktor Ox* 29 April 1882

THE DOCTOR OF ALCANTARA   Opéra-bouffe in 2 acts by Benjamin E Woolf. Music by Julius Eichberg. Boston Museum, Boston, 7 April 1862; Théâtre Français, New York, 28 May 1866.

The first American musical play to make a success both in America and abroad, *The Doctor of Alcantara*, although both derivative and imitative in text and music, is a much

more substantial and significant piece than *The Black Crook* (produced four years later) which has served so often as a starting point for histories of America's musical stage. A text written by British-born, American-bred Benjamin Woolf (who wrote texts for a series of musicals, staged mostly in Boston) and compiled from mainly familiar scenes and situations from British and Continental comic operas, and most notably those of *La Guerre ouverte, ou ruse contre ruse*, was paired with a score by German-Bostonian Julius Eichberg, musical director at the Boston Museum, the whole making up into an agreeable and much appreciated light opera.

The plot followed the student, Carlos, in his attempts to woo Isabella, daughter of the Doctor Paracelus, against the wishes of her vain and ambitious mother. When he is delivered to the house in a basket, it is dumped in the river, when he is offered wine it turns out to be a sleeping draught and the Doctor thinks he has committed murder, but, at the end of everything, the boy turns out to be – of course – the very unknown young man whom Isabella's parents had earmarked for her.

The dozen items of the first act included a pretty tenor/soprano duo 'I Love, I Love', a serenade ('Wake, lady, wake') and cavatina for the tenor (Carlos), a ballad ('The Knight of Alcantara') and a romance for the soprano, and an arietta ('When a Lover is Poor') for the contralto, as well as a basso piece declaring 'I'm Don Hypolito Lopez Pomposo' for the Alguazil, who topped up the buffo element of the piece, and some ensemble and choral work. The shorter second act included only a trio, a quartet and a finale.

After having been successfully played in its native Boston, *The Doctor of Alcantara* was taken to New York, where it was seen played by three different companies during the 1866-7 season. One group was directed by Eichberg himself (New York Theater 29 September 1866), a second was Caroline Richings's company, which toured the piece back to Boston in 1868 and gave fine coverage to Eichberg's works thereafter. *The Doctor of Alcantara* reappeared on a number of occasions over more than a decade, being seen in New York as late as 1882 when Fred Zimmerman's company played it as part of their programme at the Metropolitan Alcazar (5 July).

In Britain, the show was taken into the repertoire of the newly fledged Carl Rosa Opera Company, but it was also given a non-repertoire London showing at Holborn, under the management of J W Currans, with Blanche Ellerman, W H Woodfield, Lia Rohan, George Bassett and J A Arnold heading the cast. This set of performances gave it the distinction of being the first American musical to be played in London's commercial theatre. A few weeks later it won the same distinction in Australia when the Kelly and Leon minstrel company produced their version of *The Doctor of Alcantara* at their theatre on the corner of Sydney's King and York streets. Kelly appeared as Dr Paracelsus, with his son, Edwin Lester, as Balthazar, Leon in travesty as Inez and Emma Wangenheim as Isabel. It was well enough received to be brought back for further performances later in the minstrel season.

UK: Liverpool *The Village Doctor* 21 October 1873, Connaught Theatre, London *Alcantara* 1 November 1879; Australia: Kelly and Leon's Opera House, Sydney 26 December 1879

DO I HEAR A WALTZ? Musical in 2 acts by Arthur Laurents, based on his play *The Time of the Cuckoo*. Lyrics by Stephen Sondheim. Music by Richard Rodgers. 46th Street Theater, New York, 18 March 1965.

Do I Hear a Waltz? brought Arthur Laurents and Stephen Sondheim, who had already collaborated on book and lyrics for *West Side Story*, *Gypsy* and *Anyone Can Whistle*, together with veteran composer Richard Rodgers, whose sole Broadway show in the six years since *The Sound of Music* and the death of Oscar Hammerstein had been the 1962 *No Strings*.

Do I Hear a Waltz? was based on Laurents's play *The Time of the Cuckoo*, a Broadway success with Shirley Booth starred and already metamorphosed into a film, *Summertime*, with Katharine Hepburn in the central rôle. It followed a middle-ageing New York secretary, Leona (Elizabeth Allen), on a trip to Venice. There she at last encounters romance, in the person of the older, married and illusionless Di Rossi (Sergio Franchi). It is a kind of romance which does not fit in with her preconceptions and which, in spite of the fact that she will probably never have another such chance, she finally rejects.

With all three writers contributing of their very finest, the show boasted a feeling libretto and a memorable score ranging from the soaring tenor solos 'Stay', 'Someone Like You' and 'Take the Moment' to the crisply comic 'What Do We Do? We Fly!' and 'We're Gonna Be All Right' allotted to supporting characters, the heroine's excited 'Someone Woke Up' and 'Do I Hear a Waltz?', and a lovely trio in which three women look at the 'Moon in my Window' and think about their respective men.

In spite of all its plusses, the show was not a popular success. Its 'musical play' nature frightened both Rodgers and director John Dexter, and some more traditional Broadway elements (including dancers and dancing) were shovelled into the production on the road, leaving it to reach Broadway in a dishevelled state for a run of 220 performances.

Recording: original cast (Columbia)

DOLARO, Selina [SIMMONDS, Selina] (b London, 20 August 1849; d New York, 23 January 1889).

The daughter of the London theatrical musical director B J Simmonds, 'Dolly' Dolaro was trained at the Paris Conservatoire and made her official stage début in a matinée at the Gaiety Theatre, playing alongside Nellie Farren and John Maclean as Urgandula in Adam's *Magic Toys* (*Les Pantins de Violette*) in 1871. A few months later, in the milestone London production of *Chilpéric*, her dashing Jewish looks and fine voice swept her to stardom in the rôle of the burlesque Spanish Princess Galswinthe. She followed up by appearing in the title-rôle of *Geneviève de Brabant* and, after taking time off to bear the first of her four children, took lead rôles in the English version of *La Cour du Roi Pétaud* (Princess Girandole), the triumphant English-language *La Fille de Madame Angot* (Clairette) and the Lecocq pasticcio, *The Black Prince* (1874, Sybil).

In 1875 she went into management and presented herself as *La Périchole* and as Mlle Lange in a much altered star-vehicle version of *Madame Angot*, completing her programme with the first-ever performances of *Trial By Jury* in which she did not, however, appear. She took over in *The Duke's Daughter* (the English version of *La Timbale*

d'argent, 1876, Malvina), played in several pieces at the Alhambra in 1877-8, including Strauss's *King Indigo* (Fantasca) and, inevitably, *La Fille de Madame Angot*, and in 1878 commissioned her own original opéra-bouffe vehicle, *Belladonna*, from Alfred Cellier. It failed to reach London, but Dolaro continued as producer-star, presenting herself in the lead rôles in *Les Dragons de Villars* (Rose Friquet), the burlesque *Another Drink* and Genée's *Der Seekadet* (Cerisette), before quitting Britain for New York.

There she made her first appearance as Carmen (27 October 1879) in Bizet's opera, under the management of Colonel Mapleson. The following season she repeated that character, this time in the burlesque *Carmen, or Soldiers and Seville-ians*, and won fine notices both for her singing and her much better than usual acting. She followed this up by starring in *La Fille du tambour-major* (1880 Stella), Audran's *Les Noces d'Olivette* (1881, Olivette), *La Mascotte* (1881, Bettina), and, in breeches, as Mignapour in his *Le Grand Mogol* (*The Snake Charmer*, 1881) under the management of Fred Zimmerman, and in the British musicals *Manteaux Noirs* (1882, Girola), *Rip van Winkle* (1882, Katrina) and *The Merry Duchess* (1883, Duchess of Epsom Downs), as well as in the straight theatre, notably as Polly Eccles in *Caste*.

She turned her hand to writing and authored several books and theatrical pieces (*Justine*, *Andrea*, *Fashion*) but her fortunes flagged and, after she had been seen at the Grand Opera House in a production of *Le Pont des soupirs* (April 1885), and in the rôle of a comic opera star in *In Spite of All*, she disappeared from the scene. When she was found, ill and wretched, the Lambs Club raised $4,000 at a benefit to support her, but she died shortly after at the age of 39.

DIE DOLLARPRINZESSIN Operette in 3 acts by A M Willner and Fritz Grünbaum, based on a comedy by Gatti-Trotha. Music by Leo Fall. Theater an der Wien, Vienna, 2 November 1907.

One of the most generally popular of Leo Fall's works, *Die Dollarprinzessin* was a Ruramerican piece, written very much in the format of the British musical comedies which had been sweeping the world for the past decade and more, and almost certainly constructed with an eye to the lucrative English-language market. It had a heroine who is the daughter and deputy of a millionaire New York coal businessman (millionaires, at this period, were obligatorily American – if the rich were Continental, they were noblemen) and who describes herself as an 'echtes Selbst-mademädel'. Her feminist attitudes lead Fredy, the desirable young German she has perversely made her secretary, to proudly refuse her as a wife until he has left her employ and, in good operettic fashion, spent the interval between Acts II and III becoming a wealthy coalman in his own right.

The rôles of Alice and Fredy were created by the original stars of *Die lustige Witwe*, Mizzi Günther and Louis Treumann, immediately following their long run together in the earlier piece. The untried but soon-to-be-famous Luise Kartousch (Daisy) as a teenaged American and Karl Meister (Hans) as a penniless German aristocrat provided the soubret parallel. The latter pair's jaunty song and dance to 'Wir tanzen Ringelreih'n' was the jolliest and most popular musical moment of the entertainment, but

Fall's score included several other delightful numbers: the title quartet in waltz-time, a chorus of up-to-date typists accompanied by the clacking of their machines, and a nicely vulgar 'Olga von der Wolga' for the cabaret artist, Olga Lapinska (Mizzi Wirth), who temporarily snares Alice's father (Franz Glawatsch, also director).

Karczag and Wallner's production was taken off after two and a half months to permit the newest Lehár work, *Der Mann mit den drei Frauen*, to be staged, and the show was little played in Vienna thereafter. However, *Die Dollarprinzessin* – no little thanks to the personal triumph scored by Frln Kartousch – was accounted a definite success. The show quickly appeared in Germany, where it proved an enormous hit, passing its 500th performance on 9 October 1909, and in Hungary (ad Jenő Farágo), but the all-important (for the writers' finances) British production was slow in coming. George Edwardes, who had immediately taken up the rights to the show, had Daly's Theatre filled with the long-running *The Merry Widow*. In consequence, his version held fire and a different English *Dollar Princess*, written by George Grossmith and directed by Edwardes's stage manager Pat Malone, opened on Broadway shortly before the Basil Hood/Adrian Ross adaptation Edwardes had ordered reached London. Both were, however, considerable successes.

Broadway's *The Dollar Princess* ran to 288 performances, even though Charles Frohman's production decorated Fall's score with a wave of interpolated numbers by Jerome Kern ('A Boat Sails on Wednesday', 'Red, White and Blue', 'Not Here, Not Here'), Frank Tours, W T Francis and even by Fall's brother Richard, for a cast headed by the Broadway Danilo, Donald Brian and English performers Valli Valli, Adrienne Augarde, Louie Pounds and F Pope Stamper. *Die Dollarprinzessin* was later also seen in New York in its original form when Hans Golle's company presented it in German at the Irving Place Theater in 1926 (19 February).

Like Vienna, London also used its *Merry Widow* stars, Lily Elsie and Joe Coyne, for the leading roles of *The Dollar Princess*, but it cast the latter as the heroine's brother (here, doubtless in deference to Coyne's dashing new image, replacing her father of the original text) and gave the romantic rôle to the more legitimately voiced Robert Michaelis, who had succeeded Coyne to the rôle of Danilo. It also revamped the subplot concerning Daisy (Gabrielle Ray), added a new rôle for comedy star Bill Berry, and fresh songs by both Fall and his brother Richard (some cut following the Manchester try-out). The alterations clearly did not harm its appeal, for London appreciated the show enormously and watched *The Dollar Princess* 428 times. Australia's *Dollar Princess* opened while London's ran on. Grace Edinsell (Alice), Herbert Clayton (Freddy), Lottie Sargent (Daisy) and J Roland Hogue (Dick) followed a Melbourne season with a good six weeks at Sydney's His Majesty's Theatre (28 May 1910).

France did not take up *Die Dollarprinzessin* at all until the Olympia-Casino at Nice enterprisingly mounted a version by 'Willy' (Henri Gauthier-Villars, the husband of Colette), which actually remained fairly close to the original, in 1911, with sufficient success for it to be picked up for Paris. The Théâtre de la Scala, however, ordered yet another version, from Antony Mars and Maurice Desvallières, for its production with ex-*Veuve joyeuse* Alice

O'Brien starred opposite Dutilloy, and the young Edmée Favart as Daisy paired with the tenor Edmond Tirmont in the lighter rôles.

Die Dollarprinzessin held a place in the Continental repertoire for some time after its first series of productions but, like the majority of Fall's works, it has largely slipped from the repertoire in recent decades, even on the home front.

Hungary: Király Színház *Dollárkirálynő* 21 March 1908; Germany: Neues Schauspielhaus 6 June 1908; USA: Knickerbocker Theater *The Dollar Princess* 6 September 1909; UK: Prince's Theatre, Manchester 24 December 1908, Daly's Theatre *The Dollar Princess* 25 September 1909; Australia: His Majesty's Theatre, Melbourne 9 April 1910; France: Olympia-Casino, Nice *Princesse Dollar* 11 March 1911, Théâtre de la Scala, Paris 6 December 1911; Film: Felix Basch 1927

Recordings: selections (part-records Philips, EMI, Polydor), selection in Italian (part-record Fonit-Cetra).

DOLLY VARDEN Comic opera in 2 acts by Stanislaus Stange. Music by Julian Edwards. Herald Square Theater, New York, 27 January 1902.

Allegedly based on the character from Dickens's *Barnaby Rudge*, Stanislaus Stange's *Dolly Varden* was, in its plot, rather more a mishmash of Garrick's *The Country Girl* and its original, *The Country Wife*. Written in a comic opera style, with no low comedian featured, and Lulu Glaser starring as Dolly, it won fine initial notices from those critics who preferred the older style to up-to-date dance tunes ('a prodigious and unqualified hit', 'real comic opera'), and it had a 154-performance run in New York before producer Sam Shubert took it to the country and to Britain. In London, with two numbers from Edwardes's *When Johnny Comes Marching Home* interpolated ('Katie, My Southern Rose' became 'Dolly, My English Rose'), it was politely received for three months. Not sufficiently politely, however, for Shubert who made a furious press statement accusing British 'managers and upper-class playgoers' of being anti-American and left the embarrassed, Manchester-born librettist to explain on behalf of himself and his equally English collaborator that the outburst was nothing personal: Shubert was like that with all managers and all playgoers.

UK: Avenue Theatre 1 October 1903

DOÑA FRANCISQUITA Zarzuela in 3 acts by Federico Romero and Guillermo Fernández Shaw based on Lope de Vega's *La discreta enamorada*. Music by Amadeo Vives. Teatro Apolo, Madrid, 17 October 1923.

One of the most popular zarzuelas of the genero grande, *Doña Francisquita* has been widely played on Spanish-language stages since its first production in 1923. The tale, an updated (to 19th-century Madrid) version of a Lope de Vega work, is in the classic vein of would-be-matrimonial comedy, and the Francisquita of the title is the piece's ingénue. It is she who is the 'discreta enamorada' of the title, and the object of her affections is the student Fernando. When his widowed father, Don Matías, comes instead to offer for her hand (an offer, in time-honoured fashion, mistakenly taken to herself by the heroine's widow mother), Francisquita resorts to a useful fib and tells the gentleman that his son has been writing her love letters. Misunderstandings, misdirected love-notes and the

365

amorous frivolities of a jolly soubrette called Aurora la Beltrana from the local theatre are all mixed up with incidental song and dance and the festivities of carnival week before youth wins its way, Matías gives up his 'bride', and best-friend Cardona pairs off with the soubrette.

The favourite pieces from Vives's score included Fernando's tenor romanza 'Por el humo se sabe donde está el fuego' and a night-time street chorus of necking lovers ('Coro de románticos').

A version of *Doña Francisquita* was produced in Monaco (ad A de Badet, R Bergeret) in January 1934, and the piece was subsequently played in this French translation in Brussels and in the French provinces.

Recordings: complete (Columbia, Edigsa, Hispavox), selections (Zafiro, Columbia)

DONAHUE, Jack [DONAHUE, John J] (b Charlestown, Mass, 1892; d New York, 1 October 1930). Dancing leading man who starred in several Broadway shows before an early death.

Donohue began his career at the age of 11 in a medicine show and subsequently played in burlesque and vaudeville, making himself a place in the latter field as a speciality dancer, part of the act Donahue and Stewart. He made his entry into the musical theatre as a dancer in *The Woman Haters* as early as 1912, but had his first substantial part as Slooch in the long tour and less substantial Broadway season of *Angel Face* in 1919. He subsequently played on Broadway in *The Ziegfeld Follies* (1920), *Molly Darling* (1922, Chic Jiggs) and *Be Yourself* (1924, Matt McLean), before pairing successfully with Marilyn Miller in *Sunny* (1925, Jim Denning) and again in *Rosalie* (1928, Bill Delroy).

For some years a writer for magazines and occasionally the stage, he extended his interests when he not only starred in, but also co-wrote the 1929 success *Sons o'Guns* (1929, Jimmy Canfield) and he subsequently adapted the London version of Szirmai's *Alexandra* (*Princess Charming*) for the Broadway stage before his death at the age of 38.

1929 **Sons o'Guns** (J Fred Coots, Benny Davis, Arthur Swanstrom/w Fred Thompson, Bobby Connolly) Imperial Theater 26 November
1930 **Princess Charming** (*Alexandra*) American version of English text (Imperial Theater)

Memoirs: *Letters of a Hoofer to his Ma* (Cosmopolitan Books, New York, 1911)

DONALDSON, Walter (b New York, 15 February 1893; d Santa Monica, Calif, 15 July 1947). Highly successful resident of Tin Pan Alley who ventured only twice with a full-scale Broadway score, but hit pay dirt there as well.

The son of a musical family, Donaldson made a brief start on a career in a brokerage firm, but he soon switched to music and took a position as a pianist in a musical publishing house. He began a serious career as a songwriter at 18 and found immediate success with 'Back Home in Tennessee' and 'I've Got the Sweetest Girl in Maryland'. During the First World War he worked in the same entertainment division of the army as Irving Berlin and in 1919 he joined Berlin's music publishing company from where, for the next nine years, he turned out tunes for a regular string of popular songs including 'How Ya

Gonna Keep 'Em Down on the Farm?', 'My Mammy', 'My Sweet Hortense' (all w Sam Lewis, Joe Young) 'Carolina in the Morning', 'My Buddy', 'Beside a Babbling Brook', 'Yes, Sir, That's My Baby', 'That Certain Party', 'I Wonder Where My Baby is Tonight', 'Let's Talk About My Sweetie', 'There Ain't No Maybe in My Baby's Eyes', 'My Ohio Home' (all w Gus Kahn), 'My Sweet Indiana Home', 'Roamin' to Wyomin', 'Chili Bom Bom' and 'Let it Rain Let it Pour' (both w Cliff Friend), 'After I Say I'm Sorry', 'Where'd You Get Those Eyes', 'Sam, the Old Accordion Man', 'At Sundown', 'Just Like a Melody out of the Sky', and 'My Blue Heaven' (w George Whiting).

In 1926 he collaborated with another songsmith, Joseph Meyer, on the score of the short-lived musical *Sweetheart Time*, but another, solo try at a Broadway score brought very different results. *Whoopee*, built as a vehicle for Eddie Cantor and produced by Florenz Ziegfeld, was a major stage hit, not a little thanks to such Donaldson numbers as 'Makin' Whoopee', 'I'm Bringing a Red, Red Rose' and 'Love Me or Leave Me'. It was subsequently made into a film, by Sam Goldwyn, with Cantor starred, and without the last two named songs in 1930.

By this time Donaldson had split from the Berlin organization, founded his own publishing company and moved to Hollywood where he wrote songs for many films and planted his old successes in many more (*Kid Millions*, *The Great Ziegfeld* etc).

1926 **Sweetheart Time** (w Joseph Meyer/Irving Caesar, Ballard McDonald/H B Smith) Imperial Theater 19 January
1928 **Whoopee** (Gus Kahn/William A McGuire) New Amsterdam Theater 4 December

DON CESAR Comic Operette in 3 acts by Oscar Walther based on the play *Don César de Bazan* by Philippe Dumanoir and Adolphe d'Ennery. Music by Rudolf Dellinger. Carl-Schultze Theater, Hamburg, 28 March 1885.

An operettic version of the much-retold *Don César de Bazan* story – the most famous of all the many blindfold marriage tales of the 19th-century stage – with more than a little flavour of *La Périchole* added, Dellinger's *Don Cesar* was extremely well received on its production in Germany. After making its way from its original Hamburg production to Berlin's Walhalla Theater (22 September 1885), it went on to multiple regional productions, becoming, alongside the now-classic works of the repertoire, one of the most widely played pieces of its time, and certainly the most successful of all German 19th-century Operetten.

The disguised King of Spain, taken by the charms of the gipsy singer Maritana, finds that she will not let him have his way with her unless she is first wed to him. Since the King already has a Queen, he arranges for Don Cesar, arrested after a duel, to go through the marriage ceremony in his place. After the wedding, Cesar's friend Pueblo helps him escape, and ultimately the King is balked in his designs and Maritana and her legal husband settle down to happily ever after. The comic element was supplied by the King's Ministers, Don Onofrio and Don Fernando, and the former's wife Doña Uraca.

The show's straightforwardly merry score was at its best when galloping frankly into the bolero rhythms which Dellinger used for such pieces as the entrances of both his heroine ('Ach, ach, ach, du erster Liebestraum') and his hero ('Von altem Stamm der letzte Zweig'), spreading a

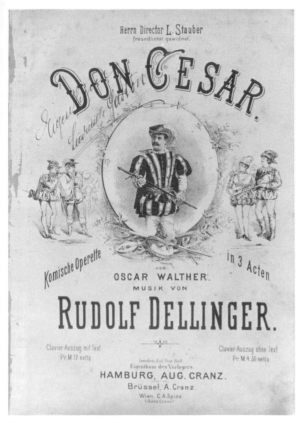

Plate 76. Don Cesar: *The most successful musical play to come out of Germany in the 19th century.*

Spanish flavour amongst a bundle of more conventional waltz measures. Both Cesar's piece and, in particular, his second-act dream-serenade ('Komm herab, o Madonna Theresa') became popular with tenors outside the show.

Don Cesar was produced in Zurich, St Petersburg, Strasbourg, Prague, Sofia, Zagreb, Stockholm and many other European centres, whilst in Vienna, following its first successful run at Carl Tatartzy's Carltheater with Adolf Brakl (Cesar), Endtreffer (King), Felix Schweighofer (Onofrio) and Gabriele Mrak (Maritana) (30 performances in 1885, and more in 1886 and 1887), it was given a new production in 1888 with Brakl, Max Monti (King), Carl Adolf Friese (Onofrio) and Frln Tischler (Maritana), and later revived at the Lustspieltheater (5 October 1902) and at the Raimundtheater (9 September 1911) with Bernard Bötel (King), Ida Russka (Maritana) and Otto Storm (Cesar).

In Budapest, the show was seen first in German, then in Ferenc Rajna's Hungarian adaptation, and it was given a major revival as late as 1906 at the Király Színház (10 April) in which Sári Fedák played a travesty Don Cesar. However, perhaps because of the enormous popularity of Vincent Wallace's English opera, *Maritana*, and of Gilbert and Sullivan's 1888 *The Yeomen of the Guard*, both of which used more or less the same story, *Don Cesar* was not staged in Britain, and when John McCaull introduced it to America (ad William von Sachs) with Bertha Ricci and Mathilde Cottrelly starring, it had but a short life. New

York German-speaking theatregoers were able to see the piece in German at the Amberg Theater in 1891.

The *Don César* story, as well as being the subject of a number of burlesques which were connected rather to *Maritana* (*Mary Turner*, *Little Don Caesar de Bazan*) than the play, was also used as the basis for an opera by Massenet (Opéra-Comique 30 November 1872).

Austria: Carltheater 20 November 1885; USA: Wallack's Theater 3 May 1886; Hungary: (Ger) 21 September 1885, Budai Színkör *Don Cészar* 7 May 1887

DON GIOVANNI, or A Spectre on Horseback Burlesque in 2 acts by Thomas Dibdin. Royal Circus and Surrey Theatre, London, 12 May 1817.

Described as a 'comic, heroic, operatic, tragic, panto-mimic burlesque burletta spectacular parody', this piece was one of the earliest of the musical pasticcio burlesques, in the rhyming couplet style, which were to become so very popular with English-language playgoers during the middle years of the 19th century. The burlesque was pinned to Mozart and Da Ponte's 1787 opera (which author Dibdin had seen a few days before penning his piece) and to Lord Byron's poem, rather than to the other main stage versions of the story of the Sevillian rake related by Tirso, Molière, Goldoni, or the musical versions by Gluck, Abertini, Gazzaniga and Carnicer. Its score was made up of melodies taken from a list of British composing royalty: Arne, Blow, Purcell, William Reeve, Stephen Storace, William Shield, Parry, Händel and the lesser known Etheridge, Davy and Sanderson, supplemented by imported melodies from the works of such as Nicolai, Zerbini, Gluck, Kreutzer and Querini, and topped off by Mozart's overture to Da Ponte's operatic version. The piece was produced at the Surrey Theatre and there it achieved a momentous record for its time, being played for 100 nights.

Contrary to later burlesque fashion, there was little travesty playing. Mr Short appeared as Giovanni, with Fitzwilliam as Leporello and Mrs Brooks as Donna Anna, and the only cross-sexual casting was that of Yarnold as the low-comedy mother of the bride (ex-Zerlina). The playbill advised that the Marble Horse of the statue was to be played by 'a real poney' and that the 'views are intended to represent several places in and near the city of Seville with (by way of a Pictorial Episode) a fine scene of Blackfriars Bridge'.

Another early pasticcio version of the *Don Giovanni* tale was William T Moncrieff's *Giovanni in London, or the Libertine Reclaimed*, an operatic extravaganza in two acts in which Giovanni ended up wedding the heroine, and the music of which included 'The Bluebells of Scotland', 'Wapping Old Stairs', 'Robin Adair', *The Beggar's Opera*'s 'Cease your funning', 'Scots What Hae' and one melody borrowed from Boieldieu's *John of Paris*.

Other English burlesque and extravaganza adaptations of the *Don Juan* story (and of Mozart's opera thereupon) have included Henry J Byron's 1865 *Little Don Giovanni* produced at the Prince of Wales Theatre with Marie Wilton as the Don, a male Zerlina and a female Masetto; the Alhambra *Don Juan* spectacular of 1873 (Frederick Clay, Georges Jacobi et al/H J Byron); two Gaiety burlesques *Don Giovanni in Venice* (Robert Reece, February 1873) with Johnnie Toole as Giovanni and Nellie Farren as Leporello, and James Tanner's Gaietyed Byron *Don Juan* (28 October 1893), and the Brothers Prendergast's *Don Juan Junior* (Royalty, 3 November 1880).

In France, Henri Varna and the Théâtre Mogador staged a piece under the title *Les Amours de Don Juan* (Juan Morata/Varna, Marc-Cab, René Richard) which professed to be 'd'après Lord Byron' and which had its Don Juan (Marcel Merkès) galloping round the world (Istanbul, Russia, Scotland etc) in a display of picturesque scenery and multinational ladies, accompanied and finally subdued by a soubrette called Antonia (Paulette Merval).

A Galt MacDermot/Derek Walcott musical, originally commissioned by Britain's Royal Shakespeare Company, was played in Trinidad as *The Joker of Seville* (1974).

DON JUAN Burlesque in 3 acts on Lord Byron's *Don Juan* by James T Tanner. Lyrics by Adrian Ross. Music by Meyer Lutz. Gaiety Theatre, London, 28 October 1893.

Conceived by the Gaiety's star comic, Fred Leslie, as a vehicle for himself and his co-star Nellie Farren, this burlesque of Byron's *Don Juan* was put aside when Leslie's death and Farren's illness ended the famous partnership. It was taken up later, when burlesque had largely given way to the new modern-dress musical comedy, and was staged at the Gaiety with Arthur Roberts, perhaps the most popular burlesque comic to follow Leslie, as Pedrillo and Millie Hylton, one of the five famous Rudge sisters and a music-hall star, as the Don. Miss Hylton successfully introduced the interpolated song 'Linger Longer Loo', which had started Sidney Jones' career and Teddy Solomon's 'Comme ça', whilst Roberts repeated his own very particular version of 'After the Ball'. Cissie (later Cecilia) Loftus, as the not-at-all-Byronic heroine, did impersonations. The show created a diplomatic incident when the Turkish Ambassador objected to the indignities suffered by a character named 'the Sultan of Turkey' and George Edwardes altered the offending personage's title to 'Jabez Pasha'.

One of the less effective of the great series of Gaiety new burlesques, *Don Juan* still had a nine-month run, but Edwardes did not repeat the experience, concentrating thereafter on his new musical comedies and leaving burlesque behind.

DONNA JUANITA Comic opera in 3 acts by F Zell and Richard Genée. Music by Franz von Suppé. Carl-theater, Vienna, 21 February 1880.

As in Suppé's earlier hit comic opera, *Fatinitza*, the lady of this show's title does not exist – she is a young man in disguise. In the context of the Spanish revolution, the army cadet René Dufour dresses up as (amongst other things) the seductive Donna Juanita, to charm and to spy on the buffoonish English governor of San Sebastian, Sir Andrew Douglas, and the Alcade, Don Pomponio, who is making himself troublesome to René's brother's fiancée. By the final curtain both the political and the amorous missions have been satisfyingly completed. The rôle of René, designed like Fatinitza as a breeches rôle, was created in Vienna by the soubrette Rosa Streitmann, with Gross and Karl Blasel as the two comic dignitaries and Therese Schäfer featured as the Alcade's libidinous wife.

Donna Juanita, with its lively score bristling with marches, polkas and waltzes, won a splendid success in Vienna. It was played again at the Theater an der Wien in 1884 with Streitmann, Blasel, Schäfer, Guttmann, and Girardi as Riego Manrique, and produced and revived in many versions throughout Europe, notably in Spain where it put up a long first run before nestling into the repertoire, and in Russia where it has remained more popular than Suppé's elsewhere more famous works. Budapest's Népszinház played *Donna Juanita* (ad Antal Radó) in 1880 and again in 1884 (17 September), and, eight years after Leterrier and Vanloo's French version had been heard at Brussels' Galeries Saint-Hubert (*Juanita* 22 October 1883), Marguerite Ugalde starred as René Belamour, alongside Louis Morlet and Maurice Lamy, in a Paris edition.

London did not venture a production of the show, but in New York Marie Geistinger scored a considerable success with her rendition of the original piece at the Thalia Theater, several months after H B Mahn had introduced the piece to Broadway in an English version with Jennie Winston starred as René/Juanita alongside Ellis Ryse (Pomponio), Arthur H Bell (Douglas) and Rose Leighton (Olympe).

A rewritten version was played at Berlin's Friedrich-Wilhelmstädtisches Theater under the title *Der pfiffige Kadett* in 1915 (30 December), and a second, by Julius Wilhelm and Gustav Beer, with a libretto reset in Paris, with a hairdresser and an actress as its leading ladies, and with Suppé's music rearranged by Karl Pauspertl, was produced by Erich Müller at the Johann Strauss-Theater 8 April 1925 as *Die grosse Unbekannte* (101 performances) and later played at Berlin's Theater des Westens (12 June 1926), whilst another rearrangement (ad Artur Bodanzky, A Mattulath) was produced at New York's Metropolitan Opera House (2 January 1932), and yet another in Koblenz (6 November 1937 ad A Treumann-Mette).

Germany: Carl-Schultze Theater, Hamburg 11 September 1880, Friedrich-Wilhelmstädtisches Theater 2 October 1880; Hungary: Népszinház 25 December 1880; USA: Fifth Avenue Theater 15 May 1881, Thalia Theater (Ger) 27 September 1881; France: Théâtre des Folies-Dramatiques *Juanita* 4 April 1891

DONNELLY, Dorothy [Agnes] (b New York, 28 January 1880; d New York, 3 January 1928). Broadway librettist and lyricist who found her greatest successes in the field of romantic operetta.

The daughter of the manager of New York's Grand Opera House, Miss Donnelly had, at first, a considerable career as an actress, playing in New York in the title-rôles of Yeats's *Kathleen-ni-Houlihan* and Shaw's *Candida*, in *Soldiers of Fortune*, *Man of Destiny*, Ibsen's *When the Dead Awaken*, *Daughters of Men*, and, most famously, in the title-rôle of the hit French play, *Madame X* (1910).

Concurrently with her performing life, she began to write libretti for the musical theatre. She collaborated on the English book for Charles Cuvillier's Franco-German *Flora Bella* (1916) and then provided the libretto for the Shuberts' production of the Marilyn Miller vehicle *Fancy Free* (1918). When the time came to readapt the existing adaptations of the hugely successful *Das Dreimäderlhaus/Lilac Time* for the Shuberts' American audiences, she was given the opportunity to work on both libretto and lyrics and, in collaboration with Sigmund Romberg, she turned out a highly romantic variant of the Franz Schubert life-and-songs show which, as *Blossom Time*, won as enduring a success throughout America as *Das Dreimäderlhaus* had done in its original form in Europe.

This success encouraged her to put an end to her acting career and to concentrate thereafter on writing. Her first collaboration thereafter was with composer Stephen Jones on the musical comedy *Poppy* (1923), a season-long success of 344 performances on Broadway with W C Fields starring, which also managed five months at London's Gaiety Theatre (1925) in the wake of the success of the not-dissimilar *Sally*. It was, however, her next effort which gave her her greatest success when she came together with Romberg a second time to adapt the old German play *Alt Heidelberg* as the libretto and lyrics for *The Student Prince*. This proved one of the most successful of all the Broadway operettas of the 1920s and put a whole bundle of its author's songs into the standards list ('Deep in My Heart Dear', 'The Drinking Song', Serenade, 'Golden Days', etc).

Miss Donnelly subsequently wrote two further shows with Romberg, the modified Barbara Frietchie tale *My Maryland*, which broke every record in Philadelphia but didn't dent them in New York, and the unsuccessful *My Princess*, as well as the unfortunate *Hello, Lola*, a piece based on Booth Tarkington's successful *Seventeen*, before her death early in 1928, during the run of *My Maryland*.

1916 **Flora Bella** (Charles Cuvillier/Percy Waxman/w Cosmo Hamilton) Casino Theater 11 September
1918 **Fancy Free** (Augustus Barratt) Astor Theater 11 April
1921 **Blossom Time** (Schubert arr Romberg) Ambassador Theater 29 September
1923 **Poppy** (Stephen Jones, Arthur Samuels) Apollo Theater 3 September
1924 **The Student Prince** (Romberg) Jolson Theater 2 December
1926 **Hello, Lola** (William B Kernell) Eltinge Theater 12 January
1927 **My Maryland** (Romberg) Jolson Theater 12 September
1927 **My Princess** (Romberg) Shubert Theater 6 October

DONOHUE, Jack [DONOHUE, John Francis] (b New York, 3 November 1908; d Marina del Rey, Calif, 27 March 1984).

Originally a dancer (*Ziegfeld Follies of 1927*, *Good News*, *Follow Thru*, *America's Sweetheart*, *Shoot the Works*, *Free for All*, as a speciality act in *Shady Lady*), Donohue began a career as a Broadway choreographer with the 1932 Fred and Dorothy Stone extravaganza *Smiling Faces*, the night-club dances featured in *Shady Lady*, and Jerome Kern's Amerikaner-strudel operetta *Music in the Air*, before spending a number of years working largely in Britain, where he made a double career as a performer of light comic rôles and a dance director.

His choreographic credits there included the Drury Lane staging of Ábrahám's *Ball im Savoy* (1933), with its celebrated soubret dances, the revue *Please*, some of the numbers for Jack Buchanan and Elsie Randolph's dance and comedy show *Mr Whittington* (w Buchanan, Buddy Bradley), the original touring production of *Jill, Darling* (*Jack and Jill*), the George Robey musical *Here's How!*, the Gaiety Theatre's *Going Greek*, in which Louise Browne performed her sylvan ballet, its successor *Running Riot*, and Firth Shephard's *Wild Oats* and *Sitting Pretty*. His stage appearances included *Here's How!* (Tim Regan), *On Your Toes* (Morrosine), *Wild Oats* (Val) and *Sitting Pretty* (Jimmy Gay).

The war occasioned Donohue's return to America, where he worked in stock and regional theatres, notably as Denikov in the St Louis première of *Balakaika* (1941, also choreography) and returned to Broadway as a performer in *Panama Hattie* (Mike), as a choreographer in the revue *The Seven Lively Arts* and *Are You with It?* (1945) and then, in a directing début, with the Phil Silvers musical *Top Banana* (1951). He subsequently directed Bobby Clark in the revised version of *Flahooley* called *Jollyanna* (1952) in Los Angeles, Sammy Davis jr's Broadway début in *Mr Wonderful* (also choreography) and *Rumple* (1957).

Outside his theatre assignments, Donohue also worked widely in film and television. Beginning with *Curly Top* (1935), he choreographed many of the Shirley Temple films, as well as the film versions of *Music in the Air* (1934), *Louisiana Purchase* (1941), *The Fleet's In* (1942), *Girl Crazy* (1943), *Best Foot Forward* (1943), *Calamity Jane* (1953) and *Babes in Toyland* (1961), and many television variety shows and specials.

DON QUIXOTE

Cervantes's 1605 tale of the chivalric Don Quixote and his faithful Sancho Panza, of the windmill which represents a giant, and the girl whom the idiosyncratic hero dreams to be his fair Dulcinea, has been translated to the stage on numberless occasions, including many in the musical theatre. Amongst the earliest were included a 1680 Venetian operatic version, *Don Chisciotte della Mancia* (Carlo Sajon/Marco Morosini), another mounted in Hamburg in 1690, a sizeable three-part affair with music by Henry Purcell put out in 1694, and a Parisian opéra of 1712.

Amongst the tidal wave of 18th-century examples were numbered Philidor's one-act *Sancho Pança [dans son île]* (Comédie-Italienne, Paris 8 July 1762), Conti's *Don Chisciotte in Sierra Morena* (Vienna, 2 February 1719), Caldara's pair of burlesque operas *Don Chisciotte in corte della duchessa* (Vienna, 6 February 1727) and *Sancho Panca, governatore dell'isola Barataria* (Vienna, 27 January 1733), Piccini's comic Singspiel *Il Don Cuiscotte* (1770), which apparently did better than a like piece by Paisiello, and the *Don Quixote und Sancho Panza* of Gerl and Giesecke (Wiedner Theater, Vienna, 17 April 1790). Henry Fielding assumed a *Don Quixote in England* (New Haymarket Theatre, 1734), whilst Karl Ditters von Dittersdorf's *Don Quixote der zweite* (Oels, 4 February 1795) and Champein's Parisian *Le nouveau Don Quichotte* (25 May 1789) went in for second-generation Dons.

The most famous retrospectively, at least, of the 19th-century works was the little *Don Quichotte et Sancho Pança* written, composed and performed by Hervé in the earliest stages of the opéra-bouffe years, but musical *Don Quixote*s continued worldwide, in equally as great numbers and in as many different languages as in the preceding era, through the 19th century. There were a number of not very successful ones in the English language. Frederic Clay composed a *Don Quixote* comic opera to a text by Harry Paulton and Alfred Maltby for London's Alhambra Theatre in 1876 (25 September) and conductor/producer Adolf Neuendorff of the New York Germania Theater composed a version to a text by someone apparently called Italianer in 1882 (9 January). Reginald De Koven and Harry B Smith ventured another English language *Don Quixote* for the Bostonians in 1889 in which celebrated comic Henry Clay Barnabee was featured as the Don alongside the Sancho of George Frothingham, but which did not make it to Broadway.

In Europe, Louis Roth and Max von Weinzierl composed the score for a 1879 comic operetta (Komische Oper 15 February) and Émile Pessard supplied a one-act *Don Quixote* to Paris's Salle Erard in Paris (lib: Deschamps, 13 February 1874) and Théâtre des Menus-Plaisirs (4 July 1889), Émile Vuillermoz gave his musical *Don Quixote* also in Paris, whilst Wilhelm Kienzl's operatic *Don Quixote* was produced at the Berlin Opera in 1898 (18 November) with more success than George Macfarren's 1846 *The Adventures of Don Quixote* (Drury Lane 3 February) or Jacques-Dalcroze's Swiss opera *Sancho Panza* (Geneva 13 December 1897). Felix Mendelssohn's first effort at an opera, *Die Hochzeit des Gamacho*, also concentrated on one of the additional episodes in Cervantes's work. Luigi Ricci gave an 1881 *Don Chisciotte* in Venice (4 February 1881), and Manuel Garcia turned out one which was later played in New York, but undoubtedly the biggest *Don Quixote* of the century was the five-act spectacular written by Sardou and Nuitter, musically illustrated by Albert Renaud, and produced on the king-sized stage of the Théâtre du Châtelet, Paris (9 February 1895). Of what might have been the most famous of *Don Quixote*s, however, no sign was seen. Rumour had it, whether jokingly or nay, in 1875–6 that Messrs Sardou and Offenbach had been engaged by Albert Vizentini of the Théâtre de la Gaîté to provide him with a *Don Quichotte* in which there would be a rôle for ... Thérésa. One wonders if the stocky, salacious chanteuse might have tried her hand at Sancho Panza.

The early years of the 20th century brought forth several more new versions of the famous tale, in all shapes and sizes, on the musical stage. New Zealand's Alfred Hill composed a *Don Quixote de la Mancha* to a text by W H Beattie (1904), Nagyvárad premièred a *Don Quijote* by Károly Liptai with music by Béla Garami (31 January 1909) later played at Budapest's Fővárosi Nyári Színház (19 August 1909), whilst Richard Heuberger's *Don Quichotte*, an Operette in two acts to a text by Reichert and Grünbaum was produced at the studio theatre Hölle in Vienna in 1910 – the same year that Massenet premièred his fine and durable operatic version (Monte Carlo 19 February) – and de Falla turned out a one-act *El retablo de maese Pedro*, another piece based on an episode from Cervantes, in Seville 23 March 1923.

In later years, far and away the most successful *Quixote* was the American musical play *Man of la Mancha* (22 November 1965, ANTA Washington Square), but its appearance and its international success did not wholly stop the flow of musicals on the subject and a more recent Russian musical, later played in East Germany (14 January 1977) as *Dulcinea von Toboso* (Gennadji Gladkov/Alexander Wolodin), followed the trend of the modern stage by giving the title to the lady of the piece.

DO RE MI
DO RE MI Musical in 2 acts by Garson Kanin. Lyrics by Betty Comden and Adolph Green. Music by Jule Styne. St James Theater, New York, 26 December 1960.

Favourite TV comedian Phil Silvers starred in *Do Re Mi* as Hubie Cram, an all-time loser with an infinite supply of crazy get-rich projects, who attempts to wade his way into the recording and juke-box market with the help of some superannuated gangsters. For once, one of his schemes works and the money rolls in. He accidentally turns a waitress, Tilda Mullen (Nancy Dussault) into a star, but she ends up falling in love with the competition, dreamboat vocalist John Henry Wheeler (John Reardon) and, with one thing and another, it is not long before Hubie ends up back where he started.

Silvers and Nancy Walker, as his loving if long-suffering wife, headed the comedy which was the show's backbone and Reardon performed the best-liked number, 'Make Someone Happy', through 400 performances for producer David Merrick without *Do Re Mi* ever getting into the black. A London version, mounted by H M Tennent Ltd and Leslie A MacDonnell, with Max Bygraves (Hubie), Maggie Fitzgibbon (Kay), Jan Waters (Tilda) and Steve Arlen (Wheeler), ran for 169 performances.

UK: Prince of Wales Theatre 12 October 1961
Recordings: original cast (RCA), London cast (Decca) etc

DORFMUSIKANTEN Operette in 3 acts by Leopold Jacobson and Robert Bodanzky. Music by Oscar Straus. Theater an der Wien, Vienna, 29 November 1919.

The village musician of the title is Friedl Pausinger (Hubert Marischka), who makes and plays his violins with a wonderful skill that wins him a 100-Thaler prize, but which risks drawing him away from his little Luisl (Luise Kartousch), the foster daughter of the villager Peterl (Ernst Tautenhayn). Alongside their tale of love and talent, the light-hearted Baron Heini von Solingen (Fritz Neumann) courted Adelheid (Betty Fischer), daughter of the violinmaker Tobias Brendl (Josef Hauschultz).

The famous team of Tautenhayn and Kartousch had their by now traditional dance duo ('Sie war siebzehn, ich war zwanzig'), whilst Friedl's prize song ('Weisst du noch? weisst du noch?') headed a busy musical evening for the show's leading man in which he partook of a whole series of duos and trios. Adelheid and Heini headed a supper waltz in the second-act entertainment at the Baron's castle, where Friedl and Luisl joined in their principal waltz duo ('Einen Mann, den muss man halten').

Dorfmusikanten had a solid run of five months and 166 performances at the Theater an der Wien, as well as being played at the Raimundtheater by the Theater an der Wien company, headed by Karl Melzer and Lotte Ferry and Tautenhayn still as old Peterl (2 May 1920), for a short season.

DAS DORF OHNE GLOCKE Singspiel in 3 acts based on the musical play *A harang* by Árpád Pásztor. Music by Eduard Künneke. Friedrich-Wilhelmstädtisches Theater, Berlin, 5 April 1919.

Eduard Künneke's first musical theatre work was a remusicked version of the Hungarian piece *A harang*, the successful three-act 'legend' set to music by Pongrác Kacsoh and Ákos Buttykay and produced at Budapest's Király Színház (1 February 1907) with Lujza Blaha in the leading feminine rôle.

The old priest, Father Benedikt (Josef Joseffy), is given 500 gulden by his parishioners which is to go towards giving the village the church bells it has lacked so many years. But Benedikt gives the money to the desperately needy blacksmith, Peter (Kurt Schönert), and his wife Eva (Katarina Garden), and trouble stirs in the village until the Baron Erwin von Lertingen (Sven Holm) comes to the rescue. When the bells he has had installed during the night ring out the next day, the villagers are reconciled to their priest.

Künneke's score was one which fitted the 'Singspiel' description of the show. The songs were not numerous, although each of the three acts – particularly the second – was endowed with a considerable concerted finale. The supporting characters had much of the music, with the soubrette, Resi (Alice von der Linden), leading several pieces and the housekeeper, Sophie (Otti Dietze), and Der Schmied (Rudolf Hilberg) pairing in two duets. The last act featured an unaccompanied Agnus Dei and Gloria.

The piece was well received through some two months of performances in Berlin and was subsequently mounted at Vienna's Volksoper.

Austria: Volksoper 2 December 1925

DORIS Comedy opera in 3 acts by B C Stephenson. Music by Alfred Cellier. Lyric Theatre, London, 20 April 1889.

This Stephenson/Cellier successor to the record-breaking *Dorothy* was another musical put together from second-hand pieces. Some of the story and more of the music was taken from Cellier's 1875 *Tower of London*, a semi-success in Manchester but unproduced after, to make up a costume drama tale which had Doris (Annette Albu from the Carl Rosa Opera), her lover, Martin (Ben Davies), and the Lady Anne Jerningham (Amy Augarde) trying to save Sir Philip Carey (Hayden Coffin) from execution and the Tower. In spite of the fact that the comic depredations of Arthur Williams in *Dorothy* had made a large part of its success, Stephenson refused to take the popular musical-low/topical-comedy route in his new show and Williams' rôle, as the foolish and bucolic Dinniver, was a less appreciable one, written with a staunchly old-style comic opera flavour.

Cellier's score was at least as good as that for the earlier piece. The tenor ballad 'I've Sought the Brake and Bracken' became enormously popular, and a recording artist's favourite as 'So Fare Thee Well', Williams's hilarious post-drinking song 'What Has Become of the Door?' was a comic opera joy and Coffin scored with a virile 'Honour Bids Me Speed Away'.

With a cast, apart from its leading lady, made up entirely from *Dorothy* veterans (Alice Barnett, Harriet Coveney, John Le Hay and John Furneaux Cook all took supporting rôles) Henry J Leslie's production of *Doris* ran 202 performances in London prefatory to a six-month touring career, but the show never threatened to repeat the monumental success of *Dorothy*.

DÖRMANN, Felix [BIEDERMANN, Felix] (b Vienna, 29 May 1870; d Vienna, 26 October 1928). Librettist and lyricist for several internationally successful Viennese Operetten of the early 20th century.

The author of a ballet scenario (w Otto Theime) for Josef Bayer at the age of 22 and later of a number of plays (*Ledige Leute* etc) before moving into the musical theatre,

Dörmann had an enormous success, first up, when he collaborated on the libretto for Oscar Straus's 1907 hit *Ein Walzertraum*. He followed up with two further fine successes in *Bub oder Mädel?* (w Adolf Altmann) for Bruno Granich-städten and the 'Altwiener Stück' *Der unsterbliche Lump*, written without a collaborator, for composer Edmund Eysler and, if Count Lubomirski's *Die liebe Unschuld* was a fortnight-long failure at the Raimundtheater, both *Majestät Mimi* at the Carltheater and *Was tut man nicht alles aus Liebe* at Ronacher had good runs at home and won exports.

During the war, Dörmann supplied a couple of little pieces to the Apollotheater programmes, but after the hostilities had ended he did not again find the success of his earlier years in the musical theatre. A version of *The Beggar's Opera* (*Der Liebling von London*) played a month at the Carltheater and inspired the authors of *Die Dreigroschenoper* to their adaptation, *Hoheit Franzl* lasted only three weeks at the same theatre, and *Die verbotene Frau*, with a Vienna run of 62 performances, proved the not-very-good best of the three. He provided the text for a one-act opera *Hagith* (Karol Szymanowski) produced in Warsaw in 1922 and, in his last work before his death, made the famous adventures of the Baron Munchhausen into the text for a musical show mounted, with Erik Wirl starred, in Berlin.

A version of his text for *Der unsterbliche Lump*, musically reset by Benatzky, was made into a film in 1953.

1907 **Ein Walzertraum** (Oscar Straus/w Leopold Jacobson) Carltheater 2 March
1908 **Bub oder Mädel?** (Bruno Granichstädten/w Adolf Altmann) Johann Strauss-Theater 13 November
1910 **Der unsterbliche Lump** (Edmund Eysler) Wiener Bürgertheater 15 October
1911 **Majestät Mimi** (Granichstädten/w Roda-Roda) Carltheater 17 February
1912 **Die liebe Unschuld** ('W Lirski') Raimundtheater 27 April
1914 **Was tut man nicht alles aus Liebe** (Leo Ascher) Ronacher 17 December
1915 **Das Finanzgenie** (Béla Zerkowitz/w Hans Kottow) Apollotheater 1 November
1916 **Arizonda** (Jean Gilbert) Apollotheater 1 February
1918 **Die Lilli vom Chor** (*Korista lány*) German version (Bundestheater)
1918 **Eriwan** (Oskar Nedbal) Wiener Komödienhaus 29 November
1919 **Die galante Markgräfin** revised version of *Das Tal der Liebe* (Straus/Rudolf Lothar) Theater in der Leopoldstadt 24 January
1920 **Zwölf Uhr nachts** (Ascher/w Kottow) Raimundtheater 12 November
1924 **Der Liebling von London** (arr Hans Ewald Heller) Carltheater 19 April
1924 **Hoheit Franzl** (Ernst Steffan) Carltheater 7 November
1926 **Die verbotene Frau** (Max Wallner/w Karl Gerold) Carltheater 5 March
1927 **Munchhausen** (Steffan) Theater am Zoo, Berlin 26 December

DOROTHY Comedy opera in 3 acts by B C Stephenson. Music by Alfred Cellier. Gaiety Theatre, London, 25 September 1886.

Following the indifferent reception of the Alfred Cellier/H B Farnie musical *Nell Gwynne* at Manchester in 1876, Farnie withdrew his libretto and he subsequently had it re-set by Planquette into a more widely played *Nell Gwynne*. Cellier was handed back his music, and he, too,

Plate 77a. **Dorothy**: *Two country wenches (Constance Drever, Louie Pounds) attract two young blades (John Bardesley, Hayden Coffin) under the eye of innkeeper John Tuppitt (Fred Vigay) …*

decided to put it to re-use. Charlie Stephenson, the librettist for his early and successful *Charity Begins at Home*, was set to write a new libretto into which the *Nell Gwynne* music might be fitted, and the resultant work was entitled *Dorothy*, that being the name of the heroine of the piece before, disguised in country clothes, she becomes Dorcas and, in time-honoured fashion, charms the naughty cousin who is refusing to marry her.

Geoffrey Wilder (Redfern Hollins) has been spreading his wild oats a little too liberally, and when he asks his uncle, Squire Bantam (John Furneaux Cook), to bail him out, the price of the rescue is that he come and live quietly in the country and marry his cousin, Dorothy. On their way to Chantecleer Hall, Geoffrey and his friend Harry Sherwood (Hayden Coffin) stop off at an inn, and there they become bewitched by two local damsels, to such an extent that Geoffrey's doubts about wedding the probably very plain Dorothy Bantam are solidified into a refusal. Of course, the two girls are Dorothy (Marion Hood) and her friend Lydia (Florence Dysart) out having a little fun as pretend milkmaids, and, back in their fine gowns and powdered wigs, they take the opportunity, that night, to win each other's rings from their gallants of the afternoon. By staging a fake robbery, the boys win enough money from the grateful Squire to pay off the comic bailiff, Lurcher (Arthur Williams), who has pursued them from town, but their getaway – in search of 'Dorcas' and 'Abigail' – is held up by a duel, a betrayal and more disguises until it is time for a happy final curtain.

In a pretty comic opera score, Wilder sang in praise of Dorcas ('With Such a Dainty Dame'), the girls warned a little country fiancée not to get tied up to a representative of the species, man ('Be Wise in Time'), and Lurcher described himself in comical couplets ('I am the Sheriff's Faithful Man') alongside some well-written ensembles and finales.

The authors had difficulty finding a producer for their show and, although it was at first announced to be produced by and with Kate Santley, it was finally staged at the Gaiety by George Edwardes, in a gap in the schedule between his newly successful burlesques and the theatre's annual French play season. Although the music was appreciated by the critics, the show was indifferently received, with Stephenson's rather deliberately old-fashioned text, with its improbable comic opera disguises and some unlikely incongruities, coming heavily under fire. Edwardes ordered alterations. Cuts were made to both book and music, Arthur Williams was given carte blanche to jolly up his rôle in an up-to-date way that made Stephenson blench, and a new song, fabricated from an old Cellier melody and some swiftly written lyrics, was introduced for the richly baritonic Coffin who, improbably, had no solo. The rewrites helped enormously. The increased comedy – notably Lurcher's amorous antics with the society widow, Mrs Privett (Harriet Coveney) – helped the book and the new song, 'Queen of My Heart', quite simply became the biggest song hit the West End had ever known. But Edwardes had more faith in the burlesque company and, when they were ready to return to the Gaiety, he decided to close *Dorothy*.

However, the theatre's accountant, Henry Leslie, purchased the production from the Gaiety and he transferred it to the Prince of Wales Theatre. There he immediately replaced the two stars, bringing in the rising young Marie Tempest and the Carl Rosa Opera's sweetly tenor Ben Davies as Dorothy and Geoffrey. Miss Tempest's arch and comic soubrette performance – replacing the coolly lovely interpretation of Miss Hood – changed the whole temper

Plate 77b. *But how should the flirty boys recognize 'Abigail' and 'Dorcas', bewigged and powdered, as the ladies of Chantecleer Hall?*

of the show and *Dorothy* simply took off at the box-office. By the time it closed, after 931 performances, it had broken every London long-run record, outstripping all the Gilbert and Sullivan shows and *Les Cloches de Corneville*, and Leslie had built Shaftesbury Avenue's Lyric Theatre on the profits.

The show toured for decades in Britain, in four or five separate and simultaneous companies during the earlier years, and for many years with Lucy Carr-Shaw, sister of George Bernard, in the rôle of Dorothy. Miss Carr-Shaw was just one of several performers who made almost a whole career out of playing *Dorothy* around the provincial towns of England, Scotland, Ireland and Wales in the later years of the century. The piece was revived in London in 1892 (Trafalgar Square Theatre 26 November) with Miss Dysart in her original rôle alongside Decima Moore (Dorothy), Joseph Tapley (Geoffrey), Leonard Russell (Harry) and William Elton (Lurcher), and again in 1908 (New Theatre, then Waldorf Theatre 21 December) with Coffin and Williams from the original cast alongside Constance Drever (Dorothy), Louie Pounds (Lydia) and John Bardesley (Geoffrey). Both revivals were, however, quick failures (15 performances and 49 performances respectively).

The show was produced on Broadway by J C Duff, with a fine cast headed by Lillian Russell (Dorothy) and Harry Paulton (Lurcher), but it proved to have no appeal for New York and folded in just 48 performances. In Australia, too, it had an indifferent start when first mounted by Williamson, Garner and Musgrove with Savoy Theatre prima donna Leonora Braham as Dorothy, supported by a top-rank London cast – W H Woodfield (Geoffrey), Federici (Harry), William Elton (Lurcher), Alice Barnett (Mrs Privett), former star tenor Albert Brennir (Bantam) – and local Aggie Kelton as Lydia. However, the Williamson

company, never one to waste costumes and scenery, brought the show back in 1888, 1889 and 1892, with Nellie Stewart and then the globetrotting American soubrette, Marie Halton, taking on the title-rôle and, as in London, the show grew into a favourite, returning regularly over a period of 20 years for further runs. *Dorothy* also surfaced in South Africa, Canada, on the Oriental circuits and almost everywhere else where English-language theatre was played, and it even made its way to Hungary (ad Bertalan Gunszt, Antal Radó) where what seems to have been its only foreign-language version was played at the Budapest Népszinház in 1888.

Australia: Princess Theatre, Melbourne 20 August 1887; USA: Standard Theater 5 November 1887; Hungary: Népszinház *Dorottya* 9 May 1888

DORSCH, Käthe (b Nuremberg, 29 December 1890; d Vienna, 25 December 1957). Singing actress who became a favourite star in the German musical theatre before going on to a substantial career on the straight stage.

Käthe Dorsch began her career as a teenage chorus singer in her native Nuremberg, and spent several years in the ensembles at the Stadttheater in Mainz and at Rotterdam before making her first appearances in Berlin under the management of Max Monti. In 1916 she created the rôle of Marie in Leo Ascher's *Der Soldat von Marie* for Jean Kren at the Theater am Schiffbauerdamm, and went on to star in such pieces as Walter Bromme's *Die Dame in Frack* (1919), *Das süsse Mädel*, as Suppé's *Boccaccio*, Winterberg's *Die Dame von Zirkus* (1919) and in Straus's *Eine Ballnacht* (1919, Riki), before making her first substantial attempts at non-musical theatre. The experiment proved a success, and thereafter she mixed the musical and non-musical theatres, scoring her most important musical successes as the original star (opposite the Goethe of Richard Tauber) of Lehár's *Friederike* ('although not gifted as a singer [she] acts and sings with such intense reality [and] the fragrance of naïveté ...'), as Boulotte to the Blaubart of Leo Slezak in the Metropoltheater's 1929 production of Offenbach's piece, as the heroine of Oscar Straus's *Marietta* and of the rewritten version of Künneke's *Liselott* (1932).

In later years she wholly abandoned the musical stage for the straight theatre in Germany and, from 1938, in Vienna, becoming a highly appreciable leading lady in both the classic and modern repertoire, and ending her career in the company at the Vienna Burgtheater where she remained up to her death. She also appeared in a number of German-language films, both straight and musical, pairing, as on the stage, on occasions with the strongest of voices (*Die Landwirtin vom Rhein* w Hans-Heinz Bollmann etc).

Biographies: Weltmann, L: *Käthe Dorsch* (1929); Thiering, H: *Käthe Dorsch* (Zinnen Verlag, Munich, 1944)

DOSTAL, Nico[laus Josef Michaël] (b Korneuberg, 27 November 1895; d Vienna, 27 October 1981).

Nico Dostal was the nephew of Hermann Dostal (1874–1930), a composer who had had some considerable sucess with Operette scores to works such as *Nimm mich mit!*, produced at the Theater an der Wien in 1919, *Das geborgte Schloss* (Leipzig, 15 May 1911), *Urschula* (Apollotheater 1 September 1916, and in Hungary as *Milliomos Kati* 30 June 1917) and the little *Eine göttliche Nacht* (Hölle, 1 March 1910, *Isteni éj* in Hungary) and *Der fliegende Rittmeister* (Apollotheater, 5 October 1912).

The young Dostal had his first Mass played at the Linzer Dom at the age of 18, before going on to follow studies in both law and music. After serving in the army for four years, he returned to begin a career in the musical theatre, first at the Innsbruck Stadttheater and then in conducting posts at St Pölten near Vienna, in Roumania and at Salzburg. In 1924 he moved to Berlin, where he began by arranging and orchestrating other people's Operetten for the stage, while at the same time turning out songs for theatre and film, and ended by composing his own first musical comedy score. The colourful movies-and-politics-in-South-American-places piece, *Clivia*, was produced at Berlin's Theater am Nollendorfplatz, where he had been a conductor since 1927, in 1933. It had a fine success and Dostal followed up with another successful piece in *Die Vielgeliebte* (1935). Like *Clivia*, *Die Vielgeliebte* starred the Viennese prima donna Lillie Claus, later to become the second Frau Dostal.

Of the regular series of mostly successful musicals which followed over the next seven years the most appreciated were *Monika* (1937), *Die ungarische Hochzeit* (1939) and *Manina* (1942). At the same time, Dostal continued to write for the cinema where his scores included a revised one of *Monika* under the title *Heimatland*. In 1943 he left Berlin for the less bomb-prone Austria and Bad Aussee and his theatre activities all but ceased. In 1947 *Manina* was staged at Vienna's Raimundtheater and in 1949 his first new work for seven years, a little musical comedy called *Süsse kleine Freundin*, was staged in Wuppertal.

The following year, *Zirkusblut*, written with his old *Monika* partner, Hermecke, and *Der Kurier der Königin*,

staged almost simultaneously at Leipzig and Hamburg respectively, set things in motion again and over the next dozen years Dostal produced, alongside revue and film music (this latter including a musical reworking of Strauss's *Eine Nacht in Venedig*), scores for a further five musicals of which *Doktor Eisenbart* (1952) was the most successful.

In 1955 his *Liebesbriefe* was given its first performance at the Vienna Raimundtheater, the only one of his works to have been premiered in Austria, and he lived into his late eighties, long enough to see his *Die ungarische Hochzeit* brought to the stage of the Volksoper in 1981 in a sign of recognition of his position as the last surviving representative of the tradition of German-language operetta.

1933 **Clivia** (Karl Amberg, 'F Maregg') Theater am Nollendorfplatz 23 December
1935 **Die Vielgeliebte** (Maregg, Rudolf Köller) Schillertheater 5 March
1936 **Prinzessin Nofretete** (Maregg, Köller) Opernhaus, Cologne 12 September
1937 **Extrablätter** (Gustav Quedtenfeld) Staatstheater, Bremen 17 February; Grosses Schauspielhaus, Berlin 30 April
1937 **Monika** (Hermann Hermecke) Staatsheater, Stuttgart 3 October
1939 **Die ungarische Hochzeit** (Hermecke) Staatstheater, Stuttgart 4 February
1940 **Die Flucht ins Glück** (Hermecke) Staatstheater, Stuttgart 23 December
1942 **Die grosse Tänzerin** (Hans Schachner) Opernhaus, Chemnitz 15 February
1942 **Eva im Abendkleid** (Fritz Maria Gribitz) Opernhaus, Chemnitz 21 November
1942 **Manina** (Hans Adler) Admiralspalast 28 November
1949 **Süsse kleine Freundin** (Gribitz) Kammerspiele, Wuppertal 31 December
1950 **Zirkusblut** (Hermecke) Volksbühne, Leipzig 3 March
1950 **Der Kurier der Königin** (Max Wallner, Kurt Feltz) Theater am Besenbinderhof, Hamburg 2 March
1952 **Doktor Eisenbart** (Hermecke) Opernhaus, Nuremberg 29 March
1954 **Der dritte Wunsch** (Hans Adler) Opernhaus, Nuremberg 20 February
1955 **Liebesbriefe** (Hubert Marischka, Rudolf Österreicher) Raimundtheater, Vienna 25 November
1961 **So macht man Karriere** (Peter Herz, Willy Fuchs) Opernhaus, Nuremberg 29 April
1963 **Rhapsodie der Liebe** (Paul Knepler) Opernhaus, Nuremberg 9 November

Autobiography: *Ans Ende deiner Träume kommst du nie* (Pinguin Verlag, Innsbruck, 1982)

LES DOUZE FEMMES DE JAPHET Vaudeville-opérette in 3 acts by Antony Mars and Maurice Desvallières. Music by Victor Roger. Théâtre de la Renaissance, Paris, 16 December 1890.

Easily the best of the many musical plays written in the decades surrounding the turn of the century which used the Mormon way of life as the basis for their comedy, *Les Douze Femmes de Japhet* was a vaudevillesque piece which had now the crazy air of *Ba-ta-clan*, now the farcical air of a *Madame Sherry* or at times the high comedy of *La Vie parisienne* about it.

Japhet Paterson (Regnard) of Salt Lake City (he of the 12 wives) is not really a Paterson. He is the once footloose Beaujolais from Paris, who married the American widow Paterson (Irma Aubrys) and her late husband's thriving preserves factory, and profited by the local customs to then wed ten other wives, chosen by the local pastor, plus a little opérette singer from home called Arabella (Alice Berthier). However, Beaujolais's rich uncle, the commissaire de police Baliveau (Bellot), having been cuckolded late in life by a young wife, has forbidden his nephew to wed on the pain of disinheritance. So each year Beaujolais goes to Paris, for a fortnight's rest from his heavy conjugal duties, and is a dutiful celibate in front of his uncle, whose chief delight in life is now uncovering other folks' marital infidelities. It is Arabella, however, who is the loose stone in this comfortable edifice. She turns out to have been the miscreant wife not only of Baliveau, but also of a singer-turned-marital agent called Cassoulet de Casabianca (Victorin) who now enjoys making mismatches which will end in disaster. Worse, she was almost the bride of Beaujolais's old friend des Toupettes (Gildès). It is des Toupettes who, hoping to get her back, pretends to the women that Japhet has gone to Paris to visit an old girlfriend, and all the wives indignantly head after him on the next steamer. After two acts of intricately ingenious comical situations, Japhet, like W S Gilbert's Bunthorne, is left the only single man around.

The musical part of the show was light, including, alongside several ensembles for the wives, a set of finales, a rondeau for Arabella ('Je viens d'ach'ter la Vie parisienne'), some regretful couplets for the aged Deborah Paterson ('Jadis je vous trouvais plus tendre'), and a further song for Arabella in the third act ('Là, vrai! Ce n'est pas amusant') which proved the musical highlight of the evening.

The Théâtre de la Renaissance production of Les Douze Femmes de Japhet played an initial season of 41 performances before the show went on to be played in Germany, in a version adapted by Julius Freund with new music by Victor Holländer, in Vienna (ad Otto Eisenschitz), and in Budapest (ad Emil Makai) where, after a first run of 26 performances in 1898, it was revived for a second run in 1901 (Népszinház 14 September).

Austria: Theater in der Josefstadt *Japhet und seine zwölf Frauen* 13 October 1897; Hungary: Népszinház *Jafet 12 felesége* 27 May 1898; Germany: Metropoltheater *Die Zwölf Frauen des Japhets* 29 November 1902

LE DRAGON DE LA REINE Opérette in 3 acts by Pierre Decourcelle and Frantz Beauvallet. Music by Leopold Wenzel. Théâtre de l'Alhambra, Brussels, 25 March 1888.

Wenzel's most widely seen piece, *Le Dragon de la reine* was premièred in Belgium before winning productions, first in Paris and then throughout Europe.

A young labourer called Sedaine has attracted the attentions of a lofty lady, the Comtesse de la Belle-Ardoise, but he has eyes only for his village lassie. During the course of the evening's action, he goes from being a manual labourer to a soldier – in which guise he goes through a series of disguises and all sorts of jiggery-pokery with a lost despatch – and ends up at one stage as a member of a troupe of strolling players. At the end of the evening, of course, he gets his sweetheart whilst the amorous Countess is paired off with his superior (elderly) officer.

Debruyère mounted *Le Dragon de la reine* at the Paris Gaîté just two months after its Brussels opening, with Juliette Simon-Girard starred in the rôle à tiroirs of

Sedaine, and Marie Gélabert, Simon-Max and Berthelier in support. It was the great Berthelier's last rôle, for he died during the 36-performance run. In spite of this discouraging record, the piece was promptly picked up to be played in Germany (ad Karl Alexander Raida), and in Britain (ad B C Stephenson, Augustus Harris, lyrics by Harry Nicholls, Harry Greenbank and Adrian Ross, additional and alternative music by John Crook). It was put on the British road by Augustus Harris as 'a burlesque opera' with American singer Tillie Wadman starred as Joe Adams alongside John Shine (Captain de Bang) and Nicholls (Sir Hercules Pettifer) and provoked one critic to comment that he thought there must be 'very little of the original left'. It did not make town. However, it did make it, some time later, to Budapest's main musical house (ad Lajos Evva, Viktor Rákosi) where it was given 12 performances in the repertoire. In the end, only the Belgians really liked it, but everyone else had had their chance.

France: Théâtre de la Gaîté 31 May 1888; Germany: Viktoriatheater *Die Dragoner der Königin* 7 October 1888; UK: Newcastle *The Young Recruit* 14 March 1892; Hungary: Népszinház *A királyné dragonyosa* 4 May 1895

LES DRAGONS DE VILLARS Opéra-comique in 3 acts by Lockroy [Joseph Simon] and Eugène Cormon. Music by Aimé Maillart. Théâtre Lyrique, Paris, 19 September 1856.

Les Dragons de Villars was one of the few opéras-comiques of the pre-opéra-bouffe era which held its own in the repertoires of the world's musical theatre companies once the rage for the works of Offenbach and Hervé and their successors had struck.

A unit of dragoons arrives in a little Provençal mountain village in search of renegade Protestants. The goat girl, Rose Friquet (Juliette Borghèse), sets the soldiers loose in the best wine cellar in the village, and helps the persecuted folk to attempt escape by an unfamiliar mountain path. In the meanwhile, the Sergeant Belamy (Grillon) makes free with Georgette (Caroline Girard), the not unwilling wife of the farmer Thibault (Girardot), who is only recalled to connubial duty by the ringing of the bell of the hermitage which, legend says, peals when a married woman is about to fall from grace. In spite of Thibault's rumour-mongering and Belamy's threats, Rose succeeds in her mission and as a bonus wins the pretty farm boy Sylvain (Scott).

Maillart's attractive, grateful music gave the principals every opportunity. Rose made her entrance with the farmer's mules she has rescued in the mountains ('Maître Thibault, vos mules sont charmantes'), and followed up with a Ronde Militaire, a disarming duo with her farm lad ('Moi! Jolie?') and an explosion of joy at the thought of being loved ('Il m'aime! Espoir charmant'), whilst Georgette featured a Chanson Provençale and the legend of the hermits' bells with its 'din, din, din, din' refrain. Sylvain begged Rose's help ('Ne parle pas, Rose, je t'en supplie') and opened the second act with a pretty Vilanelle, whilst Belamy led the Dragoons in a song in praise of their horses and courted Georgette musically, alongside a series of ensemble pieces which made up a particularly strong score.

A grand success at the Théâtre Lyrique, the piece was quickly produced in other French-language venues before going on to establish itself at the Opéra-Comique (6 June

375

1868) where Galli-Marié played Rose in the first of the 377 performances played there over the next 50 years. A German version by Ernst was mounted in Berlin and Vienna, and revived frequently thereafter, under the title of *Das Glöckchen des Eremiten* (the Hermit's bell), and it was that version that was first heard in America in 1868 introduced by Hedwig L'Arronge-Sury (Rose), Frln Haffner (Georgette), W Formes (Belamy) and Theodore Habelmann (Sylvain). Shortly after, New York was given the piece in French by Adolph Birgefeld's company in a repertoire otherwise mainly opéra-bouffe and it was regularly seen thereafter in Marie Aimée's seasons, but it was not until 1878 that an English version was played by the C D Hess Company.

Selina Dolaro introduced *The Dragoons* (ad Henry Hersee) in London in 1879, with herself as Rose Friquet to the Belamy of Frank Celli, the Thibaut of Fred Leslie and the Georgette of Alma Stanley, but, like the American version, it had apparently been preceded by an earlier English-language version, *The Hermit's Bell* (ad uncredited), first played in Melbourne in 1877 and later in Sydney (13 June 1881 Gaiety Theatre), Australia, by the Simonsen company. The English versions of the show did not have quite the same success that the long-lasting French and German ones did, but the show was translated into a bevy of other tongues, including a Hungarian version by Lajos Evva and Jenő Rákosi, played at the Népszinház as late as 1881 with Aranka Hegyi starred as Rose Friquet.

Germany: Friedrich-Wilhelmstädtisches Theater *Das Glöckchen des Eremiten* 26 November 1860; Austria: Hofoperntheater 14 September 1861; USA: Stadttheater (Ger) 22 April 1868, Grand Opera House (Fr) 10 May 1869, Union Square Theater (Eng) 6 June 1878; UK: Gaiety Theatre (Fr) 24 April 1875, Folly Theatre *The Dragoons* 14 April 1879; Australia: St George's Hall, Melbourne *The Hermit's Bell* 9 June 1877; Hungary: Népszinház *A Dragonysok* (*A remete csengetyüje*) 14 January 1881

Recording: complete (Decca)

DRAKE, Alfred [CAPURRO, Alfredo] (b New York, 7 October 1914; d New York, 25 July 1992). Compelling, rich-voiced actor and baritone vocalist who introduced several major Broadway lead rôles in the 1940s and 1950s.

Drake made his earliest stage appearances as a chorus singer, covered the rôle of Leopold in *White Horse Inn*, played supporting rôles in *Babes in Arms* (1937, Marshall Blackstone) and the Victorian pasticcio *The Two Bouquets* (1938, Albert Porter), and took part in several revues including *Two for the Show* in which he introduced 'How High the Moon', before his combination of dark good looks and a dark, easy baritone won him his first lead rôle as Curly in the original production of *Oklahoma!* ('The Surrey with the Fringe on Top', 'Oh What a Beautiful Mornin'', 'People Will Say We're in Love'). He played this rôle for more than a year before moving on to other musical leads in *Sing Out Sweet Land* (1944, Barnaby Goodchild), the remake of *The Beggar's Opera* as *The Beggar's Holiday* (1946, Macheath) and a revival of *The Cradle Will Rock* (1947, Larry Foreman), and a single musical film rôle, top-billed with Janet Blair, in *Tars and Spars* (1946).

His second major musical creation came in 1948, when he appeared as Fred Graham/Petruchio in Cole Porter's *Kiss Me, Kate*, introducing a further clutch of soon-to-be-

standard songs – 'So in Love', 'Wunderbar', 'I've Come to Wive it Wealthily in Padua' – and his third in 1953 with his memorable playing of the wily baritonic beggar, Hajj, in Wright and Forrest's musical version of *Kismet* ('The Olive Tree', 'Gesticulate', 'And This is My Beloved'), a rôle which he repeated in the show's London production. In between he succeeded Yul Brynner in the rôle of the King in *The King and I*, wrote and directed the short-lived Goldoni musical *The Liar*, and directed the charming but unsuccessful *Courtin' Time* (1951).

In his visits to the musical stage during a subsequent career spent largely in straight theatre and as a director, he did not again find as effective vehicles as his three major hits, in spite of appearing as the hero of a Wright and Forrest musical remake of *Kean* (1961), and in the rôle of Honoré (otherwise Maurice Chevalier) in a stage version of *Gigi* (1973). Other short-lived assignments included *Zenda* (1963, Richard Rassendyl/King Rudolf V), *After You, Mr Hyde* (1968) and *Gambler's Paradise* (1975).

He appeared on television in *The Adventures of Marco Polo* (1956, Marco Polo), *Naughty Marietta* (1955, Dick Warrington), *The Yeomen of the Guard* (Jack Point) and *Kiss Me, Kate* (1958) and recorded selections from a number of classic musical comedies.

As a writer, he also provided the English surtitles for the Broadway performances of the Italian musical *Rugantino* (1964), and as a director mounted the American production of *Lock Up Your Daughters* (1960).

1950 **The Liar** (John Mundy/w Edward Eager) Broadhurst Theater 18 May

DRANEM [MÉNARD, Armand] (b Paris, 23 May 1869; d Paris, 13 October 1935). Star of the French music hall who transferred to the musical theatre and there became one of the biggest comic stars of his generation.

After spending his earliest working years in a jewellery workshop, Dranem began his performing career at the age of 25 as a comic singer in the cafés-concerts, appearing at the Concert du Champ-de-Mars in 1894, at the Concert de l'Époque, the Concert Parisien (1895), the Divan Japonais (1896), the Alcazar and, from September 1899, at the Eldorado where he became, in the early years of the 20th century, one of the field's most appreciated stars in revues, playlets and songs ('Les p'tits pois', 'L'Enfant du cordonnier', 'Aglaë', 'Tu sens le menthe', 'La Boîte à clous', 'Avec mon ocarina', 'Chasseurs, sachez chassez', 'Le Beau Môme', 'Allumeur-Marche' etc).

In 1912 he made an unaccustomed appearance in the theatre when Antoine cast him in Molière's *Le Médecin malgré lui* in a matinée at the Odéon and he later guested in the small role of Buteau in the gala performance of *La Fille de Madome Angot* at the Opéra-Comique, but, from the early 1920s, he began to appear regularly in musical comedy. He starred in the title-rôle of the Paris production of *Flup...!* (1920), in *Pétoche* at the Concert Mayol, as Célestin in a revival of *Mam'zelle Nitouche* and in *Les 28 Jours de Clairette* at the Trianon-Lyrique (1921). He returned to the Mayol to play *L'Hôtel des deux amours* then made such an enormous success, opposite Maurice Chevalier, in the comical rôle of the guardian angel who brings a dead man back to earth to settle his affairs in Yvain's *Là-haut* (1923, Frisotin), that Chevalier, the top-

Plate 78. **Dranem**: *The star comic of two decades of Paris musicals.*

billed star of the show, ended by walking petulantly out of his rôle.

Over the next 12 years, through his fifties and sixties and right up to the death, Dranem doubled a continuing flow of hit songs with an almost constant presence on the Parisian musical stage, providing the comic backbone to one new musical after another as he made starring appearances in *La Dame en décolleté* (1923, Girodo, 'Les Bains de mer', 'Je n'ai pas pu', 'Si l'on réflichissait'), *En chemyse* (1924, Lahirette, 'La Girl et le homard', 'Lahirette!'), *Troublez-moi!* (1924, Picotte, 'J'ai eu tort de me mettre en toréador', 'Cordon, s'il vous plaît', 'Le Petit revenez-y'), *P.L.M.* (1925, Le Contrôleur, 'Mon coeur est un compartiment', 'On s'y fait', 'Trop nerveux', 'Paris-Lyon-Méditerranée'), *Trois jeunes filles ... nues!* (1925, Hégésippe, 'Est-ce que je te demande?'), as Mephistophélès in *Le Diable à Paris* (1926, in the title-rôle of *Louis XIV* (1929), in *Six filles à marier* (1930, 'Un million', Chanson sinueuse, 'T'as bonne mine'), *Bégonia* (1930, 'Chanson de petits bateaux', 'L'Argent', 'L'Oeil en vrille'), *Encore cinquante centimes* (1931, Hercule Boulot, 'Avec les femmes', 'Je reviendrai demain matin', 'Essayez donc'), *Un soir de reveillon* (1932, Honoré, 'Quand on perd la tête'), the Scottish spectacular *Deux sous de fleurs* (1933, Archibald), *Les Soeurs Hortensia* (1934) and *Tonton* (1935), clipping out a regular series of popular songs from their scores and contributing largely, with his adored, individual comicalities, to the successs of those which needed such contribution.

He also appeared occasionally in the classic repertoire, with marked success, playing the role of Antonio, the cor-rupted treasurer, in a major revival of *Les Brigands* at the Opéra-Comique, Frimousse in *Le Petit Duc* at the Châtelet, and Valentin in *Le Petit Faust* at the Porte-Saint-Martin.

He appeared in a number of musical films including the cinematic versions of *Ciboulette* (1935) and *La Mascotte* (1935)

DREAMGIRLS Musical in 2 acts by Tom Eyen. Music by Henry Krieger. Imperial Theater, New York, 20 December 1981.

A gotta-make-it-good-in-showbiz tale which seemed, to knowing commentators, to be based on the careers of the girls who made up the popular 1960s and early 1970s singing group, the Supremes. The *Dreamgirls* group was called the Dreams, and they, too, were operational in the decade 1962–72. Plump and powerful Effie White (Jennifer Holliday), glamorous Deena Jones (Sheryl Lee Ralph) and svelte Lorrell Robinson (Loretta Devine) are the three members of the 'Dreamettes' who work their way from Chicago and a talent contest win onto the books of the hustling agent Curtis Taylor jr (Ben Harney), and a place as a support act to the singer James Thunder Early (Cleavant Derricks). On their way up, Curtis shifts his affections from Effie to Deena, and shifts Deena into the lead vocal spot of the group. Then Effie is out, replaced by a third slim and glamorous girl (Deborah Burrell). The newly constituted group makes it to the top and, when Curtis sees Effie making a comeback as a solo act he tries to stymie her by covering her successful single with a version by the Dreams. He fails, she conquers and is on her way to stardom as the Dreams disband to allow each of the other girls to go on to the putative next stage of their careers.

The showpiece number of a score, which mostly recreated the sounds of the popular music of the period in which it was set, was the first-act curtain number for Effie, 'And I'm Telling You I'm Not Going', a piece of ripping, howling agony in which the rejected girl fought against the whole world in a wide-ranging piece of music which wrought great demands on the pop-soul voice of its performer. A number of the other pieces in the show were presented as pop songs, the repertoire of the characters in the show, notably the successful 'One Night Only' (Effie's comeback song) and the bouncy hymn to the 'Cadillac Car'.

Directed and co-choreographed by co-producer Michael Bennett in spectacular high-tech style, *Dreamgirls* had an outstanding 1,522-performance run on Broadway, but its only sightings in main centres outside America were through performances given by an American touring company which played several European cities – though, in spite of announcements, not London – before taking the show back to Broadway for a further season (28 June 1987, 168 performances) with Lillias White featured in the lead rôle.

France: Palais des Congrès 5 May 1987
Recording: original cast (Geffen)

DREI ALTE SCHACHTELN Operette in a Vorspiel and 3 acts by Hermann Haller. Lyrics by Rideamus. Music by Walter Kollo. Theater am Nollendorfplatz, Berlin, 6 October 1917.

The 'three old maids' of the title of *Drei alte Schachteln* are Ursula Krüger, her young sister Lotte, and their cook, Auguste (Claire Waldoff), and the plot is basically that of J M Barrie's *Quality Street*, with some considerable low comedy for the cook added. The three women's men all go off to the wars and, when Lotte's Klaus returns, ten years later, he finds her apparently turned into a spinsterish schoolmarm. But Lotte doffs her work-clothes and becomes young and charming again, enchanting all of Klaus's fellow soldiers in the guise of the unknown Dörte on the night of their regimental ball. Klaus falls in love with the mysterious Dörte, but when he goes to meet her again at the sisters' home, Auguste is obliged to impersonate the girl and does so so poorly that the pretence is soon made obvious. Klaus and Lotte are united for the final curtain, whilst the cook also gets back her man, Klaus's batman Cornelius Hasenpfeffer.

The action was accompanied by a lively Kollo score, from which the cook's number, 'Ach Jott, was sind die Männer dumm', proved the most popular piece, alongside a trio for the three ladies, 'Drei alte Schachteln geh'n zum Ball'. That score helped Haller's low-comedy version of Barrie to become hugely popular, running for over 450 performances in its first run at the Theater am Nollendorfplatz and being widely played for many years thereafter in Germany. The show did not, however, find many takers further afield. It was produced in Vienna at the end of the First World War with Elly Bach (Ursula), Ida Russka (Lotte), Steffi Walidt (Auguste), Karl Bachmann (Klaus) and Max Brod (Cornelius) and, a couple of years further on, on Broadway, in an adaptation by Edward Delaney Dunn under the title of *Phoebe of Quality Street* which moved back a little closer to the original play. British husband-and-wife team Dorothy Ward (Phoebe) and Shaun Glenville (Sergeant Terence O'Toole) starred alongside Warren Proctor (Valentine) and Gertrude Mudge (Patty, the cook) for 16 performances.

Quality Sheet also served as the basis for the successful British musical *Dear Miss Phoebe* (13 October 1950 Phoenix Theatre) and for a *Phoebe* (Philip Springer/Joan Javits/John Ott 23 August 1965) played for 16 performance's at Pennsylvania's Bucks County Playhouse.

Austria: Johann Strauss-Theater 1919; USA: Shubert Theater *Phoebe of Quality Street* 9 May 1921

DREI ARME TEUFEL Operette in 3 acts by Rudolf Österreicher and Heinz Reichert. Music by Karl Weinberger. Theater am Gärtnerplatz, Munich, 11 March 1916.

When violinist Nelly Wolfgang wins both an American contract to the value of $60,000 and a marriage proposal from Graf Alfred Harpen on the same day, she tries to propitiate fate by giving her meagre savings to the first poor folk she sees – the composer, Eduard Krüger, the modiste, Poldi Berndl, and the serving-man, Obermaier. When Obermaier gets the American contract she thought she had with his talking dog and Poldi proves to be promised to her would-be-fiancé, Nelly is further back than she started, but fate and the 'three poor devils' set things aright in the final act – Nelly is offered the job of musical director to the dog, and Poldi prefers her Krüger to the faithless aristocrat.

One of Weinberger's most successful Operetten in Ger-

many, *Drei arme Teufel* was also given, under the management of Oscar Fronz, at Vienna's Bürgertheater with Grete Holm (Nelly), Paul Kronegg (Alfred), Ernst Wurmser (Obermaier) and Ellie Kreith (Poldi) featured, and the interpolation of the Schrammelquartett 'Die Finken' from the Etablissement Bratwurstglöckerl into the second act. It played 51 times.

Austria: Wiener Bürgertheater 15 June 1923

DIE DREIGROSCHENOPER Piece with music in a prelude and 8 scenes, adapted from John Gay's *The Beggar's Opera* by Elisabeth Hauptmann and Bertolt Brecht. Music by Kurt Weill. Additional lyrics from the works of Rudyard Kipling and François Villon. Theater am Schiffbauerdamm, Berlin, 31 August 1928.

The hugely successful 1920 London revival of John Gay's *The Beggar's Opera* at the Lyric Theatre, Hammersmith, set the once-popular piece off on a new round of productions and on a series of fresh adaptations, amongst which were Felix Dörmann's *Der Liebling von London*, with music arranged by Hans Ewald Heller, produced at Vienna's Carltheater in 1924 (19 April), and a second German-language version, resulting from this one, but with a rather different flavour, made up from an adaptation of the English show prepared by Elisabeth Hauptmann done over and added to by Bertolt Brecht, and mounted at Berlin's Theater am Schiffbauerdamm by Josef Aufricht in 1928. Where *The Beggar's Opera* had taken a poignard to its subjects, *Die Dreigroschenoper* took a cleaver. The unaffectedly ribald and smilingly satirical tone of the original piece was replaced by a much more direct style, scornful and scathing, in a text replete with loathing, whilst the daintily incisive and often incidental musical numbers of the original gave place to a set of darkly coloured Kurt Weill pieces which were equally incisive, sometimes equally incidental, but far from dainty.

Beggar-king Jonathan Jeremiah Peachum (Erich Ponto) and his wife (Rosa Valetti) are appalled when they discover that their daughter, Polly (Roma Bahn), has married the notorious thief and womanizer Macheath (Harald Paulsen) and Peachum is determined to use his influence to get the man hanged, in spite of the highwayman's friendship with the London police chief, Tiger Brown (Kurt Gerron). Sex leads to Macheath's downfall. Mrs Peachum bribes the whore, Jenny (Lotte Lenya), to betray her customer to the law, and the thief ends up in jail, uncomfortably near to another 'wife', Brown's daughter Lucy (Kate Kühl). When she thinks Macheath prefers her to Polly, Lucy helps him escape, but another sizable dose of corruption gets him rearrested, condemned and led to the gallows before he is, at the last, reprieved in an amnesty on the occasion of a Coronation and, indeed, raised to the peerage.

The songs of the piece included several which would ultimately become great favourites, notably the opening Moritat ('Und der Haifisch, der hat Zähne), in which an unnamed street-singer introduces the deeds of the anti-hero of the tale, and Polly's vindictive pub-song 'Die Seeräuber-Jenny' ('Meine Herrn heut sehn Sie mich Gläser aufwaschen'). Polly's (or Lucy's, depending on which source you believe) Barbara-Lied, the Solomon-Lied, in which Jenny reflects on the downfall of great men, the wedding-night duet for Polly and Macheath, 'Siehst du den Mond über Soho', and a jealousy duet for Polly and

Lucy ('Komm heraus, du Schönheit von Soho') were amongst the other principal numbers of the score.

A curious mixture of a piece, with its sad conviction of and concentration on the rottenness and corruption of the entire world, and with its almost voyeuristic revelling in the representing on stage of whores and other things sexual – not with the happy enjoyment of a French comedy, but with a kind of energetic disgust – as the other motor (apart from greed) of man's deeds, and yet topped off by a fantasy or burlesque ending reeking of old-fashioned opéra-bouffe, it proved, nevertheless, to hit a spot. A success in its original Berlin production, it subsequently won further productions through Germany and Europe. It was produced at the Vienna Raimundtheater, under the management of Rudolf Beer, with Paulsen repeating his original rôle alongside Kurt Lessen (Peachum), Pepi Glöckner (Mrs Peachum), Luli Hohenberg (Polly), Walter Brandt (Brown) and Elisabeth Markus (Lucy), accompanied by the Wiener Jazz-Symphonie Orchester, for a run of just over three months, at Budapest's Vígszinház (ad Jenő Heltai) for a brief 13 performances, and then in Paris (ad André Mauprey).

In English it initially did not do well. In Britain, where the Lyric Hammersmith *The Beggar's Opera* made regular reappearances, no need was felt for the more hammer-handed *Die Dreigroschenoper*, whilst an American version (ad Clifford Cochran, Jerrold Krimsky), with Robert Chisholm (Macheath), Steffi Duna (Polly) and Rex Weber (Peachum) featured, folded in a dozen performances at Broadway's Empire Theater.

The heavily politicized Brecht, apparently embarrassed by being associated – even as just co-author/adapter – with a success which made no propaganda point, later revised his text in an attempt to make it more political and insisted, in spite of Weill's distaste for revisions which made the piece lumpenly didactic, that only the new version be permitted. However, it was not Brecht's rewrite which resulted in the show having a longer life, but a version made in English.

American musician and writer Marc Blitzstein, encouraged by the composer, wrote an adaptation which was eventually produced twice at off-Broadway's Theater de Lys (10 March 1954, 30 September 1955) with Scott Merrill (Macheath), Leon Lishner (Peachum), Jo Sullivan (Polly) and with Lotte Lenya, the composer's wife and the original Jenny, repeating her rôle of nearly 30 years earlier. The venue, the timing of the production in an era when anti-establishment feeling and the belief in wholesale corruption were high, and the skilful adaptation combined to make *The Threepenny Opera* a long-running success (2,611 performances) and 'Mack the Knife' (Moritat) a hit-parade number.

Thus relaunched, the show was given its first London production, in 1956, with a cast headed by Bill Owen (Macheath), Daphne Anderson (Polly) and Eric Pohlmann (Peachum). London did not give it more than 140 performances and, although the piece has since received regular British performances, including a starry revival in 1972 (Prince of Wales Theatre 10 January) and even a production at the National Theatre (13 March 1986), that country has never given it the welcome that it has given on several occasions to the original *The Beggar's Opera*. In America, the Blitzstein adaptation was put aside in 1976

when the New York Shakespeare Festival mounted a new adaptation by Ralph Mannheim and John Willett. Raul Julia played Macheath through 30 performances (Vivian Beaumont Theater 1 May).

Australia's semi-professional Union Theatre Company gave the piece its first Australian English-language production in 1959, and it has received intermittent Australian revivals since, including one by the Old Tote company at the Sydney Opera House's Drama Theatre in 1972. The piece also returned to Paris when Aufricht staged a version there in 1937, for which occasion Weill composed two additional songs to add to the rôle of Mrs Peachum, as played by the famous chanteuse Yvette Guilbert, and again in 1979.

Die Dreigroschenoper's determinedly aggressive sentiments and style fitted well into the grand-guignolesque production styles of Western theatre in the 1970s and 1980s, and the show found itself a multitude of productions during those decades, often played (in spite of Weill's stated wish for 'real' voices) by actors-who-sort-of-sing in a strange spit'n'snarl style at odds with both the moments of the piece which seek reality and those which ring of fanciful burlesque. With this oddly unsophisticated style stuck to it, however, it has been seen again and again, including productions at Paris's Théâtre du Châtelet in 1986 (ad Giorgio Strehler, Myriam Tannant), at Berlin's Theater des Westens in 1987, and briefly on Broadway in 1989 (Lunt-Fontanne Theater 5 November ad Michael Feingold) with popular singer Sting as Macheath and Alvin Epstein, Georgia Brown and Maureen McGovern as the Peachum family.

Die Dreigroschenoper made a quick move from the stage to the cinema screen when G W Pabst made a double film version, in German (ad Laszlo Vajda, Leo Lania, Béla Balász) with Rudolf Forster as Macheath and Carola Neher, who had left the original cast in rehearsals, as Polly, and in French (ad Solange Bussi) with Albert Préjean and Florelle. In 1962 Kurt Ulrich filmed another version with a cast headed by Curt Jurgens (Macheath) and June Ritchie (Polly), which was put out both in German and – with Sammy Davis jr performing the Moritat – in English, and in 1989 Menachem Golem issued a version under the title *Mack the Knife*, with Raul Julia repeating his previous stage performance as Macheath.

Austria: Raimundtheater 9 March 1929; Hungary: Vigszinház *A koldus operája* 6 September 1930; France: Théâtre Montparnasse *L'Opéra de quatre sous* 13 October 1930; USA; Empire Theater *The Threepenny Opera* 12 April 1933; UK: Royal Court Theatre *The Threepenny Opera* 9 February 1956; Australia: Union Theatre, Sydney *The Threepenny Opera* 8 January 1959; Films; 1930 Nero Films (Ger/Fr), 1962 Kurt Ulrich Film (Ger/Eng), 1989 21st Century Film Corp (Eng)

Recordings: complete versions (Vanguard, CBS, Polydor, Fontana, London/Decca etc), complete in French (Jacques Canetti), selections (Neue Welt, Telefunken etc), off-Broadway revival 1954 (MGM), Broadway revival 1976 (CBS), film soundtrack (London) etc

DAS DREIMÄDERLHAUS Singspiel in 3 acts by A M Willner and Heinz Reichert adapted from the novel *Schwammerl* by Rudolf H Bartsch. Music from the works of Franz Schubert selected and arranged by Heinrich Berté. Raimundtheater, Vienna, 15 January 1916.

The most widely successful, and also one of the most

Plate 79. **Das Dreimäderlhaus**: *The three little sisters of the original Vienna production – Anni Fischer (Hannerl), Else Lord (Haiderl) and Vally Ernst (Hederl).*

enduring, of all pasticcio musical plays, from *The Beggar's Opera* to *Kismet*, *Das Dreimäderlhaus* was put together, around a sentimentalized version of the love-life of Franz Schubert invented by German author Bartsch in 1912, under the aegis of producer Wilhelm Karczag of the Raimundtheater. According to one version of the story, Karczag heeded the suggestion of publisher Emil Berté that his out-of-luck composer brother, Harry, be given the opportunity to write the score to the libretto Willner and Reichert had drawn from the novel. That story goes on to tell that Karczag rejected the first score which Berté provided, as the composer had included too much of his own original music and insufficient bits of real Schubert, but the final result, even if it and its success perversely hurt the touchy composer's pride, proved a masterly transformation of gold into gold.

Poor composer Franz Schubert (Fritz Schrödter) meets Hannerl Tschöll (Anny Rainer) when she comes as a chaperone to her two sisters, Haiderl (Else Lord) and Hederl (Vally Ernst), to a rendezvous with their boyfriends, Bruneder (Louis Gross) and Binder (Alexander Nessl), under his window. She becomes his singing pupil, and he falls in love with her but, hampered by shyness, he cannot bring himself to declare his love. Hannerl, too, has warm feelings for the composer but, when the actress, Demoiselle Grisi (Therese Tautenhayn), the jealous mistress of Schubert's poet friend Franz Schober (Victor Flemming), warns the girl against the womanizing 'Franz', Hannerl mistakes her meaning and her man. Schubert writes a song to express his love for Hannerl and the easygoing Schober sings it to her, but the girl, believing that the

feelings expressed are Schober's, responds by agreeing to marry him. Schubert is left with only his music.

The song used for the key point in the plot was Schubert's Serenade ('Ich schnitt es gern in alle Rinden ein'), whilst the three little sisters of the title made their entrance to the strains of the composer's Air de ballet from *Rosamunde* as they declared themselves as 'Haiderl und Hederl und Hannerl Tschöll', Schubert's version of Shakespeare's 'Hark, Hark, the Lark' was sung by the quartet of Schubert's friends, and the A-major waltz became Schubert and Hannerl's duo 'Was Schön'res könnt's sein als ein Wiener Lied'. One of the show's best musical moments fell to father Tschöll (Franz Glawatsch), comforting his wife over the imminent marriage of their daughters in the warmly felt 'Geh, Alte, schau'.

Produced in the best tradition of the good-old-days Operette, a genre which has always proven so successful in time of war or trouble, *Das Dreimäderlhaus*, with its picturesque recreation of the Biedermeier era, was an enormous hit at the Raimundtheater. The piece ran quickly to its 100th performance (19 April) as Artur Preuss and Karl Streitmann each took a turn at the rôle of Schubert, crossed town for a Gastspiel at the Theater an der Wien, and returned home to hit 200 nights (7 September 1916), 300 nights (13 December 1916) and, with Julius Spielmann now as Schubert, its 400th night on 8 March 1917. Hans Golle and Fritz Neumann both appeared as Schubert as the show ran on to its 600th performance (13 December 1917), ultimately closing 7 February 1918 to leave the Raimundtheater stage to a soi-disant sequel, *Hannerl*, in which Glawatsch once again appeared as Tschöll and Anny Rainer as Hannerl – the daughter of her original character. *Das Dreimäderlhaus* remained in the repertoire after *Hannerl* had been and gone and it passed its 1,100th performance at the Raimundtheater on 9 April 1927, with Preuss still appearing as Schubert.

The huge Viennese success of the show was repeated in Berlin. Produced at the Friedrich-Wilhelmstädtisches Theater in 1916, the show ran until 11 September 1918 – eventually giving way to *Hannerl* as the evening entertainment, but running on in matinées to pass its 1,000th Berlin performance on 12 November 1918. Budapest, too, gave the piece a delighted welcome. *Harom a kislány* (ad Zsolt Harsányi), with the operatic tenor Béla Környei (Schubert), Emmi Kosáry (Medi, ex-Hannerl, with Erzsi Gerő and Hanna Honthy as her sisters), Gyula Csortos (Schober) and Ferenc Vendrey (Tschöll) featuring in the principal rôles, ran at the Vigszinház for 151 performances, before the piece moved on to a production at the Városi Színház (6 November 1919) with Környei and Kosáry again starred, returning to the Vígszinház as soon as 1922 (8 October), as it established itself as firmly in the repertoire in Hungary as in German-language theatres.

It was probably wartime conditions which slowed the progress of this enormous hit to the rest of the world but, when it did get to the other main theatrical centres, it thoroughly confirmed its Central-European success. *Chanson d'amour* (ad Hugues Delorme, Léon Abric), mounted at Paris's Théâtre Marigny by Constance Maille, with Henri Fabert starred as Schubert alongside Marcelle Ragon (Annette Mühl ex-Hannerl Tschöll), Louis Marie (Schober) and Max Mario (Mühl), shifted quickly to the Théâtre Apollo (1 July 1921), where it ran out a fine season. It was revived in Paris in 1928, with Gilbert Moryn as Schubert, and again in 1931 (Gaîté-Lyrique), and was later played at the Théâtre de la Porte-Saint-Martin in the original German with Richard Tauber and Irene Eisinger featured (1933). Roger Bourdin was Schubert at a revival at the Théâtre de la Porte-Saint-Martin in 1934. In France, as elsewhere, the piece has remained in the repertoire ever since.

The Shubert brothers took up *Das Dreimäderlhaus* for America but, in their normal fashion, having paid for it, they had the score remade. Dorothy Donnelly's melodramatic version of the book, which rather oddly had Schubert dying (to the sound of full-blooded angelic strains) at the final curtain, like a Viennese Jack Point, was accompanied by some semi-fresh Schubert arrangements made by Sigmund Romberg. The Unfinished Symphony provided the material for the most popular song, 'Song of Love'. Less well made than its original, *Blossom Time* was, nevertheless, no less successful. With Bertram Peacock as Schubert, Howard Marsh as Schober and Olga Cook as Mitzi Kranz (once Hannerl Tschöll), the show ran a splendid 592 performances at the Ambassador Theater before beginning a very, very long series of tours, revivals and imitations. It returned to Broadway at the Jolson Theater in 1924 (19 May) and 1926 (8 March) in Shubert seasons, was revived at its original home in 1931, again in 1943 (4 September) and once more at the 46th Street Theater in 1938 (26 December). Latterly, as in the case of *The Student Prince*, its reputation suffered slightly, simply from the number of *Blossom Time* productions and companies – often not of a very high standard – which wore a groove around the country and, eventually, it dropped from the repertoire.

Britain's *Lilac Time* (ad Adrian Ross) also had the Schu-Berté score revamped, by the well-educated G H Clutsam, but this version stayed a little closer to Berté's version, and the Viennese adapter was given a co-credit. In a masterly piece of casting, the (not-too-)ageing Courtice Pounds, once the original hero of *The Gondoliers*, was cast as Schubert alongside opera star Percy Heming (Schober) and the fine soprano Clara Butterworth (Lili Veit, a very long while back Hannerl Tschöll). Music publishers Chappell & Co produced the piece at the Lyric Theatre for a first run of 626 performances, and *Lilac Time* began a touring career almost as full as that of its American equivalent. London had return seasons in 1927 and 1928 (Daly's Theatre) with Frederick Blamey, Heming and Evelyn Laye starred, in 1930 with Blamey, Gertrude Wolfe and Thorpe Bates and in 1932 with Maurice d'Oisly as Schubert. In 1933 Richard Tauber appeared in his own personal version, followed weeks later by another season with d'Oisly and Helen Gilliland (Alhambra Theatre) who paired again three years later in a season at the London Coliseum (29 July 1936). A wartime revival at the Stoll Theatre (13 October 1942) starred Frank Titterton, Irene Eisinger and Derek Oldham, and a final West End sighting occurred in 1949 (His Majesty's Theatre 24 February) with John Lewis, Celia Lipton and Bruce Trent featured before, as in America, the show rather slid away, suffering from under-quality over-exposure.

Australia waited until 1924 before seeing *Lilac Time* (the British version was preferred to the Donnelly/Romberg one). John Ralston (Shubert), Claude Flemming (Scho-

ber), Eve Lynn (Lili) and Arthur Stigant (Veit) had to be shunted out of their theatre for a Toti dal Monte opera season and thus managed only an initial seven weeks in Sydney, but a year and a bit later Melbourne (Theatre Royal 9 January 1926) welcomed Ralston, Flemming and American soprano Harriet Bennet much more enthusiastically, and their 126-performance season established the show for a number of later returns.

The first screen version of *Das Dreimäderlhaus* came out soon after its opening when Richard Oswald produced a silent film based on the piece in 1917. An English film version was made in 1934, as *Blossom Time*, with Richard Tauber starred, and E W Emo turned out a German sound film in 1936. France's Schubert biomusical, *La Belle Meunière*, was not strictly a version of *Das Dreimäderlhaus*, but rather a piece constructed in the same way for the benefit of star tenor Tino Rossi, but in 1958 Ernst Marischka wrote and helmed one further German-language film, which featured Karlheinz Böhm as Schubert, Johanna Matz as Hannerl and Rudolf Schock as Schober, and was, musically, a touch more straight Schubert than Berté's version.

A biomusical on the fictionalized life of a composer, illustrated by arrangements of his own music, was no new idea and even Schubert himself had already been served on several occasions, notably by a distinctly successful Viennese Singspiel with a score arranged by Franz von Suppé (1864), but the triumph of *Das Dreimäderlhaus* was responsible for a worldwide flood of such pieces, as composers including Offenbach, Chopin, Mendelssohn, Grieg Tchaikovsky and Schumann found their putative love-lives transferred to the musical stage, on several occasions with no little success. None, however, managed to approach the overwhelming international fame won by *Das Dreimäderlhaus* and its national variants.

Hungary: Vígszinház *Harom a kislány* 23 April 1916; Germany: Friedrich-Wilhelmstädtisches Theater 1916; France: Théâtre Marigny *Chanson d'amour* 7 May 1921; USA: Ambassador Theater *Blossom Time* 29 September 1921; UK: Lyric Theatre *Lilac Time* 22 December 1922; Australia: Her Majesty's Theatre, Sydney *Lilac Time* 24 May 1924

Recordings: complete in French (Decca), selections (EMI, Ariola Eurodisc, Amadeo etc), selection in English (*Lilac Time*) (EMI etc), (*Blossom Time*) (RCA), selection in Italian (Fonit-Cetra), selection in Hungarian (Qualiton) etc

DREI PAAR SCHUHE Lebensbild in 3 acts and a Vorspiel by Karl Görlitz adapted by Alois Berla. Music by Carl Millöcker. Theater an der Wien, Vienna, 5 January 1871.

The German play *Drei Paar Schuhe*, as adapted to the Viennese musical stage by playwright Berla and composer Millöcker, was a major success when it was first produced at the Theater an der Wien with Marie Geistinger starred in the heavily local-accented central rôle of Leni, the wife of the shoemaker, Lorenz Flink (Jani Szika). The three pairs of shoes of the title have been made by Flink, and their delivery – respectively to the homes of the wealthy Stangelmeier family (Herr Romini, Frln Singer), to the opera singer Laura Eder (Frln Stauber), and to the variety performer Irma (Karoline Finaly) – allows the romantically inclined Leni to get mixed up in the world of wealth and of the theatre for the space of three acts as she arrives, like a good fairy, just in time to clear up the problems of each household.

The musical part of the show was mostly for the benefit of the star, who had an opening song ('O Himmelkreuzmordelement') and a lullaby ('Schlaf ein, mein Kind') in the prologue and, following the musicless first act, the hugely successful yodelling song 'I und mein Bua' in the second, and a drinking song ('Brausender Schaum') in the third, as well as a part in some extensive concerted music. There was also a song each for Laura ('Von Mozart umsäuselt, von Verdi gequält'), for Irma ('Cancan tanzt sie') and, in particular, for Carl Adolf Friese as the roué Nachtfalter – who appears in two of the three episodes – declaring in the show's second hit number 'Bei Tag, da bin ich hektisch, bei Nacht wird ich elektrisch'.

Drei Paar Schuhe was played for a whole month at the Theater an der Wien before the production of Strauss's *Indigo* forced it aside, but it was brought back again and again over the next 30 years, both at the Theater an der Wien, where it totalled 169 performances in that time, and also at other Viennese houses, at first in the original and subsequently in the inevitable 'adapted' versions. It was played in Germany and in the German theatres of America, both by local companies and by Geistinger herself on her various tours, and it was also given a successful production in Hungarian (ad Ferenc Nándori Toldy).

A second musical version of the original play, with a score by Conradi, was also produced in Vienna, whilst a third, an adaptation by Jean Kren with lyrics by Alfred Schönfeld and music by Jean Gilbert, was produced at the Berlin Thalia-Theater in 1915. An American remake, entitled *At the French Ball*, was played at Broadway's Bijou Theater in 1897.

Hungary: Budai Színkör *Harom pár cipő* 31 July 1872; USA: Germania Theater 19 May 1873

DREI WALZER Operette in 3 acts and 12 scenes by Paul Knepler and Armin Robinson. Music written and arranged by Oscar Straus with the use of music from the works of Johann Strauss I and Johann Strauss II. Stadttheater, Zurich, 5 October 1935.

The most skilful and attractive of the endless list of pasticcio works to have been made up from strippings of Strauss music, *Drei Walzer* was a piece laid out in three eras, on the lines of the successful *Wie einst im Mai*, and its score was compiled in function of this. Act 1, set in 1865 Vienna, utilized the melodies of Johann Strauss père; Act 2, which moved on to 1900, was musically illustrated by the music of Johann Strauss fils; whilst the musical part of the third act, played in the present day (ie 1935), was composed of new music from the pen of Oscar Straus.

The first act followed the ill-starred love story of dancer Fanny Pichler and Count Rudi Schwarzenegg. Realizing, with a little help from his kindly but impeccably aristocratic aunt, that marrying her would force Rudi to give up his career in the Imperial army and his social position, Fanny leaves Vienna. In the second act Rudi's son, Count Otto, seeks out Fanny's daughter, Charlotte, an Operette star, and they fall in love, but the jealousy of Otto's former mistress comes between them. The final act is set in a modern film studio where a film about Rudi and Fanny is being made, with filmstar Franzi, Charlotte's daughter,

portraying her grandmother. When the actor playing Rudi drops out, the present day Count Schwarzenegg, who has come to complain about the film, is co-opted to play the rôle. By the end of the act, the third generation are well on their way to the happy ending the first two missed. The character of the agent, Johann Brunner, linked all three stories by his presence in much the same way that the Methusalem of *Wie einst im Mai* had done.

Drei Walzer did not have a large career in its German original, but a conversation between the divette Yvonne Printemps and composer Straus resulted in it becoming a major success in France. The show and the triple-headed rôles of the lovers were adapted by Léopold Marchand and Albert Willemetz to suit the needs of Mlle Printemps and her on- and off-stage partner Pierre Fresnay. The musical part of his rôle was pruned away, whilst hers was beefed up with much of what had once been his, plus a little extra, the second act was given a different ending, and the piece, which was now set in France, linked to the years of the great Paris Exhibitions (1867, 1900, 1937). Profiting remarkably from its remake, and from the performances given to it by its two memorable stars in Willemetz's production at the Théâtre des Bouffes-Parisiens (1937), *Trois valses* became a major hit.

The highlights of a score which was built up with consummate skill and period colour, were the numbers given to Mlle Printemps, now playing Fanny, Yvette and Irène Grandpré: the first-act waltz 'C'est la saison d'amour' and the virtual solo, 'Te souvient-il?', like the first, taken from a Strauss père waltz, the dazzling waltz song 'Je t'aime' and the sprightly 'Oui, je t'aime ô Paris' of the second act, and the modern, jaunty 'Je ne suis pas ce que l'on pense' (the 'little extra' added at the last minute) and 'Mais c'est le destin peut-être' of the final part. The aged Brunner (René Dary) of the last act had the best solo opportunity outside the prima donna rôle, with a reminiscing 'Comme autrefois', alongside some small comical pieces and several ensembles, of which the anti-marriage meeting of the lofty de Chalency (ex-Schwarzenegg) family in Act I was one of the most enjoyable.

After the original season of *Trois valses*, the star pair filmed the show (ad Marchand, Hans Müller), under the direction of Ludwig Berger. Henri Guisol was Brunner, and such artists as Jean Périer and Boucot appeared in supporting rôles in a movie which remains one of the most attractive of its era and type. Printemps and Fresnay subsequently played a return season of *Trois valses* at the Théâtre de la Michodière in 1939 (31 January), and, whilst provincial productions flowed freely through the country, the show came back again in 1952 and 1959, under the management of its newest star, Germaine Roger, at the Théâtre de la Gaîté-Lyrique. It remains a regularly performed piece in France to the present day.

The Paris success provoked productions in both New York and London. Kitty Carlisle starred alongside Michael Bartlett in Broadway's *Three Waltzes* (ad Rowland Leigh, Clare Kummer), whilst in London Evelyn Laye and Esmond Knight were ideally cast at the head of another English version (ad Diana Morgan, Robert MacDermott). Neither production, however, proved as successful as the French version, the Broadway piece making 122 performances, and London's running to 189 without, in either case, establishing the show in the repertoire.

France: Théâtre des Bouffes-Parisiens *Trois valses* 22 April 1937;
USA: Majestic Theater *Three Waltzes* 25 December 1937;
UK: Prince's Theatre *Three Waltzes* 1 March 1945

Recordings: original cast recordings (EMI), complete in French (Decca), selections in French (EMI-Pathé, Decca etc)

DRESSLER, Marie [VAN KOERBER, Leila Marie] (b Coburg, Canada, 9 November 1869; d Santa Barbara, Calif, 28 July 1934). Hefty, plug-ugly singing comedienne, who led a career in burlesque and musical theatre which was topped by a later incarnation as a movie heavy.

Because of her physique and deep voice, Miss Dressler played heavies from a young age, appearing as a teenaged Katisha and on tour with Moulton and Bennett before making her first Broadway appearance in Lillian Russell's company in *The Robber of the Rhine* (1892, Cunigonde). She was seen in *Princess Nicotine* (1893, Duchess), as the Queen of Spain (a rôle created by a female impersonater) in Edward Rice's extravaganza *1492*, as the extravagantly comical mother of marriageable twins in a revival of *Giroflé-Girofla* (1894, Aurore), in *Madeleine* (1895, Mary Douclee) and *A Stag Party* (1895, Georgia West), and in 1896 she played the flashy music-hall artist Flo Honeydew (who doesn't get the man) in the American version of the British variety musical *The Lady Slavey*.

Dressler appeared alongside Eddie Foy in the Broadway version of Roger's *L'Auberge du Tohu-bohu* (1898, Flora) and in leading rôles in a series of home-made musical and revusical pieces over the next decade (*The Man in the Moon, Miss Printt, The King's Carnival, The Hall of Fame, King Highball, Higgledy Piggledy, Twiddle Twaddle, The Boy and the Girl*), after which she decided to present herself in London in a double bill of *Philpoena* (an excerpt from *Higgledy Piggledy*) and *The Collegettes*. When she won poor notices and poorer audiences she decamped furiously back to America after ten nights, leaving her cast and employees to whistle for their wages.

Justice clearly slept, for the first rôle which she took up on her return home was the one which was to give her the star status London had denied her. As the dreaming slavey of *Tillie's Nightmare* (1910, Tillie Blobbs) she delivered 'Heaven Will Protect the Working Girl' and scored her biggest Broadway success as a performer. Once again, however, she showed less credibility as an honest producer: she was hauled to court for not paying a sacked act, and walked out on her cast at the end of the run without paying their wages, obliging them to run to their union and the law to recoup their due.

With her portrayal of George Hobart's Tillie, however, Dressler had created a character which was soon transferred – with its creator – to film, a switch of medium which started her on a second career of some 20 years as the classic boot-faced harridan of MGM's films of the 1920s and 1930s. She appeared thereafter in a couple more stage musicals, being last seen in a semi-book show in 1923 as Gloria Seabright in *The Dancing Girl*, but more often her latter-day theatre appearances were in revue, and they were, in any case, much less frequent than those on the screen.

Autobiography: *The Life Story of an Ugly Duckling* (Mc Bride, New York, 1924), *My Own Story* (Little, Brown, Boston, 1934)

DREVER, Constance (b Conoor, Neilgherry Hills, Madras, ?1880; d England, 21 September 1948).

Miss Drever, who had studied voice on the Continent, made a dramatic first appearance on the musical stage when she was promoted at the very last minute, from a minor rôle, to the star part of Kenna for the opening night of Edward German's *A Princess of Kensington* (1903), replacing ailing prima donna Agnes Fraser. She subsequently worked on the concert stage, returning to the theatre to tour in the comic opera *Amasis* (1907) and later succeeding Elizabeth Firth as Natalie (Valencienne) in George Edwardes's *The Merry Widow* at Daly's Theatre. She subsequently moved up to play Sonia (Hanna) in the same production. After an appearance at the New Theatre in the title-rôle of a revival of *Dorothy*, she went to Paris where she created the part of Missia (ex-Sonia, ex-Hanna ex-*Die lustige Witwe*), otherwise *La Veuve joyeuse*, with enormous success. Her performance left such a mark on the piece and the rôle that for many years the star rôle of *La Veuve joyeuse* was – decidedly curiously, given the plot – played in France with a strong English accent.

Back in Britain, she introduced 'My Hero' to Londoners when she played the role of Nadina in the English version of *The Chocolate Soldier*, and then moved on to star as Rosalinde in a remake of *Die Fledermaus* called *Nightbirds*, as Lizzi Flora in Straus's short-lived *The Dancing Viennese* at the Coliseum, as Tatjana in Kerker's *Grass Widows* and, in succession to Gertie Millar, as Lady Babby in the rewritten *Zigeunerliebe* (*Gipsy Love*, 1912).

After appearing at the Coliseum in variety, she spent much of her time singing on similar programmes and she played out the last decade of her career as an actress and vocalist on the variety stage.

LE DROIT D'AÎNESSE Opérette in 3 acts by Eugène Leterrier and Albert Vanloo. Music by Francis Chassaigne. Théâtre des Nouveautés, Paris, 27 January 1883.

Le Droit d'aînesse had a curious career. Produced at the Paris Théâtre des Nouveautés in 1883 with a top-flight cast headed by Marguerite Ugalde (Falka), Juliette Darcourt (Edwige), Berthelier (Tancrède), Vauthier (Boléslas), Albert Brasseur (Arthur) and Scipion (Pélican), it met with little better than indifference and was removed after 49 performances, never to be seen on the Paris stage again. However, in spite of this, it was taken up for a British production and, nine months later, an H B Farnie adaptation, rechristened *Falka*, was produced by Alexander Henderson at London's Comedy Theatre. This time there was no indifference: *Falka* was an instant and very sizeable hit.

Folbach (Harry Paulton), the military governor of Mongratz, is the uncle of Tancred (Henry Ashley) and of Falka (Violet Cameron). Tancred is captured by the brigand, Boléslas (W H Hamilton), but helped to escape by the robber-maid Edwige (Tilly Wadman) when he promises her marriage, and he ends up disguised as a waiter. Falka (Violet Cameron), on the other hand, runs away from her convent school with her boy-friend, Arthur (Louis Kelleher) and, to avoid the unwelcome attentions of Uncle Folbach, she ends up disguised as Tancred, with Arthur disguised as her! In the tangling and untangling of the situations, W S Penley, in the character of the lay brother Pelican supplied much of the comedy.

Falka played for 157 performances at the Comedy Theatre, and returned to London as soon as 1885 (Avenue Theatre 19 September) whilst the first of the many touring companies which would fill the next decade or so continued round the country. In the meanwhile, Farnie's version opened on Broadway, at the Casino Theater, with Bertha Ricci (Falka), J H Ryley (Folbach), Hubert Wilke (Boléslas), Frank Tannehill jr (Tancred), Mathilde Cottrelly (Edwige) and Alfred Klein (Pelican) featured, and it once again scored a hit, compiling a run of 103 nights. Continuing its triumphal way around the world's English-speaking theatres, the show also proved a popular success in Australia. First introduced by Annette Ivanova (Falka), Edwin Kelly (Pelican), Florence Trevallyan (Edwige) and Robert Brough (Tancred), it was given a fine boost when the area's favourite opéra-bouffe prima donna, Emilie Melville returned from touring India and took over as Falka.

For many years a popular item in the repertoire of touring comic opera companies, *Falka* (which had long forgotten it had ever, briefly, existed as *Le Droit d'aînesse*) had a particularly long life in Britain where it was for many years played by Horace Lingard's provincial company which, at one stage, presented its own burlesque version of the show under the title *Brother Pelican*.

UK: Comedy Theatre *Falka* 29 October 1883; USA: Casino Theater *Falka* 4 April 1884; Australia: Opera House, Melbourne *Falka* 24 April 1886

LE DROIT DU SEIGNEUR Opérette in 3 acts by Paul Burani and Maxime Boucheron. Music by Léon Vasseur. Théâtre des Fantaisies-Parisiennes, Paris, 13 December 1878.

When the young director Debruyère took over the old Théâtre Beaumarchais and turned it into a lyric theatre, one of his first ventures was Vasseur's saucy opérette, *Le Droit du seigneur*.

The show's story lived up to its title, with Denizot featured as the Baron who tries on behalf of the local Duc (Sujol) to re-establish the old custom of the overlord's right to deflower every young bride in his fief. The villagers, in response, simply decide to do without marriage. However, Lucinette (A Humberta) and her Bibolais (Cyriali) do get wed, and spend half the evening trying to keep out of the way of the Baron. Bibolais is imprisoned and threatened with the gallows for not handing over his wife and, when he is suddenly freed, he, not unreasonably, suspects his wife of having given in. By the time the Baron and the Duc catch up with the pair, however, they've already connubed and, since the Duc can't now be first, his *droit de seigneur* is invalid. Adèle Cuinet played the Baron's wife, a former paramour of the Duc, and the mother of his long-lost child whose identity provided another complication to the plot.

Amongst the musical moments, Lucinette's gently suggestive Couplets du coquelicot with its cuckoldy refrain ('coquelicot, coquelicot'), and the Duc's song reasoning that, since all the other first fruits are reserved by vassals for their overlord, it follows that he should have the maidenhead of their wives, were both popular, as were Bibolais's romance, 'Adieu bois touffus, vert ombrages' and Lucienette's little solo ('Avec ma plus belle révérence'), sweetly thumbing her nose at the Duc after

the deed is irreparably done. Means was also found to introduce a lively hunters' chorus into the proceedings.

The show was a considerable hit, running for 229 performances and ten further in 1880, and when Debruyère took over the Théâtre de la Gaîté in 1884 he revived it again. It reappeared in 1889 at the Bouffes-Parisiens with Louise Théo starred, and again for 38 performances in 1893 at the Théâtre des Menus-Plaisirs (31 October) with Mlle Léonetti as Lucinette.

Whilst the original Paris production ran, an English version (ad Arthur Matthison) was produced in London by the gentlemen of the Comedy Opera Company, determined to make a hit following their noisy split with D'Oyly Carte over *HMS Pinafore*. Isabelle Mulholland (Marigold), George Mudie (Duc de Noces-Defendues) and Arthur Rosbey (Ferdinand) featured in *Marigold!* for a season of five weeks which put an end to the Comedy Opera Company. Whether because of this or because of the impossibility of bleaching the sexual content from the libretto, the other main centres passed, but the British provinces got the chance to hear at least a part of Vasseur's score when it was lifted to illustrate the touring burlesque *Cruel Carmen*.

UK: Olympic Theatre *Marigold!* 29 October 1879

DRUCKER, Karl (b Brünn, 3 August 1855; d Brünn, 11 January 1888).

After successes in smaller Austrian theatres and particularly in his home town, the tenor Drucker was engaged at the Carltheater in 1879. He spent several years there in leading rôles, creating such parts as Gaston Dufaure in Suppé's *Donna Juanita*, Polyphem von Croustillac in *Der Gaskogner* (1881), the tenor rôle of *Das Herzblättchen* (1882), Flagerlot in Genée's *Rosina* (1881), and Don Montiel de Carragui in his *Nisida* (1880), and appearing as Valentin in *Olivette* (1881), Tom in Émile Jonas's *Javotte* (1882), Don Luis de Rosamonte in *Drei Schwarzmäntel* (1882), Fitzo in *Kosiki* and Don Januario in *Der Seekadet* (1882).

In 1883 he quit the Carltheater and, with his companion, the soubrette Jenny Stubel, went prospecting for lucrative engagements in other Austrian and German theatres. Then, suddenly, he disappeared from view. His stage nerve had cracked and he was finally rediscovered, dying, in his home town at the age of 32.

DIE DUBARRY Operette in 9 scenes by Paul Knepler and Ignaz M Welleminsky. Music by Karl Millöcker adapted by Theo Mackeben. Admiralspalast, Berlin, 14 August 1931.

The little milliner Marie-Jeanne Beçu (Gitta Alpár) goes out one day to meet her painter boyfriend, René Lavallery (Robert Nästlberger), in the park and catches the eye of the Comte Dubarry. He follows her to René's studio, causing a breach between the young pair, and finally, after putting her through a marriage with his brother so that she can be officially the Comtesse Dubarry, takes her to court as a candidate for the important and influential post of mistress to the King. Obliged to choose between her painter and the royal bed, Jeanne, unlike most of her operettic predecessors, pragmatically chooses the King. Jeanne's actress friend, Margot (Edith Schollwer),

Plate 80. **The Dubarry**: *Grace Moore and the glamour chorus in Broadway's production of the Mackeben–Millöcker paste-up Operette.*

and her boyfriend, Brissac (Igor Gutmann), made up the soubret part of the entertainment.

An amount of the music used in this version of the semi-fictional life and loves of Madame du Barry was adapted from the score to Millöcker's earlier piece on the same subject, the indifferently successful 1879 Operette *Gräfin Dubarry* (Theater an der Wien 31 October 1879, Brünn 15 January 1879, Friedrich-Wilhelmstädtisches Theater 20 January 1879 etc). The leading lady's rôle was supplied with a fine barrage of musical numbers, beginning in the first scene with the happy 'Heut' hab ich Glück', continuing through her declaration of fidelity ('Ich schenk mein Herz'), her apprehensive first steps at court ('Ob man gefällt oder nicht gefällt') and rising to its peak in the final scene with the glittering, jaunty 'Ja, so ist sie, die Dubarry'. René supplied the tenor music, both solo and in duet with Jeanne.

Die Dubarry scored a fine success in its Berlin première, with Gitta Alpár winning a memorable triumph in the rôle of Jeanne ('the best [prima donna] Central Europe has to offer'). Further productions followed in its wake, with London the first of the major centres to take the show up (ad Rowland Leigh, Desmond Carter). Stanley Scott's production confirmed the Berlin success, and once again the show's prima donna, this time German vocalist Anny Ahlers, won enthusiastic praise, but tragedy struck when the star committed suicide during the run. With Sylvia Welling replacing, opposite the René of Heddle Nash, and such names as Farren Soutar (Chamard), Margaret Yarde (Sauterelle) and Helen Haye (Maréchale) in support, the piece ran to its 397th performance before going on the road. It was revived in the West End in 1947 (Prince's Theatre 8 October) with Irene Manning as Jeanne, John Hendrik (René) and a supporting cast including Ada Reeve (Sauterelle), Jerry Verno (de la Marche) and John Le Mesurier (Lamond).

Singing star Grace Moore was Broadway's Dubarry, in Tillie Leblang and Morris Green's production, alongside William Hain (René), Pert Kelton (Margot) and Marion Green (King Louis) for a disappointing 87 performances, whilst Alpár repeated her celebrated portrayal in her native Hungary (ad László Lakatos, Andor Szenes) alongside Dezső Kertész, Miklós Hajmássy, Ella Kertész, Klári Tabódy and László Bánát. Miss Welling repeated her London performance, paired with John Dudley (René), in an Australian production at Sydney's Theatre Royal and Melbourne's King's Theatre (31 March 1934), and Paris saw Fanély Revoil as the Dubarry in André Mouëzy-Éon and Albert Willemetz's French version for a good run. The Theater an der Wien finally mounted an 11-scene version, under the management of Hans Knappl, in 1935 with Mary Lossef starred alongside Wladimir Antscharoff (René), Olly Gebauer (Margot), Willy Stettner (Brissac) and Alfred Gerasch (Louis) for 35 performances.

Having thoroughly done the rounds of the world's stages, *Die Dubarry* returned to the Admiralspalast in 1938, and the piece remained popular in Germany, Britain and in Australia for some time. In 1935 an English-language film version was produced, under the title *I Give My Heart*, with Miss Alpár repeating her portrayal of the Dubarry opposite Owen Nares, whilst in 1951 a German film, using the Operette simply as its background but calling itself *Die*

Dubarry, was produced by Georg Wildhagen with a cast headed by Sári Bárabás, Albert Lievin and Willy Fritsch.

The rearranged Operette was itself several times subsequently rearranged, notably in a weak version by Hans Martin Cremer which added a few more wearily conventional turns to the plot – on her way from millinery to mistressing, Jeanne takes a turn as a cabaret singer! – and another new version of *Gräfin Dubarry*, made by Wilhelm Neef, was produced in Rostock in 1959 (24 March).

UK: His Majesty's Theatre 14 April 1932; USA: George M Cohan Theater 22 November 1932; Hungary: Fővarosi Operettszínház 5 September 1933; France: Théâtre de la Porte-Saint-Martin 21 October 1933; Austria: Theater an der Wien 30 August 1935; Australia: Theatre Royal, Sydney 20 January 1934; Films: *I Give My Heart* 1935, International Film *Die Dubarry* 1951 (Ger)

Recordings: selection (Eurodisc, Philips, HMV) selection in Hungarian (Qualiton) etc

DUBARRY WAS A LADY Musical comedy in 2 acts by Herbert Fields and B G De Sylva. Music and lyrics by Cole Porter. 46th Street Theater, New York, 6 December 1939.

A costume comedy musical, *Dubarry Was a Lady* used the favourite old dream-sequence trick of Victorian days with which to whisk its comedian back in time, on this occasion to the court of King Louis XV of France. Bert Lahr played little Louis Blore, a lavatory attendant in a New York nightclub, who has a passion for the place's star vocalist, May Daley (Ethel Merman). Needless to say, May has slightly loftier aims – she is more interested in the newspaperman, Alex Barton (Ronald Graham), even though he has a wife already. Encouraged to action after a big win on the sweepstakes, Louis determines to stake his claim. He spikes his rival's drink, but then mistakenly takes the mickey finn himself and finds himself dreaming that he is King Louis, and that May is his Madame du Barry. He pursues his royal suit but, just as he is about to conquer his fair French lady, he wakes up. Realizing that he is never going to win May, he spends his winnings (after tax) on helping her boyfriend get his divorce, and goes back to his old job.

Cole Porter's score for the show was far from his most memorable, but it nevertheless brought forth a couple of enduring pieces. The topical duo 'Well, Did You Evah?', performed in the show, in a supporting rôle, by the young Betty Grable and by Charles Walters, was later made a favourite by its interpolation into the film *High Society*, whilst a ditty for Lahr and Miss Merman about 'Friendship' resurfaced in several of the Porter paste-up shows of subsequent years, and now seems to have found a displaced home in the 1990s version of *Anything Goes*. Miss Merman also told of how 'Katie Went to Haiti' in an elaborate night-club number, shared the tasty but censored 'But in the Morning, No' with Lahr and, in a last-minute addition to the score, advised with surprisingly little lyrical subtlety, 'Give Him the Ooh-La-La'.

Buddy De Sylva's production of *Dubarry Was a Lady* had a fine Broadway run of 408 performances, and the show was subsequently produced by Tom Arnold and Harry Foster in London with Arthur Riscoe and Frances Day starred as Louis and his lady and Bruce Trent purveying the ballads as Alex/Alexandre. In spite of a less than

enthusiastic reception, the production ran a pretty good five months and 178 performances at His Majesty's and the Phoenix Theatres before taking a turn around the provinces.

In 1943 *Dubarry Was a Lady*, which had actually been conceived by its authors in the first instance as a possible film project, was adapted for the screen. Lucille Ball, with the assistance of dubbing vocalist Martha Mears, and Red Skelton starred in a version in which only 'Katie Went to Haiti', 'Friendship' and the ballad 'Do I Love You?' survived from the original score, alongside new numbers by Burton Lane, Ralph Freed, Lew Brown, Roger Edens and E Y Harburg ('Madame, I Like Your Crêpes Suzette', 'Salomé').

UK: His Majesty's Theatre 22 October 1942; Film: MGM 1943
Recording: selection (Decca).

THE DUCHESS OF DANTZIC Romantic light opera in 3 acts by Henry Hamilton. Music by Ivan Caryll. Lyric Theatre, London, 17 October 1903.

Written some years before its production, and at first intended as a vehicle for London's 'queen of comic opera', Florence St John, Ivan Caryll's Napoleonic musical *The Duchess of Dantzic* leaned musically towards his earliest works, in the French style, rather than to the Gaiety musical comedies which he had since made his speciality. Hamilton's version of Victorien Sardou and Émile Moreau's *Madame Sans-Gêne* story made the rôle of the outspoken washerwoman Catherine Upscher (Evie Greene) a huge leading part, which appeared even more so given the fact that the principal male rôle of Napoleon Bonaparte (Holbrook Blinn) was written as a virtually non-singing one.

Catherine is a Paris washerwoman, wed to a soldier, and the foster-mother of an aristocratic child orphaned in the revolution. One of her clients is a poor Corsican lieutenant who cannot pay his bill. Over the years, Lefèbvre, Catherine's husband, rises to a high post in the army and in court, and Napoléon orders him to divorce his untutored, rough-spoken wife and wed the imperial ward, Renée de St Mézarde (Adrienne Augarde). He refuses, and so does Renée, who is in love with Catherine's foster-son, Adhémar (Lawrence Rea). Finally, Catherine forces her way into the imperial presence and, unpaid bills in hand, reminds the Emperor of his early days and his old idealism, until Napoléon is shamed into being less high-handed. Catherine ends up as the Duchess of Dantzic, and the young couple are allowed to wed as they wish.

The remainder of the show's music, not devoted to the star, fell to the juveniles, to the stauch-voiced Denis O'Sullivan as Lefèbvre, and to the comic relief – Courtice Pounds as a parvenu milliner and Napoleon's bitchy sisters as played by Kitty Gordon and Violet Elliot. The style of the show meant that it was not written for 'hit numbers' as such, but a beautiful sobbing trio 'A Real Good Cry', Catherine's 'Mirror Song' and the vigorous baritone 'Noblesse Oblige' all demonstrated Caryll's real ability with a comic opera style he had largely forsaken in favour of popular song.

Evie Greene made an enormous success in George Edwardes's London production (236 performances) as the washerwoman who becomes a duchess through frankness. She made such a hit that, although Fritzi Scheff had originally been announced in the part, she was taken to New York to repeat the rôle through the show's 93 Broadway performances. She continued to play it in the British provinces for several years thereafter. French- and German-language theatres did not pick the show up, but Budapest's Király Színház staged *Danzigi hercegnő* in 1905 in an Hungarian version written by Adolf Merei and Jenő Heltai.

Apart from this, the show's success was all in its original language. In Australia the local star Florence Young scored strongly in the grateful title-rôle alongside the Napoleon of Wybert Stamford, and Anna Hickish and Julius Royston introduced the show to South African audiences in 1906. Dorothy Ward was Catherine when Bannister Howard revived the piece at London's Daly's Theatre in 1932 and Fay Compton starred in a major British touring revival in 1943, whilst Australia's J C Williamson Ltd equally recognized the potency of the play and its fine leading rôle and mounted a revival for one of that country's favourite musical artists, Dot Brunton, in 1931.

USA: Daly's Theater 14 January 1905; Hungary: Király Színház *Danzigi hercegnő* 15 April 1905; Australia: Her Majesty's Theatre, Sydney, 2 January 1909

THE DUENNA, or the Double Elopement

Comic opera in 3 acts by Richard Brinsley Sheridan. Music composed and arranged by Thomas Linley sr and Thomas Linley jr. Covent Garden Theatre, London, 21 November 1775.

One of the most successful British comic operas of the 18th century, *The Duenna* was played for more than 70 nights at the Covent Garden Theatre in the 1775–6 season and was continually revived on English-language stages around the world in the following decades, into the 19th century, and also mounted in several sizeable productions in Britain in the 20th century.

The duenna of the piece (Jane Green) is the guardian of Louisa (Isabella Mattocks), daughter of Don Jerome. However, instead of keeping Louisa away from her young Antonio (Charles Du Bellamy), ready for her marriage to a rich, Portuguese Jew called Isaac Mendoza (John Quick), she actually connives at the young people's meetings. When the duenna is caught and dismissed, Louisa takes her place and, disguised in her dark gown, flees her father's house. Isaac is tricked into wedding the duenna instead. The other half of the 'double elopement' concerns Jerome's son, Ferdinand (George Mattocks), and Clara d'Almanza (Miss Brown), daughter to the wealthy Don Guzman.

The 26 musical numbers which illustrated the score were part pasticcio and partly the work of the Linleys, father and son.

The show seems to have been introduced to the American stage by Lewis Hallam, who played it originally in Jamaica, and it was apparently seen in Charleston, Philadelphia and other main centres before what looks like its first New York showing at a benefit in 1787 (unless the piece played by Hallam's company previously as *The Elopement*, the title used in Charleston, was also *The Duenna*). After this introduction, it became a regularly played part of the comic opera repertoire.

The principal modern productions of *The Duenna* have been at London's Lyric, Hammersmith, where it was pro-

duced in a version with the score adapted by Alfred Reynolds in 1924 (23 October), in the wake of their success with *The Beggar's Opera*, and again in 1931 (22 April 1931), and a Bristol Old Vic production, with music by Julian Slade, brought to the Westminster Theatre (28 July 1954) and later played on a number of occasions in the British provinces.

USA: Charleston *The Elopement* 28 September 1786

DUFF, James C (b 1854; d New York, 31 August 1928).

The son of John A Duff (b 1820; d 31 March 1889), sometime operator of the Olympic and Standard Theaters and father-in-law to producer Augustin Daly, James Duff was at first manager for his father. He took over the Broadway Theater (the former Wood's Museum) in 1877 and subsequently began producing comic opera, whilst still in his twenties, on his own behalf. His J C Duff Comic Opera Company introduced many of the classics of opéra-bouffe and opéra-comique from France, Britain and Austria to American-speaking audiences in New York in the late 1870s, the 1880s and the 1890s. He produced the first New York version of *HMS Pinafore* in 1879, but when Carte began staging his own New York productions Duff tried to challenge him and the two came to blows over Broadway's versions of *The Mikado*. Duff did not win. He had another misfortune when, having secured the rights to the London musical, *Erminie*, he let them lapse and missed the biggest Broadway hit of the era.

He remained active for nearly half a century, importing such pieces as *Le Petit Duc*, *Les Noces d'Olivette*, *Le Coeur et la main* (*Hand and Heart*), *Eine Nacht in Venedig* (*A Night in Venice*), *Dorothy*, *Paola*, *A Country Girl* and *The Cingalee* to the Broadway stage, and in later years brought London's freshly revised hit version of *The Beggar's Opera* to New York, but without success.

DUHAMEL, Biana (b ?1870; d Paris, 26 October 1910). Palely pretty ingénue who scored one huge Parisian musical theatre success as Audran's *Miss Helyett*.

The 15-year-old Biana Duhamel made her first recorded appearance as Petit Poucet (Tom Thumb) in the féerie of the same name at the Paris Gaîté-Lyrique in 1885, but she made herself into a star five years later when she appeared at the Bouffes-Parisiens in two new pieces, firstly as Phrynette in André Wormser's pantomime *L'Enfant prodigue* and then, in another adolescent rôle, as the heroine of Audran's vastly successful *Miss Helyett*.

She took leading rôles in the Bouffes-Parisiens' following productions – Audran's next and slightly more musically demanding work, *Sainte-Freya* (1892, Freya), Paul Lacôme's *Le Cadeau de noces* (1893, Geneviève), and yet another Audran work, *Madame Suzette* (1893, Suzette) – without finding another rôle like Miss Helyett in which her youthful charm and limited vocal talents could shine. Her *Miss Helyett*, repeated as late as 1900 at the Théâtre de la Porte-Saint-Martin, remained a performance of choice spoken of with special warmth by old theatregoers for many years, yet the little ingénue who had enchanted le tout Paris was soon forgotten: she died aged only 40 and destitute.

DUKE, Vernon [DUKELSKY, Vladimir] (b Parafianovo, Russia, 10 October 1903; d Santa Monica, Calif, 16 January 1969). Russian-born composer, mostly for the American stage, whose few successes were undershadowed by what seems to be a record percentage of full-blooded flops.

Dukelsky underwent a classical music education in Russia but, having fled Russia's civil war, at first to America and then to Britain, he submerged his classic ambitions by writing for the more lucrative London musical theatre of the mid-1920s. He supplied sufficient additional music (nine and a half numbers including the one-step 'It's Nicer to Be Naughty') to a version of Jean Gilbert's *Uschi*, produced at the Palace Theatre by George Edwardes as *Yvonne*, to win a co-composer's credit, and he wrote his first full stage score for *The Yellow Mask*, Desmond Carter and Edgar Wallace's Oriental mystery musical in which the up-and-coming young comic Bobby Howes was paired with Phyllis Dare under the management of Laddie Cliff. In spite of two enforced changes of theatre, the spectacular mixture of romance and comedy and plotting had a reasonable career but when it was made into a film the songs were omitted.

Duke next collaborated with Carroll Gibbons on the score for the disastrous *Open Your Eyes* which stranded its company in Scotland in the third week of its tour. It somehow made it to town the next year for an anguished 24 performances, but by this time Duke had already left Britain to try his luck once again in America.

There he interpolated individual songs into several Broadway shows and collaborated on several revue scores, one of which, *Walk a Little Faster*, produced one of his most remembered songs, 'April in Paris'. It was 1940 before his first full Broadway theatre score, *Cabin in the Sky*, was heard, by which time he had come far enough from the Russian ballet to write a boogie-woogie as part of the musical illustration of Lynn Root's morality tale of the negro southlands. 'Taking a Chance on Love' was the show's take-away tune, one of three and two bits of the stage score which survived into a subsequent film version.

His subsequent musicals did not reach the same degree of success. Of his two further collaborations with lyricist John Latouche, *Banjo Eyes* turned *Three Men on a Horse* into a musical for Eddie Cantor and 128 performances, which was 125 more than their *The Lady Comes Across* managed. Three pieces with Howard Dietz, for whose *Keep Off the Grass* (1940) he had earlier provided some dance music, proved little happier, and the 1946 *Sweet Bye and Bye*, written with a royal roster of funny men, failed to get past its try-out. A revue, *Two's Company*, was played on Broadway in 1952, he composed two songs and incidental music for a production of Anouilh's play *Time Remembered* (1957), and a 1963 musical *Zenda* was played in California without progressing further.

In spite of his very limited success rate in the theatre and a relatively small number of standard songs from a large output, Duke and his material have remained favourites with fossickers, and that éminence rose of the almost forgotten show song, Ben Bagley, has shown particular favour to Duke's work in his recordings.

1926 **Yvonne** (*Uschi*) additional music for English version w Percy Greenbank (Daly's Theatre)

1928 **The Yellow Mask** (Edgar Wallace/Desmond Carter) Carlton Theatre, London 8 February

1930 **Open Your Eyes** (w Carroll Gibbons/Frederick Jackson) Piccadilly Theatre, London 8 September

1940 **Cabin in the Sky** (John Latouche/Lynn Root) Martin Beck Theater 25 October

1941 **Banjo Eyes** (Latouche, Harold Adamson/Joe Quillan, Izzy Ellinson) Hollywood Theater 25 December

1942 **The Lady Comes Across** (Latouche/Fred Thompson, Dawn Powell) 44th Street Theater 9 January

1943 **Dancing in the Streets** (Howard Dietz/Dietz, John Cecil Holm, Matt Taylor) Boston 23 March

1944 **Jackpot** (Dietz/Guy Bolton, Sidney Sheldon, Ben Roberts) Alvin Theater 13 January

1944 **Sadie Thompson** (Dietz/Rouben Mamoulian) Alvin Theater 16 November

1946 **Sweet Bye-and-Bye** (Ogden Nash/S J Perelman, Al Hirschfield) Shubert Theater, New Haven 10 October

1959 **The Pink Jungle** (Leslie Stevens) Alcazar Theater, San Francisco 14 October

1963 **Zenda** (Everett Freeman/Martin Charnin et al) Curran Theater, San Francisco 5 August

Autobiography: *Passport to Paris* (Little, Brown, Boston, 1955)

DUMANOIR, Philippe [PINEL DUMANOIR, Philippe François] (b Guadeloupe, 25 July 1806; d Pau, 13 November 1865).

A prolific playwright and vaudevillist, Dumanoir had a long list of straight theatre successes, most notably with a series of pieces written in collaboration with Jean-François Bayard, but also in tandem with Adolphe d'Ennery (*Don César de Bazan*, 1844) and with many others of the principal writers of his period. He ventured only occasionally into the musical theatre with the texts for such pieces as Louis Clapisson's one act opéra-comique *La Perruche* and, later, Hervé's *Les Folies dramatiques*, the Massé opera *La Mule de Pedro* (Opéra 4 March 1863) and opérette *La Chaise à porteurs* and the féerie *La Chatte merveilleuse* (1862).

His straight works, however, provided the bases for many libretti by other hands. *Don César de Bazan* provided the starting-point for Wallace's *Maritana* (1845), Massenet's opera *Don César de Bazan* (Opéra-Comique, 1872) and Dellinger's operetta *Don Cesar* (Hamburg, 1885) as well as, eventually, W S Gilbert's *The Yeomen of the Guard* and a long series of burlesques. Of his collaborations with Bayard, *Les Premières Armes de Richelieu* became *The Dashing Little Duke* in London and *Az ötödik pont* in Hungary (Dezső Megyeri, Népszinház, 1893), *La Vicomtesse Lolotte* became Hungary's *A titkos csok* (Bela Hegyi, Szidor Bátor, Népszinház 1888), the hugely popular *Le Vicomte de Letorrières* became *Az eleven ördög* in Hungary (Jozsef Konti, Népszinház 1885), *Der Vielgeliebte* in Germany (Eduard Künneke/Rideamus, Herman Haller Theater am Nollendorfplatz, Berlin 17 October 1919), *Der Vicomte de Letorrières* in Czechoslovakia (Bogumil Zepler/E E Taubert Neues Deutsches Theater, Prague 16 January 1903) and *El vizconde de Letorieres* in Spain, and, most successfully of all on the international stage, *Le Capitaine Charlotte* became Genée's widely played *Der Seekadett* as well as the Italian *Il Capitano Carlotta*.

His play *La Savonette impériale* (Palais-Royal 23 November 1835, w Auguste Anicet-Bourgeois) was operetticized on home ground as the successful *Ordre de l'empereur*, with a score by Justin Clérice (Théâtre des Bouffes-Parisiens, 4

March 1902), and his *La Nuit aux soufflets* (1842 w d'En-
nery) was musicalized under the same title with a score by
Hervé (ad Ferrier, d'Ennery, Théâtre de Nouveautés 18
September 1884).

1840 **La Perruche** (Louis Clapisson/w Henri Dupin) 1 act
   Opéra-Comique 18 April
1852 **Roméo et Mariette** (Hervé) 1 act Palais-Royal
1853 **Les Folies dramatiques** (Hervé/w Clairville) Palais-Royal
   2 March
1858 **La Chaise à porteurs** (Victor Massé/w Clairville) 1 act
   Opéra-Comique 28 April
1862 **La Chatte merveilleuse** (Albert Grisar/w Adolphe d'Ennery) Théâtre Lyrique 18 March

DUMAS, Alexandre [DAVY DE LA PAILLETERIE,
Alexandre] (b Villers-Cotterêts, 24 July 1802; d Puys, nr
Dieppe, 5 December 1870).

The works of the famous French novelist and playwright
provided the material for many musical plays, from the
severely operatic to the bulgingly burlesque. On the
operatic side, Donizetti set to music a version of Dumas's
Charles VII chez ses grands vassaux as *Gemma di Vergy* (1834)
and Cui reused the same work as the source of his *The
Saracen*, Saint-Saëns's *Ascanio* (1890) was based on his
play of the same title, Humperdinck set *Les Demoiselles de
Saint-Cyr* for Berlin as *Die Heirat wider willen* (1905), and
Isidore de Lara made an operatic version of *Les Trois
Mousquetaires* (1921). Samara's 1905 *Mademoiselle de Belle-
Isle* and Enna's *Gloria Arsena* (1917) were also based on
Dumas works.

Les Trois Mousquetaires (1844) went through a variety of
adaptations, both swashbuckling and burlesque, of which
Rudolf Friml's Broadway musical and the spectacular
German piece, musically set by Ralph Benatzky, proved
the most notable, whilst *Le Comte de Monte Cristo* (1844)
was made into a range of musical pieces from the Operette
Der Graf von Monte Christo (C Pleninger/Beyer, Residenztheater, Dresden January 1883) and the musical play *Monte
Cristo* (Jean-Claude Auvray, Michel Legrand, Brussels,
1975) to the highly successful British burlesque *Monte
Cristo Jr* with its Edmond Dantès in tights.

Dumas's play *Kean* (1836) became a musical both on
Broadway, as *Kean* (Robert Wright, George Forrest/Peter
Stone, Broadway Theatre 2 November 1961), and in
Romania, where it was played as *Soarele Londrei* (The sun
of London) in a version by Florian Comisel and Nicosur
Constantinescu.

Les Demoiselles de Saint-Cyr was given a comic opera
treatment by Rudolf Dellinger and Oscar Walther as *St
Cyr* (Hamburg, 1891) and the French musical *Un Mariage
au Tambour* by Paul Burani and Léon Vasseur was also
based on a Dumas work (w Adolphe de Leuven,
Brunswick). The Broadway musical *Apple Blossoms* quoted
Un Mariage sous Louis XV as its source, *La Tulipe noir*
(1850) became an opérette à grand spectacle in the hands
of André Mouëzy-Éon, Albert Willemetz and Tiarko
Richepin (Gaîté-Lyrique 19 March 1932), whilst Messager's unsuccessful comic opera *Le Chevalier d'Harmental*
was based on Dumas's 1849 piece (w Auguste Maquet) of
the same title.

Dumas's novel *Les Frères corses*, later adapted to the
stage by Eugène Grangé and Xavier de Montépin (1850)
and, in English, with huge popularity by Dion Boucicault,

was clearly not the material for a musical comedy, but it
became the subject of several English-language
burlesques, beginning as early as 1852 with *O Gemini!, or
The Brothers of Co(u)rse* by Mark Lemon and Gilbert a'
Beckett (Haymarket Theatre, 12 April) and followed by
The Corsican Bothers (Globe Theatre 1869), *The Corsican
Brothers & Co* (Gaiety Theatre, 1880), George Sims's *The
Of Course-Akin Brothers, Babes in the Wood* (Theatre
Royal, Hull 19 March 1881) and *The New Corsican
Brothers* (Royalty Theatre 1889). Its tale also filtered
through into the more modern British musical play *Blood
Brothers*.

Dumas made a small personal contribution to the lyric
stage, providing the libretti for such pieces as the opéra-
comique *Piquillo* (w Gérard de Nerval) set by Hippolyte
Monpou and played at the Opéra-Comique in 1837 (31
October), the two-act *La Bacchante* (Eugène Gautier/w de
Leuven, de Beauplan, Opéra-Comique 4 November 1858)
and Ambroise Thomas's *Le Roman d'Elvire* (w de Leuven,
Opéra-Comique 4 February 1860).

His illegitimate son, **Alexandre DUMAS** (b Paris, 28
July 1824; d Paris, 27 November 1895), known as Dumas
fils, was the author of the celebrated *La Dame aux camélias*
(Théâtre du Vaudeville, Paris 2 February 1852). Originally
produced as a 'pièce en cinq acts, mêlée de chant', with
music by Montaubry accompanying the couple of musical
numbers involved, it was later operaticized as *La Traviata*
(1853) and burlesqued by Leicester Buckingham as *La
Traviata, or The Lady Camelon* (Strand Theatre, 7 September 1857). The 'drame lyrique' *La Femme de Claude* (Louis
Gallet/Albert Cahen, Opéra-Comique 1896) was also
based on his original 1873 play of the same title.

In 1967 the pair themselves became the subject of a
musical when the San Francisco and Los Angeles Light
Opera produced a *Dumas and Son* (Dorothy Chandler
Pavilion 1 August), written by Jerome Chodorov, and with
a score by Wright and Forrest arranged from the music of
Camille Saint-Saëns.

DUNAIEVSKY [DUNAJEVSZKIJ], Isaak Osipovitch
(b Lokhvitza, Ukraine, 30 January 1900; d Moscow, 25
July 1955)

Dunaievsky studied music at the Kharkov conservatory
(piano and violin) and made his earliest composition
attempts in his late teens in the light music field, composing incidental music for a number of plays at the Kharkov
Theatre from the age of 19. He wrote incidental theatre
music, Operette scores and a considerable amount of film
music, largely in a traditional style, whilst holding several
state music posts – notably between 1936 and 1948 as
musical director of the Moscow Railways' Central Cultural
Establishment Song and Dance Ensemble. The texts
which he illustrated were often politico-didactic in intent,
but he nevertheless produced several songs which became
popular and which helped his shows to be appreciated in a
number of iron curtain countries. The most successful,
Vol'nyj veter (Moscow, 29 August 1949), was played in
Germany as *Freier Wind* (Volkstheater, Rostock 23 April
1953) and in Hungary as *Szabad szél* (Fővárósi Operettszinház 6 May 1950).

Biographies: Danilevitch, L: *Isaak Dunaievsky* (Moscow, 1947),
   Tchernov, A: *Isaak Dunaievsky* (Moscow, 1961)

DUNCAN, [Robert] Todd (b Danville, Ky, 12 February 1900).

Duncan made his first major theatrical appearance in his mid-thirties, in *Cavalleria Rusticana*, and soon after created the leading rôle in the folk opera *Porgy and Bess* (1935), introducing 'Bess, You is My Woman Now' and 'I Got Plenty o' Nutting'. He subsequently appeared in the London spectacular *The Sun Never Sets* (1938) at the Theatre Royal, Drury Lane, singing 'River God' and 'Drums', and on Broadway as the Lawd's General in *Cabin in the Sky* (1940). He later worked in opera and in films, and repeated his performance as Porgy on many occasions, but devoted himself more to the concert stage and returned only once to the Broadway musical theatre, to play Stephen Kumalo in *Lost in the Stars* (1949).

DUNCAN, William Cary (b North Brookfield, Mass, 6 February 1874; d North Brookfield, Mass, 21 November 1945). A regular contributor to the American musical stage for 17 years, Duncan, in spite of working with some top-drawer collaborators, never succeeded in getting his name on a truly top-drawer show.

An English teacher at Brooklyn Polytechnic preparatory school for the first 20 years of his working life, Duncan first surfaced in the musical theatre as the author of Joseph Gaites's touring musical *Katy Did* when already in his mid-thirties. He subsequently wrote lyrics for the same producer's unsuccessful Fritzi Scheff vehicle, a remusicked version of the Hungarian musical play *A Gyurkovicslányok* produced as *The Love Wager* (1912), and co-adapted the Vienna musical *Napoleon und die Frauen* for the American stage, under the title *The Purple Road*. He found sufficient success with his book to the Mormon musical *His Little Widows* (later filched as the text for a British piece, *Lady Luck*), to encourage him to give up English teaching, but his first success, two years later, came when George M Cohan burlesqued his Ruritanian comic opera *The Royal Vagabond* into a Broadway run.

Duncan subsequently adapted the French farce *Le Chasseur de Chez Maxims* as the libretto to *The Blue Kitten* for Friml, revised Otto Harbach's libretto for *Molly Darling*, worked with Hammerstein and Youmans on *Mary Jane McKane*, provided Gallagher and Sheen with the text for *In Dutch*, adapted Hennequin and Veber's *Le Monsieur de cinq heures* as *Sunny Days* for producer/director Hassard Short, and collaborated on *Yes, Yes, Yvette*, a version of the hit play *Nothing But the Truth* which didn't succeed in giving *No, No, Nanette* producer H H Frazee a follow-up success. He also adapted John Hunter Booth's *Rolling Home* as a libretto for Harold Orlob, and teamed with Youmans again on the romantic old-America piece *Great Day*, in the wake of the success of *Show Boat*. In spite of some fair runs, however, none of these projects scored him a genuine hit, and he ended his busy career without having produced anything enduring.

1910 **Katie Did** (Karl Hoschna/w Frank Smithson) Colonial Theater, Chicago 18 February
1912 **The Love Wager** (Charles Hambitzer/Edith Ellis) Ford's Theater, Baltimore 16 September
1913 **The Purple Road** (*Napoleon und die Frauen*) English version w Fred de Grésac (Liberty Theater)
1913 **When Love is Young** (William Schroeder/Rida Johnson Young) Cort Theater, Chicago 28 October

1916 **A Regular Girl** (Winthrop Cortelyou, Hambitzer/w Otis Drayton) Rochester, NY 18 September
1917 **Captain Cupid** (Schroeder/w Young) Shubert Theater, Minneapolis 15 April
1917 **His Little Widows** (aka *Some Little Girl*) (Schroeder/w Young) Astor Theater 30 April
1918 **Fiddlers Three** (Alexander Johnstone) Cort Theater 3 September
1919 **The Royal Vagabond** (Anselm Götzl/w Stephen Ivor Szinnyey) Cohan and Harris Theater 17 February
1919 **Sunshine** (A Johnstone) Trent Theater, Trenton 11 April
1920 **Three Showers** (Creamer and Layton) Harris Theater 5 April
1921 **The Rose Girl** (Götzl) Ambassador Theater 11 February
1922 **The Blue Kitten** (Rudolf Friml/w Harbach) Selwyn Theater 13 January
1922 **Molly Darling** (Tom Johnstone, Phil Cook/Clifford Grey, Joseph Herbert et al/Otto Harbach ad) Liberty Theater 1 September
1923 **Just Apples** (Fred J Coots) Academy of Music, Brooklyn 9 March
1923 **Mary Jane McKane** (Vincent Youmans, Herbert Stothart/w Oscar Hammerstein II) New Imperial Theater 25 December
1924 **In Dutch** (Joseph Meyer, William Daly, Alfred Newman/w Irving Caesar) Newark, NJ, 22 September
1924 **Princess April** (Monte Carlo, Alma Sanders/w Lewis Allen Browne) Ambassador Theater 1 December
1925 **Suzanne** (Harold Orlob/w John Hunter Booth) Worcester, Mass, 28 September
1927 **Talk About Girls** (revised *Suzanne*) (Orlob, Stephen Jones/Caesar/w Daniel Kusell) Waldorf Theater 14 June
1927 **Yes, Yes, Yvette** (Phil Charig, Ben Jerome, Caesar/w James Montgomery) Harris Theater 3 October
1928 **Sunny Days** (Jerome Schwartz/Clifford Grey) Imperial Theater 8 February
1929 **Moon Madness** (Sol Cohen/w Alice Barney) Figueroa Playhouse, Los Angeles 30 September
1929 **Great Day** (Youmans/w John Wells) Cosmopolitan Theater 17 October

DUNNE, Irene [Marie] (b Louisville, Ky, 20 December 1901; d Los Angeles, 4 September 1990). Charming singing ingénue who topped her half-dozen years of stage leads by a famous career in films.

At 19, Miss Dunne toured in the title-rôle of *Irene*, and she subsequently played a succession of musical ingénue rôles on Broadway in *The Clinging Vine* (1922, Tessie), *Lollipop* (1924, Virginia), *The City Chap* (1925, Grace Bartlett), *Sweetheart Time* (1926, Violet), *Yours Truly* (1927, Diana), *She's My Baby* (1928, Polly) and *Luckee Girl* (1928, Arlette) without finding a hit until she went on the road as Magnolia Hawks in the first national tour of *Show Boat* (1929).

There were hits a-plenty when she moved to movies and starred, most notably, in the celluloid versions of *Show Boat* (Magnolia), *Roberta* (Princess Stephanie) and *Sweet Adeline* (Addie), in *High, Wide and Handsome* and *The Joy of Living* as well as in many important non-musical rôles.

DUPUIS, José [DUPUIS, Joseph Lambert Édouard] (b Liège 18 March 1833; d Nogent-sur-Marne, 9 May 1900). 'The greatest of the great ... the most all-round actor I have ever known' (Yvette Guilbert). Comedian and tenor who created lead rôles in many of Offenbach's greatest works, in the early years of a long career as a Parisian musical and comedy star.

The son of a drawing master, the 18-year-old Dupuis got his first chance to perform on the stage when a rich Liégois built a private theatre and he was given a spot there as an amateur singer. He did sufficiently well with his performances of light and comic songs to progress to professional engagements and, in 1854, he made the move to Paris. His first job there was at the Bobino but, by the end of 1855, he had been given a contract at the Folies-Nouvelles where he made his first appearance in the one-acter *Jean et Jeanne* (1855) and found himself appreciated more for his talents as a light comedian than for his petite tenor singing voice. He did however, find himself cast alongside Joseph Kelm in such little musical pieces as *Les Trois Troubadours*, *La Demoiselle de la Roche-Trombelon* and de Rillé's *Le Jugement de Paris*.

He moved from the Folies-Nouvelles to the Théâtre Déjazet in 1859, playing there in such pieces as *Les Premières Armes de Figaro* and *Monsieur Garat*, and then, in 1861, joined the company at the Théâtre des Variétés where he soon became one of the principal comic players and performed in a range of pieces both with and without music (*Le Sylphe*, *Les Mille et une songes*, *L'Infortunée Caroline* etc). His still light, but now much more secure and rangy, singing voice meant that he was able to take leading rôles in musical works and in 1864 he created Hervé's *Le Joueur de Flûte* alongside the débutante Léa Silly, before being starred the following year opposite Hortense Schneider as Paris in *La Belle Hélène* ('Au Mont Ida trois déesses').

The triumph which he made in this piece was confirmed in a run of outstanding creations at the Variétés over the next four years, as Dupuis introduced some of Offenbach's most famous characters in the opéras-bouffes *Barbe-bleue* (Barbe-bleue, 'Je suis Barbe-bleue, o gué'), *La Grande-Duchesse de Gérolstein* (Fritz) and *La Périchole* (Piquillo), all as leading man to Mlle Schneider, and as the burlesque brigand-chief, Falsacappa, in *Les Brigands* alongside Zulma Bouffar. After a short detour into a Hervé piece (Robert Mouton in *Le Trône d'Écosse*) he continued in a further series of Offenbach creations (Marcassou in *Les Braconniers*, Bernadille in *La Boulangère a des écus*, Docteur Ox in *Le Docteur Ox*), other new musicals – Dunois in *Le Beau Dunois* (1870), Pierre Cargounioul in *Les Charbonniers*, Boulboum in Hervé's *La Veuve du Malabar* (1873) – and revivals, including both his own celebrated rôles and also the part of Baron Gondremarck in the first Variétés production of *La Vie parisienne*.

He subsequently starred alongside Anna Judic in the famous series of Théâtre des Variétés vaudeville-opérettes, playing the disappearing circus-owner, Casimir, in Lecocq's *Le Grand Casimir*, the dual rôle of father and son de la Boucanière in Hervé's *La Femme à Papa*, Grégoire in *Niniche*, the three ages of Plinchard in *Lili*, Médard in *La Roussotte* and Jules Primitif in *La Cosaque*, but further reprises as Paris, Fritz and Falsacappa in the mid-1880s proved that his singing voice was no longer sufficient to the task. From this time on, he had to rely on his comic abilities and the public's memories to pull him through in the musical shows which were mixed with the Variétés' regular schedule of plays (Saint-Galmier in *Mam'zelle Gavroche*, 1885, etc).

In the late eighties he tactfully abandoned the comic jeune premier rôles he had held so long, and moved across to the character tenor parts, making a particular success as the fussy pedant, Frimousse, in revivals of *Le Petit Duc*, but he retained the rôles of Gondremarck and Falsacappa into his last performances, still at the Variétés, in his sixties.

DURANTE, Jimmy [DURANTE, James Francis] (b New York City, 10 February 1893; d Santa Monica, Calif, 29 January 1980).

After an early career in vaudeville, as part of the quickly successful act Clayton, Jackson and Durante, the comedian with the famous nose – familiarly known as his 'schnozzola' – appeared on Broadway with his partners in the 1929 *Show Girl* (Snozzle) and the 1930 *The New Yorkers* (Jimmie Deegan).

The team disbanded in 1931, and, in a subsequent career which switched back and forth among theatre, film and variety performances, Durante, who had always been the featured member of the group, went on to star in the revue *Strike it Pink* (1933), as the finagling pressman Claudius Bowers in Billy Rose's circus spectacular, *Jumbo* (1935), opposite Ethel Merman as the convict, Policy Pinkle, in *Red, Hot and Blue!* (1936), in the unfortunate movieland piece *Stars in Your Eyes* (1939, Bill) and, in a last Broadway appearance, in the Shubert flop revue *Keep Off the Grass* (1940).

Durante also appeared in a number of musical films, including the movie versions of *Sally, Irene and Mary* (1938, Jefferson Twitchell) and *Jumbo* (1962, Pop Wonder) and occasionally turned his hand to songwriting, contributing several numbers to the score of *Show Girl*.

Durante, a musical based on his 'life and times', written by Frank Peppiate and John Aylesworth to a pasticcio score, was produced at the St Lawrence Center, Toronto, 12 August 1989 with Lonny Price as Durante. It folded on the road.

Biography: Fowler, G: *Schnozzola, the Story of Jimmy Durante* (Viking, New York, 1951); Robbins, J: *Inka Dinka Doo* (Paragon House, New York, 1991)

DURU, [Henri] Alfred (b Paris, 1829; d 29 December 1889). The partner of Henri Chivot in what became one of the most outstanding and fruitful libretto and lyric-writing partnerships of the French opérette and comic stages.

The pair worked only occasionally worked with other writers (*La Fille du clown*, the burlesque of the benefit system called *Les Mirlitons*, the successful comedy *Doit-on le dire?* w Labiche, etc), and their partnership endured for over 30 years, until Duru's death during an influenza epidemic and the rehearsals for their *Le Voyage de Suzette*, at the age of 60.

Duru wrote several pieces alone, notably the successful vaudeville *Les Deux Noces de M Boisjoli*, metamorphized by H B Farnie into a major London hit with a pasticcio score under the title of *Nemesis* and into *Zwei Hochzeiten und ein Brautigam* at Vienna's Carltheater (1873) where the score was provided by Conradin.

1865 **Un Rêve** (Edmond Savary/w Henri Chivot) 1 act Théâtre Lyrique 13 October
1866 **Les Chevaliers de la table ronde** (Hervé/w Chivot) 1 act Théâtre des Bouffes-Parisiens 27 December
1867 **Les Defauts de Jacotte** (Victor Robillard/w Chivot) Fantaisies-Parisiennes 27 April

1868 **Fleur de thé** (Charles Lecocq/w Chivot) Théâtre de l'Athénée 11 April

1868 **L'Île de Tulipatan** (Jacques Offenbach/w Chivot) 1 act Théâtre des Bouffes-Parisiens 30 September

1868 **Le Soldat malgré lui** (Frédéric Barbier/w Chivot) Fantaisies-Parisiennes 17 October

1868 **Le Carnaval d'un merle blanc** (Lecocq/w Chivot) Palais-Royal 30 December

1869 **Gandolfo** (Lecocq/w Chivot) 1 act Théâtre des Bouffes-Parisiens 16 January

1869 **Le Docteur Purgandi** (Robillard/w Chivot) 1 act Folies-Bergères 2 May

1869 **Le Rajah de Mysore** (Lecocq/w Chivot) 1 act Théâtre des Bouffes-Parisiens 21 September

1870 **Le Beau Dunois** (Lecocq/w Chivot) Théâtre des Variétés 13 April

1872 **Les Cent Vierges** (Lecocq/w Clairville, Chivot) Théâtre des Folies-Parisiennes, Brussels 16 March

1873 **Les Braconniers** (Offenbach/w Chivot) Théâtre des Variétés 29 January

1873 **Les Pommes d'or** (Audran/w Chivot, Henri Blondeau, Hector Monréal) Théâtre du Château d'Eau 8 February

1875 **La Blanchisseuse de Berg-op-Zoom** (Léon Vasseur/w Chivot) Théâtre des Folies-Dramatiques 27 January

1875 **Le Pompon** (Lecocq/w Chivot) Théâtre des Folies-Dramatiques 10 November

1876 **Les Mirlitons** (Auguste Coèdes/w Henri Chabrillat, Henri Bocage, Ernest Blum) Théâtre des Folies-Dramatiques 19 April

1878 **Madame Favart** (Offenbach/w Chivot) Théâtre des Folies-Dramatiques 28 December

1879 **Les Noces d'Olivette** (Edmond Audran/w Chivot) Théâtre des Bouffes-Parisiens 13 November

1879 **La Fille du tambour-major** (Offenbach/w Chivot) Théâtre des Folies-Dramatiques 13 December

1880 **La Mère des compagnons** (Hervé/w Chivot) Théâtre des Folies-Dramatiques 15 December

1880 **La Mascotte** (Audran/w Chivot) Théâtre des Bouffes-Parisiens 28 December

1882 **Boccace** French version w Chivot, Gustave Layge (Galeries St Hubert, Brussels, Théâtre des Folies-Dramatiques, Paris)

1882 **Gillette de Narbonne** (Audran/w Chivot) Théâtre des Bouffes-Parisiens 11 November

1883 **La Princesse des Canaries** (Lecocq/w Chivot) Théâtre des Folies-Dramatiques 9 February

1883 **La Dormeuse éveillée** (Audran/w Chivot) Théâtre des Bouffes-Parisiens 27 December

1884 **Le Grand Mogol** revised version w Chivot (Théâtre de la Gaîté)

1884 **L'Oiseau bleu** (Lecocq/w Chivot) Théâtre des Nouveautés 16 January

1885 **Pervenche** (Audran/w Chivot) Théâtre des Bouffes-Parisiens 31 March

1886 **La Cigale et la fourmi** (Audran/w Chivot) Théâtre de la Gaîté 30 October

1887 **Surcouf** (Robert Planquette/w Chivot) Théâtre des Folies-Dramatiques 6 October

1888 **La Petite Fronde** (Audran/w Chivot) Théâtre des Folies-Dramatiques 16 November

1889 **La Fille à Cacolet** (Audran/w Chivot) Théâtre des Théâtre des Variétés 10 July

1890 **Le Voyage de Suzette** (Audran/w Chivot) Théâtre de la Gaîté 20 January

DUVAL, Georges [RIEUX, Claude] (b Paris, 2 February 1847; d Paris, 28 September 1919).

Journalist (*L'Évènement* etc), the author of many plays and novels, the translator of the complete works of Shakespeare into French, of Bulwer Lytton and of Sheridan, and a writer on the subject of both the French and British classic stage, Duval also authored a number of opérette libretti with an unusually high percentage rate of success.

His first work, Planquette's military opérette *Les Voltigeurs de la 32ème*, won a firm success in France and an outstanding one in Britain (*The Old Guard*), the vaudevillesque *Mam'zelle Crénom* was a lively piece which lasted out its hundred metropolitan performances, and the texts for *Les P'tites Michu* and *Véronique* were admirable pieces of late classic opérette writing which, attached to Messager's sparkling scores, gave their authors worldwide success.

His highly successful play *Coquin de printemps* (w Adolphe Jaime) formed the basis for the Joseph Strauss pasticcio *Frühlingsluft* (ad Karl Lindau, Julius Wilhelm, Ernst Reiterer), for London's Gaiety Theatre musical *The Spring Chicken* and an equally successful French musical play of the same title.

1880 **Les Voltigeurs de la 32ème** (Robert Planquette/w Edmond Gondinet) Théâtre de la Renaissance 7 January

1881 **Faublas** (François Luigini/w Edouard Cadol) Théâtre Cluny 25 October

1883 **L'Education d'Achille** (Pauline Thys) 1 act Grand Théâtre, Nantes March

1888 **Mam'zelle Crénom** (Léon Vasseur/w Adolphe Jaime) Théâtre des Bouffes-Parisiens 19 January

1888 **Le Mariage avant la lettre** (Olivier Métra/w Jaime) Théâtre des Bouffes-Parisiens 5 December

1891 **Tout Paris** (Louis Ganne) Théâtre du Châlelet 16 June

1896 **Mignonette** (Georges Street) Théâtre des Nouveautés 3 October

1897 **Les P'tites Michu** (André Messager/w Albert Vanloo) Théâtre des Bouffes-Parisiens 16 November

1898 **Véronique** (Messager/w Vanloo) Théâtre des Bouffes-Parisiens 10 December

1900 **La Belle au bois dormant** (Charles Lecocq/w Vanloo) Théâtre des Bouffes-Parisiens 19 February

1905 **Les Dragons de l'Imperatrice** (Messager/w Vanloo) Théâtre des Variétés 13 February

1913 **Cocorico** (Ganne/w Maurice Soulié, P Jailly) Théâtre de l'Apollo 29 November

1918 **Mademoiselle 'Nom d'une pipe'** (Charles Cuvillier) Palais-Royal 16 July

E

THE EARL AND THE GIRL Musical comedy in 2 acts by Seymour Hicks. Lyrics by Percy Greenbank. Music by Ivan Caryll. Adelphi Theatre, London, 10 December 1903.

Having taken over the late Richard D'Oyly Carte's interests at the Savoy Theatre, William Greet attempted to continue to produce comic opera there in the traditional manner. However, in spite of such successes d'estime as *Merrie England*, he found himself obliged first to tour the Savoy company and then to bend to the all-consuming fashion for modern musical comedy. Thus the Savoy stars, long nurtured on Gilbert, Sullivan, Hood and German, were pitched into an up-to-date Seymour Hicks show, with Henry Lytton expected to play the Hicks rôle, principal tenor Robert Evett a straight juvenile called the Hon Crewe Boodle, Savoy prima donna Agnes Fraser cast to be another Ellaline Terriss, and her husband, Walter Passmore, a longtime Ko-Ko and Jack Point, to play musical-comedy comedy. The cast was completed with more regular musical comedy players in soubrette Florence Lloyd and character lady Phyllis Broughton, an American comedian, John C Dixon, and a heavy lady (Helen Kinnaird), and the show directed by Hicks, but Savoy musical director Hamish MacCunn conducted.

Fortunately for all concerned, the vehicle provided for the company was an excellent, if fairly unoriginal, one of its kind. Passmore played a little circus dog trainer, Tom Cheese, who earns some necessary money by agreeing to impersonate an earl called Dick Wargrave (Lytton), who needs an incognito to allow him to elope discreetly with his beloved Elphin Haye (Miss Fraser). The action took place to the accompaniment of a collection of colourable imitations of most of the regular kinds of musical comedy numbers, ranging from the patriotic song ('The Grenadiers') to the drawing-room ballad ('Thou Art My Rose') and something that sounded not unlike the currently ubiquitous 'Tell Me, Pretty Maiden'.

The success of *The Earl and the Girl* was helped by two elements for both of which Hicks was responsible: it came to its first night much more slickly directed and rehearsed than was normal at the time, and Caryll's score was stuffed full of bristling interpolated numbers, many from America. One of these, the naïve 'My Cosy Corner Girl' (John Bratton/Charles Noel Douglas), became a major hit for Lytton and Miss Fraser, whilst two other already-proven trans-Atlantic hits, Blanche Ring's 'Sammy', now sung by Louie Pounds, and 'In Zanzibar' also did well.

The show ran for over a year (371 performances) – during which time a number of new songs were introduced – and a string of overseas productions followed. The Shuberts' Broadway version featured Eddie Foy and Georgia Caine alongside another Savoy veteran in W H Denny for 147 performances of an americanized version in which Jerome Kern's 'How'd You Like to Spoon with Me' was amongst the pieces which replaced the already well-Broadway-exposed interpolations used in London. Scheduled for the burned and rebuilt Casino Theater, it had to be sidetracked to Philadelphia's Lyric Theater when rebuilding got behind time, but it scored well on its delayed arrival.

In Australia, the travesty comedian John Sheridan got into male attire to star as Jim Cheese alongside Maud Amber (Elphin) and Winfield Blake (Dick), but the production's singular success was ended by its star's premature death. Further afield, Sass and Nelson's company included *The Earl and the Girl* in their repertoire in South America and, later, in South Africa, whilst Greet himself toured the piece around the British provinces for several years whilst letting the secondary town rights to J Bannister Howard.

The Earl and the Girl reappeared in London in 1914 (Aldwych Theatre 4 November) and proved the most successful of the bundle of past favourites which were played in the early days of the war (107 performances). It also got a late first translation when *Hello!! Charley* (ad P-L Flers) was produced in Paris, after the end of the hostilities, under the management of Léon Volterra, in a version featuring Henri Vilbert, Aimé Simon-Girard, Felix Oudart, Rose Amy, Yvonne Yma and Thérèse Dornay, and in which the second act ended with everyone doing Herman Darewski and Arthur Wimperis's 'The Shimmy Shake'.

Australia: Criterion Theatre, Sydney 22 July 1905; USA: Casino Theater 4 November 1905; France: Théâtre Apollo *Hello!! Charley* 3 April 1919

EARLE, Virginia (b Cincinnati, Ohio, 6 August 1873; d Englewood, NJ, 21 September 1937). Turn-of-the-century star soubrette of Broadway's musical theatre.

Miss Earle made her first stage appearances in juvenile theatre, before beginning her barely adult career touring with the Pike Opera Company. She subsequently moved on into musical theatre, touring Australia as a teenager in the burlesques *Evangeline* (Evangeline) and *The Corsair* (Medora) with one of E E Rice's companies, and appearing in Melbourne as Bandini in Byron's *Cinderella* burlesque as an 1891 Christmas attraction before returning home. Although it was dramatically reported that she was likely to have a hand amputated, following a misadventure with an exploding soda bottle in Sydney, she emerged in one piece and, none the worse for the publicity, joined De Wolf Hopper's company, making her first Broadway appearance, in 1894, in revue at the Casino Theater.

She created her first sizeable rôle in T Pearsall Thorne's romantic comic opera *Leonardo*, supporting

George Devoll and Marguerite Lemon in a flop show which unhistorically married da Vinci off to a duke's daughter, before returning to the Casino for more revue and for the first of the rôles which would establish her as one of the town's favourite soubrettes – the delightful Phyllis of the Casino's botched version of *The Lady Slavey* and Miss Lotta Bonds in *The Gold Bug*.

From 1896 she appeared in a series of plays and imported musicals for Augustin Daly at his New York theatre, starring in *The Geisha* (succeding Violet Lloyd as Molly), *The Circus Girl* (Dora), *La Poupée* (Alésia) and *A Runaway Girl* (Winifred) as well as playing Ariel in Daly's *The Tempest*, befor returning to the Casino. There she featured in several home-bred musicals – *The Casino Girl* (1900, in breeches as Earl Cholmondley), *The Belle of Bohemia* (1900, Katie), *The Girl from Up There* (1901, Phrynette) – visiting Britain with the company of this last, in its attempt to repeat the success of *The Belle of New York*.

In 1902 she played Lady Holyrood in a revival of *Florodora*, the following year succeeded Blanche Ring in *The Jewel of Asia*, and in 1904 she was given star billing for the first time in Baldwin Sloane's *Sergeant Kitty*, a billing she had to relinquish when she followed up by appearing with Fay Templeton in the flop *In Newport* at Weber and Fields' Music Hall. She played in the revusical *Lifting the Lid* at the New Amsterdam's Aeriel Roof Gardens in 1905, but thereafter turned to vaudeville and was little seen in the musical theatre, although she repeated her *The Geisha* rôle at the age of 38 in a last recorded musical comedy appearance.

L'EAU À LA BOUCHE   Opérette in 3 acts by Serge Veber. Music by George van Parys and Philippe Parès. Théâtre Daunou, Paris, 5 September 1928.

Following the success of their *Lulu*, the rising team of Parès and van Parys were given a second production at the Théâtre Daunou and won a second success with their lively, up-to-date, made-for-dancing songs. Fernand Graavey scored with a spicy, self-deprecating piece declaring 'il triche au jeu, il boit mais qu'importe ... il a une belle auto, Toto', and joined Loulou Hégoburu, star of *No, No, Nanette*, in the foxtrot 'Oh! Dis! Claudie'; she glided through the bluesy 'Ce n'est qu'un mannequin' whilst Germaine Auger put across 'Donne-moi-z'en un bout' for a run of five months.

EBB, Fred   (b New York, 8 April 1932). Highly successful Broadway lyricist whose most successful material has been for a selection of female stars.

A graduate of New York and Columbia universities, lyricist Ebb did his earliest songwriting with composer Paul Klein in a collaboration which produced a novelty hit number 'Close the Door (they're coming in the window)' (1955), contributions to the revues *Put it in Writing*, *From A to Z* (1960) and *Vintage 60* (1960, 'Dublin Town'), and one short-lived 'play with music', *Morning Sun*. Ebb both adapted the libretto from a story by Mary Deasy and composed the lyrics for this piece which, with Patricia Neway and Bert Convy starring, folded in nine performances off-Broadway.

In the early 1960s Ebb teamed up with composer John Kander, and the pair had an early success with the songs 'My Colouring Book' and 'I Don't Care Much', recorded by Barbra Streisand. Their first stage musical venture together, *Flora, the Red Menace*, survived only 87 performances on Broadway, but they hit the jackpot with their second try. *Cabaret* ('Willkommen', 'Two Ladies', 'Don't Tell Mama', 'Cabaret', 'If You Could See Her') earned its writers a fine run, a Tony Award and an international career. When they topped up their score for the show's film version with some more numbers for the top-cast Liza Minnelli ('Mein Herr', 'Maybe This Time', 'Money, Money, Money'), numbers which, while perhaps less suitable to the play and the character, proved enormously popular both in and out of it, they added an Academy Award to their show's score of trophies.

Whilst *Cabaret* went on to became a major international favourite in the wake of the film's vast success, the pair moved from its acrid prewar Berlin setting to a much gentler French-Canadian one as the locale for their follow-up, the warmly coloured *The Happy Time*. David Merrick's production of this work ran only a fair 286 Broadway performances, but the same year brought the songwriters another important hit when they ventured into a different but equally colourful European setting with a musical version of the tale of *Zorba the Greek*. *Zorba*, which did not have the stage-within-a-stage from which *Cabaret* had profited to introduce stand-up material, naturally produced less in the way of popular songs than its famous predecessor, but it proved a highly successful and effective musical play with some lively, and some very affecting, song moments ('Happy Birthday'). It has won numerous overseas productions, become particularly popular in Central Europe, and survived healthily in the American repertoire.

A musical version of the English comedy *Breath of Spring* under the confusing title of *70, Girls, 70* ('Coffee in a Cardboard Cup') was a failure, but the satirical black-and-tinsel *Chicago*, a vaudevillesque retelling of a show-bizzy jazz-age murder, found Ebb and Kander back in the stand-up songs area which they had so effectively inhabited in *Cabaret* and, like *Cabaret*, *Chicago* produced some outstanding song success, ('Razzle Dazzle', 'All That Jazz', 'Mr Cellophane', 'All I Need is Love'). The musical itself also proved a long-running and enduring hit, not only in America but, notably, in both England and Australia.

A vehicle for Liza Minnelli, staged on Broadway as *The Act*, followed the act-within-a-show formula further but less successfully, but *Woman of the Year*, another show with a large and forceful central female star rôle, played first by Lauren Bacall and then by Raquel Welch and Debbie Reynolds, held the Broadway stage longer, and hosted a much-liked duet called 'The Grass is Always Greener' and an extractable '(I'm one of the girls who's just) One of the Boys'.

An emotional, double-headed female star piece, *The Rink*, with Miss Minnelli and Chita Rivera in the rôles of an eventually-reconciled daughter and mother, played for 204 performances on Broadway. It was later seen briefly in Britain and was also produced on several occasions on the Continent without establishing itself in the same way as the team's major hits, after which – give or take a revival – Ebb and his partner disappeared from the world's major stages for a surprisingly long time. They returned at the beginning of the 1990s with a musical version of the successful novel, play and film *Kiss of the Spiderwoman*, written to allow the inclusion of the glittery show-numbers which had become its songwriters' speciality within its grim prison framework. This piece side-stepped Broadway and its critic and, after a Westchester tryout, instead opted for a London opening, with Miss Rivera starring, two years later. A London journalist's review summed up what had, over the decades, become an important part of the appeal of Ebb and Kander's material: 'What was a love story about two individuals becomes a generalised monument to gay taste, with ... Rivera taking the place as icon once occupied by Judy Garland'.

Beyond the three stage musicals and the film rewrite of *Cabaret*, Ebb and his partner have written considerable further special material for Liza Minnelli, notably her television specials *Liza* and *Liza with a Z*, her pairing with Goldie Hawn in *Goldie and Liza Together*, a nightclub act, and the musical portion of the film *Lucky Lady*. They also wrote and produced Chita Rivera's nightclub act, *Chita Plus Two*, and have supplied material both for further films (notably for Barbra Streisand in *Funny Lady*, and the extremely hit title-song for *New York, New York*) and other television star vehicles (Frank Sinatra's *Ole Blue Eyes is Back*, *Baryshnikov on Broadway*, Shirley Maclaine's *The Gypsy in My Soul*).

Several compilation shows of Ebb and Kander material have been produced over the years (*2×5*, *City Lights* etc), the most successful being the 1991 off-Broadway production *And the World Goes 'Round* (Westside Theater 18 March 1991).

1963 **Morning Sun** (Paul Klein) Phoenix Theater 6 October
1965 **Flora, the Red Menace** (Kander/George Abbott, Robert Russell) Alvin Theater 11 May
1966 **Cabaret** (Kander/Joe Masteroff) Broadhurst Theater 20 November
1968 **The Happy Time** (Kander/N Richard Nash) Broadway Theater 18 January
1968 **Zorba** (Kander/Joseph Stein) Imperial Theater 17 November
1971 **70, Girls, 70** (Kander/Masteroff) Broadhurst Theater 15 April
1975 **Chicago** (Kander/w Bob Fosse) 46th Street Theater 3 June
1977 **The Act** (aka *Shine it On*) (Kander/George Furth) Majestic Theater 29 October
1981 **Woman of the Year** (Kander/Peter Stone) Palace Theater 29 March
1984 **The Rink** (Kander/Terrence McNally) Martin Beck Theater 9 February
1990 **Kiss of the Spiderwoman** (Kander/McNally) Westchester 1 May; Shaftesbury Theatre, London 20 October 1992

EDDY, Max (d 1973)

Lyricist and sometime librettist Eddy was responsible for the French versions of a number of Viennese Operetten of the years between the wars, notably the rewrite of *Walzer aus Wien* which has become a standard of the French repertoire. He also supplied the lyrics for a number of the small, light French musical comedies of the 1930s, principally in collaboration with chansonnier Gaston Gabaroche and librettist Raoul Praxy.

1919 **Les Vièrges du Nil** (Soulaire/w Maurice Rumac) Théâtre Arlequin 9 February
1920 **L'Amour à la Pacha** (Zim/w Rumac) Théâtre Arlequin 6 November
1924 **La Danse des Libellules** (*La Danza delle libellule*) French version w Roger Ferréol (Théâtre Ba-ta-clan)
1926 **Et avec ça, madame?** (Fred Pearly, Pierre Chagnon/Raoul Praxy) 26 January
1930 **Madame Pompadour** French version w Albert Willemetz and Jean Marietti (Théâtre Marigny)
1930 **Enlevez-moi** (Gaston Gabaroche/w Pierre Varenne/Praxy, Henri Hallais) Comédie Caumartin 4 October
1930 **Comtesse Maritza** (*Gräfin Mariza*) French version w Marietti (Mulhouse)
1931 **Frasquita** French version w Marietti (Théâtre du Havre, Le Havre), revised version Opéra-Comique 5 May 1933
1932 **Deux fois deux** (Gabaroche/Praxy) Théâtre Daunou 28 January
1932 **Azor** (Gabaroche, Pearly, Chagnon/Praxy) Théâtre des Bouffes-Parisiens 16 September
1932 **Violette de Montmartre** (*Das Veilchen vom Montmartre*) French version w Marietti (Théâtre des Variétés, Marseille)
1933 **Valses de Vienne** (*Walzer aus Wien*) French version w Marietti, André Mouëzy-Éon (Théâtre de la Porte-Saint-Martin)
1934 **La Princesse du cirque** (*Die Zirkusprinzessin*) French version w Marietti (Théâtre du Havre)
1935 **Quand on a vingt ans** (Michel Emer/Praxy) Théâtre Antoine 24 November
1936 **Faites ça pour moi** (Gabaroche/Praxy) Théâtre Antoine 25 January
1947 **La Bride sur le cou** (Philippe Parès/Henri Lemarchand/w André Huguet) Théâtre de la Potinière

EDDY, Nelson (b Providence, RI, 29 June 1901; d Miami Beach, Fla, 6 March 1967). Hollywood's all-time favourite operetta leading man, with a limited stage exposure.

Eddy at first led a career in commerce and studied singing with the English baritone David Bispham who had, himself, performed with notable success in both opera and light opera. He made his earliest appearances on the stage, from 1922 onwards, in both operatic and light operatic rôles, including the Gilbert and Sullivan repertoire, before – aided by a smooth profile and a tidy figure with which to complement his suave high baritone voice – he began a film career in 1931.

During the 1930s and early 1940s Eddy starred for MGM in the film versions of a number of stage musicals, including *Rose-Marie*, *Naughty Marietta*, *Rosalie*, *Sweethearts*, *Maytime*, *Balalaika*, *The New Moon*, *Bitter-Sweet*, *The Chocolate Soldier*, *I Married an Angel* and *Knickerbocker Holiday* (many of which bore only a small resemblance to their stage counterparts), mostly in partnership with soprano Jeanette MacDonald. The pair became the biggest singing film-stars of their time and Eddy's performances of such rôles as Jim Kenyon in *Rose-Marie* ('Indian Love Call'), Captain Dick in *Naughty Marietta* ('Tramp, Tramp, Tramp', 'Ah! Sweet Mystery of Life', 'I'm Falling in Love with Someone') and the hero of the severely rewritten *The New Moon* ('Stout Hearted Men') became the models for the large cinema audience who saw them and thus for future stage productions.

Eddy was commemorated in the song 'Nelson' in the American edition of the musical show *A Day in Hollywood, a Night in the Ukraine*.

EDISS, Connie (b Brighton, 11 August 1871; d Brighton, 18 April 1934). The most successful musical comedienne of the Gaiety Theatre age of British musical comedy.

A performer on the halls from the age of 12 (as Connie Coutts), plump and pleasing Connie and her comic songs were spotted by George Edwardes who sent her to America in the rôle, created by Lillie Belmore, of the phoney orphan millionairess of *The Shop Girl*. She returned to play the rôle for the last months of the show's London run and remained at the Gaiety Theatre almost unbrokenly for the next decade, building a huge following as the town's favourite musical comedienne.

Her first creation was the rôle of the Lady Mayoress in *My Girl*, performing a re-lyricked version of May Irwin's Bully Song as 'When My Husband is Sir Tom', and she followed this as the Ringmaster's wife in *The Circus Girl* ('The Way to Treat a Lady'), the Hackney Spaniard Carmenita in *A Runaway Girl* ('Society') and Mrs Bang, the mother of *The Messenger Boy* ('Comme çi, Comme ça'). She was lured away by Tom B Davis's *Florodora* finances to appear in that show's successor, *The Silver Slipper* (1901, Bella Gimper), at the Lyric, but she returned to the Gaiety as soon as that show closed to replace Claire Romaine as Mrs Malton Hoppings in *The Toreador* and to appear as Caroline Twining in *The Orchid* ('Fancy Dress'), as the suspicious Mrs Girdle in *The Spring Chicken* (equipped with one of her best songs in 'I Don't Know But I Guess') and as an overweight genie in *The New Aladdin* ('I Want to be Mortal').

When Connie left, in 1907, to go to South Africa for a healthful break, an era ended at the Gaiety Theatre, where she had become the personification of the modern musical as purveyed by George Edwardes and his imitators, and where her pairings with comedian Teddy Payne had created some of the most marvellous moments in London musical comedy.

She continued from Africa to America and was soon snapped up to play more of the weighty-lady comic rôles of which she had become the Edwardian archetype. She starred with Lew Fields in *The Girl Behind the Counter* (1907, Mrs Schniff), toured unprofitably in the Shuberts' *The Girl From the States/The Golden Widow* (1909, Madame Wowski) and returned to Broadway to play an expanded version of the rôle of Mrs Smith, created by Ada Blanche, in *The Arcadians*. Back in London, she appeared again for Edwardes in the less robustly comic rôle of Martje in *The Girl in the Train* (*Die geschiedene Frau*), toured the music-halls with the Herbert Clayton sketch *Laura Kicks* (1911), returned to the Gaiety for *Peggy* (1911, Lady Snoop) and *The Sunshine Girl* (1912, Brenda Blacker), and then appeared in both London and New York as Euphemia Knox in *The Girl on the Film*, and in New York alone in the American production of Renyi's *A kis gróf* (*Suzi*, 1914, Lina Balzer).

In 1915–18 she visited Australia and New Zealand to play in a series of musicals (Grace in *So Long, Letty*, Mrs Dick Winters in *Three Twins*, Penelope in *Oh, Boy!*, *You're in Love*, Victoria in *Tonight's the Night*, *The Girl in the Taxi*, *The Carnival Girl*, Fifi in *A Waltz Dream*, Blanche Moss in *Canary Cottage* etc) then, after another brief American interlude (*Oh, Uncle!* 1919), returned to Britain. There she developed a highly successful career in straight comedy,

appearing on the musical stage only in the revusical *The Smith Family* at London's Empire Theatre in 1922 in the last dozen years of her working life.

EDOUIN, Willie [BRYER, William Frederick] (b Brighton, 1 January 1846; d London, 14 April 1908). Star comedian of nearly 40 years and several generations of musical theatre in Britain and America.

Edouin first appeared on the London stage at the Strand Theatre at the age of five as part of a family act, performing with his brothers and sisters Eliza (d Forest Creek, Australia, 3 October 1857), John (d India, 17 December 1875), Charles (d India), Julia (d Philadelphia, 3 March 1891) and (not on this occasion) Rose (b Brighton 29 January 1844; d 24 August 1925) as 'The Living Marionettes'. He subsequently played child rôles in pantomime at Drury Lane, Sadler's Wells and the Surrey Theatre, and in burlesque at the Strand.

In 1856 the Edouin family abandoned Britain for Australia. Billed as 'The Edouin Juvenile Vaudeville and Ballet Company', they played an introductory week of their entertainment *Frolics in France* and the serio-comic ballet *Hob in the Well* with Gustavus V Brooke at Melbourne's Theatre Royal and then toured the gold rush camps in a wagon built to carry their wardrobe and props in its belly, with seats at either end for the family. 'It was drawn by three horses and painted on the side in red and white letters was "the celebrated Edouin family in farce, comedy and burlesque". We would get to a new "rush" and give a performance in the dining-tent or even on the grass – in fact anywhere we could get.' The family finally settled in Melbourne where they played at the Cremorne Gardens and appeared in pantomime ('I played clown and made the shoes for the whole family and manufactured my own properties and tricks as well as my clown's costume every Christmas'). They later travelled the Asian circuit from China, Japan and India to the West Coast of America.

In 1866, the by now solo Willie based himself in America and there performed, first on the West Coast, where he was a member of the company at San Francisco's California Theater, and then in New York, as a comedian and actor in variety and ministrel sketches (Narcissus Fritzfrizzle in *The Dancing Barber*, Murphy in *Handy Andy* with Bryant's Minstrels). In 1870 he joined up with Lydia Thompson's famous 'British Blondes' company, performing lead comic rôles with the troupe in both America and, during Miss Thompson's visits to Britain, between 1874 and 1876, at the Charing Cross, Globe and Criterion Theatres in London. Amongst the pieces in which he appeared with this famous burlesque company were *Bluebeard, or the Mormon, the Maiden and the Little Militaire* (Corporal Zoug-Zoug and, most famously, the Heathen Chinee), *Paris, or the Apple of Discord* (Pollux), *Lurline, or the Knight of the Naiads*, *Robin Hood*, *Oxygen* (Franz), *Mephisto, or the Four Sensations* (Aescalepius), *Robinson Crusoe* (Man Friday) and *Piff Paff* (Cherub).

Edouin subsequently became a prominent performer in the popular American musical farce-comedies of the late 1870s, touring, along with his wife, Alice Atherton, and young children, in Samuel Colville's Folly Company and in E E Rice's Surprise Party, the most substantial of the companies purveying this rough-shod kind of low farce with songs. Amongst the shows in which they appeared

Plate 81. **Willie Edouin** *had two careers – as a youngish 19th-century farce-comedy player (left), and then as the internationally famous comedy star of* musicals such as Les P'tites Michu *(General des Ifs, right).*

were Willie Gill's versions of *Babes in the Wood* (Tommy), and *Robinson Crusoe, Horrors* and *Revels* as well as burlesques such as *Hiawatha* (William Penn Brown) and *The Corsair* (Syng Smaul).

In 1880 he formed his own company, Willie Edouin's Sparks, which toured a similar repertoire of farcical and burlesque pieces, including the young Charles Hoyt's *A Bunch of Keys* (Littleton Snaggs) and, most successfully, *Dreams, or Fun in a Photograph Gallery* (John Antonio Binks), in both of which he also had a hand in the writing, on the circuits he had trodden with Rice. In 1883 he took his company to Britain, and ventured a season at London's Avenue Theatre. His very low-brow entertainments did not suit the West End, but they proved effective enough in the provinces for Edouin and his wife, both of whom had scored personal successes even with the London critics, to decide to remain in Britain.

Edouin continued to tour his own company, headed by himself and his wife, venturing into town occasionally with either a comedy or a musical piece or even a composite programme. In 1884 they had a splendid success with the burlesque *The Babes*, a descendant of their old American touring piece rewritten by Harry Paulton and composed by W C Levey, musical director at Drury Lane; in 1885 they introduced a little piece called *The Japs*; and in 1886 they returned with a burlesque, *Oliver Grumble*; but their biggest success was with the Mark Melford comedy *Turned Up* which they played 159 times at the Comedy Theatre and toured for many years thereafter.

On the strength of this success, Edouin took on the management of the Royalty Theatre and in the next ten years, moving from one lesser London theatre to another (Novelty, Strand, Opera Comique, Comedy), devoted his efforts largely to the straight theatre, turning up one other fine hit in *Our Flat* (1889) but also losing his shirt and his wife's on more than one occasion. Apart from Harry Paulton's only occasionally musical *Niobe* (1892), his musical productions had little success: a burlesque *Airey Annie* (on *Ariane*) had a brief life at the Strand in 1888; *Les 28 Jours de Clairette*, anglicized for his wife to play the title-rôle, lasted a month; *Jaunty Jane Shore* (1894), which he directed for Mackay Robertson, again starring Miss Atherton, made six weeks at the Strand, and another farcical Orientalism, *Quong Hi*, proved too insubstantial for London. He had little more success when he abandoned producing and instead directed and starred with his daughter, May, in the early musical comedy *All Abroad* (1896) at the Court Theatre and in the racing musical *Newmarket* for Alexander Loftus.

Edouin's career took a decisive turn upwards when Henry Lowenfeld offered him the rôle, turned down late in the day by Arthur Roberts, of the doll-maker, Hilarius, in the London edition of Audran's *La Poupée* (1897). The show was a major hit and Edouin himself 'discovered' at the age of 56. He followed up in Lowenfeld's next production, Clérice's *The Royal Star* (1898, Macready Valybow), and in a burlesque, *Great Caesar*, before taking on his most successful rôle of all, the star comic part of Anthony Tweedlepunch in *Florodora* (1899). He triumphed as the machinating old phrenologist in both Britain and America, setting himself up as a major musical comedy star of a rather more upmarket kind than previously on both sides of the Atlantic.

He appeared for *Florodora* producer Tom B Davis in his next show, *The Silver Slipper* (1901, Samuel Twanks) before moving across to the management of George Edwardes, for whom his first creation was the memorable 'Piggy' Hoggenheimer, the Yankee millionaire ('Rude? I'm not rude, I'm rich') in *The Girl from Kays*, and to Frank Curzon first for *Amorelle* and then to invest *Sergeant Brue* (1904), one of librettist Owen Hall's best creations, with stage life.

During this period Edouin also directed several touring musicals including *Black and White* (1898) for Loftus and *Bebe* (1901), but he stayed clear of the cares of management, and continued his now furiously booming and top-line performing career in the West End productions of *Les P'tites Michu* (1905, General des Ifs), *The Blue Moon* (1905, Moolraj) and *The Little Cherub* (1906, Earl of Sanctobury) before taking a turn round the variety theatres of Britain and America in sketches to cash in on his fame in what were to be the last years of his life.

His daughter May Edouin (d September 1944), who had played in Colville's company as a small child – notably as Jenny Wren in *Babes in the Wood* when barely able to walk – appeared in leading juvenile rôles alongside her father in the revival of *All Abroad*, *Newmarket* and on Broadway as Angela in *Florodora* (1900), and without him in Fred Harris's short-lived production of *Man About Town*. Of the other members of the original Edouin troupe, it was sister Rose who had the best career. She established herself in Melbourne, ahead of all the other Edouins, as a favourite player in burlesque (Morgiana in *Forty Thieves* etc), and later had a long career as a trouping actress, partially under her married name of Mrs George B Lewis. She went reciting in South Africa, and appeared in London in later life on the musical stage in the revival of *The Dairymaids* (1915) and on tour in the short-lived *The Light Blues* (1915). She also authored a musical comedy, *A Spree in Paris, and What Happened* mounted at Belfast's Theatre Royal, 25 November 1907.

EDWARDES, Felix (b London, ?1870; d London, 6 February 1954).

An actor in Britain, then from 1903 an actor and stage director in America, Edwardes worked largely with touring companies and in stock, winning his most notable credits as a director with the companies of Lily Langtry and Maxine Elliott until he was engaged by Grossmith and Laurillard to direct the American comedian Raymond Hitchcock in the London musical *Mr Manhattan* (1916). He subsequently staged *Kissing Time* and *Baby Bunting* for the same partnership, *The Cousin from Nowhere* at the Prince's, and then began a fruitful association with the Astaires with his staging of the London version of *Stop Flirting*. That association with Fred Astaire continued through *Lady, Be Good!*, *Funny Face* and *Gay Divorce*.

In 1925 he directed the London production of *Rose Marie* at the Theatre Royal, Drury Lane and, thereafter, staged the Drury Lane productions of *Show Boat*, *The New Moon*, *The Three Musketeers*, *The Land of Smiles* and *The Song of the Drum* as well as mounting *Lady Luck* for the opening of the

Carlton Theatre, *Frederica* at the Palace, *The Dubarry* at His Majesty's, Grossmith's production of *Tell Me More* at the Winter Garden and Friml's *Luana* which closed out of town. He retired from the theatre in 1934.

EDWARDES, George (b Clee, Lincs, 14 October 1852; d London, 4 October 1915). One of the most important producers of musical plays in the history of the genre, Edwardes, by his activities at the end of the 19th and in the early 20th century, set styles and standards in the musical theatre throughout the world.

He began his life in the theatre working for his cousin, the Dublin theatre manager, Michael Gunn, and subsequently held the post of acting manager at the Savoy Theatre under D'Oyly Carte for some years during the original productions of several of the Gilbert and Sullivan musicals. In 1885 he moved from the Savoy to the Gaiety Theatre, where the theatre's founder, John Hollingshead, who had established the Gaiety over its 17 years of existence as one of London's foremost light musical theatres, was preparing his retirement. Together, they produced the burlesque *Little Jack Sheppard*, before Hollingshead stepped down, leaving Edwardes to take over the running of the theatre.

Hollingshead left behind not only a burgeoning new tradition in musical shows – the new burlesque with its lively comic scenes and original songs – but also a group of stars, headed by Nellie Farren and Fred Leslie, who would, under Edwardes's guidance, bring the genre to a point where it became the principal light musical entertainment of the world for a number of years. *Little Jack Sheppard* was followed by *Monte Cristo jr*, *Miss Esmeralda*, *Frankenstein*, *Faust Up-to-Date*, *Ruy Blas and the Blasé Roué*, *Carmen Up-to-Data*, *Joan of Arc* and *Cinder-Ellen Up-Too-Late*, as Edwardes spread out his activities and influence beyond the Gaiety Theatre with national and international tours which took in Broadway, the Continent and Australia and, eventually, other London theatres.

During this period he also made a fill-in foray into the field of comic opera with the production of the B C Stephenson/Alfred Cellier *Dorothy*, but he sold off the show soon after its production to the theatre accountant H J Leslie under whose management it became the longest-running London musical of the 19th century. It was one of very few errors of judgement on Edwardes's part in a long career as a producer and theatre manager.

The new burlesque developed in such a way that eventually its title held very little relevance to its subject matter and, soon, all such pretence was given up. With Fred Leslie dead and Nellie Farren too ill to work, Edwardes produced a new kind of piece which contained all the song, dance and comedy elements of burlesque but was, rather than an extravaganza costume piece, a topical comedy entertainment of light and bright song and dance played in modern dress. *In Town* and *A Gaiety Girl* were the earliest of what came to be known as 'musical comedies' and, in the next decade, Edwardes produced a whole series of like pieces including *The Shop Girl*, *My Girl*, *A Runaway Girl*, *The Circus Girl*, *The Messenger Boy* and *The Toreador*, principally at the Gaiety Theatre, a series which became one half of the staple diet of both London's and the world's musical theatre.

Lehár's *Die lustige Witwe* (*The Merry Widow*), and *Der Graf von Luxemburg* (*The Count of Luxembourg*), Fall's *Die Dollar-prinzessin* (*The Dollar Princess*), Jean Gilbert's *Die geschie-dene Frau* (*The Girl on the Train*) and Victor Jacobi's *Leányvásár* (*The Marriage Market*). He had forward plans involving both original and imported musicals for each of the three major theatres under his management when, in 1914, his final illness forced him to hand active control over to his lieutenants. Few of those plans came to fruition without him.

After his death, the empire he had created was soon broken up as the post-war musical theatre underwent pro-found alterations in style which Edwardes, had he lived, might well have taken under his control in the same way that he had done with the variations of public taste through his 30 years as the most important figure in the musical theatre. Although Robert Evett temporarily saved Daly's Theatre with the production of *The Maid of the Mountains* (mounted under the banner 'George Edwardes presents ...'), none of his theatres was ever again to know a period of prosperity comparable to that which he had given it.

Edwardes was made the hero of a 1948 film called *Gaiety George* in which he was portrayed by Richard Greene, better known as television's Robin Hood.

Biography: Bloom, U: *Curtain Call for the Guv'nor* (Hutchinson, London, 1954)

Plate 82. **George Edwardes**: *For many years the principal purveyor of musical theatre to the world.*

The other half of that diet also stemmed from Edwardes's management. In 1893 he built and opened Daly's Theatre, in partnership with the American impresario Augustin Daly, and, from 1895, he commissioned and produced a series of musicals for that theatre which were very different in character to those at the frivolous Gaiety. The Daly's Theatre musicals, beginning with *An Artist's Model* and continuing through such pieces as *The Geisha*, *A Greek Slave*, *San Toy* and *A Country Girl*, were much more substantial both in their writing and in their music than their Gaiety fellows and, in the hands of such artists as Marie Tempest, Hayden Coffin, Huntley Wright, Letty Lind and Rutland Barrington, they provided first-class fare for theatregoers who preferred the more comic-opera kind of entertainment.

Edwardes continued to run both the Gaiety and Daly's Theatres through into the 20th century and finally enlarged his permanent empire to three by the purchase of the lease of the Adelphi Theatre. During all this time, he presided over the development of English musical comedy and led the eventual fusion of the Gaiety and Daly's style of shows into the more vertebrate musical comedies of Edwardian times – *The Spring Chicken*, *The Quaker Girl*, *The Girl from Kays*, *The Duchess of Dantzic*, *Kitty Grey* and *The Girls of Gottenberg*.

Ever watchful for a change in public taste, he encouraged the extra-light musicals of Paul Rubens (*Three Little Maids*, *Lady Madcap*), tried a dip into a quickly discontinued revival of burlesque with *The New Aladdin* and, with particular success, imported the best of the Continental pieces of the turn of the century years, scoring huge successes with Messager's *Véronique* and *Les P'tites Michu*,

EDWARDES, Paula (b Boston, 29 September 1878; d unknown). Buxom Broadway soubrette whose career went awry soon after she reached the top.

Miss Edwardes made her first Broadway appearances at the admitted age of 13 in Harrigan's *Squatter Sovereignty* and in a minor rôle and as understudy to the soubrette in Thomas Q Seabrooke's Boston musical *Tabasco* (1894). She subsequently appeared in another Seabrooke show, *The Island of Champagne*, and in Hoyt's *A Black Sheep* on the road before taking a slightly more sizeable rôle in the American version of Varney's *La Falote* at the Casino Theater (1897, Mariolle).

Her next rôle at the Casino was a tiny one in *A Dangerous Maid* (1899), but she finally came to the front as the broadly common Mamie Clancy ('Coney Island') in *The Belle of New York*. She repeated her impersonation of cock-ney Mamie in the show's enormously successful London run to such effect that on returning home she was cast in comic rôles in a series of British musicals, beginning on Broadway with the Connie Ediss rôle of Carmenita from Hackney in *A Runaway Girl* and continuing on the road in *The Circus Girl* (Lucille), *San Toy* (Dudley) and *The Geisha* (Molly). She played in *Mamselle 'awkins* (1900, Honorah) and *A Royal Rogue* with Jefferson de Angelis and returned to Broadway in *The Show Girl* (1902) and as Jelly Canvas in the 'nautico-musical extravaganza' *The Defender* (1902), before she won top-billing in the title-rôle of *Winsome Winnie* in 1903 (Winnie Walker). She had a second Broadway star rôle in *The Princess Beggar* (1907, Princess Elaine) but soon after she retired from the stage.

She was briefly seen in vaudeville in 1910 and in 1923 she unsuccessfully attempted a comeback in revue. Three years later was found kneeling in the middle of a New York street praying in the pouring rain and was removed into psychopathic care.

EDWARDS, Julian (b Manchester, England, 11 December 1855; d Yonkers, NY, 5 September 1910). Comic opera composer whose regularly produced works proved much more ephemeral than the lighter musical theatre music of his time.

The young Edwards studied at Edinburgh University and began his musical theatre career as a teenager, working as pianist-cum-musical director to the little comic operetta company run by his sister, Fanny. It was for this company that he wrote and composed his first stage works, a series of short operettas which Fanny played on the road and in occasional fringe London venues between 1873 and 1877. One, *Dorothy*, was later played as an afterpiece to *HMS Pinafore* on D'Oyly Carte's first tour.

Edwards toured as chorus master and assistant conductor with van Biene's Opera Company in 1880 and as musical director/pianist with the little Alice Barth operetta company (*The Chalet*, *Widows Bewitched* etc) before taking a pause in his conducting activities to pursue serious musical studies. He composed his first short opera, *Corinna*, in 1880, followed by a four-act opera, *Victorian, the Spanish Student*, which was published by Joseph Williams and produced at the Theatre Royal, Sheffield (6 April 1883), and took up a baton again as a conductor with the Carl Rosa Opera Company, but ultimately he returned to the musical theatre, where he was to make the bulk of his career, at first in Britain and later in America.

In 1887 Edwards toured Britain as musical director for Horace Lingard's production of *Pepita* (*La Princesse des Canaries*), but his career got the upward impetus it had been lacking when he left his home country for America. In 1888 he crossed the Atlantic to work for J C Duff, for whom he conducted the American production of Harry Paulton's *Paola*. He was subsequently musical director for A M Palmer's American production of *The Red Hussar* (1890) with Marie Tempest and, thereafter, made himself a good career as a conductor of musicals, which soon became paired with a parallel career as a theatre composer.

Edwards' first work for the musical theatre in 15 years, and his first light full-length piece, was the musical comedy *Jupiter*, produced in Washington DC with Digby Bell and his wife, Laura Joyce Bell, starring in Harry B Smith's tale of ancient Greek fooleries. In spite of his penchant for rather correct comic opera writing – something which would throughout his career bring him some appreciative nods from the critics, but also a lack of either outstanding song successes or general popularity – the music of *Jupiter* did not win particular notice. Edwards's score was, however, diluted by interpolations ranging from minstrel songs to 'Annie Rooney'. *Jupiter* visited Broadway in 1892 for a brief run.

After an attempt at something a little more effortfully artistic with an operatic version of Henrik Hertz's *King René's Daughter* (the same piece tackled by Tchaikovsky in his *Iolanta*), Edwards teamed for the first time with another English expatriate, Stanislaus Stange, a playwright and lyricist who became his chief collaborator over the next decade, and returned definitively to lighter music. Their first work together, *Friend Fritz*, a play with some songs for vocalist-turned-actress Marion Manola, was another based on a work previously used by another composer. Mascagni's version of Erckmann-Chatrian's novel as *L'amico Fritz* would remain rather more interesting than that produced by the Americo-British pair. They did, however, have rather more success with the neatly old-fashioned comic opera *Madeleine*, starring Camille D'Arville in its title-rôle as the maiden whose magic kisses bring a greybeard back down to his lovable twenties. *Madeleine* ran ten weeks in New York, toured and was revived several years later by the Castle Square Company with Louise Eissing starring.

The pair subsequently collaborated on *The Goddess of Truth*, a version of the Pygmalion legend produced with Lillian Russell in the title-rôle, and an Irish light opera for F C Whitney with *Brian Boru* for hero, revamped Audran's *La Petite Fronde* as a vehicle for the star trio of Miss Russell, Jefferson de Angelis and Della Fox, and supplied de Angelis with a touring vehicle, *The Jolly Musketeer*, for his comic opera company, in each case with respectable rather than exciting results. Edwards had a more lucrative success when he teamed with Kirk La Shelle, the former business manager of the Bostonians now turned producer, on a piece called *Princess Chic*. Although the show had a short Broadway life, it toured for two years with the young Christie MacDonald starring in its title-rôle.

In 1902 Stange and Edwards produced their two most successful pieces. The first was a rehash of Garrick's *The Country Girl* musicalized as *Dolly Varden* and played by Lulu Glaser on Broadway. Greeted with great enthusiasm by the lovers of comic opera ('a prodigious hit ... real comic opera'), it had a fine touring life in America and was given a London season – the only time one of Edwards's works was transported back to his home country. The other, generally agreed to be their best work, found these specialists of the formula old-style comic opera tackling a surprisingly verismo setting: *When Johnny Comes Marching Home* was a dramatic tale of the American Civil War with no big-name star and no low comedy. It was seen twice on Broadway and around the country and the hero's song, 'My Own United States', was the nearest that Edwards came to turning out a hit song.

The pair had sufficient reputation for the great contralto Ernestine Schumann-Heinck to make a venture into comic opera in their *Love's Lottery*, but, although Edwards subsequently composed the music for F C Whitney's production of Stange's version of *The School for Wives* (1905), they combined on only one more musical theatre piece, another rather thee-and-thou comic opera called *The Belle of London Town* in which Camille D'Arville and Orville Harrold toured for the Shuberts in 1907–8.

In the meanwhile, Edwards had had a slightly unlikely success in collaboration with songwriter-cum-producer Alfred Aarons. Their *His Honor the Mayor*, jollied up into a girls and songs show by producer Whitney, ran through the country for several seasons. Thereafter, without ever switching from his unshakeably proper musical style, Edwards had several more tries at this end of the market, the most liked of which was the Shuberts' Sam Bernard vehicle *The Girl and the Wizard*, which played for 87 performances on Broadway prior to touring. On this occasion Edwards's score was permeated with numbers by Jerome Kern, Louis Hirsch, Edward Madden, director Ned Wayburn and other representatives of the up-and-coming generation of Broadway musicals. His musical conscience, however, was probably somewhat salved by the production of his oratorio, *Lazarus*, at a Metropolitan

Opera House Sunday concert in 1910.

Edwards remained a respected and well-liked member of the Broadway establishment throughout his career, his musicianship praised by critics and his scores regularly presented by top managements over a period of nearly 20 years. Yet his style of composition was already old-fashioned when he began writing for the Broadway stage, and, lacking the essential gaiety and versatility of a Victor Herbert, he never reached that composer's level or popularity.

Edwards was married to the vocalist Philippine Seidle whose brother was co-librettist for his *The Gay Musician*. His sister, Fanny Edwards (d 1908), after a number of years running her concert party/drawing-room entertainment (latterly Miss Fanny Edwards' Entertainment and Comic Opera Company), with performers such as Michael Dwyer, Arthur Rousbey, Ethel Pierson and Redfern Hollins featured, had a good career as a contralto in comic opera. She toured as Lady Sangazure (alongside Dwyer and Rousbey) in 1878, was the first touring Little Buttercup in Britain and later took the same rôle in the Comedy Opera Company's rebel *HMS Pinafore* (1879). She toured in contralto rôles for Carte, appeared at the Alhambra as the Duchess in *La Fille du tambour-major* and was seen on Broadway in 1891 as *Patience*'s Lady Jane.

1872 **Cornarino's Mistake** (Edwards) 1 act Corn Exchange, Hereford 30 September
1874 **Love's Test** (Edwards) 1 act Victoria Hall, Norwich 4 September
1875 **May and December** (Edwards) 1 act Assembly Rooms, Tunbridge Wells 16 March
1876 **The Marquis de St Valéry** (Edwards) 1 act Reading Town Hall 20 January
1877 **Dorothy** (Edwards) Colchester 13 January, Ladbroke Hall, London 24 September
1877 **Buckingham** (Edwards) Town Hall, Northampton 28 December
1892 **Jupiter, or the Cobbler and the King** (Harry Bache Smith) Palmer's Theater 2 May
1893 **King René's Daughter** 1 act Herrmann's Theater 22 November
1893 **Friend Fritz** (Stanislaus Stange) Herrmann's Theater 20 January
1895 **Madeleine, or The Magic Kiss** (Stange) Bijou Theater 25 February
1896 **The Goddess of Truth** (Stange) Abbey's Theater 26 February
1896 **Brian Boru** (Stange) Broadway Theater 19 October
1897 **The Wedding Day** (*La Petite Fronde*) (Stange) Casino Theater 8 April
1898 **The Jolly Musketeer** (Stange) Broadway Theater 14 November
1900 **Princess Chic** (Kirk La Shelle) Casino Theater 12 February
1902 **Dolly Varden** (Stange) Herald Square Theater 27 January
1902 **When Johnny Comes Marching Home** (Stange) New York Theater 26 December
1904 **Love's Lottery** (Stange) Broadway Theater 3 October
1905 **The Pink Hussars** (later *His Honor the Mayor*) (w Alfred Aarons/Charles Campbell, Ralph M Skinner) Chicago Opera House 23 October; New York Theater 28 May 1906
1907 **The Belle of London Town** (Stange) Lincoln Square Theater 28 January
1907 **The Girl and the Governor** (S M Brenner) Manhattan Theater 4 February
1908 **The Gay Musician** (Edward Seidle, Campbell) Wallack's Theater 18 May
1909 **The Motor Girl** (Campbell, Skinner) Lyric Theater 15 June
1909 **The Girl and the Wizard** (Robert B Smith/J Hartley Manners) Casino Theater 27 September
1910 **Molly May** (Walter Browne) Hackett Theater 8 April
1911 **Two Men and a Girl** (aka *The Aero Girl*) revised *The Motor Girl* Detroit 13 February

Other title attributed: *Gringoire the Street Singer* (1901)

EGGERTH, Marta [EGGERT, Márta] (b Budapest, 17 April 1912). International Operette prima donna of stage and screen, often in partnership with her husband, tenor Jan Kiepura.

Márta Eggert began her career in her native Budapest, playing juvenile rôles at the Magyar Királyí Operaház (1924) and at the Magyar Színház in the French musical *Mannequins* (1926). She appeared in Stockholm in revue, and was then seen at the Fővárosi Operettszinház in further juvenile parts including Annuska in *Az utolsó Verebély lány* (1928), and in Egon Kemény's *Kikelet utca 3*. She was still in her teens when she succeeded Adele Kern in the title-rôle of *Das Veilchen vom Montmartre* in Vienna (1930). She also starred in Ziehrer's *Die verliebte Eskadron* and, later, in Komjati's *Ein Liebestraum* (1933, Carla) at the Theater an der Wien in the early stages of a career which – interspersed with frequent performances on film (*Ein Lied, ein Küss, ein Mädel*, the Lehár/Billy Wilder *Es war einmal ein Walzer* 1932, *Die Blume von Hawaii* 1933, *Mein Herz ruft nach dir*, as Gräfin Esterházy in *Leise flehen meine Lieder* 1934, *Das Hofkonzert* 1936, *Zauber der Bohème* 1937 etc) – spread through the world from Hamburg to Broadway, London and Paris.

She was seen in New York as Minnie Sorensen in the musical *Higher and Higher* (1940), opposite her husband in revivals of *The Merry Widow* at Majestic Theater (1943) and the City Center (1944), and again in a romantic Chopin pastiche, *Polonaise* (1945, Mariska). She appeared as Sylva Varescu in a souped-up *Princesse Czardas* in Paris (Théâtre de Paris, 1950), and also repeated her 'widow' on several occasions in five different languages (London, 1955; New York, 1957 etc).

In 1982 she appeared alongside Diana Rigg's Colette in the rôle of Sido in *Colette*, and in 1992, at 80 years of age, was seen guesting at Vienna's Volksoper in the Robert Stolz compilation show *Servus Du*.

EICHBERG, Julius (b Düsseldorf, 13 June 1824; d Boston, 18 January 1893).

German-born, Würzburg- and Brussels-educated, Eichberg taught at the Geneva conservatoire before emigrating to America in 1856. In 1859 he settled in Boston where he worked as a conductor, directed the Boston Museum concerts and later ran the local conservatoire and his own violin school. During the 1860s he composed several musical theatre pieces in the style of the earlier years of the Continental 19th century. His *The Doctor of Alcantara* was the most successful early American comic opera, being produced in Britain and Australia and toured in America for a number of years, whilst his *The Two Cadis* also won repeat productions in America, and *A Night in Rome* joined *The Doctor of Alcantara* and *The Two Cadis* in the touring repertoire of Caroline Richings's English opera company alongside such offerings as *Lucia di Lammermoor* and *The Rose of Castille*.

Eichberg also authored a number of musical teaching works, both on the violin and on musical in general, and appeared as a concert violinist and chamber musician.

1862 **The Doctor of Alcantara** (Benjamin E Woolf) Boston Museum 7 April; Théâtre Français, New York, 28 May 1866

1864 **A Night in Rome** Boston Museum 26 November; Théâtre Français, New York, 25 June 1866

1866 **The Two Cadis** Boston Museum 5 March; Théâtre Français, New York, 2 July

1868 **The Rose of Tyrol** Boston Museum 6 April

EINÖDSHOFER, Julius (b Vienna, 10 February 1863; d Berlin, 17 October 1930).

Einödshofer studied in Vienna and worked as a theatre conductor in the Austrian provinces before taking a post as conductor and house composer at the Scala Theater, Berlin, in 1892. He subsequently worked in the same capacity at the Centraltheater and at the Thalia-Theater at each of which he provided the scores for a series of musical comedies of the late 1890s and the early 1900s. Between 1906 and 1910 he was the conductor of the Kurorchester in Heringdorf and, from 1911 to 1921, at Berlin's Admiralspalast, where he composed the music for that theatre's celebrated spectacular ballets, and in wartime contributed such pieces as 'Die Welt kann ohne mich wohl sein, doch ohne Deutschland nie!' (lyric: Otto Emanuel Enskat) and 'Was hat ein Deutsches Mädchen gern' (K Schneider) to the nation's musical good. In 1921 he retired from the theatre and became a conductor for radio, and he died in 1930 after a heart attack suffered whilst he was on the air.

Although Einödshofer supplied the Berlin stage with large amounts of revue and dance music for more than 20 years, little of his work was heard further afield. A song, 'Mr Mosenstein', was, however, interpolated into George Edwardes's London musical *The Girl from Kays*.

1884 **14 Tage im Arrest** (Friedrich Rotter) 1 act Fürsttheater, Vienna 28 June

1884 **Ein Invalide von Aspern** (Wilhelm Ernst) 1 act Fürsttheater, Vienna 18 August

1889 **Die Spiritisten** (Emil Weissenturm) Stadttheater, Innsbruck April

1893 **Berliner Vollblut** (Jean Kren) Centraltheater 31 August

1894 **Ein gesunder Junge** (Kren) Centraltheater 6 March

1894 **Der neue Kurs** (Kren, Leopold Ely) Centraltheater

1894 **O, diese Berliner** (Julius Freund) Centraltheater 2 September

1895 **Unsere Rentiers** (Freund, Wilhelm Mannstädt) Centraltheater 16 February

1895 **Eine tolle Nacht** (Freund, Mannstädt) Centraltheater 4 September

1896 **1000 Jahre** (Ferdinand Maierfeld) Jantschtheater, Vienna 2 April

1896 **Eine wilde Sache** (Freund, Mannstädt) Centraltheater 20 September

1896 **Der Mandarin [von Tsing-ling-ling]** (Freund) Metropoltheater August

1897 **Ein fideler Abend** (Freund, Mannstädt) Centraltheater 7 February

1897 **Berliner Fahrten** (Freund, Mannstädt) Centraltheater 4 September

1898 **Die Tugendfalle** (Freund, Mannstädt) Centraltheater 20 January

1898 **Das Paradies der Frauen** (*Le Royaume des femmes*) German version by Freund w new music w Bertram Sänger (Metropoltheater)

1898 **Sterzl in Berlin** (Freund, Mannstädt) Theater an der Wien, Vienna 2 April

1899 **Die verkehrte Welt** (*Le Royaume des femmes*) add music for German version by Freund (Metropoltheater)

1901 **Ein tolles Geschaft** (Schönfeld/Kren) Thalia-Theater 7 September

1901 **Die Badepuppe** (Schönfeld/Kren) Thalia-Theater 26 November

1902 **Seine kleine** (Schönfeld/Kren, Ely) Thalia-Theater 18 January

1902 **Die bösen Mädchen** (Schönfeld/Kren, Ely) Thalia-Theater 23 December

1903 **Der Kamelienonkel** (w Fritz Reichmann/Leo Leipziger) Thalia-Theater 6 February

1903 **Der Posaunenengel** (w Max Schmidt/Schönfeld/Kren) Thalia-Theater 24 March

1903 **Der reicheste Berliner** (w Schmidt/Schönfeld/Kren) Belle-Alliance Theater 23 December

1904 **Götterweiber** (Kurt Kraatz, Wilhelm Jacoby) Belle-Alliance Theater 4 February

1904 **Freut euch des Lebens** (Schönfeld/Jacoby, R Stein ad Kren) Belle-Alliance Theater 8 April

1904 **Kam'rad Lehmann** (w Julius Stern/Schönfeld/Kren, Ely) Belle-Alliance Theater 7 May

1904 **Der Weiberkönig** (Schönfeld/Kren, Ely) Thalia-Theater 15 September

1904 **Rossbach** (Leo Walther Stein) Stadttheater, Bromberg 16 December

1904 **Der grosse Stern** (Schönfeld/Kren) Thalia-Theater 23 December

1909 **Tohuwabohu** (Heinz Gordon) Apollotheater 1 October

1911 **Liebesbarometer** (Max Reichert) 1 act Apollotheater 1 March

1915 **Mamas Liebling** (Ely) Rose-Theater 14 August

1915 **Aus der Jugendzeit** (Ely) Walhalla-Theater 4 October

1922 **Die Frau ohne Mann** (Erich Kaiser) Residenztheater, Dresden 6 February

1927 **Ja, ihr Mädels müsst dran glauben** (Carl Bretschneider) Theater in der Lützowstrasse 9 July

EISEMANN, Mihály (b Bács, Paripás, Hungary, 19 June 1898; d Budapest, 25 February 1966). One of the most successful Hungarian musical theatre composers of the years between the wars.

Eisemann studied law in Budapest before attending the Zeneakadémia and orientating his career towards music. Whilst working as a pianist in a coffee-house, he made his first ventures into popular songwriting in team with lyricist Imre Harmath ('Szeret-e még? csak ennyit mondjon!') and, in 1929, he produced his first theatre score, for the revusical comedy *Miss Amerika*, mounted with great success at the Fővárosi Operettszinház with Teri Fejes, Erzsi Péchy and Gyula Kabos starred and a musical part made up of blues, fox-trots and tangos. The following year, *Alvinci huszárok* ('Van aki bevallja'), produced at the Király Színház with Juci Lábass, Rózsi Bársony, Oszkár Dénes, Árpád Latabár and Dezső Kertész in the lead rôles, confirmed that success.

Eisemann contributed to the music for the same theatre's musical version of the Broadway play *The Poor Nut* (*Amerikai lányok* 7 February 1931) whose score was credited to a transatlantic team of Cowan, C I May and Albert Gumble, but a third collaboration with librettist László Szilágyi, author of his first two hits, brought him his greatest success. *Zsákbamacska*, produced at the Pesti Színház with the rising Marika Rökk starred, ran for more

Plate 83. Mihály Eisemann's *musicals of the 1920s left little doubt as to the fashionable styles of the moment.*

than 250 performances in Budapest and was subsequently played in Vienna as *Katz im Sack* (Die Komödie, 1933) and in London as *Happy Weekend* (ad Dion Titheradge, Arthur Stanley 30 May 1934), under the management of Claude B Yearsley and Percival Mackey, with Hungarians Magda Kun and Steve Geray starred.

His two following works also travelled. *Egy csók és más semmi*, originally produced in Budapest with Hanna Honthy featured, was played as *Ein Kuss – und sonst gar nichts* at Berlin's Theater am Kurfürstendamm (6 October 1932) with Friedl Schuster starring, and at Vienna's Scala Theater (14 March 1934) with Rita Georg, whilst *Vadvirág* (ad Fritz Löhner-Beda) was adapted into German and played by Rökk as *Der Sterne von Manege*. The former was filmed, and later revived at the Fővárosi Operettszinház in 1946 (22 June), whilst the latter, after an original run at the Andrássy-uti Színház and the Magyar Színház (24 May 1934), also returned in 1946 for a new run at the Márkus Park Színház.

A cirkusz csillaga (1934) had a excellent first run of 168 performances in Budapest with Rökk starred, whilst *Én és a kisöcsém*, first produced in the same year with Bársony at the top of the bill, was another Eisemann musical deemed worthy of revival, with the same star, in the post-war years (15 May 1948). *Ezüstmenyasszony*, produced at the Royal Színház with Sári Fedák as prima donna, and *Meseáruház*, first mounted at the Vigszinház with Bársony and Ella Gombaszögi featured, were also successes. In 1940 no fewer than five new Eisemann operetts were seen in Budapest, beginning with the jazz-operett *Handa-Banda* (a revised version of a piece mounted two years earlier in Szeged), including pieces written with both Szilágyi and Zsolt Harsányi, and ending, ten months after the first

première, with another piece by the same author, Gyula Halász, *Fiatalság-bolondság*, staged with considerable success at the Fővárosi Operettszínház.

Eisemann continued to write shows and popular songs through the 1940s, having perhaps his best theatrical successes of that period with *Fekete Péter* – a piece with a score still rich in such rhythms as foxtrots and rumbas – which was played 143 times at the Vígszinház with György Dénes in its title-rôle, and the fairytale operett *Őfelsége a mama*, before *Ő vagy Ő?* produced at the Fővárosi Operettszínház with Hanna Honthy, Kálmán Latabár and Andor Ajtay starred brought nearly 20 years of almost unbroken representation on the Budapest stage to an end. Thereafter, Eisemann was heard from only occasionally, contributing his last score in 1963, more than three decades after that first hit.

Eisemann was also active as a composer for the cinema, and his film scores included *Hippolyt, a lakáj*, *Lebegő szűz*, *Szerelemmel vádollak*, *Vadrózsa* and *A miniszter barátja*.

1929 **Miss Amerika** (László Szilágyi) Fővárosi Operettszínház 12 January
1930 **Alvinci huszárok** (Szilágyi) Kiraly Színház 9 April
1932 **Zsákbamacska** (Szilágyi) Pesti Színház 3 November
1933 **Egy csók és más semmi** (István Békeffy/Imre Halász) Magyar Színház 12 May
1934 **Vadvirág** (Imre Harmath/Ernő Andai) Andrássy-uti Színház 24 March
1934 **A cirkusz csillaga** (w Károly Komjáthy/László Bus Fekete) Vigszinház 22 June
1934 **Ma éjjel szabad vagyok** (Andor Szenes/János Vaszary) Andrássy-uti Színház 25 October
1934 **Én és a kisöcsém** (Szilágyi) Fővárosi Operettszínház 21 December
1935 **Ezüstmenyasszony** (Szilágyi) Royal Színház 20 December

1936 **Meseáruház** (Szilágyi) Vígszinház/Fővárosi Operett-szinház 11 April
1937 **Egy vidám éjszaka** (János Vaszary) Magyar Színház 15 May
1937 **Gólyaszanatórium** (Szilágyi, Kellér) Márkus Park Színház 25 June
1937 **Macskazene** (Gyula Halász, Károly Kristóf) Szeged 18 December
1938 **A hölgy hozzám tartozik** (Pierre Veber ad István Békeffy, Adorján Stella) Andrássy Színház 21 January
1938 **Kávé habbal** (Harmath/Pál Barabás) Royal Színház 30 November
1940 **Handa-banda** revised *Macskazene* Fővárosi Operettszinház 26 January
1940 **Tokaji aszu** (Szilágyi) Magyar Színház 15 March
1940 **Angóramacska** (Szilágyi) Vígszinház 26 April
1940 **XIV-ik René** (Zsolt Harsányi, István Zágon) Vigszinház 14 September
1940 **Fiatalság-bolondság** (G Halász) Fővárosi Operettszinház 25 October
1942 **Leány a talpán** (G Molnár) Royal Színház 28 March
1943 **Egy boldog pesti nyár** (w Denes Buday, Szabolcs Fényes/Szilágyi, Attila Orbók) Fővárosi Operettszinház 14 April
1943 **Fekete Péter** (Gyula Somogyi) Vigszinház 4 June
1944 **Mesebeszéd** (Béla Mátrai Betegh/Somogyi) Vigszinház 28 September
1944 **Őfelsége a mama** (Gábor Vaszary) Magyar Színház 29 April
1946 **Szabotál a gólya** (revised *Gólyaszanatórium*) Művesz Színház 11 May
1947 **Ő vagy Ő?** (Zágon, Vaszary) Fővárosi Operettszinház 27 September
1958 **Bástyasétány 77** (László Dalos/Géza Baróti) Lujza Blaha Színház 11 April
1959 **A princesszin** (Ferenc Felkai) Győr 6 November
1962 **Nőgyűlölő** (Sándor Balázs/László Sólyom) Szolnok 2 February
1963 **Annabál** (Baróti) Miskolc 23 December
1964 **Fel a kezekkel** revised *Leány a talpán* (László Tabi/János Erdődy) Pécs 18 November

Plate 84. **Az eleven ördög**: *Buxom little Klára Küry was the 'living devil' of the famous Hungarian operett's title. But the Vicomte de Letorrières was a devil only with the women.*

AZ ELEVEN ÖRDÖG Comic opera in 3 acts by Ántal Deréki taken from *Le Vicomte de Letorrières* by Jean-François Bayard and Philippe Dumanoir. Music by József Konti. Budai Színkör, Budapest, 8 August 1884.

One of the most successful of 19th-century Hungarian operetts, *Az eleven ördög* (the living devil) was based on Bayard and Dumanoir's highly popular play *Le Vicomte de Letorrières*, the subject for a number of other comic operas and musical plays throughout Europe.

'The living devil' is the young and penniless Vicomte de Letorrières (Emilia Pajor). Although he has not been spared by the fates of financial fortune, another kind of fortune has been granted him – the Vicomte has enormous charm, a charm that operates on both women and men alike. One day it seems that his days of pauperdom are at an end – he has received a fine inheritance. But it is not that easy. There is another claimant, the baron Tibulle de Hugéon (Aurél Follinusz). The Vicomte sets out to beat his rival to the jackpot and events rise to a duel in which our hero is wounded. But Letorrières turns the wound to his advantage – his recovery is spent in the house of the Prince Soubise (Jenő Balassa), where the Princess (Amalia Ebergényiné) soon falls under the spell of the young man. Soubise is the head of the court which is to decide the way of the will, and it is not surprising that Letorrières ends the evening triumphant.

Az eleven ördög was a hit on its production at the Budai Színkör and it played 50 performances in the repertoire there during its first 12 months (50th: 7 August 1885) before moving into the Népszínház 16 December 1885 with Lujza Blaha starred as Letorrières alongside Szilágyi (Hugéon), Szathmári (Soubise) and Ebergényiné repeating her original rôle, and with Vidor Kassai (Pomponiusz), József Németh (Desperrières), Zsofi Csatay (Veronika) and Célia Margó (Marianne) in support. Once again it was a considerable hit, played 54 times and was revived there 19 February 1897, with Klára Küry as the Vicomte, and again on 31 March 1900 when Margit Ámon took up the title-rôle alongside Imre Szirmai (Hugéon), Vince Horváth (Soubise) and Siposné (the Princess).

ELLE EST À VOUS Opérette in 3 acts by André Barde. Music by Maurice Yvain. Théâtre des Nouveautés, Paris, 22 January 1929.

One of Yvain's longest-running modern musical comedies, *Elle est à vous* was presented under the management of Benoît-Léon Deutsch at the Nouveautés, where it had an 11-month run, but for some reason it failed to endure into revivals in the manner of *Ta bouche*, *Pas sur la bouche* or *Là-haut*, or to travel as others of its contemporaries did.

A cast headed by Gabrielle Ristori ('Son Doudou'), Eliane de Creus ('Jeune fille', 'Dans une guingette'),

Urban ('Elle est à vous') and Pierre Darmant ('Honolulu, w Mlle de Creus), was topped by the comedian Milton who made a nationwide hit out of the nonsensical, slangy 'Pouèt-Pouèt' and joined Suzanne Dehelly in the brightly suggestive duet 'En auto'.

ELLINGER, Desirée (b Manchester, 7 October 1895; d London, 30 April 1951).

Born in Britain and educated in Brussels and Paris, Miss Ellinger led a theatrical career of nearly 20 years which was even more international than her early years. She first appeared in opera, starring with the Beecham Opera Company as Nedda (*Pagliacci*) at 21 and, in the years that followed, was seen with them as Butterfly, Marguerite, Susanna, Blondchen and Micaëla. She made her first appearances in the light musical theatre when she played Clairette, opposite Amy Augarde's Lange, in a 1919 revival of *La Fille de Madame Angot*, as Sylvia in the light opera *Sylvia's Lovers* (1919) and in revue at the London Hippodrome.

She subsequently toured in a third-rate piece called *The Early Girl* (1923) and as Sylva Varescu in *Die Csárdásfürstin* (1924) and appeared in the starring rôles of the short-lived Spanish musical *The First Kiss* (1924, Mariposa) and the even briefer Friml *Sometime* (1925, Enid Vaughan) in London. The last failure had its sunny side, however, when she was hurried from a subsequent engagement in Boston to New York to succeed Mary Ellis in the title-rôle of the same composer's *Rose Marie*. She won considerable publicity from the fact that this dash was bravely accomplished in an open-cockpit biplane. She remained in America to star in a third Friml piece, *The Wild Rose* (1926, Princess Elise), in Romberg's *Cherry Blossoms* (1927, O Yuki San), and *Kiss Me* (1927, Doris Durant Dodo), adding three more to her impressive collection of lead rôles in flop shows.

Things looked up, however, when she changed country again and appeared as Julie in the Paris production of *Show Boat* (*Mississippi*), but the spectacular *Silver Wings* (1930, Inez) at London's Dominion Theatre gave her her only satisfactory West End run. Her last appearances on the musical stage were in another large-scale failure, *Eldorado* (1930, Elvira), as Orestes in C B Cochran's extravagant, stellar production of a vandalized *La Belle Hélène* (*Helen!*)

Plate 85. **Desirée Ellinger** *starred in plenty of flops: London's El Dorado was one of them.*

in 1932, and as Heart's Desire in the short-lived 1935 revival of *The Rose of Persia*.

ELLIOTT, Madge [ELLIOTT, Leah Madeleine] (b Kensington, London, 12 May 1896; d New York, 8 August 1955). Cool, tall, dancing ingénue who partnered Cyril Ritchard in series of musicals in Britain and Australia.

Brought up in Australia, Miss Elliott appeared there first as a chorus dancer and later a principal dancer in such musicals as *High Jinks*, *Tonight's the Night* (Mimi), *So Long, Letty*, *Canary Cottage*, *You're in Love*, *Oh, Lady! Lady!!*, then moved through supporting rôles to progressively larger ones in *A Night Out* (Victorine), *Yes, Uncle* (Nichette), *The Girl in the Taxi* (Jacqueline), *Going Up*, *Kissing Time*, *The Cabaret Girl* (Flick Morgan), *Whirled into Happiness* (Delphine de Lavallière) and *Mary* (Madeleine).

In 1925 she went to Britain and she and her Australian dance partner, Cyril Ritchard, appeared together in the revue *Bubbly* and in the earliest cabaret in Britain, the Midnight Follies at the Metropole Hotel, before being cast by Laddie Cliff in the musical comedy *Lady Luck* (1927, Patience) at the Carlton. The elegant dancing act performed by this tall, graceful pair was a considerable success and they were built into leading dance-and-song rôles as the romantic hero and heroine of the Cliff musicals *So This is Love* (1928, Pamela Stuart), *Love Lies* (1929, Valerie St Clair), *The Love Race* (1930, Mary Dale) and *The Millionaire Kid* (1931, Gloria Devenish).

Returning to Australia, they performed in another Cliff musical *Blue Roses* (Susan Winslow), in *Hold My Hand*, *Our Miss Gibbs*, *The Quaker Girl*, *Roberta* (Stephanie), *Gay Divorce* (Mimi, with the Astaire–Luce dances), the inexhaustible *High Jinks* and the Australian musical *Blue Mountain Melody* (1934) before making a second trip to Britain.

Many of their subsequent appearances were in revue or in light comedy, but in 1943 Miss Elliott appeared at His Majesty's Theatre in the title-rôle of *The Merry Widow*, with Ritchard as Danilo, and in 1945 the two paired at the head of a production of *Tonight at 8.30* in Australia.

ELLIS, Mary [ELSAS, Mary] (b New York, 15 June 1900). Star soprano and actress who introduced a handful of important musical leads on Broadway and in London.

Miss Ellis began her career as an 18-year-old operatic singer at the Metropolitan Opera House where she appeared in the first performances of Puccini's triptych, playing a young nun in *Suor Angelica*, in Albert Wolff's *The Blue Bird* as the boy Myltyl, and as Siebel, Lauretta, the tsarevitch and Gianetta (*L'Elisir d'Amore*) alongside such artists as Chaliapine, Caruso, de Luca, Jeritza and Farrar. After three years she left the operatic world to venture into the straight theatre, but a rôle in which she had to perform a Victor Herbert song brought her to the notice of Arthur Hammerstein and, in 1924, she was hired to create the title-rôle of the Oscar Hammerstein/Rudolf Friml *Rose Marie* ('Indian Love Call').

She left the musical after a year to return to the dramatic theatre and for nearly ten years sang no more, until C B Cochran hired her to play the rôle of the prima donna Frieda Hatzfeld in the London production of *Music in the Air* (1933). Film commitments almost led her to have to turn down her next London singing rôle, but Ivor Novello

405

was willing to wait for her availability, and she returned to London in 1935 to create the star part of Militza Hájos in *Glamorous Night* ('Glamorous Night', 'Fold Your Wings'), the first of Novello's series of Drury Lane musicals. In 1939 she returned again for the best of that series, *The Dancing Years* ('I Can Give You the Starlight', 'Waltz of My Heart', 'My Dearest Dear'), and in 1943 a third time for the less successful *Arc de Triomphe*, but, in between, she occupied herself in comedy, drama and film.

She subsequently added television to these credits, and played in only one further musical, Noël Coward's adaptation of *Lady Windermere's Fan* as *After the Ball* (1954). Coward wrote the rôle of Mrs Erlynne with Miss Ellis in mind, but the Miss Ellis he had in mind was the star of *The Dancing Years*. Fifteen years on she was no longer vocally equipped for its demands and *After the Ball* was not a success.

Autobiography: *Those Dancing Years* (John Murray, London, 1982)

ELLIS, Vivian (b London, 9 October 1904).

The grandson of pianist and composer Julia Woolf, whose comic opera *Carina* had been mounted in the West End in 1888, Ellis also started his musical career studying classical piano. He began composing songs whilst in his mid-teens, and contributed to a number of revues (*The Curate's Egg*, *Yoicks!*, *The Looking Glass*), before scoring his first notable success with the basic score for the revue *By the Way*. He wrote the songs for the revues *Palladium Pleasures* and *Will o'the Whispers*, and contributed interpolated numbers to such other West End revues as *Still Dancing*, *Cochran's Revue of 1926*, *Blue Skies*, *Clowns in Clover* and *Charlot's Revue of 1928*, to the imported musicals *Mercenary Mary*, *Just a Kiss*, *Kid Boots*, the remake of Oscar Straus's *Riquette* as *My Son John*, *The Girl Friend* and *A Yankee at the Court of King Arthur*, and the British-made *Merely Molly*, but his earliest full-scale musicals were not mounted in London, but on the touring circuits.

It was one of these, however, Julian Wylie's production of *Mr Cinders* ('Spread a Little Happiness', 'On the Amazon') which gave him his biggest success to date when a London transfer topped 500 nights at the London Hippodrome and the Adelphi Theatre and the show ultimately proved itself one of the classics of its period. Thereafter, Ellis kept up a heavy schedule of writing for the West End, both for revue (contributions to *The House That Jack Built*, *Cochran's Revue of 1930*, *Folly to Be Wise*, *Over the Page*, *Please!*, *The Town Talks*, *Floodlight*) and, more particularly, for musical comedy. In three seasons he wrote much of the score for the Sophie Tucker vehicle *Follow a Star* ('If Your Kisses Can't Hold the Man You Love'), for the short-lived *Little Tommy Tucker*, the Drury Lane military spy epic *The Song of the Drum*, the Gaiety musical *Blue Roses*, Jack Buchanan and Elsie Randolph's *Stand Up and Sing*, and the musical version of *The Brass Bottle*, *Out of the Bottle*, often tied in with the fashionably (if rarely fashionable) American composers whom London managers of the period seemed unwilling to do wholly without – Ted Shapiro, Arthur Schwartz, Oscar Levant, Phil Charig. However, it was when he was left to supply the entire score for another touring piece, *Jack and Jill*, that Ellis scored another musical comedy hit. Whilst his much-admired revue *Streamline*, with its one-act parody of Gilbert and Sullivan, *Perseverance*, played at the Palace, the retitled *Jill*

Darling gave the composer a second simultaneous success at the Saville Theatre ('I'm on a See-Saw').

Success came again when he was teamed with a hydra of imported writers for the Bobby Howes–Cicely Courtneidge show *Hide and Seek*, with the Hippodrome naval piece *The Fleet's Lit Up* and the Gaiety Theatre comedy show *Running Riot* and, most lengthily, with another piece for Miss Courtneidge, *Under Your Hat*, which gave the composer his second 500-performance-plus run in the West End.

When Ellis returned to the theatre after the Second World War, he teamed again with his *Streamline* collaborator, writer A P Herbert, and the lightweight dancing shows of the previous decades gave place to a some more romantic works. The first of these, *Big Ben*, suffered from an inept libretto, but the second, *Bless the Bride*, turned out to be Ellis's most successful work of all. A pretty period comic operetta full of memorable melodies ('Ma Belle Marguerite', 'A Table for Two', 'I Was Never Kissed Before', 'This is My Lovely Day' etc) it hit the West End around the same time as the London productions of *Oklahoma!* and *Annie Get Your Gun* and held its place, alongside those two blockbusting successes, at the head of London's musical hits until Cochran, in a curious piece of managerial miscalculation, took it off to mount Ellis and Herbert's next collaboration, an oddly Ruritanian piece called *Tough at the Top*. It did not succeed.

Ellis composed a merry mock-medieval score for a musical version of J B Fagan's hit play *And So to Bed*, and collaborated one more time with Herbert on a musical version of the author's novel *The Water Gipsies*, both with some degree of success (particularly from the musical portion) before taking his distance from the musical stage. His last new show, an adaptation of Wilde's *The Importance of Being Earnest*, originally intended for a West End staging by C B Cochran but subsequently put aside, was given showings later at America's Bucks County Playhouse, at Australia's Independent Theatre and, in England, at Coventry.

Ellis supplied the music and/or songs for several British films, including Jack Hulbert and Cicely Courtneidge's *Jack's the Boy* ('The Flies Crawled Up the Window'), the original *The Water Gipsies*, *Falling for You* and *Public Nuisance Number 1*.

Throughout his career, in the face of important transatlantic influences, Ellis maintained an elegant light musical style of some class which, if it did not produce as many obvious hit numbers as were achieved by some other writers, nevertheless established him as the most important and most appreciable composer of the British musical stage in the musical comedy years between the wars before he sealed his career with *Bless the Bride* in the late 1940s.

A compilation show based on Ellis's works (*Spread a Little Happiness*, ad Sheridan Morley) was produced at London's King's Head Theatre Club (14 January 1992) and later given a West End season (Whitehall Theatre, 29 June 1992).

1927 **The Grass Widow** (William Helmore/Lauri Wylie) Bristol 8 August
1927 **The Other Girl** (Helmore, Collie Knox/Wylie) Bristol 17 October
1927 **Peg o' Mine** (w Phil Charig et al/Desmond Carter/Fred Jackson) Sunderland 31 October

1929 **Mr Cinders** (w Richard Myers/Greatrex Newman, Clifford Grey) Adelphi Theatre 11 February

1930 **Follow a Star** (w others/Douglas Furber, Dion Titheradge) Winter Garden Theatre 17 September

1930 **Little Tommy Tucker** (Carter, Caswell Garth, R P Weston, Bert Lee) Daly's Theatre 19 November

1931 **Song of the Drum** (w Herman Finck/Carter, Fred Thompson, Guy Bolton) Theatre Royal, Drury Lane 9 January

1931 **Blue Roses** (Carter, Garth) Gaiety Theatre 31 January

1931 **Stand Up and Sing** (w Charig/Furber, Jack Buchanan) London Hippodrome 5 March

1932 **Out of the Bottle** (ex- *If It Happened to You*) (w Oscar Levant/Grey, Thompson) London Hippodrome 11 June

1934 **Jill Darling** (ex- *Jack and Jill*) (Carter, Marriott Edgar) Saville Theatre 19 December

1936 **Going Places** (Bolton, Thompson) Savoy Theatre 8 October

1937 **Hide and Seek** (w Sam Lerner, Al Goodhart, Al Hoffman/Bolton, Thompson, Furber) London Hippodrome 14 October

1938 **The Fleet's Lit Up** (Bolton, Thompson, Lee) London Hippodrome 17 August

1938 **Running Riot** (Furber, Bolton, Firth Shephard) Gaiety Theatre 31 August

1938 **Under Your Hat** (Archie Menzies, Arthur Macrae, Jack Hulbert) Palace Theatre 24 November

1946 **Big Ben** (A P Herbert) Adelphi Theatre 17 July

1947 **Bless the Bride** (Herbert) Adelphi Theatre 26 April

1949 **Tough at the Top** (Herbert) Adelphi Theatre 15 July

1951 **And So to Bed** (J B Fagan) New Theatre 17 October

1955 **The Water Gipsies** (Herbert) Winter Garden Theatre 31 August

1957 **Half in Earnest** (Ellis) Bucks County Playhouse, New Hope, Pa 17 June

Autobiography: *I'm on a See-saw* (Michael Joseph, London, 1953)

ELLISON, Sydney (b 1870; d London, 21 December 1930). Director and choreographer who found fame with his staging of *Florodora*.

Originally a performer, Ellison appeared in the West End as a replacement in *An Artist's Model* (1895) and as the original George Grimston in *The Geisha* (1896), but he quickly found his métier as a director and choreographer when he reproduced George Edwardes's production of *An Artist's Model* for its Broadway season (1895). He subsequently mounted *L'Amour mouillé* for Tom Davis, and had a major success when he directed and choreographed the same producer's original production of *Florodora* (1899), creating the famous 'Tell Me, Pretty Maiden' double sextet routine which was sensationally reproduced in America, France and the colonies. He followed this up with another personal triumph when his Champagne Dance from *The Silver Slipper* scored an enormous Broadway success inside a far from unsuccessful show.

His services, thereafter, were much in demand by managers and he staged a long list of musicals over the next decade including *My Lady Molly* (1902), *The Medal and the Maid* (1903) for Davis, *The Orchid* (1903) and *The Spring Chicken* (1905) at the Gaiety Theatre, *The Gay Lord Vergy* (1905), *See See* (1906), *Two Naughty Boys* (1907), *Nelly Neil* (1907), *King of Cadonia* (1908), *The Belle of Brittany* (1908), *The Persian Princess* (1909) and *The Mountaineers* (1909), working for virtually all the top London managements. He visited America to stage *He Came from Milwaukee* (1910) for the Shuberts, *The Girl and the Kaiser*

86. **Sydney Ellison**: *The man who invented 'Tell Me, Pretty Maiden'.*

(1911, *Die Förster-Christl*), *My Best Girl* (1912) for Henry Harris and *The Lilac Domino* (1914) for Andreas Dippel, and after spending much of the war in the army continued to work through the later 1910s, mounting *Flora* for André Charlot in 1918, and the highly successful London musical, *Kissing Time*, in 1919. Soon after, however, victim of a stroke and a cab accident, he slipped from view and fell upon hard times. In his last years he lived in one room, worked as a walk-on, and, in spite of a benefit mounted for him in 1925, ended in the workhouse where his last illness claimed him.

It was said that Ellison 'revolutionized the whole style of musical comedy chorus work by putting action and special rhythm into it' but, even if the word 'revolutionized' carries things altogether too far, there is little doubt that his dance-based work, as displayed to such effect in *Florodora*, was another stage on the way from the static and elegantly strolling choruses of previous decades to a more active kind of musical comedy staging.

Ellison was married to the favourite actress and singer, Kate Cutler.

ELSIE, Lily [COTTON, Lily Elsie] (b Wortley, 8 April 1886; d London, 16 December 1962). Lovely young vocalist who shot to stardom as Britain's 'Merry Widow'.

Lily Elsie worked as a child performer in pantomime and comedy, in variety as 'Little Elsie', and made her first appearances in musical comedy touring, at 16, first in *The Silver Slipper* and then in *Three Little Maids*. She was first seen in London when, at 17, she took over the soprano rôle of Princess Soo-Soo in *A Chinese Honeymoon* at the old

Strand Theatre. Thereafter she worked exclusively for George Edwardes, rising swiftly and surely up the playbill. She succeeded to Delia Mason's soubrette rôle of Gwenny Holden in *Lady Madcap*, toured as Lady Patricia in *The Cingalee*, took a tiny rôle in *Les P'tites Michu* (1905, Madame du Tertre) and teamed up with Zena Dare and Gabrielle Ray as Willie Edouin's daughters in *The Little Cherub* (1906, Lady Agnes Congress), until the family was reduced to just two in a rewrite and she moved on to appear in a supporting rôle in the same management's *See See* instead (1906, Humming Bird).

Owing to the unavailability of Gertie Millar, she created the title-rôle in *The New Aladdin* (1906, Lally) at the Gaiety, but she was removed when Miss Millar was ready to come back to the theatre. Edwardes more than made it up to the young singer, however, when he cast her in a much more suitable rôle as the heroine of *The Merry Widow* (1907), a rôle which made her into a major star. She followed up in the starring rôles of *The Dollar Princess* (1909, Alice), *A Waltz Dream* (1911, Franzi) and *The Count of Luxembourg* (1911, Angèle Didier), as the passion for the Viennese Operette reached its peak in London, before retiring to marriage in 1911.

She returned to the musical stage in *Pamela* (1917, Pamela) and once more in *The Blue Train* (1927, Eileen Mayne) but was unable to find again the success of her five years as Edwardes's Daly's Theatre star.

ELSSLER, Fanny   *see* DIE TÄNZERIN FANNY ELSSLER

THE EMERALD ISLE, or The Caves of Carric-Cleena   Comic opera in 2 acts by Basil Hood. Music by Arthur Sullivan and Edward German. Savoy Theatre, London, 27 April 1901.

Arthur Sullivan's last work, *The Emerald Isle*, was written in collaboration with the generally accepted successor of W S Gilbert, Basil Hood, with whom the composer had already written the successful *The Rose of Persia*. However, the piece was left uncompleted at Sullivan's death, and Carte asked Edward German, who had until that time never written for the comic opera stage, to undertake the task of filling out Sullivan's sketches and composing the missing parts of the music. Before the production got to the stage, Carte, too, had died and *The Emerald Isle* was mounted by his widow, Helen, as a virtual postscript to the heyday of the Carte régime and the Savoy Theatre.

Hood's libretto was not as good as his previous one. The Lord Lieutenant of Ireland (Jones Hewson) is anglicizing the Irish, sending out elocutionists, including one Professor Bunn (Walter Passmore), to take the begorrahs out of the local speech. Would-be patriot Terence O'Brien (Robert Evett) already speaks English, for he has been brought up in London, where he has – o, incongruity! – fallen in love with Rosie Pippin (Isabel Jay), who is none other than the Lord Lieutenant's daughter. Terence hides out in the reputedly haunted caves of Carric-Cleena, and soubrette Molly (Louie Pounds) impersonates the fairy of the place to keep away the superstitious British soldiers who would capture him. Henry Lytton played Pat Murphy, the hereditary blind fiddler, Rosina Brandram was the wife of the Lord Lieutenant, to whom she spoke only in blank verse, and Robert Rous the family chaplain, Dr Fiddle,

D D, each of whom had their moments as the plot wound its way towards the union of Rosie and Terence.

The show's songs were often (and, undoubtedly, intentionally) reminiscent of the earlier Gilbert and Sullivan works, but none the worse for that, as Passmore sang about the clichés of on- and off-stage Irishness in 'The Popular Type of Pat', and the Lord Lieutenant delivered his curriculum vitae in song ('At an Early Stage of Life') and joined his wife and chaplain in a expository piece reminiscent of the introduction of the Plaza Toroi in *The Gondoliers*. Bunn pattered through a traditional comic song ('Oh, the Age in Which We're Living') and Terence got romantic over his first meeting with Rosie (''Twas in Hyde Park Beside the Row') in similar strains.

The Emerald Isle ran for 205 performances at the Savoy, during which time William Greet took over control of the theatre and the company. At the end of the London run, he sent the piece on tour, whilst Jefferson de Angelis (also Bunn) and R H Burnside put together a production for Broadway in which John Dudley (Terence), Kate Condon (Molly), Josephine Knapp (Rosie), Charles Dungan (Lord Lieutenant) and Bernard Sullivan (Pat) joined the producer/star for 50 performances in New York and more on the road. The show was subsequently played in Australia, where J C Williamson's production featured George Lauri (Bunn), Florence Young (Rosie), Reginald Roberts (Terence), Carrie Moore (Molly) and Harold Thorley (Lieutenant), and on other English-language stages, but it eventually found its place rather as a concert piece with choral societies, than as a revivable comic opera.

USA: Herald Square Theater 1 September 1902; Australia: Her Majesty's Theatre, Melbourne 17 March 1903
Recording: complete (Pearl)

EMMET, J[oseph] K[lein]   (b St Louis, Mo, 13 March 1841; d Cornwall, NY, 15 January 1891). Celebrated star of the 'Fritz' series of comico-weepie-melodramas with songs which delighted America, in particular, for a generation.

From beginnings in vaudeville and minstrelsy, latterly as a 'Dutch'-accented comic, Emmet moved into the theatre, where he made his fame in the character of the broken-Englished, curly-headed Fritz in the sentimental comedy-melodrama *[The Adventures of] Fritz, Our Cousin German* (1870). As Fritz pursued the search for his long-lost sister, battled the villainous Colonel Crafton and conducted his courtship of pretty Dutch Katarina, there were numerous opportunities for him to pause, unhitch the guitar from his back, and deliver a song. One of these songs, a Lullaby written and composed by the actor himself, became one of the most loved show songs of its time.

Emmet played Fritz for the rest of his life, the original play being switched about, expanded and altered with alternative or additional scenes, songs or musical specialities on the harmonica (five variations on 'Home, Sweet Home') or the fiddle, as it was taken round and round America by its star. In 1872 he took it as far afield as London's Adelphi Theatre in a 'London version', a couple of years later, with considerable success, he travelled his show to Australia, and in 1878 he played it again on Broadway in a 'new' version. He also tried a couple of other pieces on the same lines before his American audiences – *Carl the Fiddler* (1871), *Max, the Merry Swiss*

Boy (1873) – and introduced Australians to *Jan, the New German, or the Swiss Avalanche* (1875) and H J Byron's *Phil the Foundling* (1875), but without the same success. He inevitably returned to *Fritz, Our Cousin German*, before switching to a series of soi-disant sequels, beginning with the most durable (the original apart), *Fritz in Ireland* (1879), which allowed Emmet to sing some Irish songs and, of course, a lullaby, and continuing with *Fritz Among the Gipsies* (1882) in which he introduced another song, 'Sweet Violets', which would become a long-lived standard, *Fritz the Bohemian* (1884) and *Fritz in a Madhouse* (1889).

Hugely popular wherever he went, Emmet was the most successful of the many purveyors of the unsophisticated 'sensation-and-songs' pieces which for many years proved enormous favourites in the provincial cities and villages of America, Britain and the English-speaking colonies, and he and his character and material became the prototypes for many subsequent performers and plays in the same vein.

EMNEY, Fred (b London, 5 March 1865; d London, 7 January 1917). Character actor on the British musical and straight stages.

A nephew of the great comedian Arthur Williams, Emney originally worked in an accountant's office, but at 20 he joined a Gaiety Theatre road company, making his first appearance in the burlesque *The Forty Thieves* (Cassim) and continuing in such extravaganzas as *Ariel* and *Aladdin*. He toured in drama and farce (including Monkhouse's musical *Larks*) and made his first London musical appearance in the Jubilee curtain-raiser *Jubilation* before going on tour in Williams's famous role of Lurcher in *Dorothy*. Thereafter, he mixed musical and comedy work, sometimes in the West End (Jacques d'Arc in *Joan of Arc*, *The Baroness*, *Jaunty Jane Shore*, *Great Caesar*, *All Abroad*, *The Yashmak*, *Les Merveilleuses*, *The Antelope*) and more often on the road (*My Sweetheart*, *Captain Thérèse*, *Fun on the Bristol*, *A Gaiety Girl*, *La Mascotte*, *Madame Favart*, *The Gay Grisette*, *The Telephone Girl*, *Regina B.A*, *The Girl from Kays*, *Véronique* etc). His best new rôles in London were the burglar, Posh Jenkins, in *Lady Madcap* (1904), Nervy Nat in *The Gay Gordons* (1907) and the blackmailing sleeping car attendant, Cornelius Scrop, in *The Girl in the Train* (1910). Emney died as the result of an on-stage accident at the London Opera House, where he was appearing as Baroness de Bounce in the Christmas pantomime of *Cinderella*.

His son, who also worked as **Fred EMNEY** (b London, 12 February 1900; d Bognor Regis, 25 December 1980), began a career on the stage as a teenager and toured in musicals in Britain prior to going to America, where he remained throughout the 1920s. On returning, he appeared in *Mr Whittington* (1934) and *The Flying Trapeze* (1935) and, with his obese figure, flourishing jowls and eyeglass as a trademark, soon became established as a favourite character in musical comedy, starring in a famous team with Leslie Henson and Richard Hearne in a series of Gaiety Theatre productions (*Seeing Stars*, *Swing Along*, *Going Greek*, *Running Riot*). He supported Jack Buchanan in *It's Time to Dance*, and appeared top-billed at the Saville in 1945 in *Big Boy*, a musical tailored to his own considerable measure. He had a big success as the 'baby' in *Blue for*

a Boy and collaborated on the writing of a second musical vehicle for himself, *Happy as a King* (1954). It proved, like his previous solo star effort, less than a success.

He appeared in the film of the musical *Oliver!* and of the de-musicalized *Lock Up Your Daughters* and, in his seventies, toured as Erronius in *A Funny Thing Happened on the Way to the Forum*.

His sister, Joan Fred Emney, also appeared on the musical stage, notably as Mabel in the London production of *The Pajama Game*.

Biography: Fairlie, G: *The Fred Emney Story* (Hutchinson, London, 1960)

THE ENCHANTRESS Comic opera in 3 acts by Fred de Grésac and Harry B Smith. Lyrics by Harry B Smith. Music by Victor Herbert. New York Theater, New York, 19 October 1911.

Victor Herbert's *The Enchantress*, produced by Joseph Gaites in a spectacular staging, with a cast of 100, was played for only 72 New York performances in the Broadway season of 1911–12, but, even though it was not picked up for overseas productions, its career in the theatre was extended well beyond that by a profitable life on the American touring circuits.

Madame Fred de Grésac and Harry Smith's libretto used a familiar plot in the love-and-power genre, here set in the Ruritanian principality of Zergovia. The ambitious minister Ozir (Arthur Forrest) has his eyes on the throne of Prince Ivan (Hal Forde) and he determines to make use of the law forbidding a monarch to wed a commoner, to gain his ends. When the Prince is about to succeed to his throne, and needs to take a bride, Ozir convinces the seductive singer Vivien Savary (Kitty Gordon) to enchant the boy into a marriage. However, although she succeeds, she also falls in love with Ivan, and turns against Ozir. When it eventuates that Vivien is actually a little bit (sufficiently) royal, the happy ending is assured.

The tale of *The Enchantress* was illustrated by a shapely and attractive score entirely from the pen of Herbert, which profited greatly from not being disfigured by the unsuitable interpolations which were so liberally practised on imported shows. Herbert, not writing for a Fritzi Scheff here, tactfully kept his leger lines under control and Miss Gordon was only required to encompass an A in her principal solo and in her duo with the King, 'One Word from You', in which the lyrics (altogether better throughout than in many shows of the era) still showed traces of the libretto's original 'unhappy' ending, in which unroyal Vivien renounced her King for his own good.

The heroine's entrance song, 'The Land of My Own Romance', turned out to be the most appreciated item in the score, but otherwise the best numbers went to the supporting characters. There were comic songs for Vivien's Aunt Mamout (Hattie Arnold) and the head of the secret service (Ralph Riggs), and Nelly McCoy sang a little novelty number tracing the history of a melody ('That Pretty Little Song') as it went from its original composition around the world and ended up – oh, horror – being arranged into unrecognizableness by ragtime writers. However, it was Louise Bliss as a plump Princess insisting 'I Want to Be a Prima Donna' ('I want to be a peachy, screechy cantatrice ...'), giving as reference the fact that she is at least the same size as Tetrazzini, who had the comic gem of the evening. 'The Land of My Own Romance' got itself interpolated into a Broadway revival of *Sweethearts* in 1947, but it is 'I Want to Be a Prima Donna', re-discovered in recent years by sopranos and brought back to the concert and auditions stages, and even to record, which has proven the most enduring portion of the show.

The title *The Enchantress* had been previously used for a successful opera in 3 acts by Alfred Bunn, taken from a text by J H Vernoy de Saint-Georges, set to music by Michael Balfe, and introduced at the Theatre Royal, Drury Lane 14 May 1845, prior to productions in America and Australia.

UK: Ladbroke Hall (copyright performance) 9 October 1911

EN CHEMYSE Opérette-bouffe in 3 acts by Albert Willemetz and Cami. Music by Raoul Moretti. Théâtre des Bouffes-Parisiens, Paris, 7 March 1924.

The first stage musical by the newly popular songwriter, Raoul Moretti, *En chemyse* burlesqued the well-known story of the Burghers of Calais. *Phi-Phi* star Alice Cocéa, back in period costume as the heroine of the piece, gave several extra-light songs including 'Isoline, va dans la cuisine' whilst Dranem, dressed up in a medieval coat of mail in the chief comic rôle of Lahirette, told the tale of 'La girl et le homard'.

The piece aroused the ire of those who considered that the good burghers of Calais, though centuries dead and already the subject of several comic operas, should not be made fun of, but the merry burlesque with its dance-based score stayed on the bill for nearly three months, and set its composer on the road to more, and more successful, works.

ENCORE CINQUANTE CENTIMES Opérette in 3 acts by André Barde. Music by Henri Christiné and Maurice Yvain. Théâtre des Nouveautés, Paris, 17 September 1931.

Over a decade into the era of new-style French musical comedy, and in spite of the rise of a number of successful composers, the two who had started it all still remained at the top of the tree. For *Encore cinquante centimes*, producer Benoît-Léon Deutsch had the bright idea of bringing Christiné and Yvain together to collaborate on a score to a text by André Barde who was, with Willemetz, the most successful author of the genre.

The most popular musical comedian of the time, Dranem, starred as Hercule Boulot, a penniless circus strongman whisked off to the Balkan republic of Rouffionie to help the Queen, whose husband (José Sergy) prefers chasing butterflies, to continue the dynasty and thus save the country from the hands of the horrid Republican Prime Minister, Rapescu (Edmond Carlus). Gabrielle Ristori (Queen Stasia), soubrette Suzanne Dehelly (Boulot's girlfriend, Pirouette) and Edith Méra (Héléna Tubasek, a Rouffionian agent) provided the pulchritude and the singing voices for a delightful series of musical numbers of which Dranem contributed 'Avec les femmes', 'Je reviendrais demain matin' and 'Essayez donc' as well as the lively Parade duo 'Encore cinquante centimes' and 'L'amour est un plaisir vraiment doux' with Pirouette. The

King had a little piece explaining 'J'aime les papillons' which led naturally into a butterfly dance, and the Queen sang passionately of 'Le Sang de mes aïeux', which was eventually stirred up by a little 'Bonheur caché' with the handsome Brancomir (André Dupin), allowing Pirouette to reclaim her man unsullied ('Quand on n'a qu'un homme').

The combination of fun, tunes and top names proved a winning one, and the piece had a fine Paris run prior to touring and a production in Budapest (ad Jenő Heltai).

Hungary: Magyar Színház *A csodadoktor* 12 May 1934

ENDLICH ALLEIN Operette in 3 acts by A M Willner and Robert Bodanzky. Music by Franz Lehár. Theater an der Wien, Vienna, 30 June 1914.

An attractive Lehár score, which included a sung-through second act and which occasionally prefigured the style, if not the tone, of his later and more heftily romantic works, was set to a book which sent Dolly Doverland, a kookie American heiress (Mizzi Günther), mountain-climbing with a guide (Hubert Marischka) who turns out to be the amorous Baron Franz Hansen in disguise. The Theater an der Wien's top light-comedy team of Ernst Tautenhayn (Graf Willibald Splenningen) and Luise Kartousch (Tilly), as the offspring of the Graf Maximilian Splenningen (Paul Guttmann) and Gräfin Konstanze Dachau (Mizzi Schütz) respectively, provided a different weight of romance and the soubret music in parallel to the lyrical lovemaking.

Endlich allein did well enough through 115 performances at the Theater an der Wien, and a handful more at the Raimundtheater, to win a number of productions in areas where Germanic stage shows were not being boycotted, without ever becoming a real favourite. An American version (ad Edgar Smith, Joseph W Herbert), with John Charles Thomas as the Baron romancing Marguerite Namara, squeezed some additional numbers by Gaetano Merola and Darl Mac Boyle plus Benjamin Hapgood Burt's 'Some Little Bug is Going to Find You' into Lehár's rich score, and was compensated with a fine Broadway run of 180 performances. Zsolt Harsányi's Hungarian adaptation was performed at the Király Színház with rather less success.

The show was later revised and reproduced with considerably more success under the title of its principal waltz song, *Schön ist die Welt* (3 December 1930).

Hungary: Király Színház *Végre egyedül* 20 February 1915; USA: Shubert Theater *Alone at Last* 19 October 1915

ENGEL, Alexander (b Turocz-Neczpal, Hungary, 10 April 1868; d Vienna, 17 November 1940).

Hungarian-born journalist (sometime editor of the *Neuer Wiener Journal* and theatre correspondent for Berlin's *Klein Journal*), theatre critic, author and playwright, Engel had his first musical work, *Rhodope*, with a score by Hugo Felix, played at Carltheater and Theater des Westens (23 June 1900) without notable success. That success came, however, when he formed a writing team with Julius Horst and, although their initial musical piece, *Der Schätzmeister*, had only a disappointing 34-performance run at the Carltheater prior to an Hungarian production (*A Becsüs*), they turned out a series of often long-running comedies – several of which included some musical content – for the Raimundtheater (the highly successful *Die blaue Maus*, *Seine kleine Freundin*), the Bürgertheater (*Glück bei Frauen*, *Einheirat*), and for Munich and Berlin stages, whilst both simultaneously pursuing other collaborations. Engel paired at various times with such other successful authors as August Neidhart, Carl Lindau, Victor Léon, Leo Stein, Alfred Grünwald and Ralph Benatzky.

He did not have a success with his original libretti equivalent to that made with his plays, and although pieces such as Eysler's *Der junge Papa*, Benatzky's *Adieu Mimi* and *Pipsi* and Richard Fall's *Die Puppenbaronessen* did well enough, he did not find a musical hit to come up to the success of *Die blaue Maus*.

Die blaue Maus (Raimundtheater, 15 February 1908) was set to music in Austria by Ludwig Gruber, and again in America, under the title *The Little Blue Devil* (Central Theater 3 November 1919), where the libretto was manufactured by Harold Atteridge from Clyde Fitch's local adaptation of the play, and the songs provided by Harry Carroll, whilst Horst and Engel's hit play *Der Schrei nach dem Kind* (Theater in der Josefstadt, 7 May 1914) was used as the basis for the libretto to the Lehár/Jenbach Operette *Cloclo* (1924). In Hungary, unspecified Engel works were used as the bases for several musicals: *Rózsanyilás idején* (w Ernest Gettke) was presented as a musical comedy at the Budai Színkör (13 September 1902) as was *Marci* (w Horst) adapted by Adolf Mérei, and set to music by Alfréd Márkus (Budai Színkör 17 June 1916). *Toeff-Toeff* (Königliches Hoftheater, Berlin 6 February 1901 w Léon) in a version by Zsolt Harsányi was musicalized as *Özvegy kisasszony* by Ádorjan Ötvös (1 September 1916), a further unnamed Engel and Horst play, which seems to have been their 1903 *Der g'rade Michl*, served as the basis for the operett *Rézi* (Izsó Barna/Jenő Faragó, Árpád Abonyi Népszinház 16 September 1904) and America's Earl Carroll availed himself of an Engel and Stobitzer original when writing *The Love Mill* (1917).

1900 **Rhodope** (Hugo Felix) Carltheater 1 February
1904 **Der Schätzmeister** (Carl Michael Ziehrer/w Julius Horst) Carltheater 10 December
1906 **Der blaue Klub** (Karl Kappeller/w Horst) Theater am Gärtnerplatz, Munich 24 November
1909 **Der Ehemännerzug** (Kappeller/w Carl Lindau) Stadttheater, Nuremberg 14 November
1909 **Der Rodelbaron** (Fritz Fürst/w Horst) 2 scenes Apollotheater 1 January
1909 **Der junge Papa** (Edmund Eysler/w August Neidhart) 1 act Apollotheater 3 February
1910 **Miss Exzentrik** (Heinrich Reinhardt/w Armin Friedmann) 1 act Apollotheater 31 October
1911 **Der Liftboy** (Otto Weber) 1 act Hölle 1 March
1912 **Pariser Luft** (Martin Knopf/Louis Taufstein/w Horst) Luisen-Theater, Königsberg 22 June
1912 **Der Lockvogel** (Leo Ascher/w Horst) Walhalla-Theater, Wiesbaden 11 January
1913 **Die blaue Maus** (Ludwig Gruber/w Horst) Graben Kino 11 November
1913 **Die Bretteldiva** (Josef Snaga/w Rudolf Lothar) Stadttheater, Magdeburg 21 February
1917 **Die Puppenbaronessen** (Richard Fall/w Fritz Grünbaum) Apollotheater 1 September

1918 **Die tanzende Maske** (w Ralph Benatzky) Apollotheater 1 December
1921 **Pipsi** (Benatzky/w Horst) Wiener Bürgertheater 30 December
1921 **Die ewige Braut** (Hugo Hirsch) Volkstheater, Munich 2 March
1926 **Adieu Mimi** (Benatzky/w Horst) Johann Strauss-Theater 9 June

ENGLÄNDER, Ludwig (b Vienna, ?1851; d Far Rockaway, NY, 13 September 1914). Austrian-American composer who provided functional rather than memorable scores for a generation of Broadway shows.

Born in Vienna, Engländer left home in his late twenties and proceeded first to Paris and then, in 1882, to America. He became conductor at New York's German-language Thalia Theater, under Gustav Amberg's management, and his operetta *Der Prinz Gemahl*, written to a Viennese text by Julius Hopp and the Bohrmann–Riegen partnership, was staged there the following year. Played originally in German, it was later seen outside New York in English under the title *The Prince Consort*. His second composition, *1776*, written to a text by the brother of composer Karl Goldmark, was produced at the same theatre, briefly, early in 1884 with no less a star than Marie Geistinger and with the German Hans Junker playing a Red Indian. Less successful than the first, this, too, was ultimately seen in English, but not until more than a decade later when it was reworked under the title *A Daughter of the Revolution*. A third Operette to a German-language text, *Madelaine*, was produced in Hamburg. Englander (having abandoned his umlaut en route) subsequently became conductor at New York's Casino Theater but, after supplying George Lederer with much of the score for the successful revue, *The Passing Show* (1894), he gave up the conducting side of his work to concentrate on composing.

Over 20 years of subsequent writing he provided a steady stream of music for Broadway shows, both book musicals and revues (*A Round of Pleasure* etc), mostly as basic scores into which the comic artists and other stars of the day could interpolate individual numbers written by various popular songsmiths. In spite of providing music for stars of the popularity of Jefferson de Angelis, Francis Wilson, Sam Bernard, Eddie Foy, Blanche Ring, Fritzi Scheff, Marie Cahill, Anna Held and many others such, he did not ever succeed in composing a genuine hit show, although several of his pieces had reasonable touring lives. His most successful efforts were *The Little Corporal* (1898), played by Francis Wilson in America and subsequently produced in Vienna, and three further collaborations with *Little Corporal* author Harry B Smith – *The Rounders* (adapted from the Continental hit *Les Fêtards*), *The Strollers* (taken from another successful Continental piece, *Die Landstreicher*) and, most particularly, *The Casino Girl*, not adapted from anything but modelled closely on the Gaiety Theatre shows, which played both New York and London for respectable runs and was even briefly seen, in Hungarian, in Budapest.

Englander's longest Broadway runs came with *Miss Innocence*, in which Florenz Ziegfeld's magnificent production, built around Anna Held in the title-rôle, helped keep the show alight for 176 performances, and the 1899 spectacular extravaganza *The Man in the Moon* for which he contributed only part of the music (with Kerker and De Koven) and which again owed its run to its production values rather than its content.

In 1910 Englander returned to Vienna where (with his umlaut back on) he succeeded, over the next few years, in having a couple of short pieces and one full-length Operette produced. *Vielliebchen* was a little before its time. Although its brisk score was as waltz- and march-orientated as most European pieces, it apparently seemed disagreeably American to much of a town that had treated *The Belle of New York* as an agreeable novelty but which was not yet tuned to trans-Atlantic rhythms. *Vielliebchen* nevertheless succeeded in earning other productions in Europe following its brief Viennese run.

1883 **Der Prinz Gemahl** (*The Prince Consort*) (Julius Hopp, Bohrmann-Riegen) Thalia Theater 11 April (Ger), Wallack's Theater 4 June (Eng)

1884 **1776** (aka *Adjutant James*) (Leo Goldmark) Thalia Theater 26 February

1888 **Madelaine** (aka *Die Rose der Champagne*) (Karl Haufer) Carl-Schultze Theater, Hamburg 26 June

1893 **The Woman-King** revised score to Rudolf Aronson's *The Rainmaker of Syria* Newark, NJ 20 November

1895 **The Twentieth Century Girl** (Sydney Rosenfeld) Bijou Theater 25 January

1895 **A Daughter of the Revolution** revised *1776* (J Cheever Goodwin) Broadway Theater 27 May

1896 **The Caliph** (H B Smith) Broadway Theater 3 September

1896 **Half a King** (*Le Roi de carreau*) English version by H B Smith w new score Knickerbocker Theater 4 September

1897 **Gayest Manhattan** (H B Smith) Koster and Bial's Music Hall 22 March

1898 **The Little Corporal** (H B Smith) Broadway Theater 19 September

1899 **In Gay Paree** (Grant Stewart/ad Clay Greene) Casino Theater 20 March

1899 **The Man in the Moon** (w Gustave Kerker, Reginald De Koven/Stange, Louis Harrison) New York Theater 24 April

1899 **The Rounders** (*Les Fêtards*) American version by H B Smith with new score, Casino Theater 12 July

1900 **The Casino Girl** (H B Smith) Casino Theater 19 March

1900 **The Cadet Girl** (*Les Demoiselles de Saint-Cyriens*) American version by H B Smith, Goodwin w new score Herald Square Theater 25 July

1900 **The Monks of Malabar** (Goodwin) Knickerbocker Theater 14 September

1900 **The Belle of Bohemia** (H B Smith) Casino Theater 24 September

1901 **The Strollers** (*Die Landstreicher*) English version by H B Smith w new score Knickerbocker Theater 24 June

1901 **The New Yorkers** (Glen MacDonough/George V Hobart) Herald Square Theater 7 October

1902 **The Wild Rose** (H B Smith/Hobart) Knickerbocker Theater 5 May

1902 **Sally in Our Alley** (Hobart) Broadway Theater 29 August

1903 **The Jewel of Asia** (Frederick Ranken/H B Smith) Criterion Theater 16 February

1903 **The Office Boy** (*Le Jockey malgré lui*) English version by H B Smith w new score Victoria Theater 2 November

1904 **A Madcap Princess** (H B Smith) Knickerbocker Theater 5 September

1904 **The Two Roses** (Stanislaus Stange) Broadway Theater 21 November

1905 **The White Cat** (ad H B Smith) New Amsterdam Theater 2 November

1906 **The Rich Mr Hoggenheimer** (ad H B Smith) Wallack's Theater 22 October

1908 **Miss Innocence** (H B Smith) New York Theater 30 November

1911 **Vielliebchen** (Rudolf Österreicher, Carl Lindau) Venedig in Wien, Vienna 5 May

1912 **Kitty's Ehemänner** (Emil Kolberg, Fritz Lunzer) 1 act Hölle, Vienna 1 November

1914 **Madame Moselle** (Edward A Paulton) Shubert Theater 23 May

1914 **Seebaddrummel** (Schubert) 1 act Zirkus Schumann, Vienna 31 October

AN ENGLISH DAISY Musical comedy in 2 acts by Seymour Hicks. Music by Walter Slaughter. Royal County Theatre, Kingston, 11 August 1902.

Written for London, *An English Daisy* was eventually staged on the provincial circuits. Several love affairs, a disguised heiress, a couple of American low comics (Thomas E Murray, Will Spray), a marriage ceremony in a lion's cage and an unexceptional set of songs made up a show which introduced 15-year-old Zena Dare in the title-rôle in her first adult show. A second tour followed, but *An English Daisy* did not make it to London. In the current craze for British product, however, the show was taken up for Broadway by Weber and Fields. Rewritten by Edgar Smith, much re-musicked by expatriate Austrian composer Alfred Müller-Norden and others, and with Christie Macdonald, Templar Saxe, Charles Bigelow and Truly Shattuck heading the cast, it lasted 41 performances, winning notoriety only as one of the few British shows to have played Broadway without having reached London, and for introducing the first Broadway songs by a young composer named Jerome D Kern.

USA: Casino Theater 18 January 1904

L'ENLÈVEMENT DE LA TOLEDAD Opérette in 3 acts by Fabrice Carré. Music by Edmond Audran. Théâtre des Bouffes-Parisiens, Paris, 17 October 1894.

A welcome production for the Bouffes-Parisiens, where things had been going so poorly that bankruptcy seemed nigh, *L'Enlèvement de la Toledad* also once again gave Audran the kind of success that had, after so many years of major hits, for several seasons been avoiding him.

The La Toledad who was carried off in Fabrice Carré's libretto is a Spanish song-and-dancer (Juliette Simon-Girard) and her 'enlèvement' is not all that it might seem. The stockbroking Gaston (Charles Lamy) has romanced her and whisked her away from her extravagant mother, La Maracona (Rosine Maurel), her lover Antonio (Félix Huguenet), and a successful theatrical season solely so that the theatre she is playing will go broke, revenging him for a lost bet. Amorous and financial fortunes yo-yo up and down until the right pairings are (re-)established and the stock market has come good.

Audran's score was all that a vehicle should be. The star set things rolling with a habanera ('Je suis la Toledad'), had a letter song with Gaston's letter of intent ('Mes intentions, ma belle'), joined her 'captor' in a duo de l'enlèvement ('Un enlèvement c'est étonnant') and, in what became a celebrated duo, the third act 'Y'avait un arrêt à Dijon' with Antonio, with whom she had previously shared a duo espagnole in the second act. The soubrets of the evening had the best of the rest: Poulet (Barral) declaring his affiliations in a Chanson Naturaliste ('Le Verbe haut'), and then renouncing naturalism for symbolism before the end of the evening ('Je n'suis plus naturaliste'), whilst the Toledad's fellow actress, Mélie Cruchet (Mlle Burty), had her Couplets de la divette ('Je chant' d'un air embêté') and Germaine Gallois, in the rôle of the sculptural Baronne Trippmann had her moment with the couplets 'Faut être gentil'.

The show comfortably passed the 100-performance mark in a successful first Paris run of more than three solid months, and it was revived at the Théâtre des Menus-Plaisirs in 1896 before becoming an interminable touring vehicle for the prima donna Jenny Syril in the 1920s.

La Toledad also travelled widely, although without making any indelible marks. A German-language version (ad Victor Léon, Heinrich von Waldberg) was played in Vienna with Frln Virag as the Toledad, Viktoria Pohl-Meiser as Maracona and Karl Pfann as Tardivet, and later in Berlin with Franz Tewele and Frau Ferenczy heading her husband's troupe and in Prague. An Hungarian version (ad Béla J Fái, Emil Makai) mounted at the Népszinház with Klara Küry in the title-rôle played 17 times, an Italian version was played in Venice (11 May 1903), while an English version (ad Augustus Moore), produced in Britain at Windsor with Georgina Delmar and Roland Cunningham starring and the aged queen of the opéra-bouffe era, Emily Soldene, in the splendid rôle of La Maracona, was brought in to London's Palace Music Hall, only to be closed down by the law for playing a non-theatre venue.

Austria: Theater in der Josefstadt *Toledad* 10 October 1896; Germany: Carl-Schultze Theater, Hamburg 3 April 1897, Lessing-Theater, Berlin 17 April 1897; Hungary: Népszínház *Toledad* 24 May 1899; UK: Theatre Royal, Windsor 2 April 1903

ENLEVEZ-MOI!.. Opérette in 3 acts by Raoul Praxy and Henri Hallais. Lyrics by Pierre Varenne and Max Eddy. Music by Guy Gabaroche. Comédie Caumartin, Paris, 4 October 1930.

Enlevez-moi!.. was produced first at the Comédie Caumartin, under the management of Robert Gallois, with Eliane de Creus starring as Simone, the wife of the prefect of Issoudun, who diverts innocent young René Dargelle (Gabaroche) from his mineralogic studies for the space of three acts. Jean Devalde played best-friend Edgard Renaud, whose second thoughts over seducing the hitherto virtuous Simone in the privacy of his Parisian garçonnière, are the cause of the helpful René, deputized to cancel their culpable rendezvous, getting into his 'troubles'. Mary Richard was Edgard's interfering old nurse, Joséphine, Suzanne Préville was everything that the name of Lulu suggested, and Réda Caire was the exotic Prince Agka. The cast of 12 also included a dog.

Gabaroche's feather-light musical ('Ce n'est qu'un petit moment', 'J'hésite', 'Chagrin d'amour', Rondeau de Province, 'Je n'os'rais plus fair' ça!') was transferred to the Théâtre des Nouveautés where, with Jacqueline Francell, Christiane Dor, André Dupuis and the show's original director, Paul Villé, in its lead rôles and Réda Caire repeating as the Prince Agka, it completed a run of almost a year. It was later revived at the Folies-Wagram (13 January 1935) and again at the Théâtre Daunou (1947) as well as having a busy provincial life, proving itself in the process the most successful of Gabaroche's musical comedies.

A 1932 film version featured Mlle Francell alongside Roger Tréville, Arletty and Félix Oudart.

Film: 1932

ENRICO '61 Commedia musicale in 2 acts by Pietro Garinei and Sandro Giovannini. Music by Renato Rascel. Teatro Sistina, Rome, 23 February 1961.

A 'spettacolo patriottico' produced on the occasion of the centenary of the unification of Italy, giving star/composer/co-producer Rascel the opportunity to skip through the history of the past century with the help of a selection of hats, co-stars Clelia Matania and Gianrico Tedeschi, and what were apparently the first theatrical travellators seen in Italy. Following a Milan premiere, the show had a fine Rome run and two seasons of touring. The orchestrations of *Enrico '61* were by Enrico Morricone, soon to be known as Italy's most popular film composer.

Taken to Britain, where Garinei and Giovannini had earlier had a success with *When in Rome* (*Buona notte, Bettina*), and played there in an English version by Myers and Cass, it lasted but 86 West End performances.

UK: Piccadilly Theatre 3 July 1963; Germany: Staatsoperette, Dresden 20 October 1966
Recording: complete (RCA)

EPHRAIM, Lee (b Hopkinsville, Ky, 7 July 1877; d London, 26 September 1953). West End producer of many imported shows, and a series of successful new wartime musicals.

American Ephraim moved to Britain in 1909 and worked for a time as a theatrical agent, and then, between 1918 and 1926, in the office of producer Daniel Meyer (*The Street Singer*, *Rose Marie*, *Betty in Mayfair* etc). In 1926 he set up as a producing management on his own behalf and had his first success with the London version of *Sunny* mounted at the London Hippodrome the same year. In the late 1920s he also produced or co-produced the British productions of Broadway's *The Desert Song* (w Alfred Butt) and *Funny Face* as well as the less successful *Peggy-Ann* and *The Five o'Clock Girl* (w R H Gillespie), and initiated in London several new musicals with an American bent (*Blue Eyes* with a score by Kern, *Lady Mary* with music by Szirmai and Phil Charig).

In the 1930s he produced a version of the French musical *Toi c'est moi* as *The Gay Deceivers* with Charlotte Greenwood starred, the Robert Stolz *Venus in Seide*, which did not reach town, and other losers in *Rio Rita*, *Nina Rosa*, Rogers and Hart's *Heads Up* and *On Your Toes*, and the custom-made *Here's How* with George Robey, but he had markedly more success with *Hide and Seek* (w Moss' Empires) which presented Cicely Courtneidge and Bobby Howes together for the first and only time. He subsequently co-produced Miss Courtneidge's long-running vehicles *Under Your Hat*, *Full Swing* (w Tom Arnold), *Something in the Air* (w Arnold) and *Under the Counter* (w Emile Littler, Arnold).

He later produced several more original pieces including the Ann Ziegler–Webster Booth piece *Sweet Yesterday* (1945), the flop *The Nightingale* (1947) and the successful romantic musical *Carissima* (1949), alongside a continued touring schedule amongst which was included a stage version of the film musical *Waltz Time*.

ÉPOUSE-LA! Opérette in 3 acts by Pierre Veber. Music by Henri Hirschmann. Théâtre Fémina, Paris, 15 January 1923.

The high-living André Montrachet (Aimé Simon-Girard) and his cousin Nicolette (Germaine Webb) marry each other in order to please their rich aunt, Mme de Monbissac (Lyse Berty), but things go poorly and their respective replacement partners – Roger la Chambotte (M George) and the much-divorced Marcelline (Helène Beryll) – persuade them to divorce. However, the young lady of purchasable favours, Mlle Florise de Mézidon (Mlle Davia), who is hired to go through the motions as a professional co-respondent, does her job so curiously that the spouses end up happily reunited.

Veber's lively text and lyrics, which included a particularly jolly number for André, relating how his friend Philibert was encouraged to 'Va vit' rue Thérèse' where you can have 'tout ça pour cinq cents francs' in order to get himself caught in flagrante delicto and divorced, paired happily with Hirschmann's dance-rhythmic music. The ten-handed piece won a good run in André Gailhard's Paris production, a run which was followed by a tour in which Mlle Davia repeated the personal success she had won, in a rôle which appeared only in the very last part of the play, equipped with the saucy argot-laden 'J'ai les pieds en Valenciennes', alongside Lina Berny and Bartholomez.

ERDÉLYI, Mihály (b Szeged, 28 May 1895; d Budapest, 27 January 1979).

Actor, director, librettist and composer for the musical stage, the musically self-taught Erdélyi began his theatrical career, as a performer and writer, after wartime service in the navy. His earliest ventures in the musical theatre were as a librettist, and he supplied the texts for four original musical plays for Budapest's Budai Színkör before, from 1933, writing both text and music for his later pieces. From 1934 he became administrator of the Erzsébetvárosi Színház, the Józsefvárosi Színház and the Kisfaludy Színház – a group known as 'a kültelki színházi' or suburban theatres – and, at the first-named, mounted a series of summertime productions of his own musicals, a number with top musical-comedy star Hanna Honthy featured and often with some considerable successes.

1922 **Hazudik a muzsikaszó** (Ferenc Neumann) Budai Színkör 9 June
1923 **Mintha álom volna** (Izso Barna/Ernő Kulinyi) Budai Színkör 1 September
1929 **Mit susog a fehér akác?** (Mihály Szántó) Budai Színkör 18 May
1930 **Lehullott a rezgőnyárfa** (Szántó) Budai Színkör 17 May
1931 **Tahi Tóth Veronika** Bethlen-téri Színház October
1932 **Csókos Regiment** Bethlen-téri Színház 24 September
1933 **Fehérvári huszárok** Budai Színkör 15 August
1934 **A Dorozsmai szélmalom** Budai Színkör 5 September
1939 **Zimberi Zombori szép asszony** Erzsébetvárosi Színház 22 June
1940 **Sárgarigófészek** Erzsébetvárosi Színház 20 June
1941 **Becskereki menyecske** Erzsébetvárosi Színház 21 June
1943 **A két Kapitány** Erzsébetvárosi Színház 12 June
1944 **Cserebogár, sárga cserebogár** Erzsébetvárosi Színház 23 June

ERKEL, Elek (b Pest, 2 November 1843; d Pest, 10 June 1893).

The son of Ferenc Erkel, the composer of the celebrated Hungarian operas *Bánk Bán* and *István Király*, Elek Erkel was principal conductor at the Népszinház from 1875, and, from 1884, at the Budapest Operaház. During his time at the Népszinház he composed the scores for two successful operetts and supplied incidental music for many plays and spectaculars including Csepregi's enormously successful *A sárga csikó* (1877) and *A piros bugyellaris* and Sándor Lukácsy's *A vereshajú* (1877). He later provided the score for a musical version of Szigligeti's *Az udvari bolond*, produced under the title *A kassai diák* with Lujza Blaha starred.

1880 **Székely Katalin** (Sándor Lukácsy) Népszinház 16 January
1883 **Tempefői** (Jenő Rákosi) Népszinház 16 November
1890 **A kassai diák** (Ede Szigligeti ad Pál Vidor) Népszinház 15 November

ERLANGER, A[braham] L[incoln] (b Buffalo, NY, 4 May 1860; d New York, 7 March 1930). Long-powerful and successful American theatre-owner and producer.

After early employment as a theatre box-office manager, Abe Erlanger went into management as a producer of touring melodrama. He then joined forces with lawyer Marc Klaw and, together, the pair became influential theatrical agents under the name of the Klaw and Erlanger Exchange. They also continued their producing activities and, in 1895, they joined with some of the principal theatrical producers of the time to form the Theatrical Syndicate, an organization which aimed to put the haphazard booking practices of the country's very large and necessarily far-flung theatrical circuits into some kind of profitable (to them) order. With Erlanger effectively at its head, the Syndicate, or Trust, as it became known, quickly succeeded in its aims, taking over theatres throughout the country with a speed and efficacy which soon led to those who did not wish to do business with its organization crying out loudly about restrictive practices. Like other men in successful and powerful positions, Erlanger got bad press and became disliked by those less successful than he, the legend of his toughness being given no relief by his suaver partner, Klaw, who like to let it be believed that he was the good-hearted gentleman of the pair whilst his physically unattractive and less well-spoken partner was the forceful bully.

As producers, Klaw and Erlanger mounted a long list of musicals over a period of 23 years, and, after the dissolution of their partnership, Erlanger continued alone, remaining on the Broadway musical theatre scene for a further eight years. Their early shows included such original comic operas as Sousa's *The Bride Elect* and De Koven's *Foxy Quiller*, but they concentrated largely on the lower-brow side of the musical stage, sponsoring the Rogers Brothers series of musicals, as a challenge to non-Syndicate members Weber and Fields, pieces like *In Newport*, with former Weber and Fields' stars featured, the vaudevillesque *The Ham Tree* with McIntyre and Heath, an attempt at reviving Emmet's long-popular Fritz shows with *Fritz in Tammany Hall* for Joseph Cawthorn, the fairytale pieces *Sleeping Beauty*, *Mr Bluebeard*, *Mother Goose*, *The Pearl and the Pumpkin* and americanized versions of Drury Lane's pantomimes *Humpty Dumpty* and *The White Cat*.

In 1906 they had a considerable success with George M Cohan's *Forty-Five Minutes from Broadway*, a second with Richard Carle's version of the London musical *The Spring*

Chicken and a flop with Sousa's *The Free Lance*, in 1908 they mounted Victor Herbert's spectacular cartoon musical *Little Nemo*, and in 1911 they had their biggest success of all when they teamed up with composer Ivan Caryll, who gave them successively *The Pink Lady*, *Oh! Oh! Delphine*, *The Little Café*, *Papa's Darling* and *The Girl Behind the Gun*.

They ventured into the continental Operette on the tidal wave of hopeful grabbing which followed the success of *The Merry Widow*, and thus brought botched versions of Lehár's *The Count of Luxemburg* and *Eva* and Kálmán's *Zsuzsi kisasszony* (*Miss Springtime*) and *Die Csárdásfürstin* (*The Riviera Girl*) to Broadway. Amongst their last productions together were Louis Hirsch's delightful *The Rainbow Girl* and Victor Herbert's disappointing *The Velvet Lady*.

On his own, Erlanger mounted Vincent Youmans's *Two Little Girls in Blue*, the Ed Wynn show *The Perfect Fool*, and a made-over version of Kálmán's *Die Bajadere* played as *The Yankee Princess* on Broadway, imported the London revue *By the Way*, and had a fine success with Eddie Dowling's blithe little tale of *Honeymoon Lane* (1926). His last production of a book musical, *Happy Go Lucky* (1926), was, however, a flop.

As well as his stream of musical shows, Erlanger also produced a number of plays, and had a financial interest – often larger, sometimes smaller – in a good number of productions which did not bear his name as official producer or co-producer. The original *Ziegfeld Follies* was produced largely on Erlanger capital, and a number of celebrated Broadway producers of his era – from Nixon and Zimmerman to Ziegfeld and Dillingham – owed a good deal of their ability to continue to produce their shows through good times and, more often, bad ones, to the bad-mouthed baron of Broadway. With their acceptance of his investment, of course, came an obligation for these producers to account to Erlanger, who thus knew precisely what was going on in the accounts departments and the box offices of many of the town's most important musicals. Although the Syndicate outlived its use, and was eventually split up and replaced by other equally and, eventually, more powerful controlling interests, Erlanger remained active and important in the Broadway theatre almost up to his death.

ERMINIE Comic opera in 3 acts by Harry Paulton and Claxson Bellamy based on *L'Auberge des Adrets* by Benjamin Antier, Saint-Amand and Paulyanthe. Music by Edward Jakobowski. Comedy Theatre, London, 9 November 1885.

The melodrama *L'Auberge des Adrets*, produced at Paris's Ambigu-Comique in 1823, featured Frédéric Lemaître in the rôle of its thieving hero, Robert Macaire. However, to the authors' fury, Lemaître and his partner Firmin played their parts as the caddish exploiter and his scruffy sidekick Bertrand not for drama but for comedy, and the result (later fictionally depicted on film in the celebrated *Les Enfants du Paradis*) was a major success which resulted in a sequel, *Robert Macaire*, being produced by Lemaître and Antier (obviously reconciled once the money came pouring in) in 1834. The character of the popular thief, subsequently immortalized in the cartoons of Daumier, was thus developed from what was intended to be that of a melodrama villain.

Plate 87. *The celebrated thieves of* **Erminie** *who became the models for many other comical rogues after the show's vast world-wide success.*

*Robert Macaire*s, both serious and comical, balletic, burlesque and pantomimic, appeared thereafter all round the world. One burlesque version was said to have been produced at New York's Winter Garden Theater in 1865 by P T Barnum's company and a second, burnt-cork one was given at the Fifth Avenue Opera Theater the following season by the Griffith and Christy Minstrels. A British burlesque, written by H J Byron, was staged at London's Royal Globe Theatre in 1870, and another as *Les Deux Voleurs, or a pretty pair of purloiners* at Blackpool's Grand Theatre in July 1884. In 1885, however, author-actor Harry Paulton, aided by one Claxson Bellamy (a mysterious fellow who does not turn up anywhere else in Victorian theatre) and, according to his young son, Edward, also by him (was he Claxson Bellamy?), put together a full-scale comic opera version of the piece, *Erminie*, as a vehicle for the elder Paulton in the principal comic role of Jacques Strop.

The dashing Macaire (Frank Wyatt) and his foolish sidekick, Strop (Paulton), have escaped from prison and robbed a traveller of his clothes and papers. The traveller is the Vicomte de Brissac (Horace Bolini), son of an old friend of the Marquis de Pontvert (Fred Mervin), and he is on his way to that nobleman's home to be given in marriage to his daughter, Erminie de Pontvert (Florence St John). Macaire and Strop – here called Ravannes and Cadeau – opportunistically take on the identities of Brissac and his noble friend, the Baron, and head for the Château Pontvert, plotting to steal the jewels of the fine company gathered together to celebrate the betrothal. The evening's ball produces much comedy, as Strop bewitches the elderly Princesse de Gramponeur (Mary Ann Victor) with his comicalities and argot, a touch of melodrama as the real Vicomte, arriving late on the scene and promptly imprisoned as an impostor, attempts to prove his identity, and romance as Erminie plots to elope with her father's secretary, Eugène Marcel (Henry Bracy). Robbery, impersonations and elopement are all exposed when a strategically placed suit of armour is shifted, and the wandering Chevalier de Brabazon (Percy Compton) shocks the old Princesse to screams by accidentally invading her bedroom in the dark of night, causing the whole house to turn out at the vital moment. A happy ending is tied up when the real Vicomte turns out to be the childhood sweetheart of Eugène's sister, Cérise (Violet Melnotte).

Edward Jakobowski's score was an attractive light comic opera one, featuring, notably, two romantic numbers for Erminie – the Dream Song ('At Midnight on my Pillow Lying') and the Lullaby ('Dear Mother, in Dreams I see Her') – and one fine, despairing one for Eugène ('Darkest the Hour'), a military moment for the Marquis ('A Soldier's Life), and comical pieces for the thieves ('Downy Jailbirds of a Feather' together, and Cadeau's topical 'What the Dicky Birds Say') alongside some well-made ensemble music.

Erminie was produced by the young Violet Melnotte and brought from its provincial tryout (an unusual thing in those days) to London's Comedy Theatre. There it proved a distinct success through a run of 154 performances before being taken on the road for an enormous first tour of no less than 65 weeks in the British provinces. A second company followed, after a brief return season in the West End, and thereafter *Erminie* remained on the British touring schedules almost non-stop for five years. However, if the show was a tidy and enduring success in Britain, in America it proved a sensation. Rudolf Aronson mounted the piece at the Casino Theater, with Paulton directing Pauline Hall as Erminie, William S Daboll and Francis Wilson as the pair of thieves, and Jennie Weathersby in the plum rôle of the old Princesse. The reaction was startling. The beautiful Miss Hall made a major hit and her Lullaby, which had been politely noticed in Britain, became a major song hit in America, Wilson was boosted to stardom in the made-for-the-author comic rôle which he had embellished with some even lower comedy than originally catered for, and even the scenery proved a hit, the second-act ballroom scene, painted by Henry Hoyt in different shades of pink, being considered the last thing in sophistication.

Aronson ran the show for 150 nights before, still unaware of what had hit him, he took it off to Boston and took in Lord Lonsdale's company with Offenbach's *La Créole* (*The Commodore*) and *Kenilworth*. When that season was blasted out of town by scandalmongering and other non-theatrical problems, he quickly brought his hit show back to the Casino where it promptly settled in to run for ten further months (362 performances). He attempted to leaven what – given his past experience at the Casino – seemed like an unimaginable run with versions of two fine Parisian hits, *Jeanne, Jeannette et Jeanneton* (*The Marquis*) and *La Petite Mademoiselle*, but after these were done he brought the inexhaustible *Erminie* back again to hold the Casino boards for four months more, closing it almost exactly two years after its first performance. At the end of this chopped-about

run Aronson was able to announce a total run of 1,256 performances (774 at the Casino and 482 out-of-town in the breaks) which seems a little hard to justify. Still, even with a more conservative calculation of 648 Broadway performances during its curious, carved-up career, *Erminie* still became the theatrical phenomenon of its time.

As in Britain, the show went profitably and long on the road in America, and it returned to Broadway twice in 1889, in 1893, 1897, 1898, 1899, 1903, 1915, and finally in a major revival with Francis Wilson in his favourite rôle teamed with De Wolf Hopper, Irene Williams (Erminie) and with Jennie Weathersby, who, like Wilson, had taken part in many of the revivals and tours, still as the Princesse. This Lawrence J Anhalt production, with a libretto adapted by Marc Connolly, played 104 performances at the Park Theater (3 January 1921).

The English-speaking theatre world followed en masse where Britain and America so enthusiastically led. *Erminie* was played in Canada and in both South Africa and South America by the Edgar Perkins Co (with Alice Aynsley Cook as the Princesse), whilst Australia saw the Savoy Theatre stars Leonora Braham as Erminie and Alice Barnett as the Princesse alongside Howard Vernon (Ravannes), William Elton (Cadeau) and Jack Leumane (Eugène). The piece was also played in Amsterdam in 1889 (6 September), and the following year appeared in a German translation at Vienna's Carltheater (ad Victor Léon, Heinz von Waldberg). Producer Karl Blasel paired with Karl Tuschl as Jack and Bob, as Macaire and Strop had once again become, Frln Jules was Erminie and Wilhelm Knaack took the small rôle of the innkeeper, in a version which was, for some reason, resituated in England with the Marquis de Pontvert becoming Lord Losberne. The shift did no good, for Vienna's *Erminy* flopped in just a handful of performances. The managers of Paris, however, never very interested in the product of the British stage, turned down the opportunity to stage this musical version of 'their' Robert Macaire tale, and waited until Charles Esquier and W Salabert produced a *Robert Macaire et Cie* at the Théâtre des Mathurins in March 1901 to see their musical Macaire.

The *Auberge des Adrets* characters surfaced several more times in the musical theatre after the triumph of *Erminie*. George Fox's comic opera *Macaire* came out in 1887 (Crystal Palace 20 September) with the composer/author himself starred as Macaire, whilst Ivor Novello composed the score to a piece called *The Golden Moth* (lib: Fred Thompson, P G Wodehouse, Adelphi Theatre 5 October 1921) which had a respectable 281-performance London run with Robert Michaelis and Bill Berry playing what were now called Pierre Caravan and Dipper Tigg. In France a second local *Robert Macaire* (Marc Berthomieu/ Guillot de Saix) was produced 18 November 1933 at the Grand Théâtre du Havre. None, of course, came within coo-ee of *Erminie*'s huge success.

USA: Casino Theater 10 May 1886; Australia: Princess Theatre, Melbourne 26 December 1887; Austria: Carltheater 1 November 1890

ERROL, Leon [SIMMS, Leon Errol] (b Sydney, Australia, 3 July 1881; d Hollywood, 12 October 1951). Broadway comedy star who also worked as a director and choreographer.

Errol studied for a medical career, supporting himself through his studies by appearing as a red-nose comic singer to such effect that he abandoned an Hippocratic career for a theatrical one. He appeared in Sydney in circus, in the Rignold stock company and in musical theatre as well as in variety, prior to shifting to America in his late twenties. There, he made his way from San Francisco to Chicago, working as a comic, a director and even penning a couple of musical farces which were staged on the touring circuits. It was whilst he was appearing in one of these, *The Lilies*, that he came to notice of Abe Erlanger. Before long, he was working on Broadway in no less a show than the *Ziegfeld Follies*.

Amongst a list of revue credits in both America and Britain, Errol made only one book musical appearance in New York, in Ziegfeld's souped-up revival of *A Trip to Chinatown*, *A Winsome Widow* (1912), before he made himself into a Broadway musical comedy star in the principal comedy rôle of the down-and-out Continental ex-monarch 'Connie' in another Ziegfeld show, *Sally* (1920). His subsequent musical comedy vehicles – *Louie the 14th* (1925, Louie Ketchup), *Yours Truly* (1927, Truly) and *Fioretta* (1929, Julio Pepoli) were not in the same class, and in later years he worked largely in comedy and musical comedy films including screen versions of a Bernauer and Öster-reicher play and German-language film (*Her Majesty Love*, 1931, Baron von Schwarzdorf) with his *Sally* co-star Marilyn Miller, and *Higher and Higher* (1943, Drake).

Errol also worked throughout as a director and choreographer, notably on several editions of the *Follies*, the *Hitchy Koo* revues and, in the area of the book musical, on the 1918 *Look Who's Here*, *Lassie* (choreographer), Friml's musical comedy *The Blue Kitten* (1922) and the London musical *The Kiss Call* (1919).

ESPINOSA, Edouard [Henry] (b London, 2 February 1872; d Worthing, 22 March 1950). British choreographer who provided the dances for such hits as *Chu Chin Chow* and *The Maid of the Mountains* in a career of more than 20 years in the musical theatre.

The son of the celebrated dancer, ballet-master and choreographer Léon Espinosa (d 1 June 1903), who had choreographed and danced the male solos in the vast *Babil and Bijou* at Covent Garden (1872), Edouard Espinosa originally appeared as a dancer in Paris, London and New York, before, from 1896, beginning a career as a choreographer in the musical theatre with the dances for the musical comedy *Monte Carlo*. He, himself, later claimed that this was 'the very first production of dance ensembles with set figures and formation effects ever done in musical comedy', but reviewers of the time noted no innovation and merely nodded towards the 'pretty and lively dances'.

Whilst still, occasionally, appearing on the stage (*Hotel Topsy Turvy*, *A Good Time* etc), he choreographed the touring productions of *The New Barmaid*, *The New Mephisto*, *Billy*, *Orlando Dando*, Marie Lloyd's *The ABC* and *The Southern Belle* as well as many pantomimes and plays (a number for Beerbohm Tree), and later claimed to have set, altogether, some 180 (or, variously, 300) shows. Amongst the musical shows which he choreographed or co-choreographed for the British stage were *A Good Time*, *Great Caesar*, the revue *Pot Pourri*, *The Land of Nod*, *Castles*

in Spain, *Amasis* (1906), *Lady Tatters* (1907), *The Mousmé*, *Bonita* (1911), *The Pearl Girl* (1913), *The Laughing Husband* (1913), *Mam'selle Tralala* (1914), *The Light Blues*, *My Lady Frayle*, *Tonight's the Night* (1915), *Chu Chin Chow*, *Young England*, *The Maid of the Mountains*, *Oh, Caesar!* (1916), *A Night Out* (1920), *Cairo* (1921, replacing the dances done for New York by Fokine), *The Rebel Maid*, *The Little Girl in Red* (1921), *The Last Waltz*, *The Little Duchess* (1922), *Catherine* (1923), *Our Nell* (1924), *The Good Old Days* (1925), *Riki Tiki* (1926) and *Kong* (1931). He also visited Australia, where he directed and choreographed several productions in 1918 and 1919 (*My Lady Frayle* etc.)

Espinosa was, for a period, ballet master at Covent Garden, wrote a number of books on dance and also founded a school of dance in London which continues its activities today under the direction of Bridget Espinosa.

Autobiography: *And Then He Danced* (Sampson, Low, Marston, London, 1946)

ESSEX, David [COOK, Albert David] (b London, 23 July 1947). Bright-eyed teeny-pop idol who, in a well-maintained career of more than 20 years, has appeared in several stage musicals.

After early ventures into pop music and into repertory theatre acting, during which he was seen in several provincial musical productions, Essex came to the musical theatre fore when he appeared in the London production of the musical *Godspell* (1971). He subsequently consolidated that success on film and as a pop vocalist ('Gonna Make You a Star', 'Hold Me Close' etc), returning to the musical stage, in 1978, to create the rôle of Che in *Evita* ('O What a Circus' etc). In 1985 he wrote, composed and appeared as Fletcher Christian in a musical based on *The Mutiny on the Bounty*, the run of which was accounted due to the singer's great personal popularity rather than the merits of the show. The song 'Fallen Angels', used in the show, reached the upper regions of the pop charts attached to a video portraying highwaymen rather than mutineers.

1985 **Mutiny** Piccadilly Theatre 11 July

Biography: Tremlett, G: *The David Essex Story* (Futura, London, 1974)

ESTRELLA Comic opera in 3 acts by Walter Parke. Music by Luscombe Searelle. Prince's Theatre, Manchester, 15 May 1883; Gaiety Theatre, London, 24 May 1883.

Estrella was the most generally successful of the not-very-successful works of New Zealand's most internationally played musical theatre composer. Parke's libretto mixed quasi-tragic and comic in a tale of a Venetian lady trying against lecherous odds to remain true to her lost husband. Under the impetus of its energetic composer, the piece was produced at Manchester with an excellent cast, given a hopeful showcasing at a Gaiety matinée, and then opportunistically hurried into the Folies-Dramatiques, at a loss after Strauss's *Prinz Methusalem* had folded suddenly. It ran there for 36 performances.

A New York production got a sour reaction and was burnt out of its theatre after three nights, but when *Estrella* was introduced to Australia, with its Broadway and West End tag attached, it proved, much thanks to an extended comedy turn by Philip Day as a loopy Doge, a definite success. Australia and South Africa (under Searelle's management) both saw *Estrella* again over the years that followed, and it resurfaced at San Francisco's Tivoli Theater as late as 1892.

USA: Standard Theatre 11 December 1883; Australia: Theatre Royal, Sydney 27 September 1884

THE ETERNAL WALTZ Satirical operetta in 1 act by Austen Hurgon. Music by Leo Fall. London Hippodrome, 22 December 1911.

This 50-minute, two-scene operetta, in which an actor-manager pursues the overworked composer Féo Lahl for a waltz for his theatre, and eventually finds both it and the lovely Lulu in a cabaret, was put together by director/author Austen Hurgon to make up part of a variety bill at the London Hippodrome. It was built around melodies which Leo Fall, hugely popular in England following the productions of *The Dollar Princess*, *The Merry Peasant* and *The Girl in the Train*, provided from his trunk to make up a five-number score from which the title waltz, sung by Lulu, became a wide-selling hit and was recorded by original star, Clara Evelyn. A considerable success, the show encouraged the Hippodrome to continue to follow the operetta-in-variety-houses trend, long used in similar Continental houses, with one-act operettas commissioned from Richard Fall and Emmerich Kálmán, and other London theatres to follow where it led.

In France *La Valse Éternelle* (ad Paul Ardot) was played as part of the programme at the Folies-Bergère, with Jane Marnac performing the waltz, and the show was introduced to America at Broadway's Palace and at Chicago's Palace Music Hall (14 October 1914).

France: Folies-Bergère *La Valse Éternelle* 31 August 1912; USA: Palace 24 March 1913

L'ÉTOILE Opéra-bouffe in 3 acts by Eugène Leterrier and Albert Vanloo. Music by Emmanuel Chabrier. Théâtre des Bouffes-Parisiens, Paris, 28 November 1877.

The established stage authors Vanloo and Leterrier, struck by the musical talents of the young Chabrier, confided their libretto for *L'Étoile* to the as yet untried composer. The result was a classy opéra-bouffe score of much charm and more than a little musical complexity, which was accepted for production by Charles Comte at the Bouffes-Parisiens with some slight misgivings and by his orchestra with horror. What the composer saw as the simplest possible style of orchestration was, to players used to chipping out the uncomplicated and mostly unvarying form of musical accompaniment used in most musical shows, strewn with difficulties.

On his 40th birthday, King Ouf of the 36 realms (Daubray) is required to make a political marriage to the Princess Laoula of Mataquin (Berthe Stuart). The Princess is, all unawares, being brought to his headquarters by the extravagantly secretive ambassador Hérisson de Porc-épic (Alfred Jolly), his wife Aloès (Mlle Luch), and private secretary, Tapioca (Jannin). Another part of the birthday celebrations is supposed to be a nice public execution, and Ouf, short of a victim, is relieved when he finally manages to get an insult from the penniless peddler, Lazuli (Paola Marié), which qualifies the boy for a friendly bit of torture and impaling. But it is not to be. The royal

astrologer, Siroco (Scipion), discovers that Lazuli's fate is linked to that of the King. One day after the boy's death, the King will also die, followed at fifteen minutes' distance by Siroco himself (this crafty clause is in the King's will), and so, for the next two acts, Ouf goes to extravagant lengths to keep the love-struck Lazuli – ready to defy all dangers for the sake of the Princess – happy and safe from danger. When it seems the boy has drowned, the King and his astrologer prepare for the worst, but he turns up alive and then threatens to kill himself if Laoula cannot be his. Ouf exhaustedly gives up the girl rather than the ghost.

The score mixed solos and some particularly lovely ensembles happily, with Lazuli's romance 'O petite étoile' (a version of which had been one of the pieces which had originally attracted the librettists to their composer) being one of the most attractive moments, alongside the pretty Kissing Quartet ('Quand on veut ranimer sa belle'), the sparkling trio in which Aloès and Laoula tickle the sleeping Lazuli with straws ('Il faut le chatouiller') and the comical duo between the King and the astrologer, getting drunk on 'Chartreuse verte' at the thought of imminent death.

Comte's production of *L'Étoile* did not win a wholehearted reception. It was played 48 times and then put aside. But Berlin's Friedrich-Wilhelmstädtisches Theater picked the show up, and an Hungarian version (ad Jenő Rákosi) was played four times at Budapest's Népszinház. In spite of this unpromising start, *L'Étoile* did not, however, stop there. At least the libretto did not, for, over the years that followed, the show suffered more at the hands of rewriters and improvers than practically any other work of class. And it was the music they attacked or, more often, simply threw out.

American J Cheever Goodwin, a repeated 'borrower' of Continental libretti, turned out a piece called *The Merry Monarch* with music by Woolson Morse which was a close adaptation of the book of *L'Étoile*. It was played at New York's Broadway Theater (18 August 1890) with a cast headed by Marie Jansen as Lazuli, and Francis Wilson as the King Anso IV (and-so-forth, get it?) and subsequently by J C Williamson's comic opera company in Australia (Princess Theatre, Melbourne 26 December 1891) where Charles Ryley (Lazuli), William Elton (Anso IV) and Florence Young (Lillita) topped the bill. In Hungary a similar process took place, and the Budapest Népszinház hosted an *Uff király* (21 May 1887) in which Vanloo and Leterrier's libretto was reset musically by Béla Hegyi and Szidor Bátor. Ilka Pálmay headed the cast of a production which succeeded very much better than the original piece had done when produced at the same theatre, a decade earlier.

In England, Alexander Henderson hosted Reece and Farnie's *Stars and Garters* at London's Folly Theatre with Lydia Thompson as Lazuli, Lionel Brough as King Jingo XIX, Harry Paulton as Zadkiel (Siroco) and Annie Poole as Laoula and 'new music selected from the most popular sources' of which Chabrier was apparently not one, whilst 20 years later *The Lucky Star* with 'new English dialogue by C H E Brookfield, lyrics by Adrian Ross and Aubrey Hopwood, the whole revised and assembled by Helen Lenoir (Mrs D'Oyly Carte) with new music by Ivan Caryll' was played for 143 performances at the Savoy Theatre (7 January 1899). This piece, in its turn, was translated into Hungarian (ad Emil Makai, Adolf Mérei) and Budapest, which had already had the real *A csillag*, plus the remusicked *Uff király* now had its third *Étoile* variant with *A szerencse csillag* (Magyar Színház 1 October 1901).

The original *L'Étoile* reappeared only rarely thereafter, but in 1941 it was taken into the repertoire of the Paris Opéra-Comique (10 April) in a production which featured Fanely Révoil (Lazuli) and René Hérent (Ouf) in the lead rôles, and which was brought back in 1946. In 1984 a slightly altered version was mounted at Lyon with Colette Alliot-Lugaz and Georges Gauthier featured, and this production was subsequently played at the Opéra-Comique with Mlle Alliot-Lugaz paired with Michel Sénéchal. This exposure, and the major recording which followed it, gave *L'Étoile* a life to more than the small band of connoisseurs who had previously prized it as a forgotten gem, and in 1991 Britain finally got the 'real' *L'Étoile* (ad Jeremy Sams) when the piece was produced by Opera North with a cast headed by Pamela Helen Stephen (Lazuli), Anthony Mee (Ouf), Kate Flowers (Aloès) and Mary Hegarty (Laoula).

With the opérette and opéra-bouffe repertoire having now become largely the province of the opera houses rather than the commercial stage, *L'Étoile* and its musicianly score (with the recognizably musicianly name of Chabrier attached to it) have probably attracted more attention in the last decade than at any time since the show's original production.

Germany: Friedrich-Wilhelmstädtisches Theater, Berlin *Sein Stern* 4 October 1878, Komische Oper *Lazuli* 4 February 1909; Hungary: Népszinház *A csillag* 29 November 1878; UK: Grand Theatre, Leeds 17 September 1991
Recordings: complete Lyon cast recording 1984 (EMI), complete (MRF)

EVA (Das Fabriksmädel)

EVA (Das Fabriksmädel) Operette in 3 acts by A M Willner and Robert Bodanzky. Music by Franz Lehár. Theater an der Wien, Vienna, 24 November 1911.

Without ever being one of Lehár's most popular or enduring works, *Eva* nevertheless had a more than satisfactory career. It had a fine initial run of 226 performances at the Theater an der Wien – broken only by the summer recess and by a two-week guest season played at the Raimundtheater (26 March 1912) with Ida Russka and Ludwig Herold starred – and won itself several productions further afield in the years after its first showing.

Eva (Mizzi Günther) is a little foundling factory girl, brought up by the foreman, Larousse (Fritz Albin), and the folk who are now her fellow workers, but with a far-off memory of a lovely, bejewelled and richly gowned mother. When the new owner of the factory, man-about-Paris Octave Flaubert (Louis Treumann), takes a fancy to her, and lures her into the company of his fast-living friends from the big city, the factory folk come to the rescue. But Eva has got the taste for the high life, and she runs off to Paris where her fresh beauty soon attracts the attention of the rich, lecherous and powerful. Octave arrives with a proposal of marriage, in time to rescue her from the demimondaine fate which she now realizes was her mother's. Luise Kartousch played Pipsi Paquerette, from the men's underwear department of Printemps, who wins herself a holiday meal-ticket each year by publicly flinging herself into the protection of a gentleman and begging him to save her from a brutal husband, and Kartousch's partner of

Plate 88. **Eva.** *Pipsi Paquerette (Luise Kartousch) gets her meal ticket for the holidays in the person of Dagobert Millefleurs (Ernst Tautenhayn).*

always, Ernst Tautenhayn, was Dagobert Millefleurs, a friend of Octave, who is Pipsi's target for the year.

Amongst the romantic pieces of the music, Eva's tale of 'Das Fabrikskind' ('Im heimlichen Dämmer der silbernen Ampel') with her reminiscence of the past ('So war meine Mutter, so möchte ich sein'), and the waltzing duo with Octave, 'Wär' es auch nichts als ein Traum von Glück', were the most substantial, but the lighter moments of the score prevailed most strongly. Dagobert's besotted plea to 'Pipsi, holdes Pipsi' was the show's stand-out number, alongside the march duo (Pipsi/Octave) in praise of 'Die Geister von Montmartre', Octave's march tune in a similar vein ('O du Pariser Pflaster'), Pipsi's comical encouragements to her man to face up to his purse-closing papa ('Ziehe hin zu deinem Vater') and her jolly praises of the demi-monde ('Wenn die Pariserin spazieren geht').

Eva was played in Budapest (ad Andor Gábor) with Sári Fedák starred in the title-rôle, whilst Klaw and Erlanger's Broadway production (ad Glen MacDonough) featured Sallie Fisher alongside Walter Percival (Octave), Alma Francis (Pipsi) and Walter Lawrence (Dagobert) through an unloved 24 performances which nevertheless established 'the waltz from *Eva*' ('Wär' es auch nichts') as a popular favourite. Maurice Ordonneau and Jean Bénédict's French version was played in Belgium (Théâtre de l'Alhambra 4 December 1912) with Germaine Huber and Charles Casella starring, but when the show was mounted by Mme Rasimi in Paris, more than a decade later, with Maguy Warna (Eva), Fernand Francell (Henri Nogent, ex-Octave) and Robert Hasti (Balzar, ex-Dagobert) featured, a different version, adapted by Lucien Meyrargue, was played. None did well enough to encourage a repeat.

Hungary: Király Színház 12 October 1912; USA: New Amsterdam Theater 30 December 1912; France: Théâtre Bata-clan 13 December 1924

Recording: selection in Spanish (Montilla), etc.

EVANGELINE, or The Belle of Acadia Extravaganza in 3 acts by J Cheever Goodwin. Music by Edward E Rice. Niblo's Garden, New York, 27 July 1874.

A burlesque of Longfellow's poem of the same name, the extravaganza *Evangeline* followed the trials and tribulations of its heroine (Ione Burke) and her beloved Gabriel (Connie Thompson) after their eviction from their sweetly peaceful native village by the beastly British. This outline allowed the heroine to travel to some of the more colourful parts of the world, including darkest Africa and the wildish West, which had not been on the itinerary of her prototype, but which were distinctly and theatrically colourful. On the way she met some creatures whom Longfellow had not quite imagined either – a dancing heifer, an amorous whale and the silent but eloquent and ubiquitous Lone Fisherman – whose performances became favourite highlights of the piece. In keeping with the piece's burlesque nature, the chief low-comedy rôle of Catherine was played in travesty by Louis Mestayer.

Rice's bulging score included numbers of every shape and size. Ballads and sentimental songs were prominent ('Thinking, Love, of Thee', the jaunty 'Sweet Evangeline', the waltz 'He says I Must Go', 'Sweet the Song of the Birds' 'Come Back to the Heart that is Thine' 'Where art thou now my beloved?', The Kissing Song, 'Go Not Happy Day' etc) alongside the comical 'I Lofe you', the martial 'A Hundred Years Ago', the tale of 'Sammy Smug', a bathing trio, a soldiers' chorus, a dance for the heifer and even a chorus which nodded its recognition to 'Longfellow'.

First produced in New York, after Rice had previewed some of his music in concert in Boston the previous year, *Evangeline* was quickly dismissed after 16 performances. But the road proved friendlier and, some three years later, the still-touring piece took a second turn in the metropolis (Daly's Theater, 4 June 1877) and this time – with Lizzie Harrold (Evangeline) and Eliza Weathersby (Gabriel) featured – it found sufficient friends to stay for a good part of the not-so-fussy summer. *Evangeline* gradually became a familiar favourite, with certain artists such as James Maffitt (Lone Fisherman) and George K Fortescue (Catherine) making themselves synonomous with their rôles as *Evangeline* toured tirelessly and paid several further, brief visits to New York (Standard Theater January 1880, Niblo's Garden 3 January 1887, Star Theater March 1889). It did, however, finally have a genuine Broadway run when, now a reliable old friend, it was staged at the 14th Street Theater (7 October 1885) with Fay Templeton as Gabriel for a run of 201 performances.

The show's touring life took it as far afield as Britain,

where M B Leavitt and the Rentz–Santley Company's production appeared at Liverpool, with Nellie Larkelle starred as Gabriel. It did not appeal. Dubbing the evening a 'wet blanket' one critic went on 'Mere feminine beauty and symmetry can never prove a satisfactory substitute for wit and humour, and as a result *Evangeline* must be vetoed as not coming within the pale of legitimate stage literature'. *Evangeline* did not progress to London. A number of years later, however, it turned up in Australia, played alongside *The Corsair* in the repertoire of one of Rice's companies. Buxom local Fannie Liddiard (Gabriel) and American teenager Virginia Earle (Evangeline) were featured, and a boxing match between Jack, the fighting kangaroo, and the Lone Fisherman introduced as local colour. It then proceeded on to Tasmania and to South Africa, but although it covered plenty of ground *Evangeline*'s real and long-lived success was wholly found in America.

A staged cantata by the same name, also based on Longfellow's poem, was written by Virginia Gabriel and played in London in 1870, whilst an unsuccessful musical version of James Laver's novel *Nymph Errant* (George Posford, Harry Jacobson/Eric Maschwitz/Romney Brent), produced with Frances Day in its title-rôle at London's Cambridge Theatre (14 March 1946), also took the same title. In Belgium, *Evangeline* was a 'légende canadienne' by Louis de Gramont and André Alexandre, with music by Xavier Leroux, produced at the Théâtre de la Monnaie in Brussels 28 December 1895.

UK: Court Theatre, Liverpool 11 June 1883; Australia: Opera House, Melbourne 27 April 1891

EVERARD, Harriet[te Emily] (b 12 March 1844; d London, 22 February 1882). Favourite burlesque and comic opera contralto who created Gilbert and Sullivan's Little Buttercup.

Miss Everard (as she was always billed) first appeared on stage at the Theatre Royal, Exeter at the age of 16 and soon moved to London where she played at the Royal Alfred, Marylebone, Greenwich New Theatre, Queen's, Princess's, Olympic, Royalty and St James's Theatres and at the Theatre Royal, Drury Lane. She appeared in all types of entertainments, in rôles such as Stratonice in Bulwer Lytton's *The Last Days of Pompeii* on the one hand and Catherine in Offenbach's *Treasure Trove* (*Le Mariage aux lanternes*) or Krosascanbe to Mrs John Wood's *La Belle Sauvage* on the other, having particular success in burlesque where her rich contralto and buxom form led to her being given breeches parts and heavy-lady and character rôles from a young age.

She had an early connection with opéra-bouffe when she played Queen Greymare (otherwise Clémentine) in the English-language première of Offenbach's *Barbe-bleue* (1866), and with W S Gilbert when she appeared as the Marchioness of Birkenfelt in his early burlesque, *La Vivandière* (1868). She also appeared as Omphale in the Covent Garden spectacular *Babil and Bijou* (1872), at the Princess's Theatre in James Albery's extravaganza *The Will of Wise King Kino* (1873), and at the Philharmonic as the dragonistic Aurore in London's English-language première of *Giroflé-Girofla* (1874).

She joined D'Oyly Carte's company at the Opera Comique to appear as Mrs Partlett in the original production of *The Sorcerer* (1877) and had her most memorable success when she created the rôle of Little Buttercup in *HMS Pinafore* the following year, but a bad stage accident during the rehearsals of *The Pirates of Penzance* prevented her from opening as London's Ruth and, although she eventually recovered sufficiently to succeed Emily Cross in the rôle during the run, she was herself replaced by Alice Barnett, who was then given the equivalent part of Lady Jane in *Patience*. Although she did appear on the stage subsequently, playing Aunt Priscilla in the short-lived *Lola* (1881), she had not, in fact, wholly recovered from her accident and she died shortly after.

EVETT, Robert (b Warwickshire, 16 October 1874; d North Bucks, 15 January 1949). Star tenor of the earliest years of the 20th century who later had a successful run as a producer.

At the age of 19, Evett joined one of D'Oyly Carte's touring companies and he was subsequently promoted to the Savoy Theatre company where he succeeded Charles Kenningham in the rôle of Marco in a revival of *The Gondoliers* (1898) and appeared as Alexis in the same year's revival of *The Sorcerer*. He remained at the Savoy, appearing in Gilbert and Sullivan revivals and creating lead tenor rôles in *The Rose of Persia* (Yussuf), *The Emerald Isle* (Terence O'Brien), *Merrie England* (Walter Raleigh, 'The English Rose'), *Ib and Little Christina* (Ib) and *A Princess of Kensington* (Lt Brook Green) and, when William Greet took over the Savoy and its company, he remained with him to appear in the musical comedies *The Earl and the Girl* (Hon Crewe Boodle), *Little Hans Andersen* (Prince with the Magic Pipe) and *The Talk of the Town* (Duke of Topford).

In 1905 he joined George Edwardes to star as Gaston in *Les P'tites Michu*, Dorlis in *Les Merveilleuses*, Camille in the original London *Merry Widow* at Daly's Theatre, Niki in *A Waltz Dream*, Karel in *The Girl on the Train* (*Die geschiedene Frau*) and Frank Falconer in Kálmán's *Autumn Manoeuvres*, establishing himself as London's premier operetta tenor, before spending 18 months in the United States where he appeared on the variety stage and in the musical theatre in Fall's *The Doll Girl* (Tiborius) and Renyi's *Suzi* (Stephen).

After the death of Edwardes, with whom he had entertained a strong personal friendship, he returned to Daly's Theatre to help Edwardes's daughter run the now beleaguered theatre. Appointed as managing director of George Edwardes (Daly's Theatre) Ltd, he was responsible for the production there in 1917 of *The Maid of the Mountains* which restored the theatre's and the firm's fortunes. He followed up with other successful vehicles for *Maid of the Mountains* star José Collins (*A Southern Maid*, *Sybil*) but when James White, the chairman of the Daly's board, bought the theatre and began to take a hand in the artistic direction, Evett and Miss Collins moved on. They became based at the Gaiety where Evett produced Lehár's *Der letzte Walzer*, a Tchaikovsky pasticcio which allowed his star to appear as *Catherine* the Great, and *Our Nell* in which she played Nell Gwynne, with diminishing results. The complete failure of Lehár's *Frasquita* (1925) ended his career as a producer.

EVITA Musical in 2 acts by Tim Rice. Music by Andrew Lloyd Webber. Prince Edward Theatre, London, 21 June 1978

To follow up their initial hit with *Jesus Christ Superstar*, the team of Tim Rice (author) and Andrew Lloyd Webber (composer) found themselves another, on the surface, highly unlikely subject for a piece of modern musical theatre. Once again their show was in the way of a musical biography, and once again their central figure was one from a field in which most people kowtowed to the 'proper' way of thinking, as purveyed by the Sunday newspapers: for in the earnestly liberal atmosphere of the flaky 1970s, if anything was more touchy than religion, it was politics. Touchy, that is, if not treated in an earnestly liberal fashion, and extremely touchy when it came to Madame Eva Peron, wife of former Argentine president Juan Peron, and the much-vilified (by the foreign press) popular heroine of that country's people.

However, the writers of *Evita* looked beyond the politics of the subject, to the people involved, and most particularly to the character and tale of Eva. Madame Peron's rise from country-girl to the status of goddess of the poor, her vengeful treatment of the right-wing establishment which had long denied her everything she had finally won, and her death from cancer at what seemed like the height of her glory were the stuff of operatic drama. Later, as *Evita* went on to enormous worldwide success, some Sunday papers (and even some weekday ones) flailed furiously at Rice for his 'glorification' of this woman whom they had always painted as an unmitigated monster, and of whom many people's perception was now forever altered. But *Evita* was not a show about politics, any more than the slightly satirical musical comedies of the 1930s Broadway stage had been: like them, it was about personalities, but unlike them it did not use those personalities to produce humour but, for the large part, to produce a musical drama.

Eva Duarte (Elaine Paige) is still a teenager when she clamps on to an unbuttoned tango singer Agustin Magaldi (Mark Ryan) visiting her home town, and uses him as a means to get out of the country and up to Buenos Aires. Magaldi is soon dropped and, whilst building a fairly desultory career as an actress in the capital, she soon begins to get to know the influential and the famous, in particular the rising politician Juan Peron (Joss Ackland). Determinedly removing Peron's 16-year-old mistress (Siobhan McCarthy) from his bed, Eva moves in and, before long, she is pushing and persuading her lover towards taking over the supreme power in the country. Eva Peron is still only in her mid-twenties when Peron becomes President of Argentina. But whilst pleading his cause with the people of the country she has also established herself in their hearts with her enthusiastic promises of something for nothing. The myth of 'Saint' Eva Peron continues to grow, as she works to promote herself, her husband, and the cockeyed kind of democracy she apparently believes in, setting up a charitable Foundation which is more charitable to those who get from it than to those — largely her old 'establishment' enemies — who are virtually forced to contribute. She finally insists on recognition, on the post of Vice-President, not realizing that there are still barriers against her ambitions, but the more pragmatic Peron does not have to face her with a 'no', for her last illness is upon her. When Eva Peron died the people of Argentina were distraught, for like so many who have survived as popular icons to later ages, she did not grow old: she died at the height of her young powers.

This tale was told in a series of linked musical scenes and, through the episodes of its telling, the character of Eva was faced up to another character, a sneering, jeering narrator and commentator called Che (David Essex), who represented generally the helpless opposition to Eva Peron more than he represented that other mythicized media icon, the teenagers' wall-poster of a decade, Che Guevara.

Like *Jesus Christ Superstar*, *Evita* was first presented to the public as a two-record album, in 1976. Julie Covington (Eva) and Colm Wilkinson (Che) headed the cast on a recording which, in retrospect, showed up the key to the presentation of the show: when the protagonists are equally matched, the drama of the piece is at its best, when (as in many later productions) one or the other of the pair is the stronger performer, the excitement is dimmed. The recording produced a surprise. Eva's monologue, 'Don't Cry for Me, Argentina', spoken to the public after Peron's election victory, as performed by Miss Covington, shot to the top spot on the British hit parade. It was closely followed by the plaintive little ballad of the deposed mistress, 'Another Suitcase in Another Hall', performed on the disc by folksinger Barbara Dickson. It was many years since a musical theatre score had performed in such a way, and unprecedented in the case of the score of an unproduced musical. But the buzz around the theatre circles of the time was that *Evita* was unproduceable: what was on the record could not make up a viable stage show.

However *Superstar* producer Bob Stigwood went ahead with a stage production, the biggest hoo-ha in memory in theatrical London was staged over the selection of the girl to play Eva and, when *Evita* opened at the previously unloved Prince Edward (ex-Casino) Theatre in London's Soho in June 1978, director Hal Prince and choreographer Larry Fuller proved that not only was the show stageable, it was triumphantly so.

Highlights of the night, apart from the two already well-known songs, included the carousel of lovers parading choreographically through Eva's door as she delivered 'Good Night and Thank You', the grim musical chairs played through the Generals' 'Dice Are Rolling', Eva's approaches to Peron in 'I'd Be Surprisingly Good for You', as a pair of tango dancers danced mutely in the background, and the thrilling first-act closure with the people massed together by flare-light to hail a 'New Argentina'. Essex scored with his mockery of Eva's death in 'O What a Circus' (soon to follow the two previous hits to the charts, in his version) and of her life in 'High Flying, Adored', Eva excitingly declared herself 'Rainbow High' as she prepared to set off on what should have been her international confirmation in the 'Rainbow Tour' and the two fenced acidly through the Waltz for Eva and Che.

Evita was one of the greatest musical theatre hits ever seen in London. By the time it closed, it had played 2,900 performances in the West End, a record second only to that set up by *Jesus Christ Superstar*, and had been seen all around the world. America's production came first, beginning in Los Angeles and opening on Broadway little more than a year into the London run. In preparation for Broadway, the production of the piece (which had won some peeved criticism in London and Manchester theatre columns for not blackening its central character unambiguously) was painted in more primary colours. Eva (Patti LuPone) was played harsher, harder and less attractive, Che (Mandy Patinkin) was set up to be more entertaining. It didn't make the slightest difference. Those journalists brought up on wall-posters shrieked louder than they had or would over the most extreme violent or sexual performances on stage at what they perceived as a challenge to their perception of Eva Peron ('one of the most sinister, morally disgusting entertainments to appear on the Broadway stage in many years ...'), whilst, as in London, a public who mostly probably didn't even know where Argentina was filled the Broadway Theater for nearly four years and 1,568 performances. Theatre professionals also showed their approval: *Evita* walked off with seven Tony Awards at the end of its first season.

There was little more protest as *Evita* made its way round the world, although the piece was banned in Argentina. Australia's production featured Jennifer Murphy (until she gave out and had to be replaced, ultimately by Miss LuPone) and John O'May through its production in producer Stigwood's home town of Adelaide and some six months in Melbourne prior to a run in Sydney (Her Majesty's Theatre, 14 February 1981) and then performances around the rest of the country. Spain followed suit with the first foreign-language production (ad Ignacio Artime, Jaime Azpilicueta) at Madrid's Teatro Monumental with Paloma San Basilio and Paxti Andion in the lead rôles, and the Theater an der Wien mounted the first German-language adaptation (ad Michael Kunze) with Isabel Wiecken and Alexander Goebel top-billed. Mexico, South Africa, Japan, New Zealand, Brazil and Hungary (ad Tibor Miklós) all followed. In France, in spite of rumours being regularly floated as to a French-language production, the only version that was seen was an under-par European touring mounting sent out from America, which billed Hal Prince's name very large as director.

Another rumour (which remained just that) was over *Evita*'s film version. Over more than a decade, regular paragraphs announcing a screen *Evita* have appeared. Faye Dunaway, Liza Minnelli, Meryl Streep and Madonna were amongst the names at various times promoted in stories about a forthcoming film. At the time of writing it remains forthcoming. At the same time, however, *Evita* productions continue throughout the world as the show which was thought to be unstageable moves well into its second decade.

USA: Broadway Theater 25 September 1979; Australia: Her Majesty's Theatre, Melbourne, 2 August 1980: Hungary: Margitszigeti Vörösmarty Színpad 14 August 1980; Austria: Theater an der Wien 20 January 1981; Germany: Theater des Westens, Berlin 10 September 1982; France: Palais de Congrès 20 December 1989

Recordings: concept album (MCA), original cast (MCA), Broadway cast (MCA), Australian cast (MCA), Spanish cast (Epic), Austrian cast (Jupiter), Mexican cast (Peerless), South African cast (Gallo), Japanese cast (Trio), New Zealand cast (Stetson), Brazilian cast (Somlivree), Hungarian cast (Favorit) etc.

EVVA, Lajos (b Fegyvernek, 17 August 1851; d Budapest, 12 October 1912). Theatre director, adapter and lyricist.

Evva took over the management of the Népszinház, Budapest's most important producing house for musical theatre, from its initial manager, Jenő Rákosi, at the age of 30 (15 October 1881), and directed its fortunes for 16 years. He was later director of the Magyar Színház (11 June 1898 sq).

During his years at the Népszinház, which were initiated by a production of the French spectacular *L'Arbre de Noël*, he produced many highly successful pieces including Hungarian versions of *Le Jour et la nuit*, *Les Contes d'Hoffmann*, his new adaptation of *Orphée aux enfers*, *Lili*, *Der Bettelstudent*, *Rip van Winkle*, *Les Pilules du Diable*, *Der Zigeunerbaron*, *The Mikado*, *Mam'zelle Nitouche* and *Der Vogelhändler* and, most notably, the many Hungarian operetts – Konti's *Az eleven ördög* (1885), *Királyfogás* (1886), *A suhanc* (1888) and *A cziterás* (1894), and dramaturg György Verő's *A szúltan* (1892) and *Virágcsata* (1894) as well as works by Béla Hegyi, Szidor Bátor, Jenő Sztojanovits, Béla Szabados, Elek Erkel, Dezső Megyeri, Aladár Váradi, Miklós Forrai and others.

Having made a major hit with his first operettic adaptation for Rákosi and the Népszinház, Suppé's *Boccaccio*, Evva continued to turn out a heavy schedule of adaptations both before, and during especially the earlier years of, his direction of the theatre. Many of these were done in collaboration, notably with Rákosi and with the even more prolific Béla J Fái who often provided the textual adaptations whilst Evva worked on the lyrics.

1879 **Boccaccio** Hungarian version (Népszinház)
1897 **Madame Favart** Hungarian version w Fái (Népszinház)
1880 **A pipacs** (*Coquelicot*) Hungarian version (Népszinház)
1880 **Fatinitza** Hungarian version w Jenő Rákosi (Népszinház)
1880 **A kecskepásztor márkiné** (*Les Voltigeurs de la 32ème*) Hungarian version w Ferenc Nemes (Népszinház)
1880 **A szép perzsalány** (*La Jolie Persane*) Hungarian version (Népszinház)
1880 **A kétnejü gróf** (*Der Graf von Gleichen*) Hungarian version w Rákosi (Népszinház)
1880 **A Franciák Milánóban** (*La Fille du tambour-major*) Hungarian version w Fái (Népszinház)
1881 **Dragonyosok** (*Les Dragons de Villars*) Hungarian version w Rákosi (Népszinház)
1881 **Tiszturak a zárdában** (*Les Mousquetaires au couvent*) Hungarian version w Fái (Népszinház)
1881 **Apajune, a vizitünder** (*Apajune der Wassermann*) Hungarian version w Rákosi (Népszinház)
1881 **Az ácslegények gazdasszonykája** (*La Mère des compagnons*) Hungarian version w Fái (Népszinház)
1881 **A szélkakas** (*La Girouette*) Hungarian version w Fái (Népszinház)
1881 **Olivette lakodalma** (*Les Noces d'Olivette*) Hungarian version (Népszinház)
1881 **A királykisasszony bábui** (*Les Poupées de l'Infante*) Hungarian version (Népszinház)
1882 **Nap és hold** (*Le Jour et la nuit*) Hungarian version w Fái (Népszinház)
1882 **A furcsa háboru** (*Der lustige Krieg*) Hungarian version w Fái (Népszinház)
1882 **Viola-Ibolya** (*Giroflé-Girofla*) Hungarian version w Fái (Népszinház)
1882 **Orpheus a pokolban** (*Orphée aux enfers*) Hungarian version (Népszinház)
1882 **A denevér** (*Die Fledermaus*) Hungarian version (Népszinház)
1882 **Lili** Hungarian version w Fái (Népszinház)
1882 **A kertészleány** (*Le Coeur et la main*) Hungarian version w Fái (Népszinház)
1883 **A koldusdiák** (*Der Bettelstudent*) Hungarian version w Fái (Népszinház)
1883 **A gyürü** (*Gillette de Narbonne*) Hungarian version w 'Imre Ukki' (Népszinház)

1883 **A hercegasszony** (*Madame l'Archiduc*) Hungarian version w Fái (Népszinház)
1883 **Afrikautázo** (*Die Afrikareise*) Hungarian version w Rákosi (Népszinház)
1883 **Kanári hercegnő** (*La Princesse des Canaries*) Hungarian version w Fái (Népszinház)
1883 **Rip** (*Rip van Winkle*) Hungarian version w Fái (Népszinház)
1884 **Kék Féri** (*François les bas-bleus*) Hungarian version w Fái (Népszinház)
1884 **Gasparone** Hungarian version w Árpád Berczik (Népszinház)
1884 **A hercegnő** (*La Princesse*) Hungarian version (Népszinház)
1884 **A gerolsteini hercegnő** (*La Grande-Duchesse de Gérolstein*) Hungarian version w Fái (Népszinház)
1885 **Az ébren álmódo** (*La Dormeuse éveillée*) Hungarian version w Fái (Népszinház)
1886 **A bearni leány** (*La Béarnaise*) Hungarian version w Fái (Népszinház)
1887 **A komédiás hercegnő** (*Nell Gwynne*) Hungarian version w Fái (Népszinház)
1887 **Nebántsvirág** (*Mam'zelle Nitouche*) Hungarian version w Viktor Rákosi (Népszinház)
1887 **Fejő lány, vagy költőimádás** (*Patience*) Hungarian version w Fái (Népszinház)
1888 **Szedtevette nagysám** (*Mam'selle Crénom*) Hungarian version w Fái (Népszinház)
1889 **A gárdista** (*The Yeomen of the Guard*) Hungarian version w Ukki (Népszinház)
1890 **Szinitanoda** (*Un lycée de jeunes filles*) Hungarian version w V Rákosi (Népszinház)
1891 **A tékozló fiu** (*Le Fils prodigue*) Hungarian version w Ukki (Népszinház)
1891 **Miss Heliett** (*Miss Helyett*) Hungarian version w V Rákosi (Népszinház)
1891 **A tollkirály** (*Isoline*) Hungarian version w Fái (Népszinház)
1895 **A királyné dragonyosa** (*Le Dragon de la reine*) Hungarian version w V Rákosi (Népszinház)

EXPRESSO BONGO Musical in 2 acts taken from a story by Wolf Mankowitz. Book by Wolf Mankowitz and Julian More. Lyrics by Julian More. Music by David Heneker and Monty Norman. Saville Theatre, London, 23 April 1958.

One of the most interesting musical plays to come out of the British theatre in the 1950s, the stark and seedy *Expresso Bongo* was an adaptation of a newspaper novella written by Academy Award-winning screenplay author, Wolf Mankowitz, which was itself imaginatively based on the career of Britain's first rock-and-roll star, Tommy Steele.

Herbert Rudge (James Kenney) is discovered by agent Johnnie (Paul Scofield) playing bongo drums in a Soho coffee bar. Renamed 'Bongo' and fitted out with a loud, rhythmic song called 'Expresso Party', the boy rises quickly to the top, attracts the young and the hangers-on, and, having established his youth/sex/violence image, is then manipulated into widening his appeal to the mums and dads with a sob-stuff number dedicated to his mother. Under the influence of the sex-bent actress Dixie Collins (Hy Hazell), Bongo then begins to slip away from the agent who made him a star. He starts to become unreliable and, before Johnnie knows what is happening, the boy has deserted him for a fashionable agent. The big time is as far away as ever for Johnnie, but he will keep on trying.

Millicent Martin was the little Soho stripper, Maisie, with dreams of a singing career, Charles Grey was Captain

Mavors, the classy, shoddy club manager whose character was indubitably based on the real-life Major Donald Neville-Willing, Meier Tzelniker was Mayer, the pop record producer who only likes opera, and Aubrey Morris was 'Kakky' Katz, the down-on-his-luck ex-film producer running around Soho trying to set up just one more deal. The supporting cast included such rising performers as Susan Hampshire, Victor Spinetti, Barry Cryer, Trevor Griffiths, Anna Sharkey and Jill Gascoine as well as dancer Anne Donaghue – the future Mrs Tommy Steele.

The songs illustrated the story splendidly, with Johnnie rejoicing that 'I've Never Had it So Good' and later regretting that he has fallen off 'The Gravy Train', Dixie musing frightenedly over the ravages of 'Time' and revusically singing with a classy pal of how 'We Bought It', Bongo pounding out the acid parodies of rock-and-roll music, and little Maisie chirping out her ballads as a little ray of light in all the grey shadows.

Oscar Lewenstein and Neil Crawford's production of *Expresso Bongo* ran for 316 performances at the Saville Theatre before being toured and then made into a film with the young Cliff Richard playing the rôle of Bongo to the Johnnie of Laurence Harvey, the Dixie of Yolande Donlan and the Maisie of Sylvia Syms. Most of the music was omitted, although Richard performed the mother-loving 'The Shrine on the Second Floor' alongside a new number, 'A Voice in the Wilderness', which made it to the charts. In 1964 the show was performed in Hungary (ad Sándor Kosnár, Peter Tardos).

The first and easily the most accomplished of the low-life musicals which became for a while fashionable in the London theatre, *Expresso Bongo* encouraged other, mostly less skilful, writers into an area which proved, in the end, only spasmodically fertile.

Hungary: Fővárosi Operettszinház 18 September 1964; Film: 1959
Recording: original cast (Nixa), film songs (Columbia, EP)

EYSLER, Edmund [EISLER, Edmund] (b Vienna, 12 March 1874; d Vienna, 4 October 1949). One of the most melodiously Viennese composers of his era, with a long list of successful shows to his credit.

Born in Vienna, the son of an erratically solvent and only occasionally rich Jewish businessman, the young Eysler did sufficiently badly at his lessons to be allowed to follow the example of his schoolfriend and contemporary, Leo Fall, and pursue musical studies instead. After his years at the Vienna Conservatoire were successfully completed, he was for some while unable to find himself any more lucrative employ than as a piano teacher but, at the same time, he made his first attempts at composing for the stage. A ballet, *Schlaraffenland*, was rejected by the Hofoperntheater, where Mahler ruled, as being too expensive to stage, and Eysler turned instead to Operette, setting a libretto by Ignaz Schnitzer, the author of *Der Zigeunerbaron* and a friend of a friend. *Der Schelm von Bergen*, which had been turned down by Johann Strauss as being too similar in key areas to *The Mikado*, became *Der Hexenspiegel* in the 26 year-old Eysler's version. It evoked enough enthusiasm in the old librettist for him to sponsor Eysler sufficiently for him to quit piano teaching and take a small house at Grinzing where he might work on his composition and orches-

tration, and in publisher Josef Weinberger to earn the young man a helpful advance. Eysler had an income from his work, but had still had nothing produced.

Weinberger's efforts to convince producers to stage *Der Hexenspiegel* did not succeed. Mahler preferred to stick with Lortzing, the Prague theatre was unwilling to venture with an untried composer, and Leipzig simply didn't get round to it. Since Eysler's benefactors were unable to support him indefinitely, the composer found employment with Gabor Steiner at the adventurous summer theatre Venedig-in-Wien where, as a number-three house composer, he supplied some dance music for Ivan Caryll's *Die Reise nach Cuba* and some individual numbers for the cabaret-concerts played by members of the company. One of these was the young Frln Massari (sic), later to find fame as Fritzi Massary.

When the summer theatre season finished, Eysler moved on to Steiner's winter house, Danzers Orpheum, and there, later in the year, he had his first stage works, a one-act Operette, *Das Gastmahl der Lucullus*, and a two-scene pantomime, adapted from the French by Lindau and Louis Gundlach under the title *Das Frauenduell*, produced as sections of a five-part programme. The composer was still 'Edmund S Eisler', but the deliberately less common 'Eysler' would soon follow. Weinberger, in the meanwhile, had not forgotten the young composer and he sent Eysler another text, an Operette by Zeller's librettist, Moritz West, in which he suggested the young man could reuse the lighter portions of the unplayed *Hexenspiegel* score.

Bruder Straubinger was a text conceived to feature Alexander Girardi, the greatest star of the Viennese musical theatre and the original *Vogelhändler* of Zeller and West's famous Operette. As a result, in 1903, Eysler's first produced full-length piece was mounted at no less a venue than the Theater an der Wien with the great Girardi starring in its title-rôle. It proved an enormous success, its waltz song 'Küssen ist keine Sünd' became the the hit of the period, and Eysler was at last launched on what was to be an exceptionally busy and regularly successful career.

In the years that followed, he became one of the most popular and prolific composers of Viennese light theatre music, as he turned out a veritable shower of mostly successful shows. *Pufferl* was another successful venture with Girardi, and one which provided the artist with a second hit song, the Kirschenlied, and when after 60 performances Girardi broke his long relationship with the Theater an der Wien, he took his new favourite composer with him to the opposition Carltheater. There, together, they had two further fine successes with *Die Schützenliesel*, in which Girardi introduced his famous 'Mutterl-lied', and with the more substantial *Künstlerblut*.

After *Künstlerblut*, star and composer went different ways, but success continued for Eysler with a little one-acter, *Vera Violetta*, produced at the Apollotheater, before he met his first comparative reverses. *Das Glücksschweinchen*, with Fritzi Massary starring, had only a short summer run at Venedig-in-Wien and a Budapest appearance as *A szerencsemalac* (Budai Színkör 1 May 1909), and a modern-dress Viennese piece, *Johann der Zweite*, produced at the Carltheater was also a 28-performance disappointment. However, both pieces did altogether better when produced in Germany, and Eysler's music, shorn of Stein and Lindau's libretti, was heard in America (where the composer had been represented as early as 1905 by a waltz interpolated into Broadway's *The Rollicking Girl*) when impresario Henry Savage bought up the rights to both to top up what he saw as the undersized score of *Künsterblut* and fabricated two musicals from the three. *The Love Cure*, loudly touted by Savage as the legitimate successor to his production of *The Merry Widow* played five weeks on Broadway and toured with rather more success. *Forget-menot* apparently didn't make it to the stage, but a version of *Johann der Zweite* did ultimately appear, under the management of Weber and Fields. Adapted by Harry B Smith and E Ray Goetz as *The June Bride* (Majestic Theater, Boston 23 September 1912) it stopped short of Broadway.

After this temporary lull, a second very fine series of Viennese Eysler successes was, however, quickly under way. Oskar Fronz, director of the Wiener Bürgertheater, decided to leap on the lucrative Operette bandwagon and began his new policy with the production of Eysler's latest piece, *Der unsterbliche Lump*. It was followed by *Der Frauenfresser*, *Der lachende Ehemann* and *Ein Tag im Paradies*, all substantial successes, which between them filled Fronz's theatre for some four years, up to the outbreak of war. Eysler simultaneously turned out one last vehicle for Girardi, *Das Zirkuskind*, and also contributed to the programmes at the variety and Operette house the Apollotheater, which had introduced *Vera Violetta*, scoring notably with the little *Der Natursänger*, played 106 times in 1911–12.

It was at the Apollotheater, in fact, that was produced the most successful of the steady supply of cheerfully tuneful and mostly alt-Wienerische Operetten and musical comedies which the composer turned out through the war years. *Hanni geht tanzen* outdid, statistically at least, all of the run of successful pieces with which Eysler steadily supplied the Bürgertheater, equalled the greatest successes of his Girardi days, and was exported to fine effect. It was followed by another piece in a similar vein, *Graf Toni*, which happily confirmed that success, whilst *Die – oder keine* ran for more than 125 performances at the Bürgertheater, *Wenn zwei sich lieben* notched up 110 nights at the Theater an der Wien and *Warum geht's denn jetzt?* went through 102 performances at the Bundestheater and the Bürgertheater.

When the fashion for the more modern, foreign dance rhythms caught on in the 1920s Eysler was unable or unwilling to take them up. Although he ventured a charleston amongst the traditional rhythms in the two-month run of the 1925 Bürgertheater piece *Das Land der Liebe*, he largely stuck to what he knew and did best, and what the Viennese public seemed never to tire of hearing from him: flowing Viennese melody. It was not only Vienna, either, that wanted this mode of music. If America had fabricated its own Eysler shows, Italy preferred to purchase one ready-made and, when Fronz demurred over Eysler's new piece *Die schöne Mama*, there was a willing taker in Rome's Teatro Nazionale. Thus *Die schöne Mama* was produced as *La bella mammina* before, its credentials proven, being reimported to Vienna and the Bürgertheater to play under its original title for 111 performances.

In 1927 Eysler scored his most substantial success since *Bruder Straubinger* when he composed perhaps his most dazzling and melodious 'old Vienna' score for the 'old Vienna' story of *Die gold'ne Meisterin*. Staged at the Theater an der Wien, *Die gold'ne Meisterin* was played more than 200 times in its first run and produced several popular songs in the pre-war style.

Eysler continued to compose into the 1930s, scoring another fair success at the Bürgertheater with *Ihr erster Ball* in 1929 (76 performances), but he was forced into hiding during the 1939–45 war and, unable to work or to have his Operetten played, saw the prosperity he had achieved frittered away. When the war was over, he was once again able to compose and to conduct freely and, in his seventies, now regarded as the grand old man from the good old days, he saw his shows return to Viennese stages.

Eysler's works, an extremely large proportion of which were both popular and financial successes, won lively audiences, particularly in the Vienna of 1900–20. Most were played at that time in Germany and at least 17 were seen in Hungary, whilst several were exported further. *Der lachende Ehemann* reached London as *The Laughing Husband* and *The Girl Who Didn't*, *Vera Violetta* was played at Paris's Olympia, and, after *The Love Cure*, Broadway hosted americanized versions of *Vera Violetta*, *Der Frauenfresser* (*The Woman Haters*), *Der lachende Ehemann* (*The Laughing Husband*), *Ein Tag im Paradies* (*The Blue Paradise*), with Sigmund Romberg interpolations and considerable success, *Wenn zwei sich lieben* (*Lieutenant Gus*), and an Italian version of *Pufferl* called *Amor di Principe* played by a visiting company from Palermo. Apart from *La Bella mammina* and *Amor di Principe*, Italy also staged a number of further Eysler works including a version of *Wenn zwei sich liebe* under the title *Julicka* (Luna Palace, Rome 1922).

1901 **Das Gastmahl des Lucullus** (Carl Lindau, A Paulus) 1 act Danzers Orpheum 23 November

1903 **Bruder Straubinger** (Moritz West, Ignaz Schnitzer) Theater an der Wien 20 February

1905 **Pufferl** (Schnitzer, Sigmund Schlesinger) Theater an der Wien 10 February

1905 **Die Schützenliesel** (Leo Stein, Lindau) Carltheater 7 October

1906 **Phryne** (Fritz Grünbaum, Robert Bodanzky) 1 act Hölle 6 October

1906 **Künstlerblut** (Stein, Lindau) Carltheater 20 October

1907 **Vera Violetta** (Stein) 1 act Apollotheater 30 November

1908 **Ein Tag auf dem Mars** (Ottokar Tann-Bergler, Alfred Deutsch-German) 1 act Wiener Colosseum 17 January

1908 **Das Glücksschweinchen** (Stein, Lindau) Venedig-in-Wien 26 June

1908 **Johann der Zweite** (Stein, Lindau) Carltheater 3 October

1909 **Der junge Papa** (Alexander Engel, August Neidhart) 1 act Apollotheater 3 February

1910 **Lumpus und Pumpus** (Stein) 1 act Apollotheater 21 January

1910 **Der unsterbliche Lump** (Felix Dörmann) Wiener Bürgertheater 14 October

1911 **Der Zirkuskind** (Bodanzky, Friedrich Thelen) Raimundtheater 18 February

1911 **Der Natursänger** (Stein, Jenbach) 1 act Apollotheater 22 December

1911 **Der Frauenfresser** (Stein, Lindau) Wiener Bürgertheater 23 December

1913 **Der lachende Ehemann** (Julius Brammer, Alfred Grünwald) Wiener Bürgertheater 19 March

1913 **Ein Tag im Paradies** (Stein, Bela Jenbach) Wiener Bürgertheater 23 December

1914 **Komm, deutscher Brüder** (Lindau, Neidhart) Raimundtheater 4 October

1914 **Der Kriegsberichterstatter** (w others/Rudolf Öster-reicher, Willy Sterk) Apollotheater 9 October

1914 **Frühling am Rhein** (Lindau, Fritz Löhner-Beda) Wiener Bürgertheater 10 October

1914 **Der Durchgang der Venus** (Willner, Österreicher) Apollotheater 28 November

1915 **Die – oder keine** (Stein, Jenbach) Wiener Bürgertheater 9 October

1915 **Wenn zwei sich lieben** (Willner, Bodanzky) Theater an der Wien 29 October

1915 **Das Zimmer der Pompadour** (Eysler) 1 act Hölle 1 December

1916 **Warum geht's denn jetzt?** (Jacobson, Bodanzky) Bundes-theater 5 July

1916 **Hanni geht's tanzen** (Bodanzky) Apollotheater 7 November

1916 **Der berühmte Gabriel** (Ludwig Hirschfeld, Rudolf G Eger) Wiener Bürgertheater 8 November

1917 **Graf Toni** (Österreicher) Apollotheater 2 March

1917 **Der Aushilfsgatte** (Oskar Friedmann, Ludwig Herzer) Apollotheater 7 November

1918 **Leute von heute** (w Robert Stolz, Arthur Werau/Fritz Lunzer, Arthur Rebner) Bundestheater 22 June

1918 **Der dunkel Schatz** (Herzer, O Friedmann) Wiener Bürgertheater 14 November

1919 **Der fidele Geiger** (Louis Taufstein, Hans Herling) Wiener Bürgertheater 17 January

1920 **Rund um die Bühne** (Armin Friedmann, Gustav Beer) Apollotheater 1 March

1920 **Der König heiratet** (Beer, Ernst Marischka) 1 act Künst-lerbühne April

1920 **Wer hat's gemacht** (Willy Sterk) 1 act Variété Reclame 1 October

1921 **Die schöne Mama** (*La bella Mammina*) (Heinrich von Waldberg, Bruno Hardt-Warden) Teatro Nazionale, Rome 9 April; Wiener Bürgertheater 17 September

1921 **Die fromme Helene** (Arnold Golz, Emil Golz) Kom-odienhaus 22 December

1922 **Die Parliamentskathi** (Robert Blum, Alois Ulreich) Komödienhaus 15 April

1922 **Fräulein Sopherl, die schöne vom Markt** (Josco Schubert) Lustspieltheater 19 May

1922 **Schummel macht alles** (Karl Marfeld-Neumann) Komödienhaus 1 July

1923 **Drei auf einmal** (O Friedmann) Komödienhaus 29 March

1923 **Der ledige Schwiegersohn** (A Golz, E Golz) Wiener Bürgertheater 20 April

1923 **Vierzehn Tage (im) Arrest** (Horst, Österreicher) Raimundtheater 16 June

1923 **Lumpenlieschen** (Else Tauber) Carltheater 21 May

1926 **Das Land der Liebe** ('Habakuk' ie Gustav Tintner, Herl-ing) Wiener Bürgertheater 27 August

1927 **Die goldene Meisterin** (Brammer, Grünwald) Theater an der Wien 13 September

1929 **Ihr erster Ball** (Herling, Tintner) Wiener Bürgertheater 21 November

1930 **Das Strumpfband der Pompadour** (Lunzer, Emil von Meissner) Stadttheater, Augsburg 16 March

1930 **Durchlaucht Mizzi** (Lunzer, Beer) Neue Wiener Schauspielhaus 23 December

1931 **Die schlimme Paulette** (Stephan Walter, Karl Lustig-Prean) Stadttheater, Augsburg 1 March

1932 **Zwei alte Wiener** (Hans Borutzky, von Meissner) Neues Wiener Operetten-Theater 12 February

1932 **Die Rakete** (Fred Rhoden, Eduard Rogati) Stadttheater, Innsbruck 23 December

1932 **Donaulicbchen** (Brammer, Emil Marboth) Wiener Bürgertheater 25 December

1934 **Das ist der erste Liebe(lei)** (Beer, Hans Kottow) Volksoper 23 December

1947 **Wiener Musik** (Herz, Kosta) Wiener Bürgertheater 22 December

Biographies: Ewald, K: *Edmund Eysler: ein Musiker aus Wien* (Vienna, 1934); Prosl, R M: *Edmund Eysler* (Verlag Karl Kühne, Vienna, 1947)

EYTON, Frank (b London, 30 August 1894; d London, 1962).

City man turned lyricist and occasional playwright/librettist (*She Shall Have Music, Runaway Love, Happy Birthday*), Eyton formed an effective partnership with pianist/composer Billy Mayerl which produced the musical part of such successful shows as *Sporting Love, Twenty to One* and *Over She Goes*, and, later, with Noel Gay for the shows which followed *Me and My Girl* at the Victoria Palace.

He also wrote material for revue, additional lyrics for the shows *Love Lies* (1929), *Darling I Love You* (1929), *Silver Wings* (1930), *The One Girl* (1933), *The Flying Trapeze* (1935), *La-di-da-di-da* (1943) and *Six Pairs of Shoes* (1944), the words to Mischa Spoliansky's popular title song for the film *Tell Me Tonight*, and paired with Noel Gay on the songs for the film *Sailors Three* ('All Over the Place').

1928 **So Long, Letty!** (Billy Mayerl/Austin Melford) Birming-ham 22 October

1929 **Change Over** revised *So Long, Letty!* Hippodrome, Ports-mouth 8 April

1930 **Nippy** (Mayerl/Melford, Arthur Wimperis) Prince Edward Theatre 15 September

1931 **The Millionaire Kid** (Mayerl/Noel Scott) Gaiety Theatre 20 May

1933 **Nice Goings On** (Arthur Schwartz/Douglas Furber) Strand Theatre 13 September

1934 **Sporting Love** (Mayerl/w Carter/Stanley Lupino) Gaiety Theatre 31 March

1934 **She Shall Have Music** (Christopher Fry, Monte Crick/Ronald Frankau)

1935 **Twenty to One** (Mayerl/Arthur Rose) London Coliseum 12 November

1936 **Over She Goes** (Mayerl/w Carter/S Lupino) Saville Theatre 23 September

1937 **Crazy Days** (Mayerl/w Carter/S Lupino) Shaftesbury Theatre 14 September

1939 **Runaway Love** (Mayerl/w B Lupino) Saville 3 November book and lyrics

1940 **Present Arms** (Noel Gay/Fred Thompson) Prince of Wales Theatre 13 May

1940 **Happy Birthday** (Mayerl/w B Lupino, Arthur Rigby) Manchester 9 September

1941 **Lady Behave** (Edward Horan/S Lupino) His Majesty's Theatre 24 July

1942 **Kiki** (Mayerl/Martin Henry) Leeds 30 March

1942 **Susie** revised *Jack o' Diamonds* (Gay/w Clifford Grey/H F Maltby) Oxford 13 June

1942 **Wild Rose** revised *Sally* new lyrics (Prince's Theatre)

1943 **The Love Racket** (Gay/w others/Lupino) Adelphi Theatre 23 December

1944 **Meet Me Victoria** (Gay/Lupino Lane, Lauri Wylie) Vic-toria Palace 8 April

1944 **Ring Time** (Gay/Stanley Brightman, Melford) Glasgow 28 August

1946 **Sweetheart Mine** (Gay/Wylie, Lane) Victoria Palace 1 August

1947 **Bob's Your Uncle** (Gay, Melford) Saville Theatre 5 May

1949 **Roundabout** (ex-*Hat in the Air*) (Horan, Melford, Ken Attiwill) Saville Theatre 4 August

F

FABRAY, Nanette [FABARES, Ruby Bernadette Nanette Theresa] (b San Diego, Calif, 27 October 1922). Laughing-cheeked musical comedy juvenile of the Broadway 1940s.

Miss Fabray appeared in vaudeville and in the *Our Gang* films as a child, and made her first Broadway musical appearance at 17 in the revue *Meet the People* as Nanette Fabares ('Hurdy Gurdy Verdi'). A minor rôle the following year in Cole Porter's *Let's Face It* (1941, Jean Blanchard) was followed by a takeover of a larger one, Constance Moore's featured juvenile part of Antiope, in *By Jupiter* (1943), and rôles in two short-lived pieces, the 45-performance *My Dear Public* (1943, Jean) and as the 'demoiselle en loterie' Sally Madison in *Jackpot* (1944), before she succeeded Celeste Holm in the title-rôle of *Bloomer Girl* (1945).

She created the lead in *High Button Shoes* (1947, Sara Longstreet), introducing with Jack McCauley 'Papa Won't You Dance with Me' and 'I Still Get Jealous' and, in the following season's *Love Life* (1948, Susan Cooper), starred with Ray Middleton in Alan Jay Lerner's examination of 150 years of marriage, to Kurt Weill music ('Green-up Time') and a Tony Award. She played opposite Georges Guétary as a fourth successive period heroine in *Arms in the Girl* (1950, Jo Kirkland) and starred as the wandering French orphan of *Make a Wish* (1951, Janette) both for rather shorter runs than the previous two shows had garnered, before going to Hollywood to star in the film *The Band Wagon* with Fred Astaire and Jack Buchanan.

She subsequently had a considerable television success, and appeared only once more in a Broadway musical, as the wife of the President of the United States (Robert Ryan) in the Irving Berlin musical *Mr President* (1962, Nell Henderson). She has continued intermittently to appear in regional musical productions. (Margo Channing in *Applause*, Ruth Sherwood in *Wonderful Town, Follies* etc).

FADE OUT – FADE IN Musical comedy in 2 acts by Adolph Green and Betty Comden. Music by Jule Styne. Mark Hellinger Theater, New York, 26 May 1964.

A musical comedy set in the Hollywood of the 1930s, *Fade Out – Fade In* 100 per cent top-billed comedienne Carol Burnett, who had blundered hilariously onto the musical stage as the heroine of *Once Upon a Mattress* five years previously, as a klutzy movieland chorine accidentally cast in a starring rôle by an over-wieldy studio. In the best cinematic tradition, the unlikely movie becomes a hit and the new star can galumph off into the sunset with the boss's helpful nephew (Dick Patterson).

Jack Cassidy featured as plastic filmstar Byron Prong (a name as happily in the best burlesque tradition as that of

Miss Burnett's character, Hope Springfield), whilst characters like studio boss Lionel Z Governor (Lou Jacobi) with his plethora of despised nephews, Dora Dailey (Virginia Payne), Helga Sixtrees, Myra May Melrose, Custer Corkley, Gloria Currie (Tina Louise) and Viennese psychiatrist Dr Traurig (Rube Singer), all lived up to the expectations aroused by their names.

Miss Burnett wondered musically at how she, 'The Usher from the Mezzanine', had made it to stardom, mused on the profit of a pretty name change to 'Lila Tremaine' and imitated Shirley Temple to Tiger Haynes's version of Bojangles Robinson ('You Mustn't Be Discouraged'), whilst Jacobi pursued the ravishing Miss Louise through a nightmare ballet ('L Z in Quest of his Youth'), haunted by Hope.

The show closed down after 199 performances when Miss Burnett, discontented with a rôle which did not fulfil its paper promises, fell ill. The show's book was revamped, two replacement songs supplied for the star, and the piece remounted (15 February 1965), but it closed definitively after another 72 performances.

An Australian production mounted on the Tivoli circuit with Sheila Smith, John Stratton and H F Green featured was not a success.

Australia: Tivoli, Sydney 20 February 1965
Recording: original cast (ABC-Paramount)

FÁI, Béla [Jakab] (b Nagyvárad, 29 February 1853; d Budapest, 21 December 1904).

Journalist and theatrical translator/adapter, Fái rewrote, either alone or in collaboration, versions of the works of such authors as Sardou, Dumas, Daudet, Émile Augier, Legouvé, Ohnet, Sudermann, Meilhac and Halévy, Planché and Shirley Brooks as well as Brandon Thomas's *Charley's Aunt*, Paul Potter's *Trilby* and *Im weissen Rössl* for the Hungarian stage, many for the Nemzeti Színház, whilst also turning a vast number of texts of German-, French- and English-language musicals into the vernacular. He was secretary, in turn, to the Magyar Színház and the Népszinház, and held posts at the Nemzeti Színház and the Magyar Királyi Operaház in the last years before his death.

1879 **Kamargo** (*La Camargo*) Hungarian version (Népszinház)
1879 **A kis nagysám** (*La Petite Mademoiselle*) Hungarian version (Népszinház)
1879 **Favartné** (*Madame Favart*) Hungarian version w Lajos Evva (Népszinház)
1880 **A franciák Milánóban** (*La Fille du tambour-major*) Hungarian version w Evva (Népszinház)
1881 **Tiszturak a zárdában** (*Les Mousquetaires au couvent*) Hungarian version w Evva (Népszinház)
1881 **Az ácslegények gazdasszonykája** (*La Mère des compagnons*) Hungarian version w Evva (Népszinház)

1881 **A szélkakas** (*La Girouette*) Hungarian version w Evva (Népszinház)

1881 **A karácsonyfa** (*L'Arbre de Noël*) Hungarian version (Népszinház)

1882 **Nap és hold** (*Le Jour et la nuit*) Hungarian version w Evva (Népszinház)

1882 **A furcsa háboru** (*Der lustige Krieg*) Hungarian version w Evva (Népszinház)

1882 **Viola-Ibolya** (*Giroflé-Girofla*) Hungarian version w Evva (Népszinház)

1882 **Lili** Hungarian version w Evva (Népszinház)

1882 **A kertészleány** (*Le Coeur et la main*) Hungarian version w Evva (Népszinház)

1883 **A koldusdiák** (*Der Bettelstudent*) Hungarian version w Evva (Népszinház)

1883 **A hercegasszony** (*Madame l'Archiduc*) Hungarian version w Evva (Népszinház)

1883 **Kanári hercegnő** (*La Princesse des Canaries*) Hungarian version w Evva (Népszinház)

1883 **Rip** (*Rip van Winkle*) Hungarian version w Evva (Népszinház)

1884 **Kék Feri** (*François les bas-bleus*) Hungarian version w Evva (Népszinház)

1884 **A gerolsteini nagyhercegnő** (*La Grande-Duchesse de Gérolstein*) Hungarian version w Evva (Népszinház)

1885 **Az ébren álmodó** (*La Dormeuse éveillée*) Hungarian version w Evva (Népszinház)

1886 **A bearni leány** (*La Béarnaise*) Hungarian version w Evva (Népszinház)

1886 **Esketés dobszóval** (*Le Mariage au tambour*) Hungarian version w György Verő (Népszinház)

1886 **Százszorszép** (*La Jolie Parfumeuse*) Hungarian version w Verő (Népszinház)

1887 **Az udvari bolond** (*Der Hofnarr*) Hungarian version w Antal Radó (Népszinház)

1887 **Komédiás hercegnő** (*Nell Gwynne*) Hungarian version w Evva (Népszinház)

1887 **Az eltévedt bárányka** (*Les Brebis égarées*) Hungarian version w music by André Messager and Eduard Jakobowksi (Népszinház)

1887 **Fejő lány, vagy költőimádás** (*Patience*) Hungarian version w Evva (Népszinház)

1888 **Szedtevette nagysám** (*Mam'selle Crénom*) Hungarian version w Evva (Népszinház)

1888 **A kalózkirály** (*Surcouf*) Hungarian version w Andor Kozma (Népszinház)

1890 **A boszorkányvár** (*Das verwunschene Schloss*) Hungarian version w Ferenc Rajna (Népszinház)

1890 **A szegény Jonathan** (*Der arme Jonathan*) Hungarian version w Rajna (Népszinház)

1890 **Egy éj Velencében** (*Eine Nacht in Venedig*) Hungarian version w Rajna (Népszinház)

1891 **A madarász** (*Der Vogelhändler*) Hungarian version w Rajna (Népszinház)

1891 **A tollkirály** (*Isoline*) Hungarian version w Evva (Népszinház)

1892 **A szerencsfia** (*Das Sonntagskind*) Hungarian version w Rajna (Népszinház)

1892 **Fanchon asszony leánya** (*La Fille de Fanchon la vielleuse*) Hungarian version w Rajna (Népszinház)

1892 **Az erkölcsösök** (*Der Tugendwachter*) Hungarian version w Rajna (Budai Színkör)

1893 **A nevető örökösök** (*Lachende Erben*) Hungarian version w Rajna (Budai Színkör)

1897 **A gésák** (*The Geisha*) Hungarian version w Emil Makai (Magyar Színház)

1898 **A kék asszony** (*La Falote*) Hungarian version w Makai (Budai Színkör)

1899 **Toledad** (*L'Enlèvement de la Toledad*) Hungarian version w Makai (Népszinház)

1900 **San Toy** Hungarian version w Makai (Népszinház)

1900 **New York szépe** (*The Belle of New York*) Hungarian version w Makai (Magyar Színház)

1901 **Czirkusz-élet** (*The Circus Girl*) Hungarian version w Jenő Faragó (Népszinház)

1903 **Khinai mézeshetek** (*A Chinese Honeymoon*) Hungarian version w Faragó (Népszinház)

FAIN, Sammy [FEINBERG, Samuel] (b New York, 17 June 1902; d Los Angeles, 6 December 1989). Celebrated songwriter, particularly for film, whose stage career was less productive.

A striving songwriter from a young age, Fain found his first success when he paired with lyricist Irving Kahal to produce a series of popular songs, beginning with the 1927 'Let a Smile Be Your Umbrella' and including such numbers as 'I Left My Sugar Standing in the Rain', 'Wedding Bells are Breaking Up That Old Gang of Mine', 'You Brought a New Kind of Love' as sung by Maurice Chevalier in the film *The Big Pond* (1930), 'When I Take My Sugar to Tea', 'Sitting on a Back Yard Fence', 'By a Waterfall' (delivered by Dick Powell and a good deal of pulchritude in *Footlight Parade*), 'A Sunbonnet Blue' and 'I'll Be Seeing You', mostly for movie musicals, over a period of some 15 years. After Kahal's death in 1942 Fain continued in the film world with other partners, supplying whole or part-scores and/or title-songs for such movies as *Calamity Jane* (1953), *Love is a Many Splendoured Thing* (1955, Academy Award), *April Love* (1957) and *A Certain Smile* (1958), as well as ringing up a further series of popular songs ('Dear Hearts and Gentle People', 'I Can Dream, Can't I?', 'Home is Where the Heart Is' etc).

During his early Hollywood years, Fain also contributed one score to the musical stage, for the Shuberts' musicalization of their play hit *Up Pops the Devil* as *Everybody's Welcome* (1931). The musical was not a hit and its one song hit was not Fain's, but Herman Hupfeld's 'As Time Goes By'. Fain also supplied individual songs to a number of theatre revues and musicals (*Right This Way*, *Hellzapoppin*, *Blackbirds of 1939*, *George White's Scandals of 1939*, *Boys and Girls Together*, *Sons o' Fun*, *Ziegfeld Follies*) and, although his stage work was less considerable than his film work, subsequently wrote, over two decades, full scores for five further Broadway shows and one, Dennis King's attempt at actor-management with *She Had To Say 'Yes'*, which didn't get that far.

Toplitzky of Notre Dame, a fantasy piece about an angel who comes to earth to help a football team, and *Flahooley*, another fantasy which involved a genie, the bass-to-soprano voice of Yma Sumac (equipped with three interpolated wordless songs by Moises Vivanco) and the more normal one of Barbara Cook, were failures and though the cheerfully unsophisticated *Ankles Aweigh* lasted 176 performances at the Mark Hellinger Theater, it could not be accounted a hit. East failed to meet West in good *Geisha* fashion for just 12 performances in *Christine*, *Something More!* survived 15 showings and none of the five shows left songs which won the popularity of Fain's film music.

In 1962 he supplemented Victor Young's film score for *Around the World in 80 Days* to make it into a full-scale stage musical for the St Louis Muny and, subsequently, the Jones Beach Marine Theatre, and a stage adaptation of his *Calamity Jane* ('Black Hills of Dakota', 'Secret Love') was produced at the Muny in 1961 with Edie Adams in the title-rôle, and subsequently played in Britain with Barbara Windsor (briefly) and then Susan Jane Tanner starred.

1931 **Everybody's Welcome** (ex- *Kissable Girl*) (Harold Atteridge) Shubert Theater 13 October

1940 **She Had To Say 'Yes'** (Al Dubin/Bob Henly, Richard Pinkham) Forrest Theater, Philadelphia 30 December

1946 **Toplitzky of Notre Dame** (George Marion jr, Jack Barnett) Century Theater 26 December

1951 **Flahooley** (E Y Harburg/Fred Saidy) Broadhurst Theater 14 May

1952 **Jollyanna** (revised *Flahooley* w William Friml) San Francisco 11 August

1955 **Ankles Aweigh** (Dan Shapiro/Guy Bolton, Eddie Davis) Mark Hellinger Theater 18 April

1960 **Christine** (Paul Francis Webster/Pearl Buck, Charles Peck) 46th Street Theater 28 April

1961 **Calamity Jane** (Webster ad Charles K Freeman/James O'Hanlon) Municipal Opera, St Louis 12 June

1962 **Around the World in 80 Days** (w Victor Young/Harold Adamson/Sig Herzig) Municipal Opera, St Louis 11 June

1964 **Something More!** (Marilyn Bergman, Alan Bergman/Nate Monaster) Eugene O'Neill Theater 10 November

FAIRBROTHER, Sydney [TAPPING, Sydney Parselle Cowell]

(b Blackpool, 31 July 1872; d London, 10 January 1941). Prominent character actress in British straight and musical theatre.

Miss Fairbrother played in the straight theatre for the first 15 years of her career before creating a series of musical-comedy character rôles for Seymour Hicks between 1905 and 1907. She scored a personal success in her first musical show, playing Evelyn Snipe in *The Talk of the Town* and singing 'The Nice Young Man (who whistled down the lane)', and followed up memorably as the smitten landlady, Mrs Goodge, in *The Beauty of Bath* and then as the roustabout, Charlotte Siddons, in *The Gay Gordons*. She then returned to comedy and to the music halls in a scena with Fred Emney, but came back to the musical theatre in 1916 when she was cast as Ali Baba's shrewish wife, Mahbubah, in *Chu Chin Chow*, a part which she created, played for three and a half years at His Majesty's Theatre and made her own.

She subsequently made further musical appearances as another shrewish wife, opposite Jack Buchanan in *Battling Butler* (1922), briefly in the disastrous *All for Joy* (1932), then as the busybody Adela Teetle in *Nice Goings On* (1934) and as Mrs Flower in *Lucky Break* (1935), both with Leslie Henson, and as Miss Schnapps in the Alhambra spectacle *Tulip Time* (1935). Although her musical theatre appearances were comparatively few in an extremely busy stage and film career of 50 years, her characterful performances of often harshly spinsterish ladies were highly praised and prized. Her portrayal of Mahbubah was captured on film in the 1934 movie version of *Chu Chin Chow*.

Autobiography: *Through an Old Stage Door* (Muller, London, 1939)

FALKA *see* LE DROIT D'AÎNESSE

FALL, Leo[pold]

(b Olmütz, 2 February 1873; d Vienna, 16 September 1925). Arguably the most distinguished and, in any case, one of the most successful composers of the 20th-century Viennese Operette stage.

Leo Fall was born in what was, at that stage, part of the Austro-Hungarian Empire, the son of musician and military bandmaster Moritz Fall (1840–1922), himself the composer of several Operetten (*Prinz Bummler*, *Mirolan*, *Robin Hood*, *Das Modell* for the Berlin Theater Unter den Linden, *Leuchtkäfer*, produced at Magdeburg's Wilhelm-Theater in 1899) and theatre music for numerous Possen and other musical plays (*Berliner Spezialitaten*, *Berliner Raubthiere* etc).

A fresh posting for his father meant that the boy was brought up in Lemberg. There, from an early age, he was given a sound musical education by the elder Fall which prepared him, by the age of 14, to attend the Vienna Conservatoire, where he carried out the remainder of his studies. His first professional work thereafter was as a violinist in a military orchestra, but he returned home to work with his father, who was now retired and running a coffee-house orchestra in Berlin, and doing a little of the composing his earlier duties had limited. Fall supplemented this work by giving music lessons, as he had during his Vienna student days, but at the age of 21 he had his first working contact with the theatre when he was taken on as a junior conductor at Berlin's Centraltheater. He quickly rose to improved positions at the Belle-Alliance-Theater and then at Hamburg's Centralhallen-Theater, where he was engaged as principal conductor at the age of 23. At that house, he composed his first original music for the stage in the form of incidental music and songs for the Lokalposse *Lustige Blätter*, and the musical accompaniment to a Zeitbild by the prolific playwright and librettist George Okonkowski.

He returned to Berlin after two seasons in Hamburg, and successively held conducting posts at the Centraltheater and the Metropoltheater before taking a decided step downwards to become musical director in a cabaret, the Intimes-Theater, where apart from his principal duties he provided songs and, on one occasion, a comic opera, *Paroli*, for house production. The piece was successful enough to warrant publication, with its soprano 'Nachtigallenlied' and the tenor 'Soldatenlied' picked out as singles. During this period, Fall worked on writing a grand opera, but his ambition in that direction was kneecapped when *Irrlicht*, written with the librettist of *Paroli* and produced at Mannheim in 1905, turned out to be a failure.

Fall had, however, started working in a different direction even prior to *Irrlicht*'s stage première, and, shortly afterwards, he succeeded in placing his first Operette with no less a house than the Theater an der Wien. *Der Rebell* (1905) gave him a second resounding failure within a year. His first success was, however, not too long in coming. *Der fidele Bauer*, produced less than two years later at Mannheim, was an enormous success and just a few months after its première – and before it had yet made its appearance in Vienna – his next piece, *Die Dollarprinzessin*, was produced at the Theater an der Wien. It roundly confirmed Fall's new reputation as one of the rising stars of the European Operette, alongside Lehár, currently basking in the incomparable success of *Die lustige Witwe*, Oscar Straus, who had arrived hot on his heels with *Ein Walzertraum*, and Edmund Eysler. On the wings of the post-*lustige Witwe* craze for Viennese Operette, *Die Dollarprinzessin* was soon on its way to splendid successes in Britain and in America and Fall was quickly established as an international favourite. That favouritism was only increased by his next work, *Die geschiedene Frau*. A splendid success at the Vienna Carltheater, it also travelled the world in various tongues (*La Divorcée*, *The Girl in the Train*, *Az elvált asszony* etc) and repeated its German and Austrian success almost wherever it went.

Of his following Operetten, *Das Puppenmädel* and *Die schöne Risette* had fine successes in Vienna and central Europe without winning comparable fame overseas, and *Die Sirene*, produced in America as *The Siren*, and the one-act *Brüderlein fein*, which was played on the music halls in Britain and elsewhere, only confirmed the esteem in which their composer was held, but the next piece to win him a major international success was a rewrite of the ill-fated *Der Rebell*. Its rearranged score was matched up with a new libretto and lyrics, and the new show staged under the title *Der liebe Augustin*. One of those relyricked songs, the waltz 'Und der Himmel hängt voller Geigen', proved to be one of the most popular amongst all Fall's Operette melodies, and the show itself (played in Britain, notably, with great success as *Princess Caprice*) perhaps his most delightfully melodious and light-hearted to date.

Fall's popularity in Britain was such that he was commissioned to write an original piece for the well-paying London Hippodrome, but his activity on the home front was too great to leave him time, and the little *The Eternal Waltz* was put together from his leftovers. It was to be the last Fall musical to be seen in Britain for some time, as the coming of the war brought down the shutters on Germanic shows on the London stage, and writers such as Fall and Gilbert, for whom London had been a superb showplace for the international market, found themselves at the end of a very lucrative half-dozen years as the darlings of the world's musical theatre.

Fall's output did not shrink, however, and between 1913 and 1916 he wrote and saw staged in Berlin and Vienna a half-dozen further full-scale Operetten which, if they had, owing to circumstances, lesser international careers than the pre-war works, nevertheless included two of his musically most outstanding shows – the brilliant *Die Kaiserin* (*Fürstenliebe*), which he claimed later as his own favourite amongst his works, and the swirlingly romantic and extremely long-running *Die Rose von Stambul* with its ultimate star tenor rôle.

After the First World War, he had two further works produced at Dresden, one of which, *Der goldene Vogel*, he described as an opera, and he continued a regular more than one-per-year supply of splendid scores to the Berlin theatre. Both *Die spanische Nachtigall* and *Die Strassensängerin* played some 140 performances in Berlin, but none of these shows won the same enormous success as *Die Rose von Stambul* had done until his 1922 offering, a deliciously comical piece written around the fictional amours of Madame Pompadour, was produced at the Berliner-Theater. *Madame Pompadour* brought him once again not only European attention, but the kind of international response he had first won 15 years earlier. London welcomed the composer back with rabid enthusiasm and *Madame Pompadour* went round the world, engraving herself into the permanent repertoire at home and into international popularity for many years.

Regarded by many as Fall's most complete work, it is a piece which is as far from the deliciously frisky, up-to-date *Die Dollarprinzessin* or the winningly rural *Der fidele Bauer* as Lehár's *Das Land des Lächelns* is from his early *Die lustige*

Witwe. Unlike the later Lehár works, however, the pieces of Fall's maturer period – and most specifically the two most enduring shows of that period, *Die Rose von Stambul* and *Madame Pompadour* – contain a substantial and genuine comic element in both their music and text. Happily placed alongside their richly romantic musical part, in classic proportions, this contrasting element helps give these shows a very different feeling and flavour to the wilfully darkened tones of the pieces with which Lehár would, a few years later, take the Operette into more pretentious areas.

What Fall, some of whose own best work had been tempered by writing for a singular star in the person of prima donna Fritzi Massary, would have made of the Tauberesque fashion in musical theatre in the late 1920s and early 1930s would, on the evidence of *Die Rose von Stambul* alone, have been worth hearing, but the composer did not live that long. After just one more stage work, *Der süsse Kavalier*, produced in Vienna in 1923, he fell ill, and in 1925 he died of cancer at the age of 52. A posthumous *Jugend im Mai* was produced in Dresden the following year and in 1929 the Theater an der Wien, which had staged Fall's first Operette, staged his last – a compilation made from 16 pieces of music which the composer had left behind him, attached to a libretto by the experienced Willner and Reichert and played as *Rosen aus Florida*.

The years since his death have not treated Fall as kindly as they should have. *Madame Pompadour* and *Die Rose von Stambul* have held a place in the standard repertoire in Germany and Austria, but scarcely with the kind of prominence allotted to other, contemporary composers' works, and whilst *Die Dollarprinzessin*, *Der liebe Augustin* and *Der fidele Bauer* loiter on the fringe of that repertoire, *Die geschiedene Frau*, such an enormous hit in the wars prior to the Great War, and *Die Kaiserin* seem wholly forgotten. Perhaps through lack of an interested party to plug his works to producers of the second half of the 20th century in the style which has so profited other writers, the man who was, in the opinion of many, the most outstanding Operette composer of his period has ended up deeply in the shadow of Lehár, Straus and Kálmán, and unknown to the modern public at large.

1896 **Lustige Blätter** (Franz Fuchs) Centralhallen-Theater, Hamburg 25 July

1897 **1842** (*Der grosse Brand*) (Georg Okonkowski) Centralhallen-Theater, Hamburg 1 August

1899 **Der Brandstifter** (Okonkowski) Ostende Theater, Berlin 1 January

1900 **Die Jagd nach dem Glück** (Carl Weiss) Carl Weiss Theater, Berlin 1 February

1901 **'ne feine Nummer** (w Victor Holländer/Julius Freund) Metropoltheater, Berlin 16 February

1902 **Paroli** (*Frau Denise*) (Ludwig Fernand) 1 act Intimes-Theater 4 October

1905 **Der Rebell** (Rudolf Bernauer, Ernst Welisch) Theater an der Wien 28 November

1906 **Der Fuss** (Bernauer) 1 act Centraltheater, Chemnitz 18 September

1907 **Der fidele Bauer** (Victor Léon) Mannheim 25 July

1907 **Die Dollarprinzessin** (A M Willner, Fritz Grünbaum) Theater an der Wien 2 November

1908 **Die geschiedene Frau** (Léon) Carltheater 23 December

1908 **Brüderlein fein** (H E Falschholz) Bernhard-Rose-Theater, Berlin 31 December

1909 **Die Schrei nach der Ohrfeige**
1909 **Brüderlein fein** (Julius Wilhelm) 1 act Hölle 1 December
1910 **Das Puppenmädel** (Willner, Leo Stein) Carltheater 4 November
1910 **Die schöne Risette** (Willner, Robert Bodanzky) Theater an der Wien 19 November
1911 **Die Sirene** (Willner, Stein) Johann Strauss-Theater 5 January
1911 **The Eternal Waltz** (Austen Hurgon) 1 act London Hippodrome 22 December
1912 **Der liebe Augustin** revised *Der Rebell* Neues Theater, Berlin 3 February
1913 **Die Studentengräfin** (Léon) Theater am Nollendorfplatz, Berlin 18 January
1913 **Der Nachtschnellzug** (Léon, Stein) Johann Strauss-Theater 18 December
1914 **Jung England** (Bernauer, Welisch) Montis Operetten-Theater, Berlin 14 February
1915 **Der künstliche Mensch** (Willner, Rudolf Österreicher) Theater des Westens, Berlin 2 October
1915 **Die Kaiserin** (aka *Fürstenliebe*) (Julius Brammer, Alfred Grünwald) Metropoltheater, Berlin 16 October
1916 **Tantalus im Dachstüberl** 1 act Stadttheater, Würzburg 26 March
1916 **Seemansliebchen** (w Franz Ferdinand Warnke/Karl Hermann, Max Berger) Walhalla-Theater, Berlin 4 September
1916 **Die Rose von Stambul** (Brammer, Grünwald) Theater an der Wien 2 December
1920 **Frau Ministerpräsident** revised *Jung England* Residenztheater, Dresden 3 February
1920 **Der goldene Vogel** (Wilhelm, Paul Frank) Staatsoper, Dresden 21 May
1920 **Die spanische Nachtigall** (Schanzer, Welisch) Berliner Theater, Berlin 18 November
1921 **Die Strassensängerin** (August Neidhart, Lo Portem) Metropoltheater, Berlin 24 September
1921 **Der heilige Ambrosius** (Willner, Arthur Rebner) 1 act Deutsches Künstlertheater, Berlin 3 November
1922 **Madame Pompadour** (Schanzer, Welisch) Berliner Theater, Berlin 9 September
1923 **Der süsse Kavalier** (Schanzer, Welisch) Apollotheater 11 December
1926 **Jugend im Mai** (Schanzer, Welisch) Zentraltheater, Dresden 22 October, Städtische Oper, Berlin 1927
1929 **Rosen aus Florida** (arr Erich Wolfgang Korngold/Willner, Heinz Reichert) Theater an der Wien 22 February

Fall's brother **Richard FALL** (b Senitsch, 3 April 1882; d Auschwitz, 1943) had a regular if unspectacular career in the wake of Leo's dazzling one. He worked as a conductor, notably at Vienna's Apollotheater, and was the composer of a number of Operetten and revues, principally for Viennese theatres, of which *Der Weltenbummler* – also staged in Budapest as *Világjáró* (ad Zsolt Harsányi) and in Germany, *Die Damenparadies*, given in Hungary as *Borbála Kisasszony*, and *Die Puppenbaronessen* – were the most successful.

1909 **Goldreifchen** (Paul Wertheimer, Mia Ewers) 1 act Johann Strauss-Theater 11 December
1911 **Das Damenparadies** (Julius Brammer, Alfred Grünwald) 1 act Wiener Colosseum 19 October
1912 **Der Wiener Fratz** (Ernst Klein) 1 act Hölle 1 January
1912 **Arms and the Girl** (Austen Hurgon) London Hippodrome 29 April
1913 **Leute vom Stand** (Bodanzky, Grünbaum) 1 act Hölle 1 March
1915 **Der Weltenbummler** (Fritz Löhner-Beda, Carl Lindau) Montis Operetten-Theater, Berlin 18 November
1917 **Die Dame von Welt** (Löhner-Beda, Hans Kottow) Apollotheater 31 January
1917 **Die Puppenbaronessen** (Alexander Engel, Grünbaum) Apollotheater 1 September
1920 **Grossstadtmärchen** (Bruno Hardt-Warden, Erwin Weill) Carltheater 10 January
1921 **Im Alpenhotel** (Julius Horst, Ernst Wengraf) 1 act Apollotheater 6 August
1922 **Der geizige Verschwender** (Richard Kessler, Arthur Rebner) Deutsches Künstlertheater 24 February
1927 **Die Glocken von Paris** (Paul Knepler, Ignaz M Welleminsky) Carltheater 14 October

Biography: Zimmerli, W: *Leo Fall* (Zurich, 1957)

LA FALOTE Opérette in 3 acts by Maurice Ordonneau and Armand Liorat. Music by Louis Varney. Théâtre des Folies-Dramatiques, Paris, 17 April 1896.

The libretto of *La Falote*, one of the most successful of Louis Varney's works of the 1890s, mixed a series of particularly saucy and amusing episodes with a touch of the (apparently) supernatural. The Baronne du Hoguette (Armande Cassive) masquerades as an apparition, known as 'La Falote', to escape the discovery of her infidelities by her husband (Paul Hittemans) in a piece which was rather a cross between *Les Cloches de Corneville* and *La Dame blanche*, but none the worse for that.

The naughty Baronne has the habit of meeting her boyfriend up amongst the gothic pillars of Mont-St-Michel, and she encourages the legend of the blue-cloaked ghost to keep the inquisitive away from her trysting place. However, her husband has become fascinated by the spectre, and has, indeed, begun a serious scientific research into it which he is convinced will secure his fame. When, after many farcical incidents, he realizes the truth, he prefers to let his wife have her fling with the pretty Captain Mirasol (Baron fils) rather than compromise his scientific standing.

The young Jean Périer starred as the youthful fisherman Pierre, and made a hit with the show's most attractive number, the Chanson Bretonne, with Suzanne Elven as his country Thérèse, deeply involved, like him, in the multiple comical convolutions in the tale. Jane Evans (Mme Pigeon) was the heavy lady – Thérèse's aunt – who tries to alienate Pierre from her niece by pretending that 'La Falote' wants him for a bridegroom, and Mlle Dulaurens played the little maid who stirs up the plot by revealing the truth to the Baron.

The piece ran for a superb 190 performances in its initial run at the Folies-Dramatiques. It was similarly well received in Budapest (ad Emil Makai, Béla J Fái, as 'the blue girl') with Klára Küry starring, but an American production (ad J Cheever Goodwin) by J C Duff with a cast headed by Julius Steger, W J Le Moyne, Guy Standing, Yvonne de Tréville, May Norton and Georgia Powers was a quick Broadway failure (16 performances) in a period where the fashion for French opérette had largely passed from the American stage.

USA: Casino Theater 1 March 1897; Hungary: Népszínház *A kék asszony* 3 April 1897

FALSETTOS *see* MARCH OF THE FALSETTOS

LA FAMILLE TROUILLAT Opérette in 3 acts by Hector Crémieux and Ernest Blum. Music by Léon Vasseur. Théâtre de la Renaissance, Paris, 10 September 1874.

Léon Vasseur, struggling to follow up the enormous

success of *La Timbale d'argent*, had little luck with *La Famille Trouillat*, a sprightly period piece produced with a certain amount of pre-publicity. In spite of a cast headed by the splendid Vauthier, and with the novelty casting of the actor Paulin Ménier and the bulky, salacious café-concert star Thérésa, it was a failure, yet it was subsequently played both in Vienna and London. The English version, 'assembled' by Alfred Maltby and Richard Mansell, added music by Grevé and others to Vasseur's score, but in spite of a top-flight cast (Frank Celli, Harry Paulton, Furneaux Cook, Kate Munroe, Mme Amadi, Maria Davis), *La Belle Normande* ran just six weeks.

The 'family' of Crémieux and Blum's lively, saucy story was the Norman peasant family of little Pervenche Trouillat (Mlle Noémie). Headed by sister Mariotte (Thérésa) and her husband (Menier) they descend rageously on Paris to winkle out the culpable fellow who had his way with their Pervenche during a storm at Honfleur. Their search is complicated by a comical chap called Bobinet (Vauthier) who tries to set the 1,000-volt Mariotte onto his landlord, Cactus, before it eventuates that the 'culprit' is not the elder Cactus but his attractive nephew, Anatole. And that Pervenche had cried 'rape' only to trick her family into helping her trace her lost beloved.

The musical part of the evening gave Vauthier his share of melodies, and one song to the ingénue, but the centrepiece of the score was the group of four numbers written to feature the evening's main attraction, Thérésa, a group topped by her Norman-patriotic number explaining 'C'est les Normands, m'a dit ma mère, c'est les Normands qu'ont conquis l'Angleterre'.

Austria: Strampfertheater *Die Familie Trouillat* 29 January 1875;
  UK: Globe Theatre *La Belle Normande* 26 January 1881

FANFAN LA TULIPE Opérette in 3 acts by Paul Ferrier and Jules Prével. Music by Louis Varney. Théâtre des Folies-Dramatiques, Paris, 21 October 1882.

The character of the womanizing soldier Fanfan la Tulipe, familiar on stage and in song since his first appearance as the hero of an 1819 popular song, was woven into an opérettic intrigue by the librettists of Varney's earliest hit *Les Mousquetaires au couvent* (1880). Alongside a good deal of amorous goings-on, the principal events of their book were the challenge issued by the timid soldier Michel (Simon-Max) when he discovers Fanfan (Max Bouvet) tampering with his Pimprenelle (Juliette Simon-Girard), and the hero's subsequent adoption of the *David Garrick* technique of behaving appallingly to the girl so that she will go back to her real lover and leave him to go off and win a war or two.

Varney used the familiar old 'Fanfan la Tulipe' refrain, which Émile Debraux had originally culled from street minstrelsy, as the main motif of his attractive and eminently theatrical score and the piece won sufficient public approval to run for 100 performances in its initial season. It was revived at the Château d'Eau in 1889 and again at the Gaîté-Lyrique in 1904 (14 September) with Mme Simon-Girard in her original rôle and Lucien Noël as Fanfan.

In 1892 the Grand Théâtre at Bordeaux mounted another *Fanfan la Tulipe* (Charles Haring/Ernest Laroche) whilst in 1979 yet another opérette entitled *Fanfan la Tulipe* (Jacques Debronckart/René Wheeler, Henri Jeanson),

this one based on the successful 1952 film screenplay on which its authors had collaborated, was produced at the Opéra de Nantes (24 December). A German-language *Fanfan la Tulipe* (Thomas Bürkholz/Klaus Eidam) was produced at Rathen in 1991 (11 May).

Recording: 1991 German musical (Monopol)

FANFRELUCHE Opérette in 3 acts by Paul Burani, Gaston Hirsch and Saint-Arroman. Music by Gaston Serpette. Théâtre de la Renaissance, Paris, 16 December 1883.

The opérette which became *Fanfreluche* was first produced at the Fantaisies-Parisiennes, Brussels (20 March 1880) under the title *La Nuit de Saint-Germain* and, although it had a certain success in its Belgian première, the score was appreciated very much more than the libretto. As a result, Paul Burani was called in to doctor the piece. In fact, he did it over so thoroughly that, by the time *Fanfreluche* reached Paris, even the plot had changed. Jeanne Granier starred in a rôle which was constructed to allow her a gamut of impersonations as the virtuous Brézette, forced into all sorts of disguises to avoid the unwelcome attentions of the local potentate, alongside the baritone Louis Morlet (Saverdy) and the one-time Variétés star Léa Silly (Lucrèce de Bombonne), but neither their drawing power nor Serpette's score was able to take *Fanfreluche* beyond 60 performances.

FANNY Musical in 2 acts by S N Behrman and Joshua Logan based on the plays of Marcel Pagnol. Music and lyrics by Harold Rome. Majestic Theater, New York, 4 November 1954.

The libretto of *Fanny* was a melted-down version of the famous trio of Marseillais plays of Marcel Pagnol (*Marius, Fanny, César*), which had already been memorably adapted into a trilogy of Alexander Korda films by their author in the early 1930s. Here the plays were converted into a hurried three-into-one skeleton, scampering blandly through the atmospheric, life-paced tale of Marseillaise Fanny (Florence Henderson), who weds the kindly, ageing Panisse (Walter Slezak) when she is left alone and pregnant by Marius (William Tabbert), the son of the café owner César (Ezio Pinza), who is unable to resist the call of the sea.

With *South Pacific* director Joshua Logan at its helm and two of that show's leading players (Pinza, Tabbert) in starring rôles, *Fanny* was written and presented rather as a Rodgers-and-Hammerstein-style romantic musical, and, in spite of the fact that the adaptation and its brightly straightforward scoreful of songs wiped out virtually all of the character and depth of the original plays and films, the show as written proved a popular piece of Broadway entertainment, running for 888 performances in David Merrick and Logan's production at the Majestic Theater between 1954 and 1957.

Pinza, cast in the rôle forever connected with the great French actor Raimu, sang 'Love is a Very Light Thing' and 'Why Be Afraid to Dance?' whilst Tabbert had his best moments in the show's title-song and 'Restless Heart', but, in the inevitable comparison with *South Pacific*, they were shallowly served. Whilst Lawrence Tibbett succeeded Pinza on Broadway, a London production was staged with vocalist Ian Wallace (César) and Kevin Scott (Marius) starring alongside comic actor Robert Morley (Panisse), making an unprecedented appearance on the musical stage. It was poorly received, but was propped up for a run of 333 perfomances by the Theatre Royal, Drury Lane, which had no replacement offering to hand. A belated Australian production, mounted at the Marian Street Theatre in 1979, limited its life to Sydney.

The show has been subsequently played outside New York, the most recent revival, featuring George S Irving and José Ferrer, being played at the Paper Mill Playhouse, New Jersey, in 1990.

A film made subsequent to the appearance of the show on Broadway ignored the musical score and instead gave a similarly compressed version of the original stories.

UK: Theatre Royal, Drury Lane 15 November 1956; Australia: Marian Street Theatre, Sydney 8 June 1979
Recording: original cast (RCA)

FANTANA Musical comedy in 3 acts by Robert B Smith and Sam S Shubert. Lyrics by Robert B Smith. Music by Raymond Hubbell. Lyric Theater, New York, 14 January 1905.

Sam Shubert's production of *Fantana* with 'the Jefferson de Angelis Opera Company' came to New York from Chicago and proved a typical example of the colourful comic opera fare that the most enjoyable American writers had been turning out over the previous decade. The libretto had its principal comedian (de Angelis) playing the disguised valet of the father (Hubert Wilke) of the heroine (Adele Ritchie), who is sent sailing into hot Japanese water as a decoy duck for a condemned politician. Some jaunty, if reminiscent, numbers included plenty with waltz rhythms and had 'geisha' and 'Asia' rhymed yet again (but, less predictably, 'vile' and 'canaille' from the lips of a comic opera Jap). They included a couple of topical pieces for de Angelis ('What Would Mrs Grundy Say?', 'That's Art'), and featured such predictable titles as 'A Truculent Governor, I' for the Japanese potentate, 'Laughing Little Almond Eyes' for the heroine's baritone (Frank Rushworth), 'The Girl at the Helm' and 'A Lesson in Etiquette' for Wilke and the music-hally 'My Word' for English comedienne Katie Barry. There was also half a duet ('The Secret') attached to the rôle of 'a schoolmate of Fanny's' played by the very young Julia Sanderson.

Well made, and well run in before it was shown on the New York stage, where an up-to-date dance number ('Can-Can versus Cakewalk'), a bit more local colour ('In My Riksha of Bamboo') and the already popular 'Tammany' (Gus Edwards/Vincent Bryan) were added to the score for good measure, *Fantana* had an excellent Broadway run of 296 performances, proving one of the most effective American-bred pieces of its time. A 1906 London production announced for the Waldorf Theatre did not, however, eventuate.

THE FANTASTICKS Musical in 2 acts by Tom Jones suggested by the play *Les Romanesques* by Edmond Rostand. Music by Harvey Schmidt. Sullivan Street Playhouse, New York, 3 May 1960.

A statistical phenomenon in the musical theatre, *The Fantasticks* has, at the time of writing, recently completed its 31st consecutive year at New York's 150-seater Sullivan Street Playhouse.

The Fantasticks (the title comes from George Fleming's original English translation) is a reduction of Rostand's successful play, following the growing up of the boy Matt (Kenneth Nelson) and the girl Luisa (Rita Gardener). Brought together by the plotting of their fond fathers (William Larsen, Hugh Thomas), who pretend to wish to keep them apart, they find that they have to be disabused of their romantic notions by the harsh realities of the world before they can finally and happily come together. Jerry Orbach appeared as El Gallo, compère and tempter in turn, who won the best musical moment of the gentle, winning score in the ruefully recalling song 'Try to Remember', which opens the show. The song became a hit-parade success for Gladys Knight and a longtime cabaret favourite, whilst the girl's youthful 'Much More' and 'Soon it's Gonna Rain' also proved take-out successes.

A small-scale musical, making a virtue of being presented with simplicity on a bare stage with rudimentary properties and a cast of nine, it was originally presented in an even more compact, one-act, version by Mildred Dunnock's Summer Theater at Barnard College in 1959 with a cast including the 21-year-old Susan Watson. Expanded and reproduced in New York, under the management of Lore Noto, with a cast which included author Jones, performing under the nom de théâtre of Bruce in the rôle of henchman Henry, it proved, after a discreet beginning, to be wholly to the taste of the 1960s. While the original production began its three-decade run in the tiny venue which it life-savingly never abandoned for a larger one and the possibility of larger grosses, overseas productions proliferated. Played in a Shaftesbury Avenue theatre in London, it found the fate of virtually all off-Broadway pieces there and folded in just 44 performances, but in Britain, as in many other countries, its reduced demands in casting and staging made it a favourite with smaller provincial houses and groups. In 1990 it received a London revival from the company at the Regent's Park Open Air Theatre.

An NBC television version, mounted in 1964 (18 October), whilst the stage show ran on, featured Susan Watson and John Davidson as the youngsters, Bert Lahr and Stanley Holloway as the fathers, and Ricardo Montalban as El Gallo.

Both by its sentiments and by its staging and style, *The Fantasticks* remains a very 1960s musical, but one which has successfully carried those 1960s feelings through the 1970s and the 1980s with as much durability as, and more gentle grace than, such a piece as *Hair*.

UK: Apollo Theatre 7 September 1961; Australia: Russell Street Theatre, Melbourne 30 October 1962; Austria: Neues Theater am Kärntnertor *Die Romanticks* 1 December 1965; Germany: Ulmer Theater *Die Romantiker* 30 December 1966; France: 1966–7 season; Hungary: Fővárosi Operettszínház *Fantasztikus!* 28 January 1972
Recordings: original cast (MGM), Mexican cast (Columbia), French cast (Polydor), Japanese cast (RCA) etc

FARADAY, Philip Michael (b London, 1 January 1875; d London, 6 February 1944). Composer turned producer who had some fine London success with Continental Operette productions.

After an adventurous life, which apparently involved periods as a rating expert, a musician, an auctioneer and a surveyor, Faraday first came to theatrical notice as a composer, with the fine score for the very comic opera *Amasis* ('Little Princess, Look Up'), the surprise success of London's 1906 season, which led to him and his partner Frederick Fenn being rather hastily hailed as a new Gilbert and Sullivan. The pair later wrote a curtain-raiser for the Savoy Theatre, but Faraday's only other substantial stage score, for an indifferent piece called *The Islander*, produced in 1910, did less well. In that same year, however, he entered management and had a considerable success with his first venture, a collaboration with the American producer F C Whitney on the London version of Straus's *The Chocolate Soldier* (*Der tapfere Soldat*). The production ran 500 performances at the Lyric Theatre, of which Faraday subsequently became the lessee, and was long and profitably toured thereafter.

An adaptation of *Die Fledermaus* produced as *Nightbirds* had only a fair run, but a third Continental musical, *The Girl in the Taxi* (*Die keusche Susanne*), gave Faraday a second long-running and interminably touring success. His subsequent productions of Oscar Straus's *Love and Laughter*, Eysler's *The Laughing Husband* (*Der lachende Ehemann*), and Gilbert's *Mam'selle Tralala* (*Fräulein Tralala*) had indifferent runs before his importation of German-language musicals stopped in the face of wartime sentiments and an August 1914 bankruptcy. After the war he took the Duke of York's Theatre and again began producing, but in his remaining four years of unhighlighted activity the only musical piece which he included among his productions was the children's show *Teddy Tail* (1920).

1906 **Amasis** (Frederick Fenn) New Theatre 9 August
1908 **A Welsh Sunset** (Fenn) 1 act Savoy Theatre 15 July
1910 **The Islander** (Major Frank Marshall) Apollo Theatre 23 April

FARAGÓ, Jenő (b Budapest, 1873; d Budapest, 28 March 1940).

At first a journalist on several Budapest papers, Faragó became a librettist and lyricist for, and a prolific translator of, operettas and musical comedies. Amongst his earliest efforts were Hungarian versions of Luard Selby's little Savoy Theatre curtain-raiser *Weather or No* and of Adolphe Ferron's indifferent *Das Krokodil*, but there were more significant pieces amongst the many which he adapted first for the Magyar Színház, then for the Népszinház and, after that theatre's eclipse, for a variety of other houses. His most important successes included works from Britain (the Gaiety Theatre hit *The Circus Girl*, the record-breaking *A Chinese Honeymoon*), Vienna (Heuberger's *Der Opernball*, Fall's *Die Dollarprinzessin*, Eysler's *Bruder Straubinger*), Berlin (Paul Lincke's *Lysistrata*, Kollo's *Drei alte Schachteln*), Paris (Terrasse's *M de la Palisse*) and even a pair from New York in the shape of Harry Archer's well-travelled *Little Jessie James*, here known by the name of its hit song as *I Love You!*, and Gustave Luders's *The Sho-Gun*.

Although these translations made up a large part of his work, he also provided libretti and/or lyrics for a variegated number of original pieces, mostly with a musical content. His early works included Hungarian libretti made from French pieces ranging from musical farce to a Jules Verne spectacular, a successful operett on *Casanova* with his habitual partner, composer Izsó Barna, and another,

Katinka grofnő, with Iván Hűvös, and his later works varied from the rising revue genre to the fashionable biographical musical (*Fanny Elssler, Chopin* etc). However, in spite of his regular presence on the Budapest stage, few of his pieces were played outside Hungary. The exceptions were Komjáthy's *A kóristalány*, produced in Vienna as *Lily vom Chor*, and an Offenbach pasticcio-biography on *Dreimäderlhaus* lines which was exported to Vienna's Apollotheater in 1922 and later remade for Broadway.

1897 **Derül-Borul** (*Weather or No*) 1 act Hungarian version (Magyar Színház)
1898 **Háromláb kapitány** (Albert Kövessy) Budai Színkör 14 July
1898 **A krokodilus** (*Das Krokodil*) Hungarian version (Magyar Színház)
1898 **Az operabál** (*Der Opernball*) Hungarian version (Magyar Színház)
1899 **Vasúti baleset** (Lajos Donáth) Magyar Színház 31 May
1900 **A szerelem óvodája** (Károly Stephanides/w József Hevesi) Magyar Színház 7 June
1901 **Budapest szépe** (Izsó Barna/w Géza Márkus) Fővárosi Nyari Színház 20 July
1901 **Cirkuszélet** (*The Circus Girl*) Hungarian version (Népszinház)
1901 **Mézeshetek** (Barna/Ede Sas) Népszinház 13 April
1901 **Teréz kapitány** (*Le Capitaine Thérèse*) Hungarian version w Béla J Fái (Népszínház)
1902 **Lotty ezredesei** (Rudyard Stone ad w Adolf Mérei) Magyar Színház 17 January
1902 **Kin-Fu, egy kinai ember kalandjai** (Barna/w Márkus) Népszinház 31 May
1902 **Casanova** (Barna) Népszinház 11 October
1903 **Trouville gyöngye** (*Die Dame aus Trouville*) Hungarian version (Magyar Színház)
1903 **Khinai mézeshetek** (*A Chinese Honeymoon*) Hungarian version (Népszínház)
1903 **Makrancos hölgy** (*Lysistrata*) Hungarian version w Ferenc Molnár (Király Színház)
1903 **Hektor kisasszony** (*Die Karlsschülerin*) Hungarian version (Népszinház)
1903 **Vándorlegény** (*Bruder Straubinger*) Hungarian version (Népszinház)
1904 **Katinka grófnő** (Iván Hűvös) Népszinház 29 January
1904 **A hét Schlesinger** (w Mátyás Feld) Városligeti Nyari Színház 23 June
1904 **A lőcsei fehér asszony** (Barna) Népszinház 27 October
1904 **Rezi** (Barna/Árpád Abonyi) Népszinház 16 September
1905 **7777** (*Der Fremdenfuhrer*) Hungarian version w Dezső Bálint (Népszinház)
1906 **A Sogun** (*The Sho-Gun*) Hungarian version (Király Színház)
1906 **Mimi hercegnő** (*Messalinette/Die Ringstrassen-Prinzessin*) Hungarian version (Magyar Színház)
1907 **Az erényes nagykövet** (*Monsieur de la Palisse*) Hungarian version (Népszinház)
1907 **A dollárkirálynő** (*Die Dollarprinzessin*) Hungarian version (Király Színház)
1908 **Ezeregy éj** (*Tausend und eine Nacht*) Hungarian version (Népszinház-Vigopera)
1910 **Dudakisasszony** (*Miss Dudelsack*) Hungarian version (Városligeti Színkör)
1910 **Édes öregem** (*Brüderlein fein*) 1 act Hungarian version (Király Színház)
1911 **A lengyel menyecske** (*Polnische Wirtschaft*) Hungarian version (Városligeti Színkör)
1912 **A papa csatába megy** (Barna) Ferenczy kabaré 30 October
1913 **A csodavászon** (Barna) Népopera 22 December

1915 **Kávéházi Konrád** (Barna/Soma Guthi) Budai Színkör 30 July

1914 **Szervusz, Pest!** (Feld) Budapesti Szinház 1 July

1918 **A kóristalány** (Károly Komjáthy) Városi Színház 18 January

1918 **Pitypalaty kisasszony** (Béla Zerkovitz) Royal Orfeum 1 June

1918 **Páratlan menyecske** (Zerkovitz) Royal Orfeum 1 October

1918 **A kis szeleburdi** (*Die tolle Komtess*) Hungarian version (Városi Színház)

1918 **A táncos grofnő** (*Hanni geht tanzen*) Hungarian version (Budai Színkör)

1918 **A Marcsa katonája** (*Der Soldat der Marie*) Hungarian version (Városi Színház)

1919 **Százszorszép** (Zerkovitz) Városi Szinház 28 November

1920 **Offenbach** (Offenbach arr Mihály Nádor) Király Szinház 24 November

1920 **Három a vénlány** (*Drei alte Schachteln*) Hungarian version (Budapesti Színház)

1922 **Három a tánc** (Komjáthy/w István Szomaházy) Király Színház 20 May

1923 **Fanny Elssler** (Nádor) Király Színház 20 September

1924 **I Love You!** (*Little Jessie James*) Hungarian version (Lujza Blaha Színház)

1925 **A császárnő apródja** (Ákos Buttykay/Imre Harmath) Király Színház 24 March

1925 **A feleségem babája** (*Der Hampelmann*) Hungarian version (Lujza Blaha Színház)

1925 **A kis huncut** (*Die kleine Sünderin*) Hungarian version (Városi Színház)

1926 **Chopin** (István Bertha) Király Színház 4 December

1932 **Régi orfeum** (Lajos Lajtai/w István Békeffi) Fővárosi Operettszinház 12 March

FARKAS, Ferenc (b Nagykanizsa, 15 December 1905).

The son of an army officer, Farkas studied music first in his home region, from 1927 in Budapest and then, from 1929 to 1931, in Rome where he counted Respighi amongst his teachers at the Academia di Santa Cecilia. His earliest compositions were orchestral pieces, one of which, a 'Divertimento', was awarded the Ferenc Liszt Prize in 1933. His first venture into the dramatic world was as a composer and conductor of film scores for Sacha Films in Vienna and for Nordisk Films in Copenhagen and, in the theatre, with incidental music for the dramatic *És Pippa táncol*, *Timon of Athens* and *Madách – az ember tragédiájá*.

Farkas was for a number of years a teacher at the Budapest Zeneakadémia and in 1941 took up a post at the conservatoire in Kolozsvár where, two years later, he was appointed principal. He subsequently spent a period as chorus master at the Budapest Opera and returned to teaching at the Zeneakadémia, whilst producing occasional compositions including art songs, dance suites, and a comic opera, *Der Wunderschrank*.

His first attempt at a musical comedy, *Csinom Palkó*, originated on the radio in 1949, where it attracted sufficient interest to be revised for a stage production in 1951 with great success. It was subsequently played in Germany as *Heisse Herzen in Ungarn*, as well as in several Russian cities and in Szeged and has survived to many revivals. Amongst a varied list of compositions, including ballets, religious music, piano, instrumental and orchestral music, songs and film scores, he wrote several other dramatic pieces for radio (*Zeng az erdő*, *Májusi fenyő*, *Vidróczki* etc) and also for the theatre, of which *Vők iskolája* (played in

German as *Der Paradies der Schwiegersöhne*) was the most successful.

1938 **Bethlehembe** (Béla Paulini) 1 act Fővárosi Operettszinház 21 May

1940 **Afülemüle** (Árpád Szabados) Nemzeti Színház 9 April

1942 **A bűvös szekrény** (*Der Wunderschrank*) (Gyula Kunszery) Magyar Királyi Operaház 22 April

1951 **Csinom Palkó** (András Dékány) Erkel Színház 22 February

1955 **Zeng az erdő** (Géza Baróti/András Dékány) Miskolc 4 November

1958 **Vők iskolája** (Rezső Török, Ernő Innocent Vincze) Fővárosi Operettszinház 31 May

1964 **Vidróczki** (Ernő Innocent Vincze) Szeged 30 July

1970 **Piroschka** (H Hartung, K H Gutheim) Kaiserslautern

1971 **A Noszty fiu esete Tóth Marival** (Dezső Mészöly/Kálmán Mikszáth) Fővárosi Operettszinház 12 November

1991 **Egy úr Velencéből** (Sándor Márai) Magyar Királyi Operaház 4 July

FARKAS, Imre (b Debrecen, 1 May 1879; d Budapest, 25 March 1976).

Popular poet, novelist and composer, and sometime official of the Hungarian ministry of defence, Farkas wrote the text for Jenő Hubay's opera *Lavotta szerelme* (1906) and, later, for Buttykay's *Hamupipőke*, but he principally wrote and composed his works alone. He scored a long-lived success with his first piece, the musical student tale *Iglói diákok*, and an even better one with the musical comedy *Túl a nagy Krivánon* (1918), played for over 150 performances in two years at the Budai Színkör and at many other theatres thereafter. *Debrecenbe kéne menni!* (1920), *A kis kadett* (1921) and *A nótás kapitány* (1924) all won revivals following their original productions, and *A királyné rózsája*, mounted at the Király Színház in 1926 also had an initial run of over 100 nights.

1905 **Jeannette** 1 act Népszinház 27 April

1907 **Iglói diákok** Kolozsvár 7 October; Budai Színkör 11 September 1909

1909 **Szentgalleni kaland** Kaposvár 23 October

1910 **Narancsvirág** Uránia Színház 24 November

1912 **Hamupipőke** (Ákos Buttykay/w Károly Bakonyi) Magyar Királyi Operaház 26 October

1918 **Túl a nagy Krivánon** Budai Színkör 23 July

1920 **Pünkösdi rózsa** (w István Bródy) Revü Színház 3 January

1920 **Debrecenbe kéne menni!** (later *A cseregyerek*) Budai Színkör 6 August

1920 **Rózsika lelkem** Budai Színkör 11 August

1921 **A kis kadett** Budai Színkör 9 August

1924 **A nótás kapitány** Fővárosi Operettszinház 10 October

1925 **Májusi muzsika** (w Zsolt Harsányi) Renaissance Színház 2 May

1926 **A királyné rózsája** Király Színház 12 February

1927 **Repülj, fecském** Király Színház 5 March

1928 **A Gyurkovics fiúk** Városi Színház 7 April

1929 **Szupécsárdás** Városi Színház 28 February

1929 **Kaszárnya áristom** Andrássy-uti Színház 8 October

1930 **Poldi** Király Színház 13 September

1931 **Hajnali csók** Városi Színház 4 May

1932 **Nyitott áblak** (Károly Nóti) Fővárosi Operettszinház 6 February

1932 **Amit a lányok akarnak** Király Színház 22 December

FARKOA, Maurice (b Smyrna, 23 April 1863; d New York, 21 March 1916). Dark and originally slickly handsome light baritone, a 'professional foreigner' and matinée idol even into the days of his plumpness.

Born in Smyrna of Franco-English parentage, Farkoa went to Britain in 1892 and made his first appearance in the London theatre as part of a duet act with Alfred Nilsson Fysher, interpolated into the flexible structure of *Morocco Bound* at the Shaftesbury Theatre (1893). The team soon broke up, and Farkoa headed for the concert platform, but in 1895 he was engaged by George Edwardes for a solo spot as a bohemian artist in *An Artist's Model*. He proved popular enough to be given a fresh number, the Laughing Song, with which he made a great hit and also several gramophone records, the first of which, made in 1896, would seem to be the first example of an 'original cast recording'.

Sporting a white forelock in his dark hair, and some exotic clothes and jewellery, Farkoa followed up in a series of romantic rôles for George Edwardes: a French vicomte celebrating 'Wine, Women and Song' in *The Circus Girl* (1896), as the jeune premier (Paul Blanchard, a French student) in *Topsy Turvy Hotel* (1899), paired with Edna May as the Baron de Trègue (called Sir John Binfield until the very un-English Farkoa was cast) in *Kitty Grey* (1902), Monsieur de l'Orme, a written-to-measure rôle in *Three Little Maids* (1903), as yet another Frenchman (with French versions of the hit songs 'Sammy' and 'Bedelia' and a major hit in 'I Like You in Velvet') in *Lady Madcap* (1904), as a womanizing Indian Rajah in *The Little Cherub* (1906, 'The Supper Girl') and a romantic Chinaman in *See See* (1906).

By now over 40 and looking distinctly more corseted, but still apparently a matinée lady's delight, he visited America (where he had made a first venture in 1904) in 1906 to appear for Joe Weber in Victor Herbert's *The Dream City* (Henri d'Absinthe) and as a version of Lohengrin in *The Magic Knight*, and then returned to Britain to take over the specially expanded rôle of the amorous Dutch bandmaster in *Miss Hook of Holland* (1907). He followed up as a Niçois café owner in *My Mimosa Maid* (1908) and appeared in Lehár's *Mitislaw der moderne* (1909) at the Hippodrome before returning to the stout safety of the concert stage. He emerged again to appear as Gábor Szabo in *The Nightbirds* (1911) and repeated that rôle on Broadway (*The Merry Countess*), where he also played a small rôle in George Grossmith's production of *Tonight's the Night* (1914). He returned to appear alongside Fysher, now running the fashionable Chez Fysher nightclubs in Paris and in New York's 45th Street, in his cabaret mondaine and was playing in *Montmartre à Minuit* at the Winter Garden when he died suddenly.

His obituary described him as 'a clever singer of chansonettes, the full artistic effect of which was perhaps marred to some tastes by a rather ogling and effeminate manner; a remark that also applies to his dapper and fixedly smiling musical comedy lovers – always with a Whistlerian white curl in his black hair'.

FARNIE, H[enry] B[rougham] (b Scotland, 1820; d Paris, 22 September 1889). Adapter, 'borrower' and librettist who authored and/or pasted together and directed many major London musical successes.

Scots-born Farnie – allegedly a distant connection of Lord Brougham, and named in function of that – was educated at St Andrews University and destined for a career as a schoolmaster. However, he found his way first into journalism, as a sub-editor on the *Edinburgh Courant*, and then south to London, where he became the editor of a small journal put out by Cramer, the music publisher, called *The Orchestra*. During the early days of his period of employment with Cramer he began writing for the theatre.

His first staged work was the one-act opera *The Sleeping Queen* (1864), with music by no less a composer than Michael Balfe, and the young author continued in the best company when he wrote *The Bride of Song* for Sir Julius Benedict. He was working on a piece with Vincent Wallace, the third of the trio of important contemporary English romantic opera writers, at the time of the composer's death. Farnie also translated Gounod's opera *La Reine de Saba* for British production, but he had his biggest early success away from the stage, with the words for Arditi's hugely popular song 'The Stirrup Cup', one of the 300 or so like pieces which he lyricked during this period.

Farnie moved on to other journalistic jobs as editor of *The Paris Times* and then of his own short-lived magazine *Sock and Buskin*, whilst keeping warm his contacts with Cramer, who would prove as useful to him over the coming years as he to them. At the same time he had his introduction to the lightest part of the musical theatre when he stepped in to replace Dion Boucicault as the translator of Hervé's *Le Petit Faust* for its London production of 1870. Thereafter he was practically never out of this sphere.

His first attempt at West End burlesque, a variant of the Jack Sheppard tale called *The Idle Prentice*, produced at the Strand Theatre later in the same year, though initially criticized as being longwinded, became highly popular; one of the two Christmas entertainments written for Benjamin Webster's theatres for the 1870–1 season, *Little Gil Blas*, was acclaimed by the press for 'less puns and rhymes and more humour' than was usual, and he had his biggest success to date, adjoined to much praise for his adaptation and his direction, with the English version of *Geneviève de Brabant* staged at the Philharmonic Theatre, Islington, a few months later. Within a year, he had established himself alongside Burnand, Byron and Gilbert at the head of the town's burlesque writers and directors.

He had a further success with his version of *La Fille de Madame Angot*, in spite of the concurrence of several other anglicizations of the work, and spread his success considerably wider when he joined forces with the Henderson family. He wrote a series of burlesques for the then Mrs Henderson, better known as Lydia Thompson (*Robinson Crusoe, Bluebeard, Oxygen, Piff-Paff, Stars and Garters* etc) and directed the pieces with which she and her team of 'blondes' dazzled America and amused London. For her husband, Alexander Henderson, the lessee of the Strand Theatre, he wrote and staged a series of pasticcio pieces, the best and most successful of which were neither burlesque nor comic opera, but a combination of plot and dialogue patched together from one or more French comedies and illustrated with songs and dances from the most popular music-hall and musical theatre sources. *Nemesis* (based on Alfred Duru's *Les Deux Noces de M Boisjoli*) and *Loo and the Party who Took Miss* (from Chivot and Duru's vaudeville *Le Carnaval d'un merle blanc* but replacing most of Lecocq's music with melodies by Serpette, Offenbach and Hervé) were long-running successes which were brought back several times for repeat seasons. The close connection with his fellow-Scot, Henderson, was to prove as long and mutually beneficial as that with Cramer, for Farnie, whose greatest talent was apparently a supreme one for business, supplied both publisher and producer with the most fashionable musical pieces at just the right times.

His penchant for do-it-yourself French musicals got him a pasting in print from an angry Lecocq when he put his name to 'a new Lecocq opéra-bouffe' called *The Black Prince*, fabricated from his usual mixture of French sources (mostly *Le Voyage en Chine* in this case) and, in any case, from music that was not all Lecocq's, but he continued cheerfully to turn out these bric-à-brac entertainments and, at the same time, to consort with the best and most popular of musicians. He wrote the libretto for Offenbach's British opéra-comique *Whittington*, worked with Alfred Cellier on an adaptation of Moncrieff's *Rochester* which in his hands became the story of *Nell Gwynne*, turned out translations of several of Offenbach's works for Henderson and others and, in his greatest success of all, adapted Planquette's *Les Cloches de Corneville* which, in the version made by Farnie and Robert Reece, caused a sensation on British stages.

Several years later, he combined with Planquette on an original comic opera, *Rip van Winkle*, which won an international success and remained in the repertoire of French houses for a century. This encouraged him to continue such collaborations, and he followed up by presenting Planquette with his old *Nell Gwynne* libretto for a fresh score, and, in collaboration with the composer, metamorphosing two of his more than satisfactory but hardly major hit Parisian shows, *Surcouf* and *Les Voltigeurs de la 32ème*, into enormous English successes as *Paul Jones* and *The Old Guard*. He did the same good turn for Francis Chassaigne's unsuccessful *Le Droit d'aînesse*, anglicizing it into an international hit as *Falka*, and he paired with Edmond Audran, whose *La Mascotte* he had put into English with notable success, to write the rather less successful *Indiana* for the London and New York stages. Three further works by the pair which had been announced did not eventuate.

Paul Jones was the last big hit for the theatrical cobbler who had managed to make himself one of the most successful authors and directors of burlesque, opéra-bouffe and opéra-comique (as tastes progressively changed) in the English-speaking world. Suffering from diabetes, he died in 1889.

One newspaper summed up the attitude the press had long taken to the man whom F C Burnand (who had sued him for plagiarism) described as 'a burly swaggerer': 'most probably his like will not be seen again ... the best interests of the stage compel the admission that it can advantageously be spared'. Praised for his early works, Farnie had soon been sneered at for his theatrical borrowings ('he went to the Parisian stage for his material and to others for his translations'), and then, when the papers postulated the dying decadence of burlesque, the highly typical Farnie had become their favourite target of scorn. When the critics – many of them adapters and stage writers themselves – got tired of French opérette, Farnie got the blame for watering down the libretti which they hypocritically called 'indecent' in the original French, but nevertheless hurried across the channel to witness. But, if he was personally disliked, critically loathed and, indubitably, a journeyman as a writer, he had a theatrical skill both in writing and staging which made him and many of his works enormously popular with the world's English-speaking public for more than 20 years, which was more of a career than most of his critics could claim.

1864 **The Sleeping Queen** (Michael Balfe) 1 act Gallery of Illustration 1 September
1864 **The Bride of Song** (Julius Benedict) Covent Garden Theatre 5 December
1864 **Punchinello** (William Charles Levey) 1 act Her Majesty's Theatre 28 December
1869 **The Page's Revel, or A Summer Night's Bivouac** (pasticcio) Tammany, New York 4 January
1869 **Robinson Crusoe** (pasticcio) Tammany, New York 21 January
1869 **Sindbad, the Sailor or the Ungenial Genii and the Cabin Boy** (pasticcio) Niblo's Garden, New York 29 May
1869 **The Rose of Auvergne** (*La Rose de Saint-Flour*) English version (Gaiety Theatre)
1870 **The Forty Thieves** (pasticcio) Niblo's Garden, New York 1 February
1870 **Little Faust** (*Le Petit Faust*) English version (Lyceum)
1870 **The Idle Prentice, or High, Low, Jack and his Little Game** (pasticcio) Strand Theatre 10 September
1870 **The Mistletoe Bough, or Lord Lovel, Lady Nancy and the Milk White Steed** (pasticcio arr Frank Musgrave) Adelphi Theatre 26 December
1870 **Little Gil Blas and How He Played the Spanish D(j)euce** (pasticcio arr Musgrave) Princess's Theatre 24 December
1870 **Breaking the Spell** (*Le Violoneux*) English version (Lyceum)
1871 **Vesta** (pasticcio arr Musgrave) St James's Theatre 9 February
1871 **Les Deux Aveugles** English version (Gaiety Theatre)
1871 **Blue Beard, or The Mormon, the Maiden and the Little Militaire** (pasticcio) Wallack's Theater, New York 16 August
1871 **The Crimson Scarf** (*La Tartane*) English version (Alhambra Theatre)
1871 **Geneviève de Brabant** English version (Philharmonic Theatre)
1872 **Forty Winks** (*Une nuit blanche*) English version (Haymarket Theatre)
1872 **L'Oeil Crevé, or The Merry Toxophilites** English version (Opera Comique)
1873 **La Fille de Madame Angot** English 'Gaiety' version (Gaiety Theatre)
1873 **The Bohemians** (Offenbach pasticcio) Opera Comique 24 February
1873 **Fleur de Lys** (*La Cour du Roi Pétaud*) English version (Philharmonic Theatre)
1873 **Nemesis, or Not Wisely But Too Well** (pasticcio) Strand Theatre 17 April
1874 **Eldorado** (pasticcio arr Fitzgerald) Strand Theatre 19 February
1874 **Loo and the Party who Took Miss** (pasticcio arr Fitzgerald) Strand Theatre 28 September
1874 **The Black Prince** (pasticcio) St James's Theatre 24 October
1874 **Whittington** (Jacques Offenbach) Alhambra Theatre 26 December
1875 **Intimidad, or The Lost Regalia** (pasticcio arr Henry Reed) Strand Theatre 8 April
1875 **Antarctica, or The Pole and the Traces** (pasticcio arr Reed) Strand Theatre 26 December
1876 **Piff Paff, or The Magic Armoury** (*Le Grand Duc de Matapa*) English version w pasticcio score Criterion Theatre 31 January

1876 **Madame l'Archiduc** English version (Opera Comique)

1876 **Nell Gwynne** (Alfred Cellier) Prince's Theatre, Manchester 17 October

1876 **Robinson Crusoe** (pasticcio) Prince's Theatre, Manchester 9 October; Folly Theatre, London 11 November

1877 **Oxygen** (pasticcio arr Fitzgerald/w Robert Reece) Folly Theatre 31 March

1877 **Sea Nymphs** (*Les Ondines au champagne*) English version (Folly Theatre)

1877 **Up the River, or, The Strict Kew-Tea** (Hervé) 1 act Folly Theatre 15 September

1877 **La Créole** English version w Reece (Folly Theatre)

1877 **Champagne, or a Question of Phiz** (pasticcio arr H Reed/w Reece) Strand 29 September

1877 **Shooting Stars** (*L'Oeil crevé*) new English version (Folly Theatre)

1877 **Wildfire** (pasticcio/w Reece) Alhambra Theatre 24 December

1878 **Les Cloches de Corneville** English version w Reece (Folly Theatre)

1878 **Madcap** (*La Chaste Susanne*) (pasticcio arr A J Levey/ w Reece) Royalty Theatre 7 February

1878 **My New Maid** (Lecocq) 1 act St George's Hall 22 June

1878 **Stars and Garters** (*L'Étoile*) (pasticcio ad w Reece) Folly Theatre 21 September

1879 **Madame Favart** English version (Strand Theatre)

1879 **Rothomago, or the Magic Watch** (Edward Solomon, Procida Bucalossi, Gaston Serpette, Georges Jacobi/ad) Alhambra Theatre 22 December

1880 **The Barber of Bath** (*Apothicaire et perruquier*) 1 act English version (Olympic Theatre)

1880 **Les Mousquetaires au couvent** English version (Globe Theatre)

1880 **Olivette** (*Les Noces d'Olivette*) English version (Strand Theatre)

1880 **La Fille du Tambour-Major** English version (Alhambra Theatre)

1881 **La Boulangère** (*La Boulangère a des écus*) English version (Globe Theatre)

1881 **La Mascotte** English version w Reece (Comedy Theatre)

1882 **Manola** (*Le Jour et la nuit*) English version (Strand Theatre)

1882 **Boccaccio** English version w Reece (Comedy Theatre)

1882 **Rip van Winkle** (Robert Planquette) Comedy Theatre 14 October

1882 **Frolique** 1 act (w Henry J Byron) Strand Theatre 18 November

1883 **La Vie** altered English version of *La Vie parisienne* (Avenue Theatre)

1883 **Falka** (*Le Droit d'aînesse*) English version (Comedy Theatre)

1884 **Nell Gwynne** (Planquette) Avenue Theatre 7 February

1884 **The Grand Mogol** English version (Comedy Theatre)

1885 **Kenilworth** (pasticcio arr Michael Connelley/w Reece) Avenue Theatre 19 December

1886 **Lurline** (pasticcio arr Connelley/w Reece) Avenue Theatre 24 April

1886 **The Commodore** revised English version of *La Créole* (Avenue Theatre)

1886 **Glamour** revised *Piff Paff* w Alfred Murray and music by William M Hutchinson Edinburgh 30 August

1886 **Indiana** (Edmond Audran) Avenue Theatre 11 October

1886 **Robinson Crusoe** (John Crook/w Reece) Avenue Theatre 23 December

1887 **The Old Guard** revised English version of *Les Voltigeurs de la 32ème* (Avenue Theatre)

1889 **La Prima Donna** (Tito Mattei/w Murray) Avenue Theatre 16 October

1889 **Paul Jones** revised English version of *Surcouf* (Prince of Wales Theatre)

FARREN, Nellie [FARREN, Ellen] (b Lancashire, 10 April 1846; d London, 28 April 1904). Celebrated soubrette and 'boy', for a generation the most beloved actress on the British musical stage.

The daughter of actor Henry Farren and granddaughter of William Farren the elder, a famous actor of, in particular, elderly rôles, 'Nellie' Farren made her first appearances on the London stage at 18, at the transpontine Victoria Theatre, playing in drama, under the management of Frampton and Fenton. She moved on to Horace Wigan's Olympic Theatre, where she spent two years (1864–5) performing in every kind of entertainment from Shakespeare (Clown in *Twelfth Night* etc) and modern drama to comedy and to burlesque, one of the specialities of the house. She played supporting boy's rôles in the first British production of Offenbach's *Barbe-bleue* (*Bluebeard Repaired*, Robert) and in *Cupid and Psyche* (Bacchus) before taking over the leading boy rôles from Patti Josephs and appearing in the title-rôles of *Glaucus* and *Prince Camaralzaman* and as Zimple Zimon in *Princess Primrose*.

She moved on again, to appear next at the Queen's Theatre, and established herself to such effect that when John Hollingshead gathered together his company for the opening of the new Gaiety Theatre in December 1868, he hired Nellie Farren as his principal burlesque boy. The 22-year-old actress appeared on the first-night bill in the title-rôle of W S Gilbert's burlesque *Robert the Devil* and in the play *On the Cards*, and set in motion a 20-year association with the Gaiety Theatre, with Hollingshead and his successor, George Edwardes, which made her the most beloved performer of her time, and ended only with her retirement from the stage. Although she toured in Britain and overseas, always under the aegis of the Gaiety, she appeared very rarely away from that theatre in London except when Hollingshead's company visited the Olympic or when she was loaned to that theatre to play Giselle in Byron's burlesque of the ballet.

In the early years of the Gaiety the actress often appeared in more than one item on the two- or three-part bills but, if she sported skirts for the plays, when burlesque came on she became a boy: Christopher in *Columbus*, Henry Plantaganet in *Wat Tyler MP* and so on. With the coming of opéra-bouffe and Hollingshead's determination to make the Gaiety the main musical theatre of London, she found a little more variety in her musical rôles, appearing as Régina in *La Princesse de Trébizonde*, Ganymede in *Ganymede and Galatea* (*Die schöne Galathee*) and as the comical Eglantine in *The Island of Bachelors* (*Les Cent Vierges*) as well as playing Lubin in Dibdin's *The Quaker* and Distaffina in *Bombastes Furioso* as a contrast to a continuing run of burlesque boys (Mercury in *Thespis*, Ganem in *Ali Baba à la Mode*, Leporello in *Don Giovanni in Venice*, Lord Monteagle in *Guy Fawkes*, Young Daddles in *The Great Metropolis* ie *MM Dunanan*) and the title-rôle in the Gaiety's first original musical, *Aladdin II* (1870) in which she was paired, as so often, with Johnnie Toole at the head of the bill.

In 1876, with Toole moving on to other areas, Hollingshead constituted a new star team, matching Nellie Farren up with Edward Terry, Kate Vaughan and E W Royce. He introduced the foursome in H J Byron's burlesque of the opera *Maritana*, *Little Don Caesar de Bazan*, with Nellie in the title-rôle. Both the burlesque and the new teaming

Plate 89. **Nellie Farren** *and Fred Leslie: The most famous team of the British 19th-century musical stage, here dressed up to perform 'Ma's Advice' in* Ruy Blas and the Blasé Roué.

of George Edwardes to the Gaiety, began the third era of Gaiety burlesque, the full-length 'new burlesque'. Once again the star team changed, and once again the constant element was Nellie Farren. For the first of the genuine series of new burlesques she appeared as *Little Jack Sheppard* to the Jonathan Wild of the newest Gaiety star, Fred Leslie, and, if anything, the combination proved the most outstanding yet. Fred and Nellie immediately became the biggest thing in the London musical theatre, and they remained so through *Monte Cristo jr* (1886, Edmond Dantes), *Frankenstein* (1887, Frankenstein) and *Ruy Blas and the Blasé Roué* (1889, Ruy Blas), playing long London seasons, and touring Britain, America and Australia with their pieces whilst Edwardes's second team held the fort at the Gaiety with further popular burlesques which, though hugely successful, could not have quite the same hold on the public's heart as the Farren/Leslie pieces.

Ruy Blas turned out to be Nellie Farren's last appearance at the Gaiety. She had long suffered from an arthritic complaint which was not cured by the Australian air, as had been hoped. She opened the newest burlesque, *Cinder-Ellen Up Too Late*, in Melbourne, but when she got back to London, was unable to play there in the show that had been especially named for her.

In the 15 years of her retirement she made a brief and unfortunate essay into management at the Opera Comique but, in spite of repeated rumours, did not return to the stage.

Nellie Farren married Robert Soutar (1827–1908), a journalist turned actor, during her time at the Olympic and he moved with her to the Gaiety Theatre at the house's inception. Although he at first still appeared on the stage, and also tried his hand at authorship and at producing, it was as Hollingshead's stage director that Soutar long held an important place at the Gaiety and in the British theatre.

Their son [Joseph] Farren Soutar (b Greenwich, 17 February 1874; d London, 23 January 1962) was a successful juvenile leading man on the musical stage; whilst Nellie's brother, William Farren (1825–1908), also a highly successful actor, was the first to play the Jupiter of Offenbach's *Orphée aux enfers* in Britain (*Orpheus in the Haymarket*, Her Majesty's 1865).

were an instant and huge success, and the new Gaiety formula only increased the theatre's popularity. In the next ten years the team triumphed in one burlesque after another – *The Bohemian G'yurl* (Thaddeus), *Little Doctor Faust* (Faust, with her husband appearing as Old Faust), *Il Sonnambulo* (Alessio), *Young Fra Diavolo* (Fra Diavolo), *The Lady of Lyons Married and Settled* (Pauline), *Pretty Esmeralda* (Captain Phoebus), *Handsome Hernani* (Hernani), *Robbing Roy* (Francis Osbaldistone), *Trovatore or Larks with a Libretto* (Manrico), *The Corsican Brothers and Co. Ltd* (M de Château-Renard), *Gulliver* (Gulliver), the famous *The Forty Thieves* (Ganem), *Aladdin* (Aladdin), *Little Robin Hood* (Robert Fitzooth), *Valentine and Orson* (Valentine), *Ariel* (Ariel, wearing electric lights in her hair), *Camaralzaman* (Camaralzaman), *Our Helen*, *Der Freischutz*, *Called There and Back* (Gilbert), *Very Little Hamlet* (Hamlet), and *Mazeppa, or, Bound to Win* (Casimir).

During the same years there were many other opportunities beyond burlesque. Nellie's rôles ranged from Sam Weller in *Bardell v Pickwick* to Judic's star rôle in the vaudeville-opérette *Niniche*, and from the title-rôle of the play *La Cigale* to Angelina in Lecocq's *Le Grand Casimir*, and even when a piece was less successful than it might have been, the nimble, peaked-faced little star was always adored by the public and barely criticized by the press unless it be, perhaps, for the scantiness of a costume.

With the end of Hollingshead's tenure and the coming

FARSANGI LAKODALOM Comic opera in 3 acts by Ernő Vajda. Music by Ede Poldini. Magyar Királyi Operaház, Budapest, 16 February 1924.

'Wedding at Carnival Time' was the most significant lighter work of the Hungarian opera composer Poldini (b Pest, 13 June 1869; d Vevey, 28 June 1957) whose other credits included operatic versions of Hans Andersen's *The Princess and the Swineherd* (*Csavargó és királyleány*) and of Cinderella (*Hamupipőke*).

Country Peter and his wife (a nemzetes nagyasszony) are preparing for a big wedding feast, for today their daughter Zsuzsika is to wed Jonas Bükky. She isn't awfully keen on the idea, and doesn't mind at all when a raging snowstorm stops the bridegroom and the guests from arriving. But other folk do arrive, begging shelter from the storm, among them a Countess (a grófné), the guardsman Zoltán, and the student Kálmán. Over the six days that the storm rages, the Countess and Zoltán begin a romance, but Zsuzsika's worried mother also sees love blossoming between her daughter and Kálmán and tries to get the other pair to break it up. Her efforts are in vain, and when the bridegroom's mother finally arrives to embarrasedly explain that her son got snowed-up with a young lady and doesn't now wish to marry Zsuzsika, there is no discontent.

The piece was written to be sung through, with its heroine being a mezzo-soprano, rather than the usual soprano, and the soprano music entrusted to the rôle of the mother. Kálmán was cast as a tenor, with the Countess and Zoltán singing in the baritone/mezzo range.

Farsangi lakodalom was a major success in Hungary, being acclaimed as the greatest comic opera hit in decades, and was subsequently played on German-speaking stages, in Göteburg, Oslo, and at London's then floundering Gaiety Theatre (ad M D Calvocoressi) where Henri M Taunay and William Foss's production ran for 21 performances with a cast headed by Eva Sternroyd as Suzy and Eva van der Osten as the mother and with a young vocalist called Cavan O'Connor in a tiny rôle. It played its 50th Hungarian performance on 27 May 1926, its 75th on 20 September 1929, and was revived at Budapest's Erkel Színház in 1958.

Germany: Staatsoper, Dresden *Hochzeit im Fasching* 24 October 1925; Austria: Hofoper *Hochzeit im Fasching* 22 February 1926; UK: Gaiety Theatre *Love Adrift* 6 October 1926

DIE FASCHINGSFEE Operette in 3 acts by A M Willner and Rudolf Österreicher. Music by Emmerich Kálmán. Johann Strauss-Theater, Vienna, 21 September 1917.

Kálmán's score for the operett *Zsuzsi kisasszony* (Little Miss Susi), first heard at the Vigszinház in Budapest on 22 February 1915, attached to a libretto by Ferenc Martos and Miska Bródy, went through a curious series of wartime transformations which resulted in its turning up back in Budapest, four years and several versions later, as the accompaniment to an Operette entitled *Farsang tündere* (the carnival fairy). After playing more than 50 performances in Budapest, *Zsuzsi kisasszony* was exported by Abe Erlanger, adapted by P G Wodehouse and Guy Bolton, peppered with some additional songs by the then ubiquitous Jerome Kern, and mounted as *Miss Springtime* (New Amsterdam Theater 25 September 1916) for a fine 230 performances' worth of Broadway success and a goodly American road life. For some reason, however, the show went no further. But the score, or much of it, did. The following year, Kálmán's *Die Faschingsfee* was produced in Vienna, and there, attached to a different story by Österreicher and Willner, was a goodly amount of the *Zsuzsi kisasszony* score.

The young, widowed, re-engaged Countess Alexandra Maria (Mizzi Günther) takes refuge in a Munich artists' café when her car breaks down, and there she meets the painter Viktor Ronai (Karl Bachmann) who is celebrating having secured a 30,000-mark contract for a fresco. Viktor comes to duel-threats with the roving-handed Count Lothar Mereditt (Emil Guttmann) over this assumed chorus girl, without knowing that his rival is his patron, but Alexandra secretly assures that the artist gets his lost commission money and Viktor opens his new studio. The truth soon comes out, and the proud Viktor burns the painting he had made of Alexandra as the 'carnival fairy' rather than sell it at vast price to her future husband, the elderly Herzog Ottokar von Grevlingen (Max

Ralf-Ostermann). However, von Grevlingen, with some support from the artistic community, soon sees that it will be wise to let his bride follow her heart and her artist rather than her duty. Max Brod took the chief comic rôle of painter Andreas Lubitschek.

The favourite moments of the score included Alexandra's march song 'Was sonst verboten' which had previously done duty as a duet, 'Légy az ici, pici párocskám' in *Zsuzsi kisasszony*, Viktor went into waltz rhythms for 'Neulich sah ich eine' (formerly 'Csillag száll az égen'), whilst Alexandra joined the buffo Hubert (Oskar Sabo) in 'Sonnenglut lag auf den Feldern' which had been the popular 'Jaj Zsuzsikám' and whose lyric still made reference to a Susi. The original show's 'Suzter Nóta' became a trio ('Falsch wär die Klapperschlange'), 'Romeo és Julia' was turned into a light-comedy duo for Hubert and the soubrette Lori (Mizzi Delorm) which instead made reference to 'Lorely, schöne Zaubermaid', and 'Előre hát az angyalát' was remade as a march song for Viktor and Lubitschek (Heut' flieg' ich aus').

Erich Müller's production of *Die Faschingsfee* had a fine wartime run in Vienna but, although it was popular and published, both musically and textually, in its 'original' Viennese form, somewhere along the line the show underwent major changes to its score. In the opening act, Alexandra's entrance song 'Wenn mir der zufall Champagner kredenzt', another relic of the Hungarian show, was dropped in favour of a new 'Punkt neun – da fuhr mein Kavalier', her duo with Hubert was replaced by one for Lori and Hubert, the big first-act duet with Viktor exchanged for another ('Seh'n sich zwei nur einmal') and a comic trio added to make up an act in which only the opening, part of the finale and Ronai and Lubitschek's duo of the original score was retained. The second act suffered the same drastic rewriting, with Viktor getting a new waltz song, and a new duet ('Küss mich still'). 'Was sonst verboten', Hubert and Lori's little duo about the Loreley and bits of the finale were all that remained. It was, curiously, not even a case of getting rid of all the *Zsuzsi* music – most of what remained was from the old show – but it was seemingly the new-style *Faschingsfee* which made its way back to Hungary as *A Farsang tündére* (ad Andor Gábor). Needless to say, 'Was sonst verboten' and its fellow melodies were recognized, but otherwise *A Farsang tündére* had come a long and wandering way from *Zsuzsi kisasszony*.

Germany: Metropoltheater, Berlin 14 September 1918; Hungary: Király Színház *A farsang tündére* 3 October 1919

FATINITZA Operette in 3 acts by F Zell and Richard Genée based on the libretto to *La Circassienne* by Eugène Scribe. Music by Franz von Suppé. Carltheater, Vienna, 5 January 1876.

Suppé had been writing theatre music ranging from songs for Singspiel, burlesque, farce and spectaculars to short and medium-sized Operetten for the various Viennese theatres in which he had been engaged for 25 years before he was encouraged, in the wake of Strauss's success with *Die Fledermaus*, to compose a full-length Operette of his own. He was supplied with a well-dosed comic-romantic libretto by Richard Genée (author of the libretto to *Die Fledermaus*) and 'F Zell' (Camillo Walzel) which was adapted, like Strauss's success, from a French original, although one very different in tone: the Scribe script originally set with an Auber score as *La Circassienne.*

The young lieutenant Wladimir Samoiloff (Antonie Link) has disguised himself as a girl to escape the vigilance of the fire-breathing General Kantschukoff (Wilhelm Knaack) and thus court his niece, Lydia (Hermine Meyerhoff). Kantschukoff develops a passion for the disguised 'Fatinitza' but, when the Turks invade the Russian camp, they carry off both 'girls' to the harem of Izzet Pascha (Josef Matras) and, led by the marauding journalist Julian van Golz (Karl Blasel), the Russians are obliged to head for Isaktscha to get them back. The rescue accomplished, 'Fatinitza' disappears by simply turning back into Wladimir, while Lydia is taken home to be wed to an elderly Prince. However, the General agrees to cede his niece to Wladimir if the boy can produce the lusted-after Fatinitza. Nothing could be easier, and all ends happily.

The rôle of Fatinitza/Wladimir provided a splendid semi-travesty rôle for a leading lady – in this case Antonie Link, who also fulfilled breeches duty in her time as Strauss's Prinz Methusalem – whilst top comedians Knaack, Blasel and Matras were given plenty of comical opportunities, and the colourful Turkish settings contributed an additional visual attraction. The biggest attraction, however, was the splendid score which Suppé provided for the occasion. It produced two sizeable hits – the driving march ensemble 'Vörwarts mit frischem Mut', which became one of the most popular songs of its time, and the Pascha's comical 'Ein bisserl auffrischen' – but it also held many other delights, from Wladimir's longing 'Sie, die ich darf nie nennen' with its infectious waltz refrain, and the two-soprano duo 'Mein Herz, es zagt' to some lovely choruses and another particularly successful ensemble, the tinkling 'Silberglöckchen rufen helle'.

The immediate success of *Fatinitza* rivalled that of *Die Fledermaus.* Thirty straight nights through the month of January were followed by a further eight in February, the 50th was passed on 20 July, the 60th on 28 August, and by the end of 1879 the Carltheater had played the show a remarkable 122 times, latterly with Regina Klein in the star rôle. It remained several more seasons in the Carltheater repertoire, and was seen there again in 1892 with Anna von Bocskay and Knaack, in 1899 with Ludmilla Gaston starred and Louis Treumann as Izzet Pasha, in 1905, 1906, and in 1907 with Gabriele Mödl, Blasel and Richard Waldemar. In 1909 it was played at the Raimundtheater with Lotte Klein, Marthe Winternitz-Dorda and Gross, and in 1912 at the Johann Strauss-Theater, establishing itself through repeated performances as a classic of its kind.

Within months of its first appearance, the show had been put into production in Hungary, Czechoslovakia, the Netherlands, Sweden and in Germany, in each case with outstanding success and as a prelude to a number of revivals. Budapest's first production was mounted by Andor Gerőffy and the Fatinitza was his wife, playing alongside the Lydia of Etel Roth, but four years later the Népszinház mounted their version of the show (ad Jenő Rákosi, Lajos Evva) with Abonyiné (Wladimir), Elek Solymossy (Kantschukoff), Emilia Sziklai (Lydia) and János Kapolnai (Julian). It proved good for an initial 20 nights and a revival (29 November 1882).

In London, H S Leigh's English version was staged at the vast Alhambra Theatre with Miss Greville, Adelaide Newton and Pattie Laverne all taking turns at the lead rôle in a three-month run, whilst in America there were almost simultaneous English- and German-language versions produced in 1879 and, in 12 months, no less than five different productions of *Fatinitza* visited Broadway. The two most substantial of these featured Mathilde Cottrelly and the Boston Ideal Opera Company's Adelaide Phillips as their hero. Australia saw its first *Fatinitza* in 1881, with Eva Davenport starred alongside Miss E A Lambert (Lydia), C H Templeton (Kantschukoff) and Howard Vernon (Julian).

In Paris (ad Alfred Delacour, Victor Wilder), Mlle Preziosi (Fatinitza), Jeanne Nadaud (Lydia), Ernest Vois (Moulinot, ie Julian), Paul Ginet (Tschatchichef) and Pradeau (Makouli, a slave merchant) headed 60 spectacular performances at the Théâtre des Nouveautés of a version which seems to have differed in its details from the original text, and Marguerite Ugalde took a turn three seasons later at the now-famous star rôle. Belgium, Italy, Switzerland, Argentina, Poland and Mexico all staged their versions of *Fatinitza* which was also translated into and staged in Croatian and Estonian.

In spite of the huge vogue it enjoyed in the years after its production, the show faded from the repertoire as newer products of the blossoming Austrian Operette stage appeared and, when it reappeared in Munich in 1950, it was in one of those 'revised' versions so dear to German houses and German percentage-takers.

Hungary: Budai Színkör 26 May 1876; Germany: Friedrich-Wilhelmstädtisches Theater 16 September 1876; UK: Alhambra Theatre 20 June 1878; France: Théâtre des Nouveautés 15 March 1879; USA: Germania Theater (Ger) 14 April 1879, 5th Avenue Theater (Eng) 22 April 1879; Australia: Novelty Theatre, Melbourne 19 March 1881

Recording: Selection (Amiga, EP)

FAUST UP-TO-DATE Burlesque in 2 acts by George R Sims and Henry Pettitt. Music by W Meyer Lutz. Gaiety Theatre, London, 30 October 1888.

The overwhelmingly popular 'new burlesque' had been safely initiated at George Edwardes's Gaiety Theatre by *Little Jack Sheppard* (1885) and *Monte Cristo Jr* (1886), but *Miss Esmeralda* (1887) which had not benefited from the presence of the Fred Leslie/Nellie Farren star tandem and *Frankenstein* (1887), which had, had been a little less well received. All was set to rights, however, by *Faust Up-to-Date*, a burlesque of Gounod's opera, which scored as well or better than any of its predecessors – and that without the benefit of the drawing-power of Leslie and Farren.

E J Lonnen, the new Gaiety star comic, was Mephistopheles, declaring 'I Shall 'Ave 'Em' on the one hand and swinging into an Irish ballad ('Enniscorthy') on the other, Fanny Robina (Faust) burlesqued the opera's 'Salut, demeure chaste et pure' and showed her principal-boy legs to advantage, and Florence St John switched from straight ballad ('The Dawn of Love') to comedy adroitly, displaying, at the same time, one of the best soprano voices in town.

The story, which maintained versions of most of the plot elements and major situations of the opera, mixed prose with the old-fashioned burlesque rhyming couplets and plenty of topical and social references, amongst which Sims – the author of some strong pamphlets on social issues – was not afraid to include some urgent and unpleasant, and also left space for an acrobatic dance duel, much low comedy and a pas de quatre danced in frilly low-cut blouses, blue skirts and black silk stockings which turned out to be the hit of the show. Meyer Lutz's music for this number became a long-lived favourite, being still published in the 1950s as 'the famous barn dance'.

The show's other legacy was to the language. Sims took his title from the commercial expression 'your account up to date', and from that time on, helped by a popular song from the show, 'Up to Date', the phrase assumed a new meaning as 'the latest thing'.

The show ran for a fine 180 nights at the Gaiety, took in seasons at Islington and the Globe and returned for another month of performances before going on the road in what was to be the first of many tours over the next decade. Lonnen headed a Gaiety company to America in 1889 and another to Australia in 1892, the same year that the Gaiety welcomed a summer season of its old hit with the young Teddy Payne as Mephistopheles. Germany, too, got a glimpse of the show when Kate Santley took a company to the Continent, playing Marguerite to the Faust of Addie Conyers in English, as *Faust Up-to-Date* confirmed itself as one of the most popular of all the Gaiety burlesques.

Apart from the operas by Gounod, Meyerbeer, Boito and Spohr, there have been numerous other musical shows based on the Faust legend, including, most notably, Hervé's durable *Le Petit Faust* (1869). There were many English-language burlesques on both the subject in general and the Gounod opera in particular, the first by Halford (Olympic Theatre, 1854), four different ones by F C Burnand – *Alonzo the Brave, or Faust and the Fair Imogene* (1857, USA: *Little Faust*), *Faust and Marguerite* (St James's Theatre 1864 with Charles Mathews as Mephistopheles), *Very Little Faust* (Charing Cross, 1869) and *Faust and Loose, or Brocken Vows* (Toole's Theatre, 1886 with Toole as Mephistoolpheles) – William M Akhurst's Australian nigger minstrel piece *Faust MD, or, the Doctor, the Damsel, the Demon and the Dragoon* (1865), *Little Doctor Faust* subtitled 'the Gaiety not the Goethe version' by H J Byron (1877 with Farren as Faust), *Faust in Forty Minutes* (1885), Byron McGuinness's *Mephisto* (1886, Royalty), B L Farjeon's *Dr Faustus* (1886), and the latter-day *Faust on Toast* (1921, Gaiety Theatre with Jack Buchanan as Faust), as well as Claude Terrasse's one-act *Faust en Menage* (Théâtre de la Potinière, 1924) in France. Several 18th- and 19th-century German-language pieces also burlesqued the tale, with J Sixtus and Julius Hopp's *(Faustling und) Margarethl* (aka *Mefeles*), first produced at the Theater an der Wien, proving the most substantial. An earlier burlesque under the same title, with text by Guigno and music by the elder Adolf Müller, had been produced at the same house on the heels of the first German showing of Gounod's opera in 1862 (6 October). The Carltheater joined the burlesqueing of the opera, known in German as *Margarethe*, with a little one-person burlesque of that title in 1867 (6 July), and it too was played at the Theater an der Wien.

The British musical play *My Lady Frayle* turned the sexes around and made its Faust the Lady Frayle of the title, whilst most successful of postwar *Faust* variants – this time with a hero who sells his soul not for a girl but for an entire baseball team – has been Broadway's *Damn Yankees*.

USA: Broadway Theater 11 December 1889; Germany: Concordia Theater 1891; Australia: Opera House, Melbourne 14 May 1892

LA FAUVETTE DU TEMPLE

LA FAUVETTE DU TEMPLE Opéra-comique in 3 acts by Paul Burani and Eugène Humbert. Music by André Messager. Théâtre des Folies-Dramatiques, Paris, 17 November 1885.

In order to find the money to save her lover, Pierre (Jourdan) from being drafted, Thérèse, 'the nightingale of Le Temple' (Juliette Simon-Girard), agrees to become the pupil of the eccentric but wealthy singing teacher Saint-Angénor (Gobin). Pierre jealously refuses the money and goes off to war in Algeria and, when Thérèse follows him, accompanied by Angénor and by her friend Zélie (Mlle Vialda), she falls into the clutches of an amorous sheik (Chavrau). Pierre, and Zélie's little boyfriend Joseph (Simon-Max), are also captured, and only after two acts of comical incidents is everyone rescued for a happy and heroic ending.

Messager's first full-scale piece for the theatre, *La Fauvette du Temple* was commissioned from the young composer by Gautier of the Théâtre des Folies-Dramatiques following the success there of the late Firmin Bernicat's *François les bas-bleus*, which Messager had successfully completed for them. The new piece was all that might have been hoped for, a combination of a fine and funny libretto – full of the colourful military moments and music which were so popular at the time – and a charming and lively score. The little comedian's Chanson de la Casquette ('As-tu vu la casquette, la casquette au pèr' Bugeaud?'), the baritone's patriotic 'Je suis soldat', and the extravagant Angénor's delighted Chanson de la Musique Militaire displayed the different sides of soldierly song, while the prima donna showed off her vocal credentials to her basso captor prettily in the Chanson des blés and joined him, in suitable disguise, to pretend that they are camel-drovers (Duo des chameliers) in a score which included variations on the most of the popular kinds of numbers of the time.

Gautier's production of *La Fauvette du Temple* won a splendid Parisian success, a first run of 130 performances, and started Messager on what would be a memorable career in the musical theatre. It was revived at the Folies-Dramatiques in 1890 with Jeanne Thibault starring, and again in 1898, was played at the Théâtre de la Gaîté-Lyrique in 1914 with Jane Marnac in the title-rôle, Lucien Noël as Pierre and Henri Defreyn as Joseph and again at the Empire Théâtre in 1921 with Mlle Frémont starred. An English version (ad Alfred Rae, L Fontaine) put out by Messager's publishers, Enoch, was toured in Britain by Horace Lingard in 1891, and showcased for a week at London's Royalty Theatre, after the well-praised production of the composer's *La Basoche*, later that same year.

UK: Edinburgh *Fauvette* 18 May 1891, Royalty Theatre 16 November 1891

FAVART, Edmée (b Paris; d Marseille, 29 October 1941). Prima donna of the Paris opérette, opéra-comique and musical comedy stage.

The daughter of the baritone Edmond Favart and of the singer Zélie Weil, Mlle Favart made her first stage appearance as a child. She sang at the Casino Saint-Martin, run by her parents, and had her first significant rôle in Paris under the management of Fernand Samuel, at the Théâtre des Variétés, when she appeared in the 1904 revival of Lecocq's *Le Petit Duc* playing the little Duchess to the little Duke of Jeanne Saulier. In 1907 she joined the company at the Brussels Théâtre des Nouveautés where she created the title-rôle of the opérette *Betty* and appeared in the Belgian première of Cuvillier's *Son p'tit frère*, and then returned to Paris to play at the Boîte à Fursy. She came to the fore in Paris when she played the ingénue rôle of Daisy in the Scala production of *Princesse Dollar* (1911), featured in Redstone's *Mik 1er* and, at the Théâtre de la Gaîté the following year, confirmed herself amongst the stars of the pre-war opérette with her performances as Clairette to the Lange of Germaine Gallois (*La Fille de Madame Angot*) and as Stella in *La Fille du tambour-major*. She had a further success as Omphale in a revival of Terrasse's *Les Travaux d'Hercule* and paired with Marthe Chenal to repeat her *Fille de Madame Angot* rôle when that piece was given a special performance at the Opéra-Comique.

In spite of the fact that her excellent light soprano was an adjunct to a personality of charm and a fine actress's projection, rather than an operatic instrument, she spent some time at the Opéra-Comique (1915 sq) where she appeared as Mignon, Mimi, Manon, Micäela, Cherubino, Despina, Colette in *La Basoche*, Suzel in *Le Juif polonais*, Véronique and Rose Friquet and created the rôle of Catherine in Charles Levadé's *La Rotisserie de la Reine Pédauque* (1920) and *La Charmante Rosalie*.

In the early 1920s she appeared in revivals of *Véronique*, *Madame l'Archiduc* (Marietta) and *Le Petit Duc* (this time as the Duc to Mlle Roncey's Duchesse) at the new Théâtre Mogador, and in *Paris, ou le bon juge* (Glycère), made her début in the non-musical theatre, and created the ingénue rôles of Suzanne in Messager's semi-successful *La Petite Fonctionnaire* (1921) and Charlotte in Madame Louis Urgel's *Monsieur Dumollet* (1922), before taking up the rôle of her career as Reynoldo Hahn's *Ciboulete* (1923). In a part which had been conceived for her by the composer, as the adorable country lass who becomes a prima donna and wins herself a nobleman (Henri Defreyn, also her partner in *La Petite Fonctionnaire*) in the best old-fashioned opérette style, she introduced the winsome 'Dans ma charrette', 'Comme frère et soeur', 'Moi, je m'appelle Ciboulette', 'C'est sa banlieu' and the Chanson de route and scored a memorable success.

She subsequently starred in José Padilla's *Pépête* (1924), in Josef Szulc's successful musical comedies *Quand on est trois* (1925, Claude) and *Mannequins* (1925, Micheline) at the little Théâtre de Capucines, paired in both with her other *Ciboulette* co-star Jean Périer, in Marcel Lattès's *Le Diable à Paris* (1927) alongside Dranem and Raimu, in Cuvillier's *Boulard et ses filles* (1929) and in the title-rôle of the Châtelet's opérette à grand spectacle, *Sidonie Panache*

(1930–1). As late as 1933 she was seen as Bettina in a revival of *La Mascotte*, but she retired to being Mme Paul Gazagne in 1935 and thereafter ventured only the odd broadcast.

FEDÁK, Sári (b Beregszász, 26 September 1880; d Budapest, 5 May 1955)

The most celebrated star of the Hungarian musical theatre in the first decades of the 20th century, Sári Fedák had an outstanding career in both the musical and non-musical theatre, and created the starring rôles in several of the most important original Hungarian operetts of her time.

She was just 17 when she was cast in the soubrette rôle of Molly in the first Hungarian performances of *A gésák* (*The Geisha*) at the Magyar Színház, and, after the huge success of that production, she went on to appear in several other imported musical shows (Théa in *A bibliás asszony*, Toledad, *San Toy* etc) before, in 1902, she created the travesty title-rôle in Jenő Huszka's hit musical *Bob herceg* (Prince Bob). The following year she created the title-rôle in Huszka's next success, *Aranyvirág*, and in 1904 that of Pongrác Kacsoh's *János vitéz* (John the hero), the glorious folk-tale operett which became Hungary's most popular and admired native piece.

She appeared in a revival of another major Hungarian work, Verő's *A szultán*, and in the premières of his *Leányka* (1906), of the Károly Czobor/Ferenc Rajna *Rab Mátyás* (1906), of Jacobi's *Az istenhegyi székely leány* (1907, Lóna-

Plate 90a. **Sári Fedák:** *Budapest's greatest musical-theatre star of the early 20th century, creating the title-rôle in* János vitéz.

Szendile) and *Jánoska* (1909), as well as in the starring rôles of classic pieces such as *Gerolsteini nagyhercegnő* (*La Grande-Duchesse*), *A vig özvegy* (*Die lustige Witwe*) and *Cigányszerelem* (*Zigeunerliebe*, Ilona). In 1911 she created another durable rôle as Bessy in Victor Jacobi's internationally successful *Leányvásár*, then played the title-rôle in the Hungarian production of Lehár's *Éva* (1912), starred in Kollo and Bredschneider's *A Mozikirály* (*Filmzauber*, 1913) and as Sári in *Cigányprimás* (*Der Ziegunerprimas*) and created two further important rôles, as the richly romantic masquerading diva of Jacobi's *Szibill* (1914, Szibill) and as the soubrette of Szirmai's *Mágnás Miska* (1916, Marcsa).

Fedák spread her success abroad when she appeared at Berlin's Deutsches Theater in a version of Verő's *Kleopatra* (*Die Bettelgräfin* 1908), at the Deutsches Landestheater in Prague, in Vienna with the Király Színház company (1913) in *János vitéz*, *Leányvásár*, *Éva* and *Cigányprimás*, and again in 1920 as Rosi in *Der Pusztakavalier* (*Mágnás Miksa*), as well as visiting in America in Szirmai's *Mezeskalacs* (Manhattan Opera House, 5 October 1924) and to play the title-rôle of the play *Antonia*, one of her greatest successes. She continued, at the same time, to hold her place at the head of her profession at home, with starring appearances in such pieces as *A bajadér*, *Pompadour* (1923) and Oscar Straus's *Teresina* (1925). Latterly, however, she included more non-musical rôles in her schedule (Gárdonyi's *Fehér Anna*, Molnár's *Farsang* etc) and, although she still appeared in such musical pieces as the 1929 *Pista néni* and the Magyar Színház's 1942 *Vén diófa*, much of the latter part of her career was devoted to the straight stage.

Fedák was married to the playwright Ferenc Molnár, before the golden couple of the Hungarian theatre went through a scandal-showered divorce in 1925 after some three lively years together.

DER FELDPREDIGER Operette in 3 acts by Hugo Wittmann and Alois Wohlmuth based on the story *Der seltsame Brautgemach* by Friedrich Schilling. Music by Karl Millöcker. Theater an der Wien, Vienna, 31 October 1884.

The tale of *Der Feldprediger* is set in 1812–13 in the little Prussian border-town of Trautenfeld, which is a key point on the fighting retreat path of the Napoleonic army from Russia. The 'field-chaplain' of the title is Hellwig (Josef Joseffy), sent to this hot-spot to secretly stir up insurrection, and quartered in the house of the patriotically pliable alderman Heidekrug (Carl Adolf Friese). Hellwig quickly falls in love with Heidekrug's daughter Minna (Ottilie Collin), who has been disguised by her father as an old crone to escape unwelcome attentions. The town changes hands between Russians and French, and Hellwig escapes detection by diverting suspicion on to Heidekrug before he and his merry men bring in the Black Hussar regiment to free the town from the various invaders. Hellwig's winning of Minna was parallelled by his friend Kühnwald's (Graselli) conquest of Minna's similarly disguised sister, Rosette (Rosa Streitmann), Therese Schäfer played Heidekrug's housekeeper, and Alexander Girardi joined the comedy as the alderman's subordinate, Piffkow, who confusedly mistakes the rehearsing of the actor, Bliemchen (Alexander Guttmann), for enemy action.

Megastar Girardi, of course, topped the musical part of the show with his obligatory third-act waltz song, 'Nur ein Traum', but although the comic characters were particularly well provided-for – notably Heidekrug, with his self-descriptory 'Ein Diplomat', his lively 'Ich witt're Blut' and a jolly trio, trying to persuade his daughters that ugliness is not the 'Grösstes Unglück' – there were plenty of lyrical moments as well. Minna, with her Act-III solo 'Ich aber fühle' and a pretty, bright duo with her Hellwig ('Endlich wieder eine Sunde') had the more obviously vocal lines, whilst sister Rosette ('And're Mädchen mogen schmachten') took the soubrettier area. All three joined in another successful ensemble with Kühnwald ('Zög're nicht mein Volk erwach'). Hellwig had his main moment in a hussar song.

Der Feldprediger did not repeat the success of Millöcker's *Der Bettelstudent* in Vienna, but it did fairly well. It ran through November and into December, was brought back in 1886, with Siegmund Stelzer (Heidekrug) and Carl Lindau (Bliemchen) alongside the original stars, and reached its 50th performance on 1 April 1887. It was subsequently seen in Budapest, Berlin, Prague, Warsaw and in Madrid (as *El alcade di Strassberg*), Prague and Amsterdam, but it had its only really significant success in America.

The piece was initially played, with considerable success, in German at the Thalia Theater with Max Lube (Heidekrug), Emma Seebold (Minna), Eduard Elsbach (Hellwig), Ferdinand Schütz (Piffkow), Bernhard Rank (Bliemchen), Conrad Junker (Kühnwald) and Franziska Raberg (Rosette) in the leading rôles, but just three days after the German-language première, John McCaull

Plate 90b. **Sári Fedák** *as Szibill, alongside Ernö Király.*

opened his English production (ad Sydney Rosenfeld), at Wallack's Theater under the more swashbuckling title *The Black Hussar*. Mark Smith was Friedrich von Helbert, Edwin Hoff looked after the tenor music as his pal Hans von Waldemann, and their girls were played by Lilly Post (Minna) and Marie Jansen (Rosette). De Wolf Hopper played papa Theophil Hackenback, Mathilde Cottrelly took Schäfer's rôle and Digby Bell the Girardi part. This time the piece was a genuine hit, with Hopper, Bell and Mme Cottrelly's topical trio, 'Read the Answer in the Stars', becoming one of the song hits of the season and beyond. *The Black Hussar* played 104 straight performances, and when it closed its hit song was retained as part of the music for the following show, *Die Näherin*. It was played on Broadway again at the Star as soon as December, and the following season, while being played with great success around America, it was brought back for a further run at Wallack's (7 May). It was later remounted in the repertoire of the Castle Square company with Thomas H Persse as Helbert, Douglas Flint/William Wolff as Hackenback and Arthur Woolley as Piffkow.

In Germany, the piece found a renewed audience when its 'patriotic' subject – duly adapted to the circumstances – made it a suitable candidate for wartime revival, and Vienna also saw *Der Feldprediger* afresh when it was revived at the Raimundtheater in 1914 (December 4) and 1915 with Otto Langer (Hellwig), Rosa Mittermardi (Minna), Anton Matscheg (Heidekrug), Franz Glawatsch (Piffkow) and Paula Zulka (Rosette) featured. The Second World War saw it surface again, in a version by Rudolf Kattnigg and Hans Rainer, now entitled *Husarenstreiche* (1941, Nuremberg), before, its purpose served, it drifted from the repertoire.

Two numbers from the score survived, however, to find their remade way into the Mackeben/Millöcker pasticcio score to the longer-surviving *The Dubarry*.

Hungary: *A tábori lelkész* 20 December 1884; Germany: Walhalla Theater 10 January 1885; USA: Thalia Theater 1 May 1885, Wallack's Theater *The Black Hussar* 4 May 1885

FELIX, Hugo (b Vienna, ?19 November 1866; d Hollywood, 25 August 1934). Austrian composer of musicals for four countries.

Felix graduated from Vienna University with a Doctorate in Science, but eschewed a scientific career in favour of one in music. His first Operette, *Die Kätzchen*, was staged in Lemberg when he was but 23 years old, and had sufficient success for it to be introduced to Vienna two seasons later at the Carltheater (8 performances). He had two further pieces produced in Vienna of which *Rhodope*, on which he also collaborated on the libretto, was mounted by José Ferenczy at Berlin's Theater des Westens (23 June 1900) after its 31 performances in Vienna. He extended his libretto-writing by adapting the highly successful British musical *San Toy* for the German-language stage, but in 1902 he made good as a composer when his *Madame Sherry*, premièred in Berlin, scored him a major hit.

After the singular success of *Madame Sherry* in Europe, Felix went to Britain (where it had, notoriously, not been successful) and was commissioned by George Edwardes to compose the score for his home-made European musical play *Les Merveilleuses*, to a text by Victorien Sardou, angli-

cized by Basil Hood. The piece was well reviewed, but did only fair business at Daly's Theatre (196 performances), given the extended runs which had become the norm there under Edwardes's management, and a production at Paris's Théâtre des Variétés also had only limited success. Felix's next attempt at a musical for London, written on the French musical comedy/*Madame Sherry* lines, was an unsuccessful adaptation of the celebrated vaudeville *Le Cabinet Piperlin* called *The Antelope* (22 performances) and his only subsequent contributions to the musical stage during his London years seem to have been the supply of the pretty 'Or Thereabouts' as an interpolated number for Gertie Millar in *The Quaker Girl*, 'Der Umberrufen Guards' (w Leslie Stiles) sung by Robert Nainby and May de Souza in the revised *The New Aladdin*, and a share in the score of the latter-day old-style musical comedy *The Pearl Girl*, produced with some success by Robert Courtneidge (254 performances).

Since *Madame Sherry* had been americanized to the extent of dropping Felix's entire score for its Broadway production, the composer was first represented on Broadway by a musical version of Paul Gavault's *La Petite Chocolatière*, produced in Chicago under the title which had been given to the play in London, *Tantalising Tommy*. It was a 31-performance failure in New York, but Felix, now fixed in America, did better with *Pom-Pom*, a remake of the Hungarian operett *Csibészkirály* as a vehicle for Mitzi Hájos, *Lassie*, a version of Catherine Chisholm Cushing's play *Kitty McKay* which won enormous critical and out-of town plaudits but found the New York public diffident, and the Chicago-born *The Sweetheart Shop* which, although it had only a brief Broadway life, was a decided success on the road.

A second collaboration with Mrs Cushing produced *Marjolaine*, a musical version of Louis N Parker's popular play *Pomander Walk*, which ran 136 performances at the Broadhurst Theater and found willing American audiences, but which failed when later produced at London's Gaiety Theatre, but his last works – the music and songs to Russell Janney's comedy-with-songs version of *Don Quixote* and musical versions of the famous play *Peg o' My Heart* and of Margaret Mayo's *Polly of the Circus*, each adapted by their original author – were less appreciated.

In his last days Felix went to Hollywood to find work as an orchestrator and conductor, but it was said that in the seven months of his stay, up to his death, he earned but $15.

1890 **Die Kätzchen** (Albert Klischnegg, Ernst Niedl) Lemberg 23 January; Carltheater, Vienna 19 January 1892
1894 **Husarenblut** (Ignaz Schnitzer) Theater an der Wien 10 March
1898 **Sein Bebé** (Eugène Labiche ad H Paul) 1 act Carltheater 15 January
1900 **Rhodope** (w Alexander Engel) Carltheater 1 February
1900 **San Toy** German version (Carltheater)
1902 **Madame Sherry** (w Benno Jacobson) Centraltheater, Berlin 1 November
1906 **Les Merveilleuses** (aka *The Lady Dandies*) (Victorien Sardou, Basil Hood) Daly's Theatre, London 27 October
1908 **The Antelope** (Adrian Ross) Waldorf Theatre, London 28 November
1912 **Tantalizing Tommy** (Michael Morton, Ross) Criterion Theater, New York 2 October

1913 **The Pearl Girl** (w Howard Talbot/Hood) Shaftesbury Theatre, London 25 September
1916 **Pom-Pom** (Anne Caldwell) Cohan Theater, New York 28 February
1920 **Lassie** (Catherine Cushing) Nora Bayes Theater, New York 6 April
1920 **The Sweetheart Shop** (Caldwell) Knickerbocker Theater, New York 31 August
1922 **Marjolaine** (Cushing) Broadhurst Theater, New York 24 January
1923 **Sancho Panza** (Cervantes ad Sydney Howard, Melchior Lengyel) Hudson Theater, New York 26 November
1924 **Peg o' My Dreams** (Caldwell/J Hartley Manners) Jolson Theater, New York 5 May
1924 **Polly of the Circus** (Margaret Mayo) Alcazar, San Francisco 20 October

LA FEMME À PAPA Vaudeville in 3 acts by Alfred Hennequin and Albert Millaud. Music by Hervé. Théâtre des Variétés, Paris, 3 December 1879.

La Femme à papa marked the beginning of a second great period of success for 'the crazy composer' Hervé who, since his brilliant opéra-bouffe successes with *Chilpéric*, *Le Petit Faust* and their ilk, had been rather overshadowed by the less outrageous and less frivolous opérettes and opéras-comiques of Lecocq and his kind, whose styles he had tried to follow with narrowing results. The freely comical vaudeville style suited him much better, and his contribution to this bright-hearted comedy with songs did much to ensure its success.

Anna Judic starred as pretty Belgian Anna who is intended by the sober, 30-year-old, butterfly-fancying Aristide (José Dupuis), at the outset of things, to be his 'papa's wife'. Aristide is anxious to marry off papa, the widowed, 60-year-old Baron Florestan de la Bonnardière (also Dupuis) to stop his embarrassing gadabout of a parent running around town and getting involved with the likes of the flibberty-gibbet Coralie (Augustine Leriche), before Aristide himself gets tidily married to the daughter of his zoology professor. By the time the quiproquos of the evening are done, it is, of course, Aristide who ends up in the arms of Anna. Baron completed the star team in the rôle of Baudin-Bridet.

Judic scored a bit song hit with the tipsy couplets of the Chanson du Colonel ('Tambour, clairon, musique en tête') with its tale of a regiment quartered in a convent and its suggestive 'Ta ra ta, ta ra ta ta ta, Ra fla fla fla' refrain, and she compounded her triumph with 'Le Champagne', 'La Pensionnaire', the rondeau 'Les Parisiennes' and 'Les Inséparables', leaving little in the way of songs – after her seven solos and three duos in the final act with Dupuis – for the rest of the cast.

La Femme à papa played at the Variétés for four solid months and, after allowing space for some of the other pieces of the house's repertoire to be played, it returned for several months more, passing its 200th Parisian night before giving way to more made-for-Judic vaudevilles including Hervé's most successful pieces, *Lili* and *Mam'zelle Nitouche*. In spite of the huge success of its successors, it was by no means shelved thereafter. Judic kept *La Femme à papa* prominently in her repertoire for many years, repeating it in Paris in 1885, 1895 and in 1898, and on tour throughout the world, notably at Vienna's Theater an der Wien, (20 November 1883) and

at Broadway's Wallack's Theater and Star Theater.

La Femme à papa was subsequently given another Paris showing at the Théâtre de la Gaîté with Jeanne Pierny starring, and was played on international tour with other pieces of the Judic repertoire by the same artist (Theater an der Wien, 1900 etc). In 1909 it was revived at Paris's Trianon-Lyrique (15 November).

A German-language version was mounted at the Vienna Carltheater, with Hervé's score replaced by new music by Brandl and with Rosa Streitmann (Anna), Tewele (Aristide/Florestan), Wilhelm Knaack (Baudin-Bridet) and Karl Blasel (the butler, Tob) featured. It did not have a notable success (29th performance 4 October 1881), but it was this Brandlized version that was subsequently played in Germany. Hungary, on the other hand retained the original music for *A papa felesége* (ad Aurél Follinusz). In America, however, the show suffered an even stranger fate. The 1899 Anna Held vehicle *Papa's Wife*, although taking the title of this work, actually mixed together elements of its plot with bits of *Mam'zelle Nitouche* and replaced Hervé's music with some Reginald De Koven/Harry B Smith songs. The following year, Vienna tried a similar trick. Frln Worm appeared alongside Josef Joseffy, Carl Streitmann, Ferdinand Pagin and Giampietro in *Die Stiefmama*, a version of *La Femme à papa* written by Ludwig Held with music by Leo Held (Theater an der Wien, 20 February 1900) which ran nine performances.

Austria: Carltheater *Papas Frau* 20 March 1880; Germany: Carl-Schultze Theater, Hamburg *Papas Frau* 5 March 1881; Hungary: Népszinház *A papa felesége* 12 January 1895; USA: Wallack's Theater (Fr) 6 October 1885

THE FENCING MASTER Comic [romantic] opera in 3 acts by Harry B Smith. Music by Reginald De Koven. Casino Theater, New York, 14 November 1892.

One of Smith and De Koven's most successful successors to their biggest hit, *Robin Hood*, *The Fencing Master* had a run of 120 Broadway performances with Marie Tempest starring in breeches (most of the time) as Francesca, the daughter of a *maître d'armes* who has been brought up thinking she is a boy. She suspects she isn't when she falls in love with the deposed Fortunio, Duke of Milan (Hubert Wilke), but the non-Duke is in love with a court lady, Countess Filippa (Grace Golden), whose hand has just been bartered to a rich Venetian to boost the income of the usurper, Galeazzo Visconti (Charles Hopper). The heroine scuppers her beloved's attempt to elope and is challenged to a duel, and then things to do with gender begin to come to light amongst the fêtes and masked meetings of Venetian tradition as the tale rolls towards its predictable ending. The fencing master of the title was played by William Broderick, whilst Jerome Sykes provided the laughs as Visconti's comical astrologer, Pasquino, and Louise Pemberton-Hincks appeared as the Marchesa Goldoni, taken with the charms of the 'son' of the fencing master.

The Fencing Master toured happily, was brought back to Broadway for a brief showing in December 1893, and was subsequently played in the repertoire of the Castle Square company with Miss Golden taking over the star rôle alongside William G Stewart (Fortunio) and Arthur Woolley (Visconti).

FÉNYES, Szabolcs (b Nagyvárad, 30 April 1912; d Budapest, 12 October 1986). Composer, theatre administrator and perhaps the most important and prolific single contributor to the Hungarian musical stage of the past half-century.

Fényes studied at the Liszt Academy of Music in Budapest and began his career as a theatrical composer at the age of 19, scoring a major hit with his score for the operett *Maya* before his 20th birthday. *Maya* went on from its original production at Budapest's Fővárosi Operettszinház to be played in Vienna and throughout Europe, and Fényes also moved on, to Berlin, where he spent the next three years writing (as Peter Fényes) for the cinematic company UFA. This was the beginning of a career which ultimately totalled scores for more than a hundred films.

Both during his years in Germany and after his return to Hungary, Fényes continued to turn out a regular supply of superior popular songs and a steady list of scores for the musical stage. If none of his many subsequent musicals and operetts scored the same international success, he did, however, have home-town hits with such pieces as *Vén diófa* (1942), *Rigó Jancsi* (1947), *Szombat délutan* (1954), *Dunaparti randevú* (1957), *A csók* (1968) and *A kutya, akit Bozzi úrnak hívnak* (1976, subsequently played in Germany as *Der Hund, der Herr Bozzi hiess*).

In 1942 he took over the management of the Fővárosi Operettszínhaz which he left in 1949 to run the Vidam Színpad, returning to the Operettzínhaz in 1957 for a further period until 1960.

1931 **A hárem** (Imre Harmath/Ernő Vajda) Fővárosi Operett-színház 25 April
1931 **Maya** (Harmath) Fővárosi Operettszínház 10 November
1932 **Manolita** (Harmath) Fővárosi Operettszínház 24 September
1933 **Csipetke** (Rezső Török) Fővárosi Operettszínház 25 November
1935 **Mimi** (Iván Törs/E Solt) Royal Orfeum 21 February
1936 **Sok hűhó Emmiért** (Harmath/Károly Aszlányi) Kamara Színház 24 October
1939 **Pusztai szerenád** (István Békeffy/László Szilágyi) Fővárosi Operettszínház 29 October
1940 **Az örgög nem alszik** (Gábor Vaszary) Magyar Színház 14 September
1942 **Vén diófa** (Szilágyi) Magyar Színház 26 March
1943 **A királynő csókja** (Attila Orbók) Fővárosi Operettszínház 20 December
1947 **Rigó Jancsi** (Békeffy) Fővárosi Operettszínház 9 May
1954 **Szombat délután** (Békeffy/Dezső Kellér) Fővárosi Vigszinház 19 February
1954 **Két szerelem** (Elemér Boros) Fővárosi Operettszínház 18 June
1955 **Szerencsés flótás** (Békeffy) Fővárosi Kis Színpad 23 March
1957 **Dunaparti randevú** (A Szantó/Milály Szécsen) Szolnoki Szigligeti Színház 8 October
1958 **Majd a papa** (István Kállai) Fővárosi Kis Színpad 11 January
1958 **Ibusz kisasszony** (József Nádasi) Pécsi Színház 19 December
1962 **Légy szives Jeromos** (György Moldova) Petőfi Színház 28 September
1962 **Csacsifogat** (Imre Kertész) Déryné Színház 18 October
1963 **Cyrano házassága** (Kertész) József Attila Színház 9 November
1964 **Csintalan csillagok** (Rudolf Halász/Mátyás Czizmarek) Fővárosi Operettszinhaz 14 May

1967 **Lulu** (Iván Szenes/Michel André) József Attila Színház 20 May
1968 **A csók** (Szenes/Lajos Dóczy) Pesti Színház 29 March
1968 **Csészealj-szerenád** (Szenes/Lajos K Nagy) Győri Kisfaludy Színház 15 May
1971 **Mit vesztett et kisasszony?** (Békeffy) Fővárosi Operettszinház 26 February
1972 **Részeg éjszaka** (Gábor Görgey/Béla Gádor) Vidám Színpad 20 October
1972 **Tizenkét lakáskulcs** (Halász) Kaposvár 27 October
1976 **A kutya akit Bozzi úrnak hívnak** (Békeffy) Fővárosi Operettszinház 27 February
1979 **Florentin kalap** (Szenes/Labiche ad) Fővárosi Operettszinház 30 March
1983 **Szerdán tavasz lesz** (Péter Bacsó) Fővárosi Operettszinház 26 March
1984 **Uraim, csak egymás után** (Yves Mirande, André Mouëzy-Éon ad Adorján Stella) Városmajori Színpad 28 June
1985 **A kikapós patikárius** (*Ferdinand le noceur*) (Szenes/Léon Gandillot ad Jenő Heltai) Székesfehérvári Nyári Színház 24 June

Biography: Sugár, R; *Ugye, hogy nem felejtesz el?* (Ifjusági Lap-és Könyvkiadó, Budapest, 1987)

FERNANDEL [CONTANDIN, Fernand Joséph Désiré] (b Marseille, 8 May 1903; d Paris, 26 February 1971).

Celebrated long-faced, toothy comedian of the French stage, music-hall and cinema who appeared on the musical comedy stage in four shows during a star career of some 40: Louis Verneuil's 1935 *Le Rosier de Mme Husson*, in the star rôle of the made-to-measure military opérette *Ignace* (1936, revival 1948), at Marseille in the 1940 Vincent Scotto piece, *Hugues* (written, like *Ignace*, by his brother-in-law, Jean Manse), and again in the Théâtre du Châtelet's *Le Chasseur d'images* in 1947. Amongst his many screen credits, he appeared in the rôle of Célestin in a cinematic version of *Mam'zelle Nitouche*.

Biography: Castans, R: *Fernandel m'a raconté* (La Table Ronde, Paris, 1976)

FERRÉOL, Roger [né ROGER]

The director of the cabarets at Paris's Le Moulin de la Chanson and Les Deux-Ânes ('le théâtre le plus gai de Paris') where he was responsible for the production of many revues, notably from the pen of the nimble Rip, of the Théâtre de 10 Heures and the Théâtre de la Caricature, Ferréol also penned the French adaptations of the most successful American imports of the 1920s and 1930s.

1920 **Titin** (Joseph Szulc/w Gaston Dumestre) Théâtre Ba-ta-clan 2 October
1924 **La Danse des libellules** (*La Danza delle Libellule*) French version w Max Eddy (Théâtre Ba-ta-clan)
1926 **No, No, Nanette** French version w Robert de Simone, Paul Colline, Georges Merry (Théâtre Mogador)
1927 **Rose-Marie** French version w Saint-Granier (Théâtre Mogador)
1930 **Le Chant du désert** (*The Desert Song*) French version w Saint-Granier (Théâtre Mogador)
1931 **Halleluja!** (*Hit the Deck*) French version w Saint-Granier (Théâtre Mogador)

FERRIER, Paul [Raoul Michel Marie] (b Montpellier, 29 March 1843; d Nouan-le-Fuzelier, Loir-et-Cher, 11 September 1920).

447

Paul Ferrier threw in his career as a Montpellierain lawyer for a much more grateful one as a prolific and successful playwright and librettist and, ultimately, honorary president of the French Société des auteurs. His first piece, *La Revanche d'Iris*, was played at the Comédie Française in 1868, and he thereafter turned out a long series of plays including the musical comedy *La Chaste Suzanne* (1877), *La Vie de Bohème* (1898) and *La Troisième Lune* (1904, w Fred de Grésac) to good effect.

In 1877 he made his first full-scale contribution to the musical theatre with the libretto to Gaston Serpette's *La Petite Muette* at the Bouffes-Parisiens, and he followed this with two collaborations with Offenbach (*Maître Peronilla*, *La Marocaine*) for the same theatre. However, it was his fourth piece for Bouffes director Louis Cantin which hit the mark when *Les Mousquetaires au couvent* (1880), the first major work of the young composer Louis Varney, scored a huge hit. Several other extremely fruitful collaborations with Varney followed (*Fanfan la Tulipe*, *Babolin*, *Les Petits Mousquetaires*, *Miss Robinson*), but Ferrier's next enduringly serious musical theatre hit was a collaboration with Victor Roger on the vaudeville *Joséphine vendue par ses soeurs*, an hilarious modern retelling – with the sexes reversed – of the biblical Joseph legend, which, like *Les Mousquetaires*, became part of the standard repertoire in France and won many overseas productions.

Roger, Varney and Serpette remained Ferrier's principal musical collaborators through the most important part of his career, but he also collaborated with André Messager, Franco Leoni, Gabriel Pierné and others on works for the Opéra-Comique, co-authored several féeries including the Châtelet's *Les Mille et une nuits* (1881 w Adolphe d'Ennery), *Coco fêlé* (w Paul Burani, Floury, 1885), *Le Petit Chaperon rouge* (w Ernest Blum, Pierre Decourcelle, 1900), the particularly spectacular *Le Trésor des Radjahs* (w d'Ennery, 1894), the remarkably sexy spectacular musical fairy pieces *Le Carnet du Diable* and *Le Carillon* and the widely played latest revision of the 1833 favourite *Le Royaume des femmes*. He also supplied the libretti for several operas, notably Bemberg's *Elaine* (1892) for Nellie Melba, Xavier Leroux's *Theodora* (1907), Le Borne's *La Catalane* (1907) and Franco Leoni's *La Tsigane* (1910).

Latterly Ferrier became involved in adapting and translating and was responsible for revamping Hervé's *Chilpéric* for a major Paris revival in 1895 and for the French versions of such diverse pieces as *Die Fledermaus* and *The Quaker Girl*. His most significant success in this field was, however, in the operatic world where he supplied the standard French versions of Puccini's *La Bohème* (partly taken from his play *La Vie de Bohème*), *Tosca*, *Madame Butterfly*, *Suor Angelica* and *Gianni Schicchi* as well as new French texts for *Die Zauberflöte*, *Don Giovanni* and *The Marriage of Figaro* for the Paris Opéra.

He was also, for a period, involved with Debruyère in the management of the Théâtre de la Gaîté.

Several of Ferrier's plays were used as the bases for later musical comedies, notably the 'comédie mélée d'ariettes' *La Chaste Suzanne* which in London, shorn of its Paul Lacôme and Bariller songs, became Kate Santley's pasticcio entertainment *Madcap*, and *La Troisième Lune*, which was used as the basis for George Edwardes's English musical *See See* (1906). His libretto for *Babolin* was reset in

America (with J Cheever Goodwin taking the whole credit for it) as *The Devil's Deputy*, with a score by Edward Jakobowski (1894).

1877 **La Chaste Suzanne** (Paul Lacôme, Jules Bariller) Théâtre du Palais-Royal 4 July

1877 **La Petite Muette** (Gaston Serpette) Théâtre des Bouffes-Parisiens 4 October

1878 **Maître Peronilla** (Jacques Offenbach/w Charles Nuitter, Offenbach) Théâtre des Bouffes-Parisiens 13 March

1879 **La Marocaine** (Offenbach/w Ludovic Halévy) Théâtre des Bouffes-Parisiens 13 January

1880 **Les Mousquetaires au couvent** (Louis Varney/w Jules Prével) Théâtre des Bouffes-Parisiens 16 March

1882 **Les Beignets du roi** (Firmin Bernicat/w Albert Carré) Alcazar, Brussels 10 February

1882 **Fanfan la Tulipe** (Varney/w Prével) Théâtre des Folies-Dramatiques 21 October

1884 **Babolin** (Varney/w Prével) Théâtre des Nouveautés 19 March

1884 **La Nuit aux soufflets** (Hervé/w Adolphe d'Ennery) Théâtre des Nouveautés 18 September

1885 **La Vie mondaine** (Lecocq/w Emile de Najac) Théâtre des Nouveautés 13 February

1885 **Les Petits Mousquetaires** (Varney/w Prével) Folies-Dramatiques 5 March

1886 **Joséphine vendue par ses soeurs** (Victor Roger/w Fabrice Carré) Théâtre des Bouffes-Parisiens 20 March

1887 **Dix jours aux Pyrénées** (Varney) Théâtre de la Gaîté 22 November

1888 **Le Valet de coeur** (Raoul Pugno/w Charles Clairville) Théâtre des Bouffes-Parisiens 19 April

1888 **Les Premières Armes de Louis XV** revised *Les Beignets du Roi* (Théâtre des Menus-Plaisirs)

1889 **La Vénus d'Arles** (Varney/w Liorat) Théâtre des Nouveautés 30 January

1889 **Riquet à la houppe** (Varney/w C Clairville) Théâtre des Folies-Dramatiques 20 April

1890 **Cendrillonnette** (Roger, Serpette) Théâtre des Bouffes-Parisiens 24 January

1890 **Le Fétiche** (Roger/w C Clairville) Théâtre des Menus-Plaisirs 13 March

1890 **Samsonnet** (Roger) Théâtre des Nouveautés 26 November

1890 **La Fée aux chèvres** (Varney/w Albert Vanloo) Théâtre de la Gaîté 18 December

1891 **Le Coq** (Roger/w Ernest Depré) Théâtre des Menus-Plaisirs 30 October

1891 **Mademoiselle Asmodée** (Roger, Lacôme/w C Clairville) Théâtre de la Renaissance 23 November

1892 **Mé-na-ka** (Serpette) 1 act Théâtre des Nouveautés 2 May

1892 **Miss Robinson** (Varney) Théâtre des Folies-Dramatiques 17 December

1893 **La Prétentaine** (Vasseur/w R Bénédite) Nouveau-Théâtre 10 October

1895 **Chilpéric** revised version w Hervé (Théâtre des Variétés)

1895 **La Dot de Brigitte** (Roger, Serpette/w Antony Mars) Théâtre des Bouffes-Parisiens 6 May

1895 **Le Carnet du diable** (Serpette/w Ernest Blum) Théâtre des Variétés 23 October

1895 **Le Capitole** (Serpette/w C Clairville) Théâtre des Nouveautés 5 December

1896 **Le Royaume des femmes** (Serpette/w Blum) Eldorado 24 February

1896 **Le Chevalier d'Harmental** (Messager) Opéra-Comique 5 May

1896 **Le Carillon** (Serpette/w Blum) Théâtre des Variétés 7 November

1897 **La Peur du gendarme** (Jules Darien/w Henri Bocage) Théâtre des Bouffes-Parisiens 21 February

1898 **La Revanche de Galathée** (Edmond Diet) 1 act Théâtre Bodinière 20 April

1900 **Le Portrait magique** (Domergue) 1 act Parisiana 28 May

1900 **Mariage princier** (Ernest Gillet) Théâtre de la Renaissance 17 August

1901 **La Fille du Tabarin** (Gabriel Pierné/w Victorien Sardou) Opéra-Comique 20 February

1901 **Le Tout Petit Chaperon rouge** (Diet) 1 act Charleville 14 December

1902 **Madame la Présidente** (Diet/w Auguste Germain) Casino, Enghien-les-Bains 13 June; Théâtre des Bouffes-Parisiens 4 September 1902

1902 **L'Ordre de l'empereur** (Justin Clérice) Théâtre des Bouffes-Parisiens 4 March

1904 **La Fille de Roland** (Henri Rabaud) Opéra-Comique 16 March

1904 **Le Voyage de la mariée** (Diet, Clérice/w Ordonneau) Galeries St Hubert, Brussels 9 December

1904 **La Chauve-souris** (*Die Fledermaus*) French version (Théâtre des Variétés)

1905 **La Petite Bohème** (Henri Hirschmann) Théâtre des Variétés 19 January

1907 **La Feuille de vigne** (Hirschmann) Théâtre du Moulin-Rouge 24 February

1908 **Oeil de gazelle** (Clérice) Opéra, Monte Carlo February

1910 **Rhodope** (Louis Ganne/w Paul de Choudens) Monte Carlo 13 December

1910 **Noël** (Frédéric d'Erlanger/w Jeanne Ferrier) Opéra-Comique 28 December

1911 **La Danseuse de Tanagra** (Hirschmann/w Felicien Champsaur) Opéra, Nice 10 February

1911 **Le Voile de bonheur** (Charles Pons) 1 act Opéra-Comique 26 April

1912 **La Petite Quaker** (*The Quaker Girl*) French version w Charles Quinel

1913 **Les Merveilleuses** French version (Théâtre des Variétés)

1914 **Miousic** (Lecocq, Messager, Hahn, Redstone, Hirschmann, Xavier Leroux, Camille Erlanger, Cuvillier, Paul Vidal, Paul Letombe) L'Olympia 21 March

LES FÊTARDS Opérette in 3 acts by Antony Mars and Maurice Hennequin. Music by Victor Roger. Théâtre du Palais-Royal, Paris, 28 October 1897.

Les Fêtards, a vastly comical piece said, semi-privately, to be based on a real-life tale of Cléo de Mérode and a certain royal personage, was produced by MM Mussay and Boyer at the height of the fashion for the vaudeville or comedy with songs, and it saw a return by musical theatre to Paris's home of comedy, the Palais-Royal. A top-notch Parisian cast including Jeanne Cheirel, Charles Lamy and the greatest character lady of them all, Marie Desclauzas, played Mars and Hennequin's delightful musical comedy tale of a dancing girl who teaches a modest Marquise how to use woman's arts to woo back a straying husband, through a highly successful initial run of 74 performances.

The pious, provincial Marquise Edith de Chatellerault (Mlle Cheirel), who has brought her millions from America and wed her title (Gaston Dubosc), heads for Paris when she discovers her Marquis's tendency to duplicity and dancing girls and there, angry, troubled and at first incognito, she befriends Théa (Mlle Sidley), the dancer whom he is, so far unsuccessfully, chasing. As a lesson in how to handle a man, Théa makes Edith listen from behind a screen as her own husband tries to win something more than a kiss from the dancer. Edith, determining to win back her husband by following Théa's example, is surprised in the dressing room by the lubricious King

Ernest III of Illyria (Raimond), who has come to pay court to the famous Théa. With the dancer's connivance, Edith remains 'Théa' to the enraptured King for a night of partying and, by various stratagems, manages both to keep her husband and the dancer apart and at the same time chastely misdirect the royal clutches on to the King's old flame, the now buxom wardrobe-mistress Mme Maréchal (Desclauzas), in the dark. After a third act of the liveliest of quiproquos, the Marquise has as well and truly had her revenge, the Marquis has a rather different kind of wife, and the King realizes his 'night of bliss' has been spent with the ageing but expert duenna.

The piece gave rise to some exceptionally fine rôles – the royal roué savouring, in Victor Roger's lively song, the delights in store from 'La p'tit' Théa', the tight-laced Marquise turned coquette, with her transformation song ('Si le révérend me voyait'), her vengeful 'Vous verrez, mon cher' and her troubled duet with Théa ('C'est par la coquetterie'), the sprightly dancer, the archetypal and omnipresent silly-ass Frenchman, Duc Jéhan de Beaugeancy (Charles Lamy), the would-be marquis-of-the-world, and the show-stealing character lady, Madame Maréchal. In the part of the weighty duenna, once little 'Zozo' and the plaything of the pre-throned king, Desclauzas had, for the second time in her remarkable career, the rôle of a lifetime, with the pick of the comic songs – her advice to the coryphées of the Opéra to get into 'du bon trois pour cent', her chase after the King ('Je n'avais pas de parapluie') and her apologetic apostrophe to her late husband ('Grégoire, Grégoire') for her naughty doings.

Following its Paris success, *Les Fêtards* was played in Austria and Germany as *Wie man Männer fesselt* (how to tie up men, ad Otto Eisenschitz) and in Hungary as *A bibliás asszony* (the bible girl) with Roger's amusingly apt and tongue-in-cheek original score attached, but in English-speaking countries, producers preferred to provide their own music. George Edwardes called upon Lionel Monckton and Howard Talbot to write the score for the piece he had already successfully staged as a straight comedy, and which he called *Kitty Grey* (Apollo Theatre 7 September 1901), whilst in America, George Lederer commissioned music from Ludwig Englander to illustrate a more low-comedy version of the libretto called *The Rounders* (Casino Theater 12 July 1899). Thomas Q Seabrooke was Maginnis Pasha, an Irish Turk instead of a King of Illyria, Phyllis Rankin played Théa, Mabelle Gilman was Priscilla and Dan Daly turned the dude rôle into the Duke of Paty de Clam. The piece was an indubitable hit through 131 performances and a return season (with Joseph Herbert replacing as the Duke and Madge Lessing as Priscilla) of 35 nights the following year (25 June 1900). German-speaking New Yorkers had, however, the opportunity to hear the original score when Annie Dirkens, Georgine Neuendorff, Willy Thaller and Jo Hegyi played Eisenschitz's version at the Irving Place Theater in 1906.

That version had already scored a hit in Europe, the sensational initial season of 150 consecutive and 210 total performances at the Vienna Theater in der Josefstadt with Annie Dirkens (Edith), Adele Moraw (Théa), Karl Tuschl (Fürst Niki), Gustav Maran (Beaugency), Karl Pfann (Baron) and the little character actress Viktoria Pohl-Meiser (Mme Maréchal) being followed by a tour which included a guest season at the Munich Theater am

Gärtnerplatz, and productions at Berlin's Thalia-Theater, where Frln Dirkens teamed with Wellhof and Frln Kramm, and at Hamburg's Carl-Schultze Theater (16 September 1900). The piece's mode was even strong enough to provoke the Munich Volkstheater to come out with a Rudolf Kneisl comedy defensively entitled *Wie man Weiber fesselt*. In Hungary (ad Jenő Heltai) 'the bible girl' with Klara Küry, Gábi Bárdi and Terus Bojár, later supplanted by the young Sári Fedák as Théa, was seen for a fine 59 performances at the Népszinház in its first run, prior to widespread productions.

Hungary: Népszinház *A bibliás asszony* 4 November 1898; Austria: Theatre in der Josefstadt *Wie man Männer fesselt* 28 October 1898; Germany: Thalia-Theater *Wie man Männer fesselt* 11 May 1900; USA: Irving Place Theater *Wie man Männer fesselt* 27 December 1906

FEUER, Cy (b New York, 15 January 1911). Broadway producer of a number of major hits in the 1950s and 1960s.

Trained at the Juilliard School of Music, Feuer worked as a trumpeter in orchestras and bands, and as a musical director, before joining Republic Pictures in 1938 for a four-year stint as a film composer. He subsequently became head of the music department there (1945–7). In 1948, in partnership with Ernest Martin, he produced the Frank Loesser musical *Where's Charley?*, and the pair followed up with Loesser's next and most successful show, *Guys and Dolls* (1950) and a series of other musicals which included a high percentage rate of successes: Cole Porter's *Can-Can* (1953), the Broadway version of the London hit *The Boy Friend* (1954), Porter's *Silk Stockings* (1955), *Whoop-Up* (1958), Loesser's *How to Succeed in Business Without Really Trying* (1961), the brilliant burlesque *Little Me* (1962), *Skyscraper* (1965), a musicalized *Hobson's Choice* called *Walking Happy* (1966), and *The Act* (1977). They also produced the highly successful film version of the musical *Cabaret* and the less successful screen *A Chorus Line*.

Feuer also directed *Silk Stockings*, *Whoop-Up*, *Little Me*, *Skyscraper*, *Walking Happy*, and *I Remember Mama*, and was credited with a contribution to the libretto of *Whoop-Up*.

Between 1975 and 1980 Feuer and Martin were co-managers of the Los Angeles and San Francisco Light Opera Association and in 1989 Feuer became President of the League of American Theatres.

DAS FEUERWERK Musical comedy in 3 acts by Erik Charell and Jürg Amstein based on the comedy *De sächzigscht Giburtstag* by Emil Sautter and the musical play *Der schwarze Hecht* by Amstein. Lyrics by Jürg Amstein and Robert Gilbert. Music by Paul Burkhard. Theater am Gärtnerplatz, Munich, 16 May 1950.

Amstein and Burkhard's musical adaptation of Sauter's locally coloured Swiss play was originally produced in a small-scale version at the Zurich Schauspielhaus in 1939, and it was revived there in a revised version in 1948. This revival resulted in the show coming to the attention of the director Erik Charell, many years earlier the stager of the glitziest and grandest musical theatre spectacles in Berlin, who saw in its circus connection the possibilities for expansion into something like his London *The Flying Trapeze* of 1935. As a result, *Der schwarze Hecht* became *Feuerwerk*,

Charell's name joined Amstein's in the credits, and the revised piece was produced by the Bayerische Staatsoperette in Munich in 1950.

On the occasion of Albert Oberholzer's 60th birthday his family gather together from far and wide. Frau Oberholzer and daughter Anna greet papa's four respectable brothers and sister, whilst the cook, Kati, prepares the birthday supper. But then the black sheep of the family turns up: brother Alexander, now a circus manager called Obolski (Gustav Knuth), and his circus-artiste wife, Iduna (Rita Wottawa). Anna, enchanted by Iduna and the visions of a colourful and extraordinary life she represents, determines to go off and join the circus, and things begin to boil up. Her parents are aghast, her boyfriend, the little gardener Robert, furious, the cook gives notice because no one is eating her food, a hen-pecked husband rebels, and Obolksi and Iduna are loudly accused of bringing discontent into a well-ordered house, before the party breaks up. The family depart, and Anna opts for the safe gentility of her home, Robert, and Kati's dinner. The second act contained a long circus scenario in which all the actors took part, filling the show out into a full and highly coloured Charellish evening.

Burkhard's score produced several pretty pieces, notably Iduna's 'Ich hab' ein kleines süsses Pony', but it was her description of her father, the clown, which proved to be the hit of the evening – 'O mein Papa war eine wunderbare Clown'. It was that number, as purveyed on disc variously by Eddie Calvert, Eddie Fisher, Lys Assia and Connie Francis, which helped to spread the show further afield. Vienna's Theater in der Josefstadt welcomed 57 performances, Suzy Delair (Iduna), Jacqueline Cadet and Jean Bretonnière headed the cast of a Simone Volterra production (ad Jean Boyer, Pierre Destailles) at Paris's Théâtre Marigny, Britain's Bristol Old Vic presented *Oh, My Papa!* (ad Elizabeth Montagu) with sufficient success for it to be taken to London, with Rachel Roberts (Iduna) and Laurie Payne (Obolski) featured, for a brief run, and a film version, directed by Charell, was made by Sacha-Films and Kurt Hoffmann, with Lili Palmer (Iduna), Karl Schönböck (Obolski), Romy Schneider (Anna) and Claus Biederstädt (Robert) heading the cast. In 1983 *Feuerwerk* was reproduced at Vienna's Volksoper with Helga Papouschek (Iduna), Kurt Heumer (Obolski) and Elisabeth Kales (Anna), and it continues to win regional productions, both in its original (*Der schwarze Hecht*, Stadttheater St Gallen, 30 December 1992 etc) and its inflated forms.

Austria: Theater in der Josefstadt 15 May 1952; France: Théâtre Marigny *Feu d'artifice* 1952; UK: Bristol Old Vic *Oh, My Papa!* 2 April, Garrick Theatre, London 17 July 1957
Recordings: selection (Ariola-Eurodisc); selection in English (Parlophone EP)

FEYDEAU, Georges [Léon Jules Marie] (b Paris, 8 December 1862; d Paris, 5 June 1921).

The famous French author of farce and comedy dipped into the musical theatre early in his career with an opérette written in collaboration with Gaston Serpette. It was a two-week failure, and it was another 15 years and many of his best plays later before he tried another full-length musical show. The second piece ran just two performances longer than the first. Thereafter his only musical theatre venture was with a musical spectacular, *L'Age d'or*, for the Théâtre des Variétés, but several of his plays proved to be the material for altogether more successful musical comedies.

The most famous, *L' Hôtel du Libre-Échange* (w Desvallières) was the source of the successful 1920 London musical *A Night Out* (Willie Redstone/Clifford Grey/George Grossmith, Arthur Miller) and the less fortunate American version of that adaptation played under the same title (w Vincent Youmans/Irving Caesar). A second American adaptation, *Hotel Passionato* (Philip Springer/Joan Javits/Jerome J Schwartz, 1965), also failed.

La Dame de Chez Maxim (1899) became the successful *Das Mädel von Montmartre* with a score by Henri Berény, which was later played in America as *The Girl from Montmartre* (1912), as well as *La dama di Montmartre* (music: Ermete Liberati, 1920) in Italy and *Dama od Maxima* (Ryszard Sielicki/Antoni Marianowicz) in Romania (1967) whilst *La Duchesse des Folies-Bergère* became *Die Nachtprinzessin*, described as a musical vaudeville, with a score by Carl Weinberger (Hamburg, 4 April 1914), and *Un fil à la patte* was musicalized by Robert Winterberg as *Der letzte Kuss* (Komoedienhaus, 1925).

1887 **La Lycéenne** (Gaston Serpette) Théâtre des Nouveautés 23 December

1890 **Mademoiselle Nounou** (w Maurice Desvallières) 1 act Brussels 25 April

1902 **Le Billet de Josephine** (Alfred Kaiser/w Joseph Méry) Théâtre de la Gaîte 23 February

1905 **L'Age d'or** (Louis Varney/w Desvallières) Théâtre des Variétés 1 May

Biographies: Lorcey, J: *Georges Feydeau* (La Table Ronde, Paris, 1972), Pronko, L: *Georges Feydeau* (Ungar, New York, 1975), Gidel, H: *Feydeau* (Flammarion, Paris, 1991) etc

FIDDLER ON THE ROOF

FIDDLER ON THE ROOF Musical in 2 acts by Joseph Stein based on the stories of Sholom Aleichem. Lyrics by Sheldon Harnick. Music by Jerry Bock. Imperial Theater, New York, 22 September 1964.

The stories of the Russian-American humorist Sholom Aleichem (né Solomon Rabinowitz, 1859–1916), which had been used several years previously as the basis for a play by Arnold Perl called *Tevya and His Daughters* (Carnegie Hall Playhouse, New York 16 September 1957), were re-used to create the libretto for the most successful Broadway musical play of the 1960s. Mr Perl was given a footnoted 'by special permission of ... ' attached to an asterisk following 'based on Sholom Aleichem's stories'.

Fiddler on the Roof told a tale of the breaking-down of established, traditional ways of life – in this case, Russian Jewish traditional life – in the early 20th century, partly under the pressure of changes from the inside, where the younger generation prove no longer willing to bend their individual will to the laws of their fathers, and partly under the pressure of the jealousy, greed and hatred of people outside the community. The first crack in the hardworking, unexpansive life of Anatevka's village milkman Tevye (Zero Mostel), his wife Golde (Maria Karnilova) and their daughters comes when, in accordance with tradition, Tevye has the matchmaker Yente (Beatrice Arthur) make an advantageous match for his eldest daughter Tzeitel (Joanna Merlin), with the widowed butcher Lazar Wolf (Michael Granger). Tzeitel has, unfortunately, had time to fall in love with the poor tailor Motel (Austin

Plate 91. *Max Gillies as Tevye and Cynthia Johnston as Golde in the Australian Opera's 1988 production of* **Fiddler on the Roof**.

Pendelton), and her soft-hearted father has to go to great and shaming lengths to break off the promised match. The second daughter, Hodel (Julia Migenes), falls under the charms of the jingoistic 'student', Perchik (Bert Convy), who ends up in a labour camp, whilst little Chava (Tanya Everett) goes furthest of all and chooses as her bridegroom the Christian, Fyedka. And whilst the bewildered Tevye's world is breaking down around him, the pogroms arrive to finish off the community of Anatevka. Tevye and the remaining members of his family set off to America, taking their battered traditions with them.

Bock and Harnick's musical illustration of the tale was of a rare warmth. The gently lilting 'Sunrise, Sunset', Motel's explosion of joy in 'Miracle of Miracles', Tevye's sudden and unexpected question to his wife after 25 years of an arranged marriage, 'Do You Love Me?', Perchik and Hodel's 'Now I Have Everything' and Hodel's ballad as she leaves to follow him, 'Far From the Home I Love', were feeling moments. There were colourful ones too – the butcher and the milkman raising a tipsy paean 'To Life', the celebration of 'Tradition', the three eldest daughters taking sudden frights at the realization that 'Matchmaker, Matchmaker' might not bring them what they want in a husband, and Tevye's stand-up spot, apostrophizing God as to what would be the harm 'If I Were a Rich Man'? There was a sufficiency of Jewish and local colouring in the score to make it apt without being obtrusively ethnic, and only rarely did this most atypical of Broadway shows reach into the out-front or the showy in its music or in its staging. The principal dance routine, in a musical play set in a time and place in history where women may not dance in public, was director/choreographer Jerome Robbins's memorable version of the all-male bottle dance.

Harold Prince's production of *Fiddler on the Roof* won a clutch of Tony Awards, including that for Best Musical, and broke the Broadway long-run record for a musical play by remaining 3,242 performances at the Imperial Theater, where it used up a half-dozen Tevyes including Herschel Bernardi and singing star Jan Peerce. The first replacement, Luther Adler, headed out the initial American touring company, which travelled for more than two years. *Fiddler on the Roof* returned to Broadway in 1976 (Winter Garden Theater, 28 December), with Mostel repeating his original rôle alongside Thelma Lee (Golde) for 167 performances, and again in 1990–1 when a touring production with Topol starred was played at the Gershwin Theater (18 October 1990) for seven months.

Israeli actor Topol was the first British Tevye in Harold Prince and Richard Pilbrow's production at London's Her Majesty's Theatre. Miriam Karlin (Golde), Rosemary Nicols (Tzeitel), Jonathan Lynn (Motel), Cynthia Grenville (Yente), Paul Whitsun-Jones (Wolf), Linda Gardner (Hodel) and Caryl Little (Chava) were the initial supporting cast, and once again the show proved to be a major hit, playing through 2,030 London performances during which Alfie Bass and Lex Goudsmit were also seen as Tevye, and Avis Bunnage and Hy Hazell as Golde. Topol subsequently starred in the 1971 film version of the show, with Norma Crane (Golde), Molly Picon (Yente), Rosalind Harris (Tzeitel) and Leonard Frey (Motel), and continued thereafter to appear regularly as Tevye, notably in a revival at London's Apollo Victoria Theatre in 1983 (28 June) and again on Broadway in 1990.

Australia's *Fiddler on the Roof*, featuring Hayes Gordon and Brigid Lenihan, played 11 months in Sydney and Melbourne (Her Majesty's Theatre 28 October 1967) and the show established itself there as a perennial favourite as well, finding itself a home as a regular money-maker in the repertoire of the Australian Opera in the 1990s.

Fiddler on the Roof was one of the very few English-language musical plays of its period to make a significant and enduring mark in Europe. The first German-language version (ad Rolf Merz) was produced by Werner Schmid in Hamburg, under the title *Anatevka*, with Shmuel Rodensky as Tevye and Lilly Towska as Golde, and the show was subsequently seen in Düsseldorf and in Berlin before being mounted at Vienna's Theater an der Wien. Oddly, the credits now read 'musical based on the tale 'Tevye, the Milkman' by Sholem Aleichem with permission of Arnold Perl' – just one tale and no asterisk. Yossi Yadin was Vienna's Tevye and Lya Dulizkaya, who had already played Golde some 600 times opposite Bomba J Zur in the hugely successful Israeli production, was Golde. The Vienna season of 232 performances was the most substantial of those played by any of the series of imported musicals staged there in the later 1960s and early 1970s, and the German-language version (later played also as *Der Fiedler auf dem Dach*) maintained its position at the top of the heap through the following decades.

Helsinki, Copenhagen, Tokyo and Amsterdam were also amongst the earliest cities to mount productions of the show and in 1972 even Paris, disinterested for decades in the produce of the overseas musical theatre, mounted *Un Violon sur le toit* (ad Robert Manuel, Maurice Vidalin) with Yvan Rebroff as a richly basso Tevye and Maria Murano as Golde. In Hungary, *Hegedüs a háztetőn* (ad György Denes, István Reményi Gyenes) was produced at the Fővárosi Operettszinház in 1973, and it remains in the repertoire of the theatre to this day.

Performed incessantly around the world, *Fiddler on the Roof* is firmly fixed in the international repertoire as one of the outstanding, most frequently and widely played musicals of its or any other era.

Another musical piece included Aleichem in its credits: an adaptation of *Hard to Be a Jew* illustrated with songs by Itzak Perlow (lyrics) and Sholom Secunda (music), produced at New York's Eden Theater 28 November 1973.

UK: Her Majesty's Theatre 16 February 1967; Australia: Her Majesty's Theatre, Sydney 16 June 1967; Germany: Operettenhaus, Hamburg *Anatevka* 1 February 1968; Austria: Theater an der Wien *Anatevka* 15 February 1969; France: Théâtre Marigny *Un Violon sur le toit* 1972; Hungary: Fővárosi Operettszínház *Hegedüs a háztetőn* 9 February 1973

Recordings: original cast (RCA), London cast (CBS), German/Hamburg cast (Decca), Austrian cast (Preiser), French cast (CBS), South African Cast (RCA), Israel casts in Yiddish and Hebrew (Columbia), Japanese cast (Toho, 2 records), Mexican cast (Capitol), Hungarian cast (Qualiton), Argentine cast (PAR), Norwegian cast (Nordisc), Dutch cast (RCA), Danish cast (Decca), Icelandic cast (SG EP), Film Soundtrack (United Artists) etc

DER FIDELE BAUER Operette in a prologue and 2 acts by Victor Léon. Music by Leo Fall. Hoftheater, Mannheim, 27 July 1907; Theater an der Wien, Vienna, 1 June 1908.

In spite of being written to a text by Victor Léon, recently the co-author of the blockbusting *Die lustige Witwe*, the Operette with which the young Leo Fall first made his name was not initially produced in Vienna or in Berlin, but at the Hoftheater in Mannheim. The success of the first staging of *Der fidele Bauer* was, however, indubitable, and the show racked up an enormous number of productions throughout Germany in the years that followed. Keller's survey of the performances in Germany during the first 20 years of the century rates it statistically an all-time sixth behind *Die Fledermaus*, *Die lustige Witwe*, *Das Dreimäderlhaus*, *Die Geisha* and *Der Zigeunerbaron*. However, in spite of this rush of popularity, it was nearly 12 months before the show was given its first production in the Austrian capital – which had by then seen Fall thoroughly launched with the production of *Die Dollarprinzessin* – and more than four months more before Berlin saw its first production of *Der fidele Bauer*.

Matthäus Scheichelroither (Louis Treumann) is a peasant farmer, firmly and happily fixed in his old-fashioned ways and with ambition only that his son, Stefan (Adolf Lussmann), should have all the advantages in life. Eight years at a good school in Linz are followed by 11 years more study until Stefan becomes a doctor. But when he pays a quick visit home, it is to embarrassedly tell his father and his sister, Annamirl (Gusti Stagl), that he is to be wed to Friederike von Grunow (Nelly Ridon), the daughter of a Privy Councillor. It would not be comfortable for his peasant family to attend the wedding. When neighbour Lindoberer (Max Pallenberg) takes Matthäus and Annamirl to Vienna six months later, the meeting of the town and country families finally takes place and, thanks to Matthäus's ingenuous sincerity and the genuine goodness of Friederike and her family the ending is a happy one. Parallel to the main tale ran the little love story of Annamirl and Lindoberer's son, Vincenz (Hugo Machiau).

Fall's musical score was full of winning melodies, from the swinging Bauernmarsch ('Ich bin nix wie a Bauer') to the gentle thankfulness of Matthäus's waltz 'Jeder tragt sein Pinkerl', Stefan's more forwardly waltzing 'O frag mich nicht, mein süsser Schatz', the jolly trio for Matthäus, Lindoberer and Annamirl 'Wir waren unser drei' and a winning little folksy number ('Heinerle, Heinerle hab' kein Geld') for an incidental girl called Red Lisi (Grete Freund), explaining to her little son (Klara Meissel) that she cannot afford to buy him presents from the village fair.

Der fidele Bauer was played 54 times under Karczag and Wallner at the Theater an der Wien, before and after the summer break of 1908, and then moved on to the Raimundtheater (9 October) with Franz Gross as Matthäus and Grete Petrovits as Annamirl, for additional performances in 1908, 1909 (including a season at the Carltheater from 9 November) and again in 1910, with Ernst Tautenhayn taking the title-rôle alongside the Lindoberer of Franz Glawatsch, without, however, equalling the popularity of *Die Dollarprinzessin*. It nevertheless returned several times to the Raimundtheater, being seen there in 1914 and again in 1920. In Berlin, too, it scored heavily, racing to its 100th successive performance at the Theater des Westens on 15 September 1908 and engraving itself into the list of the time's biggest successes.

An Hungarian version (ad Ferenc Révesz, Emil Tábori) and an English adaptation (ad Cosmo Hamilton) were produced the year following the Vienna première. The London version featured one-time *Gondoliers* star Courtice Pounds as Matthäus, Julius Walther (Stefan), Marie West (Frieda) and former top-billed stars Florence St John and Arthur Williams in the small rôles of Red Lisi and Zopf and it also included additional numbers by one Theodore Holland. After a poor start it was revised by Hamilton, but it still managed only 71 performances.

Although Henry Savage announced that he would produce *A Sturdy Peasant* in the wake of *The Merry Widow*, Broadway did not see *Der fidele Bauer* in English. It was produced in New York only by Gustav Amberg at the German-speaking Garden Theater with Konrad Dreher (Matthäus), Lotte Engel (Annamirl) and Hansen (Vincent). Paris, likewise, did not take the piece up and the first French-language performances (ad Gustave Jonghbeys) were seen at Brussels's Théâtre Molière with Michel Dufour starred as Matthäus, Germaine Huber (Annamirl), Duncan (Stefan), Mlle Armel (Frida) and George (Lindoberer).

A film entitled *Der fidele Bauer* had a conventionalized screenplay by Rudolf Österreicher, Hubert and Georg Marischka in which Matthias's son Heinerle became not a doctor but a pianist, and paired off not with a middle-class German but with an American called Vivian Harrison. The music was 'arranged' by Bruno Uher. Paul Hörbiger played the merry peasant, with Erich Auer as his son, Marianne Wischmann as the American and Elisabeth Karlan as sister Resi. Annamirl (Helly Servi) was someone

else's daughter, but still romanced Vincenz (Franz Marischka), son of Lindoberer (Heinrich Gretler).

Germany: Theater des Westens 23 October 1908; Hungary: Fővárosi Nyari Szinház *A kedélyes paraszt* 25 June 1909; UK: Strand Theatre *The Merry Peasant* 23 October 1909; Belgium: Théâtre Molière, Brussels *Le Joyeux Paysan* 20 October 1910; USA: Garden Theater (Ger) 22 February 1911; Film: Donau-Berna/International films/Georg Marischka

Recordings: Selection (part-record) (Philips, EMI Columbia, Polydor) etc

FIELD, Ron[ald] (b New York, ?1934; d New York, 6 February 1989). Broadway choreographer and director.

Field worked as a child performer (*Lady in the Dark*) and a dancer (*Seventeen, Kismet, The Boy Friend*) in the theatre, but largely in television, before coming into evidence as the choreographer for the 1962 off-Broadway revival of *Anything Goes* and the St Louis Muny's Stephen Foster musical *I Dream of Jeannie* (1963, also lead dancer). His subsequent major choreography credits in a career which his biographical note claimed curiously included 'over 14 Broadway musicals' were the original productions of *Cabaret* (Tony Award), *Zorba*, *Applause* (also director, Tony Awards) and the 1971 revival of *On the Town* (also director). His subsequent work, largely away from Broadway, included the musical staging of part of the Opening Ceremony for the Los Angeles Olympic Games, and the dances for a British revival of *Kiss Me, Kate* (1987). His last Broadway credit was on the short-lived *Rags* (1987).

FIELDING, Harold (b Woking, 4 December 1916).

Originally a child prodigy violinist who appeared on touring programmes with Luisa Tetrazzini, then later an orchestral and concert promoter, Harold Fielding made his first London theatrical venture, in collaboration with C B Cochran, in the world of ballet. He entered the musical theatre with a spectacular staging of Rodgers and Hammerstein's television musical *Cinderella* at the London Coliseum in 1958 and followed that profitable production with the less successful *Aladdin* of Cole Porter and with London productions of the *Billy Barnes Revue*, *The Music Man* (1961) and *Sail Away* (1962) before launching his first original musical, the highly successful *Half a Sixpence* (1963).

Fielding subsequently produced a number of plays and revues (*Round Leicester Square, Hullaballoo, Let My People Come, Swann and Topping*) and ran Fielding's Music Hall at the Prince Charles Theatre for several years, but he concentrated largely on the musical theatre. There he scored further successes with the very long-running *Charlie Girl* (1965), the London versions of *Sweet Charity* (1967) and *Mame* (1969), the Wright and Forrest remake of *Walzer aus Wien* as *The Great Waltz* (1970) mounted at the Theatre Royal, Drury Lane, a revival of *Show Boat* (1971) which gave that show its longest-ever run, Cy Coleman's Broadway hit *I Love My Wife*, a revised version of Harry Rigby's revised *Irene*, and stage versions of the Frank Loesser *Hans Andersen* (1974) and the classic film *Singin' in the Rain* (1983), both featuring *Half a Sixpence* star, Tommy Steele. Each of these last two pieces returned for a second London season as did his highly successful production of the circus musical, *Barnum*, with Michael Crawford in its leading rôle.

A revival of *Charlie Girl* did less well, and joined the

Houdini musical *Man of Magic* (1966), a London production of *You're a Good Man, Charlie Brown*, the Percy French tale *Phil, the Fluter* (1969), a musical version of the famous *Gone With the Wind* (1972) which lost more in America than it made in London, the tiny Hollywood tale of *The Biograph Girl*, the unfortunate Italian *Beyond the Rainbow* (*Aggiungi un posto a tavola*), and a dazzling London version of the burlesque operetta *On the Twentieth Century* in the debit column.

The successive failures of the expensive extravaganza *Ziegfeld* (1988) and the Petula Clark musical *Someone Like You* (1990) drove the man widely considered as the cleverest London showman of two generations from the production arena in which he had co-produced with both the aged Cochran and the young Cameron Mackintosh (*My Fair Lady* revival) but, largely, had supplied 30 years of entertainment which, if often sniffed at as 'popular' by critics, had proven to be just that with the public.

FIELDS, Dorothy (b Allenhurst, NJ, 15 July 1905; d New York, 28 March 1974). Highly successful Broadway and Hollywood lyricist who also co-authored the libretti for several long-running musicals.

The daughter of Lew Fields, and the sister of Herbert Fields and Joseph Fields, Dorothy Fields was still in her early twenties when she formed a songwriting partnership with composer Jimmy McHugh which bore its first fruits with songs for the Cotton Club in 1927. The pair had their first hits with 'I Can't Give You Anything But Love', 'Diga, Diga, Doo' and 'Doin' the New Low-Down' as performed in the hit revue *Blackbirds of 1928*, for which Miss Fields was also credited with the 'book', and they followed up with the songs for what was virtually a Fields family show – Herbert wrote the text, Lew produced and starred in the not unsuccessful *Hello Daddy* – and for *Blackbirds* producer Lew Leslie's less successful *International Revue* (1930, 'On the Sunny Side of the Street', 'Exactly Like You'). They also interpolated a successful number into *The Vanderbilt Revue* ('Blue Again').

In the 1930s Fields and McHugh abandoned the theatre and, instead, turned to supplying songs for a long list of Hollywood films, including *Love in the Rough* ('Go Home and Tell Your Mother'), *Cuban Love Song, Singin' the Blues* ('It's the Darnedest Thing', 'Singin' the Blues'), *Dinner at Eight* ('Don't Blame Me', 'Dinner at Eight'), *Have a Heart* ('Lost in the Fog'), and *Every Night at Eight* ('I'm in the Mood for Love', 'I Feel a Song Coming On'). Miss Fields also collaborated with Jerome Kern on 'Lovely to Look At' and a revised version of 'I Won't Dance' for the film of *Roberta* (1935), and the partnership with Kern was pursued in such pieces as the Lily Pons film *I Dream Too Much*, *Swing Time* ('A Fine Romance', 'Pick Yourself Up', 'Waltz in Swing Time', 'The Way You Look Tonight [Academy Award]') and *The Joy of Living*. Amongst her other projects, Miss Fields provided the lyrics to Fritz Kreisler's melody for 'Stars in my Eyes' in the Grace Moore film *The King Steps Out*.

In 1939 she worked on her first Broadway show for nearly a decade when she supplied the lyrics for the revue *Stars in Your Eyes* (music: Arthur Schwartz), but since her return to the book musical was on a Cole Porter musical, her contribution was not to the songwords but to the libretto, on which she collaborated with brother Herbert.

Let's Face It, Something for the Boys and *Mexican Hayride* gave the lyricist three long-running successes as a librettist, and she added a fourth when she returned to lyricwriting for Sigmund Romberg's *Up in Central Park* ('Close as Pages in a Book'). When the Fieldses, brother and sister, combined with another songwriter in Irving Berlin on *Annie Get Your Gun*, Dorothy again returned to the post of co-librettist, and on this occasion won not only a long run but also an enduring hit.

She supplied lyrics and part-book for the 1950 *Arms and the Girl*, and the lyrics to Arthur Schwartz's attractive, if only moderately successful, pair of shows *A Tree Grows in Brooklyn* ('He Had Refinement') and *By the Beautiful Sea* ('I'd Rather Wake Up By Myself', also co-librettist), and again for the music-hall murder musical *Redhead*, but found her greatest success as a Broadway lyricist when she combined with composer Cy Coleman on the score for *Sweet Charity* (1966, 'Big Spender', 'If My Friends Could See Me Now', 'The Rhythm of Life', 'There's Gotta Be Something Better Than This', 'Where Am I Going?').

She contributed a score to only one further Broadway musical, Coleman's *Seesaw*, shortly before her death, turning out 'Nobody Does It Like Me', 'Welcome to Holiday Inn' and the extravagantly youthful 'It's Not Where You Start (it's where you finish)' to add to the long list of successful songs produced in a career of some 45 years in the theatre and film.

Her other credits include a television musical version of her brother Joseph's *Junior Miss* with music by Burton Lane (CBS 20 December 1957).

1928 **Hello Daddy** (Jimmy McHugh/Herbert Fields) Fields' Theater 26 December
1931 **Singin' the Blues** (McHugh/J P McGowan) Liberty Theater 16 September
1941 **Let's Face It** (Cole Porter/w H Fields) Imperial Theater 29 October
1943 **Something for the Boys** (Porter/w H Fields) Alvin Theater 7 January
1944 **Mexican Hayride** (Porter/w H Fields) Winter Garden Theater 28 January
1945 **Up in Central Park** (Sigmund Romberg/w H Fields) Century Theater 27 January
1946 **Annie Get Your Gun** (Irving Berlin/w H Fields) Imperial Theater 16 May
1950 **Arms and the Girl** (Morton Gould/w H Fields, Rouben Mamoulian) 46th Street Theater 2 February
1951 **A Tree Grows in Brooklyn** (Arthur Schwartz/Betty Smith, George Abbott) Alvin Theater 19 April
1954 **By the Beautiful Sea** (Schwartz/w H Fields) Majestic Theater 8 April
1959 **Redhead** (Albert Hague/w H Fields, Sidney Sheldon, David Shaw) 46th Street Theater 5 February
1966 **Sweet Charity** (Cy Coleman/Neil Simon) Palace Theater 29 January
1973 **Seesaw** (Coleman/Michael Stewart, Michael Bennett) Uris Theater 18 March

FIELDS, Herbert (b New York, 26 July 1897; d New York, 24 March 1958).

The son of Lew Fields, and brother of Dorothy Fields and Joseph Fields, Herbert Fields made his earliest forays into the musical theatre in college and amateur theatricals alongside the young Richard Rodgers and Lorenz Hart, variously directing, choreographing and writing as the occasion demanded. He collaborated with his two friends on a flop play, *The Melody Man*, produced by his father, and had his first successes alongside them with his contribution to the revue *The Garrick Gaieties* and the libretto for their first book musical, *Dearest Enemy* (1925).

The trio had further successes with *The Girl Friend*, and with adaptations of the favourite old play *Tillie's Nightmare* as *Peggy-Ann* and of Mark Twain's *A Connecticut Yankee (in King Arthur's Court)*, and Fields had an even bigger success when he stepped outside the team to adapt the play *Shore Leave* as the libretto for the Vincent Youmans musical *Hit the Deck*. Later musicals with Rodgers and Hart – *Present Arms*, the adaptation of Charles Pitts's *The Son of the Grand Eunuch* as the short-lived *Chee-Chee*, and the filmland burlesque *America's Sweetheart* – had less success than their earlier shows, and the songwriters and librettist went their separate ways.

Fields began an association with Cole Porter on the musical *Fifty Million Frenchmen*, and the pair continued with a series of long-running shows from *Dubarry Was a Lady* and *Panama Hattie*, both written with Buddy De Sylva, through *Let's Face It*, *Something for the Boys* and *Mexican Hayride* in which Fields was joined as co-librettist by his sister, Dorothy, with whom all his future stage musicals were written. Of these, *Up in Central Park* found a fine Broadway run, and *By the Beautiful Sea* and the posthumous *Redhead* some success, but it was the Fields's collaboration with Irving Berlin on the biomusical of sharp-shooting Annie Oakley, *Annie Get Your Gun*, which gave Herbert his biggest and most memorable hit.

1925 **Dearest Enemy** (Richard Rodgers/Lorenz Hart) Knickerbocker Theater 18 September
1926 **The Girl Friend** (Rodgers/Hart) Vanderbilt Theater 17 March
1926 **Peggy-Ann** (Rodgers/Hart) Vanderbilt Theater 27 December
1927 **Hit the Deck** (Vincent Youmans/Clifford Grey, Leo Robin) Belsaco Theater 25 April
1927 **A Connecticut Yankee** (Rodgers/Hart) Vanderbilt Theater 3 November
1928 **Present Arms** (Rodgers/Hart) Mansfield Theater 26 April
1928 **Chee-Chee** (Rodgers/Hart) Mansfield Theater 25 September
1928 **Hello Daddy** (Jimmy McHugh/Dorothy Fields) Fields' Theater 26 December
1929 **Fifty Million Frenchmen** (Cole Porter) Lyric Theater 27 November
1930 **The New Yorkers** (Porter) Broadway Theater 8 December
1931 **America's Sweetheart** (Rodgers/Hart) Broadhurst Theater 10 February
1933 **Pardon My English** (George Gershwin/Ira Gershwin) Majestic Theater 20 January
1939 **Dubarry Was a Lady** (Porter/w B G De Sylva) 46th Street Theater 6 December
1940 **Panama Hattie** (Porter/w De Sylva) 46th Street Theater 30 October
1941 **Let's Face It** (Cole Porter/w D Fields) Imperial Theater 29 October
1943 **Something for the Boys** (Porter/w D Fields) Alvin Theater 7 January
1944 **Mexican Hayride** (Porter/w D Fields) Winter Garden Theater 28 January
1945 **Up in Central Park** (Sigmund Romberg/w D Fields) Century Theater 27 January
1946 **Annie Get Your Gun** (Irving Berlin/w D Fields) Imperial Theatre 16 May

1950 **Arms and.the Girl** (Morton Gould/w D Fields, Rouben Mamoulian) 46th Street Theater 2 February
1954 **By the Beautiful Sea** (Schwartz/D Fields/w D Fields) Majestic Theater 8 April
1959 **Redhead** (Albert Hague/w D Fields, Sidney Sheldon, David Shaw) 46th Street Theater 5 February

FIELDS, Joseph [Albert] (b New York, 21 February 1895; d Beverly Hills, Calif, 3 March 1966).

Son of Lew Fields, brother of Herbert Fields and Dorothy Fields, and the co-author of the hit plays *My Sister Eileen* and *Junior Miss* (w Jerome Chodorov), Joseph Fields also worked with considerable success as a librettist in the musical theatre. He collaborated on the musical adaptation of Anita Loos's celebrated novel *Gentlemen Prefer Blondes* (1949) with its original author, on the adaptation of Chin Y Lee's novel as the Rodgers and Hammerstein musical *Flower Drum Song* (1958) with Hammerstein, on *The Girl in Pink Tights*, a piece which used the staging of the 19th-century extravaganza *The Black Crook* as its backdrop, and on the adaptation of *My Sister Eileen* as *Wonderful Town*, both with Chodorov. *Junior Miss* was also musicalized, by his sister Dorothy and Burton Lane, for CBS-TV (20 December 1957).

1949 **Gentlemen Prefer Blondes** (Jule Styne/Leo Robin/w Anita Loos) Ziegfeld Theater 8 December
1953 **Wonderful Town** (Leonard Bernstein/Betty Comden, Adolph Green/w Jerome Chodorov) Winter Garden Theater 25 February
1956 **The Girl in Pink Tights** (Sigmund Romberg/Robin/w Chodorov) Mark Hellinger Theater 5 March
1958 **Flower Drum Song** (Richard Rodgers/Oscar Hammerstein II/w Hammerstein) St James Theater 1 December 1958

FIELDS, Lew [SCHANFIELD, Lewis Maurice] (b New York, 1 January 1867; d Beverly Hills, Calif, 20 July 1941). Variety and burlesque comedian who made his fame as part of the team of Weber and Fields before going on to a solo career as a producer of, and comedy star in, musicals.

Fields made his first stage appearances at the age of ten in a dialect comedy double-act with another youngster, Joseph Weber, in minor variety theatres, and the pair continued to tour their act through the United States over the next 20 years, at first under other managements and, from 1885, with a company of their own. Fields, taller and slimmer, and Weber, shorter and stockier (and padded to emphasize the difference), both gaudily suited, derbied and whiskered, traded warm and heavily 'Dutch'-accented banter of a homely and broadly comical kind, and established themselves as considerable favourites.

In 1896 they took over the Imperial Music Hall at 29th Street and Broadway and renamed it Weber and Fields' Broadway Music Hall, and there they produced and starred in a series of variety-cum-burlesque productions which have become remembered as the most famous of their kind in the American musical theatre. Their first programme included a travesty of David Belasco's civil war drama *The Heart of Maryland* (*The Art of Maryland*), and their first big success was *The Geezer* (October 1896), a burlesque of Sidney Jones's musical play *The Geisha*, which had opened a month earlier at Daly's Theatre. The piece was written by Joseph Herbert and composed by John Stromberg, who was to be the team's resident composer for a number of years. Other recognizable-to-ostensible burlesques of popular shows followed: *Under the Red Globe* (of the Cardinal Richelieu drama *Under the Red Robe*), *The Glad Hand, or Secret Servants* (William Gillette's *Secret Service*), *Pousse Café or the Worst Born* (*La Poupée* and Belasco's *The First-Born* etc), *The Con-Curers* (Paul Potter's *The Conquerors*), *Cyranose de Bric-a-Brac* (*Cyrano de Bergerac*), but each found its mixture of low and parodic comedy in more than just its admitted target, taking potshots at all of Broadway and anything else of a topical nature in a lively, colourful and girlie-filled entertainment.

The pair made an early effort at what was less genuine burlesque and more a semi-plotless topical musical comedy with *Mister New York, Esquire* (1897) but, after a couple of years, developed what proved to be their most popular formula with a series of what were basically variety musicals: a fairly irregular plot outline filled with comic scenes, songs, specialities and topicalities and usually with a sizeable piece of up-to-date specific burlesque introduced. *Hurly Burly* (1898), *Helter Skelter* (1899), *Whir-i-gig* (1899), *Fiddle-dee-dee* (1900), *Hoity-Toity* (1901), *Twirly Whirly* (1902) and *Whoop-de-Doo* (1903) presented such artists as Sam Bernard, Lillian Russell, Fay Templeton, De Wolf Hopper, David Warfield and Bessie Clayton alongside the star comedy pair, equipped with songs including 'Dinah', 'Ma Blushin' Rosie' and 'Come Down Ma Evenin' Star', and burlesques within the burlesques in *Zaza, Barbara Fidgety, The Girl from Martin's, Sapolio, The Other Way, Quo Vass Iss?, Arizona, Exhibit II, Madame du Hurry, The Curl and the Judge, The Man from Mars, Catherine, The College Widower, The Squawman's Girl of the Golden West* and others of the ilk.

The Weber and Fields shows were enormously popular with a large section of the public but, after nearly 30 years together, Weber and Fields finally fell out over Weber's rôle in one of their burlesques and, after the run of *Whoop-de-Doo*, Fields seceded from the partnership. He combined with his long-time dramaturg, Edgar Smith, to produce one of the English musical comedies which were the rage of Broadway but he unfortunately chose one which had failed even to make London: *An English Daisy* was not a success. He then went into a producing partnership with Fred Hamlin and Julian Mitchell, and opened Fields' Theater, beginning his tenancy there with the successful production of Victor Herbert's *It Happened in Nordland* (1904) in which he took the principal comic rôle alongside Marie Cahill. Although Fields' Theater was a short-lived venture, he produced and appeared in several other musicals and burlesques, notably starring as Herman Schniff in a rewritten-to-measure version of the Willie Edouin comedy rôle in the British musical *The Girl Behind the Counter* (Herald Square, 1907) which paired him with the buxom London Gaiety comedienne Connie Ediss. He also played in his productions of *Old Dutch, The Summer Widowers* and *The Henpecks*, while at the same time turning out a full schedule of other pieces in which he did not appear, mostly of home-bred musical comedies (Victor Herbert's tuneful *The Rose of Algeria, The Jolly Bachelors, The Prince of Bohemia, The Yankee Girl,* Marie Dressler's best vehicle *Tillie's Nightmare, The Wife Hunters* etc), these totalling some dozen shows in the four years 1908–12.

In 1912 he again joined up temporarily with Joe Weber,

and they appeared together in *Hokey Pokey* and *Roly Poly* and produced the unconsummated *The June Bride (Johann der Zweite)* before separating once more. Fields continued to perform, appearing in a revival of *The Girl Behind the Counter*, rechristened *Step This Way*, and in the non-singing star comic rôle of Augustus Tripp in his 1918 production (w the Shuberts) of *A Lonely Romeo*, but his attentions were now more orientated towards production. Having staged the first more-or-less Rodgers and Hart musical, *Poor Little Ritz Girl*, in 1920, he picked up on the subsequent musicals on which they collaborated with his librettist son, Herbert, and produced *The Girl Friend* (1926), their updated *Tillie's Nightmare, Peggy-Ann* (1926), *A Connecticut Yankee* (1927), *Present Arms* (1928) and *Chee-Chee* (1928). His most successful latter-day production, however, was another of son Herbert's collaborations, this time with Vincent Youmans, *Hit the Deck* (1927).

Fields had to drop out of the production of *Wild Rose* (1924) two days before opening, through illness, and he made only one further stage musical appearance in New York thereafter, in *Hello Daddy* (1929), the suitably-named show written by his children, Herbert and Dorothy, with a score by Jimmy McHugh. He ultimately also retired from production following a two-week revue flop (*The Vanderbilt Revue*) in 1930 after more than half a century as a performer and 40 years as a manager. However, he was later seen recreating some of his famous routines on film: performing the barbershop duo routine which had helped Vernon Castle make lift-off in *The Story of Vernon and Irene Castle* and pairing with Weber in their old act in *Lillian Russell*.

Biography: Isman, F: *Weber and Fields* (Boni & Liveright, New York, 1924)

FIELDS, W C [DUKINFIELD, William Claude] (b Philadelphia, 9 April 1879; d Pasadena, Calif, 25 December 1946).

Originally a juggler in vaudeville, Fields made an isolated appearance on the Broadway musical stage in his twenties, as the juggling detective Sherlock Baffles in the McIntyre and Heath variety musical *The Ham Tree* (1905). Thereafter his fame was made in a half dozen editions of *The Ziegfeld Follies* (1915–21), but he appeared again in a musical, and with great success, as the expansively comical Professor Eustace McGargle in the 1923 show *Poppy*, before going on to the second portion of his memorable career in films. The third of his decidedly widely spaced Broadway musical performances was in 1930 when he played the rôle of Q Q Quayle in *Ballyhoo*, a show set up to feature his talents but which instead sent its producer, Arthur Hammerstein, bankrupt.

At Owing Mills, Maryland, in 1971 Fields was the subject of a musical unblushingly called *W. C.* (Al Carmines/Milton Sperling, Sam Locke) in which he was portrayed by Mickey Rooney.

Autobiography: ed Fields, R: *W C Fields by Himself: His Intended Autobiography* (Prentice Hall, Englewood Cliffs, NJ 1972), Biography: Taylor, R L: *W C Fields, his Follies and Fortunes* (Doubleday, New York, 1949)

FIFTY MILLION FRENCHMEN Musical comedy in 2 acts by Herbert Fields. Music and lyrics by Cole Porter. Lyric Theater, New York, 27 November 1929.

Songwriter Cole Porter and librettist Herbert Fields came together for what was to be the first of seven, almost always successful, shows together on this revusically constructed piece with its reminiscences of such old British musicals as *A Runaway Girl* or *After the Girl* and their Cook's Tours of picturesque places.

The girl in this case is Looloo (Genevieve Tobin), the daughter of socially overambitious Emmitt Carroll (Thurston Hall) and his wife (Bernice Mershon). Mama and Papa have destined their daughter to be the Grand Duchess of the Grand Duke Ivan Ivanovitch (Mannart Kippen), but one fine day in Paris the wealthy playboy Peter Forbes (William Gaxton) falls flamboyantly in love with her. He bets his pal Michael (Jack Thompson) that he can win Looloo away from her Duke without disclosing his own attractive financial situation and, like his predecessor of *La Vie parisienne*, takes on the rôle of a tourist guide in order to do so.

The revusical outline suited Porter's revusical style of song splendidly, and two pieces which would become Porter favourites found a home in *Fifty Million Frenchmen*: Looloo and Peter's mutual admission that 'You Do Something to Me' and Michael's duet with the soubrette Betty Compton, in the rôle of Joyce Wheeler, asserting 'You've Got That Thing'. Evelyn Hoey introduced 'Find Me a Primitive Man' and 'I'm Unlucky at Gambling' in the rôle of May de Vere, Helen Broderick, as Violet Hildegarde, delivered 'The Tale of an Oyster' (until it was cut) and 'Where Would You Get Your Coat?', and there were two songs which had Paree in the title.

Fifty Million Frenchmen had a muted reception, but it soon grew into a popular success on Broadway and ultimately had a run of 254 performances. It met with no such favour, however, in Britain. Produced at Glasgow, with Frances Day starred as Looloo, it fizzled out on the road, without making it to London.

A 1931 Warner film entitled *Fifty Million Frenchmen*, used Gaxton and Miss Broderick and the show's format, as well as Olsen and Johnson, but not the songs, whilst, conversely, a short 1934 Vitaphone film called *Paree, Paree* featuring Dorothy Stone and Bob Hope used portions of *Fifty Million Frenchmen*'s music (four songs) and its tale.

UK: King's Theatre, Glasgow 1 September 1931
Recording: Selection (New World)

LA FILLE DE FANCHON LA VIELLEUSE Opéra-comique in 4 acts by Armand Liorat, William Busnach and Albert Fonteny. Music by Louis Varney. Théâtre des Folies-Dramatiques, Paris, 3 November 1891.

It seems that the famous Fanchon has left her orphaned daughter Javotte nothing but her viol as a legacy, but the truth is that her fortune has been gambled away by the Chevalier de Saint-Florent (Lacroix) to whom she entrusted its safe-keeping and delivery. Before he succeeds in gambling it back, the action has largely concerned the farcical events surrounding the attempts of the notary Bellavoine (Gobin) to seduce Javotte (Mlle Thuillier-Leloir), those of his wife Hermine (Zélo Duran) to consummate an affair with the flautist Zéphyrin (Guyon fils), and those of Javotte's country sweetheart, Jacquot (Larbaudière), to secure his bride.

A patent attempt, in its title, to repeat the success of *La Fille de Madame Angot*, it was not in the same class or in the same style as Lecocq's great work, although Varney's pretty score, featuring the old song of 'Fanchon la vielleuse' as a sop to the title, helped the undoubtedly merry piece to be well received for 110 Parisian performances. Even though it did not establish itself in the revivable repertoire, *La Fille de Fanchon la vielleuse* nevertheless got a number of foreign-language showings. A German-language production (ad uncredited) was mounted by Alexandrine von Schönerer at Vienna's Theater an der Wien with Ilka Pálmay as Javotte, Girardi as Zephirin, Ferdinand Pagin as Jacquot and Josef Joseffy as St Florent, without success (7 performances), and again at Dresden, but an Hungarian adaptation (ad Béla J Fái, Ferenc Rajna) played a good 37 performances at the Budapest Népszinház and was well enough regarded to be given a revival in 1902 (26 September).

Austria: Theater an der Wien *Fanchons Leyer* 15 October 1892; Hungary: Népszinház *Fanchon asszony leánya* 14 October 1892; Germany: Residenztheater, Dresden *Fanchons Leier* 5 November 1892

LA FILLE DE MADAME ANGOT Opéra-comique in 3 acts by Clairville, Paul Siraudin and Victor Koning. Music by Charles Lecocq. Théâtre des Fantaisies-Parisiennes, Brussels, 4 December 1872.

Along with Planquette's *Les Cloches de Corneville*, *La Fille de Madame Angot* was the most successful product of the French-language musical stage in the postwar decades of the 19th century. Even such pieces as *HMS Pinafore* and *Die Fledermaus*, vastly successful in their original languages, did not have the enormous international careers of Lecocq's opéra-comique, which swept the theatre world with unmitigated triumph for many years before settling into a permanent and prominent place at the head of the all-time French musical theatre repertoire.

In fact, *La Fille de Madame Angot* had its first showing not in France, but in Brussels, under the management of producer Eugène Humbert, who had mounted Lecocq and Clairville's previous work, *Les Cent Vierges*. The success of *Les Cent Vierges* led wheeler-dealing Victor Koning to thinking that another original work might do equally as well in Brussels. He proposed the idea to the playwright Paul Siraudin, who came up with the thought that there might be a libretto in the series of *Madame Angot* plays, written by the dramatist Maillot, which had found such success at the turn of the 19th century. Clairville was called in to put Koning's notion and Siraudin's idea (which may, or may not, have included dipping into Dumas's 1853 historical novel, *Ange Pitou*, for a hero) into libretto form, Lecocq to set the resultant piece to music, and Humbert was only too pleased to take in a new piece by the writers who had given him his earlier hit. Koning and Siraudin both kept their names on the bill as co-authors and, naturally, in the share-out of the royalties.

Clairette (Pauline Luigini) is the orphaned daughter of the famous fishwife Madame Angot, whose gallivanting with the Grand Turk has gone down in legend. She has been brought up, with all the advantages their money can buy, by the market-folk of Les Halles and her multiple 'parents' are happy that she should wed the adoring, gentle little wig-maker Pomponnet (Alfred Jolly). But Clairette has other thoughts. She has been enraptured by the dashing political poet Ange Pitou (Mario Widmer), and so, rather than be wed to Pomponnet, she gets herself arrested, on what should have been her wedding day, for singing one of Pitou's dangerous songs in public. She is freed by the influence of a former schoolmate, the actress Mademoiselle Lange (Marie Desclauzas), who has risen to power as the mistress of Barras, a member of the ruling Directoire, but secretly part of a conspiracy to overthrow the feeble and corrupt new oligarchic government of the country.

Trouble arrives with a vengeance, however, when Lange and Pitou meet and strike instant sparks. Clairette is not slow to recognize the signs, and she sets a trap for the pair, luring each to a rendezvous at the Bal du Calypso with a forged letter. When the actress and the poet openly express their feelings amongst the hedgerows of the Calypso, Clairette is waiting, with her ever-protective 'family' at her back. But Mademoiselle Angot does not need protecting: it quickly becomes clear that she is no little violet, but the hard-tongued, strong-backed daughter of her famous mother. The two women go for each other, and when it is all over Clairette hands the faithless Pitou over to her friend and rival. She will wed the good and true Pomponnet, but given the strain of her mother that is so evident in her, one cannot fear that she will never see Ange Pitou again.

Chambéry played the financier Larivaudière, Mlle Lange's second string lover, Ernotte was the snooping policeman, Louchard, Mme Delorme played Amaranthe, the most vocal of the heroine's deputy mothers, and Touzé played the stand-out cameo rôle of the conspiring 'incroyable' Trénitz, effete and foolish in his dress and speech, but a veritable icy hero under danger.

The score of the show was a non-stop run of winning numbers, beginning in the first act with Clairette's sweetly grateful romance 'Je vous dois tout', Amaranthe's lusty description of the late Madame Angot ('Marchande de marée'), Pitou's lilting admission that although 'Certainement, j'aimais Clairette' other attentions do not leave him indifferent, and the plotworthy anti-governmental song ('Jadis les rois, race proscrit'). Lange's cleverly delayed appearance, at the top of the second act, was made all the more effective by her dazzling and difficult first number, 'Les Soldats d'Augereau sont des hommes', in which she counts on the masculine weakness of the Directoire's forces in her organization of a grand ball as a cover for a conspirators' meeting. From there, Pomponnet's featherweight 'Elle est tellement innocente', the happy duo of the old schoolfriends ('Jours fortunés de notre enfance') and the first meeting of Lange and Pitou ('Voyons, Monsieur, raisonnons politique') led up to the highlight of the act, the Conspirators' Chorus – soon to be world-famous – and the whirling waltz ('Tournez, Tournez') in which Lange leads her conspirator-guests into their cover-up dance as the government troops approach.

Unlike many contemporary third acts, that of *La Fille de Madame Angot* did not fritter away into a brisk pairing-off of its participants, and the musical part of the last portion of piece was equally as strong as its text, as Larivaudière and Pomponnet, on their way to the climax of the action in the dark alleyways at the Calypso, joined in the Duo des deux forts, and Pitou and Lange shared a Letter duet ('Cher ennemi que je devrais haïr'), on the way to the other famous moment of the night's music and drama, the blaz-

ing Quarreling Duet ('C'est donc toi, Madam' Barras') in which Clairette and Lange face up to each other at the dénouement, bringing the final act, like the preceding one, to a musical and dramatic peak.

La Fille de Madame Angot was a huge hit in Brussels. *Les Cent Vierges* was put quite in the shade by the new piece and Marie Desclauzas, in the rôle of Lange, made a veritable triumph. Koning soon had a Paris transfer underway, and Louis Cantin mounted the show at the Folies-Dramatiques less than two months after its Belgian première whilst the original production continued on towards its 400th and 500th nights in Brussels. Paola Marié was cast as Clairette for Paris, alongside Mendasti (Pitou), Luco (Larivaudière), Mme Toudouze (Amaranthe), Philippe Dupin (Pomponnet) and Legrain (Louchard) and, at Lecocq's insistence, Marie Desclauzas was brought from Brussels to recreate her rôle of Lange.

In spite of some undercasting, some sloppy staging and a fire in some paper draperies on opening night, the Brussels triumph was repeated in Paris and *La Fille de Madame Angot* became a sensation, with the Quarreling Duet and the Conspirators' Chorus proving themselves the hit songs of the time. The show ran through 411 performances, until April 1874, on its first run, was brought back following the summer recess in the same September, and remained in the repertoire at the Folies-Dramatiques continuously through the years that followed, passing its 800th performance on 17 May 1883. Parisian revivals were legion. An 1888 Eden Théâtre production put Anna Judic and Jeanne Granier together as the two rivals (10 February), and a revival at the Gaîté paired Juliette Simon-Girard's Clairette with the Lange of Yvonne Kerlord for 200 nights (1901). Germaine Gallois and Edmée Favart played another 106 performances (1912) at the same house before the Opéra-Comique's Marguerite Carré and first Raymonde Delaunois (1920) and then Jenny Syril (1921) gave their versions of the star rôles. In 1918 the piece was produced at the Opéra-Comique, first for a single performance with Mlle Favart and Marthe Chénal, and then as a full-scale repertoire piece (19 June 1919) with Mlle Favart paired with Mme Mérentié and Edmond Tirmont as Pitou. It was brought back there in 1953 with Maria Murano and Colette Riedinger, and again in 1969 with Michèle Herbé and Christiane Darbell, and it made its most recent Parisian appearance in 1984 at the Théâtre Musical de Paris.

Although Cantin reaped the rewards of the Paris season, Humbert did not let go of his hit. In May he took the original cast, with Jeanne d'Albert replacing the departed Desclauzas, to London, and these first French performances ('a success of the most unqualified character ... exactly what opéra-bouffe should be') were followed some four months later by the first English-language version. Henry Byron's adaptation, produced at the Philharmonic Theatre, added the Alcazar Dancers in a 'Nuit de Carnival' as a speciality in the third act, and popped in a song by musical director George Richardson ('Can This Be Love?') who had also reorchestrated Lecocq's score. With Julia Mathews (Lange) and Selina Dolaro (Clairette) starred, the show ran no less than 235 performances at its suburban house, as other theatres moved quickly to produce their own versions. The copyright laws of the time allowed protection only to the Philharmonic's English version and not to the French original: anyone could mount a *Fille de Madame Angot* with impunity.

The Gaiety was the first West End house to enter the ranks, six weeks after Islington's première, taking in Emily Soldene's company with an H B Farnie version, which clumsily fattened up the rôle of Lange for Soldene by having her appear in disguise as a street-singer in the first act. Soldene was again Lange to Pattie Laverne's Clairette at the Opera Comique before the year was done (26 December) for three and a half months and a quick reprise. It was no sooner done that the Globe Theatre took up a five-week season of another *Angot* (ad H F Du Terreaux) with Cornélie d'Anka as Lange, so that London had two versions of the show running concurrently for seven months.

Productions of the show flooded Britain's provincial theatres, much to the fury of W H Liston who thought he had bought the entire provincial rights for £25 down and £1 a performance only to find that all he had got was the rights to his particular English version. They also continued to bombard London: the Philharmonic, Gaiety, Criterion (Humbert's troupe), Opera Comique, Royalty (ad Frank Desprez in a dramatically reshaped star-vehicle version for Dolaro), Alexandra and the Holborn Amphitheatre all played the show in 1875, the Opera Comique took it in again in 1876 and in 1878 d'Anka and Dolaro starred in a production at the Alhambra which introduced a sabot divertissement, the French grotesques Les Quatre Bossus, the Gardes Françaises in a grand military ballet, a children's 'Dresden China minuet' and 'illuminated cascades of real water' into the final act. The Theatre Royal, Drury Lane, took in productions in 1880 and again in 1919 (ad Dion Clayton Calthrop, G Marsden), and the Criterion Theatre staged another in 1893 before the show's West End life was done.

Like London, New York saw its first *Angot* in French, with Marie Aimée starring as Clairette opposite Rosina Stani in 1873 and opposite Leontyne Minelly in 1874, and it spent most of its life – rather less outstanding here than in France and England, partly because of the system – being played by repertoire companies rather than in a continuous run. Soldene's company introduced the first English performances soon after, Paola Marié repeated her Paris performance to the Lange of Mme Angèle in 1879, Louise Théo played the piece in her repertoire, and it was part and parcel of the touring baggage of every touring opéra-bouffe and -comique company of the era. The Casino Theater mounted a production in 1890 with Marie Halton as Clairette and Camille D'Arville as Lange, Henry Hallam (Ange Pitou) and Fred Solomon (Larivaudière) which was the nearest the show got to having a straight Broadway run.

Yet another English-language *Fille de Madame Angot* was seen when the piece was given its first Australian performances. This one was the work of Fred Lyster, brother to producer W S Lyster, and known for taking large liberties with operatic scripts. Clara Thompson (Clairette), Jennie Winston (Lange), Armes Beaumont (Pitou) and Henry Bracy (Pomponnet) were starred in this version, the first of many, usually in the London adaptations, which followed in the repertoires of virtually every opéra-bouffe company which appeared in Sydney and Melbourne over the years that followed. Amongst these were included the much-

travelled Soldene, with Rose Stella as her Clairette, and Emilie Melville who cast herself in the other of the two lead rôles, and who took the show to India and the South Pacific. Luscombe Searelle exported the piece to South Africa, where it was played with his wife, Blanche Fenton, as Clairette.

Ernst Dohm's German version was produced at Berlin's Friedrich-Wilhelmstädtisches Theater, whilst a different German adaptation by Anton Langer was mounted by Franz Jauner at the Vienna Carltheater a few weeks later. Hermine Meyerhoff (Clairette) and Antonie Link (Lange) starred alongside Wilhelm Knaack (Larivaudière), Franz Eppich (Ange Pitou), Küstner (Pomponnet), Karl Blasel (Trenitz) and Therese Schäfer (Amaranthe) and the show scored up 55 almost en suite performances. The 100th was passed on 13 August 1874, the 150th July 28th 1875, and the 181st and last under Jauner's management on 19 May 1878 with Carl Streitmann playing Pomponnet. The show continued for a few performances more in repertoire under Franz Tewele's management and later got a couple of short showings at the Theater an der Wien in 1886 (13 April) and in 1901 with Ottilie Fellwock (Lange), Türk Rohn/Frln Genscher (Clairette) and Blasel in his original rôle (10 performances), but it did not attract the later revivals its fine original run might have presaged.

Hungary's version (ad Pál Tarnay) also proved a hit when produced at the Népszinház with Lujza Blaha (ie Soldosné) as Clairette, Karolin Daray as Lange, János Kápolnai as Ange Pitou and Elek Solymossy as Larivaudière, after its first performances had been seen at Kolozsvár with Ilka Medgyaszay and Zoltanné starred. A first run of 48 performances was followed by revivals in 1887 and 1897, a production at the Magyar Királyi Operaház (1887) and another at the Magyar Szinház in 1900 with Ilona Szoyer featured as Clairette. The piece was also adapted into Russian, Spanish, Italian, Swedish, Polish, Danish and Czech and a Russian-language production from the Moscow Art Theatre was seen in both Berlin and in New York in 1925. The Portuguese, however, instead of just lifting the libretto, as was the usual habit of their Spanish neighbours, turned out a *Le Fils de Madame Angot* (Angelo Frodoni) at the Theatro del Prince Royal in Lisbon (5 May 1875).

The show set loose a very flood of *Angot* parodies and spin-offs of all kinds on the Parisian stage. Armand Jallais authored a short vaudeville *Madame Angot et ses demoiselles* produced at the Folies-Marigny (19 June 1873) and Adolphe Joly provided another, *Madame Angot ou la Poissarde parvenue*, for the Ba-ta-clan (8 November 1873). A one-act opérette *Le Fils de Madame Angot* by Dorfeuil using Lecocq's music, was produced at the Gaîté-Montparnasse (25 September 1873), and *L'Héritage de Madame Angot* by Jules de Rieux and Villemer, with a Chassaigne score, at the Eldorado (24 October 1873), whilst Blondeau and Monréal went deeper and displayed *La Nuit de noces de la fille Angot* on the same stage (29 November 1873). The Funambules mounted a pantomime *La Mère Angot* by Hippolyte Demanet, the Alhambra christened its new-year revue *Pas bégueule la Mère Angot* (30 December 1873), and Clairville and Lecocq combined on a follow-up to their own piece with a saynète *La Résurrection de la Mère Angot* for the Folies-Dramatiques (24 February 1874). An Alfred Aubert vaudeville, *L'Héritage de la fille de Madame Angot*, was played at the Théâtre Sérafin (25 March 1875), a pantomime *Le Fils Angot* appeared at the Scala (9 July 1876), a vaudeville *Le Fils de Mme Angot* at the Menus-Plaisirs in 1892 (26 November) and a *L'arrière petite-fille de Madame Angot* by André Mauprey even turned up at the Théâtre des Folies-Dramatiques as late as 29 November 1912. Vienna, too, had its *Angot* parody when F Zell and Karl Pleininger combined on an *Angot und der blauen Donau* for the Strampfertheater in 1874 (13 November).

In the last half-century, productions of *La Fille de Madame Angot* have become fewer and, outside France, where it remains one of the staples of the classic repertoire, the show has not maintained the popularity which it won in the decades immediately following its production. With the movement of the operettic repertoire into the opera houses of the 1980s and 1990s, *La Fille de Madame Angot*, with its exceptionally strong dramatic, yet sophisticatedly comic, libretto and challenging star rôles, would have seemed a natural candidate for opera-house revivals, but the tendency up to date has been for such houses to stick to the frothier part of the repertoire and a handful of not always worthy shows by 'big names'.

A version of the show was filmed by Jean-Bernard Derosne in 1935.

France: Théâtre des Folies-Dramatiques 21 February 1873; UK: St James's Theatre (Fr) 17 May 1873, Philharmonic Theatre, Islington (Eng) 4 October 1873; USA: Broadway Theater (Fr) 25 August 1873, Lyceum Theater (Eng) 16 November 1873; Germany: Friedrich-Wilhelmstädtisches Theater 20 November 1873; Austria: Carltheater *Angot, die Tochter der Halle* 2 January 1874; Hungary: Kolozsvár 23 March 1875, Népszínház *Angot asszony leánya* 2 December 1875; Australia: Opera House, Melbourne 24 September 1874; Film: 1935

Recordings: complete (EMI-Pathé, Decca) selections (EMI-Pathé, Philips etc)

LA FILLE DU TAMBOUR-MAJOR Opéra-comique in 3 acts by Henri Chivot and Alfred Duru. Music by Jacques Offenbach. Théâtre des Folies-Dramatiques, Paris, 13 December 1879.

One of the outstanding works of Offenbach's late period, *La Fille du tambour-major*, like the previous year's *Madame Favart*, proved that the Empire's favourite composer could turn out opéra-comique in the style of the post-war Lecocq pieces with a potency as great as that with which he could illustrate the most extravagantly bubbling of burlesques.

The drum-major's daughter of the title is Stella (Juliette Simon-Girard) who, at the beginning of the evening, is the daughter of the exceptionally noble Italian Duc della Volta (Édouard Maugé). When the French invade northern Italy to 'liberate' the area from the Austrian empire, Stella's convent boarding school is in the path of the advancing troops and she, locked in the linen room as a punishment, is left behind when the nuns and pupils flee. This means that she gets to meet the dashing Lieutenant Robert (Lepers) whose gallant attentions to her go down badly with the jealous vivandière Claudine (Noémie Vernon). The Duc is anxious to marry Stella off to the unattractive and somewhat perverse Marquis Ernesto Bambini (Bartel), but the French are on the move and the ducal palace is invaded by the billet-seeking regiment, whose drum-major Monthabor (Luco) discovers his long-lost ex-wife is now the Duchess della Volta (Caroline Girard, mother of the

prima donna). And Stella, thus, is his equally long-lost daughter. Wartime quiproquos mix with amorous ones (with disguises included) as the action winds up to its height, but all is brought to a happy ending when the main body of the French army arrives to shock the Duc into a sudden change of loyalties.

The score of the show was in Offenbach's most tuneful mode, shot through with a delicious vein of sophisticated comedy which was a long way from the burlesque frivolities of earlier days. Stella's defiant song about the 'Petit Français' was delightful enough to put off any comparison with Clairette's rebellious song from the all-influencing *La Fille de Madame Angot*, whilst Claudine's braying song to her military donkey ('Ce n'est pas un âne ordinaire'), the Duchess's affectations of an aristocratic headache ('J'ai ma migraine'), the lovesick song of the little tailor-turned-soldier Griolet (Simon-Max), devotedly sewing a uniform for Claudine ('Un tailleur amoureux'), and the ensemble in which the officers claim their billet at the Palazzo della Volta ('Un billet de logement') were thoroughly winning musical-comic moments in a score that glittered happily from beginning to end.

La Fille du tambour-major was produced by Blandin at the Folies-Dramatiques and won a splendid success. It played all through the winter and spring, up to the summer recess and held its place at the opening of the new season, playing for more than a month and passing its 200th performance almost on the day of Offenbach's death. It was removed just short of its 250th night, but was remounted in 1884 (10 March) with Mme Simon-Girard, Simon-Max and Mlle Vernon in their original rôles alongside Péricaud (Monthabor), Mme Claudia (Duchess) and Bartel, promoted to the rôle of the Duc (46 performances). The show was repeated at the Gaîté in 1889 and 1891, again in 1907 with Juliette Méaly playing Stella, and in 1917 with Edmée Favart starred, whilst the Théâtre du Château d'Eau played a season in 1901 with Mme Simon-Girard in her original rôle. In 1920 Jenny Syril starred as the drum-major's daughter in yet another revival at the Gaîté-Lyrique which featured Lucien Fugère as Monthabor (7 October) and Roberte Jan headed the cast of a 1945 revival at the same house, as *La Fille du tambour-major* established itself firmly in the basic repertoire of the French opéra-comique.

The show also won lively appreciation outside France although, lacking the one showy central rôle of *Madame Favart*, it succeeded a little less strongly than its vivacious predecessor, and by no means in all areas and languages. Maximilian Steiner staged the first German version (ad Julius Hopp), subtitled *Die Französen in Holland*, at the Theater an der Wien. For some reason, the locality was shifted to the Netherlands, and Utrecht and Breda took the place of Novara and Milan, with the action being set back a handful of years in historical consequence. Marie Geistinger starred as Stella, alongside Carl Adolf Friese as one Van Hokenbroing (ex-Duc della Volta) and Lori Hild as his wife, Steiner as Robert, Ausim as Monthabor and Girardi as the little tailor. The change did no one any good and *Die Tochter des Tambour-Major* lasted only seven nights. In London, however, where the show opened just nine days later, the result was very different. H B Farnie's 'grand spectacular opera' adaptation for the vast Alhambra stage maintained the original setting, but added a military band and extra chorus for the 'grand entry of the French Army' which concluded the show. Constance Loseby was Stella, with Fred Leslie and Fanny Edwards as the ducal pair, Fred Mervin as the drum-major, and Fannie Leslie played Griolet in travesty to the Claudine of Edith Blande. The piece ran a magnificent ten months at the Alhambra, passing its 200th performance on 6 December and ending after 212 nights only to be remounted soon after at the Connaught Theatre with Amy Grundy, Miss Edwards, Jennie Lee (Griolet), W H Woodfield and Aynsley Cook featured, for several weeks' more performances on the London stage.

La Fille du tambour-major reached New York first in French, with Paola Marié playing Stella alongside Mary Albert (Claudine), Mezières and Mme Delorme as the ducal pair, Tauffenberger (Griolet), Duplan (Monthabor) and Nigri (Robert). Just a few weeks later an English version followed, mounted under the management of M B Leavitt, with Selina Dolaro in the title-rôle, James A Meade as Monthabor and former burlesque boy Alma Stanley, now graduated to the senior rôle of the Duchess. Nearly a decade later, the show was reprised at the Casino Theater in a new version (ad Max Freeman, Edgar Smith) under the title *The Drum Major*. Pauline Hall (Stella), Marie Halton (Claudine), James T Powers (Griolet) and Edwin Stevens (Monthabor) featured in a strong cast, but the new version proved to have only two months' life in it.

In Hungary, the title became the subtitle in Lajos Evva and Béla J Fái's tale of 'the French in Milan' for a disappointing 20 nights, but, as in so many other cases, it was Farnie's successful English translation which gave the show its other major success. Neophyte Australian producer George Musgrove mounted *La Fille du tambour-major* as his maiden venture at Melbourne's Prince of Wales Theatre just 12 months after the Paris première and eight from the first performance of the Farnie version. Pattie Laverne, the Alhambra's Fred Mervin and tenor Albert R Brennir came from London to play Stella, Monthabor and Robert alongside a local cast of 150 singers and extras in which the young Nellie Stewart made a particular success when she succeeded Jessie Grey in the rôle of Griolet. The show, staged with the utmost care and unusual splendour, proved the biggest hit the city had known. The production played for 18 weeks, creating a long-run record for Melbourne which would hold until *Florodora* arrived on the scene two decades later, and it continued on to spread its success throughout Australia. It was taken into the repertoire of J C Williamson's Royal Comic Opera Company and played in 1887 with Colbourne Baber in its title-rôle, as *La Fille du tambour-major* became established as a revivable prospect in a way that it had previously done only in France.

The show has survived through the century since its début, however, only in its original French – its last West End performances were in a French repertoire season at the Shaftesbury Theatre in 1908, and rare have been the performances since that time in any other tongue.

Austria: Theater an der Wien *Die Tochter des Tambour-Major* 10 April 1880; UK: Alhambra Theatre 19 April 1880; USA: Standard Theater (Fr) 13 September 1880, 14th Street Theater (Eng) 4 October 1880; Hungary: Népszínház *A Franciák Milanoban, or Az ezreddobos leánya* 17 December 1880; Australia: Prince of Wales Theatre, Melbourne 27

December 1880; Germany: Aachen 12 February 1881, Walhalla Theater, Berlin 11 September 1883
Recordings: Selection (EMI-Pathé) etc

LA FILLEULE DU ROI Opérette in 3 acts by Eugène Cormon and Raimond Deslandes. Music by Adolphe Vogel. Théâtre des Fantaisies-Parisiennes, Brussels, 10 April 1875.

Eugène Humbert, so successful with the works of the young Lecocq, gave opportunities to several other theatrically inexperienced composers at his Brussels theatre. Adolphe Vogel, who had studied for a career in serious music had written an opera (*Le Siège de Leyde*, 1847), a 'drame lyrique' (*La Moissoneuse*, 1853), had a one-act opérette, *Rompons!* (1857) produced by Offenbach at the Bouffes-Parisiens and another at the Folies Marigny (*Gredin de Pigoche*, 1866), supplied him with *La Filleule du Roi*. With a cast containing many veterans of the Lecocq successes (Pauline Luigini, Ginet, Alfred Jolly, Mme Delorme) it did good business in Brussels.

The show's book told the tale of the overly unbuttoned captain Phoebus (Pagès) who throws over the girl he seduced to wed another, who is supposed to be the 'goddaughter' of King Henry IV, and, as a result, is made to suffer the complicated disguised revenge of the first one's sister (Pauline Luigini) whom he ends the piece marrying. The text was a rather old-fashioned one which, paired with the not-so-young Vogel's similarly made music, did not appeal to audiences either in London, where Humbert presented it following its Brussels season, nor in Paris where it played only eleven performances with Mme Peschard playing the rôle of Phoebus in travesty opposite Mlle Luigini, nor in its German version at Vienna's Carltheater.

UK: Criterion Theatre 7 June 1875; France: Théâtre de la Renaissance 23 October 1875; Austria: Carltheater *Das Patenkind des Königs* 15 September 1877

FILMZAUBER Posse mit Gesang in 3 acts by Rudolf Bernauer and Rudolf Schanzer. Music by Walter Kollo and Willy Bredschneider. Berliner Theater, Berlin, 19 October 1912.

The first of Walter Kollo's series of original musical comedies written with Bernauer and Schanzer, and staged with great success at the Berliner Theater, *Filmzauber* used as its subject-matter the world of the newly popular cinema. The heroine of the piece, Franzi von Pappenheim, runs away from her upper-class home, disguised as a boy, to work in the cinematic firm run by Antonius Lichtenstadt and Quasta Pilsen. In the face of necessity the disguise comes off, she takes the star rôle in a film, and, in the final reel, pairs off with Antonius. The ingénue Lina Hammerschmidt and the personable Max Rademacher made up the evening's second pair to the accompaniment of much song and dance. The show's attitude to the (silent) film world was displayed by its depiction of the aptly named Italian film actress Maria Gesticulata and its comical scena of the filming of a dramatic Napoleonic movie (music: Bredschneider), with Antonius playing Napoleon and Quasta and Franzi featured, a scene ultimately broken in upon by the heroine's furious father, hot on the trail of his disobedient child.

From the lively bundle of up-to-date numbers that made up the show's score, it was Kollo's Lindenmarsch

('Unter'n Linden promenier' ich immer gern vorbei') which scored the biggest hit.

Filmzauber ran for the best part of a year at the Berliner Theater, and this success led to productions throughout the world in 1913. George Edwardes took it up for London and, rechristened *The Girl on the Film* (ad James Tanner, Adrian Ross) in order to point it up as a successor to *The Girl in the Train* (*Die geschiedene Frau*) and *The Girl in the Taxi* (*Die keusche Susanne*), it was produced during his final illness by J A E Malone, with a cast headed by Connie Ediss (Euphemia Knox of the Vioscope film company), Emmy Wehlen (Winifred, otherwise Freddy), Madeleine Seymour (Linda) and George Grossmith (Max Daly). Albert Szirmai was now credited as co-composer, and was, indeed, responsible for more than half the show's music, including the evening's principal waltz, 'Won't You Come and Waltz with Me?', and there were additional numbers by Paul Rubens and Philip Braham. The Lindenmarsch survived, but it became a song in praise of Bond Street. *The Girl on the Film* had an eight-month run (232 performances) in the West End, was sent out in two tours, and then exported to Broadway with most of its London principals for an eight-week run under the management of the Shuberts. There, as in Berlin and in London, it was closely followed on to the boards by Jean Gilbert's *Die Kino-Königin* (*The Cinema Star*, *The Queen of the Movies*) which outpointed it in each case. But *The Girl on the Film* stayed on the road in Britain through 1914 and again, in spite of wartime anti-German feelings, in 1915, and it also made its first appearance, in the London Szirmai-ed version, on the Australian stage, at Christmas 1914. Dorothy Brunton was Winifred, C H Workman played Max, Alfred Frith the General and Marie Eaton the Italian lady through not very impressive seasons in Sydney and Melbourne (Her Majesty's Theatre, 3 July 1915) which were easily bested by *The Cinema Star* shortly after. The score now included, amongst other items, Jerome Kern's 'You're Here and I'm Here', and not very much Kollo seemed to remain.

Die Kino-Königin also won out in Vienna, where *Filmzauber* was seen at Josef Jarno's Theater in der Josefstadt for only three weeks in a Viennese-localized version by Max Baer (but without the Szirmai music), and Budapest alone reversed the decision. Produced there in a version (ad Zsolt Harsányi) of the London version, with local lad Szirmai given the chief composing credit, and with Sári Fedák (Franzi) and Márton Rátkai (Antonius) starred, *A mozikirály* (the movie king) outpointed *A mozitündér* (the film fairy) which arrived a year later at the Népopera.

UK: Gaiety Theatre *The Girl on the Film* 5 April 1913; Austria: Theater in der Josefstadt 15 April 1913; Hungary: Király Színház *A mozikirály* 20 September 1913; USA: 44th Street Theater *The Girl on the Film* 24 December 1913; Australia: Her Majesty's Theatre, Sydney 19 December 1914

FINALY, Karolin[e] (b Pest, ?5 July 1852; d unknown)
Pretty, little Karoline Finaly came to Friedrich Strampfer's Theater an der Wien at the age of 16 (or 21 depending on which of her very diverse given birthdates is correct) and made her first appearance there in the little rôle of the lady-in-waiting, Olga, in *Die Grossherzogin von Gerolstein*. She rose quickly through the ranks, playing the soubrette part of Brigitte in *Genovefa von Brabant* (1868)

and the title-rôle in the production of Lecocq's *Theeblüte* (*Fleur de thé*, 1869), appearing as Irma in Millöcker's *Drei Paar Schuhe* (1871) and later the same year as Fragoletto to the Fiorella of Marie Geistinger in Offenbach's *Les Brigands* (1871).

In 1875 she created the rôle of Emilie in Johann Strauss's *Cagliostro in Wien* and won the particular approval of the composer who subsequently had her play the part of Pulcinella in the first performances of his 1877 piece *Prinz Methusalem* at the Carltheater to where she had gone previously to play in *Prinz Conti* (Friquette), the title-rôle in the Viennese première of *Graziella* (*La Petite Mariée*) and the part of Toinon in *Margot die reiche Bäckerin* (*La Boulangère a des écus*). She visited Berlin during the 1875–6 season, played the dual title rôle of *Giroflé-Girofla* at the Carltheater in 1876, and made an essay into the operatic as Gounod's Juliette (*Roméo et Juliette*, 1879) before creating the leading soprano rôles in two of Millöcker's most important works, *Apajune der Wassermann* (1880, Natalitzka) and *Der Bettelstudent* (1882, Laura), and introducing the Vienna versions of Bettina in *La Mascotte* (*Die Glücksengel*) and of Simonne in *Die Musketiere in Damenstift* (*Les Mousquetaires au couvent*).

Strauss created the brilliant soprano music of the rôle of the heroine Violetta in his 1881 *Der lustige Krieg* for Finaly, and she subsequently took the prima donna rôles of Manola in *Tag und Nacht* (*Le Jour et la nuit*), Praskovia in *Doctor Ox*, Teresina in *Der kleine Prinz* (1882) and of Titania Fanfani in the première of Suppé's *Die Afrikareise* (1883). She appeared in the title-rôle of *Boccaccio*, and, when the swiftly revised *Eine Nacht in Venedig* was brought to Vienna after its dubious Berlin première, she was given the principal soprano rôle of the fishermaid Annina. It was the last rôle she would play, for in December of 1883 she announced her marriage, and retired from the stage.

FINCK, Herman [von der] (b London, 4 November 1872; d London, 21 April 1939). London conductor and composer for the musical theatre, revue and variety stages.

The son of a theatre conductor, Finck began playing in theatre orchestras at the age of 14 and joined the orchestra of London's Palace Theatre five years later, on the house's conversion from opera house to variety theatre. He progressed from his initial place at the keyboards to rank-and-file and then first violin, to deputy and, finally, in replacement of Alfred Plumpton, conductor of the theatre's orchestra. He maintained that position through the Palace's varying phases as a theatre and a music hall until 1919, before moving on to the Queen's Theatre and then, in 1922, to the newly reconstructed Theatre Royal, Drury Lane, now run by former Palace Theatre supremo Alfred Butt. He remained in charge of the Lane's orchestra for the eight years of Butt's control.

Finck studied orchestration with Edward Solomon and, although he is credited with an interpolated number in the burlesque *King Kodak* as early as 1894 and another in the musical comedy *The Yashmak* (1897), his early work as a composer consisted largely of incidental and dance music for John Tiller's shows, for the Palace Theatre variety programmes and for musical playlets such as Amy Augarde's impersonation of *La Carmencita*, *A la Carte* for Gaby Deslys, and *Paris Frissons* for Régine Flory. In 1907 his name appeared on the bill of Vienna's Apollotheater as the composer of *Tag und Nacht (in ein Amerikanisches Knaben und Mädchenpensionat)*, an evidently saucy four-scene 'vaudeville' mounted by Tiller at the fledgling Austrian variety house. Amongst the individual pieces which he wrote and published at this time, the waltz 'In the Shadows' (1911) became a long-lived favourite.

With the coming of revue, he provided a flood of songs and scores for the revue productions at the Palace, notably for *The Passing Show* ('I'll Make a Man of You', 'Gilbert the Filbert', later used in *The Girl from Utah* in America), *Bric à Brac*, *Airs and Graces* ('Toy Town', 'Whisper to Me' w Lionel Monckton) and *Hullo! America*, as well as for similar productions at other theatres (*By Jingo if We Do*, *Round the Map*, *Its All Wrong*, *The Curate's Egg*, *Brighter London*, *The Little Revue*, *Leap Year*, *Better Days* etc). He also ventured into musical plays, contributing songs to *Bill Adams* (1903), *Winnie Brooke Widow* (1904), *Carminetta* (1917), *Flora* (1918) and Broadway's *Queen o' Hearts* (1922), collaborating with Howard Talbot on the interesting *My Lady Frayle* (1915) and the flop *The Light Blues* (1915), composing all the music for Martin Henry's touring musicals *The Love Flower* (1920) and *Kiki* (1921) and providing part of the score of the gentle *Merely Molly* and Drury Lane's picturesquely heroic *The Song of the Drum*.

At the Palace, he conducted the production of *Pamela* (1917), during an attempt to turn the revue house to musical comedy, and at Drury Lane he was musical director not only for his own *The Song of the Drum* but for the memorable series of American musicals of the 1920s – *Rose Marie*, *The Desert Song*, *The New Moon*, *Show Boat* and *The Three Musketeers*. He also conducted these shows for gramophone recordings. As late as 1935 he took the baton for a revival of *Merrie England* at the Prince's Theatre.

1900 **In Gay Paree** (J Hickory Wood, John Tiller) Palace of Varieties, Manchester 31 December

1906 **In Sunny Spain** (George R Sims, Charles Fletcher/Tiller, J R Huddlestone) Blackpool July

1907 **La Carmencita** 1 act Palace Theatre May

1912 **O-Mi-Iy** (w Frank E Tours/Seymour Hicks) 1 act London Hippodrome 25 March

1912 **Charles, his Friend** (w Harold Samuel) 1 act London Palladium

1913 **À la Carte** (Dion Clayton Calthrop) 1 act Palace Theatre 1 September

1913 **Palace Frissons** (M Tharp/L E Berman) 1 act Palace Theatre 9 December

1914 **The Slush Girl** (Arthur Wimperis) 1 act Palace Theatre 14 September

1915 **The Swiss Maid** (John Tiller) 1 act Hippodrome, Balham 9 March

1915 **The Light Blues** (w Howard Talbot/Adrian Ross/Mark Ambient, Jack Hulbert) Birmingham 13 September, Shaftesbury Theatre 14 September 1916

1915 **Vivien** (later *My Lady Frayle*) (w Talbot/Arthur Wimperis/Max Pendleton) Birmingham 27 December; Shaftesbury Theatre 1 March 1916

1920 **The Love Flower** (Adrian Ross, James Heard/Robert Marshall) Brighton 8 March

1921 **Kiki** (Reginald Arkell/José G Levy) Ramsgate 7 March

1926 **Merely Molly** (w Joseph Meyer/Harry Graham/J Hastings Turner) Adelphi Theatre 22 September

1931 **The Song of the Drum** (w Vivian Ellis/Desmond Carter/Fred Thompson, Guy Bolton) Theatre Royal, Drury Lane 9 January

Other titles credited: *The Sin of St Hulda* (1896), *A Doubtful Prospect* (1900), *Hiawatha* (1905), *Moonshine* (1905), *The Belle of Andalucia* (1908), *Amsterdam* (1909), *The Billposter* (1910), *The Comforters* (1913)

Autobiography: *My Melodious Memories* (Hutchinson, London, 1937)

FINGS AIN'T WOT THEY USED T'BE Musical in 2 acts by Frank Norman. Music and lyrics by Lionel Bart. Theatre Royal, Stratford East, London, 17 February 1959. Revised version 22 December 1959. Garrick Theatre, London, 11 February 1960.

The first original musical piece of the many which came from the Theatre Workshop, headquartered at Stratford East's Theatre Royal in the 1950s and 1960s, *Fings Ain't Wot They Used t'Be* was an attempt at an *Irma la Douce*-ish piece about life in London's Soho district. The piece had, however, none of the French musical's shapeliness or subtle comedy, but simply threw together a bunch of conventional characters including a copper (bent, of course), some whores (hearts of gold, naturally), an interior decorator (limp-wristed, needless to say) and an ex-gangman turned café-keeper and his live-in lady, who climaxed the few events of the evening by getting married, the whole topped with a set of bright and bristling songs. If the book of *Fings* was a giant step backward after the recent *Expresso Bongo*, Lionel Bart's ten songs were, on the other hand, a lively lot. It was the title song which proved the winner, but the cheery 'G'night Dearie' taken over from an earlier Bart piece, *Wally Pone*, and the langorous 'Layin' Abaht' made up for the occasional dip into banality with such as 'The Student Ponce'.

The show was successful enough to attract attention from producers Oscar Lewenstein and Donald Albery and, having been given a tightening and a larger musical content ('The Ceiling's Comin' Dahn', 'Where Do Little Birds Go?' etc) it was given a second season at Stratford, then, boosted by Max Bygraves's hoisting of the title song to number five on the charts (with nicer words), into the West End. Glynn Edwards, Miriam Karlin, Toni Palmer, Barbara Windsor, James Booth and George Sewell were amongst a cast which imbued the strangely amateurish-sounding piece and its primary-coloured characters with boundless energy through 897 performances in London, before *Fings* went on to several provincial productions.

Recording: original cast (Decca) etc

FINIAN'S RAINBOW Musical in 2 acts by E Y Harburg and Fred Saidy. Lyrics by Harburg. Music by Burton Lane. 46th Street Theater, New York, 10 January 1947.

A tale of Americo-Irish whimsy with some political points to play with was the basis of *Finian's Rainbow*, which ran to a 725-performance success in Lee Sabinson and William R Katzell's 1947 Broadway production.

Finian MacLonergan (Albert Sharpe) and his daughter Sharon (Ella Logan) arrive in America from Glocca Morra with a crock of gold, apparently stolen from the little people of Ireland, which the old man hopes to plant in the ground near Fort Knox on the principle that, if the American government's money multiplies there, so will his. They are pursued by a leprechaun called Og (David Wayne), determined to regain his people's gold. In Rainbow Valley, Missitucky they meet up with a band of sharecroppers, engaged in fighting for their land against a nasty politician called Billboard Rawkins (the name was an open reference to two American politicians of the time who were regarded as culpably ultra-conservative). Rawkins (Robert Pitkin) is made to see the error of his horrid ways when the magic of the leprechaun gold turns him black, and he has temporarily to feel the feelings of a different group of people. Whilst the big, bad lawmaker is being transformed into a good little liberal, Sharon is smiling at a handsome sharecropper, Woody Mahoney (Donald Richards), and Og romancing his mute, dancing sister, Susan (Anita Alvarez).

The songs from *Finian's Rainbow* included several which had a wider life than the show itself: Sharon and Will's 'Old Devil Moon', 'Look to the Rainbow' and 'If This isn't Love', the heroine's pretty 'How Are Things in Glocca Morra?' and the leprechaun's jaunty 'When I'm Not Near the Girl I Love' all becoming favourites.

Ten months into its Broadway run, *Finian's Rainbow* was mounted in London under the management of Emile Littler with Beryl Seton (Sharon), Patrick J Kelly (Finian), Alfie Bass (Og), Frank Royde (Rawkins) and Alan Gilbert (Woody Mahoney) in the principal rôles. It failed in 55 performances. There was no better luck for an Elizabethan Trust/Garnet Carroll Australian production with Bobby Howes (Og), Sheila Bradley (Sharon) and Bruce Barry (Will) which flopped out in six weeks in Melbourne and – a rare thing – did not then even bother to face Sydney, whilst an American revival, brought to Broadway from the City Center under the management of Robert Fryer and Lawrence Carr (46th Street Theater 23 May 1960) and featuring Jeannie Carson as Sharon did less well again, folding in 12 performances. A film version, made in 1968, kept virtually all the score but reallotted some of it to allow Fred Astaire (Finian) to share in the singing with Petula Clark (Sharon), Tommy Steele (Og) and Don Francks (Will).

UK: Palace Theatre, London 21 October 1947; Australia: Princess Theatre, Melbourne 17 December 1964; Film: Warner Brothers-Seven Arts Inc 1968

Recordings: original cast (Columbia), revival cast (RCA Victor), film soundtrack (Warner Bros) etc

FINN, William (b Boston, Mass, 1952).

Author-composer of the trio of small-scale off-Broadway musicals based on the emotional and sexual life of their central character, Marvin. After being developed at Playwrights Horizons and presented singly over a period of almost two decades to increasing, and in some quarters very enthusiastic, interest, two of the three were ultimately brought together to make up a Broadway show entitled *Falsettos*. *Falsettos* took Tony Awards for its music and libretto in the no-contest that was the 1991–2 season.

Finn has worked on several other projects which have not found the same following, nor the same success. The 1983 *America Kicks Up its Heels* did not progress from its tryout, the dance musical *Dangerous Games* played four performances on Broadway and the 1930s depression musical, *Romance in Hard Times*, six performances at New York Shakespeare Festival.

1979 **In Trousers** Playwrights Horizons 21 February, Promenade Theater 26 March 1985
1981 **March of the Falsettos** Playwrights Horizons Studio 1

April, Main Stage 20 May, Chelsea Westside Arts Theater 13 October
1983 **America Kicks Up Its Heels** (Charles Rubin) Playwrights Horizons 3 March
1989 **Dangerous Games** (Astor Piazzolla/Graciela Daniele, Jim Lewis) Nederlander Theater 19 October
1989 **Romance in Hard Times** Public Theater 28 December
1990 **Falsettoland** Playwrights Horizons 28 June, Lucille Lortel Theater 14 September
1992 **Falsettos** revised *March of the Falsettos* and *Falsettoland* (w James Lapine) John Golden Theater 29 April

FIORELLO!   Musical in 2 acts by Jerome Weidman and George Abbott. Lyrics by Sheldon Harnick. Music by Jerry Bock. Broadhurst Theater, New York, 25 November 1959.

Fiorello! was a mildly hagiographic biomusical of politician Fiorello Henry La Guardia (1882–1947), a former member of the American House of Representatives (1917–21, 1923–33) and mayor of New York between 1934 and 1945. Jerome Weidman and George Abbott's libretto did not attempt to cover the whole of their subject's life, but concentrated, in flashback, on his rise from successful lawyer to Republican congressman, via a wartime interlude and a marriage, and then, following an interval-time-skip of a decade, to his two campaigns for the mayordom of New York, the first unsuccessful and the second, which, although we don't see it, we know will be as successful as the second marriage.

The young lawyer Fiorello La Guardia (Tom Bosley) volunteers to stand on the apparently hopeless Republican ticket against the corrupt politicians of Tammany Hall. He is seen courting a labour group – and particularly the strike leader Thea (Ellen Hanley), who is later to become his wife – who are harassed by a corrupt policeman (Mark Dawson), then wooing the immigrant population, in their own pre-American languages, and, to general surprise, he wins the election. As a congressman, he supports mobilization and goes off in uniform himself to win the Great War at the end of the first act. The second act begins with his defeat in the mayoral race against the sitting candidate, Jimmy Walker. His efforts, in the time-honoured style, to show the popular mayor up as corrupt have failed. However, the administration finally has its scandal and, as the show ends, the widowed Fiorello is preparing to try again, with his faithful long-time secretary and wife-to-be, Marie (Patricia Wilson), at his side. Pat Stanley played factory-worker Dora who falls for and marries the Tammany Hall-tied policeman, Howard da Silva was Ben Marino, New York Republican leader, and Nathaniel Frey played Morris Cohen, the hero's law office manager.

The score by Bock, who at this time had one success (*Mr Wonderful*) and one flop (*The Body Beautiful*) to his Broadway credit, and Harnick, his collaborator on the second show, added some happy humour to a tale which, with its whiter-than-white hero battling shiningly against a world where everyone else in authority is dishonest and dirty, could have become a simplistic modern fairytale. The number which stood out was a piece in which Ben Marino and his cohorts joyously detailed the uses of 'The Little Tin Box' in dishonest politics. The same group had another lively piece, a polka, in which to sing about

'Politics and Poker', whilst right at the top of the show a trio of Fiorello's employees took any sanctimoniousness out of the tale with a tongue-in-cheek hymn to being 'On the Side of the Angels'. Romance was served by the waltzing "Til Tomorrow' (Thea and chorus) and 'When Did I Fall in Love?' (Fiorello/Thea), the soubrette element by Dora's admission that 'I Love a Cop', and by the Walker campaign song, 'Gentleman Jimmy', as performed by musical-comedy actress Mitzi (Eileen Rodgers) and her chorines.

Harold Prince and Robert E Griffith's production of *Fiorello!* tied for the year's Tony Award with *The Sound of Music*, followed the example set by another politically flavoured musical, *Of Thee I Sing*, in being awarded a Pulitzer Prize, and had a fine 795-performance run on Broadway, with the previously little-known Bosley making a great personal hit. A London mounting was sponsored by Donald Albery in 1962, with Derek Smith featured as Fiorello alongside Marion Grimaldi (Thea), Nicolette Roeg (Marie), Patricia Michael (Mitzi) and Peter Reeves (Ben), but the piece did not prove to have the same attractions for Britain as for Broadway and lasted only 56 performances.

La Guardia was seen again on the musical stage in the short-lived *Annie 2* (Kennedy Center, Washington 4 January 1990) when he was portrayed by Michael Cone.

The 'villain' of *Fiorello!*, Mayor James Walker, got his own show in 1969 (*Jimmy*, Winter Garden Theater 23 October) but did not manage to challenge La Guardia's record (84 performances) and another, more recent New York mayor got a musical doing-over when *Mayor*, a cabaret musical based on the autobiography of mayor Edward Koch (Charles Strouse/Warren Leigh), was played at New York's Top of the Gate (13 May 1985). Another mayor, John Lindsay, actually took to the boards as a performer, but the New York mayors still have a long way to go to catch up with the most famous musical mayor of all: London's Sir Richard Whittington.

UK: Piccadilly Theatre 8 October 1962
Recording: original cast (Capitol)

THE FIREFLY Musical comedy in 3 acts by Otto Harbach. Music by Rudolf Friml. Lyric Theater, New York, 2 December 1912.

Little street-singing Nina (Emma Trentini) escapes from a cruel master by disguising herself as a cabin-boy on the Bermuda-going yacht of wealthy socialite Mrs van Dare (Katherine Stewart). Professor Franz (Henry Vogel) thinks he has found a wonderful choirboy but, if he is disappointed when the truth comes out, Mrs van Dare's intended son-in-law Jack Travers (Craig Campbell) is not. After some Caribbean high-jinks, including a false accusation and a misdirected letter, and the passing of a little time, the jilted Geraldine van Dare (Audrey Maple) gets a more suitable husband in the comfortable 'uncle' John Thurston (Melville Stewart) and little Nina – now a famous prima donna – becomes Mrs Jack. Geraldine's maid, Suzette (Ruby Norton), and Thurston's valet, Pietro (Sammy Lee), provided the soubret song-and-dance moments and Mrs van Dare's fussy confidential secretary, Jenkins (Roy Atwell), added to the comic moments.

The Firefly was put together by producer Oscar Hammerstein as a vehicle for the former opera singer Trentini,

following her great success as the heroine of his *Naughty Marietta*. Harbach cannily cast the tiny star in another rôle where she had the opportunity to dress up as a boy, but since Victor Herbert refused to work with the temperamental and too often unprofessional vocalist a second time, Rudolf Friml was given the opportunity to compose the score. He duly supplied his star with a new hit song in the quasi-Neapolitan 'Giannina Mia', the delightfully tripping 'Love is Like a Firefly' and the showy aria 'Kiss Me and 'tis Day' to deliver in her metamorphosis as a third-act prima donna. The score, however, produced a second and even more durable standard in a different vein, in the gentle waltz song 'Sympathy', introduced by Melville Stewart, offering Geraldine a not disinterested shoulder to whimper on, as well as several other highly attractive pieces: Papa Franz's sweet 'Beautiful Ship from Toyland', the richly swimming 'In Sapphire Seas' and the lovely light-hearted ensemble 'When a Maid Comes Knocking at your Heart'.

The show ran for 120 performances at New York's Lyric Theater before taking to the road and was thereafter the subject of productions throughout America, whilst its two favourite songs got a wide recording and broadcast coverage. It did not, however, travel much abroad and the only major foreign production was mounted in Australia under the aegis of J C Williamson Ltd. Rene Maxwell starred as Nina, alongside Edith Drayson (Geraldine), George Gee (Jenkins), Ralph Errolle (Jack), Claude Flemming (Uncle John) and Ethel Morrison (Mrs Vandare) in a version which seemed to sport some unfamiliar numbers – Hugh Steyne as Pietro, for example, performed a Weston and Lee piece entitled 'The Bolshevik' – through a fine two-and-a-half months in Sydney and a disappointing month in Melbourne (Her Majesty's Theatre 29 September 1921).

A 1937 MGM film of the same title shared little with the stage show beyond a selection of its music. Jeanette MacDonald sang 'Giannina Mia' and Allan Jones made a hit with a new piece, 'The Donkey Serenade', concocted by Wright and Forrest from an old Friml melody, 'Chansonette', as illustration to a wholly different story.

In 1942 a putative revival of *The Firefly* ended up being a show with little in common with its original. Irving Actman, Leopold Spitany and composer Jean Schwartz contributed to what was ultimately called *Full Steam Ahead*, featured topical Nazis in its libretto and got no further than Philadelphia (25 December). Things were put more sanely back on the rails by a 1943 revival by Edwin Lester's Los Angeles Civic Light Opera, with Francia White starring, a cast including Al Shean (Franz), Dorothy Stone (Suzette), Odette Myrtil (Mrs van Dare) and a third-act appearance by Friml himself ('The Composer Plays'). It slipped a four-handed version of 'The Donkey Serenade' as well as three new Friml numbers ('A Composite Picture of Love', 'You're Gorgeous', 'I Give My Heart Away') into a revised book (ad Erna Lazarus, W Houston Branch) whilst cutting several principal pieces of the original score ('Beautiful Ship from Toyland', 'Tommy Atkins', 'Call Me Uncle', 'Kiss Me and 'tis Day' etc).

Australia: Her Majesty's Theatre, Sydney, 30 April 1921
Recording: selection (RCA), selection (part-record) (World Records) etc

465

FIRTH, Elizabeth (b Phillipsburg, NJ, 11 April 1884; d unknown).

Miss Firth left her native America for Britain in her late teens and was promptly engaged there by George Edwardes, for whom she first appeared in *The Duchess of Dantzic*, playing the rôle of one of Napoleon's sisters and covering Evie Greene in the title rôle, both in London (1903) and New York (1905). She took over the rôle of Agathe in Edwardes's production of *Véronique* (1906) and appeared in supporting parts in his *Les P'tites Michu* and *Les Merveilleuses* before being chosen to create the rôle of Nathalie (ie Valencienne) in the first English production of *The Merry Widow* (1907).

She starred opposite Ellaline Terriss in *The Dashing Little Duke* (1909) and returned to Edwardes's management to play the vampy Olga in *The Dollar Princess* (1910), before going back to America where she appeared as Clarisse (a rôle very close in nature to that of Valencienne in *Die lustige Witwe*) in Leo Fall's *The Siren* (1911) before ending her short but impressive career at the age of 27.

FISCHER, Betty (b Vienna, 12 October 1887; d Vienna, 19 January 1969).

Betty Fischer became the darling of the Austrian capital in the years during and following the First World War, creating starring rôles in a vast list of often memorable Operetten, notably in 13 years as prima donna at the Theater an der Wien, where she made up a celebrated star team with Hubert Marischka, Luise Kartousch and Ernst Tautenhayn.

After early work in variety and in Operette, Frln Fischer joined Wilhelm Karczag's company at the Raimundtheater at the age of 23 and, over three seasons, played leading rôles in such pieces as *Wiener Blut* (Fransizka Cagliari), *Giroflé-Girofla* (Giroflé/Girofla) *Die Dollarprinzessin* (Olga), *Casimirs Himmelfahrt* (Rudy) and *Die keusche Barbara* (Barbara) and created the rôles of Prinzessin Marie in Leo Ascher's highly successful *Hoheit tanzt Walzer* (1912), Komtesse Irene in *Die liebe Unschuld* (1912), Bessie Phelps-Butt-Johnston in Berény's *Mein Mäderl* (1913), Mitzi Hipsinger in Ziehrer's *Der Husarengeneral* (1913) and the actress, Therese Krones, in the successful Strauss père pasticcio *Die tolle Therese* (1913).

In 1914 she moved up to Karczag's flagship company at the Theater an der Wien and made her first starring appearance there in the patriotically remade version of Kálmán's *Az obsitos*, *Gold gab ich für Eisen* (Marlene). She followed up by creating the rôles of Edith Lloyd in *Die schöne Schwedin* (1915), Dina in Eysler's *Wenn zwei sich lieben* (1915), Julja Lella in Nedbal's *Die Winzerbraut* (1916), Kondja Gül in the triumphant and long-running *Die Rose von Stambul* (1916), Kitty Höfer in *Der Sterngucker* (1916), Vilma Garamy in the Vienna version of *Wo die Lerche singt* (1918), Blanka von Lossin in *Die blaue Mazur* (1920), Vera Lisaweta in *Der letzte Walzer* (1921), the title-rôle of *Frasquita* (1922), Lea – the prototype of *Das Land des Lächelns*'s Lisa – in *Die gelbe Jacke* (1923), the title-rôle in *Gräfin Mariza* (1924), Gladys Harrison in *Der Milliardensouper* (1925), Nadja Nadjakowska in the hugely successful *Der Orlow* (1925), Princess Fedora in *Die Zirkusprinzessin* (1926), Helena in *Die Königin* (1927) and the vocally wide-ranging Margarete in Eysler's *Die gold'ne Meisterin* (1927). She also appeared as Hortense in the

Plate 92. **Betty Fischer:** *Long-time prima donna of the Theater an der Wien and the creator of many famous Viennese rôles.*

1915 revival of *Der Opernball*, played alongside Marischka in *Die lustige Witwe*, as Sáffi to the Barinkay of Richard Tauber in *Der Zigeunerbaron* (1921) and in the 1923 revival of *Eine Nacht in Venedig*.

In 1928 she moved to the Johann Strauss-Theater to play the title-rôle of Miss Evelyne Bliss in Granichstädten's Operette *Die Milliardärin*, and thereafter made a long series of guest appearances at houses both in Vienna and outside, creating the part of the Countess Olga Baranskaia in *Walzer aus Wien* at the Stadttheater in 1930 and returning to the Theater an der Wien in 1931 in that part, as Yvonne Duprès in *Der Bauerngeneral* and in the title-rôle of *Viktoria und ihr Husar*.

Although the principal part of her career, as a metropolitan prima donna, was now past its peak, she continued to appear on the musical stage whilst pursuing a second career as a teacher at the Vienna Conservatoire, appearing at the Raimundtheater in character rôles over half a century after she had first starred there as a young leading lady.

FITYFIRITTY Operett in 3 acts by Rudolf Halász. Music by Dénes Buday. Fővárosi Operettszinház, Budapest, 8 March 1941.

One of the most popular of the list of operetts composed by Dénes Buday, the wartime *Fityfiritty* was written to a text by the neophyte Halász whose previous work had been largely as a lyricist for popular songs.

Fityfiritty was the nickname of the little shopgirl heroine of the piece (Manyi Kiss), but the star rôle was that of her best friend, Mária Patkay (Hanna Honthy), once a shopgirl

Plate 93.

like her, but now a rich and famous singing star. Maria's heart, however, is still in the shop – more specifically with the shop's director (György Solthy) – and it is her little friend who smooths the obstacles between stage and shop in time for a happy ending. Kálmán Latabár, Ella Gombaszögi and Lajos Hajmássy took the other principal rôles.

Buday's score featured the popular dance rhythms of the recent decades – foxtrot, tango, English waltz – and turned out a song hit in the foxtrot 'Szép hely, jó hely Teherán, de ott is teher ám a feleség' (A lovely, happy place is Teheran, but there as well as here a wife's a burden ...).

Following its successful original run at the Fővárosi Operettszinház, the show was revived there in 1946 (21 April, book now credited to Rudolf Halász and Dezső Kellér).

THE FIVE O'CLOCK GIRL Fairytale in modern clothes in 2 acts by Guy Bolton and Fred Thompson. Music by Bert Kalmar and Harry Ruby. 46th Street Theater, New York, 10 October 1927.

Alongside the French play *The 5 o'Clock Man* (which became *A Kiss in a Taxi* in Clifford Grey's American version and, subsequently, the musical *Sunny Days*) in the 1927–8 Broadway season there came also *The 5 o'Clock Girl*. Patricia Brown (Mary Eaton) is worthy of this title because 5 o'clock is the time when she, a working girl in a cleaners' shop, talks on the telephone to a young man who is clearly attractive and attracted. Since this is a fairytale in modern clothes, Gerald Brooks (Oscar Shaw) also turns out to be rich and social. In order not to lose him, Patricia pretends that she, too, is rich and social, and when she

goes out to meet him, she dresses up in clothes borrowed from her shop. However, although the deception is inevitably unmasked, a happy Cinderella-style ending is finally arrived at with some helpful interference from comical friend Susie Snow (Pert Kelton), who is striking simultaneous sparks with Brooks' valet Hudgins (Louis John Bartels), who is also pretending to be something wealthier and more social than he is.

Although the show included less dancing than was generally fashionable at the time, Kalmar and Ruby's score was in the usual dancing mode, with 'Thinking of You', Patricia and Gerald's duo 'Up in the Clouds', 'Who Did? You Did!' and Gerald's 'Happy-go-lucky' proving the favourites.

Philip Goodman's production of *The Five o'Clock Girl* played 280 performances on Broadway, and the show was taken up by R H Gillespie and Lee Ephraim to be staged at the London Hippodrome 18 months later. A fiddled-with version, which took in such additional numbers as 'Happy Little Bluebird', featured Jean Colin and Ernest Truex in the principal rôles, with Hermione Baddeley and George Grossmith providing the comedy song-and-dance, and Richard Murdoch and Ursula Jeans amongst the supporting cast. It played a rather disappointing three months (122 performances) before going out to do a little better in the provinces. An Australian production, with Alfred Frith ('and his million-dollar face') top-billed as Hudgins, Helen Paterson as Patricia, William Valentine as Gerald and a swatch of interpolated songs, had fair runs in Melbourne (eight weeks) and in Sydney (Her Majesty's Theatre, 10 August 1929, seven weeks).

A 1979 revival of a revised version, which supplemented a half-dozen of the original show's songs with rather more Kalmar and Ruby numbers from other sources, was mounted at Connecticut's Goodspeed Opera House (19 June) and it was brought back for a second season the following year. The production was then taken to Broadway (Helen Hayes Theater 28 January 1981) but lasted only 14 performances there.

UK: London Hippodrome 21 March 1929; Australia: Theatre Royal, Melbourne 18 May 1929

DIE FLEDERMAUS Comic Operette in 3 acts by [Carl Haffner and] Richard Genée based on *Le Réveillon* by Henri Meilhac and Ludovic Halévy. Lyrics by Richard Genée. Music by Johann Strauss. Theater an der Wien, Vienna, 5 April 1874.

The greatest theatrical success of composer Johann Strauss, and the most internationally enduring of all 19th-century Viennese Operetten – the second fact indubitably owing something to the first – *Die Fledermaus* has come to represent the 'golden age' of the Austrian musical stage to the modern world, much in the same way that *Die lustige Witwe* has come to represent the 'silver age' of the early 20th century Viennese theatre in the general consciousness.

Like *Die lustige Witwe*, *Die Fledermaus* had a libretto based on a French comedy by Henri Meilhac, this time written in conjunction with his habitual partner, Ludovic Halévy, and said to be taken, in its turn, from a German original, *Das Gefängnis* by Roderich Benedix. *Le Réveillon* had been produced for the first time at Paris's Palais-Royal just 18 months prior to the appearance of the Operette, with MM Geoffroy and Mme Reynold appearing as Gabriel and Fanny Gaillardin, from Pincornet-les-Boeufs, and Hyacinthe, the comedian with the famous nose, as Alfred, the chef d'orchestra of the Prince Yermontoff (played in travesty by Georgette Olivier). Alfred tracks his ex-beloved, Fanny, to her provincial home and persists in serenading her with a violin fantasy from *La Favorita* whilst awaiting her husband's condemnation to prison for insulting a garde-champêtre, before getting closer. Pellerin was Duparquet, the friend whom Gaillardin once stranded after a masked ball, still ridiculously dressed in a bluebird costume, and who now persuades him to postpone prison for a night out at the Prince's pavilion in the company of some pretty actresses from Paris. He is, in reality, plotting his revenge. Lhéritier played the prison governor, Tourillon, off in an aristocratic disguise to the same party.

Following the Palais-Royal production, Maximilian Steiner, co-director of the Theater an der Wien, ordered a German translation from the veteran playwright Carl Haffner. He did not judge the result worth producing, but subsequently he – or music publisher Gustave Lewy – had the idea of making a musical libretto from the piece instead, and handed Haffner's version over to house-composer and adapter Richard Genée. Genée was apparently no more fond of Haffner's version than Steiner, and he later asserted that nothing of that first adaptation remained in the final text of *Die Fledermaus*. However, so as not to offend the old playwright (who died in 1876), he agreed that his name should remain on the playbills. The libretto of *Die Fledermaus* contained one major alteration to the text of *Le Réveillon* (which, in other places, in spite of Genée's assertion, it followed virtually line for line) – it introduced two major female rôles into a play which was an almost wholly masculine affair. An Operette, and certainly one written for a theatre whose co-director was none other than the great Marie Geistinger, could not manage without its prima donna and its soubrette. *Le Réveillon*'s Fanny and her maid are not seen again after the first act. The gambolling of Gaillardin at the ball, and the little episode of the chiming watch, are directed on to one farmer's girl/actress, Métella, whilst the centrepiece of the third act is a long and highly comical scene between the imprisoned Alfred and Gaillardin, disguised as a lawyer in order to get to see the man who has been arrested in a compromising situation with his wife.

Die Fledermaus's Viennese Rosalinde (Marie Geistinger) is wooed by an Alfred who is a throbbing vocalist rather than a chef d'orchestre but who, like his predecessor, is bundled off to prison in place of her legitimate husband, Gabriel Eisenstein (Jani Szika). When Eisenstein turns up at the ball chez Prince Orlofsky (Irma Nittinger), he is enchanted not only by the actress Olga – who is his own maid, Adele (Karoline Charles-Hirsch), in disguise – but by a mysterious Hungarian countess who woos his watch from him. The countess is Rosalinde. After their merry evening, Eisenstein and Frank, the prison governor (Carl Adolf Friese), end up facing each other at the jail with their night's disguises torn away, and the confrontation with the 'false' Eisenstein takes place, before Rosalinde puts the cap on things by producing the watch she wooed from her husband, and Falke (Ferdinand Lebrecht) reveals that the whole thing has been a set-up. As in the play, the final act opened with a low-comedy scene for a tipsy jailer.

If the libretto replaced many of the subtleties and comicalities of the play with more conventional and well-used elements, it did, nevertheless, produce two fine – if not particularly original – leading lady's rôles, as well as many a chance for music. Strauss, to whom the libretto was given for setting, took fine and full advantage of them. Geistinger was well-served, with a showpiece csárdás ('Klänge der Heimat') in which to prove her Hungarianness, and paired with Eisenstein in a delicious sung version of the watch-scene ('Dieser Anstand, so manierlich'), whilst the soubrette had two showy coloratura pieces, a mocking laughing song ('Mein Herr Marquis') reproving the disguised Eisenstein for mistaking her for a ladies' maid, and a tacked-in ariette à tiroirs ('Spiel' ich die Unschuld vom Lande'), allowing Adele to show off her range as she demonstrates her suitability for a stage career. The bored Orlofsky summoned his guests to enjoy themselves in a loping mezzo-soprano 'Ich lade gern mir Gäste an'. The men were less showily served, although Falke led a swaying hymn to brotherly love in 'Brüderlein und Schwesterlein' and Alfred indulged in some operatic extravagances as well as an intimate supper-table duet with the almost errant wife ('Trinke, liebchen, trinke schnell'). Orlofsky's party also provided the opportunity for a display of dancing.

Many myths have grown up around the show and its original success or non-success, particularly in Vienna. The truth is that *Die Fledermaus* was well – if not extravagantly – received, and, like virtually all Strauss's pieces, was quickly taken up to be mounted in other Austrian, German and German-language houses where his name was a sure draw. In Vienna, it was played 45 times in repertoire before the summer break, and was brought back again in 1875 and in 1876, reaching its 100th performance on 17 October 1876 with Frlns Meinhardt (Rosalinde) and Steinherr (Adele) featured alongside Szika, Alexander Girardi (Falke) and Felix Schweighofer (Frank). Thereafter it remained fairly steadily in the repertoire at the Theater an der Wien, good for a regular number of performances in most years, reaching its 200th performance 15 May 1888 and the 300th on 9 December 1899. If the original run, within the repertoire system, had been less stunning than the show's later reputation might have suggested, and indeed far from the record compiled by such pieces as *Die schöne Helena* at the same house, its initial showing was above average and its (not unbroken) longevity in the repertoire exceptional. Carl Streitmann, Phila Wolff and Gerda Walde featured in a new production in 1905 (1 April), and the piece was seen at other theatres including a showing at the Hofoper, at the Volksoper for the first time in 1907, the Raimundtheater in 1908, the Johann Strauss-Theater in 1911 and the Bürgertheater in 1916, making up part of the repertoire of any self-respecting Operette theater in Vienna in the same way that it did in the provinces. Amongst the memorable Viennese *Fledermaus* productions of later years was one at the Staatsoper in 1960 which featured Hilde Güden (Rosalinde), Rita Streich (Adele) and Eberhard Wächter (Eisenstein).

In Berlin, the show was produced at the Friedrich-Wilhelmstädtisches Theater with a singular success which allegedly gave a boost to its reputation back in Vienna. The 200th performance was passed within two years of the first, and *Die Fledermaus* went on to become the most popular

Operette of the 19th century on German stages. Budapest also saw its first performance of the show in German, as did New York when the Stadt Theater mounted the piece just seven months after the Viennese première with Lina Mayr (Rosalinde), Ferdinand Schütz (Eisenstein), Schönwolff (Frank) and Antonie Heynold (Adele), but neither city proved in much haste to provide a vernacular version. It was eight years before the Hungarian capital saw an Hungarian version, and, although the piece got regular showings in New York's German theatres – including an 1881 season with Geistinger starred in her original rôle alongside Mathilde Cottrelly (Adele) and Max Schnelle (Eisenstein) – it was over a decade before New Yorkers got Die Fledermaus in an English translation.

The first English-language version was mounted on the vast stage of London's Alhambra Theatre (ad Hamilton Aidé) as a Christmas entertainment for the 1876–7 season with a cast headed by Cora Cabella, Kate Munroe, Adelaide Newton, Guillaume Loredan, Edmund Rosenthal and J H Jarvis. It ran for a good and sufficient season of some four months, and encouraged the theatre to try Strauss's earlier Indigo the following Christmas, but it was more than 30 years after this before another English Fledermaus was seen in the city. The following October, Australia was given its first glimpse of the show, under the aegis of Martin Simonsen's company (and billed, with typical local mendacity, as having played 500 nights at the Alhambra) at Sydney's Queen's Theatre. Fannie Simonsen was Rosalind and Henry Bracy Eisenstein with Minna Fischer (Adele), Maud Walton (Orlofsky), H Hodgson (Frank) and G Johnson (Falke) in support. The company left town after ten days.

New York's first English Die Fledermaus (ad uncredited) was mounted by John McCaull at the Casino Theater some eight years further down the line, with Mme Cottrelly now playing her Adele in English alongside Rosalba Beecher (Rosalinde), Mark Smith (Eisenstein) and De Wolf Hopper (Frank) and, after the split between McCaull and the Casino management, it was repeated later the same season at Wallack's Theater (14 September 1886) before, as in England, going on the shelf for several decades.

Hungary's first vernacular Denevér was mounted not in Budapest but at Kolozsvár with Sarolta Krecsányi and Béla Szombathelyi featured. It was played at Szeged the following year, but only in 1882 did a version (ad Lajos Evva) arrive in Budapest. Aranka Hegyi was the first Budapest Rosalinda with Mariska Komáromi (Ghita, ex-Adele), Elek Solymossy (Bussola), Vidor Kassai (Fujo), Pál Vidor (Crapotti) and János Kápolnai (Ritenuto, ex-Alfred) in the other major rôles. It played 54 times and was revived in 1891 (24 January) and 1907 (22 October) before going on to productions at the Népopera (1912, 1915), the Városi Színház (1926) and other houses as, in line with the rest of the world, it worked its way up past more immediately popular pieces into its present-day place at the peak of popularity.

Italy, Sweden, Russia, the Netherlands and Switzerland all took in Die Fledermaus in the first years after its début, but it was France which took the longest time to catch up with the show, and, according to one variation of the story, not without reason. In those slap-happy copyright days, nobody in Vienna, apparently, had bothered to ask Meilhac

and Halévy for permission to make a musical out of their play. Producer Victor Koning called on authors Alfred Delecour and Victor Wilder who had, to Strauss's satisfaction, heavily rewritten the libretto of Indigo for France, and ordered a brand new script to be written around some portions of Strauss's score. The story they used was a well-worn one, featuring a womanizing Prince, wed by necessity and by procuration, who goes out gallivanting with some bohemiennes on the day of his marriage. His bride-to-be gets herself into gypsy gear, goes out, and tames him. If the story was familiar, the score was less so. Many favourite pages of Die Fledermaus were missing. There was no csárdás, no Orlofsky's song, no Audition couplets and the bits that remained, often uncomfortably tacked one to another, were topped up with Lorenza Feliciana's valse brilliante 'O süsses Wörtchen' (pasted onto a Fledermaus melody) and 'Zigeunerkind wie glänzt dein Haar' ('Pourquoi pleurer') from Cagliostro in Wien and some other spare and written-for-the-occasion Strauss music. La Tzigane, with Zulma Bouffar as Princess Arabelle, the baritone Ismaël (who garnered both the 'Brüderlein' and 'Trincke liebchen' melodies as solos) as the naughty Prince, and Berthelier, Urbain and Léa d'Asco featured, was equipped with one of the most luxurious stagings Koning's theatre had ever provided. However, with Strauss himself on hand to win masses of journalistic space, although the show emerged as an uncomfortable paste-up job, it nevertheless managed 63-plus performances before Koning replaced it with the première of Le Petit Duc. It was only seen again when a German version of it (ad Hans Weigel, additional music Max Schönherr) was mounted at Graz in 1985 (16 November).

It was 1904 before a regular La Chauve-Souris (ad Paul Ferrier) was seen in Paris. Fernand Samuel's production at the Variétés featured Albert Brasseur and Max Dearly as Gaillardin and Tourillon (since the action was reset in France, the names from Le Réveillon had been resurrected for this pair), with Cécile Thévenet (Caroline, ex-Rosalinde), Jane Saulier (Arlette, ex-Adele) and Ève Lavallière as Orlofsky. It was played 56 times.

Die Fledermaus was still, even in the early days of 20th century, far from the all-obscuring international favourite it was to become, but it was a regular part of the repertoire in, in particular, German-speaking countries where it had been integrated into the repertoire of such houses as the Berlin Opera (8 May 1899). In 1905 it was produced at New York's Metropolitan Opera in German with Marcella Sembrich and Andreas Dippel featured, and in 1910 a new English version (ad Armand Kalisch) starring Carrie Tubb, Joseph O'Mara and Frederick Ranalow was played at London's Her Majesty's Theatre (4 August) in the pro-Viennese atmosphere engendered by The Merry Widow and its successors. The following year, yet another anglicized Fledermaus (ad Gladys Unger, Arthur Anderson) was produced at London's Lyric Theatre under the title Nightbirds with C H Workman and Constance Drever, Paris's Veuve joyeuse, starred for 138 performances. This version was picked up for Broadway and played with José Collins, Claude Flemming and Maurice Farkoa as The Merry Countess (20 August 1912, Casino Theater).

Another round of productions was set off by Max Reinhardt's typically big and typically botched Berlin production of 1929 (Deutsches Theater 8 June). Hermann

Thimig, Maria Rajdl, Adele Kern and Oscar Karlweis as a non-travesty Orlofsky were featured in a lavishly staged version which lyingly purported to have gone back to *Le Réveillon* for its text (ad Karl Rössler, Marcellus Schiffer) but which nevertheless did not leave Rosalinde and Adèle at home for the second and third acts! The version's vanities included some additional lyrics by Schiffer glorifying Reinhardt, whilst Strauss's music had been 'improved' by E W Korngold. The Paris Théâtre Pigalle (5 October 1929 ad Nino) played Reinhardt's version with Lotte Schöne, Jarmila Novotna, Dorville and Roger Tréville featured, whilst the Shuberts had Fanny Todd Mitchell do a version which also claimed to be a version of *Le Réveillon* and which, as *A Wonderful Night* (31 October 1929), played 125 Broadway performances with its leading ladies well and truly intact. London's Royal Opera House gave a faithful *Fledermaus* in 1930 (14 May) with Willi Wörle, Lotte Lehmann, Gerhard Hüsch and Elisabeth Schumann, whilst another American version (ad Alan Child, Robert A Simon) arrived in 1933 (14 October) with Peggy Wood (Rosalinde), Helen Ford (Adele) and John Hazzard as Frosch, to add a further 115 performances to *Die Fledermaus*'s bitty Broadway record, before the Reinhardt/Korngold version turned up, on the wings of the war, for its Broadway season under the title *Rosalinda* (44th Street Theater 28 October). Dorothy Sarnoff took the title-rôle, whilst Karlweis repeated his Berlin Orlofsky and Korngold conducted his music, and *Rosalinda* proved a perfect piece of good-old-days, richly produced wartime entertainment through 521 performances. London promptly followed up, and Tom Arnold and Bernard Delfont presented *Gay Rosalinda* (ad Austin Melford, Rudolf Bernauer, Sam Heppner 8 March 1945) at the Palace Theatre with Cyril Ritchard and Ruth Naylor featured and Richard Tauber conducting. The success was repeated for 413 London performances.

Since this late and unexpected burst of commercial theatre success for more or less botched versions of *Die Fledermaus*, the show has largely retreated – in normally less tampered-with shape – into the opera houses of those countries which do not sport repertoire Operette companies. Covent Garden, the Metropolitan, the Berlin and Vienna Opera Houses, and the Paris Opéra have all hosted the show, and divas of the ilk of Joan Sutherland and Kiri te Kanawa have played Rosalinde. Some of the lightness and gaiety which was the chief attraction of the commercial version has unavoidably been lost in this rehousing of what is basically a musical-comedy piece, but, whilst Suppé, Millöcker and Zeller are forgotten, the waltz king's most popular work has become in the process regarded as the one 'safe' 19th-century Viennese Operette for the world's operatic houses. Thus, more than a century after its première, *Die Fledermaus* is going more strongly than ever, with an international production rate that only the favourite works of Offenbach and Gilbert and Sullivan's *The Mikado* of 19th-century works can come near.

Versions of *Die Fledermaus* have been put on film on a number of occasions in the German language – in 1931 by Carl Lamac with Anny Ondra, Georg Alexander and Ivan Petrovitch, by Paul Verhoven in 1937 with Lidia Baarova and Hans Söhnker, by Geza von Bolvary in 1945 with Marte Harell, Willy Frisch and Johannes Heesters, and in 1962 by Geza von Cziffra with Peter Alexander, Marianne

Koch and Marika Rökk. Powell and Pressburger were reponsible for an English-language version (*Oh, Rosalinda!*) released in 1955 in which Michael Redgrave was paired with Anneliese Rothenberger.

An attempt at a musequel to *Die Fledermaus* was put out by Leon Treptow (text) and K A Raida (music) at Berlin's Viktoria Theater in 1882 (8 April) under the title *Prinz Orlofsky*. In fact, it was not a genuine sequel, telling a wholly conventional comic-opera tale and simply tacking the names of the characters of Genée's Operette on to its characters. Prince Orlofsky pretends he is married and a father to win financial favours from an elderly uncle. The uncle turns up, is gotten drunk for a act of revelry, Adele poses as Mrs Orlofsky and at the end, of course, becomes her for real. Frosch had become the Prince's butler, Alfred got himself a country lass who had a showy rôle in the second act, and Frank, Eisenstein and Falke put in appearances. Rosalinde had the good sense to stay at home this time.

Germany: Friedrich-Wilhelmstädtisches Theater 8 July 1874; USA: Stadt Theater (Ger) 21 November 1874, Casino Theater (Eng) 15 March 1885; UK: Alhambra Theatre 18 December 1876; Australia: Queen's Theatre, Sydney 17 October 1877; Hungary: (Ger) 14 November 1874; Kolozsvár *Denevér* 19 October 1877, Népszinház, Budapest 25 August 1882; France: Théâtre de la Renaissance *La Tzigane* 30 October 1877, Théâtre des Variétés *La Chauve-Souris* 22 April 1904; Films 1931 (Ger), 1937 (Ger), 1945 (Ger), 1955 *Oh, Rosalinda!* (Eng)

Recordings: complete (Decca, EMI, RCA, Deutsche Grammophon, HMV, Eurodicsc, Teldec, Teletheater etc), complete in French (Polydor), complete in Hungarian (Qualiton), complete in Russian (MK), complete in English (CBS) etc

FLERS, P-L [PUYOL, Pierre-Louis] (b Paris, 27 April 1865; d Antibes, 10 September 1932).

The author of more revues, plays, libretti and other diverse theatre texts than would seem possible, thanks to a very efficient team of ghost-writers and some celebrated collaborators, Flers was, nevertheless, most famed as a producer of revues, often with a British tinge, mounted at the Folies-Bergère (the annual *Le Revue des Folies-Bergère*), the Alcazar, the Moulin-Rouge, Les Ambassadeurs, La Cigale and other such houses, but also in more legitimate theatre venues.

Flers is credited with having contributed to the texts of a number of pieces which straddled the line between the revue or variety show, in which he was most active, and the book musical, but also to several regular musical plays, both in translation and but, occasionally, original. If an early collaboration with Audran was a straight-out flop, the musical comedy *Shakespeare!*, written with Paul Gavault to a score by Serpette, was both a clever piece of farce writing and reasonably successful, whilst the revusical *Messalinette, ou le tour du demi-monde en 80 nuits* was exported with success to both Vienna (*Die Ringstrassen-Prinzessin*, ad Carl Lindau, Leopold Krenn, 10 February 1905, Danzers Orpheum) and to Budapest (*Mimi hercegnő* ad Jenő Farago, 11 May 1906, Magyar Színház) before being revived at the Moulin-Rouge in 1909. He adapted another revue-house piece, *Lysistrata*, to the French stage, but also reorganized Ivan Caryll's *The Earl and the Girl* for Parisian consumption (adding the 'Shimmy Shake' to the evening's entertainment) and, in later years, he authored the text for Josef Szulc's successful musical comedy *Le Petit Choc*.

Flers ran the Moulin-Rouge through 1903, and during that time introduced there the American musical comedy *The Belle of New York*, which he had seen in Vienna, in a spectacular staging and with an enormous success. This prompted him to follow up with another opérette, written by himself. For *Voluptata* he assembled a cast including Anna Tariol-Baugé, Sulbac, Arlette Dorgère and Carlos Avril, and is reputed to have introduced ragtime dance to Paris as part of the show's choreography.

He worked on several occasions in London, staging parts of *The Passing Show* and also of the Gaiety Theatre musical play *The Beauty Spot*, in which Parisian revue star Régine Flory was starred, and for which he also took a co-librettist's and/or 'based on' credit.

1896 **La Reine des reines** (Edmond Audran) Eldorado 14 October

1898 **Un flagrant délit** (Georges Charton) 1 act Versailles 20 March; La Roulotte 11 November

1898 **Fémina** (Rodolphe Berger) 1 act La Cigale 6 May

1899 **Shakespeare!** (Gaston Serpette/w Paul Gavault) Théâtre des Bouffes-Parisiens 23 November

1899 **Ohé! Venus** (Monteux-Brissac/w Gavault) Lyon; La Cigale 24 February

1900 **Les Petits Croisés** (?/w Gavault) La Cigale 24 January

1902 **Messalinette, ou le tour du demi-monde en 80 nuits** (Berger) Concert de la Scala 19 February

1903 **Cabriole** (Laurent Halet/w Alévy) 1 act Parisiana 13 January

1904 **Voluptata** (Paul Marcelles/w Charles Clairville?) Moulin-Rouge 20 January

1904 **Lysistrata** French version (Moulin-Rouge)

1905 **Coco barmaid** 1 act Scala 2 February

1906 **Ah! Moumounte!** (Eugène Héros) La Cigale 22 March

1907 **Madame Barbe-bleue** (Georges Arnould) La Cigale 18 January

1908 **Geneviève de Brabant** revised version (Théâtre des Variétés)

1908 **La Course à l'amour** (Héros, Ondet/w André Matieux) La Cigale 17 April

1910 **Le Circuit du Leste** (Héros) Scala 16 September

1917 **The Beauty Spot** (James W Tate/Clifford Harris, Valentine/w Arthur Anderson) Gaiety Theatre, London 26 November

1919 **Hello!! Charley** (*The Earl and the Girl*) French version (Théâtre Apollo)

1921 **Les Bijoux indiscrètes** (Leo Daniderff) Théâtre Marjol 15 September

1923 **Le Petit Choc** (Joseph Szulc) Théâtre Daunou 25 May

Other title attributed: *Ma bonne cousine* (1903)

FLERS, Robert [PELLEVÉ DE LA MOTTE-ANGO, Marie Joseph Louis Camille Robert, Marquis] de (b Pont l'Évèque, 25 November 1872; d Vittel, 30 July 1927).

One of the most highly regarded French writers of light comedy of the first part of the 20th century, the Marquis de Flers collaborated for 14 years with Gaston de Caillavet on a series of plays and musical comedies. The former included such pieces as *La Montansier* (1904), *L'Ange du foyer* (1905), *Miquette et sa mère* (1906), *L'Amour veille* (1907), *Le Roi* (1908), *L'Âne de Buridan* (1909), *Primerose* (1911), and *La Belle Aventure* (1913) whilst the latter, mostly to scores by Claude Terrasse, included the young composer's two major successes, the opéras-bouffes *Le Sire de Vergy* and *M de la Palisse*.

Amongst their other musical collaborations, the pair also turned out noteworthy French-language versions of Lehár's two biggest French successes, *La Veuve joyeuse* and *Le Comte de Luxembourg*, and provided the libretti for André Messager's successful opéra-comique *Fortunio* and his 'légende lyrique', *Béatrice* (Monte Carlo, 21 March 1914).

After the death of de Caillavet, in 1915, de Flers paired up with another successful comic writer of class, Francis de Croisset, and together they compiled the pretty, genteel text for Reynaldo Hahn's consciously old-fashioned opérette *Ciboulette*, the most enduring of de Flers's original works for the musical theatre.

His plays subsequently proved popular as the bases for other people's musicals. Leo Fall's successful Operette *Das Puppenmädel* was based on de Flers and de Caillavet's *Miquette et sa mère*; the libretto written by Carlo Lombardo and Renato Simoni for the Italian operetta *Primarosa* (1926) was taken from their *Primerose*; *Le Roi* (1908), which had already been illustrated with some music by Emmanuel Arène on its original production, was made into a full-scale musical comedy by Ralph Benatzky under the title *Majestät-privat* (Theater an der Wien 18 December 1937); and *La Belle Aventure* (1914) became the source for the musical *In der Johannisnacht* (Jean Gilbert/Robert Gilbert, Thalia Theater, Hamburg 1 July 1926).

Long an influential theatrical columnist for the *Figaro*, a force in the field of organizing the laws and enforcement of copyright and other author's benefits, sometime president of the Société des Auteurs, and the author of a number of books, de Flers nevertheless won his greatest renown and respect through his writings for the stage.

1901 **Les Travaux d'Hercule** (Claude Terrasse/w Gaston de Caillavet) Théâtre des Bouffes-Parisiens 7 March

1902 **Chonchette** (Terrasse/w de Caillavet) 1 act Théâtre des Capucines 11 April

1903 **Le Sire de Vergy** (Terrasse/w de Caillavet) Théâtre des Variétés 16 April

1904 **M de la Palisse** (Terrasse/w de Caillavet) Théâtre des Variétés 2 November

1906 **Paris, ou le bon juge** (Terrasse/w de Caillavet) Théâtre des Capucines 18 March

1907 **Fortunio** (André Messager/w de Caillavet) Opéra-Comique 5 June

1908 **La Veuve joyeuse** (*Die lustige Witwe*) French version w de Caillavet (Théâtre Apollo)

1911 **Le Comte de Luxembourg** (*Der Graf von Luxemburg*) French version w de Caillavet (Théâtre Apollo)

1923 **Ciboulette** (Reynaldo Hahn/w Francis de Croisset) Théâtre des Variétés 7 April

1927 **Le Diable à Paris** (Marcel Lattès/w de Croisset) Théâtre Marigny November

FLETCHER, Percy E (b Derby, 12 December 1878; d London, 10 September 1932).

Musical director at a series of West End theatres from 1906 onwards, Fletcher made his first composing contribution to the musical stage with part of the score for the little 'conventional tragical musical absurdity', *An Exile from Home*, played as a forepiece to *The Shulamite* in 1906.

He joined Beerbohm Tree at His Majesty's Theatre in 1915 and remained there to act as the conductor of the long run of *Chu Chin Chow*. He composed the score for Oscar Asche's successor to *Chu Chin Chow*, the spectacular eastern piece produced in New York under the title

Mecca and then, under pressure from an Islamic element, in London with its title altered to *Cairo* (also conductor).

His light orchestral works won him his principal recognition as a composer, but he also composed and conducted a further, short-lived musical, the olde Englishe spectacular *The Good Old Days*, produced by Asche at the Gaiety Theatre with disastrous results.

1906 **An Exile from Home** (w R Hess/William Watson) 1 act Savoy Theatre 12 June
1920 **Mecca** (aka *Cairo*) (Asche) Century Theater, New York 4 October
1925 **The Good Old Days** (Asche) Gaiety Theatre 7 October

FLEUR DE THÉ Opéra-bouffe in 3 acts by Alfred Duru and Henri Chivot. Music by Charles Lecocq. Théâtre de l'Athénée, Paris, 11 April 1868.

When the rehearsal pianist of the Théâtre de l'Athénée showed signs of promise as a composer with his two-act *L'amour et son carquois*, the theatre director, William Busnach, gave him a Chivot and Duru libretto to set. The young Charles Lecocq's score to *Fleur de thé* proved one of its most attractive attributes, and the piece turned out to be by far the happiest of those mounted by Busnach at his unsteady little theatre.

Fleur de thé (Lucie Cabel), the daughter of the Chinese mandarin Tien-Tien (Désiré), has broken the oriental law by leaving her home to look out into the world. Her father and her future husband, Ka-o-lin (Léonce), set off in pursuit of the runaway who takes refuge in an inn, and is hidden by the ship's cook Pinsonnet (Sytter) in his room. When the cantinière Césarine (Mlle Lovato/Irma Marié), the cook's wife, jealously bundles her out, the little Chinese is captured and condemned, by another local law, to be instantly wed to the man to whom she first spoke in her flight. When it turns out that China doesn't count previous foreign marriages and that it is her husband who is nominated, Césarine takes things in hand. She disguises herself as Fleur de thé, gets re-wed to her husband, and spends the wedding night with him, but Tien-Tien discovers that his daughter has spent her night alone and, furious at this lack of marital respect, is preparing to take horrid revenge when Ka-o-lin leads on the marines. In a happy ending, everyone ends up drinking Césarine's stock of cliquot.

Lecocq's score mixed the romantic-comic and the lively with some pieces which were clearly in line of descent from the zanier moments of *Ba-ta-clan*. The rôle of Césarine, if not the title-rôle, was certainly the best and most musically substantial one. She began with a Chanson de la Cantinière, continued in the second act with an anti-man ariette ('En tous pays l'homme est un être'), joined with Pinsonnet in the duo and couplets de l'alcôve, in which he tries to convince her that nothing happened during his re-wedding night whilst she, who had taken the bride's place, knows he is lying, and ended with the jolly Ronde du cliquot. Pinsonnet spent his tenor tones on two solos, whilst the broader comicalities, such as the Chinoiserie 'Je fourre mon nez partout', or Ka-o-lin's dubious explanation of how his calm oriental temperament prevents him getting sexually over-excited, were the province of the two Chinamen.

Played at the Athénée up to the summer break, the show was brought back in the new season, and soon began to make its way both around the country and beyond its confines. However, *Fleur de thé* suffered somewhat in its overseas productions. In England, the Gaiety Theatre took the libretto and decorated its remnants, under the title *Malala* (8 April 1871), with music from the fashionable Offenbach canon instead of that by the unknown Lecocq. The French-speaking part of the population were able to see the piece as it was written later that same year at the Lyceum, but the regular English touring version (ad J H Jarvis) which finally made it to town four years later – after Lecocq had been made famous by *La Fille de Madame Angot* – with a cast headed by Alice Burville and Bessie Sudlow, was a watered-down affair which was even then considered to be too indelicate for polite consumption. Spain didn't worry about the indelicacy. It, too, took the libretto and left behind the music: the *Fior di rosa* produced in Barcelona in 1877 had a score by Galleani.

America, in spite of also getting a successful taste of the original show from Jacob Grau's troupe with Mlle Rizarelli (Fleur de thé) and Marie Desclauzas (Césarine) at its head, and also from Marie Aimée and her company, similarly put out a botched version under the tellingly burlesque title of *The Pearl of Pekin, or the Tar Outwitted by His Wife*. Charles Alfred Byrne laid claim to the libretto, and the remnants of Lecocq's score were heavily adulterated with Gustave Kerker tunelets. Thus remade for general consumption, it was produced on Broadway by E E Rice with Louis Harrison (Tyfoo), Irene Verona (Finette) and Joseph Herbert starred for 67 performances (Bijou Theater 19 March 1888), found considerable popular success on the American touring circuits, and went on to pay several further brief visits to Broadway in the years that followed.

The first German adaptation (ad Ernst Dohm) was seen in Berlin, whilst, in Vienna, F Zell's German version was given a fine Theater an der Wien cast with Karoline Finaly (Theeblütchen), Matthias Rott (Wau-wau), Carl Adolf Friese (Fi-Fi), Albin Swoboda (Pinsonnet) and Fräulein Fischer (Cäsarine) sharing the spotlight with an entr'acte of 'chinesescher Feuer und Waffenspiele' and Auguste Maywood's Chinese ballet (music by Adolf Müller) for 17 performances. Hungary, Russia, South America and, most notably, Scandinavia also welcomed Lecocq's opéra-bouffe, it being maintained in the repertoire in Sweden (*Theblomma*) past the turn of the century, long after Lecocq's later works had displaced it elsewhere.

At the turn of the century, when *A Chinese Honeymoon* became the first musical ever to run 1,000 consecutive performances in London, more than one commentator remarked on the similarity of its plot to the 30-year-old French piece, and one even referred to George Dance's libretto as an adaptation of Chivot and Duru's work. They were, perhaps, not wholly without justification, even if the plot element concerned was only one of several in the English piece, and the characters were wholly (if not nationally) different.

Fleur de thé returned to the Paris stage, first at the Théâtre des Variétés, and subsequently (17 January 1880) at the Bouffes-Parisiens, where Mme Grivot (Césarine), Mlle Burton (Fleur de thé), Paul Hittemans (Tien-Tien) and Léonce, back in his original rôle, led the cast of the now-famous composer's early work through 35 performances.

Germany: Friedrich-Wilhelmstädtisches Theater 13 January 1869; Austria: Theater an der Wien *Theeblüthe* 1 February 1869; USA: Théâtre Français (Fr) 1 February 1869; UK: Lyceum Theatre (Fr) 12 June 1871, Tyne Theatre, Newcastle-upon-Tyne (Eng) 15 March 1875, Criterion Theatre, London 9 October 1875; Hungary: Budai Színkör *Bájviräg* 13 April 1877

FLORA, THE RED MENACE

FLORA, THE RED MENACE Musical in 2 acts by George Abbott and Robert Russell based on the novel *Love is Just Around the Corner* by Lester Atwell. Lyrics by Fred Ebb. Music by John Kander. Alvin Theater, New York, May 11 1965.

Flora, the Red Menace was an unsuccessful 1965 musical (87 performances) which has become fondly remembered in retrospect as having assembled a group of Broadway's most admired talents. Amongst the proven folk were producer Harold Prince and veteran director-cum-co-author George Abbott, amongst those on their way up were songwriters John Kander and Fred Ebb and leading lady Liza Minnelli, better known at that stage as Judy Garland's teenaged daughter than for her own talents.

Fresh out of art school, Flora Mezaros (Miss Minnelli) gets a job at a department store and a fascination with a stuttering artist called Harry Toukarian (Bob Dishy) who is, himself, into communism and sex. Flora tries the communism, turns down the sex but then surprises Harry in the company of the more willing Comrade Charlotte (Cathryn Damon). Comrade Charlotte plants the *Daily Worker* in Flora's locker and she gets the sack but, although Harry clears her and she is reinstated, Flora firmly puts both him and communism behind her as she gets down to beginning her adult life. Dortha Duckworth and James Cresson played a pair of striving performers, and Mary Louise Wilson was the equally, if differently, striving Comrade Ada.

Flora's song 'A Quiet Thing' proved the favourite number from the show's score, a score which was supplemented with four new or old-new numbers when a considerably revised, small-scale version of *Flora, the Red Menace* was produced at the Vineyard Theater in 1987 (6 December) with Veanne Cox and Peter Frechette featured. The libretto (ad David Thompson) was given a major facelift, replacing the original innocence with a 1980s sophistication, the characters largely altered and the point of the piece changed.

UK: Arts Theatre, Cambridge 29 June 1992
Recordings: original cast (RCA Victor), revival cast 1987 (TER)

FLORESTAN 1er, PRINCE DE MONACO

FLORESTAN 1er, PRINCE DE MONACO Opérette in 3 acts by Sacha Guitry. Lyrics by Albert Willemetz. Music by Werner Richard Heymann. Théâtre des Variétés, Paris, 8 December 1933.

An opérette allegedly put together by Guitry around the theme of an article discovered in the *Figaro* which described how the historical Prince Florestan of Monaco (1785–1856), during youthful years passed in Paris following the deposition of his father in the French Revolution, became an actor, playing at 19 the rôle of the King of Prussia. The music for the work was composed by Heymann, best known for his score to the film *Der Kongress tanzt* (1931). With Henri Garat (then, very quickly, René Lestelly), in the rôle of the actor-prince, encouraging everyone to 'Amusez-vous, foutez-vous d'tout', serenading

'Margot', and insisting 'Je l'aime, je l'adore' and 'C'est si charmant', the grossly oversized Pauley as the extravagant and adorable actor Rosambeau singing 'Ah! si j'avais été ténor' and Jacqueline Francell (Mésange) and Geneviève Vix (La Duchesse) at the head of the feminine team, the piece had a fine Paris run under the management of Max Maurey.

FLORODORA

FLORODORA Musical comedy in 2 acts by Owen Hall. Lyrics by Ernest Boyd-Jones and Paul Rubens. Music by Leslie Stuart. Additional songs by Paul Rubens. Lyric Theatre, London, 11 November 1899.

The story goes that actor Ben Nathan and businessman Walter Weill formed a syndicate with the intention of producing a musical comedy. In something of a coup, they signed up Leslie Stuart, the highly successful songwriter, to provide the score and, somewhere along the way, got into cahoots with Tom B Davis, the newly successful producer of *Little Miss Nobody*, who put up half of the finance for the venture, became the show's nominal producer, and provided the services of a younger songwriter, the rising Paul Rubens. History does not relate who booked 'Owen Hall', the most skilful librettist of the era, for the book, but since Hall was perpetually bankrupt and wrote for cash down and no royalties, he was not, in spite of his track record, difficult to hire.

Hall's story was set in the picturesque Philippine Islands where millionaire Cyrus W Gilfain (Charles E Stevens) manufactures the profitable 'Florodora' perfume and simultaneously courts the lovely Dolores (Evie Greene), although she is but a working girl on his land. Dolores, however, loves the overseer Frank Abercoed (Melville Stewart) whom Gilfain had earmarked for his daughter Angela (Kate Cutler) who, in her turn, fancies Captain Arthur Donegal (Edgar Stevens). Gilfain's love is tactical, however, for Dolores is the rightful heir to the whole place, and he knows it. A wandering phrenologist, Tweedlepunch (Willie Edouin), is suborned by the plotting Gilfain to pair off the islanders 'suitably', but Abercoed rebels at this instant and unwanted marriage and leaves the Pacific to head back to his impoverished Welsh seat. Unfortunately for him, Gilfain has just bought his family castle as a British base for 'Florodora' and is busy settling in. However a little bit of ghostly masquerading scares the villain out of his wits and into both a confession and a happy ending.

It was scarcely the most original or well-constructed plot, but it had the merit of being malleable and, in rehearsal, it needed to be. Hall discovered that Ada Reeve was out of a job, having been effectively dropped from George Edwardes's *San Toy* at Daly's, and he offered to write her into *Florodora*. Ada became Lady Holyrood, the latest in Hall's line of brisk, modern society women, so effectively begun by Lottie Venne as Lady Virginia Forrest in *A Gaiety Girl*, and she was woven into the fabric, if scarcely the plot, of the piece.

Some of the songs for *Florodora* were a touch unusual. Stuart wrote many of his melodies rather differently from his contemporaries – with long, almost wandering lines – and his skill at the coon song meant that, alongside more English tones, a whiff of burnt cork sometimes intruded. He forebore to put a blatant coon number into his Philippine Island musical, but turned out several more suitable

Plate 94. **Florodora:** *One of the greatest hits of its era, wherever it went. Australia's production featured George Lauri as the charlatan Tweedlepunch, with the famous double-sextet here as popular as it had been everywhere else.*

songs which were winningly attractive – Angela's lovely long-limbed solo about 'The Fellow Who Might', Dolores's ballad 'The Silver Star of Love' and Abercoed's baritone hymn to 'The Shade of the Palm'. Others were swingingly so, notably Donegal's assertion that 'I Want to Be a Military Man', whilst the late-in-the-day additions for Miss Reeve, written largely by Rubens, were in the almost schoolboy-saucy vein he favoured and which she delivered so well. 'Tact' and 'I've an Inkling' both scored hits. However, the big hit of the show was not a solo but an ensemble. 'Are There Any More at Home Like You?' was, so latter-day rumour says, to have been a duet, but for some reason director/choreographer Sydney Ellison decided to make it up into a double sextet. The Big Six of his front line of chorus girls were paired with six chorus men, elegantly dressed and choreographed into a gently promenading routine to perform the number which quickly became not only the hit of the evening but the most famous single show number of its kind since the celebrated pas de quatre from *Faust Up-to-Date*.

Florodora ran 17 months and 455 performances at the Lyric Theatre. When it was secure as a hit, Davis was able to get such artists as W Louis Bradfield, Florence St John and Decima Moore to take over, whilst Ben Nathan, the initiator of the whole thing, allowed himself on occasions to go on both in the sextet and as Tweedlepunch. The cast changes brought with them new material, and the score of *Florodora* was constantly being updated. None of the replacement songs, however, found the vogue of the original ones.

John C Fisher, John W Dunne and Thomas Ryley produced *Florodora* on Broadway with Edouin repeating his London rôle in the company of his daughter May (Angela), Edna Wallace Hopper (Lady Holyrood), Sydney Deane (Abercoed), Fannie Johnstone (Dolores) and R E Graham (Cyrus). London chorus-boy Harry B Burcher restaged the famous routine, and the production was greeted with an even bigger success than the original had been, with the sextet girls becoming the celebrities of the day. The show ran 379 performances at the Casino Theater, transferred to the New York Theater for a further 122, and reopened the Monday after closing there in another production, with no less than 250 cast members, at the Winter Garden Theater (27 January 1902) for another 48 nights. By the time the show left Broadway it had totalled 549 unbroken performances, and provoked more than its quota of scandals and Broadway lawsuits. In one of these latter, a gent called Jacob Eppinger who had 'loaned' the producers $5,000 claimed he was an investor and sued for a share of the profits, whilst the producers countered that he'd been repaid with interest and was not an investor. But whilst the lawsuits ran on, and both Britain and America welcomed the first of the *Florodora* tours which would continue for many decades to come, the piece continued its way round the world.

In Australia George Lauri (Tweedlepunch), Grace Palotta (Lady Holyrood), Carrie Moore (Dolores), Wallace Brownlow (Abercoed), Charles Kenningham (Donegal, with interpolations), and Maud Chetwynd (Angela) headed the cast of J C Williamson's production to a record-breaking run of 106 performances in Melbourne as *Florodora* became as ingrained in the repertoire there as it was on the other side of the world. Mabel Nelson and Frank Danby headed the South African production to similar triumph, Budapest's Magyar Színház produced a version in Hungarian (ad Adolf Mérei, Dezső Bálint), and in 1903 *Florodora* was mounted at the Théâtre des Bouffes-Parisiens in Paris (ad Adrien Vély, F A Schwab), under the direction of Ellison, with Paulette Darty playing Dolores alongside Piccaluga as Abercoed, Simon-Max as Plum-Quick (Tweedlepunch), Edmond Roze and Mlle Dziri (Lady Holyrood). In 1907 an Italian version was mounted in Milan.

Florodora returned to New York's Broadway Theater on 27 March 1905 for four weeks, and again in 1920 when J J Shubert mounted a major revival with the script updated by Harry B Smith, the score tricked out with some Stuart numbers from his subsequent successes, a cast headed by Eleanor Painter (Dolores), Christie MacDonald (Lady Holyrood), George Hassell (Tweedlepunch) and Walter Woolf (Abercoed), a lavish production, and won a 150-performance run. In London, too, there were revivals, in 1915 and in 1932, but the show's life in Britain continued largely in the provinces. The last touch of *Florodora* to be heard in London, nearly 90 years after its opening, was in the extravaganza *Ziegfeld* which included 'The Fellow Who Might' in its score.

Officially, there was no film made of *Florodora*. However, in 1925 an Australian movie called *Painted Daughters* and boasting a cast of 100 native Australians confided in its advertising that it was 'based on *Florodora*' and Hollywood's 1930 *The Florodora Girl* included a performance of 'Tell Me, Pretty Maiden' alongside filmland's own contribution to the song content: 'Pass the Beer and Pretzels' and 'My Kind of Man'.

USA: Casino Theater 12 November 1900; Australia: Her Majesty's Theatre, Melbourne 15 December 1900; Hungary: Magyar Színház 5 December 1901; France: Théâtre des Bouffes-Parisiens 27 January 1903; Germany: Stadttheater, Leipzig 21 November 1903
Recording: archive compilation of original cast recordings (Opal)

FLORY, Régine [née ARLAZ] (b Marseille, 24 July 1894; d London, 7 June 1926). Dancer turned vocalist and actress who won a feverish following on both sides of the English channel.

Mlle Flory first appeared in Paris in revue at the Théâtre des Capucines. She played the rôle of Chiquette in the metropolitan production of the Marseille musical *La Reine s'amuse* (1913) as a teenager, but made her fame in revue in Paris (Femina, La Cigale etc) and then in London where she featured in *Paris Frissons*, *The Passing Show*, *By Jingo, if We Do ...*, and *Vanity Fair*, and in the revusical musical play *The Beauty Spot*, dancing the Haschisch Dance with Jan Oyra.

Alfred Butt, who had presented her in London, built and opened the Théâtre Mogador in Paris in 1919 and starred her there in *Hullo Paris*, a revue built on the model of the London successes *Hullo Ragtime* and *Hullo Tango*. The show failed and Butt abandoned both the venue and the star. The febrile and highly sexual performer, something of a 'special taste' with that part of the public which championed her, starred in several further revues, and also created leading rôles in two highly successful musical com-

edies, Szulc's *Le Petit Choc* (1923, Féfé Mimosa) and Yvain's *Pas sur la bouche* (1925, Gilberte Valandray) before, after one attempt at drowning herself in the Seine, she turned a gun on herself in Butt's office at the Theatre Royal, Drury Lane.

FLOSSIE Opérette in 3 acts by Marcel Gerbidon. Lyrics by Charles L Pothier. Music by Joseph Szulc. Théâtre des Bouffes-Parisiens, Paris, 9 May 1929.

A successful example of the lightest kind of French 1920s musical comedy, *Flossie* had a book in which the daughters of an English minister and a Swiss pastor swap places and thus find themselves marriage partners. The show featured Jacqueline Francell as the English Flossie ('Je m'appelle Flossie', 'Le Chemin de mon coeur'), Mireille as her Swiss equivalent and René Koval in the chief comic rôle of the Reverend Good-Bye ('Paris'). The show gave producers Quinson and Willemetz a good run both at the Bouffes-Parisiens and as a touring proposition and it still appears occasionally in the French provinces today.

An unsuccessful piece under the same title (Armand Robi/Ralph Murphy) was produced on Broadway in 1924 (Lyric Theater 3 June).

FLOTTE BURSCHE Operette in 1 act by Josef Braun. Music by Franz von Suppé. Theater am Franz-Josefs-Kai, Vienna, 18 April 1863.

One of the most successful of Suppé's early, short Operetten on the French model, *Flotte Bursche* was written whilst the musician was working as musical director and house composer at Karl Treumann's adventurous little Theater am Franz-Josefs-Kai. It proved, both on Treumann's initial production and later, to be one of the most popular of all early Viennese Operetten.

The jolly fellows of the title were the students Brand and Frinke (Anna Grobecker) and the comical Fleck (Treumann) who set out to swindle the miserly pawnbroker Hieronymus Geier out of the 500 thalers he is illegally withholding from poor Anton. Brand dresses up as an Italian painter and offers the pawnbroker an old picture. When two Englishmen – the disguised Frinke and Fleck – go into ecstasies over it and offer to buy it for 1,000 thalers, Geier hurriedly buys the worthless canvas for 700. Anton now has enough cash to wed his Lieschen and there is a bit over for jollity.

The score of the show consisted of an overture (as in so many cases with Suppé, the piece which has survived the best) and nine numbers. Frinke opened proceedings with his 'Aus dem Federn auf ihr Hechten', Fleck delivered a long comic tenor piece as an entrance song and Brand introduced an Italian-style arietta with florid passages, whilst the student song 'Gaudeamus igitur' was introduced into a first act-quartet and served again as the Schluss-gesang to the show. The disguised English pair had the evening's best fun, indulging in a cod-English duettino which gabbled 'Bless my dear, how the sun is shining, what's o'clock, at four jam dining, English Lord, English Word, English dog, English fog, Oh Cheer old England cheer'.

Flotte Bursche was played 31 times in the less than two months between its production and the destruction by fire of the Kai-Theater, and when Treumann took up at the

Carltheater two months later, Suppé's Operette was played on the opening bill (19 August 1863). It remained a regular part of the repertoire, with Wilhelm Knaack (Geier) Hermine Meyerhoff (Lieschen), Josef Matras (Fleck), Grobecker (Frinke) and Rosa Streitmann (Brand) amongst the casts which gave the piece a good dozen showings in 1869, 11 in 1870, eight in 1871, three in 1872, eight in 1873 and a handful more each year through the 1870s, whilst also putting in isolated appearances at other Vienna houses (Theater an der Wien 26 October 1863 etc).

Flotte Bursche was picked up in other Central European and Scandinavian countries, notably in Germany and in Hungary where it was played first in German and then in Hungarian (ad Endre Latabár). It was seen at the Budai Színkör in both languages in 1867 and taken into the repertoire at the Népszinház in 1877. The show returned periodically to the Viennese stage in the 20th century, being seen at the Carltheater in 1903 in a double bill with Offenbach's *Salon Pitzelberger* and again in 1911, at the Theater an der Wien in 1914 paired with *Leichte Kavallerie*, and at the Redoutensaal in 1931 (26 December).

Although translated into several other European languages, the show did not penetrate the French or English-speaking theatre and the only performances seen in New York were in the German theatres, the first being in 1867 with the dwarves Jean Petit (Geier), Jean Piccolo (Fleck) and Józsi Kiss (Anton) cast alongside full-sized women as Brand, Frincke and Lieschen. Later performances were more conventional.

Hungary: (Ger) July 1863, Budai Színkör *A pajkos diákok* 15 May 1867; Germany: Friedrich-Wilhelmstädtisches Theater 3 December 1863; USA: Stadttheater (Ger) 25 October 1867

FLOWER DRUM SONG   Musical in 2 acts by Oscar Hammerstein II and Joseph Fields based on the novel by C Y Lee. Lyrics by Oscar Hammerstein II. Music by Richard Rodgers. St James Theater, New York, 1 December 1958.

Although successful on both the American and British stage, and the source of one distinctly popular song and of a Hollywood film, Rodgers and Hammerstein's musical *Flower Drum Song* has never attained the same classic status in the public or professional mind as their, admittedly very much more successful, *The Sound of Music*, *South Pacific*, *The King and I*, *Oklahoma!* and *Carousel*.

Librettist Joseph Fields winkled out *Flower Drum Song*, C Y Lee's novel about the generation gap in the Chinese-American community, purchased the dramatic rights, and presented it to the songwriters as a possible basis for a musical. The authors themselves produced the resultant piece with song-and-dance man Gene Kelly taking on the task of directing. The story of the show, with its arranged marriage theme and its hundred-time used veiled wedding trick, had more than a little flavour of the turn-of-the-century comic opera, but *Flower Drum Song* was set firmly in the present and the tone of the piece was almost wholly a romantic, rather than a comic, one.

San Francisco bar-owner Sammy Fong (Larry Blyden) has been betrothed to Mei Li (Miyoshi Umeki), who has been sent from China for the marriage, but his tastes run rather to the nightclub stripper, Linda Low (Pat Suzuki). Determined to free himself from his obligations to Mei Li's family, Sammy sets himself to find a replacement bridegroom for her, and he chooses Wang Ta (Ed Ken-

ney), the son of the wholly traditional Wang Chi Yang (Keye Luke), who is more or less engaged to Linda. Sammy arranges for the elder Wang and his sister-in-law Madame Liang (Juanita Hall) to see Linda at work, and the damage is done. By the time that Linda and Sammy have got themselves engaged, and Wang Ta has switched his preference to Mei Li, it is too late: the elders of the community have decided that Sammy must honour his contract. The wedding goes ahead but, of course, when Sammy lifts his bride's veil he finds not Mei Li but Linda, who, in the best tradition of *The Sultan of Mocha*, *The Geisha* or *A Chinese Honeymoon*, has taken her place.

The score to the show included some attractive numbers – the gentle 'A Hundred Million Miracles', Wang Ta's ballad 'You Are Beautiful', addressed not to either girl but explaining to his aunt what he would say when the occasion arises, and the sad 'Love, Look Away' of the shoulder-to-cry-on Helen (Arabella Hong), but it was a more up-beat piece, Linda's bouncing declaration that 'I Enjoy Being a Girl', which proved to be the most enduring piece outside the show. It made its way into cabaret and variety acts around the world, and for many years became the favourite musical-comedy audition song for actresses attempting to cover vocal limitations with a wash of 'personality'.

Broadway's production of *Flower Drum Song* was played 600 times, and the authors (Williamson Music Ltd) also sponsored London's version in which Tim Herbert (Sammy), Kevin Scott (Wang Ta), Yau Shan Tung (Mei Li) and Yama Saki (Linda) featured for a good run of 464 performances, but in spite of this the show apparently went no further in its stage form. Wider viewing was left to the cinema.

In 1961 a film version was made, in which Miss Umeki and Miss Hall repeated their original rôles alongside Nancy Kwan (Linda, dubbed by B J Baker) and James Shigeta. 'Love, Look Away' was dubbed by the young singer Marilyn Horne.

UK: Palace Theatre, London 24 March 1960; Film: Universal 1961
Recordings: original cast (Columbia); London cast (HMV); Film soundtrack (Decca) etc

FLUP..!   Opérette in 3 acts by Gaston Dumestre. Music by Joseph Szulc. Théâtre de l'Alhambra, Brussels, 19 December 1913.

The Belgian production of *Flup..!*, staged under the management of Paul Clerget, introduced the Polish-born composer Szulc to the musical theatre where, in the years after the war, he was to have a prominent Parisian career. At this time, however, he was sufficiently ill-known as to be billed in the Alhambra's programme as Joseph Szule. Although the show's title had the ring of a post-war musical comedy to it, the curious word was, in fact, the name of the comic sub-hero of the piece, one Antonin Flup, a part created in Brussels by the young, rising (and very fourth-billed) André Urban.

Set amongst the colonial British on the island of Ceylon, with a suffragette heroine (Germaine Huber) and an amorous French aristocrat (Charles Casella) as hero, the show followed the comical events that occur when a French railway porter (Urban) is – in the place of the aristocrat – put in charge of the social affairs of the colony of Kandy, whilst the real Duke works his way, incognito, around to marriage with the staunchly feminist Maud. Camus appeared as Lord Archibald, the Governor of Kandy, Hélène Gérard was Edith Smithson, the vice-president of the London suffragette movement, and Mme Lepers played Mrs Flatwell, a suffragette with intentions towards what she does not suspect is a phoney 'Duke'.

The wilfully topical text was paired with a score which also introduced the first feelings of the new age. The predominant waltz and march rhythms – Maud sang waltzes when being herself, and marches when being a suffragette – were varied by such 'coming' dances as the tango (which was, nevertheless, followed immediately by a more conventional 'ballet Hindoue').

When *Flup..!* finally made its way to Paris and Mme Rasimi's Théâtre Ba-ta-clan after the First World War, the title-rôle was taken by top comedian Dranem, starred alongside Henri Defreyn (Duc de Florigny) and Maguy Warna (Maud Archibald), and supported by Saulieu (Archibald), Anne Martens (Edith) and Mary Théry (Mme Flatwell). The show scored a fine success, and was both toured and later twice revived in Paris.

Some of Szulc's music for *Flup..!* was pirated by Carlo Lombardo for the patchwork pilfered score of the successful Italian musical *Madama di Tebe*.

France: Théâtre des Célestins, Lyon 1917, Théâtre Ba-ta-clan, Paris, 18 March 1920

FÖLDES, Imre (b Kaposvár, 15 September 1881; d Budapest, 30 April 1958).

Internationally successful Hungarian playwright, (*A császár katonái, Hivatalnok urak, Hallo!, Vörös szegfű*, the hugely successful *Grün Lili* etc), Földes ventured rarely into the musical field, yet in those rare ventures produced the texts for three widely played operetts. Ákos Buttykay's *Az ezüst sirály* was played in Germany and Austria as *Liebesrausch* and was also apparently seen in America, whilst Paul Ábrahám's two most popular Operetten, *Viktória* (*Viktoria and Her Hussar*) and *Die Blume von Hawaii*, both of which he authored, won productions throughout the world and remain in the European repertoire today.

1905 **Két Hippolit** (Iván Hüvös) Népszinház 13 January
1920 **Az ezüst sirály** (Ákos Buttykay) Városi Színház 6 February
1922 **Olivia hercegnő** (Buttykay/Miksa Bródy) Fővárosi Operettszinház 23 December
1925 **Die blonde Sphinx** (Max Niederberger/ad Gustav Beer) Bürgertheater, Vienna 27 March
1930 **Viktória** (Pál Ábrahám/Imre Harmath) Király Színház 21 February
1931 **Die Blume von Hawaii** (Ábrahám/Harmath/w Grünwald, Löhner-Beda) Neues Theater, Leipzig 24 July
1946 **Fekete liliom** (Egon Kemény/w Károly Nóti) Fővárosi Operettszinház 20 December

FOLLIES Broadway legend in 2 acts by James Goldman. Music and lyrics by Stephen Sondheim. Winter Garden Theater, New York, 4 April 1971.

Built on somewhat the same kind of framework as Sondheim's successful *Company*, *Follies* similarly brought together a group of people for an occasion and then proceeded to peer into their lives. However, if *Company*'s people were a group of reasonably common-or-garden, middle-ageing New Yorkers with mostly normal-sized neuroses and personalities, those of *Follies* were anything but.

The occasion which brings the *Follies* folk together is, not unsuitably, a destruction. The theatre in which they performed as members of Weissman's Follies in their younger days is being pulled down, and Mr Weissman is giving it a wake to which several decades of the now ageing or, indeed, positively aged artistes are invited. Many of them flit briefly through the party and across the stage, their characters encapsulated in a song or a few lines, and the main focus falls on two of the less elderly ex-chorines, former best-friends Sally (Dorothy Collins) and Phyllis (Alexis Smith), who married their stage-door Johnnies and went different ways. Sally and Buddy (Gene Nelson) have a comfortable, unhappy small-town existence, whilst Phyllis and her successful businessman husband Ben (John McMartin) have an equally dissatisfied brittle-plastic, New York-stylish life. Both women – for it is the women who are the real centre of attention – are, under dissimilar façades, wallowing in more neuroses and discontent than could be justified by the worst misfortune.

The entertainment moves, first, into a flashback, showing the foursome in their young days, and introducing a whiff of the infidelity which is apparently responsible for a half-ton of the neuroses, and then into a stylized *Follies*-style series of routines in which their emotions are expressed in the exaggerated showbizzy tones of everything from torch-song and soft-shoe to low vaudeville comedy. When the four have finished having a wonderful, theatrical time mildly torturing themselves and each other with accusations of infidelities and insufficiencies ancient and modern, the party comes to an end and they head home to carry on their miserable lives.

The score of *Follies* produced a number of attractive and successful songs, written in the wide range of theatrical styles covered by its characters. Sally's powerful, self-lacerating number from the *Follies* sequence, 'Losing My Mind', went on to become a torch-singer's favourite, whilst the crackling, comical musical biography of the faded film actress Carlotta Campion (Yvonne de Carlo), 'I'm Still Here', became the century's anthem for all Carlotta's real-life equivalents and wannabes, and a cabaret standard. The vacuously satirical squeakings of an elderly 'Broadway Baby' (Ethel Shutta) also took the same trip, but like the over-the-top torch song, normally sung straight instead of tongue-in-cheek. However, some of the less larger-than-life pieces showed up more effectively than the take-out tunes in the show itself – the dainty performance of an ageing team of song-and-dance sweethearts ('Rain on the Roof'), the voice of the old Viennese soprano blending touchingly with the sounds of her young self in 'One More Kiss', the cheerfully gutsy sound of an old featured artist leading a half-remembered dance routine ('Who's That Woman?') or the still-tenor tones of the front-man Roscoe, announcing his 'Beautiful Girls' once more, were contrasted with some fresher singing from the four young folk ('Waiting for the Girls Upstairs', 'You're Gonna Love Tomorrow', 'Love Will See Us Through'), and with the bitter self-searching of the four principals, which was given an almost comical face in Buddy's Blues ('I've got those God-why-don't-you-love-me-oh-you-do-I'll-see-you-later-blues ...') or a taunting, sarcastic one in Phyllis's self-centred spiking of her husband, 'Could I Leave You?'.

Harold Prince's original production of *Follies* played 522 performances on Broadway without somehow registering in public or professional eyes as a success and, although the songs won Sondheim a Tony Award in a season where *Two Gentlemen of Verona* topped the Best Musical category, even the songs took their time to take off as favourites. They were materially helped, particularly outside America, by their exposure in the compilation revue *Side by Side by Sondheim*; Julia McKenzie's pianissimo 'Broadway Baby' and Millicent Martin's husky 'I'm Still Here' were responsible for making the numbers popular in Britain. The show itself won a boost from a highly cast concert performance at New York's Avery Fisher Hall in 1985.

Finally, carried on the increasing wave of Sondheimania in British theatre circles, *Follies* was produced in Britain in 1985, 17 years after its Broadway première, at Manchester's Wythenshawe Forum with Josephine Blake, Kevin Colson and Mary Miller in its lead rôles. It was subsequently given a London showing under the management of Cameron Mackintosh. The show was revised for the occasion, and several numbers replaced, mostly to good effect. Julia McKenzie (Sally), Diana Rigg (Phyllis), Daniel Massey (Ben) and David Healy (Buddy) played the four central characters whilst such popular British performers of yesteryear as soprano Adele Leigh and duo vocalists Pearl Carr and Teddy Johnson supported alongside London's original *Annie Get Your Gun* star, Dolores Gray. The production ran, like the first, for 522 performances without, once again, wholly convincing, and rumours of a return to Broadway had no tomorrow.

A German version (ad Michael Kunze) was produced in 1991 with Fritz Hille (Ben), Heinz Rennhack (Buddy), Australian Gaye MacFarlane (Sally), Daniela Ziegler (Phyllis), a list of well-known names in the supporting rôles which included Renate Holm (Heidi), Eartha Kitt (Carlotta), Brigitte Mira (Hattie) and with the rôle of Stella turned into two people – Ella and Stella – to feature the Kessler twins.

UK: Forum, Wythenshawe, Manchester 30 April 1985; Shaftesbury Theatre (revised version) 21 July 1987; Germany: Theater des Westens 27 September 1991

Recordings: original cast (Capitol), concert 1985 (RCA), London cast 1987 (First Night)

FOLLOW A STAR Musical comedy in 2 acts by Douglas Furber and Dion Titheradge. Music by Vivian Ellis. Additional songs by Jack Yellen and Ted Shapiro. Winter Garden, London, 17 September 1930.

A made-to-measure vehicle for cabaret singer Sophie Tucker, here cast in a minimal plot as a cabaret singer. Miss Tucker interpolated songs old and new into Ellis's score, but did best with his 'If Your Kisses Can't Hold the Man You Love (then your tears won't bring him back)'. With its star proving less 'red-hot' than might have been hoped, the show ran out 118 performances, dying on its feet when Miss Tucker left and the lead rôle was revamped for comedienne Maisie Gay.

Recording: selection (part-record) (AJA)

FOLLOW THAT GIRL Musical in 2 acts by Julian Slade and Dorothy Reynolds, based on their revue *Christmas in King Street*. Music by Julian Slade. Vaudeville Theatre, London, 17 March 1960.

Following their great success with *Salad Days* and another, lesser, with *Free as Air*, Slade and Reynolds

revamped the Bristol Old Vic revue which had been their first collaboration as a musical. In a plot which neatly spoofed Victorian musical comedy, Victoria (Susan Hampshire) was pursued round the sights of London by worried parents and suitors, an amorous policeman (Peter Gilmore) and a collection of interested Londoners, to some of Slade's best songs, including a lilting title number and an hilarious duo for two suitors who are anxious not to be forced into unattractive mourning. In spite of its attractions, the show had but a six months West End run (211 performances), and did not follow *Salad Days* to international stages.

Recording: original cast (HMV)

FOLLOW THE GIRLS Musical comedy in 2 acts by Guy Bolton, Eddie Davis and Fred Thompson. Lyrics by Dan Shapiro and Milton Pascal. Music by Philip Charig. Century Theater, New York, 8 April 1944.

Bolton and Thompson, who had been responsible in the 1910s and thereafter for a number of tightly constructed farcical libretti for the musical comedy stage, here turned out a sprawling piece of wartime foolery as the basis for a musical which was not far distant from being a variety show, and, with a little help from the war, scored one of their longest-running successes.

Follow the Girls featured nightclub vocalist Gertrude Niesen as Bubbles La Marr from burlesque, at the head of a large line of scantily-clad chorines, and comedian Jackie Gleason as Goofy Gale, who had to imitate one of them to follow her into action when she takes over the running of the soldiers' Spotlight Canteen in Great Neck, Long Island. Ballerina Irina Baronova featured as Anna Viskinova, and the score was topped by Miss Niesen's suggestive 'I Wanna Get Married'. The logically titled 'Today Will Be Yesterday Tomorrow', 'Your Perf', 'I'm Gonna Hang my Hat', 'Twelve O'Clock and All is Well' and an encouraging title-song were amongst the other musical moments of the evening.

Given the boost which wartime always seems to give to comfortably old-fashioned and picturesque entertainments, *Follow the Girls* played for no less than 882 performances at the Century and the 44th Street (12 June 1944) Theaters, and compounded its hometown success by going on, almost simultaneously, to both Australia and to London, when the helpful war was over. It turned out to be a hit all over again at London's His Majesty's Theatre with Arthur Askey heading the comedy, Evelyn Dall the nightclub glamour and Wendy Toye playing a person called Betty Deleaninnion in place of Baronova's more Russian dancer through 572 performances, and it had an agreeable run of almost four months in Sydney and nearly three in Melbourne (Her Majesty's Theatre 15 February 1947) with Don Nicol and Lois Green heading the cast.

Australia: Theatre Royal, Sydney 12 October 1946; UK: His Majesty's Theatre 25 October 1946

FOLLOW THRU Musical slice of country club life in 2 acts by Laurence Schwab and B G De Sylva. Lyrics by B G De Sylva and Lew Brown. Music by Ray Henderson. 46th Street Theater, New York, 9 January 1929.

De Sylva, Brown and Henderson, having mounted successful musical shows with footballing and boxing themes, switched to golf as the sporting element in their next musical, *Follow Thru*, and repeated that success all over again.

Lora Moore (Irene Delroy) and Ruth van Horn (Madeleine Cameron) are both in the running for the ladies' golf championship of the Bound Brook Country Club, and also for the affections of top golfer Jerry Downs (John Barker). Since Lora has and holds the latter, by musical comedy law she is quite, quite certain also to win the former. The light comedy folk were the demure Jack Martin (Jack Haley) and the very much less than demure Angie Howard (Zelma O'Neal).

The songs for *Follow Thru* included one which would become a standard, as Miss O'Neal (who had already made a hit with the team's 'Varsity Drag' in *Good News*) joined with Haley in the naïvely cute 'Button Up Your Overcoat'. Barker sang romantically of 'My Lucky Star' and joined his girl to query 'You Wouldn't Fool Me, Would You?', Miss Cameron gave out with the title-song and assured of the hero that 'He's a Man's Man', and Miss O'Neal insisted 'I Want to Be Bad'.

Schwab and Mandel's production of *Follow Thru* – well in the most modern style ('gymnastic dancing, agreeable songs, funny lines and the pace that kills everyone except musical comedy folk ... a frenzied, sufficiently original carnival') – gave them a splendid Broadway run of 403 performances and, as the show continued its run, Firth Shephard and Leslie Henson took up the piece for a London presentation at the large Dominion Theatre. Henson himself took the rôle created by Haley, giving it a rather different comic aspect, and paired himself with the American comedienne Ada May, whilst the personable Bernard Clifton played the male part of the prize sought by Ivy Tresmand and Elsie Randolph. However, in spite of the popularity of De Sylva, Brown and Henderson's songs in Britain, their shows – even with a star name like Henson attached to them – could never get off the ground there. *Follow Thru* did a little better than *Good News*, a little less well than *Hold Everything!* and, in the end, lasted only 148 performances. It proved even more disappointing in Australia where Gus Bluett appeared in the lead comedy rôle alongside Molly Fisher (Lora), Madge Aubrey, Cecil Kellaway, Robert Purdie and Michael Cole, folding in five weeks at Melbourne's Theatre Royal.

A film version of the show was produced in Hollywood in 1930 in which Haley and Miss O'Neal repeated their original rôles alongside Nancy Carroll and Charles 'Buddy' Rogers.

UK: Dominion Theatre 3 October 1929; Australia: Theatre Royal, Melbourne 8 February 1930; Film: Paramount 1930.

LES FORAINS Opérette in 3 acts by Maxime Boucheron and Antony Mars. Music by Louis Varney. Théâtre des Bouffes-Parisiens, Paris, 9 February 1894.

A musical play about sideshow folk, *Les Forains* centred on the family of the famous wrestler Toulouse (Bartel) whose daughter and star attraction, Olympia (Juliette Simon-Girard), is wed to the lion-tamer, Jules César (Charles Lamy). Unfortunately, between the civil ceremony and the wedding night, Olympia discovers that Jules César's lions are as tame as lambs and she goes right off him. Then the amateur strong-man Paul Vaubert (Félix Huguenet) declares his love, and proves it by defeating

Toulouse for the first time ever – the qualification for an ideal man his daughter had given up hope of finding. Olympia runs away with Paul and his friends Gaillac (Leriche) and Valpurgis (Dupré) and they tour Europe for two months as an act – with Olympia keeping Paul at a correct distance – before they come upon Toulouse's troupe. When Jules César turns on his strong-woman wife and wallops her, she decides to come home. Mariette Sully was Olympia's un-strong sister, Clorinde, in love with Paul throughout, and Rosine Maurel featured as a comical fortune-teller. The play, which gave a number of opportunities for wrestling-matches, weight-lifting, acrobatics and other feats, was decorated by a slim Varney score, largely for the benefit of the two girls.

Eugène Larcher's production of *Les Forains* played for 73 performances at the Bouffes-Parisiens, and the show was adjudged to share with *L'Enlèvement de la Toledad* the honours of the year's musical stage in Paris. It was featured in that year's Monte Carlo season, played through the provinces and, although it did not ultimately prove particularly enduring thereafter, it nevertheless got a good first-round coverage throughout Europe. Berlin's Theater Unter den Linden produced a version by Louis Herrmann and Julius Freund later the same year, as *Der Gaukler*, and Karl Blasel mounted another version (ad Theodor Taube) at the Vienna Carltheater, with Julie Kopácsi-Karczag starring as Olympia 'the muscle-Venus' and himself as Toulouse, for 28 performances. The Budapest Népszinház followed three seasons later with an Hungarian version (ad Emil Makai) which was played ten times.

Germany: Theater Unter der Linden *Der Gaukler* 10 November 1894; Austria: Carltheater *Olympia (die Muskelvenus)* 2 March 1895; Hungary: Népszinház *Komediások* 30 September 1898

FORD, Helen [née BARNETT, Helen Isabel] (b Troy, NY, 6 June 1897; d Glendale, Calif, 19 January 1982).

First seen on Broadway as a replacement in the 1919 production of *Sometime*, pretty, little Mrs Ford followed up in ingénue rôles in several Broadway musicals, appearing as Toinette Fontaine in *Always You* (1920, ex-*Joan of Arkansaw*), as Natalie Blythe in *The Sweetheart Shop* (1920), and as Marjorie Leeds in *For Goodness' Sake* (1922). She stuck with the slow-growing *A Man of Affairs* as it turned into *Love and Kisses* and, finally, into a success as *The Gingham Girl* (1922, Mary Thompson), took the title-rôle in the less-than-successful *Helen of Troy, New York* (who was not, apart from Mrs Ford's presence, a descendant of *Joan of Ark-ansaw*), and was Hope Franklin in another indifferent piece, *No Other Girl*. Patience was in evidence again when she stuck with another slow-moving project and reaped the reward of a fine run and a hit song ('Here in My Arms') as Betsy Burke, the heroine of Rodgers and Hart's *Dearest Enemy* (1925), produced by her husband, George Ford. She followed up with two other starring rôles in Rodgers and Hart shows: the title-rôles of *Peggy-Ann* (1926) and of the short-lived *Chee-Chee* (1928).

She returned to Broadway to appear as Adele in the version of *Die Fledermaus* known as *Champagne Sec* in 1933, and made a last Broadway musical appearance in the failed *Great Lady* in 1938. An underpowered attempt to launch an English-language version of Guitry's *Mariette*, with Mrs Ford in the lead, failed to make it to town.

FORD, Nancy   (b New York, 1 October 1935).

The composer of several off-Broadway musicals, in a collaboration with author Gretchen Cryer which had begun in University days, Ford had a first success with *The Last Sweet Days of Isaac* and major one with the long-running *I'm Getting My Act Together and Taking it on the Road* (1978). During the run of the show, she succeeded to the show's central rôle. She also supplied music to the revues *Hang on to the Good Times* (1985) and *Cut the Ribbons* (1992).

Cryer and Ford have also appeared performing their own material and on record.

1967 **Now is the Time for All Good Men** (aka *Grass Roots*) (Gretchen Cryer) Theater de Lys 26 September
1970 **The Last Sweet Days of Isaac** (Cryer) Eastside Playhouse 26 January
1973 **Shelter** (Cryer) John Golden Theater 6 February
1978 **I'm Getting My Act Together and Taking it on the Road** (Cryer) Public Theater 14 June, Circle in the Square 16 December

FOR GOODNESS' SAKE   Musical comedy in 2 acts by Frederick Jackson. Music by William Daly and Paul Lannin. Lyric Theater, New York, 20 February 1922.

The production of the musical comedy *For Goodness' Sake* was an occasion where a show made up of very limited material was turned into a singular success by the performance it was given. Frederick Jackson's story turned on one of those overly suspicious wives who, thinking her husband unfaithful, decides on a fling of her own. He fakes suicide in response, and so it continues up to a reconciliatory final curtain, accompanied by some functional songs, two of which were interpolations by the Gershwin brothers.

Comedian John E Hazzard (Perry Reynolds) and Marjorie Gateson (Vivian Reynolds) as the couple in question had to give best to the young second leads – the dance team of Fred and Adele Astaire (Teddy Lawrence and Susan Hayden) who, with the aid of some lively Teddy Royce choreography, won the plaudits for 103 performances. The next year, producer Alex Aarons whisked the show – now more provocatively retitled *Stop Flirting*, but with Perry Renolds (Jack Melford) and Vivian Marsden (Marjorie Gordon) listed as 'fiancés' instead of being married – and his light-footed stars off to London. There, he allied himself with London producers George Grossmith and J A E Malone, and theatre-manager Alfred Butt. The show's score of eight numbers, two openings and two finales was tactfully lifted by the insertion of an additional 'additional number by George Gershwin', 'Stairway to Paradise' (*George White's Scandals of 1922*), and Aarons and the Astaires repeated their American success in a broken run of 224 performances in three separate London theatres (Shaftesbury Theatre, Queens Theatre 28 July, Strand Theatre 22 October). A revival, mounted the following year (28 March 1924) added another 194 performances to the show's career and Florence Bayfield and Gerald Seymour deputized for the Astaires in a touring version of a show which its stars had well and truly established. *Stop Flirting* could still be seen on the English provincial stage in 1926 when *For Goodness' Sake* had long disappeared in America.

UK: Shaftesbury Theatre *Stop Flirting* 30 May 1923

FORREST, George   [CHICHESTER, George Forrest jr] (b Brooklyn, NY, 31 July 1915).

Forrest began a career-long partnership with fellow musician and lyricist Robert Wright whilst the two were still in their teens. In 1936 they were employed on the music staff at MGM studios, writing and/or adapting music and lyrics for a series of films which in the years that followed included cinema adaptations of *Maytime* (1937), *The Firefly* (1937), *Sweethearts* (1938), *Balalaika* (1939) and *I Married an Angel* (1942). They scored a standard with the song 'The Donkey Serenade', created from a Friml instrumental melody for *The Firefly*, and collaborated with Herbert Stothart on 'Ride, Cossack, Ride' (*Balalaika*) and on several new numbers for *I Married an Angel*. The song 'It's a Blue World', as sung by Tony Martin in *Music in My Heart*, won them one of their three Academy Award nominations.

The team's earliest theatre work consisted of similar rewrites and additions for revivals of musical shows of the past, but also of two original pieces produced at the Hollywood Playhouse in the early 1940s. Their first major musical credit, however, came with the production of *Song of Norway*, a *Dreimäderlhaus*-type treatment of the life and works of Norwegian composer Edvard Grieg, mounted by Edwin Lester in California. With a score, including 'Freddy and His Fiddle' and 'Strange Music', fabricated by Wright and Forrest from a range of Grieg melodies, *Song of Norway* went east to find success on Broadway and subsequently around the world.

An original musical, *Spring in Brazil*, produced the following year with Milton Berle starring, did not find success, but another Lester production, *Gypsy Lady*, a musical remoulding of Victor Herbert's lyrical scores for *The Fortune Teller* and *The Serenade*, was sufficiently well thought of to be taken both to New York and to London (as *Romany Love*).

The partners wrote the lyrics to Villa Lobos's score for *Magdalena*, a show which aroused considerable interest but ultimately failed, and Johann Strauss was given the *Dreimäderlhaus* treatment in *The Great Waltz*, before Wright and Forrest brought out their greatest success: an adaptation of the music of Borodin as an accompaniment to Eddie Knoblock's Oriental comedy classic *Kismet* ('The Olive Tree', 'Stranger in Paradise', 'And This is My Beloved', 'Not Since Nineveh', 'Baubles, Bangles and Beads'). Following long runs on Broadway (Tony Award) and in London, *Kismet* established itself as one of the all-time classics of the American operetta stage.

Wright and Forrest's subsequent musicals did not find the same success. They tackled Molière with *The Carefree Heart*, Vicki Baum's famous novel and film *Grand Hotel* in *At the Grand*, and the French play *Kean*, each with original scores, before turning to further musical collages, one based on the works of Rachmaninov, as the musical illustration to a version of the *Anastasia* story, another on Saint-Saëns as the musical part of the story of *Dumas and Son*. However, *The Great Waltz*, a second attempt at the Strauss story, based on the Viennese success *Walzer aus Wien*, proved altogether more successful than the first and resulted both in a long-running London production and a new 1972 film version.

Another second-time-round production gave the partnership one further satisfaction, at least from a financial point of view. Their *At the Grand* was revised and remounted in 1989, under the title *Grand Hotel*, but alterations and interpolations made by the producers on the road rendered the show a rather different piece by the time it reached New York. In spite of poor notices, it glitzed itself into a good run, nearly half a century after its originators' first success on Broadway.

1940 **Thank You, Columbus** (w Robert Wright) Hollywood Playhouse 15 November

1941 **Fun for the Money** (w Wright) Hollywood Playhouse August

1944 **Song of Norway** (Edvard Grieg ad w Wright/Milton Lazarus) Imperial Theater 21 August

1945 **Spring in Brazil** (w Wright/Philip Rapp) Shubert Theater, Boston 1 October

1946 **Gypsy Lady** (Victor Herbert ad w Wright/Henry Myers) Century Theater 17 September

1948 **Magdalena** (Villa Lobos/w Wright/Frederick Hazlitt Brennan, Homer Curran) Ziegfeld Theater 20 September

1949 **The Great Waltz** (*Walzer aus Wien*) new English adaptation w Wright (Curran Theater, San Francisco)

1953 **Kismet** (Borodin ad w Wright/Charles Lederer, Luther Davis) Ziegfeld Theater 3 December

1957 **The Carefree Heart** (aka *The Love Doctor*) (w Wright) Cass Theater, Detroit 30 September

1958 **At the Grand** (w Wright/Luther Davis) Philharmonic Theater, Los Angeles 7 July

1961 **Kean** (w Wright/Peter Stone) Broadway Theater 2 November

1965 **The Great Waltz** (*Walzer aus Wien*) new adaptation w Wright, Jerome Chodorov, Moss Hart, Lazarus San Francisco 14 September

1965 **Anya** (Rachmaninov ad w Wright/George Abbott, Guy Bolton) Ziegfeld Theater 29 November

1967 **Dumas and Son** (Camille Saint-Saëns ad w Wright/Chodorov) Dorothy Chandler Pavilion, Los Angeles 1 August

1972 **A Song for Cyrano** (w Wright/José Ferrer) Pocono Playhouse, Pa 4 September

1978 **Timbuktu!** revised *Kismet* ad Luther Davis Mark Hellinger Theater 1 March

1989 **Grand Hotel** revised *At the Grand* (w Maury Yeston/Davis) Martin Beck Theater 12 November

DIE FÖRSTER-CHRISTL
Operette in 3 acts by Bernhard Buchbinder. Music by Georg Jarno. Theater in der Josefstadt, Vienna, 17 December 1907.

Jarno's most popular Operette was set to a libretto which was one of those allegedly based on a true event, but no less thoroughly and conventionally operettic for all that.

Christl (Hansi Niese), the forester's daughter, travels from her home in the Hungarian borderlands to Vienna to beg the Kaiser, Josef II (Robert Valberg), to intercede on behalf of her lover, Franz Földessy (Kurt von Lessen), the steward to the Sternfeld estates, who has been exposed as a deserter who killed his vicious lieutenant. When feelings of love spring up between the Kaiser and the country girl, he pushes them dutifully aside and Christl goes home to her soldier. The other principal characters were the Graf Sternfeld (Louis Ralph/Alexander Beer) and his sister, the Komtesse Josefine (Betty Myra/Isa Karoly), Christl's comical suitor, Imperial tailor Peter Walperl (Max Pallenberg/Franz Stenger), the gipsy girl Minka (Käthe Krem/Hansi Reichsberg), and the courtly grande dame Baronesse Agathe von Othegraven (Viktoria Pohl-Meiser).

The show was produced in Vienna with Niese, the wife of the composer's brother Josef (himself the manager of the Theater in der Josefstadt), and the city's most popular soubrette, starring and it was an enormous success. Christl's entrance number, 'Der Christl aus dem Wiener-Wald', her detailing of how she will approach the Emperor ('Herr Kaiser, Herr Kaiser'), the waltz song 'Gebt mir die Geigen der ganzen Welt', the lusty Hungarian-flavoured ensemble 'Steht ein Mädel auf der Puszta' and Josefine and Minka's duo Ziegeuner-Marsch ('Heissa, Heissa, ihr Mädel seid bereit') were the musical highlights of an evening which, just occasionally, recalled the very special folksy simplicity of *Der Vogelhändler*, here given a dash of Hungarian spice. The rôle of the Kaiser was a non-singing one.

In spite of being produced in the same year as *Ein Walzertraum* and *Die Dollarprinzessin*, *Die Förster-Christl* ran for an excellent 62 nights at the Josefstadter Theater before being transferred to Jarno's Lustspiel Theater to carry on its run. It passed its 100th performance there in May 1908. Continually played in and out of Vienna thereafter, the show was taken in to the repertoire at the Johann Strauss-Theater on 22 December 1912 with Otto Storm and Mimi Marlow, and given further performances there with Eugene Jensen and Lisl Kurt during the run of *Der Zigeunerprimás* (1912–13), in 1914 with Fritz Schonhof and Else Adler, again with Frln Marlow. It remained steadily in the theatre's repertoire until 1925, passing its 700th performance on 2 February 1924 with Raoul Aslan and Maria Escher featured. It was revived again in Vienna in 1945.

Die Förster-Christl became one of the most popular Viennese shows of its particularly fertile decade. Its Viennese triumph was repeated in Germany, where a run at the Berliner Theater was prelude to a vast number of provincial productions (the show rates eighth on Keller's German list of silver-age musicals, edging out *Die Csárdásfürstin*, *Die Rose von Stambul* and *Polenblut*) and a revival at the Centraltheater in 1923 (2 April), and in Hungary. *Az Erdészleány* (ad Adolf Mérei, Ferenc Révész, Bertalan Országh), produced in Budapest in June 1909, passed its 100th night on 16 April 1910, was seen throughout the country and returned to town in 1927 (Városi Színház 16 April 1927) with Irén Zilahy and Jenő Törzs featured, and again in 1936 at the Király Színház (2 January).

Although the show's life was largely confined to Central Europe, it did cross the Atlantic, winning Broadway productions both in German, with Lucie Engelke and Thomas Burgarth featured, at the Irving Place Theater, and, soon after, in English (ad Leonard Liebling). Lulu Glaser starred as 'the girl' and Julius McVicker as 'the Kaiser' in *The Girl and the Kaiser*, but both had to give star billing over to Harry Conor as the comical Peter Wenzel in the Shubert brothers' production. Thomas Richards was Franz, the Baroness von Graven was played by Flavia Arcaro and Victor and Blanche Hyde contributed a 'Whirlwind Hungarian Dance' to a version which seems, otherwise, to have been remarkably close to the original. The show played for eight weeks on Broadway, and toured usefully.

Several film versions of *Die Förster-Christl* have been made, the first a silent one, and the two most recent both by Carlton films. The first sound version featured Hannerl

Matz (Christl) and Karl Schönböck (Kaiser) in a recognizable version of the tale with the music adapted by Robert Gilbert and Bruno Uher, the second starred Irene Eisinger as Christl alongside Paul Richter, Oscar Karlweis and Adele Sandrock, whilst the third featured Sabine Sinjen and Peter Weck, was musically adapted by Franz Grothe, and included interpolations by Robert Gilbert and Ronald Binge.

Germany: Berliner Theater 28 February 1908; Hungary: Városligeti Színkör *Az Erdészleány* 20 June 1909, *Die Försterchristl* (Ger) June 1912; USA: Irving Place Theatre (Ger) 13 January 1910, Herald Square Theater *The Girl and the Kaiser* 22 November 1910; Films: 1926 (silent), 1931, 1952, 1962

Recording: Selection (part-record) (Eurodisc)

FOR THE LOVE OF MIKE   Play with tunes in 3 acts, adapted from the play of the same title by H F Maltby, by Clifford Grey. Lyrics by Clifford Grey and Sonny Miller. Additional lyrics by Valentine. Music by Jack Waller and Joseph Tunbridge. Saville Theatre, London, 8 October 1931.

The first of the successful series of musical comedies – by and large, more comedy than musical – produced by Jack Waller at the Saville Theatre with Bobby Howes as their comical star, *For the Love of Mike* had been originally written by playwright H F Maltby as a vehicle for Tom Walls. Turned down by him, it was picked up by Waller, decorated with a handful of songs, and turned out to be a 239-performance West End hit with a long subsequent touring life.

Love-struck little Bob (Bobby Howes) sets out to rob the safe at the home of nasty Mr Miller (Alfred Drayton) to retrieve the power of attorney which Miller has tricked his ward, 'Mike' (Peggy Cartwright), into signing. He is caught in the act by Paton (Arthur Riscoe), Miller's private detective, who turns out to be an old school chum, and the two fake a robbery to cover the incident. Syd Walker featured as the havoc-wreaking PC Wildgoose, Wylie Watson was the local clergyman, and the lanky, aristocratic Viola Tree warbled her way through a discouragement to 'Walk with Me' as Mrs Miller. The song hit of the evening, however, fell to Howes and Miss Cartwright as they duetted through one of Waller and Tunbridge's most enduring little songs, 'Got a Date With an Angel'.

For the Love of Mike was an unusual piece for its time, putting the accent firmly on the comedy part of the entertainment rather than on the currently top-rated dancing element, or on spectacle, or even on a full-sized score. Its success proved that there was a distinct audience for musical comedy worthy of the name, and Waller followed the proven recipe for a number of years. But this first show proved the most enduring of the group, and was still to be seen on the British touring circuits 20 years after its première.

In 1932 a film version was made with Howes, Riscoe, Watson and Miss Tree repeating their original rôles alongside Constance Shotter (Mike) and Jimmy Godden (Miller).

Film: BIP 1932

THE FORTUNE TELLER   Comic opera in 3 acts by Harry B Smith. Music by Victor Herbert. Wallack's Theater, New York, 26 September 1898.

When the ambitious young soprano of the famed Bostonians company, Alice Nielsen, decided to break away from the group and start up a comic opera company in opposition, she launched her project with with a piece commissioned from Bostonians' suppliers Harry B Smith and Victor Herbert.

The Fortune Teller of the show's title was the gipsy maiden Musette (Miss Nielsen), whose amazing resemblance to the wealthy and social but long-lost Irma (also Miss Nielsen) provided what plot there was to the piece, and also enabled the canny manageress to play the two largest rôles in the show. Irma, with a little help from Musette, manages to avoid wedding the unprepossessing Polish pianist Count Berezowski (Joseph W Herbert) in favour of the handsome baritone hussar Ladislas (Frank Rushworth), whilst Musette, once everything is satisfactorily explained, pairs off with her jealous gypsy Sándor (Eugene Cowles). Joseph Cawthorn joined Herbert at the head of the comedy in the rôle of Musette's father, Richard Golden was the ballet-master of the company where Irma, before becoming un-long-lost is a dancing girl, whilst Marguerite Sylva, as the actress Pompon, picked up the crumbs of the feminine music and the heroine's hussar brother, Fedor (whom Irma, for a while, impersonates to ensure her safety from the Pole).

Four of the evening's eight solo songs (in a 16-piece score) fell to the prima donna, beginning with the schoolgirlish 'Always Do As People Say You Should' (Irma), switching to csárdás-rhythm for the more tempestuous praises of 'Romany Life' (Musette), waxing Irish, Spanish, Chinese, French and finally indulging in a coon song in the sequence 'Serenades of All Nations' whilst still in the character of the gipsy girl, and shifting back to more conventional waltz-time to finish off her multi-coloured evening. Ladislas sang in praise of 'Hungaria's Hussars' and joined Pompon in the waltz duo 'Only in the Play', but it was Cowles who scored the biggest hit of the evening – and of his career – with his basso rendition of the 'Gypsy Love Song' ('Slumber on, my little gipsy sweetheart').

Built to travel, *The Fortune Teller* did not compile a long Broadway run. It played just five weeks in New York before Miss Nielsen moved on to her next date, but there was no doubt as to its success, and its manageress-star kept the show on the road in repertoire even when she had a newer piece to play. In 1901, when she joined the rush of American companies to Britain in the wake of the success of *The Belle of New York*, it was *The Fortune Teller* which Nielsen chose to present, with Cowles (who had an extra song, 'I Sing in Praise of the Sword'), Cawthorn, Herbert and Rushworth all in their original rôles and Viola Gillette as Pompon. If notices for the piece were mixed, Miss Nielsen and, in particular, Cowles were much liked and the show stayed at London's Shaftesbury Theatre for 88 performances.

In 1903 *The Fortune Teller* was seen in Australia when George Musgrove, formerly of the Shaftesbury Theatre, mounted it with Madame Slapoffski (née Lilian Williams) in the title-rôle alongside W R Shirley (Berezowski), Lemprière Pringle (Sándor) and May Beatty (Pompon) at the Sydney Theatre Royal, the Princess, Melbourne (28 February 1903) and the Theatre Royal, Adelaide (2 May 1903).

The Fortune Teller returned briefly to Broadway when it

was remounted by the Shuberts in their series of revivals of classic pieces at the Jolson Theater in 1929 (4 November). Much later, a heavily adapted version, with bits of the score combined with some music from Herbert's earlier *The Serenade*, was produced on the West Coast as *Gypsy Lady* and subsequently seen, without success, in New York (Century Theater, 17 September 1946) and, under the title *Romany Love* (His Majesty's Theatre 7 March 1947) in London.

UK: Shaftesbury Theatre 9 April 1901; Australia: Theatre Royal, Sydney 17 January 1903

FORTY-FIVE MINUTES FROM BROADWAY

Musical play in 3 acts by George M Cohan. New Amsterdam Theater, New York, 1 January 1906.

After thoroughly establishing the vigorously here-and-now musical comedy style which would be his for more than two decades with his written-composed-directed-and-starred-in *Little Johnny Jones* (1904), George M Cohan followed up with a second nationwide hit with *Forty-Five Minutes from Broadway*. As in the earlier piece, he was author, composer and director, but he left the leading male rôle this time to Victor Moore, and the star billing to Fay Templeton.

The title of the show (a switch from the originally announced *The Maid and the Millionaire*) referred to its location – the events of the tale took place in the country-bumpkin town of New Rochelle, situated just 45 minutes away from the heart of Manhattan, where the late Mr Castleton had lived. Though defunct, he is still important in the story for, like so many plays, musical and straight, of the previous half-century, *Forty-Five Minutes from Broadway* had a plot which centred on a will. Since Mr Castleton's will cannot be found, his money goes to his nephew, Tom Bennett (Donald Brian), who is quickly pursued by the money-grubbing Mrs David Dean (Julia Ralph) and her unmarried daughter, the 'footlight favourite' Flora Dora Dean (Lois Ewell). However, when the will turns up it eventuates that the beneficiary is the old man's devoted servant girl, Mary Jane Jenkins (Miss Templeton). But such riches deter the girl's sweetheart, Tom's secretary Kid Burns (Moore), and Mary prefers to tear up the will and leave the money to Tom rather than lose her chap.

The handful of musical numbers which were inserted into the tale included the cheery title song, Tom's 'I Want To Be a Popular Millionaire', Mary's 'So Long, Mary', a male-voice chorus of four 'Gentlemen of the Press' and three reporters, and the piece which would be one of its writer's most enduring, 'Mary's a Grand Old Name'. Initially, these were supplemented by 'Retiring from the Stage' and 'Stand Up and Fight Like Hell', but they both disappeared, leaving the settled five-part song quota of the evening complemented by as much music again written by musical director Fred Solomon, whose orchestra supplied 'Reminiscences of the South', the descriptive fantasia 'Going to School' and a Spanish Dance in between the acts.

Klaw and Erlanger's production was first mounted in Chicago and took in a Broadway season of 90 performances before continuing on its way round the lucrative touring circuits with Miss Templeton and Moore holding on to their parts through into 1907. In 1912 Cohan and his partner Sam Harris revived the show and, with Cohan playing Moore's rôle, dropped into New York for 36 further performances at the Cohan Theater (14 March). In the early 1920s Charles Ray starred in a First National film version which advertised that 'It has knocked the 'o's out of gloom' and in 1959 *Forty-Five Minutes from Broadway* was given a potted showing on NBC-TV (15 March). Tammy Grimes starred as Mary alongside Russell Nype and Larry Blyden.

Film: First National 1921
Recording: TV cast (AEI)

42ND STREET

Musical in 2 acts by Michael Stewart and Mark Bramble based on the screenplay of the same name and the novel by Bradford Ropes. Lyrics by Al Dubin. Music by Harry Warren. Winter Garden Theater, New York, 25 August 1980.

A stage musical version of the 1933 musical film which became the great classic of its genre: the tale of the insignificant chorus girl who deputizes for an ailing star and wins herself stardom. Impossibly innocent Ruby Keeler and pumpkin-pie Dick Powell incarnated the singing and dancing youngsters who tap-danced and sang their way to stardom and sweetheartdom, Bebe Daniels was the displaced star, whilst Warner Baxter ground out the immortal line about going out there a youngster but coming back a star, in the rôle of the director of the show-within-a-film.

Peggy Sawyer (Wanda Richert) from Allentown, NJ, gets a last-minute job as a chorus girl in the Broadway show *Pretty Lady* and catches the eye of juvenile lead Billy Lawler (Lee Roy Reams). Producer Julian Marsh (Jerry Orbach) has financed his show by casting the professional, no-longer-juvenile Dorothy Brock (Tammy Grimes) in the ingénue rôle and thus winning backing from her sugar-daddy, Abner Dillon (Don Crabtree), but Dorothy insists on meeting up with her old boyfriend, Pat Denning (James Congdon), and Julian has to get some friendly gangsters to keep Pat out of the way, as protection for his investment. The show makes it safely to its try-out opening, but during the show Dorothy falls and breaks her ankle. The chorus persuade Marsh to give Peggy the chance to take over, and she triumphs, whilst Dorothy, discovering she prefers love to stardom, weds her Pat. Carole Cook and Joe Bova played Maggie and Bert, the comical authors of *Pretty Lady*, whilst Karen Prunczik headed the remaining chorines as soubrette Anytime Annie.

The score of the show included several numbers taken from the film of *42nd Street* ('42nd Street', 'Young and Healthy', 'You're Getting to Be a Habit with Me', 'Shuttle Off to Buffalo') but also a selection of songs from other Al Dubin and/or Harry Warren films, notably the *Gold Diggers* series ('Lullaby of Broadway', 'We're in the Money'), *Dames* ('Dames'), *Go into Your Dance* ('About a Quarter to Nine') and *The Singing Marine* ('I Know Now'). The title-song was used as the basis for an opening ensemble tap routine on which the curtain rose very slowly gradually to display the mass of frenetically auditioning feet, whilst 'Lullaby of Broadway' served for a dramatic dance scena, 'Dames' for a costume parade, and 'We're in the Money' for another large-scale tap number with Billy featured as soloist.

David Merrick's production of *42nd Street* had a dramatic opening night when the death of director/

483

choreographer Gower Champion was announced at the final curtain, and it went on from there to win the season's Tony Award as best musical and to run for 3,486 performances in some eight and a half years, following a shift to the Majestic Theater (30 March 1981). Merrick also sponsored a London edition, produced at the Theatre Royal, Drury Lane, with James Laurenson (Marsh), Clare Leach (Peggy), Michael Howe (Billy) and Georgia Brown (Dorothy) featured in its original cast, which also achieved a highly successful run of four and a half years (1,823 performances) followed by a tour and return season at the large Dominion Theatre (27 February 1991).

The show toured both in America and in Britain, and was given a successful Australian production under the management of Helen Montagu, with Barry Quin (Marsh), Leonie Page (Peggy), Nancye Hayes (Dorothy) and Toni Lamond (Maggie) in the leading rôles. This production was announced for a tour to East Berlin, but the plan was abandoned when East Germany ceased to be, prior to the trip. Germany, however, did get *42nd Street* when an American touring company with Michael Dantuono (Marsh) and Elizabeth Allen (Dorothy) top-billed and Miss Prunczik in her original rôle played an extremely outfront English-language version there, in Austria and France. The Australian version contented itself with a second round of Australia.

UK: Theatre Royal, Drury Lane 8 August 1984; Australia: Her Majesty's Theatre, Sydney 2 June 1989; Austria: Theater an der Wien (Eng) 27 June 1990; France: Théâtre du Châtelet (Eng) 6 November 1990; Germany: Deutsches Theater, Munich (Eng) 3 May 1991
Recordings: original cast (RCA), Australian cast (RCA)

FOSSE, Bob [FOSSE, Robert Louis] (b Chicago, 23 June 1927; d Washington, 23 September 1987). Choreographer-director of several major Broadway hits of the 1960s and 1970s.

Fosse began his performing life as a young teenager in vaudeville and burlesque before dancing in touring revues (*Call Me Mister, Make Mine Manhattan*) and on Broadway in *Dance Me a Song* (1950). He subsequently appeared in several films, notably in the screen version of *Kiss Me, Kate* (1953, Hortensio, co-choreographer) and as Frank in the musical film of *My Sister Eileen* (1955).

His first Broadway choreographic credit was on *The Pajama Game* (1955) in which his routines to 'Steam Heat' and 'Hernando's Hideaway' won him a Tony Award and established him presto at the forefront of his profession. In *The Pajama Game*'s follow-up, *Damn Yankees* (1956), he staged 'Who's Got the Pain?' and 'Whatever Lola Wants' and won a second consecutive Tony Award, and he subsequently shared the choreographic work of *Bells Are Ringing* with Jerome Robbins before making his début as a director in the musicalized *Anna Christie, New Girl in Town*, featuring, as had *Damn Yankees*, a dancing leading lady in Gwen Verdon. He was again director and choreographer to Miss Verdon in the music-hall murder musical *Redhead*, which won him a third Tony citation for its dances.

Fosse made a return to the stage to appear as Joey in two productions of *Pal Joey* at the City Center, but thereafter stayed strictly beyond the footlights, staging a virtually unbroken run of successful and often outstanding shows

for the Broadway stage. He choreographed *How To Succeed in Business Without Really Trying* (Broadway and London), co-directed and choreographed the swingingly funny burlesque *Little Me* (1962, Tony Award choreography, 'Rich Kids' Rag'), the conceived-and-made-for-Verdon *Sweet Charity* ('Big Spender', 'The Rhythm of Life', Tony Award choreography) and the whimsical 1960s-flavoured *Pippin* ('Magic to Do') which at last won him a first Tony Award as a director as well as his sixth as a choreographer (Broadway and London). In 1975 he directed, choreographed and co-wrote the adaptation of Maurine Dallas Watkins's *Chicago* as a 'vaudeville musical' in which Miss Verdon and Chita Rivera showed off his infallibly stylish dance numbers through a long and successful run.

The break in all this success came with the production of Frank Loesser's 1965 *Pleasures and Palaces* which failed to make it to Broadway, but he had a final Broadway success when he put together the dance revue *Dancin'* (1978). The 1986 pasticcio show, *Big Deal*, for which he took writer's, director's and choreographer's credits was a 70-performance failure, but nevertheless brought him yet another Tony Award for choreography.

Amongst an array of television and cinema credits Fosse repeated his *Pajama Game* and *Damn Yankees* (also performer) assignments in the filmed versions of the stage shows, and he both directed and choreographed the film version of *Sweet Charity* with Shirley MacLaine in the title-rôle and that of *Cabaret* (Academy Award) with Liza Minnelli and Joel Grey. In 1979 he also turned out a rather masochistic autobiographical movie called *All That Jazz* which won what comment it evoked over a scene showing open-heart surgery. Fosse himself was played by Roy Scheider.

Fosse's third wife was his oft-times collaborator, Gwen Verdon.

1975 **Chicago** (John Kander/Fred Ebb/w Ebb) 46th Street Theater 3 June
1986 **Big Deal** (pasticcio) Broadway Theater 10 April

Biographies: Boyd Grubb, K: *Razzle Dazzle: The Life and Work of Bob Fosse* (St Martin's Press, New York, 1989), Gottfried, M: *All His Jazz* (Bantam, New York, 1990)

THE FOUR MUSKETEERS Comedy musical in 2 acts by Michael Pertwee. Lyrics by Herbert Kretzmer. Music by Laurie Johnson. Theatre Royal, Drury Lane, London, 5 December 1967.

An attempt to follow up popular vocalist and comedian Harry Secombe's success as *Pickwick* cast him, with less adroitness, as a burlesque version of Dumas's musketeer D'Artagnan. Producer Bernard Delfont, director Peter Coe, and designer Sean Kenny repeated their assignments of the earlier show in a travesty tale which had Secombe as a bumbling bumpkin of a hero, achieving his heroics all unawares, and his fellow musketeers (Jeremy Lloyd, Glyn Owen, John Junkin) as a bunch of louts. They duly went off in search of missing diamonds of the Queen of France (Sheena Marshe), but not to Britain, and duly brought them back. Comedian Kenneth Connor was the King, Elizabeth Larner took over the rôle of Milady at the last minute, and Stephanie Voss was the beloved Constance Bonacieux.

With no 'If I Ruled the World' coming from its score, the show tottered suicidally through no fewer than 462 performances on its vast, rumbling sets before folding severely in the red. But the statistics just show that it ran 462 performances.

Recording: original cast (Philips)

FOX, Della [May]   (b St Louis, Mo, 13 October 1871; d New York, 16 June 1913).

Tiny soubrette who became a star as the partner of De Wolf Hopper, and helped set the fashion for bobbed hair in the 1890s.

Miss Fox worked first as a juvenile actress, appearing as the midshipmite in *HMS Pinafore* at seven and later in local productions of such pieces as *A Celebrated Case* and *Editha's Burglar* and in farce comedy. In her teens, she took employment first with the touring Bennett and Moulton opera company and then, in her first break-through, with Hans Conried for whom she appeared on Broadway as the soubrette, Yvonne, in Adolf Müller's *The King's Fool* (*Der Hofnarr*, 1890). She was then hired by John McCaull to partner the extremely tall De Wolf Hopper in his Comic Opera Company's production of Kerker's *Castles in the Air* (1890, Blanche) and she shot to stardom when she featured again alongside Hopper in the travesty rôle of another American comic opera, *Wang* (1891, Prince Mataya). She teamed with the comedian yet again, with less happy results, in *Panjandrum* (1893, Paquita), but moved on before his next big hit, *El Capitan*, to take top billing herself in the title-rôle of *The Little Trooper* (*Les 28 Jours de Clairette*, 1894, Clairette Duval), with Jefferson d'Angelis in William Furst's *Fleur de Lis* (ex-*Pervenche*, 1895, Fleur de Lis), and in 1897 in the lead rôle of the Julian Edwards/Audran *The Wedding Day* (semi-*La Petite Fronde*, Rose-Marie) alongside de Angelis and Lillian Russell.

Her next rôle was in a rather different style of piece: a low-brow musical comedy called *The Little Host* (1898, Margery Dazzle) which proved less suitable and less successful, but Miss Fox then retired to marriage, peritonitis and a nervous breakdown. She emerged again a few years later with the money of her husband, jeweller 'Diamond John' Levy backing her and the Shuberts, to star in a dual rôle as a brother and sister in an americanized version of the highly successful French musical *Toto* played at the Princess's Theater as *The West Point Cadet*. A weak adaptation, it folded quickly, taking Miss Fox's career and her husband's business with it. Thereafter she limited her performances to the vaudeville stage, where she was boasted (like several others) as being the variety theatre's highest-paid performer, until her early death at the age of 41.

FOY, Eddie [FITZGERALD, Edwin] (b New York, 9 March 1854; d Kansas City, 16 February 1928). Star little-fellow comedian of the Broadway musical stage and of vaudeville.

Foy had a career of nearly 20 years in the less upmarket backwaters of the variety and minstrel circuits and in stock theatres, changing his employment from juveniles and heavies to comedy before making his first substantial appearances in the musical theatre. In his mid-thirties he played in the extravaganzas *Aladdin*, *The Crystal Slipper*, *Bluebeard Jr*, *Sinbad the Sailor*, *Ali Baba* and *Little Robinson Crusoe* under the management of David Henderson in Chicago and this series of highly successful spectaculars,

staged by top director Richard Barker, made Foy into a comedy star. In 1894 he left Henderson to go out on his own as a performer-manager. He tried spectacular extravaganza with *Off the Earth* (1894), and the fairytale line with *Little Robinson Crusoe*, supported by Marie Cahill and Marie Dressler, but ultimately ended up renouncing the perils of producership and going to work for Klaw and Erlanger in revue.

Foy was first introduced to Broadway musical-comedy audiences at the Herald Square Theater in 1898 when he appeared alongside Miss Dressler as Lebeau in Charles Frohman's production of Victor Roger's *Hotel Topsy-Turvy* (*L'Auberge du Tohu-bohu*). He followed up in the burlesque extravaganza *The Arabian Girl and the Forty Thieves* and, more significantly, in the featured comedy rôle of Kamfer in the Knickerbocker Theater production of another made-over show, *The Strollers* (*Die Landstreicher*, 1901). He compounded his growing popularity at the Knickerbocker in *The Wild Rose* (1902, Paracelsus Noodle) and the burlesque *Mr Bluebeard* (1903), starred at the Casino Theater in 1904 in *Piff! Paff! Pouf!* (Peter Pouffle), and spent several years in New York and on the road in the Shuberts' productions of two highly successful British musical comedies – *The Earl and the Girl* and *The Orchid*. In *The Earl and the Girl* he played the part of Jim Cheese (created by Savoy comic Walter Passmore), the little dog-trainer who ends up as an earl in an evening of swapped identities, while in *The Orchid* he played a remake of Teddy Payne's classic little-chappie rôle of Meakin, rechristened Artie Choke, chasing the flower of the title around a series of lively situations.

He alternated theatre and variety engagements in the following half-dozen years, starring as Joey Wheeze in *Mr Hamlet of Broadway* (1908), in the revue *Up and Down Broadway* (1910) and in the revusical spectacular *Over the River* (1912, Madison Parke) before finally abandoning musical theatre to tour with his children in the act 'Eddie Foy and the Seven Little Foys'.

One of the 'Seven Little Foys' was **Eddie FOY jr** (Edwin FITZGERALD b New Rochelle, 4 February 1905; d Woodland Hills, Calif, 15 July 1983) who moved from variety to the musical stage in his mid-twenties. He appeared on Broadway in *Show Girl*, *Ripples*, *Smiles*, *At Home Abroad*, *All the King's Horses* and *Orchids Preferred*, and in London in the very brief *Royal Exchange* (1935), but his most notable creation as a juvenile was the salesman-turned-dancer, Alexander Sheridan, in *The Cat and the Fiddle* (1931). Towards the end of the Second World War, and after some ten years in which his musical appearances had been away from New York (Bunny in *Hit the Deck*, the Jule Styne road-folder *Glad to See You*) he returned to Broadway to pair with Michael O'Shea in the Montgomery and Stone comedy rôles of *The Red Mill* (1945). He toured in *High Button Shoes* (1948), and in 1954, after another lengthy absence from Broadway, returned to create the part of the time-and-motion-study expert, Hines, in *The Pajama Game* ('I'll Never Be Jealous Again'), a rôle he repeated in the subsequent film version (1957). Later stage rôles in *Rumple* (1957, Rumple) and *Donnybrook!* (1961, Mikeen Flynn) did not find the same level, and he was dropped from *Royal Flush* in rehearsals, before it became, without him, an even more thorough flop.

He appeared in the film versions of *Yokel Boy* (1942, Joe

Ruddy) and *Bells Are Ringing* (1960, J Otto Prantz), along-side Texas Guinan in the 1929 *Queen of the Nightclubs*, impersonated his father in the films *Lillian Russell* (1940), *Yankee Doodle Dandy* (1942), *Wilson* (1944) and *Bowery to Broadway* (1944) and narrated the tale of *The Seven Little Foys* (1955) in which Bob Hope played the rôle of Eddie Foy sr.

Autobiography: (w Harlow, A F) *Clowning Through Life* (E P Dutton & Co, New York, 1928)

FRA DIAVOLO, or L'Hotellerie de Terracina

Opéra-comique in 3 acts by Eugène Scribe. Music by Daniel Auber. Opéra-Comique, Paris, 28 January 1830.

One of the most successful works of the opéra-comique tradition of the mid-19th-century French theatre, Scribe and Auber's *Fra Diavolo*, though by no means the first work to introduce the comic-opera bandit, was largely influential in popularizing him through a vast number of works throughout the world.

Scribe's libretto followed the vicious bandit chief, Fra Diavolo, as, disguised as a Marquis, he tracks the run-away-married English couple, Lord and Lady Cokbourg, to the inn at Terracina, intending to rob them of their jewels and money. He is thwarted by the efforts of the young brigadier of carabiniers, Lorenzo, who desperately decimates the bandit band on the day his sweetheart, Zerline, is to be wed to another, and by the clumsiness of his newest recruit. If the story had its dramatic moments, it also had many comical ones, with the English pair played for comedy, and the midnight comings and goings of the brigands in the hotel's bedrooms bordering on pure farce.

Hugely popular throughout the world, *Fra Diavolo* indubitably inspired the burlesque of *Les Brigands*, as well as Burnand's comical bandits in *The Contrabandista* and W S Gilbert's teams of thieves in *Princess Toto* and *The Mountebanks*, but it also prompted some more direct burlesques including Henry J Byron's early work *Fra Diavolo, or Beauty and the Brigands* (Strand Theatre 1858) and the same author's Gaiety Theatre *Young Fra Diavolo* (17 November 1878) in Britain, and Meisl and Drechsler's *Fra Diavolo, das Gasthaus auf der Strasse* produced at Vienna's Theater in der Leopoldstadt (24 November 1830) just weeks after that city's first glimpse of Auber's work. As late as 1933 Hollywood turned out a piece entitled *Fra Diavolo* (*The Devil's Brother*) featuring the knockabout team Laurel and Hardy.

Germany: 16 July 1830; Austria: Hofoperntheater 18 September 1830; Hungary: 23 October 1830; UK: Theater Royal, Drury Lane *The Devil's Brother* 1 February 1831; USA: Park Theater 20 June 1833; Australia: Royal Victoria Theatre, Hobart 3 October 1842

FRAGONARD

Opérette in 3 acts by André Rivoire and Romain Coolus. Music by Gabriel Pierné. Théâtre de la Monnaie, Brussels, 1933.

A rare venture by the composer Pierné into the light musical theatre, *Fragonard* was greeted by the connoisseurs of the classy and refined variety of musical theatre with delight, but its production at the Paris Théâtre de la Porte-Saint-Martin under Maurice Lehmann failed to provoke more than indifference from the general public, and the show closed in 57 performances.

Marie-Anne Fragonard (Louisette Rousseau) is a patient ninny who puts up with her husband's infidelities on the excuse that he is an artist. She is a little jealous only of his model, the dancer La Guimard (Jane Marnac). In an attempt to distract him from this woman, she brings her young sister Marguerite (Simone Lencret) to town, but the distraction succeeds only too well and Fragonard (André Baugé) finds himself caught up amongst the three women until Marguerite finds herself a more suitable lover. Edmond Castel had the principal comic rôle as Soubise.

Lehmann subsequently produced *Fragonard* at the Opéra-Comique (21 February 1946) with Jacques Jansen as Fragonard, Fanély Révoil as La Guimard, Lucienne Jourfier as Marguerite and Duvaleix as Soubise for 18 performances, and the piece was also later seen in the composer's native Metz.

France: Théâtre de la Porte-Saint-Martin 17 October 1934

FRANCK, Alphonse

(b Strasbourg, 11 October 1863; d Paris, 11 February 1932). Parisian producer whose fine career included France's blockbusting *Veuve joyeuse*.

Originally a journalist, secretary at the Théâtre du Vaudeville and the Théâtre du Gymnase, and an occasional author of revues in collaboration with no less a writer than Gaston de Caillavet, Franck moved into management when he became the director, first, of Paris's little Théâtre des Capucines and then of the Théâtre du Gymnase. An excellent manager, he confirmed the latter house's reputation for top-class performances of drama, comedy and vaudeville and was sufficiently successful to branch out further by taking on the management of the Théâtre Apollo. There he changed genre, and with the most amazing results.

On 28 April 1909 he produced at his new theatre a version, written by his old collaborator Gaston de Caillavet and Caillavet's now partner, Robert de Flers, of a successful Viennese Operette based on Henri Meilhac's comedy *L'Attaché d'ambassade*. It was Franz Lehár's *La Veuve joyeuse/Die lustige Witwe*, the biggest musical theatre success Paris had seen in years. Eighty-five successive performances each took an amazing equivalent of £250 per night before Franck was obliged to close his theatre for repairs. Even the break in the run did no harm in a city used to such things. At the re-opening in September the public flocked back and, in Paris where the musical theatre had been wallowing in a considerable doldrum, Franck and the Apollo were suddenly launched as the most important producer of, and house for opérette in the city. He followed up with another splendid, if necessarily lesser, success with *Rêve de valse* (*Ein Walzertraum*), and scored again with Ganne's delightful *Hans le joueur de flûte*, produced earlier at Monte-Carlo, but Leoncavallo's *Malbrouk s'en va t'en guerre* was a failure and Franck hastened to bring back *La Veuve joyeuse*.

His 1911 productions included another Viennese success, Fall's *Die geschiedene Frau* (*La Divorcée*), as well as Terrasse's *Les Transatlantiques*, a revival of Offenbach's *Madame Favart*, and Hirschmann's *Les Petites Étoiles*, and 1912 found two other Viennese works, *Le Comte de Luxembourg* (*Der Graf von Luxemburg*) and *Le Soldat de chocolat* (*Der tapfere Soldat*) the mainstays of the programme, along-side revivals of *Les Saltimbanques*, *Les Cloches de Corneville* and the infallible *La Veuve joyeuse*. *La Veuve* had to be called on the following year again, for although another triumphant import, Jean Gilbert's *La Chaste Susanne* (*Die keusche Susanne*), played over a hundred performances, a revival of *Monsieur de la Palisse* held up for two months plus, and *La Mascotte* a little less, the two new French works Franck loyally included in his programme – Lattès's *La Jeunesse dorée* and Ganne's *Cocorico* – lasted but 17 and 28 performances respectively.

Latterly, things had not been going as well as they might at the Gymnase as well, and in 1913 Franck found himself obliged to take in there as a partner the ubiquitous Gustave Quinson, whose tentacles were spreading round a dozen Parisian houses in a manoeuvre which would make him the most powerful individual in the Paris theatre. At the Apollo, Franck tried one final new piece, Xavier Leroux's pretty *La Fille de Figaro*, and when that went under after 40 performances, he was obliged to throw in his hand. On 15 April 1914 he handed over the theatre to one M Maillart. Instead of two theatres, he now had half of one. Opérette made an unaccustomed appearance at the Gymnase when Franck and Quinson produced *La Petite Dactylo* with Yvonne Printemps in the title-rôle, but by this time Franck had had enough of partnership and, determined to be his own master again, struck out with a new theatre, the smaller Théâtre Edouard VII.

The new house was opened in November 1916 with a Rip revue, and Franck entered on a policy of 'petite opérette' with a revival of Cuvillier's *Son p'tit frère*, followed by a successful new piece, *La Folle Nuit*, composed by Marcel Pollet and a less successful one, *La Petite Bonne d'Abraham*. He returned to comedy and, after one more disastrous attempt at opérette with a fortnight's run of a piece by the young Tiarko Richepin and Albert Willemetz, *Rapatipatoum* (1919), he devoted his theatre to comedy, and especially the comedies of Sacha Guitry, full-time. The nearest he came thereafter to opérette at the Edouard VII was the production of Guitry's plays-with-song-for-Yvonne, the vehicles for Mme Guitry, otherwise Yvonne Printemps, who was the star of the delicious *L'Amour masqué* (1923, music by Messager), *Mozart* (1925, music by Hahn), *Jean de la Fontaine* (1927, music from Lully) and *Mariette* (1928, music by Oscar Straus).

In 1924 he again spread himself when he opened the little Théâtre de l'Étoile on the corner of the Champs-Élysées and the rue Balzac. Guitry's *L'Accroche-coeur* and *La Revue de printemps* (w Willemetz) and the personal attractions of Mlle Printemps kept the theatre going briefly, but subsequent pieces, including the opérette *Pouche*, of which Franck was himself the adaptor, did insufficiently well to keep the new theatre afloat. Franck sold it and it was soon transformed into the ateliers of the couturière Maggy Rouff.

In 1929 he also gave up the Théâtre Edouard VII and put the end to a career in theatrical management which had had three periods of great prominence and prosperity, one in the musical theatre and two in the non-musical, but which had also known the inevitable ration of hefty lows.

1925 **Pouche** (Henri Hirschmann/René Peter, Henri Falk ad) Théâtre de l'Étoile 18 February

FRANÇOIS LES BAS-BLEUS
Opéra-comique in 3 acts by Ernest Dubreuil, Paul Burani and Eugène Humbert. Music by Firmin Bernicat. Additional music by André Messager. Théâtre des Folies-Dramatiques, Paris, 8 November 1883.

The young composer Firmin Bernicat strove for many years for success in the theatre, and he finally achieved it when his opéra-comique *François les bas-bleus* (named for Paul Meurice's 1863 drama) was produced in Paris in 1883. But by the time the show opened, its composer was dead, and *François les bas-bleu*, instead of launching the career of Bernicat, launched that of the younger musician who had completed the score, André Messager.

François (Bouvet), the public scribe, and the little street-singer Fanchon (Jeanne Andrée) are heading cosily towards marriage when the Comtesse de la Savonnière (Mme d'Harville) recognizes the girl as her long-lost niece, the daughter of the Marquis de Pontcornet (Montrouge). Whilst Mlle de Pontcornet turns down her father's proposed suitor, de Lansac (Dekernel), and her aunt turns her glances on François, the young scribe writes out Pontcornet's newest attempt at a song. However, he makes some changes on the way, and conservative sentiments of the Marquis's lyrics are altered to ones of a liberality which earns both the men temporary popular support, social disgrace, and a trip to the Bastille. The fourteenth of July 1789 comes in time to get them released, and heading towards a happy ending.

Quite what part of the winning score of *François les bas-bleus* is to be attributed to which composer is, of course, only to be guessed, although it has been claimed (by a biographer of Messager) that Messager was responsible for a full half of the music, as well as the entire orchestration. A biographer of Bernicat might have different figures. In any case, the score as a whole contributed much to the success of the show. The strong baritone rôle of François was well served, setting off the show, after the traditional warm-up chorus and number by a minor character, with a ronde calling his profession, ('C'est François les bas-bleus'), which was soon to become popular, duetting sweetly with his Fanchon as he attempts to teach her her letters ('Avec soin formez chaque lettre'), soaring out his rewritten version of the Chanson Politique ('Peuple francais, le politique'), sadly realizing that he is no match for a rich and noble Fanchon ('Il faut bannir tout espérance'/'Espérance en d'heureux jours') and finally soliloquizing desperately over his lost love ('À toi, j'avais donné ma vie'), before the fall of the Bastille puts all right.

Fanchon's 'La complainte du petit matelot', the song of her childhood which leads to her origins being recognized, gave the ingénue her best moment, whilst the lovesick Countess had some fine and funny moments, describing her own charms to François in a rondo ('J'ai de la figure') or safely impersonating a coffee-seller ('Un barbon près de sa belle') on Bastille day. The funny moments of the Marquis came largely in the tale.

François les bas-bleus was a veritable hit at a theatre where the management was undergoing a changeover, and it was played 143 times in its first run. That first run was succeeded by others in 1887, 1895, 1896, 1900, 1908 and in 1916 as the piece established itself as a solid item in the opérette repertoire, just a touch below the most successful and famous.

The show was quickly transported to other countries and languages, with an Hungarian production (ad Lajos Evva, Béla J Fái) opening just days after the Paris season closed (10 performances), and New York getting its first glimpse of the show later in the same year when Maurice Grau included it in his season at Wallack's Theater as *Fanchon* with Louise Théo as Fanchon, Francis Gaillard as François, Mlle Delorme (Countess) and Mezières (Pontcornet). An English version called *Fantine* (ad Benjamin Woolf, Roswell Martin Field) which included additional music apparently written by Woolf was produced at the Boston Museum 1884 and in 1888 the Boston Ideal Company brought *Victor, the Bluestocking* to Broadway in their repertoire with Henry Clay Barnabee as the Marquis. Another English version, done by Justin McCarthy MP (which may have accounted for its title, *François, the Radical*), was prepared for Kate Santley who produced it at her Royalty Theatre in London, herself playing Fanchon alongside Deane Brand (François), Henry Ashley (Pontcornet) and Lizzie Mulholland (Countess). After three weeks it was withdrawn for rewrites on the book and did not reappear, but Miss Santley seems to have lifted some of its music for her own comic opera *Vetah* with which she later played several tours.

A different English version (probably Woolf's) was presented in Australia by Luscombe Searelle and Charles Harding as part of an 1886 season at Sydney's New Opera House. Gracie Plaisted, in what was now the title-rôle of *Fantine*, paired with Harding's François for ten nights. A number of years later, a German version (ad Karl Saar) which again switched the title to the heroine (*Die Strassensängerin*), was produced in Berlin, but it was only in France that the show won real popularity.

Hungary: Népszinház *Kék Feri* 14 March 1884; UK: Royalty Theatre *François the Radical* 4 April 1885; USA: Boston Museum (Eng) *Fantine* 1884, Wallack's Theater *Fanchon* 29 September 1884, Fifth Avenue Theater *Victor the Bluestocking* January 1888; Australia: New Opera House, Sydney *Fantine* 1 May 1886; Germany; Friedrich-Wilhelmstädtisches Theater *Die Strassensängerin* 1 September 1894

Recording: complete (Gaîté-Lyrique)

FRASER, Agnes [F E] (b Springfield, Scotland, 8 November 1877; d London, 22 July 1968)

Miss Fraser began her career in D'Oyly Carte's touring companies and graduated to the Savoy Theatre company in 1899. Her first rôle there was in *The Rose of Persia*, where she succeeded Isabel Jay in the supporting part of Blush-of-the-Morning when Jay herself replaced the show's quickly departed original star, Ellen Beach Yaw. She appeared as Isabel, Lady Ella and Celia in Gilbert and Sullivan revivals, and as Kathleen in *The Emerald Isle* (1901), occasionally replacing Miss Jay in leading rôles before, in 1902, taking over definitively as the Savoy company's last prima donna. In that capacity she starred in the rôles of Bessie Throckmorton in *Merrie England* ('She Had a Letter from Her Love', 'Who Shall Say That Love is Cruel') and Kenna in *A Princess of Kensington*. After the break-up of the Savoy outfit, she starred with her husband, Savoy comic Walter Passmore, in the musical comedies *The Earl and the Girl* (1903, Elphin Haye), *The Talk of the Town* (1905, Ellaline Lewin) and in the ingénue rôle of Robert Courtneidge's highly successful *The Dairymaids* (1906, Winifred) and later appeared with Passmore in musical playlets in variety houses (*Sweet William*, *Queer Fish*) before retiring from the stage.

Her daughter, Nancy Fraser, also had a career as a vocalist and appeared in her mother's rôle in *Merrie England* in a 1934 revival at the Prince's Theatre.

FRASER-SIMSON, Harold (b London, 15 August 1878; d Inverness, 19 January 1944). The musician of *The Maid of the Mountains*.

Educated at Charterhouse and King's College, Fraser-Simson was at first involved in the world of commercial shipping, successfully operating, from an office in Mincing Lane, as a ship-owner. His first appearance in the musical theatre was with the score for the colourful, if old-fashioned, comic opera *Bonita*, for which he organized a West End production, directed by no less a luminary than Granville Barker, in 1911. *Bonita* lasted only 42 performances, but its music was sufficiently well received for its composer to be offered, five years later, the opportunity of composing the score for Robert Evett's Daly's Theatre musical, *The Maid of the Mountains*.

The enormous success of this show, and of his individual songs ('Farewell', 'Love Will Find a Way', 'Husbands and Wives'), set Fraser-Simson firmly in place as one of the most touted show composers of the time, and he subsequently supplied the scores for Evett for two other vehicles for *Maid of the Mountains* star José Collins, *A Southern Maid* and *Our Peg*. The first of these followed *The Maid of the Mountains* into Daly's and had another remarkable success; the second, frozen out of Evett's London theatre by the long-running success of the other two, played only in the provinces and was later adapted into *Our Nell* (the original heroine, Peg Woffington, being replaced by Nell Gwynne for presumably commercial reasons) and played at the Gaiety.

The touring musical *Missy Jo*, a vehicle for comic W H Berry called *Head Over Heels*, and the remade *Our Nell* had only limited lives, but Fraser-Simson scored another fine success when he teamed again with Frederick Lonsdale on the romantic artists-in-Montmartre musical, *The Street Singer*, which ran nearly a year at the Lyric Theatre and toured widely thereafter.

The pretty *Betty in Mayfair* did prettily at the Adelphi the following year, but Fraser-Simson's most enduring work after *The Maid* was his last, a sprightly and lovable musical setting of Kenneth Grahame's *Toad of Toad Hall* as dramatized by A A Milne. This piece became a British Christmas annual and its success prompted the compilation in 1970 of a *Winnie the Pooh*, put together from Milne's book and Fraser-Simson's settings of the Pooh lyrics as the song-cycle *The Hums of Pooh* ('Christopher Robin is Saying His Prayers', 'They're Changing Guard at Buckingham Palace'). *Winnie the Pooh* also proved, for many years, a regular festive season favourite.

1911 **Bonita** (Wadham Peacock) Queen's Theatre 22 September
1916 **The Maid of the Mountains** (Harry Graham/Frederick Lonsdale) Prince's Theatre, Manchester 23 December; Daly's Theatre 10 February 1917
1917 **A Southern Maid** (Dion Clayton Calthrop, Graham/Harry Miller) Prince's Theatre, Manchester 24 December; Daly's Theatre 15 May 1920
1919 **Our Peg** (Graham/Edward Knoblock) Prince's Theatre, Manchester 24 December
1921 **Missy Jo** (Graham/James Clive) Folkestone 4 July
1923 **Head Over Heels** (Adrian Ross, Graham/Seymour Hicks) Adelphi Theatre 8 September

1924 **Our Nell** (revised *Our Peg*) (w Ivor Novello/Louis N Parker, Reginald Arkell) Gaiety Theatre 16 April

1924 **The Street Singer** (Percy Greenbank/Lonsdale) Lyric Theatre 27 June

1925 **Betty in Mayfair** (Graham/J Hastings Turner) Adelphi Theatre 11 November

1929 **Toad of Toad Hall** (A A Milne) Liverpool 17 December/ Lyric Theatre 17 December 1930

1970 **Winnie the Pooh** (ad Julian Slade/Milne) Phoenix Theatre 17 December

FRASQUITA Operette in 3 acts by A M Willner and Heinz Reichert based on *La Femme et le pantin* by Pierre Louÿs. Music by Franz Lehár. Theater an der Wien, Vienna, 12 May 1922.

For some reason, librettists Willner and Reichert, in setting up their heroine for Lehár's newest Operette, elected to make her not a central-European gipsy, of the kind their Hungarian composer had already proven himself expert at musicking, but a Spanish gipsy, in the *Carmen* mould, involved with a group of Frenchmen in modern-day Barcelona.

Armand Mirbeau (Hubert Marischka) has been summoned to Barcelona to meet up with his uncle Aristide Girot (Emil Guttmann) and the cousin, Dolly (Henny Hilmar), whom he hasn't seen for nearly 20 years, and whom he is now scheduled to marry. Once in Barcelona, however, he falls under the charms of the gipsy, Frasquita (Betty Fischer), who is scornfully determined only to lead him on and make a fool of him. However, she finds herself falling in love, in her turn, and she follows Armand to Paris where a happy ending is lying in wait. Dolly pairs off with best-friend Hippolyt (Hans Thimig).

Lehár's score produced one hit number in Armand's rapturous 'Hab' ein blaues Himmelbett', but it was the heroine of the piece who garnered the largest share of the score, her rôle including the sensuous waltz 'Wüsst ich, wer morgen mein Liebster ist', the introductory 'Fragst mich, was Liebe ist?' and the waltz duet with Armand 'Weisst du nicht, was ein Herz voller Sehnsucht begehrt'. The lighter numbers were largely the province of Dolly and Hippolyt, and their shimmy and polka strains were contrasted with the more romantic musical moments.

Wilhelm Karczag's Vienna production of *Frasquita* had a good run of over six months, and, with some extra performances in the months that followed, totalled 195 performances before it was replaced on the schedules. During that time a number of cast changes took place, with Harry Bauer, Karl Meister and Richard Tauber taking over, in turn, from Marischka, whilst Anny Fields, Else Kochhann and Marthe Serak replaced Fischer.

Soon after the Vienna closure, the show was mounted at the Berlin Thalia-Theater, and then in Britain (ad Fred de Grésac, Reginald Arkell) where Robert Evett took it up as a natural vehicle for gipsyish-lady specialist José Collins. Mounted in the provinces, with Miss Collins paired with Robert Michaelis and Edmund Gwenn as Hippolyt, it had an unsteady start and when it reached London, four months later, with Michaelis replaced by Thorpe Bates, it flopped briskly in 36 performances.

If the piece's fate in Britain was a sad one, it was destined to fall even further in America. The operatic singer Geraldine Farrar, the Metropolitan Opera's Carmen and a favourite star of the silent movies, was signed to make her light musical stage début as Frasquita at an unheard of salary of $6,000 a week. After two managements had withdrawn from the project, Miss Farrar opened at Hartford, Connecticut, in a version called *The (Romany) Love Spell*, which was sponsored by her own manager, C J Foley, and the music publishers, the Dreyfus brothers, prefatory to an immediate opening at Broadway's Shubert Theater. She played just one performance before announcing that she was not happy with the music and closing the production. A second attempt to get the piece away took place in Los Angeles where *The Love Call* was played for a season (1925–6) with the lovely vocalist Grace La Rue starred, but it too failed to make its way to Broadway.

In spite of these failures, Australia's J C Williamson Ltd also mounted a *Frasquita*, with Marie Burke cast in the title-rôle alongside Herbert Browne (Armand), H Barrett-Lennard (Hippolyt) and Marie Eaton (Luisa), but without succeeding in reversing the thumbs-down given the other English-language productions.

Budapest saw a version of the show at the Városi Színház (ad Zsolt Harsányi) with the operatic tenor József Gábor as Armand, whilst a French version mounted at Le Havre (ad Max Eddy, Jean Marietti) with Fanély Révoil as Frasquita continued the show's unhappy record by failing to progress to Paris. Two years later, however, a version of the show did make it to Paris when another famous singer tackled *Frasquita*, in an adaptation labelled 'opéra-comique'. Conchita Supervia was no happier in Lehár's music than Farrar had been, and the production at the Opéra-Comique, with Louis Arnoult, Annie Gueldy and René Herent supporting, was considered something of an aberration.

In 1935 Carl Lamac produced an updated film version of the show with Jarmila Novotna and Hans-Heinz Bollmann starred and some additional Lehár music introduced.

An Hungarian version of the Louÿs/Pierre Frondaie stage adaptation of *La Femme et le pantin*, with accompanying music by Károly Stephanides was produced at the Budapest Vigszinház (ad Jenő Heltai) 27 April 1918 under the title *Az asszony és a bábu* (36 performances).

Germany: Thalia-Theater, Berlin 1 February 1924; UK: Lyceum, Edinburgh 24 December 1924, Prince's Theatre, London 23 April 1925; Hungary: Városi Színház *Fraskita* 3 March 1925; USA: Parsons' Theater, Hartford *The (Romany) Love Spell* 24 November 1925; Australia: Her Majesty's Theatre, Sydney 16 April 1927; France: Théâtre du Havre, Le Havre October 1931, Opéra-Comique, Paris 5 May 1933; Film: Atlantis-Film 1935

Recordings: Supervia recording (Pacific, etc), selections in French (Decca, Véga) etc

EINE FRAU, DIE WEISS, WAS SIE WILL Musical comedy in 5 scenes by Alfred Grünwald based on *Le Fauteuil* by Louis Verneuil. Music by Oscar Straus. Metropoltheater, Berlin, 1 September 1932.

Oscar Straus's last great pre-Nazi-era hit marked the return to the musical stage of Berlin's favourite musical star, Fritzi Massary, who had avoided the Operette stage since her unhappy experience with a jazzed-up version of *Die lustige Witwe*, and who now tackled a prima-donna part which was no glamorous heroine, but a 'mother' rôle.

The revue-star Manon Cavallini (Fritzi Massary) had an

illegitimate daughter in her young days, and that child, Lucy (Ellen Schwanneke), has been brought up by her father, ignorant of her mother's identity, until she has reached the age of indiscretion, and has fallen in love. However, the young man with whom she is so taken has developed a crush on an actress, and that actress is none other than Manon. The girl decides to go and speak to her rival, to ask her to renounce the boy, and the older woman agrees to do so. Finally and inevitably the truth of the two women's relationship comes out.

Straus's score for *Eine Frau* treated its ageing prima donna gently. There were no wide-ranging vocal lines. But the composer brought forth one number which would become a world-wide hit: Manon's gentle, worldly-wise little piece 'Jede Frau hat irgendeine Sehnsucht' ('Every Woman Thinks She Wants to Wander'). She also chatted to reporters ('Was so die Gesellschaft'), as she led up to the evening's title-song ('I am a woman who knows what she wants...'), delivered a number about Ninon de l'Enclos ('Ninon, Ninon') and took part in various duos and scenes.

The show was well received in the Berlin production mounted by the Rotter brothers – 'Grünwald has treated an age-old theme with just the right modern veneer of sophistication' – and Massary's return to the musical stage was a decided success. It was also her last appearance on the Berlin stage, for soon after she – like Grünwald and Straus, and like the Rotter brothers, hounded to death by the Nazis – joined the exodus from Germany.

After the Berlin run, Massary and Frln Schwanneke headed a company at Vienna's ScalaTheater for a season (15 September–26 October 1933), by which time the show had already made its début in Budapest, played in Hungarian (ad Tamás Emőd, István Békeffy) for 32 performances at the Vígszinház, and in London where C B Cochran's punningly titled *Mother of Pearl* (ad A P Herbert) had a good run of 181 performances. Alice Delysia played Josephine Pavani, memorably singing 'Every Woman Thinks She Wants to Wander', Sepha Treble was daughter Pearl and Frederick Ranalow her father, here turned into Richard Moon, MP in a version which resituated the story in England and filled it with Lords and lieutenants. Delysia repeated her great personal success when she appeared in *Mother of Pearl* under Frank Thring's management in Australia the following year alongside Phyllis Baker as Pearl, Frank Harvey (Moon), Robert Coote (Sterling) and Cecil Scott, playing the musical in repertoire with the play *Her Past*.

In 1954 a revised version of the show (ad Leonard Steckel) was played at Vienna's Theater in der Josefstadt (23 February, 43 performances) under the title *Manon*, and in 1959 the filmstar Zarah Leander appeared at the Raimundtheater in a new production of the show under the direction of Karl Farkas.

An Arthur Maria Rabenalt film under the title *Eine Frau, die weiss, was sie will* was produced in 1958, starring Lilli Palmer both as revue-star Angela Cavallini and her granddaughter, teacher Julia Klöhn, in a routine showbiz tale which had nothing to do with the original, but which was attached to some of Straus's music.

Hungary: Vigszinház *Egy asszony, aki tudja, mit akar* 23 December 1932; UK: Gaiety Theatre *Mother of Pearl* 27 January 1933; Austria: Scala-Theater 10 October 1933; Australia: Princess Theatre, Melbourne *Mother of Pearl* 14 July 1934

DER FRAUENFRESSER

DER FRAUENFRESSER Operette in 3 acts by Leo Stein and Carl Lindau. Music by Edmund Eysler. Wiener Bürgertheater, Vienna, 23 December 1911.

The libretto of *Der Frauenfresser* ('the woman hater'), the second of the series of highly successful musical plays composed by Eysler for Oscar Fronz's Wiener Bürgertheater, was submitted to the composer by Leo Stein along with the text of another Operette. Always more at home with a wholly Austrian subject, Eysler elected to set *Der Frauenfresser*, leaving the more highly coloured *Polenblut* to make the reputation of Oskar Nedbal.

As the result of an ancestor's will, the Schloss Aichegg, left jointly to two parts of the family, is inhabited half by Major Hubertus von Murner (Fritz Werner) and half by Frau Natalie von Roffan (Viktoria Pohl-Meiser) and her daughter, the principal living room being divided down the middle. Hubertus, who was betrayed in his youth by his fiancée, Mary Wilton (Erna Fiebinger), has become a woman-hater and has founded a misogynists' club into which he is trying to induct his nephew, Camillo (Marcel Noë). The boy, however, is more interested in Tilly von Roffan (Emmy Petko) than misogyny. The widowed Mary, still in love with the fiancé of her young days, arrives on the scene to buy up the von Roffans' half of the castle and, after two acts of quiproquos and decidedly unmisogynistic behaviour by Hubertus, who at one stage even sets his sights on Tilly, the pair come happily together for the final curtain.

Eysler's score was based largely on waltz music, with Hubertus's first-act song 'Sie hiess Marie', the popular 'Junge Mädchen tanzen gern' from the first-act finale, and the second act's 'Das war Gott Amors blauer Bogen' proving the choice numbers, alongside a polka duet for Tilly and Hubertus ('Kommen Sie, kommen Sie Polka tanzen') and a jaunty quartet in which life is compared to racing – you need a little luck in both ('Ja im Leben, wie im Rennen braucht man Glück'). The musically light final act was topped by a brisk trio and dance for Mary, Tilly and Camillo ('Kinder, lasst den Kopf nicht hängen').

Der Frauenfresser gave the Bürgertheater its biggest hit to date. It passed its 100th performance on 1 April 1912, before Karl Streitmann took over as Hubertus, then shared the bill with a stage version of the Passion Play until the end of the season (159 performances). When the theatre resumed, *Der Frauenfresser* was reopened with Hans Fürst starred, before Werner returned to his original rôle as the show ran on to its 200th night (11 October). It closed its main run after 270 performances (20 December), but remained in the theatre's repertoire for two further seasons as Fronz went on to mount the next Eysler musicals with equal profit. It was seen again at the Bürgertheater in 1920, then at the Johann Strauss-Theater in 1925 with Madame Pohl-Meiser repeating alongside Fritz Imhoff as Hubertus (13 August–3 September). It was produced in Vienna once more in 1946 but, like the rest of this popular series, was effectively wiped out of the repertoire by time, aided by the wartime embargo on Eysler's music.

A Budapest production (ad Adolf Mérei) was mounted at the Budapesti Színház in 1912, and later the same year Miksa Preger's company from Berlin played the piece in German during its season at the Vigszinház, whilst a Broadway production (ad George Hobart) was staged at the Astor Theater under the management of A H Woods a few months later. Hobart altered the plot so that Major von Essenburg (Walter Lawrence) was again jilted by Marie (Sallie Fisher) in the final act, but Camillo (Joseph Santley) was allowed to keep his Tilly (Dolly Castles), now upgraded to being the daughter of a Baroness (Mrs Stuart Robson). Eysler's score won delighted praise ('lovely music'... 'a delightful score ... fresh, insinuating, soothing or inspiring as the mood of the action demands') but *The Woman Haters* was a quick failure in four weeks on Broadway. When it was sent on the road the show was given a more conventional title: *The Pretty Little Widow*.

Hungary: Budapesti Színház *Az asszonyfaló* 15 May 1912, Vigszinház *Der Frauenfresser* 22 May 1912; Germany: ?1912; USA: Astor Theatre *The Woman Haters* 7 October 1912

DIE FRAU IM HERMELIN Operette in 3 acts by Rudolf Schanzer and Ernst Welisch. Music by Jean Gilbert. Theater des Westens, Berlin, 23 August 1919.

If Jean Gilbert's most memorable successes came with his scores to those sparkling pre-war and wartime musical comedies of which *Die keusche Susanne* was the most internationally successful example, he subsequently proved his ability to write the score for pieces in the fashionable postwar romantic-costume-musical line. The most successful of these was *Die Frau im Hermelin*, which profited from the eventual loosening in anti-German feelings in the lucrative English and allied markets to run up a series of long-running productions around the world, making the piece, statistically at least, possibly Gilbert's most internationally successful work of all.

The 'woman in ermine' is a ghost, said to appear in time of danger at the Beltrami castle near Verona, and it is Mariana Beltrami, the wife of the Italian Count Adrien Beltrami, who, during the Russian invasion of 1810, sees her appear. The enemy Colonel Paltitsch imposes himself, with the support of his regiment, on the Beltrami household and before long is tempted to impose himself, equally, on the lady of the household. Count Adrien, who has been forced into disguise as a servant in his own home, reveals himself to stop the seduction and is sentenced to be shot as a spy. Mariana can buy his life with her favours, as apparently the ghostly lady in ermine did in the past in a similar situation. Events ultimately come to a happy and unbloody ending. The comical moments fell to Suitangi, an itinerant silhoutte artist, who stands in as the Count whilst he is being a servant, the visiting ballet dancer Sophie Lavalle, and Baron Kajetan Sprotti-Sprotti.

The most popular moments of Gilbert's score were, on the romantic side, the Adrien/Mariana waltz duet, 'Liebchen, du mein reizendes Liebchen', and the seductive waltz duo between Mariana and Paltitsch, 'Man sagt doch nicht gleich, "nein"', which reappeared throughout the show as the relationship between the two grew variously hotter and colder, and, on the more light-hearted side, the lively trio 'Nur an die Alten muss man sich halten' (Sophie/Suitangi/Sprotti), Suitangi's waltz number about 'Meine Silhouetten' and the polka invitation to 'Tanz mit mir den Holubiak' (apparently a kind of cossack dance).

Die Frau im Hermelin played at the Theater des Westens, under the management of Messrs Beese and Bieber, through some 300 performances before going on to further successes. Budapest was the quickest of the other main centres to take the show up, and *A hermelines nő* (ad Sándor Hevesi) was produced at the Vígszinház soon after the end of the Berlin run (31 performances), prior to its mounting in Vienna where Margit Suchy (Mariana), Harry Peyer (Adrien), Louis Treumann (Paltitsch), Luise Kartousch (Sophie), Ernst Tautenhayn (Suitangi) and Karl Tuschl (Sprotti) featured. The piece played at the Theater an der Wien through the three months till the end of the spring season, with Christl Mardayn later replacing Suchy in the star rôle, and it returned again in the autumn for a further seven weeks to bring its total run to 141 performances in Vienna.

In London, *The Lady of the Rose* (ad Frederick Lonsdale, Harry Graham) was presented by James White at Daly's Theatre, billed as a 'George Edwardes production' in spite of the fact that the great producer had been some years dead. Phyllis Dare (Mariana), Roy Royston (Adrien), Harry Welchman (Colonel Belovar), Huntley Wright (Suitangi) and Ivy Tresmand (Sophie) led the cast, the score was supplemented with a Leslie Stuart number called 'Catch a Butterfly While You Can' for Miss Tresmand, and the production proved a major hit, playing for 514 performances in the West End before going on the road and into the colonies, notably to Australia. There, after a tryout in Brisbane, it was produced in Melbourne with Edith Drayson starred alongside Howett Worster and Leslie Holland and later in Sydney (Theatre Royal, 9 May 1925) with Gladys Moncrieff teamed with Claude Flemming and John Ralston. The show was brought back briefly to London and Daly's Theatre in 1929 with Marjery Wyn playing alongside Welchman and Wright.

Another English adaptation of the libretto (ad Cyrus Wood) was apparently made for Broadway, although Harry Graham's London lyrics were again used for such of the original songs as remained. This time the beastly Colonel – still called Belovar, and played by Walter Woolf – got the girl (Wilda Bennett) in the end, for Count Adrien (Harry Fender) turned out to be not her husband, but her brother! Gilbert's score was given the usual Shubert treatment, being decorated (not to say submerged) by additional material by Sigmund Romberg ('When Hearts Are Young' etc) and by the latest addition to their botching team, Al Goodman. The resultant show ran for 232 performances.

In spite of its successes, *Die Frau im Hermelin* did not become part of the revivable repertoire, and the best of its reputation remained in England. However, the piece's story was used as the basis for a 1927 Hollywood film in which Corinne Griffith, Francis X Bushman and Einar Hansen took the star rôles, and again for a 1930 First National-Pathé musical movie starring Vivienne Segal, Lupino Lane, Allen Prior, Walter Pidgeon, Claude Flemming and Myrna Loy. Gilbert's score was replaced by numbers by Al Dubin, Al Bryan and Ed Ward, Schanzer and Welisch's title by the curious *Bride of the Regiment* and even much of their plot by Hollywooden film-flam. The Australians retitled the movie *The Lady of the Rose*, and a 1948 Hollywood remake went further back to source and called itself *That Lady in Ermine*. It didn't get much closer to the original story, however, and Friedrich Hollander and Leo Robin's musical moments included Betty Grable cooing 'Oooh, What I'll Do to That Wild Hungarian'.

Hungary: Vígszinház *A hermelines nő* 1 July 1920; Austria: Theater an der Wien 29 April 1921; UK: Daly's Theatre *The Lady of the Rose* 21 February 1922; USA: Ambassador Theater *The Lady in Ermine* 2 October 1922; Australia: Brisbane 9 August 1924, Her Majesty's Theatre, Melbourne 20 September 1924.

DAS FRÄULEIN VON AMT Operette in 3 acts by Ernst Arnold and Georg Okonkowski. Music by Jean Gilbert. Theater des Westens, Berlin, 2 September 1915.

Rich Uncle Felix Förster plans to wed his nephew to the daughter of his business partner, unaware that young Robert has already got himself married to Marie, the little lady from Amt. When Uncle Felix himself develops an unseen passion for Agathe Blutenhain, the author of a novel he has read, he is disappointed to find out that 'Agathe' is actually one Eduard Hazelhun and there is little left to do but allow himself to be prettily consoled by his new niece-in-law.

Although not one of Gilbert's biggest hits, the show was a wartime success in Germany and was also produced in both Vienna and in Budapest (ad Zsolt Harsányi).

Austria: Wiener Stadttheater 1 February 1916; Hungary: Vigszinház, *Ó Teréz!* 18 August 1917

FRAU LUNA Burlesk-phantastich Austattungs-Operette in 1 act (4 scenes) by Heinrich Bolten-Bäckers. Music by Paul Linke. Apollotheater, Berlin, 1 May 1899.

Frau Luna was a little revusical spectacular (burlesque-fantasy-spectacular-operette) written to fill the needs and a part of the bill of the popular Berlin variety house, the Apollotheater, where Emil Waldmann had earlier had a fine success with Bolten-Bäckers and Lincke's other little songs-sex-and-scenery piece, *Venus auf Erden*.

The tale of the show took the inventor Hans Steppke (Robert Steidl) up to the moon in his home-made balloon, accompanied by his friends Lämmermeier (Arnold Rieck) and Pannecke, and their landlady, Frau Iduna Pusebach (Emmy Krochert). There they meet the moon-factotum, Theophil (Harry Bender), who turns out to be the man with whom Frau Pusebach once had a little adventure when he popped down to earth during an eclipse, and the intergalactic Prinz Sternschnuppe (Siegmund Lieban), come thence in his space-automobile for one of his periodic proposals to the lady-in-the-moon, Frau Luna (Willy Walden). Frau Luna takes a violent fancy to Steppke, but the mortal man resists all temptations, remains true to his earthbound Marie, and gratefully accepts the offer from Theophil to ferry the little group back to earth. Frau Luna will become the bride of Sternschnuppe, whilst Theophil gets the space-car as a thank-you present for his happy interference.

The song hits of the show were the waltz 'Schlösser, die im Monde liegen' and Frau Luna's soprano march number 'Lasst den Kopf nicht hängen', whilst Frau Pusebach scored in the comical reminiscence of her affair in the dark, 'O Theophil', and Sternschnuppe had his moment in 'Frohe munt're Lieder' in a score which ranged from a jolly Automobile-quartet ('Des Menschen Forschungs-streben zeigt') to a grand ballet staged in Frau Luna's magic garden.

Frau Luna was a big success in Berlin, where its favourite songs became enormously popular, and the Apollo management continued with the policy of including Lincke/Bolten-Bäckers Operetten, always written with the

house's large scenic and dance possibilities in mind, in their programmes for a number of years. *Frau Luna*, however, remained the most successful of the series. The Berlin company played the piece as part of their repertoire in a season at Vienna's Danzers Orpheum in 1903 with Lucie Medlon as Luna, Felix Müller as Steppke and Helene Voss as Frau Pusebach, Budapest's Royal Orfeum was opened with *Luna asszony* (followed up by *Nakiri* and *Vénusz a földön*), and the show found a Parisian production at L'Olympia in 1904 when the Isola brothers attempted to follow the Apollotheater formula and include Operette in their variety programmes. Fabrice Lemon and Maurice de Marsan's six-scene version featured Lucien Noël (Karl), Louise Blot (Mme La Lune), Vilbert (Théophile), Yette Bertholy (Mlle Pusebach) and Colas (Prince Soleil), and the piece shared the programme with a magician, some comic acrobats, jugglers, trained animals and 'jeux athlétiques'.

It was 1911 before London got a glimpse of *Castles in the Air* (ad Mrs Cayley Robinson, Adrian Ross) when it was produced at the unfashionable Scala Theatre, paired not with variety acts but with a lecture on and demonstration of the new Kinemacolour process. What audiences there were preferred films of 'Our Farmyard Friends' and 'Picturesque North Wales' to Sybil Lonsdale, St John Hamund, Sybil Tancredi and Lincke's music, and the Operette was quickly dropped from the programme.

A new, full-length version of *Frau Luna* was subsequently put together and remounted at the Apollotheater in 1922, the original tale being expanded with more scene-changes (eleven scenes) and with some songs taken from other Lincke works. The most successful of these was the the march 'Das macht die Berliner Luft' previously heard in the composer's *Berliner Luft*, a revue which also contributed the duet 'Schenck mir doch ein kleines bisschen Lieben' to the new score. Frau Luna's 'Von Sternen umgeben' was borrowed from the rôle of Venus in *Venus auf Erden*. Yet another new version was produced at the Stadttheater, Döbeln in 1929, and more remade versions of the piece were seen in Berlin in 1935, at the Admiralspalast in 1936, at the Metropoltheater in 1957 and, again, at the same house in recent years. Yet another new version (ad Kay and Lore Lorentz, mus ad Jurgen Knieper) appeared at Nuremberg in 1972. In 1990 the Metropoltheater company took their version of what has become accepted as the 'most Berlinish of all Berlin Operetten' beyond the confines of the city and, as it heads for its 100th birthday, various versions of the show are still solidly anchored in the repertoire of its home country.

A film version was produced in 1941 with Irene von Meyerndorff, Lizzi Waldmüller, Paul Kemp and Georg Alexander featured.

Hungary: Royal Orfeum *Luna asszony* 17 March 1902; Austria: Danzers Orpheum 18 February 1903; France: L'Olympia *Madame la Lune* 1904; UK: Scala Theatre *Castles in the Air* 11 April 1911; Film: 1941
Recording: selection (revised version) (RCA)

FRAZEE, Harry H[erbert] (b Peoria, Ill, 29 June 1880; d New York, 4 June 1929).

Frazee worked in the theatre from the age of 16, first as an usher, then as an accountant, as a road advance agent and, from the age of 22, regularly as a producer. His first productions, plays and musical comedies, were confined to Chicago and the touring circuits, but his co-production of a heavily revamped and wholly re-musicked version of the Continental hit *Madame Sherry* (1910 w George Lederer, A H Woods) gave him a major success.

Thereafter, although such further musical ventures as *Jumping Jupiter* with Richard Carle, *The Happiest Night of His Life* with Victor Moore, *The Ladies' Lion* by and with Jeff de Angelis (all w Lederer) and *Modest Susanne* (w Woods) were mostly less successful, he did quite well with an adaptation of *A Contented Woman* musically mounted as *Ladies First* (1912, 164 performances) and generally prospered, as he invested in theatre building in both Chicago (Cort Theater) and New York (Longacre Theater). He also acquired the New York Lyric Theater and Wallack's Theater which he renamed the Frazee. At the same time he kept up a very high profile in the sporting world as owner of the Boston Red Sox.

Frazee continued producing plays until, in 1923, he outdid even his *Madame Sherry* success when he commissioned and produced *No, No, Nanette*, based on a play he had mounted earlier in his career. Staged first in Detroit, then in Chicago, London and ultimately on Broadway, *No, No, Nanette* was one of the greatest hits of its time. An attempt to repeat with another musical made from one of his play successes, a musical version of *Nothing But the Truth* called *Yes, Yes, Yvette*, was a failure, but the earlier show was still earning its producer plenty of money when he died a few years later, aged 48.

FREEAR, Louie (b London, 26 November 1873; d London, 20 March 1939). Tiny, munchkinnish low-comedy performer who became the rage of the London stage for several years at the turn of the century.

Louie Freear began her stage career as a child, appearing (as a boy) with the Moore and Burgess Minstrels, in pantomime, and with a touring juvenile comic opera company as well as in music hall and as a member of a midget minstrel company. At 21 she went seriously, if temporarily, legit when Ben Greet hired her to play such rôles as Puck in *A Midsummer Night's Dream* and Mopsa in *A Winter's Tale* in his Shakespearian repertoire. She next appeared in George Dance's play *Buttercup and Daisy* and the author subsequently wrote a rôle for her, as the low comedy cockney slavey Ruth, into his musical *The Gay Parisienne* when it was due to be produced in the West End after several years on the road.

Little Miss Freear became an overnight star with her rendition of Ruth's 'Sister Mary Jane's Top Note', but it did her little good when she was tacked into the London production of the American musical *Lost, Stolen or Strayed* (aka *A Day in Paris*) in a vain attempt to save an unpromising production with her new-found star status. She went to America for the starrily cast 1899 musical extravaganza *The Man in the Moon*, and, on returning home, appeared again as Puck, this time with Tree at His Majesty's, before going on the road with her own company, in a boy's rôle.

She returned to London in 1901 to play a specially enlarged version of the rôle of Fi-fi, the low-comedy cockney waitress, in the London production of Dance's *A Chinese Honeymoon* and, as in *The Gay Parisienne*, she caused a sensation with her music-hally songs 'I Want to Be a Lidy' and 'The Twiddley Bits'. After two years of the record-breaking run of *A Chinese Honeymoon* she left to cash in her zooming reputation in the lucrative music halls, but, as the momentary fashion for low-comedy munchkins oozed away, she found herself with fewer opportunities and the latter part of her career was limited to variety and to the occasional reprise of her most famous rôles.

FREE AS AIR Musical play in 2 acts by Julian Slade and Dorothy Reynolds. Music by Julian Slade. Grand Theatre, Leeds, 8 April 1957; Savoy Theatre, London, 6 June 1957.

The successor to the enormously successful *Salad Days* retained something of the naïve charm of that piece, but, being built for a London house rather than as a repertory-theatre end-of-term entertainment, it was made in a slightly more substantial form, with a plot, an orchestral accompaniment, a considerably larger cast, and a chorus.

Set on an island in the Channel Islands, *Free as Air* told the tale of the lovely and wealthy Geraldine (Gillian Lewis) who escapes both the nosy press and a pressing suitor and finds her way to the quiet island of Terhou. There she finds both peace and the handsome local Albert Postumous (John Trevor), whilst the pushy Jack (Gerald Harper) and the gushing newspaperwoman Ivy Crush (Josephine Tewson), who are ready to launch a 'development programme' on the island, are routed. Patricia Bredin was the island's little soprano Molly, co-author Miss Reynolds the booming Miss Catamole, and Michael Aldridge played the Lord of the island.

The songs were gently suitable, with the loping philosophy of the islanders, 'Let the Grass Grow Under Your Feet', contrasting with inane Jack's tales of his past conquests 'Her Mummy Doesn't Like Me Any More' and the semi-surprised love song for the formidable Miss Catamole and the gentle little Mr Potter (Howard Goorney), 'We're Holding Hands', proving the pick.

Free as Air's 417 performances in London thoroughly confirmed the authors' success with *Salad Days*, and also the fact that there was a place in the theatre for simplicity and charm alongside the increasingly loud, brash and amplified brand of musical show. The piece had a successful provincial life and was subsequently played, on the heels of *Salad Days*, in Australia and in other English-speaking regions as well as in the Netherlands.

Australia: Princess Theatre, Melbourne 11 October 1958
Recording: original cast (Oriole), Dutch cast (Philips)

FREEDLEY, Vinton (b Philadelphia, 5 November 1891; d New York, 5 June 1969). Actor turned highly successful producer of Broadway musicals through 20 years of hits.

Freedley began in the theatre as an actor and appeared as the young hero of Victor Herbert's ill-fated *Oui, Madame* (1920, Richard Ogden) and Percy Wenrich's road-folding *Maid to Love* (1920), with the Astaires in *For Goodness' Sake* (1922, Jefferson Dangerfield) and as the juvenile man of the short-lived Carlo and Sanders musical *Elsie* (1923, Harry Hammond).

He went into partnership with *Oui, Madame* and *For Goodness' Sake*'s producer, Alex Aarons, in the same year and, after initiating their new firm with the play *The New Poor*, the pair embarked on a ten-year string of musical-comedy productions which included seven George Gershwin musicals: *Lady, Be Good!* (1924) which featured

Freedley's former stage partners, the Astaires, *Tip-Toes* (1925), *Oh, Kay!* (1926), *Funny Face* (1927), *Treasure Girl* (1928), *Girl Crazy* (1930) and *Pardon My English* (1933), as well as Rodgers and Hart's *Spring is Here* and *Heads Up* (both 1929), *Here's Howe* (1928), De Sylva, Brown and Henderson's *Hold Everything!* (1928), and the 'melodrama with music' *Singin' the Blues* which they quickly hived off to the show's cast to run as a co-operative following an unimpressive opening.

The partnership with Aarons was ended in 1933, and Freedley then continued as a solo producer, beginning auspiciously with the Broadway staging of Cole Porter's *Anything Goes* (1934) which featured *Girl Crazy*'s Ethel Merman in its starring rôle. He produced three further Porter musicals in the next seven years – *Red, Hot and Blue* (1934), *Leave it to Me!* (1938) and *Let's Face It* (1941) – as well as the Vernon Duke *Cabin in the Sky* (1940), but later musical pieces did not find the same success. *Jackpot* (1945) and *Great to Be Alive!* (1950 w Anderson Lawler, Russell Markert) were Broadway failures, whilst *Dancing in the Streets* (1943) did not even get that far.

Freedley made one appearance as a Broadway director of a musical with a souped-up *HMS Pinafore* called *Memphis Bound* which failed in 1945.

DER FREMDENFÜHRER Operette in a prologue and 3 acts by Leopold Krenn and Carl Lindau. Music by Carl Michael Ziehrer. Theater an der Wien, Vienna, 11 October 1902.

The Baron Niki Schlipp (Edmund Löwe) accepts a bet from his fellow club-members that he can actually earn his living for a fortnight. He gets a job quickly, for on his way round the Ringstrasse he meets his old girlfriend, Anna Weisskopf, who is now a prima donna and calls herself Bianca Testa (Lina Abarbanell). She suggests that the apparently down-on-his-luck Niki act as a guide for her father (Siegmund Natzler) who is coming to Vienna for the wedding of her sister, Hedwig (Dora Keplinger), to the forester Hanns (Karl Meister). By the time Weisskopf's visit is done, the old man has discovered that his once-disowned daughter is rich and famous and, indeed, his own employer, whilst Niki has both won his bet and the hand of Anna-Bianca. Alexander Girardi and Mila Theren provided the soubret moments as the military bandsman Ratz and his sweetheart Gabriele, maid to Bianca.

Ziehrer's score to *Der Fremdenführer* included some locally flavoured pieces in the composer's best manner, with Bianca's entry waltz, 'Töne, Liedchen, töne durch die Nacht', Niki's waltz song in praise of Vienna, 'O Wien, mein liebes Wien', and the pretty duo for Hanns and Hedwig, 'Braucht es denn Samt und Seide', proving amongst the favourites. There were a pair of jolly numbers for Ratz, and the novelties included a yodelling duo for two bored aristocratic gentlemen and a Hannakischer dance.

Der Fremdenführer did not prove a particular success at the Theater an der Wien. It played its 40th performance on 19 November, and was replaced two days later by Lehár's maiden Operette, *Wiener Frauen*, being given just a handful of intermittent matinée performances thereafter. However, after decades of oblivion the piece was cannily remounted as a wartime good-old-days piece during the second war. Adapted by Walter Hauttmann (book) and Erik Jaksch (music), it was produced by Willy Seidl at the

Raimundtheater with a cast including ageing stars Mizzi Günther, Luise Kartousch, Fritz Imhoff and Richard Waldemar alongside Toni Niessner (Ratz), Maya Mayska (Bianca Testina) and Alfred Hülgert (Nikolaus), a programme decorated with swastikas and air-raid warnings, and considerable success. It was brought back for a further production in 1961, and in 1978 was remodelled yet again, with additional Ziehrer numbers added, for a production at the Volksoper (22 October). Alois Aichorn, Erich Kuchar, Rudolf Wasserlof, Gisela Ehrensperger and Helga Papouschek were amongst the initial cast.

It it took quite a while, and a war, to make a success out of *Der Fremdenführer* in Austria, and it did not manage the same resurrection elsewhere. It had only a fair life in Germany and in Hungary where, under the curious title of *7777* (ad Dezső Bálint, Jenő Faragó), it was played ten times at the Népszinház.

Germany: ?1903; Hungary: Népszinház *7777* 15 April 1905

THE FRENCH MAID Musical comedy in 2 acts by Basil Hood. Music by Walter Slaughter. Theatre Royal, Bath, 4 April 1896; Terry's Theatre, London, 24 April 1897.

Touring manager Milton Bode, who had trouped Hood and Slaughter's *Gentleman Joe* through Britain with great success, mounted a new piece by the same authors at Bath in 1896, for a nine-week tour. The nine were followed by a further 19, and the attractions of *The French Maid* proved so potent that Bode was able to hive off the rights for a London production of the piece the following year. Whilst Bode's tours continued, W H Griffiths mounted *The French Maid* at the unfashionable Terry's Theatre with Kate Cutler cast in the title-rôle alongside several ex-D'Oyly Carte players, and he scored a splendid success. *The French Maid* played a remarkable 480 London performances in its number-two venue.

Hood's plot was (for him) amazingly insubstantial, dealing almost entirely with the caprices and love affairs of Suzette (Andrée Corday/Kate Cutler), who is courted by the gendarme, Paul Lecuire (Arthur Watts/Herbert Standing), the waiter Charles Brown (Windham Guise/Murray King), and, more intermittently, by both Brown's twin brother Jack (Joseph Wilson) and the visiting Maharajah of Punkapore (Percy Percival). Alongside the soubrette, there was also an ingénue, Dorothy Travers (Louie Pounds), paired off, eventually, with the tenor, Lt Harry Fife (Spenser Kelly/Richard Green), and a couple of comical elders – Admiral Sir Hercules Hawser (H O Clarey) and his Lady (Caroline Ewell/Kate Talby). Instead of plot, however, Hood supplied nifty dialogue and some delightful and well-above-average lyrics for songs angled in the same popular line as those for *Gentleman Joe*.

Jack sang of 'The Jolly British Sailor' and related the music-hally tale 'I've 'er Portrait Next My 'eart' in which his life was saved from a bullet by the thickness of the packet of his various sweethearts' photos in his breast pocket, Hawser declared in Gilbertian style 'I'm an Admiral', Charles advised 'Do Not Jump at Your Conclusions', Harry got patriotic about 'Britannia's Sons' and Suzette had a selection of bright pieces to be delivered brightly, but it was a duet for the twin brothers (The Twin Duet) which turned out to be the song hit of the piece.

As *The French Maid* settled in for a very long career in

classic rôles from Cyrano de Bergerac to Don Juan await-ing him in the commercial theatre, including his memor-able stage and film portrayal of the wandering Marius in the Pagnol trilogy *Marius*, *Fanny* and *César*. His intro-duction to the musical theatre came about through his liaison à la ville with the actress and vocalist Yvonne Print-emps, opposite whom he starred, at her insistence, in London and New York in *Conversation Piece* (1934, as Paul replacing Noël Coward), in London in *O Mistress Mine* (1936, Max) and in the French stage (1937) and film (1938) versions of *Les Trois Valses*, versions specially adap-ted from the German original to allow Fresnay to play a non-singing rôle. On film, again without singing, he portrayed Offenbach to Mlle Printemps's version of Hortense Schneider (*Valse de Paris*).

FREUND, Julius (b Breslau, 8 December 1862; d Partenkirchen, 6 January 1914). Revue and musical-com-edy author at the turn of the German century.

An actor from the age of 19, Freund worked at the Vienna Burgtheater and then in various theatres in Berlin. He subsequently turned to writing and, after an early attempt at opera (*Margitta* w R Bunge, music: Erich Meyer-Hellmund, Magdeburg 5 December 1889, *Spiel-mannsglück* music: L R Herrmann), joined Richard Schultz at the Centraltheater in 1895 in the post of dramaturg. There, in collaboration with Wilhelm Mannstädt and com-poser Julius Einödshofer, he turned out text and lyrics for a series of musical comedies, including the extremely suc-cessful *Eine tolle Nacht*, before moving on, when Schulz shifted theatres, to a similar post at the newly renovated Metropoltheater.

At the Metropoltheater he supplied the texts and lyrics for a long and steady line of topical Berlin revues, written in collaboration with house composers Viktor Holländer (*Neuestes! Allerneustes!* (1903), *Ein tolles Jahr* (1904), *Auf ins Metropol* (1905), *Der Teufel lacht dazu!* (1906), *Das muss man seh'n* (1907), *Hurrah! Wir leben noch!* (1910), *Die Nacht in Berlin* (1911)) and Paul Lincke (*Donnerwetter tadellos!* (1908), *Halloh! die grosse Revue* (1909)), several of which were later mounted in other centres in suitably localized versions (*Das gündige Wien*, *Münchner Luft* etc). He also contributed texts for a number of spectacular musical plays, both adapted from the French and original, of which *Die verkehrte Welt* and *'ne feine Nummer*, with its cast of 200, were subsequently played in Viennese versions (ad Krenn, Lindau) at the Venedig in Wien summer theatre and the Theater an der Wien.

He later worked with both the American composer Gustave Kerker, in his attempt to turn out an Operette for the Continental stage, and with the indefatigable Rudolf Nelson on both Operette and revue, and his final works before his death, again for the Metropoltheater, were a rewrite of the highly successful Okonkowski/Jean Gilbert musical *Die elfte Muse* for its Berlin production as *Die Kino-Königin*, and an original piece with a score by Gilbert, the spectacular *Die Reise um die Welt in 40 Tagen*.

1894 **O, diese Berliner** (Julius Einödshofer) Centraltheater 2 September
1895 **Unsere Rentiers** (Einödshofer/w Mannstädt) Central-theater 16 February
1895 **Eine tolle Nacht** (Einödshofer/w Mannstädt) Central-theater 4 September

Plate 95. *Comedian H O Clarey as Admiral Sir Hercules Hawser in the original production of the long-running* **The French Maid**.

the British provinces and colonies, almost equalling the phenomenal records of such pieces as *The Lady Slavey*, *The New Barmaid* and *The Gay Parisienne* (all of which it had outpointed in London), it also found success in all corners of the English-speaking theatre world. On Broadway, with Marguerite Sylva in the title-rôle and Charles A Bigelow and Hallen Mostyn as the twins, E E Rice's production ran through 175 performances before going on the road and then being brought back for a three-week repeat season the following season (Herald Square Theater 12 Septem-ber 1898), whilst in Australia, after Ada Willoughby and Carrie Moore had each given their Suzette, the arrival of London variety and musical comedy star Ada Reeve gave Williamson and Musgrove's production the kind of a boost that helped to establish *The French Maid* as one of the most popular entertainments of the time.

Australia: Her Majesty's Theatre, Sydney 4 September 1897; USA: Herald Square Theater 27 September 1897

FRESNAY, Pierre [LAUDENBACH, Pierre] (b Paris, 4 April 1897; d Paris, 9 January 1975). Non-singing star of several musical shows.

Fresnay joined the Comédie-Française direct from drama school and spent the first ten years of his career (minus wartime service) playing classic and modern rôles at the 'grande maison' before buying his release at the age of 29. He found a plethora of leading juvenile parts and

1896 **Eine wilde Sache** (Einödshofer/w Mannstädt) Central-theater 20 September

1896 **Der Gaukler** (*Les Forains*) German version w Louis Herr-mann (Theater Unter den Linden)

1896 **Der Mandarin (von Tsing-ling-sing)** (Einödshofer) Metropoltheater August

1897 **Ein fideler Abend** (Einödshofer/w Mannstädt) Central-theater 7 February

1897 **Berliner Fahrten** (Einödshofer/w Mannstädt) Central-theater 4 September

1897 **Die Geisha** German version w C M Röhr (Lessing-Theater)

1898 **Die Tugendfalle** (Einödshofer/ad w Mannstädt) Central-theater 20 January

1898 **Sterzl in Berlin** (Einödshofer/w Mannstädt) Theater an der Wien, Vienna, 2 April

1898 **Das Paradies der Frauen** (*Le Royaume des femmes*) Ger-man version with new music by Einödshofer and Bertram Sänger (Metropoltheater)

1898 **Die kleine Michus** (*Les P'tites Michu*) German version w Heinrich Bolten-Bäckers (Metropoltheater)

1899 **Die verkehrte Welt** (*Le Royaume des femmes*) German ver-sion w add music by Einödshofer (Metropoltheater)

1899 **Mandanika** (Gustav Lazarus) Elberfeld 21 February

1900 **Der Zauberer von Nil** (*The Wizard of the Nile*) German version (Metropoltheater)

1901 **Schön war's doch** (Viktor Holländer) Metropoltheater 24 August

1901 **Diogenes** (Bogumil Zepler) 1 act Centraltheater 8 October

1901 **'ne feine Nummer** (Holländer, Leo Fall) Metropoltheater 26 December

1902 **Die zwölf Frauen des Japhet** (*Les douze femmes de Japhet*) German version with new music by Holländer Metropol-theater 29 November

1903 **Durchlaucht Radieschen** (Holländer) Metropoltheater 31 October

1904 **Die Herren von Maxim** (Holländer/ad) Metropoltheater 29 October

1905 **Die oberen Zehntausend** (Gustave Kerker) Metropol-theater 24 April

1905 **In Lebensgefahr** (Kerker) Walhalla-Theater 1 November

1911 **Hoheit amüsiert sich** (Rudolf Nelson) Metropoltheater 29 April

1912 **Schwindelmeier und Cie** (*The Arcadians*) German version with new music by Nelson Metropoltheater 27 April

1913 **Die Kino-Königin** revised *Die elfte Muse* w Georg Okonkowski Metropoltheater 8 March

1913 **Die Reise um die Erde in 40 Tagen** (Jean Gilbert) Metropoltheater 13 September

FRIEDERIKE Singspiel in 3 acts by Ludwig Herzer and Fritz Löhner-Beda. Music by Franz Lehár. Metropol-theater, Berlin, 4 October 1928.

Having musicalized the fictional love-lives of the com-poser Paganini and the tsarevich of Russia, Lehár took a step rather closer to home in his next Operette. Hard behind the Berlin production of what purported to be a tale about *Casanova*, his librettists picked the celebrated poet Goethe as the next victim for their romantic imaginings. It was a choice which would allow German programme-writers of later years to fill page after irrelevant page with learned pieces on the real life of the poet, but at the time the choice was regarded as a rather daring if not slightly unsavoury one. In spite of the fact that the show was a made-for-Tauber one, the authors stopped short of calling their piece *Goethe* or even *Johann Wolfgang!* and, for a change, it was *Friederike*, the little Alsacian maiden who was the other half of the love story, who became the title.

Friederike (Käthe Dorsch), the daughter of the rector of the village of Sesenheim, is the youthful sweetheart of the would-be poet Goethe (Richard Tauber), who is, for the moment, a medical student. When he wins an appointment as Court Poet to the Grand-Duchy of Saxe-Weimar, he believes that he is at last in a position to get married, but the Duke, because of past experiences, is insistent that he will hire only a bachelor. Goethe decides to refuse the post, but Friederike, knowing how important it is that he accept, pointedly flirts with his friend Lenz (Curt Wesper-mann) and, thinking that his love is rejected, Goethe duly goes off to Weimar. Eight years later, passing through Sesenheim, the now-famous poet learns the truth.

The authors called their piece a Singspiel, and displayed a rustic simplicity in the flavour of their libretto which justified that title. The ringing hit song of the piece, Goethe's 'O Mädchen, mein Mädchen', written to size for Tauber, proved to be one of Lehár's most enduring senti-mental tenor numbers, but in that song as elsewhere, echo-ing a libretto where passions did not rise and fall in the dramatically doomed fashion of the two earlier pieces, there was a pleasing simplicity to be found, whether in the poet's reciting of his poem 'Sah ein Knab' ein Röslein stehn', in the jolly Ländler of Lenz and Salomea (Hilde Wörner), 'Elsässer Kind', Lenz's little song to his 'Lämm-chen brav" or in Friederike's gently heart-broken 'Warum hast du mich wachgeküsst', the score was altogether less drivingly romantic in tone than was now usual from the composer.

In spite of the fact that Tauber's physique had nothing of the romantic to it, and that Dörsch, in the twilight of her career as a musical-theatre player prior to a second stardom as an actress, was some 20 years older than her character and rather lacking in singing voice, the two art-ists did a great deal to help the Rotter brothers' production of *Friederike* to a considerable success at the Metropol-theater and then at the Theater des Westens. He supplied the vocal values, reaching memorable heights in the hit song, whilst she gave the promise of what was to come in the straight theatre with an equally memorable acting per-formance. The piece, itself, was also largely liked, and one important Berlin critic crowed delightedly 'at last an Operette that can be listened to without mental ear-muffs on'.

The following year *Friederike* was played in Vienna, with Hans-Heinz Bollmann and Lea Seidl (later Josef Buresch, Betty Werner) starred. Again it scored a success, passing its 200th performance on 4 September 1929, before clos-ing a week later. It returned after the run of Gilbert's *Hotel Stadt-Lemberg* for a further two weeks and was given fur-ther performances in repertoire in 1930. In that same year, the show was seen widely in the rest of Europe, being mounted in Paris (ad André Rivoire) with René Gebert and Louise Dhamarys starred, in London (ad Adrian Ross, Harry S Pepper) where Lea Seidl was paired with the celebrated opera tenor Joseph Hislop for a rather dis-appointing 110-performance run under the management of Laddie Cliff, and in Hungary where Andor Szenes's version, starring Tibor Szentmihályi and Hanna Honthy, proved again a success.

America waited until 1937 before welcoming another English version (ad Edward Eliscu), produced by the Shuberts with Dennis King and Helen Gleason in the starring rôles. As in England, the hit song proved to be not enough to ensure success and the production lasted only 12 weeks on Broadway.

Käthe Dorsch subsequently played her rôle opposite Alfred Piccaver at the Volksoper, and *Friederike* was seen again in Vienna in 1945, but the piece did not establish itself as an Operette regular in the same way that the most deeply, colourfully popular of Lehár's later works did.

A film version was produced by Fritz Friedmann-Friedrich in 1932 in which Bollmann repeated the rôle he had played in Vienna alongside Mady Christians.

Austria: Johann Strauss-Theater 15 February 1929; France: Théâtre de la Gaîté-Lyrique *Frédérique* 17 January 1930; UK: Palace Theatre *Frederica* 9 September 1930; Hungary: Király Színház *Friderika* 31 October 1930; USA: Imperial Theater *Frederica* 4 February 1937; Film 1932

Recording: complete (EMI/HMV), selections (part records, Eurodisc, Telefunken etc)

FRIESE, Carl Adolf (b Bamberg, 21 October 1831; d Vienna, 24 January 1900). The creator of a long list of important comedy rôles in classic Viennese Operette.

The son of an actor/theatre director and a singer, Friese went on the stage at 12 in children's rôles. He became a chorus dancer, then a pantomime comedy-dancer in Pest, before first making his mark as a straight comedian in Temesvár. In 1852 the young comedian played at Vienna's Theater in der Josefstadt, then appeared at various theatres around Austria and Hungary before joining the companies at the Vienna Carltheater (1860) and at the Theater an der Wien under Friedrich Strampfer (1863). Along with Karl Blasel and Matthias Rott, Albin Swoboda and Marie Geistinger, Friese proved an important part of the comic backbone of this famous troupe in the years when it introduced the new repertoire of French opéras-bouffes to Vienna, along with a regular run of native Possen and the earliest important Viennese Operetten. In the Strampfer years he appeared in Offenbach's *Die schöne Helena* (1865, Agamemnon), *Blaubart* (1866, Oscar), *Die Schäfer* (Beautendon) and *Geneviève von Brabant* (Golo), in Bazin's *Die Reise nach China* (1866, Bonneteau), *Prinzessin Hirschkuh* (1866, Pelikan), *Theeblüthe* (1869, Fi-Fi) and as the theatre director in *Die falsche Carlotta Patti* (1866). Under Steiner and Geistinger's subsequent management he carried on in the same vein, playing in *Die Grossherzogin von Gerolstein* (Baron Puck) and scoring his biggest hit to date in the 1871 version of *Drei Paar Schuhe* (Julius von Nachtfalter, singing the hit song 'Bei Tag bin ich hektisch, bei Nacht werd' ich elektrisch'). He played in more Offenbach as the Caissier in *Die Banditen* (1871), Marinoni in *Fantasio* (1872), Polycarp in *Die Theaterprinzessin* (1872), Bibel in *Die Wilderer* (1873), Alfonso in *Madame Herzog* (1875) and King Vlan IV in *Der Reise in den Mond* (1876), and created lead comedy rôles in the first of Strauss's works: *Indigo* (1871, Romadour), *Karneval in Rom* (1873, Graf Falconi), *Die Fledermaus* (1874, the prison governor, Frank) and *Cagliostro in Wien* (1875, Cagliostro) as well as in Millöcker's *Abenteur in Wien* (1873, Hummel), Jonas's *Die Japanesin* (1874, Kamakuro) and Zeller's *Joconde* (Laird Dunstan Meredith), before briefly leaving the company.

He guested at the Theater an der Wien in 1877 to create the rôle of the Marquis de Marsillac in *Nanon* and again

for Millöcker's *Das verwunschene Schloss* (1878, Graf von Geiersberg) and Offenbach's *Der Brasilianer* (1879, Von Bloomberg) before again joining the company, under Maximilian Steiner, in 1880 for another long list of rôles in pieces such as *Die hübsche Perserin* (1880, Salamalek), *Apajune der Wassermann* (1880, Fürst Prutschesko), *Die Näherin* (1880, Julius von Sombar), *Die Tochter des Tambour-Major* (1880, Van Hokenbroing, ie Duc della Volta), *Der Bettelstudent* (Bogumil) and Delibes's *Ein Schotte* (1880, Ducornet). He was Lorenzo XVII in the original Vienna production of *La Mascotte* (1881), Calabazas in Lecocq's *Tag und Nacht* (1882), Chaoura in Offenbach's *Doktor Ox* (1882), Gigonnet in Millöcker's *Ein süsses Kind* (1882) and Bompan in *Lili* (1882) and also appeared as Balthasar Groot in *Der lustige Krieg* and in several other rôles created originally by Felix Schweighofer.

In 1883–4 he went to America where he appeared with Geistinger, playing principal comedy rôles in plays, musical comedies (*Der Zigeuner*, *Das tägliche Brot*, *Die Kindsfrau*) and Operetten (Ollendorf, Vicomte in *Lili* etc), but soon returned once more to the Theater an der Wien where he created a further series of often important comic rôles including Heidekrug in *Der Feldprediger*, Carnero in *Der Zigeunerbaron*, Derrick in the Viennese *Rip* (1885), Dauberval in *Zwillinge*, Philip of Navarre in *Der Hofnarr* (1886) and Graf Varoldi in Brandl's *Der liebe Augustin*, and played Casimir in *Prinzessin von Trapezunt* and such of his old roles as Frank in *Fledermaus*.

A second American season under the management of Gustav Amberg (Zsupán, Don Onofrio in *Don Cesar*, Nachtfalter, Nasoni in a remade version of *Gasparone*, Rumpelmeier in *Hundert Jungfrauen* etc), was followed by an engagement at the Carltheater under Franz Steiner, where, from 1887, he was seen as Josef Grauperl in *Die Dreizehn*, Captain Gordon in *Der Glücksritter*, Josef Lanner in the Genrebild on the composer's life and music, Don Onofrio, Doctor Track in *Die Jagd nach dem Glück*, Sergeant Meryll in *Capitän Wilson*, Don Riassa in *Farinelli* and Petrovic in Ziehrer's *Ein Deutschmeister*. He also directed many of that theatre's productions including *Tulipatan*, *Rikiki*, *Der Glücksritter*, *Der Sänger von Palermo*, *Der Freibuter* (*Surcouf*), *Die Jagd nach dem Glück*, *Ein Deutschmeister* and *Colombine*.

In 1889 he made a third voyage to America, this time accompanied by his son, with the company that opened the new Amberg Theatre in New York. They played *Farinelli* (Pancho), *Der Viceadmiral*, *Die sieben Schwaben* (Allgauerle), *Die Novize* (Severin Holberg), *Ihr Corporal*, *Boccaccio*, *Der Zigeunerbaron*, *Die Afrikarеisе*, *Der lustige Krieg*, Hopp's *Morilla* and much of the Carltheater repertoire, in many of which pieces Friese limited himself to directing and left the lead comedy to his son. When he finally returned to Vienna, however, he found that time had moved on and, after 50 years on the stage, he was forgotten and out-of-date. He took to the touring circuits until, in 1894, he was engaged as director and comic at the Theater in der Josefstadt where he had made his first Vienna appearance, 40 years earlier. It was there that he made his final stage appearances (including Bernard in the French musical comedy *Tata-Toto*) in 1895.

An outstanding comic singer, Friese also won himself first-rate laurels as a straight actor, appearing alongside Raimund in the original production of *Der Verschwender* as a young man, and ultimately developing into the best elderly comedy actor-singer of the Vienna musical theatre. In his young days, he also authored several burlesques including *Liebesqualen eines Tanzmeisters* and *Bei der Gaslanterne, oder Einer vom 57 Infanterieregiment* (music: Johann Baptiste Klerr).

A daughter, Dora Friese, and two sons, Bruno Friese and Carl Friese jr, all followed their father on to the Operette stage and appeared with him in his American trips. Several other children also went on the stage.

FRIGANZA, Trixie [O'CALLAHAN, Delia] (b Grenola, Kans, 29 November 1870; d Flintridge, Calif, 27 February 1955). Buxom soubrette who successfully carried her musical comedy career through to attractive middle-aged rôles and to comedy.

Trixie Friganza began a career in the musical theatre at the age of 19 playing in an americanized version of Lecocq's *Fleur de thé* (*The Pearl of Pekin*) and toured in *A Trip to Chinatown* (1890, Mrs Guyer) before first appearing in New York in supporting rôles in Henry Dixey's Gilbert and Sullivan company (Celia, Lady Saphir), in comic opera (*Jupiter*), and in opérette (*La Mascotte*, *The Little Trooper*, *Fleur de Lis*, *La Poupée*, *The Rounders*).

In 1900 she won her first notices when she appeared at the Casino Theatre as Mrs Muggins in *The Belle of Bohemia* and with Frank Perley's Comedians in *The Chaperons*. She played Nurse Chloe in *The Belle of Bohemia* in London the following year, toured Europe with the Casino Company in *The Belle of New York* and *The Casino Girl* and took part in the unfortunate re-opening of the Adelphi Theatre with *The Whirl of the Town* before returning home to take up her first major rôle, touring as the blackmailing Julie Bon-Bon in the American version of Ivan Caryll's *The Gay Parisienne* (*The Girl from Paris*). As her success grew, so too did her embonpoint, but her popularity on the road, where she was known as 'good value', proved solid as she took Marie Cahill's *Sally in Our Alley* and *A Trip to Chinatown* to the country and appeared regularly in vaudeville.

She created the rôle of Omee-Omi in *The Sho-Gun* (1904) in Chicago, and, while Georgia Caine took the part when the show went to Broadway, she went on to play the distinctly superior rôle of the devastating widow, Mrs Madison Crocker, in *The Prince of Pilsen* (1904) both in America and then in London. She appeared in Chicago's

Plate 96. **Trixie Friganza** *and the beauties of the American cities in* The Prince of Pilsen.

The Three Graces, *The Girl from Yama*, *Twiddle-Twaddle* and *His Honor the Mayor* and had a genuine Broadway star success when she appeared in Connie Ediss's big-lady rôle of Caroline Vokins in the American production of *The Orchid* (1907). She confirmed that success the following year in George M Cohan's *The American Idea* (1908, Mrs William Waxtapper), before returning to Chicago for *The Sweetest Girl in Paris* (1910, Mrs Ned Radcliffe).

Her later career was mostly in vaudeville, but she played in Will Hough's *Lonesome Lassies* (1915) in variety houses and on Broadway in revue on several occasions, and as late as 1929 in *Murray Anderson's Almanac* as well as on the cinema stage. She made her final New York musical-comedy appearance in *Canary Cottage* (1916, Blanche Moss), imported from the West Coast to Broadway in 1917, although she continued to appear in interstate productions for a number of years before chronic arthritis confined her largely to a bed for the last 15 years of her life.

FRIML, [Charles] Rudolf (b Prague, 8 December 1879; d Hollywood, Calif, 12 November 1972). Leading Broadway composer of romantic musical plays during the 1910s and 1920s.

The Prague-born Friml studied music in his native city from a young age, and made his early career principally as a pianist, touring the world for several years as accompanist to the violinist Jan Kubelik. He had what seems to be an isolated credit as a composer for the theatre when he wrote the music for August Berger's Tanz-Idyll *Auf Japan*, mounted at the Dresden Hoftheater in 1903 (7 June). In 1906 he settled in America where he made a career as a pianist and also as a composer of light instrumental and vocal music, winning the opportunity to write his first stage musical score when Victor Herbert refused to work for a second time with the ill-behaved *Naughty Marietta* prima donna, Emma Trentini. The score for Arthur Hammerstein's production of *The Firefly* (1912) was allotted to Friml, and songs such as 'Giannina Mia', 'Sympathy' and 'When a Maid Comes Knocking at Your Heart', widely heard in that successful show and then outside it, immediately established his reputation. The worldwide hit of the musical farce *High Jinks* (1913) gave the newcomer a second successive triumph and, if the Shuberts' production of *The Ballet Girl* – mounted for Trentini in Albany with its score attributed to Friml – turned into *The Peasant Girl*, with a score more akin to its original (Nedbal's *Polenblut*), on the road to Broadway, the slighted composer was revenged when the star walked out for lust of him and closed the show.

The 1915 *Katinka* gave him another piece which followed *High Jinks* to the corners of the English-speaking theatre world, and Arthur Hammerstein got a healthy 176 Broadway performances and an Australian sale out of *You're in Love*, but *Kitty Darlin'*, a musical version of *Sweet Kitty Bellairs* written to suit another singing star, Alice Nielsen, who had been most recently singing in opera, did less well. *Glorianna*, Catherine Chisholm Cushing's adaptation of her own *Widow by Proxy*, gave another fine soprano, Eleanor Painter only 96 performances in New York, but went onto a good touring life when taken around America by Fritzi Scheff. Friml had further good Broadway runs with the musical plays *Sometime* (1918), in which comedian Ed Wynn was the biggest draw, and *The Little Whopper* (1919, 224 performances), without producing any music or individual numbers which attracted particular attention, but of a series of further such pieces – musical versions of Mary Roberts Rinehart and Avery Hopwood's *Seven Days* as *Tumble In* (128 performances) and Charlotte Thompson's play *In Search of a Sinner* as *June Love* (50 performances), the tale of *Cinders* (31 performances) and *Bibi of the Boulevards*, which failed to reach New York – only *The Blue Kitten*, a remake of the famous French farce *Le Chasseur de Chez Maxim* (140 performances), made any kind of impression.

When Friml switched from supplying tunes for comedy musicals back to the frankly operettic style he had employed so successfully in his pieces for Trentini, his luck changed from the just all right to the extravagantly splendid. *Rose Marie* (1924, 'Rose Marie', 'The Indian Love Call') became one of the great American international operetta hits not only of its time but of all time, whilst the swashbuckling saga of *The Vagabond King* (1925, 'Only a Rose', 'Song of the Vagabonds') gave him a second major success with a romantic musical and score.

A semi-Ruritanian piece, *The Wild Rose* (61 performances), and a musical version of the play *The Squaw Man* as *The White Eagle* (48 performances) were failures, and a South Seas tale called *Luana* failed in both America and Britain, but Friml swashbuckled to the front again with another genuine romantic piece in the form of a musical version of *The Three Musketeers* ('Ma Belle'). By this time, however, the composer was headquartered in Hollywood. With lyric musicals no longer the vogue, his last Broadway show, *Music Hath Charms* (1934), developed from what was originally intended to be a botched version of *Eine Nacht in Venedig* for another operatic star, Maria Jeritza, was a failure and he abandoned the theatre to do his remaining work, including film versions of *Rose Marie* (three between 1928 and 1954), *The Vagabond King* (1930 and 1956) and *The Firefly* (1937) for the screen.

Friml was at his best in the lyrical, Continental operetta style which he managed to wrap attractively around libretti as diverse as the comedic *Katinka* and the period drama *The Vagabond King* and of which he was one of the most successful exponents in a period where the world's musical theatres were largely dominated by dance-and-comedy musicals and songwriters' shows.

1912 **The Firefly** (Otto Harbach) Lyric Theater 2 December
1913 **High Jinks** (Harbach/Leo Ditrichstein) Lyric Theater 10 December
1914 **The Ballet Girl** (*Polenblut*) Albany, NY 12 November (later *The Peasant Girl* with Nedbal's music restored)
1915 **Katinka** (Harbach) 44th Street Theater 23 December
1917 **You're In Love** (Edward Clark/Harbach) Casino Theater 6 February
1917 **Kitty Darlin'** (Harbach, P G Wodehouse) Casino Theater 7 November
1918 **Glorianna** (Catherine Chisholm Cushing) Liberty Theater 28 October
1918 **Sometime** (Rida Johnson Young) Shubert Theater 4 October
1919 **Tumble In** (Harbach) Selwyn Theater 24 March
1919 **The Little Whopper** (Bide Dudley/Harbach) Casino Theater 13 October
1921 **June Love** (Brian Hooker/W H Post, Charlotte Thompson) Knickerbocker Theater 25 April

1922 **The Blue Kitten** (Harbach, William Cary Duncan) Selwyn Theater 13 January
1922 **Bibi of the Boulevards** (Cushing) Majestic Theater, Providence 12 February
1923 **Cinders** (Clark) Dresden Theater 3 April
1924 **Rose Marie** (w Herbert Stothart/Harbach, Oscar Hammerstein II) Imperial Theater 2 September
1925 **The Vagabond King** (Hooker, Post) Casino Theater 21 September
1926 **The Wild Rose** (Harbach, Hammerstein) Martin Beck Theater 20 October
1927 **The White Eagle** (Hooker, Post) Casino Theater 26 December
1928 **The Three Musketeers** (Wodehouse, Clifford Grey/W A MacGuire) Lyric Theater 13 March
1930 **Luana** (Howard Emmett Rogers/J Keirn Brennan) Hammerstein Theater 17 September
1934 **Annina** (aka *Music Hath Charms*) (Rowland Leigh, John Schubert, G Rosener) Majestic Theater 29 December

[The Adventures of] FRITZ, OUR COUSIN GERMAN Musical play in 4 (later 3) acts by Charles Gayler. Music by various hands. Wallack's Theater, New York, 11 July 1870.

The most successful of all the comedy-melodramas with songs and dances which were popular provincial and occasionally metropolitan fare in America, Britain and in the English-speaking colonies in the second half of the 19th century, *Fritz, Our Cousin German*, was a vehicle for performer J K Emmet, which allowed its star to run the gamut from extravagant sentimentality to dashing bravado and to broad comedy, whilst pausing regularly to deliver a song, a dance or an instrumental or speciality item.

Emmet starred as the heavily accented Fritz, from Germany, who goes to the United States of America to look for his long-lost sister and the inheritance which their late father left in her charge. On his way, he falls in love with another passenger, Katrina (Georgia Langley), and she proves to be his Achilles heel, for the villainous Colonel Crafton (Charles Fisher), who has adopted Fritz's sister for all kinds of horrid motives, now kidnaps the boy's beloved. Fritz manages to rescue his sister and wed Katrina, but Crafton is not yet done. When the Fritzes have a baby, he whisks Little Fritz away, and the whole chase starts all over again.

The musical content of the show varied during its long life, but in an 1872 playbill it was announced that the third and final scene of Act 2 would comprise 'Fritz's Entertainment' including 'Dats vats de matter mit Jacob', 'Bologna Sausage Boy', 'Christine Nilsson Strauss', 'Sauer Kraut Receipt with Banjo', 'Kaiser, Don't You Want to Buy a Dog?', 'Schneider How You Vas?', 'Seven Up', 'Dat Toy Harmonic' upon which Mr J K Emmet plays Five distinct variations on 'Home, Sweet Home', 'The Brothers' Lullaby', 'Shonnie Vas a Nice Young Man' and 'Sauer Kraut is Bully'. It was, however, none of these which was the hit of the evening, but a lullaby, written by Emmet, and introduced into the piece as the key to recognition between Fritz and his sister. 'Emmet's Lullaby' became one of the favourite songs of its era.

Emmet played Fritz for the rest of his life, the original play being switched about, expanded and altered with alternative or additional scenes, songs or musical specialities on the harmonica, as it was taken round and round America and as far afield as London's Adelphi Theatre in a 'London version' (1872) and Melbourne's Theatre Royal (1874) and Opera House (18 March 1876) where the show broke every record with a run of 65 successive nights and a return later the same year. It was also played on Broadway in a 'new' version (1878). Emmet tried a couple of other pieces on the same lines without success – *Carl the Fiddler* (1871), *Max, the Merry Swiss Boy* (1873) and even *Jan, the New German* – before switching to a series of soi-disant sequels, beginning with the most durable (the original apart), *Fritz in Ireland* (1879) which allowed Emmet to sing some Irish songs and, of course, a lullaby, and continuing with *Fritz Among the Gipsies* (1882) in which he introduced another song, 'Sweet Violets', which would become a standard, *Fritz the Bohemian* (1884) and *Fritz in a Madhouse* (1889).

When Emmet had passed by, *Fritz* – or versions of it which used the famous title, if not quite its text – was often taken up by other performers, and the American smaller circuits and the Pacific and colonial theatres saw such actors as Charles Verner, Tom Buckley or, eventually, Emmet's own son (*Fritz in Ireland*, *Fritz in Prosperity*, *Fritz in Love* etc), give their versions of Fritz. The cheery hero's last Broadway appearance came in 1905 when Joseph Cawthorn starred in a new Fritz show, *Fritz in Tammany Hall* (Herald Square Theater, 16 October)

UK: Adelphi Theatre 7 December 1872; Australia: Theatre Royal, Melbourne 12 December 1874

FROHMAN, Charles (b Sandusky, Ohio, 17 June 1860; d *Lusitania* at sea, 7 May 1915). Successful and popular producer of the turn-of-the-century decades who shared his activities freely between London and New York.

The young Frohman began his working life in New York as a clerk in the offices of *New York Tribune*, and later of the *Daily Graphic*, before moving into the theatre as a member of the box office staff at Hooley's Theater in Brooklyn. He progressed to the hectic job of advance manager for a number of touring shows, notably Haverley's Minstrels, with which he toured as far afield as Britain, before joining his two brothers, Daniel and Gustave, as assistant managers at Steele MacKaye's Madison Square Theater, New York, organizing the road companies of MacKaye's productions.

He dabbled as a dramatic agent and then as a touring manager before attempting his first New York production, in 1886, with the farce-comedy *A Toy Pistol*, and he had his first success when he picked up the Boston production of Bronson Howard's *Shenandoah* and produced it at New York's Star Theater in 1889 with huge profit. Thereafter, his producing interests, often tied in with those of Al Hayman and/or Messrs Klaw and Erlanger in what became pejoratively known by competitors as 'the syndicate', grew flourishingly, at first with New York and nationwide play productions and tours, run to a standard of efficiency and quality which some circuits had not too often seen, and (after an 1891 venture with David Belasco on *Miss Helyett*) from 1895 with musicals.

Early on, Frohman developed close links with the London theatre and virtually all of his Broadway musical productions in the first dozen years of his musical theatre career were imports from London, at that time the thriving centre of musical-comedy production. With Hayman, he

hosted a Broadway season and American tour by George Edwardes's London company, playing the earliest Gaiety 'musical comedy' shows, *The Shop Girl* (1895) and *In Town* (1897), and the Daly's Theatre *An Artist's Model* (1895), as well as mounting Edwardes's production of W S Gilbert's *His Excellency* (1895) with a virtually all-English cast, the London hit *Little Miss Nobody* (1898) which folded pre-Broadway, and the English version of *L'Auberge du Tohu-bohu* (1898), before taking the opposite tack and exporting *The Girl from Up There*, an attempt to give the new star Edna May a follow-on to her West End hit in *The Belle of New York*, from New York (1901) to London. It had a limited run, but Frohman, who had been increasing his British production schedule over the previous 18 months, set up office in England and tried his hand as a producer there.

His first musical-theatre ventures on British soil, a collaboration with George Edwardes on *Kitty Grey*, and a production with Seymour Hicks and his wife, Ellaline Terriss, of the seasonal favourite, *Alice in Wonderland* (1900), were notable successes. Frohman and Hicks then teamed the following Christmas on a different kind of children's Christmas musical play. *Bluebell in Fairyland* turned out to be the most successful of its kind ever produced in England, with an appeal much wider than juvenile, and the tie-up with the Hicks family proved in the years that followed to be even more profitable for their new producer.

Over the next four years, whilst continuing his alliance with Edwardes with joint productions of *Three Little Maids* (London and Broadway), *The Girl from Kays* (USA), *The School Girl* (UK, USA solo) and *The Little Cherub* (USA), he also exported Frederick Mouillot's production of *My Lady Molly* to Broadway (but killed it by quirky casting) and took a major tumble with what should have been a good thing, the London mounting of Hugo Felix's German musical *Madame Sherry*. But at the same time he saw the Hicks connection build into a major success with *The Cherry Girl* (1903), the hit *The Catch of the Season* (1904 and Broadway 1905), a revival of *Bluebell* (1905), *The Beauty of Bath* (1906), the less successful *My Darling* (1907), *The Gay Gordons* (1908) and *The Dashing Little Duke* (1909), whilst his parallel roster of plays produced, amongst other successes, the initial performances of J M Barrie's *Peter Pan*. The profits of *The Catch of the Season* allowed Frohman to construct what he obligingly called the Hicks Theatre (nowadays the Globe) on London's Shaftesbury Avenue, where he installed his coining stars for the first time with the transfer of *The Beauty of Bath*.

He also continued to look after another lucrative star in Edna May, and starred her in the London production of *The Belle of Mayfair*, a musical commissioned from Leslie Stuart, the triumphant composer of *Florodora*. When Miss May walked out because the competition from the show-stealing Camille Clifford threatened her status, Frohman stuck by his star (whilst the money-men Stefano and Agostino Gatti stood by producers' rights to produce and by Miss Clifford) and had another show, *Nelly Neil*, written for Edna (1907). It flopped and she got married and retired.

During all this period of English and exported-English activity, Frohman produced just one almost home-bred musical as part of his continuing heavy Broadway production schedule. The so-so fate of *The Rollicking Girl* (1905, a re-adaptation of the old German Posse *Heisses Blut*, already seen on Broadway in German and English versions) did not tempt him to try very often in the future. His New York productions remained resolutely and almost exclusively British although, in a busy schedule, he later commissioned a musequel to the London piece *The Girl from Kays* for Sam Bernard from American writers (*The Rich Mr Hoggenheimer*, 1906) and in 1908 produced his first wholly native piece since *The Girl from Up There*, the cartoon musical *Fluffy Ruffles*, a vehicle for his *Rollicking Girl* and *Little Cherub* star, Hattie Williams. On one occasion he even produced a virtually British musical – a Cosmo Hamilton adaptation of the French play *La Soeur* with music by London's Paul Rubens and Frank Tours called *The Hoyden* (1907) – which had not been played in Britain, as a vehicle for Elsie Janis.

His last British productions – *The Hon'ble Phil* (1908), a collaboration with Edwardes on *A Waltz Dream* (1908, *Ein Walzertraum*) and *The Dashing Little Duke* (1909) – also did poorly to indifferently, and his only further London venture, the management of an import of Klaw and Erlanger's production of *The Pink Lady*, though a decided public favourite, proved to have its sums badly done and made a loss on full houses. After a decade straddling the Atlantic, his musical comedy activity from 1909 was wholly Broadway based.

Robert Courtneidge's productions of *The Dairymaids* (1907) and *The Arcadians* (1910) and Frank Curzon's *Miss Hook of Holland* (1907) swelled the list of Frohman imports from England alongside further Edwardes product – *The Girls of Gottenberg* (1908), *Kitty Grey* (1909), *Our Miss Gibbs* (1910), *The Sunshine Girl* (1913), *The Girl from Utah* (1914) – and, with, or rather behind Edwardes, Frohman made the switch to Viennese Operette at the moment when the massive swing in popularity away from the English musicals and towards the music of Austria occurred. In fact, he made it a little late and missed out on *The Merry Widow* which Edwardes had turned into an English-language hit, but he brought Broadway its London/Edwardes successor, *The Dollar Princess* (*Die Dollarprinzessin*, 1909), *The Marriage Market* (*Leányvásár*, 1913) which Edwardes had staged at Daly's Theatre with such success, and Eysler's *Der lachende Ehemann* (*The Laughing Husband*), and he also tried a few Continental pieces which had not come by way of Britain: Leo Fall's *Die Sirene* (*The Siren*, 1911), Berény's *Das Mädel von Montmartre* (*The Girl from Montmartre*, 1912) and Fall's *Das Puppenmädel* (*The Doll Girl*, 1913) which he had botched, Broadway-fashion, and which did not succeed.

Alongside this very full schedule of musical productions, Frohman continued to lead an equally busy life as a producer of plays which, like his musicals, were very often imported. But the overseas contact proved his undoing for, at 54 years of age and still at the height of his career in the theatre after 20 years of vast activity, he took the *Lusitania* from New York to Britain in the first year of the First World War, and was drowned when the ship was torpedoed by the Germans.

In 1916 his top musical stars, Julia Sanderson, Joseph Cawthorn and Donald Brian starred, as he had planned, in the Hungarian musical *Sybil* under the billhead 'Charles Frohman presents', a billhead which, like London's 'George Edwardes presents', lasted a little longer than was credible or, perhaps, tasteful following the two friends and collaborators' deaths.

Biography: Frohman, D, Marcosson, I: *Charles Frohman, Manager and Man* (Harper, New York, 1916)

FRÜHJAHRSPARADE Operette in 2 acts and 9 scenes by Hugo Wiener based on the screenplay by Ernst Marischka. Music by Robert Stolz. Volksoper, Vienna, 25 March 1964.

Geza von Bolvary's 1934 film *Frühjahrsparade*, featuring Paul Hörbiger, Franziska Gaal, Theo Lingen, Wolf-Albach Retty and Adele Sandrock, plus a lighthearted Viennesey score by Robert Stolz, was such a success in Europe that, in 1940, Universal Pictures decided to make a Hollywood version. *Spring Parade* starred Deanna Durbin, and the hit waltz, 'Singend, klingend ruft dich das Glück', was metamorphosed into 'Waltzing, waltzing, high in the clouds' (Academy Award nomination). A second German film version, with Romy Schneider, Paul Hörbiger, Magda Schneider and Walter Breuer starred, and a screenplay credited to Marischka and 'Gustav Holm' was produced under the title *Ein Deutschmeister* (French: *Mam'zelle Cricri*) in 1955 and, a decade later, a combination of the two films, reorganized and enlarged to make up a stage musical, was mounted at the Vienna Volksoper. It held a place in their repertoire for a decade thereafter.

Little Hungarian Marika (Guggi Löwinger), on her way to her aunt's bakery in Vienna, gets a helping hand from a handsome military bandsman and composer called Willi Sedlmeier (Erich Kuchar). Willi is hoping that the successful singer Hansi Grüber (Mimi Coertse) will introduce his new song, but when he gets tangled up in the love affair between Hansi and the aristocratic Gustl (Peter Minich), nephew of the Court Chamberlain, he finds his song banned. Marika uses her bakery connections and gets the music baked in one of the Emperor's (Fred Liewehr) favourite breakfast rolls, and the result is that Willi's 'Frühjahrsparade' march becomes a royal regular and everyone lives happily ever after.

Apart from Marika's well-known waltz, and the march-tune which makes the plot ('Frühjahrsparad' ist heut'), the score of the show also took in the lovely 'Im Frühling, im Mondschein, in Grinzing in Wien' from *Ein Deutschmeister* as a number for Hansi and a selection of numbers gathered from Stolz's song successes.

Frühlingsparade continued to find performances over the years that followed its Vienna première. A French adaptation (ad Marc-Cab, André Hornez) was mounted in Bordeaux in 1973 with Cathy Albert (Marika), Caroline Dumas (Hansi), Bernard Sinclair (Franz, ex-Willi) and Christian Borel (Fritz, ex-Gustl), whilst an Italian version (*Parata di primavera*) was premiered in 1992 at Trieste's Teatro Verdi (27 June).

France: Grand Théâtre, Bordeaux *Parade de Printemps* 26 October 1973; Films: Hunnia-Universal 1934, Universal 1940 *Spring Parade* (Eng), Erma 1955 *Ein Deutschmeister*

Recording: selection (Eurodisc)

FRÜHLINGSLUFT Operette in 3 acts by Carl Lindau and Julius Wilhelm based on the play *Coquin de printemps* by Adolphe Jaime and Georges Duval. Music taken from the works of Josef Strauss arranged by Ernst Reiterer. Venedig in Wien, Vienna, 9 May 1903.

Frühlingsluft ('spring air') was a version of the celebrated Parisian farce which also did duty for the libretti of highly successful musical shows both in Britain (*The Spring Chicken*) and France (*Coquin de printemps*). The Viennese version – the first to appear – did not let the average down.

Wilhelm and Lindau's text reset the play's action in Vienna and in the present. The lawyer Gustave Landtmann, a model of virtue two thirds of the year, gets annually frisky when spring approaches, and this year his eye falls on the Baroness Ida von Croisé whose husband he is supposed to be representing in their divorce. He attempts to rendezvous with her in the gardens at Blumenau whilst and where his equally frisky father-in-law, Knicklebein, is having a jolly time with the local young folk, headed by the clerk Hildebrandt and the maidservant Hanni. Mother-in-law Apollonia, wife Emilie, and Landtmann's client the Baron follow in pursuit, but all ultimately ends, after a lot of frisking and no fait accompli, in reunions all round, and Landtmann goes back to model living until next spring.

First produced by Gabor Steiner at his summer theatre in the Prater, *Frühlingsluft* was an immediate success. It played right through till the end of September (129 performances) and was promptly transferred to Steiner's winter house, Danzers Orpheum, to continue its run. It returned to the Prater for the summer of 1904, and was played in both houses in repertoire until 1907. It later appeared at the Theater an der Wien in 1912 (26 December), the Bürgertheater in 1920, and at the Carltheater in 1926 (16 February) with Gustave Werner starred, and was produced with considerable popularity in Germany. An Hungarian version (ad Adolf Mérei) was produced as *Tavasz* ('spring') at the Magyar Színház in 1903 and revived at the Revü Színház in 1919 (6 September) whilst the Király Színház hosted the German-language original in 1928 when the Miksa Preger/Alfred Piccaver company played it there in their repertoire.

The show does not seem to have been produced in English, perhaps hampered by the huge success of the not-very-subsequent *The Spring Chicken*, but New York's German-language theatre mounted it in 1905 with Lina Abarbanell making her American début as Hanni and Curt Weber as Gustave.

Reiterer later made up a second score, for the Operette *Frauenherz, oder die kleine Milliardärin* (lib: Carl Lindau), from Josef Strauss's music. Without equalling the popularity of *Frühlingsluft*, it was given performances in Austria (Danzers Orpheum 29 September 1905), Germany and Hungary (*A milliardos kisasszony*). He also put together a piece called *Gräfin Pepi* from Johann Strauss's *Simplicius* and *Blindekuh* (Venedig in Wien 5 July 1902).

Germany: ?1903; Hungary: Magyar Színház *Tavasz* 6 October 1903; USA: Irving Place Theater (Ger) 5 October 1905

FRYER, Robert (b Washington, DC 18 November 1920).

At first an assistant producer in theatre and television, then a casting director, Fryer moved into the production arena in partnership with George Abbott on *A Tree Grows in Brooklyn* (1951), an attractive and almost successful piece with Shirley Booth in its starring rôle. He had a fine success with his second production, Leonard Bernstein's *Wonderful Town* (1953, Tony Award), and then joined forces with Lawrence Carr with whom he produced a

second Shirley Booth piece, *By the Beautiful Sea* (1954), the unsuccessful *Shangri-La* (1956), the Tony-winning mystery musical *Redhead* (1959) and the unsuccessful *Saratoga* (1959) and *Hot Spot* (1963). The partners shared the producing credit on *Sweet Charity* (1966 w Sylvia and Joseph Harris) and the same team combined to mount *Mame* (1966), the musical version of *Auntie Mame*, which Fryer had already produced as a play.

In 1975, after almost a decade away from the musical theatre, Fryer produced another hit in *Chicago*, followed by a share in the Broadway mountings of *On the Twentieth Century* (1978 as Producers' Circle), *Sweeney Todd* (1979, Tony Award), and the unsuccessful *A Doll's Life* (1982) in a career largely now orientated towards the non-musical theatre.

He subsequently became artistic director of Los Angeles' Ahmanson Theater.

DAS FÜRSTENKIND Operette in a Vorspiel and 2 acts by Victor Léon adapted from a tale by Edmond About. Music by Franz Lehár. Johann Strauss-Theater, Vienna, 7 October 1909.

The Athenian Count of Parnes is not simply the Count of Parnes, he is Hadschi Stavros (Louis Treumann), a kind of Greek Robin Hood, sought by the police and, in particular, by the comissioner Perikles (Max Brod). The confident American commandant Bill Harris (Erich Deutsch-Haupt) bets Perikles that he will capture Stavros in ten days, little realising that the bandit is the Count and the father of his beloved Photini (Grete Freund). In the pursuit of his calling, Stavros kidnaps the comical botanist Dr Hippolyte Clérinay (Carlo Böhm), and the English tourists Mrs Gwendolyn Barley (Marie Gribl) and her daughter Mary-Ann (Mizzi Günther), with whom he falls in love. His band also overwhelms Bill and his sailors, but, preoccupied by Mary-Ann, he lets the tables be turned: he is captured by the American and thus wins him his bet. However, Perikles is balked of his prey, for when Bill realizes that the Count and the bandit are the same person, he lets him go and thus he can happily wed his Photini without her ever learning about her father's double life.

Lehár's score for his bandit musical was made up largely of ensemble music, with Stavros's 9/8 Pallikarenlied ('Lange Jahre, bange Jahre') and Mary-Ann's entrance number, beginning with a mountain echo section before segueing into the waltz 'Kindchen sei hübsch brav', being the principal solos of the piece alongside a Robber March, a pair of duets for the two stars ('Ich diene so gerne den Damen', 'Jung und alt') and another for the juveniles ('Papa, ich bin verliebt').

With the famous *Die lustige Witwe* pair of Treumann and Günther leading the cast, Leopold Müller's production of *Das Fürstenkind* brought, not unsurprisingly, a first real hit to the recently opened Johann Strauss-Theater. It passed its 100th performance on 15 January 1910 and its 200th on 28 April before closing the next night, and it was subsequently seen for a few performances at the Theater an der Wien (30 September 1911) with the leading pair supported by Betty Fischer (Photini) and Ludwig Herold (Bill), and again in 1914. In 1920 the piece was brought back at the Apollotheater (17 November) with Treumann in his original rôle.

Das Fürstenkind was rather over-shadowed by the huge

success of Lehár's *Der Graf von Luxemburg*, produced just a month later, and although the show was duly produced in most main theatre centres it was the composer's other piece which attracted the success. Andor Gábor's Hungarian *Hercegkisasszony* was produced at the Magyar Királyi Operaház, a French version (ad Maurice Ordonneau, Jean Bénédict) was staged at Brussels' Théâtre Molière (21 December 1912) as *Le Roi des montagnes* with Guillot (Stavros), Alice Favier (Mary-Ann), Eva Retty (Photini) and Nandès (Bill) and was subsequently played in the repertoire at Paris's Trianon-Lyrique the following year, whilst Henry Savage mounted a weakly-adapted version (ad Carolyn Wells), which for some reason was entitled *The Maids of Athens* – only Photini and her old nurse are Greek, the other ladies are English! – on Broadway, with a cast headed by Elbert Fretwell, Albert Pellaton, Cecil Cunningham and Leila Hughes, and was scuttled after 22 performances. London made do with just *The Count of Luxemburg*.

In 1932 a revised version of *Das Fürstenkind* entitled *Der Fürst der Berge* was produced as Berlin's Theater am Nollendorfplatz (23 September).

Hungary: Magyar Királyi Operaház *Hercegkisasszony* 20 December 1910; France: Trianon-Lyrique *Le Roi des montagnes* 1913; USA: New Amsterdam Theater *The Maids of Athens* 18 March 1914

FUGÈRE, Paul (b Paris; d Paris, 1 March 1920).

Paul Fugère made his earliest appearances as a light comedian and tenor in vaudeville and opérette, appearing through the 1880s and 1890s in rôles ranging from Prince Moutonnet in *Les Pommes d'or* at the Menus-Plaisirs (1883) to Grénicheux in *Les Cloches de Corneville*, Ichabod in *Rip!*, Fructueux in *Le Troisième Hussards*, Lamidou in *La Fée aux chèvres*, Edgard Jolicock in *Le Pays de l'or*, the comical peasant Nicolas in *Le Talisman*, Flagéolet in *Surcouf*, Cocolati in *Panurge* or the juvenile leading man Michel in *Mam'zelle Quat' sous*. His most important creation of this period was the rôle of the novice, Lancelot, in Audran's *La Poupée* (1896), but the management judging that he was playing this theoretically juvenile-lead rôle for its comedy to the detriment of its tenorizing, he was replaced soon after the opening.

Thereafter, with an ever-thickening waistline, Fugère moved on to the comic rôles of the repertoire – Larivaudière, the Abbé Bridaine, Don Boléro, Nick Vedder – whilst creating a series of new rôles in such pieces as *Les Soeurs Gaudichard* (Boniface), *La Petite Bohème* (Barbemuche), *L'Age d'or* (Louis XIV), *Capitaine Thérèse* (Duvet) and *Les Filles Jackson et Cie* (Janicot).

His elder brother, the baritone **Lucien FUGÈRE** (b Paris 22 July 1848; d Paris 15 January 1935), emerged from the cafés-concerts ('Sambre et Meuse') to play in opérette at the Bouffes-Parisiens (*La Branche cassée*, *La Boîte au lait*, *Madame l'Archiduc*, *Le Moulin du Vert-Galant*, Saint-Chamas in *La Créole* etc) before joining the company at the Opéra-Comique in 1877 for a famous career which included the premières of a handful of works by composers better known in the world of opérette, such as Messager's *La Basoche* (a famous portrayal of the comical Duc de Longueville), *Le Chevalier d'Harmental* (Buvat) and *Fortunio* (Maître André), Lecocq's *Plutus* (Plutus) and

Plate 97. **Paul Fugère** *matured from light-comedy tenor into weighty character-man.*

Missa's *Muguette* (Klotz) as well as the title-rôle in *Le Bonhomme Jadis* and de Beauval in *La Fille de Tabarin*. He also appeared at the Salle Favart as Père Mathieu in *Le Violoneux* and Jean in *Les Noces de Jeannette* as well as Papageno, Don Pasquale, Leporello and Schaunard. Late in life, he was seen back on the opérette stage, playing Monthabor in a revival of *La Fille du tambour-major* at the Gaîté-Lyrique in 1920.

Biography: Duhamel, R: *Lucien Fugère: chanteur scénique français* (Bernard Grasset, Paris, 1929)

FULLER, Loïe [FULLER, Marie Louise] (b nr Chicago, Ill, ?1863; d Paris, 2 January 1928). Variety and stage performer who made herself a star with a novelty dance act.

On the stage from childhood, Miss Fuller toured in a variety of theatre and non-theatre shows ranging from temperance lectures to Buffalo Bill's show and farce comedy with Murry and Murphy, through her teens and early twenties, before making her first appearance on the New York stage in the comedy with songs *Humbug* (1886, Nettie). She appeared for a Broadway season alongside Nat Goodwin in the title-rôle of *Little Jack Sheppard*, created in London by Nellie Farren, in a slightly musicalized version of Mark Medford's English farce *Turned Up* (1886), a revival of the on-wheels show *The Skating Rink* and in the farce-comedy *Big Pony, or the Gentlemanly Savage* (1887, Marie), and then moved to the realm of musical spectacular to play in the Chicago extravaganza *The Arabian Nights* (1887, Aladdin) and in a musical version of Rider

Haggard's *She* (1887) at Niblo's Garden. She also apparently appeared as Serpolette in *Les Cloches de Corneville* at the over-named Grand Opera House.

Miss Fuller then began her travels. She went first to the West Indies and then to England, where she presented herself at London's Globe Theatre in a comedy, *Caprice*. It failed badly, and, lowering her sights, she accepted a job as understudy to Letty Lind at the Gaiety Theatre. She played in the musical curtain-raisers traditionally given to the stars' understudies (*His Last Chance, The Woman in Pink*), deputized on occasion for Miss Lind, and repeated her Jack Sheppard at the suburban Elephant and Castle Theatre but, unwilling to wait for promotion under Edwardes's management, she struck out as a variety act with a cleverly-produced version of Miss Lind's celebrated skirt dance. Whereas Miss Lind had relied on her graceful dancing and her expertly pretty manipulation of the vast folds of her skirt, 'La Loie Fuller' added the element of light projections which were played on to the dress to make, most notably, an effect of fluttering butterfly wings.

This novelty act caught on with a vengeance and Paris, London and New York all welcomed Miss Fuller as a dancing star. Her act was interpolated into several loose-limbed shows both on Broadway (*Quack MD* (1892), *Uncle Celestin* (1892), *A Trip to Chinatown* (1892)) and in London, where she appeared in *In Town* (1892) and later, simultaneously, in *Morocco Bound* (1893), where her financial demands (50% of the gross over £138) made her a bit of a burden on the production budget. *Morocco Bound* replaced her with Letty Lind, and Miss Fuller went on to do her act as a booster for the failing *King Kodak* (1894). She appeared as an isolated act in Broadway's *Panjandrum* (1894) and London's *Little Miss Nobody* (1898), but by and large conducted the remainder of her career as performer in and promoter of dance productions.

Autobiography: *Quinze ans de ma vie* (Paris, 1908), *Fifteen Years of a Dancer's Life* (Herbert Jenkins, London, 1913); Biography: Brandstetter, G & Ochaim, B M: *Loïe Fuller*, (Rombach, Freiburg im Breisgau, 1990)

FULL SWING Musical comedy in 2 acts by Archie Menzies, Arthur Macrae and Jack Hulbert. Music by George Posford and Harry Parr Davies. Additional songs by Max Kester, Robert Probst, Harold Purcell and Kenneth Leslie-Smith. Additional lyrics by Davy Burnaby, Barbara Gordon and Basil Thomas. Palace Theatre, London, 16 April 1942.

A British wartime musical, concocted to follow the success scored by Cicely Courtneidge and Jack Hulbert in *Under Your Hat*, *Full Swing* followed the earlier piece extremely thoroughly by casting the two stars in the same characters – Kay Porter and Jack Millet – and setting them off on another secret mission, replete with disguises, on behalf of the British War Office. Once again, the luscious foreign spy, Carole Markoff (now played by Nora Swinburne), appeared as part of the opposition.

The stars appeared as able seamen, as a pair of Hampstead aesthetes called Dr and Mrs Patmore ('Lovely to Be Loose'), and Courtneidge gave an impersonation of a gross and grotesque secretary to parallel her frightful maid in the first show. She also had the most successful song, a little sentimental George Posford/Harold Purcell piece

about 'The Wedding of the Gingerbread Boy and Girl'. Most of the music, however, went to Gabrielle Brune as someone called Sally ('Mamma, Buy Me That', 'Follow My Dancing Feet', 'Cleo from Rio' etc).

Full Swing, without coming up to its predecessor as a piece, proved happy wartime entertainment and played 468 times at the Palace before the team replaced it with more of the same.

FUNNY FACE Musical comedy in 2 acts by Fred Thompson and Paul Gerard Smith. Lyrics by Ira Gershwin. Music by George Gershwin. Alvin Theater, New York, 22 November 1927.

Originally written by Thompson and drama critic-cum-humorist Robert Benchley and entitled *Smarty*, Aarons and Freedley's production opened at the Shubert Theater in Philadelphia on 11 October 1927. It didn't work. By the time that it reached their Alvin Theater on Broadway, after four weeks in Philadelphia and another in Wilmington, it had undergone some severe changes ('an almost entirely new show and score ...') which included the dropping of a bundle of songs, one of which was the later famous 'How Long Has This Been Going On?' (they had been replaced by five new ones), and the hirings of comedian Victor Moore and juvenile leading man Allen Kearns. Known play doctor Paul Gerard Smith had replaced Benchley on the bill, and the show was now called *Funny Face*, after one of its songs.

Thompson had fallen back on one of the musical theatre's most over-used plots as the basis for his book – the stolen jewels syndrome, which hadn't been precisely new when Owen Hall had used it for *A Gaiety Girl* before the turn of the century. Jimmy Reeve (Fred Astaire) has locked up the jewels belonging to his ward, June Wynne (Gertrude MacDonald), in his safe along with the diary to which another of his wards, Frankie Wynne (Adele Astaire), has confided some rather exaggerated thoughts. Frankie wants her book back, so she gets her boyfriend, aviator Peter Thurston (Allen Kearns), to help her burgle the safe. But, at the same time, there are some real thieves on the prowl. Since they were played by William Kent (Dugsie Gibbs) and Victor Moore (Herbert), there were more comical complications and disguises involved than there was menace, as the story and its characters followed the jewels – mistakenly taken from the safe by Peter – to the final curtain. Betty Compton played Jimmy's third ward, Dora, who paired off with Dugsie.

The songs for *Funny Face* included two which became firm favourites: Frankie and Peter's duet "'S Wonderful" and the oft-reprised title-song, first sung by Jimmy to Frankie. The juvenile pair had another winner in their 'He Loves and She Loves', whilst Jimmy wooed June with 'My One and Only' and donned evening dress to lead a line of top-hatted chaps and frilly-frocked chorines in 'High Hat'. The more conventional comedy was represented by Kent's send-up of psychiatry in 'Tell the Doc' and by a burlesque of the manners of the characters of Sinclair Lewis's *Babbit* in 'The Babbit and the Bromide' (Jimmy/Frankie).

Funny Face did not turn out to have quite the pull that the first Aarons/Freedley/Gershwins/Thompson/Astaires collaboration on *Lady, Be Good!*, three years earlier, had had, but it did almost as well as the producers' previous year's Gershwin production, the rather less textually conventional *Oh, Kay!*. It played a healthy 244 performances at the Alvin Theater, and soon after its producers shipped it to London where, in conjunction with Alfred Butt and Lee Ephraim, they reproduced the show at the Prince's Theatre, with the Astaires supported by Leslie Hendon (Dugsie), Sydney Howard (Herbert), Bernard Clifton (Peter) and Eileen Hatton (June). The Astaires proved as popular as they had been on their two previous visits to London with *Stop Flirting* and *Lady, Be Good!*, and the piece was played 263 times at the Prince's and later at the Winter Garden Theatre. In Australia, however, without its magnetic stars, *Funny Face* proved a flop. Ernest Rolls's production, with Janette Gilmore, Jim Gerald and Charley Sylber featured, played a season at Sydney's St James Theatre but did not go on to Melbourne, and it was five years before a brief season of *Funny Face*, mounted by the young producer Garnet Carroll, gave that city a three-week glimpse of the show (Apollo Theatre 26 September 1936).

Funny Face was revived at Connecticut's Goodspeed Opera House in 1981 (17 June) and in 1983 a 'new Gershwin musical' was produced, using the title of *Funny Face*'s 'My One and Only' as its title and five numbers from the 13 which made up the show's original score as part of its musical pasticcio. It did away with the never-very-wonderful book, but replaced it with one which was not much less conventional. However, *My One and Only*, mounted, like its predecessor, largely as a song-and-dance show, had a fine 767-performance run on Broadway with Tommy Tune and Twiggy starred and it was subsequently toured, with Sandy Duncan and Lucie Arnaz taking turns in its feminine lead rôle.

A 1957 Paramount film entitled *Funny Face* starred Audrey Hepburn and Fred Astaire who, along with four songs (supplemented by three others by Roger Edens and Leonard Gershe and one from *Oh, Kay!*), was the only element it had in common with the stage show.

UK: Prince's Theatre 8 November 1928; Australia: St James Theatre, Sydney 23 May 1931

Recordings: London cast (World Record Club); original cast reconstruction (Smithsonian)

FUNNY GIRL Musical in 2 acts by Isobel Lennart based on incidents in the life of Fanny Brice. Lyrics by Bob Merrill. Music by Jule Styne. Winter Garden Theater, New York, 26 March 1964.

A romanticized biomusical of the famous revue comedienne Fanny Brice, *Funny Girl* focused very largely on the performer's relationship with the shady but charming Nick Arnstein to whom she was, for a period, married. The first act followed Fanny (Barbra Streisand) through her early attempts to get into the theatre, and through her discovery of both her comic talent and of Arnstein (Sydney Chaplin), who turns up every so often in her life but always leaves as suddenly as he arrives. She rises to a job in the *Ziegfeld Follies*, to stardom and, with determination, to a romance with Arnstein which ends in marriage. When his interminable financial castles in the air come tumbling down, Fanny, earning star wages in the theatre, is able to pay the bills, but that is not enough for the man. He shrugs off a safe job she sets up for him to go for another big flashy gamble, and this time he ends up in prison. Fanny has waited for him to come out to take up their life

together, but when, in the final scene, he arrives in her dressing room, it is to say goodbye. Kay Medford played Fanny's mother, Danny Meehan was Eddie, her first and faithful coach, and Jean Stapleton featured as the neighbouring Mrs Strakosh.

The accompanying songs threw up two pieces which proved particularly popular outside the show. Miss Streisand made a worldwide hit out of the reaching ballad 'People', which posited that 'people who need people are the luckiest people in the world', whilst her driving double-curtain number (it closed both acts) 'Don't Rain on My Parade', a piece of blind, bull-dogging optimism, was long popular as a cabaret and concert item. There were plenty of other, less extractable, pieces which made their effect in the show: the practical point-of-view of her mother and Mrs Strakosh which queries 'If a Girl isn't Pretty' what is she going to do in show business, Fanny's first flush of optimism in 'I'm the Greatest Star', the proud 'Who Taught Her Everything She Knows?' of Eddie and Mrs Brice, and the comic-romantic supper table scene 'You Are Woman, I Am Man'. All these winning musical moments came in the first act, but the less musically weighted second part also included Fanny's 'Sadie, Sadie' in which she revels in being a married lady, as well as the final reprise of 'Don't Rain on My Parade'.

The biggest armament in the success of *Funny Girl* was, undoubtedly, its star. Barbra Streisand's funny, touching and superbly sung performance as Fanny Brice was one of the performances of an epoch and, although she left the show well before the end of its 1,348-performance Broadway run, *Funny Girl* had, by then, become thoroughly established. Whilst Mimi Hines took over on Broadway and Marilyn Michaels headed out a touring company, Miss Streisand repeated her performance in London alongside Miss Medford and Michael Craig as Nick. However, Bernard Delfont and Arthur Lewis's production folded after 112 performances when it was confirmed that the star was pregnant. In 1968 she took up the rôle of Fanny once more, in a film version which used seven of the show's numbers, topped up by such period numbers as 'Mon Homme', 'Second-Hand Rose' and 'I'd Rather Be Blue'. The film, which featured Omar Sharif as Nick and Miss Medford in her original stage rôle, was a success, and 'Second-Hand Rose' became a hit all over again.

J C Williamson Ltd mounted a production of *Funny Girl* in Australia, with Jill Perryman starred as Fanny alongside Bruce Barry and Evie Hayes, which followed a fine Sydney season with four months in Melbourne in 1966, and the show has been subsequently regularly produced in regional theatres in English-speaking countries. One of America's recent *Funny Girl*s was film nymphet Pia Zadora. The first German-language production was mounted at Coburg in 1992 with Carol Lentner as Fanny.

UK: Prince of Wales Theatre 13 April 1966; Australia: Her Majesty's Theatre, Sydney 6 March 1966; Germany: Landestheater, Coburg 22 November 1992; Film: Columbia 1968

Recording: original cast (Capitol), film soundtrack (Columbia)

A FUNNY THING HAPPENED ON THE WAY TO THE FORUM Musical comedy in 2 acts by Burt Shevelove and Larry Gelbart based on the works of Plautus. Music and lyrics by Stephen Sondheim. Alvin Theater, New York, 8 May 1962.

A musical comedy more than worthy of that description, *A Funny Thing Happened on the Way to the Forum* was constructed with the use of the standard characters and situations which had been used and reused to make up the classic Roman comedies of the Plautian age. As in the works of Plautus, the most important character is the wily slave or 'servus', whose preoccupations in life are money and that elusive dream of freedom. Several of the other characters in the piece were christened by the names of their types – the senex (old man), domina (mistress of the house), the miles gloriosus (the boastful soldier, also a Plautus play) – other names, like Erronius and Hysterium, spoke for themselves (which was just as well, for hysterium in Latin means the womb) – as did those of the leading juveniles, Hero and Philia, for all that they were Greek rather than Latin.

Pseudolus (Zero Mostel) and Hysterium (Jack Gilford) are slaves in the household of the frisky Senex (David Burns), his stringent wife Domina (Ruth Kobart), and his pubescent son Hero (Brian Davies). Hero falls in love with the maiden Philia (Preshy Marker), whom he has glimpsed at the window of the neighbouring courtesan-keeper, Marcus Lycus (John Carradine), and, during his parents' absence, he bribes Pseudolus to help him win her. Unfortunately (1) Philia has already been sold to the Miles Gloriosus (Ron Holgate) and (2) Senex arrives home unexpectedly. Pseudolus ends up trying to get the young lovers away together whilst simultaneously preparing a recondite passion-potion for the randy Senex, who thinks he has an assignation with a virgin, and staving off the pressing demands of the soldier that he produce his merchandise. When things are at their most farcically complex, a splendidly Plautian dénouement intervenes: Philia and the Miles Gloriosus are discovered to be the children of neighbour Erronius (Raymond Wallburn), stolen in childhood by pirates. Hero gets his virgin and Pseudolus his reward – freedom.

Gelbart and Shevelove's tight, farcical libretto was illustrated by some equally funny songs – the opening assertion that, although the troupe performs tragedy on other occasions, it will be 'Comedy Tonight', the old men's drooling routine 'Everybody Ought to Have a Maid', Philia's admission that she has no talent except to be 'Lovely', Hysterium's unconvinced and unconvincing declaration that 'I'm Calm', the father and son's comical sizing-up of each other's sexual potential in 'Impossible', and some ringing burlesque bass-baritone music ('Bring Me My Bride', Funeral Sequence) for the soldier which was as fine and funny as anything of its kind in musical theatre.

Harold Prince's production of *A Funny Thing* was the winner of both the 1963 Tony Award for Best Musical and a 964-performance run on Broadway, and a London mounting, which Prince co-sponsored with designer Tony Walton and Richard Pilbrow, ran almost as long. Frankie Howerd was London's Pseudolus, teamed with former Crazy Gang member 'Monsewer' Eddie Gray (Senex), *Carry On* film-star Kenneth Connor (Hysterium), famous farceur Robertson Hare (Erronius), Jon Pertwee (Lycus) and Leon Greene (Miles), and the deftly cast production played 762 performances before the show went on to become a durable favourite in provincial houses.

Paris saw *Sur le chemin du forum* (the joke of the title

didn't work in French) at the Palais-Royal in 1964, J C Williamson Ltd mounted a production in Australia also in 1964, with a cast headed by another famous musical comedy veteran, Clifford Mollison, and in 1966 United Artists and Richard Lester produced a film version. Mostel repeated his stage rôle alongside Phil Silvers, for whom the part had originally been intended, in the rôle of Lycus. Gilford was again Hysterium, Michael Hordern played Senex, Buster Keaton was a memorable Erronius and the juvenile pair were played by Michael Crawford and Annette André. Only five musical numbers were used.

In 1972 Silvers finally got to play the rôle he had been scheduled to have, when David Black mounted a revival of a slightly revised version of the show at the Lunt-Fontanne Theater (30 March, 156 performances) and, whilst the show continued a life as a solid part of the standard revivable repertoire, a Chichester Festival Theatre revival was taken to London in 1986 (14 November). Howerd repeated as a now rather aged Pseudolus alongside Ronnie Stevens (Hysterium), Patrick Cargill (Senex) and Fred Evans (Lycus) through 51 performances of an unstylish reproduction of much of the original staging.

The work of Plautus, specifically the *Miles gloriosus*, had previously been used as the basis for the German musical play *Der Weiberheld* (Erika Wilde, Magdeburg 15 September 1956).

UK: Strand Theatre 3 October 1963; France: Théâtre du Palais-Royal *Sur le chemin du forum* 1964; Australia: Theatre Royal, Sydney 18 July 1964; Germany: Theater im Reichskabarett *Ein verrückter Tag auf dem Forum* 24 February 1972; Austria: *Die Spinner de Romer* 17 June 1992; Film: United Artists 1966
Recordings: original cast (Capitol), London cast (HMV), film soundtrack (United Artists); Mexican cast

FUN ON THE BRISTOL, or A Night on the Sound [or A Night at Sea] Musical comedy oddity in 3 acts by George Fawcett Rowe (uncredited). Newport, RI, 1879, 14th Street Theater, New York, 9 August 1880.

One of the internationally most popular pieces of its kind, this American-bred 'musical comedy oddity' with its mixture of low comedy, pantomime, variety acts and concert was played for only two weeks in the sophisticated purlieus of New York. But it toured around the rest of America for years, and was played in English-language theatres throughout the world, mostly with its instigator, the actor John F Sheridan, starred famously in the dame rôle of the Widow O'Brien which would be the keystone of his career.

Such plot as there was to the piece was that of the Widow O'Brien's search for a replacement husband. The other characters of the imbroglio included the Count Menaggio, who is after Bridget's money, her two daughters by her deceased mate, and the black maid, Bella. The title came from the fact that the characters were all dumped aboard the steamer *Bristol* for the course of the evening. The story was merely 'a peg on which to hang a variety programme – comic songs, nigger sketches, grotesque dances, stump speeches, operatic selections, burlesque marches, a guitar solo etc' and its music was of the movable kind, ranging as it did from a selection from Gounod's *Faust* to 'O, Dem Golden Slippers'.

Once established at home, the show was transported to Britain by Messrs H C Jarrett and Rice's American Comedy Company with Sheridan, Carrie Daniels and Lulu Evans featured, and, after taking the country by storm, it played in the West End for a season of over three months, before returning to the provinces where Sheridan became a star and his show a durable feature of the number two (and occasionally number one) circuits. The actor also played 'his' piece in Australia on many occasions, and in both countries others took up the rôle of the Widow when he moved on.

In 1887 Sheridan reasserted himself in the rôle in Britain when he presented and starred alongside Edith Vane in a fresh London season of the show at the Gaiety (5 September) and the Opera Comique, but he then took his show back to Australia (1889) where his later days were largely spent. He carried his favourite character on into a second show, *Bridget O'Brien Esq* (aka *Mrs O'Brien Esq*) in which he played in Australia and America (Bijou Theater 31 October 1892) but the original Widow O'Brien show remained the most popular standby for its creator up to his death.

UK: Theatre Royal, Manchester 15 May 1882, Olympic Theatre 7 August 1882; Australia: Gaiety Theatre, Sydney 16 March 1884

FURBER, Douglas (b London, 13 May 1885; d London, 19 February 1961). Ubiquitous lyricist for nearly 30 years of British shows.

Furber made his earliest steps in the theatre as a writer for and performer in revues, the first of which was the 1917 piece *£150* in which he supplied the words to Australian songwriter Archie Emmett Adams's tunes and played the show's 24 performances at the Ambassadors' Theatre. Things looked up soon after, when he made his first venture into musical comedy with the lyrics for two successful C B Cochran French imports, the opéra-bouffe *Carminetta* and the slightly-less-saucy-than-before *Afgar*, and he had equally good fortune with his first original musical, Emmett Adams's touring piece *Pretty Peggy* (1919), which Cochran subsequently brought into the West End in the following year. His version of *Afgar* got a Broadway showing, *Pretty Peggy* was exported to Australia (New Princess Theatre, Melbourne 6 October 1923), and their author's career was well and truly launched.

He continued his performance career in revue, notably under the management of André Charlot, for whom he played both in London (*A to Z*) and on Broadway (*The Charlot Revue of 1926*, his last stage appearance) and also played in musical comedy on the West End stage, taking supporting rôles in the Jack Buchanan productions of *Battling Butler* (1922, Ted Spink) and *Boodle* (1925, Dixon), before giving up performing to concentrate on a solid 20-year career as a lyricist and occasional librettist for London musicals and revues.

His first West End successes were with the series of musicals produced by and for Jack Buchanan, a series with which he was associated from its beginning with *Battling Butler* through the ex-German *Toni* (co-adaptation and lyrics), *Boodle*, the three biggest successes *That's a Good Girl* (librettist, co-lyricist), *Stand Up and Sing* (lyricist, co-librettist) and *Mr Whittington*, up to the Ralph Benatzky pasticcio *The Flying Trapeze*, and the final *It's Time to Dance*, 17 years after the first.

In the late 1920s and 1930s most of London's principal musical producers had use for Furber's services at one stage or another: for Clayton and Waller he did some additional material for *Virginia* and co-wrote the book and all the the lyrics for *Silver Wings*; for Jack Hulbert he contributed lyrics and, with Dion Titheradge, the book for the Sophie Tucker vehicle *Follow a Star*; for Firth Shephard and Leslie Henson the English book and most of the lyrics for the ex-German *Nice Goings On*, an English rewrite of Broadway's *Little Jessie James* as *Lucky Break*, a bit of the book of their Gaiety shows *Swing Along*, *Going Greek* and *Running Riot*, and most of Shephard's *Wild Oats* and *Sitting Pretty*; and for Lee Ephraim part of the book of the Cicely Courtneidge/Bobby Howes *Hide and Seek*. His most singular success, however came with the songwords for his only musical for Lupino Lane, *Me and My Girl*, which produced, beyond its title-song, the celebrated 'Lambeth Walk'.

On the revue side he contributed more or less material to the Vaudeville Theatre's *Yes* and the Little Theatre's *The Little Revue Starts at 9* (1923), *Charlot's Revue* (1924), the successful Adelphi piece *The House That Jack Built* (1929, co-book, additional lyrics), the brief *Let's Raise the Curtain* (book only), the Savoy Theatre's unmemorable *And On We Go* (1937) and, following the war, giving a larger preference to revue over the musical-comedy stage for the meanwhile, George Black's triumphant London Hippodrome piece *Black Velvet* (1939), Shephard's long-running *Shephard's Pie* (1939), *Up and Doing* (1940) and *Fun and Games* (1941), the Coliseum's *It's Foolish But It's Fun*, the Prince's Theatre *The Magic Carpet* and Leslie Henson's Winter Garden *The Gaieties* (1945).

For his final work he returned to the musical theatre to provide much of the book and all of the lyrics for Fred Emney, whom he had so happily suited in Shephard's shows, in his star vehicle *Big Boy*.

Furber also made lesser contributions to *Fifinella* (1919, 'addditional witticisms by'), *Now and Then*, *A Southern Maid*, *The Cabaret Girl* and *Soldier Boy* (*Az obsitos*), supplied additional lyrics for the revival of *The Maid of the Mountains* and lyricked such popular songs as Emmett Adams's 'The Bells of Saint-Mary's' and 'God Send You Back to Me'.

He also wrote screenplays for both British and American films, including the screen versions of *The Maid of the Mountains* (1932 w Lupino Lane) and *That's a Good Girl* (1933).

1917 **Carminetta** English lyrics (Prince of Wales Theatre)
1919 **Afgar** English lyrics (London Pavilion)
1919 **Sons of the Sea** (H Sullivan Brooke/w J Peterman) 1 act Shoreditch Empire
1919 **Pretty Peggy** (Archie Emmett Adams/Charles Austin, Arthur Rose) Empire, Kilburn 25 August
1921 **Gabrielle** (G H Clutsam, Archibald Joyce/w Helen Williams, Bertrand Davis et al) Glasgow 26 December
1922 **Battling Butler** (Phil Braham/Stanley Brightman, Austin Melford) New Oxford Theatre 8 December
1923 **The Cousin from Nowhere** (*Der Vetter aus Dingsda*) English version (Prince's Theatre)
1923 **Toni** (*Der Fürst von Pappenheim*) (Hugo Hirsch/w Harry Graham) Theatre Royal, Hanley 6 August; Shaftesbury Theatre 12 May 1924
1925 **Boodle** (Braham, Max Darewski/Sydney Blow, Douglas Hoare) Empire Theatre 10 March
1925 **The Bamboula** (Albert Szirmai, Harry Rosenthal/w Irving Caesar/Guy Bolton, Harry M Vernon) His Majesty's Theatre 24 March

1925 **Cloclo** English lyrics w Graham (Shaftesbury Theatre)

1927 **Up with the Lark** (Braham/w Hartley Carrick) Adelphi Theatre 25 August

1928 **That's a Good Girl** (Phil Charig, Joseph Meyer/w Ira Gershwin, Desmond Carter) London Hippodrome 5 June

1928 **Virginia** (Jack Waller, Joseph Tunbridge/w Herbert Clayton, R P Weston, Bert Lee) Palace Theatre 24 October

1928 **Lucky Girl** (Charig/w Weston, Lee) Shaftesbury Theatre 14 November

1930 **Silver Wings** (Waller, Tunbridge/w Dion Titheradge) Dominion Theatre 14 February

1930 **Follow a Star** (Vivian Ellis/w Titheradge) Winter Garden Theatre 17 September

1931 **Stand Up and Sing** (Charig, Ellis/w Titheradge) London Hippodrome 5 March

1933 **Nice Goings On** (Arthur Schwartz/w Frank Eyton) Strand Theatre 13 September

1934 **Mr Whittington** (John Green, Tunbridge, Waller/w Clifford Grey, Greatrex Newman) London Hippodrome 1 February

1934 **Lucky Break** (*Little Jessie James*) revised version Strand Theatre 2 October

1935 **The Flying Trapeze** (Ralph Benatzky, Mabel Wayne/w Desmond Carter, Frank Eyton/Hans Müller ad) English version Alhambra Theatre 4 May

1936 **Swing Along** (Martin Broones/Graham John/w Bolton, Fred Thompson) Gaiety Theatre 2 September

1937 **Going Greek** (Sam Lerner, Al Goodhart, Al Hoffman/w Bolton, Thompson) Gaiety Theatre 16 September

1937 **Hide and Seek** (Ellis, Lerner, Goodhart, Hoffman/w Bolton, Thompson) London Hippodrome 23 September

1937 **Me and My Girl** (Noel Gay/w Rose) Victoria Palace 5 October

1938 **Wild Oats** (Gay/w Firth Shephard) Prince's Theatre 13 April

1938 **Running Riot** (Ellis, w Bolton, Shephard) Gaiety Theatre 31 August

1939 **Sitting Pretty** (Manning Sherwin) Prince's Theatre 17 August

1943 **It's Time to Dance** (Kenneth Leslie-Smith et al/w Rose) Winter Garden 22 July

1945 **Big Boy** (Carroll Gibbons/w Fred Emney, Max Kester) Saville Theatre 12 September

FURST, William W[allace] (b Baltimore, 1852; d Freeport, NY, 11 June 1917).

For many years musical director of San Francisco's Tivoli Theater, Furst subsequently became conductor at New York's Star Theater, for some 15 years at the Empire Theater (1893) for Frohman, and then with Belasco, supplying incidental music, and songs when required, for the plays on the bill. Amongst these were included J M Barrie's *The Little Minister* with Maude Adams starred, William Gillette's famous *Sherlock Holmes*, Mrs Leslie Carter's *Adrea*, the oriental spectacle *The Yellow Jacket*, Rider Haggard's *She* and Thomas Broadhurst's play version of Longfellow's *Evangeline* (1913). Furst also composed the scores for a number of stage musicals, the most successful of which was the long-touring Thomas Q Seabrooke extravaganza *The Isle of Champagne*. Others included a vehicle for Lillian Russell (*Princess Nicotine*), revue for the Casino (*The Merry World*), and major botchings of *Les 28 Jours de Clairette* as a starring piece for Della Fox (*The Little Trooper*), and of the less successful French opérettes *Pervenche* and *La Gardeuse d'oies*.

1879 **Electric Light** (William B Hazelton, Edward Spencer) Baltimore August

1892 **The Isle of Champagne** (Charles Alfred Byrne, Louis Harrison) Fifth Avenue Theater 5 December

1893 **The Honeymooners** (C M S McLellan) Columbia Theater, Boston November

1893 **Princess Nicotine** (Byrne, Harrison) Casino Theater 5 December

1894 **The Little Trooper** (*Les 28 Jours de Clairette*), new score for American version by Clay Greene (Casino Theater)

1895 **Fleur de Lis** (*Pervenche*) (ad J Cheever Goodwin) Palmer's Theater 29 August

1898 **A Normandy Wedding** (aka *Papa Gougou*) (*La Gardeuse d'oies*) new score for American version by Cheever Goodwin, Byrne Herald Square Theater 21 February

FURTH, George (b Chicago, 14 December 1932).

At first an actor on the straight and musical (*Hot Spot*, 1963) stages, and in cinema, Furth made a highly successful entry into the musical theatre as an author with the text for the 1970 musical *Company* (Tony Award). He has subsequently returned to the area twice more, providing the libretto to the Liza Minnelli vehicle *The Act* and adapting Moss Hart and George S Kaufman's play *Merrily We Roll Along* as a musical.

1970 **Company** (Stephen Sondheim) Alvin Theater 26 April

1977 **The Act** (John Kander/Fred Ebb) Majestic Theater 29 October

1982 **Merrily We Roll Along** (Sondheim) Alvin Theater 16 November

G

GABAROCHE, Gaston (b Bordeaux, 29 September 1884; d Marseille, 28 August 1961).

A popular singer and songwriter ('C'était une petite blonde', 'Le Regret', 'La Femme à la rose', 'Les Beaux Dimanches de printemps' etc), Gabaroche had a long and varied career as a performer (La Lune Rousse, Les Deux Ânes, La Pie-qui-chante etc), which included a considerable amount of work in revue and in musical comedy, starring in both Paris and/or the provinces in such successful musical theatre pieces as *Pouche, Madame, Qu'en dit l'abbé*, his own *Enlevez-Moi!..* and *Deux fois deux, Mademoiselle Star, Plume au vent* and *Au pays du soleil*.

In 1923 he contributed to the score of the highly successful musical comedy *Je t'veux* and, through the 1920s and 1930s, continued to write songs for the extremely light and small-scale musical comedies typical of the era. His most considerable success came with Robert Gallois's production of the 1929 *Enlevez-moi!..*, a piece which was subsequently revived (1935) and filmed.

In 1919 he combined with Saint-Granier to build and, briefly, operate the Théâtre de la Potinière where they produced several revues (*Danseront-ils, Vas-y-voir* etc) and other entertainments written by themselves.

1920 **Je t'adore** (Saint-Granier) 1 act Théâtre de la Potinière 1 December

1923 **Je t'veux** (w Fred Pearly, René Mercier, Albert Valsien/ Battaille-Henri/Wilned, Marcel Grandjean) Théâtre Marigny 12 February

1924 **Jean-Jean** (w Pearly, Josef Szulc, Raoul Moretti, Pierre Chagnon, Albert Chantrier, Laurent Halet/Valentin Tarault/Mme Valsamaki) Théâtre de la Potinière 2 July

1927 **Ketty Boxeur** (Pierre Varenne/Luc Mourier) Théâtre de la Potinière 1 June

1929 **Gaston** (Fernand Beissier, Louis Hennevé) Comédie Caumartin

1929 **Enlevez-moi!..** (Varenne, Max Eddy/Raoul Praxy, Henri Hallais) Comédie Caumartin 4 October

1932 **Deux fois deux** (Eddy/Praxy) Théâtre Daunou 28 January

1932 **Azor** (w Pearly, Chagnon/Eddy/Praxy) Théâtre des Bouffes-Parisiens 16 September

1936 **Faites ça pour moi** (Eddy/Praxy) Théâtre Antoine 25 January

1938 **J'hésite** (w Pearly/Praxy) Théâtre Antoine 16 February

A GAIETY GIRL Musical comedy in 2 acts by Owen Hall. Lyrics by Harry Greenbank. Music by Sidney Jones. Prince of Wales Theatre, London, 14 October 1893.

George Edwardes had tentatively heralded a move away from the 'new burlesque' and into something a little bit more like a modern musical play with his production of the up-to-date tale of London and backstage life *In Town* (1892). With *A Gaiety Girl* he took a further step towards a vertebrate comedy with songs and dances in a piece which, similarly, mixed society and theatre folk to the advantage of the latter. The story goes that lawyer-turned-journalist Jimmy Davis met Edwardes on a train and remarked unfavourably on the libretto of *In Town*, declaring he could do better. Edwardes told him to do so. The result was a text with a minimal plotline about a stolen comb, which relied for what action it had on the marital manoeuvrings of a group of social and theatrical characters. It was, however, written in a satirical, snappy and occasionally risqué style and with grateful rôles for the cast which Edwardes engaged: popular comedy actress Lottie Venne as the handsome widow, Lady Virginia Forrest, comics Eric Lewis and Harry Monkhouse as a judge and a clergyman respectively and both getting the worst of the librettist's satire, statuesque baritone Hayden Coffin as hero, French soubrette Juliette Nesville as a French maid, tall and beautiful Maud Hobson as the wrongly accused actress (it was the French maid who did it) and the Savoy Theatre's original *Gondoliers* Casilda, Decima Moore, as ingénue.

Sidney Jones, whom Edwardes had remarked as a new talent, was commissioned to write the score. He turned out a number of songs to Harry Greenbank's lyrics which actually had something to do with the show's story, but won his biggest single song success with Coffin's straightforward ballad 'Sunshine Above'. Coffin, however, in a way that characterized his career, interpolated a song he had heard in another show, Henry Hamilton's *Captain Fritz*, and it was that number, the patriotic 'Tommy Atkins', which became the hit of the show.

Edwardes had a last-minute rush to get Hall's text past the censor, but he succeeded, although he was later obliged to alter the character of the clergyman after a complaint to the Lord Chamberlain, apparently from an over-touchy but influential Archbishop. The audiences took with a will to Hall's wicked wit, Jones's lively music and Edwardes's top production values and cast, and *A Gaiety Girl* was an immediate and much-discussed success. It ran 11 months at the Prince of Wales Theatre before Edwardes shifted it to Daly's, following the definitive departure of Augustin Daly's drama company. It settled there for another three months (413 performances in all), thus setting the scene for the famous Daly's series of musicals which would follow. It also, more than either *In Town* or *Morocco Bound*, which had preceded it, set the style and tone for the species of musical comedy in which George Edwardes subsequently dealt at the Gaiety Theatre and elsewhere, and which swept the English-speaking world, in particular, as the most popular form of musical theatre entertainment in the last part of the 19th century.

Davis, under his pseudonym of 'Owen Hall', went on to have a remarkable career in the musical theatre, as did the short-lived Greenbank and, most especially, the third *Gaiety Girl* neophyte Sidney Jones who was to become resident composer to Daly's Theatre at the top of a memorable career.

Edwardes toured a British company with *A Gaiety Girl* to America and Australia (the tale of this tour is told in the little book *Round the World with A Gaiety Girl*) with a cast headed by Maud Hobson, Harry Monkhouse, Leedham Bantock, Charles Ryley, W Louis Bradfield and Decima Moore, playing a season on Broadway, where the show was later reproduced with a largely American cast (Daly's Theater 7 May 1895, 31 performances), and throughout both countries, and in 1899 he staged a London revival to fill in the gap created by Greenbank's death and the late delivery of a new Daly's show (5 June, 58 performances). Miss Venne repeated her original rôle alongside Rutland Barrington, H Scott Russell, Huntley Wright, Hilda Moody and Aileen d'Orme but, in spite of more of the updatings to which it had been subjected ever since opening, it did not have the same effect as it had had the first time round. Caught in the shadow of its more developed Daly's successors, it was nevertheless compared fondly and favourably by the press with more recent 'musical comedies'.

The show also got a production in Germany where *Ein fideles Corps* (ad Jean Kren, Eduard Jacobson) was mounted at the Adolf-Ernst Theater with London danseuse Rose Bachelor featured alongside Herrn Thielscher, Weiss, Haskerl, Klein and the Fräuleins Seemann, Fischer and Frühling.

USA: Daly's Theater 18 September 1894; Germany: Adolf-Ernst Theater *Ein fideles Corps* 25 December 1894; Australia: Princess Theatre, Melbourne 13 April 1895
Literature: Bantock, G and Aflalo, F G: *Round the World with A Gaiety Girl* (John McQueen, London, 1896)

GALLAGHER, Helen   (b Brooklyn, NY, ?1926). Lively dance and song girl who has led a fuller and more variegated career in the last half-century of American musical theatre than almost any other.

Miss Gallagher made her first Broadway appearance as a take-over in the revue *The Seven Lively Arts* (1944) and, after an early career as a chorus dancer (*Mr Strauss Goes to Boston, Billion Dollar Baby, Brigadoon*) progressed to featured rôles in *High Button Shoes* (1947, Nancy), the revue *Touch and Go* (New York and London) and *Make a Wish* (1951, Poupette), and the dance-and-comedy rôle of Gladys Bumps in the 1952 revival of *Pal Joey* (Tony Award).

She subsequently took the title-rôle in the 1953 musical *Hazel Flagg*, appeared regionally as Annie Oakley and Miss Adelaide, and as Sharon in *Finian's Rainbow* at the City Center, and replaced Carol Haney as Gladys in Broadway's *The Pajama Game* (1955). She returned to the City Center to play Meg Brockie in a revival of *Brigadoon* and Ado Annie in *Oklahoma!*, played the three Broadway performances of *Portofino* (1958, Kitty) and again went interstate to play Lola (*Damn Yankees*) and Nellie Forbush and to create the rôle of Daisy Dean in *Molly Darling* at the St Louis Muny before taking up her most memorable Broadway rôle as Nickie ('Big Spender') in *Sweet Charity* (1966). She succeeded Gwen Verdon in the title-rôle of that piece, toured with the show, and then returned to Broadway to replace Jane Connell as Agnes Gooch in *Mame* (1968).

Plate 98. **Helen Gallagher** *as the heroine of the St Louis Muny's production*, Molly Darling.

Another short-lived flop, *Cry for Us All* (1970, Bessie Legg), preceded a major success in the rôle of Lucille Early ('You Can Dance with Any Girl', 'Where Has My Hubby Gone Blues') in the 1971 revival of *No, No, Nanette* which won her a second Tony Award as best supporting actress.

She has subsequently appeared off-Broadway in the cabaret musical *Tickles by Tucholsky*, played Arisone in a musical version of *Le Misanthrope* produced at the New York Shakespeare Festival (1977), Maggie Simpson in the short-lived *A Broadway Musical* (1978), succeeded Ann Miller in the burlesque show *Sugar Babies* (1981), appeared as *Tallulah* (1983) and played a one-woman show, *Tallulah Tonight*, at off-Broadway's American Place Theater (1988). On the weather-side of 70 (her birthdate always carefully hidden) she continues an active career in the 1990s.

GALLMEYER, Josefine   [TOMASELLI, Josefina] (b Leipzig, 27 February 1838; d Vienna, 2 February 1884). One of the most popular stars of the Viennese musical stage of her time, best remembered today for the tales of her battles with fellow star, Marie Geistinger.

The daughter of theatre folk, 'Pepi' Gallmeyer began her career on the stage at 15, playing in Brünn, Budapest, Hermannstadt, between 1860 and 1862 at Temesvár, and making an appearance alongside Nestroy at the Theater in der Josefstadt. When Friedrich Strampfer moved from Temesvár to take over the Theater an der Wien, Gallmeyer was engaged to go there as soubrette, and she remained for three years starring in such Possen as *Der Goldonkel* and *Eine gezogene Kanone* until the success of Marie Geistinger led to a well-publicized rivalry and, eventually, Gallmeyer's departure. She appeared in Berlin in Geistinger's rôle of Boulotte (1867, *Barbe-bleue*) and on returning to Vienna joined the company at the Carltheater. There she came into her own, soon challenging for the position of the biggest popular singing star in town as she featured in such rôles as Vienna's original Gabrielle in *Pariser Leben*, Catherine in *Toto* and Régina in *Die Prinzessin von Trapezunt*.

In the mid-1870s she joined Julius Rosen in the direction of Strampfertheater, where she appeared, amongst others, as Ophelia to Felix Schweighofer's *Hammlet* in Julius Hopp's burlesque of Shakespeare, but the venture turned out a disaster, and she returned first to the Carltheater (*Vindobona*, Lucrezia in *Graziella/La Petite Mariée*) and then, for several years, to the Theater an der Wien to star in a series of Possen including *Die Landpomeranze*, *Ihr Corporal*, *Plausch net Pepi*, *Die Trutzige*, *Die Böhmin* and *Die Gypsfigur*, whilst also creating the rôle of Regerl, alongside Girardi, in Millöcker's successful Operette *Das verwunschene Schloss* (1878) and introducing the Viennese versions of the title-rôle of *La Mascotte* (*Der Glücksengel*) and Angelina in *Der grosse Casimir*.

In 1882 she played in *Herzblättchen* at the Carltheater, before following the example so successfully set by her old rival, Geistinger, and taking a tour to America. She appeared at New York's Thalia Theater with a repertoire of her most successful pieces and a supporting company including such stars as Tewele and Knaack and, in a season dogged by absences through illness, she was seen in *Der Goldonkel*, *Ihr Corporal*, *Die Näherin* and *Die Prinzessin von Trapezunt* as well as a selection of comedies. The illness soon proved not be a tactical one and, not long after her return home, she died.

In 1905 a Volksstuck, *Josefine Gallmeyer*, was produced at the Vienna Lustspieltheater (26 September) and in 1921 a Singspiel about her, written and composed by Paul Knepler, was mounted at the Wiener Bürgertheater by Oskar Fronz with Rosy Werginz playing the rôle of Pepi.

Biography: Waldstein, M: *Erinnerungen an Josefine Gallmeyer* (R Jacobsthal, Berlin, 1885)

GALLOIS, Germaine [GALLAIS, Jeanne] (b Paris).

Originally employed in the dressmaking business, Mlle Gallois made her first appearance on the stage as a slave-girl in *Adam et Ève* at the Nouveautés. She played in revue at the Menus-Plaisirs and appeared at the Renaissance in *Isoline* (1888) before disappearing from the stage for 'personal reasons' for several years. On her return, however, she quickly began to rise through the ranks. She played in *Madame l'Archiduc* at the Menus-Plaisirs, *Les Pilules du Diable* at the Châtelet, in two plays at the Ambigu, and then took up the rôle of Métella in Fernand Samuel's revival of *La Vie parisienne* at the Variétés. After a further venture into opéra-bouffe (Fantasia in *Le Voyage dans la lune*) and drama at the Porte-Saint-Martin, where she appeared as Madame de Pompadour in *Latude*, the Empress Marie-Louise in *Napoléon* (with a Méhul song) and as other such regal beauties, she returned to the musical stage for a long series of fine rôles in *L'Enlèvement de la Toledad* (1894, Baronne Trippmann), *La Duchesse de Ferrare* (1895, Angèle), *La Saint-Valentin* (1895), *La Dot de Brigitte* (1895, Hortense), *Monsieur Lohengrin* (1896, Cécile), *Ninette* (1896, Ninon de l'Enclos), *L'Oeil crevé* revival (Fleur de Noblesse), *Le Pompier de service* (1897, Fabienne), *Les Petites Barnett* and *La Mascotte* (1901, Bettina) at the Gaîté as well as a continuing ration of revue.

She kept up a regular presence in all areas of the theatre in the early years of the 20th century, acting as a commère in revue and being seen in such opérettes as Lincke's *Lysistrata* (1904, Lysistrata) at the Moulin-Rouge, *Les Dragons de l'imperatrice* (1905, Lucrèce), *Paris, ou le bon juge* (1906, Vénus), as Mlle Lange in *La Fille de Madame Angot* at the Variétés and the Théâtre de la Gaîté and as Isoline and Briscotte in the 1908 revival of *Geneviève de Brabant*. She moved on to slightly more senior parts (*Miousic* 1920, *Amour de Princesse*, Madame Cocardier in *J'adore ça* 1925, Madame d'Epinay in *Mozart* 1925, *Monsieur Dumollet* etc) in the later years of a full and fine career on the Parisian stage.

Mlle Gallois was equipped not only with a fine voice and notable acting charms, but also with a figure which was the marvel of Parisian womanhood. This figure, however, was not acquired without effort. She wore an amazing corset to give her a fashionable shape in spite of being, without its help, 'blonde avec une tête de poupée, un front bombé, des yeux étincélants, une bouche éblouissante ... une exquise chanteuse d'opérette ... la plus belle de toutes les belles artistes des Variétés à la grand époque'.

Mlle Gallois was married to the comedian Guy of the Variétés.

GANDOLFO Opérette in 1 act by Henri Chivot and Albert Duru. Music by Charles Lecocq. Théâtre des Bouffes-Parisiens, Paris, 16 January 1869.

An early and successful short piece by composer Lecocq and his equally up-and-coming librettists, *Gandolfo* was an old-fashioned little tale borrowed from Boccaccio and decked out with some charming music. The Gandolfo (May) of the title is a jealous old legal man with a young wife, Angela (Mlle Boulanger). Angela is rather taken by the young musician Stenio (Mlle Joly) who sings under her window, and altogether less by the pushy Captain Sabino Sabrinardi (Arnould) who pursues his suit by letter, but it is the latter who is enterprising enough to be delivered to her room in a crate in search of a kiss. When Gandolfo finally finds his wife with the musician in her room, she pretends he is being pursued by Sabrinardi and needs legal help, but the tables are turned when Sabrinardi discovers that old Gandolfo is the mysterious person who has been having an affair with his wife. The errant husband can only engage Stenio as his wife's music teacher, invite everyone to supper and promise never to be jealous again.

The score featured a little serenade for the musician ('Nina, ma bien aimée'), a trilly ariette for Angela ('L'homme est fort'), a bullocking bit for the Captain ('C'est moi qui suis l'invincible'), a quartet leading into a drinking song ('C'est le vin qui fait que soudain') and a finale.

First introduced at the Théâtre des Bouffes-Parisiens, *Gandolfo* was subsequently played in several European houses in French and in German. However, the only English-language performance seems to have been that given by an all-women's company under the management of M B Leavitt in New York in 1884 with Marie Sanger, Amy Ames, Tiny Vining, May Stembler and Marie Mülle featured, on a double bill with *An Adamless Eden*.

Austria: Strampfertheater 28 December 1872; USA: Comedy Theater 18 December 1884

GANNE, [Gustave] Louis (b Buxières-les-Mines, 5 April 1862; d Paris, 13 July 1923). French conductor and composer whose limited output of stage works included two pieces which have survived into the modern repertoire.

The young Louis Ganne made his earliest theatre venture as a composer of ballet music, and his *Les Sources du Nil* was mounted at the Folies-Bergère when he was but 20 years old. In the years that followed he composed other such pieces for the Folies-Bergère and the Casino de Paris (*Volapuk*, *Au Japon*, *Le Reveil d'une Parisienne*, *Phryné*, first produced at the Royan Casino with Cléo de Mérode starred, *L'Abeille et la fleur* etc) as well as songs, drawing-room and dance music and marches. He won particular success with the march 'Le Père la Victoire', based on a theme from *Volapuk*, and the 'Marche Lorraine'. At the same time he worked as a conductor at the Parisian Bals de l'Opéra and in several spa towns, and made his first steps as a composer of vaudeville (*Tout Paris*) and of opérette.

Ganne found an enduring success with the circus musical *Les Saltimbanques* (1899) which became a great favourite in the French provinces following its initial Paris run, and in 1906, having installed himself since the previous season at Monaco at the head of a little orchestra of what he described as 'soloists' for the 'Concerts Louis Ganne', he had his second successful opérette presented at the local Opéra. *Hans, le joueur de flûte*, artistically a much more satisfying piece than the tuppence-coloured *Saltimbanques*, went on from its Monegasque première to productions round ther world.

Hans, le joueur de flûte did not lead, however, to further successes. An ancient Egyptian comic opera *Rhodope*, also produced in Monaco, did not provoke the same interest, playing some 40 first-run Parisian performances when it eventually found a home at the Théâtre des Variétés, and the composer's last major produced piece, *Cocorico*, composed to a rather palely routine libretto about an old monarch with a young wife and the need to produce an heir, was seen only 28 times at the Théâtre Apollo in 1913.

Amongst Ganne's other theatre credits were the completion of the score for the late Robert Planquette's last work, *Le Paradis de Mahomet*, the incidental music (w Olivier Métra) for Catulle Mendès' 1906 play, *Glatigny*, and a continuing supply of dance music (*Cythère*, *Les Arles* etc). An opérette, *La Belle de Paris*, with a pasticcio score made up from Ganne's works, was mounted in Paris in 1921 for a run of 110 performances.

1891 **Tout Paris** (Georges Duval) Théâtre du Châtelet 16 June
1892 **Rabelais** (Oscar Métenier, Dubut de la Fôret) Nouveau Théâtre 25 October
1893 **Les Colles des femmes** (Henri Kéroul, Adolphe Jaime) Théâtre des Menus-Plaisirs 29 September
1899 **Les Saltimbanques** (Maurice Ordonneau) Théâtre de la Gaîté 30 December
1906 **Hans, le joueur de flûte** (Maurice Vaucaire, Georges Mitchell) Monte Carlo 14 April; Théâtre Apollo 31 May 1910
1910 **Rhodope** (Paul Ferrier, Paul de Choudens) Monte Carlo 13 December; Théâtre des Variétés, Paris 24 December 1914
1913 **Cocorico** (Georges Duval, Maurice Soulié, P Jailly) Théâtre Apollo 29 November

1916 **L'Archiduc des Folies-Bergère** (Lucien Boyer, Fernand Rouvray) 7 October
1921 **La Belle de Paris** (pasticcio/Boyer, Rouvray) Théâtre Apollo 22 October

GARINEI, Pietro (b Trieste, 25 February 1919). Italy's godfather of postwar musical theatre.

Pharmacist Garinei went into partnership with journalist [Ales]Sandro Giovannini (b Rome, 10 July 1915; d Rome, 26 April 1977) in 1944 to produce a revue, *Cantachiaro*, at Rome's Teatro Quattro Fontane, and the pair then continued their collaboration for more than 30 years, becoming Italy's foremost producers of musical theatre and co-writing and staging a number of original musical shows which found their way into productions beyond Italy.

Their earliest productions were in the field of revue, with stars such as Anna Magnani, Renato Rascel, Wanda Osiris and Enrico Viarisio topping the bills, before they moved on to more vertebrate stage shows and to the cinema. After a handful of pieces described as 'favola musicale' (*Alvaro, piuttosto corsaro*; *Tobia, la candida spia* – a piece inspired by *The Third Man*) or 'avventura musicale' (the *Amphytrion* musical *Giove in doppiopetto*), they co-wrote and produced such book-pieces as *La Granduchessa e i camerieri* (a new musical version of Savoir's *La Grande-Duchesse et le garçon d'étage*) and the footballing *La padrona di raggio di luna* with Broadway's Robert Alda starred, moving into unashamed musical comedy with their version of the Rainier–Grace Kelly romance *Carlo, non farlo*; the *Naked Truth* piece *Buona notte, Bettina*; *Un paio d'ali*; *L'adorabile Guilio*; the Aristophanean *Un Trapezio per Lisistrata*; the movieland *Un Mandarino per Teo*;, *Rinaldo in campo* which prided itself on having Italy's first musical hero-who-dies; *Enrico '61*; the old-Rome tale of *Rugantino*; *Il Giorno della tartaruga*; *Ciao, Rudy* which featured Marcello Mastroianni as Valentino; *Viola, violino e viola d'amore*; *Angeli in bandiera*; *Alleluia, brava gente*; the internationally successful *Aggiungi un posto a tavola*; the revusical *Felicibumta*; and *Anche i bancari hanno un' anima*.

After Giovannini's death, Garinei continued to produce and direct under their banner, adding *Accendiamo la lampada* (his own last credit as author), *Bravo!*, *Amore miei* and *Pardon, Monsieur Molière* to their long list of productions.

The producers were credited with the whole or part of the libretti and lyrics for most of their shows, but their most internationally successful song, 'Arriverderci, Roma' (music: Rascel) was a single. 'Domani è sempre domenica' (from *Un paio d'ali*) gave them another sizeable hit.

Buona notte, Bettina gave the producer-authors a first international success, being played in London as *When in Rome* (298 performances), in Spain as *Buenas noches Bettina*, in Budapest (*Tigris a garázsban* ie a tiger in the garage), Germany (*Gute Nacht Bettina*), South America, Czechoslovakia and Poland; *Un paio d'ali* was seen in Russia, Germany (*Ein Sonntag in Rom*) and Hungary (*Romai Vasarnáp*); *Rinaldo in campo* as *Rinaldo Rinaldini* also in Germany and in Belgrade, *Enrico '61* in Germany and London, *Rugantino* in its original Italian in New York, and *Il giorno della tartaruga* in France (*Le Jour de la tortue*) and Germany (*Amore mio*). *Alleluia, brave gente* became *Halleluja, brave Leute* in Germany but it was the mixture of low comedy and religion of *Aggiungi un posto a tavola* which –

under a rainbow of titles – travelled the most widely of all his pieces since *Buona notte, Bettina*, being produced throughout Europe and South America.

1953 **Alvaro, piuttosto corsaro** (Gorni Kramer/w Sandro Giovannini) Teatro Sistina 25 December

1954 **Giove in doppiopetto** (Kramer/w Giovannini) Teatro Lirico, Milan 27 September

1954 **Tobia, la candida spia** (Kramer/w Giovannini) Teatro Sistina 30 December

1955 **La Granduchessa e i camerieri** (Kramer/w Giovannini) Teatro Lirico, Milan 24 September

1955 **La Padrona di raggio di luna** (Kramer/w Giovannini) Teatro Alfieri 10 December

1956 **Carlo non farlo** (Kramer/ w Giovannini) Teatro Sistina 21 September

1956 **Buona notte, Bettina** (Kramer/w Giovannini) Teatro Lirico, Milan 14 November

1957 **L'adorabile Giulio** (Kramer/w Giovannini) Teatro Sistina

1957 **Un paio d'ali** (Kramer/w Giovannini) Teatro Lirico, Milan 18 September

1959 **Un Trapezio per Lisistrata** (Kramer/w Giovannini) Teatro Sistina 18 December

1960 **Un Mandarino per Teo** (Kramer/w Giovannini) Teatro Sistina 11 October

1961 **Enrico '61** (Renato Rascel/w Giovannini) Teatro Sistina 23 February

1961 **Rinaldo in campo** (Domenico Modugno/w Giovannini) Turin 13 September

1963 **Rugantino** (Armando Trovaioli/w Massimo Franciosa, Festa Campanile) Teatro Sistina 15 December

1965 **Il Giorno della tartaruga** (Rascel/w Gigi Magni, Franciosa, Giovannini) Teatro Sistina 24 October

1966 **Ciao, Rudy** (Trovaioli/w Magni, Giovannini) Teatro Sistina 7 January

1967 **Viola, violino, e viola d'amore** (Bruno Canfora/w Magni, Giovannini) Teatro Sistina 16 September

1969 **Angeli in bandiera** (Canfora/w Iaia Fiastri, Giovannini) Teatro Sistina 24 October

1970 **Alleluia, brava gente** (Rascel, Modugno/w Fiastri, Giovannini) Teatro Sistina 23 December

1974 **Aggiungi un posto a tavola** (Trovaioli/w Fiastri, Giovannini) Teatro Sistina 8 December

1979 **Accendiamo la lampada** (Trovaioli/w Fiastri) Teatro Sistina 30 December

Biography: Garinei L, Giovannini, M; *Garinei e Giovannini presentano* (Rizzoli, Milan, 1985)

GASPARONE Operette in 3 acts by F Zell and Richard Genée. Music by Carl Millöcker. Theater an der Wien, Vienna, 26 January 1884.

Millöcker's brigands-and-smugglers musical, produced little more than a year after his phenomenal success with *Der Bettelstudent*, did not come anywhere near challenging the popularity of his most famous piece, but it did well enough first time round, and proved to be made of sufficiently solid stuff to last rather better than some of his other equally or more popular pieces from around the same period. A century on, whilst shows like *Das verwunschene Schloss*, *Der Viceadmiral* and *Der Feldprediger*, and even the later and much more successful *Der arme Jonathan*, have vanished from the repertoire, various versions of *Gasparone* find their way regularly to the stage in the Operette houses of Europe.

The famous bandit Gasparone is abroad in 1820s Sicily and the Mayor of Syracuse, Baboleno Nasoni (Felix Schweighofer), has his men out hunting for him. They are unsuccessful, largely because he isn't there. It is the inn-

Plate 99. **Gasparone:** *Fun and games as the soubrets (Franz Supper, Rhonda Ann Ingle) take their turn at the stage (Landestheater, Salzburg 1987).*

keeper Benozzo (Alexander Girardi) who has started the rumours in order to distract the law's attention from his family's smuggling activities. These, however, are discovered by Count Erminio (Josef Joseffy) and, in exchange for his silence, the smugglers agree to stage an attack on the coach of the rich, beautiful and widowed Countess Carlotta della Santa Croce (Marie Theresia Massa) so that Erminio can stage a dramatic rescue and impress the lady.

The trick works, but Nasoni is furious, as he had planned to wed the Countess to his son, Sindulfo (Alexander Guttmann), and he quickly offers to help her win a lucrative lawsuit in which she is involved in exchange for the alliance. Since he knows the case is already won, he is taking no risk. But, when the betrothal has been fixed, Sindulfo is kidnapped and held for ransom by Gasparone, and the Countess's money stolen, also by Gasparone. Panic reigns, martial law is declared, and Nasoni backpedals out of the betrothal, leaving Carlotta free to turn to Erminio who can return to her the money of which he, temporarily disguised as 'Gasparone', had robbed her, whilst Sindulfo was tied up amongst the contraband in Benozzo's inn.

Millöcker's music included some delightful numbers, ranging from Erminio's dashing denial of banditry ('O, dass ich doch der Räuber wär') and Carlotta's soprano description of the attack on her coach ('Ein höchst romantisch Abenteuer') to Benozzo's comical 'Stockfinster war die Nacht' and his obligatory waltz song 'Er soll dein Herr sein!' It was, however, the tarantella of the first-act finale, 'Anzoletto sang 'komm, mia bella!'' sung by Benozzo's wife Sora (Rosa Streitmann), which proved the most popular piece of all Millöcker's score.

Gasparone played solidly for a month (30th performance, 24 February) at the Theater an der Wien, but its run was interrupted by a short French season and a revival of *Donna Juanita* and, by the time producer Steiner gave up the theatre at the end of April, it was still short of its 50th night. It was brought back in 1892 with Joseffy again starring, and was given odd performances in repertoire between 1898 and 1901, without establishing itself as a particular favourite, but it held on. In 1915 the Volksoper mounted a production (21 April) and in 1933 a revised version written by Paul Knepler with the music rearranged by Ernst Steffan, which had been introduced the previous year at Berlin's Theater am Nollendorfplatz, was mounted at the same house. This revision introduced the waltz 'Dunkelrote Rosen', plucked from the score of Millöcker's *Der Viceadmiral* (where it had been the trio 'Geh'n wir in den Garten, atmen Blumenduft'), for the character who had once been Erminio, but who was now 'The Stranger', otherwise the Governor of the area – and thus Nasoni's superior – in a good old conventional comic-opera disguise. It was this rôle which benefited most largely from the rewrite, particularly in that 'Dunkelrote Rosen' became not only the hit number of the show but a hit that went beyond the show to become a regular recital item.

Further revisions to the revisions followed. In 1980 (3 March) a new production of a *Gasparone* was mounted at the Volksoper whilst Berlin's Metropoltheater saw another version two years later, and regional theatres in Austria and Germany continued to rewrite and produce their own remakes of the show, most of which, in spite of the definite appeal of 'Dunkelrote Rosen' (now confirmed in its place in all versions), were distinctly more conventional and less fun than the original.

Gasparone quickly followed its Vienna première with productions in Germany, where it proved much more immediately popular than in Austria, following its Dresden premiere by running swiftly through to 200 performances at Berlin's Friedrich-Wilhelmstädtisches Theater, in Prague (23 March 1884), and in Budapest (ad Árpád Berczik, Lajos Evva) where the Népszinház production, with a cast headed by Aranka Hegyi, Ilka Pálmay, Pál Vidor and Elek Solymossy, played a good 36 nights. The show also made its way to the German theatre of New York, where it was mounted with Max Lube (Nasoni), Bertha Kierschner (Carlotta), Emmy Meffert (Cora), Ferdinand Schütz (Benozzo) and Eduard Elsbach (Erminio) for a fortnight. The very same night John Duff presented the show in English, with a cast featuring Richard Mansfield (Nasoni), Harrie Hilliard (Erminio), Emma Seebold (Carlotta), Mae St John (Sora) and Alfred Klein (Benozzo) with sufficient success for it to be given a further showing the following season. The German theatre also repeated the piece, first in its original form and then in what seems to have been the first of its interminable rewritten versions. *Die Banditen* (Thalia-Theater, 4 January 1887) starred Carl Adolf Friese as Nasoni, but its reception did not encourage Gustav Amberg to persevere with it, and when he played *Gasparone* again in 1892 he returned to the original version.

Although many other European cities mounted the piece during the 1880s and early 1890s, neither France nor Britain took up *Gasparone* and its career, both pre- and, in particular, post-'Dunkelrote Rosen' has been very largely in its original language. A film *Gasparone* made by George Jacoby in 1937, with Johannes Heesters and Marika Rökk featured, was even less faithful to the original than the various stage remakes.

Germany: Residenztheater, Dresden 13 April 1884, Friedrich-Wilhelmstädtisches Theater, Berlin 26 September 1884; Hungary: Népszinház 25 April 1884; USA: Standard Theater (Eng) 21 February 1885, Thalia-Theater (Ger) 21 February 1885; Film: 1937

Recordings: complete (1932 version) (EMI), selection (1932 version) (RCA) etc

GAVAULT, Paul [Armand Marcel] (b Algiers, 1 September 1865; d Paris, 25 December 1951). Comic playwright and revue writer who scored musical-theatre hits at both first- and second-hand.

A law graduate and sometime barrister, Gavault began his literary career at twenty-one whilst on the staff of the *Le National* and subsequently worked on a long list of other journals (*Petite République*, *Voltaire*, as theatre editor of *Le Soir*, *Le Gaulois* etc) whilst taking his first steps in the theatre. From the production of his first piece, the revue *Tout à la scène* (w de Cottens) at the Théâtre Moderne in 1892, he had 20 years of success as a stage author, producing a highly successful line of comedies and vaudevilles, often at first in tandem with Victor de Cottens, then with Georges Berr and a variety of other partners. He also collaborated on a long list of revues and on the libretti for several opérettes and musical comedies which found some success in their Parisian productions and were occasionally produced abroad. These latter included the four opérettes on which he collaborated with composer Louis Varney: *Le Papa de Francine* (1896), subsequently produced in Britain as *A Lucky Girl* (1898) and in Austria as *Lolas Cousin* (1898), *Les Demoiselles de Saint-Cyriens* (*Diákkisasszonyok*, Budapest 1898, *The Cadet Girl*, New York 1900), *Les Petites Barnett* (*A Barnett-lanyok*, Budapest 1899) and *Le Pompier de service* (*A tűzoltó*, Budapest 1899). Later in life he also became a theatrical administrator, spending periods at the head successively of the Nouvel-Ambigu, the Odéon (1914–21) and the Théâtre de la Porte-Saint-Martin before retiring from the theatre world.

Several of Gavault's plays were used as the bases for musical comedies during the period when established French vaudevilles and comedies were widely used as sources for libretti. In Britain, the musical comedy *The Girl for the Boy* (Duke of York's Theatre 23 Sept 1919) was based on his *La Petite Chocolatière* (1909) and the Ivan Caryll musical, *The Kiss Call* (Gaiety Theatre 8 October 1919), on *Un Coup de téléphone* (1912, w Georges Berr), whilst the long-running *Theodore and Co* (Gaiety Theatre, 19 September 1916) was taken from *Théodore et Cie*, a play to which his name was sometimes appended alongside those of Paul Armont and Nicolas Nancey. The American *Tantalizing Tommy* (1912), the German *Bezauberndes Fräulein* (1933) and the Italian *La piccola cioccolataia* also used *La Petite Chocolatière* as their starting point. Lajos Lajtai's Hungarian operett, *Az ártatlan özvegy* (the innocent widow) (Városi Színház 25 December 1925), was also based on a Gavault play, *Mademoiselle Josette, ma femme* (1906 w Robert Charvay) and Düsseldorf's 1912 musical *Eine kitzliche Geschichte* (Hugo Hirsch/Rudolf Schanzer, 31 October) was a version of the Gavault/Ordonneau play *Une affaire scandaleuse*. The libretto for Gavault's 1902 opérette *Le Jockey malgré lui* was reused as the text for the American musical comedy *The Office Boy* (Victoria Theater 2 November 1903) with the names of Harry B Smith and composer Ludwig Englander attached to it, in the same way that *Les Demoiselles de Saint-Cyriens* had been earlier stripped of its score and transformed into *The Cadet Girl*.

1896 **Le Papa de Francine** (Louis Varney/w Victor de Cottens) Théâtre Cluny 5 November

1897 **Le Pompier de service** (Varney/w de Cottens) Théâtre des Variétés 18 February

1898 **Les Demoiselles de Saint-Cyriens** (Varney/w de Cottens) Théâtre Cluny 28 January

1898 **Les Petites Barnett** (Varney) Théâtre des Variétés 8 November

1899 **Ohé Venus** (Monteux-Brissac/w P-L Flers) Lyon; La Cigale 24 February

1899 **Shakespeare!** (Gaston Serpette/w Flers) Théâtre des Bouffes-Parisiens 23 November

1900 **Les Petits Croisés** (w Flers) La Cigale 24 January

1902 **Le Jockey malgré lui** (Victor Roger/w Maurice Ordonneau) Théâtre des Bouffes-Parisiens 4 December

1903 **La Belle de New-York** (*The Belle of New York*) French version (Moulin-Rouge)

1905 **Les Poupées de M Dupont** (Charles Lecocq) 1 act Théâtre des Variétés 26 May

GAXTON, William [GAXIOLA, Arturo Antonio] (b San Francisco, 2 December 1893; d New York, 12 February 1963).

Gaxton made a start in show business as a teenager in vaudeville, and won his first Broadway appearance in *The Music Box Revue* in 1922. After several years working out of town, including musical-comedy assignments touring in the title-rôle of *All for You, John Henry* (1925), in *Betty Lee* (1925, Wallingford Speed), and in the flop *Miss Happiness* (1926, Steve Colwell), he played his first Broadway leading rôles as the heroes of Rodgers and Hart's *A Connecticut Yankee* (1927, Martin, 'My Heart Stood Still', 'Thou Swell') and of Cole Porter's *Fifty Million Frenchmen* (1929, Peter Forbes, 'You Do Something to Me'). However, his combination of leading-man good looks and edgy comic style got their best showcase when he was cast as John Wintergreen, President of the United States, in Gershwin's *Of Thee I Sing* (1931, 'Of Thee I Sing, Baby').

Of Thee I Sing paired him for the first time with comedian Victor Moore, there cast as the opaque Vice President Throttlebottom. Moore's style, as the muddled and hard-done-by little fellow, contrasted well with Gaxton's dashing, forward comic persona, and they were paired again at the top of the bill for *Let 'em Eat Cake* (1933), the sequel to *Of Thee I Sing*, and, most famously, in *Anything Goes* (1934) where Gaxton created the rôle of Billy Crocker ('You're the Top', 'All Through the Night'), opposite Ethel Merman, whilst Moore appeared as Public Enemy Number Thirteen.

Gaxton went on to star as Leopold in the Broadway version of *White Horse Inn* (1936) and joined up with Moore again for *Leave it to Me!* (1938, Buck Thomas),

Louisiana Purchase (1940, Jim Taylor), and two less successful ventures, *Hollywood Pinafore* (1945, Dick Live-Eye) and, finally, *Nellie Bly* (1946, Frank Jordan), but he was still to be seen on the musical stage as late as 1961 and 1962, when he appeared at Jones Beach, NY, in the Hawaiian musical *Paradise Island*.

He appeared on the screen in the movie versions of *Fifty Million Frenchmen* and *Best Foot Forward*.

GAY, John (b Barnstaple, September 1685; d London, 4 December 1732).

The young Gay worked as domestic steward to the Duchess of Monmouth and as secretary to the Earl of Clarendon, and during this time he made his first attempts at writing, including several pieces for the stage. For many years he hovered on the edge of court circles, making himself agreeable and useful and awaiting the comfortable position he was sure must come his way but, when, in 1727, the offer of an ushership to one of the royal princesses was made, he was disappointed and refused the post.

His disappointment was short-lived, however, for the following year Rich staged his ballad opera *The Beggar's Opera* at the theatre at Lincoln's Inn Fields, and Gay's name and fortune were made. He wrote a sequel to *The Beggar's Opera*, under the title *Polly*, but the disfavour with which he was now regarded in high places resulted in its being banned. When it finally was staged, it was clear that he had been done a favour, for the second piece was a pale imitation of the first and could very well have harmed the booming success of his one and only hit.

His opera *Acis and Galatea* (music: Handel) was produced at the Little Haymarket Theatre 28 May 1732) and an operatic *Achilles* (1735) was mounted after his death.

Gay's *Achilles in Petticoats* was subsequently adapted as a comic opera, with music by Thomas Arne (Covent Garden, 16 December 1773) but it was *The Beggar's Opera* which, of his works, was subsequently the most tampered-with by other hands. The Viennese *Der Liebling von London*, the 1928 German musical *Die Dreigroschenoper* and Broadway's *The Beggar's Holiday* (Broadway Theater, 26 December 1946) are amongst the pieces founded on the text of Gay's most famous and enduring work.

1728 **The Beggar's Opera** (pasticcio arr J C Pepusch) Lincoln's Inn Fields Theatre 29 January

1777 **Polly** (pasticcio arr Pepusch and Arnold/as George Colman) Little Haymarket Theatre 19 July

Biographies: Melville, L: *The Life and Letters of John Gay* (1921); Erving, W H: *John Gay: Favorite of the Wits* (Durham, NC, 1940)

GAY, Noel [ARMITAGE, Reginald Moxon] (b Wakefield, Yorks, 15 July 1898; d London, 4 March 1954). British songwriter who provided scores for a number of shows in the 1930s and 1940s.

A cathedral choirboy at 12, assistant organist at the Chapel Royal, St James's, and musical director at Saint Anne's church, Soho, at 18, Armitage followed a musical training at the Royal College of Music and Cambridge destining him for a career in church music. At the age of 25, however, he switched direction and within a few years the songs of 'Noel Gay' were being played in revues in London (*Stop Press, The Charlot Show of 1926, Clowns in Clover*) and in the provinces (*Merry Mexico, Jumbles* etc). He

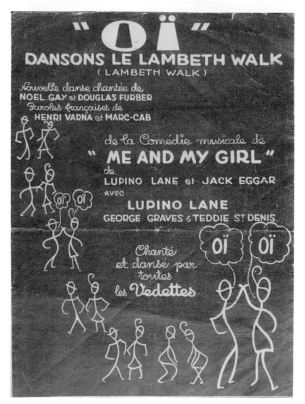

Plate 100. **Noel Gay**'s *most famous number went round the world –
but its composer got pretty poor billing.*

composed the song 'Tondeleyo' for the film *White Cargo*
(1929) but it was 'The King's Horses', performed by
Cicely Courtneidge in the revue *Folly to Be Wise* (w Harry
Graham), which gave him his first significant song-hit.

In 1931 Gay contributed to his first book musical when
he teamed with Stanley Lupino and lyricist Desmond Carter on the Gaiety musical comedy *Hold My Hand*. In the
next four years, whilst turning out regular amounts of
music for the blossoming sound-film industry, notably for
Jack Hulbert and/or Cicely Courtneidge ('There's Something About a Soldier', 'Who's Been Polishing the Sun'
etc), as well as individual numbers for the popular-song
market ('I Took My Harp to a Party' for Gracie Fields,
'Round the Marble Arch' etc), he also wrote the songs for
several similar musical plays, but it was Arthur Rose's
vehicle for another member of the Lupino family, the acrobatic little singing comedian Lupino Lane, with which he
finally hit the bullseye. Following a fine initial run at the
Victoria Palace at the edge of the war, *Me and My Girl*
(1937), with its handful of Gay songs, became a perennial
Lupino family production both in the provinces and in
regular London return seasons. Its favourite songs, 'The
Lambeth Walk' and 'Me and My Girl', turned out to be
the best-known of Gay's many popular songs.

Several further vehicles for Lane and the cheeky
cockney character he favoured followed (*La-di-da-di-da*,
revised *Twenty to One*, *Meet Me Victoria*, *Sweetheart Mine*),
along with songs for a number of other musical comedies,
for the Crazy Gang shows at the London Palladium (*Swing

is in the Air*, *These Foolish Things*, *The Little Dog Laughed*)
and their return in 1947 to the Victoria Palace (*Together
Again*), as well as for a number of further revues. Many of
these shows had long and successful London runs as Gay's
total of song successes mounted ('Leaning on a Lamp-
post', 'Run, Rabbit, Run', 'Only a Glass of Champagne',
'Hey Little Hen'). His final London show, *Bob's Your
Uncle*, produced in 1948, had to it a marked air of the pre-
war shows to which the composer had so happily contributed, but it nevertheless proved a distinct hit, seeing
out the fashion for low-comedy musical texts with light,
catchy and simple songs attached, on a high note.

Gay founded his own music-publishing company in
1938, and in 1984 the company, under the management of
his son, Richard, staged a revised version of *Me and My
Girl*. This version proved enormously successful and went
on to give Gay the kind of international exposure he had
not achieved in his lifetime. The firm subsequently produced several other, unsuccessful musical plays, and in 1992
mounted a pasticcio musical, *Radio Times* (Abi Grant,
Queen's Theatre 15 October), based on Gay's catalogue.

1931 **Hold my Hand** (Desmond Carter/Stanley Lupino) Gaiety
Theatre 23 December
1933 **That's a Pretty Thing** (ex-*Paste*) (Carter/Lupino) Daly's
Theatre 22 November
1935 **Jack o' Diamonds** (H F Maltby, Clifford Grey) Gaiety
Theatre 25 February
1935 **Love Laughs–!** (ex-*Leave it to Love*) (Grey, Greatrex Newman) London Hippodrome 25 June
1937 **Me and My Girl** (L Arthur Rose, Douglas Furber) Victoria
Palace 16 December
1938 **Wild Oats** (Furber) Prince's Theatre 13 April
1940 **Present Arms** (Frank Eyton/Fred Thompson, Bert Lee)
Prince of Wales Theatre 13 May
1942 **Susie** revised *Jack o' Diamonds* New Theatre, Oxford 13
June
1943 **La-di-da-di-da** revised *That's a Pretty Thing* (Lupino)
Victoria Palace 30 March
1943 **The Love Racket** (Eyton, Barbara Gordon, Basil Thomas,
Leslie Gibbs/Lupino) Victoria Palace 21 October
1944 **Meet Me Victoria** (Eyton/Lupino Lane, Lauri Wylie)
Victoria Palace 8 April
1944 **Ring Time** revised *Battling Butler* with new score (Eyton/
Stanley Brightman, Austin Melford) Glasgow 28 August
1946 **Sweetheart Mine** (Eyton/Lane, Wylie) Victoria Palace 1
August
1948 **Bob's Your Uncle** (Eyton/Melford) Saville Theatre 5 May

GAY DIVORCE Musical comedy in 2 acts by Dwight
Taylor based on the play *An Adorable Adventure* by
J Hartley Manners. Music and lyrics by Cole Porter. Ethel
Barrymore Theater, New York, 29 November 1932.

Fred Astaire appeared in only one further stage musical
following the retirement of his sister, Adele, to marriage.
Gay Divorce paired him with the attractive Clare Luce on a
rather different footing than that of the previous partnership. The Astaire pair's greatest musicals had never
matched them as a romantic couple – they had been
brother and sister, guardian and ward – but this time
Astaire's character was at last able to 'get' the leading lady.

Miss Luce played a certain Mimi Pratt, who is decidedly
anxious to rid herself of Mr Pratt (Roland Bottomley).
To this purpose, she hires herself a professional co-
respondent, Tonetti (Erik Rhodes), but the young novelist
Guy Holden (Astaire), who has fallen in love with Mimi,

substitutes himself for the paid separator, and performs so convincingly that Mimi, her divorce gaily achieved, is ready to go straight back into marriage again.

The score used several songs ('Mister and Missus Fitch', 'I've Got You on My Mind', 'I Still Love the Red, White and Blue') which Porter had intended for a non-starter of a musical called *Stardust*, but the song hit of the evening was the insinuating 'Night and Day' as sung by the star, and danced by him with Miss Luce.

Astaire played seven months in Dwight Deere Wiman and Tom Weatherly's production, which had shifted to the Shubert Theater a few weeks after its opening, and it was Joseph Santley who saw out the Broadway run of 248 performances in the rôle of Holden, before taking the show on tour.

As had been done successfully with the other Astaire shows from *For Goodness' Sake* (*Stop Flirting*) through *Lady, Be Good!* and *Funny Face*, *Gay Divorce* was exported to London soon after the end of its Broadway run with Astaire, Miss Luce, Rhodes and the English Eric Blore repeating their Broadway rôles. It was gussied up with three extra songs ('I Love Only You', 'Never Say No', 'Waiters v Waitresses') and Luella Gear's Broadway paean to the star-spangled banner was replaced by 'Where Would You Get Your Coat?', previously heard on Broadway in the musical *Fifty Million Frenchmen*, which had folded on the British road prior to London. Lee Ephraim's London production ran for 180 performances, during which time the show was given its Australian première. With Astaire occupied in England, Billy Milton and Mona Potts took on the lead rôles, dancing to Edward Royce's original choreography, for six weeks in Melbourne and Sydney (Theatre Royal, 28 July 1934) apiece.

The show was revived in 1960 at the Cherry Lane Theater (3 April, 25 performances).

A soi-disant 1934 film version, starring Astaire alongside Ginger Rogers, Betty Grable and Edward Everett Horton, altered the title (*The Gay Divorcée*) and retained only 'Night and Day' from Porter's score, replacing the remainder of the music with songs by Mack Gordon and Harry Revel ('Don't Let it Bother You', 'Let's K-nock K-nees') and by Con Conrad and Herb Magidson ('A Needle in a Haystack' and 'The Continental'). The last named song won an Academy Award.

This film version, however, itself became the basis for an Hungarian stage musical entitled *Vidám válás* (gay divorce) written by Iván Bradányi and Márton Karinthy and with a score credited to Gershwin, Youmans and Porter. It was produced at Budapest's Karinthy Színház on 29 October 1991 with József Bozsó (Guy) and Krisztina Simonyi (Mimi) featured.

UK: Palace Theatre 2 November 1933; Australia: King's Theatre, Melbourne 23 December 1933; Film: RKO *The Gay Divorcée* 1934

THE GAY GRISETTE Musical farce in 2 acts by George Dance. Music by Carl Kiefert. Theatre Royal, Bradford, 1 August 1898.

Written specifically for a Provincial Managers' Syndicate, to provide a musical show to fill their stages, *The Gay Grisette* was sent on tour under the management of the young Robert Courtneidge. Put together by George Dance, who had a particular flair for writing for out-of-town audiences, the piece ran through the register of comic situations as a colonel's niece disguised as a grisette galloped through Europe and through situations amorous and awkward to the accompaniment of a series of songs in all the most popular styles of the moment. The West End's favourite orchestrator, Carl Kiefert, this time supplied the tunes as well as the accompaniments.

Claire Romaine, daughter of composer Teddy Solomon, was the original Babette, but she gave way to a stream of successors as *The Gay Grisette* ran through several years of popularity on the touring and colonial circuits. Australia's *Gay Grisette* was mounted under the management of Clarke & Meynell, with Florence Imeson as Babette, and, apparently, the piece was also seen, under the management of A H Chamberlyn, in the outer-backs of America.

Australia: Theatre Royal, Melbourne 4 February 1911

THE GAY PARISIENNE Musical comedy in 2 acts by George Dance based on his play *The Barmaid*. Music by Ernest Vousden. Theatre Royal, Northampton, 1 October 1894.

The huge provincial success of *The Lady Slavey* encouraged its author, George Dance, to try another piece in the same vein – made to suit the tastes of provincial audiences rather than those of the more sophisticated West End theatre-goer. With an unerring hand, he re-mixed some of the melodramatic elements which had long been the joy of touring plays, musical and unmusical, with some classic English comedy elements, and instead of the story of the naughty, blackmailing barmaid Minnie Dew-drop, created by Louise Appleby at Manchester's Comedy Theatre three years earlier (31 August 1891), he came up with the tale of the conniving Mlle Julie Bon-Bon (Nellie Murray). Like Minnie, Julie has tricked country Canon Honeycombe (J T MacMillan) into signing a document promising her marriage, and she now turns up to sue for enough breach-of-promise cash to set her and her boy-friend, Adolphe, up for a comfortable life. But Julie mis-takes her target, and it is Amos Dingle (Alfred Fisher) who ends up in court being prosecuted by Tom Everleigh (Richard Temple jr), the fiancé of Miss Nora Honey-combe (Amy Thornton). Julie charms a verdict from the judge, but Tom comes to the rescue with some dirt on Adolphe and, as poor Honeycombe flees through a series of colourful situations and some pretty Swiss scenery, Tom manages affairs so that Julie is finally forced to back down.

Accompanied by a set of songs partly written and partly arranged by musical director Vousden, the tale of *The Gay Parisienne* proved a major provincial hit. William Greet's touring companies completed three tours, and were joined on the road by Wallace Erskine's number-two-towns company before Horace Sedger took up the show for a London production. Dance did over the libretto, introducing a new character, the little maid Ruth, in order to feature his latest discovery, tiny, cockney Louie Freear, Ivan Caryll was hired to write a new score, and *The Gay Parisienne* moved into the little Duke of York's Theatre with Ada Reeve starred as Julie and Lionel Rignold as Honeycombe. It ran there for a fine 369 performances. Miss Freear caused a sensation with her song about 'Sister Mary Jane's Top Note', W H Denny as the judge described himself happily as one of the 'Battersea Butterfly Shooters', Ada Reeve sang 'I'm All the Way from Gay Paree' and interpolated the American coon song 'Sambo', and the show's new shape and score were promptly taken up by Greet's touring company as they moved into their third, fourth and fifth years on the road. There were many more, for *The Gay Parisienne*, like *The Lady Slavey*, became a feature of the road schedules through two decades, with Greet, Erskine and Rudolph Kloss's number-three-towns companies all touring simultaneously for a number of seasons.

The London version of the show was taken up by E E Rice and, revised and rechristened *The Girl from Paris*, mounted on Broadway, with Clara Lipman (Julie), Charles A Bigelow (Honeycombe) and Josephine Hall (Ruth) in the main rôles. Again, it proved a real hit, running for 266 performances, breaking for the summer and then returning for 33 nights more before going on to another long touring career. In 1898 (Wallack's Theater 17 January) Rice even brought the show back for further Broadway month with Georgia Caine as Julie.

Ada Reeve introduced Julie Bon-Bon to Australian audiences in 1897 (popping in 'Susie-oo' instead of 'Sambo' and scoring another hit) in Williamson and Musgrove's production, played it for a season in repertoire with *The French Maid*, and took it round again in 1898. The other English-speaking venues followed suit, and all the time the British provinces welcomed returns and repeats, season after season, from *The Gay Parisienne*.

USA: Herald Square Theater *The Girl from Paris* 8 December 1896; Australia: Her Majesty's Theatre, Sydney 31 July 1897

GAY'S THE WORD Musical play in 2 acts by Ivor Novello. Lyrics by Alan Melville. Saville Theatre, London, 16 February 1951.

Cicely Courtneidge and author/composer Ivor Novello had both become firmly set into 'series' – successful runs of pieces all of a like kind – with the comedienne scoring in her versatile light comedy with bits of music, and he turning out lush and large-scale romantic operettas. Apparently, when the actress went to see the writer about a job for a friend, he jokingly (?) said he'd thought her visit might have been to ask him to compose her next show. He not only composed it, but also replaced the originally intended book-writer as well.

Miss Courtneidge starred as Gay Daventry, an actress with an out-of-town flop on her hands, who sets up a drama school in her house in Folkestone. It turns out that smugglers have been using it as an entrepôt while she's been touring, but Gay is more than a match for the miscreants, and before the evening is over she has handed them all over to justice and also has all her pupils on the professional stage in a nice, new show.

Gay's the Word had its tongue firmly in its cheek, especially when lyricist Alan Melville was let loose, and Miss Courtneidge ended up with the most comical score of all her time on the stage as she lauded 'Vitality' as a recipe for success, explained what it means when 'Bees Are Buzzin'', chortled her way through 'Gaiety Glad', mused over the prospects of her hopeless show in 'It's Bound To Be Right on the Night' before coming to the conclusion that it, of course, won't be, and gave her all in the rôle of the turkey's Ruritanian Queen, warbling semi-voicelessly about 'Guards on Parade' in a burlesque of Novello's own kind of musical. Lizbeth Webb played the show's ingénue

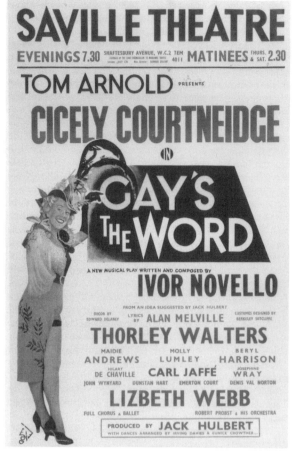

Plate 101.

alongside Courtneidge's regular (off- and on-stage) leading man, Thorley Walters.

A book which was little more than a series of set-pieces nevertheless provided endless opportunities for its star and *Gay's the Word* remained in London for 504 performances before going into the country.

Recording: selection (part-record) (WRC)

THE GEISHA, a story of a tea house Japanese musical play in 2 acts by Owen Hall. Lyrics by Harry Greenbank. Music by Sidney Jones. Additional songs by Lionel Monckton and James Philp. Daly's Theatre, London, 25 April 1896.

The most successful of the series of important musical plays produced by George Edwardes at Daly's Theatre around the turn of the century, *The Geisha* not only proved to be one of the best-loved and most enduring of all 19th-century British musicals on its home territory, but also made its mark beyond the English-speaking theatre world. It spread itself further abroad, and with more success, than any other previous English-language piece, including the works of Gilbert and Sullivan, had done, becoming one of the most popular shows in Central Europe (Keller's statistical survey rates it behind only *Die Fledermaus*, *Die lustige Witwe* and *Das Dreimäderlhaus* in 1921) and remaining in the repertoire there until quite recently.

British tar Reginald Fairfax (Hayden Coffin), on duty in

the East, spends some time in the company of the geisha O Mimosa San (Marie Tempest), at the Teahouse of Ten Thousand Joys, run by the comical little Chinaman Wun-Hi (Huntley Wright). His worried fiancée Molly Seamore (Letty Lind) gets dressed up as a Japanese girl to see if she appeals to Reggie that way, but unfortunately she is trapped as a Jap when the local overlord Marquis Imari (Harry Monkhouse), determined to have Mimosa for himself, orders Wun-Hi's establishment sold up. The wealthy Lady Constance Wynne (Maud Hobson) rescues Mimosa from his clutches in the subsequent auction, but the Marquis happily buys lot two instead – the disguised Molly. To prevent this wedding from taking place, Mimosa disguises herself as a fortune teller and predicts dire unhappiness for the superstitious Marquis in a life with an unloving wife and, when she is sent to bewitch Molly into a loving frame of mind, she uses the opportunity to substitute the eager little French interpreter, Juliette (Juliette Nesville) under the marquisal bridal canopy.

Sidney Jones's score was full of winning numbers, with the soprano rôle of Mimosa being equipped with a superb pair of waltz songs – one describing the less attractive side of 'A Geisha's Life' and the other, in her fortune-teller's disguise, singing of 'Love, Love' – as well as the rueful tale of what happened to 'The Amorous Goldfish' and a Kissing Duet with Fairfax. The other characters were also well served, with the highspots ranging from the comical antics of Wun-Hi in the enduring 'Chin-chin-chinaman' to Fairfax's baritone ballad, 'Star of My Soul', Molly's Japanese song 'Chon-kina', her anthropomorphic tale of 'The Interfering Parrot', and some delightful ensembles, including a first-act finale which gave the tenor playing Katana, Mimosa's real Japanese beloved, his one chance to burst into song. Lionel Monckton supplied several additional numbers, scoring a hit with the baritone 'Jack's the Boy' and also with the soubrette song, 'The Toy Monkey', whilst James Philp wrote the music to an interpolated piece called 'The Jewel of Asia' with which Marie Tempest scored a great success.

The Geisha was a resounding London hit, running for 760 performances at Daly's Theatre whilst the piece began to spread itself around, first, the British provinces and then the world. Edwardes had the first tour on the road by August, with Geraldine Ulmar, John Coates, Marie Studholme and Huntley Wright's brother Bert featured, whilst Mouillot and Morrell simultaneously started out their number-two-towns company with Minnie Leverentz starred. A month later, Broadway got its first *Geisha* when Augustin Daly mounted the show at his theatre with Dorothy Morton (Mimosa), Van Rensslaer Wheeler (Fairfax), Violet Lloyd (Molly) and William Samson (Wun-Hi) and with a dancer called Isadora Duncan amongst the chorus. Daly's schedule meant that the piece did not get a straight run, but it popped in and out of his theatre during the last months of 1896 and 1897, playing 194 Broadway performances (later with Nancy McIntosh as Mimosa and James T Powers as Wun-Hi) during that time, and becoming a great favourite. Such a favourite, indeed, that it won the honour of being the only musical to be granted a full-scale burlesque by the Weber and Fields team. *The Geezer* (October 1896) was one of the jolly house's first and biggest burlesque hits.

In May of 1897 the Lessing-Theater, Berlin, hosted

José Ferenczy's production of *Die Geisha, eine japanische Theehausgeschichte* (ad C M Röhr, Julius Freund). The piece became a vast success in Berlin and, before long, around the whole of Germany as Ferenczy's production, with the tiny Viennese singer Mia Werber starred as Mimosa and Emil Sondermann as Wun-Hi, became a musical must in the capital city, and , as in America, the burlesquers leapt in to give the show the compliment of a *Geisha Parodie* (H Buffe, Alexanderplatz-Theater 6 June 1897). Regularly revived thereafter, the piece had its 1,000th Berlin performance in 1904.

Vienna picked up the Berlin version of the show, and *Die Geisha* was mounted at the Carltheater later in the same year with Frln Golz (Mimosa), Betty Stojan (Molly) and Sigmund Natzler (Wun-Hi). As in America, it was not allowed a straight run. It alternated with a programme showing 'The American Biograph' and other Operetten of the theatre's repertoire, but was seen 28 times before the end of 1897 and was played the following year with the peripatetic American soubrette Marie Halton featured as it headed towards its 100th Viennese night (8 March 1900). It was held seven years in the Carltheater repertoire, during which time Mizzi Günther played Mimosa and Louis Treumann took over as Wun-Hi, played there again in 1912, and yet again in a new production in 1920 with Grete Seidlitz and Ernst Arnold (9 December, 175th night 31 December), as other Viennese and provincial houses took the show up and found it one of the most loved of all their presentations. *The Geisha*'s German version proved as popular as and even more enduring than its English one, and the show was seen in Vienna again as recently as 1954 (Raimundtheater) and 1973 (Raimundtheater), with a new version (ad Hans Herbert Pudor, Hermann Wetzlar) being mounted at Bremerhaven in 1956 (6 October).

There was a similar kind of success for the Hungarian version of the show (ad Béla J Fái, Emil Makai), first seen at the Magyar Színház with Gizella Vlád playing Mimosa, Kornél Sziklai (Wuncsi) and Sári Fédak (Molly), which ran up its first 100 performances by 31 January 1899. Amongst the subsequent Budapest revivals was one at the Király Színház (12 April 1912) in which Fédak took the star rôle (the 'title-rôle' had been cleverly designed at the beginning to apply to either Miss Tempest or Miss Lind) alongside Márton Rátkai and Lilly Berky, and another at the Fővárosi Operettszinház in 1926 (11 February).

The first French production of *La Geisha* (ad Charles Clairville, Antony Mars, Jacques Le Maire) with Jeanne Petit as Mimosa and Guyon fils as Mac-Chou-Li (ex-Wun-Hi) was a four-performance disaster, but the ubiquitous success of the show encouraged a second try and a revival at the Moulin-Rouge (14 July 1906) with Mlle Petit starring alongside Morton, Alberthal and Spinelly was followed by a Gabriel Trarieux/Georges Bravard mounting in 1920 at the Gaîté-Lyrique with Opéra-Comique diva Marguerite Carré (Mimosa), Max Dearly (Imari) and Denise Grey (Zoe, ie Molly). However, *La Geisha* never found the success of *Die Geisha*, *A gesak* or *The Geisha*.

The show was produced throughout Europe, with notable success in Italy and in Spain, but with some problems in Russia, where it was given in a rather impromptu and approximate version. Ferenczy toured his Berlin version widely, including a long trip to South America, whilst

Plate 102. **The Geisha** *was one of the most outstanding hits of the 19th-century musical stage – played and played again in France, Italy, Sweden, Yugoslavia, Hungary and many other countries throughout the world.*

J C Williamson and George Musgrove introduced Australia to *The Geisha*, and the Scandinavian countries produced adaptations in their various tongues. And, meanwhile, companies purveying the English-language *Geisha* flooded the touring circuits in Britain before the show returned to London in 1906 (18 June) when Edwardes produced a stop-gap mounting with May de Souza (Mimosa), Mariette Sully (Juliette), George Graves (Imari), Marie Studholme (Molly) and a third Wright brother, Fred Wright jr as Wun-Hi (60 performances).

The Shuberts mounted a 52-performance season of *The Geisha* in 1913 (27 March, 44th Street Theater) with Alice Zeppili, Lina Abarbanell and James T Powers featured, and several American companies mounted versions with with Japanese prima donnas – in 1919 Tamaki Maru starred in a San Francisco production and in 1931 the Civic Light Opera played a season with Hizi Koyke as Mimosa. This production was the last time the show was seen on Broadway. In the same year J Bannister Howard's season of old favourites at London's Daly's Theatre included 48 performances of *The Geisha*, and there was a barely professional production at the Garrick Theatre in 1934 (24 April, 39 performances). However, whilst the piece continued in the Continental repertoire in the postwar years, British light-opera companies preferred to play adaptations of imported works and *The Geisha* dropped from the English-language lists.

USA: Daly's Theater 9 September 1896; Germany: Lessing-Theater *Die Geisha* 1 May 1897; Hungary: Magyar Színház *A Gésak* 16 October 1897; Austria: Carltheater *Die Geisha* 16 November 1897; France: Théâtre de l'Athénée-Comique *La Geisha* 8 March 1898; Australia: Princess Theatre, Melbourne 17 December 1898
Recordings: selections in German (Decca, Urania etc), selections in Italian (Fonit-Cetra, EDM)

GEISTINGER, Marie [GEISTINGER, Maria Charlotte Cäcilia] (b Graz, 26 July 1836; d Klagenfurt, 30 September 1903). Vienna's queen of the 19th-century opéra-bouffe stage.

Born in Graz to theatrical parents, Geistinger first went on the stage as a child and had an early exposure in Vienna when, at 16, she appeared in the title-rôle of the Posse *Die falsche Pepita* (Theater in der Josefstadt, 1852). She did not follow up this success, but instead, over the next dozen years, moved on to Berlin, Hamburg, Riga and Berlin again, appearing mainly in juvenile light-comedy rôles in plays, including many with song and dance elements. She returned to Vienna in 1865 at the bidding of Friedrich Strampfer, director of the Theatre an der Wien, to introduce the title-rôle of Offenbach's *Die schöne Helena* (*La Belle Hélène*) to Viennese audiences. This show and this rôle established her as a star, and she followed up as Offenbach's Boulotte (*Blaubart*, 1866), Coscoletto (*Coscoletto*, 1866), La Sincère (*Die Schäfer* ie *Les Bergers*, 1866), *Die Grossherzogin von Gerolstein* (1867) and Drogan (*Genovefa von Brabant*), as Emma in Julius Hopp's *Die Donauweibchen* (1866) and in a whole list of smilar rôles under Strampfer's direction, before herself taking over the part-direction of the theatre in tandem with his successor, Maximilian Steiner.

She appeared in both plays and musical plays (Leni in

Plate 103. *Vienna's queen of opéra-bouffe,* **Marie Geistinger**, *as the page, Drogan, in* Genovefa de Brabant.

Alois Berla's *Drei Paar Schuhe*, Anna Birkmeier in *Der Pfarrer von Kirchfeld* etc) in a wide variety of rôles, and made another personal hit in an Operette – this time an Austrian one – when she starred as Fantasca in Johann Strauss's early piece, *Indigo und die vierzig Räuber* (1871). Continually varying plays and Operetten, she was seen the following year in the Viennese productions of Offenbach's *Le Corsair noir*, *Die Theaterprinzessin* (*La Diva*, Susi Apfelwein) and *Fantasio* (Fantasio), starred as Leokadia Blumenau in Millöcker's *Abenteuer in Wien* (1873), in Offenbach's *Die Wilderer* (*Les Braconniers*, Ginetta) and *Madame l'Archiduc* (Marietta), and as Wosana in Jonas's *Die Japanesin* (1874). She rejoined Strauss for *Carneval in Rom* (1873, Marie) and again, in 1874, to create the rôle of Rosalinde in *Die Fledermaus*, introducing 'Dieser Anstand' with Jani Szíka, and the famous csárdás 'Klänge der Heimat', and yet again as the first Lorenza Feliciani in *Cagliostro in Wien* (1875).

In spite of her considerable successes, the tenuous financial climate in Vienna following the stock-market crash found Geistinger in a parlous monetary state and, although she continued at the Theater an der Wien, playing in such pieces as Offenbach's *Les Brigands* (1875, Fiorella) and a version of *La Créole* (1876, Antoinette), she was finally obliged to give up her part of the management of the theatre.

After more than a decade as Vienna's reigning queen of musical theatre, she moved on to profit from the high fees available from guest performances and to take up dramatic rôles at the Stadttheater. She then proceeded to Leipzig where she once again mixed drama, comedy and Operette for more than two years, returning to Vienna and the Theater an der Wien in 1879 to introduce her first successful new rôle for a number of years as the German version of Offenbach's *Madame Favart*. She also played in the 'scene aus den Österreicheischen Alpen mit National-Gesängen', *Das Versprechen hinter'm Herd*, and in 1880 was seen as Lotti in *Die Näherin* and as Stella, the heroine of Offenbach's *Die Tochter des Tambour-Major*.

Gustav Amberg, the proprietor of one of New York's flourishing German-language theatres, now proposed her a long and lucrative American engagement and, in 1881, the 44-year-old star crossed the Atlantic and made her début at Amberg's Thalia Theater as Offenbach's Grande-Duchesse, to the sort of reception she had had in Vienna 20 years earlier ('she plays it as high comedy rather than rollicking bouffe', 'she is quieter than Aimée and touches the double entendres so that they are funny without being coarse', 'she sinks her personality in each character ... a great artist'). She extended her American stay over more than three years, playing across the whole country and appearing regularly in New York as Madame Favart, Boccaccio, Boulotte, Rosalinde, Fatinitza, Leni in *Drei Paar Schuhe*, the schöne Galathee and the schöne Helena, in *Carneval in Rom*, *Die Näherin*, *Der Seekadet*, *Madame Angots Tochter* and a whole range of other musical pieces whilst also playing dramatic rôles such as Camille, Therese Krones, Elizabeth I in *Graf Essex* and Donna Diana in an ever-whirling repertoire.

After two seasons she moved to the rival Germania Theater and the Thalia promptly imported her celebrated Vienna rival Josefine Gallmeyer as competition. However, Gallmeyer was mortally ill and soon returned to Europe whilst Geistinger continued to reign over the New York German theatre in a repertoire including such pieces as *Capitän Nicol* (ie *I Carbonari*), *Durchgegangene Weiber*, Lecocq's *Trompette* (ie *La Petite Mademoiselle*, Countess Cameroni), *Pariser Leben* (Gabrielle), *Leichte Kavallerie*, *Donna Juanita*, *Der Bettelstudent* (Symon), Gallmeyer's vehicle *Das verwunschene Schloss* (Regerl), Hervé's *Lili* (Lili), *Sieben Mädchen und kein Mann* (Suppé's Operette with a reduced number of maidens), *Die Afrika-reise* (Titania), *Apajune der Wassermann* (Natalitza) and Millöcker's *Die Kindsfrau* along with those already named. She also appeared in an original American-German Lokalposse, *1776* (1884, Marion), by the young Ludwig Engländer.

Back in Europe she appeared at Vienna's Carltheater and in other theatres around Austria and Germany, scoring a particular success in the title-rôle of *Therese Krones*, and otherwise still playing the famous rôles of her earlier years and such standard repertoire pieces as *Die schöne Galathee*, *Boccaccio* and *Der Bettelstudent* and, bit by bit, marginally less central parts more suited to her age. She returned in 1891 for a second American season, in 1896 for a third, and one last time in 1899 just before finally ending her memorable career at the age of 64.

In more recent times, she was musically portrayed on the stage by Elfie Mayerhofer as the heroine of the operette *Die Walzerkönigin* (Ludwig Schmidseder/Aldo Pinelli, Hubert Marischka, Wiener Bürgertheater 1948) and on the screen in Willy Forst's *Operette*, by Maria Holst. In the biomusical made on the life of Gallmeyer, however, the old rivalry was continued: although Treumann, Matras, Offenbach and Anna Grobecker were portrayed, Geistinger was left out of the tale.

Biography: Pirchan, E: *Marie Geistinger* (Verlag Wilhelm Frick, Vienna, 1947)

GÉLABERT, Marie ('Conchita') (b Madrid, 1857; d Paris, 1922).

The young Marie Gélabert was freshly out of the Paris Conservatoire when she was chosen to play a third of the title-rôle in *Jeanne, Jeannette et Jeanneton* (1876) at the Folies-Dramatiques alongside Mme Prelly and Berthe Stuart and, when the last-named singer was unable to fulfil the rôle allotted to her in the following year's *Les Cloches de Corneville* (1877), Gélabert, who had been on the point of giving up the theatre for married life, was given the creation of the part of Germaine. If the equally young Juliette Girard, in the showier rôle of Serpolette, won the most attention, Mlle Gélabert, who introduced the celebrated Chanson des Cloches, the Chanson des 'oui' et 'non' and 'Ne parlez pas de mon courage', was nevertheless thoroughly launched after two star rôles in two highly successful musicals.

She appeared in a third hit, as Suzanne to the *Madame Favart* of Girard, and then moved to the Renaissance where she appeared in the travesty rôle of the Prince in Lecocq's *La Jolie Persane* (1879), and to the Nouveautés for the vaudeville *La Beauté du Diable* (1880) in which she warmed her comedy début with some specially written songs by Coèdes. She appeared at the Théâtre de la Porte-St-Martin in 1882 as Siebel in a revival of *Le Petit Faust* and scored a huge success with one of the Spanish songs which had landed her with the life-long nickname of 'Conchita', before going on to new rôles in Audran's *Gillette de Narbonne* (1882, Rosita), *Les Pommes d'or* (1883, Princess Églantine), *La Dormeuse éveillée* (1883, Diane) and *Le Grand Mogol* (1884, Bengaline), alongside repeats of, in particular, her Germaine and Suzanne.

She was later seen creating rôles in such pieces as *Le Voyage de Suzette* (1890, Paquita), *La Fée aux chèvres* (1890, Jacotte) and *Le Pays d'or* (1892, Flora Michon) without again finding a part which reached the heights of the two great rôles of her earliest years.

GELBART, Larry [Simon] (b Chicago, 25 February 1923).

Primarily a writer for film and for television, in which areas he created the enormously successful television comedy series *M*A*S*H* and authored the screenplay for *Tootsie* (1982), Gelbart has worked only very infrequently for the theatre (*Sly Fox*, *Jump*, *Mastergate*) and for the musical stage. However, two of those infrequent musical ventures produced, at more than a quarter of a century's distance, two of the cleverest comical libretti of the postwar musical stage – the classical burlesque *A Funny Thing Happened on the Way to the Forum* (1962, Tony Award) and the parody of Hollywood's gumshoe detective films in *City of Angels* (1989, Tony Award).

1961 **The Conquering Hero** (Mark Charlap/Norman Gimbel) ANTA Theater 16 January

1962 **A Funny Thing Happened on the Way to the Forum** (Stephen Sondheim/w Burt Shevelove) Alvin Theater 8 May

1989 **City of Angels** (Cy Coleman/David Zippel) Virginia Theater 11 December

DIE GELBE JACKE *see* DAS LAND DES LÄCHELNS

GELD, Gary (b Paterson, NJ, 18 October 1935).

In a 1960s song-writing partnership with lyricist Peter Udell, Geld composed a series of hit songs, including 'Ain't Gonna Wash for a Week', 'Hurting Each Other', 'Ginny Come Lately', and 'Sealed with a Kiss', before making his début as a Broadway composer with the score for the successful musical *Purlie* ('I Got Love', 'Walk Him Up the Stairs', 'The Bigger They Are, the Harder They Fall', 'Purlie'). An even bigger success came with the adaptation to the musical stage of the screenplay *Shenandoah*, for which Geld switched from the negro-toned music of his previous work to a country style which he had used with success in his earlier songwriting. *Shenandoah* mixed some richly baritone soliloquies ('I've Heard it All Before' etc) with such numbers as the country duo 'We Make a Beautiful Pair', the affecting 'The Only Home I Know' and the rip-roaring 'Next to Lovin' (I like fightin')' in an effective and popular combination which helped the piece to a long Broadway run.

A third attempt at a musical, with a 1978 adaptation of the Thomas Wolfe novel and its subsequent play *Look Homeward, Angel* was not a success (5 performances).

1970 **Purlie** (Peter Udell/Ossie Davis, Philip Rose, Udell) Broadway Theater 15 March

1975 **Shenandoah** (Udell/James Lee Barrett, Rose, Udell) Alvin Theater 7 January

1978 **Angel** (ex-*Look Homeward, Angel*) (Udell/Ketti Frings, Rose, Udell) Minskoff Theater 10 May

GENÉE, [Franz Friedrich] Richard (b Danzig, 7 February 1823; d Baden bei Wien, 15 June 1895). The most effective librettist and lyricist of the classic Viennese theatre, the musically trained Genée also scored a major success with his most important works as a composer for the Operette stage.

Born in Danzig, where his actor father was at that time engaged at the Stadttheater, Genée was brought up in Berlin and, after initially going through the first stages of medical studies, he turned to music as a career. In 1847 he became a conductor at the Danzig Stadttheater, by then run by his father, and he subsequently held engagements at Reval, Riga, Cologne, Aachen and Düsseldorf before returning to Danzig, where his first compositions, the burlesque Operette *Polyphem oder Ein Abenteuer auf Martinique* and the comic opera *Der Geiger von Tirol*, written to a libretto by his brother Rudolf, were staged. This latter piece went on to later productions, including one at Broadway's Thalia Theater (6 December 1884).

After his father's death, Genée left Danzig and held further conducting posts at Mainz, where he provided the music for several short pieces, saw *Der Geiger von Tirol* revived (14 February 1859), and composed a two-act romantic comic opera for which he had himself written the text; then at Schwerin, where the Operette *Der Musikfeind* was produced, with sufficient success for it to be subsequently seen in Berlin and in Vienna; then at Amsterdam and, between 1863–8, at the Landestheater in Prague. Whilst working in Prague, his composing and writing output included a two-act opera, *Am Runenstein* (1868), on which he collaborated with von Flotow, and an Operette, *Der schwarze Prinz*. *Der schwarze Prinz* was subsequently taken up for production by Maximilian Steiner at the Theater an der Wien (1 February 1867), and the following year Genée was taken on to the music staff at that same theatre. He remained an employee at the Theatre an der Wien for ten years, until his success as an author finally allowed him to devote himself full-time to writing.

Although the Theater an der Wien staged another of his short Operetten soon after his arrival, and he provided such occasional music as the incidental score for the theatre's production of Sardou's *Vaterland* (*La Patrie*), Genée soon found himself heavily involved, beyond his musical duties, in another side of the theatre's business. With the huge vogue for French opéra-bouffe beginning to sweep Vienna, authors were needed to translate, adapt or largely rewrite the libretti and lyrics of these works for German-language audiences. Genée, who had written the texts for nearly all his own pieces, found himself promoted adaptor-in-chief for the Theater an der Wien, at first alongside, and then overtaking, the equally versatile Julius Hopp. Over the next five years and more he turned out not very faithful, but highly stageworthy, versions of the works of the librettists of Offenbach, Hervé, Lecocq and Jonas as well as German-language versions of such pieces as von Flotow's *L'Ombre* and *Zilda* and Massé's *Galathée*.

Genée was amongst those who persuaded and then helped dance-music composer Johann Strauss to write for the theatre in general and the Theater an der Wien in particular, and he returned to the writing of original libretti and lyrics when he supplied the texts for Strauss's *Die Fledermaus* and *Cagliostro in Wien*. On the second of these he worked with Camillo Walzel ('F Zell'), with whom he had recently formed a writing and adapting partnership. It was a partnership which would subsequently be responsible for the books and lyrics of many of the most important Viennese Operetten of the 1870s and 1880s: Suppé's *Fatinitza*, *Boccaccio* and *Donna Juanita*, Millöcker's *Apajune der Wassermann*, *Der Bettelstudent* and *Gasparone* and Strauss's *Der lustige Krieg*, *Eine Nacht in Venedig* and *Das Spitzentuch der Königin*, most, but not all, adapted from French originals.

Genée's own musical knowledge contributed greatly to his value as, in particular, a lyricist but, whilst aiding the composers with whom he worked, he also continued to write theatre music himself and he had significant success with his own first major compositions for the Theater an der Wien. The Operetten *Der Seekadett* and *Nanon* both became major international successes.

After his retirement from the staff of the Theater an der Wien in 1879, Genée moved out of the city of Vienna and settled in Pressbaum where, in a villa overflowing with all kinds of animals from the more usual dogs and cats to birds, rabbits, monkeys and even a small bear, he continued his collaboration with Walzel by post. The division of their labour left much of the plot and dialogue to Walzel and the bulk of the lyric-writing to Genée, but such a division was by no means automatic and, on occasions, Genée worked alone on libretti. When Genée was involved in a project as composer, his collaborator took full credit for the text.

When the best years of Suppé, Millöcker and Strauss were past, Genée, sometimes with Zell and sometimes without, provided texts for several of the younger generation of composers, notably for Alfons Czibulka's pair of exportable successes, *Pfingsten in Florenz* and *Der Glücksritter*, but by and large found much less success. Genée also composed several further Operetten of his own. None of these attained anything like the success of his two principal works, although *Nisida* nevertheless won itself an American production in a botched Augustin Daly version under the title *Zanina, or the Rover of Cambaye* and another in Leipzig, *Der letzte Mohikaner* was seen at Berlin's Friedrich-Wilhelmstädtisches Theater, in Prague and in many provincial houses, *Die Dreizehn* also appeared at the Friedrich-Wilhelmstädtiches Theater (10 February 1888), and *Rosina*, a musical version of the famous farce *Un Chapeau de paille d'Italie* for which he wrote text and music, was played in Hungary and Germany after its Vienna showing.

Amongst Genée's other projects in the 1880s and 1890s were an adaptation of Scribe and St-George's *La Reine d'un jour* as the text for Ignaz Brüll's opera *Königin Mariette* (w Zell, Munich 16 June 1883), the scenario for a ballet *Viola*, based on Shakespeare's *Twelfth Night* and produced at the Hamburg Stadttheater (16 March 1893, music: A Arensen), and the libretto for Tomaschek's opera *Die Teufelsbrucke* (1892, w Julius Riegen).

A pastiche Operette *Veilchenredoute* (Wiener Stadttheater 27 January 1942) by Hans Adler and Carl Cerné was later put together from Genée's music.

His brother Rudolf (b Berlin, 12 December 1824; d Berlin, 19 January 1914), with whom he wrote *Der Geiger von Tirol*, wrote several other pieces for the musical stage including the one-act musical play *Der Kapellmeister*, set with Mozart music (Krolls Theater, Berlin 13 March 1896). He also wrote on theatrical and literary history.

1856 **Polyphem, oder ein Abenteuer auf Martinique** (w Trautmann) 1 act Stadttheater, Danzig 20 September

1857 **Der Geiger von Tirol** (Rudolf Genée) Stadttheater, Danzig March

1858 **Benjamin, der seinen Vater sucht** (Theodore Hauptner/Ernst Dohm) 1 act Carltheater 17 July

1860 **Ein Trauerspiel** 1 act Mainz; Friedrich-Wilhelmstädtisches Theater, Berlin 22 June 1862

1861 **Ein Narrentraum** Mainz

1862 **Der Musikfeind** 1 act Grossherzogliches Hoftheater, Schwerin 8 February

1862 **Der Generalprobe** 1 act Friedrich-Wilhelmstädtisches Theater December

1862 **Die Herren von der Livree** (Eduard Jacobson) 1 act Berlin

1863 **Die Talismänner** (Ludwig Ullinger) Mainz March

1864 **Rosita** Mainz 1 January

1864 **Der Zopfabschneider** 1 act Schwerin 25 May

1866 **Der schwarze Prinz** (Kotzebue ad) Landestheater, Prague 14 June

1869 **Der Däumling** (*Le Petit Poucet*) German version (Theater an der Wien)

1869 **Perichole, die Strassensängerin** (*La Périchole*) German version (Theater an der Wien)

1869 **Der Schrecken des Krieges** (*Les Horreurs de la guerre*) German version (Theater an der Wien)

1869 **Schwefeles der Höllenagent** 1 act Theater an der Wien 24 November

1870 **Ein Konzertprobe** 1 act Vaudevilletheater 19 March

1870 **Der Hexensabbath** 1 act Theater an der Wien 4 May

1870 **Der schöne Ritter Dunois** (*Le Beau Dunois*) German version (Theater an der Wien)

1870 **Die Banditen** (*Les Brigands*) German version (Theater an der Wien)

1870 **Doktor Faust Jr** (*Le Petit Faust*) German version (Theater an der Wien)

1872 **Fantasio** German version w Eduard Mautner (Theater an der Wien)

1872 **Der schwarze Korsar** (*Le Corsair noir*) German version (Theater an der Wien)

1872 **Die Theaterprinzessin** (*La Diva*) German version w F Zell (Theater an der Wien)

1873 **Die Wilderer** (*Les Braconniers*) German version w Zell (Theater an der Wien)

1873 **Heloise und Abälard** German version (Theater an der Wien)

1874 **Die Japanesin** German version w Zell (Theater an der Wien)

1874 **Die Fledermaus** (Strauss/w Karl Haffner) Theater an der Wien 5 April

1875 **Cagliostro in Wien** (Strauss/w Zell) Theater an der Wien 27 February

1875 **Kleopatra** (w Carl Michael Ziehrer/J Steinherr) Komische Oper 13 November

1876 **Fatinitza** (Suppé/w Zell) Carltheater 5 January

1876 **Luftschlösser** (Wilhelm Mannstädt, A Weller ad Karl Costa) Theater an der Wien 11 July

1876 **Fliegende Blätter** (arr/Costa) Theater an der Wien 1 August

1876 **Der Seekadet** (Zell) Theater an der Wien 24 October

1877 **Die Porträtdame, oder Die Profezeiungen des Quiribi** (Max Wolf/w Zell) Theater an der Wien 1 March

1877 **Nanon, die Wirthin von 'goldenen Lamm'** (Zell) Theater an der Wien 10 March

1877 **Im Wunderland der Pyramiden** (Zell) Komische Oper 25 December

1878 **Die letzten Mohikaner** (Zell) Theater am Gärtnerplatz, Munich 10 September

1879 **Boccaccio** (Suppé/w Zell) Carltheater 1 February

1879 **Gräfin Dubarry** (Millöcker/w Zell) Theater an der Wien 31 October

1880 **Die drei Langhälse** (Josef Brandl/w Emil Pohl) Carltheater 11 December

1880 **Donna Juanita** (Suppé/w Zell) Carltheater 21 February

1880 **Die hübsche Perserin** (*La Jolie Persane*) German version w Zell (Theater an der Wien)

1880 **Das Spitzentuch der Königin** (Strauss/w Bohrmann-Riegen) Theater an der Wien 1 October

1880 **Nisida** (Zell, Moritz West) Carltheater 9 October

1880 **Apajune der Wassermann** (Millöcker/w Zell) Theater an der Wien 18 December

1881 **Der Gascogner** (Suppé/w Zell) Carltheater 22 March

1881 **Die Jungfrau von Belleville** (Millöcker/w Zell) Theater an der Wien 29 October

1881 **Der lustige Krieg** (Strauss/w Zell) Theater an der Wien 25 November

1881 **Rosina** (Eugène Labiche ad) Carltheater 25 December

1882 **Der Bettelstudent** (Millöcker/w Zell) Theater an der Wien 6 December

1883 **Tag und Nacht** (*Le Jour et la nuit*) German version (Theater an der Wien)

1883 **Die Afrikareise** (Suppe/w West) Theater an der Wien 17 March

1883 **Eine Nacht in Venedig** (Strauss/w Zell) Friedrich-Wilhelmstädtisches Theater, Berlin, 3 October

1884 **Gasparone** (Millöcker/w Zell) Theater an der Wien 26 January

1884 **Der Marquis von Rivoli** (Louis Roth/w Benjamin Schier) Theater an der Wien 13 April

1884 **Pfingsten in Florenz** (Alfons Czibulka/w Julius Riegen) Theater an der Wien 20 December

1885 **Eine gemachte Frau** (E Jacobson) Residenztheater, Dresden 6 January

1885 **Zwillinge** (w L Roth/w Zell) Theater an der Wien 14 February

1886 **Der Jagdjunker** (Czibulka/w Zell) Carltheater 20 March

1886 **Der Nachtwandler** (L Roth/w Zell) Friedrich-Wilhelmstädtisches Theater, Berlin 25 September

1886 **Der Viceadmiral** (Millöcker/w Zell) Theater an der Wien 9 October

1886 **Die Piraten** (Scribe ad w Zell) Walhalla-Theater, Berlin 8 October

1887 **Rikiki** (Josef Hellemsberger/w Mannstädt) Carltheater 28 September

1887 **Die Dreizehn** (Scribe ad w Zell) Carltheater 14 November

1887 **Der Glücksritter** (Czibulka/w Mannstädt, Bruno Zappert) Carltheater 22 December

1888 **Der Freibuter** (*Surcouf*) German version w Zappert (Carltheater)

1888 **Der Mikado** German version w Zell (Theater an der Wien)

1888 **Die Jagd nach dem Glück** (Suppé/w Zappert) Carltheater 27 October

1888 **Ein Deutschmeister** (Ziehrer/w Zappert) Carltheater 30 November

1889 **Die indische Witwe** (Gustav Geiringer/w Zell) 1 act Theater an der Wien 9 February

1889 **Capitän Fracassa** (Rudolf Dellinger/w Zell) Theater an der Wien 21 September

1889 **Page Fritz** (Max von Weinzierl, Alfred Strasser/w Alexander Landesberg) Deutsches Theater, Prague November

1889 **Die Piraten** (*The Pirates of Penzance*) German version (Theater an der Wien)

1889 **Der Königsgardist** (*The Yeomen of the Guard*) German version w Zell (Krolls Theater, Berlin)

1890 **Die Gondoliere** (*The Gondoliers*) German version w Zell (Theater an der Wien)

1890 **Mam'zelle Nitouche** German version (Theater an der Wien)

1891 **Die Basoche** (*La Basoche*) German version (Friedrich-Wilhelmstädtisches Theater, Berlin)

1891 **Madame Bonbon** (*Madame Boniface*) German version w Heinrich Thalboth (Theater an der Wien)

1891 **Miss Helyett** German version (Wallner Theater, Berlin)

1891 **Polnische Wirtschaft** (Hermann Zumpe/w West) Friedrich-Wilhelmstädtisches Theater, Berlin 26 November

1892 **Fanchon's Leyer** (*La Fille de Fanchon la vielleuse*) German version (Theater an der Wien)

1892 **Mädchenschule** (*Un lycée de jeunes filles*) German version and additional music (Thomas-Theater, Berlin)

1892 **Die Welsenbraut** (Alfred Zamara/w Max Tull) Stadttheater, Hamburg 20 March

1892 **Der Freiwillige** (Friedrich Sonkup/w Costa) Prague 27 December

1892 **Der Millionen-Onkel** (Adolf Müller jr/w Zell) Theater an der Wien 5 November

1892 **Rotkäppchen** (*La Roussotte*) German version w new score Thomas-Theater, Berlin 6 February

1892 **Signora Vendetta** (Hermann Hirschel) Wiesbaden 14 June

1893 **Die wachsame Schildwache** (Rudolf Genée) 1 act Philharmonia, Berlin 28 February

1893 **Der Taugenichts** (*Suhanc*) German version (Theater Unter den Linden, Berlin)

1893 **Das Mädchen von Mirano** (Alexander Neumann/w Zell) Carltheater 6 April

1893 **Freund Felix** (w L Herrmann) Friedrich-Wilhelmstädtisches Theater, Berlin 14 October

1894 **Mam'sell Cerevis** (*Mam'zelle Carabin*) German version w Robert Pohl (Theater am Gärtnerplatz, Munich)

1894 **Die Königin von Gamara** (Neumann/w Leo Stein) Carltheater 27 October

1895 **Engelsherz** (Raoul Mader/w Hugo Regel) Carltheater 12 January

GENEVIÈVE DE BRABANT Opéra-bouffe in 3 acts by Hector Crémieux and Étienne Tréfeu. Music by Jacques Offenbach. Original version in 2 acts by Tréfeu. Théâtre des Bouffes-Parisiens, Paris, 19 November 1859; revised version Théâtre des Menus-Plaisirs, Paris, 26 December 1867.

Of the great opéras-bouffes of Offenbach's early years, the one which has suffered the most inexplicable eclipse in the 20th century is *Geneviève de Brabant*. Whilst *Orphée aux enfers* and *La Belle Hélène* still hold the top of the market in musical and opera houses round the world, *La Grande-Duchesse* and the not-so-bouffe *La Périchole* surface from time to time, and marginally more imaginative houses are occasionally tempted into a *Barbe-bleue*, a *Pont des soupirs* or a *Les Brigands*, Tréfeu's hilarious burlesque of the medieval age has followed the other most celebrated medieval parody of the era, *Chilpéric*, into obscurity.

Geneviève de Brabant was the heroine of a favourite tale from the *Legenda Aurea* (The Golden Legend), a collection of saint's lives compiled in the 13th century by the Italian monk Jacobus de Voragine, which had won particular popularity in variant versions in Germany (by Ludwig Tieck) and in France, where it had appeared as a 'complainte bouffe' on the stage of the Palais-Royal as recently as 1851 (15 March). The wife of Count Palatine Sigfried of Brabant, in the days of Charles Martel, Geneviève was accused of infidelity and chased into the Ardennes forest where she gave birth to a son. The babe was suckled by a white doe before the Count discovered the accusations to be false and brought wife and son home.

Tréfeu stayed close to the old tale, but told it with burlesque humour rather than saintly drama. His Geneviève (Mlle Maréchal) is the victim of Duke Sifroy (Léonce)'s bosom buddy, Golo (Désiré), who has systematically distracted Sifroy from his conjugal sex life with the hope that he, Golo, will, in the absence of a legitimate heir, become the next Duke of Brabant. The pretty little pastrycook, Drogan (Lise Tautin), bakes a virility pie for the Duke which puts a fathering flicker into his eye, and Golo has to hurry to put Sifroy off his stride. He counters by accusing Drogan of dilly-dallying with Geneviève. Just to complicate things, Sifroy is dragged crossly off to the crusades by Charles Martel (Guyot), but he goes off repudiating Geneviève and leaving Golo as regent. The abandoned heroine takes refuge from the lubricious villain in the forest. There she meets a hermit and has a generally comico-melodramatic time, whilst her husband – who has got no closer to Palestine than Asnières – is holed up with Martel and his mates, having a very convivial time with a rough and tough lady called Isoline. He gets home, however, in time to checkmate Golo, rescue

525

ROYALTY THEATRE.

POWERFUL COMPANY

EVERY EVENING!

GENEVIÈVE
DE
BRABANT

OPERA BOUFFE
OFFENBACH
EVERY EVENING PRICES FROM ONE SHILLING

MISS EMILY SOLDENE.

Plate 104. **Geneviève de Brabant:** *A French artist's impressions of two scenes from the original production of the show, and an English poster showing the main attractions of the hugely successful British version – the duo of the gens d'armes, and the bulging charms of Emily Soldene.*

the blameless Geneviève, and hand over the termagent Isoline to her long-lost husband, who is none other than the horrified Golo.

In the very first version of *Geneviève*, as produced in 1859, the part which would become Drogan in the later rewrites was a multiple rôle, Mlle Tautin appearing as Mathieu, as Gracioso (a page), as Isoline and also as 'le chevalier noir' and 'la bohémienne' in the many disguises the plot involved. Another rôle, that of 'le jeune Arthur', played by Bonnet, was also due for a quick extinction, as *Geneviève* was altered and made over into its definitive version.

Offenbach's score was a delicious mixture of the broadly burlesque and the charming. What became Drogan's rondo du paté ('Salut! Noble assemblée'), vaunting his potent pie, Sifroy's nonsensical crowing Couplets de la poule and Charles Martel's arrival to a merry boléro ('J'arrive armé de pied en cap') were amongst the happiest bits of burlesque, whilst pieces such as the three-soprano Trio de la main et de la barbe and Drogan's serenade to Geneviève ('En passant sous la fenêtre') supplied the beauty, and the swingeing march finale which saw the Carolan army depart for Palestine, the booming climax. In the original layout, Mlle Tautin also indulged in a Chanson de la bohémienne, a hymn to Geneviève and a Rondo des jeux and Bonnet had a 'fable de l'enfant'. There was, as yet, no gens d'armes duo for, in this early version, the two comical law enforcers had not yet been tacked into the action.

The 1859 *Geneviève de Brabant* did not have the same huge and instant success that *Orphée aux enfers* had done. After 50 performances the composer/producer took the show off and replaced it with a hasty pasticcio revue. In spite of this, foreign producers were still interested and the first to move was the ever-ready Karl Treumann in Vienna. Treumann mounted an uncredited adaptation (possibly his own) at his Theater am Franz-Josefs-Kai under the title *Die schöne Magellone*. He himself played Sifroy – now called Siegfried, Therese Schäfer his wife, Magellone, Anton Ascher was the villainous Ulfo and Herr Grois played Charles Martell whilst Fr Majeranowska played Isoline who, in this version, was still also the page, Grazioso, the gipsy girl and the black knight. Knaack appeared as 'little Arthur' and Hopp was Narcziss, the court jester. *Die schöne Magellone*'s popularity was limited, but it nevertheless went on to be played in Berlin and in Prague in German, and in Hungary in Hungarian (ad Endre Latabár) with Véla Szilagyi, József Kovacs, Jenő Toth, Rosa Vig, János Parthenyi and Gyula Virágh featured in the Budai Népszinház's original production.

If the beginning had been only mildly promising, things soon looked up. In 1867 Offenbach, Tréfeu and Hector Crémieux put together a new, enlargened and less extravagantly burlesque three-act/nine-scene version of *Geneviève de Brabant* which was mounted by Gaspari at the new Théâtre des Menus-Plaisirs. Most of the original score was maintained, but there were some additions made, including the veritable double-act for two goonish gens d'armes ('Protéger le repos des villes') which would become the show's long-range hit, and the Asnières scene was expanded to include a tyrolienne and a dance divertissement. Once again, the piece was only a part-success in Paris, but this time the rest of the world took a little more notice, and this time (and in this form) *Geneviève de Brabant* became an international hit.

The 'new' *Geneviève* was given a rather more faithful German-language rendering under Strampfer at Vienna's Theater an der Wien (ad Julius Hopp) soon after the end of the Paris season. Albin Swoboda (Siegfried), Lori Hild (Genovefa), Jani Szika (Martell), Carl Adolf Friese (Golo), Marie Geistinger (Drogan) and Blasel and Rott as the gens d'armes headed a starry cast, and there was a spectacular ballet, 'Die drei Lebensalter', interpolated into the sixth of the seven scenes in which the high-jinks at Asnières was replaced by an 'Altdeutscher Narrenabend'. It was played 12 times. Conversely, *Geneviève*'s American production was a notable success. Joseph Grau's newly imported French opéra-bouffe company introduced the piece at the Théâtre Français with Rose Bell starring as Drogan, Marie Desclauzas as Geneviève and Bourgoin and Gabel as the gens d'armes. They were so successful that H L Bateman's previously all-conquering opéra-bouffe company, headed by Lucille Tostée, found its audiences at Pike's Opera House sadly depleted, and the canny Bateman, having reaped the rewards of *La Grande-Duchesse* swiftly sold out his interests. *Geneviève* proved to be the backbone of the new company's repertoire (*L'Oeil crevé, Fleur de thé, La Vie parisienne, La Grande-Duchesse, Chilpéric, M Choufleuri*) and it was played more than 100 times during their season.

The Broadway success, however, was nothing to that which the piece won in Britain. Music-hall manager Charles Morton and wealthy bookmaker, Charles Head, had gone into businesss producing opéra-bouffe at the old Philharmonic music hall in suburban Islington and they allied themselves with adapter/director H B Farnie, hired as artistic director to the house, to produce his version of *Geneviève de Brabant*. With Emily Soldene as Drogan, Selina Dolaro (Geneviève), John Rouse (Sifroy), Henry Lewens (Golo) and Edward Marshall and Felix Bury as the gens d'armes, Farnie's production of *Geneviève* caused the kind of sensation that *Orphée* had done in Paris (but not in London) and that only *Chilpéric* of French pieces had approached in England. The English adaptation of the 'very amusing but very indelicate' piece was lauded, and Soldene and Dolaro idolized, as the piece played on at its out-of-the-mainstream theatre for a remarkable 175 performances.

Henry Hersee hurried out another version of the show for Liverpool, but it was the Farnie version which returned to the Philharmonic in 1872 for a second run which allowed it to total an amazing 307 London nights by 30 March 1873. The following year it was back again, for a season at the Opera Comique (18 April) with Soldene, Rouse, Marshall and Bury all still in their original rôles, and, after the buxom Emily had given her version to New York – the city's first English-language performances of the show – it was mounted there again in 1876 (20 March) with the star still in her favourite rôle. In 1878 (23 January) the Philharmonic brought their big hit back, with Alice May as Drogan, but Soldene reclaimed her own when she starred in a glamorous production at the Alhambra later the same year (16 September) with Lewens, Thomas Aynsley Cook and Constance Loseby, and again, one last time, at the Royalty Theatre in 1881, a decade after she had first squeezed into the tights of the plump little page.

Australia followed Britain's example, and a local version

of *Geneviève de Brabant* was mounted there by W S Lyster (ad Garnet Walch) in 1873. Alice May (Drogan), Armes Beaumont (Sifroy) and Carrie Emmanuel (Geneviève) featured in a version which played fast and loose with both text and music, but which was undeniably successful through 15 performances. Following the Melbourne season, the show was due to be seen in Sydney, but the traditional pantomime period was nigh. Willie Gill at the Queen's solved the problem of the latest hit by simply interpolating half *Geneviève*'s music into his home-made pantomime, but the Royal Victoria Theatre's B N Jones went further and presented what was basically *Geneviève* as a putative pantomime, equipped with a harlequinade, under the title *Geneviève de Brabant, or Harlequin King of the Bakers, or Four-and-Twenty Baker Boys Baked in a Pie, When the Pie Was Opened...* (26 December 1873). Miss May repeated her Drogan alongside Henry Hallam (Sifroy), Sam Poole (Golo) and Miss Lambert (Geneviève) through a fine 24 nights. Australia later saw Soldene's Drogan, for *Geneviève de Brabant* was the prime piece in the prima donna's repertoire when she visited Australia, equipped with the usual exaggerated publicity ('as performed by her over 500 consecutive nights at the Philharmonic, London') and one of her original gens d'armes, Edward Marshall. Edward Farley (Cocorico, ie Sifroy), the lanky J H Jarvis (Golo) and Rose Stella (Geneviève) took the other main rôles.

Whilst *Geneviève* had been going on to become the rage of Britain, back in France Offenbach and Tréfeu had had another go at proving to Parisians that they should be making it an equal success there (Théâtre de la Gaîté, 25 February 1875). Adolphe Jaime joined the rewriting team on this occasion, and the piece was expanded with a goodly dose of the kind of spectacle that had served Offenbach productions well on earlier occasions. In this major production of a heavily rewritten piece, with a special rôle, Briscotte, written in to allow the appearance (with songs) of the celebrated heroine of the cafés-concerts, Mlle Thérésa, Mme Matz-Ferrare was Drogan and Lagrenay played Sifroy, whilst Scipion and Gabel were the gens d'armes. The production inspired a 'folie-vaudeville' *Geneviève de Brébant* at the Théâtre Déjazet (Grangé, Buguet, Bernard, plus some of Offenbach's music 18 March) but proved to be far too luxurious ever to break even and, although it ran more than 100 nights, it broke the bank. However, if Offenbach had failed thrice to make a success out of his witty and tuneful work, Fernand Samuel proved it could be done. In 1908 he mounted a version of the last version of *Geneviève de Brabant* for 58 nights at the Variétés with Jeanne Saulier (Drogan), Max Dearly (Golo), Guy (Sifroy), André Simon (Martell) and Geneviève Vix (Geneviève). The merits of the piece were, at last, agreed on by French audiences, but in the three-quarters of a century since, Paris has not again seen *Geneviève de Brabant*.

In habitual style, the Spanish borrowed Tréfeu's libretto and attached a fresh score to it for a *Genoveva de Brabante* produced in Madrid in 1868.

Austria: Theater am Franz-Josefs-Kai *Die schöne Magellone* 3 April 1861, Theater an der Wien *Genovefa von Brabant* 9 May 1868; Germany: Friedrich-Wilhelmstädtisches Theater 1 July 1861; Hungary: Budai Népszinház *Genoveva* 11 May 1864; USA: Théâtre Français 22 October 1868, Lyceum Theater (Eng) 2

November 1874; UK: Philharmonic Theatre, Islington 11 November 1871; Australia: Prince of Wales Theatre, Melbourne 11 September 1873

Recording: complete (Bourg)

GENNARO, Peter (b Metairie, La, 23 November 1919).

Peter Gennaro danced in a number of Broadway musicals, including *Make Mine Manhattan*, *Kiss Me, Kate*, *Guys and Dolls*, *By the Beautiful Sea* and *The Pajama Game* and had a featured rôle as Carl, dancing 'Mu-cha-cha' in *Bells Are Ringing* (1956).

His first choreographic assignment for Broadway was on the 1955 *Seventh Heaven*, and in 1957 he assisted Jerome Robbins on the celebrated dances for *West Side Story* before going on to choreograph *Fiorello!* (1959), *The Unsinkable Molly Brown* (1960 and film), *Mr President* (1962), *Bajour* (1964), *Jimmy* (1969), the 1973 version of *Irene*, the long-running *Annie*, *Carmelina*, *One Night Stand* and the 1982 *Little Me* revival for Broadway and to provide the original part of the dance content for the London stage version of *Singin' in the Rain*. He later repeated that assignment in a different show based on the same source on the road in America. In 1989 he choreographed a Broadway revival of *The Threepenny Opera*.

GENSLER, Lewis E (b New York, 4 December 1896; d New York, 10 January 1978).

In a decade as a Broadway composer, Gensler was responsible for all or part of a half-dozen musical comedy scores, which included one hit and one near-miss. A Nora Bayes vehicle, *Queen o' Hearts*, was a 39-performance flop, *Be Yourself*, a curiously uneven piece on which George S Kaufman, Marc Connelly and Ira Gershwin also worked, lasted 93 nights, and Gensler contributed the song 'Keep Smiling at Trouble' to Al Jolson's *Big Boy* (1925), before his musical version of *Captain Jinks* arrived in town with a dazzling pre-Broadway run to its credit. Under the circumstances, its 21 weeks in New York were considered a disappointment. However, the following season Gensler finally hit the target when *Queen High*, which had had almost as promising a try-out, not only won a fine Broadway run and a couple of overseas productions but also brought its composer his biggest-ever song hit with 'Cross Your Heart'.

Ups-a-Daisy, with a libretto just a little too similar to that of *Going Up*, had no song similar to 'Cross Your Heart' and a much shorter life, whilst *The Gang's All Here* lasted only three weeks and Gensler made his last Broadway venture with the revue *Ballyhoo of 1932* before moving on to Hollywood in 1933. There he operated as a composer, a writer and as a producer (*The Big Broadcast of 1937*, *Artists and Models*), turning out a series of songs of which 'Love is Just Around the Corner' (w Leo Robin), sung by Bing Crosby in *Here is My Heart*, was amongst the most successful.

Gensler also ventured as a producer on Broadway, joining with Morris Green to mount the successful 1930 show, *Fine and Dandy*, with Joe Cook starred, as well as his own *The Gang's All Here* the following year. This was apparently followed by a piece called *Hot and Bothered* which didn't make it to Broadway, and may not have, in spite of being announced, even made it to the stage. Another musical, *Melody in Spring*, also credited to him, seem to have gone the same way, leaving no trace.

He put in one posthumous reappearance when his 'Love is Just Around the Corner' resurfaced in 1986 as part of the score of the Broadway musical *Big Deal*.

1922 **Queen o' Hearts** (Oscar Hammerstein II) Cohan Theater 10 October

1924 **Be Yourself** (w Milton Schwarzwald/Ira Gershwin/Marc Connelly, George S Kaufman) Harris Theater 3 September

1925 **Captain Jinks** (w Stephen Jones/B G De Sylva/Laurence Schwab) Martin Beck Theater 8 September

1926 **Queen High** (De Sylva/Schwab) Ambassador Theater 8 September

1928 **Ups-a-Daisy** (Clifford Grey, Robert A Simon) Shubert Theater 8 October

1931 **The Gang's All Here** (w Owen Murphy/Simon/Hammerstein, Russel Crouse, Morrie Ryskind) Imperial Theater 18 February

GENTLEMAN JOE Musical farce in 2 acts by Basil Hood. Music by Walter Slaughter. Prince of Wales Theatre, London, 2 March 1895.

Gentleman Joe was written to provide comedian Arthur Roberts, the original top-biller of *In Town* and of many burlesques, with a star rôle in a reasonably legitimate musical comedy. Legitimacy was ensured by selecting the promising Basil Hood, not yet acclaimed as the successor to Gilbert, as book and lyric writer, and Hood succeeded in coming up with a character and a plot which provided the undisciplined Roberts with the finest rôle of his career.

Gentleman Joe, a cockney cabbie, goes courting his Emma while her mistress, Mrs Ralli Carr, a society 'woman who arranges things', is away. He finds himself mistaken for the poor but titled Irishman whom Mrs Carr is angling to separate from one of her poor but pretty clients (who requires a rich husband) and attach to a rich American (who requires a titled husband). Many complications emerge, first in London and then on the beach to where everyone repairs in Act II, before Joe and his Emma can, like everyone else, get safely together.

Joe was a splendid creation, and since the plot was one which allowed the popular Roberts his head with his usual and intermittently original ad-libbing, disguises and grimacing, without destroying the run of things, the star was able to make a great hit with the character and with his songs, 'In My 'Ansom', 'Gentleman Joe' and anything else he liked to ease into a minstrel show on the beach ('new scene ... "The Bathing Incident" tonight', 'Arthur Roberts' new song ... 5 recalls nightly'). The most successful of these interpolations was the smutty 'She Wanted Something to Play With', the most substantial a whole burlesque scene on the currently successful *Trilby*.

Kitty Loftus (Emma) had a hit with 'The Magic of His Eye', Aida Jenoure (Mrs Carr) stopped the show with her description of how she earns 'A Little Commission', and Kate Cutler and William Philp had the prettiest of Walter Slaughter's songs in the rôles of the Irish peer and his girl, but the big success of the score was a raucous piece for the extremely spirited American performer Sadie Jerome, playing a title-seeking, transatlantic heiress, declaring 'Lalage Potts, That's Me'. The song made a temporary star of Miss Jerome who was promptly hired for the next Roberts show but sacked when the world finally realized that she couldn't sing and couldn't act, and energy and a goodly bust only went so far.

Gentleman Joe had 391 London performances, was out in no less that four touring companies in 1896 with Frank Danby, Edwin Brett, Harry Roxbury and Fred Lyne all giving their Joes to the corners of Britain, and it cleaned up over many years on the British and colonial circuits. In America, however, it ran into trouble when a pirate production reached Broadway before the legitimate Joe was ready. Law-suits flew, in the finest American theatrical tradition, and, in the storm, not only was the pirate sunk but also James T Powers's genuine production (Bijou Theater 30 January 1896, 48 performances).

Australia saw W Louis Bradfield as Joe, when the touring Gaiety Theatre company played some performances of this non-George Edwardes production amongst their Gaiety Girls and Shop Girls later in 1895. Another Edwardes rep company introduced Gentleman Joe to South Africa around the same time, whilst London's production ran on, and though the show did not penetrate the non-English-speaking markets, it made its way to most corners of the world where there was an Anglophone audience.

Australia: Lyceum, Sydney 24 August 1895; USA: Miner's Fifth
   Avenue Theater 6 January 1896

GENTLEMEN PREFER BLONDES
Musical in 2 acts by Anita Loos and Joseph Fields based on Anita Loos's book of the same title. Lyrics by Leo Robin. Music by Jule Styne. Ziegfeld Theater, New York, 8 December 1949.

Anita Loos's comic novella Gentlemen Prefer Blondes, with its memorable blonde money-box of a heroine, Lorelei Lee, was made into a stage play by its author with (apparently very) little help from her husband, John Emerson, in 1926 (Times Square Theater 28 September), and filmed in 1928 before it went on to be made up into a stage musical in 1949.

Lorelei Lee (Carol Channing) from Little Rock, Arkansaw, is nicely looked after by Gus Esmond (Jack McCauley), the heir to a button-manufacturing fortune, who supplies her with the diamonds necessary to a girl's well-being. Business means Gus has to stay behind when they should have sailed for Europe together, and Lorelei sets off with just her good friend, a Follies girl called Dorothy Shaw (Yvonne Adair), who has curious ideas about love being more important than diamonds, as chaperone. On the voyage, Lorelei persuades one Sir Francis Beekman (Rex Evans) to sponsor her purchase of a diamond tiara, and in Paris she whizzes round the shops with fitness-freak Josephus Gage (George S Irving), the wealthy owner of the patent to the new zip-fastener. When button-man Gus turns up, the zip-fastener in Lorelei's new dress causes a breach, but, by the time an act full of incidental entertainments has passed, Lorelei has won over not only her most reliable gentleman, but also his enormously wealthy father. Zip-fasteners and buttons amalgamate, and Lorelei weds her Gus. Dorothy overcomes her principles enough to pair off with vastly wealthy Henry Spofford (Eric Brotherson). Alice Pearce played Henry's mother, converted from a careful life to hedonism under Lorelei's spell, Howard Morris and Mort Marshall were a pair of four-faced Parisian lawyers, and Anita Alvarez was a running joke of a permanently practising dancer.

The score to Gentlemen Prefer Blondes was topped by two numbers for its heroine which became favourites: 'Diamonds Are a Girl's Best Friend' and 'A Little Girl from Little Rock', but the rest of the cast were less well served, best-friend Dorothy finding her merriest moment in 'I Love What I'm Doing (when I'm doing it for love)'.

Carol Channing's bordering-on-the-burlesque portrayal of the blonder-than-a-bombshell Lorelei proved the high spot of Herman Levin and Oliver Smith's production which ran for 740 performances on Broadway before going right on back west to be made into a Hollywood film with Marilyn Monroe and Jane Russell starred as Lorelei and Dorothy. Only the star's two top songs and 'Bye Bye Baby' were retained from the score, supplemented by a pair of additional songs by Hoagy Carmichael and Harold Adamson.

In spite of its genuine success in America, Gentlemen Prefer Blondes moved very slowly abroad. It was 13 years after its première before the show was produced in London, with Dora Bryan starred as Lorelei and Anne Hart as Dorothy for a run of 223 performances, and Europe passed until a German Blondinen bevorzugt (ad Gabrielle Peter, Beate Rygiert-Schmidt, music arr by Volker M Plangg) was mounted in Pforzheim in 1988.

Broadway, however, did get a second helping. A revised Gentlemen Prefer Blondes, with Miss Channing repeating a version of her original rôle which had her looking back, 25 years on, was produced by Guber and Gross at the Civic Center, Oklahoma City under the title Lorelei (26 February 1973, billed as a 'world première'). Comden, Green and Styne wrote a number of additional and replacement songs to the revised book by Kenny Solms and Gail Parent, several of which went by the board before the show reached Broadway, nearly a year later (27 January 1974 Palace Theater), for a run of 320 performances.

UK: Prince's Theatre 20 August 1962; Germany: Stadttheater,
   Pforzheim Blondinen bevorzugt 31 December 1988; Film:
   Twentieth Century-Fox 1953
Recordings: original cast (Columbia), London cast (HMV) Lorelei
   (MGM); Film soundtrack (DRG)

GEORGE M!
Musical in 2 acts by Michael Stewart and John & Fran Pascal. Music and lyrics taken from the works of George M Cohan. Palace Theater, New York, 10 April 1968.

A biomusical put together around the songs of George M Cohan, George M! allowed Joel Grey, in the character of the actor/author/composer, Jerry Dodge (father Jerry Cohan), Betty Ann Grove (mother Nellie Cohan), Bernadette Peters (sister Josie Cohan), Jamie Donnelly (wife Ethel Levey), Jacqueline Alloway (Fay Templeton) and the rest of the cast to run through such Cohan hits as 'Mary', 'Forty-Five Minutes from Broadway', 'Give My Regards to Broadway', 'I'm a Yankee Doodle Dandy', 'Nellie Kelly, I Love You', 'Harrigan', 'Over There' and many more, to the acompaniment of a gently slanted version of his life story.

David Black, Konrad Matthaei and Lorin E Price produced George M! for a 435-performance run on Broadway, and the show was subsequently televised, with Grey repeating his stage rôle, in 1970.

Recording: original cast (Columbia)

LES GÉORGIENNES Opéra-bouffe in 3 acts by Jules Moinaux. Music by Jacques Offenbach. Théâtre des Bouffes-Parisiens, Paris, 16 March 1864.

The men of Djégani, Georgia, like a peaceful family life and are not fond of fighting, but the women of the town are furious and humiliated when 150 of their menfolk get beaten by default by only 32 of the enemy. With the perfumer's wife, Feroza (Delphine Ugalde), at their head, they take up arms to revenge and defend their city. The Pasha of the opposing forces, Rhododendron (Pradeau), caught inside the city, whence he has come to prospect for his harem, is swept up in the affair. When the two-faced Boboli (Léonce) lets it out that the men have never actually been to war, and their wounds are all sham, Feroza has them all thrown into prison, but each woman helps her own man to escape and they next appear disguised as gipsies, apparently ready to help Rhododendron in his plan to carry off a supply of harem-material. However, the Pasha's disguise has been seen through, and in the end the men and women of Djégani join happily together to celebrate his capture. Zulma Bouffar played Nani, the wife of Poterno (Jean-Paul), and Désiré was the perfumer Jol-Hiddin, both of whom partook largely of the action.

The music of *Les Géorgiennes* featured some strong and showy pieces for Feroza – on the normally masculine subjects of war and wine (Chanson de la treille, Chanson à boire, Chant de guerre) – and some gentler but equally soprano pieces for Nani ('Ah! vraiment c'est charmant', 'Sous cet uniforme modeste'), whilst the comic moments included two songs for the Pasha – one relating the tale of his depleted harem ('Je suis ce Pasha') and another a 'rataplan' piece in his second-act disguise as drummer to the female army ('Attention tapons ferme') – and a duo with Boboli discussing the relative merits of impaling or hanging as an execution. There was also plenty of martial ensemble music, varied by a fake gipsy chorus for the disguised men in the final act.

In spite of the fact that the leading lady was replaced shortly before opening, *Les Géorgiennes*, with its galaxy of tightly uniformed ladies and its glittering score, was an indubitable hit. It played for more than 100 performances for its composer/producer at the Bouffes-Parisiennes, and was soon seen throughout Europe. Karl Treumann staged his adaptation of *Die schönen Weiber von Georgien* at the Carltheater, with Frau Friedrich-Materna (Feroza), Franz Eppich (Rhododendron), Josef Matras (Paterno), Fräulein von Edelsberg (Nani) and Therese Schäfer (Zaida) featured, and the piece scored a considerable success, holding its place in the repertoire for more than six years. The German version was also played in Budapest where an Hungarian adaptation was subsequently mounted at the Budai Népszinház with Laura Istvanti, Sarolta Krecsanyi, Vizvari and Vidor Kassai. The piece's list of productions was rather cut short by the arrival, just months later, of the all-conquering *La Belle Hélène*, and it was 1871 before New York saw *Les Géorgiennes*, and then it was in French. That performance was played by Mlle Aimée's company with the star as Feroza supported by Constant Gausins (Rhododenron), Paul Hittemans (Boboli), Elise Persini (Nani) and Legros (Jol-Hiddin), and the show was later seen at the Germania in German (25 December 1873) with Frln Rindoli (Feroza), Merten (Rhododendron), Antonie Heynold (Nani) and Schutz (Boboli).

An English version (ad C J S Wilson) was produced in London in 1875 with Rose Bell (Feroza), Carlotta Zerbini (Nani) and Richard Temple (Rhododendron) featured, for a month's run. The German version later turned up at the Theater an der Wien in 1877 (18 November) for just two performances, but *Les Géorgiennes*, in spite of its successful original run, did not establish itself in the preferred Offenbach repertoire.

Austria: Carltheater *Die schönen Weiber von Georgien* 5 October 1864; Hungary: Budai *Die schönen Weiber von Georgien* (Ger) 15 July 1865, Budai Népszinház *A georgai nők* 14 February 1865; USA: Grand Opera House (Fr) 6 March 1871; UK: Philharmonic Theatre, Islington 2 October 1875

GERMAN, Edward (Sir) [JONES, German Edward] (b Whitchurch, 17 February 1862; d London, 11 November 1936). Orchestral composer who succeeded Sullivan as the purveyor of comic opera to the Savoy Theatre, but who disappeared from the musical theatre without fulfilling his potential.

A self-taught violinist and conductor, German attended the Royal Academy from the age of 18 and earned himself some spare cash by playing the violin in theatre orchestras. In 1888 he became musical director at the Globe Theatre, and he made his first notable contribution to the stage with an incidental score for their *Richard III* with Richard Mansfield (1889).

Amongst the more substantial compositions of his early years, the young composer numbered orchestral pieces, symphonies and songs, including a considerable amount of music for both for the concert and the theatrical stages. The theatre works included dance music for Henry Irving's production of *Henry VIII*, and scores for Beerbohm Tree's 1893 production of Henry Arthur Jones's *The Tempter* (Haymarket Theatre), the Forbes Robertson/Mrs Patrick Campbell *Romeo and Juliet* at the Lyceum (1895) and George Alexander's St James's Theatre *As You Like It* (1898). His dances for Anthony Hope and Edward Rose's 1900 comedy *English Nell* at the Prince of Wales Theatre won particular success and, like the *Henry VIII* dances, were subsequently made up into an orchestral suite.

When Sir Arthur Sullivan died, with his new Savoy Theatre comic opera *The Emerald Isle* incomplete, it was expected that either Savoy musical director François Cellier or Ernest Ford, both of whom had strong connections with the D'Oyly Carte régime and had previously written music for the Savoy, would be asked to finish the work. In fact, it was German, who had no experience as a composer of comic opera, who was commissioned by Mrs D'Oyly Carte to bring *The Emerald Isle* to completion. It proved a wise choice, for he won praise for his taste and tact in turning out a Sullivan score which was neither pastiche nor sturdily two-parted and *The Emerald Isle* gave the Savoy a good, if not outstanding, success.

German subsequently teamed with Basil Hood – touted as the 'new Gilbert' to German's 'new Sullivan' – on two further comic operas, the highly successful *Merrie England* (1902) ('The Yeomen of England', 'She Had a Letter from her Love', 'The English Rose', 'Who Shall Say That Love Is Cruel?') and the charming *A Princess of Kensington* (1903), produced for the Savoy company by William Greet who had, in the meanwhile, purchased the D'Oyly Carte interests. In spite of a fair run and a score which included the perennially popular 'Four Jolly Sailormen', *A Princess of Kensington* did not balance the books, and Greet gave up producing the quality English light and/or comic operas with which he had determined to continue the Savoy tradition and turned to the much more financially solid modern musical comedy. German returned, seemingly without any regret, to orchestral and concert vocal writing.

In 1907 he came back to the theatre with a commission to compose the score for another period light opera, a version of Henry Fielding's *Tom Jones* produced by Robert Courtneidge on the occasion of the Fielding bicentenary. *Tom Jones* turned out to be an expertly made piece, and its score an ideal combination of strongly made music, period flavour and tunefulness ('For Tonight', 'The Green Ribbon', 'West Country Lad', 'Dream o'Day Jill'). The show remains, almost a century later, a classic of the otherwise fairly limited English light opera repertoire.

Sadly, German returned only once more to the musical theatre, to collaborate with W S Gilbert on a musical adaptation of his 1873 play *The Wicked World* as *Fallen Fairies* (1909). Gilbert's fairies were sadly out-of-date, and the show failed utterly. Thereafter the composer withdrew from the theatre and, by and large, from composing in general.

A thorough and conservative musician, German excelled at illustrating historical subjects with a form of light operatic music which, although it was perhaps broadly uncommercial, proved both immensely singable and durable.

1901 **The Emerald Isle, or The Caves of Carric-Cleena** (w Arthur Sullivan/Basil Hood) Savoy Theatre 27 April

1901 **The Rival Poets** (W H Scott) 1 act St George's Hall (1886 by amateurs)

1902 **Merrie England** (Hood) Savoy Theatre 2 April

1903 **A Princess of Kensington** (Hood) Savoy Theatre 22 January

1907 **Tom Jones** (Charles H Taylor/Alexander M Thompson, Robert Courtneidge) Apollo Theatre 17 April

1909 **Fallen Fairies** (W S Gilbert) Savoy Theatre 15 December

Biographies: Scott, W: *Edward German* (Cecil Palmer, London, 1932), Rees, B: *A Musical Peacemaker* (Kensal Press, Bucks, 1988)

GERRARD, Gene [né O'SULLIVAN] (b London, 31 August 1892; d Sidmouth, Devon, 1 June 1971)

Gerrard first worked in variety and came to the musical theatre, by way of revue, after the First World War. His first West End show was *The Officers' Mess* (1918), his next *His Little Widows* (1919, Jack Grayson) but, after spells in variety and in Australia, he took his first important musical-comedy rôle in the West End when he was given the lead comic part of Leander in *Katja, the Dancer* (1925) at the Gaiety Theatre. This led to his being cast in the choice comic rôle of Bennie in the London production of *The Desert Song* (1927) at the Theatre Royal, Drury Lane, and top-billed in the musical comedy *Lucky Girl* (1928, Hudson Greener). He returned to Drury Lane for *The New Moon* (1929, Alexander) and a revival of *Rose Marie* (1929, Herman).

His subsequent musical rôles in such pieces as *Little Tommy Tucker* (1930, Bill Coverdale) and *The Gay Hussar* (1933, Nicola) were not in the same class as those in the three imported classics, and his last parts, in *Take it Easy* (1937, Danny Waring) and *The Silver Patrol* (1940, Albert

Stamp) were little short of disastrous. His later stage appearances were in pantomime and the occasional comedy.

Gerrard worked, in tandem with his performing, as a director, and shared the directing credit on the film of *Little Tommy Tucker* (1931). He was also the director of the original production of *Me and My Girl*, although his name had disappeared from the bills, and Lupino Lane took the credit, when the show finally opened in town.

GERSHWIN, George [GERSHVIN, Jacob] (b New York, 26 September 1898; d Hollywood, Calif, 11 July 1937). Versatile composer of everything from songs and dances to opéra-bouffe and folk opera for the Broadway stage.

After a schooling which included limited conventional musical studies, the young George Gershwin went straight to work as a pianist and song-plugger in the musical publishing firm of Jerome H Remick. During this time, he began composing songs and in 1916 he had his first piece published. This comedy number, 'When You Want 'em You Can't Get 'em', written to a lyric by Murray Roth, and performed by Sophie Tucker, ultimately appeared on the musical theatre stage more than 70 years later when it was used as part of the score for the London extravaganza *Ziegfeld*.

The young pianist/songwriter worked as a rehearsal pianist, as an accompanist to Nora Bayes for the musical *Ladies First*, and was then taken on by Max Dreyfus at Harms (a step up from the not-negligible Remicks) as a regularly-waged composer. This arrangement resulted in his having several songs interpolated into the scores of such contemporary stage shows as the British *Good Morning, Judge* (*The Boy*) and the German *The Lady in Red* (*Die Dame in Rot*) and being given the chance to write the score for a revue *Half Past Eight*. The revue folded on the road, but Harms did not have long to wait for better results. In 1919 the young songwriter scored a major song hit with 'Swanee' (lyric: Irving Caesar) and was also given the opportunity to write a full set of songs for a Broadway book show.

Whilst Al Jolson introduced 'Swanee' and 'Dixie Rose' into *Sinbad*, Alex Aarons's production of *La La Lucille*, music by George Gershwin, opened in Atlantic City. The young composer didn't make much impression on the local critic, who devoted most of his review to the physical production and merely commented 'the musical decorations are by George Gershwin'. *La La Lucille* made its way to Broadway's Henry Miller Theater where it lasted a fair 104 performances. Over the next few years, however, the book musical did not prove a profitable field for Gershwin. Whilst he had a happy time supplying songs to revue – most notably the *George White's Scandals* series ('Stairway to Paradise', 'Somebody Loves Me') – *A Dangerous Maid*, a musicalized version of Charles Bell's comedy *The Dislocated Honeymoon*, folded without making it to Broadway, a one-act tragic jazz opera, *Blue Monday*, was cut from the *George White's Scandals of 1922* after opening night, and *Our Nell*, a piece of burlesque melodrama with songs, died in five unpatronized weeks. And of the book shows into which he interpolated songs, few did better. *Dere Mabel*, composed by a Boston businessman's daughter but advertised to have additional numbers by Irving Berlin,

Plate 105. **George Gershwin** *goes Groucho for a night out with Evelyn Laye.*

instead had one by Gershwin for its short life in Baltimore and Boston, Hugo Felix's *The Sweetheart Shop* did much better on the road than in town, and 'Someone' contributed less to the success of Aarons's *For Goodness' Sake* than the young song and dance pair, the Astaires. Irene Bordoni took in Gershwin songs for the multi-source scores of her Continental plays *The French Doll* and *Little Miss Bluebeard*, both of which did better than Romberg's *The Dancing Girl* to which Gershwin again contributed a single song.

It was not until 1924, the same year that his jazz-band concerto 'Rhapsody in Blue' brought him international celebrity, that the composer achieved success with stage scores in both London and in New York. In London, where he had already contributed more or less of the songs to several revues beginning with *Mayfair and Montmartre* (on which the remainder of the music was done by Maurice Yvain, much more Montmartre than Gershwin was Mayfair), and continuing with *The Rainbow* (principal composer) and *The Punch Bowl* (one of many), he was commissioned to compose the score for George Grossmith and Pat Malone's Winter Garden show, *Primrose*. Gershwin mixed some of his already-written songs with some others written for the occasion and scored his best musical theatre run to date when his 'Wait a Bit, Susie' and 'Boy Wanted' (rescued from *A Dangerous Maid*) were heard in London for a fine run of 255 performances before *Primrose* crossed the world to represent him in Australia.

That total was soon topped by a first Broadway hit. A fairish January to April showing by Frank Mandel's production *Sweet Little Devil* (120 performances) was succeeded by Alex Aarons's new show for Adele and Fred Astaire, who had served him so well in *For Goodness' Sake*. In *Lady, Be Good!* they also served George Gershwin well, as he did them: the show was a 330-performance Broadway hit, and launched 'Oh Lady, Be Good!' and 'Fascinating Rhythm' as individual favourites.

Thereafter, whilst Gershwin continued to compose and perform instrumental music (Concerto in F, *An American in Paris*), he turned out a series of scores for Broadway which included many successes and produced many popular songs. An undercast production of *Tell Me More* managed only a round 100 performances on a Broadway struck by a heat wave, but the Winter Garden Theatre team in London got 262 performances from it and its 'Kickin' the Clouds Away', whilst the wide-eyed tale of a little girl called *Tip-Toes* ('Sweet and Low Down', 'That Certain Feeling') played 192 times on Broadway and 182 at the London Winter Garden. Just two nights after the New York opening of the *Tip-Toes*, the lavishly-staged 'romantic opera' *Song of the Flame* followed. London didn't want this one, but Broadway listened to its Russian passions and Gershwin's title-song for a fine 219 performances.

With *Oh, Kay!* (primitively titled *Cheerio!*), Gershwin left the Russian passions and returned to Aarons and Freedley and to what had become his most familiar and best-loved musical style. 'Someone to Watch Over Me', 'Maybe', 'Clap Yo' Hands' and 'Do, Do, Do' contributed effectively to a show which again had fine runs in New York (256 performances) and London (214 performances) and established itself – no small thanks to a brisker than usual comedy libretto – as arguably Gershwin's best light musical comedy.

Gershwin came together again with Aarons and Freedley and the Astaires in *Funny Face* ('Funny Face', ''S Wonderful', 'He Loves and She Loves') for 244 performances on Broadway and 263 in London, but, in the meantime, he had suffered his first out-of-town closure since *A Dangerous Maid* with a would-be political satire penned by George S Kaufman. *Strike Up the Band* and its title number went on ice, however, and a few years later the show was given a rewrite and a New York showing of 191 performances. Another piece away from the Aarons and Freedley management was another venture into the romantic, and again in collaboration. Ziegfeld's Marilyn(n) Miller vehicle, *Rosalie*, was more successful in so far as the length of its run was concerned (335 performances), and Gershwin provided a bit of the snap which characterized his best works with the number 'Oh Gee! Oh Joy!' to contrast with Romberg's more romantic moments.

The 1920s ended on a less favourable turn when *Treasure Girl* turned out a 68-performance flop and Ziegfeld's *Show Girl* ('Liza', *An American in Paris* ballet) made its way through an indifferent 111 nights, but the revised *Strike Up the Band* did better, and the Aarons/Freedley production of *Girl Crazy* ('I Got Rhythm', 'Embraceable You', 'Bidin' My Time') brought its composer back to Broadway success (272 performances). Broadway success was something which Gershwin had tasted regularly over the past half-dozen years, and which he was to find in even more appreciable doses in the years to come, but the end of the Grossmith era at the London Winter Garden and the departure of the Astaires for other spheres marked the end of the composer's London showings. From now on, his new musicals got productions only at home.

London would, in any case, perhaps not quite have known what to do with Kaufman and Ryskind's political burlesque, *Of Thee I Sing*, a zany tale of an everyday American President and Vice-President which Gershwin set with music of a twinkling burlesque humour which little in either his serious work or his dance-and-song shows had presaged. The authors of *Of Thee I Sing* won a Pulitzer

Prize, Sam Harris's production played 441 Broadway nights (Gershwin's longest-ever run) and the piece made itself a special place in the history and repertoire of America's musical theatre. The barely extractable pieces of the musical score, such as the title song ('Of Thee I Sing, Baby'), 'Who Cares?' and 'Love is Sweeping the Country', gave evidence of a differently and delightfully fun-flavoured Gershwin.

An effort to repeat the success of *Of Thee I Sing* with a musequel, *Let 'em Eat Cake*, failed, as did a final musical with Aarons and Freedley (*Pardon My English*, 46 performances), before Gershwin's 'American Folk Opera' *Porgy and Bess* (1935), a stunning amalgam of contemporary popular and serious musical and textual styles, was brought to Broadway. Once again, the composer came up with another facet of his composing talent, and *Porgy and Bess* and its songs ('It Ain't Necessarily So', 'Bess, You is My Woman Now', 'I Got Plenty of Nothin'', 'Summertime', 'My Man's Gone Now' etc) gave him yet another niche in the classic register.

Gershwin died less than two years after the première of *Porgy and Bess* without composing another score for the musical stage. His final work had been for Hollywood, where he returned to the popular songwriting style which had characterized his musical comedies of the 1920s with the songs for *Shall We Dance?* ('Let's Call the Whole Thing Off', 'Shall We Dance', 'They Can't Take That Away From Me'), *A Damsel in Distress* ('Nice Work, If You Can Get It') and the posthumous *The Goldwyn Follies*.

The three shows which stand highest as a monument to Gershwin's talents – *Oh, Kay!*, *Of Thee I Sing* and *Porgy and Bess* – are three pieces in vastly different tones: the bright, light flippancy of the first, the blithely boisterous burlesque of the second, and the strong drama of the third gave him musical opportunities of widely disparate types, and the composer encompassed all three with an enduring success which speaks volumes for his musical versatility. Yet it was the popular songwriting style of his earliest successes to which he most naturally seemed to gravitate, and the character of that style gave to his more ambitious writing melodic, rhythmic and structural qualities which helped win wide popular acceptance for pieces ranging from 'Rhapsody in Blue' to *Porgy and Bess*.

George Gershwin died young, and he won the 'future' that so many artists of all kinds who shared his fate have won. He became a show-business icon. Over the years, he has been written and rewritten about, analysed and over-analysed, appraised, praised and over-praised in a way that virtually no other writer for the American musical stage has been, and often to the exclusion of contemporaries and other songwriters of considerable talents. Yet although the name of Gershwin has become a deeply fashionable one, few of his stage musicals remain in the theatre repertoire. *Porgy and Bess* has found a home in the world's opera houses, *Oh, Kay!* and *Lady, Be Good!* have been given modest revivals, and very occasionally *Of Thee I Sing* wins a home-town production. Pasticcio shows distantly related to *Funny Face* (*My One and Only*) and *Girl Crazy* (*Crazy for You*) have cashed in on the Gershwin fashion in America where aficionados have – more and more – won rehearings (if not restagings) for such scores as *Primrose* and *Strike Up the Band*. Like Strauss in Vienna or Offenbach in France, the name of Gershwin is considered 'OK' whilst Youmans,

Hirsch, Friml, Archer, Romberg and others are largely brushed aside as part of a lightweight disposable tradition. It is a curious phenomenon and one that, in the end, does its icon no favours.

1919 **La La Lucille** (Arthur J Jackson, B G De Sylva/Frederick Jackson) Henry Miller Theater 20 April

1921 **A Dangerous Maid** (Ira Gershwin/Charles W Bell) Apollo Theater, Atlantic City 21 March

1922 **Blue Monday** (later *135th Street*) (De Sylva) 1 act in *George White's Scandals* Globe Theater 28 August

1922 **Our Nell** (w William Daly/Brian Hooker, A E Thomas) Bayes Theater 4 December

1924 **Sweet Little Devil** (ex-*A Perfect Lady*) (De Sylva/Laurence Schwab, Frank Mandel) Astor Theater 21 January

1924 **Primrose** (Desmond Carter, I Gershwin/George Grossmith, Guy Bolton) Winter Garden Theatre, London 11 September

1924 **Lady, Be Good!** (I Gershwin/Fred Thompson, Bolton) Liberty Theater 1 December

1925 **Tell Me More** (ex-*My Fair Lady*) (I Gershwin, De Sylva/Thompson, William K Wells) Gaiety Theater 13 April

1925 **Tip-Toes** (I Gershwin/Thompson, Bolton) Liberty Theater 28 December

1925 **Song of the Flame** (w Herbert Stothart/Oscar Hammerstein II, Otto Harbach) 44th Street Theater 30 December

1926 **Oh, Kay!** (I Gershwin, Howard Dietz/Bolton, P G Wodehouse) Imperial Theater 8 November

1927 **Strike Up the Band** (I Gershwin/George S Kaufman) Shubert Theater, Philadelphia 5 September

1927 **Funny Face** (ex-*Smarty*) (I Gershwin/Thompson, Paul Gerard Smith) Alvin Theater 22 November

1928 **Rosalie** (w Sigmund Romberg/I Gershwin, Wodehouse/Bolton, William Anthony McGuire) New Amsterdam Theater 10 January

1928 **Treasure Girl** (I Gershwin/Thompson, Vincent Lawrence) Alvin Theater 8 November

1929 **Show Girl** (I Gershwin, Gus Kahn/McGuire, J P McEvoy) Ziegfeld Theater 2 July

1930 **Strike Up the Band** revised version by Morrie Ryskind Times Square Theater 14 January

1930 **Girl Crazy** (I Gershwin/Bolton, Jack McGowan) Alvin Theater 14 October

1931 **Of Thee I Sing** (I Gershwin, Kaufman, Ryskind) Music Box Theater 26 December

1933 **Pardon My English** (I Gershwin/Herbert Fields) Majestic Theater 20 January

1933 **Let 'em Eat Cake** (I Gershwin, Kaufman, Ryskind) Imperial Theater 21 October

1935 **Porgy and Bess** (I Gershwin, DuBose Heyward/Heyward) Alvin Theater 10 October

Biographies etc: Goldberg, I & Garson, E: *George Gershwin: a Study in American Music* (Simon & Schuster, New York, 1931), Ewen, D: *George Gershwin: his Journey to Greatness* (Prentice Hall, New Jersey, 1956), Armitage, M: *George Gershwin: Man and Legend* (Duell Sloane, New York, 1958), Payne, R: *Gershwin* (Pyramid, New York, 1960), Jablonski, E: *George Gershwin* (Doubleday, New York, 1962), Kimball, R & Simon, A: *The Gershwins* (Athenaeum, New York, 1973), Schwartz, C: *Gershwin: His Life and Music* (Bobbs-Merrill, Indianapolis, 1973), Kendall, A: *George Gershwin* (London, 1987), Rosenberg, D: *Fascinating Rhythm* (Dutton, New York, 1991), Peyser, J: *The Memory of All That* (Simon & Schuster, New York, 1993) etc

GERSHWIN, Ira [GERSHOVITZ, Israel] (b New York, 6 December 1896; d Los Angeles, 17 August 1983).

Ira Gershwin began writing lyrics whilst at college, and

combined with his brother, George, in his first theatrical ventures – a song interpolated into Nora Bayes's *Ladies First* and the words to the songs for the quickly interred *A Dangerous Maid*, some of which would be later exhumed for the score of the London musical *Primrose* in 1924.

His first success, however, came not with his brother but under the pseudonym of 'Arthur Francis', as the lyricist for the successful *Two Little Girls in Blue* produced by George's *La La Lucille* producer Alex Aarons and composed by Vincent Youmans and Paul Lannin. He provided some additional lyrics for Kaufman and Connelly's *Be Yourself* but, following the production of *Primrose*, again joined up with brother George for the series of 1920s musical comedies which, topped with the two memorable Gershwin brothers pieces of the last days of George's career, *Of Thee I Sing* (Pulitzer Prize) and *Porgy and Bess*, made up the heart of their careers.

Ira, who had rarely worked with another composer during these years – some lyrics for Phil Charig ('Sunny Disposish') and Joseph Meyer for songs used in London's *That's a Good Girl* and the Harold Arlen revue *Life Begins at 8.40* being amongst the few theatre occasions – worked on only three stage musicals after George's premature death, although film brought him such further song successes as 'The Man That Got Away' (*A Star Is Born*) and 'Long Ago and Far Away' (*Cover Girl*). The first of those three shows, *Lady in the Dark*, brought him both kudos and success, but a second collaboration with composer Kurt Weill on *The Firebrand of Florence* brought neither, and another flop, *Park Avenue*, saw out the end of the 25 year Broadway career of Gershwin-the-words on an atypical downbeat.

A collection of his lyrics, accompanied by commentary and anecdotes, was published as *Lyrics on Several Occasions* (Knopf, New York, 1959 and Elm Tree, England, 1977).

1921 **A Dangerous Maid** (George Gershwin/Charles W Bell) Apollo Theater, Atlantic City 21 March
1921 **Two Little Girls in Blue** (Vincent Youmans, Paul Lannin/Frederick Jackson) George M Cohan Theater 3 May
1924 **Be Yourself** (Lewis Gensler, Milton Schwarzenwald/George S Kaufman, Marc Connelly) Sam H Harris Theater 3 September
1924 **Primrose** (G Gershwin/w Desmond Carter/George Grossmith, Guy Bolton) Winter Garden Theatre, London 11 September
1924 **Lady, Be Good!** (G Gershwin/Fred Thompson, Bolton) Liberty Theater 1 December
1925 **Tell Me More** (ex-*My Fair Lady*) (G Gershwin/w De Sylva/Thompson, William K Wells) Gaiety Theater 13 April
1925 **Tip-Toes** (G Gershwin/Thompson, Bolton) Liberty Theater 28 December
1926 **Oh, Kay!** (G Gershwin/w Howard Dietz/Bolton, P G Wodehouse) Imperial Theater 8 November
1927 **Strike Up the Band** (G Gershwin/Kaufman) Shubert Theater, Philadelphia 5 September
1927 **Funny Face** (ex-*Smarty*) (G Gershwin/Thompson, Paul Gerard Smith) Alvin Theater 22 November
1928 **Rosalie** (G Gershwin, Sigmund Romberg/w Wodehouse/Bolton, William Anthony McGuire) New Amsterdam Theater 10 January
1928 **That's a Good Girl** (Phil Charig, Joseph Meyer/w Douglas Furber, Carter/Furber) London Hippodrome 5 June

1928 **Treasure Girl** (G Gershwin/Thompson, Vincent Lawrence) Alvin Theater 8 November
1929 **Show Girl** (G Gershwin/w Gus Kahn/McGuire, J P McEvoy) Ziegfeld Theater 2 July
1930 **Strike Up the Band** revised version by Morrie Ryskind Times Square Theater 14 January
1930 **Girl Crazy** (G Gershwin/Bolton, Jack McGowan) Alvin Theater 14 October
1931 **Of Thee I Sing** (G Gershwin/Kaufman, Ryskind) Music Box Theater 26 December
1933 **Pardon My English** (G Gershwin/Herbert Fields) Majestic Theater 20 January
1933 **Let 'em Eat Cake** (G. Gershwin/Kaufman, Ryskind) Imperial Theater 21 October
1935 **Porgy and Bess** (G Gershwin/w DuBose Heyward/Heyward) Alvin Theater 10 October
1941 **Lady in the Dark** (Kurt Weill/Moss Hart) Alvin Theater 23 January
1945 **The Firebrand of Florence** (Weill/w Edwin Justus Mayer) Alvin Theater 22 March
1946 **Park Avenue** (Arthur Schwartz/Nunnally Johnson, Kaufman) Shubert Theater 4 November

Biography: *see* Gershwin, George

DIE GESCHIEDENE FRAU Operette in 3 acts by Victor Léon. Music by Leo Fall. Carltheater, Vienna, 23 December 1908.

Victor Léon's particularly sparky libretto for *Die geschiedene Frau* ('the divorced woman') told a tale of marital mistrust in which Jana van Lysseweghe (Mizzi Zwerenz), the lady of the title, hastily divorces her much-loved husband Karel (Hubert Marischka), after an unsatisfactorily explained episode involving him with a free-loving young actress called Gonda van der Loo (Annie Dirkens) in a railway sleeper. Shades of *Trial By Jury* hover as, after many social and railroad complications, including more than a touch of blackmail and sexual misbehaviour, the dazzling Miss van der Loo is paired off with the divorce court judge, Lucas van Deesteldonck (Richard Waldemar), whilst the foolish, loving couple who should never have been divorced are remarried. Karl Blasel was Pieter te Bakkensijl, Jana's father and the head of the Wagons-Lits company, whilst Max Rohr (Willem Krouwevliet) and Mizzi Jesel (Martje) played a simple and happily married Dutch couple, devoted to the central pair.

Leo Fall's score was in his happiest and brightest style and supplied the star soubrette, in the rôle of the sexy actress, with a splendid series of songs and duos, highlighted by the waltzes 'O Schlafcoupé, O Schlafcoupé' in which she describes the pleasures of rail travel in a sleeper berth, and the lilting 'Gonda, liebe kleine Gonda', the duo in which the unjustly divorced husband attempts to do the right thing by his blithe co-respondent by dutifully offering to marry her. Karl and Jana shared two attractive duets, a waltz in which they sing together about the time-honoured encounter between a masked husband and wife ('Kind, du kannst tanzen wie meine Frau') and the second which brings the show to a soaringly reconciled curtain ('Du, ach du bist wieder mein'). The humorous musical moments included a comical burlesque funeral march for the blackmailing sleeping-car attendant Scrop (Josef König) and a heavily-accented quintet featuring the Krouwevliets ('O Echestand, O Echestand, wie schön bist du'), and the dancing ones a display of the Roger de Coverley, a novelty dance display by Gonda to the strains of the marching 'Ich und du, Müllers Kuh' and a comical one, in tandem with Scrop, to 'Man steigt nach!'.

The Carltheater production of *Die geschiedene Frau* was a first-rate hit. With the billing of the two big female stars solved by simply placing their names in a cross formation, it played at the managerless theatre through 126 nights to the end of the season, then returned after the summer to run up its total to 227 nights under the management of newly installed Sigmund Eibenschütz. By the end of 1909 that total read 256 performances, and the show continued to be played in repertoire at the Carltheater until 1915 as it turned itself into one of the most popular musical comedies of its time, throughout Germany and Austria.

That popularity was confirmed almost everywhere else that the piece was played. Hungary, as usual, was first off the mark, with a Király Színház production starring Vilma Medgyaszay as *Elvált asszony* ('the divorced girl', ad Andor Gábor), Ilka Pálmay as Gonda, Ernő Király as Karel and Mihály Papp as Scrop. A fine success, it played its 100th night on 26 December 1916, and has continued to be revived in Hungary since. England's Adrian Ross dropped the element of 'divorce' from the title and instead turned the focus on to the little marriage-breaker who was the real star of the show, calling the piece *The Girl on the Train*. George Edwardes cast Phyllis Dare as Gonda, with Robert Evett (Karel), Clara Evelyn (Jana) and a set of top comedians – Huntley Wright (Judge), Fred Emney (Scrop) and Rutland Barrington (father, now called Lucas van Tromp), and added one Theo Wendt number to the score to allow Wright and Barrington to vocally justify their billing. The result was a 340-performance West End triumph which was followed by years of touring and productions throughout the English-language theatre world.

One of these was in America, where Charles Dillingham had the piece readapted, under – give or take a preposition – the London title, by Harry B Smith, with songs by Clare Kummer and Carter de Haven added, and played by a cast headed by Vera Michelena and Melville Stewart. It proved to be the only major production of the piece which flopped (40 performances). Australia, on the other hand, set in motion a production headed by London's Sybil Arundale (Jana) and Talleur Andrews (Karel), and locals Florence Young (Gonda), W S Percy (Judge), Jack Cannot (Scrop) and Victor Prince (Lucas) with a run of nearly two months in Sydney before *The Girl in the Train* (London version) moved on round the country.

Paris welcomed *La Divorcée* (ad Maurice Vaucaire) to Alphonse Franck's Théâtre Apollo, where Jane Marnac starred as Gonda alongside Henry Defreyn (Karl) and Jane Alba (Jana) with Colombey as Vandenparaboum (father) and Tréville as Van Plottledam (Judge) for a successful run, which earned the show a long provincial life and a reprise in 1924 at the Ba-ta-clan with Odette Darthys as Gonda.

As the stage versions of *Die geschiedene Frau* ran long and often through European theatres, two films were made, the first by Victor Janson in 1926 with Mady Christians featured as Gonda, and the second in 1953 with Marika Rökk starred alongside Johannes Heesters and Hans Nielsen.

Hungary: Király Színház *Elvált asszony* 12 March 1909; Germany: Theater des Westens 2 October 1909; UK: Vaudeville Theatre *The Girl in the Train* 4 June 1910; USA: Globe Theater *The Girl on the Train* 3 October 1910; France: Théâtre Apollo *La Divorcée* 18 February 1911; Australia: Criterion Theatre, Sydney *The Girl on the Train* 4 December 1911; Films: Victor Janson 1926, Georg Jacoby 1953
Recording: Ariola Eurodisc (EP)

GEST, Morris (b Vilna, Russia, 17 January 1881; d New York, 16 May 1942). Broadway producer who had successes with both intimate musicals and with the most extravagant and sometimes titillating of spectaculars.

Gest left Russia as a child to settle in America and he spent his early life in Boston where he made his first forays into the theatre at the age of 19. He subsequently became a ticket tout in New York, married the daughter of David Belasco, and was hired by William Hammerstein to go to Europe and scout for talent. Whilst doing so, he began to fraternize with the competition as represented by F Ray Comstock and in 1905 the two went into partnership. Over the next 23 years they produced both plays and musicals (for a while in a threesome with another Belasco son-in-law, William Elliott), often on a large scale and often with a fondness for the slightly scandalous. Amongst these were included the famous Oscar Asche musical spectaculars *Chu Chin Chow* (1917) and *Mecca* (1920), with its celebrated orgy scene, as well as the period's other major London success *The Maid of the Mountains* (1918), the homegrown *The Beauty Spot* (1909), *Sweet Kitty Bellairs* (1917) and *The Rose of China* (1919), and – on the titillating side – the lavish and scantily dressed *Aphrodite* (1919), and the fairly cleaned-up C B Cochran version of Cuvillier's opérette *Afgar* (1920).

At the other end of the spectrum, Gest was involved with the production and, more particularly, the touring of such modern musical comedies as *Oh, Boy!*, *Leave it to Jane*, *Oh, Lady! Lady!!*, *Oh, My Dear!*, the unfortunate *Zip Goes a Million*, and *Sitting Pretty*. Comstock and Gest's other productions included a number with a Russian or Continental affiliation, notably such events as the Russian ballet, seasons with Duse and the Moscow Art Theatre (1923), the fashionable Russian revue *La Chauve-Souris* (1922), Ibsen in Italian (1923), Max Reinhardt's vast production of *The Miracle* (1924) and the German Passion Plays (1929).

At various times Gest took charge of both the little La Salle Theater, Chicago, and the large Manhattan Opera House and Century Theater in New York as well as the Harmanus-Bleeker Hall in Albany and the Von Quiller in Schenectady. After the end of his association with Comstock, he continued to produce, with less éclat, joining the Shuberts to produce an unsuccessful version of Robert Katscher's Revue-Operette *Wonder Bar* for Al Jolson as one of his last projects.

GET A LOAD OF THIS A surprise musical by James Hadley Chase. Additional dialogue by Arthur Macrae. Music and lyrics by Manning Sherwin and Val Guest. Additional numbers by Arthur Young, Michael Carr and Jack Popplewell, Al Lewis, Larry Stock and Vincent Rose. London Hippodrome, 19 November 1941.

Largely a variety show, disguised as a book musical, *Get a Load of This* was hung together on a gangstery story, by *No Orchids for Miss Blandish* mystery-writer James Hadley Chase, which was usefully set in a night club. Whilst the acts flowed on to the stage of the London Hippodrome (rebuilt to reach out into the audience like a cabaret floor), in a palpable imitation of the Continental hit *Die Wunder-Bar*, the plot continued very much in the background. Vic Oliver, as the compère of the night club, and his stooge Jack Allen ran a show in which vocalist Celia Lipton featured alongside the musical clowns, the Cairoli Brothers, dancers Jeanne Ravel and Jean Barnes and a series of other acts through 698 performances.

In Australia, the show was played on the Tivoli circuit, normally reserved for variety shows, and billed as a twice-daily melodrama-revue. Jenny Howard, Arundel Nixon, Thelma Grigg, George and Joy Nichols, Teddie Scanlon and Eddie Gordon were billed alongsied the Musical Macs and the jugglers, the three Ciscos. After two and a half months of *Get a Load of This* in Melbourne and a further month in Sydney, the Tivolis returned to unadorned variety.

Australia: Tivoli, Melbourne 7 May 1945

GFALLER, Rudolf ('Rudi') (b Vienna, 10 November 1882; d Bad Ischl, 11 February 1972).

The son of a Viennese restaurateur, the young Gfaller went on the stage in children's rôles at the Carltheater under Karl Blasel's management and studied at both the Conservatoire and at drama school before electing a career as an actor. He played at the Fürstl Theater in Rudolstadt, in Wiesbaden, Darmstadt, Magdeburg and at Stralsund, and it was this last theatre which produced the 24-year-old actor's first Operette, *Der Frühlingsonkel*. There followed engagements at Olmütz and, from 1909, in Leipzig where he was engaged for buffo rôles in Operette and, soon after, Gfaller began to compose the music for what became a series of pieces successfully played in the German provinces.

In 1926 he became the resident director and Regisseur of the Leipzig Städtische Bühnen, a position he held until his retirement in 1953, and throughout this period he continued to provide musical scores for Operetten, Possen and revues and even a straight comedy (*Der verflixte Liebe*), many written in collaboration with playwright Carl Bretschneider, and almost all for the Leipzig stage. His most successful piece, however, remained the 1915 *Der dumme August*.

1906 **Der Frühlingsonkel** (Karl Schmalz) Stadttheater, Stralsund 9 February
1914 **Der Windelkavalier** (Martin Martin, Karl Dibbern) Neues Operettentheater, Leipzig 20 February
1915 **Der dumme August** (Bruno Decker, Robert Pohl) Hoftheater, Altenburg 3 November
1917 **Der Mann seiner Frau** (Decker, Pohl) Albert Schumann-Theater, Frankfurt-am-Main August
1918 **Eine Walzernacht** (Decker, Hans Bachwitz) Stadttheater, Erfurt 27 October
1919 **Wenn dich die bösen Buben locken** (Bachwitz, Hans Sturm) Residenztheater, Kassel 9 April
1921 **Der glücklichste Kiebitz** (Decker, Pohl) Stadttheater, Nuremberg 17 April
1929 **Zwischen Rossplatz und Probstheida** (w Franz Jacobs) Panorama, Leipzig 1 January
1931 **Im Hotel zum feurigen Schimmel** (Carl Bretschneider) Panorama, Leipzig 1 November
1931 **Drei Menschen suchen das Glück** Panorama, Leipzig 20 November
1933 **Die Husarenbraut** (Bretschneider) Panorama, Leipzig 1 November

1935 **Der Spürhund** (Bretschneider) Panorama, Leipzig 9 November
1935 **Runter mit'n Zylinder** (Bretschneider) Panorama, Leipzig 24 August
1935 **Immer ohne Sorgen** (*Mein Bruder und ich*) (Bretschneider) Panorama, Leipzig 21 December
1938 **Die Dorfchristel** (Bretschneider) Panorama, Leipzig 19 March
1938 **Drei werden gesucht** (Bretschneider) Panorama, Leipzig 4 November
1939 **Ossi-Ganz grosse** (w Max Neumann) Panorama, Leipzig 16 March
1939 **Die Sacher-Pepi** (Ernst Welisch) Operettentheater, Leipzig 16 September
1939 **Er und seine Frau** (Max Neal) Panorama, Leipzig 9 December
1940 **Der Star von Panorama** (Neal) Panorama, Leipzig 10 September
1941 **Venedig in Wien** (Welisch) Centraltheater, Chemnitz 29 March

Other titles attributed include *Einmal rauf – einmal runter!*, *Hallo, hier Garmisch*

GIGI Musical in 2 acts by Alan Jay Lerner based on the novel by Colette and the screenplay of its film version. Music by Frederick Loewe. Uris Theater, New York, 13 November 1973.

A 1973 attempt to revamp the score and story of the Academy Award-winning MGM musical film *Gigi* (1958) with its champagne-bucketful of hit songs ('Thank Heaven for Little Girls', 'It's a Bore', 'She is Not Thinking of Me', 'The Night They Invented Champagne', 'I Remember it Well', 'I'm Glad I'm Not Young Anymore') as a full-Broadway-sized stage musical hit trouble early on. Having shed its Gigi (lusty British performer Terese Stevens) pre-New York, it then came to grief on its arrival in town (103 performances) with Karin Wolfe replacing. Alfred Drake played Maurice Chevalier (with one of four new musical pieces), otherwise the crusty Uncle Honoré – an invention of the author of the screenplay – Agnes Moorehead and Maria Karnilova were the heroine's Aunt and Grandmother respectively, whilst Daniel Massey (Gaston) serenaded 'Gigi'. The enormous success of *My Fair Lady* on German-speaking stages encouraged productions of *Gigi* in Berlin and Vienna, and Robert Gilbert's German-language version won some success at the Theater des Westens, and the Theater an der Wien (221 performances), where the inspired casting of veteran star Johannes Heesters (Honoré) alongside the ravishing Christiane Rücker (Gigi) helped to produce the most successful stage *Gigi* to date.

Another attempt to bring *Gigi* to the theatrical big time was mounted, under Lerner's instigation, in London a dozen years after the Broadway attempt. It retained the mostly unprepossessing new musical material invented for the Broadway version, but brought the show back down to something nearer to the more intimate and manageable proportions of the original play, with a cast of 17 and an orchestra of ten. With stars Jean-Pierre Aumont (who made 'Little Girls' sound perfectly filthy), Beryl Reid (grandmother), Sîan Phillips (aunt) and Amanda Waring (Gigi) all sadly short on singing ability, an agreeable adaptation was given little chance of success (242 performances).

Austria: Theater an der Wien 10 October 1974; Germany:

Theater des Westens 1976; UK: Lyric Theatre 17 September 1985

Recordings: Original film soundtrack (MGM), French version (Columbia), Spanish version (MGM), original Broadway cast (RCA), German cast (Fair Play), London cast (Safari)

GILBERT, Jean [WINTERFELD, Max] (b Hamburg, 11 February 1879; d Buenos Aires, 20 December 1942). One of the most successful composers for the German musical stage, Gilbert won a brief but enormous world-wide vogue which was interrupted by the First World War.

Winterfeld-Gilbert studied music from an early age in Kiel, Sonderhausen, Weimar and Berlin and became a theatre conductor at the Stadttheater in Bremerhaven at the age of 18. He moved on from there to Hamburg's important Carl-Schultze Theater and then, in 1900, to the Centralhallen-Theater where his first stage work as a composer, *Das Jungfernstift*, was produced in 1901, under the newly acquired and fashionably foreign-sounding pseudonym of Gilbert. The show had sufficient success for it to remain in the provincial lists for several seasons. Gilbert worked at the Apollotheater for two seasons, and had his next two theatre works staged in Hamburg, but he lost his musical director's position in a change of management at the Centralhallen-Theater, and his career regressed as, for some six years, he found conducting engagements only in lesser and provincial venues and even with a circus, and no outlet for his writings. In this time he placed just one work, the short *Onkel Casimir* at Düsseldorf, and for that he abandoned his posh pseudonym and returned to being plain Max Winterfeld.

The turning point came with the production of his hugely successful musical comedy *Polnische Wirtschaft* at Cottbus in December 1909, a success which was followed just two months later by an even more successful musical version of the French play *Fils à Papa*, produced as *Die keusche Susanne* at Magdeburg in February 1910. The first of the famous pair ran up a vast first series in Berlin whilst the second piece proved a major hit not only in Germany but, most notably, in France (*La Chaste Susanne*), Britain (*The Girl in the Taxi*) and Spain (*La casta Suzanna*), and its favourite songs became the hits of the period.

This double triumph swiftly earned Gilbert a return to Berlin and a post at the Thalia-Theater where, replacing Victor Holländer and Max Schmidt as the purveyor of musical scores to Kren and Schönfeld's texts, he produced a veritable gusher of musical comedies over the next few years, ranging himself alongside Walter Kollo as the most prolific and popular German theatre composer of the era. His output, between 1910 and 1914, included such grand and exportable successes as the revamped metropolitan *Polnische Wirtschaft*, *Autoliebchen* ('Ja, das haben die Mädel so gern'), *Puppchen* ('Puppchen, du bist mein Augenstern'), *Die Kino-Königin* ('In der Nacht') and *Die Tangoprinzessin*. Vienna, Budapest (*Az ártatlan Zsusi*, *Lengyel menyecske*, *Az autó tündére*, *A mozitündér*, *Buksi*), Paris (*La Chaste Susanne*) and New York (*Modest Suzanne*, *The Queen of the Movies*, *A Modern Eve*) all welcomed his works and, following the enormous British success of *The Girl in the Taxi*, Gilbert became the most sought-after composer in Britain. His *Autoliebchen* (*The Joy Ride Lady*), *Fräulein Tralala* (*Mam'zelle Tralala*, *Oh! Be Careful*) and *Die Kino-Königin*

(*The Cinema Star*) were all produced in London's West End in a period of little over three months, but Gilbert's London career was cut short by the war. *Die Kino-Königin* was forced out of town at the height of what looked like being a hugely successful run, and George Edwardes, who had purchased the English-language rights to *Puppchen* and *Die Tangoprinzessin*, as well as hiring Gilbert to write the original score for a new musical for the Adelphi Theatre, was obliged to abandon all German-flavoured plans.

Although his most promising overseas outlet was now closed, Gilbert continued to produce regular and mostly successful musical comedies for the German, Austrian and Hungarian stages – *Die Döse seine Majestät* (*Jojó három võlegenye* in Budapest), *Die Fräulein von Amt* (*O, Terez!*), *Arizonda*, *Die Fahrt ins Glück* (*Az aranyfácán*), *Das Vagabundenmädel* (*A csavargolány*), *Blondinchen*, the little *Eheurlaub* – throughout the First World War, along with scores of songs for some morale-manufacturing patriotic pieces. In 1919 he essayed a slightly more substantial score with the romantic *Die Frau im Hermelin*, and the result was his biggest international success since *Die keusche Susanne*, with London in particular fêting Gilbert's return to its stages by welcoming Phyllis Dare as *The Lady of the Rose* to Daly's Theatre for more than 500 performances. This was a total reached by only two other West End musicals in the years following the War and prior to the arrival of the fashion for American musicals. One of the two was Vienna's *Lilac Time*, the other was Gilbert's most wide-flung success *Katja, die Tänzerin* which, produced in Vienna, followed up its German-language success by triumphing through Europe and from London (Daly's Theatre, 501 performances) to Australia.

Das Weib im Purpur (played in Hungary as *A biborruhás asszony*), *Die kleine Sünderin* ('In Berlin an der Ecke von der Kaiserallee', *A kis huncut* in Budapest) and the small-scale *Dorine und der Zufall*, which was played for nearly 200 nights at the Theater am Zoo, then at the Artushof-Theater, in Vienna and Budapest (*Dorine és a véletlen*), were all produced with success in 1922–3. *Geliebte seiner Hoheit* was played at the Theater am Nollendorfplatz with Fritzi Massary and in Hungary as *A nagy nö*, and the Schiller Theater happily hosted *Annemarie* ('Durch Berlin fliesst immer noch die Spree!') before Gilbert, who had sponsored tours of his own works for nearly a decade, began to expand his interests in the business side of the theatre.

He formed a firm to set up an ambitious international musical theatre circuit, but his grandiose projects failed and left him in a financially parlous state. He attempted to recoup his losses by writing for the cinema and by allowing all sorts of depredations to be practised on his works overseas. His name appeared as composer of what was virtually a new musical availing itself of some of his *Das Weib im Purpur* score, and staged by the Shuberts on Broadway as *The Red Robe*, and again on a London piece made up of a libretto apparently borrowed from his 1924 *Zwei um Eine*, some Vernon Duke songs and some of the score of his reasonably successful *Uschi*, which had already been played in Budapest (*Csak egy kislany*), all mixed together under the title *Yvonne* (280 performances). He also came up with one last success in *Hotel Stadt Lemberg* (1929), which reached Broadway as *Marching By* and Budapest under its original title. However, his best moments as a composer were now past, both at home and in the almost always supportive British theatre where his last representations were sad ones: Edward Laurillard's production of *Lovely Lady* (1932) lasted three performances, and a mishmash called *The Girl from Cooks* was unhappily served up at the Gaiety Theatre in 1927 for 34 performances.

In 1933, under the threat of Nazi rule, Gilbert left Germany and went successively to Vienna, where his *Die Dame mit der Regenbogen* was produced for 72 performances at the Theater an der Wien, and then, with his career effectively ended, to Paris, London, Barcelona and Madrid before finally emigrating in 1939 to Buenos Aires where he promoted the fourth film of his enduring *Die keusche Susanne* prior to his death in 1942.

1901 **Das Jungfernstift** (*Comtesse Marie*) (Ernest Guinot ad Max von Ritterfeld) Centralhallen-Theater, Hamburg 8 February

1903 **Der Prinzregent** (Hans Forsten) Carl-Schultze Theater, Hamburg 12 September

1903 **Jou-Jou** (Hans Buchholz) Centralhallen-Theater, Hamburg 23 October

1908 **Onkel Casimir** (as Max Winterfeld/Heinz Gorden) 1 act Apollotheater, Düsseldorf 1 November

1909 **Polnische Wirtschaft** (Alfred Schönfeld/Kurt Kraatz, Georg Okonkowski) Stadttheater, Cottbus 26 December; Thalia-Theater, Berlin 6 August 1910

1910 **Die keusche Susanne** (Schönfeld/Okonkowski) Wilhelm-Theater, Magdeburg 26 February

1910 **Die lieben Ottos** (Schönfeld/Jean Kren) Thalia-Theater 30 April

1911 **Die moderne Eva** (Schönfeld/Okonowski) Neues Operettentheater 11 November

1912 **Autoliebchen** (Schönfeld/Kren) Thalia-Theater 16 March

1912 **So bummeln wir** (Gustav Kadelburg) Theater Gross-Berlin 21 November

1912 **Puppchen** (Schönfeld/Kren, Kraatz) Thalia-Theater 19 December

1912 **Die elfte Muse** (Okonkowski) Operettentheater, Hamburg 22 November

1913 **Die Reise um die Erde in vierzig Tagen** (Julius Freund) Metropoltheater 13 September

1913 **Die Tango-Prinzessin** (Kren, Kraatz) Thalia-Theater 4 October

1913 **Die Kino-Königin** revised *Die elfte Muse* ad Julius Freund Metropoltheater 8 March

1913 **Fräulein Tralala** (Leo Leipziger/Okonkowski) Neues Luisen-Theater, Königsberg 15 November

1914 **Die Sünde der Lulatsch** (Hugo Doblin) Centraltheater, Chemnitz 15 March

1914 **Wenn der Frühling kommt!** (Schönfeld/Kren, Okonkowski) Thalia-Theater 28 March

1914 **Kam'rad Männe** (Schönfeld/Kren, Okonkowski) Thalia-Theater 3 August

1914 **Woran wir denken** (Franz Arnold, Walter Turszinksy) Metropoltheater 25 December

1915 **Drei Paar Schuhe** (Schönfeld/Carl Görlitz ad Kren) Thalia-Theater 10 September

1915 **Jung muss man sein** (Leipziger/Erich Urban) Komische Oper 27 August

1915 **Die Fräulein von Amt** (Okonowski, Ernst Arnold) Theater des Westens 2 September

1915 **Der tapfere Ulan** (Karl Herrmann) Komische Oper 20 November

1916 **Arizonda** (Felix Dörmann) Apollotheater, Vienna 1 February

1916 **Blondinchen** (Schönfeld/Jean Kren, Kurt Kraatz) Thalia-Theater 4 March

1916 **Die Fahrt ins Glück** (F Arnold, Ernst Bach) Theater des Westens 2 September

1916 **Das Vagabundenmädel** (Schönfeld/Kren, Buchbinder) Thalia-Theater 2 December

1917 **Die Dose seiner Majestät** (Leo Walther Stein, Rudolf Presber) Komische Oper 7 March

1917 **Der verliebte Herzog** (aka *Der verliebte Prinz*) (Okonkowski, Hans Bachwitz) Theater des Westens 1 September

1918 **Der ersten Liebe goldene Zeit** (Leo Kastner) Zentraltheater, Dresden 8 March, Theater des Westens 1920

1918 **Eheurlaub** (Julius Horst, Bachwitz) Liebich-Theater, Breslau 1 August; Apollotheater, Vienna 1 May 1919

1919 **Zur wilden Hummel** (Kren, Eduard Ritter) Thalia-Theater 19 March

1919 **Die schönste von allen** (Okonkowski) Centraltheater 22 March

1919 **Die Frau im Hermelin** (Rudolf Schanzer, Ernst Welisch) Theater des Westens 23 August

1920 **Der Geiger von Lugano** (Schanzer, Welisch) Wallner Theater 25 September

1921 **Onkel Muz** (Bruno Decker, Robert Pohl) Apollotheater, Halle am Saale 2 April

1921 **Die Braut des Lucullus** (Schanzer, Welisch) Theater des Westens 26 August

1921 **Princess Olala** (Schanzer, Rudolf Bernauer) Berliner Theater 17 September

1922 **Katja, die Tänzerin** (Leopold Jacobson, Rudolf Österreicher) Johann Strauss-Theater, Vienna 5 January

1922 **Dorine und der Zufall** (Grünbaum, Wilhelm Sterk) Neues Theater am Zoo 15 September

1922 **Die kleine Sünderin** (Hans Hellmut Zerlett, Willy Prager) Wallner-Theater 1 October

1923 **Das Weib im Purpur** (Jacobson, Österreicher) Wiener Stadttheater, Vienna 21 December

1923 **Der Gauklerkönig** (Presber, L W Stein, Zerlett)

1924 **Zwei um Eine** (Jacobson)

1924 **Geliebte seiner Hoheit** (Bernauer, Österreicher) Theater am Nollendorfplatz, Berlin 24 September

1925 **Uschi** (Leon Kastner, Alfred Möller) Carl-Schultze Theater, Hamburg 24 January; Theater in der Kommandantenstrasse, Berlin March

1925 **Annemarie** (Robert Gilbert/Okonkowski, Martin Zickel) Schillertheater 2 July

1925 **Das Spiel um die Liebe** (Schanzer, Welisch) Theater des Westens 18 December

1925 **Lebenskünstler** Zentraltheater, Dresden 25 December

1926 **Lene, Lotte, Liese, Josefinens Tochter** (w R Gilbert/Okonkowski) Thalia-Theater 14 January

1926 **In der Johannisnacht** (R Gilbert) Thalia Theater, Hamburg 1 July

1926 **Yvonne** pastiche of *Uschi* et al (w Vernon Duke/lib credited to Percy Greenbank) Palace Theatre, London 22 May

1927 **The Girl from Cooks** (w Raymond Hubbell/R H Burnside, Greatrex Newman) Gaiety Theatre, London 1 November

1928 **Eine Nacht in Kairo** (Bruno Hardt-Warden, Jacobson) Zentraltheater, Dresden 22 December

1928 **The Red Robe** (H B Smith) Shubert Theater, New York 25 December

1929 **Hotel Stadt Lemberg** (Ernst Neubach) Deutsches Schauspielhaus, Hamburg 1 July

1930 **Das Mädel am Steuer** (Schanzer, Welisch) Komische Oper 17 September

1932 **Lovely Lady** (Zerlett, R Gilbert ad Arthur Wimperis) Phoenix Theatre, London 25 February

1933 **Die Dame mit dem Regenbogen** (Julius Brammer, Gustav Beer) Theater an der Wien 25 August

GILBERT, Olive (b Carmarthen; d Hove, 19 February 1981). British contralto who became an institution in the musicals of Ivor Novello.

After a sizeable career in opera, mostly with the Carl Rosa touring company, Miss Gilbert appeared on the light musical stage for the first time in Ivor Novello's *Glamorous Night* (1935), playing the rôle of an opera singer. However, the stocky, middle-aged contralto eventually replaced Elisabeth Welch in the larger rôle of the seductively-toned stowaway ('Shanty Town'). Novello provided her with increasingly important and staunchly suitable rôles in each of his subsequent shows – Madame Simonetti in *Careless Rapture*, Queen Manuelita in *Crest of the Wave*, the booming singing teacher Cäcilie Kurt in *The Dancing Years* ('Fold Your Wings'), Agnes Sorel in the opera-within-a-musical in *Arc de Triomphe* (which she doubled with her rôle in *The Dancing Years* with the aid of a quick mid-evening switch of theatres), perhaps the most grateful of all, Ernestine/Mrs Bridport in *Perchance to Dream* ('Highwayman Love', 'We'll Gather Lilacs'), and, finally, the heroine's confidante, Countess Lemainken in *King's Rhapsody* ('Fly Home, Little Heart').

Between repeating her Novello rôles on tour, on film and abroad, she later appeared as Sister Margaretta in London's *The Sound of Music* (1961) for five and a half years, and as The Housekeeper in the London production of *Man of La Mancha* (1968). Her final appearance was, largely billed, in a number-three touring production of *King's Rhapsody*.

Novello's fondness for and fidelity to Miss Gilbert meant that she is largely responsible for the existence of a contralto repertoire in the post-Gilbert and Sullivan musical theatre in Britain.

GILBERT, Robert [WINTERFELD, David Robert] (b Berlin, 29 September 1899; d Minusio, 20 March 1978).

The son of Jean Gilbert, Robert Gilbert led an early career doubling playwriting and composing, providing lyrics for his father's *Annemarie*, sharing the composing of the score of *Lene, Lotte, Liese, Josefinens Tochter* with him, and adapting de Flers, de Caillavet and Rey's *La Belle Aventure* as the libretto for his musical play *In der Johannisnacht*. He also ventured book, music and lyrics for the 1928 *Aeffchen* and composed the whole music for Zerlett's *Leichte Isabell* and the Deutsches Künstlertheater's *Prosit Gipsy* ('... he has inherited as little talent as is usual'), but found a first genuine success when he supplied the lyrics and one delightfully jaunty song ('Was kann der Sigismund dafür') for the Ralph Benatzky musical *Im weissen Rössl*.

After the Second World War, he collaborated on the reorganization of *Der schwarze Hecht* into the successful *Feuerwerk*, remade some of his father's early successes, but, most successfully, became the principal adaptor of American musicals for the German-speaking stage, with the local versions of *My Fair Lady* and *Hello, Dolly!* amongst his credits.

His contribution to the musical film included the lyrics to Werner Heymann's music for the spectacular *Der Kongress tanzt* (1931, 'Just Once for All Time' etc).

1925 **Annemarie** (Jean Gilbert/Georg Okonkowski, Martin Zickel) Schillertheater 2 July
1926 **Lene, Lotte, Liese, Josefinens Tochter** (w J Gilbert/Okonkowski) Thalia-Theater 14 January
1926 **In der Johannisnacht** (J Gilbert) Thalia-Theater, Hamburg 1 July
1926 **Leichte Isabell** (Hans Hellmut Zerlett) Schillertheater 1 July
1927 **Pit-Pit** (Zerlett) Centraltheater, Dresden 19 February
1928 **Aeffchen** Centraltheater, Dresden 23 March
1928 **Die Männer von Manon** (Walter Goetze/w August Neidhart) Kleines Haus, Düsseldorf 30 September
1929 **Prosit Gipsy** (Neidhart, Henry) Deutsches Künstlertheater, Berlin 19 April
1931 **Im weissen Rössl** (Ralph Benatzky/Hans Müller) Grosses Schauspielhaus 8 November
1932 **Lovely Lady** (Gilbert/w Zerlett ad Arthur Wimperis) Phoenix Theatre, London 25 February
1933 **Zwei Herzen im Dreivierteltakt** (aka *Der verlorene Walzer*) (Robert Stolz/Paul Knepler, Ignaz M Welleminsky) Stadttheater, Zurich 30 September
1934 **Grüezi** (aka *Servus, Servus, Himmelblaue Träume*) (Stolz/'Georg Burkhard') Stadttheater, Zurich 3 November
1936 **Rise and Shine** (aka *Darling You*) original German lyrics (Theatre Royal, Drury Lane, London)
1936 **Gloria und der Clown** (Stolz/w Julius Horst) Stadttheater, Aussig 31 December
1937 **Herzen im Schnee** (Benatzky/w Henry Gilbert, Armin Robinson) Volksoper 8 September
1937 **Die Reise um die Erde in 80 Minuten** (Robert Stolz/w Hugo Wiener, H Gilbert) Volksoper 22 December
1950 **Ihr erster Walzer** (Oscar Straus/w Paul Knepler, Robinson) Bayerisches Stadttheater, Munich 31 March
1950 **Feuerwerk** (Paul Burkhard/Erik Charell, Jürg Amstein) revised *Der schwarze Hecht* Bayerische Staatsoper, Munich 16 May
1953 **Mädi** revised lyrics (Stadttheater, Zurich)
1955 **Signorina** (Stolz/w Per Schwenzen) Städtische Bühnen, Nürnberg-Fürth 23 April
1956 **Eine kleine Schwindel in Paris** (Stolz/Rudolf Weys) Theater in der Josefstadt, Vienna 25 December
1957 **Hopsa** revised version (Burkhard/w Robinson/Paul Baudisch, Robinson) Wiesbaden 12 October
1959 **Kitty und die Weltkonferenz** (aka *Die kleine und die grosse Welt*) (Stolz/Kurt Nachmann, Peter Preses) Theater in der Josefstadt, Vienna 4 February
1959 **Die Blaue von Himmel** (Friedrich Holländer/w Schwenzen) Städtische Bühnen, Nürnberg-Fürth 14 November
1961 **Die Kino-Königin** revised version (Opernhaus, Nuremberg)
1961 **My Fair Lady** German version (Theater des Westens)
1962 **Lili** (*Carnival*) German version (Stadttheater, Zurich)
1962 **Trauminsel** revised *Signorina* (Bregenz)
1962 **Die Dame mit der Brille** (Burkhard/w Karl Suter) Schauspielhaus, Zurich 31 December
1963 **Annie, schiess los!** (*Annie Get Your Gun*) German version (Theater des Westens)
1965 **Can-Can** German lyrics (Kleinen Haus, Staatstheater, Stuttgart)
1965 **Wie man was wird im Leben, ohne sich anzustrengen** (*How to Succeed in Business Without Really Trying*) German version w Gerhard Bronner (Theater an der Wien)
1966 **Hallo, Dolly!** (*Hello, Dolly!*) German version (Schauspielhaus, Düsseldorf)
1967 **Wie lernt man Liebe** (Mischa Spoliansky/ad) Bayerisches Staatsoper, Munich 5 March
1967 **Charleys Tante** (Ralph Maria Siegel/w Max Colpet) Deutsches Theater, Munich 9 March
1968 **Der Mann von la Mancha** (*Man of la Mancha*) German version (Theater an der Wien)
1969 **Hochzeit am Bodensee** revised *Grüezi* (Bregenz)
1969 **Illya Darling** German version (Schauspielhaus, Düsseldorf)

1970 **Canterbury Tales** German version (Theater am Goethe-platz, Bremen)
1970 **Cabaret** German version (Theater an der Wien)
1971 **Sorbas** (*Zorba*) German version w Bronner (Theater an der Wien)
1972 **Karusell** (*Carousel*) German version (Volksoper)
1972 **Godspell** German lyrics (Hamburg)
1973 **Oklahoma!** German version (Münster)
1980 **Brigadoon** German version (Staatstheater, Karlsruhe)

GILBERT, W[illiam] S[chwenk] (b London, 18 November 1836; d Harrow Weald, 29 May 1911). The most talented librettist and lyricist for – and, as one half of the show-writing tandem Gilbert and Sullivan, the modern flagbearer of – the 19th-century English-language theatre.

Originally destined for a legal career, Gilbert swiftly abandoned the law to take up writing. The most effective of his earliest work, mostly for humorous magazines such as *Fun*, was in the form of comic verses, and some of these, written under the pseudonym of 'Bab', brought him particular renown. They were subsequently collected into book form in 1869 under the title *The Bab Ballads*.

Gilbert began writing for the theatre in his twenties, making his début with the short play, *Hush a Bye*, produced by the eccentric W H C Nation at Astley's Theatre, but he won his first real success in the realm of burlesque. His *Dulcamara* (1866), a burlesque of Donizetti's *L'Elisir d'amore*, *La Vivandière* (1867), which took the same composer's *La Fille du régiment* as its basis, a *Bohemian Girl* parody called *The Merry Zingara*, the Gaiety Theatre's opening *Robert the Devil* (1868), a *Norma* burlesque called *The Pretty Druidess* (1869) and *The Princess* (1870), a burlesque based not, for once, on an opera but on Tennyson's poem, all won notice as particularly intelligently made and classy examples of the genre.

By the time he abandoned the pasticcio burlesque, Gilbert had already begun to branch out in different areas. In 1869 he had considerable success with some short comic operettas written for the German Reeds' Gallery of Illustration, whilst the following year he scored a hit with the play *The Palace of Truth*. This was followed by other plays equally as successful, largely based on whimsical or supernatural notions, and including *Pygmalion and Galatea* (1871) and *The Wicked World* (1873), a piece which – under the pseudonym of 'F Latour Tomline' – he used as the basis for a burlesque *The Happy Land*. *The Happy Land* won him a different kind of notice – it was stopped in mid-performance by a detective and banned by the Lord Chamberlain, allegedly for 18 pages of interpolations not in the approved script, but in reality for its ridiculing of government and the representation of Mr Gladstone on the parody stage.

On the musical comedy front, his *No Cards*, *Ages Ago*, *Our Island Home*, *A Sensation Novel* and *Happy Arcadia* all proved highly popular at the little 'drawing room entertainment' purveyed by the Reed family and their friends, and, while they prospered, Gilbert made his first venture into a full-length musical play with a piece based on the theory of metempsychosis, *The Gentleman in Black*, set to music by his preferred collaborator Frederic Clay. *The Gentleman in Black*, which held the seeds of many of the topsy-turvy ideas that Gilbert would later use repeatedly in his more famous works, played for 26 performances, but another,

Plate 106. **W S Gilbert.**

shorter piece in a similar vein, *Creatures of Impulse*, won a number of further productions, both with and without its Randegger score. Gilbert returned to the area of burlesque and extravaganza when he was commissioned to write a Christmas entertainment for the Gaiety Theatre. On this occasion, he was paired with the white hope of the light musical theatre, the young Arthur Sullivan, as his composer, and their joint effort, a jolly festive 'grotesque opera' called *Thespis* served the Gaiety's purposes more than adequately.

The author and composer were paired again when they produced a 1-act curtain-raiser, *Trial By Jury*, for Selina Dolaro's *La Périchole* company, but when the actress/manager Kate Santley commissioned a full-length comic opera from Gilbert, it was to his old collaborator of the Gallery of Illustration and *The Gentleman in Black*, Freddie Clay, that he turned for music. In spite of the special wit of some of its text and the charm of its score, the production of *Princess Toto*, dogged by backstage problems, was only a half-success.

The author's next commission came from the former company manager of the Selina Dolaro company, Richard D'Oyly Carte, and he reconstituted the Gilbert/Sullivan partnership for the occasion. The resulting piece, *The Sorcerer*, set in motion the phenomenon which would become 'the Savoy operas'. The success of the witty and whimsical English version of the opéra-bouffe form in which Gilbert excelled, and of which *The Sorcerer* was his best example to date, was confirmed with wild international success by its successor, *HMS Pinafore*, as manager Carte, author Gilbert and composer Sullivan set forth on a decade of work together which was to become one of the wonders of the theatrical world. Together, they produced, first for the old Opera Comique and then for the Savoy Theatre built by D'Oyly Carte to house his productions, *The Pirates of Penzance, Patience, Iolanthe, Princess Ida* (a remake of *The Princess*), *The Mikado, Ruddigore, The Yeomen of the Guard* and *The Gondoliers*, each of which followed its London run by an international career of greater or, just occasionally, lesser dimensions.

After *The Gondoliers*, the tensions which had grown up among the trio resulted in Gilbert breaking with the other two members of the team. He continued, however, to write for the musical stage and combined, with only limited success, with Alfred Cellier on *The Mountebanks* and with George Grossmith on a musical version of his old adaptation of *Le Chapeau de paille d'Italie* under the title *Haste to the Wedding*, before the breach at the Savoy was pasted over. He rejoined Sullivan – who had been no more successful away from him – for two final pieces, *Utopia (Limited)* and *The Grand Duke*. Neither reached the level of the earlier Savoy pieces, and, after the comparative failure of *The Grand Duke*, the collaboration was put to rest.

Gilbert subsequently wrote a libretto and lyrics worthy of his better days for the comic opera *His Excellency* (1894), set to music by Osmond Carr, the play *The Fairies' Dilemma* (1904), and an unsuccessful musical adaptation of his *The Wicked World* composed by Edward German under the title *Fallen Fairies*, but he was unable to find a producer for his last musical in a world which had moved well away from the style of Victorian comic opera in which he had made his name.

1866 **Dulcamara, or the Little Duck and the Great Quack** (pasticcio arr van Hamme) St James's Theatre 29 December
1867 **La Vivandière, or True to the Corps** (pasticcio arr Ferdinand Wallerstein) St James's Hall, Liverpool 15 June; Queen's Theatre, London 22 January 1868
1868 **The Merry Zingara, or the Tipsy Gipsy and the Pipsy Wipsy** (pasticcio) Royalty Theatre 21 March
1868 **Robert the Devil, or the Nun, the Dun and the Son of a Gun** (pasticcio arr Kettenus) Gaiety Theatre 21 December
1869 **The Pretty Druidess, or the Mother, the Maid and the Mistletoe Bough** Charing Cross Theatre 19 June
1869 **No Cards** (Thomas German Reed) 1 act Gallery of Illustration 29 March
1869 **Ages Ago** (Frederic Clay) 1 act Gallery of Illustration 22 November
1870 **The Princess** (pasticcio) Olympic Theatre 8 January
1870 **The Gentleman in Black** (Clay) Charing Cross Theatre 26 May
1870 **Our Island Home** (German Reed) 1 act Gallery of Illustration 20 June
1871 **A Sensation(al) Novel** (German Reed) 1 act Gallery of Illustration 30 January
1871 **Creatures of Impulse** (Alberto Randegger) Court Theatre 15 April
1871 **Thespis, or the Gods Grown Old** (Arthur Sullivan) Gaiety Theatre 26 December
1872 **Happy Arcadia** (Clay) Gallery of Illustration 28 October
1873 **The Happy Land** (pasticcio arr A E Bartle/w Gilbert a'Beckett) Court Theatre 3 March
1874 **Topsyturveydom** (Alfred Cellier) Criterion Theatre 21 March
1875 **Trial By Jury** (Sullivan) 1 act Royalty Theatre 25 March
1876 **Princess Toto** (Clay) Nottingham 26 June; Strand Theatre, London 2 October
1877 **The Sorcerer** (Sullivan) Opera Comique 17 November
1878 **H M S Pinafore** (Sullivan) Opera Comique 25 May

1880 **The Pirates of Penzance** (Sullivan) Fifth Avenue Theatre, New York 31 December
1881 **Patience** (Sullivan) Opera Comique 23 April
1882 **Iolanthe** (Sullivan) Savoy Theatre 25 November
1884 **Princess Ida** (Sullivan) Savoy Theatre 5 January
1885 **The Mikado** (Sullivan) Savoy Theatre 14 March
1887 **Ruddigore** (Sullivan) Savoy Theatre 22 January
1888 **The Yeomen of the Guard** (Sullivan) Savoy Theatre 3 October
1889 **The Brigands** (*Les Brigands*) English version (Casino Theater, New York)
1889 **The Gondoliers** (Sullivan) Savoy Theatre 7 December
1892 **The Mountebanks** (Cellier) Lyric Theatre 4 January
1892 **Haste to the Wedding** (George Grossmith) Criterion Theatre 27 July
1893 **Utopia (Limited)** (Sullivan) Savoy Theatre 7 October
1894 **His Excellency** (F Osmond Carr) Lyric Theatre 27 October
1896 **The Grand Duke** (Sullivan) Savoy Theatre 7 March
1909 **Fallen Fairies** (Edward German) Savoy Theatre 15 December

Biographies: Browne, E: *W S Gilbert* (London, 1907), Dark, S & Grey, R: *William Schwenk Gilbert; His Life and Letters* (Methuen, London, 1923), Pearson, H: *Gilbert: His Life and Strife* (Methuen, London, 1957), Sutton, M: *W S Gilbert* (Boston, 1975), Cox-Ife, W: *W S Gilbert: Stage Director* (Dobson, London, 1977) etc.

GILFORD, Jack [GELLMAN, Jacob] (b New York, 25 July 1913; d New York, 2 June 1990). Little comic actor whose few Broadway musical appearances included several memorable new shows and rôles.

Originally a vaudeville performer, Gilford appeared on Broadway in revue and, after an appearance at the Metropolitan Opera House as Frosch in *Die Fledermaus*, had his first musical-comedy rôle as the mute, browbeaten King Sextimus in *Once Upon a Mattress* (1959), miming his way unforgettably through a 'Man to Man Talk' about the bees and the birds with his son. His damp-eyed, put-upon kind of comedy got an even more extensive showing when he created the rôle of the fall-guy Roman slave Hysterium in *A Funny Thing Happened on the Way to the Forum* (1962, 'I'm Calm') and he had further fine rôles as the original Herr Schultz in *Cabaret* (1966, 'Meeskite') and as the wayward publisher Jimmy Smith in the 1971 revival of *No, No, Nanette* (1971). In 1985 he appeared in London in the E Y Harburg compilation show *Look to the Rainbow*.

Gilford also appeared regularly in films, repeating his *Funny Thing* rôle for the show's movie version.

Biography: Mostel, K and Gilford, M: *170 Years of Show Business* (Random House, New York, 1978)

GILL, William J

Australian author-comedian Willie Gill had a variegated career in the theatre in his native country. His name appears, in 1867, as stage director for Messrs Coker and Nish at the Melbourne Theatre of Varieties, where he directed and starred in such pieces as the London burlesque *Grin Bushes*, billed as 'Madame Celeste Gill as Miami', and in a version of Byron's *Lucy de Lammermoor*. He later surfaces, in 1871, at the Sydney School of Arts in tandem with his wife, the former Eleanor Deering, in an 'original musical entertainment' called *Laughing Faces* ('rapid changes – marvellous transformations – witty songs – grotesque dances – and faithful representation of eccentric characters') and then again as manager, stage director, sometime author and star at the Royal Victoria Theatre in Sydney in 1872–3. His appearances there included a Captain Crosstree in a remade version of Burnand's famous burlesque *Black-Eyed Susan* (here subtitled 'or All-in-the-Breakdowns'), and the title-rôle of a 'localized and adapted' (by him w S H Banks) version of the London pantomime of *The Yellow Dwarf*, for which he supplied songs ('What Will it Go the Ton?' etc) for his own use.

Gill then took over the city's Queen's Theatre, starring himself and his wife in a series of dramatic and comic rôles from Rip van Winkle to Shallabullah (*Belphegor*) and Jack Gong (*The Green Bushes*), the dramas supported by smaller comic and musical pieces, some of his own making. The season's programme also included his pantomime *The Man in the Moon* (1873, Prince of Larrikins), burlesques such as *The Orange Tree and the Humble Bee* (1873) and his own *Mephistophiles DDD*, and his comedy-drama *Ups and Downs*.

In the later 1870s, Gill crossed to the American west coast and was soon engaged as stage manager for, and an actor alongside Mr and Mrs Willie Edouin in Samuel Colville's company, playing in burlesque, extravaganza and farce comedy. His name first appeared under a title in America when he adapted the Drury Lane pantomime *Babes in the Wood*, in which he appeared as 'The Very Bad Man', as a burlesque extravaganza for Colville's Folly Company. It gained him many years of provincial royalties, and he thereafter continued a career as an author of farce-comedies, extravaganzas, melodramatic musical comedies, star-vehicles and other parti-coloured entertainments which, although roughly written and often little more than a basis on which artists and producers could embroider at will, proved to have a singular place in the less sophisticated theatres of the time.

He moved on to play with Lydia Thompson (Friday in his arrangement of Farnie's *Robinson Crusoe* etc), and with E E Rice's Surprise Party for whom he supplied the extravaganza *Horrors*, long a feature of Rice's repertoire and, like *Our Goblins*, which he wrote and played (as Benjamin Franklin Cobb) to his wife's Mrs Cobb with W C Mitchell's Pleasure Party, seen for many years on the touring circuits. These long-travelling pieces did him and his purse proud, but Gill also managed to hit the jackpot with a success of much more substantial proportions not just once, but twice during his career. The one was in America, where he collaborated with Rice on writing the burlesque *Adonis* (1884), a Broadway record-breaker and one of the most popular home-made musical pieces of its era, and the other in Britain where the American actress Minnie Palmer became an institution as she trouped his Dutch-accented variety-musical-weepie *My Sweetheart* around the provinces, into London, back into the provinces and even through the colonies.

He wrote the play *Mam'selle* (one of a number written with George H Jessop) for opéra-bouffe star Marie Aimée, and provided Tony Hart with a vehicle (*A Toy Pistol*) following the comedian's split with his author-partner Harrigan, but the piece was not successful and only served to emphasize the difference in quality between the writings of Gill and such as Harrigan. He kept on compiling his loose-limbed combinations of musical pot-pourri, low comedy and ingenuous and/or melodramatic sentiment and even bringing them to the cities, when their time was long since past. Some of his later works got short shrift, but Gill kept going, and well into the 1890s he was still around to supply (pseudonymously) the text for, and – in a still-continuing parallel career as a performer – take to the stage in, another vehicle for Minnie Palmer, *The School Girl*.

1873 **Mephistophiles DDD, or Faust and His Fair Marguerite** (pasticcio) Queen's Theatre, Sydney March
1878 **The Babes in the Wood, or Who Killed Cock Robin?** (pasticcio/w Willie Edouin) Eagle Theater 24 December
1879 **Horrors, or the Maharajah of Zogoboad** (pasticcio) Union Square Theater 28 May
1879 **Robinson Crusoe** (pasticcio/H B Farnie ad) Wallack's Theater 12 September
1880 **Our Goblins, or Fun on the Rhine** (pasticcio) Haverley's Theater 14 June
1881 **Billy Taylor** American version (Gaiety Theatre, Boston)
1882 **My Sweetheart** (pasticcio/w Clay Greene) Haverly's 14th Street Theater 14 September
1884 **Little Hendrik Hudson** Tony Pastor's Theater 14 January
1884 **Adonis** (E E Rice) Bijou Theater 4 September
1885 **A Bottle of Ink** (w George H Jessop) Comedy Theater 6 January
1886 **A Toy Pistol** (revised *A Bottle of Ink*) Comedy Theater 20 February
1886 **Arcadia** (pasticcio arr John Braham) Bijou Theater 26 April
1889 **The Seven Ages** (pasticcio) Standard Theater 7 October
1890 **Hendrik Hudson, or the Discovery of Columbus** (arr Watty Hydes, Fred Perkins/w Robert Frazer) 14th Street Theater 18 August
1892 **Miss Blythe of Duluth** Grand Opera House 26 December
1893 **The Rising Generation** Park Theater 11 September
1895 **The School Girl** (Albert Maurice et al/as 'George Manchester') Grand Theatre, Cardiff 21 September
1897 **My Boys** (pasticcio) Manhattan Theater 6 December

GILLE, Philippe [Emmanuel François] (b Paris, 10 December 1831; d Paris, 19 March 1901).

Playwright, art critic, author, journalist and librettist, Philippe Gille worked as an 'expéditionnaire' at the Préfecture de la Seine in his twenties, but found more congenial and theatrical employ in 1861 when he became secretary to the Théâtre Lyrique and a regular contributor to Paris newspapers. This latter career culminated in his taking charge of the famous *Figaro* courrier de théâtre, or theatre gossip, rubrique from 1869, under the nom de plume of 'Masque de fer'.

From his mid-twenties, when he made his entry into the musical theatre with the text for Bizet's *La Prêtresse*, Gille also became a regular supplier of texts for Offenbach's Théâtre des Bouffes-Parisiens, several of his pieces being set by the manager himself, and a number of others by Léo Delibes. If the full-length works on which he worked with Offenbach (*Les Bergers*, *Docteur Ox*) were not amongst the composer's happiest pieces, he had better fortune in his collaboration with Delibes, co-authoring the text for his *La Cour du Roi Pétaud*, and on his one work with Lecocq, the adaptation of Victorien Sardou's *Les Prés Saint-Gervais* as a light opera. However, even his most enduring texts for the light musical stage, the French adaptation of H B Farnie's London musical *Rip van Winkle* and the little one-act piece *Les Charbonniers*, were outshone by his accomplishments in the sphere of grand opera – the libretti for Massenet's

Manon (w Henri Meilhac) and for Delibes's *Lakmé* and *Jean de Nivelle* (w Edmond Gondinet).

Gille also wrote a number of non-musical theatre pieces, collaborating with Eugène Labiche on *Les 30 Millions de Gladiateur* and *Garanti dix ans*, and penned many volumes of poetry, literary criticism and humorous writing.

His *Cent mille francs et ma fille* (w Jaime fils, Théâtre Déjazet 11 April 1868), adapted by Dorn and with music composed by Ludwig Gothov-Grüneke replacing the original accompaniment provided by Costé, was played at Vienna's Theater in der Josefstadt as *100,000 Gulden und meine Tochter* (18 January 1879).

1857 **Vent du Soir, ou l'horrible festin** (Jacques Offenbach) 1 act Théâtre des Bouffes-Parisiens 16 May
1860 **Monsieur de Bonne-Étoile** (Léo Delibes/[w Adolphe Jaime]) 1 act Théâtre des Bouffes-Parisiens 4 February
1860 **L'Omelette à la Follembuche** (Delibes) 1 act Théâtre des Bouffes-Parisiens 4 February
1860 **Les Valets de Gascogne** (Alfred Dufresne) 1 act Théâtre Lyrique 2 June
1860 **Maître Palma** (Mlle Rivay/w Eugène Furpille) 1 act Théâtre Lyrique 17 June
1860 **L'Hôtel de la [Rue de la] Poste** (Dufresne) 1 act Théâtre des Bouffes-Parisiens 15 November
1861 **Les Deux Cadis** (Théodore Imbert/w Furpille) 1 act Théâtre Lyrique 8 March
1864 **Le Serpent à plumes** (Delibes/w Cham) 1 act Théâtre des Bouffes-Parisiens 16 December
1865 **Le Boeuf Apis** (Delibes/w Furpille) Théâtre des Bouffes-Parisiens 15 April
1865 **Les Bergers** (Offenbach/w Hector Crémieux) Théâtre des Bouffes-Parisiens 11 December
1866 **Tabarin duelliste** (Léon Pillaud/w Furpille) 1 act Théâtre des Bouffes-Parisiens 13 April
1866 **Le Sacripant** (Jules Duprato) Fantaisies-Parisiennes 24 September
1868 **Les Horreurs de la Guerre** (Jules Costé) Cercle des Mirlitons/Théâtre de l'Athénée 9 December
1869 **L'Écossais de Chatou** (Delibes/w Jaime) Théâtre des Bouffes-Parisiens
1869 **La Cour du Roi Pétaud** (Delibes/w Jaime) Théâtre des Variétés 26 April
1871 **La Tour du chien vert** (Duprato) Théâtre des Folies-Dramatiques 21 December
1874 **Les Prés Saint-Gervais** (Charles Lecocq/w Victorien Sardou) Théâtre des Variétés 14 November
1876 **Pierrette et Jacquot** (Offenbach/w Jules Noriac) Théâtre des Bouffes-Parisiens 13 October
1877 **Le Docteur Ox** (Offenbach/w Arnold Mortier) Théâtre des Variétés 26 January
1877 **Les Charbonniers** (Costé) 1 act Théâtre des Variétés 4 April
1882 **Rip!** (*Rip van Winkle*) French version w Meilhac (Théâtre des Folies-Dramatiques)

GILLETTE DE NARBONNE Opéra-comique in 3 acts by Henri Chivot and Alfred Duru founded on *La Femme courageuse* by Boccaccio and on Shakespeare's *All's Well That Ends Well*. Music by Edmond Audran. Théâtre des Bouffes-Parisiens, Paris, 11 November 1882.

Produced by Bouffes-Parisiens director Louis Cantin on the heels of the huge success of Audran's *La Mascotte*, *Gillette de Narbonne* gave Cantin yet another substantial success. The libretto, set in the same medieval times which had encouraged Hervé's opéra-bouffe extravagances, was comic rather than burlesque, with its story of pretty Gillette (Mlle Montbazon) who takes advantage of a favour from the King (Riga) to be granted her childhood sweetheart's hand in marriage. His masculine vanity piqued at this 'ladies' choice', her Roger (Louis Morlet) goes off to war and there asserts his bruised manhood in the dark with Rosita (Marie Gélabert), the young wife of his foolish companion, Griffardin (Édouard Maugé). When he gets home from the wars and finds Gillette has given birth he is piqued all over again, but then she produces the ring that he gave his paramour in the dark and the thwarted Roger at least knows that he is the father of his own son.

Audran's score gave its leading players plenty of opportunities, with Gillette being equipped with a waltzing Chanson Provençale, a little 3/8 'Quand on atteint un certain âge' and a reminiscing duo with Roger ('Rappelez-vous nos promenades') in the first act, the 'Chanson du Sergeant Briquet' in her wartime disguise as her own brother, and the duo wooing the ring from Roger ('A votre doigt que vois-je donc') in the second, and a charming ariette ('On m'avait dans un cage') and her final scenes of triumph in the third. Roger had no less than four numbers, and Rosita supplied the soubrette moments with her first-act ronde ('Claudine dans notre village'), the Couplets du Turlututu and a little lullaby (Couplets du Dodo). The light, high tenor music fell to the rôle of Gillette's unfavoured suitor, Prince Olivier (Charles Lamy).

Without quite attaining the huge vogue of *La Mascotte*, *Gillette* ran into the new year and right up to the summer recess, eight solid months of performances, giving Cantin another splendid success to add to those of *Les Mousquetaires au couvent* and *La Mascotte* in the previous two years. The show was not taken up again at the Bouffes, which was well supplied with new pieces and old hits, but it was liberally played in the provinces and it ultimately got a fresh Paris showing in 1935, with Fanély Revoil and André Baugé starring.

In the meanwhile it had also been produced in most of the major European centres including Geneva, Brussels and Zagreb as well as the more regular ones: Budapest (ad Imre Ukki, Lajos Evva as *A gyürü*, ie the ring); London, where Kate Santley, her production and the show (ad H Savile Clarke) were condemned as morally quite beyond the pale but still failed to run more than a few weeks; for 25 nights at Vienna's Theater an der Wien with Adolfine Ziemaier (Gillette), Rosa Streitmann (Rosita), Josef Joseffy (Robert) and Karl Blasel (Griffardin) in a season dominated by the production of Strauss's *Der Zigeunerbaron*, and in Berlin. It was also seen in Rio de Janeiro, but in New York it was performed only in German with Madame Ziemaier again taking the title-rôle alongside Selma Kronold (Rosita), Kemlitz (Roger) and Rank (Griffardin).

Hungary: Népszínház *A gyürü* 10 March 1883; UK: Royalty Theatre *Gilette* 19 November 1883; Germany: Walhalla Theater 24 October 1884; Austria: Theater an der Wien 27 March 1885; USA: Terrace Garden (Ger) 23 May 1887
Recording: complete (Gaîté-Lyrique)

GILMAN, Mabelle (b San Francisco, 1880; d unknown). Broadway leading lady of the turn of the century.

Whilst still at high school in San Francisco, Mabelle Gilman made her first venture into the professional theatre, as the in-the-wings singing voice of actress Edith Crane playing Trilby in the hit show of the moment. She soon moved east, appeared in the chorus at Daly's Theatre, New York, and at 16 played a small rôle in the Broadway production of *The Geisha* (1896, O Kinkoto San). Mixing classic plays and musical theatre, as a member of Daly's house company, she succeeded to the soubrette rôles of the Gaiety musical, *The Circus Girl* (1897, Lucille) and *The Geisha* (1898, Molly) and played the equivalent rôle in *A Runaway Girl* (1898, Alice). She appeared at the Casino Theater in 1899 as the other woman in *In Gay Paree* (Louisette) and in the famous *Les Fêtards* rôle of the demure wife in Ludwig Englander's *The Rounders* (1899, Priscilla), before she created the title-rôle in *The Casino Girl* (1900, Laura Lee) which was exported to London following its New York run in the most successful of the transatlantic attempts to repeat the success of *The Belle of New York*.

She played in the variety musicals *The King's Carnival* (1901) and *The Hall of Fame* (1902), and starred as the heroine of A Baldwin Sloane's pretty *The Mocking Bird* (1902, Yvette Millet) before taking over Lulu Glaser's rôle in *Dolly Varden* (1903, Dolly) for the London season of that piece. She remained in London to take the title-rôle in the 28 performances of Serpette's last musical *Amorelle* (1904, Amorelle) and then retired to a married life as Mrs William E Cory, wife of the President of the Steel Trust.

Perhaps the marriage did not last, for more than a decade later a Mabelle Gilman was to be seen performing on the American vaudeville circuits, alongside her performer husband, Peter Corney. This pair got more column inches over their divorce than their act: a tipsy Corney reminisced too freely over an affair with a hula dancer and his wife was sufficiently unamused to sue for separation.

GIRARDI, Alexander (b Graz, 5 December 1850; d Vienna, 20 April 1918).

The single greatest star of the heyday of the Viennese Operette stage, Girardi and his light comic, light-tenor performances became the much-loved heart of a generation of Operetten, from the earlier days of Johann Strauss and Carl Millöcker to well into the 20th century.

After teenage years spent working in his father's metal-work and locksmith business, the young Girardi made his first appearance on the professional stage in 1869 at the Kurtheater in Rohitsch-Sauerbrunn. Engagements at Krems, Karlsbad, Ischl and Salzburg followed. The last of these proved the most fortunate for the young actor, for his performance there was seen by the playwright O F Berg, who was instrumental in his being engaged, at the age of 20, as a general juvenile at the Vienna Strampfertheater. There, he played often small supporting rôles alongside the theatre's stars Pepi Gallmeyer and Felix Schweighofer, appearing in a series of Possen and Schwänke and finally getting himself properly noticed in a comical rôle as a butler in the Posse *Nur zwei Gläschen*.

When Schweighofer moved on to the Theater an der Wien, Girardi got a few of the comedy rôles that would have been his, but in 1874 he, too, made the move to the Theater an der Wien. He made his début there in June, appearing in three of the eight scenes of O F Berg and Karl Millöcker's revusical *Errinerungen an bessere Zeiten* in

Plate 107. **Alexander Girardi:** *The biggest star the Viennese musical theatre ever knew as the apparently devout Célestin in* Mam'zelle Nitouche.

turn as Hungerl, Hilarion and Morgenstern, a shoemaker. He subsequently appeared in Berg's *Der barmherziger Bruder* and as Falke in *Die Fledermaus*, then still a newish item in the theatre's repertoire, and did well enough to be given his first major creation the following February, appearing alongside Geistinger, Friese, Szika and Karoline Finaly, as the comical servant Blasoni in Johann Strauss's *Cagliostro in Wien*.

He appeared during 1875–6 as Menelaos in *Die schöne Helena*, Jockel in Léon Vasseur's *Die Perle der Wäscherinnen* (*La Blanchisseuse de Berg-op-Zoom*), First Notary in *La Créole*, Mister Bob Cadwallader in Zeller's *Joconde*, Mikroskop in Offenbach's *Der Reise in den Mond* (*Voyage dans la lune*), Pirkholzer in the Posse *Luftschlösser*, created the rôle of Don Domingos in *Der Seekadett* (the principal comedy rôle was the province of Schweighofer) and played Truck in *König Carotte*, with Schweighofer in the title rôle.

In 1877 he appeared in Max Wolf's *Der Porträt-Dame* (Hofmarschall Graf von Loos), created the juvenile light-comedy rôle of Hector de Marsillac in Genée's *Nanon*, played Grévin in *Der galante Vicomte* and Nicolas in Offenbach's *Der Jahrmarkt von Saint-Laurent*, and was given notable billing for the first time when he played Ali Baba in *Königin Indigo*, the revamped version of Strauss's first Operette which was played for just 15 performances. His line of secondary and young comic rôles continued, and 1878 brought him his best chances yet when he was cast as the sweetly gormless peasant boy Andredl, opposite no less a star than Gallmeyer, in Millöcker's *Das verwunschene Schloss*, and in the staunchly tenorial part of the cowardly Jean Grénicheux in the Viennese première of *Die Glocken von Corneville*. His status in the company was still such, however, that it was Gallmeyer, soprano Bertha Olma and comic Carl Adolf Friese who got the billing in the Millöcker piece, and Hermine Meyerhoff and Sofie König, as the two heroines, who were put above the title in Planquette's blockbuster, even though Schweighofer was cast in the main character rôle of the miser.

Strauss's *Blindekuh* (Johann) and Genée's *Der letzte Mohikaner* (Hans Graupe) did not give him similar chances, but 1879–80 saw him cast opposite Marie Geistinger as Charles Favart in Offenbach's *Madame Favart*, a substantial baritone singing rôle with more than a touch of the romantic about it, as the hairdresser Leonard in Millöcker's *Gräfin Dubarry*, as Brududur in the Viennese version of Lecocq's *La Jolie Persane*, Stefan Hoch in *Die Näherin*, the little tailor, Griolet in *Die Tochter des Tambour-Majors*, Benjamin in Adam's *Die Nürnberger Puppe*, Don Sancho d'Avellaneda in Strauss's *Das Spitzentuch der Königin* and Marcu, yet another young peasant, in *Apajune der Wassermann*.

It was 1881, however, which was the year which would finally make Girardi into a star. It was not the splendid rôles with which he opened the year which wrought this subtle transformation – Pippo to the Bettina of Karoline Finaly in *Der Glücksengel* (*La Mascotte*) with its celebrated Gobbling Duet, the overwhelming lead rôle of the baritonic musketeer Brissac in *Les Mousquetaires au couvent* or Godibert in Millöcker's *Die Jungfrau von Belleville* – but the last production of the year, Johann Strauss's *Der lustige Krieg*. Cast in the supporting comedy rôle of the Marchese Sebastiani – Schweighofer again had the best of the fun – Girardi, who had now become used to something rather better, was irked to find that Strauss had not even given him a number. He stamped his foot, threatened to walk out, and got his number. Sebastiani was still not the best rôle he had had, but the waltz song 'Nur für Natur', in spite of being only loosely linked to the plot, caused a sensation. And on the crest of that sensation, Alexander Girardi became a star.

He was, however, a member of the Theater an der Wien company and not every show, particularly the many imported ones, threw up a rôle and a song which would put the new star in evidence, so Girardi was obliged to mix the great rôles which he now held in the repertoire with some less grateful ones. Thus, while *Der lustige Krieg*, *Apajune* and *Les Cloches de Corneville* continued in repertoire, he played a mixture of fine and less fine new parts in Lecocq's *Tag und Nacht* (Don Brasiero), Millöcker's *Ein süsses Kind* (Médard), Offenbach's *Doktor Ox* (Ygèn), *Lili* (Antonin Plinchard) and Müller's *Der kleine Prinz* (Antonio Hasenlauf) before the end of the year brought him a fresh triumph. The newest piece was Millöcker's *Der Bettelstudent*, and Girardi starred in the title-rôle as Symon, the poor student sent to woo proud Laura by a rejected suitor. He launched into waltz time again in 'Ich knüpfte manche zarte Bande' and 'Ich hab' kein Geld', two splendid, thoroughly tenor pieces, even if more in the romantic and patriotic vein than the comical, and he and his songs caught the public fancy with the same enormous success that the Operette did.

In a year full of *Bettelstudent* performances, Girardi was also seen briefly in Lacôme's *Der schöne Nikolaus* (Criquet) and with more success as the explorer Miradello in Suppé's *Die Afrikareise* and as Caramello in the Viennese production of *Eine Nacht in Venedig* ('Lagunen-Walzer'). The year 1884 saw him introduce *Gasparone* (Benozzo), *Donna Juanita* (Diego Manrique), Louis Roth's *Der Marquis von Rivoli* (Breton), *Der Feldprediger* (Piffkow) and *Pfingsten in Florenz* (Fra Bombardo), 1885 brought *Zwillinge* (Adonis Duprat), new productions of *Der lustige Krieg* and *Nanon* and, finally, Strauss's *Der Zigeunerbaron*, which brought with it another first-rate rôle for Girardi, as the low-comic pig-farmer Kálmán Zsupán ('Ja, das Schreiben und das Lesen').

The series of new shows and new rôles continued, although now Girardi was in a position where he no longer had to appear in virtually every piece of the repertoire and he was able to render up some of those parts of which he was less fond to other performers. In 1886, whilst *Der Zigeunerbaron* played out its first run, he created the rôle of the jester Carillon in *Der Hofnarr*, in 1887 he took the title-rôles in Brandl's *Der liebe Augustin* and Strauss's *Simplicius* and that of the comical Spätzle in Millöcker's *Die sieben Schwaben*. The next couple of years, however, produced little – *Der Schlosserkönig* (Charles), Dellinger's unsuccessful *Kapitän Fracassa* (Fracassa) and Hellmesberger's *Das Orakel* (Dioskuros) – but in 1890 Millöcker's *Der arme Jonathan* supplied Girardi with one of his best rôles as the poor servant become suddenly and uncomfortably rich, and the Vienna production of *Mam'zelle Nitouche* gave him another splendid comic rôle as the naughty music master, Célestin.

The year 1891 brought a further triumph with the production of Zeller's *Der Vogelhändler*. In the title-rôle of Adam, the country bird-seller, Girardi was given the most winning set of songs he had yet had: the lilting entrance song with its 'flix, flux, flax Florian!' refrain, the wonderful waltz 'Schenkt man sich Rosen in Tirol' and its partner 'Wie mein Ahnl zwanzig Jahr', and the sad little song of homesickness 'Kom' ih iazt wieder ham' all went to make up a rôle full of panache, comedy and sympathy. Whilst *Der Vogelhändler* formed the backbone of the bill, Girardi also appeared in the burlesque *Krawalleria musicana* (Duriduri Salamucci), Brandl's remusicked *Die Kosakin* (Casimir) and in a distinctly minor rôle as Puycardas, the bullfighter, in *Miss Helyett*, before in 1892–3 he introduced

Das Sonntagskind (Tristan Florival), *Fanchon's Leyer* (Zephirin), *Der Millionen-Onkel* (Mihail Cakov), *Der Bajazzo* (Quadrillo), *Fürstin Ninetta* (Kassim Pacha) and *Der Schwiegerpapa* (Baptiste Maillot) without finding any new rôle to equal his best.

At the end of the year he played a revival of *Das verwunschene Schloss* with Therese Biedermann as partner, and things looked up when Zeller's *Der Obersteiger* was produced, giving him the best rôle and the best song ('Sei nicht bös') that he had had since *Der Vogelhändler*, as the rather anti-heroic mine-foreman Martin. *Husarenblut* (Streicher-Pepi), Strauss's *Jabuka* (Joschko), Millöcker's *Der Probekuss* (Hans Pfeifli), Dellinger's *Die Chansonette* (Antonio Mazzuchetti), Strauss's *Waldmeister* (Erasmus Müller), Müller's *General Gogo* (Dagobert Fragonard), Josef Bayer's *Mister Menelaus* (Septimus Wisbottle) and *Der Wunderknabe* (Kajetan Tween), which followed, did not give him anything more than ephemeral rôles.

Now, after more than 20 years at the Theater an der Wien, Girardi decided to move on. He went first to the other principal Vienna Operette house, the Carltheater, where he played during 1896 in a musical version of Meilhac and Halévy's *La Cigale* called *Bum-Bum* (Brandemayer), and then to the Deutsches Volkstheater where he put aside musical theatre to appear in Shakespeare, Raimund (notably his famous portrayal of Valentin in *Der Verschwender*), Molière and as Leopold in the play *Im weissen Rössl*. In 1899 he returned to the musical stage. He appeared at the Hofoper as Frosch in *Die Fledermaus*, starred with Marie Halton in the new Operette *Adam und Eva* at the Carltheater and appeared at the Raimundtheater and the Theater in der Josefstadt before, in 1902, he returned to the scene of his great triumphs and signed up once again with the Theater an der Wien, beginning his new contract by reappearing in one of his most famous old rôles, Zsupán in *Der Zigeunerbaron*, and as Frosch.

His first new rôles were that of little corporal Ratz in *Der Fremdenführer*, Willibald Brandl in *Wiener Frauen*, the maiden work of the young Franz Lehár, and Josef Flins in *Der Lebemann*, but February of 1903 brought him another to add to his list of great creations when he took on the title-rôle of the first work of another young composer, Edmund Eysler, in *Bruder Straubinger* and scored another huge song hit with the waltz 'Küssen ist keine Sünd'. The short or medium runs of *Die beiden Don Juans* (Mam'selle Quat'Sous, Michel Borniche), *Der Herr Professor* (Roderich Benarius), *Der neue Bürgermeister* (Jan Pieters), *Der Generalkonsul* (Peter Dingl), *Das Garnisonsmädel* (Hektor Trumpus) and Lehár's *Die Juxheirat* (Philly Kapps) were capped by a second Eysler/Girardi success with the title rôle of *Pufferl* (1905, Kirschenlied), a success which meant that Girardi went out from the Theater an der Wien on a high note. For the star had struck up a personal animosity against the theatre's director, Karl Wallner, who had refused to let Girardi run the show the way he wanted, and he had determined that he would go elsewhere.

As he had the first time, he added as much pepper to his departure as possible by choosing the rival Carltheater as his new home. Girardi had ensured that the man who had done so much to make his last two big hits was also part of the exodus from the Theater an der Wien, and Edmund Eysler was on hand to compose the score for the star's

opening attraction at the Carltheater. *Die Schützenliesel* (1905, Blasius, Mutterl-Lied) proved as big a hit as its two predecessors, and a fourth Eysler piece, *Künstlerblut* (1906, Franz Torelli), which followed it scored again, with Girardi playing a rôle which for the first time made him an ageing if not quite elderly man. In between these two Carltheater hits, Girardi took a quick trip to the Theater in der Josefstadt to star with Hansi Niese in a lucrative Posse, *Der Schusterbub*.

Raoul Mader's *Der selige Vincenz* (1907, Baron Vincenz von Rosenheim zu Schleifstein) was less successful, and Girardi once again moved on, this time to Berlin and the Thalia-Theater where he appeared for Jean Kren and Alfred Schönfeld in the Posse *Immer oben auf!* He scored a great hit with the Ackerlied from Suppé's *Bauer und Dichter* and with the famous Fiakerlied, and he remained in Berlin to perform two of his most celebrated play rôles: *Der Verschwender* and Schuster Weigl in *Mein Leopold*.

Now 40 years into his career in the theatre, Girardi was still at the top of the tree, and he was billed large when he returned to the management of Karczag and Wallner at the Raimundtheater in 1909–11 with a repertoire which mixed his best plays with his equally famous portrayals of Zsupán, Bruder Straubinger, Franz Torelli and Célestin. The once-despised Wallner directed him in some of the four new musicals he would create at the Raimundtheater: the Strauss-remake *Reiche Mädchen* (1909, Michael Karinger), *Das Glücksmädel* (1910, Andreas Lindhuber), Oscar Straus's *Mein junger Herr* (1910, Florian) and Eysler's *Das Zirkuskind* (1911, Friedl Möller). Each did well enough, but none proved memorable.

However, one final great musical starring vehicle still awaited Girardi. In October 1912, after having run through more than 200 performances as the star of Paul Ottenheimer's *Heimliche Liebe* (1911, Der Profoss) at the Johann Strauss-Theater, he appeared there as the old violinist, Pali Rácz, in Kálmán's latest Operette, *Der Zigeunerprimás*, singing 'Mein alte Stradivari' and scoring a memorable success. He appeared thereafter in *Der arme Millionär* (1913, Fridolin Stoss), *Der Nachtschnellzug* (1913, Rittmeister von Winkler) and *Das dumme Herz* (1914, Florian Strobl), and played Frosch in *Die Fledermaus*, Straubinger, Josef Drechsler in *Brüderlein fein* and *Mein Leopold* all at the same house. He created *Mein Annerl* (1916–17, Dominik Domaier) and repeated his Zsupán at the Raimundtheater, and he was still performing right up to his last days, appearing at the Burgtheater two months before his death.

Girardi died in 1918, having achieved the most outstanding career of any artist in the history of the Viennese musical theatre. Today there is a street named after him in his home town of Graz, and the Girardigasse in Vienna runs near the Theater an der Wien where so much of his fame was garnered.

Unlike his female counterparts Girardi did not get a bio-Operette named after him, but he did appear on the screen – in person in some silent Operette films, and as a character in Willy Forst's *Operette* where he was impersonated by Paul Hörbiger.

Biographies: Nowak K F: *Girardi* (Concordia, Berlin, 1908); Girardi, A M: *Das Shicksal setzt den Hobel an* (Viehweg Verlag, Braunschweig, 1942); Wutzky, Anna Charlotte: *Girardi* (Wilhelm Frick Verlag, Vienna, 1943) etc

THE GIRL BEHIND THE COUNTER Farcical musical play in 2 acts by Leedham Bantock and Arthur Anderson. Lyrics by Arthur Anderson. Additional lyrics by Percy Greenbank. Music by Howard Talbot. Additional music by Augustus Barratt and J St A Johnson. Wyndham's Theatre, London, 21 April 1906.

Using the regular motifs of the musical of the period – a shopgirl heroine who is actually a rich lady, a barrel-chested baritone hero and a plot hinging on a theft and including a lot of amorous combinations – producer Frank Curzon's team concocted with skill and taste a 'dainty and diverting' model of the genre. With Hayden Coffin singing 'In the Land Where the Best Man Wins', and Isabel Jay declaring 'I Mean to Marry a Man', it only remained for these two favourite singing stars to get through two acts to be paired off. The second act was set at a costume ball and gave comedians George Grossmith (dude), Horace Mills (little) and J P McArdle (heavy and low), soubrette Coralie Blythe and Marie Dainton, as a French girl, the chance to do speciality numbers.

After fine notices, *The Girl Behind the Counter* inexplicably failed to go beyond 141 performances in London, but a Broadway version which accentuated the low-comedy element by writing up rôles for Lew Fields and the Gaiety's Connie Ediss as Mr and Mrs Henry Schniff, rearranged the plot to give the heroine a red-blooded American instead of an English Lord as her second-act reward, and interpolated songs including Paul Lincke's Glühwurmchen Idyll from *Lysistrata* did much better (232 performances and a 1916 revival). Rupert Clarke and Clyde Meynell took *The Girl Behind the Counter* to Australia, where Ruth Lincoln and Harold Thorley headed the romance and Edwin Brett, Essie Perrin and Tom Payne the fun for seasons in Melbourne and Sydney (Criterion Theatre 27 December 1909).

(*See also* page 548.)

USA: Herald Square Theater 1 October 1907; Australia: Theatre Royal, Melbourne 17 April 1909

GIRL CRAZY Musical comedy in 2 acts by Guy Bolton and John McGowan. Lyrics by Ira Gershwin. Music by George Gershwin. Alvin Theater, New York, 14 October 1930.

The sixth of the series of Gershwin musicals produced by Alexander A Aarons and Vinton Freedley, *Girl Crazy* followed behind the unfortunate *Treasure Girl* and, statistically, succeeded better on Broadway than any of their previous collaborations excepting *Lady, Be Good!*, notching up an initial metropolitan run of 272 performances.

Its tale told of a gallivanting young New Yorker called Danny Churchill (Allen Kearns), exiled from the bright lights, bosoms and booze of the big city by his worried, wealthy father. Undeterred, Danny turns Custerville, Arizona, into an outback replica of wine, women and songland and finally finds true love with postmistress Molly Gray (Ginger Rogers). The show's comedy star, Willie Howard (a late replacement for Bert Lahr, originally slated) was cast as Jewish taxi driver Gieber Goldfarb who drives the hero to his exile and remains in Custerville with him to become town sheriff, William Kent was the town saloon keeper, Slick Fothergill, and Ethel Merman, in the rôle of his daughter, was the principal representative of the wine, women and song.

This jolly, traditional musical comedy story was illustrated by a lively score which yielded some memorable moments. The teenaged Miss Rogers had the more winsome musical numbers with the puzzled and unselfpitying 'But Not for Me' and the gliding melody of 'Embraceable You' (plucked by Gershwin from the score of an aborted musical for Ziegfeld), as well as the comical '(When it's) Cactus Time in Arizona', and Miss Merman had the lusty ones with an 'I Got Rhythm' which lived up to its title, the tale of 'Sam and Delilah' and a rather different kind of lament in 'Boy! What Love Has Done to Me!'. One of the highlights of the score, however was a rarer masculine moment: a male-voice quartet harmonizing their way winningly through the loping 'Bidin' my Time'.

Girl Crazy has won itself a special place in the historical hearts of Broadway students, partly because of its fine musical score, but largely because it gave the dazzlingly truncheon-voiced Ethel Merman her first Broadway opportunity. Without Miss Merman, and in spite of 'I Got Rhythm' and 'Embraceable You', however, the show did not travel beyond America, although elements of it went into the makings of three different film musicals. RKO produced a movie under the same title in 1932 which retained the plotline but only three of the show's songs, and MGM followed up in 1943 with a Mickey Rooney–Judy Garland vehicle which was, not unsurprisingly, unable to follow the plot but which used, instead, seven of the musical's songs plus 'Fascinating Rhythm' from *Lady, Be Good!*. A 1965 MGM film, produced as *Where the Boys Meet the Girls*, used neither the story nor much of the score (four numbers, supplemented by a half-dozen interpolations, one written by cast member Liberace).

A remake of *Girl Crazy*, done much on the same lines as the *Funny Face/My One and Only* remake of some years earlier, under the title *Crazy for You* (ad Ken Ludwig) was produced in America in 1992 (Shubert Theater, 19 February) with Harry Groener and Jodi Benson featured. A Broadway starved of light entertainment welcomed it ravenously and it quickly galloped past *Girl Crazy*'s original total, picking up a Tony Award as best musical of the utterly arid 1991–2 season before going on to give some sweetly nostalgic enjoyment to English-language theatre-goers further afield.

Germany: Pfalztheater, Kaiserslautern 19 February 1977; Films: RKO 1932, MGM 1943, MGM 1965 *Where the Boys Meet the Girls*
Recordings: complete (Electra), selection (Columbia), *Crazy For You* (EMI-Angel)

THE GIRL FRIEND Musical comedy in 2 acts by Herbert Fields. Lyrics by Lorenz Hart. Music by Richard Rodgers. Vanderbilt Theater, New York, 17 March 1926.

The Girl Friend, Rodgers and Hart's follow-up to their successful début with the period piece *Dearest Enemy*, was a show much more in the contemporary idiom. Herbert Fields's book centred around the efforts of little Leonard Silver (Sammy White) to win a bicycle race and his sweetheart Mollie (Eva Puck) in the face both of crooked gamblers, who try to nobble him, and the hoity charms of Wynn Spencer (Evelyn Cavanaugh), whilst the show's score was in the light, bright and dance-based mood of the 1920s. White and Miss Puck danced the charleston and sang the show's two most successful pieces, the lively dance number 'The Girl Friend' and the sweetly balladic

Plate 108. **The Girl Behind the Counter:** *Gowns for the girls of the front line.*

'The Blue Room'. Although Lew Fields's production of *The Girl Friend* started slowly, business gradually improved. In the end, the show remained on the Broadway boards for a highly respectable 301 performances prior to going on the road.

The Girl Friend went on to appear in London, in 1927, by which time the West End had already appreciatively tasted Rodgers and Hart's work in the made-for-London *Lido Lady*, the revue *One Dam Thing After Another* and the rather less-than-successful *Peggy-Ann*. However, the piece as seen in London differed very largely from that played on Broadway, and it could almost have been said to be sailing under false colours. Producer Jack Waller purchased two 1926 Broadway musicals, *The Girl Friend* and *Kitty's Kisses* (Con Conrad/Gus Kahn/Otto Harbach, Philip Bartholomae), and he made one out of the two. He jettisoned Fields's bicycling libretto and he replaced it with the decidedly better farcical high-jinks in a hotel suite which were the basis of *Kitty's Kisses*, done over by Bert Lee and Bob Weston. He added the plum songs ('The Girl Friend', 'The Blue Room') and title of *The Girl Friend* along with 'Mountain Greenery' and 'What's the Use of Talking?' from Rodgers and Hart's *Garrick Gaieties*, one number by local Vivian Ellis ('We Must Discover the Girl'), and a chunk of Tchaikovsky for the leading lady to dance to, to the remaining ensembles and solos of the *Kitty's Kisses* score, and produced the result at the Palace Theatre to a delighted reception and a run of precisely a year (401 performances) with Roy Royston (Robert), Louise Browne (Kitty), Clifford Mollison (Dennison), George Gee (Jerry) and Emma Haig (Jennie) featured. The 'new' *Girl Friend* (which was altogether more *Kitty's Kisses* than *Girl Friend*) subsequently had a fine provincial career in Britain and was produced in both Australia, with Annie Croft and her husband Reginald Sharland starred as Kitty and Robert, and in Budapest, hot on the heels of London's season.

A version of the London *The Girl Friend*, retaining the basic *Kitty's Kisses* libretto and with a score similarly made up from *Girl Friend*, *Kitty's Kisses* and other material, was produced at Colchester, England in 1987 as Rodgers and Hart's *The Girl Friend*.

UK: Palace Theatre 8 September 1927; Australia: Her Majesty's Theatre, Sydney 30 December 1927; Hungary: Király Színház *Puszipajtás* 21 September 1928
Recording: Colchester cast recording (UK version) (TER); selection (US version) (Fontana).

THE GIRL FROM KAYS Musical play in 3 acts by Owen Hall said to be based on *La Mariée récalcitrante* by Léon Gandillot. Lyrics by Adrian Ross and Claude Aveling. Music by Ivan Caryll and Cecil Cook. Additional numbers by Lionel Monckton, Howard Talbot, Paul Rubens, Bernard Rolt, Edward Jones, Meyer Lutz, Kitty Ashmead, Charles H Taylor and A D Cammeyer. Apollo Theatre, London, 15 November 1902.

The Girl from Kays began its life amongst some publicity, with a curious lawsuit from the Regent Street firm of Jay's Ltd who objected to the piece's original title, *The Girl from Jay's*, and injuncted George Edwardes to prevent him sullying their good name with a musical comedy. There was further bother when the names allotted to the chorus girls – each named prettily after a bishopric – aroused a storm in churchy circles. Again the producer didn't fight, he simply changed the offending words slightly and no one was fooled – merely made to look foolish. Another, much later, lawsuit was a claim for royalties from the French author, Gandillot, whose play (Théâtre Déjazet, 1 October 1897) had allegedly been used – without credit – as a basis for the script, and who had been palmed off with a £50 one-off payment when he had protested.

In spite of all this legal action, *The Girl from Kays* turned out to be a model Edwardian musical comedy. Its basic story concerned the woes of freshly wed Norah (Kate Cutler) who sees her brand new husband (W Louis Bradfield) getting a congratulatory kiss from the shopgirl Winnie (Ethel Irving), who has delivered her new hat, and floods away with her family for two acts of damp indignation and making up. Those two acts were decorated with the best of musical-theatre comedy, song and dance. The comedy was in the hands of Willie Edouin who created a memorable character as 'Piggy' Hoggenheimer, an American millionaire with social pretensions. For once, however, the audience, used to mocking these exaggerated Yankee dollar characters, laughed with and not at the brash, eager, kindly 'Mr Hoggenheimer of Park Lane' ('Rude? I'm not rude, I'm rich') who became the show's favourite character and one of its greatest assets. The song and dance was shared amongst Miss Cutler, with a delightful sobbing waltz 'Papa!', Letty Lind and America's Ella Snyder (a Howard Talbot coon song, 'Smiling Sambo') as a pair of shopgirls, Bradfield ('I Don't Care' and a charming duo with his bride, 'Semi-Detached') and Aubrey Fitzgerald in the dude rôle.

However, in spite of all its attractions, *The Girl from Kays* put up a warning sign in the Edwardes establishment. Economics were changing. Although it played happily for over a year at the Apollo and Comedy Theatres (432 performances), its lavish production led it to end its London life in the red, to the vast tune of £20,000. The piece recouped later when it proved a fine touring prospect, but production economics were now far from those of a few years earlier where a half-dozen weeks' run served to recoup the prettiest of shows.

The Girl from Kays also scored a major success on Broadway where the popular comedian Sam Bernard took up Edouin's rôle for a run of more than 200 performances at the Herald Square Theater. Having made the hit of his career as 'Piggy', Bernard returned regularly for further doses of Hoggenheimer, appearing on Broadway in 1906 in a revised version of *The Girl From Kays* called *The Rich Mr Hoggenheimer*, and again in 1914 in a rather clumsy second remake under the title of *The Belle from Bond Street*. This version was subsequently played in Britain where it had but a brief run. In 1927 Bernard starred in a fourth Hoggenheimer musical, *Piggy*, for 11 Broadway weeks, up until shortly before his death.

Australia had the treat of seeing rather a different kind of 'Piggy', when the gently endearing G P Huntley headed an exported production from Britain for a repertoire season in Australia under the Gaiety Theatre/J C Williamson banner. Delia Mason (Norah), Madge Crichton (Winnie) and Maurice Farkoa supported the comedian through three weeks of performances before the company switched to *Kitty Grey* and *Three Little Maids*.

USA: Herald Square Theater 2 November 1903; Australia: Princess Theatre, Melbourne 4 June 1904

THE GIRL FROM UTAH   Musical play in 2 acts by James T Tanner. Dialogue by James T Tanner and Paul Rubens. Lyrics by Adrian Ross, Percy Greenbank and Paul Rubens. Music by Sidney Jones and Paul Rubens. Adelphi Theatre, London, 18 October 1913.

With the production of *The Girl from Utah*, George Edwardes replaced the Lionel Monckton/Gertie Millar combination which had served him so well at the Adelphi Theatre to date. Instead, he mounted a piece of which the text had all the attributes of an old Gaiety musical, plus some music by his more substantial Daly's Theatre composer Sidney Jones, contrasted with the lightest of Paul Rubens, and a new star in America's Ina Claire, who had made a great success in Miss Millar's *Quaker Girl* rôle on Broadway.

Mormons had recently become the fashionable villains of the British theatre, in succession to wicked Uncles, Marquises and Puritans, and Tanner's book had little Una Trance (Ina Claire) fleeing to Britain from her home in Utah to avoid a Mormon marriage with a gruesome fellow of her father's choice (only the villain was different, the plot remained classic). Joseph Coyne, Phyllis Dare, Edmund Payne and Gracie Leigh were amongst the Adelphi Theatre friends who helped to rescue the breathless Una, after which everyone repaired to the Arts Ball for some costumes, half of the show's songs and a rather perfunctory ending.

Payne, as the little ham-and-beef-shop man, Trimmit, had a rôle full of disguises and comical action and a cheery number about 'The Bottom of Brixton Hill' whilst Gracie Leigh played Irish and Coyne gave another lazily suave variant of the performance his successes as Danilo and Tony Chute (*Quaker Girl*) had cast him in for ever, but it was Miss Claire, in a rôle which was little more than the classic ingénue, who won the public's biggest cheers.

The Girl from Utah's mediocre run of 195 performances in London showed that the fashion for its type of entertainment was waning very noticeably, but the show nevertheless went on the road and won itself a number of foreign performances. In New York Julia Sanderson, Donald Brian and Joseph Cawthorn starred in an americanized version with not only the inevitable Kern songs added to the London score ('Land of "Let's Pretend"', 'Alice in Wonderland', 'Same Sort of Girl'), but also such proven British pieces as 'Gilbert the Filbert' (Finck/Wimperis) which had been introduced in London's 1914 *The Passing Show*. However, this time one of the pasted-in Jerome Kern songs (in a show in which pasting was the easiest thing in the world) was the wistful 'They Didn't Believe Me' (lyric: Herbert Reynolds) and 'the botchings of a decade of Kern/Frohman British musicals could be forgiven in one wonderful song'.

In spite of this choice morsel in the score, and in spite of the undoubted success of the show, *The Girl from Utah* was played only 120 times on Broadway. Times were changing there, too, and the interest of the moment was more for anything Viennese than for what looked like just another old-fashioned British musical comedy. Nevertheless, the piece toured healthily (growing interpolations all the way) and returned to Broadway the following year.

It also got a Budapest showing (ad Frigyes Karinthy, Árpád Tóth, István Zágon) in what was basically its unbotched version. 'Brixton' even remained in the lyrics, but it was joined, in Zágon's version of the songwords, by 'Budapest'. However the mood of the times was evident in the fact that Australia, like Budapest a happy host to all that was most interesting in the musical theatre at this time, did not bother with *The Girl from Utah*. But it took 'They Didn't Believe Me' and interpolated it into the highly popular *So Long, Letty*. Britain popped it into an even bigger hit – *Tonight's the Night*.

USA: Knickerbocker Theater 24 August 1914; Hungary: Király Színház *Az Utahi Leány* 18 September 1920

THE GIRL IN THE TAXI   *see* DIE KEUSCHE SUSANNE

THE GIRL IN THE TRAIN   *see* DIE GESCHIEDENE FRAU

THE GIRL ON THE FILM   *see* FILMZAUBER

THE GIRLS OF GOTTENBERG   Musical play in 2 acts by George Grossmith and L E Berman. Lyrics by Adrian Ross and Basil Hood. Music by Ivan Caryll and Lionel Monckton. Gaiety Theatre, London, 15 May 1907.

The book for *The Girls of Gottenberg* was said to be based on a real-life and recent incident – a scandalous episode in which a German cobbler from Kopenick had masqueraded as a high-up official and got away with it for longer than was credible. In fact, when all was said and done, the show's libretto was a fairly conventional piece, with the usual kind of disguises and romances set in a pretty Prussian setting which allowed lots of uniforms to be paraded across the Gaiety stage.

Max Moddelkopf (Edmund Payne), barber and valet to Prince Otto of Saxe-Hilversum (George Grossmith), commander of the Blue Hussars, takes the place of an envoy sent to order the rival Red Hussars to the town of Gottenberg and switches the man's orders so that it is his employer's regiment which gets the posting. There is, you see, a ladies' university in Gottenberg. Otto, however, ends up romancing Elsa (May de Souza), the apparent daughter of the half-blind local innkeeper (Arthur Hatherton), who – guess what – turns out to be the very aristocrat he was supposed to wed anyway, playing at peasants in the best operettic style. The principal female rôle, however, was reserved for the theatre's star, Gertie Millar, whose Mitzi paired with Payne's Max, as the little fellow kept up his pretence of importance and caused havoc in Gottenberg with his curious commands.

The songs were not the best bunch to have come from the Gaiety, but Lionel Monckton's 'Two Little Sausages', Grossmith's rendering (to his own lyrics and Monckton's tune) of 'Otto of the Roses', Miss Millar's description of 'Berlin on the Spree' and some Wagnerian parody in 'Rheingold' all proved popular.

After the flop of *The New Aladdin*, *The Girls of Gottenberg* brought success back to the Gaiety Theatre through a fine run of 303 performances, and the show duly set off round the world. South Africa was one of the first to grab the latest Gaiety hit, and its mounting, along with J C Williamson's Australian production with George Lauri and Fanny Dango starred, and Maurice Bandmann's oriental touring edition were all under way by the end of the year, when Edwardes sent out the first British provincial company with Miss Millar at its head.

New York followed the next year, when Charles Frohman mounted his version of the show at the Knickerbocker Theater with Miss Millar supported by a star team from London headed by James Blakeley (Max) and Lionel Mackinder (Otto). The show ran 103 performances. Several years later, whilst *Girls of Gottenberg* touring companies continued to run round Britain and the colonies, a French version (ad Maurice de Marsan, Gabriel Timmory) was played with limited success at the Paris Moulin-Rouge with Marise Fairy and Jane Marnac featured.

Australia: Her Majesty's Theatre, Melbourne 26 October 1907; USA: Knickerbocker Theater 2 September 1908; France: Théâtre du Moulin-Rouge *Les Jolies Filles de Gottenberg* 17 October 1912

GIROFLÉ-GIROFLA

GIROFLÉ-GIROFLA Opéra-bouffe in 3 acts by Albert Vanloo and Eugène Leterrier. Music by Charles Lecocq. Théâtre des Fantaisies-Parisiennes, Brussels, 21 March 1874.

The immense success of *La Fille de Madame Angot* established Charles Lecocq as the new hero of the French musical theatre and his next work was impatiently awaited. It came, like the earlier piece, from the Brussels theatre run by Eugène Humbert, and was written to a Vanloo/Leterrier libretto which was in the line of the comically absurd tradition developed in opéra-bouffe and used by Lecocq in *Les Cent Vierges*, rather than in the more legitimate theatrical vein of *La Fille de Madame Angot*.

Don Boléro (Alfred Jolly), Governor of a Spanish seaside province, has arranged advantageous marriages for his twin daughters (both Pauline Luigini) – one to Marasquin, the son of the banker to whom he is indebted (Mario Widmer), the other to his belligerent Moorish neighbour, Mourzouk (Paul Ginet). When one sister is carried off by pirates on what should have been the double wedding day, the other has to act for two – with all the blushes and bother that involves – until Boléro and his wife, Aurore (Mlle Delorme), manage to get the missing virgin back from the pirates.

The delightfully extravagant and farcical libretto for *Giroflé-Girofla* (a title used 16 years earlier for Crisafulli and Devicque's Théâtre du Gymnase drama) was allied to a score in Lecocq's most light-hearted and lyrical style, which gave splendid opportunities to its leading players. The dual rôle of Giroflé and Girofla – mostly Giroflé, for Girofla gets captured fairly early on, and doesn't reappear until the dénouement – included parallel waltz couplets for the two sisters ('Père adoré', 'Petit Papa') with an orchestral break which allowed the actress to exit, change the pink bow on her shoulder for a blue one, and re-enter in her new character, and a brilliant drinking song ('Le Punch scintille'), whilst the comic tenor Marasquin, the banker's son, scored with the naïvely threatening 'Mon Père est un très gros banquier', and there were major comic rôles for both the frantic parents and for the marauding Moor, roaring lubriciously for his bride.

The concerted music of the show was particularly successful, with critics and public both approving especially the first-act sextet and finale, the quintet 'Matamoros, grand capitaine', and a humorous pirates' chorus which prefigured Gilbert and Sullivan's 'With Catlike Tread' (*The Pirates of Penzance*) in contrasting loud singing with secretive words, as the burlesque pirates stalk their feminine prey.

A triumph in Brussels (80 performances), *Giroflé-Girofla* was still at the height of its popularity when Humbert decided to take the production to London. It met with a delighted response there and was only closed after a nine-week run to permit the Philharmonic Theatre, which had been the launching pad for the huge English success of *La Fille de Madame Angot*, to produce an English-language version (ad Clement O'Neil, Campbell Clarke). Julia Mathews starred alongside E M Garden (Boléro), Harriet Everard (Aurore), Walter Fisher (Maraschino) and Edmund Rosenthal (Mourzouk) in a 14-week run and a quick revival. Before the year was out, the piece had also been seen both in Paris, with the young Jeanne Granier scoring her first big success in the title-rôle of a run of 170 performances, and in Berlin.

Hermine Meyerhoff was the double heroine, alongside Karl Blasel (Boléro), Therese Schäfer (Aurore), Albin Swoboda (Marasquin) and Ausim (Mourzouk), in a successful Vienna production (63 performances in 1875, 17 in 1876 with Karoline Finaly), whilst in New York, with Coralie Geoffroy starring, the usual opéra-bouffe routine of nightly or weekly changes in the repertoire was broken to allow *Giroflé-Girofla* to run consecutively for 50 nights at the Park Theatre. Mlle Geoffroy's French version was followed by a German one starring Lina Mayr and several English editions, including one with Julia Mathews. America's queen of opéra-bouffe, Marie Aimée, also appeared in her production of the show and, for some time, four or five companies were to be found simultaneously playing *Giroflé-Girofla*, in and out of Broadway, in a selection of languages. It returned there in 1905 with Fritzi Scheff starred (Broadway Theater 31 January) and one last time at the Jolson Theater as late as 1926 (22 November).

In Australia the piece proved equally popular. First introduced by W S Lyster's company with Clara Thompson as the twins, her husband Henry Bracy as Boléro, Mrs J H Fox (Aurore), Edward Farley (Mourzouk) and Jennie Winston as a travesty Maraschino, it scored a big success and was seen regularly in the repertoires of opéra-bouffe companies for many years thereafter.

Curiously, the usually quick-off-the-mark Hungarian stage seems to have taken eight years to mount *Viola-Ibolya* (ad Lajos Evva, Béla J Fái) and, when it did, in the wake of Lecocq's many later successes, it did not catch on. Elsewhere, however, the piece established itself firmly in the opéra-bouffe repertoire and it was regularly played as long as the vogue for that kind of piece lasted. From the 1880s, however, its revivals became rarer, and its poor (not to say negligible) place in the modern repertoire does not reflect its popularity in the years immediately following its first production, nor its value in comparison with some pieces which are still regularly played.

UK: Opera Comique (Fr) 6 June 1874, Philharmonic Theatre, Islington (Eng) 3 October 1874; France: Théâtre de la Renaissance 11 November 1874; Germany: Friedrich-Wilhelmstädtisches Theater 22 December 1874; Austria: Carltheater 2 January 1875; USA: Park Theater (Fr) 4 February 1875, Robinson Hall (Eng) 19 May 1875; Australia: Prince of Wales Opera House, Melbourne 22 May 1875; Hungary: Népszinház *Viola-Ibolya* 22 March 1882

Recordings: complete (Gaîté-Lyrique), complete in German (Urania)

LA GIROUETTE   Opérette in 3 acts by Henri Bocage and Émile Hémery. Music by Auguste Coèdes. Théâtre des Fantaisies-Parisiennes, Paris, 3 March 1880.

The most widely played of Coèdes's opérettes, *La Girouette* – apparently composed in just a few days to meet the production deadline – was played for 90 performances at the Fantaisies-Parisiennes, under the management of Debruyère, with sufficient appeal for the show to be taken up for a number of overseas productions.

The comical King Pepin de Birmenstorf (Denizot) has a daughter, Frédérique (Maria Thève) who, for reasons of state, is to wed Eustache de Tolède (Jannin). She prefers one Hildebert de Brindès (Villars). After the regulation amount of disguises and mistaken identities, she has her way, whilst the genuine Eustache is paired off with the evening's phoney Frédérique – otherwise the unaristocratic Suzanne (Mme Devaure). The other comic moments fell to the evening's third pair, Captain Colardo (Bellot) and Pélagie (Mme Tassilly).

Following its Paris run, *La Girouette* was taken up by Budapest's Népszinház (ad Lajos Evva, Béla J Fái), and by Broadway's Augustin Daly, who mounted the show (ad Fred Williams, Robert Stoepel) at his New York base with a cast from his number two company headed by William Gilbert (Pepin), May Fielding (Frédérique), Sgr Montegriffo and Harry MacDonough as the real and the false Eustache, and Francesca Guthrie as Suzanne. It did well enough, playing 44 times prior to its being taken briefly and not so successfully into the repertoire of the famous Bostonians touring company.

Paris saw the show for a second time when Debruyère revived it in 1885 at the Théâtre de la Gaîté, and Britain several years later when it was produced for the touring circuits in a Robert Reece version starring Giulia Warwick, Durward Lely, Charles Wibrow and Robert Courtneidge. A trial matinee at the Avenue Theatre did not, however, convince the management to take it to the West End.

Hungary: Népszinház *A szélkakas* 5 May 1881; USA: Daly's Theater *The Weathercock* 13 April 1882; UK: Theatre Royal, Portsmouth 25 March 1889, Avenue Theatre 24 April 1889

GIUDITTA   Musical play in 5 scenes by Paul Knepler and Fritz Löhner. Music by Franz Lehár. Staatsoper, Vienna, 20 January 1934.

Giuditta was the last of the series of darkly coloured romantic Operetten (this one purposely titled 'musikalische Komödie') composed by Lehár in the late 1920s and early 1930s and created by the star tenor, Richard Tauber. It made its first appearance, after some shocked in-house resistance from those who felt an Operette unsuitable for Vienna's famous opera theatre, on the stage of the Staatsoper, where Tauber was counted on as an enormous box-office draw.

Tauber played Octavio, an army Captain who ultimately abandons his career and his well-being for the charms of the tempestuous wife of a Mediterranean artisan, and Lehár supplied him with a violently high-pitched and showy entrance ('Freunde, das Leben ist lebenswert') and some passionate arias ('Schönste der Frauen', 'Du bist meine Sonne') to follow. However, the bon-bons of the score of *Giuditta* fell to the vamping lady of the title-rôle, created by soprano Jarmila Novotna. In the first scene she describes her frustrated longing to sink 'In einem Meer

Plate 109. **Giuditta:** *'Meine Lippen sie küssen so heiss' – Josephine Cook as Giuditta at the Landestheater, Coburg.*

von Liebe' in the third she weeps out her passionate frenzy at failing to make Octavio desert the army to stay with her ('In die Stirne fällt die Locke') and in the fourth, now a night-club performer with rich men in her bed, she hymns her own sexuality in the popular waltz song 'Meine Lippen sie küssen so heiss'.

There is some light relief to the dark main story in the parallel affair of the fruit-seller Pierrino (Erich Zimmermann) and his girlfriend Anita (Margit Bokor), and some greener comedy in the nightclub sequences, but basically *Giuditta* is an Operette of dreadful and destructive passions, set with some of the darkest and most thickly orchestrated of Lehár's music.

The original production was not well received, but it played 42 times during the season in which it was introduced. The following year, after only a few performances had been played, came the Anschluss – Tauber was gone and *Giuditta* was played no more in Vienna. It received little attention overseas. It was produced in Budapest shortly after its introduction in Vienna, and the Théâtre de la Monnaie, Brussels, staged a production (ad André Mauprey) the following season with Kate Walter-Lippert and José Janson in the leading rôles. Janson also featured in the first French performance, at Toulouse in 1936, opposite Mme Chauny-Lasson, but *Giuditta*, in spite of a handful of provincial productions, did not play Paris, nor London, nor New York.

It has subsequently twice been given major recordings, its principal numbers have been frequently performed by vocalists attempting cross-overs between opera and Operette, and it has received several stage productions in an age which prizes the heaviest and most sentimental/dramatic end of the repertoire, but it has never become popular in the way that Lehár's lighter works or *Das Land des Lächelns,* the most successful of his romantic pieces, has done.

Hungary: Magyar Kiralyi Operaház 8 April 1934; France: Théâtre du Capitole, Toulouse March 1936

Recordings: complete (EMI, Decca), selections (Eurodisc, EMI Electrola etc), selection in Hungarian (Qualiton)

GIVE ME A RING Musical in 2 acts by Guy Bolton, R P Weston and Bert Lee. Lyrics by Graham John. Music by Martin Broones. London Hippodrome, 22 June 1933.

Moss' Empires Ltd's theatre division, headed by the budding impresario George Black, put together *Give Me a Ring* with a lavish hand and with a showman's taste for the big and the fashionable name. From the world of variety, Black took the famous Scots comic Will Fyffe and the comedy duo Flanagan and Allen, from musical comedy the country's top ingénue, Evelyn Laye, from Hollywood composer Martin Broones, along with two Britons who had made themselves a name in American shows and films – John Garrick and the formidable Bertha Belmore – and the American soubrette Gina Malo. The band of Debroy Somers was topped by the harmonizing band-singers the Carlyle Cousins, a Big Ten of dancers was hired to front the Hippodrome girls, Norman Hartnell signed to dress the leading ladies, and Hungarian actor-singer Ernest Verebes was brought in to give a romantic Continental air to the rôle of the hero.

The stars were cast as employees in a hotel, Miss Laye being the telephone operator, Peggy (thus the double-meaning title), Fyffe a steward, Allen a telephone engineer and Flanagan his assistant. Verebes was Jack, the assistant manager, Miss Belmore the staff supervisor and Miss Malo the manageress of the dress shop. Garrick played a guest, radio star Cliff Reed, momentarily distracting Peggy from true-love Jack, amongst the comedy turns and numbers which were the raison d'être of a show which was really little more than a virtual variety bill. 'A Couple of Fools in Love' (Verebes/Miss Laye) proved the most catchy number of an agreeable if ephemeral score.

Give Me a Ring played 239 performances in London, and Black kept up the quality throughout. Miss Laye was succeeded by Adele Dixon and then Binnie Hale, Fyffe was replaced by none other than 64-year-old Huntley Wright, and Verebes by the young John Mills. At the end of the London season, the piece went on the road, with Flanagan and Allen top-billed, playing the Moss' Empires houses on a schedule of once- or, sometimes, twice-nightly.

GLAMOROUS NIGHT Musical play in 2 acts by Ivor Novello. Lyrics by Christopher Hassall. Music by Ivor Novello. Theatre Royal, Drury Lane, London, 2 May 1935.

The Theatre Royal, Drury Lane, had fallen into the doldrums since its great successes with American operettas in the late 1920 and early 1930s, but a lunchtime conversation between general manager Harry Tennent and actor-author-composer Ivor Novello provided the impetus that put the big theatre back on the right rails. Novello, who had not penned a musical play for some 14 years as he raced merrily on to several other successful careers, offered to write, compose and star in a suitably grandiose 'Drury Lane piece', and the piece he turned out, written to

Plate 110. **Glamorous Night:** *The gipsy wedding between Anthony (Ivor Novello) and Militza (Mary Ellis).*

measure for the house and its audiences, was *Glamorous Night.*

The young inventor Anthony Allen (Novello) blows the money advanced to him to develop a television system on taking a Ruritanian cruise-ship holiday. When they stop at Krasnia he becomes involved in drama. An attempt is made on the life of prima donna Militza Hajós (Mary Ellis), the mistress of King Stefan (Barry Jones), during the course of her show, and Anthony is on hand to foil the killer. Pushed by the ambitious republican demagogue Lydyeff (Lyn Harding), Militza takes flight on the departing cruise ship, and love blossoms as the 'republicans' pursue her and ultimately wreck the ship. Anthony and Militza escape, via a gypsy encampment and a gypsy wedding, back to Krasnia, where Lydyeff has almost got Stefan to abdicate. Anthony shoots the villain, but has finally to take his leave of Militza of whom the lonely King has the greater need in his struggle to continue to rule. Olive Gilbert of the Carl Rosa Opera played a contralto singer, and veteran actress Minnie Rayner was Militza's ex-chorus-girl maid.

The production had a vast cast and lashings of scenery (including, of course, the shipwreck), but it also had a lush, romantic score – much of it represented as part of the operetta within the operetta – which produced several standards, the soprano/contralto duo 'Fold Your Wings', the soprano's soaring title song (also the title song of the internal show), the tenor's showtime arietta, 'Shine Through My Dreams', as well as a different kind of stand-up number, 'Shanty Town', purveyed by jazz vocalist Elisabeth Welch, in a tacked-in rôle as an entertaining stowaway in the shipboard scenes.

Glamorous Night was a huge success, but the directors of the Theatre Royal, Drury Lane, closed it after seven months, at the approach of Christmas, refusing to sacrifice the traditional (and traditionally profitable) Christmas pantomime. In spite of all Novello could do, his show was bundled out and ended up passing Christmas in Glasgow. Whilst Drury Lane's productions bombed in succession, Prince Littler brought *Glamorous Night* back from 21 provincial weeks to the equally vast London Coliseum (28 May 1936) with Barry Sinclair and Muriel Barron now starred, and Miss Gilbert surprisingly doubling in the rôle of the stowaway. The impetus, however, was gone, and another 91 performances saw the end of the show's London career.

There was, however, plenty of life still left in *Glamorous Night*. It was produced at St Louis's Municipal Opera with Norma Terriss starred as Militza, Guy Robertson as Anthony and Florenz Ames as Stefan, and revived there in 1942, it was filmed, with Miss Ellis starred opposite Barry Mackay, and it was seen regularly (though with rather decreasing scenic means) in the British provinces for decades thereafter, as its favourite songs became ingrained in the repertoire of English sopranos.

USA: Municipal Opera, St Louis 24 August 1936; Film: Associated British 1937

Recordings: original cast assembly (WRC), selections (WRC, HMV, Columbia)

GLASER, Lulu [GLASER, Lilian]   (b Allegheny City, Pa, 2 June 1874; d Norwalk, Conn, 5 September 1958).

At 17 the beautiful, lithe Lulu Glaser landed her first theatrical job as a member of the chorus of Francis Wilson's company, playing a butchered version of Lecocq's *Le Grand Casimir* (*The Lion Tamer*) at the Broadway Theater. When she deputized for the ailing Marie Jansen in the starring rôle, opposite Wilson, she caused sufficient of a sensation for the manager-star immediately to promote her to larger rôles in his established repertoire, playing the boy Lazuli in another massacred masterpiece called *The Merry Monarch* (ex- *L'Étoile*) and the maid, Javotte, in *Erminie*. During nine seasons with the company, she created rôles in Wilson's productions of *The Devil's Deputy* (Elverine), Sullivan's *The Chieftain* (Rita), *Half a King* (Pierrette), *The Little Corporal* (Jacqueline) and *Cyrano de Bergerac* (Roxane), providing the ever-broadening feminine comedy opposite the very low-jinks favoured by Wilson.

She moved on to take top-billing in a couple of short-lived pieces, *Sweet Anne Page* (1900) and *The Prima Donna* (1901, Angela Chumpley), and then in *Dolly Varden* (1902), a Stanislaus Stange/Julian Edwards compound of bits of *Barnaby Rudge* and other English classics, which provided a fine vehicle for the new star in its title-rôle. She next starred as Queen Mary of England opposite William Pruette's Henry VIII in *A Madcap Princess* (1904), appeared in the title-rôles of *Miss Dolly Dollars* (1905) and of *Lola from Berlin* (1907), and found a useful vehicle when she appeared at Joe Weber's as 'Fonia' to Charles J Ross's 'Dandilo' in a burlesque version of *The Merry Widow* (1908).

She was *Mlle Mischief* in an American version of the German *Ein tolles Mädel* in 1908, Daphne Dearborn who was *The Girl from the States* (until she walked out of the dying show on the road) and Cherry Winston who was *Just One of the Boys* in 1909, she featured as Pitti Sing in the all-star *Mikado* at the Casino Theater (1910), starred in two further Continental importations, *The Girl and the Kaiser* (*Die Försterchristel*, 1910) and, sporting a sporran in Boston, *Miss Dudelsack* (1911), as well as in *First Love* (1912, Elaine Hampton) before turning her attentions to vaudeville for the last part of a career which, for all its enduring charms, had not really brought her one top-class new rôle in a top-class show.

In 1925 she married the 69-year-old De Wolf Hopper.

GLAWATSCH, Franz   (b Graz, 16 December 1871; d Vienna, 22 June 1928).

A singing comedian in the old Vienna tradition, in line of descent from Karl Blasel, Glawatsch began his career as a juvenile light comedian, winning his first big rôle at Budweis when he appeared as Adam in *Der Vogelhändler*. He moved on to Marburg (1895) and then to Graz (1896) where he was resident comedian for four years, graduating there to the older rôles in which he would specialize whilst still in his twenties.

In 1899 he was seen at Venedig in Wien, creating the rôle of Kampel in *Die Landstreicher*, and in 1900 he was engaged at the Carltheater, where he appeared in such character parts as Ollendorf (*Bettelstudent*), Marquis Imari (*Die Geisha*) and Andredl (*Das verwunschene Schloss*) and created rôles in *Die Diva* (General Menzel), *Die Primadonna* (Calignac), *Die drei Wünsche* (Fogosch) and the Viennese *Les Saltimbanques*, *Circus Malicorne* (Le Grand Pingouin). In 1902 he appeared at Danzers Orpheum in *Die beiden Blinde* and as Cosmos Bey in the Viennese version of the Gaiety Theatre's *The Messenger Boy*, and in 1903 he created the rôle of Maier in *Frühlingsluft* at Venedig in Wien before he moved to the Theater an der Wien. He made his first appearance there as Lespingot in *Venedig in Paris* (a version of Offenbach's *MM Dunanan*) and continued, under top comedians Girardi and Sigmund Natzler, as a character man/comic in *Der neue Bürgermeister* (Hulst), *Der Generalkonsul* (Giacomo di Ferrari), *Der Toreador* (Governor of Villaya), *Der Herr Professor* (Bruno Venarius), Clérice's *Ordre de l'Empereur* (Marquis de Bussière), *Der rothe Kosak* (Jorgu), *Das Garnisonsmädel* (Wenzel Placek), *Die Juxheirat* (Thomas Brodwiller) and *Pufferl* (Crispin).

After Girardi's departure from the Theater an der Wien company, he succeeded to some of the rôles which might have been his – Thomas Plumpudding in *Prince Bob* (1905), *Der Rebell* (Cretinowitsch), *Peter und Paul ins Schlaraffenland* (Schlampamprius), *Tip-Top* (1907, Colming) – taking over as director for the last-named piece. He both directed and created the rôle of John Couder in the original production of *Die Dollarprinzessin* (1907), directed and played in *Der Frauenjäger* (Sgrimazzi) and mounted the productions of *Der schöne Gardist* and *Ihr Adjutant*, and later returned to play in in *Schneeglöckchen* (Fürst Timofei) and *Die schöne Risette* (Habakuk). He also succeeded to the rôle of Baron Zeta in the original run of *Die lustige Witwe* of which he played the 500th performance in 1911.

When Karczag took over the Raimundtheater in 1908, Glawatsch moved to that house, where he was for a number of years Oberregisseur as well as principal comedian. There he played Zsupán – one of his best rôles, in which he was also seen in Berlin – Ollendorf, Ko-Ko, Joschko in

Jabuka, Couder, *Die Landstreicher*, Prosper Plewny in *Das süsse Mädel*, Lindoberer (*Der fidele Bauer*), Kagler (*Wiener Blut*), Colibrados (*Don Cesar*), Piffkow (*Der Feldprediger*), Offenbach's Jupiter, Ottokar (*Der lachende Ehemann*), Sigismund (*Prinz Methusalem*) and even the now rather young Adam (*Vogelhändler*), and created rôles in *Liebeswalzer* (Leopold Führinger), *Die Sprudelfee* (Fürst Nepomuk Wrzbrzlicky), *Das Glückmädel* (Franz Mitterer), *Die keusche Barbara* (Pittifox), *Casimirs Himmelfahrt* (Peter Paul), *Mein Mäderl* (Franz Helmer), *Der Husarengeneral* (Siegmund Weihrauch), *Die tolle Therese* (Damböck), *Die moderne Eva* (Kasimir Putschli), *Das Dreimäderlhaus* (a memorable old Christian Tschöll with his 'Geh' alte, schau!'), *Zwölf Uhr nachts* (Maringer), *Hannerl* (Christian Tschöll), *Was Mädchen traumen* (Matthias Alsdorfer), *Der Tanz ins Glück* (top-billed as Sebastian Platzer), *Die Liebe geht um!* (1922), *Vierzehn Tage Arrest* (1923, Auguste Lämmermayer) and *Das Schwalbennest* (1926, Franz Rettenbacher), latterly making guest appearances at other theatres, to play in *Die Perlen der Cleopatra* (1923, Pampylos), *Auf Befehl der Kaiserin* (1925, Johann Weisskappel) as Dominik Grüber in *Der Mitternachtswalzer* (1926), in a revival of *Der Tanz ins Glück* (1927) at the Bürgertheater and, paired with Mizzi Zwerenz, as the comical Fridolin von Gumpendorf in *Die gold'ne Meisterin* (1927), at the Theater an der Wien, shortly before his death at the age of 56.

Amongst the new and nearly new shows which he directed at the Raimundtheater were included *Das Zirkuskind* (1911), *Die keusche Barbara* (1911), *Hoheit tanzt Walzer* (1912), *Mein Mäderl* (1913), *Der Husarengeneral* (1913), *Die tolle Therese* (1913) and *Die moderne Eva* (1914).

GLÜCKLICHE REISE Operette in 3 acts by Max Bertuch. Lyrics by Kurt Schwabach. Music by Eduard Künneke. Kurfürstendamm-Theater, Berlin, 23 November 1932.

Expatriate Berliners Robert von Hartenau (Walter Jankuhn) and Stefan Schwarzenberg (Ernst Verebes), tired of life on their unproductive farms in Brazil, work their way back to Germany and there Stefan goes in search of his pen-friend, the exciting-sounding Monika Brink (Lizzi Waldmüller). Actually, Monika and her friend Lona Vonderhoff (Hilde Wörner) – under whose name Monika has also been writing to Robert – work in a shipping office. Monika tries to keep up the pretence of being a society girl, Lona – who quickly falls for Robert – is mortified when Monika admits writing to him in her name, and when their boss (Kurt Lilienn) turns up the truth soon comes out. After a few more scenes, the shipping office issues four tickets back to Brazil.

Eduard Künneke's light, modern dance-based score – in another world from the pretty, winning melodies of his *Der Vetter aus Dingsda* – featured foxtrot, rumba, tango and blues rhythms in a lively combination in which the two boys' tango song 'Drüben in der Heimat', Monika's society-girl 'Jede Frau geht so gerne mal zum Tanztee', Stefan's proposal 'Komm, mein kleines Farmerbräutchen' of a married life in Brazil, and the marching 'Glückliche Reise' were happy moments, alongside versions of such familiar musical-theatre sentiments as 'Das Leben ist ein Karussell' (Monika) or Stefan's description of life 'Am Amazonas'.

A happy success in Berlin, *Glückliche Reise* nevertheless had a career which was largely limited to Germany, where it has become accepted as the second most successful of Künneke's works, behind *Der Vetter aus Dingsda*. First filmed in 1933, the show was used again as the basis for a 1955 film which featured Paul Hubschmid, Inge Egger, Peer Schmidt and Ina Peters, swapped Brazil for a South-Sea Island called Formitosa, made Eva (Lona) into a doctor, but kept the basic shape of the piece and a revised version of what were billed as Künneke's 'world-famous songs'.

Film: Alfred Abel 1933, Thomas Engel 1955
Recordings: selections (part-record) (Fontana, EMI etc)

GO-BANG Musical farcical comedy in 2 acts by Adrian Ross. Music by F Osmond Carr. Trafalgar Square Theatre, London, 10 March 1894.

Produced by Fred Harris and C J Abud in the wake of the former's success with *Morocco Bound*, *Go-Bang* was another piece combining a colourful setting (Go-Bang is an oriental country), low comedy (John Shine, Harry Grattan, George Grossmith jr) and song and dance (Letty Lind as 'a prima ballerina assoluta, famous from St Petersburg to Utah', plus Jessie Bond and Frederick Rosse as the love interest, and Adelaide Astor as soubrette) with a rather more vertebrate story than its predecessor. It had a run of 159 performances and was accounted a success, was exported to some of the oriental and African circuits, but did not linger nor leave much in the way of traces.

GODSPELL Musical in 2 acts by John Michael-Tebelak based on the Gospel according to St Matthew. Music and lyrics by Stephen Schwartz. Cherry Lane Theater, New York, 17 May 1971; Promenade Theater, 10 August 1971; Broadhurst Theater, 22 June 1976.

Originally written by Tebelak as a college exercise, the text of *Godspell* – which, in spite of its claims, used as much material from the gospels of St Luke, St Mark and St John as from that of St Matthew – was a 1960s-style retelling of the last days of Christ, illustrated by re-enactments of some of his teachings, particularly as put over in the parables. The tone of the show was a young-teenage one, and the staging – an important element of the production, and done by the author himself – mixed styles and parodies from comic-strips, television shows and circus, in a mélange aimed at that same age-group.

The songs by Stephen Schwartz which illustrated the entertainment were in a suitably similar style, using the rock and country-and-western elements of the popular youth music of the time, and turning out several pieces which became popular: 'Day By Day', 'Prepare Ye the Way of the Lord', 'Turn Back, O Man'.

Tried first at La Mama, the show was then given an off-Broadway production by Edgar Lansbury, Stuart Duncan and Joseph Beruh at the Cherry Lane Theater where the cast of ten was headed by Stephen Nathan in the rôle of 'Jesus'. The show quickly proved to have a potential audience far beyond the lower-teens age-bracket, and it transferred to the Promenade Theater in 1971 and, soon after, whilst the off-Broadway production ran on, began its considerable international travels. H M Tennent Ltd's London production, with David Essex, Marti Webb, Julie Covington, Jeremy Irons and Verity-Ann Meldrum

Plate 111. **Godspell:** *Jeremy Irons and the London cast.*

amongst the cast, started out at a well-chosen venue in the wilfully fringe-y Roundhouse, but it quickly transferred into the thoroughly establishment Wyndham's Theatre and there it compiled a run of 1,128 performances, prefatory to a long life on the British touring circuits, in British provincial houses where its small cast and staging demands made it particularly popular, and to several returns, often from such productions, for seasons in the West End (1975, 1977, 1978, 1985). Australia's Kenn Brodziak opened that country's first *Godspell* in Melbourne just days after London's opening and its initial 12-month season ran partly alongside another in Sydney (Richbrooke Theatre, 10 April 1972), prior to repeated revivals.

Foreign-language adaptations followed in the next years. A German version (ad Robert Gilbert) was mounted in Hamburg with Heinz Ehrenfreund and Angelika Milster amongst the cast, and a French version (ad Bernard Giquel, Pierre Delanoë) was produced by Annie Fargue at Paris's Théâtre de la Porte-Saint-Martin, amongst a rush of productions, in all kinds of languages, worldwide.

In 1973 Victor Garber and Lynne Thigpen joined original cast members Dave Haskell, Joanne Jonas, Robin Lamont and Gilmer McCormick in a Columbia film version of the show made whilst the original production still ran on in its off-Broadway home. In 1976, after 2,124 performances off-Broadway, *Godspell* made the move up to Broadway's Broadhurst Theater (22 June), then to the Plymouth Theater (15 September) and to the Ambassador Theater (12 January 1977) winning, in the process, a total of 527 performances on Broadway to add to the continuing thousands played worldwide up to the present day. In 1988, when it might have been thought that its time and style were well and truly of the past, it nevertheless returned to New York's Lamb's Theater (12 June) and added yet another 225 performances to its remarkable on-and-around-Broadway tally, and in 1991 it was still to be seen in the repertoire of Budapest's Várszinház.

UK: Roundhouse 17 November 1971, Wyndham's Theatre 26 January 1972; Australia: Playbox Theatre, Melbourne 15 November 1971; Germany: Hamburg 1972; France: Théâtre de la Porte-Saint-Martin 1973; Hungary: Ódry Színpad 19 December 1986; Film: Columbia 1973

Recordings: original cast (Bell), London cast (Bell), Australian casts (SFL, HMV, Etcetera), German casts (Reprise, Backstage), French cast (Philips), film soundtrack (Bell), Swedish cast (Aksent), South African casts (ACP, Cat), Netherlands cast (Polydor), Spanish cast (Noviola), Danish cast (Hamlet), Swedish cast (Metronome) etc

GOETZ, E Ray (b Buffalo, NY, 12 June 1886; d Greenwich, Conn, 12 June 1954). Songwriter and producer of musicals and revues.

Goetz began a career as a songwriter in his teens, and he

had his earliest theatre successes as the lyricist of occasional interpolated songs in Broadway musicals: 'He Goes to Church on Sunday' in *The Orchid* (mus: Vincent Bryan, 1905), 'It's Lovely When Love Loves You' (*The Lady's Maid*), 'Don't Go in the Lion's Cage Tonight' (mus: Gilroy) in *The Blue Moon* (1906) and 'I Think I Oughtn't Auto Anymore', 'Come and Float Me, Freddie Dear' and 'Reincarnation' (Bryan) in *The Ziegfeld Follies of 1907*. He provided his first full book of show-words for B E Forrester's production of the touring musical *In Africa*, with comedians Yorke and Adams starred, and his first Broadway set to Baldwin Sloane's score for the unsuccessful *The Prince of Bohemia* (1910) and, over the next few years, followed up with several more scores, at first in collaboration with Sloane and then with some for which he provided both words and music himself. Most of these were for the musicals produced and/or performed by Lew Fields, either alone or in conjunction with his famous partner, Joe Weber, shows which became more and more like variety shows until they finally simply agreed to be honestly called revues rather than musicals.

Goetz himself turned to production with the 1917 revue *Hitchy-Koo* (w Raymond Hitchcock) in which his wife, Irene Bordoni, was featured. He subsequently co-produced the musical *Follow the Girl* (1918) and presented, solo, a series of other stage musical pieces including the much-rewritten French revue *As You Were* and the altogether less successful home-made revue *Here and There* (written w Glen MacDonough, 1920), Armont and Gerbidon's musicalized comedy *Jeunes Filles de palaces* (*The French Doll*), Cole Porter's *Paris*, and several further rewritten Continental pieces – *Little Miss Bluebeard* (1924, *Der Gatte des Fräuleins*), *A Naughty Cinderella* (1925 w Charles Frohman, *Pouche*) and Sacha Guitry and Reynaldo Hahn's *Mozart* – each with Miss Bordoni starring, and often with some of his own work appearing in the score.

His other production credits in the musical theatre included the early George Gershwin flop *Our Nell* (ex- *The Hayseed*) (1922), Porter's *Fifty Million Frenchmen* (1929) and the musical *The New Yorkers* (1930) written by Herbert Fields, son of his old mentor, as part of a highly active schedule which ranged from presenting the American seasons of the Spanish sensation vocalist Raquel Meller to operating New York's Club Mirador.

Goetz continued his songwriting activities and wrote the words to Finck's famous melody 'In the Shadows' as well as having song successes with such numbers as 'My Croony Melody' (w Joe Goodwin), 'We'll Have a Jubilee in My Old Kentucky Home' (mus Walter Donaldson), 'For Me and My Gal' (w Edgar Leslie, George Meyer) and 'Yaka Hula Hickey Dula' (w Pete Wendling, Joe Young) sung by Jolson in *Robinson Crusoe jr*. He also re-lyricked versions of several Continental song successes by Christiné ('Do I Love You?'), Kollo ('The Land of Going to Be'), Louis Alter and José Padilla (Raquel Meller's 'La Violetera' for *Little Miss Bluebeard*) as well as putting words to music by Puccini as a popular song, all to provide numbers to be performed by Miss Bordoni in her starring vehicles. He also contributed lyrics and/or music to the Shuberts' production of *Hands Up, As You Were*, to *George White's Scandals* (1922, 1923) and was credited (w Peter Arno) with the original storyline for his last Broadway production *The New Yorkers*.

1908 **In Africa** (Herbert Ingram/Aaron Hoffman)
1910 **The Prince of Bohemia** (A Baldwin Sloane/J Hartley Manners) Hackett Theater 13 January
1910 **A Matinee Idol** (Silvio Hein/w Seymour Brown/Armand, Bernard) Daly's Theater 28 April
1911 **The Hen Pecks** (Sloane/Glen MacDonough) Broadway Theater 4 February
1911 **The Never Homes** (Sloane/MacDonough) Broadway Theater 5 October
1912 **Hokey Pokey** (Sloane, W T Francis, John Stromberg/w Edgar Smith/E Smith) Broadway Theater 8 February
1912 **Bunty Bulls and Strings** (Sloane et al/E Smith) 2 scenes Broadway Theater 8 February
1912 **The June Bride** (*Johann der Zweite*) English lyrics (Majestic Theater, Boston)
1912 **Hanky Panky** (Sloane/E Smith) Broadway Theater 5 August
1912 **Roly Poly** (Sloane/E Smith) Weber and Fields Music Hall 21 November
1912 **Without the Law** (Sloane/E Smith) 1 act Weber and Fields Music Hall 21 November
1912 **The Sun Dodgers** (Sloane) Broadway Theater 30 November
1913 **All Aboard** (w Malvin Franklin/Mark Swan) 44th Street Theater 5 June
1913 **The Pleasure Seekers** (E Smith) Winter Garden 3 November
1915 **Hands Up** (w Romberg, Jean Schwartz/w William Jerome/E Smith) 44th Street Theater 22 July
1916 **Step This Way** (w Bert Grant/E Smith) Shubert Theater 29 May
1917 **Words and Music** Fulton Theater 24 December
1921 **Phi-Phi** American lyrics (Globe Theater, Atlantic City)

GOETZE, Walter W[ilhelm] (b Berlin, 17 April 1883; d Berlin, 24 March 1961).

Goetze began his musical career as a bassoon player, then worked as a theatre conductor in several German towns, and made his first mark as a musical-theatre writer when he set new music to a version of the play *Parkettsitz Nr 10* for Hermann Haller in Hamburg. The show went on to be played in Berlin and in Budapest (*Támlásszék*, Vigszinház 23 August 1913) and, thereafter, Goetze composed regular Operette scores for Berlin and for other German theatres, winning some success with the vaudeville *Zwischen zwölf und eins* played in Leipzig and at Vienna's Theater in der Josefstadt (29 March 1914), *Der liebe Pepi*, and the Hamburg Singspiel *Am Brunnen vor dem Tore*, but without any major results until the production of *Ihre Hoheit die Tänzerin* at the Bellevue-Theater, Stettin, in 1919. Produced soon after in Berlin, and subsequently at the Vienna Johann Strauss-Theater, it proved to be his biggest success, and was not topped during the 30 further years he devoted to the musical theatre, in spite of good runs with such pieces as *Der goldene Pierrot*, *Adrienne* and *Die göttliche Jette*, played at Vienna's Raimundtheater in 1934.

1911 **Parkettsitz Nr 10** (Hermann Haller, Willy Wolff) Tivoli Theater, Hamburg 24 September
1912 **Nur nicht drängeln** (Richard Nessler, Willy Prager) Walhalla-Theater 13 July
1913 **Zwischen zwölf und eins** (Georg Okonkowski, Max Neal, M Ferner) Neues Operettentheater, Leipzig 9 February
1913 **Wenn Männer schwindeln** (Robert Pohl, Bruno Decker) Stadttheater, Halberstadt 2 November
1914 **Schürzenmanöver** (R von Gatti, August Neidhart ad Hans Brennert) Neues Operettentheater, Leipzig 25 March

1914 **Der liebe Pepi** (*Der Bundesbruder*) (Decker, Otto Sprinzel) Montis Operettentheater 23 December

1917 **O schöne Zeit, o sel'ge Zeit** (Decker, Erich Platen) Deutsches Theater, Hanover 4 July

1918 **Am Brunnen vor dem Tore** (Oskar Felix) Deutsches Theater, Hanover 26 May

1919 **Ihre Hoheit die Tänzerin** (Richard Bars, Felix) Bellevue-Theater, Stettin 8 May; Friedrich-Wilhelmstädtisches Theater, Berlin 15 June 1919

1919 **Die – oder keine** (Bars) Walhalla-Theater, Halle am Saale 30 July

1920 **Amor auf Reisen** (Oskar Blumenthal, Gustav Kadelburg ad Decker) Thalia-Theater 15 April

1920 **Die Spitzenkönigin** (Felix, Bars) Bellevue-Theater, Stettin 16 June; Wallner-Theater, Berlin, 22 December 1921

1922 **Die schwarze Rose** (Bars, Felix) Neues Operettentheater 5 October

1924 **Die vier Schlaumeier** (Decker, Bars) Residenztheater 11 September

1926 **[Die schöne] Adrienne** (Günter Bibo/Felix, Alexander Pordes-Milo) Carl-Schultze Theater, Hamburg 24 April; Komische Oper, Berlin

1928 **Die Männer von Manon** (Neidhart, Robert Gilbert) Kleines Haus, Düsseldorf 30 September

1929 **Henriette Sontag** (Bibo) Landestheater, Altenberg 20 January

1930 **Komödie in Venedig** (Bibo, Felix) Zentraltheater, Magdeburg 28 April

1931 **Für eine schöne Frau** (Leo Lenz ad Bibo, Felix) Operettentheater, Braunschweig 11 March

1931 **Hochzeit auf Japata** (Jan van Hern) Zentraltheater, Magdeburg 13 November

1931 **Die göttliche Jette** (revised *Henriette Sontag*) Schillertheater 31 December

1933 **Der Page des Königs** Theater des Westens 21 February

1933 **Akrobaten des Glücks** (Emil Pohl ad Felix) Komische Oper 22 September

1934 **Der goldene Pierrot** (Felix, Otto Kleinert) Theater des Westens 31 March

1935 **Schach dem König!** (H A Schaufert, Paul Harms) Theater am Horst-Wessel-Platz 16 May

1936 **Sensation im Trocadero** (Felix) Stadttheater, Stettin 19 January

1936 **Der verliebte Wauwau** Stadttheater, Stettin

1939 **Die zwei Gesichter einer Königin** (Kurt Sauer) Stadtische Bühnen, Frankfurt-am-Main 25 March

1940 **Kleopatra die zweite** (revised *Die zwei Gesichter einer Königin*) Künstlertheater 9 February

1940 **Der Tanz der Herren** (Felix) Stadttheater, Stettin 3 November

1950 **Liebe im Dreiklang** (w Emil F Malkowsky) Städtische Bühnen, Heidelberg 15 November

Other titles attributed: *Charlie* (1923), *Eine entzückende Frau*, *Schwarze Husaren* (1931)

GOING GREEK Musical show in 2 acts by Guy Bolton, Fred Thompson and Douglas Furber. Music and lyrics by Sam Lerner, Al Goodhart and Al Hoffmann. Gaiety Theatre, London, 16 September 1937.

The team, headed by star comic Leslie Henson, which had been successfully established at the Gaiety Theatre in the mid-1930s under the management of Firth Shephard, had done very nicely with *Seeing Stars* and *Swing Along*, and in 1937 Henson followed these up with his own production of *Going Greek* which utilized most of the same team on a show of a splendid zaniness.

Little, froglike Henson and vast Fred Emney in Greek kilts (the latter still sporting his trademark monocle and

topper) played a pair of incompetent banditti, whilst the third of the comic triumvirate, Richard Hearne, was an operatic hostage no one wants to ransom until it suddenly seems he has inherited a fortune. Juveniles Roy Royston and Louise Browne performed the song and dance routines, as in the earlier shows ('A Little Co-operation from You'), in a musical where the quality was in the devising and the performance of the extravagant comedy episodes rather than in an anodine made-for-dancing score.

Going Greek ran for 303 performances at the Gaiety before being closed when Henson fell ill. It subsequently toured for a number of years, whilst Henson, Emney, Hearne and the Gaiety continued with more new shows of the same style.

GOING UP Musical comedy in 3 acts by Otto Harbach and James Montgomery based on *The Aviator* by James Montgomery. Lyrics by Otto Harbach. Music by Louis A Hirsch. Liberty Theater, New York, 25 December 1917.

James Montgomery's 1910 play, *The Aviator*, was put to musical use by its author and the now practised manufacturer of musical comedy Otto Harbach, several of whose biggest successes to date (*Three Twins*, *Madame Sherry*, *High Jinks*) had been with adaptations. The music was allotted to Louis Hirsch, composer of two recent *Ziegfeld Follies* since his well-timed incursion into London revue, but whose record with book musicals was less impressive. *Going Up* changed that.

The libretto concerned one Robert Street (Frank Craven), the author of a popular book on flying called *Going Up*. When challenged to a flying race by the jealous French aviator Jules Gaillard (Joseph Lertora), whose girlfriend, Grace Douglas (Edith Day), he has attracted, he is in a spot, for Robert's book is fiction and he has never handled an aeroplane. Grace, misunderstanding the situation, agrees to marry the winner of the challenge. Robert is given hurried flying lessons, and wins the contest, staying up in the sky longest simply because he is unable to land. When he does get down, he finds he is still a hero, and an affianced one. Frank Otto played Hopkinson ('Hoppy') Brown, Robert's comical pal, whilst Marion Sunshine was Madeleine, Grace's chum, with whom he, inevitably, paired off.

Hirsch's songs included a delicious mixture of the lightest contemporary popular strains: the jaunty titlenumber led by the flying Frenchman, a dance speciality in which everyone was exhorted to do 'The Tickle Toe', Grace's piece about the effect of 'The Touch of a Woman's Hand', Madeleine's march-time creed that 'I Want a Boy (who's determined to do what I say)' and, above all, the two girls' delightful duo 'If You Look in Her Eyes'.

Sam Harris and George M Cohan's Broadway production of *Going Up* was a first-class success and remained 351 performances at the Liberty Theater before going on the road, but an even longer run awaited Joe Sacks's London mounting, produced under the reign of Alfred Butt at the Gaiety Theatre. Evelyn Laye (Madeleine), Marjorie Gordon (Grace), Joseph Coyne (Robert), Austin Melford (Hoppy) and Henry de Bray (Gaillard) led the cast, with Arthur Chesney in the rôle of Grace's gamblingmad father. The show gave the Gaiety one of its greatest successes as wartime turned into celebration time, and it ran up 574 victory-year performances before going touring.

Australia, too, gave the show a strong welcome. Alfred Frith (Robert), Ethel Erskine (Grace), Cecil Bradley (Madeleine) and Jack Hooker (Gaillard) were featured in a very impressive 15-week run in Melbourne prior to an even more successful Sydney season of 17 weeks and 116 performances at the Criterion (23 August 1919), there was a return run in 1921, and for years half of urban Sydney was musically encouraging the other half to 'do the tickle-toe'.

In spite of its great initial success, *Going Up* was subsequently forgotten, whilst less successful shows and songs by more fashionable composers got the attention, but in 1976 it was revived in a revised version (which included the intake of other Hirsch songs, notably 'I'll Think of You' from *The Rainbow Girl*) at the Goodspeed Opera House. Successful there, it did not survive a transfer to Broadway's John Golden Theatre (19 September) where it played but 49 performances.

A 1923 film version featured Douglas McLean as Robert Street, Hallam Cooley as Hoppy, Marjorie Daw and Edna Murphy as the girls, and Mervyn Le Roy in a supporting rôle.

UK: Gaiety Theatre 22 May 1918; Australia: His Majesty's Theatre, Melbourne 19 April 1919; Film: 1923

THE GOLDEN APPLE

Musical in 2 acts by John Latouche. Music by Jerome Moross. Phoenix Theater, New York, 11 March 1954; Alvin Theater, 20 April 1954.

A virtual modern-day opéra-bouffe which used (or, rather, re-used) parts of Homer's *Iliad* and *Odyssey* in a witty and topical tale of everyday American people-in-power, *The Golden Apple* has, in spite of its relative failure in the theatre, become a cult musical amongst those who make cults of such things.

Helen (Kaye Ballard) is no longer Homer's Helen, nor indeed Meilhac and Halévy's Helen, but the weak-willed wife of the small-town Sheriff Menelaus (Dean Michener) of Angel's Roost, Washington. And Paris (Jonathan Lucas), the Prince who wins her rather too easily away and starts the Trojan war, is nothing but a banal travelling salesman, even if he does travel by balloon. The pair elope to the sea-side city of Rhododendron, pursued by Ulysses (Stephen Douglass) and the rest of Helen's former admirers, but the rescuers meet with stern opposition from the Mayor of Rhododendron, Hector (Jack Whiting). It is opposition of the insiduous kind, and it takes the hero ten whole years of resisting temptations which have nothing of the heroic to them, temptations that his friends fall prey to, before he beats Paris in a fist-fight and can traipse home to where the faithful Penelope (Priscilla Gillette) is waiting.

The show's score – virtually a series of sung scenes and with minimal dialogue – included a wide range of musical pieces in a selection of styles, from which 'Lazy Afternoon' for Helen and 'Wind Flowers' for Penelope proved the outstanding ballads, alongside the rich duo 'It's the Going Home Together', the comical 'Doomed, Doomed, Doomed' sung by Portia Nelson in the rôle of Minerva, and the scena depicting the equivalent of the Judgement of Paris, in which the salesman is called upon to make his choice among three Washington matrons and selects

Lovey Mars (Bibi Osterwald) and her promise of a good sex life.

First produced at the off-Broadway Phoenix Theater by Norris Houghton and T Edward Hambleton, *The Golden Apple* won some excited notices and the kind of attendances which encouraged Alfred de Liagre and Roger L Stevens to transfer the show (which many a Broadway producer had turned down prior to its production), after 48 performances, to Broadway's Alvin Theater. It managed only 125 performances there before closing. The show's reputation remained, however, amongst the cognoscenti, and it was given a revival, back in its off-Broadway element, in 1962 (York Playhouse 12 February 1962, 112 performances) and, most recently, by the York Theatre Company in 1990 (23 March). It was also televised in 1977.

Recording: original cast (RCA, Elektra)

GOLDEN BOY

Musical in 2 acts by Clifford Odets and William Gibson based on the play of the same name by Odets. Lyrics by Lee Adams. Music by Charles Strouse. Majestic Theater, New York, 20 October 1964.

Odets's 1937 play told the story of an Italian-American slum boy who gives up music for prize fighting but, after a promising beginning in his search for a fist-won rise in social status, sees his life go sour professionally, when he kills an opponent, and personally, when he loses his girl. After a reconciliation they are killed in a car accident.

Some of the melodrama was squeezed out of the tale when it was made over into a musical, partly by Odets and, after his death, by Gibson, and the character of the young boxer was altered to allow him to belong to a more fashionable kind of seeker-after-social-status in a 1960s context. The Joe Wellington of the musical *Golden Boy* was a negro, and the cultural-physical dilemma of the original play was replaced by a simple go-getting attitude. Sammy Davis jr was Joe, Paula Wayne played the girl, Lorna, whom he wants, but who ultimately prefers his unprepossessing manager (Kenneth Tobey), Billy Daniels was the rival manager, Eddie Satin, and Joe met his death alone.

Davis had the bulk of the evening's music ('Night Song', 'Stick Around', 'Don't Forget 127th Street', 'Colorful', 'I Want to Be With You' w Lorna, 'Can't You See It'), Lorna had the title song, Daniels delivered 'While the City Sleeps', and the boxing match which was the evening's highlight, and which resulted in the opponent's death, was a choreographed piece.

Hillard Elkins's production of *Golden Boy* played 569 performances on Broadway, and was subsequently mounted at the London Palladium with Davis repeating the performance which had encouraged much of the piece's popularity. London saw 118 performances.

A revised version with a libretto by Leslie Lee and an altered score was tested (1985, 1991) variously in Brooklyn, Florida and Connecticut without being launched on a wider scale.

UK: London Palladium 4 June 1968
Recording: original cast (Capitol)

GOLDEN RAINBOW

Musical in 2 acts by Ernest Kinoy based on *A Hole in the Head* by Arnold Shulman. Music and lyrics by Walter Marks. Shubert Theater, New York, 4 February 1968.

A vehicle for husband-and-wife singing team Steve Lawrence and Eydie Gorme, *Golden Rainbow* cast Lawrence as the unimpressive Larry Davis, a widower with a ten year-old son, Ally (Scott Jacoby), and a rather seedy Las Vegas (rather than the play's original Florida) hotel, the Golden Rainbow, on which he is having a hard time keeping up the payments. His well-off sister-in-law, Judy Harris (Miss Gorme), who starts by trying to take the child into her care, ends up by marrying Larry and supplying the needed cash. The show's songs had of-the-period titles like 'We Got Us', 'He Needs Me Now, 'How Could I Be So Wrong' and, the most successful, Larry's cop-out excuse for everything, 'I've Gotta Be Me'. Amongst the other players, only Joseph Sirola as a big-time hustler called Lou Garrity got a look in musically, with a number about 'Taste'.

Golden Rainbow served Lawrence and Miss Gorme for 385 Broadway performances.

Recording: original cast (Calendar)

DIE GOLD'NE MEISTERIN

DIE GOLD'NE MEISTERIN Operette in 3 acts by Julius Brammer and Alfred Grünwald based on the play *Die goldene Eva* by Franz von Schönthan and Franz Koppel-Ellfeld. Music by Edmund Eysler. Theater an der Wien, Vienna, 13 September 1927.

Die gold'ne Meisterin was set in 16th-century Venice, and the lady of the title was Margarete (Betty Fischer), the socially ambitious widow of a wealthy goldsmith. When she dances with an attractive stranger at a society ball, she is mortified to discover that he is only Christian (Hubert Marischka), her new goldsmith, and she petulantly permits the attentions of the gold-digging Count Jaromir von Greifenstein (Fritz Steiner) in retaliation. Christian exposes Greifenstein as a cheat and a married man, and in the gardens of the monastery at Klosterneuburg the pair are finally brought together under the guidance of the good Brother Ignatius (Richard Waldemar). Two veteran stars, Mizzi Zwerenz (Portschunkula) and Franz Glawatsch (Fridolin von Gumpendorf), provided the bulk of the comedy as Margarete's housekeeper and another penniless nobleman.

If Brammer and Grünwald's libretto was not, perhaps, their very best, the score with which Eysler illustrated it was one of his most outstanding. Margarete's dazzling entrance number ('Gräfin sein, Fürstin sein'), all excited by her success at the ball, Christian's waltz 'Du liebe, gold'ne Meisterin', their waltz-duo reminiscing over their dance together ('So tanzt man nur in Wien') and the Danube-drenched little 'In Grinzing is' ein Gasserl' were all hits, whilst the comic pieces such as the duo for the two shabby noblemen, 'Jaromir von Greifenstein', Portschunkula's reminder to Fridolin of his tipsy proposal ('Portschunkula! Portschunkula!'), and Ignatius's little homily 'Jeder Mensch hat in der Brust', gave the traditional contrast.

Die gold'ne Meisterin turned out to be one of Eysler's most successful shows. A fine success at the Theater an der Wien, it ran past its 200th performance on 19 March 1928 and closed on 4 April, but, possibly because its Alt-Wienerisch tale and tuncs sccmed old-fashioned, with the coming of jazzier strains on the one hand and the dark romanticism of latcr Lchár on the other, its future was disproportionately limited. It was revived at the Raimundtheater just after the end of the Second World War (30 November 1945) with Waldemar repeating his original rôle, at the Volksbühne in May 1946, and again at the Raimundtheater in 1955 (29 April), but has been little seen, and, sadly, little heard, otherwise.

Recording: selection (Philips)

GOLDSMITH, Oliver

GOLDSMITH, Oliver (b Pallas, Co Longford, 10 November 1730; d London, 4 April 1774).

The two principal fictional works of Oliver Goldsmith have served as the stuff of a number of musical plays. *The Vicar of Wakefield*, well-known in many versions on the straight stage, was burlesqued in Britain as *The Vicar of Wide-Awake-Field* (Gaiety Theatre, 1885) and treated more seriously in the light opera *The Vicar of Wakefield*, composed by Liza Lehmann and written by Laurence Housman (1906). *She Stoops to Conquer* became *The Two Roses* in Stanislaus Stange and Ludwig Englander's 1904 Broadway version, *O Marry Me* (Lola Pergament/Robert Kessler) at off-Broadway's Gate Theater (27 October 1961) and, updated into a wild western setting, *Liberty Ranch* in the hands of Caryl Brahms, Ned Sherrin, Dick Vosburgh and John Cameron (Greenwich Theatre 18 July 1972).

THE GONDOLIERS

THE GONDOLIERS, or The King of Barataria Comic opera in 2 acts by W S Gilbert. Music by Arthur Sullivan. Savoy Theatre, London, 7 December 1889.

The last great success of the Gilbert and Sullivan partnership, *The Gondoliers* took the favourite comic-opera location of Venice for its setting, but ignored the Doge and his Council of Ten and the other usual elements of Venetian shows – even the usually inevitable last-act masked ball – and used the city of canals only as a picturesque background for a tale, made up of largely familiar elements, which might very well have taken place anywhere.

Marco (Courtice Pounds) and Giuseppe (Rutland Barrington) Palmieri are a handsome pair of gondoliers, happily wedded before much of Act I has passed to local contadine Gianetta (Geraldine Ulmar) and Tessa (Jessie Bond). Then some disturbing news is delivered by the city's Grand Inquisitor (W H Denny). Casilda (Decima Moore), the teenaged daughter of the Duke (Frank Wyatt) and Duchess (Rosina Brandram) of Plaza Toro, was long ago betrothed to the infant King of Barataria. The little King was wet-nursed out during a revolution, but now the time has come for him – and that means one of the Palmieris – to be restored. Since it cannot be established which of Marco or Giuseppe is the apparently mislaid monarch, the two men, up to now staunch anti-royalists, go off to try to rule Barataria together, on egalitarian principles. Then the news about the wife is broken. One of them is a bigamist as well as a king. Fortunately, it turns out that the wet-nurse did a double switch, and the real King is the drummer, Luis (Wallace Brownlow), whom Casilda has been mooning over all night, and who has no nonsensically impractical ideas about the equality of men.

The Gondoliers was full of typical and delightful Gilbert and Sullivan numbers, of which Marco's serenade 'Take a

Pair of Sparkling Eyes' proved to be the bon-bon. The Ducal family were particularly well provided, with a series of numbers which were largely Gilbert's variations on well-used themes, as they arrived in shabby style 'From the Sunny Spanish Shore', with the Duke clipping out the familiar tale of the accidental hero in 'In Enterprise of Martial Kind' and trying to teach court manners to the unroyal Kings ('I am a Courtier Grave and Serious') in the same way Robert Reece's characters had done in *Cattarina* more than a decade previously. The Duchess boomed out her recipe for falling in love with an aristocratic husband on command ('On the Day That I Was Wedded') and joined with her husband in a clever piece on how to cash in on your nobility ('Small Titles and Orders'), whilst Casilda duetted forlornly with her Luis ('O Rapture! When Alone Together', 'There Was a Time'). Tessa's best opportunity came in the lively 'When a Merry Maiden Marries' and Gianetta's in 'Kind Sir, You Cannot Have the Heart', but, by and large, the four juveniles were less well served than the Inquisitor, who was featured in two bouncy basso expository tales ('I Stole the Prince', 'There Lived a King, As I've Been Told'). With its cachuca and gavotte, *The Gondoliers* also included a touch more in the way of dance than was usual in the Savoy operas.

The Gondoliers brought back the burlesque element to the Savoy after the more straight light-operatic tones of Gilbert and Sullivan's previous piece, *The Yeomen of the Guard*, and it was rewarded with excellent notices and a run of 554 performances as it joined the hard core of the Gilbert and Sullivan repertoire. Carte opened his Broadway production whilst the London one ran on, importing George Temple (Duke), Kate Talby (Duchess), Esther Palliser (Gianetta), Richard Clarke (Marco) and Barrington to head a company through 103 nights at the Park and Palmer's Theatres, and, in a Vienna still delighted over *Der Mikado*, *Die Gondoliere* (ad F Zell, Richard Genée) was produced at the Theater an der Wien in September before going on to Berlin in December. It did not, however, prove to have the same appeal to German-language audiences as its oriental predecessor, lasting only 18 performances in Vienna.

In the English language, however, the piece did splendidly. J C Williamson's Australian production, with William Elton (Duke), Maggie Moore (Duchess), Jack Leumane (Marco), Charles Ryley (Giuseppe), Flora Graupner (Gianetta) and Florence Young (Casilda) proved as successful as the London version and, as in England, the show was regularly revived throughout Australia following its first showing there. The D'Oyly Carte company brought *The Gondoliers* back to London in 1898 (22 March) with Elton repeating his Australian performance as the Duke, Rosina Brandram still the Duchess, and the young Ethel Jackson – later to be America's *Merry Widow* – in the small but demanding rôle of Fiametta (125 performances), again in 1907 (22 January, 75 performances) and thereafter in the company's repertoire seasons. After the release of the Gilbert and Sullivan copyrights, the show was played by Scottish Opera (12 December 1968) and by the New Sadler's Wells company (9 February 1984), and it has remained a steady favourite amongst the Savoy canon.

Another *Die Gondoliere*, written by Arnoldo Bonometti and Willy Kissner, was produced at the Landshut Stadttheater in 1913 (28 January).

USA: Park Theater 7 January 1890; Austria: Theater an der Wien *Die Gondoliere* 20 September 1890; Australia: Princess Theatre, Melbourne 25 October 1890; Germany: Friedrich-Wilhelmstädtisches Theater 20 December 1890
Recordings: complete (Decca, HMV) etc

GONE WITH THE WIND Musical in 2 acts by Horton Foote based on the novel by Margaret Mitchell. Music and lyrics by Harold Rome. Theatre Royal, Drury Lane, London, 3 May 1972.

The original musical version of Margaret Mitchell's celebrated civil war novel, *Gone With the Wind*, was put together under the aegis of American director and choreographer Joe Layton, and was produced in Japanese (libretto: Kasuo Kikuta), under the title *Scarlett*, at Tokyo's Imperial Theatre on 3 January 1970. Layton then took it to Britain, where its original English-language version was produced under the management of Harold Fielding at London's Theatre Royal, Drury Lane with June Ritchie in the rôle of Scarlett O'Hara, Harve Presnell as Rhett Butler, Patricia Michael as Melanie, Robert Swann as Ashley Wilkes, and the very young Bonnie Langford as Bonnie. The opening night revealed a spectacular burning of Atlanta, a misbehaved horse and a classic over-the-top performance from the very young child, provoking Noël Coward to remark drily: 'If they'd shoved the little girl up the horse's arse, they'd have solved both problems'. Horse and child both calmed down after opening night, and enough folk got used to seeing the well-known story interspersed with a long score of light musical theatre numbers for *Gone With the Wind* to turn into a distinct success (397 performances).

Fielding subsequently took the show to America, but alterations made for the Broadway-bound production, largely in an effort to try to top the big first-act ending of the famous fire with a second-act climax, proved ill-advised and, after a four-hour opening night, America's *Gone With the Wind*, with Lesley Ann Warren and Pernell Roberts featured, foundered in San Francisco.

USA: Dorothy Chandler Pavilion, Los Angeles 28 August 1973
Recordings: original Japanese production (Victor), original London cast (Columbia)

GOODHART, Al (b New York, 26 January 1905; d New York, 30 November 1955).

Variously a vaudevillian, a radio announcer, a pianist and a theatrical agent, Goodhart also had some success as a songwriter, in tandem with the already-established Al Hoffman and others, turning out 'I Apologise' (w Hoffman, Ed Nelson), 'Auf Wiederseh'n, My Dear' (w Hoffman, Nelson, Milton Ager), 'Happy Go Lucky You and Broken Hearted Me' (w Hoffman, John Murray), 'In the Dim Dawning' (w Hoffman, Stanley Adams), 'Fit as a Fiddle' (w Hoffman, Arthur Freed), later featured in *Singin' in the Rain* on screen and on stage, 'Who Walks In?' (w Hoffman, Ralph Freed) and 'I Saw Stars' (w Hoffman, Maurice Sigler) in the early 1930s.

In 1934, with the British fashion for American songwriters at its peak, he joined Hoffman and Sigler in Britain to supply songs for such early British Gaumont sound films as Jessie Matthews's *First a Girl* ('Everything's in Rhythm with My Heart'), Jack Buchanan's *Come Out of the Pantry* ('Everything Stops for Tea'), *She Shall Have Music* ('My First Thrill'), and then, with Sigler replaced by Sam

Lerner, but still in the inevitable musical troilism, for Miss Matthews's *Gangway* ('Gangway') etc.

During the same period the trios also supplied songs for Jack Buchanan's stage musical *This'll Make You Whistle* ('There Isn't Any Limit to my Love', 'I'm in a Dancing Mood', 'This'll Make You Whistle', 'You've Got the Wrong Rumba'), the Gaiety Theatre success *Going Greek* ('A Little Co-operation From You'), and the Cicely Courtneidge/Bobby Howes *Hide and Seek* (w Vivian Ellis). In 1938, when the vein of fashion ran out, the songwriters returned to America after which, apart from 'I Ups to Her and She Ups to Me' (w Hoffman, Manny Kurtz), Good-hart seems to have made no further appearance on the international songwriting scene.

1936 **This'll Make You Whistle** (w Maurice Sigler, Al Hoffman/Guy Bolton, Fred Thompson) Palace Theatre 14 September

1937 **Going Greek** (w Sam Lerner, Hoffman/Bolton, Thompson, Douglas Furber) Gaiety Theatre 16 September

1937 **Hide and Seek** (w Vivian Ellis, Lerner, Hoffman/Bolton, Thompson, Furber) London Hippodrome 14 October

GOOD MORNING, DEARIE Musical comedy in 2 acts by Anne Caldwell. Music by Jerome Kern. Globe Theater, New York, 1 November 1921.

The libretto to *Good Morning Dearie* trod paths that were not quite as well-worn as many, in its details if not in its essence. The juvenile man was rich and social Billy van Cortlandt (Oscar Shaw), doomed to be wedded to equally rich and social Ruby Manners (Peggy Kurton). But his heart has gone astray, and the object of his sighing is the little milliner's errand girl, Rose-Marie (Louise Groody). Unfortunately, Rose-Marie does not have an unblemished past. She has been associated, in not the nicest possible way, with the very dubious Chesty Costello (Harlan Dixon), to whom she is now beholden. Fortunately, Chesty's itchy fingers get the better of him. He is caught by hero and heroine in the act of stealing the jewels of a society lady and is happy to swap fiancée for liberty.

Oscar Shaw drew the hit song of the show, in the pseudo-Hawaiian 'Ka-lu-a', as well as a 'Didn't You Believe?' and a pair of watery duos with his heroine about 'Niagara Falls' and 'The Blue Danube Blues', whilst she, in turn, called herself 'Rose-Marie' and was given the title-song of the evening. William Kent, in the rôle of detective Steve, had two numbers ('Sing Song Girl', 'Melican Papa'), but the accent was as much on dancing as it was on singing and there were Sixteen Sunshine Girls (Coolie Dance, 'Le Sport American'), Six Fan-Tan Girls, a dance soloist, Marie Callahan, to perform two routines with Dixon, as well as one of the novelty dances that characterized the period, 'The Teddy Toddle'.

Even though produced at a dicky moment in theatrical time, Charles Dillingham's production of *Good Morning, Dearie* proved a jolly, multi-coloured piece of entertainment which ran through no less than 347 performances on Broadway. The public's liking, however, was not parallelled by some others. City Hall got miffed at a lyric making fun of it and refused to issue new permits for the children in the show until the offending line was altered, and then poor, silly Fred Fisher, the composer of such hits as 'Peg o' my Heart', flew into court to prosecute Kern for lifting his 'Dardanella' contra-bass for 'Ka-lu-a'. In one of those

loony theatrical lawsuits, Fisher was given eventual winner and damages of $250.

Kern made rather more than that from his song and from his show, which followed its Broadway season with a good tour, and with a production in Australia which featured Josie Melville (Rose-Marie), George Vollaire (Billy), Percy Le Fre (Steve), George Crotty (Chesty) and Dan Agar. Hailed as 'a smart American piece ... an eccentric dancing entertainment in excelsis set to daintily-scored melodic numbers and with clever dialogue and lyrics' it ran for more than two months in Sydney, and played a Christmas season in Melbourne with Miss Melville paired with George Gee.

Australia: Theatre Royal, Sydney 5 July 1924

GOOD NEWS Musical comedy in 2 acts by Laurence Schwab and B G De Sylva. Lyrics by B G De Sylva and Lew Brown. Music by Ray Henderson. 46th Street Theater, New York, 6 September 1927.

What Bordman's *The American Musical Theatre* calls 'probably the quintessential musical comedy of the era of wonderful nonsense', was a lively, ingenuous show about college kids, dating and footballing, much in the vein of the earlier *Leave it to Jane*, but without the element of parody that would appear in its post-war equivalent, *Grease*. It used a problem which is still a contemporary American one for its main plot element – Tom Marlowe (John Price Jones), the pride of the Tait College football team, isn't going to be able to play in the Big Game if he doesn't pass his examinations. He gets help and a happy final curtain from fellow student Connie Lane (Mary Lawlor). Alongside the romantic line, there was the requisite amount of light-hearted comedy from fellow footballer and funster Bobby Randall (Gus Shy), boisterous soubretting from an incidental lass called Flo (Zelma O'Neal), whilst Shirley Vernon played Patricia Bingham, the girl who is the hurdle Connie has to pass to get to Tom.

The plot of *Good News* was, however, much less important than its high-spirited production and its songs. Connie and Tom joined together to sing about being 'Lucky in Love' and declared starrily that 'The Best Things in Life Are Free', and Connie and her pals Patricia and Millie (Ruth Mayon) waxed dreamy in 'Just Imagine', whilst Flo pelted out the 'Good News', and George Olsen's band, which provided the accompaniment to the entertainment, joined in the fun in collegiate clothes. The highlight of the show, however, came with the performance of 'The Varsity Drag' ('a kind of riotous cakewalk') sung and danced, with legs aflying, by the young Miss O'Neal.

A joyful success alongside such pieces as *Rio Rita* and *Hit the Deck* and later *My Maryland*, *A Connecticut Yankee*, *Funny Face*, *The Three Musketeers* and *Show Boat* in the 1927–8 season, the Laurence Schwab/Frank Mandel production of *Good News* remained at the 46th Street Theater for a fine 557 performances.

Miss O'Neal repeated her famous dance when *Good News* was taken to London the following year, starring alongside Neil Collins (Tom), Evelyn Hoey (Connie) and Bobby Jarvis (Bobby) in a Clayton and Waller production at the Carlton Theatre. However, this very American show proved, in spite of its zingy collection of gramophoneable songs, to have less to offer to the British and it closed after 132 performances. Australia's production, mounted by the

Fullers in Melbourne and staged by Ernest Rolls, did no better. Sam Critcherson (Tom) headed the cast of a show which played a month and a half at the Princess before going on to Sydney's St James Theatre (10 November 1928) where Elsie Prince (Babe) and Jimmy Godden (Pooch) were brought in to give weight to the bill. Even with that favourite pair in place, the show did not manage to arouse any real enthusiasm.

A Budapest production (rechristened 'student love, a tale of American college life' by adaptor Lazsló Szilagyi) was successfully staged at the Király Színház, the city's home of operett, with Franziska Gaal and Kálmán Rózsahegyi starred, during Hungary's 1920s craze for musical comedy and for things American, following on behind such highly successful pieces as the blockbusting *Mersz-e, Mary?* (*Mercenary Mary*), *Rose Marie* and *The Girl Friend*, and in the atmosphere of local pieces with titles like *Hullo Amerika!*, *Miss Amerika* and *Amerikai lányok*. In France, Jane Auber and Philippe Meyer introduced 'La Chance en amour', 'Avec un peu d'imagination' and 'Tout ça, c'est pour tout le monde' and the chorus danced 'Le Drag de l'université' in Albert Willemetz's version for a short season.

Two Hollywood film versions of *Good News* were made, the first in 1930 featuring original star Mary Lawton, but utilizing only some of the show score (both 'Just Imagine' and 'Lucky in Love' were omitted) alongside some Hollywood interpolations, and the second in 1947 with Peter Lawford and June Allyson playing the young lovers and also heading the performance of 'The Varsity Drag'. This version used all the show hits (but not the rest of the score), supplemented by two in-house additions.

Following his success in bringing *No, No, Nanette* and *Irene* back to Broadway in the 1970s, Harry Rigby tried in 1974 to do the same with *Good News*. With a sizeable female film name – Alice Faye this time – again heading the bill, the new *Good News* (titivated with three numbers from *Follow Thru* and another half dozen from other shows) toured America for a year but Miss Faye, Stubby Kaye and Gene Nelson stayed in New York (St James Theater 23 December 1974) for just 16 performances.

UK: Carlton Theatre 15 August 1928; Australia: Princess Theatre, Melbourne 16 June 1928; Hungary: Király Színház *Diákszerelem* 30 March 1929; France: Palace 20 December 1929; Films: MGM 1930, MGM 1947

Recordings: selection (part record) (World Records, Allegro), film soundtrack 1947 (MGM, Columbia), cast recording 1974 (private)

GOODWIN, J[ohn] Cheever (b Boston, 14 July 1850; d New York, 19 December 1912). Broadway bricoleur of texts, many borrowed from the French, who found his greatest successes with his few original pieces.

Born in Boston and educated at Harvard, Goodwin began his working life in journalism on the *Boston Traveller*. He had his first experience in the theatre as an actor, appearing with Sothern and in opéra-bouffe with Alice Oates's company, for whom he also took a hand in the rather free 'adaptations' that that lady made to suit Continental and British musical plays to her company's sometimes outlandish needs. His progress from actor to author was completed when he had a notable writing suc-

cess in his collaboration with E E Rice on the libretto and lyrics for the enormously successful burlesque *Evangeline* (1874).

He continued to work in journalism, and as a secretary, whilst turning out a goodly list of musical theatre pieces. On the one hand, he adapted a number of French opéras-bouffes and -comiques for the American stage including some such as *La Gardeuse d'oies* (*A Normandy Wedding*), *Les Demoiselles de Saint-Cyriens* (*The Cadet Girl*), *Babolin* (*The Devil's Deputy*) and *Pervenche* (*Fleur de lis*) which – with their sources not always credited – were equipped with wholly or almost wholly new music. On the other, he wrote at first text and lyrics, and later mostly lyrics only, for a series of native musical comedies and extravaganzas (again, often, some form of adaptation), several of which had extended lives around America, although they rarely travelled beyond.

His greatest theatrical success, apart from *Evangeline*, came with the comic opera *Wang* (1891), an apparently original echo of the oriental opéras-bouffes of the French and English stages written for the comedian De Wolf Hopper, and his most popular single song hit with 'When Reuben Comes to Town'.

His musical version of the farce *Le Baptême du petit Oscar*, *Lost, Strayed or Stolen*, was played briefly at London's Duke of York's Theatre in 1897 and both his revamping of the French libretto to *L'Étoile* as *The Merry Monarch* (1891) and *Wang* (1901) were seen in Australia. *The Merry Monarch* was also used as part of the the the bases for another rehash of Chabrier's ill-treated opéra-comique, played at London's Savoy Theatre as *The Lucky Star*, with a score by Ivan Caryll.

A non-musical piece written in collaboration with Charles Bradley served as the basis for the musical comedy *The Regatta Girl* (14 March 1900), musicalized by Harry McLellan for Koster and Bial's Music Hall.

1873 **Evangeline** (E E Rice) Niblo's Garden 27 July
1881 **Cinderella at School** (Woolson Morse) Daly's Theater 5 March
1884 **Madam Piper** (Morse) Wallack's Theater 5 December
1887 **Pippins** (various) Globe Theater, Boston 24 December; Broadway Theater, New York 26 November 1890
1887 **Jacquette** (*La Béarnaise*) American version (Wallack's Theater)
1890 **The Merry Monarch** (*L'Étoile*) American version w new music by Morse (Broadway Theater)
1891 **Wang** (Morse) Broadway Theater 4 May
1892 **The Lion Tamer** (*Le Grand Casimir*) American version w new music by Richard Stahl (Broadway Theater)
1893 **Panjandrum** (Morse) Broadway Theater 1 May
1894 **Dr Syntax** (revised *Cinderella at School*) Broadway Theater 23 June
1894 **The Devil's Deputy** (*Babolin*) American version w new music by Edward Jakobowski (Abbey's Theater)
1895 **Aladdin Jr** (W H Batchelor, Jesse Williams) Chicago; Broadway Theater, New York 8 April
1895 **Fleur de lis** (*Pervenche*) American version w new music by Furst (Palmers Theater)
1896 **Lost, Strayed or Stolen** (aka *A Day in Paris*) (Morse) Fifth Avenue Theater 21 September
1897 **La Falote** English version (Casino Theater)
1898 **A Normandy Wedding** (ex-*Papa Gougou*) (*La Gardeuse d'oies*) American version w Charles A Byrne w new music by Furst (Herald Square Theater)
1899 **An Arabian Girl and the Forty Thieves** American ver-

sion (Meyer Lutz, Jesse Williams, Batchelor) Chicago; Herald Square Theater, New York 29 April

1899 **Around New York in Eighty Minutes** (Rice, John Braham/James T Waldron, Edward Fales Coward) Koster and Bial's Music Hall 27 September

1899 **The Lady from Chicago** (Richard Henry Warren, Henry K Hadley, William F Peters, Melville Ellis/w Coward, Louis Fitzgerald jr, Rupert Hughes, Robert Sands, James Barnes) Strollers' Benefit, Waldorf Astoria 15 December

1900 **The Cadet Girl** (*Les Demoiselles de Saint-Cyriens*) (Englander [and Louis Varney]/H B Smith) American version w largely new score (Herald Square Theater)

1900 **The Monks of Malabar** (ex-*Booloo Boolboom*) (Englander) Knickerbocker Theater 14 September

1900 **The Rogers Brothers in Central Park** (Maurice Levi/J J McNally) Hammerstein's Victoria 17 September

1901 **The Sleeping Beauty and the Beast** American version w Fred Solomon Broadway Theater 4 November

1902 **The Rogers Brothers at Harvard** (Levi) Knickerbocker Theater 1 September

1903 **Mr Bluebeard** American version w Solomon (mus) Knickerbocker Theater 21 January

GOODWIN, Nat [GOODWIN, Nathaniel Carl] (b Boston, 25 July 1857; d New York, 31 January 1919).

Goodwin began his career on stage at 17, in his native Boston, and he appeared at Tony Pastor's burlesque house (playing the chief comedy rôle of Captain Crosstree in the celebrated burlesque version of *Black-Eyed Susan*) and with E E Rice and his Surprise Party company (*Evangeline*, *Cruets* etc) before setting up a similar outfit of his own, the Froliques, playing farce-comedies, with varying degrees of music, around the country. Goodwin starred for long periods in specially made rôles in musical-comedy vehicles such as Professor Pygmalion in Benjamin Woolf's *Hobbies* or Delaine in *The Skating Rink*, he appeared in burlesque (Matyas Irving in *Those Bells!*, *Cinderella in School*) and was also seen in literate comedy (Onesimus Epps in *The Member for Slocum*) and in comic opera (*La Mascotte*, *Olivette*). When he stopped in New York for seven months during the 1887-8 season, he presented his old *The Skating Rink*, Meyer Lutz's London Gaiety burlesque *Little Jack Sheppard* in which Goodwin and Loie Fuller gave their versions of the roles created by Fred Leslie and Nellie Farren, a version of Mark Melford's English comedy *Turned Up*, plugged full of borrowed songs, and a standard musical farce-comedy *Big Pony, or the Gentlemanly Savage*.

In his buying-up of British successes around this time he is said to have taken the rights to a new comic opera playing at the Comedy Theatre. But he let the rights lapse, and the record-breaking *Erminie* was instead produced by the Casino Theater and Rudolf Aronson. Goodwin's subsequent fame was made in comedy and in the newspaper scandal pages.

Autobiography: *Nat Goodwin's Book* (R G Badger, Boston, 1914)

GORDON, Kitty [BLADES, Catherine] (b Folkestone, 22 April 1878; d Brentwood, NY, 26 May 1974).

Miss Gordon first appeared on stage at 23 when she was engaged for a chorus rôle in George Edwardes's pre-London production of *Kitty Grey* (1900), two weeks prior to the end of the tour. She was retained when the show opened in town several months later and, at the end of the run, filled a similarly small but picturesque rôle in Edwardes's *The Girl from Kays* (1902). Her third Edwardes

show was *The Duchess of Dantzic*, more demanding musically, and Miss Gordon's statuesque beauty and well-trained voice won her the supporting rôle of Princess Caroline Murat and the opportunity to substitute for Evie Greene in the star rôle on several occasions.

Edwardes then cast her as Agathe in London's *Véronique* (1904), a rôle she repeated on Broadway the following year, before she moved to Charles Frohman's management to play the splendidly vicious Princess Rasslova, battling against Edna May's wansome *Nellie Neil* (1907), again in London. After the quick failures of *The Three Kisses* and *The Antelope* she returned to Edwardes to play the cabaret vamp Olga Labinska in *The Dollar Princess*, and then crossed the Atlantic again. In was in America that she finally moved from second leads to starring rôles and there she spent the remainder of her career, apparently aided by publicity which claimed – with no obvious disparagement of her front – that she had 'the most beautiful back in the world'.

She appeared in lead rôles in *The Girl and the Wizard* (1909) with Sam Bernard, as the slightly scandalous heroine of the English-language production of *Alma wo wohnst du?* (1910), in *La Belle Paree* (1911, Lady Guff Jordan, a society modiste), in the title-rôle of *The Enchantress* (1911, Vivian) and in *Pretty Mrs Smith* (1914) on Broadway and in the less successful *Love For Sale* (1915) away from New York before effectively ending her stage career in vaudeville. There she appeared for a while in a Jack Lait sketch, *Alma's Return*, which featured her in her most famous rôle, as the inviting Alma, and in which she was able to command a salary of $1,500 per week.

Miss Gordon then moved to Hollywood where she became a favourite 'vampire' in such early silent movies as *The Beloved Adventuress*, *The Scar*, *The Wasp*, *The Divine Sacrifice*, *The Unveiling Hand* and *Adele* between 1916 and 1919. She was injured during the filming of a battlefield scene in *No Man's Land*, sued the company and won a week's salary ($1,250), but also effectively ended her film career.

She played in the revue *That's It* at San Francisco's Casino (1919) but an attempt to return to the musical stage in 1920 with a vehicle called *Lady Kitty Inc* came to grief on the road after just five weeks of touring. However, Miss Gordon continued to work and was seen on American television as late as 1952, in *Life Begins at Eighty*.

She was married, in her first marriage, to British producer Michael Levenston.

GORDON, Noele (b East Ham, 25 December 1923; d Birmingham, 14 April 1985).

A musical-comedy soubrette in the 1940s and 1950s, Miss Gordon was seen in London in *Let's Face It* (in place of Joyce Barbour), *The Lisbon Story*, in *Big Ben* (succeeding Gabrielle Brune) and in replacement of Julie Wilson in *Bet Your Life*, as well as introducing the rôle of Meg Brockie in London's version of *Brigadoon*.

Having established herself in the 1960s and 1970s as Britain's suppertime soap queen in the television series *Crossroads*, she was able to capitalize on that fame, after her summary removal from the screen, by appearing in the West End as Mrs Sally Adams (a rôle which she had toured in earlier days) in a revival of *Call Me Madam*. She was in the throes of following up as Sue in *No, No, Nanette* when her final illness overtook her.

GOSSE DE RICHE Comédie musicale in 3 acts by Jacques Bousquet and Henri Falk. Music by Maurice Yvain. Théâtre Daunou, Paris, 2 May 1924.

A successful example of the jazz-age Parisian musical, combining a light-hearted and gently lascivious libretto with lively up-to-date dance melodies, *Gosse de riche* told the modern-day story of Colette (Alice Cocéa), the daughter of the parvenu Patarin (Vilbert), who sets her cap at the young artist André (Henri Defreyn), only to finally discover that he has a girl, Nane (Christiane Dor), who just happens also to be her father's petite amie.

Vilbert's comedy was central to the piece, surfacing happily in the argot of his crooked 'On biase' or his blithe 'Quand on est chic', whilst Mlle Cocéa identified herself as 'gosse de riche' to foxtrot rhythm and duetted with Defreyn in waltz time ('Malgré moi') and in a java ('L'Invite à la Java'). *Ta Bouche* star Jeanne Cheirel, as a jewelled Baroness without visible means of support, growled out a song in each act, notably detailing the advantanges of 'Combine' (racketeering) in rather more open terms than *Gentleman Joe*'s Mrs Ralli Carr had done in the previous generation of shows. Yvain's score, unlike those for British and American shows of the same era, also included finely made concerted finales for each act, as well as a septet and a quartet, alongside its dance melodies and comic songs.

Parisian success was followed by a fine provincial life and an Hungarian production (ad Jenő Heltai) before the next jazz-age musical comedy took its place.

Hungary: Fővárosi Operettszinház *A Párizsi lány* 24 August 1924

DER GÖTTERGATTE *see* DIE IDEALE GATTIN

GOUBLIER, Gustave [CONIN, Gustave] (b Paris, 15 January 1856; d Paris, 27 October 1926).

The young Goublier made his first musical steps as a pianist and accompanist before becoming a conductor, at first in spa resorts and then in Parisian music halls and cafés-concerts. At the same time, he began what was to be a successful career as a songwriter from which such numbers as 'L'Angelus de la mer' and 'Le Crédo du paysan' emerged as considerable hits. He spent six years as musical director at the Eldorado, where some of his earliest one-act stage compositions were produced, then moved to the Moulin-Rouge where his activities included conducting the Paris première of *La Belle de New-York*, and then to the Folies-Bergère. In 1915, his most substantial musical, *Mam'zelle Boy Scout*, was produced at the Théâtre de la Renaissance, and the following year he took the baton at the Variétes for a revival of *La Belle de New-York*.

1890 **Chanteur et Pipelot** (Gaston Marguery) 1 act Lille 7 October
1899 **La Boule de neige** (E Verrier, G Fau) 1 act Galerie Vivienne 12 June
1899 **Par-devant le notaire** (A L'Hoste) 1 act Eldorado 4 March
1899 **Le sérum de l'amour** (H Darsay, A Trébitsch) 1 act Eldorado 7 October
1900 **Les Filles de la belle Hélène** (Gardel-Hervé) Eldorado 7 October
1909 **Ali-Bébé et les quarante voleuses** (Emil Codcy, 'Trébla' [ic A Delvaille]) Parisiana 1 May

1909 **Lucette à la caserne** (Daniel Riche, Maurice Mareuil) Parisiana 8 June
1913 **Le Roi boîte** (Ernest Depré) 1 act Théâtre Imperial 7 February
1915 **Mam'zelle Boy Scout** (Paul Bonhomme) Théâtre de la Renaissance 3 April
1919 **Les Surprises d'une nuit d'amour** (Eugène Joullot) Orléans 25 April; Théâtre Cluny, Paris 30 April 1920
1920 **Ah! Quelle nuit** (Bonhomme) Bouffes-du-Nord 19 November

GOUBLIER, Henri (b Paris, 14 March 1888; d Paris, 23 May 1951).

The younger son of Gustave Goublier, Henri made his early career as an orchestral timpanist before scoring a considerable success as the composer of the patriotic wartime musical *La Cocarde de Mimi-Pinson*, one of the rare hits of the French musical stage of the period. Thereafter he had further, if not equivalent success with *Un Mariage parisien* (1919), a piece which actually predated *La Cocarde* in its writing, but which had not found a production until the young composer had made his name, and *Le Mariage d'un Tartarin* (1921), before devoting himself to management.

He set up the Nouveau Théâtre, at the centre of a circuit of suburban theatres, to play opérette and opéra-comique, but the venture failed, as did his first attempt to return to the composing scene with *Billy-Bill* (1931). He worked as a conductor, both in France and abroad, notably on a South American tour with a repertoire of French opérettes, but it was not until 1942 that he again found success as a composer with the show *Carnaval*, a collaboration with his daughter, Jeannette Bruno ('Jean Bru'), which had a 12-month run at the Théâtre de la Gaîté-Lyrique. His subsequent works included two radio pieces, *Jour de bal* and *Le Mariage de Chiffon* (23 May 1954), the latter of which was subsequently played on the stage.

1913 **Mam'zelle Vésuve** (Fabrice Lémon, Georges Vidès) Casino, Boulogne-sur-mer 13 August
1915 **La Cocarde de Mimi-Pinson** (Maurice Ordonneau, Francis Gally) Théâtre de l'Apollo 25 November
1916 **La Demoiselle du Printemps** (Ordonneau, Gally) Théâtre Apollo 17 May
1917 **La Fiancée du lieutenant** (Gally) Théâtre Apollo 26 April
1919 **Un Mariage parisien** (Georges Léglise) Théâtre des Variétés 24 May
1920 **L'Heritière en loterie** (René Chavanne, Léglise) Théâtre Royal, Liège 4 April
1920 **La Sirène, ou la baigneuse de minuit** (Léglise, Lemon) Théâtre Apollo 30 September
1921 **Le Mariage d'un Tartarin** (Léglise, Lémon) Eldorado 6 May
1931 **Billy-Bill** (Léglise, Max Dearly) Théâtre Scala 17 January
1935 **La Nuit est belle** (Albert Sablons) Théâtre Antoine 25 September
1942 **Carnaval** (R Holt, Jean Bru) Théâtre de la Gaîté-Lyrique
1950 **Les Folies de Mylord l'Arsouille** (Eugène Joullot, Rozet) Théâtre de l'Horloge, Lyon 16 October

GRAB ME A GONDOLA Musical comedy in 2 acts by Julian More. Lyrics by Julian More and James Gilbert. Music by James Gilbert. Theatre Royal, Windsor, 30 October 1956; Lyric, Hammersmith, 27 November 1956; Lyric Theatre, London, 26 December 1956.

One of the liveliest of the small-scale musicals to emerge from British repertory theatres in the mid-1950s, *Grab Me a Gondola* won its way, by stages, to the West End

Plate 112. **Grab Me a Gondola:** *Joan Heal as the Diana Dors of a jolly parody of the world of film festivals.*

and a fine run of 673 performances. A burlesque of the film festival scene, it presented revue star Joan Heal in a virtuoso rôle as a busty blonde Diana Dors character with ambitions to become a Serious Actress ('Cravin' for the Avon') and Denis Quilley as a young reporter whose search for a scoop leads him to neglect his girl (Jane Wenham) to the extent that, in a section satirizing the veracity and methods of the press, she fabricates a newspaper story which alters the course of the plot.

Some delightful light ballads, some showy material for Miss Heal and some fine burlesque (notably a harmonized ensemble declaring 'The Motor Car is Treacherous'), teamed with a good helping of topical revusical satire, made *Grab Me a Gondola* a fine if ephemeral success on British stages.

Australia: Empire Theatre, Sydney 2 May 1959
Recording: original cast (HMV)

GRÄFIN DUBARRY *see* DIE DUBARRY

GRÄFIN MARIZA Operette in 3 acts by Julius Brammer and Alfred Grünwald. Music by Emmerich Kálmán. Theater an der Wien, Vienna, 28 February 1924.

One of the most successful of Kálmán's long list of successful Operetten, *Gräfin Mariza* has survived into the repertoire of the later years of the 20th century with marginally less strength than his *Die Csárdásfürstin* but, if it rates second of his works in general popularity, it has every claim to be the most satisfying musically.

Countess Mariza (Betty Fischer) owns an estate in the Hungarian borderlands which is managed by the handsome Béla Török (Hubert Marischka). Török is, in fact,

really the Count Tassilo Endrödy-Wirttenburg, who has been obliged to take paid employment to pay off his family debts and to earn a dowry for his sister, Lisa (Elsie Altmann). Mariza pays an unaccustomed visit to the estate to announce her engagement, but the engagement is only a ruse to deter the perpetual string of proposals she has been suffering, and she has taken the name of her prospective bridegroom, Baron Koloman Zsupán, from the cast-list of *Der Zigeunerbaron*. She is in for a surprise when a real Baron Zsupán (Max Hansen) turns up, whilst Tassilo has some covering up to do when it turns out that Lisa is part of the house party. After two acts of falling in love, misunderstandings and clearing up of the same misunderstandings, Mariza and Tassilo come together in a happy ending, alongside Lisa and the pig-farming Baron. Richard Waldemar played the interfering Fürst Moritz Dragomir Popolescu, Hans Moser was the comical valet Penizek, and Poldi Eigner took the rôle of a gipsy girl with a solo.

The score of *Gräfin Mariza* was topped by a trio of contrasting numbers which would become Operette standards: the tenor's vibrant 'Komm' Zigány!', the leading lady's csárdás 'Höre ich Zigeunergeigen', and the comically dancing invitation offered by Zsupán, first to Mariza and later to Lisa, to 'Komm mit nach Varasdin'. These were, however, only the tip of a musical iceberg. Tassilo reminisced about his wild-oat days in Vienna to suitably waltzing rhythms ('Grüss mir die Süssen, die reizende Frauen'), joined sweetly with Lisa in 'Sonnenschein, hüll dich ein', or with Mariza in the waltzing 'Einmal möcht' ich wieder tanzen' and the wooing 'Sag ja, mein Lieb, sag ja', whilst Mariza led the praises of 'Braunes Mädel von der Puszta', Zsupán mused over his change of loyalties with Lisa in 'Ich möchte träumen', and Manja opened the proceedings with her little gipsy song 'Glück ist ein schöner Traum' in a score which was effective from end to end.

Marischka's production of *Gräfin Mariza* proved a triumph. It played for 374 consecutive performances at the Theater an der Wien, using up a long list of star players as the genuinely Hungarian Ernő Király and Emmi Kosáry took turns at the lead rôles, Lea Seidl, Rosa Mittermardi, Lya Beyer and Carlotta Vanconi were seen as Mariza, Victor Flemming, Ludwig Herold, Karl Bachmann and Franz Galetta as Tassilo, and Walter Swoboda, Josef König and Josef Viktora took turns as Zsupán. Other productions quickly followed, with Budapest swiftly off the mark with a *Marica grófnő* (ad Zsolt Harsányi) with Juci Lábass (Mariza), Ferenc Kiss (Tassilo) and Márton Rátkai (Zsupán) which made its way firmly into the standard repertoire, and Berlin's Metropoltheater following, with a production featuring Adele Sandrock in the title-rôle. The first English-language production (ad Harry B Smith) was mounted by the Shuberts in New York. Kálmán's score was given the usual Shubert treatment, and songwriters Sigmund Romberg and Al Goodman got their names on the bill of a *Countess Maritza* which featured Yvonne d'Arle, Walter Woolf, Vivian Hart and Carl Randall at the Shubert Theater for a good run of 321 performances which established the show for a good life on American soil.

Elsewhere, however, the show was slower to find promoters. *Comtesse Maritza* (ad Max Eddy, Jean Marietti)

Plate 113. **Gräfin Mariza:** *Glenys Fowles (Mariza), Anthony Warlow (Zsupán) and Gordon Wilcock (Popolescu) in the Australian Opera production of 1987.*

first saw the French stage in 1930, at Mulhouse, with Anna Martens, Louis Collet, Alphonse Massart and Fanély Revoil heading the cast, and it was taken up the following year for a Paris showing with Mary Lewis, Roger Bourdin, Janie Marèse and Paul Clerget featured. It found some success there, but it did not stick, in the way that *Princesse Csárdás* had, in the French repertoire. In London, where Kálmán's works by and large got a disappointing reception, what was now just called *Maritza* (ad Robert Layer-Parker, Eddie Garr, Arthur Stanley) did not improve matters. Mara Lossef, John Garrick, Douglas Byng and Patricia Leonard headed the cast of a version which managed only 68 performances, and it was 1983 before London again saw the show, in a new and rather more listenable version by Nigel Douglas, mounted at Sadler's Wells Theatre with Marilyn Hill Smith, Ramon Remedios and Tudor Davies featured. This version was subsequently played in Australia under the auspices of the Australian Opera.

In spite of its success, and its recognized position both as one of Kálmán's best works and as one of the best and most popular romantic musicals of its era, *Gräfin Mariza* seems to have done better with the recording companies and film-makers than with the major theatres of central Europe in the years since its original productions. Filmed versions of the piece appeared in 1925 (w Vivian Gibson, Harry Liedtke), in 1932 (w Dorothea Wieck and Marischka in his original rôle) and in 1958 with Christine Görner, Rudolf Schock and Hans Moser playing his typical servant part more than 30 years on.

Hungary: Király Színház *Marica grófnő* 18 October 1924; Germany: Metropoltheater 1924; USA: Apollo Theater, Atlantic City, 29 March 1926, Shubert Theater *Countess Maritza* 18 September 1926; France: Mulhouse *Comtesse Maritza* 27 February 1930, Théâtre des Champs-Elysées, Paris, 7 May 1931; UK: Palace Theatre *Maritza* 6 July 1938

Recordings: complete (EMI, Bruno), selections (Eurodisc, CBS, Philips, RCA etc), English cast 1983 (TER), selection in Italian (EDM), selection in Hungarian (Qualiton) etc

GRAF TONI Singspiel in 2 acts by Rudolf Österreicher. Music by Edmund Eysler. Apollotheater, Vienna, 2 March 1917.

'A veritable variety-operetta, with many comical scenes and grateful rôles for the stars' was just the right kind of material for Vienna's Apollotheater which, like its Berlin namesake, had begun its life as a variety house before introducing first shorter and then longer operettes as part of its programmes. Mizzi Zwerenz starred as a Viennese cabaret star, alongside Fritz Werner and Oscar Sachs, in a production for which Eysler, who admitted to having written his score for the two acts of the show in a month, turned out a supply of joyous tunes from which one, the duo 'So küsst nur eine Wienerin', as introduced by Zwerenz and Werner, became one of his greatest hits.

Graf Toni had a good initial run, and was revived at the Jantschtheater in 1922.

DER GRAF VON LUXEMBURG Operette in 3 acts by A M Willner and Robert Bodanzky based on Willner and Buchbinder's libretto *Die Göttin der Vernunft*. Music by Franz Lehár. Theater an der Wien, Vienna, 12 November 1909.

Die Göttin der Vernunft (the goddess of reason) was the title of the libretto written by A M Willner and Bernard Buchbinder and set to music by Johann Strauss for an 1897 (13 March) production by Alexandrine von Schönerer at the Theater an der Wien. Annie Dirkens, Carl Streitmann, Josef Joseffy, Therese Biedermann, Julie Kopácsi-Karczag and Karl Blasel featured for a run of 32 performances and a handful of subsequent matinées, and the piece was put away.

A decade on, Willner exhumed the *Göttin der Vernunft* libretto, had it legally divorced from its earlier score, and rewrote it, in collaboration with Bodanzky, as *Der Graf von Luxemburg* (or, initially, Luxenberg, to avoid any protest from the Grand Duchy). Musically set by Lehár and produced, again, at the Theater an der Wien, it proved a major success this time and went on from its Vienna première to become a world-wide favourite.

The plot of the piece was one well-beloved of, in particular, French comedy writers: the marriage of convenience which turns out to be more than that. The aristocratic Fürst Basil Basilowitsch (Max Pallenberg) wishes to marry the singer Angèle Didier (Annie von Ligety) but, unable to wed an untitled lady, he arranges for her to go through a bought marriage with the penniless layabout René, Graf von Luxemburg (Otto Storm). The wedding is conducted in the studio of the artist Armand Brissard (Bernard Bötel), with the two parties hidden from each other by an easel. René breaks his bond not to return to Paris before the subsequent divorce is effected, the two wedded partners meet and fall in love, and Basil is cheated of his bride. Armand and his little Juliette (Luise Kartousch), having provided the soubrette moments of the

567

Plate 114. **Der Graf von Luxemburg:** *Angèle Didier weds René of Luxemburg in the Montmartre garret of the painter Brissac – which, in Wuppertal's production, actually looks like a garret and not the usual glamorous hotel suite.*

show, paired off at the same curtain, whilst Basil was restored to his aristocratic fiancée.

Lehár's score, still in his champagne-days *Die lustige Witwe* style, was full of melody, the first act bringing a dazzling entry for Angèle ('Heut' noch werd' ich Ehefrau'), a delightfully loping admission from Basil that 'Ich bin verliebt' and the famous marriage duet for tenor and soprano in which the pair wonder over a wedding after which 'Sie geht links, er geht rechts', as they build up into the big waltz tune of the first-act finale, 'Bist du's, lachendes Glück'. The second act gave the soubrets the pretty waltz 'Mädel klein, Mädel fein', and René his big solo number 'Es duftet nach trèfle incarnat', in which he begins to realize that the woman with whom he has fallen in love is already his 'wife', whilst the final act brought the lively march trio 'Liebe, ach, du Sonnenschein' (Basil, Juliette, Brissard).

Der Graf von Luxemburg ran 179 straight performances at the Theater an der Wien before moving out of the evening spot to give place to a visiting company from Berlin's Deutsches Theater, but it returned after the summer break and ran on through to its 226th performance on 7 October, before paying a brief visit to the Raimundtheater with Anny Mahrbach and Adolf Lutzmann featured. In 1911 Mizzi Günther and Louis Treumann gave their interpretations of Angèle and René between 10 and 30 September, and the show appeared intermittently in the house repertoire thereafter.

Hungary got its first sight of *Luxemburg grófja* (ad Andor Gábor) in March 1910 with Ernő Király, Sári Petráss and Márton Rátkai (Basil) featured. It was a huge hit, passing its 200th performance at the Király Színház on 11 Novem-

ber, and going on to major revivals at the Revü Színhaz in 1921 (22 March), and at the Fővárosi Operettszinház in 1944 (12 May ad Kálmán Kovács), 1952 (28 November ad István Békeffy, Dezső Kéller), 1957 (8 February) and 1963 (12 April) etc.

Germany's first *Graf von Luxemburg* was produced at the Neues Operettenhaus later the same year and George Edwardes's initial London production (ad Basil Hood, Adrian Ross), which followed a matter of months behind, also did well. Lily Elsie, London's *Merry Widow*, was cast as Angèle Didier, Bertram Wallis played René, W H Berry and May de Souza paired as the soubrets, and Huntley Wright followed Pallenberg's low-comedy interpretation of Basil. If its 340 London performances were considerably less than the records set up at Daly's by *The Merry Widow* and *The Dollar Princess*, the show was nevertheless a firm success, but it faded from the repertoire thereafter and a production at Sadler's Wells Theatre in 1983 (24 January, ad Nigel Douglas, Eric Maschwitz) was its first London showing since Edwardes's production.

Paris first welcomed *Le Comte de Luxembourg* in German, as given by a touring company in 1911, but the following year Alphonse Frank produced Gaston de Caillavet and Robert de Flers's French version at the theatre which had housed *La Veuve joyeuse*, with that piece's leading man, Henri Defreyn, as René. Brigitte Régent (Angèle), Angèle Gril (Juliette) and Félix Galipaux (Brissard) supported and played the show through 149 performances, followed by a further 37 the next season. A few months later, New York finally got its production of the show when Klaw and Erlanger mounted a *The Count of Luxemburg* (ad Glen MacDonough from the English version) with a cast headed by Anne Swinburne, George L Moore, Frances Cameron, Frank Moulan and Fred Walton. It had a fair, if not fabulous, run of 120 performances, sufficient to establish the piece in such a way that it was remounted at the Jolson Theater in 1930 as part of the Shubert series of classic revivals (17 February).

Australia also took up the British version and J C Williamson Ltd mounted *The Count of Luxemburg* in Melbourne in 1913. Florence Young (Angèle), Talleur Andrews (René), Phil Smith (Brissac), W S Percy (Basil) and Sybil Arundale (Juliette) featured in a regular season in the comic-opera company's repertoire.

The principal career of the show was, however, in central Europe, and in 1937 Lehár made some alterations and additions to his piece for a new production at Berlin's Theater des Volkes (ex-Metropoltheater). Amongst other alterations, the carnival opening was rearranged, whilst Basil's last-act fiancée, Gräfin Stasia Kokozow, was given something to sing. Hans-Heinz Bollmann and Elisa Illiard played the romantic leads, with Alfred Haase (Basil), Hans Hessling (Brissard) and Mara Jakisch (Juliette) in support. *Der Graf von Luxemburg*, usually in a version of this remade version, remains in repertoires in Europe, and it has regularly been produced at the Vienna Volksoper (1954, 1977, 1990).

George Walsh starred in a 1926 film version.

Hungary: Király Színház *Luxemburg grófja* 14 January 1910; Germany: Neues Operettenhaus 1910; UK: Daly's Theatre *The Count of Luxemburg* 20 May 1911; France: Théâtre du Vaudeville, Paris 1911, Théâtre Apollo *Le Comte de Luxembourg* 13 March 1912; USA: New Amsterdam Theater 16 September 1912; Australia: His Majesty's Theatre, Melbourne, 5 April 1913; Film: Celebrity Pictures 1926

Recordings: complete (EMI), selections (Decca, Eurodisc, Philips, Telefunken etc), selection in English (TER, Columbia), selection in French (Decca, Adria, Pathé, Odéon), selection in Spanish (Montilla), selection in Italian (EDM) etc

GRAHAM, Harry [Joscelyn Clive] (b London, 23 December 1874; d London, 30 October 1936). One of the most successful lyricists of the British musical stage between the two World Wars.

The son of Sir Henry Graham KCB, and educated at Eton and the Royal Military College, Graham pursued a professional military career as an officer in the Coldstream Guards before giving up the army and becoming a journalist. He had his first play produced in 1914 and, in the same year, adapted the lyrics of Jean Gilbert's *Die Kino-Königin* for Robert Courtneidge's production as *The Cinema Star*. He then went on to collaborate on the successful musical *Tina* (1915), and, the following year, had his biggest success to date when Robert Evett hired him to write the songwords for Harold Fraser-Simson's music to *The Maid of the Mountains* ('Love Will Find a Way', 'Farewell').

He became lyricist and, subsequently, librettist in chief to the Evett-Collins régime at Daly's Theatre (*A Southern Maid, Our Peg, Sybil*) and continued, after their deposition, to supply Daly's supremo, Jimmy White, with English books and lyrics for the series of Continental imports on which the inexperienced manager relied, with varying levels of success. His versions of *The Lady of the Rose* and *Madame Pompadour* were notable Daly's Theatre hits.

Although he contributed songwords and sometimes texts to several agreeable new musicals, Graham's forte was the adaptation of the colourful and musically expansive postwar Continental Operetten which were all the rage in the Britain of the 1920s and 1930s. His two most enduring successes in that area came in 1931 when he wrote the British version of *White Horse Inn*, including the English words for newly added 'Goodbye', and of Lehár's *Das Land des Lächelns*, for which he created the still sung lyric to 'You Are My Heart's Delight'.

Apart from his principal musical theatre credits, he also supplied additional lyrics for the musical plays *Sylvia's Lovers* (1919) and *Hold My Hand* (1931), and words for Richard Addinsell's songs to the stage adaptation of J B Priestly's *The Good Companions* (1931). He also adapted a number of plays from various Continental sources and languages, the most successful of which was Siegfried Geyer and Karl Farkas's *Bei Kerzenlicht* (*By Candlelight*), which later itself provided the basis for the musicals *You Never Know* (New York 1938) and *Romance in Candlelight* (London, 1955).

1914 **The Cinema Star** (*Die Kino-Königin*) English lyrics (Shaftesbury Theatre)
1915 **Tina** (Haydn Wood, Paul Rubens/w Rubens, Percy Greenbank) Adelphi Theatre 2 November
1917 **The Maid of the Mountains** (Harold Fraser-Simson/ Frederick Lonsdale) Daly's Theatre 10 February
1917 **A Southern Maid** (Fraser-Simson/Harry Miller/w Dion Clayton Calthrop) Manchester 24 December; Daly's Theatre 15 May 1920
1919 **Our Peg** (Fraser-Simson/Edward Knoblock) Manchester 24 December
1920 **A Little Dutch Girl** (*Das Hollandweibchen*) English book w Seymour Hicks and lyrics (Lyric Theatre)
1921 **Sybil** (*Szibill*) new English book and lyrics (Daly's Theatre)
1921 **Missy Jo** (Fraser-Simson/James Clive) Folkestone 4 July
1922 **The Lady of the Rose** (*Die Frau im Hermelin*) English lyrics (Daly's Theatre)
1922 **Whirled into Happiness** (*Der Tanz ins Glück*) English book and lyrics (Lyric Theatre)
1923 **Toni** (*Der Fürst von Pappenheim*) (Hugo Hirsch/w Douglas Furber) Hanley 6 August; Shaftesbury Theatre 12 May 1924
1923 **Head Over Heels** (Fraser-Simson/w Adrian Ross/ Seymour Hicks) Adelphi Theatre 8 September
1923 **Madame Pompadour** English book w Lonsdale and lyrics (Daly's Theatre)
1924 **Our Nell** (revised *Our Peg*) (Fraser-Simson, Ivor Novello/ Louis Parker, Reginald Arkell) Gaiety Theatre 16 April
1925 **Katja, the Dancer** (*Katja, die Tänzerin*) English book w Lonsdale and lyrics (Gaiety Theatre)
1925 **Cleopatra** (*Die Perlen der Cleopatra*) English lyrics (Daly's Theatre)
1925 **Cloclo** English book and lyrics w Furber (Shaftesbury Theatre)
1926 **Betty in Mayfair** (Fraser-Simson/J Hastings Turner) Adelphi Theatre 3 April
1926 **Riquette** English lyrics (tour)
1926 **My Son John** (revised *Riquette*) new book and lyrics w Graham John, Desmond Carter (Shaftesbury Theatre)
1926 **Merely Molly** (Herman Finck, Joseph Meyer/Hastings Turner) Adelphi Theatre 22 September
1927 **The Blue Mazurka** (*Die blaue Mazur*) English lyrics (Daly's Theatre)
1928 **Lady Mary** (Albert Szirmai/Lonsdale, Hastings Turner) Daly's Theatre 23 February
1931 **White Horse Inn** (*Im weissen Rössl*) English book and lyrics (London Coliseum)

1931 **The Land of Smiles** (*Das Land des Lächelns*) English book and lyrics (Theatre Royal, Drury Lane)
1931 **Viktoria and Her Hussar** (*Viktória*) English book and lyrics (Palace Theatre)
1932 **Casanova** English book and lyrics (London Coliseum)
1936 **Rise and Shine** (later *Darling You*) (Robert Stolz/w Desmond Carter etc, later w Con West, Geoffrey Orme) Theatre Royal, Drury Lane 7 May
1946 **Yours is My Heart** (*Das Land des Lächelns*) revised version of his *The Land of Smiles* by Ira Cobb and Karl Farkas (Shubert Theater, New York)

GRAIN, [Richard] Corney (b Tavisham, Cambs, 26 October 1844; d London, 16 March 1895).

A comic singer and entertainer at the piano, Grain abandoned his four-year-old legal career and joined the German Reeds' company at the Gallery of Illustration in 1870 at the age of 25. His first appearance there was with the monologue *The School Feast* (16 May 1870), his first in a musical play was as Captain Bang, the pirate, in Gilbert and Clay's *Our Island Home*, and he appeared successively in comedy 'father' rôles in such pieces as *A Sensation Novel, Ages Ago, Charity Begins at Home, Happy Arcadia*, and each and every other of the several new short operettas presented annually at the Gallery and later at St George's Hall, for a number of which he also composed the music.

He subsequently replaced the late John Parry, whose solo performances at the piano had been a feature of the Gallery's programmes, and from then on he appeared additionally at the piano, a plump figure in tails, with a musical monologue – inclusive of comic song(s) – usually between the one-acters of the evening's entertainment. He remained with the company till his death, writing, composing, performing and, from 1877, with Alfred Reed, running the business, and forming with the Reed family the continuing backbone of a company which was influential in the early development of musical comedy in Britain.

1879 **£100 Reward** (Arthur Law) 1 act St Georges Hall 27 May
1880 **A Flying Visit** (Law) 1 act St George's Hall 31 May
1881 **All at Sea** (Law) 1 act St George's Hall 28 February
1882 **That Dreadful Boy** (Gilbert a' Beckett) 1 act St George's Hall 13 December
1884 **A Double Event** (Law, Alfred Reed) 1 act St George's Hall 18 February
1884 **A Terrible Fright** (Law) 1 act St George's Hall 18 June
1885 **A Night in Wales** (Herbert Gardner) 1 act St George's Hall 1 June
1890 **Carnival Time** (T Malcolm Watson) St George's Hall 7 April
1892 **The Barley Mow** (Walter Frith) St George's Hall 16 April
1893 **Box B** (Grain) 1 act St George's Hall 22 May
1893 **The Ugly Duckling** (Grain) 1 act St George's Hall 20 November
1894 **Walls Have Ears** (Grain) 1 act St George's Hall 26 March
1894 **That Fatal Menu** (Grain) 1 act St George's Hall 15 December

Autobiography: *Corney Grain: by himself* (John Murray, London, 1883), Biography: in *The German Reeds and Corney Grain* (A D Innes & Co, London, 1895)

GRAINER, Ron[ald] (b Atherton, Australia, 11 August 1922; d Cuckfield, 21 February 1981). Composer who had his main success in television, but who, in a rare venture into the musical theatre, provided the outstanding postwar light opera score of the British stage.

Musically educated in his native Australia, Grainer sub-sequently moved to Britain where his work as a composer for television produced several widely known pieces of title-music (*Steptoe and Son, Maigret* and, above all, the theme for *Dr Who*). He made his entry into the theatre as a pianist and musical director (*The Pied Piper, Zuleika* (1957)), and subsequently as a composer when he supplied two songs for the Ned Sherrin/Caryl Brahms musical *Cindy-Ella*, but he found significant success in 1964 when director Wendy Toye brought him in to write additional music for *The Third Kiss*, the American musical version of *The Barretts of Wimpole Street*.

Ultimately, all the show's original music was thrown out and Grainer composed the whole of the score for what became *Robert and Elizabeth*. Arguably the most successful and substantial light opera written in Britain since Edwardian days, the piece had a long London run followed by tours, overseas productions and two major revivals, but Grainer and author Ronald Millar preferred to follow up with the modern, youthful *On the Level* (1966) which, in spite of many attractions, was a disappointing failure (118 performances). Grainer turned his attentions back to television and film (*The Moon Spinners* etc) until failing sight led him to leave Britain to live in Portugal. His only further efforts for the theatre were songs for two more small-scale Ned Sherrin pieces, the Marie Lloyd story *Sing a Rude Song* (1970) and, in replacement for the Arthur Schwartz score originally scheduled, *Nickelby and Me* (1975).

1962 **Cindy-Ella** (pasticcio, w Peter Knight/Caryl Brahms, Ned Sherrin) Garrick Theatre 17 December
1964 **Robert and Elizabeth** (Ronald Millar) Lyric Theatre 20 October
1966 **On the Level** (Millar) Saville Theatre 19 April
1970 **Sing a Rude Song** (w pasticcio/Sherrin, Brahms) Garrick Theatre 26 May
1975 **Nickelby and Me** (Sherrin, Brahms) Theatre Royal, Stratford East 16 December

LE GRAND CASIMIR Opérette (vaudeville) in 3 acts by Jules Prével and Albert de Saint-Albin [and Edmond Gondinet uncredited]. Music by Charles Lecocq. Théâtre des Variétés, Paris, 11 January 1879.

The Great Casimir (José Dupuis) begins the show's story as an ordinary French provincial sous-préfet, but when he catches sight of the circus performer Angélina his world turns upside down and he ends by abandoning the sous-préfecture and becoming a wild-animal trainer and director of a circus. Angélina weds him, but she still flirts with her old suitors, Gobson (Guyon) the régisseur, and Sothermann (Léonce) the juggler, and still seems able to be tempted by rich tent-flap Johnnies into some indiscretion. Casimir, whose company is in financial difficulties, decides to 'die' and leave the circus to his wife. He disappears into the depths of Corsica. There he gets unwittingly entangled with pretty local Ninetta (Mlle Baumaine) and her vendetta-making menfolk, and finds himself forcibly and bigamously remarried. Then Angélina arrives, her circus and suitors in tow, and she has to go by way of many a comical and farcical scene before the marital status quo can return in time for the final curtain.

The one and only José Dupuis, now much less of a tenor and more of a comic actor than a few years previously, added another fine creation to his impressive list as Casimir, with the lovely Céline Chaumont as his naughty wife, carrying on the series, begun and to be continued by Anna Judic, of vaudevillesque heroines who would be the stars of the Variétés in years to come. Léonce as the clown, and Baron as a burlesque of a nobleman on the ran-dan called simply Le Grand-Duc, were also featured in farcical rôles. None of these popular stars was an outstanding vocalist, and Lecocq's score took heed of the fact whilst still producing some charming numbers.

Casimir declared (Couplets du dompteur) that while he might have tamed three bears, he could not tame his wife, joined with the lady in a duo in which she displayed how she would grieve were he killed in the ring, and indulged in some Couplets de la pêche during his 'dead' period in Corsica. Angélina discovered, after Casimir's disappearance, that semi-widowhood was rather unsatisfactory, and searched for him through the accents of Europe in the rondeau: 'Il le savait bien, le perfide', then turned to waltz time with her Rondo des deux pigeons ('Deux piegons s'aimaient d'un amour tendre'). Léonce described his juggling skills merrily in the Couplets du jongleur ('Avec six balles je jonglais').

The show had a fine 113 consecutive performances in its first season at the Variétés, and was brought back the following year (12 April, 22 performances) with all its principal players in place, and again in 1884 (17 October) for further seasons, by which time Le Grand Casimir had already been picked up for other productions elsewhere. Vienna's version, mounted under Franz Tewele at the Carltheater, opened just three months after the French première. It cast the manager as Casimir opposite the thoroughly billed and much-loved Josefine Gallmeyer (Angelina), supported by a royal cast including Josef Matras as the clown, Wilhelm Knaack (Prince Charles), Karl Blasel (Picasso) and Rosa Streitmann (whose brother, Carl, played a tiny rôle) as Ninetta. However Der grosse Casimir – musically expanded by Brandl for the occasion – proved no competition for the newly produced Boccaccio and folded in 8 performances.

In London, the Gaiety Theatre produced an H S Leigh version with a cast headed by Nellie Farren (Angelina), Edward Terry (Casimir) and Edward Royce (Grand Duke), with the appelation 'vaudeville' clearly attached, but with little success, Budapest got A hórihorgas Kazimir (ad Lajos Evva) for three performances, whilst New York saw the piece performed by the Variétés company on tour and then, under the title The Lion Tamer, as a heftily rewritten vehicle for Francis Wilson and Marie Jansen. Lecocq's music had been squeezed into a corner by some local pieces by Richard Stahl.

Producer Bertrand considered the piece, with its short score of 15 musical pieces, to be a virtual 'vaudeville à couplets' and, as such, eminently suitable for his in-house team of star comedy performers, who tended to the category of actors-who-sing-a-bit, and the success of Le Grand Casimir confirmed him in the path which he was to follow at the Variétés in the next years. He followed Le Grand Casimir with such highlights of his celebrated series of Variétés vaudevilles as Lili and Mam'zelle Nitouche, and once again made his theatre one of the most flourishing centres of musical theatre in Paris.

Austria: Carltheater Der grosse Casimir 13 April 1879; UK: Gaiety Theatre The Great Casimir 27 September 1879; Hungary: Népszinház A hórihorgas Kazimir 25 October 1879; USA: Wallack's Theater (Fr) October 1885, Casino Theater The Lion Tamer 30 December 1891

THE GRAND DUKE, or The Statutory Duel Comic opera in 2 acts by W S Gilbert. Music by Arthur Sullivan. Savoy Theatre, London, 7 March 1896.

The last work of the Gilbert and Sullivan partnership, The Grand Duke, was not a success. Gilbert's libretto was based on a Blackwood's magazine story, 'The Duke's Dilemma', which had already served as the source of Tito Mattei's comic opera The Prima Donna, but it moved away from the original in many ways as Gilbert developed and then redeveloped the piece to fit the needs of the Savoy company. The fact that the company was in rather a state of flux did not help, but the libretto ended up being far from Gilbert's best in construction or in dialogue.

Theatrical manager Ernest Dummkopf (Charles Kenningham) and his comedian Ludwig (Rutland Barrington) are both part of a plot to dethrone Grand Duke Rudolph (Walter Passmore), but the two plotters fall out and – after a statutory duel, done by drawing cards, in which Dummkopf is 'killed' - Ludwig persuades the Duke to allow himself to be 'killed' until the law expires the next day, but then takes the throne and re-enacts the law. Further complications arrive when Ludwig's real wife, Lisa (Florence Perry), leading lady Julia Jellicoe (Ilka Pálmay), the Baroness of Krakenfeldt (Rosina Brandram) and the Princess of Monte Carlo (Emmie Owen) all make marital claims on the new Duke. All is resolved when it turns out that ace counts low, not high, and that, thus, Ludwig is 'dead' and Dummkopf and Rudolph 'alive'.

Hungary's greatest Operette star, Ilka Pálmay (playing the English actress in a German court with her Hungarian accent to the standard English of the rest of the cast), had the showiest musical moments of the evening with her gamut-running 'The Grand Duke's Bride' and her dramatic 'Broken Every Promise Plighted', Passmore described himself as 'a broken-down crittur', Lisa had a pretty 'Take Care of Him', and there was a curious Herald's Song which drew some attention.

The Grand Duke played a meagre 123 performances at the Savoy and attracted little in the way of takers elsewhere, apart from a German production which was whipped on at Berlin's Neues Theater whilst the piece was only some two months old in London. It wins occasional performances to this day, more as a Gilbert and Sullivan curiosity than on any real merits.

Germany: Neues Theater Der Grossherzog 20 May 1896
Recording: complete (Decca)

LA GRANDE-DUCHESSE DE GÉROLSTEIN Opéra-bouffe in 3 acts by Henri Meilhac and Ludovic Halévy. Music by Jacques Offenbach. Théâtre des Variétés, Paris, 12 April 1867.

Meilhac, Halévy and Offenbach's third great opérabouffe for the Théâtre des Variétés and for Paris's favourite diva, Hortense Schneider, La Grande-Duchesse followed the productions of La Belle Hélène and Barbebleue, and proved, if anything, the most sensational and world-wide hit of the group. Meilhac and Halévy chose to use things military and political as the main target of their fun this time round, and their heroine was the Grand Duchess of a fictional European state – who might or might not be a German, or a Luxembourgeoise (after all, the Grand Duchy?), but was – for the peace of mind of the French nobility – surely, but surely, not French.

The young Grande-Duchesse de Gérolstein (Hortense Schneider) is come of age, but her ministers, the Baron Puck (Kopp) and army chief General Boum (Couder), are not anxious to see their power diminished by an interfering girl, and are searching for a means to distract her interest from affairs of state. An attempt to wed her off to Prince Paul of Steis-Stein-Steis-Laper-Bottmoll-Schorstenburg (Grenier) has failed to occupy her attentions, so their next step is to try to enthrall their teenaged duchess with that collection of live dolls called the army. This works only too well. The Duchess takes an immediate shine to private Fritz (Dupuis), whom she quickly promotes through the ranks until he replaces Boum at the head of the army. Fritz's wham-bam tactics actually win a battle and, when he returns, the Duchess fairly delicately tries to let him know of her interest in his person. But the dense soldier simply asks her permission to wed his Wanda (Elise Garait), and his piqued sovereign promptly changes sides and begins to plot with her ministers and Prince Paul's representative, Baron Grog (Baron), to bring the new Commander-in-Chief down. Eventually the status quo is restored and the Duchess demurely agrees to marry Prince Paul.

The score to the show gave the prima donna superb opportunities, and the two principal hits from the show were her burlesque ceremonial 'Voici le sabre de mon père' in which she hands over the sword of office to the rocketingly promoted Fritz, and her winsome 'Dites-lui qu'on l'a remarqué distingué' as she relates to the boy how a certain friend of hers has developed an interest in him. But there was more to the rôle than its two bon-bons, and there was indeed a third dazzling soprano moment in the rippling Rondo Militaire ('Ah! Que j'aime les militaires'), and a fourth, the regimental song, the 'Légende de la verre' of the final act, and then still more. Amongst the men, Prince Paul had perhaps the finest and funniest moment with his dejected recital of the mockery that the scandal papers have been making of his inability to win the Duchess (Chronique de la Gazette de Hollande: 'Pour épouser une Princesse'), whilst Boum showed his credentials in the extravagantly martial 'Pif, Paf, Pouf!' and Fritz shared numbers with Wanda and related his victory in battle ('Après la victoire').

La Grande-Duchesse was pointed enough in its burlesque to attract some censorship. Mlle Schneider was forbidden to wear a splendid decoration she had had made as being too much like the real thing, the authors were obliged to remove a reference which seemed to point too acutely to the recent Austro-Prussian wars, and the 'Gérolstein' was forcibly added to the title to avoid offending Grand Duchesses in general and Luxemburg's in particular. However, neither the fun nor the éclat of the piece were in any way thus diminished and, after some heavy post-première cutting in the over-long third act and several other alterations, *La Grande-Duchesse*, having opened happily, indeed brilliantly for Mlle Schneider in particular, soon found itself the hit of the town.

In 1867, that meant something, for this was the year of the Paris Exposition and Europe, led by its crowned heads and high society, had descended upon Paris. *La Grande-*

Plate 115. La Grande-Duchesse de Gérolstein: *Even the respected musician Sir Julian Benedict jumped on the Offenbach bandwagon and ended up playing piano for a tour of* La Grande-Duchesse. *At least the manager at Barnsley gave him bigger billing than Offenbach.*

Duchesse sailed past her 100th night on 7 August, to box-office figures which outclassed even *La Vie parisienne*, passed the 200th at top speed and played on till 4 December, when Mlle Schneider deserted the Variétés for a lucrative engagement at the Châtelet. When she returned, it was as *La Périchole*, and the sabre of the sovereign of Gérolstein was not taken up again until 1878, when Paola Marié starred at the Bouffes-Parisiens (5 October) in the first major revival of Offenbach's piece. Anna Judic appeared as the Duchess at the Variétés in 1887, Jeanne Granier played her at the Gaîté-Lyrique in 1890, and Germaine Roger starred at her Gaîté-Lyrique in an unsatisfyingly adapted version (ad Albert Willemetz, André Mouëzy-Éon) in 1948. A solid vertebra in the backbone of the French opéra-bouffe repertoire, the piece has returned since at the Marigny with Suzanne Lafaye (5 May 1966) and again at the Châtelet where operatic diva Régine Crespin portrayed the teenaged Duchess in a rather different style from that used a century earlier by Mlle Schneider.

In Vienna, Friedrich Strampfer's production of *Die Grossherzogin von Gerolstein*, with Marie Geistinger following in Schneider's footsteps from her successes as Hélène and Boulotte to take the title-rôle (the Duchess had now acquired the christian name Irene), was again a major hit. Matthias Rott was General Boum, or, as he was now called, in double-barrelled fashion, General Bum-Bum, Carl Adolf Friese played Baron Puck, Jani Szika was Fritz and Karl Blasel Prince Paul – his Gazette de Hollande now become the Augsburger Allgemeine Zeitung in Julius Hopp's adaptation – and the show, and its star (in spite of a high-heeled mishap in Act Two of the opening night which meant she had to play part of Act Three sitting down) confirmed the earlier successes dazzlingly. Geistinger returned regularly in her rôle – she was still playing it at the Theater an der Wien in 1879 – and *Die Grossherzogin* proved a great favourite without quite out-pointing *Die schöne Helena* in the Viennese public's favour.

The same remained true in Germany where Lina Mayr introduced the Duchess the following year at the Friedrich-Wilhelmstädtisches Theater. Extremely popular, it tucked in behind *Die schöne Helena, Pariser Leben* and *Orpheus in der Unterwelt* in Offenbach's Germanic hit-parade, joining those three pieces in a revivable repertoire which has lasted for more than a century and a quarter. Phila Wolff played Irene at the Theater an der Wien in 1905–6, Vera Schwarz appeared at the Johann Strauss-Theater in 1911 and Fritzi Massary at Berlin's Metropol-theater in 1916 at the head of a long line of important Viennese and German Grossherzogins.

Hungary's first *Gerolsteini nagyhercegnő* (ad Károly Babos, Béla Erődi) was Antonia Hétenyi, who starred at the Budai Népszinház in 1867 alongside János Timár (Bum-Bum) and with Vidor Kassai as Baron Grog, but the show got major revivals in later years both at the Nép-szinház, with Ilka Pálmay starred (6 December 1884, ad Lajos Evva, Béla J Fái), again at the Király Színház (13 September 1906) when Sári Fédak played the Duchess with Mihaly Papp as Prince Paul and József Németh as Bum-Bum, and again at the Fővárosi Operettszinház (13 January 1950).

America saw *La Grande-Duchesse* whilst the Exposition and the Paris production still ran on. H L Bateman imported Lucille Tostée to play the piece in its original French and the production caused a sensation in New York, launching a craze for opéra-bouffe which would run for more than a decade, and establishing the show as 19th-century America's favourite amongst the Offenbach repertoire. Mlle Tostée's unreliability and a season by Ristori broke up the season somewhat, but *La Grande-Duchesse* played a remarkable 156 performances before March 25 1868, after which Tostée switched to enacting *La Belle Hélène*, with less thunderous effect. The Grand Duchesses were soon hustling each other down Broadway to challenge Tostée: Sophie Worrell was the first English Duchess (ad B A Baker) at the New York Theater (17 June 1868), Joseph Grau offered Rose Bell (5 October 1868), Mrs Howard Paul gave her version at the Théâtre Français (24 January 1870), and the all-embracing Marie Aimée, of course, arrived with her version of the show (28 March 1871) as did the west coast's Alice Oates (13 October 1873), England's Emily Soldene (30 November 1874) and the heroine of the Paris revival, Paola Marié (23 October 1879). Alongside these, the 'only' Francis Leon scored a similar hit in his 'Africanized opéra-bouffe' impersonation of *The Grand Dutch-S* at Kelly and Leon's. Later, Lillian

Russell was the star of two revivals of the show (Casino Theater 25 January 1890, Abbey's Theatre 8 December 1894) before America's taste for opéra-bouffe frittered away for the best part of a century.

It was, however, not New York but London which saw the first English-language *Grande-Duchesse*, when the 'operatic extravaganza' was mounted at Covent Garden's Theatre Royal (ad Charles Lamb Kenney) with Australian prima donna Julia Mathews in the lead rôle, Thomas Aynsley Cook as Boum and Wilford Morgan as Fritz. It was the first time that a full-length Offenbach opéra-bouffe had been given a fairly faithful British production, following hacked-up burlesquey stagings of *Orphée aux enfers, Barbe-bleue* and *La Belle Hélène*, and it was a huge hit. Tumbled out of the theatre after just 26 performances because of the all-important Christmas pantomime season, the show had, nevertheless, made its impression and, as John Russell's production set off to tour Northern England and Scotland, it quickly became the rage of the country. Mrs Howard Paul opened a production at the Olympic Theatre with Morgan again and with Henri Drayton as Boum (20 June 1868), only to find, a couple of nights after, Mlle Schneider herself delivering her original Duchess for a short season to the French-speaking population (St James's Theatre 22 June), followed by Vestris as *The Very Grand Dutch-S* in Charles Bernard's burlesque of the show. Miss Mathews touched back at London base after two years touring, then gave over her rôle to the rising Emily Soldene, but she was back again in 1871 to star in the Gaiety Theatre's version of a show which, along with *Geneviève de Brabant* and *Chilpéric*, was one of the sensations of the British opéra-bouffe stage. London saw Cor-nélie d'Anka as the Duchess in 1875 (Opera Comique 13 September) and 1878 (Alhambra, 1 April), Mary Albert in a French version in 1886 (Her Majesty's, 22 November) and 1888 (Royalty Theatre, 7 January), whilst Richard D'Oyly Carte mounted a new English version (ad C H E Brookfield, Adrian Ross) at the Savoy 4 December 1897 with Florence St John starring alongside Charles Ken-ningham (Fritz) and Walter Passmore (Boum) for 104 per-formances. The piece was seen again at Daly's Theatre in 1937 with Enid Cruickshank starred, and London's most recent Duchess, Patricia Routledge, played a Camden Festival production in 1978 which has remained a fond memory with those who saw it.

La Grande-Duchesse was, in spite of all its success, slow to find its way to Australia. In fact, New Zealand saw the Duchess, as portrayed in Dunedin, in a version by a local journalist, by Anna Forde to the Fritz of a Mr Whitworth, six months before the army of Gérolstein marched on to the stage on the other side of the Tasman sea. When it did come, the first Australian *Duchess* was not a whole-hearted success. William Lyster cast the finely singing (but not very funny) Fannie Simonsen as the Duchess alongside Armes Beaumont (Fritz), Georgia Hodson (Wanda) and Edward Farley (Boom) in Lyster and Smith's first production ('no attempt to grasp the spirit of the author ... [the piece is] more fitted for a good singing burlesque company than for an opera company ... they have made an utter mistake in producing it'), and *La Grande-Duchesse* turned out more opéra than bouffe. However the same journal completely reversed its opinion when Alice May played the Duchess for Lyster the next season, Haydée Heller followed, and

Australia later got the other side of the coin when Emily Soldene gave her buxom British Duchess to the nation and Emilie Melville her incisively comic Jewish one as the show installed itself in its rightful place in the colonial repertoire.

Still a major feature of the classic repertoire in France, *La Grande-Duchesse* has curiously (given its subject matter, and the 1970s and 1980s passion for turning defenceless classics into modern pseudo-satire) faded from the repertoire elsewhere, whilst the ancient-world burlesques *Orphée aux enfers* and *La Belle Hélène* continue to prosper.

Austria: Theater an der Wien *Die Grossherzogin von Gerolstein* 13 May 1867; USA: Théâtre Français 24 September 1867, New York Theater (Eng) 17 June 1868; Hungary: Budai Népszinház *Gerolsteini nagyhercegnő* 11 October 1867, Budai Szinkör (Ger) 28 June 1868; UK: Theatre Royal, Covent Garden 18 November 1867; Germany: Friedrich-Wilhelmstädtisches Theater 10 January 1868; Australia: Princess Theatre, Melbourne 27 February 1871

Recordings: complete (CBS, Decca, Unique Opera Records, Urania), complete in German (Philips) etc

GRAND HOTEL   Musical in 2 acts by Luther Davis. Music and lyrics by Robert Wright and George Forrest. Additional music and lyrics by Maury Yeston. Martin Beck Theater, New York 12 November 1989.

Wright and Forrest's stage musical version of the Vicki Baum book and play *Menschen im Hotel* and its celebrated Barrymore/Garbo film *Grand Hotel* (1932, Academy Award) was originally produced by California's Civic Light Opera (7 July 1958, Los Angeles) with Paul Muni starring, under the title *At the Grand*. It failed to move east, but 30 years later it was revised and reproduced by a team made up of no less than nine credited producers with Liliane Montevecchi and David Carroll in its leading rôles as the fading ballerina Grushinskaya and the aristocratic hotel thief Felix von Gaigern who brings the spring back to her fouetté.

In trouble on the road, the producers called in director Tommy Tune who solved their problem by coating the dislocated, and too often unintentionally funny, piece in sufficient revusical glamour to please audiences, negate a poor critical reception, and, against the strongest opposition for a number of years, win himself two Tony Awards and a 1,018-performance run for the show. The two most popular items of the evening were a lively legmania comedy dance routine performed by Michael Jeeter (Tony Award) as the gentle, dying Otto Kringelein and an interpolated adagio dance in semi-darkness for two uncharacterized artists.

A German production was mounted at Berlin's Theater des Westens with Leslie Caron as Grushinskaya and Helmut Baumann as Kringelein, whilst after a British production had been announced, advertised and abandoned, London instead got a three-month (135-performance) season from an American touring company with Montevecchi and Brent Barrett featured.

The same title was earlier used for the Viennese Posse with songs in 3 acts by Leopold Feldmann, music by Carl Millöcker, produced at the Theater an der Wien 7 December 1870.

Germany: Theater des Westens 25 January 1991; UK: Dominion Theatre 5 July 1992

Recording: original cast (RCA Victor)

LE GRAND MOGOL   Opéra-bouffe in 4 acts by Henri Chivot. Music by Edmond Audran. Théâtre du Gymnase, Marseille, 24 February 1877; Théâtre de la Gaîté, Paris, in a revised version by Chivot and Alfred Duru, 19 September 1884.

The libretto of *Le Grand Mogol* was entrusted to the comparatively inexperienced Audran by one of the most celebrated librettists of the French musical stage, largely because Chivot happened to be a friend of the composer's family. The resultant opéra-bouffe, however, proved to be more than just the first step in Audran's long and successful career, for *Le Grand Mogol* was, on its own merits, a considerable success throughout France where it was regularly revived and remained long in the standard repertoire, and also won a series of overseas productions.

The piece's plot centred on the young Indian Prince Mignapour who, in spite of the plottings of his Grand Vizier and the tempting Princess Bengaline, eventually succeeds in both hanging on to his Mogolship (which he would lose, should he fall from virginity before assuming his crown) and securing the hand of the pretty snake-charmer, Irma, who has been coveted by another enemy, the Britisher Captain Crackson. Audran's score, highlighted by Irma's snakecharming song ('Allons, petit serpent') and the lively Chanson du Vin de Suresnes, was in the bright, tuneful opérette style for which the composer would shortly become celebrated.

First produced in Audran's home town of Marseille with the young Jane Hading starring as Irma, it did not immediately head to Paris. Whilst the composer was swiftly signed to write a fresh opérette for the Paris stage, *Le Grand Mogol* was seen in Milan (1879), and in New York (1881) where the young Lillian Russell charmed the snakes and Selina Dolaro sang the rôle of Mignapour en travesti. In 1884 Chivot and his partner of almost always, Alfred Duru, reworked *Le Grand Mogol* for a more spectacular style of production, and it was produced on the considerable Parisian stage of the Théâtre de la Gaîté with Mlle Thuillier-Leloir (Irma), Henri Cooper (Mignapour), Mesmaecker (Nicobar) and Marie Gélabert (Bengaline) starring. It was played there again in each of the three following seasons, and its success was prelude to further overseas productions.

In London Florence St John draped herself in live snakes nightly for two months, before Berlin (ad Eduard Jacobson), Antwerp, Mexico City, Zagreb and New York, again, welcomed the piece. Austria waited until 1900 for its première when Louise Robinson (Irma) and Willy Bauer (Mignapour) played P Blumenreich's version at the Carltheater and the Theater an der Wien for three weeks. Paris, however, continued to be the friendliest, and hosted major revivals in 1895, 1901, 1914–15, 1922 and 1949.

USA: Bijou Theater *The Snake Charmer* 29 October 1881; UK: Comedy Theatre 17 November 1884; Germany: Friedrich-Wilhelmstädtisches Theater 18 April 1885; Austria: Carltheater 29 September 1900

Recording: complete (Gaîté-Lyrique)

GRANICHSTÄDTEN, Bruno   (b Vienna, 1 September 1879; d New York, 30 May 1944). Viennese writer and composer of the years between the World Wars, whose blend of traditional operettic and modern dance and 'jazz'

music proved a particularly popular accompaniment to a series of successful musicals.

The young Granichstädten worked at first as a song-writer and as a singer in concert and in Operette without causing much of a stir, but when his first attempt at a musical score for a full-scale Operette, the jaunty *Bub oder Mädel?*, was produced as the initial novelty to be played at the freshly opened Johann Strauss-Theater, the 29-year-old musician found himself with a real success on his hands. The show played over 100 performances in Vienna, with Louis Treumann starring in its early performances, and was also later successfully played in English on Broadway (*The Rose Maid*) and in Hungarian (*Fiu vagy lány*) in Budapest.

He followed up with further composing successes with the French-based musical comedy *Majestät Mimi*, another piece to be exported after its Vienna production, and with *Casimirs Himmelfahrt*, which followed six weeks at the Raimundtheater with productions in Germany and Hungary (*Abraham a mennyortszagban*). At the same time he made his full-scale début as a librettist, with a collaboration on the text for the Robert Winterberg Operette *Madame Serafin*, which did better in its initial production at Hamburg than in a subsequent mounting at Vienna's Johann Strauss-Theater (two weeks). Thererafter, he often wrote or co-wrote the libretti for his own Operetten, finding regular success with pieces such as the highly popular Theater an der Wien shows *Auf Befehl der Kaiserin* (189 performances) and *Die Bacchusnacht* (115 performances, *Bacchus-Ej* in Hungary), both later given further productions around central Europe, *Die verbotene Stadt* (*Nadmé* in Hungary), first produced in Berlin, and two Operetten for the Vienna Apollotheater, before he had the most substantial hit of his career, again at the Theater an der Wien, with the long-running 1925 piece *Der Orlow*.

He followed this success with others: *Das Schwalbennest*, for which he supplied both music and part of the text, and which played 134 performances at the Raimundtheater before going on to Germany and Hungary (*A Fecskefeszek*), *Die Königin*, on which he worked on the libretto for Oscar Straus, *Evelyne* which, after a strong Berlin start, was played for seven weeks at the Johann Strauss-Theater, and *Reklame* which ran a fine 136 performances at the Theater an der Wien.

After turning his hand to several film scores in the early 1930s, in 1932 Granichstädten surfaced again in the musical theatre when he supplied the characterful song 'Zuschau'n kann i net' to the score of *Im weissen Rössl*, but Nazi rule then forced him from Germany and then from Austria. In 1939, he fled first to Luxemburg and from there to New York. Lacking a fashionable name and reputation in America, where the hit of *The Rose Maid* was three decades old, he found himself unable to get work. Projects such as *The Singing Caesar* and a Shubert *The Life of Mozart* failed to make it to the stage, and adaptations of his Continental successes fared no better. He ended up working as a bar pianist and died four years later without having contributed further to the musical stage.

1908 **Bub oder Mädel?** (Felix Dörmann, Adolf Altmann) Johann Strauss-Theater 13 November
1909 **Wein, Weib und Gesang** (Altmann) 1 act Hölle 1 October

1910 **Lolotte** (w Alfred Schick von Markenau) 1 act Apollotheater 30 July
1911 **Majestät Mimi** (Dörmann, Roda-Roda) Carltheater 17 February
1911 **Madame Serafin** (Robert Winterberg/w Georg Okonkowski) Neues Operettentheater, Hamburg 1 September
1911 **Casimirs Himmelfahrt** (A M Willner, Robert Bodanzky) Raimundtheater 25 December
1913 **Die verbotene Stadt** (w Carl Lindau) Montis Operettentheater, Berlin 23 December
1915 **Auf Befehl der Kaiserin** (aka *Auf Befehl der Herzogin*) (Leopold Jacobson, Bodanzky) Theater an der Wien 20 March
1916 **Der Glückspilz** (Josef Königsberg/w 'Max Jungk') Carl-Schultze Theater, Hamburg 2 December
1918 **Walzerliebe** (w Bodanzky) Apollotheater 16 February
1918 **Das alte Lied** Raimundtheater 23 December
1921 **Indische Nächte** (Hardt-Warden, Bodanzky) Apollotheater 25 November
1923 **Die Bacchusnacht** (w Ernst Marischka) Theater an der Wien 18 May
1923 **Glück bei Frauen** (Victor Léon, Heinz Reichert) Carltheater 4 December
1925 **Der Orlow** (w E Marischka) Theater an der Wien 3 April
1926 **Das Schwalbennest** (w E Marischka) Raimundtheater 2 September
1927 **Die Königin** (Oscar Straus/w E Marischka) Theater an der Wien 4 February
1927 **Evelyne** (*Die Milliardärin*) (w Peter Herz/w Adolf Schütz) Deutsches Künstlertheater, Berlin 23 December
1930 **Reklame** (w E Marischka) Theater an der Wien 28 February

GRANIER, [Marie] Jeanne [Ernestine] (b Paris, 31 March 1852; d Paris, 18 December 1939). The brightest star of the Paris opérette stage, through a series of rôles composed mostly to her measure by Charles Lecocq, in the 1870s and early 1880s.

The daughter of an actress, the young Mlle Granier was performing at Étretat in the summer of 1873 when she caught the eye and the ear of Jacques Offenbach. He hired her for the company at the Théâtre de la Renaissance, where she was allotted a small rôle in *La Jolie Parfumeuse*. However, when she substituted for Louise Théo in the title-rôle of Rose Michon the 21-year-old Jeanne caused quite a stir, and it was not long before she was given a leading rôle of her own.

Her first star part in Paris was the showy double title-rôle of *Giroflé-Girofla*, created in Belgium by Pauline Luigini, and Granier confirmed all the promise of her Rose Michon dazzlingly. The delighted Lecocq composed the rôle of Graziella, the heroine of *La Petite Mariée*, particularly for her and, following that, moulded the title-rôle of *La Marjolaine* and the breeches part of the teenage Duc de Parthenay of *Le Petit Duc* around his new star.

In this last rôle, paired with the pretty soubrette, Mily-Meyer, as the little Duchess, Granier made the biggest hit of her career and she reprised the 'little Duke' many times over during the following decade. Her success led her to leave Paris for some lucrative foreign appearances and the star rôle of Lecocq's next Renaissance Theatre opérette went instead to Zulma Bouffar, but Granier returned for another triumph in *La Petite Mademoiselle* (1879, Comtesse Cameroni) before Planquette's *Les Voltigeurs de la 32ème* (1880, Nicolette) put an end to the theatre's run of large successes.

Plate 116. **Jeanne Granier:** *The famous creator of* Le Petit Duc *and many of Lecocq's other opérettes.*

After a series of revivals of her big Lecocq hits, she again attempted some new rôles, but *Janot* (1881, Janot), Raoul Pugno's *Ninette* (1882), Serpette's *Madame la Diable* (1882), *Fanfreluche* (1883, Brézette), and *Mam'zelle Gavroche* (1885, Gavroche), did not live up to her earlier pieces or rôles. Although Messager's *La Béarnaise* (1885, Jacquette) and Audran's *La Cigale et la fourmi* (1886, Thérèse) gave her two further significant successes, Lacôme's *Les Saturnales* was another failure and, in the remaining eight years of her musical theatre career, Granier, although appearing in such new pieces as *La Fille à Cacolet* (1889, Rosette Cacolet), concentrated almost wholly on the tried and triumphant works of the classical repertoire, appearing in such pieces as *La Fille de Madame Angot* (Clairette, opposite Judic's Lange), *Barbe-bleue* (Boulotte), *La Grande-Duchesse* (Grande-Duchesse), *La Belle Hélène* (Hélène), *Orphée aux enfers* (Eurydice), *La Vie parisienne* (Gabrielle), *Le Petit Faust* (Marguerite), *Le Voyage dans la lune* (Prince Caprice) and *La Périchole* (Périchole).

In 1895 she moved her star name and singular stage abilities to the straight theatre, where she had a long and successful second career as a comedienne which stretched into her seventies, before she retired from performing in 1926.

LA GRAN VÍA Zarzuela (revista madrileña comica-lirica, fantastico-callejera) in 1 act and 5 scenes by Felipe Perez y Gonzales. Music by Federico Chueca and Joaquín Valverde. Teatro Felipe, Madrid, 2 July 1886.

One of the most famous examples of the 'genero chico', the small-scale and topical Spanish musical play, *La gran vía*, did not, like most of these pieces, take a glimpse at a small slice of everyday city life, but was, rather, a revusical series of scenes set around a town-planning decision, in which many of the characters were anthropomorphic streets.

La gran vía – the main road – is a street which is planned for the centre of Madrid, demolishing some old streets and affecting others in various ways. The Caballero de Gracia (Joaquín Manini) is the least worried, as he will have a junction with the new road. It is he who, in the second scene, sets out, in the company of a passer-by to take a look at a few Madrilene scenes which may change – the poor district of La Prosperidad, where they meet the low-class Menegilda (Lucia Pastor) and a team of rats; the Puerta del Sol, the great square which will lose its celebrated central fountain in the rebuilding, and which is the setting for the introduction of a group of singing sea cadets; a cross-road where the Madrid Lyceum is situated, where two newspapers, *Lidia* and *Uncle Jindama*, are found in vigorous discussion. The final scene shows the new road. It will be a fine road.

Chueca and Valverde's score used the gamut of dance rhythms, amongst them the Caballero de Gracia's waltz ('Caballero de Gracia me llaman'), Menegilda's tango ('Pobre – chica, la que tiene que servir'), the sea cadets' mazurka ('Somos los maritanos que venimos a Madrid'), the schottische delivered by the Lyceum ('Yo soy el Elisedo'), the jota trio of the rats ('Soy el rato primero ...') as well as two further numbers, a paso doble for a pair of Sergeants and a waltz for the Chief of Police, which were censored out of the show in later days.

La gran vía was a great success in Spanish-speaking territories, but unlike the great majority of other zarzuelas, it also attracted some attention further afield. Melio le Ghassi and P F Murro's Milan zarzuela troupe played the piece in its three-show repertoire at Vienna's Carltheater in 1894, whilst in 1902 another troupe played it, also in Spanish, as part of a season at Danzers Orpheum. In France, it was another variety house, L'Olympia, which mounted Maurice Ordonneau's French version, but in London the script was put aside and the music alone used as part of the score to a comic opera put together by Anglo-French performer Harry Fragson, called *Castles in Spain* (Royalty Theatre 18 April 1906).

Austria: Carltheater 7 September 1894; France: L'Olympia 25 March 1896

Recordings: complete (Montilla, Hispavox, Columbia, Zafiro etc)

GRAU, Maurice (b Brünn, Austria, 1849; d Paris, 13 March 1907).

Brought up in America and intended for the law, Grau became involved in the theatre through his impresario uncle, Jacob Grau, with whom he worked from the age of 17. In 1872 he went into partnership with Carlo A Chizzola and, on a joint capital of $1,500, succeeded in setting up a season with the Théâtre des Variétés' Marie Aimée at the head of a company presenting the newly popular French opéras-bouffes. Under their management, Aimée became the most important and well-known performer of her kind in the country, and opéra-bouffe and its successors and imitators became firmly fixed in the American theatre repertoire, laying the bases for much of future musical theatre in that part of the world.

The pair diversified, touring Salvini, Clara Louise Kellogg in opera, Rubinstein and others, and were instrumental in taking Offenbach to America for a series of concerts in 1876 which left them $20,000 in the red. In 1879 Grau sponsored a new opéra-bouffe company, headed by Parisian star Paola Marié. This was the most successful of the latter-day opéra-bouffe troupes to play throughout northern and southern America, and Grau continued in the genre when he subsequently brought another French favourite, Louise Théo, to America.

Grau later went into partnership with Henry E Abbey and, for a period, with John B Schoeffel, and they were responsible for bringing to the American stage many Continental stars, including Bernhardt, Henry Irving, Réjane and Patti, as well as several musical companies. In 1890 they hosted a Broadway season by George Edwardes's Gaiety Theatre Company with *Faust Up-to-Date* and, in 1894, less successfully, they set up a British company, with Lillian Russell at its head, to bring Jakobowski's *Die Brillanten-Königin* from the Vienna Carltheater to America.

Grau was also, for more than a decade, co-director, with Abbey (and originally Schoeffel), of the Metropolitan Opera, New York, and at another stage involved in the management of the Royal Opera House, Covent Garden.

GRAVES, George (b London, 1 January 1876; d London, 2 April 1949). Highly popular but often destructive British comedian of the early 20th century, inclined to give his own stand-up performance regardless of the show.

Graves began his career touring in small comedy rôles in the musicals *The Shop Girl* and *The Gay Grisette* in his early twenties, and after five years of solid gagging in musical shows around the provinces, Russia and South Africa (*Kitty Grey*, *A Runaway Girl*, *The Geisha*, *Florodora* etc) made his first appearance in London, as Marie Studholme's father, in Edwardes and Frohman's production of *The School Girl*, at the Prince of Wales Theatre.

Edwardes next gave him the rôles of MacSherry in *Madame Sherry* (1904) and Coquenard in *Véronique* (1904) and took him to Daly's to succeed Willie Edouin as the comical father of the little heroines in *Les P'tites Michu*. However, it was his next rôle at Daly's which was his most famous: at 32 years of age he introduced his freely ad-libbed interpretation of *The Merry Widow*'s ageing, buffo Baron Popoff and established himself as one of the town's favourite musical comedians.

He subsequently mixed theatre, music-hall and pantomime engagements, appearing on the musical stage in *The Belle of Brittany*, *A Persian Princess*, as Bogumil in *Princess Caprice* (*Der liebe Augustin*), in *Houp-La!* with Gertie Millar (1916), *Maggie* (1919) and *Now and Then* (1921). He played with an increasing egoism, showing little concern for anything but his own performance and none for his fellow actors, and most of these shows suffered sadly from such disruption.

In the later 1920s and 1930s he appeared as Tweedlepunch in *Florodora*, General von Spatz in *The Blue Mazurka* and Tabarie in *The Vagabond King* and, now the right age for the rôles he had so long been playing, he found several congenial musical parts to which he returned regularly – Christian Veidt in *Lilac Time*, Popoff, and, from 1937, his one really significant original creation, Sir John

Tremayne in *Me and My Girl*, a rôle which he played, in tandem with Lupino Lane, as late as 1945.

Autobiography: *Gaieties and Gravities* (Hutchinson, London, 1931)

GRAY, Dolores (b Chicago, 7 June 1924). Shapely, strong-voiced leading lady of American musicals, both in the United States and in Britain.

Miss Gray first appeared in musical comedy on Broadway at 21 in a little part in a pale blue musical called *Are You With It?*, and, after a false start with the Vernon Duke book musical *Sweet Bye and Bye*, which closed on the road, moved up to the top of the bill when she took the Ethel Merman rôle of Annie Oakley in the London production of *Annie Get Your Gun* (1947).

She subsequently had lead rôles on Broadway in the revue *Two on the Aisle*, the short-lived *Carnival in Flanders* (Tony Award) and as Frenchie – the tough out-west tart created by Marlene Dietrich on film – in the musical version of *Destry Rides Again* (1959). She appeared in the unsuccessful *Sherry* (1967), returned to London to briefly succeed Angela Lansbury in the star rôle of *Gypsy* (1973) and subsequently toured and played on Broadway as Dorothy Brock in *42nd Street*. In 1987 she again appeared in London, scoring a very personal success as Carlotta Campion in the revised version of *Follies*, performing 'I'm Still Here' with lungpower that many a pre-microphone artist might have envied.

Amongst her screen appearances was numbered a lusciously blonde version of *Kismet*'s conniving Lalume.

GREASE New 50s rock 'n' roll musical by Jim Jacobs and Warren Casey. Eden Theater, New York, 14 February 1972; Broadhurst Theater, 7 June 1972.

A 1970s musical, set in the 1950s and making the most of pony-tails and beehives, ducks'-arses and Vaseline tonic, *Grease* was the ingenuous and gently parodic successor to the equally ingenuous but scarcely parodic college musicals of the *Good News* and *Leave it to Jane* school of earlier years.

High-school slicky Danny Zuko (Barry Bostwick) has spent a sweetly romantic summer at the beach with toothpaste-clean Sandy Dumbrowski (Carole Demas), but the version of the 'facts' he gives his pals in the Burger Palace Boys gang when school is back in isn't quite as handholding as the truth. When it turns out Sandy has switched to the same school, he has to keep up his image with some double-talking and double-acting. He ends up not taking her to the school dance, catches up with an invite to a drive-in movie, loses out when he gets too fresh, but finally gets his happy ending when Sandy swaps her Sandra Dee image for leather jacket, hoop-earrings, chewing-gum, cigarettes and all the other more attractive elements of 1950s sophistication.

The show's songs, a clever selection of amusing 1950s pastiches, included a selection of teenage disaster songs – Danny's 'Alone at a Drive-In Movie', Sandy's 'It's Raining on Prom Night', and the piece sung to Frenchy (Marya Small), the girl who dropped out of high-school to go to beauty-school, but then dropped out there as well, by the Guardian Angel (Alan Paul) she doesn't have ('Beauty School Drop-Out') alongside a girl-group number 'Freddy, My Love', the two different tales of the 'Summer

Nights' as allegedly spent by Sandy and Danny, and the taunting 'Look at Me, I'm Sandra Dee' sung by Betty Rizzo (Adrienne Barbeau), the head of the girls' gang, mocking Sandy's image. It was to Rizzo that the evening's only number which expressed any genuine feeling fell – her angry retort to Sandy that she'd rather be her unpretentious, slightly soiled self than something fresh out of a bubble-gum packet ('There Are Worse Things I Could Do').

First produced at off-Broadway's Eden Theater under the management of Kenneth Waismann and Maxine Fox, *Grease* shifted to Broadway's Broadhurst Theater after less than four months, and there it began a remarkable run which was clearly due to more than just 1950s nostalgia. By the time that it had done, this refreshingly simple and silly tale of tongue-in-cheek collegiate hearts, flowers and pimples had become the then longest-running Broadway musical in history. When it closed in April 1980 after nearly eight years at the Broadhurst and Royale Theaters, it had played 3,388 performances, topping the records of *My Fair Lady*, *Hello, Dolly!* and *Fiddler on the Roof*.

Like other shows – from *Erminie*, *Adonis* and *Dorothy* to *A Chorus Line* and *Salad Days* – which have set up extraordinary runs in one country, *Grease* did not confirm that record in other productions. Produced twelve months after its Broadway transfer at London's New London Theatre, under the management of Triumph Theatre Productions, with Richard Gere (Danny), Stacey Gregg (Sandy) and Jacquie-Ann Carr (Rizzo) featured, *Grease* managed only a fair 236 performances, whilst Harry Miller's Australian production showed no signs of following the vast success of his *Jesus Christ Superstar* production and was not shifted to Sydney after a disappointing Melbourne season. In Mexico, the show was called *Vaselina*, whilst in France François Wertheimer performed what can most kindly be called a rip-off by presenting his *Gomina* – which, in spite of appearances, was not Broadway's *Grease* – at the Théâtre de l'Européen.

Grease ran on and on on Broadway, but was shunned by the rest of the world until 1978. In that year, Robert Stigwood released a film version. John Travolta, Olivia Newton-John and Stockard Channing featured, the score was enriched with the interpolated songs 'You're the One That I Want' and 'Hopelessly Devoted To You', some genuine 1950s numbers were also added to the score, the three-parts-sincere, one-part-parody feeling of the piece caught to a nicety, and the result was a huge movie hit which prompted a fresh look at *Grease* in those countries which had rejected it before. London's Helen Montagu mounted a fresh production with Michael Howe and Jacqueline Reddin featured and the young Tracey Ullman as Frenchy, and once again London – which had rushed to the film – showed it had no interest in *Grease* on stage. The second coming of *Grease* did, however, win it a thorough round of the British provincial theatres which had ignored it originally. It also, ultimately, won it a showing in Sydney, Australia, when John Frost mounted a production at the Footbridge Theatre (26 September 1991) allowing the show to at last find the success which had passed it by 20 years earlier.

London followed on with its third attempt – a *Grease* mounted in the style of the recently successful London Palladium *Joseph and the Amazing Technicolor Dreamcoat*:

large and soap-starry. Australian *Neighbours* TV-star Craig McLachlan top-billed in a production mounted at the Dominion Theatre (15 July 1993) as *Grease* jived into its third decade, on the crest of a huge nostalgia boom, looking likely to stay around for at least three decades more.

Australia: Metro Theatre, Melbourne 9 September 1972; UK: New London Theatre 26 June 1973; Film: Paramount 1978

Recordings: original cast (MGM/Polygram), film soundtrack (RSO), Mexican cast (Orfeon, Raff), South African cast (EMI), London revival cast (CBS/Sony) etc

THE GREAT WALTZ *see* WALZER AUS WIEN

A GREEK SLAVE Musical comedy in 2 acts by Owen Hall. Lyrics by Harry Greenbank and Adrian Ross. Music by Sidney Jones. Additional music by Lionel Monckton. Daly's Theatre, London, 8 June 1898.

The successor to the vastly successful *The Geisha* at Daly's Theatre, written by the same team, moved its setting from the picturesque Orient to picturesque Ancient Rome. Daly's Theatre prima donna Marie Tempest was cast as Maia, the daughter of the Persian soothsayer Heliodorus (Huntley Wright) to whom all matronly Rome runs for news of her future. Amongst their slaves are the pert Iris (Letty Lind), the sculptor Archias (H Scott Russell) and the exceedingly well-proportioned Diomed (Hayden Coffin) who has served as a model for his fellow slave's marble-chipping. One day, there comes to Heliodorus's establishment the Princess Antonia (Hilda Moody) and, encouraged by the vengeful prefect Pomponius (Rutland Barrington), whom the princess has spurned, Maia announces to her customer that the God of Love has fallen in love with her. The God of Love is Archias's statue of Diomed, and the plan is to have Antonia waste her sentiments on a cold piece of marble. But Heliodorus, determined to break up the love affair between his daughter and his slave, substitutes the real slave for the statue and Diomed goes home with Antonia. It takes the entire second act to unwind the complications which end in disguises, low comedy and much music at the festival of the Saturnalia.

If the text of the piece got a little chaotic in its second half, with its burlesque of *Cyrano de Bergerac* and its bevy of topicalities, the score, on the other hand, never flagged. Miss Tempest had a delightful little piece about 'The Lost Pleiad' and a romantic ballad 'The Golden Isle', Miss Lind followed her Tomtit and Parrot tales of the two previous shows with the Aristophanic fable of 'A Frog He Lived in a Pond-O', Wright described himself patteringly as 'The Wizard', and Barrington complained, with many a modern-day reference, that 'I Want to Be Popular', whilst Coffin heroically longed for 'Freedom' in an extremely baritonic drawing-room solo, alongside some attractive ensembles.

A Greek Slave, for all its attractions, could not equal the popularity of *The Geisha*. However, on its own terms, it did well enough. It played for a year at Daly's (349 performances), went into a second edition, with the usual bundle of fresh songs and scenes, toured lengthily, and was eagerly picked up by other countries where *The Geisha* had become a favourite. Budapest's Népszinház quickly mounted *A Görög rabszolga* (ad Emil Makai, Árpád Pásztor) with a fine cast headed by Aranka Hegyi, Klara Kury, Gabi Bárdy, Imre Szirmai and József Németh, and scored one of its biggest successes of the 1890s (79 performances), Berlin mounted C M Röhr and Georg Okonkowski's *Der griechische Sklave* and Vienna's Theater an der Wien followed suit with a localized version (ad Leo Stein), with Franz Tewele featured as Heliodorus, Joseffy as Pomponius (equipped with special topical lyrics for 'Populär' provided by popular songwriter Alois Just) and Frln Reichsberg as Maia for 36 performances. On Broadway, however, Fred C Whitney's production with Dorothy Morton (Maia), Richard Carle (Heliodorus) and Herbert Sparling (Pomponius) featured, failed in just 29 performances.

In 1926 the new owner of Daly's Theatre, Jimmy White, decided to revive *A Greek Slave*, and mounted a London-bound production with José Collins starred as Maia. Dogged by squabbles and inefficiencies, the production folded on the road.

Hungary: Népszínház *A Görög rabszolga* 4 March 1899; Germany: 1899; USA: Herald Square Theater 28 November 1899; Austria: Theater an der Wien *Der griechische Sklave* 16 December 1899

GREEN, Adolph (b New York, 2 December 1915). Originally a performer, Green teamed with a fellow member of the Revuers group, Betty Comden, to form the most enduring and successful lyric- and sometimes libretto-writing partnership in Broadway-cum-Hollywood history (*see* COMDEN, BETTY).

He has also continued an intermittent career as a performer since, featuring alongside Comden in their highly successful début musical *On the Town* (1944), and coming to grief with their unsuccessful *Bonanza Bound* (1947). He appeared in the revue *A Party With Comden and Green* (1958, 1977) and also in the concert version and recording of *Follies*.

1944 **On the Town** (Leonard Bernstein/w Betty Comden) Adelphi Theater 28 December
1945 **Billion Dollar Baby** (Morton Gould/w Comden) Alvin Theater 21 December
1947 **Bonanza Bound** (Saul Chaplin/w Comden) Shubert Theater, Philadelphia 26 December
1953 **Wonderful Town** (Bernstein/w Comden/Jerome Chodorov, Joseph Fields) Winter Garden Theater 25 February
1954 **Peter Pan** (Jule Styne, Mark Charlap/w Comden, Carolyn Leigh/J M Barrie ad) Winter Garden Theater 20 October
1956 **Bells Are Ringing** (Styne/w Comden) Shubert Theater 29 November
1958 **Say, Darling** (Styne/w Comden/Richard Bissell, Marion Bissell) ANTA Theater 3 April
1960 **Do Re Mi** (Styne/w Comden/Garson Kanin) St James Theater 26 December
1961 **Subways are for Sleeping** (Styne/w Comden) St James Theater 27 December
1964 **Fade Out – Fade In** (Styne/w Comden) Mark Hellinger Theater 26 May
1967 **Hallelujah Baby** (Styne/w Comden/Arthur Laurents) Martin Beck Theater 26 April
1970 **Applause** (Charles Strouse/Lee Adams) Palace Theater 30 March
1974 **Lorelei** revised *Gentlemen Prefer Blondes* (Palace Theater)
1978 **On the Twentieth Century** (Cy Coleman/w Comden) St James Theater 19 February
1982 **A Doll's Life** (Larry Grossman/w Comden) Mark Hellinger Theater 23 September
1985 **Singin' in the Rain** (pasticcio/w Comden) Gershwin Theater 2 July

1991 **The Will Rogers Follies** (Coleman/w Comden/Peter Stone) Palace Theater 1 May

GREEN, Marion (b Janesville, Iowa, 8 March 1890; d Rye, NY, 17 March 1956). American baritone who found several fine rôles in a 25-year career.

Originally a concert vocalist in his native America, Green was selected to star opposite Maggie Teyte in the London première of Messager's *Monsieur Beaucaire* ('Red Rose'), a rôle he then repeated as his Broadway début. He went no further than Philadelphia in the romantic lead of the Anna Nichols/Werner Janssen operetta *Love Dreams* (1921, Larry Pell), but then appeared in New York in the Spanish music-drama *The Wildcat* (1921, Juanillo) and, replacing Donald Brian who had walked out in try-out, in the demanding romantic tenor rôle of Achmed Bey in the American version of Fall's *The Rose of Stamboul* (1922).

He also appeared as the leading man of the Romberg/Kummer musical *Annie Dear* (1924, John Rawson), sang Captain Corcoran in the 1926 Winthrop Ames revival of *HMS Pinafore*, closed out-of-town in *Cherry Blossoms* (1927), featured in the American production of *The Dubarry* (1932, Louis XV) and, later in his career, appeared in musical-comedy character rôles as the Secretary of State in *I'd Rather Be Right* (1937), in a revival of *Maytime*, and as the Magistrate in Kurt Weill's *The Firebrand of Florence* (1945).

GREEN, Martyn [MARTYN-GREEN, William] (b London, 22 April 1899; d Hollywood, Calif, 8 February 1975). Long-time chief comedian of the D'Oyly Carte Opera Company.

Green made his first appearances on the stage in the Daly's Theatre touring companies of *A Southern Maid*, *The Maid of the Mountains* and *Sybil*, playing the romantic tenor rôle of Petrov in the last named. He toured in *Shuffle Along* and then, in 1922, he joined the D'Oyly Carte Opera Company as a chorister and understudy, making his earliest appearances in named parts as Luiz, Major Murgatroyd, The Associate (*Trial By Jury*) and Cox. He was subsequently named understudy to Henry Lytton in the principal comedy rôles and, between 1932–4, succeeded to those rôles. With a break for war service, he remained at the comic head of the company until 1951, recording the repertoire on the first D'Oyly Carte sets of long-playing records of the Gilbert and Sullivan comic operas.

His subsequent career was in America where he repeated his well-known Savoy opera characterizations and lectured on and directed productions of the Gilbert and Sullivan repertoire. He appeared in regional productions of a number of plays, on television (voice of the Fox in *Pinocchio*) and, in spite of having lost a leg as a result of an accident in a lift in 1959, appeared as Chaucer in the Broadway production of the musical *The Canterbury Tales*. He was also, temporarily, director of the musical *Royal Flush*.

Autobiography: *Here's a How-de-Do* (Norton, New York, 1952)

GREEN, Stanley (b New York, 29 May 1923; d New York, 12 December 1990).

One of the first and few writers on the American musical theatre to approach the subject with an historical and unpretentiously analytical eye, Stanley Green authored some 30 years of writings focusing on the area of 20th-century musical theatre and film in America: *The World of Musical Comedy* (1960 and regularly updated), *The Great Clowns of Broadway*, *The Rodgers and Hammerstein Story* (1963), *Ring Bells! Sing Songs!* (1971), *Starring Fred Astaire* (1973), *The Encyclopaedia of the Musical Theatre* (1976), *The Rodgers and Hammerstein Fact Book* and *Broadway Show by Show*, as well as an *Encyclopaedia of Musical Film* and, his final book, *Broadway Musicals Year by Year* (1990).

GREENBANK, Harry [GREENBANK, Henry Harveston] (b London, 11 September 1865; d Boscombe, 26 February 1899). Short-lived lyricist to the influential British series of Daly's Theatre musicals.

The young Harry Greenbank first succeeded in placing one of his works at the Savoy Theatre, when his musical playlet *Captain Billy*, set by the company's musical director Frank Cellier, was staged there as a curtain-raiser to *The Nautch Girl*. He continued to write such small-scale pieces over the following years, both for the Savoy and for the Lyric Theatre, and it was at the latter house that Horace Sedger allotted him the job of supplying the English lyrics to F C Burnand's adaptation of the French opérette *Le Coeur et la main* (*Incognita*).

It was, thereafter, as a lyricist that Greenbank found his niche, and it was he whom George Edwardes chose, shortly after, when he put together the team of neophytes (Sidney Jones, Owen Hall and Greenbank) from whom he commissioned the musical comedy *A Gaiety Girl*. After the enormous worldwide success of that piece, the three stayed together and subsequently formed the backbone of the team which produced the famous series of Daly's Theatre musicals – *An Artist's Model*, *The Geisha*, *A Greek Slave* and *San Toy*.

Greenbank also provided lyrics for two of the most successful of the lighter brand of shows produced by Edwardes at the Gaiety Theatre – *The Circus Girl* and *A Runaway Girl* – and ventured twice as a librettist-lyricist, once with an original musical, *Monte Carlo*, and once with an adaptation of Lecocq's *La Petite Mademoiselle* as *The Scarlet Feather*. His other assignments included additional lyrics for *The Bric à Brac Will* (1895) and, posthumously, a song for the London production of *A Chinese Honeymoon* (1901, 'Roses Red and White').

Always extremely delicate of constitution, Greenbank was rarely seen in public and during the production of *A Greek Slave* moved, with his wife and son, to England's southern coast in an attempt to regain some strength. He died there whilst engaged in writing the lyrics for *San Toy*, and the piece was completed by Adrian Ross, who, with Greenbank, was largely responsible for establishing the job of lyricist (as opposed to all-in writer, or co-writer) in the modern musical theatre.

1891 **Captain Billy** (François Cellier) 1 act Savoy Theatre 24 September
1892 **Incognita** (*Le Coeur et la main*) English lyrics (Lyric Theatre)
1892 **The Young Recruit** (*Le Dragon de la reine*) English lyrics w Adrian Ross, Harry Nicholls (Newcastle)
1892 **Beef Tea** (Wilfred Bendall) 1 act Lyric Theatre 22 October
1893 **Poor Jonathan** (*Der arme Jonathan*) English lyrics (Prince of Wales Theatre)
1893 **Mr Jericho** (Ernest Ford) 1 act Savoy Theatre 24 March

1893 **A Gaiety Girl** (Sidney Jones/Owen Hall) Prince of Wales Theatre 14 October
1894 **Mirette** (André Messager/Frederick E Weatherly) Savoy Theatre 3 July
1894 **The House of Lords** (Ford, George Byng) 1 act Lyric Theatre 6 July
1895 **An Artist's Model** (Jones/Hall) Daly's Theatre 2 February
1896 **The Geisha** (Jones/Hall) Daly's Theatre 25 April
1896 **Monte Carlo** (Howard Talbot) Avenue Theatre 27 August
1896 **The Circus Girl** (Ivan Caryll/w Adrian Ross/James T Tanner, Walter Palings) Gaiety Theatre 5 December
1897 **The Scarlet Feather** (*La Petite Mademoiselle*) English book and lyrics (Shaftesbury Theatre)
1897 **Old Sarah** (F Cellier) 1 act Savoy Theatre 17 June
1898 **A Runaway Girl** (Caryll, Monckton/w Aubrey Hopwood/Seymour Hicks, Harry Nicholls) Gaiety Theatre 21 May
1898 **A Greek Slave** (Jones/Hall) Daly's Theatre 8 June
1899 **San Toy** (Jones/w Adrian Ross/Edward Morton) Daly's Theatre 21 October

GREENBANK, Percy (b London, 24 January 1878; d Rickmansworth, 9 December 1968). Harry Greenbank's younger brother, Percy, was originally intended for the law, but instead followed his celebrated brother's footsteps into the world of journalism with contributions to such journals as *Punch*, *The Sketch* and *The Tatler*, and into the theatre.

After Harry's death, George Edwardes offered the younger Greenbank the opportunity to collaborate with Adrian Ross on the lyrics for the new Gaiety show, *The Messenger Boy*, and also interpolated two of his lyrics into *San Toy*, when the score was reorganized to suit take-over Ada Reeve ('Somebody', 'All I Want is a Little Bit of Fun'). His *The Messenger Boy* contribution included one of the show's hits, its title number (and the rhyming of 'Rameses' with 'clammy seas'), and won him a firm place in the Gaiety 'team' along with composers Ivan Caryll and Lionel Monckton, Ross, and the deviser of the Gaiety show plots and outlines, James Tanner.

For the remaining 14 years of the 'Edwardes era' he worked consistently for the producer, at the Gaiety, Daly's and later the Adelphi, contributing sometimes much and sometimes only a few lyrics to most of Edwardes's shows (although the frequent credit 'additional lyrics by ...' was often no guide to quantity) and being responsible for many a fairly ephemeral song hit.

After the end of the Edwardes era, he continued for a further decade to supply songwords and occasionally libretti to the musical stage, only rarely venturing into the world of revue (*Half Past Eight*, *Vanity Fair*). His last major work for the West End was the adaptation from the German of what was to become the book to the Jean Gilbert-Vernon Duke musical *Yvonne*. He subsequently did occasional work as a play doctor (*El Dorado* et al) or an adaptor – he modernized *San Toy* with Percy Barrow for its 1931 revival – but basically settled into what proved to be a long retirement. Greenbank died at the age of 90 and, as a result, the Edwardian musical comedies to which he contributed remain in copyright well into the 21st century.

1900 **The Messenger Boy** (Lionel Monckton, Ivan Caryll/w Adrian Ross/James Tanner, Alfred Murray) Gaiety Theatre 3 February
1901 **The Toreador** (Monckton, Caryll/w Ross/Tanner, Harry Nicholls) Gaiety Theatre 17 June
1901 **The Gay Cadets** (Basil Davis/w Harold Simpson/Norman Prescott, J Thomson) Birmingham 24 June

1902 **A Country Girl** (Monckton/w Ross/Tanner) Daly's Theatre 18 January

1902 **Three Little Maids** (Paul Rubens/w Rubens/Rubens) Apollo Theatre 20 May

1903 **My Lady Molly** (Jones/w Charles H Taylor/George H Jessop) Terry's Theatre 14 March

1903 **The Orchid** (Monckton, Caryll/w Ross/Tanner) Gaiety Theatre 28 October

1903 **The Earl and the Girl** (Caryll/Seymour Hicks) Adelphi Theatre 10 December

1904 **The Blue Moon** (Talbot, Rubens/w Rubens/Harold Ellis) Northampton 29 February, Lyric Theatre, London 28 August 1905

1904 **The Cingalee** (Monckton/w Ross/Tanner) Daly's Theatre 5 March

1904 **Véronique** English lyrics w Lillian Eldee (Apollo Theatre)

1904 **Lady Madcap** (Rubens/w Rubens/N Newnham-Davis, Rubens) Prince of Wales Theatre 17 December

1905 **The Little Michus** (*Les P'tites Michu*) English lyrics (Daly's Theatre)

1905 **The Spring Chicken** (Monckton, Caryll/w Ross/George Grossmith) Gaiety Theatre 30 May

1906 **The Girl Behind the Counter** (Talbot/w Anderson/Leedham Bantock, Arthur Anderson) Wyndham's Theatre 21 April

1906 **See See** (Jones/w Ross/C H E Brookfield) Prince of Wales Theatre 20 June

1906 **The New Aladdin** (Monckton, Caryll/w others/Tanner, W H Risque) Gaiety Theatre 29 September

1906 **Two Naughty Boys** (Constance Tippett/Grossmith) Gaiety Theatre 8 January

1907 **The Three Kisses** (Talbot/w Bantock) Apollo Theatre 21 August

1908 **The Belle of Brittany** (Talbot/Bantock, P J Barrow) Queen's Theatre 24 October

1909 **Our Miss Gibbs** (Monckton, Caryll/w Ross/Tanner et al) Gaiety Theatre 23 January

1909 **A Persian Princess** (Talbot/Barrow, Bantock) Queen's Theatre 27 April

1910 **The Quaker Girl** (Monckton/w Ross/Tanner) Adelphi Theatre 5 November

1911 **The Mousmé** (Talbot, Monckton/w Arthur Wimperis/Robert Courtneidge, Alexander M Thompson) Shaftesbury Theatre 9 September

1912 **Princess Caprice** (*Der liebe Augustin*) English lyrics w Scott Craven, C M Beswick (Shaftesbury Theatre)

1912 **Autumn Manoeuvres** (*Tatárjárás*) English lyrics (Adelphi Theatre)

1912 **The Dancing Mistress** (Monckton/w Ross/Tanner) Adelphi Theatre 19 October

1913 **The Girl From Utah** (Jones, Rubens/w Rubens/Tanner, Rubens) Adelphi Theatre 18 October

1914 **The Cinema Star** (*Die Kino-Königin*) additional English lyrics w Harry Graham (Shaftesbury Theatre)

1914 **After the Girl** (Rubens/w Rubens/Rubens) Gaiety Theatre 7 February

1914 **Tonight's the Night** (Rubens/w Rubens/Fred Thompson) Shubert Theatre, New York 24 December

1915 **Tina** (Rubens, Hadyn Wood/w Graham, Rubens) Adelphi Theatre 2 November

1915 **The Miller's Daughters** (revised *Three Little Maids*) London Opera House 15 May

1916 **Houp-La!** (Nat D Ayer/w Hugh E Wright/Wright, Thompson) St Martin's Theatre 23 November

1917 **The Boy** (Talbot, Monckton/w Ross/Thompson) Adelphi Theatre 14 September

1919 **The Girl for the Boy** (Howard Carr, Bernard Rolt/Austen Hurgon, George Arthurs) Duke of York's Theatre 23 September

1919 **The Kiss Call** (Caryll/w Ross, Clifford Grey/Thompson) Gaiety Theatre 8 October

1921 **My Nieces** (Talbot) Queen's Theatre 4 October

1922 **The Little Duchess** (G H Clutsam/w Bertrand Davis/Courtneidge, Davis) Glasgow 25 December

1924 **The Street Singer** (Fraser-Simson/Frederick Lonsdale) Lyric Theatre 27 June

1926 **Yvonne** (*Uschi, Zwei um Eine* etc) English libretto and lyrics (Daly's Theatre)

1929 **Cupid and the Cutlets** (Patrick Barrow) 1 act Q Theatre 20 May

GREENE Clay M[eredith] (b San Francisco, 12 March 1850; d San Francisco, 5 September 1933).

Greene was already established as a successful stock-broker in San Francisco when he turned his hand to writing for the theatre and, from his early twenties when his first play was produced, for more than 20 years he turned out a stream of often highly popular and successful plays and libretti, mostly in a happily barnstorming style. *Hans the Boatman*, a weepie comedy-drama with movable songs, constructed around the talents of Minnie Palmer's sometime leading man Charles Arnold, was the most widely successful of his musical pieces, whilst his Dutch sentimental melodrama with musical moments, *Struck Oil* (Salt Lake City, 23 February 1874), was a long-time sure-fire vehicle for actor-producer J C Williamson and his wife Maggie Moore, in both America and Australia. In later years, after leaving the stage behind, he worked for a time with the Lubin film company and spent considerable time authoring a memoir which, although it remained unpublished, is preserved in his local library.

1887 **Hans the Boatman** (pasticcio) Theatre Royal, Sheffield, England 7 March

1889 **Bluebeard Jr** (Fred Eustis, Richard Maddern) Chicago 11 June, Niblo's Garden, New York 13 January 1890

1894 **The Maid of Plymouth** (Thomas P Thorne) Broadway Theater 15 January

1894 **The Little Trooper** (*Les 28 Jours de Clairette*) English version w music by William Furst (Casino Theater)

1899 **In Gay Paree** (Ludwig Englander/Grant Stewart) Casino Theater 20 March

1900 **Aunt Hannah** (A Baldwin Sloane/Matthew J Royal) Bijou Theater 22 February

1900 **The Regatta Girl** (Harry McLellan) Koster and Bial's Music Hall 14 March

1902 **The Little Minister and His Mash**

1902 **The Silver Slipper** revised American libretto (Broadway Theater)

GREENE, Evie [GREENE, Edith Elizabeth] (b Portsmouth, 14 January 1878; d Portsmouth, 11 September, 1917). Dark, fine-voiced West End leading lady who created major rôles in a number of highly successful musical shows.

After beginning a theatrical career as a dancer in a touring company of Slaughter's *Marjorie* at the age of 14, the young Evie was discovered to have a fine, growing soprano voice and she quickly progressed to principal rôles, touring as Annabel in *Maid Marian* (*Robin Hood*), Ethel in *Morocco Bound*, Norah in *The Gay Parisienne* (1895), Ethel Joy in *The New Barmaid*, Ethel in Bucalossi's *En Route* (1896) and opposite Little Tich as the heroine of *Billy* (1898).

At 21 she was hired by Tom Davis to star in his London production of Varney's *L'Amour mouillé*. She made a great personal success in the breeches rôle of Prince Carlo, and

Davis promptly cast her in the star rôle of his next new musical, *Florodora*. In the part of the darkly glamorous, mid-Pacific Dolores, she introduced 'Silver Star of Love' and became, overnight, one of London's favourite musical stars. After *Florodora*, she was signed up by George Edwardes who starred her in a new version of *Les Fêtards*, *Kitty Grey* (1900), in which her portrayal of the sparkling actress of the title was contrasted with the demure, betrayed Baroness of Ethel Sydney (tour) and Edna May (town). Edwardes then moved her to Daly's Theatre where she created the rôle of Nan in *A Country Girl* ('Try Again Johnnie', 'Molly the Marchioness'). After playing that rôle for most of the show's two-year run, she next starred in the title-rôle of Ivan Caryll's *The Duchess of Dantzic* (1903) as a light operatic Madame Sans-Gêne, scoring the greatest triumph of a career which had been nothing but high points.

She played Sans-Gêne through most of the London run, toured it and in 1905 repeated her performance on Broadway, before returning for new rôles under Edwardes' management in *The Little Cherub* (1906), as the elegant, directoire heroine of Hugo Felix's *Les Merveilleuses* (1906) and as another dark and dashing maiden in *Havana* (1908). After *Havana* she appeared in variety, featuring high on the bill at the Palladium, the Coliseum and the biggest provincial houses, and returned only once to the musical stage, in a revival of *Florodora* in 1915, before her death at the age of 39.

GREENWOOD, [Frances] Charlotte (b Philadelphia, 25 June 1893; d Beverly Hills, 18 January 1978).

A lanky, blonde comedienne with a talent for eccentric dance, Miss Greenwood made her first appearance on the stage, aged 12, as a dancer in *The White Cat*. She subsequently played in a minor capacity in *The Rogers Brothers in Panama* (1907) and *Nearly a Hero* (1908), toured in vaudeville and returned to Broadway to appear in *The Passing Show* and the Lehár musical *The Man With Three Wives*. Following a tour in *The Tik-Tok Man of Oz*, she won her best opportunity to date in the rôle of Letitia Proudfoot in the musical comedy *Pretty Mrs Smith* (1914). Her comical dancing and her song, 'Long, Lean, Lanky Letty', won her particular notice, and in 1915 producer Oliver Morosco had a musical built around her talents and entitled, after her previous success, *So Long, Letty*.

Letty became a running character name (though not a consistent character) through a series of musicals over the next half-dozen years which, if limited in their appeal to Broadway, proved highly successful on the road. Morosco followed *Linger Longer Letty* (1919) with *Let 'er Go, Letty* which had its title changed when Miss Greenwood abandoned it to go instead into *Letty Pepper* (1922), a musical revision of Charles Klein's successful vehicle for Rose Stahl, *Maggie Pepper*.

She played threafter in revue (*Music Box Revue*, *Ritz Revue*, her husband, Martin Broones' *Rufus Le Maire's Affairs*) and comedy, and in 1930 she filmed *So Long Letty*, but she did not return to the musical theatre until 1932, when she moved temporarily to London where her husband was establishing a career as a composer of musical-comedy songs. She played Augustc in the Drury Lane production of *Wild Violets* (*Wenn die kleinen Veilchen blühen*), Tiny Barbour in Jerome Kern's *Three Sisters* at the same house and, in a fine showy rôle, the zany Aunt Isabel of *Gay Deceivers* (*Toi c'est moi*), for which Broones had largely replaced the original French score.

Back in America, she toured extensively in one more Letty show, *Leaning on Letty* (1935), and, after a varying career including two years of *The Charlotte Greenwood Show* on radio and a trip to Australia with *Leaning on Letty*, made a final Broadway appearance as Juno in Cole Porter's *Out of This World* (1950).

As well as her 'Letty' film appearance, she appeared in the filmed version of *Flying High* (Pansy), then later in such pieces as *Tall, Dark and Handsome*, *Down Argentina Way* and *Moon Over Miami* before, in 1956, she was a memorable Aunt Eller in the film version of *Oklahoma!*.

Autobiography: *Never Too Tall* (New York, 1947)

GREET, William (b 1851; d Bournemouth, 24 April 1914).

At first an officer in the Royal Marines, then business manager for Willie Edouin, Greet ultimately became a highly successful manager of touring musical comedy. He had already made his West End début with the fairly successful burlesque *Blue-Eyed Susan* produced at the Alhambra (w C J Abud, 1892), when he picked up the second company rights of the touring musical *The Lady Slavey* from H Cecil Beryl (1893). *The Lady Slavey* turned out to be a touring phenomenon, and his production toured virtually non-stop for a dozen years, soon sharing the circuits with companies of Greet's own hugely successful made-for-touring show *The Gay Parisienne*. Whilst leaving others to take the risks of the London and New York runs, Greet toured *The Gay Parisienne* for more than a decade with great profit. He mounted *Dandy Dick Whittington* (aka *The Circus Boy*, 1895) in London and on the road, with limited success, but found another sturdy provincial annual with *The New Mephisto(pheles)* which accomplished eight years of touring from 1897.

In 1901 he returned to London, not only with a revival of the hardy *Morocco Bound* but also, on a rather different level, as the new lessee of the Savoy Theatre which the widowed Helen D'Oyly Carte was giving up. Greet took over where Carte had left off, managing *The Emerald Isle* and producing *Ib and Little Christina*, *The Willow Pattern* (1901), *Merrie England* (1902) and *A Princess of Kensington* (1903), but, finding the revenues from comic opera rather less than from his tours, he switched the Savoy company to musical comedy and scored a fine hit with *The Earl and the Girl* (1903). The Christmas entertainment *Little Hans Andersen* (1903) and *The Talk of the Town* (1905) were less successful, and Greet's name disappeared thereafter from London bills.

He was, at various times, involved in the management of the Lyric, Garrick, Comedy and Adelphi Theatres.

His younger brother, Ben Greet, was also a well-known manager and actor, initially in touring musical comedy but later and principally in the Shakespearian field.

GREGH, Louis (b Philippeville, Algeria, 16 March 1843; d St Mesme, 21 January 1915).

Conductor and composer, Gregh had his moments of success in the musical theatre with the very light musical accompaniments to the spicy *Un lycée de jeunes filles*, revived numerous times in Paris after its initial run and played in

Plate 117. **Charlotte Greenwood** *was 'Letty' for the second time in* So Long, Letty, *a musical which got her mixed up in a touch of husband-swapping.*

several other countries, with the musical comedy *Le Présomptif*, produced with success in Belgium if not in France, and with the vaudeville *Patatart, Patatart et cie* which also won itself export (*Kneisl & Co*, Vienna). He also provided the music for a number of ballets and for Fernand Beissier's play *Arlette* (1891). Latterly he devoted himself to music publishing, establishing a firm which survived in his family for three generations.

1881 **Un lycée de jeunes filles** (Alexandre Bisson) Théâtre Cluny 28 December
1883 **Le Présomptif** (Albert Hennequin, Albin Valabrègue) Galeries-Saint Hubert, Brussels 12 December; Théâtre de la Renaissance 6 June 1884
1890 **Grande vitesse, port dû** (A Philibert) 1 act La Cigale 19 September
1893 **Patatart, Patatart et cie** (André Sylvane, Charles Clairville) Théâtre des Folies-Dramatiques 9 October
1895 **Le Capitaine Roland** (Armand Laffrique) Théâtre Mondaine 29 March

GREY, Clifford [DAVIS, Percy] (b Birmingham, 5 January 1887; d Ipswich, 25 September 1941).

Highly successful British lyricist who spent prolific periods working alternately for the London and New York musical stages.

Grey first worked in the entertainment business as a performer in concert parties, where he contributed to the writing of his company's material, before Leslie Henson introduced him to the management of the Alhambra. There, in 1916, he was teamed with Nat Ayer to write lyrics for a few of the songs for the English version of the Paris revue *Les Fils Touffe sont à Paris* which that theatre had taken over from the schedule of the late George Edwardes. As *The Bing Boys Are Here* the show and its favourite songs were an enormous success ('If You Were the Only Girl in the World', 'Another Little Drink') and Grey, who had quickly ended up supplying most of the song words, including those for the two hit numbers, was launched on a series of revues which included *Pell Mell*, *The Bing Girls Are There* ('Let the Great Big World Keep Turning'), *The Bing Boys on Broadway* ('First Love, Last Love, Best Love'), *Hullo America*, *Johnny Jones* and George Gershwin's *The Rainbow*, and an even more substantial series of musical comedies.

The first of these book shows were the Gaiety Theatre's *Theodore & Co*, in which he combined with Jerome Kern to produce Leslie Henson's hit song '365 Days', and two adaptations, the London versions of the 'Roderick Freeman/Ogden Hartley' Broadway musical *High Jinks*, and of the Belgian musical *Arlette*, into which Grey and Ivor Novello interpolated the comic song 'On the Staff', with which Stanley Lupino scored his first major success.

During and after the First World War he supplied the song words to some of the most successful and long-running musical plays in London, notably Leslie Henson's *Yes, Uncle!*, the Bill Berry comedy vehicle *Who's Hooper?* and the Winter Garden musical farce *A Night Out*, as well as one virtually British musical which made its appearance on Broadway: Ivan Caryll's *The Girl Behind the Gun*, which would later become *Kissing Time* for its very successful London run.

Soon after the production of *Kissing Time*, Grey took what should have been a three-week holiday in America

and, in spite of the fact that he completed commissions for several further London shows – *Phi-Phi*, *The Smith Family*, additional lyrics for the 1921 revival of *The Maid of the Mountains* – he ended up staying in the United States for most of the 1920s. One of his earliest jobs there was a fresh collaboration with Jerome Kern, as lyricist for *Sally*, and the result was a major hit and such songs as 'Sally' and 'Wild Rose'. In the years that followed, he provided lyrics, and on several occasions libretti as well, for a series of Broadway musicals and revues. Of the book musicals, many of which did not rise above the mediocre, *Hit the Deck* ('Hallelujah!', 'Sometimes I'm Happy') and Rudolf Friml's *The Three Musketeers* were the two most notable successes, but, amongst the other, less memorable productions, Grey also had individual song credits for an English version of Kálmán's 'Komm' Zigány!' (*Gräfin Mariza*) and for José Padilla's hit song 'Valencia'.

During a spell in Hollywood he produced the lyrics for Victor Schertzinger's score to the 1929 film *The Love Parade* ('Nobody's Using it Now', 'My Love Parade', 'Paris, Stay the Same' for Chevalier, 'Dream Lover' for Jeanette MacDonald, 'March of the Grenadiers') and for the unrecognizably botched versions of Lehár's *Zigeunerliebe* entitled *The Rogue Song* (Stothart's 'When I'm Looking at You', Lehár's 'The White Dove' for Lawrence Tibbett) and of Oscar Straus's *Walzertraum*, become in Hollywood *The Smiling Lieutenant*, before returning to Britain for the final years of his career.

Those years were as busy and successful as the others. After supplying lyrics to Kern's London show *Blue Eyes* (additional), he had major song hits in Vivian Ellis's *Mr Cinders* ('Spread a Little Happiness') and Waller and Tunbridge's *For the Love of Mike* ('Got a Date With an Angel' for Bobby Howes) as he mixed musical theatre work with a good number of films, collaborating on, amongst others, the screenplays for the film versions of the musicals *For the Love of Mike* (1932), *Hold My Hand* (1938), *Yes, Madam?* (1938), and *Me and My Girl* (*The Lambeth Walk*, 1939).

During the early part of the Second World War, Grey was engaged with ENSA organizing concerts for the troops, and a contribution to the revue *Black and Blue* was his last stage offering before his death.

1916 **Theodore & Co** (Jerome Kern, Ivor Novello/w Adrian Ross/H M Harwood, George Grossmith) Gaiety Theatre 4 September
1916 **The Kodak Girl** (Grace A Vernon/Harry M Vernon) 1 act Middlesex Music Hall 27 November
1917 **Arlette** English lyrics w Ross (Shaftesbury Theatre)
1917 **Yes, Uncle!** (Nat D Ayer/Austen Hurgon, George Arthurs) Prince of Wales Theatre 29 December
1918 **The Girl Behind the Gun** (aka *Kissing Time*) (Ivan Caryll/Guy Bolton, P G Wodehouse) New Amsterdam Theater 16 September
1919 **Who's Hooper?** (Howard Talbot, Novello/Fred Thompson) Adelphi Theatre 13 September
1919 **The Kiss Call** (Caryll/w Ross, Percy Greenbank/Thompson) Gaiety Theatre 8 October
1919 **Baby Bunting** (Ayer/Thompson, Worton David) Shaftesbury Theatre 25 September
1920 **A Night Out** (Willie Redstone/Grossmith, Arthur Miller) Winter Garden Theatre 19 September
1920 **Kissing Time** (Caryll/w Philander Johnson, Irving Caesar/George V Hobart) Lyric Theater, New York 11 October

1920 **Sally** (Kern/w Wodehouse/Bolton) New Amsterdam Theater, New York 21 December

1921 **Little Miss Raffles** (Caryll/Bolton) Stamford, Conn 21 December

1922 **The Hotel Mouse** revised *Little Miss Raffles* (Caryll, Armand Vecsey/Bolton) Shubert Theater, New York 13 March

1922 **Phi-Phi** English book and lyrics w Fred Thompson (London Pavilion)

1922 **The Smith Family** (Ayer/w Stanley Logan, Philip Page) Empire Theatre 6 September

1923 **Lady Butterfly** (Werner Janssen) Globe Theater, New York 22 January

1924 **Marjorie** (Sigmund Romberg, Herbert Stothart, Stephen Jones/w Harold Atteridge) Shubert Theater, New York 11 August

1924 **Annie Dear** (Romberg, Harry Tierney/Clare Kummer) Times Square Theater, New York 4 November

1925 **June Days** (ex-*The School Maid*) (J Fred Coots/Atteridge) Astor Theater, New York 6 August

1925 **Mayflowers** (Eduard Künneke) Forrest Theater, New York 24 November

1926 **Patsy** (Isidore B Kornblum/w E Magnus Ingleton) Mason Theater, Los Angeles 8 March

1926 **Katja** (*Katja, die Tänzerin*) additional American lyrics to Harry Graham's English version (44th Street Theater, New York)

1926 **Bubblin' Over** (Richard Myers/Leo Robin) Garrick Theater, Philadelphia 2 August

1927 **Hit the Deck** (Vincent Youmans/w Robin/Herbert Fields) Belasco Theater, New York 25 April

1928 **The Madcap** (Maurice Rubens, Coots etc/Gladys Unger, Cosmo Hamilton [Gertrude Purcell]) Royale Theater, New York 31 January

1928 **Sunny Days** (Jean Schwartz/w William Cary Duncan) Imperial Theater, New York 8 February

1928 **The Three Musketeers** (Rudolf Friml/w Wodehouse/ William Anthony McGuire) Lyric Theater, New York 13 March

1928 **Ups-a-Daisy** (Lewis Gensler) Shubert Theater, New York 8 October

1929 **Mr Cinders** (Vivian Ellis, Richard Myers/w Greatrex Newman) Adelphi Theatre 11 February

1929 **Sky High** (*Der Tanz ins Glück*) additional lyrics for American version (Casino Theater)

1930 **Smiles** (*The One Girl*) (Youmans/w Harold Adamson, Ring Lardner) Ziegfeld Theater November, New York 18 and libretto revision for Britain w Frank Eyton and H M Sargent

1931 **For the Love of Mike** (Jack Waller, Joseph Tunbridge/w Sonny Miller/w H F Maltby) Saville Theatre 8 October

1932 **Out of the Bottle** (Ellis, Oscar Levant/w Thompson) 11 June

1933 **He Wanted Adventure** (Waller, Tunbridge/w Weston, Lee) Saville Theatre 28 March

1933 **Command Performance** (Waller, Tunbridge/C Stafford Dickens) Saville Theatre 17 October

1934 **Mr Whittington** (Waller, Tunbridge, John Green/Newman, Furber) London Hippodrome 1 February

1935 **Jack o' Diamonds** (Noel Gay/w Maltby) Gaiety Theatre 25 February

1935 **Love Laughs—!** (ex- *Leave It to Love*) (Gay/w Newman) London Hippodrome 25 June

1936 **At the Silver Swan** (Edmond Samuels/Bolton, Percival Mackey) Palace Theatre 19 February

1937 **Oh! You Letty** (Paul Sharon/w Geoffrey Kerr, Lee) Palace Theatre 8 December

1938 **Bobby Get Your Gun** (Waller, Tunbridge/w Bolton, Thompson, Lee, Carter) Adelphi Theatre 7 October

1942 **Susie** revised *Jack o' Diamonds* (Oxford)

1942 **Wild Rose** revised *Sally* (Prince's Theatre, London)

GREY, Joel [KATZ, Joel] (b Cleveland, Ohio, 11 April 1932).

The son of comedian Mickey Katz, Grey made his musical comedy début touring as Littlechap in *Stop the World – I Want to Get Off* and succeeded to the rôle created by Anthony Newley in the show's Broadway production in 1963. He later covered Tommy Steele in the starring rôle of *Half a Sixpence*, but came to fame with his creation of the rôle of the leering, epicene master of ceremonies in *Cabaret* (1966, 'Willkommen', 'Three Ladies', 'Money' etc) on the stage and again on film (Academy Award). He later appeared as George M Cohan in the biomusical *George M!* (1968), and with less success in the Joan of Arc musical *Goodtime Charley* (1975, Charley) and in the musicalization of *Jacobowsky and the Colonel* as *The Grand Tour* (1979, Jacobowsky). He was seen once again on Broadway in his celebrated role in *Cabaret* in a Broadway revival of 262 nights in 1987, followed by a tour.

GRIFFITH, Robert E (b Methuen, Mass, 1907; d Port Chester, NY, 7 June 1961).

Originally an actor and then, from 1935, a stage manager for George Abbott, Griffith found almost unmitigated success when he turned his hand to producing for the musical theatre. He teamed with Hal Prince (a stage-management colleague on *Touch and Go* and *Wonderful Town*) and Frederick Brisson to produce the musicals *The Pajama Game*, *Damn Yankees* and *New Girl in Town*, then with Prince only for *West Side Story*, *Fiorello!* and *Tenderloin*.

GRI-GRI Operette in 3 acts by Heinrich Bolten-Bäckers based on a play by Henriot and Jules Chancel. Music by Paul Lincke. Metropoltheater, Cologne, 25 March 1911; Friedrich-Wilhelmstädtisches Theater, Berlin, 2 November 1912.

Gaston Deligny goes to equatorial Africa to purchase the land of the King Foulamer for France and, there, falls for the daughter of one of the monarch's 200 wives, a lass who has, somehow, been born white. After a brief moment of 'married' life with the charming Gri-Gri, he returns to the Quai d'Orsay and allies himself comfortably with the niece of his Minister. But Gri-Gri and her royal father arrive in Paris in search of the missing husband, and the girl takes a job in a music-hall whilst scandal swirls around the internationally bigamous Gaston until, with the final curtain in sight, he returns to his equatorial bride.

The most successful of Lincke's latter-day Operetten, *Gri-Gri* was played in Berlin, with Traute Rose starred, given as a wartime entertainment in Vienna (ad August Neidhart) with Susanne Bachrich in the title-rôle of a localized version and Carl Pfann as the Viennese consul, Hans Heinz von Hoheneck (ex-Gaston), in Amsterdam where Beppi de Vries starred as the light-skinned lass from darkest Africa, and ultimately made its way both to Paris, where its text was credited to Chancel, and Gaby Besset starred alongside Serjius and Bever, playing the King in blackface, and to the German-language Yorkville Theater in New York. A production under the title *Mie-Mie* (ad Harry Graham) was announced for London's Adelphi Theatre in 1920 (variously under Grossmith and Laurillard, and then C B Cochran), but with anti-German feeling still strong in the wake of the war, the producer assured the press that American naturalized Englishman Howard Talbot would redo the music. Except perhaps for the ensembles. In the end, London didn't get *Gri-Gri* at all.

Austria: Wiener Stadttheater 12 February 1915; France: Gaîté-Rochechouart 6 December 1924; USA: Yorkville Theater (Ger) 26 January 1928

GRIMES, Tammy (b Lynn, Mass, 30 January 1934). Broadway soubrette of the straight and musical stages, who matured into an occasionally musical comedienne.

Miss Grimes stepped in as a stopgap in *Bus Stop*, made her regular Broadway début in the play *Look After Lulu*, and subsequently mixed musical and straight theatre appearances. She had a false start on the musical scene when the 1955 musical *The Amazing Adele*, in which she played the title-rôle, closed on the road, but she had happier times in the title-rôle of *The Unsinkable Molly Brown* (1960, the first of two Tony Awards), as the ghostly Elvira in *High Spirits* (1964), as the original Dorothy Brock in *42nd Street* (1980) and, off-Broadway, in the top-billed rôle of *Mademoiselle Colombe* (1987, Madame Alexandra).

GROBECKER, Anna [MEJO, Anna] (b Breslau, 27 July 1829; d Althofen, 27 September 1908).

The daughter of an opera singer and a member of a highly successful family of musical-theatre performers, Anna Mejo made her first stage appearances as a small child in Breslau (*Der Rattenfänger von Hameln*) in a childrens' company directed by her father. She had her first adult rôle at Magdeburg at the age of 15, and subsequently worked in Leipzig, Berlin and in Budapest with Nestroy before making her first appearances in Vienna at 19, paired with her husband Philipp Grobecker in the Posse *Einmal hunderttausend Thaler* and *Benjamin, der seinen Vater sucht* at Nestroy's Carltheater. Her performances in those pieces led Karl Treumann to choose her to play one of the two gossipy neighbours in his production of *Hochzeit bei Laternenschein*, the first German-language performance of an Offenbach work at the same house. She subsequently became a regular in Treumann's Offenbach productions, playing the first Viennese performances as Vasco in *Das Mädchen von Elisonzo*, Antoine in *Die Zaubergeige*, in *Die Savoyarden*, and as Öffentliche Meinung (L'Opinion Publique) in *Orpheus in der Unterwelt* (1860) in which her husband appeared as Orphée.

When Treumann established his own Theater am Franz-Josefs-Kai in late 1860, Grobecker went with him and during the house's existence appeared, amongst others, as first 'boy' as Daphnis in *Daphnis und Chloë*, Friquet in *Meister Fortunios Liebeslied*, Cascadetto in *Die Seufzerbrücke*, Frincke in Suppé's *Flotte Bursche* and, in skirts, as Martine in Caspers's *Ma Tante dort*, Beatrice in *Die Schwätzerin von Saragossa* (*Les Bavards*), the housekeeper Sidonia in *Zehn Mädchen und kein Mann*, Hedwig in *Die schöne Magellone* (*Geneviève de Brabant*) and Nanette in *Monsieur et Madame Denis*.

She returned to the Carltheater in 1862, and appeared there in her most successful rôles (Frincke, Friquet, Cascadetto, Daphnis), played more opéra-bouffe rôles (Pauline in *Pariser Leben*, Nani in *Les Géorgiennes*, Rigobert in *Der Regimentszauberer*, Croûte-au-Pot in *Die Damen der Halle*) and created several new ones, including her most durable rôle, Ganymede in Suppé's *Die schöne Galathee*

(1865), as well as the title-rôle in von Zaytz's *Fitzliputzli*, Max in his *Mannschaft am Bord*, Ludwig XV in *Herr von Papillon* and Der Herundhinlaufer in *Die Jungfrau von Dragant*. She retired momentarily in 1867 to wed her second husband, Count Vincente de la Rocca, made a brief return to the stage in 1869–70, but retired definitively in 1871.

Grobecker's popularity and her skill at, in particular, travesty rôles led her to be claimed as the 'perfect soubrette', 'the queen of the pants parts' and the equal of the great French actress Déjazet. Offenbach, after hearing her perform, no longer complained at the ravages Treumann had worked on his opérettes in order to fabricate rôles for her for, as the director quotably announced, 'wenn die Grobecker nicht dabei ist, ist es nicht lustig genug' ('it isn't so funny when Grobecker isn't there'). The composer is even said to have tried to persuade the actress to join the Paris Palais-Royal company. In the earliest successful Austrian works, Treumann and/or Suppé created the rôles of Frincke, Sidonia and Ganymede in *Die schöne Galathee* especially to her measure, and she thus helped set the mould for what would be the soubrette of Viennese Operette.

In the Singspiel *Josefine Gallmeyer* (Wiener Bürgertheater, 1921) Grobecker was impersonated by Paula Bäck.

GROODY, Louise (b Waco, Tex, 26 March 1897; d Canadensis, Pa, 16 September 1961).

A vivacious dancing ingénue, Miss Groody appeared on Broadway first as a chorus dancer and then in supporting rôles in Jerome Kern's *Toot-Toot!* (1918, Mrs Walter Colt), in *Fiddlers Three* (1918, Gilda Varelli) and again for Kern in *The Night Boat* (1920, Barbara) before taking leading parts as the Cinderella heroine with a Bill-Sykes fiancé in the same composer's *Good Morning, Dearie* (1921, Rose-Marie), in which she introduced the title-song and joined Harlan Dixon in 'Way Down Town' and Oscar Shaw in 'Blue Danube Blues', and again in an adaptation of Yvain's *Ta Bouche* (*One Kiss*, 1923) as Eva, the girl who keeps on practising for the action of her wedding night until parental assent can be obtained for the wedding.

Her major success came when she was brought in to replace Phyllis Cleveland in the title-rôle of *No, No, Nanette* ('I Want to Be Happy', 'No, No, Nanette', 'Tea for Two') and, after fulfilling its Chicago run, came to Broadway in the title-rôle of Youmans's hit show. She starred again in the composer's next piece, *Hit the Deck* ('Sometimes I'm Happy', 'If He'll Come Back to Me'), before disappearing from the musical scene at little more than 30 years of age to reap her rewards in the green-backed fields of vaudeville.

GROSSMITH, George (b London, 9 December 1847; d Folkestone, 1 March 1912).

George Grossmith began performing in his early twenties, following the example of his father, as a solo entertainer at the piano. He first crossed paths with author W S Gilbert when he played the rôle of the Judge in a minor London performance of *Trial By Jury* and, as a result, he was, against considerable protest from the backers, given the leading comic part of John Wellington Wells, the sorcerer of *The Sorcerer*, when Gilbert and Sullivan's first full-length opera was staged at the Opera Comique. His tentativeness and nerves were forgiven by first-night critics who did not, at this time, expect to see anything like a finished performance at a première, and Grossmith worked up his part and his courage successfully enough through the run to be retained for the following piece. He created the rôle of Sir Joseph Porter KCB in *HMS Pinafore* ('When I Was a Lad', 'Never Mind the Why and Wherefore'), played the Major General in the London version of *The Pirates of Penzance* ('I am the Very Model of a Modern Major-General'), and thereafter created the principal comedy rôles in each of the Gilbert and Sullivan works of the next decade – Reginald Bunthorne (*Patience*), the Lord Chancellor (*Iolanthe*, 'Nightmare Song', 'The Law is the True Embodiment'), King Gama (*Princess Ida*, 'If You Give Me Your Attention'), Ko-ko (*The Mikado*, 'Tit Willow', 'I've Got a Little List'), Robin/Ruthven (*Ruddigore*), and Jack Point (*The Yeomen of the Guard*, 'I Have a Song to Sing, O', 'A Private Buffoon'), becoming in the process a comic-opera institution and a huge public favourite.

After *The Yeomen of the Guard*, he retired from the stage and returned to his old form of entertaining at the piano with lucrative results. On the few occasions where he allowed himself to be lured back to the theatre through family or financial considerations – with *His Excellency* (1894), *His Majesty* (1897), *The Gay Pretenders* (1900) – his natural nervousness and friability of memory, which he had largely conquered at the Opera Comique and the Savoy, got the better of him and each experience was less and less successful.

Having for many years provided himself with monologue material and songs, Grossmith continued throughout his career to write comedy material and scenas, some of which he performed in the theatre and others in drawing-room entertainments. He also contributed the music to some little operettas of which the most successful was *Mr Guffin's Elopement*, played for many years by J L Toole and including the popular song 'The Speakers Eye', and the most substantial a full score for W S Gilbert's unsuccessful musical version of *Un Chapeau de paille d'Italie* as *Haste to the Wedding*. He was also the author of several books, of which *The Diary of a Nobody*, written in collaboration with his brother, Weedon, was the most successful.

Weedon Grossmith (b London, 9 June 1852; d London, 14 June 1919) had a fine career as an actor, and briefly appeared on the musical stage as Lord Arthur Pomeroy in the highly successful one act musical *A Pantomime Rehearsal* (1891). He also authored an autobiography, *From Studio to Stage* (Lane, London, 1913).

1878 **Cups and Saucers** 1 act Opera Comique 12 August
1880 **A Musical Nightmare** 1 act Opera Comique
1882 **Mr Guffin's Elopement** (Arthur Law) 1 act Toole's Theatre 7 October
1884 **A Peculiar Case** (Law) 1 act St George's Hall 8 December
1888 **The Real Case of Hide and Seekyll** Royalty Theatre 3 September
1892 **Haste to the Wedding** (Gilbert) Criterion Theatre 27 July

Memoirs: *A Society Clown* (J W Arrowsmith, Bristol, 1888), *Piano and I* (J W Arrowsmith, Bristol, 1910), Biography: Joseph, T: *George Grossmith: Biography of a Savoyard* (Arrowsmith/Joseph, Bristol, 1982)

GROSSMITH, George (b London, 11 May 1874; d London, 6 June 1935).

The son of the elder George, Grossmith (at this stage labelled, like his father before him, as 'jr') appeared on the London musical stage for the first time aged 18, in a small comic rôle in his father's musical collaboration with W S Gilbert, *Haste to the Wedding*. He was seen in similarly foppish parts in *The Baroness* (1892) and in the variety musical *Morocco Bound* (1893), where he built up the small rôle of Sir Percy Pimpleton with endless ad-libbing until he was one of the most prominent performers in this most elastic of musical comedies. Similar, if slightly less elastic, rôles followed in *Go-Bang* (Augustus Fitzpoop) and for George Edwardes in *A Gaiety Girl* (replacing Fred Kaye as Major Barclay), after which he was taken to the Gaiety Theatre to create the part of the gangling dude Bertie Boyd in *The Shop Girl*. The 21-year-old actor, equipped with a fine song for which he had himself supplied the lyrics, describing himself as 'Beautiful, bountiful Bertie', made a considerable hit in both London and New York.

Much of his time in the next years was spent in the straight theatre, but he returned in 1898 to take over in the musical *Little Miss Nobody* and the following year one of the producers of that piece, Yorke Stephens, staged the burlesque, *Great Caesar*, which Grossmith had written with Paul Rubens and in which he appeared as Mark Antony. The failure of that piece did not deter him, and in his next musical as an author, *The Gay Pretenders* (1900), he included rôles for both himself and his famous father, with even less happy results.

Grossmith returned to Edwardes's management to succeed G P Huntley in the lead comedy rôle of *Kitty Grey* on the road, and then moved into town with a part built to his measures in the Gaiety Theatre's hit *The Toreador* (1901). Once again he supplied some of his own lyrics ('Archie'), but did best with Paul Rubens's song 'Everybody's Awfully Good to Me'. He again succeeded Huntley in the comedy rôle of *The School Girl* and subsequently toured America in the piece, but by and large he remained at the Gaiety Theatre, as part of the basic star team, through the last decade of Edwardes's management, starring in *The Orchid* (rewriting Blanche Ring's 'Bedelia' for himself), *The Spring Chicken*, *The New Aladdin*, *The Girls of Gottenberg*, *Our Miss Gibbs* (interpolating a revised 'Yip-Ay-Addy-I-Ay'), *Peggy* and *The Sunshine Girl*. While *Havana*, which he had co-written, was produced at the Gaiety in 1908, he moved to another parallel Edwardes production to play Count Lothar in *A Waltz Dream*.

Grossmith was credited with a hand in the authorship of some of the Gaiety pieces, but always, when it was not a case of a fairly straight adaptation from a French comedy, in collaboration, and it would seem his contribution was principally one of 'putting in the jokes'. He adapted *Die Dollarprinzessin* for America (but not London) and also co-authored some of London's earliest modern revues, being named in the credits for such pieces as the Empire Theatre's 1910 *Hullo ... London!* (music: Cuthbert Clarke, lyrics CH Bovill), *Everybody's Doing It*, *Kill That Fly!*, *Eightpence a Mile*, *Not Likely*, *The Bing Boys Are Here* and *The Bing Girls Are There*, in the 1910s.

He moved from the Gaiety in 1913 to appear in London and America in *The Girl on the Film* (*Die Kino-Königin*) and, at the same time, went into partnership with Edward

Plate 118. **George Grossmith** *the younger was 'beautiful, bountiful Bertie' – one of his most popular dude creations – in* The Shop Girl.

Laurillard, who had produced his musical *The Love Birds* many years earlier, to himself produce plays and musicals. The first of these latter was the *Pink Dominos* musical *Tonight's the Night*, which was staged in New York and then in London, where Grossmith moved back into 'his' Gaiety Theatre. The piece was a great success, and over the following years, at first with Laurillard and later with ex-Gaiety stage manager Pat Malone, Grossmith established himself as a major producing force in the London musical theatre.

He continued at the Gaiety Theatre with a second hit in *Theodore & Co* but, in the power struggles following Edwardes's death, found himself outmanoeuvred by Alfred Butt, and was forced to move his operations elsewhere. Of three subsequent Grossmith-mounted successes which the Gaiety could well have done with, *Mr Manhattan* was produced at the Prince of Wales, *Arlette* at the Shaftesbury and *Yes, Uncle!* again, initially, at the Prince of Wales, before waltzing through three different theatres during its run, whilst the less successful *Oh! Joy* (*Oh, Boy!*) split its run between the Kingsway and the Apollo, before Grossmith completed the construction of his own theatre, the Winter Garden, on the site of an old music-hall in Drury Lane.

Grossmith and Laurillard opened the Winter Garden in 1919 with Grossmith and Leslie Henson starring in *Kissing Time*, and the theatre established itself as a major West End musical venue with the Grossmith/Malone productions of *A Night Out*, *Sally*, *The Cabaret Girl*, *The Beauty Prize*, a revival of *Tonight's the Night*, *Primrose*, *Tell Me More*

and *Kid Boots* between 1920 and 1926, when the operation was dissolved. *Eastward Ho!* (1919, Alhambra), *Baby Bunting* (1919, Shaftesbury) and *Faust on Toast* (Gaiety, 1921) were amongst the Grossmith/Laurillard productions staged in other venues during this period.

Grossmith had, again, a hand in the writing of the new Winter Garden pieces, directed many of his own productions, and appeared in several, notably as Otis in *Sally*. His busy producing career in the early 1920s did not lessen his performing one and, whilst those shows in which he wasn't appearing were running, he played away from home in the London version of *La Reine s'amuse* (*The Naughty Princess*) and with great success as Billy Early in Joe Waller and Herbert Clayton's original British production of *No, No, Nanette*.

After the end of his producing days he continued to perform, playing King Christian in Szirmai's *Princess Charming* (*Alexandra*) for Robert Courtneidge (a rôle he repeated several years later in New York) and appearing in the same composer's *Lady Mary* and in *The Five o'Clock Girl* at the London Hippodrome. In New York in 1930 he appeared in Ralph Benatzky's *My Sister and I* (aka *Meet My Sister*) which he persuaded his old partner, Laurillard, to bring to Britain. Grossmith directed and appeared in his New York rôle for a disastrous eight performances at the Shaftesbury, closing out his career on an unusual flop some 40 starry years after its beginning.

Grossmith's wife Adelaide Astor, one of the five sisters Rudge of whom the most celebrated was Letty Lind, had a good career in supporting rôles in both new burlesque (*Carmen Up-to-Data*, *Ruy Blas and the Blasé Roué*, *Cinder-Ellen Up-too-Late*) and in musical comedy (*The Lady Slavey*, *Go-Bang*, *The Shop Girl* (UK and USA) etc).

His younger brother **Lawrence GROSSMITH** (b London, 29 March 1877; d Hollywood, 21 February 1944) followed George onto the stage, where he had a long and successful career, often in rôles in the mould established by his brother. He first appeared in 1896 in *Nitouche*, and played in George's short-lived musical *The Love Birds* at the Savoy, before coming under the wing of George Edwardes for whom he appeared in dude rôles in *The White Chrysanthemum*, *The Girl Behind the Counter*, *Havana* and in his brother's part in *The Girl of Gottenberg*. He also appeared in de Courville's losing Leoncavallo musical *Are You There?* After a stint in straight theatre and an unfortunate attempt at management he returned to the musical theatre and appeared in *The Girl in the Taxi* and *The Joy Ride Lady* in London, and in America in the star rôle of Freddy Popple (created by G P Huntley) in *Nobody Home*, as Count Sergeiy Woronzeff in *Flora Bella* and in the revue *Hitchy Koo*. Latterly he played principally in plays and in films (including *The Girl in the Taxi*) as a character Englishman, but he appeared on the musical stage in New York in *The Cat and the Fiddle* (1931) and in London in *Command Performance* (1933), paired in this last piece with Kate Cutler as the elderly monarchs of the piece.

Lawrence's wife, Coralie Blythe (1880–1928), a sister of Vernon Castle (né Blyth), was a long-term Edwardes employee, mostly as a star understudy and sometimes in substantial soubrette rôles in town (Susie in *The Girl Behind the Counter*) and on tour. Her best new metropolitan rôle was as Césarine in *The Dashing Little Duke*.

George's daughter, Ena Grossmith (b London, 14

August 1896; d London, 20 March 1944) worked largely as a straight actress, but appeared in London in the musicals *Dear Love* (1929), *Paulette* (1932) and *Tulip Time* (1935).

1899 **Great Caesar** (Paul Rubens, Walter Rubens/w Paul Rubens) Comedy Theatre 29 April

1900 **The Gay Pretenders** (Claude Nugent) Globe Theatre 10 November

1904 **The Lovebirds** (Raymond Roze/Percy Greenbank) Savoy Theatre 10 February

1905 **The Spring Chicken** (Ivan Caryll, Lionel Monckton/Adrian Ross, P Greenbank) Gaiety Theatre 30 March

1906 **Two Naughty Boys** (Constance Tippett/P Greenbank) Gaiety Theatre 8 January

1907 **The Girls of Gottenberg** (Caryll, Monckton/Ross, Basil Hood/w L E Berman) Gaiety Theatre 15 May

1908 **Havana** (Leslie Stuart/Ross/w Graham Hill) Gaiety Theatre 25 April

1911 **Peggy** (Stuart/C H Bovill) Gaiety Theatre 4 March

1916 **Theodore & Co** (Jerome Kern, Ivor Novello/Ross, Clifford Grey/w H M Harwood) Gaiety Theatre 19 September

1920 **A Night Out** (Willie Redstone/Grey/w Arthur Miller) Winter Garden Theatre 18 September

1922 **The Cabaret Girl** (Kern/w P G Wodehouse) Winter Garden Theatre 19 September

1923 **The Beauty Prize** (Kern/w Wodehouse) Winter Garden Theatre 5 September

1924 **Primrose** (George Gershwin/Desmond Carter, Ira Gershwin/w Guy Bolton) Winter Garden Theatre 11 September

Autobiography: *GG* (Hutchinson, London, 1933), Biography: Naylor, S: *Gaiety and George Grossmith* (Stanley Paul, London, 1913)

GRÜN, Bernhard (b Starc, 11 February 1901; d London, 28 December 1972).

Grün originally studied law, but eventually became a theatre musical director in Prague, Vienna and Berlin, where he composed and arranged a number of scores for the musical stage. From 1924 he held a conducting post at Prague's Deutches Theater for some five years, and several of his earlier stage pieces were mounted in the small auditorium there, including *Miss Chocolate*, a piece which got a subsequent showing at the Établissement Ronacher in Vienna (1 February 1929). His 1930 *Böhmische Musikanten* also made its way to Vienna (Bürgertheater, 18 December 1931), as did *Musik um Suzi* (Volksoper, 2 May 1933), his first piece to be premièred in Berlin. In 1932 he arranged the score of *Freut euch das Lebens* from Johann and Josef Strauss music, and saw it progress from Leipzig to the Vienna Volksoper, whilst his 1934 Strauss pasticcio *Die Tänzerin Fanny Elssler* also found some success beyond Germany, notably in Italy.

He joined the exodus from Germany and then from Austria in the 1930s, and ended up in Britain, where he was involved in his one memorable success when he contributed some additional music to the score of George Posford's *Balalaika*. A second piece in the same vein, produced variously as *Paprika* and *Magyar Melody*, flopped utterly and twice, and his theatrical writing activity thereafter was largely limited to pasticcio work on such composers as Chopin for *Waltz Without End* (1942), Offenbach for *Can-Can* (1943) and Dvořák for *Summer Song* (1956), or as the accomplice of Eric Maschwitz in rearrangements

of classic Operette scores designed for the amateur market.

He published a number of books, including several on the musical theatre – *Prince of Vienna: the life of Oscar Straus* (1955), *Kulturgeschichte der Operette* (Munich, 1961) and *Gold und Silber: Franz Lehár und seine Zeit* (Munich, 1970), composed many radio and film scores and found a song success with the number 'Broken Wings' (1952 w John Jerome).

1923 **Onkel Perl**

1924 **Der grosse David**

1926 **Mama vom Ballett** (ad Rudolf Stadler, Ernst Stadler) Deutsches Theater, Prague 20 February

1927 **Miss Chocolate** (Hans Regina Nack, R Stadler) Deutsches Theater, Prague 19 March

1928 **Olga von der Wolga** (Nack) Neues Deutsches Theater, Prague 28 January

1928 **Abenteuer in Schottland** (Paul Frank, Peter Herz) Neues Deutsches Theater, Prague 25 December

1930 **Böhmische Musikanten** (Herz, Julius Wilhelm) Neues Operettentheater, Leipzig 30 October

1931 **Amelie**

1932 **Freut euch das Lebens** (Johann Strauss, Josef Strauss arr/Nestroy ad Wilhelm, Herz) Neues Operettentheater, Leipzig 24 October

1932 **Musik um Susi** (Frank, Herz) Komische Oper, Berlin 12 November

1932 **Marlenes Brautfahrt** (Nack, Max Bertusch) Landestheater, Wiesbaden 26 December

1934 **Die Tänzerin Fanny Elssler** (Johann Strauss arr w Oskar Stalla/Hans Adler) Deutsches Theater, Berlin 22 December

1935 **Wo die liebe blüht** (Arnold Golz, Emil Golz) Wiener Komödienhaus 20 April

1935 **Gaby Deslys**

1936 **Balalaika** revised *The Gay Hussar* (w George Posford/Eric Maschwitz) Adelphi Theatre, London 22 December

1937 **Madame Sans-Gêne** (Hans Weigel) Theater an der Wien, Vienna 1 September

1938 **Paprika** (aka *Magyar Melody*) (w Posford/Maschwitz) His Majesty's Theatre, London 15 September

1942 **Waltz Without End** (Frederic Chopin arr/Maschwitz) Cambridge Theatre 29 September

1943 **Old Chelsea** (w Richard Tauber/Fred Salo Tysh/Walter Ellis) Prince's Theatre 17 February

1946 **Can-Can** (Jacques Offenbach arr/Tysh/Max Catto) Adelphi Theatre 8 May

1956 **Summer Song** (Anton Dvořák arr/Maschwitz, Hy Kraft) Prince's Theatre 16 February

GRÜNBAUM, Fritz (b Brünn, 7 April 1880; d Dachau, 14 January 1941). Author for the Viennese silver-age theatre.

Grünbaum studied law in Vienna, but he soon switched his attentions to the theatrical world, working as a cabaret performer and stand-up comic, and also writing for all areas of the stage. He quickly scored a major success in the Operette world with his contribution to the text of *Die Dollarprinzessin* (1907), had a second success with the libretto and lyrics for Ziehrer's *Liebeswalzer*, and scored another major hit with the Hungarian tale of *Der Zigeunerprimás* in 1912, before becoming an army officer for the duration of the First World War. This did not prevent him performing his *Humoristische Vorträge* on the bill at the Apollotheater at the height of the hostilities. He emerged from the War with a decoration, but also with a number of patriotic war songs to his credit as well as a further handful of Operetten, which had been mounted in Berlin, Vienna and Budapest whilst he had been in uniform.

After the war, Grünbaum kept up his wide spread of theatrical activities. He spent a time running a cabaret in Berlin, whilst continuing to write for all corners of the musical stage. He supplied material for revues in Berlin and in Vienna, notably at the Apollotheater, teaming with composers including Benatzky, Richard Fall, Fritz Lehner and Rudolf Nelson (whose one pre-war Operette hit, *Miss Dudelsack*, he had co-authored), he wrote for cabaret and lyrics for popular songs, whilst at the same time continuing a regular flow of Operetten. However, although pieces such as *Die Csikós-Baroness*, which made its way from Hamburg to Berlin and then further afield, the little *Dorine und der Zufall*, *Des Königs Nachbarin*, and the Revue-Operette *Journal der Liebe* found some success, he did not ever again approach the level of his two big pre-war hits.

His name had ceased to appear on playbills by the Second World War, when the 60-year-old writer was imprisoned in Dachau. He died there.

1906 **Phryne** (Edmund Eysler/w Robert Bodanzky) 1 act Hölle 6 October

1906 **Peter und Paul reisen im Schlaraffenland** (Franz Lehár/w Bodanzky) Theater an der Wien 1 December

1907 **Mitislaw der Moderne** (Lehár/w Bodanzky) 1 act Hölle 5 January

1907 **Brigantino** (Béla Lazsky) 1 act Hölle 19 April

1907 **Die Dollarprinzessin** (Leo Fall/w A M Willner) Theater an der Wien 2 November

1908 **Principessa** (Rudolf Nelson/w Georg Burghard) Residenztheater, Frankfurt-am-Main 1 May

1908 **Madame Flirt** (Anselm Götzl/w Heinz Reichert) Neues Operettentheater, Hamburg 25 December

1909 **Liebeswalzer** (Carl Michael Ziehrer/w Bodanzky) Raimundtheater 24 October

1909 **Miss Dudelsack** (Nelson/w Reichert) Neues Schauspielhaus, Berlin 3 August

1910 **Die teuerste Frau von Paris** (Leo Schottländer/w Reichert) 1 act Bellevue Theater, Stettin 13 November

1910 **Der ledige Gatte** (Gustav Wanda/w Reichert) Residenztheater, Dresden ?28 October

1910 **Don Quixote** (Richard Heuberger/w Reichert) 1 act Hölle 1 December

1911 **Die weisse Fahne** (Josef Strauss arr Oskar Stalla) 1 act Hölle 18 November

1912 **Der Zigeunerprimás** (Emmerich Kálmán/w Julius Wilhelm) Johann Strauss-Theater 11 October

1912 **Der Frechling** (Carl Weinberger/w Reichert) Wiener Bürgertheater 21 December

1913 **Leute vom Stand** (Richard Fall/w Bodanzky) 1 act Hölle 1 March

1913 **Die Prinzenjagd** (Ludwig Friedmann/w Reichert) Residenztheater, Dresden 4 April

1914 **Anno 14** (Ralph Benatzky/w Benatzky) Wiener Stadttheater 22 September

1914 **General Wutzikoff** (Benatzky) 1 act Royal Orfeum, Budapest 1 December

1916 **Der Favorit** (Robert Stolz/w Wilhelm Sterk) Komische Oper, Berlin 7 April

1916 **Mein Annerl** (Georg Jarno/w Sterk) Carltheater 7 October

1917 **Die Puppenbaronessen** (R Fall/w Alexander Engel) Apollotheater 1 September

1918 **Wenn Wien wieder walzt** (Fritz Lehner) February

1918 **Das Busserlschloss** (Stolz) 1 act Ronacher 1 August

1918 **Der rote Graf** (Paul Pallos) 1 act Ronacher 3 September

1918 **Eine einzige Rettung** (Gustav Benedict/w Max (?) Reichert) Bellevue Theater, Stettin 30 July

1919 **Vox populi** (Otto Stransky) Ronacher 1 April

1919 **Die Csikós-Baroness** (Jarno) Neues Operettentheater, Hamburg 28 October

1921 **Der Frauenräuber** (Kurt Zorlig/w Herbert Steineck) Friedrich-Wilhelmstädtisches Theater, Berlin 23 December

1922 **Dorine und der Zufall** (Jean Gilbert/w Sterk) Neues Theater am Zoo, Berlin 15 September

1923 **Des Königs Nachbarin** (Leon Jessel/w Sterk) Wallner-Theater, Berlin April

1926 **Journal der Liebe** (Egon Neumann/w Karl Farkas) Wiener Bürgertheater 29 January

1926 **Ich und Du** (Lamberto Pavanelli/w Sterk) Neues Deutsches Theater, Prague 28 November

1926 **Das tanzende Märchen** (K Steininger/w Farkas) 8 December

1927 **Meine Tochter Otto** (Jessel/w Sterk) Rolandbühne 5 May

1927 **Rosen aus Schiras** (Frank Stafford/w Sterk) Johann Strauss-Theater 24 June

1930 **Tschun-Tschi** (J Gardener, Anna May Wong/ad w Jacobson) Volksoper 14 August

1931 **Der Traum-Express** (Robert Katscher/w Farkas, Geza Herceg) Theater an der Wien 5 June

1937 **Sie, Johann ...!** (P Weiss/w E Behrendt, Hans Lengsfelder, Siegfried Tisch) Volksoper 16 April

GRUNDY, Sydney (b Manchester, 23 March 1848; d London, 4 July 1914).

The son of the mayor of Manchester and a barrister in his native town until he was 28 years of age, Grundy made his first venture into theatrical writing with a version of Scribe and Duveyrier's *Oscar, ou le mari qui trompe sa femme* as *The Snowball* (1879) and subsequently became one of London's most popular playwrights with such pieces as *A Pair of Spectacles* (*Les Petits Oiseaux*), *Esther Sandraz* (*La Femme de glace*) and *The Bells of Hazelmere*.

In the early part of his career he also translated Meilhac and Millaud's text to *La Cosaque* for Kate Santley and collaborated on several musical theatre pieces with composer Edward Solomon. Following Solomon's success with *The Nautch Girl* at the Savoy, the most successful of these, *The Vicar of Bray*, was revived there by D'Oyly Carte. Grundy worked on the updating of the piece and found himself offered the next Savoy text – with Arthur Sullivan as his musical partner. The resulting *Haddon Hall*, more staid than usual Savoy fare, had a reasonable life but Grundy, after replying humorously to the critics who had in effect complained that he had not attempted to imitate Gilbert's style, was nevertheless not tempted to return again to the musical theatre.

Shortly before his death, however, he became, perhaps unwittingly, the author of another 'musical farcical comedy' when Carrie Moore appeared in Melbourne, Australia, in *Much Married* (Bijou Theatre 5 July). Grundy's play was decorated with a long list of songs, including Eysler's *Bruder Straubinger* hit 'Kissing is No Sin', 'The Chocolate Major', 'It isn't Funny But it's True', 'Mr Shadow Man' and an exasperated piece called 'Bury Alexander's Band!'.

1880 **Popsy Wopsy** (Edward Solomon) 1 act Royalty Theatre 4 October

1882 **The Vicar of Bray** (Solomon) Globe Theatre 22 July

1884 **La Cosaque** English version (Royalty Theatre)

1884 **Pocahontas** (Solomon) Empire Theatre 26 December

1892 **Haddon Hall** (Arthur Sullivan) Savoy Theatre 24 September

GRÜNWALD, Alfred (b Vienna, 16 February 1884; d Forest Hills, NY, 24 February 1951). One of the most successful librettist/lyricists of the Viennese 20th-century stage.

Long a theatre critic on *Neues Wiener Journal*, Grünwald led parallel careers as a journalist and a theatrical writer. In a pairing, established from his early twenties, with actor/writer Julius Brammer, he at first worked on small musical and non-musical pieces for studio and variety theatres, but the pair had an immediate success when they moved into writing full-length musical plays, scoring hits with *Die Dame in Rot*, *Hoheit tanzt Walzer* and *Der lachende Ehemann*, continuing with the rewrite of Lehár's *Der Göttergatte* as *Die ideale Gattin*, and peaking with a collaboration with Leo Fall on *Die Kaiserin* and on the megahit of the war years, *Die Rose von Stambul* (1916).

The collaborators ran up an amazing series of hit or near-hit shows in the years that followed – *Der letzte Walzer*, *Die Bajadere*, *Die Perlen der Cleopatra*, *Gräfin Mariza*, *Die Zirkusprinzessin*, *Die gold'ne Meisterin*, *Das Veilchen vom Montmartre* – with Grünwald only rarely taking time out to collaborate with other authors, but there too finding success (*Mädi*), before the duo separated, after some 20 years of communal work, at the beginning of the 1930s. Grünwald went on to further success, at first adapting the Hungarian texts of Pál Ábrahám's most successsful Operetten, then providing him with original texts for his later pieces, and, most successfully, adapting Louis Verneuil's play *Le Fauteuil* (1923) as the libretto to Oscar Straus's *Eine Frau, die weiss, was sie will* for *Die Kaiserin* star Fritzi Massary.

In 1940, Grünwald fled the Second World War to America, and ultimately became an American citizen, but although he worked there on much in the way of translation, notably americanizing German wartime songs for the OWI, he wrote only one Broadway show, an unfortunate attempt to produce a Johann Strauss biomusical without Strauss music called *Mr Strauss Goes to Boston*. During the 1950s, however, he saw his name appear again on several fresh pieces on Continental playbills, first when Oscar Straus set the old libretto of *Bozena*, then when the Berne Stadttheater mounted Kálmán's 'American' Operette *Arizona Lady* and, one last time, when Juan Cardona's *Festival*, like the previous piece written with fellow exile Gustav Beer, was produced in Munich.

1907 **Fräulein Sherlock Holmes** (Georges Criketown/as 'A G Wald' w Julius Brammer) Volkstheater, Munich 1 August

1908 **Die grüne Redoute** (Leo Ascher/w Brammer) 1 act Danzers Orpheum 26 March

1908 **Die lustigen Weiber von Wien** (Robert Stolz/w Brammer) 1 act Colosseum 7 November

1908 **Die kleine Manicure** (Ascher/ad w Brammer) 1 act Parisiana

1909 **Elektra** (Béla Lazsky/w Brammer) 1 act Kabarett Fledermaus 1 December

1910 **Georgette** (Lazsky/w Brammer) 1 act Kabarett Fledermaus 16 March

1910 **Vindobona, du herrliche Stadt** (Leo Ascher/w Brammer) Venedig in Wien 22 July

1911 **Das Damenparadies** (Richard Fall/w Brammer) 1 act Wiener Colosseum 16 January

1911 **Das goldene Strumpfband** (Ascher/w Brammer) 1 act Ronacher 1 May

1911 **Die Dame in Rot** (Robert Winterberg/w Brammer) Theater des Westens, Berlin 16 September

1912 **Hoheit tanzt Walzer** (Ascher/w Brammer) Raimundtheater 24 February

1912 **Eine vom Ballet** (*The Dancing Viennese*) (Oscar Straus/w Brammer) London Coliseum 3 June

1913 **Der lachende Ehemann** (Edmund Eysler/w Brammer) Bürgertheater 19 March

1913 **Die ideale Gattin** (Lehár/w Brammer) Theater an der Wien 11 October

1915 **Die schöne Schwedin** (Winterberg/w Brammer) Theater an der Wien 30 January

1915 **Die Kaiserin** (Leo Fall/w Brammer) Metropoltheater, Berlin 15 October

1916 **Fürstenliebe** revised *Die Kaiserin* Carltheater 1 February

1916 **Die Rose von Stambul** (Fall/w Brammer) Theater an der Wien 12 December

1917 **Bruder Leichtsinn** (Ascher/w Julius Brammer) Wiener Bürgertheater 18 December

1919 **Dichterliebe** (Mendelssohn arr Emil Stern/w Brammer) Komische Oper, Berlin 20 December

1920 **Der Sperrsechserl** (Stolz/w Robert Blum) Komödienhaus 1 April

1920 **Der letzte Walzer** (Straus/w Brammer) Berliner Theater, Berlin 12 February

1921 **Die Tangokönigin** revised *Die ideale Gattin* Apollotheater 9 September

1921 **Die Bajadere** (Kálmán/w Brammer) Carltheater 23 December

1923 **Mädi** (Stolz/w Leo Stein) Berliner Theater, Berlin 1 April

1923 **Die Perlen der Cleopatra** (Straus/w Brammer) Theater an der Wien 17 November

1924 **Gräfin Mariza** (Kálmán/w Brammer) Theater an der Wien 28 February

1926 **Die Zirkusprinzessin** (Kálmán/w Brammer) Theater an der Wien 26 March

1927 **Die gold'ne Meisterin** (Eysler/w Brammer) Theater an der Wien 13 September

1928 **Die Herzogin von Chicago** (Kálmán/w Brammer) Theater an der Wien 5 April

1929 **Marietta** German version (Theater an der Wien)

1930 **Das Veilchen vom Montmartre** (Kálmán/w Brammer) Johann Strauss-Theater 21 March

1930 **Viktoria und ihr Husar** (*Viktória*) German version w Fritz Löhner-Beda (Theater an der Wien)

1931 **Die Blume von Hawaii** (Pál Ábrahám/Imre Földes ad w Löhner-Beda) Neues Theater, Leipzig 24 July; Metropoltheater, Berlin 29 August

1932 **Eine Frau, die weiss, was sie will** (Straus) Metropoltheater, Berlin 1 September

1932 **Venus in Seide** (Stolz/w Ludwig Herzer) Stadttheater, Zurich 10 December

1932 **Ball in Savoy** (Ábrahám/w Löhner-Beda) Grosses Schauspielhaus, Berlin 23 December

1934 **Märchen im Grand-Hotel** (Ábrahám/w Löhner-Beda) Theater an der Wien 29 March

1934 **Die verliebte Königin** (*A szerelmes királynő*) German version w Löhner-Beda (Johann Strauss-Theater)

1935 **Das Walzerparadies** (Straus) Scala Theater 15 February

1935 **Dschainah, das Mädchen aus dem Tanzhaus** (Ábrahám/w Beda) Theater an der Wien 20 December

1937 **Roxy und ihr Wunderteam** (Ábrahám/Laszlo Szilágyi, Dezső Keller ad w Hans Weigel) Theater an der Wien 25 March

1937 **Polnische Hochzeit** (Josef Beer/w Löhner-Beda) Stadttheater, Zurich 3 April

1945 **Mr Strauss Goes to Boston** (Robert Stolz/w Géza Herczeg) Century Theater 9 June

1952 **Bozena** (Oscar Straus/w Brammer) Theater am Gärtner-platz, Munich 16 May

1954 **Arizona Lady** (Kálmán/w Gustav Beer) Stadttheater, Berne 14 February

1955 **Fiesta** (Juan Cardona/w Beer) Theater am Gärtnerplatz, Munich 11 February

Biography: Grunwald, H: *Ein Walzer muss es sein* (Überreuter, Vienna, 1991)

GUÉTARY, Georges [WORLOOU, Lamroas] (b Alexandria, Egypt, 8 February 1917). Handsome tenor who created a number of successful musical theatre rôles in nearly a half-century career in all media.

After an early working life as an accountant, Guétary made his first appearances as a vocalist with Jo Bouillon's orchestra and then, for a number of years, worked on the French music-halls. His first stage performances were in revue, and in the isolated musical comedy *La Course d'amour* (1942), but although he starred in France in the film *Le Cavalier noir* (1945) he did not find theatrical fame until he went to London to feature as the romantic Frenchman who wooed Lizbeth Webb in *Bless the Bride* (1947, 'This Is My Lovely Day', 'A Table for Two', 'Ma Belle Marguerite'). He next appeared, in Paris, in the title-rôle of the successful Francis Lopez musical *Pour Don Carlos* (1949) at the Châtelet ('C'est l'amour', 'Je suis un Bohémien') and subsequently went to America where he filmed *An American in Paris* (1950) and played on Broadway in a German rôle in the unsuccessful *Arms and the Girl*.

On his return, he teamed up with Bourvil and Annie Cordy for the enormously successful Parisian musical comedy *La Route fleurie* (1952) and starred in the French version of the film of Strauss's *Der Zigeunerbaron* (1954), but another American visit, in 1958, ended with the three performances of *Portofino*. He had to return to France for further stage success, starring with Bourvil again in the unpretentious and long-running musical comedy *Pacifico* (1958), paired with Jean Richard in the *Some Like it Hot* musical *La Polka des Lampions* (1961), in Charles Aznavour's *Monsieur Carnaval* (1965), at the Mogador as *Monsieur Pompadour* (1971), and in a musical version of *Tom Jones* (1974).

Thirty-three years after his first Francis Lopez creation he returned for two more – *Aventure à Monte-Carlo* (1981) and *Amour à Tahiti* (1983) – then starred in *Hourra Papa* (1984), Lopez's *Carnaval aux Caraïbes* (1985) and *Le Roi du Pacifique* (1986) before announcing his retirement in his 71st year on the grounds that 'operétte is not what it was'. Given the inexorably downward quality-curve of his vehicles, the comment was understandable.

GUITRY, Sacha [GUITRY, Alexandre Georges Pierre] (b St Petersburg, 21 February 1885; d Paris, 24 July 1957).

The celebrated 'boulevardier' of the Paris theatre was the author, more often than not the star, and sometimes the producer of a highly successful series of crisply literate light comedies, revues and musical plays during nearly half a century in the theatre. The most significant of his musical pieces, musically illustrated by some of the classiest composers of his time, were manufactured to feature the light comedy and outstanding soprano gifts of one of his five wives, the actress and vocalist Yvonne Printemps. *L'Amour masqué* (music by Messager), *Mozart* (Hahn) and *Mariette* (Oscar Straus) all won productions around the world after their Parisian successes, and his one rather atypical, straight-up opérette (without Mlle Printemps), the period piece *Floréstan 1er* (music by filmland's Werner Richard Heymann), also had a respectable Paris run.

Songs and incidental music were also inserted into others of his plays, in various amounts, mostly to permit Mlle Printemps to sing. Messager provided the music for his hit play *Deburau*, whilst the four-act comedy *Jean de la Fontaine* contained a musical programme which took in three pieces by Lully and one by Gilles Durant, set with words by Guitry, as well as orchestral pieces by Gluck, Haydn, Rameau and Lully. Guitry's wide-ranging musical theatre work also included revues, sometimes written with Albert Willemetz, for the Palais-Royal, the Théâtre du Vaudeville, the Étoile, the Édouard VII and the Madeleine, as well as – at the other end of the scale of grandeur – a féerie, *Charles Lindbergh*, for the vast Théâtre du Châtelet (1928).

Guitry was, slightly improbably, portrayed on film in *Si Versailles m'était conté* by Bourvil.

1902 **Le Page** (Ludo Ratz) 1 act Théâtre des Mathurins 15 April

1909 **Tell père, Tell fils** (Tiarko Richepin) 1 act Théâtre Mevisto 17 April

1923 **L'Amour masqué** (André Messager) Théâtre Édouard VII 15 February

1925 **Mozart** (Reynaldo Hahn) Théâtre Édouard VII 2 December

1928 **Mariette** (Oscar Straus) Théâtre Édouard VII 1 October

1931 **La SADMP** (Louis Beydts) 1 act Théâtre Madeleine 4 November

1933 **Florestan 1er** (Werner Richard Heymann/Albert Willemetz) Théâtre des Variétés 8 December

1933 **O, mon bel inconnu** (Hahn) Théâtre des Bouffes-Parisiens 5 October

Memoirs: *Souvenirs, ou si j'ai bonne mémoire* (1943), *Toutes réflexions faites* (1947); Biographies: Lorcey, J: *Sacha Guitry* (La Table Ronde, Paris, 1971), Benjamin, R: *Sacha Guitry, roi du théâtre* (1933), Madis, A: *Sacha* (1957); ; Harding, J: *Sacha Guitry, the Last Boulevardier* (Methuen, London, 1968) etc

GÜL BABA Zenés színjáték (musical comedy) in 3 acts by Ferenc Martos. Music by Jenő Huszka. Király Színház, Budapest, 9 December 1905.

Jenő Huszka's third hit show, after *Bob herceg* and *Aranyvirág*, and one of the most successful Hungarian musical plays of its period, *Gül Baba* helped to give a further impetus to the then speeding-up Hungarian operett tradition. It has remained in the repertoire in its native country over the decades since its initial showing, without making any impression beyond.

In this oriental tale, Gül Baba (József Németh), the saintly guardian of the sacred roses, goes to the Pasha, Kuksuk Ali (Ernő Mihályi), to beg forgiveness for the young Gábor (Lenke Szentgyörgyi), who has been condemned to death. His crime was that, in order to meet and speak secretly with Gül Baba's daughter, Leila (Biri Kazal), he climbed into the house and damaged the sacred flowers. His real crime, of course, is simply that he sought to see Leila, for the Pasha has his own eyes set on the daughter of the old guardian. Gül Baba tricks the overlord into destroying some of the plants himself and, thus, he is obliged both to withdraw the sentence on his young rival and permit a happy ending. Kornél Sziklai played the other principal rôle of Mujkó, Gábor's gipsy musician companion.

The largest part of Huszka's score fell to the leading juvenile man, originally played in travesty by a soprano but in modern times given to a tenor, with his opening song 'Rászállt a galambom a budai várra', a song on his conviction ('Az utolsó kivánságom'), a second-act drinking song ('A kulacsom kotyogós') and the third-act 'Szállj, szállj, sóhajom' being the featured solos. The heroine had a 'song of the Turkish woman's fate' to add to her first-act entrance, Mujkó had numbers in each of the last two acts, and the Pasha a single spot, alongside a regulation amount of ensemble and dance music which took fine advantage of the Turkish settings.

After its original run, *Gül Baba* was revived regularly, notably at the Fővárosi Operettszinház in 1941 (14 February) with Irma Patkós (Gábor), Kálmán Latabár (Mujkó), Biri Szondy (Leila) and György Solthy (Gül Baba), and in more recent times, televised.

Recordings: selections (Qualiton)

GUNN, Michael (b Dublin, 1840; d London, 17 October 1901).

Michael Gunn and his brother, John (d 1877), built and from 1871 operated Dublin's Gaiety Theatre and from 1874 also ran the Theatre Royal in the same town. Whilst taking in the 1876 *Grande-Duchesse* and *Trial By Jury* tour sent out by Richard D'Oyly Carte, Gunn became firm friends with the young producer, and he subsequently went into a fairly silent partnership with him, providing much of the finance to produce the early Gilbert and Sullivan shows and, later, to build the Savoy Theatre and Hotel. On a couple of occasions Gunn himself ventured as a producer, buying up the rights to the works of Edward Solomon and Henry Pottinger Stephens with the hope of establishing a second Gilbert and Sullivan team, and staging Offenbach's *Belle Lurette* at the Avenue Theatre, in neither case with marked success. Gunn's connection with Carte was instrumental in his young cousin, George Edwardes, pursuing the early part of his theatrical career at the Savoy Theatre.

Gunn's wife, Bessie Sudlow (1849–1928), was an opéra-bouffe soprano (Césarine in *Fleur de thé* 1875, and a member of Carte's 1876 tour playing the Plaintiff in *Trial By Jury*, in *La Grande-Duchesse* and the lead rôle of Carte's own *Happy Hampstead*) prior to her marriage.

Their daughter Haidée Gunn was an actress; their son, Harry, became the Gunn of the Australian producing firm of Gunn and Meynell; whilst John's son, also named John (d 1907), married the musical-comedy actress Hilda Coral and was the father of Gladys Gunn, later to be the second Mrs Leslie Henson.

GUNNING, Louise (b Brooklyn, NY, 1 April 1879; d Sierra Madre, Calif, 24 July 1960). Attractive, red-haired soprano who played several important Broadway leads in the pre-war years.

Miss Gunning, a pastor's daughter from Brooklyn, first appeared on the stage as a vocalist singing Scots songs in concert and in variety programmes. She made her earliest theatre appearances in Hoyt's *A Day and a Night*, singing those same songs, and in more conventional musical comedy in *The Circus Girl*, appeared in a featured singing spot in *The Rogers Brothers in Wall Street*, and as Violet in *The Chaperons* (with a song) before she moved up to more important rôles. In subsequent Broadway appearances, she played the principal juvenile part of Arabella in De Wolf Hopper's production of *Mr Pickwick* (1902), appeared opposite Frank Daniels in *The Office Boy* (1903), featured alongside Ernestine Schumann-Heinck in the opera star's dip into the musical theatre in *Love's Lottery* (1904, Laura Skeffington), replaced Ruth Vincent in the title-rôle of *Véronique*, and supplied the singing values in Kerker's *The White Hen* (1906, Pepi Glöckner).

In 1908 she took up another Ruth Vincent rôle, when she starred with Van Rensslaer Wheeler in Broadway production of Edward German's *Tom Jones*, and followed this with the title-rôle of the Luders/Pixley *Marcelle*, but she turned to another imported show for the kind of rôle which suited her best when she appeared opposite Robert Warwick as Princess Stephanie in *The Balkan Princess* (1911). Later the same year, she played alongside Henry Dixey, De Wolf Hopper, Eugene Cowles and Marie Cahill as Josephine in a starry revival of *HMS Pinafore* at the Casino Theater.

In 1913 she starred in Sousa's short-lived *The American Maid* and was seen once more, in a revival of *Forty-Five Minutes From Broadway*, before quitting the stage.

GÜNTHER, Mizzi (b Warnsdorf, 8 February 1879; d Vienna, 18 March 1961). One of the most memorable stars of the 20th-century Viennese Operette stage.

Mizzi Günther began her stage career working in Brünn and came to notice in Vienna in 1901 when she appeared as O Mimosa San in a revival of *Die Geisha* at the Theater an der Wien and the Carltheater. Later the same year, she was star-billed as Lotti, the heroine of the Carltheater's *Die drei Wünsche* (1901), and she followed up as the hard-done-by circus waif, Suzon, in Louis Ganne's *Circus Malicorne* (1901), as the saucy Coralie in a revival of *Das verwunschene Schloss*, and as Nina Brunet, the wife who turns actress, in *Die Debutantin*, before scoring her first major hit in a new rôle as Lola Winter, the sweet maid of the title of Reinhardt's *Das süsse Mädel* (1901), introducing the tune of the year, 'Das ist das süsse Mädel'.

Günther had a second memorable new rôle when she created the juvenile lead rôle of Suza in *Der Rastelbinder* (1902) alongside Louis Treumann, and, in the two following seasons, played opposite Klara Küry as Katharina II in *Der kleine Gunstling*, the three performances of *Der Glücklichste* (Fatime), co-starred with Treumann in a revival of *Apajune der Wassermann* (Natalitza), played the 13 performances of *Der Mameluck* (Miliora), Alkmene in *Der Göttergatte* (1904), Flora Stiebelli, the soubrette of the successful *Das Veilchenmädel*, and the 19 performances of the German Burlesque-Operette *'s Zuckersgoscherl* (Mary Parsley).

By now, after several years of sharing top rôles with Marie Halton and Betty Stojan, she had established herself as the Carltheater's leading lady, and she had also established a regular partnership with light-comedy, light-baritone, leading man Treumann. They starred together in *Der Schätzmeister*, she as the singer, Mary Elliott and he in the title-rôle, in *Der Schnurrbart* (Countess Rolly von Gumpenburg) and in the short-lived *Kaisermanöver* (Jolán), and she also appeared, without him, for 21 nights in *Der Polizeichef* (Erminia) before the arrival of megastar Alexander Girardi at the Carltheater changed the house's production policy, and the Treumann-Günther partnership decamped to Girardi's old house, the Theater an der Wien.

They made their first appearances there in Ascher's *Vergeltsgott* (Jessie) before they were cast in the lead rôles of its successor, *Die lustige Witwe* (1905). Günther's creation of the rôle of Hanna Glawari, the 'merry widow', turned her from a star into a super-star, and she carried that superstardom on through a whole series of creations in the years that followed, beginning with the self-made Mädel, Alice in *Die Dollarprinzessin* (1907), *Der Mann mit den drei Frauen* (1908, Lori) and *Der schöne Gardist* (Dorothea von Waldburghausen) at the Theater an der Wien. Günther and Treumann crossed to the Johann Strauss-Theater to create the lead rôles of Lehár's *Das Fürstenkind* (1909, Mary Ann) and she followed up there as Melitta in *Das erste Weib* (1910), Lolotte Boncourt in *Die Sirene* (1911) and Ella in *Die romantische Frau*, before returning once more to the Theater an der Wien.

In her first season back, Günther appeared in *Die schöne Helena*, *Das Fürstenkind*, *Die schöne Risette*, passed the 500th performance of *Die lustige Witwe*, played Gabrielle in *Pariser Leben*, and created the rôle of Eva in the good run of Lehár's *Eva* (1911), once again playing alongside Treumann. The pair were again seen together in *Der blaue Held* (Helene) and *Der kleine König* (1912, Anita Montarini), but Günther starred opposite Otto Storm as Reinhardt's *Prinzess Gretl* (1913) and as Dolly in *Die ideale Gattin* (which she had previously sung as *Der Gottergätte*), and appeared as Dolly Doverland in *Endlich allein* (1914) opposite the more genuinely tenorizing Hubert Marischka.

In 1915 she moved again to the Johann Strauss-Theater to create the rôle of Sylva Varescu in *Die Csárdásfürstin* (1915) and, whilst Betty Fischer moved from the Raimundtheater to take up the prima-donna spot at the Theater an der Wien, Günther followed the long run of *Csárdásfürstin* with *Liebe im Schnee* (1916, Gertrud), Straus's *Nachtfalter* (1917, Lona Valletti) and, back with Treumann, the little *Der Millionendieb* (1918, Rosannah) at Ronacher. She had a further success when she created Fürstin Alexandra Maria in *Die Faschingsfee* (1917) at the Johann Strauss-Theater before returning to the Theater an der Wien to star as Die Fremde Dame in Hermann Dostal's version of the *Official Wife* tale, *Nimm mich mit!* (1919).

After 20 years as a leading lady, some Operette leading-lady rôles were now not wholly suitable for the no-longer-juvenile star, but there were others which were. She added another fine creation to her remarkable list as Katja in *Katja, die Tänzerin* (1923) and appeared at the top of the bill in *Puzstaliebchen* (1923, Rosemarie), but, if the greatest part of her career as a star was now over, she was far from finished in the musical theatre. Mizzi Günther, like a number of the very greatest musical stars, subsequently began a second career as a character lady which was worth another quarter of a century's work on the musical stage.

In 1931 she played the Gräfin Fuchs in *Die Kaiserin* and in 1932 she appeared as Herzogin Marie Brankenhorst in *Schön ist die Welt*, paired with Gustav Charlé as the 'elders' of the piece whilst her erstwhile leading man, Marischka, played the juvenile man, and she later joined the company

at the Raimundtheater where she played in the wartime *Fremdenführer* (the written-in Excellenz Minna Freifrau von Eiseneck) and the prize 'komische Alte' rôle of Palmatica in *Der Bettelstudent*. In the 1940s she was seen there in Pepöck's *Der Reiter der Kaiserin* (1941), as Frau Anna Strauss in *Die Straussbuben* (1946), and in Fred Raymond's *Die Perle von Tokay* (1948), whilst she also appeared at the Volksoper in rôles such as the duenna, Zenobia, in *Gasparone* (1945), towards the end of one of the musical theatre's most remarkable careers.

GUTTMANN

The Operette comedian and singer **Alexander GUTTMANN** (b Budapest, 2 October 1851; d Meran, 15 February 1889), a member of the companies at the Theater an der Wien (Nakid in *Die Afrikareise*, Collinée in *Der schöne Nikolaus*, Delacqua in *Eine Nacht in Venedig*, Sindulfo in *Gasparone*, Sir Andrew Douglas in *Donna Juanita*, Dupont in *Der Marquis von Rivoli*, Bliemchen in *Der Feldprediger*, Graf Asinelli in *Pfingsten in Florenz*, Farigoul in *Zwillinge*, Cordonnier in *Gillette de Narbonne*) and at the Carltheater (Bobèche, Graf Propakoff in *Der Jagdjunker*, General Gregor Gregorovitch in *Der Vagabund* etc), fathered three sons, who would all have important careers as actors and directors in the theatre, before his death at the age of 37.

Emil GUTTMANN (d Vienna, 26 March 1934) began his career as an actor who sings very little, and appeared at the Apollotheater in such pieces as *Der Gaukler* (1909), *Lumpus und Pumpus*, *Miss Exzentrik* (1910), *Das Frauenparlament* (1911) and *Der Natursänger* (1912), at the Theater in der Josefstadt in *Die Förster-Christl* (1907, Graf Gottfried von Leoben), *Das Wäschermädel* (Fürst Josef von Kleben), *Filmzauber* (Antonius Lichtenstädt), *Die Wundermühle* (Hans Leutenfeld) and *Die Patronesse vom Nachtcafé* (Peter Schlipp), and at the Johann Strauss-Theater as the principal baddie, Graf Lothar Mereditt, in *Die Faschingsfee* (1917).

He had, by this time, already established himself in a more important career as a director, notably when he both directed and played Scharntorff in the Raimundtheater's original production of *Das Dreimäderlhaus* (1916). He directed the musequel *Hannerl* (1918) and directed and took the lead comedy rôle of Poire in *Sybill* (1919) at the Stadttheater, before taking over from his brother, Paul, as régisseur-in-chief at the Theater an der Wien.

Amongst the shows which he directed and/or played in there over the next five years were *Nimm mich mit!* (1919), *Dorfmusikanten* (1919), *Die blaue Mazur* (1920, Klemens von Reiger), *Der letzte Walzer* (1921, t/o Paul), *Frasquita* (1922, Aristide Girot), *Die Bacchusnacht* (1923) and *Gräfin Mariza* (1924), whilst he simultaneously mounted pieces at the Johann Strauss-Theater (*Das Hollandweibchen* 1920, *Rinaldo* 1921, *Die Tanzgräfin* 1921, *Eine Sommernacht* 1921), the Apollotheater (*Die Tangokönigin* 1921), the Bürgertheater (*Mädi*) and the Raimundtheater (*Zwölf Uhr Nachts*, *Der Tanz ins Glück* 1921) etc. His subsequent credits included *Das Schwalbennest* (1926, dir), *Spiel um die Liebe* (1925, Fürst Leopold von Salmannsdorf, dir) and *Mädel aus Wien* (1931, Oberst Savigny, dir).

Paul GUTTMANN (b Vienna, 1 July 1877; d Minsk, ?1941) also began his career as an actor, and played at the Venedig in Wien summer theatre and/or Danzers

Orpheum in *Die Eisjungfrau* (Scarlett, a pirate chief), *Die Ringstrassen-Prinzessin* (von Dembinsky), *Frau Luna* (Ferdinand Süss), *Eine vom 'Moulin Rouge'* (Schani), *Das Scheckbuch des Teufels* (Baron Cupido) etc. In 1911 he was hired as an actor and director at the Theater an der Wien, and over the next seven years played in and/or directed a long list of productions including a *Pariser Leben* revival (1911, Gondremarck), *Eva* (1911, Prunelles, dir), *Der blaue Held* (1912, Regent, dir), *Der kleine König* (1912, dir), *Prinzess Gretl* (1913, Fürst Aloysius, dir), *Die ideale Gattin* (1913, Marquese Columbus, dir), *Die Ballkönigin* (ie *The Catch of the Season*, 1913, Lord Dundreary), *Endlich allein* (1914, Graf Maximilian Splenningen, dir), *Leichte Kavallerie* revival (1914, dir), *Gold gab' ich für Eisen!* (1914, von Steinfeld), *Die schöne Schwedin* (1915, Axel, dir), *Der Opernball* revival (Beaubuisson, dir), *Auf Befehl der Herzogin* (1915, dir), *Wenn zwei sich lieben* (1915, von Varady, dir), *Die Winzerbraut* (dir), *Der Sterngucker* (1916, Nepomuk, dir), *Die Rose von Stambul* (1916, dir) and *Wo die Lerche singt* (1918, dir).

At the same time he directed several major hits at the Johann Strauss-Theater – *Der Zigeunerprimás* (1912), *Rund um die Liebe*, *Die Csárdásfürstin* (1915), *Die Faschingsfee* (1917) – and also staged Straus's *Nachtfalter* at Ronacher and subsequently at the Theater an der Wien. He was Oberregisseur and performer at the Apollotheater under Herbert Trau (*Der Pusztakavalier*, *Fürstenkind* revival etc) and later staged *Faschingshochzeit* (1921) at the Carltheater. After quitting the Theater an der Wien, he continued thereafter both to appear on the stage and to direct, being seen at the Bürgertheater in *Yvette und ihre Freunde* (1927, Loriot) and *No, No, Nanette* (1927, George, the butler), and at the Johann Strauss-Theater in *Der Zarewitsch* (Ministerpräsident) which he also directed as he did Kálmán's *Das Veilchen vom Montmartre* (1930).

He was deported to Minsk during the Second World War and never seen again.

Arthur GUTTMANN (b Vienna, 1 July 1877; d Vienna, 3 June 1956) worked as a comedian in plays and musicals, his best musical rôles being Lothar in *Ein Walzertraum* (1907), introducing 'Piccolo, piccolo, tsin, tsin, tsin' with his wife, soubrette Mizzi Zwerenz, and Nazi, the comical waiter of *Frühlingsluft* (1903). His other musical appearances included *Fesche Geister*, *Der schöne Rigo*, *Die Eisjungfrau* (ie *The Girl from Up There*, 1904, Angesturia Pickles) all at Venedig in Wien, Hippolit Zillinger in *Die Schützenliesel* (1905), Stanislaus Lämmermann in *Mutzi*, the marvellous dragon Schnidibumpfel in *Hugdietrichs Brautfahrt* (1906), Friedel in *Drei Musterweibchen*, Stieglitz in *Der Juxbaron* (1915), Dagobert in *Liebe im Schnee* (1916), Adolf Schmelkes in *Nachtfalter* (1918), Stepanowitsch in *Die Siegerin* (1922), Neljudow in *Das Weib im Purpur* (1924) and Jainkel in *Das Spiel um die Liebe* (1925).

He also directed musical productions at the Komödienhaus (*Der Liebesteufel*), the Neues Wiener Stadttheater (*Libellentanz*), Johann Strauss-Theater (*Ein Märchen aus Florenz*, *Das Weib im Purpur*), the Carltheater (*Hoheit Franzl*) etc.

GUYS AND DOLLS Musical fable of Broadway in 2 acts based on a story and characters by Damon Runyon. Book by Abe Burrows and Jo Swerling. Lyrics and music by Frank Loesser. 46th Street Theater, New York, 24 November 1950.

Producers Feuer and Martin were responsible for coming up with the idea that the New York short stories of Damon Runyon (1884–1946), with their strongly-defined and endearingly quirky characters and their colourful, made-to-measure jargon, might make up into a stage musical. Their first two commissions for a libretto proved unsatisfactory, but the second, written by Jo Swerling, got as far as being set with songs by Frank Loesser, the songwriter with whose *Where's Charley?* the producers had scored a fine success on their first venture into the Broadway musical sphere. When it was decided to junk book number two and replace it with a third, by Abe Burrows, the new librettist was obliged to build his tale – largely based on the story *The Idyll of Miss Sarah Brown*, but including incidents and characters from the earlier libretto – around the now-existing score. The work was so skilfully done that, in spite of this piecemeal creation, the book of *Guys and Dolls* stands out as one of the most remarkable musical plays in the English language.

Nathan Detroit (Sam Levene) runs the 'oldest established permanent floating crap game in New York'. He has been promising to give it up, and to marry night-club chantoosie, Adelaide (Vivian Blaine), his fiancée of 14 years standing, but the main chance always gets the better of him. This week he is in a pother, because the big-gambling Sky Masterson (Robert Alda) is coming to town, and Nathan hasn't got the stake money to launch a game. He tries to win it, by betting Masterson that he cannot get the holy-roller girl, Sarah Brown (Isobel Bigley), from the Save-a-Soul Mission to go with him on a day-trip to Havana. But Masterson promises Sarah to supply her enough 'souls' to make her under-attended mission pass the test of a visiting General, and she goes. While she's away, the guys have their game in the mission house. But Masterson is as good as his promise. The next day he brings the crap-players, whom he has trounced in a game, to be Sarah's souls. The Mission is saved, Sky weds Sarah and seems, at the end of affairs, to have given up gambling to bang the big drum in her band. Adelaide's psychosomatic sniffles vanish for ever as she walks, in parallel, down the aisle with Nathan. The variegated selection of guys were headed by Stubby Kaye as Nicely-Nicely Johnson, Tom Pedi as Harry the Horse, Johnny Silver as Benny Southstreet, Douglas Deane as Rusty Charlie and B S Pully as Big Jule, whilst old time Irish star Pat Rooney (Arvide Abernathy) and Netta Packer (General Matilda B Cartwright) headed the forces of virtue.

The songs for *Guys and Dolls* were in a different class to those which Loesser had written for *Where's Charley?*. Polite British pastiche was replaced by a richly individual set of thoroughly middle-to-low-life New York character songs in which even the one turn into a straight and sentimental love duet, 'I've Never Been in Love Before', seemed to take on the colour of its surroundings. On the one hand, there were the songs for the guys: three of them opening the show talking racing tips in the harmonized 'Fugue for Tinhorns', the whole gang's hymn to 'The Oldest Established Permanent Floating Crap Game in New York', their celebration of a woman's influence in 'Guys and Dolls', Sky's baritonic gambling song, 'Luck Be a Lady', and the warmly philosophical 'My Time of Day', a solo for Nicely-Nicely, testifying before the mission in the ebullient 'Sit Down You're Rockin' the Boat', and the gem of the lot, Nathan's heartfelt cry, 'Sue Me', before Adelaide's charges of infidelity in the face of a deck of cards.

Then there were the dolls: Miss Adelaide pounding out her work-time numbers, 'A Bushel and a Peck' and 'Take Back Your Mink', indulging in an orgy of post-nasal dripping as she described her fiancé's unconnubial tendencies in Adelaide's Lament or, in one of the show's most stunning numbers, joining with Sarah to decide that the answer to life is to 'Marry the Man Today' and change his ways tomorrow; and Sarah insisting to Sky that 'I'll Know' when the right man comes along, or tinkling tipsily through 'If I Were a Bell' after too many Havana-style 'milk shakes'. It was a score where there was barely a number which wasn't a stand-out.

Such was not necessarily the all-round opinion in 1950, but *Guys and Dolls* nevertheless took Tony Awards for best musical, book, score, direction (George S Kaufman) and choreography (Michael Kidd), as well as for Alda's performance, as Feuer and Martin's production settled in for 1,200 performances on Broadway. The first national tour was quickly on its way, with film-land's Allan Jones in the rôle of Masterson and Pamela Britton as Adelaide, but it was 1953 before Prince Littler and Arthur Lewis mounted a British production. Miss Blaine, Kaye, Levene, Pedi and Silver all repeated their original rôles alongside Jerry Wayne (Masterson) and Lizbeth Webb (Sarah) through a fine London run of 555 performances. A film version followed, in 1955, in which Frank Sinatra (Nathan), Marlon Brando (Masterson), Jean Simmons (Sarah) and Miss Blaine featured, alongside three fresh numbers and a fair harvest of the original ones. Australia, however, waited very much longer for its first stage *Guys and Dolls*. It was 1974 before Liz Harris, Ken Lord, Judith Roberts and Barrie Hope were seen in a three-month season at Melbourne's Total Theatre, and more than another decade before Sydney (Her Majesty's Theatre 13 May 1986) saw the show.

Although *Guys and Dolls* found its way firmly into a prized place in the English-language repertoire, for some reason it did not attract attention further afield. And, similarly, given both its qualities and the laurels and the praise it had won, its subsequent career, even in America, was more than a little disappointing. Although it was given a cast-up revival at the City Center (20 April 1955) with Walter Matthau (Nathan), Helen Gallagher (Adelaide), Leila Martin (Sarah) and Ray Shaw (Sky) heading the players, it reappeared on Broadway only in a sorely rehashed version, performed by an uneven cast of black artists (Broadway Theater 21 July 1976), before a major revival was finally mounted in 1992 (Martin Beck Theater, 14 April). Peter Gallagher (Sky), Nathan Lane (Nathan), Faith Prince (Adelaide) and Josie de Guzman (Sarah) featured in a production which won greater accolades than the piece had done first time around. The show also made a modest European début in a German version (ad Janne Furch) in Bremen.

In Britain, where Laurence Olivier had earlier projected to bring the show back in the repertoire of the subsidized National Theatre, with himself featured as Nathan, it was eventually mounted by a later management of the National

Theatre in 1982 (9 March). Julia McKenzie (Adelaide) and Bob Hoskins (Nathan) starred in an otherwise embarrassingly undersung, crudely orchestrated production which nevertheless won waves of praise from some newspaper critics, and was subsequently transferred to a commercial theatre for a run (Prince of Wales Theatre 19 June 1985, 354 performances).

UK: London Coliseum 28 May 1953; Australia: Total Theatre, Melbourne 27 July 1974; Germany: Theater der Hansestadt, Bremen 26 May 1968; Film: Goldwyn 1955
Recordings: original cast (Decca), 1976 revival (revised version) (Motown), London 1982 revival (Chrysalis), 1992 revival (RCA Victor), film soundtrack (Decca) etc

GYPSY Musical in 2 acts by Arthur Laurents suggested by the memoirs of Gypsy Rose Lee. Lyrics by Stephen Sondheim. Music by Jule Styne. Broadway Theater, New York, 21 May 1959.

The musical based on the memoirs of the celebrated peeler Gypsy Rose Lee is rather less about the titular Gypsy, and rather more about Gypsy's grotesquely ambitious stage mother, a performer manquée, who apparently pushed her children towards careers in show business less for their own good or enjoyment, than for the vicarious thrill that she found in their performances and in their ultimate success. The reason for this re-angling of the story was a very valid one: *Gypsy* was a vehicle for the middle-aged Ethel Merman, and the rôle of mother Rose provided her with one of her best-devised parts ever.

Rose (Miss Merman) has her two daughters on stage from tot-talent time, performing an act devised by her which features the blonde and bubbling 'Baby June' (the real-life June Havoc) as front kiddie. Brunette Louise supports discreetly. Stardom doesn't come, but Rose pushes on through stretches of minor engagements, with the girls and their support playing the same tatty act, decorated with any bits she can filch here and there, and twisted about to fit the latest fashions or mother's latest ideas. On the way, she wins the friendship and help of Herbie (Jack Klugman), but she loses June (Lane Bradbury) who only waits for the first twinges of puberty before running away with a boy from the act, Tulsa (Paul Wallace). Undaunted, Rose shifts her ambitions onto the previously unprized Louise (Sandra Church), who is tacked into June's place in the newest variation of the act. But one night, when they are booked into a burlesque house, the featured stripper doesn't show up. Rose shoves Louise into the spot and, within no time at all, the girl has found a métier. With the whiff of stardust up her nostrils, Rose abandons Herbie's proposal of marriage to follow 'Gypsy Rose Lee'. She can't understand that she isn't wanted – or even needed. She explodes in an agony of frustration, and Louise gives in. Momma has got at least some of what she wanted, yet again.

The score's favourite songs were Rose's raucously optimistic 'Everything's Coming Up Roses' and a song-and-dance piece for Tulsa, practising alone the double-handed routine he hopes will be his future, and announcing 'All I Need Now is the Girl'. Three strippers turned out a grossly comical routine ('You Gotta Get a Gimmick') advising Louise on how to get on in the strip business, whilst the two little girls dreamed ungrammatically of escape from the vaudeville grind in 'If Momma Was Married', and made their way through the various stages of their careers to the ever-re-orchestrated strains of the all-purpose 'Let Me Entertain You', a little song which began in Uncle Jocko's talent quest and culminated in Louise's starry strip routines. There were occasional gentler moments too – such as Louise's lonely song to her 'Little Lamb' – but the set piece of the evening was Rose's 11-o'clock number, 'Rose's Turn', the crazy ripping apart of a woman craving for recognition until it drives her round the bend.

David Merrick and Leland Hayward's Broadway production of *Gypsy* ran for 702 performances and, although Miss Merman had begun walking through her hugely demanding rôle before the end of the run, she nevertheless went on the road with it for the eight months of the national tour. A film version was made the following year, but it was made without the original star, whose rôle was taken by Rosalind Russell and the voice of Lisa Kirk. Natalie Wood was Louise and Karl Malden played Herbie.

The film was not a success, and when Miss Merman, who had agreed to go on to play her rôle in London, finally reneged, the production was shelved. It was 11 years before London saw *Gypsy*, and when it did it was Angela Lansbury who played Rose, in a production mounted by a team of American producers and London's H M Tennent Ltd, alongside Zan Charisse (Louise), Barrie Ingham (Herbie) and Bonnie Langford as a memorable Baby June. Miss Lansbury made a personal hit with a rather different reading of the rôle and, although the production folded soon after she left (300 performances), it was subsequently remounted back on Broadway with Rex Robbins (Herbie) replacing Ingham (23 September 1974). It played there for 120 performances. However, Angela Lansbury picked up the Tony Award that the show and Miss Merman had been denied first time round by *Fiorello!* and *The Sound of Music* (tied) and by Mary Martin's Maria von Trapp. Similarly, this production, although briefer in its run than the first, spawned others, including the first Australian showing. Gloria Dawn starred as Rose for four months in Melbourne and shared the rôle with Toni Lamond in a Sydney season.

In 1989 an American touring production (2 May 1989) with TV's *Cagney and Lacey* star Tyne Daly featured as Rose alongside Crista Moore (Louise) and Jonathan Hadary (Herbie), was brought to the St James Theater after some six months on the road to give Broadway its third helping of *Gypsy* in three decades (16 November 1989). It played there for 14 months, folding, as the previous revival had done, soon after the departure of its top-billed star, with whom later it returned briefly to bring its total to 582 performances. British and Australian revivals, announced off and on in its wake, have not appeared at the time of writing.

Like that of a very select handful of shows, however, the popularity of *Gypsy* seems to have grown over the years since its good, but scarcely outstanding, first runs. Reviews such as the original ' ... [the] libretto is a touch commonplace and more than a touch repetitious ... [and the star] cannot quite make the show's shortcomings seem negligible' have become forgotten, as *Gypsy* has found extravagantly fervent followers amongst a group of musical theatre fans, and amongst actresses of a certain age with an eye for a big, loud, virtuoso rôle. This new appraisal has prompted descriptions like 'one of the greatest musicals of our time' from those fans, and, as a result, *Gypsy* has found itself productions in a number of regional houses in England and America, in South America, South Africa and in other, mostly English-speaking, venues without, to date, going further afield.

UK: Piccadilly Theatre 29 May 1973; Australia: Her Majesty's Theatre, Melbourne 3 May 1975; Film: Warner Brothers 1962

Recordings: original cast (Columbia), London cast (RCA), South African cast (Philips), 1989 revival cast (Elektra-Nonsuch), film soundtrack (Warner Bros) etc

THE GYPSY BARON *see* DER ZIGEUNERBARON

GYPSY LOVE *see* ZIGEUNERLIEBE

THE GYPSY PRINCESS *see* DIE CSÁRDÁSFÜRSTIN

H

HADDON HALL Light opera in 3 acts by Sydney Grundy. Music by Arthur Sullivan. Savoy Theatre, London, 24 September 1892.

One of the musical plays produced by D'Oyly Carte at the Savoy Theatre in the period post-*The Gondoliers*, in which W S Gilbert was no longer part of the theatre's creative team, *Haddon Hall* was written by the respected playwright Sydney Grundy, whose early comic opera, *The Vicar of Bray*, Carte had just revived with some success. Like *The Vicar of Bray*, *Haddon Hall* took an old English setting and a well-known subject, the 16th-century tale of the elopement of puritan's daughter Dorothy Vernon of Haddon Hall, Derbyshire. Grundy advanced the period to the picturesque days of Cavaliers and Roundheads, leavened the romantic-dramatic story with a certain amount of humour, but made no attempt – as George Dance had done with the previous *The Nautch Girl* – to catch the special opéra-bouffe flavour of the Savoy operas. *Haddon Hall* deserved its 'light opera' description, particularly as Sullivan chose to set it musically in a style which was as near to his operatic *Ivanhoe* as to *The Yeomen of the Guard*.

Lucille Hill, the female star of *Ivanhoe*, played Dorothy, with Courtice Pounds as her romantic partner, John Manners. Rutland Barrington was the puritan Rupert Vernon and Rosina Brandram the uncomical Lady Vernon, whilst W H Denny had the most humorous moments as a Scots puritan called The McKrankie. The piece ran a respectable 204 performances in London before being taken on the road.

Recording: amateur cast recording (Pearl)

HADING, Jane [TRÉFOURET, Jeanne-Alfrédine] (b Marseille, 25 March 1859; d Neuilly-sur-Seine, 18 February 1941).

A leading lady on the Paris musical stage who went on to a more famous career in the non-musical theatre.

Having first appeared on the stage as a three-year-old child in her native Marseille, Mlle Hading (the name came from her natural father, Hadingue) attended the Conservatoire and, graduating at the age of 14, began her adult career in Algeria and in Cairo where she appeared in *La Fille de Madame Angot* and also in a number of plays. When she returned to Marseille, one of her engagements was for the leading rôle in a local opérette, *Le Grand Mogol*, to be staged at Théâtre du Gymnase. It turned out to be the first major work of Edmond Audran, who would go on to as many more successes as his teenaged star.

On going up to Paris, at the age of 18, she first worked at the Palais-Royal, but then moved to the Théâtre de la Renaissance to understudy Jeanne Granier, at that time the reigning queen of Paris opérette. She took Granier's role of Graziella in a revival of *La Petite Mariée* and played

Héloïse in a reprise of Litolff's *Héloïse et Abélard* before, during Granier's absence from the French capital, creating her first leading rôle in Lecocq's *La Jolie Persane* (1879, Namouna). She also married the director of the theatre, Victor Koning. Mlle Hading starred in Offenbach's last work, *Belle Lurette* (1880, Lurette), in a rôle written to her measure, and appeared in several other revivals, but thereafter abandoned both Koning and the musical theatre to move on to a notable career as a straight actress.

HAGUE, Albert (b Berlin, 13 October 1920). Composer of two successful 1950s Broadway musicals.

Albert Hague studied in the United States of America, and served in the Air Force during the Second World War, before settling in New York and beginning a career as a songwriter. He had a musical produced in Cleveland in 1947, and placed such songs as 'One is a Lonely Number' (w Maurice Valency, *Dance Me a Song*, 1950), before scoring a considerable success with his first full Broadway show, *Plain and Fancy*, and its song hit 'Young and Foolish'. A second success, the music-hall mystery musical *Redhead*, brought him a Tony Award for his score, but thereafter further success eluded him. He supplied two numbers for *Ziegfeld Follies of 1956*, additional music for the revue *The Girls Against the Boys* (w Arnold Horwitt, 1959), and incidental music for the play *The Madwoman of Chaillot*, but his two musicals of the 1960s closed after only a few performances, and his 1974 musicalization of Emlyn Williams's *The Corn is Green* (*Miss Moffat*) folded out of town. He subsequently had a second fine career as a character actor on television, notably in the rôle of Shorofsky in the series *Fame*.

1947 **Reluctant Lady** (Maurice Valency) Cain Park Theatre, Cleveland July
1955 **Plain and Fancy** (Arnold Horwitt/Joseph Stein, Will Glickman) Mark Hellinger Theater 27 January
1959 **Redhead** (Dorothy Fields/Herbert Fields, Sidney Sheldon, David Shaw) 46th Street Theater 5 February
1964 **Café Crown** (Marty Brill/Hy Kraft) Martin Beck Theater 17 April
1969 **The Fig Leaves Are Falling** (Allan Sherman) Broadhurst Theater 2 January
1974 **Miss Moffat** (Emlyn Williams/Joshua Logan, Williams) Shubert Theater, Philadelphia 7 October
1987 **Flim-Flam** (aka *Surprise*) (Lee Adams/Milburn Smith)

HAHN, Reynaldo (b Caracas, Venezuela, 9 August 1874; d Paris, 28 January 1947). Elegant, soigné composer whose work for the French stage, although much prized by his followers, produced only one enduring score.

A student at the Paris Conservatoire from an early age, the young and dashing Hahn made both a name and a place for himself in Parisian fin-de-siècle society, playing and singing his settings of literary verse at fashionable salons. The songs found other and more famous interpreters, and Hahn many influential and important friends, as he expanded his musical horizons to take in theatre music, ballets for both the Opéra and Diaghilev (*Le Dieu bleu*), concert works and conducting. At the same time he both began a long and highly considered period of musical criticism, and completed the composition of two substantial lyric stage works, the 3-act, Pierre Loti-based 'idylle polynésienne' *L'Île du rêve* (23 March 1898) and the 4-act *La Carmélite* (16 December 1902), both staged at the Opéra-Comique.

Other lyric works followed, including the opera *Nausicaa* (Monte Carlo/Opéra-Comique) and the 1-act 'conte lyrique japonais' *La Colombe du Bouddha* (Cannes, 1921), whilst a pantomime composed to a rhythmic poem by Edmond Rostand, *Le Bois sacré*, was produced at the Théâtre Sarah Bernhardt (20 April 1910). He had a first brush with the light musical theatre when he contributed to *Miousic*, the unsuccessful revue-opérette by ten composers fabricated for L'Olympia in 1914.

Hahn finally achieved an enduring popular theatrical success, as opposed to appreciation from artistic society, with the production of the pretty opérette *Ciboulette* at the Théâtre des Variétés in 1923. The songs which he provided for Yvonne Printemps in the musical play *Mozart*, also proved successful as an adjunct to the music of Wolfgang Amadeus and the sprightly comic romance of Sacha Guitry and another pastel period piece with *Brummell* (1931) for its hero won fond friends, but further stage ventures in opérette and musical comedy with *Le Temps d'aimer* (1926) Guitry's *O, mon bel inconnu* (1933) and *Malvina* (1935), in opera (*Le Marchand de Venise*, 1935), and in revue (*Une revue*, 1926) had an often more limited appeal and shorter lives. Having become a considerable and influential figure in Parisian musical circles, Hahn left the critic's chair at *Le Figaro*, which he had occupied for a decade, and became Director of the Paris Opéra in 1945, shortly before his death.

Hahn's refined, correct style of writing, with its tasteful shades, gentle charms and general absence of highly coloured passion or obviously popular attractions, has always appealed to commentators, who are inclined to find alibis for the quick disappearance of each of his failed works or to blame public lack of good taste for his limited success. It is perhaps that very good taste in his writing which has rendered it more interesting to and appreciated by musicians than popular with the general public.

1923 **Ciboulette** (Robert de Flers, Gaston de Caillavet) Théâtre des Variétés 7 April
1925 **Mozart** (Sacha Guitry) Théâtre Édouard VII 2 December
1926 **Le Temps d'aimer** (Hugues Delorme/Pierre Wolff, Henri Duvernois) Théâtre de la Michodière 6 November
1931 **Brummell** (Rip, Robert Dieudonné) Folies Wagram 20 January
1933 **O, mon bel inconnu** (Guitry) Théâtre des Bouffes-Parisiens 12 October
1935 **Malvina** (Maurice Donnay, Duvernois) Théâtre de la Gaîté-Lyrique 23 March
1949 **Le Oui des jeunes filles** (René Fauchois) Opéra-Comique 21 June

Biography: Gavoty, B: *Reynaldo Hahn, le musicien de la Belle Époque* (Buchet/Chastel, Paris, 1976)

HAINES, Herbert E[dgar] (b Manchester, 8 November 1879; d Manchester, 21 April 1923).

The son of Alfred Haines, musical director at the Prince's Theatre in Manchester, Haines studied music in his native town and at the age of 17 composed the dance music for Robert Courtneidge's pantomime at the Prince's Theatre. At 20, he succeeded Ernest Vousden at the baton of Courtneidge's touring musical *The Gay Grisette* before joining George Edwardes's organization as musical director for several of his road productions. He moved to London to succeed Howard Talbot as conductor of Edwardes's *Three Little Maids* and, thereafter, conducted shows at various London theatres over a period of 20 years.

Haines wrote his first musical comedy score, a vehicle for Ellaline Terriss and Seymour Hicks, for Charles Frohman in 1904. As *The Catch of the Season*, and with songs by other composers inserted freely into Haines's basic score, this piece ran 17 for months in London and went on to a series of overseas productions, whilst bringing him two individual song successes in 'The Church Parade' and 'Cigarette'. The same authorial team's *The Talk of the Town*, produced by William Greet the following year, had less success, but a second effort for Frohman, Seymour Hicks and Miss Terriss, *The Beauty of Bath*, produced a second London hit.

In 1907 Frohman set up a B team in an attempt to duplicate the Hicks/Terriss successes, and he supplied them with a show by his A team of writers: Hicks, Charles Taylor and Haines, who this time had also cornered a share in the book credit. *My Darling*, starring Henry Lytton and Marie Studholme, was not a success, and although he thereafter supplied some individual songs for interpolating in other people's scores, Haines wrote no more musical comedy scores of his own, concentrating on conducting, composing light orchestral music, and turning out such incidental scores as that for Courtneidge's production of *Paddy the Next Best Thing* (1920).

Haines won an extra Broadway credit when a Manchester Prince's Theatre pantomime to which he had supplied music was remade as a Broadway musical, *The Babes and the Baron*, and mounted at the New York Lyric Theater for Christmas 1905 (45 performances).

1904 **The Catch of the Season** (w Evelyn Baker/Charles H Taylor/Seymour Hicks, Cosmo Hamilton) Vaudeville Theatre 9 September
1905 **The Talk of the Town** (w Baker/Taylor/Hicks) Lyric Theatre 5 January
1905 **The Babes and the Baron** (w others/Taylor, Robert B Smith/A M Thompson, Robert Courtneidge) Lyric Theater, New York 25 December
1906 **The Beauty of Bath** (Taylor/Hicks, Hamilton) Aldwych Theatre 19 March
1907 **My Darling** (Taylor/Hicks) Hicks Theatre 2 March
1912 **Pebbles on the Beach** (Hicks) 1 act London Coliseum 16 December

HAIR American tribal love-rock musical in 2 acts by Gerome Ragni and James Rado. Music by Galt MacDermot. Anspacher Theater, New York, 17 October 1967; Biltmore Theater (revised version), 29 April 1968.

Less a musical, in the accepted sense, and more a semi-coherent celebration of the preoccupations of the make-love-not-war generation of the American 1960s, *Hair* moved from its off-Broadway beginnings in 50 performances at Joseph Papp's New York Shakespeare Festival (the connections with Shakespeare were not evident), via performances at the Cheetah night-club (22 December 1967 – 28 January 1968), through revisions (mostly aimed at making the piece more aggressive and more strivingly shocking), to a berth on Broadway. There it established itself as one of the theatrical phenomena of its time, and found a fine 1,742-performance run prior to a long and often successful series of productions throughout the world.

Hair – or, rather, the fact of a male person wearing it long, like a girl – is a 1960s symbol of rebellious youngsters nose-thumbing at the values of their parents. Long-haired Claude (Walker Daniels/James Rado), Berger (Ragni) and Sheila (Jill O'Hara/Lynn Kellogg), who share lodgings, Woof (Steve Dean/Steve Curry), Hud (Arnold Wilkerson/Lamont Washington) and Jeannie (Sally Eaton) are members of the hedonistic tribe of Hair. They want to be free. Free to reject responsibility, organization, and anyone or anything that stops them living a life of unspoiled pleasure. Pleasure means sleeping with whom you want, taking what drugs you like, having what you fancy and not doing anything you don't want to. Claude wants Sheila, who wants Berger, but she finally turns up the trick the night before Claude leaves the tribe to go into the real world. His hair cut short, he heads off for the draft and possibly the war in Vietnam.

The songs which illustrated the show – some of which were full-grown numbers, others merely fragments – underwent many changes during the period Hair spent off-, and on the way to, Broadway (the original 20 numbers rose to 31 between the Anspacher Theater and the Biltmore), but the score brought forth one hugely popular piece, 'Aquarius', which became the hymn of the 1960s people, with its astrologically disguised longings for the hedonistic life. 'Good Morning, Starshine' followed it into popularity outside the show, whilst the girl-group comparison of 'White Boys'/'Black Boys', and the revusical 'Frank Mills', a number describing one tribal lassie's longings for a clean-cut American man, which was amongst the most skilful of the show's musical moments, registered and lasted much better than the trendier pieces and those which were merely catalogues of 'naughty' words. It was notable that most of these, and particularly those with the carefully provocative titles ('Hashish', 'Sodomy', 'Colored Spade') were those which had been added following Hair's original success.

Hair's career on Broadway was largely boosted not only by the success of its best songs, but also by some carefully nurtured publicity over the fact that it included some nudity, both male and female. This was nothing new: Ian Richardson's buttocks had recently been on display in the Marat/Sade, and varying nudities were visible in a half-dozen Broadway and off-Broadway shows in this season, not to mention the burlesque houses. But Hair's nudity was gratuitous and thus rated as much more daring. The flashing first-act finale and the show's naughty words would have seemed to have ruled it out for a British production, but when a prospective producer submitted the script to the British censor, the results were surprising. Female nudity was not new on the London stage, but male nudity? It was the first time the censor had been asked. His office had been waiting for the point to be brought up for

many years, and there was, a priori, nothing forbidding it. As for the naughty words, virtually the only objections he had were not on sexual grounds, but on religious ones. But the list of changes required was still enough to discourage an immediate production.

Robert Stigwood and his associates, however, took up a short-term gamble. They bought the British rights to Hair and waited for the imminently expected abolition of the censor's office. When it came, they were quick off the mark with their uncensored show, little glimpse of nudity and all, and all London – as well as much of Spain and Japan – rushed to experience the new freedoms on view at the Shaftesbury Theatre. Paul Nicholas (Claude), Oliver Tobias (Berger), Annabel Leventon (Sheila), Michael Feast (Woof), Peter Straker (Hud) and Linda Kendrick (Jeannie) headed the original cast of the show, which ran for 1,998 performances. It had reached the end of its tether by the time an accident to the roof of the theatre forced it to quit the Shaftesbury, but less than a year later it surfaced again, at the Queen's Theatre (25 June 1974), this time for 111 more performances.

In 1968 a German version (ad Walter Brandin) was premièred in Munich, whilst France, which rarely showed interest in transatlantic shows, followed remarkably swiftly with a production (ad Jacques Lanzmann) at the Théâtre de la Porte-Saint-Martin, with rising pop-star Julien Clerc starred as Claude and some local topicalities slipped into the script. In Australia, Harry M Miller's production, profiting from even more publicity than had been lavished on the show's selling points elsewhere, was a major success, and Hair progressed on to Italy, the Netherlands, Mexico, Israel, Sweden, Japan and other usual and less usual corners of the theatrical and almost-theatrical world.

Hair returned to Broadway in 1977 (Biltmore Theater 5 October) with Randall Easterbrook, Michael Holt, Ellen Foley and Cleavant Derricks featured in its cast, but lasted this time only 43 performances in a rather different social and theatrical climate. Nevertheless, a film version, with a rearranged story-line, was made in 1979 with John Savage, Treat Wilson, Beverley d'Angelo and Melba Moore amongst the cast.

If Hair's time had now apparently passed in the main musical theatre centres, this did not, by any means, remain true further afield. The show has continued to be frequently produced regionally, and it toured Continental cities almost non-stop during the 1980s, provoking the same responses from audiences comprising not only middle-ageing children of the 1960s, and those who had just caught up with the 1960s, but also the young of later decades. In 1992 there were two companies trouping Hair through the short-stands of Europe, with a permanently self-renewing audience still ready and eager to partake of its music and its attitudes.

UK: Shaftesbury Theatre 27 September 1968; Germany: Theater in der Brienner Strasse, Munich 24 October 1968; France: Théâtre de la Porte-Saint-Martin 31 May 1969; Australia: Metro Theatre, Sydney 5 June 1969; Film: United Artists 1979

Recordings: original cast (RCA), London cast (Polydor), Australian casts (Spin, Festival), Japanese cast (RCA), German cast (Polydor), Dutch cast (Polydor), Mexican cast (Orfeon), Israeli cast (CBS), film soundtrack (RCA) etc

HAJOS, Mitzi [HAJÓS, Magdalena, aka Mizzi] (b
Budapest, 27 April 1891; d USA, 198–?). A little, spitfiring
soubrette who moved from Europe to America, and was
there turned into a durable musical comedy star.

After attending drama school in Budapest until 1908,
Mizzi Hajós made her earliest appearances on the stage at
the local Magyar Színház (*A Gyurkovics lányok*) and then in
Vienna. She played in the Leo Ascher burlesque *Hut ab!*
(1909, Lotte) at Venedig in Wien and starred as Mary
Gibbs in the Viennese version of *Our Miss Gibbs* at the
Établissement Ronacher before being taken to America, at
the age of 19. She appeared there at first in vaudeville and
then, with barely improved English, as Fifi Montmartre in
the Shuberts' revusical *La Belle Paree* (1911) at the Winter
Garden. Then, after touring in Christie MacDonald's rôle
of Princess Bozena in Werba and Luescher's Broadway hit
The Spring Maid (*Die Sprudelfee*), she had her first Broadway lead rôle in the same producers' production of De
Koven's *Her Little Highness* (1913, Anna Victoria). That
show disappeared quickly, but her next appearance, in the
title-rôle of the extremely Hungarian *Sari* (*Der Zigeunerprimás*, 1914) hoisted her briskly to star status. Over the
following years, with the aid of *Sari* impresario Henry
Savage, she staunchly maintained that status, billed as the
'baby star', 'the paprika primadonna' and simply as 'Mitzi'
through a series of mostly unexceptional rôles and shows
which nevertheless packed in the audiences in the long
series of tour dates she trouped year after year.

Anne Caldwell and Hugo Felix's *Pom Pom* (1916,
Paulette), a piece adapted for her benefit from the
Hungarian operett *Csibészkirály*, had her cast as another
Continental heroine, this time an actress mistaken for the
pickpocket she plays on stage, *Head Over Heels* (1918, Mitzi
Bambinetti) had her playing an acrobat to Jerome Kern
music, while Zelda Sears and Harold Levey's *Lady Billy*
(1920, Countess Antonio) cast her as an aristocrat disguised for much of the evening in boy's clothes. The same
team of writers dipped into fantasy with a second vehicle
for her in *The Magic Ring* (aka *Minnie an' Me*, 1923, Polly
Church). A move to the Shubert management for Oscar
Straus's *Naughty Riquette* (*Riquette*, 1926, Riquette Duval)
gave her some worthwhile music and yet another long and
successful tour, whilst *The Madcap* (1928, Chibi) cast the
now 37-year-old star alongside Sidney Greenstreet as a
teenager pretending to be 12 in a musical version of Régis
Gignoux and Jacques Théry's Parisian play *Le Fruit vert*.
She returned to Broadway for the last time as a star as *Sari*
in 1930, and thereafter appeared only as a featured player
on the non-musical stage.

HALE, J Robert [HALE-MONRO, John Robert] (b
Newton Abbot, 25 March 1874; d Maidenhead, Berks, 18
April 1940). Musical theatre and revue comedian, and the
father of two successful musical comedy and/or revue
stars.

Hale spent his first decade in the theatre on the road,
first in plays, and then playing for Tom Davis in the musicals *Little Miss Nobody*, *Florodora* and *The Silver Slipper*. He
made his first appearance in London in the second comic
rôle of Davis's *The Medal and the Maid* (1903, Simon Pent-
weazle). He joined George Edwardes in 1905 to tour in
Lady Madcap, subsequently taking over the same number-
two comic rôle in the show's London production, and

featured in the same producer's *Les Merveilleuses*, before
Edwardes moved him to a resident spot in the Gaiety
company, where he created good supporting comedy rôles
in *The Girls from Gottenberg* (1907, Allbrecht), *Havana*
(1908, Frank Charteris), *Our Miss Gibbs* (1909, Slithers)
and *Peggy* (1910, James Bendoyle).

Hale had a considerable success in London's early
revues, and over the next eight years played almost continuously in revue and in pantomime, returning to the
musical comedy stage to play Madame Lucy in the British
production of *Irene* (1920). He continued to appear
frequently and successfully in revue, but other book musicals with which he was involved – *Faust on Toast* (1921,
Mephistopheles), a touring musicalized version of the play
Biffy (1923, Biffy), *Open Your Eyes* (1929, Inspector
Merlin), *Sons o' Guns* (1930, Hobson), *The One Girl* (1933,
Holy Joe) and *I Can Take It* (1939) – found little or no
success. His film engagements included an appearance as
Eberseder in the 1933 British film of *Walzer aus Wien*.

His daughter **Binnie HALE** [Beatrice Mary HALE-
MONRO] (b Liverpool, 22 May 1899; d Hastings, 10
January 1984) made her earliest stage appearance alongside her father in the revue *Follow the Crowd*, at the age of
17. She made her first musical comedy appearance the
following year in a minor rôle in C B Cochran's *Houp-La!*
(Annette) and, in between revue engagements, took
increasingly important rôles in *The Kiss Call* (1920,
Charlotte), *My Nieces* (1922, Betty Culverwell) and *Katinka*
(1924, Helen Hopper). Her fame was made when she was
cast in the title-rôle of the London *No, No, Nanette* (1926),
and she followed up in a trio of star ingénue rôles in West
End musical comedy productions: Sunny Peters in *Sunny*
(1926), Jill Kemp in *Mr Cinders* (1929), introducing
'Spread a Little Happiness', and star-billed as the teahouse Nippy in *Nippy* (1930).

She toured in the much more vocally demanding rôle of
The Dubarry, returned to town and the song-and-scene
musical to succeed Evelyn Laye and Adèle Dixon as the
ingénue of *Give Me a Ring* (1933, Peggy) and then paired
with great success with her *Mr Cinders* partner, Bobby
Howes, in the comedy musical *Yes, Madam?* (1934, Sally).
Rise and Shine (1936, Anne) and *Magyar Melody* (1939,
Roszi), both quick failures, were her last appearances on
the musical stage, on which she had spent more than a
decade as a major London favourite, although she
appeared several times thereafter in revue in the fifteen
years remaining of her career.

Hale's son, **Sonnie HALE** [John Robert HALE-
MONRO] (b London, 1 May 1902; d London, 9 June
1959), also began his stage career in revue, and made his
first musical comedy appearance at the age of 21 in
Cochran's London production of George M Cohan's *Little
Nellie Kelly* (Sidney Potter). He subsequently had good
juvenile rôles in *Mercenary Mary* (1925, Jerry) and *Queen
High* (1926, Richard Johns) before playing four years of
highly successful revues in various London theatres. He
appeared in the revusical *Evergreen* (1930) and in *Hold My
Hand* with Stanley Lupino at the Gaiety in 1931 (Pop
Curry), but thereafter led an irregular stage and film
career, returning to the musical stage to appear with his
father and with his wife, the popular dancing soubrette
Jessie Matthews, in their own production of *I Can Take It*
(1939), which closed on the road, to play the comedy rôle

of Tonio in a revival of *The Maid of the Mountains* (1942), to star in a flop musical version of *When Knight's Were Bold* (1943, Sir Guy de Vere) and as comedian in the short-lived *Rainbow Square* (1951, Peppi).

Hale appeared in or directed a number of musical films in the mid-1930s, including the cinema versions of the stage shows *Evergreen* and *Head Over Heels* (director) and *Gangway* (director). He was married successively to musical-theatre star, Evelyn Laye, and to Miss Matthews.

HALÉVY, Ludovic [aka Jules SERVIÈRES] (b Paris, 1 January 1834; d Paris, 8 May 1908). One half of the partnership of librettists and lyricists who supplied Jacques Offenbach with the texts for many of his greatest successes, and the author or co-author of a long series of hit plays and musical shows on the Paris and international stage in the second half of the 19th century.

The son of the author, playwright and occasional operatic librettist Léon Halévy (1802–1883), and the nephew of Fromental Halévy [Jacques Fromental Élie LÉVY], (1799–1862), the composer of the celebrated opera *La Juive*, Ludovic began his working life in the Imperial civil service (Ministère d'État, 1852, Ministère de l'Algérie et des Colonies, 1858). However, from an early age he was taken by the theatre, and began himself to write theatrical pieces. His opportunity to break into the musical theatre came when Jacques Offenbach, needing an introductory piece for the opening of his new Théâtre des Bouffes-Parisiens, and unable to find a suitable, established author with the immediate time available, offered the nephew of his old Conservatoire professor, Fromental Halévy, the chance to write a little libretto around some lyrics which had already been prepared by Jules Méry, the recent librettist of Reyer's first opera, and around the personnel of the Bouffes company. Thus constricted, Halévy confectioned the three-handed *Entrez Messieurs, Mesdames*, to be played as the first item on the four-part programme which inaugurated the Bouffes. It was Jules Moinaux's *Les Deux Aveugles* which took the honours of the night, but the young civil servant, who had hidden his identity behind the pseudonym of 'Jules Servières' in order not to sully his chances of promotion by a connection with the stage, was launched, and over the months that followed he became a regular supplier of little opérette texts to the Bouffes-Parisiens.

Halévy's first great success came with the chaotic chinoiserie *Ba-ta-clan*, written this time without the umbrella of a pseudonym, and amongst those that followed were an adaptation of Mozart's *Der Schauspieldirektor* as *L'Impresario* (1856), the prize libretto *Le Docteur Miracle*, which was set victoriously by Lecocq and by Bizet, and Léon Gastinel's little *L'Opéra aux fenêtres* (1857), which made itself an international career (*Das Singspiel am Fenster*, *A Suitable Villa* etc) after its introduction at the Bouffes.

With the breaking down of the restrictions regarding the number of people allowed in his shows, Offenbach was able to reach out into more substantial fields, and in 1858 Halévy and Hector Crémieux provided him with the libretto for his first major work, a burlesque on which they had begun work several years earlier, *Orphée aux enfers*. When the piece was mounted, however, Halévy was not named on the playbill. Again worried by the effect of a burlesque production on his prospects in his 'real' job, he

had withdrawn from the project, only to find himself dragged back in by Offenbach. Thus, for the moment, he participated only privately in the triumph won by *Orphée*.

There were, however, plenty more triumphs to come, both in the musical theatre and in the world of the straight play. In the charming *La Chanson de Fortunio* and the burlesque *Le Pont des soupirs* he teamed again with Crémieux and with Offenbach, and the trio gave a helping hand to 'M de Saint-Rémy', otherwise the very royal Duc de Morny (whom Halévy had already provided with another little libretto), in his latest attempt at theatrical authorship with *M Choufleuri*. His co-operation helped to earn Halévy, by way of thanks, a post at the Corps Législatif. He put his hand to revue along with Eugène Grangé, Philippe Gille and Offenbach for the little *Le Carnaval des revues* (1860), but it was a further and new collaboration which brought Halévy to the peak of his career, the collaboration with fellow author Henri Meilhac.

Meilhac, Halévy and Offenbach came together first when the composer provided one number for their little Palais-Royal piece, *Le Brésilien* (1863), but they soon moved on to much more significant collaborations. Together, the soon famous pair provided Offenbach with the texts for the series of great musical plays which were the centre-piece of his oeuvre: the opéras-bouffes *La Belle Hélène*, *Barbe-bleue*, *La Grande-Duchesse de Gérolstein* and *Les Brigands*, the less burlesque *La Périchole*, and the vaudevillesque *La Vie parisienne*, as well as the almost successful, and textually delightful, *La Boulangère a des écus*. They also supplied Lecocq with the text for his charming and triumphant *Le Petit Duc*, *La Petite Mademoiselle* and, in collaboration with Albert Millaud, the internationally successful vaudeville *La Roussotte* (w Hervé). In addition, they scored huge successes in both the operatic world, with their adaptation of Prosper Mérimée's novel as the libretto for *Carmen*, and in the straight theatre, with *Frou-Frou*, *Le Mari de la débutante*, *La Cigale*, *La Petite Marquise*, *La Boule*, *Le Réveillon*, *Toto chez Tata* and *Tricoche et Cacolet*.

The year 1881 was marked by the last original Halévy musical on the Paris stage, ending a 25-year musical-theatre career which had produced some of the world's most loved and admired shows. He continued to write for the non-musical stage, and found great success as a novelist, notably with *L'Abbé Constantin* (1882), as well as such pieces as *Un Mariage d'amour*, *Une Scandale* and *Princesse*. He was elected to the Académie Française, and became a Commander of the Legion of Honour.

Halévy's works have been the bases for a long list of musical plays from other, mostly Austrian, hands, the most famous being the adaptation of his play *Le Réveillon* (w Meilhac) as the libretto for Johann Strauss's *Die Fledermaus* (1874). *La Boule* (w Meilhac) became the Posse *Von Tisch und Bett*, written and composed by Julius Hopp, (Theater an der Wien 7 September 1875), *Tricoche et Cacolet* (w Meilhac) was given songs by Karl Treumann and Franz von Suppé (Carltheater 1876) and more liberally musicalized as *Spitzbub et Cie* by Wilhelm Ascher and Robert Pohl, music by Josef Bayer, at the Vienna Lustspiel-Theater (5 July 1907). *La Cigale* (Variétés, 6 October 1877 w Meilhac) was turned by J P Burnett into a disastrous *Good Luck* for London in 1885 and remade by H Osten and Julius Stern as a Viennese *Bum-Bum* (Carltheater 24 October 1896), whilst *La Petite Marquise* (w

Meilhac) became Felix Albini's Operette *Madame Troubadour* (1907). *Le Mari de la débutante* was turned into two different Operetten at the Carltheater within eight months: Annie Dirkens played seven performances at each of the home house and the Theater an der Wien in *Die Prima Donna* (Alfred Müller-Norden/Alexander Landesberg, Ludwig Fischl 31 January 1901) and Mizzi Günther played Nina in *Die Debutantin* (Alfred Zamara/A M Willner, Waldberg 4 October 1901) for ten nights. *La Roussotte*, in one of its series of international remakings, was Germanned by Franz von Schönthan and given a new score by Karl Millöcker under the title of *Ein süsses Kind* (Theater an der Wien 1 April 1882) and the text of the Offenbach opérette *La Diva* was rewritten by Zell and Genée into a piece called *Die Theaterprinzessin* (Theater an der Wien 30 December 1872).

The 1938 French opérette *Les Petites Cardinal* (Honegger, Jacques Ibert/ad Willemetz, Paul Brach, Bouffes-Parisiens 12 February) was based on Halévy's series of sketches *M et Mme Cardinal*, *Les Petites Cardinal* and *La Famille Cardinal*.

1855 **Entrez Messieurs, Mesdames** (Jacques Offenbach/w Jules Méry) 1 act Théâtre des Bouffes-Parisiens 5 July

1855 **Une pleine eau** (Jules Costé/w d'Osmont) 1 act Théâtre des Bouffes-Parisiens 28 August

1855 **Madame Papillon** (Offenbach) 1 act Théâtre des Bouffes-Parisiens 3 October

1855 **Ba-ta-clan** (Offenbach) 1 act Théâtre des Bouffes-Parisiens 29 December

1856 **L'Imprésario** (*Der Schauspieldirektor*) French version w Léon Battu (Théâtre des Bouffes-Parisiens)

1857 **Le Docteur Miracle** (Charles Lecocq/w Battu) Théâtre des Bouffes-Parisiens 8 April

1857 **Le Docteur Miracle** (Georges Bizet/w Battu) Théâtre des Bouffes-Parisiens 8 April

1857 **L'Opéra aux fenêtres** (Léon Gastinel) 1 act Théâtre des Bouffes-Parisiens 5 October

1858 **Orphée aux enfers** (Offenbach/w Hector Crémieux) Théâtre des Bouffes-Parisiens 21 October

1859 **Voici le jour** (Jules Ward) 1 act Lyon

1860 **Titus et Bérénice** (Gastinel/w Édouard Fournier) 1 act Théâtre des Bouffes-Parisiens 11 May

1860 **Le Mari sans le savoir** ('Saint-Rémy' ie Duc de Morny/w Léon Halévy) 1 act Théâtre des Bouffes-Parisiens 31 December

1861 **La Chanson de Fortunio** (Offenbach/w Crémieux) 1 act Théâtre des Bouffes-Parisiens 5 January

1861 **Le Pont des soupirs** (Offenbach/w Crémieux) Théâtre des Bouffes-Parisiens 23 March

1861 **Les Deux Buveurs** (Léo Delibes/w Crémieux) 1 act Théâtre des Bouffes-Parisiens January

1861 **M Choufleuri restera chez lui le ...** (Offenbach/w 'Saint-Rémy', Crémieux) 1 act privately 31 May

1861 **La Baronne de San Francisco** (Henri Caspers/w Crémieux) 1 act Théâtre des Bouffes-Parisiens 27 November

1861 **Les Eaux d'Ems** (Delibes/w Crémieux) 1 act Ems; Théâtre des Bouffes-Parisiens 9 April 1863

1861 **Le Roman comique** (Offenbach/w Crémieux) Théâtre des Bouffes-Parisiens 10 December

1862 **Un fin de bail** (Adolphe Varney/w Crémieux) 1 act Théâtre des Bouffes-Parisiens 29 January

1862 **Jacqueline** (Offenbach/w Crémieux) 1 act Théâtre des Bouffes-Parisiens 14 October

1864 **La Belle Hélène** (Offenbach/w Meilhac) Théâtre des Variétés 17 December

1866 **Barbe-bleue** (Offenbach/w Meilhac) Théâtre des Variétés 5 February

1866 **La Vie parisienne** (Offenbach/w Meilhac) Palais-Royal 31 October

1867 **La Grande-Duchesse de Gérolstein** (Offenbach/w Meilhac) Théâtre des Variétés 12 April

1868 **Le Château à Toto** (Offenbach/w Meilhac) Palais-Royal 6 May

1868 **La Périchole** (Offenbach/w Meilhac) Théâtre des Variétés 6 October

1869 **La Diva** (Offenbach/w Meilhac) Théâtre des Bouffes-Parisiens 22 March

1869 **Les Brigands** (Offenbach/w Meilhac) Théâtre des Variétés 10 December

1873 **Pomme d'api** (Offenbach/w William Busnach) 1 act Théâtre de la Renaissance 4 September

1875 **La Boulangère a des écus** (Offenbach/w Meilhac) Théâtre des Variétés 19 October

1878 **Le Petit Duc** (Lecocq/w Meilhac) Théâtre de la Renaissance 25 January

1879 **La Marocaine** (Offenbach/w Paul Ferrier) Théâtre des Bouffes-Parisiens 13 January

1879 **La Petite Mademoiselle** (Lecocq/w Meilhac) Théâtre de la Renaissance 12 April

1881 **Janot** (Lecocq/w Meilhac) Théâtre de la Renaissance 21 January

1881 **La Roussotte** (Hervé, Lecocq/w Meilhac, Millaud) Théâtre des Variétés 28 January

Memoirs: *L'Invasion, souvenirs et récits* (Paris, 1872); *Notes et Souvenirs, 1871–1872* (Calmann-Lévy, Paris, 1889); Biography: Claretie, J: *Ludovic Halévy* (Quantin, Paris, 1883).

HALEY, Jack [John Joseph] (b Boston, 10 August 1899; d Los Angeles, 6 June 1979). Leading man for several song-and-dance shows of the 1920s and 1930s and many a musical film.

Haley came from vaudeville to the musical stage via revue (*Round the Town*, 1924, *Gay Paree*, 1925–6), and made his mark starring as the quiet, wealthy and ever-so-attractive hero netted by soubrette Zelma O'Neal in De Sylva, Brown and Henderson's *Follow Thru* (1929, Jack Martin). The rôle in *Follow Thru* gave him the opportunity to introduce a hit song in 'Button Up Your Overcoat', but Richard Whiting and Oscar Hammerstein II gave him no equivalent chances in a similar part in the rather less successful *Free for All* (1931, Steve Potter). In *Take a Chance* (1932, Duke Stanley) he left the dashing hero's rôle to Jack Whiting, and appeared this time as a more dubious character who, nevertheless, got to sing the best number of the evening, Whiting's 'You're an Old Smoothie', with Ethel Merman.

Having already visited Hollywood for the film of *Follow Thru* (1930, Jack Martin), he returned there for a series of more than 20 musical films including *Sitting Pretty* (1933, Peter Pendelton), *The Girl Friend* (1935, Henry), *Poor Little Rich Girl* (1936), *Alexander's Ragtime Band* (1938) and *The Wizard of Oz* (1939), in which he made a memorable appearance as the Tin Man, making his only subsequent Broadway stage ventures in Rodgers and Hart's *Higher and Higher* (1940, film 1943, Mike O'Brien), the revusical *Show Time* (1942) and the revue *Inside USA* (1948) in the latter years of his career.

HALF A SIXPENCE Musical in 2 acts by Beverley Cross based on H G Wells's novel *Kipps*. Music and lyrics by David Heneker. Cambridge Theatre, London, 21 March 1963.

Commissioned by producer Harold Fielding as a vehicle

Plate 119. **Half a Sixpence:** *James Grout (Chitterlow) knocks Tommy Steele (Kipps) flying with his bicycle.*

for rock 'n' roll singer Tommy Steele, whom he had successfully presented in Rodgers and Hammerstein's *Cinderella*, *Half a Sixpence* was based on Wells's 1905 cautionary tale of a draper's boy who finds that money and social aspirations don't bring happiness.

Arthur Kipps (Steele) works in a lowly position in a Tunbridge Wells drapery, and has an 'understanding' with the servant girl Ann Pornick (Marti Webb). But the extravagant actor Chitterlow (James Grout) arrives on the scene with the news that Kipps has inherited a fortune, and the foolish boy is soon flinging his wealth around and trying to mix with local society. The only society folk who pay any attention are those with something to gain, like the pretentious but poor Mrs Walsingham (Jessica James), her attractive daughter, Helen (Anna Barry), and her worthless son (Ian White), to whom, fatally, Kipps entrusts his money for investment. Bit by bit, the youngster comes to his senses. He renounces Helen and her kind and returns to Ann, and, when the money is lost, cashes in his assets and retires with his little wife to run a bookshop. Then Chitterlow arrives with the news that his play, in which Kipps invested in flush days, is a hit. Kipps has made a second fortune. He tells Chitterlow to keep it.

David Heneker's score for *Half a Sixpence* was one of the most warmly endearing to have appeared in the British theatre for decades. Kipps and Ann sealing their lover's pact by each taking 'Half a Sixpence' as a lover's token instead of the split sovereign that better-off folk share, the boy mooning foolishly over the comparatively sophisticated Helen in 'She's Too Far Above Me', jubilating over his first date with the lady in 'If the Rain's Got to Fall', or, still in the thrall of what money can buy, insisting that 'I'll Build

a Palace for My Girl' whilst the practical Ann, in counterpoint, insists that 'I Only Want a Little House', were memorable moments for the star. Alongside these, there were fine pieces for Ann, stubbornly refusing to go posh ('I Know What I Am'), or blazing away at the unfaithful Artie ('I'm Talking to You!'), for Kipps's pals (Anthony Valentine, Colin Farrell, John Bull) leaping joyously about imagining what life would be like if they had 'Money to Burn', for Chitterlow ('The One That Got Away') and for the whole ensemble, celebrating an outing on 'The Grand Military Canal'. Perhaps the greatest hit that came from the show, however, was a song which, like so many other show hits, was added to the score when the piece was already on its way to town: the crazy, music-hall-style wedding scene, 'Flash, Bang, Wallop!', the title of which has become a Dictionary of Quotations catch-phrase as the song continues as a favourite 35 years on.

Half a Sixpence played for 677 performances in London, being closed down to allow Steele and Grout to lead a Broadway production, mounted by Fielding in collaboration with American associates. The 'I'll Build a Palace for My Girl' sequence had to be cut when the scenery was lost en route from England, and trouble loomed as a whole series of other changes were instigated and then mostly abandoned along with the original American director before *Half a Sixpence* reached Broadway. There, with Polly James (Ann) teamed with Steele and Grout, it repeated its London success, playing in New York for 512 performances. The show toured in 1966–7, with Dick Kallman as Artie, and in 1967 Paramount mounted a film version in which Steele was teamed with Julia Foster (and the voice of Miss Webb) as Ann, Cyril Ritchard as Chitterlow, and some further alterations to the score. In spite of ending up as a pawn in a power-change at Paramount, which resulted in some clumsy cutting, the film proved an agreeable record of the show and of Steele's performance.

Australia saw *Half a Sixpence* in 1967 with Mark McManus (later of the National Theatre and TV's *Taggart*) as Artie and former Australian matinée idol Max Oldaker as Chitterlow. It ran for four months in Melbourne and three in Sydney (Theatre Royal, 16 August 1967).

USA: Broadhurst Theater 25 April 1965; Australia: Comedy Theatre, Melbourne 11 March 1967; Film: Paramount 1967
Recordings: original cast (Decca), Broadway cast (RCA), Film soundtrack (RCA) etc

HALL, Juanita [LONG, Juanita] (b Keysport, NJ, 6 November 1901; d Bay Shore, NY, 28 February 1968).

Miss Hall appeared as a chorus singer in *Sing Out Sweet Land*, the 1946 *Show Boat* revival and *Street Scene*, and in a minor part in *St Louis Woman* before creating the rôle of Bloody Mary in *South Pacific*. In spite of the fact that she was, physically, wholly the opposite to the original character description – a short, squat and chunky black woman, where a tiny, wizened Asiatic was called for – she scored an enormous success ('Bali H'ai', 'Happy Talk') and was signed to repeat her stage performance on film. On this occasion, however, her singing voice was dubbed. She later appeared on Broadway opposite Pearl Bailey in the Truman Capote/Harold Arlen musical *House of Flowers* (1954), as Madam Liang in Rodgers and Hammerstein's *Flower Drum Song* (1958) and at the Jones Beach Theater in the 1965 *Mardi Gras!* (Katie/Katherine/Marie Le Veau).

HALL, Natalie (b Providence, RI, 23 September 1904).

After a brief early career in opera, Miss Hall made her Broadway début in the leading rôle of the Shuberts' imported Operette *Three Little Girls* (1930, Beate). She subsequently starred with Guy Robertson in another Continental piece, *Marching By* (1931, Anna), on the road, as Kathleen in Vincent Youmans's briefly seen musical version of *Smilin' Through, Through the Years* (1932), and as Roxane in the St Louis Muny *Cyrano de Bergerac* (1932) before she found her biggest success as the tempestuous prima donna Frieda Hatzfeld, in Jerome Kern's Continental-style operetta *Music in the Air* (1932, 'The Song is You'). She visited London to take the lead rôle in the Theatre Royal, Drury Lane production of Ábrahám's *Ball at the Savoy* (1933), replaced Maria Jeritza in Friml's *Music Hath Charms* (1934) for its short time on Broadway, and played the rôle of Mrs Cynthia Bradley in the Gilbert and Sullivan tale *Knights of Song* (1938), performing *The Mikado*'s 'The Moon and I', but thereafter her career in the musical theatre was limited to regional productions (Bertha in *The Red Mill*, 1940 etc).

Her sister **Bettina HALL** (b North Easton, Mass, 1906) had a parallel career, playing first in Gilbert and Sullivan, then in opera, and appearing alongside Natalie in *Three Little Girls* (1930, Marie). She appeared opposite Walter Slezak in the lead rôle of an americanization of Benatzky's *Meine Schwester und ich* (*Meet my Sister*, 1930, Dolly) and starred opposite Georges Metaxa in the Harbach/Kern *The Cat and the Fiddle* (1931, Shirley Sheridan 'She Didn't Say "Yes"', 'Try to Forget'), with a success equivalent to that her sister would have the following year in *Music in the Air*. In 1934 she appeared in a souped-up Shubert revival of Herbert's *The Only Girl* (Ruth Wilson), which luckily lasted for a short enough time to allow her to take up the juvenile rôle of Hope Harcourt in the original production of *Anything Goes* (1934, 'The Gypsy in Me'). Her subsequent career in the musical theatre did not include Broadway, although she appeared in New York in non-singing rôles.

Both sisters married well and disappeared from the theatrical scene. If they are not still in the land of the living, *Variety* has not noticed the fact.

HALL, Owen [DAVIS, James] (b Dublin, 10 April 1853; d Harrogate, 9 April 1907). Style-setting librettist who authored some of the most successful musical plays of the 1890s and 1900s for the British stage.

The son of Hyman Davis, a Jewish artist, Jimmy Davis was intended to be a solicitor and, from the age of 21, he busied himself in pursuit of a legal career from an office at Mayfair's 5 Albemarle Street. Like many another young solicitor of the period, however, he had a taste for the bottle, the pen and the sporting and bohemian lives, as well as an utter incapacity to control his indulgences and an outrageous bonhomie. As a result, at the age of 29 the young solicitor went bankrupt to the vast tune of £27,385. After a dozen years of trying, and an abortive attempt to take the Dundalk parliamentary seat for the Conservative Party in 1880, he gave up the law in 1886 and went full-time into journalism, where he exercised a trippingly caustic tongue as dramatic critic on *The Sporting Times* and for two years as editor of *The Bat* (1885–7). So caustic, indeed, that he was hauled into court by musical-comedy

star Marius for what turned out to be £110 worth of rather too imaginatively libellous prose. He also continued his old way of life and, by 1888, ended up in the bankruptcy courts again.

Davis persevered both in his journalism and his vices – in which the musical theatre played a natural part – and was apparently not overly impressed when he saw George Edwardes's production of *In Town*, one of the heralds of what was to become accepted as the new-style musical comedy. Anecdote relates that, meeting Edwardes on the Brighton train, he told 'the Guvnor' what he thought of the text of his new show, adding 'I could do better myself'. Edwardes's reply is said to have been 'Then do'.

The result of this conversation was a libretto which was entitled *A Gaiety Girl*, written under the pseudonym 'Owen Hall' (said to be a reference to Davis's notorious propensity for alarming debts), which Edwardes accepted and entrusted to the young conductor and composer Sidney Jones, who had never written a full-sized musical before, and the neophyte lyricist Harry Greenbank for its songs. When it came to production, Owen Hall's book had to undergo some changes. Not to the plot, for that was a simple little affair about a stolen comb and a few tangled romances, but to the dialogue. Hall had taken a slicingly satirical tone, and the little story with its pretty girls and songs was told in lines which jabbed here and there in the style of an upmarket and particularly vicious gossip columnist. Some of the jibes were so personal that Edwardes did not dare put them on the stage. But much of the smart society back-chat was still there on opening night, and it hit its marks with such effect that Edwardes received several requests from high places for alterations. The public, on the other hand, loved it, even when the Reverend Brierly, a character depicted as a man of doubtful moral rectitude, was demoted, after pressure from Lambeth Palace, to being just plain Dr Brierly.

A Gaiety Girl was a dazzling success and confirmed Edwardes in the way he was going. It also found a new career and a new source of money for Hall, who immediately went to work on a new show with Jones and Greenbank. *An Artist's Model* kept the snappy dialogue, but twinned it with a romantic plot, tacked in at the last minute when Edwardes managed to contract favourite prima donna, Marie Tempest, and needed a rôle for her. For the £850 he was being paid this time, Hall happily made the alterations and, by this lucky chance, set up the formula for a series of successes at Daly's Theatre.

An Artist's Model was succeeded by *The Geisha*, as Hall's price climbed to a dazzling £4,000 a script – sold outright, for ready money was all the author cared about. Here Edwardes made a marvellous bargain, for *The Geisha* was to be the biggest international hit the British musical theatre had known, playing thousands of performances on the Continent (one source counts some 8,000 in Germany alone) and touring for decades in Britain.

Hall had now taken some of the sauce off his style, and happily evolved a combination of sparky, up-to-date comedy and good old-fashioned (and sometimes new-fashioned) romance, into which he was never afraid to pop some general or particular parody when the opportunity arose. For the most part his subjects were modern, but he was by no means at a loss with the citizens of Ancient Rome when he supplied Sidney Jones with the text for one of their finest works, *A Greek Slave*. They came out just like his Londoners. And all the time his honorariums were rising. He had earned £7,000 in the year *The Geisha* was produced, in the following year he netted £9,900. Astounding figures, but no less astounding was the £8,000 that he paid out to bookmakers in lost bets. A few weeks after the opening of *A Greek Slave*, Owen Hall was bankrupt again.

Given his continuing appetite for money, Hall did not confine himself to writing for Edwardes. He had already fleshed out a James Tanner plotline for ambitious touring manager Cissie Graham (*All Abroad*, £350) and when Edwardes found it a good idea to accept a libretto from the influential journalist 'E A Morton' for his next show, Hall was happy to accept the proposition from up-and-coming producer Tom Davis and his associates to write a text for a first musical by successful songwriter Leslie Stuart. The result was *Florodora*, another international hit of huge proportions.

Hall turned out two more musicals for Davis: *The Silver Slipper* with Stuart, and his one and only genuine flop, a complicated piece of nonsense, nothing like his other works in tone, called *The Medal and the Maid*, in which he came back together with Sidney Jones. For Edwardes, on the other hand, he went back to the modern society tale to turn out perhaps the most delightful of all his libretti, the sweetly silly story of a misguided kiss told with the skill of a genuine farceur in *The Girl from Kays* (allegedly based on Léon Gandillot's *La Mariée recalcitrante*), and a semi-success in *The Little Cherub* (announcedly with the use of a bit of Meilhac's *Décoré*). For Frank Curzon he created a splendid character in the amorous copper *Sergeant Brue*, which Willie Edouin, who had already made *Florodora*'s Tweedlepunch and 'Piggy Hoggenheimer' from *The Girl From Kays* into classic comic gentlemen of the theatre, turned into another memorable creation.

Life caught up with Jimmy Davis, at the age of 54, before the law did again. His last show, the farcical comedy with music *King Silly*, apparently written without a commission, seems not to have got to the stage, and his attempted launch of himself as a public company towards the end of 1906 with a capitalisation of £12,000 does not seem to have taken off. Perhaps investors knew. When he died, with the credit for two of the world's most successful ever shows and a whole series of other hits to his name, with performances of his shows taking place every day all over the world, his assets came to just £200.

Hall's non-theatrical writings included a successful novel, *The Track of a Storm* (1896), a mystery, *Jetsam* (1897), and *Hernando* (1902).

Hall's sister, Julia Frankau (?1859–1916) was a successful novelist under the name of 'Frank Danby', and the mother of author Gilbert Frankau, and the actor Ronald Frankau who appeared in London in *A Country Girl* (1914), *The Gay Princess* (1931) and a long run of 1930s and 1940s revues.

1893 **A Gaiety Girl** (Sidney Jones/Harry Greenbank) Prince of Wales Theatre 14 October
1895 **An Artist's Model** (Jones/Greenbank) Daly's Theatre 2 February
1895 **All Abroad** (Frederick Rosse/W H Risque/w James Tanner) Criterion Theatre 8 August
1896 **The Geisha** (Jones/Greenbank) Daly's Theatre 25 April

1898 **A Greek Slave** (Jones/Greenbank) Daly's Theatre 8 June
1899 **Florodora** (Leslie Stuart/E Boyd Jones) Lyric Theatre 11 November
1901 **The Silver Slipper** (Stuart/Risque) Lyric Theatre 1 June
1902 **The Girl from Kays** (Ivan Caryll, Cecil Cook/Adrian Ross, Claude Aveling) Apollo Theatre 15 November
1903 **The Medal and the Maid** (Jones/C H Taylor) Lyric Theatre 25 April
1904 **Sergeant Brue** (Liza Lehmann/J Hickory Wood) Strand Theatre 14 June
1906 **The Little Cherub** (*The Girl on the Stage*) (Caryll/Ross) Prince of Wales Theatre 13 January

HALL, Pauline [SCHMIDGALL, Pauline Fredrika] (b Cincinnati, Ohio, 26 February 1860; d Yonkers, NY, 29 December 1919). Beautiful, shapely, dark-eyed vocalist who found stardom in the title-rôle of the record-breaking *Erminie*.

Daughter of a Cincinnati druggist, Pauline Hall made a youthful start in the theatre as a dancer, then moved on to tour both with Alice Oates's and Samuel Colville's companies in comic opera and in straight plays with Mary Anderson (Lady Capulet, Widow Melnotte). In the years that followed she played with E E Rice's company (*Horrors*, *Revels*, Gabriel in *Evangeline*), with J W Norcross and with Comley and Barton (1881, Christophe in *Les Cloches de Corneville*), on Broadway in Haverley's production of *The Merry War* (Else), in *Patience*, with Rice in *Orpheus in the Underworld* (Venus), with Lila Clay's all-woman troupe in *An Adamless Eden* (1884) and as Venus – again – in Sydney Rosenfeld's all-women adaptation of *Ixion*. She appeared regularly in burlesque where, given her fine, statuesque figure, she was frequently put into tights in such boy's rôles as Gabriel in *Evangeline*, Hassan in *Bluebeard* or Ixion in *Ixion*. She was a boy again when she appeared as Prince Orlofsky in *Die Fledermaus*, in German, at the Thalia Theater.

In 1885 she joined the Casino Theater company, and appeared with them in the second-lead rôle of Ninon de l'Enclos in Genée's *Nanon*, in *Amorita* (Pfingsten in Florenz) and as Sáffi in *The Gipsy Baron*, before being allotted the title-rôle of the first English musical to be staged at the Casino. *Erminie* created theatrical history and 26-year-old Miss Hall, in the role of Erminie de Pontvert – originated in London by Florence St John – found herself with the part of a lifetime. She played it for most of the virtual two-year run at the Casino, and became identified not only with the part but also with Erminie's lullaby 'Dear Mother, In Dreams I See Her', which became a huge nation-wide hit in America, in spite of having gone for little in Britain. She toured and toured again with this piece in the following years, and returned for further *Erminie* seasons at the Casino in 1889 and 1898.

In those years that followed, Miss Hall appeared – between *Erminie* productions – on Broadway in the star rôle of a grossly rewritten version of *La Fille du tambour-major* (*The Drum Major*), in Chassaigne's *Nadgy* and Offenbach's *La Princesse de Trébizonde* (Harrigan's Theater, 1894), and toured both as Offenbach's *Belle Hélène* and, again in breeches, as Vivian Trevalyan in a comic opera vehicle called *Puritania* (1892), which she played with her own comic opera company for several years. She was later seen in New York as *Madame Favart* and *La Belle Hélène*, in *Les Cloches de Corneville* and in the

Plate 120. **Pauline Hall:** *The beautiful American star of* Erminie.

title-rôle of Harry Paulton's *Dorcas*, before she retired briefly to marriage. Although she later returned to tour with Francis Wilson and to appear as Dame Durden in the 1912 revival of *Robin Hood* and as Lady Constance Wynne in an Arthur Hammerstein revival of *The Geisha* (1913), she remained inextricably connected with *Erminie* for the rest of her long career as a singer and an actress, a career which was closed by an appearance in David Belasco's play *The Gold Diggers* (1919) in which, shortly before her death, she appeared as an ageing comic opera star.

Miss Hall's second husband was George B McLellan, theatrical manager and brother to librettist C M S McLellan.

HALLELUJAH, BABY! Musical in 2 acts by Arthur Laurents. Lyrics by Adolph Green and Betty Comden. Music by Jule Styne. Martin Beck Theater, New York, 26 April 1967

A curiously tub-thumping piece written by three of Broadway's finest writers on one of their cloudier days, *Hallelujah, Baby!* took a conventional making-it-good-in-showbiz tale (with illustrations) and gave it the gimmick of an all-in leading character who did not age in her progress from beginning-of-the-century slavey-ing up through the some 80 or 90 years to present-day success, thus standing as a symbol of the ordinary, black-maid-risen-to-showbiz-stardom in 20th-century American society.

Georgina (Leslie Uggams) opens proceedings as a poor, new-century black girl whose boyfriend, Pullman porter Clem (Robert Hooks), ruins her chance of a straightforward wedded life by losing their marriage money playing craps. So Georgina, with the surely not disinterested

help of white man Harvey (Allen Case), goes into show business, and by the 1920s she has made her way into a New York cutie line. She sings for the troops in the War, gets to the glittering gowns and glitzy clubs (owned by white man Harvey) by the 1950s, and in the 1960s starts having 1960s-type qualms about her involvement with all these non-black people. So she drops helpful Harvey and goes back to Clem (who was a civil rights yeah-man in the 1950s) for a happy(?) and racially pure ending.

Laurents and Styne, authors of the recently successful *Gypsy*, once again built their story around show business and a large – though this time young – female leading rôle, in a piece which allowed 23-year-old Miss Uggams (instead of the originally intended Lena Horne) and the other performers/characters to present numbers written in the styles of the various periods that were passed through in the course of the evening. Harry Rigby, Albert Selden, Hal James and Jane C Nusbaum sponsored the production, which played 293 times on Broadway, and picked up the season's Tony Awards for best musical, best score and best actress (tied) after it had closed.

Recording: original cast (Columbia)

HALLER, Hermann [FREUND, Hermann] (b Berlin, 24 December 1871; d London, 5 May 1943). German producer and librettist who mounted some of Berlin's most successful musicals in the 1910s, and the city's glitziest revues in the 1920s.

In turn the director of the Olympia, Berlin (1894–6), the Haller-Ensemble (1896–1907), the Centraltheater, Leipzig (1907) and the Carl-Schultze Theater, Hamburg (from 1908), Haller followed up his first tentative ventures at authorship during his Hamburg years, and had some exportable success with the musical comedy *Parkettsitz Nr 10*, which launched the young composer, Walter Goetze, and with the Walter Kollo musical comedy *Der Juxbaron*, which went on from Hamburg to a fine career around central Europe.

Haller moved back to Berlin in 1914 to take over the Theater am Nollendorfplatz, and there he produced a series of new musicals, many of which were written to his own libretti. He began with a major hit when the patriotic wartime *Immer feste druff!* marked up a run of more than 650 performances, followed up with six months of *Blaue Jungens*, more than 200 nights of *Die Gulaschkanone* and nearly 500 of the *Quality Street* musical, *Drei alte Schachteln*, before beginning a series of collaborations with Eduard Künneke, of which the highpoint was the composer's most enduring work, the delightful *Der Vetter aus Dingsda*. When the last of these Künneke pieces, *Verliebte Leute*, disappointed in 138 performances, Haller switched to importing the proven *Ta bouche* from France with only average results, and *Die Königin von Montmartre* from the Netherlands (as *Die Königin der Strasse*) with decidedly poor ones.

He promptly divested himself of the Nollendorfplatz house, and resurfaced almost immediately at the Admiralspalast, which he opened in September 1923 with *Drunter und Druber*, the first of a series of spectacular revues on Parisian lines which would become famous in 1920s Berlin: *Noch und noch, Achtung! Welle 505!, An und Aus, Wann und Wo, Schön und Schick*. Haller's revues were concocted by their director/compiler after carefully scanning the best of what was on display in London, Paris and New York. He filched material freely from all three centres, but he hired top international talent, produced lavishly, and made his opening nights at the Admiralspalast into big, publicity-bearing social events. He also prospered as he built himself a reputation as a first-class showman.

In 1930 Haller varied his programming by mounting an extravaganza-style production of *Die Csárdásfürstin*. It flopped, and once again he moved on. Soon, however, under Nazi threat, he was forced to move further and, having stuck it out in central Europe until 1936, ultimately emigrated to London, where he died before the war's end.

1902 **Cupido & Co** (*Le Carnet du diable*) German version w Maurice Rappaport (Belle-Alliance-Theater)

1911 **Parkettsitz Nr 10** (Walter Goetze/w Willy Wolff) Tivoli Theater, Hamburg 24 September

1913 **Der Juxbaron** (Walter Kollo/Wolff/w Alexander Pordes-Milo) Carl-Schultze Theater, Hamburg 14 November

1914 **Immer feste druff!** (aka *Gloria Viktoria*) (Kollo/w Wolff) Theater am Nollendorfplatz 1 October

1916 **Blaue Jungens** (Rudolf Nelson/Herman Frey/w Kurt Kraatz) Theater am Nollendorfplatz 25 August

1917 **Die Gulaschkanone** (Kollo/w Wolff) Theater am Nollendorfplatz 23 February

1917 **Drei alte Schachteln** (Kollo/w 'Rideamus' [ie Fritz Oliven]) Theater am Nollendorfplatz 6 October

1919 **Der Vielgeliebte** (Eduard Künneke/w Rideamus) Theater am Nollendorfplatz 17 October

1920 **Wenn Liebe erwacht** (Künneke/w Rideamus) Theater am Nollendorfplatz 3 September

1921 **Der Vetter aus Dingsda** (Künneke/w Rideamus) Theater am Nollendorfplatz 15 April

1921 **Die Ehe im Kreise** (Künneke/w Rideamus) Theater am Nollendorfplatz 2 November

1922 **Verliebte Leute** (Künneke/w Rideamus) Theater am Nollendorfplatz 15 April

1922 **Dein Mund** (*Ta bouche*) German version w Rideamus (Theater am Nollendorfplatz)

1930 **Der doppelte Bräutigam** (Kollo/Wolff) Theater im Schiffbauerdamm 7 March

1937 **Herzklopfen** (Willi Rosen/w Max Bertuch) Johann Strauss-Theater, Vienna 4 June

HALLIDAY, Robert (b Loch Lomond, Scotland, 11 April 1893; d California, 195–?). Scots baritone who created several memorable American operetta rôles in the 1920s and 1930s.

Halliday moved to America at the age of 20 and toured as a chorister in musicals for several years before his earliest Broadway appearances in *The Rose Girl* (1921), *Springtime of Youth* (1922) and *Dew Drop Inn* (1923, Bobby Smith). He took over the hero's rôle in *Paradise Alley* (1924, Jack Harriman) at the Casino Theater, appeared alongside the Duncan Sisters in their curious *Uncle Tom's Cabin* musical, in which they starred jointly in the title-rôles of *Topsy and Eva* (1924, George Shelby), and spent the few performances of *Holka Polka* (*Frühling im Herbst*) at the Lyric Theatre (1925, Karel Boleslaw), before taking a supporting rôle in a rather more successful show, Gershwin's *Tip-Toes* (1925–6, Rollo), duetting 'Nice Baby' with the young Jeanette MacDonald.

Later the same year he had his first major success when he created the part of Pierre Birabeau, the Red Shadow, in Romberg's *The Desert Song*, introducing 'The Desert Song', 'One Alone' and 'The Riff Song', and he confirmed that success when he followed up as Robert Misson, the

equally romantic hero of *The New Moon* (1928), introducing 'Stouthearted Men' and, with his wife Evelyn Herbert, the famous duets 'Wanting You' and 'Lover Come Back to Me'.

The pair were cast together again in Broadway's *Princess Charming* (*Alexandra*, 1930, Torelli) and in the London production of *Waltzes from Vienna* (*Walzer aus Wien*, 1931, Johann Strauss jr), and Halliday subsequently played opposite Natalie Hall in *Music Hath Charms* (1934, Charles Parker) and her sister, Bettina Hall, in a revival of *The Only Girl*, appeared as the romantic Donald Hutton (ie Dr Seidler) in the American version of *Im weissen Rössl* (1936, *White Horse Inn*) on Broadway and went through another Red-Shadowy disguise to win Nancy McCord in the American première of *Beloved Rogue* (*Venus in Seide*) in St Louis (1935, The Stranger). He also appeared at the Muny in the American première of *Teresina* (Lavalette), *The Cat and the Fiddle* (Victor), *The Desert Song*, *Madame Sherry* and *The Chocolate Soldier*.

He toured Australia in 1937–8, appearing there in the baritone rôle of *Balalaika* and in his most famous rôle of the Red Shadow, and he made a final Broadway appearance, at almost 60, in a supporting rôle (but still with third billing) in *Three Wishes for Jamie* (1952). He and Miss Herbert then went into retirement in California, where he was seen in 1954 as Archie Beaton in San Francisco Light Opera's *Brigadoon*, but apparently died soon after.

HALTON, Marie [PRENDERGAST, Mary] (b New York, 3 August 1873; d unknown). Although wholly forgotten today, the irrepressible Miss Halton had one of the most remarkable international careers of the turn-of-the-century musical theatre.

By all (her) accounts, this doctor's daughter from New York began to study music in Paris at the age of 11, and was but 14 when she was cast as the little bride, Phyllis Tuppitt, in Broadway's production of *Dorothy* (1887). In 1889 she was seen at the Standard Theater in the co-starring rôle of Inez in *The Queen's Mate* (*La Princesse des Canaries*), and then at the Casino as the vivandière Claudine in *La Fille du tambour-major*, and in the lead rôle of Babette in *The Brazilian*, in which part she rolled and smoked a cigarette whilst singing a song on the subject. The *New York Times* remarked with more venom than seems objective that 'her acting is tiresome and her singing burdensome, and her gestures and poses are without significance, her reading of the lines is commonplace and dull, her voice is limited in compass and worn in quality and her method, like the earth before the creation, without form and void'. Not for the last time the *New York Times* drama critic and the rest of the world saw things with wholly different eyes.

After the failure of *The Brazilian* Miss Halton went on to play Clairette to the Lange of Camille D'Arville in *La Fille de Madame Angot*, before departing for Australia, where she had been hired as prima donna of J C Williamson's Royal Comic Opera Company for the 1892 season, playing Marton in *La Cigale*, the title-rôle of *Dorothy* and the title-rôle of Bizet's *Carmen*. However, with a nonchalance which would characterize her extraordinarily mobile career, she cut short the successful run of *La Cigale* and sallied forth from Australia to Britain. She arrived too late to take up the rôle intended for her in Horace Sedger's production of *The Wedding Eve* and, whilst he muttered of suing, began by presenting herself in the soubrette rôle of the musical *La Rosière* (1893). The show was not successful, but Marie was well enough noticed to be given leading rôles first in Albéniz's comic opera *The Magic Ring* (Lolika, 1893), then opposite Arthur Roberts in a specially written-in rôle with written-up songs ('You've Never Seen Me Here Before', 'The Magic of Spring') in *Claude Du-val*, and finally signed to a three-year starring contract by no less a manager than George Edwardes.

Edwardes announced that this new musical star would play the title-rôle in his new 'musical comedy' *The Naughty Girl*, at the Gaiety Theatre. In the event, the landmark show was called *The Shop Girl*, and Marie played the romantic juvenile rôle of the piece, leaving the soubrettery to Ada Reeve, whilst *A Naughty Girl* became Letty Lind's vehicle at Daly's, ultimately produced under the title *An Artist's Model*. Ill on opening night, Marie missed the opportunity to introduce *The Shop Girl*'s soprano ballad 'Over the Hills and Far Away', which was left to her understudy, but she returned soon after and duly played her part in Edwardes's famous show.

Quite where she disappeared to for the next year or so one cannot tell, for she scuttled off from London soon after the show's opening, and the famous three-year contract certainly does not seem to have been adhered to. But in 1896, having given birth (or whatever she was doing), she popped up in Paris, starring alongside Marguerite Deval in the Théâtre Marigny revue *Le Dernier des Marigny* ('a young American ... who has a fine voice, but whose acting is rather too eccentric'), and in 1897 was back on Broadway again, appearing in Oscar Hammerstein's comic opera *Santa Maria*. However, it was not a long home-stop, and in the following year, now 24(?) years of age, she launched herself on the rest of the European Continent. In February 1898 she was starred at Vienna's Carltheater as O Mimosa San in *Die Geisha* in German, after which she apparently departed for Russia, and later the same year, after a return visit to Vienna, she was seen in the same rôle at Budapest's Magyar Színház, this time performing *A gésak* in Hungarian.

In 1899 the Vienna Carltheater cast her in the multiple lead rôle of *Adam und Eva* opposite no less a co-star than Alexander Girardi himself, and she played the rôles of Eve, Madame Putiphar, Xantippe to his Sokrates, Dulcinea, and Signorina Roselli for the 52 performances of the run, before going on to star at the Theater an der Wien as Winifred Grey in *Ein durchgeganges Mädel* (*A Runaway Girl*). In February 1900 she created the title-rôle of Hugo Felix's *Rhodope* at the Carltheater, and then took up the title-rôle of *San Toy*, which she played at the Carltheater in German and later both at the Népszinház (December 1900) in Hungarian, then at Berlin's Centraltheater (2 March 1901), again in German, whilst giving her O Mimosa San here and there in between times.

In October 1903 she returned to the Carltheater one more time to star as Jane MacSherry, alongside Karl Blasel and Louis Treumann, in the Vienna production of *Madame Sherry*. She had the top billing. And then, at the (admitted) age of 30, having starred for some of the greatest musical theatre managers in the greatest musical theatre centres, from one end of the world to the other, Marie Halton, now a slightly plumpish soubrette, just disappeared from the

more obvious playbills of the world. Given her record, she probably ended up starring in operetta in China.

HAMILTON, Cosmo [né GIBBS] (b 1879; d Shanley Green, Surrey, 14 October 1942).

Author, journalist, the writer of a dozen or so English plays and several more for America (amongst which a number were taken from the French), Hamilton also collaborated on the texts for several musical comedies. He began with the libretto for the highly successful Cinderella musical, *The Catch of the Season*, built around Seymour Hicks and his wife, Ellaline Terriss, as a modern-day prince and his fireside waif, and he repeated the same task for another Hicks/Terriss vehicle, *The Beauty of Bath*, but he was involved in some controversy when his name appeared on the bill for *The Belle of Mayfair*, the show from which all theatreland knew that Basil Hood had recently withdrawn his name after his book had been unsatisfactorily altered by the producer.

He was at the source of an unlikely half-success when he tacked a new plot onto some songs from the zarzuela *La gran via* and some more by the English-born Parisian music-hall star, Harry Fragson, to provide a stage vehicle for the latter as *Castles in Spain*, but thereafter, apart from a few adaptations, both while living in Britain and later in America, he worked only for the straight stage.

His play *The Hoyden*, adapted from the French comedy *La Soeur* by Tristan Bernard, was musicalized by Paul Rubens and Frank Tours for Charles Dillingham and Charles Frohman as a Broadway vehicle for Elsie Janis in 1907.

1904 **The Catch of the Season** (Herbert Haines, Evelyn Baker/Charles H Taylor/w Seymour Hicks) Vaudeville Theatre 9 September
1906 **The Beauty of Bath** (Haines/Taylor/w Hicks) Aldwych Theatre 19 March
1906 **The Belle of Mayfair** (Leslie Stuart/w C H E Brookfield) Vaudeville Theatre 11 April
1906 **Castles in Spain** (Chueca, Valverde, Harry Fragson/Eustace Ponsonby) Royalty Theatre 18 April
1907 **The Hoyden** (Paul Rubens, Frank E Tours) Knickerbocker Theater, New York 19 October
1909 **The Merry Peasant** (*Der fidele Bauer*) English version (Strand Theatre)
1916 **Flora Bella** English version w Dorothy Donnelly (Casino Theater, New York)
1917 **The Star Gazer** (*Der Sterngucker*) English version w Matthew C Woodward (Plymouth Theater, New York)

Autobiography: *Unwritten History* (Hutchinson, London, 1924)

HAMILTON, Henry (b Nunhead, Surrey, ?1853; d Sandgate, Kent, 4 September 1918).

At first an actor with J B Howard, Wilson Barrett, F Craven Robertson, the Pitt-Hamilton Company and others, then a playwright, Hamilton latterly had considerable success with his adaptation of Ouida, *Moths* (1882), and a series of dramas written with Cecil Raleigh for the Theatre Royal, Drury Lane (*The Great Ruby, The Whip, White Heather, The Sins of Society, The Hope, Sealed Orders*).

His first attempt in the musical theatre was with the grandiose *The Lady of the Locket* (1885), but he made more of mark when the song 'Private Tommy Atkins' (for which he was responsible for the lyrics), originally written for actor Charles Arnold and played by him as part of a protean musical comedy-drama *Captain Fritz*, turned out to be the interpolated hit of the musical comedy *A Gaiety Girl* (1893). He supplied words for several other successful show songs performed by baritone Hayden Coffin, including the wartime 'Hands Off!' and the rolling drawing-room-ballad 'Freedom' in *A Greek Slave*, and had a number, 'Peek-a-Boo' (music: Meyer Lutz), sung by Minnie Palmer in *My Sweetheart*. But apart from collaborating with Raleigh and Augustus Harris on the text of a Drury Lane pantomime, he did not make any further inroads on the musical theatre until 1903, when he suddenly became very visible.

In one 12-month period came the production of the successful Leslie Stuart musical *The School Girl*, on the libretto of which Hamilton had collaborated with another well-known playwright, Paul Potter; the staging of *The Duchess of Dantzic*, a piece which he had written with Ivan Caryll some years before, and which proved to be the most critically admired of all its composer's many works; and the West End production of Messager's *Véronique* for which he had prepared the English libretto.

George Edwardes used him as adaptor for a second Messager musical, *Les P'tites Michu*, with equal success, but although he subsequently provided the English text for Edwardes's production of Kálmán's *Tatárjárás* (*Autumn Manoeuvres*), his brief but highly effective spasm of work for the musical theatre was otherwise done.

1885 **The Lady of the Locket** (William Fullerton) Empire Theatre 11 March
1903 **The School Girl** (Leslie Stuart/Charles H Taylor/w Paul Potter) Prince of Wales Theatre 9 May
1903 **The Duchess of Dantzic** (Ivan Caryll) Lyric Theatre 17 October
1904 **Véronique** English version (Apollo Theatre)
1905 **The Little Michus** (*Les P'tites Michu*) English version (Daly's Theatre)
1912 **Autumn Manoeuvres** (*Tatárjárás*) English version (Adelphi Theatre)

HAMLISCH, Marvin [Frederick] (b New York, 2 June 1944). Successful film composer who turned to the stage in the 1970s and launched two major international hits on a Broadway which was sadly thin on new composing stars.

Hamlisch studied originally as a classical pianist before moving on to a songwriting career which had its first landmark in 1965 when his song 'Sunshine, Lollipops and Roses' made its way to the hit parades. He began his theatre work as a rehearsal pianist (*Funny Girl*, *Fade Out – Fade In*) and a dance-music arranger (*Golden Rainbow*, 1968), but a career as a composer of film songs intervened and, beginning with *The Swimmer* (1968), he provided songs for a series of movies including *Take the Money and Run*, *The April Fools* (1969), *Bananas*, *Kotch* (1971, 'Life is What You Make It') and *Save the Tiger* (1972), and peaking with the score (Academy Award) and title-song to the Barbra Streisand film *The Way We Were* (1973, w Marilyn and Alan Bergman, Academy Award) and the complement to and adaptation of Scott Joplin's music as heard in *The Sting* (Academy Award).

His first venture into the musical theatre was a dazzling one. In 1975 he provided the musical score for the phenomenally long-lived *A Chorus Line* ('What I Did for Love', 'At the Ballet', 'Nothing', 'One', Tony Award), but,

after this success, he once again concentrated on writing for television (*The Entertainer*) and film – *The Spy Who Loved Me* (1977, 'Nobody Does it Better'), *Same Time Next Year* (1978, 'The Last Time I Felt Like This'), *Starting Over*, *Ice Castles*, *The Champ* (1979), *Ordinary People* (1980) – and did not produce a second Broadway score until 1979.

They're Playing Our Song, a pop music-based piece with a number of its songs presented as full-frontal pop singles ('I Still Believe in Love', 'Fallin'', 'When You're in my Arms'), recounted the ups and downs of the professional and personal association of a composer and his (female) lyricist, and was said to echo the real lives of Hamlisch and his lyricist Carole Bayer Sager. If this is indeed so, that makes it the first autobiographical musical after the long line of biographical ones. It was, autobiographical or not, a major international hit.

Hamlisch's subsequent ventures into the musical theatre did not have the same outstanding success as his first. A 1983 musical on the life of actress *Jean Seberg*, staged at London's National Theatre, was an undistinguished failure which seemed to have come from a different pen, and the adaptation of the beauty-pageant screenplay, *Smile*, was a quick Broadway failure.

1975 **A Chorus Line** (Edward Kleban/James Kirkwood, Nicholas Dante) Public Theater 15 April, Shubert Theater 25 July
1979 **They're Playing Our Song** (Carol Bayer Sager/Neil Simon) Imperial Theater 11 February
1983 **Jean Seberg** (Christopher Adler/Julian Barry) National Theatre, London 15 November
1986 **Smile** (Howard Ashman) Lunt-Fontanne Theater 24 November
1993 **The Goodbye Girl** (David Zippel/Neil Simon) Marquis Theater 4 March

Autobiography: w Gardner, G: *The Way I Was* (Scribner, New York, 1992)

HAMMERSTEIN, Oscar (b Stettin, 8 May 1847; d New York, 1 August 1919).

Producer Hammerstein worked principally in the operatic world where, in a career full of financial ups and downs, he constructed and/or ran first the Harlem Opera House, then the Columbus Theater, the Manhattan Theatre (later Koster and Bial's), Hammerstein's Olympia, Hammerstein's Victoria, and finally the Manhattan Opera House (1906). He operated this last with such social – if not exactly financial – success that the Metropolitan Opera, suffering in reputation and box-office, was forced to buy him out of the operatic field (1910).

At one stage, having already – amongst his multitude of other activities – tried his composing hand at grand opera, he struck a $1,000 wager with theatre composer Gustave Kerker that he could write and compose a light musical show in 24 hours. He was satisfied enough with his effort to put *Koh-I-Noor* on the stage, and it played two weeks at Koster and Bial's before moving on to its author/composer's Harlem Opera House. He followed this first effort with others, including *Santa Maria* (1896) whose three months' run encouraged him to dip further into the light musical theatre, producing two more self-written pieces called *Mrs Rudley Bradley Ball* ('a spectacular extravaganza') and something called *War Bubbles*, which sufficed to send the Olympia (rechristened the Lyric) into receivership.

When he started up operations again, at the Victoria, he also tried authorship again. He did poorly with *Sweet Marie* (1901) and better with a variety piece called *Punch and Judy & Co*, both of which he may or may not have written himself, but after that he confined his attentions to things operatic until 1910, when he brought Ganne's delightful French opérette *Hans, le joueur de flûte* to the Manhattan Opera House. It was after the unhappy end of his operation there, however, that he produced his one big musical theatre hit, when he commissioned a vehicle for Emma Trentini, and the rest of the opera company whom he still held under contract, from Victor Herbert, and got *Naughty Marietta*.

1892 **Koh-I-Noor** Koster and Bial's Music Hall 30 October
1896 **Marguerite** Hammerstein's Olympia 10 February
1896 **Santa Maria** Hammerstein's Olympia 24 September
1897 **Mrs Radley Bradley Ball, or In Greater New York** Hammerstein's Lyric 7 March
1898 **War Bubbles** (pasticcio) Hammerstein's Lyric 16 May
1901 **Sweet Marie** Hammerstein's Victoria 10 October
1903 **Punch and Judy & Co** Paradise Roof Garden 1 June

Biography: Sheean, V: *Oscar Hammerstein I: the Life and Exploits of an Impresario* (Simon & Schuster, New York, 1956)

His son, **Arthur HAMMERSTEIN** (b New York, 21 December 1875; d Palm Beach, Fla, 12 October 1955), followed his father into the production arena, taking up where the older Hammerstein had begun with *Naughty Marietta*, and producing the second Emma Trentini operetta, *The Firefly*, with considerable success. He thereafter mounted composer Friml's *High Jinks*, *Katinka*, *You're in Love*, *Sometime* and *The Blue Kitten*, to almost unalloyed good effect, but had rather less success when he put his faith in another neophyte composer, Herbert Stothart, in whose *Somebody's Sweetheart* he himself took credit for a couple of late additional songs, and whom he later teamed with his lyric-writing nephew, Oscar Hammerstein II, on *Always You*, *Tickle Me*, *Jimmie* and *Daffy Dill*.

When Hammerstein put this, till now not particularly successful, pair together with composer Vincent Youmans for *Wildflower*, better times returned, but, when he teamed them with Friml, the result was the greatest success of his career as a producer: *Rose Marie*. It was a success which he did not really approach again. When the pair were put to work with a third prominent composer, George Gershwin, they produced the reasonably successful *Song of the Flame*, but Friml's *The Wild Rose*, Kálmán's *Golden Dawn*, *Good Boy*, *Polly*, Jerome Kern's nevertheless appreciable *Sweet Adeline*, Friml's South Seas musical *Luana* and the W C Fields flop *Ballyhoo* brought mostly diminishing returns, and Hammerstein withdrew from Broadway musical producing in 1930.

HAMMERSTEIN, Oscar [Greeley Clendenning] II

(b New York, 12 July 1895; d Doylestown, Pa, 23 August 1960).

The grandson of the first Oscar, and the son of William Hammerstein, who had also worked in the theatre as a theatre manager, Oscar II was sent to study law and graduated to work in a legal office. However, he left that office to work for his uncle, Arthur, as an assistant and then a full-blown stage manager. It was Arthur who produced his nephew's first and wholly unsuccessful attempt at playwriting, but his earliest experience of the musical theatre came with university and amateur shows, and it was only after several years of such an apprenticeship that Oscar II got his first shot at musical Broadway. Again, it was Uncle Arthur who mounted the piece which started out as *Joan of Ark-ansaw* but which finally made it to town as *Always You*. The show had a very limited amount of success, but it apparently showed sufficient signs of promise for Arthur to bring his nephew back to work with the experienced Otto Harbach and Frank Mandel on the just slightly more successful *Tickle Me* and the flop, *Jimmie*.

A collaboration with Guy Bolton on *Daffy Dill* brought no credit to either of them, and the Nora Bayes vehicle *Queen o' Hearts* passed by in just 39 Broadway nights, but Uncle Arthur's continued patronage was finally rewarded when the younger Oscar and Otto Harbach first contributed materially to the success of *Wildflower* ('Bambalina') and then supplied the book and lyrics for Arthur Hammerstein's biggest success, *Rose Marie* ('Rose Marie', 'Indian Love Call'). But, in true theatrical fashion, whilst the young man was enjoying his biggest success, he was also lending his name to a vast flop. A 'Musical Comedy Guild' backed to the tune of $2 million by a Coca-Cola magnate, who had announced his intention to 'elevate American musical comedy', called Hammerstein in to doctor their opening show, *The Purple Cow*. It limped through engagements in Washington and Pittsburg and closed. Mr Coca-Cola withdrew his guarantee and Oscar went back to (if he had ever left) *Rose Marie*.

Now thoroughly launched to the upper strata of his profession, Hammerstein followed up this huge hit by providing lyrics and libretti, either alone or in collaboration, to a series of the most successful and enduring shows of the later 1920s, from which Jerome Kern's *Sunny* (1925, 'Who?', 'Sunny', 'Two Little Bluebirds') and *Show Boat* ('Ol' Man River', 'Make Believe', 'Can't Help Lovin' Dat Man' etc), and Sigmund Romberg's *The Desert Song* ('One Alone', 'The Desert Song' etc) and *The New Moon* ('Lover, Come Back to Me', 'Softly, As in a Morning Sunrise', 'Stouthearted Men', 'One Kiss') and their songs stand out as the most memorable and enduring examples. *Show Boat* and *The New Moon* found Hammerstein the lyricist, in particular, showing enormous advances on the pretty banalities in which he and other lyric-writers had wallowed during the first part of the decade, turning out, in his best numbers, thoughtful and substantial romantic lyrics which have lasted through more than half a century with a surprising lack of visible ageing.

Show Boat marked the début of the author in another capacity, that of director, and following that stunning start he directed a large number of the 1920s and 1930s shows with which he was subsequently connected. The 1930s, however, brought little to equal his work of the 1920s. He wrote and directed two end-of-career flops for *New Moon* producer Mandel, provided one of his most unappetizing texts for Jerome Kern's kitsch-Mittel-European *Music in the Air* (but saved the affair by contributing the lyrics to 'I've Told Ev'ry Little Star' and 'The Song is You'), adapted the Continental hit *Ball im Savoy* for London's Theatre Royal, Drury Lane, and combined again with Kern for the short-lived *Three Sisters* and for *Very Warm for May* ('All the Things You Are'). He also ventured into films, working on such screen pieces as *The Night is Young, Reckless, Give Us This Night, High, Wide and Handsome, Swing High, Swing Low, I'll Take Romance, The Lady Objects* and *The Great Waltz*, in which he turned the *Zigeunerbaron* Dompfaff duo into 'One Day When We Were Young' and lyricked 'I'm in Love With Vienna' etc, in a Hollywood where his stage successes of the 1920s were now being used as the bases for musical films.

The 1940s, however, relaunched Hammerstein on a second enormously successful era in the musical theatre. With the decline and demise of Larry Hart, he began a partnership with the late lyricist's partner of always, composer Richard Rodgers. Their first work together, *Oklahoma!* ('The Surrey with the Fringe On Top', 'People Will Say We're in Love', 'I Cain't Say 'No'', 'Oh, What a Beautiful Mornin'' etc), was a major international hit, and almost single-handed it rekindled the fashion for the classic operetta, which had frittered away somewhat in the 1930s, on the American stage. After Hammerstein had taken time out to write the book and lyrics to an updated rearrangement of Bizet's *Carmen* (*Carmen Jones*), the new partnership worked solidly together for the next 16 years, up until Hammerstein's death in 1960. Their works together included four which, with *Oklahoma!*, go to make up the backbone of the surviving romantic musical play repertoire of the Broadway 1940s and 1950s – *Carousel, South Pacific, The King and I* and *The Sound of Music*.

In earlier days Rodgers had also operated as a producer, and after the production of *Allegro* he and Hammerstein began to mount productions of their own. The plays *I Remember Mama*, Anita Loos's *Happy Birthday* (for which they supplied a song) and *John Loves Mary*, a revival of *Show Boat* and the mounting of the enormously successful *Annie Get Your Gun* started things off on the right foot, and they subsequently produced the last six of their own shows, from *South Pacific* to *The Sound of Music*, on Broadway and in London.

Hammerstein's remarkable double-peaked career resulted in an enduring contribution to the Broadway stage which no other lyricist/librettist has surpassed, with pieces from both his successful periods being the corner-stones of the most revived part of their respective eras of the American musical theatre repertoire. His work as a writer came to its first peak in the songs and texts for *Show Boat* and for *The New Moon*, but he was ultimately best suited in the shows which he wrote with Rodgers, where his simple, often inspired, song ideas, his frequently sentimental but unhackneyed lyrics, and his tightly constructed libretti were popular models in Broadway's most successful years.

Two Rodgers and Hammerstein works originally written for other media were subsequently produced as stage musicals – the television version of the *Cinderella* tale, mounted at the London Coliseum with Tommy Steele as Buttons, and their fresh rewrite of the film *State Fair*, staged at St Louis with Ron Husmann and Carol Richards as its young lead players.

1920 **Always You** (ex-*Joan of Ark-ansaw*) (Herbert Stothart) Central Theater 5 January
1920 **Tickle Me** (Stothart/w Otto Harbach, Frank Mandel) Selwyn Theater 17 August

1920 **Jimmie** (Stothart/w Harbach/w Harbach, Mandel) Apollo Theater 17 November
1922 **Daffy Dill** (Stothart/w Guy Bolton) Apollo Theater 22 August
1922 **Queen o' Hearts** (Lewis Gensler, Dudley Wilkinson/w Mandel) Cohan Theater 10 October
1923 **Wildflower** (Vincent Youmans, Stothart/w Harbach) Casino Theater 7 February
1923 **Mary Jane McKane** (Youmans, Stothart/w William Cary Duncan) Imperial Theater 25 December
1924 **Rose Marie** (Rudolf Friml, Stothart/w Harbach) Imperial Theater 2 September
1925 **Sunny** (Kern/w Harbach) New Amsterdam Theater 22 September
1925 **Song of the Flame** (George Gershwin, Stothart/w Harbach) 44th Street Theater 30 December
1926 **The Wild Rose** (Friml/w Harbach) Martin Beck Theater 20 October
1926 **The Desert Song** (Romberg/w Harbach/w Harbach, Frank Mandel) Casino Theater 30 November
1927 **Golden Dawn** (Emmerich Kálmán, Stothart/w Harbach) Hammerstein's Theater 30 November
1927 **Show Boat** (Kern) Ziegfeld Theater 27 December
1928 **Good Boy** (Stothart, Bert Kalmar, Harry Ruby/w Harbach, Henry Meyers) Hammerstein's Theater 5 September
1928 **The New Moon** (Romberg/w Mandel, Laurence Schwab) Imperial Theater 19 September
1928 **Rainbow** (Youmans/w Laurence Stallings) Gallo Theater 21 November
1929 **Sweet Adeline** (Kern) Hammerstein's Theater 3 September
1930 **Ballyhoo** (Louis Alter/w Harry Ruskin, Leighton Brill) Hammerstein's Theater 22 December
1931 **The Gang's All Here** (Gensler/w Russel Crouse, Morrie Ryskind) Imperial 18 February
1931 **Free for All** (Richard Whiting/w Schwab) Manhattan Theater 8 September
1931 **East Wind** (Romberg/w Mandel) Manhattan Theater 27 October
1932 **Music in the Air** (Kern) Alvin Theater 8 November
1933 **Ball at the Savoy** (*Ball im Savoy*) English version (Theatre Royal, Drury Lane, London)
1934 **Three Sisters** (Kern) Theatre Royal, Drury Lane, London 9 April
1935 **May Wine** (Romberg/Mandel) St James Theater 5 December
1938 **Gentlemen Unafraid** (Kern/w Harbach) Municipal Opera, St Louis 3 June
1939 **Very Warm for May** (Kern) Alvin Theater 17 November
1941 **Sunny River** (ex- *New Orleans*) (Romberg) St James Theater 4 December
1943 **Oklahoma!** (Richard Rodgers) St James Theater 31 March
1943 **Carmen Jones** (Bizet arr/Henri Meilhac, Ludovic Halévy ad) Broadway Theater 2 December
1945 **Carousel** (Rodgers) Majestic Theater 19 April
1947 **Allegro** (Rodgers) Majestic Theater 10 October
1949 **South Pacific** (Rodgers/w Joshua Logan) Majestic Theater 7 April
1951 **The King and I** (Rodgers) St James Theater 29 March
1953 **Me and Juliet** (Rodgers) Majestic Theater 28 May
1955 **Pipe Dream** (Rodgers) Shubert Theater 30 November
1958 **Flower Drum Song** (Rodgers/w Joseph Fields) St James Theater 1 December
1958 **Cinderella** (Rodgers) London Coliseum 18 December
1959 **The Sound of Music** (Rodgers/Crouse, Howard Lindsay) Lunt-Fontanne Theater 16 November
1969 **State Fair** (Rodgers/Lucille Kallen) Municipal Opera, St Louis 2 June

Biographies: Taylor, D: *Some Enchanted Evenings* (Harpers, New

York, 1953); Fordin, H: *Getting to Know Him* (Random House, New York, 1977); Literature: Green, S: *The Rodgers and Hammerstein Story* (Day, New York, 1963); Rodgers, R: *Musical Stages* (Random House, New York, 1975); Nolan, F: *The Sound of Their Music* (Dent, New York, 1978); Mordden, E: *Rodgers and Hammerstein* (Abrams, New York, 1992) etc.

HANNERL Singspiel in 3 acts by A M Willner and Heinz Reichert. Music from the works of Franz Schubert arranged by Karl Lafite. Raimundtheater, Vienna, 8 February 1918.

The unprecedented success of *Das Dreimäderlhaus* at Wilhelm Karczag's Raimundtheater inevitably encouraged the theatre to try a musequel. The authors of the earlier hit were set to work on the tale of Hannerl, the daughter of Baron Schober and of Hannerl Tschöll, the pair whose wedding at the end of the first piece had broken the heart of Franz Schubert. They provided a slim and conventional little tale, which only the giving of the required second-hand names to the characters, and the very occasional reminiscence, gave *Hannerl* any connection at all with the earlier piece.

Anni Rainer, the Hannerl Tschöll of *Das Dreimäderlhaus*, now played her own daughter, grown up enough for her first ball and smitten with young Baron Hans von Gumpenberg (M de Taxi). As a result of a stone thrown at the wrong window, however, three acts of complications occur and Hannerl ends up in tears at the ball when Hans seems to be attracted by Aranka (Klara Karry), the daughter of the Countess Clementine Oroszy (Mitzi Warbeck), whose window had received the pebble. But papa Schober (Otto Langer) arrives back with the happy news that he has arranged for Hannerl's betrothal to the son of a friend. It is, of course, Hans. Fritz Neumann played Hannerl's brother, tactfully called Franz, who ran a secondary romance with her best friend, Helene (Gretl Martin), and one of the few, rather tacked in, echoes of the older piece came with the introduction of Franz Glawatsch in his original rôle of the now very old Christian Tschöll. When it came to the music for the piece, however, Harry Berté, still smarting from having to arrange rather than compose the score for the earlier piece, refused to become involved and Karczag replaced him with Karl Lafite.

Like most musequels, the piece came nowhere near living up to its original, but it passed its 100th night at the Raimundtheater (15 May 1917), and it remained in the repertoire at the house until Karczag's management ended, and the musical content of the house's programme shrank away. At the same time it also moved on to productions in other houses looking for a second *Dreimäderlhaus*. In Berlin it followed straight on behind the phenomenal run of *Das Dreimäderlhaus* at the Friedrich-Wilhelmstädtisches Theater, and the older piece actually played its 1,000th performance at a matinée during the run of *Hannerl* in the evening slot, giving the two 'episodes' of the tale in one day. The show ran a good six months.

Hungary showed no more taste for *Médi* (ad Zsolt Harsányi) than Vienna had done, when the show was produced at the Vigszinház with Ilka Pálmay featured as Médi, the mother, and Erzsi Péchey as the daughter, again on the heels of their successful mounting of *Das Dreimäderlhaus*.

Whereas the older piece had won a fine 155 performances, *Médi* made do with a milder 38.

An American performance was mounted for one night in Baltimore in 1924 under the management of the Johann Strauss-Theater Company, with a fine Austrian cast headed by Walter Jankuhn, Mizzi Delorm and Paul Dietz, playing in German. In spite of the vast success of *Blossom Time*, it did not persuade anyone to take up the show for Broadway.

Hungary: Vigszinház *Médi* 21 June 1918; Germany: Friedrich-Wilhelmstädtisches Theater 13 September 1918; USA: Lyric Theater, Baltimore 10 January 1924

HANS ANDERSEN Musical in 2 acts by Tommy Steele and Beverley Cross. Lyrics and music from the film score *Hans Christian Andersen* and other works by Frank Loesser. Additional numbers by Marvin Laird. London Palladium, 17 December 1974.

A musical put together around the well-loved score written by Frank Loesser for the 1952 film *Hans Christian Andersen* ('The Ugly Duckling', 'Wonderful Copenhagen', 'Inchworm', 'Thumbelina' etc), in which Danny Kaye had appeared as the Scandinavian poet and author of the title. Producer Harold Fielding, star Tommy Steele and librettist Beverley Cross, who had teamed a decade earlier on *Half a Sixpence*, came together again to construct and produce the piece as a vehicle for Steele, and they scored a fine success through a year's run at the Palladium, a national tour, and a subsequent return to the West End for a second season (17 December 1977), starring Steele and Sally Ann Howes, before the show went on into regional and overseas productions.

Hans Andersen (Steele), the Odense cobbler who keeps the local children amused with his tales, has ambitions as a dramatic author, but his lack of education bars him from putting anything readable on paper. When a mysterious passer-by, Otto (Milo O'Shea), takes him to the theatre, he meets the great soprano, Jenny Lind (Colette Gleeson), who encourages him to go back to school. It is she, again, years later who encourages him to put aside his attempts at 'serious' writing, and to put his children's tales into book form. Hans wins fame and fortune, but not Jenny, whose interest has been friendly but not loving.

Steele sang the famous songs, Jenny Lind (rewritten at a late stage as the singer – the character was originally to have been a ballerina, and Gillian Lynne had been hired to choreograph) was given 'Truly Loved', taken from the score of Loesser's *Pleasures and Palaces*, and joined the star in 'No Two People (have ever been so in love)', whilst several other little- or un-used Loesser pieces were topped off with some additional songs by Marvin Laird, of which a jolly piece for Steele, O'Shea (whose originally co-starring part shrank to nothing in rehearsals) and the chorus, 'Happy Days', and a spelling-song, 'Ecclesiasticus', proved lively interludes.

In spite of its success, the London version of *Hans Andersen* was prevented from playing in America, where another version, under the title *Hans Christian Andersen*, was played regionally. Yet another version, written by Irene Manning, was produced in Germany.

Recordings: original cast (Pye), London revival cast (Pye) etc

HANSEN, Max (b Mannheim, 22 December 1897; d Copenhagen, 12 November 1961). Favourite tenor/light comedian of the German stage up until the Hitler era.

Hansen was born in Mannheim, the son of a Danish actress working there, and brought up in Munich, where he made his first appearance on stage, as a child, as a dwarf in *Snow White*. He went on to work as a singer in pubs, clubs and cabarets, appearing in Denmark and Norway during and after the First World War, and made his first Viennese appearances at the Établissement Ronacher before being taken up by the Theater an der Wien as a replacement for Josef König in the rôle of Metellus in *Die Bacchusnacht* (1923). He went on to create the rôle of the comical Baron Zsupán in *Gräfin Mariza* at the same house, but his name, and the best part of his career thereafter, was made in Berlin.

He played in Berlin's *No, No, Nanette* (1926) and *Die Zirkusprinzessin* (1927, Toni), appeared alongside Rita Georg in Granichstädten's *Evelyne*, and then moved on to take part in some of the large-stage productions of Erik Charell, for whom he featured alongside Frizi Massary as Camille in the souped-up *Die lustige Witwe*, as Aramis to the Porthos of Sig Arno and the D'Artagnan of Alfred Jerger in *Die drei Musketiere* and, ultimately, in the part of his career, created the little waiter, Leopold, in *Im weissen Rössl* (1930).

Hansen appeared in the Berlin production of the unsuccessful *Hundert Meter Glück* (1932), paired with his wife, soubrette Lizzi Waldmüller, in the popular *Petite Chocolatière* musical comedy, *Bezauberndes Fräulein* (1933, Paul), in both Berlin and Vienna, and starred as the suddenly rich waiter Franz in Benatzky's *Das kleine Café* at Vienna's Deutsches Volkstheater. For a while, it seemed that his popularity on the German stage might outface his Jewishness. However, he took more and more engagements abroad, notably in Scandinavia, and ultimately quit Berlin, first for Vienna, where he scored a notable success starred opposite Zarah Leander in the Hollywooden musical comedy, *Axel an der Himmelstür* (1936), and as Seppl Huber (ski-teacher at Saint-Anton and Olympic champion!) in *Herzen am Schnee* (1937, also director), and then for Sweden.

There he appeared on the stage in a number of the classic Operette rôles of the tenor-comic repertoire (Menelaus, Calicot, Célestin), as well as in films, and did not return to Germany until the beginning of the 1950s, celebrating his return with a repeat of his most famous rôle, the Leopold of *Im weissen Rössl*, in 1951. The latter part of his career was largely devoted to film appearances.

His wife, **Lizzi WALDMÜLLER** (b Knittelfeld, Steiermark, 25 May 1904; d Vienna, 8 April 1945) was one of the most popular German musical comedy performers of her time, both on stage and film. After an early career in juvenile rôles in Austria, she made her mark when she appeared on the Berlin and Vienna stage as O Lia San in *Viktoria und ihr Husar* (1930), and subsequently created the rôle of Monika in *Glückliche Reise* and the title-rôle in *Bezauberndes Fräulein* (1933).

Autobiography: *Det måste vara underbart* (Copenhagen, 1955)

HANS, LE JOUEUR DE FLÛTE Opéra-comique in 3 acts by Maurice Vaucaire and Georges Mitchell. Music by Louis Ganne. Théâtre de Monte-Carlo, Monaco, 14 April 1906.

The most attractive of Ganne's limited output of musical plays, *Hans, le joueur de flûte*, a retelling of the tale of the pied piper of Hamelin with a difference, was first mounted in Monaco, where Ganne had made a considerable reputation at the head of the Concerts Louis Ganne and his hand-picked orchestra.

The town of Milkatz is a prosperous one and its Burgomaster, Pippermann (Poudrier), and town council have only one preoccupation – the grain trade. All else – local traditions, arts, crafts, fêtes – has been abandoned in the frantic pursuit of the benefits of commerce. Only the poet Yoris (Alberthal) yearns for the artistic past, and he has spent his time making one of the life-sized dolls with which the villagers used to compete for festival honours in days gone by. His doll shows where his heart is, for it is made in the image of Lisbeth (Mariette Sully), the burgomaster's daughter. When the strange, wandering Hans (Jean Périer) comes to town, only Yoris befriends him, and Hans takes his revenge on blinkered, profit-mad Milkatz by using his magic flute to lead all the town's cats to drown in the river, leaving the grain stores prey to a plague of mice. His price for stopping the mice is the restoration of, and a town subsidy for, the old festivals, and the doll competition. The townsfolk join in the doll-making and the fête as of yore and Yoris wins both the competition and Lisbeth before Hans, the flute-player, goes his way.

Ganne's score was full of charm and gentle parody as it brought on the bumbling town guard ('Un, deux, au pas, sacrebleu'), had Yoris apostrophizing the past in a passionate tenor ('Vous n'êtes plus, pauvres poupées') or Lisbeth regretting her father's shop-keeper mentality ('Mon cher petit père est un commerçant'), but it rose to its heights in its first-act finale, a marvellously tongue-in-cheek piece in which, to a big, romantic melody, the citizens of Milkatz bewail the fate of their protective pussies ('Adieu, petits minets, petits minous'), and in Hans's two principal numbers, the mysterious 'Je viens d'un pays lointain' and the memorable march, 'Cette flûte qui mena le monde'.

Following its Monegasque season, *Hans, le joueur de flûte* stagnated a while, but in 1910 Alphonse Franck, rich on *Veuve Joyeuse* profits, decided to mount the show at his Parisian Théâtre Apollo. Périer and Poudrier took up their original rôles with Gina Féraud as Lisbeth and Henri Defreyn as Yoris for a season of four weeks before Périer – the star and raison d'être of the production – had to move on to the Opéra-Comique. It was another 18 years before the piece was again seen in Paris, at the Gaîté-Lyrique with Gilbert Moryn starred. It was reproduced once more at the same house (17 February 1936) but, although still beloved by connoisseurs, it has not survived on the stage with the same vigour as its composer's more colourful but less worthy *Les Saltimbanques*.

The Paris season, however, quickly won the piece overseas productions. Within months, Oscar Hammerstein mounted it (ad Algernon St John Brennan) at his Manhattan Opera House, with a cast headed by Georges Chadal (Hans), Sophie Brandt (Lisbeth), Frank Pollack (Yoris) and George W Callahan (Pippermann) for a season of 79 performances, and *Hans, der Flötenspieler* (ad Felix Falzari) appeared in German in Breslau, whilst Budapest's Népopera mounted an Hungarian version (ad Miksa Bródy) early in 1912.

The pied piper of Hamelin, and variations on his theme, has been the subject of many stage pieces, of which Viktor Nessler's 1879 *Der Rattenfänger von Hameln*, first produced in Leipzig, and widely seen in German and in English over more than half a century, was the most successful. Adolf Neuendorff, conductor and sometime manager of the New York German theatres also produced his own German-language *Der Rattenfänger von Hameln* (lib: H Italianer, Germania Theater, 14 December 1880), which was played again a decade later at the Amberg Theater. In more recent times, a rock version of the tale written by Richard Jarboe, Harvey Shield and Matthew Wells under the title *Hamelin* was seen at New York's Circle in the Square Downtown (10 November 1985, 33 performances) and an hilariously awful children's entertainment in which the crippled child was characterized as an Aggressively Handicapped Person was mounted at London's National Theatre.

In 1908 De Wolf Hopper appeared on Broadway as the Piper in a sequel to the favourite tale, *The Pied Piper* (Manuel Klein/R H Burnside, Majestic Theater 3 December), which went inside the magic mountain to look at the descendents of the lost children, many years later. When the numbers of boys and girls is discovered to be unequal he has to import extra children to ensure suitable pairings, and the importation of 'foreigners' soon brings problems to his City of Innocence.

France: Théâtre Apollo 31 May 1910; USA: Manhattan Opera House 20 September 1910; Germany: Schauspielhaus, Breslau *Hans der Flötenspieler* 17 December 1910; Hungary: Népopera *Furulyás Jancsi* 19 January 1912

Recordings: complete (Gaîté-Lyrique), selection (EMI-Pathé)

HANS THE BOATMAN Musical play by Clay M Greene. Music from various sources. Theatre Royal, Sheffield, 7 March 1887.

Hans the Boatman was constructed to order by Clay Greene in his home town of San Francisco and then sent for its first production to Britain, there to showcase the American dialect actor Charles Arnold (1855–1905), who had endeared himself to British provincial audiences playing opposite Minnie Palmer as the ingenuously German-accented hero of *My Sweetheart*.

Arnold played Hans Bekel, the boatman of the title, equipped with a four-year-old child called May Hansen (playing a boy child called Fritz) and a trained St Bernard dog called Nord, in a sentimental comedy drama set on the shores of the Schroon Lake in the Adirondacks. Good-natured, lazy, dream-a-day Hans, who spends much of his time with his dog or singing songs with the country kiddies, elopes and marries Gladys (May Gurney) from the city instead of long adoring local Jeffie (Jennie Rogers), the daughter of the old boatman Thursby (Robert Medlicott). Hans proves too unsupporting for words and Gladys finally decides to go back to her father (Walter Russell), assisted by the unsavoury Darrell Vincent (Robert Morgan). Thus, it is not his disillusioned wife but Jeffie who nurses Hans when an explosion renders him blind. However, by the final curtain both Hans's eyesight and his wife have been restored and Jeffie is happily tied up elsewhere. A long list of songs and dances of uncertain authorship, mostly for the star, included 'The Boatman's Lullaby', 'Pleasures Await You, My Boy', 'Blind Man's Buff', 'The Baby Coquette',

Plate 121.

'Little Gee-Gee', 'Innocent Lilies', 'The Spirit of the Lake' and 'The Daisy Chain'. One provincial reviewer wrote, 'it abounds in scenes and incidents of pure domestic pathos, it breathes of home and of child life, of fresh bracing mountain air and of sunny gardens ...'.

Arnold toured Britain with great success for 46 weeks, played a season at London's Terry's Theatre (December 1887), and took his play, plus the all-important child and dog, on to Australia (1888), where they began with a splendid 50 nights in Melbourne, 37 in Sydney, and the biggest houses ever seen in Tasmania, as *Hans the Boatman* knocked up some 350 nights around the country. Arnold then proceeded to New Zealand (95 performances), India, China, Japan and, finally, to America, where *Hans* opened in Chicago and went on to notch up its 1,000th performance on 8 March 1890 in St Paul, Minnesota.

The show's popularity was such that Fred Reynolds (officially), the Stacy company, and the Sillitoe–Palmer company all mounted versions of *Hans* on the Pacific circuits following Arnold's departure, but the show did not find the same favour in America and, when his three-year tour contract was cancelled after one year, Arnold returned to Britain. He tried other vehicles with succeeding dogs and children (in one of which he gave an exhibition of sheep shearing), including *Captain Fritz*, in which he introduced Henry Hamilton's 'Tommy Atkins', but he always returned to *Hans*, which he toured in 1893 in a 'new version' back to the South Pacific, where it and he had found such popularity. He died in the middle of singing a song in a concert at the Savage Club.

Australia: Bijou Theatre, Melbourne 5 May 1888; USA: Mc-Vickers Theater, Chicago 9 September 1889

THE HAPPY DAY Musical play in 2 acts by Seymour Hicks. Lyrics by Adrian Ross and Paul Rubens. Music by Sidney Jones and Paul Rubens. Daly's Theatre, London, 13 May 1916.

Left with a theatre in the red at the death of George Edwardes, Robert Evett began his attempts to keep Daly's going in the Edwardes tradition with a Hicks/Ross/Rubens/Sidney Jones musical in the Ruritanian vein, into which the tried and still pretty true ingredients of the past decades of musical theatre were poured. The young soprano star Winifred Barnes and respected actor Arthur Wontner played a princess and prince in disguise, G P Huntley and Lauri de Frece were two comical villains straight out of *Erminie*, whilst soubrette Unity More from revue, Rosina Filippi, who had created a list of heart-tugging mother figures for Hicks, and concert vocalist Thorpe Bates for male vocal values all had the opportunity to do what they did best. The mixture was topped off by a glamorous gipsy queen, played by young José Collins, brought back home from a budding career on Broadway.

There was plenty of value all-round in *The Happy Day*, but it was Miss Collins who dazzled the audiences with her evocation of Rubens's 'Bohemia', and Bates, with his handsome voice (Jones's 'Yours till the End'), who edged Miss Barnes for the vocal honours. 242 performances later (the shortest run at Daly's in years) the show went on tour, with the financial situation if anything worse than before, but Evett had laid the foundation of the company which would soon turn things round with *The Maid of the Mountains*.

The Happy Day marked Jones's farewell to the kind of English musical theatre he had largely helped to boost to international supremacy, for as the new rhythms entered theatre music he, resolutely of earlier days, simply stopped writing.

HAPPY END Musical play said to be 'by Elisabeth Hauptmann based on a story by Dorothy Lane. Songs by Kurt Weill, Bertolt Brecht and Elisabeth Hauptmann'. Theater am Schiffbauerdamm, Berlin, 2 September 1929.

After the success of *Die Dreigroschenoper*, Brecht, Hauptmann and Weill came together on a second piece for the Theater am Schiffbauerdamm. An awkward, naïve little tale about a Salvation Army girl called Lillian Holliday (Carola Neher) and a Chicago gangster called Bill Cracker (Oscar Homolka), pumped up with some equally naïve and awkward political propaganda, and accompanied by a set of songs only intermittently attached to the play, it folded after three chaotic, unprofessional performances. In recent years the show has been exhumed several times in areas where its propaganda is popular, or where the incidental songs – including the slicing hymn to 'Surabaya Johnny', the 'Bilbao Song', the tango 'Matrosen Song' and 'Der Song von Mandelay' – all subsequently made widely popular through their performance by Weill's wife Lotte Lenya, have been adjudged to outweigh a libretto to which Brecht was, apparently, too canny to put his name.

London saw a version of *Happy End* (with the undoubtedly fictitious Dorothy Lane still in the credits) for a 37-performance run in 1975, and Broadway took in a Michael Feingold adaptation from the Brooklyn Academy of Music, with Meryl Streep and Bob Gunton in the principal rôles, for 75 performances at the Martin Beck Theater two years later. In 1987 it was played at London's Camden Festival (The Place, 7 April 1987) with Eric Roberts and Rosamund Shelley featured. However, if the piece has not been able to make itself a place on the non-aligned professional/commercial stage, the most popular of its songs have remained afloat, becoming often-featured standards in the repertoire of many a Lenya wannabe.

UK: Lyric Theatre 26 August 1975; USA: Brooklyn Academy of Music 8 March 1977, Martin Beck Theater 7 May 1977
Recording: complete (DGG, Capriccio), selection by Lenya (CBS) etc

HAPPY HUNTING Musical comedy in 2 acts by Howard Lindsay and Russel Crouse. Lyrics by Matt Dubey. Music by Harold Karr. Majestic Theater, New York, 6 December 1956.

The combination of librettists Crouse and Lindsay and star Ethel Merman, which had been so successful in *Anything Goes* and *Call Me Madam* and not unsuccessful with *Red, Hot and Blue*, came together yet again, along with Broadway newcomers Harold Karr and Matt Dubey, to bring *Happy Hunting* to the stage. In a plot which followed the *Call Me Madam* formula, Miss Merman was cast as Liz Livingstone, a brash and wealthy Philadelphia socialite, who is so cross at not being invited to the wedding of Prince Rainier and Grace Kelly that she heads right off for Monaco to outshine the mating of the princely couple by wedding her daughter Beth (Virginia Gibson) to a real, live Habsburg (Fernando Lamas). But the Habsburg, who clearly knows a star when he sees one, falls for mother instead.

The show's songs, topped by mother's and daughter's admission that they belong to a 'Mutual Admiration Society' and 'A New Fangled Tango', did not manage to offer the star the kind of potential standards that Cole Porter and Irving Berlin had done in the earlier shows, but Jo Mielziner's production of *Happy Hunting* held the boards for a battling, but ultimately losing, 412 performances.

Recording: original cast (RCA Victor)

THE HAPPY TIME Musical in 2 acts by N Richard Nash suggested by a character in the stories of Robert L Fontaine. Lyrics by Fred Ebb. Music by John Kander. Broadway Theater, New York, 18 January 1968.

Rodgers and Hammerstein had a 614-performance success with their production of Samuel Taylor's adaptation of Fontaine's novel *The Happy Time* as a 1950 play. Richard Nash's musical adaptation, set with songs by John Kander and Fred Ebb, and produced by David Merrick, did not do as well, but it played for 286 performances on Broadway in 1968, and found both some fond fans and intermittent regional revival.

Michael Rupert played the French-Canadian boy Bibi Bonnard, whose growing-up is coloured by the clash between his ordinary, decent father Philippe (George S Irving) and his showy photographer uncle Jacques (Robert

Goulet, Tony Award), who descends from the big city on the little town of Saint-Pierre and upsets the family's unadventurous life there with his citified ways. Grandpa Bonnard (David Wayne) succeeds in bringing back some balance between the two extremes, before dying at the approach of the final curtain, and allowing the other top-billed star, Goulet, to deliver the piece's perhaps rather dubious message – 'get out and live'.

It was a message that the songwriters would deliver with more effect later the same year in their more successful and enduring *Zorba*. Here, their most winning musical moments came with Grandpa's old-fashioned assertions that he was once 'The Life of the Party', Bibi and Jacques' duet 'Please Stay' and a lively 'Tomorrow Morning'. The rest of the winning was done by director/choreographer Gower Champion, who picked up Tonys for both assignments.

A revised version of the show was mounted at the Goodspeed Opera House in 1980 (9 April).

Recording: original cast (RCA Victor)

HARBACH, Otto [HAUERBACH, Otto Abels] (b Salt Lake City, 18 August 1873; d New York, 24 January 1963). Broadway librettist and lyricist who collaborated on many of the most important musicals of his time.

The American-born son of a Danish family, Hauerbach began his working life as a teacher of English in Washington. He moved to New York in 1901 to attend Columbia University and, whilst studying, he worked at first in insurance, then in journalism, and as a copywriter in advertising. In 1902 he began working with the young musician Karl Hoschna on a musical play but, whilst others of Hoschna's earliest works found their way to the stage, their collaboration remained unproduced. His break came when Hoschna was asked by his employer, Isidore Witmark, to set Mrs Pacheco's play *Incog* as a musical. Hoschna recommended Hauerbach for the job, and when the resultant piece, *Three Twins*, proved a considerable success in the theatre and spawned a couple of successful songs, including Harbach's 'Cuddle Up a Little Closer', the team's future seemed assured. They confirmed that first success with a major hit in the form of a remade version of the Continental musical comedy *Madame Sherry* ('Every Little Movement'), and Hauerbach felt able to give up his advertising job to concentrate full time on a theatre career. The potentially fruitful Hoschna/Hauerbach collaboration was, however, cut short by the composer's early death.

Hauerbach was fortunate enough to be quickly paired with another rising young talent. His second collaboration was with a novice composer, working on his first Broadway show, on a commission from Arthur Hammerstein for a vehicle for *Naughty Marietta* star Emma Trentini. The composer was Rudolf Friml, and the first musical which the pair turned out together was the neatly made star vehicle *The Firefly* ('Sympathy', 'Giannina Mia'). Over the years that followed, although both writers worked intermittently with other collaborators, Harbach and Friml were associated on 11 further musical shows, including the highly successful adaptation of another French comedy as the widely successful *High Jinks* (1913) and Friml's most enduring romantic operetta, *Rose Marie* (1924).

The librettist/lyricist (now billed, less Germanically, as 'Harbach') had his biggest international success to date when he paired with composer Louis Hirsch on the adaptation of James Montgomery's *The Aviator* into the musical *Going Up* (1917, 'The Tickle Toe', 'If You Look in Her Eyes'), and the pair followed this hit with another in the every-Cinderella-day tale of *Mary* (1920, 'The Love Nest'). But, in the meanwhile the author had begun another collaboration which would lead him to further significant successes. Early in 1920 he began what was to be a regular, though not exclusive, working partnership with fellow librettist and lyricist Oscar Hammerstein II. If their first work together, on two Herbert Stothart musicals, was less than distinguished, they rose several notches to turn out the pretty Mediterranean-romantic tale of *Wildflower* (1923), with a score by Vincent Youmans and Stothart, before topping all competition with *Rose Marie* ('Indian Love Call', 'Rose Marie', 'The Mounties', 'Totem Tom-Tom') the following year.

In the meantime, however, Harbach had been collecting the proceeds from another success, this one outside of New York. He had been the adapter and original lyricist for Harry H Frazee's production of the musical version of the play *My Lady Friends* as *No, No, Nanette* ('No, no, Nanette'). That piece, after having undergone some out-of-town changes at the hands of others, had been racking up a record run in Chicago since mid-1923, and when it finally came to New York Harbach had the distinction of being simultaneously involved in the authorship and the royalties of the two greatest hits the American musical theatre had known up to that time. It was estimated at the time by *Variety* that he was collecting something like half a million dollars per annum from his stage works and songs.

Whilst this pair of hits went round the world, Harbach and Hammerstein pursued their collaboration on a run of further successes: *Sunny* for Jerome Kern ('Who?', 'Two Little Bluebirds'), the dashingly romantic *Song of the Flame* for George Gershwin and the inevitable Stothart (both 1925) and, in 1926, their other major romantic operetta hit, *The Desert Song* (1926) with its hit-filled Sigmund Romberg score ('The Desert Song', 'Romance', 'The Riff Song', 'One Alone'). Their final Broadway work together was on *Good Boy* (1928), after which Harbach authored the libretto for the lavish *Nina Rosa* for Romberg, and the altogether less than convincing books, but impressive lyrics, for Kern's *The Cat and the Fiddle* ('She Didn't Say "Yes"') and *Roberta* ('Smoke Gets in Your Eyes', 'Yesterdays'), closing his Broadway record with another romantic piece, *Forbidden Melody*, again for Romberg, nearly 30 years after his first produced work. A final reunion with Hammerstein on a Civil War piece, *Gentlemen Unafraid*, musically set by Jerome Kern, played only regionally.

Alongside Harbach's successful productions there were, of course, also the failures, but the writer left very little of his work on the tryout trail, and his total of hit and near-hit shows was an impressive one, making it all the more surprising that his name has not lasted as a recognizable one in the public ear in the way that those of more fashionable writers and composers, who achieved perhaps less in the same era, have done.

Many of Harbach's libretti, including most of his biggest hits, were original texts, but a good number were also adaptations from existing plays. Although *A kis gróf* (*Suzi*) was his only straight Operette adaptation, others of his libretti were based on Continental pieces, notably Maurice Ordonneau's original libretto for *Madame Sherry*, *Les Dragées de Hercule*, which became *High Jinks*, *Le Chasseur de Chez Maxim*, the source of *The Blue Kitten*, and Hennequin and Veber's *La Présidente*, the basis for *Oh, Please!* Others, from the days of *Three Twins/Incog* onwards were adaptations of native works, including *Kitty Darlin'* (David Belasco's *Sweet Kitty Bellairs*), *Kitty's Kisses* (Bartholomae's *Little Miss Brown*), *Going Up* (James Montgomery's *The Aviator*), *Tumble In* (the Mary Roberts Rinehart/Avery Hopwood hit play *Seven Days*), *Roberta* (Alice Duer Miller's novel *Gowns by Roberta*), *June Love* (Charlotte Thompson's *In Search of a Sinner*), *Jack and Jill* (Frederick Isham's play of the same name), and the most famous, *No, No, Nanette* (*My Lady Friends*). He also – it would seem – had the novel distinction of being the first author to adapt a movie screenplay to the musical stage, when the silent screen's *Miss George Washington jr* became the libretto to his 1919 musical *The Little Whopper*.

The reverse process occurred when an unproduced play-cum-screenplay of his (w Edgar McGregor) was adapted in England by Weston and Lee as the libretto for the musical comedy *Here Comes the Bride* (Piccadilly Theatre, London 20 February 1930).

1908 **Three Twins** (Karl Hoschna) Herald Square Theater 15 June
1910 **Bright Eyes** (Hoschna) New York Theater 28 February
1910 **Madame Sherry** (Hoschna) New Amsterdam Theater 30 August
1911 **Dr Deluxe** (Hoschna) Knickerbocker Theater 17 April
1911 **The Girl of My Dreams** (Hoschna/w W D Nesbit) Criterion Theater 7 August
1911 **The Fascinating Widow** (Hoschna, later Percy Wenrich) Liberty Theater 11 November
1912 **The Firefly** (Rudolf Friml) Lyric Theater 2 December
1913 **High Jinks** (Friml) Lyric Theater 10 December
1914 **The Crinoline Girl** (Wenrich/Julian Eltinge) Knickerbocker Theater 16 March
1914 **Suzi** (*A kis gróf*) English version (Casino Theater)
1915 **Katinka** (Friml) 44th Street Theater 23 December
1917 **You're in Love** (Friml) Casino Theater 6 February
1917 **Kitty Darlin'** (Friml) Casino Theater 7 November
1917 **Going Up** (Louis Hirsch/w James Montgomery) Liberty Theater 25 December
1919 **Tumble In** (Friml) Selwyn Theater 24 March
1919 **The Little Whopper** (Friml/Bide Dudley) Casino Theater 13 October
1920 **Tickle Me** (Stothart/w Hammerstein, Frank Mandel) Selwyn Theater 17 August
1920 **Mary** (Hirsch/w Mandel) Knickerbocker Theater 18 October
1920 **Jimmie** (Stothart/w Hammerstein/w Hammerstein, Mandel) Apollo Theater 17 November
1921 **June Love** (Friml/w W H Post) Knickerbocker Theater 25 April
1921 **The O'Brien Girl** (Hirsch/w Mandel) Liberty Theater 3 October
1922 **Molly Darling** (Tom Johnstone/Phil Cook/w William Cary Duncan) Liberty Theater 1 September
1922 **The Blue Kitten** (Friml) Selwyn Theater 13 January
1923 **Wildflower** (Vincent Youmans, Stothart/w Hammerstein) Casino Theater 7 February
1923 **Jack and Jill** (Augustus Barratt/w Barratt, John Murray Anderson) Globe Theater 22 March
1923 **Kid Boots** (Harry Tierney/Joseph McCarthy/w William Anthony McGuire) Earl Carroll Theater 31 December

1924 **No, No, Nanette** (Youmans/w Irving Caesar/w Mandel) Garrick Theater, Detroit 23 April; Palace Theatre, London 11 March 1925
1924 **Rose Marie** (Friml, Stothart/w Hammerstein) Imperial Theater 2 September
1924 **Betty Lee** (Hirsch, Conrad/w Caesar) 44th Street Theater 25 December
1925 **Sunny** (Kern/w Hammerstein) New Amsterdam Theater 22 September
1925 **Song of the Flame** (Gershwin, Stothart/w Hammerstein) 44th Street Theater 30 December
1926 **Kitty's Kisses** (Con Conrad/Gus Kahn/w Philip Bartholomae) Playhouse 6 May
1926 **Criss Cross** (Kern/Caldwell) Globe Theater 12 October
1926 **The Wild Rose** (Friml/w Hammerstein) Martin Beck Theater 20 October
1926 **The Desert Song** (Romberg/w Hammerstein/w Hammerstein, Frank Mandel) Casino Theater 30 November
1926 **Oh, Please!** (Youmans/w Anne Caldwell) Fulton Theater 17 December
1927 **Lucky** (Kern, Harry Ruby, Bert Kalmar) New Amsterdam Theater 22 March
1927 **Golden Dawn** (Emmerich Kálmán, Stothart/w Hammerstein) Hammerstein's Theater 30 November
1928 **Good Boy** (Stothart, Kalmar, Ruby/w Hammerstein, Henry Meyers) Hammerstein's Theater 5 September
1930 **Nina Rosa** (Romberg/Caesar) Majestic Theater 20 September
1931 **The Cat and the Fiddle** (Kern) Globe Theater 15 October
1933 **Roberta** (Kern) New Amsterdam Theater 15 October
1936 **Forbidden Melody** (Romberg) New Amsterdam Theater 2 November
1938 **Gentlemen Unafraid** (Kern/w Hammerstein) Municipal Light Opera, St Louis 3 June

HARBURG, E[dgar] Y ('Yip') [HOCHBURG, Isidore] (b New York, 8 April 1898; d Hollywood, Calif, 5 March 1981). Longtime lyricist whose film and revue work was ultimately more productive of enduring material than his book musicals.

As a collegian the young Harburg began contributing comic verse to magazines and to newspapers such as the *New York World* and the *New York Tribune*, but on graduating he began an electrical appliance business, and it was not until that business went under in the Depression that he began a full-time professional career as a lyricist.

Although he contributed an interpolated number to *Queen High* (1926, 'Brother, Just Laugh it Off' w Arthur Schwartz, Ralph Rainger) and another to the film version of *Rio Rita* (1929, 'Long Before You Came Along' w Harold Arlen), the significant part of Harburg's career began with lyrics for the revue stage, starting with *The Earl Carroll Sketch Book* (1929 w Jay Gorney, 'Like Me Less, Love Me More') and continuing with contributions of more or less numbers to *Earl Carroll's Vanities of 1930* (w Gorney, Harold Arlen, Ted Koehler), *The Garrick Gaieties* (1930), *Americana* (1932, introducing Harburg's first major hit 'Brother Can You Spare a Dime?'), *Ballyhoo of 1932* (w Lewis Gensler), *Ziegfeld Follies of 1931* (w Gorney) and *Ziegfeld Follies of 1934* (w Vernon Duke), *Walk a Little Faster* (1932, 'April in Paris') *Life Begins at 8.40* (1934, w Harold Arlen) and *The Show is On* (1936, w Arlen). He scored another stage song hit with 'It's Only a Paper Moon' (w Arlen, Billy Rose), written for the play

The Great Magoo and later used in the film *Take a Chance* (1933).

Over the following years Harburg wrote principally for the screen, supplying songwords notably for *Stage Struck* (1936, Arlen), *At the Circus* (1939, Arlen) and for yet another Arlen score, *The Wizard of Oz*, which produced his best-remembered songs of all 'Over the Rainbow' (Academy Award), 'We're Off to See the Wizard', 'Follow the Yellow Brick Road' etc. 'God's Country', a song from Harburg's first stage book-musical *Hooray for What!*, which had run 200 performances on Broadway in 1937–8 ('Moanin' in the Mornin', 'Down With Love'), was interpolated into the 1939 film of *Babes in Arms*, and he and Arlen also provided additional songs for the film versions of the musicals *Panama Hattie* and *Cabin in the Sky* (1943, 'Happiness is a Thing Called Joe'). In 1944 Harburg penned the words to Jerome Kern's music for the Deanna Durbin musical film *Can't Help Singing*.

The post-*Oklahoma!* period piece *Bloomer Girl* (1944) gave Harburg his first significant Broadway run with a book show, and *Finian's Rainbow* (1947), in which the lyricist paired with composer Burton Lane, was even more successful on its initial production. It was also subsequently seen overseas, and its prettiest song 'How Are Things in Glocca Morra?', written in the same pleasingly ingenuous strain as 'Over the Rainbow', gave lyricist and composer one of their most enduring hits. 'Old Devil Moon', 'When I'm Not Near the Girl I Love' and 'If This Isn't Love' were also amongst the lasting part of the *Finian's Rainbow* score.

Harburg co-produced his next musical, *Flahooley*, with *Finian's Rainbow* co-librettist Fred Saidy and Cheryl Crawford, but it and his subsequent stage musicals were less successful and/or productive, even though *Jamaica*, a custom-made Harold Arlen vehicle for Lena Horne, totted up a long Broadway run, materially aided by its star's appeal. He continued to write for stage and screen through into the 1960s, providing the lyrics to the film cartoon *Gay-Purree* (1962, w Arlen), re-lyricing Offenbach for the unsuccessful stage show *The Happiest Girl in the World* (97 performances) and making his farewell to Broadway with another short-lived show, *Darling of the Day* (which, yet again, had a song with a 'rainbow' in it), in 1968 (31 performances).

A compilation show based on his work (w Saidy) was produced at the Studio Arena, Buffalo, as *I Got a Song* (26 September 1974).

1937 **Hooray for What!** (Harold Arlen/Howard Lindsay, Russel Crouse) Winter Garden Theater 1 December
1940 **Hold on to Your Hats** (Burton Lane/Guy Bolton, Matt Brooks, Eddie Davis) Shubert Theater 11 September)
1944 **Bloomer Girl** (Arlen/Sig Herzig, Fred Saidy) Shubert Theater 5 October
1947 **Finian's Rainbow** (Lane/w Saidy) 46th Street Theater 10 January
1951 **Flahooley** (Sammy Fain/w Saidy) Broadhurst Theater 14 May
1952 **Jolly Anna** revised *Flahooley* (w William Friml/w Saidy) San Francisco 11 August
1957 **Jamaica** (Arlen/w Saidy) Imperial Theater 31 October
1961 **The Happiest Girl in the World** (Offenbach/arr Saidy, Henry Myers) Martin Beck Theater 3 April
1968 **Darling of the Day** (Styne/Nunnally Johnson, Keith

Waterhouse, Willis Hall) George Abbott Theater 27 January
1971 **What a Day for a Miracle** (w Henry Myers/Larry Ornstein, Jeff Chandler) University of Vermont 29 April

HARDT-WARDEN Bruno [WRADATSCH, Bruno] (b Drachenburg, 31 August 1883; d Vienna, 21 July 1954). Prolific writer for the German-language stage through three decades.

Bruno Hardt (his earliest work was done without the double-barrel) made his first attempts as a librettist in the operatic world, providing – most often in collaboration with Ignaz Welleminsky – the texts for such pieces as Max Oberleitner's *La Vallière* (1916) and *Der eiserne Heiland* (1917), *Das Heiderntor* and *Cäcilie* (1920), Jan Brandt-Buys' *Glockenspiel* (1913), *Der Schneider von Schonau* (1916), *Der Erober* (1918), *Mi-carême* and *Der Mann in der Mond* (1922) and Franz Schmidt's *Fredegundis* (1922). However, he soon made his way into the fields of musical comedy and revue, scoring an early success with the revusical Posse *Mädel, küsse mich!* which was set to music by Robert Stolz for Vienna and later played in Hungary as *Csókbakter* (Revü Színház 18 October 1919). Hardt subsequently supplied the text (w Otto Tumlitz) for Stolz's rare attempt at an opera, *Die Rosen der Madonna* (1920).

Revues such as *Hol's der Teufel* (1916), *Wie wird man Millionär* (1918), *Wie wird man jung?* (1920), *Wien, gib acht!* (1923), a mimodrama (w Welleminsky) *Todestarantelle*, set by Julius Bittner and produced at Zurich (29 April 1920) and several Operetten apparently premièred on the Hungarian stage in translation all made up part of Hardt's busy theatrical schedule, from which the first real Operette successes came in 1921 with the productions of Eysler's *Die schöne Mama* in Rome and then in Vienna, and of Stolz's comical musical play *Der Tanz ins Glück*, which followed its Vienna première with many musically varying, but textually solid, versions in several countries.

In the 1920s Walter Kollo's *Marietta*, the good-old-days musical built around Fred Raymond's popular song *Ich hab' mein Herz in Heidelberg verloren*, and Straus's *Hochzeit in Hollywood* gave him some further musical theatre successes, whilst in the 1930s he provided the texts for Stolz's *Wenn die kleinen Veilchen blühen* (turned into the spectacular *Wild Violets* in the British Empire), Kollo's *Drei arme kleine Mädels*, Pepöck's *Hofball in Schönbrunn*, and the piece which eventually became Kattnigg's *Balkanliebe*. Hardt continued to provide libretti and/or lyrics for the musical theatre into the 1940s, as well as authoring the text for Kattnigg's opera *Donna Miranda* as late as 1953, but although his list of works contained several pieces which had some degree of popularity in their time, none has survived into the revived repertoire.

1915 **A főnyeremény kisasszony** (Ludwig Gruber/w Ignaz M Wellminsky, tr Zsigmond Rajna) Pozsony, March; Hamburg 9 November 1920
1916 **Mädel, küsse mich!** (Robert Stolz/w Emil Schwarz) Lustspiel-Theater 29 April
1917 **Lang, lang ist's her** (Stolz) Lustspiel-Theater 18 March
1917 **Tavasz és szerelem** (*Liebe und Lenz*) (Heinrich Berté) Hungarian version Városi Színház 15 September; German version w Welleminsky Hamburg 1918
1918 **Li-i-San** (Wolfgang von Bartels/w Welleminsky) Königliches Theater, Kassel 1 October

1919 **Das Liebeslied** (Ludwig Uray/w Oskar Staudigl) 1 act Opernhaus, Graz 5 April

1919 **Amor in Kasernhof** (Uray) 1 act Opernhaus, Graz 19 November

1920 **Grossstadtmärchen** (Richard Fall/w Erwin Weill) Carltheater 10 January

1920 **Dienstmann Nr 16** (Károly Hajós/Otto Hein) Hölle 1 October

1921 **Die schöne Mama** (*La bella mammina*) (Edmund Eysler/w Heinrich von Waldberg) Teatro Nazionale, Rome 9 April; Wiener Bürgertheater 17 September

1921 **A korhély gróf** (Gruber/w Welleminsky) Budai Színkör, Budapest 18 June

1921 **Der Tanz ins Glück** (later *Hallo! ist das die Liebe*) (Stolz/w Robert Bodanzky) Raimundtheater 23 December

1921 **Indische Nächte** (Bruno Granichstädten/w Bodanzky) Apollotheater 25 November

1921 **Eine Sommernacht** (Stolz/w Bodanzky) Johann Strauss-Theater 23 December

1922 **Offenbach** (aka *Der Meister von Montmartre*) German version w Bodanzky (Neues Wiener Stadttheater)

1922 **Die Liebe geht um** (Stolz/w Bodanzky) Raimundtheater 22 June

1922 **Fräulein Frau** (Max Niederberger/w Waldberg) Wiener Bürgertheater 23 December

1923 **Marietta** (Walter Kollo/w Bodanzky, Willi Kollo) Metropoltheater, Berlin 22 December

1924 **Das Fräulein aus 1001 Nacht** (Stolz/w Karl Farkas, Fritz Rotter) Robert Stolzbühne 6 October

1924 **Märchen der Liebe** (Emilie Wrana/ad Ernst Andress) Baden-bei-Wien 20 November

1926 **Das Amorettenhaus** (Leo Ascher/w Waldberg, Max Steiner-Kaiser) Carl-Schultze Theater, Hamburg January

1926 **Nur Du** (Walter Kollo/w Kollo) Berliner Theater, Berlin 23 December

1927 **Drei arme kleine Mädels** (Kollo/w Feiner) Theater am Nollendorfplatz, Berlin 22 April

1927 **Ich hab' mein Herz in Heidelberg verloren** (Fred Raymond/Ernst Neubach/w Löhner-Beda) Volksoper 29 April

1928 **Eine Nacht in Kairo** (Jean Gilbert/w Leopold Jacobson) Centraltheater, Dresden 22 December

1928 **Hochzeit in Hollywood** (Straus/w Jacobson) Johann Strauss-Theater 21 December

1929 **Die Liebesinsel** (Hans Pero/w Welleminsky) Stadttheater, Hamburg 12 March

1929 **Die Frau in Gold** (Michael Krazsnay-Krausz/w Jacobson) Neues Operettenhaus, Leipzig 28 February

1929 **Das kleine Fräulein Li** (Martin Knopf/w Hermann Feiner) Thalia-Theater, Berlin 25 December

1929 **Mädel ade!** (August Pepöck) Operettenhaus, Leipzig 14 January; Wiener Bürgertheater 4 October

1930 **Das Herrgottslied** (Krazsnay-Kraus) Neues Wiener Schauspielhaus 21 November

1930 **Die Kleine vom Zirkus** (Heinrich Strecker/w Max Leo Deutsch) 30 December

1932 **Wenn die kleinen Veilchen blühen** (Stolz) Princess Theatre, The Hague 1 April

1933 **Rosen im Schnee** (Karl Löwe arr Oscar Jascha/w Lohner-Beda) Volksoper 20 January

1937 **Mucki** (*Bub oder Mädel*) (Willy Engel-Berger) Stadttheater, Bremen 31 July

1937 **Hofball in Schönbrunn** (Pepöck/Josef Wentner) Theater des Volkes, Berlin 4 September

1937 **Die Gräfin von Durazzo** (aka *Balkanliebe*) (Rudolf Kattnigg) Neues Operetten-Theater, Lepizig 22 December

1938 **Der ewige Walzer** (Strecker/w Rudolf Köller) Staatsoper, Bremen 5 February; Volksoper, Vienna 10 May

1938 **Drei Woche Sonne** (Pepöck) Städtische Bühnen, Nuremberg 15 November

1939 **Über alles siegt die Liebe** (Edmund Nick) Stadttheater, Troppau 25 November; Theater des Volkes, Berlin 1940

1940 **Aennchen von Thurau** (Strecker/w Spirk) Raimundtheater 8 February

1941 **Die Göttin der Liebe** (Franz Drdla/w Köller) Stadttheater, Brünn 17 May

1941 **Küsse in Mai** (Strecker)

1942 **Eine kleine Liebelei** (Pepöck/w E A Iberer) Exlbühne, Vienna 2 July

1942 **Faschingstraum** (Michael Jary/w Köller) Theater des Volkes, Dresden 25 June

1942 **Der liebe Augustin** (Josef Rixner/Köller) Theater des Volkes, Berlin 18 December

1944 **Frühlingsluft** revised version w Pepöck

Other title attributed: *Die neue Mode* (1917, Aro van Leeuwen)

HARKER, Joseph C (b Levenshulme, 17 October 1855; d London, 15 April 1927).

The doyen of London's scenic artists for many years, Harker, along with his studio, was responsible for designing and/or painting the sets for Irving's productions at the Lyceum and for Beerbohm Tree at His Majesty's Theatre. In 1898 he took over as the scenic supplier for George Edwardes and, beginning with *A Greek Slave* at Daly's and with *A Runaway Girl* at the Gaiety, designed and/or made the sets for all their productions up until Edwardes's death. In 1914 he turned out the spectacular settings for Oscar Asche's *Chu Chin Chow* and was subsequently responsible for the American productions of *Chu Chin Chow* and *Mecca* as well as the Comstock/Gest *Aphrodite*, which followed that management's success with their previous spectaculars.

In later years he was partnered with two of his four sons, Joseph and Phil, who carried on the firm after his death. After Phil's death in 1933, Joseph jr continued the enterprise in partnership with the two other brothers, Roland and Colin.

Autobiography: *Studio and Stage* (Nisbet, London, 1924)

HARMATH, Imre (b Budapest, 1890; d 1940).

A prolific and successful author and adapter for the Hungarian theatre, Harmath made the most important part of his career as a lyricist for the musical stage. He supplied the songwords for such Hungarian successes as Komjáthy's *Pillangó főhadnagy*, the early works of Pál Ábrahám – beginning with *Zenebona* (*Spektakel*), *Az utolsó Verebély lány* and his jazz cabaret work, and continuing up to the internationally successful *Viktória* and *Die Blume von Hawaii* (originally presented in a German version) – and for Szabolcs Fényes's oft-revived *Maya* (book and lyrics), as well as turning out local versions of a long list of foreign hits.

Harmath died in a labour camp during the Second World War.

1916 **Fogadjunk!** (Dénes Buday) Budai Színkör 21 July

1918 **Pillangó főhadnagy** (Károly Komjáthy/w Ferenc Martos) Király Színház 7 June

1918 **Hejehuja báró** (*Bruder Leichtsinn*) Hungarian version w Adorján Ötvös (Margitszigeti Színkör)

1918 **Aranykalitka** (Béla Zerkovitz) Royal Orfeum 1 December

1919 **Beppo** (Zerkovitz) 1 act Royal Orfeum 1 February

1919 **Kalandor kisasszony** (Zerkovitz) Royal Orfeum 2 November

1920 **Csillagok csillaga** (Zerkovitz) Royal Orfeum 1 January

1920 **Zsuzsu** (Zerkovitz) Royal Orfeum 1 April
1920 **Lucia** (Zerkovitz) Royal Orfeum 1 September
1920 **Csalogánydal** (Zerkovitz) Royal Orfeum 1 November
1920 **Luna asszony** (*Frau Luna*) Hungarian version (Fővárosi Orfeum)
1921 **Kvitt** (Zerkovitz) Royal Orfeum 2 April
1921 **A bálkirálynő** (*Eine Ballnacht*) Hungarian version (Revü Színház)
1922 **Az aranymadár** (Zerkovitz) 1 act Royal Orfeum September
1923 **A hattyúlovag** (Zerkovitz) Royal Orfeum 1 April
1924 **Szegény Jonathán** (*Der arme Jonathan*) Hungarian version (Fővárosi Operettszinház)
1924 **Póstás Katica** (Zerkovitz) Lujza Blaha Színház 19 December
1925 **Dolly** Hungarian version (Városi Színház)
1925 **A császárnő apródja** (Ákos Buttykay/w Jenő Faragó) Király Színház 24 March
1925 **A fiastyúk** (Lon Sandman, Fred Froman) Royal Orfeum 1 April
1925 **Az ártatlan özvegy** (Lajos Lajtai) Városi Színház 25 December
1926 **Az alvó feleség** (Lajtai/Mátyás Feld) Budapesti Színház 13 July
1926 **Ki a Tisza vizét issza** (Buday) Kisfaludy Színház 3 September
1927 **Zsiványkirály** (Zerkovitz) Royal Orfeum 1 January
1927 **A Schlesinger-fiu este Lefkovits Katovàl** (A Red/Feld) 1 July
1927 **Az aranypók** (Zsigmond Vincze) Lujza Blaha Színház 14 October
1927 **Mersz-e-Mary?** (*Mercenary Mary*) Hungarian lyrics (Király Színház)
1928 **Huzd rá Offenbach!** (Offenbach ad Dezső Losonczy) Andrássy uti Színház 29 February
1928 **Zenebona** (Pál Ábrahám/w István Bródy, László Lakatos) Fővárosi Operettszinház 2 March
1928 **Az utolsó Verebély lány** (Ábrahám/Gábor Drégely ad) Fővárosi Operettszinház 13 October
1928 **Rose-Marie** Hungarian lyrics (Király Színház)
1928 **Yes** Hungarian lyrics (Magyar Színház)
1928 **Nizzai éjszaka** (*Lady X*) Hungarian version (Városi Színház)
1929 **Szeretem a feleségem** (Ábráhám/Adorjan Stella) Magyar Színház 15 June
1929 **Aranypáva** (Béla Neszmélyi/w László Békeffy) Városi Színház 20 April
1929 **Kikelet-utca 3** (Egon Kemény/w István Bródy) Fővárosi Operettszinház 27 April
1929 **Szökik az asszony** (Miklós Brodszky/Andor Kardos) Budai Színkör 14 June
1929 **Strandszerelem** (pasticcio/Franz Arnold, Ernest Bach ad) Nyári Operettszinház 10 July
1929 **Diákszerelem a karzaton** (pasticcio) Andrássy uti Színház 30 August
1929 **Miss Europa** (Losonczy/László Bús Feketé) Andrássy uti Színház 30 August
1930 **A biarritzi Vénusz** (Dezső Szenkár/Andor Kardos) Városi Színház 30 January
1930 **A csúnya lány** (Alfréd Márkus/László Vadnai) Fővárosi Művész Színház 7 February
1930 **Viktória** (Ábráhám/Imre Földes) Király Színház 21 February
1930 **Huszárfogás** (Vincze/w Rezső Török) Fővárosi Művész Színház 4 April
1930 **Dunabár** (Otto Vincze) Bethlen-téri Színház 14 May
1930 **Sanyikát örökbe fogadják** (pasticcio) 1 act Andrássy uti Színház 29 May
1930 **Jobb mint otthon** (arr Vincze/w Adorján Stella) Nyári Operettszinház 5 July

1930 **Az első tavasz** (Brodszky/Ernő Andai) Budai Színkör 16 July
1931 **Lámpaláz** (Kálmán Rozsnyai/Adorján Stella) Magyar Színház 24 January
1931 **Katóka** (*Peppina*) Hungarian version (Fővárosi Operettszinház)
1931 **Viharos nászéjszaka** (pasticcio/Albert Acremant ad János Vaszary) Magyar Színház 4 April
1931 **Falu végén kurta kocsma** (Zerkovitz) Bethlen-téri Színház 10 April
1931 **A hárem** (Szabolcs Fényes/Ernő Vajda) Fővárosi Operettszinház 24 April
1931 **Die Blume von Hawaii** (*Hawaii Rózája*) original Hungarian lyrics (Neues Theater, Leipzig, in German; Király Színház 28 January 1932)
1931 **Maya** (Fényes) Fővárosi Operettszinház 10 December
1932 **Nyiott ablak** (Imre Farkas/Károly Nóti) Fővárosi Operettszinház 6 February
1932 **Manolita** (Fényes) Fővárosi Operettszinház 24 September
1933 **A kék lámpás** (Brodszky/w Szilágyi) Király Színház 3 March
1933 **Dinom-dánom** (József Hajós) Pesti Színház 22 April
1934 **Vadvirág** (Mihály Eisemann/Ernő Andai) Andrássy uti Színház 24 March
1934 **Music Hall** (Fényes, Támás Bródy/Charles Méré) Fővárosi Operettszínház 13 October
1934 **Szeressen kedves** (Komjáthy/Ernő Andai) Fővárosi Operettszinház 1 April
1934 **Oh! Papa** Hungarian lyrics (Andrássy uti Színház)
1935 **Mimi** (Fényes/Endre Solt, Iván Törs) Royal Színház 13 February
1935 **Leányálom** (*La Madone du promenoir*) Hungarian version (Andrássy uti Színház)
1936 **Madame Bajazzo** (Ferenc Földes/Kardos) Kamara Színház 27 June
1936 **Sok hűhó Emmiért** (Fényes/Károly Aszlányi) Kamara Színház 24 October
1936 **3:1 a szerelem javára** (Ábráhám/Szilágyi, Dezső Kellér) Royal Színház 18 December
1937 **Antoinette** (Károly Komjáthy/Armand Szánthó, Mihály Szécsén) Művész Színház 23 December
1938 **Dinasztia** (Brodszky/w István Békeffi) Magyar Színház 16 April
1938 **Szomjas krokodil** (Markús/Szilágyi) Márkuspark Színház 11 June
1938 **Kávé habbal** (Eisemann/Pál Barabás) Royal Színház 30 November
1939 **Egy bolond százat csinál** (László Walter/Mihály Szüle) Royal Színház 29 January

HARNICK, Sheldon [Mayer] (b Chicago, 27 December 1924). Lyricist for several Broadway successes and one international hit.

Early on a violinist in a dance orchestra, then a songwriter ('The Boston Beguine'), Harnick did much of his first work as a writer for the theatre in the world of revue, contributing lyrics and/or music for songs in *New Faces of 1952*, *Two's Company* (1952), *John Murray Anderson's Almanac* (1953), *Shoestring Revue* (1955), *The Littlest Revue* (1956), *Shoestring '57* (1957), *Kaleidoscope* (1957), *Take Five* (1959) and *Vintage '60* (1960). During this time, following some contributions to regional book shows, he also made his first ventures into the world of the Broadway musical when he proffered some additional lyrics to the scores of the flop shows *The Amazing Adele* (1955) and *Shangri La* (1956). In 1958, in collaboration with composer Jerry Bock, he wrote the songs for the 60-performance musical

The Body Beautiful, and also shared the lyric-writing credit on the briefly seen *Portofino*, but he found his first considerable success soon after when he rejoined Bock to write the songs for the award-winning biomusical *Fiorello!* ('Little Tin Box').

The two subsequently collaborated on the scores for five further stage musicals, each of which found at least some degree of success on Broadway, and the greatest of which, *Fiddler on the Roof* ('If I Were a Rich Man', 'Sunrise, Sunset', 'Do You Love Me?', 'Matchmaker, Matchmaker' etc), became one of the most important international hits of its era. Beyond Broadway, they also produced the score for the marionette show *The Man in the Moon* for Bill Baird's puppets (1963) and, away from their own shows, supplied additional material to the score of *Her First Roman* (1968).

When Bock withdrew from the musical theatre scene in 1970 after *The Rothschilds*, Harnick continued with a variety of other projects, including a superior English adaptation of the libretto and lyrics of *Die lustige Witwe* and the English-language version of the widely acclaimed Parisian production of *La Tragédie de Carmen*, as well as an *Alice* (1975, w Joe Raposo) for the Baird puppets, for which he supplied not only the words but the voice of the White Rabbit. He also ventured into the operatic world, supplying the texts for the one-act operas *That Pig of a Molette* and *A Question of Faith*, with music by Thomas Z Shepard.

He has also returned intermittently to the musical theatre, most recently with a stage musical version of the Frank Capra film *A Wonderful Life*, again written with Raposo and produced in Washington in 1991.

1953 **High Time** Andover, NJ
1954 **Horation** Margo Jones Theater, Dallas 8 March
1958 **The Body Beautiful** (Jerry Bock/Joseph Stein, Will Glickman) Broadway Theater 23 January
1958 **Portofino** (Louis Bellson, Will Irwin/w Richard Ney/Ney) Adelphi Theater 21 February
1959 **Fiorello!** (Bock/Jerome Weidman, George Abbott) Broadhurst Theater 23 November
1960 **Tenderloin** (Bock/Abbott, Weidman) 46th Street Theater 17 October
1961 **Smiling the Boy Fell Dead** (David Baker/Ira Wallach) Cherry Lane Theater 19 April
1963 **She Loves Me** (Bock/Joe Masteroff) Eugene O'Neill Theater 23 April
1964 **Fiddler on the Roof** (Bock/Stein) Imperial Theater 22 September
1966 **The Apple Tree** (Bock/w Bock, Jerome Coopersmith) Shubert Theater 16 October
1970 **The Rothschilds** (Bock/Sherman Yellen) Lunt-Fontanne Theater 19 October
1975 **Captain Jinks of the Horse Marines** (Jack Beeson) Kansas City 20 September
1976 **Rex** (Richard Rodgers/Yellen) Lunt-Fontanne Theater 25 April
1978 **The Merry Widow** (*Die lustige Witwe*) new English version (New York City Opera)
1979 **The Umbrellas of Cherbourg** (*Les Parapluies de Cherbourg*) English version (Public Theater)
1981 **Penny by Penny** (Michel Legrand) Playhouse, Wilmington 9 November
1982 **A Christmas Carol** revised *Penny by Penny* Stamford, Conn 10 December
1991 **A Wonderful Life** (Joe Raposo) Arena Stage, Washington 15 November

HARRIGAN, Edward [Green] (b New York, 26 October 1845; d New York, 6 June 1911). Performer and author of a series of colourful and popular comedies with songs played on Broadway over a period of some 20 years.

The young Ned Harrigan made his beginnings in show business on America's west coast, playing in minstrelsy and in variety, as he teamed up, in turn, with Alex O'Brien, then Sam Rickey, and then with the man who would be his partner through the largest part of his career, Tony Hart. This pair, performing comic sketches which were written to their measure by Harrigan, soon rose to a prominent and profitable place in their profession, and in August 1876 they took over the old Theatre Comique as a permanent New York base. Their programmes there, for the most part, were made up of an olio, followed by one of their now considerably extended comic and musical sketches, the whole illustrated with numbers in which Harrigan's lyrics were set musically by his father-in-law and musical director, David Braham.

Eventually, the olio was done away with and Harrigan's sketches expanded to the size of a full-length musical comedy, to fill the whole evening of Harrigan and Hart entertainment. These sketches and comedies were aimed squarely at a variety-house audience. Harrigan's characters were European immigrants – particularly Irish or German – or blacks, and his plots often used the ridiculous rivalries and the comical mistrust between the various over-exclusive bands of 'new Americans' as the source of their fun. His own most popular character was that of Irishman Dan Mulligan, and he wrote a whole series of pieces in which he appeared as Dan, alongside his upwardly-striving wife Cordelia (Annie Yeamans), his son, Tommy (Hart) and their mouthy black maid, Rebecca Allup (also Hart). The Mulligans battled it out socially with the German Lochmullers or physically with the black Skidmore Guards, the rival factions prancing up and down in uniform in pseudo-military parades which made up for there being no war to get dressed for, getting into a regular run of fistfights and barneys, all to the accompaniment of a series of songs which turned out a whole set of popular hits ('The Babies on the Block', 'The Mulligan Guards', 'Maggie Murphy's Home', 'Hush, the Bogie', 'McNally's Row of Flats', 'O, Never Drink Behind the Bar' etc).

The run of shows, which is usually agreed to have reached its peak with *Cordelia's Aspirations* in 1884, ended soon after. The Theatre Comique was burned down and, in the wake of the disaster, as the partners transferred their operations to the Park Theater, Harrigan and the increasingly unstable Hart fell out. After revivals of *The Major* and *Cordelia's Aspirations*, covering the dates which should have been used by Harrigan's newest piece, *McAllister's Legacy*, which, uncharacteristically, had failed, the partnership ended.

Harrigan continued on in the same vein, but not with quite the same élan. He suffered a one-week flop with *Are You Insured?*, in which he did not play, did slightly better when he appeared as a Civil War colonel in *The Grip*, and better again when he went back to his oldest formula and appeared as a comic Irishman, with Mrs Yeamans as ever his shrewish wife, in *The Leather Patch* ('Denny Grady's Hack', 'Baxter Avenue'). He remained Irish to appear as O'Reagan and McNooney in the next two pieces, and then tried himself out in blackface (with occasional lapses into

Irish) as the servant of the title in *Pete*. *Pete* did well, but nevertheless, Harrigan stuck thereafter to the Googans and the Hogans and the Reillys winning his last big success with *Reilly and the Four Hundred* in 1890.

After a decade of going it alone, however, things began to weaken seriously. One new show Harrigan was preparing for Broadway, *My Son Dan*, was abandoned on the road, and he announced his retirement, only to return later the same year as *Marty Malone*. The Irish sailor was his last home-made creation. He reappeared from time to time thereafter, as a producer and a performer, but the 20-year series of Harrigan shows, which had won vast and enthusiastic audiences for its genuinely popular brand of theatre, was over.

When Harrigan died, some 15 years later, an obituary summed up his work: 'Harrigan's plays were intensely local; the types were true studies of New York life, but the story of the play was often extravagant and was intended to serve the purposes of character, drollery, comedy and song and dance. The social point of view, if it could be called a point of view, was democratic in the extreme. Harrigan's "Four Hundred" was a conglomeration of all races, colors and creeds. The negro was a welcome guest in the parlours of the socially ambitious of the Fourth Ward. The incongruity of it finally became too much of a burden for the nimble feet and rollicking songs to carry. Harrigan himself, Tony Hart, Annie Yeamans, Collier, Quilter and others of the company were individually very clever and inimitable, but the plays as a whole meant nothing. True in character and details of life, often touching in incident and episode, they suddenly plunged into a whirlwind of social extravaganza. Harrigan was not a very good actor, but he had the genius of sympathy for poor, unlettered and odd people. He caught the passing types of the day and he knew how, as a stage manager, to reproduce them to the life in manners and dress and speech and thought. No adequate account can be given in print of his plays or, to speak with more accuracy, of his productions and performances, but they contained genius, some of which will remain in the music and songs of Braham.'

The obituarist was right. His description was inadequate. It tried to analyse what was little more than the appeal of a modern-day, working-class television comedy series: the joy of seeing familiar everyday folk, colourfully exaggerated, up there doing extravagantly silly and funny and foolish and sentimental and picturesque things. Whatever else, Harrigan knew his audiences, and he pleased them hugely for most of two happy decades. For that achievement, William Dean Howells gave him the rather curious soubriquet 'The American Dickens', and the description has been glibly quoted frequently since. I can think of no British dramatist who portrayed his countrymen to themselves with such goodhumoured, pointed burlesquery, teetering somewhere between the satirical and the surreal and, almost always, the successful.

A biomusical on Harrigan and Hart was produced at the Goodspeed Opera House in 1984 and subsequently played for five performances at Broadway's Longacre Theater (31 January 1985). The score included a selection of Harrigan's songs, and the part of Harrigan was played by Harry Groener.

1873 **The Mulligan Guards** (David Braham) 1 act Theatre Comique

1874 **The Donovans** (Braham/w John Woodard) Theatre Comique 31 May

1875 **The Doyle Brothers** (Braham/w Woodard) Theatre Comique 17 May

1877 **Old Lavender** (Braham) Theatre Comique 3 September (revised version 22 April 1878)

1877 **The Rising Star** (Braham) 1 act Theatre Comique 22 October

1877 **Sullivan's Christmas** (Braham) 1 act Theatre Comique 24 December

1878 **A Celebrated Hard Case** (Braham) 1 act Theatre Comique 18 March

1878 **The Mulligan Guards' Picnic** (Braham) Theatre Comique 23 September

1878 **The Lorgaire** (Braham) Theatre Comique 25 November

1879 **The Mulligan Guards' Ball** (Braham) Theatre Comique 13 January

1879 **The Mulligan Guards' Chowder** (Braham) Theatre Comique 11 August

1879 **The Mulligan Guards' Christmas** (Braham) Theatre Comique 17 November

1880 **The Mulligan Guards' Surprise** (Braham) Theatre Comique 16 February

1880 **The Mulligan Guards' Nominee** (Braham) Theatre Comique 22 November

1881 **The Mulligans' Silver Wedding** (Braham) Theatre Comique 21 February

1881 **The Major** (Braham) Theatre Comique 29 August

1882 **Squatter Sovereignty** (Braham) Theatre Comique 9 January

1882 **The Blackbird** (Braham) Theatre Comique 26 August

1882 **Mordecai Lyons** (Braham) Theatre Comique 26 October

1882 **McSorley's Inflation** (Braham) Theatre Comique 27 November

1883 **The Muddy Day** (aka *Bunch o' Berries*) (Braham) Theatre Comique 2 April

1883 **Cordelia's Aspirations** (Braham) Theatre Comique 5 November

1884 **Dan's Tribulations** (Braham) Theatre Comique 7 April

1884 **Investigation** (Braham) Theatre Comique 1 September

1885 **McAllister's Legacy** (Braham) Park Theatre 5 January

1885 **Are You Insured?** (Braham) 14th Street Theater 11 May

1885 **The Grip** (Braham) Park Theater 30 November

1886 **The Leather Patch** (Braham) Park Theater 15 February

1886 **The O'Reagans** (Braham) Park Theater 11 October

1887 **McNooney's Visit** (Braham) Park Theater January

1887 **Pete** (Braham) Park Theater 22 November

1888 **Waddy Googan** (Braham) Park Theater 3 September

1889 **4–11–44** (Braham) (revised *McNooney's Visit*) Park Theater 21 March

1890 **Reilly and the Four Hundred** (Braham) Harrigan's Theater 29 December

1891 **The Last of the Hogans** (Braham) Harrigan's Theater 21 December

1893 **The Woolen Stocking** (Braham) Harrigan's Theater 9 October

1894 **Notoriety** (Braham) Harrigan's Theater 10 December

1896 **My Son Dan** (Braham)

1896 **Marty Malone** (Braham) Bijou Theater 31 August

Biographies: Kahn, E J: *The Merry Partners* (Random House, New York, 1955), Moody, R: *Ned Harrigan; From Corlear's Hook to Herald Square* (Nelson Hall, Chicago, 1980)

HARRIS, Charles (b London, ?1855; d London, 23 February 1897).

The brother of Augustus Harris, supremo of the Theatre Royal, Drury Lane, and a sometime writer of plays and libretti, Charles Harris found his niche in the theatre as the most important and influential director on the English-language musical stage of his time. He initiated the Gilbert and Sullivan era, at the age of 22, with his direction of *The Sorcerer*, and went on to mount the original production of *HMS Pinafore* before Gilbert decided to take on the single-handed direction of his shows himself ('produced under the direction of the author and composer'). He later directed the record-breaking comedy opera *Dorothy* for George Edwardes, and set the 'new burlesque' on its way to triumph at the Gaiety Theatre with his productions of *Monte Cristo Jr*, with its long-famous escape scene over the roofs of London, and *Miss Esmeralda*, before staging the highspots of the new burlesque era – *Faust Up-to-Date* and *Carmen Up-to-Data*. When Gilbert walked out of the Savoy Theatre, Harris returned to direct D'Oyly Carte's latter-day productions, including the two last Gilbert and Sullivan comic operas. He died at the age of 42, whilst directing the London production of the comic opera *His Majesty*.

Harris was, without doubt, the outstanding British stager of musical plays of the 19th century, and he did more than any other 'stage manager' in establishing the metier of director, as it later became known, as a separate and creative position, as opposed to the post of a stage manager, overseeing the day-to-day physical running of a show.

Amongst the shows which Harris directed, in an age when a 'stage manager' or 'stage director' was often not given a programme credit, were *The Sorcerer* (1877), *The Spectre Knight* (1878), *Billee Taylor* (1880, USA 1881), *Claude Duval* (1881), *Patience* (USA), *Manteaux Noirs* (USA 1882), *Dorothy* (1886), *Monte Cristo Jr* (1886, USA 1888), *The Sultan of Mocha* (revival 1887), *Jack in-the-Box* (1887), *Miss Esmeralda* (1887), *Frankenstein* (1887), *Carina* (1888), *Faust Up-to-Date* (1888), *Doris* (1889), *The Red Hussar* (1889), *Captain Thérèse* (1890), *Carmen Up-to-Data* (1890), *The Rose and the Ring* (1890), *The Nautch Girl* (1891), *The Vicar of Bray* (1892 revival), *Haddon Hall* (1892), *Jane Annie* (1893), *Utopia (Ltd)* (1893, USA 1894), *The Queen of Brilliants* (1894), *The Chieftain* (1894) and *The Grand Duke* (1896).

HARRIS, Sam[uel] H[enry] (b New York, 3 February 1872; d New York, 3 July 1941). Long successful Broadway producer and theatre owner.

After a variegated youthful life which included running a steam laundry during his teens, Harris ended up becoming the manager of prize-fighter called Terry McGovern. When McGovern, like many boxers of his day, moved into a different area of show business, touring in the burlesque *The Gay Morning Glories*, Harris took a part share in the show, and thus began his career as a theatrical producer. He subsequently went into partnership with Paddy Sullivan and A H Woods staging slightly more substantial touring plays, before, in 1904, he mounted the production of the young George M Cohan's musical comedy, *Little Johnny Jones*. Cohan and Harris subsequently formed a partnership which presented all of Cohan's later pieces, as well as a quantity of other musical shows and plays, over a period of some 16 years. Amongst the most successful of their many productions were Cohan's own *Forty-Five Minutes from Broadway* (1912) and the international hit musical comedy *Going Up* (1917).

After the ending of his alliance with Cohan in 1920,

Harris continued a lively production schedule in the straight theatre as well as staging both revues (notably *The Music Box Revues*) and musical comedy. He mounted the Marx Brothers' vehicles *The Cocoanuts* (1925) and *Animal Crackers* (1928), George Gershwin's *Of Thee I Sing* (1931) and its sequel *Let 'em Eat Cake* (1933), Cole Porter's *Jubilee* (1935), Irving Berlin's *I'd Rather Be Right* (1937) and, just before his death, Moss Hart and Kurt Weill's *Lady in the Dark* (1941).

Harris built the Music Box Theater (w Irving Berlin), which housed his series of revues, and ran Sam H Harris Theaters in both New York and in Chicago.

HARSÁNYI, Zsolt (b Korompa, 27 January 1887; d Budapest, 29 November 1943).

Journalist, librettist and playwright, Harsányi adapted a vast number of foreign pieces for the Hungarian stage, including the long-surviving local versions of *Das Dreimäderlhaus*, *Das Land des Lächelns*, *Der Zigeunerprimás* and *Gräfin Mariza*, but he also contributed to several successful original works of the Hungarian musical stage – notably the libretto for the Zsigmond Vincze musical comedy *Limonádé ezredes*, and the lyrics for Huszka's *Nemtudomka*, both pieces which were seen beyond their country of origin.

Alongside his other musical theatre works he also provided Hungarian versions of Mozart's *Don Giovanni*, Rossini's *Il barbiere di Siviglia* and Strauss's *Ariadne auf Naxos*, and wrote the libretto for Kodály's *Háry János*.

1911 **Kreolvér** (*Kreolenblut*) Hungarian version (Budai Színkör)
1911 **A provanszi vándor** (Alfred Rieger/Franz Wolf) Hungarian version (Ujpesti Népszinház)
1911 **A nőtlen férj** (*Der ledige Gatte*) Hungarian version (Ujpesti Népszinház)
1912 **Limonádé ezredes** (Zsigmond Vincze) Király Színház 15 September
1913 **A cigányprimás** (*Der Zigeunerprimás*) Hungarian version (Király Színház)
1913 **Buksi** (*Puppchen*) Hungarian version (Király Színház)
1913 **A mozikirály** (*Filmzauber*) Hungarian version (Király Színház)
1913 **A tökeletes feleség** (*Die ideale Gattin*) Hungarian version (Király Színház)
1914 **Nemtudomka** (Jenő Huszka/Károly Bakonyi) Király Színház 14 January
1915 **Nad-Mé** (*Die verbotene Stadt*) Hungarian version (Király Színház)
1915 **A pirosruhás hölgy** (*Die Dame in Rot*) Hungarian version (Budai Színkör)
1915 **Link báró** (*Der Juxbaron*) Hungarian version (Royal Orfeum)
1915 **A költő éjzsakája** (*Die verschenkte Nacht*) Hungarian version (Royal Orfeum)
1915 **A bolondok háza** (*Der Narrenhaus*) Hungarian version (Royal Orfeum)
1916 **Vagy ő, vagy senki** (*Die, oder keine*) Hungarian version (Népopera)
1916 **Az artistabál** ('FG') Royal Orfeum 1 April
1916 **Dicsőfalvi** (Miklós Balázs) 1 act Kolozsvár May
1916 **Végre egyedül** (*Endlich allein*) Hungarian version (Király Színház)
1916 **Egyszer volt** (*Wie einst im Mai*) Hungarian version (Fővárosi Nyári Színház)
1916 **Három a kislány** (*Das Dreimäderlhaus*) Hungarian version (Vigszinház)
1916 **Özvegy kisasszony** (*Toeff-Toeff*) Hungarian version with music by Adorjan Ötvös (Budai Színkör)

1916 **A derék Fridolin** (*Der brave Hendrik*) Hungarian version (Budai Színkör)

1916 **A mecénás** (*Der Natursänger*) Hungarian version w Albert Kövessy (Royal Orfeum)

1916 **A világjaró** (*Der Weltenbummler*) Hungarian version (Budai Színkör)

1917 **Vandergold kisasszony** (Aladár Rényi/w Sándor Hevesi) Városi Színház 24 October

1917 **Ó Teréz!** (*Das Fräulein von Amt*) Hungarian version (Vígszínház)

1917 **Milliomos Kati** (*Urschula*) Hungarian version (Budai Színkör)

1917 **A Favorit** (*Der Favorit*) Hungarian version (Budai Színkör)

1917 **Tessék szellőztetni** (*Eheurlaub*) Hungarian version (Budai Színkőr)

1918 **Hóvirág** (*Liebe im Schnee*) Hungarian version (Városi Színház)

1918 **Csalni jó** Margitszigeti Színkör 18 May

1918 **Médi** (*Hannerl*) Hungarian version (Vígszínház)

1918 **A szép Saskia** (*Die schöne Saskia*) Hungarian version (Városi Színház)

1918 **Háztűznéző** (Béla Reinitz/w Gábor Drégely) 1 act Medgyaszayszinház 17 December

1920 **A kislány** (Károly Stefanides/w Emil Szomory) Revű Színház 20 March

1920 **Búcsúkeringő** (*Der letzte Walzer*) Hungarian version (Városi Színház)

1921 **Csókos asszony** (*Clary-Clara*) Hungarian version w new music by Béla Zerkovitz (Eskütéri Színház)

1921 **Az erénycsősz** (*Die keusche Barbara*) Hungarian version (Budai Színkör)

1923 **Marinka, a tancosnő** (*Katja, die Tänzerin*) Hungarian version (Fővárosi Operettszinház)

1923 **A diadalmas asszony** (*Die Siegerin*) Hungarian version (Városi Színház)

1923 **A három grácia** (*Libellentanz*) Hungarian version (Fővárosi Operettszínház)

1923 **Pompadour** (*Madame Pompadour*) Hungarian version (Fővárosi Operettszínház)

1924 **Amerika lánya** (László Kiszely/w Sándor Szilágyi) Városi Színház 17 May

1924 **Apukám!** (*Cloclo*) Hungarian version (Fővárosi Operett-szinház)

1924 **Dorina és a véletlen** (*Dorine und der Zufall*) Hungarian version (Renaissance Színház)

1924 **A párizsi lány** (*Gosse de riche*) Hungarian version (Fővárosi Operettszínház)

1924 **Marica grófnő** (*Gräfin Mariza*) Hungarian version (Király Színház)

1925 **Frasquita** Hungarian version (Városi Színház)

1925 **Hármackskán** (*Quand on est trois*) Hungarian version (Vigszinház)

1925 **Az Orlov** (*Der Orlow*) Hungarian version (Fővárosi Operettszínház)

1925 **Terezina** (*Teresina*) Hungarian version (Fővárosi Operett-szinház)

1926 **Párizsi kirakat** (*Mannequins*) Hungarian version (Magyar Színház)

1927 **Nachtmusik** (Mihály Nádor) 1 act Uj Színház 2 December

1928 **Szeretlek** (*J'aime*) Hungarian version (Király Színház)

1928 **Lulu** Hungarian lyrics (Fővárosi Operettszínház)

1928 **Jolly Joker** (*Le Petit Choc*) Hungarian version (Belvárosi Színház)

1929 **Libavásár** (*Le Renard chez les poules*) Hungarian version (Belvárosi Színház)

1929 **Volga-bar** Hungarian version of comedy with songs (Vígszínház)

1929 **Régen és most** (*Bitter-Sweet*) Hungarian version (Király Színház)

1930 **Csodabár** (*Wunder-Bar*) Hungarian version (Fővárosi Operettszinház)

1930 **A mosoly országa** (*Das Land des Lächelns*) Hungarian version (Magyar Királyi Operaház)

1933 **Ez a kislány nem eladó** (*Un soir de reveillon*) Hungarian version (Vigszínház)

1934 **Giuditta** Hungarian version (Magyar Királyi Operaház)

1937 **Szabó a kastélyban** Hungarian version of a play by Paul Armont and Leopold Marchand with songs by Alexander Steinbrecher (Vigszínház)

1940 **XIV René** (Mihaly Eisemann/w István Zágon) Vigszinház 14 September

1941 **A tizedik kérő** (pasticcio ad Tamás Bródy/w Sándor Hunyady) Vigszinház 7 May

HART, Lorenz [Milton] (b New York, 2 May 1895; d New York, 22 November 1943). Lyricist of the Rodgers and Hart team through two decades of successful musical comedies.

From his college days, lyricist Hart formed a songwriting partnership with composer Richard Rodgers and, after a slow beginning, during which Hart worked as a translator for the German-language Irving Place Theater and for the Shuberts, the pair took their first Broadway steps under the wing of producer Lew Fields. They broke through with their songs for the revue *The Garrick Gaieties* ('Manhattan') and became established, in the mid-1920s, as regular contributors to the Broadway musical stage. Beginning with the costume piece *Dearest Enemy* ('Here in My Arms'), they provided the scores for a sequence of musical comedies, of which a version of *The Girl Friend* ('The Blue Room'), *Peggy-Ann* and *A Connecticut Yankee* ('My Heart Stood Still', originally heard in the London revue *One Dam Thing After Another*) provoked productions beyond America, and which produced a number of individual songs that became popular: 'Mountain Greenery' (*Garrick Gaieties* 1926, *The Girl Friend* UK), 'You Took Advantage of Me' (*Present Arms*), 'With a Song in My Heart' (*Spring Is Here*) and 'Ten Cents a Dance' (*Simple Simon*).

After a spell in Hollywood the partners returned to Broadway, and in the eight years before the dissolution of their partnership and Hart's death, they turned out a flow of scores covering an eclectic range of established musical comedy styles and, on some occasions, as in the dance-based *On Your Toes* (1936) and in their most remarkable and most retrospectively admired piece, the wryly misanthropic *Pal Joey*, taking altogether less usual tones. Alongside these two shows, a standard-studded let's-do-a-show show, *Babes in Arms*, the Hungarian fantasy *I Married an Angel*, and the classical burlesque *By Jupiter*, gave the partnership their best Broadway runs of this period, a period which brought forth many of Hart and Rodgers's most enduring songs, including 'Where or When', 'My Funny Valentine', 'The Lady is a Tramp', 'Johnny One Note', 'I Wish I Were in Love Again' (all *Babes in Arms*), 'There's a Small Hotel', 'Glad to Be Unhappy' (*On Your Toes*), 'Falling in Love With Love', 'This Can't Be Love' (*The Boys from Syracuse*), 'I Could Write a Book' and 'Bewitched' (*Pal Joey*).

The Rodgers and Hart partnership broke down when the lyricist's erratic private life and drinking habits made him into an impossibly unreliable collaborator. Rodgers himself, in desperation, supplied some lyrics which Hart was supposed to have written in their last days together.

The composer, unable to rein in his energies to cope with his partner's failures to provide, joined Oscar Hammerstein II to write *Oklahoma!*, whilst producing a revival of a revised version of *A Connecticut Yankee*, for which Hart supplied some additional songs. The comically revusical 'To Keep My Love Alive' proved the pick of what were to be his last theatre songs. Hart died later the same year, having survived long enough to see *Oklahoma!* become a bigger hit than anything he and Rodgers had written together.

At their best, Hart's songs were unusually attractive in their ideas, with lyrics that were unostentatiously clever and complex, easy and pleasantly ingenious in their rhyming, and sufficiently general to allow them a life away from the shows in which they were introduced.

1920 **Poor Little Ritz Girl** (Richard Rodgers, Sigmund Romberg/Lew Fields, George Campbell) Central Theater 28 July

1925 **Dearest Enemy** (Rodgers/Herbert Fields) Knickerbocker Theater 18 September

1926 **The Girl Friend** (Rodgers/H Fields) Vanderbilt Theater 17 March

1926 **Lido Lady** (Rodgers/Guy Bolton, Bert Kalmar, Harry Ruby) Gaiety Theatre, London 1 December

1926 **Peggy-Ann** (Rodgers/ad H Fields) Vanderbilt Theater 27 December

1926 **Betsy** (Rodgers/Irving Caesar, David Friedman) New Amsterdam Theater 28 December

1927 **She's My Baby** (Rodgers/Kalmar, Ruby) Globe Theater 3 January

1927 **A Connecticut Yankee** (Rodgers/H Fields) Vanderbilt Theater 3 November

1928 **Present Arms** (Rodgers/H Fields) Lew Fields Mansfield Theater 26 April

1928 **Chee-Chee** (Rodgers/H Fields) Lew Fields Mansfield Theater 25 September

1929 **Spring is Here** (Rodgers/Owen Davis) Alvin Theater 11 March

1929 **Heads Up!** (Rodgers/John McGowan, Paul Gerard Smith) Alvin Theater 11 November

1930 **Simple Simon** (Rodgers/Bolton, Ed Wynn) Ziegfeld Theater 18 February

1931 **America's Sweetheart** (Rodgers/H Fields) Broadhurst Theater 10 February

1935 **Jumbo** (Rodgers/Ben Hecht, Charles McArthur) Hippodrome Theater 16 November

1936 **On Your Toes** (Rodgers/w Rodgers, George Abbott) Imperial Theater 11 April

1937 **Babes in Arms** (Rodgers/w Rodgers) Shubert Theater 14 April

1937 **I'd Rather Be Right** (Rodgers/Moss Hart, George S Kaufman) Alvin Theater 2 November

1938 **I Married an Angel** (Rodgers/ad w Rodgers) Shubert Theater 11 May

1938 **The Boys from Syracuse** (Rodgers/Abbott) Alvin Theater 23 November

1939 **Too Many Girls** (Rodgers/George Marion jr) Imperial Theater 18 October

1940 **Higher and Higher** (Rodgers/Gladys Hurlbut, Joshua Logan) Shubert Theater 4 April

1940 **Pal Joey** (Rodgers/John O'Hara) Ethel Barrymore Theater 25 December

1942 **By Jupiter** (Rodgers/w Rodgers) Shubert Theater 2 June

Literature: Hart, D & Kimball, R: *Complete Lyrics of Lorenz Hart* (Knopf, New York, 1986), Rodgers, R: *Musical Stages* (Random House, New York, 1975), Marx, S and Clayton, J: *Rodgers & Hart: Bewitched, Bothered and Bedevilled* (Putnam,

New York, 1976); Hart, D: *Thou Swell, Thou Witty: the Life and Lyrics of Lorenz Hart* (Harper & Row, New York, 1976).

HART, Moss (b New York, 24 October 1904; d Palm Springs, Calif, 20 December 1961).

The winningly comical author of such highly successful plays as *Once in a Lifetime, Merrily We Roll Along, You Can't Take it with You, The Man Who Came To Dinner* (all w George S Kaufman) and *Light Up the Sky*, and of what is arguably the best theatrical autobiography of the post-war period (*Act One*), Hart had a rather less memorable career as an author in the musical theatre. His first and rather untypical work, *Jonica*, was a quick flop, collaborations with Irving Berlin (165 performances), Cole Porter (169 performances) and Rodgers and Hart (290 performances) gave him respectable rather than fine results, and he hit the jackpot only with his final work, the libretto for *Lady in the Dark*, in which an up-to-date skin of psychoanalysis was cleverly used to give an appearance of modernity to an old-fashioned romantic tale, decorated here with some particularly fine sung-through dream sequences by Ira Gershwin and Kurt Weill.

Hart supplied sketches for Berlin's successful revue *As Thousands Cheer* (1933) and for the 1938 *Sing Out the News* (w Kaufman), a Music Box Theater revue which he also co-produced and which was played for 105 performances, but, in the end, his memorable success in the musical theatre came not as a writer, but as a director: the original stager of *My Fair Lady* (1956) and of *Camelot* (1960, also co-producer). His only other venture as a producer of musical theatre was on the Irving Berlin *Miss Liberty* (1949, also director).

Musicals have been made from several of the plays which Hart wrote with Kaufman, *Merrily We Roll Along* (*Merrily We Roll Along* Stephen Sondheim/George Furth 1981, 16 performances) and *The Man Who Came to Dinner* (*Sherry!* Laurence Rosenthal/James Lipton 1967, 72 performances) being musicalized for brief Broadway stays, and *You Can't Take it with You* (*Így élni ... Ó!* mus: Charles Bradley, Magyar Színház, Budapest 26 June 1948) for the Hungarian stage.

Hart was married to musical leading lady Kitty Carlisle.

1930 **Jonica** (Joseph Meyer, William Friedlander/William Moll/w Dorothy Heyward) Craig Theater 7 April

1932 **Face the Music** (Irving Berlin/w Berlin) New Amsterdam Theater 17 February

1934 **The Great Waltz** (*Walzer aus Wien*) American version (Center Theater)

1935 **Jubilee** (Cole Porter) Imperial Theater 12 October

1937 **I'd Rather Be Right** (Richard Rodgers/Lorenz Hart/w George S Kaufman) Alvin Theater 2 November

1941 **Lady in the Dark** (Kurt Weill/Ira Gershwin) Alvin Theater 23 January

Autobiography: *Act One* (Random House, New York, 1959); Literature: Hart, K C: *Kitty* (Doubleday, New York, 1988)

HART, Tony [CANNON, Anthony J] (b Worcester, Mass, 25 July 1855; d Worcester, Mass, 4 November 1891). Half of the celebrated musical-comedy team of Harrigan and Hart.

The young Hart worked in a circus and in minstrel troupes in his youth before, at the age of 16, joining forces with Ned Harrigan in what was to become the famous double act of Harrigan and Hart. The pair worked at first in variety, and then, when Harrigan expanded their sketches into full-sized variety-based musical comedies, in a decade of mostly successful theatre shows. Hart starred opposite Harrigan's Dan Mulligan in blackface as the big-mouthed maid Rebecca Allup or, on occasions, as the Mulligan family's son, Tommy or, on yet other occasions, as both in the course of the same evening, and, in the later non-Mulligan shows, mostly as a selection of tough-talking little Irish dames such as Widow Nolan (*Squatter Sovereignty*), Mrs Bridget McSorley (*McSorley's Inflation*), Mary Ann O'Leary (*The Muddy Day*) and Molly McGouldrich (*McAllister's Legacy*). It was the sassy Rebecca, however, who remained the public's favourite amongst his creations.

When the partnership broke up, soon after the destruction by fire of their Theatre Comique base, Hart went on to appear in the farce-comedy *The Toy Pistol* (1886, Isaac Roost), opposite Lillian Russell in the Charles Hoyt/Edward Jakobowski musical comedy *The Maid and the Moonshiner* (1886, Upton O Dodge), and in the slightly musical comedy *Donnybrook*, but none of these pieces succeeded, and his increasingly unstable behaviour finally led him to be committed. He died, insane, at the age of 36.

Biography: Kahn, E J: *The Merry Partners* (Random House, New York, 1955)

HASSALL, Christopher (b London, 24 March 1912; d London, 25 April 1963). Lyricist to the Ivor Novello canon.

At first an actor, Hassall had supplied some lyrics to his Oxford University revue (*The Oxford Blazers*), but only made his professional debut as a musical comedy writer when Ivor Novello, to whom he had acted as understudy, and with whom he was then appearing in *Murder in Mayfair*, gave him the opportunity to write the lyrics for his Drury Lane commission *Glamorous Night* ('Glamorous Night', 'Fold Your Wings', 'Shine Through My Dreams', 'Shanty Town'). He subsequently worked on Novello's *Careless Rapture* ('Music in May'), *Crest of the Wave* ('Rose of England'), *The Dancing Years* ('Waltz of My Heart', 'The Wings of Sleep', 'I Can Give You the Starlight', 'My Dearest Dear'), *Arc de Triomphe* ('Dark Music') and *King's Rhapsody* ('Some Day My Heart Will Awake', 'Fly Home, Little Heart', 'The Mayor of Perpignan').

In 1950 he adapted J M Barrie's *Quality Street* as the libretto for the successful musical play *Dear Miss Phoebe* ('I Leave My Heart in an English Garden'). His film work included the screenplay of the 1955 film version of *King's Rhapsody*.

Hassall committed suicide at the age of 51.

1935 **Glamorous Night** (Ivor Novello/Novello) Theatre Royal, Drury Lane 2 May
1936 **Careless Rapture** (Novello/Novello) Theatre Royal, Drury Lane 11 September
1937 **Crest of the Wave** (Novello/Novello) Theatre Royal, Drury Lane 1 September
1939 **The Dancing Years** (Novello/Novello) Theatre Royal, Drury Lane 23 March
1943 **Arc de Triomphe** (Novello/Novello) Phoenix Theatre 9 November
1949 **King's Rhapsody** (Novello/Novello) Palace Theatre 15 September
1950 **Dear Miss Phoebe** (Harry Parr Davies) Phoenix Theatre 13 October

HAVANA Musical comedy in 3 acts by George Grossmith jr and Graham Hill. Lyrics by Adrian Ross and George Arthurs. Music by Leslie Stuart. Gaiety Theatre, London, 25 April 1908.

When George Edwardes decided that it was time for a change of policy at the Gaiety Theatre he contracted Leslie Stuart of *Florodora* fame to compose the theatre's new musical in the place of the Ivan Caryll–Lionel Monckton team, which had served him so well for more than a decade. *Havana* had a mite more substance to it than some of the earlier Gaiety shows, and it had no made to measure rôle for the theatre's usual star, Gertie Millar. Evie Greene starred in the substantial leading soprano rôle of Cuban Consuelo, in a fairly traditional tale in which the heroine, due to marry her influential cousin, Don Adolfo (Lawrence Grossmith, in a rôle tailored for his brother, co-author George), spends her last day of freedom romancing steam-yacht captain Jackson Villiers (Leonard Mackay) with predictable results. The comedy came from Villiers's crew, especially the bosun Nix (Alfred Lester) and the ship's boy, Reginald Brown (W H Berry). Nix had unwisely 'married' a Cuban girl on an earlier trip, and is now faced by the gorgonic Isabelita (Gladys Homfrey), claiming her rights. Fortunately, pretty Anita (Jean Aylwin) turns out to be the real bride.

Stuart's score – which boasted an amount of ensemble music and concerted finales of a kind not seen for many years at the Gaiety – did not have the kind of hit numbers that *Florodora* had, but Evie Greene scored with a weightless piece called 'Little Miquette', Grossmith had his best moment with a jolly 'Hello, People!', contralto Jessie Broughton sang of 'Zaza', Bill Berry had a topical 'How Did the Bird Know That?', and there was a cautionary comical quartet which warned 'It's a Bomb!'.

Havana had a good, if not outstanding, 221-performance run at the Gaiety before going on the road with the young Dorothy Ward featured at the head of one of the two companies, and then round the world. It had a notable success in America, where James T Powers had the text rearranged to corner all of the comedy in the rôle of Nix. The Shubert brothers' production, with Edith Decker as Consuelo, William Pruette (Diego) and Eva Davenport (Isabelita) caused a sensation in its Philadelphia tryout, and *Mr Hamlet of Broadway*, currently on show at the Casino, was bundled out to allow the piece to move swiftly to Broadway, where it was anticipated that it would out-*Florodora* its famous predecessor. It didn't, but it turned out to be one of the biggest hits of its time, played 236 Broadway performances (with a short summer break) and 'Hello, People!' and 'How Did the Bird Know That?' became decided hits. Stuart, a fanatical fighter against the interpolation habit had, however, no chance with the inveterately interpolating Shuberts, and he had to listen to 'My Little Deutscher Girl' and other such 'improvements' sung alongside his numbers.

Havana exported well. Berlin saw the show at the Belle-Alliance Theatre, J C Williamson mounted an Australian production with Florence Young (Consuelo), Victor Gouriet (Nix), W S Percy (Reginald, restored to his British-sized rôle), Fanny Dango (Anita) and Susie Vaughan (Isabelita) featured, and it was toured in repertoire in South Africa, but, in spite of the show's international popularity, Edwardes did not pursue the new line he had announced. For his next Gaiety show he returned to Monckton and Miss Millar and scored one of his biggest ever hits with *Our Miss Gibbs*.

Germany: Belle-Alliance-Theater 17 October 1908; USA: Casino Theater 11 February 1909; Australia: Her Majesty's Theatre, Sydney 13 March 1909

HAYDON, Ethel   (b Melbourne, 13 June 1878; d England, January 1954). Australian soubrette who played several important rôles for George Edwardes in a very short stage career.

After a youthful career in Australia, where she moved from being the star of the local amateur group to playing in pantomime at Melbourne's Princess Theatre with Robert Courtneidge, and in Arthur Garner's comedy company alongside Jennie Lee in *Jo* and in *The Morals of Marcus*, Miss Haydon travelled to Britain. There, at the age of 17, she made her first West End appearance, under the management of William Greet, as the the juvenile heroine of the comic opera *Dandy Dick Whittington* (1895), opposite May Yohé's Dick. George Edwardes then took her to the Gaiety, to succeed Ellaline Terriss as the fifth heroine of the long run of *The Shop Girl*, and subsequently cast her as second girl alongside Miss Terriss in *My Girl* and in *The Circus Girl* (1896, La Favorita, the circus girl), in which she succeeded to the star rôle during the show's run. To all intents and purposes she terminated what looked like becoming a significant career before her 19th birthday, but continued to appear occasionally in pantomime and variety, sometimes alongside her husband, star comedian George Robey.

HAYWARD, Leland   (b Nebraska City, Neb, 13 September 1902; d Yorktown Heights, NY, 18 March 1971).

After spells in film and as a theatrical agent, Hayward turned theatrical producer in 1944 and, over the next two decades had a high profile career in both the musical and straight theatre.

His first venture into the musical theatre was as co-producer with Rodgers, Hammerstein and Joshua Logan of the enormously successful *South Pacific*, and he followed up with further successes in *Call Me Madam*, *Wish You Were Here* (w Logan), *Gypsy* (w David Merrick) and *The Sound of Music* (w Rodgers, Hammerstein, Richard Halliday), before ending this remarkable run of hits on a less successful note with his final venture, *Mr President* (1962).

Biography: Hayward, B: *Haywire* (Knopf, New York, 1977)

HAZELL, Hy [O'HIGGINS, Hyacinth Hazel] (b London, 4 October 1922; d London, 10 May 1970). Favourite character actress of the London musical stage of the 1950s and 1960s.

Hy Hazell made her first appearance on the London stage in the chorus of *On Your Toes* (1937), and her first mark as a noticeably lush and glamorous principal boy in a long series of pantomimes. She won notice in her first major musical rôle as the middle-ageing filmstar, Dixie Collins in *Expresso Bongo* (1958), introducing the sultry 'Time' and the revusical 'We Bought It', and confirmed largely the following year when she created the part of another sexually ravenous dame, Mrs Squeezum, in *Lock Up Your Daughters* ('When Does the Ravishing Begin', 'I'll Be There') at the Mermaid Theatre. She repeated this rôle

in America, in Australia, and in London's West End, but subsequent engagements in *Innocent as Hell* (1960, Inez Packard) and *No Strings* (1962, Mollie Plummer) in Britain and in the Broadway-bound *Pleasures and Palaces* (1965, Catherine) in America were short lived.

In 1965 she created the rôle of the brash American Kay Connor opposite Anna Neagle in the long-running *Charlie Girl*, in 1968 was seen as Mrs Peachum in a revival of *The Beggar's Opera*, and in 1969 played the rôle of Miss Miniver in the musicalization of H G Wells's *Anne Veronica*. She succeeded to the rôle of Golde in London's *Fiddler on the Roof* later the same year, and was playing that part when her accidental death occurred.

HAZZARD, John E[dward]   (b New York, 22 February 1881; d Great Neck, NJ, 2 December 1935). Popular Broadway musical comedian of the 1910s and 1920s.

John Hazzard mixed plays and musicals in the earliest part of his career (1901 ssq) before landing his first Broadway musical engagement when he appeared at the Knickerbocker Theater in a comic rôle in *The Hurdy Gurdy Girl* (1907, Judge van Coover). He took a supporting rôle in the American production of *The Girls of Gottenberg* (1908, Sergeant Brittlbottl), a larger one in the less successful *The Echo* (1910) and gave out further prominent helpings of dialect comedy in *The Red Rose* (1911), Victor Herbert's *The Duchess* (1911, Adolphe de Paravente), Luders and Pixley's *The Gypsy* (1912), and *Miss Princess* (1912, t/o). In *The Lilac Domino* (1914) he appeared without the accent as Prosper Woodhouse, and in 1915 had perhaps his best opportunity to date when he took the principal low-comic rôle in Kern's *Very Good Eddie* (Al Cleveland) at the Princess Theater.

Thereafter Hazzard had a whole series of fine starring comedy rôles in major musical shows, appearing in the americanization of Kálmán's *Zsuzsi kisasszony* (*Miss Springtime*, 1916, Michael Robin), in Ivan Caryll's *The Girl Behind the Gun* (1918, Paul Bréval) and in George Gershwin's début show *La La Lucille* (1919, John Smith), taking the central (if not very musical) rôle of Kern's *The Night Boat* (1920, Bob White) and, with considerable success, the principal comedy rôle of the colourful *Tangerine* (1921). He was top-billed over the up-and-coming Astaires in Gershwin's *For Goodness' Sake* (1922, Perry Reynolds), and appeared as Pas de Vis in the American version of Yvain's slickly comical *Ta bouche* (One Kiss, 1923) before his musical appearances largely gave way to straight comic rôles. However, he later appeared as Sir Joseph Porter in Winthrop Ames's 1926 revival of *HMS Pinafore* and in the version of *Die Fledermaus* presented in 1933 as *Champagne Sec*.

In 1916, following his success in *Very Good Eddie* (to which he had supplied a handful of songwords), Hazzard collaborated with Anne Caldwell and John Golden on an unsuccessful rewrite of Charles Hoyt's *A Milk White Flag*, produced by F Ray Comstock at the Princess Theater as *Go to It*, and he later ventured as an author again with the musical *The Houseboat on the Styx* in which he played alongside Blanche Ring's Queen Elizabeth I to a Carlo and Sanders score. He did, however, have some success as a stage author, notably with the comedy *Turn to the Right!* (w Winchell Smith, 18 August 1916), and with the songs 'Ain't it Awful, Mabel?' and 'Queenie Was There with Her

Hair in a Braid'. He also wrote and published books of poetry and vaudeville material.

1916 **Go to It** (w John Golden, Anne Caldwell) Princess Theater 24 October
1928 **The Houseboat on the Styx** (Monte Carlo, Alma Sanders/w Kenneth Webb) Liberty Theater 25 December

HEADS UP! Musical comedy in 2 acts by John McGowan and Paul Gerard Smith. Lyrics by Lorenz Hart. Music by Richard Rodgers. Alvin Theater, New York, 11 November 1929.

In spite of the indifferent run of *Spring is Here* (1929), producers Aarons and Freedley again teamed librettist Owen Davis and songwriters Rodgers and Hart as the authors of their next production, prematurely titled *Me for You*. Davis's text cast lovable comedian Victor Moore as a bootlegger who puts his daughter (Betty Starbuck) under the control of his partner-in-booze (Jack Whiting) to get her away from her legal-eagle boyfriend (John Hundley). As in *Spring is Here*, Daddy wins out and Hundley loses the girl, but this time he did not have the compensation of a song like the earlier piece's 'With a Song in My Heart'.

Produced out-of-town in Detroit, *Me for You* showed up unmistakeably as a potential flop. The producers closed the show, called in John McGowan (who had given them the text for the successful De Sylva, Brown and Henderson musical *Hold Everything!* the previous year) and Paul Gerard Smith, who had doctored *Funny Face* into a hit for them a couple of seasons back, and set them to writing a new libretto around the same sets, costumes and songs. The result was *Heads Up!*, which had Whiting as a coast-guard chasing the yacht belonging to socialite Mrs Trumbell (Janet Velie) which is apparently running bootleg liquor. He proves his point and also wins Miss Mary Trumbell (Barbara Newberry). Moore played the yacht's cook, Skippy Dugan, a nervous fellow who is given to tinkering about with inventions. In a scene set in 'Skippy's galley aboard the *Silver Lady*', he was able to go through a kitchen routine, in the vein of the traditional British pantomime, before arriving at a happy ending, when one of his inventions finally came good.

Miss Starbuck became incidental to the plot and sang 'The Lass Who Loved a Sailor' and half the old title-song, while Hundley was left with nothing to sing at all. Additions to the cast included Ray Bolger, who sang about being a 'Play Boy' and, with Alice Boulden, about 'Knees' in the rôle of Georgie, and the dance team of Atlas and La Mar who did a speciality just before each finale, the second with the Reynolds Sisters (who'd already done their own speciality in the first act). Whiting got the best musical moment, 'A Ship Without a Sail', and also the most plugged, his duet with Mary, 'Why Do You Suppose?'.

Heads Up! opened in the earliest weeks of the Depression, but was voted 'a lively diversion' and managed to run up a total of 144 Broadway performances before moving on to the touring circuits. A London production, however, mounted under the management of Lee Ephraim, with Sydney Howard in Moore's rôle supported by Louise Browne, Clarice Hardwicke, Jack Hobbs and Arthur Margetson, was mildly noticed by one newspaper as 'not the best America has sent us' and folded in 19 performances.

UK: Palace Theatre 1 May 1930

HEARN, George (b St Louis, Mo, 18 June 1934). Rich-voiced baritone and actor who has rarely found Broadway rôles to allow him to display his talents.

In a career which has regularly mixed musical rôles with non-musical engagements (*An Almost Perfect Person*, *The Changing Room*), Hearn had early musical theatre parts in *1776*, *Camelot*, and *Wonderful Town* (w Lauren Bacall) on the road, and in *A Time for Singing* (1966), a musical based on *How Green is My Valley* and featuring Ivor Emmanuel and Tessie O'Shea, in New York. His first high-billed rôle in a Broadway musical was as Papa to the Mama of Liv Ullman in Richard Rodgers's musical version of *I Remember Mama* (1979), and he subsequently succeeded to the title-rôle of *Sweeney Todd*, following his Broadway performances with the national tour and with the made-for-television film of the show.

In the musical portion of a subsequent career which also saw him on Broadway in Lillian Hellman's *Watch on the Rhine*, the short-lived *Whodunnit*, and *Ghetto* at the Circle in the Square, he appeared as Torvald in the short-lived Ibsen musequel *A Doll's Life* (1982), created the rôle of the female impersonator Albin in the musical version of *La Cage aux Folles* (1983, Tony Award), introducing 'I Am Who I Am' in both New York and London, played Hajj (*Kismet*, 1985) for the New York City Opera, appeared as Long John Silver in an unsuccessful musical version of *Treasure Island* in Canada, and was seen as Alonzo Smith, the father of the family, in *Meet Me in St Louis* (1989).

Hearn also appeared as Ben in the celebrity concert of *Follies* and its subsequent recording.

HEARNE, Richard (b Norwich, 30 January 1909; d Bearstead, Kent, 25 August 1979). Acrobatic comedian who had a successful career of nearly 20 years in West End musicals.

Hearne began his life on the stage as a child and worked in circus, variety, revue and pantomime before moving into musical comedy in the farcical *Nice Goings On* (1933, Lehmann) and *Lucky Break* (1934, Wilkins), alongside Leslie Henson. He went to the Alhambra to appear in the unsuccessful circus musical *The Flying Trapeze* (1935, Clown) with Jack Buchanan, but returned to join Henson at the head of comical affairs at the Gaiety Theatre. There, the gangling, long-faced, acrobatic comedian formed a comically-contrasting team with obese Fred Emney and frog-like Henson through a series of successful musicals (Stefan in *Seeing Stars*, Alphonse in *Swing Along*, Mogolini in *Going Greek*, Burkinshaw in *Running Riot*), introducing with singular success a comedy routine in which he danced the lancers, alone, in a variety of characters.

He subsequently appeared in revue, but returned to the musical stage to play Maxie in a revised version of *Sally* (for which he took a share in the book credit) under the title *Wild Rose*, as Loppy in the London production of *Panama Hattie* (1943), and alongside his old team-mate, Emney, as Mr Pastry in *Big Boy* (1945), creating a character whose name would remain with him for the rest of his life. He appeared with Emney again in the long-running *Blue for a Boy* (1950, Dickie Skippett), but thereafter left the musical stage, although he remained active as a performer in variety and in television (still performing the old lancers routine) until his death.

HEDLEY, H B   (b ?1890; d 2 June 1931).

Hedley worked as a pianist in concert party and touring revue, and composed music for some of Harry Day's provincial revues and for the music halls before he made his first metropolitan appearance as a composer, part of the songwriting team put together by producers Laddie Cliff and Firth Shephard when they ventured into the musical theatre with *Dear Little Billie* (1925). He teamed again with lyricist Desmond Carter and co-composer Jack Strachey on Cliff's next venture, *Lady Luck* (1927), and also appeared in the show heading a trio of speciality pianists, but he was forced to hide under a pseudonym (along with his composing colleagues) for *So This is Love*, Cliff's biggest success to date, when the producer guessed – apparently with some justice – that the public would come to hear music by even an unknown composer as long as he was given out to be fashionably American, rather than the work of a handful of local boys. 'Hal Brody' lasted only two shows, as Cliff could not resist triumphantly unveiling his trick, and Hedley went back to being himself for Cliff's following shows – *So Long, Letty!* (1928, additional songs), *Darling, I Love You* (1930), *The Love Race* (1931, additional songs) and *The Millionaire Kid* (1931, additional song) – before a premature death at the age of 41.

1920 **Fruit Salad** (Ernest Melvin) 1 act Penge Empire 29 November
1925 **Dear Little Billie** (w Jack Strachey/Desmond Carter/ Firth Shephard) Shaftesbury Theatre 25 August
1927 **Lady Luck** (w Strachey/Carter/Shephard) Carlton Theatre 27 April
1928 **So This is Love** (as part of 'Hal Brody'/Carter/Stanley Lupino, Arthur Rigby) Winter Garden Theatre 25 April
1929 **Love Lies** (as part of 'Hal Brody'/Carter/Lupino, Rigby) Gaiety Theatre 20 March
1930 **Darling, I Love You** (w Harry Acres/Carter/Stanley Brightman, Rigby) Gaiety Theatre 22 January

HEESTERS, Johannes [VAN HEESTERS, Jan] (b Amersfoort, Netherlands, 5 December 1903). Matinée and movie idol, longtime star of the German-language musical stage and screen, and Lehár's 'ideal Danilo'.

Heesters began his working life in a bank before becoming an actor and singer in the Dutch theatre. He appeared in Amsterdam, Rotterdam and The Hague in a mixture of classics and new productions (*Ein Walzertraum*, *Die Glocken von Corneville*, *Der Zarewitsch*, *Das Milliardensouper*, *Die Bajadere*, *Susi*, *Die blaue Mazur*, *Gräfin Mariza*, *Der liebe Augustin*, *Die Teresina*, *Das Veilchen vom Montmartre* [*Violetta*], Hirsch's *Dolly*) and original works (*Die Königin von Montmartre*, *Feminola*, *Der blaue Mantel*, *Seppl*, *Roszi der Zigeuner*) as well as such enterprising productions as the Hungarian *Éjféli tangó* and Friml's *Der Vagbundkönig*.

In 1934 he joined the company at the Vienna Volksoper for a season (*Der Bettelstudent*, *Das Hollandweibchen*, *Wiener G'schichten*, *Polenblut*, *Die erste Liebelei*, *Orpheus in der Unterwelt*, *Valentino*) before going on to the Scala to appear – still as Jan Heesters – as film director Karl Hell in Robert Stolz's *Servus! Servus!* (1935) and to play in his first German-language film *Die Leuchter des Kaisers*. He made his first appearance in Berlin in the Operette *Tatanja* at the Theater am Nollendorfplatz at the end of 1935, and there-

after his career was centred in Berlin, where he became a major film and stage star in musical shows.

His stage shows in the late 1930s and early 1940s included Stolz's *Der süsseste Schwindel der Welt* (1937), Benatzky's *Meine Schwester und ich*, and the first performances of the rôle which he would become so very identified: Danilo in *Die lustige Witwe*. He also created the part of tennis-playing Ulrich, the bridegroom of *Hochzeitsnacht im Paradies*. His film credits in the same period included *Der Bettelstudent*, *Das Hofkonzert* (1936), *Wenn Frauen schweigen*, *Gasparone* (1937), *Manon*, *Das Abenteuer geht weiter* (1938), *Hallo Janine*, *Meine Tante, deine Tante* (1939), *Liebesschule*, *Die lustigen Vagabunden*, *Rosen in Tirol* (1940), *Immer nur du*, *Jenny und der Herr in Frack*, *Illusion* (1941), *Karneval der Liebe* (1942), *Glück bei Frauen*, *Es lebe die Liebe* (1943), *Es fing so harmlos an*, *Frech und verliebt* (1944) and *Die Fledermaus* (1945).

He moved to Vienna in 1948, and in 1949 he created another new part in the title-rôle of Kattnigg's *Bel Ami* at the Raimundtheater. In 1950 he repeated *Hochzeitsnacht im Paradies* in Vienna, in Frankfurt and on both the film and television screens, and in the years that followed he returned to the rôle of Ulrich frequently throughout Europe, along with his other favourite parts – *Die lustige Witwe*, *Der Graf von Luxemburg*, *Meine Schwester und ich* (also television) – whilst keeping up a regular schedule of films including versions of the stage musicals *Die Csárdásfürstin* (1951) with Marika Rökk, *Der Tanz ins Glück* (1951), *Im weissen Rössl* (1952), *Die geschiedene Frau* (1953) and *Der Opernball* (1956). He also starred in a German version of *The Moon is Blue* in the rôle simultaneously taken by David Niven in the English version, and in the 1957 remake of *Viktor und Viktoria*.

In 1956 he appeared in *Kiss Me, Kate* in Munich, in 1959 in a revival of *Der Orlow* at the Raimundtheater, and in 1960 in a second *Bel Ami*, this one by Kreuder, at the same house. Thereafter he mixed straight and musical rôles, the latter including a Dutch version of *The Sound of Music* in Amsterdam, further *Hochzeitsnacht im Paradies* and *Die lustige Witwe* performances, and a *Viktoria und ihr Husar* (1973) at the Mörbisch lake-theatre. He scored one final success when he took on the rôle created by Maurice Chevalier in the stage adaptation of *Gigi* in Vienna, Berlin, Hamburg and Munich.

Autobiography: *Es kommt auf die Sekunde an* (Blanvalet Verlag, Munich, 1978)

HÉGOBURU, Loulou

A popular singing, dancing revue and musical comedy ingénue of the French années folles.

Pop-eyed, pop-cheeked Loulou Hégoburu made a major hit as Nanette in the Théâtre Mogador's *No, No, Nanette* ('Heureux, tous les deux', 'Thé pour deux', 'No, no, Nanette') and thereafter was seen starred with Fernand Graavey in *L'Eau à la bouche* (1928, 'Ce n'est qu'un mannequin'), as the Parisian star of Gershwin's *Tip-Toes* (1929, 'Petit Boby' ie 'Looking for a Boy', 'Le Petit Capitaine' ie 'Virginia'), and alongside Edmée Favart, Bach and Géo Bury in the spectacular Théâtre du Châtelet *Sidonie Panache* (1931, 'C'est Rosalie', 'La cantinière'). Later in her career, she appeared in *Un petit bout de femme* (1936) and *Ma petite amie* (1937) before ceasing to be an ingénue.

Plate 122. **Aranka Hegyi:** *The Népszinház's most skilful soprano swapped happily between male rôles (left) and such feminine parts as the title-rôle of* Katalin *(right) in a long and dazzling career.*

HEGYI, Aranka (b Pest, 25 May 1855; d Pest, 9 June 1906).

One of the outstanding performers of the Hungarian musical theatre of the last two decades of the 19th century, soprano Aranka Hegyi shared the limelight and the star rôles – particularly those which required the strongest vocal skills – at Budapest's Népszinház with Lujza Blaha and Ilka Pálmay, without following the former to a vaster celebrity, or the latter to fame abroad.

The daughter of a gipsy musician, she lived her early life in the wilds before, after her father's death, being adopted and brought up first by his fellow musician Sándor Herczenberger and then by the famous gipsy musician and composer Ferenc Sárközi. She appeared early on as a dancer at the Nemzeti Színház, but her singing talents soon became evident and in 1880 Jenő Rákosi hired her for the Népszinház, where she made her début in the title-rôle of *La Jolie Persane*. Amongst the other pieces which she introduced in the following decades were local versions of *Les Dragons de Villars* (Rose Friquet), *La Marquise des rues*, *Les Noces d'Olivette* (Bathilde), *Les Poupées de l'Infante*, *Le Jour et la nuit* (Béatrix), the enormously successful *Lili* (Lili), *Der Bettelstudent* (Laura, with Blaha as Symon and Pálmay as Bronislawa), *Der lustige Krieg* (Violetta), *Gasparone*, *Les Contes d'Hoffman* (Antonia, a particular success for her), *Les Pilules du Diable*, *Le Fils prodigue* (Pierrot), *Der Zigeunerbaron* (Sáffi), *La Fille de Madame Angot* (Lange), *The Mikado* (Nanki Poo), *Der arme Jonathan* (Harriet), *The Geisha* (O Mimosa San), *A Runaway Girl* and

Bruder Straubinger, and she also reprised rôles originally played by Blaha and others, including Rosalinde, Serpolette and Boccaccio, in the Népszinház repertoire. The arrival of the new wave of Hungarian musical stars, Sári Fedák and Klára Küry at their head, still found her firmly entrenched at the top of the tree, and whilst younger stars came and went she remained to the fore until after the turn of the century, retiring in 1903 at nearly 50 years of age.

Hegyi created leading rôles in a number of Hungarian operetts, including Lajos Serly's *Világszép asszony Marica* (Marica), *Peking rózsája*, the title-rôle of Verő's successful *A szultán*, *Virágcsata*, *A libapásztor*, Konti's *A Talmi hercegnő*, József Bokor's *A kis alamuszi* (Vicomte Renaud), and, in one of her last appearances, the title-rôle in the record breaking *Katalin*.

HEGYI, Béla (b Pápa, 1858; d Budapest, 19 April 1922).

Conductor and composer, Hegyi was trained at the Budapest Zeneakadémia and thereafter wrote a number of orchestral and instrumental works which, like his stage pieces, and unlike the operetts of some of his contemporaries, had a distinct Hungarian flavour to them. His stage opus comprised six operetts and a one-act opera (*Yvonne és Loïc* aka *A falu csúfja*, 27 March 1893), as well as incidental music and songs to the play *Az árendás zsidó* (1884). The two most successful of his lighter musical theatre works, both composed in collaboration with Szidor Bátor, were a re-musicked version of Leterrier and

Vanloo's libretto for *L'Étoile*, produced at the Népszinház as *Uff király* (King Ouf), and *A titkos csók*, a musical adaptation of Bayard and Dumanoir's French play *La Vicomtesse Lolotte*. *Pepita*, composed alone, was a version of another French original, *Ne touchez pas à la reine*.

1886 **A milliomosnő** (w Szidor Bátor/Ferenc Rajna) 1 act Népszinház 27 December

1887 **Uff király** (w Bátor/Vanloo, Leterrier ad Jenő Rákosi) Népszinház 21 May

1888 **A titkos csók** (w Bátor/Sándor Lukácsy) Népszinház 7 December

1890 **Pepita** (Rajna, Antal Radó) Népszinház 21 January

1899 **A liliputi hercegnő** (József Márkus) Magyar Színház 25 March

1904 **Boris király** (Zsigmond Szőllősi) Király Színház 18 March

HEIMLICHE LIEBE Operette in 3 acts by Julius Bauer. Music by Paul Ottenheimer. Johann Strauss-Theater, Vienna, 13 October 1911.

The most successful work of the composer Ottenheimer, *Heimliche Liebe* was mounted in Vienna under the management of Leopold Müller, with Alexander Girardi and Gerda Walde starred for a run of 200 consecutive performances. This first run record outdid that of the much more famous *Der Zigeunerprimás*, in which same the two stars followed up the following year, and was as good or better than anything yet produced at the three-year-old Johann Strauss-Theater, or anything that followed until the house's long-running production of *Rund um die Liebe* in 1914–15. Like the latter piece, however, and unlike *Zigeunerprimás*, *Heimliche Liebe* did not prove to have much of an afterlife following its fine initial run.

The piece was set in a Viennese fashion-factory 'Zur schöne Wienerin' run by Madame Gruber. The heroine, her niece Toni (Gerda Walde), profits from her aunt's profession, disguising herself as a boy on her way to discovering the heimliche Liebe of the title.

The centre of attraction, however, was not the plot but Girardi who played Der Profoss equipped with a Basteilied, which slipped from march-time into his preferred waltz refrain ('Was jetzt die Mäderln machen'), and a little Vogellied at the top of the final act which took in some twittering bird imitations. The military Egon von Romberg supplied a Gondellied ('Lieblich leuchtet das Himmelszelt') and a women-and-war piece ('Nur durch die Liebe kamen wir ums Paradies'), while the dancer Rositta ('from the Opera at Milan') made her entrances to the showy strains of a mazurka and the waltz 'Wie sie alle mich umschmachten'. Toni culled a little Veilchenlied in the first act and a Trommellied in the second ('Ich ging in Männerkleidern') in a musically well-furnished evening which served its purposes admirably and was then forgotten.

HEIN, Silvio (b New York, 15 March 1879; d Saranac Lake, NY, 19 December 1928).

A pleasant, popular and prolific member of the Broadway establishment in the early years of the 20th century, Hein worked widely as a musical director whilst also turning his hand to a steady stream of straightforward and prettily functional scores, written over a period of some 15 years. He provided the songs for solid comedy touring vehicles for such stars as Marie Cahill, for whom he musicked *Nancy Brown*, *Moonshine*, *Marrying Mary* ('The Hottentot Love Song', 'He's a Cousin of Mine'), *Judy Forgot* and *The Boys and Betty* ('Marie Cahill's Arab Love Song'), De Wolf Hopper (*A Matinée Idol*), Blanche Ring (*The Yankee Girl*), Joseph Santley (*When Dreams Come True*, featuring a song called 'Dear World' and another advising 'Come Along to the Movies') and for the popular touring team of Cecil Lean and Cleo Mayfield (*Look Who's Here*). He won his longest Broadway run, however, with the 1917 musical comedy surprise *Flo-Flo* (220 performances), which boasted no such starry aid.

Outside his principal scores he also wrote for a number of revues from *The Ziegfeld Follies of 1907* ('I Want to Be a Drummer Boy') to *Some Party* (1922), composed various scores of incidental music, ranging from that for the 1917 Park Theater revival of Shakespeare's *The Merry Wives of Windsor* to 'music and cabaret songs' for George Hobart's play *Experience* (27 October 1914), and interpolated isolated songs into a range of musicals. Amongst these last were found some of his more successful numbers: 'Some Little Bug is Going to Find You Someday' (w Benjamin Hapgood Burt, Roy Attwood), introduced in Broadway's version of Lehár's *Endlich Allein*, and 'All Dressed Up and No Place to Go' (w Burt), which was performed by Raymond Hitchcock in Broadway's *The Beauty Shop* and in London's *Mr Manhattan*.

1903 **Nancy Brown** (w Henry Hadley/Frederick Ranken, George Broadhurst) Bijou Theater 16 February

1905 **Moonshine** (Benjamin Hapgood Burt/George V Hobart) Liberty Theater 30 October

1906 **Marrying Mary** (Burt/Edward Milton Royle) Daly's Theater 27 August

1908 **The Boys and Betty** (Hobart) Wallack's Theater 2 November

1910 **The Yankee Girl** (Hobart) Herald Square Theater 10 February

1910 **A Matinée Idol** (Seymour Brown, E Ray Goetz/Armand, Barnard) Daly's Theater 28 April

1910 **Judy Forgot** (Avery Hopwood) Broadway Theater 6 October

1913 **Glorianna** (Hobart/Philip Bartholomae) Cort Theater, Chicago 12 October

1913 **When Dreams Come True** (Bartholomae) Lyric Theater 18 August

1914 **The Model Maid** (Bartholomae) Opera House, Providence 17 August

1914 **Miss Daisy** (revised *The Model Maid*) Shubert Theater 9 September

1914 **At the Ball** (Bartholomae, Alice Gerstenberg) Van Curler Opera House, Schenectady 12 December

1915 **All Over Town** (Harry B Smith/Joseph Santley) Shubert Theater, New Haven 26 April

1915 **One of the Boys** (Bartholomae) Palace Theater 24 May

1917 **The Red Clock** (Schuyler Greene/Val Crawford) Buffalo

1917 **Furs and Frills** (Edward Clark) Casino Theater 9 October

1917 **Flo-Flo** (Edward A Paulton/Fred de Grésac) Cort Theater 20 December

1917 **The Golden Goose** (Herbert Reynolds, Schuyler Greene/Edgar Smith) Apollo Theater, Atlantic City 29 November

1918 **The Bride Shop** (w Walter Rosemont/de Grésac)

1918 **He Didn't Want to Do It** (Broadhurst) Broadhurst Theater 20 August

1918 **Miss Blue Eyes** (Hobart) Apollo Theater, Atlantic City 3 October

1920 **Look Who's Here** (E A Paulton/Frank Mandel) 44th Street Theater 2 March

1920 **The Girl from Home** (ex- *The New Dictator*) (Frank Craven) Globe Theater 3 May

Plate 123.

and others (one Edmund Eysler song was featured). Hattie Williams starred as *The Rollicking Girl*, still called Ilona, alongside Sam Bernard as her comical helpmate, the wigmaker Schmalz, and Joe Coyne as Panagl. Charles Frohman's production played a splendid 169 performances at the Herald Square Theater. Shortly after this Ilka Pálmay appeared at the city's German-speaking theatre, playing the original version of *Heisses Blut* (7 December 1905).

USA: Casino Theater *A Dangerous Maid* 12 November 1898, Herald Square Theater *The Rollicking Girl* 1 May 1905

HELD, Anna (b ?Warsaw, 18 March 1873; d New York, 13 August 1918). Broadway's favourite 'parisienne' of the turn-of-the-century years.

After beginning her career as a music-hall performer in Europe, the Polish-born – or, at the least, partly-Polish descended – Miss Held was taken to America by Florenz Ziegfeld, whilst in her early twenties. She also (although it has been suggested that the official deed might have been overlooked) married the famous showman. She first

HEISSES BLUT Posse mit Gesang in 3 acts and 7 scenes by Carl Lindau and Leopold Krenn. Music by Heinrich Schenk. Theater an der Wien, Vienna, 17 April 1892.

A highly successful musical play built as a showpiece for its central female character, *Heisses Blut* allowed the winsome Ilona to partake of a multiplicity of disguises as she runs away from her country home on her wedding day, through a series of adventures, including a spectacular duel, before, inevitably, ending her cavalcade by becoming a theatre star in Vienna. Her progress was accompanied by a bright score, much of it in 3/4 time, from which the waltz 'Schön sind die Veilchen' proved to be the favourite musical moment.

Vienna's original production of *Heisses Blut* was a decided success. It played from Easter through to the summer break and was brought back again to re-open the new season in the autumn, playing through until 14 October. It was kept in the house's repertoire until 1895, and ended up totalling 100 performances in all at the Theater an der Wien.

The show was subsequently widely reprised in other German-language houses, but it proved particularly popular in America. Sydney Rosenfeld's English-language adaptation, under the title *A Dangerous Maid* (add ly Louis Harrison, add mus Fred J Eustis), was produced by George Lederer and George B McLellan at the Casino Theatre for a run of 65 performances in 1898, with Cissie Loftus popping her famous impersonations into the rather loose-jointed proceedings. It surfaced on Broadway again in 1905 in a much more comedy-orientated version (still credited to Rosenfeld), with new music by W T Francis

Plate 124. **Anna Held**: *Florenz Ziegfeld promoted the pretty soubrette as the epitome of Paris and also – according to all the evidence – married her.*

appeared on the American musical stage in the farce-comedy *A Parlour Match*, then starred as the girl-doll in a version of Audran's *La Poupée* and, under Ziegfeld's management, in a compôte of two shows made famous by Anna Judic, *Mam'zelle Nitouche* and *La Femme à papa*, which called itself *Papa's Wife* (1899). In the process, she established herself prettily in the eyes of New York theatregoers as the epitome of all that was invitingly French. In the years that followed, it was the star's 'naughty' Continental charm and a good deal of expensive staging that were the main ingredients of what became known as 'an Anna Held show'.

Quickly publicized into a solid above-the-title name, she starred in a series of Broadway musicals in the space of a decade: a made-over version of another Anna Judic vehicle, *Niniche*, called *The Little Duchess* (1901), a musical allegedly custom-made from a Jean Richepin play and entitled *Mam'selle Napoléon*, Joe Weber's variety musical *Higgledy-Piggledy* (1904, Mimi de Chartreuse), as *A Parisian Model* (1906, 'It's Delightful to Be Married', 'I Just Can't Make My Eyes Behave') and as *Miss Innocence* (1908, 'I Wonder What's the Matter with My Eyes').

Her marriage to Ziegfeld ended, but Miss Held's Broadway career had one further chapter when, in 1916, she appeared for the Shuberts in a piece that had once been a Leo Ascher musical but was now a pot-pourri called *Follow Me*, singing 'I Want to Be Good But My Eyes Won't Let Me', the last of the parade of 'eyes' songs she had featured during her American stage life.

Anna Held was portrayed on film in *The Great Ziegfeld* (1936) by Luise Rainer, and on the musical stage in the London extravaganza *Ziegfeld* (1988) by French actress and singer Fabienne Guyon.

Biography: *Anna Held: Une Étoile française au ciel de l'Amérique* (La Nef de Paris, Paris, 1954) – although the cover and first-person narration give the impression that this is an autobiography, it was apparently written by Held's daughter

HELD, Ludwig (b Regensberg, 14 April 1837; d Vienna, 2 March 1900).

The author of a number of successful comedies, Held had a memorable hit on the musical stage with his Posse *Die Näherin*, in which Marie Geistinger scored as the chatterbox seamstress of the title. He later joined with Moritz West to provide three libretti for Karl Zeller – including the composer's two most successful pieces, the inimitable *Der Vogelhändler* and *Der Obersteiger* – and co-wrote three texts for Suppé, of which *Bellman* and *Das Modell* found some success.

Although *Die Näherin* and *Der Obersteiger* were both original creations, many of Held's libretti were, in fact, adaptations from French originals. *Der Vagabund* was taken from an original by Émile Souvestre, *Der Vogelhändler* from Charles Varin and de Biéville's *Ce qui deviennent les roses*, *Der Cognac-König* from Eugène Scribe and Bayard's *La Frontière de Savoie*, *Der Schlosserkönig* similarly from Scribe, whilst *Die Stiefmama* was a version of the famous Hennequin and Millaud vaudeville *La Femme à papa*.

His son, **Leo HELD** (b Vienna, 1874; d Vienna, 16 May 1903) was the composer of several short-lived Operetten, and the music for a number of Possen, including the successful *Die Goldtante* at the Theater an der Wien (1897). He also composed additional pieces for the Vienna version

of the German hit *Eine tolle Nacht*, and one short opera, *Gina, die Ziegunerin*. He committed suicide before the age of 30.

1880 **Die Näherin** (Carl Millöcker) Theater an der Wien 13 March
1884 **Gefundenes Geld** (Julius Stern) Theater an der Wien 18 October
1886 **Der Vagabund** (Karl Zeller/w Moritz West) Carltheater 30 October
1887 **Bellman** (Franz von Suppé/w West) Theater an der Wien 26 February
1889 **Der Schlosserkönig** (Eduard Kremser/w Benjamin Schier) Theater an der Wien 12 January
1891 **Der Vogelhändler** (Zeller/w West) Theater an der Wien 10 January
1894 **Der Obersteiger** (Zeller/w West) Theater an der Wien 5 January
1895 **Der Schnuffler** (Leo Held) Raimundtheater 1 February
1895 **Das Modell** (Suppé/w Victor Léon) Carltheater 4 October
1897 **Die Schwalben** (Leo Held/w West) Theater an der Wien 12 February
1897 **Der Cognac-König** (Franz Wagner/w Léon) Carltheater 20 February
1898 **Die Pariserin** (Suppé/w Léon) Carltheater 26 January
1900 **Die Stiefmama** (Leo Held) Theater an der Wien 20 February

HELDEN, HELDEN Musical comedy in 2 acts by Helmut Gmür based on *Arms and the Man* by George Bernard Shaw. Lyrics by Eckart Hachfeld, Walter Brandin and Gmür. Music by Udo Jürgens. Theater an der Wien, Vienna, 23 October 1972.

After the success of *My Fair Lady* in Vienna, the Theater an der Wien had, as so many others did, the idea of making another musical out of a Shaw play. In spite of the existence of *Der tapfere Soldat*, Rolf Kutschera and his team selected an existing German-language version of *Arms and the Man* written by Peter Goldbaum, which was subsequently revised textually by Hans Gmür. The score to this piece, the work of Udo Jürgens – best known for his Eurovision song 'Warum nur, warum', which had been taken to number four in the English charts by Matt Monro – was re-worked over by its composer, and *Helden, Helden* (Heroes, heroes) was produced in 1972 with Michael Heltau as Bluntschli and Gabriele Jacoby (Vienna's Eliza Doolittle) as Raina. Amongst the rest of the cast were opera star Irmgard Seefried as Catherine and the rising Julia Migenes as Louka. *Helden, Helden* was played 130 times in Vienna in 1972–3, and later also appeared in Hamburg with Frln Jacoby and Paul Hubschmid featured, and in Leipzig (10 October 1975).

Germany: Operettenhaus, Hamburg 23 February 1973
Recordings: Hamburg cast (Ariola)

HELLMESBERGER, Josef (b Vienna, 9 April 1855; d Vienna, 26 April 1907). Viennese composer of the turn-of-the-century years.

A descendant of a celebrated Viennese musical family, Josef (known as 'Pepi') was the son of the elder Josef Hellmesberger, longtime director of the Vienna Conservatorium, and famous for his 40 years at the head of the Hellmesberger quartet. Josef the younger played the violin and performed, often with his father's groups, from an early age, appearing in popular concerts and with dance groups, becoming in the process a personality on the Vienna music scene. His career as a violinist took him, in his early twenties, to solo work and also to a teaching post at the Vienna Conservatorium, and it was while he was engaged there that he began to compose more substantial work than the small dance pieces which had been his first efforts as a writer.

His earliest Operetten were produced by Adolf Grünwald at the then-billed Ronachers Operetten-Theater im KK Prater, and one of them, *Der Graf von Gleichen*, proved sufficiently successful there to be later staged in both Germany and in Hungary (*A kétnejü gróf*). However, during the 1880s and 1890s it was as a conductor that Hellmesberger made his principal career, working first at the Carltheater, then at the Hofoper, as well as at the head of the Philharmonic society. He nevertheless produced a considerable amount of theatre music, including a lyric-dance-drama, *Fata Morgana*, played at the Hofoper, the ballets *Meissner Porzellan*, *Das Licht* and *Der Blumen rachen*, incidental music and arrangements of such pieces as Grisar's *Gute Nacht, Herr Pantalon* and London's *Manteaux Noirs* for the Carltheater, and several Operette scores, without finding any one particular success. One Operette, *Das Orakel*, was, however, given a brief production at New York's Casino Theater, following its Viennese run, under the title *Apollo*.

Hellmesberger lost his position in the royal music establishment through an amorous misdemeanour and was forced to leave town. He found a post at the Stuttgart Hoftheater, but the timely Carltheater success of his Operette *Das Veilchenmädel* (1904) and of the popular Posse ('ein Episode aus der Grossstadt') *Wien bei Nacht* later the same year salvaged him both financially and professionally, and he was soon back in Vienna. Although his 'phantastiches Operette' *Der Triumph des Weibes* was taken up by Berlin's Apollotheater after its month's run in Vienna and reproduced there with added music by Lincke, Hellmesberger was unable to repeat the success of *Das Veilchenmädel* in a list of subsequent works for the Operette stage. *Mutzi* flopped in seven performances at the Carltheater, and his last years were spent mostly supplying piece-work music to Gabor Steiner at his two Viennese houses and in increasingly less prominent positions in musical society, before his death at the age of 52.

A well-regarded piece called *Letzter Fasching*, arranged from Hellmesberger's musical leavings, was later mounted in Graz, and a second posthumous piece, a soi-disant sequel to *Das Veilchenmädel* entitled *Der Veilchenkavalier*, was played at Ronacher in Vienna. Many years later his work was used as the basis for a third made-up piece, *Wiener G'schichten*, played at the Volksoper in 1934.

1880 **Kapitän Ahlström** (Albert Hofmann) Ronachers Operetten-Theater 15 May

1880 **Der Graf von Gleichen [und seine beiden Frauen]** (Alois Just) Ronachers Operetten-Theater 31 July

1886 **Der schöne Kurfürst** (Böhrmann-Riegen) Theater am Gärtnerplatz, Munich 15 May

1887 **Rikiki** (Richard Genée, Wilhelm Mannstädt) Carltheater 28 September

1889 **Das Orakel** (Ignaz Schnitzer) Theater an der Wien 30 November

1890 **Der bleiche Gast** (w Alfred Zamara/Victor Léon, Heinrich von Waldberg) Carl-Schultze Theater, Hamburg 6 September

1895 **Die Doppelhochzeit** (Léon, Waldberg) Theater in der Josefstadt 21 September

1904 **Das Veilchenmädel** (Leopold Krenn, Carl Lindau) Carltheater 27 February

1904 **Die Eisjungfrau** revised version of *The Girl from Up There* (w Gustave Kerker/M Band, Lindau, Julius Wilhelm) Venedig in Wien 3 June

1904 **Wien bei Nacht** (Lindau, Wilhelm) Danzers Orpheum 28 October

1906 **Die drei Engel** (ad Lindau, F Antony) Venedig in Wien 4 May

1906 **Mutzi** (Wilhelm, Robert Pohl) Carltheater 15 September

1906 **Der Triumph des Weibes** (August Neidhart) Danzers Orpheum 16 November

1906 **Eine vom 'Moulin-Rouge'** (Leopold Krenn) Danzers Orpheum 21 December

1909 **Letzter Fasching** (arr Ludwig Prechtl/Louis Windhopp) Stadttheater, Graz 10 February

1911 **Der Veilchenkavalier** (Krenn) Ronacher 16 April

1934 **Wiener G'schichten** (arr Oskar Jascha/Wilhelm Sterk) Volksoper 27 October

Other title attributed: *Der Wunderkaftan* (1902)

Biography: Prosl, R M: *Die Hellmesberger* (Gerlach & Wiedling, Vienna, 1947)

HELLO, DOLLY! Musical in 2 acts by Michael Stewart based on Thornton Wilder's *The Matchmaker*. Music and lyrics by Jerry Herman. St James Theater, New York, 16 January 1964.

Thornton Wilder's successful play *The Matchmaker* (Royale Theater 1955, 486 performances), a rewritten version of his unsuccessful 1938 piece *The Merchant of Yonkers*, had a long pedigree, being a descendant of the classic Viennese comedy *Einen Jux will er sich machen* by Johann Nestroy, itself apparently taken from an earlier (English) play, John Oxenford's *A Day Well Spent*. The musical comedy version followed the reshaping done by Wilder in making Mrs Dolly Levi, the matchmaker, the central character of the piece.

Widowed Mrs Levi (Carol Channing) of Yonkers, NY, is a 'woman who arranges things' in the best tradition of such musical-theatre ladies as Mrs Ralli-Carr of *Gentleman Joe*. Employed to find a suitable wife for rich Horace Vandergelder (David Burns), she decides that the most suitable candidate is not, after all, her pretty milliner client Irene Molloy (Eileen Brennan), but herself. She succeeds in turning Vandergelder both from thoughts of Mrs Molloy and an exasperated dislike of her bossy, managing self, to a frame of mind which brings a proposal, all in the space of two comedy-packed acts. When Vandergelder heads for New York for the day out which will change his life, his young employees Cornelius Hackl (Charles Nelson Reilly) and Barnaby Tucker (Jerry Dodge) take the opportunity to skive off for a jaunt to town themselves. They fall in with Irene and her assistant Minnie Fay (Sondra Lee) and, after a farcical series of events which peak in a night out at the ritzy Harmonia Gardens (a scene echoing closely the famous centrepiece of the 19th-century American musical comedy *A Trip to Chinatown*), ends up with all the characters hauled up in court, everyone heads back to Yonkers and a happy – or at least matrimonial – ending.

Jerry Herman's score did more than just illustrate the farcical incidents of the play, for it turned out a whole set of numbers which would become favourites, topped by the extravagant welcome proffered to Mrs Levi on her 'return' to the Harmonia Gardens after many years of widowly absence. 'Hello, Dolly!', with a certain amount of help from Louis Armstrong's hugely popular broken-glass-voiced recording, became one of the most popular Broadway songs of its era. The two boys excitedly planned their day out in 'Put on Your Sunday Clothes' and joined with their girls pretending to know what 'Elegance' is. Irene primped prettily through her plans for the summer in 'I'll Be Wearing Ribbons Down My Back', and Cornelius pleaded, in an incoherent defence in a semi-surreal court, that 'It Only Takes a Moment' to fall in love. Mrs Levi led a bewildering march in praise of 'Motherhood, [America and a hot lunch for orphans]', squalled out her determination to get something more out of life 'Before the Parade Passes By' (whilst *Funny Girl*, up the street, was simultaneously instructing the world 'Don't Rain on My Parade'), and closed her talons around Vandergelder with a succulent 'Goodbye, Dearie' which had no intention of meaning 'goodbye'.

David Merrick's production of *Hello, Dolly!* scored a triumph on Broadway, with Carol Channing – in the rôle originally designed for Ethel Merman – shooting back to and even beyond the level of fame she had achieved many years earlier in *Gentlemen Prefer Blondes*. She shared the accolades with director/choreographer Gower Champion, whose arangement of the Harmonia Gardens scene with its famous Waiter's Galop and its splendid display of traditional dinner-table and dance-floor low comedy, was the high-point of the evening.

Hello, Dolly! broke America's musical comedy long-run record with a stay of no less than 2,844 performances in its first run on Broadway. Miss Channing was succeeded by a parade of often well-known names in the title-rôle as the performances and the years passed by – Ginger Rogers, Martha Raye, Betty Grable, Bibi Osterwald, Pearl Bailey at the head of a wholly recast all-black version, Phyllis Diller and, in 1970, Miss Merman, who finally got to play the rôle she had originally been offered. For the occasion, two additional songs were added, but they did not succeed in impinging on the public consciousness in the way that virtually the entire original score had. Not for the first time, however, a major hit show and a major hit song brought forth a plagiarism lawsuit. This time it was 'Hello, Dolly!' which was the subject of the accusations, songwriter Mack David claiming that the main theme had been lifted from his 'Sunflower'. As in so many past cases, the challenge proved worth his while, to the tune of a quarter of a million dollars, when Herman found it advisable to settle rather than face the kind of costly litigation which has scared so many away from properly defending themselves in a Broadway court.

Fifteen months after the show's opening, the first touring company of *Hello, Dolly!* went out in America with Mary Martin in the role of Mrs Levi, and it was Miss Martin who went on to head H M Tennent Ltd's London production at the Theatre Royal, Drury Lane, later the same year. London, for some reason, did not display the same enthusiasm for *Hello, Dolly!* that Broadway had done, and after some five months the musical was on the verge of being closed. However, when (at Miss Martin's suggestion) local favourite Dora Bryan took over the part of Mrs Levi, the show picked up well enough to remain in the

West End for 794 performances after which Miss Bryan took it on tour. Before Britain had welcomed *Dolly*, however, the first overseas production had already been launched, in Australia, with rather more positive reactions. Carole Cook starred as Dolly alongside Jill Perryman (Eileen) and Bill Mulliken (Cornelius) for ten months in Sydney and Melbourne (Her Majesty's Theatre 27 August 1965) prior to a tour of New Zealand and a long series of other dates.

A German-language version of the show (ad Robert Gilbert) was produced in Düsseldorf in 1966 with Tatania Iwanow starring, and the show went on to establish itself as a firm favourite in German-speaking countries, with Marika Rökk appearing in the title-rôle in Berlin and at Vienna's Theater an der Wien, and Gisela May leading the company in East Germany's production. The first French-language performance (ad Jacques Collard, Marc-Cab, André Hornez) was played in Liège, Belgium (26 March 1971), but the piece was brought to Paris the following year with Annie Cordy starring as a Dolly less abrasive than some and Jacques Mareuil as Vandergelder. The Paris season was not a whole-hearted success, but the show nevertheless won a number of regional productions in France in the years that followed. Its only return to Paris, however, was in a season by one of the American touring companies which took to the European roads in the 1980s and 1990s, playing the show in English. French jazz-singer Nicole Croisille took the rôle of Mrs Levi (Théâtre du Châtelet, 12 November 1992).

A film version, produced in 1969, with Barbra Streisand playing a much younger-seeming and altogether rather different (but probably more valid) Dolly alongside Walter Matthau (Vandergelder) and the young Michael Crawford (Cornelius), made some alterations to the show's score, adding two numbers which had been cut prior to the show's Broadway opening and slimming out some others. It did not ever become as popular as the stage show, which has continued to be a world-wide favourite, but which has nevertheless not made anything like the impression made in its record-breaking original run in several returns to the main centres. Broadway had a second black-cast version, again with Pearl Bailey starred, in 1975 (Minskoff Theater 6 November, 42 performances), whilst Miss Channing played 147 more performances in her famous rôle at the Lunt-Fontanne Theater in 1978 (5 March) before going on to a disappointingly tatty London reproduction at the Shaftesbury Theatre (21 September 1979, 170 performances). The most recent London production perhaps provided the answer to this apparent droop in favour when it showed the way that the rôle of Dolly Levi and, by extension, the show, had gone. At the Prince of Wales Theatre in 1984 (3 January), female impersonator Danny La Rue appeared briefly as a travesty Dolly. Around the same time, London's National Theatre was triumphing with a new and trippingly legitimate version of *Einen Jux* (*On the Razzle* ad Tom Stoppard).

Australia: Her Majesty's Theatre, Sydney 27 March 1965; UK: Theatre Royal, Drury Lane 2 December 1965; Germany: Schauspielhaus, Düsseldorf 26 November 1966; Hungary: Fővárosi Operettszinház 23 February 1968; Austria: Theater an der Wien 10 September 1968; France: Théâtre Mogador 29 September 1972; Film: Twentieth Century-Fox 1969

Recordings: original cast (RCA), London cast (RCA Victor),

London cast replacement stars (HMV), Broadway black cast (RCA), film soundtrack (Twentieth Century-Fox), German cast (Columbia), French cast (CBS), Israeli cast (CBS), Austrian cast (Metronome), East German cast (Amiga), Russian cast (Melodiya), Mexican cast (RCA Victor) etc

HELOÏSE ET ABÉLARD Opérette in 3 acts by Clairville and William Busnach. Music by Henri Litolff. Théâtre des Folies-Dramatiques, Paris, 19 October 1872.

Coralie Geoffroy appeared as Heloïse, alongside an Abélard who remained intact at the final curtain, in an opérettic version of the famous tale which gave all the discomfort to the villain. The villain in Clairville and Busnach's text was Chanoine Fulbert, Heloïse's clerical uncle, a nasty, worldly fellow who is proposing to make free with the wife of his tenant in retaliation for his being behind with the rent, but who nevertheless has no intentions of allowing his bluestocking niece to cast sweet glances at her teacher. When Heloïse arranges for Abélard to carry her off, the Chanoine summons his men to kidnap and chastise the 'ravisher'. Unfortunately for him, they get the wrong man.

A fine score by opérettic novice Litolff supported the piece through a good Parisian run, after which the show was given an Austrian production (ad Richard Genée) with Irma Nittinger and Jani Szika in the title-rôles and Matthias Rott as Fulbert. The piece was revived at the Théâtre de la Renaissance in 1879 with Jane Hading, Vauthier and Urbain.

Austria: Theater an der Wien 27 September 1873

HELTAI, Jenő (b Budapest, 11 August 1871; d Budapest, 3 September 1957).

Journalist Heltai had his first short play staged when he was 23, and he passed on through jobs at the Paris Exposition and as secretary at the Vigszinház, as well as in various capacities in the newspaper world, as his theatrical career as a writer and, most particularly, as an adaptor began to flourish. He subsequently worked as a dramaturg, directed the Belvárosi Színház, and held a number of other theatrical posts over the nearly forty years in which he turned out a vast amount of writing for the Hungarian stage.

Heltai's original works included only a few for the musical stage, but he was responsible for the lyrics for the most important original Hungarian work of the early 20th century, *János vitéz*, and his early operett *Egyptom gyöngye* was sufficiently successful to be adapted and played in Germany under the title *Das heilige Krokodil* (Elberfeld 28 February 1911). A wide-ranging and very lengthy list of adaptation credits, most particularly from the French, but including *Abie's Irish Rose*, *The Constant Wife*, *Le Mariage de Mlle Beulemans*, *Coralie et Cie*, *Romance*, *Pillangókisasszony* (*Madame Butterfly*), *La Petite Chocolatière* and Xavier Leroux's *Le Chemineau* also included a varying selection of musical pieces, ranging from Gaiety musical comedy and French opéra-bouffe to postwar French jazz-age musicals and a number of 'comedies with songs'.

Heltai had two posthumous musical theatre credits. Ernő Innocent Vincze adapted one of his works as the libretto for Albert Szirmai's *A tündérlaki lányok* (Fővárosi Operettszinház 29 January 1964), and his translation of

Léon Gandillot's *Ferdinand le noceur* was musicalized (ly: Iván Szenes, mus: Szabolc Fényes) for the Székesfehérvári Nyári Színház in 1985 (24 June).

1898 **A bibliásasszony** (*Les Fêtards*) Hungarian version (Népszínház)

1899 **Egyptom gyöngye** (Miklós Forrai) Magyar Színház 17 February

1900 **El Párizsba!** (pasticcio/w Emil Makai) Magyar Színház 16 May

1902 **Az aranyos** (*The Casino Girl*) Hungarian version (Népszinház)

1902 **A sötét kamra** (*Joli sport*) Hungarian version of comedy with added songs (Magyar Színház)

1902 **Soh'se halunk meg!** Hungarian version of Horst/Stein comedy with added songs (Városligeti Nyári Színkör)

1902 **Az izé** (*Das gewiss etwas*) Hungarian version w Miska Marton (Népszinház)

1904 **A királynő férje** (*Le Prince Consort*) Hungarian version with songs by László Kun Vigszinház 8 April

1904 **János vitez** (Jenő Huszka/Károly Bakonyi) Király Színház 18 November

1904 **Az ezüstpapucs** (*The Silver Slipper*) Hungarian version (Népszinház)

1904 **Én, te, ő** (*Le Sire de Vergy*) Hungarian version (Király Színház)

1904 **A szalmaözvegy** (*Les Vacances de mariage*) Hungarian version of comedy with added songs (Népszinház)

1904 **A rátartós királykisasszony** (*Der var en Gang*) Hungarian version with songs by Viktor Jacobi (Népszinház)

1904 **Muki** Hungarian version of Pierre Wolff comedy with songs by Géza Chorin (Budai Színkör)

1905 **Mulató istenek** (*Der Göttergatte*) Hungarian version (Magyar Színház)

1905 **A kedves bácsi** (*The Wrong Mr Wright*) Hungarian version of comedy with added songs (Magyar Színház)

1905 **A danzigi hercegnő** (*The Duchess of Dantzic*) Hungarian version (Király Színház)

1905 **Bohémszerelem** (*La Petite Bohème*) Hungarian version (Magyar Színház)

1905 **A férjhezment kisasszony** (*Le Voyage de la mariée*) Hungarian version (Magyar Színház)

1906 **Tengerszem tündére** (Victor Jacobi/Zoltán Thury) Magyar Színház 7 November

1906 **A császárné legyezője** (*Les Dragons de l'imperatrice*) Hungarian version (Népszinház)

1907 **Miciszlav** (*Mitislaw der moderne*) Hungarian version (Király Színház)

1907 **Bernát** (Imre Kálmán) Vígszinház 1 June

1907 **A balkiralynő** (*The Catch of the Season*) Hungarian version (Népszinház)

1908 **Naftalin** (Albert Szirmai) Vigszínház 6 June

1909 **Édes teher** (various) Vígszínház 5 June

1911 **A ferencvárosi angyal** (Szirmai/w Ferenc Molnár) Royal Orfeum 31 December

1911 **As ezred apja** (*Le Papa du régiment*) Hungarian version of comedy with songs by Károly Stephanides (Vígszinház)

1912 **Ábraham a mennyországban** (*Casimirs Himmelfahrt*) Hungarian version w Molnár (Budai Színkör)

1914 **Napsugár kisasszony** (*The Sunshine Girl*) Hungarian version (Király Színház)

1914 **Leni néni** (*Le Portait de ma tante*) Hungarian version of comedy, with songs by Zsigmond Vincze (Magyar Színház)

1917 **A márványmenyasszony** (*Niobe*) Hungarian version (Vigszinház)

1917 **Tavasz és szerelem** (*Liebe und Lenz*) Hungarian version (Városi Színház)

1921 **Fi-fi** (*Phi-Phi*) Hungarian version (Lujza Blaha Színház)

1922 **Cserebere** (*Ta bouche*) Hungarian version (Vigszinház)

1923 **Dédé** Hungarian version (Lujza Blaha Színház)

1924 **A párizsi lány** (*Gosse de riche*) Hungarian version (Fővárosi Operettszinház)

1924 **Csókoljon meg!** (*Embrassez-moi!*) Hungarian version (Renaissance Színház)

1927 **Csókról-csókra** (*Pas sur la bouche*) Hungarian version (Magyar Színház)

1928 **Enyém az első csók** (Szirmai) Andrássy uti Színház 16 May

1933 **Bál a Savoyban** (*Ball im Savoy*) Hungarian version (Magyar Színház)

1934 **A csodadoktor** (*Encore cinquante centimes*) Hungarian version (Magyar Színház)

HENDERSON, Alexander (b ?1829; d Cannes, 1 February 1886). Successful London producer of burlesque, opéra-bouffe and -comique.

Henderson began life working in the post-office. He left postage to work as a secretary for Sothern, but made his first significant steps as a theatre manager in Australia, where he was lessee and manager of Melbourne's Princess Theatre in the late 1850s, before moving on first to India and then to Liverpool, where he was involved in the construction of the Prince of Wales Theatre. He was subsequently manager and sometime stage director for Lydia Thompson's famous company of touring burlesque actresses and actors in Britain and America, and the fair Lydia herself became his fourth wife (he was her second husband).

He had his first London success as a manager when, after the Lydia Thompson company followed its Manchester season with one at the not-very-loved Folly Theatre playing *Blubeard*, *Robinson Crusoe* (1876) and *Oxygen* (1877), he retained the theatre (whilst losing Lydia) and mounted a triple-bill of French opérettes: *Up the River*, *La Créole* and *Sea Nymphs*/*Shooting Stars* (1877). They did well enough for him to venture again into the French, this time with a contemporary Paris hit, *Les Cloches de Corneville* (1878). It proved the longest-running musical show in London theatre history, and Henderson's career as a manager was made. Part way through the show's record-breaking run he transferred out of the Folly to the slightly better and bigger Globe Theatre, leaving the smaller house to Selina Dolaro and her attempts to capitalize on the place's new reputation as a home for opérette whilst he collected the extra coin produced by the move.

Over the next few years Henderson became omnipresent in the London musical theatre. He announced plans to build an Alcazar Theatre in Leicester Square to house his opérette productions, but ultimately he leased the existing Strand Theatre, for so long the home of burlesque under the management of the Swanborough family, as his principal arena of operations. There, with his friend Henry Brougham Farnie as adaptor, director and artistic advisor, he launched a series of successful productions of opéras-comiques and opérettes, beginning with the 1879 *Madame Favart*, another truly triumphant success which gave him a second hit to run alongside the seemingly inexhaustible *Les Cloches de Corneville*. He also took the Comedy Theatre and there mounted another major French hit, *La Mascotte*, which was succeeded by *Boccaccio* (129 performances), then by Henderson's one real home-made hit, *Rip van Winkle* (328 performances), and by *Falka* (157 performances).

Whilst *Les Cloches* gave way at the Globe to an unsuc-

cessful *The Naval Cadets*, *Les Mousquetaires au couvent*, six weeks of *La Belle Normande* (*La Famille Trouillat*, 1881), *La Boulangère (a des écus)* (1881, 40 performances) and a *Cloches* revival (1881), the Strand ran on with another huge hit in *Olivette* (466 performances), then *Manola* (1882, three months) and a *La Mascotte* revival, as Henderson shifted the centre of his activities to the new Avenue Theatre, opening there with a revival of *Madame Favart* (11 March 1882). The Avenue subsequently housed *Olivette*, *Lurette*, *Barbe-bleue*, *La Vie*, a second original musical in the Planquette/Farnie *Nell Gwynne*, further revivals of *La Mascotte* and *Barbe-bleue*, and London's first sight of *The Grand Mogol*.

Henderson's biggest successes were a year or two behind him when he died, still in the saddle. With Farnie's aid and expertise as a potent arm, and a largely wise choice of the biggest Continental hits as material, he gave himself half a dozen years at the very top of the managerial tree. However, his record as an instigator of original material was a very short one, even though the version of *Rip*, manufactured to star Fred Leslie, turned out to be an enduring item in the opérette repertoire.

Henderson's son, Alexander F Henderson, worked as general manager for Charles Wyndham, and his granddaughter, Meggie Albanesi (1899–1923), was a much-loved young actress on the London stage, who ensured herself a fond place in many memories by dying at a very early age.

HENDERSON, Ray [BROST, Raymond] (b Buffalo, NY, 1 December 1896; d Greenwich, Conn, 31 December 1970). One-third of the famous songwriting team of De Sylva-Brown-n-Henderson.

The son of a musician, and set from early on for a musical career, Henderson studied in Chicago and made his first money as a piano player in a dance band, as an accompanist in variety, and as a publisher's arranger. He worked as a song-plugger and pianist for several publishers and, at the same time, turned out a number of songs of which 'Humming' (ly: Louis Breau) which was interpolated into *Tip Top* on Broadway for the Duncan Sisters, and then found its way into the short-lived London musical *Faust on Toast*, got the most exposure.

Henderson first collaborated with lyricist Lew Brown (no relation to Lou Breau) in 1922 on a song called 'Georgette', which was sung with success in the *Greenwich Village Follies*, and the two continued to turn out songs together in the years that followed ('Why Did I Kiss That Girl?', 'Don't Bring Lulu', 'If You Hadn't Gone Away' w Billy Rose). Both continued, however, also to work with other writers, and in 1923 Henderson had a success with 'That Old Gang of Mine' written with Billy Rose and Mort Dixon, with whom he also wrote 'Follow the Swallow' for the *Ziegfeld Follies of 1924*. He followed up with such pieces as ''Bam, 'Bam, 'Bammy Shore' and 'Bye, Bye, Blackbird' with Dixon, 'Five Foot Two, Eyes of Blue' and 'I'm Sitting on Top of the World' (both 1926 w Joe Young, Sam Lewis) and 'Keep Your Skirts Down Mary Ann' (w Andrew Sterling, Robert King). In 1925, he had a first success in a collaboration with Buddy De Sylva, when the pair put their names alongside each other's and the title of the song 'Alabamy Bound' (w Bud Green).

The songwriting team that was to become famous to a

generation as 'De Sylva-Brown-n-Henderson' came wholly together for the first time on Broadway with a contribution to Al Jolson's *Big Boy* (1925, 'It All Depends on You') before they went on to find substantial theatrical success with their score for the 1926 edition of the revue *George White's Scandals*. The one hit of the previous edition, for which they had also written the score, had been Irving Berlin's second-hand 'All Alone', but the 1926 show included a Blues section in which several famous blues numbers, Gershwin's 'Rhapsody in Blue' and bits of Schubert and Schumann were all topped by De Sylva, Brown and Henderson's new 'The Birth of the Blues', and Ann Pennington danced frenetically to their Charlestonny 'The Black Bottom'. 'The Girl is You and the Boy is Me', from the same score, went on to become a London hit when played, along with their 'Tweet Tweet', in the musical *Up with the Lark* in 1927.

Song successes continued apace ('I Wonder How I Look When I'm Asleep', 'Magnolia' etc), and it was not long before the trio turned out their first Broadway score for a book musical, the college show *Good News* (1927, 'The Best Things in Life Are Free', 'The Varsity Drag'). *Good News* was a major hit, and over the next four years, whilst continuing to supply the *George White Scandals* with annual material (some of which, such as 'I'm On the Crest of a Wave' [*Love Lies*], was pilfered for London musicals and for the voracious Paris revue stage), they turned out four further book shows. They were a quartet of variable value, but all of them proved popular through good Broadway runs and were mostly exported – with uneven results – to London, and on several occasions to France, where the team's up-to-date musical style had become decidedly popular.

Manhattan Mary, a vehicle for comedian Ed Wynn, was short on song hits but long on personality; *Hold Everything!* invaded the world of boxing, introduced 'You're the Cream in My Coffee', and made a star of Bert Lahr; *Follow Thru* turned to golf and produced 'Button Up Your Overcoat'; whilst *Flying High* gave Lahr the opportunity to take comically to the skies, if without any songs as durable as the best of those in the earlier shows.

What had now become the hottest songwriting team on Broadway was naturally courted by Hollywood, and the trio moved west, where they quickly scored outstanding filmland successes with songs for such early sound pieces as *The Singing Fool* (1928, 'Sonny Boy') and *Sunny Side Up* (1929, 'If I Had a Talking Picture of You', 'Sunny Side Up'). However, the combination broke up when De Sylva moved on to an executive position in the film industry and Brown and Henderson returned to Broadway. The pair turned out a score for the *Scandals of 1931*, in which 'Life is Just a Bowl of Cherries' was the take-away tune, but they did not succeed in producing anything of the same kind of lasting value for either of the subsequent revusical book shows to which they contributed scores: *Hot-Cha*, even with Bert Lahr, was a 15 week semi-flop, and *Strike Me Pink*, which Brown and Henderson produced themselves, had Jimmy Durante, a lot of limp material and an unimpressive life.

Brown then followed De Sylva back to Hollywood, but Henderson remained in the theatre to compose and co-produce one more musical, the short-lived *Say When*, on which he collaborated with Ted Koehler, and to contribute the score to one more edition of *George White's Scandals* (1935). His most successful individual number from this period came, however, from a film – 'Animal Crackers in my Soup' (1935, w Koehler, Irving Caesar) as performed by top tot Shirley Temple in *Curly Top*.

Henderson continued to write songs through the 1940s including the score of the *Ziegfeld Follies of 1943* (w Jack Yellen), before he retired to Connecticut, where he devoted himself to some more serious composition in his later days.

A 1956 Hollywood biopic of the threesome, *The Best Things in Life Are Free*, had Henderson portrayed by Dan Dailey.

1927 **Good News** (Lew Brown, B G De Sylva/Laurence Schwab, De Sylva) 46th Street Theater 6 September
1927 **Manhattan Mary** (Brown, De Sylva/William K Wells, George White) Apollo Theater 26 September
1928 **Hold Everything!** (Brown, De Sylva/Jack McGowan, De Sylva) Broadhurst Theater 10 October
1929 **Follow Thru** (Brown, De Sylva/Schwab, De Sylva) 46th Street Theater 9 January
1930 **Flying High** (Brown, De Sylva/McGowan) Apollo Theater 3 March
1932 **Hot-Cha!** (Brown, Hy S Kraft, Mark Hellinger) Ziegfeld Theater 8 March
1933 **Strike Me Pink** (ex-*Forward March*) (McGowan, Mack Gordon) Majestic Theater 4 March
1934 **Say When** (Ted Koehler/McGowan) Imperial Theater 8 November

HENEKER, David (b Southsea, 31 March 1906). Songwriter who turned out some of the most delightful work of the British 1950s and 1960s, and who kept at it even when his style had been made to seem outdated by the fashion for large-scale spectaculars.

A brigadier in the regular army, Heneker found sufficient success as a popular songwriter ('There Goes My Dream' etc) to encourage him to resign his commission and take up a job as a club pianist to allow himself to concentrate on writing. He provided material for several revues (*Scoop* etc) before combining with lyricist Julian More and singer-songwriter Monty Norman to turn out the music and lyrics for *Expresso Bongo* (1958), the best of the British wave of 'realistic' musicals of the 1950s ('Time', 'The Shrine on the Second Floor'). The songwriting team won a wider success with their remarkably characterful English adaptation of the French low-life slang of the Paris hit *Irma la Douce* (1958), and Heneker and Norman had a third successive hit with a second show with *Expresso Bongo* author, Wolf Mankowitz, on *Make Me an Offer*, before Heneker went solo on a commission to turn H G Wells's *Kipps* into a stage musical for rock star Tommy Steele. As *Half a Sixpence*, the show gave its songwriter his greatest success ('Half a Sixpence', 'She's Too Far Above Me', 'If the Rain's Got to Fall', 'Flash, Bang, Wallop') and put the phrase 'Flash, Bang, Wallop' into the world's dictionaries.

His 1965 show *Charlie Girl* was a very long-running West End hit, but the fox-hunting tale of R G Surtees's *Jorrocks*, a Percy French biomusical, for which he supplemented the Irish songwriter's popular numbers with others mostly more plotworthy ('They Don't Make Them Like That Any More') and a musicalized version of the Ben Travers farce *Rookery Nook* (*Popkiss*) did not find extended success. After a gap of some eight years, Heneker returned to the West End with the songs for the small-scale history of soundless Hollywood, *The Biograph Girl*, and at the age of 78 he provided one final score, for a musical version of J Hartley Manners's *Peg o'My Heart* ('When a Woman Has to Choose'). Once again, these failed to find the success of his early work, in a theatrical world where his combination of unambitious musical elegance and precise lyrical charm were no longer the order of the day.

1958 **Expresso Bongo** (w Monty Norman/w Norman, Julian More/More, Wolf Mankowitz) Saville Theatre 23 April

1958 **Irma la Douce** English version w Norman, More (Lyric Theatre)

1959 **Make Me an Offer** (w Norman/Mankowitz) New Theatre 16 December

1963 **Half a Sixpence** (Beverley Cross) Cambridge Theatre 21 March

1965 **Charlie Girl** (w John Taylor/Hugh & Margaret Williams, Ray Cooney) Adelphi Theatre 15 December

1966 **Jorrocks** (Cross) New Theatre 22 September

1969 **Phil the Fluter** (w Percy French/Cross, Donal Giltinan) Palace Theatre 15 November

1972 **Popkiss** (w John Addison/Michael Ashton) Globe Theatre 22 August

1980 **The Biograph Girl** (Warner Brown) Phoenix Theatre 19 November

1984 **Peg** (Robin Miller, Ronald Millar) Phoenix Theatre 8 March

HENNEQUIN, Alfred [Néocles] (b Liège, 13 January 1842; d Épinay, 7 August 1887). Prominent author of comedies and vaudevilles for the French 1870s and 1880s stage.

Hennequin studied for a career in civil engineering, and he was employed on the Belgian state railways when, at the age of 25, he began writing for the theatre. His first play, *J'attends mon oncle* (1869), was produced at Brussels's Galeries Saint-Hubert and, when Hennequin moved on to Paris as the manager of a tramway company, he soon found notable success as a playwright with his contributions to such Parisian pieces as *Le Procès Veauradieux*, the celebrated *Les Dominos roses*, *Bébé* and *La Poudre de l'escampette*. He did not, however, write for the musical stage until 1878 when he began a collaboration with Albert Millaud which produced the internationally successful vaudevilles *Niniche*, *La Femme à papa* and *Lili* for Anna Judic and the Théâtre des Variétés. The other few libretti which he helped pen did not find the same success, and his last contributions to the musical stage were in the form of French adaptations of a couple of the most successful Viennese Operetten of the time. Both, however, proved less successful on the French-language stage than they had at home. In 1886 Hennequin suffered a breakdown, said to have been caused by overwork, and he died, insane, the following year.

Hennequin's comedies subsequently proved fertile ground for adaptors. *Les Dominos roses* (Vaudeville 17 April 1876, w Alfred Delacour) became *Tonight's the Night* in America and Britain, *Der Opernball* in Vienna, and *Három légyott* (text and music by József Bokor 22 October 1897 Népszinház) in Budapest; *Bébé* (Gymnase 10 March 1877 w de Najac, known in its hit English translation as *Betsy*) was the source for the British musical *Oh, Don't, Dolly!*

(1919) and for Hungary's *Kis fiu* (Aladár Váradi/Hugó Ilosvai Népszinház 30 January 1895), and *Les Petites Correspondences* (Gymnase 2 July 1878) became *Kleine Anzeigen* in a musicalized German-language form (mus: Josef Brandl, Carltheater 22 April 1880). *Niniche* and *La Femme à papa* also underwent all kinds of transsubstantiations, attached to all sorts of scores, notably those by the same Brandl, in several languages.

1878 **Niniche** (Marius Boullard/w Albert Millaud) Théâtre des Variétés 15 February

1878 **Fleur d'Oranger** (Auguste Coedès/w Victor Bernard) Théâtre des Nouveautés 7 December

1879 **La Femme à papa** (Hervé/w Millaud) Théâtre des Variétés 3 December

1882 **Lili** (Hervé/w Millaud, Ernest Blum) Théâtre des Variétés 10 January

1882 **Ninetta** (Raoul Pugno/w Alexandre Bisson) Théâtre de la Renaissance 26 December

1883 **Le Présomptif** (Louis Gregh/w Albin Valabrègue) Galeries Saint-Hubert, Brussels 12 December, Théâtre de la Renaissance 6 June 1884

1884 **Les Trois Devins** (Edouard Okolowicz/w Valabrègue) Théâtre de l'Ambigu-Comique 11 June

1885 **L'Étudiant Pauvre** (*Der Bettelstudent*) French version w Valabrègue (Brussels)

1885 **La Guerre joyeuse** (*Der lustige Krieg*) French version w Maurice Hennequin (Brussels)

HENNEQUIN, [Charles] Maurice (b Liège, 10 December 1863; d Montreux, Switzerland, 3 September 1926).

The son of Alfred Hennequin, Maurice made his début as a writer modestly refusing to capitalize on his father's name, and his first piece, the one-act comédie-vaudeville *L'Oiseau bleu*, was put out at the Théâtre de la Renaissance in 1882 under the nom de plume 'Maurice Debrun'. He soon abandoned this pseudonym and, from 1886, under his own name, turned out a long list of highly successful comedies and vaudevilles in collaborations with such authors as Paul Bilhaud, Georges Duval, Georges Feydeau, Pierre Veber and Antony Mars. That list included such durable favourites as *Vous n'avez rien à declarer?*, *La Présidente*, *Le Système Ribadier* and *Madame et son filleul*.

Hennequin ventured intermittently into the musical theatre, scoring a major international success in 1897 with the uproarious musical comedy *Les Fêtards*, which went on to become the basis for successful musicals in Britain (*Kitty Grey*) and America (*The Strollers*), whilst conquering central Europe in its original form, and a second appreciable success, with the same partners, in *La Poule blanche*. Thereafter he concentrated almost entirely on the non-musical stage, but in 1926 he returned to collaborate on the libretto for the highly successful André Messager musical comedy *Passionnément*.

Hennequin's comedies and vaudevilles proved widely popular as the bases for musical shows by other hands, *Coralie et Cie* (Palais-Royal 30 November 1899 w Valabrègue) being made into a musical for Lottie Collins in Britain (*The Dressmaker*), *Les Dragées d'Hercule* (1904) turning into Rudolf Friml and Otto Harbach's international hit *High Jinks*, *Madame et son filleul* (Palais-Royal 12 September 1916, w Veber) becoming *The Girl Behind the Gun* on Broadway and then *Kissing Time* (1919) in Britain and

English-speaking areas beyond, *Le Monsieur de cinq heures* (Palais-Royal 1 October 1924 w Veber) the source for the American play *A Kiss in a Taxi* and for the musical comedy *Sunny Days* developed therefrom, the farce *Aimé des femmes* (Palais-Royal 2 May 1911 w Georges Mitchell) being taken as the source for Broadway's Henry Blossom/Alfred Robyn *All for the Ladies*, and an earlier Palais-Royal piece, *Place aux femmes!* (8 October 1898 w Valabrègue), making it to the German musical stage as *Die moderne Eva* (1911), with a score by Jean Gilbert.

Elsewhere, in a gust of such nebulous credits, such as 'from the French' or 'based partly on a play by', both *Oh, Please!* and *Oh, Kay!* were claimed at one stage to be based on *La Présidente* (Bouffes-Parisiens 12 September 1902 w Veber), which Italy's *La Presidentessa* (a Robert Stolz pasticcio made by Carlo Lombardo) certainly was, whilst Vienna's *Fräulein Präsident*, perversely, had a heroine called Nelly Rozier, and may have been based, rather, on Hennequin's popular play of that name (w Bilhaud). The Frankfurt musical *Angst vor der Ehe* (Emil Reznicek/ Erich Urban, Louis Taufstein, 28 November 1913) was announced as based on a Hennequin and Veber play known in German as *Der Taubenschlag* (*Le Colombier*). Vienna's Theater in der Josefstadt admitted that its musical play *Die Kindsfrau* was based on 'Hennequin' without identifying which Hennequin or which play, and Italy also borrowed something of Hennequin's – presumably *Le Paradis* (w Bilhaud, Barré) – for a 1924 Mario Ferrarese musical called *Paradiso*. In Hungary, Jenő Heltai adapted what seems to have been Hennequin's *Les Vacances du Mariage* (Menus-Plaisirs 12 February 1887 w Valabrègue) as a musical comedy under the title *A szalmaözvegy* (Népszinház, 10 June 1904).

1885 **La Guerre joyeuse** (*Der lustige Krieg*) French version w Alfred Hennequin (Brussels)
1891 **La Petite Poucette** (Raoul Pugno/w Maurice Ordonneau) Théâtre de la Renaissance 5 March
1893 **Les Cousins de Nanette** (P Rougnon/w V Meusy) tour
1894 **Le Troisième Hussards** (Justin Clérice/w Antony Mars) Théâtre de la Gaîté 14 March
1894 **Le Régiment qui passe** (Lucien & Paul Hillemacher) 1 act Royan 11 September
1896 **Sa majesté l'amour** (Victor Roger/w Mars) Eldorado 24 December
1897 **Les Fêtards** (Roger/w Mars) Palais-Royal 28 October
1899 **La Poule blanche** (Roger/w Mars) Théâtre Cluny 13 January
1907 **Betty, ou L'entente cordiale** (Eustache de Lorey/w Paul Bilhaud) Théâtre des Nouveautés (Olympia), Brussels 4 October
1914 **La Fille de Figaro** (Xavier Leroux/w Hugues Delorme) Théâtre Apollo 10 March
1916 **Le Poilu** (Maurice Jacquet/w Pierre Veber) Palais-Royal 14 January
1916 **Cyprien, ôte ta main d'la** (André Messager) 1 act Concert Mayol
1917 **La Petite Dactylo** (Jacquet/w Georges Mitchell) Gymnase 19 October
1926 **Passionnément** (Messager/w Albert Willemetz) Théâtre de la Michodière 15 January

HENSON, Leslie (b London, 3 August 1891; d Harrow Weald, 2 December 1957). Frog-featured star comedian, long one of the reigning favourites of the West End musical stage.

Henson worked in concert party and in pantomime before landing his first musical comedy rôle at the age of 21, touring as Jeremiah in *The Quaker Girl* for George Dance. Two years later he had a minor rôle in Grossmith and Laurillard's New York company of *Tonight's the Night*, a part he enlarged sufficiently successfully to be given a larger one when the show was produced at London's Gaiety Theatre the following year.

Grossmith hired him for the star soubret rôle of *Theodore & Co* (1916, Pony Twitchin), a part which was increased to even greater size when the manager/star departed the show to join the war effort, and in the company's next and equally successful piece, *Yes, Uncle!* (1917, Bobby Summers), Henson showed up as the top comic of the evening. He had, however, an odd contract: wishing himself to join up, he agreed to go into the show just to create the rôle and its comical stage business before departing with a royalty in his pocket to find a uniform.

After the war Henson returned to Grossmith and Laurillard's (later Grossmith and Malone's) management for a seven-year series of mostly successful musicals at the Winter Garden Theatre, taking star comic rôles in *Kissing Time* (1919, Bibi St Pol), *A Night Out* (1920, Pinglet), as the shorn Grand Duke Connie in *Sally*, *The Cabaret Girl* (1923, Mr Gravvins), *The Beauty Prize* (1923, Odo Philpotts), a revival of *Tonight's the Night*, *Primrose* (1924, Tony Mopham), *Tell Me More!* (1925, Monte Sipkin) and *Kid Boots* (1926, Kid Boots), making up a comical team with slim, dudey Grossmith and big Davy Burnaby, which equalled any musical comedy combination in town. When the Winter Garden series terminated he appeared as the star of *Lady Luck* at the new Carlton Theatre (1927, Windy Bleugh), with the Astaires in *Funny Face* (1928, Dugsie Gibbs), and in *Follow Through* (1929, Jack Martin) at the Dominion Theatre. He then left the musical stage temporarily to appear in the comedies *It's a Boy* (*Hurra! Eine Junge!*) and *It's a Girl* under his own management, on London's 'comedy corner'.

Henson took up afresh his long run of musical comedy successes in the musical farces *Nice Goings On* (1933, Olaf Henscuttle) and *Lucky Break* (1934, Tommy Turtle), and then began at the Gaiety Theatre what turned out to be a new series of shows, a series which teamed him this time with gross, monocled Fred Emney, acrobatic Richard Hearne, and dance-and-song juveniles Louise Browne and Roy Royston: *Seeing Stars* (1935, Jimmy Swing), *Swing Along* (1936, Maxie Mumm), *Going Greek* (1937, Alexander Saggappopolous) and *Running Riot* (1938, Cornelius Crumpet). In each of these he took a share of the direction, as he had, credited or uncredited, in all his own shows since Winter Garden days and several others besides (*So This is Love*, *On Your Toes* etc).

This Gaiety Theatre series came to an end with the Second World War, and although Henson came back once more with success in the postwar *Bob's Your Uncle* (1948), it was to a world where tastes had changed. They had not changed sufficiently, however, for audiences to allow their favourite, free-wheeling, frog-faced little comedian of the inter-war years to change his coat and, when he attempted the rôle of Samuel Pepys in a well-made musical version of *And So to Bed* (1951), playing the script and just the script without his usual ad-libbing and antics, his public could not accept it. His last appearance on the musical stage was

Plate 125. **Leslie Henson** *and the girls of the Gaiety Theatre in* Seeing Stars.

in 1955, when he played the role of Eccles in a musical version of *Caste* at the Theatre Royal, Windsor.

His son, **Nicky HENSON** (b London, 12 May 1945) has had a successful career as an actor in musical and non-musical shows, appearing in his young days as Mordred in London's *Camelot*, in *Passion Flower Hotel*, as the original juvenile man of *Canterbury Tales*, as Toad in *Toad of Toad Hall* and as Jack Sheppard in *Stand and Deliver*. He returned to the musical stage in 1990 in the short-lived *Matador* (El Panama) as part of a later career angled towards the non-musical stage.

Autobiography: *My Laugh Story* (Hodder & Stoughton, London, 1926), *Yours Faithfully* (John Long, London, 1948)

HENTSCHKE, Heinz   (b Berlin, 20 February 1895; d Berlin, 3 July 1970).

After an early career spent in and with all kinds of theatre-related organizations, Hentschke made good when he earned himself a fortune as a theatre-ticket broker. At the same time, he won his way into the confidence of the Rotter brothers, who were then in control of most of Berlin's musical theatre, rising to be their managing director during the 1920s. When the brothers fell into, first, financial difficulties and then, in 1933, Nazi difficulties, Hentschke moved in to to take over their holdings and their position in the Berlin theatre. He was the manager of Berlin's Metropoltheater from 1934, directing and also

writing the libretti for the shows played there during the era of National Socialism. His term at the Metropoltheater came to an end in 1944, and his subsequent theatrical activities were on a less prominent scale.

Amongst his writings, he found greatest success with the banal but surprisingly enduring *Maske in Blau*, and with the rather more adeptly constructed *Hochzeitsnacht im Paradies*, two from a group of pieces of mostly very limited value, cobbled together as isn't-life-jolly type entertainments for the Hitlerian years.

1934 **Lauf ins Glück** (Fred Raymond/Paul Beyer) Metropoltheater 24 September

1935 **Ball der Nationen** (Raymond/Beyer) Metropoltheater 27 September

1936 **Auf grosser Fahrt** (Raymond/Günther Schwenn) Metropoltheater 21 August

1936 **Marielu** (Raymond/Schwenn/w Theo Halton) Centraltheater, Dresden 19 December

1937 **Maske in Blau** (Raymond/Schwenn) Metropoltheater 27 September

1938 **Melodie der Nacht** (Ludwig Schmidseder/Schwenn) Metropoltheater 21 September

1939 **Die, oder keine** (Schmidseder/Schwenn) Metropoltheater 20 September

1940 **Frauen im Metropol** (Schmidseder) Metropoltheater 27 September

1942 **Hochzeitsnacht im Paradies** (Friedrich Schröder/Schwenn) Metropoltheater 24 September

1943 **Der goldene Käfig** (Theo Mackeben/Schwenn) Admiralspalast 23 September

HERBERT, (Sir) A[lan] P[atrick] (b Elstead, Surrey, 24 September 1890; d London, 11 November 1971). British librettist and lyricist whose reputation for fine writing was not always upheld by his musical theatre work.

Lawyer, journalist, novelist and longtime Member of Parliament, Herbert began writing for the stage in his thirties whilst working for *Punch* magazine. His earliest pieces, all written for the Lyric Theatre, Hammersmith, included a short operetta, the revue *Riverside Nights*, and what cannot strictly be called an adaptation of, but rather a new show loosely based on bits of, Offenbach's *La Vie parisienne*. He combined with Sir Thomas Dunhill to write the original musical *Tantivy Towers* (1931) and with Alfred Reynolds on the pompous *Derby Day* (1932) for the same theatre, and did an almost as devastating a hatchet job on *La Belle Hélène* as he had done on *La Vie parisienne* for a spectacular C B Cochran production, based on a German Max Reinhardt remake and staging, and called *Helen!*.

He successfully, and much less drastically, adapted Oscar Straus's *Eine Frau, die weiss, was sie will* (*Mother of Pearl*, 'Every Woman Thinks She Wants to Wander') for the English stage, Englished Franz Lehár's less fortunate *Paganini* for London and, in 1934, he collaborated for the first time in the theatre with composer Vivian Ellis to turn out the successful C B Cochran revue *Streamline* ('Other People's Babies'). That collaboration with Ellis was restarted after the war, when Ellis composed the scores to Herbert's texts for the effortfully political *Big Ben* (1946), for his least 'meaningful' and by far his most successful musical, the period piece *Bless the Bride* (1947, 'This is My Lovely Day', 'Ma Belle Marguerite', 'I Was Never Kissed Before'), *Tough at the Top* (1949) and *The Water Gipsies* (1955), the last of these based on Herbert's own novel and screenplay.

1927 **Plain Jane** (Richard Austin) Greyhound Theatre, Croydon 26 December
1929 **La Vie parisienne** rewritten English version (Lyric Theatre, Hammersmith)
1931 **Tantivy Towers** (Thomas Dunhill) Lyric Theatre, Hammersmith 16 January
1931 **The Gay Princess** (Robert Katscher/Siegfried Geyer) English lyrics (Kingsway Theatre)
1932 **Helen!** rewritten English version of *La Belle Hélène* (Adelphi Theatre)
1932 **Derby Day** (Alfred Reynolds) Lyric Theatre, Hammersmith 24 February
1933 **Mother of Pearl** (*Eine Frau, die weiss, was sie will*) English version (Gaiety Theatre)
1937 **Paganini** English version w Reginald Arkell (Lyceum)
1946 **Big Ben** (Vivian Ellis) Adelphi Theatre 17 July
1947 **Bless the Bride** (Ellis) Adelphi Theatre 26 April
1949 **Tough at the Top** (Ellis) Adelphi Theatre 15 July
1955 **The Water Gipsies** (Ellis) Winter Garden 31 August

Autobiography: *A.P.H.: His Life and Times* (Heinemann, London, 1970)

HERBERT, Evelyn [HOSTETTER, Evelyn Herbert] (b Philadelphia, 1898; d California, 195–?). Soprano star of several Broadway musicals of the 1920s and 1930s.

After a brief attempt at an operatic career (Mimi with the Chicago Grand Opera Company etc), Miss Herbert lost her voice. When she returned to the stage she switched to the musical theatre where her fine, and now less overworked, soprano quickly won her leading rôles. Her first Broadway appearance was in support (with two solos and several ensembles to sing) of Fred and Dorothy Stone in Charles Dillingham's production *Stepping Stones* (1923); her second, after the withdrawal of Marguerite Namara, was in the Hungarian Offenbach pasticcio, *The Love Song* (1925), playing the rôle of Mrs Offenbach. In the same year, following a second rehearsal-time flit by Miss Namara, and an out-of-town interlude by Mary Mellish, she took up the title-rôle in *Princess Flavia*, the musical version of *The Prisoner of Zenda*, for Broadway, and confirmed that she was one of the most impressive vocalists in the musical theatre of her time.

She appeared in revue for Charles Dillingham, and then created further operettic leading rôles in Sigmund Romberg's *My Maryland*, in which she appeared as a young and glamorized Barbara Frietchie, and in *The New Moon* (1928) where, in the rôle of Marianne, she introduced 'One Kiss', 'Lover, Come Back to Me' and 'Wanting You', the last in partnership with her husband, Robert Halliday, cast opposite her in the rôle of Robert Misson.

She followed up, again paired with Halliday, in the title rôle of Szirmai's *Princess Charming* (*Alexandra*) and in London's large-scale presentation of the Strauss pasticcio *Waltzes from Vienna* (*Walzer aus Wien*), and she essayed another Romberg score in *Melody* (1933), with rather less return than on previous occasions. Her final appearance on the New York stage was in the leading role of Noël Coward's *Bitter-Sweet* on the occasion of a short Shubert revival at the 44th Street Theater in 1934. In 1935 she starred at the St Louis Municipal Opera as Rio Rita, and in the title-rôle of the American première of *Teresina*.

HERBERT, Joseph W (b Liverpool, 1867; d New York, 18 February 1923). A tall, gangling, comic actor, who had a considerable career in the Broadway theatre both as a performer and as a writer.

Herbert's acting career began in the non-musical theatre and, over the years, he mixed appearances in classic plays (*The Merry Wives of Windsor*, Tranio in *The Taming of the Shrew* etc) and modern successes with a vast range of comedy rôles in the musical theatre. In 30 years of comic-musical credits, his Broadway credits included E E Rice's *The Pearl of Pekin* (1888), Carillon in *The King's Fool* (1890), Jacques in *Miss Helyett* (1891), Prince Gregory of Montenegro in *The Algerian* (1893) with Marie Tempest, *Rob Roy*, Count Giulio Cesario in *La Tzigane* with Lillian Russell, the Chicago extravaganza *Aladdin Jr* (1895, Ki-Yi), two different rôles in his own *Thrilby* (1895), Courte-Botte de Roquencourt in the Cheever Goodwin/Woolson Morse success *Lost, Strayed or Stolen* (1896), Ringmaster Drivelli in Daly's revival of *The Circus Girl*, Captain Carmona of the Mexican army in *Mexicana*, Auguste Pompier in *The Girl from Paris* (1896), Marquis Imari in a Daly revival of *The Geisha* (1898), Count Berezowski in Alice Nielsen's production of *The Fortune Teller* (USA and London) and Prince Pumpernickel in her *The Singing Girl* (1899), as replacement for Dan Daly in *The Rounders* (1900, Duke of Paty de Clam), *The Little Duchess* (1901), *Mam'selle Napoleon* (1903, Miche), *The West Point Cadet* (1904) with Della Fox, Victor Herbert's *It Happened in Nordland* (1904, Duke of Toxen), Harry Canting in his own *Music Master* burlesque for Lew Fields, *The Great Decide* (1906), The Laird o'Finnan Haddock in his own

About Town alongside his son, Joseph W Herbert jr (1906), *The Honeymoon Express* (1907), *Fascinating Flora* (1907), Lothar in *A Waltz Dream* (1908), Count Buzot in *Oh, I Say!* (1913), *The Gay White Way* (1913), *The Beauty Shop* (1914), and The Duke of Cambridge in *Betty* (1916), before, in 1919, he turned for the last years of his life to acting in films.

Herbert's first work as a musical-theatre writer was the text for the *Trilby* burlesque *Thrilby*, which was produced on Broadway in 1905. He collaborated with *Erminie* composer Jakobowski on an apparently unproduced piece called *The Birth of Venus*, authored several other burlesques, and a musical play *The Prince of Borneo*, which was staged in three different versions in three different continents under three different titles in search of a ration of success. He was lyricist and co-librettist for the Casino Theater's *The Social Whirl* and the revusical *About Town*, wrote adaptations of several Continental Operetten, including *Ein Walzertraum* and the successful Broadway version of *Endlich Allein*, and supplied the text for the Al Jolson vehicle *Honeymoon Express*, whilst also turning out pieces, such as a successful English version of Léon Gandillot's *La Tortue* for Sadie Martinot (1898), for the non-musical stage. In later years his parody of highblown operetta, *The Scourge of the Sea*, was adapted straight-facedly as the text for the Ephraim Zimbalist musical *Honeydew*.

In his later days Herbert also worked as a director, and his credits include the staging of the Broadway production of the *King of Cadonia*, of the 1910 revival of *The Mikado* and his own adaptation of Albini's *Madame Troubadour* (1910) for the Shuberts, and of the Jerome Kern musicals, *The Red Petticoat* (1912) and *Nobody Home* (1915).

1895 **Thrilby** (Charles Puerner) Garrick Theater 3 June
1896 **The Geezer** (John Stromberg) Weber & Fields Music Hall 8 October
1897 **Under the Red Globe** (Stromberg) Weber & Fields Music Hall 18 February
1898 **Le Rêve** (Max Gabriel) Koster & Bial's Music Hall 23 May
1899 **The Prince of Borneo** (Edward Jones) Strand Theatre, London 5 October
1902 **Cryris** (Henry Waller) 1 act in *Fad and Folly* Mrs Osborn's Playhouse 21 October
1902 **Tommy Rot** (Safford Waters/w Rupert Hughes, Paul West, Kirk La Shelle) Mrs Osborn's Playhouse 21 October
1903 **Mam'selle Napoleon** (Gustav Luders/w Charles Doty) Knickerbocker Theater 8 December
1905 **The Music Master** (burlesque) 1 act in *It Happened in Nordland* (Hans Siegfried Linne) Lew Fields Theater 21 September
1906 **The Social Whirl** (Gustave Kerker/w Doty) Casino Theater 7 April
1906 **About Town** (Melville Ellis, Raymond Hubbell) Herald Square Theater 30 August
1907 **Fascinating Flora** (Kerker/w R H Burnside) Casino Theater 20 May
1907 **The Orchid** American adaptation (Herald Square Theater)
1908 **The Waltz Dream** (*Ein Walzertraum*) American version (Broadway Theater)
1908 **Morning, Noon and Night** (Jean Schwartz/William Jerome) Yorkville Theater 5 October
1909 **The Beauty Spot** revised *The Prince of Borneo* with music by Reginald De Koven Herald Square Theater 10 April
1909 **The Golden Widow** (Melville Gideon, Louis A Hirsch, Jerome D Kern/ad Glen MacDonough) Belasco Theater, Washington 26 October

1910 **Madame Troubadour** English version (Lyric Theater)
1911 **The Duchess** (ex- *The Rose Shop*, *Mlle Rosita*) (Victor Herbert/w H B Smith) Lyric Theater 16 October
1913 **The Honeymoon Express** (Schwartz/w Harold Atteridge) Winter Garden 6 February
1915 **Alone at Last** (*Endlich Allein*) English version w Edgar Smith (Shubert Theater)
1916 **Husbands Guaranteed** (August Kleinecke) Rochester 30 November
1920 **Honeydew** (aka *What's the Odds*) (Ephraim Zimbalist) Casino Theater 6 September
1923 **Sue Dear** (Frank Grey/Bide Dudley/w Dudley, C S Montayne) Times Square Theater 10 July

HERBERT, Victor [August] (b Dublin, 1 February 1859; d New York, 24 May 1924). The most substantial and versatile composer for the Broadway musical stage of the early 20th century.

The grandson of Samuel Lover, the novelist, portrait painter and author of such Irish songs as 'The Low-backed Car', 'Rory O'More' and 'Molly Bawn', Herbert was born in Dublin, but brought up and educated in Germany. He began his musical career as an orchestral cellist, and became a member of the Court Orchestra in Stuttgart, but in 1886 he left Germany for America, where his wife, vocalist Therese Förster, had secured a contract at the Metropolitan Opera House. Herbert worked in New York as a cellist at first at the Metropolitan and then elsewhere before subsequently, and with considerable success, making himself a place in the musical world as a popular conductor of classical works and a bandmaster. In 1894 he became Regimental Bandmaster of the 22nd Regiment Band, New York.

Herbert's earliest compositions were in the form of classical and light classical orchestral and instrumental works, and, although he contributed pieces of music to Charles Hoyt's musical play *The Midnight Bell* and other such shows, it was some time before he turned his attentions to the musical theatre. His first extended lyric work was, in fact, an oratorio, *The Captive*. His initial full score for the musical theatre, the comic opera *La Vivandière*, was submitted to Lillian Russell, but it was rejected and never performed. Thus it was the composer's second effort, *Prince Ananias*, produced in 1894 by the Boston Ideal Opera Company and played in their repertoire in a Broadway season (55 performances) that introduced him to the New York stage. Having arrived on Broadway, Herbert was rarely long away from its theatres during the rest of his considerable career.

Over the next 30 years Herbert composed a long list of musical scores for the theatre, scores ranging from burlesque to romantic operetta and to the light-hearted dance-and-song pieces that subsequently became the popular musical theatre fodder. He scored a number of fine successes, but also a large number of flops – flops which were, it must be emphasised, not always such because of any lack in their musical content. In the process (and also in hindsight) he became regarded as the most important figure in Broadway's composing fraternity in the first decades of the 20th century.

After the modest beginnings made with *Prince Ananias*, Herbert quickly found success when his next work, the burlesque comic opera *The Wizard of the Nile* ('Star Light, Star Bright'), was given a fine 105 performances on Broadway. It went on to productions in Britain and on the Continent – a rare thing for an American work of the period – and to a revival in New York. It was an impressive beginning, but the international record compiled by *The Wizard of the Nile* was one which, amazingly, none of Herbert's later shows would ever equal. In spite of occasional showings abroad, even his greatest successes in the musical theatre were successes only within the United States.

A farcical piece called *The Gold Bug* foundered in a week on Broadway, and favourite soprano Camille D'Arville's self-starring production of his *Peg Woffington* failed to make it that far, but in the same year, 1897, Herbert scored his second important success with the romantic comic opera *The Serenade* ('I Love Thee, I Adore Thee'), again produced by the Bostonians. This more musically substantial work was followed by two further pieces which had good lives – another burlesquey vehicle for *The Wizard of the Nile* star, Frank Daniels, called *The Idol's Eye* ('The Tattooed Man'), and a piece commissioned by *Serenade* star, Alice Nielsen, with which to launch her own company. *The Fortune Teller* ('Slumber On, My Little Gypsy Sweetheart') served Miss Nielsen well in America and in a season in London's West End, and confirmed its composer's now pre-eminent position in American comic opera.

Herbert's rate of writing thereafter became demential. In a period of little more than seven months in 1899–1900 he had four new works premièred. It was, perhaps, a salutory warning that none came near the best of his earliest pieces in popularity. An attempt to wed comic opera and burlesque in a version of *Cyrano de Bergerac* for Francis Wilson and Lulu Glaser was a 28-performance flop, but another piece for Miss Nielsen, *The Singing Girl*, while not coming up to the standard of *The Serenade* or *The Fortune Teller*, served its star for a while in New York (77 performances) and on the road. A fresh work for Daniels, this time cast as *The Ameer*, did better on tour than in New York, and *The Viceroy*, another piece written for the Bostonians, also had an indifferent life.

After this burst of composing activity Herbert disappeared from the bills for a while, fulfilling a three-season contract as conductor of the Pittsburgh Symphony Orchestra and of a season at Chicago's Grand Opera House. He did not return to Broadway until 1903, when he was commissioned to provide the score for a grandiose musical extravaganza produced by Julian Mitchell and Fred Hamlin. *Babes in Toyland* was a fairytale spectacular which was designed specifically as a Broadway entertainment and not, like virtually every other one of Herbert's works to date, as a vehicle for a touring company or star. Lavishly staged, as a successor to the producers' previous *The Wizard of Oz*, it turned out to be a splendid success, and Herbert's score rendered up several pieces which have long remained popular in America (The March of the Toys, 'I Can't Do The Sum', 'Toyland').

The comic opera *Babette*, with ex-opera star Fritzi Scheff starred in its title-rôle, won only 55 Broadway performances, but Herbert scored a fresh success the following year with another commission from Hamlin and Mitchell (teamed this time with producer-star Lew Fields), when he composed the score for the Ruritanian musical comedy *It Happened in Nordland* ('Absinthe frappée'). It ran long into 1905, joined by two further Herbert shows, *Miss Dolly Dollars* and another fairytale piece called *Wonderland*

(73 performances), each of which had only a moderate New York run, but a regular touring life. This time the high rate of activity to which he had returned did not seem to have any adverse effect on the quality of Herbert's scores. His third new work of 1905, again a vehicle for Fritzi Scheff, cast her as *Mlle Modiste* ('Kiss Me Again', 'I Want What I Want When I Want It') with great success, whilst his first score of 1906, written for a blatantly low comedy musical, as opposed to the Frenchified light opérette of the previous show, brought him an equally fine success in *The Red Mill* ('Moonbeams', 'The Streets of New York', 'Every Day is Ladies' Day with Me'). Both these two very differently flavoured pieces remained favourites for decades in America, proving themselves amongst the most durable of Herbert's works.

It was, however, a few years and rather more shows before such success came again. Herbert continued to turn out scores of all kinds, ranging through a rather classy burlesque on *Lohengrin* (*The Magic Knight*) for Joe Weber, a free-wheeling bit of low comedy for Daniels (*The Tattooed Man*), a spectacular children's show based on the comic strip *Little Nemo*, a fine romantic musical score ('Rose of the World') to the comic opera *Algeria* (later *The Rose of Algeria*), a disappointing *The Prima Donna* for Fritzi Scheff, and a short-lived Lew Fields dialect comedy show, *Old Dutch*, without notching up another major hit. In 1910, however, he hit the heights once more when he provided a score for another refugee from the world of opera, Emma Trentini, as *Naughty Marietta*. The show scored a fine success in America, and its title and songs ('Ah! Sweet Mystery of Life', ''Neath the Southern Moon', 'I'm Falling in Love with Someone', 'Tramp! Tramp! Tramp!' etc) later won worldwide recognition with the aid of the cinema.

Herbert kept up a resolute and regular output through the 1910s. The light musical comedy *When Sweet Sixteen* proved to be more to the taste of the provinces than the city, and *The Duchess*, another piece modelled around Fritzi Scheff, and of which enough was expected to have it tried out in a copyright performance at London's Ladbroke Hall (as *The Rose Shop*), went through out-of-town agonies as its star abandoned ship before Broadway proffered its thumbs down. *The Enchantress* ('The Land of my Own Romance', 'I Want to Be a Prima Donna') also played only a medium season on Broadway (72 performances) but, like several other Herbert shows with similar metropolitan records, it lived out a good and highly profitable life on the touring circuits, where in most years several of the composer's works could be seen and heard, going round the country for the first, second, third or umpteenth time.

The composer's voluminous and ever-rebounding career soon brought forth a number of further successes. Montgomery and Stone, whom Herbert had served so well in *The Red Mill*, had a fine run with the Cinderella tale of *The Lady of the Slipper*, and another Ruritanian operetta, *Sweethearts* ('Sweethearts'), in spite of a cute, confused and confusing libretto, played 136 performances in New York and proved to have more staying power than some of Herbert's other and better pieces in the same vein. *The Madcap Duchess*, accounted a little too musically ambitious by some, failed to catch on, but the musical comedy *The Only Girl*, composed to an adaptation of Ludwig Fulda's

Jugendfreude done by Herbert's most appreciable collaborator, Henry Blossom, gave him one of the longest Broadway runs of his career (240 performances) as well as one of his rare British productions.

Herbert paired with Blossom again for the pretty *The Princess Pat* ('Love is Best of All'), the Ziegfeld revue *The Century Girl* (w Irving Berlin), the Irish light opera *Eileen*, and a version of a Frederick Jackson farce, *A Full House*, which had started in Boston with a score by Uda Waldrop and the title *She Took a Chance*, but arrived in New York as Herbert's *The Velvet Lady*. From this group *Eileen* brought him the most praise, for its pretty Irishy melodies and superior concerted music. He worked on a second Ziegfeld revue, *Miss 1917*, but several other pieces to which he provided music proved poor stuff, and the resultant shows had short Broadway lives. In 1920, for only the second time in nearly 30 years of composing, a Victor Herbert show closed on the road. The small-scale *Oui Madame*, announced as the show which would revive the George Edwardes kind of musical, underwent some last-minute efforts to gussy it up to more conventional proportions with Ned Wayburn girls, glitz and dances, but went under without making Broadway.

His 1919 *Angel Face*, a curious modern musical comedy with a plot about monkey-glands, had to fight its way to some kind of success through strikes and lockouts, but there was a real disappointment when Fred de Grésac made over her elegant play *La Passerelle* as what should have been an ideal Herbert libretto. *Orange Blossoms* (1922, 'A Kiss in the Dark'), the last Herbert musical produced in his lifetime, played only 95 times in New York. The composer was represented once more, posthumously, on Broadway when *The Dream Girl*, a musical version of the reincarnation play *The Road to Yesterday*, played 117 performances for the Shuberts without establishing itself or its songs amongst Herbert's best. Amongst Herbert's other dramatic compositions were two operas, *Natoma* (1911) and *Madeleine* (1914), and incidental music for the accompaniment of silent films.

The popularity ultimately won throughout the English-speaking world by the songs from *Naughty Marietta* would seem to indicate that Herbert's music should have had an appeal reaching beyond America, but apart from *The Wizard of the Nile*, Miss Nielsen's touring season of *The Serenade*, two unsuccessful attempts at *The Red Mill*, a production of *The Only Girl* and a handful of performances of *Angel Face*, the only Victor Herbert score to have been heard in London's West End was a musical mélange of *The Serenade* and *The Fortune Teller*, originally produced on America's west coast as *Gypsy Lady* (George Forrest, Robert Wright/Henry Myers, Century Theater 17 September 1946), which briefly played on Broadway, and in Britain as *Romany Love*.

Australia proved no more enthusiastic – although *The Fortune Teller* was given a brief showing there – and only *The Wizard of the Nile* seems to have penetrated into Europe. It must remain a mystery why Broadway's acknowledgedly most appreciable, versatile and prolific composer of the turn-of-the-century years failed to 'travel', leaving what overseas laurels there were to be won and the position of international flagbearcr to the era's American musical stage to Gustave Kerker and his *Belle of New York*.

A Hollywood film, *The Great Victor Herbert* (1939), which had little or nothing to do with the composer or his life story, had Walter Connolly starred as Herbert.

1894 **Prince Ananias** (Francis Neilson) Broadway Theater 20 November
1895 **The Wizard of the Nile** (H B Smith) Casino Theater 4 November
1896 **The Gold Bug** (Glen MacDonough) Casino Theater 21 September
1897 **The Serenade** (H B Smith) Knickerbocker Theater 16 March
1897 **Peg Woffington** (H B Smith) Lyceum, Scranton, Pa, 18 October
1897 **The Idol's Eye** (H B Smith) Broadway Theater 25 October
1898 **The Fortune Teller** (H B Smith) Wallack's Theater 26 September
1899 **Cyrano de Bergerac** (H B Smith) Knickerbocker Theater 18 September
1899 **The Singing Girl** (H B Smith/Stanislaus Stange) Casino Theater 23 October
1899 **The Ameer** (Frederick Ranken/Kirk La Shelle) Wallack's Theater 4 December
1900 **The Viceroy** (H B Smith) Knickerbocker Theater 30 April
1903 **Babes in Toyland** (MacDonough) Majestic Theater 13 October
1903 **Babette** (H B Smith) Broadway Theater 16 November
1904 **It Happened in Nordland** (MacDonough) Lew Fields Theater 5 December
1905 **Miss Dolly Dollars** (H B Smith) Knickerbocker Theater 4 September
1905 **Wonderland** (MacDonough) Majestic Theater 24 October
1905 **Mlle Modiste** (Henry Blossom) Knickerbocker Theater 25 December
1906 **The Red Mill** (Blossom) Knickerbocker Theater 24 September
1906 **The Dream City** (Edgar Smith) Weber's Theater 25 December
1906 **The Magic Knight** (E Smith) Weber's Theater 25 December
1907 **The Tattooed Man** (H B Smith, A N C Fowler) Criterion Theater 18 February
1907 **The Song Birds** (George V Hobart) 1 act Lambs' Club; New York Theater in *The Land of Nod* 1 April
1907 **Miss Camille** (Hobart) 1 act Lamb's Club 14 April
1908 **Algeria** (MacDonough) Broadway Theater 31 August
1908 **Little Nemo** (H B Smith) New Amsterdam Theater 20 October
1908 **The Prima Donna** (Blossom) Knickerbocker Theater 30 November
1909 **Old Dutch** (E Smith/Hobart) Herald Square Theater 22 November
1910 **Naughty Marietta** (Rida Johnson Young) New York Theater 7 November
1911 **When Sweet Sixteen** (Hobart) Daly's Theater 14 September
1911 **The Duchess** (Joseph Herbert/H B Smith) Lyric Theater 16 October
1911 **The Enchantress** (H B Smith/Fred de Grésac) New York Theater 19 October
1912 **The Lady of the Slipper** (James O'Dea/Anne Caldwell, Lawrence McCarty) Globe Theater 28 October
1912 **The Village Blacksmith** (Hobart) 1 act Lambs' Club 29 December
1913 **Sweethearts** (R B Smith/de Grésac, H B Smith) New Amsterdam Theater 8 September
1913 **The Madcap Duchess** (Justin Huntly McCarthy, David Stevens) Globe Theater 11 November
1914 **The Only Girl** (Blossom) 39th Strcet Thcatcr 2 November
1914 **The Débutante** (R B Smith, H B Smith) Knickerbocker Theater 7 December

1915 **The Princess Pat** (Blossom) Cort Theater 29 September

1917 **Eileen** (ex-*Hearts of Erin*) (Blossom) Shubert Theater 9 March

1917 **Her Regiment** (William Le Baron) Broadhurst Theater 12 November

1919 **The Velvet Lady** (Blossom) New Amsterdam Theater 3 February

1919 **Angel Face** (R B Smith/H B Smith) Knickerbocker Theater 30 December

1920 **My Golden Girl** (Frederick Kummer) Nora Bayes Theater 2 February

1920 **Oui, Madame** (R B Smith/'G M Wright') Little Theater, Philadelphia 22 March

1920 **The Girl in the Spotlight** (ex- *The Miracle Maid*) ('Richard Bruce' ie R B Smith/H B Smith) Knickerbocker Theater 12 July

1922 **Orange Blossoms** (B G de Sylva/de Grésac) Fulton Theater 19 September

1924 **The Dream Girl** (Young, Harold Atteridge) Ambassadors Theater 20 August

Biographies: Waters, E N: *Victor Herbert: a Life in Music* (New York, 1955); Kaye, J: *Victor Herbert* (G Howard Watt, New York, 1931)

HERE COMES THE BRIDE

Musical farcical comedy in 2 acts by Robert P Weston and Bert Lee adapted from an original by Otto Harbach and Edgar McGregor. Lyrics by Desmond Carter. Music by Arthur Schwartz. Opera House, Blackpool, 7 October 1929; Piccadilly Theatre, London, 20 February 1930.

Here Comes the Bride was producer Julian Wylie's attempt – in the wake of the British success of his botched American musical comedy *Merry, Merry* – to manufacture his own American musical in the British provinces. He purchased an unproduced screenplay which had been turned into an unproduced play (and which, in any case, had strong reminiscences of a certain French musical comedy) from American writers Otto Harbach and Edgar McGregor, had it turned into a libretto by the English adaptors of *Merry, Merry*, and equipped it with a set of new and nearly new songs composed by the young American songwriter Arthur Schwartz.

Rich Mexican Maria (Maria Minetti) will inherit even more money if she is still Mrs Tile at the end of a certain period. Having split with her husband, she pays well to wed impoverished and dejected Frederick Tile (Clifford Mollison) who has, apparently irrevocably, been forbidden to wed his beloved Kitty (Jean Colin). But Kitty defies her daddy, turns up in time to take part in a lot of farcical now-you wed me now you-don't action, and everything ends up being resolved when the original Mr Tile turns up to claim back his wife. The songs which lightly accompanied all the action included one, 'High and Low', sung by Miss Colin and Mollison, which would remain one of its composer's popular favourites.

After a four-month tour Wylie's production was taken to London, where it lasted a reasonable to good 175 performances at the Piccadilly Theatre and the Lyceum (26 May).

A different musical, entitled with less comprehensible grammar *Here Goes the Bride*, written by Peter Arno and with music by Edward Heyman, John W Green and Richard Myers, was a quick fold at Broadway's 46th Street Theater in 1931 (3 November).

HERE'S HOWE

Musical comedy in 2 acts by Fred Thompson and Paul Gerard Smith. Lyrics by Irving Caesar. Music by Roger Wolfe Kahn and Joseph Meyer. Broadhurst Theater, New York, 1 May 1928.

Aarons and Freedley sponsored the production of this slightly unusual piece, which told the tale of one Joyce (Irene Delroy) a secretary who is encouraged by her boyfriend (Allen Kearns) to accept her boss's offer to accompany him on a world trip. When Joyce gets to Havana, she finds her Billy is there having lots of luck as a gambler. The two of them end up back where they started, still dreaming of the future, but with a bit of colourful past behind them.

The one bit of *Here's Howe* which lasted beyond its 71 Broadway performances was the song 'Crazy Rhythm', introduced by June O'Dea, Peggy Chamberlain and Ben Bernie. The rest of the show did not make London, but the song did, interpolated into the 1928 show *Lucky Girl*.

HERE'S LOVE

Musical in 2 acts by Meredith Willson based on *Miracle on 34th Street* by Valentine Davies and the screenplay by George Seaton. Shubert Theater, New York, 3 October 1963.

What happens when Macy's department-store Santa Claus falls down, incapable, just before the big parade, and personnel's Doris Walker (Janis Paige) hires an ideal looking replacement (Laurence Naismith) who just happens to be ... Santa Claus? He spreads goodwill more extravagantly than seems real, helps get rid of the store's impossible surplus stock of plastic alligators by pure bonhomie, gets into all sorts of modern mix-ups and ends up besting a prosecuting District Attorney (Larry Douglas) who doesn't believe in Santa Claus, but whose little boy does. Valerie Hall played little Susan Walker, daughter of the personnel lady, who befriends lawyer Fred Gailly (Craig Stevens), who defends Santa and who wins Doris.

Santa and the little girl sang of 'Pine Trees and Holly Berries', Susan and her mum got on 'Arm in Arm', and R H Macy (Paul Reed) sang a eulogy of the jolly man in red in 'That Man Over There' in a score and show which mixed warmth and spectacle in well-judged doses for 338 performances.

The show was revived at the Goodspeed Opera House in 1991 (2 October).

Recording: original cast (Columbia)

HERMAN, Jerry

[HERMAN, Gerald] (b New York, 10 July 1933). Highly successful Broadway songwriter with a winningly popular touch.

Born in New York, brought up in Jersey City and schooled in Florida, Herman was at first orientated towards a career as a designer and architect but, whilst studying at New York's Parsons School of Design, he changed direction and moved on to take a theatre course at the University of Miami. There he wrote several stage shows, one of which, the revue *I Feel Wonderful*, gave him his first professional credit when it was reproduced at the off-Broadway Theater de Lys for a run of 49 performances.

In the years that followed, Herman wrote special material and individual songs for artists including Jane Froman and Hermione Gingold and for Tallulah Bankhead's *Welcome Darlings*, as well as supplying the songs for two further off-Broadway revues, *Nightcap* (1958) and *Parade* (1960, also director). The latter was produced by Lawrence Kasha, who simultaneously announced that he would produce Herman's first full-scale Broadway musical, *Spirit of the Chase*. *Spirit of the Chase* did not eventuate, but the following year Herman's first Broadway show did appear, under the banner of producer Gerald Oestreicher. *Milk and Honey* had an upbeat modern Israeli setting, a story about middle-aged love, and a warmly attractive and effective score, and it proved a fine first-up success for its composer. Whilst it built up a 543-performance run on Broadway, another Herman musical, the off-Broadway *Madame Aphrodite*, came and went in an unobtrusive 13 performances.

In 1964 Herman's second Broadway musical was produced, and it easily outran his not negligible first. In fact, *Hello, Dolly!*, Michael Stewart's musicalized version of *The Matchmaker* with Carol Channing starring as Mrs Dolly Levi, easily outran any and every Broadway musical up to that time in a first run of 2,844 performances. It also walked off with the season's Tony Award, and spread itself around the world to become one of the half-dozen major international classics of the modern Broadway stage, as its title-song became first a hit and then a standard.

One extravagant leading lady followed another as Dolly Levi was followed on to the musical stage, with further great success by *Mame*. Angela Lansbury personified the musical version of Patrick Dennis's much-portrayed Auntie at the top of a long Broadway run prior to Ginger Rogers taking up the relay at London's Theatre Royal, Drury Lane, before *Mame* went on to several other international productions ('Mame','If He Walked into My Life', 'My Best Girl', 'Bosom Buddies').

After three fine hits in a row, things went rather less well for Herman for a number of years. An attempt to turn the winsomely unworldly old heroine of Giraudoux's *The Madwoman of Chaillot* into a further starring rôle for Lansbury saw Herman reaching out beyond the effectively straightforward songwriting of his earlier scores towards some characterful solos and interesting ensemble writing, but the public did not take to the more complex central character of *Dear World* as they had to the straightforwardly outfront ladies of the earlier shows, and the show lasted only 132 Broadway performances. *Mack and Mabel*, the filmland story of the unpleasant Mack Sennett and the foolish Mabel Normand, lasted even less time (66 performances) but, unlike *Dear World*, it left behind several numbers which, after some diligent plugging, became popular with theatrical folk, in particular ('I Won't Send Roses', 'Look What Happened to Mabel', 'Time Heals Everything', 'Wherever He Ain't'). *The Grand Tour*, a musical *Jacobowsky and the Colonel* proved the shortest lived of all its composer's Broadway shows (61 performances) and left no re-usable parts behind.

Following this run of by no means unmitigated (commercial) failures, Herman again connected with success when he contributed some additional numbers to the score of the British revue-musical *A Day in Hollywood – A Night in the Ukraine* (as he had earlier done for the 1964 *Ben Franklin in Paris*), and even more extensively in 1983 with a musical version of the popular French play and film *La Cage aux Folles* (Tony Award, 'I Am Who I Am', 'Song on the Sand'). Gene Barry and George Hearn played out the

crises which sweep down upon the ménage who run and perform in the Riviera nightclub 'La Cage aux Folles' through a Broadway run of 1,761 performances, and the show went on to win more overseas productions than virtually any other Broadway musical of its period, running up a record second, of the composer's works, only – for the moment – to the inexhaustible *Hello, Dolly!*

Herman's shows have produced a good number of take-out songs which have become popular material in the cabaret and concert world, and many of these, with the notable exception of 'Hello, Dolly', which was growled and gurgled up the charts by Louis Armstrong, have been habitually performed (if not necessarily written) in the one, same late-night idiom. 'If He Walked into My Life', 'Time Heals Everything', 'Wherever He Ain't' and their fellows and, most recently and extravagantly, *La Cage aux Folles*'s 'I Am Who I Am' have been blazed into liberally by ladies no longer young but still strong-lunged. It was no surprise, given this, that when a compilation show made up of numbers from Herman's works was produced in 1985, its cast was entirely feminine. *Jerry's Girls* ran 141 performances at New York's St James Theater, had several successful productions, under the management of John Frost, in Australia, and was later seen on the Continent.

1961 **Milk and Honey** (Don Appell) Martin Beck Theater 10 October
1961 **Madame Aphrodite** (Tad Mosel) Orpheum Theater 29 December
1964 **Hello, Dolly!** (Michael Stewart) St James Theater 16 January
1966 **Mame** (Jerome Lawrence, Robert E Lee) Winter Garden Theater 24 May
1969 **Dear World** (Lawrence, Lee) Mark Hellinger Theater 6 February
1974 **Mack and Mabel** (Stewart) Majestic Theater 6 October
1979 **The Grand Tour** (Stewart, Mark Bramble) Palace Theater 11 January
1983 **La Cage aux Folles** (Harvey Fierstein) Palace Theater 21 August

HERMECKE, Hermann (b Magdeburg, 29 May 1892; d Oberaudorf, 15 October 1961).

At first an actor, Dresden-based Hermecke then became a stage writer, scoring his first success with the musical comedy *Liebe in der Lerchengasse*, produced in Magdeburg in 1936. He subsequently paired with composer Nico Dostal to turn out five pieces, including the pre-war *Monika* and *Die ungarische Hochzeit*, and *Doktor Eisenbart*, written after Hermecke's return to (East) Germany after the War, each of which found some success, principally in Germany.

1934 **Venezia** (Arno Vetterling) Deutsches Grenzland Theater, Görlitz 18 November
1936 **Die Dorothee** (Vetterling) Stadttheater, Fürth 18 April
1936 **Liebe in der Lerchengasse** (Vetterling, Heinrich Strecker) Magdeburg 31 December
1937 **Monika** (Nico Dostal) Staatstheater, Stuttgart 3 October
1939 **Die ungarische Hochzeit** (Dostal) Staatstheater, Stuttgart 4 February
1939 **Das Mädchen aus der Fremde** (Vetterling) Opernhaus, Nuremberg 23 October
1940 **Die Flucht ins Glück** (Dostal) Staatstheater, Stuttgart 23 December
1942 **Die Erntebraut** (new version) Opernhaus, Chemnitz 3 May

1949 **Die Rosenhochzeit** (Eva Engelhardt) Stadttheater, Bautzen 3 June
1950 **Zirkusblut** (Dostal) Volksbühne, Leipzig 3 March
1952 **Doktor Eisenbart** (Dostal) Opernhaus, Nuremberg 29 March
1957 **Der ideale Geliebte** (Gerhard Winkler) Städtische Bühne, Nuremberg-Fürth 5 March

HERVÉ [RONGER, Louis Auguste Joseph Florimond] (b Houdain, 30 June 1825; d Paris, 3 November 1892).

Florimond Ronger, known to the musical and theatrical world simply as Hervé, was one of the great characters in, and one of the moving influencers and inspirers of the course of, the French and world musical theatre in the 19th century. It was he who was at the root of the tradition of opéra-bouffe which developed in France in the mid-19th century, as an author, a composer, as a theatre manager and even, on a variety of occasions, as a performer. In a career which included more than the regulation amounts of ups and downs, he was still around more than 30 years on to take a significant part in an important wave of wholly different musical plays, the vaudevilles or musical comedies produced at the Théâtre des Variétés in the late 1870s and early 1880s, a series which gave their composer a second and highly popular 'tour du monde' of successes.

Born in the Pas de Calais near Arras, the son of a French gendarme and his Spanish wife, Hervé lost his father at the age of ten. His mother moved to Paris, and there the child became a choirboy at Saint-Roch whilst following a regular course of musical studies, which allowed him, as a young teenager, to become organist at the chapel of the mental asylum at Bicêtre. During his time in this post he began to work musically with the asylum's inmates, setting up an orchestra and, in 1842, writing a little opérette, *L'Ours et le pacha*, based on the popular vaudeville by Scribe and Saintine, for his pupils to perform. He subsequently became organist at Saint-Eustache and, around this time, also made his first appearances on the professional stage, working as a comedian and vocalist in several of Paris's suburban theatres.

In 1848, Hervé the performer, the writer and the composer concurrently made their first notable appearance on the Parisian stage when the young man wrote, composed and played in a little two-handed saynète devised as an occasional piece for the short, stout actor Désiré, and his tall, gangling self in the rôles of Sancho Panza and Don Quixote. *Don Quichotte et Sancho Pança*, played for the first time at Adolphe Adam's Théâtre National, has been quoted in retrospect as being the starting point for the new French musical theatre tradition.

Hervé, still doubling as church organist and theatrical writer and performer, went on to write and play in a number of other short pieces before he forsook the stage for the pit and took up appointments as chef d'orchestre at, respectively, the Palais-Royal and the Odéon. There he duly turned out a number of other little musical playlets – variously described in such terms as vaudeville-opérette, parodie-opérette or opéra-bouffe – and of wordless pantomimes to be played on the composite programmes which made up the habitual bills at those houses. It was, however, his burlesque ('fantaisie bouffe') *Les Folies dramatiques*, an extravagant five-act parody of all things theatrical which had a strong flavour of the topical revue about it,

Plate 126. **Hervé**

which gave him his first important impetus. The show aroused the interest of the powerful and stage-struck Duc de Morny, and in consequence Hervé was offered a position under royal patronage. He asked, instead, for permission to operate a theatre, and as a result the Folies-Concertantes (soon renamed the Folies-Nouvelles) was opened under his management in the Faubourg du Temple in 1854.

Hervé himself was the main supplier of the quickly turning-over repertoire played at his little theatre, writing and/or composing more than 30 short musical playlets, pochades, vaudevilles and pantomimes during the first three years of his operation. However, he also encouraged and mounted works by other composers, amongst whom Jacques Offenbach – in whose *Oyayaye* Hervé took the travesty title-rôle – and Léo Delibes, whose music the manager interpreted in such pieces as the little two-hander *Deux sous de charbon* (Bigarreau), were prominent. Hervé took part, in fact, in a large number of his own productions, playing opposite Joseph Kelm in the title-rôle of the 'autobiographical' *Le Compositeur toqué* (Fignolet), and in such other little pieces as *La Belle Espagnole* and *La Fine Fleur de l'Andalousie*.

In 1858 the multiple workload became too much for the producer-house author-star performer of the Folies-Nouvelles. Hervé fell ill and had to leave his theatre. He went abroad, touring around, taking employment where he could and would, and spending some time as musical director to the theatre in Cairo, before finally returning to

Paris to take up posts as musical director at the Eldorado, where he turned his hand to supplying the vast number of songs needed for the ever-changing programmes of a café-concert, and at the Délassements-Comiques, for which he composed a further run of the musical playlets and scenes which he had favoured at the Folies-Nouvelles.

During Hervé's absence, however, the musical theatre in Paris had taken strides ahead. Offenbach had produced his famous full-length opéra-bouffe, *Orphée aux enfers*, and in 1864, whilst the Théâtre des Variétés mounted Hervé's winning one-act *Le Joueur de flûte*, they also premièred Offenbach's sensational three-act *La Belle Hélène*. Hervé, whilst still continuing his parallel career as a performer, soon followed Offenbach into the field of the full-length opéra-bouffe. His mock-Arthurian *Les Chevaliers du table ronde*, composed to a text by Chivot and Duru, eased him into the genre with a medium ration of of success, and the following year he topped it with a loopy burlesque of *William Tell*, *Robin Hood* and of anything else in flight for which he himself supplied the text. *L'Oeil crevé* scored a major success in Paris and was soon exported around the world.

Chilpéric, the next year, saw Hervé, the librettist and the composer, in his very top form. This burlesque of things medieval won him a second triumph, compounded this time by his triumph as a performer, for Hervé himself starred in the title-rôle of his thoroughly crazy opéra-bouffe, introducing the famous horseback Chanson du Jambon in his character as the mad Merovingian monarch. His third major work, *Le Petit Faust*, came out only months later. Once more, Hervé the composer and Hervé the actor – appearing here in the dual rôle of the young and the aged Faust – scored a major hit, and *Le Petit Faust* proved internationally the most popular of all his pieces to date. Offenbach, who had turned out *Barbe-bleue*, *La Vie parisienne* and *La Grande-Duchesse de Gérolstein*, in the same period and Hervé were now at the peak of their glory, and the Parisian stage was the centre of the musical theatre world.

Adolphe Jaime and Hector Crémieux, the librettists of *Le Petit Faust*, supplied Hervé with the text for the less successful *Les Turcs*, but this time Hervé did not appear in his show, for he made his way across the Channel to Britain and there, as the Franco-Prussian war raged at home, introduced London to English versions of, first, *Chilpéric* and then *Le Petit Faust*. London was stunned by *Chilpéric*, and Hervé was demanded on all sides. He toured Britain as Chilpéric, and turned his composing talents to supplying the emerging British opéra-bouffe with one of its earliest substantial scores in the Gaiety Theatre's parody of the Aladdin tale, *Aladdin II*. He also contributed to the vast spectacle that was Dion Boucicault's *Babil and Bijou* at Covent Garden, and to the Covent Garden pantomime of 1870, *The Sleeping Beauty, or Harlequin and the Spiteful Fairy* (w Betjemann/Gilbert a' Beckett, C H Ross). At the same time, however, the indefatigable writer continued to hold up a presence in Paris, where another extravagantly burlesque piece, the Scottish saga *Le Trône d'Écosse (et la difficulté de s'asseoir dessus)*, had a fairly successful run.

After Hervé's postwar return to Paris, things went, at first, rather less well. The end of the Empire had more or less spelled the end of opéra-bouffe and its crazy follies,

and Hervé's surreal, imaginative style was no longer what the public demanded. His *La Veuve du Malabar*, with Hortense Schneider starred, and *Alice de Nevers*, in which he himself took the rôle of the Prince de Ferrare alongside Milher, Marie Périer and Marie Desclauzas, were not successes, and if Hortense Schneider's impersonation of *La Belle Poule* and *La Marquise des rues* (68 Paris performances and an Hungarian showing as *Az utszéli grófkisasszony*) did a little better, the composer seemed to have passed his most popular days. When he again took to the stage as an actor in one of someone else's shows, it was in a pre-war piece, in the rôle of Jupiter in Offenbach's revival of his early *Orphée aux enfers*.

However, renewed success arrived before the end of the decade. The Théâtre des Variétés had enjoyed a great success with the vaudeville-opérette *Niniche*, with Anna Judic starred in its oversized title-rôle and a score put together by Marius Boullard. Manager Bertrand decided to continue with more productions in the same vein, and it was Hervé to whom he went for the scores for the three subsequent pieces (and a share in the fourth, *La Roussotte*), conceived and written in a similar vein, with which the star and the theatre triumphed in the years that followed. *La Femme à papa*, with its famous 'Chanson du Colonel', *Lili* and *Mam'zelle Nitouche* brought Hervé three of the biggest successes of his long career, with the last two pieces, in particular, surviving into revivals long after virtually all of his rather more special opéras-bouffes had virtually vanished from the repertoire.

With *La Cosaque*, the vogue for vaudeville-opérette passed, but Hervé continued to write for the musical stage. There were, however, no further hits, and several echoing flops, after the last of which the composer put down his pen, left Paris and returned to England, where he became musical director at the Empire Theatre. He rarely returned to France in his last years, and although he composed several ballets for his London house and possibly a three-act comic opera called *Frivoli* (1886) staged at London's Theatre Royal, Drury Lane, under the name 'Louis Hervé' (which may, perhaps, actually have been the work of his son) with a fine cast but a short run, only a small handful of further Hervé compositions, the last posthumously, were produced in Paris. It was in Paris, however, that he died at the age of 67 after an asthmatic attack.

His son (b Paris, 1847; d nr Paris, 18 July 1926), professionally known as **GARDEL**[-Hervé], had an eclectic career in the theatre. He worked as a performer (playing Médor in his father's *Les Chevaliers de la table ronde* and featuring in the Paris production of *Le nouvel Aladin*, as Raab in *La Timbale d'argent*, Le Rougeaud in *L'Auberge du Tohu-bohu* etc), in management, (for a period director of the Menus-Plaisirs), as a stage director (notably at the Théâtre de la Gaîté and at the Eldorado) and also as an intermittent author and composer. He wrote and/or composed several small musical playlets (*Un Choriste amoureux* [Folies-Nouvelles 23 December 1871], *Dans le bain* [w Hermil, Eldorado 7 April 1873], *Le Roi Topino* [Excelsior 18 November 1898], *Le Brasseur* [Variétés, 18 April 1896], *La Demoiselle de chez Maxim* [Parisiana, 2 March 1899], *Les Aventures de Télémaque* [w Hervé, Scala, 9 March 1900], *Les Filles de la belle Hélène* [w Goublier, Eldorado, 6 January 1900], *La Môme Grenouille*, *Le Voyage d'amour* etc), burlesques, revues, ballet scenarii, sketches, vaudevilles, and even dramas.

1842 **L'Ours et le pacha** (Eugène Scribe, 'Saintine' [ie Xavier Boniface]), Bicêtre, March

1848 **Don Quichotte et Sancho Pança** (Hervé) 1 act Théâtre National 5 March

1849 **Les Gardes Françaises** (Hervé) 1 act Théâtre de l'Odéon 16 December

1849 **Les Parisiens en voyage** (Jules Méry, Gérard de Nerval, Paul Bocage) 1 act Théâtre de l'Odéon

1851 **Passiflor et Cactus** (Hervé) Palais-Royal 6 May

1852 **L'Enseignement mutuel** (Théodore Barrière, Adrien Decourcelle) 1 act Palais-Royal 20 January

1852 **Roméo et Mariette** (Philippe Dumanoir) 1 act Palais-Royal

1853 **Les Folies dramatiques** (Dumanoir, Clairville) Tuileries 1 March, Palais-Royal 2 March

1854 **Prologue d'ouverture** (Charles Bridault) Folies-Concertantes 8 February

1854 **La Perle d'Alsace** (Hervé) 1 act Folies-Concertantes 24 February

1854 **Le Compositeur toqué** (Hervé) 1 act Folies-Concertantes 11 April

1854 **[Amour], Poésie et turlupinade** (Hervé) 1 act Folies-Concertantes 20 June

1854 **La Fine Fleur de l'Andalousie** (Hervé) 1 act Folies-Nouvelles 21 October

1854 **La Caravane d'Amour** (Théodore de Banville) 1 act Folies-Nouvelles 10 December

1855 **La Belle Créature** (Bridault) 1 act Folies-Nouvelles 8 January

1855 **Vadé au cabaret!** (Henri de Kock) 1 act Folies-Nouvelles 20 January

1855 **L'Intrigue espagnole** (A Ruiz) 1 act Folies-Nouvelles 22 January

1855 **Le Sergent Laramé** (Émile Durandeau) 1 act Folies-Nouvelles 3 February

1855 **La Fanfare** (de Banville) 1 act Folies-Nouvelles 29 March

1855 **Un Drame de 1779** (Hervé) 1 act Folies-Nouvelles 21 April

1855 **Latrouillat et Truffaldini** (Jules Petit, Ernest Blum) 1 act Folies-Nouvelles 10 May

1855 **Un Ténor très léger** (René Lordereau) 1 act Folies-Nouvelles 27 July

1855 **Le Testament de Polichinelle** (Armand Montjoie) 1 act Folies-Nouvelles 17 November

1855 **Le Trio d'enfoncés** (Hervé) 1 act Folies-Nouvelles 27 December

1856 **Fifi et Nini** (Albert Monnier) 1 act Folies-Nouvelles 15 January

1856 **Agamemnon, ou le chameau à deux bosses** (Hervé) 1 act Folies-Nouvelles 24 April

1856 **Toinette et son carabinier** (Michel Delaporte) 1 act Folies-Nouvelles 15 September

1856 **Femme à vendre** (Paul de Kock) 1 act Folies-Nouvelles 4 October

1857 **La Dent de sagesse** (Édouard Morin) 1 act Folies-Nouvelles 25 April

1857 **Le Pommier ensorcelé** (Morin) 1 act Folies-Nouvelles 28 April

1857 **Brin d'Amour** (Achille Eyraud) 1 act Folies-Nouvelles 23 September

1857 **Phosphorus** (Hervé) 1 act Folies-Nouvelles 21 November

1858 **Le Voiturier** (Hervé) 1 act Bouffes-Deburau 3 September

1858 **La Belle Espagnole** 1 act Bouffes-Deburau 22 September

1858 **Simple Histoire** (Hervé) 1 act Bouffes-Deburau 10 October

1858 **Les Noces de Bigaro** (Hervé) 1 act Délassements-Comiques 24 December

1860 **La Belle Nini** (Hervé) Palais-Royal 28 January

1862 **L'Alchimiste** (Hervé) 1 act Délassements-Comiques 22 February

1862 **Le Hussard persecuté** (Blum) 1 act Délassements-Comiques 30 May

1862 **La Fanfare de Saint-Cloud** (Blum, Paul Siraudin) 1 act Délassements-Comiques 30 May

1862 **Le Retour d'Ulysse** (Édouard Montagne) 1 act Délassements-Comiques 21 August

1863 **Les Toréadors de Grenade** (Hervé) 1 act Palais-Royal 15 June

1863 **Les Troyens en Champagne** (w Jules Renard) 1 act Palais-Royal 30 December

1864 **Moldave et Circassiène** (Hervé) 1 act Eldorado

1864 **Le Joueur de flûte** (Jules Moinaux) 1 act Théâtre des Variétés 16 April

1864 **La Liberté des Théâtres** (Clairville) Théâtre des Variétés 10 August

1864 **La Revue pour rire/Roland à Rongeveaux** (Clairville, Siraudin, Blum) 1 act Théâtre des Bouffes-Parisiens 27 December

1865 **Une Fantasia** (Nuitter, Nérée Desarbes) 1 act Théâtre des Variétés 12 November

1866 **Les Chevaliers de la table ronde** (Chivot, Duru) Théâtre des Bouffes-Parisiens 17 November

1867 **La [Nouvelle] Biche au bois** (w Jean-Jacques de Billemont, Amédée Artus/Cogniard frères) Théâtre de la Porte-Saint-Martin 15 June

1867 **Le Pédicure** (Hippolyte Bedeau) 1 act Eldorado 14 July

1867 **L'Oeil crevé** (Hervé) Théâtre des Folies-Dramatiques 12 October

1867 **L'Enfant de la troupe** (Félix Baumaine, Charles Blondelet) 1 act Eldorado December

1868 **Le Gardien de sérail** (Hervé) 1 act Théâtre des Variétés 8 March

1868 **Trombolino** (Paul Renard, Charles de St Piat) 1 act Eldorado 9 May

1868 **Chilpéric** (Hervé) Théâtre des Folies-Dramatiques 24 October

1868 **Le Roi Amatibou** (Eugène Labiche, Edmond Cottinet) Palais-Royal 27 November

1868 **Entre deux vins** (René Lugot) 1 act Eldorado

1868 **Nini c'est fini** (Taratte) 1 act Théâtre Molière

1868 **Chilméric** (Renard, de Saint-Piat) 1 act Eldorado 10 December

1868 **Juliette et Dupiton** (Hervé) 1 act Comédie-Parisien

1869 **Deux portières pour un cordon** (w Charles Lecocq, Isidore Legouix, G Martin/'Lucian') 1 act Palais-Royal 15 March

1869 **Les Metamorphoses de Tartempion** (Léon Quentin) 1 act Comédie Parisien 8 April

1869 **Le Petit Faust** (Hector Crémieux, Adolphe Jaime) Théâtre des Folies-Dramatiques 28 April

1869 **Faust passementier** (Hervé) 1 act Eldorado 4 June

1869 **Une Giboulée d'amoureux** (Hippolyte Lefèbvre) 1 act Grand Comédie-Parisien 8 August

1869 **Les Turcs** (Crémieux, Jaime) Théâtre des Folies-Dramatiques 23 December

1870 **Aladdin II** (Alfred Thompson) Gaiety Theatre, London, 24 December

1871 **Les Contes de fées** (w G Raspail, Maximilien Graziani/Oswald François, E Bloch) Délassements-Comiques 5 March

1871 **Le Trône d'Écosse** (Crémieux, Jaime) Théâtre des Variétés 17 November

1872 **Babil and Bijou** (w Frederic Clay, Jules Rivière et al/Dion Boucicault) Covent Garden Theatre, London, 29 August

1873 **La Veuve du Malabar** (Crémieux, Delacour) Théâtre des Variétés 26 April

1873 **La Cocotte aux oeufs d'or** (w Auguste Coèdes,

Raspail/Clairville, Grangé, Victor Koning) Théâtre des Menus-Plaisirs 31 December

1873 **Le Hussard persecuté** revised 2-act version Palais-Royal

1874 **La France et la chanson** (Hippolyte Bideau) 1 act Eldorado 28 February

1874 **La Noce à Briochet** (Ange Hermil) Délassements-Comiques 26 April

1875 **Alice de Nevers** (Hervé) Théâtre des Folies-Dramatiques 22 April

1875 **Dagobert** (arr/Frank W Green/R Sellman) Charing Cross Theater, London 30 August

1875 **La Belle Poule** (Crémieux, Saint-Albin) Théâtre des Folies-Dramatiques 30 December

1876 **Estelle et Némorin** (Amédée de Jallais, Gardel-Hervé) Théâtre des Menus-Plaisirs 2 September

1877 **Up the River, or the Strict Kew-Tea** 1 act Folly Theatre, London 15 September

1879 **La Marquise des rues** (Siraudin, Gaston Hirsch) Théâtre des Bouffes-Parisiens 22 February

1879 **Les Sphinx** (Hervé) Folies-Bergère 29 April

1879 **Panurge** (Clairville, Octave Gastineau) Théâtre des Bouffes-Parisiens 10 September

1879 **La Femme à papa** (Alfred Hennequin, Albert Millaud) Théâtre des Variétés 3 December

1880 **Le Voyage en Amérique** (Maxime Boucheron, Hippolyte Raymond) Théâtre des Nouveautés 16 September

1880 **La Mère des compagnons** (Chivot, Duru) Théâtre des Folies-Dramatiques 15 December

1881 **La Roussotte** (w Charles Lecocq, Marius Boullard/Henri Meilhac, Ludovic Halévy, Millaud) Théâtre des Variétés 28 January

1881 **Les Deux Roses** (Clairville, Victor Bernard, Eugène Grangé) Théâtre des Folies-Dramatiques 20 October

1882 **Lili** (Millaud, Hennequin, Blum) Théâtre des Variétés 10 January

1883 **Mam'zelle Nitouche** (Meilhac, Millaud) Théâtre des Variétés 26 January

1883 **Le Vertigo** (Henri Bocage, Henri Crisafulli) Théâtre de la Renaissance 29 September

1884 **La Cosaque** (Meilhac, Millaud) Théâtre des Variétés 1 February

1884 **La Nuit aux soufflets** (Paul Ferrier, Adolphe d'Ennery) Théâtre des Nouveautés 18 September

1885 **Mam'zelle Gavroche** (Edmond Gondinet, Blum, Saint-Albin) Théâtre des Variétés 24 January

1886 **Fla-Fla** (Hirsch) Théâtre des Menus-Plaisirs 4 September

1887 **La Noce à Nini** (Émile de Najac, Millaud) Théâtre des Variétés 19 March

1890 **Les Bagatelles de la porte** (Baer) 1 act Théâtre des Menus-Plaisirs 14 August

1892 **Bacchanale** (Georges Bertal, Julien Lecocq) Théâtre des Menus-Plaisirs 22 October

1897 **Le Cabinet Piperlin** (Hippolyte Raymond, Paul Burani) Théâtre de l'Athénée-Comique 17 September

1900 **Les Aventures de Télémaque** (arr Gardel-Hervé) 1 act Scala 9 March

Biographies: Schneider, L: *Les Maîtres de l'Opérette Française: Hervé, Charles Lecocq* (Perrin, Paris, 1924); Cariven, R and Ghesquière, D: *Hervé, un musicien paradoxale* (Édition des Cendres, Paris, 1992); Rouchouse, J: *Hervé, ou l'Opérette, une histoire* (Michel de Roule, Paris, 1992)

HERZER, Ludwig [HERZL] (b Vienna, 18 March 1872; d St Gallen, 17 April 1939).

Gynaecologist, author and playwright, Herzer apparently owed at least one production amongst his earlier works to a quid pro quo – having treated the daughter-in-law of theatre director Oskar Fronz, he effectively put him in obligation to mount his *Der dunkle Schatz*. *Der dunkle Schatz* was Herzer's third collaboration with Oskar Friedmann and Edmund Eysler, and it did rather less well than their *Der Aushilfsgatte*, which had topped 100 nights at the Apollotheater in 1917–18 and was subsequently played in Hungary as *A potférj* (ad Imre Harmath).

Herzer also wrote texts for Miska Herczel, leader of the Budapest Opera orchestra, who composed under the pseudonym of 'Max J Milian' and whose *Die goldene Tochter* was seen in Germany, Austria (Wiener Bürgertheater 22 April 1916, 55 performances) and Hungary (*Az aranyos*, Budai Színkör 14 June 1918), and for Louis Grünberg, a composer who showed the colour of his ambitions in the musical theatre by calling himself 'George Edwards' and whose *Lady X*, similarly, won plays throughout central Europe (*Nizzai éjszaka* in its Hungarian production). However, the aspiring librettist had his first real success when he worked on the text to the Singspiel *Friederike*, Lehár's setting to music of Goethe's putative love-life, with Fritz Löhner-Beda. The pair subsequently provided Lehár with the rewrites which turned *Die gelbe Jacke* into *Das Land des Lächelns*, and *Endlich Allein* into *Schön ist die Welt*.

A Strauss pasticcio for the Berlin Metropoltheater and Richard Tauber, and an attempt, with composer Ernst Steffan, to repeat the success of the remade *Die Dubarry* with a Catherine the Great musical, *Katharina*, were not in the same class, and the swashbuckling, romantic *Venus in Seide*, musically set by Robert Stolz, proved the best of Herzer's later pieces.

1913 **Gräfin Fifi** (Albert Chantrier/w Oskar Friedmann) Theater des Westens, Berlin 20 September

1914 **Die weisse Gefahr** (Max J Milian/w Friedmann) Wilhelm Theater, Stuttgart 1 July

1914 **Die goldene Tochter** (Milian/w Friedmann) Wilhelm Theater, Stuttgart 15 July, Wiener Bürgertheater 22 April 1916

1915 **Das Zimmer der Pompadour** (Edmund Eysler/w Friedmann) 1 act Hölle 1 December

1917 **Der Aushilfsgatte** (Eysler/w Friedmann) Apollotheater 7 November

1918 **Der dunkle Schatz** (Eysler/w Friedmann) Wiener Bürgertheater 14 November

1926 **Lady X** (George Edwards) Apollotheater 17 September

1927 **Cagliostro in Wien** revised text (Bürgertheater)

1928 **Friederike** (Lehár/w Löhner-Beda) Metropoltheater, Berlin 4 October

1929 **Das Land des Lächelns** revised *Der gelbe Jacke* (Lehár/w Löhner-Beda) Metropoltheater, Berlin 10 October

1930 **Hallo Tommy** (Edwards) Kleines Haus, Düsseldorf 4 October

1930 **Schön ist die Welt** revised *Endlich allein* (Lehár/Löhner-Beda) Metropoltheater, Berlin 3 December

1931 **Das Lied der Liebe** (Johann Strauss arr Erich Wolfgang Korngold) Metropoltheater, Berlin 23 December

1932 **Venus in Seide** (Robert Stolz/w Alfred Grünwald) Stadttheater, Zurich 10 December

1932 **Katharina** (Ernst Steffan) Admiralspalast, Berlin 22 August

1934 **Der Prinz von Schiras** (Josef Beer/w Löhner-Beda) Theater an der Wien 20 November

1937 **Verzeih' das ich dich lieb'** (*Esö után köpönyeg*) German version w Karl Farkas (Scala Theater)

DIE HERZOGIN VON CHICAGO Operette in 2 acts, a Vorspiel and Nachspiel, by Julius Brammer and Alfred Grünwald. Music by Emmerich Kálmán. Theater an der Wien, Vienna, 5 April 1928.

The 'Duchess of Chicago' is the wealthy Mary Lloyd (Rita Georg) who, during a visit to a Budapest dance-hall, throws a public tantrum when the Crown Prince Sándor of the Ruritanian kingdom of Sylvarien requests that the band play a waltz when she wants only the Charleston and a 'heisses Jazzband'. She buys up the band to get her own way, then invades Sylvarien and promptly proceeds to buy up not only the royal family's castle but the Crown Prince himself. Hans Moser (King Pankraz XXVII) and Hans Thimig (Benjamin Lloyd) were, respectively, the poor royal and wealthy hot-dog-selling fathers. Elsie Altmann as the Sylvarien Princess Rosemarie Sonjuschka von Morenien and Fritz Steiner as Mary's secretary, James Jacques Bondy, provided the soubret part of the entertainment. The Nachspiel to the show, set in the 'Grill American' in Budapest, was, naturally, entitled 'Happy End!' If you call being married to a woman like that 'happy'.

As the tale suggested, the score was a mixture of traditional Austro-Hungarian music and American-style dance music. The evening opened with the chorus demanding that everyone 'Charleston! Charleston!', and the Prince responded with a Viennese song 'In Grinzing steht ein kleines Haus'. By the time things come to a peak he has convinced her that 'Den Walzer hat der Herrgott für verliebte nur gemacht', and she has convinced him of the interest of 'Ein kleiner Slow-Fox mit Mary' and his father of the virtues of a brisker foxtrot ('Voulez-vous, Papachen?').

Hubert Marischka produced and directed, and although the musical mixture provoked such comments as 'has Kálmán sold Austria's musical birthright for a mess of bad American jazz pottage?' the show found plenty of takers. Anny Coty and Juci Lábass succeeded to the rôle of Mary, Harry Bauer, as usual, succeeded Marischka, and was in turn suceeded by Willy Thunis and Willy Degner, as the show ran past its 200th performance (28 September) and, with only a brief pause for a visiting company's season, ran on to 21 February 1929 (287 performances).

Die Herzogin von Chicago followed Kálmán's other successes abroad, but it did not make a significant mark. Budapest's Király Színház mounted a season of an Hungarian version (ad Adorján Stella, Ernő Kulinyi), whilst an American production (ad Edward Eliscu), staged under the Shubert management with Lilian Taiz and Walter Woolf in the starring rôles, started out from Newark but did not make it to Broadway.

Hungary: Király Színház *Csikágói hercegnő* 21 December 1928; USA: Shubert Theater, Newark *The Duchess of Chicago* 11 November 1929

HEUBERGER, Richard [Franz Joseph] (b Graz, 18 June 1850; d Vienna, 28 October 1914). Austrian composer who scored a major hit with his first venture into the Operette world.

Originally an engineer, Heuberger abandoned that career to become a professional musician in his mid-twenties. His subsequent working life combined a notable career as a music critic on the *Allgemeine Zeitung* and the *Neue freie Presse*, wide work as a choral conductor and as a music teacher, with the composition of a variety of works including six Operetten and several operas (*Abenteuer ein Neujahresnacht/Prinz Bummler*, Leipzig 13 January 1886, *Manuel Benegas*, Leipzig 27 March 1889, *Maienacht*, 1894, *Mirjam*, 1894).

His first Operette, *Der Opernball*, produced at the Theater an der Wien when its composer was nearly 50, was a musical version of the hugely successful French comedy *Les Dominos roses*. It proved to be an enormous favourite at home, threw up an all-time hit in 'Im Chambre separée', and was freely exported, establishing Heuberger, on its strength alone, amongst the most in-view composers of his time. The Theater an der Wien hosted two further works which Heuberger and his librettists again based on solidly successful French stage pieces – Hennequin and Millaud's *Niniche* (already set with success by Marius Boullard, not to mention Brandl, twenty years earlier) was remade as *Ihre Excellenz* (48 performances), and Henri Meilhac's *Decoré* musicalized as *Der Sechsuhrzug* (20 January 1900, 25 performances) – and in 1902 he turned to British comedy with a musical, *Das Baby*, based on Pinero's *The Magistrate*. However, none of these well-made musicals, in spite of reasonable runs, approached the success of his first work.

Heuberger was, apparently, the originally intended composer for another French derivative, Léon and Stein's *Die lustige Witwe* libretto, but the job eventually went to Lehár with the well-known happy results, and Heuberger's only subsequent light musical pieces came nowhere near the success of his first. An original Operette, *Der Fürst von Düsterstein*, mounted at the new Johann Strauss-Theater, flopped in 13 performances, whilst his folk opera, *Barfüssele*, first produced at the Dresden Königliches Operntheater (11 March 1905, lib: Victor Léon) and posthumously played at the Vienna Volksoper (22 December 1915), left no mark.

1898 **Der Opernball** (Victor Léon, Heinrich von Waldberg) Theater an der Wien 5 January
1899 **Ihre Excellenz** (aka *Die kleine Excellenz*) (Léon, Waldberg) Theater an der Wien 28 January
1900 **Der Sechsuhrzug** (Léon, Leo Stein) Centraltheater, Berlin 17 January
1902 **Das Baby** (Waldberg, A M Willner) Carltheater 3 October
1909 **Der Fürst von Düsterstein** (Gaudeamus) Johann Strauss-Theater 3 March
1910 **Don Quichotte** (Heinz Reichert, Fritz Grünbaum) 1 act Hölle 1 December

HE WANTED ADVENTURE Musical fantasy in 3 acts by Robert P Weston and Bert Lee based on *Ambrose Applejohn's Adventure* by Walter Hackett. Additional lyrics by Clifford Grey. Music by Jack Waller and Joseph Tunbridge. Saville Theatre, London, 28 March 1933.

After their successful adaptation of *Nothing But the Truth* as *Tell Her the Truth*, the Jack Waller team put together another musical comedy based on a well-liked play for comedian Bobby Howes and the Saville Theatre company. Walter Hackett's 1921 piece *Ambrose Applejohn's Adventure* was adapted to Howes's measure, and the usual short order of musical pieces (seven songs, two choruses and a finale) added.

Howes played Bobby Bramstone (ex-Ambrose Applejohn), a rich chappie who longs for picture-book adventure and who gets it, first in a dream in which he is a pirate chief, and then in real life when jewel-robbers get at a treasure hidden in his stately home. Darkly dramatic Marie Burke and villainous Raymond Newell were a harem girl and a mutineer in the pirate scenes and a pair of Russian crooks in the home ones. Abraham Sofaer and Winifred Izard imitated, in turn, a pair of phony psychics and a couple of Indian mystics, whilst Wylie Watson, a slave-master at sea, became a bumbling scoutmaster, Eustace Didcott, on land, and scored the musical hit of the evening with the tongue-in-cheek boy-scout song 'Smile and Be Bright'. The show played 152 West End performances, toured well, and was remounted on the road in 1943 as *Smile and Be Bright*.

HICKMAN, Charles (b Snaresbrook, Essex, 18 January 1905; d London, 3 April 1983).

At first an actor, Hickman found success as a director from the 1930s, notably with the *Sweet and Low* series of revues, and he went on to direct a number of West End musicals, including the local editions of *Song of Norway*, *The Red Mill* (revival) and *Annie Get Your Gun*, and the mostly successful British musicals *Cage Me a Peacock* (1948), *Dear Miss Phoebe* (1950), *Zip Goes a Million* (1951), *Love from Judy* (1952), *Wedding in Paris* (1954), *The Water Gipsies* (1955) and the pasticcio *Summer Song* (1956) for the London stage. He subsquently went on to direct musicals in both Australia (*The Sound of Music* etc) and South Africa.

Autobiography: *Directed By ...* (New Horizon, London, 1981)

HICKS, [Edward] Seymour (Sir) (b St Helier, Jersey, 30 January 1871; d Fleet, Hampshire, 6 April 1949). Suave, light comedy leading man of the British musical stage.

An actor from the age of 16, Hicks played in the British provinces and appeared with the Kendals in their Broadway season with *The Squire* and *The Queen's Shilling* before his performance as a kind of comical Sherlock Holmes in the revue *Under the Clock* at the Court Theatre brought him to the attention of George Edwardes. Hicks was hired to star in a Gaiety Theatre revival of *Little Jack Sheppard*, in the rôle famously created by Fred Leslie, and he put sufficient individuality into his part to win himself the lead juvenile rôle, opposite Ada Reeve, in Edwardes's next production, the musical comedy *The Shop Girl* (1894, Charlie Appleby). The pair, comedy players both, gave an unaccustomed light-hearted air to the show's juvenile rôles for, until that time, sentimentality rather than fun had been de rigueur in such parts, and Hicks scored a hit with the first of the many borrowed songs he would perform in shows over the years, Felix McGlennon's 'Her Golden Hair Was Hanging Down Her Back'. The emphasis on charming light comedy was increased when Hicks's wife, Ellaline Terriss, took over as 'the shop girl', and together this attractive, bright pair of young performers helped materially to seal the fate of the drooping/sighing, tenor/soprano lovers in London musical plays.

Hicks repeated his *Shop Girl* rôle on Broadway, but refused the 'unsuitable' juvenile part of Edwardes's *My Girl* (1895), which drove the angry manager to court to bar

Hicks from breaking his contract by appearing anywhere else. However, all was back in order in time for him to join his wife in the starring juvenile rôles of the next Gaiety show, *The Circus Girl* (1896, Dick Capel). It was Hicks's last appearance at the Gaiety, but he maintained sufficiently good relations with Edwardes to work as co-author on one of the house's most successful shows, *A Runaway Girl*, in which Miss Terriss played the lass of the title.

A Runaway Girl was, in fact, Hicks's second venture into authorship. He had 'adapted' an Armenian operetta, *Leblébidji Horhor* (which had caused a sensation in Constantinople) for the London stage as *The Yashmak* the previous year. The adaptation seemed more like a total rewrite, and the piece was, in any case, not a success.

The Hickses then joined forces with producer Charles Frohman and, in his company, over a period of some seven years, they played in a series of musicals written by Hicks and designed as vehicles for them: *Bluebell in Fairyland* (1901, Dicky), *The Cherry Girl* (1902, Moonshine), *The Catch of the Season* (1904, Duke of St Jermyns), *The Beauty of Bath* (1906, Richard Alington), which opened the Frohman-sponsored Hicks Theatre, and *The Gay Gordons* (1907, Angus Graeme). Hicks, as author, also ventured further pieces on similar lines. For William Greet he wrote the highly successful *The Earl and the Girl* and the indifferent *The Talk of the Town*, for Frohman, *My Darling*, a piece destined, unsuccessfully, to be played by a B-team of would-be Terriss and Hicks clones.

Hicks and Miss Terriss established themselves, during this period, not only as the town's favourite musical comedy hero and heroine, but also as the theatre's 'ideal couple'. As with most such couples, the ideal was a pretty fictional one, but Miss Terriss tactfully ignored Hicks's repeated trips to the ladies' chorus, and their charming public image lasted happily, to the great good of their popularity.

An attempt to put Miss Terriss into breeches as the hero of *The Dashing Little Duke* did only fairly, but gave place to an interesting incident when Hicks played some performances for his indisposed wife (surely the only case in the history of the musical where a husband succeeded to his wife's rôle), and the 1910 *Captain Kidd*, a version of the American comedy, *The Dictator*, adapted by Hicks, was a smart flop, marking the end of the Hicks/Terriss era of supremacy in the musical theatre in post-*Merry Widow* London. Hicks put his hand to several more not unsuccessful libretti, and the pair appeared together on the halls in *Pebbles on the Beach*, singing and dancing 'Alexander's Ragtime Band', as well as in the Palace Theatre musical *Cash on Delivery*, but, although Hicks remained a respected theatrical figure and, indeed, was awarded a knighthood in 1935, he did not appear further on the musical stage.

Amongst a limited list of film appearances, Hicks starred as Sir John Tremayne in the 1939 *The Lambeth Walk*, the film based on the stage musical *Me and My Girl*.

1895 **Papa's Wife** (Ellaline Terriss/w F C Phillips) 1 act Lyric Theatre 26 January
1897 **The Yashmak** (Napoleon Lambelet/w Cecil Raleigh) Shaftesbury Theatre 31 March
1898 **A Runaway Girl** (Ivan Caryll, Lionel Monckton/Aubrey Hopwood, Percy Greenbank/w Harry Nicholls) Gaiety Theatre 21 May

1901 **Bluebell in Fairyland** (Walter Slaughter/Hopwood, C H Taylor) Vaudeville Theatre 18 December

1903 **The Earl and the Girl** (Caryll/Greenbank) Adelphi Theatre 10 December

1903 **The Cherry Girl** (Caryll/Hopwood et al) Vaudeville Theatre 21 December

1904 **The Catch of the Season** (Herbert Haines, Evelyn Baker/Taylor/w Cosmo Hamilton) Vaudeville Theatre 9 September

1905 **The Talk of the Town** (Haines, Baker/Taylor) Lyric Theatre 5 January

1906 **The Beauty of Bath** (Haines/Taylor/w Hamilton) Aldwych Theatre 19 March

1907 **My Darling** (Haines, Baker/Taylor, P G Wodehouse) Hicks Theatre 2 March

1907 **The Gay Gordons** (Guy Jones/several) Aldwych Theatre 11 September

1907 **A Dress Rehearsal** (Frank E Tours, 'A Lotte'/w A C Robatt) 1 act Tivoli 2 December

1909 **The Dashing Little Duke** (Tours/Adrian Ross) Globe Theatre 17 February

1910 **Captain Kidd** (Leslie Stuart/Ross) Wyndhams Theatre 12 January

1912 **O-Mi-Iy** (Tours, Herman Finck) 1 act London Hippodrome 25 March

1912 **Pebbles on the Beach** (Haines) 1 act London Coliseum 16 December

1916 **The Happy Day** (Sidney Jones, Rubens/Ross) Daly's Theatre 13 May

1917 **Cash on Delivery** (Haydn Wood/H E Wright, Davy Burnaby, James Heard) Palace Theatre 13 October

1918 **Jolly Jack Tar** (Herman Darewski/Burnaby, Heard, J Harrington/w Arthur Shirley) Princes Theatre 29 November

1920 **The Little Dutch Girl** (*Das Hollandweibchen*) English version w Harry Graham (Lyric Theatre)

1923 **Head Over Heels** (Harold Fraser-Simson/Ross, Graham) Adelphi Theatre 8 September

Autobiographies: *Seymour Hicks: 24 Years of an Actor's Life* (Alston Rivers, London, 1910), *Between Ourselves* (Cassell, London, 1930), *Me and My Missus* (Cassell, London, 1939) etc

HIDE AND SEEK Musical play in 2 acts by Guy Bolton, Fred Thompson and Douglas Furber. Lyrics and music by Vivian Ellis, and Sam Lerner, Al Goodhart and Al Hoffman. London Hippodrome, 14 October 1937.

Lee Ephraim's production of *Hide and Seek* teamed comedians Cicely Courtneidge, returning to the theatre after having remade her name in movies, and Bobby Howes in a slightly confusing piece in which they played both themselves and their respective parents. The parents were a jockey and a barmaid, and the jockey wins some shares in a wager on the Derby before they run away to Montana together, and he finally walks out on her. The children – her daughter and his son – are a pair of seaside pierrots, before the daughter becomes a cabaret star. In the course of the evening – when not performing their routines – they outwit some Yankee gangsters and finally get hold of those 'worthless' shares ... in the original 'horseless carriage'.

Hide and Seek was a piece designed to get in the maximum of opportunities for the two stars – plus such currently over-fashionable elements as cabaret stars and American gangsters – and the filmland team of Lerner, Goodhart and Hoffman turned out some suitably functional songs as musical relief. However, the score leaped onto a different level when Howes delivered a song by co-composer Vivian Ellis. 'She's My Lovely' was the little comedian's greatest ever hit. Ellis also supplied Miss Courtneidge with her best opportunity, the stand-up solo for her cabaret act, 'I Follow the Bride'. The two hit songs, and the two favourite stars – not an ideal match, and it was not repeated – ensured 200 West End performances for *Hide and Seek* prior to two seasons touring with other players in the made-to-measure star rôles.

HIGH BUTTON SHOES Musical in 2 acts by Stephen Longstreet based on his *The Sisters Liked Them Handsome*. Lyrics by Sammy Cahn. Music by Jule Styne. Century Theater, New York, 9 October 1947.

Stephen Longstreet's tales of his youth in pre-First-World-War New Brunswick, NJ, made up prettily into a period picture-post-card musical play in which comedian Phil Silvers appeared as Harrison Floy, a home-town boy made small-time bad. Returning to New Brunswick he befriends the Longstreet family – Mama Sara (Nanette Fabray), Papa Henry (Jack McCauley), maiden Auntie Fran (Lois Lee), and young Stevie (Johnny Stewart) – and gets them involved in a scheme to sell a piece of swampland they own, intending to decamp with the cash. A jolly picnic is the scene of the sale, after which Floy, his helper, Mr Pontdue (Joey Faye), and the bewitched Fran run off to Atlantic City with the loot. After ups and downs which go via a football match to an attempt to sell the swampland clay as mud-packs, Floy judges it safer to leave town, while the wiser and not much sadder Fran goes back to her first love, local footballer Hubert 'Oggle' Ogglethorpe (Mark Dawson).

The highlight of the piece was the second-act scene in Atlantic City in which the chase after the stolen money – involving all the principals plus the police and a chorus of seaside holidaymakers – was set by choreographer Jerome Robbins as a dance routine performed in a frenetic Keystone Kops style. The favourite moments of the score fell to Mama and Papa, she persuading him to come and dance with her at the picnic ('Papa, Won't You Dance With Me?') and he, looking sideways at Floy, reminding her that after years of happy marriage 'I Still Get Jealous'. The star, too, had his musical moments. Silvers flashed out 'There's Nothing Like a Model "T"', sang about 'Sunday by the Sea', and tried to get the local team to throw their football match in 'Nobody Ever Died for Dear Old Rutgers'.

Indifferently received by the critics, *High Button Shoes* nevertheless proved to be friendly and colourfully enjoyable entertainment and, in a period in which the musical theatre was flourishing brightly on Broadway, it drew no less than 727 performances, and was then sent on the road with Eddie Foy jr starring as Floy, as well as being mounted in London under the management of Jack Hylton with Lew Parker (Floy), Kay Kimber (Mama), Sid James (Papa) and Hermene French (Fran) featured, for a run of 291 performances. It was recorded for American television in 1956 with Miss Fabray and Faye teamed with Hal March and Don Ameche, and again in 1966 with Jack Cassidy, Carol Lawrence and Maureen O'Hara, and has reappeared on the stage in a number of regional productions, including one at the Goodspeed Opera House (16 June 1982).

The Keystone Kops sequence was seen again on Broadway when it was recreated as part of the compilation show, *Jerome Robbins' Broadway*.

UK: London Hippodrome 22 December 1948
Recording: original cast (RCA)

HIGH JINKS Musical farce (musical jollity) in 3 acts by Leo Ditrichstein and Otto Harbach based on *Les Dragées d'Hercule* by Maurice Hennequin and Paul Bilhaud. Lyrics by Otto Harbach. Music by Rudolf Friml. Lyric Theater, New York, 10 December 1913.

Harbach and Friml followed up their success with the comic operetta *The Firefly* by writing a piece for producer Arthur Hammerstein which was wholly different in tone. *High Jinks* was based on Leo Ditrichstein's *Before and After* (1905), an adaptation of the 1904 French comedy *Les Dragées d'Hercule*, and used the famous 'magic potion' element so beloved of the old fairytale spectaculars and W S Gilbert as the basis of its plot. The 'lozenge' in this case was a perfume which, supposed to cure 'all kinds of spiritual distempers', instead has strange effects on people, and it is in the hands not of a sorcerer, but of Dr Gaston Thorne (Robert Pitkin), a fashionable Parisian neurologist. It has effects on explorer Dick Wayne (Burrell Barbaretto), his girlfriend Sylvia Dale (Mana Zucca), a Spanish couple called M et Mme Rabelais (Ignacio Martinetti, Edith Gardiner), American Lumber King Mr J J Jeffreys (Tom Lewis) and runaway wife Adelaide Fontaine (Elizabeth Murray), as a criss-cross of romances gets bundled up with rumours of a long-lost daughter through three acts.

Friml's score had moments when it launched into the lyrical, but they were mainly moments of gentle burlesque, and the score of *High Jinks* was almost entirely a dancing one. Dick described the symptoms of the 'high jinks' in 'Something Seems a Tingle-ingle-ingling' and joined with Sylvia to waltz about 'Love's Own Kiss' in the two most often repeated numbers of the score, Adelaide mooned over her big, Irish 'Jim' and got come-hitherish with Mr J J Jeffreys in 'She Says it with Her Eyes' (aka 'Come Hither Eyes') and, with little care for the setting, encouraged 'All Aboard for Dixie!' in Cobb and Yellen's interpolation, whilst the inevitable femme du demi-monde, Chi-Chi (Emilie Lea), sang of 'The Bubble'.

High Jinks had a sticky start. Produced in Syracuse in October, it looked far from promising on the road and Hammerstein toyed with the idea of abandoning it. Ultimately, however, he took it to Broadway's Lyric Theater in December and found himself with the season's most successful new show on his hands. *High Jinks* ran for 213 performances on Broadway, and it was swiftly taken up by J C Williamson for Australia, and by Alfred Butt for a London production as a vehicle for comedian W H Berry in the rôle of Dr Thorne. It was wartime and London was touchy about foreign-sounding names, so Butt tried a little dissembling. He masked the largely Central European creative team of the piece under the credit 'by Ogden Hartley and Roderick Freeman' and then – as if that was not enough – wiped them right off the bill, declaring simply that the French play was 'adapted by Frederick Lonsdale'. He also inserted five Howard Talbot numbers, and other pieces by Paul Rubens, Jerome Kern, Jimmy Tate et al into the score. Maisie Gay (Adclaidc), Marie Blanche (Mrs Thorne), Peter Gawthorne (Dick), Nellie Taylor (Sylvia), Saffo Arnay (Chi-Chi) and W H Rawlins (Jeffreys) supported the star,

and the production turned out a major hit which lasted 383 performances in wartime London before touring in 1917 and 1918 (2 companies).

Australia gave an equally warm and long welcome to the show. Williamson's initial production featured Field Fisher (Thorne), Dorothy Brunton (Sylvia), C H Workman (Dick), W H Rawlins (Jeffreys), Gertrude Glyn (Chi-Chi) and Florence Vie (Adelaide) through six weeks in Sydney and ten in Melbourne, but that was far from the end of the show's career in Australia. It was played again in Sydney in September of the same year, and thereafter was revived regularly for many years as one of the handful of staple musical comedies of which there never seemed to be too many performances for Australian audiences. Local favourites Cyril Richard and Madge Elliott were featured in a major revival as late as 1935 (Theatre Royal, Sydney 18 May).

Australia: Her Majesty's Theatre, Sydney 6 February 1915; UK: Adelphi Theatre 24 August 1916

HIGH SPIRITS Musical comedy in 2 acts by Hugh Martin and Timothy Gray based on Noël Coward's play *Blithe Spirit*. Alvin Theater, New York, 7 April 1964.

An attempt to make a musical play out of Noël Coward's *Blithe Spirit* appeared to be an unnecessary exercise – there seemed little that songs, extra scenes and choruses of singers and dancers in the living-room could add to the piece – and, indeed, the show as produced proved little more than a vehicle for revue star Beatrice Lillie in which to display her comic talents. In the now heavily featured rôle of the zany spiritualist Madame Arcati, arriving on the traditional bicycle ('Bicycle Song'), touching filmland parody with a scene in which she advised a chorus to 'Go into Your Trance', calling up her ouija board ('Talking to You') and frothing with excitement over the prospect of meeting a real, live spirit in 'Something is Coming to Tea', Miss Lillie made the most of the many opportunities with which her once supporting rôle was now endowed. Edward Woodward appeared as Charles Condomine, whose marriage to Ruth (Louise Troy) is disrupted when Madame Arcati raises the ghost of his first wife, the extravagant Elvira (Tammy Grimes). Coward himself directed Lester Osterman, Robert Fletcher and Richard Horner's production which played 375 performances on Broadway.

Elsewhere, Lillie-less, thing went less well. A London production, mounted by Geoffrey Russell, featured Cicely Courtneidge as a rather more traditional Madame Arcati alongside Denis Quilley (Charles), Jan Waters (Ruth) and Marti Stevens (Elvira) and played 93 times, whilst an Australian production, a few months later, did even less well. Stuart Wagstaff, Amanda Fox, Dossie Hollingsworth and Betty Kean played a month and a half in Melbourne before the show was shuttered.

UK: Savoy Theatre 3 November 1964; Australia: Princess Theatre, Melbourne 13 March 1965
Recordings: original cast (ABC-Paramount), London cast (Pye)

HIRCHMANN, Henri *see* HIRSCHMANN, HENRI

HIRIGOYEN, Rudy (b Mendionde, 29 August 1919). Heroically voiced French tenor of the postwar romantic musical.

Having worked as a hotel page and envisaged a career in hairdressing, the young Hirigoyen, who had won several singing competitions, ultimately went into the theatre. He was obliged to wait until after the war, however, to begin his stage career as a chorister and second understudy in *Valses de Vienne*. He appeared at the Casino de Paris in revue, in the musical comedy *La Concièrge est dans l'escalier* and in *Le Pays de sourire* at the Gaîté-Lyrique (1949), created the leading rôle of Louis Gasté's *La Rose de Bengale* (1948) out of town, then toured in the star tenor rôles originally created by Luis Mariano in *La Belle de Cadix* and in *Andalousie*, as well as making several visits to Canada.

He subsequently created rôles in *Le Brigand d'amour* (Lyon, 1951) and *Les Caprices de Vichnou* (1952) and made his first film appearance in *Musique en fête* (1951) before succeeding Mariano in the star rôle of *Le Chanteur de Mexico* at the Châtelet. The presence of the idolized Mariano and Rossi in Paris kept Hirigoyen largely to reproducing their rôles in the provinces, but he starred in revivals of *Andalousie* and of *Méditerranée* and introduced the leading tenor rôle of *Maria Flora* at the Châtelet in 1957. Out of town, he created the star rôle of Georges Dherain's *Pour toi* (1955), as well as those of *Farandole d'amour* (1962) and *Rendezvous à Paris* (1968), neither of which was to brave Paris, but he finally got his metropolitan reward with the grand dual lead rôle of the Francis Lopez opérette *Viva Napoli* (1969), in which he appeared as Napoléon to the stirring strains of 'Soldats, je suis content de vous'. Hirigoyen continued to tour, mostly in the Mariano/Rossi/Lopez repertoire, well into his sixties, whilst appearing in Paris in the latter-day Lopez productions.

Over the years Hirigoyen recorded many of the French postwar shows, proving, in a remarkable display of rash singing, that it was certainly not any lack of vocal capacities, but presumably name value that kept him largely in the provinces whilst Mariano and Rossi triumphed in Paris.

HIRSCH, Hugo (b Birnbaum, 12 March 1884; d Berlin, 16 August 1961). Prolific composer for the Berlin stage of the 1920s.

Hirsch briefly studied medicine in Breslau before switching his attentions to music. He moved to Berlin in 1906, and in 1911 he began writing for the theatre. He had his first success with the Revue-Posse *Gehn Sie bloss nicht nach Berlin!*, but his consecration as a part of the Berlin composing world did not come until after the war, when Victor Barnowski produced his vaudeville *Die Scheidungsreise* at the Deutsches Künstlertheater. *Die Scheidungsreise*, from which the song 'Wer wird denn weinen, wenn man auseinander geht' became quickly popular, went on from Berlin to be seen in Vienna, with Annie Dirkens and Otto Storm starred, for six weeks at the Bürgertheater (30 March 1922).

Other successes followed, and at the peak of his activities in the mid-1920s Hirsch was turning out four or five musical comedy and revue scores a season, with a good number proving successful throughout Germany and several getting exposure further afield. The musical Schwank *Die tolle Lola* went from Berlin to a guest season at Vienna's Raimundtheater (2 August 1924), to an American production, under the management of F C Coppicus, as *Lola in Love* (ad Irving Caesar, Scranton, 25 December 1922), then to a revival as *Die Bolero-Prinzessin* in Vienna in 1945 and onto film in 1954, whilst *Dolly* (Johann Strauss-

Plate 127. *One of* **Hugo Hirsch***'s swathe of songs which flooded on to Berlin's stages between the wars.*

Theater 1 October 1924) and the vaudeville *Der Fürst von Pappenheim* (Bürgertheater 5 September 1924) also got Vienna showings, within two months of *Die tolle Lola*. At the same time, his music was heard on the London stage when, after a tour in which the entire score had been his, five Hirsch numbers were eventually combined with some by Broadway composer Stephen Jones to make up the score of Jack Buchanan's *Toni* (Shaftesbury Theatre, 12 May 1924), a piece which seems to have been an uncredited variant on *Der Fürst von Pappenheim*.

His flush of fame was largely over when Hirsch joined the exodus from Berlin in 1933, and moved first to Belgium and then to Paris, where he lived until well after the war, returning in 1950 to settle in Wiesbaden and, later, Berlin. Although still active as a musician, he never succeeded in making a comeback to the popularity that had been his in the 1920s.

1912 **Die Broadway-Girls** 1 act Viktoria Theater, Breslau 1 July

1912 **Eine kitzliche Geschichte** (Rudolf Schanzer/Erich Urban) Lustspielhaus, Düsseldorf 31 October

1913 **Die Hoflieranten** (Leo Walther Stein/Rudolf Presber) Deutsches Theater, Hannover 1 May

1913 **Bummelmädels** (w Schreyer/Max Heye) Berlin Pratertheater 11 May

1914 **Tanzfieber** [*Tangofieber*] (Schanzer, Theo Halton, Heye/Urban) Walhalla-Theater 15 January

1916 **'ne feine Familie** (Alfred Müller-Förster) Metropoltheater, Cologne 10 December

1918 **Die Scheidungsreise, oder Wer wird denn weinen..!** (L W Stein) Deutsches Künstlertheater

?1919 **Die tolle Lola** (Gustav Kadelburg, Arthur Rebner) Neues Operetten-Theater

1921 **Die ewige Braut** (Robert Liebmann/Alexander Engel, Ernst Gettke) Volkstheater, Munich 2 March

1922 **Die erste Nacht** (Heye/Urban, Hans Hellmut Zerlett) Deutsches Künstlertheater 1 June

1922 **Señora** (Alfred Berg/Presber)

1923 **Der Fürst von Pappenheim** (Berg/Franz Arnold, Ernst Bach) Deutsches Künstlertheater 16 February

1923 **Dolly** (Rudolf Bernauer/Arnold, Bach) Berliner Theater 16 October

1925 **Komm doch endlich** (Richard Kessler, Rebner) Operettenhaus am Schiffbauerdamm 27 February

1925 **Der blonde Traum** (Kessler, Rebner) Theater am Schiffbauerdamm 5 March

1925 **Monsieur Trulala** (Kessler) Deutsches Künstlertheater 1 May

1925 **Wenn man verliebt ist** (Rebner, Martin Zickel) Theater in der Kommandantenstrasse 1 November

1925 **[Die Abenteuer des Herrn] Maiermax** (Rudolf Österreicher, Leopold Jacobson) Lessing-Theater 31 December

1925 **Der Weg zu Hölle** (Rebner)

1926 **Yvonne** (August Neidhart, Rebner) Theater am Kurfürstendamm 1 August

1928 **Fräulein Mama** (Kessler)

Other titles attributed: *Pippin der kleine, Die vertauschte Braut, Charleys Tante* (1925), *Kyritz-Pyritz* (1926)

HIRSCH, Louis A[chille] (b New York, 28 November 1881; d New York, 13 May 1924). One of the most happily light-fingered of the group of Broadway composers who carried the popular dance-rhythms of the 1910s into the musical theatre and revue.

Hirsch, apparently at first self-taught as a musician, studied classical piano in New York and in Berlin, but on his return to America in 1906 he devoted himself to popular music, becoming a pianist and arranger to the Tin Pan Alley music publishing houses of Gus Edwards and, subsequently, of Shapiro-Bernstein. At the same time he began to place the songs he was writing, and he became a regular purveyor of material to the Lew Dockstader Minstrels whilst interpolating numbers into such Broadway shows as *The Gay White Way* (1907), *Miss Innocence* (1908) and the Sam Bernard show, *The Girl and the Wizard* (1909 w Edward Madden). He collaborated with his neighbour Jerome Kern and with Melville Gideon on the score for a misbegotten Shubert production called *The Golden Widow* (ex- *The Girl from the States*) which folded on the road and, as a result, he had to wait two years further for his first representation as a full-blown show composer on Broadway. This came when he collaborated with Ben Jerome on the music for the Shubert brothers' *He Came from Milwaukee*, another successful vehicle for comedy star Sam Bernard.

Hirsch joined the Shubert staff in 1911 and, over the nearly two years which he spent as a musical pieceworker on their large turnout of shows, he contributed songs to a variety of musicals, including interpolations for the imported *Vera Violetta* ('The Gaby Glide' w Harry Pilcer), *The Siren* and *The Kiss Waltz* ('Elevation') and pieces for such revues as *The Revue of Revues*, two editions of *The Passing Show* and *The Whirl of Society* ('My Sumurun Girl'). When Hirsch abandoned his place in the musical production line at the Shubert organization in 1912 he was replaced by the young Sigmund Romberg.

Hirsch then moved to London, where he immediately scored a significant hit with his score to the London Hippodrome revue *Hullo, Ragtime!*, one of the earliest shows to emphasise the 'new' American dance rhythms before the British public. He supplied much of the music (w J Rosamond Johnson) for *Come Over Here* at the London Opera House, the scores for *Hullo, Ragtime!*'s successor *Hullo, Tango* and for *Honeymoon Express* at the Oxford, as well as scores and interpolated numbers for various variety house musical playlets, establishing himself as the most visible supplier of the now hugely fashionable American kind of dance/stage music to the London revue and variety theatre, before the outbreak of war sent him back to America.

Hirsch's first years back home saw him still concentrating largely on revue work, supplying songs for such pieces as Klaw and Erlanger's Broadway production of the London revue *Around the Map* (1915), the *Ziegfeld Follies of 1915* ('Hello, Frisco!' w Gene Buck, 'A Girl for Each Month in the Year' w Channing Pollock, Rennold Wolf, 'Marie Odile') and the *Ziegfeld Follies of 1916*, whilst also taking a turn back to the musical play. His first efforts in that field were not, however, successful. Neither Chicago's *Molly and I*, in which Lina Abarbanell starred, nor *My Home Town Girl*, a vehicle for popular touring stars John Hyams and Leila McIntyre, produced by Perry J Kelly, ventured to Broadway, while *The Grass Widow*, a musicalization of the French comedy *Le Péril jaune* produced by Madison Corey with Howard Marsh, George Marion and Natalie Alt featured, which did, stayed there for only six weeks.

The kind of success Hirsch had enjoyed in his time in London, and in revue, was, nevertheless, soon to come. Whilst *The Grass Widow* was stumbling through its Broadway run, a second Hirsch score got its first airing on Broadway. *Going Up*, a musical version of James Montgomery's play *The Aviator*, scored a splendid success and the dance song 'The Tickle Toe', the pretty ballad 'If You Look in Her Eyes' and the lively title number were swiftly added to the composer's growing list of song successes. Whilst *Going Up* went on to international success, its composer's hometown triumph was consolidated by Klaw and Erlanger's production of *The Rainbow Girl*. Based on Jerome K Jerome's play *Lady Fanny and the Servant Problem*, this musical featured another delightfully tuneful and rhythmic score from which the lilting 'I'll Think of You' proved the stand-out number. *The Rainbow Girl* had a good Broadway run and a subsequent life on the road, though without winning *Going Up*'s popularity outside America.

This vein of success, however, soon faded out temporarily. Of his next three book musicals, one – a ragtimey reunion show for Weber and Fields – failed to make it to Broadway, whilst the other two left no mark. *Oh! My Dear*, a small-scale piece constructed for the Princess Theater, on which Hirsch deputised for his old friend Jerome Kern in a collaboration with P G Wodehouse and Guy Bolton, was a disappointment. The show survived six months in its little auditorium. This was more than the life garnered by the indifferent *See-Saw*, a piece originally intended as a vehicle for the irrepressible Mitzi, but ultimately played with a starless cast for 11 Broadway weeks.

The composer was at work on other fronts as well. He continued his contribution to revue (*Ziegfeld Follies of 1918*) and wrote a musical show for the Friars' Club (*The Hit of the Season*, 17 December 1917), but it was again a musical comedy which gave him his next major hit. *Mary*, produced by George M Cohan, followed *Irene* and preceded *Sally* in the hit parade of poor, pretty girls of the 1920s American musical theatre who made good to the accompaniment of the catchy, light-hearted melodies of the period. Hirsch turned out 'The Love Nest', 'Anything You Want to Do, Dear' and 'We'll Have a Wonderful Party', and both the show, which racked up 217 performances on Broadway, and its songs, became widespread favourites.

The same team of writers and producer Cohan attempted to repeat *Mary*'s success with *The O'Brien Girl*, a piece built rather transparently on the same lines, the following year. It found a fair degree of popularity, but did not bring forth the same kind of enduring response which had been evoked by *Mary*. Hirsch then turned back to revue to write for *The Ziegfeld Follies of 1922* and *The Greenwich Village Follies of 1922* and *of 1923* (w Con Conrad), and he was to return only once more to the musical theatre, with the score for a version of Paul Armstrong and Rex Beach's comedy *Going Some*, produced in 1924 under the title *Betty Lee*. Like *The O'Brien Girl*, it won its due measure of success at home and as an export to Australia, but Hirsch was not around to accept its rewards. He died that year, at the age of 42, and *Betty Lee*'s Broadway season was played posthumously.

The composer of some of the most infectiously attractive theatre melodies of his era, Hirsch has suffered an eclipse under the shadow of the big, well-plugged names of, mostly, a slightly later period, but his *Going Up* was revived by the Goodspeed Opera House in 1976 and his favourite songs are still occasionally heard. Historically, he holds a firmer position in the British theatre where, in spite of his brief stay, he was an important figure in encouraging the spread of modern American popular dance and song music into the English theatre on the eve of the First World War.

1909 **The Golden Widow** (ex- *The Girl From the States*) (w Jerome Kern, Melville Gideon/Edward Madden/Glen MacDonough, Joseph Herbert) Belasco Theater, Washington 26 October

1910 **He Came From Milwaukee** (w Ben Jerome/Madden/Mark Swan, Edgar Smith) Casino Theater 21 September

1914 **Dora's Doze** (George Arthurs) 1 act London Palladium 6 July

1915 **The Magic Touch** (w Leon Bassett, Maxwell Brunell/Arthurs, Charles Danvers) 1 act Walthamstow Palace, London 18 January

1915 **Go to Jericho** (w Fred Godfrey/Arthurs) 1 act Oxford Theatre, London 22 February

1915 **Molly and I** (Frank R Adams) La Salle Theater, Chicago 31 August

1915 **My Home Town Girl** (Frank M Stammers) Empire Theater, Syracuse 15 November

1917 **The Grass Widow** (Channing Pollock, Rennold Wolf) Liberty Theater 3 December

1917 **Going Up** (Otto Harbach) Liberty Theater 25 December

1918 **The Rainbow Girl** (Jerome K Jerome ad Wolf) New Amsterdam Theater 1 April

1918 **Back Again** (George V Hobart, Stammers) Chestnut Street Theater, Philadelphia 29 April

1918 **Oh! My Dear** (ex- *Ask Dad*) (P G Wodehouse, Guy Bolton) Princess Theatre 26 November

1919 **See-Saw** (Earl Derr Biggers) George M Cohan Theater 23 September

1920 **Mary** (ex- *The House That Jack Built*) (Harbach, Frank Mandel) Knickerbocker Theater 18 October

1921 **The O'Brien Girl** (Mandel, Harbach) Liberty Theater 3 October

1924 **Betty Lee** (Harbach, Irving Caesar) 44th Street Theater 25 December

[CHARLES]-HIRSCH, Karoline [HIRSCH, Karoline] (b Vienna, 28 August 1848; d Vienna, 13 March 1932). Viennese operatic soprano, who created Strauss's Adele on an infrequent visit to the Operette stage.

After graduating with the top award from the Vienna Conservatorium, Karoline Charles-Hirsch performed coloratura soprano rôles at Graz, Dresden, Budapest and at the Vienna Hofoper, where she made her début in the rôle of Mozart's Queen of the Night. She broke her Viennese contract to go off to sing in Leipzig, and made her Operette début at the Theater an der Wien, where she created the rôles of Gräfin Falconi in Strauss's *Carneval in Rom* (1873) and Adele in *Die Fledermaus* (1874), introducing the famous laughing song ('Mein Herr Marquis') and its companion audition song 'Spiel' ich die Unschuld vom Lande'. She subsequently returned to operatic rôles, playing throughout central Europe, before retiring and becoming a singing teacher.

HIRSCHMANN, Henri [HERBLAY, Henri Louis] (b St Mandé, 30 April 1872; d Paris, 3 November 1961). French composer of opéra-comique and musical comedy scores.

Hirschmann began his composing life with operatic ambitions, and he placed a short piece, *Amour à la Bastille*, at the Opéra-Comique at the age of 25. A more ambitious opéra-comique, *Lovelace*, was staged briefly at the Théâtre des Variétés, but before long the composer was purveying short musical scenes and ballet and pantomime music to such light music venues as the Olympia (*Néron*, *Les Sept Péchés capitaux* etc) and the Bôite à Musique (*Le Siècle*, *Le Retour*). His first success came in that lighter musical theatre when his opérette *Les Hirondelles* was produced in Berlin in 1904. The piece went on to be played in Budapest (*Fecskefészek* 1904 Magyar Színház), in Vienna (*Das Schwalbennest* 1905 Venedig in Wien) and in Brussels before it finally made its way to Paris in 1907. By that time Hirschmann had already made himself a home reputation with the highly successful production of his *La Petite Bohème*, a musical comedy variant on the Murger/Puccini tale, mounted at the Théâtre des Variétés.

In the years that followed he continued to write scores for lyric drama (*Rolande* 1905, *Hernani* 1908, *La Danseuse de Tanagra* 1911), and was considered one of the country's great musical theatre hopes by those to whom the line of French opérette represented by Messager and *Ciboulette* was the legitimate one. Hirschmann lived up neither to their hopes nor to his early promise. Lightening his musical style to approach that of the fashionable and potentially lucrative dance-rhythmed shows of the wartime and postwar years, he supplied some agreeable music to a series of further musical shows in the next 20 years without achieving either a standard repertoire piece nor, in spite of reasonable home success with such pretty pieces as *Pouche* (its foreign versions were given new scores), any particularly long runs.

He was represented briefly on Broadway in 1912 when the Léon Pavi mimodrama *Seostrata*, for which he had composed the music, was played on the bill at the Winter Garden with *The Whirl of Society*.

1897 **Amour à la Bastille** (Lucien Augé de Lassus) 1 act Opéra-Comique 14 December

1898 **Lovelace** (Jules Barbier, Paul de Choudens) Théâtre des Variétés 15 September

1898 **Les Favorites** (Octave Pradels) 1 act Olympia 28 May

1898 **Folles amours** (w Oscar de Lagoanère/Max Maurey) 1 act Olympia 11 September

1904 **Les Hirondelles** (Maurice Ordonneau ad Maurice Rappaport) Centraltheater, Berlin 9 January

1905 **La Petite Bohème** (Paul Ferrier) Théâtre des Variétés 19 January

1907 **La Feuille de vigne** (Ferrier) Théâtre du Moulin-Rouge 24 February

1910 **Mam'zelle Don Juan** (Antoine Yvan) Théâtre Grévin 26 January

1910 **La Vie joyeuse** (Antony Mars, Alfred Barré) Valence 17 November

1911 **La Danseuse de Tanagra** (Ferrier, Felicien Champsaur) Opéra, Nice 10 February

1911 **Les Petites Étoiles** (Pierre Veber, Léon Xanrof) Théâtre Apollo 23 December

1913 **La Petite Manon** (Ordonneau, Henze) Théâtre Royal, Ghent 15 March

1920 **La Princesse Carnaval** (Maurice Desvallières, Paul Moncousin) Théâtre Apollo 24 January

1923 **Épouse-la!** (Veber) Théâtre Fémina 15 February

1924 **La Dame du Pesage** (André Leroy) Théâtre Michel 24 May

1925 **Pouche** (René Peter, Henri Falk ad Alphonse Franck) Théâtre de l'Étoile 18 February

1927 **La Dame au domino** (Henri de Gorsse, Victor Darlay) Théâtre de la Gaîté-Lyrique 28 October

HIS LITTLE WIDOWS Musical comedy in 3 acts by Rida Johnson Young and William Cary Duncan. Music by William Schroeder. Astor Theater, New York, 30 April 1917.

Rida Johnson Young, recently successful with her adaptation of the Hungarian *Az obsitos* as *Her Soldier Boy*, and her collaborator William Cary Duncan took up a much older tale, which had served for a number of earlier musicals, as the plot for their 1917 musical, *His Little Widows*. However, whereas 19th-century pieces like *The Terrible Turk* and *Black and White* had used Eastern harems to supply the bevy of 'wives' necessary to the storyline, Mrs Young and her partner went more local and, following the line used by the French vaudeville *Les Douze Femmes de Japhet*, set their piece in the Mormon centre, Salt Lake City.

Robert Emmett Keane played Jack Grayson, a member of the brokerage firm of Lloyd (Carter de Haven), Grayson and Hale (Harry Tighe), who has inherited from his uncle. The conditions of the will, however, state that Jack must marry the dead man's widows. There are eight of them, for Uncle was a Mormon. They are, after three acts of comic convolutions, eventually disposed of to Harry Jolson (Charles Prince), who runs a revue company, and each fellow pairs off with the girl he has been singing duets with most of the night – Pete Lloyd with Blanche (Frances Cameron), Biff Hale with Annabelle (Flora Parker) and Jack with Marilla (Hattie Burks). Frank Lalor featured as a Mormon called Abijah Smith, and the better songs included a song-and-dance quartet 'I'm Crazy About the Way You Dance with Me', and a trio led by Abijah about 'A Wife for Each Day in the Week'.

His Little Widows had an indifferent Broadway run of 72

performances and changed its title before being shown to the rest of the country (*Some Little Girl* Empire, Syracuse 14 March 1918), but London's Bernard Hishin took it up and mounted it (ad Firth Shephard) at Wyndham's Theatre with a cast headed by Gene Gerrard (Jack), Eric Blore (Biff), Laddie Cliff (Pete), Joan Hay (Blanche) and Mabel Green (Annabelle) and achieved a thoroughly respectable 172 performances before putting the show on the road. Shephard and Cliff were clearly amongst those who remembered it fondly, for a few years later they lifted the show's libretto, even more blatantly than its authors had lifted the earlier pieces for theirs, and attached it to a fresh score, under the title *Lady Luck*, scoring a 324-performance West End hit.

The first English version of *His Little Widows* also got a showing in Australia, produced on the Tivoli circuit with William Valentine (Jack), Muriel Cathcart (Marilla), Hugh Steyne (Biff), Marie La Varre (Annabelle), Rex London (Pete) and Vera Pearce, then Minnie Love (Blanche). It ran for around six weeks in Melbourne, and was then seen in Sydney (17 July 1920).

UK: Wyndham's Theatre 16 June 1919; Australia: Tivoli, Melbourne 24 April 1920

HITCHCOCK, Raymond (b Auburn, NY, 22 October 1871; d Beverly Hills, Calif, 24 November 1929). Popular star comedian of the Broadway musical stage in the early years of the 20th century.

After playing first as an amateur Hitchcock began his professional career as a comic actor in the straight theatre, and did not appear in his first musical until he was in his early thirties. He played in the chorus of W T Carleton's touring *Les Brigands* and *The Golden Wedding*, but later moved up to take leading comedy rôles in the Castle Square Opera Company: Bicoquet in Planquette's *Paul Jones*, the Lord Chancellor (*Iolanthe*), Don Alhambra (*Gondoliers*), Ko-ko (*Mikado*), Bunthorne (*Patience*), Flapper (*Billee Taylor*), Baron Puck (*La Grande-Duchesse*), Lambertuccio (*Boccaccio*), Duc de Ifs (*Les Noces d'Olivette*), Lurcher (*Dorothy*), Nicola (*Sinbad*), Enterich (*Der Bettelstudent*), Fanfani Pasha (*Die Afrikareise*), Corrigan (*Lily of Killarney*) and even Antonio (*Mignon*). He continued this musical line in George Lederer's production of the German musical comedy *A Dangerous Maid* (1899), teamed with Marie Cahill as one of the crooked protaganists of the revamped Boston musical *Three Little Lambs* (1899, David Tooke), appeared in *The Belle of Bridgeport* (1900, Bokhara Skitbolliski) and toured in Luders and Pixley's successful Chicago musical *The Burgomaster* (E Booth Talkington) and in *Miss Bob White*, establishing himself as a solid principal musical comedian and a touring name.

Back on Broadway he appeared in the American version of the Strauss pasticcio *Wiener Blut* as the merry-go-round proprietor, Kagler, before displacing William Norris in the title-rôle of the next Luders/Pixley piece, *King Dodo* (1902), for his first Broadway starring rôle. When the great success of that piece was ultimately exhausted, producer Henry Savage starred him as the comical Abijah Booze, American consul in Puerto Plata, in an even more successful musical *The Yankee Consul* (1904, 'Ain't it Funny What a Difference Just a Few Hours Makes', 'In the Days of Old', 'In Old New York').

He toured with his wife in the play *Easy Dawson* and in

De Koven's *The Student King* (1906, Rudolph) before the authors of *The Yankee Consul* successfully supplied him with another useful Broadway vehicle in *The Yankee Tourist* (1907, Copeland Schuyler). He missed a few performances of this piece when he was sent to jail after a run-in with some blackmailers, and was deputized for by one Wallace Beery. Hitchcock then switched first to revue and then back to French opérette to play Laurent in a revival of *La Mascotte* (1909) before moving on to further Broadway musical star rôles in *The Red Widow* (1914, Cicero Hannibal Butts) and *The Beauty Shop* (1914, Dr Arbutus Budd). He won a personal success when he appeared in London in the title-rôle of the custom-made *Mr Manhattan* (1916, 'All Dressed Up and No Place to Go') before coming back to one more musical in New York – the British piece *Betty* (1916), in which he gave his version of the rôle of Lord Playne created by G P Huntley. Thereafter his musical stage appearances were largely in revue – notably his own series of *Hitchy-Koo* shows – although he returned once more, a decade later, to the musical theatre to play a minor rôle in *Just Fancy* (1927) at the Casino Theater, at the age of 62.

His wife, **Flora ZABELLE** (née MANGASARIAN, b Armenia, 1880; d New York, 7 October 1968), having begun her career in Chicago, graduated to second soubrette rôles on the Broadway stage, appearing as Poppy in *San Toy* for Daniel Frohman and singing 'Maisie' in *The Messenger Boy* (1901, Isabel Blythe) for Nixon and Zimmerman. She took the juvenile rôles opposite Hitchcock in *King Dodo* (Annette), *The Yankee Consul* (Bonita) and *The Yankee Tourist* (Grace Whitney) and starred as Bettina in *La Mascotte* as well as playing in revue and straight theatre. Later musical appearances included the Viennese Operette *The Kiss Waltz* (1911, Nella), *Have a Heart* (tour 1917), *Toot Toot* (1918, Mrs James Wellington), the short-lived *The Girl from Home* (1920, Juanita Arguilla) and a tour of *The Rose Girl*. She collapsed during this last engagement and was taken to hospital, reportedly dying. However, although she retired from the stage, she lasted for nearly half a century more. After her husband's death she pursued a career as a designer.

HIT THE DECK Musical comedy in 2 acts by Herbert Fields based on the play *Shore Leave* by Hubert Osborne. Lyrics by Leo Robin and Clifford Grey. Music by Vincent Youmans. Belasco Theater, New York, 25 April 1927.

In 1927 Vincent Youmans, miffed at what he considered a lack of consideration by his latest producer, decided to mount his next show himself. He went into partnership with Lew Fields, optioned the 1922 play *Shore Leave*, and gave it to Fields's son, Herbert, to adapt. Young Fields turned the plain, demure heroine of the original into a bouncy stunner, shifted the action from seaside New England to the much more picturesque venues of a battleship and far-off China, and christened the piece with the rather more jazzy title of *Hit the Deck*.

Looloo Martin (Louise Groody), who runs a dockside café, takes an enduring shine to sailor Bilge Smith (Charles King) who has spent one of his evenings ashore romancing her. When Bilge goes back to sea, Looloo waits until she can wait no more, and then, since she has come into some money, sets out to find the forgetful gob. She invites all the Smiths in the navy to a party on board a battleship, and then chases up Bilge's trail all the way to colourful China. This impresses him quite a lot, but her money doesn't, and he will only say 'yes' when he thinks she is poor again.

Youmans supplied a score full of happy songs, topped by Looloo and Bilge's duo 'Sometimes I'm Happy' and 'Hallelujah', a decidedly tacked-in revivalist number for Looloo's negro pal, Lavinia (Stella Mayhew in blackface), both of which became lasting hits. Neither, however, was precisely a new number: the former had already gone unappreciated in the composer's rewrite of the London hit *A Night Out*, which had folded on the American road, whilst the latter was also a melody he had composed some years earlier, although not previously used. Looloo also duetted through 'The Harbour of My Heart' and 'If He'll Come Back to Me', Lavinia had a second spot with the comical 'Lucky Bird', and three supporting characters (Bobbie Perkins, Madeleine Cameron, John McCauley) sang and danced their way through 'What's a Little Kiss Between Friends?'.

Hit the Deck was a fine Broadway success, running for 352 performances as its first touring company headed by Queenie Smith and Charles Purcell set out to cover the country. The show made its London début under the management of Britain's *No, No, Nanette* producers Clayton and Waller and the Moss' Empires organisation in a version adapted, and with one interpolated song, by R P Weston and Bert Lee, which more politely rechristened Bilge Smith as Bill (Stanley Holloway). Ivy Tresmand played Looloo and Alice Morley was Lavinia, and the show was again a thorough success through 277 London performances, prior to going on tour in triplicate the following season. It was, perhaps, fortunate for Youmans that Britain's production of *Two Little Girls in Blue* had folded on the road a few months earlier – otherwise some further pieces of the show's reorganized musical score might have been too readily recognized as second-hand.

Australia followed suit, presenting the English version of the show with English ingénue Annie Croft cast as Looloo alongside comic Gus Bluett (Battling), Lance Fairfax (weeks away from becoming the country's favourite Red Shadow) as Bill, and comedienne May Beatty blacked up to play Lavinia. It played seven weeks in Melbourne, and rather more the following season (Theatre Royal, 26 January 1929) without becoming a real hit.

The Parisian success of *No, No, Nanette* and, to a lesser extent, of subsequent American shows, encouraged the Isola brothers to mount a version of *Hit the Deck* at the Théâtre Mogador. Adapted by Roger Ferréol and Saint-Granier as *Hallelujah*, the piece was produced with local *Rose-Marie* star Coecilia Navarre as Looloo, Géo Bury as Bilge and Gesky belting out 'Hallelujah!', a male chorus of a hundred, a vast battleship, and the Borah Minevitch musical comedians and an acrobatic danseuse, Olympe Bradna, tacked in as extra attractions. In spite of the decided effect made by Minevitch's harmonica-playing team, it didn't take, and after a month the management returned to their reliable *Rose-Marie*.

Two film versions of *Hit the Deck* appeared, the first in 1930, with Polly Walker and Jack Oakie in the lead rôles, the second in 1955 with Debbie Reynolds, Jane Powell and Tony Martin in a version which used more of the show's score (seven of ten numbers, complemented by several

Plate 128. 'He's never, never sick at sea'. Paul Bentley as Captain Corcoran receives the homages of Dick Deadeye (John Kavanagh) and Ralph Rackstraw (William Relton) in Noel Pearson's Dublin production of **HMS Pinafore**.

other Youmans numbers and 'Ciribiribin'!) than its story. The show was also televised (1950), but in spite of its original popularity, it has been rarely seen on the stage since. Characteristic revivals were seen at the Jones Beach Marine Theater in 1960 (23 June) and at the Goodspeed Opera House in 1977.

UK: London Hippodrome 3 November 1927; Australia: Her Majesty's Theatre, Melbourne 28 July 1828; France: Théâtre Mogador *Hallelujah* 15 December 1929; Films: RKO 1930, MGM 1955

Recordings: London cast recordings assembled (WRC), selection (HMV, Fontana), film soundtrack 1955 (MGM)

HMS PINAFORE, or the Lass That Loved a Sailor
Comic opera in 2 acts by W S Gilbert. Music by Arthur Sullivan. Opera Comique, London, 25 May 1878.

Following the success of his Comedy Opera Company production of *The Sorcerer*, Richard D'Oyly Carte mounted a second comic opera written by W S Gilbert and Arthur Sullivan. The new piece abandoned the familiar English rustics and rural nobles of its predecessor and, instead, devoted itself to having some burlesque fun at the expense of things nautical and theatrical-nautical, much as F C Burnand had done with such felicity a decade or so earlier

in his hugely successful burlesque *Black-Eyed Susan*. Gilbert's libretto, which recycled many ideas and elements first used in his comic poetry, had much more of the flavour of the Gallery of Illustration and of English operetta to it than Burnand's combination of low comedy, puns and pantihose, and the text of *HMS Pinafore* wittily mocked the conventions of the nautical melodrama in an altogether more sophisticated manner than the celebrated burlesque had done, following naturally, but more joyously, in the path rather politely set out by the English comic tale of *The Sorcerer*.

Extremely able seaman Ralph Rackstraw (George Power) is in love with Josephine (Emma Howson), the daughter of his Captain (Richard Temple), but she is intended as a bride for the Admiral, Sir Joseph Porter KCB (George Grossmith), a curious gentleman who has never been to sea and who has trendy liberal ideas about equality amongst all men – himself, of course, excepted. Josephine is not long able to mask her reciprocal yearnings for the pretty tar, and the two plan to elope. Alas, they are betrayed by the standard villain of melodrama, the hunch-backed Dick Deadeye (Rutland Barrington). But the bumboat woman, Little Buttercup (Harriet Everard), comes to the rescue. Once wet-nurse to Captain Corcoran and

Ralph, she mixed the two babes up, and thus Ralph is Corcoran and Corcoran is Ralph. Since birth is the all-important consideration in such things, Ralph is promptly promoted to Captain and is quite able to wed the daughter of his inferior, now disdained by the Admiral, for love and liberalism (trendy or otherwise) do not level all ranks quite that much.

The score of *HMS Pinafore* was in every way the equal of its libretto. On one hand, Sullivan clipped through the pattering notes of Sir Joseph's comical curriculum vitae ('When I was a lad I served a term...') as the Admiral told of how he had 'polished up the handle of the big, front door' on his way to becoming 'ruler of the Queen's Navee', and of Corcoran's jolly self-introduction ('I Am the Captain of the Pinafore') claiming that he was 'never, never sick at sea'. On the other, he turned out some soaringly romantic, but sufficiently twinkle-in-the-eyed, pieces for the romantic and dramatic moments: Josephine's primadonna soliloquy over giving up riches and rank for the sake of a sailor ('The Hours Creep on Apace'), Ralph's lyrical praises of 'A Maiden Fair to See' for whom he is prepared to blow his brains out, their sub-operatic confrontation, with the lady not yet willing to drop her pretence of indifference ('Refrain, Audacious Tar'), and their last farewell ('Farewell, My Own') which, of course, turns out not to be the last. Captain Corcoran had his lyrical moment, too, serenading the moon in not quite traditional style ('Fair Moon, to Thee I Sing'), before joining in one of the show's light-hearted highlights, the trio song-and-dance 'Never Mind the Why and Wherefore', which introduced the most famous theatrical dance in years in Johnny D'Auban's tripping little routine for Grossmith, Temple and Miss Howson. Little Buttercup had her musical moment in her entry song ('I'm Called Little Buttercup'), whilst memories of many a nautical night in the theatre were echoed in the glee which Sullivan composed for a quartet of sailors – a piece presented as the philanthropic work of the Admiral, intended as a morale-boosting piece for the lower ranks – 'A British Tar'.

After a mediocre beginning, *HMS Pinafore* soon established itself as a major hit in London and, in spite of managerial problems and a broken run, it ended by playing a total of 571 performances at the Opera Comique, a record for a British musical to that time, even though the London production of *Les Cloches de Corneville* was at the same time notching up an even longer run. At one stage there were two *Pinafores* playing in the West End for, when Carte successfully outmanoeuvered and outbattled his backers for control of the show, those gentlemen set up a rival production of *HMS Pinafore* at the Imperial Theatre. It lasted 12 weeks before they were obliged to give best, but the suings and counter-suings continued for a long time.

Two concurrent productions was, however, nothing compared to what happened when *HMS Pinafore* hit Broadway. R M Field of Boston (with a female Ralph), Mrs Alice Oates of San Francisco (with an interpolated tenor rôle – to make up for the fact she played Ralph – and several interpolated songs) and John T Ford of Baltimore all got versions of the copyright-free show onto the stage before the end of 1878, and in January 1879 James C Duff mounted New York's first production. Thomas Whiffen played Sir Joseph, Eva Mills and Henri Laurent the lovers,

and Eugene Clarke the Captain, and Duff's production ran for a fine 175 nights in the metropolis, as a perfect tidal wave of royalty-free *Pinafores* swept the stages of New York and the rest of the country. There was Edward Rice's *Pinafore* with George Fortescue playing a travesty Buttercup, there was Gorman's Philadelphia Church Choir Company with a cast of church vocalists, there was the Coloured Opera Troupe's negro version, a juvenile version, an all-women one, a German-language version (*Ihre Majestats Schiff Pinafore*), a Pennsylvania Dutch version (*HMS Pinafore, oder das Mädel und ihr Sailor Kerl* ad Alfred Charles Moss), and there was the Boston Ideal Opera Company's impeccably vocal version, which was set up to be the ideal production, not to mention such burlesques as *TPS Canal Boat Pinafore* and *No Pinafore*. At one stage, in 1879, there were said to be 150 companies playing the show throughout America, although it is a fair bet that some of these productions were very far from the original in both text and in music, and were largely cashing in on what had become the most famous stage title in decades. Finally, Carte himself brought a company to Broadway to show America how superior a faithful version of the piece, correctly done, could be, but his company was largely there to launch his next show and it played only four weeks of *Pinafore* in New York.

The rest of the English-speaking world followed Britain's, and America's, lead. Australia and New Zealand saw several approximate and pirated productions before J C Williamson's officially licensed production was mounted there, venues as far apart as India and Cuba saw the show before 1879 was out, and everywhere the response was the same: *HMS Pinafore* was the most successful English-language musical play ever – everything from *The Beggar's Opera* to *Maritana* had to take second place. It was, perhaps, difficulties in adapting Gilbert's humour to other tongues which led to such a great hit being largely ignored in Europe. Ernst Dohm's German-language version, *Amor am Bord*, was mounted in Berlin in 1881, and Budapest saw but four performances of Jenő Rákosi's Hungarian version the same year, but there seems to have been little else in the way of Continental takers.

America and Australia both hosted burlesque *Pinafores*, but Britain satisfied itself with the real thing until a down-under piece called *The Wreck of the Pinafore* (Dunedin, New Zealand, 29 November 1880) was mounted on the London stage in 1882 (Opera Comique 27 May). It lasted but four nights. Another sequel, *Sir Joseph at Sea*, was mounted by the Kelly and Leon minstrels after the Australian courts had prevented them continuing their popular but pirated performances of the real show.

If the show's popularity and influence was small in Europe, however, it was enormous in the English-speaking theatre. *HMS Pinafore* set the style and standard for English-language comic opera in the decades to come, and gave an impetus to the musical theatre in Britain and America at least equivalent to that given by *Orphée aux enfers* in France, or by *Die Fledermaus* in Vienna. Like those two shows, it has remained a staple in the English-language repertoire, and one of the most popular amongst the Gilbert and Sullivan shows.

Whilst other Gilbert and Sullivan shows – notably *The Mikado* and *The Pirates of Penzance* – have been staged in more or less gimmicky productions or 'versions' in the twentieth century, *HMS Pinafore* has proved remarkably resistant to such treatment. An attempt in America, in the wake of the first flush of souped-up *Mikado*s in the 1930s resulted in a *Tropical Pinafore* being unsuccessfully mounted in Chicago in the 1939–40 season, and there were two simultaneous Broadway flops on the same lines in 1945: a black-cast *Memphis Bound!* (Broadway Theater 24 May) and a filmland burlesque *Hollywood Pinafore* (Alvin Theater 31 May). London, in its turn, later proffered a slightly modern *Pinafore* at the Collegiate Theatre, with Alec McCowen as Corcoran, following the great success of the enlivened American *Pirates of Penzance*. The most successful such production, however, was one mounted in Dublin and subsequently played at London's Old Vic (22 April 1986), which took few liberties with the text, but swapped the 19th-century burlesque idiom for a vigorously hyperactive 20th-century one.

USA: Boston Museum 25 November 1878, Standard Theater, New York 15 January 1879, Germania Theater *IMS Pinafore* 22 March 1879; Australia: School of Arts, Sydney 3 May 1879; Hungary: Népszinház *A Pannifor kapitánya* 21 June 1881; Germany: Friedrich-Wilhelmstädtisches Theater 1881; France: St Edmund's College, Douai January 1901
Recordings: complete (Decca, HMV), selections (ALP, TER) etc

HOBART, George V [PHILPOTT, George Vere Hobart] (b Cape Breton, Nova Scotia, 16 January 1867; d Cumberland, Md, 23 January 1926). A prolific supplier of texts of all kinds to the Broadway stage over some 25 years.

Hobart did his first writing as a journalist, becoming managing editor of the Cumberland *Scimitar* in 1895, and then, during his years living and working in Baltimore, a contributor to the local *American* and *News* ('Dinkelspiel' papers). He made his Broadway début as a dramatist in 1897 when he adapted the Philadelphia success *Miss Philadelphia* as *Miss Manhattan* for New York audiences, and for more than a quarter of a century thereafter he was engaged in turning out the texts for a string of plays, revues and musicals for the New York stage, directing in the theatre and also writing books, in a busy career which, whilst it ensured him a constant presence in the theatres of the time, did not produce any enduring successes.

On the revue front he provided material for six editions of the *Ziegfeld Follies* between 1911 and 1917, for the *Music Box Revues*, *The Greenwich Village Follies*, *Hitchy Koo of 1919* and others, on the straight stage his plays *Wildfire* (1908) and *Experience* (1914) proved his most popular, whilst his musical shows – for which he wrote sometimes book and lyrics, and at other times just one or the other – ranged through the whole spectrum of current styles. The fairly traditional musical-play mode of pieces such as *The Wild Rose*, *The Jersey Lily* or *Glorianna* however, seemed to suit him less well than the frankly musical-comic genre, in which he provided adaptations of such German pieces as Jean Kren's Posse *Im Himmelshof* (*Hodge, Podge & Co*), the Viennese hit musical *Der Frauenfresser* and the spicily farcical and extremely successful *Alma, wo wohnst du?*, vehicles for such stars as May Irwin or Marie Cahill, variety-house pieces like the little *Peaches* toured by Stella Mayhew and William Courtleigh, and texts for negro musical comedy, alongside burlesque and such broadly low-brow entertainments as the Rogers Brothers shows. At one stage, he even

combined with Gitz Rice in writing miniature radio musical comedies plugging Goodrich Silverton Cord.

Several of Hobart's shows found a solid popularity on the American circuits, but probably the most generally successful amongst them was the sentimental post-wartime musical tale of *Buddies*, which provoked its author to a kind of musequel in *Sonny*. His rewrite of Adolf Phillip and Edward Paulton's musical comedy *Mimi* as the libretto for Ivan Caryll's *Kissing Time* and the adaptation of the Charles Klein play *Maggie Pepper* as *Letty Pepper* for Charlotte Greenwood were amongst the other works of the later part of his career.

A number of Hobart's non-musical works were subsequently turned into musical plays by his own or other hands. His farce *What's Your Husband Doing?* became *Miss Blue Eyes*, a piece with a Silvio Hein score which folded on the road to Broadway in 1918, as did the 1920 musical *Dearie* (Malvin Franklin/John Wilson, Detroit 5 September), based on the horse-racing play *Wildfire* by Hobart and George Broadhurst. Hobart's book *Up the Line, John Henry* became the source for the musicals *It's Up to You, John Henry* (Grand Opera House 23 October 1905) and *All for You* (Mason Opera House, Los Angeles 24 October 1925, music by Arthur Freed).

1897 **Miss Manhattan** (F Puehringer, Herman Perlet et al/ Edgar Smith ad) Wallack's Theater 23 March
1900 **Broadway to Tokio** (Reginald De Koven, A Baldwin Sloane/w Louis Harrison) New York Theater 23 January
1900 **A Million Dollars** (Sloane/w Harrison) New York Theater 27 September
1900 **The Military Maid** (Alfred E Aarons) Savoy Theater 8 October
1900 **Hodge, Podge & Co** (John Bratton/Walter Ford) Madison Square Theater 23 October
1900 **Nell Go In** (Sloane) 1 act New York Theater 31 October
1900 **Miss Printt** (John Golden) Victoria Theater 25 December
1900 **After Office Hours** (Sloane) 1 act New York Theater 24 December
1901 **The King's Carnival** (Sloane/w Sydney Rosenfeld/ Rosenfeld) New York Theater 13 May
1901 **The New Yorkers** (Ludwig Englander/Glen MacDonough) Herald Square Theater 7 October
1902 **The Hall of Fame** (Sloane/Rosenfeld) New York Theater 3 February
1902 **The Belle of Broadway** (Sloane et al/Rosenfeld) 1 scene Winter Garden Theater 17 March
1902 **The Wild Rose** (Englander/w H B Smith) Knickerbocker Theater 5 May
1902 **Sally in Our Alley** (Englander) Broadway Theater 29 August
1903 **The Darling of the Gallery Gods** (Matt C Woodward, John Gilroy) Crystal Gardens 22 June
1903 **The Rogers Brothers in London** (Max Hoffman, Max Ellis, Melville Ellis/w Edward Gardenier/J J McNally) Knickerbocker Theater 7 September
1903 **Peaches** (various)
1903 **The Jersey Lily** (De Koven) Victoria Theater 14 September
1903 **Mother Goose** (Fred Solomon/McNally) New Amsterdam Theater 2 December
1904 **The Smiling Island** (Albert von Tilzer, J Sebastian Hiller, K S Clark) Casino Theater, Philadelphia 15 December
1904 **Mrs Black is Back** (several) Bijou Theater 7 November
1904 **The Rogers Brothers in Paris** (Hoffman/McNally) New Amsterdam Theater 5 September
1905 **The Athletic Girl** (Jean Schwartz) 1 act Colonial Music Hall 15 February

1905 **A Yankee Circus on Mars** (Manuel Klein, Schwartz/ Harry Williams) New York Hippodrome 12 April

1905 **The Ham Tree** (Schwartz/William Jerome) New York Theater 28 August

1905 **Moonshine** (Silvio Hein/Edward Milton Royle) Liberty Theater 30 October

1906 **Comin' Through the Rye** (Sloane/Hiller) Herald Square Theater 9 January

1906 **Mrs Wilson That's All** (various) Bijou Theater 5 November

1907 **The Land of Nod** (Joseph E Howard/Frank Adams, Will Hough) adaptation for New York (New York Theater)

1907 **The Song Birds** (Victor Herbert) 1 act Lamb's Club; New York Theater in *The Land of Nod* 1 April

1907 **Miss Camille** (V Herbert) 1 act Lamb's Club 14 April

1908 **The Merry Widow** burlesque (Lehár arr) Weber's Music Hall 2 January

1908 **The Boys and Betty** (Hein) Wallack's Theater 2 November

1908 **The Merry Widow and the Devil** West End Theater 16 November

1909 **The Candy Shop** (Golden) Knickerbocker Theater 27 April

1909 **Old Dutch** (V Herbert/Edgar Smith) Herald Square Theater 22 November

1909 **The Big Stick** (uncredited) West End Theater 24 February

1910 **The Yankee Girl** (Hein) Herald Square Theater 10 February

1910 **Girlies** (Egbert van Alstyne) New Amsterdam Theater 13 June

1910 **Alma, Where Do You Live?** (*Alma, wo wohnst du?*) English version (Weber's Theater)

1911 **When Sweet Sixteen** (V Herbert) Daly's Theater 14 September

1912 **Over the River** (Schwartz, John Golden/w H A du Souchet) Globe Theater 8 January

1912 **A Polish Wedding** (*Polnische Wirtschaft*) English version (Empire Theater, Syracuse)

1912 **The Woman Haters** (*Der Frauenfresser*) English version (Astor Theater)

1912 **The Village Blacksmith** (V Herbert) 1 act Lamb's Club 29 December

1913 **Glorianna** (Hein/Philip Bartholomae) Cort Theater, Chicago 12 October

1918 **Back Again** (Louis Hirsch/w Frank Stammers) Chestnut Street Theater, Philadelphia 29 April

1918 **Just Around the Corner** (various/w Herbert Hall Winslow) Atlantic City 9 May; Longacre Theater, New York 5 February 1919

1918 **Miss Blue Eyes** (Hein) Apollo Theater, Atlantic City 3 October

1919 **Buddies** (B C Hilliam) Selwyn Theater 27 October

1920 **Kissing Time** (Ivan Caryll/Philander Jones, Clifford Grey, Irving Caesar) Lyric Theater 11 October

1921 **Sonny** (Raymond Hubbell) Cort Theater 16 August

1922 **Letty Pepper** (Werner Janssen/Leo Wood, Irving Bibo/ w Oliver Morosco) Vanderbilt Theater 10 April

1923 **That Casey Girl** (Schwartz/Jerome/w Willard Mack) Lyceum Theater, Paterson, NJ 22 October

HOCHZEITSNACHT IM PARADIES
Operette in 6 scenes by Heinz Hentschke. Lyrics by Günther Schwenn. Music by Friedrich Schröder. Metropoltheater, Berlin, 24 September 1942.

On the day of her wedding to tennis-playing Ulrich Hansen (Johannes Heesters), Regine (Hilde Seipp) succumbs to a fit of jealousy over a piece of his past, the extravagant Spanish dancer Doña Dolores, otherwise known as Dodo (Gretl Schörg), and a quarrel ends with the bridegroom going to spend his wedding night at the Hotel Paradies. The repentant Regine follows, but finds Ulrich with a woman – of whom she does not see enough to know it is her innocent friend Veronika (Ingeborg von Kusserow) – and floods out again. So Ulrich takes Veronika on what should have been his honeymoon in Venice. There, amongst the picturesque accoutrements of a gondoliers' festival, all is sorted out. Walter Müller was Poldi, who gets Veronika, whilst Paul Westermaier played friend Felix, who pairs off with the harmful Dodo.

A little less feeble than most of Hentschke's libretti, *Hochzeitsnacht im Paradies* had the advantage of a delightful, dancing score by Schröder, a score topped by matinée idol Heesters's rendition of the joyful, pre-wedding 'Es kommt an die Sekunde an', a number which became his theme-song and the title for his autobiography. In fact, *Hochzeitsnacht im Paradies* and the rôle of Ulrich became one of the actor's staple shows and parts. He repeated it over and over for nearly thirty years all around Germany and Austria as well as playing it on both film and television.

The first film version was made in 1950 with Heesters now playing the drearily inevitable 'film-und-revuenstar' of contemporary German films rather than a sportsman alongside Claude Farell (Clarisse, the wife) and Frln Schörg (Rosita, eine revusängerin), and in the same year the star introduced his show to Vienna, where he was now headquartered. Franz Stoss's mounting at the Bürgertheater featured the matinée idol alongside Friedl Loor (Regine), Herta Staal (Veronika), Hedy Fassler (Dodo), Fritz Imhoff (Felix) and Josef Menschik (Poldi). Heesters played Berlin again in 1952 (Titaniapalast w Ilse Hülper, Paul Westermeier and Frln Staal), during which time the show passed what was announced as its 1,000th performance, and Frln Loor and Imhoff took up their rôles again alongside Heesters when the show was revived at the Raimundtheater in 1957 with Rosy Bársony playing Dodo. The theatre repeated the piece with Heesters, Raoul Retzer and Eleanore Bauer in 1961, and in 1971 when the now rather aged but still dashing star teamed with Inge Karstens, Peter Gerhard and Ossy Kolomon. When, in 1962, a second film version was put out, Heesters had terminated his film career and it was Peter Alexander, who had had a tiny rôle in the 1950 Vienna revival, who played the hard-done-by tennis player, starred alongside Waltraut Haas and Marika Rökk (Ilonka Davarosch, eine revuesängerin).

With more than a little help from the always popular Heesters, *Hochzeitsnacht im Paradies* has remained one of the favourite German-language shows of its period, and has won the honours of recordings as well as revivals and films.

Austria: Wiener Bürgertheater 8 December 1950; Films: International Films 1950, Sascha Films 1962

Recordings: selection (part-record) (EMI Electrola, Polydor, SMS, Telefunken)

HOCKRIDGE, Edmund
(b Vancouver, BC, 1919). Baritone leading man of the British editions of several Broadway musicals in the 1950s.

At first a concert and radio vocalist, Hockridge came to the theatrical fore when he succeeded Stephen Douglass in the rôle of Billy Bigelow in London's *Carousel*. He subsequently took over as Sky Masterson in *Guys and Dolls*, and then appeared as London's Aristide Forrestier in *Can-Can* and as Sid Sorokin in *Pajama Game*. Thereafter seen largely in revue, variety and pantomime, he latterly played in musicals in the British provinces and made his last West End appearance in the rôle of Buffalo Bill in a revival of *Annie Get Your Gun*.

HOEY, Iris (b London, 17 July 1885; d London, ?April 1979). Leading ingénue of the pre-war and wartime British stage.

In the early part of her career Miss Hoey alternated appearances in straight theatre with Beerbohm Tree and in musical comedy with George Edwardes, appearing at first in minor rôles in *Les P'tites Michu* and the 1906 revival of *The Geisha*. She had her first major part in the musical theatre as the ingénue of *Butterflies* (1908, Elsie Podmore), alongside Ada Reeve and Hayden Coffin, and appeared as juvenile lady in the unfortunate *The Pigeon House* (1911, Leontine), before taking a run of lead rôles in West End musicals: Anna in *Princess Caprice* (1912), Delphine in Ivan Caryll's *Oh! Oh! Delphine* (1913), Miranda Peploe in *The Pearl Girl* (1913), Beatrice in the English company of *Tonight's the Night* which played on Broadway (1914), Peggy in *The Miller's Daughters* (1915), Lolotte in *Mr Manhattan* with Raymond Hitchcock, and Edna May's famous rôle in a revival of *The Belle of New York* (1916 revival). She subsequently concentrated her work on a long career in the straight theatre.

HOFFMAN, Al (b Minsk, 25 September 1902; d New York, 21 July 1960). Successful songwriter who supplied material to both theatre and film during a brief stay in Britain.

Seattle-bred and -based Hoffman went to New York to try to break into the songwriting world. He soon managed to get his first songs published, finding successes with a series of partners and such numbers as 'Heartaches' (1930, w John Klenner), 'I Apologise' (w Al Goodhart, Ed Nelson), 'Auf Wiederseh'n, My Dear' (w Goodhart, Nelson, Milton Ager), 'Happy Go Lucky You and Broken Hearted Me' (w Goodhart, John Murray), 'In the Dim Dawning' (w Goodhart, Stanley Adams), 'Little Man, You've Had a Busy Day' (w Maurice Sigler, Mabel Wayne), 'Fit as a Fiddle' (w Goodhart, Arthur Freed), later featured in *Singin' in the Rain* on screen and stage, 'Who Walks In?' (w Goodhart, Ralph Freed) and 'I Saw Stars' (w Goodhart, Sigler).

In 1934 he left America for Britain, when he was hired by Gaumont-British pictures to write for their musical films. His film credits over the following years included *Squibs*, *Jack of All Trades*, Jessie Matthews's *First a Girl* ('Everything's in Rhythm With my Heart'), Jack Buchanan's *Come Out of the Pantry* ('Everything Stops for Tea'), *When Knights Were Bold*, *She Shall Have Music* ('My First Thrill') and Miss Matthews's *Gangway* ('Gangway').

During the same period he and his collaborators also supplied songs for Jack Buchanan's stage musical *This'll Make You Whistle* ('There Isn't Any Limit to My Love', 'I'm in a Dancing Mood', 'This'll Make You Whistle', 'You've Got the Wrong Rumba'), the Gaiety Theatre success *Going Greek* ('A Little Co-operation from You'), and the Cicely Courtneidge/Bobby Howes *Hide and Seek*. He returned to

America in 1937, and thereafter severed his connection with the musical theatre, but continued to turn out rather more characterful numbers than he had contributed to the stage for some 20 further years: 'Story of a Starry Night', 'Mairzy Doats and Doazy Dotes', 'If I Knew You Were Comin' I'd've Baked a Cake', 'Hot Diggity', 'Me and My Imagination', 'Gilly Gilly Ossenfeffer Katzenelenbogen-by-the-Sea', 'I Can't Tell a Waltz from a Tango', 'Papa Loves Mambo', 'Where Will the Dimple Be', 'You Can't Be True to Two', 'Allegheny Moon', 'My House is Your House' and the score of Walt Disney's cartoon *Cinderella* ('Bibbidi-Bobbidi-Boo!', 'A Dream is a Wish Your Heart Makes' w Jerry Livingston, Mack David).

1936 **This'll Make You Whistle** (w Maurice Sigler, Al Goodhart/Guy Bolton, Fred Thompson) Palace Theatre 14 September

1937 **Going Greek** (w Sam Lerner, Goodhart/Bolton, Thompson, Douglas Furner) Gaiety Theatre 16 September

1937 **Hide and Seek** (w Vivian Ellis, Lerner, Goodhart/Bolton, Thompson, Furber) London Hippodrome 14 October

DER HOFNARR Romantic comic opera in 3 acts by Hugo Wittmann and Julius Bauer. Music by Adolf Müller jr, Theater an der Wien, Vienna, 20 November 1886.

Camillo Walzel's 1886–7 season at Vienna's Theater an der Wien saw the production of new works by Millöcker (*Der Viceadmiral*), Suppé (*Bellman*) and Brandl (*Der liebe Augustin*), but the theatre's young conductor Adolf Müller topped all their efforts with the most important Operette of his career, *Der Hofnarr*.

The 'royal fool' of Wittmann and Bauer's 16th-century story is Carillon (Alexander Girardi), and like his more famous operatic counterpart, Rigoletto, he vows a fine revengeful hatred to his employer, the usurping Philip, King of Navarre (Carl Adolf Friese). But Philip is actually a no-holds-barred Bad King, who is unlovingly known simply as 'Philip the Bad', and the Jester is not the only one plotting to unseat him. Both the army, headed by Oberst Graf Rivarol (Josef Joseffy) and Lieutenant Archibald de Zornoza (Siegmund Stelzer), and the Home Office, under the manipulation of Der Protonotarius (Franz Eppich) and Der Kanzler (Carl Lindau), are intent on winkling out the hiding place of the legal heir to the crown of Navarre, Prince Julius (Karl Streitmann). Baby Julius was hurried away from danger by the Gräfin Corisdanda von Pompignan (Antoine Hartmann) in good comic-opera fashion, and brought up, disguised as a girl, equipped with a gold chain bearing the star of Navarre for the day when he needed to be refound. The diplomats get the right Prince, the Military – trusting the chain, which the home-going Prince has left with his beloved Felisa d'Amores (Ottilie Collin) and her soubrette foster-sister Yvonne (Frln Stein) – get the wrong one, but, after an act and a half of ins-and-outs, and largely thanks to the machinations of the Jester, Philip gets his lot and the juveniles their throne in time for the final curtain.

Müller illustrated the largely comico-romantic, but also, occasionally, dramatic tale with a score which was more substantial but none the less melodious than those he had turned out for such pieces as his other hit of the season, *Die Wienerstadt in Wort und Bild*, and Walzel provided a fine production with 'neuen Dekorationen' by Hoftheatermalern Carlo Brioschi and Burghart, 'neuen Costüme' by

M Czibak and B Grünbaum, and a much-admired dance speciality 'Grand Assauts' for eight danseuses in the second-act setting of 'a military Camp near Pampeluna'.

Der Hofnarr won a fine reception from press and public and was played for an excellent 51 performances on its first run. It was brought back for a few additional performances in the Theater an der Wien repertoire in most of the next dozen or so seasons (85 performances to 1900) as it went on to be seen in Berlin, St Petersburg (7 February 1887), Budapest, Prague (24 May 1887), at Munich's Theater am Gärtnerplatz (10 September 1887) and throughout central Europe. It continued to find productions into the 20th century, and in 1920 Sigmund Eibenschütz mounted a major Vienna revival at the Carltheater (1 April), with director Louis Treumann in the rôle of Carillon supported by Grete Sedlitz (Felisa), Mizzi Egerth (Yvonne) and Victor Norbert (Julius), through 53 successive nights.

Although the show does not seem to have had a German-language production in New York, America did get *Der Hofnarr* when Heinrich Conried mounted an English-language version of the piece at Niblo's Gardens. His casting, however, did add one more string to the skein of the intrigue, for to play Julius – the boy disguised temporarily as a girl – he hired burlesque actress Helen Bertram. J P McGovern (Philip of Navarre), Della Fox (Yvonne), Ada Glasca (Felice), Jennie Reiffarth (Constantia) and Joseph W Herbert (Carillon) took the other principal rôles in a production which failed in two weeks.

Germany: Friedrich-Wilhelmstädtisches Theater 7 January 1887; Hungary: Király Színház *Az udvari bolond* 26 March 1887; USA: Niblo's Garden *The King's Fool* 15 February 1890

HOHEIT TANZT WALZER Operette in 3 acts by Julius Brammer and Alfred Grünwald. Music by Leo Ascher. Raimundtheater, Vienna, 24 February 1912.

The librarian Dominik Gaudenzdorf (Otto Langer) wants his daughter Lisi (Mimi Marlow) to wed the rich hotelier Plunderer (Anton Matschegg), of the 'Zum Goldenen Ochsen'. Lisi, however, is in love with the poor but striving Aloisius Strampfl (Bernhard Bötel), who has been unable to save enough cash to purchase the lease on an inn. The girl's music-teacher Peperl Gschwandner (Otto Storm) comes to the rescue. He is about to be named a Hofkapellmeister, with all that means financially, so he gives his savings to the young pair to allow them to lease the 'Zur silbernen Bretze' and to be wed. Alas, the horrid Plunderer devotes himself to their ruin, and all looks black until two pretty ladies stop off one day at the Strampfls' inn. Peperl, whose appointment never came through, and who now works as a waiter for his friends, takes a shine to one of them, and a jolly, musical hour is had by all. Even Plunderer's big drawcard, the famous Lanner quartet, deserts his hotel to join in the music-making. But the joyous session has to end when a coach draws up to take the Princess Marie (Betty Fischer) and her Hofdame (Luise Lichten) back to court. In that hour, however, the name and fame of the 'Zur silbernen Bretze' have been made, and the Strampfls are saved. Back at the castle, the Princess, preparing for her state wedding, thinks longingly of her waltz at the inn and of sweet, happy Peperl. But all she can do is ensure that he, at last, gets his Hofkapellmeister's post.

Brammer and Grünwald's pretty, alt-Wienerisch story

was illustrated by suitably Viennese music, in which waltz tempo reigned supreme. Peperl's first act 'Drunten am blauen Donaustrand', the duo for Lisi and Strampfl ('Erst zog ich bloss galant den Hut'), Lisi's second act 'Man preist in tausend Liedern dich', Marie's regretful 'Das ist die Prinzessin Tralala', and the key duo for the Princess and Peperl, at the heart of their happy hour, 'Das Lercherl von Hernals', were amongst the waltz-time features of a score in which most of what was not in 3/4 time was in the form of march music, give or take a moment or two of 9/8 or a gavotte.

Hoheit tanzt Walzer had a fine Viennese run on its initial production. It was played for a month at the Raimundtheater before swapping theatres for a few performances with the Theater an der Wien's *Eva*. The run was broken again for the brief life of *Die liebe Unschuld*, and yet again for the summer recess, but the show continued on undiminished to pass its 100th night on 10 September, then, with the management now fully aware they had a hit, its 200th on 20 December, finally ending its first run eleven months after its première with 230 performances to its credit.

The show became Ascher's most successful piece in Germany, outstripping even his big Berlin hit of a few years later, *Der Soldat der Marie*, and it was mounted at Budapest's Népopera in 1913 in a Hungarian version (ad Adolf Merei). An American adaptation was prepared and published, under the title of *Princess Tralala* (ad Matthew Woodward), but does not seem to have been performed, and New York saw *Hoheit tanzt Walzer* only at the Irving Place Theater in its original German. In Europe, the piece was played regularly for many years. It was given a librettolift in 1937 for a production in Zurich under the title *Hochzeitswalzer*, returned to Vienna in 1945 and again at the Rextheater in 1946, and still wins occasional performances when a 'Biedermeier-era' Operette is chosen for revival.

A film version, which used some of Ascher's music, but also a bit of Beethoven, made the hero a handsome young waltz composer in a libretto which was very different from and altogether less charming than the stage-book. Hans Jaray played him and Irene Agay was the Princess who danced the waltz and sang 'Das Lercherl von Hernals'.

Hungary: Népopera *Budagyöngye* 5 September 1913; Germany: Friedrich-Wilhelmstädtisches Theater ?1920; USA: Irving Place Theater; Film: Max Neufeld 1935

HOLD EVERYTHING! Musical comedy in 2 acts by B G De Sylva and John McGowan. Lyrics by Lew Brown and B G De Sylva. Music by Ray Henderson. Broadhurst Theater, New York, 10 October 1928.

In 1928 Aarons and Freedley, whose productions in the musical theatre up to that time had been almost all from the pen of George Gershwin, ventured with a show from the De Sylva-Brown-Henderson combination, a team at the top of the theatrical tree since their hit with *Good News*. *Hold Everything!* took the fashionable world of boxing as its venue, and its little tale told of the ups and downs of the love match between stalwart boxer 'Sonny Jim' Brooks (Jack Whiting), who is punching his way through college, and a tiresome little lady called Sue (Ona Munson), who keeps telling him how to fight his matches. Betty Compton played the rich (and therefore threatening and undesirable

– only rich men were theatrically OK at this time, girls had to be poor and virtuous) Norine Lloyd, who gets after Sonny Jim whilst Sue is sulking over the boxer's preference for taking orders from his trainer. The comedy was provided by Victor Moore as boxing-camp cook Nosey Bartlett, equipped with a surefire drunk scene, and Bert Lahr as a punch-drunk and ever overweight boxer called Gink Schiner. In spite of bribery, corruption and the women battling over him, Jim punches his way through, pulling out the knock-down blow when the champ (understandably?) casts aspersions at his Sue.

The show's score brought up one De Sylva, Brown and Henderson standard in Whiting and Miss Munson's 'You're the Cream in My Coffee' alongside a sort of antititle song, in which Alice Boulden as an incidental person called Betty Dunn insisted 'Don't Hold Everything', and a number of pieces with reference to boxing ('Footwork') or, more frequently, love-making ('An Outdoor Man for My Indoor Sports', 'When I Love, I Love', 'To Know You is to Love You'). There was also 'much breathless dancing'.

Hold Everything! had the longest Broadway life of any Aarons and Freedley production, running up a splendid 413 performances at the Broadhurst Theater before going on the road. Even before that happened, a British production had already been opened in London, where Clayton and Waller's production of a version which had been anglicized by R P Weston and Bert Lee was mounted at the Palace Theatre. Owen Nares was the boxer, Mamie Watson the pouting beloved, Pamela Carne the opposition, and George Gee headed the comedy as Spike Skinner for a run of 173 performances. The anglicized version also put in an appearance on the J C Williamson Ltd Australian circuits, where speciality dancers Terry and Patricia Kendall starred as Sonny Jim and Sue, with Mary Lawson (Toots) as the feminine rival, and Alfred Frith (Gink), Cecil Kellaway (Chubby) and Pop Cory heading the comedy. It played a month in Sydney and nearly two in Melbourne (Theatre Royal 2 November 1929).

A film version produced in 1930 with 35-year-old former world light-heavyweight boxing champion Georges Carpentier starred alongside Winnie Lightener, Joe E Brown and Sally O'Neil used only two numbers from the original score, topped up by five by Al Dubin and Johnny Burke.

UK: Palace Theatre 12 June 1929; Australia: Her Majesty's Theatre, Sydney 28 September 1929; Film: Warner Brothers 1930

HOLLAND, Fanny (b London, ?1847; d London, 18 June 1931). Soprano with the German Reed company through their most prosperous period.

Londoner Fanny Holland joined the German Reed company at the Gallery of Illustration in 1869 and she created almost all the soprano rôles in their subsequent pieces, beginning with the ingénue, Rose, in Clay and Gilbert's *Ages Ago* and continuing in the librettist's *Our Island Home*, *A Sensation Novel* and *Happy Arcadia*, Cellier's *Charity Begins at Home* and *Dora's Dream*, Burnand's *Very Catching* and *Mildred's Well*, and many others. She left the group momentarily to play in the 'real' theatre in Gilbert's *Topsyturveydom* at the Criterion in 1874, temporarily leaving her place at the Reeds' establishment to Leonora Braham, and departed again when, having married Arthur

Law, actor and author for the organization, the couple toured with a drawing room entertainment. She also, briefly, took over the rôle of Josephine in the original *HMS Pinafore*. She was seen performing as late as 1895, when she took up the rôle of Daphne in *Happy Arcadia* during Rutland Barrington's attempt to revive the German Reed entertainments at the St George's Hall.

A charming and dignified young woman with a fine, uncomplicated soprano voice, her characters and performances at the Gallery can be considered the prototype for the English comic-opera heroines created by Gilbert at the Opera Comique and the Savoy.

HOLLÄNDER, Viktor (b Leobschütz, 20 April 1866; d Hollywood, 24 October 1940). Widely travelled all-purpose German theatre composer, more prolific than memorable.

After an early career conducting at, and intermittently composing for, several theatres both in and around Germany, the young Viktor Holländer went to America to act as musical director at the German theatre in Milwaukee (1890). After a brief time back in Berlin, some of it spent working at the Wallner-Theater, he tried his luck abroad again, first in Chicago, then in London. He has been credited with being musical director of the so-called Royal Opera Comique during his six-years' stay in Britain, and with having at least two shows produced there (*The Bey of Morocco* (Karl Norden) 1894, *Double Dealings* (Fred Vigay), 1898). However, he conducted no musical at the run-down and very unroyal old Opera Comique theatre – although he was, for a period, musical director for Richard Mansell at the suburban Coronet Theatre – and he certainly had no work produced for a run in the London theatre.

On his return from England in 1901, however, he landed the post of musical director and house composer at Berlin's Metropoltheater. There he provided the music for a highly successful series of revues (*Ein tolles Jahr*, *Auf ins Metropol*, *Der Teufel lacht dazu*, *Das muss man seh'n!*, *Hurra! Wir leben noch!*, *Die Nacht von Berlin* etc) and Possen for several years before succeeding Paul Lincke in the same position at the Thalia-Theater (1908–9). This second experience was not a success, and he was soon replaced by Jean Gilbert. He continued to supply scores for revues and musical plays to not only German theatres but also, occasionally, abroad for another decade, providing the music for George Lederer's Broadway flop *The Charity Girl* and, in a small tit-for-tat for his replacement at the Thalia, almost an entire replacement score for the American production of Gilbert's *Die moderne Eva*.

Holländer's attempts at musical plays were, by and large, not very successful. A little piece called *San Lin*, set in Chinese San Francisco, won several productions, his musical of H G Wells's *The Time Machine*, *Der Sonnenvogel*, was toured through Europe, his *Der rote Kosak* ('Katzerl und Kater') was seen in Berlin and Vienna, his 1914 *Die Schöne vom Strand* turned up as *A korzéo szépe* at Budapest's Vigszinház (4 September 1915) and as *The Belle of the Beach* at New York's Yorkville Theater, and his 1915 piece *Die Prinzessin von Nil*, probably the most successful of his Operetten, was played at New York's Irving Place Theater also in German (31 March 1916). None of them, however, went as far afield as his incidental music for the oriental

pantomime *Sumurun* (Kammerspiele, Berlin 1910), which
was played in Budapest, in New York and around Europe,
indeed everywhere Max Reinhardt's much admired spectacular travelled.

His son **Friedrich HOLLÄNDER** [later Frederick
Hollander] (b London, 18 October 1896; d Munich, 18
January 1976), originally a theatre conductor, became a
successful film composer in Germany and in America
(1933–56). His principal screen credits included *Der blaue
Engel/The Blue Angel* (1930, 'Ich bin vom Kopf bis Fuss auf
Liebe eingestellt' aka 'Falling in Love Again'), *Die grosse
Sehnsucht* (1930), Deanna Durbin's *One Hundred Men and
a Girl* (1937), *Destry Rides Again* (1939, 'The Boys in the
Backroom'), *The Man Who Came to Dinner* (1942), *A Foreign Affair* ('Black Market') and *Das Spukschloss im Spessart*
(1962). In his early European days he also composed
revues, Possen, vaudevilles and Operetten, including the
1929 *Ich tanze um die Welt mit dir* (Darmstadt 26 December, Deutsches Künstlertheater w Marcellus Schiffer etc)
and *Hetärengespräche* and the 1930 *Höchste Eisenbahn* (w
Schiffer). A later Operette, written after his eventual
return to Germany, *Das Blaue von Himmel* (Per
Schwenzen), was produced at the Nuremberg-Fürth
Städtische Bühnen in 1959 (14 November).

1882 **Der Gesangvereinsprobe** (Holländer) 1 act Cologne July
?1885 **Schloss Calliano** (Gustav Kadelburg) Carl-Schultze
Theater, Hamburg 8 September
1887 **Carmosinella** (Rudolf Hirschsohn) Saalbau, Frankfurt-
am-Main December
1891 **König Rhampsinit** (Leo Winternitz) Milwaukee 19 April;
Residenztheater, Breslau 24 June 1893
1892 **König Krause** (Jan Keller, Louis Hermann) Wallner-
Theater January
1892 **Der berühmte Mitburger** (Karl Laufs, Wilhelm Jacoby) 1
act Wallner-Theater 10 February
1892 **Yvette** (Laufs, Max Krämer) Wallner-Theater 10 February
1897 **The Fair in Midgetown** (Robert Breitenbach) Star
Theater, New York 20 September
1898 **San Lin** (Holbrook Blinn) 1 act Breslau 28 January
1901 **Schön war's doch** (Julius Freund) Metropoltheater 24
August
1901 **Der rote Kosak** (Hermann, Hermann Hirschel)
Friedrich-Wilhelmstädtisches Theater 21 December
1901 **'ne feine Nummer** (w Leo Fall/Freund) Metropoltheater
26 December
1902 **Die Zwölf Frauen des Japhet** (*Les Douze Femmes de
Japhet*) German version by Freund w new score (Metropoltheater)
1903 **Der Sonnenvogel** (aka *Der Phönix*) (Rudolf Schanzer,
Georg Okonkowski) St Petersburg 22 August
1903 **Durchlaucht Radieschen** (Freund) Metropoltheater 31
October
1904 **Die Herren von Maxim** (ad Freund) Metropoltheater 29
October
1906 **Kadettenstreiche** (Heinrich Bolten-Bäckers) Eden-
Theater, Aachen 19 July
1906 **La Plus Belle** (Léon Xanrof, Pierre Veber) 1 act Casino de
Paris, Paris 29 October
1907 **Die schöne Vestalin** revised *La Plus Belle* by Bolten-
Bäckers 1 act Apollotheater 31 October
1908 **Das Mitternachtsmädchen** (Jean Kren, Arthur Lippschitz) Thalia-Theater 14 August
1908 **Schneider Fips** (Kotzebue ad Hans von Wentzel) 1 act
Hoftheater, Weimar 17 November
1909 **Der Jockeyklub** (Robert Misch) Neues Operetten-
Theater, Mannheim 8 January; Theater des Westens 27
March

1909 **Meister Tutti** (Alfred Schönfeld/Kren) Thalia-Theater
15 January
1909 **Wo wohnt sie denn?** (Kren, Okonkowski) Thalia-Theater
12 February
1909 **Prinz Bussi** (Schönfeld/Kren) Thalia-Theater 13 August
1909 **Revanche** (Louis Windhopp, Loebel) 1 act Hölle, Vienna
31 October
1909 **Die süsse Cora** (Kren, Lippschitz) Thalia-Theater 11
December
1910 **Hupf mein Mäderl!** (Krenn, Lindau) Ronacher, Vienna
13 August
1912 **The Charity Girl** (Edward Peple) Globe Theater, New
York 2 October
1913 **Die Königin der Nacht** (Arnold Golz, Emil Golz) 1 act
Apollotheater, Vienna 1 February
1914 **Der Regimentspapa** (Richard Kessler, Heinrich Stobitzer) Residenztheater 4 March
1914 **Und Michel lacht dazu** (Ely, Otto) Nationaltheater 2
November
1914 **Freiwillige vor** (Louis Taufstein) Kristallpalast, Leipzig 1
December
1915 **Die schöne vom Strand** (Oskar Blumenthal, Kadelburg)
Reisdenztheater 5 February
1915 **Die Prinzessin vom Nil** (Franz Cornelius, Arthur Lands-
berger) Residenztheater 18 September
1916 **Loge nr 7** (Kurt Kraatz, Theo Halton) Residenztheater 28
January
1916 **Fliegende Blätter aus dem Jahrgang 1850** (Hans Gaus,
Theo Halton/Gaus) Residenztheater, 12 May
1916 **Der Patentküss** (Stein-Wildegans) Stadttheater, Schweid-
nitz 20 October
1917 **Der Zigeuner** (Liszt arr/Ferdinand Bonn) Walhalla-
Theater 31 May
1917 **Die Liebesgeige** Theater an der Westfront 17 May
1919 **Der Jäger von der Kurpfalz** (Bonn) Walhalla-Theater 2
April
1920 **Der Schwan von Siam** (Bruno Decker, Robert Pohl)
Olympia-Theater, Dortmund 25 December
1921 **Der Marmorgraf** (Kessler, Gerhard Schätzler-Perasini)
Residenztheater, Wiesbaden 12 March

Other titles attributed: *Die Rosiere, Primanerliebe* (1885), *Tulipan
von Panama* (1891), *Der Kerzverführer, Bitte recht freundlich, Die
Blümenkönigin, An der schönen blauen Donau*

Autobiography (F Hollander): *Von Kopf bis Fuss, mein Leben mit
Text und Musik* (Munich, 1965)

DAS HOLLANDWEIBCHEN Operette in 3 acts by
Leo Stein and Béla Jenbach. Music by Emmerich Kálmán.
Johann Strauss-Theater, Vienna, 30 January 1920.

Quite what decided Kálmán, the most Austro-
Hungarian of composers, to treat a demi-semi-Dutch tale
is a mystery, but the resultant piece, if a slightly curious
variation on the usual Ruritanian Operette (the few
moments of Dutch music sound rather Tyrolean, and the
Dutch-accented dialogue as if it were burlesque) nevertheless provided the composer and his librettists, Stein and
Jenbach, with a distinct success. *Das Hollandweibchen* ran
up no fewer than 362 performances in its first run of over a
year at Vienna's Johann Strauss-Theater, returning later in
1921 for several further weeks of performances. It also
played some performances in-between times at the
Raimundtheater.

The Princess Jutta of Sonnenburg-Glücksburg (Ida
Russka) is all ready to be married to Crown Prince Paul
Roderich of Usingen (Karl Bachmann), but on the day of
the ceremony only an envoy, Dr Udo von Sterzel (Fritz
Werner), turns up, for the Prince has apparently no inten-

tion of losing his freedom. The charming persuadings of the Baroness Elly von der Weyde (Steffi Walidt) convince Sterzel to stand proxy for his Prince, and it is only after the wedding that Jutta discovers that her bridegroom is not truly indisposed, he is just indisposed to getting wed, and is actually off yachting around Holland. She swears her revenge, heads for Holland in disguise as a little Dutch girl, hooks and catches her Prince, then dumps him, and makes him wait till the very end of the third act for a reconciliation and a happy, waltzing ending.

Kálmán's score proved that Sonnenburg-Glücksburg was not too far from Vienna and that, most certainly, waltzes were in favour there but, given that the piece was set in 1920, there was also space for such modern (if not very Dutch) musical moments as a tango.

Das Hollandweibchen quickly found its way from Vienna to Berlin's Metropoltheater, where, with Claire Dux starring, it had a fine run of a little over six months up to March 1921, before being replaced by Lehár's *Die blaue Mazur*, by which time Seymour Hicks and Joe Sacks had mounted an English version in London (ad Seymour Hicks, Harry Graham). *A Little Dutch Girl* featured no less a star than opera diva Maggie Teyte as Princess Julia of Sylvania alongside Martin Iredale (Paul), Jack Hulbert (Posch), Cicely Debenham (Eloise) and Lauri de Frece (Bomba) for a run of 215 performances. That English version was also seen in Australia, where, after a tryout in Adelaide with Sheila Gale and J Roland Hogue featured, the piece was recast for Sydney (Her Majesty's Theatre 15 April 1922) with René Maxwell and Savoy veteran Claude Flemming. Its six weeks there were followed by a respectable seven in Melbourne (Her Majesty's Theatre 3 June 1922). In Hungary a local adaptation (ad Ernő Kulinyi), *Hollandi menyeckske*, was mounted at the Budapest Király Színház, but in America the show flopped, when a different English version (ad Guy Bragdon, Joe Burrows) made it no further towards Broadway than Boston's Majestic Theater.

Germany: Metropoltheater 4 September 1920; UK: Lyric Theatre *A Little Dutch Girl* 1 December 1920; Hungary: Király Színház *Hollandi menyeckske* 21 October 1921; Australia: Theatre Royal, Adelaide *A Little Dutch Girl* 25 March 1922; USA: Majestic Theater, Boston *The Dutch Girl* 22 January 1925

HOLLIDAY, Judy [TUVIM, Judith] (b New York, 21 June 1922; d New York, 7 June 1965). Very blonde star of one Broadway musical whose performance won a Tony Award and, with the help of its film, some cult following.

A member of the night-club act 'The Revuers' with Adolph Green and Betty Comden, in which capacity she was briefly a member of the cast of *My Dear Public*, Miss Holliday appeared in several films (including the screen version of *Something for the Boys*) before making her Broadway bow in the 1945 *Kiss Them for Me*. She hit the headlines with her dumb blonde performance in the play *Born Yesterday* and its subsequent film, for which she won an Academy Award and, after other successful films, returned to the musical theatre to star in the comical *Bells Are Ringing*, written by her revue days partners. She scored a second oversized hit as the ministering angel of the ansaphone service who was the piece's heroine and introduced 'The Party's Over' and 'Just in Time'. She filmed

Bells are Ringing in 1960 but returned to the theatre for just one further musical, *Hot Spot* (Sally Hopwinder), in 1963, before her early death.

Biographies: Holtzman, W: *Judy Holliday* (Putnam, New York, 1982); Carey, G: *Judy Holliday* (Seaview Books, New York, 1982)

HOLLINGSHEAD, John (b Hoxton, 9 September 1827; d 10 London, October 1904). The man who made the London Gaiety Theatre.

The young Hollingshead began his working life as a clerk, and spent periods as a rent collector, a printer's devil and a commercial traveller before settling into a career as a journalist. He worked on *Household Words* and *All the Year Round* under Charles Dickens, for Thackeray on the *Cornhill Magazine* and for a period as dramatic critic of the *Daily News* before he switched from writing to the theatre, initially as stage-manager at the Alhambra. He moved from there, and into management, when he applied for and was given the tenancy of the newly built Gaiety Theatre.

Hollingshead opened the Gaiety in December 1868 and ran it for 17 years, making it into one of London's most popular and famous houses. From the start he put a particular accent on musical pieces, and was one of the earliest and most enterprising British producers in the field, mounting fine productions of French opéra-bouffe as well as some of the earliest important musical shows of the British tradition – *Aladdin II*, *Thespis*, *Cinderella the Younger* – and a long and substantial run of superior burlesque, notably as played by J L Toole and Nellie Farren, and then by the famous quartet of Farren, Edward Terry, Edward Royce and Kate Vaughan. Hollingshead also mounted opéra-comique, classic British comic- and ballad-opera, and even operatic productions, as well as taking in visiting, mostly French, companies, both musical and dramatic, during the summer months. In 1885, following an illness, he took George Edwardes into partnership and, soon after, left the Gaiety to develop into the home of Victorian musical comedy in the younger man's hands.

In collaboration with the financier Henry Osborne O'Hagan and the actor John L Shine, Hollingshead also for a time ran the Empire Theatre in Leicester Square, but success proved difficult to find there, and ultimately he gave up that house, and returned his full attentions to the Gaiety. After leaving the Gaiety, however, everything seemed to go wrong for Hollingshead. He lost all the money that he had made over the years, and was eventually reduced to being given a benefit by the profession.

Autobiographies: *My Lifetime* (Law, Marston, London, 1895), *Gaiety Chronicles* (Archibald Constable, London, 1898)

HOLLOWAY, Stanley [Augustus] (b London, 1 October 1890; d Littlehampton, 1 October 1982). Comic stage and film actor who played in musicals at each end of his career, and made his biggest hit in his sixties.

Holloway spent most of his early career as a concert party performer, but he made the first of his few widely spaced appearances in musical comedy at the Winter Garden under George Grossmith, appearing in supporting roles in *Kissing Time* (1919, Captain Wentworth) and *A Night Out* (1920, René). For the next decade he was an important member of the celebrated Co-Optimists concert party, taking time out to play leading rôles in the London productions of *Hit the Deck* (Bill Smith) and *The Song of the Sea* (*Lady Hamilton*, Lieutenant Manners), but over the next decade he interrupted his revue and film successes only for the chief comic rôle in Jerome Kern's short-lived *Three Sisters* (1934). It was 22 years after this flop before he returned to the musical stage, at the age of 65, to create the rôle for which he is now mostly remembered, the cockney dustman Alfred P Doolittle in *My Fair Lady*, introducing 'With a Little Bit o' Luck' and 'I'm Getting Married in the Morning'. He made, thereafter, just one further incursion on the musical stage, in 1964, in a *Faust*-based musical *Cool Off!*, which folded at Philadelphia.

Holloway also performed and recorded a series of comic monologues ('Albert and the Lion', 'Sam, Pick Up Thy Musket' etc) which remained long popular in Britain, and appeared in a vast number of films over more than 40 years, notably in his original rôle in *My Fair Lady* (1964), as Lockit in the 1952 film of *The Beggar's Opera* and in the filmed *The Co-Optimists* (1929) and *The Lily of Killarney* (1934).

Autobiography: *Wiv a Little Bit o' Luck* (Stein & Day, New York, 1967)

HOLM, Celeste (b New York, 29 April 1919).

In a career in which the musical theatre played but a small part, Miss Holm achieved celebrity when she created the rôle of Ado Annie in *Oklahoma!* (1943), introducing 'I Cain't Say No' and 'All er Nuthin''. As a result, she was starred as Evelina, the titular lady of *Bloomer Girl*, the following year. Later in her career as a stage and film comedienne and dramatic actress she made intermittent musical theatre appearances, stepping in briefly to play Anna in Broadway's *The King and I*, touring as *Mame* (1967), starring in the short-lived *The Utter Glory of Morrissey Hall*, and playing the rôle of Liza Elliott in Britain's first performances of *Lady in the Dark* (Nottingham, 1981). In a film career which cast her mainly as smart ladies, she was given a rare musical moment in *High Society* (1956), introducing 'Who Wants to Be a Millionaire' with Frank Sinatra.

HOLM, Grete

Operette leading lady of two Viennese decades who created several important rôles for Straus, Lehár and Kálmán.

Grete Holm made her first appearances in the musical theatre at Brünn, where, at the age of 22, she created the leading rôle in Robert Stolz's *Manöverliebe* (1904). Both she and the musician (to whom she was later, if briefly, married) were subsequently hired for the Theater an der Wien, but it was the lady who did the better out of the engagement. She had her first major success in Vienna when she created the rôle of Nadina in Oscar Straus's *Der tapfere Soldat* (1908), introducing 'Held meine Träume', the song which was to become internationally known as 'My Hero' in Stanislaus Stange's English version. She then took the principal soprano rôle in the highly successful Vienna production of Kálmán's *Tatárjárás* (*Ein Herbstmanöver*, 1909) and played Risette/Jeanette in Fall's *Die schöne Risette* (1910), but she had her two most important new parts when she moved across to the Carltheater and created the musically and dramatically substantial star rôle

Plate 129. **Grete Holm** *as the Marie of Ascher's* Der Soldat der Marie.

of Zorika in Lehár's *Zigeunerliebe* (1910) and that of Juliska in Kálmán's *Der Zigeunerprimás* (1912).

She appeared at the Theater an der Wien as Tatjana von Nadaschkin in *Schneeglöckchen* (1910) and as Erna von Hardenstein in *Ihr Adjutant* (1911), and at the Venedig in Wien summer theatre in *Eine Nacht in Venedig* (1912), spent several years in Germany and returned to Vienna, to the Bürgertheater, in 1916. She was seen there as Coralie (*Das verwunschene Schloss*), as the star of *Der Soldat der Marie* (1917), as Laura in *Der Bettelstudent*, and Heiderose in *Die Glocken von Corneville* and subsequently created rôles in Eysler's *Der fidele Geiger* (1919), in *Hasard* (1920, Steffi) and in *Drei arme Teufel* (1923, Nelly Wolfgang), as well as appearing as Titania in *Afrikareise*, in her most famous rôle of Zorika and in *Herbstmanöver* again in 1924.

HOLM, Hanya [ECKERT, Johanna] (b Worms, Germany, 3 March 1893; d New York, 3 November 1992).

Dancer, teacher and choreographer in all areas of stage and screen performance.

Miss Holm had several major successes as a choreographer for the musical theatre in the years following her emigration from Germany to America in 1931, beginning, after a contribution to the 1948 *Broadway Ballads*, with the dances for *Kiss Me, Kate* ('Too Darn Hot', New York 1948 and London 1951) and continuing, most notably, with those for *My Fair Lady* (The Ascot Gavotte, 'The Rain in Spain', New York 1956, London 1958) and for *Camelot*. Other credits included *Out of This World* (1950), *My Darlin' Aïda* (1952), *The Golden Apple* (1954), *Reuben, Reuben* (1955), *Where's Charley?* (London, 1958), *Christine* (1960) and *Anya* (1965).

Biography: Sorrell, W: *Hanya Holm: The Biography of an Artist* (Wesleyan University, Middletown, Conn, 1969)

HOMFREY, Gladys [HUMPHRIES, Alice] (b ?1849; d Kingston-on-Thames, 10 March 1932). Tall, imposing actress who became one of Victorian London's favourite musical comedy dragons.

Miss Homfrey came to the theatre at the age of 34 and made her first musical theatre appearance in London as the Princess Badoura in Jakobowski's *Dick* (1884), but thereafter, apart from two stints with Minnie Palmer's company in *My Sweetheart* and *My Brother's Sister*, she played mainly in the straight theatre for more than a decade. In 1897 George Edwardes contracted her to succeed Maud Hobson in the important, but barely sung, rôle of Lady Constance Wynne in *The Geisha*, and subsequently she became highly popular as the reigning heavy lady of the musical theatre, creating the rôles of Melanopis (*A Greek Slave*), Wun-Lung (*San Toy*), Isabelita (*Havana*), the Duchess of Minster (*Our Miss Gibbs*) and Countess Kokozeff (*The Count of Luxemburg*, London and New York) for Edwardes, and appearing as the formidable Martha Sliggs in *Naughty Nancy* (1902). She continued in the musical theatre under George Grossmith, playing dragonistic ladies in *Tonight's the Night* (Angela Lovitt-Lovitt) on Broadway and then in London, in *Theodore & Co* (1916, Lady Theresa Wye), *Yes, Uncle!* (1917, Bébé) and in *The Shop Girl* revival (Lady Appleby), into her 70th year.

HONEYMOON LANE Musical comedy in 2 acts by Eddie Dowling. Lyrics by Eddie Dowling and Irving Caesar. Music by James T Hanley. Knickerbocker Theater, New York, 20 September 1926.

An ingenuous Irishy musical with songs with titles like 'The Little White House (at the end of Honeymoon Lane)', and a cutesy-pie hero (author Dowling) and heroine (Pauline Mason) who dream that they encounter the horrid temptations of the big world outside – including the ghastly possibility that little Mary might make a career in show business – but wake up at the end of the nightmare, heading for their cosy love-nest for two. The evil world was represented by the son of the owner of the pickle factory where our hero works, a wicked fellow who plans to hamstring the lead dancer of a show to allow Mary to have her big chance for stardom, thus entrenching her deep in the mire of Broadway.

The real raison d'être of the show was a lavish production, heavily featuring Bobby Connolly's dancers and a series of variety acts which included 250lb coon shouter Kate Smith and tiny pratfalling Gordon Dooley. Bernard Randall played the manager of the Broadway theatre which belonged to the dream-plot, made up to resemble Florenz Ziegfeld. The combination provided entertainment for Broadway audiences for a highly satisfactory 364 performances.

HONTHY, Hanna [HÜGEL, Hajnalka] (aka HAJNAL, Hajnalka) (b Budapest, 21 February 1893; d Budapest, 30 December 1978). The most important musical comedy star on the Hungarian stage in the years between the wars.

Hanna Honthy worked in the theatre as a child before taking such rôles as Juliette in *Der Graf von Luxemburg*, Gonda van der Loo in *Elvált asszony* (*Die geschiedene Frau*), and the soubrette rôle of Tengerész Kató (*Die Marinen-Gustl*) during her teenage years. She made a big success in the lead rôle of Hungary's version of *Das Dreimäderlhaus* (Médi), and in her twenties played in a wide range of classic pieces, including *Ein Walzertraum*, *Az obsitos*, *Mam'zelle Nitouche*, *Leányvásár*, *Der letzte Walzer*, as Adele in *Die Fledermaus* and, most particularly, in the title-rôle of *Die Csárdásfürstin*, as well as the less enduring *Niobe*, *Rund um die Liebe*, Kollo's *Der selige Balduin* etc.

She appeared at the Orfeum in *Frau Luna* and *Lysistrata* and in several original operetts, and scored a major hit as Aspasie in Hungary's version of *Fi-fi*, before joining the Király Színház as leading lady in 1922. There she starred in a series of musical shows, including Komjáthy's *Három a tánc* (Maca), the local operett on the life and love of Offenbach, *Die Bajadere* (Mariette), *Die gelbe Jacke* (Mi), Nádor's *Fanny Elssler* (Fanny), Szirmai's *Mézeskalács* (Queen), *Mädi*, Buttykay's *A császárnő apródja* and a revival of *Szibill*, before moving to the Budai Színkör to star in *A nóta vége*, and then, in 1925, to the Fővárosi Operettszínház where she was starred in Jacobi's *Miámi* and Straus's *Teresina* at the top of an extended association of nearly a quarter of a century with what by then was Budapest's principal musical house.

Amongst the Hungarian operetts in which she subsequently created leading rôles were *Csókos asszony*, *Muzsikus Ferkó*, *A királyné papucsa*, *Asszonykám*, *Kiss és Kis*, *Mesék az irógépről*, *A régi nyar*, *Szökik az asszony*, *Lámpaláz*, *A balerina*, *Pillangó*, Fényes's highly successful *Maya*, *Egy csók és más semmi*, *Sárga Liliom*, *Aki mer, az nyer*, *Csárdás*, *Hulló falevél*, *Romantikus asszony*, *Julia*, *Zimberi Zombori szép asszony*, *Sárgarigó fészek*, *Fityfiritty*, *Száz piros rózsa*, *Mária főhadnagy*, *Egy boldog pesti nyár* and *Cserebogár, sárga cserebogár*.

She played the Hungarian versions of Lehár's *Die lustige Witwe* and *Zigeunerliebe* and, in the mid-1940s, she still appeared in such rôles as the 'vig özvegy', or merry widow, in *Das Dreimäderlhaus*, as Szibill or the Grande-Duchesse de Gérolstein, whilst adding ever more new rôles in local pieces such as *Barbara* (1948), and *Bécsi diákok* (1949). When age crept on, a special star-sized rôle, that of Cecilia, the ex-chorine mother of Prince Edwin, was created for her in a new libretto for *Die Csárdásfürstin*, and a similar one, as Madame Fleury, garde-dame to Angèle Didier, in a new version of *Der Graf von Luxemburg* (1952). Eventually, like all the best Hungarian senior stars, she began to play Lujza Blaha's famous 'grandmother' rôle in the musical version of Csiky's *Nagymama*, in the twilight of a long and memorable career in the musical theatre.

Biography: Molnár Gál, P: *Honthy Hanna és kora* (Színháztudományi Intézet, Budapest 1967), Gál, G S: *Honthy Hanna* (Zenemükiadó, Budapest, 1973)

HOOD, Basil (b Yorkshire, 5 April 1864; d London, 7 August 1917). Librettist and lyricist acclaimed as the 'new Gilbert', but who turned out to have a much wider range than his famous predecessor at the Savoy.

The younger son of Sir Charles Hood, Basil Hood was educated at Wellington and Sandhurst and joined the army at the age of 19, rising to be a Captain (1893) in the Prince of Wales's Own Regiment of Yorkshire. He began writing for the theatre in his mid-twenties, and a first little piece, *The Gypsies*, was mounted as a curtain-raiser at the Prince of Wales Theatre in 1890. He provided the lyrics to Lionel Monckton's song 'What Will You Have to Drink?', interpolated into the Gaiety burlesque *Cinder-Ellen Up-too-Late*, and wrote two other short operettas before authoring his first full-scale musical comedy, *Gentleman Joe*, as a vehicle for comedian Arthur Roberts.

Gentleman Joe was a serious hit, and when his army duties threatened to take him away from London just when the time had come to enjoy his success, Hood promptly handed in his commission. He followed up his first winner with another major nationwide hit in the musical comedy *The French Maid*, and a second successful vehicle for Roberts, *Dandy Dan, the Lifeguardsman*, before swapping the kind of popular musical comedy at which he had proven so adept for light opera and becoming the partner of Sir Arthur Sullivan, in the place of the estranged W S Gilbert, at the Savoy Theatre. The pair had a fine success with their first collaboration on *The Rose of Persia*, and the literate and intelligent librettist/lyricist was hailed as a worthy successor to Gilbert, but their second work together was interrupted by the composer's death, and Hood completed *The Emerald Isle* with Edward German. The new Savoy pairing continued, and together Hood and German turned out *Merrie England* and *A Princess of Kensington* before producer William Greet moved out of the light operatic area, effectively ending what looked like becoming a memorable collaboration.

Hood next set to work on a musical comedy based on *Romeo and Juliet*, but when producer Charles Frohman started chopping up his work to suit casting considerations he withdrew his name from the libretto of what was produced as *The Belle of Mayfair*. He adapted Sardou's Directoire play as the libretto for George Edwardes's Daly's Theatre musical *Les Merveilleuses*, supplied the Gaiety Theatre with lyrics for *The Girls of Gottenberg*, and found himself a new area of expertise when, with the onset of the fashion for the Continental Operette, Edwardes hired him to do the English versions of what became *The Merry Widow*, *A Waltz Dream*, *The Dollar Princess*, *The Count of Luxemburg* and *Gipsy Love*.

His original works were few in these years of Continental domination, but in 1913 he authored a superior but only half-successful musical comedy, *The Pearl Girl*, for Robert Courtneidge. It turned out to be his last work: four years later he was found dead one morning in his bachelor chambers in St James Street, his death brought on, apparently, 'from overwork at the War Office coupled with an indifference to eating'.

Hood directed a number of his own short and provincial pieces.

1890 **The Gypsies** (Wilfred Bendall) 1 act Prince of Wales Theatre 18 October

1892 **Donna Luiza** (Walter Slaughter) 1 act Prince of Wales Theatre 23 March

1893 **The Crossing Sweeper** (Slaughter) 1 act Gaiety Theatre 8 April

1895 **Gentleman Joe** (Slaughter) Prince of Wales Theatre 2 March

1896 **The French Maid** (Slaughter) Bath 4 April, Terry's Theatre, London 24 April 1897

1896 **Belinda** (Slaughter/w B C Stephenson) Prince's Theatre, Manchester 5 October

1897 **The Duchess of Dijon** (Slaughter) Portsmouth 20 September

1897 **Dandy Dan, the Lifeguardsman** (Slaughter) Lyric Theatre 4 December

1897 **Hans Andersen's Fairytales** (Slaughter) Terry's Theatre 23 December

1898 **Orlando Dando** (Slaughter) Grand Theatre, Fulham 1 August

1898 **Her Royal Highness** (Slaughter) Vaudeville Theatre 3 September

1899 **The Rose of Persia** (Arthur Sullivan) Savoy Theatre 29 November

1901 **The Emerald Isle** (Sullivan, Edward German) Savoy Theatre 27 April

1901 **The Willow Pattern** (Cecil Cook) 1 act Savoy Theatre 14 November

1901 **Ib and Little Christina** (Franco Leoni) 1 act Savoy Theatre 14 November

1902 **Merrie England** (German) Savoy Theatre 2 April

1903 **A Princess of Kensington** (German) Savoy Theatre 22 January

1903 **Little Hans Andersen** revised *Hans Andersen's Fairytales* Adelphi Theatre 23 December

1905 **The Golden Girl** (Hamish MacCunn) Prince of Wales Theatre, Birmingham 5 August

1906 **The Belle of Mayfair** (Leslie Stuart/w C H E Brookfield) Vaudeville Theatre 11 April

1906 **Les Merveilleuses** (Hugo Felix/Victorien Sardou ad) Daly's Theatre 27 October

1907 **The Girls of Gottenberg** (Ivan Caryll, Lionel Monckton/w Adrian Ross/L E Berman, George Grossmith) Gaiety Theatre 15 May

1907 **The Merry Widow** (*Die lustige Witwe*) English version (Daly's Theatre)

1908 **The Dollar Princess** (*Die Dollarprinzessin*) English version (Daly's Theatre)

1911 **A Waltz Dream** (*Ein Walzertraum*) new English version (Daly's Theatre)

1911 **The Count of Luxemburg** (*Der Graf von Luxemburg*) English version (Daly's Theatre)

1912 **Gipsy Love** (*Zigeunerliebe*) English version (Daly's Theatre)

1913 **The Pearl Girl** (Felix, Howard Talbot) Shaftesbury Theatre 25 September

HOOD, Marion [ISAAC, Marion] (b ?1853; d London, 14 August 1912). Leading lady of the Savoy and Gaiety Theatres in the 1880s, playing star rôles in comic opera or burlesque with equal facility.

The elegant, blonde, 26-year-old Miss Hood was studying at the Royal Academy of Music when she accompanied Harriet Coveney to a rehearsal at the Opera Comique and was given the opportunity to audition for Gilbert and D'Oyly Carte. She sang the Shadow Song from *Dinorah*, and found herself cast, for what was billed as her 'first appearance on any stage', as the original Mabel of London's production of *The Pirates of Penzance*. It was, in fact, not her first appearance on 'any' stage, for she had previously been seen, under her own name, singing soprano songs in the music halls, but it was her first appearance as Marion Hood, and her first on the legitimate stage. At the end of that first engagement she married and retired from the stage, but she returned after six months' absence and was seen as Constance to the *Claude Duval* of Frank Celli in Solomon's comic opera (1881), starred both as Casquette in *The Golden Ring* (1883) and as Laura in the first London production of *The Beggar Student* at the Alhambra, and as Girola in a revival of *Manteaux Noirs* (1885).

Having attempted Gounod's Marguerite at the Crystal Palace and found its operatic demands too strenuous, she took the opposite direction and instead went to the Gaiety to play Phoebe in *Billee Taylor*. She followed up there in her first burlesque rôle as Winifred Wood in *Little Jack Sheppard* (1885) and then created the title-rôle in Cellier's *Dorothy* (1886), but when the show transferred to the Prince of Wales she remained behind to become the leading lady of the Gaiety new burlesques. She took over as Mercedes in *Monte Cristo Jr* (1887) and created the rôles of Tartina in *Frankenstein* (1887), Esmeralda in *Miss Esmeralda* (1887) and the Queen of Spain in *Ruy Blas and the Blasé Roué* (1889) alongside Nellie Farren and Fred Leslie, and toured with them through Britain, to America and Australia.

She later took over the title-rôle of the burlesque *Joan of Arc* in London, and in 1892 made another trip to Australia with the Gaiety company, playing Carmen (*Carmen Up-to-Data*), Marguerite (*Faust Up-to-Date*) and *Joan of Arc* for George Musgrove. On her return Miss Hood took over the title-rôle of Alma Somerset in Edwardes's tour of *A Gaiety Girl*, but she seems then to have gone into retirement, bringing to an end a dozen years as a leading lady in the musical theatre in which she had been at the front end of all the most active elements in the theatre of the time – Gilbert and Sullivan, the Alhambra Operettes, the record-breaking *Dorothy*, the Gaiety new burlesque and the new-style musical comedy.

HOOKER, [William] Brian (b New York, 2 November 1880; d New London, Conn, 28 December 1946).

A university English professor, Hooker served up English versions of such classics as *Cyrano de Bergerac* and *Ruy Blas* for the Broadway stage whilst also writing libretti and/or lyrics for a series of musicals in the 1920s and the early 1930s. His first musical ventures included the lyrics for Rudolf Friml's music in the adaptation of *In Search of a Sinner* as *June Love* (1921) and for Mrs Cushing's *Pomander Walk* musical, *Marjolaine* (1922), and he collaborated with A E Thomas on the burlesque melodrama of *Our Nell*, this time having his words set by George Gershwin.

In 1925 he compiled a pastiche score for a musical version of W S Gilbert's play *Engaged*, before scoring his one memorable success with an adaptation of Justin Huntly McCarthy's *If I Were King* as the libretto for Friml's *The Vagabond King* ('Song of the Vagabonds', 'Only a Rose'). Musical versions of two further plays, *The Squaw Man* (*The White Eagle*) and *Smiling Through* (*Through the Years*), did not confirm that success, and another attempt at a swashbuckler, *The O'Flynn*, was a quick flop, ultimately leaving *The Vagabond King* as Hooker's one claim to musical theatre fame.

An opera entitled *Der weisse Vogel* by Hooker and Ernest Carter was produced at Osnabrück, Germany, in 1927 (15 November).

1921 **June Love** (Rudolf Friml/W H Post, Charlotte Thompson, Otto Harbach) Knickerbocker Theater 25 April
1922 **Marjolaine** (Hugo Felix/Catherine Cushing) Broadhurst Theater 24 January
1922 **Our Nell** (ex-*The Hayseed*) (George Gershwin, William Daly/w A E Thomas) Bayes Theater 4 December
1925 **Engaged** (pasticcio) 52nd Street Theater 18 June
1925 **The Vagabond King** (Friml/w Post) Casino Theater 21 September
1927 **The White Eagle** (Friml/w Post) Casino Theater 26 December
1932 **Through the Years** (Vincent Youmans/Edward Heyman) Manhattan Theater 21 November
1934 **The O'Flynn** (Franklin Hauser/w Russell Janney) Broadway Theater 27 December

HOPE, Bob [HOPE, Leslie Townes] (b Eltham, London, 26 May 1903). Celebrated film comedian whose early career included a rising curve of musical comedy rôles.

Originally a performer in vaudeville, the young Hope appeared in the chorus of the musical *The Ramblers* (1926), in *The Sidewalks of New York* (1927, Monk), *Ups-a-Daisy* (1928, Screeves), *Smiles* (1930) and in the revue *Ballyhoo of 1932*, whilst working his way to the top in variety. When he returned to the musical theatre, in *Roberta*, it was in the lead comic rôle of Huck Haines, and he followed up in a similar capacity in *Say When* (1934, Jimmy Blake), in the *Ziegfeld Follies* and as Bob Hale in *Red, Hot and Blue* (1936), introducing 'It's De-Lovely', before definitively abandoning the musical stage to make his fame in films.

Amongst those films – from *The Big Broadcast of 1938* and *Thanks for the Memory* through the celebrated series of *Road to ...* films with Bing Crosby and Dorothy Lamour – were included many in which music was a part of the entertainment, and in 1941 he played the rôle of Jim Taylor in the film adaptation of Irving Berlin's stage musical *Louisiana Purchase*.

Autobiographies: *Have Tux Will Travel* (Simon and Schuster, New York, 1954), *The Road to Hollywood* (New York, 1977); Biography: Morelli, J, Epstein, E, Clarke, E: *The Amazing Careers of Bob Hope* (1973)

HOPP, Julius (b Graz, 18 May 1819; d Vienna, 28 August 1885). Versatile and prolific author of texts and scores for the mid-19th-century Vienna stage.

From his teenage years Hopp composed incidental music and songs for the Viennese theatre, beginning with scores for a half-dozen Possen written by his father, the actor and author Friedrich Hopp (1789–1869), for the Theater an der Wien, and continuing for some 40 years with incidental music and songs for most of the principal Vienna houses. Apart from regular scores for Possen, Volksstücke, Lebensbilder and other musical-comedy variants, a list that included Johann Grün's *Die letzte Fahrt* and Anton Langer's *Zwei Mann von Hess*, both of which would find later revivals, he also wrote and/or composed a number of more substantial musical pieces of his own. These included the popular five-act burlesque of the Faust legend (*Fäustling und*) *Margarethl* (the second of its title) which won productions throughout central Europe

(Debrecen 1870, Budai Színkör 26 May 1872 ad Emil Follinusz), and the Operette *Morilla*, for which he wrote both text and music, and which was staged in Austria, Germany, Hungary and in America. However, his most notable contribution to the musical stage was his adaptation into German of many of the most important works of the French opéra-bouffe stage during the 1860s and 1870s, at a time when they dominated and influenced the development of the Viennese musical theatre.

Later works from more than 150 included:

1863 **Ein Deutschmeister** (*Der Köchin ihr Schatz*) (Karl Elmar) 1 act Fürsts Singspiel-Halle 6 April

1863 **Kein Taschentuch** 1 act Carltheater 7 May

1863 **Der Tugendpreis** (*Flotte Mädchen*) (Berger) Theater an der Wien 6 June

1863 **Zehntausend Gulden** (Karl Bayer) 1 act Fürsts Singspiel-Halle 11 August

1863 **Aurora's Geheimnis** (Julius Megerle) Theater an der Wien 27 August

1863 **Eine leichte Person** (O F Berg) Theater an der Wien 10 November

1863 **Novara** (Therese Megerle) Thalia-Theater 13 September

1864 **Er nimmt auf seine Frau Geld auf** (Franz Biringer) 1 act Theater an der Wien 18 January

1864 **Herr Arthur Gareissl** (Adolf Bahn) Theater an der Wien 1 June

1864 **Der halbe Mensch** (Berg) Theater an der Wien 17 June

1864 **Ein Matrose von der Fregate Schwarzenberg** (Kies) 1 act Theater an der Wien 30 August

1864 **Der Postillion von Langelois** (Anton Bittner) Theater an der Wien 20 September

1864 **Ein Wiener Findelkind** (Megerle) Theater an der Wien 19 November

1864 **(Fäustling und) Margarethl** (later *Mefeles*) (Julius Sixtus) Strampfertheater 20 September

1864 **Herr Maier** (ad Alois Blank) Theater an der Wien 26 December

1865 **Die verwandelete Katze** (*La Chatte metamorphosée en femme*) German version w music by Hopp (Theater an der Wien)

1865 **Dinorah** (burlesque) (Franz von Suppé) Carltheater 4 May

1865 **Der geheimnisvolle Dudelsack** (O F Berg) 1 act Theater an der Wien 27 May

1865 **Die fesche Godel** (Ferdinand Hein) Theater an der Wien 3 June

1865 **Die schöne Helena** (*La Belle Hélène*) German lyrics w F Zell (Theater an der Wien)

1866 **Coscoletto** German version (Theater an der Wien)

1866 **Die Schäfer** (*Les Bergers*) German version (Theater an der Wien)

1866 **Das Donauweibchen und der Ritter vom Kahlenberg** (w Paul Krone) Theater an der Wien 14 April

1866 **Ein dutzend Naturkind** (*Les Douze Innocents*) German version (Theater an der Wien)

1866 **Blaubart** (*Barbe-bleue*) German version (Theater an der Wien)

1867 **Auf einem Vulkan** (Alois Berla) Theater an der Wien 22 March

1867 **Die Ohren des Midas** (*Les Oreilles de Midas*) German version (Theater an der Wien)

1867 **Dorfschönheiten** (Poly Henrion) 1 act Theater an der Wien 6 April

1867 **Die Piraten von Savannah** (pasticcio) Theater an der Wien 18 June

1867 **Die Grossherzogin von Gerolstein** (*La Grande-Duchesse*) German version (Theater an der Wien)

1867 **Der Freischütz** (burlesque) Theater an der Wien 13 August

1868 **Genovefa von Brabant** (*Geneviève de Brabant*) German version (Theater an der Wien)

1868 **Morilla** Theater an der Wien 13 November

1868 **Der Pfeil im Auge** (*L'Oeil crevé*) German version (Theater an der Wien)

1869 **Toto** (*Le Château à Toto*) German version (Carltheater)

1869 **Tulipatan** (*L'Île de Tulipatan*) German version (Carltheater)

1869 **Nach Mitternacht** 1 act Fürsts Singspiel-Halle 10 July

1869 **In der Sackgasse** (aka *In der Kramergasse*) 1 act Carltheater 27 November

1869 **Einer von der Südbahn** (L Meier) 1 act

1870 **Kakadu** (*Vert-Vert*) German version (Carltheater)

1871 **Die Ente mit den drei Schnäbeln** (*Le Canard à trois becs*) German version (Strampfertheater)

1871 **Die Prinzessin von Trapezunt** (*La Princesse de Trébizonde*) German version (Carltheater)

1872 **Javotte, das neue Aschenbrödel** (*Cinderella the Younger*) German version (Strampfertheater)

1872 **Schneeball** (*Boule de Neige*) German version (Carltheater)

1872 **Confusius IX** (*La Cour du Roi Pétaud*) German version (Carltheater)

1872 **Am Fasching Dienstag** (w Franz Roth) Strampfertheater 30 January

1873 **Der Goldchignon** (*Chignon d'or*) German version (Strampfertheater)

1873 **Wiener Blut** (Bittner) Strampfertheater 3 October

1874 **Hammlet** (burlesque) Strampfertheater 29 January

1875 **Madame 'Herzog'** (*Madame l'Archiduc*) German version (Theater an der Wien)

1875 **Die Perle die Wäscherinnen** (*La Blanchisseuse de Berg-op-Zoom*) German version (Theater an der Wien)

1875 **Vom Tisch und Bett** Theater an der Wien 7 September

1876 **Die Creolin** (*La Créole*) German version (Theater an der Wien)

1876 **Seit Mittag vermählt** (*Mariée depuis midi*) German version (Carltheater)

1876 **König Carrotte** (*Le Roi Carotte*) German version (Theater an der Wien)

1876 **Die Reise in den Mond** (*Le Voyage dans la lune*) German version (Theater an der Wien)

1877 **Der Jahrmarkt von St Laurent** (*La Foire St Laurent*) German version (Theater an der Wien)

1877 **Dorothea** (*Jacqueline*) German version (Theater an der Wien)

1878 **Der Teufel auf Erden** (Suppé/w Karl Juin) Carltheater 5 January

1878 **Hotel Klingebusch** (w C F Conradin/Rudolf Kneisl, Eduard Jacobson) Carltheater 16 March

1878 **Jeanne, Jeannette, Jeanneton** German version (Carltheater)

1878 **Atlantic-Pacific-Company** (M V Kautsky) Theater an der Wien 16 September

1879 **Unruhige Nachbarn** 1 act Ronacher 23 August

1879 **Der Abenteuer des Seekapitäns** (Arendorf) Theater in der Josefstadt 28 September

1879 **König Wenzel in Wien** (Franz von Radler) Theater in der Josefstadt 23 October

1879 **Die letzte Fee im Orient** (Carl Elmar) Theater in der Josefstadt 8 November

1879 **In China** 1 act Theater in der Josefstadt 29 November

1880 **Eine ruhige Partei** (Friedrich Wimmer) 1 act Theater in der Josefstadt 1 January

1880 **Die lieben Schwiegereltern** (Wimmer) 1 act Theater in der Josefstadt 24 January

1880 **Tausend und eine Nacht** (Renard) Theater in der Josefstadt 25 January

1880 **Eine Parforcejagd durch Europa** (Bruno Zappert) Theater in der Josefstadt 14 February

1880 **Doktor und Friseur** (Friedrich Kaiser) Theater in der Josefstadt 28 March

1881 **Musketiere in Damenstift** (*Les Mousquetaires au couvent*) German version w Eduard Mautner (Theater an der Wien)

1883 **Der Prinz-Gemahl** (Ludwig Engländer/w Bohrmann-Riegen) Thalia-Theater, New York 11 April

1884 **In der Einöd** (Karl Gründorf) Theater in Rudolsheim 15 March

HOPPER, De Wolf [HOPPER, William d'Wolf] (b New York, 30 March 1858; d Kansas City, 23 September 1935). Tall (very), slim and deep-voiced comedy star who spent 40 years on the American musical stage, many of them as a well-loved star.

Hopper at first attemped a theatrical career as a serious actor, but he soon found his niche in comedy and then, with the help of a basso voice with which he at one time had considered setting himself towards an operatic career, in musical comedy. He appeared with John McCaull's company in a series of leading comic rôles in mostly imported comic operas – as Theophil Hackenback in *The Black Hussar* (*Der Feldprediger*), Ollendorf in *Der Bettelstudent*, Gaspard in *Lorraine*, Lambertuccio in *Boccaccio*, Lord Middleditch in Czibulka's *The May Queen* (*Der Glücksritter*), Frank in *Die Fledermaus*, Folbach in *Falka*, as Elvegaard in *Bellman*, Jeremiah Hackett in *Chatter* (*Die Näherin*), Gavadeau in *The Crowing Hen* (*Serment d'amour*), Onofrio in *Don Cesar*, Alfred Pharaon Pasha in *Josephine vendue pas ses soeurs*, Pomponio in *Jacquette* (*La Béarnaise*), *Prinz Methusalem*, in which he apparently introduced (apropos of nothing) his famous recitation 'Casey at the Bat', Casimir in Suppé's *Clover* (*Die Jagd nach dem Glück*) and Fracasse in Dellinger's *Capitän Fracasse* – but also in some of the earliest American comic operas (Howja-Dhu in *The Begum*, Pausanias in *The Lady or the Tiger*).

He left McCaull in 1890 to star as Filacoudre in Kerker's *Castles in the Air*, and was by now sufficient of a draw for the company to go under the title of the De Wolf Hopper Comic Opera Company. It was under that same banner that he appeared in the most successful of his new pieces to date, as the comical regent of a very Rurasian Siam in *Wang* (1891). *Panjandrum* (1893, Pedro) and *Dr Syntax* (1894, Dr Syntax) provided him with further vehicles, but neither could approach the effectiveness of *Wang* or of John Philip Sousa's comic opera *El Capitan* (1896, Don Errico Medigua) in which, in the part of the South American regent who disguises himself as his own enemy, Hopper found the best original rôle of his career. He repeated *El Capitan* and another useful vehicle, Sousa's *The Charlatan* (1898, Demidoff) as *The Mystical Miss*, in London in 1899.

Thereafter he appeared on Broadway and on the American road with a regular series of new pieces – Weber and Fields's revusical *Fiddle-Dee-Dee* (1900, Hoffman Barr/Petrolius) and *Hoity-Toity* (1901, General Steele), as Dickens's *Mr Pickwick* (1903), in *Happyland* (1905, King Ecstaticus), *The Pied Piper* (1908, Piper) and in a soi-disant musical adaptation of *Le Medecin malgré lui* called *A Matinee Idol* (1910, Medford Griffin) – as well as reprising his former successes, most particularly and frequently *Wang*.

In his fifties he ceased this town-to-country routine, and appeared in New York as Dick Deadeye in the All-Star *HMS Pinafore* at the Casino before essaying a series of

Plate 130. **De Wolf Hopper** *(centre) as Colonel Popoff to the Bumerli of Donald Brian (right) in* The Chocolate Soldier.

Gilbert and Sullivan rôles (Bunthorne, Sergeant, Ko-Ko, Lord Chancellor, Jack Point, John Wellington Wells) and appearing once more in the rôle of General Ollendorf in *Der Bettelstudent*, which he had first played 30 years earlier at the Casino. He also appeared as Bogumil in the American version of Fall's *Der liebe Augustin*, in the festive show *Hop o' my Thumb* (1913, King Mnemonica) at Oscar Hammerstein's Manhattan Opera House, played in revue in *The Passing Show of 1917* and in Hippodrome spectacular (*Everything*, 1918). In 1919 he succeeded Charles Coburn as Old Bill in the British wartime musical *The Better 'Ole* and, in his sixties, paired with Francis Wilson as Ravannes in a revival of Wilson's enduring vehicle *Erminie*, whilst continuing to tour successfully both in his old successes and in a selection of operettas. His last appearances in the Broadway musical theatre were as a take-over in *The Student Prince* (Lutz) and, at the age of seventy, in the 1928 musical *White Lilacs* (Debusson), although he continued to perform, in rôles of decreasing size, almost up to his death.

Hopper's third wife (of six), the diminutive **Edna Wallace HOPPER** (b San Francisco, 17 January 1864; d New York, 14 December 1959) began a stage career as an actress in Boston and with Frohman, then joined Hopper's company to take over opposite him as Paquita in *Panjandrum*. She subsequently teamed her bright little singing voice with his comic basso as Merope Mallow in *Dr Syntax* and Estrelda in *El Capitan* before the marriage was over. She appeared as Orestes in the Casino Theater's revival of *La Belle Hélène*, in *Yankee Doodle Dandy* and took the title-rôle in *Chris and the Wonderful Lamp* before being cast in Ada Reeve's role of Lady Holyrood ('Tact', 'When I Leave

Town') for the Broadway production of *Florodora*. Her personal success in this enormous hit was followed over the next decade by more rôles in musical comedies British (Wrenne in *The Silver Slipper*, *The Lady's Maid* ie *Lady Madcap*, Betty in *The White Chrysanthemum*, *The School Girl*) and American (*About Town*, *Fifty Miles from Boston*, Chicago's *The Three Graces*, *Jumping Jupiter*), before she turned her activities mostly to vaudeville. In 1918 she appeared at Broadway's Bijou Theater in *Girl o'Mine* (Lulu) prior to retiring from the stage in 1920. She subsequently decided on a facelift, had the operation filmed, and went touring with the resultant film for eight years. She then retired to play the stockmarket into her nineties.

Hopper's last wife, wed when he was in his sixties, was another musical-theatre star, Lulu Glaser.

Autobiography (w Winan-Stout, W): *Once a Clown, Always a Clown* (Little, Brown, Boston, 1927)

HORST, Julius [HOSTASCH, Josef] (b Innsbruck, 12 November 1864; d Vienna, 12 May 1943).

Playwright and librettist Horst combined on a careerful of plays, mostly written in collaboration with Alexander Engel, but also with Arthur Lippschitz, Leo Stein and other successful writers. The most notable of these was the internationally played 1908 comedy *Die blaue Maus* (w Engel), and other successes included the 1900 Posse *Man lebt ja nur einmal* played by Girardi, *Der g'rade Michl* (w Engel) and *Der Schrei nach der Kinde* (w Engel). He also provided the texts for a long list of pieces for the musical stage, both Possen and Operette libretti, of which *Der Pumpmajor*, a piece based on Gogol's *Der Revisor* and played in both Vienna and Berlin (Theater Unter den Linden 24 October 1896), and two pieces written with Ralph Benatzky (*Pipsi*, *Adieu Mimi!*) were amongst the more successful. None of these, however, proved to be an international piece on a par with his most famous play.

Die blaue Maus was made over as a musical play with a score by Ludwig Gruber, and also became the American musical comedy *The Little Blue Devil* (Harry Carroll/ Harold Atteridge, Central Theater 3 November 1919), whilst *Der Schrei nach der Kinde* was later used as the basis for Lehár's musical comedy *Cloclo* and his *Der Himmel auf Erden* was remade as the 1914 musical *Unser Frauchen* (Georg & Emil Pipping/ad Victor & Julius Pipping, Stadttheater, Katowice) and again, under its original title, in 1943. Two other, unidentified, plays, one written with Arthur Lippschitz and the other with Engel, were musicalized for the Hungarian stage as the highly successful *Limonádé ezredes* (mus: Zsigmond Vincze, Király Színház 15 September 1912) and *Marci* (mus: Alfred Márkus, Fővárosi Nyári Színház 17 June 1916) respectively.

1885 **Die Pechvogel** (Paul Mestrozzi/w Fritz Waldau) Theater in der Josefstadt 14 November
1886 **Der Pascha von Podiebrad** (Franz Roth/w Waldau) 1 act Fürsttheater 2 June
1886 **Pfingsten in Wien** (F Roth/w Waldau) 1 act Fürsttheater 12 June
1887 **Münchhausen** (Hanns Krenn/w Waldau) Theater in der Josefstadt 10 April
1890 **Angelor** (Carl Weinberger) 1 act Troppau 15 January
1892 **Lachende Erben** (Weinberger/w Leo Stein) Carltheater 24 October
1896 **Der Pumpmajor** (Alexander Neumann/w Stein) Theater in der Josefstadt 11 January

1896 **Der Pfiffikus** (Adolf Müller jr/w Stein) 1 act Raimundtheater 18 April
1897 **Der Sergeant** (Friedrich von Thul/Charles Berger ad) Theater in der Josefstadt 2 April
1898 **Frau Reklame** (Louis Roth/w Stein) Venedig in Wien 6 August
1898 **Lolas Cousin** (*Le Papa de Francine*) German version (Theater in der Josefstadt)
1898 **Der Blondin von Namur** (A Müller jr/w Stein) Theater an der Wien 25 October
1899 **Die wahre Liebe ist das nicht** (Fritz Skallitzky/w Stein) Raimundtheater 9 November
1900 **Ein besserer Herr** (Ludwig Gothov-Grüneke/w Eduard Lunzer) Jantschtheater 19 October
1900 **Der Wundertrank** (Weinberger/w Benjamin Schier) 1 act Hotel Continental 17 March
1900 **Man lebt nur einmal** (w Stein) Raimundtheater 14 November
1902 **Ninettens Hochzeit** (von Thul) Jantschtheater 21 February
1902 **Der Mann ohne Kopf** (Heinrich Müller/w Lunzer) Jantschtheater 5 July
1902 **Die kleine Witwe** (Julius Eibenschütz) Stadttheater, Magdeburg 10 December
1904 **Der Polizeichef** (Josef Bayer/w Robert Pohl) Theater am Gärtnerplatz, Munich 12 November
1904 **Der Schätzmeister** (Carl Michael Ziehrer/w Alexander Engel) Carltheater 10 December
1905 **Uns gehört die Welt** (Karl Josef Fromm) Jantschtheater 20 January
1905 **Der Strohwitwer** (Rudolf Ehrich/w Emil Norini) Stadttheater, Brünn 7 March; Theater des Westens 1 June
1905 **Champagner** (Ehrich) Raimundtheater 14 November
1906 **Der blaue Klub** (Karl Kappeller/w Engel) Theater am Gärtnerplatz, Munich 24 November
1906 **Das Mädchen für Alles** (Karl F Adolfi) 1 act Wiener Colosseum November
1909 **Der Rodelbaron** (Fritz Fürst/w Engel) 2 scenes Apollotheater 1 January
1909 **Der Liebeskongress** (arr Wilhelm Eckstein) 1 act Apollotheater 1 December
1910 **Der Schwimmlehrer** (Josef Heller) 1 act Wiener Colosseum 1 September
1911 **Das Frauenparlament** (Rudolf Raimann) Apollotheater 1 March
1911 **Die Mumien** (von Thul) 1 act Wiener Colosseum 1 March
1912 **Der Lockvogel** (Leo Ascher/w Engel) Walhalla-Theater, Wiesbaden 11 January
1912 **Pariser Luft** (Martin Knopf/Louis Taufstein/w Engel) Luisen-Theater, Königsberg 22 June
1913 **Die blaue Maus** (Ludwig Gruber/w Engel) Graben Kino 11 November
1918 **Eheurlaub** (Jean Gilbert/w Horst Bachwitz) Breslau August; Apollotheater, Vienna 2 May 1919
1919 **Der Künstlerpreis** (Ascher/w Rudolf Österreicher) Apollotheater 1 October
1920 **Glück bei Frauen** (Knopf/w Oskar Engel) Neues Operetten-Theater, Munich 14 August
1920 **Die Witwe aus Indien** (Arthur M Werau/w Ernst Wengraf) 1 act Künstlerspiele Pan 1 November
1921 **Pipsi** (Ralph Benatzky/w Engel) Wiener Bürgertheater 30 December
1921 **Im Alpenhotel** (Richard Fall/w Wengraf) 1 act Apollotheater 6 August
1923 **Vierzehn Tage Arrest** (Edmund Eysler/w Österreicher) Raimundtheater 16 June
1926 **Adieu Mimi!** (Benatzky/w Engel) Johann Strauss-Theater 9 June
1927 **Glück in der Liebe** (Michael Krasznay-Krausz/w Peter Herz) Johann Strauss-Theater 25 February

1930 **Aber Otty** (Egon Baderle/w Erwin Spahn) Deutsches Theater, Prague 10 March

1931 **Frau, für die man schwärmt** (Camillo Faust/w Spahn) Stadttheater, Troppau 17 October

1931 **Die göttliche Jette** (revised *Henriette Sonntag*) (Walter Goetze/Günther Bibo, Emil Rameau ad) Schillertheater, Berlin 31 December

1936 **Gloria und der Clown** (Robert Stolz/w Robert Gilbert) Stadttheater, Aussig 31 December

1941 **Immer sind die Männer schuld** (Hans Lang) Residenz-bühne 13 June

1943 **Der Himmel auf Erden** (Nowosad-Nissen/w Josef Petrak) Zur Neuen Welt 6 July

HOSCHNA, Karl L (b Kuschwarda, 16 August 1877; d New York, 22 December 1911). Composer for the Broadway stage whose few years of activity, before an early death, produced two hit shows.

Born in Bohemia and trained musically at the Vienna Conservatoire, Hoschna was originally an oboeist in an Austrian army band. He moved to America at the age of 19 and worked initially as an instrumentalist, notably in Victor Herbert's celebrated orchestra. He became quickly convinced, however, that the continual pressure on the brain involved in playing the oboe was damaging his health, and he wrote to Isidore Witmark of the music publishing firm of Witmark Brothers asking for any kind of employment, no matter how menial or poorly paid, which would permit him to give up playing. Witmark employed him on arranging, copying and preparing piano reductions of show music for publication, and during this employment Hoschna began himself composing for the theatre.

In 1902 he met would-be lyricist and librettist Otto Hauerbach (later Harbach), then working in advertising, and the two men began to collaborate on a comic opera which, although finished, was never staged. Several other of Hoschna's attempts, however, did make the stage, but they were made-for-travelling pieces of little pretension – B F Forrester's production of *The Belle of the West* featuring Florence Bindley in the title-rôle, and Samuel E Rork's mounting of *Prince Humbug* with Frank Lalor starred – as were the pieces like *Captain Careless* (1907), to which he contributed additional numbers under Witmark's umbrella. It was not until Witmark commissioned his in-house employee, who had risen inexorably from over-qualified copyist to the position of friend, confidant and advisor, to provide the songs for a musical version of the play *Incog*, which he had himself adapted into a libretto (w Charles Dickson), that one of Hoschna's scores finally reached Broadway. *Three Twins* turned out to be a fine success, gave Hoschna his first song hits in 'Cuddle Up a Little Closer' (ly: Hauerbach) and 'The Yama Yama Man' (ly: Collin Davis), and was seen on the American touring circuits for many seasons.

Hoschna contributed to the score for the Adeline Genée musical *The Silver Star*, and followed up with a fresh collaboration with Hauerbach and Dickson on a musical version of the play *Mistakes Will Happen*, entitled *Bright Eyes*. *Bright Eyes* was a one-month Broadway failure, and Joseph Gaites's production of the next Hoschna musical, *Katie Did*, did not even succeed in crossing the continent, but six months later Hoschna and Harbach came up with their most successful piece as a team when they revamped the Berlin hit *Madame Sherry* for an American production.

Hoschna replaced the whole of Hugo Felix's score with music of his own, came up with an agreeable set of songs, which included one genuine hit number in 'Every Little Movement [Has A Meaning All Its Own]', and, with its score filled out with one or two interpolated numbers, *Madame Sherry* proved both a singular Broadway success and a long-lived touring proposition.

The rash of Hoschna shows which followed over the next 12 months – vehicles for Richard Carle, Ralph Herz (star of *Madame Sherry*), variety performer Leila McIntyre, and female impersonator Julian Eltinge as *The Fascinating Widow* – did not produce anything which looked like equalling the success of their two earlier winners and Hoschna's one remaining show, *The Wall Street Girl*, produced by Frederick McKay the year after the composer's death at the age of 34, did little better, in spite of Blanche Ring's presence at the top of the bill and that of Will Rogers ('who did the most extraordinary lassoing feats') lower down.

1905 **The Belle of the West** (Harry B Smith) Great Northern Theater, Chicago 29 October

1906 **The Girl from Broadway** (Chas Noel Douglas/Herbert Hall Winslow) Chicago; 14th Street Theater 14 January 1907

1908 **Prince Humbug** (Mark Swan) Springfield, Mass 31 August

1908 **Three Twins** (Otto Harbach/Charles Dickson, Isidore Witmark) Herald Square Theater 15 June

1910 **Bright Eyes** (Harbach/Dickson) New York Theater 28 February

1910 **Katie Did** (William Cary Duncan, Frank Smithson) Colonial Theater, Chicago 18 February

1910 **Madame Sherry** (Harbach/Maurice Ordonneau ad Harbach) New Amsterdam Theater 30 August

1911 **Jumping Jupiter** (Richard Carle, Sydney Rosenfeld) Criterion Theater 6 March

1911 **Dr Deluxe** (Harbach) Knickerbocker Theater 17 April

1911 **The Girl of My Dreams** (Harbach, Wilbur Nesbit) Criterion Theater 7 August

1911 **The Fascinating Widow** (Harbach) Liberty Theater 11 September

1912 **The Wall Street Girl** (Benjamin Hapgood Burt/Margaret Mayo, Edgar Selwyn) George M Cohan Theater 15 April

HOTEL STADT LEMBERG Musical play [musikalisches Schauspiel] in 3 acts and an epilogue adapted from Lajos Biró's novel and play by Ernst Neubach. Music by Jean Gilbert. Deutsches Schauspielhaus, Hamburg, 1 July 1929.

Set in Galicia during the First World War, *Hotel Stadt Lemberg* centred on the attempts of Anna, housemaid at the Hotel of the title, to stave off the attentions of, and otherwise outwit, the Russian General Juschkiewitsch and, at the same time, to help the Austrian hussar lieutenant Almasy to safety and a happy ending. The lighter moments were provided by the General's adjutant, Sascha Suchalow, and his wife Zinotschka, and the spectacle by the insertion of an 'original-russische-Tanz-und-Balalaika-Truppe' into the proceedings. Jean Gilbert's score of dance-based songs featured the waltz duet 'Du liebst mich' (Anna/Almasy), the foxtrot duo 'Hab' heut' die Sternlein am Himmel gezählt' (Sascha/Zinotschka), Anna's opening slow-fox 'Bin nichts und hab' nichts', and the General and Anna's duo 'Nur diese Nacht'.

First mounted in Hamburg, the show was later played

for two months at Vienna's Johann Strauss-Theater with Anny Ahlers (Anna), Walter Jankuhn (Almasy), Franz Höbling (General), Victor Colani (Sascha) and Mimi Gyenes (Zinotschka) featured, and an Hungarian version (ad Ernő Andai, István Zágon) was subsequently played at Budapest's Király Színház. An American version (ad Ernest Clarke, H B Smith, add songs Mack Gordon, Harry Revel) featuring the Continental star Emmi Kosáry was mounted in Philadelphia in 1930. It did not progress from there, but the piece was done over and produced by the Shuberts a year later, rechristened *Marching By* (ad Harry Clarke, Harry B Smith, Edward Eliscu, George Hirst). It got fine initial notices and played a good Chicago season, with Natalie Hall and Guy Robertson in the leading rôles, but it lasted only 12 nights when it moved to Broadway.

Austria: Johann Strauss-Theater 13 September 1929; Hungary: Király Színház *Hotel Lemberg* 6 June 1930; USA: Chestnut Street Opera House, Philadelphia *Arms and the Maid* 1 December 1930; 46th Street Theater *Marching By* 3 March 1932

HOUGH, Will M (b Chicago, 23 August 1882; d Carmel, Calif, 20 November 1962).

Hough collaborated with Frank Adams, his contemporary at the University of Chicago, and with Joe Howard on a series of musicals, the earliest of which had outstanding runs in Chicago, and helped to make that city for a period a strong centre of musical theatre production. The Hough/Adams/Howard shows toured long and successfully, but, in spite of inherent values often as worthwhile as those the east-coast shows had to offer, they were not accepted by New York's critics and public, and had limited Broadway runs. Hough and Adams split with Howard in 1910 and, shortly after, the vein of Chicago musical hits ran out. Hough continued to work for another decade in the musical theatre, writing three pieces with composer William B Friedlander, the last of which, a musical adaptation of the William Collier comedy *Caught in the Rain*, had a fair run on Broadway under the title *Pitter Patter*.

1904 **His Highness the Bey** (Howard/w Adams) La Salle Theater, Chicago 21 November
1905 **The Isle of Bong-Bong** (Howard/w Adams) La Salle Theater, Chicago 14 March
1905 **The Land of Nod** (Howard/w Adams) Opera House, Chicago 7 June; New York Theater, New York 1 April 1907
1905 **The Umpire** (Howard/w Adams) La Salle Theater, Chicago 2 December
1906 **The Time, the Place and the Girl** (Howard/w Adams) La Salle Theater, Chicago 20 August; Wallack's Theater, New York 5 August 1907
1907 **The Girl Question** (Howard/w Adams) La Salle Theater, Chicago 24 August; Wallack's Theater, New York 3 August 1908
1908 **The Honeymoon Trail** (Howard/w Adams) La Salle Theater, Chicago 23 March
1908 **A Stubborn Cinderella** (Howard/w Adams) Princess Theater, Chicago 1 June; Broadway Theater, New York 25 January 1909
1909 **The Prince of Tonight** (Howard/w Adams) Princess Theater, Chicago 9 March
1909 **The Golden Girl** (Howard/w Adams) La Salle Theater, Chicago 16 March
1909 **The Goddess of Liberty** (Howard/w Adams) Princess Theater, Chicago 15 August; Weber's Theater, New York 22 December

1909 **The Flirting Princess** (Harold Orlob, Howard/w Adams) Princess Theater, Chicago 1 November
1910 **Miss Nobody From Starland** (Howard/w Adams/Howard Johnstone Mitchell) Princess Theater, Chicago 31 January
1911 **The Heartbreakers** (Orlob, Melville Gideon) Princess Theater, Chicago 30 May
1912 **The Girl at the Gate** (Ben Jerome/w Frederick Donaghey) La Salle Theater, Chicago 1 September
1915 **Lonesome Lasses** Colonial Theater 18 January
1915 **A Modern Eva** (*Die moderne Eva*) English version w Benjamin Hapgood Burt (Casino Theater)
1916 **Tickets Please** (William B Friedlander) Victoria Theater, Wheeling, Va 3 April
1917 **The Naughty Princess** (Friedlander) Palace Theater 24 September
1919 **Honeymoon Town** (Byron Gay, Felix Rice) La Salle Theater, Chicago 17 June
1920 **Pitter Patter** (Friedlander) Longacre Theater 28 September

Other title attributed: *The Lady from the Lake* (Frederick Donaghey, 1915)

HOUSE OF FLOWERS Musical in 2 acts by Truman Capote based on his story of the same title. Lyrics by Truman Capote and Harold Arlen. Music by Harold Arlen. Alvin Theater, New York, 30 December 1954.

Set under the hot sun of the West Indies, *House of Flowers* told the tale of two rival brothel-keepers, Madame Tango (Juanita Hall) and Madame Fleur (Pearl Bailey), proprietor of the titular 'House of Flowers'. Madame Fleur's establishment is temporarily knocked out of commission by a mumps epidemic, and she has to put her hopes of regained supremacy in taking under her management the saleable attractions of pretty, un-mumped Ottilie (Diahann Carroll). Ottilie ends up marrying her young man, Royal (Rawn Spearman), but Madame Tango's triumph is cut short when she, too, is put out of action, for her girls are all whisked away on a world cruise by an obliging passing liner and its captain.

Harold Arlen's score included some attractive numbers, both Caribbean-lively ('Two Ladies in de Shade of de Banana Tree') and Caribbean-gentle ('A Sleeping Bee', 'I Never Has Seen Snow' both for Ottilie), which won more praise and popularity than the show as a whole. After a rocky ride in from Philadelphia, where – in obeisance to the star's demands – some cuts (to other folk's rôles) had been, perhaps unwisely, introduced, Saint Subber's original Broadway production ran for only 165 performances. *House of Flowers*, however, lingered. In 1968 Subber mounted a revised version, with five new songs, and with Novella Nelson (Tango), Josephine Premice (Fleur) and Yolande Bavan (Ottilie) featured, at off-Broadway's Theater de Lys (28 January), but the show failed a second time in 57 performances. Its score and its subject nevertheless continued to encourage repeated attempts to bring it back to the stage, and in 1990–1 the piece was still to be seen regionally in America.

Recordings: original cast (Columbia), revival cast (United Artists), composer's demo recording (Mark 56)

HOWARD, Joseph E[dgar] (b New York, 12 February 1867; d Chicago, 19 May 1961). Lifelong performer and songwriter who spent a while in the musical comedy spotlight in Chicago.

A vaudeville performer as a child soprano, then as a teenager, Howard began writing songs not only for his own use, but to supplement his uncertain stage income. He composed a rash of cheerfully rhythmic and down-to-earth numbers in the later years of the 19th century, from which 'Goodbye, My Lady Love' (re-used by Jerome Kern as a period number in *Show Boat*) and 'Hello, Ma Baby' (lyrics: Ida Emerson) have survived the most strongly.

Howard entered the musical theatre in Chicago when he supplied first some additional songs for Raymond Hubbell's score to the burlesque *Chow Chow* (1902) and then two full scores, written in collaboration with lyricist Raymond Peck, for the local shows *The Paraders* and *Tom Tom* (1903). Real success, however, came when he joined two young local writers, Will Hough and Frank Adams, to write the musical comedy *His Highness, the Bey* (1904), for what was still then the quiescent Chicago theatre. The show was distinctly successful, and the trio followed up with a whole series of lucrative hit musicals which were largely responsible for putting the city on the map as a producing centre. These shows toured long and extensively with popular road performers and some rising stars in the main rôles (the young John Barrymore played juvenile in *A Stubborn Cinderella*), but they were, not unexpectedly, sneered at by determinedly parochial New York, in spite of being as tuneful, as amiably foolish and, occasionally, more original than the bulk of east coast musicals of the time.

Howard, in the meanwhile, continued his own career as a performer, expending an attractive tenor voice and an appealing personality on a variety of vehicles, including several musical comedy-dramas of his own writing and/or composing (*The District Leader*, *The Flower of the Ranch* etc). At one stage, in 1907, when he was making his official début as a star (ie billed above the title) in Chicago, he had his name showing on the bills of three of the city's theatres at once – his appearance as Jack Farnum in his musical comedy melodrama *The Flower of the Ranch*, plus his scores for *A Stubborn Cinderella* (Princess Theater) and *Honeymoon Trail* (La Salle Theater).

Although Howard's songs, topped by *The Time, The Place and The Girl's* 'The Waning Honeymoon', were whistled for a decade throughout Chicago, the nearest thing to a single hit song, on a wider basis, which he produced during the years of his Chicago collaborations was 'What's the Use of Dreaming?'. This did not, in fact, come from one of the team's shows, and when the Adams/Hough/Howard series finally did come up with a real hit, in *The Prince of Tonight*, the first of their shows not to be enthusiastically received by Chicago, it finally ended up as the subject of a lawsuit. It eventuated that Howard – in a manner not uncommon at the time – had bought the tune of 'I Wonder Who's Kissing Her Now' from the penniless Harold Orlob and had put his name to it. Orlob was brought in as part of the writing team the following year and, soon after, Howard split away and went back to writing and performing in his old style. He did so for another 50 years, right up till his death in his nineties, and finished his days literally on the stage, collapsing and dying during a performance.

Howard was married to performer **Mabel BARRISON** [Eva FARRANCE] (d Toronto, 31 October 1912), who starred alongside him in several of his shows and who was

one of the original 'babes' of *Babes in Toyland*, and later to Ida Emerson.

A film of his life, rather unfortunately (given the facts) entitled *I Wonder Who's Kissing Her Now*, was produced in 1947. Mark Stevens played the part of Howard, with his singing voice being provided by Buddy Clark.

1902 **The Paraders** (Raymond Peck) La Salle Theater, Chicago 21 December

1903 **Tom Tom** (Peck) La Salle Theater, Chicago 1 February

1904 **His Highness the Bey** (Hough, Adams) La Salle Theater, Chicago 21 November

1905 **The Isle of Bong-Bong** (Hough, Adams) La Salle Theater, Chicago 14 March

1905 **The Land of Nod** (Adams, Hough ad Hobart) Opera House, Chicago 17 June; New York Theater, New York 1 April 1907

1905 **The Umpire** (Hough, Adams) La Salle Theater, Chicago 2 December

1906 **The Time, the Place and the Girl** (Hough, Adams) La Salle Theater, Chicago 20 August; Wallack's Theater, New York 5 August 1907

1906 **The District Leader** (w Collin Davis, Arthur Gillespie) Wallack's Theater 30 April

1907 **The Flower of the Ranch** Kansas City 15 September; Majestic Theater, New York, 20 April 1908

1907 **The Girl Question** (Hough, Adams) La Salle Theater, Chicago 24 August; Wallack's Theater, New York 3 August 1908

1908 **Honeymoon Trail** (Hough, Adams) La Salle Theater, Chicago 23 March

1908 **A Stubborn Cinderella** (Hough, Adams) Princess Theater, Chicago 1 June; Broadway Theater, New York 25 January 1909

1909 **The Prince of Tonight** (Hough, Adams) Princess Theater, Chicago 9 March

1909 **The Golden Girl** (Hough, Adams) La Salle Theater, Chicago 16 March

1909 **The Goddess of Liberty** (Hough, Adams) Princess Theater, Chicago 15 August; Weber's Theater, New York 22 December

1909 **The Flirting Princess** (w Orlob/Hough, Adams) Princess Theater, Chicago 1 November

1910 **Miss Nobody from Starland** (Hough, Adams/Howard Johnstone Mitchell) Princess Theater, Chicago 31 January

1910 **The Sweetest Girl in Paris** (Colin Davis, Addison Burkhardt) La Salle Theater, Chicago 29 August

1910 **Lower Berth Thirteen** (Davis, Arthur Gillespie) Whitney Opera House, Chicago 16 October

1912 **Frivolous Geraldine** (w Herbert Stothart/Theodore Stempfeldt) Olympic Theater, Chicago 21 December

1913 **Broadway Honeymoon** (w Stothart/Davis/Davis, Thomas T Reilley) Joe Howard's Theater ?3 October

1914 **The Manicure Shop** (w Stothart/Stempfeldt) Suburban Garden, St Louis 29 June

1915 **The Girl of Tomorrow** La Salle Theater, Chicago 18 October

1917 **What is Love?** National Theater, Washington 2 July

1918 **In and Out** (Davis) ?22 January

1920 **Chin Toy** (Isidore Benjamin Kornblum)

HOWARD, Sydney (b Yeadon, 7 August 1885; d London, 12 June 1946). Plump comedian of the British revue and musical-comedy stage between the wars.

Howard began his performing career in his late twenties in the concert party world, and was seen in London for the first time in the revue *Box o' Tricks*. After more than a decade of revue and variety work, he made his first appearance in the musical theatre when he played the rôle of Battling Smith in the London production of *Hit the Deck* (1927). He followed up in *Funny Face* (1928, Herbert), *The Co-Optimists*, *Dear Love* (1930, Maurice Gerard) and *Heads Up* (1930, Skippy Dugan) and, after a period playing in farce and in films, returned to the musical stage to feature as Moonface Mooney in London's production of *Anything Goes* (1935). He subsequently appeared in leading comedy rôles in Firth Shephard's productions of *Oh! You Letty* (1937, Mr Simmons), *Wild Oats* (1938, Samuel Cloppitt) and *Sitting Pretty* (1939, Wilberforce Tuttle), and in several of the same producer's wartime revues.

Howard also appeared in a regular schedule of films in the 1930s and 1940s, most of which were comedies, but occasionally – as in the Gracie Fields movie *Shipyard Sally* (1939) – contained a musical element.

HOWARD, Willie [LEVKOWITZ, Wilhelm] (b Neustadt, Germany, 13 April ?1886; d New York, 12 January 1949). Popular vaudeville comedian who featured in a handful of Broadway musicals.

After an early career as a boy singer, Willie Howard found success in a vaudeville comedy act with his brother, Eugene Howard (1880–1965), and the pair appeared in several editions of *The Passing Show* and in more than two decades of subsequent revues on Broadway. In 1925 Willie was cast in the star comedy rôle of Jimmy, the theatre-usher, in *Sky High* (*Der Tanz ins Glück*), and he subsequently returned to the musical stage for a second fine rôle when he created the part of the comical taxi-driver, Gieber Goldfarb, in *Girl Crazy* (1930). After his brother's retirement from the stage, he returned again to the musical theatre, appearing in the short-lived *My Dear Public* (1943, Barney) and as Connie in a 1948 revival of *Sally*.

HOWES, Bobby [HOWES, Robert William] (b London, 4 August 1895; d London, 27 April 1972). Brash little comedian who became a star of the London musical stage between the wars.

Howes made his earliest appearances in variety and in concert parties, and was first seen in London in revue before moving on to take rôles in the London productions of *The Blue Kitten* (1925, Octave) and *The Blue Train* (1927, Mädi, Freddie Royce). He established himself as a rising comic star with his performance in the musical melodrama *The Yellow Mask* (1928, Sam Slider), and took off thoroughly when he created the title-rôle of the long-running musical comedy *Mr Cinders* (1929, Jim). He played in the London edition of *Sons o' Guns* (1930, Jimmy Canfield) and the Drury Lane spectacular *The Song of the Drum* (1931, Chips Wilcox), and scored a series of starring successes in three musicalized comedies written to his measure and mounted at the Saville Theatre by Jack Waller: *For the Love of Mike* (1931, Bobby Seymour), in which he introduced 'Got a Date With an Angel', *Tell Her the Truth* (1932, Bobby) and *He Wanted Adventure* (1933, Bobby Bramstone).

Howes had another major success when he paired again with his *Mr Cinders* co-star, Binnie Hale, in *Yes, Madam?* (1934, Bill Quinton), and yet another as the comical little hero of *Please, Teacher!* (1935, Tommy Deacon). If *Big Business* (1937, Jimmy Rackstraw) proved less successful than its predecessors, he nevertheless came back to the top with a good run and a hit song ('She's My Lovely') in *Hide*

Plate 131. **Bobby Howes** *(right) gets mixed up with pirates Marie Burke and Raymond Newell in* He Wanted Adventure.

and Seek (1937), in which he was paired for a single occasion with comedienne Cicely Courtneidge.

Howes subsequently appeared in *Bobby Get Your Gun* (1938, Bobby Lockwood), took over from the ailing Stanley Lupino in *Lady Behave* (1941, Tony Meyrick) and then toured the show, played Jerry Walker in London's production of *Let's Face It* (1942) and took part in several revues. He had an unusual taste of failure in the quick 1949 flop *Roundabout*, and his resultant haranguing of the unappreciative audience left him for several years out of favour in London. He toured in *Good Night Vienna* (1952), and made his last London appearance in the musical theatre as Ben Rumson, alongside his daughter, Sally Ann, in the London version of *Paint Your Wagon* (1953). In 1960 he appeared as Og in a short-lived New York revival of *Finian's Rainbow*, a rôle he repeated in 1964 in the flop Australian production of the show.

Howes appeared in film versions of several of his stage successes – *For the Love of Mike* (1932), *Please, Teacher!* (1937) and *Yes, Madam?* (1938).

Sally Ann HOWES (b London, 20 July 1930) began her career on stage and film as a child, and appeared in leading ingénue rôles in *Caprice* (1950, Joan), *Bet Your Life* (1952, Jane), *Paint Your Wagon* (1953, Jennifer), *Romance in Candlelight* (1955, Margaret) and *Summer Song* (1956, Karolka), before going to America to take over the rôle of Eliza Doolittle in *My Fair Lady*. She remained in America

Plate 132. *Baritone* **John Howson** – *London's first Marquis de Corneville – and his sister Emma, the creator of* HMS Pinafore*'s Josephine, pictured in their early days in the Australian theatre.*

to take leading rôles in *Kwamina* (1961) and *What Makes Sammy Run?* (1964), and was subsequently seen in England as Anna in a revival of *The King and I* (1973) and as Jenny Lind in *Hans Andersen* (1976). In 1991 she appeared in New York as Désirée in a revival of *A Little Night Music*.

She was for a period married to songwriter and producer Richard Adler.

HOWSON, John [Jerome] (b Hobart, Tasmania, 17 November 1844; d Troy, NJ, 16 December 1887).

Francis Howson (1817–1869), his wife Emma (ex-Richardson), and his brother John emigrated to Australia in 1842, and thereafter were involved in some of Tasmania's (and Australia's) earliest theatricals, working on the stage when there was a stage to work on and giving dance and music lessons when there was not. Frank was star and stage director at Mrs Clarke's Royal Victoria Theatre whilst it existed (dancer Emma was, at the time, mostly giving birth to children in rapid succession), whilst John sr worked as vocalist, violinist, tenor trombonist, composer, actor and recitalist as required. Their children were given a full theatrical upbringing, and went forth, eventually, from their home island to win fame in the most competitive of musical-theatre arenas.

As professional theatrical activity came and went somewhat in Tasmania, Frank's son – the young John Howson – worked in a lawyer's office, in a chandlers', as assistant to a dance-master, as an operatic chorister, as a violinist and, with the members of his family, took part in a concert party with which they visited the Australian gold-fields before the family took to the metropolitan theatres of the Australian mainland to deliver a substantial programme of English operas. Many such operas got their first Australian performances in this way, and John featured in them alongside his sisters, Emma and Clelia, and father Frank.

In 1866 the Howsons left Australia for America, pausing in Tahiti to give the island their repertoire. They began their American career in San Francisco, toured for several years until father Frank's death, then moved on to New York. John worked there at first in stock before going on to play at Booth's Theater in drama with Joseph Jefferson (*Rip van Winkle*) and with Edwin Booth (*Richelieu*). He attempted a family tour as the Howson English Opera Company with *La Grande-Duchesse*, played comic rôles with Alice Oates (Boléro in *Giroflé-Girofla* etc) and sometimes worked as an orchestral violinist, before moving on in 1877 to see what London had to offer. There luck struck with a vengeance, for after being cast at the unfashionable Folly Theatre in *La Créole* (Commodore) and *L'Oeil crevé* (Chamberlain), he was given the main baritone rôle in that house's next production: London's première of its most enormous hit to date, *Les Cloches de Corneville* (Henri). When the piece later went on the road, however, he dropped the star singing rôle to take up the showy character part of Gaspard the miser.

Howson returned to America in 1880 and appeared on

Broadway as Cornwallis Algernon Prout in *Lawn Tennis* and in some classic plays, revisited Britain for the disastrous *Gibraltar* (1881, *La Reine des Halles*, Major), and then definitively settled in America. He starred as John Wellington Wells in *The Sorcerer*, as Bunthorne (made up as Oscar Wilde) to the Patience of Lillian Russell, in *Olivette* for Comley and Barton, in *Madame Favart* and in *Manola*, but ultimately he abandoned singing and returned to the comedy stage, appearing musically in later days only as King Cole in the musical comedy *Madame Piper* (1884). His last engagement was on tour with Lotta, during which he died in harness aged just 43.

John's sister **Emma HOWSON** (b Hobart, Tasmania, 28 March 1844; d New York, June 1928), the prima donna of the Howson family company, crossed to America with her brother, and at first used her fine soprano as a member of the Caroline Richings troupe (1870–1). She appeared in the musical drama *Paul Clifford*, at Niblo's as Eily in *The Colleen Bawn* (1871), and took the title-rôle in the family tour of *Grande-Duchesse*, a rôle she repeated on several occasions. She also appeared as Arline in *Bohemian Girl* and Lucy in *Guy Mannering* with the Conway Company, in the star rôle of J M Loretz's new opera *The Pearl of Baghdad*, as Princess Cunégonde in Augustin Daly's starry production of *King Carrot* and in the revue *Round the Clock*.

Like John, however, it was in Britain that she found her greatest success, when she was cast as the original Josephine in *HMS Pinafore*. Oddly, she did not follow that success up, and although she toured with Sims Reeves in the little operetta *The Gay Cavalier*, she was little seen in Britain thereafter. In 1881 she was back in America, touring in *La Mascotte* and in 1883 she was to be seen playing alongside John in *Olivette* through America, but thereafter her voice and her career thinned down.

John and Emma's brother, Frank A[lfred] Howson (1841–1926), who had been on the stage from the age of three, when he played Cupid to his father's Silenus in a 'mythological ballet' at the Royal Victoria, later worked as a musical director in America and in Britain. He conducted the family tour of *La Grande-Duchesse* and Alice Oates's company in early days, later worked with Irving at the Lyceum in London and ended up as musical supervisor for Charles Frohman. Amongst his composing credits were the incidental music for America's first production of the play *Im weissen Rössl* (At the White Horse Tavern, 1899) and for Daniel Frohman's 1902 *Notre Dame*.

A second sister, Clelia (b Hobart, 8 June 1845), also worked in the theatre, alongside Frank, John and Emma, in Australia and, briefly, in America. In later life, when Emma's singing career was done, she moved in with her long-retired sister and her husband and spent her later years keeping house for them whilst giving occasional voice lessons at Carnegie Hall.

HOW TO SUCCEED IN BUSINESS WITHOUT REALLY TRYING

Musical in 2 acts by Abe Burrows, Jack Weinstock and Willie Gilbert based on the book by Shepherd Mead. Music and lyrics by Frank Loesser. 46th Street Theater, New York, 14 October 1961.

Producers Feuer and Martin, songwriter Frank Loesser and librettist Abe Burrows, who had all worked together to such outstanding effect on *Guys and Dolls* a decade earlier, came together for a second time with a very different style of musical comedy in *How To Succeed in Business Without Really Trying*, and scored a second major hit.

Whereas *Guys and Dolls* had wallowed wonderfully in its very special period downtown atmosphere and lingo, *How To Succeed* was a here and now musical, a brisk, bristling, big-business affair which drew its unbitter fun from the game of city office politics, and how to play it. Robert Morse appeared as J Pierrepont Finch, an ambitious window-cleaner who, equipped with a manual on 'How to Succeed in Business ...', sets out to make his way to the top of the corporate steeple. The firm on which he clips his pitons is World Wide Wickets and with a little help from a gentle distortion of the truth he gets a foot-in-the-door job in the mail-room. From there, in spite of the rivalry and enmity of boss's nephew, Bud Frump (Charles Nelson Reilly), and aided by his all-foreseeing manual, 'Ponty' quickly begins to rise through the echelons of management, treading with innocently smiling guile on the faces of his superiors as he leapfrogs over their superiors. By the end of the first act, having carefully spiked a handful of rivals in the eyes of big boss Biggley (Rudy Vallée), he is Vice-President in Charge of Advertising, with his own office and his own secretary, the very Rosemary (Bonnie Scott) who has been his admiring supportrice from the start. Trouble arrives, however, when a televised advertising stunt featuring Biggley's bit-on-the-side, Hedy la Rue (Virginia Martin), goes horribly wrong, compromising not only Finch but big boss Biggley. But, summoned before even Bigger Boss Womper, our hero somehow pulls out of it all shining-white; and before Biggley knows it, Womper has disappeared off into the sunset with Hedy, and Finch has leapfrogged him into the position of biggest boss of all. Biggley is going to telegraph to the President of the United States to look out for his job.

The tale was illustrated with a scoreful of bright and funny songs. The office setting brought forth some – the retiring head of the mail-room sang a hymn to 'The Company Way', the men and girls of the office insisted, some with more conviction than others, that 'A Secretary is Not a Toy' – but the happiest musical moments of the evening came in Finch's self-admiratory 'I Believe in You', Rosemary's vision of suburban bliss as Mrs Finch, 'Happy to Keep His Dinner Warm', and the after-hours song 'Been a Long Day', in which the two young folk mutter going-home platitudes at each other whilst the older secretary, Miss Jones (Ruth Kobart), interprets the real thoughts behind their words.

How To Succeed In Business Without Really Trying was a first-rate hit on Broadway. It walked away with the Tony Award for best musical of its season, as well as the awards for libretto, lyrics, Burrows's direction and Morse's performance, and garnered a handful of other awards (including a pre-devaluation Pulitzer Prize) as it settled in to the 46th Street Theater for a grand run of 1,417 performances. The other main centres, even those which had not picked up on *Guys and Dolls*, moved in cohort to stage *How to Succeed*. As the first American tour company took to the road, with Dick Kallman as Finch and Dyan Cannon as Rosemary, Arthur Lewis opened the first foreign production, in London. Warren Berlinger was seen as Finch, alongside Patricia Michael (Rosemary), Billy de Wolfe (Biggley), Eileen Gourlay (Hedy) and David Knight (Frump), the piece was again directed by Burrows, and it

Plate 133. **How to Succeed in Business Without Really Trying:** *Billy de Wolfe happily belies the maxim that 'a secretary is not a toy'. Carole Buck and Monte Amundsen are the toys in this St Louis Muny production, 1966.*

again scored a fine success with a West End run of 520 performances.

Australia's production of the show, with Len Gochman, Edwin Steffe, Jay Gerber, Betty McGuire and Annabelle Adams featured, played some five months in Melbourne and more than six months further in Sydney (Her Majesty's Theatre 15 February 1964), and then the foreign-language mountings began. Paris got its *Comment réussir dans les affaires sans vraiment se fatiguer* (ad Raymond Castans), under the management of Elvire Popesco, Hubert de Malet and Lars Schmidt in 1964, with Jacques Duby (Finch), André Luguet (Biggley), Evelyne Dandry (Rosemary) and such countable-with names as Jacqueline Mille, Roger Tréville and Arlette Didier amongst the supporting cast. The following year Vienna saw a German-language adaptation (ad Robert Gilbert, Gerhard Bronner), with Harald Juhnke starred as Hannibal Fink, veteran character actor Theo Lingen as Biggley, Inge Brück as Rosemary and Franco Steinberg as Fred Strunk (ex-Bud Frump), through 62 performances at the Theater an der Wien.

The show was seen at New York's City Center in 1966, and in 1967 a film version was made, with Morse, Vallée and Miss Kobart repeating their original rôles alongside Broadway take-over Michelle Lee as Rosemary, as *How to Succeed* made itself a regular home in regional theatres.

Perhaps surprisingly, given its recognized merits, and its continued topicality in a world where office practices and big-to-medium business haven't changed that much (give or take a computer or two), it has taken nearly a quarter of a century for *How to Succeed* to return to one of the major musical theatre centres, in a full first-class production. In 1993 Australia got a fresh production of the piece, mounted under the management of John Frost (Footbridge Theatre, Sydney, 9 January) with Tom Burlinson starred as Ponty alongside a high-energy selection of local veterans – Noel Ferrier (Biggley), Johnny Lockwood (Twimble), ballet star Garth Welch (Bratt) and June Bronhill (Miss Jones) – and soap star Georgie Parker (Rosemary).

UK: Shaftesbury Theatre 28 March 1963; Australia: Her Majesty's Theatre, Melbourne 16 August 1963; France: Théâtre de Paris *Comment réussir dans les affaires sans vraiment se fatiguer* 1964, Austria: Theater an der Wien *Wie man was wird im Leben, ohne sich anzustrengen* 21 December 1965; Germany: Theater der Stadt, Trier 17 December 1968; Film: United Artists 1967

Recordings: original cast (RCA), London cast (RCA), French cast (Philips), Austrian cast (Ariola-Eurodisc), film soundtrack (United Artists) etc

HOYT, Charles [Hale] (b Concord, NH, 26 July 1860; d New York, 20 November 1900). Author of some of the soundest and most successful farce-comedies of the American musical stage during the 1890s.

For five years the drama and music editor of the Boston *Post*, Hoyt made his first attempt as a dramatist when he cobbled up a play to fill an empty week at a local theatre. He got his first musical theatre credit when he worked over Willie Edouin's mixture of low comedy and a patchwork of new and borrowed (and ever-changing) songs, *Dreams*. He turned the until-then-dubious piece into a durable vehicle for the famous farce-comedian and, as a result, Edouin commissioned a second piece. He got a second long-lived touring piece, built on pretty much the same principles, in the knock-about variety farce *A Bunch of Keys*.

In 1884 the playwright joined with Eugene Tomkins, owner of the Boston Theater, and Charles H Thomas to present his next musical play, *A Rag Baby*, himself. Tomkins dropped out of the partnership after two seasons, but Thomas remained with Hoyt, producing his series of musically mobile farce comedies for extended tours, until his death in 1894, after which Frank McKee took his place. During this period Hoyt had his greatest success, scoring a huge and international hit with his 1891 piece *A Trip to Chinatown*, and more than satisfactory runs with such pieces as *A Milk White Flag* and *A Texas Steer*. He continued to turn out regular new works, scoring a fresh success with *A Black Sheep*, as his companies of 'Hoyts Comedians' toured his plays as far afield as Australia. His later shows, however, began to show signs of a mental disorder, brought on by venereal disease, and in 1899 McKee had his partner committed to an asylum. The wealthy Hoyt soon let himself out and tried to return to the theatre, but he died shortly after.

Hoyt's appeal was largely to American playgoers, and most particularly to the touring circuits rather than more sophisticated venues. Apart from *A Trip to Chinatown* (Toole's Theatre 29 September 1894), which held up its popularity throughout Britain for many years, his pieces did not go down well in London. Edouin's production of *A Bunch of Keys* (Avenue Theatre, 25 August 1883, 'pitiful trash ... decidedly more of a pantomime than anything else') was a quick failure, and *A Stranger in New York* (Duke of York's Theatre 21 June 1898) and *A Parlour Match* (Terry's Theatre 4 October 1900 'old music-hall jokes ... stale and puerile ... two hours of nothing in particular disguised as an excuse for presenting entertainment more or less humorous') were no more happy, counting their runs in a few weeks. However, the former was later seen in the British provinces, remade under the more saleable title *In Gay Paree*.

Australia was rather more welcoming, and Hoyt was well represented on the colonial stages by his own productions of *A Trip to Chinatown* (Lyceum, Sydney 27 June 1896) and *A Milk White Flag* (1896), female impersonator Francis Leon and the Coghill brothers' version of *A Parlour Match* (St Georges Hall, Melbourne 23 January 1886), followed by a fresh production by Frank Clark in 1894, Harry Rickards's *A Bunch of Keys* (Opera House, Brisbane 18 September 1897) and J C Williamson's mounting of *A Rag Baby* (Theatre Royal, Adelaide 22 September 1899).

When long years of touring popularity finally wore them a touch thin, several of Hoyt's shows were later remade by other hands, with a more regular musical content. *A Texas Steer* became *A Trip to Washington* (La Salle Theater, Chicago 24 August 1913) and later, under the management of Elisabeth Marbury and Frederick McCay, *We Should Worry* (Apollo, Atlantic City 25 October 1917, A Baldwin Sloane/Henry Blossom), *A Trip to Chinatown* was remade and remounted by Florenz Ziegfeld as *A Winsome Widow* (Moulin Rouge 11 April 1912), and *A Milk White Flag* was turned without success into *Go to It* (Princess Theater 24 October 1916, ad Anne Caldwell, John E Hazzard, John L Golden). His *A Contented Woman* became *Ladies First* (Broadhurst Theater 24 October 1918) in the hands of adapter Harry B Smith and composer A Baldwin Sloane, whilst *Dreams* also underwent many further alterations, and Edouin presented a version of some of its elements on the English and Australian stage under the title of *Binks, the Downy Photographer*.

1883 **A Bunch of Keys** (various) San Francisco Opera House, New York 26 March
1884 **A Rag Baby** (various) Tony Pastor's 14 April
1884 **A Parlour Match** (various) Tony Pastor's 5 October
1885 **A Tin Soldier** (various) Standard Theater 3 May
1886 **The Maid and the Moonshiner** (Edward Solomon) Standard Theater 16 August
1887 **A Hole in the Ground** (various) 14th Street Theater 12 September
1888 **A Brass Monkey** (various) Bijou Theater 15 October
1888 **A Midnight Bell** (various) San Francisco 4 April; Bijou Theater 5 March 1889
1890 **A Texas Steer** (various) Bijou Theater 10 November
1890 **A Trip to Chinatown** (Percy Gaunt et al) Harlem Opera House 8 December; Madison Square Theater 9 November 1891
1893 **A Temperance Town** (various) Madison Square Theater 18 September
1894 **A Milk White Flag** (various) Boston Theater, Boston 5 February; Hoyt's Theater, New York 8 October
1895 **A Runaway Colt** (various) American Theater 2 December
1896 **A Black Sheep** (Richard Stahl) Hoyt's Theater 6 January
1897 **A Contented Woman** (Stahl) Hoyt's Theater 4 January

1897 **A Stranger in New York** (various) Garrick Theater 13 September
1898 **A Day and Night in New York** (Stahl) Garrick Theater 30 August
1899 **A Dog in a Manger** (various) Washington

Biography: Hunt, D L: *The Life and Work of Charles H Hoyt* (Joint University Libraries, Nashville, 1945)

HUBBELL, [John] Raymond (b Urbana, Ohio, 1 June 1879; d Miami, Fla, 13 December 1954). Composer of two decades of functional rather than memorable scores for the American theatre.

Hubbell moved to Chicago from his native Ohio to study, and he first entered the music world there as a dance-band conductor and as an employee of the music publishing house of Charles K Harris. At the age of 23 he composed his first score for the musical theatre, a Chicago extravaganza called *Chow Chow* which mixed comedy, songs (not all by Hubbell) and a South Seas setting in traditional style with sufficient success for the show to be transported to Broadway the following season. Played there as *The Runaways*, under the management of Sam Shubert and Nixon and Zimmerman, it was scorned by sophisticated critics, ran up 167 metropolitan performances, and toured thereafter for five years. Hubbell had a second success with the score for another Sam Shubert piece on similar, but slightly more substantial, lines in *Fantana* (1905). He subsequently became a prolific composer of show music both for the Shubert management and for other producers through 20 years of occasionally attractive if utilitarian writing which, if it produced no memorable music or enduring shows, kept many a Broadway theatre musicked for considerable periods.

Hubbell was principal composer on five editions of the *Ziegfeld Follies* (1911 to 1914, 1917) and composed the scores for six of the Hippodrome spectaculars produced by Charles Dillingham (*Hip! Hip! Hooray!*, *The Big Show*, *Cheer Up*, *Happy Days*, *Good Times*, *Better Times*), the second of which produced his most successful single song, 'Poor Butterfly' (lyric: R H Burnside), a number written as a vehicle for a Japanese soprano who ultimately did not join the cast.

In the realm of the book musical he rarely equalled the success of his earliest pieces. Sam Shubert failed to repeat *Fantana*'s run with *Mexicana*, but although John C Fisher's starring vehicle for Sallie Fisher was rejected as *Mam'selle Sallie* it rebounded a season later as *A Knight for a Day* and ran for 176 nights on Broadway, prior to a healthy life on the road and an export to Australia. Hubbell suffered a couple of quick failures with *The Girl from the States*, which was totally rewritten (without his music) yet still folded out of town, and *The Air King*, which opened at Buffalo and got only as far as Chicago before collapsing, whilst *The Girl at the Helm* pleased Chicago for a five-month run in the wake of the Howard, Hough and Adams shows, but went no further. However, a collaboration with Glen MacDonough on a piece for Lew Fields, *The Midnight Sons*, won a fine success as a summer musical — that traditionally loose-limbed and undemanding form of entertainment which was played during the hot months of the year when people didn't feel like concentrating on anything but the lightest and most frivolous of entertainments.

Fields's follow-up production of the same team's *The*

Jolly Bachelors starred Nora Bayes (instead of last time's Blanche Ring), who brought her own successful songs with her, whilst *The Bachelor Belles* featured another artist, Adeline Genée, who was also inclined to bring her own music with her, to the detriment of the show's nominal composer. Hubbell shared the score on a further indifferent Lew Fields vehicle, *The Never Homes*, and had little joy with the equally indifferent *Three Romeos* and with Ziegfeld's attempt to update the old hit *A Trip to Chinatown* as *A Winsome Widow*. Another summer musical, the allegedly French-farce-based *The Man from Cook's*, had some success in the hot part of 1912.

After several years of writing only for revue (*Fads and Fancies*, *Hitchy-Koo*, *Ziegfeld Follies* and the Hippodrome), Hubbell essayed a handful more musicals. *The Kiss Burglar* used a smidgin of a wartime theme in its Frenchified farce book and won a respectable run, but a piece written to launch swimming-star Annette Kellerman as a musical performer and a tiny musical called *Miss Millions*, written with his Hippodrome colleague R H Burnside, both failed, as did a sentimental wartime piece called *Sonny*, which attempted too blatantly to cash in on the success of its author's previous Franco-weepie, *Buddies*. Hubbell's music was now becoming regarded more as an appendage to a show than an advantage, but he persevered with a respectable Leon Errol comedy vehicle, *Yours Truly* (127 performances), and a show for the slightly fading Fred Stone, *Three Cheers*. He also saw quite a bit of his music tacked in alongside some bits of Jean Gilbert in an R H Burnside concoction, apparently partially remade from *The Man from Cook's*, called *The Girl from Cook's*, mounted at London's Gaiety Theatre, before quitting the theatre and moving to Miami in retirement.

1902 **Chow Chow** (Addison Burkhart) New Orpheon Theater, Chicago 4 October
1903 **The Runaways** revised *Chow Chow* Casino Theater 11 May
1905 **Fantana** (Robert B Smith) Lyric Theater 14 January
1906 **Mexicana** (Clara Driscoll, R B Smith) Lyric Theater 29 January
1906 **Mam'selle Sallie** (R B Smith) Grand Opera House 26 November
1907 **A Knight for a Day** revised *Mam'selle Sallie* Wallack's Theater 26 November
1908 **A Girl at the Helm** (R B Smith) La Salle Theater, Chicago 5 September
1909 **The Midnight Sons** (Glen MacDonough) Broadway Theater 22 May
1909 **The Girl from the States** (w A Baldwin Sloane/MacDonough) Adelphi Theater, Philadelphia 11 October
1909 **The Air King** (Harry B Smith) Star Theater, Buffalo November
1909 **Spirit Land** 1 act Fifth Avenue Theater 8 February
1910 **The Jolly Bachelors** (MacDonough) Broadway Theater 6 January
1910 **The Bachelor Belles** (H B Smith) Globe Theater 7 November
1911 **The Never Homes** (w Sloane/E Ray Goetz/MacDonough) Broadway Theater 5 October
1911 **The Three Romeos** (H B Smith) Globe Theater 13 November
1912 **The Man from Cook's** (Henry Blossom) New Amsterdam Theater 25 March
1912 **A Winsome Widow** (Charles Hoyt ad) Moulin Rouge 11 April
1915 **The Model Maid** (Anne Caldwell) Atlantic City 26 January

1918 **The Kiss Burglar** (MacDonough) George M Cohan Theater 9 May
1919 **Among the Girls** (Blossom, MacDonough/Blossom, Roi Cooper Megrue) Shubert Theater, New Haven 9 May; Park Square Theater, Boston 19 May
1919 **Miss Millions** (R H Burnside) Punch and Judy Theater 9 December
1921 **Sonny** (George V Hobart) Cort Theater 16 August
1922 **The Elusive Lady** (MacDonough) Baltimore 2 October
1927 **Yours Truly** (Caldwell/Clyde North) Shubert Theater 25 January
1927 **The Girl from Cook's** (w Jean Gilbert/Burnside, Greatrex Newman) Gaiety Theatre, London 1 November
1928 **Three Cheers** (Caldwell, Burnside) Globe Theater 15 October

HUGDIETRICHS BRAUTFAHRT Komische Märchen-Operette in 3 acts by 'Rideamus'. Music by Oscar Straus. Carltheater, Vienna, 10 March 1906.

The second collaboration of 'Rideamus' (Fritz Oliven) and the rising Oscar Straus, following their joyous burlesque on things legendary in *Die lustigen Nibelungen*, *Hugdietrichs Brautfahrt* was an imaginative fairytale piece, told with genuine burlesque wit and humour.

Hugdietrich (Mizzi Zwerenz), the ruler of Byzantium, is in need of a wealthy wife, as the expenses of running his country and his court and the upkeep on the royal mistresses are proving burdensome. Whilst a Royal Commission is set under way to solve the problem, however, he gets an unexpected hand from the out-of-favour fairy Belladonna (Betti Seidl). She has been semi-seduced by the neighbouring and seriously rich King Ladislaus (Karl Blasel), and has sworn to be revenged on him through his daughter, Miki (Helene Merviola). Ladislaus has locked up Miki in a tower, which is guarded by a perpetually hungry dragon called Schnidibumpfl (Arthur Guttmann), and has engaged her, against her will, to the pillocky but profitable Prince Kakerlack (Ferdinand Pagin). Belladonna disguises Hugdietrich as a girl, Hughlinde, who attracts lascivious Ladislaus's attention and is made lady-in-waiting to Miki. Tower-bound Miki is delighted to have a lady-in-waiting who will share a cigarette with her and even more delighted when 'she' exposes her manhood. Of course, the inevitable happens. The helpful Schnidibumpfl gets rid of the local League of Virtue and eats Kakerlack before everything comes to a messy but happy end.

The score included some jolly numbers for the dragon, reminiscing smokily over an unfaithful girlfriend, and for Miki, whose wistful sighings for romance and a knight ('Prinzessin sass träumend auf duftiger Halde') gave way to a whoop of joyous 4/4 ('Er ist ein Mann') on Hugdietrich's self-revelation, whilst Belladonna made her fairy appearance to the waltzing strains of 'Sorgloser Schläfer', in one of the evening's prettiest, but nonetheless amusing, moments.

Mounted, like *Die lustigen Nibelungen*, at Vienna's Carltheater under the management of Andreas Aman, *Hugdietrichs Brautfahrt* started rather more promisingly than its predecessor, running for 53 straight performances (to 4 May), and being brought swiftly back after the brief run of Kubler's *Der Rosenjungling* to play out the last weeks of the season, and then again to open the new one in the autumn (75th performance, 16 September). It remained in the repertoire in 1907, but was overwhelmed by the theatre's big hit of that year, Straus's own *Ein Walzertraum*, and disappeared from the schedules.

The show was afterwards seen in Germany, but does not seem to have travelled any further, nor to have returned to the Viennese stage.

Germany: ?1907

HUGO, Victor [Marie] (b Besançon, 26 February 1802; d Paris, 22 May 1885).

The famous French novelist and dramatist did not actually dip his own pen into the musical theatre, but his works proved the inspiration for other writers, of all degrees and kinds, to do so. At first this was in the operatic field, and Verdi's 1844 opera *Ernani* (*Hernani*, 1830), his *Rigoletto* (*Le Roi s'amuse*, 1832), Donizetti's *Lucrezia Borgia* (*Lucrèce Borgia*, 1833), Ponchielli's *La Gioconda* (*Angelo*, 1835) and many other less-celebrated operas were based on Hugo's works. These operas, in their turn, prompted burlesques, and London saw revamped Hugo in an *Ernani* by William Brough (Alexandra Theatre 1859) and Henry Byron's *Handsome Hernani, or the Fatal Penny Whistle* (Gaiety Theatre 30 August 1879), Lester Buckingham's *Lucrezia Borgia!, at Home and All Abroad* (St James's Theatre 1860), Sydney French's *Lucrezia Borgia* (Marylebone Theatre 1867) and Byron's *Lucrezia Borgia MD or the Grand Doctoress* (Holborn Theatre 28 October 1868). By far the most popular of Hugo's works amongst the burlesquers, however, was *Notre Dame*, many times operaticized from 1836 onwards without a standard opera emerging, which was parodied as *Esmeralda* (Adelphi Theatre 5 June 1850), *Esmeralda, or the Sensation Goat* (Strand Theatre 28 September 1861), *Pretty Esmeralda, and Captain Phoebus of Ours* (Gaiety Theatre 2 April 1879), and in the highly successful new Gaiety Theatre burlesque, *Miss Esmeralda* (1887). *Ruy Blas* also came under the hands of both operatic and burlesque-writers and parodies appeared in London as *Ruy Blas Righted* (Vaudeville Theatre 3 January 1874) and as *Ruy Blas and the Blasé Roué* (Gaiety Theatre 21 September 1889).

Quatre-vingt-treize became *Los hijos del batallón* in the hands of Spain's Ruperto Chapí and Guillermo Fernández Shaw as early as 1898, but it was nearly a century more before Hugo's most successful moment in the non-operatic musical theatre arrived. With the fashion for dramatic musical plays replacing that for the comic, in the 1980s Hugo finally moved, unparodied, into the English-language musical theatre when *Les Misérables* was musicalized by Claude-Michel Schönberg, Alain Boublil and Jean-Marc Natel with vast international success. It was a success which, perhaps surprisingly, did not produce a huge flood of musical Hugo from other sources, although several versions of *Notre Dame*, notably a British one by Mark Bramble and Callum McLeod (Oxford, 1991), a French and a German one (Schauspielbühne, Munich 1988), both entitled *Quasimodo*, and an Hungarian (Hevesi Sándor Színház, Zalaegerszeg, Gabor Kemény/Peter Tömöry, 1989) were added to the vast list of former years. The last-named piece was subsequently mounted in Bruchsal, Germany, as *Der Glöckner von Notre Dame* (ad Franz Csiky, 1992).

HULBERT, Jack (b Ely, 24 April 1892; d London, 25 March 1978). A light-comic actor, singer and dancer with a well-known shovel-chin whose biggest successes as a performer were made in partnership with his wife, Cicely Courtneidge.

Hulbert moved into the professional musical theatre direct from his Cambridge University show *Cheer-Oh! Cambridge* (also author), which was given a West End showing at the Queen's Theatre (12 June 1913) after its local performances. He joined Robert Courtneidge's company to play a light comedy supporting rôle in *The Pearl Girl* (Robert Jaffray), and appeared consecutively in the same producer's *The Cinema Star* (Billy), *The Arcadians* revival (Bobby) and the disastrous *The Light Blues* (Arthur Hobbs), another Cambridge musical, for which the young man collaborated on the book.

He played in several revues, took the soubret rôle of Posch in the London version of *Das Hollandweibchen* (1920), made an appearance on Broadway with Miss Courtneidge in their successful London revue *By the Way* (1925), and then, following his managerial ambitions, joined with Paul Murray to commission and produce the musical comedy *Lido Lady* with a score by the young Rodgers and Hart. Both he (Harry Bassett) and his wife appeared in the piece, which Hulbert also directed with a fair degree of success. Thereafter he co-produced and occasionally appeared in several revues (*Clowns in Clover*, *The House That Jack Built*, *Folly to Be Wise*, *On with the Show*), whilst directing (*The Blue Train*, *Song of the Sea*) and choreographing (*Lady Mary*) musicals for other producers. Hulbert produced only one musical play himself, the Sophie Tucker vehicle *Follow a Star*, a virtual cabaret show in which he appeared opposite his star in the rôle of Bobby Hillary whilst also directing and choreographing it.

When his producing ventures finally sent him broke, Hulbert turned to the film world to help him recuperate, and he starred in a number of successful musical movies (*Sunshine Susie*, *Jack's the Boy* etc), returning to the theatre to direct and choreograph his wife in *Hide and Seek* and then to team up with her on stage in a successful trio of musicals, *Under Your Hat* (1938, film 1940, Jack Millett), *Full Swing* (1942) and *Something in the Air* (1943), which he also co-wrote, directed and co-choreographed. He then distanced himself once more from performing, but he continued to direct Miss Courtneidge's musicals (*Under the Counter*, *Her Excellency* also co-producer w Val Parnell, *Gay's the Word*, *Star Maker*) and her revue *Over the Moon*, as well as such other musical plays as *Sweet Yesterday*, *The Nightingale* and a stage version of the radio series *Life with the Lyons*, mounted as a Blackpool holiday entertainment.

He made a late return to the stage to appear with his wife in a compilation entertainment based on their lives at the Yvonne Arnaud Theatre, Guildford (*Words and Music*).

His brother, **Claude Hulbert** (b London, 25 December 1900; d London, 22 January 1964), also had a career as a light-comic actor in musicals, appearing in London in *Primrose*, *Tell Me More!*, *Kid Boots*, *Sunny*, *Oh, Kay!*, *Song of the Sea*, *Dear Love*, *Follow a Star* and *Panama Hattie*. He also made a small contribution to the songs of *Under Your Hat*.

1914 **The Cinema Star** (*Die Kino-Königin*) English libretto (Shaftesbury Theatre)
1915 **The Light Blues** (Howard Talbot, Herman Finck/Adrian

Ross/w Max Pemberton) Prince of Wales Theatre, Birmingham 13 September; Shaftesbury Theatre, London 14 September 1916

1919 **Too Many Girls** (Arthur Wood/G Hartley Milburn/w Harold Simpson, Robert Courtneidge) Hippodrome, Liverpool 22 December

1938 **Under Your Hat** (Vivian Ellis/w Archie Menzies, Arthur Macrae) Palace Theatre 24 November

1942 **Full Swing** (George Posford, Harry Parr-Davies/w Menzies, Macrae) Palace Theatre 16 April

1943 **Something in the Air** (Manning Sherwin/Max Kester, Harold Purcell/w Macrae, Menzies) Palace Theatre 23 September

1952 **Life with the Lyons** (w others) Hippodrome, Blackpool 28 June

Autobiography: *The Little Woman's Always Right* (W H Allen, London, 1975)

HUMBERT, Eugène   (b ?1835; d May 1886).

For many years the hugely enthusiastic director of Brussels' Théâtre des Fantaisies-Parisiennes (later known as the Théâtre Alcazar), Humbert brought himself, for a period of several years, to the very centre of the world of the musical theatre by a diligent choice of première productions.

His first major success came as a result of the siege of Paris and the period of the Commune. With Paris a dubiously healthy place to be, a number of writers and composers had gone to Britain or elsewhere away from the capital. Charles Lecocq, whose first full-scale success, *Fleur de thé*, had recently been staged at the Théâtre de l'Athénée, was amongst these, and when his latest collaboration with librettists Chivot and Duru (and, this time, also Clairville) was complete, it was offered not to Paris but to the respected and reliable Humbert in Brussels. Humbert staged Lecocq's *Les Cent Vierges* in 1872 with great success, and the piece was subsequently played and revived throughout the world. However, even before this had happened Humbert had started on the work which would be his greatest triumph. A dinner with wheeler-dealer Victor Koning brought forth the suggestion of a libretto set in the Directoire period and – so one version of the tale goes – when, three months later, the libretto was brought to Humbert he handed it on to 'his' composer for a musical setting. *La Fille de Madame Angot* was to turn out to be one of the greatest and most enduring musicals of its century. From its rapturous reception in Brussels it went on to Paris and to the rest of the world with unalloyed success, spreading the fame of Humbert and his theatre. In 1878 the old Parisian Théâtre Beaumarchais, altered by director Debruyère into a musical house, was christened the 'Fantaisies-Parisiennes' in imitation of Humbert's theatre.

During the summer recess of 1873, whilst his theatre was being redecorated, Humbert took his company to Britain, where they played *La Fille de Madame Angot*, *Les Cent Vierges*, *La Belle Hélène*, *Les Brigands* and Britain's only ever performances of *Les Braconniers*. On his return home Humbert then followed up *La Fille de Madame Angot* at the Fantaisies-Parisiennes with another outstanding Lecocq work, *Giroflé-Girofla*, and caused a sensation when he took the piece (still unseen in Paris) to London's Opera-Comique. Their season there had to be ended when Humbert and Lecocq sold the English rights to the piece, but

the experience had been a paying one, and the Fantaisies-Parisiennes company returned to London in 1875 with their new piece, Vogel's *La Filleule du roi*, and in 1876 with *La Petite Mariée* and, again, *Giroflé-Girofla*.

La Filleule du roi was one of the new pieces, often by newer (but not always younger) composers, with which Humbert attempted to keep up the high profile won all around the world by his three Lecocq productions. It failed in Paris, whilst *Le Chignon d'or* by the better-known Jonas, Grangé and Tréfeu, produced in 1874, went to Vienna but not Paris. Apart from a French version of Suppé's *Fatinitza*, it was Vasseur's *Le Roi d'Yvetot* (1876) which proved the best of Humbert's later productions – a group which included such pieces as *La Princesse Marmotte* (de Rillé, 1880), *La Petite Reinette* (Varney, 1882), *Les Beignets du roi* (Bernicat, 1882), *Le Présomptif* (Gregh, 1883) – but none of them came up to the expectations fulfilled and fuelled by those first hits.

Humbert had, however, given his first significant opportunity to the composer Bernicat, and he took part in supplying the promising young man with his next libretto, *François les bas-bleus*, which he co-produced not at his home base, but at Paris's Théâtre des Folies-Dramatiques. It proved the success that he had not found again in Brussels. Bernicat's death, prior to the completion of the show, meant that Humbert and his partner, Dubreuil, had to find someone to complete it and their choice fell on another promising young man, André Messager. When Messager proved to be a real find they commissioned him to write his own first full-length work, *La Fauvette du Temple*, and Humbert, who had already experienced a notable first co-authorial success (although with how much input is unknown) with the libretto for *François*, again collaborated on the text, winning a second strong writing credit.

In 1884 he took on the management of Brussels' new Bourse Theatre, but illness prevented him from effectively running it for the two years between his appointment and his death at the age of 51.

1883 **François les bas-bleus** (Firmin Bernicat/w Ernest Dubreuil, Paul Burani) Théâtre des Folies-Dramatiques 8 November

1885 **La Fauvette du Temple** (André Messager/w Burani) Théâtre des Folies-Dramatiques 17 November

HUNTINGTON, Agnes   (b Kalamazoo, Mich, ?1864; d New York, 10 March 1953). Statuesque American contralto who briefly became a huge star in Victorian London.

Miss Huntington studied voice in Germany and made her earliest appearances on the concert stage in Dresden, London, at the Paris Trocadero and with the New York Philharmonic. She played several seasons with the Boston Ideal Comic Opera Company, appearing with them in *Alidor* at the St Paul Opera House (1887) and in the contralto rôles of their light operatic repertoire, before she crossed the Atlantic and starred at London's Prince of Wales Theatre with the newly formed Carl Rosa Light Opera Company, in the travesty title-rôle of Planquette's *Paul Jones* (1889), a part which had been created in the provinces by baritone Michael Dwyer. She caused a sensation in London, and *The Era* reported 'a more brilliant début has not been known in connection with comic opera'. George Edwardes was amongst those dazzled by the lady and her performance, and he announced plans to build the Agnes Huntington Theatre, where he would feature Ms Huntington at the centre of her own company.

At the end of the run of *Paul Jones* she was cast by the Carl Rosa to play another male rôle, Wilfred, in the medieval comic opera *Marjorie* (1890), a rôle again played in tryout by a male performer. After one week of performances, however, she walked out and, when taken to court by theatre-owner Henry Leslie, claimed that the rôle was unsuited to her voice. Since she refused to go on tour with *Paul Jones* as an alternative, Leslie was granted an injunction that prevented her from singing. Ultimately she was fined £1,000 and costs, and she then announced she was returning to America to play *Paul Jones*. When news filtered back to Britain that she was being paid a salary of $7,500 a week to do so, the degree of 'unsuitability' of *Marjorie* became evident.

The 'stately, handsome American girl' caused something of a stir back in America as well, but maybe a touch less in singing circles than in social ones. It was noted that the President himself came to her Washington first night of *Paul Jones*. She appeared on Broadway both as Paul Jones and in the title-rôle of *Captain Thérèse*, the new Planquette piece commissioned by Carl Rosa especially to highlight her talents, and then in 1892 she vanished from the world of the light musical theatre as suddenly as she had come, into marriage as the exceedingly wealthy Mrs Paul D Cravath, wife of a rich, social and distinguished lawyer and patron of the arts. In the 60 years of her retirement she maintained her interest in musical theatre, founding the Little Theater Opera Company and encouraging young singers.

Edwardes built his theatre, but its first leading lady was Ada Rehan, and it was called after his American partner in the venture, Augustin Daly.

HUNTLEY, G[eorge] P[atrick] (b Fermoy, Co Cork, 13 July 1868; d London, 21 September 1927). Warmly dotty star comedian of the British 1900s and 1910s.

Huntley had been 13 busy years on the stage before he appeared in the musical theatre for the first time, touring in *The Circus Boy* (ex- *Dandy Dick Whittington*) in the travesty rôle of Lady Fitzwarren, created by the celebrated dame-comic, John F Sheridan. He was then hired for George Edwardes's touring company of *The Circus Girl* (1897, Sir Titus) and was subsequently brought to the Gaiety to succeed Harry Monkhouse as Brother Tamarind in *A Runaway Girl*. This he did with such success that Edwardes gave him the top comic rôle of Lord Plantaganet in his new musical *Kitty Grey*, both for its touring production and its subsequent London season.

Kitty Grey established Huntley as one of the best and most endearing comedians of the British musical stage. His subsequent creations in *Three Little Maids* (1902, Lord Cheyne), *The School Girl* (1903, Sir Ormesby St Leger) and *Lady Madcap* (1904, Trooper Smith) – each of which he repeated in America and Australia – and, above all, in *Mr Popple of Ippleton* (1905, Freddy Popple) and *Miss Hook of Holland* (1907, Mr Hook) confirmed his position. *My Mimosa Maid* (1908, Victor Guilbert), the successor to *Miss Hook*, was not successful and neither was Huntley's venture into actor-authorship in *The Hon'ble Phil* (1908, Phil Giffard), but success returned when he took up his old rôle in *Kitty Grey* for a season on Broadway.

Huntley stayed in America for several non-musical engagements, and on returning home appeared in several musical playlets (including Fall's *Arms and the Girl*) in variety before his next musical theatre successes in Edwardes's production of Jacobi's *The Marriage Market* (*Leányvásár*, 1913, Lord Hurlingham) and *Betty* (1914, Lord Playne). He subsequently appeared in *The Happy Day* (1916, Captain), *Pamela* (1917, Toby Woodhouse) and *The Kiss Call* (1919, Allsop Bibby), until the pre-show tippling which had long aided his amiable, laid-back comedy style rendered him unemployable.

He subsequently appeared in *Hitchy-Koo*, with Raymond Hitchcock, and in the musical comedy *Be Yourself* (1924, Joseph Peabody Prescott) in America, where he also created the rôle of *Gentlemen Prefer Blondes*'s Sir Francis Beekman in the non-musical theatre version of Anita Loos' novel (1926), but he did not again return to the London musical stage.

His American-born wife **Eva Kelly** (b Lockhaven, Pa, 18 September 1880; d Los Angeles, 16 March 1948), who had begun her musical career in the chorus of the Alice Nielsen opera company and at the Casino Theater (*The Rounders* etc), went to Britain and the Continent with the Casino company, playing in *An American Beauty* and *The Casino Girl* in London, and *The Belle of New York* (Mamie Clancy) through Europe, and she remained in Britain to take over from Florence Collingbourne as Nancy in *The Toreador*. She appeared as Nephele Noggs in *Naughty Nancy*, and then, with Huntley, in soubrette rôles of varying sizes in the London *Kitty Grey* (Sadie), *Three Little Maids* (t/o Venetia), *The School Girl* (t/o Mrs Marchmont), *Mr Popple* (t/o Louise), *Miss Hook of Holland* (Gretchen), *My Mimosa Maid* (Mme de Pilaine), *The Hon'ble Phil* (Didine), *Kitty Grey* on Broadway, *Betty* (Rawlins) and *The Happy Day* (Luna d'Étoile).

Their son, G P Huntley jr, was also an actor, who made occasional appearances on the musical stage (*The Golden Moth*, *Gay Divorce* etc).

1897 **Turpin à la Mode** (H C Barry/w 'George Grey' [ie George Graves]) Royalty Theatre, Chester 29 March

HURGON, Austen A [HORGAN, Richard Cornelius] (b Netherlands, 1867; d Folkestone, 24 June 1941). Director and librettist for several successful West End musicals of the 1900s and 1910s.

Hurgon began his career as an actor and appeared in a supporting rôle in the musical *Miss Wingrove* (1905, Alberto), which he produced and directed in conjunction with Frank Curzon. Curzon then employed him to direct *The White Chrysanthemum* (1905) and *The Girl Behind the Counter* (1906), and he subsequently became stage director for the producer at the Prince of Wales Theatre. When Paul Rubens fell ill during the preparation of *Miss Hook of Holland*, Curzon brought Hurgon in to complete the writing of the piece, and the success that the show, which Hurgon also directed, achieved, led to his collaborating with Rubens on its successor, *My Mimosa Maid*. However, both *The Three Kisses* (1907) and *My Mimosa Maid* (1908) which he directed for Curzon were failures, and the alliance ended. Hurgon directed *The Hon'ble Phil* (1908) for *Miss Hook* star G P Huntley, and then made another attempt at producing when he took on the management of the failing musical *Two Merry Monarchs* (1909), which he had also directed. His management lasted four performances.

Hurgon subsequently went to the London Hippodrome, where he directed the famous revue *Hullo, Ragtime!* and its sequels for Albert de Courville, and wrote both revue books and the libretti for the one-act operettas which were included in those revues for a period. He also penned a travesty of his own revue hit in the Chiswick Empire revue *What Ho! Ragtime*. At the same time, he found himself in demand as a director in New York, and in 1910 he mounted two musicals with British connections, Ivan Caryll's *Marriage à la Carte* and Leslie Stuart's *The Slim Princess*, on Broadway.

In 1915 he began an association with producers Grossmith and Laurillard, directing *Tonight's the Night* for Broadway and London, and following up with *Theodore & Co* and with *Yes, Uncle!*, both, like the first, considerable successes. He also continued to write, in collaboration with George Arthurs, and their musicals *Suzette*, the English version of *Arlette*, *Yes, Uncle!* (taken from Armont and Nancey's *Le Truc du Brésilien*), and *The Girl for the Boy*, adapted from Paul Gavault's *La Petite Chocolatière* as a vehicle for Gina Palerme, all had good to fine runs.

He tried production/direction again with Ivor Novello's comic opera *The Golden Moth* (1921), and with his own musical *His Girl* (1922), but although they suceeded better than his first attempts, neither was a *Miss Hook* or a *Hullo, Ragtime!* and, thereafter, he retired from the musical theatre scene.

1907 **Miss Hook of Holland** (Paul Rubens/w Rubens) Prince of Wales Theatre 31 January

1908 **My Mimosa Maid** (Rubens/w Rubens) Prince of Wales Theatre 21 April

1911 **The Eternal Waltz** (Leo Fall) 1 act London Hippodrome 22 December

1913 **Arms and the Girl** (Richard Fall) 1 act London Hippodrome 29 April

1913 **The Blue House** (Emmerich Kálmán) 1 act London Hippodrome 28 October

1916 **Girl Wanted** (w Herbert C Sargent) 1 act

1917 **Suzette** (Max Darewski, George Arthurs) Globe Theatre 29 March

1917 **Arlette** (Jane Vieu, Novello, Guy Lefeuvre/w Arthurs) English version (Shaftesbury Theatre)

1917 **Yes, Uncle!** (Nat D Ayer/Clifford Grey/w Arthurs) Prince of Wales Theatre 29 December

1919 **The Girl for the Boy** (Howard Carr, Bernard Rolt/Percy Greenbank/w Arthurs) Duke of York's Theatre 23 September

1922 **His Girl** (M Darewski, Ernest Longstaffe/C E Burton/w F W Thomas) Gaiety Theatre 1 April

HUSZKA, Jenő   (b Szeged, 24 April 1875; d Budapest, 2 February 1960). One of the earliest, most successful and longest active composers of Hungarian musical theatre.

Huszka studied music in Budapest and Paris and worked originally as a violinist. He was later employed at the Hungarian Ministry of Culture, and it was there that he first made contact with the playwright and librettist Ferenc Martos, who would be his most fruitful collaborator.

He made his first contribution as a theatre composer at the age of 24, when he supplied the songs and incidental music for Adolf Mérei's short musical play *Tilos a bemenet* at the Magyar Színház, and his first full-scale operett, *Bob*

herceg, with a libretto by Martos and another established writer, Károlyi Bakonyi, was staged three years later at the Népszinház. *Bob herceg* proved to be the most successful Hungarian operett produced to date, and Huszka went on to compose several other major successes – *Aranyvirág, Gül Baba, Nemtudomka* (played in Vienna as *Die Patronesse vom Nachtcafé*), *Lili bárónő* and, 40 years after his first great success, *Mária főhadnagy* – many of which have remained in the repertoire in Hungary up to the present day, without being heard further afield.

1899 **Tilos a bemenet** (Adolf Mérei) 1 act Magyar Színház 2 September

1902 **Bob herceg** (Károly Bakonyi, Ferenc Martos) Népszinház 20 December

1903 **Aranyvirág** (Martos) Király Színház 6 November

1905 **Gül Baba** (Martos) Király Színház 9 December

1907 **Tündérszerelem** (Martos) Népszinház 20 December

1909 **Rébusz báró** (Ferenc Herczeg) Király Színház 20 November

1914 **Nemtudomka** (Zsolt Harsányi/Bakonyi) Király Színház 14 January

1919 **Lili bárónő** (Martos) Városi Színház 7 March

1926 **Hajtóvadászat** (Martos) Városi Színház 22 October

1939 **Erzsébet** (László Szilágyi) Magyar Színház 5 January

1941 **Gyergyói bál** (Szilágyi) Magyar Színház 4 January

1942 **Mária főhadnagy** (Szilágyi) Fővárosi Operettszinház 23 September

1955 **Szép juhászné** (Károly Kristóf) Nemzeti Színház, Szeged 8 May

1955 **Szabadság, szerelem** (Mór Jókai ad Gyula Háy) Fővárosi Operettszinház 1 April

Biography: Huszka, A M: *Szellő szárnyán* (Zenemükiadó, Budapest, 1977)

HYLTON, Jack   (b Great Lever, Lancs, 2 July 1892; d London, 29 January 1965). Busy, canny producer in all areas of the postwar London theatre.

Originally a pianist and subsequently one of Britain's most popular dance-band leaders of the 1930s, Hylton gave up his band in 1940 and switched to theatrical production for a second, and equally successful, career. His first musical theatre production was the popular wartime musical comedy *Lady Behave* (1941), and he followed up with a mass of both musical and straight theatre productions, including revivals of *The Merry Widow, The Lilac Domino* and *Irene, Follow the Girls*, the pasticcii *Can-Can* and *Romany Love*, and London's productions of *High Button Shoes, Kiss Me, Kate, Call Me Madam, Paint Your Wagon, Wish You Were Here, Pal Joey, Wonderful Town, Kismet, Oh, My Papa!, Simply Heavenly* and *When in Rome*, and a mass of revue and variety productions, notably those of the Crazy Gang at the Victoria Palace.

Most of his musical productions were reproductions of proven, usually imported, material and he mounted very few original pieces (*Bet Your Life, Happy as a King, School*). Even his most successful single show, the British musical *Salad Days*, was brought in from an independent production in Bristol, in collaboration with the firm of Linnit and Dunfee.

In earlier days Hylton also composed the music for a musical play *Mutt and Jeff*, produced by Alexander Loftus and Wilfred Jessop at the King's Theatre in Hammersmith (Con West/Bud Fisher).

HYLTON, Millie   *see* LIND, LETTY

I

I CAN GET IT FOR YOU WHOLESALE Musical in 2 acts by Jerome Weidman based on his novel of the same name. Music and lyrics by Harold Rome. Shubert Theater, New York, 22 March 1962.

Weidman wrote the novel *I Can Get It for You Wholesale* (1937) at the age of 22, basing it on a real-life character, a bankrupt young dress manufacturer who had gone astray in the unreal world of paper finance in the 1930s, and whom he had encountered during his teen years working as an accountant's clerk.

The charming Harry Bogen (Elliott Gould) of the musical comedy version of the book is an unprincipled, egoistic go-getter. He makes his way up the money ladder by wickedly taking advantage of a labour strike to provide privately the services the strikers refuse, backed by cash wooed from rich and loving Ruthie (Marilyn Cooper). He does down his best friend (James Hickman) by selling him a half of what he knows will soon be a worthless company, and he woos away the designer (Ken LeRoy), salesman (Harold Lang) and secretary (Barbra Streisand) from his old boss to start his own nastily competitive dress firm. He throws money about to set his business going, acquires a Broadway showgirl (Sheree North), then proceeds to milk the company's bank accounts whilst making sure that someone else is lined up for the blame. When everything goes bust, Harry is theoretically clean, and he goes back to his first employer to await a fresh start with the money won from marrying Ruthie.

Harold Rome's score, which made no concessions to the 1930s, included few obvious numbers. Harry expounded his uncompromising business creed in 'The Way Things Are', his reasonably perspicacious Momma (Lillian Roth) warned Ruthie not to expect too much 'Too Soon', and the girl hinted at a first-act marriage in 'Who Knows?', but the number which proved the show's solo highlight was the lament of the taken-for-functional secretary 'Miss Marmelstein'. As sung by the 19-year-old Barbra Streisand, wife-to-be to the leading man and, like him, making her Broadway début in a principal rôle, it marked the beginning of what was to be a notable career.

David Merrick's production of *I Can Get It for You Wholesale* played 300 performances on Broadway, but the show did not establish itself as the kind of success which would go on to productions in other centres. It was, however, revived in 1991 by New York's American Jewish Theater (Susan Bloch Theater 23 February).

Recording: original cast (Columbia)

ICH HAB' MEIN HERZ IN HEIDELBERG VERLOREN Singspiel in 3 acts by Bruno Hardt-Warden and Fritz Löhner-Beda. Lyrics by Ernst Neubach. Music by Fredy Raymond. Volksoper, Vienna, 29 April 1927.

Ich hab' mein Herz in Heidelberg verloren was a musical christened after Fred(y) Raymond's successful 1925 song of the same title, a song which became an international hit as 'I Left My Heart in Heidelberg'. The number in question was used as the keystone of a score of which another part was made up of arrangements of existing folk tunes and student songs, in the fashion of the days of Zaytz and his contemporaries, 60 or 70 years earlier.

The story into which the famous song was slipped was a fairly conventional operettic one, with more than a touch of *Hoheit tanzt Walzer* and other such pieces to its outline. Max Schneckenroither (Heinz Kroegler), philosophy student and poet, and Karl Wilhelmi (Otto Glaser), law student, share rooms whilst they attend Heidelberg University in the year of 1825. Max is beloved by the innkeeper, Veronika Laubenthaler (Steffi Walidt), but he dreams romantically over a picture of the Princess Auguste (Paula Bäck), child of the local duke. When the Duke (Géza Brand) and his court visit the University, Auguste, her lady Christiane (Vally Frank) and their company are freed to spend some time with the students. The young folk gather at Veronika's inn, and when a song contest is proposed, the starry-eyed Max wins himself a kiss from his dreamgirl with his rendition of 'I Left My Heart...'. But the royal afternoon of freedom is soon over, and if Christiane and Karl have some hope that they may see each other again, Max knows he will be left with only the memory of the kiss. His heart will remain in Heidelberg all his days. The supporting rôle of Hieronymus Strudelmayer was played by former star juvenile Josef König.

Directed by Rainer Simons, conducted by Oskar Jascha, and choreographed with a ballet 'Reigen' in the second act by Grete Führer, the show proved to be well liked in its first run at the Volksoper, was filmed in 1927 with Werner Fütterer and Dorothea Wieck starred, was seen at the Bürgertheater (30 March 1928), where it passed its 300th Viennese performance, and then, briefly, at the Carltheater (2 July 1928), with Mimi Vesely and Otto Storm featured. It was revived in Vienna in 1946.

Warden, Beda and the Volksoper were not the only, nor even the first, to capitalize on the title of the hit song. The Leipzig Kleines Theater came out with a Thilo Schmidt Volksstuck of the same name in September 1926.

DIE IDEALE GATTIN Operette in 3 acts by Julius Brammer and Alfred Grünwald. Music by Franz Lehár. Theater an der Wien, Vienna, 11 October 1913.

Die ideale Gattin was the second, and probably the most successful, of the three Operetten produced to more or less the same Franz Lehár score, which had begun its life as an appendage to *Der Göttergatte* (Operette in a Vorspiel and two acts, Carltheater 20 January 1904). *Der Göttergatte*, which followed on behind Lehár's first real success with *Der Rastelbinder*, was set in Ancient Greece, and Victor

Léon and Leo Stein's libretto was a version of the Amphytrion legend purposely written 'in the style of the Offenbachiade'. Working on the Boccaccio principle that the best way to find a tale is to live it oneself, Jupiter (Willy Bauer) and Mercury (Friderich Becker) go down to earth to find themselves the subject-matter for a new Olympian Operette. Juno (Mizzi Günther) is wise to her husband's antics, however, and when the two Olympian mashers disguise themself as Amphytrion (Karl Streitmann) and his valet Sofias (Louis Treumann), she takes the place of Alcmene, Amphytrion's wife, and allows herself to be seduced by her own husband. If the book had something of the frothy foolery of opéra-bouffe about it, however, Lehár's score was not a burlesque one, and it was this apparent failure on the composer's part to adapt his style to the right kind of humour that, later, made Léon doubt whether the man who had composed *Der Rastelbinder* was the right collaborator for him on *Die lustige Witwe*.

Der Göttergatte proved something of a disappointment, and played only 37 consecutive performances on its first run, followed by a German production and a Hungarian version (*Mulató istenek* ad Jenő Heltai, Maygar Színház 10 February 1905), neither of which did anything to boost its popularity to the level attained by *Der Rastelbinder*. However, a revised version was remounted on 25 March 1905, and the show remained in the repertoire at the Carltheater until as late as 1913, when Lehár reclaimed and reused this first of the many wasted scores which he would, during his career, recycle to a different libretto. His revised music was attached to a new book by Brammer and Grünwald which, although it was now set in Spain, retained the same premise of the wife winning her own husband (it was an almost tiresomely popular theme added, notably, to *Die Fledermaus* in its conversion from *Le Réveillon*) as the *Göttergatte* book.

With the Theater an der Wien's new star tenor, Hubert Marischka, in the rôle of the Visconde Pablo de Cavaletti, supported by a top-line cast including soubrette Luise Kartousch (Carmen), comic Ernst Tautenhayn (Don Gil de Tenorio de Sevilla), Otto Storm (Sergius Sartrewsky-Goifrin) and Mizzi Günther, who had played in the original *Göttergatte* nearly a decade earlier once again in the principal soprano rôle of Elvira, the 'perfect' wife, *Die ideale Gattin* was played for 105 consecutive performances. It was a respectable rather than a good run (*Eva*, two years earlier, had run twice as long), and although the show was subsequently played at the Raimundtheater for a few performances with Ludwig Herold, Rosa Mittermardi, Therese Tautenhayn and Anton Matscheg, then in Hungary (*Tökéletes feleség* [later *A tökeletes asszony*], Király Színház 26 November 1913) and, with some considerable success, in Germany with Else Adler featured in its title-rôle, it did not establish itself as an enduring repertoire piece.

The second metamorphosis of the show took place another seven years on. Brammer and Grünwald's libretto was amended to take Lehár to the Argentine and the then fashionable world of the tango – a Hispanic shift of venue which meant that the names of some of the characters did not even have to be changed. Produced by Herbert Trau at the Apollo-Künstlertheater, *Die Tangokönigin* (Operette in 3 acts, 9 September 1921 and advertised as being 'mit teilweiser Benützung von Motiven aus der *Idealen Gatten*') followed, again, the same basic plot to which the score had

always been attached. Manolita (Ida Russka) needs to sprighten the failing ardour of her husband, Graf Leandro de Cavaletti (Robert Nästlberger), so, like *Quality Street*'s Phoebe, she pretends to be her own, highly seductive, sister, and by woman's wiles reawakens her husband's lust. Josef König (Don Gil di Tenorio), Eugen Günther (Marquese Columbus de Serranti), Willi Strehl (Sergius Sartrewski) and Mme Olga Bartos-Trau (Coletta) completed the principal cast, and Lehár himself conducted a performance which showed novelty films in the interval, in the variety tradition of the Apollo. After two and a half months the piece gave way to Granichstädten's *Indische Nächte* and, whilst Hungary braved the third version of Lehár's score (*Tangokiralynő* ad Ernő Kulinyi 23 July 1923), Germany this time passed.

I DO! I DO! Story of a marriage in 2 acts by Tom Jones based on Jan de Hartog's play *The Fourposter*. Music by Harvey Schmidt. 46th Street Theater, New York, 5 December 1966.

A two-handed musical play set in the bedroom of the home of Michael (Robert Preston) and Agnes (Mary Martin), *I Do! I Do!* followed the pair through half a century of married life. Starting with their youthful wedding-night and passing through two doses of childbirth (off-stage – this was 1966!), professional success, brief infidelity for him and difficulties and fury for her, it included all the other little ups and downs of everyday life in a picture of a marriage which is, for all that we see here largely just its most colourful moments, based on a real affection. The children get married, Michael and Agnes are brought closer together by being once again on their own, and ultimately they leave their big house and the four-poster bed, in which they have spent 50 years together, for the use of the next generation.

Schmidt and Jones's songs and duets illustrated happily what was, in its essence, a warmly simple tale, with the couple's loving duet 'My Cup Runneth Over' proving the highlight of the score. Michael sang and danced a tipsily barefoot, night-shirted wedding-night 'I Love My Wife', Agnes had a showy moment threatening, with the help of a garish hat, to become 'Flaming Agnes', the pair bickered in 'Nobody's Perfect', and contrasted dreams ('When the Kids Get Married') and reality ('The Father of the Bride', 'What is a Woman') before finally bidding farewell to 'This House'.

David Merrick's Broadway production of *I Do! I Do!* ran for 561 performances, and, as it ran on, a London production was mounted by H M Tennent with Anne Rogers and Ian Carmichael featured. It ran for 115 performances. The show's one-set, two-star-character dimensions helped to make it a popular piece in regional houses, and London saw it for a second time when Rock Hudson and Juliet Prowse appeared in a brief season at the Phoenix Theatre in 1976. Australia saw the musical first in 1969, for a three months' Sydney season followed by a similar run in Melbourne (Her Majesty's Theatre 21 June 1969) with Stephen Douglass and Jill Perryman starred, and later, for a second time, in a 1976 revival at the Marian Street Theatre, Sydney (21 July 1976). A German-language version (ad Peter Goldbaum, Walter Brandin) was produced

Plate 134. **I Do! I Do!** *Carol Burnett and Rock Hudson say the words that bind in the St Louis Muny's production of Schmidt and Jones's musical comedy of marriage.*

initially in Düsseldorf in 1968. In 1982 *I Do! I Do!* was filmed for American television with Lee Remick and Hal Linden in its rôles.

UK: Lyric Theatre 16 May 1968; Germany: Schauspielhaus, Düsseldorf *Das musikalisches Himmelbett* 24 August 1968; Australia: Theatre Royal, Sydney 15 February 1969
Recordings: original cast (RCA), London cast (RCA), Japanese cast (Toshiba), German cast (Ariola).

I'D RATHER BE RIGHT   Musical show in 2 acts by George S Kaufman and Moss Hart. Lyrics by Lorenz Hart. Music by Richard Rodgers. Alvin Theater, New York, 2 November 1937.

One of the run of 1930s American musicals (this one called itself successively 'a revue' and 'a musical show') written and staged by men who had apparently decided that the field of national politics was a fertile one for musical comedy subject-matter, *I'd Rather Be Right* went so far as to present on stage ('with merriment rather than vicious satire') a character who represented the current President of the United States, Franklin D Roosevelt. Any real sting that might have been intended in this lampoon of the New Deal was, however, removed by the casting of George M Cohan, the ageing musical comedy megastar and former business partner of producer Sam H Harris, in the rôle of the President of the United States in a story which had two young lovers (Austin Marshall, Joy Hodges) petitioning the President to balance the budget so that the boy can have a raise in wages(!) and they can get married. The President's comical efforts to find ways to raise money, beginning with a call to women to give up cosmetics and ending with a broadcast White House Jamboree Hour, made up much of the evening's revusical entertainment.

Although the show's four writers were all Roosevelt supporters, they had unfortunately chosen a man to impersonate him who, although in many ways an inspired choice, was not. He was, likewise, not at home with 1930s musical comedy styles in songwriting, which were far from the driving ditties which he had written for his own greatest shows. On the run-in to Broadway, Cohan not only edged in as much as he could of the old-style Cohan, he also decided, unilaterally, to rewrite some lines in one of his songs ('Off the Record') to his own political colour, assuring, via an audience aside, that his lines were known to be his own. The writers exploded, but the newspapers, who were covering every step in the development of this well-publicized show – which was doing what no other country would ever think of doing, in showing its leader in mildly critical song and dance – had a field day.

I'd Rather Be Right was ultimately met on Broadway with modified rapture. It was almost entirely political and topical in its text and songs, and thus of limited interest to many theatregoers, and, in any case, the subject-matter had not propelled the composers to some of their easiest efforts. 'Have You Met Miss Jones?', the nearest thing to a purposeless number in the piece, was, perhaps not surprisingly, also the nearest to being a success. Cohan himself who 'aroused wild applause with each new song and each familiar and beloved step' had 'Off the Record' and 'Tune Up, Bluebird' in which to score, as well as joining in the title trio with the two young people. Other actors were recognizable as members of Congress, notably Taylor Holmes as Treasurer Morgenthau crooning out a plea to the nation to buy 'A Baby Bond', whilst the Supreme Court, headed by Chief Justice Johnny Cherry, disported themselves in 'Not Such Innocent Fun'. *I'd Rather Be Right* played five and a half months at the Alvin Theater before transferring to the little Music Box to run out the last of its 290 performances.

IGNACE   Opérette in 3 acts by Jean Manse. Music by Roger Dumas. Théâtre des Variétés, Marseille, 1935; Théâtre de la Porte-Saint-Martin, Paris, 4 February 1936.

Ignace was a vaudevillesque piece written as a stage vehicle for the music-hall and film star Fernandel by his brother-in-law Jean Manse, who had previously written lyrics for a number of the films in which the comedian had appeared. It was produced at Marseille in 1935, with Fernandel cast in the military-vaudeville character so popular on the French stage of an exorbitantly innocent and foolish private soldier, mixed up in a network of fidelities and, mostly only attempted, infidelities. Colonel Durozier looks sideways at the danseuse Loulette, his boomingly authoritarian wife attracts the comical Baron des Orfraies, his niece Monique (Simone Rouvière) sighs after the young lawyer Serge de Montroc but is being tied up with Captain Boisdelisle, whilst little Ignace himself gets friendly with their maid Annette.

Dumas's suitably music-hally score consisted largely of dance-rhythmed ballads and a love duet for the principal girl (the foxtrot/blues 'Un mari', the waltz 'Lequel des deux?', the letter song 'Je vous écris ces quelques mots'), and of comical numbers for the star (Java des p'tits galons, the one-step 'Quelle famille!', two duets with his Annette,

Plate 135. **Ignace** *is Fernandel.*

a reprise of Monique's waltz and a last-act waltz of his own). There was also a one-step for Mlle Loulette and a dance called La Mexicana.

Originally intended for the Théâtre Mogador, the piece was forced by circumstances to move from Marseille to the big Théâtre de la Porte-Saint-Martin, but there, largely thanks to the appeal of the popular young comedian, it scored an undeniable success with a run of almost a year. Fernandel subsequently filmed the show alongside Andrex and Nita Raya, and returned to Paris in 1947 to star in a revival of a revised two-act version at the Théâtre de l'Étoile.

Film: 1937
Recording: complete w Fernandel (Decca)

IHRE HOHEIT DIE TÄNZERIN Operette in 3 acts by Richard Bars and Oskar Felix. Music by Walter Goetze. Bellevue Theater, Stettin, 8 May 1919.

The 18th-century Herzogin von Tyllberg disguises herself as a Spanish dancer called Marietta and, in that disguise, wins and tests the love of the officer Hans von Mayburg. In parallel to this main romantic plot, her steward's nephew Bolko von Wellhofen falls in love with a girl he thinks is the Countess's maid, only to find out in the end that she is really the Baroness Helma. Goetze's score and the star rôle of the Countess were highlighted by the song 'Im Rausch des Glücks' and the duo 'Dich hat Frau Venus geboren', and the show gave the composer his first and most considerable stage success.

After a fine reception in Stettin and in Hanover, *Ihre Hoheit die Tänzerin* was taken to Berlin the following year and mounted at the Thalia-Theater (22 June 1920). It transferred to the Friedrich-Wilhelmstädtisches Theater before passing its 100th night (29 September), and ran on there until 13 May, totalling nearly 300 performances. A Viennese production at Erich Müller's Johann Strauss-Theater with Elly Kreith as the Countess, Gisa Kolbe as

Helma, Georg Kober as Hans and Fritz Imhoff as Bolko, played for 86 performances in 1922.

The show has continued to appear intermittently in German theatres, and a revised version was produced in 1952.

Austria: Johann Strauss-Theater 7 July 1922

L'ÎLE DE TULIPATAN Opéra-bouffe in 1 act by Henri Chivot and Alfred Duru. Music by Jacques Offenbach. Théâtre des Bouffes-Parisiens, Paris, 30 September 1868.

Even after the success of his full-length opéras-bouffes and the disappearance of the constrictions which had limited him in earlier days to writing and producing one-act pieces with tiny casts, Offenbach continued to turn out musical playlets of the kind with which he had originally made his fame. Of those few written in the last dozen years of his life, the most widely successful was the mini opéra-bouffe *L'Île de Tulipatan*.

Chivot and Duru's libretto was a full-strength, crazy burlesque based on that favourite theme, that things are seldom what they seem, which overflowed with sexual ambiguity, treated, as was usual at this time, with a laughing freedom rather than the pink-lipped purposefulness of a century later. The action was extravagantly set on the island of Tulipatan, '24,000 sea-miles from Nanterre, 473 years before the invention of the spittoon'. Alexis (Mlle Castello), son and heir of King Cacatois XXII (Berthelier), is actually a girl, whom the seneschal, Romboïdal (Bonnet), has had brought up as a boy for dynastic reasons. Hermosa (Victor), Romboïdal's daughter, on the other hand, is a boy whom his mother, Théodorine (Mme Thierret), has brought up as a girl to avoid military service. Bouffe bit by bouffe bit, sexes and things get sorted out and, by the end, the two can be wed.

L'Île de Tulipatan was musically more substantial than some of the very shortest Offenbach pieces, with a score of a dozen numbers that included Cacatois's zany and incidental burlesque barcarolle ('Dans Venezia la belle') and the Couplets du canard ('Prince doux et fort debonair') in which the monarch denies the bad press he has been getting, Théodorine's nonsensically important-sounding excuse for an exit ('Je vais chercher les petites cuillières'), a lively piece for the 'girl' ('Vive le tintamarre') and a pretty one for the 'boy' ('J'ai perdu mon ami'), as well as three duets.

Tulipatan was a success first up in Paris, and it was seen the following year in Germany (ad Emil Pohl), in Hungary (ad Emil Follinusz) and in Austria (ad Julius Hopp), where it was staged on double-bills with *Die schöne Galathee* or *Flotte Bursche* with a royal cast featuring Josef Matras (Cactus), Hermine Meyerhoff (Oleander), Karl Blasel (Ficus) and Therese Schäfer (Aloe) for the earliest of 35 performances in four years in the repertoire at the Carltheater. It also made its way to Britain, where it was played first at Leeds and then at the Opera Comique as an afterpiece to *Le Canard à trois becs* as *Kissi-Kissi* (ad F C Burnand), subtitled 'a Persian operatic bouffonerie', with Pattie Laverne appearing in the title-rôle. It was 'better received by the audience than anything ever produced at the Opera Comique', maintained on the bill when the main piece was withdrawn, and brought back later in the year. In Australia, when the piece was finally shown there, it was in a different version, entitled *Alexis*, played by Amy Horton's burlesque company with the lady as Alexis and John L Hall as Cactus. America, on the other hand, seems, curiously, to have passed the piece by.

In Europe, *L'Île de Tulipatan* won numerous revivals over the years, being, amongst others, revived at the Carltheater by Franz Steiner (24 January 1889) with a cast including Karl Streitmann (Azalea/Hermosa), Wilhelm Knaack (Ficus/Romboïdal) and Frln Seebold (Oleander/Alexis), given at the Berlin Opera in 1917, and at the Vienna Staatsoper in 1918. In Hungary it appeared under a different title (*XII Cactus*) in 1891, but apparently in the same Follinusz translation in which it had been originally played 30 years earlier in Arad. The piece was most recently played in Paris in 1982, originally at the Festival du Marais and subsequently at the Théâtre de la Gaîté-Montparnasse (16 July), with Christian Pernot, Kay Fender and Pierre Jacquemont.

Germany: Friedrich-Wilhelmstädtisches Theater 21 July 1869; Austria: Carltheater *Tulipatan* 5 May 1869; UK: Leeds *King Kokatoo, or Who is who and which is which?* 4 March 1872, Opera Comique *Kissi-Kissi* 12 July 1873; Hungary: Arad 1869, Budai Színkör *Tulipatan szigete* 6 June 1872, *XII Cactus (herceg)* 1891; Australia: St George's Hall, Melbourne *Alexis* 3 June 1886

Recording: complete (TLP)

ILLYA DARLING

ILLYA DARLING Musical in 2 acts by Jules Dassin based on his film screenplay *Never on Sunday*. Lyrics by Joe Darion. Music by Manos Hadjidakis. Mark Hellinger Theater, New York, 11 April 1967.

The enormous success of the film *Never on Sunday*, from which Melina Mercouri's performance as a Greek prostitute and Manos Hadjidakis's hit-parade-worthy title-song emerged memorably, prompted author Jules Dassin and United Artists to bring a fully musicalized version of the show to Broadway. Mercouri starred in her film rôle as the free-living and paid-loving Illya of the title (which had nothing to do with Russian spies, as British *Man from Uncle* watchers might have thought) who is lit upon by a well-meaning American teacher called Homer Thrace (Orson Bean) who attempts to turn her into a virtuous creature. It is soon obvious that a conventionally 'virtuous' life does not come naturally to Illya and, ultimately, even Homer has to admit that it is right for the unhappy harlot to go uncomplicatedly back to her old job.

Hadjidakis supplemented his film song with four more for the star, two of which used the word 'love' in the title, a couple for the leading man ('Golden Land', 'I Think She Needs Me') and some lively Greek pieces for the lively Greek characters who peopled the rest of a sex-centred story, a story which began to the sound of bouzouki music and ended to a massed 'Ya chara'. Titos Vandis performed a title-song which did not make up for the loss of the better known *Never on Sunday* as the show's title.

As in the case of the film, the now widely popular 'Never on Sunday' and the performance of Miss Mercouri proved the highlights and the drawcards of the show, aided a little by the fairly sustained (political) newsworthiness of composer Hadjidakis. The colourful Kermit Bloomgarden/United Artists production held the stage for 320 Broadway performances, but the musical did not ever succeed in obliterating memories of a film version which was perhaps

a little too close in the recent past. A German version (ad Robert Gilbert) was staged at Düsseldorf in 1969, and Mexico hosted a Spanish-language version which helped itself to a vernacular version of the more famous title, *Nunca en Domingo*.

Germany: Schauspielhaus, Düsseldorf 24 May 1969

Recordings: original cast (United Artists), Mexican cast (Private label)

I LOVE MY WIFE

I LOVE MY WIFE Musical in 2 acts by Michael Stewart from a play by Luis Rego. Music by Cy Coleman. Ethel Barrymore Theater, New York, 17 April 1977.

Purchased by Stewart, who had seen it on stage in Paris, the play which became the basis of the Broadway musical *I Love My Wife* was metamorphosed into a likeable, almost four-handed, comic story which gently mocked the permissive age in a tale of attempted wife-sharing in Trenton, New Jersey. The 'almost' came about because author Stewart conceived the idea of involving the orchestra in the action, along with the four principal actors. Thus, the four distinctly oddball musicians who made up the accompanying band wandered in and out of, and commented on, the story in which the endearing and not awfully bright Alvin (Lenny Baker) and his old pal Wally (James Naughton) tentatively set up a festive season foursome. Their mini-orgy collapses under the weight of inexpertness, an intrusive banana cream pie and the ultimate admission that 'I Love My Wife'.

Coleman's lively and catchy score was at is best when able to escape the naïvely sexual subjects imposed by the plot ('Love Revolution', 'Sexually Free', 'Everybody Today is Turning On', 'Married Couple Seeks Married Couple'). It turned out moments both infectiously swinging, as in the chorused 'Hey There, Good Times' and countryfied, as in the duet for the two wives (Joanna Gleason, Ilene Graff) wondering if there was 'Someone Wonderful I Missed' in Nashvillistic harmonies, both gently lilting, as in Alvin's explanation that 'I Love My Wife', or lugubriously comic as in the musicians' whimsical description of 'A Mover's Life'.

Harry Rigby and Terry Allen Kramer's Broadway production was well received, with the lanky, comical Baker winning particular kudos for his portrayal of eager-beaver Alvin, and the show settled down for an 857 performance run. Baker and Naughton were succeeded during the run by the television comedy duo the Smothers Brothers. The show was still running on Broadway when Harold Fielding opened a London version, with television sitcom star Richard Beckinsale (Alvin) and Ben Cross (Wally) featured alongside Deborah Fallender (Cleo) and Liz Robertson (Monica). If the show did not catch on quite as it had in America, it nevertheless ran profitably until Beckinsale left. With Robin (*Confessions of a Windowcleaner*) Asquith replacing, the atmosphere became more panting than endearing and the production closed after 410 performances.

The fact that both Baker and Beckinsale died very prematurely, shortly after their starring spells in *I Love My Wife*, did not deter other producers and actors, and the show's success and its economic proportions won it further English-language showings, including productions in both South Africa, and later (disastrously) in Australia, under the management of Louis Burke.

UK: Prince of Wales Theatre 6 October 1977; Australia: Her Majesty's Theatre, Sydney 22 September 1982

Recordings: Original cast (Atlantic/DRG), South African cast (EMI), Australian cast (Festival)

I MARRIED AN ANGEL Musical comedy in 2 acts by Richard Rodgers and Lorenz Hart adapted from the play *Angyalt vettem feleségül* by János Vaszary. Shubert Theater, New York, 11 May 1938.

Richard Rodgers and Lorenz Hart were first introduced to the Hungarian musical play *Angyalt vettem feleségül* (Király Színház, 23 April 1932, lyrics: Andor Szenes, music: Dawies), which was to become *I Married an Angel*, in 1933, during their second period as Hollywood screen composers at MGM. Following their success with *Love Me Tonight*, Irving Thalberg set the pair to work with playwright Moss Hart to turn the piece, which had been purchased by the studio, into a musical film in which Jeanette MacDonald would play the angel who comes to earth to be the wife of a Budapest banker and shows him that perfection is not always devoutly to be wished for in a wife. The score was written, but the film was cancelled at the last moment.

Some years later, Dwight Deere Wiman, the co-producer of Rodgers and Hart's *On Your Toes* and *Babes in Arms*, succeeded in winkling the stage rights for the piece out of MGM. The songwriters, who had done well enough as self-librettists on *Babes in Arms*, adapted the piece from scratch themselves (it was subsequently given a going over by director Josh Logan), and the resultant show was produced with Dennis King playing the rôle of Walter Palaffi, the banker, and Vera Zorina (who had played in *On Your Toes* in London) appearing as the angel. Since Miss Zorina danced more than she sang, the show contained a solid dance element. She danced gracefully to Balanchine's ballet 'The Modiste' and in a Honeymoon Ballet in the first act, drew comedy from the second-act 'Angel Without Wings', and fooled about in a sea-nymph's costume with the rest of the girls in a burlesque piece which, apropos of nothing at all, sang about what goes on 'At the Roxy Music Hall'.

The short ration of songs went mostly to King, to Vivienne Segal in the rôle of his worldly-wise sister, Countess Peggy Palaffi, who knocks some of the dust off the angel's wings, and to Audrey Christie as Walter's rejected girlfriend, Anna Murphy. King had the pick of the numbers in the flowing title-song, and joined Miss Segal in 'Spring is Here' (a number which had nothing to do with the songwriters' earlier musical of the same name), whilst he and she and Charles Walters queried comically of one another 'Did You Ever Get Stung?'.

I Married an Angel's Broadway life of 338 performances gave Rodgers and Hart their longest New York run since *A Connecticut Yankee* – better than *Babes in Arms* or *On Your Toes* – and the musical went on to tour America through 1939. Perhaps because of the failure there of *On Your Toes*, it was not taken up for London. However, Ernest C Rolls, who had recently come to the top-spot in Australia's all-powerful J C Williamson Ltd, gave the show a lavish production in Melbourne with Jack Arthur (Willy), Helen Denizon (Angel) and Bernice Claire (Peggy) in the starring rôles. It was a spectacular and utter four-week failure. A Sydney season was nevertheless persevered with (Theatre Royal, 13 May 1939) with Katrin Rosselle taking over as the angel, and its equivalent failure – one of the most dire in Australian musical theatre history – shook the foundations of the famous old firm badly.

The tale went back to source when Vaszary produced and directed *I Married an Angel* under its original title (lyrics: Mihály Szécsen) at his Budapest Andrássy Színház whilst the show still ran on Broadway, but otherwise the show's export came only in film form. The film version starred Miss MacDonald and Nelson Eddy, and primped up the score with three new studio-made numbers by Herbert Stothart, a piece called 'Little Work-a-Day World' which Rodgers had written for a play, and a barrage of fresh lyrics from the studio's Wright and Forrest. Rodgers didn't like it, and neither did many other people.

Hungary: Andrássy Színház *Angyalt vettem feleségül* 17 September 1938; Australia: Her Majesty's Theatre, Melbourne 26 November 1938; Film: MGM 1942

Recording: original cast (AEI), film soundtrack (Pelican) etc

I'M GETTING MY ACT TOGETHER AND TAKING IT ON THE ROAD Musical by Gretchen Cryer. Music by Nancy Ford. Anspacher Theater, New York, 16 May 1978; Circle in the Square, 16 December 1978.

The title of Gretchen Cryer and Nancy Ford's five-handed musical largely summed up its content. The central character was Heather Jones (Miss Cryer), 39 years old, a TV afternoon soap actress and singer-songwriter who once made number 89 on the charts. She is putting together a programme of new songs with which to go on tour, accompanied by her Liberated Man's Band and her backing singers Cheryl (Betty Aberlin) and Alice (Margot Rose). Heather's new songs are different to the ones she used to sing. They are tougher and less obviously attractive, and they reflect her own life as an obviously strong, intelligent and independent woman whose personal life has been unsatisfying. By the time she has said her strong, intelligent and independent say and done her thing, during the course of the evening, even her old friend and manager, Joe (Joel Fabiani), is alienated – just another man running away from commitment is the way Heather sees it – but she thinks there may be hope for the future and for that enduring relationship, in the young guitarist, Jake (Don Scardino). If, that is, Heather can ever sustain a one-to-one relationship.

Many of the songs of the show were the songs of Heather's act ('Natural High', 'Miss America', 'Old Friend', 'Feel the Love', 'Lonely Lady'), others illustrated events in her earlier life, but were equally presented as songs written by her. Of these the lightly attractive 'In a Simple Way I Love You', sung here by Jake and representing Heather's younger and more optimistic style of writing and thinking – a style which is for the moment his – proved the pick.

Produced by the New York Shakespeare Festival at the Public Theater, the show was shifted to off-Broadway's Circle in the Square after its initial season and remained there for 1,165 performances, during which time composer Nancy Ford, Carol Hall, composer of the score to *The Best Little Whorehouse in Texas*, and Betty Buckley each took a turn at the rôle of Heather. The handily-sized piece got a wide showing at home and abroad, but largely fared less well outside America. A London version, which showed a number of textual alterations since the original American performances, was sponsored by Celia Bogan Ltd and Richard Denning, with Diane Langton as Heather and Ben Cross as Joe, and failed in 62 performances, whilst an Australian production was mounted by the Sydney Theatre Company with Nancye Hayes featured. A German version (ad Erika Gesell, Helmut Baumann) was produced at Berlin's Schlossparktheater in 1980, and was followed by other German-language productions on smaller stages, and adaptations were seen from Scandinavia to the Orient.

Australia: Recording Hall (Opera House) April 1980; Germany: Schlossparktheater *Ich steig aus und mach ne eigene Show* 18 October 1980; UK: Apollo Theatre 31 March 1981

Recordings: original cast (CBS), London cast (TER), Japanese cast (Sony), Norwegian cast *Det er jo mitt show!* (DNS), Swedish cast *Det av ju min show!* (Europa), Danish cast *I Morgen er jes påkej ...* (Wilhem Hansen) etc.

IM REICHE DES INDRA
Operette in 1 act by Heinrich Bolten-Bäckers and Leopold Ely. Music by Paul Lincke. Apollotheater, Berlin, 18 December 1899.

Im Reiche des Indra was a piece made to order for the specific and spectacular needs of the Berlin Apollotheater, the variety house where the Lincke/Bolten-Bäckers *Frau Luna* had been such a splendid success. This time, instead of going to the moon like the hero of *Frau Luna*, the ordinary Berliner – in this tale reporter Gustave Steinbock – turned up in the almost as far-away kingdom of Brahmaputra, and became mixed up in the affairs of King Menelek and his Queen, Sita. Steinbock helps out the little page, Bhimo, who has been caught out sighing over his mistress, incurs the King's wrath when he photographs Sita in her bath, but ends up improving matters between the ill-matched royal spouses, with the help of some magic rings, before heading back home to his newspaper. The plot was mainly an opportunity for some often revusical songs and some spectacular dance and costume scenes, and *Im Reiche des Indra*, with its three scenes and 'Schlussapotheose' of oriental splendour, fulfilled its purpose on the Apollo programme almost as well as its famous predecessor had done. Lincke's seductive invitation to 'Nimm mich mit in dein Kämmerlein' proved the favourite piece of the score.

In 1903 the Apollotheater company played *Im Reiche des Indra* in their season at Vienna's Danzers Orpheum with Müller (Steinbock), Lucie Medlon (Sita) and Harnisch (Menelek) in the leading rôles, and with the 'electric ballet' 'Leuchtende Brillanten' interpolated into the first act, and in 1906 an Hungarian version was played at Budapest's equivalent of the Apollo, the Royal Orfeum, where Lincke's *Luna asszony*, *Nakiri* and *Vénus a földön* had already been featured.

The show was later readapted by Hans Brennecke into a two-act version on the lines of the enlarged *Frau Luna*, but without the same enduring success. Another 'Neufassung' was mounted at Chemnitz in 1938.

Austria: Danzers Orpheum 14 March 1903; Hungary: Royal Orfeum *Indra* 31 January 1906

IM WEISSEN RÖSSL
Singspiel (Revue-Operette) in 3 acts by Hans Muller based on the play of the same name by Oscar Blumenthal and Gustav Kadelburg. Lyrics by Robert Gilbert. Music by Ralph Benatzky. Additional songs by Robert Stolz, Bruno Granichstädten, Robert Gilbert et al. Grosses Schauspielhaus, Berlin, 8 November 1930.

The Schwank *Im weissen Rössl*, originally produced at Berlin's Lessing-Theater (30 December 1897), was a highly successful comico-romantic play which was revived frequently on German-language stages following its first production. The story is told that director Erik Charell was given the idea of turning it into a musical spectacular when the actor Emil Jannings, who had appeared in Berlin in the piece's starring comic rôle of Giesecke, took the occasion of a luncheon with the director on the lakeside terrace of the real Weisses Rössl hotel in St Wolfgang, in the Austrian Salzkammergut, to lurch into some jokey backchat from the show with a waiter.

The book for the musical *Im weissen Rössl* was reorganized by Charell and rewritten by Hans Müller to fit Charell's and the Grosses Schauspielhaus's large-stage Revue-Operette requirements, the score was composed and collected by Ralph Benatzky, the theatre's house composer, with additional songs from Bruno Granichstädten, Robert Stolz, lyricist Robert Gilbert and others tacked in in the then and there accepted fashion, and the piece was staged with even more than usual in the way of the spectacular accoutrements (if, given the subject, altogether less of the glitter) for which the Schauspielhaus had become famous.

Camilla Spira played Josefa Vogelhuber, the landlady of the *Zum weissen Rössl*, whose amorous sights are set on the handsome city lawyer Otto Siedler, much to the distress of her adoring head-waiter, Leopold (Max Hansen). When Siedler comes to stay at the hotel, Josefa does everything to make his stay comfortable whilst Leopold does just the opposite, and ends up getting himself sacked. But Siedler is unaware of Josefa's attachment and he is soon sighing behind the cowshed with Ottilie (Trude Lieske), the daughter of the belligerent ladies' underwear manufacturer, Giesecke (Otto Wallburg). A commercial marriage is proposed between Ottilie and Sigismund (Sig Arno), son of Giesecke's business competitor, but in the end bald and beautiful Sigismund falls for little, stuttering Klärchen, Siedler gets Ottilie, and, after some homespun truth from no less a guest than the Emperor Franz Josef (Paul Hörbiger) himself, Josefa sees the sense in marrying the adoring Leopold. The musical realigned the emphasis of the piece towards the Josefa/Leopold relationship, rather than, as originally, towards Giesecke and his commercial and family problems, and Leopold, a rôle built in the good, old Girardi mould, became the principal comic character of the piece. There was also a small stand-out comic rôle for a little hotel busboy – something of a mini Hans Moser part – in which Gustl Stark Gstettenbauer pulled the notices in the original production.

The score was a friendly, catchy one, from its yodelling overture and a buzzing opening, with Leopold organizing crowds of tourists in and out of the hotel, to its final waltzing happily-ever-after finale. Leopold serenaded his employer with 'Es muss was Wunderbares sein' and stood his amorous ground, in the face of dismissal, in Granichstädten's delightful 'Zuschau'n kann i net', Josefa welcomed Siedler 'Im weissen Rössl am Wolfgangsee' in waltz time and urged Giesecke into good temper with the thigh-slapping rhythms of 'Im Salzkammergut'. Sigismund wondered over his unobvious (to everyone else) good looks in Gilbert's 'Was kann der Sigismund dafür', the romantic pair wallowed in the tuneful sentimentality of Stolz's 'Die ganze Welt ist himmelblau' and the waltzing 'Mein Liebeslied muss ein Walzer sein', and the Emperor delivered rich philosophy in the Sprechgesang of 'Es ist einmal in Leben so'.

The lavish production, designed by Ernst Stern to include anything and everything Salzkammerguttish that moved, included a boat, a train, an arkful of animals, a vast cast and real rain. All this, added to the charming music and the homely, countrified and familiar tale, made up a combination which was irresistible to Berliners of the Depression years ('Stern catches the gaiety of the country, and the Schuhplattler is a breath of fresh air after all that dreary revue dancing'), and *Im weissen Rössl* scored a huge success through a first run of more than 400 performances.

The Berlin production was still at its peak when the foreign versions of the show started to come thick and fast. The first of these was in London, where Oswald Stoll imported Charell to stage an English adaptation of the show (ad Harry Graham, with plot variations) at the vast London Coliseum. Clifford Mollison (Leopold) and Vienna's Lea Seidl (Josefa) starred, with Bruce Carfax (here anglicized from Otto Siedler into Valentine Sutton) and Rita Page (now the daughter of an English north-country businessman) providing the romantic music, and comedian George Gee as Sigismund. The London version of *White Horse Inn* boosted the popular musical content of the show by adding another song for Mollison. Declaring that, having been sacked, he would go off and join the Foreign Legion, he delivered Graham's version of Robert Stolz's already familiar march song 'Adieu, mein kleiner Garde-offizier', borrowed from the film score *Das Lied ist aus* (1930), as 'Goodbye', and scored, alongside the title song, the hit of the evening. Another Stolz number, 'You Too' ('Auch du wirst mich einmal betrügen'), taken from the film *Zwei Herzen im Dreivierteltakt* (1930), was also added, and his contribution, which had now mounted to four numbers, was judged sufficient by the British publishers of the show to give him a co-composer's credit with Benatzky. The picturesque lashings of Tyrolean scenery, largely reproduced from Stern's Berlin designs, the dancing and the yodelling, and the happy score and story proved equally as popular in London as in Berlin. The show remained in London just over a year and played 650 twice-daily performances in its king-sized home. It was revived at the same theatre during the war with Derek Oldham and Nita Croft (20 March 1940) in the lead rôles.

The London version and staging, with its revolving stage and all, was subsequently produced in Australia. Popular primadonna Strella Wilson starred as Josefa and palliated the part's lack of music by introducing Ivor Novello's song 'Lend Me a Dream'. Arthur Stigant (Giesecke), Charles Norman (Leopold) and Sydney Burchall (Valentine) supported, and the piece was, yet again, a vast hit, playing nearly four months in Sydney and four in Melbourne (Her Majesty's Theatre/King's Theatre 28 July 1934) before being sent out to tour Australia. The cast travelled by one train – the revolve went on ahead on a second.

In Vienna the show was staged at the Stadttheater with Hubert Marischka and Paula Brosig in the leading rôles

and Fritz Imhoff as Giesecke. The 'Blue-Boys' jazz band was heavily featured, there was a 'Wäschentanzer' scene, a 'Schützenfest am Wolfgangsee', a scene on the Bad Ischl esplanade (how did we get there?) featuring a song called 'Ischl' (Anton Paulik/Karl Farkas) and a 'Quodlibet' by the same pair, and there was a second contribution from Granichstädten ('Ich hab' es fünfzigmal geschworen') to swell the decidedly in-and-out score. Again – in spite of some mumbles about the propriety of representing Franz Josef on the musical stage – the show was a huge hit, which ended up alternating no fewer than three Josefas and two Emperors, and it returned two seasons later to pass its 700th Viennese performance during a week's stand at the Theater an der Wien.

Adorján Stella and Imre Harmath's Hungarian version also scored the show's now habitual fine success when it was mounted at Budapest's Király Színház with Márton Rátkai (Giesecke), Emmi Kosáry (Ottilie), Erzi Pechy (Josefa), Jenő Nádor (Siedler), Dezső Kertesz (Leopold), Teri Fejes (Klärchen) and Gyula Kabos (Sigismund) featured, and Josef Jarno, longtime head of Vienna's Theater in der Josefstadt, stealing the show in the rôle of the Emperor.

It was several years before *White Horse Inn* arrived in New York. When it did it was mounted at the enormous Center Theater (ad David Freeman, Irving Caesar) with Kitty Carlisle and William Gaxton starred, with Robert Halliday providing the romance, and with a bundle of the most un-Austrian numbers ever inserted into the score: Will Irwin and Norman Zeno's 'In a Little Swiss Chalet' (!), 'White Souls', 'Leave it to Katarina' and 'I Would Love to Have You Love Me'. It pleased New York for 223 performances.

Meanwhile, however, the Paris production had given the show one of its most successful outings of all. As Stoll had done in London, the Isola Brothers imported Charell to supervise the staging of a version of his singular hit, on the less vast stage of the Théâtre Mogador (ad Lucien Besnard, René Dorin). Again, like Stoll, they used a version of Stern's designs, which had, like the show itself, been once again adapted. As far as the score was concerned, 'Goodbye' had been retained from the London version, but 'You Too' was replaced by a delicious duet 'Je vous emmènerai dans mon joli bateau', a piece gallicized from a 1929 song, 'Am Sonntag will mein Süsser mit mir segeln gehn', written by Robert Gilbert and composed by Anton Profès, which gave the score yet one more highlight. Several numbers from the original score, including Granichstädten's song, had, however, vanished. The comedians Milton (Léopold) and Charpin (Bistagne/Giesecke) and Gabrielle Ristori (Josépha) headed the cast, with André Goavec (Guy Florès/Siedler) and Rose Carday (Sylvabelle/Ottilie) as a pair of sweethearts here turned as French, as the British production had made them British. Paris gave *L'Auberge du Cheval Blanc* its longest run of all, with a first series of over 700 performances, during which Hélène Regelly and Lucien Dorval replaced the original stars, and France also proved to be the show's most appreciative foreign home thereafter.

L'Auberge du Cheval Blanc returned to Paris and the Mogador in 1935. It then migrated to the Châtelet under Maurice Lehmann, where Luc Barney famously took possession of the rôle of Léopold, which he played again in the

1948 and 1953 revivals. The show returned once more in 1960, and in 1968 the Châtelet presented a revised version (ad Marcel Lamy, Jean Valmy) which raked up and replaced in the show the bits of the German score that had got dropped on the way to the definitive French version. Granichstädten's song went back in, along with a heurige song by Hans Frankowski which had become part of the German show in the meantime, and two 'lost' Benatzky pieces. The Mogador repeated the show they had introduced nearly half a century earlier in 1979, and in 1987 Paris had its most recent *Auberge du Cheval Blanc* at the considerably smaller Eldorado, with the ageing Barney now playing Bistagne.

In Vienna, *Im weissen Rössl* was re-introduced at the Volksoper in 1976 (1 March, w Christiane Hörbiger, Peter Minich), where its spectacular side was well catered for but, although Berlin's *Im weissen Rössl* was conceived as a spectacle, and owed much of its original success to its visual side, it has been often and successfully played, since its establishment as an international hit, in much smaller and virtually scenery-free productions without suffering, largely thanks to the positive charm of its Leopold/Josefa tale and the popularity of its well-known score.

Im weissen Rössl has been several times filmed, the first in 1934 with Christl Mardayn, Hermann Thimig and Theo Lingen, the second in 1952 with Hannerl Matz, Walter Müller and Johannes Heesters. The third, a distinctly up-to-date one with Peter Alexander, Waltraud Haus, Adrian Hoven, Gunther Philipp and Karin Dor, is still played daily as a tourist attraction at the cinema in St Wolfgang, just along from the real Weisses Rössl on the Wolfgangsee.

UK: London Coliseum *White Horse Inn* 8 April 1931; Hungary: Király Színház *A 'Fehér Ló'* 20 October 1931; Austria: Wiener Stadttheater 25 September 1931, France; Théâtre Mogador *L'Auberge du Cheval Blanc* 1 October 1932; USA: Center Theater *White Horse Inn* 1 October 1936, Australia: Theatre Royal, Sydney *White Horse Inn* 31 May 1934; Films: Carl Lamac 1934, Willi Forst 1952, Tobik/Jupiter Films

Recordings: complete (various versions) (Amadeo, Eurodisc, HMV), complete French version (EMI, Festival), selections (Telefunken etc), selections in French (CBS, Barclay, Philips etc), selections in English (MFP etc), selections in Italian (EDM, RCA) etc

IN DAHOMEY Negro musical comedy in a prologue and 2 acts by Jesse A Shipp. Lyrics by Paul Laurence Dunbar and others. Music by Will Marion Cook and others. New York Theater, New York, 18 February 1903.

In Dahomey was the first American musical comedy written almost entirely by black writers and played entirely by black artists to be presented at a regular Broadway house, rather than the more fringe establishments which normally catered for such shows and their particular audiences. Conceived specifically to feature the popular vaudeville team of Bert Williams and George Walker, its delightfully free-wheeling libretto portrayed the two comedians as the comical Shylock Homestead, or Shy to his friends (Williams), and Rareback Pinkerton, his buddy and adviser (Walker). The two get involved with the Get-the-Coin Syndicate, led by Hustling Charley (played by author Shipp), which is raising cash to back the Dahomey Colonisation Society set up by Hamilton Lightfoot (Peter Hampton) and his brother Moses (William Barker). The idea is to export all the down-and-out blacks of America

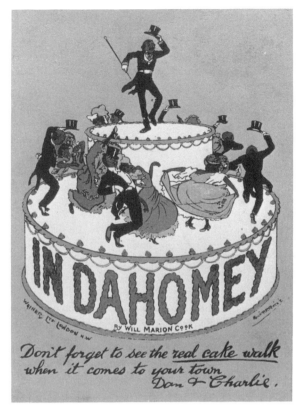

Plate 136.

to a promised land on the African continent. Rareback swindles the money out of the simple Shy, and puts most of it on his own slick back before Nemesis starts to tweak his coat-tails.

The original basic songs of the piece, the majority written by the respected black poet Paul Dunbar and composed by Will Marion Cook, featured such pieces as 'Emancipation Day' (on which 'white folk try to pass fo' coons'), 'The Czar' and a song called 'Society', with lyrics that sounded like Victorian parlour words, but these soon proved insufficient and the score developed as *In Dahomey* developed out of town. With the help of lyricist Cecil Mack, Cook made over his earlier 'The Little Gipsy Maid' to the only barely more coloured-sounding 'Brown-skinned Baby Mine', wrote a waltz song 'Molly Green', and teamed up with James W Johnson on a piece about the 'Leader of the Colored Aristocracy'. The most effective numbers, however, came from other sources: cast member J Leubrie Hill and Frank B Williams's 'My Dahomian Queen', Hill's later addition explaining catchily 'That's How the Cake Walk's Done', Alex Rogers's 'I'm a Jonah Man' and Harry von Tilzer's infectious 'I Wants to Be an Actor Lady' and 'Chocolate Drops' cakewalk. Williams himself supplied the music for a jig.

The show had, in fact, been originally constructed to tour those variety houses which had specifically black audiences, and an eyebrow or two was raised when producers Jules Hurtig and Harry Seamon took the unusual step of opening their show on Broadway. Their gamble did not come off. Williams and Walker were appreciated, but *In Dahomey* – the lingoistic fun of which seemed altogether on a happier level than much of the music and lyrics – was not considered up to very much as a piece, and the producers could not hold it up in New York for more than 53 performances.

A second gamble, however, did work. The whole cast and production of *In Dahomey* was promptly shipped to London, where the show opened less than three months after its Broadway première to a very different reaction. There, where the nearest thing to a black show ever seen was the Christy Minstrels, *In Dahomey* was a genuine novelty, if nothing else in the unbridled energy with which the black artists played ('its vitality, quaint comedians, catchy music, and its unique environment should make it one of the dramatic sensations of the London season'). The show settled in and, boosted very usefully by a command performance at Buckingham Palace for the young Prince's birthday celebration, swelled. Fifteen extra American blacks were brought in to expand the line of the cakewalk dancers, and the cast tasted a kind of theatrical and social success they had never before had through the 251 performances between May and the Boxing Day closure. Later the piece went on tour in Britain, but ultimately the *In Dahomey* folk had to go home, and the bubble burst. The show had no tomorrow, and not until the coming of the fashion for ragtime and revue to the international stage did black artists, again Americans, again win such wide attention, either in Britain or America.

UK: Shaftesbury Theatre 16 May 1903

INDIANA Comic opera in 3 acts by H B Farnie. Music by Edmond Audran. Avenue Theatre, London, 11 October 1886.

After the enormous successes he had won working with Planquette, both on the original *Rip van Winkle* and then with the transformation of *Les Voltigeurs de la 32ème* and *Surcouf* into the long-lived moneymakers *The Old Guard* and *Paul Jones*, the oft-(critically)-despised librettist and director H B Farnie was anything but despised by the French musical establishment. It was announced that he had been signed to write four musicals with no less a composer than Edmond Audran and, eventually, *Indiana* appeared. It was, allegedly, based on a French vaudeville – the title was not disclosed, but the show had been originally announced in mid-1884 as *The Miller of Dee*, which didn't sound very French – which made up into a passable, but not terribly original, comic-opera book.

American Indiana Grayfaunt (American Mathilde Wadman) comes to Civil War England to secretly look over her unknown fiancé, cavalier Philip Jervaulx (W T Hemsley), herself disguised as a cavalier. Jervaulx, under the pressure of current events, is also at this time disguised, hiding as a servant in the house of his cousin (Phyllis Broughton), whose foolish husband, Sir Mulberry Mullitt (Henry Ashley) is actually in charge of finding him. The principal comedy rôle was that of Matt o' the Mill (Arthur Roberts), whose mill Indiana uses as her headquarters and which Mullitt attacks, thinking she is Jervaulx. There was also a sexy sub-plot concerning the designing, lubricious Lord Dayrell (Charles Ryley) and the miller's young wife (Mary Duggan).

Audran wrote an attractive score to the piece, but one which was less obviously popular than the Planquette scores had been, and after the out-of-town try-out the piece

was given a going-over to try to make it more catchily colourful. The up-and-coming comic Roberts was given his head, and some extra material, including a song 'The Plain Potato', composed by musical director John Crook, added to his rôle. He added more himself, but even his popular low comedy efforts failed to make *Indiana* better than a half-success, and it closed after 70 performances. It returned to London briefly (with extra songs again) as a stopgap when a revival of *Madame Favart* was forced to close through star illness. It was also given two tours, as well as a brief showing (32 performances) and a briefer return season (16 performances, 11 July 1888 Wallack's Theater) on Broadway, produced under John McCaull's management with Digby Bell and Lilly Post/Marion Manola starred. It never reached the degree of success hoped for, and the other three musicals did not eventuate.

USA: Star Theater 18 January 1887

INDIGO UND DIE VIERZIG RÄUBER Comic Operette in 3 acts 'by Maximilian Steiner'. Music by Johann Strauss. Theater an der Wien, Vienna, 10 February 1871.

In the early 1870s Johann Strauss, widely famed for his popular orchestral music, was persuaded by his wife and by Maximilian Steiner of the Theater an der Wien to make an attempt to write for the stage. With some guidance from the Theater an der Wien's multi-talented and experienced in-house playwright/lyricist/composer Richard Genée, he at length completed the score for his first Operette, a score which was written to a libretto ultimately cobbled up from the Arabian Nights' tale of 'Ali Baba' by Steiner himself, after several uncredited collaborators and play doctors had failed to get the piece into satisfactory order.

The book of *Indigo und die vierzig Räuber* was flavoured liberally with Offenbachian elements. The heroine, Fantasca (Marie Geistinger), was a Viennese-born maiden, shipwrecked as a child on Macassar's shores, and now become the monarch's favourite bajadere. The country's High Priest, Romadour (Carl Adolf Friese), is another Viennese risen to high place with the help of his native wits, and a third Viennese, the young voyager Janio (né Schani, Albin Swoboda), who is to be the 'hero' and love interest of the piece, makes up the *Ba-ta-clan*nish total of strayed Austrians.

The land ruled over by Indigo (Matthias) is in a shabby state, and practically run – or run down – by his ministers' wives. The court is also threatened by a robber band, and Indigo offers Fantasca as a prize to whomsoever shall rid him of these worrisome intruders. It is Fantasca herself, however, who discovers the secret of the robbers' cave and its 'sesame' key-word, and she resolves to lead the ladies of the harem to the cave, stack up the donkey of the donkey-man, Ali Baba (Jani Szika) with as many sacks of riches as it can carry, and flee. In the event, she finally flees with Janio, leaving the harem in a drugged sleep in the cave of the robbers (who are never seen in this 'version' of the tale!), and after an extra act of quiproquos and a great deal of dancing (Sclaven-Tanz, Mohren-Tanz, Mulatten-Tanz, Tanz-Finale), the pair head off back to the city of their birth.

The most successful single number in the evening's score was a waltz trio for Fantasca, Janio and Romadour, 'Ja, so singt man in der Stadt wo ich geboren', but there was a selection of attractive music to fit all the styles of the

Theater an der Wien's lead players. The romantic pair, Fantasca and Janio, were particularly well-equipped with some virtuoso vocal pieces, including a vast, showy duo, 'Wir haben uns schon gern g'habt', Fantasca's first-act finale aria 'In des Harems Heiligthume' and second-act military number 'Folget eures Ruf und Gebot', and a waltz song for Janio. Toffana, Ali Baba's wife (Frln Stauber), was endowed with an ariette and a romanze in the soubrette style, whilst Ali, at the head of the comical side of things, had several numbers, beginning with his first-act entrance song, and including a duettino with Janio. Elsewhere, the music ran from a bacchanale and valse-brindisi, full of ornaments and runs, to a soldiers' chorus and back, two or three times.

The opening night of the first Operette by the beloved Viennese waltz king was quite an occasion, but the reaction to *Indigo* was at best mixed. The music was admired as music, if not necessarily as theatrical music, but the text came in for heavy criticism. The show was played 46 times at the Theater an der Wien before being withdrawn. Strauss's reputation, however, ensured that it had far more future than many shows with such a track record. Later the same year *Indigo* was played in Graz, then it appeared in Berlin, with its libretto revised by Ernst Dohm, and over the next decade was seen, in various revisions, in Prague, Pressburg, Magdeburg and several other European cities, resurfacing at Berlin's Theater Unter den Linden as late as 1897 in yet another revised version (ad Eduard Jacobson).

In Paris, the unfancied libretto was given more than its usual cosmetic overhaul, and the piece produced as *La Reine Indigo* at the Théâtre de la Renaissance sported a largely different book written by Victor Wilder and Adolphe Jaime. Zulma Bouffar played Fantasca, Vauthier was Romadour, Daniel played Babazouk, Félix Puget was Janio and Madame Alphonsine played the queen of the title, a jealous creature who has vowed to sell off her late husband's harem, a job lot which includes Fantasca. She also has her eyes on Fantasca's beloved Janio. The lad proves of sufficient mettle, however, to duck the Queen's passion, and to reach a happy ending in time for the final curtain. The score of the original *Indigo* was not taken note for note into the new show, and the composer was on hand to provide extra numbers, especially in view of the libretto's introduction of another major feminine character. The bon-bons were there, of course: 'So singt man' even kept its sentiments, letting forth curiously in joyous trio about the Danube and the joys of Vienna, but Babazouk's 'Ronde du marchand des quatre saisons' replaced Miraka's Auftrittslied, 'Geschmiedet fest an starre Felsenwand' gave way to the 'Couplets du merle blanc', Toffana's aria and Janio's waltz song both disappeared, and Fantasca was given a little youp-la! tyrolienne which wasn't familiar. The Queen's rôle was supplied with a new number and, in the final act of the French show, non-*Indigo* music came thick and fast.

Paris did not take with any great vigour to the waltzing Viennese Operette, nor to the book which the French librettists had patched around Strauss's score. Not even a luxurious production could persuade them to favour *La Reine Indigo* for more than 80 performances, although it was brought back for 18 further performances as a compliment to Strauss when the composer visited Paris to conduct, and to negotiate the production of *Die Fledermaus* with the Théâtre de la Renaissance management. If Parisians didn't care overly for *La Reine Indigo*, however, Strauss and his partners clearly did, for a revised German-language version, translated from Wilder and Jaime's French was subsequently produced at the Theater an der Wien as *Königin Indigo* (ad Josef Braun, 9 October 1877) with Marie Stolle (Indigo), Jenny Heisler (Fantasca) Alexander Girardi (Ali Baba), Felix Schweighofer (Romadour) and Josef Eisenbach (Janio) in the lead rôles. Two weeks and 15 performances saw it out again. America, too, had a chance to see the alternative *Indigo* when Marie Aimée introduced it briefly into her ever-touring repertoire (14 December 1877).

The first English language performance of *Indigo* was played at London's Alhambra Theatre in a version which, like the French one, kept the principals' names but advertised 'an entirely new libretto' by F C Burnand. It nevertheless seemed to have some bones of the Viennese *Indigo* left in it. Selina Dolaro (Fantasca, a young Hungarian wrecked on the Indigonian Isles and made chief Maid of Honour), Harry Paulton (King Indigo), J H Ryley (Babazouk, a descendant of Ali Baba), Guillaume Loredan (Janio, the King's Private Musician), Adelaide Newton (Princess Radamanta) and Emma Chambers (Zoe) were featured in a show whose text ran to no less than 40 pages of printed libretto, included a Hungarian ballet and a bayadere divertissement, and still (after being chopped to $2\frac{1}{4}$ hours after opening night) shared the evening programme with a farce and a full-length ballet. It also managed to fit in an arrangement of the Blue Danube waltz. Like all its fellow makes and remakes, it failed, closing in just seven weeks.

America hosted its first performances of the show in German, when Lina Mayr starred as Fantasca alongside Witt (Indigo), Merten (Ali Baba) and Ferdinand Schütz (Janio) at the Germania Theater in 1875, and the piece was also seen in New York in its French alternative version, and in an 1891 revival at the Terrace Garten (25 August), before the Casino Theater finally tried an *Indigo* in English, 20 years after the original production (ad Max Freeman, Edgar Smith). Jefferson de Angelis (Ali), Pauline L'Allemand (Fantasca), Louise Beaudet (Toffana), Ferdinand Schütz (Janio) and Edwin Stevens (Indigo) starred, and it ran five weeks.

Hungary saw its first brief production in 1874 (ad Jenő Rákosi) and the Népszinház brought the show back nearly 20 years later in a revised version without notable success. Russia, Italy, Poland, Spain, South America and even Malta all had a go with *Indigo* over 20 years of bootless efforts to make a success out of it, and Berlin's Friedrich-Wilhelmstädtisches Theater tried it again in 1887 (9 April), but the sole real successes which emerged from the piece were Strauss's own arrangements of some of his melodies as dance music ('Tausend und eine Nacht', 'Indigo-Marsch' etc).

The attempts to re-use Strauss's *Indigo* music (and, not coincidentally, his saleable name) continued after his death. In 1906 the score was largely borrowed to be set by Ernst Reiterer to a wholly different libretto by Leo Stein and Carl Lindau, albeit one which maintained the Middle-Eastern flavour, under the title *Tausend und eine Nacht* (fantastic Operette in a prologue and two acts, Venedig in

Wien, 15 June). An extremely indifferent tale about a fisherman (Rauch) and a Prince (Willy Bauer) who take each other's places, and the Leila (Phila Wolff) they both love, made place in its action for a Viennese soubrette (Fella Schreiter) who was able to make reasonable sense of singing 'Ja so singt man' without changing the lyrics. In spite of a libretto which did not seem even as convincing as the original, *Tausend und eine Nacht* did better than *Indigo*. It was picked up by the Volksoper for the following season, and was subsequently given there as late as the 1970s. It was played in several mid-European countries and became a favourite (probably partly because of its opportunity for water-based scenes) at the lakeside theatre at Bregenz (1949, 1959, 1978). The revamping continued, however, and in 1936 *Tausend und eine Nacht* was itself given a reworking as *Eine Nacht am Bosporus* (ad G Heidrich, Ernst Schliepe, Nuremberg 30 August).

Germany: Victoria-Theater, Berlin 1 September 1871; Hungary: Budai Színkör *Indigo* (Ger) 12 September 1874, Népszinház *Indigo és a nagyven rabló* 28 April 1893; France: Théâtre de la Renaissance *La Reine Indigo* 27 April 1875; USA: Germania Theater 12 April 1875; UK: Alhambra *Indigo* 24 September 1877

Recording: *Tausend und eine Nacht* complete (Urania)

INTO THE WOODS Musical in 2 acts by James Lapine. Music and lyrics by Stephen Sondheim. Martin Beck Theater, New York, 5 November 1987.

A piece in the vein of the fairytale burlesques of Victorian times, *Into the Woods* brought together some familiar nursery tale characters – along with some other less familiar ones – in a jolly adventure of the Quest variety which didn't stop at its happy ending.

The quest is one imposed upon the Baker (Chip Zien) and his wife (Joanna Gleason) by their neighbouring witch (Bernadette Peters), who cursed their family with childlessness after the Baker's naughty father (Tom Aldredge) stole her magic beans. The Baker sets out to get his hands on the cow of Jack the Giantkiller (Ben Wright), the golden slipper of Cinderella (Kim Crosby), the hair of Rapunzel (Pamela Winslow) and the hood of Little Red Riding-Hood (Danielle Ferland). Several dead bodies and a lot of lying and cheating later, the magic is concocted and everyone gets what they wanted – the Baker's Wife gets pregnancy, the Witch gets youth and beauty, Jack a fortune, Rapunzel and Cinderella a Prince apiece (Chuck Wagner, Robert Westenberg), and Cinderella's Ugly Sisters some self-improvement. Unfortunately for them, however, there is another act to go. Happiness cannot be ever-after. One of Jack's beanstalks produces a fresh giant (Merle Louise), the spouse of the last one killed, and as everyone heads off into the woods again, under the pressures of a few more deaths, more lying and more cheating, the happy ending starts to crack up. A little co-operation between Jack and the Baker eventually finishes off Mrs Giant, and at the end of the act the depleted band are left to mull over their experiences and the lessons they have (or ought to have) learned.

The score of the piece included some fine comic moments, topped by a duo for the two Princes suffering egoistic 'Agony' as they lust over Rapunzel and Cinderella in Act One, and then over the Sleeping Beauty and Snow White in Act Two, Little Red Riding-Hood's encounter

with an X-rated wolf ('Hello, Little Girl'), Cinderella's Prince's polished line of seduction as practised on the Baker's Wife ('Any Moment'), and Cinderella's monologue over the same Prince's dirty trick of laying pitch on the palace steps to stop her running away at midnight as per literary tradition. Little Red Riding-Hood headed a lively title-song, and the Baker's Wife and the Witch performed the more contemplative and lyrical pieces, of which the Witch's melodious waltz, 'The Last Midnight', stood out.

Although the show had moral and social points to make, it stood up – particularly in its first act – perfectly well as a face-value fairy story and, helped by this double-level possibility of appreciation, Broadway's production (which billed six producers above its title) played for almost two years (764 performances) before, in November 1988, the show went out into the regions. The touring cast included Cleo Laine (Witch), Charlotte Rae (Jack's mother), Kathleen Rowe McAllen (Cinderella), Ray Gill (Baker) and Mary Gordon Murray (Baker's Wife).

David Mirvisch's British production, with Julia McKenzie (Witch), Ian Bartholomew (Baker), Imelda Staunton (Baker's Wife), Mark Tinkler and Clive Carter (Princes) and Jacqueline Dankworth (Cinderella) featured was not given the kind of breath-for-breath restaging usual in recent years. However, it, fared less well than its American counterpart, lasting only 186 performances at the Phoenix Theatre. After a German version (ad Michael Kunze) was first seen in Heilbronn in 1990 with Tom Zahner (Baker), Thea Schnering (Baker's Wife) and Esther Stein (Witch), and then at Munich's Theater am Gärtnerplatz (14 April 1991) with Erich Hallhuber, Noemi Nadelmann and Marianne Larsen featured, several other German houses showed interest in the piece, which seems, at the time of writing, to have found its most appreciative theatre-directors in the land of the Brothers Grimm. *Into the Woods* has also been taken up for regional production both in America and in Britain, appeared on stage and television in Denmark as *Langt ud i Skoven* and, after a disastrous saga of walkouts, breakdowns amongst actors and the mechanical scenery, and postponements, in Sydney, Australia. Philip Quast, Tony Sheldon, Judi Connelli and Geraldine Turner featured in a truncated season.

Germany: Stadttheater, Heilbronn *Ab in den Wald* 31 March 1990; UK: Phoenix Theatre 25 September 1990; Australia: Drama Theatre, Opera House, Sydney 18 March 1993

Recording: original cast (RCA Victor), London cast (RCA Victor)

IN TOWN Musical farce in 2 acts by Adrian Ross and James Leader (ie James T Tanner). Music by F Osmond Carr. Prince of Wales Theatre, London, 15 October 1892.

In Town, one of the several shows quoted loosely in the past as being 'the first musical comedy', may not have been precisely that, but it was indeed a show which marked a change in policy on the part of George Edwardes, at that time the most powerful and perspicacious producer in a London theatre which had been successfully producing exportable pieces for a number of years. Edwardes and his Gaiety Theatre company, headed by Nellie Farren and Fred Leslie, had run through the heyday of the 'new burlesque' genre which he and they had initiated, but already, although Leslie was still pulling them in for *Cinder-Ellen Up-too-Late* at the Gaiety (without Miss Farren, who was ill), Edwardes's antennae told him that the appeal of the new burlesque – which was no real burlesque, but a series of songs, dances and comic scenes played in fantastical costume – was faltering.

He decided on a shift of gear and, in the Prince of Wales Theatre production of *In Town*, he simply presented comic Arthur Roberts and star soprano Florence St John, two solid top-of-the-bill names featured large above the title, in a piece which made no pretence of being a parody or burlesque of anything. It merely presented the same kind of songs and dances as were used in the burlesques in the loose, revusical framework of a little tale peopled by contemporary folk, costumed not in fantastic or period clothes but in modern dress. Roberts was Captain Arthur Coddington, an easy-going man-about-town whose jokey charm is his passe-partout. In the style of a meneur de revue, he leads the young Lord Clanside (Phyllis Broughton in breeches) around the backstage of the Ambiguity Theatre and other important holes of London life, in spite of the restrictions imposed by the lad's suspicious mother, the Duchess of Duffshire (Maria Davis). Miss St John played Kitty Hetherton, former governess to the Duchess's daughter, who has become an actress, after being sacked for attracting the attention of the Duke (Eric Lewis). The second act brought everyone together backstage at the Ambiguity for a barrage of traditional disguises and mistakes, illustrated by the usual parade of songs and dances, before Coddington and Kitty were safely united in time for the final curtain. There was still sufficient real burlesque for those who liked it, for the second act managed to squeeze in a parody of *Romeo and Juliet* as performed on the stage of the Ambiguity Theatre.

The contemporary text joined up the songs and dances at least as well as, if not better than, the old burlesque libretti had done, and it had the advantage of comfortably taking in the large topical element of both the comedian's dialogue and of the song lyrics much better than had the old type of books. Roberts described himself as a 'Typical Man About Town' in an Adrian Ross lyric which wholly fitted his character, and dilated over the effects of alcohol in 'Drinks of the Day' as well as going through all the extravagances as a Scots Friar Lawrence ('Friar Larry') in the burlesque and parodying the balcony scene with his co-star. She, as usual, stuck largely to ballads, scoring best with Osmond Carr's pretty 'Dreamless Rest'. Lewis, too, had a character number, describing his unfortunate penchant for serving girls ('My Propensities Are All the Other Way') and a topical number about 'The House of Lords', a pair of pieces which pretty well exemplified the range of entertainment the show had to offer.

In Town was far from being a finished musical farce. It had characters, with some songs and scenes which matched their characterisations, but at other times it leaned strongly towards being as much of a variety show as the later burlesques had been. This tendency was not diminished by Roberts who, often tipsy and almost always unbridled in his performances, ad libbed and interpolated fairly fresh and frankly old material freely. One of his additions was his own version of Vesta Victoria's music-hall hit 'Daddy Wouldn't Buy Me a Bow-Wow', to which he added topical verses, often of his own making. Later, in a frankly revusical manner, Edwardes added some specialities into the theatrical scenes of the second act.

Amongst these were included skirt-dancer Loie Fuller and 17-year-old impressionist Cissie Loftus.

The new mixture confused and displeased some of the critics, but it pleased the public, who were also pleased by the display of up-to-date fashion in which both the beautiful girls and the men of the cast were displayed. The clothes were from London fashion houses, and thus the stalls audience, at least, could, if they wished, purchase copies of the models worn by their favourite performers.

The death of Leslie precipitated the end of the new burlesque and, more immediately, the closure of *Cinder-Ellen* at the Gaiety Theatre. Edwardes had planned his all-important Gaiety Christmas show around his biggest star, and now he was stuck. So he transferred *In Town* from the Prince of Wales to the Gaiety, where it broke the line of burlesques which had held the stage there since *Dorothy* and where it played happily through till the summer (292 performances) before being sent on the road in two companies. Its success encouraged the producer to continue the modern-dress style of show – although he persisted with burlesque, in parallel, a little longer – and it was his second and rather more vertebrate musical comedy, *A Gaiety Girl*, with a score by *In Town*'s conductor, Sidney Jones, again produced at the Prince of Wales Theatre, which confirmed the way that he would go in his later productions.

In Town's out-of-town assignments soon took in the colonies, notably with Edwardes's own tour of 1895 which, having played *A Gaiety Girl* in America, continued to Australia with a repertoire including *In Town*. Louis Bradfield, who had succeeded Roberts at the Gaiety, starred alongside Gilbert and Sullivan's Casilda, Decima Moore. Two years later Edwardes put together another company to take the show to America, with Bradfield sharing top-billing with Minnie Hunt. It played two weeks in London, then crossed the Atlantic, but Edwardes himself had by now shown Broadway his later pieces and *In Town* seemed already démodé. It closed after only 40 Broadway performances.

Australia: Princess Theatre, Melbourne 4 May 1895; USA: Knickerbocker Theater 6 September 1897

IOLANTHE, or The Peer and the Peri Comic (fairy) opera in 2 acts by W S Gilbert. Music by Arthur Sullivan. Savoy Theatre, London, 25 November 1882.

The first new Gilbert and Sullivan opera to be produced at Richard D'Oyly Carte's freshly built Savoy Theatre, *Iolanthe* came along behind the team's great run of international successes with *HMS Pinafore*, *The Pirates of Penzance* and *Patience*, and, if it did not prove quite as exportable as they, it became equally as popular as its predecessors on the home front. Following the nautical, melodramatic and aesthetic burlesques of the previous three shows, Gilbert decided on a burlesque of faërie, an area to which he had always shown a particular attachment (*The Wicked World*, *The Palace of Truth*, *Creatures of Impulse*), and – with a little re-use of some of the conceits from his older fairy-cum-politics burlesque *The Happy Land* – he built his characters and plot around the now fairly settled core of D'Oyly Carte's Savoy Theatre company.

Jessie Bond was Iolanthe, a fairy who had married a mortal and borne him a son. This sort of thing being against fairy law, the Queen (Alice Barnett) was forced to banish her, but after a quarter of a century she feels able to relent and Iolanthe is summoned back to fairyland, still looking not a fairy day over the age of 16. This causes a problem when Phyllis (Leonora Braham), an Arcadian shepherdess beloved by Iolanthe's Arcadian shepherd son, Strephon (Richard Temple), as well as by the entire House of Lords, sees the pair embracing. The distraught Phyllis, believing Strephon unfaithful, agrees to marry the House of Lords, and the vengeful Fairy Queen promptly uses her magic powers to get Strephon into Parliament, there to wreak havoc amongst British Institutions with the use of fairy logic. When the Lord Chancellor of England (George Grossmith) finally decides that it is commensurate with his position to marry Phyllis himself, Iolanthe can be quiet no longer, for the Chancellor is her long-lost husband and Strephon's father. But by breaking her silence she has again broken fairy law and her Queen must doom her to die. However, it seems that all her fellow sisters have been busy breaking fairy law with the House of Lords as well. A swift redrafting of fairy law serves to avert wholesale slaughter in fairyland and to legalize the tie-up of peers and peris for a happy ending.

Grossmith had one of his best rôles as the Lord Chancellor, equipped with some of Gilbert and Sullivan's nippiest patter songs: his self-explanatory 'The Law is the True Embodiment', his declaration of principle 'When I Went to the Bar (as a very young man)' and, most memorably, his nonsensical Nightmare Song, a cacophony of images of a sleepless, love-racked night. The imposing Alice Barnett as the booming Queen of the Fairies was also equipped with some of the Gilbert and Sullivan canon's best contralto moments, powering down her thunders on the naughty peers or giving her fairies a lesson in sexual self-control ('O Foolish Fay'). Baritone Temple, used to playing fathers, and most recently Captain Corcoran, the Pirate King and Colonel Calverley, found himself unusually cast as the juvenile lead, since tenor Durward Lely and Rutland Barrington played the most forward members of the House of Lords, a group burlesqued with the green vigour that Gilbert always applied to the inherited position he clearly longed for. In an unusual step, however, Gilbert wrote just one of his characters in an entirely un-burlesque manner. The rôle was that of Iolanthe herself, who was presented as a sentimental character with genuine emotions, and whose love was presented in a wholly different way to that of the peers and even the juveniles. And yet neither her character nor her sentiments seemed out of place in the show's inherently comical tale.

Carte's production of Iolanthe was a splendid one. The settings of Arcadia and, particularly, of the Thames Embankment and the Houses of Parliament, Johnnie D'Auban's show-stopping dance routine to the three peers' trio 'Nothing Venture, Nothing Win', and the little electric lights which glittered in the hair of the fairies, all added to the success of the show. This success, however, did not stop some post-production alterations. Temple and Barrington both lost solos in the aftermath of opening night as the piece was trimmed to svelter proportions, preparatory to a run of 13 months and 398 performances at the Savoy.

As part of his continuing battle against theatrical piracy, Carte opened Iolanthe simultaneously in Britain and America. On Broadway J H Ryley added another Gros-

smith rôle to his list and several other British artists, Lyn Cadwaladr (Tolloller), Augusta Roche (Queen) and Arthur Wilkinson (Mountararat), were joined by Americans Marie Jansen (Iolanthe), Sallie Reber (Phyllis) and the expatriate William T Carleton (Strephon) at the head of the cast under the direction of Charles Harris and the baton of Alfred Cellier. The show was well received, but the fairies and the British Parliament did not succeed in raising the same enthusiasm or merriment amongst New Yorkers that the lustier burlesque of *Pinafore* and *Pirates* or the particular parody of *Patience* had done. *Iolanthe* played a respectable 105 performances at the Standard Theater and a return season at the Fifth Avenue whilst the British production continued. In later years, however, *Iolanthe*'s American popularity grew. It returned several times to Broadway, being produced by the Shuberts and William Brady at the Casino (12 May 1913) with De Wolf Hopper as the Chancellor (40 performances) and, with the genuine success that it had rather lacked first time round, by Winthrop Ames at the Plymouth Theater (19 April 1926), when it notched up 355 performances in a run rarely bettered by a Gilbert and Sullivan production on Broadway.

Iolanthe quickly became and remained a favourite in the Gilbert and Sullivan repertoire in Britain and the colonies. It was particularly successful in Australia, where a largely imported cast featuring Robert Brough (Chancellor), his wife Florence Trevallyan (Queen), returned Australian star Emma Chambers (Iolanthe) and W H Woodfield (Mountararat), with local heroine Nellie Stewart as Phyllis, set the piece rolling in 1885. Over the next half-century J C Williamson and his associates played the piece regularly, with both Alice Barnett and Leonora Braham repeating their original rôles in different seasons as the piece established itself as one of the most popular of all comic operas on the Australian stage.

Following the release of the Gilbert and Sullivan copyrights in Britain, *Iolanthe* was the first of the Savoy canon to be given a major London production, when the Sadler's Wells Opera staged a production (24 January 1962) featuring Eric Shilling (Chancellor), Heather Begg (Queen) and Elizabeth Harwood (Phyllis), and *Iolanthe* hoisted another first when it was selected to open the initial season of the re-formed D'Oyly Carte Opera Company in 1987, subsequently becoming the most effective part of the new company's repertoire.

USA: Standard Theater 25 November 1882; Australia: Theatre Royal, Melbourne 9 May 1885
Recordings: complete (Decca, Angel, HMV, TER), Sadlers Wells 1962 (HMV) etc

IRENE Musical comedy in 2 acts by James Montgomery based on his play *Irene O'Dare*. Lyrics by Joseph McCarthy. Music by Harry Tierney. Vanderbilt Theater, New York, 18 November 1919.

The most successful American musical comedy of its time, *Irene* was a powerful force in setting in motion the fashion for the ingenuous, modern-day Cinderella shows (poor-girl-wins-rich-boy) which inundated Broadway in the early and middle 1920s, and from which *Sally* and *Mary* emerged as some of the other happiest examples.

The show was evolved from a James Montgomery play, *Irene O'Dare*, which had foundered on the road to Broadway in 1916 but which, like many another contemporary play of limited success, was nevertheless picked up to be made into a musical. The picking up was done by producer Carle Carleton, whose lady friend, ingénue Edith Day, had been appearing in the highly successful musical version of another Montgomery play, *Going Up*, and the author remoulded his play into a libretto with the young performer in mind. Miss Day was also instrumental in the choice of the show's songwriters, for it was her friend Anna Held who suggested – and she suggested to Carleton – that an opportunity be given to the little-tried composer Harry Tierney, who had provided Miss Held with a bundle of songs for her 1916 vehicle, *Follow Me*, and his newest lyric-writing partner, Joseph McCarthy.

Irene O'Dare (Miss Day) is an unmoneyed New York-Irish lass from Ninth Avenue who attracts the attentions of the wealthy Donald Marshall (Walter Regan) when she is sent to his Long Island mansion on an upholstering job. Donald arranges for Irene and her friends Helen (Eva Puck) and Eleanor (Bernice McCabe) to go to work as models in the fashion-house run by Madame Lucy (Bobbie Watson), and the girls are obliged to pass themselves off as ladies at a society party as part of Donald's efforts to launch the couturier. The upwardly striving J P Bowden (Arthur Burckly) pursues Irene, but when the truth of her origins emerges he wriggles away, leaving her to a happy ending with Donald. Dorothy Walters played Irene's canny Irish mother and Florence Hills was the aristocratic Mrs Marshall.

The highlight of *Irene*'s pretty score was the heroine's description of her 'Alice-Blue Gown' (alice-blue was a shade of pale blue, allegedly linked to Alice Roosevelt), which became an enduring favourite, and a lilting title-song, the remake of a bit of Chopin's Minute Waltz as 'Castle of Dreams', the jolly determination of the girls to be 'The Talk of the Town' and a neat variation on the party type of song, 'The Last Part of Every Party', were other popular musical items.

Carleton's production of *Irene* played for 670 performances at the little Vanderbilt Theater, setting up a long run record on Broadway as Edith Day was succeeded first by Adele Rowland and then by Patti Harrold in the title-rôle. Miss Day, in the meanwhile, crossed to London and there starred in Joe Sacks's production of her show, at the Empire Theatre, alongside Pat Somerset (Donald), Robert Hale (Mme Lucy), Robert Michaelis (Bowden), Margaret Campbell (Helen) and Daisy Hancox (Eleanor). It was another successful production, which played for over a year in the West End (399 performances) before it went on the road.

Even before this, *Irene* had made her way into Europe, where Budapest's Lujza Blaha Színház mounted what sounded like a rather unfamiliar version of the show. It was entitled *A tündérek cselédje* (the fairy-like servant-girl, ad Ernő Kulinyi), and advertised as a 'latvanyos amerikai operett' (spectacular American operetta). However, although the show was also, and much later, played in Vienna, it was in the English language that it made and maintained its greatest popularity.

In Sydney, Australia, where *Irene* was produced by the Tait brothers with Dorothy South as its heroine, Chester Clute as Lucy and Robert Jewett as Donald, the show was hit by an opening night chorus strike. The handful of the chorus who went on were lustily cheered, the evening was an enormous hit and the production went on to pass its 100th night (1 November) before moving on in December to the rest of the country, and to a Melbourne season (Her Majesty's Theatre 9 April 1921) under the J C Williamson banner.

In spite of being followed onto the Broadway and British stages by a regular band of like shows, *Irene* survived as the most appealing of her kind, and she returned to the main English-speaking centres on a number of occasions. London impresario Jack Hylton followed in Carleton's steps when he mounted a revival of *Irene* in London in 1945 with his girlfriend Pat Taylor starred in the title rôle, but, if the show ran less long this time, he had better luck than Carleton on the personal front. In spite of marrying Miss Day, her producer had quickly (if briefly) lost her to her West End leading man, Pat Somerset, in a shower of newspaper paragraphs. Hylton was already married ... to someone else.

More than 50 years after its original production, the show had a second success, equal to that of its first run, when, encouraged by Montgomery's widow, Harry Rigby, Albert Selden and Jerome Minskoff mounted a revised version of *Irene* on Broadway in 1973 (Minskoff Theater 13 March). The libretto had been adapted by Rigby, Hugh Wheeler and Joseph Stein, with boring old J P Bowden disappearing completely from a story which was otherwise largely the same, and the score had been enlarged from its original 13 pieces (six of which vanished) with the addition of a number of other songs to which lyricist McCarthy had contributed ('What Do You Want to Make Those Eyes at Me For?', 'They Go Wild, Simply Wild Over Me', 'You Made Me Love You', and another Chopin derivative 'I'm Always Chasing Rainbows') and several pieces by Charles Gaynor and Otis Clements and other modern hands.

Debbie Reynolds starred as Irene (now a piano-tuner rather than an upholsterer), alongside Monte Markham (Donald), George S Irving (Mme Lucy) and Patsy Kelly (Mrs O'Dare), and the colourful production of this new version played 605 Broadway performances, with Jane Powell succeeding Miss Reynolds in the later part of the run. The new *Irene* underwent further revisions before it was produced in Australia (Her Majesty's Theatre, Sydney, 25 May 1974) with Julie Anthony (Irene), Noel Ferrier (Mme Lucy) and Robert Colman (Donald) featured, and with very considerable success. After a two months' Sydney season, it toured, played seven months in Melbourne (Her Majesty's Theatre 14 September 1974), and ultimately returned for a second Sydney season (2 May 1975), this time of five months. Further revisions to this version set in prior to Harold Fielding's production being mounted in London, with Miss Anthony repeating her down-under rôle in the West End alongside Jon Pertwee (Mme Lucy) and Eric Flynn (Donald). Patricia Michael succeeded to the title-rôle as the show ran out the 974 performances which gave *Irene* its longest ever run.

Irene was filmed in 1926 by First National with Colleen Moore as a silent Irene and George K Arthur as a silent Madame Lucy, and again in 1940 with Anna Neagle starred alongside Ray Milland, Alan Marshal and Roland Young.

UK: Empire Theatre 7 April 1920; Hungary: Lujza Blaha Színház *A tündérek cselédje* 23 October 1921; Austria: Rextheater 24 June 1946; Australia: Criterion Theatre, Sydney 7 August 1920; Films: First National 1926, RKO 1940

Recordings: original London cast (Monmouth-Evergreen), 1973, revival cast (Columbia), London revival cast (EMI)

IRMA LA DOUCE Musical play in 2 acts by Alexandre Breffort based on his story of the same name. Music by Marguerite Monnot. Théâtre Gramont, Paris, 12 November 1956.

The tale of Irma la Douce, the ultimate tart with the heart of gold, began as a short story written by Alexandre Breffort (d Paris, 23 February 1971) for the strivingly satirical French newspaper *Le Canard enchaîné*. Breffort subsequently adapted the piece as a sketch, and then finally as a stage musical illustrated with songs by Marguerite Monnot, whose only previous venture into the domain had been with a scoreful of songs for Edith Piaf's musical comedy venture *La P'tite Lili*.

The show is narrated by Bob le Hotu (René Dupuy, also director), the patron of the Bar des Inquiets in the back streets of Pigalle, the hangout of the folk of the 'milieu', the 'poules' (whores) and their flashy 'mecs' (chaps/pimps). Nestor-le-Fripé (Michel Roux), a law student studying the milieu, comes to the bar one day and before he leaves finds he has, in the nicest possible way, become the mec of a little poule called Irma la Douce (Colette Renard). The lovers settle down together, but Irma does not give up her lucrative employment. Nestor tries not to be niggled, but he is. Finally, he disguises himself behind a beard as an elderly gent called Oscar and books Irma exclusively, paying out 10,000 francs which go from Oscar, to Irma, to Nestor, to Oscar, and so forth. He has to take a job cleaning floors to bring in the money Irma thinks she is bringing in, and finally the double schedule becomes too much. He decides to kill Oscar off. It all goes wrong. Nestor is arrested for murder, tried in a surreal court and sentenced to Devil's Island along with all the other mecs. They escape, paddle across the seas to Paris, and reach home. But since they had no razors on their raft, Nestor gets home bearded, and Irma greets him ... as Oscar! If Oscar is alive, then Nestor has been wrongly condemned. When he is pardoned, the razor comes out and Oscar can disappear once more. The happy ending is crowned by Irma giving birth to twins, one for each father.

Monnot's songs were a characterful, winning lot in the pure tradition of the French chanson which she had exploited so brilliantly in her work with Piaf. Irma fell in love over 'Me v'là, te v'là' and 'Avec les anges' (both w Nestor), bounced out a joyous 'Ah! Dis-donc, dis-donc' at finding her rich protector, and came to the imprisoned Nestor in his dreams with 'Irma la Douce'. Nestor looked at his overworked double-self in 'La cave à Irma' and beamoaned his imprisonment in 'L'aventure est morte', and the mecs indulged in the 'Valse milieu', doubled as Irma's admiring customers with 'Elle a du chien', chorused their admiration of her working-girl's success in 'To Be or Not to Be' and of her double-giving birth in 'Il est né, le Môme à Irma', and longed for home in 'Y'a que Paris pour ça'.

Irma la Douce proved a singular hit at the little Théâtre Gramont, band singer Colette Renard became a star in short time, the show's songs became the rage and, as *Irma la Douce* ran through its more than two years of Parisian

performances, shifting up to the larger Théâtre de l'Athénée part way through the run, it was taken up by overseas producers in a way that few French shows had been since the passing of the jazz-age musical comedy.

A year and a half into the Paris run, an English-language version of *Irma la Douce* opened in London. Bandleader Henry Hall had seen the show in Paris and snapped up the English rights, and he sublet them to Donald Albery's Donmar Productions and to H M Tennent Ltd, who mounted the piece at the West End's Lyric Theatre. The very special argot which gave the French *Irma la Douce* so much of its character had seemed almost impossible to reproduce in another language, but David Heneker, Julian More and Monty Norman not only succeeded in this tricky task, but succeeded so well that eventually the English-language *Irma* went on to become even more popular than the original French one. Britain's *Irma*, directed by Peter Brook, featured Elizabeth Seal in its title-rôle, with Keith Michell as Nestor, Clive Revill as Bob and Ronnie Barker, Frank Olegario, Julian Orchard and Gary Raymond amongst the mecs, 'Avec les anges' became 'Our Language of Love', and the show proved a copper-bottomed hit through 1,512 performances in the West End before going around Britain.

The London production was remounted (with a handful of alterations, including some more Broadwayish orchestrations) in America, with Michell, Revill and Miss Seal repeating their rôles in a cast which also included George S Irving, Elliott Gould and Stuart Damon, under the management of David Merrick. The London success was repeated, Miss Seal took the year's Tony Award (in a season which included *Bye Bye Birdie*, *Camelot* and *Carnival*) and *Irma la Douce* graced Broadway for 524 performances before going on the road, with Taina Elg and Denis Quilley in the starring rôles.

Australia's *Irma la Douce* underwent a postponement when leading lady Judith Bruce fell ill, but show and star both proved worth waiting for, and when *Irma* opened, with Kevin Colson (Nestor) and Noel Ferrier (Bob) sharing top-billing, at Sydney's Theatre Royal, it ran 12 weeks before moving on to Melbourne's Comedy Theatre (17 June 1961) and to cities beyond.

Translation proved to be no problem at all, and the English language was not the only one to have its *Irma* adaptation. In 1961 a German-language version (ad Ivo Kohorte, Hanns Bernhardt) was produced at Baden-Baden, then, the following year, at Munich's Theater die kleine Freiheit (14 February 1962) and under the management of Rolf Kutschera at Berlin's Theater des Westens with Violetta Ferrari in the title-rôle. In 1964 the Hungarian *Irma, te édes* (ad Erzsébet Mágori, Tamás Ungvári, Tamás Blum) was produced in Budapest, and in 1966 the Theater an der Wien hosted a 45-performance season of the German production with Ferrari and Ernst Stankovsky (Nestor).

After widespread regional productions all round the world through a decade, *Irma* made reappearances in several main centres. Colette Renard took up her old rôle, alongside Dupuy and Franck Fernandel as Nestor, in a revival at the Théâtre de l'Athénée in 1967, which brought *Irma*'s Parisian total up to 932 performances, a total which was further increased by another mounting, at the Théâtre Fontaine, in 1977 (18 June), in which Joëlle Vauthier and

Georges Belier teamed with the still present Dupuy. Sydney saw the piece again when it was staged at the Marian Street Theatre in 1975 (31 January), and London witnessed a brief second showing in 1979 when an under-par production featuring Helen Gelzer, Charles Dance and Bernard Spear was mounted at the Shaftesbury Theatre (27 November). Although the show has not appeared subsequently in metropolitan revivals, it continues to be played regionally, and was the subject of a major provincial revival in France in 1992, with Sophie Destaing and Eric Boucher in the leading rôles, and of a Budapest revival in 1991 (Józsefvárosi Színház) with Éva Vándor as Irma and Imre Harmath as Nestor.

A film version of *Irma la Douce*, which featured Shirley MacLaine and Jack Lemmon as Irma and Nestor, dropped both the concept of the stage piece and the songs.

UK: Lyric Theatre 17 July 1958; USA: Plymouth Theater 29 September 1960; Australia: Theatre Royal, Sydney 25 February 1961; Germany: Theater der Stadt, Baden-Baden 24 January 1961, Theater des Westens, Berlin 6 March 1962; Hungary: Fővárosi Operettszínház *Irma, te édes* 4 November 1964; Austria: Theater an der Wien 9 March 1966

Recordings: original cast star, French revival cast, complete w dialogue (Véga), London cast (Philips), Broadway cast (Columbia), South African cast (Plum), Israeli cast (CBS), Dutch cast (Artone) etc

IRVING, Ethel (b England, 5 September 1869; d Bexhill, 3 May 1963). Dancer and soubrette in turn-of-the-century musicals who went on to a fine career in plays.

'Birdie' Irving began her career in the chorus at the Gaiety Theatre at the age of 16, appearing in *The Vicar of Wideawakefield* and in the minor rôle of Valentine in *Monte Cristo Jr*. She took over the small dance rôle of Lady Betty in *Dorothy* at the Prince of Wales, played in Ivan Caryll's supporting operetta *Jubilation*, and appeared for George Edwardes as principal dancer in *Ruy Blas and the Blasé Roué* (1889) and for Henry Leslie in *The Red Hussar* (1890), both in London and on Broadway. She remained in America for six years, and on returning to Britain, now billed as Ethel Irving, returned to the management of George Edwardes, who sent her on tour in Letty Lind's rôle of Molly in *The Geisha*, and then brought her to Daly's to replace Gracie Leigh in the comedy rôle of Dudley in *San Toy*.

Edwardes then featured her as Sophie in *A Country Girl* (1902, 'Two Little Chicks') and in the title-rôle of *The Girl from Kays* (1902, Winnie Harborough), and she starred opposite Willie Edouin in *Sergeant Brue* (1904, Lady Bickenhall) for Frank Curzon before being inveigled into an amateurish flop called *Ladyland* (1904, Alma Molyneux). At this stage she began to mix plays with her musicals and, after playing the part of the tempting actress La Boléro in *Mr Popple of Ippleton* (1905) and the Contessa di Ravolgi in Curzon's unsuccessful *The Three Kisses* (1907), she was cast in a part which, legend insists, nobody wanted: the startling title-rôle of Somerset Maugham's *Lady Frederick*. The sensation which she caused in this rôle set her on a major career as a straight actress, and she did not return to the musical theatre.

IRVING, George S [SHELASKY, George Irving] (b Springfield, Mass, 1 November 1922). Versatile Broadway character man who has compiled the kind of substantial musical theatre career which has become rare in an era of long runs and shy actors.

After working in musical shows on the road, at the St Louis Muny (The Foreign Gentleman in America's première of *Glamorous Night* etc) and New Jersey's Paper Mill Playhouse, Irving first played in New York in the choruses of *Oklahoma!* and *Lady in the Dark*. After the Second World War he appeared in London and Paris with the company playing Menotti's *The Telephone* and *The Medium*, and subsequently mixed revue and musical appearances, appearing in a multiple rôle in the fantasy *That's the Ticket* (1948), creating the rôles of Roger Gage in *Gentlemen Prefer Blondes* (1949) and Dario in *Me and Juliet* (1953), taking over from Hans Conried as Boris in *Can-Can*, and introducing the rôle of the producer, Larry Hastings, in *Bells Are Ringing* (1956).

He subsequently appeared in *The Beggar's Opera* (Peachum), *Shinbone Alley* (Big Bill), *Lock Up Your Daughters* (Sotmore), the 1960 revival of *Oh, Kay!* (t/o McGee), *Irma la Douce* (Inspector), *Tovarich* (Charles Davis), *Bravo Giovanni* (Bellardi), *Street Scene* (Carl Olsen), and in *Anya* (Chernov), as well as in the road-closed *Comedy* (Captain Cockalorum) and a number of plays. He made a hit within a hit when he played the principal comedy rôle of Madame Lucy in the long-running revival of *Irene* (1973, Tony Award), before going on to star alongside Liv Ullmann in Richard Rodgers's *I Remember Mama*. He succeeded to the rôle of the Major-General in *The Pirates of Penzance* (1981) and played Mr Micawber in the short-lived *Copperfield* (1981) on Broadway, appeared at the New York City Opera in *Regina*, *The Good Soldier Schweik*, *Street Scene* and *The Ballad of Baby Doe*, and was then featured as Sergei Alexandrovitch in the 1983 revival of *On Your Toes* and as Sir John Tremayne in Broadway's *Me and My Girl* (1986–8). He has also appeared regionally in a number of other musicals, including a 1990 production of *Fanny* at the Paper Mill Playhouse.

Irving is married to actress and dancer Maria Karnilova.

IRWIN, May [CAMPBELL, Georgia] (b Whitby, Ontario, 27 June 1862; d New York, 22 October 1938). Top-notch coon-shouter and comedienne, the energetic Miss Irwin spent a decade of stardom touring in custom-made vehicles.

May Irwin began performing at the age of 12, in a vaudeville act with her sister, Flo Irwin [Ada May CAMPBELL] (b Whitby, Ontario; d Los Angeles, 20 December 1930), and the pair joined Tony Pastor's burlesque company two years later. May remained with Pastor for six years, singing, dancing and occasionally playing the cornet in such pieces as the burlesque *The Pie-Rats of Penn Yan* and as Lady Angela in Pastor's almost straight production of *Patience*. She moved on from Pastor's to spend three years playing comic soubrettes with Augustin Daly's famous dramatic company (Popham in *The Magistrate*, Susan in *A Night Off*, Becky in *Nancy and Co* etc) before returning to vaudeville. When she came back to the theatre it was in a completely different form of entertainment, the musical farce-comedy.

Her first lead rôle in this combination of home-made low comedy and punchy, music-hall songs, which had become increasingly popular around America, was under the management of Rich and Harris in *A Country Sport* (1893, Elizabeth Alwright). However, it was in *The Widow Jones*, played at the Bijou Theater in 1895, that she made her name, scoring a huge hit with the splendidly vigorous coon song known as the – or very quickly, as May Irwin's – Bully Song. She followed up in a string of like vehicles: *Courted into Court* (1896), *The Swell Miss Fitzswell* (1897), *Kate Kip, Buyer* (1898), *Sister Mary* (1899), *Madge Smith, Attorney* (1900), *Mrs Black is Back* (1904) and *Mrs Wilson That's All* (1906), all played at Broadway's Bijou Theater and toured under her own management, all of which gave further opportunities to the plump and popular comedienne to supply her public with the lusty, loud and low-comic mixture expected from her.

When her most popular days as a star-billed singing comedienne were over, she continued to play in comedy and vaudeville. Her 1919 vehicle *Raising the Aunty* (Alicia Penn) had to be closed out of town, but she returned to New York for her last Broadway appearance in a musical, *The 49ers*, in 1922.

ISIDORA Comic opera in 3 acts by Mr Morley. Music by Luscombe Searelle. Bijou Theatre, Melbourne, 7 July 1885.

A dramatic-comic spectacular light opera from the pen of New Zealand's Luscombe Searelle, *Isidora* was first seen in Australia at the beginning of a career which would take it first to New Zealand, then to South Africa, and finally to the West End of London, under the guidance and promotion of its extravagant creator. The story of the piece was a hotch-potch of operatic elements. Set in Cuba in the year 1550, it had for its heroine Isidora, the supposed daughter of estate owner Patronio, who is in love with fisherman Felix but is intended by her father for a wealthy nobleman. Felix and chief comedian Jacob set out to find the legendary treasure of the Black Rover, but the mysterious Rover appears and carries everyone off to his ship for what threatens to be a sticky end. Then Isidora opportunely remembers a song she's been trying to remember all night. It is the lullaby her mother sang to her before she sank to her death under the prow of the Black Rover's ship, and its singing breaks the spell which binds the Rover to earth. He comes back in the third act, however – after Isidora's mad scene – to protect her from a local revolution, and all ultimately ends happily.

Australian producers Majeroni and Wilson produced *Isidora* in Melbourne with Gracie Plaisted in the title-rôle, Edwin Kelly (once of Kelly and Leon's ministrels) as the Black Rover, Charles Harding as Felix, Kelly's son, Edwin Lester as Jacob and the composer at the baton. It won some praise and went on to be played alongside such pieces as *La Périchole* and *Maritana* in the Majeroni/Wilson company's repertoire in Sydney (New Opera House, 23 August), before Searelle pushed on with further productions, mostly under his own management. He ultimately got the piece to the stage in London in 1890 under the title *The Black Rover*. London proved less attracted to the melo-dramatic fate of Isidora as played by Mrs Searelle (Blanche Fenton) and William Ludwig (The Rover), and after six weeks the production folded.

UK: Globe Theatre *The Black Rover* 23 September 1890

ISOLA, Émile (b Blida, Algeria, 1860; d Paris, 17 May 1945).
ISOLA, Vincent (b Blida, Algeria, 1862; d Paris, September 1947). Parisian impresarii of the first half of the 20th century.

Originally illusionists on the music-hall stage, the Isola brothers went into management in 1892, presenting their own programme at the Théâtre des Capucines, which they rechristened the Théâtre Isola for the occasion. They moved on to take over the Parisiana, and it was there, amongst their music-hall programmes, that they first dipped into the musical theatre, producing a number of opérettes and revues, from which the spectacular *Madame Méphisto* proved perhaps the most successful. They subsequently extended their control to the Olympia where, following the trends in Vienna, they mounted a series of imported musicals that included America's *The Prince of Pilsen* and *The Belle of New York*, Berlin's *Frau Luna* and Britain's *The Country Girl* with some success, and to the Folies-Bergère.

In 1903 they moved to more legitimate areas when they took over the big Théâtre de la Gaîté-Lyrique from Debruyère and, in the following decade, they mounted many productions of classic operas and opérettes there before again moving up the ladder and taking over the control of the Opéra-Comique, in a team with the playwright Pierre-Barthélmy Gheusi. Their most notable period as producers of musical theatre came, however, in the decade 1926–36 when they managed the Théâtre Mogador, sponsoring Paris's productions of *Die Bajadere, No, No, Nanette, Rose Marie, The Desert Song, Hit the Deck, Im weissen Rössl* and the original opérette *Mandrin*.

When the ever-rising pair eventually stopped rising and fell on hard times, largely thanks to their attempts at staging prestigious pieces at the Théâtre Sarah Bernhardt, they took up once more the illusion act of their young days and, at nearly 80 years of age, played engagements in theatres and casinos in France and Switzerland. Both died at the age of 85.

Biography: Andrieu, P: *Souvenirs des Frères Isola: cinquante ans de vie parisienne* (Flammarion, Paris, 1943)

IT HAPPENED IN NORDLAND Musical comedy in a prologue and 2 acts by Glen MacDonough. Music by Victor Herbert. Lew Fields Theater, New York, 5 December 1904.

The first Lew Fields production following his split from the Weber and Fields partnership had all the right ingredients. His producing associates were Fred R Hamlin and Julian Mitchell, the men behind *The Wizard of Oz* and *Babes in Toyland* of the two previous seasons, and the authors were those of the second-named piece, librettist and lyricist Glen MacDonough and composer Victor Herbert. As far as its book was concerned, *It Happened in Nordland* was a marginally more adult piece than *Babes in Toyland*, but it relied, like its predecessor, rather more on plenty of comedy and a glamorous and spectacular production than on anything else. Herbert's attractive score came, as it had in *Babes in Toyland*, as the lace on the hankie.

Queen Elsa of Nordland is to be wed against her royal will to the Czar's choice, Prince George of Nebula (Harry Davenport), and she takes the obvious way out: she runs away. Nordland's face is saved when the new American ambassadress, Katherine Peepfogle (Marie Cahill), turns out to be the queen's double, and she is corralled into standing in for the missing monarch for the length of the evening's entertainment. Fields himself played Hubert, Katherine's brother, who surfaces unexpectedly during her impersonation to cause considerable embarrassment to the new 'queen', with Joseph Herbert in the supporting comic rôle of the Duke of Toxen, May Robson as the Queen's comical aunt and Pauline Frederick in the small part of a lady-in-waiting.

Herbert supplied one of his musical-comedy style of scores for the show, with Prince George's hymn to 'Absinthe frappé' proving the favourite number of the evening, but Miss Cahill had a fine *Grande-Duchesse de Gérolstein* finale to the first act, proclaiming herself 'Com-anderess in Chief' as well as a coon song routine that included 'Bandana Land' and 'The Coon Banshee', which gave her some unaccustomed coloratura moments. May Naudain, as an incidental Marchioness, sang in waltz time about 'The Knot of Blue', the Prince flirted with a maid (Bessie Clayton), threatening to sail her away on 'My Catamaran', and a pretty second-act opening entitled 'Al Fresco' proved popular enough to later become an orchestral favourite. There was also an Indian Squaws' chorus, which raised a few questions as to where precisely Nordland was supposed to be situated.

It Happened in Nordland opened at Harrisburg on 21 November 1904, but its New York opening was delayed a few days when producer Hamlin died. When it opened, as the first entertainment at the new Lew Fields Theater, it won pleased notices, and settled in for what looked like being a trouble-free run. In her usual style, however, Miss Cahill soon began to bring in her own material to interpolate into the musical part of the show. This caused a showdown with Herbert and, when Lew Fields backed up his composer, Miss Cahill walked out of the show. Miss Frederick stepped in for five weeks and caught enough eyes and ears to help set in motion what would be a notable career before, incomprehensibly, Fields went and hired Blanche Ring as a star replacement. If there was one leading lady on Broadway more famous for her interpolations than Marie Cahill, it was Blanche Ring. She naturally interpolated, and she too was effectively fired. Amongst all this brouhaha *It Happened in Nordland* managed 154 successful Broadway performances, followed by a summer-break tour and a return to New York (31 August 1905) for a further 100 nights.

Recording: selection (part record) (AEI)

IT'S TIME TO DANCE Musical play (musical show) in 2 acts by Douglas Furber and L Arthur Rose. Lyrics by Harry Roy, Gaby Rogers, Harry Phillips and James Dyrenforth. Music by Kenneth Leslie-Smith, Roy, Rogers and Phillips. Winter Garden Theatre, London, 22 July 1943.

Jack Buchanan and Elsie Randolph returned, six years after their previous London musical together, with a piece whose title summed up the essence not of the era they were now in, but of that in which they had known their greatest success. *Me and My Girl* authors Rose and Furber supplied them with a conventional gangstery plot in which Buchanan played Willmott Brown who, assisted by the bulky comedian Fred Emney, infiltrates a gang of baddies

and pops in and out of a series of melodramatic-comic situations until the inevitable missing jewels are saved and the girl (Miss Randolph) won. The light, dancing score was topped by the star pair's 'I'm Looking for a Melody', and the all-important choreographic content of the show was given variety by the inclusion of both American dancer, Buddy Bradley, and adagio pair Daria Luna and Nevill Astor, who were featured alongside the more characterful dances of Randolph and Buchanan and the massed effects of the dancing chorus.

It's Time to Dance played three wartime months out of town, 259 performances in London, and then returned to the road. It played one more week in London in 1944 when a Manchester date had to be cancelled because of bombing, and that week represented Buchanan and Randolph's last London dance-and-comedy appearance as a West End pair.

IXION, or The Man at the Wheel Burlesque in 1 prologue, 4 scenes and ever so many tableaux by F C Burnand. Royalty Theatre, London, 28 September 1863.

One of the most successful of all the vast output of musical burlesques in the 1860s, *Ixion* brought its young author firmly to the forefront of burlesque writing, where he would remain for a quarter of a century. The story he chose to parody here was the classical tale of Ixion, King of the Lapiths and the father of the Centaurs, who drew down Zeus' wrath by trying to imitate his thunders and by paying court to the goddess Hera, and who was in consequence condemned to turn forever on a burning wheel in the depths of Hades.

Burnand's Ixion was a pretty, if inefficient, fellow ('though a King with a prefix of an 'X', it does not alphabetically follow that he has a *Wise Head* on his shoulders') who was played in travesty by Jenny Willmore. Bumped from his throne by his disloyal spouse, Queen Dia (Mrs Charles Selby), and a trio of conspiring Thessalian democrats, he nevertheless wins the favour of the Olympian family. Much of the evening's entertainment thereafter was found in the burlesqued qualities of the Roman gods – Mercury, 'the celestial telegraph boy', Apollo, 'secretary to the Imperial "Sun" Fire Insurance Co (Ltd)', Minerva ('a quiet lady, though appearing with an "owl"'), Bacchus ('promoter and chief director of the Celestial Light Wine Association') and the central Jupiter, Juno, Venus and Cupid, this last a short-tunicked travesty rôle reserved for the prettiest young actress of the company. The rôle of Minerva was also played in travesty, by the company's chief comedian, as were those of Mercury and Apollo. Jupiter's pretty cupbearer, Ganymede, however, was played as a fat boy, by a comic.

Staged at the Royalty Theatre under the management of Mrs Selby, *Ixion* was played for a remarkable 153 consecutive nights. The next season, when the Misses Pelham took over the theatre, they reprised the show (5 September 1864), themselves playing Ixion and Mercury, and provincial theatres were quick off the mark with their productions of the hottest burlesque in years. Burnand supplied the Royalty with a musequel, *Pirithous, Son of Ixion*, which played there, with Harriet Pelham in the title-rôle, whilst the original piece did a return season at the New Theatre, Greenwich (17 April 1865), with Florence Johnson as Ixion and the young Harriet Everard as Queen Dia. Then

Miss Pelham brought it back to the Royalty (5 August 1865) for a third successive season, with Ada Cavendish again playing her original rôle of Venus and Harriet Pelham now playing Jupiter. The Alexandra Theatre mounted its production with Eliza Hamilton as Ixion (21 October 1865) and the Pelhams' production was played at Astley's (9 October 1865), whilst in Nottingham the demand for seats was such that the local producer was obliged to play the show twice daily.

Amongst the companies which toured *Ixion* in 1865 was one headed by the planturous Lydia Thompson, and it was she who, although not the first to play the piece in New York, ended by spreading her americanized and topicalized version of *Ixion* through America. Supported by her famous troupe of British Blondes (many of whom were neither British nor blonde), she materially helped the show to win the same kind of popularity throughout America that it had won at home. In Britain, as in America, the piece held its place in the provinces for many years, in spite of the deluge of burlesques which competed for attention in the 1870s, and it even returned to London for further seasons at the Alexandra (March 1866), Sadlers Wells (2 April 1866) with Lizzie Willmore, at the Charing Cross Theatre (1870) with Edith Fowler starred, and in a revised version by Burnand as *Ixion Re-Wheeled* at the Opera Comique (21 November 1874).

The rest of the English-speaking world took to *Ixion* with equal vigour, and it became one of the half-dozen principal standards in the repertoires of burlesque companies throughout the globe. In Australia it seems to have been mounted for the first time by John Hall, with his wife Emily Wiseman as Ixion, supported by Julia Edouin (Venus), Tilly Earl (Cupid) and William Gill (Mercury), and it was later played by Bland Holt and his wife Lina Edwin, by San Francisco's three travelling Zavistowski 'sisters' (the two real sisters played Ixion and Mercury, the third – their mother – was Jupiter) and by many other lesser burlesque companies.

USA: Washington Hall, Williamsburgh 21 June 1866, Booth's Theater (revised version) 28 September 1868; Australia: 1866

J

JABUKA, or Das Apfelfest Operette in 3 acts by Max Kalbeck and Gustav Davis. Music by Johann Strauss. Theater an der Wien, Vienna, 12 October 1894.

One of the series of essentially disappointing Operetten for which Johann Strauss composed the music in the later years of his career, *Jabuka* was nevertheless mounted throughout central Europe following its original run at the Theater an der Wien. The choice of a libretto set in Serbian Hungary, not the most obvious for the composer of Viennese waltzes, was apparently dictated by Strauss's admiration for Smetana's *Prodaná nevsta* (*The Bartered Bride*), which had been played for a season at the Theater an der Wien in 1893, but the tale concocted by the neophyte librettists Gustav Davis and Max Kalbeck was a comico-amorous affair, of a different flavour to that of the Smetana piece.

Farmer's daughter Jelka (Jenny Pohlner) is heading for the local marriage market, the Apfelfest, dolled up in her finest and riding in an over-grand carriage, when she gets stuck in the mud. She is rescued by the less-than-wealthy but instantly lovestruck Count Mirko von Gradinaz (Karl Streitmann) whom she haughtily spurns, but she reacts more favourably to Mirko's pal, the comical bailiff Joschko (Alexander Girardi), who fools her into believing that he is a wealthy nobleman. Joschko whisks her off in Mirko's coach, but instead of delivering her to the city where the Apfelfest is taking place, he takes her to Mirko's castle and, indeed, to the gentleman's very bedroom. The lady's reaction when she discovers that she's been abducted is as predictable as is her ultimate winning over. Mirko's brother, Vasil (Herr Felix) and Annita (Therese Biedermann), daughter of the starch-manufacturing Bambora (Josef Joseffy), were the evening's number-two pair, whose amours reached their apotheosis at the same time as those of the number-one pair.

The three principal characters had the bulk of the music, with Girardi topping his first-act 'Im ganzen Land bin ich bekannt', and his comical description of Mirko's ancestral portraits, 'Alle uns're Ahnen waren, so zusagen, Gospodars', with the third-act 'Das Comität geht in der Höh', and Streitmann and Frln Pohlner leading the romantic numbers. The second pair had a pair of duets.

Jabuka was played 45 times before being removed in favour of a version of the French vaudeville *Patatart, Patatart et Cie*. When that flopped in a week, the standard repertoire was brought back and, amongst the *Der arme Jonathan*s and *Bettelstudent*s, a handful of *Jabuka* performances helped it to pass its 50th performance (an important figure in rights and publishing contracts) on 18 December. It was a disappointing record, well below that achieved by such recent Theater an der Wien successes as *Heisses Blut*, *Ein armes Mädel* and *Der Obersteiger*, and even less than Strauss's last and already disappointing work, *Fürstin*

Ninetta, the previous year. But the composer's reputation and name ensured *Jabuka* productions in Berlin, where Ottilie Collin appeared as Jelka alongside Steiner (Mirko) and Wellhof (Joschko), in Hamburg (Stadttheater, 17 January 1895), in Prague, Poland and in Budapest (ad Dezsö Megyeri, 8 performances), before it returned for a week of further performances (13 November 1895) in another Theater an der Wien repertoire period, following the flop of Louis Roth's *Der goldene Kamarad*.

The piece proved to have a little more subsequent appeal than *Fürstin Ninetta* amongst the minor Strauss works. In 1909 it was seen again in Vienna, at the Raimundtheater, with Franz Glawatsch as Joschko, Carl Streitmann as Mirko and Marthe Dorda-Winternitz as Jelka, and in 1942 a revised version, under the title *Das Apfelfest* (ad Karl Schleifer) was mounted at the Stadttheater in Kassel (22 September).

Germany: Friedrich-Wilhelmstädtisches Theater 7 November 1894; Hungary: Népszinház 21 September 1895

JACK O' LANTERN Musical comedy (musical extravaganza) in 2 acts by Anne Caldwell and R H Burnside. Music by Ivan Caryll. Globe Theater, New York, 16 October 1917.

After the splendid success of his version of *Aladdin* (*Chin-Chin*), producer Charles Dillingham ordered another vehicle on similar lines for comedians Montgomery and Stone from the same team of author Caldwell, author/director Burnside and composer Ivan Caryll. He got a piece which was, if anything, an even better prospect than his previous hit. *Jack o' Lantern* was another fairytale-based piece, leaning largely on the tale of *The Babes in the Wood*, with Montgomery and Stone cast in the famous British pantomime rôles of the two murderers and robbers – the nasty one and the kind-hearted one – who are hired by a beastly uncle to do away with his young wards.

The show was all prepared to go into rehearsal when Montgomery died. The authors hurriedly reorganized their piece, cutting down the two star rôles and making them up into one, and Stone starred in the resulting piece as Jack o' Lantern, a whimsical little fellow who is mistaken for the hired assassin by wicked Uncle George (Oscar Ragland) and who, thereafter, helps the threatened children to escape from Appledale Farm, through a series of pretty pantomime-extravaganza places, until safety is assured and Uncle George reformed and repentant. The trio passed by the Banquet Hall in Jack's villa (scenery: Homer Emens, mechanical properties by Charles T Aldrich), to the Cave of Dreams, to Candyland and to a place Outside the Lines (all by Joseph Urban), to Camp Nowhere for an army scene in which Allene Crater as Villainessa led a Signal Corps March (Emens), to Clowntown (Urban), where the Six Brown Brothers did their speciality, and finally to an Ice Carnival, designed by Ernest Albert, where Misses Ellen Dallerup and Katie Smith were able to get in their ice-skating speciality and Stone to give his impersonation of the skater, Charlotte, prior to the happy ending.

Caryll's score illustrated the fun and spectacle in the gay vein that he had so successfully practised at London's Gaiety Theatre, and he came up with one patent hit, and several other pieces which became highly popular. The hit, oddly enough, did not fall to Stone, but to Helen Falconer and Douglas Stevenson, jauntily singing and dancing their way through 'Wait Till the Cows Come Home'. Miss Falconer also had another success with 'A Sweetheart of My Own', Harold West and Kathleen Robinson as the two kiddies, Bobbie and Babbie, advised 'Take a Trip to Candyland', whilst Stone had his jolliest musical moment with the comical 'Follow the Girls Around'. The show used little in the way of interpolated songs, but Stone and Tessa Valerio performed one piece, 'I'll Take You Back to Italy', credited to the by now risen Irving Berlin.

Jack o' Lantern played 265 performances on Broadway before Stone went off to cash in on a lucrative engagement out west, but he returned to Dillingham in time to relaunch *Jack o' Lantern* at Boston's Colonial Theater for Christmas 1918 ('America's greatest entertainer in the incomparable musical extravaganza...') prior to a long and successful tour. In later days, when Stone had moved on to his next show with Dillingham, *Jack o' Lantern* continued to be a favourite on the touring circuits in a version which restored the script to its original state and featured two 'murderers' rather than one.

JACKSON, Ethel (b New York, 3 February 1877; d East Islip, NY, 23 November 1957). Broadway's *Merry Widow*, who never found another worthwhile vehicle.

Miss Jackson originally studied piano in America and in Vienna, but went on the stage at the age of 20 in the chorus of the D'Oyly Carte company at London's Savoy Theatre, appearing in a chorus rôle in *The Beauty Stone*, in the 1898 revival of *The Gondoliers* as Fiametta and understudying Emmie Owen as Gianetta and Florence Perry (Wanda) in *The Grand Duchess*. She was taken back to America by Charles Frohman to take the title-rôle in the British musical *Little Miss Nobody*, which closed on the road, but thereafter made several appearances in New York, taking over from Virginia Earle in *A Runaway Girl*, appearing as Little Red Riding-Hood in the Casino Theater's piece of that title in 1899, at Koster and Bial's in *The Regatta Girl*, as Cécile in *Hotel Topsy-Turvy* and as Gabriele in *Wiener Blut*. She also played in Philadelphia in the successful *Miss Bob White* before retiring from the stage after what had been a fairly unimpressive career. Four years later, however, she returned to Broadway in the rôle of the Indian singing-girl Chandra Nil, created by London's Florence Smithson, in a Broadway version of *The Blue Moon*, and the following year she won the title-rôle in the American production of *The Merry Widow*. With its success she made a name for herself.

She did not, however, go on to genuine stardom but, in a career which stretched to some 40 years, appeared spasmodically on the musical stage in such pieces as *The Wild Goose* (1912, Princess Violetta) and *The Purple Road* (1913), but never again in a rôle to equal her one big

success. She worked latterly in the non-musical theatre, making her last Broadway appearance in 1939 in *Key Largo*.

Miss Jackson married, and later divorced producer Fred Zimmerman. She then married the lawyer who had represented her in the divorce. When she subsequently divorced him, too, she doubtless used a different lawyer.

JACOBI, Georges (b Berlin, 13 February 1840; d London, 13 September 1906). Famous conductor and sometime director and composer for the British Victorian theatre.

Jacobi studied music in Brussels, attending the Conservatoire from the age of nine, and then in Paris, where he later played in the orchestra at the Opéra before becoming, at the age of 29, a conductor at the Théâtre des Bouffes-Parisiens. In that post he conducted a number of important Offenbach premières. There, also, his one-act opérettes *Le Feu aux poudres, La Nuit du 15 Octobre* and *Mariée depuis midi* were played, the last of which – starring Anna Judic – with sufficient success to be later played at Vienna's Carltheater (*Seit mittag vermählt*). The second appeared, as *The Fifteenth of October*, at London's Alhambra (1875) and Prince of Wales (1891) Theatres.

Jacobi moved to London during the Franco-Prussian War and, in 1871, he was appointed musical director of the Alhambra Theatre under John Baum. There he composed and arranged a vast amount of music for the spectacular shows of which the Alhambra made a speciality: full and part-scores, single songs, short operettas and, above all, over a hundred ballets and dance interludes. He also organized and arranged the pasticcio and part-pasticcio scores which for a long time made up the musical part of the Alhambra book-musical shows. Before he had been long at the Alhambra, Jacobi took over the stage direction of these shows, and many of the most spectacular of London's opéra-bouffe productions with their vast cohorts of extras and dancers and their monumental scenery were, in fact, staged by their musical director.

Amongst the shows which, apart from his own compositions and concoctions, he conducted during more than 16 years at the head of the Alhambra's orchestra were the London productions of many of Offenbach's works, including the original production of his London piece, *Whittington*, and other large-scale French opéras-bouffes, Clay's *Don Quixote* and the grand opéra-bouffe féerie *La Poule aux oeufs d'or* (for both of which he also supplied the dance music) and the aggrandized revival of Burnand's *Black-Eyed Susan* (1884).

Jacobi appeared occasionally as a conductor in other theatres (St James's Theatre *Le Voyage dans la lune*, Avenue Theatre *La Vie, Nell Gwynne* etc) but the largest part of his career was spent in the service of the Alhambra until he departed from that theatre, the functions of which had severely altered, in 1897. He subsequently directed the orchestra at the Crystal Palace.

1869 **Le Feu aux poudres** (N Fournier, Élie Frébault) 1 act Concert performance 21 March; Théâtre des Bouffes-Parisiens 11 April
1869 **La Nuit du 15 Octobre** (Eugène Leterrier, Albert Vanloo) 1 act Théâtre des Bouffes-Parisiens 15 October
1872 **The Black Crook** (w Frederic Clay/Harry Paulton, Joseph Paulton) Alhambra Theatre 23 December

1873 **Mariée depuis midi** (William Busnach, Armand Liorat)
1 act Marseille 20 August, Théâtre des Bouffes-Parisiens
6 March 1874

1874 **The Demon's Bride** (Leterrier, Vanloo ad H J Byron)
Alhambra Theatre 7 September

1876 **Le Ruy Blas des Batignolles** (Clerc brothers) Fantaisies-
Parisiennes 4 April

1879 **Rothomago** (w Edward Solomon, Procida Bucalossi,
Gaston Serpette/H B Farnie) Alhambra Theatre 22
December

1882 **Le Clairon** (Gaston Marot, Frébault, Édouard Philippe)
Lyon; Théâtre de la Renaissance, Paris 7 November 1883

1885 **Chirruper's Fortune** (w others/Arthur Law) Portsmouth
31 August

1886 **The Two Pros** (Frederick Bowyer) 1 act Prince of Wales
Theatre 4 December

1886 **Vetah** arranged and supplemented the late Firmin Bernicat's score (tour)

1895 **The Newest Woman** (H Chance Newton) 1 act Avenue
Theatre 4 April

JACOBI, Viktor [JAKABFI, Viktor] (b Budapest, 22
October 1883; d New York, 10 December 1921). One of
the group of successful Hungarian composers who dominated the European musical stage in the early 20th century,
who lost his way when he left his native country.

Jacobi studied at the Budapest Zeneakadémia, alongside
Kálmán and Szirmai, and was still a student when his first
work was produced at no less a venue than the Budapest
Népszinház (as Jakabfi). *A rátartós királykisasszony* (the
proud princess), described as a mesejáték (fable, fairytale)
in 5 scenes, and based on Holger Drachmann's *Der var en
Gang* (once upon a time) was written by Jenő Heltai, the
lyricist of the recently produced *János vitéz*. It played a
respectable 33 times with Klára Küry in its title-rôle.

Still in his early twenties, Jacobi collaborated for the first
time with librettist Ferenc Martos on *A legvitézebb huszár*
(the bravest hussar), in which Ákos Ráthonyi appeared
with great success at the Magyar Színház, and set Heltai's
lyrics for the fairy play *A tengerszem tündére* (the sea fairy)
('Ha én rózsa volnék', 'Ki vagy te gyönyörűségem', 'Be
sokat ígér s ki tudja mier?') in which Ráthonyi paired with
Olga Turchányi at the same house. He also gained a considerable success with his score to Martos's musicalization
of Mór Jókai's poetic fairytale *Az istenhegyi székeley leány*,
produced at the Király Színház under the title *Tüskerózsa*
(prickly rose) with a top-class cast including Sári Fedák,
Márton Rátkai, József Németh and Kornél Sziklai.

In 1908 Jacobi supplied the accompanying music for
Martos's ten-scene *100 év mulva* (100 years after), and the
Király Színház also mounted his Operette *Van de nincs*
(there is, but there isn't) in which Vilma Medgyaszay
scored a hit with the gavotte 'Szökellő keskeny ici-pici láb',
as well as another Martos fairytale Operette, *Jánoska*, again
with Fedák featured ('Tul, tul, tul az óperencian'), which
initially ran rather less long than its predecessors, but
which was brought back as late as 1925 for a revival at the
Király Színház (24 October).

In spite of the fact that he had been collaborating with
some of the finest names in the Hungarian theatre, the
breakthrough into wider success only came when Jacobi
moved on from the *János vitéz*-influenced style of mythi-
cal/fairytale subject which these early works had followed,
and into something more attractive to the strivingly up-to-
date theatres of the outside world. That success was

Plate 137. **Viktor Jacobi***'s earliest works were in the fairytale vein
popularized by the success of* János vitéz.

accomplished with *Leányvásár*, a piece which took the
American west as its setting, the well-used fair-wedding
plot, most famously used in Flotow's *Martha*, as its basic
element, and which the composer filled to the brim with
the kind of dancing melodies the English-speaking theatre
currently favoured, the whole coloured with an individual
and, above all to the foreigner, exotic Hungarian tint. A
major hit on its production in Hungary, *Leányvásár* went on
to become a worldwide property, a veritable smash in
London, and it remains a solid element of the basic
Hungarian repertoire up to the present day.

The musical-comedy-styled *Leányvásár* was followed up
by an even bigger success when Martos, Miksa Bródy and
Jacobi collaborated on a second outward-looking piece,
but this time one which had more of the romantic operetta
element mixed with its lively dances and songs and its
comic moments. Even in the face of the competition coming from Vienna, in particular, on the eve of the First
World War, *Szibill* proved to be one of the outstanding
musical plays of its time, and Jacobi's newly established
international reputation was well and truly confirmed.

The composer was not slow to follow up this success
and, in 1914, he was to be found in London, where *The
Marriage Market* (*Leányvásár*) was still running, and where
it was rumoured that he would write the score for George
Edwardes's next piece, when the war broke out. There was
no question of Edwardes or anyone else employing any
Central European composer whilst Britain was at war with
Central Europe, and people like columnist and aspiring
composer Jimmy Glover were busy rooting anyone with a
remotely Germanic name out of every seaside band in

Britain. Jacobi's British prospects went down the drain along with those of Jean Gilbert who, like him, had recently become a West End favourite. When another rumour was spread to the effect that perhaps he had composed some music for Edwardes already, and that Paul Rubens had accommodatingly put his name to it, Rubens took the rumour-monger to court, and won.

Jacobi, in the meantime, moved on to America, where it was still possible for an Hungarian composer with a few hits to his name to find work. He quickly became naturalized as an American citizen, and his name soon appeared on a Broadway bill, as the composer of *Rambler Rose* (1917). Broadway's *Szibill* star Julia Sanderson featured, but Harry B Smith's book was a now-you-marry-money-now-you-don't sort of piece, far from the colourful romance of the Hungarian show, and *Rambler Rose* lasted only 72 performances on Broadway. *Apple Blossoms*, two seasons later, was based on a similarly slight tale of the road to marriage. This time, Jacobi shared the composing credit with Fritz Kreisler, but it was his 'You Are Free' and 'Little Girls, Goodbye' which proved the pick of the score through the show's seven months of Broadway run and subsequent life on the road.

It was this taste of success which apparently encouraged Jacobi to stick with the marriage-and-money type of libretto (and with librettist Le Baron) which seemed so alien to his style of composition, and it proved a mistake. *The Half Moon* was a quick flop in spite of a cast headed by Joseph Cawthorn, Joseph Santley and Ivy Sawyer, and an attempt by Dillingham to give the composer an opportunity to work in his Hungarian element also failed. Le Baron's emasculation of Molnár's *A Farkas* as *The Love Letter* did not inspire the now extremely nerve-racked composer to the heights of a *Szibill* and the show was again a quick failure (31 performances).

Jacobi's American episode had been an almost unmitigated failure. In the few years since his departure from Budapest he had fallen from a pre-eminent place, on a par with Fall, Lehár, Kálmán and Gilbert, in the European musical theatre, and at the same time he had destroyed his health. He died shortly after the failure of *The Love Letter*.

An operett called *Miámi*, with Jacobi music arranged by Zsigmond Vincze, and attached to an Hungarian-authored libretto set in Florida, was mounted in Budapest several years after the composer's death. A top-flight trio of local performers in Sári Petráss, Hanna Honthy and Teri Féjes featured, but the local opinion was that Jacobi's 'American' music was only a shadow of that of his pre-war works. A few weeks later the Theater an der Wien in Vienna mounted a half-dozen performances of a version of *Jánoska* as a children's Christmas entertainment, as one of the most promising careers of the 20th-century musical theatre went sadly out on the proverbial whimper.

1904 **A rátartós királykisasszony** (Jenő Heltai) Népszinház 17 December
1905 **A legvitézebb huszár** (Ferenc Martos) Magyar Színház 30 December
1906 **A tengerszem tündére** (Heltai/Zoltán Thury) Magyar Színház 7 November
1907 **Tüskerózsa** (Martos) Király Színház 23 March
1908 **Van, de nincs** (Martos) Király Színház 30 October
1909 **Jánoska** (Martos) Király Színház 7 May

1911 **Leányvásár** (Martos, Miksa Bródy) Király Színház 14 November
1914 **Szibill** (Martos, M Bródy) Király Színház 27 February
1917 **Rambler Rose** (Harry B Smith) Empire Theater, New York 10 September
1919 **Apple Blossoms** (w Fritz Kreisler/William Le Baron) Globe Theater, New York 7 October
1920 **The Half Moon** (Le Baron) Liberty Theater, New York 1 November
1921 **The Love Letter** (Le Baron) Globe Theater, New York 4 October
1925 **Miámi** (pasticcio/István Bródy, László Vajda) Fővárosi Operettszinház 27 November

JACOBSON, Leopold (b Czernowitz, 30 June 1878; d Theresienstadt, 23 February 1943).

Theatre critic, chief editor of the *Neues Wiener Journal*, dramatist and operettic librettist, Jacobson began his career in the musical theatre with a fine series of successes: Oscar Straus's *Ein Walzertraum* and *Der tapfere Soldat*, Nedbal's *Die keusche Barbara* and Granichstädten's *Auf Befehl der Herzogin*. If his first great success with Straus remained his most memorable, he nevertheless worked with the composer later on such long-running pieces as *Eine Ballnacht* and *Dorfmusikanten*, teamed profitably with Robert Stolz on *Die Tanzgräfin* and with Künneke on *Lady Hamilton*, and had a particularly fruitful alliance with Jean Gilbert, for whom he supplied the texts for *Katja, die Tänzerin* and *Das Weib im Purpur*.

His many-highlighted career in the theatre was over well before the Second World War, in which he was deported and then murdered.

1907 **Ein Walzertraum** (Oscar Straus/w Felix Dörmann) Carltheater 2 March
1908 **Der tapfere Soldat** (Straus/w Rudolf Bernauer) Theater an der Wien 14 November
1910 **Die keusche Barbara** (Oscar Nedbal/w Bernauer) Theater Weinberge, Prague 14 September; Raimundtheater 7 October 1911
1912 **Adam und Eva** (Schweiger) 1 act Ronacher 1 March
1913 **Fürst Ypsilon** (Friedrich Bermann/Somerset Maugham ad) Schauburg, Hannover 15 March
1915 **Auf Befehl der Herzogin** (Bruno Granichstädten/w Robert Bodanzky) Theater an der Wien 20 March
1915 **Die schöne Unbekannte** (Straus/w Leo Stein) Carltheater 15 January
1916 **Warum geht's denn jetzt?** (Edmund Eysler/w Bodanzky) Bundestheater 5 July
1917 **Nachtfalter** (Straus/w Bodanzky) Ronacher 13 March
1918 **Eine Ballnacht** (Straus/w Bodanzky) Johann Strauss-Theater 11 October
1919 **Der Liebesteufel** (Julius Bistron/w Bodanzky) Wiener Komödienhaus 17 October
1919 **Dorfmusikanten** (Straus/w Bodanzky) Theater an der Wien 29 November
1919 **Was Mädchen träumen** (Leo Ascher/w Bodanzky) Raimundtheater 6 December
1920 **Yuschi tanzt** (Ralph Benatzky/w Bodanzky) Wiener Bürgertheater 3 April
1921 **Die Tanzgräfin** (Robert Stolz/w Bodanzky) Wallner-Theater, Berlin 18 February
1923 **Katja, die Tänzerin** (Jean Gilbert/w Rudolf Österreicher) Johann Strauss-Theater 5 January
1923 **Das Weib im Purpur** (Gilbert/w Österreicher) Wiener Stadttheater 21 December
1924 **Der Tanz um die Liebe** (Straus/w Heinz Saltenburg) Deutsches/Künstlertheater, Berlin 25 September

1925 **Maiermax** (Hugo Hirsch/w Österreicher) Lessing-Theater, Berlin 31 December

1926 **Lady Hamilton** (Eduard Künneke/w Richard Bars) Schauspielhaus, Breslau 25 September

1927 **Eine einzige Nacht** (Stolz/w Österreicher) Carltheater 23 December

1928 **Eine Nacht in Kairo** (Gilbert/w Bruno Hardt-Warden) Centraltheater, Dresden 23 December

1928 **Hochzeit in Hollywood** (Straus/w Hardt-Warden) Johann Strauss-Theater 21 December

1929 **Die Frau in Gold** (Michael Krasznay-Krausz/w Hardt-Warden) Neues Operetten-Theater, Leipzig 28 February

1930 **Tschun-Tschi** (W Cliffords/John Gardener, Anna Mae Wong ad w Grünbaum) Neues Wiener Schauspielhaus 14 August

DIE JAGD NACH DEM GLÜCK Comic Operette in a Vorspiel and 3 acts by Richard Genée and Bruno Zappert. Music by Franz von Suppé. Carltheater, Vienna, 27 October 1888.

Suppé's *Die Jagd nach dem Glück* had only a fair introduction to Vienna, with a run of little more than a month at the Carltheater, but its more substantial than usual musical content won it praise from the critics and it was given a number of productions abroad, going through some curious permutations on the way.

Genée and Zappert's original text told of the 'chase after happiness' of Bavarian Rudolf, the foster-son of Graf Wilfried. Rudolf (Carl Streitmann) is engaged to be wed to Wilfried's daughter Stella (Frln Seebold), but he suddenly decides that he is not ready for marriage, and, with his servant Casimir (Herr Wittels) in supportive tow, quits his home town and heads off to Paris in search of fame and fortune. Stella, a wise lass, follows him in the disguise of a street-singer, accompanied by Casimir's sweetheart Fanny (Frln Augustin). In Paris, Rudolf squanders his money and falls ruinously under the spell of the danseuse Florinde (Frln Tischler). In a last impoverished stroke he gambles all but the fare home, and loses. Unfortunately, in the meanwhile Casimir has been robbed of the fare-money by a highwayman. Deserted by all his fairweather French friends, Rudolf joins the Swedish army and leads them to a fine victory over the Danes, but the old Swedish king dies and he wins no reward. Venice in carnival time sees him fall once again into feminine webs and Rudolf – finally convinced that the 'chase after happiness' in the form of money and fame is a vain one – returns home. Stella, who has watched over him all the way, will be there to welcome him.

In Germany Suppé's score was detached from its text and tacked on to another libretto by Hermann Hirschel under the title *Die Brautjagd*, and the resultant piece was produced at the Friedrich-Wilhelmstädtisches Theater (16 February 1894), whilst in America the show was produced by John McCaull under the meaningless title of *Clover*. The reason for this was that librettist Harry B Smith had promised the members of New York's Clover Club that he would give them a plug, and this was his way of doing so. Perhaps the club's members were responsible for repaying Smith by attending Palmer's Theatre, for *Clover*, with a cast headed by De Wolf Hopper (Casimir), Jeff de Angelis (Don Cristoval), Eugene Oudin (Rudolf), Marion Manola (Stella) and Mathilde Cottrelly (Petronella) became a solid hit, unmarred by a row between Oudin and Miss Manola which caused them to walk out. McCaull got a run of 173 Broadway performances from the show, a success which encouraged the Amberg Theater to try the original German version. With original star Streitmann (Rudolf), Friese jr (Casimir), Guste Zimmermann (Stella) and Carola Englander featured, it ran for an initial week and was reprised later in the season.

Another show of the same title, composed by Leo Fall, was produced at the Carl Weiss-Theater, Berlin 1 February 1900.

USA: Palmer's Theater *Clover* 8 May 1889, Amberg Theater 10 April 1890

J'AIME Opérette in 3 acts by Albert Willemetz and Saint-Granier. Music by Henri Christiné. Théâtre des Bouffes-Parisiens, Paris, 22 December 1926.

The Théâtre des Bouffes-Parisiens and producers Gustave Quinson and Edmond Roze (also director) staged Willemetz and Christiné's *J'aime* at the continuing height of the vogue for the up-to-date musical comedy which had been inaugurated at the same theatre, and by the same authors, eight years previously. Now there were other writers and composers on the same wagon – the Bouffes itself had just had an enormous success with Raoul Moretti's *Trois jeunes filles ... nues!* written to a libretto by Yves Mirande and the inevitable Willemetz – but Christiné and Willemetz proved surefire winners once again with their new piece, one which re-used many of the creative team from the previous show.

The penniless Baron (Le Gallo) and Baroness (Nina Myral) de Malassis de la Panouille inherit a vast fortune from his late and disgraced sister who ran away to become a circus rider. But – horror! – they can touch the money only when they have spent a year and a day working in a circus. They become comically incompetent jugglers, but they win through with the aid of the little black-bottom dancing dog of the lawyer (Koval) who is overseeing their calvary. Of course, the sister (Marguerite Peuget) is not dead at all, she has married a duke and is merely wreaking her revenge on her snooty relatives before helping them out. Pretty Sim-Viva, baritone Géo Bury, soubrette Christiane Dor and Gustave Nellson, all from the *Trois jeunes filles ... nues!* cast, were the singing and dancing younger generation, whilst Gabin père as a comical General completed the star line up.

Christiné's score was in his inexhaustibly lively, tuneful and modern style, ranging from Koval's description of 'L'Inventeur du Charleston', comically detailing the alleged origins of the dance, and his syncopated song of the soundless 'Biniou', to lightsome ballads and the music of the circus. Sim-Viva described the joys of the telephone for long-distance lovemaking in spite of intrusive operators, whilst Le Gallo and Myral, in rôles made on the Dranem and Jeanne Cheirel format, sang in an embarrassed and brisk pianissimo of what to do 'Quand on n'a pas d'argent' and made a middle-aged attempt to dance the polka. Bury discovered the aristocratic delight of having a 'de' in his name and romanced over 'Djibouti', Myral comically demanded that her marriageable daughter choose between 'le Rolls Royce, les chapeaux d'Lewis, l'château en Anjou, la villa à Nice, l'hiver en Tunis' or the pawnshop and her sweetheart, and whooped out the joys of circus life as opposed to aristocratic leisure ('Quand on en a goûté'), whilst Mlle Dor swooped saucily through 'J'attends' and 'Pour faire son trou', in a score which also boasted real concerted finales and some delightful ensembles.

A good Paris life, a longer touring one, and a production as far afield as Budapest (ad Zsolt Harsányi, Adorján Stella) all went to help add *J'aime* to Christiné and Willemetz's list of hit shows.

Hungary: Király Színház *Szeretlek* 26 May 1928

JAIME, [Louis] Adolphe [né GEM] (b Paris, 1824; d Paris, March 1901).

A prolific author of vaudevilles and opérettes, Adolphe Jaime had his name attached – along with those of some of the most imaginative comic writers of the time – to a good number of important musical theatre pieces of the second half of the 19th century and, posthumously, to one or two 20th-century adaptations of his work.

Jaime's earliest little pieces for the musical stage (a number of which – such as Delibes' *Maître Griffard* and *M de Bonne-Étoile* and Jonas's *Le Manoir des Larenadière* – he did not sign) included Offenbach's *Croquefer* and *Une Demoiselle en loterie*, Jonas's most successful short piece *Les Petits Prodiges* and, above all, *Six Demoiselles à marier*, originally set with some success by Delibes but later and memorably reset in a German translation by von Suppé as his highly successful *Zehn Mädchen und kein Mann*.

The playwright's entry into the full-length opéra-bouffe was equally as successful, his earliest works being a collaboration with Philippe Gille on the text for Delibes' *La Cour du Roi Pétaud*, with Hector Crémieux on the libretti and lyrics for Hervé's extravagant burlesque *Le Petit Faust*, the parody of *Bajazet*, *Les Turcs*, and the Scots high-jinks of *La Trône d'Écosse*, and yet another with Jules Noriac, on the sweetly scabrous and hugely successful *La Timbale d'argent*.

In latter years his success rate in the musical – if not the comic – theatre fell somewhat, as the burlesque style of pre-war years gave way to a more moderate comic opera variety of libretto, and the best of Jaime's musical theatre ventures proved to be his remade libretto, *La Reine Indigo*, for Johann Strauss's *Indigo und die vierzig Räuber* score, and a new and enlarged remake of Étienne Tréfeu's *Geneviève de Brabant* text for an 1875 revival.

Several of his vaudevilles and comedies were later adapted to the musical stage elsewhere, the most notable being his *Coquin de printemps* (Folies-Dramatiques 13 June 1888 w Georges Duval) which was made into London's *The Spring Chicken* and Vienna's *Frühlingsluft*, both highly successful pieces, and much later into a French musical comedy. His vaudeville *Cent mille francs et ma fille* (w Gille) was musicalized as *100,000 Gulden und meine Tochter* by Edvard Dorn, music by Ludwig Gothov-Grüneke, for Vienna's Theater in der Josefstadt (18 January 1879).

1856 **Six Demoiselles à marier** (Léo Delibes/w Adolphe Choler) 1 act Théâtre des Bouffes-Parisiens 12 November
1857 **Le Roi boit** (Émile Jonas/w Eugène Mestépès) 1 act Théâtre des Bouffes-Parisiens 9 April
1857 **Les Petits Prodiges** (Jonas/w Étienne Tréfeu) 1 act Théâtre des Bouffes-Parisiens 19 November
1857 **Croquefer** (Offenbach/w Tréfeu) 1 act Théâtre des Bouffes-Parisiens 12 February
1857 **Dragonette** (Offenbach/w Mestépès) 1 act Théâtre des Bouffes-Parisiens 30 April
1857 **Une Demoiselle en loterie** (Offenbach/w Hector Crémieux) 1 act Théâtre des Bouffes-Parisiens 27 July
1858 **La Harpe d'or** (Félix Godefroid/w Ernest Dubreuil) Théâtre Lyrique 8 September
1859 **Les Vivandières de la grande armée** (Offenbach/w Pittaud de Forges) 1 act Théâtre des Bouffes-Parisiens 6 July
1862 **Zehn Mädchen und kein Mann** (*Six Demoiselles à marier*) (Franz von Suppé/w Choler tr Karl Treumann) 1 act Theater am Franz-Josefs-Kai 25 October
1863 **L'Argent et l'amour** (Eugène Déjazet/w Colin, Auguste Polo) Théâtre Déjazet 5 February
1863 **La Mère de la débutante** (Eugène Moniot) 1 act Théâtre des Folies-Dramatiques 13 July
1869 **L'Écossais de Chatou** (Delibes/w Philippe Gille) 1 act Théâtre des Bouffes-Parisiens 16 January
1869 **La Cour du Roi Pétaud** (Delibes/w Gille) Théâtre des Variétés 24 April
1869 **Le Petit Faust** (Hervé/w Crémieux) Théâtre des Folies-Dramatiques 28 April
1870 **Les Turcs** (Hervé/w Crémieux) Théâtre des Folies-Dramatiques 23 December
1871 **Le Barbier de Trouville** (Charles Lecocq/w Jules Noriac) 1 act Théâtre des Bouffes-Parisiens 19 November
1871 **Le Trône d'Écosse** (Hervé/w Crémieux) Théâtre des Variétés 17 November
1872 **Un fi, deux fi, trois figurants** (Léon Vasseur) 1 act Alcazar 1 April
1872 **La Timbale d'argent** (Vasseur/w Noriac) Théâtre des Bouffes-Parisiens 9 April
1872 **Mon mouchoir** (Vasseur) 1 act Théâtre des Bouffes-Parisiens 9 May
1873 **L'Exemple** (Moniot) 1 act Théâtre des Bouffes-Parisiens 1 January
1873 **La Petite Reine** (Vasseur/w Noriac) Théâtre des Bouffes-Parisiens 9 January
1873 **La Casque de Thémistocle** (Fouqué) la Théâtre du Tivoli 18 April
1873 **Le Mouton enragé** (Lacôme/w Noriac) 1 act Théâtre des Bouffes-Parisiens 27 May
1873 **Les Amours d'un pierrot** (Georges Rose) 1 act Délassement-Comiques 6 October
1874 **La Branche cassée** (Gaston Serpette/w Noriac) Théâtre des Bouffes-Parisiens 23 January
1874 **Madame de Rabucor** (Mme de Ste Croix) 1 act Théâtre des Bouffes-Parisiens 5 February
1874 **Paille d'avoine** (Robert Planquette/w Adolphe Lemonnier, Rozale) 1 act Délassements-Comiques 12 March
1875 **Geneviève de Brabant** (Offenbach/revised version w Tréfeu) Théâtre de la Gaîté 25 February
1875 **La Reine Indigo** (*Indigo und die vierzig Räuber*) French replacement libretto w Victor Wilder (Théâtre de la Renaissance)
1886 **Il était une fois...** (Oscar de Lagoanère/Doré-Simiane) Théâtre des Menus-Plaisirs 1 May
1888 **Mam'zelle Crénom** (Vasseur/w Georges Duval) Théâtre des Bouffes-Parisiens 19 January
1888 **Le Mariage avant la lettre** (Olivier Métra/w Duval) Théâtre des Bouffes-Parisiens 5 December
1889 **Le Diable à quatre** (Monteux-Brissac) 1 act La Cigale 4 October
1892 **Eros** (Paul Vidal/w Noriac, Maurice Bouchor) Théâtre des Bouffes-Parisiens 22 April
1893 **Les Colles des femmes** (Louis Ganne/w Henri Kéroul) Menus-Plaisirs 29 September

JAKOBOWSKI, Edward [aka BELLEVILLE, Edward or Edouard] (b London, 17 April 1858; d London 29 April 1929). The composer of the score for one vast international hit, which was never confirmed.

Born in Hanover Street, Islington, the son of a Polish-born commercial traveller, Israel Jakobowski, and his Viennese wife, Fanny Schenheit, Jakobowski spent his youth in Vienna where he studied music under Hellmesberger and saw his first small operetta, *Le Réveil* (1873), played privately. He moved first to Paris, and then back to Britain, where a showcase production of a burlesque *Little Carmen* (1884), written with another novice, Alfred Murray, attracted the attention of Gaiety Theatre manager John Hollingshead who, as a result, co-commissioned and staged the collaborators' comic-opera version of the Dick Whittington tale, *Dick* (1884), at the Globe Theatre.

The following year, Jakobowski leapt to fame when he composed the score for Violet Melnotte's production of *Erminie*. *Erminie* proved to be one of the outstanding shows of its era. The most successful of all comic operas on the 19th-century American stage, it toured incessantly in Britain for many years, won a variety of overseas productions, and its Lullaby ('Dear Mother, In Dreams I See Her') became a popular American hit.

The celebrity Jakobowski found, particularly in America, as 'the composer of *Erminie*' gradually frittered away as he failed to come up with another winner. A well-made piece built by and for the *Erminie* team, *Mynheer Jan* (1887), went under amidst backstage squabbles, a bandit musical called *Paola* (1889) found a limited success touring in Britain and America, a Broadway score for *Erminie* star Francis Wilson, *The Devil's Deputy* (1894), written to the libretto of the French opérette *Babolin*, was played 72 times in New York before touring, and a musical comedy for comedian Arthur Roberts, *Milord Sir Smith* (1898), based on another borrowed Continental text, had only an average success.

Jakobowski had, perhaps, his most satisfying result of the post-*Erminie* period with the well-considered *Die Brillanten-Königin*. Written for the Vienna Carltheater, it was played there for 34 performances in 1894 before going on to Prague (1 July 1894) and then being heavily rewritten for London and New York. However, the composer's affairs were by this stage in a sad state. A much-touted commission for another musical for Wilson never eventuated, in 1902 Jakobowski was declared bankrupt, and a final attempt for the American stage ended in embarrassment. His score for *Winsome Winnie* was abandoned on the road in favour of some routine music by Kerker, as the man who had been the toast of Broadway in the late 1880s vanished into professional oblivion.

Several other compositions from his pen appeared over the following decade or so, but they were played by provincial amateurs and did not get a professional performance.

Amongst his minor credits is included additional music for the British touring show *Pat*, whilst his name appears, along with that of André Messager, as the composer of the incidental music for a production of the Eugène Grangé/Victor Bernard play *Az eltévedt bárányka (La Brebis égarée)* at the Budapest Népszinház in 1887.

1883 **The Three Beggars** (Sinclair Dunn) 1 act Royal Academy of Music 28 July

1884 **Little Carmen** (Alfred Murray) Globe Theatre 7 February
1884 **Dick** (Murray) Globe Theatre 17 April
1885 **Erminie** (Harry Paulton, Claxson Bellamy) Comedy Theatre 9 November
1886 **Mass-en-yell-oh** (Paulton, Mostyn Tedde) Comedy Theatre 23 March
1886 **The Palace of Pearl** (w Frederick Stanislaus/Murray, Willie Younge) Empire Theatre 12 June
1887 **Mynheer Jan** (Paulton, Mostyn Tedde) Comedy Theatre 14 February
1889 **Paola** (Paulton, Mostyn Tedde) Fifth Avenue Theater, New York 26 August
1893 **La Rosière** (Harry Monkhouse) Shaftesbury Theatre 14 January
1893 **The Venetian Singer** (B C Stephenson) 1 act Court Theatre 25 November
1894 **Die Brillanten-Königin** (Theodore Taube, Isidore Fuchs) Carltheater, Vienna 25 March
1894 **The Queen of Brilliants** (Brandon Thomas, new version of *Die Brillanten-Königin*) Lyceum, London 8 September
1894 **The Devil's Deputy** (J Cheever Goodwin) Abbey's Theater, New York 10 September
1898 **Milord Sir Smith** (ex-*Campano*) (George Day, Adrian Ross) Comedy Theatre 15 December
1899 **La Tarantella** Chicago August
1912 **The Myrtle Maiden, or the Girl of Granada** (O'Reilly) Ladbroke Hall (copyright performance) 13 July

JAMAICA Musical in 2 acts by E Y Harburg and Fred Saidy. Lyrics by Harburg. Music by Harold Arlen. Imperial Theater, New York, 31 October 1957.

Jamaica was a slice of Caribbean romance originally conceived as a vehicle for Harry Belafonte (as *Pigeon Island*) but subsequently re-invented as a vehicle for singing star Lena Horne, in the rôle of luscious Miss Savannah from the said Pigeon Island. For most of the evening Savannah refused to make do with the equally luscious local fisherman Koli (Ricardo Montalban), for she had her eye firmly fixed on getting out of Pigeon Island and up to New York. The get-rich-quick slicker, Joe Nashua (Joe Adams), seems like her ticket north but, thanks to a timely hurricane, she comes to her senses, stays home and marries the fisherman. A good half of the show's songs, both romantic ('Cocoanut Sweet') and comic ('Push de Button', 'Ain't it the Truth', 'Napoleon') were devoted to the star, with Montalban ('Monkey in the Mango Tree', 'Savannah'), Josephine Premice ('Leave the Atom Alone') and Adelaide Hall ('For Every Fish') sharing the remainder, but none of the numbers found the favour that Arlen's greatest and best songs had done.

The piece, however, served its star and its purpose well enough for David Merrick's shrewdly publicized production to run for 558 performances on Broadway.

Recording: original cast (RCA)

JANIS, Elsie [BIERBOWER, Elsie] (b Columbus, Ohio, 16 March 1889; d Los Angeles, 26 February 1956). Revue and musical comedy soubrette, specializing in impersonations.

Miss Janis began her career as 'Little Elsie', a child performer, in vaudeville. With one of the most famous stage mothers of all time behind and beside her, she made her first move into the legitimate theatre at the age of 15, making her earliest musical comedy appearance as Fifi in a touring company of *The Belle of New York*, then in productions of *The Fortune Teller* and *The Little Duchess* on the road. She was seen on Broadway for the first time in the burlesque *When We Were Forty-One*, performing the impersonations which were her speciality act and touted as America's answer to Cissie Loftus. She also managed to squeeze this 'spot' into the more legitimate musical comedy *The Vanderbilt Cup*, in which she was cast as the juvenile heroine, in her book-musical début on Broadway the following season.

A musical comedy version of Tristam Bernard's *La Soeur* produced on Broadway as *The Hoyden* (1907), a piece which cast her as *The Fair Co-Ed* (1909), Leslie Stuart's *The Slim Princess* (1910–11) and the rôle of Cinderella in Victor Herbert's *The Lady of the Slipper* alongside Montgomery and Stone (1912) provided further and similarly above-the-title opportunities. In 1914 she appeared in London in *The Passing Show* before returning home to play her last Broadway musical rôle in *Miss Information* (1915). Thereafter she appeared widely in revue in both America and Britain, latterly often performing material of her own making, and was seen again in musical comedy only when she toured America in the latter stages of her career, playing the title rôle in *Oh, Kay!*

During the war she was prominent amongst the troops' entertainers, taking the soubriquet 'The Sweetheart of the AEF', and after the hostilities were over she trouped with a group of ex-servicemen in a variety show entitled *Elsie Janis and her Gang* (1919). She retired from the stage in 1929 and for some years worked in the film industry as a writer (*Close Harmony, Madam Satan*) and production supervisor (*Paramount on Parade*).

Autobiographies: *So Far, So Good!* (Dutton, New York, 1932), *The Big Show, My Six Months with the American Expeditionary Forces* (Cosmopolitan, New York, 1919)

JÁNOS VITÉZ

JÁNOS VITÉZ   A play with songs (daljaték) in 3 acts by Károly Bakonyi based on the dramatic poem by Sándor Petőfi. Lyrics by Jenő Heltai. Music by Pongrác Kacsoh. Király Színház, Budapest, 18 November 1904.

János vitéz (brave John), the most celebrated and loved of all Hungarian musical plays, has been revived regularly and widely in its country of origin in the nearly 90 years since its first production, and it has become regarded virtually as the Hungarian national show, without attracting the attention of the rest of the world.

The shepherd, János (Sári Fedák), is in love with the orphaned Iluska (Vilma Medgyaszay), and she returns his love, to the despair of the devoted Bagó (Mihály Papp). Iluska's cruel stepmother (Janka Csatay) causes János's flock to stray whilst he is playing his pipes to his beloved, and the disgraced shepherd has to leave the village. He joins the army in the hope of winning fame and fortune, rises to command, comes to the aid of the beleaguered French King (József Németh) and leads his army to victory over the Turks, but he turns down the prize of half the French kingdom and the hand of the French Princess (Elza Szamosi) in order to return home, only to learn from Bagó that Iluska is dead, murdered by her jealous stepmother. With Bagó as his companion, he sets out for the afterworld and the Lake of Life, determined to find his love. Defeating the witch – for that indeed was what the stepmother was – he succeeds in calling up Iluska from her place, deep in the lake, as the queen of fairyland. She would have him stay there, to rule by her side, but Bagó

Plate 138. **János vitéz**: *Miska Papp (Bagó) encourages János, the hero (Sári Fedák), to seek out his lost love.*

insists that János belongs to the real world and, ultimately, Iluska leaves the fairy realms to return to the mortal world at János's side.

Kacsoh's score illustrated the tale with a warm, rich simplicity, producing some beautiful folk-toned melodies for his leading characters, with János's entrance song 'Én a pásztorok királya' and Iluska's introductory 'Van egy szegény kis árva lány' being amongst the gems of the score. The French characters, the only 'foreigners' of the piece, are pointedly given music of a different type. The Princess has a stylized showpiece of a waltz (the only one in the score), 'Oh csak ne volnék gyönge leányka', whilst the King, traditionally played as a croaking ancient, wheezes through his two numbers in a depiction of decadent foreignness.

József Bokor's mounting of *János vitéz* at the Király Színház was a huge success. The piece was played 100 times by 17 February 1905, passed its 200th performance on 10 June 1905, its 300th on 6 April 1906, its 400th on 23 May 1913, its 500th on 22 January 1920 and its 600th on 19 October 1921. A burlesque, *Kukorica Jónás* (Géza Vágó, Adolf Mérei) was seen at the Városligeti Színkör 21 June 1905, the show was produced in Helsinki (4 January 1913) in Finnish, and was played in Vienna, with Fedák and Csatay in their original rôles, by the Király Színház company (Carltheater 6 May 1913).

Played, in all, 689 times at Király Színház, it has since been seen at the Népopera, the Városi Színház and, after many other productions and performances, most recently in the repertoire at the Erkel Színház.

In 1985 a souped-up version, *János a vitéz*, subtitled a 'pop-dal-játék' with Kacsoh's music rearranged by Maté Victor, was produced at Szeged (9 August).

Austria: Carltheater 6 May 1913
Recordings: complete, selections (Qualiton), 1985 version (Hungaraton)
Literature: Bódis, M: *Két színházi siker a századelőn* (Magyar Színházi intezet, Budapest, 1984)

JANSEN, Marie [JOHNSON, Hattie] (b Boston, 1857; d Milford, Mass, 20 March 1914). Broadway musical leading lady of the 1880s and 1890s.

Miss Jansen made her first Broadway appearance in the musical comedy *Lawn Tennis* in 1881. She next joined the Comley-Barton company, with whom she took a small rôle in *Olivette* (Veloutine) at the Bijou Theater (though she was promoted to the principal soprano part of Bathilde when the show moved to Boston), and, alongside Catherine Lewis, the second lead as Béatrice in *Manola* (*Le Jour et la nuit*). She played leading ingénue rôles in *Madame Favart* (Suzanne), *The Vicar of Bray* (Dorothy) and *Billee Taylor* (Phoebe), before in 1883 she joined John McCaull's comic opera company to appear in *Der Bettelstudent*. After a trip to London with a play called *Featherbrain* (1884), she returned to McCaull to play Rosetta in *The Black Hussar* (1884) and the star rôle in the successful *Nadgy*, a rôle which fell to her lot when Sadie Martinot walked out in rehearsals.

She subsequently joined Francis Wilson's comic opera company and appeared as leading lady opposite the comedian in the American versions of three French opérettes *La Jolie Persane/The Oolah* (1889, Tourouloupi), *L'Étoile/ The Merry Monarch* (1890, Lazuli) and *Le Grand Casimir-/The Lion Tamer* (1891, Colombe), before taking advantage of her now considerable popularity to go out as the top-billed star of Glen MacDonough's play with songs, *Miss Dynamite* (1894). She top-billed in *The Merry Countess* (ie *Niniche*, 1895), in the flop play *A Florida Enchantment* and then in the farce *The Nancy Hanks* in which, in the rôle of a music-hall artist, she interpolated several songs.

She toured at the head of her own company after the turn of the century, before tactfully retiring when her ventures proved that, although still a drawing favourite, she had begun to wane in public favour.

JARNO, Georg [KOHNER, György] (b Budapest, 3 June 1868; d Breslau, 25 May 1920). Composer for turn-of-the-century central European stages who scored one major hit.

In the first part of his life in the musical theatre, Jarno led parallel careers as a conductor and a composer. He worked in the former capacity in Bremen, Gera, Halle, Metz, Liegnitz, Chemnitz and Magdeburg, and then as régisseur at Kissingen, whilst his early composing work included the music for a piece called *Die schwarze Kaschka* (lib: Viktor Blüthgen, Breslau 27 May 1895), the incidental music for a comedy produced at Ischl, and an Operette, *Juno von Tarent*, which does not seem to have been staged.

His *Der Richter von Zalamea/A zalameai biró* (lib: Blüthgen), at first described as an opera, was seen in Posen and at the Breslau Stadttheater (14 March) in 1899, and his first genuine Operette, *Der zerbrochene Krug*, based on the play by Heinrich von Kleist, although it took some while to find a producer, was ultimately mounted at Hamburg four years later. He had some success with the Operette *Der Goldfisch*, which went on from Breslau to be seen in Nagyvárad and other mid-European centres, but he was just short of his 40th birthday before he broke through to significant success with the score for the 1907 musical play *Die Förster-Christl*, mounted at Vienna's Theater in der Josefstadt by his brother Josef Jarno, with his sister-in-law, star soubrette Hansi Niese, in the title-rôle.

He repeated the *Förster-Christl* formula with *Das Musikantenmädel* and *Die Marinen-Gustl*, both vehicles for the hugely popular Niese and both produced with success (57 performances, 30 performances) at the Theater in der Josefstadt before going on to productions in Germany and in Hungary (*A Muzsikuslány*, Budai Színkör 4 June 1911, *Tengerész Kató*, Népopera 21 September 1912), and with a Berlin piece *Das Farmermädchen*. He then he had a further ration of success with a wartime piece *Mein Annerl*, mounted by Sigmund Eibenschütz at the Vienna Carltheater, with Alexander Girardi in the starring rôle, for a five months' run.

Jungfer Sonnenschein, with no Girardi to assist the box-office, was, nevertheless, another Carltheater success before going on to a fine 140-performance run at Berlin's Thalia-Theater (5 July 1919), and his last work, *Die Csikós-Baroness*, a piece based on a Sándor Petőfi tale, kept up the composer's fine latter-day record, playing 50 nights in Hamburg and in Breslau before going on to Munich, Leipzig and to Berlin's Neues Theater (28 August 1919) for 112 performances, playing there whilst his previous piece still filled the Thalia. Jarno was still at the peak of his late-found success when he died at the age of 52.

His brother, the actor and theatre director **Josef JARNO** [József KOHNER] (b Budapest, 24 August 1866; d Vienna 11 January 1932) was the manager of Vienna's Theater in der Josefstadt from 1899. During his management, he premièred a number of musical plays, including a German version of the French vaudeville-opérette *La Dot de Brigitte, Auch so eine!*, *Das Wäschermädl*, *Der Schusterbub*, *Die Förster-Christl*, *Paula macht alles*, *Das Musikantenmädel*, *Die Frau Gretl*, *Die Marinen-Gustl*, *Die Wundermühle* and *Botschafterin Leni*. He also, for a period, concurrently ran the Lustspieltheater (*Tolle Wirtschaft*, *Alma, wo wohnst du?* etc). Jarno made an enormously successful appearance as an actor on the musical stage when he appeared in his native Budapest, in his sixties, as the Emperor in the Hungarian première of *Im weissen Rössl*.

1903 **Der zerbrochene Krug** (Heinrich Lee) Stadttheater, Hamburg 15 January
1907 **Der Goldfisch** (Richard Jäger) Schauspielhaus, Breslau 20 January
1907 **Die Förster-Christl** (Bernhard Buchbinder) Theater in der Josefstadt 17 December
1910 **Das Musikantenmädel** (Buchbinder) Theater in der Josefstadt 18 February
1912 **Die Marinen-Gustl** (Buchbinder) Theater in der Josefstadt 22 March
1913 **Das Farmermädchen** (Georg Okonkowski) Grosses Operetten-Theater, Berlin 22 March

1916 **Mein Annerl** (Fritz Grünbaum, Wilhelm Sterk) Carltheater 7 October
1918 **Jungfer Sonnenschein** (Buchbinder) Volksoper, Hamburg 16 February; Carltheater, Vienna 18 May
1919 **Die Csikós-Baroness** (Grünbaum) Neues Operetten-Theater, Hamburg 28 October

JAUNER, Franz (b Vienna, 14 November 1832; d Vienna, 23 February 1900). Important Vienna producer of the last decades of the 19th century.

At first an actor of some repute, Jauner turned to production when he took over the management of the Carltheater from Anton Ascher in 1872. He continued the theatre's policy of local musical comedies and imported opéras-bouffes and -comiques, bringing Vienna such pieces as German versions of *La Cour du Roi Pétaud* (*Confusius IX*), *Les Cent Vierges* (*Hundert Jungfrauen*), *La Fille de Madame Angot* (*Angot die Tochter der Halle*), *La Permission de dix heures* (*Urlaub nach Zapfenstreich*), *La Jolie Parfumeuse* (*Schönroschen*), *La Belle Bourbonnaise* (*Die schöne Bourbonnaise*), *Les Prés Saint-Gervais* (*Prinz Conti*), *La Petite Mariée* (*Graziella*), *Giroflé-Girofla* and Verne's spectacular *Die Reise um die Erde in 80 Tagen*, as well as Suppé's *Cannebas*, *Die Frau Meisterin*, the reorganized *Banditenstreiche* and, above all, the première of his *Fatinitza*, and a number of short new native pieces by such composers as Löw, Zaytz and Brandl.

Jauner moved on to take over the management of the Vienna Hofoper (1877–80), which he left in 1881 to go to the Ringtheater. He had been in charge there but a short time when the destruction of the full theatre by fire occurred in December 1881. This deathly disaster put a frost on Jauner's ostensible activities for a number of years, although, during the management of Franz Steiner at the Theater an der Wien in the early 1880s, it was actually Jauner who was the owner of that famous house. In 1884 he sold the bricks and mortar to Alexandrine von Schönerer, but he remained an active co-director of the Theater an der Wien with her, through the artistic managements of Camillo Walzel and of Schönerer herself, for more than another decade, until Frau von Schönerer took over the management alone in 1895.

At that same time, Jauner returned to take over again the management of the Carltheater. In the five years that followed, however, he did not find a great deal of good fortune. He survived largely on revivals of repertoire pieces, as none of his wide selection of new works proved to be the kind of hit he had housed in his first period at the theatre: Suppé's *Das Modell*, Victor Herbert's *Der Zauberer von Nil* (*The Wizard of the Nile*), the new German version of *König Chilperich*, the attempt to make a musical of *La Cigale* as *Bum-Bum* for Girardi, Ludwig and Leon Held's *Der Cognac-König*, Ferron's *Das Krokodil*, Suppé's *Die Pariserin*, Weinberger's *Adam und Eva*, a German version of *Les P'tites Michu*, Englander's American comic opera *Die kleine Corporal* and Gilbert and Osmond Carr's *Der Herr Gouverneur* (*His Excellency*). Even *Wiener Blut*, a Johann Strauss pasticcio, which would later find its way into the revivable repertoire, was a failure on its first showing at Jauner's house.

Jauner committed suicide at his desk in the Carltheater in February of 1900.

Willi Först's film *Operette* used Jauner as its central character. As played by Först himself, he was depicted as the 'König der Wiener Operette' leading a battle from the Carltheater for supremacy over Marie Geistinger and the Theater an der Wien.

JAVOTTE *see* CINDERELLA THE YOUNGER

JAY, Isabel (b London, 17 October 1879; d Monte Carlo, 26 February 1927). Star soprano of the London comic opera and musical comedy stage.

Miss Jay joined D'Oyly Carte's company at the age of 18 and made her first important appearance deputizing for Ilka Pálmay, as Elsie in *The Yeomen of the Guard*, before being sent out with the Carte touring companies. She returned to the Savoy the following year, playing the Plaintiff in *Trial By Jury*, understudying Ruth Vincent and Emmie Owen, and then appearing as Aloès in *The Lucky Star* (1899). In the following production, *The Rose of Persia*, she was cast in the supporting rôle of Blush-of-Morning, but when the American vocalist Ellen Beach Yaw proved insufficient in the star rôle of the piece, she was promoted to leading lady, and remained in that position at the Savoy for two years (Mabel, Patience, Phyllis, Lady Rosie Pippin in *The Emerald Isle*, Gipsy in *Ib and Little Christina*) before retiring to a brief marriage to an African explorer.

She returned less than two years later, under the management of George Edwardes, to take over Lillian Eldée's rôle of Marjory Joy in *A Country Girl* for the final part of the show's long London run, and she remained with Edwardes to play the lead soprano rôle of *The Cingalee* (1904, Lady Patricia Vane) and to succeed Miss Vincent as *Véronique*, before moving to the management of Frank Curzon for the leading rôles in a series of musicals between 1906 and 1911, during which time she also became Mrs (1910), and later Lady, Curzon.

Amongst the musicals which she created under Curzon's management were *The White Chrysanthemeum* (1905, Sybil Cunningham), *The Girl Behind the Counter* (1906, Winnie Willoughby), *Miss Hook of Holland* (1907, Sally Hook), *My Mimosa Maid* (1908, Paulette), *King of Cadonia* (1908, Princess Marie), *Dear Little Denmark* (1909, Christine) and *The Balkan Princess* (1910, Princess Stephanie). She also appeared with great critical success as Olivia in the Liza Lehmann/Laurence Housman musicalization of *The Vicar of Wakefield* (1906).

JEAN DE PARIS Opéra-comique in 2 acts by C Godard d'Aucour de Saint-Just. Music by Adrien Boieldieu. Opéra-Comique, Paris, 1 April 1812.

The opéra-comique *Jean de Paris*, written and composed at a time when the beginnings of the modern musical theatre were still some half a century in the future, is a fine example of a work which might easily have belonged to a later generation. Even given the style and substance of its musical part, its relationship to the opéras-comiques of the end-of-the-century years and, indeed, to later musical comedy is, in retrospect, clearly visible.

The action is set in a country inn, which, to its owner's exaggerated delight, has been wholly reserved by the travelling Princesse de Navarre. But, before the Princess arrives, one Jean de Paris turns up, with a great retinue, and takes over the whole accommodation. Whilst the innkeeper suffers agonies, Jean then invites the Princess to

JEANNE, JEANNETTE ET JEANNETON

partake of his hospitality. Her Chamberlain is horrified, but the Princess is pre-warned – Jean de Paris is none other than the disguised Prince of France, the friend of her childhood, whom her brother, the King, hopes she will wed and who has come to try to win her heart in disguise. Whilst the comical antics of their servants and the inn folks buzz on around them, the Princess leads her suitor on, and only after she has made him suffer for his trickery does she admit that she always had every intention of wedding him.

Long a favourite amongst Boieldieu's works, and amongst French opéras-comiques of the early 19th century, *Jean de Paris* was given regular revivals in Paris and further productions around the world, both in opera houses and also in regular musical theatres. Following its earliest Viennese showings (ad Johann von Seyfried) at the Hoftheater, it was seen at the Theater an der Wien (ad Castelli) and the Theater in der Josefstadt and, as late as 1879, returned for a fresh showing at the Hofoper. London's and New York's first *John of Paris* (ad I Pocock) was a botched affair to which Henry Bishop added some music of his own, whilst the Australians, half a century on, presented a lively English version which also went in for a touch of botching, as it allowed the final curtain to come down on a rondo for the Princess 'composed expressly by A Reiff'. The piece was played in London at all the principal theatres – Covent Garden, Drury Lane, the Haymarket – and reappeared as late as 1869, as part of an opera in English season at the Olympic Theatre (31 July), in a version topped up with 'several solos and concerted pieces by W F Taylor'.

Italian, Spanish, Russian, Hungarian (ad E Pály), Czech and Scandinavian adaptations and productions were all also seen in the decades following the show's first productions.

Austria: Hoftheater *Johann von Paris* 28 August 1812 Germany: Stuttgart *Johann von Paris* 28 September 1812, Berlin 25 March 1813; UK: Theatre Royal, Covent Garden *John of Paris* 14 November 1814; USA: Park Theater 25 November 1816 (Eng); Australia: Melbourne 1862
Recording: complete (Gaîté-Lyrique)

JEANNE, JEANNETTE ET JEANNETON

JEANNE, JEANNETTE ET JEANNETON Opéra-comique in 3 acts by Clairville and Alfred Delacour. Music by Paul Lacôme. Théâtre des Folies-Dramatiques, Paris, 27 October 1876.

Lacôme's most successful work, *Jeanne, Jeannette et Jeanneton* was a welcome hit at the Folies-Dramatiques, which had suffered through several previous years of flops. It was played for 104 successive performances at Louis Cantin's theatre before being forcibly withdrawn in order to fulfil the theatre's contract to produce Offenbach's *La Foire Saint-Laurent*. Clairville and Delacour's fine libretto, however, sat long on Cantin's desk without being set. The manager originally offered it to Offenbach, who thought it might work well, but that it would require three top-of-the-bill prima donnas in the triple title-rôle. The idea of Judic, Théo and Granier together in one show gave Cantin sufficient of a turn (doubtless both financially and in anticipation of the backstage dramas involved) to back off, and Offenbach returned *Jeanne, Jeannette et Jeanneton* unset. Thereafter, Cantin used the text as an audition piece for aspiring composers, doling them out three or four numbers to set as a trial. When he did this to Lacôme, the composer

instead set almost the whole piece in record time, and won his production.

The three poor girls of the title meet on a coach on their way to Paris, and make a promise to meet up again in five years time, on 3 June 1765. Jeanneton (Marie Gélabert) works at, and then inherits, her godfather's restaurant, and there she is courted by the soldier Laramée, who is none other than the Marquis de Nocé (Ernest Vois) in disguise. She fixes her marriage for the night of the reunion, but marriage is not what de Noce had in mind, and though Jeannette (Berthe Stuart) and Jeanne (Mlle Prelly) turn up for the big night, the bridegroom doesn't – there is just a letter, saying his colonel has forbidden the marriage. But Jeannette is now the famous dancer, La Guimard, and Jeanne has become the Comtesse du Barry, and they have influence. More, it eventuates that Jeannette is also being courted by the Marquis/Colonel de Noce, under his real name, whilst Jeanne finds herself in trouble with the King when a newspaper accuses her of a rendez-vous galant with the same nobleman at Jeanneton's inn. De Noce has the vengeance of all three to cope with. The girls manage things so that Jeanneton ends up in the arms of faithful little Briolet (Simon Max), who has managed to turn up in a different guise in each act, Jeannette makes peace with her principal protector, the Prince de Soubise (Ange Milher), and Jeanne sets the King's mind at rest – whilst de Noce is bundled off to the womanless battle-front.

The three girls shared the finale of the prologue ('Jeanne, Jeannette et Jeanneton, nous commençons un grand voyage avec un bien léger bagage ...'), and thereafter also shared the show's main musical moments. Jeanneton had a romance ('Depuis longtemps') and a duo with de Noce in the first act, before Jeanne and Jeannette entered to join in a series of reunion Couplets. A second series of Couplets followed on their departure, when, in a neat piece of theatre, the announcement of each lady's carriage gives away, for the first time, her new station in life. In the second act, at her home, Jeannette sang of her double life ('On sait que j'ai deux amoureux'), and Jeanne bewailed the depredations of the gutter press ('La chronique médisante'), whilst in the third, at Jeanne's headquarters at Versailles, she delivered the air 'Oui, c'en est fait, me voilà reine!', Jeanneton the Couplets 'Je suis femme et cabaretière' and Jeanette faced up to the slimy Marquis with 'Ah! tu prêtes l'orcille'.

The men were less largely served, though Briolet, having opened the prologue, turns up as a chef de cuisine at the Cabaret de Bancelin, with some jolly Act I moments, then as Jeannette's cook, equipped with a sorry romance ('Dieu! quelle faiblesse est le nôtre') in the second part, and as a soldier in the third when Édouard Maugé, in the rôle of his Sergeant La Grenade, joined him in the comic duo 'Obéissance à la consigne' and a quartet. The Marquis rendered the couplets 'En jeune et galant militaire' in Act One, and the rondeau of excuses 'Vous allez comprendre peut-être' in Act Two.

Following its Paris success, the show was seen throughout Europe. A German version (ad Georg Friedrich Reiss) was played in Hamburg, Berlin, and in Vienna, where Hermine Meyerhoff (Jeanne), Rosa Streitmann (Jeannette) and Frln Schindler (Jeanneton) were paired with Franz Eppich (de Noce), Karl Blasel (Briolet) and Grün (Prince). The piece failed to appeal to the

Viennese and was dropped after ten performances, but it continued on to be played in Graz, Nuremberg and elsewhere, whilst Italian and Spanish versions were mounted.

The first English version (ad Robert Reece) was produced in Britain, where Alice May, Lizzie St Quinten and Constance Loseby appeared as the three ladies of the title, W S Penley the Prince, W H Woodfield the Marquis and Fred Leslie as Briolet, and a 'grand mythological ballet' called *Endymion*, music by Georges Jacobi, was pasted into the second act for 'the renowned Alhambra corps de ballet'. It played a respectable three months in the big Alhambra auditorium. In America, where the piece had been seen in 1878 in French with Rosina Stani and Zélie Weil heading the cast, Reece's adaptation, readapted by Max Freeman, was produced in 1887 retitled *The Marquis*. The girls were now Mae (Isabelle Urquhart), Marie (Bertha Ricci) and Marion (Lucie Grubb), Mark Smith played the Marquis, James T Powers was Briolet and Courtice Pounds the Prince de Soubise, through some 70 performances.

In Hungary, a version by 'Imre Ukki' (Mrs Csepreghy) was mounted at the Népszinház in 1885 for five performances.

Another opérette, in one act (Julien Nargeot/Émile Abraham, Marc Constantin) was produced under the same title at the Folies-Marigny on 31 October 1876.

Germany: Carl-Schultze Theater, Hamburg 30 September 1877, Friedrich-Wilhelmstädtisches Theater, Berlin 9 October 1877; Austria: Carltheater 24 February 1878; USA: Booth's Theater 28 October 1878, Casino Theater *The Marquis* 19 September 1887; UK: Alhambra Theatre 28 March 1881; Hungary: Népszinház 20 February 1885

JEANNE QUI PLEURE ET JEAN QUI RIT Opérette in 1 act by Charles Nuitter and Étienne Tréfeu. Music by Jacques Offenbach. Bad Ems, 19 July 1864; Théâtre des Bouffes-Parisiens, Paris, 3 November 1865.

The Jeanne who snivels (Zulma Bouffar) is actually a lively little miller's daughter, and the Jean who is jolly is also her, in disguise. It is all part of a plot to dissuade the local viticulteur, Cabochon (Désiré), from purchasing the mill which she has inherited and the new owner of which she must marry, so that her own boyfriend can become both boss and spouse. Jean-Paul, as Cabochon's offspring, and Pelva completed the cast as the two young men.

First produced, like a number of other one-act Offenbach pieces, in the spa resort of Ems, the little four-hander reached Vienna before it reached Paris, and with positive results. It became particularly popular in its German-language version (ad uncredited) and Vienna's Carltheater played *Hanni weint, Hansi lacht* in its repertoire regularly for five years, and intermittently for another ten, with Karl Blasel making the most of the rôle of the outwitted Sebastian Mosthuber (ex-Cabochon) with its grotesque leap into feminine clothes. The German version was seen in Hungary and in America, and an Hungarian version (ad Jenő Rákosi) was also later played in Budapest.

An English version, mounted at London's Adelphi Theatre with Johnny Toole as Popinoff (ex-Cabochon), Mrs Mellon as Jenny and Johnny, Miss Furtado as Jocrisse (the son), and William H Eburne as the favoured Jollibois had less of an afterlife.

Austria: Carltheater *Hanni weint und Hansi lacht* 4 February 1865;

UK: Adelphi Theatre *Crying Jenny and Laughing Johnny* 16 April 1866; Hungary: Budai Színkör *Die Hanni weint, der Hansi lacht* 26 September 1869, Népszinház *Ancsi sir, ancsi nevet* 18 January 1878; USA: Terrace Garten *Hanni weint, Hansi lacht* 17 May 1872

JEANS, Ronald (b Birkenhead, 10 May 1887; d London, 16 May 1973). Lyricist and adapter, mainly for the London revue stage.

A former stockbroker, Jeans was involved in the founding of the Liverpool Repertory Company, but subsequently became a prolific writer of West End revue material, contributing to the modern revue stage from its earliest days through the 30-plus years to the virtual disappearance of the genre from the London theatre. He was responsible for all or a part of a number of the most famous such shows of the period, notably the series of André Charlot revues, and such other like pieces as *Buzz Buzz* (w Arthur Wimperis), *Puss Puss*, *Pot Luck*, *Rats*, *London Calling* (w Noël Coward), *Charlot's Revue*, *By the Way*, *One Dam Thing After Another* (w Rodgers and Hart), *Clowns in Clover*, *The House That Jack Built*, *Bow Bells*, *Streamline*, *Follow the Sun*, *Lights Up*, *Flying Colours* et al.

His involvement in book-based musical theatre was mostly limited to doctoring other people's works. He heavily adapted two of the more sprightly French musicals for the less than sprightly London stage, revamped Kalmar and Ruby's original *Lido Lady* libretto into the form in which it was set by Rodgers and Hart, and provided some additional lyrics for Liverpool Repertory Theatre's children's musical *Fifinella*, when it was produced in London (1919).

1919 **Hustle** (Philip Braham) 1 act Finsbury Park Empire
1920 **Wild Geese** (*Son p'tit frère*) English version (Comedy Theatre)
1922 **Dédé** English version (Garrick Theatre)
1926 **Lido Lady** (Richard Rodgers/Lorenz Hart/Bert Kalmar, Harry Ruby ad w Guy Bolton) Gaiety Theatre 1 December

JENBACH, Béla [JAKOBOVITS, Béla] (b Miskolcz, 1 April 1871; d Vienna, 21 January 1943). Successful librettist/lyricist to, in particular, Kálmán, Eysler and Lehár in the 1910s and 1920s.

Originally an actor, the Vienna-based Jenbach was nearly 40 before he made his first attempts as a librettist, and he had something of a success with his early text for the Operette *Die Liebesschule*, which did well enough in Germany to be taken up for productions in Hungary (*Don Juan hadnagy* Városligeti Színkör 4 November 1910) and, under the Shubert management, in America (*The Love School* ad Howard Jacott, Wilkes-Barre, closed pre-Broadway).

An Operette written with Carl Weinberger and Carl Lindau, *Die romantische Frau*, ran for 73 performances at the Johann Strauss-Theater, before Jenbach notched up a more substantial success – although mainly in Britain – with his libretto to the Charles Cuvillier piece *Der lila Domino*, and his first real Vienna hit, in collaboration with Leo Stein, with the libretto for Edmund Eysler's *Ein Tag im Paradies* (1913). *Ein Tag im Paradies* went on to considerable Broadway success, attached to a botched score, as *The Blue Paradise*. Jenbach and Stein topped that success two seasons later when they supplied the libretto for Kálmán's enormously popular *Die Csárdásfürstin*, and they continued on to further successes with the same composer's *Das Hollandweibchen* and with Lehár's *Die blaue Mazur*.

Jenbach later continued the association with Lehár when he adapted Horst and Engel's play *Der Schrei nach der Kinde* as the libretto for his *Cloclo*, revised Paul Knepler's original *Paganini* libretto into its definitive version, and turned Gabryela Zapolska's play *A Cárevics* into the libretto for *Der Zarewitsch*. Like this piece, his other late works were also largely in the line of adaptations from the Hungarian.

1909 **Biribi** (Fritz Korolanyi/w Robert Pohl) Neues Operetten-theater, Mannheim 5 February

1909 **Die Liebsschule** (Korolanyi/w R Pohl) Stadttheater, Leipzig 13 March

1911 **Die romantische Frau** (Carl Weinberger/w Carl Lindau) Johann Strauss-Theater 17 March

1911 **Der Natursänger** (Edmund Eysler/w Leo Stein) 1 act Apollotheater 22 December

1912 **Der lila Domino** (Charles Cuvillier/w Emmerich von Gatti) Stadttheater, Leipzig 3 February

1912 **Der tolle Kosak** (Siegwart Ehrlich/w Hans Hall) Neues Operetten-Theater, Leipzig 28 September

1912 **Die Premiere** (J G Hart/w Stein) 1 act Apollotheater 10 August

1912 **Der fliegende Rittmeister** (Hermann Dostal/w Stein) Apollotheater 5 October

1913 **Ein Tag im Paradies** (Eysler/w Stein) Wiener Bürger-theater 23 December

1915 **Liebesgeister** (Ernst Steffan/w Rudolf Österreicher) 1 act Apollotheater 1 March

1915 **Die Csárdásfürstin** (Emmerich Kálmán/w Stein) Johann Strauss-Theater 13 November

1916 **Die – oder keine** (Eysler/w Stein) Wiener Bürgertheater 9 October

1916 **Urschula** (H Dostal/w Julius Wilhelm) Apollotheater 1 September

1920 **Das Hollandweibchen** (Kálmán/w Stein) Johann Strauss-Theater 30 January

1920 **Die blaue Mazur** (Lehár/w Stein) Theater an der Wien 28 May

1921 **Rinaldo** (*Grof Rinaldo*) German version w Österreicher (Johann Strauss-Theater)

1922 **Die Siegerin** (Tchaikovsky arr Josef Klein/w Oskar Friedmann, Fritz Lunzer) Thalia-Theater 7 November

1923 **Die Ballkönigin** (Karl Stigler/w von Gatti) Löwinger-bühne 21 September

1924 **Cloclo** (Lehár) Wiener Bürgertheater 9 March

1925 **Paganini** (Lehár/w Paul Knepler) Johann Strauss-Theater 30 October

1928 **Der Zarewitsch** (Lehár/w Heinz Reichert) Johann Strauss-Theater 18 May

1930 **Sisters** German version (Johann Strauss-Theater)

1931 **Die kluge Mama** (*Az okos mama*) German version (Volksoper)

1933 **Fahrt in der Jugend** (Eduard Künneke/w Ludwig Hirschfeld) Stadttheater, Zurich 26 March

JEROME, Ben[jamin M] (b New York; d Huntingdon Station (Brightwater), NY, 27 March 1938). Composer principally for the Chicago stage during that city's days as a prominent musical production centre.

For many years the conductor at Chicago's La Salle Theater, Ben Jerome was also one of the chief purveyors of music to the Chicago theatre during its heyday as a home of original musicals in the early years of the 20th century.

The Whitneys' production of his first piece, *The Isle of Spice*, had a fine run of 143 performances in Chicago, another good season in Boston and took in 80 performances on Broadway as part of a considerable touring life and, if others of his Chicago pieces did less well on the east coast, they also had extended lives on the touring circuits.

From 1908 Jerome also provided music for several shows at New York's Casino Theater, including the 1908 revue *The Mimic World*, *Mr Hamlet of Broadway* (54 performances) and the successful Sam Bernard piece *He Came from Milwaukee* (117 performances), but he returned west for his later work. Of one of these later pieces, *Louisiana Lou*, featuring the young Sophie Tucker, an east coast journal remarked, in what was clearly intended as a compliment, that it 'comes closer to Broadway standards of glitter and girls than anything that has worn the trademark of Chicago in recent memory'.

He subsequently provided individual songs to the scores of several new and several made-over shows, including the German *A Modern Eve* ('A Quiet Evening at Home') and the local *Queen High* ('My Lady'), but he returned only once more to Broadway in a more substantial way when he collaborated on the music for H H Frazee's production of *Yes, Yes, Yvette*.

Jerome's most popular individual songs included 'By the Pale Moonlight', 'Melancholy Mose', 'Take Me Back to Chicago', 'The Gumshoe Man' and 'Lamb, Lamb, Lamb'.

1903 **Lifting the Cup** (Matt Woodward, N H Biddle, George V Hobart) 1 act Crystal Gardens 27 July

1903 **The Isle of Spice, or His Majesty of Nicobar** (w Paul Schindler/Allen Lowe, George E Stoddard) La Salle Theater, Chicago, 12 September; Majestic Theater, New York 23 August 1904

1903 **The Belle of Newport** (revised *The Defenders*) (Charles F Dennee) La Salle Theater, Chicago 21 December

1904 **The Royal Chef** (Stoddard, Charles S Taylor) La Salle Theater, Chicago 28 March

1905 **The Yankee Regent** (Charles Adelman, I C Blumenstock) La Salle Theater, Chicago 19 August

1908 **Mr Hamlet of Broadway** (Edward Madden/Edgar Smith) Casino Theater 23 December

1910 **He Came from Milwaukee** (w Louis Hirsch/Madden/Mark Swan) Casino Theater 21 September

1911 **Louisiana Lou** (Addison Burkhardt, Frederick Donaghey) La Salle Theater, Chicago 3 September

1912 **The Girl at the Gate** (Will Hough, Donaghey) La Salle Theater, Chicago 1 September

1913 **A Trip to Washington** (Henry Blossom) La Salle Theater, Chicago 24 August

1927 **Yes, Yes, Yvette** (w Phil Charig/Irving Caesar/James Montgomery) Harris Theater 3 October

JEROME, Jerome K[lapka] (b Walsall, 2 May 1859; d Northampton, 14 June 1927).

The author of *Three Men in a Boat* had a number of successes as a playwright, but not in the musical-comedy field. His *(John Jenkins in) Biarritz*, written as a vehicle for Arthur Roberts, was a failure, in spite of the popular comedian's name on the bill. Subsequently, several musicals were based on Jerome's works, including the Broadway piece *The Rainbow Girl* and a curious German musical called *Lady Fanny* with a score by Theo Mackeben, both based on *Fanny and the Servant Problem* (1908, US: *The New Lady Bantock*). His name also appeared on the credits for the very short-lived *I Love a Lassie* (Shubert Theater,

New Haven 15 May 1919), as the author of an original piece adapted by one Erwin Connelly with songs by its producer-star, Scottish-American actor Clifton Crawford.

1896 **Biarritz** (F Osmond Carr/Adrian Ross) Prince of Wales Theatre 11 April

Memoirs: *On the Stage and Off: The Brief Career of a Would-be Actor* (Holt, New York, 1891), *My Life and Times* (Harper, New York, 1926) etc

JEROME, William [FLANNERY, William] (b Cornwall-on-Hudson, NY, 30 September 1865; d New York, 25 June 1932). Highly successful songwriter of the earliest part of the 20th century, who also had some notable successes in the theatre.

Renouncing law studies, the young Jerome became at first a minstrel man and vaudevillian, then subsequently a facile lyricist, forming a team with composer Jean Schwartz which led them to a long run of song hits in the earliest years of the 20th century. Their songs, fresh and/or slightly used, were liberally interpolated into both Broadway and West End shows – although it was rumoured that publishers Shapiro, Bernstein initially paid producers for the privilege – the same song being, on a number of occasions, used in more than one show. 'Rip van Winkle was a Lucky Man' appeared in Broadway's *The Sleeping Beauty and the Beast* and in London's *The Cherry Girl*, 'Mr Dooley' in America's *A Chinese Honeymoon* and London's *The Toreador*, 'Bedelia' was sung by Blanche Ring in *The Jersey Lily* (1903) and *When Claudia Smiles* (1914) in America and by George Grossmith in *The Orchid* in Britain, and 'Cordalia Malone', heard in *Glittering Gloria* on Broadway, was also put into *The Orchid* in London. All four were considerable hits in both countries.

The pair interpolated numbers into other shows such as *San Toy*, *An English Daisy*, *The Show Girl* ('In Spotless Town'), *The Echo* ('The Newport Glide'), the Rays' *Down in the Pike*, *The Little Cherub* ('My Irish Rose'), *A Winsome Widow* and several editions of the *Ziegfeld Follies*, provided seven numbers to soup up the Drury Lane pantomime *The White Cat* (1905) for Broadway, and had further show song hits with 'When Mr Shakespeare Comes to Town' (*Hoity-Toity*), 'Hamlet Was a Melancholy Dane' (*Mr Bluebeard*), 'My Irish Molly O' (*Sergeant Brue*) and 'Any Old Time at All' (*The Rich Mr Hoggenheimer*). They also supplied the full scores for a series of Broadway shows, of which the comical *Piff! Paff! Pouf!* was a long-running hit, composed the songs for two shows for blackface comedians McIntyre and Heath (*The Ham Tree*, *In Hayti*) and for the 1909 revue *Up and Down Broadway* ('Chinatown, My Chinatown'), and founded their own music publishing company to publish both their own and other folks' work.

Jerome also had song hits in his collaborations with other composers, scoring with such numbers as 'Row, Row, Row' (*Ziegfeld Follies of 1912* w Jimmy Monaco), 'Back Home in Tennessee' (w Walter Donaldson) and 'Get Out and Get under the Moon' (w Larry Shay, Charles Tobias), and provided non-Schwartz interpolated numbers for such shows as *Betty* ('Sometime' w Harry Tierney) and *Step This Way* (1916), where another Chinatown lyric encouraged the world to 'Take me down to blinky, winky, Chinky Chinatown'.

1903 **Mrs Delaney of Newport** (Jean Schwartz) Grand Opera House 3 November

1904 **Piff! Paff! Pouf!** (Schwartz/Stanislaus Stange) Casino Theater 4 April

1905 **Lifting the Lid** (Schwartz/J J McNally) Aerial Gardens 5 June

1905 **The Ham Tree** (Schwartz/George V Hobart) New York Theater 28 August

1905 **Fritz in Tammany Hall** (Schwartz/McNally) Herald Square Theater 16 October

1907 **Lola from Berlin** (Schwartz/McNally) Liberty Theater 16 September

1908 **Morning, Noon and Night** (Schwartz/Joseph Herbert) Yorkville Theater 5 October

1909 **In Hayti** (Schwartz/McNally) Circle Theater 30 August

1915 **Hands Up** (Schwartz, Sigmund Romberg, Goetz et al/w E Ray Goetz/Edgar Smith) 44th Street Theater 22 July

JESSEL, Leon (b Stettin, 22 January 1871; d Berlin, 4 January 1942). Composer of one of Germany's most enduring Operetten.

A conductor from the age of 20 in such venues as Gelsenkirchen (1891), Mühlheim (1892) and in Celle (1894), where his first short stage piece was produced, then later in Freiberg (1899), at Stettin's important Bellevue-Theater, Chemnitz's Stadttheater and at the Wilhelm-Theater, Lübeck, Jessel won some considerable success as a composer of piano and instrumental music, producing, in particular, a little orchestral piece called 'Die Parade der Zinnsoldaten' which would go round the world. It was heard in the Russian revue *Chauve-Souris*, in Charell's Berlin revue *An Alle*, recorded by the Andrews Sisters (the soldiers became 'wooden' in Ballard McDonald's lyric) and remains the composer's single best-known piece of work internationally.

Jessel did not make any headway as an Operette composer until after he settled in Berlin in 1911. There he contributed two numbers to the successful Posse *Grosse Rosinen* and had his first full-sized piece, *Die beiden Husaren*, produced at the Theater des Westens before it went on to be seen in other German houses and in an Hungarian version in Budapest (*Ikrek a táborban*, Fővárosi Nyari Színház 24 July 1915). It was, however, the enormously successful wartime Operette *Das Schwarzwaldmädel* produced at the Komische Oper two years later which gave him the theatrical hit of his life and the basis and impetus for a career in the musical theatre.

In the 15 years that followed this singular hit Jessel turned out a regular stream of stage works, finding a willing acceptance for his works in the wake of the triumph of *Schwarzwaldmädel*, and several of these shows did well without, however, producing a second major success. *Die närrische Liebe* had a 127-performance run at the Berlin Thalia-Theater, *Die Postmeisterin*, another collaboration with *Schwarzwaldmädel* librettist Neidhart, was played for over 100 nights in Berlin and is generally regarded as the composer's best work after his big hit, *Das Detektivmädel*, which followed it, played some 60 nights and went on to be *Detektiv kisasszony* (Budai Színkör 15 September 1922 ad Ernő Kulinyi) in Hungary, whilst *Des Königs Nachbarin* played two months in Berlin and 88 performances at Vienna's Johann Strauss-Theater (6 June 1924).

Of his later pieces, *Meine Tochter Otto* did the best when it was played for 50 nights at Vienna's Rolandbühne, but in 1933, with the coming of National Socialism, the Jewish composer found his music banned. Although he stuck it out in Germany, his last Operette, *Die goldene Mühle*, was produced in Switzerland. It went on to a production at the Vienna Volksoper and a guest season at the Johann Strauss-Theater (21 April 1937), but it was not seen in his native land.

Jessel died in 1942 after having been knocked about by the Gestapo.

1894 **Die Brautwerburg** (Else Gehrke) 1 act Schlosstheater, Celle 1 August

1896 **Kruschke am Nordpol** (Max Reichardt) 1 act Tivoli Theater, Kiel 18 August

1911 **Die grosse Rosinen** (w Willi Bredschneider, Bogumil Zepler et al/Rudolf Bernauer, Rudolf Schanzer) Berliner Theater 31 December

1913 **Die beiden Husaren** (Wilhelm Jacoby, Schanzer) Theater des Westens 6 February

1914 **Wer zuletzt lacht** (Arthur Lippschitz, A Bernstein-Sawersky) Deutsches Schauspielhaus 31 December

1917 **Das Schwarzwaldmädel** (August Neidhart) Komische Oper 25 August

1918 **Ein modernes Mädel** (Neidhart) Volkstheater, Munich 28 June

1918 **Ohne Mann kein Vergnügen** (Neidhart) Komische Oper, Berlin

1919 **Die närrische Liebe** (Jean Kren) Thalia Theater 28 November

1920 **Verliebte Frauen** (Alexander Pordes-Milo) Thalia Theater, Königsberg

1921 **Schwalbenhochzeit** (Pordes-Milo) Theater des Westens 28 January

1921 **Die Postmeisterin** (Neidhart) Centraltheater, Berlin 3 February

1921 **Das Detektivmädel** (*Miss Nobody*) (Neidhart) Central-theater, Berlin 28 October

1923 **Des Königs Nachbarin** (Fritz Grünbaum, Wilhelm Sterk) Wallner-Theater, Berlin 15 April

1923 **Der keusche Benjamin** (Max Steiner-Kaiser, Hans Bodenstädt) Carl-Schultze Theater, Hamburg 1 September

1925 **Prinzessin Husch** (Neidhart) Operettenhaus, Hamburg, 22 December; Theater des Westens, Berlin 11 March 1926

1926 **Die kleine Studenten** (Leo Kastner, Alfred Möller) Bellevue Theater, Stettin 22 December

1927 **Meine Tochter Otto** (Grünbaum, Sterk) Rolandbühne, Vienna 5 May

1927 **Mädels, die man liebt** (Kastner, Möller) Volksoper, Hamburg 17 April

1929 **Die Luxuskabine** (Neidhart) Neues Operetten-Theater, Leipzig 20 October

1933 **Junger Wein** (Neidhart) Theater des Westens 1 September

1936 **Die goldene Mühle** (Hugo Wiener, Carl Costa ad Sterk) Städtebundtheater, Olten, Switzerland 29 October; Volksoper, Vienna 2 March 1937

Biography: Dümling, A: *Die verweigerte Heimat* (Die kleine Verlag, Düsseldorf, 1992)

JESSOP, George H (b Ireland, ?1850; d Hampstead, London, 21 March 1915). Popular dramatist for America's country circuits who later produced two successful musicals for the London stage.

Irish-born Jessop moved to the western American seaboard on the proceeds of an inheritance in 1873, and there, over some 20 years, he wrote mostly plays of a colourfully basic but highly effective kind for the touring circuits. Several, written either alone or with such collaborators as William Gill or Brander Matthews, had long, profitable careers (*Sam'l of Posen*, Aimée's vehicle

Mam'zelle, A Gold Mine, Stolen Money, The Power of the Press). Some, notably the farce comedy *A Bottle of Ink*, which was played in America and Britain, Scanlan's Irish vehicles *Myles Aroon* and *Mavourneen*, or *An Irish Artist*, written for Scanlan's successor at the head of the stage-Irish circuits, Chauncey Olcott, also included varying amounts of musical illustration and songs. At the other end of the scale, he also ventured a stage adaptation of Dumas's *Edmund Kean*.

In the mid-1890s Jessop returned to Ireland, where he had inherited an estate, and his first work for the British stage was the fine libretto for C V Stanford's light opera *Shamus O'Brien*, which the authors and Stanford's publisher, Boosey & Co, produced at the Opera Comique, with some success, with the young Louise Kirkby Lunn and Denis O'Sullivan starring.

A later collaboration with Sidney Jones produced the highly successful comedy opera *My Lady Molly*, which was, like *Shamus O'Brien*, a piece more substantial and play-like in its libretto than many of the musical comedies of its time. Although not ultimately credited, he is also said to have had a hand in the writing of a musical version of *The Scarlet Letter*, composed by Walter Damrosch with a text credited only to George P Lathrop.

Jessop also wrote a number of novels (*Check and Counter Check, Judge Lynch, A Tale of the Californian Vineyards, Gerald Ffrench's Friends*).

1885 **A Bottle of Ink** (w William Gill) Comedy Theater 6 January

1889 **Myles Aroon** (w Horace Townsend) 14th Street Theater 21 January

1891 **Mavourneen** (w Townsend) 14th Street Theater 28 September

1894 **An Irish Artist** 14th Street Theater 1 October

1896 **Shamus O'Brien** (Charles Villiers Stanford) Opera Comique, London 2 March

1902 **My Lady Molly** (Sidney Jones/w Percy Greenbank, C H Taylor) Theatre Royal, Brighton 11 August; Terry's Theatre, London 14 March 1903

JESUS CHRIST SUPERSTAR rock opera in 2 acts with lyrics by Tim Rice. Music by Andrew Lloyd Webber. Mark Hellinger Theater, New York, 12 October 1971.

The first musical by Rice and Lloyd Webber to be produced on the professional stage, following their happy beginning with the children's cantata *Joseph and the Amazing Technicolor Dreamcoat*, *Jesus Christ Superstar* made its way into the theatre by stages. The first part of it to be heard was the title-song, 'Superstar', which was issued as a record single. Then, after a search for a producer who was interested in putting a cantata-form sung-through bio-musical of Jesus Christ, with a pop/rock music score, on to the stage had, perhaps not unsurprisingly, failed, David Land, the representative of the piece, instead settled for the offer by MCA Records' Brian Brolly to put the score of the show on record instead. The two-record album, costing £20,000 to produce, and starring Murray Head (Judas), Ian Gillam (Jesus) and Yvonne Elliman (Mary Magdalene) in its central rôles, encouraged producer Harold Fielding to take the piece up, but whilst Land was dealing with Fielding, the young producer and pop music man, Robert Stigwood, had approached the authors direct. From having no producer, *Jesus Christ Superstar* suddenly had two. It also had a growing success, for the recording

Plate 139. **Jesus Christ Superstar:** *Two different kinds of 'superstar' – London's 'traditional' one, and a fierce-looking oriental Jesus Christ.*

had caught on, particularly in the United States, and the double album three times topped the American album charts. In Britain, the response was more mitigated, but 'Superstar' and Mary Magdalene's 'I Don't Know How to Love Him' both made it into the British top 50 as singles.

It was Stigwood who eventually got *Superstar*, but MCA had covered their big investment well, and he had to share his producer's credit with the recording firm whose contract stipulated their right to first option on any staged version. The producers chose, given the record sales, to mount the show in America rather than in Britain, where there were, in any case, more worries over the tender subject matter. But there was still another stage to pass through before *Jesus Christ Superstar* was seen in a full theatrical production. The popularity of the recording had resulted in concert performances of the show's music – some authorised through ASCAP, others simply pirated – springing up around America. To protect their investment, Stigwood and MCA launched their own concert series, and whilst the music of *Superstar* was sung round the country, they took the final steps towards getting the show into the theatre.

Broadway's *Jesus Christ Superstar*, directed by Tom O'Horgan of *Hair* celebrity, featured Ben Vereen (Judas), Jeff Fenholt (Jesus) and Miss Elliman in the middle of a wildly extravagant and gimmicky production which did almost as much as the subject matter to arouse the not unexpectedly howls of disapproval in some quarters. However, as had happened with the recording, the show

found a large number of enthusiastic fans and, as this initial production ran on towards a 711-performance Broadway record, it was clear that the stage version of *Jesus Christ Superstar* was a success equal to that of *Jesus Christ Superstar* on record.

The text of the show dealt with the last days of the life of Jesus Christ, as seen through the eyes of his disciple, Judas. Not the two-dimensional Judas of mythology, the archetypical betrayer, but a man, a follower of Christ who has become severely worried by the hysterical behaviour of his fellow followers and also by the effect of all this adulation on Christ himself, and on his clear seeing of the way events are going. He disapproves of Jesus's consorting so familiarly with the whore, Magdalene, but, more seriously, he sees a real and growing danger of a lashback, a civil disturbance which may destroy them all, and what they all believe in. As Christ sweeps into Jerusalem to the hosannas of the crowd, routs the moneylenders from the temple, and quails from the hordes of out-of-control cripples and beggars, crying out for the eternal something for nothing, for magic, Judas sees not a messiah or a magician but an overstretched and tiring man who is losing control. So, rather than let Jesus drag their whole enterprise down, he goes to the priests, Caiaphas (Bob Bingham) and Annas (Phil Jethro), and informs. Christ is taken prisoner by the soldiers of the state in the Garden of Gethsemane, and brought first before Pontius Pilate (Barry Dennen), who refuses to judge him, and then before a sybaritic, mocking King Herod (Paul Ainsley). As the 'king of the Jews' heads on towards conviction and crucifixion, Judas, shattered by the part the designs of God have had him play in the whole affair, hangs himself.

The score, part pop, part rock, and withal, based in many of its parts firmly on classical tenets and styles, had already seen its favourite numbers climb the charts, but alongside the urging 'Superstar' and the plangent country melody of 'I Don't Know How to Love Him' (originally written, to a different lyric, as a country song), there were other memorable moments, most particularly Jesus's night-time monologue in the garden of Gethsemane, Pilate's puzzled relation of his dream, some dramatically effectively wide voice part-writing for a menacing counter-tenor and basso profundo pair of priests, and the searing moments of Judas's evening-long dilemma. Amongst all the drama, only Herod's sneeringly epicene interrogation, of all the score, loaned itself to an exaggerated comic staging, and that was what it would ever get.

The British representative of Australia's *Hair* producer, Harry M Miller, was a London colleague of Fielding, and even before the opening of *Superstar* on Broadway, he had secured the show for Miller in Australia. Thus, six months after the Broadway première, it was Australia which was first off the mark with another English-language production of the show. This was a very different production. In Jim Sharman's staging, the colourful, tricksy trimmings of Broadway's production were banished in favour of an almost spartan, space-age production, with stark, clear plastic pieces of scenery, spare, galactic costumes, and an altogether more essentially reverent style. Launched, after a concert series, at Sydney's big Capitol Theatre, *Superstar* style two, with Jon English (Judas), Trevor White (Jesus) and Michele Fawdon (Magdalene) featured, proved an even bigger success than it had on Broadway. It stayed for nine months in Sydney before moving on to another and even larger house, Melbourne's St Kilda Palais (30 March 1973), where it proved not a whit affected by a local attempt to pre-empt it with a piece called *Jesus Christ Revolution* (Comedy Theatre 8 January 1972). After going to the rest of the country, the show was soon back in both main centres, in a revival, as early as 1976.

Productions began to sprout in all corners of the world. A German version (ad Anja Hauptmann) made its way from Munster to Berlin, a French adaptation (ad Pierre Delanoë) with Farid Dali (Judas), Daniel Beretta (Jesus) and Anne-Marie David (Mary) starred was played in Paris, and Scandinavia saw its first versions, whilst London still held back. Finally, however, the West End version came. The stylishness and success of the Australian production had not gone unnoticed, and it was Sharman who was called upon to mount the piece for London. This time there was, however, not even any plastic: the British *Superstar* was, by order, pictorially traditional and both sensitive and dramatic in its mood. The judgement which ensured this uncluttered, serious style of direction proved to be wholly sound. London's *Jesus Christ Superstar*, with Stephen Tate (Judas), Paul Nicholas (Jesus) and Dana Gillespie (Mary) as its original stars, was the most successful version of all. By the time it closed, after some eight years and 3,358 performances, it had become the longest running musical in West End history.

Whilst the London *Superstar* ran on, Broadway, like Australia, took in a second season (Longacre Theater, 23 November 1977, 96 performances), and a filmed version, with Ted Neely (Jesus), Carl Anderson (Judas) and Miss Elliman again as Mary was also produced, as the show spread itself to the regions and touring circuits and to just about every country where musical theatre is played – Japan, Brazil, Mexico, Spain, Hungary – except for South Africa. There it was banned as irreligious.

Jesus Christ Superstar has been reproduced regularly, around the world, in the 20 years since its first appearance and, at the time of writing, it seems that, in the footsteps of the renewed success of *Joseph and the Amazing Technicolor Dreamcoat* in London, it may soon return to the principal musical theatre centres in a major production. Australia has taken the lead, mounting a series of vastly successful Harry M Miller staged concerts of the show with local megastar Johnny Farnham in the rôle of Jesus, the record-breaking returns of which would seem to signify that, in the nostalgia-drenched musico-theatrical world of the 1990s, *Jesus Christ Superstar* is a sure thing for a big return engagement.

Australia: Capitol Theatre, Sydney 4 May 1972; Germany: Munsterlandhalle, Munster 18 February 1972, Deutschlandhalle, Berlin 31 March 1972; France: Théâtre National du Palais de Chaillot, 1972; UK: Palace Theatre 9 August 1972; Hungary; Open Air Theatre, Szeged 25 June 1986; Film: Universal 1973

Recordings: original concept recording, 2 records (MCA), original cast (MCA), London cast (MCA), Australian cast (MCA), French cast (Philips), German cast (Decca), Spanish cast (Pronto), film soundtrack, 2 records (MCA), Japanese cast (Express), Swedish cast (Sonet), Hungarian cast (Qualiton) etc

JE T'VEUX Opérette-revue in 3 acts by Wilned and Marcel Grandjean. Lyrics by Bataille-Henri. Music by Gaston Gabaroche, Fred Pearly, Albert Valsien and René Mercier. Théâtre Marigny, Paris, 12 February 1923.

Madeleine (Jane Pyrac) is obliged, for political reasons, to sell her successful couture business, the Maison Tapin, before wedding the rising young sous-préfet, Pierre Vignac (Adrien Lamy). However, her first husband, Tapin, demands that his name be removed from the firm on its sale, and that demand is a deal-breaker with Madeleine's American buyers. To get round the problem she temporarily marries an available and jolly little china-mender, who is also called Tapin (Milton), thus extending her claim to the name. But then Tapin number two falls for his temporary wife, and decides that he doesn't want to divorce her, until just before the final curtain.

The bright comedy of the piece was supported by a score by four popular songwriters which threw up several lively pieces in varying up-to-date dance rhythms – Gabaroche and Pearly combined on 'La Java-Javi-Java', sung and danced by Milton and Denise Grey as his rejected girlfriend, Adrien Lamy performed Valsien's 'schimmy oriental' 'Là-bas'; and Marguerite Pierry, as a seamstress called Zou-zou, who tries to snaffle the temporarily available Pierre once Madeleine is apparently inextricably re-wed, got tipsy to the tango strains of Mercier's 'C' coquin d'porto' – alongside a selection of more regular waltzes, foxtrots and one-steps.

Je t'veux proved a decided hit for producer Abel Deval and for the Théâtre Marigny. It ran there through to the summer, then reappeared at the Ba-ta-clan for a further run in the autumn, with Marthe Ferrare now playing

Plate 140. **Jill Darling:** *Juveniles John Mills and Louis Browne set out to confirm 'I'm on a See-Saw' with the assistance of 16 Saville chorus girls.*

Madeleine, as well as being sent on the road under the experienced eye of Charles Montcharmont, with Lerner, Pastore and Gaby Dargelle in the lead rôles. In the year following its first production it was seen as far afield as Budapest's Lujza Blaha Színház (ad István Zágon).

Hungary: Lujza Blaha Színház *Gyere be rozsam* 24 April 1924

JILL DARLING Musical comedy (all musical to tell a tale of laughter) in 2 acts by Marriott Edgar. Additional scenes and lyrics by Desmond Carter. Music by Vivian Ellis. Alhambra Theatre, Glasgow (as *Jack and Jill*), 23 December 1933; Saville Theatre, London, 19 December 1934.

Produced by the Moss' Empires and Howard and Wyndham's touring organization to help fill their chain of provincial theatres, *Jack and Jill* was a swiftly written light comedy piece which starred Arthur Riscoe in a dual rôle as a prohibitionist parliamentary candidate and his gormless double who steps in for him when he gets merry before a speech. Vivian Ellis provided a score including one song, the dancing 'I'm on a See-Saw' (introduced by Marjery Wyn and Roy Royston), which would become an enduring hit.

Jack and Jill was a fine success on the road, and Riscoe determined to bring 'his' show to town. Both he and Ellis were intent on using Riscoe's *Out of the Bottle* co-star, Frances Day, as leading lady and, with the help of lyricist Desmond Carter, they changed the leading rôle into a vehicle for the unusual Miss Day as a flapper masquerading as an Hungarian chanteuse, equipped her with four made-to-measure new numbers (including 'Pardon My English' and 'Dancing with a Ghost'), and dug up their own producer in the person of rich South African, Jack Eggar, who had a singing and dancing wife. The wife joined the cast alongside American dancer Louise Browne, Viola Tree, the young John Mills and Eddie Molloy, the piece was produced at the downmarket Saville Theatre, and it promptly became a hit. Mills and Miss Browne's 'I'm on a See-Saw', Riscoe's comedy and Miss Day's Hungarian version of Minnie Mouse were the highlights of a show which ran strongly till Miss Day flitted off to make a film and a bit of inept recasting (real Hungarian star Irene Palasty as the phoney Hungarian!) closed the show after 242 performances.

Jill Darling returned to the provinces, where it toured for four years, but in 1944 Riscoe (in partnership with Alfred Zeitlin and Paul Murray) brought a revamped version (ad Caswell Garth) of the show back to London. This time Riscoe directed and starred opposite Carole Lynne, but the moment for *Jill Darling* was past and its revival folded in 67 performances.

Australia saw *Jill Darling* in 1936 with Nellie Barnes and Leo Franklyn featured alongside Frank Leighton, Diana du Cane, Marie La Varre and Cecil Kellaway for five weeks in Melbourne and seven at Sydney's Theatre Royal (11 April 1936).

Australia: Her Majesty's Theatre, Melbourne 22 February 1936
Recording: original cast recordings (WRC)

JOAN OF ARC

The historical tragedy of Jeanne d'Arc has been the subject of a number of serious stage pieces, including Schiller's 1801 play (*Die Jungfrau von Orleans*), the operas of Hovens and Volkert which were based on it, and Honegger's *Jeanne d'Arc au bûcher* (1938/1950). G B Shaw's *Saint Joan* drew some humour from the tale, but even the play of this most promising of musical comedy librettists has never seemed likely source material for the musical theatre. Nevertheless, Joan has served as the subject of a handful of musical shows, of which the first and the nearest to successful were burlesques: an early Olympic Theatre piece *Joan of Arc, or the Maid of all Hell'uns*, a William Brough piece staged at the Strand Theatre (29 March 1869) in which Thomas Thorne starred as Joan at the head of an Amazon ballet, and another *Joan of Arc* produced by George Edwardes at the Opera Comique (17 January 1891).

Authored by new-found writing team Adrian Ross and composer F Osmond Carr in collaboration with the comedian John L Shine, this last piece had a Joan (Emma Chambers) from the village of Do-re-mi pursued by the King (Shine) to use her talent for visions to find a winning system for him to use at Monte Carlo. Joan and her boyfriend de Richemont (Arthur Roberts) go off to war equipped with the great sword of Charlemagne, but Joan is captured and condemned to the stake only to be saved when the British troops succumb to their national malady and go on strike. The coster number 'Round the Town' performed by Roberts and Charles Danby as Joan's father, and Roberts's burlesque of a solar-topeed Stanley, describing how 'I Went to Find Emin', were high spots of the evening. Neither of them, of course, had anything more to do with Joan of Arc than did an episode in which the whole French court crept up on the English, disguised in blackface, to sing a coon chorus 'De Mountains ob de Moon', but all three songs became hits. The show enjoyed some scandalous moments, firstly when the 'strike' part of the plot offended some loud (and allegedly planted) members of the first-night audience, and then through the fact that shapely Alma Stanley wore no trunks over her tights. Politics proved more powerful than propriety. The tights stayed, the strikes were cut, and the show became a jolly, anodine and successful entertainment until the 'new edition' alterations went in. This time it was Roberts's new hit song 'Randy, Pandy O' which was seen as being offensive – to Randolph Churchill (which it was undoubtedly intended to be). The words were changed to 'Jack the Dandy, O' and no one was fooled. The show had a fine run at the Opera Comique (181 performances) and subsequently moved to the Gaiety Theatre for another 101 nights, prior to a strong career in the provinces and in the colonies.

After this rather undignified treatment, Joan was left alone by the musical theatre for a good, long time, but she surfaced on Broadway in 1975 as the heroine of what seemed to be a new burlesque, *Goodtime Charley* (Palace Theater 3 March), in which Joan was portrayed by the leggy, glamorous dancer Ann Reinking and the Dauphin by Joel Grey, and then again in the era of 'serious' musical plays in both Ireland and in England. Gráinne Renihan was Ireland's Joan to 'the witness' of Colm Wilkinson in the musical *Visions* (T C Doherty, Olympia Theatre, Dublin 24 May 1984), whilst first Siobhan McCarthy and then Rebecca Storm went to the stake along with England's unfortunate *Jeanne* (Shirlie Roden, Birmingham Repertory Theatre 16 September 1985, Sadler's Wells Theatre, 22 February 1986).

JOHN, Graham [COLMER, Graham John] (b London, 13 July 1887; d London, 16 January 1957). Librettist, lyricist and adapter for the British musical stage between the wars.

Educated at Rugby and Corpus Christi, John worked on the Stock Exchange for a number of years, and during this time he began writing material for the revue stage. Amongst his early musical theatre assignments, he interpolated a number for George Grossmith and Leslie Henson into *Tonight's the Night*, provided the lyrics for Vivian Ellis's songs in the revue *By the Way*, additional dialogue for the London production of *Mercenary Mary* and lyrics for London's *Just a Kiss* (*Pas sur la bouche*), as well as the complete lyrics for the English version of Bruno Granichstädten's Viennese hit *Der Orlow* (*Hearts and Diamonds*).

He subsequently rewrote the book of Oscar Straus's *Riquette* as *My Son John* for comedian Billy Merson, and collaborated with Guy Bolton on the book and lyrics of *Blue Eyes*, the romantic tale of how Evelyn Laye saved Scotland, before shifting to America. There he supplied the lyrics for Busby Berkeley's Broadway musical *The Street Singer* (1929) and the Fred Stone vehicle *Ripples* (1930), and spent several years working in Hollywood.

On his return to Britain he collaborated with Hollywood's Martin Broones on the scores for *Give Me a Ring*, *Seeing Stars* and *Swing Along*, and adapted Robert Stolz's romantic *Venus in Seide* as a vehicle for Carl Brisson, before taking up an administrative entertainments post through the length of the war. He subsequently wrote material for several more revues, but not for the book musical.

1924 **Mam'zelle Kiki** (Max Darewski/w Douglas Hoare/Hoare, Sydney Blow) Portsmouth 25 August
1926 **Hearts and Diamonds** (*Der Orlow*) English lyrics (Strand Theatre)
1926 **Just a Kiss** (*Pas sur la bouche*) English lyrics w Desmond Carter, Vivian Ellis (Shaftesbury Theatre)
1928 **Blue Eyes** (Jerome Kern/w Guy Bolton) Piccadilly Theatre 27 April
1929 **The Street Singer** (Niclas Kempner, Sam Timberg/Edgar Smith) Shubert Theater, New York 17 September
1930 **Ripples** (Albert Szirmai, Oscar Levant/w Irving Caesar/William Anthony McGuire) New Amsterdam Theater, New York 11 February
1933 **Give Me a Ring** (Martin Broones/Bolton, R P Weston, Bert Lee) London Hippodrome 22 June
1935 **Seeing Stars** (Broones/Bolton, Fred Thompson) Gaiety Theatre 31 October
1936 **Swing Along** (Broones/Bolton, Thompson, Douglas Furber) Gaiety Theatre 2 September
1937 **Venus in Silk** (*Venus in Seide*) English version w J Hastings Turner (tour)

JOHNSON, Bill (b Baltimore, Md, 22 March 1918; d Flemington, NJ, 6 March 1957). Short-lived American leading man who starred in two major imported hits in Britain.

After an early career in stock, Johnson first appeared on Broadway in revue (*Two for the Show*, *All in Fun*) and in the musical comedy *Banjo Eyes* (1941, Charlie). He moved up the bill to feature opposite Ethel Merman in *Something for the Boys* (1943, Rocky Fulton), and to play a leading rôle in Lerner and Loewe's *The Day Before Spring* (1945) before going to London to play the part of Frank Butler in *Annie Get Your Gun* (1947). He played this rôle throughout the show's long West End run, and remained in Britain to star as Fred/Petruchio in *Kiss Me, Kate* (1951). Back in America he toured as Hajj in *Kismet*, and appeared once more on Broadway, as Doc in *Pipe Dream* (1955), before an accidental death at the age of 38.

Johnson was married to actress and vocalist Shirl Conway, who featured on Broadway in *Plain and Fancy* and in London in *Carissima*.

JOHNSON, J[ohn] Rosamund (b Jacksonville, Fla, 11 August 1873; d New York, 11 November 1954).

The son of a Florida minister, Johnson studied music at the New England conservatory before going on tour with John Isham's Oriental America troupe in 1896. His first attempt at writing for the musical stage was a piece called *Toloso*, written in collaboration with his brother James W Johnson, but when the pair went to New York to try to sell their work, they were unsuccessful. Johnson joined up with song and dance man Bob Cole, performing a vaudeville act for which they wrote their own material, and the three men began to make themselves known as a characterful songwriting team, interpolating numbers – sometimes several, sometimes just one – and often of the imitation-negro coon song variety, into such shows as *The Belle of Bridgeport*, *Humpty Dumpty*, *In Newport*, *The Little Duchess*, *The Rogers Brothers in Central Park*, *Sally in Our Alley* ('Under the Bamboo Tree'), *Sleeping Beauty and the Beast*, *The Girl from Dixie*, *Mr Bluebeard*, *Nancy Brown*, *Mother Goose*, Peter Dailey's *Hello, My Lulu* and *An English Daisy* in the first years of the 20th century.

Cole and Johnson supplied the basic scores for two all-

Plate 141.

negro musical comedies, *The Shoofly Regiment* and A L Wilbur's mounting of *The Red Moon*, and Johnson also contributed material to F Ray Comstock's production of *Mr Lode of Koal* (40 performances), but all of these pieces were unsuccessful and the pair returned to performing in vaudeville. After Cole's death Johnson held several musical directorial posts, and continued to compose, arrange and to perform, sometimes for the theatre (Alice Lloyd's 'If You'll Be My Eve, I'll Build an Eden for You' etc), but mostly in other areas. Some of Johnson's music was used, along with that of Louis Hirsch, to compile the score of the London revue *Come Over Here* (London Opera House, 19 April 1913) at the dawning of the fashion for 'new' American dance rhythms on the budding London variety-revue stage.

Amongst his other activities, Johnson authored a volume on negro song, compiled a collection of spirituals and wrote both dance and vocal music. He also appeared on the stage as a performer in *Porgy and Bess* (1935 and 1942, Frazier) and *Cabin in the Sky* (1940, Brother Green).

His brother, **James W[eldon] JOHNSON** (b Jacksonville, Fla, 17 June 1871; d Wiscasset, Maine, 26 June 1938), was trained as a lawyer and later became a diplomat and author (*Black Manhattan* 1930, *Along this Way* 1933). He joined his brother and Cole in their songwriting during their most successful years before going to Venezuela on a consular posting in 1906, a posting which did not stop him from continuing to partner his brother in the manufacture of popular songs. He was killed in an accident in Maine in 1938. He was posthumously represented at off-Broadway's Astor Place Playhouse in 1963 by a Vinette Carroll compilation of sermons and gospel music under the title *God's Trombone* (21 December, 160 performances), repeated at the New Federal Theater in 1989 (4 October, 45 performances).

1900 The Belle of Bridgeport (w Accoe, Bob Cole, James William Jefferson, Cissie Loftus etc/Glen MacDonough) Bijou Theater, 29 October
1907 The Shoofly Regiment (James Weldon Johnson/Cole) Bijou Theater 6 August
1909 The Red Moon (Cole) Majestic Theater 3 May
1909 Mr Lode of Koal (w Bert Williams/Jesse A Shipp, Alexander Rogers) Majestic Theater 1 November

LA JOLIE PARFUMEUSE Opéra-comique in 3 acts by Hector Crémieux and Ernest Blum. Music by Jacques Offenbach. Théâtre de la Renaissance, Paris, 29 November 1873.

The tale of the pretty perfumeress, and her struggles to hold on to her virtue in the face of the worst the operettic world could fling at her, brought Offenbach his first genuine success in the two years since the Franco-Prussian War and the end of the Empire. To win this success, however, the composer and his authors had had to change their ways. Crémieux, the co-author of the fantastical burlesque texts of *Orphée aux enfers* and *Le Pont des soupirs*, abandoned the grotesqueries of the opéra-bouffe for a bright little farcical libretto of sexual quiproquos, and Offenbach went with him in illustrating a tale that seemed to owe more than a little to Sauvage and Grisar's 1850 opéra-comique *Les Porcherons* and others of its kind. Some of the success of *La Jolie Parfumeuse* was, however, due to one of the composer's other talents – that of discovering new leading ladies. This opérette served to launch charming, teenaged, pretty-voiced Louise Théo, previously seen only in the one-act *Pomme d'api*, who scored a huge personal success as the parfumeuse of the title.

Rose Michon (Théo), the pretty perfumeress, has to pass by some of the wickedest spots and folk in Paris on her way from her wedding to her nuptial bedding. As part of a surprise arranged by her new husband, she is whisked from her wedding reception amid the dizzy gaiety of the unbuttoned part of town known as les Porcherons by the wealthy financier and uncle of the groom, La Cocardière (Daubray). La Cocardière leads her to her old home, newly done up by her husband as a wedding gift, but once they are there, the naughty uncle, who all the time has had a bit of brisk, instant adultery on his mind, switches out the lights and pretends to be the new husband. Next, he leads the little bride to his own luxurious mansion, where the more usual company are such abandoned women as the danseuse Clorinde (Mlle Fonti), and lays siege to her again. When her unwealthy, unlubricious little husband, Bavolet (Mlle Laurence Grivot), turns up inopportunely, the far from unskilled Rose salves his hurt by pretending to be his wife's double, a dancer called Dorothée Bruscambille. Clorinde helps in the deception and, the next morning, she uses the fact that the real Bruscambille is fifty and a mother of several, to pin down the still hopefully prowling La Cocardière, whilst the two newlyweds go their way, the cunning little wife still in one piece and the innocent little husband none the wiser.

Much of the appeal of *La Jolie Parfumeuse* was in its high-jinks: the country wedding-style first act, the sexual fencing of the second act, Rose's impersonation of the dancer, and the farcical japes of the final act with the persistent La Cocardière trying to rendezvous with Rose in her perfumery and subjected to all sorts of pretences, indignities and sudden exits. But the music played its part.

Théo had, as intended, the best moments of the score, topped by the pretty Couplets de la vertue, with their message that a girl loses nothing by waiting to lose her virtue, a tickling number, and the jolly Chanson de la Bruscambille in her disguise as the opera danseuse ('A Toulouse en Toulousain'). One of the other favourite moments fell to the supporting comedy character of Poirot, La Cocardière's accomplice in foolery in the first act, who finally falls for Rose after everyone else has been doing so for two acts, and delivers up his feelings in a comical letter-song.

La Jolie Parfumeuse was a grand success, playing for more than 200 nights under the management of Hostein at the Théâtre de la Renaissance on its first run. In 1875 Charles Comte revived the piece at the Bouffes-Parisiens, where Théo triumphed all over again as Rose Michon, and the now well-known show appeared in Paris yet again in 1876, as it simultaneously spread itself around the world. In 1892 *La Jolie Parfumeuse* was given a revival at the Renaissance with Juliette Simon-Girard as Rose Michon, and in 1898 Mariette Sully played the title-rôle in a production at the Théâtre de la Gaîté, but, in spite of its early popularity, *La Jolie Parfumeuse*, like almost all Offenbach's shows of the postwar 1870s, did not survive into the 20th century as part of the standard repertoire.

London's Alhambra Theatre was the first overseas house to snap up the latest Offenbach hit (ad H J Byron). In a programme shared with the ballet *Flick and Flock*, Kate Santley starred as Rose Michon to the Clorinde of Rose Bell, the La Cocardière of Harry Paulton and the Bavolet of Lennox Grey, through a good run of 94 straight performances, and the following year Emily Soldene took the piece on the British road. America was slower to take up an English version, and the first performances that were seen in New York were in the original French, with Marie Aimée leading her company as a particularly successful Rose Michon. She kept the work in her repertoire for four seasons, during which time the show appeared as *The Pretty Perfumer* in English in the repertoire of the ever-anglicizing Alice Oates. In 1883 (17 March) New York got the original pretty perfumeress, when a now slightly older Louise Théo repeated her most famous rôle, expanded for the occasion with a rendition of Judic's famous song 'Piii-ouit!', on Broadway, and, like Aimée, she subsequently kept the show as a feature of her repertoire through her several seasons of performances through America.

Australia swiftly welcomed its first *Jolie Parfumeuse* when Clara Thompson introduced Rose Michon to Melbourne and then (23 May 1876) to Sydney, with Jennie Winston as her Bavolet, and the colonies later got a variant version when Kelly and Leon's troupe introduced their *Rose Michon, or The Little Bride* (School of Arts, Sydney 1879) with Leon impersonating Rose Michon in a version where the quiproquos took on rather a different flavour.

Austria, too, took to *Schönröschen* (ad Carl Treumann, add mus Brandl) with a will. Produced by Franz Jauner at the Carltheater with Hermine Meyerhoff (Rose), Wilhelm Knaack (La Cocardière), Frln Wiedermann (Clorinde), Karl Blasel (Persiflage) and Antonie Link (Bavolet) featured, the piece was played 22 times en suite, 40 times in its first 12 months in the repertoire, and 63 times (with Rosa Streitmann taking over the lead rôle) before Jauner quit the house in 1878. The new manager, Tewele,

immediately mounted a fresh production (4 December 1878), and *Schönröschen* reappeared in Vienna as late as 1907, when Kurt von Lessen starred himself briefly alongside Frln Blank at the Lustspieltheater.

In spite of its general success, however, Hungary seems curiously to have largely ignored the show, and a version mounted as late as 1886 at the Népszinház (ad György Verő, Jenő Rákosi) was played just four times.

UK: Alhambra Theatre 18 May 1874; Austria: Carltheater *Schönröschen* 6 November 1874; Germany: Wallner Theater *Schönröschen* 16 January 1875; USA: Lyceum Theater (Fr) 31 March 1875, Brooklyn Theater *The Pretty Perfumer* 5 October 1876; Australia: Prince of Wales Opera House, Melbourne 17 November 1875; Hungary: Népszinház *Százszorszép* 22 May 1886

LA JOLIE PERSANE Opérette in 3 acts by Eugène Leterrier and Albert Vanloo. Music by Charles Lecocq. Théâtre de la Renaissance, Paris, 28 October 1879.

Nadir (Lary) and Namouna (Jane Hading), who have only just wed, quarrel and promptly get themselves divorced by Moka (Vauthier), the Cadi. The local Prince (Marie Gélabert) is anxious to marry Namouna himself, but the hasty young pair have already made up their differences and decided that they prefer to be married to each other after all. Unfortunately for them, the law of the land says they can only re-wed after having, in between, been wed elsewhere. As in most countries with silly laws, there is an equally silly traditional way of subverting this one. The hulla, old Broudoudour (Ismaël), is available, for the 115th time, to go through a marriage of convenience with Namouna prior to a quick divorce. The Prince, however, determines to take the hulla's place. There are plenty of comings and goings before the youngsters get back together, the Prince ultimately switching his affections to Moka's wife (obliging the Cadi to hastily divorce) and Broudoudour, who had been momentarily determined to have and hold Namouna as well, ending up with the buxom Babouche (Marie Desclauzas), the orange-seller.

Lecocq's score had some attractive moments, including Moka's suggestive Couplets des pêches ('L'été, quand la pêche est mure'), Namouna's Rondeau du petit ange, a lilting entrance number for the Prince, casting his eyes around the village girls for a prospective bride ('J'aime l'oiseau'), and a third-act waltz ('Voyons d'abord') for the same character, whilst the Opéra-Comique's Ismaël was given the Chanson de la brune et de la blonde on which to expend his rich basso voice.

In spite of its top-drawer cast, Victor Koning's Paris production of *La Jolie Persane* was not a genuine success, and although the producer tried hard to get a run out of it, he was obliged to withdraw it on 4 January, after a little over two months of performances. This less-than-a-half success, however, did not stop other venues from taking up Lecocq's latest show. Vienna saw Hermine Meyerhoff as *Die hübsche Perserin* (ad F Zell, Richard Genée) alongside Felix Schweighofer (Moka), Carl Adolf Friese (Salamalek), Alexander Girardi (Brududur) and Frln König (Schrias-Kuli-Khan) 23 times, Germany saw a different German version at Aachen, then at Hamburg (17 April 1881) and ultimately in Berlin, and Budapest got *A szép perzsalány* (ad Lajos Evva), with Aranka Hegyi starred as its heroine, 11 times. However, the piece finally did find

Plate 142. **Al Jolson** *in* Robinson Crusoe Jr.

genuine success when it was done over and into English by
Sydney Rosenfeld, under the title *The Oolah*, as a Broadway vehicle for comedian Francis Wilson.

The change in title clearly showed the change in
emphasis, away from the music and towards low comedy,
but it was a shift that also ensured the show a run. Wilson
(Hoolah Goolah), Marie Jansen (Tourouloupi), Hubert
Wilke (Prince) and Harry MacDonough (Cadi) headed the
cast of the show past its 100th Broadway night on 19
August, and *The Oolah* ran on merrily until October (156
performances) before going into the American regions.

Austria: Theater an der Wien *Die hübsche Perserin* 16 January
1880; Hungary: Népszinház *A szép perzsalány* 10 September
1880; Germany: Aachen *Die schöne Perserin* 29 May 1880,
Carl-Schultze Theater, Hamburg 17 April 1881, Belle-
Alliance-Theater, Berlin 3 January 1887; USA: Broadway
Theater *The Oolah* 13 May 1889

JOLSON, AL [YOELSON, Asa] (b Srednike, Lithu-
ania, 26 March 1886; d San Francisco, 23 October 1950).
Famous blackface Mammy-singer of the stage and screen,
whose run of successful theatrical vehicles can only barely
be regarded as book musicals.

Jolson ran away from home to go into show business,
and he made his first appearances in variety, in circus and,
at the age of 13, in the play *The Children of the Ghetto*. He
eventually made himself a career in minstrel shows and in
vaudeville, and made his first Broadway appearance in a
musical show when the Shuberts cast him in the blackface
rôle of Erastus Sparkler, alongside some of the more

glamorous ladies of the musical and revue stage, in the
revusical *La Belle Paree* at the Winter Garden. His extravagantly emotional delivery of sentimental, patriotic and
exuberant songs quickly made him popular, and he rose
through a series of revusical musical plays, beginning with
an adaptation of the Viennese hit *Vera Violetta* ('Rum Tum
Tiddle'), and then continuing, in the character of the black
'boy', Gus, through *The Whirl of Society*, *The Honeymoon
Express* ('Who Paid the Rent for Mrs Rip van Winkle'),
Dancing Around, *Robinson Crusoe jr* ('Yackey Hula Hickey
Dula', 'Down Where the Swanee River Flows', 'Where the
Black-Eyed Susans Grow') and *Sinbad* ('Rock-a-Bye Your
Baby with a Dixie Melody', 'My Mammy', 'Chloe', 'You
Ain't Heard Nothin' Yet'), to major stardom in the Ameri-
can theatre.

Eventually, Jolson's shows developed into a two-part
affair – a sketchy little musical comedy in the first act, and
a second act in which the audience got little more than
Jolson, singing his songs with blithe disregard for any dramatic coherence which the first half might have pretended,
and with a consummate ability to hold an audience in the
palm of his hand. On his way through a decade and more
of celebrity, Jolson made enduring hits of some of the
handsful of songs which he interpolated into the scores of
his various shows, some of which numbers bore his name
as co-author much on the same principle as that adopted
by the 19th-century music-hall stars, who considered that
'creating' a song earned them a co-authorial credit, not to
mention a share in the royalties.

Jolson abandoned the character of Gus to play the title-rôle in *Bombo* ('April Showers', 'Toot Toot Tootsie', 'California, Here I Come') at the Jolson Theater, but he returned to his old all-purpose character once more in 1925 in *Big Boy*. His illness cut short *Big Boy*'s run, but the show went on the road and returned to Broadway when the star had recovered. After 15 years at the top, however, Jolson's position in public favour had now become slightly wobbly, but he returned vigorously to the forefront with the coming of the sound film, starring in the famous *The Jazz Singer* and a series of similar films in the next few years (*The Singing Fool, Sonny Boy, Mammy, Big Boy*).

In 1931 he returned to Broadway to appear, this time without the famous blackface, in a version of the Austrian hit cabaret musical *Die Wunder-Bar* (*Wonder Bar*). The production was not a success, and Jolson turned back to films to continue through another decade of movies (*Wonder Bar, Go into Your Dance, The Singing Kid, Rose of Washington Square, Swanee River* etc) with mostly decreasing results. In 1940 he made one last return to the stage, this time in a regular musical play, *Hold on to Your Hats*, with an end-to-end construction and no second-half Jolson concert. He took the part of a radio cowboy character who is set to performing real-life heroics, but he found the limitations of a straight script and the fact that he was not the solo star of the show more than he could take for too long, and *Hold on to Your Hats* was scuppered after five months on Broadway.

Jolson had a third period in the limelight when Hollywood made a highly successful biopic of his life as *The Jolson Story* in 1946. To Jolson's disappointment, Larry Parks appeared as him, but it was his singing voice which was heard both in that film and in a sequel, *Jolson Sings Again* (1949).

Although he had no monopoly on the genre, even in his own latter-day period, Jolson became accepted throughout the world as the archetype of the blackface singer, much in the same way that Marie Lloyd came facilely to represent virtually the whole of the English music-hall tradition to later generations, and he was imitated many times in later revues and musical shows. Several attempts were made in the 1970s to mount a stage biomusical based on Jolson's life, using much of the star's old material. Neither *Al Jolson Tonight!* (Kansas City, 1978) nor *Joley* (Northstage Theater, Glen Cove 2 March 1979), with Larry Kert starred as Jolson, found its intended way to Broadway.

Jolson was married for a time to stage and film ingénue Ruby Keeler.

Biography: Jolson, H & Emley, A: *Mistah Jolson* (House-Warren, New York, 1951), Seiben, P: *The Immortal Jolson* (Fell, New York, 1962), Anderton, B: *Sonny Boy* (1975), Freedland. M: *Jolson* (fictionalized biography) (Stein & Day, New York, 1972), Oberfirst, R: *Al Jolson* (A S Barnes, New York, 1980), Goldman, H: *Jolson: The Legend Comes to Life* (OUP, New York, 1988) etc

JONAS, Émile (b Paris, 5 March 1827; d Saint-Germain-en-Laye, 22 May 1905). Composer for the early French opéra-bouffe stage.

A teacher at the Paris Conservatoire for some 20 years, musical director at Paris's Portuguese synagogue and, subsequently, bandmaster of the Garde Nationale, Jonas was an early contributor to the programmes mounted by

Offenbach at the Théâtre des Bouffes-Parisiens, providing the scores for a number of one-act opérettes, of which *Les Petits Prodiges* (add mus Offenbach), played both at home and by the Bouffes company on its European tours, was the most generally popular. His little *Les Deux Arlequins* was also exported, and had the distinction of being played as part of the opening programme at London's Gaiety Theatre (ad Gilbert a' Beckett 21 December 1868), whilst *Avant la noce* was played in London as *Terrible Hymen* (Covent Garden 26 December 1866).

Jonas had his greatest success with his first full-scale opéra-bouffe, the extravagantly comical *Le Canard à trois becs*, and he confirmed that success with an opéra-bouffe score written for John Hollingshead and London's Gaiety Theatre as *Cinderella the Younger*. Under the title of *Javotte*, that piece – still arguably the best version of the Cinderella tale written for the light musical stage – was also seen throughout Europe. But if *Javotte* made its way back to Paris, as part of its international exposure, Jonas's next two pieces did not. *Die Japanesin* and *Goldchignon*, although originally written to French texts, were both premièred in translation in Vienna and, although the second named went on to productions in Brussels (Fantaisies-Parisiennes, Brussels 17 October 1874), where Pauline Luigini and Alfred Jolly starred, and in Budapest (*Az arany chignon*, Budai Színkör 6 June 1874) following its introduction at the Strampfertheater, Jonas could not find either of them a place in his home town. The two amongst his pieces which were mounted there, *La Bonne Aventure* and *Le Premier Baiser*, were both unsuccessful, and it was *Le Canard à trois becs*, his two little pieces, and *Javotte* which remained his principal references as a theatre composer.

1855 **Le Duel de Benjamin** (Eugène Mestépès) 1 act Théâtre des Bouffes-Parisens October
1856 **La Parade** (Jules Barbier) 1 act Théâtre des Bouffes-Parisiens 2 August
1857 **Le Roi boit** (Mestépès, Adolphe Jaime) 1 act Théâtre des Bouffes-Parisiens 9 April
1857 **La Momie de Roscoco** (w E Ortolan/Émile de Najac) 1 act Théâtre des Bouffes-Parisiens 27 July
1857 **Les Petits Prodiges** (Jaime, Étienne Tréfeu) Théâtre des Bouffes-Parisiens 19 November
1863 **Job et son chien** (Mestépès) 1 act Théâtre des Bouffes-Parisiens 6 February
1864 **Le Manoir des Larenardière** (Mestépès) 1 act Théâtre des Bouffes-Parisiens 29 September
1865 **Avant la noce** (Mestépès, Paul Boisselot) 1 act Théâtre des Bouffes-Parisiens 24 March
1865 **Le Roi Midas** (Charles Nuitter) privately
1865 **Les Deux Arlequins** (Mestépès) 1 act Fantaisies-Parisiennes 29 December
1867 **Marlbrough s'en va-t-en guerre** (w Georges Bizet, Isidore Legouix, Léo Delibes/William Busnach, Paul Siraudin) Théâtre de l'Athénée 15 December
1869 **Le Canard à trois becs** (Jules Moinaux) Théâtre des Folies-Dramatiques 6 February
1869 **Désiré, Sire de Champigny** (Désiré) 1 act Théâtre des Bouffes-Parisiens 11 April
1871 **Cinderella the Younger** (*Javotte*) (Alfred Thompson) Gaiety Theatre, London 23 September
1873 **Goldchignon** (*Chignon d'or*) (Eugène Grangé, Tréfeu) Strampfertheater, Vienna 20 May
1874 **Die Japanesin** (Grangé, Victor Bernard ad Richard Genée, F Zell) Theater an der Wien, Vienna 24 January
1882 **La Bonne Aventure** (Henri Bocage, de Najac) Théâtre de la Renaissance 3 November

1883 **Le Premier Baiser** (de Najac, Raoul Toché) Théâtre des Nouveautés 21 March

JONES, Edward (b ?1859; d London, 10 August 1917). A regular West End musical director for more than 20 years, who also composed scores for the theatrical and variety stages.

Over the years, Jones the conductor worked for Wilson Barrett at the Princess's Theatre, at the Court Theatre, and with both George Edwardes and with Charles Frohman in musical comedy. He composed incidental music for a number of Barrett's most famous productions (*The Silver King, The Lights o' London, Claudian, Hamlet, Junius, Hoodman Blind, Lord Harry, The Romany Rye* etc) and, most notably, for the famous Lyric Theatre production of *The Sign of the Cross* ('Shepherd of Souls'), and he subsequently conducted such major London shows as *The Girl from Kays, The Belle of Mayfair* and *The Catch of the Season*, and such revues as *Odds and Ends* and *More* at the Ambassadors Theatre.

Jones also made a number of very varied attempts at composing for the musical theatre, beginning with the grandiose but short-lived medieval tale of *The Fay o' Fire*, including an indifferent prewrite of the Broadway musical *The Beauty Spot* for London, and ending with a collaboration with the infallibly popular George Dance on his one and only wholly unsuccessful musical. Latterly he composed music for provincial shows, for musical playlets and sketches for variety houses, and for revue (the early *Under the Clock, Odds and Ends*, three editions of *More* etc) as well as incidental music ranging from the children's fairy play *Where Children Rule* at the Garrick Theatre to the drama.

His one enduring success came with his smallest work for the regular theatre, a short score of light-hearted songs composed for the musical playlet *A Pantomime Rehearsal*, which became the most popular one-act piece of its time in a long West End run (as part of a triple bill of which it was the feature), and regular productions, professional and amateur, for decades after.

Jones's presence on the musical scene has been said to have been the reason why the more celebrated composer Edward German (real name: German Edward Jones) was forced to take up his pseudonym. The anecdote is a dubious one, however, given that German was known by his first name, and not as Edward.

1885 **The Fay o' Fire** (Henry Herman) Opera Comique 14 November
1891 **A Pantomime Rehearsal** (Cecil Clay) 1 act Terry's Theatre 6 June
1895 **A Near Shave** (George D Day) 1 act Court Theatre 6 May
1895 **Giddy Galatea** (Henry Edlin) 1 act Duke of York's Theatre 15 November
1896 **Playing the Game** (w Fred Eplett/Willie Younge, Arthur Flaxman) Strand Theatre 12 June
1899 **The Prince of Borneo** (Joseph W Herbert) Strand Theatre 5 October
1901 **The Thirty Thieves** (aka *Miss Mariana*) (William H Risque) Terry's Theatre 1 January
1902 **The West End** (Ernest Boyd-Jones/George Dance, George Arliss) Norwich 29 September
1904 **The Marchioness** (Charles Dickens ad) 1 act His Majesty's Theatre 23 June
1905 **The Varsity Belle** (George Porrington/Frederick Jarman) Theatre Royal, Dover 20 February

1907 **The Blossom of Brittany** (Sutton Vane) Theatre Royal, Brighton 25 June
1909 **The Queen of the Fairies** (Sydney Blow) 1 act London Coliseum 15 February
1912 **Maid Marjorie** Theatre Royal, Halifax 7 October
1913 **Mam'zelle Champagne** (Leslie Stiles) 1 act Oxford Music Hall 22 June
1914 **Dusk** (Robert Vansittart) 1 act Little Theatre 24 April
1914 **England Expects** (Seymour Hicks, Edward Knoblock) 1 act London Opera House 17 September

JONES, [James] Sidney (b London, 17 June 1861; d London, 29 Jan 1946). The most internationally successful composer of the Victorian British romantic musical theatre.

Islington-born Sidney Jones was the son of the bandmaster and conductor, also called Sidney Jones, who was for many years a prominent figure in the musical life of the city of Leeds, where he held not only the position of musical director at the Grand Theatre but also presided over the city band. The younger Sidney began his musical life playing clarinet under his father's baton, but he soon found his own feet and left Leeds, while still in his early twenties, to go on the road as musical director with a company playing the popular American 'musical comedy oddity' *Fun on the Bristol*. He subsequently worked in a similar capacity with the Vokes family, touring their enduring farcical entertainment *In Camp*, and it was for this low comic tale of amateur theatricals in a military camp that Jones composed his first theatre music, in the shape of fresh incidental music and songs to be added to what was virtually the Vokes's 'act'.

In 1886 the young Jones's talents as a musical director came under the ever discerning eye of actress/producer Kate Santley, who hired him as musical director for the tour of her musical *Vetah*, and his next employer was the newly rich Henry Leslie, for whom he worked for nearly four years as conductor of the number one touring companies of the phenomenally successful *Dorothy* (starring Lucy Carr-Shaw, sister to George Bernard), *Doris* and *The Red Hussar*. He next took musical control of a tour of the Gaiety Theatre success *Little Jack Sheppard* under the management of comedian J J Dallas, and this last engagement resulted in his coming to the notice of George Edwardes, who hired him as musical director for the Gaiety Theatre's prestigious 1891 tour of America and Australia, conducting a company which included Nellie Farren and Fred Leslie, and playing the burlesque *Ruy Blas and the Blasé Roué*. When the company produced *Cinder-Ellen Up-too-Late* in Australia, Jones contributed a dance number to Meyer Lutz's score.

On his return to London Jones remained in Edwardes's employment, and took up the baton for the first time in the West End as conductor of the new musical comedy *In Town* at the Prince of Wales Theatre. He was obliged to give up this position when the show transferred to the Gaiety Theatre, and resident musical director, Meyer Lutz, took over command of the orchestra, but now established as one of the principal conductors of the West End theatre he was soon engaged for another important new musical comedy, *Morocco Bound*, produced under the management of Fred Harris at the Shaftesbury Theatre.

In the meanwhile, Jones had also begun to establish himself as a composer. He composed original music for the pantomime *Aladdin II* at Leeds (1889), an operetta, *Our Family Legend*, written with Reginald Stockton, was staged at the Brighton Aquarium, and he also supplied some individual numbers for interpolation into London and touring scores. One of these, 'Linger Longer, Loo', was taken up by Edwardes and subsequently became a hit at the Gaiety in the burlesque *Don Juan* (1893), but by that time Jones had already made his mark in a more substantial manner. The society journalist Jimmy Davis ('Owen Hall') had spoken disparagingly to Edwardes of the qualities of *In Town*, and Edwardes had challenged him to come up with a better script. When Hall produced the book of *A Gaiety Girl* it was given to Jones to set to music and the result was a show which, even more than *In Town* and *Morocco Bound*, set the trend for a new era of light musical theatre. It was music which had a popular ring, no doubt gleaned from the composer's early years with the touring variety combinations, allied to something of the substance of the classic light theatre music of Sullivan and, more particularly, of Cellier, which he had so long conducted for Leslie.

Whilst continuing to work as a conductor, both for his own works and for such pieces as the hit London production of Ivan Caryll's *The Gay Parisienne*, and while continuing to provide additional pieces of music both for touring musicals such as *Giddy Miss Carmen* and his old employer J J Dallas's *One of the Girls*, and for town shows (*Lost, Strayed or Stolen* etc), Jones settled down to a steady career as what eventually became house composer to George Edwardes's new Daly's Theatre. When *A Gaiety Girl* finished its run, at Daly's, Jones again combined with Hall and lyricist Harry Greenbank on a successor, *An Artist's Model*, and this, in turn, was followed by the three most substantial light musical pieces of the era: *The Geisha*, *A Greek Slave* and *San Toy*.

With Edwardes's famous Daly's star team to write for, Jones turned out ever more masterly scores, including a fine supply of individual hit songs ('The Amorous Goldfish', 'Chin, Chin, Chinaman' etc.). Soprano solos, such as 'A Geisha's Life' and the waltz song 'Love, Love' from *The Geisha* or 'The Golden Isle' from *A Greek Slave* and baritone ballads such as 'The One in the World' (*San Toy*) and 'The Girl of My Heart' (*Greek Slave*), were outstanding examples of late-19th-century romantic show music, set in shows which could still dip near to the music hall in some of their point numbers, such as the insistently anthropomorphic fables of 'The Interfering Parrot' or 'A Frog He Lived in a Pond', and rise to some magnificently tuneful concerted finales, such as that ending the first act of *A Greek Slave*, a piece of ensemble music which bordered on the light operatic without ever becoming too heavy for the kind of musical play which housed it.

Both *The Geisha* and *San Toy* became international hits, being played over several decades not only in Britain and the colonies but all round the world. Both were played in Germany, in Hungary and in Austria, where *The Geisha* became the most successful English-language musical of all time, being played regularly in metropolitan and provincial houses for more than half a century and taking a firm place in the regular repertoire, as it did also, in a lesser way, in Italy. If *A Greek Slave* took a definite third place to these two works, this was in no way due to any failings in its musical score, which held some of Jones's most attractive work.

After his series of successes at Daly's, Jones tried his hand at a comedy opera, *My Lady Molly*, an old-fashioned costume musical with strong affiliations with *Dorothy*. Given that the vogue for such pieces had long been drowned in the tide of success created by Jones's own musicals, on the one hand, and the lighter fare purveyed at the Gaiety Theatre on the other, the show was a fine success, but when Jones and Hall were hired by Tom Davis, grown rich on the triumph of *Florodora*, to write him a piece for his Lyric Theatre, the resultant *The Medal and the Maid*, again rather more by Hall's fault than Jones's, was a failure – the first in the composer's and the author's careers. A return to oriental topics in the pretty *See See* did rather better, but Jones had to wait for a further success until 1908, when he combined with the young Frederick Lonsdale in another trend-setting show, *King of Cadonia*, the archetypal modern Ruritanian musical, mounted with singular success under the management of Frank Curzon. Its successor, *A Persian Princess*, failed, but when Jones changed direction yet again he once more found at least a measure of success, back with Edwardes, this time at the more light-hearted Gaiety Theatre, with *The Girl from Utah*.

It was now 1913, and musical tastes were taking a very heavy turn away from Victorian ballads and point songs towards the syncopated dance-based rhythms coming from America. Jones was not at home in this musical atmosphere. He turned one last time back to Daly's Theatre to supply the score for the post-Edwardes production of the thoroughly Ruritanian *The Happy Day*, with José Collins and Bertram Wallis starring where Marie Tempest and Hayden Coffin had been, but although this last show fared well enough it was no *Geisha*, and it had nothing like the success of his most famous piece. At the age of 55 Jones withdrew from the world of the musical theatre and, for the last 30 years of his life, he wrote no more.

1892 **Our Family Legend** (Reginald Stockton) 1 act Brighton Aquarium 8 October
1893 **A Gaiety Girl** (Harry Greenbank/Owen Hall) Prince of Wales Theatre 14 October
1895 **An Artist's Model** (H Greenbank/Hall) Daly's Theatre 2 February
1896 **The Geisha** (H Greenbank/Hall) Daly's Theatre 25 April
1898 **A Greek Slave** (H Greenbank, Adrian Ross/Hall) Daly's Theatre 8 June
1899 **San Toy** (H Greenbank, Ross/Edward Morton) Daly's Theatre 21 October
1902 **My Lady Molly** (C H Taylor, Percy Greenbank/George H Jessop) Theatre Royal, Brighton 11 August; Terry's Theatre, London 14 March 1903
1903 **The Medal and the Maid** (Taylor/Hall) Lyric Theatre 25 April
1906 **See See** (Ross, P Greenbank/C H E Brookfield) Prince of Wales Theatre 20 June
1908 **(The) King of Cadonia** (Ross/Frederick Lonsdale) Prince of Wales Theatre 3 September
1909 **A Persian Princess** (P Greenbank/Leedham Bantock, P J Barrow) Queen's Theatre 27 April
1913 **The Girl from Utah** (w Paul Rubens/Ross, P Greenbank, Rubens/James Tanner) Adelphi Theatre 18 October
1916 **The Happy Day** (w Rubens/Ross, Rubens/Seymour Hicks) Daly's Theatre 13 May

His brother **[John] Guy [Sidney] JONES** (b 1875; d Surbiton, 8 February 1959) also pursued a career as a musical director (*The Lady Slavey*, *The French Maid*,

Bilberry of Tilbury, The Medal and the Maid, The Blue Moon, The Grass Widows) and as a composer, his one substantial score being that for Charles Frohman's production of the successful Seymour Hicks musical *The Gay Gordons* (1907).

1898 **Bilberry of Tilbury** (George D Day, Silvanus Dauncey) Criterion Theatre 8 August
1899 **The American Heiress** (w Herbert Simpson et al/Day, Arthur Branscombe) Birmingham 3 April
1907 **The Gay Gordons** (Seymour Hicks/Arthur Wimperis) Aldwych Theatre 11 September
1911 **Belle of the Skies** (Graham Squiers) 1 act Theatre Royal, Birmingham 22 May
1912 **The Democrats** (St John Hamund, Squiers) 1 act Theatre Royal, Birmingham 13 May
1915 **Menari, the Malay Dancing Girl** (Charles Ward-Jackson) 1 act Golders Green Empire 15 March

JONES, Tom (b Littlefield, Tex, 17 February 1928).

Jones teamed up with songwriting partner Harvey Schmidt during their university days and the pair made their earliest stage ventures in college shows. They placed songs in such revues as Julius Monk's *Demi-Dozen* and *Pieces of Eight*, and *Shoestring '57* before their first book musical *The Fantasticks* ('Try to Remember') was brought to the stage. The immense success of this little piece won Schmidt and Jones the opportunity to work on a very much larger show, the adaptation of the play *The Rainmaker* into the musical *110 in the Shade* but, although the piece had a certain success, they intelligently returned to what they recognized they did best and produced another intimate piece, the two-handed musical adaptation of Jan de Hartog's *The Fourposter* as *I Do! I Do!* This time, however, the piece was not staged like an intimate musical. It was mounted not in a tiny house like that which housed *The Fantasticks*, but on a regular Broadway-sized plateau, but the result was, just the same, another long-running hit.

Thereafter, however, success deserted the pair and, as *The Fantasticks* continued its run into the record books, their several attempts at a biomusical on the French writer and music-hall artist, Colette, a small-scale allegoric piece, with multiple echoes of *The Fantasticks* and of its 1960s era, entitled *Celebration* (110 performances), and a classical burlesque, *Philemon*, failed to confirm their popularity, as established by their first three shows. Like the largest version of *Colette*, mounted in 1982 with Diana Rigg starred as the novelist, their most recent work, a musical version of the Thornton Wilder play *Our Town*, produced under the title *Grovers Corners*, did not make it to Broadway.

Schmidt and Jones were responsible for establishing Portfolio Theater, a small-scale experimental musical theatre for workshopping new pieces.

1960 **The Fantasticks** (Harvey Schmidt) Sullivan Street Playhouse 3 May
1960 **Anatol** City Hall Theater, Hamilton, Bermuda
1963 **110 in the Shade** (Schmidt/w N Richard Nash) Broadhurst Theater 24 October
1966 **I Do! I Do!** (Schmidt) 46th Street Theater 5 December
1969 **Celebration** (Schmidt) Ambassador Theater 22 January
1970 **Colette** (Schmidt/w Elinor Jones) Ellen Stewart Theater 6 June
1975 **The Bone Room** (Schmidt) Portfolio Studio 28 February
1975 **Philemon** (Schmidt) Portfolio Studio 8 April
1982 **Colette** revised version 5th Avenue Theater, Seattle 9 February
1983 **Colette Collage** revised version of *Colette* York Players 31 March
1987 **Grovers Corners** (Schmidt) Marriott's Lincolnshire Theater, Chicago 29 July

JOSEFFY, Josef [ICHHÄUSER, Josef] (later JOSEPHI) (b Kracow, 15 July 1852; d Berlin, 8 January 1920). Longtime leading man of the Viennese stage who created many notable Operette roles.

Joseffy came to Vienna from his home town in 1873 to work in a bank, but it was not long before he abandoned money to begin a career as an actor. When he was thrown on, without rehearsal, in a provincial theatre to play Ange Pitou in *La Fille de Madame Angot*, he scored a considerable success and he thereafter began to orientate himself towards musical theatre. In 1878 he was engaged by Strampfer for the Ringtheater, but he soon moved on, first to the Carltheater (Evangelista in *Donna Juanita*, Duc des Ifs in *Olivette*, Marquis des Millefleurs in *Rosina*), and then to the Theater an der Wien where, from 1882 he began a long series of important rôles in Operetten, including both dashing tenor/baritone heroes and some more comical characters.

Amongst the rôles he created were leading parts in Zeller's *Die Carbonari* (1880, Bruto), Suppé's *Der Gaskogner* (1881, James, Duke of Monmouth), *Herzblättchen* (1882), *Die Afrikareise* (1882, Antarsid), *Der Bettelstudent* (1883, as Jan Janicki to the Symon of Girardi), *Gasparone* (1884, Graf Erminio) and *Der Feldprediger* (1884, Hellwig), and he also appeared as Lotteringhi (*Boccaccio*) and later as Gaston Dufaure in *Donna Juanita*, whilst his original rôle was taken by the young Girardi. He created a number of rôles in Johann Strauss Operetten, appearing in the premières of *Der Zigeunerbaron* (Homonay, introducing the celebrated Recruiting Song, though he would later play both Zsupán and Barinkay), *Simplicius* (Der Einsiedler), *Fürstin Ninetta* (Baron Mörsburg), *Jabuka* (Bambora), *Waldmeister* (Tymoleon) and *Die Göttin der Vernunft* (Furiaux), as well as playing variously Eisenstein or Falke in *Die Fledermaus*, Sebastiani in *Der lustige Krieg*, Hesse in *Carneval in Rom* and the Duke of Urbino in the first Vienna performances of *Eine Nacht in Venedig*.

Other important creations included the rôle of the poet, Carl Bellman, in *Bellman* (1887), further Millöcker rôles as Godibert in *Die Jungfrau von Belleville*, Sir Lothar in *Das Sonntagskind* (1892), Rodomonte in *Der Probekuss* and Jussupov in *Nordlicht*, and the leading rôle of Paul Aubier in Heuberger's *Der Opernball* (1898). He also appeared in the French repertoire as the Marquis in *Les Cloches de Corneville*, in the title-rôle of Planquette's *Rip van Winkle* (*Rip-Rip*, 1885), as Matthieu in *Die Zaubergeige*, as Fortunio, as Champlâtreux in *Mam'zelle Nitouche* (1890), as Lorémois in *La Poupée* (*Die Puppe*) and as Coquenard in Vienna's version of *Véronique* (*Brigitte*), as well as in the British musicals *Weather or No* with Annie Dirkens, *A Runaway Girl* (Tamarinde Dubois) and *A Greek Slave* (Marcus Pomponius). He also played in revivals of such pieces as *Nanon* (d'Aubigné), *Drei Paar Schuhe* (Flink), *Der arme Jonathan* (Jonathan), *Der Vogelhändler* (Adam), *Die sieben Schwaben* (Theophrastus) and *Leichte Kavallerie* (Janos).

Alongside these more successful or noteworthy pieces, Joseffy also took part in the theatre's premières of the less enduring *Der kleine Prinz* (Paolo), *Der schöne Nikolaus* (Pastorel), *Zwillinge* (Blondeau), *Gillette de Narbonne* (Robert de Lignolles), *Der Hofnarr* (Graf Rivarol), Brandl's *Der liebe Augustin* (von Hocher), *Madame Bonbon* (Hannibal), *Krawelleria musicana* (Assio), Weinberger's *Pagenstreiche* (von Himmel), Geiringer's *Die indische Witwe* (Dschihan), Kremser's *Der Schlosserkönig* (Luiz von Robello), the Viennese version of *Miss Helyett* (Paul Landrin), *Fanchons Leyer* (Chevalier de St Florent), *Der Millionenonkel* (Wunibald), *Der Schwiegerpapa* (Hassan), *Husarenblut* (Michael Barna), Dellinger's *Die Chansonette* (Marchese Bonelli), *Die Karlsschulerin* (Major von Seeger), *Die Blumen-Mary* (Geza Budai), *Der goldene Kamerad* (Fred Hamlin), *General Gogo* (Florian Ducôt), *Mister Menelaus* (Johnny Tackleton), *Der Wunderknabe* (Patricio Gordoni), *Der Löwenjäger* (Casimir Brisson), *Die Schwalben* (Sykora), *Die Küchen-Komtesse* (Franz von Wuck), *Der Dreibund* (Kurt Koller), *Der Blondin von Namur* (Leroche), *Fräulein Hexe* (Graf Stelzenberg), *Katze und Maus* (Baron Montrichard), *Ihre Excellenz* (Prince Santiago de Merimac), *Fräulein Präsident* (Don Abricolaves), *Die Strohwitwe* (Snopper), *Der Sechs-Uhr Zug* (Camille Colineau), *Die Stiefmama* (Bodin Bridet) and a continuing list of others.

One of the mainstays of the Theater an der Wien company through its golden age, progressing from juvenile rôles to principal comedy parts in direct competition with Girardi (some of whose rôles he subsequently played), he ultimately left Vienna in 1900 and moved to Berlin, where he appeared at the Friedrich-Wilhelmstädtisches Theater and at the Metropoltheater, most especially in revue, with great success. In 1909 he was again seen on the Viennese stage when he played at the Johann Strauss-Theater in *Der Fürst von Düsterstein* and as Eisenstein, and in 1911 when he starred as Simplicitas in Vienna's version of *The Arcadians*, as Fierabras in Straus's *Venus im Grünen*, and in the two-handed singspiel *Verliebte Plakate*. As late as 1917 he was seen at the Bürgertheater as Ollendorf, and in the new pieces *Brüderlein und Schwesterlein* (August Better) and *Bruder Leichtsinn* (Karl Pampinger), and in 1919 created a final major rôle as Vater Benedikt in Künneke's *Das Dorf ohne Glocke* at Berlin's Friedrich-Wilhelmstädtisches Theater.

JOSEPH AND THE AMAZING TECHNICOLOR DREAMCOAT

Musical in 1 act with lyrics by Tim Rice. Music by Andrew Lloyd Webber. Haymarket Ice Rink, Edinburgh, 21 August 1972; Young Vic Theatre, London, 16 October 1972.

The first produced stage piece by Tim Rice and Andrew Lloyd Webber, *Joseph and the Amazing Technicolor Dreamcoat* was originally written as a 15-minute staged cantata, to be performed by the pupils of Colet Court School (1 March 1968). It was given a second performance at Westminster's Central Hall (12 May 1968) and, gathering momentum and additional pieces of music each time, on several other occasions, profiting from the enthusiasm of music critic Derek Jewell (father of a Colet's Court pupil), music publishers Novello, and recording man Norrie Paramor. By the time the piece made it onto its first record, it had become 35 minutes in length.

After the success of *Jesus Christ Superstar*, *Joseph* was given its first professional performance by the Young Vic

company at the Edinburgh Festival of 1972, with Gary Bond featured as Joseph. That production was transferred to London's Young Vic (14 performances) and, under the management of *Superstar* producer Robert Stigwood, to the Roundhouse (43 performances). Early the next year Stigwood and Michael White remounted the production at the Albery Theatre, with *Joseph* sharing the bill with another Rice/Lloyd Webber one-acter *Jacob's Journey*, but a run of 243 performances proved disappointingly brief.

However, in spite of this semi-failure, *Joseph* continued to grow. Now a full, if short, evening's entertainment, it was played in provincial and overseas English-speaking theatres with great success, and a West End Christmas season in 1978 with Paul Jones as Joseph (Westminster Theatre 27 November) did well enough for a repeat season to be mounted by the same management the following year, followed in 1980 by a colourful Bill Kenwright production, starring former pop star Jess Conrad, which emphasized the family entertainment aspect of the show. This production became a provincial phenomenon, setting up a record as the longest-lived touring show of the post-war era and returning regularly to London for holiday seasons. By this time the text and music of the piece had become reasonably settled, and the originally all-male casting had been eased open not only to include the Potiphar's Wife of the early expansion, but to give the large rôle of the narrator, originally written for a man, to a female voice.

The story of Joseph and his brothers is acted out by a group of performers featuring a Joseph, a Pharoah, a Narrator and the team of brothers, with a children's choir supplying a backing without normally physically taking part in the action. The sung-through tale is told in a lively, modern fashion, with Joseph sharing with the Narrator the bulk of the music, but only occasionally bursting into what might be a full-scale song ('Close Every Door to Me'). Pharoah introduces himself as a pseudo-Elvis Presley, and the additions of the years included a burlesque Western carol, 'There's One More Angel in Heaven', a parody of the French chanson ('Those Canaan Days') and calypso for the brothers (Benjamin calypso).

Joseph had been staged regularly in American school productions from 1969 (Cathedral College, Douglaston, Long Island, 3 October) onwards, and had been given its first professional productions at the Brooklyn Academy of Music in 1976 and 1977 with David James Carroll in the rôle of Joseph. However, in 1981, following a successful production in Baltimore, the show was given at off-Broadway's Entermedia Theater under the management of Zev Bufman and Susan Rose and, after 77 performances, transferred uptown to Broadway's Royale Theater. There it played for a fine run of 747 performances, with original Joseph Bill Hutton being succeeded by several other performers, including the pop world's Andy Gibb and David Cassidy, as the show, more than a decade on from its original production, established itself as a favourite in America.

Oddly, given the enthusiasm the show aroused in Britain and America, it simply did not go in Australia. A first production, at Sydney's York Theatre in 1975 with Mark Holden as Joseph, failed, and a later attempt to stage a version of the all-conquering Kenwright production also went under in a barrage of financial question marks.

However, *Joseph* proved popular virtually everywhere else it went, appearing around the world translated into a number of languages, but ever most popular in the original English.

In 1991, after the publishing rights to the show had been recuperated from Novello by Lloyd Webber's Really Useful Company, London saw a new production of *Joseph*, mounted with great splendour in the large auditorium of the London Palladium (12 June 1991). Australian teeny-idol Jason Donovan (later Philip Schofield) starred as Joseph, the children were brought out of their choir bleachers to join in the action for the first time, and the now enormous and spectacular show at last proved to be the West End hit that it had not been, in its more reduced shape, the first time around. This version of the show was also mounted on the American touring circuits with a teeny-idol of a slightly earlier period, Donny Osmond, in its title-role, and also throughout Australia.

USA: Brooklyn Academy of Music 22 December 1976, Entermedia Theater 18 November 1981, Royale Theater 27 January 1982; Australia: York Theatre, Sydney 26 November 1975

Recordings: original cast (RSO), London cast (MCA), Irish cast (RAM), South African cast (EMI), Israeli cast (Hed-Arzi), Mexican cast (Melody), Broadway cast (Chrysalis), Austrian cast (Ha-Ha), London revival cast (Polygram) etc

JOSÉPHINE VENDUE PAR SES SOEURS Opérabouffe in 3 acts by Paul Ferrier and Fabrice Carré. Music by Victor Roger. Théâtre des Bouffes-Parisiens, Paris, 20 March 1886.

Joseph and the Amazing Technicolor Dreamcoat was not the first musical to utilize the biblical tale of Joseph for its libretto, but the 1886 *Joséphine vendue par ses soeurs* treated the tale rather differently. Ferrier and Carré called their piece an opéra-bouffe, and there was little doubt that it treated Joseph's story in a burlesque fashion, even if the result was a finished and funny French farce with little of the burlesque extravagance of earlier years about it. To start with, as the title made plain, *Joséphine* had its sexes reversed.

The widowed concièrge Madame Jacob (Mme Macé-Montrouge) has twelve daughters but, whilst the others have to tighten their belts and go out to work, Joséphine (Jeanne Thibault) is the spoiled darling of the family who wants for nothing. For Joséphine is at the Conservatoire and she is practising to be a musical theatre star. The exasperated sisters plot together and they work it so that Joséphine is finally 'sold' to the love-struck Egyptian Alfred Pharaon Pasha (Édouard Maugé), with a contract to star at the Cairo opera. However, when Joséphine gets to Egypt she finds that it is the Pasha's harem rather than his theatre that is in store for her. Madame Jacob and her daughters are, however, hot on the trail, pursued in turn by Joséphine's beloved baritone, Montosol (Piccaluga), and the wily concièrge soon takes control. She is determined that Joséphine will indissolubly wed the fabulously wealthy Pasha before bedtime, and that Alfred, who ultimately ends up being sacked from his post for neglecting his offices for the sake of his amours, shall spend his fortune on getting her dozen daughters good (rich) husbands.

Plate 143. **Joséphine vendue par ses soeurs:** *Ilka Pálmay as Benjamine in Hungary's version.*

Eventually the poor Pasha retreats from Paris, his bank balance battered and his masculinity thoroughly tried, Joséphine weds her persevering baritone, and Madame Jacob settles down in a nice new concièrgerie without any daughters, all of whom have been nicely married off, thanks to the dowries supplied by Alfred. The principal soubret parts of the show were youngest sister, Benjamine (Mily-Meyer), and Alfred's traditionalist, anti-French nephew, Putiphar Bey (Charles Lamy), whom she ultimately subdues.

The humour of the text permeated the whole of the show's score. Even the nominal lovers of the play, Joséphine and Montosol, gave forth with humorous numbers, albeit in a lyrical mode. Joséphine justified her choice of a baritone in the first act Couplets du conservatoire, pleaded with Alfred to let her return to Paris (the conservatoire, the rain, and the omnibus accidents) in a rondeau-valse, launched into extravagant operatic duo with Montosol in a first-act rehearsal and again in the second act ('Je lui disait encore'), on both occasions to splendidly funny effect, and repulsed poor Alfred in a third-act ronde. Montosol gave forth with operatic fervour, beginning with a romance in the first act ('Je ne vois que vous seule') and topping his second-act solo with what he vowed would be his last high A flat in what he vowed would be his last serenade, before launching into the big duo of the evening. The soubrette rôle of Benjamine also had a large share in the music, with a number in each of the first two acts, a duo with Putiphar in the third, and, above all, the famous section of the first act's quartet in which she downed the operaticizing of her sister and Montosol with a brisk little bit of sexy nonsense illustrating her own rather lighter taste in music: 'Ugène, Ugèn' tu me fais languir, Où y a d'hygiène y a plus de plaisir'. Alfred, Putiphar and, briefly, Madame Jacob, all took a share in the music, which included several ensembles and concerted finales alongside its principal numbers.

Joséphine was a great success on its production in Paris, with Mily-Meyer, in particular, winning a triumphant reception as the perky and highly-featured little baby of the family. It played through till the summer break, and took up its place again as soon as the house reopened, passing its 100th performance on 20 September and its 200th on 22 December before being replaced by Lecocq's newest piece in the first week of January. The show became a regular part of the French repertoire and it was brought back, with Mily-Meyer always repeating her famous performance as Benjamine, in 1889 and 1890, at the Eldorado in 1896, at the Château d'Eau in 1903, and once more at the Bouffes in 1906.

The first foreign productions followed quickly behind the remarkable Parisian success, and before the end of 1886 *Joséphine* had been seen in New York, Budapest, London and Vienna, but, for some strange reason, without causing anything like the merry stir it had done at home. America's *Josephine Sold By her Sisters* (ad William von Sachs) featured De Wolf Hopper (Alfred), Emily Soldene (Madame Jacob), Herndon Morsell (Putiphar) and Mathilde Cottrelly (Benjamine), with Louise Parker (Josephine) and the novice Eugene Oudin (Montosol) as the operettic lovers. Colonel McCaull's production was well received and played through the six weeks' slot allotted to it in his season at Wallack's, but it was not a major hit. In Budapest (ad Viktor Rákosi) Ilka Pálmay (Benjamine), Aranka Hegyi (Josephine), Zsófi Csatay (Mme Jacob), Pál Vidor, József Németh and Vidor Kassai headed a top-flight Népszinház cast for just a dozen performances, whilst in London a C M Rae adaptation/production called *Our Diva*, which featured Frank Celli (Montosol), Frank Wyatt (Alfred), Madame Amadi (Madame Jacob), Effie Clements (Caroline ie Josephine) and Minnie Marshall (Fifine ie Benjamine), and which chastely removed the biblical parallels, lasted only from the end of October till mid-December (48 performances). It did better, however, than the disappointing production (ad Heinrich Osten) mounted by Carl Tatartzy at the Vienna Carltheater. Wilhelm Knaack (Alfred), Adolf Brackl (Montosol) and Sophie Link (Josephine) were featured in a version which interpolated some pieces of music by Louis Lackenbacher, had the director's wife in the plum rôle of Madame Jacob, and folded in a fortnight.

USA: Wallack's Theater *Josephine Sold By her Sisters* 30 August 1886; Hungary: Népszinház *Jozefa Egyptomban* 9 October 1886; UK: Opera Comique *Our Diva* 28 October 1886, Austria: Carltheater *Josephine und ihre Schwestern* 25 December 1886

LE JOUR ET LA NUIT Opéra-bouffe in 3 acts by Albert Vanloo and Eugène Leterrier. Music by Charles Lecocq. Théâtre des Nouveautés, Paris, 5 November 1881.

When Lecocq and producer Koning broke up their long and profitable association after the failure of *Janot*, the composer moved on to the Théâtre des Nouveautés and promptly turned out two of the best works of the later part of his career in *Le Jour et la nuit* and *Le Coeur et la main* for manager Brasseur. The first of these two works started out with the advantage of a fine, farcical libretto from the top team of Leterrier and Vanloo.

Manola (Marguerite Ugalde) is the intended of Miguel (Montaubry), who is employed as steward to Don Brasiero de Tra os Montes (Berthelier), Governor of a Portuguese province. She is also, however, lusted after by the ubiquitously lustful Portuguese prime minister, Prince Picrates de Calabazas (Jules Brasseur). Brasiero has just been proxy wed to a new wife, Béatrix (Juliette Darcourt), selected by his trusted and aristocratic cousin Degomez (Scipion), but since a little war has happened on his frontier, he is away from home when she is due to arrive. Before she does, however, Manola turns up, fleeing from the fingers of Calabazas, and Miguel's defence against the slavering prime minister is to pretend that it is Manola who is, untouchably, the new wife of the governor. Good friend Béatrix helps keep up the charade, so whilst Manola plays wife to the duly returned nobleman by day, it is Béatrix, with the lights out, who enjoys the night-time part of marriage. The trick almost works, but then Calabazas switches his amorous intentions on to Béatrix, and the deceptions and avoidances multiply until the truth comes out. But the vengeance of the furious prime minister is stifled by his sacking – he has been off chasing skirt too long and the King has decided to get a new prime minister.

Lecocq's score was in his most attractive vein, popularly topped by Calabazas's lively if unlikely insistence that 'Les Portugais sont toujours gais'. Manola's rôle was a particularly well-served one, featuring a first-act air ('Eh bien! oui, je suis la baronne') in which she challenged her would-be seducer with her false rank, a series of numbers in which she frantically attempted to recall a tune sung to Brasiero by his night-time wife, the seductive 'J'ai vu le jour dans un pays' and Chanson Indienne, with which, after the turn of the plot, she attempts to distract Calabazas from Béatrix, and her last act waltz duo with Miguel, 'Nous sommes deux amoureux'. Miguel's romantic moments included a charming romance, 'Laissez-moi rallumer, ma belle', and his despairing ones a duct with Manola in the opening act deciding that the only way out of the situation is a quick double suicide ('Tuons-nous'). The two comedians both had fine moments, Calabazas regretting his unstoppable lascivious tendencies ('Les femmes! ne m'en parlez pas!') and walloping out his Portuguese number, and Brasiero proffering his act-now philosophy ('Mon cher ami, sache bien qu'ici-bas') or rapturizing over his new bride (Ballade de la lune) in a first-act finale of particular quality and appeal.

Le Jour et la nuit was a major hit for Brasseur's theatre. Its first run totalled 197 performances, and it was brought back in 1883 (20 September) for a further 34 performances. It was later seen again at the Athénée-Comique in 1897 (27 April) with Jeanne Petit (Manola), Édouard

Maugé (Calabazas), Dekernel (Brasiero) and Piccaluga (Miguel), at the Château d'Eau in 1911 (3 November) and in 1923 at the Gaîté. In the meanwhile, it had spread itself around the world, though not always with the kind of success it had found at home.

In Hungary (ad Lajos Evva, Béla J Fái) *Nap és hold* was a major hit, with Ilka Pálmay (Manola), Aranka Hegyi (Béatrix), Vidor Kassai (Calabazas), Elek Solymossy (Brasiero) and János Kápolnai (Miguel) heading the cast through an initial season of 69 performances, followed by revivals in 1899 (9 September) and 1906 (28 December). In America the piece did not get a regular Broadway run, as both the English and French-language productions were played only in repertoire companies. An English *Manola* with Catherine Lewis (Manola), Marie Jansen (Beatrice), John Howson (Calabazas), Fred Leslie (Brasiero) and C J Campbell (Miguel) was quickly followed (1 May) by Maurice Grau's French company with Paola Marié (Manola), Mlle Grégoire (Béatrix), Mezières (Calabazas), Nigri (Miguel) and Duplan (Brasiero), and both proved to be well-enough liked.

London's English version (ad H B Farnie) opened just a few days after New York's, with a cast that did not match the starry teams chosen for the piece elsewhere. Rosa Leo, Irene Verona, Henry Ashley, Eugène Desmonts and W J Hill featured in Alexander Henderson's production (which allowed the interpolation of a number by Leopold Wenzel) and ran for just a respectable three months at the Strand Theatre. Its relative failure can probably be put down to the bowdlerizing practised on a libretto judged too sexual for English-hearing ears, as much as to its undercasting. It is hard to believe that the same kind of sanitization went on in Vienna, but the result there was even poorer. Franz Steiner's production of an uncredited German version at the Theater an der Wien, with Carl Adolf Friese (Calabazas), Alexander Girardi (Brasiero), Rosa Streitmann (Béatrix), Karoline Finaly (Manola) and Hubert Wilke (Miguel), was played only six times.

Hungary: Népszinház *Nap és hold* 7 January 1882; USA: Fifth Avenue Theater *Manola* 6 February 1882; UK: Strand Theatre *Manola* 11 February 1882; Austria: Theater an der Wien *Tag und Nacht* 13 March 1882; Australia: Opera House, Melbourne *Manola* 13 September 1882

Recording: complete (Gaîté-Lyrique)

JUBILEE Musical comedy in 2 acts by Moss Hart. Music and lyrics by Cole Porter. Imperial Theater, New York, 12 October 1935.

Apparently suggested by the silver jubilee of King George V of Britain, Moss Hart's libretto for *Jubilee* took up the once favourite, very old comic opera theme of disguised princes and princesses out for adventure in the real world. On this occasion, the whole royal family goes gallivanting at once, because some minor royal has got greedy and decided to have a little revolution, putting them out of a job. Leaving the now unburdened King Henry (Melville Cooper) at home to play the parlour games which are his chief delight, the Queen (Mary Boland), Princess Diana (Margaret Adams) and Prince James (Charles Walter) leave behind the luxuries and responsibilities of royalty and dash off in search of a bit of unspied-upon romance. The Queen does well enough in batting her eyelashes at movie star Charles Rausmiller (Mark Plant), the Princess

becomes briefly involved with the writer Eric Dare (Derek Williams), whilst the Prince sings and dances the night away with the dancer Karen O'Kane (June Knight) before the revolution fizzles out and they all have to go back home to work. The show's innish-joke was that Rausmiller was a Johnny Weismuller copy, Dare modelled on Noël Coward, another character on Elsa Maxwell, and one was supposed to think, for example, of Queen Mary having a flirt with Tarzan.

The score to *Jubilee* produced one of Porter's best-loved songs, when June Knight led off a dance number with her prince telling what happens when they 'Begin the Beguine'. The same pair also had the show's other most successful song, the enduring 'Just One of Those Things', as well as the description of 'A Picture of You Without Me', whilst the Princess demanded of herself 'Why Shouldn't I?' at the first whisperings of romance, and her writer sang in the Cowardesque Samolan fashion of 'The Kling-Kling Bird on the Divi-Divi Tree'.

The songs which became standards and the Queen-meets-Tarzan joke did not prove sufficient to keep *Jubilee* afloat for very long. Sam H Harris and Max Gordon's production played just 169 performances on Broadway, but *Jubilee* nevertheless rendered up more re-usable musical parts than many shows which lasted twice or thrice as long.

Recording: composer (Columbia)

JUDIC, Anna [DAMIENS, Anna Marie Louise] (b Semur, 17 July 1850; d Nice, 14 April 1911). Saucy, skilful megastar of the Parisian opérette and vaudeville stage.

The young Mlle Damiens made her first stage appearance in 1868, at the Théâtre du Gymnase in the one-act *Les Grandes Demoiselles*. She then went on to work as a chanteuse at the Eldorado café-concert and, whilst there, she married the régisseur Israël, known as Judic, whose name she used thereafter for her stage appearances in various theatres and cafés-concerts in Belgium and France, including a period at the Folies-Bergère in 1872. She returned to the theatre later the same year, when she was hired for the company at the Théâtre de la Gaîté, and there she created her first important opéra-bouffe rôle as the Princess Cunégonde in Offenbach's *Le Roi Carotte* (1872).

Mlle Judic was subsequently snapped up by the Théâtre des Bouffes-Parisiens, and she made a sensation in her very first rôle there, as the innocently scabrous heroine of Vasseur's hit musical, *La Timbale d'argent*. Over the next three years she created a series of lead rôles at the Bouffes in often less than successful shows, including the title-rôle of the café-chanteuse in Offenbach's little *Bagatelle*, Vasseur's *La Petite Reine*, Léon Roques's *La Rosière d'ici*, *La Branche cassée*, *Les Parisiennes*, as Marietta in Offenbach's successful *Madame l'Archiduc*, and, stained black, as his *La Créole*, Dora, before moving on to the Théâtre des Variétés and the management of Eugène Bertrand.

There, she became quickly established as one of Paris's top musical comedy players as she appeared in a mixture of classic opérettes (Hélène, Périchole etc) and new pieces (*Le Docteur Ox*, *Les Charbonniers* etc), before causing a second sensation – six years after the first – in the starring rôle of the vaudeville *Niniche*, in which she shocked public opinion deliciously by appearing on stage in a bathing suit.

Plate 144. **Anna Judic:** *Paris's musical-comedy megastar of the 1880s.*

The successors of *Niniche*, constructed specially in the same play-with-songs manner and each made to feature its star in a vast, bravura rôle, hoisted Judic to her highest popularity. *La Femme à papa* (1879), *La Roussotte* (1881), *Lili* (1882) and *Mam'zelle Nitouche* (1883) were each a long-running triumph for her, and each supplied her with at least one all-pervading hit song, in five solid years at the very top of her profession. In 1883 she visited London's Gaiety Theatre, Vienna – where in five hectic days she introduced the Theater an der Wien to *Niniche*, *La Femme à papa*, *Lili* and supporting programmes including *Les Charbonniers* and *La Princesse* – and Budapest (23 November) but, on her return, her series of successes came to an end with the rather less than triumphant production of the latest made-to-measure piece, *La Cosaque* (1884).

With the fashion having turned away from the now rather too similar run of vaudeville-opérettes, Judic left the Variétés to try her hand as an actress, but after a couple of flops she returned once more to the musical stage, to star in revivals of her earlier hits, the co-author of which, Albert Millaud, she had in the meanwhile married. In 1885 she travelled to America where she played her staple rôles (*La Femme à papa*, *Mam'zelle Nitouche*, *Niniche*, *Lili*, *La Cosaque*) and also appeared in pieces such as *La Mascotte*, *Le Grand Casimir* and the comedy *Divorçons*, to new audiences, appearing throughout the country and in a season at New York's Star, Wallack's and Casino Theaters for Maurice Grau with considerable success. It had to be a

success, as Judic – the biggest French musical star to visit America in years – had apparently extorted quite a deal from her manager: a reported guarantee of the equivalent of £42,000 for the eight months (25% payable to her Paris bank in advance), travel and hotels paid, and her own personal train for touring.

Back in France the now rather portly actress subsisted over the years that followed largely on further reprises of her Variétés hits and on revivals of such pieces as *La Belle Hélène* and *La Grande-Duchesse* (paired in both with the even more ageing original star of those pieces, José Dupuis), *Madame l'Archiduc*, *Madame Favart*, and notably, opposite Jeanne Granier, who had succeeded to her prima-donna assoluta's crown in Parisian eyes, as Lange in *La Fille de Madame Angot*. She visited Vienna and Budapest again in 1889 with the Variétés company and Dupuis, playing *Niniche*, *Lili*, *La Femme à papa*, *Les Charbonniers* and *Mam'zelle Nitouche*, then again the following year, in 1891 and in 1892, with *La Roussotte* and the little *Joséphine* added to her repertoire. She visited Budapest's Népszinház to play Nitouche in 1892 and repeated her famous rôles in Paris in 1894, but she latterly made her Paris appearances largely on the straight stage, although she continued to perform her famous songs out of their theatrical context. She appeared on the Paris stage as Niniche as late as 1901. She subsequently took a turn at management, taking over the Palais-Royal in 1906, but without notable success.

Judic's granddaughter, Simone Judic, originally a shop-girl in her family's hairdressing business, also took to the stage (at first as Simone Reva) performing her grandmother's numbers, but later in revue at the Cigale and the Folies-Bergère and then as a leading lady in 1920s musical comedy (Fourdrain's *Cadet-Roussel*, *Mariage princier*, *Marché d'amour*, *Rapatipatoum*, *La Princesse Carnaval*, *La Belle du Far-West*, *La Sirène*, *La Ceinture de Vénus*, *You-You*, *Dolly*, *Pouick*, *Prends-moi*, *Les Rendezvous clandestins* etc).

JUMBO Musical comedy in 2 acts by Ben Hecht and Charles MacArthur. Lyrics by Lorenz Hart. Music by Richard Rodgers. Hippodrome, New York, 16 November 1935.

Jumbo was conceived by producer Billy Rose as a gigantic circus-spectacular-cum-musical, to be built around the greatest circus acts in the world which he, characteristically, had little doubt he could secure. What he did secure, in order of importance, was the vast old New York Hippodrome – the home of so many spectacular Charles Dillingham shows in the early years of the century – George Abbott, who had never staged a musical, as book director (John Murray Anderson was already hired with a 'production staged by' credit), Rodgers and Hart for the songs, and Hecht and MacArthur, the authors of *The Front Page* and *Twentieth Century*, as neophyte librettists.

Having acquired the Hippodrome, Rose proceeded to tear its interior to pieces to make the place resemble a circus tent and, in place of the most famous acts in the world (which were, not wholly surprisingly, not available at short notice), he hired a mass of jugglers, trapeze artists, clowns, riders and a female elephant to play Jumbo, all of who rehearsed their way in and around the musical comedy portion of the show for rather longer than was usual. Rose, who was flinging money around wildly on some areas of the production, made a saving when he somehow persuaded Actor's Equity to agree that the show was not a musical but a circus and that, therefore, he had no reason to pay rehearsal wages to his cast. In spite of this economy, the production budget rose to the then enormous amount of $340,000.

Hecht and McArthur's libretto was a run of the mill affair about two rival circus owners (W J McCarthy, Arthur Sinclair) one of whom has a son (Donald Novis), the other a daughter (Gloria Grafton), and both of whom have a predictable ending. Top-billed comedian Jimmy Durante was cast as Claudius B Bowers, a circus press agent. Rather better were the songs. McCarthy and Miss Grafton had the best, the waltzing 'The Most Beautiful Girl in the World', but the heroine's 'Little Girl Blue' and her duo with her boy, 'My Romance', also found popularity, alongside the ensemble 'The Circus is on Parade'. Durante's contribution was 'Laugh'. One song did not make it to opening night, and Rodgers and Hart put aside 'There's a Small Hotel' for later (but not much later) use.

Jumbo's spectacle and songs earned it a fine reception, but Rose's limits as a producer soon showed up. He had done his sums ridiculously poorly and, even playing to good houses, the show could not make ends meet. It had to be closed after 233 performances, and there was little chance that it could ever be staged again. In fact, it was, but on the screen: 27 years later MGM made a movie version which they christened *Billy Rose's Jumbo*. They threw out the bulk of the Hecht/MacArthur book and Sidney Sheldon developed a new story on not dissimilar lines, featuring Durante as the circus owner and Doris Day as his daughter who falls in love with the son (Stephen Boyd) of the rival proprietor (Dean Jagger), who has come in disguise to try to steal Jumbo from them (steal an elephant?). Martha Raye was Durante's love interest, as a circus lady called Madame Lulu. The half-dozen principal numbers of the *Jumbo* scored were topped up with 'This Can't Be Love' (*On Your Toes*) and 'Why Can't I?' (*Spring is Here*) and a number by associate producer Roger Edens, and film gave production values to the piece which even the New York Hippodrome couldn't hold.

Film: MGM 1962

Recordings: film soundtrack (CBS), selection (RCA)

JUNE [TRIPP, June Howard] (b London, 11 June ?1900; d unknown) British dancing ingénue of the 1920s.

Trained as a dancer, June at first appeared at the Palace Theatre as an allegedly 11-year-old chorus girl, then later at the Folies-Bergère, and in revue in London (*Watch Your Step, Buzz Buzz*). She had her first featured rôle in a musical playing the part which ended up being called Aspasia in C B Cochran's unrecognizable version of the Parisian hit *Phi-Phi* (1922), and followed up in the title-rôle of the London production of George M Cohan's *Little Nellie Kelly* under the same management. She played juvenile leads opposite Jack Buchanan in *Toni* (1924) and *Boodle* (1925), and – although she was at one stage announced to lead the cast of Broadway's *Riquette* – in two imported musicals in London, the highly successful *Mercenary Mary* (1925) and the very quick flop *Happy-Go-Lucky* (1926).

Thereafter she played principally in revue, although she visited America to play the title-rôle of the unsuccessful *Polly* (1929) and replaced the insufficient Lili Damita

opposite George Robey in *Here's How!* (1934). She subsequently became – for a period – Lady Inverclyde.

Autobiography: *The Glass Ladder* (Heinemann, London, 1960)

DIE JUNGFRAU VON BELLEVILLE Operette in 3 acts by F Zell and Richard Genée based on *La Pucelle de Belleville* by Paul de Kock and its stage version, *Agnès de Belleville*, by de Kock and the Cogniard brothers. Music by Carl Millöcker. Theater an der Wien, Vienna, 29 October 1881.

Although never as popular or as successful as Millöcker's most famous works, *Die Jungfrau von Belleville* nevertheless attracted plenty of producers in the 1880s, and was seen throughout the world in a variety of languages. The text was based on the vaudeville *Agnès de Belleville* (Folies-Dramatiques 1835), itself a stage version of the novel of the same title, which told the tale of a rather Mam'zelle Nitouche-like creature called Virginie Troupeau (Rosa Streitmann), daughter of a rich manufacturer (Felix Schweighofer) and tyrannically guarded by her aunt, the dragonistic Mdlle Javotte Bergamotte (Therese Schäfer). Virginie, whose virtue is the pride of all Belleville, is anxious to marry anyone at all to escape life with her aunt, and has been practising love-making with goofy neighbour Doudoux (Schütz) in preparation. Her father proposes the ageing rake Count Archibald de Châteaurien (Grève), his friend Vaudoré (Ausim) proposes his son, and Virginie gets her pitter-pats from a visiting Sergeant Godibert (Alexander Girardi). When she is nearly caught out 'practising', her poor cousin Adrienne (Frln Scholz) takes the blame, but finally all is sorted out: Adrienne gets the painter Émile Montreux (Steiner) she adores, and Virginie settles for the Count who will, at least, be a complaisant husband. The piece was set with some typically attractive Millöcker music, with a first-act march proving popular, along with some of the more lyrical numbers which illustrated the love affairs in the second act.

The Theater an der Wien's production was played 35 times during its first twelve months in the repertoire, and it ultimately passed the 50 mark as the show went on to be mounted successively in Dresden, Hamburg, Berlin and at New York's Thalia Theater. Max Lube, Emmy Meffert, Habrich, Bertha Schulz, Junker, Elsbach, Rank and Schütz featured for a handful of performances in America's German-language production, and although the subsequent English version mounted at the Star Theatre was a frank flop, *Die Jungfrau von Belleville* turned up again, in 1891, at the German-language Terrace Garten.

Paris briefly saw a French version (ad Alexandre Beaumont, Charles Nuitter) with Mily-Meyer as Virginie more than six years after the show's première, and later the same year Budapest got an Hungarian version (ad Andor Kozma). Neither won any particular favour. But *Die Jungfrau von Belleville* carried on. It was seen at the Johann Strauss-Theater in 1910, and it continued to hold a revivable place in the Millöcker repertoire which was not really in line with its lack of real theatrical success.

La Pucelle de Belleville was used as the basis for another Operette, *Die Jungfrau von Paris*, written by Günther Schwenn, composed by Friedrich Schröder and produced at the Vienna Raimundtheater in 1969.

Germany: Residenztheater, Dresden 25 June 1882, Friedrich-

Wilhelmstädtisches Theater, Berlin 29 September 1882; USA: Thalia Theater 6 May 1886, Star Theatre *The Maid of Belleville* 24 June 1886; France: Théâtre des Folies-Dramatiques *La Demoiselle de Belleville* 29 February 1888; Hungary: Népszinház *A bellevillei szüz* 3 November 1888

DER JUXBARON Operette in 3 acts by Alexander Pordes-Milo and Herman Haller. Lyrics by Willi Wolff. Music by Walter Kollo. Carl-Schultze Theater, Hamburg, 14 November 1913.

The 'joke-baron' of Pordes-Milo's title is the vagabond Blaukehlchen. When Hans von Grabow and his new little wife Hilda go off to enjoy their honeymoon they are threatened with the company of Hilda's parents and her sister, Sophie, so they pretend that the only other available room in the house is taken up by their friend Alexander Christlieb, Baron von Kimmel. When the family turn up anyhow, and Alexander has not arrived, they have quickly to find a deputy. Blaukehlchen agrees to play the part. He plays it with extravagant gusto, drags the in-laws off to a vagabond's ball, gets engaged to Sophie and then, when the real Baron arrives and all is revealed, shrugs happily off on the road once more.

Kollo's jolly score ranged through such made-for-dancing pieces as 'Bubi, mein lieber süsser Bubi', 'Wozu hast du denn die Beene, kleine Maus', 'Kleine Mädchen müssen schlafen geh'n' and 'Wenn ein Mädel einen Herrn hat', with soubrette Sophie and the phoney baron winning the best of the song and dance moments.

A fine success in Hamburg, *Der Juxbaron* was seen in Berlin first at the Berliner Theater and, later, for a two-month revival at the other bastion of Kollo's fame, the Theater im Nollendorfplatz (25 December 1918), then run by co-librettist Haller. It was produced in Vienna during the war in a 'localized' version by Oskar Fronz and his Bürgertheater company, with Ludwig Herold and Emmy Petko as the newly-weds, Arthur Guttmann as the false baron, now called Stieglitz, and Alexander Hernfeld and Victoria Pohl-Meiser as the interfering in-laws. It played for a month at that house, then moved to the Colosseum when the Berliner Theater ensemble arrived for a season (50th 4 April 1915), returning to play its last performances at the Bürgertheater in May. The show was also played at the German-language Irving Place Theater in New York in 1918, with Christian Rub starring as the vagabond, supported by Lotte Engel, Hanns Unterkirchner, Flora Arndt and Bruno Schlegel.

Hungary: Royal Orfeum *Link báró* 11 February 1915; Austria: Wiener Bürgertheater 23 February 1915; USA: Irving Place Theater 1 February 1918

K

KACSOH, Pongrác (b Budapest, 15 December 1873; d Budapest, 18 December 1923). Composer of Hungary's most popular and enduring folk operett.

Brought up in Kolozsvár, the young Kacsoh spread his studies between mathematics and science on the one hand, and a musical education at the local conservatoire on the other. He later became a secondary-school teacher, teaching mathematics and science in Budapest and, whilst pursuing a continuing scientific career, he also furthered his musical studies and ultimately became a music critic, editor of the musical paper *Zenevilág* (1905–7), and both a writer and a composer.

His first contribution to the theatre was in the form of a set of songs for the musical play *Csipkerózsika*, but in 1904 he composed the score for the light opera *János vitéz*, the Hungarian folk-tale of John the Hero as told in the dramatic poem by Sándor Petőfi and adapted to the stage by Károly Bakonyi, and with that piece he won an outstanding musical theatre success. The half-fairytale of the shepherd boy János who is chased from his home and his beloved Iluska by her murderous stepmother, and who, after becoming a military hero, throws up glory and sets out to the afterworld to find his lost love, was illustrated with a richly constructed, movingly wistful score of folk-based music which complemented its subject perfectly. *János vitéz*, regularly played throughout Hungary ever since its first production, has become virtually the country's national operett.

Kacsoh's two other principal works, in a small output, were *Rákóczi*, another Hungarian piece authored by Bakonyi, based on the tale of Ferenc Rákóczi, the 18th-century monarch who spread his Protestant power over Hungary and Transylvania, but who was subsequently defeated and exiled by the Austrians (a subject simultaneously used for an operatic trilogy by Zichy at the Magyar Királyi Operaház); and an operettic adaptation of Israel Zangwill's 1904 London play, *Merely Mary Ann*. He also supplied part of the music for the Árpád Pásztor Singspiel *A harang* which became better known in a subsequent musical setting, by Eduard Künneke, as *Das Dorf ohne Glocke*. All of these pieces were produced at the Király Színház, where *János vitéz* had established Kacsoh's reputation, and each found some success, but thereafter he limited his stage compositions to such assignments as the incidental music for Ferenc Molnár's plays *Liliom* (1909) and *Fehér felhő* (1916).

His final work, *Dorottya*, a comic opera based on a classic Hungarian poem, was produced posthumously. An 18th-century tale of a spinster who herself finds love whilst trying to settle the amorous affairs of her younger sister, it was well regarded although its music was judged more ambitious and less individual than that of *János vitéz*.

Kacsoh also wrote several historical works on music.

1904 **Csipkerózsika** no production traced
1904 **János vitéz** (Jenő Heltai/Károly Bakonyi) Király Színház 18 November
1906 **Rákóczi** (Sándor Endrődi, Árpád Pásztor/Bakonyi) Király Színház 20 November
1907 **A harang** (w Ákos Buttykay/Pásztor) Király Színház 1 February
1908 **Mary Ann** (Andor Gábor/Sándor Hajó) Király Színház 5 December
1929 **Dorottya** Szeged 9 January

KAHN, Gus (b Koblenz, 6 November 1886; d Beverly Hills, Calif, 8 October 1941). Lyricist for popular songs and films and for a small but song-productive group of stage shows.

Brought up in Chicago, and at first employed in the hotel supplies trade, Kahn had his first song published at the age of 21. Thereafter he became a prolific popular-music lyric writer and supplied the songwords for four Broadway shows, of which the comical Eddie Cantor vehicle *Whoopee* (1928, 'Makin' Whoopee', 'I'm Bringing a Red, Red Rose', 'Love Me or Leave Me'), written in collaboration with his most frequent songwriting partner, Walter Donaldson, remains the outstanding example. The first Broadway show for which he took a major credit was an adaptation of the German light opera *Frühling im Herbst* (1920), played by *Naughty Marietta* star Orville Harrold and his daughter Patti with only limited success in the 1925–6 season, the second the lively musical farce *Kitty's Kisses*, in which his words were paired with Con Conrad's music to rather better effect and a much more enduring life, and the last, before Kahn's abandonment of Broadway in favour of Hollywood, a collaboration with George and Ira Gershwin, amongst others, on the indifferent Ziegfeld spectacular *Show Girl*, the hit of which, 'Liza' ('All the Clouds'll Roll Away') fell not to Kahn but to the Gershwins.

Although Kahn had but few full-scale Broadway credits, many of his songs were individually interpolated in musical comedies and revues of the 1910s and 1920s, the more memorable including 'Toot, Toot, Tootsie' (w Dan Russo, Ernie Erdman) for Al Jolson in *Bombo*, 'I'll Say She Does', ''N' Everything' and 'You Ain't Heard Nothin' Yet' (w Jolson, B G De Sylva) for the same star in *Sinbad*, *Whoopee*'s 'Love Me or Leave Me' (w Walter Donaldson) recycled into *Simple Simon*, 'Pretty Baby' (w Egbert van Alstyne, Tony Jackson) in *The Passing Show of 1916*, *A World of Pleasure* and London's *Houp-La* and 'Carolina in the Morning' (w Donaldson) in *The Passing Show of 1922*. A good number of his *Kitty's Kisses* songs were interpolated into the show that London preferred to call *The Girl Friend* (although it contained much more of *Kitty's Kisses*), and his 'I Wonder Where My Baby is Tonight' was used in the British revue *The Co-Optimists*. 'Ain't We Got Fun' (w

Raymond Egan, Richard Whiting) and 'It Had to Be You' (w Isham Jones) turned up, many years later, in pasticcio London shows – *A Day in Hollywood, A Night in the Ukraine* and *Ziegfeld* respectively.

Kahn also introduced songs into many film scores of the period, including the screen versions of the stage musicals *The Chocolate Soldier* ('While My Lady Sleeps'), *The Merry Widow* ('Tonight Will Teach Me to Forget'), and *Rose Marie* ('Just for You', 'Pardon Me, Madame'), as well as providing several fresh numbers for the cinematic *Whoopee* ('My Baby Just Cares for Me').

Of Kahn's other songs, many of which have been used repeatedly in revues, theatrical compilation shows and musical films, the most successful included 'Yes Sir, That's My Baby', 'That Certain Party', 'There Ain't No Maybe in My Baby's Eyes', 'My Blackbirds Are Bluebirds Now', 'Beside a Babbling Brook' (all w Donaldson),'Some Sunday Morning' (w Egan, Whiting), 'The Shores of Minnetonka' (w Percy Wenrich), 'The One I Love Belongs to Somebody Else', 'I'll See You in my Dreams' (w Isham Jones) and 'Chloe' (w Neil Moret).

During the 1930s in Hollywood, Kahn supplied the words for many film songs for artists such as Grace Moore, Eddie Cantor, Dick Powell and Jeanette MacDonald: *Flying Down to Rio* ('Flying Down to Rio', 'Carioca' w Youmans, Edward Eliscu), *One Night of Love* (w Victor Schertzinger), *Kid Millions, The Girl from Missouri, On Wings of Song, Thanks a Million* and Jeanette MacDonald's celebrated title-song to *San Francisco* (w Walter Jurmann, Bronislav Kaper).

Kahn was impersonated by Danny Thomas in the 1951 musical biofilm *I'll See You in My Dreams*.

1925 **Holka Polka** (aka *Spring in Autumn, Nobody's Girl*) (*Frühling im Herbst*) English lyrics (Lyric Theater)
1926 **Kitty's Kisses** (Con Conrad/Philip Bartholomae, Otto Harbach) Playhouse Theater 6 May
1928 **Whoopee** (Walter Donaldson/William Anthony Maguire) New Amsterdam Theater 4 December
1929 **Show Girl** (George Gershwin/w Ira Gershwin/J P McEvoy ad Maguire) Ziegfeld Theater 2 July

DIE KAISERIN (aka *Fürstenliebe*) Operettenspiel in 2 acts by Julius Brammer and Alfred Grünwald based partly on a work by Franz von Schönthan. Music by Leo Fall. Metropoltheater, Berlin, 15 October 1915.

Leo Fall's *Die Kaiserin* owed its production in Berlin to censorship. In the same manner that Rodgers and Hammerstein's projected musical about Queen Victoria was banned from the British stage, the Austrian authorities would not allow a piece which presented an ancestor of their then reigning monarch to appear as a singing and dancing character in the musical theatre. In fact, as it proved, the story was a fairly harmless one, and one which had no need to be tacked on to the character of the Empress Maria Theresia, but *Die Kaiserin* was given its first production at the Berlin Metropoltheater, with Fritzi Massary starring in its title-rôle, instead of in Vienna.

Having defied her advisers and married the Prinz August Franz von Lothringen (Rolf Brunner), the young monarch discovers the difficulty of being both queen and wife to her husband. Her lively friend the Countess Adelgunde (Rosa Valetti) gives some worldly, womanly advice which helps matters to a happy end. The book was

credited as being based on a work by Franz von Schönthan, but the backbone of the text was not so very different from that of the French hit *Le Prince consort* nor even of *Ein Walzertraum*.

The score to *Die Kaiserin* gave its prima donna every opportunity she could wish, from the twinkling light-footed 'Zwei Füsserl zum Tanzen' to the soaring showpiece aria 'Du, mein Schönbrunn', in which the Empress serenades her magnificent Viennese palace and all that it represents, and a huge waltz duet with her Franz ('Mir hat heute Nacht'). The show is, however, composed in classic Operette proportions: the tenor Franz has his big moment in the lively 'Dir gehört mein Herz', and Adelgunde and her light-comic partner, Graf Pepi Cobenzl, have contrastingly tripping numbers to set off the more romantic and seriously sung pieces of the score.

Following its German première, the work, delicately remade as *Fürstenliebe*, was played at Vienna's Carltheater, under the description 'ein Operettenspiel aus dem fröhlichen Rokoko'. Mizzi Zwerenz starred as 'the Princess' and later as 'the Regent' to the Franz von Baldrigen of Victor Norbert, in a piece which was described as taking place 'at the court of a principality of the rococo era'. The non-royal Countess Adelgunde (Gerda Walde) was allowed to remain the Countess Adelgunde. *Fürstenliebe* played for 119 performances at the Carltheater, a respectable but ultimately slightly disappointing run, particularly in the eyes of Fall, who considered his score one of the best that he had ever written, as well as his own personal favourite.

Die Kaiserin was repeated, in its original version, at the same house for three weeks in 1925, after the end of the Habsburg years, with manager's wife Dora Keplinger-Eibenschütz starring as Maria Theresia alongside Norbert, Mimi Vesely (Adelgunde) and Oscar Karlweis (Pepi), and again at the Bürgertheater in 1935 with Maria Horstwig, Walter Kochner and Mimi Shorp, and former prima donna Mizzi Günther as Gräfin Fuchs, but it never succeeded in establishing itself as part of the standard repertoire.

Austria: Carltheater (as *Fürstenliebe*) 1 February 1916, (as *Die Kaiserin*) 4 December 1925
Recording: Radio cast (RCA, Germany)

KÁLMÁN, Emmerich [KÁLMÁN, Imre] (b Siófok, Hungary, 24 October 1882; d Paris, 30 October 1953). One of the principal composers for the Hungaro-Viennese 'silver age' of Operette.

Balked in his hopes of becoming a concert pianist by meagre finances and a hand injury, the young Kálmán subsequently led parallel studies at Budapest University's law faculty and in music theory and composition at the Budapest Zeneakadémia under János Koessler, through whose classes had passed such musicians as Bartók, Dohnányi and Kodály. His first musical compositions were largely in the form of orchestral and vocal concert works, written in the late romantic style. One of them, a song cycle, won him a civic award, the Franz-Josef Prize (1907), whilst another, the symphonic poem 'Saturnalia', was performed in concert at the Magyar Királyi Operaház (1904).

Between 1904 and 1908 Kálmán worked as a répétiteur at Budapest's Vigszinház and as a music critic for the *Pesti Napló*, and, following a dip into the popular-music world with some pseudonymous cabaret music, he made his first essay as a theatre composer with songs for Samuel Fényes's musical comedy *A pereszlényi juss* (1906) at the Magyar Színház. After contributing to another piece in a similar vein, he then ventured, at the age of 26, his first full-scale operett, *Tatárjárás*, to a libretto by the celebrated author of *János vitéz* and *Bob herceg*, Károly Bakonyi. Produced at the Vigszinház, *Tatárjárás* proved to be one of the most successful of all Hungarian operetts at a time when, with Kacsoh's *János vitéz* and *Rákóczi*, Huszka's *Gül Baba* and *Bob herceg* and Buttykay's *A bolygo görög* and *A csibészkirály* all having appeared in the few years before its production, the native musical theatre in Budapest was beginning to flourish merrily.

Unlike these earlier works, the success of which had been large but limited almost entirely to their country of origin, Kálmán's piece found a considerable audience not only in Hungary but beyond its frontiers. Eighteen months after its Budapest première, *Tatárjárás* was produced in Austria under the title of *Ein Herbstmanöver* by Wilhelm Karczag, the Hungarian director of Vienna's Theater an der Wien, in an adaptation by Robert Bodanzky. *Ein Herbstmanöver* scored a major Viennese success, totting up a total of over 250 performances in its first run and setting the show off on an international career which took the young composer's work to London (*Autumn Manoeuvres*) and New York (*The Gay Hussars*) as well as to Moscow, Berlin and most other European theatre capitals.

Kálmán's second piece, another if rather differently styled military piece entitled *Az obsitos*, also produced at the Vigszinház, thoroughly confirmed his rising star. After its home-town success, it followed *Tatárjárás* to Vienna where, under the title *Der gute Kamarad*, it was played at the Bürgertheater. And this time the composer went with it. Kálmán left Hungary and settled in Vienna, where he became 'Emmerich' instead of 'Imre' and where he remained for the large part of the rest of his life.

Kálmán's first works for the Viennese theatre appeared towards the end of 1912. One, *Der kleine König* (*A kis király*), produced at the Theater an der Wien, still bore its Hungarian origins in the form of a libretto by Bakonyi and Ferenc Martos, which had been translated into German for its première. However, it was his other offering of this season, Kálmán's first genuinely Viennese piece, in spite of having a deeply Hungarian story and score, which gave the composer his next big success. *Der Zigeunerprimás*, with Alexander Girardi starring as the old gipsy violinist of the title ('Mein alte Stradivari'), was a Viennese hit which was soon exported with singular success around Europe as well as to Broadway where, under the title of *Sari*, it proved to be one of the most successful of all Kálmán's works on the New York stage.

In 1914, *Gold gab' ich für Eisen*, a new version of *Az obsitos*, was staged in Vienna, its libretto heavily revised to make it into a piece of morale-boosting wartime propaganda and, perhaps surprisingly, it was picked up and played (admittedly in a thoroughly botched form) both in America (*Her Soldier Boy*) and in Britain (*Soldier Boy*). In addition to this remake, Kálmán brought three new pieces to the stage during the war. The first, *Zsuzsi kisasszony*, began its life in Hungary, but, in the wake of the success of *Sari*, it was quickly picked up for Broadway where it was staged, to genuine success, as *Miss Springtime*. In 1917

Kálmán re-used some of the *Zsuzsi kisasszony* score in his successful Vienna musical *Die Faschingsfee*.

In the interim, however, Vienna had seen the production of the composer's most successful Operette to date – *Die Csárdásfürstin*, produced at the Johann Strauss-Theater in November 1915. With its text-book combination of lushly romantic and light comic elements in both script and score, spiced with the gutsy Hungarian flavour which permeated all the best of Kálmán's works and gave them just that spicy iota of a difference from their Viennese fellows, and with a star performance from Mizzi (*Die lustige Witwe*) Günther in its title-rôle, *Die Csárdásfürstin* clocked up nearly 600 performances in the two years of its original run and became one of the greatest European successes of its time. Although, initially, badly botched in America (*The Riviera Girl*) and meeting an odd indifference in Britain (*The Gipsy Princess*) the show has, nevertheless, remained a member of the basic Austrian Operette repertoire, and won recent revivals even outside Continental Europe.

After the war, Kálmán continued to turn out often outstanding, and outstandingly successful, new musicals. The not-terribly-Dutch *Das Hollandweibchen* was perhaps a mite more discreet than his biggest successes, but it nevertheless ran for 13 months and 362 performances at the Johann Strauss-Theater, went round the world, and was the subject of a notable production in London where the *Little Dutch Girl* of the title was impersonated by opera star Maggie Teyte. However, his next two works, *Die Bajadere* and *Gräfin Mariza*, represented some of the best – and perhaps the very best – of all the composer's musical theatre output. *Die Bajadere* mixed a tale of romance between an Indian prince and an Operette star with a joyously comical one-wife/two-husbands ménage and a combination of lush Viennese melodies ('O Bajadere' etc) and lively up-to-date song-and-dance numbers, in a score which was probably the most outstanding, musically, of the composer's 'Viennese' works. *Gräfin Mariza*, conversely the most thoroughly Hungarian of all the scores of Kálmán's peak years, rendered up some of his most memorable individual numbers, from the striking tenor 'Komm' Zigán!' to the loopy 'Komm mit nach Varasdin', in a tempestuous Magyar love story lightened judiciously with a little fun.

Both pieces were splendid successes in Vienna, where *Die Bajadere* initially played a full year (353 performances) at the Carltheater and · *Gräfin Mariza* even longer (374 performances) at the Theater an der Wien. Both also triumphed throughout Europe but, of the two, *Gräfin Mariza* had a much more significant career in the decades which followed. Neither, however, truly won its due outside Europe. America, still not having learned that botching the big European hits of Kálmán (or anyone else, for that matter) almost invariably led to failure, turned *Die Bajadere* into *The Yankee Princess*, and London quite simply passed. *Countess Maritza* suffered less defacing and, probably not uncoincidentally, was rewarded with a splendid 321 Broadway nights. It did not, however, turn out a genuine hit in London. In Europe, however, both pieces had their due firmly and first time round, and *Gräfin Mariza* settled solidly into the backbone repertoire.

Success struck for Kálmán yet again with the Viennese production of the scenically nifty and musically joyous *Die Zirkusprinzessin* ('Zwei Märchenaugen'), but the composer finally faced disappointment, after years of virtually unshadowed triumph, when he attempted an original musical for the Broadway which had been so prodigal with its reception of its versions of his earliest shows and, so recently, *Gräfin Mariza*. *Golden Dawn*, concocted with a handful of Hammersteins and various other folk whilst the composer was in America for the local production of *The Circus Princess*, was a ludicrous piece – a custom-made botched show – which nevertheless played for 184 performances at the new Hammerstein's Theater. It produced one number (the villain's baritone exhibition of 'The Whip') which left memories with some audience members, and it was subsequently filmed. It was not, however, the kind of hit that Kálmán had produced so regularly at home. As Jacobi and Szirmai had so sadly found, even the greatest Hungarian talent often did not flourish under Broadway conditions.

Back in Europe, Kálmán next turned out an Operette with an American tinge in the Yankee-meets-Ruritania tale of *Die Herzogin von Chicago*. Some critics found the show's mixture of traditional Kálmán style and modern dance rhythms uncomfortable, but the show gave the composer another Viennese success. *Das Veilchen vom Montmartre*, a flimsy period piece of La-Bohèmerie in the composer's least virile Viennese style, also had a fair two-part run at the Johann Strauss-Theater and the Theater an der Wien, as well as some subsequent overseas productions, but the composer had now given all his best and even his second-best work, and the shows he turned out in the later part of his career were the least impressive and enjoyable of his opus.

Kálmán composed the score for the 1931 Reinhold Schünzel and Emmerich Pressburger film *Ronny*, one last Operette for Vienna, *Der Teufelsreiter*, and one which was produced in Zurich, before quitting Europe in 1938 to take shelter from Hitler in the United States. There, the composer of *Gräfin Mariza* and *Sari* found himself in a theatrical atmosphere in which more of his projects were aborted than came to fruition, but he had one further score heard on Broadway when the 1945 musical *Marinka*, the umpteenth rehash of the Mayerling tale (but this time given a happy ending), was played for some five months at the Winter Garden Theater and subsequently exported to a brief showing in Australia.

Kálmán returned to Europe after the Second World War but his only subsequent stage work, another American-flavoured piece called *Arizona Lady*, was not produced until after the composer's death in 1953.

A 1958 CCC-Farbfilm entitled *Der Csárdáskönigin*, which insisted in its sub-title that it was 'Die Emmerich-Kálmán-Story', featured Gerhard Riemann as the composer, alongside Camilla Spira (original star of *Im weissen Rössl*) as Frau Kálmán, Marina Orschel as Vera, and Rudolf Schock as a tenor János.

Kálmán's son, Charles Kálmán (b Vienna, November 1929), has also composed several Operetten including *Der grosse Tenor* (Wiesbaden, 1955), *Wir reisen um Welt* to a text by his sister, Elisabeth (Wiesbaden, 1955), *Rendezvous mit dem Leben* (Würzburg, 1969), *Antonia* (Vienna, 1970) and *Der Glöckner von Notre Dame*.

1906 **A pereszlényi juss** (Samuel Fényes) Magyar Színház, Budapest 7 April
1907 **Bernát** (Jenő Heltai) Vigszínház, Budapest 1 June

1908 **Tatárjárás** (Károly Bakonyi, Andor Gábor) Vigszinház, Budapest 22 February
1910 **Az obsitos** (Bakonyi) Vigszinház, Budapest 16 March
1912 **Der Zigeunerprimás** (Fritz Grünbaum, Julius Wilhelm) Johann Strauss-Theater 11 October
1912 **The Blue House** (Austen Hurgon) 1 act London Hippodrome 28 October
1912 **Der kleine König** (Bakonyi, Ferenc Martos ad Robert Bodanzky) Theater an der Wien 27 November
1913 **Kivándorlók** (Gábor) Modern Színház, Budapest 28 September
1914 **Gold gab ich für Eisen** revised version of *Az obsitos/Der gute Kamerad* (Theater an der Wien)
1915 **Zsuzsi kisasszony** (Martos, Miska Bródy) Vigszinház, Budapest 23 February
1915 **Die Csárdásfürstin** (Leo Stein, Béla Jenbach) Johann Strauss-Theater 17 November
1917 **Die Faschingsfee** (A M Willner, Rudolf Österreicher) Johann Strauss-Theater 21 September
1920 **Das Hollandweibchen** (Stein, Jenbach) Johann Strauss-Theater 31 January
1921 **Die Bajadere** (Julius Brammer, Alfred Grünwald) Carl-theater 23 December
1924 **Gräfin Mariza** (Brammer, Grünwald) Theater an der Wien 28 February
1926 **Die Zirkusprinzessin** (Brammer, Grünwald) Theater an der Wien 26 March
1927 **Golden Dawn** (w Herbert Stothart/Otto Harbach, Oscar Hammerstein) Hammerstein's Theater, New York, 30 November
1928 **Die Herzogin von Chicago** (Brammer, Grünwald) Theater an der Wien 5 April
1930 **Das Veilchen vom Montmartre** (Brammer, Grünwald) Johann Strauss-Theater 21 March
1932 **Der Teufelsreiter** (Rudolf Schanzer, Ernst Welisch) Theater an der Wien 10 March
1936 **Kaiserin Josephine** (Paul Knepler, Géza Herczeg) Stadttheater, Zurich 18 January
1945 **Marinka** (aka *Song of Vienna*) (Karl Farkas, George Marion jr) Winter Garden Theater, New York 18 July
1954 **Arizona Lady** (Grünwald, Gustav Beer) Stadttheater, Berne 14 February

Biographies: Österreicher, R: *Emmerich Kálmán: der Weg eines Komponisten* (Amalthea-Verlag, Vienna, 1954) Bistron, J: *Emmerich Kálmán* (Karczag, Leipzig, 1932); Kálmán, V: *Grüss' mir die süssen, die reizenden Frauen* (Hestia Verlag, Bayreuth, 1966)

KALMAR, Bert (b New York, 16 February 1884; d Los Angeles, 18 September 1947). Song, stage and film wordsmith whose teaming with Harry Ruby left some fine numbers.

Bert Kalmar began his theatre career as a child, performing firstly as a magician, then as a comedian in vaudeville and even on occasion in musical comedy (Frank D Weyman in *Li'l Mose*, 1908). He later turned to songwriting, and had his earliest efforts heard in the Chicago musical theatre before, in 1918, he joined songwriting forces with composer-author Harry Ruby. He made his first Broadway appearance as a lyricist with individual songs in revues such as *The Ziegfeld Follies of 1920* ('I'm a Vamp from East Broadway' w Irving Berlin) *The Passing Show of 1921* ('My Sunny Tennessee') and *The Greenwich Village Follies of 1922* ('Beautiful Girls'), and contributed to Chicago's *Arabian Knights*, before the pair provided the score for George S Kaufman and Marc Connelly's *Helen of Troy, New York* (1923). It was one of those rare cases where the book of a musical won better notices than its songs.

Whilst regularly turning out material for the ubiquitous revues of the time over the next half-dozen years, Kalmar also supplied the songs or lyrics and/or libretti for ten musicals, of which the lively 'fairytale in modern clothes' *The Five o'Clock Girl* (1927, 'Thinking of You') was the only one to attract attention in theatres beyond America. The Marx Brothers show *Animal Crackers* (1928, 'The Musketeers', 'Hooray for Captain Spalding') was another popular success which, if its international potential was negated by its being so very much a custom-made vehicle, was made into a film by its inseparable stars, two years after its Broadway run.

The other Kalmar and Ruby shows, if less than memorable in the theatre, nevertheless produced both some good runs and some popular individual numbers. In spite of bad notices, *The Ramblers* (1926), a loose-limbed piece with a film-land setting, was helped to a 290-performance Broadway run and a long afterlife by the antics of comics Clarke and McCullough, and gave the songwriters a hit with 'All Alone Monday'. *Good Boy* (1928) lasted 253 performances and produced the song 'I Wanna Be Loved By You', famously squeaked out by Helen Kane, the 'boop-a-doop' girl.

Kalmar and Ruby were, along with Guy Bolton, given a 'based on' credit on the London Rodgers and Hart musical *Lido Lady*, after Ronald Jeans had worked over an unused libretto of theirs to create a new 'American' musical to order for Cicely Courtneidge and Jack Hulbert. The piece had a 259-performance London run, toured merrily and was exported to Australia and to Paris's Théâtre Apollo, where it was staged 'à grand spectacle'.

Less fortunate Kalmar and Ruby ventures included three attempts to get an adaptation of Aaron Hoffman's *Nothing But Lies* into musical-comedy shape in 1924–5, a share in the adaptation of the 'rather serious' German musical *Frühling im Herbst* (at various times called *Holka Polka*, *Spring in Autumn* and *Nobody's Girl*), and a disappointing collaboration with Jerome Kern on a piece called *Lucky*, which failed to live up to its title in 71 performances on Broadway. A genuine pairing with Rodgers and Hart on *She's My Baby* had all the star values of *Lido Lady* (Clifton Webb, Jack Whiting, Beatrice Lillie, Irene Dunne) but none of the same success.

During the 1930s Kalmar and Ruby spent a period in Hollywood, during which they provided the scores for further Marx Brothers films (*Duck Soup*, *Horsefeathers*) which included such songs as 'Show Me a Rose' and 'Timbuctoo', for Eddie Cantor's *The Kid from Spain* and for *Three Little Words* ('Three Little Words'). Kalmar continued to write film songs up to his death in 1947, returning only once to Broadway for *High Kickers* (1941), a vehicle for George Jessel and Sophie Tucker.

Some of Kalmar's songs were used in the briefly displayed off-Broadway musical *The Cockeyed Tiger* (1977).

In the 1950 musical biofilm *Three Little Words*, Fred Astaire played Kalmar to the Ruby of Red Skelton.

1914 **One Girl in a Million** (Ted Snyder/w Edgar Leslie/Addison Burkhard, Charles Collins) La Salle Theater, Chicago 6 September
1923 **Helen of Troy, New York** (Harry Ruby/George S Kaufman, Marc Connelly) Selwyn Theater 19 June

1924 **The Town Clown** (Ruby/Aaron Hoffman) Illinois Theater, Chicago 6 January
1924 **The Belle of Quakertown** revised *The Town Clown* Stamford, Conn July
1924 **No Other Girl** revised *The Town Clown* Morosco Theater 13 August
1925 **Holka Polka** (aka *Spring in Autumn*) (*Frühling im Herbst*) English version w Ruby (Lyric Theater)
1926 **The Ramblers** (ex-*The Fly-by-Knights*) (Ruby/w Guy Bolton) Lyric Theater 20 September
1926 **Lido Lady** (Richard Rodgers, Lorenz Hart/w Bolton, Ruby ad Ronald Jeans) Gaiety Theatre, London 1 December
1927 **Lucky** (Jerome Kern/w Harbach, Ruby) New Amsterdam Theater 22 March
1927 **The Five o'Clock Girl** (Ruby/Bolton, Fred Thompson) 44th Street Theater 10 October
1928 **She's My Baby** (Rodgers/Hart/w Bolton, Ruby) Globe Theater 3 January
1928 **Good Boy** (Herbert Stothart/w Ruby/Harbach, Oscar Hammerstein, Henry Meyers) Hammerstein's Theater 5 September
1928 **Animal Crackers** (Ruby/Kaufman, Morrie Ryskind) New York Theater 23 October
1929 **Top Speed** (w Ruby/Bolton) 46th Street Theater 25 December
1941 **High Kickers** (w Ruby/w George Jessel) Broadhurst Theater 31 October

KANDER, John [Harold] (b Kansas City, 18 March 1927). Composer of several hit shows of the Broadway 1960s and 1970s.

Kander's earliest musical theatre assignments were as pianist for the try-out of the futureless musical *The Amazing Adele* and for a tour of *An Evening with Beatrice Lillie*, and as musical director for the Barbizon Plaza revival of Noel Coward's *Conversation Piece*. He arranged the dance music for *Gypsy* and for the Broadway version of *Irma la Douce*, before he had his first theatre score as a composer heard in 1962 when Andrew Siff produced *A Family Affair* at the Billy Rose Theater. With a cast headed by Shelley Berman, Eileen Heckart and *West Side Story* star Larry Kert, the show ran for 65 performances.

Kander supplied incidental music for a production of *It's Never Too Late* at the Playhouse, before he moved into the most successful phase of his career when he teamed up with lyricist Fred Ebb to write, at first a number of successful songs ('My Colouring Book' etc) and then a series of stage musicals. After an indifferent beginning with the tale of *Flora the Red Menace*, the pair scored a major international hit with *Cabaret* ('Cabaret', 'Willkommen' etc), a success magnified hugely by its transformation into one of the most successful musical films of the postwar era ('Maybe This Time', 'Money'). After a switch into gentler tones for the not-unsuccessful *The Happy Time*, the team found further international success with the virile tale of *Zorba* ('Happy Birthday') and with the darkly comic, bitingly glittery vaudeville *Chicago* ('Razzle Dazzle, 'All That Jazz', 'All I Care About is Love', 'Cell Block Tango' etc).

Having, in their earlier shows, demonstrated a considerable versatility, as well as a particularly sure touch with what might best be described as stand-up or out-front material, the pair, who had throughout their association also provided a considerable amount of special material and songs to cabaret, nightclub and television performers, now put themselves at the service of the oversized female star-name for a series of shows. If *The Act*, a show about a show manufactured for vocalist Liza Minnelli, the enormously successful star of their *Cabaret* film, had only a medium run, a musicalization of the screenplay *Woman of the Year*, with further film names, Lauren Bacall and later Raquel Welch and Debbie Reynolds featured, played rather longer in town and also found its way to Europe. A third piece, *The Rink*, which paired Miss Minnelli with Chita Rivera, had a fair Broadway run and proved popular in Germany, but, like its two predecessors, it did not have either the attractions or the wide success of the team's three major shows.

In the decade since *The Rink*, Kander and Ebb have been represented on Broadway only by a reprise of *Cabaret*, although at the time of writing a musical version of the film and play *Kiss of the Spiderwoman* – another piece allowing the introduction of performance material into the fabric of its story and, yet again, featuring a large and now slightly grotesque feminine star personality – has been tried out out-of-town in America and, side-stepping Broadway, mounted in London with Miss Rivera top-billed.

A five-handed compilation show of Kander and Ebb songs, *And the World Goes Round: The Songs of Kander and Ebb*, has been played at off-Broadway's Westside Theater and in other venues around America.

1962 **A Family Affair** (James Goldman, William Goldman) Billy Rose Theater 27 January
1965 **Flora, the Red Menace** (Fred Ebb/George Abbott, Robert Russell) Alvin Theater 11 May
1966 **Cabaret** (Ebb/Joe Masteroff) Broadhurst Theater 20 November
1968 **The Happy Time** (Ebb/N Richard Nash) Broadway Theater 18 January
1968 **Zorba** (Ebb/Joseph Stein) Imperial Theater 17 November
1971 **70, Girls, 70** (Ebb/Joe Masteroff) Broadhurst Theater 15 April
1975 **Chicago** (Ebb/Ebb, Bob Fosse) 46th Street Theater 3 June
1977 **The Act** (aka *Shine It On*) (Ebb/George Furth) Majestic Theater 29 October
1981 **Woman of the Year** (Ebb/Peter Stone) Palace Theater 29 March
1984 **The Rink** (Ebb/Terrence McNally) Martin Beck Theater 9 February
1990 **Kiss of the Spiderwoman** (Ebb/McNally) Westchester 1 May; Shaftesbury Theatre, London 20 October 1992

KÁPOLNAI, János [KIRCHNER, János] (b 1842; d Budapest, 11 December 1907).

The handsome, curly-headed principal tenor of the Népszinház, Budapest, from its earliest days, Kápolnai introduced many of the principal rôles of the French and Viennese classic repertoire to the Budapest theatre. He was seen during the 1870s and 1880s as Offenbach's Barbe-bleue, Ange Pitou, Pygmalion, Grénicheux, Fritellini, Lotteringhi, Jan Janicki to the Symon of Lujza Blaha, Lamberto (*Kapitány kisasszony* ie *Der Seekadett*), Miguel (*Nap és hold* ie *Le Jour et la nuit*), Frikkel (*Kisasszony feleségem* ie *La Marjolaine*), Ritenuto (ie Alfred) in *Denevér* (*Die Fledermaus*), in *A furcsa háború* (*Der lustige Krieg*), Háromcsőrű kacsa (*Le Canard à trois becs*), Kanári hercegnö (*La Princesse des Canaries*) and many such other pieces. He played Sándor Barinkay in Hungary's first *Zigeunerbaron* at Kolozsvár and introduced the Hungarian version of Offenbach's Hoffman, as well as creating roles in some of

the earliest Hungarian operetts (Bruno in Erkel's *Katalina Székely* (1880) etc).

KARCZAG, Wilhelm [KRAMMER, Vilmos] (b Karcag, Hungary, 15 August 1859; d Baden bei Wien, 11 October 1923). Manager of the Theater an der Wien through some of its greatest hours.

The son of an Hungarian grain merchant, Karczag made his earliest steps in the theatre as a writer, placing his first one-act play, *Szent a béke*, with the theatre in his home town of Debrecen at the age of 18. He wrote a number of other stage pieces over the following 17 years, including several comedies, a five-act drama, and, most successfully, the three-act *Lemondás*, the majority of which were produced at Budapest's Nemzeti Színház. He also authored one operett, *A leánypapa*, with music by Isidor Dreysach, which was produced in 1881. In 1894 he moved from Budapest to Vienna and, over the following years, worked as a writer and a journalist whilst his wife, the highly popular soubrette Juliska Kopácsi-Karczag, reaped the family's theatrical honours as one of the city's favourite Operette performers.

The most successful part of Karczag's theatrical life began on 9 May 1901. The Theater an der Wien had been going through a low time since the decline of the kind of Viennese Operette which had been its staple diet under the management of the Steiners and Alexandrine von Schönerer. With Strauss, Suppé and Millöcker no longer supplying the theatre with their popular works, it had begun to lose its way, and its last manager, Karl Langkammer, had lasted only part of a season before throwing in his hand. The theatre was for the taking, and Karczag took it. He acquired a long lease and set himself to work to get the house playing the best of Operette to the best effect, as it had in its palmiest days.

The opposition in 1901 didn't seem too great. The Carltheater had found itself a hit with Reinhardt's *Das süsse Mädel* to compensate for the lesser runs of Millöcker's *Die Damenschneider* and Zamara's *Die Debutantin*; the Raimundtheater had been living on revivals of classic pieces before getting round to producing *Der Kellermeister*; and the adventurous Gabor Steiner had tried Kappeller's version of the French spectacle *Die verkehrte Welt* (*Le Royaume des femmes*) at Venedig in Wien, gone to Germany for Lincke's *Venus auf Erden* and to Britain for a score from Ivan Caryll for *Die Reise nach Cuba*, and produced Eysler's *Das Gastmahl des Lucullus* at Danzers Orpheum, none with particular success. Most of the other houses were relying on repeats. But the best Karczag could manage, for the moment, was a revival of *The Geisha*, which, for all its several-years-old charms, was not about to challenge the sprightly *Das süsse Mädel*.

However, the new manager hung on, and 1902 got better. He landed one of the best new Operetten that had turned up in Vienna for several years with Ziehrer's *Der Fremdenführer* and, although no one was yet to know it, the best new composer as well. If Steiner went to Berlin, Paris and London for his material and inspiration, Karczag went home to Hungary. Or rather, Hungary, as represented by the young Franz Lehár, came to him, and Karczag produced the young composer's first major Operette, *Wiener Frauen*, at the Theater an der Wien, with Girardi starring. The good luck, or good management, continued. The year

1903 brought the first work and first hit of another young composer, Edmund Eysler's *Bruder Straubinger*. With Girardi again in the starring rôle, this delightful piece gave the theatre one of the biggest successes it had ever known. Then, after a curious flop with another début work, Leo Fall's *Der Rebell*, in 1905, Karczag produced Lehár's *Die lustige Witwe*. The show made all its participants rich – and the most important the richest – and it soon propelled the Theater an der Wien right back to the top, as the leading musical theatre of Europe. Fall's *Die Dollarprinzessin* (1907), Lehár's *Der Mann mit den drei Frauen* and Oscar Straus's *Der tapfere Soldat* (1908), the Vienna début of another Hungarian composer, Emmerich Kálmán with the hugely successful *Ein Herbstmanöver* (1909), Lehár's *Der Graf von Luxemburg* (1909) and Fall's *Die schöne Risette* (1910) nearly all helped – some less, some very much more – to continue the newly refound prosperity of the Theater an der Wien, and, in 1908, Karczag took the opportunity to spread himself, with the financial backing of Karl Wallner, into the management of the Raimundtheater, recently fallen into disastrous straits.

He brought to the failing theatre not only the Theater an der Wien repertoire but also its stars, notably the one-and-only Girardi, and he even produced several new Operetten there, including one of the biggest hits Vienna had ever seen. But, although he got the Raimundtheater back on its financial feet in 12 years of management, he found himself constantly obstructed by a faction on the theatre's board of directors (who were, of course, not paying the bills) who insisted that the theatre should play the traditional old Vienna repertoire it had been originally founded to house. And so, what the productions of the plays of Raimund and Nestroy, mounted to appease these 'businessmen', lost, the Operette productions the gentlemen of the board so artsily despised earned back, to keep their theatre alive.

At the Theater an der Wien, Karczag continued to produce the same fine fare as before: Lehár's *Die ideale Gattin* (1913) and *Endlich allein* (1914), Kálmán's war-effort *Gold gab' ich für Eisen*, and, most particularly, Leo Fall's *Die Rose von Stambul* (1916), a wartime triumph which provided the producer with his biggest success since *Die lustige Witwe*. In fact 1916 was a spectacular year for him, for, across town at the Raimundtheater, in the same year, he produced the biggest hit that theatre had ever had or would ever have: the Schubert biomusical *Das Dreimäderlhaus*. And in the euphoria thus created, Karczag took on a third house, the Wiener Stadttheater.

The Theater an der Wien continued with *Wo die Lerche singt* (1918), *Die blaue Mazur* (1920), the superb success of Oscar Straus's splendid *Der letzte Walzer* (1921), Lehár's *Frasquita* (1922) and *Die gelbe Jacke* (1923), the Raimundtheater followed *Das Dreimäderlhaus* with its musequel *Hannerl*, Granichstädten's *Das alte Lied*, Künneke's *Das Dorf ohne Glocke*, a Berlin Mendelssohn pasticcio *Dichterliebe*, Ascher's *Was Mädchen träumen* and Stolz's *Der Tanz ins Glück*, whilst the Stadttheater also joined in Karczag's Operette blitz.

After a few years of this triple burden, however, Karczag started to shed his enormous workload. More and more of the responsibility at the Theater an der Wien fell onto his son-in-law, the longtime principal tenor of the house, Hubert Marischka, and in 1921, after nearly 13 years of fighting to keep a solvent ship at the Raimundtheater, he

turned in his management there. It was ironic that, now given their heads, the conservative gentlemen of the Raimundtheater quickly got into difficulties. Only a few years later, they would call Hubert Marischka and Operette back to rescue them from bankruptcy once again.

In fact, Karczag now had little time left to live but when he died in 1923 his record over two decades of musical theatre production made him unchallengedly the most remarkable and internationally successful producer of his era.

KARNILOVA, Maria [DOVGOLENKO, Maria Karnilovitch] (b Hartford, Conn, 3 August 1920). Dancer and character actress on the modern Broadway stage.

In the early part of her career, Miss Karnilova appeared as a dancer at the Metropolitan Opera, with the Ballet Theater, and in a number of musicals and revues (*Stars in Your Eyes*, *Hollywood Pinafore*, *Call Me Mister*, *High Button Shoes*, *Miss Liberty*, *Out of This World*, *Two's Company*, *Kaleidoscope*) both on Broadway and elsewhere. Her first notable rôle came in the 1959 musical *Gypsy*, in which she created the part of the stripper Tessie Tura ('You Gotta Have a Gimmick').

She moved into non-dancing, accented-acting rôles in *Bravo Giovanni* (1962, Signora Pandolfi), and followed this up with a famous creation as the milkman's wife, Golde, starred opposite Zero Mostel in the original production of *Fiddler on the Roof* (1964). Four years later she had another fine rôle, as the sweetly heart-wringing cocotte Hortense ('Happy Birthday') in *Zorba* (1968). In 1973 she took the part of Mamita in an attempt to put the Loewe/Lerner film score *Gigi* on to the stage, in 1981 appeared briefly in the effort to *Bring Back Birdie*, and subsequently played opposite Herschel Bernardi in a revival of *Fiddler on the Roof*.

She appeared as Daphne in the film version of *The Unsinkable Molly Brown*.

Miss Karnilova is married to actor George S Irving.

KARTOUSCH, L[o]uise (b Linz, 17 August 1886; d Vienna, 13 February 1964). The favourite soubrette of the heyday of 20th-century Viennese Operette.

After studying music in her home town and in Vienna, the young Luise Kartousch worked at first in provincial theatres, moving from children's rôles in Linz to adult ones in Graz where, from 1902, she played soubrette parts in Operette and the occasional opéra-comique and even, in repertoire, such small operatic rôles as Mercedes in *Carmen* and a minor Walküre in *Die Walküre*.

Before long, however, she made her way back to Vienna and to the Theater an der Wien where, at the age of 21, she created first the rôle of Mary in Stritzko's short-lived *Tip-Top*, and then the juvenile soubrette, Daisy, in the highly successful first performances of *Die Dollarprinzessin*, joining with Karl Meister to introduce the jolly song and dance of 'Wir tanzen ringelreih'n' to the Viennese public. Show by show thereafter she established herself as the adored little favourite of the Theater an der Wien audiences: *Der Mann mit den drei Frauen* (Coralie), *Der schöne Gardist* (Franziska), *Der Frauenjäger* (Fioretta), as the pining cousin Masha in *Der tapfere Soldat* (1908), as the lively Juliette in *Der Graf von Luxemburg* (1909) and, in a personal triumph which outdid all her previous efforts, in

Plate 145. **Luise Kartousch:** *Vienna's favourite soubrette through the years of the Austrian stage's greatest supremacy.*

and scored in a fine run of rôles in the early 1920s: Gretl Aigner in *Die blaue Mazur*, Sophie Lavalle in *Die Frau im Hermelin* and, at the Carltheater, the sparky Marietta who only fancies her husbands when she is not married to them in *Die Bajadere* ('Schatzi, ich möchte einen Zobel von dir!', 'Der kleine Bar dort am Boulevard'). Back at the Theater an der Wien she created the rôle of Mi – the prototype of *Das Land des Lächelns'* Chinese princess – in *Die gelbe Jacke*, but, after a last appearance there in Granichstädten's *Die Bacchusnacht*, she put an end to some 15 years' association with the Theater an der Wien and moved on, still the eternal soubrette, to perform in musical and non-musical shows at most of Vienna's other principal theatres.

An appearance at the Raimundtheater in Schnitzler's play *Vermächtnis* led the critics delightedly to compare her to Hansi Niese, the great comic soubrette of the Vienna stage of earlier years. However, she returned to Operette at the Bürgertheater in the title-rôle of Robert Stolz's successful *Mädi* (1923), in *Agri* (1924, Violet), as Lehár's little cabaret girl in *Cloclo* (1924) and in the juvenile lead of Dorothy in *Revanche* (1924). A second period at the Raimundtheater had her starring in Jerome K Jerome's play *Lady Fanny and the Servant Problem*, pairing with Tautenhayn in the operette *Ich hab' dich Lieb*, playing Nettl in *Das Schwalbennest* and Denise in *Mam'zelle Nitouche*, whilst on a visit to Ronacher she appeared in *Spiel um die Liebe* (Erzherzogin Immaculata) and in the title-rôle of Straus's *Teresina*. In 1927 she appeared in the title-rôle of *Dorine und der Zufall* at the Rolandbühne, at the Carltheater in *Eine einzige Nacht* and, in her oddest male rôle yet, in the part of the detective, Mister Quick, alongside Tautenhayn in the Revue-Operette *Die Lady vom Lido* at the Johann Strauss-Theater.

Still just a little over 40, Kartousch returned briefly to the Theater an der Wien in 1930 to take over from Hella Kürty the role of Mi in *Das Land des Lächelns* and she appeared there again, as a guest artist, in 1933 for Straus's *Zwei lachende Augen* (Grossfürstin Maria Helene) and as Prinz Orlofsky, and in 1935 as Madame Sauterelle in *Die Dubarry*. In 1934 she played at the Scala Theater in *Ein Kuss – und sonst gar nichts* (*Ein aufgeregte Frau*), and in 1936 in *Warum lügst du, Chérie* (Erszy Körmendi). She later returned also to the Raimundtheater, playing there in both Operette and plays during the war (Resi-Tante in *Der Fremdenführer* etc), and appeared in several musical films (*Zauber der Bohème* etc).

She was still to be seen on the Operette stage in her sixties (Kathi the Haushälterin in *Abschiedswalzer* etc) after a long career in which the difficult years between soubrette and character parts (she never became a komische Alte comedienne) had been covered without any real break in activity.

KASSAI, Vidor [KOSSITZSKY] (b Gyála, 16 February 1840; d Vác, 29 July 1928).

Comedian and operettic buffo at Budapest's Népszínház for many years, Kassai introduced many celebrated opéra-bouffe and opéra-comique rôles to Hungarian audiences from the 1860s onwards. He was Budapest's first Baron Grog in *La Grande-Duchesse*, the first Frank (Fujo) in the Hungarian *Die Fledermaus*, played Madame Madou in *Mesdames de la Halle* (aged 25), Sebastiani in *Der lustige Krieg*, von Bontrouche in *Le Canard à trois becs*, Calabazas

travesty as the highly featured little army cadet Marosi in the extremely successful Viennese production of Emmerich Kálmán's *Ein Herbstmanöver* (1909). It was this rôle and this production which marked the real confirmation of Kartousch's position as one of the city's favourite musical stars.

In the years that followed she appeared as Honoria Leontieff in Kerker's *Schneeglöckchen* (1910), Orestes in a revival of *Die schöne Helena*, Pauline in *Pariser Leben* and Pedro in *Giroflé-Girofla*, and created such rôles as Princess Margot in *Die schöne Risette*, Milli Gärtner in *Ihr Adjutant* (1911) and the piquant Pipsi Paquerette who lends the liveliness to Lehár's tale of *Eva* (1911). She played in *Der kleine König* (Zaza) and *Der blaue Held* (Lottenbusch) and, in 1913, got into boy's clothes again as Prince Max in *Prinzessin Gretl*. She created the rôles of Carmen de Serrantis in *Die ideale Gattin* and Tilly in Lehár's *Endlich allein*, played Xaver in the patriotic wartime *Gold gab' ich für Eisen* and, again in pants, the boy Henri in a revival of *Der Opernball*, before returning to skirts as Hilma, the title-lass of *Die schöne Schwedin* (1915). In 1916 she created the rôle of Lilly in Lehár's *Der Sterngucker* and found one of the best parts of her career as the harem-girl Midili Hanum in the long-running *Der Rose von Stambul*, introducing 'Fridolin, ach wie dein Schnurrbart sticht', the Schnucki-Duett and 'Papachen, Papachen' with her partner of almost always, Ernst Tautenhayn.

Continuing to mix girls' and boys' rôles, Kartousch returned to Lehár for *Wo die Lerche singt* (Margit), played little Baron Boris in the 'official wife' musical *Nimm mich mit!* (1919) and the soubrette Louisl in *Dorfmusikanten*,

Plate 146. *The cast of Broadway's* **Katinka** *assemble as events rise to their finale. Olga (Edith Decker), Boris (Count Lorrie Grimaldi), Katinka (May Naudain), Thaddeus Hopper (Franklin Ardell), Mrs Hopper (Adele Rowland), Ivan Dimitri (Samuel Ash), Arif Bey (Edward Durand) and Knopf (W J McCarthy).*

(*Le Jour et la Nuit*), Laurent (*La Mascotte*), Lambertuccio (*Boccaccio*), Menélaos, John Styx and Saint Hypothèse (*Lili*) and also created rôles in a number of original Hungarian works, including Pomponius in *Az eleven ördög* (1885), Marx in Konti's *Királyfogás* (1886), Rettenetes in *A kis alamuszi* (1894) and Tamás Pöl in *A citerás* (1894). At the other end of the repertoire, he was also seen as the Fool in *King Lear*.

KATALIN Operett in 3 acts by Izor Béldi. Music by Jenő Féjer. Népszinház, Budapest, 4 October 1901.

The earliest original Hungarian operett to be played for 100 performances in Budapest – even though they were spread over five years – *Katalin* was first produced at the Népszinház with Aranka Hegyi as Katalin and Klára Küry, József Németh and Imre Szirmai in the other principal rôles. By the time the record-making 100th performance arrived, however, the first famous works of Huszka and Kacsóh had come to the stage and *Katalin* and its record run were soon eclipsed.

Küry took over the lead rôle alongside two other star ladies, Mizzi Günther (Katharina II) and Mizzi Zwerenz (Anita), when the piece was played in Vienna as *Der kleine Günstling* for a run of 17 performances in 1902.

Austria: Carltheater *Der kleine Günstling* 12 April 1902

KATINKA Musical play in 3 acts by Otto Hauerbach (Harbach). Music by Rudolf Friml. 44th Street Theater, New York, 23 December 1915.

Produced by Arthur Hammerstein in the wake of his

Friml/Hauerbach (as the latter was then still spelling his name) successes with *The Firefly* and *High Jinks*, *Katinka* gave the team of producer, composer and librettist a third successive hit. Hauerbach's libretto was altogether more old-world-Operette than the previous two pieces he had written or adapted, with Viennese and Turkish harem settings, a hero and villain and chorus of dancers who were Russians, and a foolish American for its low comedy.

Katinka (May Naudain) wants to marry Ivan Dimitri (Samuel Ash), an attaché at the Russian embassy in Vienna, but it is the ambassador himself, Boris Strogoff (Lorrie Grimaldi), who is leading her unhappily to the altar as the piece begins. Rather than consummate the marriage, she climbs out of the window of her nuptial bower on her wedding night and is helpfully hidden away by comical Yankee Thaddeus Hopper (Franklin Ardell), much to the annoyance of his suspicious wife (Adele Rowland). However, after the process of hiding the fleeing bride has led the action through some harem high-jinks, a certain Olga Nashan (Edith Decker), bigamous Boris's already wife, turns up to claim her husband, and Katinka and her Ivan can be united.

The show's score, again laid out on traditional Operette lines, with full-scale finales to the first two acts, solos and ensembles and at least one dance speciality per act, included several numbers which became popular: Katinka's song of the pigeon 'Rackety-Coo', Olga's Eastern number 'Allah's Holiday', and Ivan's maestoso solo 'My Paradise' and his first act farewell duet with Katinka, ''Tis the End'. The quota of comical numbers featured Mrs Hopper's declaration that 'I Want to Marry a Male Quartet' (not because there are four of them, you understand, but because they are good at harmony) and her 'Your Photo' in which she encourages her beloved to hurry home, because his glossy picture is nasty and chilly against her bosom.

Brought swiftly from its tryout at Morristown, New Jersey, to open at the 44th Street Theater on the same night that the decidedly different *Very Good Eddie* made its début at the Princess, *Katinka* was swiftly established as a solid success. It ran for 220 performances on Broadway before heading for the touring circuits and, eventually, to overseas productions. J C Williamson's wartime Australian production (first actually produced in Wellington, New Zealand), which starred the young Gladys Moncrieff (Katinka), Florence Young (Mrs Hopper) and Phil Smith (Hopper), was a genuine hit and the piece earned regular revivals in Australia as a vehicle for the idolized Miss Moncrieff up until 1944. But, in spite of the fine London success of *High Jinks*, it was not until 1923 that *Katinka* appeared in Britain, produced by Robert MacDonald (ad Bertram Davis) at the Shaftesbury Theatre, with Helen Gilliland and George Bishop as the lovers, Joe Coyne and Binnie Hale heading the fun, and Peter Gawthorne as the libidinous Russian. It lasted only a disappointing 108 performances, although it proved good for two seasons in the provinces.

Like Friml's other early hits, *Katinka* was not produced in Europe, but another piece under the same title was staged with some success by Louis Brigon at Paris's Théâtre de l'Empire (22 February 1933). This was, in effect, an adaptation of the Hungarian operette *Őfelsége frakkja* (Budapest, 1931), with text by István Békeffy (ad André Barde, Pierre Varenne, Robert Delamare) and music by Lajos Lajtai. The Viennese diva Rita Georg, Adrien Lamy, Saint-Granier and Lynne Clevers starred in Brigon's production, a production which led to some French composers publicly stamping their feet and accusing managers of jiggery-pokery on the royalty front, or, worse, of unpatriotically preferring foreign-made foxtrots, tangos, waltzes and marches to their own efforts at foxtrots, tangos, waltzes and marches.

Two further *Katinka*s – the first and the last of the group – were produced, logically enough, in Hungary, where Zoltán Thury and Árpád Orbán turned out an 1898 operett (Budai Színkör 21 August), and Nándor Bihary (text) and István Máthé (music) combined on a piece premièred at the Városi Színház in February 1938, its title-rôle played by the young Sári Bárabás.

Australia: Her Majesty's Theatre, Melbourne 8 June 1918; UK: Shaftesbury Theatre 30 August 1923

KATJA, DIE TÄNZERIN
Operette in 3 acts by Leopold Jacobson and Rudolf Österreicher. Music by Jean Gilbert. Johann Strauss-Theater, Vienna, 5 January 1923.

The Princess Katja Karina (Mizzi Günther) has been deposed from her Ruritanian throne and has ended up, like all the best deposed operettic monarchs, working as a dancer and singer in a Paris nightclub. One night, at a reception, she encounters the aristocratic and attractive Eusebius von Koruga (Karl Bachmann) and, before that evening and the Operette are over, the two have not only

fallen in love but discovered that Eusebius is the very prince who deposed Katja. While the romance was going on, the light-hearted part of the evening involved the American ambassador Lallan Webster (Max Brod), his daughter Maud (Gisela Kolbe) and his private secretary, Leander Bill (Fritz Imhoff) and the efforts of the last-named pair to get together in spite of Papa's objections.

Gilbert's score spread itself in less than classic proportions between the romantic moments and the soubret and comic ones: the bulk of the music was the property of the soprano and her tenor. Katja introduced herself ('Spiel' auf, Kamerad ...'), and whilst Eusebius soliloquized 'O du verflixte Politik! Du nimmst uns Menschen soviel Glück ...', her soprano tones could be heard outside serenading in 'Heut' Nacht beim Mondenschein'. She was soon inside and joining him in their first duet ('Sie dachten, da ist eine Tänzerin') and the stage was only left for the space of a duo to Maud and Leander ('Komm morgen zu mir') before the romantic principals were back with a long and strong finale. In the second act Maud got a little more of a look-in, with duets with both Eusebius and Leander, but although Katja and Eusebius with a duo, a trio, another big finale and even a solo (him) dominated again, it was that little duo which invited 'Komm, Liebchen, wander mit deiner Leander...' which proved the takeaway gem not only of the act but of the piece. As in so many Operetten, the third act was little more than a perfunctory wind-up, holding only a trio, a number for a supporting character and a couple of little pieces before the evening was played out on a replay of the jaunty 'Leander' duo.

Produced by Erich Müller at the Johann Strauss-Theater, *Katja die Tänzerin* was played for 207 performances in its first run, and for several further nights in a break between productions some months later. Herbert Trau produced the piece at Berlin's Neues Operetten-Theater less than a month after the Vienna première with Margit Suchy (Katja), Erik Wirl (Sacha), Jacob Wiedtke (Webster), Ilse Muth (Maud) and Harald Paulsen (Leander Bill) starred, and Budapest's Fővárosi Operettszinház was close behind, with a production in which Marinka (as she had now become in Zsolt Harsányi's version) was played by Sári Petráss, and which ran up its first 100 performances in repertoire in just five months. In 1927 *Marinka, a tancosnő* was played at the Budai Színkör (9 September) and in 1938 it was revived at the Royal Színház (12 November).

In Britain, James White produced *Katja the Dancer* (ad Harry Graham, Frederick Lonsdale) in Manchester, under the cheekily appropriated 'George Edwardes presents' banner, with soprano Lilian Davies and Gregory Stroud in the romantic rôles, Gene Gerrard and Ivy Tresmand as soubrets, and Rene Mallory as a new 'heroine's friend' character with two re-allotted songs. When the Gaiety Theatre fell free through the failure of *Poppy*, he quickly moved the clearly successful show to London, where it proved a rare hit for the now rather sad Gaiety, and where Gerrard and Miss Tresmand saw their 'Leander' become a major hit. However, after a seven-month run, White elected to transfer the show to Daly's, provoking a vicious strike against the continued employment of their Gaiety colleagues by the current Daly's choristers, who expected to go unchallenged from one show into the next at 'their' theatre, and leaving the Gaiety once again to its woes. As no fewer than three touring companies took to the road,

Katja the Dancer sailed on for another eight months at Daly's, closing only after a total of 501 West End performances, and joining *Lilac Time* and Gilbert's other most recent hit *The Lady of the Rose* as one of the three longest-running London musicals of the post-war period.

In Australia, with Marie Burke starring alongside Marjorie Hicklin (Maud) and R Barrett-Lennard (Leander), *Katja the Dancer* and 'Leander', as delivered by the last two named artists, once again made a hit. It played a splendid 131 performances in Sydney, before setting off round the country and to New Zealand. In America, however, things went a little less well. The Shuberts, inevitably, botched the British version of *Katja* (who was no longer titularly a dancer) with 'additional scenes by Isobel Leighton', 'additional lyrics by Clifford Grey' and 'additional music by Vernon Duke'. The additional numbers ('Try a Little Kiss', 'Back to My Heart'), which actually had lyrics by London's Percy Greenbank and Arthur Wimperis, seemed to be left-overs from Duke's London botching of another Gilbert piece as *Yvonne*.

Having originally announced the show (interestingly if curiously given its vocal demands) as a vehicle for dancer Marilyn Miller, the producers finally imported the British soprano Lilian Davies to repeat her rôle opposite the Prince Carl of Allen Prior in a version set in Monte Carlo. Denis Hoey was the villanous Ivo and soubrette Doris Patston (Patricia) and Jack Sheehan headed 'Leander'. *Katja* was adjudged 'a worthy and respectable candidate for Shubert operatic honours, containing as many virtues and fewer faults than most of such enterprises' and it ran for 112 Broadway performances without winning the larger popularity it had elsewhere.

Germany: Neues Operetten-Theater 2 February 1923; Hungary: Fővárosi Operettszinház *Marinka a táncosnő* 24 February 1923; UK: Gaiety Theatre *Katja the Dancer* 21 February 1925; Australia: Theatre Royal, Sydney 19 December 1925; USA: 44th Street Theater *Katja* 18 October 1926

KATSCHER, Robert (b Vienna, 20 May 1894; d Hollywood, 23 February 1942). Songwriter with a revusical bent who scored one sizeable international success.

Viennese-born Katscher wrote music for revue and, in particular, for what became known as the Revue-Operette, during the late 1920s and early 1930s, scoring a particular and international success with the nightlife-with-numbers tale of the cabaretty goings-on in *Die Wunder-Bar* ('Elizabeth', 'Tell Me I'm Forgiven'). His other major musical theatre productions had mixed fortunes. The Revue-Operette *Die Lady vom Lido* lasted only a month and a half in spite of a cast led by patented Vienna stars Luise Kartousch (as a male detective) and Ernst Tautenhayn, and was bundled off the Johann Strauss-Theater stage to be replaced by a visit from a certain *Dreimal Hochzeit* (otherwise *Abie's Irish Rose*). Katscher and his collaborators did, however, find some later success with another up-to-date and picturesque piece, *Der Traum-Express*, a revusical show developed from an earlier work that Katscher and Herczeg had had staged in Budapest. Set on the Blue Train between Paris and Nice and with an American film man (Hubert Marischka) as hero, what was described as an 'unbeabsichte (unintentional) Operette' ran 136 performances at the Theater an der Wien.

Plate 147. **Robert Katscher** *supplied words and/or music to many revusical entertainments in central Europe between the wars.*

Katscher's other principal showing, however, came not only after his flight from Hitlerian Europe back towards the film-lands of America (which he had visited previously in the early 1930s) but largely after his death. He was responsible for the original musical setting of *Bei Kerzenlicht*, an internationally produced small-scale play written by Siegfried Geyer, with whom Katscher had previously combined on a comedy with songs produced disastrously in London as *The Gay Princess* and a little 'Märchen aus Wien' *Essig und Öl* played in Budapest as *Ecet és olaj* (ad István Békeffy, János Vaszary Andrássy-úti Színház, Budapest 27 November). *Bei Kerzenlicht* ('Bei Kerzenlicht', 'Wenn's Mai wird', 'Ich bin nur eine Mizzi!', 'Wo bist du?', 'Es ist nicht leicht, Mondän zu sein', 'Mit Klavierbegleitung'), to all evidence first produced not in German, but in Hungarian in Budapest (*Gyertyafényél* Royal Színház 1 October 1937), later won productions in Vienna, in a heavily botched version in New York (*You Never Know* with Katscher still slightly credited but mostly with new material by Cole Porter) and, almost entirely rewritten, in London where the piece was ill-treated by Eric Maschwitz (text) and Sam Coslow (replacement music) and, as *Romance by Candlelight*, was a quick failure.

Katscher's second American episode was not a success. He found little work in Hollywood, where his only real reference turned out to be the fact that his song 'Madonna' had found some currency in a version by Buddy De Sylva called 'Day is Done', and he died soon after from a liver ailment, apparently a legacy of his maltreatment in a German concentration camp.

1924 **Das Mädel mit dem Storch** (Wolfgang Pollaczek) Kammerspiele 4 March

1924 **Was Frauen träumen** (Katscher, Karl Farkas) Kammerspiele 27 June

1924 **Küsse am Mitternacht** (Katscher, Farkas) Kammerspiele 30 October

1925 **Frauenträume am Mitternacht** (Katscher) Carltheater 29 April

1927 **Die Lady vom Lido** (Katscher, Otto Florian) Johann Strauss-Theater 17 August

1929 **Riviera Express** (Géza Herczeg) Fővárosi Operettszinház, Budapest 30 March

1930 **Die Wunder-Bar** (Herczeg, Farkas) Kammerspiele 17 February

1931 **The Gay Princess** (Siegfried Geyer ad A P Herbert, Harold Simpson) Kingsway Theater, London, February

1931 **Traum-Express (Paris-Nizza)** revised *Riviera-Express* (Herczeg, Farkas, Fritz Grünbaum) Theater an der Wien 5 June

1932 **Essig und Öl** (w Geyer/Geyer, Paul Frank) Kammerspiele 2 September

1933 **Pech muss man haben** (Julius Berstl) Kammerspiele 24 February

1937 **Gyertyafényél** (*Bei Kerzenlicht*) (Geyer ad Farkas) Hungarian version by Armand Szántó, Mihály Szécsen (Royal Színház)

KATTNIGG, Rudolf (b Oberdorf, Switzerland, 9 April 1895; d Klagenfurt, Austria, 2 September 1955). Dusktime composer in the Viennese tradition.

Kattnigg began by studying law in Graz, but in the years after the war he turned his ambitions to the world of music and, after further studies in Vienna, he became first a répétiteur and then a theatrical conductor. He spent some years in this capacity in Innsbruck (1928–34) and then, after four years of fairly constant movement from one town and theatre to another, returned to Vienna and took up a teaching post at the Akademie für Musik.

During his years as a conductor in the provinces, Kattnigg had taken his first steps as a composer of Operette, and in 1937 his *Kaiserin Katharina* won a production at Berlin's Admiralspalast. However, his most successful piece was the lushly romantic Operette *Die Gräfin von Durazzo*, first produced in Leipzig but later, as *Balkanliebe*, played widely in Germany and Austria. In 1942 he composed a three-act fairytale piece as a Christmas entertainment for the Vienna Opera, in 1949 he supplied the score for an Operette, *Bel Ami*, based on the work by de Maupassant, in which Johannes Heesters, as the hero of the title, and Gretl Schörg starred at Vienna's Raimundtheater, and in 1953 turned out an opera, *Donna Miranda*. A final piece for the musical stage, *Rendezvous um Mitternacht*, was produced posthumously at the Raimundtheater in 1956.

Kattnigg was conductor of the Wiener Symphoniker and Opernhaus orchestra from 1939 and also wrote orchestral and chamber music and several film scores, including the arrangement of Suppé's music for the 1953 biopic *Hab ich nur deine Liebe*.

1936 **Der Prinz von Thule** (Oskar Walleck, 'Erik Kahr') Stadttheater, Basel 13 December

1937 **Kaiserin Katharina** (Hans Fritz Beckmann, Paul Beyer) Admiralspalast, Berlin 3 February

1937 **Die Gräfin von Durazzo** (aka *Balkanliebe*) ('Erik Kahr', Bruno Hardt-Warden) Neues Operetten-Theater, Leipzig 22 December

1938 **Mädels vom Rhein** (Gustav Quedtenfeldt) Staatstheater, Bremen

1939 **Die Mädel von St Goar** (Quedtenfeldt) Staatstheater, Bremen 4 February

1941 **Der Feldprediger** musical revision of Millöcker's Operette (Opernhaus, Nuremberg)

1942 **Hansi fliegt zum Negerkral** (Hera Kassmekat) Opernhaus 16 December

1949 **Bel Ami** (Fritz Eckhardt) Raimundtheater 18 January

1956 **Rendezvous um Mitternacht** (Otto Emmerich Groh) Raimundtheater 20 May

KAUFMAN, George S[imon] (b Pittsburgh, 14 November 1889; d New York, 2 June 1961). Comic playwright and stage director who had several hits, in each capacity, in the musical theatre.

Originally a newspaper writer in Washington and then in New York, at first as a humourist and later as a drama critic, Kaufman began to write for the theatre in his twenties and had his first important success with the play *Dulcy* (1922, w Marc Connelly). He and Connelly subsequently collaborated on other successful plays (*To the Ladies*, *Merton of the Movies*) before being commissioned to write what was for Kaufman a first musical play. The producer of the piece had as a predestined title a not-very-novel joke which had served, notably, as a plot device in Harry Paulton's famous play *Niobe*, and wanted the piece called *Helen of Troy, New York* (there is a place called Troy in New York state). If the piece's book was rather funnier than the title, it was still not enough to give what was basically a formula musical comedy more than a 191-performance run, a record which was pale beside those the pair had compiled with their three hit plays.

Kaufman joined Robert Benchley to supply sketches for Irving Berlin's *Music Box Revue* (1923) and ventured with Connelly on a second musical, *Be Yourself*, based on an unproduced play called *Miss Moonshine* which the two had written in the years before their first success. With the great British comedian G P Huntley starring as the satirized Joseph Peabody Prescott alongside veteran Georgia Caine and the dances of Queenie Smith and Jack Donahue, it was noticed as having 'a screamingly funny first act', but apparently little thereafter. Its story of a Tennessee feud was seen only 93 times on Broadway.

As the play hits continued through the mid-1920s (*Beggar on Horseback*, *The Butter and Egg Man*, *The Royal Family*), Kaufman also produced his first musical comedy successes – the scripts for the Marx Brothers' vehicles *The Cocoanuts* and *Animal Crackers* – but in between these two he ventured an interesting failure. *Strike Up the Band* was a burlesque-satire which struck out at politicians, businessmen, warmongers-for-profit, other peripheral moneygrubbers and anyone else who had a whiff of 'have' about him, to the accompaniment of a set of Gershwin songs. It didn't interest Longbranch, New Jersey, and was closed down on the road, but three years later, with some of its pricklier thorns removed, it won a showing on Broadway. It ran for precisely the same time as had *Helen of Troy, New York*.

In spite of this, the following year Kaufman, collaborator Morrie Ryskind, and the Gershwins tried another piece in a similar vein. *Of Thee I Sing*, a gently but highly comical burlesque of the American political system and people, gauged public and critical taste rather better than had *Strike Up the Band*. It was rewarded with a long Broadway run, a Pulitzer Prize award, and respected places in

American musical theatre history and on the fringe of the standard repertoire.

Around the same time Kaufman turned out one of his most famous plays, *Once in a Lifetime* (w Moss Hart), and contributed further and with some success to revue (*The Little Show*, 1929, *The Bandwagon*, 1931), but, in the musical theatre, things went less well. The success of *Of Thee I Sing* was not repeated when, in 1933, he and Ryskind essayed a musequel, *Let 'em Eat Cake*, nor, after further play successes (*Merrily We Roll Along, Stage Door, You Can't Take it with You*), when he went to the well yet again, with another Presidential musical, *I'd Rather Be Right* (1937).

Kaufman made several further, if intermittent, musical theatre ventures in the next 20 years, turning out a comical if perhaps rather too in-jokey rewrite of *HMS Pinafore* in a Hollywood setting, and a confused and confusing flop called *Park Avenue* (1946). He collaborated, with rather better results, on the musicalization of the cold-war tale of *Ninotchka* as *Silk Stockings*, as well as contributing to such revues as *Sing Out the News* (1938, w Hart) and *Seven Lively Arts* (1944), whilst continuing, all the time, to make play hits with such pieces as *The Man Who Came to Dinner* and *The Solid Gold Cadillac*.

Parallel to his life as a playwright, Kaufman led a second career, virtually as successful, as a director, principally of plays, but also of some musicals. He staged *Of Thee I Sing, Let 'em Eat Cake, Hollywood Pinafore* and *Park Avenue* of his own works, and also Irving Berlin's 1932 *Face the Music* (w Hassard Short) and, with the most singular success, the original production of *Guys and Dolls* (1950).

Two of Kaufman's plays have been adapted to the American musical stage with rather less success than their originals: *The Man Who Came to Dinner* became *Sherry!* (Alvin Theater, 27 March 1967, Laurence Rosenthal/James Lipton), whilst *Merrily We Roll Along* was musicalized under the same title by George Furth and Stephen Sondheim (Alvin Theater 16 November 1981). *You Can't Take it with You* was produced as a musical play in Budapest under the title *Így élni ... Ö!* (Magyar Színház, 26 June 1948, music Charles Bradley).

1923 **Helen of Troy, New York** (Harry Ruby/Bert Kalmar/w Marc Connelly) Selwyn Theater 19 June
1924 **Be Yourself** (Lewis Gensler, Milton Schwarzwald/w Ira Gershwin/w Connelly) Harris Theater 3 September
1925 **The Cocoanuts** (Irving Berlin) Lyric Theater 8 December
1927 **Strike Up the Band** (George Gershwin/I Gershwin) Broadway Theater, Longbranch, NJ 29 August
1928 **Animal Crackers** (Kalmar, Ruby/w Morrie Ryskind) 44th Street Theater 23 October
1930 **Strike Up the Band** revised version w Ryskind Times Square Theater 14 January
1931 **Of Thee I Sing** (G Gershwin/I Gershwin/w Ryskind) Music Box Theater 26 December
1933 **Let 'em Eat Cake** (G Gershwin/I Gershwin/w Ryskind) Imperial Theater 21 October
1937 **I'd Rather Be Right** (Richard Rodgers/Lorenz Hart/w Moss Hart) Alvin Theater 2 November
1945 **Hollywood Pinafore** adaptation of *HMS Pinafore* Alvin Theater 31 May
1946 **Park Avenue** (Arthur Schwartz/I Gershwin/w Nunnally Johnson) Shubert Theater 4 November
1955 **Silk Stockings** (Cole Porter/w Leueen McGrath, Abe Burrows) Imperial Theater 24 February

Biographies: Goldstein, M: *George S Kaufman: His Life, His Theatre* (OUP, New York, 1979); Teichmann, H: *George S*

Kaufman: an Intimate Portrait (Angus & Robertson, London, 1973); Meredith, S: *George S Kaufman and His Friends* (Doubleday, New York, 1974)

KAYE, Danny [KOMINSKY, David Daniel] (b Brooklyn, NY, 18 January 1913; d Los Angeles, 3 March 1987). Lightning-lipped comedian who starred in a handful of musicals.

Previously part of a vaudeville act, The Three Terpsichoreans, the quick-fire comic first appeared on Broadway in *The Straw Hat Revue* (1939), but made his musical theatre name as the effeminate Russell Paxton in *Lady in the Dark*, in which he performed the frenetic catalogue of composers' names entitled 'Tschaikowsky'. He subsequently starred in the Dorothy and Herbert Fields/Cole Porter musical *Let's Face It* (1941, Jerry Walker) performing a similar piece of material, interpolated this time ('Melody in Four F', later included in the film *Up in Arms*), before moving on to a starring film career. Kaye returned to the stage in 1970 to star in the Rodgers and Charnin musical *Two By Two*, appearing as a 600-year-old Noah faced with worldly problems and an ark. Much in the way of the old-time musical comedians, he turned the show into a festival of individual gags (aided for a while, following an accident, by a wheelchair and a plaster-cast) for the year of its run.

Kaye's musical film credits included the title-rôle of Frank Loesser's *Hans Christian Andersen*, a score later turned several times into a stage musical.

Biography: Singer, K: *The Danny Kaye Saga* (Hale, London, 1957), Richards, D: *The Life Story of Danny Kaye* (Convoy, London, 1949); Freedland, M: *The Secret Life of Danny Kaye* (St Martin's Press, W H Allen, 1985)

KEARNS, Allen (b Brockville, Ontario, 1893; d Albany, NY, 20 April 1956). A juvenile and leading man on both sides of the Atlantic in the 1910s and 1920s.

The Canadian actor and singer worked as a child in Gus Edwards's juvenile troupe, and first appeared on Broadway as a teenager, in the chorus of the Marie Dressler vehicle *Tillie's Nightmare* (1910), and in very minor parts in Jerome Kern's *The Red Petticoat* (1912, Slim) and the sweetly slightweight *Miss Daisy* (1914, Fred). After a stint as a second-class cook in the navy during the war, he returned with a supporting rôle in uniform (Private Barker) in the short-lived *Come Along* and then replaced Ward de Wolf as the young man forced to pretend to be a boy in the musical version of *The Magistrate*, here retitled *Good Morning, Judge* (1919).

He followed up in *Tickle Me* (1920, Jack Barton), *Tangerine* (1921, t/o Lee Loring), in the unfortunate Jimmy Powers show *The Little Kangaroo* (1922, Billy Irving), *Lady Butterfly* (1923, Billy Browning), and in the second lead of *Little Jessie James* (1923, Tommy Tinker) before having his first singing/light-comedy leading rôle in *Mercenary Mary* (1925, Jerry). He took the last, confirming step to leading-manhood playing Steve Burton, the rich man who falls for the dancing heroine (Queenie Smith) and who sings 'That Certain Feeling' in Gershwin's *Tip-Toes*. He played this piece in America and, opposite Dorothy Dickson, in Britain, took another jeune premier rôle, in Ziegfeld's production of *Betsy*, on Broadway and then returned to London for two more similar parts, in the short-lived import from Chicago *Castles in the Air* (Monty

Blair) and in the slightly more successful local musical, *Up with the Lark* (Freddy van Bozer).

Broadway gave Kearns some better quality stuff than these with the leading juvenile/romantic rôles in *Funny Face* (1927, Peter Thurston, introducing 'He Loves and She Loves' and ''S Wonderful'), *Here's Howe* (1928, Billy Howe), *Hello Daddy* (1928, Lawrence Tucker) and, still well short of his fortieth birthday, in *Girl Crazy* (1930, Danny Churchill, singing 'Embraceable You' to and with Ginger Rogers). For some reason, this, one of his better rôles, was his last on Broadway. He appeared once more in London, as the hero of the not-very-successful *Love Laughs—!* (1935, Tony Thornton), but in later years confined himself largely to television appearances.

KEEL, Howard [KEEL, Harold Clifford] (b Gillespie, Ind, 13 April 1919). Handsome musical leading man largely lost to films and television.

The richly baritonic Keel succeeded to the rôles of Billy Bigelow (*Carousel*) and Curly (*Oklahoma!*) on Broadway and (still billed as 'Harold Keel') introduced the latter rôle to London audiences in 1947. Thereafter he was seen exclusively in film musicals for almost a decade, appearing notably in the screen versions of *Annie Get Your Gun* (1948, Frank Butler), *Show Boat* (1951, Gaylord Ravenal), *Kiss Me, Kate* (1953, Fred), *Rose Marie* (1954, Jim Kenyon) and *Kismet* (1955, Hajj). His combination of heroic singing, impressive physique and willingness for a comic touch helped to steam his image onto these rôles forever for much of the cinema-going world. He also played the leading male rôles of the screen's *Calamity Jane* (1953) and *Seven Brides for Seven Brothers* (1954), both pieces later to be remade as stage musicals.

On the stage, he did not find the same kind of opportunities. He appeared in a further production of *Carousel* (1957), as the raffish and vengeful hero of Harold Arlen's *Saratoga* (1959, Clint Maroon), succeeded Richard Kiley as the leading man of *No Strings* (1963), and performed regionally in such pieces as *Kiss Me, Kate, South Pacific, Camelot, Show Boat, On a Clear Day You Can See Forever, I Do! I Do!*, and *Man of La Mancha*, creating his last stage rôle as the star of an unsuccessful musical based on Henry James's *The Ambassadors* (*Ambassador*, London 1971, New York 1972).

His subsequent television success as the older love interest of the serial *Dallas* brought him a second period of fame which included concert tours as a vocalist, but no further musical-theatre rôles either on Broadway or in London.

KEELER, Ruby [KEELER, Ethel Hilda] (b Halifax, Nova Scotia, 25 August 1909; d Rancho Mirage, Calif, 28 February 1993). Dancing ingénue of the musical screen.

After some small beginnings as a dancer in Broadway musicals, starting with *The Rise of Rosie O'Reilly* (1923) at the age of 14, then in increasingly important rôles in *Bye, Bye Bonnie* (1927, Ruby), *Lucky* (1927, Mazie), *The Sidewalks of New York* (1927, Mamie) and *Show Girl* (1929, Dixie Dugan), in which she featured the show's most successful song, 'Liza (all the clouds'll roll away)', the small and young-looking Miss Keeler came to international fame as the show-must-go-on heroine of the film *42nd Street* (1933). Her career in the 1930s was made in similar

Warner Brothers films (*Gold Diggers of 1933, Dames, Go Into Your Dance*) in which her frenetic tap-dancing and angelic features combined to make her the ideal girl of a hundred thousand households next door. She made a return to the musical stage in later life star-billed in Harry Rigby's revival of *No, No, Nanette*, performing a dancer's 'I Want to Be Happy' and 'Take a Little One Step' in the rôle of Sue.

Miss Keeler was married for a period to performer Al Jolson.

KELLY, Edwin (b Dublin, Ireland, 1831; d Adelaide, Australia, 1 January 1899).

The American minstrel team of Edwin Kelly and Francis Leon had a considerable success in America during the 1860s and 1870s, performing high-class minstrel programmes of which the usual highlight was a spectacularly produced burlesque of a currently popular show, featuring the square and sober-looking Kelly, the interlocutor of the troupe, in the leading male rôles and the blondly softer and shorter Leon as prima donna. Their burlesques included a home-made version of *The Black Crook, The Grand Dutch-S, La Belle LN, Barber-Blu, Orphée, Frow-Frow, Cinder-Leon, Kill Trovatore* and *Ginnevieve de Graw*, and in 1870 they presented their version of Hervé's burlesque *Le Petit Faust* (with Leon as Marguerite) before the show itself reached America. They later added such opérettes as Offenbach's *Lischen et Fritzchen, Ba-ta-clan, Monsieur Choufleuri* and *La Rose de Saint-Flour*, Suppé's *Die schöne Galathee* and Legouix's *The Crimson Scarf* (*La Tartane*) to their repertoire, but still played these in their usual, genuinely burlesque manner with Leon as the feminine star. In this way, they introduced a number of important French opéra-bouffe pieces to the American theatre.

In spite of several attempts, various alliances, and a genuine popularity, the pair did not manage to establish themselves permanently in New York where competition was high (Kelly was acquitted after shooting and killing the brother of a rival manager in 1867, and in 1872 their theatre was burned down), and they spent part of their year on the road. In 1878 Hayman and Hiscocks took them to the south Pacific where, after introducing their programmes – including such pieces as *M Choufleuri, Belles of the Kitchen, Galatea, La Rose de Saint-Flour*, their own musical comedy *His Grace, the Duke* and a burlesque of *Norma*, a number of these new to Australia – in Sydney, Melbourne, the Australian provinces and New Zealand with great success, they won a triumph and a certain notoriety when they produced early pirated versions of *HMS Pinafore* and later *The Sorcerer*, played in the burlesque manner. When J C Williamson came on the scene with the legal rights to the pieces, Kelly negotiated to sublet those rights for certain areas, but shortly afterwards the Kelly and Leon team split up.

Leon returned, at first, to America whilst Kelly remained in Australia and, after attempts at launching further minstrel entertainments, he mounted a comic opera company playing straight versions of *Fatinitza* (Kantschukoff), *Giroflé-Girofla* (Mourzouk), *La Fille de Madame Angot* (Larivaudière) and *Les Cloches de Corneville* (Gaspard). He soon renounced management, however, joining up with Williamson, Garner and Musgrove's

Plate 148. **Edwin Kelly** *as Rocco in J C Williamson's production of* La Mascotte.

powerful comic-opera company to play the Major General and later the Pirate King (*Pirates of Penzance*), Major Murgatroyd and later Grosvenor (*Patience*), Monthabor (*La Fille du tambour-major*), Gaspard (*Les Cloches de Corneville*), Merimac (*Olivette*), Rocco (*La Mascotte*), Mincing Lane (*Billee Taylor*) and other leading character/comic rôles in opéra-bouffe and -comique.

He continued a flourishing comic-opera career in Australia through the 1880s, starring with Majeroni and Wilson's company as the Black Rover in Luscombe Searelle's local comic opera *Isidora* and Pomposo in his *Estrella*, and being seen as Brother Pelican in *Falka*, as Sir Lothbury Jones in *The Merry Duchess*, Don Jose in *Manteaux Noirs*, Lotteringhi in *Boccaccio*, Nick Vedder in *Rip van Winkle*, King Portico in Gilbert and Clay's *Princess*

Toto, Pietro in *Les Brigands*, the old Prisoner in *La Périchole*, Larivaudière in *La Fille de Madame Angot*, Montefiore in *Maritana*, the Beadle in *Nell Gwynne*, Mourzouk in *Giroflé-Girofla*, Hannibal Grosgrain in *Babiole*, the Chevalier de Brabazon in *Erminie*, the Mikado, Nicholas in *Marjorie*, Bumpus in *Charity Begins at Home* as well as in pantomime (King Broken-down-o in *Cinderella*, Fitzwarren in *Dick Whittington*), before gradually turning more and more to straight theatre rôles.

In the 1890s, whilst still appearing on the musical stage (Baron Badde in *Randolph the Reckless* with Coppin, Trenchard in *Little Jack Sheppard*), he became a regular elderly character player with J C Williamson, George Darrell, Bland Holt, Arthur Garner, Mrs Brown Potter and Kyrle Bellew and other major companies, and he died, still in harness, whilst on tour in Adelaide, 'from failure of the heart's action'.

Without specific credit, Kelly wrote, co-wrote and adapted a number of the burlesque pieces and songs played by the Kelly and Leon troupe, notably *His Grace the Duke*, a musical comedy featuring Leon as a husband-hunting dame and Kelly as a theatrical manager whom she mistakes for a Duke, which the company announced as having been played for over 1000 performances in America and Australia.

Kelly's eldest son, who worked under the name of Edwin Lester, was a member of the Kelly and Leon troupe and went with his father to Australia, where he appeared in the minstrels (Babylas in *Choufleuri*, Ganymede in *Galatea*, Smith in *La Rose de St-Flour* etc), the short-lived opera company (Julian in *Fatinitza* etc) and in other musical (*Isidora* etc) and non-musical shows. He remained in Australia with his father and step-mother and in later life became a popular and praised character actor there.

1871 **Matrimony** Hooley's Opera House 9 January
1875 **His Grace, the Duke** Darling's Opera House 1 May

KELLY, Gene [KELLY, Eugene Curran] (b Pittsburgh, 23 August 1912). Screen dance star with a handful of theatre credits.

Kelly made his first appearance on the Broadway stage as a dancer in *Leave it to Me!* (1938), played in revue, and directed the shows at the Diamond Horseshoe before he was cast in the title-rôle of the original production of *Pal Joey* (1940, 'I Could Write a Book'). The following year he choreographed the musical *Best Foot Forward*, but from 1942 his career was made in films where he became the epitome of the Hollywood song-and-dance man. He took starring rôles in a long series of movies which included celluloid versions of *Dubarry Was a Lady*, *Anchors Aweigh*, *The Three Musketeers*, *On the Town* (also co-director) and *Brigadoon*, as well as the made-for-film musicals *The Pirate*, *An American in Paris*, *Singin' in the Rain*, *Les Girls* and many others.

He later returned to the musical theatre intermittently as a director (*Flower Drum Song*) and, regionally, as a performer (*Take Me Along*, 1974 etc), and in 1969 he directed the film version of *Hello, Dolly!*.

Biography: Hirschhorn, C: *Gene Kelly* (W H Allen, London, 1974)

KENNEY, Charles Lamb (b 1823; d London, 25 August 1881).

The son of James Kenney and the godson of Charles

Lamb (thus the name, which F C Burnand insisted 'did a great deal for him'), Kenney worked as a journalist from the age of 19, but still found time to become involved in all sorts of other projects, notably with de Lesseps on launching the scheme for the Suez canal, and with Joseph Paxton on organizing the transport services during the Crimean War. Kenney moved comfortably in high London literary circles, and he worked latterly as a dramatic author and a critic, writing a number of successful pieces for the West End stage, including the play *The Spitalfields Weaver* and the English versions of the operas *The Mock Doctor* (Gounod's *Le Medecin malgré lui*) and *L'Africaine* for the Theatre Royal, Covent Garden.

This theatre was also the venue for the landmark British production of Offenbach's *La Grande-Duchesse de Gérolstein* for which Kenney supplied the English version, a version which became the standard English text of this most popular of pieces and which brought his estate returns many years after his death. It also brought him, living, a series of further commissions for opéra-bouffe adaptations. 'Epigrammatically brilliant and invariably, because constitutionally, lazy', Kenney nevertheless published a number of works on a variety of subjects, which included *The Gates of the East*, a *Life and Letters of Balzac* and a biography of the composer Balfe.

His son, **Charles H KENNEY** (b 1857; d London, 18 September 1909), had a successful career as a performer, appearing as Flint in Lydia Thompson's London production of *The Sultan of Mocha* (1888), as the Mayor in *Rhoda* and as Favart in *Madame Favart* at the Avenue Theatre, as a dame in pantomime and burlesque, and on tour in *Newmarket*, *The American Heiress* and other musical and non-musical pieces. He also co-directed and played in Marie Lloyd's one attempt at a musical, *The ABC* (1898), in the provinces.

1867 **La Grande-Duchesse** English version (Theatre Royal, Covent Garden)
1870 **La Princesse de Trébizonde** English version (Gaiety Theatre)
1870 **Barbe-bleue** English version (Gaiety Theatre)
1871 **La Belle Hélène** English version (Gaiety Theatre)
1873 **The Wonderful Duck** (*Le Canard à deux becs*) English version (Opera Comique)
1875 **La Jolie Parfumeuse** English version (Birmingham)

KENNY, Sean (b Portroe, Ireland, 23 December 1932; d 11 June 1973).

Architect turned theatrical designer, Kenny made his name with the sets for Peter Coe's London production of *Lock Up Your Daughters* – a series of non-representational, skeletal constructions which served as a multiplicity of settings – and, most particularly, for Coe's subsequent *Oliver!* His collection of moving rostra and stairs, which came swiftly together in different groupings to make up the many settings of Bart and Dickens's tale, helped materially in keeping the impetus of the show's story going, and *Oliver!*'s scenery, re-used over and over in revival, was long quoted as an outstanding piece of theatre mechanics and design.

In the 1960s he then designed, amongst others, the productions of *Stop the World – I Want to Get Off* (London and New York), the hugely scenic *Blitz!*, *The Roar of the Greasepaint – the Smell of the Crowd* (New York), *Pickwick* (London and New York), *Maggie May* and *The Four*

Musketeers, by which time the qualities which had made his early work so interesting had, through repetition and imitation, themselves become clichés.

Kenny also worked on a number of theatre buildings, conceiving and designing his 'theatre of the future', the New London Theatre, from the ground up, on the site of the old Winter Garden Theatre. The theatre of the future seemed, for a long time, as if it had no future. Its many movable stage and auditorium parts lay idle for years before Cameron Mackintosh, already reponsible for successfully redisplaying Kenny's *Oliver!* sets to a new generation, put *Cats* into the New London. *Cats* not only utilized a number of Kenny's stage machines and concepts for the first time, it also virtually saved the theatre from dwindling away into non-use.

KENT, William (b St Paul, Minn, ?1886; d New York, 5 October 1945). Agile, spindle-shanked comedian who had more than a decade of starring rôles on the musical stage.

Kent began his career working in music-hall (Looey from Louisville in *The Athletic Girl*, 1905 etc) and in stock, where he was first noticed by Arthur Hammerstein. After a number of youthful years in regional and touring productions (*Miss Hook of Holland*, *Have a Heart*, *Look Who's Here* etc), he had his first Broadway rôle as the campy Hyperion Buncombe in Jerome Kern's *Toot-Toot!* (1918). There then followed a succession of larger comic parts in Broadway musicals: as the show-stealing, hen-pecked Uncle Toby alongside Nora Bayes in *Ladies First* (1919), the best man in a spot, Sam Benton in *Somebody's Sweetheart* (1919, until he walked out) and the comical hero, Dick Crawford, in *Pitter Patter* (1920), but he came to grief with the 'ultimate in intimate musicals' when Victor Herbert's *Oui Madame*, which featured him as a janitor singing about being 'Sincopated', folded out of town.

Kent took a rather plot-incidental rôle as Steve Simmons in the long-running *Good Morning, Dearie*, performing 'Sing Song Girl' and 'Melican Papa' and getting to imitate a Chinese waiter, and he played Hozier in support of Charles Ruggles's *Battling Butler* in the musical comedy of that title, before landing his most memorable rôle as the anything but Hard-Boiled Herman of Friml's *Rose Marie* (1924, 'Hard-Boiled Herman', 'Why Shouldn't We?'). He made a dumb decision when he elected to come out of *Rose Marie* to take the principal comedy rôle in an americanization of Lehár's *Frasquita* alongside opera star Geraldine Farrar, for it folded after one night out of town. But Kent was still riding high: in 1926 he took Walter Catlett's rôle of Watty Watkins alongside the Astaires in the London version of *Lady, Be Good!*, and in 1927 he shared the stage with the same pair as he created the part of the comical crook Duggsie Gibbs, in a double act with Victor Moore, in *Funny Face*.

He appeared as the phoney mountain climber Billings in a rip-off of *Going Up* called *Ups-a-Daisy* (1928), visited Australia to star in the revue *Clowns in Clover*, and then, on his return, landed another fine rôle as Ethel Merman's father in *Girl Crazy* (1930). His later Broadway shows and parts were less happy (*A Little Racketeer*, *Music Hath Charms*, *Revenge with Music*) although he toured and/or played regionally in such proven pieces as *Show Boat* (Cap'n Andy), *Blossom Time* (Tscholl), *The Merry Widow*

(Nisch), *Balalaika* (Nicki) and *Anything Goes* (Moonface) in the latter years of his career, being seen as Nisch, in his last appearance, in the year before his death.

KERKER, Gustave [Adolph] (b Westphalia, Germany, 28 February 1857; d New York, 29 June 1923). Prolific illustrator and botcher of Broadway shows who popped out one worldwide novelty hit show.

A descendant of a family of German musicians, Kerker was taken to America at the age of ten and settled with his family in Louisville, where he began his career in the theatre as an orchestral cellist. He subsequently became a theatrical conductor and at the same time began composing with an eye to the stage, and before long a regional touring production of his first operetta, *Cadets*, won the 22-year-old composer the notice of and a position with E E Rice, as musical director of his touring opéra-bouffe company.

Kerker's first engagement in New York, also under Rice, was as conductor at the Bijou Theater, and it was at that house that he had his first music presented on the Broadway stage. It took the form of some considerable interpolations in a successful adaptation of Lecocq's *Fleur de thé*, there played under the title *The Pearl of Pekin*. He continued to double as a composer and a conductor and, when he was subsequently engaged as musical director at the Casino Theater (1888), his own music straightaway began to find its way, in varying amounts, into the scores of most of the imported opérettes presented there. In 1890, he wrote his first full score to a libretto by Charles Alfred Byrne, the adaptor of *Fleur de thé*, and the resulting piece, a rip-off of Offenbach's *Les Bavards* entitled *Castles in the Air*, was produced by the De Wolf Hopper Comic Opera Company with a fine cast including Della Fox, Thomas Q Seabrooke, Marion Manola and the future Mrs Kerker, Rose Leighton, for a respectable three-months-plus Broadway run.

The young composer's name appeared nebulously on the bills of a mysterious Casino piece called *The Brazilian* which claimed to be the work of the then red-hot Francis Chassaigne, but it was several seasons before Kerker's next own Broadway musical, *Prince Kam*, a revised version of an extravaganza played for a fine season in Boston as *Venus* the previous year, was produced at the Casino in 1894. It proved to have rather less appeal for New York, whilst another effort called *Kismet*, with a libretto as deeply indebted to Offenbach's *L'Île de Tulipatan* as *Castles in the Air* had been to *Les Bavards*, lasted but three weeks on the Broadway stage. A second sizeable piece of botching for the Casino, a revamped *The Lady Slavey*, did rather better. Producer George Lederer had had this long-running English variety musical comedy rewritten to such an extent that little remained of the original show except its joyously comical Cinderella storyline and characters, and Kerker was responsible for the songs which replaced almost all of the original British score. If the new version did not in any way approach the original *Lady Slavey*'s vast success in Britain, it nevertheless did well enough, without the musical score gaining any particular kudos.

Kerker and his fellow 'adapter', Hugh McLellan, followed up their remade *The Lady Slavey* with a series of original musicals for the Casino, beginning with the revusical *In Gay New York* (1896) and continuing with the

musical comedy *An American Beauty*, featuring Lillian Russell in its title-rôle, the revue *The Whirl of the Town* (1897), and a jolly rag-bag of a variety musical, built on *Lady Slavey* lines and called *The Belle of New York*. *The Belle of New York* ('The Belle of New York', 'Teach Me How to Kiss', 'They All Follow Me') lasted only 56 performances at the Casino, but it pleased Boston much better and, when the Australian impresario George Musgrove took the gamble of transporting the show and its company to London, the piece became a novelty hit of huge proportions at the Shaftesbury Theatre, leading to years of productions throughout Europe and around the world where the piece was accepted as the epitome of the American musical-comedy stage.

Gaston Serpette's French vaudeville *La Demoiselle du téléphone* was given the same treatment as had been meted out to *The Lady Slavey* and Kerker supplied the Casino with one last revue, *Yankee Doodle Dandy* (1898), before, on the strength of the reputation won by *The Belle of New York* overseas, moving out to work with other managements and theatres. Amongst a series of mostly serviceable but scarcely memorable musicals, over the following years, he collaborated with Ludwig Englander and Reginald De Koven on the score for the successful extravaganza *The Man in the Moon* and composed a new show for his *Belle of New York* star, Edna May, *The Girl From Up There* (1900). Although this piece came nowhere near the earlier one in the extent of its success, it nevertheless had fair runs in both New York and London and was played in Vienna (*Die Eisjungfrau*), where *The Belle* had had the same kind of novelty effect as in London, in a revised version, with Kerker's score revamped by Josef Hellmesberger in much the same way Kerker had earlier botched so many Continental scores for the American stage.

Two further musicals, *The Tourists* (124 performances) and *The White Hen*, fared respectably in America and a third, *Schneeglöckchen*, premièred at Vienna's Theater an der Wien (which had previously hosted *Die Schöne von New-York*), during Kerker's short-lived attempt to establish himself as a composer in Europe, was later played on Broadway as *Two Little Brides* (1912) and also won a brief London showing in the same year as *The Grass Widows*. London also saw one of Kerker's less likely works, the little burlesque *Burning to Sing*, originally written for a benefit performance in New York, and subsequently mounted by J C Williamson in Australia and by George Edwardes, as part of a bill at the London Empire, as *Very Grand Opera* (1906). Kerker's last Broadway songs were heard in the revue *Some Party* the year before his death.

Kerker was often dismissed by commentators as a hack, and there is no doubt that he did his own cause little good by placing his melodies alongside those of the Continental masters of the period in his days of botching imported shows at the Casino Theater. However, unlike some interpolating songwriters, whose frankly simplistic music-hally songs, with their endlessly repeated phrases and refrains, could be relied on to catch only an undemanding ear, Kerker did in fact more or less aspire to writing in the same kind of strains as the composers he was 'supplementing'. As a result, he neither had 'hit' songs, nor, lacking the class of an Offenbach or a Lecocq, won any critical acclaim. His one hit, with *The Belle of New York*, may indeed have been due largely to the novelty of its style for overseas audiences, but its score alone contains sufficient in the way of lively, attractive music to show that Kerker at his uncomplicated best was indeed capable of writing both charming and catchy music.

Kerker was married to comic-opera contralto **Rose LEIGHTON** who had a prominent Broadway career in the last decades of the 19th century. She appeared with Lydia Thompson in *The Babes in the Wood* (1877, Queen of Tragedy), for Edward Rice in *Evangeline* and *HMS Pinafore* (Hebe), with Colville's company in *The Magic Slipper* (1879, Elfina), *Oxygen* and *Ill-Treated Travatore* and in a long series of comic-opera character rôles at New York's principal musical houses: Donna Olympia in *Donna Juanita*, Germaine in *Les Cloches de Corneville*, Gypsy Queen in *The Bohemian Girl*, Lady Allcash in *Fra Diavolo*, Palmatica in *The Beggar Student*, Lady Saphir in *Patience*, Thomas Darrell in *Little Jack Sheppard*, Mrs Privett in *Dorothy*, Catarina in *The Queen's Mate*, Buccametta in *A Trip to Africa*, Inez in *The Gondoliers*, Angélique in her husband's *Castles in the Air*, Aurore in *Giroflé-Girofla* etc.

1879 **Cadets** (Morris Warner) tour
1890 **Castles in the Air** (Charles Alfred Byrne) Broadway Theater 5 May
1893 **Venus** (Byrne, Louis Harrison) Park Theater, Boston, 11 September
1894 **Prince Kam, or a Trip to Venus** revised version of *Venus* Casino Theater 29 January
1894 **Kismet** (Richard F Carroll) Boston, July; Herald Square Theater, New York 12 September 1895
1896 **The Lady Slavey** (George Dance ad ?George Lederer, ?C M S McLellan) American version w new songs Casino Theater 3 February
1896 **In Gay New York** (McLellan) Casino Theater 25 May
1896 **An American Beauty** (McLellan) Casino Theater 28 December
1897 **The Belle of New York** (McLellan) Casino Theater 28 October
1897 **The Telephone Girl** (*La Demoiselle du téléphone*) (McLellan) American version w new songs Casino Theater 27 December
1899 **The Man in the Moon** (w Ludwig Englander, Reginald De Koven/Stanislaus Stange, Harrison) New York Theater 24 April
1900 **The Girl from Up There** (McLellan) Herald Square Theater 7 January
1902 **The Billionaire** (Harry B Smith) Daly's Theater 29 December
1903 **The Blonde in Black** (aka *The Sambo Girl*) (H B Smith) Knickerbocker Theater 8 June
1903 **Winsome Winnie** (Frederick Ranken) Casino Theater 1 December
1904 **Die Eisjungfrau** revised version of *The Girl from Up There* (ad Carl Lindau, Julius Wilhelm) Venedig in Wien, Vienna 3 June
1904 **Burning to Sing** (aka *Very Grand Opera*) (R H Burnside) 1 act Lyric Theater 10 May (Lamb's Club Gambol)
1905 **Der oberen Zehntausend** (Julius Freund) Metropoltheater, Berlin 24 April
1905 **In Lebensgefahr** (Freund) Walhalla-Theater, Berlin 1 November
1906 **The Social Whirl** (Joseph Herbert, Charles V Doty) Casino Theater 7 April
1906 **The Tourists** (Burnside) Majestic Theater 25 August
1905 **The Great Decide** (Glen MacDonough) 2 scenes Herald Square Theater 15 November
1907 **The White Hen** (aka *The Girl from Vienna*) (Paul West/Roderic C Penfold) Casino Theater 16 February
1907 **Fascinating Flora** (Burnside, Herbert) Casino Theater 20 May
1907 **The Lady from Lane's** (George Broadhurst) Lyric Theater 19 August
1910 **Schneeglöckchen** (A M Willner, Wilhelm) Theater an der Wien, Vienna 14 October

KERN, Jerome D[avid] (b New York, 27 January 1885; d New York, 11 November 1945).

A major figure in the American musical theatre for more than two decades, Jerome Kern composed, during a long career, music and songs for a wide variety of musical plays, ranging from additional material for the musical comedies of the heyday of the London Edwardian stage, through sets of numbers for the comedy musicals of the American wartime years, to full-scale scores for more musically ambitious projects such as *Show Boat* and *Sweet Adeline* and, in the 1930s, a kind of mid-Atlantic brand of operetta.

Kern became an adept pianist at an early age, was composing songs for school and amateur shows in his early teens, and had his first piece of music published at the age of 17, whilst he was working in the accounts section of the music publishers Edward Marks. He soon moved on to work for another publisher, Max Dreyfus, in a more congenial position as a staff writer (later becoming a junior partner in Dreyfus's T B Harms when an inheritance allowed him to buy a share in the firm), and in that capacity he had his first opportunity to write songs which could, in the rather haphazard manner of the time, be interpolated by the plugging publisher in Broadway musical comedies.

The first of these shows were three British imports, two of which, *An English Daisy* and *Mr Wix of Wickham*, had never made it to London's West End. Nevertheless, in the scrabble amongst American producers for the popular and fashionable British-made entertainments that were the backbone of Broadway entertainment at the turn of the century, they won themselves a showing in New York. The third was the post-Broadway tour of the London and New York success *The Silver Slipper*. Kern had two songs heard in *An English Daisy*, but by the time *Mr Wix* arrived in town no less than a dozen of his numbers had been crammed in to the score, virtually ousting the show's original songs. Neither show proved popular.

Kern then began an association with producer Charles Frohman, which resulted in his placing numbers in Frohman shows both on Broadway (*The Catch of the Season, The Babes and the Baron*) and in London (*The Beauty of Bath*), whither Kern moved temporarily in 1905. It was clearly not an exclusive engagement, as Kern was soon supplying songs to London's William Greet (*The Talk of the Town*) and George Edwardes (*The Spring Chicken, The Little Cherub*), and the composer's first song hit 'How'd You Like to Spoon with Me?' was first heard in the Shuberts' Broadway production of the imported *The Earl and the Girl*. In the years that followed, Kern continued to provide a flood of additional material for the Broadway and, occasionally, the London stage, contributing sometimes just one song, at others a significant part of the show's song schedule. Many of these shows were American versions of the fairly elastically constructed contemporary British musical comedies – *The Rich Mr Hoggenheimer, The Little Cherub, My Lady's Maid, The White Chrysanthemum, The Orchid, The Dairymaids, Kitty Grey, King of Cadonia, The*

Girls of Gottenberg, Our Miss Gibbs – whilst others were fresh-made American material (Kerker's *Fascinating Flora*, the revue *The Gay White Way*, *Fluffy Ruffles*, Julian Edwards's *The Girl and the Wizard*, *The Hen Pecks*, *The Echo* and a shortlived Shubert production called *The Golden Widow*). In the wake of *The Merry Widow*, some were also from the newly super-popular Austrian theatre (*A Waltz Dream*, *The Dollar Princess*, *The Gay Hussars*). By and large, these more consistently constructed and composed shows took interpolations much less happily. But several of the botched-in numbers nevertheless proved popular. In London George Edwardes's unsuccessful production of *A Waltz Dream*, *The Dollar Princess* and the Frohman costume piece *The Dashing Little Duke* all took in a ration of Kern songs.

In 1906 Seymour Hicks announced that he would write his next musical, *The Lady of Bath*, with Kern as his partner – but the composer ultimately contributed only a little music to Herbert Haines's score for *The Beauty of Bath*. Then in 1908 George Grossmith announced the forthcoming production of a musical comedy, *The President's Daughter*, to be written by his *Girls of Gottenberg* associate L E Berman and composed by Kern, but this project never saw stagelight. It was to be three further years before, after nearly a decade of successful if rarely enduring songwriting, Kern finally got billing for the first time as the principal composer of a show when he contributed to the revusical piece *La Belle Paree* not in London but in New York. Amongst the cast of *La Belle Paree* were included ex-Edwardes employees Jeannie Aylwin and Kitty Gordon, the newly arrived Hungarian starlet Mizzi Hajós (aka Mitzi) and the young Al Jolson and, played as an item on a Winter Garden programme, the piece had a respectable run. Although Kern would continue for many years to be one of Broadway's busiest interpolaters and, most notably, one of the more active botchers of the Continental Operetten which were then crowding onto American stages (Fall's *The Siren*, Berény's *The Girl from Montmartre*, Ziehrer's *The Kiss Waltz*, Heuberger's *The Opera Ball*, Jean Gilbert's *A Polish Wedding*, Eysler's *The Woman Haters*, Fall's *The Doll Girl* and *Lieber Augustin*, Victor Jacobi's *The Marriage Market*), he was at last on the road to becoming a successful show composer in his own right.

The success did not come immediately. The Shubert production of *The Red Petticoat*, an adaptation of a Rida Johnson Young play, failed in 61 Broadway performances, and a version of the French comedy *Une nuit de noces*, previously a hit play as *Oh, I Say!*, lasted just 68. It did, however, confirm the trend, already seen in Ivan Caryll's French-comedy-based shows (*The Pink Lady*, *Oh! Oh! Delphine* etc) and in George Grossmith's earlier adaptations of Paris's *Le Coquin de printemps* (*The Spring Chicken*) and *L'Amorçage* (*Peggy*), towards a very satisfying kind of musical comedy; a type of piece on the lines of the French vaudeville in which a coherent and, in these cases, proven farcical tale provided the solid theatrical-comical basis for a set of lively and up-to-date songs and ensembles in a show which had no extravagant production, no large 'beauty' chorus and/or glued-in 'pop' songs to cover weaknesses in plot, character or score. It was a kind of show to which the composer would return regularly over the following years.

At the same time, however, Kern was himself still supplying such 'pop' songs, although often of a more soigné character than those by some of his contemporaries – whether for use in Viennese Operetten (*The Laughing Husband*, *The Queen of the Movies*, *A Modern Eve*), home-made star vehicles (*When Claudia Smiles*, *When Dreams Come True*) or in the now-dwindling selection of imports from Britain (*The Sunshine Girl*, *The Girl from Utah*). It was one of these last, however, which gave him his most serious song hit since 'How'd You Like to Spoon with Me?' when Julia Sanderson and Donald Brian introduced 'They Didn't Believe Me' in Sidney Jones and Paul Rubens's score for *The Girl from Utah*. There were fine songs, too, in Kern's own next show, *Ninety in the Shade*, a ramshackle creation tailored for ageing stars Richard Carle and Marie Cahill that quickly went under, and the composer rescued the best of the slightly used numbers for later re-use. Re-use, in the meanwhile was already going on in London, where Frohman took up some Kern material to bolster Herman Darewski's score for J M Barrie's curious, revusical *Rosy Rapture*.

Kern's next Broadway assignment started out as another fairly routine botching job, but it ended up as something rather better. Hired to do over the music of *Mr Popple of Ippleton*, Paul Rubens's charming London comedy with songs, for the new, tiny and financially limited Princess Theater, he ended up composing an entire set of songs (with the inevitable interpolations) to a revised Guy Bolton libretto to effectively make up a nearly new and necessarily 'intimate' musical on the lines of *Oh, I Say!* and its predecessors. The piece was no longer *Mr Popple*, and in some ways it was less good than *Mr Popple*, but *Nobody Home* (as it was now called) proved an attractive, enjoyable, small-scale piece, and it caught on so happily that its producers, F Ray Comstock and Bessie Marbury, soon moved it to a larger house to cash in. Naturally, they also followed up *Nobody Home* with more of the same, and Kern was next hired to provide the songs for a musical adaptation of a successful farce, *Over Night*.

Whilst Kern busily manufactured short scores for two star-vehicles – Julian Eltinge's *Cousin Lucy* and Elsie Janis and Irene Bordoni's *Miss Information* – *Over Night* was turned into *Very Good Eddie* ('Babes in the Wood'), and Kern and his producers found themselves with a second, and more considerable, success on their hands, one which, once again, ultimately moved into a lucrative house. However, there was no sign as yet of making these 'intimate' musical shows larger. They retained their musical-farce-in-two-sets layout and their limited production values and they continued to be popular and fashionable in their little home and after it. However, Bolton and Kern were not involved with the next of Comstock's productions: they turned down his plan to musicalize Charles Hoyt's *A Milk White Flag*, and Kern instead supplied half a score to his old friend George Grossmith for his musical of the hugely successful French farce *Theodore & Co* (503 performances) at London's Gaiety Theatre, some interpolations for Klaw and Erlanger's version of Kálmán's Budapest show *Zsuzsi kisasszony* (*Miss Springtime*), and the scores for two new works which opened almost simultaneously on Broadway.

One of this pair was the first piece to come from what was to be a not very prolific but fondly remembered three-sided partnership, Kern–P G Wodehouse–Bolton. However, Henry Savage's production of their *Have a Heart* – written for the Princess Theater but given to Savage after a law suit – had only a disappointing two-month run on Broadway, and the fashionably dance-filled Shubert production of *Love o' Mike* did much better. Neither, however, topped *Very Good Eddie*, and the new trio had to wait for a return to the Princess Theater for that kind of success. Back in the cradle of the small-scale musical they together provided Comstock with the two best pieces written for his little house: *Oh, Boy!* (1917, 'Till the Clouds Roll By'), and *Leave it to Jane* (1917, 'The Siren's Song', 'The Crickets are Calling') which arrived before *Oh, Boy!* had done its run and ended up, probably to its disadvantage, being played at the Longacre Theater instead of at the little house whose kind of entertainment it characterized. When *Oh, Boy!* was done, the team were ready with another delightful hit to take its place in *Oh, Lady! Lady!!*, and then, to all intents and purposes, the little series which had looked so promising halted. Kern split from the team, and after two more productions Comstock gave up intimate musicals to continue with pieces like the vastly spectacular *Mecca* (1920).

Kern, who had, in the meanwhile, contributed to the unhappy Dillingham revue *Miss 1917*, moved on through several unexceptional works – *Toot-Toot!* and a Mitzi-vehicle called *Head Over Heels* for Savage, *Rock-a-Bye Baby*, a version of the successful if rather distasteful Margaret Mayo play *Baby Mine* for the Selwyns, and *She's a Good Fellow* for Dillingham – before suffering the indignity, for the first time in his long and full career, of having a show fold on the road. It was a reunion with Bolton and Comstock, an adaptation of the hugely successful farce *Brewster's Millions* apparently intended to carry on the Princess Theater line of shows, and it ground to a halt after three weeks on the road.

Kern bounced back quickly. His delightful score to Anne Caldwell's adaptation of Alexandre Bisson's *Le Controlleur des Wagons-lits* as *The Night Boat* ('Whose Baby Are You?', 'Good Night Boat', 'Left All Alone Again Blues') helped materially towards a 313 performance Broadway run, before, following another brief interlude writing for revue with the indifferent *Hitchy Koo of 1920*, he moved to an ever bigger success with the winsome tale of *Sally* (1920). Ziegfeld's favourite star Marilyn Miller sang of being 'A Wild Rose' and duetted that one should 'Look for the Silver Lining' to enormous effect, and *Sally* gave Kern his most substantial international hit up to that time.

It was a level of attainment which could not come every year, and in fact it was seven years before an equivalent triumph again came his way. Those years, nevertheless, brought forth some highly agreeable results and some happy songs. He composed the scores for two London musicals for George Grossmith of which *The Cabaret Girl* proved the better, and he took part in no less than five further collaborations with Ms Caldwell. Of these, *Good Morning, Dearie* ran for 347 performances and ended Kern up in court, charged (at the eventual cost of $250) with plagiarizing the hit song 'Dardanella' for his 'Ka-lu-a'; *The Bunch and Judy*, in spite of the Astaires, folded in 63 nights; *The City Chap* did no better; and two pieces for Fred Stone, *Stepping Stones* and *Criss-Cross*, if less distinguished than the comedian's best and earlier shows, nevertheless

served his purposes. A final, disappointing attempt to team once more with Bolton and Wodehouse in *Sitting Pretty* (95 performances), *Lucky* (71 performances) and *Dear Sir* (14 performances) resulted in three straightforward failures. Amongst this mixed bag, however, the most sizeable success amongst Kern's new shows of this period was Dillingham's production of *Sunny* (1925), another Marilyn Miller vehicle, which topped 500 Broadway performances, brought 'Who?', 'Sunny' and 'Two Little Bluebirds' to the standards list, and which followed *Sally* on to the international circuits without having quite the same qualities or the same success.

Kern had for many years threatened to go 'serious', to abandon foxtrots and one-steps for more dramatically and lyrically substantial forms. When he did, it proved to be in combination with a superlative text by the librettist of the textually indifferent *Sunny*, Oscar Hammerstein II, and the most extravagantly fearless of producers, Florenz Ziegfeld. The result was *Show Boat* – not only perhaps the most artistically complete and impressive, but also the most popularly enduring Broadway musical show of its era. In *Show Boat* ('Ol' Man River', 'Can't Help Lovin' Dat Man o' Mine', 'Bill', 'Make Believe' etc), Kern turned out a score which was in a different mode to the light-footed dance-and-songs of *Sally* or *Sunny* and proved, once for all, that this songwriter had more than one colour of ink in his pen.

After *Show Boat* he never turned back to his old style of songwriting as musical theatre. A rather limp Scottish operetta, *Blue Eyes*, written for London before *Show Boat*'s opening, had a fair life without leaving Britain, but for New York henceforth Kern supplied more consciously substantial fodder. *Sweet Adeline*, a rather downbeat vehicle for *Show Boat* star Helen Morgan, produced the plangent 'Why Was I Born?' but fell victim to the stock market crash. However, two considered attempts to write operetta in the Continental manner did better. The Parisian love story of *The Cat and the Fiddle* ('She Didn't Say "Yes"', 'The Night Was Made for Love') was rather happier libretto material than the saccharine operettic tale of *Music in the Air* ('I've Told Ev'ry Little Star'), but both produced some memorable music, had fine runs, foreign productions and considerable lives thereafter. Kern struck libretto problems again in the uninteresting frock-shop tale of *Roberta* (in the après-*Show Boat* period, libretti mattered more than before), but the piece's score simply rustled with good things ('Yesterdays', 'Smoke Gets in your Eyes', 'I'll Be Hard to Handle', 'You're Devastating') from a man who, 30 years into his career, seemed to be enjoying himself exploring a new register of musical theatre. *Roberta*'s future, after a disappointing 259 Broadway performances, turned out to be in films rather than in further stage productions.

The same went for Kern. Whilst London's *Three Sisters* (1934, 'I Won't Dance'), the St Louis Municipal Opera's *Gentlemen Unafraid* (1938) and Broadway's *Very Warm for May* (1939, 'All the Things You Are') failed in the theatre, Kern was having a simultaneous success (mostly) with film versions of *Roberta* (1933) and *Show Boat* (1936) and the scores for such original films as *Swing Time* (1936), *High, Wide and Handsome* (1937) and *Joy of Living* (1938). This celluloid success continued (mostly) with *One Night in the Tropics* (1940), *You Were Never Lovelier* (1942), *Cover Girl*

(1944), *Can't Help Singing* (1944) and his final, posthumously released film, *Centennial Summer* (1946). At the time of his death, he was preparing to embark on one more Broadway score, a score to a Herbert and Dorothy Fields libretto about the sharp-shooting Annie Oakley.

Only one Jerome Kern work, *Show Boat*, has remained actively in the standard repertoire – a repertoire which has always preferred the musically more substantial, operetta kind of musical to the lighthearted comedy-with-songs style of piece to which Kern devoted most of his career. On the other hand, the most popular of his individual show songs have held a continuing and prominent place in the recital and recording repertoire. In recent years, however, his work – again, most often the songs separated from their shows rather than whole shows – has been given detailed and appreciative attention by theatre writers and by performers, and his songs have been used as the material for several of the rash of compilation shows which have been seen on musical stages. This attention has come mainly in America where Kern has become perceived as 'the recognized father of the modern [American] musical theatre' and 'the father of the American popular theater song'. In an era when the kind of songwriting which he practised, most particularly in the first 20 years of the century, has virtually ceased, a large number of his previously forgotten show numbers, which had been hidden behind those that became standards, have been brought out, and performed and recorded with an energy devoted to few other composers.

If tags such as those quoted, and the others which have been glibly attached to his works – notably *Show Boat* and the song 'They Didn't Believe Me' – have a simplistic and, therefore, debatable ring to them, they cannot mask the fact that Kern supplied the musical theatre, principally in America but also in Britain, with some of the happiest show songs of the 1910s and 1920s, helped produce one of the great romantic stage musicals of all time with his score to *Show Boat*, and continued, virtually to the end of his life to give of his very best material in a way that so many other writers, after a handful of successes, have failed to do. To call him the 'father of the modern [American] musical' is to do poor service both to those who preceded and those who were contemporary with him, but if a sole paternity has to be established, Kern would certainly have to be queueing for a blood test.

1911 **La Belle Paree** (Edward Madden et al/Edgar Smith) Winter Garden Theater 20 March

1912 **The Red Petticoat** (Paul West/Rida Johnson Young) Daly's Theater 13 November

1913 **Oh, I Say!** (aka *Their Wedding Night*) (Harry B Smith/Sydney Blow, Douglas Hoare) Casino Theater 30 October

1915 **Ninety in the Shade** (H B Smith/Guy Bolton) Knickerbocker Theater 15 January

1915 **Nobody Home** (Paul Rubens ad Bolton) Princess Theater 20 April

1915 **Rosy Rapture, the Pride of the Beauty Chorus** (w Herman Darewski, John Crook/'F W Mark' (E V Lucas)/J M Barrie) Duke of York's Theatre, London 22 March

1915 **Cousin Lucy** (Schuyler Greene/Charles Klein) George M Cohan Theater 29 August

1915 **Miss Information** (Paul Dickey, Charles W Goddard) George M Cohan Theater 5 October

1915 **Very Good Eddie** (Greene/Philip Bartholomae, Bolton) Princess Theater 22 December

1916 **Theodore & Co** (w Ivor Novello/Adrian Ross, Clifford Grey/H M Harwood, George Grossmith) Gaiety Theatre, London 4 September

1917 **Have a Heart** (P G Wodehouse/Bolton) Liberty Theater 11 January

1917 **Love o' Mike** (ex *Girls Will Be Girls*) (H B Smith/T Sidney) Shubert Theater 15 January

1917 **Oh, Boy!** (Wodehouse/Bolton) Princess Theater 11 January

1917 **Leave it to Jane** (Wodehouse/Bolton) Longacre Theater 28 August

1918 **Oh, Lady! Lady!!** (Wodehouse/Bolton) Princess Theater 1 February

1918 **Toot-Toot!** (Edgar A Woolf, Berton Braley) George M Cohan Theater 11 March

1918 **Rock-a-Bye Baby** (Herbert Reynolds/Woolf, Margaret Mayo) Astor Theater 22 May

1918 **Head Over Heels** (Woolf) George M Cohan Theater 29 August

1919 **She's a Good Fellow** (ex *A New Girl*) (Anne Caldwell) Globe Theater 5 May

1919 **Zip Goes a Million** (B G De Sylva/Bolton) Worcester Theater, Worcester, Mass 8 December

1920 **The Night Boat** (Caldwell) Liberty Theater 2 February

1920 **Sally** (Clifford Grey/Bolton) New Amsterdam Theater 21 December

1921 **Good Morning, Dearie** (Caldwell) Globe Theater 1 November

1922 **The Cabaret Girl** (Wodehouse/George Grossmith) Winter Garden Theatre, London 19 September

1922 **The Bunch and Judy** (Caldwell, Hugh Ford) Globe Theater 28 November

1923 **The Beauty Prize** (Wodehouse/Grossmith) Winter Garden Theatre, London 5 September

1923 **Stepping Stones** (Caldwell, R H Burnside) Globe Theater 6 November

1924 **Sitting Pretty** (Wodehouse/Bolton) Fulton Theater 8 April

1924 **Dear Sir** (Howard Dietz/Edgar Selwyn) Times Square Theater 23 September

1925 **Sunny** (Hammerstein, Otto Harbach) New Amsterdam Theater 22 September

1925 **That City Chap** (Caldwell/James Montgomery) Liberty Theater 26 October

1926 **Criss Cross** (Caldwell, Harbach) Globe Theater 12 October

1927 **Lucky** (Harbach, Bert Kalmar) New Amsterdam Theater 22 March

1927 **Show Boat** (Oscar Hammerstein) Ziegfeld Theater 27 December

1928 **Blue Eyes** (Graham John/Bolton) Piccadilly Theatre, London 27 April

1929 **Sweet Adeline** (Hammerstein) Hammerstein Theater 2 September

1931 **The Cat and the Fiddle** (Harbach) Globe Theater 15 October

1932 **Music in the Air** (Hammerstein) Alvin Theater 8 November

1933 **Roberta** (Harbach) New Amsterdam Theater, 18 November

1934 **Three Sisters** (Hammerstein) Theatre Royal, Drury Lane, London 9 April

1938 **Gentlemen Unafraid** (Hammerstein, Harbach) Municipal Opera, St Louis 3 June

1939 **Very Warm for May** (Hammerstein) Alvin Theater 17 November

Biography: Bordman, G: *Jerome Kern* (OUP, New York 1980); Lamb, A: *Jerome Kern in Edwardian England* (ISAM, City University of New York 1985) etc

Plate 149. **Henri Kéroul** *and Albert Barré's* Une nuit de noces *made up into the musical* Telling the Tale *in London. Marie Blanche starred as Sidonie de Matisse and her gentlemen included Arthur Margetson, Bruce Winston, C Denier Warren, Douglas Blore and Gerald Kirby.*

KÉROUL, Henri [QUEYROUL, Henri] (b Corte, Corsica, 8 February 1857; d Paris, 14 April 1921).

The successful author of many Parisian songs, libretti and plays, Kéroul confined his musical theatre work largely to the early part of his career, during which he collaborated with a half-dozen different composers on as many works, and turned out amongst them two pretty sizeable hits. *L'Oncle Célestin*, a lively vaudeville with a score by Audran, had a great Paris success through 150 performances in its first season and subsequently went round the world, whilst *Cousin-Cousine*, a collaboration with composer Gaston Serpette and, like the earlier success, with co-librettist Maurice Ordonneau, also had an international career following a 90-performance Paris run. His *L'Élève de Conservatoire*, a vehicle for star soubrette Mily-Meyer, once again had an agreeable career but, at the other end of the scale, his earliest musical effort *Le Sosie* was an 18-night flop, a rather tasteless piece called *Les Colles des femmes* folded in 36 performances at the Menus-Plaisirs and a

disappointing collaboration with Varney on *La Belle Épicière* also failed. Following one further attempt, Kéroul abandoned the musical theatre for more than 20 years, during which period he turned out a number of highly successful plays, notably in a long collaboration with Albert Barré.

Several of these plays proved the meat for other men's musicals. Kéroul and Barré's 1904 Paris hit *Une nuit de noces* became the British play *Oh, I Say!* (ad Sidney Blow, Douglas Hoare) which made up into a musical of the same name (Casino Theater 1913, music by Jerome Kern, aka *Their Wedding Night*) in America, another, *Telling the Tale* (Ambassadors Theatre 1918, music by Philip Braham) in Britain, and yet another *La Supermoglie* (music by G F Checcacci, Teatro Fossati, Milan 13 January 1920) in Italy. The pair's *Le Portrait de ma tante* became *Léni néni* in the hands of Hungarian adapter Jenő Heltai and composer Zsigmond Vincze (Magyar Színház 2 May 1914), whilst Paul Lincke's Berlin musical *Ihr Sechs-Uhr Onkel* (w

Alfred Schönfeld/Jean Kren, Thalia Theater 15 August 1907) also allowed that it was based on an unidentified Kéroul and Barré work.

Apart from concocting a festive season féerie for the Châtelet in 1907, the Kéroul and Barré combination collaborated on just one musical piece during their partnership, the libretto for *Les Maris de Ginette*, an unpretentious piece which, with a score by Félix Fourdrain and Mariette Sully starring, played successfully at the Théâtre Apollo in 1916–17.

1879 **La Sarbacane** (Chatau) 1 act Scala 30 August

1887 **Le Sosie** (Raoul Pugno/w Albin Valabrègue) Théâtre des Bouffes-Parisiens 8 October

1891 **L'Oncle Célestin** (Edmond Audran/w Maurice Ordonneau) Théâtre des Menus-Plaisirs 24 March

1893 **Les Colles des femmes** (Louis Ganne/w Adolphe Jaime) Théâtre des Menus-Plaisirs 29 September

1893 **Cousin-Cousine** (Gaston Serpette/w Ordonneau) Théâtre des Folies-Dramatiques 23 December

1894 **L'Élève de Conservatoire** (Leopold de Wenzel/w Paul Burani) Théâtre des Menus-Plaisirs 29 November

1895 **La Belle Épicière** (Louis Varney/w Pierre Decourcelle) Théâtre des Bouffes-Parisiens 16 November

1896 **La Noce de Grivolet** (Marius Carman/w Charles Raymond) Théâtre Déjazet 24 October

1907 **La Princesse Sans-Gêne** (Marius Baggers/w Albert Barré) Théâtre du Châtelet 16 November

1916 **Les Maris de Ginette** (Félix Fourdrain/w Barré) Théâtre Apollo 18 November

KERT, Larry [KERT, Frederick Lawrence] (b Los Angeles, 5 December 1930; d New York, 5 June 1991).

After early experience as a child actor, stuntman and stand-in in films (he doubled for Roddy McDowell in *Lassie Come Home*), in variety, in revue and in stock companies, Kert made his first Broadway appearances in the revues *Tickets Please* (1950) and *John Murray Anderson's Almanac* (1953). After the *Ziegfeld Follies of 1956* closed pre-Broadway, he took over a supporting part in *Mr Wonderful* (1956) before winning his one memorable Broadway creation as Tony, the West Side Romeo of *West Side Story* ('Maria', 'Something's Coming', 'Tonight'). He appeared regionally in Menotti's *The Medium* and *The Telephone*, in *The Merry Widow* and in his *West Side Story* rôle, and after John Kander's maiden musical, *A Family Affair* (1962, Gerry Seigel), had closed its brief run, he replaced Elliot Gould as the young 'hero' of *I Can Get it for You Wholesale* (1962).

Kert suffered a second out-of-town closure in *Holly Golightly* (1966), the musical version of *Breakfast at Tiffany's*, and a quick Broadway flop in *La Strada* (1969, Mario), in between which he spent a period playing the rôle of Cliff in Broadway's *Cabaret*. He similarly took over, this time very soon after the show's opening, in the central part of Robert in *Company* (1970), a rôle which he subsequently played in London's production of the show (1972). He appeared on tour in *Gentlemen of Verona* (Proteus), in *Music! Music!*, *Sugar*, *Irma la Douce* and *La Cage aux Folles* (Georges), succeeded David Kernan in the cast of the compilation show *Side by Side by Sondheim* and played the rôle of Al Jolson in a series of attempts to put together a biomusical about *Joley* (1979 aka *Al Jolson Tonight*, 1978) which stopped short of Broadway. In 1980 he appeared at off-Broadway's Theater de Lys in the

short-lived *Changes*, and in 1986, for the last time on Broadway, in another failure, *Rags*. He was again seen in the off-Broadway piece *The Rise of David Levinsky* before his final illness.

DIE KEUSCHE BARBARA Operette in 3 acts by Rudolf Bernauer and Leopold Jacobson. Music by Oskar Nedbal. Theater Weinberge, Prague, 14 September 1910.

Nedbal's first Operette was a piece set in England in the 'Gainsborough period', and the virtuous Barbara was little Miss Knox, daughter of the landlord of the alehouse 'Zur keuschen Barbara' who is sighed over by the whole House of Lords. Most unoperettically, she weds her preferred Lord Halifax by the end of Act I, but for all the wrong reasons. Halifax is the promoter of a law by which a gentleman who compromises a lady must wed her, and he is accidentally caught in his own clauses. It takes two more acts for the marriage to turn from forced to full-blooded, thanks to the interference of Halifax's tenant, the House of Commonser Pittifox, who suspects the Lord of writing suggestive letters to his wife, Mabel. Pittifox's young niece, Kitty, and her sailorboy Jony Burns get mixed up in the resulting moral and amorous misunderstandings, all of which are happily cleared up for the final curtain.

Halifax rendered a waltz on morals ('Grossvater in seiner Jugend') and a march song with a sextet of supporting Lords ('Weib den braven Mann verlässt'), Barbara a not-very-English mazurka ('Ich zügte meine Leidenschaft') and the comic pair duetted to the strains of the waltz, the minuet, the can-can, the cakewalk and the maxixe.

First produced in Prague, *Die keusche Barbara* was quickly picked up by Wilhelm Karczag for the Raimundtheater where, with Betty Fischer, Otto Storm, Ernst Tautenhayn and Franz Glawatsch starring and the composer conducting, it was played for 33 performances. After the success of Nedbal's later *Polenblut*, it was also produced in Hungary (ad Zsolt Harsányi) but, if its runs were generally limited, its several productions in central Europe nevertheless marked Nedbal out as a promising writer.

Germany: ?1911; Austria: Raimundtheater 7 October 1911; Hungary: Budai Szinkör *Az Erénycsősz* 22 April 1921

DIE KEUSCHE SUSANNE Operette in 3 acts by Georg Okonkowski adapted from the farce *Fils à papa* by Antony Mars and Maurice Desvallières. Music by Jean Gilbert. Wilhelm-Theater, Magdeburg 26 February 1910; Neues Operetten-Theater, Berlin, 6 August 1911.

One of the outstanding and outstandingly successful shows of its era, *Die keusche Susanne* was a germanicized version of a Parisian Palais-Royal vaudeville set with a score of sparkling dance-and-song music by German composer Jean Gilbert. Very serious commentators and writers of programme copy like to see in its text a 'satire of middle-class values in France' (and, by transfer, Germany or anywhere else), but this musicalized version of *Fils à Papa* is, of course, simply a rattling good sex comedy which its composer fitted out with delightful melodies well adapted to the more popular and enduring dance rhythms of the day.

Apparently model papa des Aubrais strictly refuses to allow his daughter Jacqueline to wed the womanizing René Boislurette, yet he himself – unbeknown to all – has the habit of sneaking off for jolly, disguised evenings in the company of various ladies at the Moulin-Rouge. Unfortunately, on this particular occasion, he there encounters not only Jacqueline, out on the town with René, but his son Hubert in the company of the advertisedly 'virtuous' Susanne Pomarel, the wife of a provincial friend. A panoply of disguises and hidden identities entwine their way through an action which hots up dangerously when Monsieur Pomarel, egged on by the jealous moral crusader Charencey, brings in the police, only to discover that des Aubrais's partner of that evening is ... Madame Charencey. The next morning mutual interest ensures that everything is 'forgotten', René and Jacqueline are allowed to become engaged, Pomarel is reassured of his wife's modesty, and Madame des Aubrais – who never got out of the house – remains sweetly unaware that her children clearly, if secretly, take after their father.

The 14-piece score was a lively affair, topped by a waltz 'Wenn die Füsschen sich heben und schweben' for Jacqueline and René and by a march duo for Aubrais and Hubert, 'Wenn der Vater mit dem Sohne auf den Bummel geht', both of which duly became popular outside the show as well as in it.

Die keusche Susanne was a great success on its initial showing at Magdeburg, and it quickly took its first steps onwards in what was to be a long and high-profile international career. The earliest foreign production – mounted before the show had even made its way to Berlin's Neues Operetten Theater – was Sigmund Eisenschütz's Austrian one, at the Carltheater, which starred Mizzi Zwerenz as Susanne with Karl Blasel as her husband, Richard Waldemar as the naughty des Aubrais, handsome Josef König and Olga Barco-Frank as his children and Willi Strehl as the tenor lieutenant. After a first run of 128 performances, straddling the summer break, the show was held in the repertoire for the next two seasons. During this time Budapest welcomed Juci Lábass as *Az artálan Zsuzsi*.

The musical's most ringing success to date, however, came in Britain. Produced by Philip Michael Faraday, the happy London co-producer of *The Chocolate Soldier*, in a version by Frederick Fenn and Arthur Wimperis, it swapped its slightly sexy title for the less apt *The Girl in the Taxi*, the title used for the American production of the source play. The reference was to Madame Charencey (now called Charcot) whom the Baron Dauvray (*sic*) encounters when they share a taxi to the Restaurant 'Jeunesse Dorée' (no longer the Moulin-Rouge), but the change in name was really an attempt to capitalize on the major London success of the recent *The Girl in the Train*, a more apt title for Fall's *Die geschiedene Frau*, with another 'girl' title. Yvonne Arnaud (Suzanne), ex-D'Oyly Carte comic C H Workman (Pomarel), Arthur Playfair (Dauvray), Amy Augarde (Mme Dauvray) and Alec Fraser (René) were the name artists in a production which kept pretty close to the original and which scored an immense success with its fun, its songs – notably 'Waltzing' ('Wenn die Füsschen') – and its tangos and one-steps, and which played for 385 performances in a year at London's Lyric Theatre.

The Girl in the Taxi was sent out in triplicate on the road, and returned quickly to London (1 November 1913) following the failure of Straus's *Love and Laughter* for another six weeks at the Lyric Theatre, and again in 1915 – in spite of the virtual ban on all German shows – for another 155

performances at the Garrick (23 January), the New and the Criterion. This series of repeats brought its record to a total of nearly 600 metropolitan performances in two and a half years, a figure which ranked it alongside *The Chocolate Soldier* as the most successful imported show of the decade. When Australia took in the same version of *The Girl in the Taxi* two years later it found a similar welcome. A cast headed by Maggie Jarvis (Suzanne), Dorothy Brunton (Jacqueline), Millie Engler (Delphine), W H Rawlins (Dauvray) and Workman in his London rôle totted up 60 consecutive Sydney performances – one of the best musical comedy records of the time – before the show went on to Melbourne (Her Majesty's Theatre 24 October 1914) and to a number of return visits to both cities over the following years.

America's A H Woods produced a rather different version of the show (ad Harry and Robert B Smith) which he entitled *Modest Suzanne* (the *Girl in the Taxi* title having, of course, been pre-empted on Broadway). Sallie Fisher starred as Suzanne and a couple of Jean Schwartz numbers, 'The Tangolango Tap' and 'I Would Like to See the Peaches', were tacked into the score. What remained of its Palais-Royal gaiety was found 'vulgar' and 'debauched' – though the music was spared such critical quiverings – and it still flopped in 24 Broadway performances.

France, on the other hand, took a predictably distinct and unprudish liking to *La Chaste Suzanne*, a liking which ultimately outstripped even London's enthusiasm. The show was mounted at Lyon, in a version by the authors of the original play, under the management and direction of Montcharmont, the producer and agent who had his French finger firmly on central Europe's output. Montcharmont then sold it briskly to Alphonse Franck, Paris's *Veuve joyeuse* producer, for his Théâtre Apollo. With American actress Bella Atkins (Suzanne) featured alongside Tréville (des Aubrais), *Veuve joyeuse* star Henri Defreyn (Hubert) and the future opéra-comique tenor Edmond Tirmont (René), and with Josef Szulc at the baton, the show had a stunning première with 'almost the entire score played twice, given the encores demanded for the songs and, above all, the dances', and a popular success which led to its being played 108 consecutive times as a first run. Thereafter it toured limitlessly, reappeared in Paris in 1913 (Théâtre Cluny), 1921 (Théâtre de l'Eden under the management of Léon Volterra, with Max Dearly starred), and at the Théâtre de la Gaîté-Lyrique in 1935, in 1945 and again in 1960 with manageress Germaine Roger starring as Suzanne. In the 30 years since, *La Chaste Suzanne* has remained an active item in the French repertoire – almost the only German musical comedy so to do – just as it has in the Spanish (*La casta Susanna*).

The success of *Die keusche Susanne* on the international stage was almost equalled by its cinematic success. A German film was issued in 1926 with Lillian Harvey starred, in 1937 André Berthommier made parallel French and English versions – the former starring Meg Lemonnier, Henri Garat and Raimu, the latter teaming Garat with the blonde bit of shrapnel that was Frances Day and with Lawrence Grossmith. Another, Spanish-language version was made in the Argentine, where Gilbert spent his last days, and further films appeared in 1950 (*La P'tite Femme du Moulin-Rouge*) and in 1951 (*La Chaste Suzanne*, with the voice of Mathé Altéry).

Gilbert's son, Robert Gilbert, rewrote *Die keusche Suzanne* in 1953 rather in the same way that Kollo junior had done with his father's most profitable pieces. He plucked the hit songs from Jean Gilbert's other shows – 'Puppchen du bist mein Augenstern' from *Puppchen* became a duo for the Baron Conrad von Felsneck and Rosa Hintzmeier (as Aubrais and Mme Charency had become in a curious shift of national setting) and 'Das haben die Mädchen so gerne' from *Autoliebchen* was a duo for René (who actually kept his first name) and Pauline (ex-Jacqueline) – squeezing out some of the original material in the process, and the rather over-egged Neubearbeitung was republished as a fresh copyright.

Austria: Carltheater 18 March 1911; USA: Liberty Theater *Modest Suzanne* 1 January 1912; Hungary: Budai Színkör *Az ártatlan Zsuzsi* 11 May 1912, Király Színház (Ger) May 1913; UK: Lyric Theatre *The Girl in the Taxi* 5 September 1912; France: Théâtre des Célestins, Lyon *La Chaste Susanne* 7 February 1913, Théâtre Apollo, Paris 29 March 1913; Australia: Her Majesty's Theatre, Sydney *The Girl in the Taxi* 8 August 1914; Films: 1926, 1937 (Fr), 1937 (Eng), 1950, 1951 etc.

KEYS, Nelson (b London, 7 August 1886; d London, 26 April 1939).

Principally known for his performances in revue, the diminutive and sometimes rather disagreeable comedian created several musical-comedy rôles in the early part of his career. Amongst these were the small rôle of Bobby, the jockey, in *The Arcadians* in which he introduced the song 'Back Your Fancy', originally intended for another artist, the comic little Lieutenant Makei, opposite Cicely Courtneidge, in *The Mousmé*, and the non-singing Ensign Pips in *Princess Caprice* – all three pieces produced under the Courtneidge management – as well as Lieutenant Skrydloff in Oscar Straus's unfortunate London musical *Love and Laughter*. He also took over as the out-on-the-town youngster Hubert des Aubrais in Phillip Michael Faraday's production of *The Girl in the Taxi*.

Keys's diminutive stature later made him a natural for the rôle of Eddie Kettle in the botched and brief London version of *Very Good Eddie* (1918), but thereafter he stuck to revue, and less prominently film, only returning to the West End musical stage for a period to play, in succession to Billy Merson, the part of Hard-Boiled Herman in the Drury Lane production of *Rose Marie* (1926).

Biography: Carstairs, J P: *Bunch* (Hurst & Blackett, London, 1941)

KID BOOTS Musical comedy of 'Palm Beach and Golf' in 2 acts by William Anthony McGuire and Otto Harbach. Lyrics by Joseph McCarthy. Music by Harry Tierney. Earl Carroll Theater, New York, 31 December 1923.

Eddie Cantor starred in Florenz Ziegfeld's first musical comedy production since *Sally* in what was a patent attempt to repeat the formula of that show: the successful teaming of one star comedian and one blonde, dancing ingénue. The billing values, between the two shows, were about equal for if Cantor was a priori a bigger draw than Leon Errol, pretty little Mary Eaton, the principal dancer of the last *Ziegfeld Follies*, did not have the pull of a Marilyn Miller. She got the same sized billing as Ziegfeld and

Cantor, but they (and Ziegfeld first) were above the title, whilst she was blessed with a 'with' prefix and followed underneath the title.

Cantor was featured as 'Kid' Boots, a down-South golf-club caddy-chief who is into bootlegging and fixing golf balls (for a small sum) to help the undertalented defeat the overtalented at this newly mass popular sport. Unfortunately, his pal Tom Sterling (Harry Fender), the most accomplished golfer in the whole place, accidentally gets hold of one of Kid's doctored balls and uses it in his big match against the Champion of Hudson River Golf Club (Robert Barrat). Mary Eaton played Polly Pendleton, Tom's love interest and the daughter of sporting-goods manufacturer Herbert Pendleton (Paul Everton), whose business rivalry with fellow club-member Peter Pillsbury (Robert Cummings) was another, parallel portion of the plot. Marie Callahan played Kid's girlfriend Jane Martin ('in charge of ladies' lockers'), Ethelind Terry was a glamorous soprano Carmen Mendoza, whilst Jobyna Howland played a lady doctor, Dr Josephine Fitch, whose main part in the proceedings was a pair of comical routines with the star: one in the club gymnasium, featuring some electrical treatment, and the other a golf lesson. There were also three principal dancers, not including Miss Eaton, and George Olsen and his orchestra to supply both the accompaniment and their own spot ('The Cocoanut Ball').

Harry Tierney and Joseph McCarthy, still floundering somewhat in trying to repeat the success and attractions of the score of *Irene*, didn't do much better for *Kid Boots* than they had for the short-lived *Up She Goes* and *Glory* the previous year. The juveniles duetted 'If Your Heart's in the Game', whilst Cantor advised 'Keep Your Eye on the Ball', delivered a 'Rain Song' and topped up the not terribly impressive basic score with a winning interpolation in 'Dinah' (Joe Young, Harry Akst, Sam Lewis). 'Dinah (is there anyone finah ...)' gave *Kid Boots* a genuine hit which would go on to be liberally recorded and performed outside the show, used in two films, and become the theme song of popular vocalist Dinah Shore.

Ziegfeld's production of the show was mounted in picturesque style, with its lavish sets depicting scenes of the Floridean golf club's putting green, club-house, trophy room ('the tarpon in this scene caught at Palm Beach by Miss Billie Burke-Ziegfeld') and the final Cocoanut Ball, but Cantor remained the main attraction. He clowned his way through the action in what was thought his 'best performance to date' without the aid of his usual blackface make-up, until he arrived at the moment where he was due to do what was little more than his 'act'. A timely explosion then sufficed to get him into smut-soiled blackface. Largely thanks to its star, *Kid Boots* proved to have sufficient mainly comical attractions to last through a whole season and it eventually ran up a total of 482 Broadway performances before going on the road.

An English production, sponsored by Grossmith and Malone as the latest in their series of American musical shows at the Winter Garden Theatre, starred their enormously popular regular comedian, Leslie Henson, in Cantor's rôle. The score was again topped up, this time by Vivian Ellis, but *Kid Boots* proved to have few of the attractions of the Winter Garden's recent imports or virtual imports: Kern's *Sally*, *The Cabaret Girl* and *The Beauty Prize*, Gershwin's *Primrose* or even *Tell Me More!* It dwindled away in 163 performances, effectively putting Grossmith out of the producing business.

In Australia, George Gee took the show's title-rôle alongside Josie Melville (Polly), George Vollaire (Tom), Fiole Allen (Jane) and Jean Newcombe (Dr Fitch) through 11 weeks in Sydney and two months in Melbourne (Her Majesty's Theatre 25 June 1925).

In 1926 Cantor ventured into films for the first time to put *Kid Boots* on celluloid. Clara Bow, Billie Dove, and Lawrence Gray as Tom supported.

Australia: Her Majesty's Theatre, Sydney 4 April 1925; UK: Winter Garden Theatre 2 February 1926; Film: 1926

KIDD, Michael [GREENWALD, Milton] (b New York, 12 August 1919). Choreographer in Broadway's peak postwar years.

Kidd danced with Ballet Caravan, the Eugene Loring Dancers and, between 1942 and 1947 as a member of the Ballet Theatre, with whom he created a principal rôle in *Fancy Free*, latterly taking some choreographic assignments in addition to performing. He made his Broadway début as a choreographer with *Finian's Rainbow* (1947), and continued with the short-lived college musical *Hold It!* (1948), Kurt Weill and Alan Jay Lerner's *Love Life* (1948), and *Arms and the Girl* (1950) before creating the dances for the original production of *Guys and Dolls* (1950) and for Cole Porter's *Can-Can* (1953) with its Montmartre dances and its spectacular Garden of Eden ballet sequence.

For the successful production of *L'il Abner* (1956) he turned both producer and director, and he doubled again as director and choreographer on his three subsequent shows: the comical western *Destry Rides Again*, the Lucille Ball vehicle *Wildcat* and the less successful *Subways Are for Sleeping*. Latterly, however, he failed to find the success of the best of his earlier pieces and although *Here's Love* had both charm and a year's run, *Ben Franklin in Paris* (director and co-producer), *Skyscraper*, *Holly Golightly*, *The Rothschilds*, *Cyrano* and the 1974 revival of *Good News* were less than hits. In 1993 he directed the musical version of *The Goodbye Girl* on Broadway.

His Broadway record and its five accompanying Tony Awards (*Finian's Rainbow*, *Guys and Dolls*, *Can-Can*, *Li'l Abner*, *Destry Rides Again*) were equalled only by his success in the cinema where he choreographed the screen versions of *Where's Charley?* and *The Band Wagon*, the memorably masculine routines of *Seven Brides for Seven Brothers*, *Guys and Dolls* and *Hello, Dolly!*.

Kidd was seen as an actor – playing the rôle of a choreographer – in the film *Smile*.

KIEFERT, Carl (d ?Manchester, 1937). The man who made the sound of the British theatre orchestra of the Victorian and Edwardian musical comedy.

Originally a cellist, the German-born Kiefert visited London in 1880 as a member of the Saxe-Meiningen court orchestra for a series of performances at the Theatre Royal, Drury Lane. He remained in Britain thereafter, working as an arranger and then a conductor, and became an important if low-profile contributor to the success of the British musical comedy during the 1890s and 1900s. Osmond Carr, then Lionel Monckton, and subsequently almost all of the principal musical-comedy composers of the time confided their theatre scores to him for orchestration and, as a result, he set the tone and style for the sound of theatre music of the era. Such was his popularity that eventually all the theatre orchestras of London began to sound the same, because their music had been arranged and orchestrated either by Kiefert himself or else by others who copied his effective, classic if, perhaps, unadventurous style.

Carr also got Kiefert off the ground as a conductor, and he led the orchestra for that composer's *Morocco Bound* (1893), *Go-Bang* (1894) and *His Excellency* (1894) before taking up the baton at Daly's Theatre for *An Artist's Model* (1895), at the Court Theatre for *All Abroad* (1896) and *The Belle of Cairo* (1896), and joining Tom Davis as the original conductor and orchestrator of *Florodora* (1899). Amongst a series of end-to-end assignments, he also led the orchestra for Stuart's *The School Girl* (1903), joined Charles Frohman as musical director for *The Catch of the Season* (1904), *Bluebell in Fairyland* (1905) and *The Beauty of Bath* (1906), and moved to the Gaiety to conduct a third Leslie Stuart musical, *Havana* (1908). After *A Persian Princess* (1909), he succeeded Ivan Caryll as conductor of *Our Miss Gibbs* (1909), and remained with George Edwardes to be the initial conductor/orchestrator of *The Quaker Girl* (1910), *The Dancing Mistress* (1911) and *The Girl from Utah* (1912).

Beyond his conducting and orchestrating activities, Kiefert was one of the most popular arrangers of published dance music over many years. He also ventured as a composer, initially with single songs for use in such touring musicals as *A Village Venus* (1895), *A Merry Madcap* (1896) and *The Dandy Detective* (1898), and then with two scores, also for the road, but which nevertheless found considerable success. *The Ballet Girl* (with additional numbers by Stuart) had two good tours and was produced in America by E E Rice, whilst *The Gay Grisette*, written with George Dance, toured Britain for many years and won a number of overseas productions.

1897 **The Ballet Girl** (James T Tanner/Adrian Ross) Wolverhampton 15 March
1898 **The Gay Grisette** (George Dance) Bradford 1 August
1901 **Hidenseek** (w others/Arthur Eliot, Edward Granville) Globe Theatre 10 December
1907 **The Zuyder Zee** (comp and arr/W H Risque) 1 act London Hippodrome 24 June

KIEPURA, Jan (b Sonowicz, Poland, 6 May 1902; d Rye, NY, 15 August 1966). Film and stage tenor, often in tandem with his wife.

Kiepura spent the early part of his career in opera in Poland, Austria, Italy and America before appearing in 1943 opposite his wife, Marta Eggerth, as Danilo in a revival of *The Merry Widow* at New York's Majestic Theater. He followed up on Broadway, again with his wife, in a romantic Chopin pastiche, *Polonaise* (1945, General Thaddeus Kosciusko), as Edwin to her Sylva in a souped-up *Princesse Czardas* in Paris (Théâtre de Paris, 1950), as the Tauber-touched heroes of *Der Zarewitsch* (1954) and *Paganini* (1956) at Vienna's Raimundtheater, and repeated his Danilo to Eggerth's *Merry Widow* in London in 1955.

In spite of limited acting talents, Kiepura played in films in Austria (*Zauber der Bohème*), Britain (*Farewell to Love*, *My*

769

Song for You, Be Mine Tonight), America (*Give Us This Night*) and Italy (*Her Wonderful Lie*).

KILEY, Richard [Paul] (b Chicago, 31 March 1922). One of the most impressive actor-vocalists of the postwar Broadway stage, only rarely served with winning rôles.

After an early career in radio, in stock and in touring plays (Stanley Kowalski in the national tour of *A Streetcar Named Desire*), and an appearance on Broadway in Shaw's *Misalliance*, Kiley had his first musical rôle in the road-closing *A Month of Sundays* (1951, Joe Ross). He won his first musical success soon after when he was cast in the part of the Caliph in *Kismet* (1953) in which he created 'And This Is My Beloved', 'Stranger in Paradise' and 'Night of My Nights'.

After several years of non-musical assignments he returned to the musical stage in 1959 to play the rôle of hero Tom Baxter, paired with Gwen Verdon, in the music-hall mystery musical *Redhead* (Broadway and tour, Tony Award). He then appeared opposite Diahann Carroll as David Baxter, the hero of *No Strings* (1962), introducing 'The Sweetest Sounds' with his co-star, took over from Craig Stevens as the straight man in Meredith Willson's Santa-Claus musical *Here's Love* (1963) and played along-side Buddy Hackett as Sam the Shpieler in *I Had a Ball* (1964) before creating his second major musical rôle as Don Quixote in *Man of La Mancha* (Tony Award), singing 'The Impossible Dream' and 'Man of La Mancha' into the standards list.

He subsequently played the part of Julius Caesar in a musical version of Shaw's *Caesar and Cleopatra*, *Her First Roman* (1968), and repeated his *Man of La Mancha* rôle in a revival of the show in London (1969). Thereafter, however, Broadway gave him no further new musical rôles. He played the aviator in the Lerner and Loewe musical film of *The Little Prince* (1975), appeared as Peter Stuyvesant in a season of *Knickerbocker Holiday* at Town Hall (1977), reprised his *Man of La Mancha* rôle at the Vivian Beaumont Theater in 1972 and again in a 1977 revival which toured the following year, and appeared in the Michel Legrand/Sheldon Harnick musical version of Dickens's *A Christmas Carol* (1981) outside New York, but has played in the last two decades mostly in non-musical productions.

THE KING AND I Musical play in 2 acts by Oscar Hammerstein II based on Margaret Landon's novel *Anna and the King of Siam*. Music by Richard Rodgers. St James Theater, New York, 29 March 1951.

The historical tale of the British governess Mrs Anna Leonowens and her 19th-century adventures in the differently civilized land of Siam had been metamorphosed – in a suitably romanticized form – into a successful novel and into a Hollywood film (1946) in which Rex Harrison starred as the King of Siam, Irene Dunne as Mrs Leonowens and Linda Darnell as the erring royal wife, before Gertrude Lawrence approached Rodgers and Hammerstein, the reigning monarchs of the musical stage, with the suggestion that the tale be adapted into a musical play with the rôle of Mrs Leonowens tailored to suit her own talents. The show that resulted followed the lines of the film screenplay, although it eventually developed a lighter touch to its warmly sentimental plot, a touch which

Plate 150. **The King and I:** *Hayley Mills and Tony Marinyo in the title-rôles of John Frost's Australian revival.*

was perhaps not unconnected with its star's natural comedic style.

The no-nonsense, widowed Anna (Miss Lawrence) goes to Siam as governess to the royal household of a king (Yul Brynner) who is tentatively willing to adapt his and his country's ways to Western values. He allows himself to be tactfully guided in this 'progress' by the governess, but the wild, proud ways of traditional kinghood inevitably assert themselves from time to time and it is the morally hidebound Anna who is unable to understand his values when he orders the execution of a Burmese emissary, Lun Tha (Larry Douglas), who has been planning to run away with one of the royal concubines (Doretta Morrow). The warm personal relationship between the willing but still royal King and the rather less flexible Anna seems damaged, but she returns to him as he lies on his death-bed and promises to remain at the side of his young son as the boy makes his first steps in what will, under the influence of Anna's teachings, be a new style of rule in Siam.

The score, laid out rather differently to that of the three earlier Rodgers and Hammerstein successes, *Oklahoma!*, *Carousel* and *South Pacific*, reflected the casting. Whereas the authors' heroines in the first two pieces had been light soprano ingénues or, in *South Pacific*, a soubrette, here they had as a leading lady a light-comedy actress with romantic possibilities and not much of a voice. They supplied her with vocally limited, charming songs: the chin-up 'I Whistle a Happy Tune', the wistful 'Hello, Young Lovers', the almost coy invitation to the King 'Shall We Dance?' and, added on the road to town with the express intention of lightening the mood of the piece, a children-and-chorus number 'Getting to Know You', fabricated from a cut-out melody from *South Pacific*. The King's rôle, too, was vocally truncated for a Brynner who semi-talked his way through 'A Puzzlement', and the lyrical values of the piece were sidewound into the supporting parts. The ill-fated romance between Tuptim and Lun Tha was illustrated by two thoroughly sentimental soprano-tenor duets ('We Kiss in a Shadow' and the pre-Broadway addition 'I Have Dreamed') which, by their arioso nature and plot placing, held more of the musical-dramatic in them than the writers had previously used, and Lady Thiang (Dorothy Sarnoff), the King's devoted chief wife, hymned her understanding of her lord in the mezzo-soprano 'Something Wonderful', perhaps the most beautifully worded of the series of big songs for big ladies' voices with which Rodgers and Hammerstein followed *Carousel*'s 'You'll Never Walk Alone'.

The dance element of the show, in line with its strongly book-based nature, was limited, but it nevertheless threw up one of the evening's highlights. Introduced in the 19th-century variety-musical manner as 'an entertainment for the king', it took the form of a dance-play, 'The Small House of Uncle Thomas' which related in Eastern terms the tale of *Uncle Tom's Cabin*: a meaningful story about a cruel despot whose slave runs away. Jerome Robbins's dance piece, assisted by a sincerely humorous narration, made its serious point whilst impressing both with its beauty and its fun. Robbins and director John van Druten also made a major effect with the simply staged presentation of the King's children ('The March of the Siamese Children') in a classic piece of winning kiddie display.

The King and I was an enormous Broadway success, giving Miss Lawrence her most outstanding musical comedy rôle and launching Brynner (who had won the part at audition only after Rex Harrison and Alfred Drake had been sounded out) as a star. Sadly, Miss Lawrence was not to profit from her winning idea. Ill with cancer, she died during the show's run and, having already been temporarily substituted by Celeste Holm, was succeeded by Rodgers's lady friend, Constance Carpenter, as the show ran on to a 1,246 performance record in over three years. The rich-voiced Drake also took a brief turn at the rôle of the King, playing – and singing – it in rather a different style from Brynner.

Whilst *The King and I* ran on on Broadway, a London production was mounted at the Theatre Royal, Drury Lane, again under the management of the authors, with van Druten reproducing his Broadway direction, prematurely blocked in by a stage manager. Herbert Lom (King) and Valerie Hobson (Anna) starred, with Muriel Smith as a memorable Lady Thiang, and Drury Lane, which had already hosted extended runs of *Oklahoma!*, *Carousel* and *South Pacific*, continued to be the home away from home of the Rodgers and Hammerstein opus for a further 926 performances, bringing the pair's tenancy at London's famous house to nearly a decade. London's success was ultimately repeated in Australia, but only after that country's chief producing house, J C Williamson Ltd, had turned the show down, put off by the exhausting prospect of organizing multiple casts of children. Garnet Carroll took up the rights and staged the show – ten years after its Broadway première – and, with Jeff Warren and Sheila Bradley starring, scored a major hit through nearly seven months in Melbourne and, with Susan Swinford as Anna, four more in Sydney (Tivoli 17 July 1963).

In the meantime, thanks to a particularly successful 1956 film version which used almost the whole original score without interpolations, *The King and I* had already become an integral part of the international musical show bank of memories and song standards. The filmed version saw Brynner repeat his stage rôle opposite an ideally cast Deborah Kerr (dubbed by Marni Nixon) and, if the lyric rôles were less well served, the two stars gave memorable performances which helped to disseminate *The King and I* and its songs around the world. However, like other musi-

cals of the period, it received only few and delayed productions in Europe. Germany, where the show has since gained some currency, was the first to venture its version, in 1966, whilst the Belgian Opéra Royal de Wallonie, whose management have in recent years followed a policy of presenting American musicals in the French language, initiated *Le Roi et moi* as late as 1985, with opérette diva Nicole Broissin starred as Anna. Like its source book and the original film, however, stage and screen versions of *The King and I* are banned in Thailand.

The King and I has maintained a high profile in the basic repertoire and on English-speaking stages in the decades since its production, and it has been given several major revivals. New York's City Center hosted reprises in 1960, 1963 and 1968, the Music Theater of Lincoln Center produced the piece in 1964 with opera star Risë Stevens as Anna, and in 1990 former ballet superstar Rudolf Nureyev toured America in the rôle of the King without making it to Broadway. In London a 1973 revival featured television detective Peter Wyngarde as a stirring King (260 performances) and a 1991 tour and Sadler's Wells season starred Japan's Koshiro Matsumoto and Susan Hampshire. In 1991–2 Australia also saw *The King and I* afresh when John Frost mounted a spectacular new production with Hayley Mills starred as Anna and Tony Marinyo as the King with notable success.

However, the show's most substantial revival owed its existence to Brynner who, through a subsequent film and stage career, never shook off the image or the rôle of the King of Siam. In 1977 he returned to Broadway in a *King and I* which had undoubtedly reversed the show's original hierarchy of star values, with Brynner's King now both very much the centrepiece of the attention and also a much broader and barnstorming characterization. He trouped the show with enormous success through America, to London's Palladium (where the adept casting of Virginia McKenna as Anna went a long way towards re-establishing the old balance) and finally back to Broadway where he appeared for a second season (7 January 1985) shortly before his death.

One of the finest musical plays of its period, *The King and I* has, ironically, profited by being constructed with sympathetic rôles at its heart for two star actors-who-sing-a-bit, and its indelible connection with Brynner seems not to have hamstrung its continuing production prospects around the world.

UK: Theatre Royal, Drury Lane 8 October 1953; Australia: Princess Theatre, Melbourne 22 December 1962; Germany: Theater am Gärtnerplatz, Munich *Der König und ich* 17 April 1966; Belgium: Opéra Royal de Wallonie, Verviers *Le Roi et moi* 22 March 1985; Film: Twentieth Century-Fox 1956
Recordings: original cast (Decca), original London cast (Philips), German cast (Philips), New York revival 1964 (RCA), South African cast (RCA), Israeli cast (CBS), selections (MFP, Philips, RCA, Columbia etc), film soundtrack (Capitol) etc

KING, Charles (b New York, 31 October 1889; d London, 11 January 1944). Broadway leading man who introduced several durable songs.

Originally a player in minstrelsy and vaudeville, King was engaged in the chorus of *The Yankee Prince* and *The Mimic World* before winning his first Broadway rôle alongside Elsie Janis in *The Slim Princess* (1911, Tom Norcross).

He appeared as Wilder Daly in the Ziegfeld rehash of *A Trip to Chinatown* (*A Winsome Widow*, 'Be My Little Baby Bumble Bee') and as Dick Cunningham in the Arthur Hammerstein/Shubert revival of *The Geisha*, before playing in and out of Broadway in revue (*The Passing Show*, *The Honeymoon Express*) and featuring in New York in two further revusical productions: Irving Berlin's *Watch Your Step* (1917, Algy Cuffs) and Ziegfeld's ill-fated *Miss 1917*.

In 1919 he took over as the boy Hughie in the musical version of Pinero's *The Magistrate*, *Good Morning Judge*, then toured in the leading rôle of *Buddies*, starred as Ned Spencer in the flop *It's Up to You* (1921) and won his best rôle to date when he created the part of Jerry Conroy, the Irish lad who defeats the rich chap in the contest for the hand and heart of George M Cohan's *Little Nellie Kelly* ('Nellie Kelly, I Love You').

After a number of years working in vaudeville and revue, King returned to the musical stage to create the not-very-romantic lead rôle of Bilge Smith in Vincent Youmans's *Hit the Deck* ('Sometimes I'm Happy') and the heroic Chick Evans who gets the girl in Rodgers and Hart's *Present Arms* (1928) before heading to Hollywood, where he appeared in *The Broadway Melody* and a number of other early musical films. He returned to the stage to star as the bootlegger Al Spanish in *The New Yorkers* (1930) and, one last time, in a character rôle in *Sea Legs* (1937, Captain Nordstrom).

KING, Dennis [PRATT, Dennis] (b Coventry, England, 2 November 1897; d New York, 21 May 1971). British vocalist and actor who made himself a fine career in both capacities in America.

King first worked on the professional stage at Birmingham Repertory Theatre, aged 19, and he made his first musical theatre appearance touring in Robert Courtneidge's *Oh, Caesar!* (Dick Hamilton) in the same year. Three years later he played in London for the first time when he appeared in a supporting rôle in Messager's *Monsieur Beaucaire* (1919, Townbrake). When the company took the show to America his part was given to André Brouard, but King soon followed, taking up the rôle of Rakell in the show's tour, and from 1921 onwards was based in America, performing not in the musical theatre but in plays. His first musical leading rôle came in 1924 when he was cast as Jim Kenyon in *Rose Marie* ('Rose Marie', 'The Indian Love Call'), and this performance established him as one of Broadway's most prized operetta stars. He subsequently used his combination of classic acting experience and a rich, firm baritone in creating further romantic musicals – as François Villon in the Broadway production of Friml's *The Vagabond King* (1925, 'Song of the Vagabonds', 'Only a Rose' and on film), and in both America and Britain as D'Artagnan in the same composer's *The Three Musketeers*. In 1932 he appeared as Gaylord Ravenal opposite Norma Terris in a revival of *Show Boat*, and the following year he was the hero of the unfortunate London musical of C Stafford Dickens's Broadway play *Command Performance*.

King's musical appearances were spaced thereafter through a career in often ambitious straight theatre, but they included, in 1937, Richard Tauber's rôle of Goethe in

Lehár's *Friederike*, Count Willi Palaffi who married Vera Zorina's angel in *I Married an Angel* (1938), the disreputable though Ducal hero of his own production of *She Had to Say 'Yes'* which folded on the road in 1940, the heroically singing hero of the 1951 revival of *Music in the Air* and, finally, an unfortunate musicalization of *Lost Horizon* under the title *Shangri La* (1956, Hugh Conway).

On film, as well as re-creating his *Vagabond King*, he appeared with Laurel and Hardy in a low comic version of *Fra Diavolo*, and on television he starred as Peter Stuyvesant in *Knickerbocker Holiday* (1950).

His son, John Michael King, also appeared on the Broadway musical stage, creating the rôle of Freddy Eynsford Hill in *My Fair Lady* ('On the Street Where You Live').

KING, Walter Woolf *see* WOOLF, WALTER

KING DODO Musical comedy in 3 acts by Frank Pixley. Music by Gustave Luders. Daly's Theater, New York, 12 May 1902.

The first work of the Luders/Pixley combine, *King Dodo* failed to find a producer until the success of the pair's *The Burgomaster* suddenly made them and their show saleable. Henry Savage secured *King Dodo* and produced it in Chicago, where it duly had as big a success as its predecessor, and sent it off round the touring circuits on a long run which finally led it to an appearance in New York.

Set in the kind of crazy fantasy land, derived from extravaganza, that was the favourite setting of turn-of-the-century American musicals, the show told the story of King Dodo of Dodo Land, 'a ruler by divine right only' (William Norris), who attempts to boost his courtship of lovely Queen Lili of Spoojus (Maude Lambert) by seeking out a fountain of youth which rejuvenates him by 30 years, only to find that the lady prefers to take an older, and therefore wiser, husband. He changes back in time for a happy ending. The court historian (Charles W Meyer) decreed in topical song that he'd 'Look in the Book and See', the court physician introduced himself as 'The Eminent Doctor Fizz', the King's ward Angela (Celeste Wynne) and her beloved 'Lad Who Leads', Piola (played in travesty by Lillian Green), supplied the pretty romantic music ('Two Hearts Made One'), and the soon-to-be-famous basso William Pruette as the Queen's Prime Minister declared himself a 'True, Barbaric Soldier' in rich tones, but the score's two veritable hits came in Angela's jaunty, raggy 'Diana' and in Dodo's 'The Tale of a Bumble-Bee', a comical piece with a throbbingly tongue-in-cheek refrain.

Broadway's version of *King Dodo* introduced the eccentric comedian Raymond Hitchcock as a grotesque, white-faced, spiky-haired Dodo, in a performance which set him off on a star career, and the show was pronounced 'a genuine success', but when the summer break arrived, 64 performances later, the musical headed back to the touring circuits where it remained for a number of years. An Australian version (ad J Francis), well botched and reorganized into two acts, was later produced by John F Sheridan, featuring himself as Dodo and Maud Amber as Lili, as part of a 1905 repertoire season.

Australia: Criterion Theatre, Sydney 10 June 1905

KING KONG Jazz opera in 2 acts by Harry Bloom. Lyrics by Pat Williams. Music by Todd Matshikiza.

A South African musical, apparently based on a real character, but with his story conventionally romanticized, *King Kong* told the tale of a boxer (Nathan Mdlele) who gets jailed for a killing and thereafter goes on the skids, finally murdering the girl, Joyce (Miriam Makeba), whom he had in better days attracted away from gang leader Lucky (Joseph Mogotsi). Sentenced to prison, King Kong kills himself.

Highly successful on its original production in South Africa, *King Kong* was taken to Britain by Jack Hylton, and produced in a revised version with its two original lead men and Peggy Phango starred. Its enormous zest, and such novelties as the Gumboot Dance, won it favour and, although the management found that the performers' exuberant energies meant they couldn't sell the front stalls, it played for 201 performances.

UK: Prince's Theatre 23 February 1961
Recordings: Original cast (Gallotone), London cast (Decca)

[THE] KING OF CADONIA Musical play in 2 acts by Frederick Lonsdale. Lyrics by Adrian Ross. Music by Sidney Jones. Prince of Wales Theatre, London, 3 September 1908.

Frederick Lonsdale had his first piece produced on the London stage when Frank Curzon hurried on a musical of which the young playwright had written the libretto, to replace an unexpected flop.

Nobody wants to be the King of Cadonia, because the population have a habit of getting rid of their kings in unpleasant fashion. The current young monarch, Alexis (Bertram Wallis), is watched over nervously by his official heir, the comical Duke of Alasia (Huntley Wright), whose daughter Marie (Isabel Jay) has been nominated as future Queen. To his horror, however, the young folk – who object to all the restrictions placed on them for their safety – both run away, meet, fall in love, and ultimately, because the incognito King has become chummy with the populus, are able to return to take up the throne together unmolested.

Lonsdale's libretto was more imaginative and literate in its style than many musical-comedy books, and Sidney Jones's score was similarly classy, from its romantic baritone and soprano music for the handsome Wallis and former D'Oyly Carte prima donna, Miss Jay ('There's a King in the Land Today', 'Castles in the Air'), to some happily comic numbers for Wright ('Do Not Hesitate to Shoot') and for Gracie Leigh ('Situations') as a Balkan wench called Militza.

Critical praise was warm, success considerable, and *King of Cadonia* won a fine 333-performance London run, quickly sent out three British touring companies, and was briskly and successfully opened in Australia, before the year was out, with Herbert Clayton and Dorothy Court starring and Susie Vaughan featured as the Duchess of Alasia in a production which included an interpolated performance of the latest craze, the danse apache. The Shuberts took the piece for New York and then proceeded to dismember it. They featured Robert Dempster (Alexis), Marguerite Clarke (Marie), William Norris (Alasia) and Clara Palmer (Militza) in a version which did over Lonsdale's text, dropped great chunks of Jones's score and

replaced them by a virtual actful of M E Rourke/Jerome Kern numbers which had precious little to do with Cadonia. They had no latitude for surprise when the resultant show folded expensively after 16 performances.

Australia: Her Majesty's Theatre, Melbourne 12 June 1909; USA: Daly's Theater 10 January 1910

THE KING'S DRAGOONS Comic opera in 3 acts by J Wilton Jones. Music by John Crook. Theatre Royal, Manchester, 1 November 1880.

Produced in the same year as *The Pirates of Penzance* and *Billee Taylor*, *The King's Dragoons* did not take their sophisticated burlesque tone, but instead looked back to the classic comic-opera style of earlier years in its tale of pretty 18th-century Alice (Gertrude Cave-Ashton) who vows to wed the man who will take the place of her rash young brother (Fred J Stimson) in the army. It is not the horrid Marquis (Richard Cummings) but his son, handsome Edgar (Henry Walsham), who – after some tricky ins and outs – wins the prize. John Crook's score, in a ballad opera strain, served the piece well and, produced with a distinguished cast, *The King's Dragoons* scored well at Manchester, in several other Midlands productions, and in Australia and New Zealand where it was produced by Alfred T Dunning with Knight Aston, Annette Ivanova and Thomas B Appleby starred.

Australia: Opera House, Melbourne 18 November 1882

KING'S RHAPSODY Musical romance in 3 acts by Ivor Novello. Palace Theatre, London, 15 September 1949.

King's Rhapsody was the last of the highly successful series of large-scale romantic musicals with which Ivor Novello filled the Theatre Royal, Drury Lane before the war, and other houses around London and Britain thereafter. Novello himself starred (as he had in all but one of the series), as the newly acceded King Nikki of Murania, unwillingly called back from Paris and his actress mistress, Marta Karillos (Phyllis Dare), to rule his country and to wed an unknown bride of state, the Princess Cristiane (Vanessa Lee). Aware of his unwillingness, Cristiane, disguised as a peasant, gets herself seduced by the King before the wedding. But the rather unroyal Nikki is so irked by the way the women around him – in particular his mother, Queen Elena (Zena Dare) – take him for a kingly cypher, simply to be managed, that he refuses to conform and runs back to Marta. Whilst the king becomes more and more unpopular, Cristiane – the mother of his child – becomes adored by the people, and when he tries to interfere in government and is forced to flee Murania, she stays behind to bring up their child to be king.

The return to the Ruritania which Novello had so successfully mined with *Glamorous Night*, the first of his series, proved a great success. The libretto of *King's Rhapsody* was arguably the best of its kind that he had written, and the score which he attached to it – for once, not pretending to be show-songs within a show – turned out his now almost inevitable ration of, in particular, lovely soprano ballads. Vanessa Lee's crystal rendition of 'Someday My Heart Will Awake' was the highlight of the show, and contralto Olive Gilbert as her duenna boomed out the lullaby 'Fly Home, Little Heart' to great effect. The soprano had further lovely melodies in 'When the Violin Began to Play'

773

and 'If This Were Love', and Phyllis Dare sang of 'The Mayor of Perpignan' whose situation – with his wife liked so much better than he by his people – is a lesson to the sullen King.

King's Rhapsody was as great a success in London as *The Dancing Years* and *Perchance to Dream* had been, and it seemed likely to become Novello's longest running musical play, but its prospects were sadly damaged when, 18 months into the run, the author/star died. Another middle-ageing star, Jack Buchanan, took over his rôle, but in spite of Buchanan's popularity, the show was not the same without Novello and it closed after a total of a little over two years at the Palace Theatre (839 performances). It had an extended touring life thereafter, both in its full-sized version and, later, in a scaled-down one, and was both filmed (w Errol Flynn as Nikki and Martita Hunt as Elena) and televised (1957 w Griffith Jones and Miss Lee) without being given a major production outside Britain. In 1988 a small-cast rewritten version (ad Michael Pertwee), which replaced much of the libretto's romanticism with humour and scattered the score with numbers from other Novello shows, was seen outside the West End.

Film: Everest (1955).
Recording: original cast recordings (HMV, WRC), selection (Columbia), film selection (Parlophone).

DIE KINO-KÖNIGIN Operette in 3 acts by Georg Okonkowski (and Julius Freund). Music by Jean Gilbert. Deutsches Operettentheater, Hamburg (as *Die elfte Muse*) 23 November 1912; Metropoltheater, Berlin, 8 March 1913.

The noble Victor von Gardennes (Karl Bachmann), who moonlights as a clandestine film actor, inadvertently compromises Annie (Helene Ballot), the daughter of Josias Clutterbuck (Guido Thielscher), President of the Temperance League, Vice-President of the Crusade Against Trashy Books, and an anti-cinema advocate, on the day of her wedding to the apparently Quakerish Boppi Lopp (Victor Norbert) and he is thus, by the laws of Operette, obliged to marry her. The jealous movie star Delia Gill (Ida Russka) tricks the old man into being seen with her in public and thus ruins his credibility as a moral crusader, but Victor has a change of heart and he turns things round by announcing that Josias is going to make a useful marriage between morals and movies – he will use film productions to bring poverty and injustice to general notice. Victor keeps his little bride, and the slightly slighted Delia has to make do with the arms of a less aristocratic actor.

Gilbert's work came hot on the heels of Walter Kollo's widely played *Filmzauber*, the first significant German piece to use the newly popular silent movies and their performers as subject matter. Originally called *Die elfte Muse* (the eleventh muse ... cabaret was supposed to be the tenth!) in its Hamburg production, the Operette was revised by Julius Freund and rechristened with the more commercial title *Die Kino-Königin* for Berlin where it joined *Polnische Wirtschaft*, *Autoliebchen*, *Puppchen* and *Die Reise um die Erde in 40 Tage* to establish Gilbert at the forefront of the German musical comedy scene in just a few brief seasons.

Gilbert's score for *Die Kino-Königin* was filled with dancing melodies, and one – the march song 'In der Nacht (wenn die Liebe erwacht)' – became a major song hit. Amongst the remainder, the Kino-Walzer 'Man lacht, man lebt, man liebt!', the heroine's dance-duet with her 'victim', 'Ach, Amalia!' and Victor's lighthearted 'Liebliche kleine Dingerchen' topped the musical list, and all gave opportunities for a display of the dance element which was now so liberally emphasized in local musical shows.

Die Kino-Königin proved a great success far beyond Hamburg. Following its initial season in Berlin it went on to run up a long series of productions in the German provinces where it was subsequently rated second in popularity only to *Die keusche Susanne* in the long list of Gilbert's works and, whilst its record overseas was not quite as fine, given that it appeared in time of war, it nevertheless was played widely and well.

In Vienna Mizzi Freihardt (Delia), Paul Harden (Victor) and Oskar Sachs (Josias) played a season at the Établissement Ronacher before the show was moved up to the temporarily at-a-loss Carltheater (2 June 1914), where it soon passed its 100th performance (30 June). It had to be withdrawn when the theatre got a production of its own together, and it moved back to Ronacher, but such was its popularity that the following year, in an almost unprecedented move, Carltheater director Eibenschütz remounted the piece, again directed by Miksa Preger, with the theatre's own star Mizzi Zwerenz as Delia alongside Richard Waldemar's Josias. It ran right through the summer and closed after its 286th performance. The wartime playbills credited the music to 'Max Winterfeld' but reminded patrons in brackets that he was the same person who once liked to pretend he was the French 'Jean Gilbert' when being French was all right. In 1924 *Die Kino-Königin* was again seen at the Carltheater, with Freihardt and Fritz Imhoff starred.

Thomas Ryley's American production of *The Queen of the Movies* (ad Glen MacDonough, Edward Paulton), starring Valli Valli (Delia) and Frank Moulan (Josias) and featuring additional numbers by Leslie Stuart ('Whistle') and Irving Berlin ('Follow the Crowd'), ran a good 106 nights at the Globe Theater and popularized 'When the Moon Slyly Winks in the Night' ('In der Nacht') around America, whilst in Britain, Robert Courtneidge's staging of *The Cinema Star* (ad Jack Hulbert, Harry Graham) with Dorothy Ward playing the title-rôle alongside Lauri de Frece, Harry Welchman, Cicely Courtneidge and Hulbert, seemed set for a long run, when it was hit by considerations of loyalty (Gilbert was, after all, actually reported to be fighting on the war's other side) and had to be closed after 109 performances. Courtneidge nevertheless managed to keep his show going on the road, where apparently such considerations of origin counted for less, for four seasons.

Australia, similarly, had no foolish qualms about the sources of its entertainment, and *The Cinema Star* was mounted there in 1916 with Ethel Cadman (singing 'On the Beach at Waikiki'), Florence Young, Minnie Love (performing Louis Hirsch's 'My Radium Girl' and 'The Broken Doll'), Reginald Roberts, Derek Hudson and Phil Smith declaring 'I Want to Go Back to Honolulu' (Sonny Cunha/William Warren) as Clutterbuck at the head of its cast. A fine eight weeks in Melbourne and six as a Christmas entertainment in Sydney (Her Majesty's Theatre, 23 December 1916) compensated a show which did not, by this stage, seem to be very largely *Die Kino-Königin*, in its music at least.

There was a Berlin revival at the Metropoltheater in 1948 and a fresh German version of the piece, heavily rewritten by Gilbert's son Robert and Per Schwenzen, and with numbers from other Gilbert shows introduced, was produced at the Opernhaus, Nuremberg in 1961, thus creating a new copyright for the show. This version was played at the Metropoltheater in 1964.

USA: Globe Theater *The Queen of the Movies* 12 January 1914; Austria: Ronacher 1 April 1914; UK: Shaftesbury Theatre *The Cinema Star* 4 June 1914; Hungary: *A mozitündér* Népopera 31 October 1914; Australia: Her Majesty's Theatre, Melbourne *The Cinema Star* 7 October 1916

KIRÁLY, Ernő (b Kiskeszi, 26 April 1884; d New York, 1953). Fine-featured high baritone who starred in two decades of Hungarian operetts and musical comedies.

Király joined the Népszinház company as a chorus singer at the age of 18, and subsequently worked his way up to principal rôles in provincial houses before returning in 1907 to Budapest and the Király Szinház. There, with his elegant style and pleasing light baritone, he quickly became one of the favourite stars of Budapest's musical stage. In 1908 he succeeded Ákos Ráthonyi as Danilo in *A vig özvegy* (*Die lustige Witwe*) and played Papp in *Hollandi lány* (*Miss Hook of Holland*), and he subsequently appeared as Hungary's first Karel van Lysseweghe in *Elvált asszony* (1909, *Die geschiedene Frau*), as René in *Luxemburg grófja* (*Der Graf von Luxemburg*), as Edwin in *Csárdáskirálynö* (1916, *Die Csárdásfürstin*), as Sándor in the world première of Lehár's *Pacsirta* (*Wo die Lerche singt*, 1918) and, later, as Tassilo in *Marica grófnö* (1925, *Gräfin Mariza*). He also created starring rôles in some of the most important Hungarian operetts of the time: the title-rôle of Rényi's *A kis gróf* (1911), the cowboy Tom Miggles in *Leányvásár* (1911), the Grand Duke to Sári Fedák's *Szibill* (1914), Iván Baracs in *Mágnás Miska* (1916), the title-rôle of Szirmai's *Gróf Rinaldo* (1918) and the Count Dániel Cziráky, opposite Emmi Kosáry's Xenia, in Buttykay's *Az ezüst sirály* (1920). In 1921 he directed the successful Budapest production of Stolz's *Die Tanzgräfin* (*A kis grizett*) at the Vigszinház.

His other rôles included the Marquis in *Kornevillei harangok* (*Les Cloches de Corneville*), Tom in *Aranyhattyu*, Mihajlovics in *Bíborruhás asszony* (*Das Weib im Purpur*), Bagó in *János vitéz*, Lászlo Tassy in *Párizsi divat* and György Honti in *Mesék az irógépről*.

Király visited the Vienna Carltheater in 1913 (Bagó, Prinz Georg in *Limonádé ezredes*, Octave in *Eva*), played *Ezüst sirály* in Vienna as *Liebesrausch* and appeared in both Austria and Germany in 1922 with Hungarian companies. He was later seen in New York, where he eventually settled and opened a Hungarian restaurant (1935).

KIRK, Lisa [KIRK, Elise Marie] (b Brownsville, Pa, 25 February 1926; d New York, 11 November 1990)

Best known as a nightclub and recording vocalist, tough-voiced Lisa Kirk created the rôles of Emily in *Allegro* (1947, 'The Gentleman is a Dope'), the delectable Lois Lane in *Kiss Me, Kate* (1948, introducing 'Always True to You in My Fashion' and 'Why Can't You Behave?') and, 26 years on, that of Lottie Ames in *Mack and Mabel*, invit-

ing the world to 'Tap Your Troubles Away'. She also appeared on Broadway in *Here's Love* (1964), replacing Janis Paige in the feminine lead, closed out of town with *Home Again, Home Again* (1979) and loaned her voice to Rosalind Russell to dub parts of her rôle as Rose in the film version of *Gypsy* (1963).

KIRKWOOD, Pat (b Manchester, 24 February 1921). British soubrette of the 1940s and 1950s.

After teenage successes in pantomime and revue, Miss Kirkwood played principal soubrette rôles opposite Stanley Lupino in *Lady Behave* (1941) and in London's edition of *Let's Face It* (1942). In a subsequent career similarly dominated by revue and pantomime, she had a nervous breakdown over her role in America's *Sweet Bye and Bye* and went home, leaving the later performances to Dolores Gray, and later took leading parts in the short-lived *Roundabout* (1949), as the cabaret vocalist Pinkie Leroy in Noël Coward's *Ace of Clubs* (1950, 'Chase Me Charlie'), as Ruth in the London edition of *Wonderful Town* (1955) and as Chrysanthemum Brown, the dashingly persecuted heroine of *Chrysanthemum* (1958, 'Love Is a Game'). Intermittent provincial musical appearances in later years included Mrs Squeezum in *Lock up Your Daughters* and Vera Simpson in *Pal Joey*.

She was for a time married to Hubert Gregg (b 19 July 1916), actor, director, sometime lyricist and broadcaster, who appeared with her in *Chrysanthemum* and *Lock up Your Daughters*.

A KIS GRÓF Operett in 3 acts by Ferenc Martos. Music by Aladár Rényi. Király Színház, Budapest, 9 September 1911.

Produced in 1911, in a period when the blossoming Hungarian operett tradition was turning out some of the most interesting works in Europe, *A kis gróf*, composed to a libretto by top text-writer Ferenc Martos, was premièred on the 23rd (or, according to some sources, 26th) birthday of the hitherto untried Aladár Rényi.

The tale was a very simple one, finding its virtue in Martos's telling. The little count of the story was Count Laci d'Ennery (Ernő Király), son of the Count Guidó Agárdy (Imre Szirmai), whose father has decided that he shall wed the decidedly attractive and rich American widow Dorothy Howard (Anna Lonzay). Unfortunately, Laci is a very inexperienced young man so, prior to marriage with a woman who has already experienced all an American millionaire has to offer, he sets out to get some practice with a lady of the stage. Rózsi (Sári Fedák) is the chosen one. Of course the practice soon turns serious. Papa intervenes determinedly, Rószi tries some self-sacrificing pretences, but by the end of the evening young love has its way, especially as Dorothy, who likes older men, has both given the 'little count's' romance a helping hand, and turned her attractions most successfully onto her intended's father.

The score was in the traditional mode, featuring Hungarian-flavoured waltzes and marches – as in Rózsi's 'Kettesben csókok közt ...' and her Katonasári induló respectively – whilst Dorothy tra-la-laed out the refrain to a tale of 'Daphnis és Chloé' in soubrette style and the fun was looked after by star comic Márton Rátkai (Roth) with such pieces such as the 'Csetneki Roth' couplets.

A kis gróf ran straight through to its 50th performance at the Király Színház on 28 October and, in spite of the fact that it was succeeded in November by an even bigger success in the shape of Jacobi's *Leányvásár*, it maintained its popularity, was played at the Budai Színkör (25 May 1912), and reached its 250th Budapest performance in November 1913. In the meanwhile it had begun to be seen elsewhere. Vienna's Carltheater production (ad Julius Wilhelm), which reallotted the characters' names and rechristened the work *Susi*, starred Mizzi Zwerenz as Susi alongside Hubert Marischka (Stefan), Dora Keplinger (Aglaia), Blasel (Dr Häring) and Richard Waldemar (Szigetváry) and opened for the 1912 Christmas season. It proved a distinct hit, running right through the winter and spring – with a slight break for the visit of the Budapest Király Színház company, during which it emigrated to Ronachers 'Établissement Parisien' – till the summer recess (143 performances). It returned again both to open the new season and as an occasional matinée during the 1913–14 hit run of Nedbal's *Polenblut*. It was brought out again in 1917 for further performances.

Suzi was produced in Stockholm (1 April 1913) and in Leipzig, later the same year, and Lew Fields staged a version on Broadway, with José Collins (Suzi), Connie Ediss (Fritzi von Busing), Robert Evett (Stefan), Lew Hearn (Herr Horn) and Melville Stewart (Count Emmerich) starred, which, in spite of being greeted as 'far above the average musical comedy' was bumped from the Casino to the Shubert Theater and then out of town after just 55 performances. In true Broadway style, it was a version (ad Otto Harbach) which had been regularly botched, but Fields showed a little more taste than some of his fellow producers by taking his 'additional songs' from the best Continental sources. The interpolations, whose melodies at least melded stylistically with the original score, included a Lehár melody relyricked as 'The Best Toast of All' and a piece of Lincke performed under the gulpful title 'Teenie, Eenie, Weenie'.

Austria: Carltheater *Susi* 20 December 1912; Germany: Leipzig *Susi* May 1913; USA: Casino Theater *Suzi* 3 November 1914

KISMET Musical Arabian Night in 2 acts by Charles Lederer and Luther Davis based on Edward Knoblock's play of the same title. Music, adapted from the works of Alexander Borodin, and lyrics by George Forrest and Robert Wright. Ziegfeld Theater, New York, 3 December 1953.

Like their first great success, *Song of Norway*, Wright and Forrest's musical *Kismet* was written for and produced by Edwin Lester's Los Angeles and San Francisco Light Opera Company, opening its initial west coast run at the San Francisco Philharmonic Auditorium on 17 August 1953 before going on to establish itself as one of the outstanding Broadway operettas of the postwar period at the top of a long international career.

The libretto for the show was based on Eddie Knoblock's successful London *Kismet* of 1911, a play in which Oscar Asche had made a sensation in the expansively comic-dramatic rôle of the rogue beggar Hajj, before it went on to play Broadway, with Otis Skinner starred, to Paris, where Lucien Guitry was Hajj, and round the world in a multitude of languages. By and large, the original tale was adhered to in the libretto for the musical.

The opportunistic street poet Hajj (Alfred Drake), with the help of a fine set of coincidences, works his way into the confidence of the power-crazy Wazir of Baghdad (Henry Calvin), who is plotting, for his own benefit, to wed the young Caliph (Richard Kiley) to several wealthy foreign princesses. But the Caliph has fallen in love with, and then lost track of, pretty Marsinah (Doretta Morrow), Hajj's daughter, and the rhymester does not realize that in aiding the Wazir he is risking losing a royal son-in-law. After some dramatic ups and downs and a visit to the harem of the Wazir, the lovers are united, the villain is suppressed, and Hajj goes off to purge his punishment in exile, in the company of the Wazir's lush widow, Lalume (Joan Diener).

The score which Wright and Forrest evolved for this story included several pieces which would become musical theatre standards. Hajj's vibrantly baritonic parable of 'The Olive Tree', the quartet 'And This is My Beloved', Marsinah's realization that she can afford 'Baubles, Bangles and Beads', and the love duet 'A Stranger in Paradise' (derived from the famous Polovtsian Dances) were set alongside the supremely comical mezzo-soprano recital of the debaucheries of Baghdad, 'Not Since Nineveh' (another portion of the Polovtsian Dances), and the Wazir's gloating 'Was I Wazir' in a score full of hit songs which brought Borodin's melodies to a wider audience than they might ever have expected.

The $400,000 production of *Kismet* moved from the west coast to the east in December, under the co-management of Charles Lederer and Lester, and arrived in the middle of a newspaper strike. The strike and its resultant lack of reviews certainly seemed to do no harm: word soon got round that *Kismet* was a good thing and, come the time of year for prize-giving, the prize-givers nodded their assent. *Kismet* garnered Tony Awards as best musical, libretto and score, as well as for Drake's Hajj, as it settled in for 583 performances at Broadway's Ziegfeld Theater before beginning its touring life. Earl MacVeigh and William Johnson were the earliest road Hajjs.

Drake and Misses Morrow and Diener repeated their original characters in Jack Hylton's London production (1955) which stretched to an even longer 648 performances, and Garnet Carroll's Australian mounting, with Hayes Gordon (Hajj), Madge Stephens (Marsinah) and Morgan St John (Lalume) in the leading rôles scored such a hit in its nine months in Melbourne and subsequent Sydney season (20 August 1956) as to launch its producer on an important career in the Australian musical theatre.

A film version was issued in the same year, featuring Howard Keel in one of his outstanding film appearances as Hajj supported by Ann Blyth (Marsinah), Vic Damone as a croony Caliph and Dolores Gray as a voluptuous if vocally truncated Lalume. It included much of the stage score (the Wazir's song being a notable casualty) and added one fresh number ('Bored').

Kismet swiftly settled itself firmly into the standard English-language repertoire. It was played and recorded regularly, televised (1967 w José Ferrer) and given major revivals in America both in 1962, with Drake teamed with Calvin, Anne Jeffreys, Lee Venora and Richard Banks and again in 1965 (Lincoln Center w Drake and Anne Jeffreys) and back at the Civic Light Opera in 1976 with John Reardon starred. This last production, with Reardon repeating his memorable Hajj, was exported to London's Shaftesbury Theatre in a scenically cut-down version the following year. Around the same time, *Kismet* was first heard in German (ad Janne Furch) in Koblenz, and also suffered a racial and musical reorganization (which admitted that it was 'based on' *Kismet*) to be produced on Broadway as *Timbuktu!* (Mark Hellinger Theater, 1 March 1978). Ira Hawkins played Hadji, Melba Moore was Mars, Gilbert Price the Mansa of Mali, and Eartha Kitt's Sahleem La-lume provided the marquee value through 243 performances.

An earlier musical *Kismet* subtitled *or Two Tangled Turks*, written by Richard Carroll jr and composed by Gustave Kerker, was seen on Broadway in 1895. This Kismet, although suitably Eastern, had nothing to do with 'fate'. It was the name of the heroine (Lizzie MacNichol) who was disguised as a male child, in good operettic fashion, in order to succeed to a throne. It lasted but three Broadway weeks.

UK: Stoll Theatre 20 April 1955; Australia: Princess Theatre, Melbourne 10 November 1955; Germany: Theater der Stadt, Koblenz 22 January 1977; Film: MGM 1955
Recordings: original cast (Columbia, USA), 1965 revival cast (RCA, USA), film soundtrack (MGM, USA), complete (TER), selections (London, Sony, Capitol) etc

KISSING TIME

Perhaps the only example in the musical theatre of a composer writing two almost contemporaneous shows with different scores but with the same title. And, just to make things even more difficult, both shows were actually played under other titles before they were called *Kissing Time*.

The first *Kissing Time* was a musical comedy in 2 acts by Guy Bolton and P G Wodehouse based (uncredited) on the wartime farce *Madame et son filleul* by Maurice Hennequin and Pierre Veber (Palais-Royal 12 September 1916). Additional lyrics by Clifford Grey. Music by Ivan Caryll. However, by the time it became *Kissing Time*, it had already run its Broadway life under Klaw and Erlanger's management and the wartime title of *The Girl Behind the Gun* (New Amsterdam Theater, New York 16 September 1918).

The actress Georgette Bréval (Ada Meade) has patriotically 'adopted' a serving soldier, Brichoux (John E Young). However, Lambrissac (Donald Brian), a fellow soldier and aspiring dramatist, decides to substitute himself for Brichoux and pay a visit to the actress in the hope of making a connection or two that will help get his play produced. Amorous complications follow, with Georgette's uncle, the Colonel Servan (Frank Doane), assuming that Lambrissac is Georgette's husband until the real Brichoux, the real husband (John E Hazzard) and Madame Lucienne Lambrissac (Wilda Bennett) all arrive on the scene and complicate matters further.

Lucienne drew the plum of the score, the yearning 'Some Day the Waiting Will End', duetted 'There's a Light in Your Eyes' with her husband at the show's end and gave the title song, 'The Girl Behind the Gun'. Bréval had a comical 'Women Haven't Any Mercy on a Man' and Georgette headed a piece about '[Godsons and] Godmothers' alongside a pleasing ration of ensembles ('I Like It', 'How Warm it is Today', 'Back to the Dear Old Trenches').

Plate 151. **Kissing Time:** *Leslie Henson, Tom Walls, George Grossmith and Yvonne Arnaud line up a cue for a song-and-dance of mistaken identities.*

The show ran a fine 160 performances in New York, during which time it was seen by George Grossmith, over in America and freshly free from the cares of war. He realized there was a good part for himself in the show, and snapped up *The Girl Behind the Gun* for a London production. He cast it royally, with himself (Max, ie Lambrissac) and Leslie Henson (Bibi, ie Brichoux) playing the two comic rôles, Yvonne Arnaud (Georgette) and Phyllis Dare (Lucienne) as principal ladies, and such rising names as Tom Walls (Colonel Bollinger) and Isobel Jeans (Lady Mercia) and a young seaside comic called Stanley Holloway (Captain Wentworth) in his first West End appearance in supporting rôles.

Kissing Time (as it was now rechristened) opened Grossmith and Laurillard's brand new theatre, the Winter Garden, risen on the site of the famous old 'Mogul' music hall. It rose a little slowly, which meant that *Kissing Time* got five months of rehearsals, but when it did open, on 20 May 1919, it proved just the kind of show London wanted for its continuing victory celebrations.

The brisk comic tale was attached to a score of of-the-moment songs including 11 of the original 17, now topped up by some new ones. Miss Dare sang 'Some Day' and the new 'Thousands of Years Ago', Henson gave a light-hearted 'My Motors' (replacing Brichoux's 'True to Me') and filched 'Women Haven't Any Mercy on a Man', Grossmith detailed his 'Desertions' in another new piece, and spent his light comic-romantic moments with Miss Dare in 'There's a Light in Your Eyes' and another fresh number, 'Joan and Peter'. The whole was topped off by a French song for the French Mlle Arnaud ('Oh, ma chérie') written by the Winter Garden's French md, Willie Redstone. It all proved just the ticket, and it remained the ticket for no less than 430 performances in London's West End as a preface to a long career in the provinces and the colonies.

Australia, in particular, took a strong shine to *Kissing Time*. It saw its first performance (Theatre Royal, Melbourne 31 January 1920) only eight months after the London première, with Maud Fane (Lucienne), Gladys Moncrieff (Georgette), Leslie Holland (Max), Arthur Stigant (Bollinger) and Theodore Leonard (Bibi) playing in the lead rôles through no less than four months in two theatres in Melbourne, before going on to Sydney (Her Majesty's Theatre, 29 May 1920) for nearly three months more. It was brought back several times thereafter, notably in 1924 with Madge Elliott and Alfred Frith and again as late as 1941, for another wartime showing, and proved itself one of the favourite musical comedies of its era.

Soon after the Australian opening of *Kissing Time* Mark I, *Kissing Time* Mark 2 began its career. This one was described as 'a musical comedy in 2 acts by George V Hobart based on the libretto *Mimi* by Adolf Philipp and Edward A Paulton, with music by Ivan Caryll', and was produced at the Lyric Theatre, New York, on 11 October 1920. Before it was produced in New York, however, it had actually been produced as *Mimi*, without Caryll's music, but with a score by the multi-talented Philipp and by Frank E Tours, patently trying to repeat the formula of Philipp's earlier hit show *Alma, Where Do You Live?* Having started out on its try-out at the Shubert Belasco in Washington on 14 March 1920, *Mimi* soon vanished from the road schedules. But seven months later *Kissing Time*, equipped with no Tours or Philipp songs but a whole score of Caryll ones, a libretto credited to Hobart based on Philipp and Paulton's alleged 'translation from the French' and lyrics by a journalist called Philander Johnson (who made no other mark on the musical stage), Clifford Grey and Irving Caesar, surfaced on Broadway. Broadway, of course, hadn't had a *Kissing Time*, because *Kissing Time* Mark I had still been *The Girl Behind the Gun* when it had played New York, and since it *had* played New York, there was no likelihood of it doing so again with its new title. The title was up for grabs, and Caryll, at least, clearly though it was worth saving.

The story that had, similarly, been thought worth saving (from *Mimi*) was barely an original one, and soubrette Mimi (Dorothy Maynard) of the Maison Mimi wasn't quite the central figure in it. That was 'the other Mimi', otherwise Clarice (Edith Taliaferro), a little lass from Dijon, who poses as the wife of an unmarried man so that he can get a married man's rise. William Norris (Polydore Cliquot, Mimi's admirer) was chief comic, Frank Doane (Armand Moulanger, another Mimi admirer) number two comic, Paul Frawley (Robert Perronet, admired by Mimi) the juvenile man, and Carl Hyson and Evelyn Cavanaugh a ubiquitous pair of speciality dancers. Caryll's songs included three duos for Miss Taliaferro and Frawley – an invitation to 'Bill and Coo', the tale of 'Love's Telephone' (an instrument already investigated in Caryll's *The Little Cherub*) and their assertion of being 'Absolutely Certain' – whilst the real Mimi sang of being 'Mimi', headed the 'Mimi Jazz' and joined the juveniles and Cliquot in 'So Long as the World Goes Round'. Frawley had a solo title-song (which London's *Kissing Time* hadn't had), whilst Norris described himself as 'An Absolute Son of a Juan' and the dancers encouraged 'Keep a Foxtrot For Me'.

The plot of *Kissing Time* actually won critical praise, simply for being a plot in an age where a musical didn't always have one, Caryll's 'pleasant, singable and danceable melodies' didn't demerit, and one critic also found to his surprise that 'the ladies of the chorus manage to look more like intelligent human beings than is usually the case ...'. All these elements put together, however, earned *Kissing*

Time but nine weeks on Broadway, and this time there was no export.

KISS ME, KATE Musical comedy in 2 acts by Sam and Bella Spewack. Music and lyrics by Cole Porter. New Century Theater, New York, 30 December 1948.

Following the successful quintet of colourful, light song-and-dance shows which he had written with Herbert Fields in the late 1930s and the early 1940s, Cole Porter switched to a rather more substantial kind of show and, in collaboration with the authors of his earlier *Leave it to Me*, turned out the musical which was to be his most successful and most enduring of all in *Kiss Me, Kate*.

Fred Graham (Alfred Drake) and Lilli Vanessi (Patricia Morison) were once married, but they are now divorced. However, they are stage stars and the forces of show business and the pursuit of profit mean that they still work together. At the moment they are starring in a production of a musical based on *The Taming of the Shrew*, directed by Fred, which is being got into shape at Ford's Theater in Baltimore. Fred has, for not entirely blameless reasons, cast a perky cabaret performer called Lois Lane (Lisa Kirk) in the rôle of Bianca, and the other half of her double-act, Bill Calhoun (Harold Lang), has been found a rôle as Lucentio. Lilli – who is being intensely courted by a wealthy politician – nevertheless gets miffed by Fred's attentions to Lois, but it is Bill who really upsets the applecart. Heavily done down in a rough game of cards, he has signed the IOU as 'Fred Graham', and on opening night a pair of gangsters (Harry Clark, Jack Diamond) turn up to collect their boss's winnings from Fred. The evening is a tough one, as Fred has more than just gangsters on his plate: he has an ex-wife. Lilli is in a rage, for a bouquet from Fred has been delivered to her, and, having let down her guard and admitted that she still loves her ex-husband, she has discovered that the flowers were meant for Lois. She glowers through the first act, until Fred takes advantage of the play's script to administer his temperamental co-star a good spanking. Lilli refuses to continue the show, but Fred reminds the gangsters that they won't get their money if the box-office has to be returned, so the leading lady is frogmarched through the last act, up to the inevitable happy ending all round.

Cole Porter's brimming-over scoreful of songs illustrated both the Fred-and-Lilli and Bill-and-Lois tales and also show-within-the-show, allowing the songwriter to spread himself over a much wider variety of numbers than was usual in his theatre scores. In the former group, Fred and Lilli reminisced about their early touring days in a burlesque of Viennese Operette, 'Wunderbar' ('gazing down on the Jungfrau ...' is a physical impossibility) and Lilli gave out one of Porter's warmest romantic numbers, admitting that she is 'So In Love' with her ex-husband, whilst Lois bemoaned Bill's irresponsibility in 'Why Can't You Behave?' and excused her own in the revusical 'Always True to You in My Fashion'.

The *Taming of the Shrew* had Petruchio/Fred thinking over his old conquests in 'Where is the Life That Late I Led' whilst admitting 'I've Come to Wive it Wealthily in Padua' and rudely wooing Kate/Lilli in 'Were Thine That Special Face', Lilli spitting out 'I Hate Men' with virulent overtones whilst Bianca/Lois played with her suitors in

Plate 152. **Kiss Me, Kate:** *Lilli Vanessi (Elisabeth Kalès) ignores the chorused advice to kiss her ex-husband, Fred Graham (Peter Minich), in spite of the plot of their play, at the Vienna Volksoper, 1989.*

'Tom, Dick or Harry', alongside a choral introduction 'We Open in Venice' and, a rare thing in a Porter score, a winning concerted finale, 'Kiss Me, Kate'. On top of all this, there was still space for a front-cloth kind of Gallagher-and-Shean number for the gangsters, advising in more typical, cataloguing, Porter tones that you should 'Brush Up Your Shakespeare' to make a wow with the ladies, a lazy dance number performed by the stage-door keeper as an opener to the second act ('Too Darn Hot'), and a choral opening, hymning the out-of-town tryout in 'Another Op'nin', Another Show'.

Saint Subber and designer Lemuel Ayres's production of *Kiss Me, Kate* was a full-scale Broadway hit. It picked up, in the days before the proliferation of award categories, the initial Tony Award for best musical as well as the citations for best book and best score, and went on to a run of 1,077 performances. Keith Andes and Anne Jeffreys headed out the first touring company, before moving into town to replace the original stars, whilst the same company's Julie Wilson (Lois) also left what was to eventually be an almost two-year tour to go to London, where the first overseas *Kiss Me, Kate* was mounted, under the management of Jack Hylton, early in 1951. Miss Morison repeated her original rôle alongside Bill Johnson's Fred, Danny Green paired with Sidney (later to be famous as just Sid) James as the gangsters, and the show repeated its Broadway success, running for just short of 12 months (400 performances) as Helena Bliss (Lilli) and Valerie Tandy (Lois) took over from the original stars.

The following year, Australia welcomed its production of *Kiss Me, Kate* with Hayes Gordon (Fred), Joy Turpin (Lilli), Maggie Fitzgibbon (Lois) and Alec Kellaway and Morgan Davis (gangsters) featured, for five months in Melbourne and then four more in Sydney (Theatre Royal, 2 August 1952), before Hollywood issued its 1953 celluloid version with Howard Keel (Fred), Kathryn Grayson (Lilli), Ann Miller (Bianca) and Tommy Rall (Bill) starred.

In 1955 the show made something of a breakthrough when it was produced at Frankfurt (ad Günter Neumann), the first postwar American musical to have made its way to the Continental stage. From Frankfurt, the show slowly but surely worked its way through Europe, becoming, in the process, not only a ground-breaker, but also the most

popular and enduring of all the trans-Atlantic musical shows of the 1950s and 1960s which then began, tentatively at first, to follow in its wake. In 1963 *Csókolj meg Katám* became the first American musical to be played at Budapest's main musical house, the Fővárosi Operettszinház (ad Tamás Ungvári, György Dénes), opening the way for Britain's *Expresso Bongo* and France's *Irma la Douce* the following year, and for *My Fair Lady* two seasons later. That season saw a Budapest revival of *Kiss Me, Kate*, which also made its first appearance in Berlin in the same year.

In 1973 a version directed, designed and revised by Helmut Käutner was mounted at the Theater an der Wien, Vienna (which had begun its Broadway period with a visit from *My Fair Lady* in 1963) with Harald Serafin (Fred), Naëmi Priegel (Lilli), Olivia Molina (Chiquita!) and Joachim Kemmer (Bill) featured, and a vast amount of ballet tacked in for the theatre's corps de ballet (78 performances). Nearly a decade later (5 March 1982) the show was taken into the repertoire at the Volksoper, with Peter Minich (Fred), Dagmar Koller (Lilli) and Melanie Holliday (Bianca) featured in rôles which they were still playing a further decade on as *Kiss Me, Kate* confirmed itself as one of the pillars of American musical theatre repertoire in Austria, in the same way that it had in Germany and in Hungary.

Kiss Me, Kate has held its place firmly in the repertoire in English-language countries as well, but in the regional theatre rather than in the main centres. Although it has been seen at New York's City Center, and on American television (1970, with Robert Goulet and Carol Lawrence), there has been, in spite of the enormous push for Porter productions in recent decades, no Broadway revival of this most complete (and, thus, least fiddleablewith) of his shows. London, on the other hand, has seen the show twice, but each time in most unlikely circumstances and in the subsidized rather than the commercial theatre. In 1970 the English National Opera produced a semi-operatic version (London Coliseum 24 December) with its members Émile Belcourt (Fred) and Ann Howard (Lilli) supported by musical comedy players Judith Bruce (Lois) and Teddy Green (Bill), and some 17 years later the Royal Shakespeare Company followed suit (Old Vic 19 May 1987) with a production which barely used their company at all – just their name and their subsidy. Paul Jones (Fred), Nichola McAuliffe (Lilli) and Fiona Hendley (Lois) featured in a revival which followed its Old Vic season with a run at the Savoy Theatre (18 January 1988).

In 1992 a French-language version (ad Alain Marcel) made its first appearance in Geneva with Bernard Alane (Fred), Marie Zamora (Lilli), Fabienne Guyon (Lois) and Jacques Verzier (Bill) featured. It was subsequently shown in Paris at the Théâtre Mogador the following year.

UK: London Coliseum 8 March 1951; Australia: His Majesty's Theatre, Melbourne 2 February 1952; Germany: Städtische Bühnen, Frankfurt, 19 February 1955, Metropoltheater, Berlin 9 April, 1965; Hungary: Fővárosi Operettszinház *Csókolj meg Katám* 15 November 1963; Austria: Theater an der Wien 6 February 1973, Volksoper 5 March 1982: France: Théâtre Mogador 26 January 1993; Film: MGM 1953.

Recordings: original cast (Columbia), London cast on *Cole Porter in London* (WRC), London cast 1987 (First Night), Dutch cast (Philips, CNR), complete (EMI), film soundtrack (MGM, CBS), selection (Reprise etc), selection in German (Ariola) etc.

KITTY GREY Musical comedy in 3 acts adapted by J Smyth Piggott from *Les Fêtards* by Antony Mars and Maurice Hennequin. Music by Lionel Monckton, Howard Talbot, Augustus T Barratt and Victor Roger. Bristol, 27 August 1900; Apollo Theatre, London, 7 September 1901.

George Edwardes first produced his British version of the dazzling French musical comedy *Les Fêtards* (ad J Smyth Piggott) as a non-musical play (*Kitty Grey*, Vaudeville Theatre, 25 April 1900). However, he changed his mind in mid-run and, closing the production after 107 West End performances, he had the play briskly re-musicalized so that, less than three weeks after the London closure, he was able to open a new, musical version of *Kitty Grey* in Bristol with several of the same players still holding their London rôles.

In a very strong Edwardes cast, Ethel Sydney played the Quakerish Baronne de Trègue and Maurice Farkoa (whose Smyrnese accent was responsible for this character being made French instead of English as in the play version) her philandering husband, with Evie Greene as Kitty, the actress who teaches the lady about sex and how to use it to control an errant mate. Plump and funny Lillie Belmore took the plum character rôle of the wardrobe lady which had been created by Marie Desclauzas, Harry Monkhouse was the sex-seeking King of Illyria and G P Huntley the goofy and scene-stealing Lord Plantaganet. If the strong text of the original play was well adhered to, the musical part was a bit of a patchwork, a little of Roger's Parisian music being retained, and other songs being supplied by Edwardes's loyal Lionel Monckton, conductor Howard Talbot and others mostly less eminent. Monckton came out with the most successful song, a piece for expansive Mrs Bright, describing how she was once 'Little Zo-Zo' of the circus.

The new *Kitty Grey* proved such a success on the road that Edwardes decided to bring it back to town. Evie Greene, in spite of the fact that a special rôle had been written for her in Edwardes's upcoming *Three Little Maids*, stayed on and was paired with suitably American Edna May (the Baronne de Trègue was an American in the original script) for whom extra songs were supplied to make her part the co-lead, with Huntley repeating his road success alongside Farkoa, Charles Angelo (King) and Gladys Homfrey (Mrs Bright). In spite of the fact that it was Mars and Hennequin's delicious play and characters that were the heart of *Kitty Grey*, the version with music outran the play comprehensively: 220 London performances, umpteen tours (as soon as Farkoa was gone his rôle reverted to being 'Sir John Binfield'), and productions throughout the colonies over many years.

For the first of these, in Australia, George Edwardes sent out almost an entire principal cast from Britain. The 'Gaiety Company' carried *The Girl from Kays* and *Three Little Maids* as well as *Kitty Grey*, and the cross-casting was done in function of *Three Little Maids*, but Huntley and Farkoa were both there in their original rôles, alongside two of the three little maids, Madge Crichton (Kitty) and Delia Mason (Baronne), J Edward Fraser as the King and Clara Clifton as Mrs Bright. The show was not given for a run, but played for limited seasons in repertoire with its two fellows.

America had already had its own version of *Les Fêtards*

(*The Strollers*) some time previously, but a number of years later when Charles Frohman needed a Broadway vehicle for Huntley and Julia Sanderson, he produced the comedian's old hit for 50 New York performances at the New Amsterdam Theater. For that occasion the London 'balance' between the lady stars was abolished: Miss Sanderson sang five songs and a duet (including Jerome Kern's 'If a Girl Wants You' and 'Just Good Friends'), Valli Valli (Lady Binfield) had half a duet and 'Little Zo-Zo' had been suppressed. Only Angelo, now living in America and repeating his London rôle, got much of a sing otherwise.

An atypical musical in turn-of-the-century Britain, the very libretto-orientated *Kitty Grey* was an important forerunner to the farcical musical comedies of the postwar years. Unlike them, it did not make a feature of modern dance fashions, and its music was the music of the standard Victorian musical comedy rather than of the dance floor, but its long and wide popularity showed that there was a market for reasonably sophisticated musical plays on the lines of the French vaudeville, as opposed to extravaganza, to spectacle or to the styles practised by Edwardes at either the Gaiety or Dalys. Yet, in spite of the fact that several successful pieces based more or less on good French plays followed it (*The Girl from Kays*, *Madame Sherry*, *The Spring Chicken*, *Peggy*), it was a style of piece that was oddly slow finding its feet in the English-speaking world.

Australia: Princess Theatre, Melbourne 25 June 1904; USA: New Amsterdam Theater 25 January 1909

KITTY'S KISSES Musical comedy in 2 acts by Philip Bartholomae and Otto Harbach adapted from Bartholomae's play *Little Miss Brown*. Lyrics by Gus Kahn. Music by Con Conrad. Playhouse Theater, New York, 6 May 1926.

A musical version of Bartholomae's 14-year-old play *Little Miss Brown*, the less accurately but more catchily titled *Kitty's Kisses* told the tale of little Kitty Brown (Dorothy Dilley) who, through a little bit of almost French misunderstanding, unintentionally spends a night asleep in a hotel room which is also (if chastely and elsewhere) occupied by Robert Dennison (Mark Smith), a perilously married man. However, the divorce lawyer summoned the next morning by Mrs Dennison (Frances Burke) to deal with the situation turns out to be a young man called Robert Mason (John Boles) who had fallen for Kitty during her eventful trip to the hotel the previous day, and, when all the farcical doings are sung and done, he is able to sort things out to everybody's satisfaction. William Wayne and Ruth Warren as a couple of hotel employees supplied the traditional soubretteries.

Kitty's Kisses was a piece well in the 1920s fashion for frantic and funny farce with loads of lively dances which were not obliged to take too much notice of the locations or the story: 'a rough and tumble of dancing men and women, individually and in chorus, at the pace that exhilarates while it kills ... as soon as the first curtain goes up the chorus begins ecstatically dancing between the railroad tracks and, from then on, it glides, pops, swoons, careens and charlestons through hotel corridors, lobbies, bedrooms and gardens indiscriminately ... ', The show also sported some light and bright summer fashions and some jolly songs, including a bright title number put over by Kitty and Robert who also joined to romantically sigh over 'Whenever I Dream', the hero's admission that 'I'm in Love', Kitty's tale of 'Two Fellows and a Girl', her duo with Dennison ('Early in the Morning') and her insistence in the face of the rest of the Dennison family that 'I Don't Want Him'. The soubrets bounced out a 'Thinking of You' and the second act danced to its feet 'Steppin' on the Blues'. It was all lively, well-constructed, harmlessly tuneful fun and, as a result, spent a fine 22 weeks on Broadway.

A sizeable portion of the show also made its way to London. Producer Jack Waller, on a shopping trip to New York, purchased both *Kitty's Kisses* and another of the season's successes, *The Girl Friend*, with a score by Rodgers and Hart. In one of history's better bits of botching, he then took the solid comical libretto of *Kitty's Kisses* plus 'Steppin' on the Blues','I'm in Love' and a number of other pieces of Con Conrad's score, welded them to some of the score of *The Girl Friend*, added a couple of Rodgers and Hart songs from *The Garrick Gaieties* ('Mountain Greenery', 'What's the Use of Talking?'), filled up the gaps with some local numbers by Vivian Ellis, had the whole lot shaken and stirred by musical comedy men-of-all-work Bert Lee and R P Weston and presented the show – which was altogether more *Kitty's Kisses* than it was *The Girl Friend* – at the Palace Theatre under the title of the latter. The hybrid show, with Roy Royston, Louise Browne and Clifford Mollison starred, proved delightful. It ran for a year (421 performances) in London, toured, was successfully produced in Australia with Annie Croft starred as Kitty, adapted into Hungarian and staged in Budapest, and went on to be given periodic revivals throughout Britain for many decades thereafter, all in and under the name of *The Girl Friend*.

The most recent production of a version of this version, at Colchester's Mercury Theatre in 1987, used five *Kitty's Kisses* numbers alongside just two and a half by Rodgers and Hart who nevertheless had their names billed above the title for a piece which, even more than Britain's original production, was more *Kitty's Kisses* than *The Girl Friend*. And altogether the better for it.

Recording: Colchester cast (as *The Girl Friend*) (TER)

KLAW, Marcus (b Paducah, Ky, 29 May 1858; d Bracken Fell, Hassocks, 14 June 1936). Powerful Broadway producer of the early 20th century.

Lawyer Klaw had his first connection with the theatre when he dealt with a suit against theatrical pirates for Gus Frohman. He soon made serious inroads into the show business world, however, when, after first having tried his hand at touring management, he moved to New York and joined with Abe Erlanger to take over an important theatrical agency (1888). Their influence and power soon spread, and the partners were the moving force in the establishment of the Theatrical Syndicate, a body which sought to bring order to the touring booking systems of the time and which was regarded (by those who were not part of it) as an attempt to monopolize the management of the American theatre.

During the years in which they had an effective control of a large section of the New York and regional theatres, Klaw and Erlanger produced many musical shows as product for their houses. These included the *Rogers Brothers*

series, dialect low-comedy shows intentionally set up to challenge the productions of the unsubdued Weber and Fields on their own ground, Sousa's *The Bride Elect* (1898) and *The Free Lance* (1906), the McIntyre and Heath musical *The Ham Tree* (1905), George M Cohan's *Forty-Five Minutes from Broadway* (1906), Victor Herbert's cartoon musical *Little Nemo* (1908), *The Silver Star* (1909) with Adeline Genée as star, such imports as *Véronique*, *The Count of Luxemburg*, *The Spring Chicken*, *La Mascotte*, *Eva*, Kálmán's *Miss Springtime* (*Zsuzsi kisasszony*) and *The Riviera Girl* (*Die Csárdásfürstin*), and the series of Ivan Caryll musicals beginning with the vastly successful *The Pink Lady* (1911) and *Oh! Oh! Delphine* (1912), the first of which they also presented in Britain.

The thin-faced, droopy-moustachioed Klaw appeared as the gentlemanly and receptive half of the feared and disliked (by their rivals) partnership with the pugnacious, pudgy and bald Erlanger. However, there can be little doubt, for all that he liked to have it believed otherwise, that the former lawyer had as much to do as his more openly dislikeable – and equally efficacious – partner with the policies and actions that earned Klaw and Erlanger their hated position.

In 1919 the partnership broke up, and Klaw, who built the Klaw Theater in the following year, continued to produce on his own for several more years. His first, and sole musical, venture, *Dere Mabel* (1920), a piece written by the daughter of a Bostonian businessman and produced in her home town, folded there. In 1927 he sold up and, two years later, moved to Britain where he lived in retirement for his last ten years.

KLEIN, Charles (b London, 7 January 1867; d at sea, 7 May 1915). Playwright and librettist to the turn-of-the-century Broadway stage.

An actor from the time of his moving to America from his native Britain in 1882, Klein had his first play as an author, *By Proxy*, produced in the United States in 1891. He ventured into the musical theatre at first by way of pasticcio farce-comedy, sometimes apparently without allowing his name on the programme, and by adaptation, turning out one of the many versions of *Niniche* which found their way to the world's stages following the vaudeville's original Paris production. *The Merry Countess* starred Marie Jansen and Dan Daly in its leading rôles for 10 Broadway performances.

He found significant success with his first original libretto, the text for John Philip Sousa's enduring comic opera *El Capitan*, and thereafter wrote several highly successful plays (*Heartsease*, *The Music Master*, *The Lion and the Mouse*) and the odd play with some music (*Happy Little Home*, 14th Street Theater 25 November 1895), whilst returning regularly to the genuine musical stage. *The Charlatan*, a second collaboration with Sousa, proved an excellent vehicle for De Wolf Hopper and his company, and *Mr Pickwick*, with a score by Klein's brother Manuel, gave the comedian a fine Dickens rôle in a musical which was liked on the road if not in New York. Of his other very varying musical shows *A Royal Rogue* was mounted for the 'Jefferson de Angelis Musical Comedy Company', *The Red Feather* was a Ziegfeld romantico-swashbucker of a piece starring the specifically soprano Grace van Studdiford, whilst *Cousin Lucy* was written to feature female impersonator Julian Eltinge.

Klein was travelling to Europe with Charles Frohman, for whom he had once worked as play-reader, when the *Lusitania* was sunk and both men were drowned.

Klein's play *Maggie Pepper* (1913), which had originally housed a notable performance by Rose Stahl as the lady of the title, was subsequently turned into a musical comedy vehicle for Charlotte Greenwood as *Letty Pepper* (1922).

1891 **A Mile a Minute** (pasticcio) People's Theater 9 February
1895 **The Merry Countess** (*Niniche*) American version w Thomas Frost (Garrick Theater)
1896 **El Capitan** (John Philip Sousa/Frost) Broadway Theater 20 April
1898 **The Charlatan** (aka *The Mystical Miss*) (Sousa) Knickerbocker Theater 5 September
1900 **A Royal Rogue** (W T Francis/Grant Stewart) Broadway Theater, 24 December
1903 **Mr Pickwick** (Manuel Klein) Herald Square Theater 19 January
1903 **The Red Feather** (Reginald De Koven/Charles Emerson Cook) Lyric Theater 9 November
1915 **Cousin Lucy** (Jerome Kern et al) George M Cohan Theater 29 August

KLEIN, Manuel (b London, 6 December 1876; d Yonkers, NY, 1 June 1919).

Manuel Klein followed his brother, Charles, to America at 20 years' distance and worked there as a conductor, notably for ten years at the New York Hippodrome (1905–15), and as a composer of musical scores and occasionally lyrics. Most of these were intended to accompany the vast spectacles staged at the Hippodrome, but his credits also included two children's musicals and a Dickensian vehicle for De Wolf Hopper. He was sacked by the Shuberts in 1915, apparently for 'insubordination', and subsequently returned to Britain where he acted as musical director for Grossmith and Laurillard's Gaiety Theatre production of *Tonight's the Night*. He suffered a traumatism when the theatre came under fire from a German zeppelin and was forced to give up work, returning to America where he died a few years after, having never recovered from the shock. The Klein family subsequently sued the German government for encompassing the deaths of the two brothers.

In 1921 some of the songs he had written for the out-of-town flop *High and Dri* were posthumously used to make up the score of the musical *It's Up to You* at the Casino Theater. His of-the-moment song successes included 'Moon Dear' and 'Red Sky', whilst his 'Lucia' made its way back to Britain to be interpolated in the score of Seymour Hicks's *The Gay Gordons*.

1903 **Mr Pickwick** (Charles Klein) Herald Square Theater 19 January
1905 **A Yankee Circus on Mars** (w Jean Schwartz/Harry Williams/George Hobart) Hippodrome 12 April
1905 **Tomorrowland** (John Kendrick Bangs) Hippodrome in *A Yankee Circus on Mars*
1905 **A Society Circus** (w Gustave Luders/Sydney Rosenfeld) Hippodrome 13 December
1906 **The Man from Now** (Vincent Bryan/Bangs) New Amsterdam Theater 3 September
1906 **Pioneer Days** (Carrol Fleming) Hippodrome 28 November

1906 **Neptune's Daughter** (Edward P Temple) 1 act Hippodrome 28 November
1907 **The Top of the World** (Anne Caldwell/James O'Dea/Mark E Swan) Hippodrome 19 October
1907 **The Auto Race** (Temple) Hippodrome 25 November
1908 **The Battle of Port Arthur** (Owen Davis) 2 scenes Hippodrome 13 January
1908 **Sporting Days** (R H Burnside) Hippodrome 5 September
1908 **The Land of Birds** (Burnside) ballet with songs in *Sporting Days*
1908 **The Battle in the Skies** (Burnside) in *Sporting Days*
1908 **The Pied Piper** (Burnside) Hippodrome 3 December
1909 **A Trip to Japan** (Burnside) Hippodrome 4 September
1910 **The International Cup** (Burnside) Hippodrome 3 September
1911 **Bow Sing** (Carroll Fleming) 1 act Winter Garden 20 March
1911 **Around the World** (Fleming) Hippodrome 2 September
1911 **Undine** (M Klein) 1 act Winter Garden 20 November
1912 **Under Many Flags** (Fleming, Arthur Voegtlin) Hippodrome 31 August
1913 **America** (Voegtlin, John P Wilson) Hippodrome 30 August
1913 **Hop o' My Thumb** (George Sims et al ad Sydney Rosenfeld) Manhattan Opera House 26 November
1914 **The Wars of the World** (Voegtlin) Hippodrome 5 September
1919 **High and Dri** (Augustus McHugh, Edward Paulton, A Douglas Leavitt)
1921 **It's Up to You** (revised *High and Dri*) Casino Theater 24 March

A third of the four Klein brothers, Alexander, also worked in the theatre, as a performer, spending a considerable amount of his career with De Wolf Hopper's companies.

KNAACK, Wilhelm (b Rostock, Germany, 1823; d Vienna, 29 October 1894). Top-rank comic of the mid-19th century Vienna stage.

On the stage from his early twenties, Knaack played in Stralsund, Greifswalde, Güstrow, Lübeck and, from 1852, at the Friedrich-Wilhelmstädtisches Theater in Berlin before he moved in 1857 to Vienna and was engaged at the Carltheater. He remained there for virtually the whole of the rest of his life, apart from a brief period with Treumann at the Theater am Franz-Josefs-Kai and another which he spent playing in German-language theatre in America, and in harness with Karl Blasel and Josef Matras he made up the trio of great and enormously popular Viennese comedians of the time.

Knaack introduced the German versions of a plethora of Offenbach rôles in the earliest days of the composer's introduction to Vienna including Crécy-Crécy (*Toto*), Boboli (*Die schöne Weiber von Georgien*), Baron Gondremarck (*Pariser Leben*, a part which he played into his seventies), Sparadrap (*Princesse de Trébizonde*), John Styx (*Orphée aux enfers*), Trompeter und Näherin, Romboïdal (*L'Île de Tulipatan*), Tschin-Tschin (*Tschin-Tschin*), Der kleine Arthur (*Die schöne Magellone*), Baptist (*Die Seufzerbrücke*), Christobal (*Die Schwätzerin von Saragossa*), Frau Hetschepetsch (*Die Damen von Stand*), Jean Brösel (ie Petermann, *Salon Pitzelberger*), Ignazio (*Tromb-al-ca-zar*), Plumotzeau (*Apotheker und Friseur*), Bellecoeur (*Kakadu*), Arsenico (*Coscoletto*), Marquis von Fontrose (*Die Schäfer*), Balabreloque (*Schneeball*), Chrisostome (*Schönröschen*) and von Tricasse (*Doktor Ox*). He succeeded Nestroy in the rôle of Pan in *Daphnis und Chloë*, as well as appearing in other Viennesed French works in such parts as Alcidor von Rosenville (*Die Reise nach China*), Wetterhahn (*Confusius IX*), Larivaudière (*Angot*), Grison (*Die schöne Bourbonnaise*), Casteldémoli (*Graziella*), Graf Cornisti (*Niniche*), Prinz Charles (*Der grosse Casimir*) and Bodin-Bridet (*Papas Frau*).

Knaack also took part in some of the earliest original Viennese works, appearing as Hieronymus Geier in *Flotte Bursche*, Svermazet in *Mannschaft am Bord*, Ritter Hannibal vom Bisamberg (*Das Donauweibchen*), Nicodemus Violette (*Isabella*), Breselmaier (*In der Sackgasse*) and Lord Blessington (*Fitzliputzli*) and he created, amongst others, the more important rôles of Graf Kantschukoff in *Fatinitza* (1876), Herzog von Ricerac in *Prinz Methusalem*, Mephisto in *Der Teufel auf Erden*, Bob Chester in *Die Mormonen* (1879), Muzinard in *Der Kukuk* and Barnacle in *Nisida* (1880).

After his trip to America, where he appeared at the Thalia Theater with the Gallmeyer-Tewele combination, in challenge to Geistinger and her company, in his rôles in *Niniche*, *Die Prinzessin von Trapezunt* and a series of comedies, he returned to the Carltheater in 1886 to carry on with a series of new shows and rôles: Iwan der Schrecklich (*Der Vagabund*), Alfred Pharoa Pascha (*Josefine und ihre Schwestern*), Van der Putt-Putt (*Rikiki*), Eustachio fa Presto (*Die Dreizehn*), Lord Middleditch (*Der Glücksritter*), Prince Prostamento (*Der Sänger von Palermo*), Wilfred Shadbolt (*Capitän Wilson*), Campistrel (*Colombine*), Bluff (ie Dufois) (*Erminie*), Schnerb (*Die Uhlanen*), Pierre Josua Favart (*Die Kätzchen*), Pichard (*Das Fräulein vom Telephone*), Verduron (*Susette, oder Zweihundert millionen*) and Van der Beerenboom (*Lachende Erben*). Turned 70, he was still to be seen as Gondremarck, Kantschukoff and Sparadrap, as well as in the occasional new rôle such as Borgos in *Edelweiss* or the American David Osteborn in the French spectacular *Das Goldland*. Shortly before his death, he played Spettigue to the Fancourt Babberly of the equally veteran Blasel in the play *Charley's Aunt*.

KNEPLER, Paul [KNÖPLER, Paul] (b Vienna, 29 October 1879; d Vienna, 17 December 1967). Viennese composer turned librettist.

Like Genée and Hopp before him and others since, Paul Knepler set out to be a composer for the musical theatre and yet had his most considerable success as a librettist and lyricist. Nevertheless, he did well enough with his first produced work as a composer-author, a romanticized bio-musical of the favourite Viennese 19th-century soubrette Josefine ('Pepi') Gallmeyer. Produced at the Wiener Bürgertheater with Rosy Werginz (Gallmeyer) and Fritz Schrödter (Josef Matras) starring, and with such old-time favourites as Anna Grobecker (Paula Bäck), Karl Treumann (August Nietl) and Offenbach himself (Heinrich Pirk) represented on the stage, it ran for 139 performances.

In 1924 Knepler teamed with librettist Ignaz Michael Welleminsky on a second Operette *Wenn der Hollunder blüht*, which was produced in Berlin, and at the same time he sent a libretto he had written based on the putative love-life of another historical character, the violinist Paganini, to Lehár. Lehár accepted it with some delight and put Knepler to work on the text with the proven Béla Jenbach. The success of the resultant Operette established its

author as a librettist, and thereafter, often in collaboration with Welleminsky, he turned out books for many of the best composers of the time, including Leo Ascher, Eduard Künneke, Oscar Straus and Emmerich Kálmán. However, although he had a certain success with yet another text set in theatreland, the tale of the actor Devrient and his Spanish dancer as told in Künneke's *Die lockende Flamme*, and again with his adaptation to the stage of the filmscript *Zwei Herzen im Dreivierteltakt* (yet another show about a show), of his original texts it was his only other collaboration with Lehár, on the grimly passionate libretto for the composer's last work, *Giuditta* (1935), which won him, at length if at not at the time of production, any kind of lasting laurels.

Knepler also translated the zarzuela *El barberillo de Lavapiès* (w Fred Salo Tysh) as *Lamparilla* for the German-language stage, and worked on adaptations of several classic Operetten. He had notable success with his rewrite of Millöcker's *Gasparone* (which introduced the famous 'Dunkelrote Rosen') and also of the fresh book for Theo Mackeben's musical remake of Millöcker's *Gräfin Dubarry* as *Die Dubarry*. Both versions, conforming more readily to operettic styles of the years between the wars than their originals, found themselves a place in the repertoire they would not otherwise have recovered.

1921 **Josefine Gallmeyer** (Knepler) Wiener Bürgertheater 22 March
1924 **Wenn der Hollunder blüht** (Knepler/w Ignaz M Welleminsky) Bundestheater (Metropoltheater), Berlin 1 July
1925 **Paganini** (Franz Lehár/w Béla Jenbach) Johann Strauss-Theater 30 October
1927 **Die Glocken von Paris** (Richard Fall/w Welleminsky) Carltheater 14 October
1931 **Bei der Wirtin Rosenrot** (Leo Ascher/w Fritz Löhner-Beda) Theater des Westens, Berlin 14 March
1931 **Die Toni aus Wien** (Ernst Steffan/Willner, Rubricius ad w Steffan)
1932 **Tanz durchs Leben** (R Düringer/w Welleminsky) Stadttheater, Danzig 13 November
1933 **Gasparone** revised version w Steffan (Volksoper)
1933 **Zwei Herzen im Dreivierteltakt** (*Der verlorene Walzer*) (Robert Stolz/w Welleminsky) Opernhaus, Zurich 30 September
1933 **Die lockende Flamme** (Eduard Künneke/w Welleminsky) Theater des Westens 25 December
1934 **Giuditta** (Lehár/w Löhner-Beda) Operntheater 20 January
1935 **Die Dubarry** (Carl Millöcker arr Theo Mackeben/w Welleminsky) Theater an der Wien 30 August
1936 **Kaiserin Josephine** (Emmerich Kálmán/w Geza Herczeg) Stadttheater, Zurich 18 January
1950 **Ihr erster Walzer** (Oscar Straus/w Armin Robinson, Robert Gilbert) Bayerische Staatsoper, Munich 31 March
1963 **Rhapsodie der Liebe** (Nico Dostal/w Peter Herz) Städtische Bühnen, Nuremberg-Furth 9 November

KNICKERBOCKER HOLIDAY Musical comedy in 2 acts by Maxwell Anderson based on Washington Irving's *Father Knickerbocker's History of New York*. Music by Kurt Weill. Barrymore Theater, New York, 19 October 1938.

A costume musical which utilized the low-comedy 'Dutch' accent, popular on the musical stage 30 to 50 years earlier, in a tale of old New York, *Knickerbocker Holiday* told the story of knifegrinder Brom Broeck (Richard Kollmar) who has to fight against both a peremptory town council and the Governor, Pieter Stuyvesant (Walter Huston), in order to get the girl he wants (Tina, played by Jeanne Maddern). In fact, he succeeds not by his own exertions but only when author Washington Irving (Ray Middleton) century-hops and deters Stuyvesant from hanging the insubordinate fellow by threatening him with the thumbs-down verdict of posterity.

Anderson's libretto and dialogue included some tetchily social, political and even jingoistic moments in the unrolling of its standard comic-opera story, whilst taking time off for such personal jibes as calling one buffoonish councillor Roosevelt and another Vanderbilt. Weill's score, on the other hand, was sometimes adventurous in its form, but it scored best when following the traditional song patterns that produced Stuyvesant's 'September Song', crackled out by Huston in a rueful look at approaching age. 'September Song', which found its way into the score only when Huston requested a number that would give his rather one-dimensional character some personality, has remained the most popular single number composed by Kurt Weill for a Broadway show.

The show was dubbed 'unwieldy ... the light fantastic vein of musical comedy does not become [Anderson's] serious mind – or vice versa' and, in spite of a memorable performance by top-billed Huston, who negated some of Anderson's intent by making the Governor a warmly likeable character as he danced along peg-legged at the head of a line of little Dutch girls, the Playwrights' Company production of the rather ill-assorted *Knickerbocker Holiday* lasted only 168 performances on Broadway.

It was subsequently filmed, with Charles Coburn starred as Stuyvesant, Constance Dowling as Tina and Nelson Eddy as Broeck, in a version which used but four numbers from the original score, topped up with contributions from Werner Richard Heymann, Jule Styne, Sammy Cahn, Theodore Paxton and with both Forman Brown and Eddy himself having a go at lyricking Weill's music. In 1950 (17 November) it was televised with Dennis King, Doretta Morrow and John Raitt featured, and its writers' reputations and political standpoint have helped ensure it regular regional and occasional performances since. An attempt at a major Broadway-bound revival, mounted at the San Francisco Light Opera in 1971 with Burt Lancaster starred as Stuyvesant and Anita Gillette and David Holliday in support did not, in the end, make it to the east coast.

Germany: Thalia-Theater, Hamburg 25 September 1976; Film: United Artists 1944
Recordings: original cast compilation (AEI), film soundtrack (Joey)

A KNIGHT FOR A DAY Musical comedy in 2 acts by Robert B Smith. Music by Raymond Hubbell. Wallack's Theater, New York, 16 December 1907.

Musical-comedy star Sallie Fisher's Chicago successes earned her a fairly transparent title-rôle in *Mam'selle Sallie*, a musical manufactured by Robert B Smith with songs by Raymond Hubbell, which was duly trouped from Chicago around the country and eventually, and almost incidentally, towards New York. Miss Fisher played a Mittel-European washerwoman disguised as a brigand who is trying to get back the missing proofs of her pals' noble birth, to the accompaniment of a set of lively songs which had little of

the Continental about them, and of a good deal of low comedy from British star Katie Barry and John Slavin.

A week at the combination house grandly known as the Grand Opera House (26 November 1906), and 16 performances at the New York Theater saw the show out of town and back on the road, but producer John C Fisher did not give up. *Mam'selle Sallie* was given a wash and brush-up and turned up again the following season under the title *A Knight for a Day*. The plot was much as before, Miss Fisher and Slavin still starred (with May Vokes replacing Miss Barry) and the score had simply been jollied up with more of the same, but this time Broadway liked it well enough to keep it running for 176 performances. Equipped with this record – a much longer run than many of the most memorable shows of its time – it headed out onto the roads again with the cachet of Broadway success attached. One road even led as far as Australia where W S Percy, Bert Gilbert, Herbert Clayton, Toby Claude and Grace Edinsell featured in a brief production under the banner of the J C Williamson comic-opera company.

Australia: Her Majesty's Theatre, Sydney 9 July 1910

KNOBLOCK, Edward [KNOBLAUCH, Edward] (b New York, 7 April 1874; d London, 19 July 1945). Writer for all fields who had some success in the musical theatre.

Knoblock began his working life as an actor in the British theatre, but he soon switched to play-writing and had memorable successes on the London stage with *Kismet* (1911) and *Milestones* (1912). He wrote several short musical pieces for the variety theatre, including a musical sketch on the *Kismet* character of Hajj for Oscar Asche and Lily Brayton, before, in 1919, he combined with the *Maid of the Mountains* composer and lyricist Harold Fraser-Simson and Harry Graham to provide a new vehicle for their show's star, José Collins. The resultant *Our Peg*, based exceedingly loosely on the loves of the historical Irish actress Peg Woffington, was tried out successfully in Manchester, but the long runs of its predecessors in London shut it out from Daly's Theatre and, although it toured extensively, without Miss Collins, the piece never played town.

The following year the East End musical *Cherry* which Knoblock wrote for C B Cochran had only a limited run, and he had thereafter but an intermittent connection with the musical theatre. In 1931, in collaboration with J B Priestley, he authored a stage version of *The Good Companions* with songs by Richard Addinsell and in 1944 he did a hatchet-job of an adaptation on *Merrie England* for a highly successful revival of Edward German's musical.

The author of several screenplays, he wrote the well-devised film version of *Chu Chin Chow* (w L du Garde Peach, Sidney Gilliatt), a piece which had been written very much along the lines of his *Kismet* by original *Kismet* star, Oscar Asche. *Kismet* was, in its turn, most successfully adapted into a musical comedy by Charles Lederer and Luther Davis, with a score compiled by George Wright and Robert Forrest from the melodies of Borodin, putting Knoblock posthumously into the repertoire of classic musical theatre.

1914 **England Expects** (Edward Jones/w Seymour Hicks) 1 act London Opera House 17 September

1915 **Hajj** (Christopher Wilson) 1 act Palace Theatre 22 February

1919 **Our Peg** (Harold Fraser-Simson/Harry Graham) Prince's Theatre, Manchester 24 December

1920 **Cherry** (Melville Gideon) Apollo Theatre 22 July

Autobiography: *Round the Room* (Chapman & Hall, London, 1939)

KNOPF, Martin (b Treuenbrietzen, 2 February 1876; d unknown).

A prolific composer of musical plays, most often for the German provinces. Knopf's work was long present on the stages of his own country but only rarely played further afield. The little one-acter *Décolleté und cie*, originally seen at Vienna's Établissement Ronacher, was exported to London and, as *Maison Décolleté* (ad George Arthurs, Sydney Morgan) played on a bill at the London Pavilion during the brief pre-war fashion for Continental musical playlets in variety theatres, and *Der blonde Zieguener* made it to Rotterdam's Tivoli Theater (*Roszi de zigeuner*) in 1931.

1908 **Venus auf Seide** (Hans Brennert) Apollotheater, Cologne 1 October

1908 **Das Heiratsbad** (M Nowak, E Beuth) Residenztheater, Dresden 5 December

1909 **Suzette** (Max Epstein) Neues Operettentheater, Mannheim 21 October

1910 **Die Dame von Moulin-Rouge** (Louis Taufstein) 1 act Intimes Theater 7 April

1911 **Im Schlafcoupé** (Taufstein) 1 act Apollotheater 1 April

1911 **Wir tanzen durchs Leben** (Dora Duncker, Hans Gaus) Kurtheater, Freienwalde 18 June

1912 **Décolleté und cie** (Taufstein, Erich Urban) 1 act Ronacher, Vienna 1 April

1912 **Pariser Luft** (Taufstein/Alexander Engel, Julius Horst) Luisen-Theater, Königsberg 23 June

1912 **Der Zaungast** (Gaus, Taufstein) Kurtheater, Freienwalde 23 June

1912 **Die Bajadere** (Taufstein) Residenztheater, Dresden 6 December

1914 **Die kleine Motte** (Taufstein) Luisen-Theater, Königsberg 21 March

1915 **Das kommt davon** (Otto Härting) Thalia-Theater, Elberfeld 6 February

1916 **Gräfin Mumm** (Urban, Taufstein) 1 act Theater des Westens 6 April

1919 **Meine Frau, deine Frau** (Taufstein, Theo Halton) Stadttheater, Brandenburg 11 May

1919 **Helenes Ehemänner** (Taufstein) Stadttheater, Brandenburg 27 September, Eden Theater, Berlin, 1920

1920 **Glück bei Frauen** (Julius Horst, Oskar Engel) Neues Operetten-Theater, Munich 14 August

1921 **Die Mädels von Davos** (Hans Bühler, Halton) Centraltheater 22 April

1921 **Die Nädelprinzess** (Wilhelm von Österen, Adolf von Körber) Volkstheater, Munich 30 April

1921 **Die kleine Hoheit** (Gaus) Neues Operetten-Theater 9 January

1922 **Die Tochter der Leda** (Cornelius) Thalia-Theater, Hamburg 3 June

1922 **Traum von Glück** (Eduard von der Beck) Wallner-Theater 2 May

1924 **Der Liebling der Frauen** (Willy Kaufmann) Deutsches Theater, Hannover 31 December

1926 **Der blonde Zigeuner** Bellevue-Theater, Stettin 20 November

1927 **Die ungeküsste Eva** Bellevue-Theater, Stettin 25 December

1929 **Das kleine Fräulein Li** (Hardt-Warden, Hermann Feiner) Thalia-Theater 25 December

1932 **Rutschbahn der Liebe** revised *Die Mädels von Davos* by H Bühler Thalia-Theater 23 December

KOLLO, Walter [KOLLODZIEJSKI, Elimar Walter] (b Neidenburg, Germany, 28 March 1878; d Berlin, 30 September 1940). One of German's leading composers of musical comedy in the early decades of the 20th century.

Intended by his father to follow him in the shopkeeping trade, Kollo worked effectively enough on his mother to be allowed at the age of 16 to go, instead, to study at the conservatoire at Sondershausen. Although his first bent was towards church music, he ended up working in a more popular area, writing songs and cabaret music, before moving on to become a répétiteur and then a conductor at the Luisen-Theater in Königsberg. It was in that town that his name appeared for the first time on a theatre-bill as composer, when the local Tivoli produced a little burlesque called *Die versunkene Glocke* with 'music by W Kollodziejski'. Thereafter his pieces were signed more succinctly.

He subsequently moved on to the very active Bellevue Theater at Stettin and then to Berlin, where he worked as a cabaret pianist as he began placing his songs in cabaret and revue, and he and his song-writing partner, Hermann Frey, saw their Operette *Ali Ben Mocca* produced at the Apollotheater. Kollo had further songs and small theatrical pieces played when Frey briefly and disastrously opened his own little cabaret theatre, but if the experience ruined his friend, it gave the composer sufficient exposure for him to be asked to set a little playlet written by the well-placed authors Rudolf Schanzer and August Neidhart. *Sein Herzensjunge* was well enough received at Elberfeld and in Vienna to ease Kollo further into the musical theatre establishment, and within little more than a year his first significant successes had begun.

After re-setting of the saucy American success *Alma, wo wohnst du?* for the German stage, he moved on to join the co-founder of the newly activated Berliner Theater, Rudolf Bernauer, and his collaborator, Schanzer, on their highly successful New Year's Eve Posse *Grosse Rosinen* and then on the manufacture of a series of musical comedies, the first of which, capitalizing on the new craze for moving pictures, was entitled *Filmzauber*. *Filmzauber* was a grand Berlin success, and it was subsequently exported throughout the world (*The Queen of the Movies*, *A Mozikirály* etc), giving the composer his first general international exposure.

Kollo remained resident composer at the Berliner Theater for seven years, providing the scores (often in collaboration with the musical director Willi Bredschneider) for a series of a further seven more-or-less annual musical comedies and Operetten which began with the most widely-played, *Wie einst im Mai* (1913), then continued, end-to-end through the war years, with *Extrablätter*, the 'Scherzspiel mit Gesang' *Wenn zwei Hochzeit machen* ('Hindenburg-Marsch', 'Ein Jüngling kann nicht gut allein', 'Puppe, sei nicht so neutral!', 'Du süsses Gulaschmägdelein'), *Auf Flügeln des Gesanges*, and peaked with the longest-running, the Operette *Die tolle Komtess* (more than 350 performances in 1917–18, revival 1919, 'Dein auf ewig', 'Edelweiss-Marsch', 'Junges Herz lass die Liebe ein'), *Blitzblaues Blut* (nearly 300 performances, 'Immer hinterdrein', 'Jeder Mann hat einen dunkeln

Plate 153.

Punkt', 'Liebe auf den ersten Blick', 'Mädchen, Ihr seid wie das Mailicht') and seven months of *Sterne, die wieder leuchtet*.

During this pre-war and wartime period, however, the composer spread himself and his music far beyond the Berliner Theater. A commission from Hamburg produced *Der Liebesonkel* which duly made its way to Berlin and ultimately to New York's Irving Place Theater under the title *Die tolle Dolly* (1918), and a second Hamburg piece, the comical *Der Juxbaron*, followed it with even wider success. Then, with the triumph of *Wie einst im Mai* at its height, Kollo began simultaneously supplying Hermann Haller with what was to become a second wartime series of not quite end-to-end Operetten for his Theater am Nollendorfplatz. The patriotic four-act 'Vaterländisches Volksstück' *Immer feste druff!* ('Unser Kaiser', 'Der Soldate', 'Marine und Zeppeline', 'Auf der Banke an der Panke', 'Wenn man ein Mädchen küsst') set things rolling with a run of nearly two years and more than 650 performances, and after Nelson's *Blaue Jungens* (with lyrics by Kollo's old friend, Frey) had run through six months, Kollo followed up with *Die Gulaschkanone* and a second long-running hit, a version of J M Barrie's *Quality Street*, with its wartime message couched in music. As *Drei alte Schachteln* ('Ach Jott, was sind die Männer dumm', 'Drei alte Schachteln geh'n zum Ball') it ran for over 450 performances, went on to Vienna, and even eventually ended up (briefly) on Broadway. And amongst all this activity, on two fronts, Kollo found time to supply a further hit, *Der selige Balduin* ('Rechts im Arm', 'Mausi, wenn's dunkel ist', 'Dolores', 'Ja, wen der Storch im Mai gebracht') to Max Monti's Operetten-Theater.

The hugely successful composer now began to diversify his interests. Whilst still composing such pieces as the distinctly popular *Fräulein Puck*, produced in Munich for 150 performances before moving on to Berlin, he founded his own publishing house and then took on first the management of the Bellevue-Theater in Stettin (1919–22), then that of the Theater in der Kommandantenstrasse, where he revived Bromme's *Die Dame in Frack* and produced his own *Das verjungte Adolar*, and finally the Neues-Operetten-Theater am Schiffbauerdamm where he staged his *Die Königin von Nacht* and *Lady Chic*. He had, however, ill chosen his moment to venture into business. By 1922 his ventures had been flattened by the postwar inflation of the mark, but he continued to cling to a managerial chair just a little longer with the tiny Kabarett Pot-Pourri until that, too, finally went under.

If his career as a businessman was more or less done, Kollo, however, continued to compose. He returned to Haller to write the music for the vastly popular and glitzy revues which the manager staged at the Admiralspalast between 1923 and 1927 (*Drunter und Drüber, Noch und Noch, Achtung, Welle 505!, An und Aus, Wann und Wo, Schön und Schick*), scoring one of his greatest song hits with 'Solang noch Untern Linden' in the 1923 *Drunter und Drüber*, and he continued to turn out a regular supply of Operetten, both for Haller and for other managers. In 1924 his 20-year-old son Willi made his theatrical début as a lyricist in tandem with his father in *Die Frau ohne Kuss*, which followed its Berlin production with 80 performances at Vienna's Rolandbühne in 1927.

However, although Berlin welcomed several of Kollo's pieces over the next 15 years, and a handful ventured as far as Vienna, and although he continued to turn out a regular supply of popular Berliner songs, he was never again to taste the kind of theatrical success he had had during the whirlwind war years. Only *Marietta* and the 1927 Operette

Drei arme kleine Mädels, a piece written in blatant imitation of *Wie einst im Mai*, which reached Vienna, Budapest and America as the Shuberts' *Three Little Girls* (1930, ad Marie Armstrong Hecht, Gertrude Purcell) came anywhere near drawing the attention Kollo had attracted in the half-dozen years he had spent challenging Jean Gilbert at the forefront of the German Operette, during its most effective period.

In fact, even during that time, Kollo never found the grand overseas success that his contemporary did. In Britain, he was represented only by a revamped version of *Filmzauber*, played as *The Girl on the Film* (add mus Szirmai), and although a number of his pieces were staged in America, he came out of the action very poorly. *Wie einst im Mai* became a huge hit as *Maytime*, but Kollo's entire score had been replaced by Sigmund Romberg. *Alma, wo wohnst du?* had won success with a score by librettist Adolf Philipp (masquerading as 'Jean Briquet'), before Kollo remusicked it for Germany, *Sterne, die wieder leuchtet* underwent a major botching before flopping as *Springtime of Youth*, *Drei alte Schachteln* lived for even less time as *Phoebe of Quality Street*, and only *Three Little Girls* (103 performances) and *Queen of the Movies* of the American versions of his plays, plus the German-language presentation of *Der Juxbaron*, gave him any kind of worthwhile New York representation. The nearest he came to a hit song on Broadway was when one of his songs was hijacked into Eysler's *Die Frauenfresser* as 'Come on Over Here'.

In Hungary, Kollo was represented by *Pintyöke* (*Alma*), *A mozikirály* (*Filmzauber*), *A csaladfö* (*Der selige Balduin*), *Harom a venlány* (*Drei alte Schachteln*), *Egyszer volt* (*Wie einst im Mai*), *Ej királynö* (*Die Königin der Nacht*), *Link báró* (*Der Juxbaron*), *Katicabogár* and *A kis szelburdi* (*Die tolle Komtess*), whilst France got a brief glimpse of *Pour plaire aux femmes* (*Frauen haben das gerne*) in the late 1930s.

His son, **Willi Kollo**, wrote several plays, screenplays, songs and theatre lyrics, and adapted his father's *Wie einst im Mai* for a second copyright life by adding other pieces of his own and of Walter's music to the score and removing Bredschneider's contribution. He also composed music for both the stage and screen. His son, René Kollo, became celebrated as an Operette and opera singer.

1897 **Die versunkene Glocke** (Paul Kasten) Tivoli, Königsberg 27 July

1907 **Ali Ben Mocca** (Hermann Frey, F W Hardt, Louis Hermann) Apollotheater 2 March

1909 **Der süsse Leutnant** (Henry Bender/Robert Breitenbach, Leopold Ely) 1 act Passage-Theater 2 October

1909 **Meyer mit 'n Hängeboden** (Paul Bendix) 1 act Buggenhagen 1 October

1909 **Sherlock Holmes in Treuenbrietzen** 1 act Buggenhagen

1911 **Sein Herzensjunge** (Rudolf Schanzer, August Neidhart) Thalia-Theater, Elberfeld 1 April

1911 **Der Brettlkönig** Liebichs Établissement, Breslau 18 September

1911 **Alma wo wohnst du?** (Adolf Philipp) Luisen-Theater 17 October

1911 **Grosse Rosinen** (w Willi Bredschneider, Bogumil Zepler, Leon Jessel/Schanzer, Rudolf Bernauer) Berliner Theater 31 December

1912 **Ein aufgelegtes Geschäft** (Frey, Hardt) Komische Oper 7 April

1912 **Der Liebesonkel** (aka *Die tolle Dolly*) (w Walter Schütt/ Frey, Alexander Pordes-Milo) Neues Theater, Hamburg 3 August; Walhalla-Theater, Berlin 13 August 1913

1912 **Filmzauber** (Schanzer, Bernauer) Berliner Theater 19 October

1912 **So wird's gemacht** (Frey, Hardt) Neues Theater, Hamburg December

1913 **Wie einst im Mai** (w Willi Bredschneider/Bernauer, Schanzer) Berliner Theater 4 October

1913 **Der Juxbaron** (Willy Wolff/Pordes-Milo, Hermann Haller) Carl-Schultze Theater, Hamburg 14 November

1914 **Extrablätter** (w Bredschneider/Schanzer, Heinz Gordon) Berliner Theater 24 October

1914 **Immer feste druff!** (aka *Gloria Viktoria*) (Haller, Wolff) Theater am Nollendorfplatz 1 October

1915 **Wenn zwei Hochzeit machen** (w Bredschneider/ Bernauer, Schanzer) Berliner Theater 23 October

1916 **Auf Flügeln des Gesanges** (w Bredschneider/Bernauer, Schanzer) Berliner Theater 9 September

1916 **Der selige Balduin** (Erich Urban, Wolff) Montis Operetten-Theater 31 March

1917 **Die tolle Komtess** (Bernauer, Schanzer) Berliner Theater 21 February

1917 **Die Gulaschkanone** (Haller, Wolff) Theater am Nollendorfplatz 23 February

1917 **Drei alte Schachteln** (Rideamus/Haller) Theater am Nollendorfplatz 6 October

1918 **Blitzblaues Blut** (Bernauer, Schanzer) Berliner Theater 9 February

1918 **Sterne, die wieder leuchtet** (Bernauer, Schanzer) Berliner Theater 6 November

1919 **Fräulein Puck** (Franz Arnold, Ernst Bach) Volkstheater, Munich 25 June

1920 **Der verjungte Adolar** (Kurt Kraatz, Richard Kessler, Frey) Theater in der Kommandantenstrasse 4 October

1921 **Die Königin der Nacht** (Arnold, Bach) Neues Operetten-Theater 2 September

1922 **Lady Chic** (Kraatz, Kessler, Willy Steinberg) Neues Operetten-Theater 11 March

1924 **Die Frau ohne Kuss** (Willi Kollo/Kessler) Schillertheater, Berlin 6 July

1923 **Marietta** (Willi Kollo/Robert Bodanzky, Bruno Hardt-Warden) Metropoltheater 22 December

1924 **Die vertauschte Frau** (Arnold, Bach) Operettenhaus am Schiffbauerdamm 22 December

1925 **Olly Polly** (Arnold, Bach) Theater am Zoo 3 September

1926 **Nur Du** (Hardt-Warden, Willi Kollo) Berliner Theater 23 December

1927 **Drei arme kleine Mädels** (Bruno Hardt-Warden, Feiner) Theater am Nollendorfplatz 22 April

1927 **Gaby und die Drei** (Kurt Robitschek, Paul Morgan) 1 act Johann Strauss-Theater, Vienna 26 May

1928 **Die grosse Kaiserin** (Robitschek, Morgan) 1 act Theater der Komiker 1 April

1928 **Kitty macht Karriere** Kabarett (Robitschek, Morgan) der Komiker 1 September

1928 **Arme Ritter** (Arnold, Bach) Volkstheater, Munich 22 September

1928 **Jettchen Gebert** (Wolff, Martin Zickel) Theater am Nollendorfplatz 22 December

1930 **Der doppelte Bräutigam** (Haller, Wolff) Theater am Schiffbauerdamm 7 March

1930 **Majestät lässt bitten** (Rideamus) Komische Oper 5 April

1934 **Derfflinger** (Karl Bretscneider) Metropoltheater 17 February

1933 **Die Männer sind mal so** (Halton, Rideamus) Schillertheater 4 January

1934 **Lieber reich – aber glücklich** (Arnold, Bach) Johann Strauss-Theater, Vienna 11 May

1935 **Heirat nicht ausgeschlossen** (Kessler) Komische Oper 4 January

1935 **Ein Kaiser ist verliebt** (Theo Halton) Deutsches National-altheater, Osnabrück 22 August

1935 **Frauen haben das gerne** (Arnold, Bach) Residenzbühne, Vienna 17 December

1936 **Die wilde Auguste** (Halton) Volksoper, Hamburg 18 February

1936 **Mädel Ahoi!** (Halton) Deutsches Nationaltheater, Osnabrück 17 April

1938 **Besuch am Abend** (Willi Kollo, Engelbrecht) Theater am Schiffbauerdamm 23 September

1940 **Das Schiff der schönen Frauen** Apollotheater, Cologne

1942 **Ich bin in meine Frau verliebt** (w Willi Kollo) Raimundtheater December

KOMJÁTI, Károly (b Budapest, 8 May 1896; d Budapest, 3 July 1953). Hungarian composer for his local and for Viennese stages.

Komjáti studied at the Budapest Zeneakadémia and went on to a fine career in the musical theatre, beginning as a répétiteur, chorusmaster and theatrical conductor at Kolozsvár, Bremen and, ultimately, Budapest's Magyar Színház. He was 22 when his first operett, *A kóristalány*, written to a text by top librettist Jenő Faragó, was staged at the Városi Színház and later at Vienna's Bundestheater (*Lily vom Chor* ad Felix Dörmann), but it was his second piece, produced just a few months later, that made his name. *Pillangó főhadnagy* (Lieutenant Butterfly), a military operett in the vein of the recent Kálmán hit *Tatárjárás*, was composed to a text by another expert librettist, Ferenc Martos, and with lyrics by the equally respected Imre Harmath. It was produced at Budapest's principal musical house, the Király Színház, where the last new native work mounted had been Szirmai's highly successful *Mágnás Miska*, and the premières since had been of no lesser works than *Liebeswalzer*, *Die Csárdásfürstin*, *Die Rose von Stambul* and *Wo die Lerche singt*.

The young composer's show was a wild success, reached its 200th Budapest performance within two years and was given a major revival in 1926 (Király Színház, 22 May) whilst further productions proliferated round the country. He followed up with several other well-regarded and successful pieces, of which *A harapós férj* (the snapping husband) was twice revived in various forms following its original production at the Fővárosi Operettszinház, *Fizessen nagysád*, a tale of the French Riviera, clocked up a fine 44 performances at the Vigszinház, and the 1932 *Éjféli tangó*, his most popular piece since his first great hit, travelled on from its original Király Színház production through Hungary, Germany (*Tango um Mitternacht* Neues Operetten-Theater, Leipzig 25 August 1932), Holland (*Tango der Liebe* Scala Theater, The Hague 1933 with Beppi de Vries and Johannes Heesters) and Austria (Volksoper 8 April 1933). Vienna, in fact, saw two Komjáti Operetten in 1933, for Hubert Marischka also produced *Ein Liebestraum* at the Theater an der Wien (27 October 1933) with Hungarian soprano Marta Eggerth and Wilhelm Klitsch starred for a season of 49 performances.

The Király Színház produced one further Komjáti piece, *A szegény ördög* (the poor devil), a piece based on Machiavelli, in 1934, the Városi Színház presented his *Bécsi tavasz* (spring in Vienna) with Hanna Honthy and Árpád Latabár the following year, and the Fővárosi Operettszinház produced both his *Antoinette* with Gitta Alpár starring in the rôle of Marie Antoinette (as perceived in Max Bertuch's novel), and his final work, *Csicsónének három lánya*, with Hanna Honthy starred, but in spite of

fulfilling more than 20 highly satisfying years of a writing career, Komjáti's single most successful piece remained the work he had written at 22 years of age.

1918 **A kóristalány** (Jenő Faragó) Városi Színház January

1918 **Pillangó főhadnagy** (Imre Harmath/Ferenc Martos) Király Színház 7 June

1922 **Három a tánc** (Istvan Szomaházy, Faragó) Király Színház 20 May

1931 **A harapós férj** (Tamás Emőd, Rezső Török) Fővárosi Operettszinház 22 March

1931 **Phryné a fótárgyaláson** (Endre Nagy, Viktor Lányi) 1 act Vigszínház 31 December

1932 **Fizessen nagysád** (Emőd, Török) Vigszinház 23 January

1932 **Éjféli tangó** (István Békeffy, László Vadnai) Király Színház 27 February

1933 **Ein Liebestraum** (Martos, László Szilagyi ad Heinz Reichert) Theater an der Wien 27 October

1934 **Szeressen kedves!** (Ernő Andai) Fővárosi Operettszinház 1 April

1934 **A cirkusz csillaga** (w Mihály Eisemann/Békeffy/László Bús Fekete) Vigszinház 22 June

1934 **A szegény ördög** (Emőd, Török) Király Színház 29 September

1935 **Grand Café** (Török, Andor Kellér) Fővárosi Operettszinház 21 March

1935 **Bécsi tavasz** (Harmath/Török, Adorján Stella) Városi Színház 15 November

1937 **Antoinette** (Harmath/Armand Szántó, Mihály Szécsén) Fővárosi Operettszinház 23 December

1945 **Vannak még férfiak** Márkuspark Színház 3 July

1946 **Csicsónének három lánya** (Dezső Keller, Békeffy) Fővárosi Operettszinház 5 October

1949 **Ipafai lakodalom** revised version of *A harapós férj* Fővárosi Operettszinház 25 May

KÖNIG, Josef (b 1877; d Vienna, 26 February 1938). Viennese song-and-dance man who created several important rôles in a busy career in the 1910s and 1920s.

Unless he was the Herr König who played the young Fredy in *Ein tolles Mädel* at Danzers Orpheum in 1907, it would seem that Josef König began the visible part of his career at the Carltheater where he played six years of soubret and light-comic rôles from 1908 onwards. Amongst the best of these were the character rôle of the naughty sleeping-car attendant Scrop in *Die geschiedene Frau* (1908), the desperate-to-gallivant young Hubert in *Die keusche Susanne* (1910), and the hero's best friend, Bronio von Popiel of *Polenblut*. During this period he also created rôles in *Der schwarze Tenor* (1908, Mister Tom), *Johann der Zweite* (1908, Bobby), *Der Glücksnarr* (1908, Prince Alberich), *Das Puppenmädel* (1910, Romuald Talmi), *Majestät Mimi* (1911, Fürst von Lepanto), *Alt-Wien* (1911, Franz Stelzer), *Der liebe Augustin* (1912, Nicola), *Susi* (1912, Horn), *Fürst Casimir* (1913), *Der erste Kuss* (1914, Dr Rottermann) and played Pietro in *Boccaccio* and other mostly light-comedy and youthful parts in the revived repertoire.

In 1915 he moved to the Johann Strauss-Theater where he took over the part of Vincenz in *Rund um die Liebe*, played Schmink in *Er und sein Schwester* and then created his most enduring rôle as Gróf Boni Káncsiánu in *Die Csárdásfürstin* ('Die Mädis vom chantant'). From 1917 he teamed with Mizzi Zwerenz at the Apollotheater, playing in *Der Aushilfsgatte* (1917), *Walzerliebe* (1918), as Rosenstock in *Rosenstock und Edelweiss*, in Jean Gilbert's *Die Fahrt ins Glück* (1918, Kurt von Bodegg), *Der Favorit* (1919,

Peter Heller) and *Die Dame von Zirkus* (1919). He played alongside Sári Fedák in *Der Pusztakavalier* (1920) and was seen in *Fräulein Puck* (1920), *Die Tangoprinzessin* (1921, Don Gil de Tenorio), *Indische Nächte* (1921), *Der Geiger von Lugano* (1921), *Apachen* (1921, Redingote) and *Die Strassensängerin* (1922, Martin Schurf) before abandoning the Apollo and moving on to more profitable houses.

In the 1920s he appeared in most of Vienna's principal musical houses: at the Carltheater in *Faschingshochzeit* (1921, Gustl Engel) and *Das Milliardensouper* (1925, Jimmy Twinkle), at the Wiener Stadttheater in *Die Siegerin* (1922, Wassili Bronin), *Offenbach* (Basco) and *Libellentanz* (Bouquet), at the Theater an der Wien in *Bacchusnacht* (1923, Metellus) and *Die gelbe Jacke* (1923, Claudius) and, in succession to Max Hansen, as Zsupán in *Gräfin Mariza* (1924), at the Johann Strauss-Theater in *Ein Märchen aus Florenz* (1923, Don Carlos y Riminez), *Bajazzos Abenteuer* (1923, Cyprian Gunkel), *Marietta* (1924, Nicolo Tromboni), and *Des Königs Nachbarin* (1924, Major von Fehlow), at the Bürgertheater in *Das Land der Liebe* (1926, Martin) then in *Ich hab' mein Herz in Heidelberg verloren* (1927, Hieronymus Strudelmayer) at the Volksoper, in *Eine einzige Nacht* (1927, Fürst Severin) and *Prinzessin Ti-Ti-Pa* (1927, Arpad Basarhely) both back at the Carltheater and in Straus's *Hochzeit in Hollywood* (1928, Ein Filmregisseur), taking increasingly more senior and, finally, less important rôles.

DIE KÖNIGIN Operette in 3 acts by Ernst Marischka and Bruno Granichstädten. Music by Oscar Straus. Deutsches Künstlertheater, Berlin, 5 November 1926.

After *Riquette* in 1925 and *Teresina* in 1926, *Die Königin* was the last in the series of 1920s Operetten composed by Oscar Straus and produced by Heinz Saltenburg at Berlin's Deutsches Künstlertheater as a vehicle for Berlin's queen of Operette, Fritzi Massary. *Die Königin* featured the star as ex-Königin Helena, who comes together in a 'fashionables Berghotel in der Schweiz' with the President who has replaced her at the head of her country. She is a soprano, he a tenor, and it is quite clear that by the end of the evening they will, in the best operettic fashion, get together. Hopefully, Präsident Nikola Tonitscheff has fallen sufficiently in love not to regret the fact that his short-sighted republican actions have deprived him of a royal crown. There were plenty of other guests at the hotel – Willibald Netzerle and his pals, Harry and Fred, Miss Mabel Rostaslowitsch, her papa Vlasta and her pals, Mary and Gerda, and a group of military gents – who joined the staff members in supplying the comic and soubret material which offset the romantic plot.

Saltenburg gave only three months of performances of *Die Königin* before removing the piece to produce Lehár's *Der Zarewitsch*, but when *Die Königin* was produced the following year in Vienna it got a much better run. Vienna's production was mounted at the Theater an der Wien, under the management of Hubert Marischka, with Betty Fischer as Königin Helena, Marischka as Präsident Nikola Tonitscheff, Fritz Steiner as Willibald Netzerle, Richard Waldemar as Vlasta Rostaslowitsch and Lizzi Holzschuh as Mabel. Marischka himself directed, and the dances were arranged by Franz Bauer of the Staatsoper and George Shurley from London's Palace Theatre. The piece proved a definite success, running for 177 straight performances as understudy Ernst Nadherny, Raoul Aslan and then no less a star than Louis Treumann succeeded the manager-director-star, Maria Schwarz and Anny Coty relieved Frln Fischer, and Elsie Altman stepped into the soubrette rôle. After a revival of *Der Orlow*, *Die Königin* returned, and passed its 200th performance on 11 August.

Austria: Theater an der Wien 4 February 1927

KONING, Victor (b 1842; d Paris, 1 October 1894). Wheeler-dealer turned top Parisian producer of the 1880s.

Koning began work at the age of 15 as a Parisian journalist and was soon purveying his own particular brand of witticisms and theatrical gossip in *Le Figaro*. He quickly made his name by making his columns the nastiest and most viciously personal in town, and wielded his journalistic influence in such a way as to compel all but the bravest members of the theatrical establishment to 'collaborate' with him, whether journalistically or in the furtherance of his own ambitions in the theatre.

One of those ambitions was to run his own theatre and, in 1869, he rashly took over the management of the large Théâtre de la Gaîté. The experience was a short and costly one – the power he wielded over the profession could not be wielded over the public – but Koning hung on in the theatrical world and attempted to turn himself into an author, most particularly in a curious collaboration with Paul Siraudin and the celebrated vaudevillist Clairville. The curiosity came from the fact that apparently Siraudin – a lazy but bright writer – provided the ideas, the indefatigable Clairville wrote the pieces, and Koning put in the odd witticism and sold them. He placed several of the team's revues at the Théâtre des Variétés and a couple of comic féeries, *La Cocotte aux oeufs d'or* and *La Reine Carotte*, at the Théâtre des Menus-Plaisirs, but his biggest success came when he got his collaborators together with the composer Lecocq and theatre manager Eugène Humbert in Brussels. The result was the writing and the production of *La Fille de Madame Angot* (1872). Koning took up the provincial and touring rights to the show himself, and when *La Fille de Madame Angot* proved to be the most successful musical stage piece of its time he was thoroughly launched on a managerial career.

In 1876 he took over the management of the Théâtre de la Renaissance in Paris and there, for a number of years, he presided over what quickly became one of the most thriving centres of musical theatre in the Paris of the late 1870s, proving himself an extraordinarily talented, if thoroughly loathed, producer. Reading between the contemporary lines, however, it seems that at least a part of the loathing was caused by his tight-ship, letter-of-the-contract, nothing-for-nothing style of management in a Parisian theatre all too used to less worldly and more easy-going employers.

At the Renaissance Koning produced a long series of internationally successful Lecocq opérettes, beginning with *La Petite Mariée* (1876) and continuing over the next five years with *Kosiki*, *La Marjolaine*, *Le Petit Duc*, *La Camargo*, *La Petite Mademoiselle*, *La Jolie Persane* and, finally, *Janot*, the series being interspersed with the occasional new work from other composers such as Humbert's latest Brussels production, Vogel's *Le Filleule du Roi*, the adaptation of Johann Strauss's *Die Fledermaus* as *La Tzi-*

gane, Planquette's *Les Voltigeurs de la 32ème* and Offenbach's posthumous *Belle Lurette*.

Le Petit Duc, with Jeanne Granier starring in the title-rôle, gave him his most outsized success since *La Fille de Madame Angot*, and the combination Koning–Lecocq–Granier was for several years the most potent musical theatre force in town. After a while, however, the formula of their shows became rather too predictable and, following the comparatively only good-to-fair showings of *La Petite Mademoiselle* and *La Jolie Persane*, the unequivocal failure of *Janot* in 1881 resulted in a breach between the manager and the composer.

Lecocq moved on to the Théâtre des Nouveautés to produce some of his best works for Jules Brasseur (*Le Jour et la nuit*, *Le Coeur et la main*) and, after staging a handful of revivals (*Le Canard à trois becs*, *L'Oeil crevé* etc), Koning, in timely fashion, gave up his lease on the Théâtre de la Renaissance, having lost in the last days a deal of the fortune he had made with his string of early Lecocq hits. He moved his centre of activity to the Théâtre du Gymnase, where Montigny had just given up his lease, and away from musical productions. After some initial success and, from 1889 on, a subsequent and swift failure, he once more moved on, this time to build a theatre of his own, the Comédie-Parisienne (later the Théâtre de l'Athenée). The venture took the last of his fortune and he died in 1894 both in want and insane, aged 52. One of his obituaries read 'no man in our theatrical world had so many enemies, nor was so thoroughly detested ...'.

KONTI, József (b Warsaw, 24 October 1852; d Budapest, 23 October 1905).

The composer of the earliest group of successful Hungarian operetts.

Konti studied music from the age of 12, first at the Warsaw conservatoire and later in Vienna, and he began his working life in the theatre as an assistant conductor at the Theater in der Leopoldstadt and as a conductor at Salzburg. He subsequently held theatre posts as chef d'orchestre in Debrecen (1876) and then in Kolozsvár (1878) before settling in Budapest where he became, at first, conductor at the Várszinház.

In 1884 his first significant stage work as a composer was produced. *Az eleven ördög* (the living devil) was a comic opera treatment of Bayard and Dumanoir's long-popular play *Le Vicomte de Letorrières*, a piece already musicalized by several other writers, written to a libretto by Antal Deréki and produced initially at Ödenburg. The piece was subsequently brought to Budapest's Budai Színkör where it scored a fine success and the following year both the show and its composer were taken up by the city's most important musical house, the Népszinház. There had been, intermittently, good and successful Hungarian musical plays and operetts before, but *Az eleven ördög* was a landmark both in its quality and in the success it won, and its Népszinház production with the darling of the Hungarian stage, Lujza Blaha, starring in travesty as the Vicomte – even though it was a French-style work written by a Polish composer trained in Vienna – was an important step in the development of native musical theatre in Hungary.

In the 18 years that Konti remained as chief conductor at the Népszinház, he turned out, between regular revivals of his first work (1897, 1900 etc), five further major operetts and the incidental music for innumerable plays, establishing himself as the first major composer of the Hungarian musical theatre. Of his principal pieces, *Király-fogás* (the king's capture), first mounted with Pál Vidor as Count Radziwill and Blaha as Fjóra in the starring rôles, was played 50 times over five years in the Budapest repertoire whilst winning productions throughout the country, and *A suhanc*, for which he returned to the works of Bayard, with an adaptation of the French playwright's *Le Gamin de Paris* (w Emile Vanderburch), was another considerable success. Blaha starred again, this time in trousers as the 'gamin' of the title. Its hometown reception – a first run of 94 performances – was sufficient, this time, to win Konti's piece notice abroad, and *A suhanc* was produced at Berlin's Theater Unter den Linden (*Der Taugenichts* ad Genée 9 June 1893), before being given a major Budapest revival in 1904 (Népszinház 23 April).

A kópé (the crafty one), an adaptation of August Kotzebue's *Pagenstreiche*, did less well (9 performances), apparently hampered by an unadventurous book which had done even worse a few years previously when adapted by Hugo Wittmann for a Carl Weinberger Operette at Vienna's Theater an der Wien, but Konti had further success with *A citerás* (the zither-player), which featured the Népszinház's new star Klára Küry through a first run of 33 nights, and *Talmi hercegnő* (the counterfeit countess) which brought the theatre's two old-guard stars, Blaha and Aranka Hegyi, together again to give the composer a final Népszinház run of 29 performances.

In 1903 Konti moved as musical director to the newly opened Király Színház. There his final operett *Fecskék*, a musical version of Dumas's *Les Demoiselles de Saint-Cyr*, was produced as one of the three new Hungarian operetts introduced in an eclectic first year's production which included the British musical *The Toreador*, the American *Robin Hood* and Germany's *Lysistrata* alongside Austrian and French musical pieces, *Il barbiere di Siviglia*, an Hungarian version of Shaw's *Arms and the Man* and a visit from Sarah Bernhardt. Konti's new position was, however, of short duration: he died in 1905 at the age of 53.

Amongst the long list of plays for which Konti supplied varying degrees of music were *Szeget szeggel* (1883, Aurél Follinusz), *Szikra Panna* (1885, Mihály Kiss) *A cigányprinc* (1885, József Szigeti), *A tunikás leányok* (1886, Károly Gerő), *A dezentor* (1886, Viktor Rákosi), *Rokolyás biró* (1887, Szigeti), *Az ezres bankó* (1887, Dezső Margitay), *A kupéban* (1888, Ede Kabos), *Kisvárosi hirességek* (1888, Hippolyte Raymond, Maxime Boucheron ad), *Haluska Benedek* (1889, Lajos Bartók), *A szép Darinka* (1892, Ilka Klárné Angyal), *Holtomiglan* (1896, György Ruttkay, Miska Rothauser), *Nászuton* (1896, Ferenc Herczeg) and the highly successful *A gyimesi vadvirág* (1897, István Géczsy).

1878 **A vadászok** 1 act Nagyvárad August
1883 **Ein Wachsfigurenkabinett** (K Bayer) 1 act Fürsttheater, Vienna 15 May
1884 **Az eleven ördög** (Antal Deréki) Ödenburg 3 March, Budai Színkör 8 August
1886 **Királyfogás** (Gergely Csiky) Népszinház 29 October
1888 **A suhanc** (Ignác Nagy) Népszinház 12 January
1890 **A kópé** (August Kotzebue ad) Népszinház 7 February
1894 **A citerás** (Károly Murai ad Csiky) Népszinház 23 February
1898 **Talmi hercegnő** (Emil Makai, Albert Kövessy) Népszinház 4 February
1904 **A fecskék** (Árpád Pásztor) Király Színház 20 January

KOPÁCSI-KARCZAG, Juliska [née KOPÁCSI] (b Komárom, 13 February 1868; d Budapest, 20 February 1957).

A joyously fresh-faced soubrette, Julie Kopácsi was engaged at Budapest's Népszinház between 1890 and 1894, beginning there in *Der arme Jonathan* and *Die schöne Helena* and creating leading rôles in Miklós Forrai's *A libapásztor*, and, in her last appearance there, as Sarah, opposite the Vicomte Renard of Aranka Hegyi, in Bokor's successful *A kis alamuszi* (1894). She married the rising Wilhelm Karczag and, after the couple's move to Vienna in 1894, she was employed at the Carltheater (1894–5), creating leading rôles in Jakobowski's *Die Brillantenkönigin* (Betta), *Die Königin von Gamara* (Polly), *Lady Charlatan* (Emma Lion), *Coeur d'Ange* (Gräfin Ilona), *Olympia die Muskelvenus* (ie Varney's *Les Forains*, Olympia), *Die Lachtaube* (Tatjana), Suppé's *Das Modell* (Coletta) and *Die Prima Ballerina* (Rosita Tremelli) and appearing as Hélène and Adele. In 1896–7 she appeared at the Theater an der Wien, prior to her husband's takeover of that house, creating Jeanette Millefleur in Weinberger's *Der Schmetterling*, Marina in Millöcker's *Nordlicht* and Ernestine in *Die Göttin der Vernunft* and again playing Hélène.

In 1898 she visited America where she repeated her Adele and starred in *Die Lachtaube* at the Irving Place Theater, and in 1899 she appeared once more at the Carltheater in the title-rôle of Ludwig Englander's *Der kleine Korporal*. In 1901 she starred in her old part, at the Theater in der Josefstadt, in the remade version of *Die Prima Ballerina* (*Auch so eine!*). She took some of the leading rôles at the Theater an der Wien in the first days of her husband's management (King in *Das Spitzentuch der Königin*, Adele, Eurydice) and was seen on the Vienna stage as late as 1909, still appearing in such decidedly juvenile rôles as Denise in *Mam'zelle Nitouche*.

During her starring years as a soubrette, although she made a particular and repeated success as Offenbach's *La Belle Hélène*, first and foremost a personality rôle, Kopácsi-Karczag was also able to encompass the vocal difficulties of a rôle like *Die Fledermaus*'s Adele. This duality was also evident in her appearances in opéra-comique, where she was seen, amongst others, as Bizet's *Carmen*.

KORNGOLD, Erich Wolfgang (b Brünn, 29 May 1897; d Hollywood, 29 November 1957). Operettic arranger whose main career was in film music.

Korngold had a promising beginning to a career as an operatic composer when his operas *Der Ring des Polykrates* and *Violanta* were produced at the Vienna Hofoper in 1916 when the composer was still under 20, and he confirmed that promise with *Die tote Stadt*, his best known work, in 1920. However, after *Das Wunder der Heliane* (1927) he produced just one more opera, *Kathrin* (Stockholm, 1939), devoting his attentions rather to a career in the light musical theatre and film.

Korngold, in fact, wrote no original score for the Operette stage, but limited himself to remaking the already-famous works of other composers. He rearranged such classics as *Eine Nacht in Venedig*, *Die schöne Helena* – a major reworking with a quantity of Offenbach music culled from other shows inserted into the score – and *Die Fledermaus* – a remake which did similar things to Strauss's work – as spectaculars for Max Reinhardt and sub-sequently stages further afield, and his continuing name value was emphasized by the vast above-the-title billing given him by the Theater an der Wien when he conducted his reconstitution of the Leo Fall (billed small) Operette *Rosen aus Florida* which had been left uncompleted at the celebrated composer's death. He was also responsible for the musical manufacture of both the Strauss pasticcio *Das Lied der Liebe* played in Berlin by Richard Tauber, and of the widely successful *Walzer aus Wien*, a biomusical illustrated by a score compiled from the music of the Strausses, father and son, done for the Wiener Stadttheater in 1930 and subsequently played around in the world in various further reworked versions.

In 1934 he moved to Hollywood where he became a favourite composer of scores for more than a decade of pictures including *Captain Blood*, *Anthony Adverse*, *A Midsummer Night's Dream*, *The Adventures of Robin Hood*, *Elizabeth and Essex*, *The Sea Wolf*, *King's Row*, *The Constant Nymph*, *Of Human Bondage* and *Escape Me Never*, winning two Academy Awards in the process.

In 1951 he provided incidental music and songs for the musical radio play *Die stumme Serenade*, subsequently produced on the stage at Dortmund.

1923 **Eine Nacht in Venedig** revised version w Ernst Marischka (Theater an der Wien)

1927 **Cagliostro in Wien** revised version w Ludwig Herzer (Wiener Bürgertheater)

1929 **Rosen aus Florida** (Leo Fall arr/A M Willner, Heinz Reichert) Theater an der Wien 22 February

1929 **Die Fledermaus** revised version (Deutsches Theater, Berlin)

1929 **Eine Nacht in Venedig** second revised version (Hofoper, Vienna)

1930 **Walzer aus Wien** (Johann Strauss arr w Julius Bittner/Willner, Reichert, Ernst Marischka) Wiener Stadttheater 30 October

1931 **Die schöne Helena** revised version (Theater am Kurfürstendamm, Berlin)

1931 **Das Lied der Liebe** (Johann Strauss arr/Ludwig Herzer) Metropoltheater, Berlin 23 December

1933 **Die geschiedene Frau** (*Abenteuer im Schlafcoupé*) revised version w Max Colpet (Theater am Nollendorfplatz, Berlin)

1954 **Die stumme Serenade** (Bert Reisfeld, William Okie/Victor Clement ad Raoul Auernheimer) Städtische Bühnen, Dortmund 10 November

KOSÁRY, Emmi (b Kisszeben, 31 May 1889; d Budapest, 22 October 1964). Hungarian prima donna who created important rôles in two Lehár Operetten and also in many home-made ones.

After early experience in the chorus at the Király Színház, Kosáry at first made a career in opera in Berlin and Budapest and appeared, aged 23, as the heroine of the *Hamupipőke* (Cinderella) written by her husband, composer Ákos Buttykay, at the Budapest Opera. She scored a great success when she turned to the musical theatre and appeared as Budapest's Sylva Varescu in *Die Csárdásfürstin* at the Király Színház (1916), and she followed this up by creating the rôle of Juliska in Lehár's *Pacsirta* (*Wo die Lerche singt*), and the prima donna part of Szirmai's *Gróf Rinaldo* (1918). She also played Germaine to the Serpolette of Juci Lábass (1919) and Médi in *Három a kislány* (*Das Dreimäderlhaus*) as well as introducing the star rôle of Xenia, opposite her *Csárdáskirályné* and *Pacsirta* partner, Ernő Király, in Buttykay's highly successful *Ezüst sirály* (1920, the silver seagull). The pair repeated their performances when the show was staged shortly after in Vienna, under the title *Liebesrauch*, running for 200 performances at the Carltheater.

She starred in Budapest in Stolz's *A kis grizett* (*Die Tanzgräfin*, Városi Színház, 1921), created the title-rôle in her husband's *Olivia hercegnő* (Fővárosi Operettszinház, 1922) and apparently also visited America to repeat her *Ezüst sirály* rôle (1923) and to appear as Catherine the Great in the tryout of the Tschaikowsky pasticcio *Die Siegerin*. In 1924 she succeeded to the rôle of *Gräfin Mariza* at the Theater an der Wien and she remained in Vienna to create her first major rôle there, starring opposite Carl Clewing, as Maria Anna Elisa in Lehár's *Paganini* at the Johann Strauss-Theater (1925). She went on to appear at the same house in the Viennese version of Szirmai's *Alexandra* (1926) and at the Carltheater for the 160 performances as the top-billed star of Stolz's Black-Bottomful *Eine einzige Nacht* (1927, Ora Kolorewna) alongside Luise Kartousch, Josef König and Ernst Tautenhayn.

She then returned to Hungary where she appeared at the Városi Színház in *A biborruhás hölgy* (*Das Weib im Purpur*), but took on another major Lehár rôle in Vienna in 1928 when she appeared as Sonja to *Der Zarewitsch* of Hans-Heinz Bollmann at the Johann Strauss-Theater. She subsequently appeared in Germany, America (a Philadelphia tryout of *Arms and the Maid*, ie *Hotel Stadt Lemberg*) and in Budapest, in pieces such as *Die Csárdásfürstin*, *Das Land des Lächelns*, as the original Ottilie in Hungary's version of *Im weissen Rössl*, and in home-made pieces including Lajtai's *Amikor a kislányból nagylány lesz* (1931) and *Őfelsége frakkja* (1931), *A kék lámpás* (Király Színház 1933, Nagyhercegnő) with Hanna Honthy, *Marion* (1940) and as Katinka in Tamás Hegedűs's *Kata, Kitty, Katinka* at the Operettszinház in 1942 in the latter part of a fine career.

KOSIKI Opéra-comique in 3 acts by William Busnach and Armand Liorat. Music by Charles Lecocq. Théâtre de la Renaissance, Paris, 18 October 1876.

Zulma Bouffar, back in trousers yet again, starred in Lecocq's opéra-comique as Kosiki, 'the son of the sun' and the boyish inheritor of the throne of the eastern principality of Yeddo. The new monarch finds both politics and married life tricky. He cannot bear to be surrounded by counsellors like the pompous Xicoco (Berthelier) and he causes a scandal by appointing a little juggler called Fitzo (Félix Puget) to be his closest minister. Similarly, duly wed to Xicoco's pretty daughter, Nousima (Marie Harlem), much to the despair of her kissing cousin, Sagami (Urbain), he finds that he can get up no interest in things marital. The reason is, of course, is that the 'he' is a girl and the real sovereign is apparently Namitou (Vauthier), a state prisoner who is employed decorating hats and who now proposes to wed Kosiki as he ascends the throne. She refuses him, and goes off to be a fairground performer with Fitzo who, by the end of the third act, is naturally found to be the real heir.

Both the soprano rôle of Kosiki and the tenor part of Fitzo – a rôle which required Puget to juggle, balance and do a knife-throwing act with Mlle Bouffar as his target –

were equipped with vocally demanding numbers and ensembles in Lecocq's best style, ranging from her discovery of the 'drôle d'effet' of his presence, and his romance with its final high C, to their balancing solo and knife-throwers' duet, whilst Namitou's baritone tale of the baby-swapping ('Jadis certaine altesse') – a sort of Franco-Japanese equivalent to Gilbert's 'I Stole the Prince' in *The Gondoliers* – and his over-drinking song, 'Dans la forteresse où naguère', headed the comic moments.

Kosiki was a fine Paris success, without equalling the popularity of the top group of Lecocq favourites. It ran to the end of 1876 at the Théâtre de la Renaissance and was revived the following year when, during the illness of the theatre's star, Jeanne Granier, Koning remounted *Kosiki* with Mlle Bouffar. He saw it pass its 100th performance on 11 September, before being replaced a week or so later by another Lecocq revival. In the meanwhile the show had already been seen with some considerable success in Budapest, with Lujza Blaha starring, and it was subsequently played in Germany and in Vienna (ad Carl Treumann) where Lori Stubel (Kosiki), Karl Drucker (Fitzo) and Kühle (Namitou) headed the not very starry cast for Strampfer's production at the Carltheater without establishing *Kosiki* in the revivable repertoire. English-language theatres, however, seem to have passed the tale of the androgynous 'son of the sun' by.

Hungary: Népszinház 27 April 1877; Germany: Centraltheater, Hamburg *Mikado Kosiki* 11 July 1880, Krolls Theater, Berlin 16 October 1880; Austria: Carltheater 28 November 1882

KOSTA, Tessa (b Chicago, 1893; d New York, 23 August 1981).

Recognized as having one of the loveliest soprano voices on the American musical stage in the years after the First World War, the beautiful, dark-haired Miss Kosta starred on Broadway in a number of famous Continental and British musicals which did not equal their original success in their American versions, and in a number of original musicals of which only the picturesque *Song of the Flame* gave her the kind of opportunities on which she could capitalize.

She played early on in *The Pink Lady* on the road, and made her first appearances on Broadway in *The Beauty Shop* (1914) and as a take-over in Irving Berlin's *Stop! Look! Listen!* (1916). Her first leading rôles came in 1917 when she was cast first as Peggy in Andreas Dippel's touring *The Love Mill* and then as Marjanah in the American production of *Chu Chin Chow* (1917). She subsequently played heroines in George M Cohan's burlesque operetta *The Royal Vagabond* (1919, Anitza Chefchek), the highly rated *Lassie* (1920, Kitty McKaye) and *Princess Virtue* (1921, Lane Demarest) before taking on the very vocal starring rôles of Nadina in a revival of *The Chocolate Soldier*, Kondja Gül in Leo Fall's *The Rose of Stambul* and Caroline Lee in *Caroline* (*Der Vetter aus Dingsda*). She appeared in the title-rôle of the Carlo and Sanders musical play *Princess April*, as Princess Ida in a revival of Gilbert and Sullivan's comic opera (1925) and as the romantic Russian heroine of Gershwin's *Song of the Flame* (1925, Aniuta), and starred in Alice Nielsen's double-rôle in *The Fortune Teller* in the Shubert's operetta season of 1929, before disappearing from Broadway playbills.

KOVAL, [René] (b ?1886; d 17 August 1936). Tall, slim and dapper character man of the French musical comedy stage.

Koval, who had appeared as the essence of Parisianness in the London revue *Kill That Fly* as early as 1912, later created more than a decade of comic Americans, Englishmen and, much less frequently, Frenchmen in Paris musicals of the 1920s and 1930s. He made an early mark with his last-act portrayal of the composer Olivier Métra in the original production of *Ciboulette* (1923), appeared alongside that show's star, Edmée Favart, in the 1924 revival of *Madame l'Archiduc* and went on to create such featured comedy rôles as the American ex-husband of the heroine of *Pas sur la bouche* (1925, Eric Thompson, 'Pas sur la bouche') who will never allow himself to be kissed on the lips, the tipsy American millionaire with a young wife to lose in *Passionnément* (1926, William Stevenson) and a third American in Christiné's *J'aime* (1926, Harry Stonc). He was the English Reverend Good-Bye, father to the heroine of *Flossie* (1929), singing of 'Paris', another Englishman as Bob, the bemused host of *Un soir de reveillon* (1932), and even one Spaniard, Pedro Hernandez, the plantation owner, performing the celebrated Duo des palétuviers with Pauline Carton, in *Toi c'est moi* (1934).

Koval played an American in a genuine American piece when *Mercenary Mary* came to Paris, taking the top-billed rôle of the money-seeking Charley, and he also appeared in *J'adore ça* (1925, André de Saint-Assise), *Le Madelon de la Victoire* (1925), *Elle ou moi* (1925, Siegfried), *La Marraine de l'Escouade* (1927), *Déshabillez-vous* (1928, 'Breton, Bretonne'), Honegger's *Les Aventures du Roi Pausole* (1930, Taxis), *Arsène Lupin Banquier* (1930, the tricksy banker, Lord Turner with his 'Marche de Lupin'), *La Pouponnière* (1932), *Azor* (1932), Guitry's *O mon bel inconnu* (1933, Hilarion Lallumette), *Pour ton bonheur* (1935), *Trente et quarante* (1935) and *Simone est comme ça* (1936), and was last seen in a revival of *Flossie* shortly before his death.

KRAATZ, Kurt (b Berlin, 2 September 1856; d Wiesbaden, 30 April 1925).

A German playwright, whose considerable output was largely in the non-musical theatre, Kraatz nevertheless also authored a number of successful musical comedies.

His earliest significant venture in the musical comedy field seems to have been the musical adaptation of his own Schwank *Eine lustige Doppel-Ehe*, a play originally mounted in Cologne in 1904 and later turned into a musical for Berlin's Thalia-Theater. This was swiftly followed by the highly successful *Eine tolles Mädel*, which went on from its initial production in Wiesbaden to be seen in Berlin, in Vienna (Danzers Orpheum 8 November 1907) and in America (*Mlle Mischief*), and then by his biggest hit of all, the Posse *Polnische Wirtschaft*, which moved from Cottbus to Berlin's Thalia-Theater, scored a huge success there, launched its author and composer Jean Gilbert to the top of their professions, and went on to be played internationally.

Kraatz subsequently teamed with the Thalia's Kren and Schönfeld, and also with Gilbert, on several other shows which were housed for good runs at the theatre where *Polnische Wirtschaft* had scored its great Berlin triumph, and also paired with Hermann Haller to produce the text

for *Blaue Jungens*, played for a run of six months at the Theater am Nollendorfplatz.

1896 **Olympische Spiele** (Max Schmidt/w Max Neal) Cologne 11 November

1903 **Der Hochtourist** (Schmidt/w Neal) Thalia-Theater September

1904 **Götterweibe** (Julius Einödshofer/w Wilhelm Jacoby) Belle-Alliance Theater 4 February

1906 **Eine lustige Doppel-Ehe** (Paul Lincke/Alfred Schönfeld) Thalia-Theater 27 November

1907 **Ein tolles Mädel** (Carl Michael Ziehrer/Wilhelm Sterk/w H Stobitzer) Walhalla-Theater, Wiesbaden 24 August

1909 **Polnische Wirtschaft** (Jean Gilbert/ w Georg Okonkowski) Stadttheater, Cottbus 26 December

1912 **Die Millionenbraut** (Johannes Döbber/Schönfeld/w Jean Kren) Wilhelm-Theater, Magdeburg 17 February

1912 **Puppchen** (Gilbert/Schönfeld/w Kren) Thalia-Theater 19 December

1913 **Die Tangoprinzessin** (Gilbert/Schönfeld/w Kren) Thalia-Theater 4 October

1915 **Des Kaisers Rock** (Döbber/w Kren) Residenz-Theater 19 February

1916 **Blondinchen** (Gilbert/Schönfeld/w Kren) Thalia-Theater 4 March

1916 **Blaue Jungens** (Rudolf Nelson/Hermann Frey/w Hermann Haller) Theater am Nollendorfplatz 25 August

1916 **Loge nr 7** (Victor Hollänäder/w Theo Halton) Residenztheater 28 January

1918 **Inkognito** (Nelson/w Richard Kessler) Berlin Kammerspiele 4 June

1919 **Die Kabarett-Diva** (Rudolf Kaiser/w Kessler) Schauspielhaus, Potsdam 30 April

1920 **Die Löwenbraut** (Otto Gaze/w Halton) Albert-Schumann-Theater, Frankfurt am Main 12 February

1920 **Der verjungte Adolar** (Walter Kollo/w Kessler, Frey) Theater in der Kommandantenstrasse 4 October

1921 **Der Alpenrosenkavalier** (Karl Grandauer/w Neal) Orpheum, Darmstadt 7 August

1922 **Lady Chic** (Kollo/w Kessler, Willy Steinberg) Neues Operetten-Theater 11 March

1928 **Zu Befehl – schöne Frau** (Ottberg/w Kessler) Neues Theater am Zoo 23 March

Other title attributed: *Lolas Rache* (Josef Snaga/w Halton)

[KRASZNAY]-KRAUSZ, Michael **[KRASZNAI-KRAUSZ, Mihály]** (b Pancsova, 11 April 1897; d during the Second World War). Composer for European stages between the wars.

Krausz studied at the Budapest Zeneakadémia, and in his twenties wrote for the operatic stage (*Marika* 1919, *Táncosnö*) before moving to Vienna and to Berlin and devoting himself to the musical theatre. His first Viennese Operette, *Bajazzos Abenteuer*, produced at the Johann Strauss-Theater, was in a very different idiom from his early efforts, featuring such items as the shimmy and the Aequetor-Java in a score which wed traditional musical styles with popular and foreign dance rhythms. It played for only two months, but a second piece for the same house, *Pusztaliebchen*, outran it comprehensively with a fine run of 110 nights. *Glück in der Liebe*, with Gisela Werbezirk starred, had a good run of 103 performances, also at the Johann Strauss-Theater, and was later seen at Berlin's Metropoltheater, whilst *Eine Frau von Format*, successfully introduced along with its hit song 'Wir wollen tun, als ob wir Freunde wären' in Berlin in 1927, was later played in Vienna (21 April 1935 27 performances), and in Budapest,

Plate 154.

as *A fenséges asszony* (ad Andor Szenes, Király Színház, 8 May 1935).

The latter part of Krausz's career in the theatre was less fulfilling than the previous decade. His *Yvette und ihre Freunde* managed only a little over a month at the Bürgertheater, and his most successful subsequent pieces, a musical adaptation of the Hungarian *Sárga liliom*, first produced in Budapest, then in Teplitz-Schönau (12 May) and later an 81-performance semi-success at the Theater an der Wien, and the musical crime-story *Dixie* (42 performances) were also less long-lived. Another musical comedy, *Eső után köpönyeg*, otherwise *Verzeih', das ich dich lieb'*, which played an initial 56 performances at Vienna's Johann Strauss-Theater (1 March 1937) was however, well enough liked to be revived in 1946. His last work, *Marion* produced in Budapest nearly 20 years after his first, was mounted with the end-of-career Emmi Kosáry in its title-rôle.

Krausz supplied two additional songs for the Berlin production of *The Student Prince* (1932) and also wrote for the musical screen (*Die Lindwirtin vom Rhein* for Käthe Dorsch, etc).

1923 **Bajazzos Abenteuer** (Ludwig Stärk, Adolf Eisler) Johann Strauss-Theater 22 December
1924 **Pusztaliebchen** (Wilhelm Sterk) Johann Strauss-Theater 19 December
1927 **Glück in der Liebe** (Julius Horst, Peter Herz) Johann Strauss-Theater 25 February
1927 **Eine Frau von Format** (Rudolf Schanzer, Ernst Welisch) Theater des Westens, Berlin, 22 September
1927 **Yvette und ihre Freunde** (Sterk, Rudolf Österreicher) Bürgertheater 18 November
1929 **Die Frau in Gold** (Leopold Jacobson, Bruno Hardt-Warden) Neues Operettenhaus, Leipzig 28 February

1930 **Das Herrgottslied** (Hardt-Warden) Neues Wiener Schauspielhaus 21 November
1933 **Die Lindenwirtin** (Schanzer, Welisch) Metropoltheater, Berlin 30 March
1933 **A papucs** (Paul Armont, Marcel Gerbidon ad Sándor Lestyán) Pesti Színház 18 November
1934 **Sárga liliom** (*Die gelbe Lili*) (Lajos Biró ad Géza Herczeg, István Zágon) Fővárosi Operettszinház, Budapest 5 January
1936 **Eső után köpönyeg** (Mihály Szécsén/István Békeffy) Andrássy úti Színház, Budapest 6 November
1938 **Dixie** (Farkas, Schürz) Theater an der Wien 8 February
1940 **Marion** (Maurice Dekobra ad Attila Orbók) Városi Színház, Budapest

KREISLER, Fritz (b Vienna, 2 February 1885; d New York, 29 January 1962).

Fritz Kreisler studied under Hellmesberger in Vienna and Delibes in Paris, and made a famous career as a virtuoso violinist, using melodies composed and arranged by himself as a popular part of his concert repertoire. He put some of these melodies to use in two musical plays, an updated version of Dumas's *Un Mariage sous Louis XV* called *Apple Blossoms* (w Victor Jacobi) produced by Charles Dillingham at Broadway's Globe Theater in 1919, during Kreisler's wartime and post-wartime decade in America, and the 1932 *Sissy*, a costume Operette staged at Vienna's Theater an der Wien after the violinist's return to Europe, and later expanded and reorganized for a spectacular production in France as *Sissi, future imperatrice*. His music was also put to use in Broadway's *Rhapsody* (John Latouche, Russell Bennett/Leonard Levinson, Arnold Sundgaard, Century Theater 22 November 1944) in arrangements by Bennett.

1919 **Apple Blossoms** (w Victor Jacobi/William le Baron) Globe Theater, New York 7 October
1932 **Sissy** (Ernst Marischka, Hubert Marischka) Theater an der Wien, Vienna 23 December

KREN, Jean (b Berlin, 31 March 1862; d Berlin, 11 September 1922). Manager and author who turned out a series of Berlin's most successful-ever shows.

Kren began his theatrical career as an actor, but successes with his earliest attempts at a musical play, *Im siebenten Himmel* and *Leute von heute*, each played first at Berlin's Centraltheater and later as far afield as the German Amberg Theater in New York (1892), set him off on a career as a playwright instead. He collaborated with the Centraltheater's resident dramaturg, Alfred Schönfeld, and musical director/composer Julius Einödshofer on several further musical Possen and Schwänke, but when the theatre's management preferred to turn to Julius Freund and Wilhelm Mannstädt for more and more of their shows, Kren and Schönfeld decided to move on. Their first stop was at the Adolf-Ernst-Theater, where they wrote the German version of Audran's opérette *Madame Suzette* for Ernst, and then a series of pieces including the successful Posse *Im Himmelshof* for his successor. Then, at the turn of the century, Kren and Schönfeld began the next phase of their theatre life by taking over the direction of the theatre themselves. They rebuilt it into a 1,200-seat house and called it the Thalia-Theater.

The Thalia-Theater became the home of a long series of successful Kren/Schönfeld Possen and Schwänke, usually with libretti written or adapted by Kren and with lyrics by his partner. The musical part, whether it be arranged, additional or new was supplied, successively, by Einöd-shofer, Max Schmidt, Paul Lincke and Viktor Holländer, before the partners hired the young Jean Gilbert, fresh from his first success with *Polnische Wirtschaft* at Cottbus, as their resident composer. Together Kren, Schönfeld and Gilbert wrote, and the managers produced, such success-ful musical comedies as *Autoliebchen* and *Puppchen*, and the Thalia-Theater prospered on a continuous run of their works. Their pieces were produced, in principal, twice yearly although some, like *Blondinchen*, ran beyond their allotted six months and others, such as the later *Zur wilden Hummel* and *Die närrische Liebe*, managed only three.

Kren and Schönfeld also produced pieces by other writers, but although many of these proved at least adequate propositions, no major successes arose from their productions of such as *Jungfer Sonnenschein*, Goetze's very short-lived *Amor am Reisen*, *Der dumme Franzl*, *Botschafterin Leni* or *Schäm dich, Lotte*, although Gellért's very respect-able *Unter den blühenden Linden* and Walter Bromme's *Mascottchen* both had good runs, and Goetze's *Ihre Hoheit die Tänzerin*, brought in from Hanover, began a fine run at the Thalia before being transferred to the Friedrich-Wilhemstädtisches Theater.

Business was good enough at the Thalia that when Max Monti, one of their most serious rivals in the Berlin musi-cal theatre, went into retirement, Kren (Schönfeld had died in 1916) was able to take over his Montis Operetten-Theater which he ran thereafter as the Neues Operetten-haus playing, again, a mixture of his own and other people's musicals. His own most notable contribution to the Spielplan of the new house was his first production there, Leo Ascher's hugely successful wartime musical comedy *Der Soldat der Marie*, which ultimately proved to be one of Kren's greatest successes as both an author and as a producer. A collaboration with Robert Winterberg on *Die Dame von Zirkus* brought another six months' success, and it was Winterberg who was Kren's partner on his last profitable work, *Die Herrn von und zu*, produced at the Thalia-Theater in January 1922 and still running there until just a few days before its author and producer's death in September.

In 30 years as a prolific writer, Kren had many successes in the Berlin theatre, but few followed *Im Himmelshof* (adapted by George V Hobart as *Hodge, Podge and Co* for the American stage) and *Autoliebchen* to productions out-side central Europe. As a producer, whilst giving obvious attention to his own work, he nevertheless used and pro-moted local talent – Gilbert being the most successful example – and new local shows, and almost never hosted imported and/or translated pieces in his theatres.

1891 **Im siebenten Himmel** (Johannes Döbber) Thomas-theater 31 July

?1891 **Leute von heute** (Gustav Steffens) Centraltheater

1892 **Das grosse Los** (Döbber/w Alfred Schönfeld) Tivoli Theater, Bremen 6 August

1893 **Berliner Vollblut** (Julius Einödshofer/w Schönfeld) Centraltheater 31 August

1894 **Ein gesunder Junge** (Einödshofer/w Schönfeld) Central-theater 6 March

1894 **Der neue Kurs** (Einödshofer/w Leopold Ely) Central-theater

1894 **Ein fideles Corps** (*A Gaiety Girl*) German version w Eduard Jacobson (Adolf-Ernst-Theater)

1895 **Madame Suzette** German version w E Jacobson (Adolf-Ernst Theater)

1896 **Mamsell Vielliebchen** (revised *Im siebenten Himmel*) (arr Steffens) Belle-Alliance-Theater 8 October

1897 **Ein fideler Abend** (Einödshofer/w Wilhelm Mannstädt) Centraltheater 7 February

1897 **Heirath auf Probe** (*Próbaházasság*) (Leopold Kühn/Károly Gerő ad Bernhard Buchbinder, Ferenc Rajna) Berlin ver-sion w G Görss Thalia-Theater 10 April

1899 **Im Himmelshof** (Max Schmidt/Schönfeld) Thalia-Theater 23 December

1899 **Der Platzmajor** (Gustav Wanda/w Schönfeld) Thalia-Theater 9 September

1900 **Der Liebesschlüssel** (Schmidt/Schönfeld) Thalia-Theater September

1900 **Der Amor von heute** (Wanda/w Schönfeld) Thalia-Theater 30 November

1901 **Der Cadetten-Vater** (Schmidt, Conradi/Schönfeld) Thalia-Theater 9 March

1901 **Ein tolles Geschaft** (Einödshofer/Schönfeld) Thalia-Theater 7 September

1901 **Die Badepuppe** (Einödshofer/Schönfeld) Thalia-Theater 26 November

1902 **Seine kleine** (Einödshofer/Schönfeld/w Ely) Thalia-Theater 18 January

1902 **Die bösen Mädchen** (Einödshofer/Schönfeld/w Ely) Thalia-Theater 23 December

1903 **Der Posaunenengel** (Einödshofer, Schmidt/Schönfeld) Thalia-Theater 24 March

1903 **Der reicheste Berliner** (Einödshofer, Schmidt/Schön-feld) Belle-Alliance-Theater 23 December

1904 **Der Weiberkönig** (Einödshofer/w Schönfeld, Ely) Thalia-Theater 15 September

1904 **'s Zuckersgocherl** (J Wolffsgruber/Schönfeld) Carl-theater, Vienna

1904 **Freut euch des Lebens** (Einödshofer/Schönfeld/Wilhelm Jacoby, Robert Stein ad) Belle-Alliance-Theater 8 April

1904 **Der grosse Stern** (Einödshofer/Schönfeld) Thalia-Theater 23 December

1904 **Kam'rad Lehmann** (Einödshofer, Julius Stern/Schön-feld/F Zell ad w Ely) Belle-Alliance-Theater 7 May

1905 **Der beste Tip** (Schmidt) Belle-Alliance-Theater 9 February

1905 **Noch einmal so leben** (Schmidt/Schönfeld) Belle-Alliance-Theater 1 April

1905 **Madame Tip-Top** (Karl Woytschach/Arthur Lippschitz, Fritz Friedmann-Friedrich ad) Belle-Alliance-Theater 31 May

1905 **Bis früh um Fünfe** (Lincke/w Lippschitz) Thalia-Theater 26 August

1906 **Hochparterre-Links** (Lincke/Schönfeld/w Arthur Lipp-schitz) Thalia-Theater 7 April

1906 **Wenn die Bombe platzt** (Lincke/Schönfeld/w Lipp-schitz) Thalia-Theater 25 August

1907 **Wo die Liebe hinfallt** (Schmidt/w Lippschitz) Thalia-Theater 20 April

1907 **Ihr sechs-Uhr Onkel** (Lincke/Schönfeld/Henri Kéroul, Albert Barré ad) Thalia-Theater 25 August

1908 **Immer obenauf** (Lincke/Schönfeld/Buchbinder ad) Thalia-Theater 22 January

1908 **Doktor Klapperstorch** (Schmidt/Schönfeld/w Georg Okonkowski) Thalia-Theater 28 March

1908 **Das Mitternachtsmädchen** (Viktor Holländer/Schön-feld/w Lippschitz) Thalia-Theater 14 August

1909 **Meister Tutti** (Holländer/w Schönfeld) Thalia-Theater 15 January

1909 **Wo wohnt sie denn?** (Holländer/Schönfeld/w Okonkow-ski) Thalia-Theater 12 February

1909 **Prinz Bussi** (Holländer/Schönfeld) Thalia-Theater 13 August

1909 **Die ewige Lampe** (Max Schmidt/Schönfeld) Thalia-Theater 30 October

1909 **Die süsse Cora** (Holländer/w Lippschitz) Thalia-Theater 11 December

1910 **Die lieben Ottos** (Jean Gilbert/Schönfeld) Thalia-Theater 30 April

1912 **Autoliebchen** (Gilbert/Schönfeld) Thalia-Theater 16 March

1912 **Puppchen** (Gilbert/Schönfeld/w Kurt Kraatz) Thalia-Theater 19 December

1913 **Die Millionenbraut** (Döbber/Schönfeld/w Kraatz) Wilhelm-Theater, Magdeburg 17 February

1913 **Die Tangoprinzessin** (Gilbert/w Kraatz) Thalia-Theater 4 October

1914 **Wenn der Frühling kommt** (Gilbert/Schönfeld/w Georg Okonkowski) Thalia-Theater 28 March

1914 **Kam'rad Männe** (Gilbert/Schönfeld/w Okonkowski) Thalia-Theater 3 October

1915 **Des Kaisers Rock** (Döbber/w Kraatz) Residenztheater 19 February

1915 **Drei Paar Schuhe** (Gilbert/Schönfeld) Thalia-Theater 10 September

1916 **Blondinchen** (Gilbert/Schönfeld/w Kraatz) Thalia-Theater 4 March

1916 **Der Soldat der Marie** (Leo Ascher/Schönfeld/w Buchbinder) Neues Operettenhaus 2 September

1916 **Das Vagabundenmädel** (Gilbert/Schönfeld/w Buchbinder) Thalia-Theater 2 December

1917 **Egon und seine Frauen** (Ascher/w Buchbinder) Thalia-Theater 25 August

1918 **Graf Habenichts** (Robert Winterberg/w Buchbinder) Wallner-Theater 4 September

1919 **Zur wilden Hummel** (Gilbert/w Eduard Ritter) Thalia-Theater 10 March

1919 **Die Dame von Zirkus** (Winterberg/w Buchbinder) Neues Operettenhaus 31 May

1919 **Die närrische Liebe** (Leon Jessel) Thalia-Theater 28 November

1920 **Prinzessin Friedl** (Ascher/w Buchbinder) Neues Operettenhaus 14 May

1922 **Die Herrn von und zu** (Winterberg/w Richard Bars) Thalia-Theater 3 January

KRENN, Leopold (b Vienna, 6 December 1851; d Vienna, 2 October 1930).

Krenn led a career as an official in the Austrian railways whilst contributing texts, over more than 30 years, to the Viennese stage. The large part of these were in the musical theatre, initially in the form of Possen, written first in collaboration with Karl Wolff and then, most productively of all, with Carl Lindau. This pair had singular successes with their musical comedies *Ein armes Mädel* and *Heisses Blut* before going on to work with Gabor Steiner, adapting foreign musical plays and revues for his theatres and writing the texts for a number of new Operetten, of which *Die Landstreicher*, musically set by Carl Michael Ziehrer, turned out to be the most popular. The pair also supplied the libretti and lyrics to Ziehrer's other most enduring work, *Der Fremdenführer*, produced at the Theater an der Wien, and for Hellmesberger's one big hit, *Das Veilchenmädel*, mounted at the Carltheater two years later.

The collaboration ended in 1911, and Krenn subsequently provided several more texts to Steiner, now based at the Établissement Ronacher, and to the Raimundtheater, both on his own and with other, occasional collaborators, before, in his sixties, virtually retiring. His name returned on a playbill, however, in 1926, half a century after its first appearance, along with that of Lindau, the pair being credited as authors of the revusical *Donauweibchen* at the Bürgertheater.

1876 **Ein falsches Spiel** (Franz Roth/w Karl Wolff) Theater in der Josefstadt 25 November

1877 **Schwere Zeit, leichte Leut** (Roth/w Wolff) Theater in der Josefstadt 10 February

1877 **Ein Mann für alles** (Roth/w Wolff) Theater in der Josefstadt 7 July

1878 **Helden von heute** (Adolf Müller/w Wolff) Ringtheater 7 December

1878 **Schwester Lori** (Henrik Delin/w Wolff) Theater in der Josefstadt 13 April

1878 **Die Vorstadtprinzessin** (Roth/w Wolff) Fürsttheater 22 June

1879 **Die Jockeys** (Roth/w Wolff) 1 act Ronacher 23 August

1880 **Die Liebe war daran schuld** (Max von Weinzierl/w Wolff) 1 act Ronacher 20 May

1880 **Lorely** (von Weinzierl/w Wolff) 1 act Ronacher 11 May

1881 **Wiener Kinder** (Carl Michael Ziehrer/w Wolff) Carltheater 19 February

1883 **Auf goldenem Boden** (Louis Roth/w Wolff) Theater in der Josefstadt 19 January

1883 **Ein schieches Ding** (Paul Mestrozzi/w Wolff) Theater in der Josefstadt 7 December

1885 **Ein alter Junggeselle** (Mestrozzi) Theater in der Josefstadt 3 November

1886 **Husar und Grenadier** (Mestrozzi/w Engel) Fürsttheater 28 August

1890 **Die Frau Sopherl von Naschmarkt** (C W Löw/w Vincenz Chiavacci) Theater in der Josefstadt 25 January

1892 **Einer von der Burgmusik** (Karl Kleiber/w Chiavacci) Theater in der Josefstadt 14 January

1892 **Heisses Blut** (Heinrich Schenk/w Carl Lindau) Theater an der Wien 17 April

1893 **Der letzte Kreuzer** (Kleiber/w Chiavacci) Theater in der Josefstadt 28 January

1893 **Ein armes Mädel** (Leopold Kuhn/w Lindau) Theater an der Wien 6 May

1893 **Die Wiener in Amerika** (Fritz Lehner/w Chiavacci) Theater in der Josefstadt 21 October

1895 **Der Nazi** (L Kuhn/w Lindau) Theater an der Wien 3 October

1896 **Im siebenten Himmel** (Ferdinand Pagin/w Lindau) Theater an der Wien 29 April

1897 **Die Fesche Pepi** (Wilhelm Argauer/w Lindau) Theater an der Wien 23 January

1897 **Der Herr Pomeisl** (von Weinzierl/w Lindau) Raimundtheater 23 October

1898 **Moderne Weiber** (L Kuhn/ad w Lindau) Carltheater 10 April

1898 **Der schöne Rigo** (Ziehrer/w Lindau) Venedig in Wien 24 May

1899 **Ein durchgegangenes Mädel** (*A Runaway Girl*) German version w Lindau (Theater an der Wien)

1899 **Die Landstreicher** (Ziehrer/w Lindau) Venedig in Wien 29 July

1900 **Die Schöne von New-York** (*The Belle of New York*) German version w Lindau (Venedig in Wien)

1901 **Die verkehrte Welt** (*Le Royaume des femmes*) (Karl Kappeller/ad w Lindau) Danzers Orpheum 22 February

1901 **Die drei Wünsche** (Ziehrer/w Lindau) Carltheater 9 March

1901 **Die Reise nach Cuba** (Ivan Caryll/w Lindau) Venedig in Wien 3 August

1902 **(Ei)ne feine Nummer** Austrian version w Lindau (Venedig in Wien)

1902 **Der Fremdenführer** (Ziehrer/w Lindau) Theater an der Wien 11 October

1902 **Das Cirkusmädel** (*The Circus Girl*) German version w Lindau (Danzers Orpheum)

1902 **Der Laufbursche** (*The Messenger Boy*) German version w Lindau (Danzers Orpheum)

1903 **An der schönen blauen Donau** (pasticcio) Danzers Orpheum 4 November

1904 **Das Veilchenmädel** (Josef Hellmesberger/w Lindau) Carltheater 27 February

1904 **Ein nasses Abenteuer** (F Roth/w Lindau) Deutsches Volkstheater 27 August

1904 **Jung Heidelberg** (Millöcker arr Reiterer/w Lindau) Venedig in Wien 9 July

1905 **Die Ringstrassenprinzessin** (*Messalinette*) German version w Lindau (Danzers Orpheum)

1905 **Fesche Geister** (Ziehrer/w Lindau) Venedig in Wien 7 July

1905 **Der Nabob** (Felix Albini) Carltheater 23 September

1906 **Eine vom 'Moulin-Rouge'** (Hellmesberger) 1 act Danzers Orpheum

1907 **Es gibt nur a Kaiserstadt** (Leo Ascher) 1 act Danzers Orpheum 27 September

1909 **Die arme Lori** (Ascher) Raimundtheater 12 March

1909 **Miss Gibbs** (*Our Miss Gibbs*) German version w Lindau, Max Baer (Ronacher)

1910 **Hupf mein Mädel** (Viktor Holländer/w Lindau) Ronacher 13 August

1910 **Der Dumme hat's Glück** (Béla von Ujj/w Lindau) Raimundtheater 10 September

1910 **Chantecler** (von Ujj/w Lindau) 1 act Ronacher 25 October

1911 **In fünfzig Jahren** (pasticcio arr Ziehrer/w Lindau) 1 act Ronacher 7 January

1911 **Der Veilchenkavalier** (Hellmesberger) Ronacher 16 April

1911 **Die schöne Helena von heute** (Offenbach arr Ludwig Gothov-Grüneke/w Gabor Steiner) Ronacher 1 September

1912 **Der Teufelswalzer** (Hans May/Ernst Ress) Ronacher February

1913 **Die tolle Therese** (Strauss père arr Otto Römisch/w Julius von Ludassy) Raimundtheater 21 November

1926 **Donauweibchen** (Egon Neumann/w Lindau ad Karl Farkas) Wiener Bürgertheater 22 May

KREOLENBLUT Operette in 3 acts by Ignaz Schnitzer and Emmerich von Gatti. Music by Heinrich Berté. Neues Operetten-Theater, Hamburg, 25 December 1910.

A comical piece, centred on the President of one of those comic-operatic exotic isles so popular on turn-of-the-century stages. This head of state, however, unlike most of his fellows, is actually encouraging revolution. He is keen to be deposed so that he can go off to the kind of luxurious exile in France which was (and still is) the lot of the deposed.

Produced in Hamburg, *Kreolenblut* had a rather curious afterlife. Although it apparently played neither Berlin or Vienna, it was later given in an Hungarian version (ad Zsolt Harsányi) in Budapest, in a French version (ad Maurice Ordonneau, Bénédict) in Lille, and even produced in America, by John Cort, in a version written by the unlikely combination of London comedian John L Shine and wheeler-dealer-adapter Sydney Rosenfeld, with Chapine and Forrest Huff in the leading rôles and with speciality interpolations enlivening the evening. None of the three adaptations proved successful.

Hungary: Budai Színkör *Kreolvér* 7 July 1911; USA: Daly's Theater *The Rose of Panama* (*Jacinta*) 2 January 1912; France: Lille *Coeur de créole* 1913

KRETZMER, Herbert (b Kronstadt, South Africa, 5 October 1925).

For many years the dramatic critic of London's *Daily Express*, Kretzmer authored and/or lyricked several adaptations for the musical stage, beginning with a version of *The Admirable Crichton* in which Tweeny became the principal character, continuing with a burlesque-style *The Four Musketeers* which featured Harry Secombe above the title, and, most successfully, the final English version of the French musical play *Les Misérables*.

He has also written the lyrics for a number of songs, most notably Charles Aznavour's 'She', Peter Sellers's 'Goodness Gracious Me' and 'Yesterday When I Was Young'.

1964 **Our Man Crichton** (David Lee) Shaftesbury Theatre 22 December

1967 **The Four Musketeers** (Laurie Johnson/Michael Pertwee) Theatre Royal, Drury Lane 5 December

1985 **Les Misérables** English version (Barbican Theatre)

KREUDER, Peter [Paul] (b Aachen, 18 August 1905; d Salzburg, 28 June 1981). Composer of several of the more popular musical comedies of the German and Austrian stages of the postwar period.

Son of an Operette singer, Kreuder had a musical education from a young age and performed as a juvenile pianist. He studied music in Munich and Hamburg, was musical director to Max Reinhardt in Berlin at 23, and composed both for cabaret and for the theatre. His earliest stage works were an Operette *Bis hierher und nicht weiter* and a new musical version of the British farce *Tons of Money*, played under the title *Geld wie Heu* at the Neues Theater am Zoo. From 1929, with plenty of songwriting success already under his belt, he began composing music for film, and in the years that followed, although he turned out a certain amount of incidental theatre music, he wrote but few pieces for the musical stage.

In 1930 he moved to Munich, where he spent several years as musical director at the Schauspielhaus, and then, with the coming of National Socialism, shifted successively to America and to the Argentine, where he worked as a radio conductor, whilst continuing to supply music to the German screen (*Es lebe die Liebe*, *Es fing so harmlos an*, *Frech und verliebt* etc). He returned to Munich in 1951, and it was in this later part of his career that he composed the scores of his best known stage works. Vienna's Raimundtheater staged *Madame Scandaleuse* with Zarah Leander in the title-rôle, followed (in spite of having produced a Kattnigg Operette on the same subject a decade earlier) by his musical version of Guy de Maupassant's *Bel Ami*, a piece which then went on to be seen in Germany (Dresden Staatsoperette, 1961). The Raimundtheater also produced his version of *Lady Windermere's Fan*, under the title *Die Lady aus Paris*, with Leander in the rôle of Mrs Erlynne. This piece of musical Oscar Wilde subsequently played at Berlin's Theater des Westens (19 March 1965). He had a further success with his final work for the adult musical stage, *Wedding Mary*, first mounted in Schleswig-Holstein. His last piece, *Silla, Pupsi und Kulline*, was a piece for children.

1925 **Bis hierher und nicht weiter** (w Walter Basny/Gustav Quedtenfeldt) Cherubintheater, Munich 7 March

1930 **Geld wie Heu** (Leo Walther Stein/Anton Exl) Neues Theater am Zoo, Berlin 11 November

1938 **Liebe, Trommeln und Fanfaren** (Arthur Wagner) Bayerische Staatsoper, Munich 8 July

1939 **Frackkomoedie** (Fritz Schwiefort) Deutsches Volkstheater 13 May

1940 **Franzi** (Ernst Marischka) Leipzig 12 September

1941 **Lips** (*Der Zerissene*) (Hans Martin Kremer) Stockholm 15 September

1957 **Unsere Träume** (Johannes Majo) Städtische Bühnen, Nuremberg-Fürth 29 June

1958 **Madame Scandaleuse** (Ernst Nebhut) Raimundtheater, Vienna 3 September

1960 **Bel Ami** (Therese Angeloff/Angeloff, Franz Gribitz) Raimundtheater, Vienna 27 May

1964 **Die Lady aus Paris** (Karl Farkas) Raimundtheater, Vienna 22 October

1976 **Wedding Mary** (Schwenn/Erika Lanz) Landestheater, Schleswig-Holstein 25 December

1977 **Silla, Pupsi und Kulline** (Rosita Magnus)

Autobiography: w Sailer, A: *Schön war die Zeit* (Munich, 1955), *Nur Püppen haben keine Tränen* (Percha, 1971)

KRIEGER, Henry (b New York, 9 February 1945). The composer of two long-running Broadway musicals of the early 1980s.

Krieger initially worked off- and off-off-Broadway before first having his music played on Broadway as interlude music to the hit comedy *Same Time Next Year*. He had a major hit in America with his first full-scale book musical, the pop-music saga of *Dreamgirls* ('And I'm Telling You I'm Not Going', 'One Night Only') which played for 1,522 performances in its first run in New York, and he followed up that success two seasons later with the songs for a second successful gotta-make-it-good-in-showbiz musical, the rather less high-powered tale of *The Tap Dance Kid* (669 performances).

In the decade since, he has provided music for children's theatre (a rewrite of the French musical *Le Cochon qui voulait maigrir*) and television (the songs for CBS's *Captain Kangaroo*), and collaborated again with his *Dreamgirls* partner, Tom Eyen, on one further musical.

1975 **(Tom Eyen's) Dirtiest Musical** (Tom Eyen) Truck and Warehouse Theater

1981 **Dreamgirls** (Eyen) Imperial Theater 20 December

1983 **The Tap Dance Kid** (Robert Lorick/Charles Blackwell) 21 December

1988 **Dangerous Music** (Eyen) Burt Reynolds Theater, Jupiter, Fla 18 October

1988 **Fat Pig** (*Le Cochon qui voulait maigrir*) ad Mark Bramble, Jenny Hawkesworth with new score Haymarket Theatre, Leicester 20 November

KÜNNEKE, Eduard (b Emmerich-am-Rhein, 27 January 1885; d Berlin, 27 October 1953). The most appreciable German composer for the mid-20th-century musical stage.

Born at Emmerich, near the German border with the Netherlands, Künneke studied music in Berlin and became, at the age of 22, chorus-master at Victor Palfi's Neues Operetten-Theater and later a conductor at the Deutsches Theater. During this period, he won his first professional stage production as a composer with an opera, *Robins Ende*, which was mounted at the Mannheim Hoftheater (5 May 1909) and later at the Komische Oper (23 March 1910). A second piece, *Coeur-As*, was produced several years later at the Dresden Hofoper (November 1913), before Künneke joined the wartime army as a horn-player in an infantry regiment.

In 1916 he put aside the horn when he was engaged as a conductor at Berlin's Friedrich-Wilhelmstädtisches Theater. There he acted as a musical director for the extremely long run of the Schubert pasticcio *Das Dreimäderlhaus* and, thus inspired, decided himself to compose a piece which, like the Viennese work, called itself a Singspiel. He took as his libretto a 12-year-old Hungarian piece by Árpád Pásztor, already set with no little success by Pongrác Kacsoh and Ákos Buttykay as *A harang* (the bell) for Lujza Blaha and Budapest's Király Szinház, and made it into *Das Dorf ohne Glocke*. The piece was produced at the Friedrich-Wilhelmstädtisches Theater following the more than a thousand performances of *Das Dreimäderlhaus* and the rather shorter run of its sequel, *Hannerl*. Although it did not achieve anything like that kind of a run, it was sufficiently well liked not only to win itself a Vienna production (Volksoper, 2 December 1925) but also to arouse the interest of Hermann Haller, the new manager of the Theater am Nollendorfplatz.

Haller commissioned Künneke to set an umpteenth version of Bayard's celebrated play *Le Vicomte de Letorrières*, written by himself and lyricist 'Rideamus', and the resultant Operette, produced at Haller's theatre under the title *Der Vielgeliebte*, was a six-month success. Whilst Bromme's *Eine Nacht im Paradies* followed *Der Vielgeliebte* on to the Nollendorfplatz stage, Haller, Rideamus and Künneke concocted a second Operette, *Wenn Liebe erwacht* – this time an original piece – and they were gratified with another six-month run (218 performances). When *Wenn Liebe erwacht* had left Berlin to move on to other productions, as well as several other countries and other versions, the team were ready with a third piece. It was this third little Operette – a piece which shunned both the classic glamour of *Le Vicomte de Letorrières* and the colourful romanticism of *Wenn Liebe erwacht*, and returned to something like the winning simplicity of *Das Dorf ohne Glocke* – which was to turn out to be the highlight of their collaborating years. *Der Vetter aus Dingsda*, with its intimate family story, its cast of nine, and its delightfully dreamy and comical score, was a major hit. It duly ran out its allotted six-month spot in the theatre's calendar but, when its successor, *Die Ehe im Kreise*, took over, it continued its life with much more vigour than its predecessors, heading to productions in the provinces, through Europe and to almost every major country where musical theatre was played.

Die Ehe im Kreise duly ran out its six months without winning a comparable afterlife, but its successor *Verliebte Leute* did less well (138 performances) and it marked the end of the Künneke series at the Theater am Nollendorfplatz, for Haller decided to produce the French hit *Ta bouche* and, soon after, he was obliged to give up his theatre. Künneke moved on to supply one piece to the rival Metropoltheater before, in 1924, setting off to pick up some of the gold lying in the streets of America.

In New York he worked for the Shuberts on the adaptation of an Hungarian pasticcio *Offenbach*, a biomusical with which they hoped to imitate the success of *Das Dreimäderlhaus/Lilac Time*, and he composed a part of the original score for a musical version of Arthur Richman's play *Not So Long Ago*, produced as *Mayflowers* with Ivy Sawyer and Joseph Santley starred. Neither piece was a success, and Künneke's subsequent commission to write a piece for London resulted in an even worse failure when *Riki-Tiki* folded after only 18 performances.

Back in Germany, he did rather better with *Die hellblauen Schwestern*, and he returned to something like his old level of success with *Lady Hamilton*, a piece dealing with an operetticized version of the lady in question's relationship with Lord Nelson. First produced at Breslau, *Lady Hamilton* eventually made it to London where, either through respect or because the story was too patently unhistorical for British consumption, the leading characters had their names changed and the title became *Song of the Sea*.

Künneke had a number of Operetten produced in the following years at Breslau, Altenberg and Prague, and an opera, *Nadja* (1931), was played at Kassel, but it was five years since his last metropolitan production when his music was once again heard in the Berlin theatre. Once again, it was under the management of his old collaborator Haller, who was now at the head of the Admiralspalast and who had become celebrated over recent years as the purveyor of glitzy revue to Berlin society. The piece Haller mounted was *Liselott*, a revision of one of Künneke's out-of-town pieces, with Käthe Dorsch starring as a royal Austrian lady who saves her home country from war by being nice to her bellicose brother-in-law, the King of France. *Liselott* did well enough, but it was Künneke's next piece which gave him his biggest hit since *Der Vetter aus Dingsda*.

Glückliche Reise was altogether different in tone from his first big hit. It was a bright, modern musical comedy with bright up-to-date music, light years away from the charmingly stylish and atmospheric *Vetter*, but it proved, in this day and age, almost equally as popular. *Glückliche Reise* began its career at the Theater am Schiffbauerdamm and has been 'journeying happily' around European theatres ever since.

Künneke continued to turn out regular new works for another decade without finding a third major success, but he nevertheless produced several works, widely varying in style and tone, which evoked more than passing interest during years when the flight of Jewish writers from Nazi Germany left him at the head of a now miniscule group of able Operette composers. The comfortably old-world Singspiel *Die lockende Flamme*, with its theatrical tale of the actor Devrient and the poet Hoffmann and their unrequited rivalry for the love of a Spanish dancer; one of most vocally challenging of all costume Operettes, *Die grosse Sünderin*, produced at the Berlin Staatsoper Unter den Linden with Helge Roswaenge and Tiana Lemnitz; the spectacular *Hochzeit in Samarkand*, Künneke's last Berlin work; and the more modern-sounding movieland musical comedy *Traumland*, all had their moment.

Apart from the thoroughly international career of *Der Vetter aus Dingsda*, Künneke's works were seen largely only in Germany. Alongside his unfortunate American and British commissions, *Wenn Liebe erwacht* was played in Vienna and, for a brief 35 performances, as *Love's Awakening* in London, where *Lady Hamilton/Song of the Sea* had a rather longer life. His two principal works, however, have remained in the German-language repertoire up to the present day, whilst the best of his other works still win occasional attention.

Künneke also wrote scores for the screen, and a certain amount of instrumental and piano music.

1919 **Das Dorf ohne Glocke** (Árpád Pásztor) Friedrich-Wilhelmstädtisches Theater 5 April
1919 **Der Vielgeliebte** (Herman Haller, 'Rideamus') Theater am Nollendorfplatz 17 October
1920 **Die Schöne von Baden-Baden** (Hermann Beutten arr/August Neidhart) Kurhaustheater, Baden-Baden 12 June
1920 **Wenn Liebe erwacht** (Haller, Rideamus) Theater am Nollendorfplatz 3 September
1921 **Der Vetter aus Dingsda** (Haller, Rideamus) Theater am Nollendorfplatz 15 April
1921 **Die Ehe im Kreise** (Haller, Rideamus) Theater am Nollendorfplatz 2 November
1922 **Verliebte Leute** (Haller, Rideamus) Theater am Nollendorfplatz 15 April
1923 **Casino-Girl** (Georg Okonkowski) Metropoltheater 15 September
1925 **The Love Song** (*Offenbach*) musical revision, American version w Offenbach arr, Century Theater, New York 13 January
1925 **Die hellblauen Schwestern** (Albert Salfeld, Franz Richthoff) Theater am Nollendorfplatz 22 August
1925 **Mayflowers** (Clifford Grey) Forrest Theater, New York 24 November
1926 **Riki-Tiki** (Leslie Stiles) Gaiety Theatre, London 16 April
1926 **Lady Hamilton** (Richard Bars, Leopold Jacobson) Schauspielhaus, Breslau 25 September
1927 **Die blonde Liselott** (Richard Kessler) Landestheater, Altenburg 25 December
1928 **Die singende Venus** (Gustav Beer, Fritz Lunzer) Schauspielhaus, Breslau, 9 June
1930 **Der Tenor der Herzogin** (Kessler) Deutsches Theater, Prague 8 February
1932 **Lieselott** revised *Die blonde Liselott* (Kessler, Carl Stobitzer) Admiralspalast 17 February
1932 **Glückliche Reise** (Max Bertusch, Kurt Schwabach) Theater am Kurfürstendamm 23 November
1933 **Die Fahrt in die Jugend** (Bela Jenbach, Ludwig Hirschfeld) Stadttheater, Zurich 26 March
1933 **Die lockende Flamme** (Paul Knepler, Ignaz Welleminsky) Theater des Westens 25 December
1933 **Klein Dorrit** (Franz von Schönthan, Kessler) Stadttheater, Stettin 28 October
1934 **Liebe ohne Grenzen** (Bertusch, Schwabach) Neue Wiener Stadttheater 29 March
1935 **Herz über Bord** (Eduard van der Becke) Opernhaus, Zurich 30 March
1935 **Die grosse Sünderin** (Katharina Stoll, Hermann Rommer) Staatsoper Unter den Linden 31 December
1937 **Zauberin Lola** (Alfred Brieger, Sigmund Graff) Stadttheater, Dortmund 24 April
1938 **Hochzeit in Samarkand** (Kessler) Theater des Volkes, Berlin 14 February
1938 **Der grosse Name** (Ferdinand Julius, Ursula Renate Hirt) Städtische Bühnen, Düsseldorf 14 May
1941 **Die Wunderbare** (Kurt Aadalbert, Just Scheu) Stadttheater, Fürth 25 January
1941 **Traumland** (Eduard Rhein) Theater des Volkes, Dresden 15 November
1949 **Hochzeit mit Erika** (Willi Webel) Opernhaus, Düsseldorf 31 August

Biography: Schneidereit, O: *Eduard Künneke der Komponist aus Dingsda* (Henschelverlag, Berlin, 1978)

KÜNSTLERBLUT Operette in 2 acts by Leo Stein and Carl Lindau. Music by Edmund Eysler. Carltheater, Vienna, 20 October 1906.

Künstlerblut was written by Stein and Lindau as a vehicle in which Vienna's most important musical star, Alexander Girardi, might follow up his great Carltheater success in their *Schützenliesel* (1905). Whilst the star took a turn to the Theater in der Josefstadt to appear in the Posse *Der Schusterbub* with Hansi Niese, and whilst the Carltheater found only Oscar Straus's *Hugdietrichs Brautfahrt* of their five new shows capable of standing up more than a few performances, the authors dreamed up and wrote down a piece which ˇcast Girardi as an ageing comedy actor-manager called Franz Torelli − a rôle modelled on the famous Raimund himself. They also took a slightly daring turn: this time, at the end of the evening, the star did not come to a happy ending with the show's female star Mizzi Zwerenz, who was cast in their play as Nelli Leitner, the beloved soubrette of Torelli's company. It was the tenor, Max Rohr, in the rôle of the star-struck Alfred Blank who got the girl who had originally set out to disillusion him, but finally fell in love with him. The curtain fell on Torelli looking sadly in the mirror at his greying hair as the younger man won Nelli from him.

Shooting the bullets apparently forged by his wife, who was altogether indignant at the idea of her megastar husband appearing grey-haired and defeated, the 55-year-old Girardi announced that he was not old enough to play such a part, and turned the show down. However, the authors persuaded their star of the benefits of sympathetic, tragic scenes and a heart-tugging ending, and he ultimately agreed to go ahead. Composer Eysler played his part once more by supplying the rôle with a dainty Schmetterlingslied which which Girardi could follow up his famous hit with the Mutter-Lied in *Schützenliesel*, and *Künstlerblut* turned out to be every bit as big a success as its predecessor. Girardi's impersonation of Torelli was acclaimed as one of his best, and he played *Künstlerblut* for 101 successive nights in its first run. Unlike so many of his nevertheless highly successful shows, this one was also a piece to which the star would return. He played Torelli again in 1910 in a Girardi season at the Raimundtheater (30 April), and again in 1915, back at the Carltheater, as it became more and more what even his wife could not deny was a 'suitable' rôle for him.

The score of *Künstlerblut* proved a fine adjunct to its solid story. If the Schmetterlingslied was the evening's biggest hit, Mizzi Zwerenz's march-tempo Gassen-bubenlied ('Ein jeder, der mich näher kennt') ran a close second, and the tenor was given a fine waltz, 'Wie scheint das Leben mir so wonnig'. The bulk of the music, of course, nevertheless fell to the show's star, and it ranged with Eyslerian tunefulness from the score's biggest and most oft-repeated waltz theme, 'So vergehen der Tage gar viel', via another waltz ('Einst und jetzt'), to Torelli's big Rauschszene, leading into the first-act finale, and the Schmetterlingslied.

Whilst *Künstlerblut* established itself through the years as a thorough Viennese hit, it also won itself a good showing elsewhere. Germany, Hungary (ad Adolf Mérei) and Italy (*Sangue d'artista*) all produced versions, whilst America's Henry Savage picked up not only *Künstlerblut* but also Eysler's less successful *Johann der Zweite* and *Das Glücks-*schweinchen which he dismembered for additional numbers to make up what was considered a more Broadway-sized score for his show. Even then he called on Augustus Barratt for additional bits. Oliver Herford's adaptation, entitled *The Love Cure*, was produced with great fanfare, with Charles J Ross (Torelli) and Craig Campbell (Alfred) starred alongside Elgie Bowen − although Annie Dirkens had been announced − as Nelly. The 'haunting and bewitching melodies' won praise, but *The Love Cure* stretched to only 70 Broadway performances before it went on the road with now-exported Theater an der Wien ingénue Lina Abarbanell taking over the role of Nelly.

Germany: Centraltheater 22 December 1906; Hungary: Fővárosi Nyari Színház *Szinésvér* 30 July 1909; USA: New Amsterdam Theater *The Love Cure* 1 September 1909

KULINYI, Ernő (b Szeged, 18 June 1893; d Bruck 2 February 1945). Successful Hungarian lyricist and adaptor.

A journalist from his late teens, Kulinyi became, in his twenties, a prolific adaptor of foreign musicals of all kinds for the Hungarian stage. He also provided lyrics, and less frequently, libretti for a number of native musical plays, amongst which his adaptation of Gyula Pekár's comedy *Kölcsönkért kastély* as the libretto to Vincze's *A hamburgi menyasszony* had a fine run of over 100 nights at the Városi Színház in 1922 and Károly Czobor's *Szépasszony kocsisa* also scored over 100 performances at the Lujza Blaha Színház the following year. As a lyricist, too, he scored a number of hits, providing the songwords to popular songwriter Béla Zerkovitz's *Árvácska*, which ran up its century as it moved from the Budai Színkör to the Király Színház in 1924, and for his score to Bús-Fekete's adaptation of his own play as *A nóta vége*, a 100-night success at the Budai Színkör before going on to top 300 nights in an outstanding run at the Városi Színház.

Kulinyi died in a concentration camp in 1945.

1918 **Pintyőke** (*Alma, wo wohnst du?*) Hungarian version (Margitszigeti Színház)

1920 **A cigánygrófné** (Zsigmond Vincze/Ferenc Martos) Király Színház 13 March

1920 **Yu-shi** (*Yushi tanzt*) Hungarian version (Eskü-téri Színház)

1921 **A tündérek cselédje** (*Irene*) Hungarian version (Scala Színház)

1921 **A reichstadti herceg** (*Der Graf von Reichstadt*) Hungarian lyrics (Városi Színház)

1921 **A hollandi menyecske** (*Das Hollandweibchen*) Hungarian version (Király Színház)

1922 **A hamburgi menyasszony** (Vincze) Városi Színház 31 January

1922 **Babavásár** (Mihály Nádor/Andor Kardos) Király Színház 16 February

1922 **Vigyen el az ördög** (*Hol' mich der Teufel*) Hungarian version w Imre Liptai (Lujza Blaha Színház)

1922 **Az éj királynője** (*Die Königin der Nacht*) Hungarian version w Liptai (Renaissance Színház)

1922 **Detektivkisasszony** (*Das Detektivmädel*) Hungarian version (Fővárosi Nyári Színház)

1922 **A bajadér** (*Die Bajadere*) Hungarian version (Király Színház)

1923 **Cowboy** (Alfréd Márkus) 1 act Várszinház 26 January

1923 **A gárdista** (Vincze) Városi Színház 15 February

1923 **A sárga kabát** (*Die gelbe Jacke*) Hungarian version (Király Színház)

1923 **Tangókirálynő** (*Die Tango-Prinzessin*) Hungarian version (Budai Színkör)

1923 **Szépasszony kocsisa** (Károly Czobor/Ferenc Rajna) Lujza Blaha Színház 19 May

1923 **Mintha álom volna** (Izsó Barna/w Mihály Erdélyi) Budai Színkör 1 September

1924 **A balga szűz** (*Die torichte Jungfrau*) Hungarian version (Lujza Blaha Színház)

1924 **A nóta vége** (Zerkovitz/Bús Fekete) Budai Színkör 24 June

1924 **Árvácska** (Béla Zerkovitz/László Bús Fekete) Budai Színkör 1 July; Király Színház 13 September

1924 **Egy éj Velencében** (*Eine Nacht in Venedig*, revised version) Hungarian version (Városi Színház)

1924 **Krizantém** (Nador/Gustav Beer, Hans Kottow ad) Városi Színház 19 December

1925 **Anna-bál** (Robert Volkmann ad Vincze/Ferenc Martos) Király Színház 30 September

1925 **A nagy nő** (*Geliebte seiner Hoheit*) Hungarian version (Városi Színház)

1926 **Csuda Mihály szerencséje** (Zerkovitz/Bús Fekete) Magyar Színház 22 May

1926 **Paganini** Hungarian version (Városi Színház)

1926 **A cirkuszhercegnő** (*Die Zirkusprinzessin*) Hungarian version (Király Színház)

1926 **Asszonykám** (Béla Nagypál/Dezső Uray) Városi Színház 18 December

1927 **Kiss és Kis** (Vincze/Bús Fekete) Városi Színház 22 January

1927 **A biborruhás asszony** (*Das Weib im Purpur*) Hungarian version (Városi Színház)

1927 **A cigánykirály** (Nagypál/Uray) Városi Színház 30 December

1928 **Bocáanat felseg** (Laura Lengyel Dánielné) Andrássy uti Színház 9 January

1928 **A cárevics** (*Der Zarewitsch*) Hungarian version (Városi Színház)

1928 **A csikágói hercegnő** (*Die Herzogin von Chicago*) Hungarian version w Adorján Stella (Király Színház)

1929 **A palatinus rózsái** (Nagypál/Uray) Városi Színház 1 February

1929 **Naplopó** (Géza Marton/Imre Liptai, Gábor Drégely) Pécs 27 April

1929 **Aranyszőrű bárány** (Vincze/Ferenc Móra) Szeged 15 November

1932 **Vőlegényem a gazember** (Sándor Szlatinay/w Imre Füredi/Uray) Budai Színkör 24 May

1933 **Kék Duna** (Johann Strauss ad Nagypál/Gyula Halász, Károly Kristóf) Király Színház 23 December

1936 **Urilány szobát keres** (Pál Zsigmondi/Jenő Rejtő) Kamara Színház 23 December

KUMMER, Clare [née BEECHER, Clare Rodman] (b Brooklyn, NY, 9 January ?1888; d Carmel, Calif, 22 April 1958)

A cousin of actor William Gillette and a relation of Henry Ward Beecher and of Harriet Beecher Stowe, Miss Beecher married playwright Frederick Arnold Kummer and, although they subsequently divorced, she kept his name, under which she had made her first success as a songwriter. That first success came with the song 'Dearie' (1906), originally written as a valentine card greeting, which was interpolated along with her 'On the Rialto' into Broadway's version of the British musical *Sergeant Brue*. Mrs Kummer had several other song successes in the first decade of the 20th century, both as a composer and a lyricist, and she had songs displayed in a number of musical plays including *Lonesome Town* ('Diana'), *Noah's Ark* ('Wilderness', 'My Very Own' for Sallie Fisher), *The Girl from Kays* ('Egypt', 'Sufficiency'), *The Girl in the Train*, *Ninety in the Shade* ('Lonely in Town'), *The Rollicking Girl*

('Miranda') and even in Edward German's comic opera *Tom Jones* ('The Road to Yesterday') in New York, as well as in the occasional London show ('Egypt' in *A Chinese Honeymoon*).

She ventured in the theatre more substantially with her adaptation of the text of Heuberger's *Der Opernball*, but she had her greatest stage success as a straight playwright with the comedy *Good Gracious Annabelle*, into which Lola Fisher nevertheless inserted the authoress's song, 'Other Eyes', and soon found herself acclaimed as one of the most promising and skilful modern playwrights of the American theatre. Although she adapted several other Continental musicals for the Broadway stage, and authored what she called a 'play with songs' titled *Amourette* in 1933, her sole venture as a musical-comedy librettist in over 30 years of theatrical activity was with an adaptation of her own hit play, set to a Sigmund Romberg score, as *Annie Dear*.

1912 **The Opera Ball** (*Der Opernball*) English version w Sydney Rosenfeld (Liberty Theater)

1921 **The Choir Rehearsal** 1 act Funch and Judy Theater 28 February

1921 **Chinese Love** 1 act Punch and Judy Theatre 28 February

1923 **One Kiss** (*Ta bouche*) American version (Fulton Theater)

1924 **Annie Dear** (Sigmund Romberg) Times Square Theater 4 November

1924 **Madame Pompadour** American version (Martin Beck Theater)

1933 **Amourette** (Kummer) Henry Miller Theater 27 September

1937 **Three Waltzes** (*Drei Walzer*) American version w Rowland Leigh (Majestic Theater)

KÜRY, Klára [aka HAJNAL, Klárika] (b Jászkisér, 27 March 1870; d Budapest, 27 April 1935). Hungary's favourite musical soubrette of the turn of the century.

Plumply pretty Klára Küry made her earliest stage appearance at the Nemzeti Színház in Kolozsvár, under the name Klárika Hajnal, playing Louise in *Les Mousquetaires au couvent*, and there earned herself the attention of Lajos Evva, manager of the Budapest Népszinház. As a result, in October 1892 she made her début at the capital's most important musical house in the star rôle of Denise de Flavigny in *Mam'zelle Nitouche*. She followed up a week later in the title-rôle of Varney's *La Fille de Fanchon la vielleuse* and, less than another week later, created the rôle of Roxelán, the heroine of one of the most important Hungarian operetts of the time, György Verő's *A szultán*, hoisting herself at 22 to an immediate popularity and a place alongside the most important stars of the Hungarian musical theatre.

Over the following years she appeared at the Népszinház in leading rôles in both plays and musicals in a repertoire which introduced Konti's newest work *A citerás* (1894, Rozetta), the Hungarian versions of Roger's *Clari-Clara*, Serpette's *Le Dot de Brigitte*, Banès's *Toto*, Wenzel's *Le Dragon de la Reine*, Varney's *La Falote*, and another successful Hungarian operett, Szabados's *Rika*. She also succeeded to some of the star rôles in the standard repertoire such as La Belle Hélène, Serpolette, Eurydice and Hervé's Lili, whilst continuing to add to her credits new ones French (Alésia in *La Poupée*, the title-rôle of Audran's *La Toledad*, *Les Fêtards*), British (Molly in *The Geisha*, *San Toy*, *A Greek Slave*, Winifred Grey in *A Runaway Girl*, *A Chinese Honeymoon*, *The Silver Slipper*) and home-made (Pásztor's

Kadétkisasszony, Barna's *Casanova*, Hűvös's *Katinka grófnő*), the most important of which was the rôle of the tzarina's page, Germain Duplessis, in Izor Béldi's highly successful *Katalin* (1901). It was this piece which gave Küry her first Vienna exposure, when she visited the Carltheater to star as Katalin in the retitled *Der kleine Günstling* in 1902.

Just as Küry had moved in a decade earlier to challenge Ilka Pálmay and Aranka Hegyi for their musical comedy throne, she herself, in her mid-thirties, now saw the arrival of a new challenger in the young Sári Fedák. Intrigue reigned at the Népszinház and, in 1904, Küry left. It was, to all intents and purposes, the end of her reign as Budapest's princess of musical comedy. She visited Vienna again in 1906 to star opposite Mizzi Zwerenz as Ilka Etvös in a short-lived musical version of the famous play *Krieg im Frieden*, and was seen again on the Budapest stage in local versions of *Die Förster-Christl* (1906, Városligeti Nyári Színház), in the rôle created by Hansi Niese, in *The Sho-Gun*, *Die lustige Witwe*, *Die keusche Susanne* and *Die Musikantenmädel*, but without regaining the popularity she had known in her twenties.